CIVIL PROCEDURE

CIVIL PROCEDURE

The Civil Procedure Rules 1999

Second Edition

LONDON
SWEET AND MAXWELL
1999

Published in 1999 by Sweet & Maxwell Limited of
100 Avenue Road, London NW3 3PF.
Typeset by Mendip Communications Ltd, Frome, Somerset.
Printed in England by Clays Ltd, St Ives plc.

No natural forests were destroyed to make this product; only farmed timber was used and replanted.

British Library Cataloguing in Publication Data
A catalogue record for this book is available from the British Library

ISBN 0–421–69260X

GENERAL EDITOR

THE RIGHT HON. LORD JUSTICE MAY

EDITOR-IN-CHIEF OF SUPREME COURT PRACTICE

THE RIGHT HON. SIR RICHARD SCOTT
The Right Hon. The Vice-Chancellor and Head of Civil Justice

EMERITUS EDITOR

SIR JACK I. H. JACOB, LL.B., Hon. LL.D. (Birmingham; London; Staffordshire), Hon. Dr.Jur. (Wurzburg)
One of Her Majesty's Counsel; Former Senior Master of the Supreme Court and Queen's Remembrancer; Fellow of University College London; Honorary Bencher of Gray's Inn; Honorary Fellow of the University of Westminster; former Director, Institute of Advanced Legal Studies

EDITOR OF SUPREME COURT PRACTICE NEWS

I. R. SCOTT, LL.B. (Melb.), Ph.D. (Lond.)
Barber Professor of Law, University of Birmingham; Barrister; Honorary Bencher of Gray's Inn

EDITORS OF CIVIL PROCEDURE

J. D. R. ADAMS, LL.B.
Circuit Judge, Barnett County Court

A. R. S. BASSETT CROSS
District Judge of the Principal Registry, Family Division

N. W. BRAGGE, LL.B.
A Master of the Supreme Court, Chancery Division

N. CHAMBERS
One of Her Majesty's Counsel, Deputy High Court Judge and Recorder

B. M. M. DAWSON, LL.B., B.A. (Adel.)
Solicitor, Supreme Court Chancery Chambers; Barrister and Solicitor of the Supreme Court of South Australia

A. FERRIGNO
The Admiralty Marshal and Chief Clerk of the Admiralty and Commercial Registry

R. N. HILL
District Judge, Kingston-upon-Hull County Court; Visiting Professor of Law, Leeds Metropolitan University

G. H. HODGSON, LL.B.
A Master of the Supreme Court, Queen's Bench Division

P. T. HURST, LL.B.
Chief Taxing Master of the Supreme Court Taxing Office

THE HON. MR JUSTICE LADDIE
Judge of the Chancery Division of the High Court

N. MADGE, M.A. (Cantab.)
District Judge, West London County Court

P. M. MILLER, M.A. (Oxon.)
Admiralty Registrar and a Master of the Supreme Court, Queen's Bench Division

J. A. MONCASTER
A Master of the Supreme Court, Queen's Bench Division

N. MURRAY
A Master of the Supreme Court, Queen's Bench Division

J. O'HARE
A Master of the Supreme Court Taxing Office

G. H. ROSE, M.A. (Oxon.)
A Master of the Supreme Court, Queen's Bench Division

I. R. SCOTT, LL.B. (Melb.), Ph.D. (Lond.)
Barber Professor of Law, University of Birmingham; Barrister; Honorary Bencher of Gray's Inn

R. L. TURNER, M.A.
Senior Master of the Supreme Court Q.B.D. and Queen's Remembrancer

R. A. VENNE
Head of the Civil Appeals Office

D. WILCOX
A Judge of the Technology and Construction Court

J. WINEGARTEN
Chief Master of the Supreme Court, Chancery Division

B. YOUNG
Chief Associate, Queen's Bench Division

PREFACE TO SECOND EDITION

I am delivering this Preface to Sweet & Maxwell three months to the day after the Civil Procedure Rules 1998 came into effect. If we were not so conditioned to affect the idea that rules of court must be dull, we would say that these three months have been exciting times. Litigation practitioners have made great efforts to adapt their thought processes and their practices to a new way of life: judges have been trained and are striving to take the much more active part in civil litigation which the new rules require. There have been problems, many of them practical and most of these, I trust, temporary.

Meanwhile what is the publisher of a standard work which comprises and seeks to comment on the Civil Procedure Rules and all related statutory material to do? We no longer have separate rules for civil litigation in the High Court and the County Court. Indeed, any remaining procedural distinction between litigation in the two civil courts is largely illusory. There is a single procedure for multi-track cases wherever they are started. The new Civil Procedure Rules are as yet only partly written and in force. Substantial parts of the former Rules of the Supreme Court and the County Court Rules have a twilight existence in Schedules to the new rules. Practice directions now feature far more prominently than before. They may be expected to change, at least initially, more frequently than the rules. A thoughtful commentator has to try to achieve an insight into the balance which will in practice be achieved between the rules and the practice directions. The advent of new rules makes for initial uncertainty, the more so when the comfortable security of fossilised systems is replaced by an overriding objective encouraging judges to do justice without the restraint of outmoded regulation.

Although the introduction of the new rules is incomplete, it is already obvious that the culture of civil litigation has changed radically. There is a discernible tension between judge imposed discipline and the freedom of those who litigate to do so as they wish. But the judicial message is clear. The judges have been given the responsibility to manage cases with the aim of reducing cost and delay and by this means affording more people better access to justice. In this context the rules themselves are almost secondary, and in theory each case could be managed by judges applying Part 1 of the new rules alone. But of course any system of this kind needs a structure and the certainty and stability which the structure can provide. A proper appreciation of the details will take time to evolve and the culture should mean that the structure as eventually understood will be less rigid and less angular than its predecessors.

The editorial policy of Civil Procedure is to embrace the "new procedural code" and to recognise that no one would expect us to achieve a full, mature editorial commentary on the new rules and practice directions overnight. Embracing the new procedural code means starting the process of commentary from scratch and only bringing back material from the past if the principles which it contains really do survive as being relevant to the new rules. So we aim to offer you, not old material recycled, but new material thought out to the best of our combined abilities. We also aim to achieve, as soon as may be, the full and mature commentary which we cannot achieve overnight. We shall do this by continuing the process, which this publication has undertaken for the new Civil Procedure Rules, with further rules and practice directions as they are brought into force: and we shall develop the present work as practical experience and reported decisions enable us to produce a commentary which has the support of authority.

Implementing this policy has placed a great demand on individual editors to whom Sweet & Maxwell and I are most grateful. They have put in extraordinary efforts preparing the commentary for both editions of Civil Procedure. Changes and additions to the rules and practice directions have made things particularly difficult and meant that editorial material has had to be produced with great speed. The publishers are particularly grateful for the team's continuing enthusiasm and good humour. Invidious though it may seem to highlight the contribution of an individual, Professor Ian Scott has undertaken a greater burden than most and deserves grateful recognition for doing so.

Anthony May
Royal Courts of Justice
London
July 26, 1999

PREFACE TO FIRST EDITION

The Civil Procedure Rules 1998

On April 26, 1999 a revolutionary set of Civil Procedure Rules and Practice Directions came into force and governs the handling of *all* civil cases in the High Court and the county courts. These Rules have no equivalents in the former Rules of the Supreme Court (RSC) and the County Court Rules (CCR). They have signalled a substantial change in the handling of all civil cases in the courts whilst at the same time reinforcing certain "procedural values" which, although acknowledged in the past, were not always put into effect.

A number of Orders of the former RSC and CCR—notably those relating to the more specialist aspects of litigation—have been re-enacted (with nominal "plain English" amendments) in Schedules attached to CPR. The bulk of the surviving provisions relate to:

1. Proceedings in relation to land;
2. Foreign proceedings and enforcement of foreign judgments;
3. Enforcement of domestic judgments and orders;
4. Appeals of various kinds;
5. Proceedings under miscellaneous statutes.

The new Rules are supplemented by Practice Directions which take on a far more prominent character than was the case with former Directions. Each Part of the new Rules will eventually be supported by its own Practice Direction—except, perhaps, Part 1. Most of these Practice Directions have been published. Practical Guides for the Queen's Bench and Chancery Divisions will be published soon to assist practitioners and will deal with many of the practical matters covered formerly by the Practice Directions and Masters Practice Directions of their Divisions. Practitioners should also note Part 49 of the Rules which provides that the CPR are to apply to specialist proceedings subject to Practice Directions which are yet to be finalised.

Practitioners must realise that the *approach* of CPR is new: the Rules will set out *general principles*, whilst the *detailed application* will in future be found in the Practice Directions.

Minor amendments have been made to the Rules published in January 1999 by the Civil Procedure Rules (Amendment) Order 1999 and the Access to Justice Act 1999 will make substantive changes to the appeals procedure.

* * * * * *

One of the most radical features of the Rules is that the *reactive judge* (for centuries past at the heart of the English Common Law concept of the independent judiciary) has gone. Instead, we have a *proactive judge*, whose task is to take charge of the action at an early stage and manage its conduct in a way we have never seen before in this jurisdiction.

Hardly less radical, is the introduction of a written definition of the *aim governing the interpretation of the Rules*. The first Rule, or "Part", as it is called, requires judges and practitioners alike to bear in mind the Overriding Objective.

Part 1 states that the Rules have the *Overriding Objective* of enabling the court to deal with cases *justly*. Whenever the court exercises a power under the Rules or interprets them, it *must* seek to give effect to this Overriding Objective by trying to ensure that the parties are on an equal footing, that expense is saved, by dealing with the case in ways which are proportionate to the amount of money involved, the importance of the case, the complexity of the issues and the parties' financial position. All this must be done to ensure that the case is dealt with expeditiously and fairly whilst only allotting to it an appropriate share of the court's resources, having taken into account the need to allot resources to other cases.

The Rules of Court state for the first time that litigation must be handled in a manner that is both proportionate to the amount at issue and expeditious.

One very significant late addition to the Rules was the provision in Part 1 that these are a "new Procedural code". This was no accident. It was intended to give a clear message to the courts at all levels that interpretation of the Rules was to be tackled afresh without reference to earlier precedent. This will of course not be the case where there are clear and unambiguous earlier decisions, but the Court of Appeal is likely to interpret the new Rules in the light of the new culture which they seek to promote.

Two new features of the Rules need some mention. In the pre-litigation stages, parties are now encouraged to adopt practices which conform to the "pre-action protocols" where such exist—ignoring them may be to the financial detriment of the defaulter. For the first time it is the practitioners, not the Rules Committee, who draft these protocols.

The other feature is the role and use of the Allocation Questionnaire, sent out by the court once a defence is made to a claim. This requires from the parties a very detailed assessment of the nature of the case which the Procedural Judge must take into acount when he/she makes the vital Allocation decision. He/she might, in appropriate cases, give the directions necessary to bring the case to trial in the small claims court or in the Fast Track.

The information in the Allocation Questionnaire and the statements of case (the "pleadings") are the start of the matrix of the case which the procedural judge will have to acquire as he/she reads the papers and plans how to design the case management directions of that particular action.

The Procedural Judge under the new scheme will *normally* be the same person as that performing the role at present: that is to say, a High Court Master or District Judge.

The aim of the Procedural Judge is to fix a "*trial window*" or "*trial date*" and to do everything necessary to bring the action *either* to a settlement *or* to a state of readiness for trial at a time which coincides with that window.

The idea of fixing a trial window very early in the life of an action is a major innovation—but it is seen as a key element in the fight to cut down delay.

Cases allocated to the Small Claims Track will follow the well-trodden track which many will know well and, in the Fast Track, the court will generally be giving fairly standard directions. However, once a case has been allocated to the Multi-Track, the significant starting point for the proactive judge will be the first case management conference.

The judge has now to read in depth the available papers and supporting documents and get to grips with the case in a way which, in the past, he has never done before trial. Why? Because under the new system it is his job to further the *Overriding Objective* by *active* case management: by encouraging co-operation, identifying the issues, deciding which issues need a trial and which can be dealt with summarily, considering whether ADR is appropriate, deciding the order for rolling determination (the order in which different issues should be determined with a view to shortening the proceedings and the fixing of timetables). Moreover, the judge must act with regard to the value of the case, the means of the parties, and the complexity of the issues. This may mean considering whether a step proposed by one party should be permitted (or, for example, refused on the ground that it is unlikely to produce benefits proportional to the costs it will generate), dealing with as many aspects of the case on the same occasion, dealing with the case if possible without requiring the parties to attend court and using IT. Nevertheless, the judge must *still* deal with the cases quickly and fairly.

And what does this new approach mean for practitioners? First, the profession is going to have to work much harder at the early stages of the case. Counsel and solicitors who come to the case management conference will have to think through the various problems highlighted above and, wherever possible, reach agreement with their opponents on the approach to be taken. No longer will it be enough to agree not to use ADR because you "do not understand what it can achieve" as happens all too often at present. No more will you be able to go at your own speed, tackling one stage at a time and explaining to your client that that is how the courts work.

Now the client may have to attend the hearings in chambers. I see nothing wrong in the case management hearing being a five-party meeting between the judge, and the lawyers and clients on both sides. Often it is not a bad thing for the opposing clients to meet on relatively neutral ground and to consider ways of settling their differences. Most clients usually want to get the litigation behind them and to get back into the marketplace to resume trading—litigation may be our chosen livelihood, but is it theirs?

But the key to making *any* case management conference effective is thorough preparation: it is a *conference* at which, allotted tasks having already been performed, decisions can be made about the next steps in the action.

New ways for settling differences are explicitly encouraged and one with a proven track record is ADR. Judges are already inviting litigants, as a matter of routine, in the Commercial Court to take a three-month break from the procedural treadmill, to explore the possibility of using ADR to settle the dispute—and then to come back and report. Recourse to ADR procedures after legal proceedings have been started can be expected to increase—not least because the overriding objective states that active case management includes encouragement of such procedures. The parties have a duty to help the court further that objective, and thus have a duty to consider seriously the possibility of ADR procedures being utilised for the purposes of resolving their dispute when encouraged by the court to do so. Since the discharge of the parties' duty in this respect may be relevant to the question of costs, compliance can be expected.

The court cannot monitor every stage of the case. The court will limit this monitoring to the essential Milestones in the life of the case.

The Milestones are likely to be the Case Management Conference, the Listing Questionnaire, the Second Case Management Conference or Pre-Trial Review and the Trial.

The Listing Questionnaire has two purposes. First, to check that the timetable/directions have been complied with and, if not, to discover why. Secondly, it will lead to a firm date for trial being given. Completion and return of the questionnaire on time is therefore essential. Failure to do so will lead to a listing hearing before a Procedural Judge, the cost of which will be borne by the party in default—and this is one place in which a wasted costs order may prove to be appropriate.

Once listed, the trial date will only be vacated on very good grounds. The expectation is that the parties must be ready to proceed with the claim and the Court Service must provide a court room and judge to enable the case to proceed on that day.

In many multi-track cases a *pre-trial review* will be fixed about eight weeks before trial to be conductd wherever practicable by the trial judge. The expectation will be that the *trial advocates* should attend wherever possible. The parties or someone authorised to settle the action should also attend. The purpose of the pre-trial will be to give an opportunity for settlement before the full costs of trial are incurred and, where settlement is not possible, to prepare an agenda for the trial.

In the last twenty years we have come a long way from trial by ambush to the concept of "cards on the table"—and the new Rules will cement this process.

These rules seek to make litigation *less adversarial*—meaning that there should in future be more co-operation between the opposing parties lawyers. Apart from anything else, this is intended to save time and money. And preparation for trial is an activity which, to a large extent, should be undertaken jointly.

There must, for example, be agreement on the outstanding issues for determination at trial and, of course, on the documents which it is *necessary* to put before the court in connection with them.

The judges will require not only *skeleton arguments* and *chronologies* but also *reading plans*. These too should be discussed and agreed between the parties in advance. As to *witnesses*, the court will, again, wish to consider in advance which ones it will agree to hear from each side and why—because, of course, the extent of the oral evidence will have a major impact on the *length of the trial* and the time allotted to each side to present its case. A *timetable* for the trial will have to be agreed with the court AND ADHERED TO, particularly by the advocates.

Civil litigation will be trimmed of its inessential features in order to concentrate on the search for the true issues at stake. It is to this end, that the courts wish to see the parties being more open from the start with clear protocols before the litigation commences, with statements of case (especially defences) which do not try to fudge the true nature of the case and with the clients being properly advised as to the advantages of settling their differences by alternative means, if they can.

At an early stage, a target date for the trial must be set and all directions tailored to achieving it. The Procedural Judge's task is to determine all issues that can be determined summarily, and indeed devise a rolling agenda for resolving issues as so often two or three key issues can, if determined early on, cause the parties to settle the whole dispute and thus avoid an expensive trial.

If, however, there has to be a trial, then the aim must be to restrict the amount of oral evidence, disclosure of documents, and reliance on experts to the right amount to ensure a fair and just trial.

But none of this can be achieved unless the courts and the judges realise that it is a partnership. The role played by the profession—meaning the manner in which they co-operate and work with the courts—will be vital.

This new edition of Civil Procedure by Sweet and Maxwell, part of the *White Book* Service, will enable the practitioner prepare for the new culture which will govern all civil litigation in the future.

R. L. Turner
The Senior Master and Queen's Remembrancer

January 1999

SERVICE INFORMATION

Civil Procedure, 2nd Edition is provided free of charge to subscribers to the Supreme Court Practice 1999. Additional copies can be purchased for £85. Subscribers to the Supreme Court Practice also receive a free subscription to the Civil Procedure News. This newsletter will be automatically sent to all purchasers of the second edition who register with Sweet and Maxwell.

This Volume updates the first edition of Civil Procedure. The Rules and Practice Directions are up-to-date to October 20, 1999. Changes to the Rules and Practice Directions will be noted in Civil Procedure News and on our web updater service at http://www.smlawpub.co.uk/whitebook.

The schedules to the Civil Procedure Rules are now fully annotated so this edition fully replaces Volume One of the Supeme Court Practice 1999.

HOW TO USE THIS VOLUME

Civil Procedure, 2nd Edition is divided into five parts:

Part A: Contains the Civil Procedure Rules **and the Practice Directions supplementing those Rules.** Practice Directions can be found after the relevant Part. Miscellaneous Practice Directions (*i.e.* those not relating to any particular Rule) are located at the end of Part A.

Part B: contains Pre-action Protocols. Each protocol is number B1, B2, etc.

Part C: contains the forms prescribed under the Civil Procedure Rules. Forms are numbered C1, C2, etc., and also carry an official number.

Part D: contains Court Guides, which are numbered D1, D2, etc.

Part E: contains fees legislation.

Commentary is included in the standard White Book style in a smaller typeface to the text of the primary law. Introductory comments and references to related sources appear at the beginning of each Part within the Civil Procedure Rules. Paragraph numbers for commentary will follow the Part and Rule and then have an additional suffix. For example, 27.9.1 refers to the first paragraph of commentary immediately after Rule 27.9.

CUSTOMER SERVICES

If you have a query relating to your subscription or you wish to purchase extra copies of Civil Procedure, 2nd Edition, please call our Customer Services team in Swiss Cottage on:

U.K. Direct customers: (0171) 449 1111

U.K. Trade customers: (0171) 449 1104

International customers: +44 1264 343032

Or you can write to:

Customer Services
Sweet & Maxwell Limited
100 Avenue Road
London
England NW3 3PF
DX: 38861 Swiss Cottage

COMMENTS AND FEEDBACK

We are always pleased to receive comments and suggestions from customers. Address correspondence to: Publishing Editor, The White Book Service, Sweet & Maxwell, 100 Avenue Road, London, NW3 3PF or e-mail to *whitebook@smlawpub.co.uk*

CONTENTS

TABLE OF STATUTES

1640 Habeas Corpus Act (16 Car. 1, c. 10) R54.1.2
1679 Habeas Corpus Act (31 Car. 2, c. 2) R54.1.2
1706 Union with Scotland Act (6 Ann, c. 11)
art. XIX R57.1.3
1709 Landlord and Tenant Act (8 Ann, c. 18) R17.1.13
ss.6–7 .... R45.1.12
1803 Habeas Corpus Act (44 Geo. 3, c. 102) R54.9.2
1805 Writ of Subpoena Act (45 Geo. 3, c. 92)
s.3 .... R57.5.3, R57.5.6
1816 Habeas Corpus Act (56 Geo. 3, c. 100) R54.1.2
s.3 .... R54.7.4
1838 Judgments Act (1 & 2 Vict. c. 110) C66–001
s.12 .... R45.1.19
s.17 .... 36.13.2, 36.21.2, 40.8.1, 40.8.6, 44.12.2, C25.5A.1
(1) 44.12.2
1840 Loan Societies Act (3 & 4 Vict., c. 110) R49.1.16
1845 Evidence Act (8 & 9 Vict. c. 113)
s.1 .... 2.6.3
1846 County Courts Act 27.0.2
1849 Distress for Rates Act (12 & 13 Vict. 14)
s.2 .... R45.1.34
1852 Common Law Procedure Act (15 & 16 Vict. c. 76) R11.0.5
1853 Criminal Procedure Act (16 & 17 Vict. c. 30) R54.9.2
s.9 .... R54.9.2
Evidence Amendment Act (16 & 17 Vict. c. 83)
s.3 .... 31.3.34
1854 Attendance of Witnesses Act (17 & 18 Vict. c. 34) R57.5.3, R57.5.5
1856 Mercantile Law Amendment Act (19 & 20 Vict. c. 97)
s.5 .... R46.2.7
1857 Summary Jurisdiction Act (20 & 21 Vict. c. 43)
s.6 .... R56.5.13
s.7 .... R56.5.11
1860 Solicitors Act (23 & 24 Vict. c. 127)
s.28 .... R49.3.14
1862 Habeas Corpus Act (25 & 26 Vict. c. 20) R54.1.2
1864 Naval Prize Acts Repeal (27 & 28 Vict. c. 23) R59.1.81
1868 Judgments Extension Act (31 & 32 Vict. c. 54) R23.3.8, R49.1.9, R71.0.2, R71.0.3
1869 Debtors Act (32 & 33 Vict. c. 62) R45.1.2, R45.5.1, R52.1.10, C28.0.4, C28.0.5
1869 Debtors Act—*cont.*
s.4 ..... R45.1.29, R45.1.38, R45.1.41, R45.1.46, R45.1.47, R47.1.5
s.5 .... R45.1.49, R48.3.5, R49.1.10, C28.0.3
s.6 .... R45.1.50, R45.1.51
1870 Wages Attachment Abolition Act (33 & 34 Vict. c. 30)
s.1 .... R49.1.73
1874 East India Annuity Funds Act (37 & 38 Vict. c. 12) R46.5.7
1877 Colonial Stock Act (40 & 41 Vict. c. 59)
s.20 .... R77.15.2
1878 Bills of Sale Act (41 & 42 Vict. c. 31) R95.0.2
s.8 .... R95.6.2
s.10 .... R95.6.1
(2) R95.1.2
s.11 .... R95.1.3
ss.14–15 .... R95.0.2
s.14 .... R95.0.4, R95.1.3, R95.1.5, R.95.5.1
s.15 .... R95.2.1
Debtors Act (41 & 42 Vict. c. 54) .. R45.1.2, R45.1.46, R45.1.47, R45.3.1, R52.1.10
1879 Bankers Books Evidence Act (42 & 43 Vict. c. 11) 31.18.2
s.7 .... R59.1.75
Supreme Court of Judicature (Officers) Act
s.4 .... 2.3.11
1881 Army Act (45 & 45 Vict. c. 58) R51.3.22
Fugitive Offenders Act (44 & 45 Vict. c. 69) R59.1.75
s.5 .... R54.1.2
s.7 .... R54.1.2
s.10 .... R54.1.7, R59.0.2
s.35 .... R59.0.2
1882 Bills of Sale Act (1878) Amendment Act (45 & 46 Vict. c. 43) R95.0.2
s.7 .... R95.0.2
s.11 .... R95.1.2
Bills of Exchange Act (45 & 46 Vict. c. 61) R23.3.20
1883 Bankruptcy Act (46 & 47 Vict. c. 52)
s.27 .... 31.3.12
s.44(2) R45.1.2
1887 Sheriffs Act (50 & 51 Vict. c. 55)
s.10 .... R45.1.5
s.20 .... R47.4.2
s.25 .... R45.1.9
s.28(3) R47.2.1
s.29 .... R45.1.9, R47.4.2, R52.1.25

1954 Landlord and Tenant Act—*cont.*
s.25 .... R97.10.1, C43.0.2
s.26 .... R97.10.1, C43.0.2
s.29 .... C43.0.2
(1) R97.6.3
(3) R97.6.4
s.30(1)(d)–(f) R97.10.1
s.31(2) R97.10.1
(b) R97.10.1
s.33 .... R97.6.3
s.34 .... R97.6.3
s.37(1) R97.9.1
(4) R97.9.1, R97.10.1
s.38(4) R97.2.1
s.45 .... R97.1, C43.1
s.47(5) R97.1, C43.1
s.67 .... R97.1.1
s.68(1) R97.1, C43.1
Sched. 7 .... R97.1, C43.1
1955 Army Act (3 & 4 Eliz. 2, c. 18)
s.101 .... R52.1.37
s.203 .... R49.1.73, R51.3.21
Air Force Act (3 & 4 Eliz. 2, c. 19)
s.101 .... R52.1.37
1956 Administration of Justice Act (4 & 5 Eliz. 2, c. 46)
s.36(1) R50.1.18
s.51 .... R71.1.6
Copyright Act (4 & 5 Eliz. 2, c. 74)
s.30 .... R56.7.2
1957 Naval Discipline Act (5 & 6 Eliz. 2, c. 53)
s.65 .... R52.1.37
1958 Adoption Act (7 & 8 Eliz. 2, c. 5)
s.9 .... 2.1.9
Variation of Trusts Act (6 & 7 Eliz. 2, c. 53) 39.2.4, D1–029, D1–295, D1–384, D1–385
Agriculture Act (6 & 7 Eliz. 2, c. 71)
Sched. 1,
Pt 1,
para. 27 .... R94.7.1
1959 Nuclear Installations (Licensing and Insurance) Act (7 & 8 Eliz. 2, c. 46)
Sched. 1,
para. 4 .... R52.1.37
1960 Caravan Sites and Control of Development Act (8 & 9 Eliz. 2, c. 62)
s.34 .... R56.7.2
Sched. 3,
para. 4 .... R56.7.2
Administration of Justice Act (8 & 9 Eliz. 2, c. 65) R56.5.13, R57.1.7, C29.0.3
s.1 ..... R53.14.22, R54.1.7, R56.1.12, R57.1.8, R59.1.75
(2) R54.1.7, R59.1.110
s.2(1) R54.1.7
(3) R54.1.7
s.5 .... R54.1.7
s.13 .... R52.0.2, R52.1.38, R57.1.8, R59.1.74, R59.1.76, R59.1.110
(2) R52.1.38, C29.3.2

1960 Administration of Justice Act—*cont.*
s.13(2)(a) R59.1.76
(b) R59.1.98
(3) ... R52.1.4, R52.1.38, R52.3.2
s.14(1) R54.1.3
(2) R54.1.3
(3) R54.1.7
s.15 .... R54.1.7, R57.1.8
(1) R54.1.7
(2) R54.1.7, R59.1.75
(3) R54.1.7, R59.1.75
(4) R54.1.7
s.45 .... R52.0.3
1961 Carriage by Air Act (9 & 10 Eliz. 2, c. 27) 19.4.4, R11.4.51
Land Compensation Act (9 & 10 Eliz. 2, c. 33) R62.0.8
s.4 .... R62.0.12
s.40(3) R61.1
Sched. 5 .... R61.1
Criminal Justice Act (9 & 10 Eliz. 2, c. 39)
s.29 .... R54.9.3
Army & Air Force Act (9 & 10 Eliz. 2, c. 52)
s.128G R49.1.73
Public Health Act (9 & 10 Eliz. 2, c. 64)
s.66 .... R56.7.2
1962 Carriage by Air (Supplementary Provisions) Act (10 & 11 Eliz. 2, c. 43) R11.4.51
Law Reform (Husband and Wife) Act (10 & 11 Eliz. 2, c. 48) 12.10.1
Pipeline Act (10 & 11 Eliz. 2, c. 58)
Sched. 5,
para. 7 .... R52.1.37
1963 Betting, Gaming and Lotteries Act (c. 2) C56.1.2
Purchase Tax Act (c. 9)
s.24(6) 31.3.31
1964 Licensing Act (c. 26) R56.1.2
Diplomatic Privileges Act (c. 81) R11.0.4
1965 Administration of Justice Act (c. 2)
s.36(4) R92.2, C49.20
Sched. 3 .... R92.2, C49.20
Carriage of Goods by Road Act (c. 37) R11.4.51
Backing of Warrants (Republic of Ireland) Act (c. 45)
s.2A R56.12A.2
Commons Registration Act (c. 64)
s.18(2) R59.1.29
Criminal Procedure (Attendance of Witnesses) Act (c. 69)
s.2 .... R57.5.8, R79.0.2, R79.0.3
s.3(1) R52.1.27
s.4 .... R79.0.2, R79.0.3
1967 Industrial and Provident Societies Act (c. 48)
s.1(5) R95.0.1, R95.0.2, R95.5.1
Criminal Justice Act (c. 80)
s.22 .... R56.1.6, R56.5.6, R79.0.3, R79.9.2

TABLE OF STATUTORY INSTRUMENTS

1925 Deeds of Arrangement Rules (S.R. & O. 1925 No. 795) R94.4.1
1926 Supreme Court Documents (Production) Rules (S.R. & O. 1925 No. 461) 5.2.8
1936 Reciprocal Enforcement of Foreign Judgments (France) Order in Council (S.R. & O. 1936 No. 609) R71.1.5
Reciprocal Enforcement of Foreign Judgments (Belgium) Order in Council (S.R. & O. 1936 No. 1169) R71.1.5
1939 Prize Court Rules (S.I. 1939 No. 1466) 2.1.6, 23.3.27
1950 Legal Aid (General) Regulations (S.I. 1950 No. 1359)
reg. 16 .... R49.1.19
1958 Reciprocal Enforcement of Judgments (Pakistan) Order (S.I. 1958 No. 141) R71.1.6
Reciprocal Enforcement of Judgments (India) Order (S.I. 1958 No. 425) R71.1.6
1960 Bills of Sale (Local Registration) Rules (S.I. 1960 No. 2326) R95.1.2
1961 Reciprocal Enforcement of Foreign Judgments (Germany) Order (S.I. 1961 No. 1199) R71.1.5
1962 Reciprocal Enforcement of Foreign Judgments (Norway) Order (S.I. 1962 No. 636) R71.1.5
Reciprocal Enforcement of Judgments (Austria) Order (S.I. 1962 No. 1339) R71.1.5
1967 Rules of the Supreme Court (Amendment No. 1) (S.I. 1967 No. 829) R94.2.1, R94.6.1
Rules of the Supreme Court (Amendment No. 2) (S.I. 1967 No. 1809) R79.9.1, R94.2.1
1968 Rules of the Supreme Court (Amendment No. 1) (S.I. 1968 No. 1244) R55.1.1, R55.7.1, R94.6.1
Magistrates' Courts (Forms) Rules (S.I. 1968 No. 1919) Form 148 .... R56.1.9
1968 Magistrates' Court Rules (S.I. 1968 No. 1920)
r.68 .... R56.1.9
1969 Reciprocal Enforcement of Judgments (The Netherlands) Order (S.I. 1969 No. 1063) R71.1.5
Rules of the Supreme Court (Amendment) (S.I. 1969 No. 1105) R94.2.1
1971 Judgment Debts (Rate of Interest) Order (S.I. 1971 No. 491) 40.8.1
Sheriffs Fees (Amendment) Order (S.I. 1971 No. 808) R47.4.4
Rules of the Supreme Court (Amendment No. 4) (S.I. 1971 No. 1269) R54.1.1, R54.11.1, R56.1.1, R56.4A.1, R56.5.1, R57.2.1, R57.3.1, R57.4.1, R57.5.1, R58.1.1, R77.8A.1, R106.2.1
Blood Tests (Evidence of Paternity) Regulations (S.I. 1971 No. 1861) R112.6.1, **R112.6.13**, C47.0.3, C47.0.4
Rules of the Supreme Court (Amendment No. 5) (S.I. 1971 No. 1955) R79.9.1, R106.2.1
Rules of the Supreme Court (Amendment No. 2) (S.I. 1972 No. 1194) R106.2.1
1972 European Communities (Enforcement of Community Judgments) Order (S.I. 1972 No. 1590) R71.0.4
Rules of the Supreme Court (Amendment No. 3) (S.I. 1972 No. 1898) R71.24.1
1973 Reciprocal Enforcement of Foreign Judgments (Guernsey) Order (S.I. 1973 No. 610) R71.1.6
Reciprocal Enforcement of Foreign Judgments (Isle of Man) Order (S.I. 1973 No. 611) R71.1.6
Reciprocal Enforcement of Foreign Judgments (Jersey) Order (S.I. 1973 No. 612) R71.1.6
1974 Land Charges Rules (S.I. 1974 No. 1286) R94.4.1
1975 Rules of the Supreme Court (Amendment) (S.I. 1975 No. 128) R106.1.1, R106.6.1, R106.7.1, R106.8.1, R106.12.1, R106.13.1, R106.14.1, R106.17.1

TABLE OF CIVIL PROCEDURE RULES

TABLE OF RULES OF THE SUPREME COURT

TABLE OF COUNTY COURT RULES

TABLE OF PRACTICE DIRECTIONS

TABLE OF CASES

SECTION A

CIVIL PROCEDURE RULES 1998

CONTENTS

PART 1

OVERRIDING OBJECTIVE

Contents **1.0.1**

Editorial Introduction

The rules in this Part have no equivalents in the former Rules of the Supreme Court (RSC) and the County Court Rules (CCR). In terms, they are unusual. Their principal purpose is to signal a substantial change in the handling of civil cases in the courts whilst at the same time reinforcing "procedural values" which, although acknowledged in the past, have not always been put into effect. The Civil Procedure Rules 1998 (CPR) bring into force many new procedural rules but also re-enact much that was found in the RSC and the CCR (see, respectively, Scheds 1 and 2). In many respects the success of the new procedural regime will depend on the attitudes of judges and lawyers to the underlying policies. The rules in this Part, which are directed as much to the judges of the courts as to parties and their legal representatives, summarise the policies expounded in the "Access to Justice" Reports and which should inform the operation in practice of the rules of civil procedure as stated in the CPR and related practice directions. **1.0.2**

Related Sources

- Rule 3.1 (Court's general powers of case management). **1.0.3**

The overriding objective

1.1—(1) These Rules are a new procedural code with the overriding objective of enabling the court to deal with cases justly. **1.1**

(2) Dealing with a case justly includes, so far as is practicable—

(a) ensuring that the parties are on an equal footing;

(b) saving expense;

(c) dealing with the case in ways which are proportionate—

(i) to the amount of money involved;

(ii) to the importance of the case;

(iii) to the complexity of the issues; and

(iv) to the financial position of each party;

(d) ensuring that it is dealt with expeditiously and fairly; and

(e) allotting to it an appropriate share of the court's resources, while taking into account the need to allot resources to other cases.

Application by the court of the overriding objective

1.2 The court must seek to give effect to the overriding objective when it— **1.2**

(a) exercises any power given to it by the Rules; or

(b) interprets any rule.

Duty of the parties

1.3 The parties are required to help the court to further the overriding objective. **1.3**

Effect of rules 1.1 to 1.3—In the Final Report it was said (at p. 274) that, ultimately, the purpose of rules of court "is to guide the court and the litigants towards the just resolution of the case". Rules of court contain detailed directions for the steps which must be taken. The effectiveness of those steps "depends upon the spirit in which they are carried out". That, in turn, "depends on an understanding of the fundamental purpose of the rules and of the underlying system of procedure". It was further said in the Final Report (*ibid.*) that the "overriding objective", as stated in r.1.1 and r.1.2, encapsulates that fundamental purpose. The CPR are deliberately not **1.3.1**

designed expressly to answer every question which could arise. The statement of the overriding objective in those rules "provides a compass to guide courts and litigants and legal advisers as to their general course" (Final Report, p. 275).

1.3.2 **The overriding objective**—The court must seek to give effect to the overriding objective when it (a) "exercises any power" given to it by the CPR, or (b) interprets any rule (r.1.2). Consequently, the elaboration of the overriding objective cannot be treated as amounting merely to a set of pious aspirations. The aspects of the overriding objective as particularised in r.1.1(2) are likely to be given operational effect. There is a risk that the objectives listed in that provision will be used selectively and merely for the purpose of giving added weight to particular exercises of powers and of interpretations of rules. There is also a risk that the terms of r.1.1(2) will be subjected to over-elaborate analysis. The listed objectives are not mutually exclusive and, in a given situation, a course taken by the court to meet one objective may yield a different result to a course taken to meet another. The provenance of rr.1.1 and 1.2 is the Final Report (p. 274) (see also Interim Report, p. 216).

As to overriding objective as guide to interpretation of rules (r.1.2(b)), see notes to r. 2.3 below.

1.3.3 **Justice and fairness**—It is perhaps obvious that the fundamental purpose of civil procedure should be to enable the court "to deal with cases justly" (r.1.1(1)) and, so far as is practicable, "fairly" (r.1.1(2)(d)). The classic explanation of the role of civil procedure is that it should be the "handmaiden of justice" (*Re Coles and Ravenshear* [1906] 1 K.B. 1, CA, at 4, *per* Collins M.R.). However, these sentiments cannot be allowed to hide the fact that procedural rules are not "value free". They are based on policy choices, they have their own objectives and, in the adversary context, for good reason individual rules may reflect a bias towards one party or another. Further, in a given situation, what is just and what is fair may be a matter on which reasonable persons may reasonably differ. Clearly, the overriding consideration must be the doing of justice in the individual case and the application of the several aspects of the overriding objective as particularised in r.1.1(2) are subject to that consideration.

1.3.4 **Cost and delay**—The "Access to Justice" Reports were concerned to recommend cures to the time-honoured twin scourges of civil justice; they are cost and delay. Paragraphs (b) and (d) of r.1.1(2) state that the furthering of the overriding objective of dealing with a case justly includes "so far as is practicable", amongst other things, saving expense and ensuring that it is dealt with expeditiously and fairly. The matter of expense is also referred to in para. (c)(iv) which requires the court to deal with the case in ways which take account of the financial position of each party (see further "Proportionality", para. 1.3.5, below). In these respects r.1.1 echoes the Arbitration Act 1996, s.1. That section states that the provisions of Pt 1 of that Act are founded on certain principles "and shall be construed accordingly". One of the principles is that "the object of arbitration is to obtain the fair resolution of disputes by an impartial tribunal without unnecessary delay or expense" (see SCP 1999, Vol. 2, para. 21D–7).

1.3.5 **Proportionality**—See also "Ensuring parties on equal footing" below, para. 1.3.6.

Rule 1.1(2)(c) introduces one of the most important principles underlying the new approach to civil procedure heralded by the bringing into force of the CPR, that is, the principle of proportionality. Dealing justly with a case (*i.e.* furthering the overriding objective) includes, so far as is practicable, dealing with the case in ways which are proportionate (i) to the amount of money involved, (ii) to the importance of the case, (iii) to the complexity of the issues, and (iv) to the financial position of each party.

There is nothing new in the concept of proportionality. Civil procedures have always been designed in a manner which took account of the fact that cases vary enormously in these respects. However, as a practical matter, in important respects the mechanisms that existed for matching claims with appropriate procedures and for ensuring that procedures designed for the heavier cases were not routinely used in ordinary cases were ineffective. In the "Report of the Civil Justice Review Body" (Cm. 394, 1988) it was said (p. 14) that the cost of litigation was often quite disproportionate to the amount of the claim, that too many cases were dealt with according to High Court procedures when county court procedures would suffice, and that procedures for handling smaller cases (including debts, other small claims and many housing cases) were disproportionately complex. These findings were confirmed in the "Access to Justice" Reports.

To a significant extent, the principle of proportionality is implemented by the procedure for allocation of cases to one or other of the three case management tracks, the small claims track, the fast track, and the multi-track (see Pts 26 to 29). Allocation is controlled by the court. The procedures applied in the several tracks are significantly different. The procedures applicable to cases on the small claims track are similar to those which formerly applied in cases referred to arbitration under former CCR, O.19, Pt I. The fast track is designed to accommodate cases in the middle range. The procedures applicable to cases proceeding on this track are limited and in this way proportionality is assured. Nothing comparable to the fast track existed in the rules formerly applicable to actions proceeding in the High Court or the county courts. (Historically speaking, the county courts were meant to offer procedures which were proportionate to smaller cases but meaningful distinctions between High Court and county court procedures disappeared as the jurisdictional limits on the county courts were raised for the purpose of relieving the High Court of business. The introduction of the fast track may be seen as an effort to re-invent the county courts.) The multi-track is designed to accommodate the heavier cases and the full range of procedures is available. At this level proportionality is assured by the court's power to control the development of the case by directions given in exercise of the powers given to the court by rules of court and practice directions (all of which should be exercised with the overriding objective, and therefore the need for proportionality, in mind). Rule 26.8 states the matters which the court should take into account when deciding whether to allocate a case to one track or another. As would be expected, paras (i) to (v) of r.1.1(2)(c) are reflected in that provision. Paragraphs (i) to (v), or some of them, are referred to, either expressly or impliedly, in a number of other provisions in the CPR; *e.g.* r.30.3 (Criteria for transfer order), r.31.3 (Right of inspection of a disclosed document), r.31.7 (Duty of search), and r.44.5 (Matters to be taken into account in deciding the amount of costs); note also Practice Direction relating to Part 44 (General Rules about Costs) para. 3.1 (44PD–003). The financial position of each party is a relevant factor where the court is considering whether to exercise its discretion under r.44.3(8) to order an amount to be paid on account before costs are assessed (*Mars (U.K.) Ltd v. Teknowledge Ltd (No. 2), The Times,* July 8, 1999. Applicants for wasted costs orders must bear in mind the principle of proportionality (*Re Merc Property Ltd, The Times,* May 19, 1999).

The concept of proportionality is also relevant to the taking of appeals, both from interlocutory and from final orders. The concept of proportionality is also relevant to the taking of appeals, both from interlocutory and final orders; see *Piglowska v. Piglowski* [1991] 1 W.L.R. 1360, HL (wisdom of granting successive permissions to appeal important point of principle at expense of parties with very limited resources doubted by Lord Hoffmann), *Walker v. Home Office,* April 16, 1999, CA, unrep. (permission to appeal striking out order refused where point of principle trivial in circumstances).

Ensuring parties on equal footing—Dealing with a case justly includes, so far as is **1.3.6** practicable, "ensuring that the parties are on an equal footing" (r.1.1(2)(a)). Obviously, this aspect of the overriding objective is closely related to that of dealing with a case in ways which are proportionate "to the financial position of each party" (r.1.1(2)(c)(iv)). However, equality is not limited to the respective capacities of the parties to finance the litigation in which they are involved.

In the "Access to Justice" Reports it was said that one of the defects in the civil justice system was the "lack of equality" between the powerful, wealthy litigant and the under-resourced litigant and amongst the specific objectives of the reforms proposed in those Reports was the need to establish "equality of arms" between the parties involved in civil cases so as to ensure, so far as possible, that there should be "a level playing field between litigants of unequal financial or other resources" (see Final Report, pp. 2 and 146 and Interim Report, p. 26). It was said that financially stronger and more experienced parties could exploit rules of court so as to intimidate weaker parties by spinning out proceedings and escalating costs. In the Interim Report it was said that the overriding objective should include "making allowances for any inequality between the parties" (p. 216) but in the Final Report this formula was abandoned in favour of that now found in r.1.1(2)(a) (p. 274).

The procedures introduced by the CPR are simpler than those which previously prevailed and their application in individual cases is subject to supervision by the court through the case management system. Consequently, the scope for a wealthy or experienced party using intimidatory tactics against a party weaker in either or both of those respects is now reduced. Thus, the overall system goes a long way towards ensuring that in individual cases the parties are "on an equal footing".

The provisions introduced by the CPR as to costs should have the effect of reducing the burden on a party who is financially weaker than his opponent. In fast track cases the costs recoverable by a successful party are limited. As this limitation accrues to the benefit of both financially strong and financially weak losing parties it has been suggested that it may have the effect of favouring the stronger party and introducing inequality. However, fast track cases are subject to limited procedures and to strict timetables and this reduces both the scope for a strong party to push up the amount of work required by his weaker opponent and the extent to which the strong party will be able to spend money extravagantly on his own case (see Final Report, pp. 28 and 45).

Where one party can afford to instruct a large firm of experienced and expensive solicitors, whereas the other can afford only small and relatively inexperienced advisers, the court may make orders designed to rectify this imbalance; for example, orders allowing the smaller firm more time to carry out necessary work, or requiring the larger firm to prepare bundles of documents needed for court hearings (*Maltez v. Lewis, The Times,* May 4, 1999). However, the court has no power, either under r.1.1(2) or under any other provision, to prevent a party from instructing the legal representatives of his choice, simply on the ground that he is able to afford more powerful representation than his opponent.

A potential source of inequality between parties may lie in their respective access to expert evidence. Some of the provisions as to experts now found in Pt 35 (particularly r.35.8) are designed to remedy this imbalance (see Final Report, p. 146).

When deciding the track for a claim, the matters to which the court should have regard include "the circumstances of the parties" (r.26.8(1)(i)).

1.3.7 **Court's resources**—Dealing with a case justly includes, so far as is practicable, "allotting to it an appropriate share of the court's resources, while taking into account the need to allot resources to other cases" (r.1.1(2)(e)). This provision is inelegant, but its meaning is tolerably clear. An underlying theme in the "Access to Justice" Reports is that the harmful impacts of excessive and disproportionate costs, and of delays brought about by the behaviour of parties, are not confined to the parties themselves. The burden of costs can fall on publicly provided funds and can harm the economic health of businesses. Where delays occur in one case, parties in other cases can be inconvenienced, subject to delays not of their own making, and put to additional expense. Further, court resources can be wasted where parties make unnecessary applications, or where time is taken up by hearings provoked or made necessary by one party's failure to comply with court rules or orders. In modern times, concerns about these wider effects have influenced decisions made by the courts in cases involving applications for late adjournments, to extend time, to relieve from the normal consequences of defaults of various kinds (including failures to comply with "unless" orders), and to strike out for want of prosecution or abuse of process (*e.g. Mortgage Corporation Ltd v. Sandoes, The Times*, December 27, 1996, CA; *Hytec Information Systems Ltd v. Coventry City Council* [1997] 1 W.L.R. 1666, CA; and *Arbuthnot Latham Bank Ltd v. Trafalgar Holdings Ltd, The Times*, December 29, 1997, CA). Rule 1.1(2)(e) recognises that court resources are limited, that demand is always likely to outstrip supply, that justice has to be "rationed". The overall scheme of the CPR and the case management system in particular is designed to ensure that each case is allotted its "appropriate share of the court's resources" (see further "Proportionality", para. 1.3.5 above). The significance of r.1.1(2)(e) is that it states that, in allotting each case its share of resources, the court should take into account "the need to allot resources to other cases". It would seem that what is meant by determining the share of court resources which should be allotted to a case is determining what is the appropriate form of management for that case. This is not confined to determining the appropriate case management track but also includes the manner in which all of the other powers which the court has to control the development of the case (including the power to impose sanctions for procedural failures) is exercised. In determining the appropriate form of management the court should have regard to the need to prevent any one case being conducted in a way that interferes with the resolution of other disputes and wastes the resources of the court (see Interim Report, p. 39). Litigants and their advisers should recognise that any delay which occurs will be assessed, not only from the point of view of the prejudice caused in their case, but also in relation to other litigants and the prejudice which is caused to the due administration of justice (*Arbuthnot Latham Bank Ltd v. Trafalgar Holdings Ltd, op. cit., per* Lord Woolf M.R.).

The allocation to a case of an appropriate share of the court's resources may also be a consideration in the handling of appeals by the Court of Appeal (*Adoko v. Jemal, The Times*, July 8, 1999, CA, *Stephenson (S.B.J.) Ltd v. Mandy, The Times*, July 21, 1999, CA).

1.3.8 **Duty of the parties (r.1.3)**—The structure of the rules in Pt 1 suggests that the achievement of the overriding objective is the duty of the court. The rules are designed to enable "the court" to deal with cases justly (r.1.1), it is "the court" that must seek to give effect to the overriding objective (r.1.2), and it is "the court" that must further that objective by actively managing cases (r.1.4). (Note also r.3.1(2)(m).) No such duty is directly imposed on the parties. However, r.1.3 states that the parties are required "to help the court" to further the overriding objective (r.1.3). This may be contrasted with the Arbitration Act 1996, s.40 which is expressed in rather more forceful and pointed language and states that the parties "shall do all things necessary for the proper and expeditious conduct of the arbitral proceedings". This includes "complying without delay with any determination of the tribunal as to procedural or evidential matters, or with any order or directions of the tribunal" (see SCP 1999, Vol. 2, para. 21D–87). In the final draft of the CPR (and in previous drafts) r.1.3 stated that parties were "expected" rather than "required" to help the court further the overriding objective. Civil proceedings in the courts differ from arbitration proceedings (and other ADR procedures) in that they are not optional but mandatory. If parties agree to arbitrate they know that the Arbitration Act 1996, s.40 will apply and therefore it is not unreasonable to expect that they will conduct themselves accordingly. If a party is brought into civil proceedings in the courts against his wishes and interests he will find that the procedural rules to which the proceedings are subject provide plenty of sanctions to ensure that he cannot frustrate the process. It may not be unreasonable for rules of court to say that, in addition to being exposed to such penalties, he is also "expected" to help the court in furthering the overriding objective. But to say that he is "required" to do so may be regarded as excessive and unnecessary.

One important way in which parties can assist the court in furthering the objective of dealing with cases fairly and expeditiously is by cooperating with the court in the fixing of trial dates, particularly by providing timely and accurate information as to the availability of expert witnesses (*Matthews v. Tarmac Bricks and Tiles Ltd, The Times*, July 1, 1999, CA).

Court's duty to manage cases

1.4 1.4—(1) The court must further the overriding objective by actively managing cases.

(2) Active case management includes—

(a) encouraging the parties to co-operate with each other in the conduct of the proceedings;

(b) identifying the issues at an early stage;

(c) deciding promptly which issues need full investigation and trial and accordingly disposing summarily of the others;

(d) deciding the order in which issues are to be resolved;

(e) encouraging the parties to use an alternative dispute resolution[GL] procedure if the court considers that appropriate and facilitating the use of such procedure;

(f) helping the parties to settle the whole or part of the case;

(g) fixing timetables or otherwise controlling the progress of the case;

(h) considering whether the likely benefits of taking a particular step justify the cost of taking it;

(i) dealing with as many aspects of the case as it can on the same occasion;

(j) dealing with the case without the parties needing to attend at court;

(k) making use of technology; and

(l) giving directions to ensure that the trial of a case proceeds quickly and efficiently.

Effect of rule—Rule 1.4(1) states that the court's duty to further the overriding objective (rr.1.1 and 1.2) includes the duty actively to manage cases. The concept of "case management" was the single most important recommendation to emerge from the "Access to Justice" Reports. This recommendation was based on the conclusion that the problems in the civil justice system could be remedied if many detailed changes were made to existing practices and procedures and that those changes could only be rendered effective in the context of a "managed system of dispute resolution" (see notes to rr.1.1 to 1.3 above). In the "Access to Justice" Reports, the concept of case management was not defined and it was used in broad and narrow senses depending on the context in which it was applied (for a statement of the objectives of case management in the broad sense, see Interim Report, p. 30). To an extent, the inconsistency which resulted is perpetuated in the CPR. 1.4.1

It is perhaps understandable that, having stated in r.1.4(1) that the overriding duty is to be furthered by a case management system, the rules should go on to give some indication as to what is meant by "actively managing cases". Thus r.1.4(2) contains a list of what could be called case management "elements" or "objectives"; it is not exhaustive. The list is not prescriptive. It summarises objectives which are implemented in many and various ways by provisions found throughout the CPR and related practice directions. The list has no logic about it. Further, the matters stated are not at the same level of abstraction; some are quite general, others quite detailed. Rule 1.4(2) does not confer powers on the court. In this respect it may be contrasted with r.3.1(2) which lists the court's "general powers of case management". Those powers are in addition to any other powers given to the court (including those derived from the inherent jurisdiction) and include the power "to take any other step or make any or order for the purpose of managing the case and furthering the overriding objective" (r.3.1(2)(m)). The powers listed in r.3.1(2) include powers not generally thought of as being properly described as aspects of the "management" of cases and which have long been part of English civil procedure (*e.g.* the powers to consolidate proceedings or to direct the separate trial of any issue).

As is explained below, the provenance for much of what is said in r.1.4(2) is a passage in the Final Report. In that report it was said (p. 18) that the principal "essential element" of the recommended case management system is the procedure by which each case is allocated to an appropriate "track" and court (whether High Court or a county court). Detailed provisions relating to this element are found in Pts 26 to 29 and related practice directions. It was said, further, that other essential elements of the recommended case management system include (a) "encouraging and assisting the parties to settle cases or, at least, to agree on particular issues", (b) "identifying at an early stage the key issues which need full trial", (c) "summarily disposing of weak cases and hopeless issues", (d) "fixing and enforcing strict timetables for procedural steps leading to trial and for the trial itself", and (e) "encouraging the use of ADR". Detailed provisions reflecting these elements are found throughout the CPR and cannot be easily summarised.

In the list of case management objectives given in r.1.4(2) no mention is made of the principal essential element but the other essential elements are covered in paras (a) to (c) and (e) to (g). The remaining paragraphs in r.1.4(2) refer to other matters which may be regarded as "elements" of the case management system introduced by the CPR. However, the means by which these elements have been identified and the reasoning behind their inclusion (and the exclusion of other possible elements) is not immediately apparent. The result is that the purpose of r.1.4(2) is rendered obscure. It at least has the advantage of drawing to the attention of parties, lawyers and judges important aspects of the wholesale reforms in civil justice introduced by the CPR. Some Practice Directions speak of r.1.4 as imposing "duties" on the court.

1.4.2 **Controlling progress of case**—In the common law world, the expression "case management" is used in various senses. The significance of case management procedures is that they mark a change from the traditional position under which the progress of cases was left largely in the hands of the parties. In its narrow sense, "case management" means the exercise by the court of powers given to it to enable it, and not the parties, to dictate the progress of cases at the pre-trial stage, ensuring that the practices and procedures applicable during that stage are complied with promptly and not abused. Under the CPR, the expression "case management" is used in a much wider sense. The powers given to the court go far beyond those necessary merely to ensure the avoidance of unnecessary delay and include powers to manipulate the application of pre-trial procedures on a case by case basis, principally in the interest of saving costs and reducing delays. Case management in its narrow sense is encapsulated by r.1.4(2)(g) which states that active case management includes the "controlling" of "the progress of the case" by the court by "fixing timetables or otherwise".

As was the case in the RSC and CCR (and in former practice directions), many provisions in the CPR (and related practice directions) stipulate that particular steps in the proceedings must be taken within time limits. Traditionally, these time limits were not self-enforcing and, on the whole, securing compliance was regarded as a matter for the party disadvantaged or inconvenienced by the delay. The case management Practice Directions issued in 1995 marked a shift towards a court controlled approach to case progress (see SCP 1999, Vol. 2, para. 2C–22). Under the new scheme, the court is able to monitor the progress of cases from an early stage in the proceedings and compliance with time limits stipulated in rules, practice directions and bespoke orders is not solely a matter for the parties, even where they are in agreement. The power to control case progress "by fixing timetables or otherwise" is a power which complements and supplements the time limits stipulated by rules and practice directions. Rule 28.2(1) states that, when the court allocates a case to the fast track, the court will give directions (dealing with the matters listed in r.28.3) for the management of the case and set a timetable for the steps to be taken between the giving of directions and the trial and r.29.2 has a similar effect in relation to multi-track cases. These are the most obvious of the provisions implementing the power referred to in r.1.4(2)(g). Other opportunities for the court to give case progress directions (of its own initiative if necessary), including directions laying down timetables, arise at various points in the pre-trial process; for example, after determining a summary judgment application (r.24.6(b)), after expiration of a stay to allow for settlement (r.26.4(5)), and after a defence to a Pt 20 claim is filed (r.20.13). Where a party fails to comply with a rule, practice direction or court order, including a rule etc. imposing a time limit, any sanction for that failure has effect unless the party in default applies for and obtains relief from the sanction (r.3.8(1)). Where a party is required to do something within a specified time and a consequence for failing to comply is specified, the time may not be extended by agreement between the parties (r.3.8(2)).

Note also "Dealing simultaneously with as many aspects of case as practicable" below, para. 1.4.14.

1.4.3 **Trial directions**—Active case management includes the court "giving directions to ensure that the trial of a case proceeds quickly and efficiently" (r.1.4(2)(l)). It is important that the time of judges available for the hearing of trials should be used as efficiently as possible. Various provisions in the CPR are designed to ensure that trials are not prolonged. Perhaps the most striking is the provision (formerly found in practice directions) that normally a witness's statement should stand as his evidence in chief (see now r.32.5(2)). Further, in cases allocated to the fast track, the expectation is that the trial will last for no longer than one day (r.26.6(6)). Obviously, the time taken to try a case can be affected by orders made before trial, for example, orders as to the number of expert witnesses, and as to the extent of disclosure of documents. Illustrations of the power of the court to give directions specifically designed to ensure that the trial of a case proceeds not only quickly but also efficiently are found in rr.28.6 and 29.8; these rules deal, respectively, with fast track and multi-track cases, and include power to give any directions for the trial, including a trial timetable. Such timetables are to be set by the court in consultation with the parties (r.39.4). Unless the trial judge otherwise directs, the trial will be conducted in accordance with any order previously made (rr.28.7 and 29.9).

1.4.4 **Encouraging co-operation between parties**—Active case management includes encouraging the parties to co-operate with each other in the conduct of the proceedings (r.1.4(2)(a)). In the Interim Report it was recommended that the court should use its power over costs to encourage co-operative conduct on the part of litigants and to discourage unreasonable conduct, both before and after proceedings have been commenced (p. 204, see also Final Report, p. 79). These recommendations are brought into effect by rr.44.3 and 44.5 and by other provisions in the CPR. The objective is to make the court's powers as to the award of costs more effective as incentives for responsible party behaviour and more compelling as deterrents against unreasonable behaviour (see further "Cost-benefit of taking particular step" below, para. 1.4.10). It may be noted that r.44.3(4) makes particular mention of the extent to which the parties followed any relevant pre-action protocol. The increased powers given to the court to order disclosure of documents or inspection of property before a claim is made (brought about by amendments to the Supreme Court Act 1981, s.33 and the County Court Act 1981, s.52) have been introduced partly for the purpose of encouraging co-operation between the parties (Interim Report, p. 151) (see further notes to rr.25.1 and 25.4). Rule 1.4(2)(a) can be regarded as a pointed illustration of the duty of the parties to help the court further the overriding objective imposed by r.1.3.

Various provisions in the CPR encourage party co-operation once proceedings have been commenced. A good illustration is provided by r.29.4 which states that the court may approve without a hearing proposals agreed by the parties for the management of proceedings on the multi-track and give directions in the terms proposed. Other illustrations include r.15.5 (agreement extending period for filing defence) and r.26.4 (agreement to request stay to allow for settlement of case), and r.35.7 (agreement on single joint expert). The efforts made by the parties to resolve their dispute is a factor to which the court should have regard in deciding the amount of costs (r.44.5(3)(a)).

Identification, clarification and ordering of issues—Paragraphs (b) to (d) of r.1.4(2) go together. The court must further the overriding objective by actively managing cases. In a given case, this includes the court doing the following things in relation to the issues: (1) at an early stage in the proceedings, "identifying the issues" (para. (b)); (2) promptly classifying those issues according to whether (a) they "need full investigation and trial" or (b) they may be disposed of summarily (para. (c)); and (3) deciding "the order in which issues are to be resolved" (para. (d)). The provenance of paras (b) to (d) is a passage in the Final Report (pp. 14 and 16) in which the matters mentioned therein are said to be "essential elements" of the recommendations made as to case management. These elements are made operational by their incorporation in the provisions of the CPR and related practice directions in various ways. **1.4.5**

Early identification of issues—Under the case management system introduced by the CPR and related practice directions, the court is involved in the process of identifying and clarifying the issues between the parties from an early stage in the proceedings. In recent years, the involvement of the court in the early identification of issues has become a feature of the interlocutory procedure applied in certain types of proceedings (*e.g. Practice Direction (Medical Negligence)*; see SCP 1999, Vol. 2, para. 2A–123). Under the CPR proceedings are started when a claim form is issued. The expression "statements of case" is used to describe what were formerly known as "pleadings". Such statements include "particulars of claim", "defence" and "reply to defence" (see Pt 16). It is important that the parties should state plainly the factual ingredients of their case so that the true nature of the dispute can be identified because, on the basis of the information given in the statement of claim and the defence, the court will allocate the case to an appropriate case management track (Pt 26). For the purpose of clarifying the issues so that the case may be allocated to an appropriate track, the court may require a party to provide further information about his case and may hold an allocation hearing. The court's concern with identifying issues does not cease once a case is allocated to a case management track but, in the interests of encouraging settlement and of minimising the burden on the court at trial, continues throughout the pre-trial process generally. **1.4.6**

Full investigation or summary disposal of issues—In Practice Direction (Case Management—Preliminary Stage: Allocation and Re-Allocation) (see para. 26PD–001) it is explained in para. 5.2 that the court's powers to make orders for the summary disposal of issues which do not need "full investigation and trial" include the power under r.3.4 to strike out a statement of case, or part of a statement of a case, and the power to give summary judgment where a claimant or defendant has no reasonable prospect of success in accordance with the provisions in Pt 24. The court may use these powers on an application or of its own initiative. The court's general powers of case management as listed in r.3.1(2) includes the power to "exclude an issue from consideration". **1.4.7**

Order in which issues resolved—The court's general powers of case management as listed in r.3.1(2) includes the power to direct that part of any proceeding be dealt with as separate proceedings and to decide the order in which issues are to be tried (paras (e), (i) and (j)). These powers are familiar. When utilised they have the effect of adjusting the order in which issues are resolved. (As to trial of counterclaim, see r.20.9.) Rule 3.1(2) also states that the court may consolidate proceedings or try two or more claims on the same occasion (paras (g) and (h)). Again, these are familiar powers. They may be used to enable the resolution together of issues which otherwise would be resolved separately. **1.4.8**

Helping parties to settle—Active case management includes helping the parties to settle the whole or part of the case (r.1.4(2)(f)). Two significant aims of the recommendations made in the "Access to Justice" Reports are (1) that of encouraging the resolution of disputes before they come to litigation, and (2) that of encouraging the settlement of claims commenced (Final Report, p. 16). Provisions in the CPR designed to achieve the former aim include those expanding pre-litigation disclosures (r.25.1(1)(i) and (j) and rr.31.16 and 31.17) and those encouraging greater use of alternative dispute resolution procedures (see "Encouraging use of alternative dispute resolution (ADR) procedure" below). Provisions designed to achieve the latter aim include those providing for claimants' offers to settle (Pt 36) and for the summary disposal of issues so as to narrow the dispute. All of these devices are intended to divert cases from **1.4.9**

the court system or to ensure that those cases which do go through the system are disposed of as rapidly as possible (Final Report, *ibid.*).

1.4.10 **Cost-benefits of taking particular step**—Active case management includes considering whether the likely benefits of taking a particular step justify the cost of taking it (r.1.4(2)(h)). This can be regarded as an aspect of "proportionality" (see "Proportionality", para. 1.3.5 above). Virtually all of the recommendations made in the "Access to Justice" Reports and implemented by the CPR are designed to tackle the problem of costs. In the Interim Report it was recommended that the court's discretion as to costs should be exercised so that parties were encouraged to conduct litigation "in a proportionate manner" and to discourage "excess" (see too Final Report, p. 80). Rule 44.3 now provides that in exercising its costs discretion the court should consider the conduct of all the parties and this includes taking into account the several matters listed in r.44.3(4) (see too r.43.6). In terms, that paragraph does not repeat r.1.4(2)(h). However, it achieves a similar result by stating that the conduct of a party includes the manner in which he has pursued or defended his case or a particular allegation or issue, and whether it was reasonable for him to raise, pursue or contest a particular allegation or issue. Cases allocated to the small claims track or to the fast track are conducted according to limited procedures. Necessarily, the question whether the benefits of a particular step justified the taking of it is more likely to arise in multi-track cases. All cases on all case management tracks proceed according to a pre-trial timetable. The effect of this discipline alone is likely to discourage parties from attempting to take steps where their likely benefits do not justify the cost of taking it.

Despite the futurity apparent in the terms of r.1.4(2)(h) that provision does not give the court a general power to prevent a party form taking a particular step otherwise open to him (whether it involves making an application to the court or not). The rules as to costs constitute the principal mechanism by which parties are encouraged to conduct litigation in a proportionate manner and by which excess is discouraged and those rules take effect after the event (but, of course, their expected application may modify party conduct prospectively). However, in particular contexts the court does have specific powers clearly aimed at these ends. The best illustrations are found in the powers given to the court in Pt 31 to regulate the disclosure of documents. Further, to an extent, a party can protect himself from demands made on him by his opponent as to disclosure on the grounds that they make expectations of him which are onerous and which are not justified in the circumstances of the case (see rr.31.3(2) and 31.7(3)).

Where the "particular step" taken by a party consists of an application to the court and that application fails the costs of the application would normally be awarded against that party. Where the application was clearly unjustified the court may assess those costs and order them to be paid forthwith.

1.4.11 **Encouraging use of alternative dispute resolution (ADR) procedure**—The furthering of the overriding objective (of enabling the court to deal with cases justly) by "actively managing cases", includes encouraging the parties to use an alternative dispute resolution (ADR) procedure "if the court considers that appropriate" and facilitating the use of such procedure (r.1.4(2)(e)) (see Interim Report, pp. 136 *et seq.*). In the Glossary, the meaning given to the expression "alternative dispute resolution" is "collective description of methods of resolving disputes otherwise than through the normal trial process".

By definition, disputes between parties are adversarial in the sense that one party is opposed to another. A large proportion of the business of the courts (but by no means all) consists of the adjudication of disputes. Adjudication involves the intervention of a third party in the form of a judge. Adjudication takes place according to law (substantive, jurisdictional and adjectival). Disputes may be, and usually are, resolved by the parties themselves, and this is so even where legal proceedings have been commenced by one party or another. Broadly speaking, where the culmination of the adjudicative process (*i.e.* a trial at law) is avoided, whether in the course of trial, on the steps of the court, or at some earlier stage, it is because the parties negotiated a resolution to their dispute. Procedural law encourages resolution by negotiation. Indeed, the pre-trial process (though preparatory to trial) can be regarded as an alternative method to trial for the resolution of disputes (and a highly effective one).

Negotiation is a dispute resolution procedure and it is the principal "alternative" method to adjudication by the courts. It is a method which may, or may not, involve the assistance of others, for example, legal representatives of the parties. In modern times, increasing attention has been given to dispute resolution procedures alternative to adjudication by the courts (ADR) and involving third parties, for example, mediators. Such methods are many and various. Some are very much akin to negotiation and others are virtually informal forms of adjudication. As dispute resolution methods, they have some attributes not shared, on the one hand, by simple negotiation between the parties, and, on the other, by adjudication by the courts (and attendant pre-trial procedures). Not least of these attributes are the possibility of reducing the costs incurred by parties and the potential for relieving the courts of business. In the Interim Report it was said that the range and availability of ADR procedures should be increased.

As was explained in the Final Report (p. 11), for some time before the CPR came into force, resort by parties involved in litigation to ADR methods had been encouraged by the courts. By *Practice Statement* [1994] 1 W.L.R. 14, a practice was introduced in the Commercial Court, and developed subsequently, under which parties were expected to take seriously the possibility of resolving particular issues in the case, if not the whole claim, by ADR procedures, particularly where the costs of the litigation were likely to be wholly disproportionate to the amount at stake. In providing information to the court on the summons for directions, and in completing pre-trial check-lists, parties were required to indicate whether they had considered ADR (see SCP 1999, Vol. 2, paras 72/2/4, 72/A24, 72/A38, 72/A41, 72/A50 and 72/A52). Later on, a similar practice was introduced elsewhere in the High Court, notably by the two case management practice directions issued in 1995, *Practice Direction (Civil Litigation: Case Management)* [1995] 1 W.L.R. 508, and *Practice Direction (Chancery Division: Procedure and Case Management)* [1995] 1 W.L.R. 785 (see SCP 1999, Vol. 1, paras 25/4/16 and 33/3/2, and Vol. 2, paras 2B–205, 2B–298, 2B–306 and 2B-307 and 2C–22), and in the Central London county court business list (see SCP 1999, Vol. 2, paras 2D–131 and 2D–153). (As to ADR in the Court of Appeal, see SCP 1999, Vol. 1, para. 59/9/68.) The CPR and the practice directions build on these earlier developments.

Once legal proceedings are commenced, the rules of court which apply and the case management powers available to the court, in various ways encourage settlement by simple negotiation between the parties. There is a belief that the quality of settlements might be improved and the incidence of settlements increased if recourse was had to ADR procedures during the pre-trial process. Accordingly, r.1.4(2)(e) states that active case management includes the court's encouragement of the parties to use ADR procedures "if the court considers that appropriate". Such encouragement may be given at various points in the procedure laid down in the CPR and related practice directions and may be given, either on the court's own initiative, or in response to an initiative of the parties (as to the latter, see r.26.4). The Glossary explains that ADR is a collective description of methods of resolving disputes "otherwise than through the normal trial process". In terms, this includes simple negotiation between the parties not involving third parties (apart from the parties' legal representatives). However, it would seem that the purpose of r.1.4(2)(e) is to draw attention to methods other than simple negotiation.

The hallmark of ADR procedures, and perhaps the key to their effectiveness in individual cases, is that they are processes voluntarily entered into by the parties in dispute with outcomes, if the parties so wish, which are non-binding. Consequently, the court cannot direct that such methods be used but may merely encourage and facilitate. Obviously, encouragement should not be given as a matter of course but only in the light of the overriding objective. A balance has to be struck. If the encouragement is perfunctory there is a risk that the parties will not take the possibility of using an ADR procedure seriously; if the encouragement is heavy-handed there is a risk that the parties' participation in an ADR procedure may not be truly voluntary.

The court may facilitate the use of an ADR procedure in two main ways. First, by ensuring that the opportunity to explore ADR prospects are not prejudiced by the rigours of case management procedures generally. Thus, for example, r.26.4 provides that a party, when completing the allocation questionnaire required by r.26.3, may make a written request for the proceedings to be stayed while the parties try to settle the case "by alternative dispute resolution or other means" (see Form N150 (Allocation Questionnaire) Section A). Secondly, the court can act as a source of information about professional and commercial bodies providing ADR services.

The encouragement and facilitating of ADR by the court is an aspect of active case management which in turn is an aspect of achieving the overriding objective. The parties have a duty to help the court in furthering that objective and, therefore, they have a duty to consider seriously the possibility of ADR procedures being utilised for the purpose of resolving their claim or particular issues within it when encouraged by the court to do so. The discharge of the parties' duty in this respect may be relevant to the question of costs because, when exercising its discretion as to costs, the court must have regard to all the circumstances, including the conduct of all the parties (r.44.3(4), see too r.44.5).

In a given case it is quite conceivable that, before legal proceedings were commenced, the parties may have made a genuine but unsuccessful attempt to reach agreement on an ADR procedure or, indeed, may have participated in such a procedure in an unsuccessful (or only partly successful) effort to settle their dispute. The failures in these respects should not blind the parties or the court to the possibility that an opportunity may arise during the pre-trial process (or even on appeal) when an ADR procedure might yet be used to good effect.

Recourse to ADR procedures after legal proceedings have been started may be expected to increase as litigation lawyers becomes more familiar with them and, in particular, with the ways in which they may be used to complement the adjudication process once proceedings have been started. (The prospects for developing ADR falls within the remit of one of the Civil Justice Council sub-committees.)

The Commercial Court Guide (5th ed.) Section G explains the approach of the Commercial Court to ADR and makes special reference to the use of "early neutral evaluation" facilities available in that Court (see para. D2–330). Similarly, the Chancery Guide (April 1999) explains the approach of the Chancery Division in ADR (see Chap. 17, para. D1–237).

Attendance at court—The furthering of the overriding objective (of enabling the court to deal with cases justly) by "actively managing cases", includes "dealing with the case without the parties needing to attend court" (r.1.4(1)(j)). Obviously, it is to the advantage of the court and of the parties and their legal advisers if attendances at court can be minimised. In certain circumstances, applications to the court may be dealt with without a hearing (*e.g.* r.23.8 & r.40.6(6)). **1.4.12**

Note also "Use of technology" below.

1.4.13 **Use of technology**—In the "Access to Justice" Reports, much was made of the importance of using computer-assisted technology to improve the efficiency of the administration of civil justice at all levels (see Interim Report, pp. 82 *et seq.* and Final Report, pp. 284 *et seq.*). Such technology may be used to advantage (1) by practitioners to assist them in the management of their cases, (2) by courts (a) for the purpose of recording information about individual cases, tracking their progress and ensuring deadlines are met, and (b) for the purpose of providing management information about pending business to aid forward planning of sittings and listing, and (3) by courts and parties to aid communication between one another. In addition, technology may be used in the court room itself to facilitate the presentation of evidence and argument. It could be argued that the very success of the reforms introduced by the CPR depends on technology, particularly on court-based technology to facilitate case management.

The furthering of the overriding objective (of enabling the court to deal with cases justly) by "actively managing cases", includes "making use of technology" (r.1.4(1)(k)). This objective is carried forward by rules and practice directions. The court's general powers of case management include the power to hold a hearing and receive evidence by telephone or by using any other method of direct oral communication (except where the rules provide otherwise) (r.3.1(2)(d)). As to telephone hearings of applications to the court and video conferencing, see *Practice Direction (Applications)* paras 6 and 7 (see para. 23PD–001). A further illustration of the use of technology is provided by r.32.3 which states that the court may allow a witness to give evidence through a video link or by other means.

As to use of information technology in the Chancery Division, see Chancery Guide (April 1999), Chap. 14 (para. D1–202).

1.4.14 **Dealing simultaneously with as many aspects of case as practicable**—See also "Order in which issues resolved" (para. 1.4.8 above).

The furthering of the overriding objective (of enabling the court to deal with cases justly) by "actively managing cases", includes "dealing with as many aspects of the case as is practicable on the same occasion" (r.1.4(1)(i)). During the pre-trial stages of cases the court stands ready to react to the needs of the parties by making necessary orders and directions. Further, under the case management system introduced by the CPR and related practice directions, the court is able to intervene of its own initiative in the pre-trial development and progress of cases. Usually, when the court reacts or intervenes it will be for a particular purpose; for example, to deal with an application made by one party and an application made by his opponent in response. Clearly, costs and delays would be increased and court resources wasted if, in dealing with a case for one purpose (whether by a hearing or otherwise), the court did not deal with other matters which had arisen or were looming and which required or justified the court's attention. Obviously, it is important that rules of court or practice directions should not be drafted in a way which prevents the court from dealing with multiple pre-trial issues on the same occasion. Further, it is important that parties and judges should not be encouraged to deal (perhaps for reasons of their own convenience only) with several "aspects" of a case on successive "occasions" where it would be practicable to deal with them on one "occasion". This aspect of case management is not new. However, it gains new significance now that the court has greater powers than heretofore to intervene in cases of its own initiative. Various provisions in the CPR illustrate the policy stated in r.1.4(2)(i) in operation. Examples include those rules which state that, when dealing with particular pre-trial matters, the court may, in addition, give directions as to the further progress of the case (see "Controlling progress of case", para. 1.4.2 above).

PART 2

Application and Interpretation of the Rules

Contents 2.0.1

Editorial Note

The rules in this Part contain provisions similar to those formerly found in RSC, O.1 and O.3 and CCR, O.1. 2.0.2

Part 2 is supplemented by Practice Direction (Court Offices) (see 2PD–001). Paras 2.1, 3.2 and 3.3 of this Practice Direction deal with court office opening hours and are relevant to r.2.8 (Time); the provenance of these provisions is explained in para. 2.8.4 below. Other provisions are not related to any of the rules in Pt. 2. Thus, para. 1 replaces RSC, O.63, r.1 (Distribution of business in the Central Office) (see SCP 1999, Vol. 1, para. 63/1/2), para. 2.2 replaces RSC, O.63, r.3 (Practice Master) (see SCP 1999, Vol. 1, para. 63/2/1) and r.3.1 replaces CCR, O.2, r.1 (County courts to have offices).

Part 2 is also supplemented by Practice Direction (Allocation of Cases to Levels of Judiciary) (see para. 28PD–001 below); for explanation, see notes following r.2.4 below.

Application of the Rules

2.1—(1) Subject to paragraph (2), these Rules apply to all proceedings in— 2.1

(a) county courts;

(b) the High Court; and

(c) the Civil Division of the Court of Appeal.

(2) These Rules do not apply to proceedings of the kinds specified in the first column of the following table (proceedings for which rules may be made under the enactments specified in the second column) except to the extent that they are applied to those proceedings by another enactment—

	Proceedings	Enactments
1.	Insolvency proceedings	Insolvency Act 1986, ss.411 and 412[1]
2.	Non-contentious or common form probate proceedings	Supreme Court Act 1981, s.127[2]

[1] 1986 c. 45.
[2] 1981 c. 54.

3.	Proceedings in the High Court when acting as a Prize Court	Prize Courts Act 1894, s.3[3]
4.	Proceedings before the judge within the meaning of Part VII of the Mental Health Act 1983[4]	Mental Health Act 1983, s.106
5.	Family proceedings	Matrimonial and Family Proceedings Act 1984, s.40[5]
6.	Adoption proceedings	Adoption Act 1976, s.66

2.1.1 **General note on application of rules (r.2.1)**—The Civil Procedure Rules 1998 (CPR) are made under the Civil Procedure Act 1997, s.1 (see SCP 1999, Vol. 2, para. 20A–5) and, in accordance with that provision, are to govern "the practice and procedure to be followed" in the courts mentioned in para. (1). Accordingly, they are "rules of court" as defined by the Interpretation Act 1978, s.5, Sched. 1. In r.1.1(1) they are described as "a new procedural code". Previously, proceedings in county courts were governed by the County Court Rules and in the High Court and Court of Appeal (Civil Division) by the Rules of the Supreme Court (RSC). The CPR constitute a single set of rules replacing the RSC and the CCR. The CPR contain much that is new (implementing recommendations made in the Access to Justice Reports) but also much that is the same as that formerly found in the RSC and the CCR. Most of what is new is found in Pts 1 to 49. The rules found in the Schedules (see Pt 50) incorporate in the CPR rules formerly found in the RSC and CCR (see, respectively, Scheds 1 and 2). The CPR are divided, not into Orders, but into Parts. A number of the Parts are supplemented by Practice Directions.

In terms, the RSC and CCR have not been repealed. To an extent they remain relevant to civil proceedings in the High Court and the county courts beyond the date when the CPR come into force (see Pt 51—Transitional Arrangements). Further, in so far as the RSC and CCR are incorporated by reference into other sets of rules they remain in effect.

2.1.2 **Specialist proceedings**—In r.49(1) it is said that the CPR shall apply to "specialist proceedings" subject to the provisions of the relevant practice direction which applies to those proceedings. In this context, "specialist proceedings" means the proceedings listed in r.49(2). They are: (a) admiralty proceedings, (b) arbitration proceedings, (c) commercial and mercantile actions, (d) Patents Court business, (e) Technology and Construction Court business (formerly Official Referees' business), (f) proceedings under the Companies Act 1985, and (g) contentious probate proceedings. Note also r.2.3(3) (definition of "specialist list"). See further notes to Pt 49 (Specialist Proceedings).

2.1.3 **Proceedings to which CPR do not apply**—Proceedings of the type referred to in the first column of the Table in r.2.1(2) may be taken either in the High Court or a county court (sometimes exclusively one or the other) and in the Court of Appeal. Such proceedings may be subject to rules of court made under the enactments referred to in the second column (see further below).

Paragraph (2) states that the CPR "do not apply to proceedings of the kinds specified in the first column" of the Table. This formulation follows that formerly found in RSC, O.2, r.2 (*cf.* CCR, O.1, r.2). Clearly, in certain circumstances rules in the CPR can and do apply to proceedings of the type referred to in the first column of the Table either expressly or by necessary implication.

2.1.4 ***Insolvency proceedings***—Under the Insolvency Act 1986, s.411 rules may be made in relation to England and Wales by the Lord Chancellor with the concurrence of the Secretary of State for the purposes of giving effect to Parts I to VIII of that Act (company insolvency and companies winding-up), and under s.412 for the purpose of giving effect to Parts VII to IX (insolvency of individuals, bankruptcy). Nothing in the Insolvency Act, s.411 or 412 prejudices any power to make rules of court. The Lord Chancellor is required to consult the Insolvency Rules Committee

[3] 1894 c. 39.
[4] 1983 c. 20.
[5] 1984 c. 42. Section 40 was amended by the Courts and Legal Services Act 1990 (c. 41), Schedule 18, paragraph 50

before making any rules under IA, s.411 or 412. The Insolvency Rules 1986 (S.I. 1986 No. 1925) were made under the Insolvency Act, s.411 and 412; numerous other sets of rules have been made, or are deemed to have been made, under IA, s.411. The former RSC were not excluded completely from winding-up proceedings. Indeed the RSC were incorporated by express reference into the Insolvency Rules 1986 by virtue of r.7.33 (O.62 to apply to insolvency proceedings in the High Court), r.7.59 (RSC to apply to payments into and out of court of money lodged as security for costs in insolvency proceedings in the High Court) and r.7.51 of those Rules (RSC and the practice of the High Court to apply to insolvency proceedings in the High Court except in so far as the same may be inconsistent with the Insolvency Rules).

Probate proceedings—Probate rules may be made under the Supreme Court Act 1981, s.127 for regulating and prescribing the practice and procedure of the High Court with respect to non-contentious or common form probate business. The Non-contentious Probate Rules 1987 (S.I. 1987 No. 2024) were made in exercise of this power (see SCP 1999, Vol. 2, para. 11B–1). **2.1.5**

Prize Court proceedings—Under the Prize Courts Act 1894, s.3, rules of court may be made for regulating, subject to the provisions of the Naval Prize Act 1894 and the 1894 Act, the procedure and practice of prize courts; see the Prize Court Rules 1939 (S.R. & O. No. 1466). **2.1.6**

Court of Protection proceedings—Proceedings for the management of property and affairs of patients may be taken before the Court of Protection in accordance with the Mental Health Act 1983, Pt VII. Section 106 provides that proceedings before the judge are to be conducted in accordance with rules of procedure; see Court of Protection Rules (S.I. 1994 No. 3046) (see SCP 1999, Vol. 2, para. 10C–1). **2.1.7**

Family proceedings—The Matrimonial and Family Proceedings Act 1984, s.40 gives power to make rules of court for the purposes of family proceedings in the High Court or county courts (see SCP 1997, Vol. 2, para. 7–773). The Family Proceedings Rules 1991 (S.I. 1991 No. 1247) were made in exercise of this power (see SCP 1997, Vol. 2, para. 7–002). Rule 1.3 of the FPR states that, subject to the provisions of those rules and any enactment, the CCR and the RSC shall apply, with the necessary modifications, to family proceedings in a county court and the High Court respectively. Further, for these purposes, any provision of the FPR authorising or requiring anything to be done in family proceedings shall be treated as if it were, in the case of proceedings pending in a county court, a provision of the CCR and, in the case of proceedings pending in the High Court, a provision of the RSC. **2.1.8**

Adoption proceedings—The Adoption Act 1976 was a consolidating measure, bringing together the law of adoption as found in several Acts of Parliament, including the Adoption Act 1958. Section 9 of the 1958 Act consolidated several former rule-making powers and provided that Adoption Rules shall be made by the Lord Chancellor; see now section 66 of the 1976 Act. Former CCR, O.1, r.2(2) stated that, in relation to proceedings of a particular kind in county courts (*e.g.* adoption proceedings), the CCR should have effect subject to any rules made by an authority other than the County Rules Committee (*e.g.* the Adoption Rules). As a result of the Civil Procedure (Amendment) Rules 1999 (S.I. 1999 No. 1008), r.2, the effect of that provision is preserved in this context by r.2.1(2). **2.1.9**

The glossary

2.2—(1) The glossary at the end of these Rules is a guide to the meaning of certain legal expressions used in the Rules, but is not to be taken as giving those expressions any meaning in the Rules which they do not have in the law generally. **2.2** p.1470

(2) Subject to paragraph (3), words in these Rules which are included in the glossary are followed by “GL”.

(3) The words “counterclaim”, “damages”, “practice form” and “service”, which appear frequently in the Rules, are included in the glossary but are not followed by “GL”.

Interpretation

2.3—(1) In these Rules— **2.3**

“child” has the meaning given by rule 21.1(2);

“claim for personal injuries” means proceedings in which there is a claim for damages in respect of personal injuries to the claimant or any other person or in respect of a person’s death, and “personal injuries" includes any disease and any impairment of a person's physical or mental condition;

"claimant" means a person who makes a claim;

"CCR" is to be interpreted in accordance with Part 50;

"court officer" means a member of the court staff;

"defendant" means a person against whom a claim is made;

"defendant's home court" means—

(a) if the claim is proceeding in a county court, the county court for the district in which the defendant's address for service, as shown on the defence, is situated; and

(b) if the claim is proceeding in the High Court, the district registry for the district in which the defendant's address for service, as shown on the defence, is situated or, if there is no such district registry, the Royal Courts of Justice;

(Rule 6.5 provides for a party to give an address for service.)

"filing", in relation to a document, means delivering it, by post or otherwise, to the court office;

"judge" means, unless the context otherwise requires, a judge, Master or district judge or a person authorised to act as such;

"jurisdiction" means, unless the context requires otherwise, England and Wales and any part of the territorial waters of the United Kingdom adjoining England and Wales;

"legal representative" means a barrister or a solicitor, solicitor's employee or other authorised litigator (as defined in the Courts and Legal Services Act 1990[6]) who has been instructed to act for a party in relation to a claim;

"litigation friend" has the meaning given by Part 21;

"patient" has the meaning given by rule 21.1(2);

"RSC" is to be interpreted in accordance with Part 50;

"statement of case"—

(a) means a claim form, particulars of claim where these are not included in a claim form, defence, Part 20 claim, or reply to defence; and

(b) includes any further information given in relation to them voluntarily or by court order under rule 18.1;

"statement of value" is to be interpreted in accordance with rule 16.3;

"summary judgment" is to be interpreted in accordance with Part 24.

(2) A reference to a "specialist list" is a reference to a list[GL] that has been designated as such by a relevant practice direction.

(3) Where the context requires, a reference to "the court" means a reference to a particular county court, a district registry, or the Royal Courts of Justice.

2.3.1 **General note on interpretation of rules (rr. 2.2 and 2.3)**—In the Interim Report it was said (at p. 215) that the exercise of drafting the single procedural code involved three specific objectives. They were: (a) to identify the core propositions in the rules and to cut down the number of interconnecting provisions which are used; (b) to provide procedures which apply to the broadest possible range of cases and to reduce the number of instances in which a separate regime is provided for a special type of case; and (c) to reduce the size of the rules and the number of propositions contained in them, to remove verbiage and to adopt a simpler and plainer style of drafting. The Interim Report said (*ibid.*) that these specific objectives can only be fully achieved if a new approach is taken by the judges applying the rules under a managed system of litigation. Instead of the over-technical way the rules have been applied in the past, "the new rules will have to be used in a different way: they will have to be read as a whole, not dissected and viewed word by word under a microscope". The new rules have been deliberately framed so that the approach of those construing them can be more purposive and less technical. It will thus be the responsibility of the judiciary to make the new system work. In *James Buchanan & Co. Ltd v. Babco Forwarding and Shipping (UK) Ltd* [1977] Q.B. 208, Lord Denning M.R. explained that under

[6] 1990 c. 41.

the purposive method of interpretation the judges do not go by the literal meaning of the words or by the grammatical structure of the sentence. They go by the design or purpose behind it. When they come upon a situation which is to their minds within the spirit but not the letter of the legislation, they solve the problem by looking at the effect it was sought to achieve. "They then interpret the legislation so as to produce the desired effect. This means they fill in gaps, quite unashamedly, without hesitation. They ask simply: what is the sensible way of dealing with this situation so as to give effect to the presumed purpose of the legislation?"

In the Interim Report it was said (at p. 217) that it will be of fundamental importance that the new rules "are not hidebound by previous authorities on the old rules". It was also said that the procedural innovations in the CPR "will make most of the old authorities redundan". Doubtless that is an exaggeration. However, to the extent that provisions in the CPR are shorter and more clearly expressed than the provisions in the RSC and CCR they replace, the task of the judge and practitioner should be made easier. Furthermore, the plainer, simpler form of drafting of the new rules should mean "that there should be less need to seek instructions from the courts on what the rules mean" (Interim Report, p. 217). It is clear that many provisions in the CPR have been drafted on the assumption that previous case law will continue to apply. This is particularly true of provisions that simply re-enact in simpler language procedural rules which drew no criticism in the "Access to Justice" Reports. It is also largely true of the case law on former RSC and CCR provisions incorporated in Scheds 1 and 2 of the CPR. The case law on extending time limits and procedural sanctions (striking out, etc.) has always been of particular concern to practitioners. Such case law will continue to provide the most relevant source of guidance on the application of procedural sanctions in the many and various situations which arise. Clearly, in some respects such case law may cease to be applicable where the new rules incorporate new tests.

In the Final Report it was said (at p. 275) that the CPR are deliberately not designed expressly to answer every question which could arise. The statement of the overriding objective in those rules (see rr.1.1 and 1.2 and notes thereto) "provides a compass to guide courts and litigants and legal advisers as to their general course" (see further "Interpretation to give effect to overriding objective", para. 2.3.3 below).

The Civil Procedure Act 1997, s.2(7) states that the rule committee when making rules must "try to make rules which are both simple and simply expressed". The former RSC and CCR contained provisions of general application giving definitions of particular expressions (see former RSC, O.1, r.4 and CCR, O.1, r.3) and particular expressions were specially defined in the context of particular rules. Further, definitions were incorporated by reference from the Supreme Court Act 1981 and the County Courts Act 1984. Also, certain expressions in the former RSC and CCR received authoritative definition in decided cases.

The definitions given in r.2.3 apply throughout the CPR. Other words and phrases are defined in context. For example, in the text of Pt 23 (General rules about applications for court orders) "application notice" and "respondent" are defined in r.23.1.

Glossary—The Glossary at the end of the rules contains a number of legal expressions, some of which were defined in rules replaced by the CPR. It is expressly provided that the meanings given there are meant as guides only and do not give those expressions "any meaning in the Rules which they do not have in the law generally". **2.3.2**

Interpretation to give effect to overriding objective—The overriding objective is stated in r.1.1. It is specifically provided that the court must seek to give effect to the overriding objective, not only when it exercises any power given to it by the CPR, but also when it interprets any rule (r.1.2(b)). In the Final Report it was said (at p. 274) that every word in the rules of court should have a purpose, but every word cannot be given "a minutely exact meaning". Civil procedure involves more judgment and knowledge than rules can directly express. Ultimately their purpose is to guide the court and litigants towards the just resolution of the case. Although rules of court can offer detailed directions for the technical steps to be taken, the effectiveness of those steps depends upon the spirit in which they are carried out. That in turn depends on an understanding of the fundamental purpose of the rules and of the underlying system of procedure. **2.3.3**

Interpretation Act 1978—Former RSC, O.1, r.3 stated that the 1978 Act should apply to the interpretation of those rules. The CPR contain no such provision but, for the reasons which follow, the effect is the same. The provisions of the 1978 Act, except ss.1 to 3 and 4(b), apply, so far as applicable and unless the contrary intention appears, to subordinate legislation made after January 1, 1979 (s.23(1)). In this context, "subordinate legislation" includes rules made under any Act (s.21(1)). Consequently, those provisions in the 1978 Act apply to the CPR. Section 5 of the Act states that, in any Act (or subordinate legislation), unless the contrary intention appears, words and expressions listed in Sched. 1 to the Act are to be construed according to that Schedule. Several words and expressions in Sched. 1 are relevant to matters of practice and procedure dealt with by the CPR. Note also s.7 (references to service by post). **2.3.4**

Section 11 of the 1978 Act states that, where an Act confers power to make subordinate legislation, expressions used in that legislation have, unless the contrary intention appears, the meaning which they bear under the Act. By operation of this section, expressions used in the CPR have, unless the contrary intention appears, the meaning which they bear under the Civil Procedure Act 1997. It would seem that IA 1978, s.11 does not have the effect of incorporating into the CPR meanings assigned to expressions found in the Supreme Court Act 1981 (particularly by s.151) or in the County Courts Act 1984 (particularly by s.147).

Words and expressions defined in r.2.3(1)

2.3.5 *"child"*—The words "child", "infant" and "minor" have been used to describe a person who has not attained the age of 18 years (Family Law Reform Act 1969, ss.1(1) and 1(2). Since the enactment of the Children Act 1989, in the drafting of legislation "child" appears to be the preferred word and is used throughout the CPR (see particularly Pt 21).

2.3.6 *"claim for personal injuries"*—By this definition (which follows that given in RSC, O.1, r. 4(1)), a "claim for personal injuries" means proceedings in which one or other of the following claims for damages are made: (1) a claim in respect of personal injuries to the claimant, (2) a claim in respect of personal injuries to any other person, and (3) a claim in respect of a person's death. Proceedings raising claims of this nature form a significant proportion of the courts' caseloads and, for case management purposes, are subject to special rules of practice and procedure in a number of respects.

Claims for personal injuries are referred to at various places in the CPR (see *e.g.* r.16.3(3) (statement of value in claim form), r.19.4(4) (addition or substitution of parties after limitation period), r.25.7(2) (interim payments) and r.26.6(1)(a) & (2) (allocation of claims to small claims track)).

The expression "personal injuries" includes, not only personal injuries in the strict sense, but also"any disease and any impairment of a person's physical or mental condition". In this respect the definition follows important statutory provisions of long-standing (*e.g.* Law Reform (Miscellaneous Provisions) Act 1934, s.3 (as amended) (interest on damages), Law Reform (Personal Injury) Act 1948, ss.2 and 3 (measure of damages), Supreme Court Act 1981, s.35(5) and Limitation Act 1980, s.38(1)).

A "claim for personal injuries" includes proceedings in which a claim for damages is made in respect of personal injuries, not to the claimant, but to "any other person". This follows the definition given in the Limitation Act 1980, s.11 (special time limit for actions in respect of personal injuries). For an illustration of such a claim, see *Howe v. David Brown Tractors (Retail) Ltd* [1991] 4 All E.R. 30, CA, at 42, *per* Nicholls L.J.

A "claim for personal injuries" includes proceedings in which a claims for damages is made "in respect of a person's death". It would seem that what is meant here is an action under the Fatal Accidents Act 1976 (see Limitation Act 1980, s.12, *cf.*, Limitation Act 1963, s.3(2)).

The claim for damages must be "in respect of" personal injuries or a person's death. Guidance as to what is meant by "in respect of" in this context may be gained from cases on statutory provisions containing this phrase. For example, *Ackbar v. C.F. Green & Co. Ltd* [1975] Q.B. 582; *Pattison v. Hobbs, The Times*, November 11, 1985, CA; and *Howe v. David Brown Tractors (Retail) Ltd* [1991] 4 All E.R. 30, CA, dealing with the Limitation Act 1980, s.11 (special time limit for actions in respect of personal injuries), and *Paterson v. Chadwick* [1974] 1 W.L.R. 890, dealing with the Supreme Court Act 1981, s.34 and County Courts Act 1984, s.53 (power of court to order disclosure of documents etc. by non-party in proceedings in which claim made in respect of personal injuries). See further SCP 1999, Vol. 1, para. 1/4/9.

2.3.7 *"claimant" "defendant"*—Whereas previously proceedings were started by the court issuing a writ or a summons (or some other form of originating process) under the CPR proceedings are started by the court issuing a "claim" in the prescribed form (Final Report, p. 116). A person who makes a claim is referred to in these rules as a "claimant" and the person against whom a claim is made as a "defendant" (see r.7.2). Part 23 contains general rules about applications for court orders. An application is made by an "application notice" against a "respondent". Both of these terms are defined in r.23.1. By necessary implication, an application is made by an "applicant", but that term is not defined in Pt 23.

2.3.8 *"court officer"*—See r.2.5 and notes thereto.

2.3.9 *"defendant's home court"*—The concept of the "home court" was used in the CCR (see CCR, O.1, rr.3 and 13) and is carried forward into the CPR with modifications. References to "the defendant's home court" are found in Pt 14 (Admissions) (rr.14.12 and 14.13) and in CCR, O.22, r.10 (Variation of payment), a CCR provision which survives in Sched. 2 of the CPR. See also r.13.4 (Application to set aside or vary judgment procedure), where the definition of "defendant's home court" is varied slightly (by r.13.4(1A)).

2.3.10 *"statement of value"*—A claimant claiming an unspecified amount of money must include on the claim form a certificate, known as a "statement of value", stating that he believes that there is good reason for him to expect to recover amounts falling in particular bands (r.16.3). The purpose of the statement is to facilitate the allocation of the claim to an appropriate case management track.

"the court"—Rule 2.3(3) states that, where in these rules the context requires, a reference to "the court" means a reference to a particular county court, a district registry, or the Royal Courts of Justice. On the face of it, this seems a curious provision. However, in certain contexts in the CPR it is convenient. (It provides good illustration of the difficulties inherent in marrying together rules of court applicable to a superior court with those applicable to inferior courts.) The CPR apply to all proceedings in county courts, in the High Court and in the Civil Division of the Court of Appeal (r.2.1(1)). The High Court is a superior court and, therefore, notionally, there is one High Court and, though it is based at the RCJ in London, its business (and the business of the Court of Appeal) may be conducted at "any place in England and Wales" (Supreme Court Act 1981, ss.57 and 67). The principal registry of the High Court, known as the Central Office of the Supreme Court (Supreme Court Act 1981, s.96) is located at the RCJ in London. (The Central Office was established by the Supreme Court of Judicature (Officers) Act 1879, s.4 (see SCP 1999, Vol. 2, para. 63/0/2).) By the Supreme Court Act 1981, s.99, the Lord Chancellor has power by order to direct that there will be a district registry of the High Court at such places and for such county court district as are specified in the order to support the business of the High Court conducted at provincial court centres (see Civil Courts Order 1983 (S.I. 1983 No. 713) (as amended) (see SCP 1999, Vol. 2, para. 18C–1). 2.3.11

The county courts, on the other hand, are inferior courts with limited legal jurisdiction and limited territorial jurisdiction, and, therefore, there are many county court districts, each with at least one county court. Over the years, the limits on the legal jurisdiction of county courts have been relaxed and the problems inherent in the territorial limits on jurisdiction have been largely overcome, mainly by rules enabling the easy movement of cases from court to court. The CPR contain rules of court applicable to proceedings both in the High Court and in the county courts. In various contexts it is convenient if the expression "the court" can be taken to mean, not only the county courts (wherever located) and the High Court, but also the High Court either at the RCJ or at a location where a district registry of the High Court is situated (see, particularly, Pt 30 (Transfer)).

"legal representative"—Note also distinction between "a lawyer" and "a lay representative" in Practice Direction (Small Claims Track) para. 3.1 (27PD–001). 2.3.12

"statement of case"—It would seem that there may be further statements of case subsequent to a reply to a defence, even though the definition in r.2.3(1) does not extent to this (see r.15.9 and note para. 22.1.7 below). 2.3.13

Specialist lists (r.2.3(2))—The Glossary explains that cases are allocated to different "lists" depending on the subject-matter of the proceedings. Such lists are used for administrative purposes and may also have their own procedures and judges. Rule 2.3(2) states that a reference in the CPR to a "specialist list" is a reference to a list that has been designated as such by a relevant practice direction. The most obvious of the specialist lists are those that relate to what are called "specialist proceedings"; see Pt 49. The provisions of the CPR are to be applied subject to the practice directions which apply to those proceedings. Numerous references to "specialist lists" are found throughout the CPR and related practice directions (*e.g.* r.16.3(5) (Statement of value in claim form issued in High Court) and r.30.5 (Transfer between Divisions and to and from a specialist list)). For the purposes of the CPR, the list of a Mercantile Court and the business list of an authorised county court is a "specialist list" (Practice Direction (Mercantile Courts and Business Lists) para. 1.4 (see 49HPD–001). 2.3.14

Power of judge, Master or district judge to perform functions of the court

2.4 Where these Rules provide for the court to perform any act then, except where an enactment, rule or practice direction provides otherwise, that act may be performed— 2.4

(a) in relation to proceedings in the High Court, by any judge, Master or district judge of that Court; and

(b) in relation to proceedings in a county court, by any judge or district judge.

Effect of rule—Throughout the CPR, references are made to the "court", rather than to a judge or to a particular court (whether the High Court, a county court, or the Court of Appeal) except where it is necessary to do otherwise (*e.g.* r.29.9 (Powers of "trial judge" in relation to orders previously made), r.30.2 (Transfer between county courts and within the High Court), r.34.13 (High Court's power to order letter of request) and r.43.2(1) (defining "costs judge")). Where the context requires, a reference to "the court" means a reference to a particular county court, a district registry or the Royal Courts of Justice (r.2.3(2)). Rule 2.3 states that "judge" means, unless the context otherwise requires, a judge, Master or district judge or a person 2.4.1

authorised to act as such. Rule 2.4 states the general rule that where "the court" may perform any act then that act may be performed, not only by the judges of the court, but also by lesser judicial officers. Rule 2.4 draws a clear distinction between proceedings in the High Court and proceedings in a county court. The rule is confined to circumstances in which these Rules refer to the performance of an "act" by the court. The general principle is that Masters and district judges should have power to act.

The expression "the High Court" or "the court" or "the court or a judge" if used in a statute does not include lesser judicial officers unless jurisdiction is expressly conferred upon them by rules of court (see SCP 1999, Vol. 1, para. 1/4/7).

In various circumstances it is necessary to be clear about the limits of the powers and jurisdiction of Masters and district judges in relation to proceedings in the High Court, and about the limits of the powers and jurisdiction of district judges in relation to proceedings in a county court. Practice Direction (Allocation of Cases to Levels of Judiciary) (see para. 28PD–001 below) conveniently sets out the matters over which masters and district judges do not have jurisdiction or which they may deal with only on certain conditions. The Supreme Court Act 1981, s.19(3) states that in the High Court any jurisdiction of the court shall be exercised only by a single judge of that court, except in so far as it is by rules of court made exercisable by a Master, district judge or other officer of the court, or by any other person (note also SCA, s.68) (see SCP 1999, Vol. 2, paras 20A–180 and 20A–451). The County Courts Act 1981, s.62 states the general rule that, subject to other provisions in the Act and rules of court, the judge of a county is the sole judge in all proceedings and shall determine all questions of fact and law and CCA 1981, s.37(1) states that any jurisdiction and powers conferred by that Act or any other Act on a county court or on the judge of a county court may be exercised by any judge of the court (see SCP 1999, Vol. 2, paras 20A–696 and 20A–735). Rules of court may prescribe cases in which any jurisdiction of a county court is to be exercised by a district judge or by some other officer of the court (County Courts Act 1981, s.75(3)(d), see SCP 1999, Vol. 2, para. 20A–748). In former RSC, O.1, r.4(2) "the court" was defined as including a judge, a Master or a district judge (see SCP 1999, Vol. 1, para. 1/4/7). The CCR contained no such general provision (but see CCR, O.1, r.8).

It is not possible in a short compass to state the limits of the jurisdiction and powers of Masters and district judges. However, it may be noted that a broad distinction can be drawn between the exercise of any jurisdiction or power conferred on the court by rules of court (1) at the trial or hearing of a claim, and (2) at any other stage of the proceedings (see *e.g.* former CCR, O.1, r.8). Historically speaking, the exercise of jurisdiction and powers in the first circumstance were reserved to the judge (whether of the High Court or a county court) and in the second, subject to some exceptions, were readily delegated to lesser judicial officers in the form of Masters and district judges (see *e.g.* former CCR, O.1, r.8 and O.13, r.1(6) and RSC, O.32, rr.11 and 14). However, in modern times the jurisdiction of lesser judicial officers to hear and determine claims has been established and increased (see *e.g.* former CCR, O.19, r.5 and O.21, r.5 (note also O.50, r.2) and RSC, O.14, r.6(2), O.33, r.2(e), O.36, r.11 and O.37, r.1). Most of the acts which the court may perform in accordance with rules of court are not performed at the trial or hearing of a claim but at other stages of proceedings. Consequently, the circumstances in which such acts cannot be performed by a lesser judicial officer, and must be performed by a judge, can be regarded as exceptional. Such circumstances may be stipulated by statute, by rules of court or by practice directions (*e.g. Practice Direction (Case Management—Preliminary Stage, etc.)* para. 12.10 (jurisdiction of Masters and district judges)).

As to Practice Directions, see notes to Civil Procedure Act 1997, s.5 (SCP 1999, Vol. 2, paras 20A–6/7 and 20A–6/8).

2.4.2 **"district judge of that Court"**—Formerly, at court centres out of London where district registries of the High Court are located, the functions of Master were discharged by selected county court registrars each designated as "a district registrar of the High Court". By the Courts and Legal Services Act 1990, s.74, the offices of county court registrar and of district registrar became the office of district judge. Thereafter, the proper designation for a district registrar became "a district judge of the High Court" (Supreme Court Act 1981, s.100, see SCP 1999, Vol. 2, para. 509). For each district registry of the High Court the Lord Chancellor is required to appoint at least one district judge for a county court district as district judge of the High Court (*ibid.*), hence the distinction between district judges generally and district judges of the High Court.

2.4.3 **Masters**—For appointment of Masters of the Queen's Bench and Chancery Divisions of the High Court, see the Supreme Court Act 1981, s.89 (SCP 1999, Vol. 2, para. 20A–482; note also SCP 1997, Vol. 1, para. 1/4/2). Under r.2.4, except where otherwise provided, Masters may perform any act which may be performed by the court "in relation to proceedings in the High Court"; no distinction is drawn between High Court cases proceeding at the Royal Courts of Justice or in a district registry. The jurisdiction of Masters in relation to proceedings in county courts granted by former RSC, O.107 is now dealt with under Pt 30 (Transfer) of the CPR.

2.4.4 **Performance of "acts ... provided for" by CPR**—Rule 2.4 speaks of circumstances in which "these Rules provide for the court to perform any act" and provides that generally such acts may be performed by lesser judicial officers. This formula has no exact counterpart in former rules. The former provisions spoke variously of the exercise by lesser judicial officers of power, authority, and jurisdiction, and their transaction of business. Further, they were not always limited to the exercise of power etc. conferred by the RSC and the CCR. In the CPR, sometimes the source of the court's power to perform particular acts is found within the CPR and sometimes the power has a provenance without (Pt 3 (Court's case management powers) and Pt 25 (Interim remedies) contain illustrations of both categories). It would seem that, whatever the provenance of the court's power to perform an "act" if it is mentioned in the CPR the Rules "provide for" it and, therefore, unless excepted by statute, rule or practice direction, it may be performed by a lesser judicial officer.

Court staff

2.5—(1) Where these Rules require or permit the court to perform an act of a formal or administrative character, that act may be performed by a court officer. 2.5

(2) A requirement that a court officer carry out any act at the request of a party is subject to the payment of any fee required by a fees order for the carrying out of that act.

(Rule 3.2 allows a court officer to refer to a judge before taking any step.)

Effect of rule—The CPR may provide for the exercise of the jurisdiction of any court within the scope of the rules by officers or other staff of the court (Civil Procedure 1997, s.1 and Sched. 1, para. 2, see SCP 1999, Vol. 2, para. 20A–13). 2.5.1

"act of a formal or administrative character"—A court officer means a member of the court staff (r.2.3(1)). In modern times the trend has been towards devolving to civil servants working in the Court Service, tasks that formerly were thought proper for discharge only by a judge, Master or district judge. Under the former CCR, various functions were to be performed by "the proper officer" by which was meant the district judge or, in relation to any act of a formal or administrative character which was not by statute the responsibility of the district judge, the court manager or any other officer of the court acting on his behalf in accordance with directions given by the Lord Chancellor (O.1, r.3). Further, the chief clerk court manager (or officer authorised on his behalf) could discharge certain listed functions which were not obviously merely formal or administrative (*e.g.* the oral examination of debtors in county courts) (*ibid.*). Rule 2.5 is confined to acts of a formal or administrative character and is not in terms restricted to such acts as are not by statute the responsibility of the district judge or any other judicial officer. The Civil Procedure Act 1997, s.1 and Sched. 1, para. 2 provides that rules in the CPR may provide for the exercise "of the jurisdiction of any court within the scope of the rules" by officers or other staff of the court. Thus, for example, r.14.11 provides that in certain circumstances, a court officer may exercise the powers of the court under r.14.10 to determine the rate of payment where a defendant has admitted a money claim and requested time to pay, and r.46.3. Further, under Pt 43 the Lord Chancellor may authorise court officers to exercise certain powers in relation to the assessment of costs (see r.46.3). 2.5.2

Rule 3.2 provides that, where in the exercise of the court's case management powers, "a step is taken" by a court officer, the court officer may consult a judge before taking that step, and the step may be taken by the judge instead of by the court officer.

Court documents to be sealed

2.6—(1) The court must seal[GL] the following documents on issue— 2.6

(a) the claim form; and

(b) any other document which a rule or practice direction requires it to seal.

(2) The court may place the seal[GL] on the document—

(a) by hand; or

(b) by printing a facsimile of the seal on the document whether electronically or otherwise.

(3) A document purporting to bear the court's seal[GL] shall be admissible in evidence without further proof.

Effect of rule—A seal on a document indicates that it has been issued by the court (see Glossary). Formerly, the County Courts Act 1984, s.134(1) (now omitted, see "Sealed documents as evidence" below) stated that all summonses issued out of a county court, and all such other documents so issuing as may be prescribed, should be"sealed and stamped" with the seal of the court. Under the RSC, various forms of process were validly issued only when sealed (*e.g.* RSC, O.6, r.7(3) (Issue of writ)). Rule 2.6(1) replaces these and other provisions. 2.6.1

Proceedings are started when the court issues a claim form at the request of the claimant (r.7.2(1)). A claim form must be sealed on issue (r.2.6(1)(a)). The date of issue of a claim form is the date entered on the form by the court (r.7.2(2)).

Where a form set out in a practice direction includes the word "seal", the court must seal the form "when issuing it for use" (r.4(6)).

As to sealing of judgments and orders, see r.40.2(2)(b) and rr.40.2 to 40.6.

As to the signature of documents used in court proceedings, see r.5.3.

2.6.2 **Placing of seal**—The court may place the seal in the manner provided by r.2.6(2). Claim forms issued by the Summons Production Centre (r.7.10) may be sealed electronically and means of sealing otherwise than by hand may be more widely used in the future as the courts gain the benefits of information technology.

2.6.3 **Sealed documents as evidence**—The general rule is that a party wishing to rely on a document must adduce primary evidence of its contents. At common law, by way of exception to the general rule, the contents of most public documents could be proved by copies of various kinds on account of the inconvenience that would have been occasioned by production of the originals. This common law rule is declared in many specific contexts by statutes. Examples include the Supreme Court Act 1981, s.132 (see SCP 1999, Vol. 2, para. 20A–525), which states that any document purporting to be"sealed or stamped" by the Supreme Court shall be received in evidence "in all parts of the United Kingdom without further proof". The County Courts Act 1984, s.134(2) (see SCP 1999, Vol. 2, para. 20A–809) was to similar effect, but limited to "all parts of England and Wales", and has been omitted from that Act by the Civil Procedure (Modification of Enactments) Order 1998 (S.I. 1998 No. 2940).

Former RSC, O.38, r.10(2) stated that every document purporting to be sealed with the seal of any office or department of the Supreme Court should be received in evidence without further proof. This sub-rule further stated that any document purporting to be so sealed and to be a copy of a document filed in, or issued out of, that office or department should be deemed to be an office copy of that document without further proof unless the contrary is shown. Rule 2.6(3) follows former RSC, O.38, r.10(2) and declares that a sealed document is admissible in evidence without further proof in the courts to which the CPR apply (see further SCP 1999, Vol. 1, paras 38/10/1 *et seq.*). The effect of the Evidence Act 1845, s.1 is that, when a statute permits a document to be proved by certified or sealed copy, it is unnecessary to prove certification or sealing; the mere production of the copy suffices.

Court's discretion as to where it deals with cases

2.7 **2.7** The court may deal with a case at any place that it considers appropriate.

2.7.1 **Effect of rule**—The County Courts Act 1984, s.3(3) stated that county court proceedings (whether heard by a judge or a district judge) or any question arising in proceedings "may be heard or determined at any place either within or without the district". The exercise of this power was subject to the consent of the parties. This provision could be explained in historical terms but in modern times its purpose and scope had become matters for doubt, largely because its original objectives had come to be met by other provisions. The sub-section was omitted by the Civil Procedure Act 1997, s.10 and Sched. 2, para. 2. However, it would seem that it is revived by r.2.7. In terms, the rule grants the court a wide power as to venue. In contrast to former CCA 1984, s.3(3), the rule makes no mention of the consent of the parties. Further, it is not limited to sittings of county courts but applies to all courts covered by the CPR. However, the need to give effect to the overriding objective stated in r.1.1 may impose some restraint and ensure that, in a given case, the power is not exercised purely for the convenience of the court. It would seem that, formerly, CCA 1984, s.3(3) was used, not for the purpose of moving cases from a court in one county court district to a venue in another district, but for the purpose of enabling the court, with the consent of the parties, to sit at a location within its district which was not a court house. It may be that the intention is that r.2.7 should be interpreted in a similarly restricted manner.

Rule 2.7 states that the court may deal with "a case" at any place that it considers appropriate. This would include holding a hearing of any kind provided for by the CPR (including case management events) and not merely (as provided by CCA 1984, s.3(3)) a hearing for the determination of "any question arising in proceedings".

Rule 2.7 is not concerned with the transfer of proceedings between one court and another. Provisions as to transfer are found in Pt 30. It may be noted that r.30.6 states that the court may specify the place (for instance a particular county court) where the trial or some other hearing in any proceedings is to be held and may do so without ordering the proceedings to be transferred (see further Practice Direction (The Fast Track) para. 8.1 (28PD–004) and Practice Direction (The Multi-Track) para. 10.1 (29PD–005)). It may be noted that Practice Direction (Miscellaneous Provisions Relating to Hearings) para. 1.7 states that the hearing of small claim "in premises other than the court will not be a hearing in public". That rule has a different provenance. Its relationship with r.2.7 is not obvious.

There is some doubt as to whether r.2.7 lies within the rule-making power. The question is unlikely to arise unless an attempt is made to exercise it without the consent of the parties. The rule-making power for the CPR includes power to make rules about any matters which were governed by the former CCR (Civil Procedure Act 1997, s.1 and Sched. 1, para. 1). As explained above, formerly, the power now granted by r.2.7 was not granted by rule but by the County Courts Act 1984, s.3(3). Section 75 of that Act (now omitted) stated that the rule making power extended to prescribing the circumstances in which proceedings may be transferred from one court to another court (but not to a non-court location).

Time

2.8—(1) This rule shows how to calculate any period of time or doing any act which is specified— **2.8**

(a) by these Rules;
(b) by a practice direction; or
(c) by a judgment or order of the court.

(2) A period of time expressed as a number of days shall be computed as clear days.

(3) In this rule "clear days" means that in computing the number of days—

(a) the day on which the period begins; and
(b) if the end of the period is defined by reference to an event, the day on which that event occurs

are not included.

Examples

(i) Notice of an application must be served at least 3 days before the hearing.
An application is to be heard on Friday 20 October.
The last date for service is Monday 16 October.

(ii) The court is to fix a date for a hearing.
The hearing must be at least 28 days after the date of notice.
If the court gives notice of the date of the hearing on 1 October, the earliest date for the hearing is 30 October.

(iii) Particulars of claim must be served within 14 days of service of the claim form.
The claim form is served on 2 October.
The last day for service of the particulars of claim is 16 October.

(4) Where the specified period—

(a) is 5 days or less; and
(b) includes—
(i) a Saturday or Sunday; or
(ii) a Bank Holiday, Christmas Day or Good Friday,

that day does not count.

Example

Notice of an application must be served at least 3 days before the hearing.
An application is to be heard on Monday 20 October.
The last date for service is Tuesday 14 October.

(5) When the period specified—

(a) by these Rules or a practice direction; or
(b) by any judgment or court order,

for doing any act at the court office ends on a day on which the office is closed, that act shall be in time if done on the next day on which the court office is open.

Effect of rule—Circumstances in which periods of time for doing any act are specified or may be specified are many and various. Under a case management system the circumstances in which time limits may be fixed are increased and the attitude of the court to compliance with time limits is more strict than under a system in which case progress is largely controlled by the wishes of parties. Further, the circumstances in which time limits may be varied are restricted and the procedures enabling variation are likely to involve monitoring by the court. **2.8.1**

Formerly, any periods of time fixed by the RSC or the CCR or "by any judgment, order or direction" for doing any act were reckoned in accordance with the provisions in, respectively, RSC, O.3, rr.2 and 4 and CCR, O.1, r.9. The calculation of periods of time is now dealt with by the provisions in r.2.8. Rule 2.8(1) states that the provisions which follow are to be used for the purpose of calculating any period of time for doing any act which is specified by the CPR, by a practice direction, or by "a judgment or order" of the court. In terms, this does not include times specified by directions other than practice directions but this omission would appear to be an oversight (see rr.2.9(1) and 2.10). Depending on the circumstances, an act may have to be done within a specified period, or after or from a specified date or it may have to be done within or not less than a specified period before a specified date. Where expressly so provided, a time limit fixed by a rule may be varied by a practice direction (see *e.g.* r.26.3(7)).

See generally, SCP 1999, Vol. 1, paras 3/2/2 *et seq.*

2.8.2 **Number of days as "clear" days**—A period of time expressed as a number of days may be calculated in different ways. Rule 2.8(2) states that such periods shall be "computed as clear days". In itself, this is not entirely free from ambiguity. Consequently, r.2.8(3) explains that what is meant is that (a) the day on which the period begins shall not be included, and that (b) if the end of the period is defined by reference to an event, the day on which that event occurs is not included either. The explanation is followed by examples. The first and the last are based on, respectively, r.23.7(1)(b) and r.7.4(1)(b). The second relates to those many rules which provide that the court must give parties a minimum period of notice of a hearing (*e.g.* r.27.4(2)). It should be noted that these provisions are not concerned with periods of time expressed otherwise than as numbers of days, *e.g.* expressed in weeks (*e.g.* r.28.6(2)) or months (*e.g.* r.7.5(2)).

In the past, the language used by draftsmen of rules of court to express periods of time has not been consistent. Clearly, drafting styles have changed from time to time. Many of the rules now found in the CPR are based on former provisions of the RSC and CCR. The unfortunate result is that the old inconsistencies are perpetuated. Thus, for example, where providing that a party must take a particular action before a certain event occurs, rules state variously that he must do so "at least", "no later than", "not less than", or "not more than" a certain number of days before that event. Rules providing that certain actions must be taken after particular events show similar disparities in addition to providing in a number of rules that action should be taken "within" a number of days "of" or "after" an event. In some rules, periods of time are expressed in elaborate terms and this complexity is not always made necessary by the context. If one of the goals of the CPR was to standardise and simplify rules of court they have failed in this respect.

2.8.3 **Specified periods of five days or less**—Where a period of time is expressed as a number of days and the number does not exceed five, it is conceivable that such short period may as a practical matter be further reduced by the fact that it includes days falling on weekends, etc. Consequently, r.2.8(4) provides that in these circumstances such days shall not count. The provision follows former RSC, O.3, r.1(5) (which applied to periods of seven days or less) and CCR, O.1, r.9(3) (which applied to periods of three days or less). See SCP 1999, Vol. 1, para. 3/2/11. Provisions in the CPR specifying time periods of seven days are quite common but provisions imposing limits of five days or less are rare: examples are r.23.7(1)(b) and r.24.5(2). Certain provisions in Sched. 1, CCR, O.24, Pt II (Interim possession orders) require parties to act "within 24 hours" and it is expressly provided that r.2.8(4) does not apply to the calculation of this period of time (*ibid.* r.8(2)).

2.8.4 **Specified period ending on day on which court office closed**—Rule 2.8(5) states that, where a specified period of time, whether expressed in a number of days or otherwise, for doing an act at the court office ends on day on which the office is closed, that act shall be done in time if done on the next day on which the court office is open. A similar dispensation was given by former RSC, O.1, r.4 and CCR, O.1, r.9(5); see SCP 1999, Vol. 1, para. 3/4/2. Presumably, this rule applies where the period of time is specified by a direction other than a practice direction (see "Effect of rule", para. 2.8.1 above).

The days on which court offices are open, and the hours during which they are open on those days, are stipulated by Practice Direction (Court Offices) para. 2.1 (offices of the Supreme Court) and paras 3.2 and 3.3 (county court offices) (2PD–001). Formerly, comparable provisions were found in, respectively, RSC, O.64, rr.7 and 8 (see SCP Vol. 1, paras 64/7/2 and 64/8/1) and CCR, O.2, rr.2 and 3.

Dates for compliance to be calendar dates and to include time of day

2.9 **2.9**—(1) Where the court gives a judgment, order or direction which imposes a time limit for doing any act, the last date for compliance must, wherever practicable—

(a) be expessed as a calendar date; and

(b) include the time of day by which the act must be done.

(2) Where the date by which an act must be done is inserted in any document, the date must, wherever practicable, be expressed as a calendar date.

2.9.1 **Effect of rule**—It is important that the court, lawyers and parties should be clear as to the final dates for compliance with time limits imposed by judgments, orders or directions for doing particular acts. This is especially true under a case management system. A date expressed as a calendar date is much more satisfactory than one which has to be calculated in relation to another date or the occurrence of a particular event. Rule 2.9 provides that calendar dates should be used wherever practicable. This rule has no counterpart in the former RSC or CCR.

In certain circumstances it may be convenient or necessary to stipulate that an act must be done by a particular time on a particular day. Rule 2.9 states that this should be done wherever practicable, whether or not there is any obvious reason for doing so. See SCP 1999, Vol. 1, para. 3/2/6 (Time of day) and 3/2/7 (Fractions of a day).

Meaning of "month" in judgments, etc.

2.10 Where "month" occurs in any judgment, order, direction or other document, it means a calendar month. 2.10

Effect of rule—Rule 2.10 follows former RSC, O.3, r.1. For explanation of significance of this rule, see SCP 1999, Vol. 1, para. 3/1/2. 2.10.1

In the CPR, examples of periods of time being specified in terms of months are not common. Most are found in the provisions relating to procedures for assessment of costs (see r.46.8, r.46.16(1), r.46.19(2), r.47.10(5)). Other examples include r.7.5(2)(3) (service of a claim form), r.15.11 (claim stayed if not defended or admitted), r.40.8(1) (default judgment against State).

Time limits may be varied by parties

2.11 Unless these Rules or a practice direction provides otherwise or the court orders otherwise, the time specified by a rule or by the court for a person to do any act may be varied by the written agreement of the parties. 2.11

(Rules 3.8 (sanction to have effect unless defaulting party obtains relief), 28.4 (variation of case management timetable—fast track), 29.5 (variation of case management timetable—multi-track) and RSC O.59, r.2C (appeals to the Court of Appeal) in Schedule 1, provide for time limits that cannot be varied by agreement between the parties.)

Effect of rule—Formerly, except where otherwise provided, the period within which a person was required or authorised by rules or by any judgment, order or direction to do any act in any proceedings could be extended or abridged by consent of all the parties or by order of the court on the application of any party (RSC, O.3, r.5(1) and CCR, O.13, r.4). Former RSC, O.3, r.5(2) stated that the period within which a person was required by court rules, or by any order of direction, to serve, file or amend any pleading or other document could be extended by consent given in writing without an order of the Court being made for that purpose. Now, the general power of the court to shorten or extend the time for complying with any rule, practice direction or court order is found in r.3.1(2)(a). An express power in the hands of the court to extend time for serving a claim form is found in r.7.6 and Sched. 1, O.59, r.15 states that certain time limits relating to appeals to the Court of Appeal may be abridged or extended by the court below. Under the CPR, the scope for variation of time limits by agreement between parties is curtailed. 2.11.1

Under r.2.11, variation by agreement between the parties of times specified is limited to the variation of times specified "by a rule or by the court". This phrase would include a time specified in a judgment, direction or order of the court. It does not in terms include a time specified by other means, for example, in a practice direction. However, presumably it could be argued that a time specified by a practice direction is a time specified "by the court". The rule speaks of "a person" being required to do any act; such person may or may not be a party in the proceedings (*e.g.* an expert witness). In the interests of case management, parties should not be permitted to vary certain time limits without the permission of the court. Rules containing provisions expressly forbidding variation by agreement are referred to in r.2.11.

One example of a situation in which a time limit may be varied by agreement of the parties is provided by r.15.5 which states that the defendant and the claimant may agree that the period for filing a defence specified in r.15.4 shall be extended by up to 28 days; the defendant must notify the court in writing of any such agreement (r.15.5(2)).

One of the circumstances in which a time limit may not be varied by written agreement between parties is where "the court orders otherwise". When the court makes an order, not only may it make it subject to conditions, including conditions as to the time within which acts must be done, but also it may specify the consequence of failure to comply with the order (r.3.1(3)). In this situation the order comes within r.3.8 and, consequently, by operation of r.3.8(2) the time specified may not be varied by written agreement between the parties (r.3.8(2)) and the order need not contain an express term to that effect. Where a court order contains a term specifying a period of time for a person to do an act, but specifies no consequence for failure to comply with that or any other term of the order, variation of the specified time period by written agreement between the parties is permitted unless the order contains an express term to the contrary (or unless not permitted by a rule or practice direction).

Practice Direction (The Fast Track) para. 4.5 and Practice Direction (The Multi-Track) para. 6.5 state that where the parties take advantage of r.2.11 and vary a time limit, thereby affecting directions previously given by the court, the parties need not file the written agreement (see, respectively, paras 28PD–003 and 29PD–004).

Rule 2.11 is incorporated by reference in Sched. 1, RSC, O.45, r.5(1)(a) and r.7(5) (Enforcement of judgment to do or abstain from doing any act). Formerly, these provisions contained no express reference to extension of time by agreement, whether written or otherwise.

Sched. 1, O.59, r.2C (noted in the text of r.2.11) states that any date "set by the court" or by O.59 (Appeals to the Court of Appeal) "for doing any act" may not be varied by the parties. Presumably, in this context "set by the court" includes set by the court below, insofar as that court may fix O.59 time limits (*e.g.* a time limit varied under O.59, r.15), and "doing any act" means taking any step in relation to an appeal to the Court of Appeal.

PRACTICE DIRECTION—COURT OFFICES

2PD–001 *This Practice Direction supplements CPR Part 2*

Central Office of the High Court at the Royal Courts of Justice

1 The Central Office shall be divided into such departments, and the business performed in the Central Office shall be distributed among the departments in such manner, as is set out in the Queen's Bench Division Guide.

Business in the Offices of the Supreme Court

2.1 (1) The offices of the Supreme Court shall be open on every day of the year except

- (a) Saturdays and Sundays,
- (b) Good Friday and the day after Easter Monday,
- (c) Christmas Day and, if that day is a Friday or Saturday, then 28th December,
- (d) Bank Holidays in England and Wales under the Banking and Financial Dealings Act 1971, and,
- (e) such other days as the Lord Chancellor, with the concurrence of the Lord Chief Justice, the Master of the Rolls, the President of the Family Division and the Vice-Chancellor ("the Heads of Division") may direct.

(2) The hours during which the offices of the Supreme Court shall be open to the public shall be as follows:

- (a) at the Principal Probate Registry at First Avenue House, 42–49 High Holborn, London WC1V 6HA, from 10 a.m. to 4.30 p.m.,
- (b) at the Supreme Court offices at the Royal Courts of Justice (including the Construction & Technology Court Registry in St. Dunstan's House, 133–137 Fetter Lane, London EC4A 1HD), from 10 a.m. to 4.30 p.m., except during the month of August in every year, when the hours shall be from 10 a.m. to 2.20 p.m.,
- (c) such other hours as the Lord Chancellor, with the concurrence of the Heads of Division, may from time to time direct.

(3) Every District Registry shall be open on the days and during the hours that the Lord Chancellor from time to time directs and, in the absence of any such directions, shall be open on the same days and during the same hours as the county court offices of which it forms part are open.

2.2 One of the Masters of the Queen's Bench Division (the "Practice

Master") shall be present at the Central Office every day on which the office is open for the purpose of superintending the business performed there and giving any directions which may be required on questions of practice and procedure.

County Courts

3.1 Every County Court shall have an office or, if the Lord Chancellor so directs, two or more offices, situated at such place or places as he may direct, for the transaction of the business of the court.

3.2(1) Every County Court office, or if a court has two or more offices at least one of those offices, shall be open on every day of the year except—
- (a) Saturdays, and Sundays,
- (b) the day before Good Friday from noon onwards and Good Friday,
- (c) the Tuesday after the Spring bank holiday,
- (d) Christmas Day and, if that day is a Friday or Saturday, then the 28th December,
- (e) bank holidays, and
- (f) such other days as the Lord Chancellor may direct.

(2) In this paragraph "bank holiday" means a bank holiday in England and Wales under the Banking and Financial Dealings Act 1971 and "Spring holidays" means the bank holiday on the last Monday in May or any day appointed instead of that day under section 1(2) of that Act.

3.3 Subject to paragraph 3.2(1)(b), the hours during which any court office is open to the public shall be from 10 a.m. to 4 p.m. or such other hours as the Lord Chancellor may from time to time direct.

PRACTICE DIRECTION—ALLOCATION OF CASES TO LEVELS OF JUDICIARY

1.1 Rule 2.4 provides that Judges, Masters and District Judges may exercise any function of the court except where an enactment, rule or practice direction provides otherwise. This Practice Direction sets out the matters over which Masters and District Judges do not have jurisdiction or which they may deal with only on certain conditions. It does not affect jurisdiction conferred by other enactments. Reference should also be made to other relevant Practice Directions (*e.g.* Part 24, paragraphs 3 and Part 26, paragraphs 12.1–10). References to Circuit Judges include Recorders and Assistant Recorders and references to Masters and District Judges include Deputies. **2BPD–001**

1.2 Wherever a Master or District Judge has jurisdiction, he may refer the matter to a Judge instead of dealing with it himself.

The High Court

Injunctions

2.1 Search orders (rule 25.1(1)(h)), freezing orders (rule 25.1(1)(f)), an ancillary order under rule 25.1(1)(g) and orders authorising a person to enter land to recover, inspect or sample property (rule 25.1(1)(d)) may only be made by a Judge.

2.2 Except where paragraphs 2.3 and 2.4 apply, injunctions and orders relating to injunctions, including orders for specific performance where these involve an injunction, must be made by a Judge.

2.3 A Master or a District Judge may only make an injuction
(a) in terms agreed by the parties;
(b) in connection with or ancillary to a charging order;
(c) in connection with or ancillary to an order appointing a receiver by way of equitable execution; or

(d) in proceedings under RSC Order 77 rule 16 (order restraining person from receiving sum due from the Crown).

2.4 A Master or District Judge may make an order varying or discharging an injunction or undertaking given to the court if all parties to the proceedings have consented to the variation or discharge.

Other pre-trial Orders and Interim Remedies

3.1 A Master or District Judge may not make orders or grant interim remedies:

(a) relating to the liberty of the subject;

(b) relating to criminal proceedings or matters except procedural applications in appeals to the High Court (including appeals by case stated) under any enactment;

(c) relating to proceedings for judicial review, except applications under RSC Order 53 rule 8 (interlocutory applications);

(d) relating to appeals from Masters or District Judges;

(e) in appeals against a costs assessment under Parts 43–48, except—

(i) on an appeal under rule 47.22 against the decision of an authorised court order; or

(ii) on an application for the grant of permission where rule 47.24 requires this.

(f) in applications under section 42 of the Supreme Court Act 1981 by a person subject to a Civil or a Criminal or an All Proceedings Order (vexatious litigant) for permission to start or continue proceedings.

3.2 This Practice Direction is not concerned with family proceedings. It is also not concerned with proceedings in the Family Division except to the extent that such proceedings can be dealt with in the Chancery Division or the Family Division, *e.g.* proceedings under the Inheritance (Provision for Family and Dependants) Act 1975 or under section 14 of the Trusts of Land and Appointment of Trusts Act 1996. District Judges (including District Judges of the Principal Registry of the Family Division) have jurisdiction to hear such proceedings, subject to any Direction given by the President of the Family Division.

Trials and Assessments of damages

4.1 A Master or District Judge may, subject to any Practice Direction, by a case which is treated as being allocated to the multi-track because it is proceeding under Part 8 (see rule 8.9(c)). He may try a case which has been allocated to the multi-track under Part 26 only with the consent of the parties. Restrictions on the trial jurisdiction of Masters and District Judges do not prevent them from hearing applications for summary judgment or, if the parties consent, for the determination of a preliminary issue.

4.2 A Master or a District Judge may assess the damages or sum due to a party under a judgment without limit as to the amount.

Chancery Proceedings

2BPD–002 **5.1** In proceedings in the Chancery Division, a Master or a District Judge may not deal with the following without the consent of the Vice-Chancellor:—

(a) approving compromises (other than applications under the Inheritance (Provisions for Family and Dependants) Act 1975) (i) on behalf of a person under disability where that person's interest in a fund, or if there is no fund, the maximum amount of the claim, exceeds £100,000 and (ii) on behalf of absent, unborn and unascertained persons;

(b) making declarations, except in plain cases;

(c) making final orders under section 1(1) of the Variation of Trusts Act 1958, except for the removal of protective trusts where the interest of the principal beneficiary has not failed or determined;

(d) where the proceedings are brought by a Part 8 claim form in accordance with paragraph A.1(2) or (3) of the Part 8B Practice Direction (statutory or other requirement to use originating summons), determining any question of law or as to the construction of a document which is raised by the claim form;

(e) giving permission to executors, administators and trustees to bring or defend proceedings or to continue the prosecution or defence of proceedings, and granting an indemnity for costs out fo the trust estate, except in plain cases;

(f) granting an indemnity for costs out of the assets of a company on the application of minority shareholders bringing a derivative action, except in plain cases;

(g) making an order for rectification, except for rectification of the register under the Land Registration Act 1925 in plain cases;

(h) making orders to vacate entries in the register under the Land Charges Act 1972, except in plain cases;

(i) making final orders on applications under section 19 of the Leasehold Reform Act 1967, section 48 of the Administration of Justice Act 1985 and sections 21 and 25 of the Law of Property Act 1969;

(j) making final orders under the Landlord and Tenant Acts 1927 and 1954, except (i) by consent, (ii) orders for interim rents under section 24A of the 1954 Act and (iii) on applications to authorise agreements under section 38(4) of the 1954 Act;

(k) making orders in proceedings in the Patents Court except (i) by consent, (ii) to extend time, (iii) on applications for permission to serve out of the jurisdiction and (iv) on applications for security for costs.

5.2 A Master or District Judge may only give directions for early trial after consulting the Judge in charge of the relevant list.

5.3 Where a winding-up order has been made against a company, any proceedings against the company by or on behalf of debenture holders may be dealt with, at the Royal Courts of Justice, by a Registrar and, in a District Registry with insolvency jurisdiction, by a District Judge.

Group or Multi-Party Claims

6.1 In group or multi-party claims the Lord Chief Justice and/or the Vice-Chancellor may give directions that all pre-trial applications in the group or multi-party act claims must be made to and heard by a designated High Court Judge, Circuit Judge, Master or District Judge.

6.2 A party seeking a direction under paragraph 6.1 must apply to the Senior Master, the Chief Master or the appropriate Designated Civil Judge for the matter to be referred to the Lord Chief Justice and/or the Vice-Chancellor for such a direction. Any judge may on his own initiative refer a case for such a direction to be made.

6.3 When a direction has been made under paragraph 6.1, all pre-trial applications must be made in accordance with it.

Assignment of Claims to Masters and Transfer between Masters

7.1 The Senior Master, and the Chief Master will make arrangements for proceedings to be assigned to individual Masters. They may vary such arrangements generally or in particular cases, for example, by transferring a case from a Master to whom it had been assigned to another Master.

7.2 The fact that a case has been assigned to a particular Master does not prevent another Master from dealing with that case if circumstances require, whether at the request of the assigned Master or otherwise.

Freezing Orders: Cross Examination of Deponents about Assets

8 Where the court has made a freezing order under rule 25.1(f) and has **2BPD–003**

ordered a person to make a witness statement or affidavit about his assets and to be cross-examined on its contents, unless the Judge directs otherwise, the cross-examination will take place before a Master or a District Judge, or if the Master or District Judge directs, before and examiner of the Court.

County Courts

Injunctions and Committal

9.1 Injunctions which a county court has jurisdiction to make may only be made by a Circuit Judge, except:—

(a) where the injunction is to be made in proceedings which a District Judge otherwise has jurisdiction to hear (see paragraph 11.1 below);

(b) where the injunction is sought in a money claim which has not yet been allocated to a track, where the amount claimed does not exceed the fast track financial limit;

(c) in the circumstances provided by paragraph 2.3.

9.2 A District Judge may make orders varying or discharging injuctions in the circumstances provided by paragraph 2.4.

9.3 A District Judge may not make an order committing a person to prison except where an enactment authorises this: see section 23 of the Attachment Earnings Act 1971, sections 14 and 18 of the County Courts Act 1984, sections 152–157 of the Housing Act 1996, section 3 of the Protection from Harassment Act 1997, and the relevant rules.

Other pre-trial Orders and Interim Remedies

10.1 In addition to the restrictions on jurisdiction mentioned at paragraphs 9.1–3, paragraph 3.1(d) and (e) above applies.

Trials and Assessments of Damages

11.1 A District Judge has jurisdiction to hear the following:

(a) any claim which has been allocated to the small claims track or fast track or which is treated as being allocated to the multi-track under rule 8.9(c) and Table 2 of the Practice Direction to Part 8, except proceedings under:—

(i) CCR Order 43 rules 4, 6 and 18 (certain applications under the Landlord and Tenant Acts 1927 and 1954);
(ii) CCR Order 43, rule 20 (Landlord and Tenant Act 1987);
(iii) CCR Order 44, (Agricultural Holdings Act 1986);
(iv) CCR Order 46, rule 1 (Legitimacy Act 1976);
(v) CCR Order 49, rule 5 (Fair Trading Act 1973);
(vi) CCR Order 49 rule 10 (Local Government and Finance Act 1982);
(vii) CCR Order 49, rule 12 (Mental Health Act 1983);

(b) proceedings for the recovery of land;

(c) the asssessment of damages or other sum due to a party under a judgment without any financial limit;

(d) with the consent of the parties and the permission of the Designated Civil Judge in respect of that case, any other proceedings.

11.2 A case allocated to the small claims track may only be assigned to a Circuit Judge to hear with his consent.

Freezing Orders: Cross Examination of Deponents about Assets

2BPD–004 **12** To the extent that a county court has power to make a freezing order, paragraph 8 applies as appropriate.

Distribution of Business between Circuit Judge and District Judge

13 Where both the Circuit Judge and the District Judge have jurisdiction in respect of any proceedings, the exercise of jurisdiction by the District Judge is subject to any arrangements made by the Designated Civil Judge for the proper distribution of business between Circuit Judges and District Judges.

14.1 In District Registries of the High Court and in the county court, the Designated Civil Judge may make arrangements for proceedings to be assigned to individual District Judges. He may vary such arrangements generally or in particular cases.

14.2 The fact that a case has been assigned to a particular District Judge does not prevent another District Judge from dealing with the case if the circumstances require.

PART 3

THE COURT'S CASE MANAGEMENT POWERS

3.0.1 **Contents**

Editorial Introduction

3.0.2 The contents of this Part are almost entirely new. They provide the powers which it is essential for the court to have in order to undertake active case management. The powers fall into three main categories:

(1) General powers, including notably, power for the court to make orders of its own initiative (rr.3.1, 3.2, 3.3 and 3.10);
(2) Coercive powers (r.3.1(3) and (5), rr.3.4, 3.5 and 3.7);
(3) Power to give relief against sanctions (rr.3.6, 3.8 and 3.9).

Related Sources

3.0.3
- Part 24 (summary judgment).
- Practice Direction supplementing r.3.4 (see para. 3PD–001).
- Practice Direction supplementing r.3.7 (see para. 3BPD–001).

The court's general powers of management

3.1 **3.1**—(1) The list of powers in this rule is in addition to any powers given to the court by any other rule or practice direction or by any other enactment or any powers it may otherwise have.

(2) Except where these Rules provide otherwise, the court may—

(a) extend or shorten the time for compliance with any rule, practice direction or court order (even if an application for extension is made after the time for compliance has expired);
(b) adjourn or bring forward a hearing;
(c) require a party or a party's legal representative to attend the court;
(d) hold a hearing and receive evidence by telephone or by using any other method of direct oral communication;
(e) direct that part of any proceedings (such as a counterclaim) be dealt with as separate proceedings;
(f) stay[GL] the whole or part of any proceedings either generally or until a specified date or event;
(g) consolidate proceedings;
(h) try two or more claims on the same occasion;
(i) direct a separate trial of any issue;
(j) decide the order in which issues are to be tried;
(k) exclude an issue from consideration;
(l) dismiss or give judgment on a claim after a decision on a preliminary issue;

(m) take any other step or make any other order for the purpose of managing the case and furthering the overriding objective.

(3) When the court makes an order, it may

(a) make it subject to conditions, including a condition to pay a sum of money into court; and

(b) specify the consequence of failure to comply with the order or a condition.

(4) Where the court gives directions it may take into account whether or not a party has complied with any relevant pre-action protocol[GL].

(5) The court may order a party to pay a sum of money into court if that party has, without good reason, failed to comply with a rule, practice direction or a relevant pre-action protocol.

(6) When exercising its power under paragraph (5) the court must have regard to—

(a) the amount in dispute; and

(b) the costs which the parties have incurred or which they may incur.

(6A) Where a party pays money into court following an order under paragraph (3) or (5), the money shall be security for any sum payable by that party to any other party in the proceedings, subject to the right of a defendant under rule 37.2 to treat all or part of any money paid into court as a Part 36 payment.

(Rule 36.2 explains what is meant by a Part 36 payment)

(7) A power of the court under these Rules to make an order includes a power to vary or revoke the order.

Effect of rule—The powers listed in r.3.1(2) enable the court to carry out its duty to *actively* manage cases (r.1.4(1)) so as to further the overriding objective (r.1.1). The list of powers is not exhaustive (see r.3.1(1) and r.3.1(2)(m)). An order exercising these powers is not irrevocable; the court may later make different orders varying the position as the case develops (r.3.1(7)). **3.1.1**

In order to encourage a party to carry out his duty to help the court to further the overriding objective (r.1.3) an order may be made subject to conditions and may specify the consequence of failure to comply with an order or a condition (r.3.1(3)). The court is not required to impose an express sanction for failing to comply with an order or condition. However, when making an order requiring somebody to do something for the first time, the court may be less reluctant than it previously was to impose an express sanction in the event of non-compliance. Even if no express sanction is stated the court may later strike out all or part of a statement of case of a party who fails to comply with the order (see further r.3.4).

If an order against a defendant includes a condition as to the payment of a sum of money into court, the defendant may treat a sum paid into court following that order as a Part 36 payment (r.3.1(6A) and, for a definition of Part 36 payments, see r.36.2).

Ordering security—If a party has, without good reason, failed to comply with a rule, practice direction or a relevant pre-action protocol, the court may order him to pay a sum of money into court (r.3.1(5)). The sum of money will be security for any sum payable by that party to any other party in the proceedings (r.1(6A)). An order such as this can be made against a claimant or a defendant. In exercising this power the court must have regard to the amount in dispute and the costs incurred and to be incurred (r.3.1(6)). In the case of claimants, an order under r.3.1(5) significantly broadens the court's powers to order security for costs (as to which, see generally RSC, O.23, see R23.A1). As to defendants and defendants to counterclaims they may be ordered to give security for costs and also for any money remedy claimed against them. However, the defendant or defendant to counterclaim may later treat any sums paid into court following an order under r.3.1(5) as a Part 36 payment (r.3.1(6A) and for a definition of Part 36 payments, see r.36.2). **3.1.2**

In deciding whether to require security the court may anticipate the arguments which may be raised on an application under r.3.9 "relief from sanctions" including in particular r.3.9(1)(i) "the effect which the granting of relief would have on each party". Difficult questions may arise where the court is considering making an order under r.3.1(5) against a legally aided party, or a party who has entered into a conditional fee agreement, or a litigant in person. In such cases an order for security may in practice amount to an order of strike out.

In *Mealey Horgan plc v. Horgan, The Times,* July 6, 1999, Buckley J. held that it would be inappropriate to order a defendant to give security either as a condition of an order extending time for service of witness statements or as a penalty for failing to serve witness statements in time. In that case the defendant's default had not prejudiced the trial and had not significantly prejudiced the claimant. In his lordship's view, an order for security might be appropriate where there was a history of repeated breaches of timetables or court orders or where the conduct of one party was such as to raise a suspicion that it was not bona fide and the court thought the other side should have protection.

Court officer's power to refer to a judge

3.2 **3.2** Where a step is to be taken by a court officer—

(a) the court officer may consult a judge before taking that step;

(b) the step may be taken by a judge instead of the court officer.

3.2.1 **Effect of rule**—"Court officer" means a member of the court staff (r.2.3(1)). Many steps taken by court officers concern the filing of documents, the issue of claim forms and the entry of default judgments. This rule enables court officers to refer to a judge any such document, form or request for judgment which appears to be irregular or inappropriate. In respect of that matter the judge may give directions to the court officer as to the step to be taken, or may take the step himself. In either case the judge may also exercise the court's power to make orders of its own initiative (see r.3.3).

Court's power to make order of its own initiative

3.3 **3.3**—(1) Except where a rule or some other enactment provides otherwise, the court may exercise its powers on an application or of its own initiative.

(Part 23 sets out the procedure for making an application.)

(2) Where the court proposes to make an order of its own initiative—

(a) it may give any person likely to be affected by the order an opportunity to make representations; and

(b) where it does so it must specify the time by and the manner in which the representations must be made.

(3) Where the court proposes—

(a) to make an order of its own initiative; and

(b) to hold a hearing to decide whether to make the order,

it must give each party likely to be affected by the order at least 3 days' notice of the hearing.

(4) The court may make an order of its own initiative, without hearing the parties or giving them an opportunity to make representations.

(5) Where the court has made an order under paragraph (4)—

(a) a party affected by the order may apply to have it set aside[GL], varied or stayed[GL]; and

(b) the order must contain a statement of the right to make such an application

(6) An application under paragraph (5)(a) must be made—

(a) within such period as may be specified by the court; or

(b) if the court does not specify a period, not more than 7 days after the date on which the order was served on the party making the application.

(CCR, O.42, in Schedule 2, sets out the circumstances when the court may not make an order of its own initiative against the Crown.)

3.3.1 **Effect of rule**—The court's duty of active case management includes narrowing the issues, controlling the timetable and moving the case forward quickly and efficiently (r.1.4(2)(b), (c), (g) and (l)). By giving him power to make orders on his own initiative, r.3.3 enables the judge to manage cases proactively as well as reactively. The judge has power to:

(1) make a provisional order containing a procedure for representations and a hearing (r.3.3(2)); or

(2) convene a hearing to decide whether to make a specified order (r.3.3(3)); or

(3) make an order without hearing the parties or giving them an opportunity to make representations (r.3.3(4)). In this instance the parties may later apply to set aside that order (r.3.3(5) and (6)).

Power to strike out a statement of case

3.4 **3.4**—(1) In this rule and rule 3.5, reference to a statement of case includes reference to part of a statement of case.

(2) The court may strike out[GL] a statement of case if it appears to the court—

(a) that the statement of case discloses no reasonable grounds for bringing or defending the claim;

(b) that the statement of case is an abuse of the court's process or is otherwise likely to obstruct the just disposal of the proceedings; or

(c) that there has been a failure to comply with a rule, practice direction or court order.

(3) When the court strikes out a statement of case it may make any consequential order it considers appropriate.

(4) Where—

(a) the court has struck out a claimant's statement of case;

(b) the claimant has been ordered to pay costs to the defendant; and

(c) before the claimant pays those costs, he starts another claim against the same defendant, arising out of facts which are the same or substantially the same as those relating to the claim in which the statement of claim was struck out,

the court may, on the application of the defendant, stay[GL] the second claim until the costs of the first claim have been paid.

(5) Paragraph (2) does not limit any other power of the court to strike out[GL] a statement of case.

Effect of rule—"Statement of case" means "a claim form, particulars of claim where these are not included in the claim form, defence, Pt 20 claim, or a reply to a defence" (r.2.3(1)). "Strike out" is defined in the Glossary. This rule enables the court to strike out statements of case in whole or in part and then make consequential orders. A statement of case may be struck out (in whole or in part) if: **3.4.1**

(a) it discloses no reasonable grounds for bringing or defending the claim;

(b) it is an abuse of the court's process or is otherwise likely to obstruct the just disposal of the proceedings; or

(c) there has been a failure to comply with a rule, practice direction or court order.

Grounds (a) and (b) cover statements of case which are unreasonably vague, incoherent, vexatious, scurrilous or obviously ill-founded and other cases which do not amount to a legally recognisable claim or defence. This power can be exercised at the stage of issuing a claim and thus defendants against whom an ill-founded action is sought to be brought will be spared needless expense in having to initiate "strike out" proceedings.

Ground (c) covers cases where the abuse lies not in the statement of case itself but in the way the claim or defence (as the case may be) has been conducted. The strike-out can be made even where there was nothing in the rule, practice direction or court order breached which specified that this might happen as a consequence of breach. In many circumstances such a strike-out would seem unduly harsh unless the party concerned was warned (possibly in writing by another party) of the risk of his statement of case being struck out if he did not comply with the rule, practice direction or court order in question.

In the case of non-compliance with a rule or practice direction the court may instead order the non-complying party to pay a sum of money into court (see r.3.1(5) and (6)). In the case of non-compliance with a court order the court may instead repeat its order, this time imposing conditions and/or specifying the consequences of failure to comply with the order or condition (r.3.1(3)).

In *Biguzzi v. Rank Leisure plc* (Court of Appeal, Civil Division, Transcript July 26, 1999) the Court of Appeal drew attention to several alternatives to a strike out under r.3.4 which may be appropriate to deal with non-compliance with time limits laid down by rules or orders: awarding costs on the indemnity basis payable forthwith, ordering a party to pay money into court and awarding interest at a higher or lower rate.

Applications under r.3.4 should be made as soon as possible and before allocation if possible (Practice Direction supplementing r.3.4, para. 5.1, see para. 3PD–001).

The court may make an order under r.3.4 of its own initiative (r.3.3). The most likely occasion for such an order would be on the filing of a claim form or defence which appears to fall within grounds (a) or (b) above (Practice Direction supplementing r.3.4, paras 2.2 and 3.2, see para. 3PD–001). The fact that the court allows such a claim or defence to proceed does not prejudice the right of any other party to apply for an order under r.3.4 (Practice Direction supplementing r.3.4, paras 2.6 and 3.5, see para. 3PD–001).

Overlap with Part 24 (summary judgment)—Many cases falling within r.3.4 also fall within Pt 24 which provides for the summary disposal of claims or defences which have no reasonable prospect of success (see r.24.2). However, the overlap between r.3.4 and Pt 24 is not complete: **3.4.2**

(1) Unlike Pt 24, r.3.4 also applies to cases of non-compliance with a rule, practice direction or court order.
(2) Unlike r.3.4, Pt 24 also applies to the summary disposal of issues including preliminary issues.
(3) There are various procedural requirements in Pt 24 which do not apply to r.3.4.

3.4.3 **Consequential orders after striking out**—If the court has struck out a claim form or defence of its own initiative shortly after that document was filed the court may give directions permitting, for example the filing of an amended document (Practice Direction supplementing r.3.4, paras 2 and 3, see para. 3PD–001).

Where an order of strike out has been made the court may enter such judgment for the other party as that party appears entitled to (Practice Direction supplementing r.3.4, para. 4.2, see para. 3PD–001). Where the strike out relates only to part of a statement of case the court may also give directions for the management of any remaining parts of the proceedings, for example allocating them to a case management track (r.3.1).

3.4.4 **Staying subsequent claim until costs paid**—Rule 3.4(4) applies where a claimant's statement of case has been struck out, the claimant has been ordered to pay costs to the defendant and before paying those costs he starts another claim against the same defendant arising out of facts which are the same or substantially the same as those relating to the first claim. In such a case the defendant may apply for a stay of the second claim until the costs of the first claim have been paid. The term "stay" is defined in the Glossary. As to the expression "arising out of facts which are the same or substantially the same" see the commentary to r.17.4 in which similar words are used.

3.4.5 **Vexatious litigants**—The term "vexatious litigant" is used to describe a person who has habitually and persistently and without reasonable ground instituted vexatious proceedings, whether in the High Court or an inferior court, made vexatious applications in such proceedings or instituted vexatious prosecutions. In respect of such a person an order may be made under SCA 1981, s.42 requiring him to obtain the permission of a High Court judge to begin or continue or to make any application in proceedings covered by the order (see SCP 1999, Vol. 2, para. 20A–253).

An application by a vexatious litigant for permission to begin or continue, or to make any application in, any civil proceedings must be made by application notice issued in the High Court and will be determined by a High Court Judge (Practice Direction supplementing r.3.4, paras 7.2 and 7.6). Similarly, an application to set aside the grant of permission by a person against whom the vexatious litigant wishes to take proceedings can be made by application notice if the permission was granted other than at a hearing of which the applicant was given notice (Practice Direction supplementing r.3.4, paras 7.9 and 7.10). As to the meaning of "application notice" see r.23.1.

Judgment without trial after striking out

3.5 **3.5**—(1) This rule applies where—

(a) the court makes an order which includes a term that the statement of case of a party shall be struck out if the party does not comply with the order; and
(b) the party against whom the order was made does not comply with it.

(2) A party may obtain judgment with costs by filing a request for judgment if—

(a) the order referred to in paragraph (1)(a) relates to the whole of a statement of case; and
(b) where the party wishing to obtain judgment is the claimant, the claim is for—
 (i) a specified amount of money;
 (ii) an amount of money to be decided by the court;
 (iii) delivery of goods where the claim form gives the defendant the alternative of paying their value; or
 (iv) any combination of these remedies.

(3) The request must state that the right to enter judgment has arisen because the court's order has not been complied with.

(4) A party must make an application in accordance with Part 23 if he wishes to obtain judgment under this rule in a case to which paragraph (2) does not apply.

3.5.1 **Effect of rule**—This rule applies where a striking out occurs automatically because of non-compliance with the terms of a court order, for example an unless order. In such circumstances this rule enables the other party to obtain judgment with costs.

In the cases falling within r.3.5(2) the judgment can be obtained by filing a request stating that the right to enter judgment has arisen because the court's order has not been complied with. In other cases the party entitled to judgment under this rule must make an application in accordance with Pt 23 (General rules about applications for court orders).

Where the court makes an order directly striking out a statement of case it may also make any consequential order it thinks appropriate (r.3.4(3)) including entering such judgment for the other party as that party appears entitled to (Practice Direction supplementing r.3.4, para. 4.2, see para. 3PD–001). Rule 3.5 does not apply in these circumstances.

Setting aside judgment entered after striking out

3.6—(1) A party against whom the court has entered judgment under rule 3.5 may apply to the court to set the judgment aside. **3.6**

(2) An application under paragraph (1) must be made not more than 14 days after the judgment has been served on the party making the application.

(3) If the right to enter judgment had not arisen at the time when judgment was entered, the court must set aside[GL] the judgment.

(4) If the application to set aside[GL] is made for any other reason, rule 3.9 (relief from sanctions) shall apply.

Effect of rule—This rule applies to a judgment entered under r.3.5, *i.e.* a judgment with costs entered where a statement of case has been struck out automatically as a consequence of non-compliance with the terms of a court order. It does not apply to orders directly striking out a statement of case (for example, a striking out under r.3.4). **3.6.1**

The party against whom the judgment under r.3.5 was entered may apply to the court to set the judgment aside (r.3.6(1)). The application must be made promptly, within 14 days of service of the judgment on the applicant (r.3.6(2); as to the calculation of time periods under these rules, see r.2.8 and the commentary thereto). If the judgment was entered prematurely, the court must set it aside. In other cases the court has a discretion, to be exercised after considering all the circumstances (r.3.6(4) which refers to r.3.9 (relief from sanctions)).

Where the court has made an order directly striking out a statement of case (for example, an order under r.3.4(2)(c) the party against whom that order was made may apply under r.3.9 for relief from that order.

Sanctions for non-payment of certain fees

3.7—(1) This rule applies where— **3.7**

(a) an allocation questionnaire or a listing questionnaire is filed without payment of the fee specified by the relevant Fees Order; or

(b) the court dispenses with the need for an allocation questionnaire or a listing questionnaire or both; or

(c) these Rules do not require an allocation questionnaire or a listing questionnaire to be filed in relation to the claim in question.

(Rule 26.3 provides for the court to dispense with the need for an allocation questionnaire and rules 28.5 and 29.6 provide for the court to dispense with the need for a listing questionnaire.)

(2) The court will serve a notice on the claimant requiring payment of the fee which the relevant Fees Order specifies as being due—

(a) on the filing of the allocation questionnaire or the listing questionnaire; or

(b) in the circumstances where the claimant is not required to file an allocation questionnaire or a listing questionnaire,

if, at the time the fee is due, the claimant has not paid the fee or made an application for exemption from or remission of the fee.

(3) The notice will specify the date by which the claimant must pay the fee.

(4) If the claimant does not—

(a) pay the fee; or

(b) make an application for an exemption from or remission of the fee,

by the date specified in the notice—

(i) the claim shall be struck out; and

(ii) the claimant shall be liable for the costs which the defendant has incurred unless the court orders otherwise.

(Rule 44.12 provides for the basis of assessment where right to costs arises under this rule.)

(5) Where an application for exemption from or remission of a fee is refused, the court will serve notice on the claimant requiring payment of the fee by the date specified in the notice.

(6) If the claimant does not pay the fee by the date specified in the notice—

(a) the claim shall be struck out; and

(b) the claimant shall be liable for the costs which the defendant has incurred unless the court orders otherwise.

(7) If—

(a) a claimant applies under rule 3.9 (relief from sanctions) to have the claim reinstated; and

(b) the court grants relief under that rule,

the relief shall be conditional on the claimant—

(i) paying the fee; or

(ii) filing evidence of exemption from payment or remission of the fee,

within 2 days of the date of the order.

(c) evidence of exemption from payment or remission of the fee has not been filed.

3.7.1 **The relevant fees**—This rule makes provisions concerning the court fees payable on the filing of an allocation questionnaire (as to which, see r.26.3) or a listing questionnaire (as to which see r.28.5 (fast track cases) and r.29.6 (multi-track cases)). These fees are payable by the claimant.

3.7.2 **Consequences of non-payment**—If the claimant fails to pay these fees or to apply for exemption or remission in respect of them, the court will serve a notice on him requiring payment and specifying the date of payment. If the claimant fails to pay the fee or apply for exemption or remission by the date specified in the notice:

(1) the claim will be struck out, and

(2) the claimant will be liable for the defendant's costs of the claim unless the court orders otherwise.

The striking out is automatic but the claimant can apply under r.3.9 (relief from sanctions) to have the claim reinstated on the strict terms set out in r.3.7(7)).

If a claim is struck out under this rule the court will send a notice to the defendant stating that the claim has been stuck out and explaining the effect that has upon any interim injunction granted (Practice Direction supplementing rule 3.7, see para. 3BPD–001). The defendant must file this notice if it becomes necessary to commence proceedings for a detailed assessment of costs (see r.44.12 and Directions relating to Part 47, para. 4.5, see 47PD–011).

Sanctions have effect unless defaulting party obtains relief

3.8 **3.8**—(1) Where a party has failed to comply with a rule, practice direction or court order, any sanction for failure to comply imposed by the rule, practice direction or court order has effect unless the party in default applies for and obtains relief from the sanction.

(Rule 3.9 sets out the circumstances which the court may consider on an application to grant relief from a sanction.)

(2) Where the sanction is the payment of costs, the party in default may only obtain relief by appealing against the order for costs.

(3) Where a rule, practice direction or court order—

(a) requires a party to do something within a specified time, and

(b) specifies the consequence of failure to comply,

the time for doing the act in question may not be extended by agreement between the parties.

3.8.1 **Effect of rule**—This rule confirms the validity of any sanction imposed by a rule, practice direction or court order whilst at the same time providing that the party in default may apply for relief from the sanction. In most cases an application for relief can be made under r.3.9. However, if the sanction is an order for the payment of costs the party in default may obtain relief only by way of appealing against the order for costs (r.3.8(2)).

This rule also removes the right which the parties would otherwise have (r.2.11) to extend by agreement the time for doing an act specified in a rule, practice or court order where the rule, practice direction or court order also specifies the time for doing that act and the consequences of failure to comply (r.3.8(3)).

Relief from sanctions

3.9—(1) On an application for relief from any sanction imposed for a failure to comply with any rule, practice direction or court order the court will consider all the circumstances including— 3.9

(a) the interests of the administration of justice;
(b) whether the application for relief has been made promptly;
(c) whether the failure to comply was intentional;
(d) whether there is a good explanation for the failure;
(e) the extent to which the party in default has complied with other rules, practice directions and court orders and any relevant pre-action protocol[GL];
(f) whether the failure to comply was caused by the party or his legal representative;
(g) whether the trial date or the likely date can still be met if relief is granted;
(h) the effect which the failure to comply had on each party; and
(i) the effect which the granting of relief would have on each party.

(2) An application for relief must be supported by evidence.

Effect of rule—This rule sets out the court's general discretion to give relief against any sanction imposed for failure to comply with any rule, practice direction or court order. Rule 3.9(1) lists various circumstances the court must consider. The list is not exhaustive; the court must consider "all the circumstances". 3.9.1

Rule 3.9(2) requires the application for relief to be supported by evidence. The applicant cannot rely upon oral evidence unless the court so permits (r.32.6). Instead he may rely upon written evidence set out in his statement of case or application notice or in a witness statement. Each item of written evidence relied on must contain a statement of truth (as to which, see further Pt 22 and the Practice Direction supplementing it at para. 22PD–001). An applicant may also rely upon affidavit evidence if he so wishes. However, if he does so, he may not recover any additional costs thereby incurred unless the court orders otherwise (r.32.15 and, as to affidavits generally, r.32.16, r.32.17 and the Practice Direction supplementing Pt 32, see para. 32PD–001).

General power of the court to rectify matters where there has been an error of procedure

3.10 Where there has been an error of procedure such as a failure to comply with a rule or practice direction— 3.10

(a) the error does not invalidate any step taken in the proceedings unless the court so orders; and
(b) the court may make an order to remedy the error.

Effect of non-compliance—In these rules, as under the previous rules, non-compliance with a rule, or (under these rules) a practice direction, does not nullify the proceedings or any step taken in the proceedings unless the court so orders. Instead the court has power to make an order to remedy the error, *i.e.* deal with the non-compliance. This power is additional to its power to strike out a statement of case (r.3.4) or order a party to pay a sum of money into court (r.3.1(5)) in cases in which such orders would be appropriate where there is some failure to comply with a rule or practice direction. (The power in r.3.4 also applies on non-compliance with a court order. The power in r.3.1(5) also applies on non-compliance with a pre-action protocol.) 3.10.1

Remedying procedural errors—An application for an order to remedy an error of procedure may be made by application notice (as to which see r.23.1) or in response to an application to strike out a statement of case under r.3.4. The court may also make the order of its own initiative (r.3.3). 3.10.2

The court has a discretion as to whether to remedy the error and, if so, on what terms including terms as to costs. Alternatively, the court may make a dispensing order waiving the error. In many cases the way in which the discretion is exercised will depend on whether it appears that the other parties have suffered prejudice as a consequence of the error, but the rule gives the court the widest possible discretion and the court can look at all the circumstances. Hence, although prejudice or lack of prejudice to the other party will often be the all important factor in the exercise of discretion, it will not always be so. For case illustrations under the previous rules (which had similar effect) see *Leal v. Dunlop Bio-Processes International Ltd* [1984] 1 W.L.R. 874, CA, *Metroinvest Anstalt v. Commercial Union Assurance Co. Plc* [1985] 1 W.L.R. 513; [1985] 2 All E.R. 318, CA, *Oyston v. Blaker* [1996] 1 W.L.R. 1326, CA; [1996] 2 All E.R. 106.

PRACTICE DIRECTION—STRIKING OUT A STATEMENT OF CASE

3PD–001 *This Practice Direction supplements CPR Rule 3.4*

1. Introductory

1.1 Rule 1.4(2)(c) includes as an example of active case management the summary disposal of issues which do not need full investigation at trial.

1.2 The rules give the court two distinct powers which may be used to achieve this. Rule 3.4enables the court to strike out the whole or part of a statement of case which discloses no reasonable grounds for bringing or defending a claim (rule 3.4(2)(a)), or which is an abuse of the process of the court or otherwise likely to obstruct the just disposal of the proceedings (rule 3.4(2)(b)). Rule 24.2 enables the court to give summary judgment against a claimant or defendant where that party has no real prospect of succeeding on his claim or defence. Both those powers may be exercised on an application by a party or on the court's own initiative.

1.3 This practice direction sets out the procedure a party should follow if he wishes to make an application for an order under rule 3.4.

1.4 The following are examples of cases where the court may conclude that particulars of claim (whether contained in a claim form or filed separately) fall within rule 3.4(2)(a):

(1) those which set out no facts indicating what the claim is about, for example "Money owed £5,000",

(2) those which are incoherent and make no sense,

(3) those which contain a coherent set of facts but those facts, even if true, do not disclose any legally recognisable claim against the defendant.

1.5 A claim may fall within rule 3.4(2)(b) where it is vexatious, scurrilous or obviously ill-founded.

1.6 A defence may fall within rule 3.4(2)(a) where:

(1) it consists of a bare denial or otherwise sets out no coherent statement of facts, or

(2) the facts it sets out, while coherent, would not even if true amount in law to a defence to the claim.

1.7 A party may believe he can show without a trial that an opponent's case has no real prospect of success on the facts, or that the case is bound to succeed or fail, as the case may be, because of a point of law (including the construction of a document), is bound to fail. In such a case the party concerned may make an application under rule 3.4 or Part 24 (or both) as he thinks appropriate.

1.8 The examples set out above are intended only as illustrations.

2. Claims which appear to fall within rule 3.4(2)(a) or (b)

2.1 If a court officer is asked to issue a claim form which he believes may fall within rule 3.4(2)(a)or (b) he should issue it, but may then consult a judge (under rule 3.2) before returning the claim form to the claimant or taking any other step to serve the defendant. The judge may on his own initiative make an immediate order designed to ensure that the claim is disposed of or (as the case may be) proceeds in a way that accords with the rules.

2.3 The judge may allow the claimant a hearing before deciding whether to make such an order.

2.4 Orders the judge may make include:

(1) an order that the claim be stayed until further order,

(2) an order that the claim form be retained by the court and not served until the stay is lifted,

(3) an order that no application by the claimant to lift the stay be heard unless he files such further documents (for example a witness statement or an amended claim form or particulars of claim) as may be specified in the order.

2.5 Where the judge makes any such order or, subsequently, an order lifting the stay he may give directions about the service on the defendant of the order and any other documents on the court file.

2.6 The fact that a judge allows a claim referred to him by a court officer to proceed does not prejudice the right of any party to apply for any order against the claimant.

3. Defences which appear to fall within rule 3.4(2)(a) or (b)

3.1 A court officer may similarly consult a judge about any document filed which purports to be a defence and which he believes may fall within rule 3.4(2)(a) or (b). **3PD–002**

3.2 If the judge decides that the document falls within rule 3.4(2)(a) or (b) he may on his own initiative make an order striking it out. Where he does so he may extend the time for the defendant to file a proper defence.

3.3 The judge may allow the defendant a hearing before deciding whether to make such an order.

3.4 Alternatively the judge may make an order under rule 18.1 requiring the defendant within a stated time to clarify his defence or to give additional information about it. The order may provide that the defence will be struck out if the defendant does not comply.

3.5 The fact that a judge does not strike out a defence on his own initiative does not prejudice the right of the claimant to apply for any order against the defendant.

4. General Provisions

(1) The court may exercise its powers under rule 3.4(2)(a) or (b) on application or on its own initiative at any time.

(2) Where a judge at a hearing strikes out all or part of a party's statement of case he may enter such judgment for the other party as that party appears entitled to.

5. Applications for orders under rule 3.4(2)

5.1 Attention is drawn to Part 23 (General Rules about Applications) and to the practice direction that supplements it. The practice direction requires all applications to be made as soon as possible and before allocation if possible.

5.2 While many applications under rule 3.4(2) can be made without evidence in support, the applicant should consider whether facts need to be proved and, if so, whether evidence in support should be filed and served.

6. Applications for summary judgment

Applications for summary judgment may be made under Part 24. Attention is drawn to that Part and to the practice direction that supplements it.

7. Vexatious Litigants

7.1 This Practice Direction applies where a "civil proceedings order" or an "all proceedings order" (as respectively defined under section 42(1A) of the Supreme Court Act, 1981) is in force against a person ("the litigant").

7.2 An application by the litigant for permission to begin or continue, or to make any application in, any civil proceedings shall be made by application notice issued in the High Court and signed by the litigant.

7.3 The application notice must state:

(1) the title and reference number of the proceedings in which the civil proceedings order or the all proceedings order, as the case may be, was made,

(2) the full name of the litigant and his address,

(3) the order the applicant is seeking, and

(4) briefly, why the applicant is seeking the order.

7.4 The application notice must be filed together with any written evidence on which the litigant relies in support of his application.

7.5 Either in the application notice or in written evidence filed in support of the application, the previous occasions on which the litigant made an application for permission under section 42(1A) of the said Act must be listed.

7.6 The application notice, together with any written evidence, will be placed before a High Court judge who may:

(1) without the attendance of the applicant make an order giving the permission sought;

(2) give directions for further written evidence to be supplied by the litigant before an order is made on the application;

(3) where the remedy sought, or the grounds advanced, substantially repeat those submitted in support of a previous application which has been refused, make an order dismissing the application without a hearing; or

(4) in any case where (3) does not apply, give directions for the hearing of the application.

7.7 Directions given under paragraph 7.6(4) may include an order that the application notice be served on the Attorney General and on any person against whom the litigant desires to bring the proceedings for which permission is being sought.

7.8 Any order made under paragraphs 6 or 7 will be served on the litigant at the address given in the application notice. CPR Part 6 will apply.

7.9 A person may apply to set aside the grant of permission if:

(1) the permission allowed the litigant to bring or continue proceedings against that person or to make any application against him, and

(2) the permission was granted other than at a hearing of which that person was given notice under paragraph 7.

7.10 Any application under paragraph 9 must be made in accordance with CPR Part 23.

PRACTICE DIRECTION—SANCTIONS FOR NON-PAYMENT OF FEES

This Practice Direction supplements CPR Rule 3.7

3BPD–001 **1.** If a claim is struck out under rule 3.7, the court will send notice that it has been struck out to the defendant.

2. The notice will also explain the effect of rule 25.11. This provides that any interim injunction will cease to have effect 14 days after the date the claim is struck out under rule 3.7. Paragraph (2) provides that if the claimant applies to reinstate the claim before the interim injunction ceases to have effect, the injunction will continue until the hearing of the application unless the court orders otherwise. If the claimant makes such an application, the defendant will be given notice in the ordinary way under rule 23.4.

PART 4

Forms

Editorial Introduction

The forms which may be used in conjunction with these Rules are not prescribed by rule, as was formerly the case under the RSC and CCR. As practice forms they can be varied to accommodate the particular circumstances of a case provided that any instruction or guidance to the recipient are always included. The Part 4 practice direction contains three tables. Listed in table 1 are the "N" forms—new forms referred to in and required by the practice directions supporting the Rules, in table 2 forms that were previously prescribed forms in the High Court, Queen's Bench Masters' practice forms and Chancery Masters' practice forms, and in table 3 forms that were previously prescribed or practice forms in the county courts. Most of the forms in table 1 are published in Section C. The forms in tables 2 and 3 are those which are still appropriate for use and are undergoing amendment to ensure consistency with the Rules. Until they are published in amended form, litigants and practitioners may use the existing forms suitably amended. **4.0.1**

4—(1) The forms set out in a practice direction shall be used in the cases to which they apply. **4.1**

(2) A form may be varied by the court or a party if the variation is required by the circumstances of a particular case.

(3) A form must not be varied so as to leave out any information or guidance which the form gives to the recipient.

(4) Where these Rules require a form to be sent by the court or by a party for another party to use, it must be sent without any variation except such as is required by the circumstances of the particular case.

(5) Where the court or a party produces a form shown in a practice direction with the words "Royal Arms", the form must include a replica of the Royal Arms at the head of the first page.

Use of forms—Rule 4(1), "The forms ... shall be used ..."; certain forms must be used in connection with the Rules, but other forms are referred to in the Rules which are provided or suggested for use. For example, the Part 7 practice direction at paragraph 3.1 states that forms N1 or N208 *must* be used to start a claim, on the other hand, for an application notice referred to in Part 23, the practice direction at para. 2.1 states that form N244 *may* be used. **4.1.1**

PRACTICE DIRECTIONS—FORMS

This Practice Direction Supplements Part 4 of the Civil Procedure Rules

Scope of this practice direction:

1.1 This practice directions lists the forms to be used in civil proceedings on or after 26th April 1999, when the Civil Procedure Rules (CPR) come into force. **4PD–001**

1.2 The forms may be modified as the circumstances require, provided that all essential information, especially information or guidance which the form gives to the recipient, is included.

1.3 This practice direction contains 3 tables—

- Table 1 lists forms required by CPR Parts 1–48 and therefore applicable in both the High Court and county court
- Table 2 lists High Court forms in use before 26th April 1999 that will remain in use on or after that date (see paragraph 4 below)
- Table 3 lists county court forms in use before 26th April 1999 that will remain in use on or after that date (see paragraph 5 below)

Other forms:

2.1 Other forms may be authorised by practice directions supplementing

Part 49 (specialist proceedings). For example the forms relating to Admiralty proceedings are authorised by, and annexed to, the Admiralty practice direction.

Table 1 "N" Forms

Contents:

4PD–002 **3.1** This table lists the "N" forms that are referred to and required to be used by Practice Directions supplementing particular Parts of the CPR. A Practice Direction and its paragraphs are abbreviated by reference to the Part of the CPR which it supplements and the relevant paragraph of the Practice Direction, for example; PD 34 1.2.

No.	Title
N1	Part 7 (general) claim form (Pt 7 PD 3.1)
N1 CPC	Claim Production Centre ("CPC") claim form—rule 7.10)
N1A	Notes for claimant
N1C	Notes for defendant
N1(FD)	Notes for defendant (Consumer Credit Act cases)
N9	Ackinowledgment of service/response pack (Pt 10 PD 2)
N9 CPC	CPC acknowledgment of service/response pack (Pt 10 PD 2)
N9A	Admission and statement of means (specified amount) (Pt 14 PD 2.1)
N9B	Defence and counterclaim (specified amount) (Pt 15 PD 1.3)
N9C	Admission and statement of means (unspecified amount and non money claims) (Pt 14 PD 2.1)
N9D	Defence and counterclaim (unspecified amount and non money claims) (Pt 15 PD 1.3)
N10	Notice that acknowledgment of service has been filed—rule 10.4
N17	Judgment for claimant (amount to be decided by court)—rules 12.5(3), 14.6(7) and 14.7(10)
N20	Witness summons (Pt 34 PD 1.2)
N21	Order for Examination for Deponent before the hearing (Pt 34 PD 4.1)

No.	Title
N24	Blank form of order or judgment
N30	Judgment for claimant (default HC)—rule 12.5(2)
N30	Judgment for claimant (default CC)—rule 12.5(2)
N30(1)	Judgment for claimant (acceptance HC) (Pt 14 PD 4.2)
N30(1)	Judgment for claimant (acceptance CC) (Pt 14 PD 4.2)
N30(2)	Judgment for claimant (after determination HC) (Pt 14 PD 10(4)
N30(2)	Judgment for claimant (after determination CC) (Pt 14 PD 10(4))
N30(3)	Judgment for claimant (after re-determination HC)—rule 14.13
N30(3)	Judgment for claimant (after re-determination CC)—rule 14.13
N32	Judgment for return of goods
N32(1) HP/CCA	Judgment for delivery of goods
N32(2) HP/CCA	Judgment for delivery of goods (suspended)
N32(3) HP/CCA	Judgment for delivery of goods
N32(4)	Variation order (return of goods)
N32(5) HP/CCA	Order for balance for purchase price
N33	Judgment for delivery of goods
N34	Judgment for claimant (after amount decided by court HC)
N34	Judgment for claimant (after amount decided by court CC)
N150	Allocation Questionnaire (Pt 26 PD 2.1)
N150A	Master/DJ's directions on allocation
N151	Allocation Questionnaire (amount to be decided by court)
N151A	Master/DJ's directions on allocation

No.	Title
N152	Notice that [defence][counterclaim] has been filed (Pt 26 PD 2.5)
N153	Notice of allocation or listing hearing (Pt 26 PD 6.2)
N154	Notice of allocation to fast track (Pt 26 PD 4.2 and 9)
N155	Notice of allocation to multi track (Pt 26 PD 4.2 and 10)
N156	Order for further information (for allocation) (Pt 26 PD 4.2(2))
N157	Notice of allocation to small claims track (Pt 26 PD 4.2 and 8)
N158	Notice of allocation to small claims track (preliminary hearing) (Pt 26 PD 4.2 and 8)
N159	Notice of allocation to small claims track (no hearing) (Pt 26 PD 4.2 and 8)
N160	Notice of allocation to small claims track (with parties consent) (Pt 26 PD 4.2 and 8)
N170	Listing questionnaire (Pt 26 PD 6.1 and Pt 28 PD 8.1)
N171	Notice of date for return of listing questionnaire (Pt 26 PD 6.1 and Pt 28 PD 8.1)
N172	Notice of trial date
N173	Notice of non-payment of fee—rule 3.7
N205A	Notice of issue (specified amount)
N205B	Notice of issue (unspecified amount)
N205C	Notice of issue (non-money claim)
N208	Part 8 claim form (Pt 8 PD 2.2)
N208A	Part 8 notes for claimant
N208C	Part 8 notes for defendant
N209	Part 8 notice of issue
N210	Part 8 acknowledgment of service (Pt 8 PD 3.2)
N211	Part 20 claim form—rule 20.7

No.	Title
N211A	Part 20 notes for claimant
N211C	Part 20 notes for defendant
N212	Part 20 notice of issue
N213	Part 20 acknowledgment of service—rule 20.12
N215	Certificate of service—rule 6.10
N216	Notice of non-service—rule 6.11
N217	Order for substituted service—rule 6.8
N218	Notice of service on a partner (Pt 6 PD 4.2)
N225	Request for judgment and reply to admission (specified amount) (Pt 12 PD 3)
N225A	Notice of part admission (specified amount)—rule 15.5
N226	Notice of admission (unspecified amount)—rule 14.7
N227	Request for judgment by default (amount to be decided by the court)—rule 12.5
N228	Notice of admission (return of goods) (Pt 7 PD Consumer Credit Act 8.5)
N235	Certificate of suitability of litigation friend (Pt 21 PD 2.3)
N236	Notice of defence that amount claimed has been paid—rule 15.10
N242A	Notice of payment into court (in settlement)—rule 36.6(2)
N242B	Notice of payment into court (by order)
N243	Notice of acceptance of payment into court (Pt 36 PD 7.7)
N244	Application notice (Pt 23 PD 2.1)
N244A	Notice of hearing of application (Pt 23 PD 2.2)
N252	Notice of commencement of assessment (Pt 47 PD 2.3)

4PD–002

No.	Title
N253	Notice of amount allowed on provisional assessment (Pt 47 PD 6.5)
N254	Request for default costs certificate (Pt 47 PD 3.1)
N255	Default costs certificate HC (Pt 47 PD 3.3)
N255	Default costs certificate CC (Pt 47 PD 3.3)
N256	Final costs certificate HC (Pt 47 PD 5.11)
N256	Final costs certificate CC (Pt 47 PD 5.11)
N257	Interim costs certificate (Pt 47 PD 5.11)
N258	Request for assessment hearing (Pt 47 PD 4.3)
N259	Notice of appeal against a detailed assessment (Pt 47 PD 8.16)
N265	List of documents (Pt 31 PD 3.1)
N266	Notice to admit facts/admission of facts—rule 32.18
N268	Notice to prove documents at trial—rule 32.19
N271	Notice of transfer of proceedings—rule 30
N279	Notice of discontinuancee—rule 38.3
N292	Order on settlement on behalf of child or patient (Pt 21 PD 11.3)
N294	Claimants application for a variation order
N367	Notice of hearing to consider why fine should not be imposed—rule 34.10
N434	Notice of change of solicitor—rule 42.2

Table 2 Practice Forms

Contents:

4PD–003 **4.1** This table lists the Practice Forms that may be used under this Practice Direction. It contains forms that were previously—

- Prescribed Forms contained in Appendix A to the Rules of the Supreme Court 1965
- Queen's Bench Masters' Practice Forms
- Chancery Masters' Practice Forms

4.2 The former prescribed forms are shown as "No 00". The former practice forms where they are appropriate for use in either the Chancery or Queen's Bench Division (or where no specific form is available for use in the county court, in that court also) are prefixed "PF" followed by the number. Where the form is used mainly in the Chancery or Queen's Bench Division, the suffix CH or QB follows the form number.

4.3 Where a rule permits, a party intending to use a witness statement as an alternative to an affidavit should amend any form in this Table to be used in connection with that rule so that "witness statement" replaces "affidavit" wherever it appears in the form.

4.4 The forms in this list are reproduced in an Appendix to the Chancery and Queen's Bench Guides, and in practitioners' text books.

No 8A	Arbitration application/claim form
No 15	Acknowledgment of service on non-party
No 15A	Acknowledgment of service of Arbitration application
No 32	Order for examination within jurisdiction of witness before trial (rule 34.8)
No 33	Application for issue of letter of request to judicial authority out of jurisdiction (Pt 34 PD 5.2)
No 34	Order for issue of letter of request to judicial authority out of jurisdiction (Pt 34 PD 5.1)
No 35	Letter of request for examination of witness out of jurisdiction (Pt 34 PD 5.3(1))
No 37	Order for appointment of examiner to take evidence of witness out of jurisdiction (rule 34.13(4))
No 41	Default judgment in claim relating to detention of goods
No 42	Default judgment in claim for possession of land
No 42A	Order for possession (sched. 1—RSC O.113)
No 44	Judgment under Part 24
No 45	Judgment after trial before judge without jury (Pt 40 PD 14)
No 46	Judgment after trial before judge with jury (Pt 40 PD 14)
No 47	Judgment after trial before a master/technology & construction court judge (Pt 40 PD 14)
No 48	Judgment after decision of preliminary issue
No 49	Judgment against personal representatives (Pt 40 PD 14)

No 50	Judgment for defendant's costs on discontinuance
No 51	Judgment for costs after acceptance of money paid into court
No 52	Notice of [claim] [proceedings]
No 52A	Notice of judgment or order to an interested party
No 53	Writ of fieri facias (sched. 1—RSC O.46 and 47)
No 54	Writ of fieri facias on order for costs (sched. 1—RSC O.46 and 47)
No 55	Notice of seizure (sched. 1—RSC O.45)
No 56	Writ of fieri facias after levy of part (sched. 1—RSC O.45)
No 57	Writ of fieri facias against personal representatives (sched. 1—RSC O.45)
No 58	Writ of fieri facias de bonis ecclesiasticis (sched. 1—RSC O.45)
No 59	Writ of sequestrari de bonis ecclesiasticis (sched. 1—RSC O.45)
No 62	Writ of fieri facias to enforce Northern Irish or Scottish judgment (sched. 1—RSC O.45)
No 63	Writ of fieri facias to enforce foreign registered judgment (sched. 1—RSC O.45)
No 64	Writ of delivery: delivery of goods, damages and costs (sched. 1—RSC O.45)
No 65	Writ of delivery: delivery of goods or value, damages and costs (sched. 1—RSC O.45)
No 66	Writ of possession (sched. 1—RSC O.45)
No 66A	Writ of possession (sched. 1—RSC O.113)
No 67	Writ of sequestration (sched. 1—RSC O.45)
No 68	Writ of restitution (sched. 1—RSC O.46)
No 69	Writ of assistance (sched. 1—RSC O.46)
No 71	Notice of renewal of writ of execution (sched. 1—RSC O.46)

No 72	Garnishee order to show cause (sched. 1—RSC O.49, r.1)
No 73	Garnishee order absolute: garnishee owes more than judgment debt (sched. 1—RSC O.49, r.1)
No 74	Garnishee order absolute: garnishee owes less than judgment debt (sched. 1—RSC O.49, r.1)
No 75	Charging order: notice to show cause (sched. 1—RSC O.50, r.1)
No 76	Charging order absolute (sched. 1—RSC O.50, r.3)
No 79	Stop order on capital and income of funds in court (sched. 1—RSC O.50, r.10)
No 80	Affidavit and notice under RSC O.50, scheduled to Part 50 CPR
No 81	Order on claim to restrain transfer of stock (sched. 1 RSC O.50)
No 82	Application for appointment of a receiver (sched. 1—RSC O.51, r.3)
No 83	Order directing application for appointment of receiver and granting injunction meanwhile (sched. 1—RSC O.51, r.3)
No 84	Order for appointment of receiver by way of equitable execution (S37 of Supreme Court Act and sched. 1—RSC O.51)
No 85	Order of committal (sched. 1—RSC O.52)
No 86	Claim form for judicial review (sched. 1 RSC O.53, r.5(2A))
No 86A	Application for permission to apply for judicial review (sched. 1—RSC O.53, r.3)
No 86B	Renewal application for permission to apply for judicial review (sched. 1—RSC O.53, r.3)
No 87	Claim form for writ of habeas corpus ad subjiciendum
No 88	Notice of adjourned application for writ of habeas corpus
No 89	Writ of habeas corpus ad subjiciendum

No 90	Notice to be served with writ of habeas corpus ad subjiciendum
No 91	Writ of habeas corpus ad testificandum
No 92	Writ of habeas corpus ad respondendum
No 93	Order under the Evidence (Proceedings in Other Jurisdictions) Act 1975
No 94	Order for production of documents in marine insurance action (Pt 49 PD 49D.7.1)
No 95	Certificate of order against the Crown (sched. 1—RSC O.77, r.15)
No 96	Certificate of order for costs against the Crown (sched. 1—RSC O.77, r.15)
No 97	Claim form to grant bail (criminal proceedings) (sched. 1—RSC O.79, r.9)
No 97A	Claim form to vary arrangements for bail (criminal proceedings) (sched. 1—RSC O.79, r.9)
No 98	Order to release prisoner on bail (sched. 1—RSC O.79, r.9)
No 98A	Order varying arrangement for bail (sched. 1—RSC O.79, r.9)
No 99	Order of Court of Appeal to admit prisoner to bail (sched. 1—RSC O.59, r.20)
No 100	Notice of sureties for bail
No 101	Witness summons—Crown Court
No 103	Witness summons—Crown Court
No 104	Attachment of earnings order (Attachment of Earnings Act 1971)
No 105	Notice under s.10(2) of the Attachment of Earnings Act 1971
No 108	Application for reference to the European Court (sched. 1—RSC O.114, r.2(2))
No 109	Order for reference to the European Court (sched. 1—RSC O.114, r.2)

No 110	Certificate under s.12 of the Civil Jurisdiction and Judgments Act 1982 (sched. 1—RSC O.71, r.36(3))
No 111	Certificate of money provisions contained in a judgment for registration under Schedule 6 to the Civil Jurisdiction and Judgments Act 1982 (sched. 1—RSC O.71, r.37(3))
No 112	Certificate of non-money provisions contained in a judgment under Schedule 7 to the Civil Jurisdiction and Judgments Act 1982 (sched. 1—RSC O.71, r.38(2))
PF1	Application for time (rule 3.1(2)(a))
PF2	Order for time (rule 3.1(2)(a))
PF3	Application for an extension of time for serving a claim form (rule 7.6(1))
PF4	Order for an extension of time for serving a claim form (rule 7.6(1))
PF5	Order as to service in claim for possession where premises empty (sched. 1—RSC O.10, r.4)
PF6	Order for service out of the jurisdiction (rule 6A.4)
PF7QB	Request for service of document abroad (rule 6A.11)
PF8	Application for judgment for possession
PF9	Order for possession
PF11	Application for Part 24 judgment (whole claim)
PF12	Application for Part 24 judgment (one or some of several claims)
PF13	Order under Part 14 (No 1)
PF14	Order under Part 14 (No 2)
PF15	Order under Part 14 (for assessment of solicitor's bill of costs) (Part 48)
PF20	Application for Part 20 directions
PF21	Order for Part 20 directions
PF23QB	Notice of claim to goods taken in execution (sched. 1—RSC O.17)

PF24QB	Notice by claimant of admission or dispute of title of interpleader claimant (sched. 1—RSC O.17)
PF25QB	Interpleader application by defendant (sched. 1—RSC O.17)
PF26QB	Interpleader application by sheriff (sched. 1—RSC O.17)
PF27QB	Evidence in support of interpleader application (sched. 1—RSC O.17)
PF28QB	Interpleader order (1) claim barred where Sheriff interpleads (sched. 1—RSC O.17)
PF29QB	Interpleader order (1a) Sheriff to withdraw (sched. 1—RSC O.17)
PF30QB	Interpleader order (2) interclaimant substituted as defendant (sched. 1—RSC O.17)
PF31QB	Interpleader order (3) trial of issue (sched. 1—RSC O.17)
PF32QB	Interpleader order (4) conditional order for Sheriff to withdraw and trial of issue (sched. 1—RSC O.17)
PF34QB	Interpleader order (6) summary disposal (sched. 1—RSC O.17)
PF43	Application for security for costs
PF44	Order for security for costs
PF48	Court record available for use before and at hearing
PF49	Request to parties to state convenient dates for hearing
PF50	Application for directions (Part 29)
PF52	Order for directions following an application or otherwise (Part 29)
PF53	Order for trial of an issue
PF56	Request for further information or clarification with provision for response (Pt 18 PD 1.6(2))
PF57	Application for further information or clarification (Pt 18 PD 5)

PF58	Order for further information or clarification (rule 18.1)
PF63	Interim order for receiver in pending claiom (sched. 1—RSC O.30)
PF67	Evidence in support of application to make order or House of Lords an order of the High Court (Pt 40B PDD 13.2)
PF68	Order making an order of the House of Lords an order of the High Court (Pt 40B PD 13.3)
PF72	List of exhibits
PF74	Order for trial by Master
PF78QB	Solicitor's undertaking as to expenses (re letter of request) (rule 6A.11 and Pt 34 PD 5.3(5))
PF79	Default judgment for possession of land, damages and costs (Part 12)
PF83	Judgment (non attendance of party) (rule 39.3)
PF84	Judgment as a consequence of failure to comply with an order or condition (rules 3.1(3) and 3.5)
PF86	Praecipe for writ of fieri facias (sched. 1—RSC O.46 and 47)
PF87	Praecipe for writ of sequestration (sched. 1—RSC O.46)
PF88	Praecipe for writ of possession (sched. 1—RSC O.45)
PF89	Praecipe for writ of possession and fieri facias combined (sched. 1—RSC O.45)
PF90	Praecipe for writ of delivery (sched. 1—RSC O.45)
PF91	Evidence in support of application to enforce judgment for possession (sched. 1—RSC O.45)
PF97QB	Order for sale by Sheriff by private contract (sched. 1—RSC O.47)
PF98	Evidence in support of application for order for examination of judgment debtor or officer (sched. 1—RSC O.48)
PF99	Order for oral examination of judgment debtor or officer (sched. 1—RSC O.48)

PF100	Evidence in support of garnishee order (sched. 1—RSC O.49)
PF101	Evidence in support of charging order (sched. 1—RSC O.49)
PF103	Warrant of committal (general) (sched. 1—RSC O.52)
PF104	Warrant of committal (in face of court) (sched. 1—RSC O.52)
PF105	Warrant of committal (failure of witness to attend) (sched. 1—RSC O.52)
PF110	Notice of appeal to judge from Master or district judge (sched. 1—RSC O.58)
PF113	Evidence in support of application for service by an alternative method (Pt 6 PD 9.1)
PF114	Order for service by an alternative method (rule 6.8)
PF130	Form of advertisement
PF141	Evidence of personal service
PF147	Application for order declaring solicitor ceased to act (death etc) (rule 42.4)
PF148	Order declaring solicitor has ceased to act (rule 42.4)
PF149	Application by solicitor that he has ceased to act (rule 42.3)
PF150	Order that solicitor has ceased to act (rule 42.3)
PF152QB	Evidence in support of application for examination of witness under the Evidence (Proceedings in Other Jurisdictions) Act 1975
PF153QB	Certificate witness under the Evidence (Proceedings in Other Jurisdictions) Act 1975 (sched. 1—RSC O.70)
PF154QB	Order for registration of foreign judgment under the Foreign Judgments (Reciprocal Enforcement) Act 1933 (sched. 1—RSC O.71)
PF155QB	Certificates under s.10 of the Foreign Judgments (Reciprocal Enforcement) Act 1933 (sched. 1—RSC O.71)
PF156QB	Evidence in suppport of application for registration of a Community judgment (sched. 1—RSC O.71)

PF157QB	Order for registration of a Community judgment (sched. 1—RSC O.71)
PF158QB	Notice of registration of a Community judgment (sched. 1—RSC O.71)
PF159QB	Evidence in support of application for registration of a judgment of another Contracting State (sched. 1—RSC O.71)
PF160QB	Order for registration of a judgment of another Contracting State under s.4 of the Civil Jurisdiction and Judgments Act 1982 (sched. 1—RSC O.71)
PF161QB	Notice of registration of a judgment of another Contracting State (sched. 1—RSC O.71)
PF163QB	Evidence in support of application for certified copy of a judgment for enforcement in another Contracting State (sched. 1—RSC O.71)
PF164QB	Evidence in support of application for certificate as to money provisions of a judgment of the High Court for registration elsewhere in the United Kingdom (sched. 1—RSC O.71)
PF165QB	Evidence in support of application for registration of a judgment of a court in another part of the United Kingdom containing non-money provisions (sched. 1—RSC O.71)
PF166QB	Certificate as to finality etc. of Arbitration Award for enforcement abroad (Arbitration Act 1996, s.58)
PF167QB	Order to stay proceedings under s.9 of the Arbitration Act 1996
PF168	Order to transfer claim to county court (County Courts Act 1984)
PF170	Application for child or patient's settlement in personal injury or fatal accident claims (Pt 21 PD 6 and 7)
PF172QB	Application in respect of funds in court or to be brought into court (Pt 21 PD 8)
PF177	Order for written statement as to partners in firm (sched. 1—RSC O.81, r.2)
PF179QB	Evidence in support of an application for registration of a Bill of Sale (sched. 1—RSC O.95)

PF180QB	Evidence in support of an application for registration of an Absolute Bill of Sale, Settlement and Deed of Gift (sched. 1—RSC O.95)
PF181QB	Evidence in support of an application for re-registration of a Bill of Sale (sched. 1—RSC O.95)
PF182QB	Order for extension of time to register or re-register a Bill of Sale (sched. 1—RSC O.95)
PF183QB	Evidence in support of an application for permission to enter a memorandum of Satisfaction on a Bill of Sale (sched. 1—RSC O.95)
PF184QB	Claim form for entry of satisfaction on a registered Bill of Sale (sched. 1—RSC O.95)
PF185QB	Order for entry of Satisfaction on a registered Bill of Sale (sched. 1—RSC O.95)
PF186QB	Evidence in support of application for registration of Assignment of Book Debts (sched. 1—RSC O.95)
PF187	Application for Solicitor's Charging order (sched. 1—RSC O.106, r.2)
PF188	Charging order: Solicitor's costs (sched. 1—RSC O.106, r.2)
PF197	Application for order for transfer from the Royal Courts of Justice to a district registry or vice-versa or from one district registry to another (rule 30.2(4))
PF198	Order under PF197
PF200	Notice of proposed order to transfer to county court or strike out (s.40(1) and (8) of the County Courts Act 1984)
PF201	Notice of hearing to decide whether to order transfer to county court or strike out
PF202	Notice of proposed order to transfer to county court (s.40(2) of the County Courts Act 1984)
PF203	Notice of objection to proposed transfer to county court (s.40(2) of the County Courts Act 1984)
PF205	Evidence in support of application for permission to execute for earlier costs of enforcement under s.15(3) and (4) of the Courts and Legal Services Act 1990
PF5CH	Order for possession on mortgaged property

PF6CH	Certificate on application for leave to issue execution on suspended order for possession where defendant in default of acknowledgment of service
PF7CH	Inquiry for persons entitled to the property of an intestate dying on or after 1st January 1926
PF8CH	Summons after masters findings on kin enquiry for re benjamin order giving leave to distribute estate upon footing
PF9CH	re benjamin order giving leave to distribute estate upon footing
PF10CH	Judgment in beneficiaries administration action where deceased died on or after 1st January 1926
PF11CH	Judgment in creditors administration action where deceased died on or after 1st January 1926
PF12CH	Advertisement for creditors
PF13CH	Advertisement for claimants other than creditors
PF14CH	Affidavit verifying list of creditors claims
PF15CH	List of claims sent in pursuant to advertisement by persons claiming to be creditors
PF16CH	List of claims by persons claiming to be creditors other than those sent in pursuant to advertisement
PF17CH	List of sums of money which may be due in respect of which no claim has been received
PF18CH	Notice to creditor to prove claim
PF19CH	Notice to creditor or other claimant to produce documents
PF20CH	Notice to creditor of allowance of claim
PF21CH	Notice to creditor of disallowance of claim
PF22CH	Order for administration: beneficiaries action reconstituted as creditors claims
PF23CH	Affidavit verifying list of claims other than creditors claims
PF24CH	List of claims not being creditors' claims sent in pursuant to advertisement

PF25CH	List of claims not being creditors' claims other than those sent in pursuant to advertisement
PF26CH	Notice to claimant other than a creditor to prove claim
PF27CH	Affidavit verifying accounts and answering usual enquiries in administration action
PF28CH	Executors (or administrators account)
PF29CH	Masters order stating the results of proceedings before him on the usual accounts and inquiries in an administration action
PF30CH	Security of receiver or administrator
PF31CH	Consent to act as trustee
PF32CH	Affidavit in support of application for appointment of new next friend of minor plaintiff
PF33CH	Order for cross examination of deponents on their affidavits
PF34CH	Order in inquiry as to title in proceedings to enforce charging order where the defendants title is not disclosed
PF35CH	Subpoena to bring in a script
PF36CH	Order appointing administrator
PF37CH	Affidavit of testamentary scripts
PF38CH	Order approving compromise in probate action

Table 3

Contents

4PD–004 **5.1** This table lists county court forms in use before 26 April 1999 that will continue to be used on or after that date.

5.2 Where a rule permits, a party intending to use a witness statement as an alternative to an affidavit should amend any form in this Table to be used in connection with that rule so that "witness statement" replaces "affidavit" wherever it appears in the form.

No.	Title
N5	Summons for possession of property

No.	Title
N5A	Application for accelerated possession (assured tenancies) s.8 HA 1988
N5B	Application for accelerated possession (assured tenancies) s.21 HA 1988
N6	Possession Summons (forfeiture and right of re-entry)
N8	Notice to Respondent when a matter will be heard
N8(1)	Notice to Respondent when a matter will be heard under Order 24
N8(2)	Notice to Respondent in application under section 53
N8(4)	Notice to respondent in application under section 17 and 18 of the Leasehold Reform Act
N11	Form of Reply—Possession Summons
N11A	Form of Reply to application for accelerated possession (assured tenancies) s.8 HA 1988
N11(B)	Acknowledgment of Service Business List Actions
N11B	Form of reply to application for accelerated possession (assured tenancies) s.21 HA 1988
N11M	Form of Reply (mortgaged property)
N11R	Form of Reply (Rented property)
N16	General form of injunction
N16(1)	General form of injunction (formal parts only)
N16A	General form of application for injunction
N26	Order for possession (Rented property)
N26A	Order that claimant have possession (assured tenancies)
N27	Judgment for claimant in Action of Forfeiture for non payment of rent
N27(1)	Judgment for claimant—Forfeiture for Non Payment of Rent where order refused under Rent Acts
N27(2)	Judgment for claimant—for Non Payment of Rent where Order suspended under Rent Acts

No.	Title
N28	Order for Possession (possession suspended) (rented property)
N29	Order for Possession (mortgaged property)
N31	Order for Possession of mortgaged property suspended uner s.36 of the Administration of Justice Act 1970
N35	Variation Order
N35A	Variation Order (determination)
N36	Order for Possession under Order 24
N37	Oral Examination of Judgment Debtor
N38	Oral Examination (person other than Judgment Debtor)
N39	Order for Defendants Attendance at an adjourned hearing of an Oral Examination
N40	Warrant of Committal (Oral Examination)
N41	Order suspending judgment or Order, and/or Warrant of execution/Committal
N41A	Order suspending warrant (determination)
N42	Warrant of Execution
N46	Warrant of Delivery and Execution for damages and Costs
N48	Warrant of Delivery, where, if goods are not returned, Levy is to be made for their value
N49	Warrant for Possession of Land
N50	Warrant of Restitution (Order 26 rule 17)
N51	Warrant of Restitution (Order 24, rule 6(1))
N52	Warrant of Possession under Order 24
N53	Warrant of Execution or Committal to District Judge of Foreign Court
N55	Notice of Application for Attachment of Earnings Order

No.	Title
N55A	Notice of application for attachment of earnings order (maintenance)
N56	Form for replying to an attachment of Earnings application (statement of means)
N58	Order for Defendants attendance at an adjourned Hearing of an Attachment of Earning Application (maintenance)
N59	Warrant of Committal under section 23(1) of the Attachment of Earnings Act 1971
N60	Attachment of Earnings Order (Judgment Debt)
N61	Order for production of Statement of Means
N61A	Order to employer for production of statement of earnings
N62	Summons for Offence under Attachment of Earnings
N63	Notice to show Cause section 23 of the Attachment of Earnings Act 1971
N64	Suspended Attachment of Earnings Order
N64A	Suspended Attachment of Earnings Order (maintenance)
N65A	Attachment of Earnings Arrears Order
N65	Attachment of Earnings Order (Priority Maintenance)
N66	Consolidated Attachment of Earnings Order
N66A	Notice of Application for Consolidated Attachment of Earnings Order
N67	Judgment Summons under the Debtors Act 1869
N68	Certificate of Service (Judgment Summons)
N69	Order for Debtors Attendance at an Adjourned Hearing of Judgment Summons
N70	Order of Commitment under section 110 of the County Court Act 1984

No.	Title
N71	Order revoking an Order of Commitment under section 110 of the County Courts Act 1984
N72	Notice to Defendant where a Committal Order made but directed to be suspended under Debtors Act
N73	New Order on Judgment Summons
N74	Warrant of Committal Judgment Summons under the Debtors Act 1869
N75	Indorsement on a warrant of Committal sent to a Foreign Court
N76	Certificate to be indorsed on duplicate Warrant of Committal issued for re-arrest of Debtor
N77	Notice as to consequences of disobedience to Court Order
N78	Notice to show good reason why an order for your committal to prison should not be made (Family proceedings only)
N79	Committal of other Order upon proof of disobedience of a court order or breach of undertaking
N80	Warrant for Committal to Prison
N81	Notice to solicitor to show cause why an undertaking should not be enforced by committal to prison
N82	Order for committal for failure by solicitor to carry out undertaking
N83	Order for discharge from custody under warrant of committal
N84	Garnishee order to show cause
N85	Garnishee Order Absolute
N86	Charging Order nisi
N87	Charging Order absolute
N88	Interpleader Summons to Execution Creditor
N88(1)	Interpleader Summons to Claimant claiming goods or rent under an execution

No.	Title
N89	Interpleader summons to persons making adverse claims to debt
N90	Summons for assaulting an officer of the court or rescuing goods
N91	Order of Commitment and or Imposing a fine for assaulting an officer of the court or rescuing goods
N92	Request for Administration Order
N93	List of Creditors furnished under the Act of 1971
N94	Administration Order
N95	Order revoking an administration order
N95A	Order suspending or varying an administration order
N110	Power of arrest attached to injunction under section 2 Domestic Violence and Matrimonial Proceedings Act 1976
N110A	Anti social behaviour injunction—power of arrest s.152 and 153 HA 1996
N112	Order for Arrest under section 110 of County Courts Act 1984
N112A	Power of arrest, section 23 Attachment of Earnings Act 1971
N117	General form of undertaking
N118	Notice to Defendant where committal order made but directed to be suspended
N119	Particulars of claim for possession (rented property)
N120	Particulars of claim for possession (mortgaged property)
N130	Application for possession including application for interim possession order
N131	Notice of application for interim possession order
N132	Affidavit of Service of notice of application for interim possession order

No.	Title
N133	Affidavit to occupier to oppose the making of an interim possession order
N134	Interim possession order
N135	Affidavit of Service of interim possession order
N136	Order for possession
N138	Injunction order
N139	Application for warrant of arrest
N140	Warrant of arrest
N206	Notice of Issue of fixed date claim
N206A	Notice of Issue of application (assured tenancies)
N207	Plaint note (Adoption freeing for Adoption)
N200	Petition—Note old number was N208
N201	Request for entry of appeal—Note old number was N209
N202	Order for party to sue or defend on behalf of others having the same interest—**Note old number was N210**
N203	Notice to persons on whose behalf party has obtained leave to sue or defend—**Note old number was N211**
N204	Notice to person against whom party has obtained leave to sue or defend on behalf of others—**Note old number was N212**
N220	Request for service of Possession Summons on Defendants Representative
N220(1)	Notice to Representative of Defendant in Action for recovery of land
N224	Request for Service out of England and Wales through the Court
N229	Notice of Admission in Possession Action
N245	Application for suspension of a warrant and/or variation of an instalment order

No.	Title
N246	Claimant's Reply to Defendant's application to vary instalment order
N246A	Claimant's reply to Defendant's application to suspend warrant of execution
N270	Notes for guidance (application for administration order)
N276	Notice of Hearing of Interpleader Proceedings transferred from High Court
N277	Notice of Pre Trial Review of Interpleader proceedings transferred from the High Court
N280	Order of reference of proceedings or questions for inquiry and report
N285	General form of affidavit
N288	Order to produce prisoner
N289	Judgment for Defendant
N291	Judgment for Defendant in action for recovery of land
N293	Certificate or judgment or order
N293A	Combined certificate of judgment and request for writ of fi fa.
N295	Order for sale of land
N296	Notice of Judgment or order to party directed to be served with notice
N297	Order for accounts and Inquiries in Creditors Administration Action
N298	Order for Administration
N299	Order for foreclosure nisi of legal mortgage of land
N300	Order for sale in action by equitable mortgagee
N302	Judgment in action for specific performance (vendors action title accepted)
N303	Order for dissolution of partnership

No.	Title
N304	Notice to parties to attend upon taking accounts
N305	Notice to creditor to prove his claim
N306	Notice to creditor of determination of claim
N307	District Judges order (accounts and inquiries)
N309	Order for foreclosure absolute
N310	Partnership order on further consideration
N311	Administrative action order on further consideration
N312	Claim form for possession under Order 24
N313	Indorsement on certificate of judgment (transfer)
N316	Request for oral examination
N317	Bailiff's report
N317A	Bailiff's report to the claimant
N319	Notice of execution of warrant of committal
N320	Request for return of, or to, warrant
N322	Order for recovery of money awarded by tribunal
N322A	Application for an order to recover money awarded to a tribunal or other body
N322H	Request to register a High Court Judgment or order for enforcement
N323	Request for warrant of execution
N324	Request for warrant of goods
N325	Request for warrant for possession of land
N326	notice of issue of warrant of execution
N327	notice of issue of warrant of execution to enforce a judgment or order
N328	notice of transfer of proceedings to the high court

No.	Title
N329	notes for guidance on completion of N.79
N330	Notice of sale or payment under execution in respect of a judgment for a sum exceeding £500
N331	Notice of withdrawal from poss. or payment of moneys on notice of receiving or winding up order
N332	Inventory of goods removed
N333	Notice of time when and where goods will be sold
N335	Request to hold walking possession and authority to re-enter
N336	Request and result of search in the attachment of earnings index
N337	Request for attachment of earnings order
N338	Request for statement of earnings
N339	Discharge of attachment of earnings order
N340	Notice as to payment under attachment of earnings order made by the High Court
N341	Notice of intention to vary attachment of earnings oreer under section 10(2) of AE Act 1971
N342	Request for judgment summons
N343	Notice of result of hearing of a judgment summons issued on a judgment or order of the High Court
N344	Request for warrant of committal on judgment summons
N345	Certificate of payment under the Debtors Act 1869
N349	Affidavit in support of application for Garnishee order
N353	Order appointing receive of real and personal property
N354	Order appointing receiver of partnership
N355	Interim order for appointment of receiver
N356	Order for appointment of receiver by way of equitable execution

No.	Title
N358	Notice of claim to goods taken in execution
N359	Notice to claimant to goods taken in execution to make deposit or give security
N360	Affidavit in support of interpleader summons other than an execution
N361	Notice of application for relief in pending action
N362	Order on interpleader summons under an execution where the claim is not established
N363	Order on interpleader summons under an execution where the claim is established
N364	Order on interpleader summons (other than execution) where there is an action
N365	Order on interpleader summons (other than execution) where there is no action
N366	Summons for neglect to levy execution
N368	Order fining a witness for non-attendance
N370	Order of commitment or imposing a fine for insult or misbehaviour
N372	Order for rehearing
N373	Notice of application for an administration order
N374	Notice of intention to review an administration order
N374A	Notice of intention to revoke an administration order
N375	Notice of further creditors claim
N376	Notice of hearing administration order (by direction of the court)
N377	Notice of dividend
N388	Notice to probate registry to produce documents
N390	Notice that a claim has been entered against the Crown

No.	Title
N391	Crown Proceedings Act affidavit in support of application directing payment by Crown to judgment creditor
N392	Crown Proceedings Act notice of application for order directing payment by the Crown to the judgment creditor
N394	Claim form for determining the right to compensation for improvement (Landlord and Tenant Act 1927)
N395	Claim form for certificate or determination of question other than compensation (Landlord and Tenant Act 1927)
N396	Claim form for statutory tenancy under part I of the Landlord and Tenanct Act 1954
N397	Claim form for new tenancy under part II of the Landlord and Tenant Act 1954
N398	Order on application for certificate as to improvement (Landlord and Tenant Act 1927)
N399	Final order (Landlord and Tenant Act 1927)
N400	Answer to claim form for new tenancy under part II of the Landlord and Tenant Act 1954
N401	Order on application for a new tenancy under part II of the Landlord and Tenant Act 1954
N402	Order substituting date in Landlord's or tenant's request
N403	Application for certificate of ground for refusing new tenancy
N404	Certificate of ground for refusing new tenancy
N404(1)	Order authorising agreement excluding act
N405	Notice of proceedings
N425	Notice to repair
N426	Notice of proceedings
N432	Affidavit on payment into court under section 63 of the Trustee Act 1925

No.	Title
N436	Order for sale of land under charging order
N437	District Judges report
N438	Notice to charge holder under Matrimonial Homes Act 1983
N440	Notice of application for time order by debtor or hirer—CC Act 1974
N441	Notification of request for certificate of satisfaction or cancellation
N441A	Certificate of satisfaction or cancellation of judgment debt
N444	Details of sale under a warrant of execution
N445	Request for re-issue of warrant
N446	Request for re-issue of post-judgment process (other than warrant)
N447	Notice to claimant of date fixed for adjourned hearing
N448	Request to defendant for employment details, attachment of earnings
N449	Notice to employer, failure to make deductions under attachment of earnings order

PART 5

COURT DOCUMENTS

Contents 5.0.1

Editorial Introduction

This Part deals with three quite disparate matters concerning court documents. Rules 5.2 and 5.3 follow very closely former provisions found in the CCR. The provenance of r.5.4 is also obvious. This Part is supplemented by Practice Direction (Court Documents), see para. 5PD–001 below. The Practice Direction does much more than merely supplement the provisions in Pt 5 (*e.g.* it deals with the supply of documents to new parties joined to existing proceedings). 5.0.2

Related Sources

- Rule 2.6 (Court documents to be sealed) 5.0.3
- Rule 4(5) (Forms including replica of Royal Arms)
- Rule 32.13 (Availability of witness statements for inspection)
- Rule 39.7 (Impounded documents)
- CCR, O.25, r.5(3) (reissue of enforcement proceedings) (CPR Sched. 2)
- CCR, O.25, r.8(9) (reissue of warrant where condition upon which warrant was suspended or not complied with) (CPR Sched. 2)
- CCR, O.28, r.11(1) (issue of warrant of committal) (CPR Sched. 2)

Scope of this Part

5.1 This Part contains general provisions about— 5.1

(a) documents used in court proceedings; and

(b) the obligations of a court officer in relation to those documents.

Preparation of documents

5.2—(1) Where under these Rules, a document is to be prepared by the court, the document may be prepared by the party whose document it is, unless— 5.2

(a) a court officer otherwise directs; or

(b) it is a document to which—

(i) CCR Order 25, rule 5(3) (reissue of enforcement proceedings);

(ii) CCR Order 25, rule 8(9) (reissue of warrant where condition upon which warrant was suspended has not been complied with); or

(iii) CCR Order 28, rule 11(1) (issue of warrant of committal), applies.

(2) Nothing in this rule shall require a court officer to accept a document which is illegible, has not been duly authorised, or is unsatisfactory for some other similar reason.

Effect of rule—The CPR cover proceedings in the High Court and proceedings in the county courts. Historically speaking, the two levels of court were meant to operate in quite distinctive ways. In particular, the county courts were meant to be easily accessible to litigants who did not have the benefit of legal representation. Consequently, under the rules of court applicable, it was provided that most documents which had to be prepared for the purpose of proceedings (*e.g.* a summons) were prepared, not by the parties, but by the court at the request of the parties. In 1991, when the jurisdiction of the county courts was expanded significantly, enabling these courts to deal with many matters formerly falling within the exclusive jurisdiction of the High Court, the 5.2.1

CCR were amended to permit parties to prepare court documents. These amendments were contained in CCR, O.3, r.3 (originating process) and CCR, O.50, r.4A (documents generally) (see SCP 1999, Vol. 1, paras C3/3 and C50/4A). Rule 5.2 follows the terms of former CCR, O.50, r.4A.

5.2.2 **Excluded documents**—Certain county court documents are excluded and may not be prepared by a party (r.5.2(1)(b)). In this respect, r.5.2 follows exactly the terms of former CCR, O.50, r.4A(2)(b). The exclusions are contained in certain provisions in the CCR which are included in Sched. 2 to the CPR and continue in force. Consequently, documents prepared under those scheduled provisions are documents which "under these Rules" are to be prepared by the court.

5.2.3 **"document... unsatisfactory"**—A court officer is not required to accept a document "which is illegible, has not been duly authorised, or is unsatisfactory for some other similar reason" (r.5.2(2)). This is an improvement on the wording of former CCR, O.50, r.4A(2)(a), which was open to the interpretation that the proper officer could reject a document as being unsatisfactory for reasons not necessarily similar to illegibility or lack of authorisation.

5.2.4 **Court officer**—A "court officer" is a member of the court staff (r.2.3(1)). Where the CPR require or permit the court to perform an act of a formal or administrative character, that act may be performed by a court officer (r.2.5(1)). Under the former rules, it was the "proper officer" who had power to allow a party to prepare a document.

5.2.5 **Court documents to be sealed**—Rule 2.6 states that the court must seal on issue claim forms and any other documents which a rule or practice direction requires it to seal. A document purporting to bear the court's seal shall be admissible in evidence without further proof.

5.2.6 **Form of court documents**—Every document prepared by a party for filing or use at court must comply with the provisions of Practice Direction (Court Documents) para. 2.2 (see para. 5PD–001 below). As to signature of documents, see notes following r.5.3.

5.2.7 **Filing of documents at court**—Former RSC, O.63, r.3 (Date of filing to be marked, etc.), r.5 (Deposit of documents) and r.9 (Restriction on removal of documents) are replaced by, respectively, Practice Direction (Court Documents) paras 5.3 and 5.4, para. 5.5, and para. 5.6 (see para. 5PD–001 below).

5.2.8 **Production of court documents to tribunal, arbitrator or other court**—The Supreme Court Documents (Production) Rules 1926 (see SCP 1999, Vol. 1, para. 63/9/4), made under the Supreme Court Act 1981 s.136, are replaced by Practice Direction (Court Documents) para. 5.7 (see para. 5PD–001 below) and this provision applies to documents held in any court office.

5.2.9 **Enrolment of instruments—change of name by deed poll**—The Supreme Court Act 1981, s.133 provides that the Master of the Rolls may make regulations for authorising and regulating the enrolment or filing of instruments in the Supreme Court (see SCP 1999, Vol. 2, para. 20A–527). Practice Direction (Court Documents) para. 2.2 (replacing former RSC, O.63, r.10) states that deeds to be enrolled in the Supreme Court may be enrolled at the Central Office (see para. 5PD–001 below). Deeds evidencing change of name form the bulk of deeds enrolled at the Central Office. Regulations made by the Master of the Rolls concerning these deeds are the Enrolment of Deeds (Change of Name) Regulations 1994 (S.I. 1994 No. 604). These Regulations are attached as an Appendix to the Practice Direction, see para. 5PD–004 below (see further SCP 1999, Vol. 1, paras 63/10/1 *et seq.*).

Signature of documents by mechanical means

5.3 **5.3** Where any of these Rules or any practice direction requires a document to be signed, that requirement shall be satisfied if the signature is printed by computer or other mechanical means.

5.3.1 **Effect of rule**—This rule is based on CCR, O.50, r.6A. That provision was introduced into the CCR in 1991 when the Summons Production Centre was established (see CCR, O.2, Pt II) (there was no comparable provision in the RSC). The wording in r.5.3 is not quite the same. Rule 6A said a requirement that any document should "bear a person's signature" would be satisfied if "that person's name" was printed by computer or other mechanical means.

For Production Centre, see now r.7.10 and note Practice Direction (Court Documents) para. 1 (see 5PD–001 below). Practice Direction (Production Centre), para. 1.4(5) makes special provision for the signature by mechanical means of statements of truth where a party files with the Production Centre a batch of requests for the issue of claim forms (see 7CPD–001).

As to the sealing of court documents otherwise than by hand, see r.2.6 (Court documents to be sealed).

Note also r.4(5) (Forms including replica of Royal Arms).

The rule refers to any requirement that "a document" be signed. The question what is, and what is not, a "document" for these purposes is not free from doubt. Provisions in the CPR require the following to be signed: acknowledgments of service (r.10.5), statements of truth (verifying statements of case, witness statements, and application notices) (r.22.1), witness statements (r.32.4), written consents of trustees to act (r.33.8), certificates of witness's failure to attend for examination (r.34.10), and draft consent orders (r.40.6(5)). Practice Direction (Court Documents) para. 2.1 states that, not only statements of case, but also "other documents drafted by a legal representative", should bear his signature and, if they are drafted by a legal representative as a member or employee of a firm, they should be signed in the name of the firm (see para. 5PD–001 below). For meaning of "legal representative", see r.2.3(1). **5.3.2**

Supply of documents from court records

5.4—(1) Any party to proceedings may be supplied from the records of the court with a copy of any document relating to those proceedings (including documents filed before the claim was commenced), provided that the party seeking the document— **5.4**

(a) pays any prescribed fee; and

(b) files a written request for the document.

(2) Any other person who pays the prescribed fee may, during office hours, search for, inspect and take a copy of the following documents, namely—

(a) a claim form which has been served;

(b) any judgment or order given or made in public;

(c) any other document if the court gives permission.

(3) An application for permission under paragraph (2)(c) may be made without notice.

(4) This rule does not apply in relation to any proceedings in respect of which a practice direction makes different provision.

Effect of rule—Former RSC, O.63, r.4 defined the nature and extent of the right to search for, inspect and take copies of documents filed in the Central Office or a district registry (see SCP 1999, Vol. 1, para. 63/4/2). A distinction was drawn between the rights of parties and of other persons in this respect. By an amendment made to the RSC in 1998 non-parties were prevented from searching for, etc., originating process by which arbitration applications were made. Former CCR, O.50, r.10 provided for the supply of documents from county court records upon written application and was more restrictive than the RSC rule. The supply of documents to non-parties under this rule was made subject to the permission of the district judge. CCR, O.22, r.8 made separate provision for supplying certificates of judgment. **5.4.1**

Rule 5.4 governs the supply of documents in the records of the High Court and county courts. It is based on the former RSC provision but may be disapplied in relation to certain proceedings by practice direction (see below). The rule is more restrictive than former RSC, O.63, r.4 in that a non-party may not search for etc. a claim form which has been issued but not served. The general rule is that a claim form must be served within four months after the date of issue (r.7.5(2)). As previously, the documents which may be supplied to a party to proceedings include documents filed before the proceedings were started but made with a view to their being started (*e.g.* relating to an order for discovery before claim made).

For the time being, rr.5.4(2) and 5.4(3) do not apply to proceedings in a county court. It is intended that they will apply once facilities for computer search of court records have been installed in county courts (Practice Direction (Court Documents) para. 4.5, see 5PD–001 below).

A person wishing to inspect and copy from the records of the court a document other than a claim form which has been served, or a judgment or order given or made in public, requires the permission of the court (r.5.4(2)(c)). Application for permission, even if made without notice, must be made under Pt 23 (General rules about applications for court orders) and the application notice must identify the documents in respect of which permission is sought and the grounds relied on (Practice Direction (Court Documents) para. 4.4 (see 5PD–001 below)).

For availability of witness statements for inspection, see r.32.13.

For release of documents impounded by the court, see r.39.7(Impounded documents).

It should be noted that r.5.4 and the provisions in Practice Direction (Court Documents) supplementing the rule are concerned with the supply of copies of documents from court records. Increasingly, in making their decisions in cases coming before them judges rely on papers filed by the parties and not read out in open court (including disclosed documents, witness statements and skeleton arguments) as much as on documents revealed and referred to in court open court. This modern practice raises new questions as to (1) the extent to which parties may make collateral use of such documents (see r.31.22 and note *Smithkline Beecham Biologicals S.A. v. Connaught Laboratories Inc., The Times,* July 13, 1999, CA) and (2) the extent to which non-parties should be given access to such documents in the hands of parties (copies of which may or may not also be in the hands of the court) (*GIO Personal Investment Services Ltd v. Liverpool and London Steamship Protection and Indemnity Association Ltd* [1999] 1 W.L.R. 984, CA).

5.4.2 **Supply of documents to parties, including new parties**—Under the conditions stipulated in r.5.4(1), any party to proceedings may be supplied from the records of the court with a copy of any document relating to those proceedings (including documents filed before the claim was commenced).

Parties may be removed, added or substituted in existing proceedings either on the court's own initiative or on the application of either an existing party or a person who wishes to become a party (r.19.3 and Practice Direction (Addition and Substitution of Parties) para. 1.1, see 19PD–001). Obviously, a party joined to existing proceedings, as well as an original party, may take advantage of r.5.4(1), but, for reasons which are immediately explained, he may not have to.

Practice Direction (Court Documents) para. 3.1 states that, where a party is joined to existing proceedings, the party joined shall be entitled to require "the party joining him" to supply, without charge, copies of all statements of case, written evidence and any documents appended or exhibited to them which have been served in the proceedings by or upon the joining party which relate to any issues between the joining party and the party joined, and copies of all orders made in those proceedings (see para. 5PD–001 below). Presumably, "the party joining him" is an existing party (to existing proceedings) who has made a successful application for a party to be joined. The documents should be supplied within 48 hours after a written request for them is received (*ibid*).

PRACTICE DIRECTION—COURT DOCUMENTS

This Practice Direction supplements CPR Part 5

Signature of Documents by mechanical means

5PD–001 **1** Where, under rule 5.3, a replica signature is printed electronically or by other mechanical means on any document, the name of the person whose signature is printed must also be printed so that the person may be identified. This paragraph does not apply to claim forms issued through the Claims Production Centre.

Form of Documents

2.1 Statements of case and other documents drafted by a legal representative should bear his/her signature and if they are drafted by a legal representative as a member or employee of a firm the should be signed in the name of the firm.

2.2 Every document prepared by a party for filing or use at the Court must

(1) Unless the nature of the document renders it impracticable, be on A4 paper of durable quality having a margin, not less than 3.5 centimetres wide,

(2) be fully legible and should normally be typed,

(3) where possible be bound securely in a manner which would not hamper filing or otherwise each page should be endorsed with the case number,

(4) have the pages numbered consecutively,

(5) be divided into numbered paragraphs,

(6) have all numbers, including dates, expressed as figures, and

(7) give in the margin the reference of every document mentioned that has already been filed.

2.3 A document which is a copy produced by a colour photostat machine or other similar device may be filed at the court office provided that the coloured date seal of the Court is not reproduced on the copy.

Supply of Documents to New Parties

3.1 Where a party is joined to existing proceedings, the party joined shall be entitled to require the party joining him to supply, without charge, copies of all statements of case, written evidence and any documents appended or exhibited to them which have been served in the proceedings by or upon the joining party which relate to any issues between the joining party and the party joined, and copies of all orders made in those proceedings. The documents must be supplied within 48 hours after a written request for them is received.

3.2 If the party joined is not supplied with copies of the documents requested under paragraph 3.1 within 48 hours, he may apply under Part 23 for an order that they be supplied.

3.3 The party by whom a copy is supplied under paragraph 3.1 or, if he is acting by a solicitor, his solicitor, shall be responsible for it being a true copy.

Supply of documents from court records

4.1 Where a person makes a search for the documents mentioned in CPR rule 5.4(2), that search may be conducted by means of a computer, if the court office has a computer with the appropriate search facility.

4.2 When the document searched for under CPR rule 5.4(2) is identified and upon payment of the prescribed fee, the document will be produced for inspection by a member of the Court staff.

4.3 If, in the course of a computer search, the computer identifies documents held on the Court file, other than those which the person searching is entitled to inspect, that person may not, without the Court's permission, inspect, take a copy or make any note of, or relating to, those documents.

4.4 An application for inspection of a document under CPR rule 5.4(2)(c), even if made without notice, must be made under CPR Part 23 and the application notice must identify the document in respect of which permission is sought and the grounds relied upon.

4.5 CPR rules 5.4(2) and 5.4(3) do not apply to proceedings in a county court. (It is intended that these rules will be applied to county courts once the facilities for a computer search have been installed.)

Documents for Filing at Court

5.1 The date on which a document was filed at court must be recorded on the document. This may be done by a seal or a receipt stamp. 5PD–002

5.2 Particulars of the date of delivery at a court office of any document for filing and the title of the proceedings in which the document is filed shall be entered in court records, on the court file or on a computer kept in the court office for the purpose. Except where a document has been delivered at the court office through the post, the time of delivery should also be recorded.

5.3 Where the Court orders any document to be lodged in Court, the document must, unless otherwise directed, be deposited in the office of that Court.

5.4 A document filed, lodged or held in any court office shall not be taken out of that office without the permission of the Court unless the document is to be sent to the office of another court (for example under CPR Part 30 (Transfer)), except in accordance with CPR rule 39.7 (impounded documents) or in accordance with paragraph 5.5 below.

5.5(1) Where a document filed, lodged or held in a court office is required to be produced to any Court, Tribunal or arbitrator, the document may be produced by sending it by registered post (together with a Certificate as in paragraph 5.5(8)(b)) to the Court, Tribunal or arbitrator in accordance with the provisions of this paragraph.

(2) Any Court, Tribunal or arbitrator or any party requiring any document filed, lodged or held in any court office to be produced must apply to that court office by sending a completed request (as in paragraph 5.5(8)(a)), stamped with the prescribed fee.

(3) On receipt of the request the court officer will submit the same to a Master in the Royal Courts of Justice or to a District Judge elsewhere, who may direct that the request be complied with. Before giving a direction the Master

or District Judge may require to be satisfied that the request is made in good faith and that the document is required to be produced for the reasons stated. The Master or District Judge giving the direction may also direct that, before the document is sent, an official copy of it is made and filed in the court office at the expense of the party requiring the document to be produced.

(4) On the direction of the Master or District Judge the court officer shall send the document by registered post addressed to the Court, Tribunal or arbitrator, with:

(a) an envelope stamped and addressed for use in returning the document to the court office from which it was sent;

(b) a Certificate as in paragraph 5.5(8)(b);

(c) a covering letter describing the document, stating at whose request and for what purpose it is sent, referring to this paragraph of the Practice Direction and containing a request that the document be returned to the court office from which it was sent in the enclosed envelope as soon as the Court or Tribunal no longer requires it.

(5) It shall be the duty of the Court, Tribunal or arbitrator to whom the document was sent to keep it in safe custody, and to return it by registered post to the court office from which it was sent, as soon as the Court, Tribunal or arbitrator no longer requires it.

(6) In each court office a record shall be kept of each document sent and the date on which it was sent and the Court, Tribunal or arbitrator to whom it was sent and the date of its return. It shall be the duty of the court officer who has signed the certificate referred to in para (8)(b) below to ensure that the document is returned within a reasonable time and to make inquiries and report to the Master or District Judge who has given the direction under paragraph (3) above if the document is not returned, so that steps may be taken to secure its return.

(7) Notwithstanding the preceding paragraphs, the Master or District Judge may direct a court officer to attend the Court, Tribunal or arbitrator for the purpose of producing the document.

(8)(a) I, of , an officer of the Court/Tribunal at /an arbitrator of /the Claimant/Defendant/Solicitor for the Claimant/Defendant *[describing the Applicant so as to show that he is a proper person to make the request]* in the case of v. [19 No.]

REQUEST that the following document [or documents] be produced to the Court/Tribunal/arbitrator on the day of 19 [and following days] and I request that the said document [or documents] be sent by registered post to the proper officer of the Court/Tribunal/arbitrator for production to that Court/Tribunal/arbitrator on that day.

(Signed).

Dated the day of 1999/2 .

(b) I, A.B. an officer of the Court of certify that the document sent herewith for production to the Court/Tribunal/arbitrator on the day of 1999/2 in the case of v. and marked "A.B." is the document requested on the day of 1999/2 and I FURTHER CERTIFY that the said document has been filed in and is produced from the custody of the Court.

(Signed)

Dated the day of 1999/2 .

Enrolment of Deeds and other Documents

6.1 (1) Any deed or document which by virtue of any enactment is required or authorised to be enrolled in the Supreme Court may be enrolled in the Central Office of the High Court. **5PD–003**

(2) Attention is drawn to the Enrolment of Deeds (Change of Name) Regulations 1994 which are reproduced in the Appendix to this Practice Direction.

6.2 The following paragraph of the Practice Direction describes the practice to be followed in any case in which a child's name is to be changed and to which the 1994 Regulations apply.

6.3 (1) Where a person has by any order of the High Court, County Court or Family Proceedings Court been given parental responsibility for a child and applies to the Central Office, Filing Department, for the enrolment of a Deed Poll to change the surname (family name) of a child who is under the age of 18 years (unless a child who is or has been married), the application must be supported by the production of the consent in writing of every other person having parental responsibility.

(2) In the absence of that consent, the application will be adjourned generally unless and until permission is given in the proceedings, in which the said order was made, to change the surname of the child and the permission is produced to the Central Office.

(3) Where an application is made to the Central Office by a person who has not been given parental responsibility for a child by any order of the High Court, County Court or Family Proceedings Court for the enrolment of a Deed Poll to change the surname of the child who is under the age of 18 years (unless the child is or has been married), permission of the Court to enrol the Deed will be granted if the consent in writing of every person having parental responsibility is produced or if the person (or, if more than one, persons) having parental responsibility is dead or overseas or despite the exercise of reasonable diligence it has not been possible to find him or her for other good reason.

(4) In cases of doubt the Senior Master or, in his absence, the Practice Master will refer the matter to the Master of the Rolls.

(5) In the absence of any of the conditions specified above the Senior Master or the Master of the Rolls, as the case may be, may refer the matter to the Official Solicitor for investigation and report.

Appendix

Regulations made by the Master of the Rolls, Sir Thomas Bingham M.R. on March 3, 1994 (S.I. 1994 No. 604) under s.133(1) of the Supreme Court Act 1981. **5PD–004**

1 (1) These regulations may be cited as the Enrolment of Deeds (Change of Name) Regulations 1994 and shall come into force on April 1, 1994.

(2) These Regulations shall govern the enrolment in the Central Office of the Supreme Court of deeds evidencing change of name (referred to in these Regulations as "deeds poll").

2 (1) A person seeking to enrol a deed poll ("the applicant") must be a Commonwealth citizen as defined by section 37(1) of the British Nationality Act 1981.

(2) If the applicant is a British citizen, a British Dependent Territories citizen or a British Overseas citizen, he must be described as such in the deed poll, which must also specify the section of the British Nationality Act under which the relevant citizenship was acquired.

(3) In any other case, the applicant must be described as a Commonwealth citizen.

(4) The applicant must be described in the deed poll as single, married, widowed or divorced.

3(1) As proof of the citizenship named in the deed poll, the applicant must produce

(a) a certificate of birth; or
(b) a certificate of citizenship by registration or naturalisation or otherwise; or
(c) some other document evidencing such citizenship.

(2) In addition to the documents set out in paragraph (1), an applicant who is married must

(a) produce his certificate of marriage; and
(b) show that the notice of his intention to apply for the enrolment of the deed poll had been given to his spouse by delivery or by post to his spouse's last known address; and
(c) show that he has obtained the consent of his spouse to the proposed change of name or that there is good reason why such consent should be dispensed with.

4(1) The deed poll and the documents referred to in regulation 3 must be exhibited to a statutory declaration by a Commonwealth citizen who is a householder in the United Kingdom and who must declare that he is such in the statutory declaration.

(2) The statutory declaration must state the period, which should ordinarily not be less than 10 years, during which the householder has known the applicant and must identify the applicant as the person referred to in the documents exhibited to the statutory declaration.

(3) Where the period mentioned in paragraph (2) is stated to be less than 10 years, the Master of the Rolls may in his absolute discretion decide whether to permit the deed poll to be enrolled and may require the applicant to provide more information before so deciding.

5 If the applicant is resident outside the United Kingdom, he must provide evidence that such residence is not intended to be permanent and the applicant may be required to produce a certificate by a solicitor as to the nature and probable duration of such residence.

6 The applicant must sign the deed poll in both his old and new names.

7 Upon enrolment the deed poll shall be advertised in the London Gazette by the clerk in charge for the time being of the Filing and Record Department at the Central Office of the Supreme Court.

8(1) Subject to the following provisions of this regulation, these Regulations shall apply in relation to a deed poll evidencing the change of name of a child as if the child were the applicant.

(2) Paragraphs (3) to (8) shall not apply to a child who has attained the age of 16, is female and is married.

(3) If the child is under the age of 16, the deed poll must be executed by a person having parental responsibility for him.

(4) If the child has attained the age of 16, the deed poll must, except in the case of a person mentioned in paragraph (2), be executed by a person having parental responsibility for the child and be endorsed with the child's consent signed in both his old and new names and duly witnessed.

(5) The application for enrolment must be supported

(a) by an affidavit showing that the change of name is for the benefit of the child, and
  (i) that the application is submitted by all persons having parental responsibility for the child; or
  (ii) that it is submitted by one person having parental responsibility for the child with the consent of every other person; or
  (iii) that it is submitted by one person having parental responsibility for the child without the consent of every other such person, or

by some other person whose name and capacity are given, for reasons set out in the affidavit; and

(b) by such other evidence, if any, as the Master of the Rolls may require in the particular circumstances of the case.

(6) Regulation 4(2) shall not apply but the statutory declaration mentioned in regulation 4(1) shall state how long the householder has known the deponent under paragraph (5)(a) and the child respectively.

(7) Regulation 6 shall not apply to a child who has not attained the age of 16.

(8) In this regulation "parental responsibility" has the meaning given in section 3 of the Children Act 1989.

9 The Enrolment of Deeds (Change of Name) Regulations 1983 and the Enrolment of Deeds (Change of Name) (Amendment) Regulations 1990 are hereby revoked.

PART 6

Service of Documents

6.0.1 **Contents**

I. General Rules about Service

Editorial Introduction

6.0.2 Part 6 gathers into one part rules previously contained in RSC, O.10 and O.65 and CCR, O.7 as well as other provisions previously scattered throughout the rules such as service on persons under disability (O.80) and service on partners (O.81).

Part 6, together with its related Practice Direction, is a simple, straight-forward and comprehensive code. It is modelled more on the former service rules of the county courts (CCR, O.7) than on the former High Court rules. In particular, the High Court used not to make provision for service by the Court whereas the county court always did.

Part I of Pt 6 deals with service generally whereas Part II deals with service of the claim form (The "claim form" has replaced the writ—see Pt 7).

"Personal service" was the traditional method of service. In many instances (*e.g.* service of an injunction or any order endorsed with a penal notice) personal service is still the necessary or most appropriate method of service (see further, *e.g.* Sched. 1, RSC, O.52 and commentary). Subject to these important exceptions it can fairly be said that personal service has been replaced by postal service as the traditional method of service.

Part 6 continues all but one of the methods of service previously in use under the RSC and CCR. Thus, service by post, personal service, service on solicitor and, where appropriate, by fax or through a document exchange are all provided for in Part 6.

The method of service which has disappeared is "bailiff service". The High Court does not, and never has, provided for "bailiff service" but, before the CCR 1981, "bailiff service" was the main method of service in the County Court and, after the CCR 1981 until April 26, 1999, was an important (and cheap) method of service in the County Court (see the now redundant CCR, O.7, r.2). Bailiff service is not provided for under the CPR.

There is no longer a rule titled "substituted service" but see now r.6.8—"service by an alternative method"—which is to similar effect. (Confusingly, Form N217 is titled "Order for Substituted Service").

Related Sources

6.0.3 • Practice Direction (Service)—see para. 6PD–001

- Sched. 1, RSC, O.11 (Service out of the jurisdiction)

Forms 6.0.4

- N215—Certificate of service
- N216—Notice of non-service
- N217—Order for substituted service
- N218—Notice of service on partner

I. GENERAL RULES ABOUT SERVICE

Part 6 rules about service apply generally

6.1 The rules in this Part apply to the service of documents, except where— 6.1
(a) any other enactment, a rule in another Part, or a practice direction makes a different provision; or
(b) the court orders otherwise.

"Court orders otherwise"—See r.6.8—service by an alternative method 6.1.1

Other rules which deal with service—RSC, O.11 and O.77, r.4 and CCR, O.7, rr.15 and 15A and O.42, r.7 are all expressly re-enacted in the Schedules to the CPR. RSC, O.10, r.4 is not in Schedule 1 and has been repealed: this will have no practical consequences as CCR, O.7, r.15(4) deals with the same topic (service in as action for recovery of premises which are vacant or occupied only by the presence of furniture or other goods). 6.1.2

Methods of service—general

6.2—(1) A document may be served by any of the following methods— 6.2
(a) personal service, in accordance with rule 6.4;
(b) first class post; See 6.7
(c) leaving the document at a place specified in rule 6.5;
(d) through a document exchange in accordance with the relevant practice direction; or
(e) by fax or other means of electronic communication in accordance with the relevant practice direction.

(Rule 6.8 provides for the court to permit service by an alternative method)

(2) A company may be served by any method permitted under this Part as an alternative to the methods of service set out in—
(a) section 725 of the Companies Act 1985[1] (service by leaving a document at or posting it to an authorised place);
(b) section 695 of that Act(service on overseas companies); and
(c) section 694A of that Act(service of documents on companies incorporated outside the UK and Gibraltar and having a branch in Great Britain).

Effect of rule—Rule 6.2 sets out methods of service and reflects practice already established by RSC, O.10 and O.65 and CCR, O.7. Note that by r.6.2(1)(b) first class post must be used for postal service. The Practice Direction which supplements Pt 6 deals in particular with r.6.2(1)(d)—service through document exchange and r.6.2(1)(e)—service by fax. 6.2.1

Service on a company—Rule 6.2(2) expressly provides that a company may be served by any method permitted in Pt 6 as an alternative to the methods of service provided for under sections 725, 695 and 694A of the Companies Act 1985. Service under the CPR will invariably be simpler and cheaper than service under the Act (though there is overlap between the rules and s.725). 6.2.2

Registered companies—Companies Act 1985, s.725—Section 725 of the 1985 Act states that a document may be served on a company by leaving it at, or sending it by post to, the company's registered office (subs. (1)) (see *Addis Ltd v. Berkeley Supplies Ltd* [1964] 1 W.L.R. 913, [1964] 2 All E.R. 753). By the Interpretation Act 1978, s.7, service by post is "deemed to be effected by properly addressing, prepaying, and posting a letter containing the document". The 6.2.3

[1] 1985 c. 6.

word "post" in s.725 of the Companies Act 1985, is wide enough to include both ordinary and registered post and therefore a company is properly served with a document (including a claim form) which is sent by registered post to its registered office (*T. O. Supplies (London) v. Jerry Creighton* [1952] 1 K.B. 42). However, service pursuant to r.6.2 is less technical and invariably cheaper and simpler than other forms of service.

6.2.4 **Personal service on a company**—See r.6.4 and, in particular, the Practice Direction which supplements Part 6 (6PD–001) at paras 6.1 and 6.2.

6.2.5 **Service on foreign corporation in England—Companies Act 1985, s.695**—Section 691 of the 1985 Act states that when a company incorporated outside Great Britain establishes a place of business in Great Britain (an "oversea company", as defined in s.744), it shall within one month of doing so deliver to the registrar of companies for registration a return in the prescribed form containing, *inter alia*, "a list of the names and addresses of some one or more persons resident in Great Britain authorised to accept on the company's behalf service of process and any notices required to be served on it". Alterations in the name, etc., must be duly notified (*ibid.*, s.692(1)).

The mode of service for any process required to be served on an overseas company is provided for by section 695 of the 1985 Act. The section states that such service is sufficiently made if the process is addressed to any person whose name has been delivered to the registrar under s.691 and is "left at or sent by post to the address which has been so delivered" (s.695(1)). Section 695 further provides that (a) where an oversea company makes default in delivering to the registrar the name and address of a person resident in Great Britain who is authorised to accept on behalf of the company service of process or notices, or (b) if at any time all the persons whose names and addresses have been so delivered are dead or have ceased so to reside, or refuse to accept service on the company's behalf, or for any reason cannot be served, a document may be served on the company by leaving it at, or sending it by post to, any place of business established by the company in Great Britain (s.695(2)).

Once having established a place of business in Great Britain, the duty remains with an oversea company, even if it ceases to carry on business there, to keep the name on the register (*Sabstier v. Trading Co.* [1927] 1 Ch. 495). As to the service of the document (including a claim form) in such a case, the essential point is that it shall be served at that address. Where a document (including a claim form) has been served upon an overseas company and addressed to a person whose name had been delivered to the registrar of companies in compliance with the Companies Act 1985 as a person authorised to accept that service of notice on the company's behalf, it was sufficient service within the meaning of s.695(1) of the Act (*Rome v. Punjab National Bank (No. 2)* [1989] 1 W.L.R. 1211; [1990] 1 All E.R. 58, CA). Where service cannot be effected on the person whose name has been delivered to the registrar, a document (including a claim form) may under Act be served on the company by leaving it at the established place of business (see *ibid.*, s.695(2) and *The Madrid* [1937] P. 40 at 45, *per* Bucknill J.). Where the foreign corporation has failed to register the name and address of a person who will accept service on its behalf, or all the persons whose names and addresses so registered have died or ceased to reside in Great Britain or refuse to accept service or for any reason cannot be served, service may be effected by leaving the document (including a claim form) or other document at or by posting it to an established place of business of the corporation in Great Britain (*ibid.*, s.695(2)). See also *Employers' Liability Assurance Corp. v. Sedgwick, Collins & Co.* [1927] A.C. 93, where it was held that the service of the document (including a claim form) on a person appearing on the file of the registry was valid, notwithstanding that he had done his best to have his name removed from the file. Where, however, the individual served sought himself to have the service set aside, it was held by Tucker J. in Court as Chambers on February 21, 1940 in *Emil Rind v. Anglo-Prague Credit Bank*, that he had no *locus standi* in the matter. Service on an employee of a foreign state airline at their London offices was effective because the employee was a "similar officer" of the airline within the meaning of O.65, r.3(1). (*Kuwait Airways Corp v. Iraqi Airways Co.* [1995] 1 W.L.R. 1147; [1995] 3 All E.R. 691, HL(E).)

Note that it is expressly provided by r.6.2(2) that service can be effected under Part 6 "as an alternative to" service under s.695.

6.2.6 **Service on foreign corporation in England—Companies Act 1985, s.694A**—For a document (including a claim form) to be validly served on an overseas company at its London branch it is not necessary that the case should be wholly or even substantially "in respect of the carrying on of the business of" the London branch, so long as it is at least partly in respect of that business (see *Saab and anor v. Saudi American Bank, The Times*, July 29, 1999, CA).

Who is to serve

6.3 **6.3**—(1) The court will serve a document which it has issued or prepared except where—

(a) a rule provides that a party must serve the document in question;

(b) the party on whose behalf the document is to be served notifies the court that he wishes to serve it himself;

(c) a practice direction provides otherwise;

(d) the court orders otherwise; or
(e) the court has failed to serve and has sent a notice of non-service to the party on whose behalf the document is to be served in accordance with rule 6.11.

(2) Where the court is to serve a document, it is for the court to decide which of the methods of service specified in rule 6.2 is to be used.

(3) Where a party prepares a document which is to be served by the court, that party must file a copy for the court, and for each party to be served.

Effect of rule—Service by the Court is the general rule. This is an important change of practice for the High Court but continues established County Court Practice. The Court decides which method of service is to be used (r.6.3(2)): service by first class post will be the most usual save that solicitors will usually be served through a document exchange. A party preparing a document to be served by the court must provide the necessary copies for service (r.6.3(3)). **6.3.1**

Where the court has failed to effect service it will send a "notice of non-service" under r.6.11. The party then has the option of providing the court with further information so that the court can try again (*e.g.* a new address) or arranging service himself (r.6.3(1)(e)) including, where appropriate, obtaining an order for service by an alternative method under r.6.8.

Personal service

6.4—(1) A document to be served may be served personally, except as provided in paragraph (2). **6.4**

(2) Where a solicitor—
(a) is authorised to accept service on behalf of a party; and
(b) has notified the party serving the document in writing that he is so authorised,

a document must be served on the solicitor, unless personal service is required by an enactment, rule, practice direction or court order.

(3) A document is served personally on an individual by leaving it with that individual.

(4) A document is served personally on a company or other corporation by leaving it with a person holding a senior position within the company or corporation.

(The service practice direction sets out the meaning of "senior position")

(5) A document is served personally on a partnership where partners are being sued in the name of their firm by leaving it with—
(a) a partner; or
(b) a person who, at the time of service, has the control or management of the partnership business at its principal place of business.

Effect of rule—Rule 6.4 is a comprehensive rule on personal service. As a general rule personal service on a party is disallowed where that party has a solicitor: the only method of service in such a situation is service on the solicitor. This means, for example, that a solicitor "on the record" cannot refuse service. If the solicitor finds himself without instructions and cannot continue to act he must promptly apply for an order declaring that he has ceased to be the solicitor acting for a party: see r.42.3. Until this is done the solicitor will be considered to be acting for that party (r.42.1) and service must be effected upon him (r.6.4(2)). **6.4.1**

The court is only likely to order personal service on a party represented by a solicitor where the order, to be enforceable, requires personal service: *e.g.* an injunction or other order endorsed with a penal notice (see RSC, O.52 and CCR, O.29, both re-enacted in the Schedules to the CPR).

Practice Direction—See the Practice Direction on service at para. 6PD–001. In particular it amplifies r.6.4(4) and r.6.4(5). **6.4.2**

Address for service

6.5—(1) Except as provided by RSC Order 11 (service out of the jurisdiction) a document must be served within the jurisdiction. **6.5**

("Jurisdiction" is defined in rule 2.3)

(2) A party must give an address for service within the jurisdiction.

(3) Where a party—
(a) does not give the business address of his solicitor as his address for service; and

(b) resides or carries on business within the jurisdiction,
he must give his residence or place of business as his address for service.

(4) Any document to be served—
(a) by first class post;
(b) by leaving it at the place of service;
(c) through a document exchange; or
(d) by fax or by other means of electronic communication,
must be sent or transmitted to, or left at, the address for service given by the party to be served.

(5) Where—
(a) a solicitor is acting for the party to be served; and
(b) the document to be served is not the claim form;
the party's address for service is the business address of his solicitor.

(Rule 6.13 specifies when the business address of a defendant's solicitor may be the defendant's address for service in relation to the claim form.)

(6) Where—
(a) no solicitor is acting for the party to be served; and
(b) the party has not given an address for service,
the document must be sent or transmitted to, or left at, the place shown in the following table.

(Rule 6.2(2) sets out the statutory methods of service on a company)

Nature of party to be served	**Place of service**
Individual	• Usual or last known residence.
Proprietor of a business	• Usual or last known residence; or • Place of business or last known place of business.
Individual who is suing or being sued in the name of a firm	• Usual or last known residence; or • Principal or last known place of business of the firm.
Corporation incorporated in England and Wales other than a company	• Principal office of the corporation; or • Any place within the jurisdiction where the corporation carries on its activities and which has a real connection with the claim.
Company registered in England and Wales	• Principal office of the company; or • Any place of business of the company within the jurisdiction which has a real connection with the claim.
Any other company or corporation	• Any place within the jurisdiction where the corporation carries on its activities. • Any place of business of the company within the jurisdiction.

(7) This rule does not apply where an order made by the court under rule 6.8(service by an alternative method) specifies where the document in question may be served.

Effect of rule—Rule 6.5 is clearly drafted and is a comprehensive code for a party's address for service. The rule draws a clear distinction between parties who act through a solicitor and those who do not. **6.5.1**

"Service out of the jurisdiction"—The rules for service out of the jurisdiction continue to be provided for by RSC, O.11 which is re-enacted to the Schedule 1 to the CPR. **6.5.2**

Address for service—Every party must have an address for service. If not the address of his solicitor it must be his residential address or the address of his place of business if he carries on business within the jurisdiction (r.6.5(3)). **6.5.3**

Service Table—Rule 6.5(6) sets out in useful tabular form the appropriate address to which to send a document in cases where no solicitor is acting for the party to be served and the party has not given an address for service. **6.5.4**

Service on registered companies—The use of methods of service allowed by the new rules as an alternative to those prescribed by the Companies Act 1985 should be exercised with caution where the consequences of failing to prove good service of originating process could be serious for the claimant (such as service at the end of a limitation period). Service using the statutory procedure is usually conclusive. However, the court will interpret Part 6 in accordance with the "overriding objective" in Part 1. Service is not an end in itself but a means of bringing process, or a document, to the attention of the company. The important point is to prove that the process was brought to the attention of the company. See further commentary to rr.6.3 and 6.4. Rule 6.2(4) expressly provides that service under Part 6 is "an alternative to" service under the Companies Act. **6.5.5**

Service of documents on children and patients

6.6—(1) The following table shows the person on whom a document must be served if it is a document which would otherwise be served on a child or a patient. **6.6**

Type of document	Nature of party	Person to be served
Claim form	Child who is not also a patient	• One of the child's parents or guardians; or • If there is no parent or guardian, the person with whom the child resides or in whose care the child is.
Claim form	Patient	• The person authorised under Part VII of the Mental Health Act 1983[2] to conduct the proceedings in the name of the patient or on his behalf; or • if there is no person so authorised, the person with whom the patient resides or in whose care the patient is.

[2] 1983 c. 20.

Application for an order appointing a litigation friend, where a child or patient has no litigation friend	Child or patient	See rule 21.8.
Any other document	Child or patient	The litigation friend who is conducting proceedings on behalf of the child or patient.

(2) The court may make an order permitting a document to be served on the child or patient, or on some person other than the person specified in the table in this rule.

(3) An application for an order under paragraph (2) may be made without notice.

(4) The court may order that, although a document has been served on someone other than the person specified in the table, the document is to be treated as if it had been properly served.

(5) This rule does not apply where the court has made an order under rule 21.2(3) allowing a child to conduct proceedings without a litigation friend.

(Part 21 contains rules about the appointment of a litigation friend.)

6.6.1 **"Children and patients"**—Part 21 is entitled "Children and Patients" and deals generally with this topic.

"Child" means a person under 18 (r.21.1(2)(c)) and "patient" means a person who by reason of mental disorder within the meaning of the Mental Health Act 1983 is incapable of managing and administering his own affairs (r.21.1(2)(b)).

Generally, a patient or child must have a "litigation friend" (see r.21.2).

The terms "Disability" (the title of RSC, O.80) and "Persons under Disability" (the title of CCR, O.10) are no longer in use.

Deemed service

6.7 **6.7**—(1) A document which is served in accordance with these rules or any relevant practice direction shall be deemed to be served on the day shown in the following table.

Method of service	**Deemed day of service**
First class post	The second day after it was posted.
Document exchange	The second day after it was left at the document exchange.
Delivering the document to or leaving it at a permitted address	The day after it was delivered to or left at the permitted address.
Fax	• If it is transmitted on a business day before 4 p.m., on that day; or • in any other case, on the business day after day on which it is transmitted.

Other electronic method	The second day after the day on which it is transmitted.

(2) If a document (other than a claim form) is served after 5 p.m. on a business day, or at any time on a Saturday, Sunday or a bank holiday, the document shall be treated as having been served on the next business day.

(3) In this rule—

"business day" means any day except Saturday, Sunday or a bank holiday; and

"bank holiday" includes Christmas Day and Good Friday.

Scope of provision—Although entitled "deemed service", r.6.7 deals rather with the date upon which service is deemed to have occurred. 6.7.1

"Bank holiday"—The term "bank holiday" is well-known and understood. Technically it means a day which is, or is to be observed as, a bank holiday, or a holiday, under the Banking and Financial Dealings Act 1971, in England and Wales. "Bank holiday" includes Christmas Day and Good Friday for the purposes of r.6.7 (see r.6.7(3)). 6.7.2

"Business day"—The term "business day" is defined by r.6.7(3). 6.7.3

Time—The basic rule for computation of time is r.2.8. Previously the rule for computation of time in RSC, O.3 differed from the computation of time when calculating date of service in RSC, O.10. This unnecessary complication has disappeared in the CPR. See the examples in r.2.8 and below examples: 6.7.4

Examples—Document posted on Monday, January 8 by first class post: deemed date of service Wednesday, January 10 (see Table in r.6.7). 6.7.5

Document posted on Friday, January 12 by first class post: deemed date of service Monday, January 15 (see Table in r.6.7 and r.6.7(2)).

Document transmitted by fax on Friday, January 12 after 4.00pm: deemed date of service Monday, January 15 (see Table in r.6.7).

Document transmitted by fax on Friday, January 12 before 4.00pm: deemed date of service Friday, January 12 (see Table in r.6.7).

Service by an alternative method

6.8—(1) Where it appears to the court that there is a good reason to authorise service by a method not permitted by these Rules, the court may make an order permitting service by an alternative method. 6.8

(2) An application for an order permitting service by an alternative method—

(a) must be supported by evidence;

(b) may be made without notice.

(3) An order permitting service by an alternative method must specify—

(a) the method of service; and

(b) the date when the document will be deemed to be served.

Scope of provision—Rule 6.8 deals with the topic previously known as "substituted service" and previously governed by RSC, O.65, r.4 and CCR, O.7, r.8. In all situations where it would have been possible to obtain an order for substituted service it is now possible to obtain an order for "service by an alternative method". The order must specify both the method and the date when the document will be deemed to be served. Obviously the order is applied for without notice (r.6.8(2)(b)) and the application must be supported by evidence (r.6.8(2)(a)). The better practice is for that evidence to be reduced to writing in the form of written evidence. The written evidence is placed on the court file to provide a record of the evidence upon which the court relied. 6.8.1

Power of court to dispense with service

6.9—(1) The court may dispense with service of a document. 6.9

(2) An application for an order to dispense with service may be made without notice.

6.9.1 **Scope of provision**—Rule 6.9 is a new provision giving the court a general power on application (made without notice but preferably on affidavit) to dispense with service of a document. There was no such general power in the RSC or CCR (RSC, O.65, r.9 did not require service where a defendant was in default as to acknowledgment of service or had no address for service and the document was not required to be served personally. No order dispensing with service was necessary). There has always been a power to dispense with service in the Family jurisdiction (see r.2.9(11), F.P.R. 1991) and it is sensible that there should be a general rule as now provided for by r.6.9.

The most likely use of r.6.9 in practice (though it is not limited to such cases) will be to dispense with re-service. For example, where a document is served with an application to amend, on granting the application the court could dispense with service of that document.

Certificate of service

6.10 **6.10** Where a rule, practice direction or court order requires a certificate of service, the certificate must state—

(a) that the document has not been returned undelivered; and

(b) the details set out in the following table—

Method of service	**Details to be certified**
Post	Date of posting
Personal	Date of personal service
Document exchange	Date of delivery to the document exchange
Delivery of document to or leaving it at a permitted place	Date when the document was delivered to or left at the permitted place
Fax	Date and time of transmission
Other electronic means	Date of transmission and the means used
Alternative method permitted by the court	As required by the court

6.10.1 **Scope of provision**—The certificate of service has been the standard method of proving service in the county courts (CCR, O.7, r.6). The certificate was not of general use, however, and could be given only by the county court bailiff or other court officer who effected service. In other cases (and in the High Court: RSC, O.10, r.1(3); O.65, r.8) an affidavit of service was required.

Rule 6.10 provides for the form and details of a certificate of service where one is required by any rule, practice direction or court order. See, for example, r.6.14(2) as to certificate of service of the claim form.

Notice of non-service

6.11 **6.11** Where—

(a) a document is to be served by the court; and

(b) the court is unable to serve it,

the court must send a notice of non-service stating the method attempted to the party who requested service.

6.11.1 **Scope of provision**—The RSC contained no equivalent rule to r.6.11 simply because, formerly, the High Court did not effect service on behalf of parties. Notice of non-service has always been provided for by the CCR (CCR, O.7, r.6(2) and r.10(4)). The county court provision

is, in effect, now incorporated into the combined CPR as service by the court is now a feature of the unified system (see r.6.3). Clearly there has to be a procedure for notifying the party where the court has tried to effect service but failed. That procedure is the "notice of non-service" provided for by r.6.11. For the effect of such a notice see r.6.3(1): the party may now wish to proceed with personal service (see r.6.4 and r.6.12). As a claim form is valid for service for only 4 months it may be necessary or prudent to seek an order extending its validity under r.7.6.
See also the Practice Direction on Service at para. 6PD–001.

II. SPECIAL PROVISIONS ABOUT SERVICE OF THE CLAIM FORM

General rules about service subject to special rules about service of claim form

6.12 The general rules about service are subject to the special rules about service contained in rules 6.13 to 6.16. **6.12**

Scope of provision—The RSC had two Orders dealing with service namely RSC, O.10—Service of Originating Process and RSC, O.65—Service of Documents, whereas the CCR had just one Order, CCR, O.7, divided into two parts. Part 6 of the CPR follows exactly the model of the CCR with just one part divided into two. Thus, there continue to be special rules for service of the claim form (the new form of originating process in the CPR—see Pt 7) and general rules about service are subject to these special rules. **6.12.1**

Service of claim form by the court—defendant's address for service

6.13—(1) Where a claim form is to be served by the court, the claim form must include the defendant's address for service. **6.13**

(2) For the purposes of paragraph (1), the defendant's address for service may be the business address of the defendant's solicitor if he is authorised to accept service on the defendant's behalf but not otherwise.

(Rule 6.5 contains general provisions about the place of service)

Scope of provision—The normal method of service is now service by the Court (see r.6.3). Rule 6.13 necessarily requires the claimant to provide the defendant's "address for service" so that the Court can effect service. Rule 6.13(2) is self-explanatory as to service on the defendant's solicitor. See r.6.5 for general provisions about the address for service. **6.13.1**

The normal method of service by the court is service by first class post (see r.6.2and the Practice Direction on Service at para. 6PD–001).

Certificate of service relating to the claim form

6.14—(1) Where a claim form is served by the court, the court must send the claimant a notice which will include the date when the claim form is deemed to be served under rule 6.7. **6.14**

(2) Where the claim form is served by the claimant—

(a) he must file a certificate of service within 7 days of service of the claim form; and

(b) he may not obtain judgment in default under Part 12unless he has filed the certificate of service.

(Rule 6.10 specifies what a certificate of service must show)

Effect of rule—The normal method of service is now service by the Court (see r.6.3). Though this is new to the High Court it has always been a feature of the county courts. Therefore, the CCR have always had a procedure whereby the court gives notice of service (CCR, O.7, r.21). **6.14.1**

The "claim form" is the form of originating process under the CPR and clearly it is essential that the Court notifies the claimant not only that service has been effected but also when so that the claimant can calculate the relevant date for the taking of the next step (which may be, for example, the entry of judgment in default). That is provided for by r.6.14(1).

Rule 6.14(2) provides for the claimant to file a certificate of service in those cases where the claimant has effected personal service. The certificate must be filed within seven days of service of the claim form.

Rule 6.10 deals with the form of the certificate of service. This certificate has replaced the affidavit of service.

Service of claim form by contractually agreed method

6.15 **6.15**—(1) Where—

(a) a contract contains a term providing that, in the event of a claim being issued in relation to the contract, the claim form may be served by a method specified in the contract; and

(b) a claim form containing only a claim in respect of that contract is issued,

the claim form shall, subject to paragraph (2), be deemed to be served on the defendant if it is served by a method specified in the contract.

(2) Where the claim form is served out of the jurisdiction in accordance with the contract, it shall not be deemed to be served on the defendant unless—

(a) permission to serve it out of the jurisdiction has been granted under RSC Order 11, r.1(1); or

(b) it may be served without permission under RSC Order 11, r.1(2).

6.15.1 **Scope of provision**—There has long been provision for service pursuant to a contract. Rule 6.15 is a modernised version of RSC, O.10, r.3. The rule makes it clear that service of a claim form (which has replaced the writ) pursuant to a provision in a contract is good service where the English court has jurisdiction to try the claim whether jurisdiction is conferred by a term in the contract or vests or is assumed by the court apart from such contract, for example, by virtue of RSC, O.11, r.1 (which is still in force—see Sched. 1).

The rule covers service pursuant to a contract within the jurisdiction as well as out of the jurisdiction. However, permission (formerly described as "leave") to serve out of the jurisdiction is required under RSC, O.11, r.1(1) unless permission is not required by virtue of RSC, O.11, r.1(2).

RSC, O.11 is re-enacted in Schedule 1 to the CPR.

Service of claim form on agent of principal who is overseas

6.16 **6.16**—(1) Where—

(a) the defendant is overseas; and

(b) the conditions specified in paragraph (2) are satisfied,

the court may, on an application only, permit a claim form relating to a contract to be served on a defendant's agent.

(2) The court may not make an order under this rule unless it is satisfied that—

(a) the contract to which the claim relates was entered into within the jurisdiction with or through the defendant's agent; and

(b) at the time of the application either the agent's authority has not been terminated or he is still in business relations with his principal.

(3) An application under this rule—

(a) must be supported by evidence; and

(b) may be made without notice.

(4) An order under this rule must state a period within which the defendant must respond to the particulars of claim.

(Rule 9.2 sets out how a defendant may respond to particulars of claim)

(5) The power conferred by this rule is additional to the power conferred by rule 6.8(service by an alternative method).

(6) Where the court makes an order under this rule, the claimant must send to the defendant copies of—

(a) the order; and

(b) the claim form.

(Other rules about service can be found—

(a) in Schedule 1, in the following RSC—O.10 (certain actions for the possession of land); O.11 (service out of the jurisdiction); O.30 (receivers); O.52(application for committal order); O.54(writ of habeas corpus); O.69 (foreign process); O.77 (service on the Crown); O.97 (Landlord and Tenant Acts); O.106 (Solicitors Act 1974); O.113 (summary proceedings for possession of land);

(b) in Schedule 2, in the following CCR—O.3 (appeal to the county court); O.7 (recovery of land and mortgage possession claims); O.24 (summary proceedings for recovery of land and interim possession orders); O.33 (interpleader); O.42 (service on the Crown); O.43(Landlord and Tenant Acts); O.45 (application for detailed assessment of returning officer's account); O.47 (application for direction for use of blood tests); O.48B (order for enforcement of parking penalties); O.49 (notice to repair under Chancel Repairs Act 1932; applications under various statutes); and

(c) in relation to certain enforcement proceedings, in the provisions in the Schedules dealing with those proceedings.)

Effect of rule—Rule 6.16 is derived from RSC, O.10, r.2. The rule is clear. It enables service to be effected on a principal residing and carrying on business out of the jurisdiction but who has entered into a contract by or through an agent residing or carrying on business within the jurisdiction. The effect of the rule is to enable the claimant to serve the agent without having to obtain an order for service on the principal out of the jurisdiction under RSC, O.11. Permission must first be obtained under this rule and the order authorising service must state the period within which the defendant must respond to the particulars of claim. Note that the response is required to the particulars of claim not the claim form (see Pt 7). In addition to effecting service on the agent the claimant must also send to the defendant copies of the order under r.6.16 and the claim form. **6.16.1**

The application should be made without notice but supported by written evidence (see r.6.16(3)).

A Practice Direction dealing with the then equivalent rule was published by the Senior Master in 1920. It is set out in SCP 1999, Vol. 1, para. 10/2/3 but is now only of historical or background interest.

PRACTICE DIRECTION—SERVICE

This Practice Direction supplements CPR Part 6 **6PD–001**

Methods of Service

1.1 The various methods of service are set out in rule 6.2.

1.2 The following provisions apply to the specific methods of service referred to.

Service by non-electronic means

Service by Document Exchange

2.1 Service by document exchange (DX) may take place where;

(1) the party's address for service[3] includes a numbered box at a DX, or

(2) the writing paper of the party who is to be served or of his legal representative[4] sets out the DX box number, and

(3) the party or his legal representative has not indicated in writing that they are unwilling to accept service by DX.

2.2 Service by DX is effected, unless the contrary is proved, by leaving the document addressed to the numbered box;

[3] See rule 6.5.

[4] See rule 2.3 for the definition of legal representative.

(1) at the DX of the party who is to be served, or
(2) at a DX which sends documents to that party's DX every business day.

Service by Electronic Means

Service by Facsimile (Fax)

3.1 Subject to the provisions of paragraph 3.2 below, where a document is to be served by facsimile (fax);

(1) the party who is to be served or his legal representative must previously have indicated in writing to the party serving—
(a) that he is willing to accept service by fax, and
(b) the fax number to which it should be sent,

(2) if the party on whom the document is to be served is acting by a legal representative, the fax must be sent to the legal representative's business address, and

(3) a fax number
(a) provided in writing expressly for the purpose of accepting service where the party to be served is acting in person, or
(b) set out on the writing paper of the legal representative of the party who is to be served, or
(c) set out on a statement of case or a response to a claim filed with the court,

shall be taken as sufficient written indication for the purposes of paragraph 3.1(1).

3.2 A legal representative's business address must be within the jurisdiction and is the physical location of his office. Where an electronic address or identification is given in conjunction with the business address, the electronic address will be deemed to be at the business address.

3.3 Service by other electronic means may take place only where;

(1) the party serving the document and the party on whom it is to be served are both acting by legal representative,

(2) the document is served at the legal representative's business address, and

(3) the legal representative who is to be served has previously expressly indicated in writing to the party serving his willingness to accept service by this means and has provided
(a) his e-mail address, or
(b) other electronic identification such as an ISDN or other telephonic link number.

3.4 Where a document is served by fax or other electronic means, the party serving the document is not required in addition to send a copy by post or document exchange, but if he does not do so and the document is proved not to have been received then the court may, on any application arising out of that non-receipt, take account of the fact that a hard copy was not sent.

Service on certain individuals

Personal service on partners

4.1 Where partners are sued in the name of a partnership, service should be in accordance with rule 6.4(5)and the table set out in rule 6.5(5)where it refers to an "individual who is suing or being sued in the name of a firm".

4.2 A claim form or particulars of claim which are served by leaving them with a person at the principal or last known place of business of the partnership, must at the same time have served with them a notice as to whether that person is being served;

(1) as a partner,

(2) as a person having control or management of the partnership business, or

(3) as both.

Service on Members of H.M. Forces and United States Air Force

5. The Lord Chancellor's Office issued a memorandum on 26 July 1979 as to service on members of H.M. Forces and guidance notes as to service on members of the United States Air Force. The provisions annexed to this practice direction are derived from that memorandum and guidance notes. **6PD–002**

Service generally

Personal service on a Company or other corporation

6.1 Personal service on a registered company or corporation in accordance with rule 6.4(4)service is effected by leaving a document with "a person holding a senior position".

6.2 Each of the following persons is a person holding a senior position;

(1) in respect of a registered company or corporation, a director, the treasurer, secretary, chief executive, manager or other officer of the company or corporation, and

(2) in respect of a corporation which is not a registered company, in addition to those persons set out in (1), the mayor, chairman, president, town clerk or similar officer of the corporation.

Change of address

7. A party or his legal representative who changes his address for service shall give notice in writing of the change as soon as it has taken place to the court and every other party.

Service by the court

8.1 Where the court effects service of a document in accordance with rule 6.3(1) and (2), the method will normally be by first class post.

8.2 Where a party receives a notice of non-service of a document by the court, he should take steps to effect service of the document himself as the court is under no further duty to effect service.

Content of Evidence

The following applications relating to service require evidence in support

9.1 An application for an order for service by an alternative method[5] should be supported by evidence stating;

(1) the reason an order for an alternative method of service is sought, and

(2) what steps have been taken to serve by other permitted means.

9.2 An application for service of a claim form relating to a contract on the agent of a principal who is overseas should be supported by evidence setting out;

(1) full details of the contract and that it was entered into within the jurisdiction with or through an agent who is either an individual residing or carrying on business within the jurisdiction, or is a registered company or corporation having a registered office or a place of business within the jurisdiction,

[5] See rule 6.8.

(2) that the principal for whom the agent is acting was, at the time the contract was entered into and is at the time of making the application, neither an individual, registered company or corporation as described in (1) above, and

(3) why service out of the jurisdiction cannot be effected.

Annex

Service on Members of H.M. Forces

6PD–003 **1.** The following information is for litigants and legal representatives who wish to serve legal documents in civil proceedings in the courts of England and Wales on parties to the proceedings who are (or who, at the material time were) regular members of Her Majesty's Forces.

2. The proceedings may take place in the county court or the High Court, and the documents to be served may be both originating claims, interim applications and pre-action applications. Proceedings for divorce or maintenance and proceedings in the Family Courts generally are subject to special rules as to service which are explained in a practice direction issued by the Senior District Judge of the Principal Registry on 26 June 1979.

3. In these instructions, the person wishing to effect service is referred to as the "claimant" and the person to be served is referred to as the "serviceman"; the expression "overseas" means outside the United Kingdom.

Enquiries as to address

4. As a first step, the claimant's legal representative, will need to find out where the serviceman is serving, if he does not already know. For this purpose he should write to the appropriate officer of the Ministry of Defence as specified in paragraph 10, below.

5. The letter of enquiry should in every case show that the writer is a legal representative and that the enquiry is made solely with a view to the service of legal documents in civil proceedings.

6. In all cases the letter should give the full name, service number, rank or rating, and Ship, Arm or Trade, Regiment or Corps and Unit or as much of this information as is available. Failure to quote the service number and the rank or rating may result either in failure to identify the serviceman or in considerable delay.

7. The letter should contain an undertaking by the legal representative that if the address is given, it will be used solely for the purpose of issuing and serving documents in the proceedings and that so far as is possible the legal representative will disclose the address only to the court and not to his client or to any other person or body. A legal representative in the service of a public authority or private company should undertake that the address will be used solely for the purpose of issuing and serving documents in the proceedings and that the address will not be disclosed so far as is possible to any other part of his employing organisation or to any other person but only to the court. Normally on receipt of the required information and undertaking the appropriate office will give the service address.

8. If the legal representative does not give the undertaking, the only information he will receive will be whether the serviceman is at that time serving in England or Wales, Scotland, Northern Ireland or overseas.

9. It should be noted that a serviceman's address which ends with a British

Forces Post Office address and reference (BFPO) will nearly always indicate that he is serving overseas.

10. The letter of enquiry should be addressed as follows:

a. Royal Navy Officers

The Naval Secretary
Room 161
Victory Building
HM Naval Base
Portsmouth
Hants PO1 3LS

RN Ratings

Commodore Naval Drafting
Centurion Building
Grange Road
Gosport
Hants PO13 9XA

RN Medical and Dental Officers

The Medical Director General (Naval)
Room 114
Victory Building
HM Naval Base
Portsmouth
Hants PO1 3LS

Officers of Queen Alexandra's Royal Naval Nursing Service

The Matron-in-Chief
QARNNS
Room 139
Victory Building
HM Naval Base
Portsmouth
Hants PO1 3LS

Naval Chaplains

Director General
Naval Chaplaincy Service
Room 201
Victory Building
HM Naval Base
Portsmouth
Hants PO1 3LS

b. Royal Marine Officers and Ranks Personnel Section

West Battery
Whale Island
Portsmouth
Hants PO2 8DX

RM Ranks HQRM

(DRORM)
West Battery
Whale Island
Portsmouth
Hants PO2 8DX

c. Army Officers and Other Ranks

Ministry of Defence
Army Personnel Centre
Secretariat, Public Enquiries
RM CD424
Kentigern House
65 Brown Street
Glasgow G2 8EH

d. Royal Air Force Officers and Other Ranks

Personnel Management Agency (RAF)
Building 248
RAF Innsworth
Gloucester GL3 1EZ

Assistance in serving documents on servicemen

11. Once the claimant's legal representative has learnt the serviceman's address, he may use that address as the address for service by post, in cases where this method of service is allowed by the Civil Procedure Rules. There are, however, some situations in which service of the proceedings, whether in the High Court or in the county court, has to be effected personally; in these cases an appointment will have to be sought, through the Commanding Officer of the Unit, Establishment or Ship concerned, for the purpose of effecting service. The procedure for obtaining an appointment is described below, and it applies whether personal service is to be effected by the claimant's legal representative or his agent or by a court bailiff, or, in the case of proceedings served overseas (with the leave of the court) through the British Consul or the foreign judicial authority.

12. The procedure for obtaining an appointment to effect personal service is by application to the Commanding Officer of the Unit, Establishment or Ship in which the serviceman is serving. The Commanding Officer may grant permission for the document server to enter the Unit, Establishment or Ship but if this is not appropriate he may offer arrangements for the serviceman to attend at a place in the vicinity of the Unit, Establishment or Ship in order that he may be served. If suitable arrangements cannot be made the legal representative will have evidence that personal service is impracticable, which may be useful in an application for service by an alternative method.

General

13. Subject to the procedure outlined in paragraphs 11 and 12, there are no special arrangements to assist in the service of process when a serviceman is outside the United Kingdom. The appropriate office will however give an approximate date when the serviceman is likely to return to the United Kingdom.

14. It sometimes happens that a serviceman has left the service by the time that the enquiry is made. If the claimant's legal representative confirms that the proceedings result from an occurrence when the serviceman was in the Forces and he gives the undertaking referred to in paragraph 7, the last known private address after discharge will normally be provided. In no other case however will the Department disclose the private address of a member of H.M. Forces.

Service on members of United States Air Force

15. In addition to the information contained in the memorandum of the 26 July 1979, the Lord Chancellor's Office, some doubts having been expressed as to the correct procedure to be followed by persons having civil claims against members of the United States Air Force in this country, issued the following notes for guidance with the approval of the appropriate United States authorities:

16. Instructions have been issued by the U.S. authorities to the commanding officers of all their units in this country that every facility is to be given for the service of documents in civil proceedings on members of the U.S. Air Force. The proper course to be followed by a creditor or other person having a claim against a member of the U.S. Air Force is for him to communicate with the commanding officer or, where the unit concerned has a legal officer, with the legal officer of the defendant's unit requesting him to provide facilities for the service of documents on the defendant. It is not possible for the U.S. authorities to act as arbitrators when a civil claim is made against a member of their forces. It is, therefore, essential that the claim should either be admitted by the defendant or judgment should be obtained on it, whether in the High Court or a county court. If a claim has been admitted or judgment has been obtained and the claimant has failed to obtain satisfaction within a reasonable period, his proper course is then to write to: Office of the Staff Judge Advocate, Headquarters, Third Air Force, R.A.F. Mildenhall, Suffolk, enclosing a copy of the defendant's written admission of the claim or, as the case may be, a copy of the judgment. Steps will then be taken by the Staff Judge Advocate to ensure that the matter is brought to the defendant's attention with a view to prompt satisfaction of the claim.

PART 7

How to Start Proceedings—The Claim Form

7.0.1 **Contents**

Editorial Introduction

7.0.2 The user-friendly term "claim form" has replaced the ancient terms "writ" and "summons". A person who wishes to make a claim no longer issues a High Court writ or a county court summons but instead issues a "claim form". Part 7 deals with starting proceedings in the High Court or a county court. Matters formerly dealt with in RSC, O.5 to O.9, CCR, O.3 and in various provisions of the County Courts Act 1984 are now dealt with in Pts 7, 8 and 9 of the CPR.

The rules in Part 7 should be read together with the rules in Parts 9, 10, 11 and 15. To overcome the perceived weakness in the former system of pleadings the system is simplified. The new code of rules in Part 7 *et seq.* is much simpler and shorter than that previously found in RSC, O. 5 to 9. The new code contains some important innovations (*e.g.* the requirement to plead affirmative defences).

Proceedings are commenced by a claimant (formerly a plaintiff) making a claim. A defendant may respond by filing a defence; a claimant may file a reply to a defendant's defence. The "claim", "defence" and "reply" are no longer to be described generically as "pleadings" but as "statements of case" (see r.2.3(1)). The former High Court term "statement of claim" is abandoned in favour of the county court term "particulars of claim" (see r.7.4).

Statements of case should enable the court and the parties to identify and define the real issues in dispute. In particular they should enable the court to allocate the case to the appropriate track, to give appropriate case management directions, to direct trial of specific issues, to direct summary trial of specific issues and to limit matters which will eventually need to be tried.

The former rules of court as to pleadings set out in RSC, O.18 and CCR, O.6 were a mixture of general and specific requirements. Some of the specific provisions dealt with issues which the courts had had to resolve from case to case over the years. But, as the lengthy commentary to RSC, O.18 reveals, there were many more such points which were not explicitly covered by the rules. Many of these points were reflections of an over-technical approach which should not survive in a case-management system under which "statements of case" ("pleadings") are subject to judicial scrutiny. For this reason, the new provisions are fairly short. Detailed provisions are limited to those situations where more general provisions cannot guide the parties as to what they should put in their statements of case (Interim Report, p. 158).

Note also r.3.4 (Courts power to strike out a statement of case) and r.18.1 (Court's power to obtain further information).

In the majority of cases the claimant will issue a "claim form" to commence legal proceedings. The claim form is the main (but not the only) form of originating process under the CPR. See also r.25.4 (application for an interim remedy where there is no related claim) which requires an application under Part 23, and, in particular, Part 8—Alternative Procedure for Claims. Although basically sound, it is nonetheless an oversimplification to say that claims which would have been brought by writ (High Court) or summons (county court) should now be brought by claim form under Part 7 and claims which would bave been brought by originating summons (High Court) or originating application (county court) should now be brought under the alternative procedure of Part 8. Some claims of a sort frequently before the court *e.g.* mortgage possession actions and rent possession actions which used to be by fixed date action in the county court (and ought logically to have been dealt with by way of Practice Direction pursuant to r.7.9) must now be brought under Part 8. (Contrast claims for return of goods which were, and still are, fixed-date actions 7BPD–001). It is worth verifying, therefore, that a case is not one which could or should be commenced under Part 8 before issuing a claim form pursuant to Part 7. (Unfortunately the Practice Direction supplementing Part 8 is the most badly drafted and unnecessarily complicated Direction of all). The original intention of having just one simple and straightforward way to commence any case in any court has not materialised.

Nevertheless, for the majority of claims, the "claim form" issued pursuant to Part 7 has replaced the High Court writ and the county court summons.

Pre-action protocols—Before issuing a claim form it is necessary to consider Practice Direction—Protocols, B0–001 the Pre-Action Protocol for Personal Injury Claims and the Pre-Action Protocol for the Resolution of Clinical Disputes (all reproduced in this volume at Section B). Litigation should no longer be regarded as the first or main method of resolving disputes. Lord Woolf in his final "Access to Justice" Report recommended the development of pre-action protocols "to build on and increase the benefits of early but well informed settlement which genuinely satisfy both parties to dispute". The CPR enable the court to take into account compliance or non-compliance with pre-action protocols (rr.3.1(4) and 5, 3.9(e), 44.3(5)(a)). Both prospective claimants and prospective defendants should comply with the substance of an approved protocol. Although, currently, there are only two more one anticipated and the existing protocols are relevant in *all* cases. Para. 4 of the Practice Direction—Protocols (B0–001) states "In cases not covered by any approved protocol, the court will expect the parties, in accordance with the overriding objective and the matters referred to in CPR, r.1.1(2)(a)(b) and (c), to act reasonably in exchanging information and documents relevant to the claim and generally in trying to avoid the necessity for the start of proceedings". Thus, for all cases, the pre-action protocols indicate the sort of behaviour now expected of lawyers and potential litigants. 7.0.3

Interest—Obviously the new procedural code has not, of itself, changed the law on interest: see section 35A of the SCA 1981 and section 69 of the CCA 1984. Nevertheless, there is one important matter which will now require re-consideration by the courts. 7.0.4

The law on interest is fully explained in SCP 1999, Vol. 1 at para 6/L/1 *et seq.* As explained at 6/L/26(7) interest on general damages for pain and suffering and loss of amenities has been awarded from the date of service of the writ (now a claim form) until the date of trial (*Wright v. B.R.B.* [1983] 1 A.C. 352, HL, approving *Birkett v. Hayes* [1982] 1 W.L.R. 816, CA). It is submitted that this rule is inconsistent with the philosophy and tenor of the CPR. Claimants are now expected to settle the dispute without proceedings and comply with pre-action protocols (see para. 7.0.3 above) whereas awarding interest from the date of *service* of a claim form pulls in the opposite direction by encouraging early issue and service of proceedings. This inconsistency will have to be addressed. It cannot be right to award interest to a claimant who has served a claim form promptly without compliance with the pre-action protocol but deny it to a claimant who has done everything required by the protocol and issued only as a last resort. It is submitted that a new rule is required and that, in future, interest should run not from the date of service of the writ (claim form) but from the date of the "letter before action" or even from the date of the accident itself.

Related Sources

- Part 1 (Overriding Objective) 7.0.5
- Rule 3.4 (Power to strike out statement of case)
- Part 8 (Alternative Procedure for Claims)
- Part 9 (Responding to Particulars of Claim—General)
- Part 10 (Acknowledgment of Service)
- Part 11 (Disputing the Court's Jurisdiction)
- Part 15 (Defence and Reply)
- Part 16 (Statements of Case)
- Part 17 (Amendments to Statements of Case)
- Part 18 (Further Information)
- Part 19 (Addition and Substitution of Parties)
- Part 20 (Counterclaims and other additional claims)
- Rule 21.10 (Compromise etc. by or on behalf of child or patient)
- Part 23 (General Rules about Applications for Court Orders)
- Rule 25.4 (Application for an interim remedy where there is no related claim)
- RSC, O. 17 (Interpleader)—re-enacted in Sched. 1, CPR
- CCR, O. 33 (Interpleader)—re-enacted in Sched. 2, CPR

Forms

- Form N1—Part 7 Claim Form (para. C1–001) 7.0.6

Practice Direction

Part 7 is supplemented by a Practice Direction (see paras 7PD–001 *et seq.*). Some of the detail formerly in rules (particularly CCR, O.6) is now repeated in this Practice Direction. 7.0.7

Where to start proceedings

7.1 **7.1** Restrictions on where proceedings may be started are set out in the relevant practice direction.

7.1.1 **Practice Direction**—See paras 7PD–001 *et seq.*; in particular para. 2 of the Practice Direction.

How to start proceedings

7.2 **7.2**—(1) Proceedings are started when the court issues a claim form at the request of the claimant.

(2) A claim form is issued on the date entered on the form by the court.

(A person who seeks a remedy from the court before proceedings are started or in relation to proceedings which are taking place, or will take place, in another jurisdiction must make an application under Part 23.)

(Part 16 sets out what the claim form must include.)

7.2.1 **Effect of rule**—This rule is at the heart of the CPR reforms. It introduces the "claim form"—a single form of originating process for all claims in the High Court and county court. (The concept is diluted somewhat by Pt 8—Alternative Procedure for Claims which is akin to the originating summons/originating application procedure and is for use only in appropriate cases as provided by r.8.1).

The plethora of originating process previously available in the High Court (writ, originating summons, originating motion and petition) and in the county court (summons, originating application, petition and notice of appeal) are all abolished and replaced by the "claim form" for all types of case governed by the CPR.

7.2.2 **Claim Form**—The expression "statement of case" (which, broadly, has replaced the term "pleadings") includes a claim form (r.2.3(1)).

7.2.3 **Part 23**—General Rules about applications for court orders. Part 23 is referred to in the note in brackets immediately after r.7.2. The "application notice" referred to in r.23.1 is a further dilution of the principle that all claims are made by one simple claim form in the sense that Pt 23 applies where an application is made before a claim has been started (r.23.2(4)) or in relation to proceedings which are taking place in another jurisdiction.

7.2.4 **Prescribed Forms**—See Practice Direction at paras 7PD–001 *et seq.*; and the list of forms at para. 48PD–017.

Right to use one claim form to start two or more claims

7.3 **7.3** A claimant may use a single claim form to start all claims which can be conveniently disposed of in the same proceedings.

7.3.1 **Starting two or more claims**—In the simplest case, in a single claim form one claimant (C) brings one claim against one defendant (D). The more complicated situations are these (or some mixture of them); in a single claim form—

(1) C brings two (or more) claims against D
(2) C brings a claim (or claims) against D1 and D2
(3) C1 and C2 bring a claim (or claims) against D (or against D1 and D2)
(4) C1 brings a claim against D1 and C2 brings a claim against D2

Traditionally, by a mixture of procedural and substantive rules applying various tests the law has regulated the circumstances in which parties and claims may be joined in the same originating process. The assumption has been that, for a variety of reasons, there should be limits. On the whole, constraints on party joinder have been more severe than constraints on claims joinder. Further, with some exceptions, the joinder rules have been permissive and not mandatory. However, a party who failed to join a claim when he might have done so may run the risk that, on limitation grounds or on *res judicata* or issue estoppel grounds, he will be prevented from pursuing it subsequently on separate originating process. Obviously, the parameters of a claim are not fixed by rules regulating the joinder of claims and parties in originating process but may be expanded or contracted subsequently by amendment (see particularly Pt 19 (Addition and substitution of parties) and Pt 17 (Amendments to statements of case)).

Over the years, the trend has been towards liberalising the rules restraining joinder and encouraging the joinder in the same proceedings of all claims and interested parties. This has had the advantages of (1) avoiding a multiplicity of proceedings (and attendant costs and delays), and (2) minimising the risk that claims might be defeated on technical grounds. The liberalising trend is continued by r.7.3. (The Civil Procedure Act 1997, s.1(3) states that the rule-making power shall be exercised "with a view to securing that the civil justice system is accessible fair and efficient". Joinder provisions can be regarded as being consistent with that policy.)

Multiple claims against the same defendant—Former RSC, O.15, r.1(1) and CCR, O.5, r.1 stated that, with the leave of the court, a plaintiff could in one action claim relief against the same defendant in respect of more than one cause of action and, in certain circumstances (concerning the capacities of the parties), without the leave of the court relief for more than one cause of action could be claimed in the one action. These provisions were subject to the court's power to order separate trials or to make such other order as may be expedient where it appeared to the court that the joinder of the causes of action "may embarrass or delay the trial or is otherwise inconvenient" (RSC, O.15, r.5(1), CCR, O.5, r.3). **7.3.2**

Rule 7.3 provides that a claimant may use a single claim form "to start all claims which can be conveniently disposed of in the same proceedings". Under this rule the joinder in the one claim form of several claims against a defendant does not require the permission of the court and does not depend on the capacities in which the parties sue or are sued. However, the claimant's freedom to include more than one claim is limited by the test of convenience.

As noted above, the former rules contained an express provision stating that the court had power to order separate trials where several "causes of action" were joined in one action. The CPR contain no such express provision as to "claims". However, r.3.1(2)(i) states that the court may direct a separate trial "of any issue".

Claims involving multiple claimants or defendants—Former RSC, O.15, r.4(1) and CCR, O.5, r.1 stated that, with the leave of the court, two or more persons could be joined together in one action as plaintiffs or as defendants and, in certain circumstances (concerning the relationship between the issues raised in the several claims and the rights to relief claimed), they could be joined without the leave of the court. These provisions were subject to the court's power to order separate trials or to make such other order as may be expedient where it appeared to the court that the joinder of the causes of action "may embarrass or delay the trial or is otherwise inconvenient" (RSC, O.15, r.5(1), CCR, O.5, r.3). **7.3.3**

Under r.7.3 the joinder in the one claim form of two or more persons as claimants or as defendants does not require the permission of the court and does not depend on the relationship between the issues raised in the several claims and the rights to relief claimed. However, the joinder of parties is limited by the test of convenience.

Joinder of persons jointly entitled to a remedy—Rule 19.2 (which is derived from RSC, O.15, r.4(2)) provides that where a claimant seeks a remedy to which some other person is jointly entitled with him, all persons jointly entitled to the remedy must be parties unless the court otherwise orders. (See further Rule 19 and commentary thereon.) The procedure for adding parties is in r.19.3. If a jointly entitled person does not agree to be a claimant, he must be made a defendant unless the court orders otherwise (r.19.2(2)). **7.3.4**

"Claims which can be conveniently disposed of in the same proceedings" (the convenience test)—The test for joinder in r.7.2 is merely whether the several claims "can be conveniently disposed of in the same proceedings". In terms neither the rule nor its related practice direction provides any further test. **7.3.5**

Many matters may be relevant to the question whether two or more claims "can be conveniently disposed of in the same proceedings". It may be inconvenient to attempt to try the claims together. In this event, there is no need to impugn the validity of the initial joinder of the claims in the one claim form; instead reliance may be placed on the court's powers to order separate trials to mitigate the inconvenience (see r.3.1(2)(e) and (i)). It may also be inconvenient to attempt to handle two or more claims together throughout all or part of the pre-trial process. If the expression "disposed of" is given a broad meaning and is not confined to those steps in the procedural process which will (*e.g.* a trial) or may (*e.g.* an application for summary judgment) result in the disposal of the claim, but is interpreted as including the pre-trial process generally, additional inconvenience concerns may arise. However, even in these circumstances, having regard to the "overriding objective" in Pt 1, the court's case management powers should be adequate and it is unlikely that there should be need to impugn the validity of the initial joinder of the claims in the one claim form.

Causes of Action, Counterclaims and Parties (O.15)—The following rules in RSC, O.15 are re-enacted in Schedule 1 to the CPR: **7.3.6**

- O.15, r.6A (Proceedings against estates)
- O.15, r.7 (Change of parties by reason of death, etc.)
- O.15, r.8 (Provisions consequential on making of order under r.6 or r.7)
- O.15, r.9 (Failure to proceed after death of party)
- O.15, r.11 (Relator actions)
- O.15, r.12 (Representative proceedings)
- O.15, r.12A (Derivative claims)

- O.15, r.13 (Representation of interested persons who cannot be ascertained, etc.)
- O.15, r.13A (Notice of claim to non-parties)
- O.15, r.14 (Representation of beneficiaries by trustees, etc.)
- O.15, r.15 (Representation of deceased person interested in proceedings)
- O.15, r.16 (Declaratory judgment)
- O.15, r.17 (Conduct of proceedings)

Particulars of claim

7.4 **7.4**—(1) Particulars of claim must—

(a) be contained in or served within the claim form; or
(b) subject to paragraph (2) be served on the defendant by the claimant within 14 days after service of the claim form.

(2) Particulars of claim must be served on the defendant no later than the latest time for serving a claim form.

(Rule 7.5 sets out the latest time for serving a claim form.)

(3) Where the claimant serves particulars of claim separately from the claim form in accordance with paragraph (1)(b), he must, within 7 days of service on the defendant, file a copy of the particulars together with a certificate of service.

(Part 16 sets out what the particulars of claim must include.)

(Part 22 requires a particulars of claim to be verified by a statement of truth.)

(Rule 6.10 makes provision for a certificate of service.)

7.4.1 **Effect of rule**—It is important to distinguish between what the claim form must contain and what the particulars of claim must contain. Part 7 deals with the claim form; Pt 16 with the particulars of claim. Broadly, the claim form has replaced the High Court writ and Particulars of Claim have replaced the former Statement of Claim. County court procedure is now the same. In effect, the CPR have here merged High Court and County Court Practice by adopting the old county court jargon of the CCR and applying it to the High Court procedure of the RSC to create the current CPR.

7.4.2 **Extension of time for serving particulars of claim**—See commentary at 7.6.3

7.4.3 **Particulars of claim**—Rule 7.4 provides for three possible ways of dealing with the Particulars of Claim:

(i) C may include his particulars of claim on the claim form itself (r.7.4(1)(a)).
(ii) C may prepare his particulars of claim as a separate document and serve them with the claim form (r.7.4(1)(a)).
(iii) C may prepare his particulars of claim as a separate document and serve them later (r.7.4(1)(b) and r.7.4(3)).

The first option is likely to be used where particulars of claim are short and can be stated in a few lines: typically a straightforward debt claim (where previously a "specially indorsed writ" would have been used).

Options (ii) and (iii) reflect the old "generally indorsed writ". Given the importance of pre-action preparation (and, in particular, the importance of complying with pre-action protocols) it is hoped that option (ii) will be more common and preferred to option (iii). Option (iii) could be used where the claim form has to be issued quickly, for example for limitation purposes.

Service of a claim form

7.5 **7.5**—(1) After a claim form has been issued, it must be served on the defendant.

(2) The general rule is that a claim form must be served within 4 months after the date of issue.

(3) The period for service is 6 months where the claim form is to be served out of the jurisdiction.

Effect of rule—Rule 7.5 is self-explanatory and effects no change in the former service rules of RSC, O.6, r.8 and CCR, O.7, r.20. 7.5.1

Extension of time for serving a claim form

7.6—(1) The claimant may apply for an order extending the period within which the claim form may be served. 7.6

(2) The general rule is that an application to extend the time for service must be made—

(a) within the period for serving the claim form specified by rule 7.5; or
(b) where an order has been made under this rule, within the period for service specified by that order.

(3) If the claimant applies for an order to extend the time for service of the claim form after the end of the period specified by rule 7.5 or by an order made under this rule, the court may make such an order only if—

(a) the court has been unable to serve the claim form; or
(b) the claimant has taken all reasonable steps to serve the claim form but has been unable to do so; and,
(c) in either case, the claimant has acted promptly in making the application.

(4) An application for an order extending the time for service—

(a) must be supported by evidence; and
(b) may be made without notice.

Effect of rule—Whilst r.7.6 is self-explanatory and effects no change in practice it nevertheless provides welcome clarification to the previous provisions found in RSC, O.6, r.8(2) *et seq.* and CCR, O.7, r.20(2) and (3). 7.6.1

The general rule is that the claim form should be served within its initial period of validity (generally, 4 months: see r.7.5). If it is not so served, an application to extend its validity should be made within that same initial period (r.7.6(2)(a)). If no such application is made, an order is required under r.7.6(3) and the court can only make the order if the three requirements of r.7.6(3) are met.

Supported by evidence—It always was the better practice when applying to extend or re-new a writ under RSC, O.6, r.8(2) or to extend or renew a summons under CCR, O.7, r.20(2) to do so by application supported by affidavit although an affidavit was not a strict requirement of either rule. Rule 7.6(4) clarifies the former procedure and requires an application to be "supported by evidence". Although this new rule requires "evidence" it is clearly the better practice for that evidence to be reduced to writing in the form of an affidavit. An affidavit is placed on the court file and provides a permanent record of the evidence on which the court relied. 7.6.2

Under the old rules one clear case where non-service of a writ during its period of validity was excused was where there was a clear agreement that service should be deferred. Examples would be, particularly where a limitation period was about to expire:

(a) in a serious personal injury case where liability was not in dispute but where the nature and extent of the claimant's injuries were still not resolved
(b) where an action proceeding elsewhere, either in this country or abroad, would determine all or some of the issues between the parties
(c) where a serious scientific investigation was being carried out in attempt to determine the cause of the alleged damage to the claimant.

Under the CPR it is submitted that it is appropriate to serve the claim form promptly in all cases. Where necessary, a stay can then be obtained (see, *e.g.*, rr.1.4(2) and 26.4).

Extension of time for serving particulars of claim—The particulars of claim need not be indorsed on the claim form but can be in a separate document served subsequently (r.7.4). Having served the claim form the parties can agree in writing to extend the period for service of the particulars of claim (see r.2.11). 7.6.3

Application by defendant for service of claim form

7.7—(1) Where a claim form has been issued against a defendant, but has not yet been served on him, the defendant may serve a notice on the claimant requiring him to serve the claim form or discontinue the claim within a period specified in the notice. 7.7

(2) The period specified in a notice served under paragraph (1) must be at least 14 days after service of the notice.

(3) If the claimant fails to comply with the notice, the court may, on the application of the defendant—
 (a) dismiss the claim; or
 (b) make any other order it thinks just.

7.7.1 **Effect of rule**—Rule 7.7 is clearly derived from RSC, O.12, r.8A. Once a claim form has been issued it may, depending on the circumstances, be served on the defendant by the claimant or by the court (see r.6.3). In either event, it must be served within the time limits imposed by r.7.5 unless extended under r.7.6. Circumstances may arise in which it is in the interests of the defendant, against whom a claim form has been issued but not yet served, to compel service by the claimant so that he can respond to the claim form in accordance with r.9.2. Before 1979, when the process of "acknowledgment of service" was substituted for the time honoured process of "entry of appearance", it was possible for a defendant to appear to a writ even though it had not been served upon him by the so-called "appearance gratis". After 1979 it was held that the "appearance gratis" did not survive the abolition of "entry of appearance"; there was no such thing as "acknowledgment of service gratis" (*Abu Dhabi Helicopters v. Aeradio Plc* [1986] 1 W.L.R. 312, CA). As a result, in 1987 the RSC were amended by the addition of RSC, O.12, r.8A from which the current r.7.7 is derived. The usefulness of the provision can be questioned and its practical application is expected to be rare. The provision was more useful in the days when writs were valid for 12 months and readily extended for further periods. There was no equivalent provision in the CCR (though the county court, prior to the CPR, never had "acknowledgment of service").

Under the new r.7.7, where the claimant issues a claim form but delays serving it, the defendant may by notice require the claimant to serve the claim form or discontinue the action within a period of at least 14 days after service of the notice. Where the claimant complies by serving the claim form the defendant must acknowledge service within the time limit for so doing (see r.8.3).

Form for defence, etc., must be served with particulars of claim

7.8 **7.8**—(1) When particulars of claim are served on a defendant, whether they are contained in the claim form, served with it or served subsequently, they must be accompanied by—
 (a) a form for defending the claim;
 (b) a form for admitting the claim; and
 (c) a form for acknowledging service.

(2) Where the claimant is using the procedure set out in Part 8 (alternative procedures for claims)—
 (a) paragraph (1) does not apply; and
 (b) a form for acknowledging service must accompany the claim form.

7.8.1 **Effect of rule**—The High Court has always had a system for acknowledging service of originating process. In 1979 the "acknowledgment of service" replaced "entry of appearance" and this procedure is retained in the CPR.

In contrast, the county courts never had an acknowledgment of service. This stage was omitted. The common procedure of the CPR now brings county courts into line with the High Court on this aspect of procedure.

However, it is important to note that the acknowledgment of service is served with the "particulars of claim". The defendant is required to acknowledge service of the particulars of claim, not the claim form. As r.7.8(1) repeats (see also r.7.4) the particulars of claim can be contained in the claim form, served with the claim form or served separately and subsequently.

Rule 7.8 requires not only service of "a form for acknowledging service" but also "a form for defending the claim" and "a form for admitting the claim". This aspect of procedure is new to the High Court but reflects established county court practice and is derived from CCR, O.9. The new forms are based on well established count court forms.

7.8.2 **Prescribed forms**—See Practice Direction at paras 7PD–001 *et seq.* and list of forms at paras C1–001 *et seq.*

Fixed date and other claims

7.9 **7.9** A practice direction—
 (a) shall set out the circumstances in which the court may give a fixed date for a hearing when it issues a claim;
 (b) may list claims in respect of which there is a specific claim form for use and set out the claim form in question; and
 (c) may disapply or modify these Rules as appropriate in relation to such claims.

Fixed date actions—Prior to 1981 all county court actions were classified as "default actions" or "ordinary actions". Since 1981 all actions excluded from the definition of "default action" in CCR, O.3, r.2 were classified as "fixed date actions". **7.9.1**

There are some types of claim which, by their nature, require a court trial but do not require an extensive, or any, pre-trial procedure. The most common examples are mortgage possession actions, rent possession actions, and actions for the return of goods. These—and some other—claims have long had special forms of county court summons each specifically for the type of fixed date claim. Clearly this has to continue in the unified CPR.

Because there are a variety of different fixed date claims, which can change, it is sensible not to expand the CPR with all necessary detail but instead provide for this to be done by practice direction. Unfortunately, whereas the Practice Direction supplement r.7.9 is clear and straightforward, the Practice Direction supplementing Pt 8 is not.

Practice Direction—See paras 7PD–001 and 8PD–001. **7.9.2**

Production Centre for claims

7.10—(1) There shall be a Production Centre for the issue of claim forms and other related matters. **7.10**

(2) The relevant practice direction makes provision for—

(a) which claimants may use the Production Centre;

(b) the type of claims which the Production Centre may issue;

(c) the functions which are to be discharged by the Production Centre;

(d) the place where the Production Centre is to be located; and

(e) other related matters.

(3) The relevant practice direction may disapply or modify these Rules as appropriate in relation to claims issued by the Production Centre.

Production Centre—A "Summons Production Centre" was established in 1989 specifically to cater for the bulk issue of hundreds (sometimes thousands) of summonses by water companies, credit card companies and the like. The procedure was regulated by CCR, O.6, Pt II, *i.e.* O.6, rr.6–12, on which the new Practice Direction is based. **7.10.1**

Practice Direction—See para. 7CPD–001. **7.10.2**

PRACTICE DIRECTION—HOW TO START PROCEEDINGS—THE CLAIM FORM

This Practice Direction supplements CPR Part 7 **7PD–001**

General

1. Subject to the following provisions of this practice direction, proceedings which both the High Court and the county courts have jurisdiction to deal with may be started in the High Court or in a county court.

Where to start proceedings

2.1 Proceedings (whether for damages or for a specified sum) may not be started in the High Court unless the value of the claim is more than £15,000.

2.2 Proceedings which include a claim for damages in respect of personal injuries must not be started in the High Court unless the value of the claim is £50,000 or more article 9 of the High Court and County Courts Jurisdiction Order 1991 (S.I. 1991 No. 724 as amended) describes how the value of a claim is to be determined).

2.3 A claim must be issued in the High Court or a county court if an enactment so requires.

2.4 Subject to paragraphs 2.1 and 2.2 above, a claim should be started in the High Court if by reason of—

(1) the financial value of the claim and the amount in dispute, and/or

(2) the complexity of the facts, legal issues, remedies or procedures involved, and/or

(3) the importance of the outcome of the claim to the public in general, the claimant believes that the claim ought to be dealt with by a High Court judge.

(CPR Part 30 and the practice direction supplementing Part 30 contain provisions relating to the transfer to the county court of proceedings started in the High Court and vice-versa.)

2.5 A claim relating to Chancery business (which includes any of the matters specified in paragraph 1 of Schedule 1 to the Supreme Court Act 1981) may, subject to any enactment, rule or practice direction, be dealt with in the High Court or in a county court. The claim form should, if issued in the High Court, be marked in the top right hand corner "Chancery Division" and, if issued in the county court, be marked "Chancery Business".

(For the equity jurisdiction of county courts, see County Courts Act 1984, s.23.)

2.6 A claim relating to any of the matters specified in sub-paragraphs (a) and (b) of paragraph 2 of Schedule 1 to the Supreme Court Act 1981 must be dealt with in the High Court and will be assigned to the Queen's Bench Division.

2.7 Practice directions which supplement CPR Part 49 (Specialist Proceedings) will contain provisions relating to the commencement and conduct of the specialist proceedings listed in that Part.

2.8 A claim in the High Court for which a jury trial is directed will, if not already being dealt with in the Queen's Bench Division, be transferred to that Division.

2.9 The following proceedings may not be started in a county court unless the parties have agreed otherwise in writing:

(1) a claim for damages or other remedy for libel or slander, and

(2) a claim in which the title to any toll, fair, market or franchise is in question.

The claim form

3.1 A claimant must use practice form N1 or practice form N208 (the Part 8 claim form) to start a claim (but see paragraphs 3.2 and 3.4 below).

3.2 Rule 7.9 deals with fixed date claims and rule 7.10 deals with the Production Centre for the issue of claims; there are separate practice directions supplementing rules 7.9 and 7.10.

3.3 If a claimant wishes his claim to proceed under Part 8, or if the claim is required to proceed under Part 8, the claim form should so state. Otherwise the claim will proceed under Part 7. But note that in respect of claims in specialist proceedings (listed in CPR Part 49) and claims brought under the RSC or CCR set out in the Schedule to the CPR (see CPR Part 50) the CPR will apply only to the extent that they are not inconsistent with the rules and practice directions that expressly apply to those claims.

3.4 To commence specialist proceedings (listed in CPR Part 49) it may be necessary to use the practice form approved for that purpose by the practice direction relating to the specialist proceedings in question. Reference should be made to that practice direction.

3.5 Where a claim which is to be served out of the jurisdiction is one which the court has power to deal with under the Civil Jurisdiction and Judgments Act 1982, the claim form and, when they are contained in a separate document, the particulars of claim should be endorsed with a statement that the court has power under that Act to deal with the claim and that no proceedings based on the same claim are pending between the parties in Scotland, Northern Ireland or another Convention territory.[1]

[1] "Convention territory" means the territory or territories of any Contracting State as defined by s.1(3) of the Civil Jurisdiction and Judgments Act 1982, to which the Brussels Conventions or Lugano Convention apply.

3.6 If a claim for damages or for an unspecified sum is started in the High Court, the claim form must—
(i) state that the claimant expects to recover more than £15,000 (or £50,000 or more if the claim is for personal injuries); or
(ii) state that some enactment provides that the claim may only be commenced in the High Court and specify that enactment; or
(iii) state that the claim is to be in one of the specialist High Court lists (see CPR Part 49) and specify that list.

3.7 If the contents of a claim form commencing specialist proceedings complies with the requirements of the specialist list in question the claim form will also satisfy paragraph 3.6 above.

3.8 If a claim for damages for personal injuries is started in the county court, the claim form must state whether or not the claimant expects to recover more than £1,000 in respect of pain, suffering and loss of amenity.

3.9 If a claim for housing disrepair which includes a claim for an order requiring repairs or other work to be carried out by the landlord is started in the county court, the claim form must state—
(i) whether or not the cost of the repairs or other work is estimated to be more than £1,000, and
(ii) whether or not the claimant expects to recover more than £1,000 in respect of any claim for damages.[2]

If either of the amounts mentioned in (i) and (ii) is more than £1,000, the small claims track will not be the normal track for that claim.

Title of Proceedings

4.1 The claim form and every other statement of case, must be headed with the title of the proceedings. The title should state:
(1) the number of proceedings,
(2) the court or Division in which they are proceeding,
(3) the full name of each party,
(4) his status in the proceedings (i.e. claimant/defendant).

4.2 Where there is more than one claimant and/or more than one defendant, the parties should be described in the title as follows:

(1) AB
(2) CD
(3) EF Claimants
and
(1) GH
(2) IJ
(3) KL Defendants

Start of proceedings

5.1 Proceedings are started when the court issues a claim form at the request of the claimant[3] (see rule 7.2) but where the claim form as issued was received in the court office on a date earlier than the date on which it was issued by the court, the claim is "brought" for the purposes of the Limitation Act 1980 and any other relevant statute on that earlier date. 7PD–002

5.2 The date on which the claim form was received by the court will be recorded by a date stamp either on the claim form held on the court file or on the letter that accompanied the claim form when it was received by the court.

5.3 An enquiry as to the date on which the claim form was received by the court should be directed to a court officer.

5.4 Parties proposing to start a claim which is approaching the expiry of the limitation period should recognise the potential importance of establishing the date the claim form was received by the court and should themselves make arrangements to record the date.

[2] See rules 16.3(4) and 26.6.
[3] See rule 7.2.

5.5 Where it is sought to start proceedings against the estate of a deceased defendant where probate or letters of administration have not been granted, the claimant should issue the claim against "the personal representatives of A.B. deceased". The claimant should then, before the expiry of the period for service of the claim form, apply to the court for the appointment of a person to represent the estate of the deceased.

Particulars of claim

6.1 Where the claimant does not include the particulars of claim in the claim form, particulars of claim may be served separately—

(1) either at the same time as the claim form, or

(2) within 14 days after service of the claim form[4] provided that the service of the particulars of claim is not later than 4 months from the date of issue of the claim form[5] (or 6 months where the claim form is to be served out of the jurisdiction[6]).

6.2 If the particulars of claim are not included in or have not been served with the claim form, the claim form must contain a statement that particulars of claim will follow.[7]

(These paragraphs do not apply where the Part 8 procedure is being used. For information on matters to be included in the claim form or the particulars of claim, see Part 16 (statements of case) and the practice direction which supplements it.)

Statement of Truth

7.1 Part 22 requires the claim form and, where they are not included in the claim form, the particulars of claim, to be verified by a statement of truth.

7.2 The form of the statement of truth is as follows:

"[I believe] [the claimant believes] that the facts stated in [this claim form] [these particulars of claim] are true."

7.3 Attention is drawn to rule 32.14 which sets out the consequences of verifying a statement of case containing a false statement without an honest belief in its truth.

(For information regarding statements of truth see Part 22 and the practice direction which supplements it.)

Extension of time

8.1 An application under rule 7.6 (for an extension of time for serving a claim form under rule 7.6(1)) must be made in accordance with Part 23 and supported by evidence.

8.2 The evidence should state—

(1) all the circumstances relied on,

(2) the date of issue of the claim,

(3) the expiry date of any rule 7.6 extension, and

(4) a full explanation as to why the claim has not been served.

(For information regarding (1) written evidence see Part 32 and the practice direction which supplements it and (2) service of the claim form see Part 6 and the practice direction which supplements it.)

[4] See rule 7.4(1)(b).
[5] See rules 7.4(2) and 7.5(2).
[6] See rule 7.5(3).
[7] See rule 16.2(2).

PRACTICE DIRECTION—CONSUMER CREDIT ACT CLAIM

This Practice Direction supplements CPR Rule 7.9

1.1 In this practice direction "the Act" means the Consumer Credit Act 1974, a section referred to by number means the section with that number in the Act, and expressions which are defined in the Act have the same meaning in this practice direction as they have in the Act. **7BPD–001**

1.2 "Consumer Credit Act procedure" means the procedure set out in this practice direction.

When to use the Consumer Credit Act procedure

2.1 A claimant must use the Consumer Credit Act procedure where he makes a claim under a provision of the Act to which paragraph 3 of this practice direction applies.

2.2 Where a claimant is using the Consumer Credit Act procedure the CPR are modified to the extent that they are inconsistent with the procedure set out in this practice direction.

2.3 The court may at any stage order the claim to continue as if the claimant had not used the Consumer Credit Act procedure, and if it does so the court may give any directions it considers appropriate.

2.4 This practice direction also sets out matters which must be included in the particulars of claim in certain types of claim, and restrictions on where certain types of claim may be started.

The provisions of the Act

3.1 Subject to paragraph 3.2 and 3.3 this practice direction applies to claims made under the following provisions of the Act—

(1) section 141 (claim by the creditor to enforce regulated agreement relating to goods, etc.);

(2) section 129 (claim by debtor or hirer for a time order);

(3) section 90 (creditor's claim for an order for recovery of protected goods);

(4) section 92(1) (creditor's or owner's claim to enter premises to take possession of goods);

(5) section 139(a) (debtor's claim for a credit agreement to be reopened as extortionate); and

(6) creditor's or owner's claim for a court order to enforce a regulated agreement relating to goods or money where the court order is required by—

- (a) section 65(1) (improperly-executed agreement)
- (b) section 86(2) of the Act (death of debtor or hirer where agreement is partly secured or unsecured)
- (c) section 111(2) (default notice, etc., not served on surety);
- (d) section 124(1) or (2) (taking of a negotiable instrument in breach of terms of section 123); or
- (e) section 105(7)(a) or (b) (security not expressed in writing, or improperly-executed).

3.2 This practice direction does not apply to any claim made under the provisions listed in paragraph 3.1 above if that claim relates to the recovery of land.

(Provisions governing the procedure for such claims can be found in CPR Schedule 2, CCR, O.49, r.4 and related rules about the matters to be included in the particulars of claim can be found in CPR Schedule 2, CCR, O.6).

3.3 This practice direction also does not apply to a claim made by the creditor under section 141 of the Act to enforce a regulated agreement where the agreement relates only to money. Such a claim must be started by the issue of a Part 7 claim form.

Restrictions on where to start some Consumer Credit Act claims

4.1 Where the claim includes a claim to recover goods to which a regulated hire purchase agreement or conditional sale agreements relates, it may only be started in the county court for the district in which the debtor, or one of the debtors—

(1) resides or carries on business; or

(2) resided or carried on business at the date when the defendant last made a payment under the agreement.

4.2 In any other claim to recover goods, the claim may only be started in the court for the district—

(1) in which the defendant, or one of the defendants, resides or carries on business; or

(2) in which the goods are situated.

4.3 A claim of a debtor or hirer for an order under section 129(1)(b) of the Act (a time order) may only be started in the court where the claimant resides or carries on business.

(Costs rule 45.1(2)(b) allows the claimant to recover fixed costs in certain circumstances where such a claim is made.)

(Paragraph 7 sets out the matters the claimant must include in his particulars of claim where he is using the Consumer Credit Act procedure.)

The Consumer Credit Act procedure

5.1 In the types of claim to which paragraph 3 applies the court will fix a hearing date on the issue of the claim form.

5.2 The particulars of claim must be served with the claim form.

5.3 Where a claimant is using the Consumer Credit Act procedure, the defendant to the claim is not required to—

(1) serve an acknowledgment of service; or

(2) file a defence, although he may choose to do so.

5.4 Where a defendant intends to defend a claim, his defence should be filed within 14 days of service of the particulars of claim. If the defendant fails to file a defence within this period, but later relies on it, the court may take such a failure into account as a factor when deciding what order to make about costs.

5.5 Part 12 (default judgment) does not apply where the claimant is using the Consumer Credit Act procedure.

5.6 Each party must be given at least 28 days' notice of the hearing date.

5.7 Where the claimant serves the claim form, he must serve notice of the hearing date at the same time, unless the hearing date is specified in the claim form.

Powers of the court at the hearing

6.1 On the hearing date the court may dispose of the claim.

6.2 If the court does not dispose of the claim on the hearing date—

(1) if the defendant has filed a defence, the court will—

(a) allocate the claim to a track and give directions about the management of the case; or

(b) give directions to enable it to allocate the claim to a track;

(2) if the defendant has not filed a defence, the court may make any order or given any direction it considers appropriate.

6.3 Rule 26.5(3) to (5) and rules 26.6 to 26.10 apply to the allocation of a claim under paragraph 6.2.

Matters which must be included in the particulars of claim

7.1 Where the Consumer Credit Act procedure is used, the claimant must state in his particulars of claim that the claim is a Consumer Credit Act claim.

7.2 A claimant making a claim for the delivery of goods to enforce a hire purchase agreement or conditional sale agreement which is—

(1) a regulated agreement for the recovery of goods; and

(2) let to a person other than a company or other corporation; must also state (in this order) in his particulars of claim—

(a) the date of the agreement;
(b) the parties to the agreement;
(c) the number or other identification of the agreement (with enough information to allow the debtor to identify the agreement);
(d) where the claimant was not one of the original parties to the agreement, the means by which the rights and duties of the creditor passed to him;
(e) the place where the agreement was signed by the defendant (if known);
(f) the goods claimed;
(g) the total price of the goods;
(h) the paid up sum;
(i) the unpaid balance of the total price;
(j) whether a default notice or a notice under section 76(1) or section 88(1) of the Act has been served on the defendant, and, if it has, the date and the method of service;
(k) the date on which the right to demand delivery of the goods accrued;
(l) the amount (if any) claimed as an alternative to the delivery of goods, and
(m) the amount (if any) claimed in addition to—
(i) the delivery of the goods; or
(ii) any claim under subparagraph (l) above

with the grounds of each such claim.

7.3 A claimant who is a debtor or hirer making a claim for an order under section 129(1)(b) of the Act (a time order) must state (in the following order) in his particulars of claim—

(1) the date of the agreement;
(2) the parties to the agreement;
(3) the number or other means of identifying the agreement;
(4) details of any sureties;
(5) if the defendant is not one of the original parties to the agreement then the name of the original party to the agreement;
(6) the names and addresses of the persons intended to be served with the claim form;
(7) the place where the claimant signed the agreement;
(8) details of the notice served by the creditor or owner giving rise to the claim for the time order;
(9) the total unpaid balance the claimant admits is due under the agreement, and—
(a) the amount of any arrears (if known); and
(b) the amount and frequency of the payments specified in the agreement;
(10) the claimant's proposals for payments of any arrears and of future instalments together with details of his means;
(11) where the claim relates to a breach of the agreement other than for the payment of money the claimant's proposals for remedying it.

7.4(1) This paragraph applies where a claimant is required to obtain a court order to enforce a regulated agreement by—

(a) section 65(1) (improperly-executed agreement);
(b) section 105(7)(a) or (b) (security not expressed in writing, or improperly-executed)

(c) section 111(2) (default notice, etc., not served on surety)
(d) section 124(1) or (2) (taking of a negotiable instrument in breach of terms of section 123); or
(e) section 86(2) of the Act (death of debtor or hirer where agreement is partly secured or unsecured.)

(2) The claimant must state in his particulars of claim what the circumstances are that require him to obtain a court order for enforcement.

Admission of certain claims for recovery of goods under regulated agreements

8.1 In a claim to recover goods to which section 90(1)[8] applies—

(1) the defendant may admit the claim; and

(2) offer terms on which a return order should be suspended under section 135(1)(b).

8.2 He may do so by filing a request in practice form N9C.

8.3 He should do so within the period for making an admission specified in rule 14.2(b). If the defendant fails to file his request within this period, and later makes such a request, the court may take the failure into account as a factor when deciding what order to make about costs.

8.4 On receipt of the admission, the court will serve a copy on the claimant.

8.5 The claimant may obtain judgment by filing a request in practice form N228.

8.6 On receipt of the request for judgment, the court will enter judgment in the terms of the defendant's admission and offer and for costs.

8.7 If—

(1) the claimant does not accept the defendant's admission and offer; and

(2) the defendant does not appear on the hearing date fixed when the claim form was issued,

the court may treat the defendant's admission and offer as evidence of the facts stated in it for the purposes of sections 129(2)(a)[9] and 135(2).[10]

Additional requirements about parties to the proceedings

9.1 The court may dispense with the requirement in section 141(5) (all parties to a regulated agreement and any surety to be parties to any proceedings) in any claim relating to the regulated agreement, if—

(1) the claim form has not been served on the debtor or the surety; and

(2) the claimant either before or at the hearing makes an application (which may be made without notice) for the court to make such an order.

9.2 In a claim relating to a regulated agreement where—

(1) the claimant was not one of the original parties to the agreement; and

(2) the former creditor's rights and duties under the agreement have passed to him by—

(a) operation of law; or
(b) assignment,

the requirement of section 141(5) (all parties to a regulated agreement and

[8] Section 90(1) provides that—"At any time when—(a) the debtor is in breach of a regulated hire-purchase or a regulated conditional sale agreement relating to goods, and (b) the debtor has paid to the creditor one-third or more of the total price of the goods, and (c) the property in the goods remains in the creditor, the creditor is not entitled to recover possession of the goods from the debtor except on an order of the court."

[9] Section 129(2) provides that—"A time order shall provide for one or both of the following, as the court considers just—(a) the payment by the debtor or hirer or any surety of any sum owed under a regulated agreement or a security by such instalments, payable at such times, as the court, having regard to the means of the debtor or hirer and any surety, considers reasonable; (b) the remedying by the debtor or hirer of any breach of a regulated agreement (other than non-payment of money) within such period as the court may specify."

[10] Section 135(2) provides that—"The court shall not suspend the operation of a term [in an order relating to a regulated agreement] requiring the delivery up of goods by any person unless satisfied that the goods are in his possession or control."

any surety to be parties to any proceedings) does not apply to the former creditor, unless the court otherwise orders.

9.3 Where a claimant who is a creditor or owner makes a claim for a court order under section 86(2) (death of debtor or hirer where agreement is partly secured or unsecured) the personal representatives of the deceased debtor or hirer must be parties to the proceedings in which the order is sought, unless no grant of representation has been made to the estate.

9.4 Where no grant of representation has been made to the estate of the deceased debtor or hirer, the claimant must make an application in accordance with Part 23 for directions about which persons (if any) are to be made parties to the claim as being affected or likely to be affected by the enforcement of the agreement.

9.5 The claimant's application under paragraph 9.4—
(a) may be made without notice; and
(b) should be made before the claim form is issued.

Notice to be given to re-open a consumer credit agreement

10.1 Where a debtor or any surety intends to apply for a consumer credit agreement to be reopened after a claim on or relating to the agreement has already begun, and—
(1) section 139(1)(b)[11]; or
(2) section 139(1)(c),
applies, the debtor or surety must serve written notice of his intention on the court and every other party to the proceedings within 14 days of the service of the claim form on him.

10.2 If the debtor or surety (as the case may be) serves a notice under paragraph 10.1 he will be treated as having filed a defence for the purposes of the Consumer Credit Act procedure.

Notes on Practice Direction supplementing CPR, Pt 7 (see para. 7PD–001 et seq.)

2.4 Not all cases over the financial limits specified by paras 2.1 and 2.2 will be suitable for trial in the High Court and some will be transferred elsewhere. The guidelines in this paragraph will assist the court in this exercise. **7BPD–002**

2.6 This refers to writs of *habeas corpus* and claims for judicial review.

3.3 A large number of procedures under the RSC and CCR are preserved in the Schedules to the CPR and the old rules with some modification continue to apply. These proceedings include in the High Court:

• Relator actions	O.15, r.11
• Derivative claims	O.15, r.12A
• Interpleader Proceedings	O.17
• Appointment of Receivers	O.30
• Committal	O.56
• Claims against the Crown	O.77
• Criminal Proceedings	O.79
• Partnership proceedings	O.81
• Defamation claims	O.82
• Administration Actions	O.85
• Debenture holders actions	O.87
• Mortgage claims	O.88
• Revenue proceedings	O.91
• Various statutory proceedings	O.93
• Landlord and Tenant Acts 1927, 1954 and 1987 proceedings	O.97
• Applications Under Local Government Finance Act 1982 Pt III	O.98
• Claims for Provisions for Dependants out of estates	O.99

[11] Section 139(1) provides that—(1) A credit agreement may, if the court thinks just, be reopened on the ground that the credit bargain is extortionate—(a) on an application for the purpose made by the debtor or any surety to the High Court, county court or sheriff court; or (b) at the instance of the debtor or a surety in any proceedings to which the debtor and creditor are parties, being proceedings to enforce the credit agreement, any security relating to it or any linked transaction; or (c) at the instance of the debtor or a surety in other proceedings in any court where the amount paid or payable under the credit agreement is relevant.

- Pension Appeals O.101
- Proceedings under Solicitors Act 1974 O.106
- Proceedings under Charities Act 1993 O.108
- Environmental Control Proceedings O.110
- Application for Blood Tests O.112
- Summary Proceedings for Possession O.113
- Criminal Confiscation Orders O.115

4.1 and 4.2 As it will be necessary to open a court file in respect of every claim it will not always be possible to issue a claim form on the date of receipt by the court. These paragraphs make it clear that for limitation purposes it is the date of receipt that is determinative. Paragraphs 4.3 and 4.4 illustrate how this may be established.

PRACTICE DIRECTION—PRODUCTION CENTRE

This Practice Direction supplements CPR Rule 7.10

General

7CPD–001 **1.1** In this Practice Direction

"the Centre" means the Production Centre.

"Centre user" means a person who is for the time being permitted to issue claims through the Centre, and includes a solicitor acting for such a person.

"officer" means the officer in charge of the Centre or another officer of the Centre acting on his behalf.

"national creditor code" means the number of reference allotted to a Centre user by the officer.

"Code of Practice" means any code of practice which may at any time be issued by the Court Service relating to the discharge by the Centre of its functions and the way in which a Centre user is to conduct business with the Centre.

"data" means any information which is required to be given to the court or which is to be contained in any document to be sent to the court or to any party.

1.2 For any purpose connected with the exercise of its functions, the Centre will be treated as part of the office of the court whose name appears on the claim form to which the functions relate, or in whose name the claim form is requested to be issued, and the officer will be treated as an officer of that court.

1.3(1) The functions of the Centre include the provision of a facility which, through the use of information technology, enables a Centre user to have claim forms issued and served, whether or not those claim forms are to be treated as issued in the Northampton County Court or in another county court.

(2) If a Centre user issues claim forms in the name of Northampton County Court, the functions of the Centre also include:

(a) the handling of defences and admissions,

(b) the entry of judgment in default, on admission, on acceptance, or on determination,

(c) the registration of judgments,

(d) the issue of warrants of execution,

(e) the transfer to the defendant's home court of any case which is to continue following the filing of a defence or where a hearing is required before judgment, and

(f) the transfer to the defendant's home court, in the circumstances to which CCR Order 25 rule 2 (transfer for enforcement) applies, of any case for an oral examination or where enforcement of a judgment (other than by warrant of execution) is to follow.

1.4(1) Where the officer is to take any step, any rule or Practice Direction which requires a document to be filed before he does so will be treated as complied with if the data which that document would contain is delivered to the Centre in computer readable form in accordance with the Code of Practice.

(2) Data relating to more than one case may be included in a single document or delivery of data.

(3) CPR Rule 6.3(3) (copies of documents to be served by court) does not apply to any document which is to be produced by electronic means from data supplied by a Centre user.

(4) Paragraph 10.3 of the practice direction supplementing CPR Part 16 (statements of case), which requires documentation to be attached to the particulars of contract claims, does not apply to claims to be issued by the Centre.

(5) The practice direction supplementing CPR Part 22 (statements of truth) is modified as follows:

(a) a single statement of truth may accompany each batch of requests to issue claim forms and may be in electronic form,

(b) the form of such a statement should be as follows: 'I believe that the facts stated in the attached claim forms are true.', and

(c) the signature of the appropriate person (as to which see section 3 of the practice direction supplementing CPR Part 22) may be in electronic form.

Claims which may not be issued through the Centre

2.1 The Centre will not issue any claim form which is to be issued in the High Court.

2.2 The Centre will only issue a claim form if the claim is for a specified sum of money less than £100,000.

2.3 The Centre will not issue any of the following types of claim:

(1) a claim against more than two defendants,

(2) a claim against two defendants where a different sum is claimed against each of them,

(3) a claim where particulars of claim separate from the claim form are required,

(4) a claim against the Crown,

(5) a claim for an amount in a foreign currency,

(6) a claim where either party is known to be a child or patient within Part 21 of the Civil Procedure Rules,

(7) a claim where the claimant is a legally assisted person within the meaning of the Legal Aid Act 1988,

(8) a claim where the defendant's address for service as it appears on the claim form is not in England or Wales.

(9) a claim which is to be issued under Part 8 of the Civil Procedure Rules.

Centre users

3.1 Only a Centre user may issue or conduct claims through the Centre.

3.2 The officer may permit any person to be a Centre user.

3.3 The officer may withdraw the permission for any person to be a Centre user.

3.4 A Centre user must comply with the provisions of the Code of Practice in his dealings with the Centre.

3.5 The officer will allot a national creditor code to each Centre user.

The Code of Practice

4.1 The Code of Practice will contain provisions designed to ensure that the Centre can discharge its functions efficiently, and it may in particular provide for:

(1) the forms of magnetic media that may be used,

(2) the circumstances in which data may or must be supplied in magnetic form,
(3) the circumstances in which data may or must be supplied in a document and the form that such a document must take,
(4) how often data may be supplied,
(5) the numbering of cases and data relating to cases,
(6) data to be given to the Centre by the Centre user about cases which have been settled or paid or are otherwise not proceeding, and
(7) accounting arrangements and the method of payment of fees.

4.2 The Court Service may change the Code of Practice from time to time.

Other Modifications to the Civil Procedure Rules

Power of the officer to make orders:

5.1 The officer may make the following orders:
(1) an order to set aside a default judgment where, after that judgment has been entered, the claim form in the case is returned by the Post Office as undelivered,
(2) an order to set aside a judgment on application by a Centre user,
(3) an order to transfer the case, in the circumstances to which CCR Order 25 rule 2 applies (transfer for enforcement or oral examination), of any case to another county court on the application of a Centre user.

Procedure on the filing of a defence

5.2(1) This paragraph applies where a Centre user has issued a claim in the Northampton County Court and the defendant has filed a defence to the claim or to part of the claim.
(2) On the filing of the defence the officer will serve a notice on the Centre user requiring the Centre user to notify him within 28 days whether he wishes the claim to proceed.
(3) If the Centre user does not notify the officer within the time specified in the notice that he wishes the claim to proceed the claim will be stayed, and the officer will notify the parties accordingly.
(4) The proceedings will not be transferred to the defendant's home court under CPR rule 26.2, and no allocation questionnaires will be served under CPR rule 26.3(3) until the Centre user notifies the officer that he wishes the claim to continue.

PRACTICE DIRECTION—CLAIMS FOR THE RECOVERY OF TAXES

This Practice Direction supplements CPR Rule 7.9

Scope

7DPD–001 **1.1** This practice direction applies to claims by the Inland Revenue for the recovery of—
(a) Income Tax,
(b) Corporation Tax,
(c) Capital Gains Tax,
(d) Interest, penalties and surcharges on Income Tax, Corporation Tax or Capital Gains Tax which by virtue of section 69 of the Taxes Management Act 1970 are to be treated as if they are taxes due and payable,
(e) National Insurance Contributions and interest, penalties and surcharges thereon.

Procedure

2.1 If a defence is filed, the court will fix a date for the hearing.

2.2 Part 26 (Case management—preliminary stage) apart from CPR rule 26.2 (automatic transfer) does not apply to claims to which this practice direction applies.

At the hearing

3.1 On the hearing date the court may dispose of the claim.
(Section 70 of the Taxes Management Act 1970 and section 118 of the Social Security Administration Act 1992 provide that a certificate of an officer of the Commmissioners of Inland Revenue is sufficient evidence that a sum mentioned in such a certificate is unpaid and due to the Crown.)

3.2 But exceptionally, if the court does not dispose of the claim on the hearing date it may give case management directions, which may, if the defendant has filed a defence, include allocating the case.

PART 8

ALTERNATIVE PROCEDURE FOR CLAIMS

8.0.1 Contents

Editorial Introduction

8.0.2 The rules in this Part deal with the alternative procedure for claims. It was the subject of an "Access to Justice" Consultation Paper.

The main difference between the general procedure and the Pt 8 procedure is that a defence is not required (Pt 15) default judgment (Pt 12) is not available and the claim is treated as allocated to the multi-track.

The rules in this Part should be read together with the general rules. The general rules apply subject to express contrary provisions.

Accordingly, the rules relating to striking out (Pt 3), addition and substitution of parties (Pt 19) and summary judgment (Pt 24) apply. Part 50 contains as schedules to the rules former rules of Court which are re-enacted without substantial changes. Accordingly, Pt 8, will be generally suitable for use in situations where previously proceedings were commenced by originating summons. Examples would be declarations as to construction of documents and questions of law and administration of estates and kin enquiries.

The Pt 8 procedure replaces, in a simplified form, the former High Court originating summons procedure in RSC, O.7 and O.28. Rule 8.1 and para. 1 of the Pt 8 Practice Direction (see para. 8PD–001) provides for the types of claim in which the Pt 8 procedure may be followed. These are claims for the court's decision on a question which is unlikely to involve a substantial dispute of fact or where a practice direction or rule requires or permits the use of alternative procedure. Paragraph 1.4 of the Practice Direction includes, for example, applications for summary possession of land (RSC, O.113), but note that RSC Order 113 is one of those parts of the RSC which have been retained in Schedule 1 to the CPR.

Further Part 8 Practice Direction

8.0.3 A further Pt 8Practice Direction has been issued described as supplementing Pt 8 and Scheds 1 and 2 to the CPR. This Practice Direction is divided into three sections, A, B and C. If a claim is of a type described in para. A1, then Section A is to be used, if described in Section B, Section B and if described in Section C (which deals with appeals) Section C. Section A applies if the claim is either a claim listed in Table 1, *or* where an Act provides such a claim is one if brought in the High Court would have been by originating summons (other than those listed in Section C) *and* no other method of bringing the claim is specified by the CPR or Practice Directions.

Table 1—Table 1 lists a large number of proceedings under the Scheduled RSC order including applications for charging orders, stop orders, mortgage claims, proceedings under the Landlord and Tenant Acts 1927, 1954 and 1987 and proceedings under the Inheritance (Provisions for Family and Dependants) Act 1975 and summary proceedings for possession of land (RSC, O.113).

Section B—Section B applies if the claim (1) is listed in Table 2 (2) in the County Court is for or includes a claim for recovery of possession of land or for damages for harassment under section 3 of the Protection from Harassment Act 1973 (3) would have been brought prior to the operation of the CPR in the High Court by originating motion (other than those listed in Section C) or in the county court by originating application or petition *and* no other proceeding is specified by the CPR or Practice Direction.

Table 2 lists a large number of applications and appeals and including summary proceedings for the possession of land under CCR, O.24, r.1(1), CCR, O.24, r.10(2)(a) and applications for Charging Orders, CCR, O.31, r.4(1).

Section C is concerned with appeals listed in Table 3 including appeals in the Court of Appeal (RCS, O.59, r.3(1)).

Practice—This is a complicated Practice Direction and practitioners will in particular need to refer to the Tables in the sections in order to determine which section applies. In broad terms, Section A applications are to follow Part 8 procedure subject to any necessary modifications in a particular case (Section A.2(2)). A similar approach governs Section B applications but it is to be noted that para. B.6 contains restrictions on where to start claims listed in Table 2 as both are provisions concerning the claim form, (B.8), the court fixing a hearing date (B.9) and service of the claim form (B.1C, B.4). Section B is elaborate and generally it provides that a modified version of the Pt 8 proceudre is to be followed but all such claims are dealt with as multi-track proceedings.

The wording "unlikely to involve substantial dispute of fact" is similar to the former O.5, r.4(2)(b) of the RSC. Contentious claims involving substantial factual dispute were not suitable under the former procedure and nor will they be under the Pt 8 procedure.

In essence, the Pt 8 procedure, like its predecessor originating summons procedure, is designed for the determination of relevant claims without elaborate pleadings. If the procedure is misused, the defendant can object and equally the court of its own motion, and as part of its function to manage claims, will order the claim to proceed under the general procedure and allocate a track and give appropriate directions.

Managing the Claim

All Pt 8 claims are allocated to the multi-track. Accordingly, there is no allocation questionnaire in Pt 8 claims. The court may give directions immediately after the procedural judge reviews the court file in an appropriate case and the Practice Direction at para. 4.1 (see para. 8PD–001) gives examples. If the court does not fix a hearing date when the claim is issued and give directions immediately then it will do so "as soon as practicable" after the defendant has acknowledged service or the time for acknowledgment of service has expired. In practice it is unlikely that in any substantial Pt 8 case the court will be able to give effective directions until that stage of the proceedings. The court can order a directions hearing (case management conference) if appropriate. The multi track rules in para. 29 apply to Pt 8. **8.0.4**

Related Sources

- Practice Direction (Alternative Procedure for Claims), see para. 8PD–001, below **8.0.5**
- Practice Direction—Part 8, see para. 8BPD–001, below
- Part 8 claim form (N208)
- N208A—Part 8 notes for claimants (see para. C42–001)
- N208C—Part 8 notes for defendant (see para. C43–001)
- N212—Part 8 notice of issue (see para. C50–001)
- Part 8 acknowledgment of service
- Chancery Guide April 1999 (General Commentary)

Types of claim in which Part 8 procedure may be followed

8.1—(1) The Part 8 procedure is the procedure set out in this Part. **8.1**

(2) A claimant may use the Part 8 procedure where—

(a) he seeks the court's decision on a question which is unlikely to involve a substantial dispute of fact; or

(b) paragraph (6) applies.

(3) The court may at any stage order the claim to continue as if the claimant had not used the Part 8 procedure and, if it does so, the court may give any directions it considers appropriate.

(4) Paragraph (2) does not apply if a practice direction provides that the Part 8 procedure may not be used in relation to the type of claim in question.

(5) Where the claimant uses the Part 8 procedure he may not obtain default judgment under Part 12.

(6) A rule or practice direction may, in relation to a specified type of proceedings—

(a) require or permit the use of the Part 8 procedure; and

(b) disapply or modify any of the rules set out in this Part as they apply to those proceedings.

(Rule 8.9 provides for other modifications to the general rules where the Part 8 is being used.)

Types of claim in which Part 8 procedure may or must be followed—Rule 8.1 specifies the types of claim for which the alternative procedure may be followed. **8.1.1**

Rule 8.1(2)(a) provides that the procedure may be used where a claimant seeks the court's decision on a question which is unlikely to involve a substantial dispute of fact, for example a declaration as to construction of a document or a question of law.

Rule 8.1(2)(b) is important as setting out the authority of the practice direction by providing that such direction can require or permit the use of the Pt 8 procedure and further by r.8.1(6)(b) by providing that the practice direction may disapply or modify any Pt 8 rule.

The other types of claim for which the Pt 8 procedure is expressly permissible are set out in para. 1.4 of the Practice Direction. They include claims for a summary order for possession against named or unnamed defendants occupying land or premises without licence or consent. The former RSC, O.113 is annexed to Pt 50 under heading RSC, O.113.

If there is a common theme in the types of Pt 8 claim set out in the Practice Direction at para. 1.4, it is that such claims are likely to be capable of disposal without there being substantial disputes of fact.

If any substantial dispute of fact is anticipated then the Pt 8 procedure should not be followed, similarly the court will assess the suitability of the procedure at the stage it gives directions. This is particularly recognised in paras 1.5 and 1.6 and 4 of the Practice Direction which underlines the court's function in managing Pt 8 claims.

The RSC, O.88 in Sched. 1 of the CPR claims are suitable for commencement under Pt 8.

See also under Editorial Introduction and the further Practice Direction.

8.1.2 **Ex parte Part 8 claims**—The Pt 8 rules and practice direction do not appear to provide, at any rate expressly, for situations where there is no party to be served, *e.g.* applications for the payment or transfer of monies in court (see notes to former RSC, O.7(7) in SCP 1999).

Directions should be sought from the court in such situations, a practice direction will it is presumed provide, in due course, for Pt 8 claims where there is no party to be served.

Contents of the claim form

8.2 **8.2** Where the claimant uses the Part 8 procedure the claim form must state—

(a) that this Part applies;
(b) (i) the question which the claimant wants the court to decide; or
 (ii) the remedy which the claimant is seeking and the legal basis for the claim to that remedy;
(c) if the claim is being made under an enactment, what that enactment is;
(d) if the claimant is claiming in a representative capacity, what that capacity is; and
(e) if the defendant is sued in a representative capacity, what that capacity is.

(Part 22 provides for the claim form to be verified by a statement of truth.)
(Rule 7.5 provides for service of the claim form.)

8.2.1 **Contents of the Claim Form**—Claims to which Pt 8 apply are commenced by the issue of a claim form.

The claim form should, in general, not contain the same amount of detail as a claim form for other claims and should set out in summary form only the question or issue the claimant wants the court to decide or the remedy that is sought, as the case may be.

Paragraph 2.2 of the Practice Direction provides that the claim form must be in practice form N208. The claim form must state that Pt 8 applies. The burden is put upon the claimant that the claim is suitable for Pt 8 procedure. It is a requirement that the claim must state that it is suitable for Pt 8.

The claim form contains guidance notes on the completion of the form and the description and details of parties, for example minors, companies and unincorporated associations.

Acknowledgment of service

8.3 **8.3**—(1) The defendant must—

(a) file an acknowledgment of service in the relevant practice form not more than 14 days after service of the claim form; and
(b) serve the acknowledgment of service on the claimant and any other party.

(2) The acknowledgment of service must state—

(a) whether the defendant contests the claim; and
(b) if the defendant seeks a different remedy from that set out in the claim form, what that remedy is.

(3) The following rules of Part 10 (acknowledgment of service) apply—
(a) rule 10.3(2) (exceptions to the period for filing an acknowledgment of service); and
(b) rule 10.5 (contents of acknowledgment of service).

(4) Part 11 (disputing the court's jurisdiction) applies subject to the modification that in rule 11(4)(a) and (5)(b) (time limit for application disputing court's jurisdiction) references to the period for filing a defence are treated as if they were references to a period of 14 days from the filing of an acknowledgment of service.

Rule 8.3—Does not apply to applications listed in section B, Table 2 to the Part 8 Practice Direction. **8.3.1**

Consequence of not filing an acknowledgment of service

8.4—(1) This rule applies where— **8.4**
(a) defendant has failed to file an acknowledgment of service; and
(b) the time period for doing so has expired.

(2) The defendant may attend the hearing of the claim but may not take part in the hearing unless the court gives permission.

Responding to claim—The combined effect of r.8.3 and para. 3 of the Practice Direction is that if a defendant wishes to *respond* to a Pt 8 claim he must acknowledge service within 14 days of service of the claim form using Form N210. **8.4.1**

Although r.8.3 is expressed in mandatory language, para. 3.2 of the Practice Direction (see para. 8PD–001) makes clear that a defendant can acknowledge service informally in such a document as a letter.

It is at this stage that, in practice, a defendant must either respond to the claim, for example if a different remedy to the remedy claimed is sought he should set this out with particulars, *or* seek to dispute the court's jurisdiction (a directions hearing will then be appointed) *or* object to the use of the Pt 8 procedure, for example, on the ground that a substantial dispute of fact needs to be considered by the court in the particular claim.

Directions already given—If the court has already given directions, a copy of the court order will be served on the defendant with the claim form. In that case the defendant must not only file and serve his acknowledgment of service but also comply with the directions. If a defendant wishes to seek to vary any directions already given he should in most cases ask for a variation at a directions hearing and state the variation sought in his written evidence accompanying his acknowledgment of service. **8.4.2**

Agreed Directions—It is sensible practice for the parties to seek to agree directions and submit them to the court immediately after the time limited for filing or acknowledge by the defendant. CPR, r.29.4 applies to Pt 8 claims and the Guidance in the Practice Direction supplementing CPR, Pt 29 encourages the parties to agree suitable Directions. **8.4.3**

Filing and serving witness statements

8.5—(1) The claimant must file any written evidence on which he intends to rely when he files his claim form. **8.5**

(2) The claimant's evidence must be served on the defendant with the claim form.

(3) A defendant who wishes to rely on written evidence must file it when he files his ackowledgment of service.

(4) If he does so, he must also, at the same time, serve a copy of his evidence on the other parties.

(5) The claimant may, within 14 days of service of the defendant's evidence on him, file further written evidence in reply.

(6) If he does so, he must also, within the same time limit, serve a copy of his evidence on the other parties.

(7) The claimant may rely on the matters set out in his claim form as evidence under this rule if the claim form is verified by a statement of truth.

(Rule 2.11 allows the parties to agree in writing to vary time limits specified by a rule unless a rule, practice direction or court order provides otherwise.)

Filing and serving written evidence

8.5.1 *Claimant's evidence*—Rule 8.5 is important as providing that if the claimant wishes to file any written evidence this must be filed with the claim form unless the evidence is contained on the claim form itself and is supported by a statement of truth.

8.5.2 *Defendant's evidence*—Similarly, the defendant must file his evidence with his acknowledgment of service and serve it on all parties. Rule 8.5(4) gives 14 days in which the claimant can serve evidence in reply. The former originating summons procedure allowed 28 days after receipt of the plaintiff's evidence and 14 days may prove short for a defendant. The 14 days for Pt 8 is a fixed period.

Evidence for the purposes of Pt 8 is in the form of an affidavit or a witness statement, subject to the court's power to admit oral evidence.

8.5.3 *Timings*—Timings are important and are set out in this part. In summary the claimant must be ready to serve all his evidence with his claim form. The defendant then has 14 days from service of evidence served on him to file his acknowledgment of service and any evidence in reply to be filed by the claimant must be within 14 days of service of the acknowledgment of service by the defendant.

Evidence—general

8.6 **8.6**—(1) No written evidence may be relied on at the hearing of the claim unless—

(a) it has been served in accordance with rule 8.5; or

(b) the court gives permission.

(2) The court may require or permit a party to give oral evidence at the hearing.

(3) The court may give directions requiring the attendance for cross-examination[GL] of a witness who has given written evidence.

(Rule 32.1 contains a general power for the court to control evidence.)

8.6.1 **Evidence**—Rule 8.6 governs the position in relation to evidence in Pt 8 claims. Generally, the position is that no written evidence may be filed unless it has been served in accordance with the rules or the court gives permission.

Rule 8.6(2) gives the court power to authorise a party to adduce oral evidence at the hearing and r.8.6(3) gives to the court power to make an order requiring the attendance of a person who has given written evidence to attend for cross examination.

It is thought that, in practice, it is unlikely that the court will permit oral evidence unless it has been foreshadowed in earlier written evidence. Equally, if it becomes apparent that the claim is one that is going to involve substantial cross examination involving disputed matters of fact, it is likely that the court will take the view that the case is not suitable for the Pt 8 procedure and will give directions accordingly.

Part 20 claims

8.7 **8.7** Where the Part 8 procedure is used, Part 20 (counterclaims, third party claims and other similar claims) applies except that a party may not make a Part 20 claim (as defined by rule 20.2) without the court's permission.

Procedure where defendant objects to use of the Part 8 procedure

8.8 **8.8**—(1) Where the defendant believes that the Part 8 procedure should not be used because—

(a) there is a substantial dispute of fact; and

(b) the use of the Part 8 procedure is not required or permitted by a rule or practice direction, he must state his reasons when he files his acknowledgment of service.

(Rule 8.5 requires a defendant who wishes to rely on written evidence to file it when he files his acknowledgment of service.)

(2) When the court receives the acknowledgment of service and any written evidence it will give directions as to the future management of the case.

(Rule 8.1(3) allows the court to make an order that the claim continue as if the claimant had not used the Part 8 procedure.)

Procedure where defendant objects to use Part 8 procedure—This provision is set out in r.8.8. An objection will be considered by the court. Even if no objection is taken by a defendant the court officer may bring to the attention of the judge any case where he considers that the procedure is being used inappropriately. **8.8.1**

In practice, the judge will consider the appropriateness or otherwise of the use of the alternative procedure when the claim comes before him either initially or at the directions hearing.

Modifications to the general rules

8.9 Where the Part 8 procedure is followed— **8.9**

(a) provision is made in this Part for the matters which must be stated in the claim form and the defendant is not required to file a defence and therefore—
   (i) Part 16 (statements of case) does not apply;
   (ii) Part 15 (defence) does not apply;
   (iii) any time limit in these Rules which prevents the parties from taking a step before a defence is filed does not apply;
   (iv) the requirement under rule 7.8 to serve on the defendant a form for defending the claim does not apply;

(b) the claimant may not obtain judgment by request on an admission and therefore—
   (i) rules 14.4 to 14.7 do not apply;
   (ii) the requirement under rule 7.8 to serve on the defendant a form for admitting the claim does not apply; and

(c) the claim shall be treated as allocated to the multi-track and therefore Part 26 does not apply.

PRACTICE DIRECTION—ALTERNATIVE PROCEDURE FOR CLAIMS

This Practice Direction supplements CPR Part 8 **8PD–001**

Types of claim in which Part 8 procedure may be used

1.1 A claimant may use the Part 8 procedure where he seeks the court's decision on a question which is unlikely to involve a substantial dispute of fact.

1.2 A claimant may also use the Part 8 procedure if a practice direction permits or requires its use for the type of proceedings in question.

1.3 The practice directions referred to in paragraphs 1.2 and 1.3 above may in some respects modify or disapply the Part 8 procedure and, where that is so, it is those practice directions that must be complied with.

1.4 The types of claim for which the Part 8 procedure may be used include;

(1) a claim by or against a child or patient which has been settled before the commencement of proceedings and the sole purpose of the claim is to obtain the approval of the court to the settlement,

(2) a claim for provisional damages which has been settled before the commencement of proceedings and the sole purpose of the claim is to obtain a consent judgment,

(3) provided there is unlikely to be a substantial dispute of fact, a claim for a summary order for possession against named or unnamed defendants

occupying land or premises without the licence or consent of the person claiming possession.

1.5 Where it appears to a court officer that a claimant is using the Part 8 procedure inappropriately, he may refer the claim to a judge for the judge to consider the point.

1.6 The court may at any stage order the claim to continue as if the claimant had not used the Part 8 procedure and, if it does so, the court will allocate the claim to a track and give such directions as it considers appropriate.[1]

Issuing the claim

2.1 Part 7 and the practice direction which supplements it contain a number of rules and directions applicable to all claims, including those to which Part 8 applies. Those rules and directions should be applied where appropriate.

2.2 Where a claimant uses the Part 8 procedure, the claim form (practice form N208) should be used and must state the matters set out in rule 8.2 and, if paragraphs 1.2 or 1.3 apply, must comply with the requirements of the practice direction in question. In particular, the claim form must state that Part 8 applies; a Part 8 claim form means a claim form which so states.

Responding to the claim

3.1 The provisions of Part 15 (defence and reply) do not apply where the claim form is a Part 8 claim form.

3.2 Where a defendant who wishes to respond to a Part 8 claim form is required to file an acknowledgement of service, that acknowledgment of service should be in practice form N210[2] but can, alternatively, be given in an informal document such as a letter.

3.3 Rule 8.3 sets out provisions relating to an acknowledgment of service of a Part 8 claim form.

3.4 Rule 8.4 sets out the consequence of failing to file an acknowledgment of service.

3.5 The provisions of Part 12 (obtaining default judgment) do not apply where the claim form is a Part 8 claim form.

3.6 Where a defendant believes that the Part 8 procedure should not be used because there is a substantial dispute of fact or, as the case may be, because its use is not authorised by any rule or practice direction, he must state his reasons in writing when he files his acknowledgment of service.[3] If the statement of reasons includes matters of evidence it should be verified by a statement of truth.

Managing the claim

4.1 The court may give directions immediately a Part 8 claim form is issued either on the application of a party or on its own initiative. The directions may include fixing a hearing date where;

(1) there is no dispute, such as in child and patient settlements, or

(2) where there may be a dispute, such as in claims for mortgage possession or appointment of trustees, but a hearing date could conveniently be given.

4.2 Where the court does not fix a hearing date when the claim form is issued, it will give directions for the disposal of the claim as soon as practicable after the defendant has acknowledged service of the claim form or, as the case may be, after the period for acknowledging service has expired.

4.3 Certain applications, such as a consent application under s.38 of the Landlord and Tenant Act 1954, may not require a hearing.

4.4 The court may convene a directions hearing before giving directions.

[1] Rule 8.1(3).
[2] Rule 8.3(1)(a).
[3] Rule 8.8(1).

Evidence

5.1 A claimant wishing to rely on written evidence should file it when his Part 8 claim form is issued[4] (unless the evidence is contained in the claim form itself).

5.2 Evidence will normally be in the form of a witness statement or an affidavit but a claimant may rely on the matters set out in his claim form provided that it has been verified by a statement of truth.

(For information about (1) statements of truth see Part 22 and the practice direction that supplements it, and (2) written evidence see Part 32 and the practice direction that supplements it.)

5.3 A defendant wishing to rely on written evidence, should file it with his acknowledgment of service.[5]

5.4 Rule 8.5 sets out the times and provisions for filing and serving written evidence.

5.5 A party may apply to the court for an extension of time to serve and file evidence under Rule 8.5 or for permission to serve and file additional evidence under Rule 8.6(1).

(For information about applications see Part 23 and the practice direction that supplements it).

5.6(1) The parties may, subject to the following provisions, agree in writing on an extension of time for serving and filing evidence under Rule 8.5(3) or Rule 8.5(5)

(2) An agreement extending time for a defendant to file evidence under Rule 8.5(3)—

(a) must be filed by the defendant at the same time as he files his acknowledgment of service; and

(b) must not extend time by more than 14 days after the defendant files his acknowledgment of service.

(3) An agreement extending time for a claimant to file evidence in reply under Rule 8.5(5) must not extend time to more than 28 days after service of the defendant's evidence on the claimant.

PRACTICE DIRECTION—PART 8

This Practice Direction supplements CPR Part 8, and Schedule 1 and Schedule 2 to the CPR **8BPD–001**

Terminology

1.1 In this practice direction "Schedule rules" means provisions contained in the Schedules to the CPR, which were previously contained in the Rules of the Supreme Court (1965) or the County Court Rules (1981).

Contents of this Practice Direction

2.1 This practice direction explains—

(1) how to start the claims referred to in Sections A and B;

(2) which form to use as the claim form;

(3) the procedure which those claims will follow; and

(4) how to start the appeals referred to in Section C.

(Further guidance about Forms other than claim forms can be found in the practice direction supplementing Part 4.)

[4] Rule 8.5.

[5] Rule 8.5(3).

(Forms to be used when making applications under Schedule 1, RSC, O.53 for judicial review and under Schedule RSC, O.54 for writs of habeas corpus are forms 86 and 87 (modified as necessary). Reference should be made to the relevant existing Crown Office practice directions for further guidance on procedure).

How to use this Practice Direction

3.1 This Practice Direction is divided into three sections—Section A, Section B and Section C. Only one section will be relevant to how to make a particular claim or appeal.

3.2 If the claim is described in paragraph A.1—use section A.

3.3 If the claim is described in paragraph B.1—use section B.

3.4 If the appeal is described in paragraph C.1—used section C.

Section A

Application

A.1 Section A applies if—

(1) the claim is listed in Table 1 below;

(2) an Act provides tha a claim or application in the High Court is to be brought by originating summons; or

(3) before 26 April 1999, a claim or application in the High Court would have been brought by originating summons, and is not listed in Section C, and no other method for bringing the claim or application on and after 26 April 1999 is specified in a Schedule rule or practice direction.

A.2(1) The claimant must use the Part 8 procedure unless an Act, Schedule rule, or practice direction, makes any additional or contrary provision.

(2) Where such additional or contrary provision is made the claimant must comply with it and modify the Part 8 procedure accordingly.

Claim form

8BPD–002 **A.3** The claimant must use the Part 8 claim form.

Table 1

RSC, O.11, r.8A	Service of process etc., out of the jurisdiction: Applications for interim remedy under section 25(1) of the Civil Jurisdiction and Judgments Act 1982
RSC, O.17, r.3(1)	Interpleader (Mode of application)
RSC, O.50, r.9A	Charging orders, Stop orders etc., Enforcement of charging order by sale
RSC, O.50, r.10(2)	Charging orders, Stop orders etc., Funds in court: Stop order
RSC, O.50, r.14(4)	Charging orders, Stop orders etc., Withdrawal etc. of Stop Notice
RSC, O.50, r.15(2)	Charging orders, Stop orders etc., Order prohibiting transfer, etc., of securities

Table 1

RSC, O.71, r.2(1)	Reciprocal Enforcement of Judgments and Enforcement of European Community Judgments and Recommendations etc. under The Merchant Shipping (Liner Conferences) Act 1982 (III Reciprocal Enforcement: The Administration of Justice Act 1920 and the Foreign Judgments (Reciprocal Enforcement) Act 1933—Application for registration)
RSC, O.71, r.38	Reciprocal Enforcement of Judgments and Enforcement of European Community Judgments and Recommendations etc. under The Merchant Shipping (Liner Conferences) Act 1982 (III Reciprocal Enforcment: The Civil Jurisdiction and Judgments Act 1982—Enforcement of United Kingdom Judgments in other Parts of the United Kingdom: Non-money Provisions)
RSC, O.71, r.41	Reciprocal Enforcement of Judgments and Enforcement of European Community Judgments and Recommendations etc. under The Merchant Shipping (Liner Conferences) Act 1982 (IV Enforcement of Recommendations etc. under the Merchant Shipping (Liner Conferences) Act 1982—Application for registration)
RSC, O.77, r.11	Proceedings by and against the Crown (Interpleader: Application for order against Crown)
RSC, O.77, r.16(2)	Proceedings by and against the Crown (Attachment of debts, etc.)
RSC, O.77, r.17(1)	Proceedings by and against the Crown (Proceedings relating to postal packets)
RSC, O.77, r.18(1)	Proceedings by and against the Crown (Applications under sections 17 and 29 of the Crown Proceedings Act)
RSC, O.79, r.8(2)	Criminal Proceedings (Estreat of recognizances)
RSC, O.79, r.9(2)	Criminal Proceedings (Bail)
RSC, O.79, r.10(2)	Criminal Proceedings (Issue of witness summons, etc.)
RSC, O.79, r.11(1)	Criminal Proceedings (Application for warrant to arrest witness)
RSC, O.81, r.10(1)	Partners (Applications for orders charging partner's interest in partnership property)

Table 1

RSC, O.82, r.8(2)	Defamation claims (Fulfilment of offer of amends under section 4 of the Defamation Act 1952)
RSC, O.88, r.3	Mortgage claims (Commencement of claim)[6]
RSC, O.92, r.5(2)	Lodgment, Investment etc. of Funds in Court: Chancery Division (Applications with respect to funds in court)
RSC, O.93, r.5(2)	Applications and Appeals to High Court under Various Acts: Chancery Division (Applications under section 2(3) of the Public Order Act 1936)
RSC, O.93, r.6(2)	Applications and Appeals to High Court under Various Acts: Chancery Division (Application under the Variation of Trusts Act 1958)
RSC, O.93, r.18(2)	Applications and Appeals to High Court under Various Acts: Chancery Division (Proceedings under section 86 of the Civil Aviation Act 1982)
RSC, O.93, r.20(2)	Applications and Appeals to High Court under Various Acts: Chancery Division (Proceedings under section 50 of the Administration of Justice Act 1985)
RSC, O.93, r.21	Applications and Appeals to High Court under Various Acts: Chancery Division (Proceedings under section 48 of the Administration of Justice Act 1985)
RSC, O.93, r.23(2)(a)	Applications and Appeals to High Court under Various Acts: Chancery Division (Proceedings under the Banking Act 1987: applications under sections 26(3), 71(3) and (5) and 77(3) and (5))
RSC, O.94, r.5	Applications and Appeals to High Court under Various Acts: Queen's Bench Division (Exercise of jurisdiction under Representation of the People Acts)
RSC, O.95, r.2(1)(b)	Bills of Sale Act 1878 and 1882 and the Industrial and Provident Societies Act 1967 (Entry of satisfaction)
RSC, O.95, r.3	Bills of Sale Acts 1878 and 1882 and the Industrial and Provident Societies Act 1967 (Restraining removal on sale of goods seized)
RSC, O.96, r.1	The Mines (Working Facilities and Support) Act 1966 etc. (Assignment to Chancery Division)

[6] This type of claim may also be brought by the Part 8 procedure in Section B.

Table 1

RSC, O.96, r.3	The Mines (Working Facilities and Support) Act 1966 etc. (Issue of claim form)
RSC, O.97, r.2	The Landlord and Tenant Acts 1927, 1954 and 1987 (Assignment of proceedings to Chancery Division etc.)
RSC, O.97, r.5	The Landlord and Tenant Acts 1927, 1954 and 1987 (Proceedings under Part I of the Act of 1927)
RSC, O.97, r.6(1)	The Landlord and Tenant Acts 1927, 1954 and 1987 (Application for new tenancy under section 24 of the Act of 1954)
RSC, O.97, r.6A(1)	The Landlord and Tenant Acts 1927, 1954 and 1987 (Application to authorise agreement)
RSC, O.97, r.9A(1)(b)	The Landlord and Tenant Acts 1927, 1954 and 1987 (Application to determine interim rent)
RSC, O.97, r.14	The Landlord and Tenant Acts 1927, 1954 and 1987 (Application under section 19 of the Act of 1987)
RSC, O.97, r.15(3)	The Landlord and Tenant Acts 1927, 1954 and 1987 (Application for order under section 24 of the Act of 1987)
RSC, O.97, r.16(3)	The Landlord and Tenant Acts 1927, 1954 and 1987 (Application for acquisition order under section 29 of the Act of 1987)
RSC, O.99, r.3(1)	Inheritance (Provision for Family and Dependants) Act 1976 (Application for Financial Provision) (High Court and County Court Cases)
RSC, O.106, r.3(2)	Provisions Relating to Solicitors: The Solicitors Act 1974 (Power to order solicitor to deliver cash account etc.)
RSC, O.106, r.6(2)	Proceedings Relating to Solicitors: The Solicitors Act 1974 (Applications under schedule 1 to the Act)
RSC, O.106, r.8(1)	Proceedings Relating to Solicitors: The Solicitors Act 1974 (Interim order restricting payment out of banking account)
RSC, O.109, r.1(3)	Administration Act 1960 (Applications under Act)
RSC, O.113, r.1	Summary proceedings for possession of land (Proceedings to be brought by claim form)

Section B

Application

8BPD–003 **B.1** Section B applies if the claim—

(1) is listed in Table 2;

(2) in the county court is for, or includes a claim for:

(a) the recovery of possession of land; or

(b) for damages for harassment under Section 3 of the Protection for Harassment Act 1997

(3) would have been brought before 26 April 1999—

(a) in the High Court, by originating motion and is not listed in Section C;

(b) in the county court—

(i) by originating application; or

(ii) by petition, and

no other procedure is prescribed in an Act, a Schedule rule or a practice direction.

Table 2

Schedule Rule		**Claim Form**
RSC, O.56, r.8(1)	Appeals, etc., to High Court by Case Stated: General (Application for order to state a case)	
RSC, O.56, r.10(1)	Appeals, etc., to High Court by Case Stated: General (Proceedings for determination of case)	
RSC, O.71, r.24[7]	Preciprocal Enforcement of Judgments and Enforcement of European Community Judgments and Recommendations etc., under The Merchant Shipping (Liner Conferences) Act 1982, II Enforcement of European Community Judgments. (Application for enforcement of Euratom inspection order)	
RSC, O.77, r.8(2)[8]	Proceedings by and against the Crown (Summary applications to the court in certain revenue matters)	
RSC, O.93, r.19(1)	Applications and Aspects to High Court under Various Acts: (Proceedings under section 85(7) of the Fair Trading Act 1973 and the Control of Misleading Advertisements Regulations 1988)	

[7] This type of claim may also be brought by the Part 8 procedure.
[8] These types of claim may also be brought by the Part 8 procedure.

Table 2

Schedule Rule		Claim Form
RSC, O.93, r.22(3)	Applications and Appeals to High Court under Various Acts: Chancery Division (Proceedings under the Financial Services Act 1986) (Applications by inspectors under section 94 or 178)	
RSC, O.94, r.1(2)	Applications and Appeals to High Court under Various Acts: Queens Bench Division (Jurisdiction of High Court to Quash Certain Orders, Schemes etc.)	
RSC, O.94, r.7(2)	Applications and Appeals to High Court under Various Acts: Queens Bench Division (Reference of Question of Law by Agricultural Land Tribunal)	
RSC, O.94, r.11(4)	Applications and Appeals to High Court under Various Acts: Queens Bench Division (Case stated by Mental Health Review Tribunal)	
RSC, O.94, r.12(5)(c)	Applications and Appeals to High Court under Various Acts: Queens Bench Division Applications for permission under section 289(6) of the Town and Country Planning Act 1990 and section 65(5) of the Planning (Listed Buildings and Conservation Areas) Acts 1990	
RSC, O.94, r.13(5)	Applications and Appeals to High Court under Various Acts: Queens Bench Division Proceedings under sections 289 and 290 of the Town and Country Planning Act 1990 and under section 65 of the Planning (Listed Buildings and Conservation Areas) Act 1990	
RSC, O.94, r.14(2)	Applications and Appeals to High Court under Various Acts: Queens Bench Division Applications under section 13 of the Coroners Act 1988	
RSC, O.94, r.15(2)	Applications and Appeals to High Court under Various Acts: Queens Bench Division Applications under section 42 of the Supreme Court Act 1981	

Table 2

Schedule Rule		Claim Form
RSC, O.98, r.2(1)	Local Government Finance Act 1982, Part III (Application by auditor for declaration)	
RSC, O.109, r.2(4)	Administration of Justice Act 1960 (Appeals under section 13 of Act)	
RSC, O.114, r.2(2)	References to the European Court (Making of order)	
RSC, O.115, r.2B(1)	Confiscation and Forfeiture in Connection with Criminal Proceedings (I. Drug Trafficking Act 1994 and Criminal Justice (International Co-operation) Act 1990—Application for confiscation Order)	
RSC, O.115, r.3(1)	Confiscation and Forfeiture in Connection with Criminal Proceedings (I. Drug Trafficking Act 1994 and Criminal Justice (International Co-operation) Act 1990—Application for restraint order or charging order)	
RSC, O.115, r.7(1)	Confiscation and Forfeiture in Connection with Criminal Proceedings (I. Drug Trafficking Act 1994 and Criminal Justice (International Co-operation) Act 1990—Realisation of property)	
RSC, O.115, r.26(1)	Confiscation and Forfeiture in Connection with Criminal Proceedings (III. Prevention of Terrorism (Temporary Provisions) Act 1989—Application for restraint order)	
RSC, O.116, r.5(1)	The Criminal Procedure and Investigations Act 1996 (Application under section 54(3))	
CCR, O.24, r.1(1)	Summary proceedings for the recovery of land (Part I—Land: proceedings to be by claim form)	N312
CCR, O.24, r.10(2)(a)	Summary proceedings for the recovery of land (Part II—Interim possession orders—issue of the applications)	N130

Table 2

Schedule Rule		**Claim Form**
CCR, O.31, r.4(1)	Charging orders (Enforcement of charging order by sale)	
CCR, O.43, r.2(1)	The Landlord and Tenant Acts 1927, 1954, 1985 and 1987 (Commencement of proceedings and answer)	
CCR, O.43, r.4(1)	The Landlord and Tenant Acts 1927, 1954, 1985 and 1987 (Proceedings under Part I of the Act of 1927)	N394 N395 N396
CCR, O.43, r.6(1)	The Landlord and Tenant Acts 1927, 1954, 1985 and 1987 (Application for a new tenancy under section 24 of the Act of 1954)	N397
CCR, O.43, r.16	The Lord and Tenant Acts 1927, 1954, and 1985 and 1987 (Application under section 12(2) of the Act of 1985)	
CCR, O.43, r.18(1)	The Landlord and Tenant Acts 1927, 1954, 1985 and 1987 (Application for order under section 24 of the Act of 1987)	
CCR, O.43, r.19(1)	The Landlord and Tenant Acts 1927, 1954, 1985 and 1987 (Application for acquisition order under section 29 of the Act of 1987)	
CCR, O.43, r.20(1)	The Landlord and Tenant Acts 1927, 1954, 1985 and 1987 (Application for order under section 38 or 40 of the Act of 1987)	
CCR, O.44, r.1(1)	The Agricultural Holdings Act 1986 (Special case stated by arbitrator)	
CCR, O.44, r.3(1)	The Agricultural Holdings Act 1986 (Removal of arbitrator or setting aside award)	
CCR, O.45, r.1(1)	The Representation of the People Act 1983 (Application for detailed assessment of returning officer's account)	N408
CCR, O.46, r.1(1)	The Legitimacy Act 1976 (Manner of application)	

Table 2

Schedule Rule		Claim Form
CCR, O.49, r.1(2)	Miscellaneous Statutes: (Access to Neighbouring Land Act 1992)	
CCR, O.49, r.4(5)	Miscellaneous Statutes: (Consumer Credit Act 1974—claim relating to land (Application under section 129(1)(b)))	N440
CCR, O.49, r.4(9)	Miscellaneous Statutes: (Consumer Credit Act 1974—claim relating to land (Application for enforcement order))	
CCR, O.49, r.4(14)	Miscellaneous Statutes: (Consumer Credit Act 1974—claim relating to land (Application under section 139(1)(a) for a credit agreement to be reopened))	
CCR, O.49, r.4(15)	Miscellaneous Statutes: (Consumer Credit Act 1974—claim relating to land (proceedings as are mentioned in section 139(1)(b) or (c)))	
CCR, O.49, r.5(1)	Miscellaneous Statutes: Fair Trading Act 1973 (Proceedings under section 35, 38 or 40)	
CCR, O.49, r.6(5)	Miscellaneous Statutes: Housing Act 1988: assured tenancies (application for accelerated possession)	N5A
CCR, O.49, r.6A(5)	Miscellaneous Statutes: Housing Act 1988: assured shorthold tenancies (application for accelerated possession)	N5B
CCR, O.49, r.6B(1)	Miscellaneous Statutes: Housing Act 1996: Injunctions and Powers of Arrest (Application for injunction order section 152)	N16A
CCR, O.49, r.7(2)	Miscellaneous Statutes: Injunctions to Prevent Environmental Harm: Town and Country Planning Act 1990 etc. (Application for injunction)	
CCR, O.49, r.9(3)	Miscellaneous Statutes: Leasehold Reform, Housing and Urban Development Act 1993	
CCR, O.49, r.10(3)	Miscellaneous Statutes: Local Government Finance Act 1982	

Table 2

Schedule Rule		Claim Form
CCR, O.49, r.12(2)	Miscellaneous Statutes: Mental Health Act 1983 (Application)	
CCR, O.49, r.13(1)	Miscellaneous Statutes: Mobile Homes Act 1983 (Applications and questions)	
CCR, O.49, r.15(1)	Miscellaneous Statutes: Post Office Act 1969 (Application under section 30(5))	

Possession Proceedings

Under the County Court Rules possession proceedings were fixed date actions (CCR, O.3, r.2). That procedure has been abolished, with no direct replacement in the CPR.

However CPR 7.9 provides that:

> "A practice direction may set out the circumstances in which the court may give a fixed date for a hearing when it issues a claim."

The Second PD to Part 8 issued on April 1, 1999 does this.

Paragraph B.1 of the Second PD to Part 8 provides that the practice direction applies to proceedings for the recovery of possession of land. They must be begun in the court for the district in which the property is situated (PD, para. B.7). Claimants must use the form prescribed in the PD supplementing CPR Part 4 (Forms) (PD para. B8(2)). That PD retains the familiar N5 (summons for possession of property), N119 (possession proceedings including a claim for arrears of rent) and N120 (mortgage possession proceedings).

Does the landlord have to complete a statement of truth? The intention of the LCD was that there should, at this stage, be no change to the procedure for initiating possession proceedings. None of the forms prescribed for possession proceedings includes a statement of truth. Accordingly many people assumed that no statement of truth is necessary. However CPR 22.1(1) provides that a statement of case must be verified by a statement of truth. CPR 2.3(1) provides that "statement of case" means "... particulars of claim where these are not included in a claim form ...". CPR 22.1(7) and PD to CPR 22 para. 2.3 both envisage situations where the statement of truth is included in a separate document. The better view is that a statement of truth should be prepared. The consequences of failure to comply with CPR 22.1(1) are not necessarily fatal to proceedings. CPR 22.2(1) provides that proceedings remain effective but the claimant cannot rely upon the contents as proof of the facts alleged without calling evidence and the court may strike out the statement of case.

Particulars of claim must:

(1) identify the land sought to be recovered;
(2) state whether the claim relates to residential premises;
(3) state whether the rent exceeds the amount specified in Rent Act 1977 s.4(4)(b) (*i.e.* £25,000 p.a.);
(4) if the claim is for non-payment of rent for residential premises, state the amount due at the start of proceedings, details of all payments that have been missed, steps taken to recover arrears, relevant information about the defendant's circumstances and whether payments are made directly to the claimant under Social Security Contributions and Benefits Act 1992;
(5) give details of the agreement or tenancy, state whether it has been determined and the amount of money payable as rent or licence fee;
(6) state the daily rate if County Courts Act 1984, s.138 (forfeiture for non-payment of rent) applies;
(7) state the ground on which possession is claimed; and
(8) give the name and address of any person entitled to apply for relief from forfeiture.

(See PD to Part 16, para. 6. See too CCR O.6, rr.3 and 5 which are retained in CPR Sched. 2.)

There is no requirement in the Rules or the PD that a Defence must be filed or served (cf CPR Part 15.1.). But N.B. the standard wording on Form N5. Part 12 (judgment in default) cannot apply to possession proceedings.

The PD to CPR Part 8 also preserves the use of existing forms for summary possession proceedings (CCR O.24, Form N312), interim possession orders (Form N130) and accelerated possession proceedings (CCR O.49, rr.6 and 6A, Forms N5A and N5B).

The PD to Part 8 provides that the court will fix a date for the hearing (para. B.9) and, except in cases where other rules provide for a shorter period, not less than 21 days notice must be given before the hearing. Hearings of possession claims by mortgagees and where landlord's claims are based upon rent arrears should in the first instance be listed in private (CPR Part 39.2(3)(c) and

PD to Part 39 para. 1.5(1) and (2). See too Human Rights Act 1998, Sched. 1, Article 6.) The fact that a hearing is in private does not affect existing rights of audience (PD to Part 39, para. 1.12).

At the hearing the court may proceed to hear the case and dispose of the claim or give case management directions, including allocation to track (PD, paras B.13 and 14). When allocating to track the normal principles apply—see CPR 26.6 to 26.10. Note especially CPR 26.8(1)(b)—the nature of the remedy sought. The value of any counterclaim or other Part 20 claim and the complexity of any matters relating to it should be taken into account (see CPR 26.8(1)(e), and, in relation to counterclaims for breach of repairing obligations, CPR 26.6, discussed above). The norm will be for possession proceedings with a counterclaim for significant works to be carried out to be allocated to the fast track or multi track. (N.B. too the PD to CPR 26, para. 8.1(c).)

Defended mortgage possession claims are relatively rare but there is no guidance in the CPR or in any PD as to how the court should assess the financial value of such a case. Is it to be based on the level of the arrears, the amount of the outstanding balance or the value of the property? In view of CPR 26.8(2)(a) it could be argued that the amount in dispute is what matters, but the potential loss of a borrower's home which will inevitably be worth more than £15,000 is a strong pointer towards allocation to multi track. There can be little doubt that undue influence cases, where the whole of the outstanding balance is in issue will be allocated to multi track.

The hearing of a possession claim is a trial. The normal rules about evidence in CPR Part 32 apply. It is unlikely that a court will have directed exchange of witness statements before the initial hearing and so if the case is heard as a simple undefended matter, it is likely that evidence will be given orally (CPR Part 32.2(1)).

A PD on Allocation of Cases to levels of Judiciary provides that district judges have jurisdiction to hear possession actions, irrespective of track.

Costs in possession proceedings

As possession proceedings are issued under Part 8, they are treated as multi track cases (CPR 8.9(c)) unless allocated to another track. Fixed advocacy costs do not apply (CPR 46.2).

Suspended possession orders. Part 45 (fixed costs) does not include any reference to possession proceedings. However Appendix B to CCR Order 38 is retained, providing for fixed costs on the making of a suspended possession order for rent arrears where the defendant has neither delivered a defence, admission or counterclaim.

Arrears £25 to £600	Fixed costs £38.50p
Arrears £600 to £3,000	Fixed costs £57.25p
Arrears exceeding £3,000	Fixed costs £70.75p

"unless the court orders otherwise"—CCR Ord. 38 r.18(2).

Special provisions take precedence

8BPD–004 **B.2** The claimant must first comply with any special provision set out in the Schedule rules, practice direction or any Act relating to the claim.

(In Schedule 2, CCR, O.6 makes special provisions about particulars of claim and CCR, O.7 makes special provision for service, for certain types of claim.)

B.3 Special provisions contained in Schedule rules or an Act may set out—

(1) where the claim may be started;

(2) the contents of the claim form;

(3) whether a hearing is required;

(4) the nature of evidence required in support of the claim, and when it must be filed or served;

(5) the method of service of the claim form and evidence;

(6) persons on whom service must or may be effected;

(7) the form and content of Notices, and when they must or may be filed, and on whom served;

(8) the form and content of any affidavit, answer, or reply and when they must or may be filed or served;

(9) persons who may apply to be joined as parties to the claim;

(10) minimum periods of notice before the hearing date.

B.4 Where a Schedule rule makes special provision for the contents of particulars of claim, those particulars must be attached to the claim form and served with it.

B.5 Subject to any special or contrary provision in an Act or Schedule rule, the claimant must use the procedure set out in the remainder of this section.

Restrictions on where to start the claim

B.6 Where the claimant is bringing a claim in a county court that claim may only be started—

(1) in the county court for the district in which—

(a) the defendants or one of the defendants lives or carries on business; or

(b) the subject matter of the claim is situated; or

(2) if there is no defendant named in the claim form, in the county court for the district in which the claimant or one of the claimants lives or carries on business.

B.7 Where the claimant is making a claim in the county court for—

(1) the recovery of land;

(2) the foreclosure or redemption of any mortgage;

(3) enforcing any charge or lien on land;

(4) the recovery of moneys secured by a mortgage or charge on land,

the claim must be started in the court for the district in which the land, or any part of it, is situated.

Claim form

B.8 This paragraph sets out which Form is to be used as the claim form—

(1) where a claim form number is listed against a particular claim in Table 2, the claimant must use that numbered form as the claim form;

(2) where the claimant intends to make a claim in the county court which is for, or includes, the recovery of possession of land, the claimant must use the claim form numbered in the practice direction supplementing Part 4 (Forms), and

(3) in every other claim, the claimant must use the Part 8 claim form.

Court will fix a date

B.9 When the court issues the claim form it will—

(1) fix a date for the hearing; and

(2) prepare a notice of the hearing date for each party.

Service of the claim form

B.10 The claim form must be served not less than 21 days before the hearing date.

B.11 Where the claimant serves the claim form, he must serve notice of the hearing date at the same time, unless the hearing date is specified in the claim form.

(CPR, Rule 3.1(2)(a) and (b) provide for the court to extend or shorten the time for compliance with any rule or practice direction, and to adjourn or bring forward a hearing.)

Defendant is not required to respond

B.12 The defendant is not required to serve an acknowledgment of service.

At the hearing

B.13 The court may on the hearing date—

(1) proceed to hear the case and dispose of the claim; or

(2) give case management directions.

B.14 Case management directions given under paragraph B.13 will, if the defendant has filed a defence, include the allocation of a case to a track, or directions to enable the case to be allocated.

B.15 CPR rule 26.5(3) to (5) and CPR rules 26.6 to 26.10 apply to the allocation of a claim under paragraph B.14.

C.1 Section C applies if the appeal is listed in Table 3. 8BPD–005

C.2 The Schedule rules provide—

(1) that the appeal must be started by Notice of Appeal; and

(2) the procedure the appeal should follow.

(Further information on the procedure to be followed, and the form of the

Notice of Appeal for Appeals to the Court of Appeal can be found in the Practice Direction for the Court of Appeal (Civil Division).)

Table 3

Schedule Rule		**Claim Form**
RSC, O.55, r.3(1)	Appeals, etc., to High Court from Court, Tribunal or person: general (Bringing of Appeal)	
RSC, O.59, r.3(1)	Appeals to the Court of Appeal	
RSC, O.60, r.1	Appeals to the Court of Appeal from Restrictive Practices Court	
RSC, O.61, r.3(1)	Appeals from Tribunals to Court of Appeal by Case Stated. (Proceedings on case stated)	
RSC, O.91, r.2(2)	Revenue proceedings (Appeal under section 222 of the Inheritance Tax Act 1984)	
RSC, O.93, r.11(3)	Applications and Appeals to High Court under various Acts: Chancery Division (Appeal under section 17 of the Industrial Assurance Act)	
RSC, O.93, r.12(1)	Applications and Appeals to High Court under Various Acts: Chancery Division (Appeals, etc., affecting Industrial and Provident Societies, etc.)	
RSC, O.93, r.23(2)(b)	Applications and Appeals to High Court under Various Acts: Chancery Division Appeal (Proceedings under the Banking Appeal Act 1987—appeals under section 31(1).)	
RSC, O.94, r.10	Applications and Appeals to High Court under Various Acts: Queens Bench Division (Tribunals and Enquiries Act 1971: Appeal from Minister of Transport)	
RSC, O.94, r.10A(2)	Applications and Appeals to High Court under Various Acts: Queens Bench Division (Consumer Credit Act 1974: Appeal from Secretary of State)	
RSC, O.101, r.4(1)	The Pensions Appeal Tribunals Act 1943 (Appeal)	

Table 3

Schedule Rule		**Claim Form**
RSC, O.106, r.12(1)	Proceedings relating to Solicitors: The Solicitors Act 1974 (Title, service etc., of Notice of Appeal)	
RSC, O.108, r.5(2)	Proceedings relating to Charities: the Charities Act 1993 (Appeal against order, etc., of Commissioners)	
RSC, O.111, r.4(3)	Society Security Administration Act 1992 (Reference of question of law)	

PART 9

Responding to Particulars of Claim—General

9.0.1 **Contents**

Editorial Introduction

9.0.2 The two rules in this very short Part are general and do no more than foreshadow procedures found in five other Parts of the CPR. They are Pt 10 (Acknowledgment of Service), Pt 11 (Disputing the Court's Jurisdiction), Pt 12 (Default Judgment), Pt 14 (Admissions) and Pt 15 (Defence and Reply). Which one these five other Parts becomes relevant to the particular case depends on the choices made by the defendant.

There has always been a default procedure in the High Courts and county courts. Default judgment is now governed by Pt 12 and, broadly speaking, if the defendant chooses to ignore the proceedings, the claimant can obtain judgment in default as before.

Formerly, the procedures which immediately followed service of originating process (assuming the defendant did not choose to ignore the proceedings) were not the same in the High Court and county courts. Under the RSC the defendant could acknowledge service and give notice of intention to defend (RSC, O.2 and O.3) and then (after service upon him of a statement of claim) serve a defence (RSC, O.18). Under the CCR the defendant was invited to admit liability in whole or in part and, if admitting, make an offer to pay; or if denying liability in whole or in part deliver a defence accordingly. Under both sets of Rules different responsive procedures applied in particular circumstances (*e.g.* summary proceedings for recovery of land: CCR, O.24 (still in force having been re-enacted in Schedule 2 to the CPR)). Obviously a combined procedural code for both the High Court and county courts required a choice to be made between the former procedures or a newly designed procedure. Features of both former codes can be recognised. Essentially, the procedure for responding to the service of process under the CPR is based on the former RSC but incorporates some features previously found only in the CCR.

The rules contained in Pt 7 (How to start proceedings—The Claim Form) have the effect of injecting a degree of urgency into the civil process. The rules designed for the purpose of dictating how a defendant should respond to a claim form keep up the momentum. The various routes which the defendant may take, and which are briefly outlined in this Part, are foreshadowed in r.7.8 which states that when particulars of claim are served on a defendant they must be served with a form for defending the claim, a form for admitting the claim and a form for acknowledging service. (See further, Pt 7 and commentary thereon).

Related Sources

9.0.3
- Part 7 (How to Start Proceedings—the claim form)
- Part 8 (Alternative Procedure for Claims)
- Part 10 (Acknowledgment of Service)
- Part 11 (Disputing the Court's Jurisdiction)
- Part 12 (Default Judgment)
- Part 14 (Admissions)
- Part 15 (Defence and Reply)

Forms

9.0.4 None—but see generally, list of forms at section C.

Scope of this Part

9.1 **9.1**—(1) This Part sets out how a defendant may respond to particulars of claim.

(2) Where the defendant receives a claim form which states that particulars of claim are to follow, he need not respond to the claim until the particulars of claim have been served on him.

9.1.1 **"Claim form"**—The claim form is the new form of originating process (see Pt 7). Note that Pt 9 does *not* require a response to the claim form as such. The defendant must respond to the "particulars of claim" (the term previously found in the CCR and now adopted by the CPR to replace the RSC's "statement of claim"). The particulars of claim can be indorsed on the claim form, contained in a separate document served with the claim form or separately later. Rule 9.1(2) applies where the particulars of claim are served separately: the defendant need not respond to the claim form but must respond to the particulars of claim.

Defence, admission or acknowledgment of service

9.2 When particulars of claim are served on a defendant, the defendant may— 9.2

(a) file or serve an admission in accordance with Part 14;

(b) file a defence in accordance with Part 15,

(or do both, if he admits only part of the claim); or

(c) file an acknowledgment of service in accordance with Part 10.

(RSC O.15, r.12A in Schedule 1 makes special provision where the defendant in a derivative claim responds to particulars of claim.)

Effect of rule—If the defendant admits the claim he must, as r.9.2(a) provides, file *or* serve an admission in accordance with Pt 14. This procedure essentially follows the former CCR, O.9, rr.2, 3 and 4. See further, Pt 14 and commentary therein. The defendant should also make an appropriate admission where part of the claim is admitted. 9.2.1

If the defendant wishes to defend (in whole or in part) he has a choice: he can file a defence within 14 days (see r.15.4 and Pt 15 generally) or he can acknowledge service within 14 days (see r.10.3 and Pt 10 generally). If the defendant adopts the latter course and files an acknowledgment of service he must serve his defence later: the period is 28 days after service of the particulars of claim (see r.15.4(1)(b)).

Consequences of not responding—If the defendant does none of the things required by r.9.2 the claimant can proceed to obtain a default judgment (see Pt 12). 9.2.2

PART 10

Acknowledgment of Service

10.0.1 **Contents**

Editorial Introduction

10.0.2 The concept of an "acknowledgment of service" is already well known to practitioners in the High Court (RSC, O.12). However, the concept will be new to those familiar only with practice in county courts. (The exception is those practitioners in the "Business List" of the Central London County Court: CCR, O.48c. This rule came into force in June 1994 and is closely modelled on the RSC; a clear recognition that practice in the High Court was preferable in business cases.) All procedural codes have to have a machinery for requiring a defendant to respond to service of process and signal his intentions. It can be no surprise that the CPR adopt closely the model of the RSC, O.12 as modernised in 1979. There are, however, two significant changes to note. First, the defendant is not required to acknowledge the claim form as such ("claim form" has replaced "writ" as the High Court's originating process: see Pt 7). Rather, the defendant has to acknowledge the "particulars of claim" (which can be on the claim form, served separately either with the claim form or subsequently). Secondly, the defendant can choose to omit the acknowledgment of service stage altogether by instead filing an admission in accordance with Pt 14 or a defence in accordance with Pt 15 (see r.9.2).

Related Sources

10.0.3
- Part 10 is supplemented by a Practice Direction (Acknowledgment of Service): see para. 10PD–001.
- Rule 6.5 (Address for Service)
- Rule 9.2 (Defence, admission or acknowledgment of service)
- Rule 12.2 (Claims in which default judgment may be obtained)
- Part 12 (Default Judgment)
- Part 11 (Disputing the Courts Jurisdiction)
- Part 15 (Defence)
- Part 14 (Admissions)
- Part 24 (Summary Judgment) (note in particular r.24.4—claimant may not apply for summary judgment until defendant has filed acknowledgment of service or defence)
- Rule 25.2(2)(c) (defendant may not apply for interim remedy until he has filed an acknowledgment of service)

Forms

10.0.4 For form of Acknowledgment of Service see Practice Direction at para. 10PD–001 and list of forms at para. 48PD—005.

Acknowledgment of service

10.1 **10.1**—(1) This Part deals with the procedure for filing an acknowledgment of service.

(2) Where the claimant uses the procedure set out in Part 8 (alternative procedure for claims) this Part applies subject to the modifications set out in rule 8.3.

(3) A defendant may file an acknowledgment of service if—

(a) he is unable to file a defence within the period specified in rule 15.4; or

(b) he wishes to dispute the court's jurisdiction.

(Part 11 sets out the procedure for disputing the court's jurisdiction.)

"Filing"—Means delivering, by post or otherwise, to the court office. The defendant delivers the acknowledgment of service to the court office; the court office notifies the claimant (see r.10.4). 10.1.1

"a form for acknowledging service"—see r.7.8(c): the form must be served by the claimant with the particulars of claim. See also the list of forms at para. 48PD–005. 10.1.2

"alternative procedure for claims"—The "alternative procedure" (akin to the former originating summons under the RSC) is governed by Pt 8. In such cases Pt 10 applies subject to the modifications in r.8.3. 10.1.3

"defendant ... unable to file a defence within the period specified"—A defendant must respond to service of the particulars of claim in accordance with r.9.2. One of the three choices given to the defendant by r.9.2 is to "file an acknowledgment of service in accordance with Part 10". Rule 10.1(3)(a) by the use of the words "unable to file a defence within the period specified in rule 15.4" clearly implies that a defendant who is able to file a defence within the period specified should do so (in which case no acknowledgment of service is required). The period for filing a defence is 14 days after service of the particulars of claim or 28 days after service of the particulars of claim if the defendant files an acknowledgment of service within 14 days after service of the particulars of claim (see rr.15.4 and 10.3). Thus, a defendant who does acknowledge service has twice as long to do so as a defendant who chooses to file a defence without first filing an acknowledgment. The CPR contain no incentives to encourage a defendant to file a defence within the shorter period rather than the acknowledgment of service. However, a defendant who is merely playing for time and who has no defence can be immediately subjected to an application for summary judgment under Pt 24 as soon as he has filed an acknowledgment of service (see r.24.4 and Pt 24 generally). If a claimant applies for summary judgment against a defendant who has not yet filed a defence that defendant need not do so before the hearing of the application (r.24.4(2)). This is significant in that the court cannot proceed to allocate a case to a track in accordance with Pt 26 (Case Management—Preliminary Stage) so that if the claimant obtains summary judgment the case concludes without having ever become subject to the costs limitations of the small-claims track or the fast-track. (Costs would be governed by Pt 45.) 10.1.4

Summary judgment—See above note and Pt 24. 10.1.5

Default judgment—See Pt 12. Basically, a claimant has the opportunity to obtain a default judgment at two distinct stages. First, if the defendant does not file an acknowledgment of service or otherwise respond in accordance with r.9.2. Secondly, if the defendant does file an acknowledgment of service but then fails to file a defence within the specified period. 10.1.6

"dispute the court's jurisdiction"—This important topic is in Pt 11. A defendant who wishes to dispute the jurisdiction of the court does not submit to the jurisdiction and thereby lose the opportunity to do so merely by acknowledging service (*aliter* if he served a defence). Indeed, as r.10.1(3) makes clear, a defendant who does wish to dispute jurisdiction must file an acknowledgment of service. He then proceeds in accordance with Pt 11. 10.1.7

"notice of intention to defend"—This term, used in RSC, O.12 in the context of the acknowledgment of service, is not used in the CPR and is now redundant. 10.1.8

Consequence of not filing an acknowledgment of service

10.2 If— 10.2

(a) a defendant fails to file an acknowledgment of service within the period specified in rule 10.3; and

(b) does not within that period file a defence in accordance with Part 15 or serve or file an admission in accordance with Part 14,

the claimant may obtain default judgment if Part 12 allows it.

"default judgment"—See note under r.10.1 and Pt 12 generally. If the defendant does not file an acknowledgment of service within the specified period or otherwise respond as mentioned in r.10.2(b), a default judgment is the usual consequence. However, there is nothing to prevent a defendant filing a late acknowledgment of service if the claimant has not entered a default judgment in the interim. 10.2.1

The period for filing an acknowledgment of service

10.3—(1) The general rule is that the period for filing an acknowledgment of service is— 10.3

(a) where the defendant is served with a claim form which states that particulars of claim are to follow, 14 days after service of the particulars of claim; and
(b) in any other case, 14 days after service of the claim form.

(2) The general rule is subject to the following rules—
(a) RSC Order 11, r.1A (which specifies how the period for filing an acknowledgment of service is calculated where the claim form is served out of the jurisdiction); and
(b) rule 6.16(4) (which requires the court to specify the period for responding to the particulars of claim when it makes an order under that rule).

10.3.1 **"general rule"**—"Particulars of claim" (see r.7.4) is a term formerly used in the CCR and now adopted by the CPR instead of the former RSC term "statement of claim". The particulars of claim can be indorsed on the claim form (in essence the equivalent of the former specially indorsed writ), or contained in a separate document served with or subsequently to the claim form. As the general rule in r.10.3 makes clear, therefore, that the defendant is required to acknowledge service of the particulars of claim. He is not required to respond to service of the claim form if it states that the particulars of claim are to follow (see r.10.3(1)(a) and compare r.10.3(1)(b)).

10.3.2 **"RSC, O.11"**—Service of process out of the jurisdiction in High Court cases was, and still is, governed by RSC, O.11. That Order is re-enacted in Sched. 1 to the CPR. However, the former CCR, O.8 ("Service out of England and Wales") is not so re-enacted. It follows that the provisions of RSC, O.11 now apply to all cases in both the High Court and county courts.

Where a claim form is to be served in a country listed in the table at the end of the Practice Direction to Order 11 in Sched. 1, RSC, O.11, it must be accompanied by the particulars of claim.

10.3.3 **"Rule 6.16"**—This rule is entitled "Service of claim form on agent of principal who is overseas". It is, in the cases to which it applies, an alternative to serving the overseas principal. See the rule and commentary therein, especially r.6.16(4).

Notice to claimant that defendant has filed an acknowledgment of service

10.4 **10.4** On receipt of an acknowledgment of service, the court must notify the claimant in writing.

10.4.1 **Effect of rule**—Rule 10.4 is essentially a simplified version of RSC, O.12, r.4. As before, the responsibility of telling the claimant that the defendant has acknowledged service is placed on the court. The court's duty arises "on receipt of an acknowledgment of service". It is the defendant's duty to file the acknowledgment. "Filing" is defined in r.2.3 and means "delivering it, by post or otherwise, to the court office". When sent by post, the date of filing is the date on which it is received by the office (and not the date of posting or a fixed number of days after that). A defendant who sends an acknowledgment by post cannot call in aid the provisions of s.7 of the Interpretation Act 1978: the risk of loss or delay in the post lies entirely upon the defendant using this mode of acknowledging service. The duty of the court arises "on receipt".

Contents of acknowledgment of service

10.5 **10.5** An acknowledgment of service must—
(a) be signed by the defendant or his legal representative; and
(b) include the defendant's address for service.

(Rule 6.5 provides that an address for service must be within the jurisdiction.)

(RSC Order 81, in Schedule 1, makes special provision in relation to the acknowledgment of service in a claim against a firm.)

(The Contentious Probate Proceedings Practice Direction provides that a defendant who wishes to defend a contentious probate claim, must file an acknowledgment of service.)

10.5.1 **Form of acknowledgment**—See para. C9–001.

10.5.2 **"must ... be signed by the defendant or his legal representative"**—See further the

Practice Direction at para. 10PD–001. Rule 10.5(a) is clear and mandatory. The acknowledgment of service can be signed by the defendant being sued or his "legal representative" (a term defined in r.2.3—"a barrister or a solicitor, solicitor's employee or other authorised litigator (as defined in the Courts and Legal Services Act 1990)"). Thus it is *not* a compliance with r.10.5(a) if the form is signed by, *e.g.*, the defendant's accountant, estate agent, debt collector, probation officer or anyone else not within the definition.

A form of acknowledgment purporting to be signed otherwise than in accordance with r.10.5(a) is irregular and should not be accepted by the court. The court should return it and insist upon compliance with the rule.

"must . . . include the defendant's address for service"—The note in brackets immediately after r.10.5 is a reminder that an address for service must be within the jurisdiction. See generally r.6.5. Where a solicitor is acting for the defendant, the address for service will be the business address of the solicitor. **10.5.3**

Formal requirements—Rule 10.5 clearly states the only two mandatory formal requirements of an acknowledgment of service. As noted above, the court must insist on strict compliance and return a purported acknowledgment which does not comply with the rule. See further the Practice Direction at para. 10PD–001. If the court is forced to return a purported acknowledgment which is irregular, the claimant can enter a default judgment upon expiry of the specified period (see r.10.2) if no valid acknowledgment is received by the court before then. **10.5.4**

PRACTICE DIRECTION—ACKNOWLEDGMENT OF SERVICE

This Practice Direction supplements CPR Part 10 **10PD–001**

Responding to the claim

1.1 Part 9 sets out how a defendant may respond to a claim.

1.2 Part 10 sets out the provisions for acknowledging service (but see rule 8.3 for information about acknowledging service of a claim under the Part 8 procedure).

The Form of Acknowledgment of Service

2. A defendant who wishes to acknowledge service of a claim should do so by using form N9.

Address for Service

3.1 The defendant must include in his acknowledgment of service an address for the service of documents.[1]

3.2 Where the defendant is represented by a legal representative[2] and the legal representative has signed the acknowledgment of service form, the address must be the legal representative's business address; otherwise the address for service that is given should be as set out in rule 6.5 and the practice direction which supplements Part 6.

Signing the Acknowledgment of Service

4.1 An acknowledgment of service must be signed by the defendant or by his legal representative.

4.2 Where the defendant is a company or other corporation, a person holding a senior position in the company or corporation may sign the acknowledgment of service on the defendant's behalf, but must state the position he holds.

4.3 Each of the following persons is a person holding a senior position:

(1) in respect of a registered company or corporation, a director, the treasurer, secretary, chief executive, manager or other officer of the company or corporation, and

[1] See rule 6.5.
[2] See rule 2.3 for the definition of legal representative.

(2) in respect of a corporation which is not a registered company, in addition to those persons set out in (1), the mayor, chairman, president, town clerk or similar officer of the corporation.

4.4 Where the defendant is a partnership, the acknowledgment of service may be signed by:

(1) any of the partners, or

(2) a person having the control or management of the partnership business.

4.5 Children and patients may acknowledge service only by their litigation friend or his legal representative unless the court otherwise orders.[3]

General

5.1 The defendant's name should be set out in full on the acknowledgment of service.

5.2 Where the defendant's name has been incorrectly set out in the claim form, it should be correctly set out on the acknowledgment of service followed by the words "described as" and the incorrect name.

5.3 If two or more defendants to a claim acknowledge service of a claim through the same legal representative at the same time, only one acknowledgment of service need be used.

5.4 An acknowledgment of service may be amended or withdrawn only with the permission of the court.

5.5 An application for permission under paragraph 5.4 must be made in accordance with Part 23 and supported by evidence.

[3] See Part 21.

PART 11

Disputing the Court's Jurisdiction

Contents 11.0.1

Editorial Introduction

Part 11 is short and simple, containing just one rule prescribing the procedure for disputing the court's jurisdiction. Though short, it is eminently sensible to have this important topic in this readily identifiable rule rather than tucked away in a rule primarily dealing with a different matter altogether, as was formerly the case. 11.0.2

Part 11 is derived from RSC, O.12, r.8.

Practice Direction

This Part is not supplemented by a Practice Direction. 11.0.3

Procedure for disputing the court's jurisdiction

11—(1) A defendant who wishes to— 11.1

(a) dispute the court's jurisdiction to try the claim; or

(b) argue that the court should not exercise its jurisdiction,

may apply to the court for an order declaring that it has no such jurisdiction or should not exercise any jurisdiction which it may have.

(2) A defendant who wishes to make such an application must first file an acknowledgment of service in accordance with Part 10.

(3) A defendant who files an acknowledgment of service does not, by doing so, lose any right that he may have to dispute the court's jurisdiction.

(4) An application under this rule must—

(a) be made within the period for filing a defence; and

(b) be supported by evidence.

(Rule 15.4 sets out the period for filing a defence.)

(5) If the defendant—

(a) files an acknowledgment of service; and

(b) does not make such an application within the period for filing a defence,

he is to be treated as having accepted that the court has jurisdiction to try the claim.

(6) An order containing a declaration that the court has no jurisdiction or will not exercise its jurisdiction may also make further provision including—

(a) setting aside the claim form;

(b) setting aside service of the claim form;

(c) discharging any order made before the claim was commenced or before the claim form was served; and

(d) staying[GL] the proceedings.

(7) If on an application under this rule the court does not make a declaration—

(a) the acknowledgment of service shall cease to have effect; and

(b) the defendant may file a further acknowledgment of service within 14 days or such other period as the court may direct.

(8) If the defendant files a further acknowledgment of service in accordance with paragraph (7)(b) he shall be treated as having accepted that the court has jurisdiction to try the claim.

(9) Where a defendant makes an application under this rule he need not file a defence before the hearing of the application.

(10) Where the claimant uses the procedure set out in Part 8 (alternative procedure for claims) this Part applies subject to the modifications set out in rule 8.3.

11.1.1 **Effect of Part 11**—Although most obviously of relevance to service out of the jurisdiction and applications to stay proceedings with an extraterritorial element, the procedure is available in all cases where the court's jurisdiction is challenged or its exercise opposed. The High Court has a universal and unrestricted jurisdiction to decide the existence and limits of its own jurisdiction (*Canada Trust Co. v. Stolzenberg* [1997] 1 W.L.R. 1582, CA; [1997] 4 All E.R. 983, CA).

A defendant does not submit to the jurisdiction of the court by reason only of having acknowledged service of the proceedings for the purpose of disputing the court's jurisdiction to try the claim or by arguing that the court should not exercise its jurisdiction (*e.g.* on the grounds that the dispute should be submitted to arbitration). Nevertheless the rule is strict: the application must be promptly made and be supported by evidence (r.11(4)). If the application is successful the court will grant a declaration (see r.11(6)); if the application is not successful the acknowledgment of service ceases to have effect but the defendant may file a further acknowledgment which does then amount to a submission to the jurisdiction (see r.11(7) and (8)). Not every issue of jurisdiction has to be disposed of at this stage and the court may postpone a question of jurisdiction to a later stage where it is convenient to do so; as for instance, where the justiciability of an issue may be disputed (*Kuwait Airways Corpn v. Iraqi Airways Co.* [1995] 1 W.L.R. 1147; [1995] 3 All E.R. 694, HL). Although not expressly stated in Part 11, the relief granted by the court may relate to only part of the case (*Kuwait Airways Corpn.* above).

Applications are governed by Part 23 and will normally be decided on the written evidence of the parties, although the court does have power to allow cross-examination of a signatory of written evidence and to order disclosure. Where the challenge is against service out of the jurisdiction the general burden of proof is upon the claimant to establish the necessary elements of his case (*Canada Trust Co. v. Stolzenberg (No. 2)* [1998] 1 W.L.R. 547, CA). The relevant elements are set out in the notes to Sched. 1, O.11. Where a defendant seeks the stay of proceedings brought as of right within the jurisdiction, the general burden of proof is upon him to make his case, except to the extent that a claimant alleges that there is a special aspect of his case that takes it outside the general principles (*Spiliada Maritime Corporation v. Cansulex Ltd* [1987] A.C. 460; [1986] 3 All E.R. 843). Where a claimant has served a defendant pursuant to permission obtained without notice, the claimant will be under the normal obligation to fully inform the court of all relevant circumstances and will be liable to have his permission set aside where there has been a breach of that duty if the situation warrants it.

When permission to serve out of the jurisdiction has been properly given, it cannot be discharged simply because circumstances have changed, unless further evidence throws a new light on what should have been a relevant consideration at the time that permission was granted (*I.S.C. Technologies v. Guerin* [1992] 2 Lloyd's Rep. 430).

PART 12

DEFAULT JUDGMENT

Contents 12.0.1

Editorial Introduction

The former position in the High Court, was that judgment in default of acknowledgment of service was covered by RSC, O.13 and judgment in default of defence by RSC, O.19. Under the CCR there was no acknowledgment of service so judgment in default thereof could not exist. Judgment in default of defence was covered by CCR, O.9. Part 12 has gathered together in one place the essence of these three Orders without any fundamental changes or surprises. Subject to having introduced the "acknowledgment of service", the CPR follow the CCR model of default judgment. 12.0.2

A default judgment is obtained by procuring an administrative act rather than by judicial decision. A defendant who fails to file an acknowledgment of service, or having filed an acknowledgment of service then fails to file a defence, is liable to have a default judgment entered against him save in those specific cases where it is prohibited.

Forms

The forms mentioned in the relevant Practice Direction, namely forms N203A, N255 (see para. C69–001), N225B and N227 (see para. C59–001). 12.0.3

Related Sources

- Practice Direction (Default Judgment), para. 12PD–001. 12.0.4
- Part 13 (Setting Aside or Varying Default Judgment)
- Part 24 (Summary Judgment)
- Practice Direction supplementing Part 26 (Disposal hearings) 26PD–001

Meaning of "default judgment"

12.1 In these Rules, "default judgment" means judgment without trial where a defendant— 12.1

(a) has failed to file an acknowledgment of service; or

(b) has failed to file a defence.

(Part 10 contains provisions about filing an acknowledgment of service and Part 15 contains provisions about filing a defence)

Scope of provision—Rule 12.1 lays down the only two situations where a default judgment can be obtained. The period for filing an acknowledgment of service is prescribed by r.10.3 (14 12.1.1

days after service of the claim form or service of the particulars of claim if later). The period for filing a defence is prescribed by r.15.4 (14 days after service of the particulars of claim or 28 days if the defendant has first filed an acknowledgment of service under Pt 10). If the defendant fails to do either of these things the claimant may, subject to the rules in Pt 12, enter a default judgment.

Claims in which default judgment may not be obtained

12.2 **12.2** A claimant may not obtain a default judgment—

(a) on a claim for delivery of goods subject to an agreement regulated by the Consumer Credit Act 1974[1];

(b) where he uses the procedure set out in Part 8 (alternative procedure for claims); or

(c) in any other case where a practice direction provides that the claimant may not obtain default judgment.

12.2.1 **Scope of provision**—There is a risk of being misled by the brevity of r.12.2. See also r.12.3 (conditions to be satisfied), and r.12.10 which deals with cases where default judgment can be obtained only on application.

This rule prohibits obtaining default judgment on a claim for delivery of goods subject to an agreement regulated by the Consumer Credit Act (such a claim would in any event be a "fixed date claim"—see r.7.9); in cases where the claim was begun not by a claim form pursuant to Pt 7 but by the alternative procedure for claims governed by Pt 8 (a procedure derived from the former "originating summons"); and in any other case pursuant to a practice direction. The Practice Direction's provisions are set out below and extend to mortgage claims and those subject to Pt 49. (See para. 1.2 of the Practice Direction (see para. 12PD–001) and the examples given in para. 1.3.)

Conditions to be satisfied

12.3 **12.3**—(1) The claimant may obtain judgment in default of an acknowledgment of service only if—

(a) the defendant has not filed an acknowledgment of service or a defence to the claim (or any part of the claim); and

(b) the relevant time for doing so has expired;

(2) The claimant may obtain judgment in default of defence only if—

(a) the defendant has filed an acknowledgment of service but has not filed a defence; and

(b) the relevant time for doing so has expired.

(Rules 10.3 and 15.4 deal respectively with the period for filing an acknowledgment of service and the period for filing a defence.)

(3) The claimant may not obtain a default judgment if—

(a) the defendant has applied for summary judgment under Part 24, and that application has not been disposed of;

(b) the defendant has satisfied the whole claim (including any claim for costs) on which the claimant is seeking judgment; or

(c) (i) the claimant is seeking judgment on a claim for money; and

(ii) the defendant has filed or served on the claimant an admission under rule 14.4 or 14.7 (admission of liability to pay all of the money claimed) together with a request for time to pay.

(Part 14 sets out the procedure where a defendant admits a money claim and asks for time to pay.)

(Rule 6.14 provides that, where the claim form is served by the claimant, he may not obtain default judgment unless he has filed a certificate of service.)

12.3.1 **"judgment in default of an acknowledgment of service"**—Judgment obtained in default under the former RSC, O.13 was technically a "judgment in default of notice of intention to defend" although it was invariably referred to by practitioners as "judgment in default of acknowledgment of service". The former colloquialism is now the correct title of a default judgment pursuant to r.12.3(1). Acknowledgment of service is governed by Pt 10. The time for acknowledging service is prescribed by r.10.3 (14 days from service of the claim form or from

[1] 1974 c. 39.

service of the particulars of claim if later). Subject to the provisions of Pt 12 (see in particular r.12.4, r.12.8, r.12.10 and r.12.11), if the defendant fails to file an acknowledgment of service the claimant can enter default judgment.

The acknowledgment of service did not exist in county courts under the CCR so those rules never made provision for judgment in default of it. Under the CPR the procedure is, of course, now the same in the county courts as in the High Court.

"judgment in default of defence"—Judgment in default of defence used to be obtainable in the High Court under RSC, O.19 and in county courts under CCR, O.9, and is now obtainable in both under r.12.3(2). The defendant must have filed an acknowledgment for service but then failed to file a defence within the time limit prescribed by r.15.4 (28 days from service of the particulars of claim). **12.3.2**

"summary judgment"—Summary judgment was a well-known concept under the RSC where it was also often referred to as "Order 14 judgment". It did not exist in the county courts until introduced as CCR, O.9, r.14 in 1981. It is now governed by Pt 24. For the purposes of r.12.3 it is necessary to note one fundamental distinction between Pt 24 and the former rules, namely that it is now possible for a defendant as well as a claimant to apply for summary judgment. (Formerly, a defendant could only seek summary judgment on a counterclaim.) Hence r.12.3(3)(a), which prevents a claimant obtaining a default judgment where the defendant has applied for summary judgment. Summary judgment is obtained by judicial decision only upon application; if the defendant makes such an application it effectively stays the claim pending disposal thereof. See further Part 24 and commentary thereon. **12.3.3**

"satisfied the whole claim (including any claim for costs)"—Rule 12.3(3)(b) is self-explanatory. If the defendant has paid the claim and costs there is now nothing to enter judgment for. For the position where the defendant has paid the claim but not the costs, see r.12.9—procedure for obtaining default judgment for costs only. **12.3.4**

"admission ... together with a request from time to pay"—Admitting a claim and requesting time to pay it has always been a feature of the county courts (CCR, O.9, r.3). It had no direct equivalent in the High Court. The former county court practice is now of general application under the CPR. When served with the claim form the defendant will also be served with "a form for admitting the claim" in accordance with r.7.8(1). The defendant uses that form to make an admission in accordance with Pt 14 (see rr.14.4 and 14.7). Where such an admission is filed the claimant cannot obtain a default judgment. He can instead obtain judgment on the admission: see rr.14.10, 14.11 and 14.12. For a list of the relevant forms see para. 48PD–017. **12.3.5**

"certificate of service"—The normal method of proof of service is by a certificate of service. Usually the claim form is served by the court but where it has been served by the claimant he must file a certificate of service. By r.6.14 the claimant cannot obtain a default judgment unless he has done so. **12.3.6**

Procedure for obtaining default judgment

12.4—(1) Subject to paragraph (2), a claimant may obtain a default judgment by filing a request in the relevant practice form where the claim is for— **12.4**

(a) a specified amount of money;
(b) an amount of money to be decided by the court;
(c) delivery of goods where the claim form gives the defendant the alternative of paying their value; or
(d) any combination of these remedies.

(2) The claimant must make an application in accordance with Part 23 if he wishes to obtain a default judgment—

(a) on a claim which consists of or includes a claim for any other remedy; or
(b) where rule 12.9 or rule 12.10 so provides.

(3) Where a claimant—

(a) claims any other remedy in his claim form in addition to those specified in paragraph (1); but
(b) abandons that claim in his request for judgment,

he may still obtain a default judgment by filing a request under paragraph (1).

"request in the relevant practice form"—See Forms N205A (see para. C38–001), N255 (see **12.4.1**

para. C69–001) and N227 (see C59–001). There is a different prescribed form for each of the cases described in r.12.4(1).

12.4.2 **Scope of r.12.4(1)**—In the types of case described—and most claims issued do fit one of these descriptions—the claimant obtains a default judgment simply by filing a request in the relevant practice form. "Request" has been the name of a type of form used in county courts for many years, the former name "praecipe" having been abandoned, but the term is new in the High Court.

12.4.3 **"a specified amount of money"**—The former term "liquidated sum" is replaced by "specified amount of money". Default judgment can be entered for the specified sum, plus interest pursuant to r.12.6, plus fixed costs pursuant to r.45.4. However, it is important to note that "a specified sum of money" is wider than the old term "liquidated sum". Clearly it covers a case where the claim is for a debt. However, it appears that "a specified amount of money" covers any case where the claimant puts a figure on the amount of his claim whether it is debt, damages or any other sum. If the claimant chooses to put a value on his claim in a specified sum, the claimant can request a default judgment in that sum (plus interest if claimed: see r.12.6) and fixed costs (see r.45.4). The term "specified amount of money" is used not only in r.12.4 but throughout the CPR, see, *e.g.* r.26.2 on automatic transfer. Claiming a specified amount of money will cause the rules for automatic transfer to the defendant's home court to apply if the claim is defended. This change in practice accords with the system in Commonwealth countries where the law is based on Roman-Dutch principles.

12.4.4 **"an amount of money to be decided by the court"**—In a claim which is not for "a specified amount of money" (see above) the amount has to be decided by the court. This was formerly known as "interlocutory judgment for damages to be assessed" and was obtainable under RSC, O.13, r.2 and CCR, O.9, r.6(2). Default judgment is obtained by filing a request in Form N225B or N227. The judgment is final on the issue of liability but the sum to be paid still has to be decided by the court. Directions for assessing the damages will be given when judgment is entered, see r.12.7(2)(a) and if necessary the case will be allocated to the appropriate track. (See Pt 26)

12.4.5 **"delivery of goods where the claim form gives the defendant the alternative of paying their value"**—Default judgment in such a case is obtained by a request in Form N255; if the claim form does not give the alternative mentioned an application is required in accordance with r.12.4(2). Note that in neither case can default judgment be obtained if the goods are subject to an agreement regulated by the Consumer Credit Act 1974 (r.12.2(a)).

12.4.6 **Scope of r.12.4(2)**—Rule 12.4 distinguishes between those cases where a default judgment is obtained by filing a request and those where an application is required. If the case does not fall within r.12.4(1) then an application in accordance with Pt 23 is required in order to obtain a default judgment under r.12.4(2). Also an application is required if r.12.9(1)(b) (default judgment for costs only where costs are not fixed) or r.12.10 applies.

12.4.7 **Scope of r.12.4(3)**—Only claims within r.12.4(1) are susceptible to default judgment by request. If an additional remedy is claimed, the claimant can obtain default judgment if that remedy is abandoned in the request for default judgment. It has long been the practice to allow this.

Nature of judgment where default judgment obtained by filing a request

12.5 **12.5**—(1) Where the claim is for a specified sum of money, the claimant may specify in a request filed under rule 12.4(1)—

(a) the date by which the whole of the judgment debt is to be paid; or
(b) the times and rate at which it is to be paid by instalments.

(2) Except where paragraph (4) applies, a default judgment on a claim for a specified amount of money obtained on the filing of a request, will be judgment for the amount of the claim (less any payments made) and costs—

(a) to be paid by the date or at the rate specified in the request for judgment; or
(b) if none is specified, immediately.

(Interest may be included in a default judgment obtained by filing a request if the conditions set out in Rule 12.6 are satisfied.)

(Rule 45.4 provides for fixed costs on the entry of a default judgment.)

(3) Where the claim is for an unspecified amount of money a default

judgment obtained on the filing of a request will be for an amount to be decided by the court and costs.

(4) Where the claim is for delivery of goods and the claim form gives the defendant the alternative of paying their value, a default judgment obtained on the filing of a request will be judgment requiring the defendant to—

(a) deliver the goods or (if he does not do so) pay the value of the goods as decided by the court (less any payments made); and

(b) pay costs.

(Rule 12.7 sets out the procedure for deciding the amount of a judgment or the value of the goods.)

(5) The claimant's right to enter judgment requiring the defendant to deliver goods is subject to rule 40.14 (judgment in favour of certain part owners relating to the detention of goods).

Scope of provision—Rule 12.5 deals with the nature of the default judgment and is self-explanatory. The rule is modelled on county court practice. When entering a default judgment the claimant can enter judgment for payment "immediately" (replacing the former term "forthwith"), on a specified date or by instalments, the amount and frequency of which will be decided by the claimant. **12.5.1**

A judgment pursuant to r.12.5(3) was formerly known as "interlocutory judgment for damages to be assessed".

Interest

12.6—(1) A default judgment on a claim for a specified amount of money obtained on the filing of a request may include the amount of interest claimed to the date of judgment if— **12.6**

(a) the particulars of claim include the details required by rule 16.4;

(b) where interest is claimed under section 35A of the Supreme Court Act 1981[2] or section 69 of the County Courts Act 1984,[3] the rate is no higher than the rate of interest payable on judgment debts at the date when the claim form was issued; and

(c) the claimant's request for judgment includes a calculation of the interest claimed for the period from the date up to which interest was stated to be calculated in the claim form to the date of the request for judgment.

(2) In any case where paragraph (1) does not apply, judgment will be for an amount of interest to be decided by the court.

(Rule 12.7 sets out the procedure for deciding the amount of interest.)

Effect of rule—Rule 12.6 is derived from CCR, O.9, r.8 but effects no change in practice for claiming interest. The rule is self-explanatory. **12.6.1**

Rate of interest payment on judgment debts—The rate is 8% and has been since April 1993 (Judgment Debts (Rate of Interest) Order 1993 (S.I. 1993 No. 564)). For the table showing rates prior to April 1, 1993 see SCP, Vol. 1, 1999, para. 42/1/17. **12.6.2**

Procedure for deciding an amount or value

12.7—(1) This rule applies where the claimant obtains a default judgment on the filing of a request under rule 12.4(1) and judgment is for— **12.7**

(a) an amount of money to be decided by the court;

(b) the value of goods to be decided by the court; or

(c) an amount of interest to be decided by the court.

(2) Where the court enters judgment it will—

[2] 1981 c. 54. Section 35A was inserted by the Administration of Justice Act 1992 (c. 53), section 15(1), Schedule 1, Part I.

[3] 1985 c. 28. Section 69 was amended by the Courts and Legal Services Act 1990 (c. 41), Schedule 18, paragraph 46.

(a) give any directions it considers appropriate; and
(b) if it considers it appropriate, allocate the case.

12.7.1 **Scope of provision**—Judgments entered pursuant to r.12.4(1) may be final both as to liability and the amount of the judgment (judgment for "a specified amount of money": see r.12.4(1)(a)) or final only as to liability leaving a further issue to be decided by the court. The latter is governed by r.12.7. The rule is helpfully straightforward. Judgment will be obtained by filing a request in Form N227 (see para. C59–001).

12.7.2 **Interlocutory Judgment**—The expression "interlocutory judgment, previously used in both the RSC and the CCR, is no longer in use: see now "judgment for an amount to be decided by the court" obtained pursuant to r.12.7.

12.7.3 **Judgment for an amount to be decided by the court**—This expression, in r.12.7, has replaced the former term "interlocutory judgment".

12.7.4 **Assessment of Damages**—There is no equivalent of the former rule, RSC, O.37, Part I. See now "disposal hearings".

12.7.5 **Disposal hearings**—This term is used in the Practice Direction which supplements Part 26 (26PD–006): see paras 12.1 to 12.10, especially para. 12.8.

The term "disposal" was not previously in use in the High Court and was in use in the county court only to describe a hearing to decide mode of payment of a judgment debt.

Paragraph 12.7 of the Practice Direction which supplements Part 26 provides "on the entry of the judgment the court will list a disposal hearing" referring to a judgment in default for an amount of money to be decided by the court. Para. 12.8(1) provides that "at a disposal hearing the court will give directions or decide the amount payable in accordance with this sub-paragraph". This paragraph needs to be read in conjunction with r.12.7(2), and both the paragraph and the rule need to be borne in mind when filing the request for judgment to be entered for an amount to be decided. Although not a requirement of either the rule or the practice direction, it is helpful to give the court all appropriate information so that directions can be given without a hearing and the case can then proceed straight to a disposal hearing where damages can be assessed. If such information is not provided the court is unlikely to be able to give meaningful directions and may have to convene a disposal hearing to do so. The default judgment is final on the issue of liability but the "default" process plays no part in deciding the amount to be paid. This aspect of the case has to be proved.

12.7.6 **Allocation**—It is not always necessary to allocate to a track and the case can proceed to a disposal hearing without allocation. Allocation to the small claims track brings into operation the limited costs regime for such cases (rr.27.4 and 44.9(2)). The court will allocate the case "if it considers it appropriate" (r.12.7(2)(b)). Allocation is governed by Part 26 and its supplementary Practice Direction.

Claim against more than one defendant

12.8 **12.8**—(1) A claimant may obtain a default judgment on request under this Part on a claim for money or a claim for delivery of goods against one of two or more defendants, and proceed with his claim against the other defendants.

(2) Where a claimant applies for a default judgment against one of two or more defendants—

(a) if the claim can be dealt with separately from the claim against the other defendants—
   (i) the court may enter a default judgment against that defendant; and
   (ii) the claimant may continue the proceedings against the other defendants;
(b) if the claim cannot be dealt with separately from the claim against the other defendants—
   (i) the court will not enter default judgment against that defendant; and
   (ii) the court must deal with the application at the same time as it disposes of the claim against the other defendants.

(3) A claimant may not enforce against one of two or more defendants any judgment obtained under this Part for possession of land or for delivery of goods unless—

(a) he has obtained a judgment for possession or delivery (whether or not obtained under this Part) against all the defendants to the claim; or

(b) the court gives permission.

Effect of rule—Rule 12.8 helpfully gathers in one rule (unlike the RSC and CCR) the practice on default judgment where the claim is against more than one defendant. The rule reflects established practice since the Civil Liability (Contribution) Act 1978 and is self-explanatory. For the background law see the 1978 Act and SCP 1999, Vol. 1, para. 13/0/16. **12.8.1**

Procedure for obtaining a default judgment for costs only

12.9—(1) Where a claimant wishes to obtain a default judgment for costs only— **12.9**

(a) if the claim is for fixed costs, he may obtain it by filing a request in the relevant practice form;

(b) if the claim is for any other type of costs, he must make an application in accordance with Part 23.

(2) Where an application is made under this rule for costs only, judgment shall be for an amount to be decided by the court.

(Part 45 sets out when a claimant is entitled to fixed costs.)

Effect of rule—The lack of a clear specified procedure for obtaining a default judgment for costs only in either the RSC or CCR has been a source of confusion and irritation for years. This gap in the old rules is sensibly filled by r.12.9. It is common for a defendant who does not dispute liability for, say, a debt to pay the debt on being served with the claim form (or, formerly, a writ or summons) but to refuse to pay costs typically because he was "going to pay anyway" or because he alleges that proceedings were issued prematurely. A claimant who is content with payment of the debt and is prepared to write-off costs incurred need do no more. A claimant who wishes to obtain a default judgment for costs only can do so pursuant to r.12.9. The judgment, if granted, will be "for an amount to be decided by the court". The use of this phrase invokes the procedure for deciding an amount in r.12.7. **12.9.1**

Default judgment obtained by making an application

12.10 The claimant must make an application in accordance with Part 23 where— **12.10**

(a) the claim is—

(i) a claim against a child or patient;

(ii) a claim in tort by one spouse against the other; or

(iii) a claim against the Crown.

(b) he wishes to obtain a default judgment where the defendant has failed to file an acknowledgment of service—

(i) against a defendant who has been served with the claim out of the jurisdiction under RSC Order 11, r.1 (2) (a) (service without leave under the Civil Jurisdiction and Judgments Act 1982[4]);

(ii) against a defendant domiciled in Scotland or Northern Ireland or in any other Convention territory;

(iii) against a State;

(iv) against a diplomatic agent who enjoys immunity from civil jurisdiction by virtue of the Diplomatic Privileges Act 1964[5]; or

(v) against persons or organisations who enjoy immunity from civil jurisdiction pursuant to the provisions of the International Organisations Acts 1968 and 1981.[6]

Effect of rule—"Child" is defined in r.21.1 (2) and is the expression which has replaced the old terms "infant" or "minor". "Patient" is defined in r.21.1 (2) but the meaning is the same as in the RSC. (The former term "persons under disability" referring to both has been abandoned.) **12.10.1**

[4] 1982 c. 27.
[5] 1964 c. 81.
[6] 1968 c. 48; 1981 c. 9.

It has never been possible to obtain a default judgment by administrative act against either a child or a patient and the established practice has been carried forward into the CPR. See also Pt 21—Children and Patients. The court will have to consider whether a defendant who is a child or patient needs a "litigation friend" (formerly a guardian *ad litem* in this context). The court will not grant a default judgment even on an application in accordance with Pt 23 until this has been done.

Apart from children and patients, all other situations in r.12.10 are governed by specific statutory provisions. A claim in tort by one spouse against another was governed by the Law Reform (Husband and Wife) Act 1962 (see SCP 1999, Vol. 1, para. 89/2/2) which obliged a court to consider the stay of proceedings between husband and wife in an action in tort. However paragraph 4 of the Civil Procedure (Modification of Enactments) Order 1998 (S.I. 1988 No. 2940) has abrogated this rule so the purpose of r.12.10(a)(ii) is not clear unless it be to protect a spouse from a malicious action. A claim against the Crown is governed by the Crown Proceedings Act 1947 (see also RSC, O.77, which is re-enacted in Schedule 1 to the CPR). The several situations in r.12.10(b) are governed by the statutes mentioned in the rule: hence the need for an application under Pt 23 before the claimant can obtain judgment.

Rule 12.10 needs to be read in conjunction with r.12.11.

Supplementary provisions where applications for default judgment are made

12.11 **12.11**—(1) Where the claimant makes an application for a default judgment, judgment shall be such judgment as it appears to the court that the claimant is entitled to on his statement of case.

(2) Any evidence relied on by the claimant in support of his application need not be served on a party who has failed to file an acknowledgment of service.

(3) An application for a default judgment on a claim against a child or patient or a claim in tort between spouses must be supported by evidence.

(4) An application for a default judgment may be made without notice if—

(a) the claim was served in accordance with the Civil Jurisdiction and Judgments Act 1982;

(b) the defendant has failed to file an acknowledgment of service; and

(c) notice does not need to be given under any other provision of these Rules.

(5) Where an application is made against a State for a default judgment where the defendant has failed to file an acknowledgment of service—

(a) the application may be made without notice, but the court hearing the application may direct that a copy of the application notice be served on the State;

(b) if the court—

(i) grants the application; or

(ii) directs that a copy of the application notice be served on the State,

the judgment or application notice (and the evidence in support) may be served out of the jurisdiction without any further order;

(c) where paragraph (5)(b) permits a judgment or an application notice to be served out of the jurisdiction, the procedure for serving the judgment or the application notice is the same as for serving a claim form under RSC Order 11 except where an alternative method of service has been agreed under section 12(6) of the State Immunity Act 1978.[7]

(6) For the purposes of this rule and rule 12.10—

(a) "domicile" is to be determined in accordance with the provisions of sections 41 to 46 of the Civil Jurisdiction and Judgments Act 1982;

(b) "Convention territory" means the territory or territories of any Contracting State, as defined by section 1(3) of the Civil Jurisdiction and Judgments Act 1982, to which the Brussels Conventions or Lugano Convention apply;

[7] 1978 c. 33.

(c) "State" has the meaning given by section 14 of the State Immunity Act 1978; and
(d) "Diplomatic agent" has the meaning given by Article 1(e) of Schedule 1 to the Diplomatic Privileges Act 1964.

Scope of provision—Rules 12.11(1) and 12.11(2) are of general application and are self-explanatory. 12.11.1

Rule 12.11(3) supplements r.12.10(a): see commentary thereon. Rules 12.11(4), 12.11(5) and 12.11(6) supplement r.12.10(b).

PRACTICE DIRECTION—DEFAULT JUDGMENT

This Practice Direction supplements CPR Part 12

Default Judgment

1.1 A default judgment is judgment without a trial where a defendant has failed to file either; 12PD–001

(1) an acknowledgment of service, or
(2) a defence.

For this purpose a defence includes any document purporting to be a defence.

(See Part 10 and the practice direction which supplements it for information about the acknowledgment of service, and Parts 15 and 16 and the practice directions which supplement them for information about the defence and what it should contain.)

1.2 A claimant may not obtain a default judgment under Part 12 (notwithstanding that no acknowledgment of service or defence has been filed) if:

(1) the procedure set out in Part 8 (Alternative Procedure for Claims) is being used, or
(2) the claim is for delivery of goods subject to an agreement regulated by the Consumer Credit Act 1974, or
(3) the claim is one to which RSC Order 88 (Schedule 1 to the CPR) (mortgage claims) applies or if proceeding in a county court, is a claim for money secured by mortgage, unless, in either case, the claimant obtains the permission of the court; or
(4) the claim is made in proceedings in respect of which, under CPR Part 49 and practice directions supplemental to that Part, either there is no requirement for an acknowledgment of service or a defence to be filed or special provision is made about the obtaining of a default judgment.

1.3 Examples of proceedings where default judgment under Part 12 cannot be obtained are:

(1) admiralty proceedings;
(2) arbitration proceedings;
(3) contentious probate proceedings;
(4) claims for provisional damages.

Obtaining default judgment

2.1 Rules 12.4(1) and 12.9(1) describe the claims in respect of which a default judgment may be obtained by filing a request in the appropriate practice form.

2.2 A default judgment on;

(1) the claims referred to in rules 12.9(1)(b) and 12.10, and
(2) claims other than those described in rule 12.4(1),

can only be obtained if an application for default judgment is made and cannot be obtained by filing a request.

2.3 The following are some of the types of claim which require an application for a default judgment:

(1) against children and patients,[8]

(2) for costs (other than fixed costs) only,[9]

(3) by one spouse against the other[10] on a claim in tort,[11]

(4) for delivery up of goods where the defendant will not be allowed the alternative of paying their value,

(5) against the Crown, and

(6) against persons or organisations who enjoy immunity from civil jurisdiction under the provisions of the International Organisations Acts 1968 and 1981.

Default judgment by request

3. Requests for default judgment;

(1) in respect of a claim for a specified amount of money or for the delivery of goods where the defendant will be given the alternative of paying a specified sum representing their value, or for fixed costs only, must be in Form N205A or N225, and

(2) in respect of a claim where an amount of money (including an amount representing the value of goods) is to be decided by the court, must be in Form N205B or N227.

Evidence

12PD–002 **4.1** Both on a request and on an application for default judgment the court must be satisfied that;

(1) the particulars of claim have been served on the defendant (a certificate of service on the court file will be sufficient evidence),

(2) either the defendant has not filed an acknowledgment of service or has not filed a defence and that in either case the relevant period for doing so has expired,

(3) the defendant has not satisfied the claim, and

(4) the defendant has not returned an admission to the claimant under rule 14.4 or filed an admission with the court under rule 14.6.

4.2 On an application against a child or patient[12];

(1) a litigation friend[13] to act on behalf of the child or patient must be appointed by the court before judgment can be obtained, and

(2) the claimant must satisfy the court by evidence that he is entitled to the judgment claimed.

4.3 On an application where the defendant was served with the claim either:

(1) outside the jurisdiction[14] without leave under the Civil Jurisdiction and Judgments Act 1982, or

(2) within the jurisdiction but when domiciled[15] in Scotland or Northern Ireland or in any other Convention territory,[16]

and the defendant has not acknowledged service, the evidence must establish that;

[8] See rule 12.10(a)(i).

[9] See rule 12.9(b).

[10] See rule 12.10(a)(ii).

[11] Tort may be defined as an act or a failure to do an act which causes harm or damage to another person and which gives the other person a right to claim compensation without having to rely on a contract with the person who caused the harm or damage.

[12] As defined in rule 21.1(2).

[13] As defined in the practice direction which supplements Part 21.

[14] As defined in rule 2.3.

[15] As determined in accordance with the provisions of ss.41 to 46 of the Civil Jurisdictions and Judgments Act 1982.

[16] Means the territory of a Contracting State as defined in s.1(3) of the Civil Jurisdiction and Judgments Act 1982.

(1) the claim is one that the court has power to hear and decide,
(2) no other court has exclusive jurisdiction under the Act to hear and decide the claim, and
(3) the claim has been properly served in accordance with Article 20 of Schedule 1, 3C or 4 of the Act.

4.4 On an application against a State[17] the evidence must:
(1) set out the grounds of the application,
(2) establish the facts proving that the State is excepted from the immunity conferred by section 1 of the State Immunity Act 1978,
(3) establish that the claim was sent through the Foreign and Commonwealth Office to the Ministry of Foreign Affairs of the State (unless the State agreed to a different form of service), and
(4) establish that the time for acknowledging service, which is extended to two months by section 12(2) of the Act, has expired.

(See rule 40.8 for when default judgment against a State takes effect.)

4.5 Evidence in support of an application referred to in paragraphs 4.3 and 4.4 above must be by affidavit.

4.6 On an application for judgment for delivery up of goods where the defendant will not be given the alternative of paying their value, the evidence must identify the goods and state where the claimant believes the goods to be situated and why their specific delivery up is sought.

General

5.1 On all applications to which this practice direction applies, other than those referred to in paragraphs 4.3 and 4.4 above, [18]notice should be given in accordance with Part 23.

5.2 Where default judgment is given on a claim for a sum of money expressed in a foreign currency, the judgment should be for the amount of the foreign currency with the addition of "or the Sterling equivalent at the time of payment".

[17] As defined in s.14 of the State Immunity Act 1978.
[18] See rule 12.11(4) and (5).

PART 13

SETTING ASIDE OR VARYING DEFAULT JUDGMENT

13.0.1 **Contents**

Editorial Introduction

13.0.2 A default judgment is invariably obtained by an administrative act (see Pt 12). This puts default judgments in a different category from summary judgment (see Pt 24) or a judgment following a trial. These latter judgments cannot be "set aside"; the unsuccessful party has a right of appeal. In contrast a default judgment will not usually have been subject to judicial scrutiny and there is no right of appeal. Hence the need for a procedure to apply to set aside or vary a default judgment.

Part 13 is limited in scope to the setting aside (or varying) of a default judgment. Unlike CCR, O.37 it is not a comprehensive code for setting aside generally. Setting aside a default judgment was formerly covered by CCR, O.37, r.4 and RSC, O.13, r.9 and O.19, r.9. Part 13 has not effected any changes in practice under the old rules.

Related Sources

13.0.3
- Rule 39.3(3) (Setting aside on application of party who failed to attend)
- Rule 40.9 (Application to set aside by a person who is not a party but who is directly affected by judgment)
- Part 12 (Default Judgment)
- Part 23 (General Rules for Applications)
- See O.22, r.10 (Varying the rate at which a judgment debt is paid)

Forms

13.0.4 None are currently prescribed. See list of forms at para. 48PD–005.

Practice Direction

13.0.5 Part 13 is not supplemented by a practice direction.

Scope of this Part

13.1 **13.1** The rules in this Part set out the procedure for setting aside or varying judgment entered under Part 12 (default judgment).

(CCR Order 22, r.10 sets out the procedure for varying the rate at which a judgment debt must be paid.)

13.1.1 **Effect of rule**—Part 13 is not a comprehensive code for setting aside judgments generally but is confined to the setting aside of a default judgment which has been obtained pursuant to Pt 12.

CCR, O.22, r.10 is re-enacted in Schedule 2 to the CPR. It deals with an application to vary the rate at which a judgment debt must be paid on the application of either the judgment creditor or the judgment debtor.

Cases where the court must set aside judgment entered under Part 12

13.2 **13.2** The court must set aside[GL] a judgment entered under Part 12 if judgment was wrongly entered because—

(a) in the case of a judgment in default of an acknowledgment of service, any of the conditions in rule 12.3(1) and 12.3(3) was not satisfied;

(b) in the case of a judgment in default of a defence, any of the conditions in rule 12.3(2) and 12.3(3) was not satisfied; or

(c) the whole of the claim was satisfied before judgment was entered.

Effect of rule—Practitioners familiar with either the RSC or the CCR will know of the distinction between "regular" and "irregular" judgments. Rule 13.2 refers to judgment being "wrongly entered" *i.e.* the judgment is irregular. The court must set aside the wrongly entered judgment in the three situations specified in the rule. For general principles see the discussion of irregular judgments in SCP 1999, Vol. 1, para. 13/9/8. It should be noted that the decision in *Faircharm Investments Limited v. Citibank International plc, The Times*, February 20, 1998, CA (which is fully considered therein) would appear to no longer be able to support an argument against setting aside an irregular judgment as the word "must" is used in the new rule. **13.2.1**

Cases where the court may set aside or vary judgment entered under Part 12

13.3—(1) In any other case, the court may set aside[GL] or vary a judgment entered under Part 12 if— **13.3**

(a) the defendant has a real prospect of successfully defending the claim; or
(b) it appears to the court that there is some other good reason why—
 (i) the judgment should be set aside or varied; or
 (ii) the defendant should be allowed to defend the claim.

(2) In considering whether to set aside[GL] or vary a judgment entered under Part 12, the matters to which the court must have regard include whether the person seeking to set aside the judgment made an application to do so promptly.

(Rule 3.1(3) provides that the court may attach conditions when it makes an order.)

Effect of rule—Rule 13.3 deals with the setting aside of a regular judgment (*cf.* r.13.2—cases where the court must set aside). **13.3.1**

The use of the word "may" shows that the court has a discretion but act in accordance with Pt 1 (the Overriding Objectives).

The defendant applying to set aside the judgment must come within r.13.3(1)(a) or (b). The phrase "real prospect of success" is a re-statement of the principles laid down by the Court of Appeal in *Alpine Bulk Transport Co. Inc. v. Saudi Eagle Shipping Co. Inc., The Saudi Eagle* [1986] 2 Lloyd's Rep. 221. It is not enough to show an "arguable" defence; the defendant must show that he has "a real prospect of successfully defending the claim". This is discussed fully in SCP 1999, Vol. 1, para. 13/9/18.

Rule 13.3(2) gives added emphasis to the need to act promptly in seeking to set aside. Indeed the need to comply with time-limits and generally to act promptly is a feature of the CPR. In applying to set aside the court has always considered delay and the reasons for it (*Evans v. Bartlam* [1937] A.C. 437). An application to set aside must be supported by evidence (see r.13.4(3)). If a defendant has not acted promptly he would be well advised to address the reason for this in his witness statement or affidavit having regard to r.13.3(2).

The discretionary power to set aside is unconditional. The purpose of the power is to avoid injustice. The major consideration on an application to set aside is whether the defendant has shown a real prospect of successfully defending the claim or some other good reason why judgment should be set aside or he should be allowed to defend the claim. The defendant is seeking to deprive the claimant of a regular judgment which the claimant has validly obtained in accordance with Pt 12: this is not something which the court will do lightly.

Application to set aside or vary judgment—procedure

13.4—(1) Where— **13.4**

(a) the claim is for a specified amount of money;
(b) the judgment was obtained in a court which is not the defendant's home court;
(c) the claim has not been transferred to another defendant's home court under rule 14.12 (admission—determination of rate of payment by judge) or rule 26.2 (automatic transfer); and
(d) the defendant is an individual;

the court will transfer an application under this Part to set aside[GL] or vary judgment to the defendant's home court.

(1A) In this rule, "defendant's home court" has the meaning given to it by rule 2.3, except that reference to the defendant's address for service shall be a reference to that address shown on the last of the following documents to be filed at court giving an address for service for the defendant—

(a) the application to set aside[GL];
(b) any acknowledgment of service; and
(c) the claim form.

(2) Paragraph 1 does not apply where the claim was commenced in a specialist list.

(3) An application under rule 13.3 (cases where the court may set aside[GL] vary judgment) must be supported by evidence.

13.4.1 **Effect of rule**—Rule 13.4(1) is derived from CCR, O.37, r.4(2) but is modified. Under the CCR automatic transfer to the defendant's home court occurred "in a default action for a liquidated sum". Automatic transfer to the defendant's home court (defined in r.2.3) now occurs only if the four specified conditions in the rule are satisfied. The phrase "a specified amount of money" is wider than the old expression "liquidated sum" and includes any claim where the claimant has put a specific figure on his claim rather than claim damages. Automatic transfer now only occurs where the defendant "is an individual" not, for example, where the defendant is a company or partnership sued as a firm.

There is no automatic transfer where the claim was commenced in a specialist list.

Rule 13.4(3) reflects existing practice on an application to set aside a regular judgment obtained in default. It has been the rule that the application must be supported by an affidavit of merits (see SCP 1999, Vol. 1, para. 13/9/7). The new rule does not expressly require an affidavit but does require the application to be "supported by evidence". The filing and service of a witness statement or an affidavit to support the application is undoubtedly the better practice. In a clear case the service of the witness statement or the affidavit may induce the claimant not to oppose the application. Even where the claimant does wish to oppose the service of the witness statement or the affidavit gives time for the claimant to consider his position and file and serve a witness statement or an affidavit in reply.

Claimant's duty to apply to set aside judgment

13.5 **13.5**—(1) This rule applies where—

(a) the claimant has purported to serve particulars of claim; and
(b) the claimant has entered judgment under Part 12 against the defendant to whom the particulars of claim were sent.

(2) If a claimant who has entered judgment subsequently has good reason to believe that the particulars of claim did not reach the defendant before the claimant entered judgment, he must—

(a) file a request for the judgment to be set aside[GL]; or
(b) apply to the court for directions.

(3) The claimant may take no further step in the proceedings for the enforcement of the judgment until the judgment has been set aside[GL] or the court has disposed of the application for directions.

13.5.1 **Effect of rule**—Rule 13.5 imposes a duty on the claimant to apply to set aside his own judgment (or apply for directions) where he has served (or rather, as the rule puts it, purported to serve) particulars of claim then entered a default judgment under Pt 12 and now "has good reason to believe" that the particulars of claim did not reach the defendant before judgment was entered. Though in different terms, the rule is derived from RSC, O.13, r.7(3) which placed a duty on the plaintiff to request set aside of his default judgment (or apply for directions) where a writ served by post was subsequently returned undelivered. The rule is not based on CCR, O.37, r.3 whereby the *court* would set aside judgment on failure of postal service. Rule 13.5 puts the onus on the claimant.

Surprisingly there is no express provision in the CPR equivalent to CCR, O.37, r.3 whereby the court sets aside judgment of its own motion on failure of postal service. It is surprising because the CPR adopt the CCR rather than the RSC on service so that the general rule is service by the court by first class post. It follows that if postal service fails the claim form/particulars of claim will be returned to the court. Could the court set aside of its own initiative under r.3.3? It could not do so under r.3.3(1) which begins "except where a rule ... provides otherwise ..." r.13.5 does "provide otherwise" by placing the onus on the claimant. However, r.3.3(4) is wide enough—"the court may make an order of its own initiative without hearing the parties or giving them the opportunity to make representations".

Abandoned claim restored where default judgment set aside

13.6 Where— 13.6

(a) the claimant claimed a remedy in addition to one specified in rule 12.4(1) (claims in respect of which the claimant may obtain default judgment by filing a request);

(b) the claimant abandoned his claim for that remedy in order to obtain default judgment on request in accordance with 12.4(3); and

(c) the default judgment is set aside[GL] under this Part,

the abandoned claim is restored when the default judgment is set aside.

Effect of rule—Default judgment is not available on the filing of a request in all cases: only the claims specified in r.12.4(1). Claimants will sometimes claim remedies where it is not possible to enter judgment in default on request but a claimant is entitled, if he so chooses, to abandon the claim for that remedy and enter judgment for the remainder of the claim: see r.12.4(3). If a claimant does this but his default judgment is subsequently set aside; the abandoned claim is automatically restored pursuant to r.13.6 when the default judgment is set aside. 13.6.1

PART 14

ADMISSIONS

14.0.1 **Contents**

Editorial Introduction

14.0.2 Part 14 has no equivalent Order in the RSC and is not based on RSC, O.27—Admissions. Part 14 is therefore new to practitioners familiar only with the RSC but will be instantly recognised by practitioners familiar with the CCR as based upon the "admissions" part of CCR, O.9—Admission, defence, counterclaim and answer. Typically of the CPR, however, Pt 14 represents a considerable drafting improvement over the former CCR and it is eminently sensible and useful to have the important and common topic of admissions dealt with in one self-contained Part.

Part 14 essentially covers two distinct situations. First, "formal admissions" (typically an admission of liability in a defence) and, secondly, a defendant debtor's admission of a debt (usually accompanied by an offer to pay by instalments) on a form provided by the court and served with the claim form. In the first case the appropriate judgment can be obtained by an application to the court under r.13.3: the application will be heard by the district judge or, if in the High Court in London, by a Master. In the second case there is usually no judicial input and judgment is obtained administratively.

Related Sources

14.0.3
- Practice Direction (Admissions), see para. 14PD–001
- Rule 7.8 (Form for defence [and admitting the claim] to be served with claim form)
- Part 15 (Defence and Counterclaim)
- Part 23 (General Rules About Applications for Court Orders)
- Part 16 (Statements of Case)

Forms

14.0.4
- N9A—Admission (specified amount) (see para. C5–001)
- N9C—Admission (unspecified amount and non-money claims) (see para. C7–001)
- N225—Request for judgment and reply to admission (specified amount) (see para. C56–001)
- N225A—Notice of part admission (specified amount) (see para. C57–001)
- N226—Notice of admission (unspecified amount) (see para. C58–001)
- N228—Notice of admission (return of goods) (see para. C60–001)

Making an admission

14.1 **14.1**—(1) A party may admit the truth of the whole or any part of another party's case.

(2) He may do this by giving notice in writing (such as in a statement of case or by letter).

(3) Where the only remedy which the claimant is seeking is the payment of money, the defendant may also make an admission in accordance with—

(a) rule 14.4 (admission of whole claim for specified amount of money);

(b) rule 14.5 (admission of part of claim for specified amount of money);

(c) rule 14.6 (admission of liability to pay whole of claim for unspecified amount of money); or

(d) rule 14.7 (admission of liability to pay claim for unspecified amount of money where defendant offers a sum in satisfaction of the claim).

(4) Where the defendant makes an admission as mentioned in paragraph (3), the claimant has a right to enter judgment except where—

(a) the defendant is a child or patient; or

(b) the claimant is a child or patient and the admission is made under rule 14.5 or 14.7.

(Rule 21.10 provides that, where a claim is made by or on behalf of a child or patient or against a child or patient, no settlement, compromise or payment shall be valid, so far as it relates to that person's claim, without the approval of the court.)

(5) The court may allow a party to amend or withdraw an admission.

(Rule 3.1(3) provides that the court may attach conditions when it makes an order.)

Formal admission—In various ways, for the purposes of reducing costs and delay and of narrowing the issues in dispute, the CPR encourage parties, where appropriate, to make admissions of fact and to concede claims (or parts of a claim) and not to contest the incontestable throughout the pre-trial process. **14.1.1**

"notice in writing"—Rule 14.1(2) does not require an admission to be in any particular form, merely that it be "in writing". If it is not in writing it may still be admissible in evidence but it is not a formal admission for the purposes of Pt 14. **14.1.2**

"statement of case"—This is a new phrase (defined in r.2.3(1)) which has replaced the former term "pleadings" and is not to be confused with "statement of claim" (a term used in the RSC but not used in the CPR where the term "particulars of claim", borrowed from the CCR, is used instead). **14.1.3**

A defendant who wishes to admit the whole or part of the claim should do so in his defence. See further r.16.5.

"admissions of fact"—An admission may be express or implied but must be clear (*Ellis v. Allen* [1914] 1 Ch. 904 at 909; *Ash v. Hutchinson and Co. (Publishers)* [1936] Ch. 489 at 503; *Technistudy v. Kelland* [1976] 1 W.L.R. 1042; *Murphy v. Culhane* [1977] Q.B. 94). Where the defendant admits a document but does not admit that its terms are fully or correctly pleaded, the claimant may obtain judgment if the document, on production, clearly establishes the claim (*Barnard v. Wieland* (1882) 30 W.R. 947; but see *Rutter v. Tregent* (1879) 12 Ch.D. 758 and *Smith v. Davies* (1884) 28 Ch.D. 650). **14.1.4**

An admission in a defence in one action has been held not to be binding in other proceedings between the same parties on a different issue (*Re Walters* (1889) 61 L.T. 872).

Judgment on admission—See r.14.3. Where an admission is made pursuant to r.14.1(1)(2) an application to the court for judgment is necessary. This contrasts with the claimant's right to enter judgment under r.14.1(4) whereby judgment is obtained administratively without judicial involvement. **14.1.5**

"claimant . . . seeking . . . the payment of money"—Rule 14.1(3) sets out the four situations where the defendant can make an admission on the relevant practice form. See further the four specific rules referred to. Usually, an admission under any of these rules will be accompanied by a request for time to pay (see r.14.9). If the defendant makes an offer to pay by instalments which the claimant accepts, judgment can be entered accordingly. If the claimant rejects the offer, rr.14.10 *et seq.* provides for determination of the rate of payment. **14.1.6**

"claimant has a right to enter judgment"—The claimant's right to enter judgment on an **14.1.7**

admission pursuant to r.14.1(3) is subject only to the usual requirement, pursuant to r.21.10, where the defendant is a child or patient or the claimant is a child or patient and the admission is under r.14.5 or r.14.7 (but note, not if the admission is under r.14.4 or r.14.6). In these cases, involving a child or patient, an application to the court is necessary. (See Pt 21—Children and Patients, and Pt 23—General Rules about applications for court orders.) Otherwise—*i.e.* in the vast majority of cases—the claimant has a right to enter judgment. Judgment is obtained merely by completing the appropriate court form (the CPR retain the CCR term "request": see rr.14.4(3), 14.5(6), 14.6(4) and 14.7(5)). Judgment is entered administratively by a member of the court staff: there is no judicial input.

14.1.8 **"amend or withdraw an admission"**—The court does not normally permit the withdrawal of an admission consciously made (see *Hollis v. Burton* [1892] 3 Ch. 226). Nevertheless, it was established practice under RSC, O.27 to permit a defendant to resile from an admission in an appropriate case (see *Bird v. Birds Eye Walls Ltd, The Times,* July 24, 1987, CA; *Gale v. Superdrug Stores* [1996] 1 W.L.R. 1089, CA; *Heggarty v. Murray* [1993] C.L.Y. 3296, a county court case). Rule 14.1(5) now, sensibly, specifically gives the court an express power to allow a party to amend or withdraw an admission. Rule 3.1(3) provides that the court may attach conditions when it makes an order. Inevitably the court will have to consider costs and the party seeking to withdraw or amend an admission will usually have to do so at his own expense as well as having to pay the other party's costs of the application.

Period for making an admission

14.2 **14.2**—(1) The period for returning an admission under rule 14.4 or for filing it under rules 14.5, 14.6 or 14.7 is—

(a) where the defendant is served with a claim form which states that particulars of claim will follow, 14 days after service of the particulars; and

(b) in any other case, 14 days after service of the claim form.

(2) Paragraph (1) is subject to the following rules—

(a) RSC Order 11, r.1A (which specifies how the period for filing or returning an admission is calculated where the claim form is served out of the jurisdiction); and

(b) rule 6.16(4) (which requires the court to specify the period for responding to the particulars of claim when it makes an order under that rule).

(3) A defendant may return an admission under rule 14.4 or file it under rules 14.5, 14.6 or 14.7 after the end of the period for returning or filing it specified in paragraph (1) if the claimant has not obtained default judgment under Part 12.

(4) If he does so, this Part shall apply as if he had made the admission within that period.

14.2.1 **Effect of rule**—Rule 14.2 has no application to an admission made in a statement of case pursuant to r.14.1(1) and (2), but is confined to the four situations in r.14.1(3) re-stated in r.14.2(1). It is therefore concerned with four situations where the claimant seeks the payment of money as the only remedy, *i.e.* admission of whole claim for a specified amount of money (r.14.4); admission of part of claim for specified amount of money (r.14.5); admission of liability to pay whole of claim for unspecified amount of money (r.14.6) and admission of liability to pay claim for unspecified amount of money where defendant offers a sum in satisfaction (r.14.7). The effect of r.14.2(1) is to give the defendant 14 days from service of the particulars of claim. The "claim form" (which has replaced the county court summons and High Court writ) may be endorsed with the particulars of claim or contained in a separate document served with the claim form; in either case, r.14.2(1)(b) applies and the defendant has 14 days from service of the claim form. Where the claimant has elected to serve particulars of claim separately but subsequently to the claim form, r.14.2(1)(a) applies and the defendant has 14 days after service of the particulars.

14.2.2 **RSC, O.11, r.1A**—RSC, O.11 (which deals with service out of the jurisdiction) is re-enacted in Schedule 1 to the CPR.

14.2.3 **Rule 6.16**—This rule (service of claim form on agent of principal who is overseas) provides a procedure whereby an agent within the jurisdiction can be served instead of serving the principal under the provisions of RSC, O.11. Rule 6.16(4) requires the court to specify the period for responding to the particulars of claim.

"default judgment"—Where a defendant fails to respond to service of the particulars of claim as required by the rules, the claimant can enter a default judgment (see further Pt 12). If, however, the claimant is slow to seek judgment and in the interim the defendant files a late admission the admission is treated as if it were in time (r.14.2(3) and (4)). **14.2.4**

Admission by notice in writing—application for judgment

14.3—(1) Where a party makes an admission under rule 14.1(2) (admission by notice in writing), any other party may apply for judgment on the admission. **14.3**

(2) Judgment shall be such judgment as it appears to the court that the applicant is entitled to on the admission.

"admission by notice in writing"—This is a new phrase not found in the former RSC or CCR and is the only formal requirement of the rule. It is clearly envisaged that no particular form is required so long as the admission is in writing: it could be in a statement of case (typically, the defence), by letter or in any written form so long as it is clear. **14.3.1**

Effect of rule—Rule 14.3 is derived from RSC, O.27, r.3. By admitting a fact a party can save costs by obviating the need to call evidence to prove that fact. Where a party has made admission of fact, r.14.3 enables the court to give his opponent such judgment that he is entitled to without waiting for the determination of any other questions between the parties. If the relief claimed is an injunction, application should be made to the judge. In other cases application should normally be to the district judge or Master as appropriate. **14.3.2**

"any other party"—Either claimant or defendant can apply. It was held in *Re Wright, Kirke v. North* [1895] 2 Ch. 747 that one only of several plaintiffs could not apply. There is no reason why application could not be made against one of several defendants. **14.3.3**

Admission of liability—If the defendant in a damages action admits the claim, the claimant can obtain judgment for "damages to be assessed" (one reason for doing so is to enable the claimant to obtain an order for an interim payment: see r.25.7(1)(b) and Pt 25 generally). The court giving judgment will give case-management directions for the assessment of damages (there is no equivalent in the CPR to the former RSC, O.37). **14.3.4**

For the claimant to obtain judgment in a negligence action the defendant must have admitted both that he was negligent and that the claimant thereby suffered damage: an admission of the negligence only is not sufficient (*Blundell v. Rimmer* [1971] 1 W.L.R. 123; [1971] 1 All E.R. 1072, approved in *Rankine v. Garton Sons and Co. Ltd* [1979] 2 All E.R. 1185 and *Parrott v. Jackson* (1996) *The Times*, February 14). The reason is that an admission of negligence without an admission that the claimant suffered injury thereby is not an admission of liability. The claimant, therefore, cannot obtain judgment on an application under r.14.3 but may be able to obtain, in an appropriate case, summary judgment under Pt 24 (see *Dummer v. Brown* [1953] 1 Q.B. 710; [1953] 1 All E.R. 1158 and Pt 24 generally).

Claim and counterclaim—Where a defendant admits a claim but pleads a counterclaim the usual practice has been to grant judgment on terms. For example, there may be judgment on the claim with a stay of execution pending trial of the counterclaim (if not already done, the court will give case-management directions for the trial of the counterclaim). Alternatively, the defendant could be required to pay money into court pending trial of the counterclaim. **14.3.5**

"may apply for judgment"—Unless the defendant consents to a judgment being entered (in which case a consent judgment can be obtained in accordance with r.40.6) the claimant will have to make an application to the court. See, generally, Pt 23. **14.3.6**

Admission of whole of claim for specified amount of money

14.4—(1) This rule applies where— **14.4**

(a) the only remedy which the claimant is seeking is the payment of a specified amount of money; and

(b) the defendant admits the whole of the claim.

(2) The defendant may admit the claim by returning to the claimant an admission in the relevant practice form.

(3) The claimant may obtain judgment by filing a request in the relevant practice form and, if he does so—

(a) if the defendant has not requested time to pay, the procedure in paragraphs (4) to (6) will apply;

(b) if the defendant has requested time to pay, the procedure in rule 14.9 will apply.

(4) The claimant may specify in his request for judgment—

(a) the date by which the whole of the judgment debt is to be paid; or

(b) the times and rate at which it is to be paid by instalments.

(5) On receipt of the request for judgment the court will enter judgment.

(6) Judgment will be for the amount of the claim (less any payments made) and costs—

(a) to be paid by the date or at the rate specified in the request for judgment; or

(b) if none is specified, immediately.

(Rule 14.14 deals with the circumstances in which judgment under this rule may include interest.)

14.4.1 **Scope of provision**—As the title to the rule, re-inforced by r.14.4(1), makes clear, this rule only applies where the claimant has sued for a specified sum and the defendant admits the claim in full.

14.4.2 **"specified amount of money"**—This term, found in r.14.4(1)(a) and in many other rules in the CPR, is a new term which has replaced the former term "liquidated sum". It is not a synonym for the old term, however, and is wider. Clearly it covers a case where the claim is for a debt (which, in practice, will be the most common use of r.14.4). However, "specified amount of money" is wide enough to cover any case where the claimant has put a figure on the amount of his claim, *e.g.* a claim for damages arising out of a road traffic accident where the claimant has not claimed "damages" but a "specified amount of money" such as the repair bill. In this case, or indeed any other where the claimant claims a "specified amount of money" if the defendant admits not only the claim but also the specified sum he can make an admission and r.14.4 applies.

14.4.3 **"an admission in the relevant practice form"**—The relevant form is served on the defendant with the particulars of claim: see r.7.8. Rule 14.4(2) requires the defendant to send the admission "to the claimant", not to the court.

14.4.4 **"claimant may obtain judgment"**—Rule 14.4(3), (4), (5) and (6) are clearly drafted and are self-explanatory. If the defendant has not requested time to pay, r.14.4(4) to (6) apply. The claimant has the choice of requesting judgment payable forthwith, payable on a specified date or payable by instalments, the frequency and size of which is determined by the claimant.

If, as is more usual, the defendant is making an offer to pay by instalments and the claimant is accepting that offer, r.14.9 applies (if the claimant is *not* accepting the instalments offered, r.14.10 applies).

Note that under r.14.4(6) if the claimant fails to request payment by instalments or on a specified date, the judgment will be payable immediately. This rule only applies where the defendant is not requesting time to pay.

14.4.5 **Interest**—Judgment can include interest: see r.14.14.

14.4.6 **Costs**—Judgment will include fixed costs: see further Pt 45.

Admission of part of a claim for a specified amount of money

14.5 14.5—(1) This rule applies where—

(a) the only remedy which the claimant is seeking is the payment of a specified amount of money; and

(b) the defendant admits part of the claim.

(2) The defendant may admit part of the claim by filing an admission in the relevant practice form.

(3) On receipt of the admission, the court will serve a notice on the claimant requiring him to return the notice stating that—

(a) he accepts the amount admitted in satisfaction of the claim;

(b) he does not accept the amount admitted by the defendant and wishes the proceedings to continue; or

(c) if the defendant has requested time to pay, he accepts the amount admitted in satisfaction of the claim, but not the defendant's proposals as to payment.

(4) The claimant must—

(a) file the notice; and

(b) serve a copy on the defendant,

within 14 days after it is served on him.

(5) If the claimant does not file the notice within 14 days after it is served on him, the claim is stayed[GL] until he files the notice.

(6) If the claimant accepts the amount admitted in satisfaction of the claim, he may obtain judgment by filing a request in the relevant practice form and, if he does so—

(a) if the defendant has not requested time to pay, the procedure in paragraphs (7) to (9) will apply;

(b) if the defendant has requested time to pay, the procedure in rule 14.9 will apply.

(7) The claimant may specify in his request for judgment—

(a) the date by which the whole of the judgment debt is to be paid; or

(b) the time and rate at which it is to be paid by instalments.

(8) On receipt of the request for judgment, the court will enter judgment.

(9) Judgment will be for the amount admitted (less any payments made) and costs—

(a) to be paid by the date or at the rate specified in the request for judgment; or

(b) if none is specified, immediately.

(If the claimant files notice under paragraph (3) that he wishes the proceedings to continue, the procedure which then follows is set out in Part 26.)

Scope of provision—Rule 14.5(1) clearly sets out the limited situation to which r.14.5 applies, *i.e.* only where the claimant seeks a specified sum of money and the defendant admits part of the claim. It is based on CCR, O.9, r.3 though the two distinct situations governed by the former rule are more sensibly dealt with by separate rules in the CPR. **14.5.1**

"specified amount of money"—This term is wider than the former term "liquidated sum". See commentary to r.14.4. **14.5.2**

"relevant practice form"—The form is served on the defendant with the particulars of claim: see r.7.8. Rule 14.5(2) requires the defendant to file the admission with the court (*cf.* an admission under r.14.4 which the defendant must send "to the claimant". This unnecessary distinction will surely lead to confusion). **14.5.3**

"filing an admission"—The defendant by filing an admission, albeit of part of the claim, prevents the claimant entering a default judgment. **14.5.4**

"the court will serve a notice"—The defendant, by filing an admission of part of the claim has notified the court, but not the claimant. It is therefore the court's task to notify the claimant of the partial admission. The claimant must return the notice, in accordance with r.14.5(3) stating his response to the partial admission. The three options open to the claimant are clearly set out in that rule. The claimant has 14 days to respond (r.14.5(4)) and if he does not do so the action is stayed (r.14.5(5)). **14.5.5**

Acceptance of partial admission—If the claimant accepts the partial admission note that it is not sufficient to merely return the notice in accordance with r.14.5(3) and (4). He must also file "a request in the relevant practice form" in accordance with r.14.5(6) in order to obtain judgment. See the list of forms at para. 48PD–017. **14.5.6**

Request for time to pay—See rr.14.9 and 14.10. **14.5.7**

Non-acceptance of partial admission—The claimant can refuse the partial admission and **14.5.8**

continue his claim for the whole sum. He must file the notice of partial admission sent to him by the court pursuant to r.14.5(3) and (4). The court will then proceed to allocate the case to the appropriate track (see further, Pt 26).

14.5.9 **Rule 14.5(6), (7), (8) and (9)**—Rule 14.5(6) is a necessary modification of r.14.4(3). Rule 14.5(7), (8) and (9) are in identical terms to r.14.4(4), (5) and (6).

14.5.10 **Interest**—See r.14.14 and commentary thereon. That rule, surprisingly, does not apply and r.14.5 contains no provision for including interest.

14.5.11 **Costs**—See Pt 45—fixed costs.

Admission of liability to pay whole of claim for unspecified amount of money

14.6 **14.6**—(1) This rule applies where—

(a) the only remedy which the claimant is seeking is the payment of money;
(b) the amount of the claim is not specified; and
(c) the defendant admits liability but does not offer to pay a specified amount of money in satisfaction of the claim.

(2) The defendant may admit the claim by filing an admission in the relevant practice form.

(3) On receipt of the admission, the court will serve a copy on the claimant.

(4) The claimant may obtain judgment by filing a request in the relevant practice form.

(5) If the claimant does not file a request for judgment within 14 days after service of the admission on him, the claim is stayed[GL] until he files the request.

(6) On receipt of the request for judgment the court will enter judgment.

(7) Judgment will be for an amount to be decided by the court and costs.

14.6.1 **Scope of provision**—Rule 14.6 is clear and self-explanatory. It applies only where the claimant sues to recover an "unspecified amount of money", the defendant does not dispute liability to pay and the court's task is therefore limited to deciding the amount to be paid and costs.

14.6.2 **"relevant practice form"**—A form to admit the claim must be served on the defendant with the particulars of claim: see r.7.8.

14.6.3 **"filing an admission"**—The rule requires the defendant to file the admission with the court and the court to serve a copy on the claimant.

14.6.4 **"filing a request"**—The claimant, on receipt of a copy of the admission from the court, can request judgment on the relevant practice form which he obtains from the court. He should do so within 14 days (r.14.6(4), (5) and (6)) and r.14.8(1)).

14.6.5 **Judgment**—As provided by r.14.6(7), judgment is for "an amount to be decided by the court". The court will give case-management directions including allocating the case to the relevant track if it is necessary.

14.6.6 **Disposal hearing**—Paragraph 12.6 of the Practice Direction which supplements Part 26 (26PD–006) enables the court to order a disposal hearing. At a disposal hearing the court "may give directions or decide the amount payable" (see para. 12.8 at 26PD–006).

Admission of liability to pay claim for unspecified amount of money where defendant offers a sum in satisfaction of the claim

14.7 **14.7**—(1) This rule applies where—

(a) the only remedy which the claimant is seeking is the payment of money;
(b) the amount of the claim is not specified; and
(c) the defendant—

(i) admits liability; and
(ii) offers to pay a specified amount of money in satisfaction of the claim.

(2) The defendant may admit the claim by filing an admission in the relevant practice form.

(3) On receipt of the admission, the court will serve a notice on the claimant requiring him to return the notice stating whether or not he accepts the amount in satisfaction of the claim.

(4) If the claimant does not file the notice within 14 days after it is served on him, the claim is stayed[GL] until he files the notice.

(5) If the claimant accepts the offer he may obtain judgment by filing a request in the relevant practice form and if he does so—

(a) if the defendant has not requested time to pay, the procedure in paragraphs (6) to (8) will apply;
(b) if the defendant has requested time to pay, the procedure in rule 14.9 will apply.

(6) The claimant may specify in his request for judgment—

(a) the date by which the whole of the judgment debt is to be paid; or
(b) the times and rate at which it is to be paid by instalments.

(7) On receipt of the request for judgment, the court will enter judgment.

(8) Judgment will be for the amount offered by the defendant (less any payments made) and costs—

(a) to be paid on the date or at the rate specified in the request for judgment; or
(b) if none is specified, immediately.

(9) If the claimant does not accept the amount offered by the defendant, he may obtain judgment by filing a request in the relevant practice form.

(10) Judgment under paragraph (9) will be for an amount to be decided by the court and costs.

Scope of provision—Rule 14.7 is the longest rule in Pt 14 and the least used in practice. The rule only applies if the three conditions in r.14.7(1) apply. The rule then goes on to provide for all possible permutations that can arise if r.14.7(1) is satisfied: hence the length of the rule. However, the rule is clearly drafted and self-explanatory. All relevant forms referred to are available from the court. **14.7.1**

Allocation of claims in relation to outstanding matters

14.8—(1) Where the court enters judgment under rule 14.6 or 14.7 for an amount to be decided by the court it will— **14.8**

(a) give any directions it considers appropriate; and
(b) if it considers it appropriate, allocate the case.

Scope of provision—Rule 14.6 applies where the claim is for an "unspecified amount of money" and the defendant admits liability. One of the permutations which can arise under r.14.7 is a judgment for an amount to be decided by the court. In either case, the court's only task is to decide the amount to be paid by the defendant. Rule 14.8 requires the court to give necessary directions for that issue to be tried. Directions for trial of the issue of damages will always be necessary and appropriate. In particular the court will have to consider the need for disclosure, exchange of witness statements and permission for either party to call expert evidence or rely on an expert's report. (See generally, Pt 31—Disclosure and Inspection of Documents; Pt 32—Evidence and Pt 35—Experts and Assessors.) Clearly the giving of directions is important. As r.14.8(b) recognises it may not always be appropriate to allocate the case to a specific track. Allocation could be important, however, as it can have costs consequences. For the scope of each track see r.26.6. A case will only be allocated to the fast-track if within the financial limits (generally £5,000 to £15,000) and if it can be concluded in one day. There will be costs limitations if the case is allocated to the small-claims track (see r.27.14). Although the court can allocate a case to a higher track than its "normal track" it cannot allocate a case to a lower track than its normal track unless all parties consent (r.26.7(3)). See generally Pt 26. **14.8.1**

Request for time to pay

14.9—(1) A defendant who makes an admission under rules 14.4, 14.5 or **14.9**

14.7 (admission relating to a claim for a specified amount of money or offering to pay a specified amount of money) may make a request for time to pay.

(2) A request for time to pay is a proposal about the date of payment or a proposal to pay by instalments at the times and rate specified in the request.

(3) The defendant's request for time to pay must be served or filed (as the case may be) with his admission.

(4) If the claimant accepts the defendant's request, he may obtain judgment by filing a request in the relevant practice form.

(5) On receipt of the request for judgment, the court will enter judgment.

(6) Judgment will be—

(a) where rule 14.4 applies, for the amount of the claim (less any payments made) and costs;

(b) where rule 14.5 applies, for the amount admitted (less any payments made) and costs; or

(c) where rule 14.7 applies, for the amount offered by the defendant (less any payments made) and costs; and

(in all cases) will be for payment at the time and rate specified in the defendant's request for time to pay.

(Rule 14.10 sets out the procedure to be followed if the claimant does not accept the defendant's request for time to pay.)

14.9.1 **"request for time to pay"**—A request by the defendant for time to pay an admitted claim is a very common occurrence in practice. Rule 14.9 applies to three distinct situations which all have the common feature of a defendant's request for time to pay, *viz.* under r.14.4 admission of whole of claim for a specified amount of money; under r.14.5 admission of part of claim for a specified amount of money which the claimant is accepting in full settlement of the claim; under r.14.7 admission of liability in a claim for an unspecified amount of money where the defendant also offers a sum in satisfaction of the claim which the claimant is accepting. A "request for time to pay" is defined in r.14.9(2).

14.9.2 **Scope of provision**—Rule 14.9 applies to the three situations specified in r.14.9(1) (see commentary above) where the defendant has made a request for time to pay and the claimant is agreeing to that request (if he is not agreeing to it see r.14.10). The rule enables judgment to be obtained administratively without the need for a hearing or any judicial input.

14.9.3 **"request for time to pay must be served or filed . . ."**—An admission under r.14.4 must be served on the claimant (r.14.4(2)). An admission under r.14.5 or r.14.7 must be filed with the court (rr.14.5(2) and 14.7(2)). In all cases the request for time to pay must accompany the admission. It will be on the relevant practice form which will have been served on the defendant with the particulars of claim (r.7.8).

Determination of rate of payment

14.10 **14.10**—(1) This rule applies where the defendant makes a request for time to pay under rule 14.9.

(2) If the claimant does not accept the defendant's proposals for payment, he must file a notice in the relevant practice form.

(3) Where the defendant's admission was served direct on the claimant, a copy of the admission and the request for time to pay must be filed with the claimant's notice.

(4) When the court receives the claimant's notice, it will enter judgment for the amount admitted (less any payments made) to be paid at the time and rate of payment determined by the court.

14.10.1 **"request for time to pay under rule 14.9"**—Rule 14.9 applies to three distinct situations where the defendant has requested time to pay an admitted sum. See r.14.9 and commentary thereon. Essentially, r.14.9 applies where the claimant is agreeing to the request for time to pay in the terms offered by the defendant and r.14.10 applies where the claimant is not so agreeing.

14.10.2 **"request for time to pay"**—This phrase is defined in r.14.9(2).

"admission ... served ... on the claimant"—An admission under r.14.4 (admission of whole claim for a specified amount of money) should be served on the claimant (r.14.4(2)). The claimant must file it with the court pursuant to r.14.10(3) when he is giving notice of non-acceptance of the defendant's proposals for payment pursuant to r.14.10(2). 14.10.3

"relevant practice form"—All such forms can be obtained from the court office. See the list of forms at para. 48PD–017. 14.10.4

"time and rate of payment determined by the court"—In most cases this is done by a court officer, not a judge (see r.14.11). The court officer works to prescribed guidelines. For the right to have the payment rate re-determined by a judge see r.14.13. For variation of orders to pay by instalments see CCR, O.22, r.10 which is re-enacted in Schedule 2 to the CPR. 14.10.5

Determination of rate of payment by court officer

14.11—(1) A court officer may exercise the powers of the court under rule 14.10(4) where the amount outstanding (including costs) is not more than £50,000. 14.11

(2) Where a court officer is to determine the time and rate of payment, he must do so without a hearing.

Scope of provision—Rule 14.10 applies where the defendant has requested time to pay an admitted sum but the claimant does not agree to the defendant's request for time to pay in the terms offered. The only issue for determination by the court is the time and rate of payment to be made by the defendant. Rule 14.10(4) requires the court to enter judgment for the amount admitted "to be paid at the time and rate of payment determined by the court". Rule 14.11 entrusts this task to a court officer (not a judge) where the amount outstanding is not more than £50,000. This is a paper exercise: no hearing is involved. The court officer works to prescribed guidelines and has regard to the statement of means filed by the defendant with the admission. For the right to have the court officer's decision redetermined by a judge see r.14.13. 14.11.1

"including costs"—The £50,000 limit in r.14.11(1) expressly includes costs. Costs will be fixed costs (see Pt 45). The rule does not mention interest. However, it is submitted that interest too must be included within the £50,000 limit for the purposes of this rule. The rule refers to "the amount outstanding" (not, *e.g.* the amount claimed or amount admitted) and interest added to the claim pursuant to r.14.14 is just as much part of the "amount outstanding" as the sum claimed. 14.11.2

Variation—Variation of an order is still governed by CCR, O.22, r.10 which is re-enacted in Schedule 2 to the CPR. 14.11.3

Determination of rate of payment by judge

14.12—(1) Where a judge is to determine the time and rate of payment, he may do so without a hearing. 14.12

(2) Where a judge is to determine the time and rate of payment at a hearing, the proceedings must be transferred automatically to the defendant's home court if—

(a) the only claim is for a specified amount of money;
(b) the defendant is an individual;
(c) the claim has not been transferred to another defendant's home court under rule 13.4 (application to set aside[GL] or vary default judgment—procedure) or rule 26.2 (automatic transfer);
(d) the claim was not started in the defendant's home court; and
(e) the claim was not started in a specialist list.

(Rule 2.3 explains which court is a defendant's home court.)

(3) If there is to be a hearing to determine the time and rate of payment, the court must give each party at least 7 days' notice of the hearing.

Scope of provision—In most cases determination of the rate of payment is by a court officer and not a judge (see r.14.11). There are two distinct situations where determination is by a judge: first, where the amount outstanding is more than £50,000 (see r.14.11(1)) and, secondly, where the court officer is unable to make a determination in accordance with the prescribed guidelines (typically where the information provided by the defendant is inadequate or his income, having 14.12.1

regard to necessary outgoings, is a "negative income" so that apparently the defendant has no means to pay the admitted sum).

14.12.2 **"without a hearing"**—Wherever possible the judge will determine the time and rate of payment as a paper exercise without the need for the expense and inevitable delay of a court hearing. It is a judicial exercise: there are no prescribed guidelines. For the right to seek a re-determination at a hearing see r.14.13 and commentary thereon.

14.12.3 **With a hearing**—Where the judge is not able to make a determination as a paper exercise, or considers it inappropriate to do so, the court will give each party at least 7 days notice of the hearing (r.14.12(3)) so that each can attend to make representations and/or provide further evidence. Rule 14.12(2) provides that the case is to be transferred to another court if the five specified conditions are all met. The transfer is to the "defendant's home court" (a quaint term defined in r.2.3 and previously used in the CCR).

Right of re-determination

14.13 **14.13**—(1) Where—

(a) a court officer has determined the time and rate of payment under rule 14.11; or

(b) a judge has determined the time and rate of payment under rule 14.12 without a hearing,

either party may apply for the decision to be re-determined by a judge.

(2) An application for re-determination must be made within 14 days after service of the determination on the applicant.

(3) Where an application for re-determination is made, the proceedings must be transferred to the defendant's home court if—

(a) the only claim (apart from a claim for interest or costs) is for a specified amount of money;

(b) the defendant is an individual;

(c) the claim has not been transferred to another defendant's home court under rule 13.4 (application to set aside[GL] or vary default judgment—procedure) or rule 26.2 (automatic transfer);

(d) the claim was not started in the defendant's home court; and

(e) the claim was not started in a specialist list.

(Rule 2.3 explains which court is a defendant's home court.)

14.13.1 **Scope of provision**—Where the claimant has not accepted the defendant's proposal for payment determination of the time and rate of payment is carried out by the court and in the vast majority of cases this is done as a paper exercise without a court hearing. Most determinations are by a court officer under r.14.11 but a significant number are by a judge under r.14.12.

Where the time and rate of payment have been determined as a paper exercise (whether by court officer or judge) either party can apply for re-determination at a hearing by a judge pursuant to r.14.13(1).

Rule 14.13 does not apply to a determination by a judge at a hearing pursuant to r.14.12(2). In such a case a dissatisfied party must accept the decision or appeal. For variation of an order see CCR, O.22, r.10 which is re-enacted in Schedule 2 to the CPR.

14.13.2 **"within 14 days"**—Rule 14.13(2) prescribes a 14 day time period in which to seek a re-determination.

14.13.3 **"defendant's home court"**—This term is defined in r.2.3. If the case is not already proceeding there and if the five conditions set out in r.14.13(3) are met, the proceedings will be transferred to that court for the re-determination to take place there. This is so whether it is the claimant or defendant who seeks re-determination and is something the claimant should have in mind as he may find he has to travel to the "defendant's home court" for the re-determination.

14.13.4 **Evidence of means**—The initial determination will be based on the statement of means filed by the defendant with the admission. A claimant is entitled to adduce evidence that the means are greater than stated. Indeed if the claimant is unable to do so he should consider carefully whether it is worth seeking a re-determination. There is little the court can do where the means are plainly inadequate to justify a higher order and a claimant's plea that "it will take eight years to pay the debt at that rate" is, of itself, likely to be insufficient to justify a higher order.

Interest

14.14—(1) Judgment under rule 14.4 (admission of whole of claim for specified amount of money) shall include the amount of interest claimed to the date of judgment if— 14.14

(a) the particulars of claim include the details required by rule 16.4;
(b) where interest is claimed under section 35A of the Supreme Court Act 1981[1] or section 69 of the County Courts Act 1984,[2] the rate is no higher than the rate of interest payable on judgment debts at the date when the claim form was issued; and
(c) the claimant's request for judgment includes a calculation of the interest claimed for the period after the date up to which interest was stated to be calculated in the claim form to the date of the request for judgment.

(2) In any case where judgment is entered under 14.4 and the conditions in paragraph (1) are not satisfied judgment shall be for an amount of interest to be decided by the court.

(3) Where judgment is entered for an amount of interest to be decided by the court, the court will give directions for the management of the case.

Scope of provision—Rule 14.14(1) sets out the requirements for interest to be included in a judgment based on an admission. The law on interest in s.35A of the Supreme Court Act 1981 and s.69 of the County Courts Act 1984 obviously remains unaffected by the new procedural code introduced by the CPR and therefore r.14.14 continues established practice under the RSC and CCR and is based on CCR, O.9, r.8. Under SCA 1981, s.35A and CCA 1984, s.69 the court has power to award interest in all cases. Whether interest should be awarded, and if so, at what rate and for what period, are all at the discretion of the court. However, the court invariably does award interest nowadays. The rate of interest payable on judgment debts, for the sake of uniformity and simplicity, has been the rate adopted by rules of court for many purposes including default judgments and judgment on admissions. 14.14.1

"details required by rule 16.4"—See this rule, in particular r.16.4(2) and commentary thereon, which clearly sets out the necessary detail to be included in a statement of case when claiming interest. 14.14.2

"Judgment under rule 14.4"—Somewhat surprisingly r.14.14 applies only to judgment on admission under r.14.4. It does not apply (surely it should!) to judgment on admission under either r.14.5 or r.14.7. Clearly it is not necessary for r.14.14 to apply to judgment under r.14.6 (where, in any event, there will be a hearing to assess damages so that interest can be considered then) but it is odd that r.14.14 is confined to judgments under r.14.4. For the sake of simplicity and consistency, and to avoid hearings purely to determine the issue of interest, it is submitted that r.14.14 should be amended to extend it to judgments under rr.14.5 and 14.7 subject, of course, to the existing reasonable requirements set out in paragraphs (a), (b) and (c) in r.14.14(1). 14.14.3

"conditions in paragraph (1) are not satisfied"—Rule 14.14(1) is strict in its requirements and judgment on admission cannot include interest unless they are met. A hearing is necessary. Unfortunately (see above commentary), r.14.14(2) also applies only to judgments under r.14.4 (not under rr.14.5 or 14.7). 14.14.4

[1] 1981 c. 54. Section 35A was inserted by the Administration of Justice Act 1982 (c. 53), section 15(1), Schedule 1, Part I.

[2] 1984 c. 28. Section 69 was amended by the Courts and Legal Services Act 1990 (c. 41), section 125(3), Schedule 18, paragraph 46.

PRACTICE DIRECTION—ADMISSIONS

14PD–001 *This Practice Direction supplements CPR Part 14*

Admissions generally

1.1 Rules 14.1 and 14.2 deal with the manner in which a defendant may make an admission of a claim or part of a claim.

1.2 Rules 14.3, 14.4, 14.5, 14.6 and 14.7 set out how judgment may be obtained on a written admission.

Forms

2.1 When particulars of claim are served on a defendant the forms for responding to the claim that will accompany them will include a form[3] for making an admission.

2.2 If the defendant is requesting time to pay he should complete as fully as possible the statement of means contained in the admission form, or otherwise give in writing the same details of his means as could have been given in the admission form.

Returning or filing the admission

3.1 If the defendant wishes to make an admission in respect of the whole of a claim for a specified amount of money, the admission form or other written notice of the admission should be completed and returned to the claimant within 14 days of service of the particulars of claim.[4]

3.2 If the defendant wishes to make an admission in respect of a part of a claim for a specified amount of money, or in respect of a claim for an unspecified amount of money, the admission form or other written notice of admission should be completed and filed with the court within 14 days of service of the particulars of claim.[5]

3.3 The defendant may also file a defence under rule 15.2.

Request for time to pay

4.1 A defendant who makes an admission in respect of a claim for a specfied sum of money or offers to pay a sum of money in respect of a claim for an unspecified sum may, in the admission form, make a request for time to pay.[6]

4.2 If the claimant accepts the defendant's request, he may obtain judgment by filing a request for judgment contained in Form N225A[7]; the court will then enter judgment for payment at the time and rate specified in the defendant's request.[8]

4.3 If the claimant does not accept the request for time to pay, he should file notice to that effect by completing Form N225A; the court will then enter judgment for the amount of the admission (less any payments made) at a time and rate of payment decided by the court (see rule 14.10).

Determining the rate of payment

5.1 In deciding the time and rate of payment the court will take into account:

(1) the defendant's statement of means set out in the admission form or in any other written notice of the admission filed,

(2) the claimant's objections to the defendant's request set out in the claimant's notice,[9] and

[3] Practice forms N9A (specified amount) or N9C (unspecified amount).
[4] Rules 14.2 and 14.4.
[5] Rules 14.2, 14.5, 14.6 and 14.7.
[6] Rule 14.9.
[7] Rule 14.9(4).
[8] Rule 14.9(5) and (6).
[9] Practice form N225A.

(3) any other relevant factors.

5.2 The time and rate of payment may be decided:

(1) by a judge with or without a hearing, or

(2) by a court officer without a hearing provided that—

(a) the only claim is for a specified sum of money, and

(b) the amount outstanding is not more than £50,000 (including costs).

5.3 Where a decision has been made without a hearing whether by a court officer or by a judge, either party may apply for the decision to be re-determined by a judge.[10]

5.4 If the decision was made by a court officer the re-determination may take place without a hearing, unless a hearing is requested in the application notice.

5.5 If the decision was made by a judge the re-determination must be made at a hearing unless the parties otherwise agree.

5.6 Rule 14.13(2) describes how to apply for a re-determination.

Varying the rate of payment

6.1 Either party may, on account of a change in circumstances since the date of the decision (or re-determination as the case may be) apply to vary the time and rate of payment of instalments still remaining unpaid.

6.2 An application to vary under paragraph 6.1 above should be made in accordance with Part 23.

[10] Rule 14.13(1).

PART 15

Defence and Reply

15.0.1 **Contents**

Editorial Introduction

15.0.2 Those parts of the CPR concerned with commencing an action and identifying the issues between the parties which will have to be determined by the court, are closely modelled on the RSC. However, some important changes, including new terminology, have been introduced and the basic procedure is outlined here so as to set Pt 15 in context.

The "claimant" (a term which has replaced "plaintiff") commences his action by issuing a "claim form" (a term which has replaced "writ" in the High Court and "summons" in the county court).

The "particulars of claim" (a term derived from the CCR and which, in the High Court has replaced "statement of claim") must be either endorsed on the claim form or contained in a separate document served with, or subsequently to, the claim form.

The defendant is not required to respond to service of the claim form as such but must respond to service of the particulars of claim.

The defendant does not have to file an acknowledgment of service as a prerequisite to filing a defence but can omit the acknowledgement stage and file a defence within 14 days of service of the particulars of claim. However, a defendant can file an acknowledgment of service in which case a defence must be filed within 28 days of service of the particulars of claim.

The claimant can file a reply to the defence. For further details of the basic procedure outlined above see the Parts of the CPR referred to in "Related Sources" below.

Related Sources

15.0.3
- Practice Direction (Defence and Reply), see para. 15PD–001, below
- Part 7 (How to Start Proceedings—the Claim Form)
- Part 8 (Alternative Procedure for Claims)
- Part 9 (Responding to Particulars of Claim—General)
- Part 10 (Acknowledgment of Service)
- Part 12 (Default Judgment)
- Part 16 (Statements of Case)
- Part 17 (Amendments to Statements of Case)
- Part 20 (Counterclaims and Other Additional Claims)
- Part 22 (Statements of Truth)

Practice Direction

15.0.4 Part 15 is supplemented by a Practice Direction: see para. 15PD–001.

Part not to apply where claimant uses the Part 8 procedure

15.1 **15.1** This Part does not apply where the claimant uses the procedure set out in Part 8 (alternative procedure for claims).

15.1.1 **"alternative procedure for claims"**—The alternative procedure for claims (see Pt 8 and commentary thereon) is akin to the procedure commenced under the previous rules by originating summons or originating application. Where the Pt 8 procedure is used the defendant is not required to file a defence, but is required to file and serve an acknowledgment of service (r.8.3).

Filing a defence

15.2 A defendant who wishes to defend all or part of a claim must file a defence. 15.2

(Part 14 contains further provisions which apply where the defendant admits a claim.)

"must file a defence"—"Filing" is defined in r.2.3 and simply means delivering it (by post or otherwise) to the court office. Rule 15.2 is based on established practice in county courts. Hitherto, in the High Court, a defendant did not file, but merely served, his defence. The change in High Court practice effected by r.15.2 means, of course, that the High Court must now keep a file for every defended case. Clearly this is necessary for effective case-management. 15.2.1

Service of defence—See r.15.6. 15.2.2

Contents of defence—See r.16.5. Note also Pt 22—Statements of Truth. 15.2.3

Consequence of not filing a defence

15.3 If a defendant fails to file a defence, the claimant may obtain default judgment if Part 12 allows it. 15.3

"default judgment"—See Pt 12 and commentary thereon. 15.3.1

The period for filing a defence

15.4—(1) The general rule is that the period for filing a defence is— 15.4

(a) 14 days after service of the particulars of claim; or

(b) if the defendant files an acknowledgment of service under Part 10, 28 days after service of the particulars of claim.

(Rule 7.4 provides for the particulars of claim to be contained in or served with the claim form or served within 14 days of service of the claim form.)

(2) The general rule is subject to the following rules—

(a) RSC Order 11, r.1B (which specifies how the period for filing a defence is calculated where the claim form is served out of the jurisdiction);

(b) rule 11 (which provides that, where the defendant makes an application disputing the court's jurisdiction he need not file a defence before the hearing);

(c) rule 24.4(2) (which provides that, if the claimant applies for summary judgment before the defendant has filed a defence, the defendant need not file a defence before the summary judgment hearing); and

(d) rule 6.16(4) (which requires the court to specify the period for responding to the particulars of claims when it makes an order under that rule).

Effect of rule—The period for filing a defence runs from service of the particulars of claim, a document which may be endorsed on the claim form or served with, or subsequently to, the claim form (for time limit see r.7.4). The period for filing a defence is 14 days after service of the particulars of claim or 28 days after service of the particulars of claim if the defendant files an acknowledgment under Pt 10. Rule 2.8 sets out how to calculate any period of time under the CPR. A defendant who first files an acknowledgment of service has twice as long to file a defence as one who does not. However, as r.10.1(3)(a) states, a defendant may file an acknowledgment of service if "he is unable to file a defence within the period specified in rule 15.4". The reference in r.10.1(3)(a) to r.15.4 is clearly intended to be a reference to r.15.4(1)(a). Having regard to the detail now required in a defence (see r.16.5) in anything but the most straightforward of cases, 14 15.4.1

days from service of particulars of claim is likely to be too short leading to most defendants first acknowledging service so as to obtain a total of 28 days for filing a defence. See r.15.5 for extending the period for the defence.

In four exceptional cases, listed in r.15.4(2) a longer period for filing a defence is specified by another rule:

(1) where the claim form has been served out of the jurisdiction (as to the time for filing a defence in such a case see RSC, O.11, r.1B, see below para. R11.1B);

(2) where a defendant applies to the court for an order declaring that it has no jurisdiction to try the claim or should not exercise any jurisdiction which it may have (as to the time for filing a defence in such a case see r.11(9), see above para. 11.1);

(3) where, before the defence is filed, the claimant or defendant applies for summary judgment on the whole of a claim or on a particular issue (as to the time for filing a defence in such cases see r.24.4(2) and r.12.3(3) respectively;

(4) where the court makes an order for service of a claim form on an agent of a principal who is overseas (as to the time for filing a defence in such a case see r.16(4)).

15.4.2 **Filing of a late defence**—Part 14—Admissions contains specific rules (rr.14.2(3) and (4)) expressly dealing with filing of a late admission. Provided the claimant has not already obtained a default judgment the admission is effective and treated as if it were in time. There is no equivalent provision in Pt 15 dealing with filing of a late defence. Nevertheless, it is submitted that the onus is on the claimant to act promptly if he wishes to obtain a default judgment. In practice, if the time for filing a defence has expired but the claimant has taken no step to obtain default judgment and the defendant then files a late defence, the court office will accept the defence, file it and proceed as usual so that the claimant will not now be able to obtain default judgment. Note also, r.15.11 which provides for an automatic stay. If no defence has been filed and the claim has been stayed pursuant to r.15.11, the defendant would need to apply under r.15.11(2) to lift the stay before filing a defence. The reality is that the court office will accept a late defence unless the claim has been stayed.

Agreement extending the period for filing a defence

15.5 **15.5**—(1) The defendant and the claimant may agree that the period for filing a defence specified in rule 15.4 shall be extended by up to 28 days.

(2) Where the defendant and the claimant agree to extend the period for filing a defence, the defendant must notify the court in writing.

15.5.1 **"period for filing a defence . . . shall be extended by up to 28 days"**—One aim of the CPR is to set a tight but realistic timetable and insist on compliance with it. There is, in general, limited scope for the parties to extend time periods by consent (see, *e.g.*, rr.28.4 and 29.5). The court cannot allocate the case to its appropriate track, nor proceed to give case-management directions and timetable the case, until the defence is filed and then allocation questionnaires filed (see Pt 26). There is therefore some urgency in requiring the defence to be filed.

Rule 15.5(1) allows the claimant and defendant to agree that the period for filing a defence be extended "by up to 28 days". Although the agreement need not be in writing the defendant must give written notice of it to the court.

15.5.2 **Extension beyond 28 days**—Rule 15.5 is silent as to the position if the parties wish to extend the period beyond 28 days. It is submitted that the parties cannot agree an extension beyond 28 days and that the onus is on the defendant to apply to the court for an order extending time for filing a defence beyond 28 days. Whether or not the application is made by consent of all parties, the court may deal with it without a hearing (see r.23.8 and the commentary thereto). If the application is opposed, the court's decision whether or not to grant more time will depend on the circumstances of the case and, in particular, whether the claimant has complied with any relevant Pre-Action Protocol (see paras B1–001 *et seq.*). If the claimant has not, the court will certainly be more sympathetic to the defendant's application and may penalise the claimant in costs.

15.5.3 **Holding defence**—A defendant cannot legitimately obtain more time for preparing his defence by filing the so-called "holding defence" such as "I deny this debt: full defence to follow". Such a defence does not comply with r.16 (contents of defence). A defence which consists of a bare denial may be struck out under r.3.4 (see Practice Direction supplementing r.3.4, para. 1.6, see above para. 3PD–001). Indeed on the filing of such a defence a court officer may refer it to a judge and the court may strike it out on its own initiative (see rr.3.2 and 3.3).

15.5.4 **Filing of a late defence**—See commentary to r.15.4 under this heading.

15.5.5 **"defendant must notify the court in writing"**—Once the time limit for filing a defence has expired the claimant can enter a default judgment under Pt 12. It is therefore in the defendant's interest—and r.15.5(2) so provides—for the defendant to notify the court of any extension of time agreed under r.15.5(1).

Automatic stay—Note the provisions of r.15.11 imposing an automatic stay after 6 months inactivity. 15.5.6

Service of copy of defence

15.6 A copy of the defence must be served on every other party. 15.6

(Part 16 sets out what a defence must contain.)

"a copy of the defence must be served"—Rule 15.6 is disappointingly vague about who should serve a copy of the defence. Nor is it followed by any helpful cross-reference. The forms themselves refer only to the filing of a defence (see response pack, N9 *et seq.*, para. C4–001 and *cf.* r.9.2). The former practice under the RSC was for the defendant to serve the defence (RSC, O.18, r.2). However, unlike CPR, r.15.2, there was no requirement to file the defence. The former practice under the CCR was for the defendant to file the defence and for the court to serve a copy of it on the plaintiff (CCR, O.9, r.2(6) and (7)). Who then is to serve a copy of the defence under r.15.6? The rule does not expressly require the court to serve it but it will do so in practice provided that the defendant sends the necessary copy to the court. The court will then serve it pursuant to r.6.3(3). It is not for the court to make an extra copy for service so if the defendant does not provide a copy for service the court may assume that the defendant has done so direct. It is therefore suggested that defendants should either serve copies direct and, on filing the defence, inform the court that they have done so or, on filing the defence, supply sufficient copies for the court to serve pursuant to r.6.3(3). The court will then serve form N152 on all parties enclosing with it a copy of the defence and an allocation questionnaire (see para. C26–001). 15.6.1

Making a counterclaim

15.7 Part 20 applies to a defendant who wishes to make a counterclaim. 15.7

"counterclaim"—This term is defined in the glossary (see para. G1.1). A defendant may make a counterclaim against a claimant by filing particulars of the counterclaim (r.20.4). Practice directions state that "the defence and counterclaim should normally form one document with the counterclaim following on from the defence". (Practice Direction supplementing Pt 15, para. 3.1 (see para. 15PD–001) and Practice Direction supplementing Pt 20, para. 6.1 (see para. 20PD–001)). 15.7.1

Defence to counterclaim—A counterclaim is treated for certain purposes as if it were a claim (r.20.3). Thus, a claimant served with a counterclaim must file a defence in accordance with r.15.4 or risk judgment in default if Pt 12 allows it (r.15.3). If the claimant also wishes to serve a reply see para. 15.8.3 below. 15.7.2

Reply to defence

15.8 If a claimant files a reply to the defence, he must— 15.8

(a) file his reply when he files his allocation questionnaire; and

(b) serve his reply on the other parties at the same time as he files it.

(Rule 26.3(6) requires the parties to file allocation questionnaires and specifies the period for doing so.)

(Part 22 requires a reply to be verified by a statement of truth.)

"If a claimant files a reply"—Rule 15.8 makes clear that a reply is optional. A claimant need not serve a reply unless he wishes to allege facts in answer to the defence which were not included in his claim. See further as to the contents of a reply r.16.7 and the commentary thereto. 15.8.1

Time for reply—The claimant must file a reply "when he files his allocation questionnaire". The allocation questionnaire is served by the court pursuant to r.26.3. It states on it the date by which it is to be returned which will be "at least 14 days after the date when it is deemed to be served" (r.26.3(6)). 15.8.2

Rule 15.8(b)—unlike r.15.6—expressly states who is to serve the reply: *i.e.* the claimant not the court.

Serving a reply and defence to counterclaim—Practice Directions state that "the reply and defence to counterclaim should normally form one document with the defence to counterclaim following on from the reply" (Practice Direction supplementing Pt 15, para. 3.2 (see para. 15PD–001) and Practice Direction supplementing Pt 20, para. 6.2 (see para. 20PD–001)). 15.8.3

Reply served by defendant—A counterclaim is treated for certain purposes as if it were a 15.8.4

claim (r.20.3). Thus, in receipt of defence to counterclaim the defendant may serve a reply if he wishes to allege facts in answer to the defence to counterclaim which were not included in his counterclaim. See further as to the contents of a reply, r.16.7 and the commentary thereto.

No statement of case after a reply to be filed without court's permission

15.9 **15.9** A party may not file or serve any statement of case after a reply without the permission of the court.

15.9.1 **Effect of rule**—No party has a right to file or serve a statement of case subsequent to a reply. This rule acknowledges that the court may permit such a step but such permission will be appropriate only in the most exceptional circumstances. Instead of permitting further statements of case, the court is more likely to permit amendments to earlier statements of case.

For a case illustration under the previous rules in which parties were permitted to serve pleading subsequent to a reply see *Tito v. Waddell (No. 2)* [1977] Ch. 106; [1977] 3 All E.R. 129.

Claimant's notice where defence is that money claimed has been paid

15.10 **15.10**—(1) Where—

(a) the only claim (apart from a claim for costs and interest) is for a specified amount of money; and

(b) the defendant states in his defence that he has paid to the claimant the amount claimed,

the court will send notice to the claimant requiring him to state in writing whether he wishes the proceedings to continue.

(2) When the claimant responds, he must serve a copy of his response on the defendant.

(3) If the claimant fails to respond under this rule within 28 days after service of the court's notice on him the claim shall be stayed[GL].

(4) Where a claim is stayed under this rule any party may apply for the stay[GL] to be lifted.

(If the claimant files notice under this rule that he wishes the proceedings to continue, the procedure which then follows is set out in Part 26.)

15.10.1 **Effect of rule**—Rule 15.10 had no equivalent in the RSC and is based on the so-called "states paid" defence previously covered by CCR, O.9, r.2(7). The new rule is an improved version of the old and will be easier to apply.

15.10.2 **"specified sum of money"**—In respect of all money claims, whether debt or damages, the claimant may if he wishes, put a precise figure on the amount of his claim: see further para. 12.4.3 above.

15.10.3 **States paid**—The rule is intended to provide a simple procedure where the defendant has in fact paid the debt before receiving the claim form. When the court receives a "states paid" defence it sends a notice to the claimant which, in effect, asks the claimant whether the defence is correct. The claimant must respond within 28 days and the claim is stayed if he does not do so. Whatever his response, the claimant must serve a copy on the defendant. If the claimant does not wish to continue that is the end of the case. If the claimant does wish to continue (because he does not agree that the debt has been paid or because, for example, he still wishes to recover interest and costs) the court will proceed to allocate the case to the appropriate track and give directions pursuant to Pt 26.

Claim stayed if it is not defended or admitted

15.11 **15.11**—(1) Where—

(a) at least 6 months have expired since the end of the period for filing a defence specified in rule 15.4;

(b) no defendant has served or filed an admission or filed a defence or counterclaim; and

(c) the claimant has not entered or applied for judgment under Part 12 (default judgment), or Part 24 (summary judgment), the claim shall be stayed[GL].

(2) Where a claim is stayed[GL] under this rule any party may apply for the stay to be lifted.

Effect of rule—This rule imposes an automatic stay after 6 months if the defendant fails to file an admission, defence or counterclaim and the claimant has not sought default judgment or summary judgment. **15.11.1**

There was no equivalent rule in the RSC and the rule caters for the same situation previously covered by CCR, O.9, r.10. However, under CCR, O.9, r.10 the relevant period was 12 months (now reduced to 6 months) and the action was automatically struck out (not stayed).

Any party can apply for the stay to be lifted.

PRACTICE DIRECTION—DEFENCE AND REPLY

This Practice Direction supplements CPR Part 15

Defending the claim

1.1 The provisions of Part 15 do not apply to claims in respect of which the Part 8 procedure is being used. **15PD–001**

1.2 In relation to specialist proceedings (see CPR Part 49) in respect of which special provisions for defence and reply are made by the rules and practice directions applicable to those claims, the provisions of Part 15 apply only to the extent that they are not inconsistent with those rules and practice directions.

1.3 Form N9B (specified amount) or N9D (unspecified amount or non-money claims) may be used for the purpose of defence and is included in the response pack served on the defendant with the particulars of claim.

1.4 Attention is drawn to rule 15.3 which sets out a possible consequence of not filing a defence.

(Part 16 (statements of case) and the practice direction which supplements it contain rules and directions about the contents of a defence.)

Statement of Truth

2.1 Part 22 requires a defence to be verified by a statement of truth.

2.2 The form of the statement of truth is as follows:

"[I believe] [the defendant believes] that the facts stated in this defence are true."

2.3 Attention is drawn to rule 32.14 which sets out the consequences of verifying a statement of case containing a false statement without an honest belief in its truth.

(For information about statements of truth see Part 22 and the practice direction which supplements it.)

General

3.1 Where a defendant to a claim serves a counterclaim under Part 20, the defence and counterclaim should normally form one document with the counterclaim following on from the defence.

3.2 Where a claimant serves a reply and a defence to counterclaim, the reply and defence to counterclaim should normally form one document with the defence to counterclaim following on from the reply.

3.3 Where a claim has been stayed under rules 15.10(3) or 15.11(1) any party may apply for the stay to be lifted.[1]

3.4 The application should be made in accordance with Part 23 and should give the reason for the applicant's delay in proceeding with or responding to the claim.

[1] Rules 15.10(4) and 15.11(2).

PART 16

STATEMENTS OF CASE

16.0.1 **Contents**

Editorial introduction

16.0.2 The rules in this part deal with the contents of "statements of case", a term which means "a claim form, particulars of claim where these are not included in the claim form, defence, Part 20 claim or a reply to a defence" (r.2.3(1)). Parts 7, 15 and 20 deal with the filing and serving of these documents and Pt 12 deals with the consequences of failing to file a defence or defence to counterclaim.

The main differences between the previous rules and these rules are:

(1) Statements of case must be verified by a statement of truth.

(2) A defence must provide a comprehensive response to the particulars of claim; a simple denial of an allegation will not suffice.

(3) The defence of tender before action (which has been renamed "tender before claim") is available in response to claims for damages as well as debts.

Part 16 and the Practice Direction supplementing it offers little guidance on drafting statements of case and contain no precedents or specimens. Two specimen forms of particulars of claim are listed in the Practice Direction supplementing Pt 4. Both were in use in the county courts before April 26, 1999; N119 (particulars of claim for possession of rented property) and N120 (particulars of claim for possession of mortgaged property). Useful guidance on drafting statements of case is set out in Appendix 1 of the Chancery Guide (April 1999). Although this Guide applies only to proceedings in the Chancery Division of the High Court much of the guidance as to statements of case will be useful in other divisions of the High Court and in the county courts.

Related sources

16.0.3
- Part 7 (How to start proceedings—the claim form)
- Part 15 (Defence and reply)
- Part 20 (Counterclaims and other additional claims)
- Part 22 (Statements of truth)
- Chancery Guide (April 1999)

Part not to apply where claimant uses Part 8 procedure

16.1 **16.1** This Part does not apply where the claimant uses the procedure set out in Part 8 (alternative procedure for claims).

16.1.1 **Part 8 procedure**—Part 8 provides an alternative procedure for claims which largely reproduces the procedure applicable to cases commenced under the previous rules by originating summons or originating application. Rule 8.2 deals with the contents of the claim form for use in cases under the alternative procedure and there is no requirement for particulars of claim, defences or replies in such cases.

16.1.2 **Part 20 claims**—Counterclaims, third party proceedings and other similar claims are referred to collectively in these rules as "Part 20 claims" (see r.20.2). Part 16 applies to Pt 20 claims as if they were claims. A Pt 20 claim is a statement of case (r.2.3). The person on whom it is served must file a defence (see r.15.2 and r.15.6) and the Pt 20 claimant may then serve a reply (r.15.8).

16.1.3 **Specialist proceedings**—Part 49 and the Practice Direction supplementing it (see para.

49PD–001) deal with various types of specialist proceedings and make some special provisions for statements of case in such proceedings. Part 16 and the Practice Directions supplementing it (see para. 16PD–001) apply to specialist proceedings only to the extent that they are not inconsistent with Pt 49 and the Practice Directions supplementing it (para. 1.2 of the Practice Direction supplementing Pt 16).

Contents of the claim form

16.2—(1) The claim form must— 16.2

(a) contain a concise statement of the nature of the claim;
(b) specify the remedy which the claimant seeks;
(c) where the claimant is making a claim for money, contain a statement of value in accordance with rule 16.3; and
(d) contain such other matters as may be set out in a practice direction.

(2) If the particulars of claim specified in rule 16.4 are not contained in, or are not served with the claim form, the claimant must state on the claim form that the particulars of claim will follow.

(3) If the claimant is claiming in a representative capacity, the claim form must state what that capacity is.

(4) If the defendant is sued in a representative capacity, the claim form must state what that capacity is.

(5) The court may grant any remedy to which the claimant is entitled even if that remedy is not specified in the claim form.

(Part 22 requires a claim form to be verified by a statement of truth.)

"a concise statement of the nature of the claim"—This phrase is derived from the description of an indorsement on a writ under the previous rules. Such indorsements, formerly called general indorsements, will often provide useful precedents. 16.2.1

"specify the remedy which the claimant seeks"—In respect of money claims (whether debt or damages) the claimant may, if he wishes, put a precise figure on the amount of his claim. If he does so the claimant, even a claimant in a personal injury claim, may later obtain a default judgment for that sum, plus costs and interest, if the defendant does not respond (see Pt 12 and the commentary thereto and in particular para. 12.4.3). Another consequence of specifying the amount claimed in a damages claim is that, if no other remedies are claimed and if the defendant responds, the rules for automatic transfer to the defendant's home court will apply (see r.26.2). 16.2.2

The court may grant any remedy to which the claimant is entitled even if that remedy is not specified in the claim form (r.16.2(5)).

"a statement of value in accordance with rule 16.3"—See the commentary to r.16.3. 16.2.3

"such other matters as may be set out in a practice direction"—Examples are the indorsement which is required in certain cases where a claim is to be served out of the jurisdiction (see Practice Direction supplementing Pt 7, para. 3.5 (para. 7PD–001)) and the statement which is required where a claim is for a sum of money expressed in a foreign currency (see Practice Direction supplementing Pt 16, para. 12.1 (para. 16PD–001)). 16.2.4

Particulars of claim—As to the content of the particulars of claim, see r.16.4 and the commentary thereto. The particulars of claim must be contained in or served with the claim form or served within 14 days after service of the claim form, or within the time allowed for service of the claim form, if less (r.7.4). Where the particulars of claim are served separately the claim form must state that the particulars of claim will follow (r.16.2(2) and see further, para. 3.2 of the Practice Direction supplementing Pt 16 (para. 16PD–001)) and when served, a copy must be filed together with a certificate of service (r.7.4(3)). 16.2.5

The Practice Direction supplementing Pt 16 states that, if practicable, the particulars of claim should be set out in the claim form (see para. 3.1). The time limits for filing an acknowledgment of service and a defence both run from the date of service of the particulars of claim, not the claim form (see r.10.3 and r.15.4 respectively). It therefore follows that a claimant cannot obtain a default judgment before serving his particulars of claim (see r.12.3).

"a representative capacity"—If the claimant is claiming in, or the defendant is being sued in, a representative capacity, the claim form must state what that capacity is (r.16.2(3) and (4)). Under RSC, O.15, r.12 representative proceedings are appropriate where the persons to be represented were numerous and where they and the person representing them have the same interest in the proceedings (see further R15.12). 16.2.6

16.2.7 **Statement of truth**—A claim form must be verified by a statement of truth (r.22.1) in the following form "[I believe] [the claimant believes] that the facts stated in this claim form are true" (para. 6.2 of the Practice Direction supplementing Pt 7 (see para. 7PD–001)). If the statement of truth is contained in a separate document, it should specify the date on which the claim form was issued (para. 2.3 of the Practice Direction supplementing Pt 22 (see para. 22PD–001)).

The statement of truth must be signed by the claimant or his legal representative (para. 3.1 of the Practice Direction supplementing Pt 22, para. 3.1; and the subsequent paras also make provision for signing where the claimant is a child, a patient or a company or other corporation and where the claim form is issued on behalf of a partnership).

A claim form verified by a statement of truth may be used as evidence by the claimant at any hearing other than the trial (r.32.6).

As to the significance of a statement of truth signed by a legal representative, see para. 3.8 of the Practice Direction supplementing Pt 22. As to the consequence of verifying a claim form containing a false statement without an honest behalf in its truth, see r.32.14.

The court may strike out a claim form which is not verified by a statement of truth (r.22.2(2)).

16.2.8 **Supply of documents from court records**—Rule 5.4 entitles members of the public to inspect and take a copy of any claim form which has been served in High Court proceedings (but not in county court proceedings, see r.5.4(4) and the Practice Direction supplementing Pt 5 (para. 4.5, see 5PD–001)). Rule 5.4 appears also to apply to particulars of claim stapled or otherwise attached to a claim form. However, r.5.4(2)(c) prevents inspection of particulars of claim filed in court which were served separately from a claim form unless the court grants permission.

Statement of value to be included in the claim form

16.3 **16.3**—(1) This rule applies where the claimant is making a claim for money.

(2) The claimant must, in the claim form, state—
- (a) the amount of money which he is claiming;
- (b) that he expects to recover—
  - (i) not more than £5,000;
  - (ii) more than £5,000 but not more than £15,000; or
  - (iii) more than £15,000; or
- (c) that he cannot say how much he expects to recover.

(3) In a claim for personal injuries, the claimant must also state in the claim form whether the amount which he expects to recover as general damages for pain, suffering and loss of amenity is—
- (a) not more than £1,000; or
- (b) more than £1,000.

(4) In a claim which includes a claim by a tenant of residential premises against his landlord where the tenant is seeking an order requiring the landlord to carry out repairs or other work to the premises, the claimant must also state in the claim form—
- (a) whether the estimated costs of those repairs or other work is—
  - (i) not more than £1,000; or
  - (ii) more than £1,000; and
- (b) whether the financial value of any other claim for damages is—
  - (i) not more than £1,000; or
  - (ii) more than £1,000.

(5) If the claim form is to be issued in the High Court it must, where this rule applies—
- (a) state that the claimant expects to recover more than £15,000;
- (b) state that some other enactment provides that the claim may be commenced only in the High Court and specify that enactment;
- (c) if the claim is a claim for personal injuries state that the claimant expects to recover £50,000 or more; or
- (d) state that the claim is to be in one of the specialist High Court lists and state which list.

(6) When calculating how much he expects to recover, the claimant must disregard any possibility—
- (a) that he may recover—

(i) interest;
(ii) costs;
(b) that the court may make a finding of contributory negligence against him;
(c) that the defendant may make a counterclaim or that the defence may include a set-off; or
(d) that the defendant may be liable to pay an amount of money which the court awards to the claimant to the Secretary of State for Social Security under section 6 of the Social Security (Recovery of Benefits) Act 1997.[1]

(7) The statement of value in the claim form does not limit the power of the court to give judgment for the amount which it finds the claimant is entitled to.

Effect of rule—A statement of value must be included in the claim form if the claimant is making a claim for money. The statement may prevent the claim form being issued in the High Court (see r.16.3(5) and the Practice Direction supplementing Pt 7, paras 2.1 to 2.9 (see para. 7PD–001)). The statement will be considered by the court before the case is allocated to a case management track (see Pt 26 and the commentary thereto). The statement of value does not limit the amount the court may later award (r.16.3(7)). **16.3.1**

Matters to be disregarded in calculation of value—Rule 16.3(6) states that in calculating how much he expects to recover the claimant must disregard the following matters: **16.3.2**
(1) claims for interest
(2) claims for costs
(3) any defence of contributory negligence which may be raised against him
(4) any set off or counterclaim which may be made against him
(5) the value of any state benefits received which the defendant may be liable to pay under the Social Security (Recovery of Benefits) Act 1997.

Money claim expressed in a foreign currency—Where a claim is for a sum of money expressed in a foreign currency the claim form must expressly state a variety of matters including the Sterling equivalent of the sum at the date of the claim and the source of the exchange rate relied on to calculate the Sterling equivalent (para. 11.1 of the Practice Direction supplementing Pt 16 (see para. 16PD–001)). **16.3.3**

Contents of the particulars of claim

16.4—(1) Particulars of claim must include— **16.4**
(a) a concise statement of the facts on which the claimant relies;
(b) if the claimant is seeking interest, a statement to that effect and the details set out in paragraph (2);
(c) if the claimant is seeking aggravated damages[GL] or exemplary damages[GL], a statement to that effect and his grounds for claiming them;
(d) if the claimant is seeking provisional damages, a statement to that effect and his grounds for claiming them; and
(e) such other matters as may be set out in a practice direction.

(2) If the claimant is seeking interest he must—
(a) state whether he is doing so—
(i) under the terms of a contract;
(ii) under an enactment and if so which; or
(iii) on some other basis and if so what that basis is; and
(b) if the claim is for a specified amount of money, state—
(i) the percentage rate at which interest is claimed;
(ii) the date from which it is claimed;
(iii) the date to which it is calculated, which must not be later than the date on which the claim form is issued;
(iv) the total amount of interest claimed to the date of calculation; and

[1] 1997 c. 27.

(v) the daily rate at which interest accrues after that date.

(Part 22 requires particulars of claim to be verified by a statement of truth.)

16.4.1 **"concise statement of facts"**—The primary function of the particulars of claim is to state concisely the facts on which the claimant relies (*cf.* the claim form which should contain a concise statement of the nature of the claim, see r.16.2(1)(a)). The claimant should state all the facts necessary for the purpose of formulating a complete cause of action. A claimant may also:

(1) refer in his particulars of claim to any point of law on which his claim is based;
(2) give in his particulars of claim the name of any witness whom he proposes to call; and
(3) attach to or serve with the particulars of claim a copy of any document which he considers is necessary to his claim (including any expert's report to be filed in accordance with Pt 35) (para. 16.3 of the Practice Direction supplementing Pt 16).

16.4.2 **"if the claimant is seeking interest"**—If the claimant is seeking interest, the particulars of claim must contain a statement to that effect and details as to the basis on which the right to interest is said to arise. If the interest is claimed in respect of a specified amount of money the particulars of claim must also include various details such as the percentage rate at which interest is claimed (r.16.(1)(b) and (2)).

16.4.3 **"aggravated damages ... exemplary damages ... provisional damages"**—The terms "aggravated damages" and "exemplary damages" are defined in the Glossary. As to provisional damages, see Pt 41 and the commentary thereto.

16.4.4 **"such other matters as may be set out in a practice direction"**—Paragraphs 4 to 8 of the Practice Direction supplementing Pt 16 set out lengthy details of matters which must be included in the particulars of claim in the following types of claim:

(1) Personal injury claims
(2) Fatal accident claims
(3) Recovery of land claims
(4) Mortgage claims
(5) Hire purchase
(6) Defamation claims

Paragraph 9 of the Practice Direction supplementing Pt 16 sets out other matters to be included in particulars of claim in the following circumstances:

(1) where a claim is made for an injunction or declaration in respect of or relating to any land or the possession, occupation, use or enjoyment of any land;
(2) where a claim is brought to enforce a right to recover possession of goods;
(3) where a claim is based upon a written agreement;
(4) where a claim is based upon an oral agreement;
(5) where a claim is based upon an agreement by conduct;
(6) where a claim relating to a Consumer Credit Agreement is issued in the High Court.

Paragraph 10.1 of the Practice Direction supplementing Pt 16 (see para. 16PD–001) states certain matters which must be specifically set out in the particulars of claim if the claimant wishes to rely on evidence under section 11 or 12 of the Civil Evidence Act 1968.

Paragraph 10.2 of the Practice Direction supplementing Pt 16 requires the claimant to specifically set out the following matters in his particulars of claim where he wishes to rely on them in support of his claim:

(1) any allegation of fraud:
(2) the fact of any illegality;
(3) details of any misrepresentation;
(4) details of all breaches of trust;
(5) notice or knowledge of a fact;
(6) details of unsoundness of mind or undue influence;
(7) details of wilful default; and
(8) any facts relating to mitigation of loss or damage.

As to further matters which are specifically required to be set out, see para. 3.8 of the Practice Direction supplementing Pt 16 (16PD–001) (see "Particulars of claim served separately from the claim form" below), the Practice Direction supplementing r.7.9 (Consumer Credit Act claims) at para. 7BPD–001 and the Practice Directions supplementing Pt 49 (Specialist Procedures) at paras 49PD–001 *et seq.*

16.4.5 **Particulars of claim served separately from the claim form**—The Practice Direction supplementing Pt 16 (see para. 16PD–001) states that if practicable, the particulars of claim should be set out in the claim form (para. 3.1). If not so set out they should be served separately with the claim form or alternatively within 14 days after service of the claim form or within four months from the date of issue of the claim form (six months where the claim form is to be served out of the jurisdiction) whichever is the earlier (para. 3.20).

Where particulars of claim are not contained in or served with the claim form, the claimant must, within seven days of service of the particulars on the defendant, file a copy of them together with a certificate of service (r.7.4(3)).

Particulars of claim served separately from the claim form must be verified by a statement of truth (see "Statement of truth" below) and must contain details as to the court in which the claim is proceeding, the claim number, the title of the proceedings and the claimant's address for service (para. 3.8 of the Practice Direction supplementing Pt 16 (see para. 16PD–001)).

Serving particulars of claim separately from the claim form may prevent members of the public inspecting and taking copies of them: see further "supply of documents from court records" under r.16.2 above.

Statement of truth—Particulars of claim which are not included in the claim form must be verified by a statement of truth (r.22.1) in the following form "[I believe] [the claimant believes that the facts stated in these particulars of claim are true" (para. 3.4 of the Practice Direction supplementing Pt 16 (see para. 16PD–001)). If the statement of truth is contained in a separate document it should specify the date on which the particulars of claim were issued (para. 2.3 of the Practice Direction supplementing Pt 22 (see para. 22PD–001)). **16.4.6**

The statement of truth must be signed by the claimant or his legal representative (para. 3.1 of the Practice Direction supplementing Pt 22 (see para. 22PD–001); para. 3.1 and the subsequent paras also make provision for signing where the claimant is a child, a patient or a company or other corporation and where the particulars of claim are issued on behalf of a partnership).

Particulars of claim verified by a statement of truth may be used as evidence by the claimant at any hearing other than the trial (r.32.6).

As to the significance of a statement of truth signed by a legal representative, see para. 3.8 of the Practice Direction supplementing Pt 22. As to the consequences of verifying particulars of claim containing a false statement of fact without an honest belief in its truth, see r.32.14.

The court may strike out particulars of claim which are not verified by a statement of truth (r.22.2(2)).

Contents of defence

16.5—(1) In his defence, the defendant must state— **16.5**

(a) which of the allegations in the particulars of claim he denies;

(b) which allegations he is unable to admit or deny, but which he requires the claimant to prove; and

(c) which allegations he admits.

(2) Where the defendant denies an allegation—

(a) he must state his reasons for doing so; and

(b) if he intends to put forward a different version of events from that given by the claimant, he must state his own version.

(3) A defendant who—

(a) fails to deal with an allegation; but

(b) has set out in his defence the nature of his case in relation to the issue to which that allegation is relevant;

shall be taken to require that allegation to be proved.

(4) Where the claim includes a money claim, a defendant shall be taken to require that any allegation relating to the amount of money claimed be proved unless he expressly admits the allegation.

(5) Subject to paragraphs (3) and (4), a defendant who fails to deal with an allegation shall be taken to admit that allegation.

(6) If the defendant disputes the claimant's statement of value under rule 16.3 he must—

(a) state why he disputes it; and

(b) if he is able, give his own statement of the value of the claim.

(7) If the defendant is defending in a representative capacity, he must state what that capacity is.

(8) If the defendant has not filed an acknowledgment of service under Part 10, he must give an address for service.

(Part 22 requires a defence to be verified by a statement of truth.)

(Rule 6.5 provides that an address for service must be within the jurisdiction.)

16.5.1 **Contents of defence**—The defence must

(1) provide a comprehensive response to the particulars of claim;
(2) state any representative capacity in which the defendant is defending;
(3) include any other matters required by a practice direction;
(4) unless an acknowledgment of service has been filed, give an address for service.

The defence may also refer to any point of law on which it is based, or name any witnesses whom the defendant proposes to call or have attached to it or served with it a copy of any document considered essential to it (para. 16.3 of the practice direction supplementing Pt 16 (see para. 16PD–001)). There are also some specific requirements as to points of law and documents (see "Other matters required by a practice direction" below).

The defence must be verified by a statement of truth (see "Statement of truth" below).

16.5.2 **Comprehensive response to the particulars of claim**—In respect of each allegation in the particulars of claim there should be an admission, a denial or a requirement for proof (r.16.5(1)). Denials must be explicit; the defendants must state his reasons for denying the allegation and, if he intends to put forward a different version of events from that given by the claimant, he must state his own version (r.16.5(2)). Similarly, if he disputes the statement of value included in the claim form he must state why he disputes it and, if he is able, must give his own statement of the value of the claim (r.16.5(3)).

16.5.3 **Defending in a representative capacity**—If the defendant is defending in a representative capacity, he must state what that capacity is (r.16.5(7)). As to the term "representative capacity" see further the commentary to r.16.2 under the heading "a representative capacity" (para. 16.2.6).

16.5.4 **Other matters required by a practice direction**—Paragraphs 14 to 16 of the Practice Direction supplementing Pt 16 (see para. 16PD–001) set out various matters (including in some cases an obligation to deal with points of law or annex documents) which must be dealt with in the defence in the following circumstances:

(1) where the claim is for personal injuries;
(2) where the claim is for defamation;
(3) where the defendant relies on a limitation period as a defence.

16.5.5 **Give an address for service**—If the defendant has not filed an acknowledgment of service under Pt 10 he must give an address for service (r.16.5(8)). As to addresses for service see r.6.5 and the commentary thereto (para. 6.5.3).

16.5.6 **Defence of tender**—The expression "defence of tender" is defined in the Glossary. The defence may be raised in response to any money claim, whether or not a specified amount is claimed. Where the defendant wishes to rely on this defence he must make a payment into court of the amount he says was tendered (r.37.3).

16.5.7 **Filing a defence and counterclaim**—A defendant who wishes to defend must file a defence (r.15.2) and a copy of it must be served on every other party (r.15.6). A defendant may make a counterclaim against a claimant by filing particulars of the counterclaim (r.20.4). Practice Directions state that "the defence and counterclaim should normally form one document with the counterclaim following on from the defence" (Practice Direction supplementing Pt 15, para 3.1 (see para. 15PD–001) and Practice Direction supplementing Pt 20, para 6.1 (see para. 20PD–001)).

16.5.8 **Consequences of not dealing with an allegation**—In two cases allegations in the particulars of claim which are not expressly dealt with in the defence will be treated as allegations which the claimant is required to prove:

(1) where the allegations are inconsistent with the nature of the case set out in the defence (this appears to be the effect of r.16.5(3)); and
(2) in money claims allegations relating to the amount of money claimed (r.16.5(4)).

Save in those two cases a defendant who fails to deal with an allegation shall be taken to admit that allegation (r.16.5(5)).

16.5.9 **Statement of truth**—A defence must be verified by a statement of truth (r.22.1) in the following form "[I believe] [the defendant believes] that the facts stated in the defence are true" (para. 14.2 of the Practice Direction supplementing Pt 16). If the statement of truth is contained in a separate document it should specify the date on which it was served and the name of the party on whom it was served (para. 2.3 of the Practice Direction supplementing Pt 22 (see para. 22PD–001)).

The statement of truth must be signed by the defendant or his legal representative (para. 3.1 of the Practice Direction supplementing Pt 22; para. 3.1 and the subsequent paras also make provision for signing where the defendant is a child, a patient or a company or other corporation and where the defence is served on behalf of a partnership).

A defence verified by a statement of truth may be used as evidence by the defendant at any hearing other than the trial (r.32.6).

As to the significance of a statement of truth signed by a legal representative, see para. 3.8 of the Practice Direction supplementing Pt 22 (para. 22PD–001). As to the consequence of verifying a defence containing a false statement of fact without an honest belief in its truth, see r.32.14.

The court may strike out a defence which is not verified by a statement of truth (r.22.2(2)).

Defence of set-off

16.6 Where a defendant— **16.6**

(a) contends he is entitled to money from the claimant; and

(b) relies on this as a defence to the whole or part of the claim, the contention may be included in the defence and set off against the claim, whether or not it is also a Part 20 claim.

Effect of rule—This rule makes wide provisions for monetary cross-claims "to be included in the defence and set-off against the claim" whether or not the cross-claim is a claim in debt or is inter-related with the claimant's claim. The previous High Court rules contained a provision (RSC, O.18, r.17) which was almost identical to this rule. However, when that provision was in force there was established case law to the effect that the question whether or not a cross-claim amounted to a set-off was a "matter of law" and did not depend upon the form in which it was pleaded. ("The question as to what is a set off is to be determined as a matter of law and is not in any way governed by the language used by the parties in their pleadings" (*per* Morris L.J. in *Hanak v. Green* [1958] 2 Q.B. 9 at 26 and see SCA 1981, s.49(2)(a)). That "matter of law" was both complex and restrictive and from time to time attracted judicial criticism (see for example *Axel Johnson Petroleum AB v. MG Mineral Group AG* [1992] 1 W.L.R. 270, CA). It is possible that the court will take the opportunity which the wide words of r.16.6 allows to define "set-offs" differently in future. Even if the widest possible definition was given, the court would still be able to summarily dispose of issues raised by the claimant's claim which do not need full investigation and trial. In all such cases the defendant's position would have to be protected by an order delaying enforcement of judgment on the claim until after the trial of any cross-claim (see r.24.2, and the commentary thereto and r.24.6 under "Judgment on the claim or on an issue therein"). **16.6.1**

Reply to defence

16.7—(1) A claimant who does not file a reply to the defence shall not be taken to admit the matters raised in the defence. **16.7**

(2) A claimant who—

(a) files a reply to a defence; but

(b) fails to deal with a matter raised in the defence,

shall be taken to require that matter to be proved.

(Part 22 requires a reply to be verified by a statement of truth.)

Where reply necessary—A reply is optional (see r.15.8). A claimant need not serve a reply unless he wishes to allege facts in answer to the defence which were not included in his claim. **16.7.1**

No implied admission of the defence—Unless the claimant makes an express admission, the defendant will be required to prove facts raised in his defence whether the claimant files a reply (r.16.7(2)) or does not file a reply (r.16.7(1)). **16.7.2**

Reply must not contradict the claim—A reply must not contradict or be inconsistent with the claim; for example it must not bring in a new claim. If the claimant wishes to depart from the case set out in his claim he should seek to amend that claim rather than serve a reply (see generally para. 11.2 of the Practice Direction supplementing Pt 16 (para. 16PD–001)). **16.7.2A**

Serving a reply and defence to counterclaim—A claimant who wishes to rely on a reply must file it (r.15.8). A claimant who wishes to defend a counterclaim must file a defence and a copy of it must be served on every other party (see r.15.2, r.15.6 and r.20.2). Practice Directions state for service of a reply by providing that "the reply and defence to counterclaim should normally form one document with the defence to counterclaim following on from the reply" (Practice Direction supplementing Pt 15, para. 3.2 (see para. 15PD–001) and Practice Direction supplementing Pt 20, para. 6.2 (see para. 20PD–001)). **16.7.2B**

16.7.3 **Statement of truth**—A reply must be verified by a statement of truth (r.22.1) in the following form "[I believe] [the claimant believes] that the facts stated in this reply are true" (para. 2.1 of the Practice Direction supplementing Pt 22 (see para. 22PD–001)). If the statement of truth is contained in a separate document it should specify the date on which it was served and the name of the party on whom it was served (para. 2.3).

The statement of truth must be signed by the claimant or his legal representative (para. 3.1 of the Practice Direction supplementing Pt 22; para. 3.1 and the subsequent paras also make provision for signing where the claimant is a child, a patient, or a company or other corporation and where the reply is served on behalf of a partnership.

A reply verified by a statement of truth may be used as evidence by the claimant at any hearing other than the trial (r.32.6).

As to the significance of a statement of truth signed by a legal representative, see para. 3.8 of the Practice Direction supplementing Pt 22. As to the consequences of verifying a reply containing a false statement of fact without an honest belief in its truth, see r.32.14.

The court may strike out a reply which is not verified by a statement of truth (r.22.2(2)).

16.7.4 **Statements of case subsequent to a reply**—No party may file or serve a statement of case after the reply without the court's permission (r.15.9).

Court's power to dispense with statements of case

16.8 **16.8** If a claim form has been—

(a) issued in accordance with rule 7.2; and

(b) served in accordance with rule 7.5,

the court may make an order that the claim will continue without any other statement of case.

(Other rules about the contents of statements of case can be found—

(a) in Schedule 1, in the following RSC—O.77 (proceedings against the Crown); O.82 (defamation claims); O.88 (mortgage claims); O.97 (claims under section 1 of the Landlord and Tenant Act 1927); and

(b) in Schedule 2, in the following CCR—O.6 (recovery of land; mortgage claims; mortgage claims—dwelling house and hire purchase); O.42 (proceedings against the Crown); O.43 (applications under sections 13 or 24 of the Landlord and Tenant Act 1954 and sections 24, 29, 30 or 40 of the Landlord and Tenant Act 1987); O.49 (applications under various statutes).)

16.8.1 **Effect of rule**—This rule gives the court express power to make an order which dispenses with all statements of case other than the claim form. The power is first exercisable once the claim form has been issued and served. On making the order the court may give further directions as to case management including perhaps the allocation of the claim to a particular case management track.

A claim in which there are no statements of case other than the claim form is analogous to the alternative procedure for claims (Pt 8). Where that procedure is followed the claim is treated as allocated to the multi-track (r.8.9(c)).

PRACTICE DIRECTION—STATEMENTS OF CASE

This Practice Direction supplements CPR Part 16

General

16PD–001 **1.1** The provisions of Part 16 do not apply to claims in respect of which the Part 8 procedure is being used.

1.2 In relation to specialist proceedings (see CPR Part 49 in respect of which special provisions for statements of case are made by the rules and practice directions applicable to those claims, the provisions of Part 16 and of this practice direction apply only to the extent that they are not inconsistent with those rules and practice directions.

The claim form

2. Rule 16.2 refers to matters which the claim form must contain. Where the claim is for money, the claim form must also contain the statement of value referred to in rule 16.3.

(For information about how and where a claim may be started see Part 7 and the practice direction which supplements it.)

Particulars of claim

3.1 If practicable, the particulars of claim should be set out in the claim form.

3.2 Where the claimant does not include the particulars of claim in the claim form, particulars of claim may be served separately:

(1) either at the same time as the claim form, or

(2) within 14 days after service of the claim form[2] provided that the service of the particulars of claim is not later than 4 months from the date of issue of the claim form[3] (or 6 months where the claim form is to be served out of the jurisdiction[4]).

3.3 If the particulars of claim are not included in or have not been served with the claim form, the claim form must also contain a statement that particulars of claim will follow.[5]

3.4 Particulars of claim which are not included in the claim form must be verified by a statement of truth, the form of which is as follows:

"[I believe] [the claimant believes] that the facts stated in these particulars of claim are true."

3.5 Attention is drawn to rule 32.14 which sets out the consequences of verifying a statement of case containing a false statement without an honest belief in its truth.

3.6 The full particulars of claim must include:

(1) the matters set out in rule 16.4, and

(2) where appropriate, the matters set out in practice directions relating to specific types of claims.

3.7 Attention is drawn to the provisions of rule 16.4(2) in respect of a claim for interest.

3.8 Particulars of claim served separately from the claim form must also contain:

(1) the name of the court in which the claim is proceeding,

(2) the claim number,

(3) the title of the proceedings, and

(4) the claimant's address for service.

Matters which must be included in the particulars of claim in certain types of claim

Personal injury claims

4.1 The particulars of claim must contain:

(1) the claimant's date of birth and

(2) brief details of the claimant's personal injuries.

4.2 The claimant must attach to his particulars of claim a schedule of details of any past and future expenses and losses which he claims.

4.3 Where the claimant is relying on the evidence of a medical practitioner the claimant must attach to or serve with his particulars of claim a report from a medical practitioner about the personal injuries which he alleges in his claim.

4.4 In a provisional damages claim the claimant must state in his particulars of claim:

[2] See rule 7.4(1)(b).
[3] See rules 7.4(2) and 7.5(2).
[4] See rule 7.5(3).
[5] See rule 16.2(2).

(1) that he is seeking an award of provisional damages under either section 32A of the Supreme Court Act 1981 or section 51 of the County Courts Act 1984,

(2) that there is a chance that at some future time the claimant will develop some serious disease or suffer some serious deterioration in his physical or mental condition and

(3) specify the disease or type of deterioration in respect of which an application may be made at a future date.

(Part 41 and the practice direction which supplements it contain information about awards for provisional damages.)

Fatal Accident claims

16PD–002 **5.1** In a fatal accident claim the claimant must state in his particulars of claim:

(1) that it is brought under Fatal Accidents Act 1976,

(2) the dependants on whose behalf the claim is made,

(3) the date of birth of each dependent, and

(4) details of the nature of the dependency claim.

5.2 A fatal accident claim may include a claim for damages for bereavement.

5.3 In a fatal accident claim the claimant may also bring a claim under the Law Reform (Miscellaneous Provisions) Act 1934 on behalf of the estate of the deceased.

(For information on apportionment under the Law Reform (Miscellaneous Provisions) Act 1934 and the Fatal Accidents Act 1976 or between dependants see Part 37 and the practice direction which supplements it.)

Recovery of land

6. In a claim for recovery of land the particulars of claim must:

(1) identify the land sought to be recovered,

(2) state whether the claim relates to residential premises,

(3) if the claim relates to residential premises, and the tenancy is one which otherwise would be a protected tenancy within the meaning of the Rent Act 1977, state whether the rateable value of the premises on every day specified by section 4(2) of the Rent Act 1977 in relation to the premises exceeds the sum so specified or whether the rent for the time being payable in respect of the premises exceeds the sum specified in section 4(4)(b) of the Act,

(4) where the claim relates to residential premises and is for non-payment of rent, state

- (a) the amount due at the start of the proceedings,
- (b) details of all payments which have been missed,
- (c) details of any history of late or under-payment,
- (d) any previous steps taken to recover the arrears of rent with full details of any court proceedings, and
- (e) any relevant information about the defendant's circumstances, in particular whether any payments are made on his behalf directly to the claimant under the Social Security Contributions and Benefits Act 1992,

(5) give details about the agreement or tenancy, if any, under which the land was held, stating when it determined and the amount of money payable by way of rent or licence fee,

(6) in a case to which section 138 of the County Courts Act 1984 applies (forfeiture for non-payment of rent), state the daily rate at which the rent in arrear is to be calculated,

(7) state the ground on which possession is claimed whether statutory or otherwise, and

(8) in a case where the claimant knows of any person entitled to claim relief

against forfeiture as underlessee (including a mortgagee) under section 146(4) of the Law of Property Act 1925 (or in accordance with section 38 of the Supreme Court Act 1981), give the name and address of that person.

(See also further rules about recovery of land in RSC, Orders 88 and 113 (Schedule 1 to the CPR) and CCR, Orders 6 and 24 (Schedule 2 to the CPR)

Hire Purchase Claims

7.1 Where the claim is for the delivery of goods let under a hire-purchase agreement or conditional sale agreement to a person other than a company or other corporation, the claimant must state in the particulars of claim: **16PD–003**

(1) the date of the agreement,

(2) the parties to the agreement,

(3) the number or other identification of the agreement,

(4) where the claimant was not one of the original parties to the agreement, the means by which the rights and duties of the creditor passed to him,

(5) whether the agreement is a regulated agreement, and if it is not a regulated agreement, the reason why,

(6) the place where the agreement was signed by the defendant,

(7) the goods claimed,

(8) the total price of the goods,

(9) the paid-up sum,

(10) the unpaid balance of the total price,

(11) whether a default notice or a notice under section 76(1) or 98(1) of the Consumer Credit Act 1974 has been served on the defendant, and if it has, the date and method of service,

(12) the date when the right to demand delivery of the goods accrued,

(13) the amount (if any) claimed as an alternative to the delivery of goods, and

(14) the amount (if any) claimed in addition to

(a) the delivery of the goods, or

(b) any claim under (13) above

with the grounds of each claim.

(If the agreement is a regulated agreement the procedure set out in the practice direction relating to consumer credit claims (which supplements Pt 7) should be used.)

7.2 Where the claim is not for the delivery of goods, the claimant must state in his particulars of claim:

(1) the matters set out in paragraph 7.1(1) to (6) above,

(2) the goods let under the agreement,

(3) the amount of the total price,

(4) the paid-up sum,

(5) the amount (if any) claimed as being due and unpaid in respect of any instalment or instalments of the total price and

(6) the nature and amount of any other claim and how it arises.

Defamation

8.1 If the claim form starting a claim:

(1) for libel does not include or have served with it the full particulars of claim, at least sufficient detail must be given of the publications which are the subject of the claim to enable them to be identified, and

(2) for slander does not include or have served with it the full particulars of claim, at least sufficient detail must be given of the words complained of, including to whom they were spoken and when, to enable them to be identified.

8.2 Where in a claim for libel or slander the claimant alleges that the words or matters complained of were used in a defamatory sense other than their ordinary meaning, the particulars of claim must describe that defamatory sense.

8.3 Where a defendant to a claim for libel or slander alleges that the words complained of are true, or are fair comment on a matter of public interest, or similar, the claimant must serve a reply specifically admitting or denying the allegation and giving the facts on which he relies, unless they are set out elsewhere.

8.4 In a claim for libel or slander the claimant need not set out specific details of malice in his particulars of claim. However if the defendant contends that any of the words or matters:

(1) are fair comment on a matter of public interest, or

(2) were published on a privileged occasion

and the claimant intends to allege that the defendant acted with express malice, the claimant must serve a reply giving details of the facts or matters relied on.

8.5 A claimant must give full details of the facts and matters on which he relies in support of his claim for damages and of any conduct of the defendant which the claimant alleges has increased the loss suffered (and see rule 16.4(1)(c) in respect of aggravated or exemplary damages).

8.6 In a claim for slander the precise words used and the names of the persons to whom they were spoken must be set out in the particulars of claim.

8.7 RSC, Order 82 (Schedule 1 to the CPR) contains additional requirements relating to defamation claims.

Other matters to be included in particulars of claim

16PD–004 **9.1** Where a claim is made for an injunction or declaration in respect of or relating to any land or the possession, occupation, use or enjoyment of any land the particulars of claim must:

(1) state whether or not the injunction or declaration relates to residential premises, and

(2) identify the land (by reference to a plan where necessary).

9.2 Where a claim is brought to enforce a right to recover possession of goods the particulars of claim must contain a statement showing the value of the goods.

9.3 Where a claim is based upon a written agreement:

(1) a copy of the contract or documents constituting the agreement should be attached to or served with the particulars of claim and the original(s) should be available at the hearing, and

(2) any general conditions of sale incorporated in the contract should also be attached (but where the contract is or the documents constituting the agreement are bulky this practice direction is complied with by attaching or serving only the relevant parts of the contract or documents).

9.4 Where a claim is based upon an oral agreement, the particulars of claim should set out the contractual words used and state by whom, to whom, when and where they were spoken.

9.5 Where a claim is based upon an agreement by conduct, the particulars of claim must specify the conduct relied on and state by whom, when and where the acts constituting the conduct were done.

9.6 In a claim issued in the High Court relating to a Consumer Credit Agreement, the particulars of claim must contain a statement that the action is not one to which section 141 of the Consumer Credit Act 1974 applies.

Matters which must be specifically set out in the particulars of claim if relied on

10.1 A claimant who wishes to rely on evidence:

(1) under section 11 of the Civil Evidence Act 1968 of a conviction of an offence, or

(2) under section 12 of the above mentioned Act of a finding or adjudication of adultery or paternity,
must include in his particulars of claim a statement to that effect and give the following details:
(1) the type of conviction, finding or adjudication and its date,
(2) the court or Court-Martial which made the conviction, finding or adjudication, and
(3) the issue in the claim to which it relates.

10.2 The claimant must specifically set out the following matters in his particulars of claim where he wishes to rely on them in support of his claim:
(1) any allegation of fraud,
(2) the fact of any illegality,
(3) details of any misrepresentation,
(4) details of all breaches of trust,
(5) notice or knowledge of a fact,
(6) details of unsoundness of mind or undue influence,
(7) details of wilful default, and
(8) any facts relating to mitigation of loss or damage.

General

11.1 Where a claim is for a sum of money expressed in a foreign currency it must expressly state:
(1) that the claim is for payment in a specified foreign currency,
(2) why it is for payment in that currency,
(3) the Sterling equivalent of the sum at the date of the claim, and
(4) the source of the exchange rate relied on to calculate the Sterling equivalent.

11.2 A subsequent statement of case must not contradict or be inconsistent with an earlier one; for example a reply to a defence must not bring in a new claim. Where new matters have come to light the appropriate course may be to seek the court's permission to amend the statement of case.

The defence

General

12.1 Rule 16.5 deals with the contents of the defence. **16PD–005**
12.2 A defendant should deal with every allegation in accordance with rule 16.5(1) and (2).
12.3 Rule 16.5(3), (4) and (5) sets out the consequences of not dealing with an allegation.

Statement of truth

13.1 Part 22 requires a defence to be verified by a statement of truth.
13.2 The form of the statement of truth is as follows:
"[I believe] [the defendant believes] that the facts stated in the defence are true."
13.3 Attention is drawn to rule 32.14 which sets out the consequences of verifying a statement of case containing a false statement without an honest belief in its truth.

Matters which must be included in the defence

Personal injury claims

14.1 Where the claim is for personal injuries and the claimant has attached a medical report in respect of his alleged injuries, the defendant should:
(1) state in his defence whether he
(a) agrees

(b) disputes or
(c) neither agrees nor disputes but has no knowledge of, the matters contained in the medical report,

(2) where he disputes any part of the medical report, give in his defence his reasons for doing so, and

(3) where he has obtained his own medical report on which he intends to rely, attach it to his defence.

14.2 Where the claim is for personal injuries and the claimant has included a schedule of past and future expenses and losses, the defendant should include in or attach to his defence a counter-schedule stating:

(1) which of those items he
(a) agrees
(b) disputes, or
(c) neither agrees nor disputes but has no knowledge of, and

(2) where any items are disputed, supplying alternative figures where appropriate.

Defamation

15. Where in a claim for libel or slander a defendant alleges that the words complained of are true or are fair comment on a matter of public interest he must give specific details in support of that allegation. RSC, Order 82 (Schedule 1 to the CPR) contains requirements relating to defamation claims.

Other matters

16.1 The defendant must give details of the expiry of any relevant limitation period relied on.

16.2 Rule 37.3 and paragraph 2 of the practice direction which supplements Part 37 contains information about a defence of tender.

16.3 A party may:

(1) refer in his statement of case to any point of law on which his claim or defence, as the case may be, is based,

(2) give in his statement of case the name of any witness he proposes to call, and

(3) attach to or serve with this statement of case a copy of any document which he considers is necessary to his claim or defence, as the case may be (including any expert's report to be filed in accordance with Part 35).

PART 17

AMENDMENTS TO STATEMENTS OF CASE

Contents 17.0.1

Editorial Introduction

The rules in this Part deal with amendments to "statements of case", a term which means "a claim form, particulars of claim where these are not included in the claim form, defence, Part 20 claim or a reply to a defence" (r.2.3(1)). 17.0.2

The main differences between the previous rules and these rules are:

(1) The wide latitude parties previously enjoyed concerning the amendment of pleadings without leave has not been applied to the amendment of statements of case (the successors to pleadings under the new rules). It is well to bear in mind the increased attention the court now gives to statements of case at an early stage of the proceedings in order to allocate them to the appropriate case management track (see Pt 26 and the commentary thereto).

(2) Whilst still permitting parties to prepare amendments by the traditional method employing colour coding to distinguish between successive amendments, the new rules also allow the parties to:

(a) omit superseded text unless the court otherwise orders;

(b) adopt the method first introduced in 1992 in the Commercial Court. When this method is used, amended and re-amended documents can be printed and photocopied in monochrome whilst still distinguishing between successive amendments.

Related Sources

- Practice Direction (Amendments to Statements of Case) (see para. 17PD–001) 17.0.3
- Part 19 (Addition and substitution of parties)
- Part 23 (General rules about applications for court orders)

Amendments to statements of case

17.1—(1) A party may amend his statement of case at any time before it has been served on any other party. 17.1

(2) If his statement case has been served, a party may amend it only—

(a) with the written consent of all the other parties; or

(b) with the permission of the court

(Part 19 also applies where the amendment relates to the addition, substitution or removal of a party.)

(Part 22 requires amendments to a statement of case to be verified by a statement of truth unless the court orders otherwise.)

Effect of rule—Once a party has served his statement of case he cannot amend it unless: 17.1.1

(1) all other parties give written consent, or

(2) the court gives permission.

Accordingly the right to amend without consent or permission arises only in respect of statements of case which are filed but not served. Even in those cases permission is required if the amendment involves adding, substituting or removing a party (see r.19.1 and r.19.3).

17.1.2 **Practice on amendment**—A party amending his statement of case is not required to retain the superseded text in the amended document unless the court directs him to do so. If the superseded text is included it should be shown either:

(1) struck through in the appropriate colour: new text should be inserted or underlined in the same colour (see Practice Direction supplementing Pt 17, para. 2.3 (para. 17PD–001): the order of colours is, as previously, red, green, violet and then yellow),

(2) printed in monochrome document in a different type-face from the new text: the document must include a numerical code defining the different typefaces (see Practice Direction supplementing Pt 17, para. 2.2 (see para. 17PD–001), and see further the method used for amendments in the Commercial Court, Commercial Court Guide (5th ed.)).

A statement of case amended without permission must be endorsed as follows "Amended [Particulars of Claim *or as may be*] under CPR [' 17.1(1)(c) or (2)(a)] dated ..." and should be filed as well as served.

A statement of case amended by order must be endorsed as follows "Amended [Particulars of Claim *or as may be*] by Order of [Master ...] [District Judge ... *or as may be*] dated ..." and should be filed within 14 days of the date of the order or within such other period as the court may direct (Practice Direction supplementing Pt 17, paras 1.3 and 2.1 (see para. 17PD–001).

If the substance of the statement of case is changed by reason of the amendment, the statement of case should be re-verified by a statement of truth (Practice Direction supplementing Pt 17, para. 1.4 which, strictly, applies only to amendments by permission). The court may strike out a statement of case which is not verified by a statement of truth (r.22.2).

Power of court to disallow amendments made without permission

17.2 **17.2**—(1) If a party has amended his statement of case where permission of the court was not required, the court may disallow the amendment.

(2) A party may apply to the court for an order under paragraph (1) within 14 days of service of a copy of the amended statement of case on him.

17.2.1 **Effect of rule**—An application under this rule is appropriate if the amendment challenged is one which, if permission to amend it had been necessary, that permission would not have been granted. The clearest examples of such amendments are those which are scurrilous, vexatious or shown to be dishonest. In such cases an application might also be made under r.3.4 (Power to strike out a statement of case) or Pt 24 (summary judgment).

If an amendment is irregular, *i.e.* made without permission where permission was necessary, a party wishing to challenge it should apply under r.3.4 (Power to strike out a statement of case).

17.2.2 **Time limit for application**—A party wishing to apply under r.17.2 should do so within 14 days of service of a copy of the amended statement of case (r.17.2(2)).

Amendments to the statements of case with the permission of the court

17.3 **17.3**—(1) Where the court gives permission for a party to amend his statement of case, it may give directions as to—

(a) amendments to be made to any other statement of case; and

(b) service of any amended statement of case

(2) The power of the court to give permission under this rule is subject to—

(a) rule 19.1 (change of parties—general);

(b) rule 19.4 (special provisions about adding or substituting parties after the end of a relevant limitation period[GL]); or

(c) rule 17.4 (amendments of statement of case after the end of a relevant limitation period).

17.3.1 **When permission needed**—Once it has been served, a statement of case can be validly amended only with permission unless the amendment is made with the written consent of all the other parties (r.17.1). Even before service, a statement of case which has been filed cannot be amended without permission if the amendment involves adding, substituting or removing a party (r.19.1 and r.19.3).

For limits on the court's power to allow amendments after the end of a relevant limitation period, see r.17.4.

17.3.2 **Procedure on application**—On an application under r.17.3 a copy of the statement of case should be filed with the application notice (as to which, see r.23.6 and the Practice Direction supplementing Pt 23, para. 2.1 (para. 23PD–001)). If the application is made at an early stage of the proceedings it may be appropriate to request the court to deal with it without a hearing (r.23.8 and see the Practice Direction supplementing Pt 23, para. 2.1).

If the court gives permission to amend it may give directions as to consequential amendments to other statements of case and as to the service of the amended statement of case (r.17.3(1)). Unless the court otherwise orders the applicant should file the amended statement of case within 14 days of the order and must serve a copy of the order and the amended statement of case on every other party to the proceedings (Practice Direction supplementing Pt 17, paras 1.3 and 1.5 (see para. 17PD–001)).

Practice on amendment—See this heading under r.17.1. 17.3.3

Effect of amendment—Under the previous rules, an amendment duly made, with or without leave, took effect, not from the date when the amendment was made, but from the date of the original document which it amended. This rule applied to every successive amendment of whatever nature and at whatever stage the amendment was made. Thus, when an amendment was made to the writ, the amendment dated back to the date of the original issue of the writ and the action continued as if the amendment had been inserted from the beginning: "the writ as amended becomes the origin of the action, and the claim thereon endorsed is substituted for the claim originally endorsed" (*per* Collins M.R. in *Sneade v. Wotherton, etc.* [1904] 1 K.B. 295 at 297). Similarly in the pleadings: "once pleadings are amended, what stood before amendment is no longer material before the court and no longer defines the issues to be tried" (*per* Hodson L.J. in *Warner v. Sampson* [1959] 1 Q.B. 297 at 321). The fact that a pleading had been amended could sometimes affect the orders for costs which the court would make at trial: "As a general rule, where a plaintiff makes a late amendment, as here, which substantially alters the case the defendant has to meet and without which the action will fail, the defendant is entitled to the cost of the action down to the date of the amendment" (*per* Stuart-Smith L.J. in *Beoco Ltd v. Alfa Laval Co. Ltd* [1995] Q.B. 137). It is likely that the same principles will be applied under these rules. 17.3.4

General principles for grant of permission to amend—Under the previous rules the court would refuse permission to amend only in exceptional cases where an amendment could not be made without doing injustice to the other party: "it is a well established principle that the object of the court is to decide the rights of the parties, and not to punish them for mistakes they make in the conduct of their cases by deciding otherwise than in accordance with their rights . . . I know of no kind of error or mistake which, if not fraudulent or intended to overreach, the court ought not to correct, if it can be done without injustice to the other party. Courts do not exist for the sake of discipline, but for the sake of deciding matters in controversy, and I do not regard such amendment as a matter of favour or grace . . . it seems to me that as soon as it appears that the way in which a party has framed his case will not lead to a decision of the real matter in controversy, it is as much a matter of right on his part to have it corrected if it can be done without injustice, as anything else in the case is a matter of right" (*per* Bowen L.J. in *Cropper v. Smith* (1884) 26 Ch.D. 700 at 710–711) "however negligent or careless may have been the first omission, and however late the proposed amendment, the amendment should be allowed if it can be made without injustice to the other side. There is no injustice if the other side can be compensated by costs" (*per* Brett M.R. in *Clarapede v. Commercial Union Association* (1883) 32 W.R. 262 at 263). Under the new rules the court must apply the overriding objective which "includes, so far as is practicable (*e*) allotting to [the case] an appropriate share of the court's resources, while taking into account the need to allot resources to other cases" (s.1.1(2)). Amendments can cause waste, the repetition of work, delay and the adjournment of existing appointments. The obligation of the court to have regard to the effect the amendment, if allowed, would have on the court's resources and on other cases before the court may lead the court to grant permission to amend in fewer cases than it did previously. 17.3.5

Amendments to statements of case after the end of a relevant limitation period

17.4—(1) This rule applies where— 17.4

(a) a party applies to amend his statement of case in one of the ways mentioned in this rule; and

(b) a period of limitation has expired under—

(i) the Limitation Act 1980[1];

(ii) the Foreign Limitation Periods Act 1984[2];

(iii) section 190 of the Merchant Shipping Act 1995[3]; or

(iv) any other statutory provision.

[1] 1980 c. 58.
[2] 1984 c. 16.
[3] 1995 c. 21.

(2) The court may allow an amendment whose effect will be to add or substitute a new claim, but only if the new claim arises out of the same facts or substantially the same facts as a claim in respect of which the party applying for permission has already claimed a remedy in the proceedings.

(3) The court may allow an amendment to correct a mistake as to the name of a party, but only where the mistake was genuine and not one which would cause reasonable doubt as to the identity of the party in question.

(4) The court may allow an amendment to alter the capacity in which a party claims if the new capacity is one which that party had when the proceedings started or has since acquired.

(Rule 19.4 specifies the circumstances in which the court may allow a new party to be added or substituted after the end of a relevant limitation period[GL].)

17.4.1 **Effect of rule**—The term "limitation period" is defined in the Glossary. This rule limits the court's power to allow amendments after a relevant limitation period has expired unless the application is to amend in one of the following ways:

(1) Adding or substituting a new claim arising out of the same facts or substantially the same facts as an existing claim;
(2) Correcting a mistake as to the name of a party;
(3) Altering a capacity in which a party claims.

These three occasions for amendments derive from s.35 of the Limitation Act 1980 and therefore case law on the previous High Court rule (RSC O.20, r. 5) which was similar to r.17.4, may still be applicable and is summarised below.

A related topic, adding or substituting a new party after expiry of a relevant limitation period is dealt with by r.19.4.

17.4.2 **Power to amend after expiry of limitation period**—The provisions of this rule empower the court to grant permission to amend a statement of case in the particular circumstances mentioned in paras (2), (3) or (4) even though the application for such amendment is made after the expiry of any relevant period of limitation current at the date of the issue of the claim. The principle underlying the powers of the court under this rule is that if the proceedings had been, from the beginning, properly formulated or constituted in the circumstances specified in paras (2), (3) and (4) the defence of limitation would not have been available to the defendant; and accordingly, if in its discretion, the court thinks it just to grant permission to amend defects in the statement of case within the scope of the circumstances specified in this paragraph, so that such defects in the proceedings are treated as having been cured *ab initio*, the defendant is not being deprived of the benefit of a defence which he would not have had if the proceedings had been so properly formulated or constituted in the first place. To contend in the cases specified in these paras, that the defendant has an existing right which will be prejudiced by the amendment is to argue in a circle, since he only has an existing right if one pre-supposes that the court will not use its powers to amend under this rule or r.19.4. (For pre-CPR case authorities on these principles, see *Pontin v. Wood* [1962] 1 Q.B. 594; [1962] 1 All E.R. 294; and *Rodriguez v. Parker* [1967] 1 Q.B. 116; [1966] 2 All E.R. 349.)

This rule deals with the making of amendments even though the current limitation period has expired in the particular circumstances specified in the three classes of cases mentioned in paras (2), (3) and (4) and must be read closely with and subject to the provisions of section 35 of the Limitation Act 1980 (see SCP 1999, Vol. 2, para. 14–42 and r.19.4).

Under s.35(2) of the Limitation Act 1980, which deals with new claims in pending actions, a "new claim" includes any claim involving the addition or substitution of a new cause of action or the addition or substitution of a new party and any such new claim is deemed to be a separate action and to have been commenced on the same date as the original action (s.35(1)(b)). The Act is imperative in its terms that the Court must not allow such a new claim to be made in the course of any action after the expiry of any time limit under the Act which would affect a new action brought to enforce that claim, except as provided by s.33 of the Act which provides a discretionary power to extend the time-limits in respect of actions for damages for personal injuries or death or as provided by rules of the Court. The effect of this provision is to support the view expressed in *Braniff v. Holland & Harman and Cubitts (Southern)* [1969] 1 W.L.R. 1533; [1969] 3 All E.R. 959, CA; *Brickfield Properties Ltd v. Newton* [1971] 1 W.L.R. 862, *per* Edmund Davies L.J. at 879 and *per* Cross L.J. at 881, and expressly and pointedly to negative any decision, dictum or notion that O.20, rr.5(1) and (2) provide a wide discretion, and in some way allow a general relaxation against the governing principle that any amendment after the expiry of the limitation period will not be allowed, thus negativing *per* Lord Denning in *Chatsworth Investments Ltd v. Cussins (Contractors) Ltd* [1969] 1 W.L.R. 1 at 5; [1969] 1 All E.R. 143 at 145 and in *Sterman v. E. W. & W. J. Moore* [1970] 1 Q.B. 596 at 604; *per* Salmon L.J. *ibid.*, at 605; and *per* Sachs L.J. in *Brickfield Properties Ltd v. Newton* [1971] 1 W.L.R. 863 at 874; [1971] 3 All E.R. 328 at 339.

Where it is reasonably arguable that the relevant limitation period has expired before an amendment is made, the onus is on the applicant to show that the amendment falls within the provisions of s.35(5) of the Limitation Act 1980 and r.17.4(2). Further a new claim under s.35(3) is not made until the statement of case is actually amended which by definition cannot be earlier than the date upon which permission to amend is given and unless the case falls within one of the exceptions such permission cannot be given after the relevant time limit has expired. Such is the case even though such time limit had not expired when the application to amend was made, see *Welsh Development Agency v. Redpath Dorman Long Ltd* [1994] 1 W.L.R. 1409, CA; [1994] 4 All E.R. 10, CA.

Under r.17.4, the power to amend extends to a time limit which applies to the proceedings in question by virtue of the Foreign Limitation Periods Act 1984, *i.e.* any English proceedings in which the law of a foreign country falls, in accordance with the applicable rules of private international law, to be taken into account in the determination of any matter, since for the purposes of such proceedings, the law of that foreign country relating to limitation will apply in respect of that matter (*ibid.*, s.1).

For the cases specified in paras (2), (3) and (4) of this rule, see, "Adding or substituting new cause of action", "Correcting name of party", and "Altering capacity of party" below.

Amendments to allow new claims—Rules of Court for allowing new claims can be made only if the conditions specified by the Limitation Act 1980 are satisfied (s.35(4)). This provision seems to emphasise that the principle underlying the provisions of s.35 and the rules made thereunder is restrictive. 17.4.3

In relation to a claim involving a new cause of action the conditions which the rules of Court must satisfy are specified in s.35(5)(a), which provides as follows:

"(a) in the case of a claim involving a new cause of action, if the new cause of action arises out of the same facts or substantially the same facts as are already in issue on any claim previously made in the original action."

These words are substantially the same as the words in r.17.4(2).

In relation to a claim involving a new party, the conditions which the rules of Court require to be satisfied are specified in s.35(5)(b) which provides as follows:

"(b) in the case of a claim involving a new party, if the addition or substitution of the new party is necessary for the determination of the original action"

and s.35(6) of the Act provides that this will not be regarded as necessary unless either:

"(a) the new party is substituted for a party whose name was given in any claim made in the original action in mistake for the new party's name; or

(b) any claim already made in the original action cannot be maintained by or against an existing party unless the new party is joined or substituted as plaintiff or defendant in that action."

So far as s.35(6)(a) is concerned the terms are not significantly different from the provisions of r.17.4(3), because they simply provide for correcting the name of the party—what is technically called "a misnomer".

So far as the addition or substitution of new parties is concerned, r.19.4 follows the requirement of s.35(5)(b) that the addition or substitution of such a new party should be allowed only if it is necessary for the determination of the original claim.

So far as the capacities in which a party may sue are concerned, r.17.4(4) follows the provisions of s.35(3).

Adding or substituting new cause of action (rule 17.4(2))—The Court has power to grant or allow an amendment after the expiry of any relevant period of limitation notwithstanding that the effect of the amendment will be to add or substitute a new cause of action provided that the new cause of action arises out of the same facts or substantially the same facts as a cause of action in respect of which relief has already been claimed in the proceedings by the party applying for permission to make the amendment (r.17.4(2) and see *Collins v. Herts. C.C.* [1947] K.B. 598; *Dornan v. J. W. Ellis & Co. Ltd* [1962] 1 Q.B. 583; [1962] 1 All E.R. 303, CA; *Robinson v. Unicos Property Corp. Ltd* [1962] 1 W.L.R. 520; [1962] 2 All E.R. 24, CA and for a like principle in a criminal case *cf. R. v. Newcastle-upon-Tyne Justices, ex p. John Bryce (Contractors) Ltd* [1976] 1 W.L.R. 517; [1976] 2 All E.R. 611, DC. 17.4.4

An amendment which relies on the same facts but alleges a novation of a contract as between the claimant, the defendant and the other original contracting party may be allowed after the expiry of the period of limitation (*Chatsworth Investments Ltd v. Cussins (Contractors) Ltd* [1969] 1 W.L.R. 1; [1969] 1 All E.R. 143, CA).

An allegation of negligence against an architect in the *design* of a building arises out of the same or substantially the same facts as an allegation of negligence against him in the *supervision* of the building and will be allowed after the expiry of the current period of limitation, even though it may thereby be adding a new cause of action (*Brickfield Properties Ltd v. Newton* [1971] 1 W.L.R. 862; [1971] 3 All E.R. 328, CA). But in an action for breach of a written contract to modify a ship's engines and fuel system, in the face of a defence that the alleged breach was not covered by the written term, the Court of Appeal dismissed an appeal to allow the plaintiff to amend to add an allegation of breach of a duty of care in the design of and the carrying out of the modifications either in contract or in tort, but allowed an appeal and gave leave to amend to add an allegation of breach of an implied contractual term that the modifications would be reasonably fit for their purpose. The Court held that all these allegations were new causes of action, but only in respect of the last was it satisfied that there was little or no prejudice to the defendant and that it was just to do so (*The "Casper Trader"* [1991] 2 Lloyd's Rep. 237).

So also, an allegation of negligence in respect of the *design* of drawings and specification may be added to a claim for negligence in respect of building works not in accordance with the drawings and specifications (*Circle 33 Housing Trust Ltd v. Fairview Estates (Housing) Ltd* (1984–1985) 1 Const.L.J. 282, CA). But see *Balfour Beatty Construction v. Parsons Brown and Newton* (1991) 7 Const.L.J. 205, CA.

An amendment will be allowed to add fresh allegations complaining of defects in the roof of a building to earlier allegations of defects in the building, principally faults in the brickwork (*Idyll v. Dineman Davidson and Hillman* (1984–1985) 1 Const.L.J. 294, CA).

An amendment which relies on the same facts but seeks to substitute a new date on which an accident is alleged to have happened, being a date over a year after that pleaded, will be allowed, as it does not substitute a new cause of action, since the date itself is not a material part of the cause of action (*Hay v. London Brick Co. Ltd* (1981) *The Times*, May 12, CA).

In each case the question is, are the facts alleged in the amendments sought to be made the same or substantially the same as those alleged to support a cause of action already pleaded?

In *Hydrocarbons Great Britain v. Cammell Laird Shipbuilders* (1991) 58 B.L.R. 123, 25 Con.L.R. 131, H.H. Judge Forbes, Q.C. held that a proposed amendment to allege a claim for negligent misstatement was not within the language of the unamended statement of claim which pleaded negligence in act, that accordingly the proposed amendment was in respect of a new cause of action, that it did not arise out of the same or substantially the same facts as the cause of action pleaded and thus there was no jurisdiction pursuant to s.35 of the Limitation Act 1980 to allow the amendment.

There is power under rule 17.4(2) to give permission to amend a statement of case after the limitation has expired in order to add or substitute a new cause of action arising out of the same facts as those already pleaded but which in fact disclosed no sustainable cause of action (*Sion v. Hampstead Health Authority* , *The Times*, June 10, 1994, CA).

On the other hand, the Court will refuse to allow an amendment of a claim form which would introduce a new cause of action against a foreign defendant in respect of which the Court would have refused leave for service out of the jurisdiction under O.11 (*Beck v. Value Capital Ltd (No. 2)* [1975] 1 W.L.R. 6; [1974] 3 All E.R. 442; affirmed [1976] 1 W.L.R. 572; [1976] 2 All E.R. 102, CA, distinguishing *Holland v. Leslie* [1894] 2 Q.B. 450). See too *Beecham Group plc v. Norton Healthcare Ltd* , *The Times*, October 11, 1996.

An amendment to add a new allegation of intentional wrongdoing by pleading fraud where previously mere negligence had been alleged constituted the introduction of a new cause of action and would not be allowed after the expiry of any relevant limitation period since the new cause of action did not arise out of the same facts or substantially the same facts as a cause of action in respect of which relief had already been claimed in the action. Nor was it possible to circumvent the effect under this sub-rule of the expiry of a period of limitation in respect of a common law claim by seeking to invoke a concurrent equitable jurisdiction where the claims in equity were not different causes of action but merely equitable counterparts of the claims at common law: see *Paragon Finance plc v. Thakerar* [1999] 1 All E.R. 400, CA.

Where the claim was based on a breach of duty whether arising from contract or in tort, the question whether an amendment raised a new cause of action required comparison with the unamended claim to determine (a) whether a different duty was alleged; (b) whether the breaches alleged differed substantially and, where appropriate, (c) the nature and extent of the damage of which complaint was made; see *Darlington Building Society and Another v. O'Rourke, James Scourfield & McCarthy (a Firm)*, *The Times*, November 20, 1998, CA.

17.4.5 **Correcting name of party (r.17.4(3))**—An amendment to correct the name of a party may be allowed, even if made after the expiry of any relevant period of limitation and even if it is alleged that the effect of the amendment will be to substitute a new party, provided the Court is satisfied that the mistake sought to be corrected was a genuine mistake and was not misleading, or such as to cause any reasonable doubt as to the identity of the person intending to sue or to be sued; *Rodriguez v. Parker* [1967] 1 Q.B. 116; [1966] 2 All E.R. 349; *Mitchell v. Harris Engineering Co. Ltd* [1967] 2 Q.B. 703; [1967] 2 All E.R. 682, CA; and see *Davies v. Elsby Brothers, Ltd* [1961] 1 W.L.R. 170; [1960] 3 All E.R. 672, CA; *Whittam v. W. J. Daniel & Co. Ltd* [1962] 1 Q.B. 271; [1961] 3 All E.R. 796, CA). See also *Katzenstein Adler Industries (1975) Ltd v. Borchard Lines Ltd* [1988] 2 Lloyd's Rep. 274; (1988) 138 New L.J. 94 (correcting names of plaintiffs as well as the country in which they are incorporated and carry on business).

An amendment to correct the name of a party may be allowed, even after a final default judgment has been entered, *e.g.* to substitute the correct name of the defendant for the incorrect name in which he was sued where it is plain that the mistake was genuine and that the defendant knew that the plaintiff intended to sue him as the person against whom the claim was being made (*Singh v. Atombrook Ltd* [1989] 1 W.L.R. 810; [1989] 1 All E.R. 395, CA, distinguishing *Davies v. Elsby Bros. Ltd* [1961] 1 W.L.R. 170; [1960] 3 All E.R. 672).

The transposition of the names of the parties in the claim form, *e.g.* that of the defendants as the claimants and that of the claimants as the defendants does not render the claim form a nullity but it is an irregularity, and if it is made by a genuine mistake and is not misleading, permission to amend may be given, even after the expiry of the current period of limitation (*Teltscher Brothers v. London and India Dock Investments Ltd* [1989] 1 W.L.R. 770).

The word "mistake" in r.174(5) should not be narrowly construed to mean error without fault (*per* Russell L.J. in *Mitchell v. Harris Engineering Co. Ltd* [1967] 2 Q.B. 703, CA).

The power to amend after the expiry of the limitation period to correct the name of a party is not limited to making mere variations in the names of parties to an action but allows the substitution of a different party if it is plan that the new party is the party that the person making the mistake intended to sue and therefore a lessee who was applying to the Court for the grant of a new tenancy under the Landlord and Tenant Act 1954 and who by a genuine mistake gave the name of "Charrington & Co. Ltd" as its landlord is entitled to have the error corrected by having its actual landlord "Bass Holdings Ltd" substituted as the respondent to its application, since both Charringtons and Bass Holdings, who were both familiar with the circumstances could not have been misled and could not have had any real doubt as to the identity of the person to be sued (*Evans Constructions Co. Ltd v. Charrington & Co. Ltd and Bass Holdings Ltd* [1983] Q.B. 810; [1983] 1 All E.R. 310, CA). See too *Murray v. Hibernian Dance Club* (1996) *The Times*, August 12—amendment allowed where defendants named under a collective title apt to describe them but devoid of personality at English law since there was no reasonable doubt claim was being asserted and intended to be asserted against the entire membership. See, however, *Beardmore Motors Ltd v. Birch Brothers (Properties) Ltd* [1959] Ch. 298; [1958] 2 All E.R. 311.

Where an action is mistakenly commenced in the name of a claimant company which had ceased to exist as a result of a merger, the Court has power, to correct the name of the claimant company, since the mistake had gone to the name rather than the identity of the claimant, and such amendment would relate back to the date of commencement of proceedings so that there never was a non-existent claimant (*Owners of Sardinia Sulcis v. Owners of Al Tawwab* (1990) *The Times*, November 21, CA).

Altering capacity of party (r.17.4(4))—An amendment to alter the capacity in which a party sues may be allowed under r.17.4(4) if the new capacity is one which that party had at the commencement of the proceedings or has since acquired. This will allow a party to amend the capacity in which he or she sues as executor or executrix after the grant of probate, since this would relate back to the date of death (see *Stebbings v. Holst & Co. Ltd* [1953] 1 W.L.R. 608; [1953] 1 All E.R. 925; *Bowler v. Mowlem (John) & Co.* [1954] 1 W.L.R. 1445; [1954] 3 All E.R. 556, CA) but it will also allow a party to amend the capacity in which he or she sues as administrator or administratrix after the grant of administration even though this may take place after the issue of the claim. **17.4.6**

PRACTICE DIRECTION–AMENDMENTS TO STATEMENTS OF CASE

This Practice Direction supplements CPR Part 17

Applications to amend where the permission of the court is required

1.1 The application may be dealt with at a hearing or, if rule 23.8 applies, without a hearing. **17PD–001**

1.2 When making an application to amend a statement of case, the applicant should file with the court;

(1) the application notice, and

(2) a copy of the statement of case with the proposed amendments.

1.3 Where permission to amend has been given, the applicant should within 14 days of the date of the order, or within such other period as the court may direct, file with the court the amended statement of case.

1.4 If the substance of the statement of case is changed by reason of the amendment, the statement of case should be re-verified by a statement of truth.[4]

1.5 A copy of the order and the amended statement of case should be served on every party to the proceedings, unless the court orders otherwise.

General

2.1 The amended statement of case and the court copy of it should be endorsed as follows;

(1) where the court's permission was required:

[4] See Part 22 for information about the statement of truth.

"Amended [Particulars of Claim *or as may be*] by Order of [Master ....] [District Judge .... *or as may be*] dated ...."

(2) Where the court's permission was not required:

"Amended [Particulars of Claim *or as may be*] under CPR [rule 17.1(1) or (2)(a)] dated ...."

2.2 The statement of case in its amended form need not show the original text. However, where the court thinks it desirable for both the original text and the amendments to be shown, the court may direct that the amendments should be shown either;

(1) by coloured amendments, either manuscript or computer generated, or

(2) by use of a numerical code in a monochrome computer generated document.

2.3 Where colour is used, the text to be deleted should be struck through in colour and any text replacing it should be inserted or underlined in the same colour.

2.4 The order of colours to be used for successive amendments is; (1) red, (2) green, (3) violet and (4) yellow.

(For information about changes to parties see Part 19 and the practice direction which supplements it.)

PART 18

Further Information

Contents 18.0.1

Editorial Introduction

Under former RSC, O.18, r.12 and CCR, O.6, r.7, the court could order a party to serve on any other party further particulars of any claim, defence or other matter stated in his pleadings. Further, a pleader who alleged as a fact that a person had knowledge or notice of some fact, matter or thing could be required, on such terms as the court thought just, to serve particulars of such knowledge or notice. Parties were expected to seek further and better particulars first by request and not to apply for an order except where no particulars, or insufficient particulars were forthcoming. 18.0.2

A major objective of the new system is that the pleadings (now statements of case) system should be made more effective than heretofore. The rules as to the contents of statements of case have been made simpler and they are now subject to "judicial scrutiny" at an early stage. As part of its responsibility for managing cases, the court will ensure that the parties plainly state the factual ingredients of their case so that the true nature and scope of the dispute can be identified. The claim and defence will be considered by the procedural judge after the defence is filed and, if the issues cannot be readily identified from the pleadings, directions will be given with a view to rectifying this. Where there is a case management conference, a major aim will be to produce a statement of the issues in dispute (Interim Report, pp. 116 *et seq.*). The objective is to get the issues clarified quickly without the need for further exchanges between the parties in the form of the old requests for further and better particulars, notices to admit and interrogatories (*ibid.*).

The power to order a party to provide further information given by r.18.1 can be seen as the successor to the power formerly given to order particulars of pleading, but it is a broader power than that. If the judicial scrutiny system is effective then recourse by parties to r.18.1 should be infrequent.

The provisions in Pt 18 do not apply to small claims (r.27.2(1)(f)).

Related Sources 18.0.3

- Part 22 (Statements of truth)
- Part 23 General rules about applications for court orders)
- Rule 26.5(3) (Information about case for case allocation purposes)
- Rule 35.9 (Power of court to direct a party to provide information)
- Practice Direction (Further Information) (see para. 18PD–001)
- Practice Direction (Applications) (see para. 23PD–001)

Forms 18.0.4

- N156—Order for further information (for allocation) (see para. C30–001)

Obtaining further information

18.1—(1) The court may at any time order a party to— 18.1

(a) clarify any matter which is in dispute in the proceedings; or

(b) give additional information in relation to any such matter,

whether or not the matter is contained or referred to in a statement of case.

(2) Paragraph (1) is subject to any rule of law to the contrary.

(3) Where the court makes an order under paragraph (1), the party against whom it is made must—

(a) file his response; and

(b) serve it on the other parties

within the time specified by the court.

(Part 22 requires a response to be verified by a statement of truth.)

Effect of rule—Rule 2.3(1) states that a "statement of case" (formerly "pleading") includes: (1) a claim form, including a claim form used under the Pt 8 procedure, (2) particulars of claim 18.1.1

where these are not included in a claim form, (3) a defence, (4) a Pt 20 claim, and (5) a reply to defence. Rule 18.1(1) states that the court may order a party to clarify or give additional information in relation to any matter which is "in dispute in the proceedings". In most instances whether or not a matter is "in dispute" will be apparent only from a reading of the parties' statements of case and, therefore, the disputed matter will be "contained or referred to in, a statement of case". However, in terms r.18.1 gives the court power to order a party to clarify, or give additional information in relation to, any disputed matter even though the matter is not contained or referred to in a statement of case (*e.g.* in a notice verified by a statement of truth).

The court may exercise its powers under this rule at any time.

It is said in r.18.1(2) that the power to require a party to give further information in accordance with r.18.1(1) is "subject to any rule or law to the contrary". This makes it clear that the power cannot be used to order the disclosure of information which, as a matter of law, cannot be compelled (*e.g.* on grounds of privilege).

The court may vary or revoke an order made under this rule (r.3.1(7)).

This rule should be distinguished from r.35.9 (Power of court to direct a party to provide information) which has a different provenance.

18.1.2 **Application by party**—A party may apply for an order under r.18.1. Rule 18.1 is supplemented by Practice Direction (Further Information) (see para. 18PD–001) in which, amongst other things, the practice for making an application for an order for clarification or further information and the position as to costs is explained. The Practice Direction states that, before making an application to the court, the party seeking clarification or information should first serve on the party from whom it is sought a written request.

The provisions in Pt 23 (General rules about applications for court orders) apply to an application under r.18.1. An application notice must state (a) what order the applicant is seeking, and (b) briefly, why the applicant is seeking the order. Under former procedure, applications for "further and better particulars" of pleadings tended to be unfocused. It would be consistent with the new approach to civil procedure if the courts required applications for further information to state precisely the information sought.

In cases allocated to the fast track, directions as to requests for further information will normally be included in the Standard Directions; see Practice Direction (The Fast Track) Appendix paras 2 and 7 (see para. 28PD–001). As to such directions in multi-track cases, see Practice Direction (The Multi-Track) para. 4.10 (see para. 29PD–001).

18.1.3 **Order on court's own initiative**—The court may exercise its powers under this rule on an application or of its own initiative (r.3.3(1)). Where acting on its own initiative the provisions of r.3.3 apply.

The court has a duty to actively manage cases (r.1.4) and this duty includes, amongst other things, identifying the issues at an early stage, and deciding promptly which issues need full investigation and trial and accordingly disposing summarily of the others (so-called "rolling adjudication") (r.1.4(2)(b)(c)). If the court has recourse to r.18.1 on its own initiative it is likely to be for the purpose of enabling it to discharge this aspect of its case management duties.

When a defence is filed, a case will be allocated to a case management track (see Pt 26). Rule 26.5(3) states that, before deciding the track to which to allocate proceedings or deciding whether to give directions for an allocation hearing to be fixed, the court may order a party "to provide further information about his case". (This power is in addition to that given to the court by r.18.1.) In this situation, the further information is not confined to matters contained or referred to in the party's statement of case. The matters which the court may be particularly interested in obtaining further information about will be those listed in r.26.8 (Matters relevant to allocation to a track).

18.1.4 **Court's discretion**—In early drafts of this rule it was said that an order for further information should not be made unless it is necessary in order to dispose fairly of the claim or to save costs. Further, when considering whether to make an order the court must have regard (a) to the likely benefit which will result if the information is given; and (b) to the likely cost of giving it; and (c) to whether the financial resources of the party against whom the order is sought are likely to be sufficient to enable that party to comply with such an order. These considerations, though not stated in r.18.1, are consistent with the "overriding objective" stated in r.1.1, and which the court is obliged to give effect to when exercising any power given to it by the CPR.

18.1.5 **Response to order**—Where the court makes an order under r.18.1(1) the party against whom it is made must (a) file his response, and (b) serve it on the other parties within the time specified by the court.

A response is filed if it is delivered by post or otherwise to the court office (r.2.3(1)). As to service, see Pt 6.

18.1.6 **Verification of response**—Under r.22.1(1) a statement of case is included among the documents that must be verified by a statement of truth. Rule 2.3(1) states that a "statement of case" includes, not only the documents listed therein (claim form, defence, etc.), but also any "further information given in relation to them voluntarily or by court order under rule 18.1". Thus, where a party responds to an order under r.18.1, and the "further information" he provides by way of clarification or additional information is "given in relation to" a statement of case, then the response must be verified by a statement of truth. (For further information about statements of truth, see Pt 22 and notes therein.)

Consequences of failure to respond—When the court makes an order it may make it subject to conditions, and specify the consequences of failure to comply with the order (r.3.1(3)). The court may strike out a statement of case if it appears to the court that there has been a failure to comply with a court order (r.3.4(2)(c)). Where a party fails to comply with an order made under r.18.1 requiring him to provide further information in relation to a disputed matter contained or referred to in a statement of case the sanction of striking out some or all of the statement of claim might be imposed. Presumably, a failure to provide information may be treated as conduct relevant to the question of costs (see r.44.3(4)). **18.1.7**

Practice Direction—Rule 18.1 is supplemented by Practice Direction (Further Information) (see para. 18PD–001) in which various matters of practice relating to written requests and applications for clarification or further information are dealt with. **18.1.8**

Restriction on the use of further information

18.2 The court may direct that information provided by a party to another party (whether given voluntarily or following an order made under rule 18.1) must not be used for any purpose except for that of the proceedings in which it is given. **18.2**

(RSC Order 82, in Schedule 1, provides for circumstances in which further information is not allowed in defamation claims.)

Effect of rule—When the court makes an order it may make it subject to conditions (r.3.1(3)). This rule specifically provides that, where the court makes an order under r.18.1 ordering a party to give further information, it may direct that the information provided must not be used for any purpose "except for that of the proceedings in which it is given". Consequently, for example, the information could not be used in other proceedings. Whether or not it will be appropriate for the court to give a direction restricting use will depend on the nature of the further information which the party is ordered to provide. If it is in the nature of, what used to be called, further and better particulars of pleading, then no restriction should be imposed. **18.2.1**

The meaning of the phrase "proceedings in which it is given" may require consideration. It may be appropriate to limit the use that may be made of "further information" to proceedings within the proceedings, as it were. For example, it may be appropriate to limit use to proceedings for an interim remedy thereby prohibiting use at trial.

Other provisions in the CPR impose restrictions on the use that may be made by one party of information provided by another (possibly under compulsion). For example, r.31.22 states that, subject to exceptions, a party to whom a document has been disclosed may use the document "only for the purpose of the proceedings in which it is disclosed" (see former RSC, O.24, r.14A). Further, r.34.12 states that, subject to exceptions, where the court orders a party to be examined about his or any other assets for the purpose of any hearing except the trial, the deposition may be used "only for the purpose of the proceedings in which the order was made" (see former RSC, O.29, r.1A). Also, r.32.12 states that, subject to exceptions, a witness statement may be used "only for the purpose of the proceedings in which it is served" (see former RSC, O.38, r.2A(11) and CCR, O.20, r.12A(11)). Rule 35.9 states that where a party has access to information which is not reasonably available to the other party, the court may direct the party who has access to the information to (a) prepare and file a document recording the information, and (b) to serve a copy of that document on the other party. In terms, this rule does not impose any restriction on the use that may be made of information provided but restrictions could be imposed by the court under r.3.1(3)).

PRACTICE DIRECTION—FURTHER INFORMATION

This Practice Direction supplements CPR Part 18

Attention is also drawn to Part 22 (Statement of Truth)

1. Preliminary Request for Further Information or Clarification

1.1 Before making an application to the court for an order under Part 18, **18PD–001**

the party seeking clarification or information (the first party) should first serve on the party from whom it is sought (the second party) a written request for that clarification or information (a Request) stating a date by which the response to the Request should be served. The date must allow the second party a reasonable time to respond.

1.2 A Request should be concise and strictly confined to matters which are reasonably necessary and proportionate to enable the first party to prepare his own case or to understand the case he has to meet.

1.3 Requests must be made as far as possible in a single comprehensive document and not piecemeal.

1.4 A Request may be made by letter if the text of the Request is brief and the reply is likely to be brief; otherwise the Request should be made in a separate document.

1.5 If a Request is made in a letter, the letter should, in order to distinguish it from any other that might routinely be written in the course of a case,

(1) state that it contains a Request made under Part 18, and

(2) deal with no matters other than the Request.

1.6(1) A Request (whether made by letter or in a separate document) must

(a) be headed with the name of the court and the title and number of the claim,

(b) in its heading state that it is a Request made under Part 18, identify the first party and the second party and state the date on which it is made,

(c) set out in a separate numbered paragraph each request for information or clarification,

(d) where a Request relates to a document, identify that document and (if relevant) the paragraph or words to which it relates,

(e) state the date by which the first party expects a response to the Request,

(2)(a) A Request which is not in the form of a letter may, if convenient, be prepared in such a way that the response may be given on the same document.

(b) To do this the numbered paragraphs of the Request should appear on the left hand half of each sheet so that the paragraphs of the response may then appear on the right.

(c) Where a Request is prepared in this form an extra copy should be served for the use of the second party.

2. Responding to a Request

2.1 A response to a Request must be in writing, dated and signed by the second party or his legal representative.

2.2(1) Where the Request is made in a letter the second party may give his response in a letter or in a formal reply.

(2) Such a letter should identify itself as a response to the Request and deal with no other matters than the response.

2.3(1) Unless the Request is in the format described in paragraph 1.6(2) and the second party uses the document supplied for the purpose, a response must:

(a) be headed with the name of the court and the title and number of the claim,

(b) in its heading identify itself as a response to that Request,

(c) repeat the text of each separate paragraph of the Request and set out under each paragraph the response to it.

(d) refer to and have attached to it a copy of any document not already in the possession of the first party which forms part of the response.

(2) A second or supplementary response to a Request must identify itself as such in its heading.

2.4 The second party must when he serves his response on the first party serve on every other party and file with the court a copy of the Request and of his response.

3. Statements of Truth

Attention is drawn to Part 22 and to the definition of a statement of case in Part 2 of the rules; a response should be verified by a statement of truth. **18PD–002**

4. General Matters

4.1 (1) If the second party objects to complying with the Request or part of it or is unable to do so at all or within the time stated in the Request he must inform the first party promptly and in any event within that time.

(2) He may do so in a letter or in a separate document (a formal response), but in either case he must give reasons and, where relevant, give a date by which he expects to be able to comply.

4.2 (1) There is no need for a second party to apply to the court if he objects to a Request or is unable to comply with it at all or within the stated time. He need only comply with paragraph 4.1(2) above.

(2) Where a second party considers that a Request can only be complied with at disproportionate expense and objects to comply for that reason he should say so in his reply and explain briefly why he has taken that view.

5. Applications for Orders under Part 18

5.1 Attention is drawn to Part 23 (Applications) and to the Practice Direction which supplements that Part.

5.2 An application notice for an order under Part 18 should set out or have attached to it the text of the order sought and in particular should specify the matter or matters in respect of which the clarification or information is sought.

5.3 (1) If a Request under paragraph 1 for the information or clarification has not been made, the application notice should, in addition, explain why not.

(2) If a Request for clarification or information has been made, the application notice or the evidence in support should describe the response, if any.

5.4 Both the first party and the second party should consider whether evidence in support of or in opposition to the application is required.

5.5 (1) Where the second party has made no response to a Request served on him, the first party need not serve the application notice on the second party, and the court may deal with the application without a hearing.

(2) Sub-pararaph (1) above only applies if at least 14 days have passed since the Request was served and the time stated in it for a response has expired.

5.6 Unless paragraph 5.5 applies the application notice must be served on the second party and on all other parties to the claim.

5.7 An order made under Part 18 must be served on all parties to the claim.

5.8 Costs—(1) Attention is drawn to the Costs Practice Direction and in particular the court's power to make a summary assessment of costs.

(2) Attention is also drawn to rule 43.5(5) which provides that if an order does not mention costs no party is entitled to costs relating to that order.

PART 19

ADDITION AND SUBSTITUTION OF PARTIES

19.0.1 **Contents**

Editorial Introduction

19.0.2 Part 19 provides simple rules for the addition and substitution of parties which give the judge a wide discretion. Particular rules apply after the expiry of a relevant limitation period—see r.19.4.

Related Sources

19.0.3
- Practice Direction to Pt 19 (see para. 19PD–001)
- Part 1 (Overriding objective)
- Limitation Act 1980
- Foreign Limitation Periods Act 1984
- Merchant Shipping Act 1995
- Part 17, especially r.17.4 (other changes after the end of a limitation period)
- Practice Direction to Pt 17 (Amendments) (see para. 17PD–001)

Changes of parties—general

19.1 **19.1**—(1) This rule applies where a party is to be added or substituted except where the case falls within rule 19.4 (special provisions about changing parties after the end of a relevant limitation period[GL]).

(2) The court may order a person to be added as a new party if—

(a) it is desirable to add the new party so that the court can resolve all the matters in dispute in the proceedings; or

(b) there is an issue involving the new party and an existing party which is connected to the matters in dispute in the proceedings, and it is desirable to add the new party so that the court can resolve that issue.

(3) The court may order any person to cease to be a party if it is not desirable for that person to be a party to the proceedings.

(4) The court may order a new party to be substituted for an existing one if—

(a) the existing party's interest or liability has passed to the new party; and

(b) it is desirable to substitute the new party so that the court can resolve the matters in dispute in the proceedings.

19.1.1 **"court" (r.19.1)**—The power may be exercised by a judge or district judge in a county court or by a judge, Master or district judge in the High Court—r.2.4. It may be exercised on application or on the court's own initiative. See Practice Direction para. 1.1 and r.3.3. An application may be dealt with without a hearing where all the parties are in agreement (r.1.4(2)(j) and Practice Direction 1.2).

19.1.2 **"The court may order" (r. 19.1(2))**—*cf.* RSC, O.15, r.6. See the commentary at SCP 1999, Vol. 1, paras 15/6/1 to 15/6/18.

19.1.3 **"resolve all the matters in dispute" (r. 19.1(2)(a))**—See too r.1.1.

19.1.4 **"order any person to cease to be a party" (r.19.1(3))**—*cf.* RSC, O.15, r.6(1)(2)(a). When the court makes an order for the removal of a party, the claimant must file (see r.2.3) with the court an amended claim form (Pt 7)and particulars of claim and serve a copy of the order on every party to the proceedings and on any other person affected by the order (Practice Direction para. 4).

Provisions applicable where two or more persons are jointly entitled to a remedy

19.2—(1) Where a claimant claims a remedy to which some other person is jointly entitled with him, all persons jointly entitled to the remedy must be parties unless the court orders otherwise. **19.2**

(2) If any person does not agree to be a claimant, he must be made a defendant, unless the court orders otherwise.

(3) This rule does not apply in probate proceedings.

"claimant" (rr.19.2 and 19.3)—See r.2.3. **19.2.1**

"claims a remedy to which some other person is jointly entitled" (r.19.2(1))—See RSC, O.15, r.4(2) and the commentary at SCP 1999, Vol. 1, paras 15/4/1 to 15/4/16. **19.2.2**

Procedure for adding and substituting parties

19.3—(1) An application for permission to remove, add or substitute a party may be made by— **19.3**

(a) an existing party; or
(b) a person who wishes to become a party.

(2) An application for an order under rule 19.1(4) (substitution of new party where existing party's interest or liability has passed)—

(a) may be made without notice; and
(b) must be supported by evidence.

(3) Nobody may be added or substituted as a claimant unless—

(a) he has given his consent in writing; and
(b) that consent has been filed with the court.

(4) An order for the removal, addition or substitution of a party must be served on—

(a) all parties to the proceedings; and
(b) any other person affected by the order.

(5) When the court makes an order for the removal, addition or substitution of a party, it may give consequential directions about—

(a) filing and serving the claim form on any new defendant;
(b) serving relevant documents on the new party; and
(c) the management of the proceedings.

"application" (r. 19.3)—See Pt 23. **19.3.1**

"evidence" (r.19.3)—See Practice Direction, para. 1.3 (see para. 19PD–001), Pt 32 and the Practice Direction to Pt 32 (see para. 32PD–001). **19.3.2**

"filed" (r.19.3(3))—See r.2.3. **19.3.3**

"Nobody may be added or substituted as a claimant unless . . . he has given his consent in writing" (r. 19.3(3))—*cf.* RSC, O.15, r.6(4). Where an application is made to add or substitute a new party as claimant, the party applying must file (see r.2.3) the application notice, the proposed amended claim form and the signed, written consent of the new claimant (see Practice Direction, para. 2.1 (see para. 19PD–001)). **19.3.4**

"serving" (r. 19.3(5))—See Pt 6. **19.3.5**

Special provisions about adding or substituting parties after the end of a relevant limitation period

19.4—(1) This rule applies to a change of parties after the end of a period of limitation under— **19.4**

(a) the Limitation Act 1980[1];
(b) the Foreign Limitation Periods Act 1984[2];
(c) section 190 of the Merchant Shipping Act 1995[3]; or
(d) any other statutory provision.

(2) The court may add or substitute a party only if—
(a) the relevant limitation period[GL] was current when the proceedings were started; and
(b) the addition or substitution is necessary.

(3) The addition or substitution of a party is necessary only if the court is satisfied that—
(a) the new party is to be substituted for a party who was named in the claim form in mistake for the new party;
(b) the claim cannot properly be carried on by or against the original party unless the new party is added or substituted as claimant or defendant; or
(c) the original party has died or had a bankruptcy order made against him and his interest or liability has passed to the new party.

(4) In addition, in a claim for personal injuries the court may add or substitute a party where it directs that—
(a) (i) section 11 (special time limit for claims for personal injuries); or
(ii) section 12 (special time limit for claims under fatal accidents legislation),

of the Limitation Act 1980 shall not apply to the claim by or against the new party; or
(b) the issue of whether those sections apply shall be determined at trial.

(Rule 17.4 deals with other changes after the end of a relevant limitation period[GL].)

(Other rules about parties can be found—
(a) in Schedule 1, in the following RSC—O.15 (proceedings against estates; relator and representative parties); O.17 (interpleader); O.81 (partners); O.85 (administration claims); O.93 (proceedings under the Administration of Justice Act 1985); O.97 (Landlord and Tenant Acts); O.98 (proceedings under the Local Government Finance Act 1982); O.106 (proceedings under the Solicitors Act 1974); and
(b) in Schedule 2, in the following CCR—O.5 (representative proceedings; representation of person or class; representation of estate where no personal representative; proceedings against estates; partners; defendant carrying on business in another name; failure to proceed after death of party; claim to money in court where change in parties after judgment).)

19.4.1 **Addition or substitution of Defendant**—The CPR apply to a new defendant who has been added or substituted as they do to any other defendant—see in particular Pt 9 (Responding to Particulars of Claim), Pt 10 (Acknowledgment of Service), Pt 11 (Disputing the Court's Jurisdiction) and Pt 15 (Defence and Reply).

A new defendant does not become a party to the proceedings until the amended claim form has been served (see Pt 6) on him—Practice Direction, para. 3.4. Practice Direction, para. 3.3, see para. 19PD–001 deals with the making of directions when making an order adding or substituting a defendant.

19.4.2 **Transfer of interest or liability**—See Practice Direction, para. 5, see para. 19PD–001.

19.4.3 **Special provisions ... after the end of a relevant limitation period (r.19.4)**—Parties may

[1] 1980 c. 58.
[2] 1984 c. 16.
[3] 1995 c. 21.

only be added or substituted after the end of a period of limitation if the limitation period was current when proceedings were started (see r.7.2) and the addition or substitution is necessary. The circumstances in which it is "necessary" are prescribed by r.19.4(3) and (4). This is an exhaustive list. If none of the circumstances in r.19.4(3) or (4) applies, the court has no jurisdiction to add or substitute.

"any other statutory provision" (r.19.4(1)(d))—for example, the Carriage by Air Act 1961. 19.4.4

"claim for personal injuries" (r.19.4(4))—See r.2.3. 19.4.5

PRACTICE DIRECTION—ADDITION AND SUBSTITUTION OF PARTIES

This Practice Direction supplements CPR Part 19

A party applying for an amendment will usually be responsible for the costs of and arising from the amendment.

Changes of parties—general

1.1 Parties may be removed, added or substituted in existing proceedings either on the court's own initiative or on the application of either an existing party or a person who wishes to become a party. 19PD–001

1.2 The application may be dealt with without a hearing where all the existing parties and the proposed new party are in agreement.

1.3 The application to add or substitute a new party should be supported by evidence setting out the proposed new party's interest in or connection with the claim.

1.4 The application notice should be filed in accordance with rule 23.3 and, unless the application is made under rule 19.1(4),[4] be served in accordance with rule 23.4.

1.5 An order giving permission to amend will, unless the court orders otherwise, be drawn up. It will be served by the court unless the parties wish to serve it or the court orders them to do so.

Addition or substitution of claimant

2.1 Where an application is made to the court to add or to substitute a new party to the proceedings as claimant, the party applying must file;

(1) the application notice,

(2) the proposed amended claim form and particulars of claim, and

(3) the signed, written consent of the new claimant to be so added or substituted.

2.2 Where the court makes an order adding or substituting a party as claimant but the signed, written consent of the new claimant has not been filed;

(1) the order, and

(2) the addition or substitution of the new party as claimant,

will not take effect until the signed, written consent of the new claimant is filed.

2.3 Where the court has made an order adding or substituting a new claimant, the court may direct;

(1) a copy of the order to be served on every party to the proceedings and any other person affected by the order,

(2) copies of the statements of case and of documents referred to in any statement of case to be served on the new party,

[4] See rule 19.3(2)(a).

(3) the party who made the application to file within 14 days an amended claim form and particulars of claim.

Addition or substitution of defendant

3.1 The Civil Procedure Rules apply to a new defendant who has been added or substituted as they apply to any other defendant (see in particular the provisions of Parts 9, 10, 11and 15).

3.3 Where the court has made an order adding or substituting a defendant whether on its own initiative or on an application, the court may direct;

(1) the claimant to file with the court within 14 days (or as ordered) an amended claim form and particulars of claim for the court file,

(2) a copy of the order to be served on all parties to the proceedings and any other person affected by it,

(3) the amended claim form and particulars of claim, forms for admitting, defending and acknowledging the claim and copies of the statements of case and any other documents referred to in any statement of case to be served on the new defendant.

(4) unless the court orders otherwise, the amended claim form and particulars of claim to be served on any other defendants.

3.4 A new defendant does not become a party to the proceedings until the amended claim form has been served on him.[5]

Removal of party

4. Where the court makes an order for the removal of a party from the proceedings;

(1) the claimant must file with the court an amended claim form and particulars of claim, and

(2) a copy of the order must be served on every party to the proceedings and on any other person affected by the order.

Transfer of interest or liability

5.1 Where the interest or liability of an existing party has passed to some other person, application should be made to the court to add or substitute that person.[6]

5.2 The application must be supported by evidence showing the stage the proceedings have reached and what change has occurred to cause the transfer of interest or liability.

For information about making amendments generally, see the practice direction supplementing Part 17.

[5] *Kettleman v. Hansel Properties Ltd* [1987] A.C. 189, HL.
[6] See rule 19.1(4).

PART 20

COUNTERCLAIMS AND OTHER ADDITIONAL CLAIMS

Contents **20.0.1**

Editorial Introduction

Part 20 applies not only to counterclaims but also to claims by a defendant for a contribution, an indemnity or any other remedy against any other person, whether or not that person is already a party. Permission is not generally needed to bring a Part 20 claim but see rr.20.4(2)(b), 20.5(1) and 20.7(3)(b). Permission is needed if a case is proceeding under Part 8 (see r.8.7). **20.0.2**

Related sources

- Practice Direction to Part 20 (see para. 20PD–001) **20.0.3**
- Parts 1, 9, 10, 11 and 15
- Parts 2.3, 22.1, 26.8
- RSC, O.77, r.6 and CCR, O.42, r.9 (restrictions on Pt 20 claims where the Crown is claimant).
- The County Court Fees Order 1999

Forms

- N9B—Defence/counterclaim (specified amount) (see para. C6–001) **20.0.4**
- N9D—Defence/counterclaim (unspecified amount and non-money claim) (see para. C8–001)
- N211—Part 20 claim form (see para. C46–001)
- N211A—Part 20 notes for claimant (see para. C47–001)
- N211C—Part 20 notes for defendant (see para. C49–001)
- N212—Part 20 notice of issue (see para. C50–001)
- N213—Part 20 acknowledgment of service (see para. C51–001)

Purpose of Part 20

20.1 The purpose of Part 20 is to enable Part 20 claims to be managed in the most convenient and effective manner. **20.1**

"most convenient and effective manner" (r.20.1)—See too r.1.1 (Overriding objective). **20.1.1**

Meaning of "Part 20 claim"

20.2 **20.2**—(1) A Part 20 claim is any claim other than a claim by a claimant against a defendant and includes—

(a) a counterclaim by a defendant against the claimant or against the claimant and some other person;

(b) a claim by a defendant against any person (whether or not already a party) for contribution[GL] or indemnity[GL] or some other remedy; and

(c) where a Part 20 claim has been made against a person who is not already a party, any claim made by that person against any other person (whether or not already a party).

(2) In this "Part 20 claimant" means a person who makes a Part 20 claim.

20.2.1 **"claimant" (20.2(1))**—See r.2.3.

20.2.2 **Fee**—On the filing of a counterclaim the same fee is payable as if the relief or remedy sought were the subject matter of separate proceedings. See the County Court Fees Order, Sched. 1, para. 1.5. On the filing of proceedings against a party or parties not named in the originating proceedings a fee of £30 is payable. See the County Court Fees Order, Sched. 1, para. 1.4.

Part 20 claim to be treated as a claim for the purposes of the Rules

20.3 **20.3**—(1) A Part 20 claim shall be treated as if it were a claim for the purposes of these Rules, except as provided by this Part.

(2) The following rules do not apply to Part 20 claims—

(a) rules 7.5 and 7.6 (time within which a claim form may be served);

(b) rule 16.3(5) (statement of value where claim to be issued in the High Court); and

(c) Part 26 (case management—preliminary stage).

(3) The following rules do not apply to Part 20 claims except where the Part 20 claim is a counterclaim—

(a) Part 12 (default judgment); and

(b) Part 14 (admissions) except rules 14.1(1) and (2) (which provide that a party may admit in writing the truth of another party's case) and 14.3 (admission by notice in writing—application for judgment).

(Rule 20.11 makes special provision for default judgment on a Part 20 claim.)

20.3.1 **"A Part 20 claim shall be treated as if it were a claim for the purposes of this Rule" (r.20.3(1)**—See too Practice Direction, para. 3 (see para. 20PD-001)). Note Pts 9 (Responding to Particulars of Claim), Pt 11 (Disputing The Court's Jurisdiction) and Pt 15 (Defence and Reply). For example a person served with a Pt 20 claim must file a defence in accordance with r.15.2. However there are exceptions—for example, rr.7.5and7.6 (time within which a claim form may be served), r.16.3(5) (statement of value) and Pt 26 (case management—preliminary stage do not apply. Default judgment under Pt 12 applies to counterclaims against claimants, but not to other Pt 20 claims (r.20.3(3)(a)). However a person served with a Pt 20 claim which is not a counterclaim against a claimant who fails to respond by failing an acknowledgment of service or defence is deemed to admit the Pt 20 claim—see r.20.11. See too r.22.1(1)(a) and r.2.3 and PD to Pt 20, para. 4. A Pt 20 claim must be accompanied by a statement of truth.

Defendant's counterclaim against the claimant

20.4 **20.4**—(1) A defendant may make a counterclaim against a claimant by filing particulars of the counterclaim.

(2) A defendant may make a counterclaim against a claimant—

(a) without the court's permission if he files it with his defence;

(b) at any other time with the court's permission.

(Part 15 makes provision for a defence to a claim and applies to a defence to a counterclaim by virtue of rule 20.3.)

(3) Part 10 (acknowledgment of service) does not apply to a claimant who wishes to defend a counterclaim.

Time—The normal time for making a Part 20 claim is the same time as the defence, but permission may be given at other times—see below. 20.4.1

Permission (rr.20.4(2)(b), 20.5(1) and 20.7(3)(b))—A counterclaim against a claimant may be made without the court's permission if it is filed with the defence (r.20.4(2)(a)). Similarly, a defendant may claim a contribution or indemnity against another defendant without the permission of the court (r.20.6). However the court's permission is needed if a defendant wants to make a counterclaim against the claimant at any other time (r.20.4(2)(b)), where a defendant wishes to counterclaim against someone other than the claimant (r, 20.5(1)) or where he seeks to make any other claim after filing his defence (r.20.7(3)(b)). Applications under rr.20.5(1) and20.7(3)(b) may be made without notice (rr.20.5(2) and 20.7(5)—see too r.23.9). 20.4.2

An application for permission must be supported by evidence (see Pt 32 and the Practice Direction to Pt 32 (see para. 32PD–001)) stating the stage that the action has reached, the nature of the Pt 20 claim, a summary of facts and the name and address of the Pt 20 defendant (Practice Direction, para. 2.1 (see para. 20PD–001)). Where there has been delay an explanation should be given. Where possible the applicant should provide a time table of the action to date (Practice Direction, paras 2.2 and 2.3 (see para. 20PD–001)).

If permission is given, directions as to service should be given at the same time (r.20.8(3)).

"court" (rr.20.4(2)(b), 20.5(1) and 20.7(3)(b))—The power may be exercised by a judge or district judge in a county court or by a judge, Master or district judge in the High Court—(r.2.4). It may be exercised on application or on the court's own initiative. See Practice Direction 1.1 (para. 20PD–001). An application for permission may be dealt with without a hearing where all the parties are in agreement (r.1.4(2)(j)). 20.4.3

Form of counterclaim and titles of proceedings where there are Pt 20 claims—See Practice Direction, paras 6.1–7.5 (para. 20PD–001). 20.4.4

Statement of truth—The contents of a Pt 20 claim should be verified by a statement of truth ("[I believe] [the [Pt 20 claimant] believes] that the facts stated in this statement of case are true.") (see Practice Direction para. 4.1 (para. 20PD–001), Pt 22 and r.32.14). 20.4.5

Counterclaim against a person other than the claimant

20.5—(1) A defendant who wishes to counterclaim against a person other than the claimant must apply to the court for an order that that person be added as defendant to the counterclaim. 20.5

(2) An application for an order under paragraph (1) may be made without notice unless the court directs otherwise.

(3) Where the court makes an order under paragraph (1), it will give directions as to the management of the case.

Counterclaim against a person other than a claimant—An application to add a person as a defendant to a counterclaim should be accompanied by a copy of the proposed counterclaim. It must be supported by evidence stating the stage which the action has reached, the nature of the Part 20 claim, a summary of facts upon which it is based and the name and address of the proposed Part 20 defendant. If there has been delay, an explanation must be given. Where possible the applicant should provide a timetable of the action to date. (See PD to Pt 20, paras 2.1 to 2.4). Such an application may be made without notice unless the court directs otherwise (r.20.5(2)). 20.5.1

Allocation questionnaire—If a party intends to make a Part 20 claim, or to apply to add another party, this should be stated on the allocation questionnaire (see PD to Pt 26, para. 2.2(3)(b)). 20.5.2

Defendant's claim for contribution or indemnity from co-defendant

20.6 A defendant who has filed an acknowledgment of service or a defence may make a Part 20 claim for contribution[GL] or indemnity[GL] against another defendant by— 20.6

(a) filing a notice containing a statement of the nature and grounds of his claim; and

(b) serving that notice on the other defendant.

Procedure for making any other Part 20 claim

20.7—(1) This rule applies to any Part 20 claim except— 20.7

(a) a counterclaim; and
(b) a claim for contribution[GL] or indemnity[GL] made in accordance with rule 20.6.

(2) A Part 20 claim is made when the court issues a Part 20 claim form.

(3) A defendant may make a Part 20 claim—
(a) without the court's permission if the Part 20 claim is issued before or at the same time as he files his defence;
(b) at any other time with the court's permission.

(Rule 15.4 sets out the period for filing a defence.)

(4) Particulars of a Part 20 claim must be contained in or served with the Part 20 claim.

(5) An application for permission to make a Part 20 claim may be made without notice, unless the court directs otherwise.

20.7.1 **Claim form**—A Part 20 claim must be made on Form N211—see r.4(1) and PD to Pt 4. If the Part 20 claim is a counterclaim, the defence and counterclaim should normally be in one document—see PD to Pt 20, para. 6.1.

20.7.2 **Titles of proceedings where there are Part 20 claims**—See PD to Pt 20, para. 7.

Service of a Part 20 claim form

20.8 **20.8**—(1) Where a Part 20 claim may be made without the court's permission, the Part 20 claim form must—
(a) in the case of a counterclaim, be served on every other party when a copy of the defence is served;
(b) in the case of any other Part 20 claim, be served on the person against whom it is made within 14 days after the date on which the party making the Part 20 claim files his defence.

(2) Paragraph (1) does not apply to a claim for contribution[GL] or indemnity[GL] made in accordance with rule 20.6.

(3) Where the court gives permission to make a Part 20 claim it will at the same time give directions as to the service of the Part 20 claim.

20.8.1 **Service of a Part 20 claim form (r.20.8)**—See also Pt 6 and, for documents which must accompany it where service is upon a non-party, r.20.12. Defendants to counterclaims should file admissions or defences within 14 days from service, or 28 days if an acknowledgment of service is filed—see r.15.4. Judgment may be obtained in default (Pt 12) but see r.20.11 below.

Matters relevant to question of whether a Part 20 claim should be separate from main claim

20.9 **20.9**—(1) This rule applies where the court is considering whether to—
(a) permit a Part 20 claim to be made;
(b) dismiss a Part 20 claim; or
(c) require a Part 20 claim to be dealt with separately from the claim by the claimant against the defendant.

(Rule 3.1(2)(e) and (j) deal respectively with the court's power to order that part of proceedings be dealt with as separate proceedings and to decide the order in which issues are to be tried.)

(2) The matters to which the court may have regard include—
(a) the connection between the Part 20 claim and the claim made by the claimant against the defendant;
(b) whether the Part 20 claimant is seeking substantially the same remedy which some other party is claiming from him;
(c) whether the Part 20 claimant wants the court to decide any question connected with the subject-matter of the proceedings—
(i) not only between existing parties but also between existing parties and a person not already a party; or

(ii) against an existing party not only in a capacity in which he is already a party but also in some further capacity.

Matters relevant—See too rr.1.1 (overriding objective), 1.4 (court's duty to manage case—especially 1.4(2)(i)) and 3.1 (court's general powers of case management—especially 3.1(2)(e) and (i)). **20.9.1**

Effect of service of a Part 20 claim

20.10—(1) A person on whom a Part 20 claim is served becomes a party to the proceedings if he is not a party already. **20.10**

(2) When a Part 20 claim is served on an existing party for the purpose of requiring the court to decide a question against that party in a further capacity, that party also becomes a party in the further capacity specified in the Part 20 claim.

Special provisions relating to default judgment on a Part 20 claim other than a counterclaim or a contribution or indemnity notice

20.11—(1) This rule applies if— **20.11**

(a) the Part 20 claim is not—

(i) a counterclaim; or

(ii) a claim by a defendant for contribution[GL] or indemnity[GL] against another defendant under rule 20.6; and

(b) the party against whom a Part 20 claim is made fails to file an acknowledgment of service or defence in respect of the Part 20 claim.

(2) The party against whom the Part 20 claim is made—

(a) is deemed to admit the Part 20 claim, and is bound by any judgment or decision in the main proceedings in so far as it is relevant to any matter arising in the Part 20 claim;

(b) subject to paragraph (3), if default judgment under Part 12 is given against the Part 20 claimant, the Part 20 claimant may obtain judgment in respect of the Part 20 claim by filing a request in the relevant practice form.

(3) A Part 20 claimant may not enter judgment under paragraph (2)(b) without the court's permission if—

(a) he has not satisfied the default judgment which has been given against him; or

(b) he wishes to obtain judgment for any remedy other than a contribution[GL] or indemnity[GL].

(4) An application for the court's permission under paragraph (3) may be made without notice unless the court directs otherwise.

(5) The court may at any time set aside[GL] or vary a judgment entered under paragraph (2)(b).

Procedural steps on service of a Part 20 claim form on a non-party

20.12—(1) Where a Part 20 claim form is served on a person who is not already a party it must be accompanied by— **20.12**

(a) a form for defending the claim;

(b) a form for admitting the claim;

(c) a form for acknowledging service of the claim; and

(d) a copy of—

(i) every statement of case which has already been served in the proceedings; and

(ii) such other documents as the court may direct.

(2) A copy of the Part 20 claim form must be served on every existing party.

20.12.1 **"form for defending the claim" (r.20.12(1)(a))**—Forms N9B and N9D at paras C6–001 and C8–001.

20.12.2 **"form for admitting the claim" (r.20.12(1)(b))**—Forms N9A and N9C at paras C5–001 and C7–001.

20.12.3 **"form for acknowledging service" (r.20.12(1)(c))**—Form N213 at para. C51–001.

20.12.4 **Supply of documents to new parties**—Where a party is joined to existing proceedings, the party joined is entitled to require the person joining him to supply, without charge, copies of all statements of case, written evidence and any documents appended or exhibited to them. They should be supplied within 48 hours after reciept of any written request (see PD to Pt 5, para. 3).

Case management where there is a defence to a Part 20 claim form

20.13 **20.13**—(1) Where a defence is filed to a Part 20 claim the court must consider the future conduct of the proceedings and give appropriate directions.

(2) In giving directions under paragraph (1) the court must ensure that, so far as practicable, the Part 20 claim and the main claim are managed together.

(CCR Order 42, in Schedule 2, makes provision for a Part 20 claim against the Crown where the Crown is not a party.)

20.13.1 **Case management where there is a defence to a Pt 20 claim form (20.13(1))**—See also Practice Direction paras 5.1 to 5.4 and Pts 1, 28 and 29.

20.13.2 **Case management**—The court must consider case management when a defence to a Pt 20 claim is filed. A hearing should be arranged unless the defence is a defence to a counterclaim (PD to Pt 20, para. 5.1 which was amended in March 1999.)

20.13.3 **Allocation to track**—The Pt 20 claim and the main claim should normally be managed together and allocated to the same track. The financial value of the Pt 20 claim and its complexity are to be taken into account when considering allocation to track—see r.26.8(1)(e).

20.13.4 **The Crown**—See too RSC, O.77, r.6 and CCR, O.42, r.9 (restrictions on Pt 20 claims where the Crown is claimant).

PRACTICE DIRECTION—COUNTERCLAIMS AND OTHER PART 20 CLAIMS

This Practice Direction supplements CPR Part 20

A Part 20 claim is any claim other than the claim by the claimant against the defendant.

Cases where court's permission to make a Part 20 claim is required

20PD–001 **1.1** Rules 20.4(2)(b), 20.5(1) and 20.7(3)(b) set out the circumstances in which the court's permission will be needed for making a Part 20 claim.

1.2 Where an application is made for permission to make a Part 20 claim the application notice should be filed together with a copy of the proposed Part 20 claim.

Applications for permission to issue a Part 20 claim

2.1 An application for permission to make a Part 20 claim must be supported by evidence stating;

(1) the stage which the action has reached,
(2) the nature of the claim to be made by the Part 20 claimant or details of the question or issue which needs to be decided,
(3) a summary of the facts on which the Part 20 claim is based, and
(4) the name and address of the proposed Part 20 defendant.
(For further information regarding evidence see the practice direction which supplements Part 32.)

2.2 Where delay has been a factor contributing to the need to apply for permission to make a Part 20 claim an explanation of the delay should be given in evidence.

2.3 Where possible the applicant should provide a timetable of the action to date.

2.4 Rules 20.5(2) and 20.7(5) allow applications to be made to the court without notice unless the court otherwise directs.

General

3. The Civil Procedure Rules apply generally to Part 20 claims as if they were claims.[1] Parties should be aware that the provisions relating to failure to respond will apply.

Statement of Truth

4.1 The contents of a Part 20 claim should be verified by a statement of truth. Part 22 requires a statement of case to be verified by a statement of truth.

4.2 The form of the statement of truth should be as follows:

"[I believe] [the [Part 20 claimant]* believes] that the facts stated in this statement of case are true."

*(For the purpose of this practice direction the Part 20 claimant means any party making a Part 20 claim.)

4.3 Attention is drawn to rule 32.14 which sets out the consequences of verifying a statement of case containing a false statement without an honest belief in its truth.

(For information regarding statements of truth see Part 22 and the practice direction which supplements it.)

Case management where there is a Part 20 defence

5.1 Where the Part 20 defendant files a defence, other than to a counterclaim, the court will arrange a hearing to consider case management of the Part 20 claim. **20PD–002**

5.2 The court will give notice of the hearing to each party likely to be affected by any order made at the hearing.

5.3 At the hearing the court may;
(1) treat the hearing as a summary judgment hearing,
(2) order that the Part 20 proceedings be dismissed,
(3) give directions about the way any claim, question or issue set out in or arising from the Part 20 claim should be dealt with,
(4) give directions as to the part, if any, the Part 20 defendant will take at the trial of the claim,
(5) give directions about the extent to which the Part 20 defendant is to be bound by any judgment or decision to be made in the claim.

5.4 The court may make any of the orders in 5.3(1) to (5) either before or after any judgment in the claim has been entered by the claimant against the defendant.

Form of counterclaim

6.1 Where a defendant to a claim serves a counterclaim under this Part, the

[1] Rule 20.3 but note the exceptions set out in rule 20.3(2)and(3).

defence and counterclaim should normally form one document with the counterclaim following on from the defence.

6.2 Where a claimant serves a reply and a defence to counterclaim, the reply and the defence to counterclaim should normally form one document with the defence to counterclaim following on from the reply.

Titles of proceedings where there are Part 20 claims

7.1 The title of every Part 20 claim should contain:

(1) the full name of each party and

(2) his status in the proceedings (*e.g.* claimant, defendant, Part 20 claimant, Part 20 defendant etc.). For example:

AB	Claimant
CD	Defendant/Part 20 Claimant
EF	Part 20 Defendant

7.2 Where a defendant makes a counterclaim not only against the claimant but also against a non-party the title should show this as follows:

AB	Claimant/Part 20 Defendant
CD	Defendant/Part 20 Claimant
and	
XY	Part 20 Defendant

7.3 Where there is more than one Part 20 claim, the parties to the first Part 20 claim should be described as "Part 20 Claimant (1st claim)" and "Part 20 Defendant (1st claim)", the parties to the second Part 20 claim should be described as "Part 20 Claimant (2nd claim)" and "Part 20 Defendant (2nd claim)", and so on. For example:

AB	Claimant and Part 20 Defendant (2nd claim)
CD	Defendant and Part 20 Claimant (1st claim)
EF	Part 20 Defendant (1st claim) and Part 20 Claimant (2nd claim)
GH	Part 20 Defendant (2nd claim)

7.4 Where the full name of a party is lengthy it must appear in the title but thereafter in the statement of case it may be identified by an abbreviation such as initials or a recognised shortened name.

7.5 Where a party to proceedings has more than one status, *e.g.* Claimant and Part 20 Defendant (2nd claim) or Part 20 Defendant (1st claim) and Part 20 Claimant (2nd claim) the combined status must appear in the title but thereafter it may be convenient to refer to the party by name, *e.g.* Mr Smith or, if paragraph 7.3 applies, by initials or a shortened name.

7.6 Paragraph 4 of the practice direction supplementing Part 7 contains further directions regarding the title to proceedings.

PART 21

CHILDREN AND PATIENTS

Contents **21.0.1**

Editorial Introduction

Litigation friends—Formerly, rules of court as to children and patients were found mainly in RSC, O.80 and CCR, O.10. The former Order was convoluted and, in parts, descended into unnecessary detail, and the latter Order was incomplete in its coverage of the subject. **21.0.2**

There are two types of legal disability, namely minority and mental incapacity. CCR, O.10 used the term "minor" to describe someone under the age of 18, rather than the term "infant" used in the RSC, and "mental patient" rather than just "patient" used in the RSC. However, both sets of rules used "person under disability" to refer to both. The differences between the two Orders were more than merely terminological; for example, the documents that had to be filed under RSC, O.80 were not the same as those under CCR, O.10.

Previously, the general rule was that a person under disability could not bring proceedings except by his "next friend" and could not defend except by his "guardian ad litem". Under Pt. 21, persons under disability are to have a "litigation friend" to "conduct proceedings" on their behalf, whether they are bringing proceedings or defending. The dropping of the distinction between next friends and guardians ad litem does much to simplify the structure of the rules. It is possible, of course, that, before proceedings are started, there will be a person already involved in the affairs of a person under disability and well-placed to act as his litigation friend (whether he is claimant or defendant) (*e.g.* a child's guardian ad litem).

The expression "person under disability" and the word "disability" are not used in Pt. 21. The word "child" is used to describe a person under 18 and "patient" means a person, who by reason of mental disorder within the Mental Health Act 1983 is incapable of managing and administering his own affairs (see s.94(2)).

Judgments and settlements—Rules 21.2 to 21.9 of this Part are concerned with the matters outlined above. Rule 21.10 deals with the approval by the court of settlements of claims on behalf of children and patients. **21.0.3**

A number of provisions in other Parts of the CPR and Practice Directions have to be borne in mind where a child or patient is a party to proceedings. For example, r.

14.1(4) restricts the right of a claimant to enter judgment on an admission made by a defendant "where a party is a child or patient" (presumably, what is meant here is that the defendant is the party under disability). Further, under r.12.10 a default judgment cannot be obtained against a child or patient except on an application to the court supported by evidence (r.12.11(3)). It may be noted that the Practice Direction supplementing Pt 12 (Default Judgment) the Pt 12 Practice Direction states that a litigation friend must be "appointed by the court" (see r.21.6) before the claimant can obtain default judgment in these circumstance (Practice Direction (Obtaining Default Judgment) para. 4.2 (see para. 12PD–001). In terms, this direction is not satisfied where a litigation friend acts without a court order (see r.21.4).

Related Sources

21.0.4
- Practice Direction (Children and Patients), see para. 21PD–001.
- Part 8 (Alternative procedure for claims).
- Part 23 (General rules about applications for court orders).
- Rule 6.6 (Service of documents on children and patients).
- Rule 14.1(4) (Entering judgment on admission where party child or patient).
- Rules 12.10 and 12.11 (Application for default judgment in claim against child or patient).
- Rule 21.1(5)(6) (Statement of truth by litigation friend).
- Rule 39.2(3)(d) (Hearings in private to protect interests of child or patient).
- Rule 48.5 (Costs where money is payable by or to a child or patient).
- Mental Health Act 1983, Pt VII (see SCP 1999 Vol. 2, para. 10B–3).
- SCP 1999, Vol. 2, Section 10 (Court of Protection), paras 10A–1 *et seq.*
- Practice Direction (Obtaining Default Judgment).
- Practice Direction (Statement of Truth), para. 3.1, see para. 22PD–001.
- Mental Health Act 1983, Pt VII (see SCP 1999, Vol. 2, paras 10B–3 *et seq.*).
- Court of Protection Rules (see SCP 1999, Vol. 2, paras 10C–1 *et seq.*).

Forms

21.0.5
- N235—Certificate of suitability for litigation friend (see para. C61–001)
- N292—Court of Protection Form (see para. C79–001)
- Court Funds Office Forms 200 and 320 (see SCP 1999, Vol. 2, paras 5C–123 and 5C–139)

Scope of this Part

21.1 **21.1**—(1) This Part—

(a) contains special provisions which apply in proceedings involving children and patients; and

(b) sets out how a person becomes a litigation friend.

(2) In this Part—

(a) "child" means a person under 18; and

(b) "patient" means a person who by reason of mental disorder within the meaning of the Mental Health Act 1983[1] is incapable of managing and administering his own affairs.

(Rule 6.6 contains provisions about the service of documents on children and patients.)

(Rule 48.5 deals with costs where money is paid to a child or patient.)

Requirement for litigation friend in proceedings by or against children and patients

21.2 **21.2**—(1) A patient must have a litigation friend to conduct proceedings on his behalf.

(2) A child must have a litigation friend to conduct proceedings on his behalf unless the court makes an order under paragraph (3).

(3) The court may, on the application of a child, make an order permitting the child to conduct proceedings without a litigation friend.

(4) An application for an order under paragraph (3)—

(a) may be made by the child;

(b) if the child already has a litigation friend, must be made on notice to the litigation friend; and

(c) if the child has no litigation friend, may be made without notice.

(5) Where—

(a) the court has made an order under paragraph (3); and

(b) it subsequently appears to the court that it is desirable for a litigation friend to conduct the proceedings on behalf of the child,

the court may appoint a person to be the child's litigation friend.

21.2.1 **Effect of rule**—See former RSC, O.80, r.2(1) and CCR, O.10, r.1(1)(2).

A patient must have a litigation friend "to conduct proceedings on his behalf". Normally, a child should have a litigation friend but the court may make an order permitting him to conduct the proceedings himself, even if the child already has a litigation friend. The County Courts Act

[1] 1983 c. 20.

1984, s.47 stated that a child may bring proceedings in a county court for sums due to him as wages; this section has been omitted by the Civil Procedure (Modification of Enactments) Order 1998 (S.I. 1998 No. 2940), art 6(a). Former CCR, O.10, r.8 stated that, where a minor was sued for a liquidation sum, a guardian ad litem need not be appointed.

Any step taken before a child or patient has a litigation friend, shall be of no effect, unless the court otherwise orders (r.21.3(4)); see further notes following r.21.3.

The meaning of "conduct proceedings on his behalf" is not elaborated in the rules (*cf.* RSC, O.80, r.2(2) and CCR, O.10, r.12) but doubtless would include doing anything which in the ordinary conduct of any proceedings is required or authorised by a provision of the CPR to be done by a party to the proceedings (see further, "Powers of next friend and guardian ad litem" SCP 1999, Vol. 1, para. 80/2/18).The duties of a litigation friend are outlined in Practice Direction (Children and Patients), para. 2.1 (see para. 21PD–001).

There is no requirement that a litigation friend must act by a solicitor in High Court proceedings (*cf.* RSC, O.80, r.2(3)).

The Official Solicitor will act on behalf of a child or patient where there is no-one else able and willing to do so (see SCP 1999, Vol. 2, para. 20A–490/3).

Rule 3.1(2)(c) states that the court may require a party or a party's legal representative to attend court. Presumably, this extends to a litigation friend and his legal representative.

Stage of proceedings at which a litigation friend becomes necessary

21.3—(1) This rule does not apply where the court has made an order under rule 21.2(3). **21.3**

(2) A person may not, without the permission of the court—

(a) make an application against a child or patient before proceedings have started; or

(b) take any step in proceedings except—

(i) issuing and serving a claim form; or

(ii) applying for the appointment of a litigation friend under rule 21.6

until the child or patient has a litigation friend.

(3) If a party becomes a patient during proceedings, no party may take any step in the proceedings without the permission of the court until the patient has a litigation friend.

(4) Any step taken before a child or patient has a litigation friend, shall be of no effect, unless the court otherwise orders.

Effect of rule—A claimant may issue and serve a claim form against a child or patient who does not have a litigation friend; however, unless r.21.2(3) applies, he may take no further step in the proceedings without the permission of the court until a litigation friend has been appointed apart from applying to have an appointment made (should that be necessary). A step taken before a child or patient has a litigation friend shall be of no effect, unless the court otherwise orders (r.21.3(4)). **21.3.1**

Rule 21.3(2) is concerned with the situation where it is the defendant who is the party under disability. It provides the necessary protection for the defendant child or patient and does so in much simpler terms than those used in former RSC, O.80, r.6(1) to (4), made possible, in part, by the substitution of the single claim form for the multiplicity of originating process formerly permitted by the RSC.

Generally, a Pt 20 claim is to be treated as if it were a claim for the purposes of the CPR (r.20.3(1)). Consequently, r.21.3 applies where a Pt 20 claim is brought against a child or patient, for example, for an indemnity.

Party becoming a patient during proceedings—Rule 21.3(3) follows former RSC, O.80, r.3(5) but is different in certain respects. Where, after any proceedings have been begun, a party to the proceedings (whether as claimant, defendant or as a party in some other capacity) becomes a patient, no party (including the party becoming a patient) may take any step in the proceedings until that party has a litigation friend. However, pending the appointment of a litigation friend, further steps in the proceedings may be taken with the permission of the court. In these circumstances it is likely that the litigation friend will be appointed by the court upon an application being made by another party under r.21.6. Under former RSC, O.80, r.3(5), upon a party becoming a patient during proceedings, an application had to be made to the court for the appointment of a next friend or guardian ad litem. In terms, r.21.3(3) imposes no such requirement. Thus, where a person is authorised under the Mental Health Act 1983, Pt VII to conduct legal proceedings on behalf of a person who is, at the time of that authorisation, already a party to proceedings, no application to the court is required (but note r.21.5(2)). Provided a litigation friend comes on the scene, whether as a result of court order or not, further steps in the proceedings can be taken. **21.3.2**

Former RSC, O.80 did not deal expressly with the validity of any step taken in proceedings after a party became a patient, but before a guardian ad litem or next friend was appointed (see SCP 1999, Vol. 1, para. 80/2/12). Rule 21.3(4) deals with the point directly and states that any step taken before a patient has a litigation friend shall be of no effect, unless the court otherwise orders. Presumably, where the court has given its permission under r.21.3(3) no further order under r.21.3(4) is required to secure validity.

Who may be a litigation friend without a court order

21.4 **21.4**—(1) This rule does not apply if the court has appointed a person to be a litigation friend.

(2) A person authorised under Part VII of the Mental Health Act 1983 to conduct legal proceedings in the name of a patient or on his behalf, is entitled to be the litigation friend of the patient in any proceedings to which his authority extends.

(3) If nobody has been appointed by the court or, in the case of a patient, authorised under Part VII, a person may act as a litigation friend if he—

- (a) can fairly and competently conduct proceedings on behalf of the child or patient; and
- (b) has no interest adverse to that of the child or patient; and
- (c) (where the child or patient is a claimant) undertakes to pay any costs which the child or patient may be ordered to pay in relation to the proceedings, subject to any right he may have to be repaid from the assets of the child or patient.

How a person becomes a litigation friend without a court order

21.5 **21.5**—(1) If the court has not appointed a litigation friend, a person who wishes to act as litigation friend must follow the procedure set out in this rule.

(2) A person authorised under Part VII of the Mental Health Act 1983 must file an official copy[GL] of the order or other document which constitutes his authorisation to act.

(3) Any other person must file a certificate of suitability stating that he satisfies the conditions specified in rule 21.4(3).

(4) A person who is to act as litigation friend for a claimant must file—

- (a) the authorisation; or
- (b) the certificate of suitability,

at the time when the claim is made.

(5) A person who is to act as litigation friend for a defendant must file—

- (a) the authorisation; or
- (b) the certificate of suitability;

at the time when he first takes a step in the proceedings on behalf of the defendant.

(6) The litigation friend must—

- (a) serve the certificate of suitability on every person on whom, in accordance with rule 6.6 (service on parent, guardian, etc.), the claim form should be served; and
- (b) file a certificate of service when he files the certificate of suitability.

(Rule 6.10 sets out the details to be contained in a certificate of service.)

21.5.1 **Effect of rules 21.4 and 21.5**—For practice relevant to appointment of a litigation friend without order, see Practice Direction (Children and Patients), para. 2.3 (see 21PD–001). Neither of these rules applies if the court has already appointed a litigation friend (see former RSC, O.80, r.3(4)), nor presumably, if the court has made an order under r.21.2(3) permitting a child to conduct proceedings without a litigation friend.

A litigation friend may be appointed by order of the court and in some instances a court order is necessary (see r.21.6). Rule 21.5 shows how a person may become a litigation friend (of either a plaintiff or a defendant) without a court order appointing him as such where no order is required. Obviously, limits must be placed on the persons who may become a litigation friend without court order; r.21.4 imposes the necessary controls.

In this context, the former rules did not draw a clear distinction between who may? and how may? However, it can be seen that, in relation to the former question, r.21.4(2) follows RSC, O.80, r.3(3) and CCR, O.10, rr.1(3), 2(a) and 5(a). And r.21.4(3) follows RSC, O.80, r.3(3) and CCR, O.10, r.5(b). Rule 21.4(3) follows RSC, O.80, r.3(8)(c)(iii) and CCR, O.10, rr.2(b) and 5(b).

As previously, a litigation friend who undertakes to conduct proceedings on behalf of a claimant must undertake to pay any costs which the claimant may be ordered to pay in relation to the proceedings (for termination of this costs liability, see r.21.9(6)). Former CCR, O.10, r.9 declared the rule that a guardian ad litem should not be liable for any costs "not occasioned by his personal negligence or misconduct". Strictly speaking, a rule to this effect is not necessary; no comparable provision appeared in the RSC and none is in the CPR (but see, generally, r.47(5) (Costs where money is payable by or to child or patient).

If the court has not appointed a litigation friend, a person who is able to fulfil the conditions stated in r.21.4 and wishes to act as litigation friend, must follow the procedure set out in r.21.5. This rule replaces provisions formerly found in RSC, O.80, r.3(8) and CCR, O.10, rr.2 and 5, and in so doing removes the distinctions which formerly existed between county court and High Court practice (and, within the High Court, in practice between the divisions). The procedure is self-explanatory. It includes the filing and serving of certain documents, including (for persons other that those authorised under the Mental Health Act 1983) a "certificate of suitability" satisfying the conditions stated in r.21.4(3). (As to filing, see r.2.3(1), and as to service, see r.6.10).

Any step taken by a person intermeddling as a litigation friend before rr.21.4 and 21.5 have been complied with shall be of no effect, unless the court otherwise orders (r.21.3(4)).

The court may, by order, direct that a person who wishes to act as a litigation friend and who follows the procedure stated in r.21.5 may not so act (r.21.7(1)).

It may be noted that former RSC, O.80, r.3(4) said that where, in any proceedings, a person "has been or is" (what would now be called a litigation friend) no other person should be entitled to act as a litigation friend in those proceedings except by order of the court appointing him in substitution for the person previously acting in that capacity. Clearly, where the first litigation friend was appointed by an order of the court another person could not become a litigation friend under r.21.5 (see r.21.5(1)). Presumably, the position would be the same where the person previously acting had become a litigation friend without a court order.

Certificate of suitability—For form, see certificate of suitability of litigation friend (N235) (see para. C61–001). **21.5.2**

How a person becomes a litigation friend by court order

21.6—(1) The court may make an order appointing a litigation friend. **21.6**

(2) An application for an order appointing a litigation friend may be made by—

(a) a person who wishes to be the litigation friend; or
(b) a party.

(3) Where—

(a) a person makes a claim against a child or patient;
(b) the child or patient has no litigation friend;
(c) the court has not made an order under rule 21.2(3) (order that a child can act without a litigation friend); and
(d) either—
  (i) someone who is not entitled to be a litigation friend files a defence; or
  (ii) the claimant wishes to take some step in the proceedings.

the claimant must apply to the court for an order appointing a litigation friend for the child or patient.

(4) An application for an order appointing a litigation friend must be supported by evidence.

(5) The court may not appoint a litigation friend under this rule unless it is satisfied that the person to be appointed complies with the conditions specified in rule 21.4(3).

Effect of rule—A child or patient must have a litigation friend to conduct proceedings on his behalf, whether as claimant or defendant. A litigation friend may be appointed by order of the court and in some instances a court order is necessary. In certain circumstances a person may act as a litigation friend without a court order so appointing him (see rr.21.4 and 21.5). Further, the court may make an order permitting a child to conduct proceedings without a litigation friend (r.21.2(3)). Rule 21.6 contains provisions dealing with the appointment of a litigation friend by the court where this is desired on request (see former RSC, O.80, r.6(5) to (7), and CCR, O.10, r.3 and 6). **21.6.1**

Rule 21.6(1) states the general proposition that the court may make an order appointing a litigation friend. An application of a court order may be made by (a) a person who wishes to be the litigation friend, or (b) a party (r.21(2)). Rule 21.6(3) states the circumstances in which a party who is a claimant must make an application for the appointment of a litigation friend by court order where the defendant is under a disability. Generally, a Pt 20 claim is to be treated as if it were a claim for the purposes of the CPR (r.20.3(1)). Consequently, r.21.6(3) applies where a Pt 20 claim is brought against a child or patient.

Rule 3.1(7) states that where the court has a power under the CPR to make an order, for example, the power to make an order appointing a litigation friend under r.21.6, that power includes a power to vary or revoke the order. For specific powers to vary where a litigation friend is appointed, see r.21.7 below.

As nothing in r.21.6 provides otherwise, the court may exercise its powers under this rule of its own initiative (r.3.3(1)) but, in terms, the rule envisages the powers being exercised on application by the persons referred to in r.21.6(2).

21.6.2 **The application**—For practice relevant to appointment of a litigation friend by court order, see Practice Direction (Children and Patients), para. 3 (see para. 21PD–001).

An application for an order appointing a litigation friend must be supported by evidence (r.21.6(4)). For rules as to applications for court orders, see Pt 23 (General rules about applications for court orders) and note r.32.6 (Evidence in proceedings other than trial). The application notice must state what order is sought and state why it is sought (r.23.5). The application must be served on the persons referred to in r.21.8(1) and (2). The implication is that the application must state, not only that a litigation friend should be appointed, but also propose that a particular person should be appointed. The court may appoint the person proposed or any other person (r.21.8(4)) (see former CCR, O.10, r.6(4)).

Court's power to change litigation friend and to prevent person acting as litigation friend

21.7 **21.7**—(1) The court may—

(a) direct that a person may not act as a litigation friend;

(b) terminate a litigation friend's appointment;

(c) appoint a new litigation friend in substitution for an existing one.

(2) An application for an order under paragraph (1) must be supported by evidence.

(3) The court may not appoint a litigation friend under this rule unless it is satisfied that the person to be appointed complies with the conditions specified in rule 21.4(3).

21.7.1 **Effect of rule**—A person may become a litigation friend without court order (r.21.5) or by court order (r.21.6). The court has general power to vary or revoke any order which it makes (r.3.1(7)). Consequently, it may vary or revoke an order appointing a litigation friend. Rule 21.7 deals specifically with the powers of the court to alter or vary such an order in specific ways which, between them, take account of all eventualities. But these powers are not restricted to circumstances in which a litigation friend has been appointed by court order, but extend also to circumstances in which he has become a litigation friend without a court order.

The general rule is that, once a person has become a litigation friend (whether by court order or otherwise) his position may not be usurped by another. However, the court may make an order (a) directing that he may not act as a litigation friend, (b) terminating his appointment, (c) appointing a new litigation friend in substitution for him.

The court may exercise its powers under this rule of its own initiative (r.3.3(1)).

21.7.2 **The application**—For relevant practice, see Practice Direction (Children and Patients), para. 4 (see para. 21PD–001).

An application for an order under r.21.7 must be supported by evidence (r.21.7(2)). (If the court is dissatisfied with the actions of a litigation friend it is not obvious who should provide the evidence in support of an application under r.21.7.) The application must be served on the persons referred to in r.21.8(1) and (3).

See further "The application" in notes following r.21.6 at para. 21.6.2.

Appointment of litigation friend by court order—supplementary

21.8 **21.8**—(1) An application for an order under rule 21.6 or 21.7 must be served on every person on whom, in accordance with rule 6.6 (service on parent, guardian, etc.), the claim form should be served.

(2) Where an application for an order under rule 21.6 is in respect of a patient, the application must also be served on the patient unless the court orders otherwise.

(3) An application for an order under rule 21.7 must also be served on—
(a) the person who is the litigation friend, or who is purporting to act as the litigation friend, when the application is made; and
(b) the person who it is proposed should be the litigation friend, if he is not the applicant.

(4) On an application for an order under rule 21.6 or 21.7, the court may appoint the person proposed or any other person who complies with the conditions specified in rule 21.4(3).

Effect of rule—The provisions in this rule supplement two previous rules. See notes following rr.21.6 and 21.7. **21.8.1**

Procedure where appointment of litigation friend ceases

21.9—(1) When a child who is not a patient reaches the age of 18, a litigation friend's appointment ceases. **21.9**

(2) When a party ceases to be a patient, the litigation friend's appointment continues until it is ended by a court order.

(3) An application for an order under paragraph (2) may be made by—
(a) the former patient;
(b) the litigation friend; or
(c) a party.

(4) The child or patient in respect of whom the appointment to act has ceased must serve notice on the other parties—
(a) stating that the appointment of his litigation friend to act has ceased;
(b) giving his address for service; and
(c) stating whether or not he intends to carry on the proceedings.

(5) If he does not do so within 28 days after the day on which the appointment of the litigation friend ceases the court may, on application, strike out[GL] any claim or defence brought by him.

(6) The liability of a litigation friend for costs continues until—
(a) the person in respect of whom his appointment to act has ceased serves the notice referred to in paragraph (4); or
(b) the litigation friend serves notice on the parties that his appointment to act has ceased.

Effect of rule—For relevant practice, see Practice Direction (Children and Patients), para. 5 (see para. 21PD–001). **21.9.1**

A patient must have a litigation friend to conduct proceedings on his behalf and, generally, so must a child. If a party ceases to be a child or a patient the need for a litigation friend ceases; indeed, his further involvement in the conduct of the proceedings should not be permitted. This rule states the procedure to be followed in this event.

In terms, this rule speaks of an "appointment" as litigation friend ceasing. Strictly speaking, a person who became a litigation friend otherwise than by court order was not "appointed" as such. However, the rule would seem to apply whether the litigation friend has been acting under a court order or otherwise.

After the appointment of a litigation friend to conduct proceedings on their behalf, a child may become of full age and a patient may recover and become capable of managing his own affairs. By operation of r.21.9(1), the appointment of a litigation friend for a party who is a child ceases when the party (provided he is not a patient) attains full age. Application to the court must be made for an order to terminate the appointment of a litigation friend acting for a patient who has recovered (r.21.9(2)).

See, "Infant defendant coming of age" and "Patient defendant recovering", SCP 1999, Vol. 1, paras 80/2/15 and 80/2/16.

An application for a court order ending the appointment of a litigation friend for a patient may be made by the persons referred to in r.21.9(3). The provisions of Pt 23 (General rules about applications for court orders) apply; see, generally, "The application" in notes following r.21.6.

The duties of a party in respect of whom the appointment of a litigation friend has ceased by operation of r.21.9, and the possible consequences of his failure to discharge them, are stated in r.21.9(4)(5).

The liability of the former litigation friend for costs ceases as provided by r.21.9(6).

Part 21 contains no provision comparable to former RSC, O.80, r.7 (Application to discharge or vary certain orders).

Compromise, etc., by or on behalf of child or patient

21.10 **21.10**—(1) Where a claim is made—

(a) by or on behalf of a child or patient; or

(b) against a child or patient,

no settlement, compromise or payment and no acceptance of money paid into court shall be valid, so far as it relates to the claim by, on behalf of or against the child or patient, without the approval of the court.

(2) Where—

(a) before proceedings in which a claim is made by or on behalf of, or against child or patient (whether alone or with any other person) are begun, an agreement is reached for the settlement of the claim; and

(b) the sole purpose of proceedings on that claim is to obtain the approval of the court to a settlement or compromise of the claim,

the claim must—

(i) be made using the procedure set out in Part 8 (alternative procedure for claims); and

(ii) include a request to the court for approval of the settlement or compromise.

(Rule 48.5 contains provisions about costs where money is payable to a child or patient.)

21.10.1 **Effect of rule**—For relevant practice, see Practice Direction (Children and Patients), para. 6 (see para. 21PD–001).

Former RSC, O.80, r.10(1) provided that, in proceedings where money was claimed by or on behalf of a person under disability, no settlement, compromise or payment, and no acceptance of money paid into court, so far as it related to that person's claim was valid without the approval of the court (see also former CCR, O.20, r.11(1)). Rule 21.10(1) is to the same effect, but in two respects it is different. First, it is not confined to proceedings in which money is claimed. Secondly, it applies, not only where a claim is made by or on behalf of a child or patient, but also where it is made against a child or patient. For rules as to offers to settle and payments into and out of court, see Pt 36 (in particular, r.36.18).

Agreements for the settlement of claims involving children and patients may be reached before proceedings are begun. In these circumstances it will be necessary to obtain the court's approval of the settlement or compromise. Rule 21.10(2) states that proceedings for such approval are to be brought by a claim under the procedure stipulated in Pt 8 (Alternative procedure for claims) (see further Practice Direction (Alternative Procedure for Claims) para. 1.4 (see para. 21PD–001 below). Formerly, this matter was dealt with by RSC, O.80, r.11 and CCR, O.20, r.10(2). Rule 21.10(2) differs from its predecessors in that the approval of the court may be sought whether or not a claim for money is made and where the claim is made against the child or patient as well as by or on his behalf.

See generally, SCP 1999, Vol. 1, paras 80/11/2 *et seq.*

Rule 48.5 replaces former RSC, O.62, r.16 and contains provisions about costs where money is claimed or recovered etc. by a child or patient.

For information about structural settlements and provisional damages, see, respectively, the practice directions supplementing Pt 40 (Judgments and Orders) (see para. 40BPD–001) andPt 41 (Provisional Damages) (see para. 41PD–001). Note also SCP 1999, Vol. 2, para. 104–118 (Structural settlements involving patients).

Control of money recovered by or on behalf of child or patient

21.11 **21.11**—(1) Where in any proceedings—

(a) money is recovered by or on behalf of or for the benefit of a child or patient; or

(b) money paid into court is accepted by or on behalf of a child or patient,

the money shall be dealt with in accordance with directions given by the court under this rule and not otherwise.

(2) Directions given under this rule may provide that the money shall be wholly or partly paid into court and invested or otherwise dealt with.

21.11.1 **Effect of rule**—For relevant practice and further information, see Practice Direction (Children and Patients), paras 8 to 12 (see para. 21PD–001).

This rule replaces former RSC, O.80, r.12 and CCR, O.10, r.11. See generally, SCP 1999, Vol. 1, paras 80/12/1 *et seq.*

See also r.37.4 (apportionment by court in Fatal Accidents Act 1976 and Law Reform (Miscellaneous Provisions) Act 1934 proceedings), replacing former RSC, O.80, r.15 (see SCP 1999, Vol. 1, paras 80/15/2 *et seq.*) and note Practice Direction (Children and Patients), para. 7, see para. 21PD–001.

Appointment of guardian of child's estate

21.12—(1) The court may appoint the Official Solicitor to be a guardian of a child's estate where— **21.12**

(a) money is paid into court on behalf of the child in accordance with directions given under rule 21.11 (control of money received by a child or patient);

(b) the Criminal Injuries Compensation Board or the Criminal Injuries Compensation Authority notifies the court that it has made or intends to make an award to the child;

(c) a court or tribunal outside England and Wales notifies the court that it has ordered or intends to order that money be paid to the child;

(d) the child is absolutely entitled to the proceeds of a pension fund; or

(e) in any other case, such an appointment seems desirable to the court.

(2) The court may not appoint the Official Solicitor under this rule unless—

(a) the persons with parental responsibility (within the meaning of section 3 of the Children Act 1989[2]) agree; or

(b) the court considers that their agreement can be dispensed with.

(3) The Official Solicitor's appointment may continue only until the child reaches 18.

Effect of rule—This rules replaces former RSC, O.80, r.13. See generally, SCP 1999, Vol. 1, para. 80/13/1. **21.12.1**

PRACTICE DIRECTION—CHILDREN AND PATIENTS

This Practice Direction supplements CPR Part 21

General

1.1 In this practice direction "child" means a person under 18 years old and "patient" means a person who by reason of mental disorder within the meaning of the Mental Health Act 1983 is incapable of managing and administering his own affairs.[3] **21PD–001**

1.2 A patient must bring or defend proceedings by a litigation friend (see paragraph 2 below for the definition of a litigation friend).

1.3 In the proceedings referred to in paragraph 1.2 above the patient should be referred to in the title as "A.B. (by C.D. his litigation friend)".

1.4 A child must bring or defend proceedings by a litigation friend unless the court has made an order permitting the child to do so on his own behalf.[4]

1.5 Where;

(1) the child has a litigation friend, the child should be referred to in the title to proceedings as "A.B. (a child by C.D. his litigation friend)", and

(2) the child is conducting proceedings on his own behalf, the child should be referred to in the title as "A.B. (a child)".

1.6 The approval of the court must be obtained if a settlement of a claim by or against a child or patient[5] is to be valid. A settlement includes an agreement on a sum to be apportioned to a dependent child under the Fatal Accidents Act 1976.

[2] 1989 c. 41.
[3] See rule 21.1(2).
[4] See rule 21.2(3).
[5] See rule 21.10.

1.7 The approval of the court must also be obtained before making a voluntary interim payment to a child or patient.

1.8 A hearing of an application under Part 21 will take place in private unless the court directs otherwise.

The litigation friend

2.1 It is the duty of a litigation friend fairly and competently to conduct proceedings on behalf of a child or patient. He must have no interest in the proceedings adverse to that of the child or patient and all steps and decisions he takes in the proceedings must be taken for the benefit of the child or patient.

2.2 A person may become a litigation friend;

(1) of a child

(a) without a court order under the provisions of rule 21.5, or

(b) by a court order under rule 21.6, and

(2) of a patient

(a) by authorisation under Part VII of the Mental Health Act 1983, or

(b) by a court order under rule 21.6.

2.3 In order to become a litigation friend without a court order the person who wishes to act as litigation friend must:

(1) if he wishes to act on behalf of a patient, file an official copy of the order or other document which constitutes the authorisation referred to in paragraph 2.2(2)(a) above, or

(2) if he wishes to act on behalf of a child, or on behalf of a patient without the authorisation referred to in (1) above, file a certificate of suitability[6]—

(a) stating that he consents to act,

(b) stating that he knows or believes that the [claimant] [defendant] is a [child] [patient],

(c) in the case of a patient, stating the grounds of his belief and if his belief is based upon medical opinion attaching any relevant document to the certificate,

(d) stating that he can fairly and competently conduct proceedings on behalf of the child or patient and has no interest adverse to that of the child or patient,

(e) where the child or patient is a claimant, undertaking to pay any costs which the child or patient may be ordered to pay in relation to the proceedings, subject to any right he may have to be repaid from the assets of the child or patient, and

(f) which he has signed in verification of its contents.

2.4 The litigation friend must serve a certificate of suitability[7]:

(1) in the case of a child (who is not also a patient) on one of the child's parents or guardians or if there is no parent or guardian, on the person with whom the child resides or in whose care the child is, and

(2) in the case of a patient on the person authorised under Part VII of the Mental Health Act 1983 to conduct proceedings on behalf of the patient or if there is no person so authorised, on the person with whom the patient resides or in whose care the patient is.

2.4A The litigation friend is not required to serve the documents referred to in paragraph 2.3(2)(c) when he serves a certificate of suitability on the person to be served under paragraph 2.4.

2.5 The litigation friend must file either the certificate of suitability together with a certificate of service[8] of it, or the authorisation referred to in paragraph 2.3(1) above:

[6] See rule 21.5(3).
[7] See rule 21.5(6) and rule 6.9 (service).
[8] See rule 6.10 for the certificate of service.

(1) where the litigation friend is acting on behalf of a claimant, when the claim form is issued, and

(2) where the litigation friend is acting on behalf of a defendant, when he first takes a step in the action.

Application for a court order appointing a litigation friend

3.1 Rule 21.6 sets out who may apply for an order appointing a litigation friend. **21PD–002**

3.2 An application should be made in accordance with Part 23 and must be supported by evidence.[9]

3.3 The application notice must be served:

(1) on the persons referred to in paragraph 2.4 above, and

(2) where the application is in respect of a patient, on the patient unless the court orders otherwise

3.4 The evidence in support must satisfy the court that the proposed litigation friend:

(1) consents to act,

(2) can fairly and competently conduct proceedings on behalf of the child or patient,

(3) has no interest adverse to that of the child or patient, and

(4) where the child or patient is a claimant, undertakes to pay any costs which the child or patient may be ordered to pay in relation to the proceedings, subject to any right he may have to be repaid from the assets of the child or patient.

3.5 Where a claimant wishes to take a step in proceedings against a child or patient who does not have a litigation friend he must apply to the court for an order appointing a litigation friend.

3.6 The proposed litigation friend must satisfy the conditions in paragraph 3.4(1), (2) and (3) above and may be one of the persons referred to in paragraph 2.4 above where appropriate, or otherwise may be the Official Solicitor. Where it is sought to appoint the Official Solicitor, provision should be made for payment of his charges.

Change of litigation friend and prevention of person acting as litigation friend

4.1 Rule 21.7(1) states that the court may;

(1) direct that a person may not act as a litigation friend,

(2) terminate a litigation friend's appointment,

(3) substitute a new litigation friend for an existing one.

4.2 Where an application is made for an order under rule 21.7(1), the application notice must set out the reasons for seeking it. The application must be supported by evidence.

4.3 If the order sought is the substitution of a new litigation friend for an existing one, the evidence must satisfy the court of the matters set out in paragraph 3.4 above.

4.4 The application notice must be served;

(1) on the persons referred to in paragraph 2.4 above, and

(2) on the litigation friend or person purporting to act as litigation friend.

Procedure where the need for a litigation friend has come to an end

5.1 Rule 21.9 deals with the situation where the need for a litigation friend comes to an end during the proceedings because either:

(1) a child who is not also a patient reaches the age of 18 (full age) during the proceedings, or

(2) a patient ceases to be a patient (recovers).

[9] See rule 21.6(4).

5.2 A child on reaching full age must serve on the other parties to the proceedings and file with the court a notice:

(1) stating that he has reached full age,

(2) stating that his litigation friend's appointment has ceased,[10]

(3) giving an address for service,[11] and

(4) stating whether or not he intends to carry on with or continue to defend the proceedings.

5.3 If the notice states that the child intends to carry on with or continue to defend the proceedings he shall subsequently be described in the proceedings as:

"A.B. (formerly a child but now of full age)"

5.4 Whether or not a child having reached full age serves a notice in accordance with rule 21.9(4)(a) and paragraph 5.2(2) above, a litigation friend may at any time after the child has reached full age serve a notice on the other parties that his appointment has ceased.

5.5 The liability of a litigation friend for costs continue until a notice that his appointment to act has ceased is served on the other parties.[12]

5.6 Where a patient recovers, an application under rule 21.9(3) must be made for an order under rule 21.9(2) that the litigation friend's appointment has ceased.

5.7 The application must be supported by the following evidence:

(1) a medical report indicating that the patient has recovered and that he is capable of managing and administering his property and affairs,

(2) where the patient's affairs were under the control of the Court of Protection, a copy of the order or notice discharging the receiver, and

(3) if the application is made by the patient, a statement whether or not he intends to carry on with or continue to defend the proceedings.

5.8 An order under rule 21.9(2) must be served on the other parties to the proceedings. The patient must file with the court a notice:

(1) stating that his litigation friend's appointment has ceased,

(2) giving an address for service,[13] and

(3) stating whether or not he intends to carry on with or continue to defend the proceedings.

Settlement or compromise by or on behalf of a child or patient

21PD–003 **6.1** Where a claim by or on behalf of a child or patient has been dealt with by agreement prior to the start of proceedings and only the approval of the court to the agreement is sought, the claim:

(1) must be made using the Part 8 procedure,

(2) must include a request for approval of the settlement or compromise, and

(3) in addition to the details of the claim, must set out the terms of the settlement or compromise or have attached to it a draft consent order in practice form N292.

6.2 In order to approve the settlement or compromise, the information concerning the claim that the court will require will include:

(1) whether and to what extent the defendant admits liability,

(2) the age and occupation (if any) of the child or patient,

(3) the litigation friend's approval of the proposed settlement or compromise, and

(4) in a personal injury case airising from an accident—

(a) the circumstances of the accident,

(b) any medical reports,

[10] Rule 21.9(4)(a).
[11] See rule 6.5.
[12] Rule 21.9(6).
[13] See rule 6.5.

(c) where appropriate, a schedule of any past and future expenses and losses claimed and any other relevant information relating to personal injury as set out in the practice direction which supplements Part 16 (statement of case), and
(d) where considerations of liability are raised—
(i) any evidence or police reports in any criminal proceedings or in an inquest, and
(ii) details of any prosecution brought.

6.3(1) An opinion on the merits of the settlement or compromise given by counsel or solicitor acting for the child or patient should, except in very clear cases, be obtained.

(2) A copy of the opinion and, unless the instructions on which it was given are sufficiently set out in it, a copy of the instructions, must also be supplied to the court.

6.4 Applications for the approval of a settlement or compromise will normally be heard by a Master or district judge.

(For information about structured settlements see the practice direction on structured settlements supplementing Part 40 (Judgments and Orders).)

(For information about provisional damages claims see Part 41 and the practice direction which supplements it.)

Apportionment under the Fatal Accidents Act 1976

7.1 A judgment on or settlement in respect of a claim under the Fatal Accidents Act 1976 must be apportioned between the persons by or on whose behalf the claim has been brought.

7.2 Where a claim is brought on behalf of a dependent child or children, the money apportioned to any child must be invested on his behalf in accordance with rules 21.10 and 21.11 and paragraphs 8 and 9 below.

7.3 In order to approve an apportionment of money to a dependent child, the court will require the following information:
(1) the matters set out in paragraph 6.2(1), (2) above, and
(2) in respect of the deceased
(a) where death was caused by an accident, the matters set out in paragraph 6.2(3)(a), (b) and (c) above, and
(b) his future loss of earnings, and
(3) the extent and nature of the dependency.

Control of money recovered by or on behalf of a child or patient

8.1 Money recovered or paid into court on behalf of or for the benefit of a child or patient shall be dealt with in accordance with directions of the court under rule 21.11.

8.2 The court:
(1) may direct the money to be paid into the High Court for investment,
(2) may also direct that certain sums be paid direct to the child or patient, his litigation friend or his legal representative[14] for the immediate benefit of the child or patient or for expenses incurred on his behalf, and
(3) may direct the applications in respect of the investment of the money be transferred to a local district registry.

8.3 The Master or district judge will consider the general aims to be achieved for the money in court (the fund) by investment and will give directions as to the type of investment.

8.4 Where a child is also a patient, and likely to remain so on reaching full age, his fund shall be administered as a patient's fund.

8.5 Where a child or patient is legally aided the fund will be subject to a first charge under s.16 of the Legal Aid Act 1988 (the legal aid charge) and an

[14] See rule 2.3 for a definition of legal representative.

order for the investment of money on the child or patient's behalf must contain a direction to that effect.

Guardian's Accounts

9. Paragraph 8 of the practice direction supplementing Part 40 (Judgments and Orders) deals with the approval of the accounts of a guardian of assets of a child.

Investment on behalf of a child

21PD–004 **10.1** At the hearing of the application for the approval of the agreement the litigation friend or his legal representative should provide a CFO form 320 (request for investment) for completion by the Master or district judge.

10.2 On receipt of that form in the Court Funds Office the investment managers of the Public Trust Office will make the appropriate investment.

10.3 Where an award of damages for a child is made at trial the trial may direct:

(1) the money to be paid into court and placed in the special investment account, and

(2) the litigation friend to make an application to a Master or district judge for further investment directions.

10.4 If the money to be invested is very small the court may order it to be paid direct to the litigation friend to be put into a building society account (or similar) for the child's use.

10.5 If the money is invested in court it must be paid out to the child when he reaches full age.

Investment on behalf of a patient

11.1 The Court of Protection is responsible for protecting the property of patients and is given extensive powers to do so under the Mental Health Act 1983. Fees are charged for the administration of funds by the Court of Protection and these should be provided for in any settlement.

11.2 Where the sum to be administered is:

(1) over £30,000, the order approving the settlement will contain a direction to the litigation friend to apply to the Court of Protection for the appointment of a receiver, after which the fund will be transferred to the Court of Protection,

(2) under £20,000, it may be retained in court and invested in the same way as the fund of a child, or

(3) in intermediate cases the advice of the Master of the Court of Protection should be sought.

11.3 A form of order transferring the fund to the Court of Protection is set out in practice form N292.

11.4 In order for the Court Funds Office to release a fund which is subject to the legal aid charge to the Court of Protection the litigation friend or his legal representative should provide the appropriate area office of the Legal Aid Board with an undertaking in respect of a sum to cover their costs, following which the area office will advise the Court Funds Office in writing of that sum, enabling them to transfer the balance to the Court of Protection on receipt of a CFO form 200 payment schedule authorised by the court.

11.5 The CFO form 200 should be completed and presented to the court where the settlement or trial took place for authorisation, subject to paragraphs 11.6 and 11.7 below.

11.6 Where the settlement took place in the Royal Courts of Justice the CFO form 200 should be completed and presented for authorisation:

(1) on behalf of a child, in the Masters' Secretary's Office, Room E214, and

(2) on behalf of a patient, in the Action Department, Room E15.

11.7 Where the trial took place in the Royal Courts of Justice the CFO form 200 is completed and authorised by the court officer.

Payment out of funds in court

12.1 Applications to a Master or district judge;

(1) for payment out of money from the fund for the benefit of the child, or

(2) to vary an investment strategy,

may be dealt with without a hearing unless the court directs otherwise.

12.2 When the child reaches full age, his fund in court:

(1) where it is a sum of money will be paid out to him, and

(2) where it is in the form of investments other than money (for example shares or unit trusts), will be transferred into his name.

12.3 An application for payment out of funds being administered by the Court of Protection must be made to the Court of Protection.

(For further information on payments into and out of court see the practice directions supplementing Parts 36 and 37.)

PART 22

Statements of Truth

22.0.1 **Contents**

Editorial Introduction

22.0.2 Rule 22.1 states that any statement of case (formerly "pleadings"), a response complying with an order under r.18.1 to provide further information, and any witness statement must be verified by a statement of truth. Certain other documents, not mentioned in r.22.1, also may or must be verified by a statement of truth (*e.g.* an notice of application) (see further notes following r.22.1). Pt 22 is supplemented by Practice Direction (Statement of Truth) (see 22PD–001). This Practice Direction is modified by the Practice Direction supplementing r.7.10. Some other practice directions also refer to statements of truth.

In certain circumstances, a false statement made in a document verified by statement of truth may lead to a liability for contempt of court (see further notes following r.22.1).

The justification for the requirement that a witness statement should be verified is obvious; it provides some guarantee that the statement is made with an honest belief as to the accuracy of its contents. There are two justifications for the requirement that a statement of case should be verified. First, if a party is required to certify his belief in the accuracy and truth of the matters put forward the statement of case is less likely to include assertions that are speculative and fanciful and designed to obfuscate (Interim Report at p. 161). Secondly, in certain circumstances, a statement of case may be relied on as evidence. If it is to be used as such it is right that the facts asserted in it should be verified. The same can be said of facts asserted in a notice of application.

Under the old pleadings practice, often pleaders strove to keep their options open and to avoid restricting issues, leaving room for manoeuvre as the case developed (see Interim Report at p. 153). The pleader was assisted in doing this by the fact that pleadings could include assertions based on facts of which (perhaps unbeknownst to the opponent) the party had no actual knowledge or was not in a position to prove when the pleading was made (but hoped that proof would be forthcoming). To an extent, the pleader's scope for prevarication and obfuscation, and for pleading alternative positions that may come perilously close to flat contradictions, is restricted by the verification requirement in r.22.1. The rule falls short of requiring the claimant to verify his statement of case by affidavit.

Rules 22.2 and 22.3 explain the consequences which may follow from a failure to verify any statement of case or witness statement and r.22.4 sets out the court's power to require a document to be verified.

Related Sources

22.0.3
- Practice Direction (Statements of Truth)—see para. 22PD–001.
- Rule 8.2 (contents of claim form where Pt 8 procedure used).
- Rule 16.2(1) (contents of claim form).
- Rule 16.5 (contents of defence).
- Rule 16.7 (reply to defence).
- Rule 32.8 (Form of witness statement).
- Rule 32.14 (False statements).
- Part 17 (Amendments to statements of case).
- Part 18 (Further information).
- Part 20 (Counterclaims, etc.).
- Part 21 (Children and patients).
- Practice Direction (How to Start Proceedings), para. 7 (see para. 7PD–001).
- Practice Direction (Production Centre), para. 1.4(5) (see para. 7CPD–001).
- Practice Direction (Statement of Case), para. 14 (see para. 16PD–001).
- Practice Direction (Defence and Reply), para. 2 (see para. 15PD–001).
- Practice Direction (Counterclaims and Other Part 20 Claims), para. 4.1 (see para. 20PD–001).
- Practice Direction (Further Information), para. 3 (see para. 18PD–001).

- Practice Direction (Experts and Assessors) (see para. 35PD–001).
- Practice Direction supplementing Pt 40 (Judgments and Orders) (see para. 40BPD–001).

Documents to be verified by a statement of truth

22.1—(1) The following documents must be verified by a statement of truth— **22.1**

(a) a statement of case;

(b) a response complying with an order under rule 18.1 to provide further information; and

(c) a witness statement.

(2) Where a statement of case is amended, the amendments must be verified by a statement of truth unless the court orders otherwise.

(Part 17 provides for amendments to statements of case.)

(3) If an applicant wishes to rely on matters set out in his application notice as evidence, the application notice must be verified by a statement of truth.

(4) Subject to paragraph (5), a statement of truth is a statement that—

(a) the party putting forward the document; or

(b) in the case of a witness statement, the maker of the witness statement,

believes the facts stated in the document are true.

(5) If a party is conducting proceedings with a litigation friend, the statement of truth in—

(a) a statement of case;

(b) a response; or

(c) an application notice,

is a statement that the litigation friend believes the facts stated in the document being verified are true.

(6) The statement of truth must be signed by—

(a) in the case of a statement of case, a response or an application—

(i) the party or litigation friend; or

(ii) the legal representative on behalf of the party or litigation friend; and

(b) in the case of a witness statement, by the maker of the statement.

(7) A statement of truth which is not contained in the document which it verifies, must clearly identify that document.

(8) A statement of truth in a statement of case may be made by—

(a) a person who is not a party; or

(b) by two parties jointly,

where this is permitted by a relevant practice direction.

Effect of rule—The following are to be verified by a statement of truth: (1) a statement of case; (2) a response complying with an order under r.18.1 to provide further information; (3) a witness statement; and (4) a notice of application (where the applicant wishes to rely on matters stated in it as evidence). In the notes below these four are dealt with in turn. An expert's report should also be verified by a statement of truth (see Practice Direction supplementing Pt 35) and so should a notice of objections to an account being taken by the court (unless verified by an affidavit or witness statement) (see Practice Direction supplementing Pt 40). **22.1.1**

In the case of documents required to be verified by r.22.1, the statement of truth is made by the person (or persons, see r.22.1(8)) referred to in r.22.1(6) as appropriate and is to the effect that he believes that the facts stated are true (r.22.1(4)). If the statement of truth is not contained in the document which it verifies, it must clearly identify that document (r.22.1(7)) in the manner provided by Practice Direction (Statement of Truth), para. 2.3 (see 22PD–001).

For appropriate form of statement of truth, see para. 22.1.14 "Form of Statement of Truth" below.

Statement of case—A "statement of case" is one of the documents which, under the provisions of this Part, "must be verified by a statement of truth" (r.22.1(1)). (For former law as to signing of pleadings, see RSC, O.18, r.6(5) and CCR, O.50, r.6A, and note SCP 1999, Vol. 1, paras 18/6/2 and 50/6/1). A "statement of truth" is a statement that "the party putting forward the document" believes the facts stated in the document are true (r.22.1(4)). **22.1.2**

The statement of truth verifying a statement of case must be signed by either the party or the legal representative on behalf of the party (r.22.1(6)). In either event, it is the party, and not the legal representative, who is "putting forward the document". Where a party is conducting proceedings with a litigation friend (see Pt 21 (Children and Patients), the statement of truth is a statement that the litigation friend believes the facts stated are true (r.22.1(5)(a)) and must be signed by him or his legal representative (r.22.1(6)(a)).

A "statement of case" is one or other of the following documents (see r.2.3(1)): (1) a claim form, including a claim form used under the Pt 8 procedure, (2) particulars of claim where these are not included in a claim form, (3) a defence, (4) a Part 20 claim; or (5) a reply to defence. (A statement of case, also includes "further information" given in relation to any of these documents, see further below.)

Note Practice Direction (How to Start Proceedings), para. 7 (see para. 7PD–001) and Practice Direction (Statements of Case), para. 13 (see para. 16PD–001).

22.1.3 **Claim form**—Rule 16.2(1) states that the claim form must contain: (a) a concise statement of the nature of the claim; (b) specify the remedy which the claimant seeks; (c) where the claimant is making a claim for money, containing a statement of value in accordance with r.16.3; and (d) contain such other matters as may be set out in a practice direction. Particulars of claim must be contained in or served with the claim form (r.7.4(1), but in certain circumstances may be served subsequently (r.7.4(2)). Rule 16.4 states that the particulars of claim must include, amongst other things, "a concise statement of the facts on which the claimant relies". As a practical matter, the signficance of the particulars being verified by a statement of truth is confined to this "concise statement of the facts" in the particulars of claim, whether contained in the claim form or served separately.

Rule 8.5 states that, under the alternative procedure for claims set out in Pt 8, a claimant must file any "written evidence" on which he intends to rely when he files his claim form. A claimant may rely on the matters set out in his claim form as evidence under that rule if the claim form is verified by a statement of truth (r.8.5(7)). Where the Pt 8 procedure is being used, the claim form must state the matters set out in r.8.2.

22.1.4 **Defence**—Rule 16.5 states that, in his defence, a defendant must state: (a) which of the allegations in the particulars of claim he denies; (b) which allegations he is unable to admit or deny, but which he requires the claimant to prove; and (c) which allegations he admits; further, (d) where he denies an allegation he must state his reasons for doing so and, (e) if he intends to put forward a different version of events from that given by the claimant, he must state his own version. As a practical matter, the significance of the defence being verified by a statement of truth is confined to the defendant's own "version of events".

Note Practice Direction (Defence and Reply), para. 2 (see para. 15PD–001).

22.1.5 **Part 20 claim**—A Pt 20 claim is defined in r.20.2(1) and includes a counterclaim, a claim against a third party and similar claims. By r.20.2(1), a Pt 20 claim, generally, is to be started as if it were a claim. This provision, together with the inclusion of Pt 20 claims in the definition of a "statement of case" (r.2.3(2)), makes it clear that any statement of case generated under Pt 20 must be verified.

See further Practice Direction (Counterclaims and Other Part 20 Claims), para. 4.1 (see para. 20PD–001).

22.1.6 **Reply**—Should a claimant file a reply to defence (r.15.8), the reply should be verified.

22.1.7 **Statement of case subsequent to reply**—With the permission of the court, a party may serve a statement of case after a reply (r.15.9). Such further statement of case does not fall within the definition of "statement of case" given in r.2.3(1) and this omission may create doubts as to whether a further statement is included among the documents which must be verified by a statement of truth by virtue of r.22.1(1). It would be surprising if it were not. In any event, the court, in giving permission for a further statement to be served, could direct that it should be verified.

22.1.8 **Verification of amendments to statement of case**—A statement of case may be amended as provided by the rules in Pt 17 (Amendments to statements of case). In certain circumstances the permission of the court is required. Obviously, as a party's statement of case has to be verified by a statement of truth any amendment thereto must also be verified (r.22.1(2)). However, the court may order otherwise and is likely to do so in cases where amendment cannot be made without the court's permission and the amendment does not involve any allegations of fact by the party.

22.1.9 **Any "further information" of statement of case to be verified**—A "statement of case" includes, not only (1) a claim form, including a claim form used under the Pt 8 procedure, (2) particulars of claim where these are not included in a claim form, (3) a defence, (4) a Pt 20 claim, (5) a reply to defence, but also any "further information" given in relation to them voluntarily or by court order under r.18.1 (r.2.3(1)). Rule 18.1 states that the court may at any time order a party to (a) clarify any matter which is in dispute in the proceedings, or (b) give additional information in relation to any such matter, whether or not the matter is contained or referred to in a statement of case. It is clear from the terms of r.22.1(1)(b) that where a party provides further information in relation to his statement of case by way of a response to a court order under r.18.1 it must be verified by a statement of truth. This proposition is repeated in Practice Direction (Statement of Truth) para. 1.1(2). But neither the rule nor the Practice Direction requires a voluntary response to be so verified. By indirect (but not wholly successful) means, Practice Direction (Further Information) para. 3 attempts to deal with this apparent gap (see 18PD–002). Clearly, the intention is that voluntary responses should be verified by statements of truth.

Verified statement of case as evidence—At hearings other than trial, a party (whether claimant or defendant) may in support of his application, rely on matters set out in his statement of case if it is verified by a statement of truth (r.32.6(2)(a)); an example is provided by r.25.6(5) (application for interim payment). **22.1.10**

Rule 8.5 states that, under the alternative procedure for claims set out in Pt 8, a claimant must file any "written evidence" on which he intends to rely when he files his claim form. The claimant may rely on matters set out in his claim form as evidence under r.8.5 if the claim form is verified by a statement of truth (r.8.5(7)).

Witness statement—A witness statement is a written statement signed by a person which contains the evidence, and only that evidence which that person would be allowed to give orally (r.32.4(1)). (For form of witness statement, see r.32.8.) Rule 22.1(1) states that a witness statement is a document which must be verified by a statement of truth. The statement of truth must state that the maker of the statement "believes the facts stated in the document are true" (r.22.1(4)(b)) and it must be signed by the maker of the statement (r.22.1(6)(b)). (For former law, see RSC, O.38, r.2A(4) and CCR, O.20, r.12A(4).) **22.1.11**

By definition, a written statement signed by a witness, though not verified by a statement of truth, is a witness statement. It would seem therefore that a requirement to serve a witness statement is satisfied if a statement that is signed but not verified is served.

In certain circumstances, a "witness summary" may be permitted in lieu of a "witness statement" (r.32.9). Because of the limited nature of these circumstances, there is no requirement for a witness summary to be verified.

Application notice—An application notice is a written document in which the applicant states his intention to seek a court order (r.23.1), for example, an order for an interim remedy. An application notice must state (a) what order the applicant is seeking, and (b) briefly, why the applicant is seeking the order (r.23.6). At the hearing of the application the applicant may in support of his application rely on matters set out in his statement of case, provided it is verified by a statement of truth (r.32.6(2)(a)). If an applicant wishes to rely on matters set out in his application notice, the application notice must be verified by a statement of truth (r.22.1(3) and r.32.6(2)(b)), otherwise the notice need not be verified. Verification is by the party (r.22.1(4)(a)) and the statement of truth must be signed by him or by his legal representative (r.22.1(6)(a)). Where a party is conducting proceedings with a litigation friend (see Pt 21 (Children and Patients), verification is by the litigation friend and the statement of truth is signed by him or by his legal representative (r.22.1(5)(c) and r.22.1(6)(a)). **22.1.12**

Rule 5.3 states that, where it is required that "a document" should be signed, the signature may be "printed by computer or other mechanical means". It would seem that this does not apply to statements of truth because a statement of truth is not "a document" but a statement in a document.

Expert's report—An expert's report must comply with the requirements set out in the relevant practice direction (r.35.10(1)). Practice Direction (Experts and Assessors) para. 1.3 states that an expert's report must be verified by a statement of truth and para. 1.4 indicate the form such verification should take (see 35PD–001). **22.1.13**

Form of statement of truth—The form of statement of truth verifying a statement of case should be as stated in Practice Direction (Statements of Truth) para. 2.1 (see 22PD–001); see also Practice Direction (How to Start Proceedings—The Claim Form) para. 7 (see 7PD–002), Practice Direction (Statements of Case) para. 13 (see 13PD–005), Practice Direction (Defence and Reply) para. 2 (see 15PD–001), and Practice Direction (Counterclaim and Other Part 20 Claims) para. 4.1 (see 20PD–001). **22.1.14**

In certain circumstances, claim forms may be issued through the Production Centre. Practice Direction (Production Centre) (see 7CPD–001) modifies the Practice Direction (Statements of Truth) *op. cit.* in a manner which facilitates the preparation of statements of truth where a party files with the Centre a batch of requests for the issue of claim forms (*ibid.* para. 1.4(5)).

The form of statement of truth verifying an application notice, a response to a further information order, or a notice of objections should be as stated in Practice Direction (Statements of Truth) para. 2.1 (see 22PD–001); see also Practice Direction (Further Information) para. 3 (see 18PD–002) and Practice Direction (Accounts, Inquiries, etc.) para. 3.3 (40PD–001).

For form of statement of truth verifying a witness statement, see Practice Direction (Written Evidence) para. 20 (20PD–004).

For form of statement of truth verifying expert's report, see para. 22.1.13 "Expert's report" above.

22.1.15 **Who may sign the statement of truth**—In the case of documents referred to in r.22.1, the statement of truth is to be signed by the persons referred to in r.22.1(5) to (7). The matter is amplified in Practice Direction (Statements of Truth) paras 3.1 *et seq.* (see 22PD–001) where the appropriate person to verify a notice of objections to an account is also explained. The Practice Direction contains important provisions concerning the conclusions which the court may draw where a legal representative signs a statement of truth on behalf of the party (*ibid.* paras. 3.7 and 3.8).

Special provision is made in the Practice Direction for cases in which the party verifying a document by a statement of truth is a company or a partnership (*ibid.* paras 3.4 to 3.6). In the case of a company or corporation verification is to be by "a person holding a senior position" and, in effect, this is a person who could swear an affidavit.

22.1.16 **False statements**—In certain circumstances, a false statement made in a document verified by statement of truth may lead to a liability for contempt of court. Provisions to this effect are found, not in this Part, but in r.32.14. Proceedings for contempt of court may be brought against a party if he makes, or causes to be made, a false statement in a document verified by a statement of truth. This applies, not only to the documents referred to in r.22.1, but also to other documents which may or must be verified by a statement of case or a notice of application verified by a statement of truth.

Failure to verify a statement of case

22.2 **22.2**—(1) If a party fails to verify his statement of case by a statement of truth—

(a) the statement of case shall remain effective unless struck out; but

(b) the party may not rely on the statement of case as evidence of any of the matters set out in it.

(2) The court may strike out[GL] a statement of case which is not verified by a statement of truth.

(3) Any party may apply for an order under paragraph (2).

22.2.1 **Effect of rule**—See notes following r.22.3.

Failure to verify a witness statement

22.3 **22.3** If the maker of a witness statement fails to verify the witness statement by a statement of truth the court may direct that it shall not be admissible as evidence.

22.3.1 **Effect of rules 22.2 and 22.3**—Statements of case (and amendments thereto) and witness statements should be verified by a statement of truth (r.22.1(1)(2)). Rules 22.2 and 22.3 deal with the consequences that may follow if they are not verified. A notice of application should be verified if a party wants to rely on it as evidence in those circumstances where the contents of a notice can be relied on as evidence. Rules 22.2 and 22.3 are not concerned with the consequences that may follow if a notice of application is not verified (see notes following r.22.1).

22.3.2 **Failure to verify a statement of case**—See Practice Direction (Statements of Truth), para. 4 (see para. 22PD–002) (Consequences of failure to verify).

The rule is that a statement of case must be verified by a statement of truth (r.22.1(1)). Rule 22.1(a) makes it clear that if a statement of case is not verified it is not a nullity. The lack of verification is an irregularity which may be cured. The court may strike out a statement of case (or part of a statement of case) on the grounds stated in r.3.4(2). Under r.22.2(2) the court may strike out a statement of case on the additional ground that it is not verified by a statement of truth, and any party may apply for a striking out order on this ground (r.22.2(3)).

In certain circumstances, a party may rely on matters set out in a statement of case as evidence (see r.32.6(2) and r.8.5(7)). However, where a statement of case remains unverified the party may not rely on it as evidence of any matters set out in it (r.22.2(1)(b)) (for unverified witness statements as evidence, see below).

For costs consequences of failure to verify statement of case, see Practice Direction (Statement of Truth), para. 4.3 (see para. 22PD–002 below).

In certain circumstances, a party may rely on matters set out in an application notice where the notice is verified by statement of truth (see notes following r.22.1).

Failure to verify a witness statement—A witness statement must at least be signed by the maker (r.32.4), must comply with the requirements of the relevant practice direction (r.32.8), and must be verified by a statement of truth (r.22.1(1)). The general rule is that evidence at hearings other than at trial is to be by witness statement (r.32.6(1)). In certain circumstances, witness statements may also be used as evidence at trial (r.32.5). Rule 22.3 provides that a witness statement which is not verified by a statement of truth, signed by the maker of the statement, may be rendered inadmissible as evidence if the court so directs. The lack of verification does not render it *ipso facto* inadmissible (*cf.* unverified statement of case, *supra*). 22.3.3

Power of the court to require a document to be verified

22.4—(1) The court may order a person who has failed to verify a document in accordance with rule 22.1 to verify the document. 22.4

(2) Any party may apply for an order under paragraph (1).

Effect of rule—The documents referred to in r.22.1 are statements of case and witness statements. In terms, this rule does not give the court power to require verification of an application notice. 22.4.1

PRACTICE DIRECTION—STATEMENTS OF TRUTH

This Practice Direction supplements CPR Part 22

Documents to be verified by a statement of truth

1.1 Rule 22.1(1) sets out the documents which must be verified by a statement of truth. The documents include: 22PD–001

(1) a statement of case,

(2) a response complying with an order under rule 18.1 to provide further information, and

(3) a witness statement.

1.2 If an applicant wishes to rely on matters set out in his application notice as evidence, the application notice must be verified by a statement of truth.[1]

1.3 An expert's report should also be verified by a statement of truth. For the form of the statement of truth verifying an expert's report (which differs from that set out below) see the practice direction which supplements Part 35.

1.4 In addition, a notice of objections to an account being taken by the court should be verified by a statement of truth unless verified by an affidavit or a witness statement.[2]

1.5 The statement of truth may be contained in the document it verifies or it may be in a separate document served subsequently, in which case it must identify the document to which it relates.

1.6 Where the form to be used includes a jurat for the content to be verified by an affidavit then a statement of truth is not required in addition.

Form of the statement of truth

2.1 The form of the statement of truth verifying a statement of case, a response, an application notice or a notice of objections should be as follows:

"[I believe] [the (*claimant or as may be*) believes] that the facts stated in this [*name document being verified*] are true."

2.2 The form of the statement of truth verifying a witness statement should be as follows:

"I believe that the facts stated in this witness statement are true."

2.3 Where the statement of truth is contained in a separate document, the document containing the statement of truth must be headed with the title of the proceedings and the claim number. The document being verified should be identified in the statement of truth as follows:

(1) claim form: "the claim form issued on [*date*]",

(2) particulars of claim: "the particulars of claim issued on [*date*]",

(3) statement of case: "the [*defence or as may be*] served on the [*name of party*] on [*date*]",

[1] See rule 22.1(3) .

[2] See the Accounts and Enquiries practice direction supplementing Part 40 (Judgments and Orders).

(4) application notice: "the application notice issued on [*date*] for [*set out the remedy sought*]",

(5) witness statement: "the witness statement filed on [*date*] or served on [*party*] on [*date*]".

Who may sign the statement of truth

22PD–002 **3.1** In a statement of case, a response or an application notice, the statement of truth must be signed by:

(1) the party or his litigation friend,[3] or

(2) the legal representative[4] of the party or litigation friend.

3.2 A statement of truth verifying a witness statement must be signed by the witness.

3.3 A statement of truth verifying a notice of objections to an account must be signed by the objecting party or his legal representative.

3.4 Where a document is to be verified on behalf of a company or other corporation, subject to paragraph 3.7 below, the statement of truth must be signed by a person holding a senior position[5] in the company or corporation. That person must state the office or position he holds.

3.5 Each of the following persons is a person holding a senior position:

(1) in respect of a registered company or corporation, a director, the treasurer, secretary, chief executive, manager or other officer of the company or corporation, and

(2) in respect of a corporation which is not a registered company, in addition to those persons set out in (1), the mayor, chairman, president or town clerk or other similar officer of the corporation.

3.6 Where the document is to be verified on behalf of a partnership, those who may sign the statement of truth are;

(1) any of the partners, or

(2) a person having the control or management of the partnership business.

3.6A An insurer or the Motor Insurers' Bureau may sign a statement of truth in a statement of case on behalf of a party where the insurer or the Motor Insurers' Bureau has a financial interest in the result of proceeding brought wholly or partially by or against that party.

3.7 Where a party is legally represented, the legal representative may sign the statement of truth on his behalf. The statement signed by the legal representative will refer to the client's belief, not his own. In signing he must state the capacity in which he signs and the name of his firm where appropriate.

3.8 Where a legal representative has signed a statement of truth, his signature will be taken by the court as his statement:

(1) that the client on whose behalf he has signed had authorised him to do so,

(2) that before signing he had explained to the client that in signing the statement of truth he would be confirming the client's belief that the facts stated in the document were true, and

(3) that before signing he had informed the client of the possible consequences to the client if it should subsequently appear that the client did not have an honest belief in the truth of those facts (see rule 32.14).

3.9 The individual who signs a statement of truth must print his full name clearly beneath his signature.

3.10 A legal representative who signs a statement of truth must sign in his own name and not that of his firm or employer.

3.11 The following examples of the possible application of this practice direction describing who may sign a statement of truth verifying statements in documents other than a witness statement. These are only examples and not an indication of how a court might apply the practice direction to a specific situation.

[3] See Part 21 (Children and Patients).
[4] See rule 2.3 for the definition of legal representative.
[5] See rule 6.4(4).

Managing Agent

An agent who manages property or investments for the party cannot sign a statement of truth. It must be signed by the party or by the legal representative of the party.

Trusts

Where some or all of the trustees comprise a single party one, some or all of the trustees comprising the party may sign a statement of truth. The legal representative of the trustees may sign it.

Insurers and the Motor Insurers' Bureau

If an insurer has a financial interest in a claim involving its insured then, if the insured is the party, the insurer may sign a statement of truth in a statement of case for the insured claimant. Paragraphs 3.4 and 3.5 apply to the insurer if it is a company. The claims manager employed by the insurer responsible for handling the insurance claim or managing the staff handling the claim may sign the statement of truth for the insurer (see next example). The position for the Motor Insurers' Bureau is similar.

Companies

Paragraphs 3.4 and 3.5 apply. The word manager will be construed in the context of the phrase "a person holding a senior position" which it is used to define. The court will consider the size of the company and the size and nature of the claim. It would expect the manager signing the statement of truth to have personal knowledge of the content of the document or to be responsible for managing those who have that knowledge of the content. A small company may not have a manager, apart from the directors, who holds a senior position. A large company will have many such managers. In a larger company with specialist claims, insurance or legal departments the statement may be signed by the manager of such a department if he or she is responsible for handling the claim or managing the staff handling it.

In-house legal representatives

Legal representative is defined in rule 2.3(1). A legal representative employed by a party may sign a statement of truth. However a person who is not a solicitor, barrister or other authorised litigator, but who is employed by the company and is managed by such a person, is not employed by that person and so cannot sign a statement of truth. (This is unlike the employee of a solicitor in private practice who would come within the definition of legal representative.) However such a person may be a manager and able to sign the statement on behalf of the company in that capacity.

Consequences of failure to verify

4.1 If a statement of case is not verified by a statement of truth, the statement of case will remain effective unless it is struck out,[6] but a party may not rely on the contents of a statement of case as evidence until it has been verified by a statement of truth.

4.2 Any party may apply to the court for an order that unless within such period as the court may specify the statement of case is verified by the service of a statement of truth, the statement of case will be struck out.

4.3 The usual order for the costs of an application referred to in paragraph 4.2 will be that the costs be paid by the party who had failed to verify in any event and forthwith.

Penalty

5. Attention is drawn to rule 32.14 which sets out the consequences of verifying a statement of case containing a false statement without an honest belief in its truth.

PART 23

General Rules about Applications for Court Orders

23.0.1 Contents

Editorial Introduction

23.0.2 Part 23 is the successor to former RSC, O.32 (Applications and proceedings in chambers) and CCR, O.13 (Applications and orders in the course of proceedings), especially rr.1 and 3.

RSC, O.32, grouped together in a convenient way court rules relating to proceedings "in chambers", mainly of an interlocutory nature. It consisted of 32 separate rules and had to deal with differences in practice within the several Divisions of the High Court and the district registries. The general provisions as to the making of applications stated in CCR, O.13, r.1, had effect in relation to any application "authorised by or under any Act or rule to be made in the course of an action or matter before or after judgment" in a county court, except as otherwise provided. By the County Courts Act 1984, s.38, subject to certain restrictions, in any proceedings a county court was (and still is) authorised to "make any order which could be made in the High Court if the proceedings were in the High Court" (see SCP 1999, Vol. 2, para. 20A–696).

Part 23 contains general provisions relating to applications. They are supplemented by Practice Direction (Applications) (see para. 23PD–001 below). (It should be noted that that Practice Direction also contains directions concerning consent orders supplemental to Pt 40 (Judgments and Orders) (specifically r.40.6).) In certain proceedings, it may be necessary to read the provisions of Pt 23 and supplementing Practice Directions in conjunction with the appropriate court guide (see further para. 23.0.11 below). Where a particular application is to be made in accordance with Pt 23 it should be made on an "application notice". Application should be made to the appropriate court as explained in r.23.2. Rule 23.6 indicates what the notice should include. Other rules are concerned with the filing (r.23.3) and service of the application notice (rr.23.4, 23.7 and 23.9). The court may proceed with the hearing of an application in the absence of a party (r.23.11) and, in certain circumstances, the court may deal with an application without a hearing (r.23.8).

An application notice is not necessary where an application for a court order may be made orally.

Where an application should be made with notice to the respondent it must be served on the respondent. Where an application may be made without notice to the respondent it need not be served.

The circumstances in which an application for a court order (a) may be made orally rather than by application notice or (b) should be made with notice or may be made without notice may vary depending upon the nature of the court order sought. Consequently, reference may have to be made, not only to the rules in Pt 23 and to the terms of the supplementing practice direction (see Practice Direction (Applications) at para. 23PD–001 below) but also to provisions specifically relating to the court order sought (see r.23.3(2) and r.23.4(2)).

The provisions in Pt 23 are, as it were, "default provisions" which generally apply to applications for court orders but which are subject to any express provisions which may apply to applications for specific court orders (see further below).

Under the new procedures introduced by the CPR, defended cases will proceed under directions issued by the court and will be constantly subject to court control at case management hearings such as case management conferences, allocation hearings, listing hearings, or pre-trial reviews (as well as by other means). In a given case, matters that otherwise might have to be raised by application notice may be dealt with at a case management hearing.

It should be noted that r.3.3(1) states that the court may exercise its powers, not only "on an application" (*e.g.* in accordance with Pt 23), but also of its own initiative, except where a rule (*e.g.* r.42.8) or some other enactment provides otherwise.

When does Part 23 apply?

In civil procedure, "application" is not a term of art. The circumstances in which a person may **23.0.3**
make an application to the court for "a court order" are many and various. Further, the legal basis upon which such an application is made may be statute, case law, rules of court or practice direction.

As a practical matter, many applications are made in the course of proceedings already on foot, having been started (usually) by claim form (r.7.2(1)). However, in certain circumstances, proceedings in court may be originated by an application. Whether an application is made in the course of proceedings or is an originating application, the provisions of Pt 23 may apply.

Some rules draw a distinction between (1) an application made at trial and (2) an application made at any other time in the course of the proceedings, and stipulate that an application of the latter variety (but not the former) should be made in accordance with Pt 23 (or in some other special way); examples are Practice Direction (Committal Applications) paras 2.2 and 2.3, Sched. 1, RSC, O.77, r.18 (applications under Crown Proceedings Act 1947 ss.17 and 29) and Sched. 1, RSC, O.97, r.14 (application under the Landlord and Tenant Act 1954, s.16, etc.).

In some circumstances, CPR rules provide that a particular application may be made either before or after proceedings have been commenced and, in the former event, the application is made by claim form and, in the latter event, is made in accordance with Pt 23 (*e.g.* Sched. 1, RSC, O.50, r.10 (funds in court: stop order)). However, in some other circumstances, an application made before proceedings have been commenced is made, not by claim form, but in accordance with Pt 23 (*e.g.* r.25.4 (application for interim remedy where there is no related claim)).

In some instances, in the "core" CPR rule or in Practice Directions supplementing those rules it is expressly provided that, if an application is to be made to the court, it should be made "in accordance with Part 23"; *e.g.* r.12.4 (procedure for obtaining default judgment), and Practice Direction (Transfer) paras 5.1 and 6.2 (see 30PD–001). Similarly, such express references are found in some "schedule" rules (*viz.*, former RSC and CCR rules); *e.g.* Sched. 1, RSC, O.97, r.9A(1) (application under Landlord and Tenant Act 1954, s.24A to determine an interim rent where tenant has begun proceedings for new tenancy) and Sched. 2, CCR, O.39, r.12 (application by creditor under County Courts Act 1984, s.112(4) to present bankruptcy petition).

In other instances, it is merely implied that the application should be made in accordance with Pt 23; sometimes the implication is strong (*e.g.* r.24.4 (summary judgment procedure)), but on other times it is weak (*e.g.* Practice Direction (Allocation and Re-Allocation) para. 11.1 (application for case track re-allocation), r.27.11 (application to set aside small claims judgment) and r.28.4 (variation of fast-track case management timetable) and Practice Direction (The Fast Track) para. 4.3, see para. 28PD–003). In r.7.6 (extension of time for serving a claim form) the implication is weak but is made strong by the practice direction supplementing that rule (Practice Direction (The Claim Form) para. 8.1, see para. 7PD–002); see also r.24.4 (procedure for summary judgment) and Practice Direction (The Summary Disposal of Claims) r.2 (procedure for making an application).

An application for an extension of a stay of proceedings directed under r.26.4 to allow for settlement of a case may be made by letter (Practice Direction (Case Management—Preliminary Stage: Allocation and Re-allocation) para. 3.1, see 26PD–002). A letter will also suffice as an application notice where a party applies under r.40.12 for the correction of an accidental slip or omission in a judgment or order (Practice Direction (Judgments and Orders) para. 4.2). p. 538

In certain circumstances, an application may be made by witness statement or affidavit (Sched. 1, RSC, O.71, r.36 (enforcement of High Court judgments in other Contracting States)).

It should be noted that Pt 23 is not confined to proceedings at the trial level. Sched. 1, RSC, O.59, r.14(1) states that, unless otherwise directed, every application to the Court of Appeal, a single judge or the registrar must be made by application notice in accordance with CPR Pt 23.

Where it is proposed to make an application to the court for a court order, whether in the course of proceedings or not, care has to be taken in inquiring whether the application should be made in accordance with Pt 23 (and, therefore, by way of application notice) or by some other means. Further, if Pt 23 does apply, care has to be taken to inquire as to the extent to which the provisions of that Part and of the Practice Direction which supplements it must be varied in the light of rules specifically enacted in relation to the particular application which is to be made. These specific rules are likely to deal with such matters as the grounds upon which the application is made, the time when it may be made, the service of the application notice, and the nature and extent of the evidence required in support, and may be quite elaborate.

Application under "schedule" rules

Many of the former RSC and CCR rules re-enacted in the Schedules to the CPR (the **23.0.4**
"schedule" rules) (see Pt 50) provide for the making of applications to the court (see further para. 50.1.7). Some but by no means all of these provisions expressly incorporate Pt 23.

Application in specialist proceedings

The CPR, including Pt 23, apply to the "specialist proceedings" listed in r.49(2) subject to the **23.0.5**
provisions of the relevant practice direction which applies to those proceedings. Consequently, Pt 23 must be read in the light of any provisions as to applications which may be made in those

practice directions. Note also Commercial Court Guide (5th ed), section F. Applications pp. 52 *et seq.*

The basic procedure—applications with notice (rr.23.3, 23.4, 23.6 and 23.7)

23.0.6 An application notice must state (a) what order the applicant is seeking, and (b) briefly, why the applicant is seeking the order (r.23.6). Generally, the applicant must:

(1) file an application notice (r.23.3(1)) with the appropriate court (r.23.2);
(2) upon receiving from the court a time and date for the hearing, serve a copy of the application notice on each respondent (r.23.4(1)) as soon as practicable (r.23.7(1)(a), but see following paragraph) and, in any event, at least 3 days before the court is to deal with the application (except where another time limit is specified) (r.23.7(1)(b));
(3) serve with the application notice a copy of (a) any written evidence in support (if it has not already been served) and (b) any draft order attached to the notice (r.23.7(3) and (5)).

It may be noted that r.23.7(1)(a) states that the applicant must serve the notice of application "as soon as practicable after it is filed" whereas para. 4.1 of Practice Direction (Applications) (see para. 23PD–001 below) says, more realistically, it must be served "as soon as practicable after it is has been issued". Presumably an application notice is "issued" when it has been so processed by the court.

Where service of the application notice is to be made by the court, rather than by the applicant, r.23.7(2) applies.

Applications without notice

23.0.7 An application may be made without serving a copy of the application notice if this is permitted by (a) a rule, (b) a practice direction, or (c) a court order (r.23.4(2)). An example of such permission is provided by r.25.3, which states that the court may grant an interim remedy on an application made without notice if it appears to the court that there are good reasons for not giving notice. Other circumstances in which an application may be made without service of application notice are (a) where the court permits, (b) where the parties consent, (c) where there is "exceptional urgency" and (d) where the overriding objective is best furthered by doing so; see Practice Direction (Applications) para. 3 (see para. 23PD–001 below). See also notes following r.23.4 below. The general rule that the applicant must file the application notice applies to applications made without notice (r.23.3(1)).

The provisions of r.23.9 apply where the court has disposed of an application which it permitted to be made without service of a copy of the application notice. A person served, in accordance with r.23.9, with an order made on an application but on whom a copy of the application notice was not served may apply to the court for the order to be set aside or varied (r.23.10).

Time when application should be made

23.0.8 Every application should be made as soon as it becomes apparent that it is necessary or desirable to make it. Wherever possible, applications should be made so that they can be considered at any other hearing for which a date has already been fixed or for which a date is about to be fixed (particularly where case management conferences, allocation hearings, listing hearings, or pre-trial reviews have been fixed); see Practice Direction (Applications) paras 2.7 and 2.8 (see para. 23PD–001 below). This is consistent with the court's duty to manage cases as stated in r.1.4(2)(j)).

Hearing of application

23.0.9 Normally, where an application for a court order is made in accordance with Pt 23, it will be dealt with at a hearing. However, the court may deal with the application without a hearing in the circumstances stated in r.23.8.

Where the court holds a hearing for the purposes of dealing with an application made in the course of proceedings the parties must anticipate that the court may wish to review the conduct of the case as a whole and give any necessary case management directions. Consequently, at such a hearing the parties should be ready to assist the court in doing so and to answer questions the court may ask for this purpose; Practice Direction (Applications) para. 2.9 (see para. 23PD–001 below).

Except in the most simple application, the applicant should bring to any hearing a draft of the order sought; see further Practice Direction (Applications) para. 6.1 (see para. 23PD–003 below).

The judge should keep a note of the proceedings on the application; Practice Direction (Applications) para. 8 (see para. 23PD–002 below).

As to the disposal of an application by a "telephone hearing" or without a hearing, see notes following r.23.6 and r.23.8 below.

Hearing of application "in public" or "in private"

23.0.10 It was explained above (see "Editorial Introduction") that Pt 23 is the successor to provisions formerly found in RSC, O.32 and CCR, O.13. Those Orders dealt with proceedings for applications normally held "in chambers". The term "chambers" was not defined in the RSC or the CCR. Court hearings were held either "in chambers" or "in court". Commonly, but not necessarily, a hearing of the former type was held in the judge's room (literally, in his chambers) whereas a hearing of the latter type was held in a court room. The principal significance of the distinction was that hearings in chambers (whether held in a court room or not) were in private and hearings in court were in public.

The hearing of applications to which the provisions of Pt 23 apply may be heard either in chambers or in court. The "core" CPR make no reference to "chambers". However, they do draw a distinction between hearings "in private" and hearings "in public". References to "chambers" in RSC and CCR provisions re-enacted in Scheds 1 and 2 (the "schedule" rules) have been amended accordingly (see *e.g.* RSC, O.52, r.6 (provisions as to committal hearings) and Practice Direction (Committal Applications) para. 9). The general rule is that, wherever held, hearings will be in public and this includes hearings of Pt 23 applications (r.39.2(1)). But there are exceptions (see r.39.2(3) and they are amplified in Practice Direction (Miscellaneous Provisions Relating to Hearings) para. 1.5 (para. 39PD–001 below)). For example, the hearing may be in private (a) if publicity would defeat the object of the application, (b) the application involves confidential information and publicity would damage that confidentiality, or (c) the application was made without notice and it would be unjust to any respondent for there to be a public hearing; see further r.39.2 and notes following. In many instances, hearings of Pt 23 applications will fall within one or other of the exceptions and will be held in private.

Practice Direction (Miscellaneous Provisions Relating to Hearings) para. 1.5 (para. 39PD–001 below) lists various proceedings which, conceivably, may be dealt with in private in accordance with the principles stated in r.39.2(3). A number of the proceedings listed there may arise on a Pt 23 application. Para. 1.5 states that the proceedings shall in the first instance be listed by the court as hearings in private.

The court's general powers of case management include the power to hold a hearing and receive evidence by telephone or by using any other method of direct oral communication (except where the rules provide otherwise) (r.3.1(2)(d)). The court may order that an application or part of an application should be dealt with by a "telephone hearing"; for practice, see Practice Direction (Applications) paras 6.1*et seq* (see para. 23PD–001 below). It may be expected that this power will prove particularly useful in relation to the hearing of certain Pt 23 applications where it is not necessary for the hearing to be held in public.

Costs on application

Note Practice Direction (Applications) paras 13.1 and 13.2 (see para 23PD–003 below) and the further sources referred to there. In the Access to Justice Reports it was recommended that the courts should make more use of their powers to assess costs on an interlocutory application and order them to be paid immediately where this was appropriate (see Interim Report p. 8 and Final Report, p. 75). The objective is to ensure that applications in the course of proceedings are not made unless necessary and that orders made on such applications are effective (and that further applications are not required for the purpose of securing compliance). **23.0.11**

When, in dealing with an application, the court orders a party to pay costs to another party (other than fixed costs) it may make a summary assessment of the costs of the application (r.44.7), that is to say, the court may order the payment of a sum of money instead of ordering fixed costs or a detailed assessment (formerly, taxation) (r.43.3). The general rule is that the court will make a summary assessment at the conclusion of any application hearing which has lasted less than one day (Practice Direction (General Rules about Costs) para. 4.4 , see 48PD–005). The present approach is for all interlocutory applications to have their "costs in any event" orders summarily assessed. The court may order that costs summarily assessed should be paid by some specified date or by instalments. If no such orders is made the costs will be payable within 14 days (r.44.8).

Appeal to judge from order made by Master or district judge on application notice

CPR Sched. 2, CCR, O.13, r.1(10) states that, in county court proceeding (see r.50.1(4)(c)), an appeal shall lie to a judge from any order made by a district judge on an application in the course of proceedings. Many of the circumstances in which application may be made to the court in accordance with Pt 23 may properly be described as made in the course of proceedings and, consequently, under r.1(10) an appeal will lie to a judge from orders made by district judges on such applications. An appeal under r.1(10) shall be made on notice, which shall be filed and served on the opposite party within five days after the order appealed from or such further time as the judge may allow. **23.0.12**

CPR Sched. 1, RSC, O.58, r.1(1) states that, in High Court proceedings (see r.50.1(3)(c)), an appeal shall lie to a judge from any judgment, order or decision of a master or district judge. The appeal shall be brought by serving on every other party to the proceedings a notice of appeal; the notice must be issued within five days of the judgment etc. and served within five days after issue (r.1(2) and (3)). An appeal shall not be heard sooner than two clear days after such service (r.1(3)). When the court issues the notice of appeal, it will fix a date for the hearing (r.1(3A)).

Court Guides and general rules about applications—Where applications are made in proceedings in the Commercial Court, and in proceedings in the Chancery Division of the High Court, the provisions of Pt 23 and the practice directions supplementing that Part must be read in conjunction with, respectively, the Commercial Court Guide (5th ed.), Section F, and the Chancery Guide (April 1999 ed.), Chap. 7, and the practice directions referred to there. In some respects, the modifications to Pt 23 practice made by these Guides are significant. **23.0.13**

Related Sources

23.0.14
- Practice Direction (Applications) (see para. 23PD–001 below)
- Practice Division Interim Injunctions paras 2 & 3 (see 25PD–003 below)
- Rule 3.3 (Court's power to make order of its own initiative)
- Rule 22.1 (Documents to be verified by a statement of truth)
- Rule 32.6 (Evidence in proceedings other than at trial)
- Rule 39.2 (General rule—hearing to be in public)
- Part 12 (Default judgment)
- Part 25 (Interim remedies)
- Part 30 (Transfer of proceedings)
- Chancery Guide (April 1999) Chap. 7
- Commercial Court Guide (5th ed.), Section F

Forms

23.0.15
- Practice Direction (Forms) Table 1
- N244 (Application Notice)
- N244A (Notice of hearing of application)

Forms relevant to particular applications made in accordance with Pt 23 are also found in Tables 2 and 3 of this Practice Direction; *e.g.* PF3 (application for an extension of time for serving a claim form (r.7.6(1)).

Meaning of "application notice" and "respondent"

23.1 **23.1** In this Part—

"application notice" means a document in which the applicant states his intention to seek a court order; and

"respondent" means

(a) the person against whom the order is sought; and

(b) such other person as the court may direct.

Where to make an application

23.2 **23.2**—(1) The general rule is that an application must be made to the court where the claim was started.

(2) If a claim has been transferred to another court since it was started, an application must be made to the court to which the claim has been transferred.

(3) If the parties have been notified of a fixed date for the trial, an application must be made to the court where the trial is to take place.

(4) If an application is made before a claim has been started, it must be made to the court where it is likely that the claim to which the application relates will be started unless there is good reason to make the application to a different court.

(5) If an application is made after proceedings to enforce judgment have begun, it must be made to any court which is dealing with the enforcement of the judgment unless any rule or practice direction provides otherwise.

23.2.1 **Effect of rule**—Proceedings may be transferred between county courts, between the High Court and the county courts, and within the High Court in accordance with the provisions of Pt 40 and, in certain circumstances, proceedings may be transferred automatically (see r.26.2). An application to set aside a transfer order is made in accordance with Pt 23 (Practice Direction (Transfer) para. 6.2, see 30PD–001).

Proceedings arising on an application may be transferred from one court to another in accordance with r.30.2(1). A county court may order proceedings before that court, or any part of them (such as an application made in the proceedings), to be transferred to another county court. An application for an order to transfer such proceedings must be made to the court where the claim in which the application arises is proceeding and, presumably, should be made in accordance with Pt 23.

Application notice to be filed

23.3 **23.3**—(1) The general rule is that an applicant must file an application notice.

(2) An applicant may make an application without filing an application notice if—

(a) this is permitted by a rule or practice direction; or
(b) the court dispenses with the requirement for an application notice.
See further "Editorial Introduction" above.

Effect of rule—On receipt of an application notice containing a request for a hearing, the court will notify the applicant of the time and date for the hearing of the application; see Practice Direction (Applications) para. 2.2 (see para. 23PD–001 below). For practice where hearing not requested, see r.23.8 below and notes following. 23.3.1

Notice of an application

23.4—(1) The general rule is that a copy of the application notice must be served on each respondent. 23.4

(3) An application may be made without serving a copy of the application notice if this is permitted by—
(a) a rule;
(b) a practice direction; or
(c) a court order.
(Rule 23.7 deals with service of a copy of the application notice.)

Effect of rule—In a case where an application is made against one party only, and there are other parties to the proceedings, only the party against whom the order is sought should be addressed in the notice of application. It is prudent practice to send a copy to other parties stating, in the covering letter, that it is sent for information only and that if other parties attend they do so at their own risk as to costs. 23.4.1

The circumstances in which application may be made to the court without notice first being given to the respondent by service of the application notice upon him are set out in Practice Directions (Applications) para. 3 (see 23PD–001) and they include "exceptional urgency" and the furthering of the "overriding objective". Commonly, applications for certain interim remedies (see Pt 25) are made without notice. Rule 25.3 states that an application for a court order in the form of an order for an interim remedy may be made without notice "if it appears to the court that there are good reasons for not giving notice". If the applicant makes an application without giving notice, the evidence in support of the application must state the reasons why notice was not given. Under the former rules, provision for application without notice was made in relation to some but not all interim remedies dealt with in RSC, O.29. Now, in terms, applications for an interim remedy may be without notice if there appear to the court to be good reasons for dispensing with notice. However, mandatory requirements as to notice are retained by r.25.5 in relation to the interim remedies specifically referred to in that rule (inspection of property before claim or against non-party).

Where the court has dealt with an application made without notice, service of a copy of the application notice and any evidence in support is generally required in accordance with r.23.9 below.

For practice where party does not have time to serve a notice of an application and wishes to make an oral application at a hearing already fixed, see notes following r.23.7 below.

"copy must be served on each respondent"—In this context, "respondent" means (a) the person against whom the order is sought, and (b) such other person as the court may direct (r.23.1). In terms, the general rule stated in r.23.4(1) does not direct service on every person who is a party to the litigation (*Re Creehouse Ltd* [1983] 1 W.L.R. 77; [1982] 3 All E.R. 659, CA (service of application by solicitor to remove his name from the record, see now r.42.3)). 23.4.2

See further r.23.7 (Service of a copy of an application notice) below.

Time when an application is made

23.5 Where an application must be made within a specified time, it is so made if the application notice is received by the court within that time. 23.5

What an application notice must include

23.6 An application notice must state— 23.6
(a) what order the applicant is seeking;
(b) briefly, why the applicant is seeking the order.
(Part 22 requires an application notice to be verified by a statement of truth if the applicant wishes to rely on matters set out in his application notice as evidence.)

23.6.1 **Effect of rule**—An application notice must, in addition to the matters set out in r.23.6, be signed, contain a request that the application be dealt with either by a hearing or without a hearing and include the other information listed in Practice Direction (Applications) para. 2.1 (see para. 23PD–001 below). If the application is to be made to a judge, the application notice should so state (*ibid.* para. 2.6)).

Grounds for the application should be stated "briefly", but they must also be adequate and, in particular, must be stated in a manner that complies with any special provisions relating to the application made.

23.6.2 **Evidence on an application**—A hearing of an application is a hearing "other than a trial" within r.32.6 and, therefore, the general rule is that evidence is to be by witness statement unless the court, a practice direction or any other enactment requires otherwise (r.32.6(1)). A party may, in support of his application, rely on the matters set out in (a) his statement of case, or (b) his application notice, if the statement of case or application notice is verified by a statement of truth (r.32.6). See further r.22.1(3) and notes following.

For filing and service of evidence on applications for court orders, see Practice Direction (Applications) paras 9.1 *et seq* (see para. 23PD–002 below).

Service of a copy of an application notice

23.7 **23.7**—(1) A copy of the application notice—

(a) must be served as soon as practicable after it is filed; and

(b) except where another time limit is specified in these Rules or a practice direction, must in any event be served at least 3 days before the court is to deal with the application.

(2) If a copy of the application notice is to be served by the court, the applicant must, when he files the application notice, file a copy of any written evidence in support.

(3) When a copy of an application notice is served it must be accompanied by—

(a) a copy of any witness statement in support; and

(b) a copy of any draft order which the applicant has attached to his application.

(4) If—

(a) an application notice is served; but

(b) the period of notice is shorter than the period required by these Rules or a practice direction,

the court may direct that, in the circumstances of the case, sufficient notice has been given, and hear the application.

(5) This rule does not require written evidence—

(a) to be filed if it has already been filed; or

(b) to be served on a party on whom it has already been served.

(Part 6 contains the general rules about service of documents including who must serve a copy of the application notice.)

23.7.1 **Effect of rule**—The general rule is that the applicant must serve the application notice on each respondent (r.23.4(1)) as soon as practicable after filing (r.23.7(1)(a)) (but see para. 23.0.6 above where Practice Direction (Applications) para. 4.1 is noted, see 23PD–001) and, in any event, at least three days before the court is to deal with the application (except where another time limit is specified) (r.23.7(1)(b)). Practice Direction (Applications) para. 4.2 supplements these provisions and state that, where an application notice should be served but there is not sufficient time to do so, informal notification of the application should be given unless the circumstances of the application require secrecy (see para. 23PD–001 below).

Where a date for a hearing has been fixed (*e.g.* a case management conference or a pre-trial review) and a party wishes to make an application for a court order at that hearing, but does not have sufficient time to serve an application notice in accordance with r.23.7, he should inform the other party and the court (if possible in writing) as soon as he can of the nature of the application and the reason for it and should then make the application orally at the hearing; Practice Direction (Applications) para. 2.10 (see para. 23PD–001 below).

23.7.2 **Service out of jurisdiction**—Schedule 1, RSC, O.11, r.1 applies to the service out of the jurisdiction of an application notice as it applies to service of a claim form (*ibid.* r.9(1)).

Applications which may be dealt with without a hearing

23.8 The court may deal with an application without a hearing if— 23.8

(a) the parties agree as to the terms of the order sought;

(b) the parties agree that the court should dispose of the application without a hearing, or

(c) the court does not consider that a hearing would be appropriate.

Effect of rule—The court must further the overriding objective (see r.1.1) by actively managing cases (r.1.4(1)) and this includes dealing with "the case" without the parties needing to attend at the court (r.1.4(2)(j)). 23.8.1

An application notice must include either a request for a hearing or a request that the application be dealt with without a hearing; see Practice Direction (Applications) para. 2.1(5) (see para. 23PD–001 below). Where the request is for the application to be dealt with without a hearing, the practice stated in Practice Direction (Applications) paras 2.3 to 2.6 is to be followed by the court (see para. 23PD–001).

Where applications are considered without a hearing in the circumstances provided for by rr.23.8(b) and 23.8(c) the directions in Practice Direction (Applications) para. 11.1 and 11.2 apply (see para. 23PD–003 below).

Service of application where application made without notice

23.9—(1) This rule applies where the court has disposed of an application which it permitted to be made without service of a copy of the application notice. 23.9

(2) Where the court makes an order, whether granting or dismissing the application, a copy of the application notice and any evidence in support must, unless the court orders otherwise, be served with the order on any party or other person—

(a) against whom the order was made; and

(b) against whom the order was sought.

(3) The order must contain a statement of the right to make an application to set aside[GL] or vary the order under rule 23.10.

Application to set aside or vary order made without notice

23.10—(1) A person served with an order made on an application but on whom a copy of the application notice was not served may apply to the court for the order to be set aside[GL] or varied. 23.10

(2) An application under this rule must be made within 7 days after the date on which the order was served on the person making the application.

Effect of rules 23.9 and 23.10—The title to r.23.9 is misleading as it does not accurately encapsulate the scope of the rule. 23.10.1

Where the court makes an order on an application made without notice, the applicant must serve on the respondent the material referred to in r.23.9(2). This includes service of the order and of a copy of the application notice. Rule 23.10(2) states that a person "on whom the application was not served" may apply for the order to be set aside or varied. This is inept. What is meant is that a person on whom a copy of the application notice was not served before the court made the order disposing of the application may apply for the order to be set aside or varied.

Rule 23.10 replaces former RSC, O.32, r.6 which stated, simply, that the court could set aside an order made *ex parte*. An application under r.6 had to be made timeously (see SCP 1999, para. 32/6/30). Under r.23.10(2) it is to be made within seven days of service of the order. The order must contain a statement of the respondent's right to make an application under r.23.10 to set aside or vary the order (r.23.9(3)).

Part 40.4 deals with the service of orders.

Part 6 contains rules as to who is to serve, etc.

Power of the court to proceed in the absence of a party

23.11—(1) Where the applicant or any respondent fails to attend the hearing of an application, the court may proceed in his absence. 23.11

(2) Where—

(a) the applicant or any respondent fails to attend the hearing of an application; and

(b) the court makes an order at the hearing,
the court may, on application or of its own initiative, relist the application.
(Part 40 deals with the service of orders.)

23.11.1 **Effect of rule**—This rule deals with two related matters (dealt with in turn in the notes following); first, the power of the court to proceed with the hearing of an application for a court order in the absence of a party to the application and, secondly, the power of the court to re-consider any court order made at such hearing. The cross-reference to Pt 40 appears to have slipped and should have been inserted at the end of r.23.10.

23.11.2 **"the court may proceed in his absence" (r.23.11(1))**—Rule 23.11(1) follows former RSC, O.32, r.5(1) and former CCR, O.13, r.1(5) (see SCP 1999, para. 32/6/26). Those provisions said that the court could proceed in the absence of any party "if, having regard to the nature of the application", the court thought it "expedient to do so". These words no longer appear but their effect is more than adequately retained by the fact that the court must seek to give effect to the overriding objective when exercising the power to proceed in a party's absence given by r.23.11(1) (see rr.1.1 and 1.2). Former RSC, O.32, r.5(2) stated that, before proceeding with the first or any resumed hearing of a summons in the absence of any party, the court "may require to be satisfied that the summons or, as the case may be, notice of the time appointed for the resumed hearing was duly served on that party". It was held that this provision did not empower the court to dispense with service (*Westminster City Council v. Government of Iran* [1986] 1 W.L.R. 979).
As to court's power to proceed with a trial in the absence of party, see r.39.2.

23.11.3 **"the court may re-list the application"**—Rule 23.11(2) replaces with modifications former RSC, O.32, r.5(3) and (4). Under the former provisions, where the party who failed to attend the hearing of the summons was the applicant the normal outcome was that the summons was dismissed. In these circumstances, the court could allow the summons to be restored to the list if satisfied that it was just to do so (r.5(4)) (see SCP 1999, para. 36/6/27). In terms, this power is not retained by r.23.11(2). Under the former provisions, where the party failing to attend was not the applicant and the court proceeded with the summons and made an order the court had power "to re-hear the summons". The general rule was that this power could not be exercised after the order had been perfected unless the parties consented (r.5(4)), but there were some important exceptions to this restriction (see SCP 1999, para. 32/6/28). Rule 23.11(2) imposes no such restriction: the exceptions have become the rule. Presumably, what is meant by "re-list the application" is "re-hear the application". It should be noted that an application may be re-listed on application or on the court's own initiative (*cf.* r.3.3).
In certain circumstances default judgments are to be obtained by application under Pt 23 (see Editorial Introduction at para. 23.0.2 above). As to setting aside and varying default judgments, see Pt 13.

PRACTICE DIRECTION—APPLICATIONS

This Practice Direction supplements CPR Part 23

Reference to a judge

23PD–001 **1.** A Master or district judge may refer to a judge any matter which he thinks should properly be decided by a judge, and the judge may either dispose of the matter or refer it back to the Master or district judge.

Application notices

2.1 An application notice must, in addition to the matters set out in rule 23.6, be signed and include:
(1) the title of the claim,
(2) the reference number of the claim,
(3) the full name of the applicant,
(4) where the applicant is not already a party, his address for service, and
(5) either a request for a hearing or a request that the application be dealt with without a hearing.
(Practice Form N244 may be used.)

2.2 On receipt of an application notice containing a request for a hearing the court will notify the applicant of the time and date for the hearing of the application.

2.3 On receipt of an application notice containing a request that the application be dealt with without a hearing, the application notice will be sent to a Master or district judge so that he may decide whether the application is suitable for consideration without a hearing.

2.4 Where the Master or district judge agrees that the application is suitable for consideration without a hearing, the court will so inform the applicant and the respondent and may give directions for the filing of evidence. (Rules 23.9 and 23.10 enable a party to apply for an order made without a hearing to be set aside or varied.)

2.5 Where the Master or district judge does not agree that the application is suitable for consideration without a hearing, the court will notify the applicant and the respondent of the time, date and place for the hearing of the application and may at the same time give directions as to the filing of evidence.

2.6 If the application is intended to be made to a judge, the application notice should so state. In that case, paragraphs 2.3, 2.4 and 2.5 will apply as though references to the Master or district judge were references to a judge.

2.7 Every application should be made as soon as it becomes apparent that it is necessary or desirable to make it.

2.8 Applications should wherever possible be made so that they can be considered at any other hearing for which a date has already been fixed or for which a date is about to be fixed. This is particularly so in relation to case management conferences, allocation and listing hearings and pre-trial reviews fixed by the court.

2.9 The parties must anticipate that at any hearing the court may wish to review the conduct of the case as a whole and give any necessary case management directions. They should be ready to assist the court in doing so and to answer questions the court may ask for this purpose.

2.10 Where a date for a hearing has been fixed and a party wishes to make an application at that hearing but he does not have sufficient time to serve an application notice he should inform the other party and the court (if possible in writing) as soon as he can of the nature of the application and the reason for it. He should then make the application orally at the hearing.

Applications without service of application notice

3. An application may be made without serving an application notice only:

(1) where there is exceptional urgency,

(2) where the overriding objective is best furthered by doing so,

(3) by consent of all parties,

(4) with the permission of the court,

(5) where paragraph 2.10 above applies, or

(6) where a court order, rule or practice direction permits.

Giving notice of an applications

4.1 Unless the court otherwise directs or paragraph 3 of this practice direction applies the application notice must be served as soon as practicable after it has been issued and, if there is to be a hearing, at least 3 clear days before the hearing date (rule 23.7(1)(b)).

4.2 Where an application notice should be served but there is not sufficient time to do so, informal notification of the application should be given unless the circumstances of the application require secrecy.

Pre-action applications

5. All applications made before a claim is commenced should be made under Part 23 of the Civil Procedure Rules. Attention is drawn in particular to rule 23.2(4). 23PD–002

Telephone hearings

6.1 The court may order that an application or part of an application be dealt with by a telephone hearing.

6.2 An order under 6.1 will not normally be made unless every party entitled to be given notice of the application and to be heard at the hearing has consented to the order.

6.3(1) Where a party entitled to be heard at the hearing of the application is acting in person, the court—

(a) may not make an order under 6.1 except on condition that arrangements will be made for the party acting in person to be attended at the telephone hearing by a responsible person to whom the party acting in person is known and who can confirm to the court the identity of the party; and

(b) may not give effect to an order under 6.1 unless the party acting in person is accompanied by a responsible person who at the commencement of the hearing confirms to the court the identity of the party.

(2) The "responsible person" may be a barrister, solicitor, legal executive, doctor, clergyman, police officer, prison officer or other person of comparable status.

(3) If the court makes an order under 6.1 it will give any directions necessary for the telephone hearing.

6.4 No representative of a party to an application being heard by telephone may attend the judge in person while the application is being heard unless the other party to the application has agreed that he may do so.

6.5 If an application is to be heard by telephone the following directions will apply, subject to any direction to the contrary:

(1) The applicant's legal representative must arrange the telephone conference by the British Telecom conference call "call out" system or by some other comparable system for precisely the time fixed by the court.

(2) He must tell the operator the telephone numbers of all those participating in the conference call and the sequence in which they are to be called.

(3) It is the responsibility of the applicant's legal representative to ascertain from all the other parties whether they have instructed counsel and, if so the identity of counsel, and whether the legal representative and counsel will be on the same or different telephone numbers.

(4) The sequence in which they are to be called will be:

(a) the applicant's legal representative and (if on a different number) his counsel,

(b) the legal representative (and counsel) for all other parties, and

(c) the judge.

(5) The applicant's legal representative must arrange for the conference to be recorded on tape by the telecommunications provider whose system is being used and must send the tape to the court.

(6) Each speaker is to remain on the line after being called by the operator setting up the conference call. The call may be 2 or 3 minutes before the time fixed for the application.

(7) When the judge has been connected the applicant's legal representative (or his counsel) will introduce the parties in the usual way.

(8) If the use of a "speakerphone" by any party causes the judge or any other party any difficulty in hearing what is said the judge may require that party to use a hand held telephone.

(9) The telephone charges debited to the account of the party initiating the conference call will be treated as part of the costs of the application.

Video conferencing

7. Where the parties to a matter wish to use video conferencing facilities, and those facilities are available in the relevant court, they should apply to the Master or district judge for directions.

Note of proceedings

8. The procedural judge should keep, either by way of a note or a tape recording, brief details of all proceedings before him, including the dates of the proceedings and a short statement of the decision taken at each hearing.

Evidence

9.1 The requirement for evidence in certain types of applications is set out in some of the rules and practice directions. Where there is no specific requirement to provide evidence it should be borne in mind that, as a practical matter, the court will often need to be satisfied by evidence of the facts that are relied on in support of or for opposing the application.

9.2 The court may give directions for the filing of evidence in support of or opposing a particular application. The court may also give directions for the filing of evidence in relation to any hearing that it fixes on its own initiative. The directions may specify the form that evidence is to take and when it is to be served.

9.3 Where it is intended to rely on evidence which is not contained in the application itself, the evidence, if it has not already been served, should be served with the application.

9.4 Where a respondent to an application wishes to rely on evidence which has not yet been served he should serve it as soon as possible and in any event in accordance with any directions the court may have given.

9.5 If it is necessary for the applicant to serve any evidence in reply it should be served as soon as possible and in any event in accordance with any directions the court may have given.

9.6 Evidence must be filed with the court as well as served on the parties. Exhibits should not be filed unless the court otherwise directs.

9.7 The contents of an application notice may be used as evidence (otherwise than at trial) provided the contents have been verified by a statement of truth.[1]

Consent orders

10.1 Rule 40.6 sets out the circumstances where an agreed judgment or order may be entered and sealed. **23PD–003**

10.2 Where all parties affected by an order have written to the court consenting to the making of the order a draft of which has been filed with the court, the court will treat the draft as having been signed in accordance with rule 40.6(7).

10.3 Where a consent order must be made by a judge (*i.e.* rule 40.6(2) does not apply) the order must be drawn so that the judge's name and judicial title can be inserted.

10.4 The parties to an application for a consent order must ensure that they provide the court with any material it needs to be satisfied that it is appropriate to make the order. Subject to any rule or practice direction a letter will generally be acceptable for this purpose.

10.5 Where a judgment or order has been agreed in respect of an application or claim where a hearing date has been fixed, the parties must inform the court immediately. (Note that parties are reminded that under rules 28.4 and 29.5 the case management timetable cannot be varied by written agreement of the parties.)

Other applications considered without a hearing

11.1 Where rule 23.8(b) applies the parties should so inform the court in

[1] See Part 22.

writing and each should confirm that all evidence and other material on which he relies has been disclosed to the other parties to the application.

11.2 Where rule 23.8(c) applies the court will treat the application as if it were proposing to make an order on its own initiative.

Miscellaneous

12.1 Except in the most simple application the applicant should bring to any hearing a draft of the order sought. If the case is proceeding in the Royal Courts of Justice and the order is unusually long or complex it should also be supplied on disk for use by the court office. [The current word processing system to be used is WordPerfect 5.1.]

Costs

13.1 Attention is drawn to the costs practice direction and, in particular, to the court's power to make a summary assessment of costs.

13.2 Attention is also drawn to rule 44.13(i) which provides that if an order makes no mention of costs, none are payable in respect of the proceedings to which it relates.

23PD–004 **Notes on Practice Direction supplementing CPR Pt 23 (see para. 23PD–001)—1.** This embodies the former practice in RSC, O.32, r.12 (Q.B.D.) (applied to Chancery Division by O.32, r.14(3)) and CCR, O.13, r.2. Out of London it has formerly been the practice to make such references readily but with the abolition of local practice directions it is anticipated that this practice will cease and "difficulty" and "the losing party is bound to appeal regardless of the court's judgment" will no longer be regarded as good reasons for reference in accordance with the current practice of masters. If another application is pending before the judge and the outstanding application can be dealt with conveniently at the same time then a reference can properly be made. Also where the application is likely to affect an early fixed date for trial.

2.9 This means that the relevant documents must be brought to the hearing and the person attending should be familiar with the solicitor's file.

7. Video Conferencing has been used experimentally with some success in the Queen's Bench Division; see QBM PD 50, SCP 1999, Vol. 2, para. 2A–124 for guidance as to practice. Telephone hearings are new and it is not anticipated that they will find much favour. A new pilot scheme for video applications is now in place in Room E109. Further details should be sought from the Masters' Support Unit Room E14.

8. In the Chancery Division the RSC prescribed, by RSC, O.32, r.22, an obligation on masters to keep a note; save for recording oral there was no such obligation in the Q.B.D. The practicality of doing so in all hearings is doubted. Fortunately the word "should" appears to recognise this.

9.2 See SCP 1999, Vol. 1, paras 14/2/3 for an example of former practice.

PART 24

SUMMARY JUDGMENT

Contents **24.0.1**

Editorial Introduction

The rules in this Part provide a procedure by which the court may carry out part of its duty of active case management, the summary disposal of issues which do not need full investigation and trial (r.1.4(2)(c)). The issues disposed of may arise in claims (including claims under the alternative procedure for claims), counterclaims, third party proceedings or similar proceedings. **24.0.2**

The rules in this Part permit summary disposal in three types of cases which under the previous High Court rules were dealt with by separate provisions; summary judgment (RSC, O.14), summary disposal of a case on a point of law (RSC, O.14A) and striking out pleadings (RSC, O.18, r.19).

Part 24 also permits the court to summarily dispose of cases and issues in three additional types of case:

(1) allowing summary judgment against a claimant where, on all the facts, the claim would be bound to be dismissed at trial;

(2) allowing summary disposal of preliminary issues where the court is satisfied that those issues do not need full investigation and trial; and

(3) allowing the court to fix summary judgment hearings of its own initiative.

There is a substantial overlap between Pt 24 and r.3.4 (Power to strike out a statement of case). As with Pt 24 the court's powers under r.3.4 may be exercised on the application of a party or on the court's own initiative. Rule 3.4(2)(a) and (b) cover the strike out of claims or defences which are unreasonably vague, incoherent, vexatious, scurrilous or obviously ill-founded and other cases which do not amount to a legally recognisable claim or defence. For a more detailed discussion of the extent to which r.3.4 overlaps with Pt 24 see the commentary to r.3.4.

Related Sources

- Rule 3.3 (Court's power to make order of its own initiative). **24.0.3**
- Rule 3.4 (Power to strike out a statement of case).
- Part 23 (General rules about applications for court orders).
- Practice Directions supplementing:
  —Part 23 (General rules about applications for court orders);
  —Part 24 (Summary judgment); and
  —Part 26 (Case management—preliminary stage).

Forms

- N.244—Application notice **24.0.4**
- No.44—Judgment under Pt 24
- No.48—Judgment after decision of preliminary issue
- PF11—Application for Pt 24 judgment (whole claim)
- PF12—Application for Pt 24 judgment (one or some of several claims)
- PF13—Order under Pt 24 (No. 1)
- PF14—Order under Pt 24 (No. 2)
- PF15—Order under Pt 24 (for assessment of solicitor's bill of costs) (Pt 48)

Scope of this Part

24.1 This Part sets out a procedure by which the court may decide a claim or a particular issue without a trial. **24.1**

"a claim or a particular issue"—These words are not defined in the rules. The word "claim" **24.1.1**

when used as a noun in other rules usually refers to the whole of a case in question (see, for example, r.8.1 and r.26.2). However, in some rules the word is used to refer to separate causes of action raised in the case in question (see, for example, r.7.3). On the assumption that the usual meaning of "claim" applies in Pt 24, an application for summary judgment which relates to only one of several causes of action raised in a case could be characterised as an application concerning "a particular issue". In case law under the previous rules the word "issue" was defined as "a disputed point of fact or law relied on by way of claim or defence" (*Koiso Finance Establishment Anstalt v. John Wedge*, unrep., February 15, 1994, CA, Transcript no. 94/387).

The word "issue" is also apt to refer to any preliminary issue, *i.e.* a disputed point upon which a claim or defence depends in part; for example, in a negligence claim the issue of carelessness if determined separately from the issues of causation and quantum. If a party applies for summary judgment on a preliminary issue and is unsuccessful the court will make an order as to that issue which is adverse to the case of the applicant, unless it appears to the court that the preliminary issue needs full investigation and trial.

Grounds for summary judgment

24.2 **24.2** The court may give summary judgment against a claimant or defendant on the whole of a claim or on a particular issue if—

(a) it considers that—

(i) that claimant has no real prospect of succeeding on the claim or issue; or

(ii) that defendant has no real prospect of successfully defending the claim or issue; and

(b) there is no other reason why the case or issue should be disposed of at a trial.

(Rule 3.4 makes provision for the court to strike out[GL] a statement of case or part of a statement of case if it appears that it discloses no reasonable grounds for bringing or defending a claim.)

24.2.1 **"on the whole of a claim or on a particular issue"**—See the commentary to r.24.1.

24.2.2 **"no real prospect of succeeding/successfully defending"**—In order to defeat the application for summary judgment it is sufficient for the respondent to show some "prospect", *i.e.* some chance of success. That prospect must be "real", *i.e.* the court will disregard prospects which are false, fanciful or imaginary. The respondent is not required to show that his case will probably succeed at trial. A case may be held to have a "real prospect" of success even if it is improbable. However, in such a case the court is likely to make a conditional order (as to which, see the commentary to r.24.6).

The hearing of application for summary judgment is not a summary trial. The court at the summary judgment application will consider the merits of the respondent's case only to the extent necessary to determine whether it has sufficient merit to proceed to trial.

24.2.3 **"no other reason [for] a trial"**—Words similar to r.24.2(b) were included in former RSC, O.14. Under those rules the following circumstances were held to afford "some other reason for trial": where the claimant's case appears to be "devious and crafty" and not "plain and straightforward" *Miles v. Bull* [1969] 1 Q.B. 258; [1968] 3 All E.R. 632); where the defendant is an executor or administrator who can raise facts by reference to the existence or absence of letters, accounts or such like of the deceased which make it reasonable to require full investigation (*Harrison v. Bottenheim* [1878] 26 W.R. 362) where the claimant's case tended to show that he had acted harshly and unconscionably and it is thought desirable that if he were to get judgment at all it should be in the full light of publicity (*per* Cairns L.J. in *Bank für Gemeinwirtschaft Aktiengesellschaft v. City of London Garages* [1971] 1 W.L.R. 149 at 158; [1971] 1 All E.R. 541 at 548).

The previous rule did not apply to proceedings which included a claim by the plaintiff for libel, slander, malicious prosecution or false imprisonment. Cases such as these are not expressly excluded from the current rule. However, the fact that in such cases the respondent may have a right to trial by jury may, of itself, be a reason for trial (see SCA 1981, s.69 and CCA 1984, s.66; see SCP 1999, Vol 2, paras 20A–454 and 20A–737, respectively.

24.2.4 **Burdens of proof**—The burdens of proof in summary judgment applications may be deduced from paras 4.1 and 4.2 of the Practice Direction supplementing Pt 24 (see para. 24PD–001 below) which set out the court's approach when deciding such applications.

In all cases there is a burden of proof on the claimant to show a case which, if unanswered, would entitle him to judgment on the claim or issue raised in the application (see paras 4.1(a) and 4.2(a) of the Practice Direction supplementing Pt 24 (at para. 24PD–001 below)).

Where the application for summary judgment was made by the claimant there is also a burden on the defendant to show "any reason why the claim or issue should be dealt with at trial" (see para. 4.1(b) of the Practice Direction supplementing Pt 24 (at para. 24PD–001 below)). Presumably the clearest reason would be that he has a real prospect of successfully defending the relevant claim or issue (see r.24.2(a)(ii) and the note "no real prospect of succeeding/successfully defending" above). Alternatively he may show some "other reason why the case or issue should be disposed of at a trial" (see r.24.2(b) and the note "no other reason [for] a trial" above).

Where the application for summary judgment was made by the defendant for judgment on the claimant's claim in his favour, summary judgment will be awarded if either:

(a) the claimant has failed to show a case which, if unanswered, would entitle him to judgment; or
(b) the defendant has shown that the relevant claim or issue would be bound to be dismissed at trial.

(See para. 4.2 of the Practice Direction supplementing Pt 24 (at para. 24PD–001 below)). Presumably the court would still refuse summary judgment if the claimant could show "some other reason why the case or issue should be disposed of at a trial" (see r.24.2(b)). However, if the claimant has no real prospect of succeeding on the claim or issue the "other reason [for] a trial" would have to be strong enough to outweigh the court's desire to decide "promptly which issues need full investigation and trial and accordingly [dispose] summarily of others" (r.1.4(2)(c)).

Effect of a set off or counterclaim—As to the meaning of the term "set off" see r.16.6 and the commentary thereto. As to the meaning of the term "counterclaim" see the Glossary and r.20.2 and the commentary thereto. 24.2.5

The question which arises here is whether a defendant can rely upon a set off or counterclaim as a "reason why the claim should be dealt with at trial" (see para. 4.1(b) of the Practice Direction supplementing Pt 24 at para. 24PD–001 below)) and thereby defeat a claim for summary judgment. The case law under the previous rules on this point was not coherent. Often the court refused to give summary judgment in such cases or granted summary judgment subject to a stay on enforcement pending trial of a counterclaim (see *Morgan & Son Ltd v. S Martin Johnson & Co* [1949] 1 K.B. 107, CA; *Hanak v. Green* [1958] 2 Q.B. 9; *United Overseas Ltd v. Peter Robinson Ltd* March 26, 1991, CA, Transcript no. 91/0297). In some exceptional cases the claimant obtained summary judgment which was enforceable immediately even though the defendant intended to raise a counterclaim (see "No set off in action on dishonoured bill or cheque" below).

It is possible that, under the new rules, the court may grant summary judgment more frequently than hitherto and may impose a delay on enforcement more frequently than hitherto. Such an approach would appear to be in harmony with the overriding objective to ensure that cases are dealt with "expeditiously and fairly" (r.1.1(2)(d))) and with the court's duty to actively manage cases by "deciding promptly which issues need full investigation and trial and accordingly disposing summarily of the others" (r.1.4(2)(c)).

If a claim is otherwise suitable for summary disposal, the court may prefer to deal with a defence of set off by entering summary judgment on the claim expressing that judgment to be subject to the determination of the defendant's cross claim or until further order, and stating that the summary judgment would not be enforceable until determination of the cross claim or until a further order was made. See further "Judgment on the claim or an issue therein" under r.24.6, para 24.6.3..

No set off in action on dishonoured bill or cheque—Under the previous rules a wholly different practice prevailed concerning the setting up of a defence of set off in proceedings on a dishonoured bill of exchange, or cheque or promissory note. In such proceedings, save in exceptional circumstances or upon strong grounds (*per* Stephen J. in *Newman v. Lever* [1887] 4 T.L.R. 91) the defendant was not allowed to set up a set off or counterclaim for damages for breach of some other contract or the commission of a tort, and the plaintiff was entitled to judgment for the amount of his claim without a stay of execution (*Brown Shipley & Co. Ltd v. Alicia Hosiery Ltd* [1966] 1 Lloyd's Rep. 668, CA; *James Lamont & Co Ltd v. Hylands Ltd* [1950] 1 K.B. 585, CA; *Montebianco Industrie Tessili SpA v. Carlyle Mills (London) Ltd* [1981] 1 Lloyd's Rep. 509, CA (summary judgment on dishonoured bill without a stay pending determination of counterclaim for defective goods)). This practice applied whether the counterclaim was connected with or arose out of or was independent of the contract in respect of which the bill, cheque or note was given, and whether or not the proceedings were between the immediate parties to the bill (*Anglo-Italian Bank v. Wells & Davies* [1878] 38 L.T. 197, CA). The principle is that a bill, cheque or note is given and taken in payment as so much cash, and not as merely given a right of action for the creditor to litigate a counterclaim (see *Jackson v. Murphy* [1887] 4 T.L.R. 92n). 24.2.6

"We have repeatedly said in this court that a bill of exchange or a promissory note is to be treated as cash. It is to be honoured unless there is some good reason to the contrary" (see *per* Lord Denning M.R. in *Fielding & Platt Ltd v. Selim Najjar* [1969] 1 W.L.R. 357 at 361; [1969] 2 All E.R. 150 at 152, CA).

In an action on a dishonoured bill of exchange by one of the immediate parties to the bill against the other, a claim for an unspecified amount of damages under a contract for the sale of goods did not afford a defence, nor was it available as a set off or counterclaim, nor did it afford a ground for a stay of execution (*Nova (Jersey) Knit Ltd v. Kammgarn Spinnerei GmbH* [1977] 1 W.L.R.

713; [1977] 2 All E.R. 463, HL). "[A seller] may demand payment in cash; but if the buyer cannot provide this at once, he may agree to take bills of exchange payable at future dates. These are taken as equivalent to deferred instalments of cash. Unless they are to be treated as unconditionally payable instruments . . . which the seller can negotiate for cash, the seller might just as well give credit. And it is for this reason that English law . . . does not allow cross claims, or defences, except such limited defences as those based on fraud, invalidity, or failure of consideration, to be made." (*per* Lord Wilberforce at 721). In *Esso Petroleum Co. Ltd v. Milton* [1997] 1 W.L.R. 938; [1997] 2 All E.R. 593, CA the special rule precluding a defence of set off was applied to direct debit mandates which were treated as equivalent to cheques.

Types of proceedings in which summary judgment is available

24.3 **24.3**—(1) The court may give summary judgment against a claimant in any type of proceedings.

(2) The court may give summary judgment against a defendant in any type of proceedings except—

- (a) proceedings for possession of residential premises against—
  - (i) a mortgagor; or
  - (ii) a tenant or a person holding over after the end of his tenancy whose occupancy is protected within the meaning of the Rent Act 1977[1] or the Housing Act 1988[2] and;
- (b) proceedings for an admiralty claim in rem; and
- (c) contentious probate proceedings.

24.3.1 **"any type of proceedings"**—A valid application for summary judgment can be made in any type of proceedings except the three mentioned in r.24.3; *i.e.* applications against a defendant in certain types of proceedings for possession of residential premises, for an admiralty claim *in rem* and contentious probate proceedings. In the three exceptional types of proceedings there are no restrictions on applications for summary judgment against the claimant.

The new rules do not repeat the provisions contained in the old rules which excluded applications for summary judgment in proceedings which included a claim by the plaintiff for libel, slander, malicious prosecution or false imprisonment (former RSC, O.14, r.1(2) and CCR, O.9, r.14(1)(c)). However in these cases, the defendant may have a right to trial by jury and this may amount to some "other reason for a trial"; see para. 24.2.3 above.

The new rules do not repeat the provision contained in the old rules which excluded applications for summary judgment in proceedings automatically referred for determination as small claims (former CCR, O.9, r.14(1)(a)). Therefore, an application for summary judgment may be made in a claim allocated to the small claims track (however, see further "Ideal time for application", para. 24.4.1, below).

24.3.2 **Accounts and inquiries**—Paragraph 6 of the Practice Direction supplementing Pt 24 (see para. 24PD–001 below) confirms that, where a remedy sought by a claimant in his claim form includes, or necessarily involves, taking an account or making an inquiry, an application can be made under Pt 24 by any party to the proceedings for an order directing any necessary accounts or inquiries to be taken or made. This provision replaces RSC ,O.43, r.1 but applies to county court proceedings as well as to High Court proceedings. An application for an order for accounts and inquiries may also be made under Pt 25 (see Practice Direction (Accounts and Inquiries) supplementing Pt 25 (para. 25BPD–001 below)).

Paragraph 6 is limited to claims brought by claim form but see further "Counterclaims, third party proceedings and other similar claims" below.

24.3.3 **Specific performance**—Paragraph 7 of the Practice Direction supplementing Pt 24 (see para. 24PD–001) provides for summary judgment applications in respect of the remedy of specific performance and similar remedies in cases in which in the High Court were formerly governed by RSC, O.86, rr.1 and 2. The paragraph modifies the provisions otherwise applicable as to the earliest time for application, the documentation to be served with the application notice and the time for service of that documentation (see further "Earliest time for applications in certain specific performance cases", "Evidence in support of the application" and "Timetable for Evidence", under r.24.4).

Paragraph 7 is limited to claims brought by claim form but see further "Counterclaims, third party proceedings and other similar claims" below.

[1] 1997 c. 42.
[2] 1988 c. 50.

Counterclaims, third party proceedings and other similar claims—Counterclaims, third party proceedings and other similar claims are referred to collectively in these rules as "Pt 20 claims" (see r.20.2). Part 24 applies to Pt 20 claims as if they were claims (see r.20.3). **24.3.4**

Alternative procedure for claims—Part 8 provides an alternative procedure for claims which largely reproduces the procedure applicable to cases commenced under the previous rules by originating summons or by originating application. There is no restriction on applications under Pt 24 in cases in which the claimant uses the Pt 8 procedure. However, that procedure is itself intended to provide a simple and expeditious means of determining cases. Indeed, summary proceedings for the possession of land (cases governed by RSC, O.113 or CCR, O.24, now re-enacted in the Schedules to the CPR) now fall within the Pt 8 procedure (see the Practice Direction supplementing Pt 8, para. 1.4 (para. 8PD–001)). **24.3.5**

Procedure

24.4—(1) A claimant may not apply for summary judgment until the defendant against whom the application is made has filed— **24.4**

(a) an acknowledgment of service; or

(b) a defence,

unless—

(i) the court gives permission; or

(ii) a practice direction provides otherwise.

(Rule 10.3 sets out the period for filing an acknowledgment of service and rule 15.4 the period for filing a defence.)

(2) If a claimant applies for summary judgment before a defendant against whom the application is made has filed a defence, that defendant need not file a defence before the hearing.

(3) Where a summary judgment hearing is fixed, the respondent (or the parties where the hearing is fixed of the court's own initiative) must be given at least 14 days' notice of—

(a) the date fixed for the hearing; and

(b) the issues which it is proposed that the court will decide at the hearing.

(Part 23 contains the general rules about how to make an application.)

(Rule 3.3 applies where the court exercises its powers on its own initiative.)

Ideal time for application—A party intending to apply for summary judgment should do so before or when filing his Allocation Questionnaire. If he does so, the court will not usually allocate the claim to a track before the hearing of the application. Where a party files an Allocation Questionnaire stating that he intends to apply for summary judgment but has not done so, the case will usually be listed for an Allocation Hearing. The application for summary judgment may be heard at that Allocation Hearing if the application notice has been issued and served in sufficient time (see generally the Practice Direction supplementing Pt 26, para. 5.2 (at para. 26PD–001 below) and, as to Allocation Questionnaires and Allocation Hearings, rr.26.3 and 26.5, respectively). **24.4.1**

Effect on time for service of defence—If a claimant applies for summary judgment before a defendant against whom the application is made has filed a defence, that defendant need not file a defence before the hearing (r.24.4(2)). **24.4.2**

If a defendant applies for summary judgment the claimant cannot obtain a default judgment before that application has been disposed of (r.12.3(3)).

Earliest time for application: general rules—Unless a practice direction provides otherwise a claimant cannot validly apply for summary judgment until: **24.4.3**

(1) the defendant against whom the application is made has filed an acknowledgment of service (as to which, see Pt 10); or

(2) the defendant against whom the application is made has filed a defence (as to which, see Pt 15); or

(3) the court gives permission (r.24.4(1)).

The time limits for filing an acknowledgment of service and a defence both run from the date of service of the claimant's particulars of claim (see rr.10.3 and 15.4, respectively). It therefore follows that a claimant cannot validly apply for summary judgment before serving his particulars of claim unless the court gives permission under (3) above.

If, after service of the particulars of claim, no acknowledgment of service or defence is filed the claimant should, before seeking the court's permission under (3) above, consider whether he can obtain a default judgment (as to which see Pt 12).

A defendant can apply for summary judgment in his favour on the claimant's claim at any time after the proceedings have been commenced. There is no requirement for him to file an acknowledgment of service or a defence before doing so.

The rules make no special provision as to the earliest time for application in respect of a Pt 20 claim (as to which see r.20.2). Presumably the earliest time to apply in such claims is after the Pt 20 claim has been served (see r.20.10).

24.4.4 **Earliest time for application in certain specific performance cases**—In specific performance cases and similar cases which fall within the limits of para. 7 of the Practice Direction supplementing Pt 24 (see para. 24PD–001 below), a claimant may apply for summary judgment at any time after the claim form has been served, whether or not the defendant has acknowledged service of the claim form, whether or not the time for acknowledging service has expired and whether or not any particulars of claim have been served.

24.4.5 **Earliest time for application where Part 8 procedure used**—The earliest time for an application for summary judgment by a claimant who has used the alternative procedure for claims set out in Pt 8 differs from the general rules set out above because:

(1) the claimant is not required to file particulars of claim (see r.8.9);
(2) the defendant is not required to file a defence (see r.8.9); and
(3) if the defendant fails to acknowledge service of the claim form the claimant cannot obtain a default judgment (r.12.2(b)).

Therefore a claimant seeking summary judgment where the Pt 8 procedure has been used must either await the filing of an acknowledgment of service or seek the court's permission to apply (see r.24.4(1)).

24.4.6 **Hearings concerning summary judgment fixed of the court's own initiative**—Part of the court's duty of active case management is the summary disposal of issues which do not need full investigation and trial (r.1.4(2)(c)). Its case management powers include power to make orders, including orders under Pt 24 of its own initiative (see generally r.3.3).

Paragraph 5.4 of the Practice Direction supplementing Pt 26 (see para. 26PD–001 below) makes specific provision for cases in which the court wishes to consider whether, before allocating a case to a track, whether any claim or issue in that case should be summarily disposed of. In such cases, the court will fix a hearing and give the parties notice of the issues which it is proposed that the court will decide or, alternatively, the court will make an order directing a party to take the steps described in the order within a stated time and specifying the consequences of not taking those steps.

24.4.7 **Minimum period of notice of hearing**—The minimum period of notice to be given to the respondent (or to the parties where the hearing is fixed of the court's own initiative) is 14 days (r.24.4(2)). For precise details as to the calculation of that time period see r.2.8 and the commentary thereto.

24.4.8 **Contents of an application notice**—An applicant may use Practice Form N244 suitably completed so as to:

(1) comply with the formal requirements set out in para. 2.1 of the Practice Direction supplementing Pt 23 (see para. 23PD–001 below),
(2) state that it is an application for summary judgment made under Pt 24 (para. 2(2) of the Practice Direction supplementing Pt 24 at para. 24PD–001 below)),
(3) state what order the applicant is seeking and, briefly, why he is seeking that order (see r.23.6),
(4) identify the written evidence on which the applicant relies, unless no evidence is relied on or the application notice itself contains all such evidence (see para. 2(4) of the Practice Direction supplementing Pt 24 (at para. 24PD–001 below)), and
(5) draw the attention of the respondent to r.24.5(1) (see para. 2(5) of the Practice Direction supplementing Pt 24 (at para. 24PD–001 below)). The Practice Direction supplementing Pt 4 (see 4PD–001) lists two forms of application; PF11 (for Pt 24 judgment, whole claim) and PF12 (for Pt 24 judgment, one or some of several claims).

If the application is intended to be made to a Judge other than a Master or District Judge the application notice should so state (para. 2.6 of the Practice Direction supplementing Pt 23 at para. 23PD–001 below). The hearing of a summary judgment application will normally take place before a Master or District Judge but:

(a) the Master or District Judge may direct that the application be heard by a High Court Judge (if the case is in the High Court) or a Circuit Judge (if the case is in a county court) (see para. 3 of the Practice Direction supplementing Pt 24 at para. 24PD–001 below);
(b) the jurisdiction of Masters and District Judges to grant injunctions is limited (see Practice Direction (Interim Injunctions) supplementing Pt 25, paras 1.1 to 1.4 at para. 25CPD–001 below).

In specific performance cases and similar cases which fall within the limits of para. 7 of the Practice Direction supplementing Pt 24 (see para. 24PD–001 below), the application notice must have attached to it the text of the order sought by the claimant (see para. 7.2).

Evidence in support of the application—An applicant cannot rely upon oral evidence unless the court so permits (r.32.6). Instead he may rely upon written evidence set out in his claim form, statement of case, or application notice or in a witness statement. Each item of written evidence relied on must contain a statement of truth (as to which, see further the Practice Direction supplementing Pt 22 (see para. 22PD–001) and the Practice Direction supplementing Pt 8, para. 5.2 (see para. 8PD–001). An applicant may also rely upon affidavit evidence if he so wishes. However, if he does so, he may not recover any additional costs thereby incurred unless the court orders otherwise (r.32.15 and as to affidavits generally, r.32.16, r.32.17 and the Practice Direction which supplements Pt 32 at para. 32PD–001 below). 24.4.9

Evidence relied on which is not set out in the application notice itself must be served with the application notice (unless already served) and must also be filed (Practice Direction supplementing Pt 23, paras 9.3 and 9.6, respectively (see para. 23PD–001 below)).

Paragraph 2(3) of the Practice Direction supplementing Pt 24 (see para. 24PD–001 below) provides that the application notice or the evidence contained or referred to in it or served with it must:

(a) identify concisely any point of law or provision in a document on which the applicant relies; and/or
(b) state that it is made because the applicant believes that on the evidence the respondent has no real prospect of succeeding on the claim or issue or (as the case may be) of successfully defending the claim or issue to which the application relates,

and in either case must state that the applicant knows of no other reason why the disposal of the claim or issue should await trial.

Given the burdens of proof in summary judgment applications (see "Burdens of proof" under r.24.2) the evidence in support of an application should also contain:

(1) if the applicant is the claimant, evidence verifying the relevant claim or issue;
(2) if the applicant is the defendant, evidence showing that the relevant claim or issue is bound to be dismissed at trial.

Effect of non-compliance with the requirements of rules and practice directions—The court has general power to rectify matters where there has been an error of procedure such as defects or omissions in the documents supporting an application or a failure to serve documents within the time limits applicable (see r.3.10 and the commentary thereto). 24.4.10

Evidence for the purposes of a summary judgment hearing

24.5—(1) If the respondent to an application for summary judgment wishes to rely on written evidence at the hearing, he must— 24.5

(a) file the witness statement; and
(b) serve copies on every other party to the application,

at least 7 days before the summary judgment hearing.

(2) If the applicant wishes to rely on a witness statement in reply, he must—

(a) file the written evidence; and
(b) serve a copy on the respondent,

at least 3 days before the summary judgment hearing.

(3) Where a summary judgment hearing is fixed by the court of its own initiative—

(a) any party who wishes to rely on written evidence at the hearing must—
 (i) file the written evidence; and
 (ii) unless the court orders otherwise, serve copies on every other party to the proceedings,

 at least 7 days before the date of the hearing;
(b) any party who wishes to rely on written evidence at the hearing in reply to any other party's written evidence must—
 (i) file the written evidence in reply; and
 (ii) unless the court orders otherwise serve copies on every other party to the proceedings,

 at least 3 days before the date of the hearing.

(4) This rule does not require written evidence—

(a) to be filed if it has already been filed; or
(b) to be served on a party on whom it has already been served.

Evidence in support of the application—See the annotation under this heading in the commentary to r.24.4. 24.5.1

24.5.2 **Evidence in response and further evidence in reply**—Given the burdens of proof in summary judgment applications (see "Burdens of proof" under r.24.2), the evidence in response to an application should contain:

(1) if the respondent is the defendant, evidence of facts justifying any reason relied on showing why the claim or issue should be dealt with at trial;

(2) if the respondent is the claimant, evidence of facts showing a case which, if unanswered, would entitle him to judgment on the relevant claim or issue.

If the respondent files and serves written evidence the applicant may, if he wishes, rely on written evidence in reply. There is no requirement for evidence in reply to be identified in the application notice (Practice Direction supplementing Pt 24, para. 2(4) at para. 24PD–001 below).

No party can rely upon oral evidence unless the court so permits (r.32.6). Instead, a party may rely on written evidence set out in his statement of case (if any) or in a witness statement. Each item of written evidence relied on must contain a statement of truth (as to which, see further Pt 22 and the Practice Direction supplementing it at para. 22PD–001). A party may also rely upon affidavit evidence if he so wishes. However, if he does so he may not recover any additional costs thereby incurred unless the court orders otherwise (r.32.15 and, as to affidavits generally, see rr.32.16, 32.17 and the Practice Direction which supplements Pt 32 at para. 32PD–001 below).

24.5.3 **Timetable for serving evidence**—Unless the summary judgment hearing was fixed by the court of its own initiative:

(1) The evidence in support of the application must either be contained in the application notice itself or must be served with the application notice (unless already served) (Practice Direction supplementing Pt 23, para. 9.3 (see para. 23PD–001). The evidence in support must also be filed (Practice Direction supplementing Pt 23, para. 9.6 (see para. 23PD–001)).

(2) Evidence in response to the application must be filed and served on every other party to the application at least seven days before the hearing (r.24.5(1)).

(3) Evidence in reply must be filed and served on the respondent at least three days before the hearing (r.24.5(2)).

Where a summary judgment hearing is fixed by the court of its own initiative:

(1) In specific performance cases and similar cases which fall within the limits of para. 7 of the Practice Direction supplementing Pt 24 (see para. 24PD–001 below), the claimant must file and serve on every other party to the application any written evidence he wishes to rely on at least four days before the hearing (para. 7.3).

(2) In all other cases any party who wishes to rely on written evidence at the hearing must file and serve it on every other party to the proceedings at least seven days before the date of the hearing (r.24.5(3)(a)).

(3) Any party who wishes to rely on written evidence at the hearing in reply to any other party's written evidence must file and (unless the court otherwise orders) serve it on every other party to the proceedings at least three days before the date of the hearing (r.24.5(3)(b)).

As to the effect of late service of evidence and other failures to comply with the requirements of the rules or Practice Directions, see r.3.10 and the commentary thereto.

Court's powers when it determines a summary judgment application

24.6 **24.6** When the court determines a summary judgment application it may—

(a) give directions as to the filing and service of a defence;

(b) give further directions about the management of the case.

(Rule 3.1(3) provides that the court may attach conditions when it makes an order.)

24.6.1 **The court's approach**—The court's approach to the question whether or not to grant summary judgment is described in paras 4.1 to 4.3 of the Practice Direction supplementing Pt 24 (see para. 24PD–001 below). The effect of these paragraphs is explained below in relation to the orders which the court may make.

24.6.2 **Orders which the court may make**—The orders which the court may make on an application under Pt 24 include:

(a) judgment on the claim or on an issue therein;

(b) the striking out or dismissal of the claim or of an issue therein;

(c) the dismissal of the application;

(d) a conditional order; and

(e) an order dealing with costs.

(See paras 5 and 9 of the Practice Direction supplementing Pt 24 (para. 24PD–001 below); a marginal note to para. 5 states that the court will not follow its former practice of granting leave to a defendant to defend a claim, whether conditionally or unconditionally.)

24.6.3 **Judgment on the claim or on an issue therein**—This order will be made if:

(a) the claimant has shown a case which, if unanswered, would entitle him to that judgment; and
(b) the defendant has not shown any reason why the claim or issue should be dealt with at trial (see para. 4.1 of the Practice Direction supplementing Pt 24 (para. 24PD–001 below)).

The judgment given may be the grant of remedies sought, an order for damages to be assessed or an order amounting to declaratory relief finally determining a preliminary issue in the proceedings in favour of the claimant (see further, the commentary to r.24.1).

In some cases the court will give judgment with a stay of enforcement. Where the claimant has succeeded on his claim but the defendant has shown a plausible counterclaim of a value which equals or exceeds the claim the court may stay enforcement on the claim until after the trial of the counterclaim. Under the previous rules the circumstances in which the court would make such an order were limited. Counterclaims amounting to set-offs would often prevent the entry of summary judgment in the first place. Under the new rules the court may make an order disposing of the issues raised by the claimant by giving summary judgment on his claim subject to the determination of the defendant's cross claim (see further "Effect of a set-off or counterclaim" under r.24.2).

An order amounting to declaratory relief finally determining a preliminary issue in the proceedings in favour of the defendant will be made if, in respect of that issue:
(a) the claimant has failed to show a case which, if unanswered, would entitle him to judgment; or
(b) the defendant has shown that the claimant's case would be bound to be dismissed at trial (see para. 4.2 of the Practice Direction supplementing Pt 24 at para. 24PD–001 below).

On a claim by a solicitor against his former client for non-payment of costs, the court may, if there is no real prospect of defending the claim, give summary judgment for a sum to be determined by means of a detailed assessment under Pts 47 and 48. For the form of order see PF 15 listed in the Practice Direction supplementing Pt 4. Such an order can be made even if the former client has lost the opportunity to apply for a detailed assessment of the solicitor's bill under Part III of the Solicitors Act 1974 (*Thomas Watts & Co. v. Smith*, March 16, 1998, CA (unreported)). If, in addition to challenging items in the bill, the defendant also counterclaims for negligence, an order in Form PF 15 can be made with a stay of proceedings after the detailed assessment pending the determination of the counterclaim.

The striking out or dismissal of the claim or of an issue therein—This order will be made in favour of the defendant if, in respect of the relevant claim or issue: **24.6.3A**
(a) the claimant has failed to show a case which, if unanswered, would entitle him to judgment; or
(b) the defendant has shown that the claimant's case would be bound to be dismissed at trial (see para. 4.2 of the Practice Direction supplementing Pt 24 at para. 24PD–001 below).

An order striking out or dismissing a preliminary issue in the proceedings in favour of the claimant will be made if, in respect of that issue:
(a) the claimant has shown a case which, if unanswered, would entitle him to judgment; and
(b) the defendant has not shown any reason why the claim or issue should be dealt with at trial (see para. 4.1 of the Practice Direction supplementing Pt 24 at para. 24PD–001 below).

The dismissal of the application—This order will be made if it appears to the court that the conditions set out in paras 4.1 or 4.2 (as the case may be) of the Practice Direction supplementing Pt 24 (see para. 24PD–001 below) have not been satisfied in such a way as to justify the grant of summary judgment on a claim or defence or on any preliminary issue upon which a claim or defence depends. **24.6.4**

A conditional order—This order will be made if it appears to the court that, in respect of some claim or defence or issue, it is possible that that claim, defence or issue may succeed but it is improbable that it will do so (see para. 4.3 of the Practice Direction supplementing Pt 24 at para. 24PD–001 below). **24.6.5**

Paragraph 5.2 of the Practice Direction supplementing Pt 24 (see para. 24PD–001 below) defines a conditional order as an order which requires a party:
(a) to pay a sum of money into court; or
(b) to take a specified step in relation to his claim or defence as the case may be, and which provides that that party's claim will be dismissed or his statement of case will be struck out if he does not comply.

An order dealing with costs—The court may make an order for costs, for example, an order for fixed costs (as to which see Pt 45) or an order for costs, to be assessed by way of summary assessment or detailed assessment (as to which, see Pt 43). **24.6.6**

Fixed costs may be applicable where the only claim in the proceedings is a claim for a specified sum of money or a claim to which the Practice Direction supplementing r.7.9 applies (Consumer Credit Act claims) and where, in either case, the value of the claim exceeds £25. In all cases the court has power to allow costs other than fixed costs.

Where the court makes an order on an application under Pt 24 which does not mention costs, no party is entitled to costs relating to that order (r.44.4(5)).

24.6.7 **Setting aside order for summary judgment**—If an order for summary judgment is made against a respondent who does not appear at the hearing, the court may later (whether on the application of that respondent or of its own initiative) make such order as it thinks just setting aside or varying its previous order (see rr.3.3, 23.11 and para. 8 of the Practice Direction supplementing Pt 24 (para. 24PD–001 below)).

24.6.8 **Case management**—Where the court dismisses the application or makes an order that does not completely dispose of the claim, the court will give case management directions as to the future conduct of the case (para. 10 of the Practice Direction supplementing Pt 24 (see para. 24PD–001 below)).

Special provision is made for a case in which an order is made for an amount of damages or interest to be decided by the court or for the taking of an account or the making of an inquiry as to any sum due or any similar order (other than certain orders for the assessment of costs). In order to deal with such cases para. 12 of the Practice Direction supplementing Pt 26 (see para. 26PD–001 below) provides (amongst other things) that the court may:

(a) give directions for the assessment;
(b) make the assessment immediately (if the claimant's evidence for that assessment has been served on the defendant at least 3 days in advance of the hearing);
(c) allocate the claim to the small claims track (if the financial value of the claim is within the scope of that track).

PRACTICE DIRECTION—THE SUMMARY DISPOSAL OF CLAIMS

This Practice Direction supplements CPR Part 24

1. Applications for summary judgment under Part 24

24PD–001 **1.1** Attention is drawn to Part 24 itself and to:
Part 3, in particular rule 3.1(3) and (5),
Part 22,
Part 23, in particular rule 23.6,
Part 32, in particular rule 32.6(2).

1.2 In this paragraph, where the context so admits, the word "claim" includes:
(1) a part of a claim, and
(2) an issue on which the claim in whole or part depends.

1.3 An application for summary judgment under rule 24.2 may be based on:
(1) a point of law (including a question of construction of a document),
(2) the evidence which can reasonably be expected to be available at trial or the lack of it, or
(3) a combination of these.

1.4 Rule 24.4(1) deals with the stage in the proceedings at which an application under Part 24 can be made (but see paragraph 7.1 below).

2. Procedure for making an application

(1) Attention is drawn to rules 24.4(3) and 23.6.

(2) The application notice must include a statement that it is an application for summary judgment made under Part 24.

(3) The application notice or the evidence contained or referred to in it or served with it must—

(a) identify concisely any point of law or provision in a document on which the applicant relies, and/or
(b) state that it is made because the applicant believes that on the evidence the respondent has no real prospect of succeeding on the claim or issue or (as the case may be) of successfully defending the claim or issue to which the application relates,

and in either case state that the applicant knows of no other reason why the disposal of the claim or issue should await trial.

(4) Unless the application notice itself contains all the evidence (if any) on which the applicant relies, the application notice should identify the written evidence on which the applicant relies. This does not affect the applicant's right to file further evidence under rule 24.5(2).

(5) The application notice should draw the attention of the respondent to rule 24.5(1).

3. The hearing

(1) The hearing of the application will normally take place before a Master or a District Judge.

(2) The Master or District Judge may direct that the application be heard by a High Court Judge (if the case is in the High Court) or a Circuit Judge (if the case is in a county court).

4. The court's approach

Where it appears to the court possible that a claim or defence may succeed but improbable that it will do so, the court may make a conditional order, as described below.

5. Orders the court may make

5.1 The orders the court may make on an application under Part 24 include: 24PD–002

(1) judgment on the claim,
(2) the striking out or dismissal of the claim,
(3) the dismissal of the application,
(4) a conditional order.

5.2 A conditional order is an order which requires a party:

(1) to pay a sum of money into court, or
(2) to take a specified step in relation to his claim or defence, as the case may be,

and provides that that party's claim will be dismissed or his statement of case will be struck out if he does not comply.

(Note—the court will not follow its former practice of granting leave to a defendant to defend a claim, whether conditionally or unconditionally.)

6. Accounts and inquiries

If a remedy sought by a claimant in his claim form includes, or necessarily involves, taking an account or making an inquiry, an application can be made under Part 24 by any party to the proceedings for an order directing any necessary accounts or inquiries to be taken or made.

(This paragraph replaces RSC, Order 43, rule 1, but applies to county court proceedings as well as to High Court proceedings. The Accounts practice direction supplementing Part 40 contains further provisions as to orders for accounts and inquiries.)

7. Specific performance

7.1 (1) If a remedy sought by a claimant in his claim form includes a claim—

(a) for specific performance of an agreement (whether in writing or not) for the sale, purchase, exchange, mortgage or charge of any property, or for the grant or assignment of a lease or tenancy of any property, with or without an alternative claim for damages, or
(b) for rescission of such an agreement, or
(c) for the forfeiture or return of any deposit made under such an agreement,

the claimant may apply under Part 24 for judgment.

(2) The claimant may do so at any time after the claim form has been served, whether or not the defendant has acknowledged service of the claim

form, whether or not the time for acknowledging service has expired and whether or not any particulars of claim have been served.

7.2 The application notice by which an application under paragraph 7.1 is made must have attached to it the text of the order sought by the claimant.

7.3 The application notice and a copy of every affidavit or witness statement in support and of any exhibit referred to therein must be served on the defendant not less than 4 days before the hearing of the application.

(Note—the 4 days replaces for these applications the 14 days specified in rule 24.4(3). Rule 24.5 cannot, therefore, apply.)

(This paragraph replaces RSC ,Order 86, rules 1 and 2 but applies to county court proceedings as well as to High Court proceedings.)

8. Setting aside order for summary judgment

8.1 If an order for summary judgment is made against a respondent who does not appear at the hearing of the application, the respondent may apply for the order to be set aside or varied (see also rule 23.11).

8.2 On the hearing of an application under paragraph 8.1 the court may make such order as it thinks just.

9. Costs

9.1 Attention is drawn to Part 44 (Fixed Costs).

9.2 Attention is drawn to the Costs Practice Direction and in particular to the court's power to make a summary assessment of costs.

9.3 Attention is also drawn to rule 43.5(5) which provides that if an order does not mention costs no party is entitled to costs relating to that order.

10. Case management

Where the court dismisses the application or makes an order that does not completely dispose of the claim, the court will give case management directions as to the future conduct of the case.

PART 25

Interim Remedies

Contents 25.0.1

Editorial Introduction

The rules in this part deal with two matters formerly treated quite separately: (1) the granting of orders for interim remedies (including interim injunctions) and (2) the granting of orders for interim payments. General rules about applications for court orders, including orders for interim remedies and interim payments, are found in Pt 23. Detailed procedures applicable on applications for interim remedies and interim payments are found in this Part. 25.0.2

Formerly, rules of court relating to many of the interim remedies listed in r.25.1 were found in RSC, O.29 and were made applicable in county court procedures by CCR, O.13, rr.6 and 7.

Formerly, rules of court relating to applications for interim payments (implementing the statutory scheme in the Supreme Court Act 1981, s.32) were found in RSC, O.29, Pt II, and with minor modifications, these provisions were applied in county courts by CCR, O.13, r.12 (implementing the statutory scheme in the County Courts Act 1984, s.50).

Related Sources

- Practice Direction (Interim Payments) (see para. 25PD–001 below). 25.0.3
- Practice Direction (Accounts and Inquiries) (see para. 25BPD–002 below).
- Practice Direction (Interim Injunctions) (see para. 25CPD–003 below).
- Practice Direction (Applications) (see para. 23PD–001).
- Part 23 (General rules about applications for court orders).
- Practice Direction (Allocation of Cases to Levels of Judiciary) (see para. 2B–001).
- Commercial Court Guide (5th ed.), Section F (see para. D2–001).
- Chancery Guide (April 1999 ed.), Chap. 7 (see para. D1–001).
- Rule 39.2(1) (General rule—hearing to be in public).
- This Part (except as it relates to interim injunctions) does not apply to small claims (r.27.2(1)(a)).
- A claimant needs permission from the court if he wishes to discontinue all or part of a claim in relation to which the court has granted an interim injunction (r.38.2(2)(a)(i)).
- Civil Procedure Act 1997, s.7 (see SCP 1999, Vol. 2, para. 20A–7).
- Supreme Court Act 1981, s.32 (see SCP 1999, Vol. 2, para. 20A–209).
- Supreme Court Act 1981, ss.33 and 34 (see SCP 1999, Vol. 2, paras 20A–215 and 20A–219).
- Supreme Court Act 1981, s.37 (see SCP 1999, Vol. 2, para. 20A–231).
- County Courts Act 1984, s.50 (see SCP 1999, Vol. 2, paras 20A–723).
- County Courts Act 1984, ss.52 and 53 (see SCP 1999, Vol. 2, paras 20A–725and 20A–726).
- Torts (Interference with Goods) Act 1977, s.4.
- Civil Jurisdiction and Judgments Act 1982, ss.24 and 25 (see SCP 1999, Vol. 2, paras 7B–18 and 7B–19).

Practice Directions

25.0.4 The provisions of this Part are supplemented by several Practice Directions. From a practical point of view, the most important of them is Practice Direction (Interim Injunctions) (see para. 25CPD–001 below) replacing *Practice Direction (Mareva Injunctions and Anton Piller Orders)* [1994] 1 W.L.R. 1233 (see SCP 1999, Vol. 2, para. 2C–42).

The other Practice Directions supplementing Pt 25 are: Practice Direction (Interim Payments) (para. 25PD–001) and Practice Direction (Accounts and Inquiries) (para. 25BPD–001).

Forms

25.0.5 See further para. 25.1.8 (Form of order for interim injunction) below.

- N244 (Application notice).

The following county court forms in use before the CPR came into effect on April 26, 1999, continue in use (see Practice Direction (Forms) Tables 1 and 3):

- N16A (General form of application for injunction)
- N361 (Notice of application for relief in pending action)

Forms for orders for freezing injunctions (formerly Mareva injunctions) both domestic and worldwide, and for search orders (formerly Anton Piller orders), previously found in *Practice Direction (Mareva Injunctions and Anton Piller Orders: Forms)* [1996] 1 W.L.R. 1522 (see SCP 1999, Vol. 2, para. 2C–46) are replaced by forms annexed to the Practice Direction supplementing this Part (see paras 25CPD–005 *et seq.*) and referred to above.

See also Commercial Court Guide (5th ed.) Appendix 5 (draft freezing injunctions and search order).

Court Guides and interim remedies procedure

25.0.6 It was noted above (para. 23.0.13) that where applications are made in accordance with the Pt 23 procedure in proceedings in the Commercial Court, and in proceedings in the Chancery Division of the High Court, the provisions of Pt 23 and the practice directions supplementing that Part must be read in conjunction with, respectively, the Commercial Court Guide (5th ed.), Section F, and the Chancery Guide (April 1999), Chap. 7, and the practice directions referred to there. In some respects, the modifications to Pt 23 practice made by these Guides are significant.

As is explained below (para. 25.2.1), when an application is made for an interim remedy, the provisions of Pt 23 and the practice directions supplementing that Part are subject to the provisions of Pt 25 and supplementing practice directions. It should also be noted that the Court Guides referred to above deal specifically with applications for certain kinds of interim remedies, in particular, interim injunctions, freezing injunctions and search orders; see the Commercial Court Guide (5th ed.), Section F, paras F19 *et seq.* and the Chancery Guide (April 1999 ed.) Chap. 7, paras 7.12 *et seq.*

Powers of Masters and district judges in relation to interim remedies

25.0.7 Masters and district judges may exercise any function of the High Court except where an enactment, rule or practice direction provides otherwise (r.2.4). The circumstances in which Masters and district judges may exercise the jurisdiction of the High Court in relation to the interim remedies listed in r.25.1(1) is restricted by Practice Direction (Allocation of Cases to Levels of Judiciary) paras 2.1 *et seq.* (see para. 2B–001).

District judges may exercise any function of the county courts except where an enactment, rule or practice direction provides otherwise (r.2.4). The jurisdiction of the county courts to grant the interim remedies listed in r.25.1(1) is not as great as that enjoyed by the High Court (see para. 25.1.2 below). The circumstances in which district judges may exercise that limited jurisdiction is restricted by Practice Direction (Allocation of Cases to Levels of Judiciary) paras 2.1 *et seq.* (see para. 2B–001).

Note also Practice Direction (Interim Injunctions) paras 1.1 to 1.4 (see para. 25CPD–001 below).

Orders for interim remedies

25.1 **25.1**—(1) The court may grant the following interim remedies—

(a) an interim injunction[GL];

(b) an interim declaration;

(c) an order—

(i) for the detention, custody or preservation of relevant property;

(ii) for the inspection of relevant property;

(iii) for the taking of a sample of relevant property;

(iv) for the carrying out of an experiment on or with relevant property;

(v) for the sale of relevant property which is of a perishable nature or which for any other good reason it is desirable to sell quickly; and

(vi) for the payment of income from relevant property until a claim is decided;

(d) an order authorising a person to enter any land or building in the possession of a party to the proceedings for the purposes of carrying out an order under sub-paragraph (c);

(e) an order under section 4 of the Torts (Interference with Goods) Act 1977[1] to deliver up goods;

(f) an order (referred to as a "freezing injunction[GL]")—

(i) restraining a party from removing from the jurisdiction assets located there; or

(ii) restraining a party from dealing with any assets whether located within the jurisdiction or not;

(g) an order directing a party to provide information about the location of relevant property or assets or to provide information about relevant property or assets which are or may be the subject of an application for a freezing injunction[GL].

(h) an order (referred to as a "search order") under section 7 of the Civil Procedure Act 1997[2] (order requiring a party to admit another party to premises for the purpose of preserving evidence, etc.);

(i) an order under section 33 of the Supreme Court Act 1981[3] or section 52 of the County Courts Act 1984[4] (order for disclosure of documents or inspection of property before a claim has been made);

(j) an order under section 34 of the Supreme Court Act 1981[5] or section 53 of the County Courts Act 1984[6] (order in certain proceedings for disclosure of documents or inspection of property against a non-party);

(k) an order (referred to as an order for interim payment) under rule 25.6 for payment by a defendant on account of any damages, debt or other sum (except costs) which the court may hold the defendant liable to pay;

(l) an order for a specified fund to be paid into court or otherwise secured, where there is a dispute over a party's right to the fund;

(m) an order permitting a party seeking to recover personal property to pay money into court pending the outcome of the proceedings and directing that, if he does so, the property shall be given up to him; and

(n) an order directing a party to prepare and file accounts relating to the dispute.

(Rule 34.2 provides for the court to issue a witness summons requiring a witness to produce documents to the court at the hearing or on such date as the court may direct.)

(2) In paragraph (1)(c) and (g), "relevant property" means property (including land) which is the subject of a claim or as to which any question may arise on a claim.

(3) The fact that a particular kind of interim remedy is not listed in paragraph (1) does not affect any power that the court may have to grant that remedy.

[1] 1977 c. 32; section 4 was amended by the Supreme Court Act 1981 (c. 54), section 152(1), Schedule 5; by the County Courts Act 1984 (c. 28), section 148(1), Schedule 2, Part V, paragraph 64 and by S.I. 1980/397 (NI3).

[2] 1997 c. 12.

[3] 1981 c. 54. Section 33 was amended by S.I. 1998/2940.

[4] 1984 c. 28. Section 52 was amended by the Courts and Legal Services Act 1990 (c. 41), Schedule 18, paragraph 43, and by S.I. 1998/2940.

[5] 1981 c. 54. Section 34 was amended by S.I. 1998/2940.

[6] 1984 c. 28. Section 53 was amended by the Courts and Legal Services Act 1990 (c. 41), Schedule 18, paragraph 44 and by S.I. 1998/2940.

(4) The court may grant an interim remedy whether or not there has been a claim for a final remedy of that kind.

25.1.1 **Effect of rule**—In r.25.1(1) an attempt is made to list all of the interim remedies for which a party may wish to apply (including some available before proceedings are commenced) and which the court, in the exercise of discretion, may be prepared to grant. It is possible that the list is not exhaustive. Consequently, r.25.1(3) states that the fact that a particular kind of interim remedy is not listed in para. (1) does not affect any power that the court may have to grant that remedy. (The power to appoint a receiver granted by the Supreme Court Act 1981, s.37(1) might be regarded as an example.) In certain circumstances, some of the remedies listed in r.25.1, and described as "interim", may be granted after final judgment (r.25.2(1)(b)). Thus the power to grant "a freezing injunction" after judgment is preserved; see SCP 1999, Vol. 1, paras 29/L/49 and 29/L68 for the former practice.

Formerly, rules of court relating to many of the remedies listed in r.25.1 were found in RSC, O.29. In that Order, a distinction was drawn between those interim remedies for which the sources of the court's jurisdiction were the rules of court themselves; *e.g.* r.3 (Power to order samples to be taken, etc.) and those for which the sources were found in common law rules or statute; *e.g.* r.1 (Application for injunction) (see now, respectively, r.25.1(1)(c)(iii) and r.25.1(1)(a) in this Part). Rules dealing with interim remedies falling within the former category stated in terms that "the court may grant" the remedy (or contained words to similar effect) whereas rules dealing with interim remedies falling in the latter category acknowledged that the jurisdiction was derived from outside the RSC and stated simply that "application may be made". No such distinction is drawn in r.25.1. The rule states that "the court may grant" the remedies listed therein. It is unfortunate that the distinction has disappeared in the CPR but no harm is done so long as it is remembered that the source of the court's jurisdiction to grant many of the interim remedies listed is not to be found in r.25.1; *e.g.* the source of the court's jurisdiction to grant an interim injunction (r.25.1(1)(a)) is the Supreme Court Act 1981, s.37 (see SCP 1999, Vol. 2, para. 20A–231).

Where, by application to the court, remedies may be granted before final order, that is to say, as interim remedies, various procedural issues concerning the handling of such applications and the conditions in which relief may be granted arise. Those that are not dealt with in Pt 23 (General rules about applications for court orders), or not dealt with completely in that Part, are dealt with in r.25.1 and following rules. Some interim remedies were developed as purely interim remedies and not as interim versions of final remedies.

25.1.2 **Jurisdiction of county courts to grant interim relief**—The County Courts Act 1984, s.38 (as amended in 1990) (see SCP 1999, Vol. 2, para. 20A–697) provides that, generally, in any proceedings in a county court the court may make any order (final or interlocutory and absolute or conditional) which could be made by the High Court if the proceedings were in the High Court (see also *Burris v. Azadani* [1995] 1 W.L.R. 1372, CA). The circumstances in which county courts may grant relief in the form of freezing injunctions and search orders (see, respectively paras 25.1.19 and 25.1.21 below) is restricted by the County Court Remedies Regulations 1991, reg. 3 (see SCP 1999, Vol. 2, para. 20B–163).

25.1.3 **Interim remedies and the overriding objective**—The court must seek to give effect to the overriding objective stated in r.1.1 when it "exercises any power given to it by the Rules" or when it "interprets the meaning of any rule" (r.1.2). Further, the court is required to further the overriding objective by actively managing cases (r.1.4), and this includes considering "whether the likely benefits of taking a particular step justify the cost of taking it". So far as is practicable, the court must deal with cases so as to save expense, to ensure that they are dealt with expeditiously as well as fairly, and in a manner which is proportionate to what is at stake, etc. It is not immediately clear how these duties relate to the granting of interim remedies (as distinct from the procedures by which the remedies may be sought and granted). The sources of the court's jurisdiction to grant the more important of the interim remedies lie outside the CPR. When considering whether to grant such remedies the court is not merely exercising a "power given to it by the Rules" or deciding whether "a particular step" should be taken. Further, the power to grant interim remedies is not listed among the court's "general powers of management" (see r.3.1), which are to be exercised in a manner which further the overriding objective, unless it is caught by r.3.1(2)(m) (court's power to "take any other step or make any other order for the purpose of managing the case and furthering the overriding objective"). Nevertheless, it seems clear that the intention is that the various elements in the overriding objective should be applied to the granting of interim remedies. The interim remedies are discretionary and the discretion is exercised judicially within a framework of case law. In the past, many factors now formally adopted by the rules in Pt 1 as elements of the overriding objective have routinely influenced the exercise of the discretion and will continue to do so.

25.1.4 **Inherent jurisdiction**—It is expressly provided that the fact that a particular kind of interim remedy is not listed in r.25.1(1) does not affect any power that the court may have to grant that remedy (r.25.1(3)). This provision was inserted principally for the purpose of making it clear that the court's inherent jurisdiction is not limited by r.25.1 but it also has the effect of ensuring that it does not cast doubt on the powers derived from statute (*e.g.* the power to appoint a receiver derived from the Supreme Court Act 1981, s.37(1)). The description interim remedy is not a term of art and doubts may arise as to whether or not a particular power of the court is properly described as such.

The High Court has an inherent jurisdiction to make an order for the purpose of preventing abuse of its procedures. This jurisdiction is a fertile source for procedural development. For example, in *Ebert v. Birch* (1999) 149 New L.J. 608, CA, it was held that the High Court has jurisdiction to make an order (which may, perhaps, properly be described as an order for an "interim remedy") restraining a person from initiating civil proceedings without the permission of the court where those proceedings would be vexatious (an "extended *Grepe v. Loam* order"). The jurisdiction may be exercised where proceedings against the respondent for a civil proceedings order under the Supreme Court Act 1981, s.42 are pending.

Interim remedy order in cases of doubtful jurisdiction—The Civil Jurisdiction and Judgments Act 1982, s.24(1)(a) (see SCP 1999, Vol. 2, para. 7B–20) states that the power of any court in England to grant "interim relief" pending trial, or pending the determination of an appeal, shall extend to a case where the issue to be tried, or which is the subject of the appeal, relates to the jurisdiction of the court to entertain the proceedings (*e.g.* where there is a question whether the court has jurisdiction under the Brussels Convention) or to entertain the application for the interim relief itself (note also s.24(1)(b)). As defined by s.25.7, in this context "interim relief" would appear to include all of the forms of relief listed as "interim remedies" in r.25.1(1). **25.1.5**

See also, para. 25.4.2 "Interim remedy order in support of foreign proceedings" below.

Interim remedies in judicial rview—Rules for applications for judicial review are found in Sched. 1, RSC, O.53. Rule 3(10) of that Order states that, where permission to apply for judicial review is granted, then, depending on the relief sought, the court may at any time grant in the proceedings "interim remedies in accordance with CPR Part 25" (see para. R53.3). Formerly, r.3(10) stated, more broadly, that the court could grant "such interim relief as could be granted in an action begun by writ". It would seem that the narrower formulation now found in r.3(10) is not intended to effect any change in the law. **25.1.6**

Interim remedy not limited by claim form (r.25.1(4))—Interim remedies are of two broad varieties (but some are a mixture). First there are those which are temporary versions of final remedies. In the interests of fairness and justice they are granted pending trial; *e.g.* a claimant issues a claim for an injunction and is granted a temporary injunction to the same or similar effect. Secondly, there are those which are purely interlocutory; *e.g.* an order permitting one party to inspect relevant property in the possession of another party. The effect of r.25.1(4) is to make clear that a party may apply for an interim remedy falling in the first category even though he has made no claim in his claim form for a final remedy of that kind. The rule follows former rule RSC, O.29, r.1(1) but is cast in broader terms (see also former CCR, O.13, r.6(1)). **25.1.7**

Interim injunction (r.25.1(1)(a))—The Glossary attached to the CPR states that an injunction is "a court order prohibiting a person from doing something or requiring a person to do something". For former rules, see RSC, O.29, r.1 and CCR, O.13, r.6. **25.1.8**

An injunction granted by judicial decision at trial after the plaintiff has established the existence of his right in law and the fact that the defendant has infringed it or is about to do so may be described as a *perpetual injunction.* An order other than a final judgment, whether such order be made before judgment or not, may properly be described as an interlocutory order. Under the CPR, "interim" is preferred to "interlocutory". Consequently, an injunction granted by interlocutory order as so defined is an *interim injunction.*

A claim form must specify the remedy the claimant seeks (r.16.2) and therefore should include any claim for an injunction as a final order. However, an application for the grant of an interim injunction may be made by any party, whether or not a claim for an injunction was included in that party's claim form or Part 20 claim (*e.g.* counterclaim), as the case may be (r.25.1(4)). Where the defendant is the applicant the relief sought need not necessarily arise in respect of the claimant's claim. An interim injunction may be in terms which would not be appropriate, or given the nature of the parties' allegations, possible, at the final trial (*Fresh Fruit Wales Ltd v. Halbert, The Times,* January 29, 1991, CA).

Subject to certain limits, an interim injunction may be granted at any time (r.25.2) (see further paras. 25.2.3 *et seq.,* below).

For "freezing injunctions" (formerly Mareva injunctions) see para. 25.1.19 below.

As to the granting of an injunction on an application for judicial review see Sched. 1, RSC, O.53, r.1 and para. 25.1.6 "Interim remedies in judicial review" above.

As to applicant's duty to make full and frank disclosure when applying without notice for interim injunction, see para. 25.3.5 "Applicant's duties where application made without notice to respondent" below.

As to discharge of intrim injunctions, see note r.25.10 (Interim injunction to cease if claim stayed) and r.25.11 (Interim injunction to cease after 14 days if claim struck out under r.3.7).

Jurisdiction—The Supreme Court Act 1981 s.37 (see SCP 1999, Vol. 2, para. 20A–231) states that the High Court may by order, whether interlocutory or final, grant an injunction in all cases in which it appears to the court to be just and convenient to do so (s.37(1)). Any such order may be made either unconditionally or on such terms and conditions as the court thinks just (s.37(2)).

The County Courts Act 1984 s.38 (see SCP 1999, Vol. 2, para. 20A–697) provides that, generally, in any proceedings in a county court the court may make any order (final or interlocutory and absolute or conditional) which could be made by the High Court if the proceedings were in the High Court (see also *Burris v. Azadani* [1995] 1 W.L.R. 1372, CA).

See also Civil Jurisdiction and Judgments Act 1982 s.25 (see SCP 1999, Vol. 2, para. 7B–20) explained in para. 25.4.2 "Interim remedy order in support of foreign proceedings" below.

In the High Court, in certain circumstances, interim injunctions may be granted by Masters or district judges. Similarly, in county courts, in certain circumstances, interim injunctions may be granted by district judges. For conditions under which Masters and district judges may exercise jurisdiction in relation to interim injunctions, see "Powers of Masters and district judges in relation to interim remedies" para. 25.0.7 above and note Practice Direction (Interim Injunctions) paras 1.1 to 1.4 (see 25CPD–001 below) (where, misleadingly, interim and final injunctions are not distinguished). Note also Sched. 1, RSC, O.50, r.9, O.51, r.2 and O.77, r.16.

Principles and guidelines to be applied—The leading authority is *American Cyanamid Co. v. Ethicon Ltd* [1975] A.C. 396, HL. For an extensive discussion of the principles and guidelines stated in this case and related matters, see SCP 1999, Vol. 1, paras 29/L/2 *et seq.*

Practice—See also "Relationship between Pt 23 and rr. 25.2 to 25.5" (para. 25.2.1 below) and "Court Guides and interim remedies procedure" para. 25.0.6 above.

An application for an interim injunction is made on an application notice in accordance with the provisions of Pt 23 (General rules about applications for court orders) (see para. 23.0.1). The practice and procedure to be followed is as stated in the rules of that Part and the provisions of the practice direction supplementing that part (see 23PD–001) as complemented and modified by rules in Pt 25 and the provisions of Practice Direction (Interim Injunctions) (see 25PD–003 below). Despite its title, this last-mentioned Practice Direction is concerned, not merely with applications for interim injunctions (r.25.1(1)(a)), but also with applications for "freezing injunctions" (r.25.1(1)(f)) and "search orders" (r.25.1(1)(g)) (see further, respectively, paras 25.1.16 and 25.1.18 below). Indeed, in terms, the Practice Direction appears to regard "freezing injunctions" and "search orders" as forms of interim injunction.

When the provisions (1) of Pt 23 and the practice direction supplementing that Part and (2) of Pt 25 and the practice direction supplementing that Part are put side by side, it is not easy to discern to what extent the former are complemented and modified by the latter where applications for interim injunctions are made. Some of the Pt 23 provisions are unaffected by the Pt 25 provisions; *e.g.* r.23.2 (where to make an application). A degree of repetition is apparent; *e.g.* the several provisions relating to the service of an application notice (r.23.7(1) and 25PD para. 2.2, but note that the former speaks of filing and the latter of issuing) and to the providing of a draft order (r.23.7(3)(b), 23PD para. 2.1 and 25PD para. 2.4). Rule 23.6 and 23PD para. 2.1 (what an application notice must include) are modified very slightly by 25PD para. 2.1.

The principal modifications and additions to the Pt 23 provisions made by the Pt 25 provisions, in so far as they relate to the applications for interim injunctions (and for freezing injunctions and search orders), are (1) those concerning applications made without notice to the respondent, and made either before or after the issue of a claim form, and (2) those concerning evidence in support of applications. An application may be made without notice if it appears to the court that there are good reasons for not giving notice (r.25.3(1)). Except in cases where secrecy is essential, the applicant should take steps to notify the respondent informally of the application (25PD para. 4.3(3)). It follows from r.25.2(2)(b) that an application should not made before a claim has been made unless (i) the matter is urgent, or (ii) it is otherwise necessary to do so in the interests of justice (and the same obtains in a case where the respondent has been given notice).

The significant modifications and additions made by Pt 25 provisions relating to evidence in support of applications for intrim injunctions (and for freezing injunctions and search orders) include provisions relating to the filing and serving of evidence (see 25PD paras 2.2 and 2.3). Further, it is provided that an application must be supported by evidence unless the court orders otherwise (r.25.3(2)). Where an application is made without notice to the respondent, the evidence must set out why notice was not given (25PD para. 3.4). In certain circumstances the evidence should be in affidavit form (25PD paras 3.1 and 3.2). The evidence must set out the facts on which the applicant relies for the claim being made against the respondent, including all material facts of which the court should be made aware (25PD para. 3.3) (see further "Applicant's duties where application made without notice to respondent" para. 25.3.5 below).

Form of order for interim injunction—For forms for orders for "freezing injunctions" and "search orders", see paras 25CPD–003 *et seq.* and para. 25CPD–005; note also Commercial Court Guide (5th ed.) Appendix 5.

The following county court forms in use before the CPR came into effect on April 26, 1999, continue in use (see Practice Direction (Forms) Table 3):

- N16 (General form of injunction)
- N16(1) General form of injunction (formal parts only)
- N138 (Injunction orders)

Standard forms for the following orders were annexed to *Practice Direction (Interim Injunctions: Forms)* [1996] 1 W.L.R. 1551 (see Queen's Bench Practice Direction No. 12A, S.C.P. 1999, Vol. 2, para. 2C–97) and were for use in the Chancery Division and the Queen's Bench Division:

(1) injunctions before the issue of a writ of summons,
(2) order for injunction,
(3) order containing undertaking instead of injunction,
(4) adjournment of application for an injunction,
(5) application for an injunction treated as trial of the action.

This Practice Direction further provided that all such orders made in the Chancery motions court or by the Queen's Bench judge in chambers should, in the absence of good reason to the contrary, follow these forms. Where possible a draft should be provided and a word-processing disk containing the draft should also be made available to the court (for technical details, see para. 4 of the Practice Direction). These forms were not re-furbished in time for the commencement of the CPR in April 1999. However, it was made known that these and other forms were being re-drafted for use in the Chancery Division and the Queen's Bench Division and in the county courts, and that, for the time being, the old forms should be used, adapted as necessary.

Interim declaration (r.25.1(1)(b))—The statement "Interim declaratory relief is unknown to English law and consequently the court has no jurisdiction to grant an interim delcaratory order" (*Riverside Mental Health NHS Trust v. Fox* [1994] 1 F.L.R. 614, CA), has been overruled by this provision. It represents a new development in the law. "Declaration" is not in the Glossary to the CPR and therefore will retain its subsisting meaning. Although it is not anticipated that this relief will often be sought in practice its value will lie in protecting a party wishing to perform some act, such as demolishing a building, with the approval of the court. However, in most instances, a speedy trial will be more satisfactory. (It is submitted that an interim declaration may be granted by a Master or district judge under r.2.4; albeit the Practice Direction is silent thereon. However under RSC, O.14A almost the same relief could be obtained from a Master or district judge, albeit such declaration was final.) 25.1.9

Orders in relation to relevant property (r.25.1.(1)(c))—The court (this would normally be a Master or district judge; see r.2.4) may grant as interim remedies a number of different orders relating to "relevant property". (For other orders as to property, see r.25.1(1)(g), (i) and (j).) In r.25.1(1)(c), relevant property means "property (including land) which is the subject of a claim or as to which any question may arise on a claim" (r.25.1(2)). 25.1.10

Detention, custody or preservation of relevant property (r.25.1(1)(c)(i)—The court may grant an interim remedy in the form of an order for the detention, custody or preservation of relevant property (r.25.1(1)(c)(i)). For former rules, see RSC, O.29, r.2(1) and CCR, O.13, r.7(1)(b) (part). 25.1.11

Inspection of relevant property (r.25.1(1)(c)(ii))—The court may grant an interim remedy in the form of an order for the inspection of relevant property (r.25.1(1)(c)(ii)). For former rules, see RSC, O.29, r.2(1) and CCR, O.13, r.7(1)(b) (part). It may be noted that, under former RSC, O.29, r.2(1), inspection could be ordered of property "in the possession of a party" only. (See "in the possession of a party" SCP 1999, Vol. 1, para. 29/8A/8.) No such limitation was imposed by former CCR, O.13, r.7(1)(b) and no such limitation is now imposed by r.25.1(2). 25.1.12

Taking of a sample of relevant property (r.25.1(1)(c)(iii))—The court may grant an interim remedy in the form of an order for the taking of a sample of relevant property (r.25.1(c)(iii)). For former rules, see RSC, O.29, r.3(1) (part) and CCR, O.13, r.7(1)(e) (part). 25.1.13

Carrying out of an experiment on or with relevant property (r.25.1(1)(c)(iv))—The court may grant an interim remedy in the form of an order for the carrying out of an experiment on or with relevant property (r.25.1(1)(c)(iv)). For former rules, see RSC, O.29, r.3(1) (part) and CCR, O.13, r.7(1)(e) (part). 25.1.14

25.1.15 *Sale of property where desirable to sell quickly (r.25.1(1)(c)(v))*—The court may grant an interim remedy in the form of an order for the sale of relevant property which is of a perishable nature or which for any other good reason it is desirable to sell quickly (r.25.1(1)(c)(v)). "Relevant property" in this context includes land (r.25.1(2)). Former RSC, O.29, r.4(1) dealt with the sale of property other than land (including any interest in, or right over, land); see also former CCR, O.13, r.7(f). Former RSC, O.31, r.1 dealt with sales of land; see SCP 1999, Vol. 1, paras 29/8A/14 *et seq.* and paras 31/1/1 *et seq.*

25.1.16 *Payment of income until a claim is decided (r.25.1(1)(c)(vi))*—The court may grant an interim remedy in the form of an order for the payment of income from relevant property until a claim is decided (r.25.1(1)(c)(vi)). This is based on former RSC, O.29, r.8 (Allowance of income of property *pendente lite*). That rule stated that, where any real or personal property formed the subject-matter of any proceedings, and the Court was satisfied that it would be more than sufficient to answer all the claims thereon for which provision ought to be made in the proceedings, "the Court could at any time allow the whole or part of the income of the property to be paid, during such period as it may direct, to any or all of the parties who have an interest therein or may direct that any part of the personal property be transferred or delivered to any or all of such parties." See SCP 1999, Vol. 1, para. 29/8A/24.

25.1.17 **Order authorising entry on land for carrying out interim remedy orders as to relevant property (r.25.1(1)(d))**—Where the court grants an interim remedy in the form of any of the orders listed in r.25.1(1)(c) the court (this would normally be at the same judicial level as that granting the primary interim remedy) may grant a further interim remedy in the form of an order authorising a person to enter any land or building in the possession of a party to the proceedings for the purposes of carrying out the first order (r.25.1(d)). This accords with former rules found in RSC, O.29, rr.2 and 3 and made applicable in county court proceedings under CCR, O.13, r.7. However, the former RSC, O.29, r.4, which dealt with the sale of perishable property, etc., other than land, did not permit the making of a supplementary order authorising the entry on any land in the possession of a party for the purpose of enabling the order for sale to be carried out. Of course, r.4(1) did not include sales of land but r.25.1(1)(c)(v) does.

An order granting an interim remedy of this type may be made only by a judge (Practice Direction (Allocation of Cases to Levels of Judiciary) para. 2.1, see para. 2B–001 above).

25.1.18 **Order for delivery up of goods under Torts (Interference with Goods) Act 1977, s.4 (r.25.1(1)(e))**—The court (again, a Master or district judge in accordance with former practice; see SCP 1999, Vol. 1, paras 29/8A/3 and 29/8A/13) may grant an interim remedy in the form of an order under s.4 of the Torts (Interference with Goods) Act 1977 to deliver up goods (r.25.1(1)(e)). According to the statute an application for an interim remedy of this type may be made either before or after a claim is started. Rule 25.1(e) is based on former RSC, O.29, r.2A and CCR, O.13, r.7(1)(d). In terms, r.2A did not permit applications before proceedings were commenced (see SCP 1999, Vol. 1, para. 29/8A/13) but now no such limitation is imposed. Section 4(2) of the 1977 Act states that, in proceedings for wrongful interference, the court shall have power to make an order "providing for the delivery up of goods which are or may become the subject-matter of subsequent proceedings". Former RSC, O.29, r.2A was broader than the statute and said that an application under s.4 of the 1977 Act could be made for the delivery up of any goods which are the subject-matter of the cause or matter "or as to which any question may arise therein" (former CCR, O.13, r.7(1)(d) was to the same effect). Rule 25.1(1)(e) contains no definition of goods.

25.1.19 **Freezing injunction (Mareva injunction) (r.25.1(1)(f))**—The court may grant an interim remedy in the form of an order (i) restraining a party from removing from the jurisdiction assets located there, or (ii) restraining a party from dealing with any assets whether located within the jurisdiction or not (r.25.1(1)(f)). Such an order is referred to as a "freezing injunction" in r.25.1(1)(f) and r.25.1(1)(g). Formerly, "freezing injunctions" were known as "Mareva injunctions".

An order granting an interim remedy of this type may be made only by a judge (Practice Direction (Allocation of Cases to Levels of Judiciary) para. 2.1, see para. 2B–001 above).

Since the late 1970s, the jurisdiction of the High Court to grant "freezing" injunctions by way of interim relief has been significantly expanded and refined by case law, practice directions and legislation. The creation of this form of injunction was a judicial innovation. The existence of the jurisdiction to grant such injunctions is recognised by the Supreme Court Act 1981, s.37(3) (first enacted in 1981). However, s.37(3) did not, as is sometimes said, turn the common law freezing injunction into a statutory remedy; rather it assumed that the remedy existed, and tacitly indorsed its validity (*Mercedes-Benz A.G. v. Leiduck* [1995] 3 W.L.R. 718; [1995] 3 All E.R. 929, PC, at 728 and 938 *per* Lord Mustill).

The power of county courts to grant freezing injunctions is restricted by the County Court Remedies Regulations 1991 (see SCP 1999, Vol. 2, para. 20B–163) made under the County Courts Act 1984, s.38 (as amended in 1990) (*ibid.* para. 20A–697). The general rule is that a county court may not grant a freezing injunction. Exemption from this restriction is enjoyed by nominated circuit judges sitting in patents county courts and mercantile courts and by High Court judges sitting as judges for any county court district (*ibid.* reg. 3(2)). Further, a county court may grant such relief in the circumstances listed in reg. 3(3) and these include (a) for the purpose of making an order for the preservation, custody or detention of property which forms or may form the subject matter of proceedings (*i.e.* where the property is subject to a proprietary claim), and (b) in aid of execution of a judgment or order made in proceedings in a county court to preserve assets until execution can be levied upon them. A county court may not vary or revoke a freezing injunction granted by the High Court but may vary (but not revoke) such an injunction where all the parties are agreed on the terms of the variation (reg. 3(1) and (4)(b)).

An application for a freezing injunction is made on an application notice in accordance with the provisions of Pt 23 (General rules about applications for court orders) as modified by the provisions of Practice Direction (Interim Injunctions) (see 25PD–003 below). The modifications are substantial. This Practice Direction replaces Practice Direction (Mareva Injunctions and Anton Piller Orders) [1994] 1 W.L.R. 1233. Note also "Court Guides and interim remedies procedure", para. 25.0.6 above.

As to applicant's duty to make full and frank disclosure when applying without notice for interim injunction, see para. 25.3.5, "Applicant's duties where application made without notice to respondent" below.

Forms for freezing injunctions, both worldwide and domestic, formerly found in Practice Direction (Mareva Injunctions and Anton Piller Orders: Forms) [1996] 1 W.L.R. 1552, are replaced by the forms in annexures 2 and 3 to the Practice Direction supplementing Pt 25 (see 25PD–005 and 25PD–006 below). The 1994 Practice Direction said that the forms contained in the 1996 Practice Direction were "standard forms" and should be used "save to the extent that the judge hearing a particular application considers there is good reason for adopting a different form". In the Practice Direction supplementing Pt 25 it is said, simply, that the annexed forms are "examples". This change acknowledges the fact that, although it is desirable that a consistent approach should in general be adopted in relation to the form and carrying out of such orders, it is important that freezing injunctions be carefully tailored to meet the circumstances of each case.

In a claim in which the claimant seeks to recover his property, the court has jurisdiction to grant an interim injunction restraining the disposal of property over which the claimant has a proprietary claim. Such an injunction was not properly called a "Mareva injunction". A Mareva injunction goes further and enables the court to grant the claimant an interim injunction restraining the defendant from disposing of, or even merely dealing with, his assets, being assets over which the claimant asserts no proprietary claim but which after judgment may be granted to satisfy a money judgment. (Frequently, one injunction will achieve both objectives.) The definition of "freezing injunction" in r.25.1(f) would seem not to cover the interim injunction restraining the disposal of property over which the claimant has a proprietary claim.

An interim order in the form of a freezing injunction may contain an order requiring the defendant to provide information about his assets (see r.25.1(1)(g) below).

For further information on freezing injunctions, see SCP 1999, Vol. 1, paras 29/1A/12 and 29/L/36 *et seq.*

For basis of High Court's jurisdiction to grant a freezing injunction, see SCP 1999, Vol. 1, paras 29/1A/12 and 29/L/36.

For basis of County Court's jurisdiction to grant a freezing injunction, see SCP 1999, Vol. 1, para. 29/1A/9. It is unclear if the County Court Remedies Regulations 1991, restricting county court power to grant *Marevas* (and *Anton Pillers*) are going to survive but the requirement of a "duly authorised" judge (discussed above) will, in practice, restrict the availability of such relief in the county court.

In a claim in which the claimant seeks to recover his property, the court has jurisdiction to grant an interim injunction restraining the disposal of property over which the claimant has a proprietary claim. Such an injunction is not properly called a "*Mareva* injunction". A *Mareva* injunction goes further and enables the court to grant the claimant an interim injunction restraining the defendant from disposing of, or even merely dealing with, his assets, being assets over which the claimant assets no proprietary claim but which after judgment may be satisfied to satisfy a money judgment. (Frequently, one injunction will achieve both objectives.) The definition of "freezing injunction" in this rule woud seem not to cover the interim injunction restraining the disposal of property over which the claimant has a proprietary claim. Such limited relief is merely an interim injunction under r.25.1(1)(a) and, pursuant to para. 1.3 of the Practice Direction (see para. 25PD–003) can be granted by a judge having jurisdiction to try the action.

An interim order in the form of a freezing injunction may contain an order requiring the defendant to provide information about the location of relevant property or his assets (see r.25.1(1)(g) below). The purpose of the general power in relation to restraining a party from removing or dealing with his "assets" is to preserve them for execution of a judgment subsequently obtained; it is wider than "relevant property" which is property relevant to the action.

Order to provide information about property or assets (r.25.1(1)(g))—The court may grant an interim remedy in the form of an order directing a party to provide information about the location of relevant property or assets or to provide information about relevant property or assets which are or may be the subject of an application for a freezing injunction (r.25.1(1)(g)). 25.1.20

This interim remedy complements that stated in r.25.1(1)(f) and in terms is restricted to "freezing injunctions" as defined there. An interlocutory injunction, even when seeking preservation of relevant property only, may not have such an order attached unless such a power could be invoked under r.25.1(3).

The jurisdiction to grant an order ancillary to an order preventing a party from removing or otherwise dealing with assets by requiring the party to make disclosures applies both in cases where the claimant makes a proprietary claim over the assets and where he does not (see SCP 1999, Vol. 1, paras 29/1A/35 and 29/L/51). The jurisdiction was recognised in RSC, O.29, r.1A (Cross-examination on assets disclosure affidavit) but, otherwise the RSC made no specific reference to the jurisdiction. (Order 29, r.1A contained rules as to the conduct of the cross-examination of a defendant on his disclosure affidavit. Comparable provisions are now found in rr.32.6 and 32.7.)

In certain circumstances, a party may refuse to provide information on grounds of privilege, see *Den Norske Bank A.S.A. v. Antonatos* [1998] 3 W.L.R. 711, CA; see further Pt 31.

In r.25.1(1)(g), relevant property means "property which is the subject of a claim or as to which any question may arise on a claim" and includes land (r.25.1(2)).

As to power of court to make against third party order ancillary to interim order against party requiring the third party (*e.g.* the party's bank) to make disclosures, etc., *e.g.* Bankers Trust order (*Bankers Trust Co. v. Shapira* [1980] 1 W.L.R. 1274; [1980] 3 All E.R. 353, CA), see Pt 31, and note SCP 1999, Vol. 2, para. 29/L/48.

25.1.21 **Search order (Anton Piller order) (r.25.1(1)(h))**—The jurisdiction of the High Court to grant a "search order" (formerly Anton Piller order) was put on a statutory basis by the Civil Procedure Act 1997, s.7 (see SCP, Vol. 2, para. 20A–7). In any proceedings in a county court the court may make an order which could be made by the High Court if the proceedings were in the High Court (County Courts 1984, s.38 (see SCP 1999, Vol. 2, para. 20A–697). However, the power of county courts to grant search orders is restricted by the County Court Remedies Regulations 1991 (see SCP 1999, Vol. 2, para. 20B–163) made under s.38 (as amended in 1990). The general rule is that a county court may not grant a search order. Exemption from this restriction is enjoyed by a nominated circuit judge sitting in a patents county court and by a High Court judge sitting as judge for any county court district (*ibid.*, reg. 3(2)). A county court may not vary or revoke a search order granted by the High Court but may vary (but may not revoke) such an order where all the parties are agreed on the terms of the variation (reg. 3(1) and (4)(b)).

An order granting an interim remedy of this type may be made only by a judge (Practice Direction (Allocation of Cases to Levels of Judiciary) para. 2.1, see para. 2B–001 above).

An application for a search order is made on an application notice in accordance with the provisions of Pt 23 (General rules about applications for court orders) as modified by the provisions of Practice Direction (Interim Injunctions) (see 25PD–003 below). The modifications are substantial. This Practice Directive replaces Practice Direction (Mareva Injunctions and Anton Piller Orders) [1984] 1 W.L.R. 1233. Note also "Court Guides and interim remedies procedure", para. 25.0.6 above.

For further information on search orders, see SCP 1999, Vol. 1, paras 29/L/77 *et seq.*

25.1.22 **Order for disclosure before claim made of documents by prospective party (r.25.1(1)(i))**—There has been a major alteration to the power of the court (normally exercised by a Master or a district judge) to grant an interim remedy in the form of an order under the Supreme Court Act 1981, s.33(2) or the County Courts Act 1984, s.52(2) (r.25.1(1)(i)).

These subsections state (see SCP 1999, Vol. 2, paras 20A–215 and 20A–725) that a person who appears to the court to be likely to be a party to subsequent proceedings *in which a claim in respect of personal injuries to a person, or in respect of a person's death, is likely to be made,* the court shall have power to order a person *who appears to the court to be likely to be a party to the proceedings* and to be likely to have *or to have had* in his possession, custody or power any documents which are relevant to an issue arising or likely to arise out of that claim (a) to disclose whether those documents are in his possession, custody or power, and (b) to produce such of those documents as are in his possession, custody or power to the applicant or, on such conditions as may be specified in the order (i) to the applicant's legal advisers, or (ii) to the applicant's legal advisers and any medical or other professional adviser of the applicant, or (iii) if the applicant has no legal adviser, to any medical or other professional adviser of the applicant.

These sub-sections deal with discovery before proceedings are commenced against "a person who appears to the court to be likely to be a party to the proceedings". For discovery after proceedings are commenced against "non-parties" (or "third parties"), see s.34(2) of the 1981 Act and s.53(2) of the 1984 Act explained below.

Under the Civil Procedure Act 1997, s.8, s.33(2) and s.52(2) may be extended by the Lord Chancellor to new situations (see SCP 1999, Vol. 1, para. 20A–8 and notes therein).

Under The Civil Procedure (Modification of Enactments) Order 1998 (S.I. 1998 No. 2940) (which comes into force at the same time as the CPR) the power has been extended to order discovery of documents against a potential party before proceedings have started and to non-parties in all proceedings. This accords with the recommendations in the Final Report.

Formerly, rules of court supporting s.33(2) of the 1981 Act and s.52(2) of the 1984 Act were found, respectively, in RSC ,O.24, r.7A and CCR, O.13, rr.7(1)(g), 7(2A) and 7(3). See now rr.25.2 *et seq.* and notes following those rules. Note in particular r.25.4(b) and para. 25.4.3 "Interim remedy order for disclosure, inspection, etc., before a claim started" and para. 25.2.2 "Disclosure of documents by interim remedy order".

Application should be made under Pt 23 (r.25.4) and be supported by evidence (r.31.16(2)). As to the circumstances in which an order may be made and the terms of the order, see r.31.16(3) to (5).

Order to inspect, etc., and to take samples, etc., of property before claim made (r.25.1(1)(i))—The court may grant an interim remedy in the form of an order under the Supreme Court Act 1981, s.33(1) or the County Courts Act 1984, s.52(1) (r.25.1(1)(i)). 25.1.23

These subsections state that on the application of any person the court has power to make an order providing for (a) the inspection, photographing, preservation, custody and detention of property which appears to the court to be property *which may become the subject-matter of subsequent proceedings in the court*, or as to which any question may arise in any such proceedings, and (b) the taking of samples of any such property and the carrying out of any experiment on or with any such property (see SCP 1999, Vol. 2, paras 20A–215 and 20A–725).

In effect, these subsections enable the court to make orders similar to those referred to in r.25.1(1)(c)(i) to (iv). The significant feature of the subsections is that they specifically empower the court to make such order before proceedings are commenced. It may be noted that r.25.2(1)(a) states that an order for an interim remedy, including the remedies referred to in paras (i) to (iv) of r.25.1(1)(c), may be made before proceedings are started (that is to say, before the court issues a claim form).

Formerly, rules of court supporting s.33(1) of SCA 1981 and s.52(1) of CCA 1984 were found, respectively, in RSC, O.29, r.7A and CCR, O.13, rr.7(1)(g), 7(2A) and 7(3). See now rr.25.2 *et seq.* and notes following those rules.

Order to inspect, etc., and to take samples, etc., of non-party's property after claim made (r.25.1(1)(j))—The comments made as to r.25.1(1)(i) as to extension of jurisdiction are also applicable under this head. The court (normally a Master or district judge) may grant an interim remedy in the form of an order under the Supreme Court Act 1981, s.34(3) or the County Courts Act 1984, s.53(3) (r.25.1(1)(j)). 25.1.24

These subsections state that in any proceedings on the application of a party the court has power to make an order providing for (a) the inspection, photographing, preservation, custody and detention of property which appears to the court to be property *which is not the property of, or in the possession of any party to the proceedings* but which is the subject-matter of the proceedings or as to which any question may arises in the proceedings, and (b) the taking of samples of any such property and the carrying out of any experiment on or with any such property (see SCP 1999, Vol. 2, paras 20A–219 and 20A–727). Previously these subsections applied only to proceedings in which a claim was made in respect of personal injuries, or in respect of a person's death. This restriction was removed by the Civil Procedure (Modifications of Enactments) Order 1998 (S.I. No. 2940).

In effect, these subsections enable the court to make orders similar to those referred to in r.25.1(1)(c)(i) to (iv). The significant feature of the subsections is that they specifically empower the court to make such orders after proceedings are commenced against persons who are not parties to the proceedings.

Formerly, rules of court supporting s.34(3) of the SCA 1981 and s.53(3) of the CCA 1984 were found, respectively, in RSC, O.29, r.7Aand CCR, O.13, rr.7(1)(g), 7(2A) and 7(4). See now rr.25.2 *et seq.* and notes following those rules.

Order for disclosure of documents by non-party after claim (r.25.1(1)(j))—The court may grant an interim remedy in the form of an order under the Supreme Court Act 1981, s.34(2) or the County Courts Act 1984, s.53(2) (r.25.1(1)(j)). 25.1.25

These subsections state (see SCP 1999, Vol. 2, paras 20A–219 and 20A–727) that in any proceedings the court shall have power to order a person *who is not a party to the proceedings and who appears to the court* to be likely to have in his possession, custody or power any documents which are relevant to an issue arising out of that claim (a) to disclose whether those documents are in his possession, custody or power, and (b) to produce such of those documents as are in his possession, custody or power to the applicant or, on such conditions as may be specified in the order (i) to the applicant's legal advisers, or (ii) to the applicant's legal advisers and any medical or other professional adviser of the applicant, or (iii) if the applicant has no legal adviser, to any medical or other professional adviser of the applicant. Previously these subsections applied only to proceedings in which a claim was made in respect of personal injuries, or in respect of a person's death. This restriction was removed by the Civil Procedure (Modifications of Enactments) Order 1998 (S.I. No. 2940).

The significant feature of the subsections is that they specifically empower the court, in the proceedings to which they apply, to make orders for disclosure against persons who are not parties.

Formerly, rules of court supporting s.34(2) of the SCA 1981 and s.53(2) of the CCA 1984 were found, respectively, in RSC, O.24, r.7A and CCR ,O.13, rr.7(1)(g), 7(2A) and 7(4). See now r.25.2 *et seq.* and commentary following those rules.

Note in particular r.25.4(b) and para. 25.4.3 "Interim remedy order for disclosure, inspection etc. before a claim started" and para. 25.2.2 "Disclosure of documents by interim remedy order".

Application should be made under Pt 23 (r.25.4) and be supported by evidence (r.31.17(2)). As to the circumstances in which an order may be made and the terms of the order, see r.31.17(3) to (5).

25.1.26 **Interim payment order r.25.1(1)(k))**—The court (normally a Master or district judge) may grant an interim remedy in the form of an order (referred to as an order for interim payment) under r.25.6 for payment by a defendant on account of any damages, debt or other sum (except costs) which the court may hold the defendant liable to pay (r.25.1(1)(k)).

See the commentary to r.25.6 to r.25.9 below.

25.1.27 **Order for securing of specified fund (r.25.1(1)(l))**—The court (normally a Master or district judge) may grant an interim remedy in the form of an order for a specified fund to be paid into court or otherwise secured, where there is a dispute over a party's right to the fund (r.25.1(1)(l)). This is based on former RSC, O.29, r.2(3); see also CCR, O.13, r.7(1)(c).

25.1.28 **Order for recovery of personal property subject to lien, etc. (r.25.1(1)(m))**—The court (normally a Master or district judge) may grant an interim remedy in the form of an order permitting a party seeking to recover personal property to pay money into court pending the outcome of the proceedings and directing that, if he does so, the property shall be given up to him (r.25.1(1)(m)). This is based on former RSC, O.29, r.6 (Recovery of personal property subject to lien, etc.) but is rather cryptic by comparison. Rule 6 stated as follows: "Where the plaintiff, or the defendant by way of counterclaim, claims the recovery of specific property (other than land) and the party from whom recovery is sought does not dispute the title of the party making the claim but claims to be entitled to retain the property by virtue of a lien or otherwise as security for any sum of money, the Court, at any time after the claim to be so entitled appears from the pleadings (if any) or by affidavit or otherwise to its satisfaction, may order that the party seeking to recover the property be at liberty to pay into court, to abide the event of the action, the amount of money in respect of which the security is claimed and such further sum (if any) for interest and costs as the Court may direct and that, upon such payment being made, the property claimed be given up to the party claiming it." However, as in practice doubtless, the former sensible inhibitions will continue to apply the abbreviation will make little difference; this rule seems clear enough.

It would seem that the purpose of the form of interim remedy stated in r.25.1(1)(m) is to alleviate difficulties caused by the exercise of possessory liens in general. It does not affect the jurisdiction of the court to grant relief in equity against the exercise of a solicitor's lien (see *Ismail v. Richards Butler* [1996] 3 W.L.R. 129; [1996] 2 All E.R. 506, where the authorities are examined).

25.1.29 **Order directing a party to prepare and file accounts (r.25.1(1)(n))**—The court may grant an interim remedy in the form of an order directing a party to prepare and file accounts relating to the dispute (r.25.1(1)(n)). Former RSC, O.43, r.1 stated that in proceedings where a party made a claim for an account, or made a claim which necessarily involved taking an account, he could apply for an order "that an account be taken". Former RSC, O.43, r.2(1) said that in any action the court could at any stage "direct any necessary accounts *or inquiries* to be taken or made" whether such relief was claimed or necessarily involved in the action. See also CCR, O.13, r.7(1)(h), which spoke of "the taking or making of any necessary accounts or inquiries". It would seem that r.25.1(1)(n) is based on RSC, O.43, r.2(1), but is more narrowly drawn (being in terms restricted to directing a party to file accounts). The practice formerly stated in RSC, O.43, r.2(2) is continued in Practice Direction (Accounts and Inquiries) para. 3 (see para. 25PD–002). The court may direct any account to be taken or inquiry to be made on its own initiative (*ibid.*, para. 3). Generally, an application for an account or inquiry may be made at any time (r.25.2).

The power of the court formerly found in former RSC, O.43, r.1 (see above) to order summarily that an account be taken in cases where a party made a claim for an account, or made a claim which necessarily involved taking an account, was quite distinct from the power of the court to grant such remedy on the claimant's application for summary judgment under former RSC, O.14. Summary judgment is now dealt with by the provisions of Pt 24. The Practice Direction supplementing that Part provides that, if a remedy sought by a claimant in his claim form, includes, or necessarily involves, taking an account or making an inquiry, "an application can be made under Part 24" by any party to the proceedings for an order directing any necessary accounts or inquiries to be taken (Practice Direction (The Summary Disposal of Claims) para. 6; see 24PD–002).

Provisions as to the taking of accounts and making inquiries after judgment or order, comparable to those formerly found in RSC, O.44 (Proceedings under judgment and inquiries: Chancery Division) and CCR, O.23 (Accounts and inquiries in equity proceedings), are now found in one of the Practice Directions supplementing Pt 40 (Practice Direction (Accounts, Inquiries etc.), see 40PD–001).

Time when an order for an interim remedy may be made

25.2—(1) An order for an interim remedy may be made at any time, including— 25.2

(a) before proceedings are started; and

(b) after judgment has been given.

(Rule 7.2 provides that proceedings are started when the court issues a claim form.)

(2) However—

(a) paragraph (1) is subject to any rule, practice direction or other enactment which provides otherwise;

(b) the court may grant an interim remedy before a claim has been made only if—

(i) the matter is urgent; or

(ii) it is otherwise necessary to do so in the interests of justice; and

(c) unless the court otherwise orders, a defendant may not apply for any of the orders listed in rule 25.1(1) before he has filed either an acknowledgement of service or a defence.

(Part 10 provides for filing an acknowledgment of service and Part 15 for filing a defence.)

(3) Where the court grants an interim remedy before a claim has been commenced, it may give directions requiring a claim to be commenced.

(4) In particular, the court need not direct that a claim be commenced where the application is made under section 33 of the Supreme Court Act 1981 or section 52 of the County Courts Act 1984 (order for disclosure, inspection, etc., before commencement of a claim).

Relationship between Pt 23 and rr.25.2 to 25.5—Formerly, in the High Court, interlocutory applications were made in accordance with rules found in RSC, O.32 (Applications and proceedings in chambers), supplemented by provisions in RSC, O.25 (Summons for directions). In addition, reference had to be made to RSC, O.29, the Order which contained detailed rules about most of the remedies now known, compendiously, as "interim remedies". In county court proceedings, the analogue to RSC, O.32 was CCR, O.13 (Applications and orders in the course of proceedings). In that Order applications for interim injunctions were dealt with in r.6 and most of the other provisions found in RSC, O.29 dealing with interim remedies were incorporated by reference by r.7. In the RSC, important rules as to applications for interim remedies in the form of discovery of documents (whether against prospective parties before proceedings were commenced, or against non-parties after commencement) were found elsewhere in RSC, O.24 (Discovery and Inspection of Documents) but in the CCR were subsumed in CCR, O.13. 25.2.1

Under the CPR, application for court orders, including orders for interim remedies, are to be made in accordance with the general rules found in Pt 23. Further, they apply when an application is made for an interim remedy before a claim is made (see r.25.4 and notes following). Provisions in Pt 23 provide, generally, that an applicant must file an application notice (r.23.3(1)), that the notice must state (a) what order the applicant is seeking, and (b) briefly, why the applicant is seeking the order (r.23.6). (Note also the rules as to service and notice, rr.23.4 and 23.9, and as to where applications should be made, r.23.2.) In relation to applications for certain interim remedies, the provisions of Parts other than Pts 23 and 25 are important. For example, rr.31.16 and 31.17 apply to applications for orders for disclosure of documents before proceedings are started and against non-parties (r.25.1(i) and (j)). In some instances, such provisions significantly alter or enhance provisions found in Pts 23 and 25 (and their supplementing Practice Directions) which would otherwise apply unalloyed, but in other instances they do little more than repeat them.

Rule 25.2 and r.25.3 apply where an application for an interim remedy is made. Particular rules as to certain interim remedies are found in rr.25.4 and 25.5. All of these provisions have to be read against the background of the rules found in Pt 23. An application for an interim payment order is an application for an interim remedy (r.25.1(k)). In terms, rr.25.2 and 25.3 would apply to an application for an interim payment order. However, particular rules for such an application are found in rr.25.6 to 25.9 and, presumably, those provisions would prevail in the event of any inconsistency between them and rr.25.2 and 25.3.

Disclosure of documents by interim remedy order—The court may grant an interim remedy order in the form of an order requiring the disclosure of documents before a claim has been made by a prospective party or by a "non-party" (under the Supreme Court Act 1981, s.33(2), or the County Courts Act 1984, s.52(2)), or for an order requiring disclosure by a non-party after a claim has been made (under, respectively, s.34(2) and s.53(2) of these Acts). 25.2.2

Detailed provisions for such applications are found in Pt 31 (Disclosure and inspection of documents) (see rr.31.16 and 31.17). Note also r.25.4(1)(b) and r.25.4(2). The advantages of a *Norwich Pharmacal* (see SCP 1999, Vol. 1, para. 15/4/7 order (identifying the proper defendant to an action) may now, it seems, be obtained by an application in an action without the need to join the proposed information provider or bring separate proceedings for this purpose.

25.2.3 **Effect of rule r.25.2**—Generally speaking, an interim remedy is a remedy applied for and granted in the intervening period between the commencement of the proceedings and final judgment or order, and having effect for the duration of that period and no longer. However, in some instances it may be possible for a party to apply for, and appropriate for the court to grant, before proceedings are started or after judgment has been given, one or other of the remedies listed as "interim remedies" in r.25.1(1). Whether or not any one of those remedies may be applied for and granted before proceedings are started or after judgment has been given depends primarily on the law relating to the jurisdiction of the court to grant the remedy. Rule 25.2(1) should not be interpreted as meaning that, subject only to the constraints imposed by r.25.2(2), the court has jurisdiction to grant all of the interim remedies listed in r.25.1(1) at any time. This is acknowledged by r.25.2(2)(a) which states that r.25.2(1) is "subject to any rule, practice direction or other enactment which provides otherwise". (It may be noted that r.23.5 states that, where an application must be made within a specified time, it is so made if the application notice is received by the court within that time.)

It would appear that r.25.2(1) is derived from former RSC, O.29, r.1(1) which stated that an application for the grant of an injunction could be made "before or after the trial of the cause or matter" (see also CCR, O.13, r.6(1)).

An application made before a claim is commenced should be made under Pt 23 (Practice Direction (Applications) para. 5, see para. 23PD–002) and, generally, should be made to the court where it is likely that the claim to which it relates will be started (r.23.2(4)).

Practice Direction (Mercantile Courts and Business Lists) paras 2.2 and 2.3 apply where it is proposed to make an application to the court for an interim remedy before the making of a mercantile claim in a mercantile court or a county court business list (see para. 49HPD–001).

25.2.4 **Interim remedy granted before claim made—urgency and the interests of justice (r.25.2(2)(b))**—The general rule is that an order for an interim remedy may be made at any time; but the court may grant an interim remedy before a claim has been made only if (i) the matter is urgent, or (ii) it is otherwise necessary to do so in the interests of justice (r.25.2(2)(b)).

Some interim remedies have been designed specifically for use before a claim has been made (*cf.* "before proceedings are started" in r.25.2(1)(a)). A good example is an interim remedy in the form of an order under the Supreme Court Act 1981, s.33(1) or the County Courts Act 1984, s.52(1) (Order to inspect, etc., and to take samples, etc., of property before claim made) (see r.25.1(1)(i)). Former rules of court did not suggest that orders granting such remedies could only be made on a showing that the matter was "urgent". It may be said that they could not be granted unless "necessary to do so in the interests of justice". To that extent the former practice and r.25.2(2)(b) are in accord.

Strictly speaking, timing and urgency are quite separate matters (and both are separate from the question whether application should be made on notice or not). However, it is not surprising that, at least in relation to some interim remedies, they should be mixed. Circumstances can arise when it is in the interests of justice that a person should be able to obtain an order for an interim remedy before beginning his claim, even though that remedy is not specifically designed for use before a claim has been made. Thus, former RSC, O.29, r.1(3) stated that a plaintiff could make an application for an injunction before the issue of originating process provided the case was "one of urgency" (see also CCR, O.13, r.6(4)–(6)). (By analogy, the same rule was applied, not only to *Mareva* injunctions, but also to *Anton Piller* orders.) Similarly, former RSC, O.29, r.2A (see also CCR, O.13, r.7(1)(d)) stated that an application could be made for an order under the Torts (Interference with Goods) Act 1977, s.4 for the delivery up of goods before issue of originating process on grounds of urgency (see now r.25.1(1)(e)).

Previously, under the rules urgency was not an essential condition for the granting of other forms of interim relief. Rule 25.2(2)(b)(i) re-enacts former RSC, O.29, r.1(3). However, as stated therein, the urgency rule does not have quite the same effect as previously. It is both broader and narrower in its applications. Rule 25.2(2)(b) says that the court may grant any interim remedy before claim (including an interim remedy in the form of an interim injunction) only if (i) the matter is urgent, or (ii) it is otherwise necessary to do so in the interests of justice. In terms, a finding of urgency is no longer essential for the granting of an interim injunction. Further, other forms of interim relief can be denied on the ground that they are not urgent. However, it is doubtful whether any change in the former practice is intended. It could be argued that no harm would be done if the urgency rule were deleted entirely from r.25.2(2)(b). Clearly, there are some interim remedies that ought not to be granted before a claim has been made unless they are urgent. If they are urgent it is in the interests of justice that they should be granted.

25.2.5 **No application by defendant before acknowledgment of service or defence (r.25.2(2)(c))**—Rule 25.2(1) states the general rule that an order for an interim remedy may be made at any time. However, r.25.2(2)(c) states that a defendant may not apply for any of the orders listed in rule 25.1(1) before he has responded to the claim by filing either an acknowledgment of service or a defence. This rule has a limited application because most of the interim remedies are remedies available to the claimant. Rule 25.2(2)(c) follows former RSC, O.29, r.2 (Detention, preservation, etc., of subject-matter of cause or matter), a rule which was incorporated by reference into other rules relating to interim remedies available to defendants (*viz.*, RSC, O.29, r.3 (Power to order samples to be taken, etc.), and RSC, O.29, r.4 (Sale of perishable property, etc.)). Should a defendant wish to apply for an interim injunction he will be subject to r.25.2(2)(c). However it will be easy to obtain leave so as to disapply the operation of the rule where the defendant can show a sufficiently strong case for obtaining relief. Although r.25.2(2)(c) speaks of "orders" listed in r.25.1(1) it seems clear that what is intended is that, generally, a defendant should not be able to apply for any of the interim remedies listed there, whether described as "orders" or not, before he has filed either an acknowledgment of service or a defence.

Directions requiring claim to be commenced (r.25.2(3) and (4))—Former RSC, O.29, r.1(3) stated that, where an interim injunction was granted before originating process was issued it "may be granted on terms providing for the issue of the writ or summons and such other terms, if any, as the court thinks fit" (see also CCR, O.13, r.6(4)(b)). (By analogy, the same rule was applied, not only to *Mareva* injunctions, but also to *Anton Piller* orders.) The rule was incorporated by reference in former RSC, O.29, r.2A (Delivery up of goods under s.4 of Torts (Interference with Goods) Act 1977) (see also CCR, O.13, r.7(1)(d)) (see now r.25.1(1)(e)). **25.2.6**

Former RSC, O.29, r.1(3) forms the basis of r.25.2(3) and, in terms, is made applicable to all interim remedies that may be granted before claim made. Where an application is made before a claim is made for an interim remedy in the form of an interim injunction, r.25.2(3) is supplemented by Practice Direction (Interim Injunctions) para. 4.4 (see 25CPD–001). In the penultimate draft of r.24.2(3) it was stated that "the court must give" directions requiring a claim to be commenced and r.24.2(4) created obvious exceptions. In its final form r.24.2(3) was made permissive and r.24.2(4) rendered merely illustrative.

How to apply for an interim remedy

25.3—(1) The court may grant an interim remedy on an application made without notice if it appears to the court that there are good reasons for not giving notice. **25.3**

(2) An application for an interim remedy must be supported by evidence, unless the court orders otherwise.

(3) If the applicant makes an application without giving notice, the evidence in support of the application must state the reasons why notice has not been given.

(Part 3 lists general powers of the court.)

(Part 23 contains general rules about making an application.)

Effect of rule—Note commentary at para. 25.2.1—"Relationship between Pt 23 and rr.25.2 to 25.5" following r.25.2 (Time when an order for an interim remedy may be made). **25.3.1**

This rule modifies and amplifies provisions found in Pt 23 (General rules about applications for court orders) in two respects. The general rule is that an application for a court order must be made to the court where the claim was started (or is likely to be started) (r.23.2), it must generally be made by filing an application notice (r.23.3(1)), and the notice must state (a) what order the applicant is seeking, and (b) briefly, why the applicant is seeking the order (r.23.6). The two modifications made in the rule relate to notice and evidence.

(For special rules as to notice and evidence on applications for interim remedy order for disclosure of documents, see rr.31.16 and 31.17, and note "Disclosure of documents by interim remedy order" at para. 25.2.2.)

Notice—The general rule is that a copy of an application notice for a court order must be served on each respondent (r.23.4(1)) but application may be made without serving a copy of the application notice where this is permitted by rule, practice direction or court order (r.23.4(3)); for other circumstances in which applications may be made without notice, see Practice Direction (Applications) para. 3 (para. 23PD–001 above) and para. 23.0.7 "Applications without notice" para. 23.0.7. **25.3.2**

Such an exception to the general rule is found in r.25.3. An application for a court order in the form of an order for an interim remedy may be made without notice "if it appears to the court that there are good reasons for not giving notice" (r.25.3(1)) (*i.e.* serving a copy of the notice of application under Pt 23). If the applicant makes an application without giving notice (*i.e.* without serving a copy of the notice of application under Pt 23), the evidence in support of the application (see further below) must state the reasons why notice was not given (r.25.3(3)).

Under the former rules, provision for application without notice was made in relation to some but not all interim remedies dealt with in RSC, O.29. Now, in terms, applications for any interim remedy may be made without notice if it appears to the court that there are good reasons for dispensing with notice. However, mandatory requirements as to notice are retained by r.25.5 in relation to the interim remedies specifically referred to in that rule.

In Practice Direction (Interim Injunctions) paras 4.1 to 4.5 appear under the heading "urgent applications and applications without notice" (see 25CPD–001). It is not immediately clear what these paragraphs intend. They distinguish applications made before a claim form is issued and after a claim form is issued. It would seem that they are meant to apply to applications for interim remedies in the form of interim injunctions, freezing injunctions and search orders and that they apply where (1) the application is urgent, and (2) notice is not to be given, either (a) because the urgency makes this impossible or (b) because there are other reasons which justify dispensing with notice (see Practice Direction (Applications) para. 3, see para. 23PD–001). Para. 4.5 states the practice where, because of extreme urgency, the application for an interim injunction, freezing injunction or search order has to be made by telephone.

See also para. 25.2.4 (Interim remedy granted before claim made—urgency and the interests of justice) above.

Where an interim application needs to be dealt with urgently in a case in the list of a mercantile court or in the business list of an authorised county court and a mercantile judge of the court in question is not available, the application may be dealt with by another judge, including a district judge (Practice Direction (Mercantile Courts and Business Lists) para. 5.3 (see para. 49HPD–001).

25.3.3 **Evidence**—An application for an interim remedy must be supported by evidence unless the court orders otherwise (r.25.3(2)).

Rule 32.6(1) states that the general rule is that evidence "at hearings other than the trial" (*e.g.* proceedings for an interim remedy before or after trial) is to be by witness statement unless the court, a practice direction or any other enactment requires otherwise.

However, at such hearings a party may, if he wishes, in support of his application rely solely on the matters set out in (a) his statement of case, or (b) his application, provided that the statement of case or application is verified by a statement of truth (r.22.1(1) and (3) and r.32.6(2)). (A "statement of truth" is a statement that the party putting forward the document believes the facts stated in the document are true (r.22.1(4)). (See Pt 22 for provisions regarding statement of truth.) Proceedings for contempt of court may be brought against a party if he makes or causes to be made a false statement in an application verified by a statement of truth without an honest belief in its truth (r.32.14(1)).

Special requirements as to evidence are imposed by r.25.5 in relation to the interim remedies specifically referred to in that rule.

For particular requirements as to evidence on applications for interim injunctions, freezing injunctions and search orders, see Practice Direction (Interim Injunctions) para. 3 (25CPD–001).

25.3.4 **Interim remedy order hearings in private**—Rule 39.2(1) states that the general rule is that a hearing (including a hearing other than a trial) is to be in public. However, a hearing, or any part of it, may be in private in the circumstances listed in r.39.2(3). Exceptional circumstances which may be particularly apposite to the hearing of an application for an order for an interim remedy are: that publicity would defeat the object of the hearing; that it is a hearing on an application without notice and it would be unjust to any respondent for there to be a public hearing; that the hearing involves confidential information (including information relating to personal financial matters) and publicity would damage that confidentiality. In certain circumstances, the important thing is that what transpires at a hearing for an interim order, whether held in public or in private, should not be revealed, either by publicity or otherwise, at least for the time being. That objective may be achieved by the court's sitting in private, but that cannot be assured. The court has an inherent power to order that information should not be disclosed and certain rules of court are to similar effect (see r.25.9; this imposes a restriction on disclosure of an interim payment).

25.3.5 **Applicant's duties where application made without notice to respondent**—It is well-established that an applicant who applies for an interim remedy without notice to the respondent is under a duty to investigate the facts and fairly to present the evidence on which he relies. (This duty is obliquely referred to in para. 3.3 of 25PD, but in terms which are misleading and not confined to applications without notice.)

The duty has always been important. The emergence and development of freezing injunctions and search orders as forms of interlocutory relief has given the courts occasion to re-affirm it. Most of the modern case law arises out of applications for relief of this kind. The principles were reviewed by Ralph Gibson L.J. in *Brink's MAT Ltd v. Elcombe* [1988] 1 W.L.R. 1350; [1988] 3 All E.R. 188, CA, at 1356 and 192. In *Marc Rich & Co. Holding GmbH v. Krasner*, January 15, 1999, CA (unrep.), the Court of Appeal said the duty was clearly described on the basis of the principal authorities by Bingham J. in *Siporex Trade S.A. v. Comdel Commodities* [1986] 2 Lloyd's Rep. 428, at 437. (1) The applicant must show the utmost good faith and disclose his case fully and fairly. (2) He must, for the protection and information of the defendant, in the evidence in support of the application summarise his case and the evidence on which it is based. (3) He must identify the crucial points for and against the application, and not rely on general statements and the mere exhibiting of numerous documents. (4) He must investigate the nature of the claim asserted and the facts relied on before applying and must identify any likely defences. (5) He must disclose all facts which reasonably could or would be taken into account by the judge in deciding whether to grant the application. This duty should be distinguished from the duty of the advocate for an applicant to bring all relevant legal authorities as to law and practice to the attention of the court (*Memory Corporation Plc. v. Sidue, The Times*, May 31, 1999 (Hart J.)).

In an interim injunction case, if the duty of full and fair disclosure is not observed, the court may discharge the injunction. It is no excuse for an applicant to say that he was not aware of the importance of the matters he omitted to state. Further, where the duty is not observed, the court may discharge the injunction even if after full enquiry the view is taken that the order made was just and convenient and would probably have been made even if there had been full disclosure. This last proposition was authoritatively restated by Scrutton L.J. in *R. v. Kensington Income Tax Commissioners, ex p. de Polignac* [1917] 1 K.B. 486, CA (at 514) (the authorities were reviewed by Jacob J. in *O.M.V. Supply & Training AG. v. Clarke*, January 14, 1999 (unrep.)). This rule has a two-fold purpose. It deprives the wrongdoer of an advantage improperly obtained. Further, it serves as a deterrent to ensure that persons who make applications without notice realise that they have this duty and the consequences (which may include a liability in costs) if they fail (see *Brink's-MAT Ltd v. Elcombe, op. cit.*, at 1358 *per* Balcombe L.J.). (For recent examples of injunctions being discharged on grounds of material non-disclosures, see *CME-Centers for Medical Innovation GmbH v. Phytopharm Plc.*, July 23, 1998 (unrep.) (Laddie J.), *Gulf Interstate Oil Corporation v. Ant Trade & Transport Ltd of Malta (The "Giovanna")* [1999] 1 Lloyd's Rep. 867 (Rix J.), *Dora v. Simper*, May 7, 1999, unrep. (Buckley J.), *I.C.F.I. Corporate Securities Fund v. International Corporation for Finance & Investment*, April 20, 1999, unrep. (Timothy Walker J.).

However discharge of the order is not automatic on any non-disclosure being established of any fact known to the applicant which is found by the court to have been material. In these circumstances, the court has a discretion whether or not to discharge and a discretion whether or not to grant fresh injunctive relief (*Dubai Bank v. Galadari* [1990] 1 Lloyd's Rep. 120, CA at 127 *per* Dillon L.J.; *Kuwait Oil Tanker Co. v. Al Bader*, November 27, 1995, CA (unrep.), *per* Hobhouse L.J.). It should be remembered that the borderline between material facts and non-material facts may be a somewhat uncertain one, particularly in heavy commercial cases. Further, by their very nature, applications without notice usually necessitate the dealing with and taking of instructions and the preparation of the requisite drafts in some haste (*Brink's-MAT Ltd v. Elcombe, op. cit.*, at 1359 *per* Slade L.J.).

In modern cases judges have been critical of a growing tendency among litigants against whom interim injunctions had been granted "to allege non-material disclosure on rather slender grounds" (*Brink's-MAT Ltd v. Elcombe, op. cit.*, at 1359 *per* Slade L.J.) and to seek discharge "on the grounds of the most trifling errors" (*Worldcom International v. Home Communications Ltd*, September 16, 1998 (unrep.), *per* Timothy Walker J.).

For a fuller account of the authorities on the applicant's duty to make full and frank disclosures, see SCP 1999, Vol. 1, para. 29/1A/24.

Application for an interim remedy where there is no related claim

25.4—(1) This rule applies where a party wishes to apply for an interim remedy but— **25.4**

(a) the remedy is sought in relation to proceedings which are taking place, or will take place, outside the jurisdiction; or

(b) the application is made under section 33 of the Supreme Court Act 1981 or section 52 of the County Courts Act 1984 (order for disclosure, inspection, etc., before commencement) before a claim has been commenced.

(2) An application under this rule must be made in accordance with the general rules about applications contained in Part 23.

(The following provisions are also relevant—

Rule 25.5 (inspection of property before commencement or against a non-party)

Rule 31.16 (orders for disclosure of documents before proceedings start)

Rule 31.17 (orders for disclosure of documents against a person not a party).)

Effect of rule—An application for an interim remedy order may be made in circumstances "where there is no related claim". Two circumstances are identified in paras (a) and (b) of r.25.4(1). Where either of those circumstances exists "an application under this rule" must be made in accordance with the general rules about applications for court orders contained in Pt 23. The general rules in Pt 23 proceed on the assumption that a claim has been commenced or will be commenced (as did former CCR, O.13 (Applications and orders in the course of proceedings)). **25.4.1**

This rule makes it clear that those rules apply when an application for an interim remedy is made before a claim is made in the two circumstances stated in paras (a) and (b) of r.25.4(1). The particular significance of this is that these remedies are to be applied for by notice of application without the prior issue of a claim form.

25.4.2 **Interim remedy order in support of foreign proceedings (r.25.4(1)(a))**—The Civil Jurisdiction and Judgments Act 1982, s.25 (see SCP 1999, Vol. 2, para. 7B–20) enables the High Court to grant "interim relief" in cases proceeding in courts other than the courts of England and Wales. In such circumstances, an order is sought "where there is no related claim" in the sense that there is no claim made over which the English court has jurisdiction. See former RSC, O.29, r.8A, and note SCP 1999, paras 29/1A/8, 29/L/44 and 29/L/71.

As defined by s.25.7, in this context "interim relief" would appear to include all of the forms of relief listed as "interim remedies" in r.25.1(1), including "freezing injunctions" (*cf. Mercedes Benz AG v. Leiduck* [1996] 1 A.C. 284, PC). Initially, s.25 was confined to cases proceeding in courts in jurisdictions within other constituent parts of the U.K. and within the E.C., but was subsequently extended, notably by the Civil Jurisdiction and Judgments Act 1982 (Interim Relief) Order 1997 (S.I. 1997 No. 302) (for fuller explanation, see SCP 1999, Vol. 1, paras 29/1A/8 and 29/L/71).

Section 25(2) of the 1982 Act states that, on an application for interim relief under this jurisdiction, the court may refuse to grant relief if in the opinion of the court, the fact that the court has no jurisdiction apart from s.25 in relation to the subject-matter of the proceedings in question "makes it inexpedient for the court to grant it" (on this aspect of s.25, see *Crédit Suisse Fides Trust S.A. v. Cuoghi* [1997] 3 W.L.R. 871, CA; [1997] 3 All E.R. 724, CA, and *Refco Inc. v. Eastern Trading Co.* [1999] 1 Lloyd's Rep. 159, CA).

Rule 25.2(3) states that, where the court grants an interim remedy before a claim has been commenced, "it must give directions requiring a claim to be commenced". In terms this rule applies where the court grants an interim remedy in support of foreign proceedings yet to be commenced (perhaps on the undertaking recited in the order that proceedings will be commenced in the foreign jurisdiction).

Former RSC, O.29, r.8A stated that an application for interim relief under s.25 was to be made by originating summons. This rule is not included amongst the RSC rules re-enacted in Sched. 1 of the CPR. It would seem that, by virtue of Practice Direction (Pt 8 and Sched. 1 and Sched. 2 to the CPR) a claimant applying for relief under s.25 must use the Pt 8 claim form and follow the Pt 8 procedure. It is likely that the applicant will wish to serve this claim form on the respondent out of the jurisdiction and will require the permission of the court to effect such service. Formerly, an applicant in this position would apply for leave by summons under RSC, O.11, r.8A, a provision which appears among the CPR "schedule" rules (see para. R11.8A). It might be expected that, now, the applicant would apply for the court's permission by application notice and that the Pt 23 procedure should be followed, subject to the express terms of r.8A (relating to written evidence in support, etc.) and it seems that this is the correct practice. However, the Practice Direction referred to above suggests that an application for such permission should now be made, not on an application notice, but on a Pt 8 claim form and the Pt 8 procedure should be followed.

25.4.3 **Interim remedy order for disclosure, inspection etc. before a claim started (r.25.4(1)(b))**—Some interim remedy orders may be sought before a claim has been started. In this circumstance, an order is sought "where there is no related claim" in the sense that, as yet, no claim has been made. An interim remedy may be applied for before proceedings are started (r.25.2(1)(a)). Two particular interim remedies orders are referred to in r.25.4(1)(b). They are (1) an order to inspect, etc., and to take samples, etc., of property before claim made under the Supreme Court Act 1981, s.33(1) or the County Courts Act 1984, s.52(1) and (2) an order for disclosure before claim made of documents by a prospective party under s.33(2) or s.52(2) of those Acts respectively (see r.25.1(1)(i)). The distinguishing feature of these two remedies is that they cannot be granted after the claim has been started (but other remedies are available having that effect). Rule 25.4(1)(b) states that, where an application is made for one or other of these interim remedies, the general rules in Pt 23 apply. Thus the remedies are sought by an application whereas, previously, they were sought, in the High court, by originating summons (see RSC, O.24, r.7A and O.29, r.7A), and in the county courts by originating application (see CCR, O.13, r.7(3)). The provisions in rr.25.2 to 25.5 are also relevant to such applications (see para. 25.2.1 "Relationship between Pt 23 and rr.25.2 to 25.5" and note r.31.16). For obvious reasons, where the court grants the interim remedy applied for it is not required to give directions "requiring a claim to be commenced" (see r.24.2(3) and (4)).

Inspection of property before commencement or against a non-party

25.5 **25.5**—(1) This rule applies where a person makes an application under—

(a) section 33(1) of the Supreme Court Act 1981 or section 52(1) of the County Courts Act 1984 (inspection, etc., of property before commencement);

(b) section 34(3) of the Supreme Court Act 1981 or section 53(3) of the County Courts Act 1984 (inspection, etc., of property against a non-party).

(2) The evidence in support of such an application must show, if practicable by reference to any statement of case prepared in relation to the proceedings or anticipated proceedings, that the property—

(a) is or may become the subject matter of such proceedings; or
(b) is relevant to the issues that will arise in relation to such proceedings.

(3) A copy of the application notice and a copy of the evidence in support must be served on—

(a) the person against whom the order is sought; and
(b) in relation to an application under section 34(3) of the Supreme Court Act 1981 or section 53(3) of the County Courts Act 1984, every party to the proceedings other than the applicant.

Effect of rule—General rules as to the giving of notice of applications for court orders and for the providing of evidence on such applications are found in Pt 23. The effect of these rules on applications for court orders in the form of interim remedies is modified by r.25.3 and it is further modifed by this rule in relation to applications for the particular remedies mentioned in r.25.5(1). They are: an order to inspect etc. and to take samples, etc., of property before claim made (s.33(1) of SCA 1981 or s.52(1) of CCA 1984), and (2) an order to inspect etc. and to take samples etc. of non-party's property after claim made (s.34(3) or s.53(3)). The provisions in this rule are based on former RSC, O.29, r.7A and CCR, O.13, r.7(3)(4). **25.5.1**

Interim payments—general procedure

25.6—(1) The claimant may not apply for an order for an interim payment before the end of the period for filing an acknowledgement of service applicable to the defendant against whom the application is made. **25.6**

(Rule 10.3 sets out the period for filing an acknowledgement of service.)

(Rule 25.1(1)(k) defines an interim payment.)

(2) The claimant may make more than one application for an order for an interim payment.

(3) A copy of an application notice for an order for an interim payment must—

(a) be served at least 14 days before the hearing of the application; and
(b) be supported by evidence.

(4) If the respondent to an application for an order for an interim payment wishes to rely on written evidence at the hearing, he must—

(a) file the written evidence; and
(b) serve copies on every other party to the application,

at least 7 days before the hearing of the application.

(5) If the applicant wishes to rely on written evidence in reply, he must—

(a) file the written evidence; and
(b) serve a copy on the respondent,

at least 3 days before the hearing of the application.

(6) This rule does not require written evidence—

(a) to be filed if it has already been filed; or
(b) to be served on a party on whom it has already been served.

(7) The court may order an interim payment in one sum or in instalments.

(Part 23 contains general rules about applications.)

Effect of rule—The statutory bases for rules of court as to interim payments are the Supreme Court Act 1981, s.32 and the County Courts Act 1984, s.50 (see SCP 1999, Vol. 2, paras 20A–209 and 20A–723). The court has no inherent power to order an interim payment (*Moore v. Assignment Courier Ltd* [1977] 1 W.L.R. 638, CA). (Interim payment orders must be distinguished from orders for provisional damages in personal injuries claims provided for by the Supreme Court Act 1981, s.32A and, formerly, by rules in RSC, O.37, rr.7 to 10, see now CPR, r.41.) **25.6.1**

Formerly, rules giving effect to the statutory provisions mentioned above, were found in RSC, O.29, Pt II, and with minor modifications, these provisions were applied in county courts by CCR, O.13, r.12. In this and the following rules the general procedure for interim payment applications is stated (r.25.6), then provision is made for the conditions to be satisfied and matters to be taken into account by the court (r.25.7), and the powers of the court subsequent to the making of an order (r.25.8). In the former rules, the principal distinction drawn was between orders in respect of damages (especially in actions for personal injuries) and orders in respect of sums other than damages. That distinction was, and remains to be taken into account by the court (see r.25.7).

Interim payment orders were introduced in 1969, partly because it was recognised that delays between cause of action and disposal could be so long, even in cases where liaiblity seemed clear, as to make it unjust to keep the plaintiff out of all of his damages for the duration. Under a system in which cases are managed, such delays should be much reduced. The interim payment rules do not apply to cases on the small claims track (r.27.2(1)(a)). Applications in cases proceeding on the fact track should be rare, except in damages cases where judgment is granted on liability or liability is admitted.

Contrary to what is said in this rule, "interim payment" is not defined by r.25.1(1)(k); it merely repeats the definition given by the Supreme Court Act 1981 s.32(5). That subsection gives the following definition: "a payment on account of any damages, debt or other sum (excluding any costs) which that party may be held liable to pay to or for the benefit of another party to the proceedings if a final judgment or order of the court in the proceedings is given or made in favour of that other party" (see SCP 1999, Vol. 2, para. 20A–209). The last part of the s.32(5) definition (see also RSC, O.29, r.9) was crucial to the decision in *Securities and Investments Board v. Scandex Capital Management A/S* [1998] 1 W.L.R. 712, CA, but is not included in the definition rendered in r.25.1(1)(k).

25.6.2 **Application for an order for interim payment**—The interim payment procedure is not suitable where the factual issues are complicated or where difficult points of law arise which may take many hours and the citation of many authorities to resolve (*Schott Kem Ltd v. Bentley* [1990] 3 W.L.R. 397, CA, at 406, and *Chiron Corporation v. Murex Diagnostics Ltd (No. 13)* [1996] F.S.R. 578).

Rule 25.7 has to be read in conjunction with Pt 23 (see also notes following r.25.3 (How to apply for an interim remedy)) and with the provisions of Practice Direction (Interim Payments), one of the Practice Directions supplementing Pt 25 (see 25PD–001).

Formerly, specific provisions as to the making of applications for interim payment were found in RSC, O. 29, r.10. As is immediately explained, now they are found (with modifications) partly in r.25.6 and partly in Pt 23. Under the CPR, applications for court orders are made in accordance with the general rules contained in Pt 23. Particular rules relating to specific applications appear elsewhere in the CPR and amplify or modify the provisions found in Pt 23 according to need. The general rule is that a copy of the application notice must be served on each respondent (r.23.4(1)). The respondent is "the person against whom the order is sought"' (r.23.1(a)). (In the case of an application for interim payment it is obvious whom the respondent should be.) The copy notice of application must be served as soon as practicable after it is filed (r.23.7(1)(a)); however, an application for an order for interim payment cannot be made before the time stated in r.25.6(1). The general rule is that a copy notice of application must in any event be served at least three days before the court is to deal with the application (r.23.7(1)(b)); however, where the application is for an order for interim payment it should be served at least 14 days before the hearing (r.25.6(3)(a)). Pt 6 contains the general rules about service of documents, including applications.

25.6.3 **Time of application**—Every application, whether made for an interim remedy or for some other purpose, should be made as soon as it becomes apparent that it is necessary or desirable to make it (Practice Direction (Applications) para. 2.7; see 23PD–001). The general rule is that, subject to any limiting provisions, an application for an interim remedy may be made at any time (r.25.2(1)) and r.25.6(1) states that the claimant may not apply for an order for an interim payment before the end of the period for filing an acknowledgment of service applicable to the defendant against whom the application is made. It is not necessary to wait until all defendants have been served. Rule 25.6(1) is copied from former RSC, O.29, r.10(1) and fails to take account of the fact that, under the CPR, the function of the acknowledgment is changed. The period within which a defendant should file an acknowledgment of service, if he is going to do so (taking advantage of r.10.1(3)), is calculated in accordance with r.10.3. Where the Pt 8 procedure is being used, r.8.3 applies. (A claimant may not apply for summary judgment until the defendant has filed an acknowledgment of service or defence; r.24.4.)

25.6.4 **Evidence**—As to evidence in applications for interim orders generally, note, in addition to r.25.6(4)(5), rr.22.1(3), and r.32.6.

As to the service and filing of evidence, see, in addition to r.25(3) to (6), Practice Direction (Applications) paras 9.1 to 9.7 (see para. 23PD–002).

The application notice must be supported by evidence (r.25.6(3)). The evidence should be by witness statement (r.32.6(1)), but may be by affidavit, subject to r.32.15(2). The claimant may, in support of his application, rely on the matters set out in his statement of case or his application notice, if they are verified by a statement of truth (rr.25.6(3) and 32.6(2)). The evidence should deal with the matters listed in Practice Direction (Interim Payments) para. 2 (see para. 25PD–001).

See further SCP 1999, Vol. 1, paras 29/10/6 to 29/10/8.

Prerequisite orders—No special preliminary orders require to be obtained if the application for interim payment for damages or some other sum of money is based on an admission of liability (r.25.7(1)(a)), or on the likelihood of recovery of a substantial sum of money (r.25.7(1)(c)) or a sum of money in a possession case (r.25.7(1)(d)). If it is desired to apply on the ground that the claimant has obtained judgment for damages to be assessed or a sum of money to be assessed (r.25.7(1)(b)), the claimant must obtain the judgment or order before the hearing. It is possible to do this at the same appointment but immediately before the hearing. Thus, in the one application the claimant may apply for (1) summary judgment, and (2) interim payment of part of that judgment, ahead of the assessment of damages. **25.6.5**

Payment by instalments (r.25.6(7))—See former RSC, O.29, r.13(3)(4). **25.6.6**
The court may order an interim payment in one sum or in instalments (r.25.6). Where an interim payment is to be paid in instalments, the order should set out the matters listed in Practice Direction (Interim Payments) para. 3 (see para. 25PD–001). Former RSC, O.29, r.13(4) stated that, where a payment is ordered in respect of the defendant's use and occupation of land under, what is now, r.25.7(1)(d), the order may provide for periodical payments to be made "during the pendency of the action". It would seem that, although "periodical payments" are not the same as "instalments", they too are now covered by r.25.6.

"claimant may make more than one application"—Rule 25.6(2) states that a claimant may make more than one application for an order for interim payment. This would appear to be based on former RSC, O.29, r.10(5) which stated, rather more particularly, that, notwithstanding the making or refusal of an order for an interim payment, a second or subsequent application "may be made upon cause shown". Obviously, where there are several defendants it may prove to be necessary for the claimant to make more than one application. But successive applications should not be made against the same defendant unless the circumstances have changed materially; for instance because of unexpected delay in bringing the case to trial, underestimation of the plaintiff's needs, or some special expense. The witness statement in support of the further application should bring the story up to date but the court file should be bespoken if it is necessary for the judge to see any previous statement. **25.6.7**

Interim payments—conditions to be satisfied and matters to be taken into account

25.7—(1) The court may make an order for an interim payment only if— **25.7**
(a) the defendant against whom the order is sought has admitted liability to pay damages or some other sum of money to the claimant;
(b) the claimant has obtained judgment against that defendant for damages to be assessed or for a sum of money (other than costs) to be assessed;
(c) except where paragraph (3) applies, it is satisfied that, if the claim went to trial, the claimant would obtain judgment for a substantial amount of money (other than costs) against the defendant from whom he is seeking an order for interim payment; or
(d) the following conditions are satisfied—
(i) the claimant is seeking an order for possession of land (whether or not any other order is also sought); and
(ii) the court is satisfied that, if the case went to trial, the defendant would be held liable (even if the claim for possession fails) to pay the claimant a sum of money for the defendant's occupation and use of the land while the claim for possession was pending.

(2) In addition, in a claim for personal injuries the court may make an order for the interim payment of damages only if—
(a) the defendant is insured in respect of the claim;
(b) the defendant's liability will be met by—
(i) an insurer under section 151 of the Road Traffic Act 1988[7]; or
(ii) an insurer acting under the Motor Insurers Bureau Agreement, or the Motor Insurers Bureau where it is acting itself; or
(c) the defendant is a public body.

(3) In a claim for personal injuries where there are two or more defendants,

[7] 1988 c. 52. Section 151 was amended by the Road Traffic Act 1991 (c. 40), s.83, Sched. 8.

the court may make an order for the interim payment of damages against any defendant if—

(a) it is satisfied that, if the claim went to trial, the claimant would obtain judgment for substantial damages against at least one of the defendants (even if the court has not yet determined which of them is liable); and

(b) paragraph (2) is satisfied in relation to each of the defendants.

(4) The court must not order an interim payment of more than a reasonable proportion of the likely amount of the final judgment.

(5) The court must take into account—

(a) contributory negligence; and

(b) any relevant set-off or counterclaim.

25.7.1 **Effect of rule**—This rule contains provisions reflecting mainly those formerly found in RSC, O.29, rr.11 and 12. The court may make an order for an interim payment in the several circumstances listed in r.25.7(1), but not otherwise, and special conditions apply to personal injury claims.

25.7.2 **Judgment obtained**—The most obvious circumstance is where the claimant has *obtained judgment* against the defendant, either (1) for damages to be assessed, or (2) "for a sum of money to be assessed (other than costs)" (r.25.7(1)(b)). The first of these is based on former RSC, O.29, r.11(1)(b) and the second on RSC, O.29, r.12(a), which stated that an order could be made where the claimant had obtained "an order for an account to be taken as between himself and the defendant and for any amount certified due on taking the account to be paid".

25.7.3 **Liability admitted**—Next there is the situation where the defendant has admitted liability to pay to the claimant either (1) damages (see former RSC, O.29, r.11(1)(a)), or (2) "some other sum of money" (in neither event need the sum be substantial) (r.25.7(1)(a)). The second of these did not figure in the former rules.

25.7.4 **Judgment predicted**—Finally, there is the situation where the court is satisfied that, *if the case went to trial*, either (1) the claimant would obtain judgment for "a substantial amount of money (other than costs)" or, (2) in a claim for possession, the defendant would be held liable "to pay the claimant a sum of money" for occupation and use whilst the claim was pending (r.25.7(1)(c)) (see, respectively, former RSC, O.29, rr.11(1)(c) and 12(b)).

25.7.5 **Personal injuries claims**—In practice, many applications for interim payment orders are made in personal injuries cases. Such claims are subject to the special provisions in r.25.7(2) and (3) (see further below). A given personal injuries case may fall within any one of the three categories mentioned above, with the claimant seeking an order on the basis (1) that he has obtained judgment on liability, or (2) that liability has been admitted, or (3) that, if the case went to trial, he would obtain judgment for substantial damages. Obviously, it is the third of these three situations which creates the greatest difficulty (especially where there are several defendants) and which has attracted the bulk of the case law. If progress can be made towards securing earlier admissions of liability, the difficulty will be reduced.

25.7.6 **Discretion**—Whether or not an order is made is a matter of discretion. In the former RSC rules, it was said that the court could make an interim payment order "if it thinks fit" and the amount of the payment was expressed to be "of such amount as [the court] thinks just". It was these phrases which encouraged the courts to emphasise that the discretion is extremely wide (*Crimpfil Ltd v. Barclays Bank plc*, *The Times*, February 24, 1995, CA) and that no limitations on its exercise (over and above those imposed by the rules themselves) should be implied (see *Schott Kem Ltd. v. Bentley* [1990] 3 W.L.R. 397, CA, at 406, where it was held that it is not necessary for the claimant to satisfy the court of his need for an interim payment or that he will suffer prejudice if he does not obtain one). These phrases do not appear in r.25.7 but no restriction on the wide discretion should be implied from their omission.

Special conditions in personal injury claims (r.25.7(2))

25.7.7 **Defendant insured**—Rule 25.7(2) provides that an interim payment order cannot be made in a claim for personal injuries (see definition of such claim in r.2.3) unless the defendant is a public body or an insurer is involved. The reasons for this limitation are clear. Former RSC, r.11(2) was not so limiting, see para. 25.7.18 "Defendant's resources" below.

25.7.8 **Motor Insurers' Bureau**—An order for an interim payment may be made where the defendant's liability will be met by an insurer "acting under" the MIB agreement, as well as by the MIB "where it is acting for itself". The drafting here is different to that found in former RSC, O.29, r.11(2)(a) and is designed to implement the decision of the Court of Appeal in *Sharp v. Pereira* [1998] 4 All E.R. 145, CA.

Two or more defendants—Rule 25.7(1)(c) provides that the court must be satisfied that, if the claim proceeds to trial, the claimant will obtain judgment for a substantial amount of money (whether damages or some other sum of money) "against the defendant from whom he is seeking an order for interim payment" (formerly, RSC, O.29, r.11(1)(c)) said "against the respondent or, where there are two or more defendants against any of them"). Interim payment orders may be made against two or more defendants in respect of the same liability and in respect of the same sum, if the court is satisfied as to the liability of each of the defendants against whom the order is made (*Schott Kem Ltd v. Bentley* [1991] 1 Q.B. 61; [1990] 3 All E.R. 850, CA). There is no objection in principle to the making of orders for interim payments against two or more defendants for different fractions of the total amount thought to be just, provided (a) it is made clear in the order that, if the aggregate of the fractions awarded against the defendants exceeds the "just amount," the sum actually recoverable by the plaintiff cannot exceed the "just amount"; (b) in the case of a claim for damages, it is made clear that the sum actually recoverable by the plaintiff cannot exceed the "reasonable proportion of the damages"; and (c) the order otherwise complies with the rules (*ibid.*). 25.7.9

Difficulties may arise where the court is satisfied that if a claim against two defendants proceeds to trial the claimant would obtain judgment for a substantial amount of money against one or other of the defendants but not against both. Cases on the former rules held that proof of success to the necessary standard against a particular defendant is required before an order can be made against him (*Breeze v. McKennon* (1985) Build.L.R. 41; (1985) 135 New L.J. 1233, CA; *Ricci Burns Ltd. v. Toole* [1989] 1 W.L.R. 993; [1989] 3 All E.R. 478, CA) and, although r.25.7(1)(c) is not in the same terms as former RSC, O.29, r.11(10)(c) or 4.12(c), the law remains the same in this respect. However, r.25.7(3) now provides that, in a claim for personal injuries against several defendants, the court may make an order for the interim payment of damages against any defendant if it is satisfied that the claimant would obtain judgment against at least one defendant "even if the court has not yet determined which of them is liable".

Judgment "for a substantial amount of money" (r.25.7(1)(c))—The court is empowered to have regard to all the circumstances of the case, including the statements of case, any documents disclosed or exhibited and any other relevant material and any admissions made by the defendant, and to determine on such material whether it is satisfied that the claimant will at the trial obtain judgment for a substantial sum of money. This could arise in a claim for a quantum meruit, where the defence is that the claim is excessive or for work done and materials supplied where the defence is that some of the work was defective or was not done, and situations of a like character. 25.7.10

The application should be considered by the court in two stages *Schott Kem Ltd. v. Bentley* [1990] 3 W.L.R. 397, CA, at 404). The court must first be satisfied that, if the action proceeds to trial, the claimant will obtain judgment for a substantial sum, and, if so, the court should then consider whether, in its discretion, it should order an interim payment. At the first stage the claimant must satisfy the court on the balance of probabilities, but to a high standard, that he will obtain judgment for a substantial sum; the likelihood of a set-off or any other defence succeeding must be considered by the court. At the second stage the rules also require (r.25.7(5)) the court to take into account any set-off claimed by the defendant, and any counterclaim arising out of some other transaction and not available as a defence (*Shanning International Ltd v. George Wimpey International Ltd* [1989] 1 W.L.R. 981; [1988] 3 All E.R. 475, CA).

Alternative claims in debt and damages (r.25.7(1)(c))—Rule 25.7(1)(c) states that the court may order an interim payment if it is satisfied that, if the claim went to trial, the claimant would obtain judgment for a substantial sum of money, whether (1) damages or (2) some other sum of money. Formerly, these two forms of money judgment were dealt with in quite separate provisions in RSC, O.29, specifically, in r.11(1)(c) (damages) and in r.12(c) (apart from damages). In *Shearson Lehman Brothers Inc. v Maclaine Watson & Co. Ltd* [1989] Q.B. 842; [1987] 2 All E.R. 181, CA, it was held that the two provisions should be read together to permit the court to make an order for interim payment where it is satisfied that, if the action proceeded to trial, the claimant would obtain judgment either for substantial damages or for a substantial sum of money apart from damages, even though thought not to be certain which. It would seem, however, that if there is doubt whether the sum claimed will prove to be recoverable as damages or under some other heading the court should apply a discount when ordering an interim payment to take account of the provision as to "a reasonable proportion of the likely amount of the final judgment" in r.35.7(4) (*Schott Kem Ltd v. Bentley* [1990] 3 W.L.R. 397, CA, at 405). 25.7.11

Claim for possession of land (r.25.7(1)(d))—The object of r.25.7(1)(d) (formerly RSC, O.29, r.12(b)) is to enable the Court, during the pendency of the action, to order the defendant to make an interim payment to the plaintiff in respect of his continued use and occupation of the land, whoever should ultimately succeed on the claim for possession of the land itself. This rule 25.7.12

operates to negative the decision in *Moore v. Assignment Courier Ltd* [1977] 1 W.L.R. 638; [1977] 2 All E.R. 842, CA. (For fuller explanation, see SCP 1999, Vol. 1, para. 29/12/3) This rule applies to an action for possession of land, on whatever ground it is based. An application for interim payment in these circumstances should be distinguished from an application to determine the amount of the interim rent under the Landlord and Tenant Act 1954, s.24A (see Sched. 1, RSC, O.97, r.9A).

25.7.13 **Interim payment sought in counterclaims and other proceedings**—Interim payments can be sought in all proceedings, whether commenced under Pt 7 or Pt 8.

25.7.14 **Amount of interim payment (r.25.7(4))**—Rule 25.7(4) consolidates provisions formerly found in the RSC and, as a result, some subtle changes emerge. In all cases, the court must not order an interim payment of more than "a reasonable proportion of the likely amount of the final judgment". Former RSC, O.29, rr.11(1) and 12 stated that, if it thought fit, the court should order a payment "of such amount as it thinks just" and, in cases of damages (but not in cases of sums other than damages) the amount was not to exceed a reasonable proportion, etc. In the reported cases, the requirement that the court should award "such amount as it thinks just" figures prominently and, presumably, despite its omission from these rules will continue to do so.

The court should take into account contributory negligence and any relevant set-off or counterclaim (r.25.7(5)).

The court must not risk over-paying the claimant, since a final adjustment under r.25.8 may not be effective in such a case. Particular care has to be taken where the claimant is impecunious and a large interim payment is asked for. See further, para. 25.7.18 "Defendant's resources" below.

25.7.15 **Personal injury claims**—Considerable uncertainty may exist as to the quantum of damages likely to be awarded in the event. The claimant does not have to demonstrate that a certain sum is required to cover any particular need over and above the general need that a claimant has to be paid his damages as soon as reasonably may be done (*Stringman v. McArdle* [1994] 1 W.L.R. 1653, CA, *cf.*, *Schott Kem Ltd v. Bentley* [1991] 1 Q.B. 61; [1990] 3 All E.R. 850, CA). The court is not concerned with what the claimant proposes to do with the money received (*Campbell v. Mylchreest* [1998] P.I.Q.R. P20). In the case of a child or patient, the money will normally be paid into court and then the litigation friend will apply to the district judge for payment out as and when the money is required. Where the Court of Protection is concerned, it is for that court to decide how and when the money is to be spent (*Stringman v. McArdle, op. cit.*).

25.7.16 **Recoverable benefits and interim payments**—The Social Security (Recovery of Benefits) Act 1997 replaces (with some modifications) the legislative scheme formerly found in the Social Security Administration Act 1992, Pt IV, providing for the recoupment by the Secretary of State from persons making compensation payments of certain benefits paid to the injured parties. An interim payment, whether made voluntarily or under a court order, appears to fall within the definition of a compensation payment under s.29 of this Act. Consequently, a person making an interim payment is liable to the Secretary of State for an amount equal to the total certified recoverable benefits (s.6(1)). (Certain payments are exempted and "small payments" as fixed by regulations may be disregarded.) In these circumstances, where an application for an interim payment is otherwise than by consent, and practice stated in Practice Direction (Interim Payments) paras 4.1 and 4.2 should be followed (see para. 25PD–001). The order will set out the amount by which the payment to be made has been reduced and the payment made to the claimant will be the net amount (*ibid.* paras 4.3 and 4.4).

25.7.17 **Costs**—An interim payment order is an order for payment on account of any sum which a party may be held liable to pay if final judgment is given against him. However, such an order cannot be made for the purpose of requiring a party to make a payment on account of any costs for which he may be required to indemnify his opponent by an order for costs made upon final judgment (see Supreme Court Act 1981, s.31(5)). In certain circumstances, a party may be required, not to make a payment on account of expected orders for costs, but to provide security for his opponent's costs. For example, where an application for summary judgment fails, the court may order that a party with a weak case should pay a sum of money into court as security for costs (see rr.3.1(3) and 24.6).

25.7.18 **Defendant's resources**—Former O.29, r.11(2)(c) stated that an interim payment order could not be made against a defendant who, assuming he was not insured, was not "a person whose means and resources are such as to enable him to make the interim payment". In terms, this provision was confined to personal injury actions but its sentiment was thought to be relevant in other cases as well (see SCP 1999, para. 29/1/9). This provision does not appear in r.25.7 because, now, an order cannot be made against an uninsured defendant (see r.25.7(2)) (though an order can be made against a public body). This leaves open the question whether the adequacy of the defendant's means and resources is a condition to be satisfied before an interim payment order can be made in claims other than claims for personal injuries. The former rules contained no specific provision to this effect but it was assumed, by way of analogy with the rule formerly found in 11(2)(c), that it was a relevant factor to be taken into account in other claims (see SCP 1999, para. 29/11/9, and note *Jones v. Tower Hamlets*, May 21, 1996, CA (unrep.)). It has been held that, if the defendant's resources are such that an order for interim payment will cause irremediable harm which cannot be made good by eventual repayment, that is a very relevant factor to be taken into account in fixing the amount of any interim payment (*British & Commonwealth Holdings plc v. Quadrex Holdings Inc.* [1989] 3 All E.R. 492, CA).

"financial position of each party"—Rule 1.1 states that the "overriding objective" of the CPR is to enable the court "to deal with cases justly" and dealing with a case justly includes, so far as is practicable, dealing with it in ways which *inter alia* are proportionate "to the amount of money involved" and "to the financial position of each party" (r. 1.1(2)(c)). The question whether or not an interim remedy in the form of an order for interim payment should be made is not a mere matter of practice or procedure but a matter of substantive remedy. It may be doubted, therefore, whether r.1.1 strictly applies. However, it has always been the case that the court has taken into account the financial position of each party (see SCP 1999, paras 29/11/2 and 29/11/6 *et seq.*). **25.7.19**

Delay to trial—The power to grant orders for interim payments was introduced by legislation at a time when delays before trial had become so significant that the injustice that could be inflicted on personal injury plaintiffs was patent. Obviously, the length of time before a claim may be settled or tried is an important consideration. Under the new "case management" system the hope is that the incidence of early settlements will be increased and delays to trial very much reduced. In those circumstances, the need for interim payment orders may decline. **25.7.20**

Interest—Where an order for an interim payment is made in respect of expenditure already incurred and paid for, the court has power to award interest in its discretion. If the court should think it desirable to award interest on the amount of the interim payment, *e.g.* where the amount awarded is substantial or the trial is unlikely to come on for a long time, it should clearly and precisely specify the rate of interest awarded and the period or periods for which it is awarded, so that if the trial judge should award a different rate or rates or for a different period or periods, the necessary adjustments can be made to determine the correct total amount of interest which the trial judge has awarded. The rates at which, and the periods for which, interest may have been awarded in respect of an interim payment ordered before trial are not binding on the trial judge. **25.7.21**

Form of order—Where an interim payment is to be paid by instalments, the order should contain the information stated in Practice Direction (Interim Payments) para. 3 (see para. 25FPD–001 below). **25.7.22**

Manner of payment—Former RSC, O.29, r.13 contained some express provisions as to the manner in which an interim payment should be paid. These provisions are not repeated in Pt 25 but the practice remains the same. The order should specify to whom the payment is to be made and fix a time for payment. Normally payment is to the claimant. If the claimant is legally aided an interim payment is exempted from the first charge in favour of the Legal Aid Fund (Legal and General Regulations 1989, reg. 94(a)) it may be made to the claimant or, if more convenient, to his solicitor on his behalf. If the claimant is a child or patient the money should be dealt with in accordance with directions given by the court under r.21.11. **25.7.23**

Former RSC, O.29, r.13 stated that the court had power to order payment into court of an interim award. This power (which was seldom used) may now be derived from r.3.1(3).

Payment is usually in a lump sum, but the court may order payment by instalments. In the case of payments for the occupation of land, it is usual to order periodical payments as if they were of rent in arrear. In personal injury cases the payment may, in appropriate cases, be expressly ordered to be made in respect of the special damages and loss of wages claimed; this may simplify the calculation of interest at the end of the day.

Directions for further conduct of case—Former RSC, O.29, r.14 provided that, on an application for interim payment, whether or not an order was made, the court could give directions as to the further conduct of the case, particularly where the issue of liability still remained to be tried and the hearing of the application revealed that an early trial was desirable. Under the case management system introduced by the CPR, no express provision to that effect is required. The court has ample powers to adjust the management of the case in the light of any order as to interim payment. **25.7.24**

Part 36 payment before or after interim payment order application—There is no objection to the Court being told, on an application for an interim payment order, of any payment into court (*Fryer v. London Transport Executive, The Times*, December 4, 1982, CA). If an interim payment order is made, it is usual to order that payment should be made out of any money in court. **25.7.25**

Where, after making an interim payment, whether voluntarily or pursuant to a court order, a defendant offers to settle a money claim by paying a sum into court under Pt 36, the notice of payment in must state that the defendant has taken into account the interim payment (r.36.6(2)(d)).

25.7.26 **Interim payment and summary judgment**—The court may give summary judgment against a defendant on the whole of a claim or a particular issue (r.24.2). Summary judgment is not available in certain possession proceedings (r.24.3(2)) but otherwise may be granted in cases where an interim payment order may be made. Depending on the circumstances, an application for summary judgment and for an interim payment order may conveniently be made and dealt with together (*Associated Bulk Carriers Ltd v. Koch Shipping Inc.* [1978] 2 All E.R. 254, CA) (see also SCP 1999, Vol. 1, para. 14/1/3).

The court may now give a claimant summary judgment if it considers that the defendant has "no real prospect of successfully defending" the claim or issue (r.24.2). The court may make an interim payment order if it is satisfied that the claimant "would obtain judgment for a substantial amount of money", if the claim went to trial. If the court is so satisfied it is likely that it will also consider that the defendant has no real prospect of defending. Under the former law, a defendant could be granted unconditional leave to defend where the court was satisfied that he had an arguable defence. In *Andrews v. Schooling* [1991] 1 W.L.R. 783; [1991] 3 All E.R. 723, CA, the Court of Appeal examined the earlier authorities (which were not *ad idem*) and said that it was inconsistent to order an interim payment at the same time as giving unconditional leave to defend and approved the practice of making such leave conditional on the making of an interim payment (see SCP 1999, Vol. 1, paras 14/1/3 and 29/11/4). There is authority for the proposition that the mere fact that the defendant lodges a bona fide appeal against an order for summary judgment is not, of itself, a sufficient ground for refusing to award the claimant an interim payment order (*Halvanon Insurance Co. Ltd v. Central Reinsurance Corp.* [1984] 2 Lloyd's Rep. 420).

25.7.27 **Enforcement**—An order for an interim payment falls within Sched. 1, RSC, O.45, r.1 (see para. R45.1) and unless time to pay has been given can be enforced forthwith by the means there set out, and, no doubt, may found winding-up proceedings.

25.7.28 **Grounds for contesting interim payment**—The defendant against whom an order for interim payment is sought may show cause against the making of the order in the following ways:

(a) *by a technical objection, e.g.* that the claim is for damages for personal injuries and he is not within the categories of r.25.7(2).

(b) *on the merits* by showing that there is a serious doubt whether the claimant will recover anything. In a claim for a sum of money, the court must be "satisfied" that the claimant "would obtain judgment for a substantial amount of money". In determining whether it is so satisfied the Court should apply the civil standard of proof; the Court is not required to be sure in the sense of being satisfied beyond reasonable doubt (*Shearson Lehman Bros. Inc. v. Maclaine Watson & Co. Ltd* [1989] Q.B. 842; [1987] 2 All E.R. 181, CA; *Gibbons v. Wall, The Times*, February 24, 1988, CA). It should be observed, however, that the test prescribed by r.25.7(1)(c) is whether the court is satisfied that the claimant will succeed in his claim against the defendant, rather than whether he is likely to succeed (*British & Commonwealth Holdings plc v. Quadrex Holdings Inc.* [1989] Q.B. 842; [1989] 3 All E.R. 492, CA; *Andrews v. Schooling* [1991] 1 W.L.R. 783; [1991] 3 All E.R. 723, CA).

(c) *on quantum*, r.25.7(5) expressly provides that the court must take into account any set-off or counterclaim as well as any allegation of contributory negligence. Thus the court must be satisfied, whatever the description of the bar relief on in opposition that the claimant would obtain judgment for a substantial amount at trial. *Smallman Construction v. Redpath Dorman Long* (1992) 47 B.L.R. 15, 25 Con.L.R. 105, CA. "Substantial" will mean different amounts in different situations and real need of the plaintiff may be taken into account in this context; however, to say that its meaning extends to sums that are, in absolute terms, trivial would be straining the flexibility of the Order. Applications for small sums are discouraged but if made should be coupled with an application to transfer to the appropriate county court.

Powers of court where it has made an order for interim payment

25.8 **25.8**—(1) Where a defendant has been ordered to make an interim payment, or has in fact made an interim payment (whether voluntarily or under an order), the court may make an order to adjust the interim payment.

(2) The court may in particular—

(a) order all or part of the interim payment to be repaid;

(b) vary or discharge the order for the interim payment

(c) order a defendant to reimburse, either wholly or partly, another defendant who has made an interim payment.

(3) The court may make an order under paragraph (2)(c) only if—

(a) the defendant to be reimbursed made the interim payment in relation to a claim in respect of which he has made a claim against the other defendant for a contribution[GL], indemnity[GL] or other remedy; and

(b) where the claim or part to which the interim payment relates has not been discontinued or disposed of, the circumstances are such that the court could make an order for interim payment under rule 25.7.

(4) The court may make an order under this rule without an application by any party if it makes the order when it disposes of the claim or any part of it.

(5) Where—

(a) a defendant has made an interim payment; and

(b) the amount of the payment is more than his total liability under the final judgment or order,

the court may award him interest on the overpaid amount from the date when he made the interim payment.

Effect of rule—Most of the provisions in this rule are traceable to former RSC, O.29, r.17, a rule which had a title which did not adequately reflect its contents. Rule 25.8 goes beyond the former rule in that it contains specific provisions as to interest. The rule provides for the adjustment of interim payment orders in the light of subsequent events, particularly, final judgment or discontinuance. **25.8.1**

Discharge, variation, repayment—The court has wide powers to discharge or vary an interim payment order, including the power to order any money paid repaid. Further, in certain circumstances the court may order a defendant to reimburse, either wholly or partly, another defendant who has made an interim payment (r.25.8(3)). The court may adjust an order that has been made but not yet paid. **25.8.2**

The court may make an order under this rule without an application by any party if it makes the order when it disposes of the claim or any part of it (r.25.8(4)) by final judgment or grant of leave to discontinue. Otherwise an application for the relief permitted under this rule may be made by any party at any time.

Interest—Former RSC, O.29, r.17 contained no specific provisions as to interest; the matter was dealt with by case law (see SCP 1999, para. 29/17/1). It is clear that, where, following final judgment or order, the court orders that part of the interim payment should be repaid to the defendant, the court may award him interest on the overpaid amount from the date when he made the interim payment (r.25.8(5)); that is to say, when his "total liability" is less than the interim payment. Presumably, where a defendant is found not liable at all he would be entitled to interest on the full amount of the interim payment. The court may award interest on an interim payment made voluntarily as well as under an order of the court. **25.8.3**

Payment into court and interim payment—Former RSC, O.29, r.16 stated that a notice of payment into court must indicate whether it takes into account an interim payment, whether made voluntarily or pursuant to a court order (applied in county court proceedings by CCR, O.13, r.12(1)). A notice of payment into court is now known as a "Part 36 payment notice" and the former rule is now found in r.36.6(2)(d). **25.8.4**

Adjustment on final judgment or order or on discontinuance

Final judgment—Where an action proceeds to trial either on the issue of liability or of damages or both after the defendant or one of two or more defendants has made an interim payment whether voluntarily or pursuant, to order, the court may, before the final judgment or order is given or made, make such adjustments with respect to the interim payment as may be necessary, for the purpose of giving effect to its determination of that defendant's liability. Such adjustments may become necessary (a) as between the plaintiff and that defendant, and (b) as between that defendant and any co-defendant of his (r.25.8(2)(b) and (c)). **25.8.5**

As between the claimant and the defendant, the first and obvious adjustment that needs to be made is that the amount of the interim payment should be deducted from the amount of the total award of damages, and subject to any further adjustment with regard to the interest on the damages (see para. 25.8.3) judgment should be entered for the plaintiff only for the difference between these two amounts. The form of the judgment should recite the amount of the final judgment or the assessment of the damages and should further recite the order for interim payment and payment made thereunder or the amount paid voluntarily. The judgment or order should then provide for entry of judgment and payment of the balance (see Practice Direction (Interim Payments) paras 5.2 and 5.3 (25PD–001) and, to same effect, Practice Direction (Judgments and Orders) paras 6.1 and 6.2 are to same effect (para. 40BPD–001)).

In the unlikely event that the amount of the interim payment should exceed the amount of the final award for damages, debt or other sum, the court will order the claimant to repay the difference to the defendant who made the payment (see r.25.8(2)(c)). In addition, the court may award the defendant interest on the overpaid amount in accordance with r.25.8(5) (putting into legislative form *Mercers Co. v. New Hampshire Insurance Co.* [1991] 1 W.L.R. 1173; [1991] 4 All E.R. 542). For form of judgment in this event, see Practice Direction (Interim Payments) paras 5.2 and 5.3 (25D–001) and, to same effect, Practice Direction (Judgments and Orders) paras 5.4 and 5.5 (40BPD–001).

25.8.6 *Discontinuance*—The court's power to adjust an interim payment may also be exercised where the court grants leave to the claimant to discontinue his action or to withdraw the claim in respect of which the interim payment was made. Rule 38.2(2)(b) states that where the claimant has received an interim payment, whether voluntarily or pursuant to order, in relation to the whole or part of his claim he may discontinue that claim or that part of it only if (1) the defendant who has made the payment consents in writing, or (2) the court gives permission. It should be noted that leave to discontinue is required when the claimant "has received an interim payment", and not where such payment has been ordered but not paid, and leave may be dispensed with where the "defendant who has made the payment" consents, and the consent of all other parties is not required. In these two respects, r.38.2(2)(b) differs from former RSC, O.21, r.2(2A). Presumably, "has received an interim payment" includes having received any instalment where the interim payment was to be paid by instalments.

25.8.7 **Adjustment between co-defendants**—As between the defendant who makes the interim payment and his co-defendants, the court may order any defendant to pay the whole or part of the interim payment to the defendant who made it.

The effect of r.25.8 in this context is as follows. Where (1) a defendant has been ordered to make an interim payment, or has in fact made an interim payment (either voluntarily or under an order), and (2) he made that payment in relation to a claim or part of a claim in respect of which he has made a claim against the co-defendant for a contribution, indemnity or other relief (former RSC, O.29, r.17 added here "relating to or connected with the plaintiff's claim"), then (3) the court may order the co-defendant to reimburse him either wholly or partly. Obviously, such an order is likely to be made on or after final judgment or discontinuance of the claim or the part of the claim to which the interim payment related. However, subject to r.25.8(3)(b), such order for re-imbursement may be made at an earlier stage in the proceedings.

Restriction on disclosure of an interim payment

25.9 **25.9** The fact that a defendant has made an interim payment, whether voluntarily or by court order, shall not be disclosed to the trial judge until all questions of liability and the amount of money to be awarded have been decided unless the defendant agrees.

25.9.1 **Effect of rule**—This provision is derived from RSC, O.29, r.15, which was applied to county court proceedings by CCR, O.13, r.12.

Under the former rule, two things could not be disclosed by pleadings or otherwise: (1) the fact that an order for interim payment had been made, and (2) the fact that an interim payment had been made (either voluntarily or by court order). In terms, r.25.9 is confined to the latter.

Under the former rule, the disclosure prohibited was disclosure "to the Court at the trial, or hearing, of any question or issue as to liability or damages". Under r.25.9 disclosure "to the trial judge" is prohibited. Under the case management system introduced by the CPR, cases on the multi-track are managed by "teams of judges" (Interim Report p. 66 and Final Report p. 91) and the court is encouraged (in appropriate cases) to resolve issues that have been identified at the pre-trial stage by "rolling adjudication" instead of leaving all issues alive until trial (Interim Report p. 50 and Final Report p. 63). Under this system, the chances of the prohibited disclosures being made inadvertently are enhanced.

Formerly, the chances of prohibited disclosures being made by any person, whether advertently or inadvertently, were restricted by the fact that most orders were made in chambers and therefore in private. However, following recent developments in the law, the general rule now is that, subject to exceptions, the hearing of applications is to be in public (r.39.2).

By way of exception, disclosures may be made if the party that has made the interim payment agrees. In terms, the former rule provided a further exception to the effect that disclosure could be made if the court so directed.

Although, almost invariably, applications for interim payments will be held in chambers that does not mean that they will be held in private (see r.39.2 and Practice Direction (Miscellaneous Provisions Relating to Hearings) para. 1.5 (39PD–001). This creates a risk that the fact that the defendant has made an interim payment may come to the attention of the judge. Circumstances may arise in which a judge would be entitled to make public his reasons for granting an interim payment order for a large amount (*British & Commonwealth Holdings plc v. Quadrex Holdings Inc.* [1989] Q.B. 842; [1989] 3 All E.R. 492, CA).

Where a Master or district judge makes an order for an interim payment at the same time as any other order, the order for the interim payment should be sealed as a separate order. This order must not be included in the setting down bundle.

Obviously, once the court has decided all questions of liability, and the amount of money to be awarded, the fact that an order for interim payment has been made, what its amount was, the date it was paid and by which of two or more defendants, and all other relevant facts, should be communicated to the court immediately, and before the judgment is perfected by entry, so as to enable the court to make any necessary adjustments under r.25.8, including interest, and to deal with the question of costs.

Interim injunction to cease if claim is stayed

25.10 If— 25.10

(a) the court has granted an interim injunction[GL]; and

(b) the claim is stayed[GL] other than by agreement between the parties, the interim injunction[GL] shall be set aside[GL] unless the court orders that it should continue to have effect even though the claim is stayed.

Effect of rule—An interim injunction (see r.25.1(1)(a)) is granted on the assumption that the claim will be actively pursued. It should not be continued for longer than is necessary. This rule provides that an interim injunction "shall be set aside" where a claim is stayed (other than by agreement between the parties) unless the court orders otherwise. It would seem that what is intended is that, where the court orders the stay of a claim, it should turn its attention to the question whether any interim injunction should be continued and, on its own initiative, should set it aside if it should not be continued. (For explanation of "stay", see Glossary.) In terms, the rule is confined to an interim remedy in the form of an interim injunction and does not extend to other forms of interim remedy as listed in r.25.1(1). A party who obtains an interim remedy in the form of a freezing injunction should promptly apply to the court for its discharge if the time comes when it is no longer needed (*Detect Sea Enterprises Ltd v. O'Connor*, unrep., October 14, 1997, *per* Sir Richard Scott V.-C.). 25.10.1

A claimant needs permission from the court if he wishes to discontinue all or part of a claim in relation to which the court has granted an interim injunction (r.38.2(2)(a)(i)).

Interim injunction to cease after 14 days if claim struck out

25.11—(1) If— 25.11

(a) the court has granted an interim injunction[GL]; and

(b) the claim is struck out under rule 3.7 (sanctions for non-payment of certain fees).

the interim injunction shall cease to have effect 14 days after the date that the claim is struck out unless paragraph (2) applies.

(2) If the claimant applies to reinstate the claim before the interim injunction ceases to have effect under paragraph (1), the injunction shall continue until the hearing of the application unless the court orders otherwise.

Effect of rule—This rule provides for the special situation where an interim injunction is in place, whether in favour of the claimant or the defendant, but the claim is struck out automatically (not merely stayed) for non-payment of certain court fees by the claimant under r.3.4(4)(b)(i). The rule provides that, in that event, after a period the interim injunction will cease to have effect. Where, within the period, a claimant applies under r.3.9 for re-instatement of his claim (see para. 3.7.2) by operation of the rule that interim injunction remains in effect beyond the period until the hearing of the application. If, at the hearing, the claim is not re-instated, the interim injunction lapses; if the claim is re-instated the interim injunction (whether in favour of the claimant or the defendant) will not continue unless the court orders that it should. 25.11.1

PRACTICE DIRECTION—INTERIM PAYMENTS

This Practice Direction supplements CPR Part 25

General

1.1 Rule 25.7 sets out the conditions to be satisfied and matters to be taken into account before the court will make an order for an interim payment. 25PD–001

1.2 The permission of the court must be obtained before making a voluntary interim payment in respect of a claim by a child or patient.

Evidence

2.1 An application for an interim payment of damages must be supported by evidence dealing with the following;

(1) the sum of money sought by way of an interim payment,

(2) the items or matters in respect of which the interim payment is sought,

(3) the sum of money for which final judgment is likely to be given,

(4) the reasons for believing that the conditions set out in rule 25.7 are satsified,

(5) any other relevant matters,

(6) in claims for personal injuries, details of special damages and past and future loss, and

(7) in a claim under the Fatal Accidents Act 1976, details of the person(s) on whose behalf the claim is made and the nature of the claim.

2.2 Any documents in support of the application should be exhibited, including, in personal injuries claims, the medical report(s).

2.3 If a respondent to an application for an interim payment wishes to rely on written evidence at the hearing he must comply with the provisions of rule 25.6(4).

2.4 If the applicant wishes to rely on written evidence in reply he must comply with the provisions of rule 25.6(5).

Instalments

3. Where an interim payment is to be paid in instalments the order should set out;

(1) the total amount of the payment,

(2) the amount of each instalment,

(3) the number of instalments and the date on which each is to be paid and

(4) to whom the payment should be made.

Compensation Recovery Payments

4.1 Where in a claim for personal injuries there is an application for an interim payment of damages;

(1) which is other than by consent,

(2) which falls under the heads of damage set out in column 1 of Schedule 2 of the Social Security (Recovery of Benefits) Act 1997 in respect of recoverable benefits received by the claimant set out in column 2 of that Schedule and

(3) where the defendant is liable to pay recoverable benefits to the Secretary of State,

the defendant should obtain from the Secretary of State a certificate of recoverable benefits.

4.2 A copy of the certificate should be filed at the hearing of the application for an interim payment.

4.3 The order will set out the amount by which the payment to be made to the claimant has been reduced according to the Act and the Social Security (Recovery of Benefits) Regulations 1997.

4.4 The payment made to the claimant will be the net amount but the interim payment for the purposes of paragraph 5 below will be the gross amount.

Adjustment of Final Judgment Figure

5.1 In this paragraph "judgment" means;

(1) any order to pay a sum of money,

(2) a final award of damages,

(3) an assessment of damages.

5.2 In a final judgment where an interim payment has previously been made which is less than the total amount awarded by the judge, the order should set out in a preamble;

(1) the total amount awarded by the judge, and

(2) the amounts and dates of the interim payment(s).

5.3 The total amount awarded by the judge should then be reduced by the total amount of any interim payments, and an order made for entry of judgment and payment of the balance.

5.4 In a final judgment where an interim payment has previously been made which is more than the total amount awarded by the judge, the order should set out in a preamble;

(1) the total amount awarded by the judge, and

(2) the amounts and dates of the interim payment(s).

5.5 An order should then be made for repayment, reimbursement, variation or discharge under rule 25.8(2) and for interest on an overpayment under rule 25.8(5).

5.6 A Practice Direction supplementing Part 40 provides further information concerning adjustment of the final judgment sum.

PRACTICE DIRECTION—ACCOUNTS AND INQUIRIES

This Practice Direction supplements CPR Part 25

An application for an order for accounts and inquiries may also be made under Part 24 (summary judgment). Reference should be made to paragraph 6 of the practice direction that supplements that Part. 25BPD–001

1. The remedies that the court may grant under Part 25 include orders directing accounts to be taken and inquiries to be made.

2. The court may, on application or on its own initiative, at any stage in the proceedings, whether before or after judgment, make an order directing any necessary accounts to be taken or inquiries to be made.

3. Every direction for an account to be taken or an inquiry to be made shall be numbered in the order so that, as far as possible, each distinct account and inquiry is given its own number.

(This practice direction replaces RSC Order 43, rule 2 and applies to county court proceedings as well as to High Court proceedings.)

(The Accounts and Inquiries Practice Direction supplementing Part 40 contains provisions regarding the taking of an account or conduct of an inquiry after the order for the account or inquiry has been made.)

PRACTICE DIRECTION—INTERIM INJUNCTIONS

This Practice Direction supplements CPR Part 25

General

Jurisdiction

1.1 High Court Judges and any other Judge duly authorised may grant "search orders"[8] and "freezing injunctions".[9] 25CPD–001

1.2 In a case in the High Court, Masters and District Judges have the power to grant injunctions:

[8] Rule 25.1(1)(g).
[9] Rule 25.1(1)(f).

(1) by consent,
(2) in connection with charging orders and appointments of receivers,
(3) in aid of execution of judgments.

1.3 In any other case any Judge who has jurisdiction to conduct the trial of the action has the power to grant an injunction in that action.

1.4 A Master or District Judge has the power to vary or discharge an injunction granted by any Judge with the consent of all the parties.

Making an Application

2.1 The application notice must state;
(1) the order sought, and
(2) the date, time and place of the hearing.

2.2 The application notice and evidence in support must be served as soon as practicable after issue and in any event not less than 3 days before the court is due to hear the application.[10]

2.3 Where the court is to serve, sufficient copies of the application notice and evidence in support for the court and for each respondent should be filed for issue and service.

2.4 Whenever possible a draft of the order sought should be filed with the application notice and a disk containing the draft should also be available to the court. This will enable the court officer to arrange for any amendments to be incorporated and for the speedy preparation and sealing of the order. The current word processing system to be used is WordPerfect 5.1.

Evidence

3.1 Applications for search orders and freezing injunctions must be supported by affidavit evidence.

3.2 Applications for other interim injunctions must be supported by evidence set out in either:
(1) a witness statement, or
(2) a statement of case provided that it is verified by a statement of truth,[11] or
(3) the application provided that it is verified by a statement of truth,
unless the court, an Act, a rule or a practice direction requires evidence by affidavit.

3.3 The evidence must set out the facts on which the applicant relies for the claim being made against the respondent, including all material facts of which the court should be made aware.

3.4 Where an application is made without notice to the respondent, the evidence must also set out why notice was not given.

(See Part 32 and the practice direction that supplements it for information about evidence.)

Urgent applications and applications without notice

4.1 These fall into two categories:
(1) applications where a claim form has already been issued, and
(2) applications where a claim form has not yet been issued,
and, in both cases, where notice of the application has not been given to the respondent.

4.2 These applications are normally dealt with at a court hearing but cases of extreme urgency may be dealt with by telephone.

4.3 Applications dealt with at a court hearing after issue of a claim form:
(1) the application notice, evidence in support and a draft order (as in 2.4 above) should be filed with the court two hours before the hearing wherever possible,

[10] Rule 23.7(1) and (2) and see Rule 23.7(4) (short service).
[11] See Part 22.

(2) if an application is made before the application notice has been issued, a draft order (as in 2.4 above) should be provided at the hearing, and the application notice and evidence in support must be filed with the court on the same or next working day or as ordered by the court, and

(3) except in cases where secrecy is essential, the applicant should take steps to notify the respondent informally of the application.

4.4 Applications made before the issue of a claim form:

(1) in addition to the provisions set out at 4.3 above, unless the court orders otherwise, either the applicant must undertake to the court to issue a claim form immediately or the court will give directions for the commencement of the claim,[12]

(2) where possible the claim form should be served with the order for the injunction,

(3) an order made before the issue of a claim form should state in the title after the names of the applicant and respondent "the Claimant and Defendant in an Intended Action".

4.5 Applications made by telephone;

(1) where it is not possible to arrange a hearing, application can be made between 10.00 am and 5.00 pm weekdays by telephoning the Royal Courts of Justice on 0171 936 6000 and asking to be put in contact with a High Court Judge of the appropriate Division available to deal with an emergency application in a High Court matter. The appropriate district registry may also be contacted by telephone. In county court proceedings, the appropriate county court should be contacted.

(2) where an application is made outside those hours the applicant should either

- (a) telephone the Royal Courts of Justice on 0171 936 6000 where he will be put in contact with the clerk to the appropriate duty judge in the High Court (or the appropriate area Circuit Judge where known) or
- (b) the Urgent Court Business Officer of the appropriate Circuit who will contact the local duty judge,

(3) where the facility is available it is likely that the Judge will require a draft order to be faxed to him,

(4) the application notice and evidence in support must be filed with the court on the same or next working day or as ordered, together with two copies of the order for sealing,

(5) injunctions will be heard by telephone only where the applicant is acting by counsel or solicitors.

Orders for Injunctions

5.1 Any order for an injunction, unless the court orders otherwise, must contain; 25CPD–002

(1) an undertaking by the applicant to the court to pay any damages which the respondent(s) (or any other party served with or notified of the order) sustain which the court considers the applicant should pay,

(2) if made without notice to any other party, an undertaking by the applicant to the court to serve on the respondent the application notice, evidence in support and any order made as soon as practicable,

(3) if made without notice to any other party, a return date for a further hearing at which the other party can be present,

(4) if made before filing the application notice, an undertaking to file and pay the appropriate fee on the same or next working day, and

(5) if made before issue of a claim form

- (a) an undertaking to issue and pay the appropriate fee on the same or next working day or

[12] Rule 25.2(3).

(b) directions for the commencement of the claim.

5.2 An order for an injunction made in the presence of all parties to be bound by it or made at a hearing of which they have had notice, may state that it is effective until trial or further order.

5.3 Any order for an injunction must set out clearly what the respondent must do or not do.

Freezing Injunctions

Orders to restrain disposal of assets worldwide and within England and Wales

6. Examples of Freezing Injunctions are annexed to this practice direction.

Search Orders

Orders for the preservation of evidence and property

7.1 The following provisions apply to search orders in addition to those listed above.

The Supervising Solicitor:

7.2 The Supervising Solicitor must be experienced in the operation of search orders. A Supervising Solicitor may be contacted either through the Law Society or, for the London area, through the London Solicitors Litigation Association.

Evidence:

7.3(1) the affidavit must state the name, firm and its address, and experience of the Supervising Solicitor, also the address of the premises and whether it is a private or business address, and

(2) the affidavit must disclose very fully the reason the order is sought, including the probability that relevant material would disappear if the order were not made.

Service:

7.4(1) the order must be served personally by the Supervising Solicitor, unless the court otherwise orders, and must be accompanied by the evidence in support and any documents capable of being copied,

(2) confidential exhibits need not be served but they must be made available for inspection by the respondent in the presence of the applicant's solicitors while the order is carried out and afterwards be retained by the respondent's solicitors on their undertaking not to permit the respondent

(a) to see them or copies of them except in their presence, and

(b) to make or take away any note or record of them,

(3) the Supervising Solicitor may be accompanied only by the persons mentioned in the order,

(4) the Supervising Solicitor must explain the terms and effect of the order to the respondent in every day language and advise him of his right to

(a) legal advice, and

(b) apply to vary or discharge the order,

(5) where the Supervising Solicitor is a man and the respondent is likely to be an unaccompanied woman, at least one other person named in the order must be a woman and must accompany the Supervising Solicitor, and

(6) the order may only be served between 9.30 am and 5.30 pm Monday to Friday unless the court otherwise orders.

Search and custody of materials:

7.5(1) no material shall be removed unless clearly covered by the terms of the order,

(2) the premises must not be searched and no items shall be removed from them except in the presence of the respondent or a person who appears to be a responsible employee of the respondent,
(3) where copies of documents are sought, the documents should be retained for no more than 2 days before return to the owner,
(4) where material in dispute is removed pending trial, the applicant's solicitors should place it in the custody of the respondent's solicitors on their undertaking to retain it in safekeeping and to produce it to the court when required,
(5) in appropriate cases the applicant should insure the material retained in the repondent's solicitors' custody,
(6) the Supervising Solicitor must make a list of all material removed from the premises and supply a copy of the list to the respondent,
(7) no material shall be removed from the premises until the respondent has had reasonable time to check the list,
(8) if any of the listed items exists only in computer readable form, the respondent must immediately give the applicant's solicitors effective access to the computers, with all necessary passwords, to enable them to be searched, and cause the listed items to be printed out,
(9) the applicant must take all reasonable steps to ensure that no damage is done to any computer or data,
(10) the applicant and his representatives may not themselves search the respondent's computers unless they have sufficient expertise to do so without damaging the respondent's system,
(11) the Supervising Solicitor shall provide a report on the carrying out of the order to the applicant's solicitors.
(12) as soon as the report is received the applicant's solicitors shall—
(a) serve a copy of it on the respondent, and
(b) file a copy of it with the court, and
(13) where the Supervising Solicitor is satisfied that full compliance with paragraph 7.5(7) and (8) above is impracticable, he may permit the search to proceed and items to be removed without compliance with the impracticable requirements.

General

8.1 The Supervising Solicitor must not be an employee or member of the applicant's firm of solicitors.
8.2 If the court orders that the order need not be served by the Supervising Solicitor, the reason for so ordering must be set out in the order.
8.3 The search order must not be carried out at the same time as a police search warrant.
8.4 There is no privilege against self incrimination in Intellectual Property cases (see the Supreme Court Act 1981, section 72) therefore in those cases, paragraph (4) of the Respondent's Entitlements and any other references to incrimination in the Search Order, should be removed.
8.5 Applications in intellectual property cases should be made in the Chancery Division.
8.6 An example of a Search Order is annexed to this Practice Direction.

Annex

25CPD–003

****Freezing Injunction** Order to restrain assets in England and Wales**	**IN THE [HIGH COURT OF JUSTICE] [CHANCERY DIVISION] [Strand, London WC2A 2LL]**

Before The Honourable Mr Justice [ ]

Claim No.

Dated

Applicant

Seal

Respondent

Name, address and reference of Respondent

PENAL NOTICE

IF YOU THE WITHIN NAMED [ ] DISOBEY THIS ORDER YOU MAY BE HELD TO BE IN CONTEMPT OF COURT AND LIABLE TO IMPRISONMENT OR FINED OR YOUR ASSETS SEIZED

IMPORTANT

Notice to the Respondent

You should read the terms of the Order and the Guidance Notes very carefully. You are advised to consult a Solicitor as soon as possible.
This Order prohibits you, the Respondent, from dealing with your assets up to the amount stated in the Order, but subject to any exceptions set out at the end of the Order. You have a right to ask the Court to vary or discharge this Order. If you disobey this Order you may be found guilty of Contempt of Court and may be sent to prison or fined. In the case of a Corporate Respondent, it may be fined, its Directors may be sent to prison or fined or its assets may be seized.

THE ORDER

An application was made today [*date*] by [Counsel] [Solicitors] [*or as may be*] for the Applicant to Mr Justice [ ] who heard the application. The Judge read the affidavits listed in Schedule A and accepted the undertakings set out in Schedule B at the end of this Order. As a result of the application **IT IS ORDERED** that until [[ ] ("the return date")] [or further Order of the Court]:—

1. The Respondent must not remove from England and Wales or in any way dispose of or deal with or diminish the value of any of his assets which are in England and Wales whether in his own name or not and whether solely or jointly owned up to the value of £ .
This prohibition includes the following assets in particular:—
(a) the property known as [*title/address*] or the net sale money after payment of any mortgages if it has been sold:
(b) the property and assets of the Respondent's business known as (or carried on at [*address*]) or the sale money if any of them have been sold; and
(c) any money in the account numbered [*a/c number*] at [*title/address*]

2. If the total unincumbered value of the Respondent's assets in England and Wales exceeds £ , the Respondent may remove any of those assets from England and Wales or may dispose of or deal with them so long as the total unincumbered value of his assets still in England and Wales remains above £ .

3. Exceptions to this Order:—
(1) This Order does not prohibit the Respondent from spending £ a week towards his ordinary living expenses [and £ a week towards his ordinary and proper business expenses] and also £ a week [*or* a reasonable sum] on legal advice and representation. But before spending any money the Respondent must tell the Applicant's legal representatives[7] where the money is to come from.
[(2) This Order does not prohibit the Respondent from dealing with or disposing of any of his assets in the ordinary and proper course of business.]
(3) The Respondent may agree with the Applicant's legal representatives that the above spending limits should be increased or that this Order should be varied in any other respect, but any agreement must be in writing.

[7] For the definition of legal representative see the glossary in Part 2.

(4) The Respondent may cause this Order to cease to have effect if the Respondent provides security by paying the sum of £ into Court or makes provision for security in that sum by another method agreed with the Applicant's legal representatives.

4. The Respondent must:—

(1) Inform the Applicant in writing at once of all his assets in England and Wales and whether in his own name or not and whether solely or jointly owned, giving the value, location and details of all such assets.

[The Respondent may be entitled to refuse to provide some or all of this information on the grounds that it may incriminate him. *This sentence may be inserted in cases not covered by the Theft Act 1968, s.31.*]

(2) Confirm the information in an affidavit which must be served on the Applicant's legal representatives within [ ] days after this Order has been served on the Respondent.

[**5.** *Where an Order for service by alternative means or service out of the jurisdiction has been made—*

(1) The Applicant may issue and serve a Claim Form on the Respondent at [*address*] by [*method of service*]

(2) If the Respondent wishes to defend the Claim where the Claim Form states that Particulars of Claim are to follow he must complete and return the Acknowledgment of Service within [ ] days of being served with the Claim Form. Where the Particulars of Claim are served with the Claim Form, and the Respondent wishes to defend part or all of the Claim he must complete and return an Acknowledgment of Service within [ ] days of being served with the Claim Form or a Defence within [ ] days.

GUIDANCE NOTES

Effect of this Order

(1) A Respondent who is an individual who is ordered not to do something must not do it himself or in any other way. He must not do it through others acting on his behalf or on his instructions or with his encouragement.

(2) A Respondent which is a corporation and which is ordered not to do something must not do it itself or by its directors, officers, employees or agents or in any other way.

Variation of discharge of this Order

The Respondent (or anyone notified of this Order) may apply to the Court at any time to vary or discharge this Order (or so much of it as affects that person), but anyone wishing to do so must first inform the Applicant's legal representatives.

Parties other than the Applicant and Respondent

1. Effect of this Order:—
It is a Contempt of Court for any person notified of this Order knowingly to assist in or permit a breach of this Order. Any person doing so may be sent to prison, fined or have his assets seized.

2. Set off by Banks:—
This injunction does not prevent any bank from exercising any right of set off it may have in respect of any facility which it gave to the Respondent before it was notified of this Order.

3. Withdrawals by the Respondent:—
No bank need enquire as to the application or proposed application of any money withdrawn by the Respondent if the withdrawal appears to be permitted by this Order.

Interpretation of this Order

(1) In this Order, where there is more than one Respondent, (unless otherwise stated) references to "the Respondent" means both or all of them.
(2) A requirement to serve on "the Respondent" means on each of them. However, the Order is effective against any Respondent on whom it is served.
(3) An Order requiring "the Respondent" to do or not to do anything applies to all Respondents.

Communications with the Court

All communications to the Court about this Order should be sent, where the Order is made in the Chancery Division, to [Room TM 510], Royal Courts of Justice, Strand, London WC2A 2LL quoting the case number. The telephone number is 0171 936 [6827]; and where the order is made in the Queen's Bench Division, to Room W11 (0171 936 6009). The offices are open between 10 am and 4.30 pm Monday to Friday.

Schedule A

Affidavits:—
The Applicant relied on the following affidavits:

[*name*]	[*number of affidavit*]	[*date sworn*]	[*filed on behalf of*]
(1)			
(2)			

Schedule B

Undertakings given to the Court by the Applicant:—

(1) If the Court later finds that this Order has caused loss to the Respondent, and decides that the Respondent should be compensated for that loss, the Applicant will comply with any Order the Court may make.
(2) The Applicant will on or before [*date*] cause a written guarantee in the sum of £ to be issued from a bank having a place of business within England or Wales, such guarantee being in respect of any Order the Court may make pursuant to paragraph (1) above. The Applicant will further, forthwith upon issue of the guarantee, cause a copy of it to be served on the Respondent.
(3) As soon as practicable the Applicant will [issue and serve on the Respondent a Claim form in the form of the draft produced to the Court] [serve on the Respondent the Claim Form] claiming the appropriate relief, together with this Order.
(4) The Applicant will cause an affidavit to be sworn and filed [substantially in the terms of the draft affidavit produced to the Court] [confirming the substance of what was said to the Court by the Applicant's Counsel/Solicitors].
[(5) *Where a return date has been given*—As soon as practicable the Applicant will serve on the Respondent an Application for the return date together with a copy of the affidavits and exhibits containing the evidence relied on by the Applicant.]
(6) Anyone notified of this Order will be given a copy of it by the Applicant's legal representatives.
(7) The Applicant will pay the reasonable costs of anyone other than the Respondent which have been incurred as a result of this Order including the costs of ascertaining whether that person holds any of the Respondent's assets and if the Court later finds that this Order has caused such person loss, and decides that such person should be compensated for that loss, the Applicant will comply with any Order the Court may make.
(8) If for any reason this Order ceases to have effect (including in particular where the Respondent provides security as provided for above or the Applicant does not provide a bank guarantee as provided for above), the Applicant will forthwith take all reasonable steps to inform, in writing, any

person or company to whom he has given notice of this Order, or who he has reasonable grounds for supposing may act upon this Order, that it has ceased to have effect.

Name and Address of Applicant's Legal Representatives
The Applicants Legal Representatives are:—
[Name, address, reference, fax and telephone numbers both in and out of office hours.]

25CPD–004

****Freezing Injunction** Order to restrain assets worldwide**	**IN THE [HIGH COURT OF JUSTICE] [CHANCERY DIVISION] [Strand, London WC2A 2LL]**

Before The Honourable Mr Justice [ ]

Claim No.

Dated

Applicant

Seal

Respondent

Name, address and reference of Respondent

PENAL NOTICE

IF YOU THE WITHIN NAMED [ ] DISOBEY THIS ORDER YOU MAY BE HELD TO BE IN CONTEMPT OF COURT AND LIABLE TO IMPRISONMENT OR FINED OR YOUR ASSETS SEIZED

IMPORTANT

Notice to the Respondent

You should read the terms of the Order and the Guidance Notes very carefully. You are advised to consult a Solicitor as soon as possible.

This Order prohibits you, the Respondent, from dealing with your assets up to the amount stated in the Order, but subject to any exceptions set out at the end of the Order. You have a right to ask the Court to vary or discharge this Order. If you disobey this Order you may be found guilty of Contempt of Court and may be sent to prison or fined. In the case of a Corporate Respondent, it may be fined, its Directors may be sent to prison or fined or its assets may be seized.

THE ORDER

An application was made today [*date*] by [Counsel] [Solicitors] [*or as may be*] for the Applicant to Mr Justice [ ] who heard the application. The Judge read the affidavits listed in Schedule A and accepted the undertakings set out in Schedule B at the end of this Order. As a result of the application **IT IS ORDERED** that until [[ ] ("the return date")] [further Order of the Court]:—

1. The Respondent must not:—
(1) remove from England and Wales or in any way dispose of or deal with or diminish the value of any of his assets which are in England and Wales whether in his own name or not and whether solely or jointly owned up to the value of £ or
(2) in any way dispose of or deal with or diminish the value of any of his assets whether
they are in or outside England or Wales whether in his own name or not and whether solely or jointly owned up to the same value. This prohibition includes the following assets in particular:—
(a) the property known as [*title/address*] or the net sale money after payment of any mortgages if it has been sold;
(b) the property and assets of the Respondent's business known as (or carried on at [*address*]) or the sale money if any of them have been sold; and
(c) any money in the account numbered [*a/c number*] at [*title/address*]

2. (1) If the total unincumbered value of the Respondent's assets in England and Wales exceeds £ , the Respondent may remove any of those assets from England and Wales or may dispose of or deal with them so long as the total unincumbered value of his assets still in England and Wales remains above £ .
(2) If the total unincumbered value of the Respondent's assets in England and Wales does not exceed £ , the Respondent must not remove any of those assets from England and Wales and must not dispose of or deal with any of them, but if he has other assets outside England and Wales the Respondent may dispose of or deal with those assets so long as the total unincumbered value of all his assets whether in or outside England and Wales remains above £ .

3. Exceptions to this Order:—

(1) This Order does not prohibit the Respondent from spending £ a week towards his ordinary living expenses [and £ a week towards his ordinary and proper business expenses] and also £ a week [*or* a reasonable sum] on legal advice and representation. But before spending any money the Respondent must tell the Applicant's legal representatives where the money is to come from.
[(2) This Order does not prohibit the Respondent from dealing with or disposing of any of his assets in the ordinary and proper course of business.]

(3) The Respondent may agree with the Applicant's legal representatives that the above spending limits should be increased or that this Order should be varied in any other respect, but any agreement must be in writing.
(4) The Respondent may cause this Order to cease to have effect if the Respondent provides security by paying the sum of £ into Court or makes provision for security in that sum by another method agreed with the Applicant's legal representatives.

4. The Respondent must:—
(1) Inform the Applicant in writing at once of all his assets whether in or outside England and Wales and whether in his own name or not and whether solely or jointly owned, giving the value, location and details of all such assets.
[The Respondent may be entitled to refuse to provide some or all of this information on the grounds that it may incriminate him. *This sentence may be inserted in cases not covered by the Theft Act 1968, s.31.*]
(2) Confirm the information in an affidavit which must be served on the Applicant's legal representatives within [ ] days after this Order has been served on the Respondent.

[**5.** *Where an Order for an alternative means or service out of the jurisdiction has been made:—*
(1) The Applicant may issue and serve a Claim Form on the Respondent at [*address*] by [*method of service*]
(2) If the Respondent wishes to defend the Claim he must complete and return the Notice of Intention to Defend within [ ] days of being served with the Claim Form.]

GUIDANCE NOTES

Effect of this Order

(1) A Respondent who is an individual who is ordered not to do something must not do it himself or in any other way. He must not do it through others acting on his behalf or on his instructions or with his encouragement.
(2) A Respondent which is a corporation and which is ordered not to do something must not do it itself or by its directors, officers, employees or agents or in any other way.

Variation or discharge of this Order

The Respondent (or anyone notified of this Order) may apply to the Court at any time to vary or discharge this Order (or so much of it as affects that person), but anyone wishing to do so must inform the Applicant's legal representatives.

Parties other than the Applicant and Respondent

1. Effect of this Order:—
It is a Contempt of Court for any person notified of this Order knowingly to assist in or permit a breach of this Order. Any person doing so may be sent to prison, fined or have his assets seized.

2. Effect of this Order outside England and Wales:—
The terms of this Order do not affect or concern anyone outside the jurisdiction of this Court until it is declared enforceable by or is enforced by a Court in the relevant country and then they are to affect him only to the extent they have been declared enforceable or have been enforced **UNLESS** the person is:
(i) a person to whom this Order is addressed or an officer or an agent appointed by power of attorney of that person; or
(ii) a person who is subject to the jurisdiction of this Court and (a) has been given written notice of this Order at his residence or place of business within the jurisdiction of this Court and (b) is able to prevent acts or omissions outside the jurisdiction of this Court which constitute or assist in a breach of the terms of this Order.

3. Set off by Banks:—
This injunction does not prevent any bank from exercising any right of set off it may have in respect of any facility which it gave to the Respondent before it was notified of this Order.

4. Withdrawals by the Respondent:—
No bank need enquire as to the application or proposed application of any money withdrawn by the Respondent if the withdrawal appears to be permitted by this Order.

Interpretation of this Order

(1) In this Order, where there is more than one Respondent, (unless otherwise stated) references to "the Respondent" means both or all of them.
(2) A requirement to serve on "the Respondent" means on each of them. However, the Order is effective against any Respondent on whom it is served.

(3) An Order requiring "the Respondent" to do or not to do anything applies to all Respondents.

Communications with the Court

All communications to the Court about this Order should be sent, where the Order is made in the Chancery Division, to [Room TM 510], Royal Courts of Justice, Strand, London WC2A 2LL quoting the case number. The telephone number is 0171 936 [6827]; and where the order is made in the Queen's Bench Division, to Room W11 (0171 936 6009). The offices are open between 10 am and 4.30 pm Monday to Friday.

Schedule A

Affidavits:—
The Applicant relied on the following affidavits:

[*name*]	[*number of affidavit*]	[*date sworn*]	[*filed on behalf of*]
(1)			
(2)			

Schedule B

Undertakings given to the Court by the Applicant:—

(1) If the Court later finds that this Order has caused loss to the Respondent, and decides that the Respondent should be compensated for that loss, the Applicant will comply with any Order the Court may make.

(2) The Applicant will on or before [*date*] cause a written guarantee in the sum of £ to be issued from a bank having a place of business within England or Wales, such guarantee being in respect of any Order the Court may make pursuant to paragraph (1) above. The Applicant will further, forthwith upon issue of the guarantee, cause a copy of it to be served on the Respondent.

[(3) As soon as practicable the Applicant will [issue and serve on the Respondent a Claim Form in the form of the draft produced to the Court] [serve on the Respondent the Claim Form] claiming the appropriate relief, together with this Order.]

(4) The Applicant will cause an affidavit to be sworn and filed [substantially in the terms of the draft affidavit produced to the Court] [confirming the substance of what was said to the Court by the Applicant's Counsel/Solicitors].

[(5) *Where a return date has been given*— As soon as practicable the Applicant will serve on the Respondent an application for the return date together with a copy of the affidavits and exhibits containing the evidence relied on by the Applicant.]

(6) Anyone notified of this Order will be given a copy of it by the Applicant's legal representatives.

(7) The Applicant will pay the reasonable costs of anyone other than the Respondent which have been incurred as a result of this Order including the costs of ascertaining whether that person holds any of the Respondent's assets and if the Court later finds that this Order has caused such person loss, and decides that such person should be compensated for that loss, the Applicant will comply with any Order the Court may make.

(8) If for any reason this Order ceases to have effect (including in particular where the Respondent provides security as provided for above or the Applicant does not provide a bank guarantee as provided for above), the Applicant will forthwith take all reasonable steps to inform, in writing, any person or company to whom he has given notice of this Order, or who he has reasonable grounds for supposing may act upon this Order, that it has ceased to have effect.

[(9) The Applicant will not without the leave of the Court begin proceedings against the Respondent in any other jurisdiction or use information obtained as a result of an Order of the Court in this jurisdiction for the purpose of civil or criminal proceedings in any other jurisdiction.]

[(10) The Applicant will not without the leave of the Court seek to enforce this Order in any country outside England and Wales [or seek an Order of a similar nature including Orders conferring a charge or other security against the Respondent or the Respondent's assets].]

Name and Address of Applicant's Legal Representatives

The Applicants Legal Representatives are:—

[Name, address, reference, fax and telephone numbers both in and out of office hours.]

25CPD–005

**** Search Order ****
Order to preserve evidence and property

IN THE [HIGH COURT OF JUSTICE]
[CHANCERY DIVISON]
[Strand, London WC2A 2LL]

Before The Honourable Mr Justice [ ]

Claim No.

Dated

Applicant

Seal

Respondent

Name, address and reference of Respondent

PENAL NOTICE

IF YOU THE WITHIN NAMED [ ] DISOBEY THIS ORDER YOU MAY BE HELD TO BE IN CONTEMPT OF COURT AND LIABLE TO IMPRISONMENT OR FINED OR YOUR ASSETS SEIZED

IMPORTANT
Notice to the Respondent

You should read the terms of the Order and the Guidance Notes very carefully. You are advised to consult a Solicitor as soon as possible.
This Order orders you, the Respondent, to allow the persons mentioned in the Order to enter the premises described in the Order and to search for, examine and remove or copy the articles specified in the Order. The persons so named will have no right to enter the premises or, having entered, to remain at the premises, unless you give your consent to their doing so. If, however, you withhold your consent you will be in breach of this Order and may be held to be in Contempt of Court.
The Order also requires you to hand over any of such articles which are under your control and to provide information to the Applicant's Solicitors, and prohibits you from doing certain acts.
If you, the Respondent, disobey this Order you may be found guilty of contempt of Court and may be sent to prison or fined. In the case of a Corporate respondent, it may be fined, its Directors may be sent to prison or fined or its assets may be seized.

THE ORDER

AN APPLICATION was made today [*date*] by [Counsel] [Solicitors] for the Applicant to Mr Justice [ ] who heard the application. The Judge read the affidavits listed in Schedule F at the end of this Order and accepted the undertakings by the Applicant, the Applicants's Solicitors and the Supervising Solicitor set forth in the Schedules at the end of this Order. As a result of the application **IT IS ORDERED** that until [[ ] ("the return date")] [or further Order of the Court]:—

1. (1) The Respondent must allow Mr/Mrs/Miss [ ] ("the Supervising Solicitor"), together with Mr [ ] a Solicitor of the Supreme Court, and a partner in the firm of [ ] the Applicant's Solicitors and up to [ ] other persons being [*their capacity*] accompanying them, to enter the premises mentioned in Schedule A to this Order and any other premises of the Respondent disclosed under paragraph 4(1) below and any vehicles under the Respondent's control on or around the premises so that they can search for, inspect, photograph or photocopy, and deliver into the safekeeping of the Applicant's Solicitors all the documents and articles which are listed in Schedule B to this Order ("the listed items") or which Mr [ ] believes to be listed items.
(2) The Respondent must allow those persons to remain on the premises until the search is complete, and to re-enter the premises on the same or the following day in order to complete the search.

2. (1) No item may be removed from the premises until a list of the items to be removed has been prepared, and a copy of the list has been supplied to the person served with the Order, and he has been given a reasonable opportunity to check the list.

(2) The premises must not be searched, and items must not be removed from them, except in the presence of the Respondent or a person appearing to be a responsible employee of the Respondent or in control of the premises.

(3) If the Supervising Solicitor is satisfied that full compliance with paragraph 2(1) or (2) above is impracticable, he may permit the search to proceed and items to be removed without compliance with the impracticable requirements.

3. (1) The Respondent must immediately hand over to the Applicant's Solicitors any of the listed items which are in his possession or under his control save for any computer or hard disk integral to any computer.

(2) If any of the listed items exists only in computer readable form, the Respondent must immediately give the Applicant's Solicitors effective access to the computers, with all necessary passwords, to enable them to be searched, and cause the listed items to be printed out. A print-out of the items must be given to the Applicant's Solicitors or displayed on the computer screen so that they can be read and copied. All reasonable steps shall be taken by the Applicant to ensure that no damage is done to any computer or data. The Applicant and his representatives may not themselves search the Respondent's computers unless they have sufficient expertise to do so without damaging the Respondent's system.

4. (1) The Respondent must immediately inform the Applicant's Solicitors:—
(a) where all the listed items are; and
(b) so far as he is aware:—
(i) the name and address of everyone who has supplied him, or offered to supply him, with listed items,
(ii) the name and address of everyone to whom he has supplied, or offered to supply, listed items, and
(iii) full details of the dates and quantities of every such supply and offer.

(2) Within [ ] days after being served with this Order the Respondent must swear an affidavit setting out the above information.

5. (1) Except for the purpose of obtaining legal advice, the Respondent or anyone else with knowledge of this Order must not directly or indirectly inform anyone of these proceedings or of the contents of this Order, or warn anyone that proceedings have been or may be brought against him by the Applicant until [[ ] the return date] [or further Order of the Court].

(2) The Respondent must not destroy, tamper with, cancel or part with possession, power, custody or control of the listed items otherwise than in accordance with the terms of this Order.

(3) [*Insert any negative injunctions.*]

[**6.** *Insert any further order.*]

GUIDANCE NOTES

Effect of this Order

(1) A Respondent who is an individual who is ordered not to do something must not do it himself or in any other way. He must not do it through others acting on his behalf or on his instructions or with his encouragement.
(2) A Respondent which is a corporation and which is ordered not to do something must not do it itself or by its directors officers employees or agents or in any other way.
(3) This Order must be complied with either by the Respondent himself or by an employee of the Respondent or other person appearing to be in control of the premises and having authority to permit the premises to be entered and the search to proceed.
(4) This Order requires the Respondent or his employee or other person appearing to be in control of the premises and having that authority to permit entry to the premises immediately the Order is served upon him, except as stated in paragraph six below.

Respondent's Entitlements

(1) Before you the Respondent or the person appearing to be in control of the premises allow anybody onto the premises to carry out this Order you are entitled to have the solicitor who serves you with this Order explain to you what it means in everyday language.
(2) You are entitled to insist that there is nobody [or nobody except Mr] present who could gain commercially from anything he might read or see on your premises.
(3) You are entitled to refuse to permit entry before 9.30 am or after 5.30 pm or at all on Saturday and Sunday unless the Court has ordered otherwise.
(4) Except in certain cases, you may be entitled to refuse to permit disclosure of any documents which may incriminate you ("incriminating documents") or to answer any questions if to do so may incriminate you. It may be prudent to take advice, because if you so refuse, your refusal may be taken into account by the Court at a later stage.
(5) You are entitled to refuse to permit disclosure of any documents passing between you and your Solicitors or Patent or Trade Mark Agents for the purpose of obtaining advice ("privileged documents").
(6) You are entitled to seek legal advice, and to ask the Court to vary or discharge this Order, provided you do so at once, and provided you do not disturb or move anything in the interim and that meanwhile you permit the Supervising Solicitor (who is a Solicitor acting independently of the Applicant) to enter, but not start to search.
(7) Before permitting entry to the premises by any person other than the Supervising Solicitor, you (or any other person appearing to be in control of the premises) may gather together any documents you believe may be [incriminating or] privileged and hand them to the Supervising Solicitor for the Supervising Solicitor to assess whether they are [incriminating or] privileged as claimed. If the Supervising Solicitor concludes that any of the documents may be [incriminating or] privileged documents or if there is any doubt as to their status the Supervising Solicitor shall exclude them from the search and shall retain the documents of doubtful status in his possession pending further order of the Court. While this is being done, you may refuse entry to the premises by any other person, and may refuse to permit the search to begin, for a short time (not to exceed two hours, unless the Supervising Solicitor agrees to a longer period). If you wish to take legal advice and gather documents as permitted, you must first inform the Supervising Solicitor and keep him informed of the steps being taken.

Restrictions on Service

Paragraph 1 of the Order is subject to the following restrictions:—
(1) This Order may only be served between 9.30 am and 5.30 pm on a weekday unless the Court has ordered otherwise.
(2) This Order may not be carried out at the same time as a police search warrant.
(3) This Order must be served by the Supervising Solicitor, and paragraph 1 of the Order must be carried out in his presence and under his supervision. Where the premises are likely to be occupied by an unaccompanied woman and the Supervising Solicitor is a man, at least one of the persons accompanying him as provided by paragraph 1 of the Order shall be a woman.
(4) This Order does not require the person served with the Order to allow anyone [or anyone except Mr] to enter the premises who in the view of the Supervising Solicitor could gain commercially from anything he might read or see on the premises if the person served with the Order objects.

Variation or Discharge of this Order

The Respondent (or anyone notified of this Order) may apply to the Court at any time to vary or discharge this Order (or so much of it as affects that person), but anyone wishing to do so must first inform the Applicant's Solicitors.

Interpretation of this Order

(1) In this Order, where there is more than one Respondent, references to "the Respondent" means both or all of them.
(2) A requirement to serve on "the Respondent" means on each of them. However, the Order is effective against any Respondent on whom it is served.
(3) An Order requiring "the Respondent" to do or not to do anything applies to all Respondents.
(4) Any other requirement that something shall be done to or in the presence of "the Respondent" means to or in the presence of any one of them or in the case of a firm or company a director or a person appearing to the Supervising Solicitor to be a responsible employee.

Communications with the Court

All communications to the Court about this Order should be sent, where the Order is made in the Chancery Division, to [Room TM 510], Royal Courts of Justice, Strand, London WC2A 2LL quoting the case number. The telephone number if 0171 936 [6827]; and where the order is made in the Queen's Bench Division, to Room W11 (0171 936 6009). The offices are open between 10 am and 4.30 pm Monday to Friday.

Schedule A

The premises

Schedule B

The listed items

Schedule C

Undertakings given by the Applicant:—

(1) If the Court later finds that this Order or carrying it out has caused loss to the Respondent, and decides that the Respondent should be compensated for that loss, the Applicant will comply with any Order the Court may make. Further, if the carrying out of this Order has been in breach of the terms of this Order or otherwise in a manner inconsistent with the Applicant's Solicitors' duties as Officers of the Court the Applicant will comply with any order for damages the Court may make.
[(2) As soon as practicable to issue a Claim Form [in the form of the draft produced to the Court] [claiming appropriate relief.]]
[(3) To [swear and file an affidavit] [cause an affidavit to be sworn and filed] [substantially in the terms of the draft produced to the Court] [confirming the substance of what was said to the Court by the Applicant's Counsel/Solicitors].]
(4) To serve on the Respondent at the same time as this Order is served upon him,

(i) the Claim Form, or if not issued, the draft produced to the Court,
(ii) an Application for hearing on [*date*],
(iii) copies of the affidavits [or draft affidavits] and exhibits capable of being copied containing the evidence relied on by the Applicant. [Copies of the confidential exhibits need not be served, but they must be made available for inspection by or on behalf of the Respondent in the presence of the

Applicant's Solicitors while the Order is carried out. Afterwards they must be provided to a Solicitor representing the Respondent who gives a written undertaking not to permit the Respondent to see them or copies of them except in his presence and not to permit the Respondent to make or take away any note or record of the exhibits.], and

(iv) a note of any allegation of fact made orally to the Judge where such allegation is not contained in the affidavits or draft affidavits read by the Judge.

(5) To serve on the Respondent a copy of the Supervising Solicitor's report on the carrying out of this Order as soon as it is received.

(6) Not, without the leave of the Court, to use any information or documents obtained as a result of carrying out this Order nor to inform anyone else of these proceedings except for the purposes of these proceedings (including adding further Respondents) or commencing civil proceedings in relation to the same or related subject matter to these proceedings until after the return date.

[(7) To maintain pending further order the sum of £ in an account controlled by the Applicant's Solicitors.]

[(8) To insure the items removed from the premises.]

Schedule D

Undertakings given by the Applicant's Solicitors:—

(1) To answer at once to the best of their ability any question whether a particular item is a listed item.

(2) To return the originals of all documents obtained as a result of this Order (except original documents which belong to the Applicant) as soon as possible and in any event within two working days of their removal.

(3) While ownership of any item obtained as a result of this Order is in dispute, to deliver the article into the keeping of Solicitors acting for the Respondent within two working days from receiving a written undertaking by them to retain the article in safe keeping and to produce it to the Court when required.

(4) To retain in their own safe keeping all other items obtained as a result of this Order until the Court directs otherwise.

Schedule E

Undertakings given by the Supervising Solicitor:—

(1) To offer to explain to the person served with the Order its meaning and effect fairly and in everyday language, and to inform him of his right to seek legal advice (such advice to include an explanation that the Respondent may be entitled to avail himself of [the privilege against self-incrimination or] [legal professional privilege]) and apply to vary or discharge the Order as mentioned in the Respondent's Entitlements above.

(2) To make and provide to the Applicant's Solicitors and to the Judge who made this Order (for the purposes of the Court file) a written report on the carrying out of the Order.

Schedule F

Affidavits:—

The Applicant relied on the following affidavits:—

[*name*] [*number of affidavit*] [*date sworn*] [*filed on behalf of*]

Name and Address of Applicant's Solicitors

The Applicant's Solicitors are:—

[Name, address, reference, fax and telephone numbers both in and out of office hours.]

PART 26

Case Management—Preliminary Stage

Contents 26.0.1

Editorial Introduction

The preliminary stage of case management is mainly concerned with the allocation of a defended claim to the appropriate track. There is no "automatic" allocation; each case requires a judicial decision. However, the general rule for allocation is in r.26.7. Note in particular that the court will not allocate a claim to a "lower" track unless all the parties consent (r.26.7(3)). 26.0.2

The court will allocate a defended claim to one of three tracks: the small claims track, the fast track or the multi-track. These tracks are dealt with, respectively, in Pts 27, 28 and 29 and each of those Parts contains rules about case management and conduct of the claim following allocation. The aim is to ensure that each case is dealt with proportionately to its size and complexity.

Rule 26.6 sets out the normal scope of each track. The court will normally send an "allocation questionnaire" to each party on the filing of a defence. The claim will be allocated when the questionnaires have been filed or when the period for filing has expired (see r.26.5). The court will normally deal with allocation on the basis of the information provided but can, if necessary, hold an "allocation hearing" (r.26.5(4)).

Allocation to the correct track is the main, but not the only, function at this preliminary stage of case management. The court will also consider striking out a statement of case (see r.3.4), summary judgment (see r.24.4) and whether to give case management directions pursuant to Pt 27, 28 or 29 as appropriate.

Related Sources

- Practice Direction—Case Management—Preliminary Stage: Allocation and Re-Allocation—para. 26PD–001 26.0.3
- Part 1 (The Overriding Objective)
- Part 3 (The Court's Case Management Powers)
- Part 24 (Summary Judgment)
- Part 27 (The Small Claims Track)
- Part 28 (The Fast Track)
- Part 29 (The Multi-Track)
- Part 30 (Transfer)
- Part 31 (Disclosure and Inspection of Documents)
- Part 32 (Evidence)
- The County Court Fees Order 1999

Forms

- N150—Allocation questionnaire (see para. C25–001) 26.0.4
- N153—Notice of allocation or listing hearing (see para. C27–001)
- N154—Notice of allocation to fast track (see para. C28–001)
- N155—Notice of allocation to multi-track (see para. C29–001)
- N157—Notice of allocation to small claims track (see para. C31–001)
- N158—Notice of allocation to small claims track (preliminary hearing) (see para. C32–001)
- N159—Notice of allocation to small claims track (no hearing) (see para. C33–001)
- N160—Notice of allocation to small claims track (with parties' consent) (see para. C34–001)
- N151—Allocation questionnaire (amount to be decided by court)
- N151A—Master/DJ's directions on allocation

- N152—Notice that [defence] [counterclaim] has been filed (Pt 26 PD2.5)
- N156—Order for further information (for allocation) (Pt 26 PD4.2(2))

Practice Direction

26.0.5 Part 26 is supplemented by a Practice Direction. See para. 26PD–001.

Scope of this Part

26.1 **26.1**—(1) This Part provides for—

(a) the automatic transfer of some defended cases between courts; and

(b) the allocation of defended cases to case management tracks.

(2) There are three tracks—

(a) the small claims track;

(b) the fast track; and

(c) the multi-track.

(Rule 26.6 sets out the normal scope of each track. Part 27 makes provision for the small claims track. Part 28 makes provision for the fast track. Part 29 makes provision for the multi-track.)

26.1.1 **Effect of rule**—The automatic transfer provision of r.26.1(1) and r.26.2 is a modified version of CCR, O.1, r.13 (which had no direct equivalent in the RSC). Transfer on application of a party is governed by Pt 30.

Rule 26.1(2) creates the three tracks which are a fundamental feature of the new rules. Each track is also governed by its own Part and practice direction.

26.1.2 **The small claims track**—See too PD to Pt 26, para. 8.

26.1.3 **The fast track**—See too PD to Pt 26, para. 9.

26.1.4 **The multi track**—See too PD to Pt 26, para. 10.

Automatic transfer

26.2 **26.2**—(1) This rule applies to proceedings where—

(a) the claim is for a specified amount of money;

(b) the claim was commenced in a court which is not the defendant's home court;

(c) the claim has not been transferred to another defendant's home court under rule 13.4 (application to set aside[GL] or vary default judgment—procedure) or rule 14.12 (admission—determination of rate of payment by judge); and

(d) the defendant is an individual.

(2) This rule does not apply where the claim was commenced in a specialist list[GL].

(3) Where this rule applies, the court will transfer the proceedings to the defendant's home court when a defence is filed, unless paragraph (4) applies.

(Rule 2.3 defines "defendant's home court".)

(4) Where the claimant notifies the court under rule 15.10 and rule 14.5 that he wishes the proceedings to continue, the court will transfer the proceedings to the defendant's home court when it receives that notification from the claimant.

(Rule 15.10 deals with a claimant's notice where the defence is that money claimed has been paid.)

(Rule 14.5 sets out the procedure where the defendant admits part of a claim for a specified amount of money.)

(5) Where—

(a) the claim is against two or more defendants with different home courts; and

(b) the defendant whose defence is filed first is an individual,

proceedings are to be transferred under this rule to the home court of that defendant.

(6) The time when a claim is automatically transferred under this rule may be varied by a practice direction in respect of claims issued by the Production Centre.

(Rule 7.10 makes provision for the Production Centre.)

Effect of rule—It has always been a feature of the county court system that justice should be "local". This is now of general application. However, "local" means local to the defendant rather than the claimant. Automatic transfer applies only when the defendant is an "individual" (r.26.2(1)(d)) not, for example, a limited company. 26.2.1

This rule deals sensibly with automatic transfer as a preliminary case management issue. It is a self-contained code for automatic transfer and gathers in one place rules previously scattered through the CCR (CCR, O.1, r.13; CCR, O.9, r.2(8); CCR, O.22, r.10(4); CCR, O.37, r.4(2)). Any application by either party to transfer to a more convenient court must be made to the defendant's home court after automatic transfer there. Transfer on the application of a party is governed by Pt 30.

Specialist list—See Pt 49. 26.2.2

Allocation questionnaire

26.3—(1) When a defendant files a defence the court will serve an allocation questionnaire on each party unless— 26.3

(a) rule 15.10 or rule 14.5 applies; or

(b) the court dispenses with the need for a questionnaire.

(2) Where there are two or more defendants and at least one of them files a defence, the court will serve the allocation questionnaire under paragraph (1)—

(a) when all the defendants have filed a defence; or

(b) when the period for the filing of the last defence has expired,

whichever is the sooner.

(Rule 15.4 specifies the period for filing a defence.)

(3) Where proceedings are automatically transferred to the defendant's home court under rule 26.2, the court in which the proceedings have been commenced will serve an allocation questionnaire before the proceedings are transferred.

(4) Where—

(a) rule 15.10 or rule 14.5 applies; and

(b) the proceedings are not automatically transferred to the defendant's home court under rule 26.2,

the court will serve an allocation questionnaire on each party when the claimant files a notice indicating that he wishes the proceedings to continue.

(5) The court may, on the application of the claimant, serve an allocation questionnaire earlier than it would otherwise serve it under this rule.

(6) Each party must file the completed allocation questionnaire no later than the date specified in it, which shall be at least 14 days after the date when it is deemed to be served on the party in question.

(7) The time when the court serves an allocation questionnaire under this rule may be varied by a practice direction in respect of claims issued by the Production Centre.

(Rule 7.10 makes provision for the Production Centre.)

(Rule 6.7 specifies when a document is deemed to be served.)

Effect of rule—Allocation of defended cases to the appropriate track is a crucial preliminary case management issue. Allocation is not automatic; an "allocation questionnaire" is sent by the court to each party. Parties are required to file (not serve) the allocation questionnaire; the court will serve a copy of the other party's allocation questionnaire with the allocation decision under r.26.9. The Practice Direction which supplements Pt 26 (see para 26PD–001) encourages consultation and exchange of information between the parties. 26.3.1

Allocation Questionnaire—See Form NI50 (see para. C25–001). The court will send copies of completed allocation questionnaires to other parties on allocation—see r.26.9(2). 26.3.2

26.3.3 **Each party must file the completed questionnaire no later than the date specified**—For the court's powers and approach if any party fails to return an allocation questionnaire, see r.26.5(5) and PD to Pt 26, paras 2.5 and 6.6.

A fee of £80 is payable by a claimant filing an allocation questionnaire or where the court dispenses with the need for an allocation questionnaire, unless the case is proceeding on a counterclaim alone in which case the fee is payable by the defendant. (The County Court Fees Order, Sched. 1, para. 2.1). If a claimant fails to pay the fee, the court may send out a notice requiring payment (Form N173). If after receipt of the notice the claimant does not pay the fee or make an application for exemption, the claim shall be struck out and the claimant shall be liable for the costs of the defendant (r.3.7).

26.3.4 **Estimate of costs**—Note that para. 4.5(1) to the Costs PD requires parties to file estimates of costs already incurred and likely to be incurred with completed allocation questionnaires. See too question I to Form N150.

26.3.5 **The court dispenses with the need for a questionnaire**—See *e.g.* PD to Pt 26, para. 2.4(1).

26.3.6 **Pre-Action Protocols**—When completing allocation questionnaires parties must state whether a pre-action protocol applies and, if there has been less than complete compliance with it, give an explanation. This should be taken into account when case management directions are given and may be relevant to the question of costs. (See PD to Pre Action Potocols paras 2.1 and 2.3.)

26.3.7 **Summary judgment**—When completing allocation questionnaires parties should state whether they intend to apply for summary judgment or make any other application. (See question D.)

26.3.8 **Agree case management directions**—When consulting each other about allocation questionnaires, parties should attempt to agree case management directions and invite the court to make them (PD to Pt 26, para. 2.3(2). See too r.1.4(2)(a)).

Stay to allow for settlement of the case

26.4 **26.4**—(1) A party may, when filing the completed allocation questionnaire, make a written request for the proceedings to be stayed[GL] while the parties try to settle the case by alternative dispute resolution[GL] or other means.

(2) Where—

(a) all parties request a stay[GL] under paragraph (1); or

(b) the court, of its own initiative, considers that such a stay would be appropriate,

the court will direct that the proceedings be stayed for one month.

(3) The court may extend the stay[GL] until such date or for such specified period as it considers appropriate.

(4) Where the court stays[GL] the proceedings under this rule, the claimant must tell the court if a settlement is reached.

(5) If the claimant does not tell the court by the end of the period of the stay[GL] that a settlement has been reached, the court will give such directions as to the management of the case as it considers appropriate.

26.4.1 **Effect of rule**—The new rules aim to encourage parties to settle a dispute without a judicial decision if possible (see *e.g.* r.1.4(2)(f)). Rule 26.4 is an example of this. Stay is, in effect, automatic under r.26.4(2) and the short stay of one month can be extended by judicial decision under r.26.4(3). Any stay must be seen in the context of case management: it is not possible for a case to "go to sleep" or evade case management. The onus is on the claimant to tell the court if a settlement is reached (r.26.4(4)) and if he does not do so the court will give directions under r.26.4(5). If an action is stayed, any interim injunction is automatically set aside unless the court orders that it should continue—see r.25.10.

Allocation

26.5 **26.5**—(1) The court will allocate the claim to a track—

(a) when every defendant has filed an allocation questionnaire, or

(b) when the period for filing the allocation questionnaires has expired,

whichever is the sooner, unless it has—

(i) stayed[GL] the proceedings under rule 26.4; or

(ii) dispensed with the need for allocation questionnaires.

(Rules 12.7 and 14.8 provide for the court to allocate a claim to a track where the claimant obtains default judgment on request or judgment on admission for an amount to be decided by the court.)

(2) If the court has stayed[GL] the proceedings under rule 26.4, it will allocate the claim to a track at the end of the period of the stay.

(3) Before deciding the track to which to allocate proceedings or deciding whether to give directions for an allocation hearing to be fixed, the court may order a party to provide further information about his case.

(4) The court may hold an allocation hearing if it thinks it is necessary.

(5) If a party fails to file an allocation questionnaire, the court may give any direction it considers appropriate.

Effect of rule—Allocation will be by the Master or district judge on the filing of the allocation questionnaires or when time for filing them has expired. It is envisaged that most cases will be allocated on the basis of the "statements of case" (pleadings) and the information given in the questionnaires. However, there is provision in r.26.5(3) for the court to order a party to provide further information (see Form N156 and PD to Pt 26, paras 2.2 and 4.2). If necessary the court will hold an "allocation hearing" (r.26.5(4)) which would be held within a matter of a few days. An allocation hearing would be necessary, for example, if the court were minded to seek the consent of the parties under r.26.7(3) to allocation to the fast track of a claim which is financially within the multi-track. Generally, however, allocation will be on paper by the court and allocation hearings are expected to be rare. **26.5.1**

Allocation hearing—See PD to Pt 26 para. 6. A court will only hold an allocation hearing on its own initiative if it considers it necessary to do so. A legal representative who attends an allocation hearing should be the person responsible for the case or must be familiar with it and must have sufficient authority to deal with any issues likely to arise. At least seven days notice of such a hearing should be given (see PD to Pt 26, para. 6.2(1)). **26.5.2**

Scope of each track

26.6—(1) The small claims track is the normal track for— **26.6**

(a) any claim for personal injuries where—

(i) the financial value of the claim is not more than £5,000; and

(ii) the financial value of any claim for damages for personal injuries is not more than £1,000;

(b) any claim which includes a claim by a tenant of residential premises against his landlord where—

(i) the tenant is seeking an order requiring the landlord to carry out repairs or other work to the premises (whether or not the tenant is also seeking some other remedy);

(ii) the cost of the repairs or other work to the premises is estimated to be not more than £1,000; and

(iii) the financial value of any other claim for damages is not more than £1,000.

(Rule 2.3 defines "claim for personal injuries" as proceedings in which there is a claim for damages in respect of personal injuries to the claimant or any other person or in respect of a person's death.)

(2) For the purposes of paragraph (1) "damages for personal injuries" means damages claimed as compensation for pain, suffering and loss of amenity and does not include any other damages which are claimed.

(3) Subject to paragraph (1), the small claims track is the normal track for any claim which has a financial value of not more than £5,000.

(Rule 26.7(4) provides that the court will not allocate to the small claims track certain claims in respect of harassment or unlawful eviction.)

(4) Subject to paragraph (5), the fast track is the normal track for any claim—

(a) for which the small claims track is not the normal track; and
(b) which has a financial value of not more than £15,000.

(5) The fast track is the normal track for the claims referred to in paragraph (4) only if the court considers that—

(a) the trial is likely to last for no longer than one day; and
(b) oral expert evidence at trial will be limited to—
(i) one expert per party in relation to any expert field; and
(ii) expert evidence in two expert fields.

(6) The multi-track is the normal track for any claim for which the small claims track or the fast track is not the normal track.

26.6.1 **Effect of rule**—The three tracks, which are the essence of the CPR, are defined by r.26.6. The rule starts at the bottom by defining the small claims track (generally, claims valued at not more than £5,000 and personal injury claims valued at not more than £1,000: see r.26.6(1)), then the fast track (claims not on the small claims track valued at not more than £15,000: see r.26.6(4)) and finally the multi-track (any claim not on the small claims track or the fast track: see r.26.6(6)).

26.6.2 **Personal injuries**—Note the definition of "claim for personal injuries" in r.2.3 and the restrictive meaning given to "damages for personal injuries" in r.26.6(2) ("damages claimed as compensation for pain, suffering and loss of amenity. . ."). For example, a claim for £4,000 for loss of earnings and other losses plus a claim for £800 for damages for pain and suffering is a claim which would be allocated to the small claims track (see r.26.6(1)(a)).

26.6.3 **Claim by a tenant of residential premises**—If proceedings include a claim requiring the landlord to carry out works or other repairs, the claim form must state whether the cost of repairs is estimated to be more than £1,000 and whether or not the claimant expects to recover more than £1,000 in respect of any claim for damages (CPR 16.3(4) and PD to Pt 7, para. 3.9).

Irrespective of their value, harassment and unlawful eviction claims must be allocated either to the fast track or multi-track. (See r.26.7(4) and the note to CPR 27.1(2).)

The position relating to disrepair cases is less straightforward. If there is simply an action for damages for breach of repairing obligations, with no claim for an order requiring works to be carried out, the case will be allocated to the small claims track unless

(1) the financial value of the claim is £5,000 or more, *or*
(2) the financial value of any claim for personal injuries is £1,000 or more (see CPR Pt 26.6(1)(a)(ii), *or*
(3) there are abnormal circumstances.

The case will be allocated to fast track if the financial value of the case is £5,000 or more or to multi track if the financial value is £15,000 or more. A claim for damages for disrepair (without a claim for specific performance) may be allocated to the fast track if there are abnormal factors—*e.g.* the likely complexity of the facts, law or evidence, the number of parties, the amount of oral evidence or the importance to persons who are not parties to the proceedings. (See CPR, Pt 26.8 which sets out matters relevant to allocation to track and which states that it is for the court to assess the financial value of a claim.)

If there is a claim for both damages and an order for works to be carried out, the case will *not* be allocated to the small claims track if *either* the cost of works *or* the damages claim is more than £1,000. In such circumstances the case will be allocated to the fast track, unless the financial value of the claim is more than £15,000. Claims for both damages and an order for works to be carried out will only be allocated to the small claims track if the cost of work is less than £1,000 *and* the claim for damages is less than £1,000. This interpretation is borne out by PD to Pt 7, para. 3.9 (see above) and the note to CPR Pt 27.1(2).

There is no pre-action protocol for disrepair claims, but see para. 4 of the PD to the Pre Action Protocols.

26.6.4 *Other landlord and tenant disputes*—The PD to Pt 26, para. 8.1(2)(c) states that "most disputes between a landlord and a tenant other than those for possession" are suitable for the small claims track. This does not however apply to cases "involving a disputed allegation of dishonesty" (PD to Pt 26, para. 8.1(2)(d)), or to possession proceedings (see below).

There is a particular form of Standard Directions for use in small claims track cases where tenants are suing for the return of deposits or where landlords are suing for damage caused by tenants—see PD to Pt 27 Appendix A, Form D.

26.6.5 **Small claims track**—Allocation to the small claims track has replaced "reference to arbitration" under former CCR, O.19. Subject to r.26.6(1) the small claims track is the normal track for any claim which has a financial value of not more than £5,000. Unlike the fast track there is no envisaged maximum length of trial (compare r.26.6(5)(a)). This is unlikely to matter in practice. District judges are already experienced in estimating the length of small claims hearings. The fast track, in contrast, is a new concept and it is necessary for the rules to be more specific.

See also Pt 27 and its related Practice Direction (see para. 27PD–001).

Fast track—Basically, the fast track is the normal track for claims valued between £5,000 and £15,000. The fast track is undoubtedly one of the main innovations of the CPR. See also Pt 28 and its related Practice Direction. Part 26.6(5) is silent as to what will happen when it appears that the trial will last longer than one day and/or extensive expert evidence is required. The court could allocate the case to the multi-track. However, before doing this the court will consider whether it is more appropriate to order a split trial so that, for example, the issue of liability is tried first. Having regard to the "overriding objective" in Pt 1 it is likely that "split trial" will be the rule rather than the exception in fast track cases, and certainly split trial must be anticipated in a fast track case which would not otherwise conclude in one day. **26.6.6**

Note the limitation on expert evidence in r.26.6(5).

Multi-track—The multi-track is the normal track for any claim not allocated to the small claims track or the fast track. See also Pt 29 and its related Practice Direction (para. 29PD–001). **26.6.7**

Claims on the small claims or fast track will be in a county court. Claims on the multi-track will be in either a county court or the High Court. Apart from cases in a "specialist list", this makes no difference: the main purpose of the CPR is to repeal and replace both the RSC and CCR with a common code.

General rule for allocation

26.7—(1) In considering whether to allocate a claim to the normal track for that claim under rule 26.6, the court will have regard to the matters mentioned in rule 26.8(1). **26.7**

(2) The court will allocate a claim which has no financial value to the track which it considers most suitable having regard to the matters mentioned in rule 26.8(1).

(3) The court will not allocate a claim to a track if the financial value of the claim, assessed by the court under rule 26.8, exceeds the limit for that track unless all the parties consent to the allocation of the claim to that track.

(4) The court will not allocate a claim to the small claims track, if it includes a claim by a tenant of residential premises against his landlord for a remedy in respect of harassment or unlawful eviction.

Effect of rule—This short "general rule for allocation" is self-explanatory. Note that r.26.7(3) prevents the court allocating a claim to a lower track (*i.e.* multi-track claim to the fast track or fast track claim to the small claims track) unless all parties consent. If the court felt that a simple multi-track case ought to be on the fast track no doubt parties would be invited to consent. If one party refused consent, although the court could not then proceed to allocate to the fast track, it could give a timetable and directions of the sort that would be given in a fast track case. **26.7.1**

Matters relevant to allocation to a track

26.8—(1) When deciding the track for a claim, the matters to which the court shall have regard include— **26.8**

(a) the financial value, if any, of the claim;
(b) the nature of the remedy sought;
(c) the likely complexity of the facts, law or evidence;
(d) the number of parties or likely parties;
(e) the value of any counterclaim or other Part 20 claim and the complexity of any matters relating to it;
(f) the amount of oral evidence which may be required;

(g) the importance of the claim to persons who are not parties to the proceedings;

(h) the views expressed by the parties; and

(i) the circumstances of the parties.

(2) It is for the court to assess the financial value of a claim and in doing so it will disregard—

(a) any amount not in dispute;

(b) any claim for interest;

(c) costs; and

(d) any contributory negligence.

(3) Where—

(a) two or more claimants have started a claim against the same defendant using the same claim form; and

(b) each claimant has a claim against the defendant separate from the other claimants,

the court will consider the claim of each claimant separately when it assesses financial value under paragraph (1).

26.8.1 **Matters relevant to allocation**—See too PD to Pt 26, para. 7.

26.8.2 **Length of trial**—Note that in addition to the factors set out in r.26.8, when deciding whether or not to allocate to fast track, the court should take into account the limits likely to be placed on disclosure, the extent to which expert evidence may be necessary and whether the trial is likely to last more than five hours, although the likely length of trial is not necessarily conclusive—see r.26.6(5) and PD to Pt 26 para. 9.1.

26.8.3 **Claims with no monetary value**—See r.26.7(2). A claim which has no financial value should be allocated to the most suitable track.

26.8.4 **Effect of rule**—It is for the court to allocate a case to the relevant track. The rule does not expressly require the court to have regard to "all the circumstances" but the use of the word "include" in r.26.8(1) before the nine specific matters (a) to (i) shows that the matters mentioned are not exhaustive.

In the majority of cases the appropriate track will be obvious and largely determined by the financial value of the claim. In all cases the "allocation questionnaire" must be appropriately and fully completed (see Form N150) to enable the court to perform correctly the essential case management task of allocation.

Notice of allocation

26.9 **26.9**—(1) When it has allocated a claim to a track, the court will serve notice of allocation on every party.

(2) When the court serves notice of allocation on a party, it will also serve—

(a) a copy of the allocation questionnaires filed by the other parties; and

(b) a copy of any further information provided by another party about his case (whether by order or not).

(Rule 26.5 provides that the court may, before allocating proceedings, order a party to provide further information about his case.)

26.9.1 **Effect of rule**—The rule requires the court to serve "notice of allocation" as soon as it has allocated the case. It serves with the notice a copy of the allocation questionnaires filed by other parties (hence r.26.3(6) requires a party merely to file, not file and serve, his allocation questionnaire). See Forms N153 to 160.

Appeals against allocation are likely to be very rare and r.26.9 makes no reference to it. Appeal is still governed by CCR, O.37 and RSC, O.58—both re-enacted in the Schedules to the CPR.

Re-allocation

26.10 **26.10** The court may subsequently re-allocate a claim to a different track.

26.10.1 **Re-allocation**—See too PD to Pt 26, para. 11. If a claim initially allocated to the small claims track is re-allocated to a different track, the limitations on costs cease to apply from that date (see r.27.15).

Assessment of damages—See too PD to Pt 26, para. 12. 26.10.2

Effect of rule—This short rule provides for re-allocation. It seems that it is not possible to allocate different parts of a claim to different tracks simultaneously. However, sequential allocation is possible. Thus, for example, a very large claim where the issue of liability is not complex and could be tried within a day, could (with consent: see r.26.7(3)) be allocated to the fast track for trial on liability. If the claimant succeeds the case could be re-allocated to the multi-track under r.26.10. 26.10.3

PRACTICE DIRECTION—CASE MANAGEMENT—PRELIMINARY STAGE: ALLOCATION AND RE-ALLOCATION

This Practice Direction supplements CPR Part 26

1. Reminders of Important Rule Provisions other than Parts 26–29

Attention is drawn in particular to the following provisions of the Civil Procedure Rules: 26PD–001

Part 1	The Overriding Objective (defined in Rule 1.1). The duty of the court to further that objective by actively managing cases (set out in Rule 1.4). The requirement that the parties help the court to further that objective (set out in Rule 1.3).
Part 3	The court's case management powers (which may be exercised on application or on its own initiative) and the sanctions which it may impose.
Part 24	The court's power to grant summary judgment
Parts 32–35	Evidence, especially the court's power to control evidence.

Attention is also drawn to the practice directions which supplement those Parts and Parts 27–29, and to those which relate to the various specialist jurisdictions.

2. The Allocation Questionnaire

2.1 Form—The allocation questionnaire referred to in Part 26 will be in Form N150.

Attention is drawn to the Costs Practice Direction, paragraph 4.5(1) which requires an estimate of costs to be filed and served when an allocation questionnaire is filed.

2.2 Provision of Extra Information—(1) This paragraph sets out what a party should do when he files his allocation questionnaire if he wishes to give the court information about matters which he believes may affect its decision about allocation or case management.

(2) The general rule is that the court will not take such information into account unless the document containing it either:

(a) confirms that all parties have agreed that the information is correct and that it should be put before the court, or

(b) confirms that the party who has sent the document to the court has delivered a copy to all the other parties.

(3) The following are examples of information which will be likely to help the court:

(a) a party's intention to apply for summary judgment or some other order that may dispose of the case or reduce the amount in dispute or the number of issues remaining to be decided,

(b) a party's intention to issue a Part 20 claim or to add another party,

(c) the steps the parties have taken in the preparation of evidence (in particular expert evidence), the steps they intend to take and whether those steps are to be taken in co-operation with any other party,

(d) the directions the party believes will be appropriate to be given for the management of the case,

(e) about any particular facts that may affect the timetable the court will set,

(f) any facts which may make it desirable for the court to fix an allocation hearing or a hearing at which case management directions will be given.

2.3 Consultation—(1) The parties should consult one another and co-operate in completing the allocation questionnaires and giving other information to the court.

(2) They should try to agree the case management directions which they will invite the court to make. Further details appear in the practice directions which supplement Parts 28 and 29.

(3) The process of consultation must not delay the filing of the allocation questionnaires.

2.4 Hearings Before Allocation—Where a court hearing takes place (for example on an application for an interim injunction or for summary judgment under Part 24) before the claim is allocated to a track, the court may at that hearing:

(1) dispense with the need for the parties to file allocation questionnaires, treat the hearing as an allocation hearing, make an order for allocation and give directions for case management, or

(2) fix a date for allocation questionnaires to be filed and give other directions.

2.5 Consequences of Failure to File an Allocation Questionnaire—(1) If no party files an allocation questionnaire within the time specified by Form N152:

(a) the file will be referred to a judge for his directions,

(b) the judge will usually order that unless an allocation questionnaire is filed within 3 days from service of that order the claim and any counterclaim will be struck out, but he may make a different order.

(2) Where a party files an allocation questionnaire but another party does not, the court may:

(a) allocate the claim to a track if it considers that it has enough information to do so, or

(b) order that an allocation hearing is listed and that all or any parties must attend.

3. Stay to Allow for Settlement of the Case

26PD–002 **3.1 Procedure for the parties to apply to extend the stay**

(1)(a) The court will generally accept a letter from any party or from the solicitor for any party as an application to extend the stay under Rule 26.4.

(b) The letter should—

(i) confirm that the application is made with the agreement of all parties, and

(ii) explain the steps being taken and identify any mediator or expert assisting with the process.

(2)(a) An order extending the stay must be made by a judge.

(b) The extension will generally be for no more than 4 weeks unless clear reasons are given to justify a longer time.

(3) More than one extension of the stay may be granted.

3.2 Position at the end of the stay if no settlement is reached—(1) At the end of the stay the file will be referred to a judge for his directions.

(2) He will consider whether to allocate the claim to a track and what other directions to give, and may require any party to give further information or fix an allocation hearing.

3.3 Any party may apply for a stay to be lifted.

3.4 Position where settlement is reached during a stay—Where the whole of the proceedings are settled during a stay, the taking of any of the following steps will be treated as an application for the stay to be lifted:

(1) an application for a consent order (in any form) to give effect to the settlement,

(2) an application for the approval of a settlement where a party is a person under a disability,

(3) giving notice of acceptance of money paid into court in satisfaction of the claim or applying for money in court to be paid out.

4. Allocation, Re-Allocation and Case Management

4.1 The court's general approach—The Civil Procedure Rules lay down the overriding objective, the powers and duties of the court and the factors to which it must have regard in exercising them. The court will expect to exercise its powers as far as possible in co-operation with the parties and their legal representatives so as to deal with the case justly in accordance with that objective.

4.2 Allocation to track—(1) In most cases the court will expect to have enough information from the statements of case and allocation questionnaires to be able to allocate the claim to a track and to give case management directions.

(2) If the court does not have enough information to allocate the claim it will generally make an order under rule 26.5(3) requiring one or more parties to provide further information within 14 days.

(3) Where there has been no allocation hearing the notice of allocation will be in Forms N154 (fast track), N155 (multi-track) or N157–160 (small claims).

(4)(a) The general rule is that the court will give brief reasons for its allocation decision, and these will be set out in the notice of allocation.

(b) The general rule does not apply where all the allocation questionnaires which have been filed have expressed the wish for the claim to be allocated to the track to which the court has allocated it.

(5) Paragraph 6 of this practice direction deals with allocation hearings and Paragraph 7 deals with allocation principles.

(6) Paragraph 11 of this practice direction deals with re-allocation.

4.3 The practice directions supplementing Parts 27, 28 and 29 contain further information about the giving of case management directions at the allocation stage.

5. Summary Judgment or Other Early Termination

5.1 Part of the court's duty of active case management is the summary disposal of issues which do not need full investigation and trial (rule 1.4(2)(c)).

5.2 The court's powers to make orders to dispose of issues in that way include:

(a) under rule 3.4, striking out a statement of case, or part of a statement of case, and
(b) under Part 24, giving summary judgment where a claimant or a defendant has no reasonable prospect of success.

The court may use these powers on an application or on its own initiative. The practice direction "Summary Disposal of Claims" contains further information.

5.3(1) A party intending to make such an application should do so before or when filing his allocation questionnaire.

(2) Where a party makes an application for such an order before a claim has been allocated to a track the court will not normally allocate the claim before the hearing of the application.

(3) Where a party files an allocation questionnaire stating that he intends to make such an application but has not done so, the judge will usually direct that an allocation hearing is listed.

(4) The application may be heard at that allocation hearing if the application notice has been issued and served in sufficient time.

5.4(1) This paragraph applies where the court proposes to make such an order of its own initiative.

(2) The court will not allocate the claim to a track but instead it will either:
(a) fix a hearing, giving the parties at least 14 days notice of the date of the hearing and of the issues which it is proposed that the court will decide, or
(b) make an order directing a party to take the steps described in the order within a stated time and specifying the consequence of not taking those steps.

5.5 Where the court decides at the hearing of an application or a hearing fixed under paragraph 5.4(2)(a) that the claim (or part of the claim) is to continue it may:

(1) treat that hearing as an allocation hearing, allocate the claim and give case management directions, or

(2) give other directions.

6. Allocation Hearings

26PD–003 **6.1 General Principle**—The court will only hold an allocation hearing on its own initiative if it considers that it is necessary to do so.

6.2 Procedure—Where the court orders an allocation hearing to take place:

(1) it will give the parties at least 7 days notice of the hearing in Form N153, and

(2) Form N153 will give a brief explanation of the decision to order the hearing.

6.3 Power to treat another hearing as an allocation hearing—Where the court may treat another hearing as an allocation hearing it does not need to give notice to any party that it proposes to do so.

6.4 The notice of allocation after an allocation hearing will be in Form N154, N155 or N157.

6.5 Representation—A legal representative who attends an allocation hearing should, if possible, be the person responsible for the case and must in any event be familiar with the case, be able to provide the court with the information it is likely to need to take its decisions about allocation and case management, and have sufficient authority to deal with any issues that are likely to arise.

6.6 Sanctions—(1) This paragraph sets out the sanctions that the court will usually impose for default in connection with the allocation procedure, but the court may make a different order.

(2)(a) Where an allocation hearing takes place because a party has failed to file an allocation questionnaire or to provide further information which the court has ordered, the court will usually order that party to pay on the indemnity basis the costs of any other party who has attended the hearing, summarily assess the amount of those costs, and order them to be paid forthwith or within a stated period.

(b) The court may order that if the party does not pay those costs within the time stated his statement of case will be struck out.

(3) Where a party whose default has led to a fixing of an allocation hearing is still in default and does not attend the hearing the court will usually make an order specifying the steps he is required to take and providing that unless he takes them within a stated time his statement of case will be struck out.

7. Allocation Principles

7.1 Rules 26.6, 26.7 and 26.8—(1) Rule 26.6 sets out the scope of each track,

(2) Rule 26.7 states the general rule for allocation, and

(3) Rule 26.8 sets out the matters relevant to allocation to a track.

7.2 Objective of this paragraph—The object of this paragraph is to explain what will be the court's general approach to some of the matters set out in rule 26.8.

7.3 "the financial value of the claim"—(1) Rule 26.8(2) provides that it is for the court to assess the financial value of a claim.

(2) Where the court believes that the amount the claimant is seeking exceeds what he may reasonably be expected to recover it may make an order under rule 26.5(3) directing the claimant to justify the amount.

7.4 "any amount not in dispute"—In deciding, for the purposes of rule 26.8(2), whether an amount is in dispute the court will apply the following general principles:

(1) Any amount for which the defendant does not admit liability is in dispute,

(2) Any sum in respect of an item forming part of the claim for which judgment has been entered (for example a summary judgment) is not in dispute,

(3) Any specific sum claimed as a distinct item and which the defendant admits he is liable to pay is not in dispute,

(4) Any sum offered by the defendant which has been accepted by the claimant in satisfaction of any item which forms a distinct part of the claim is not in dispute.

It follows from these provisions that if, in relation to a claim the value of which is above the small claims track limit of £5,000, the defendant makes, before allocation, an admission that reduces the amount in dispute to a figure below £5,000 (see CPR Part 14), the normal track for the claim will be the small claims track. As to recovery of pre-allocation costs, the claimant can, before allocation, apply for judgment with costs on the amount of the claim that has been admitted (see CPR rule 14.3 but see also paragraph 5.1(3) of the Costs Directions relating to CPR Part 44 under which the court has a discretion to allow pre-allocation costs).

7.5 "the views expressed by the parties"—The court will treat these views as an important factor, but the allocation decision is one for the court, to be taken in the light of all the circumstances, and the court will not be bound by any agreement or common view of the parties.

7.6 "the circumstances of the parties"—See paragraph 8.

7.7 "the value of any counterclaim or other Part 20 claim"—Where the case involves more than one money claim (for example where there is a Part 20 claim or there is more than one claimant each making separate claims) the court will not generally aggregate the claims. Instead it will generally regard the largest of them as determining the financial value of the claims.

8. The Small Claims Track—Allocation and Case Management

26PD–004 **8.1 Allocation**

(1)(a) The small claims track is intended to provide a proportionate procedure by which most straightforward claims with a financial value of not more than £5,000 can be decided, without the need for substantial pre-hearing preparation and the formalities of a traditional trial, and without incurring large legal costs. (Rule 26.6 provides for a lower financial value in certain types of case.)

(b) The procedure laid down in Part 27 for the preparation of the case and the conduct of the hearing are designed to make it possible for a litigant to conduct his own case without legal representation if he wishes.

(c) Cases generally suitable for the small claims track will include consumer disputes, accident claims, disputes about the ownership of goods and most disputes between a landlord and tenant other than those for possession.

(d) A case involving a disputed allegation of dishonesty will not usually be suitable for the small claims track.

(2) Rule 26.7(3) and rule 27.14(5)

(a) These rules allow the parties to consent to the allocation to the small claims track of a claim the value of which is above the limits mentioned in rule 26.6(2) and, in that event, the rules make provision about costs.

(b) The court will not allocate such a claim to the small claims track, notwithstanding that the parties have consented to the allocation, unless it is satisfied that it is suitable for that track.

(c) The court will not normally allow more than one day for the hearing of such a claim.

(d) The court will give case management directions to ensure that the case is dealt with in as short a time as possible. These may include directions of a kind that are not usually given in small claim cases, for example, for Scott Schedules.

8.2 Case management—(1) Directions for case management of claims allocated to the small claims track will generally be given by the court on allocation.

(2) Rule 27.4 contains further provisions about directions and the practice direction supplementing Part 27 sets out the standard directions which the court will usually give.

9. The Fast Track

9.1 Allocation—(1) Where the court is to decide whether to allocate to the fast track or the multi-track a claim for which the normal track is the fast track, it will allocate the claim to the fast track unless it believes that it cannot be dealt with justly on that track.

(2) The court will, in particular, take into account the limits likely to be placed on disclosure, the extent to which expert evidence may be necessary and whether the trial is likely to last more than a day.

(3)(a) When it is considering the likely length of the trial the court will regard a day as being a period of 5 hours, and will consider whether that is likely to be sufficient time for the case to be heard.

(b) The court will also take into account the case management directions (including the fixing of a trial timetable) that are likely to be given and the court's powers to control evidence and to limit cross-examination.

(c) The possibility that a trial might last longer than one day is not necessarily a conclusive reason for the court to allocate or to re-allocate a claim to the multi-track.

(d) A claim may be allocated to the fast track or ordered to remain on that track although there is to be a split trial.

(e) Where the case involves a counterclaim or other Part 20 claim that will be tried with the claim and as a result the trial will last more than a day, the court may not allocate it to the fast track.

9.2 Case management—(1) Directions for the case management of claims which have been allocated to the fast track will be given at the allocation stage or at the listing stage (in either case with or without a hearing) or at both, and if necessary at other times. The trial judge may, at or before the trial, give directions for its conduct.

(2) The practice direction supplementing Part 28 contains further provisions and contains standard directions which the court may give.

10. The Multi-Track

10.1 The following paragraphs do not apply to a claim which is being dealt with at the Royal Courts of Justice. **26PD–005**

10.2 Venue for allocation and case management—(1) The case management of a claim which is allocated to the multi-track will normally be dealt with at a Civil Trial Centre.

(2) In the case of a claim to which Part 49 (specialist proceedings) applies, case management must be dealt with at a Civil Trial Centre. Sub-paragraphs (4) to (10) do not apply to such a claim. The claim will be allocated to the multi-track irrespective of its value, and must be transferred to a Civil Trial Centre for allocation and case management if not already there.

(3) Where a claim is issued in or automatically transferred to a Civil Trial Centre it will be allocated and managed at that court.

(4) The following *sub-paragraphs* apply to a claim which is issued in or automatically transferred to a court which is not a Civil Trial Centre. Such a court is referred to as a "feeder court".

(5) Where a judge sitting at a feeder court decides, on the basis of the allocation questionnaires and any other documents filed by the parties, that the claim should be dealt with on the multi-track he will normally make an order:

(a) allocating the claim to that track,
(b) giving case management directions, and
(c) transferring the claim to a Civil Trial Centre.

(6) If he decides that an allocation hearing or some pre-allocation hearing is to take place (for example to strike out a statement of case under Part 3 of the Rules) that hearing will take place at the feeder court.

(7) If, before allocation, a hearing takes place at a feeder court and in

exercising his powers under paragraph 2.4(1) above the judge allocates the claim to the multi-track, he will also normally make an order transferring the claim to a Civil Trial Centre.

(8) A judge sitting at a feeder court may, rather than making an allocation order himself, transfer the claim to a Civil Trial Centre for the decision about allocation to be taken there.

(9) When, following an order for transfer, the file is received at the Civil Trial Centre, a judge sitting at that Centre will consider it and give any further directions that appear necessary or desirable.

(10) Where there is reason to believe that more than one case management conference may be needed and the parties or their legal advisers are located inconveniently far from the Civil Trial Centre, a judge sitting at a feeder court may, with the agreement of the Designated Civil Judge and notwithstanding the allocation of the case to the multi-track, decide that in the particular circumstances of the case it should not be transferred to a Civil Trial Centre, but should be case managed for the time being at the feeder court.

(11) A Designated Civil Judge may at any time make an order transferring a claim from a feeder court to a Civil Trial Centre and he may do so irrespective of the track, if any, to which it has been allocated.

(12) No order will be made by a feeder court fixing a date for a hearing at a Civil Trial Centre unless that date has been given or confirmed by a judge or listing officer of that Centre.

10.3 Case management—Part 29 of the Rules and the practice direction supplementing that Part set out the procedure to be adopted.

11. Re-Allocation of Claims and the Variation of Directions

11.1 (a) Where a party is dissatisfied with an order made allocating the claim to a track he may appeal or apply to the court to re-allocate the claim.

(b) He should appeal if the order was made at a hearing at which he was present or represented, or of which he was given due notice.

(c) In any other case he should apply to the court to re-allocate the claim.

11.2 Where there has been a change in the circumstances since an order was made allocating the claim to a track the court may re-allocate the claim. It may do so on application or on its own initiative.

The practice directions supplementing Parts 28 and 29 contain provisions about the variation of case management directions.

12. Allocation and Case Management of Assessment of Damages and Allied Proceedings

26PD–006 **12.1 Scope**—(1) In the following paragraphs a "relevant order" means an order or judgment of the court which requires the amount of money to be paid by one party to another to be decided by the court.

(2) A relevant order may have been obtained:

(a) by a judgment in default under Part 12,
(b) by a judgment on an admission under Part 14,
(c) on the striking out of a statement of case under Part 3,
(d) on a summary judgment application under Part 24,
(e) on the determination of a preliminary issue or on a trial as to liability, or
(f) at trial.

(3) A relevant order includes an order for an amount of damages or interest to be decided by the court, an order for the taking of an account or the making of an inquiry as to any sum due, and any similar order.

(4) A relevant order does not include an order for the assessment of costs except where the court has made an order for the assessment of costs payable under a contract other than a contract between a solicitor and client for legal services.

12.2 Directions—(1) Directions which may be given under the following paragraphs may include:

(a) a direction allocating or re-allocating the claim,
(b) a direction that allocation questionnaires be filed by a specified date,
(c) a direction that a date be fixed for a hearing or a further hearing,
(d) an order that the claim be stayed while the parties try to settle the case by alternative dispute resolution or other means.

(2) Directions may specify the level or type of judge before whom a hearing or a further hearing will take place and the nature and purpose of that hearing.

12.3 Allocation—Where a claim has not been allocated to a track at the time a relevant order is made, the court will not normally consider it to be appropriate to allocate it to a track (other than the small claims track) unless the amount payable appears to be genuinely disputed on grounds which appear to be substantial. It may instead direct that a disposal hearing (referred to in paragraph 12.8) be listed.

12.4 Orders and judgments made at hearings—Where a relevant order is made by a judge at a hearing, the judge should at the same time give such directions as the information about the case available to him enables him to give.

12.5 Orders made by consent without a hearing—(1) Where a relevant order is made by consent without a hearing a judge will give directions.

(2) The parties should where possible file with the draft consent order agreed directions which they invite the court to give.

12.6 Judgments entered on admissions without a hearing—(1) Where a relevant order is a judgment entered without a hearing under Part 14 the court will give directions.

(2) The court may in particular direct that a disposal hearing be listed.

12.7 Judgments entered in default—(1) This paragraph applies where the relevant order is a judgment entered under Part 12 without a hearing.

(2) On the entry of the judgment the court will list a disposal hearing.

12.8 Disposal hearings—(1) At a disposal hearing the court may give directions or decide the amount payable in accordance with this sub-paragraph.

(2) If the financial value of the claim (determined in accordance with Part 26) is such that the claim would, if defended, be allocated to the small claims track, the court will normally allocate it to the track and may treat the disposal hearing as a final hearing in accordance with Part 27.

(3) If the court does not give directions and does not allocate the claim to the small claims track, it may nonetheless order that the amount payable is to be decided there and then without allocating the claim to another track.

(4) Rule 32.6 applies to evidence at a disposal hearing unless the court otherwise directs.

(5) The court will not exercise its powers under sub-paragraph 12.8(3) unless any written evidence on which the claimant relies has been served on the defendant at least 3 days before the disposal hearing.

12.9 Costs—(1) Attention is drawn to the costs practice directions and in particular to the court's power to make a summary assessment of costs.

(2) Attention is drawn to rule 44.13(1) which provides that if an order makes no mention of costs, none are payable in respect of the proceedings to which it relates.

(3) Attention is drawn to rule 27.14 (special rules about costs in cases allocated to the small claims track).

(4) Attention is drawn to Part 45 (fixed trial costs in cases which have been allocated to the fast track). Part 45 will not apply to a case dealt with at a disposal hearing whatever the financial value of the claim. So the costs of a disposal hearing will be in the discretion of the court.

12.10 Jurisdiction of Masters and district judges—Unless the court otherwise directs, a Master or a district judge may decide the amount payable under a relevant order irrespective of the financial value of the claim and of the track to which the claim may have been allocated.

PART 27

THE SMALL CLAIMS TRACK

Contents **27.0.1**

Editorial Introduction

Although derived from CCR, O.19, Pt 27 represents a considerable improvement not only in drafting style but also in the manner of dealing with small claims. **27.0.2**

The county courts were created by the County Courts Act 1846 to provide a local, cheap and simple system for the recovery of small debts which were disproportionately expensive or uneconomic to recover in the then Court of Queen's Bench. The jurisdiction in 1846 was limited in contract and tort cases not exceeding £20. The county courts were given an ever higher jurisdiction over the years. As a result it again became necessary to consider a cheap and simple system for small claims and so small claims arbitration was introduced into the county court in 1973, initially for claims not exceeding £100. The small claims limit had increased to £1,000 by the time of Lord Woolf's "Access to Justice" Report and as a result of that Report, was further increased to £3,000. The "small claims track" has now replaced small claims arbitration.

The small claims track is created by r.26.1(2). The scope of the small claims track is defined by r.26.6. The small claims track is the normal track for any claim which has a financial value of not more than £5,000 (r.26.6(3): note the special provisions for personal injury claims in r.26.6(1)(a) and certain claims by a tenant of residential premises in r.26.6(1)(b)).

There are already over 95,000 small claims hearings a year and that number must increase with the higher small claims track limit. It is anticipated that over 85 per cent of final hearings will be of cases on the small claims track.

In comparing Pt 27 with its predecessor, CCR, O.19, there are a number of differences to note:

(i) The term "arbitration" is no longer used in the context of small claims. It was an inappropriate term which had frequently been criticised (see, *e.g.*, Sir Thomas Bingham M.R. in *Joyce v. Liverpool City Council* [1996] Q.B. 252).

(ii) There is no "automatic reference". All claims, including small claims, are allocated to the appropriate track as a case-management decision. This occurs in accordance with Pt 26 following completion of the "allocation questionnaire" (see r.26.3).

(iii) The special costs rules on the small claims track (see r.27.14) apply as from allocation to the small claims track but cease to apply if the case is re-allocated to another track (see r.27.15).

(iv) Summary judgment under Pt 24 is not prohibited in claims on the small claims track.

(v) The application of other Parts of the CPR is governed by r.27.2. The excluded rules differ.

(vi) No expert evidence is admissible without permission (r.27.5).

(vii) The machinery for giving directions is formalised (r.27.4). It is anticipated that in most cases directions will be given without requiring the parties to attend.

(viii) Preliminary hearings will be rare and only for the purposes stated in r.27.6(1). There is no longer a general power to give judgment at a preliminary hearing: the court's power to do so is prescribed by r.27.6(1)(b) and (c) and by r.27.6(4).

(ix) The court can propose that the claim be dealt with on paper without a hearing (r.27.4(1)(e) and r.27.10). There is no right to apply to set aside if the court does deal with the claim without a hearing (r.27.11(5)).

(x) A party can give written notice that he will not attend whereupon the court will take into account his statement of case and any documents filed (r.27.9(1)). Such a party cannot apply to have judgment set aside (r.27.11(1)).

(xi) The judge conducting the hearing "may adopt any method of proceeding" that he "considers to be fair". The court may limit cross-examination. The hearing continues to be "informal" and "the strict rules of evidence do not apply" (r.27.8).

(xii) The general rule is that the hearing is to be in public (r.39.2).

(xiii) There is no general provision to apply to set aside. There is a very limited provision in r.27.11.

(xiv) A right of appeal is introduced but it is restricted in scope (r.27.12).

(xv) The rules are supplemented by a detailed Practice Direction (see para. 27PD–001).

Related Sources

27.0.3
- Practice Direction—Small Claims Track—para. 27PD–001.
- Part 26 (Case Management—The Preliminary Stage).

Forms

27.0.4 See list of forms at section C.

Scope of this Part

27.1 **27.1**—(1) This Part—

(a) sets out the special procedure for dealing with claims which have been allocated to the small claims track under Part 26; and

(b) limits the amount of costs that can be recovered in respect of a claim which has been allocated to the small claims track.

(Rule 27.14 deals with costs on the small claims track.)

(2) A claim being dealt with under this Part is called a small claim.

(Rule 26.6 provides for the scope of the small claims track. A claim for damages for harassment or unlawful eviction relating, in either case, to residential premises shall not be allocated to the small claims track whatever the financial value of the claim. Otherwise, the small claims track will be the normal track for—

- any claim which has a financial value of not more than £5,000 subject to the special provisions about claims for personal injuries and housing disrepair claims;
- any claim for personal injuries which has a financial value of not more than £5,000 where the claim for damages for personal injuries is not more than £1,000; and
- any claim which includes a claim by a tenant of residential premises against his landlord for repairs or other work to the premises where the estimated cost of the repairs or other work is not more than £1,000 and the financial value of any claim for damages in respect of those repairs or other work is not more than £1,000.)

27.1.1 **Effect of rule**—Allocation to the small claims track has replaced small claims arbitration. The small claims track is the normal track for claims mentioned above. Costs limitations apply to cases allocated to the small claims track (rr. 27.14 and 44.9).

Extent to which other Parts apply

27.2 **27.2**—(1) The following Parts of these Rules do not apply to small claims—

(a) Part 25 (interim remedies) except as it relates to interim injunctions[GL];

(b) Part 31 (disclosure and inspection);

(c) Part 32 (evidence) except rule 32.1 (power of court to control evidence);

(d) Part 33 (miscellaneous rules about evidence);

(e) Part 35 (experts and assessors) except rules 35.1 (duty to restrict expert evidence), 35.3 (experts—overriding duty to the court) and 35.8 (instructions to a single joint expert);

(f) Part 18 (further information);
(g) Part 36 (offers to settle and payments into court); and
(h) Part 39 (hearings) except rule 39.2 (general rule—hearing to be in public).

(2) The other Parts of these Rules apply to small claims except to the extent that a rule limits such application.

Effect of rule—It is a fundamental principle of the CPR that cases should be dealt with proportionately, expeditiously, fairly and as cheaply as possible (see Pt 1—Overriding Objective). Rule 27.2 is no more that the application of that principle to small claims. All parts of the CPR apply to small claims save those expressly listed in r.27.2(1). The excluded rules are the more elaborate features of the adversarial system. The old CCR, O.19, r.6(9) similarly excluded rules: although it did not specifically exclude summary judgment, O.9, r.14(1)(a) did. However, this provision is not repeated in the new rule on summary judgment (see Pt 24). Thus it is possible for either party to apply for summary judgment. In the majority of cases it will not be necessary to do so as the small claims directions will be simple and the hearing date promptly given. In some cases, however, where it would be otherwise relatively expensive to collect and collate evidence, it may be quicker and cheaper to apply for summary judgment under Pt 24. Indeed, if an application is made promptly the claim may never be allocated to the small claims track thus avoiding the costs restrictions of r.27.14, and a successful applicant who obtains a summary judgment can expect to recover costs (see further Part 24). **27.2.1**

Court's power to grant a final remedy

27.3 The court may grant any final remedy in relation to a small claim which it could grant if the proceedings were on the fast track or the multi-track. **27.3**

Scope of provision—Rule 27.3 makes it clear that no party is disadvantaged as to final remedy by having the claim allocated to the small claims track. The court has the same powers as in other cases and can grant whichever final remedy is appropriate, *e.g.* damages, injunction, specific performance, rectification, etc. **27.3.1**

Preparation for the hearing

27.4—(1) After allocations the court will— **27.4**

(a) give standard directions and fix a date for the final hearing;
(b) give special directions and fix a date for the final hearing;
(c) give special directions and direct that the court will consider what further directions are to be given no later than 28 days after the date the special directions were given;
(d) fix a date for preliminary hearing under rule 27.6; or
(e) give notice that it proposes to deal with the claim without a hearing under rule 27.10 and invite the parties to notify the court by a specified date if they agree the proposal.

(2) The court will—

(a) give parties at least 21 days' notice of the date fixed for the final hearing, unless the parties agree to accept less notice; and
(b) inform them of the amount of time allowed for the final hearing.

(3) In this rule—

(a) "standard directions" means—
(i) a direction that each party shall, at least 14 days before the date fixed for the final hearing file and serve on every other party copies of all documents (including any expert's report) on which he intends to rely at the hearing; and
(ii) any other standard directions set out in the relevant practice direction; and
(b) "special directions" means directions given in addition to or instead of the standard directions.

Scope of provision—It is expected that the court will be able to give appropriate directions without the attendance of the parties in the majority of small claims cases. Indeed the court will consider its four options ((a), (b), (c) and (d)) in r.27.4(1) in the order in which they are listed. **27.4.1**

Rule 27.4(1)(e) is a new provision whereby the court can give notice inviting the parties to consent to its proposal to deal with the claim without a hearing. There are three types of case where the court might take the initiative in suggesting this: first, where the case is clearly one which can be decided solely on the basis of documents; secondly, where it would be disproportionately expensive for parties to attend; and, thirdly, in cases where the court knows from experience that a particular litigant never attends. Note r.27.11(5) prevents a party applying to set aside if the court deals with the claim without a hearing.

27.4.2 **"standard directions"**—This term is defined in r.27.4(3)(a). Note the reference to "expert's report". Permission is always required to adduce any expert evidence (see r.27.5). Where it is clear that expert evidence is required the court will give permission as part of its standard directions. See also the Practice Direction at para. 27PD–001.

27.4.3 **"special directions"**—Note the meaning of "standard directions" as set out above and in the Practice Direction at para. 27PD–001. Special directions will be specially tailored by the district judge to the needs of the case.

27.4.4 **"time allowed for the final hearing"**—As all practitioners know, estimating the length of a final hearing is a difficult task and one which most litigants in person find impossible. Litigants in small claims cases have little option but to go along with the district judge's time allocation. However, to prevent adjournments part-heard, if a solicitor feels that the "time allowed" is inadequate or excessive he should immediately so inform the court so that it can be re-considered. The rules impose no restriction on the maximum time to be allowed. However, the court will bear in mind r.26.6(5)(a) (fast track trials "likely to last for no longer than one day"), the overriding objective in Pt 1 and the specific rules in r.27.8 (conduct of hearing). It will be rare for any trial of a case on the small claims track to last as long as a day.

Experts

27.5 **27.5** No expert may give evidence, whether written or oral, at a hearing without the permission of the court.

(Rule 27.14(3)(d) provides for the payment of an expert's fees.)

27.5.1 **Effect of rule**—Bringing about a change of culture and a new approach to the use of expert evidence is one of the aims of the reforms effected by the CPR: see Pt 35. There is always a risk of expert evidence being disproportionately expensive. Many claims on the small claims track will require expert evidence (*e.g.* allegations of defective goods or repairs, typically involving cars). Many claimants will already have obtained expert evidence before issuing proceedings as a way of ascertaining whether or not they have a good claim.

There have always been limitations on the sums that could be recovered from the other party by way of experts' fees (see now r.27.14(3)(d) and the Practice Direction at para. 27PD–001).

Rule 27.5 prevents oral or written expert evidence without permission of the court. Permission should be given, where appropriate, at directions stage. If there is a preliminary hearing permission should be sought then. If the court has given some directions and directed (pursuant to r.27.4(1)(c) that it will consider further directions within 28 days, that too provides an opportunity for a party to seek permission. If none of these apply, permission has not been given and a party wishes to have it, a letter to the court will be necessary. The district judge will then re-consider. A hearing to consider the matter would be held only exceptionally. The specimen forms of "standard directions" prescribed by the Practice Direction which supplements Pt 27 (see paras 27PD–003 *et seq.*) include directions giving permission to use experts' reports.

Preliminary hearing

27.6 **27.6**—(1) The court may hold a preliminary hearing for the consideration of the claim, but only—

(a) where—

(i) it considers that special directions, as defined in rule 27.4, are needed to ensure a fair hearing; and

(ii) it appears necessary for a party to attend at court to ensure that he understands what he must do to comply with the special directions; or

(b) to enable it to dispose of the claim on the basis that one or other of the parties has no real prospect of success at a final hearing; or
(c) to enable it to strike out[GL] a statement of case or part of a statement of case on the basis that the statement of case, or the part to be struck out, discloses no reasonable grounds for bringing or defending the claim.

(2) When considering whether or not to hold a preliminary hearing, the court must have regard to the desirability of limiting the expense to the parties of attending court.

(3) Where the court decides to hold a preliminary hearing, it will give the parties at least 14 days' notice of the date of the hearing.

(4) The court may treat the preliminary hearing as the final hearing of the claim if all the parties agree.

(5) At or after the preliminary hearing the court will—
(a) fix the date of the final hearing (if it has not been fixed already) and give the parties at least 21 days' notice of the date fixed unless the parties agree to accept less notice;
(b) inform them of the amount of time allowed for the final hearing; and
(c) give any appropriate directions.

Effect of rule—The court will try to avoid a preliminary hearing and give all necessary directions without the need for parties to attend. Nevertheless there are some cases where it is not possible to do this. Even so, the court can hold a preliminary hearing for the purpose of giving directions only if the case falls within r.27.6(1)(a). **27.6.1**

Unlike most fast track and multi-track cases, where parties have solicitors, most small claims track cases are brought and defended by litigants in person. It follows that there are many more small claims where it is clear that one party has no prospect of success or part or all of the statement of case should be struck out. Hence r.27.6(1)(b) and (c) to enable this to be done quickly with even less expense than would be involved at a small claims hearing.

It is important to note that the purpose of a preliminary hearing is limited by r.27.6(1). In particular there is no general power (there used to be: CCR, O.19, r.6(6) and O.17) to give judgment. The courts' power to finally determine the case at a preliminary hearing is limited by r.27.6(1)(b) and (c) and r.27.6(4).

Power of court to add to, vary or revoke directions

27.7 The court may add to, vary or revoke directions. **27.7**

Effect of rule—Rule 27.7 is short, simple and self-explanatory. For an example of when and why the court may need to add a direction see commentary to r.27.5 above. **27.7.1**

Conduct of the hearing

27.8—(1) The court may adopt any method of proceeding at a hearing that it considers to be fair. **27.8**

(2) Hearings will be informal.

(3) The strict rules of evidence do not apply.

(4) The court need not take evidence on oath.

(5) The court may limit cross-examination[GL].

(6) The court must give reasons for its decision.

Effect of rule—Rule 27.8 follows the new style of the CPR but is closely modelled on CCR, O.19, r.7. Rule 27.8(1)(2)(3)(4) and (6) were in the previous rules. It had been held that parties must be given the opportunity to cross-examine (*Chiltern v. Saga Holidays* [1986] 1 All E.R. 841). Rule 27.8(5) now expressly gives the court power to "limit cross-examination" (but not to exclude it). See further the Practice Direction at para. 27PD–001 and note in particular para. 4.3 thereof. **27.8.1**

The Court of Appeal described the former small claims arbitration as necessarily "brisk and efficient": *Starmer v. Bradbury, The Times*, April 11, 1994.Trial of a claim on the small claims track no doubt merits the same description.

In fact the most significant change in the conduct of hearings on the small claims track is effected not by r.27.8 but by r.39.2 (which is not excluded, though the rest of Pt 39 is: r.27.2(1)(h)). Rule 39.2 provides for all hearings to be in public. This is dealt with further in the

Practice Direction at para. 39PD–001. The hearing can be in private if all parties agree but the Practice Direction restates the general rule that "a small claims hearing will be in public". One consequence of this is that all hearings will be recorded.

Non-attendance of parties at a final hearing

27.9 **27.9**—(1) If a party who does not attend a final hearing—

(a) has given the court written notice at least 7 days before the date of the hearing that he will not attend; and

(b) has, in that notice, requested the court to decide the claim in his absence,

the court will take into account that party's statement of case and any other documents he has filed when it decides the claim.

(2) If a claimant does not—

(a) attend the hearing; and

(b) give the notice referred to in paragraph (1),

the court may strike out[GL] the claim.

(3) If—

(a) a defendant does not—

(i) attend the hearing; or

(ii) give the notice referred to in paragraph (1); and

(b) the claimant either—

(i) does attend the hearing; or

(ii) gives the notice referred to in paragraph (1),

the court may decide the claim on the basis of the evidence of the claimant alone.

(4) If neither party attends or gives the notice referred to in paragraph (1), the court may strike out[GL] the claim and any defence and counterclaim.

27.9.1 **Effect of rule**—Rule 27.9 spells out the various options available to the court when either or both parties fails to attend the final hearing. Rule 27.9(1) is new and usefully regulates the position where a party decides not to attend the final hearing and wishes the court to consider his case in his absence.

See also r.27.10.

For the possibility of a party who failed to attend applying to set aside the judgment see r.27.11.

Disposal without a hearing

27.10 **27.10** The court may, if all parties agree, deal with the claim without a hearing.

27.10.1 **Effect of rule**—Rule 27.10 had no equivalent in CCR, O.19 and is a useful innovation. The court may take the initiative in suggesting that the claim be dealt with without a hearing: see r.27.4(1)(e) and commentary thereon.

It is not possible for a party who has agreed pursuant to r.27.10 to apply to set aside the judgment under r.27.11: see r.27.11(5).

Setting judgment aside and re-hearing

27.11 **27.11**—(1) A party—

(a) who was neither present nor represented at the hearing of the claim; and

(b) who has not given written notice to the court under rule 27.9(1),

may apply for an order that a judgment under this Part shall be set aside[GL] and the claim re-heard.

(2) A party who applies for an order setting aside a judgment under this rule must make the application not more than 14 days after the day on which notice of the judgment was served on him.

(3) The court may grant an application under paragraph (2) only if the applicant—

(a) had a good reason for not attending or being represented at the hearing or giving written notice to the court under rule 27.9(1); and
(b) has a reasonable prospect of success at the hearing.

(4) If a judgment is set aside[GL]—
(a) the court must fix a new hearing for the claim; and
(b) the hearing may take place immediately after the hearing of the application to set the judgment aside and may be dealt with by the judge who set aside[GL] the judgment.

(5) A party may not apply to set aside[GL] a judgment under this rule if the court dealt with the claim without a hearing under rule 27.10.

Effect of rule—Rule 27.11 gives a very limited right to apply to have a judgment set aside and the case re-heard. The right to so apply is not available to a party who attended the hearing, was represented at the hearing, who gave notice under r.27.9(1) or who agreed to the case being dealt with without a hearing under r.27.10 **27.11.1**

"neither present nor represented"—The term "present" requires no explanation but "represented" does. "Represented" is not confined to representation by solicitor or counsel but includes any form of representation by, *e.g.*, employee or lay representative, (see para. 3 of the Practice Direction at 27PD–001). **27.11.2**

The Lay Representatives (Rights of Audience) Order 1999 (S.I. 1999 No. 1225)—This Order has revoked and replaced the Lay Representatives (Rights of Audience) Order 1992 (S.I. 1992, No. 1966), as from 18 May 1999. Any person may exercise rights of audience in proceedings dealt with as a small claim except where the client does not attend the hearing; at any stage after judgment; or on any appeal brought against any decision made by a district judge. **27.11.3**

"good reason for not attending"—The court will require evidence of the "good reason", *e.g.* medical certificate. **27.11.4**

"a reasonable prospect of success"—There is no purpose in setting aside if the unsuccessful party has no case. Accordingly the applicant must show that he has "a reasonable prospect of success". This term is new in the context of setting aside a small claims judgment but is a familiar term in the context of setting aside a default judgment. See *Alpine Bulk Transport Co. Inc. v. Saudi Eagle Shipping Co. Inc.; The Saudi Eagle* [1986] 2 Lloyd's Rep. 221 and commentary to Pt 13, especially r.13.3. **27.11.5**

Deliberate absence—In *Shocked v. Goldschmidt* [1988] 1 All E.R. 373 the Court of Appeal held that a party who deliberately chooses to be absent from a hearing is not entitled to a rehearing even if the party has a good claim or defence. Clearly such a party, even if able to comply with r.27.11(3)(b), could not comply with r.27.11(3)(a) **27.11.6**

Right of appeal under Part 27

27.12—(1) A party may appeal against an order under this Part only on the grounds that— **27.12**
(a) there was serious irregularity affecting the proceedings; or
(b) the court made a mistake of law.

(2) On an appeal the court may make any order it considers appropriate.

(3) The court may dismiss an appeal without a hearing.

(4) This rule does not limit any right of appeal arising under any Act.

Effect of rule—There was no right of appeal under CCR, O.19, though the term was often used incorrectly. Rule 27.12 introduces a limited right of appeal for cases on the small claims track. **27.12.1**

There are only two grounds of appeal set out in r.27.12(1). Ground (a) is "serious irregularity affecting the proceedings". Note the use of the word "serious". Given that hearings are conducted by judges a "serious irregularity" would be highly unusual and nothing like as usual as unsuccessful parties will allege. It is important to note that the general rule is that all hearings are in public (see r.39.2) and that generally all hearings will be tape recorded. (See Practice Direction at para. 27PD–001.) A party who wishes to appeal on the ground of a "serious irregularity affecting the proceedings" should therefore obtain a transcript of the hearing for consideration by the appeal judge.

The other ground of appeal is "the court made a mistake of law".

Note the court's power to dismiss (but not allow) the appeal without a hearing in r.27.12(3).

Most small claims trials are conducted by a district judge. Appeal is therefore to a circuit judge. If the small claims trial was conducted by a circuit judge or High Court judge, appeal is to the Court of Appeal. However, it is intended to change the law so that an appeal from a circuit judge will go to a High Court Judge (see Foreword).

Procedure for appealing is in r.27.13.

In practice the majority of small claims hearings are conducted by a district judge. A case allocated to the small claims track may only be assigned to a circuit judge to hear with his consent (Practice Direction: Allocation of cases to levels of Judiciary). High Court judges have consented to hear small claims but this is rare.

Procedure for making an appeal

27.13 **27.13**—(1) A party who wishes to appeal must file a notice of appeal not more than 14 days after the day on which notice of the order was served on him.

(2) Notice of appeal—

(a) must be filed at the court which made the order; and

(b) must set out the grounds for the appeal with particulars of the serious irregularity or mistake of law alleged.

27.13.1 **Effect of rule**—A limited right of appeal is given by r.27.12. Notice of appeal, stating grounds and particulars, must be filed at the court which made the order not more than 14 days after the day on which notice of the order was served (not 14 days from the date the order was made).

Appeal from a district judge is to the circuit judge.

Costs on the small claims track

27.14 **27.14**—(1) This rule applies to any case which has been allocated to the small claims track unless paragraph (5) applies.

(Rules 44.9 and 44.11 make provision in relation to orders for costs made before a claim has been allocated to the small claims track.)

(2) The court may not order a party to pay a sum to another party in respect of that other party's costs except—

(a) the fixed costs payable under Part 45, attributable to issuing the claim which—

(i) are payable under Part 45; or

(ii) would be payable under Part 45 if that Part applied to the claim;

(b) in proceedings which included a claim for an injunction[GL] or an order for specific performance a sum not exceeding the amount specified in the relevant practice direction for legal advice and assistance relating to that claim;

(c) costs assessed by the summary procedure in relation to an appeal under rule 27.12; and

(d) such further costs as the court may assess by the summary procedure and order to be paid by a party who has behaved unreasonably.

(3) The court may also order a party to pay all or part of—

(a) any court fees paid by another party;

(b) expenses which a party or witness has reasonably incurred in travelling to and from a hearing or in staying away from home for the purposes of attending a hearing;

(c) a sum not exceeding the amount specified in the relevant practice direction for any loss of earnings by a party or witness due to attending a hearing or to staying away from home for the purpose of attending a hearing; and

(d) a sum not exceeding the amount specified in the relevant practice direction for an expert's fees.

(4) The limits on costs imposed by this rule also apply to any fee or reward for acting on behalf of a party to the proceedings charged by a person exercising a right of audience by virtue of an order under section 11 of the Courts and Legal Services Act 1990[1] (a lay representative).

[1] 1990 c. 41.

(5) Where—

(a) the financial value of a claim exceeds the limit for the small claims track; but

(b) the claim has been allocated to the small claims track in accordance with rule 26.7(3),

the claim shall be treated, for the purposes of costs, as if it were proceeding on the fast track except that trial costs shall be in the discretion of the court and shall not exceed the amount set out for the value of the claim in rule 46.2 (amount of fast track trial costs).

(Rule 26.7(3) allows the parties to consent to a claim being allocated to a track where the financial value of the claim exceeds the limit for that track.)

History of rule—Amended by the Civil Procedure (Amendment) Rules 1999 (S.I. 1999 No. 1008). 27.14.1

Effect of rule—There have always been restrictions on costs recoverable in small claims cases. The former CCR, O.19, r.4 was often wrongly referred to as the "no costs rule": it imposed restrictions on costs but never was a no costs rule. The same principle is carried forward into r.27.14. 27.14.2

Rules 44.9 and 44.11 make provision for costs before a claim is allocated to the small claims track. There is no automatic referring of cases to the small or any track (see Pt 26—Case Management—Preliminary Stage). Special rules relating to a particular track apply to the period before, as well as after, allocation except where the court or a practice direction provides otherwise (r.44.9(2) as amended by the Civil Procedure (Amendment) Rules 1999 (S.I. 1999 No. 1008)).

"fixed costs ... attributable to issuing the claim"—Costs of issue were always allowable. Rule 27.14(2)(a) reflects CCR, O.19, r.4(2)(a). Fixed costs are dealt with in Pt 45. 27.14.3

"proceedings which included a claim for an injunction ..."—Rule 27.14(2)(b) reflects CCR, O.19, r.4(2)(aa) (introduced in 1995) and caters for the obvious need for legal advice in such cases. The Practice Direction is at para. 27PD–001. 27.14.4

"costs assessed by the summary procedure in relation to an appeal"—There is a limited right of appeal given by r.27.12. The practice is for the judge to summarily assess costs of the appeal. 27.14.5

"such further costs as the court may assess by the summary procedure and order to be paid by a party who has behaved unreasonably"—Rule 27.14(2)(d) reflects CCR, O.19, r.4(2)(c). There is very little authority on the old rule and no case reported in the mainstream law reports. The Court of Appeal said in *Martin v. Sherwood*, June 9, 1995 (unrep.) that the fabrication of an untruthful defence may be "unreasonable". In *Bloomfield v. Roberts* [1989] C.L.Y. 2948 it was held to be "unreasonable conduct" to defend proceedings when there is no arguable defence. If costs are awarded under r.27.14(2)(d) they will be summarily assessed by the judge at the conclusion of the hearing. 27.14.6

"... fees ... expenses ... loss of earnings ... experts' fees"—Rule 27.14(3) simply adapts to the new terminology the provisions of CCR, O.19, r.4(3). Reserving the detail to a Practice Direction (set out at para. 27PD–001) creates greater flexibility in changing the sums when required. 27.14.7

"financial value ... exceeds the limit for the small claims track"—Where a claim has a financial value which exceeds the limit for the small claims track the court cannot allocate the case to the small claims track unless the parties consent. If they do consent (see r.26.7(3)) the costs rules which apply are not those of r.27.14 but rather those applicable to the fast track (see Pt 46). Thus parties who wish to have the informality and finality of a trial on the small claims track do not suffer a costs disadvantage by doing so. 27.14.8

Claim reallocated from the small claims track to another track

27.15 Where a claim is allocated to the small claims track and subsequently reallocated to another track, rule 27.14 (costs on the small claims track) will cease to apply after the claim has been reallocated, and the fast track or multi-track costs rules will apply from the date of reallocation. 27.15

27.15.1 **Effect of rule**—Rule 27.15 is self-explanatory. It merely emphasises the point that the costs limitations of the small claims track only apply while a claim is on that track and not afterwards. (As to before see rr.44.9 and 44.11.)

PRACTICE DIRECTION—SMALL CLAIMS TRACK

This Practice Direction supplements CPR Part 27

1. Judges

27PD–001 The functions of the court described in Part 27 which are to be carried out by a judge will generally be carried out by a district judge but may be carried out by a Circuit Judge.

2. Case Management Directions

2.1 Rule 27.4 explains how directions will be given, and rule 27.6 contains provisions about the holding of a preliminary hearing and the court's powers at such a hearing.

2.2 Appendix A sets out the Standard Directions which the court may give.

3. Representation at a Hearing

3.1 In this paragraph:

(1) a lawyer means a barrister, a solicitor or a legal executive employed by a solicitor, and

(2) a lay representative means any other person.

3.2(1) A party may present his own case at a hearing or a lawyer or lay representative may present it for him.

(2) The Lay Representatives (Right of Audience) Order 1999 provides that a lay representative may not exercise any right of audience:—

(a) where his client does not attend the hearing;

(b) at any stage after judgment; or

(c) on any appeal brought against any decision made by the district judge in the proceedings.

(3) However the court, exercising its general discretion to hear anybody, may hear a lay representative even in circumstances excluded by the Order.

(4) Any of its officers or employees may represent a corporate party.

4. Small Claim Hearing

4.1(1) The general rule is that a small claim hearing will be in public.

(2) The judge may decide to hold it in private if:

(a) the parties agree, or

(b) a ground mentioned in rule 39.2(3) applies.

(3) A hearing or part of a hearing which takes place other than at the court, for example at the home or business premises of a party, will not be in public.

4.2 A hearing that takes place at the court will generally be in the judge's room but it may take place in a courtroom.

4.3 Rule 27.8 allows the court to adopt any method of proceeding that it considers to be fair and to limit cross-examination. The judge may in particular:

(1) ask questions of any witness himself before allowing any other person to do so,

(2) ask questions of all or any of the witnesses himself before allowing any other person to ask questions of any witnesses,

(3) refuse to allow cross-examination of any witness until all the witnesses have given evidence in chief,

(4) limit cross-examination of a witness to a fixed time or to a particular subject or issue, or both.

5. Recording Evidence and the Giving of Reasons

5.1 The judge may direct that all or any part of the proceedings will be tape recorded by the court. A party may obtain a transcript of such a recording on payment of the proper transcriber's charges.

5.2 Attention is drawn to section 9 of the Contempt of Court Act 1981 (which deals with the unauthorised use of tape recorders in court) and to the Practice Direction ([1981] 1 WLR 1526) which relates to it.

5.3 The judge will make a note of the central points of the oral evidence unless it is tape recorded by the court.

5.4 The judge will make a note of the central reasons for his judgment unless it is given orally and tape recorded by the court.

5.5(1) The judge may give his reasons as briefly and simply as the nature of the case allows.

(2) He will normally do so orally at the hearing, but he may give them later either in writing or at a hearing fixed for him to do so.

5.6 Where the judge decides the case without a hearing under rule 27.10 or a party who has given notice under rule 27.9(1) does not attend the hearing, the judge will prepare a note of his reasons and the court will send a copy to each party.

5.7 A party is entitled to a copy of any note made by the judge under sub-paragraphs 5.3 or 5.4.

5.8 Nothing in this practice direction affects the duty of a judge at the request of a party to make a note of the matters referred to in section 80 County Courts Act 1984.

6. Non-attendance of a Party at a Hearing

6.1 Attention is drawn to rule 27.9 (which enables a party to give notice that he will not attend a final hearing and sets out the effect of his giving such notice and of not doing so), and to paragraph 3 above. **27PD–002**

6.2 Nothing in those provisions affects the general power of the court to adjourn a hearing, for example where a party who wishes to attend a hearing on the date fixed cannot do so for a good reason.

7. Costs

7.1 Attention is drawn to rule 27.14 which contains provisions about the costs which may be ordered to be paid by one party to another

7.2 The amount which a party may be ordered to pay under rule 27.14(2)(b) (for legal advice and assistance in claims including an injunction or specific performance) is a sum not exceeding £260.

7.3 The amounts which a party may be ordered to pay under rule 27.14(3)(c) (loss of earnings) and (d) (experts' fees) are:

(1) for the loss of earnings of each party or witness due to attending a hearing or staying away from home for the purpose of attending a hearing, a sum not exceeding £50 per day for each person, and

(2) for expert's fees, a sum not exceeding £200 for each expert.

(As to recovery of pre-allocation costs in a case in which an admission by the defendant has reduced the amount in dispute to a figure below £5,000, reference should be made to paragraph 7.4 of the Practice Direction supplementing CPR Part 26 and to paragraph 5.1(3) of the Costs Directions relating to CPR Part 44.)

8. Appeals from decisions of District Judges

8.1 An appeal from a decision of a district judge under Part 27 will be dealt with by a Circuit Judge.

8.2 Attention is drawn to rule 27.12 and 13 and in particular to the limited grounds of appeal and the time limits for giving notice of appeal.

8.3 A notice of appeal must set out particulars of the serious irregularity or mistake of law relied on.

8.4 When a notice of appeal is filed it will be put before a Circuit Judge as soon as possible after it is filed and he will decide how to deal with the appeal.

8.5 The court will serve a copy of the notice on all other parties.

8.6 The Circuit Judge may either:

(1) dismiss the appeal without a hearing if no sufficient ground is shown in the notice of appeal, or

(2) order that the appeal is to be listed for hearing.

8.7 The Circuit Judge will give any necessary directions:

(1) about the filing of any evidence concerning any allegation of serious irregularity, and

(2) about the supply to the parties of copies of any document (including any note made by the judge who heard the case) which he has taken or may have taken into account in dealing with the appeal.

8.8 Where the Circuit Judge dismisses the appeal without a hearing his order will contain brief reasons for his decision.

8.9 Where the Circuit Judge directs that the appeal is to be listed for hearing the court will give at least seven days notice of the hearing to all parties.

8.10 If the appeal is allowed, the Circuit Judge will if possible dispose of the case at the same time without ordering the claim to be reheard. He may do so without hearing further evidence.

Appendix

27PD–003

FORM A—THE STANDARD DIRECTIONS

(for use where the district judge specifies no other directions)

THE COURT DIRECTS:

1. Each party shall deliver to every other party and to the court office copies of all documents (including any experts' report) on which he intends to rely at the hearing no later than [ ] [14 days before the hearing].
2. The original documents shall be brought to the hearing.
3. [Notice of hearing date and time allowed.]
4. The court must be informed immediately if the case is settled by agreement before the hearing date.

27PD–004

FORM B—STANDARD DIRECTIONS FOR USE IN CLAIMS ARISING OUT OF ROAD ACCIDENTS

THE COURT DIRECTS:

1. Each party shall deliver to every other party and to the court office copies of all documents on which he intends to rely at the hearing. These may include:

   - experts' reports (including medical reports where damages for personal injury are claimed),
   - witness statements,
   - invoices and estimates for repairs,
   - documents which relate to other losses, such as loss of earnings,
   - sketch plans and photographs.

2. The copies shall be delivered no later than [ ] [14 days before the hearing].

3. The original documents shall be brought to the hearing.

4. Before the date of the hearing the parties shall try to agree the cost of the repairs and any other losses claimed subject to the court's decision about whose fault the accident was.

5. Signed statements setting out the evidence of all witnesses on whom each party intends to rely shall be prepared and copies included in the documents mentioned in paragraph 1. This includes the evidence of the parties themselves and of any other witness, whether or not he is going to come to court to give evidence.

6. The parties should note that:

   a) in deciding the case the court will find it very helpful to have a sketch plan and photographs of the place where the accident happened,

   b) the court may decide not to take into account a document or the evidence of a witness if no copy of that document or no copy of a statement or report by that witness has been supplied to the other parties.

7. [Notice of hearing date and time allowed.]

8. The court must be informed immediately if the case is settled by agreement before the hearing date.

27PD–005

FORM C—STANDARD DIRECTIONS FOR USE IN CLAIMS ARISING OUT OF BUILDING DISPUTES, VEHICLE REPAIRS AND SIMILAR CONTRACTUAL CLAIMS

THE COURT DIRECTS:

1. Each party shall deliver to every other party and to the court office copies of all documents on which he intends to rely at the hearing. These may include:
    - the contract,
    - witness statements,
    - experts' reports,
    - photographs,
    - invoices for work done or goods supplied,
    - estimates for work to be done.
2. The copies shall be delivered no later than [ ] [14 days before the hearing].
3. The original documents shall be brought to the hearing.
4. [The shall deliver to the and to the court office [no later than] [with his copy documents] a list showing all items of work which he complains about and why, and the amount claimed for putting each item right.]
5. [The shall deliver to the and to the court office [no later than] [with his copy documents] a breakdown of the amount he is claiming showing all work done and materials supplied.]
6. Before the date of the hearing the parties shall try to agree about the nature and cost of any remedial work required, subject to the court's decision about any other issue in the case.
7. [Signed statements setting out the evidence of all witnesses on whom each party intends to rely shall be prepared and included in the documents mentioned in paragraph 1. This includes the evidence of the parties themselves and of any other witness, whether or not he is going to come to court to give evidence.]
8. The parties should note that:

    a) in deciding the case the judge may find it helpful to have photographs showing the work in question,

    b) the judge may decide not to take into account a document or the evidence of a witness if no copy of that document or no copy of a statement or report by that witness has been supplied to the other parties.
9. [Notice of hearing date and time allowed.]
10. The court must be informed immediately if the case is settled by agreement before the hearing date.

27PD–006

FORM D—TENANTS' CLAIMS FOR THE RETURN OF DEPOSITS/ LANDLORDS CLAIMS FOR DAMAGE CAUSED

THE COURT DIRECTS:

1. Each party shall deliver to every other party and to the court office copies of all documents on which he intends to rely at the hearing. These may include:

   - the tenancy agreement and any inventory,
   - the rent book or other evidence of rent and other payments made by the to the ,
   - photographs,
   - witness statements,
   - invoices or estimates for work and goods.

2. The copies shall be delivered no later than [ ] [14 days before the hearing].
3. The original documents shall be brought to the hearing.
4. The shall deliver with his copy documents a list showing each item of loss or damage for which he claims the ought to pay, and the amount he claims for the replacement or repair.
5. The parties shall before the hearing date try to agree about the nature and cost of any repairs and replacements needed, subject to the court's decision about any other issue in the case.
6. [Signed statements setting out the evidence of all witnesses on whom each party intends to rely shall be prepared and included in the documents mentioned in paragraph 1. This includes the evidence of the parties themselves and of any other witness whether or not he is going to come to court to give evidence.]
7. The parties should note that:

   a) in deciding the case the judge may find it helpful to have photographs showing the condition of the property,

   b) the judge may decide not to take into account a document or the evidence of a witness if no copy of that document or no copy of a statement or report by that witness has been supplied to the other parties.

8. [Notice of hearing date and time allowed.]
9. The court must be informed immediately if the case is settled by agreement before the hearing date.

27PD–007

FORM E—HOLIDAY AND WEDDING CLAIMS

THE COURT DIRECTS:

1. Each party shall deliver to every other party and to the court office copies of all documents on which he intends to rely at the hearing. These may include:
   - any written contract, brochure or booking form,
   - photographs,
   - documents showing payments made,
   - witness statements,
   - letters.
2. The copies shall be delivered no later than [ ] [14 days before the hearing].
3. The original documents shall be brought to the hearing.
4. Signed statements setting out the evidence of all witnesses on whom each party intends to rely shall be prepared and copies included in the documents mentioned in paragraph 1. This includes the evidence of the parties themselves and of any other witness, whether or not he is going to come to court to give evidence.
5. If either party intends to show a video as evidence he must:
   (a) contact the court at once to make arrangements for him to do so, because the court may not have the necessary equipment, and
   (b) provide the other party with a copy of the video or the opportunity to see it (if he asks) at least 2 weeks before the hearing.
6. The parties should note that the court may decide not to take into account a document or the evidence of a witness or a video if these directions have not been complied with.
7. [Notice of hearing date and time allowed.]
8. The court must be told immediately if the case is settled by agreement before the hearing date.

27PD–008

FORM F—SOME SPECIAL DIRECTIONS

The must clarify his case. He must do this by delivering to the court office and to the no later than [a list of] [details of] [ ]

The shall allow the to inspect by appointment within days of receiving a request to do so.

The hearing will not take place at the court but at .

The must bring to court at the hearing the .

Signed statements setting out the evidence of all witnesses on whom each party intends to rely shall be prepared and copies included in the documents mentioned in paragraph 1. This includes the evidence of the parties themselves and of any other witness, whether or not he is going to come to court to give evidence.

The court may decide not to take into account a document [or video] or the evidence of a witness if these directions have not been complied with.

If he does not [do so] [ ] his [Claim] [Defence] [and Counterclaim] and will be struck out and [(specify consequence)].

It appears to the court that expert evidence is necessary on the issue of [ ] and that that evidence should be given by a single expert [ ] to be instructed by the parties jointly. If the parties cannot agree about who to chose and what arrangements to make about paying his fee, either party may apply to the court for further directions.

If either party intends to show a video as evidence he must

(a) contact the court at once to make arrangements for him to do so, because the court may not have the necessary equipment, and

(b) provide the other party with a copy of the video or the opportunity to see it at least [ ] before the hearing.

PART 28

The Fast Track

28.0.1 **Contents**

Editorial Introduction

28.0.2 The "fast track" is an innovation of the CPR and had no equivalent in either the RSC or the CCR. One of the unintended consequences of the reforms effected by the CCR 1981 (accentuated by the High Court and County Courts Jurisdiction Order 1991 which further increased the jurisdiction of county courts) was to make litigation in the county courts ever more complex and expensive. Trial in a county court was not simpler and not necessarily cheaper than trial in the High Court. The old CCR, O.19 (see now Pt 27 of the CPR) provided a system and limited costs regime for "small claims". For many years it has been obvious that the county court needed a new procedure rather more detailed than the "small claims" procedure but rather less detailed than the full procedural code necessitated by more complex cases. The "fast track" has been designed to meet that need. Cases on the fast track have more pre-trial stages than cases on the small claims track (compare Pts 27 and 28) but less than most cases on the multi-track (compare Pts 28 and 29).

The fast track is intended as a limited procedure designed to take straightforward cases to trial within a short but reasonable timescale. It is designed for cases which exceed the limit for the small claims track and which do not need the more detailed procedure of the multi-track, *i.e.* generally cases valued at over £5,000 but less than £15,000. This bracket theatre contains the majority of personal injury cases and a very significant proportion of county court cases.

Initially district judges and circuit judges have concurrent jurisdiction to hear trials of cases on the fast track.

Related Sources

28.0.3
- Practice Direction (The Fast Track) para. 28PD–001
- Part 3 (The Courts Case Management Powers)
- Part 26 (Case Management—Preliminary Stage)
- Part 31 (Disclosure and Inspection of Documents)
- Part 32 (Evidence)
- Part 35 (Experts and Assessors)
- Part 39 (Miscellaneous Provisions Relating to Hearings)
- Part 43 (Scope of Costs Rules and Definitions)
- Part 44 (General Rules about Costs)
- Part 46 (Fast Track Trial Costs)

Forms

28.0.4
- N170—Listing questionnaire (see para. C35–001)

Scope of this Part

28.1 **28.1** This Part contains general provisions about management of cases allocated to the fast track and applies only to cases allocated to that track.

(Part 27 sets out the procedure for claims allocated to the small claims track.)

(Part 29 sets out the procedure for claims allocated to the multi-track.)

Effect of rule—There is no "automatic allocation" to a track. Cases are allocated by the judge upon receipt of the "allocation questionnaire" (see rr.26.3 and 26.5). See r.26.6 for the scope of each of the three tracks and in particular r.26.6(4) for the scope of the fast track. 28.1.1

General provisions

28.2—(1) When it allocates a case to the fast track, the court will give directions for the management of the case and set a timetable for the steps to be taken between the giving of the directions and the trial. 28.2

(2) When it gives directions, the court will—

(a) fix the trial date; or

(b) fix a period, not exceeding 3 weeks, within which the trial is to take place.

(3) The trial date or trial period will be specified in the notice of allocation.

(4) The standard period between the giving of directions and the trial will be not more than 30 weeks.

(5) The court's power to award trial costs is limited in accordance with Part 46.

"the court will give directions for the management of the case . . ."—It is of the essence of the fast track that pre-trial preparation should be the minimum necessary for the particular case (see further the "overriding objective" in Pt 1). 28.2.1

Pre-action protocols—The pre-action protocols have a significant role in the new regime enacted by the CPR. Nowhere is this role more significant than in the context of fast track cases. As a general rule parties will have to comply with the pre-action protocol relevant to the case. The courts will expect this and will use the case management powers (see Pt 3) to ensure that no party can take advantage of another or suffer a disadvantage, by non-compliance with the spirit of the pre-action protocols. In practice, both parties will have to undertake significant preparation of a case before proceedings are issued in anticipation of the court setting a strict timetable on allocation of the case and insisting that it be complied with. As to variation of the case management timetable see r.28.4, but note in particular that parties cannot agree any variation which would delay the trial. 28.2.2

There are only two protocols at the moment (set out at paras B0–001 *et seq.*) but more are anticipated.

"the court will fix the trial date or fix a period ... within which the trial is to take place"—In practice it is far more likely that the court will fix a "trial window" of two or three weeks rather than give a fixed trial date. Of course, the court can be asked to fix a trial date at the allocation stage if there is a particular reason why it should do so. Fixing the trial date or "trial window"—and insisting upon it—is of the essence of the fast-track. 28.2.3

"not more than 30 weeks"—The aim of this rule is clear. All fast track cases should be compromised or tried within a period of 30 weeks from the giving of directions. 28.2.4

Split trial—One inevitable consequence of the fast track regime will be an increase in the number of cases where liability is ordered to be tried separately from and before the issue of quantum. The power to order a split trial is found in r.3.1(2)(i). If the claimant fails on liability a significant costs saving is invariably achieved and the case is concluded at a much earlier stage. If the claimant succeeds on liability it is more probable than not that quantum will be agreed without a further hearing. Often, due to non-availability of experts, it will not be possible to fix a trial date within the 30 week period and ordering a trial on liability only is one way to overcome this difficulty. Furthermore, a case is allocated to the fast track only if the trial is likely to last for no longer than one day and oral expert evidence is limited to one expert per party in relation to any expert field and expert evidence in two fields only (see r.26.6(5)). By narrowing the issue for trial the court will be able to allocate to the fast-track a case that might otherwise have had to be allocated to the multi-track. It must be anticipated that, where a case is within the financial limits of the fast-track, the court will make every effort to allocate it to the fast-track. 28.2.5

"trial costs"—See Pt 46. One of Lord Woolf's "Access to Justice" recommendations which has not yet been enacted in the CPR is a recommendation for a fixed costs regime for fast-track cases. 28.2.6

Directions

28.3 **28.3**—(1) The matters to be dealt with by directions under rule 28.2(1) include—

(a) disclosure of documents;
(b) service of witness statements; and
(c) expert evidence.

(2) If the court decides not to direct standard disclosure, it may—

(a) direct that no disclosure take place; or
(b) specify the documents or the classes of documents which the parties must disclose.

(Rule 31.6 explains what is meant by standard disclosure.)

(Rule 26.6(5) deals with limitations in relation to expert evidence and the likely length of trial in fast track cases.)

28.3.1 **Scope of provision**—In a fast-track case, when giving directions the only matters which need to be addressed are the fixing of the trial date or "trial window" and the three matters mentioned in r.28.3(1): disclosure, witness statements, expert evidence. Parties will have to undertake more pre-issue preparation than was formerly the case under the RSC and CCR (see above commentary on "Pre-action protocols" and "Split trial" at paras 28.2.2 and 28.2.5 respectively). Disclosure will be "standard disclosure" (see r.31.6) or less. Exchange of witness statements will always be ordered. If either party is relying on expert evidence (note the limitations in r.26.6(5) and see generally Pt 35) the court will have to give directions as to service of experts reports. Permission is always required to adduce expert evidence (r.35.4(1)). The court will bear in mind that normally trial of a fast-track case "is likely to last for no longer than one day" (see r.26.6(5)).

28.3.2 **Cases valued at over £15,000**—A case which is valued at over £15,000 is normally allocated to the multi-track. The court cannot allocate it to the fast track "unless all the parties consent to the allocation ..." (see r.26.7(3)). However, directions on the multi-track are specific to the case and therefore, for example, if the case only just exceeds £15,000 and the court considers the case otherwise suitable for the fast track the court could give directions in a multi-track case which are identical to the directions it could have given had it been on the fast track.

28.3.3 **Split trial**—See above commentary to r.28.2 at para. 28.2.5.

28.3.4 **Agreed directions**—Parties are encouraged to agree directions so as to avoid attendance at a directions hearing. Specimen directions are set out in the Practice Direction which supplements Pt 28: para. 28PD–001.

Variation of case management timetable

28.4 **28.4**—(1) A party must apply to the court if he wishes to vary the date which the court has fixed for—

(a) the return of a listing questionnaire under rule 28.5;
(b) the trial; or
(c) the trial period.

(2) Any date set by the court or these Rules for doing any act may not be varied by the parties if the variation would make it necessary to vary any of the dates mentioned in paragraph (1).

(Rule 2.11 allows the parties to vary a date by written agreement except where the rules provide otherwise or the court orders otherwise.)

28.4.1 **Effect of rule**—A case management timetable, once set, should be complied with. The aim of the rules is to set a realistic timetable which all must then honour. However, minor variations (*e.g.* extending by a few days time for exchange of witness statements) can be agreed by the parties without troubling the court: see r.2.11 and note that any such agreement must be in writing. However, the trial date (or "trial window" if the trial date is not yet fixed: see r.28.2 above) is immutable. Accordingly so is the date for return of the listing questionnaire.

These dates cannot be varied by agreement and a party who wishes to vary any of the dates listed in r.28.4(1) must apply to the court. (See Pt 23 for general rules regarding applications.) It must be anticipated that the court will not be pre-disposed to delaying the trial and very cogent arguments and reasons will be required in order to achieve it.

Listing questionnaire

28.5—(1) The court will send the parties a listing questionnaire for completion and return by the date specified in the notice of allocation unless it considers that the claim can be listed for trial without the need for a listing questionnaire. **28.5**

(2) The date specified for filing a listing questionnaire will not be more than 8 weeks before the trial date or the beginning of the trial period.

(3) If—

(a) a party fails to file the completed questionnaire by the date specified;

(b) a party has failed to give all the information requested by the listing questionnaire; or

(c) the court considers that a hearing is necessary to enable it to decide what directions to give in order to complete preparation of the case for trial,

the court may fix a listing hearing or give such other directions as it thinks appropriate.

Effect of rule—The court will have fixed a trial date or (more likely) a "trial window" of two or three weeks when it gave directions upon allocation (see r.28.2). The trial date or window will be not more than 30 weeks from the directions. The court needs to make final listing arrangements (especially where a fixed date has not yet been given) as the period draws to a close. Further, it is anticipated that a significant proportion of cases will have been settled during the trial preparation period and will not now require a trial. Rule 28.5 therefore requires the court to send out a "listing questionnaire". This will be done about 10 weeks before the trial date or beginning of the trial window. The precise date for the return of the listing questionnaire is specified in the notice of allocation and that date "will not be more than 8 weeks before the trial date or beginning of the trial window". **28.5.1**

In effect the rules envisage directions being given in two stages. The first and the main stage is upon allocation. However, listing provides a second and final opportunity to deal with further directions.

It is essential for all parties to return the listing questionnaire by the specified date. No advantage—and certainly no delay—follows from a failure to do so. Indeed there are likely to be adverse costs consequences from such a failure and the court is likely to fix a "listing hearing" with a defaulting party being ordered to pay the costs of it. Similarly, if a party returns the listing questionnaire without giving all requested information.

Fixing or confirming the trial date and giving directions

28.6—(1) As soon as practicable after the date specified for filing a completed listing questionnaire the court will— **28.6**

(a) fix the date for the trial (or, if it has already done so, confirm that date);

(b) give any directions for the trial, including a trial timetable, which it considers appropriate; and

(c) specify any further steps that need to be taken before trial.

(2) The court will give the parties at least 3 weeks' notice of the date of the trial unless, in exceptional circumstances, the court directs that shorter notice will be given.

"listing questionnaire"—See r.28.5. **28.6.1**

"fix the date for trial"—Although the court has the option of fixing a trial date at the **28.6.2**

allocation stage it is more likely that the court will have fixed a trial window of one, two or three weeks, not more than 30 weeks ahead. Accordingly all parties and witnesses will have knowledge of the approximate trial date. Upon the filing of a completed listing questionnaire the court will now fix the precise trial date and give the parties at least 3 weeks' notice of it (in exceptional circumstances, shorter notice: see r.28.6(2)).

28.6.3 **"directions for the trial"**—As noted in the commentary to rule 28.5 (see para. 28.5.1), the "listing stage" provides a second and final opportunity for the court to give directions. It is envisaged that in many cases the only further directions required will be for the trial timetable.

28.6.4 **"trial timetable"**—A "fast track" was recommended in Lord Woolf's Interim Report, confirmed in the final "Access to Justice" Report and now enacted by the CPR. The final rules differ somewhat from the original draft but a constant feature throughout has been the recognition that fast-track trials will occupy a limited amount of court time. Rule 26.6(5) provides that the fast track is the normal track for cases within its financial limit ("not more than £15,000") "only if the court considers that the trial is likely to last for no longer than one day". The Practice Direction supplementing Pt 28 states that "one day" means five hours (*i.e.* 10.30 a.m. to 4.30 p.m. or thereabouts). It has always been envisaged that, for fast-track cases, in addition to the case-management rules, some firm judicial control of the trial itself will be required. Parties—and especially advocates—need to know in advance how much time has been allocated to the case. Accordingly a trial timetable is necessary and will be given at the listing stage. Rule 26.6(1) requires the court to give a trial timetable. See also Pt 39 and in particular note that r.39.4 provides that when the court sets a timetable for trial it will do so in consultation with the parties. The Practice Direction supplementing Pt 28 (see para. 28PD–001) contains the format for a trial timetable.

28.6.5 **Specimen Trial Timetable for trial of a case allocated to the Fast Track**—Neither r.28.6 nor the Practice Direction supplementing Part 28 contains a specimen timetable although r.28.6(1)(b) requires the court to give one. A typical timetable is as follows:-

Claimant's opening	10 min
Defendant's opening	10 min
Cross-examination of Claimant's witnesses	1 hr 10 min
Re-examination	15 min
Cross-examination of Defendant's witness	1 hr 10 min
Re-examination	15 min
Defendant's submissions	20 min
Claimant's submissions	20 min
Judge's "thinking time" and judgment	30 min
Costs and consequential orders	20 min
	5 hr 00 mins

This timetable makes no provision for evidence in chief as witness statements stand as evidence in chief (r.32.5) and expert evidence is generally given in the form of a written report (r.35.5).

A period of five hours is the maximum for a trial on the fast-track: not all cases will require as long as this and the timetable will be varied accordingly.

A fast-track trial concludes with a summary assessment of costs (see 48PD-005).

Conduct of trial

28.7 **28.7** Unless the trial judge otherwise directs, the trial will be conducted in accordance with any order previously made.

28.7.1 **Effect of rule**—In fast-track cases a "trial timetable" will have been given at the allocation stage or the listing stage (see r.28.6). Many other rules have consequences for the conduct of the trial (*e.g.* an order under r.35.4 giving—or refusing—permission to a party to call an expert witness).

If a party is dissatisfied with a direction the proper course is to appeal, not wait until the trial in the hope that the trial judge will take a different view.

The general rule is that "the trial will be conducted in accordance with any order previously made". Rule 28.7 does enable the trial judge to "otherwise direct". The trial judge is likely to do that only in non-controversial circumstances. Time is limited at a fast-track trial and the trial judge is most unlikely to allow part of it to be used up by what is, in effect, an application to vary or appeal directions previously given. Nevertheless the principle remains that the trial judge is in charge of his/her own court and in an exceptional appropriate case has power to depart from an order previously made.

Trial bundle—See r.39.5. Directions as to what the trial bundle should contain will be given at allocation or listing. See further the Practice Direction supplementing Pt 28 at para. 28PD–001. **28.7.2**

PRACTICE DIRECTION—THE FAST TRACK

This Practice Direction supplements CPR Part 28

1. General

1.1 Attention is drawn in particular to the following Parts of the Civil Procedure Rules: **28PD–001**

Part 1	The overriding objective
Part 3	The court's case management powers
Part 26	Case management—preliminary stage
Part 31	Disclosure and inspection of documents
Parts 32–34	Evidence
Part 35	Experts and assessors

and to the practice directions which relate to those Parts.

1.2 Attention is also drawn to:

Rule 26.6(5)—which makes provision about limitation on expert evidence and the length of trial in fast track cases.

Part 46—Fast Track Trial Costs.

2. Case Management

2.1 Case management of cases allocated to the fast track will generally be by directions given at two stages in the case:

(1) at allocation to the track, and

(2) on the filing of listing questionnaires.

2.2 The court will seek whenever possible to give directions at those stages only and to do so without the need for a hearing to take place. It will expect to do so with the co-operation of the parties.

2.3 The court will however hold a hearing to give directions whenever it appears necessary or desirable to do so, and where this happens because of the default of a party or his legal representative it will usually impose a sanction.

2.4 The court may give directions at any hearing on the application of a party or on its own initiative.

2.5 When any hearing has been fixed it is the duty of the parties to consider what directions the court should be asked to give and to make any application that may be appropriate to be dealt with at that hearing.

2.6 When the court fixes a hearing to give directions it will give the parties at least 3 days notice of the hearing.

2.7 Appendix A contains forms of directions. When making an order the court will as far as possible base its order on those forms. Agreed directions which the parties file and invite the court to make should also be based on those forms.

2.8 Where a party needs to apply for a direction of a kind not included in the case management timetable which has been set (for example to amend his statement of case or for further information to be given by another party) he must do so as soon as possible so as to minimise the need to change that timetable.

2.9 Courts will make arrangements to ensure that applications and other hearings are listed promptly to avoid delay in the conduct of cases.

3. Directions on Allocation

28PD–002 **3.1** Attention is drawn to the court's duty under rule 28.2(2) to set a case management timetable and to fix a trial date or a trial period, and to the matters which are to be dealt with by directions under rule 28.3(1)

3.2 The court will seek to tailor its directions to the needs of the case and the steps of which it is aware that the parties have already taken to prepare the case. In particular it will have regard to the extent to which any pre-action protocol has or (as the case may be) has not been complied with.

3.3 At this stage the court's first concern will be to ensure that the issues between the parties be identified and that the necessary evidence is prepared and disclosed.

3.4 The court may have regard to any document filed by a party with his allocation questionnaire containing further information provided that the document states either that its contents has been agreed with every other party or that it has been served on every other party and when it was served.

3.5 If:

(1) the parties have filed agreed directions for the management of the case, and

(2) the court considers that the proposals are suitable,

it may approve them and give directions in the terms proposed.

3.6(1) To obtain the court's approval the agreed directions must:

(a) set out a timetable by reference to calendar dates for the taking of steps for the preparation of the case,
(b) include a date or a period (the trial period) when it is proposed that the trial will take place,
(c) include provision about disclosure of documents, and
(d) include provision about both factual and expert evidence.

(2) The latest proposed date for the trial or the end of the trial period must be not later than 30 weeks from the date the directions order is made.

(3) The trial period must not be longer than 3 weeks.

(4) The provision in (1)(c) above may:

(a) limit disclosure to standard disclosure between all parties or to less than that, and/or
(b) direct that disclosure will take place by the supply of copy documents without a list, but it must in that case either direct that the parties must serve a disclosure statement with the copies or record that they have agreed to disclose in that way without such a statement.

(5) The provision in (1)(d) may be to the effect that no expert evidence is required.

3.7 Directions agreed by the parties should also where appropriate contain provisions about:

(1) the filing of any reply or amended statement of case that may be required,

(2) dates for the service of requests for further information under the practice direction supplementing Part 18 and questions to experts under rule 35.6 and when they are to be dealt with,

(3) the disclosure of evidence,

(4) the use of a single joint expert, or in cases where the use of a single expert has not been agreed the exchange and agreement of expert evidence (including whether exchange is to be simultaneous or sequential) and without prejudice discussions of the experts.

3.8 If the court does not approve the agreed directions filed by the parties but decides that it will give directions on its own initiative without a hearing, it will take them into account in deciding what directions to give.

3.9 Where the court is to give directions on its own initiative and it is not aware of any steps taken by the parties other than the service of statements of case, its general approach will be:

(1) to give directions for the filing and service of any further information required to clarify either party's case,

(2) to direct standard disclosure between the parties,

(3) to direct the disclosure of witness statements by way of simultaneous exchange,

(4) to give directions for a single joint expert unless there is good reason not to do so,

(5) in cases where directions for a single expert are not given:

(a) to direct disclosure of experts' reports by way of simultaneous exchange, and

(b) if experts' reports are not agreed, to direct a discussion between the experts for the purpose set out in rule 35.12(1) and the preparation of a report under rule 35.12(3).

3.10(1) If it appears to the court that the claim is one which will be allocated to the fast track but that it cannot properly give directions on its own initiative or approve agreed directions that have been filed, the court may either:

(a) allocate the claim to the fast track, fix a trial date or trial period and direct that a case management hearing is to be listed and give directions at that hearing, or

(b) direct that an allocation hearing is to be listed and give directions at that hearing.

(2) In either case the hearing will be listed as promptly as possible.

3.11 Where the court is proposing on its own initiative to make an order under rule 35.15 (which gives the court power to appoint an assessor), the court must, unless the parties have consented in writing to the order, list a directions hearing.

3.12 The table set out below contains a typical timetable the court may give for the preparation of the case.

Disclosure	4 weeks
Exchange of witness statements	10 weeks
Exchange of experts' reports	14 weeks
Sending of listing questionnaires by the court	20 weeks
Filing of completed listing questionnaires	22 weeks
Hearing	30 weeks

These periods will run from the date of the notice of allocation.

3.13(1) Where it considers that some or all of the steps in that timetable are not necessary the court may omit them and direct an earlier trial.

(2) This may happen where the court is informed that a pre-action protocol has been complied with or that steps which it would otherwise order to be taken have already been taken.

(3) It may also happen where an application (for example for summary judgment or for an injunction) has been heard before allocation and little or no further preparation is required. In such a case the court may dispense with the need for a listing questionnaire.

4. Variation of Directions

4.1 This paragraph deals with the procedure to be adopted: 28PD–003

(1) where a party is dissatisfied with a direction given by the court,

(2) where the parties agree about changes they wish made to the directions given, or

(3) where a party wishes to apply to vary a direction.

4.2(1) It is essential that any party who wishes to have a direction varied takes steps to do so as soon as possible.

(2) The court will assume for the purposes of any later application that a party who did not appeal and who made no application to vary within 14 days of service of the order containing the directions was content that they were correct in the circumstances then existing.

4.3(1) Where a party is dissatisfied with a direction given or other order made by the court he may appeal or apply to the court for it to reconsider its decision.

(2) He should appeal if the direction was given or the order was made at a hearing at which he was present or represented, or of which he had due notice.

(3) In any other case he should apply to the court to reconsider its decision.

(4) If an application is made for the court to reconsider its decision:

(a) it will usually be heard by the judge who gave the directions or another judge of the same level,

(b) the court will give all parties at least 3 days notice of the hearing, and

(c) the court may confirm its decision or make a different order.

4.4 Where there has been a change in the circumstances since the order was made the court may set aside or vary any direction it has given. It may do so on application or on its own initiative.

4.5 Where the parties agree about changes to be made to the directions given:

(1) If rule 2.11 (variation by agreement of a date set by the court for doing any act other than those stated in the note to that rule) or rule 31.5, 31.10(8) or 31.13 (agreements about disclosure) applied the parties need not file the written agreement.

(2)(a) In any other case the parties must apply for an order by consent.

(b) The parties must file a draft of the order sought and an agreed statement of the reasons why the variation is sought.

(c) The court may make an order in the agreed terms or in other terms without a hearing, but it may direct that a hearing is to be listed.

5. Failure to Comply with Case Management Directions

5.1 Where a party has failed to comply with a direction given by the court any other party may apply for an order to enforce compliance or for a sanction to be imposed or both of these.

5.2 The party entitled to apply for such an order must do so without delay but should first warn the other party of his intention to do so.

5.3 The court may take any such delay into account when it decides whether to make an order imposing a sanction or whether to grant relief from a sanction imposed by the rules or any practice direction.

5.4(1) The court will not allow a failure to comply with directions to lead to the postponement of the trial unless the circumstances of the case are exceptional.

(2) If it is practicable to do so the court will exercise its powers in a manner that enables the case to come on for trial on the date or within the period previously set.

(3) In particular the court will assess what steps each party should take to prepare the case for trial, direct that those steps are taken in the shortest possible time and impose a sanction for non-compliance. Such a sanction may, for example, deprive a party of the right to raise or contest an issue or to rely on evidence to which the direction relates.

(4) Where it appears that one or more issues are or can be made ready for trial at the time fixed while others cannot, the court may direct that the trial will proceed on the issues which are or will then be ready, and order that no costs will be allowed for any later trial of the remaining issues or that those costs will be paid by the party in default.

(5) Where the court has no option but to postpone the trial it will do so for the shortest possible time and will give directions for the taking of the necessary steps in the meantime as rapidly as possible.

(6) Litigants and lawyers must be in no doubt that the court will regard the postponement of a trial as an order of last resort. The court may exercise its power to require a party as well as his legal representative to attend court at a hearing where such an order is to be sought.

6. Listing Questionnaires and Listing

6.1 (1) The listing questionnaire will be in Form N170. 28PD–004

(2) Unless it has dispensed with listing questionnaires, the court will send Forms N170 and N171 (Notice of date for return of the listing questionnaire) to each party no later than 2 weeks before the date specified in the notice of allocation or in any later direction of the court for the return of the completed questionnaires.

(3) When all the listing questionnaires have been filed or when the time for filing them has expired the file will be placed before a judge for his directions.

(4) Although the Rules do not require the parties to exchange copies of the questionnaires before they are filed they are encouraged to do so to avoid the court being given conflicting or incomplete information.

Attention is drawn to the Costs Practice Direction, paragraph 4.5(2), which requires a costs estimate to be filed and served at the same time as the listing questionnaire is filed.

6.2 Attention is drawn to rule 28.6(1) (which sets out the court's duty at the listing questionnaire stage) and to rule 28.5(3) (which sets out circumstances in which the court may decide to hold a listing hearing).

6.3 Where the judge decides to hold a listing hearing the court will fix a date which is as early as possible and the parties will be given at least 3 days notice of the date.

The notice of a listing hearing will be in Form N153.

6.4 The court's general approach will be as set out in the following paragraphs. The court may however decide to make other orders, and in particular the court will take into account the steps, if any, which the parties have taken to prepare the case for trial.

6.5 (1) Where no party files a listing questionnaire the court will normally make an order that if no listing questionnaire is filed by any party within 3 days from service of the order the claim and any counterclaim will be struck out.

(2) Where a party files a listing questionnaire but another party does not do so, the court normally will give listing directions. These will usually fix or confirm the trial date and provide for steps to be taken to prepare the case for trial.

7. Directions the Court will Give on Listing

7.1 Directions the court must give:

(1) The court must confirm or fix the trial date, specify the place of trial and give a time estimate. The trial date must be fixed and the case listed on the footing that the hearing will end on the same calandar day as that on which it commenced.

(2) The court will serve a notice of hearing on the parties at least 3 weeks before the hearing unless they agree to accept shorter notice or the court authorises shorter service under rule 28.6(2), and

(3) The notice of hearing will be in Form N172.

7.2 Other directions:

(1) The parties should seek to agree directions and may file the proposed order. The court may make an order in those terms or it may make a different order.

(2) Agreed directions should include provision about:

(a) evidence,
(b) a trial timetable and time estimate,
(c) the preparation of a trial bundle,
(d) any other matter needed to prepare the case for trial.

(3) The court will include such of these provisions as are appropriate in any order that it may make, whether or not the parties have filed agreed directions.

(4)(a) A direction giving permission to use expert evidence will say whether it gives permission for oral evidence or reports or both and will name the experts concerned.
(b) The court will not make a direction giving permission for an expert to give oral evidence unless it believes it is necessary in the interests of justice to do so.
(c) Where no without prejudice meeting or other discussion between experts has taken place the court may grant that permission conditionally on such a discussion taking place and a report being filed before the trial.

7.3 The principles set out in paragraph 4 of this practice direction about the variation of directions apply also to directions given at this stage.

8. The Trial

8.1 The trial will normally take place at the court where the case is being managed, but it may be at another court if it is appropriate having regard to the needs of the parties and the availability of court resources.

8.2 The judge will generally have read the papers in the trial bundle and may dispense with an opening address.

8.3 The judge may confirm or vary any timetable given previously, or if none has been given set his own.

8.4 Attention is drawn to the provisions in Part 32 and the following parts of the Rules about evidence, and in particular—

(1) to rule 32.1 (court's power to control evidence and to restrict cross-examination), and

(2) to rule 32.5(2) (witness statements to stand as evidence in chief).

8.5 At the conclusion of the trial the judge will normally summarily assess the costs of the claim in accordance with rule 44.7 and Part 46 (fast track trial costs). Attention is drawn to the steps the practice directions about costs requires the parties to take.

8.6 Where a trial is not finished on the day for which it is listed the judge will normally sit on the next court day to complete it.

Appendix

Fast Track Standard Directions

Further Statements of Case

28PD–005 The must file a and serve a copy on no later than .

Requests for Further Information

Any request for clarifications or further information based on another party's statement of case shall be served no later than .

[Any such request shall be dealt with no later than].

Disclosure of Documents

[No disclosure of documents is required]

[[Each party] [The] shall give [to the] [to every other party] standard disclosure of documents [relating to] by serving copies together with a disclosure statement no later than].

[Disclosure shall take place as follows:

[Each party shall give standard discovery to every other party by list]

[Disclosure is limited to [standard] [disclosure by the to the] [of documents relating to damage] [the following documents]

[The latest for delivery of the lists is]

[The latest date for service of any request to inspect or for a copy of a document is]]

Witnesses of Fact

Each party shall serve on every other party the witness statements of all witnesses of fact on whom he intends to rely.

There shall be simultaneous exchange of such statements no later than .

Expert Evidence

[No expert evidence being necessary, no party has permission to call or rely on expert evidence].

[On it appearing to the court that expert evidence is necessary on the issue of [ ] and that that evidence should be given by the report of a single expert instructed jointly by the parties, the shall not later than inform the court whether or not such an expert has been instructed].

[The expert evidence on the issue of shall be limited to a single expert jointly instructed by the parties.

If the parties cannot agree by who that expert is to be and about the payment of his fees either party may apply for further directions.

Unless the parties agree in writing or the court orders otherwise, the fees and expenses of such an expert shall be paid to him [by the parties equally] [ ] and be limited to £ .

[The report of the expert shall be filed at the court no later than].

[No party shall be entitled to recover by way of costs from any other party more than £ for the fees or expenses of an expert].

The parties shall exchange reports setting out the substance of any expert evidence on which they intend to rely.

[The exchange shall take place simultaneously no later than].

[The shall serve his report(s) no later than the and the shall serve his reports no later than the].

[The exchange of reports relating to [causation] [ ] shall take place simultaneously no later than . The shall serve his report(s) relating to [damage] [ ] no later than and the shall serve his reports relating to it no later than].

Reports shall be agreed if possible no later than [days after service] [ ].

[If the reports are not agreed within that time there shall be a without prejudice discussion between the relevant experts no later than to identify the issues between them and to reach agreement if possible.

The experts shall prepare for the court a statement of the issues on which they agree and on which they disagree with a summary of their reasons, and that statement shall be filed with the court [no later than] [with] [no later than the date for filing] [the listing questionnaire].

[Each party has permission to use [ ] as expert witness(es) to give [oral] evidence [in the form of a report] at the trial in the field of provided that the substance of the evidence to be given has been disclosed as above and has not been agreed].

[Each party has permission to use in evidence experts' report(s) [and the court will consider when the claim is listed for trial whether expert oral evidence will be allowed].]

Questions to Experts

28PD–006 The time for service on another party of any question addressed to an expert instructed by that party is not later than days after service of that expert's report.

Any such question shall be answered within days of service.

Requests for Information etc.

Each party shall serve any request for clarification or further information based on any document disclosed or statement served by another party no later than days after disclosure or service.

Any such request shall be dealt with within days of service.

Documents to be filed with Listing Questionnaires

The parties must file with their listing questionnaires copies of [their experts' reports] [witness statements] [replies to requests for further information].

Dates for filing Listing Questionnaires and the Trial

Each party must file a complete listing questionnaire no later than .

The trial of this case will take place [on] [on a date to be fixed between and].

Directions following filing of Listing Questionnaire

Expert Evidence

The parties have permission to rely at the trial on expert evidence as follows:

The claimant:	Oral evidence—
	Written evidence—
The defendant:	Oral evidence—
	Written evidence—

Trial Timetable

The time allowed for the trial is .

[The timetable for the trial may be agreed by the parties, subject to the approval of the trial judge].

[The timetable for the trial (subject to the approval of the trial judge) will be that].

[The evidence in chief for each party will be contained in witness statements and reports, the time allowed for cross-examination by the defendant is limited to and the time allowed for cross-examination by the claimant is limited to].

[The time allowed for the claimant's evidence is . The time allowed for the defendant's evidence is].

The time allowed for the submissions on behalf on each party is .

The remainder of the time allowed for the trial (being) is reserved for the judge to consider and give the judgment and to deal with costs].

Trial Bundle Etc.

The claimant shall lodge an indexed bundle of documents contained in a ring binder and with each page clearly numbered at the court not more than 7 days and not less than 3 days before the start of the trial.

[A case summary (which should not exceed 250 words) outlining the matters still in issue, and referring where appropriate to the relevant documents shall be included in the bundle for the assistance of the judge in reading the papers before the trial].

[The parties shall seek to agree the contents of the trial bundle and the case summary].

Settlement

Each party must inform the court immediately if the claim is settled whether or not it is then possible to file a draft consent order to give effect to their agreement.

PART 29

THE MULTI-TRACK

29.0.1 **Contents**

Editorial Introduction

29.0.2 The rules in this Part set out the procedure to be followed from allocation to trial in multi-track cases. The major innovations made or demonstrated in this Part are set out below.

(1) The court will actively manage each case, running it according to a timetable set by the court and from time to time adjusted if necessary.

(2) The parties may be required to prepare a case summary, a document not normally exceeding 500 words in length which sets out a brief chronology of the claim, the issues of fact which are agreed or in dispute and evidence needed to decide them.

(3) The parties will be expected to co-operate with each other in the conduct of the proceedings so as to facilitate the court in giving directions suitably tailored to the needs of the case.

(4) The parties must each file a costs estimate of the costs incurred to date and to be incurred. The estimate may affect the maximum costs recoverable from other parties.

Related Sources

29.0.3
- Part 3 (The court's case management powers).
- Part 26 (Case management—preliminary stage).
- Part 32 (Evidence).
- Part 35 (Experts and assessors).

Forms

29.0.4 Form N155 (Notice of allocation to the multi-track)
Form N170 (Listing questionnaire)
Form N171 (Notice of date for return of listing questionnaire)
Form N172 (Notice of trial date)
Form PF49 (Request to parties to state convenient dates for hearing)
Form PF50 (Application for directions) (Pt 29)
Form PF53 (Order for trial of an issue)
Form PF74 (Order for trial by Master)
Form PF168 (Order to transfer claim to county court (County Courts Act 1984))

Scope of this Part

29.1 **29.1** This Part contains general provisions about management of cases allocated to the multi-track and applies only to cases allocated to that track.

(Part 27 sets out the procedure for claims allocated to the small claims track.)

(Part 28 sets out the procedure for claims allocated to the fast track.)

29.1.1 **The multi-track**—The multi-track is one of the three management tracks to which a case may be allocated. The other two tracks are the small claims track and the fast track. As to the scope of each track, see r.26.6. Cases allocated to the multi-track includes cases with a financial value exceeding the limit for the fast track (*i.e.* exceeding £15,000) and also cases with a lower financial value if the court considers that the trial is likely to last longer than one day or that the oral expert evidence at the trial will not be limited to one expert per party in not more than two expert fields.

All claims concerned by way of the alternative procedure for claims are treated as allocated to the multi-track (r.8.9(c)). The Practice Direction supplementing Pt 29, para. 3.2 (see para. 29PD–001 below) states that the hallmarks of the multi-track are:

(1) the ability of the court to deal with cases of widely differing values and complexity; and
(2) the flexibility given to the court in the way it will manage a case in a way appropriate to its particular needs.

Case management

29.2—(1) When it allocates a case to the multi-track, the court will— 29.2

(a) give directions for the management of the case and set a timetable for the steps to be taken between the giving of directions and the trial; or
(b) fix—
  (i) a case management conference; or
  (ii) a pre-trial review,

or both, and give such other directions relating to the management of the case as it sees fit.

(2) The court will fix the trial date or the period in which the trial is to take place as soon as practicable.

(3) When the court fixes the trial date or the trial period under paragraph (2), it will—

(a) give notice to the parties of the date or period; and
(b) specify the date by which the parties must file a listing questionnaire.

Management on allocation—Rule 29.2(1) sets out the ways in which the court may give case management directions at the time of allocation: 29.2.1

(1) by setting out comprehensive directions immediately on allocation; and
(2) by fixing a case management conference, a pre-trial review, or both (as to these, see r.29.3).

It should not be thought that every case on the multi-track will go straight to a case management conference. It is envisaged that, in many cases, the court will be able to give comprehensive directions whether on its own initiative (as to which, see r.3.3) or as agreed by the parties and approved by the court (as to which, see r.29.4).

Paragraphs 4.1 to 4.13 to the Practice Direction supplementing Pt 29 (see para. 29PD–001 below) set out in detail the approach the court will take to giving directions on allocation and the steps the parties should take.

Controlling the timetable—Rule 29.2(2) states that the court will fix the trial date or trial period "as soon as practicable". This major innovation in general civil procedure comprises a key element in furthering the overriding objective, *i.e.* ensuring that cases are dealt with expeditiously (see r.1.1(1) and (2)(d)). 29.2.2

A party who considers that a case management conference should be held before any directions are given should complete question J in the allocation questionnaire requesting an appointment, giving reasons justifying the request and supplying a realistic time estimate for the appointment with a list of any dates or times which are inconvenient. In the Chancery Division of the High Court so much is provided for in the Chancery Guide (April 1999) para. 5.4. In the Queen's Bench Division of the High Court Form PF49 (Request to parties to state convenient dates for hearing) will be sent to the parties together with the allocation questionnaire so that, in the event of the Master requiring a case management conference, he can fix the hearing having regard as far as possible to the parties' convenience.

If it is appropriate to do so the court will order an early trial on a fixed date (and consequently dispense with the need for listing questionnaires; see further on this, r.29.6(1)). In other cases the court may set a timetable by reference to calendar dates for the taking of steps for the preparation of the case and, if practicable, specifying the period in which the trial will take place (see Practice Direction supplementing Pt 29, para. 4.10 (at para. 29PD–001 below)).

Active case management means that the court will manage the case at the speed and on the dates which the court thinks appropriate. Once started the court will be reluctant to let the case slow down except to facilitate the parties to reach settlement. "Litigants and lawyers must be in no doubt that the court will regard the postponement of a trial as an order of the last resort" (Practice Direction supplementing Pt 29, para. 7.4(6) (see para. 29PD–001 below)).

Jurisdiction of Masters and District Judges—Case management will generally be dealt with by a Master (cases proceeding in London) or a District Judge (cases proceeding in a District 29.2.3

Registry of the High Court and cases proceeding in a country court). However, a Master or District Judge may consult and seek directions of a judge of a higher level about any aspect of case management (Practice Direction supplementing Pt 29, para. 3.10 (see para. 29PD–001 below)). A Master or District Judge may refer to a judge any application which he thinks should properly be decided by a judge (Practice Direction supplementing Pt 23, para. 1 (see para. 23PD–001)).

29.2.4 **Case management in the Royal Courts of Justice and elsewhere**—A claim with an estimated value of less than £15,000 which is commenced in the Central Office of the Royal Courts of Justice will normally be transferred to a county court unless:

(1) it is required by an enactment to be tried in the High Court,
(2) it falls within Part 49 (specialist proceedings), or
(3) it falls within one of the following categories or is otherwise within the criteria of article 7(5) of the High Court and County Courts Jurisdiction Order 1991:
 (a) professional negligence claims;
 (b) Fatal Accident Act claims;
 (c) fraud or undue influence;
 (d) defamation claims;
 (e) claims for malicious prosecution; or
 (f) claims against the police.

(See Practice Direction supplementing Pt 29, paras 2.1 and 2.2 (para. 29PD–001 below).) The decision to transfer should be made as soon as possible. However, if an application is made under r.3.4 (striking out) or under Pt 24 (Summary judgment) or under Pt 25 (Interim remedies) that application will usually be dealt with before a decision to transfer is taken (paras 2.4 and 2.5).

The provisions summarised above (likelihood of transfer of cases to a county court if suitable) apply only to claims issued in the Central Office of the Royal Courts of Justice. Therefore, they do not apply to claims issued in Chancery Chambers in London.

Unless and until an order of transfer is made the case management of a claim which is proceeding at the Royal Courts of Justice will be undertaken there (Practical Direction supplementing Pt 29, para. 3.1 (see para. 29PD–001 below)).

The case management of any other claim which has been allocated to the multi-track will normally be undertaken at a Civil Trial Centre (para. 3.2; for a list of Civil Trial Centres see SCP 1999, Vol 2, Section 18B). In some cases this will necessitate transfer to a Civil Trial Centre (as to which, see Practice Direction supplementing Pt 26para 10.2, (para. 26PD–001)).

29.2.5 **Listing arrangements in the Royal Courts of Justice**—The Royal Courts of Justice suffer unique problems in terms of fixing trial dates because of the number of Judges and Masters involved, the absence of a fully integrated IT support system, and the obligations of judges to go on circuit. To meet these problems a Practice Direction has been made governing the fixing of trial dates and windows in multi-track cases in the Chancery and Queen's Bench Divisions (excluding the Admiralty and Commercial Court and the Technology and Construction Court). The Practice Direction is set out in the Chancery Guide (April 1999). Instead of fixing the trial date or window the Master may direct that the trial shall not begin earlier than a specified date (calculated to provide enough time for the parties to complete any necessary preparations for trial) and/or direct that the trial date be within a specified period. Where either direction is given the Master will order the parties to attend before the listing officer within a specified number of days in order to fix a date of trial. The obligation to take out an appointment with the listing officer falls upon the claimant. If no appointment is made the listing officer will appoint a date for a listing hearing and give notice of the date to all parties. Further details as to the listing hearing and details of an appeal against a decision made by the listing officer are given in the Practice Direction.

Case management conference and pre-trial review

29.3 **29.3**—(1) The court may fix—
 (a) a case management conference; or
 (b) a pre-trial review,
at any time after the claim has been allocated.

(2) If a party has a legal representative, a representative—
 (a) familiar with the case; and
 (b) with sufficient authority to deal with any issues that are likely to arise,
must attend case management conferences and pre-trial reviews.

(Rule 3.1(2)(c) provides that the court may require a party to attend the court.)

29.3.1 **The case management conference**—The date of the first case management conference will often be stated in Form N155 (Notice of allocation to the multi-track). Paragraphs 5.1 and 5.3 of the Practice Direction supplementing Pt 29 (see para. 29PD–001 below) explain the court's approach to a case management conference and set out the topics the court is likely to consider at it. Paragraphs 5.6 to 5.8 describe the steps the parties should take in preparation for the conference. These include the preparation of a case summary, a document which should not normally be more than 500 words in length which may be prepared by the claimant and agreed with the other parties if possible. Especially in the first few years of the new rules, a direction for the preparation of a case summary may be made at the time the claim is allocated to the multi-track.

The first case management conference in a claim is likely to be allotted between one and two hours of court time.

The court will give the parties at least three days' notice of the hearing (para. 3.7). Where a party wishes to obtain an order not routinely made at a case management conference and believes that his application will be opposed, he should issue and serve the application in time for it to be heard at the case management conference. If this is likely to require the conference to last longer than the court time already allotted, the applicant should inform the court so that a new appointment can be made. Failure to apply promptly or to inform the court of the need for extra time may result in a costs sanction (para. 5.8).

Rule 29.3(2) indicates the personal involvement and seniority of the representative who should attend the case management conference on behalf of a represented party. If non-compliance with this sub-rule leads to an adjournment the court will expect to make a wasted costs order (para. 5.2(3); as to wasted costs orders see r.48.7). In some cases it may be appropriate for the represented party to attend also (see para. 5.6(2)). In some cases it may be appropriate for the case management conference to be conducted by way of a telephone conference or a video conference (as to these, see further the Practice Direction supplementing Pt 23, paras 6 and 7 (para. 23PD–001)).

Directions as to expert evidence—Several topics concerning expert evidence are likely to be considered at a case management conference (paras 4.10 and 4.11). **29.3.2**

(1) Directions for a single joint expert on any appropriate issue unless there is good reason to the contrary.
(2) Otherwise, simultaneous exchange of each side's reports.
(3) Directions for a discussion between experts and for the preparation by them of a statement of agreed issues and disputed issues.
(4) Directions for sequential exchange of reports where appropriate.

The court will not at this stage give permission to use expert evidence unless it can identify each expert by name or field in its order and say whether his evidence is to be given orally or by the use of his report (para. 5.5(1)).

Failure to comply with case management directions—A party who fails to keep to the timetable fixed by the court is in real jeopardy of orders imposing severe sanctions upon him, including: **29.3.3**

(1) the payment of a sum of money into court (r.3.1(5) and (6));
(2) the striking out of the whole or part of his statement of case plus judgment against him accordingly (r.3.4(2) and (3));
(3) a short extension of time specifying the consequence of non-compliance, *e.g.* depriving him of the right to raise or contest an issue or rely on evidence to which the direction relates (Practice Direction supplementing Pt 29, para. 7(3); and
(4) where a trial can proceed as to some issues only, an order disallowing any costs in respect of any later trial of the remaining issues (para. 7(4)).

Paragraph 7(2) of the Practice Direction supplementing Pt 29 (see para. 29PD–001 below) states that a party who is entitled to apply for a sanction against another party is required to do so without delay but should first warn the party in default of his intention so to apply.

Pre-trial review—See the commentary to r.29.7. **29.3.4**

Steps taken by the parties

29.4—(1) If— **29.4**

(a) the parties agree proposals for the management of the proceedings (including a proposed trial date or period in which the trial is to take place); and
(b) the court considers that the proposals are suitable;

it may approve them without a hearing and give directions in the terms proposed.

Effect of rule—If the parties agree proposals for the management of the case they should so notify the court. If the court considers them suitable, much time and expense will be saved. Even if the court does not consider them suitable, some time and expense may be saved because the court will take the agreed proposals into account in deciding what directions are appropriate. **29.4.1**

Guidance as to the approach the parties should take is given in the Practice Direction supplementing Pt 29, paras 4.6 to 4.10 (see para. 29PD–001 below).

This rule provides a practical demonstration of one of the biggest cultural changes made by the new rules. Parties are expected to co-operate with each other in the conduct of the proceedings. Co-operation of this sort is something the court must encourage in order to further the overriding objective (see r.1.4(2)(a)). The parties are expected to help the court to further the overriding objective (r.1.3). Parties who take reasonable steps to co-operate will be rewarded in costs if they later obtain an order for costs (see r.44.3(4)(a)). Parties who persist in the old combative style of litigation can expect to be penalised in costs whether or not their case succeeds at trial.

Variation of case management timetable

29.5 **29.5**—(1) A party must apply to the court if he wishes to vary the date which the court has fixed for—

(a) a case management conference;
(b) a pre-trial review;
(c) the return of a listing questionnaie under rule 29.6;
(d) the trial; or
(e) the trial period.

(2) Any date set by the court or these Rules for doing any act may not be varied by the parties if the variation would make it necessary to vary any of the dates mentioned in paragraph (1).

(Rule 2.11 allows the parties to vary a date by written agreement except where the rules provide otherwise or the court orders otherwise.)

29.5.1 **Effect of rule**—This rule clearly indicates the extent to which the court controls the timetable of the proceedings (see further "Controlling the timetable" under r.29.2).

Paragraphs 6.1 to 6.5 of the Practice Direction supplementing Pt 29 (see para. 29PD–001 below) deal generally with the procedure to be adopted in order to obtain any variation in the directions given. The first method of variation mentioned is an appeal (as to which see Pt 50). Alternatively, a party can reapply to the court which gave the direction requesting it to reconsider it if:

(1) there has been a change of circumstances since the order was made; and/or
(2) all parties agree about the changes they wish to make to the directions given.

Listing questionnaire

29.6 **29.6**—(1) The court will send the parties a listing questionnaire for completion and return by the date specified in directions given under rule 29.2(3) unless it considers that the claim can be listed for trial without the need for a listing questionnaire.

(2) Each party must file the completed listing questionnaire by the date specified by the court.

(3) If—

(a) a party fails to file the completed questionnaire by the date specified;
(b) a party has failed to give all the information requested by the listing questionnaire; or
(c) the court considers that a hearing is necessary to enable it to decide what directions to give in order to complete preparation of the case for trial,

the court may fix a date for a listing hearing or give such other directions as it thinks appropriate.

29.6.1 **Form and purpose of the listing questionnaire**—The listing questionnaire will be in form N170. It has two purposes. The first is to check that the case management directions previously given have been complied with (and if not to give the court an opportunity to give further directions, see "Failure to comply with case management directions" under r.29.3). Secondly, it will lead to a firm date for trial being given (r.29.8). Completion and return of the questionnaire on time is, therefore, essential. Failure to do so will lead to a listing hearing, the cost of which will be borne by the party in default (r.29.6(3)). Whether or not the defaulting party attends that hearing, the court will normally fix or confirm the trial date and make other orders about the steps to be taken to prepare the case for trial (Practice Direction supplementing Pt 29, para. 8.3(2) (see 29PD–001 below)). If no party files a listing questionnaire the court will normally make a conditional order striking out the proceedings unless a listing questionnaire is filed by any party within three days of service of the order (para. 8.3(1)).

Timetable for listing questionnaires—Unless this stage of the proceedings has been dispensed with the court will, at the earliest opportunity practicable, specify the date upon which the parties must file completed questionnaires (Practice Direction supplementing Pt 29, para 8.1(2) (see para. 29PD–001 below)). That date will be a date at least eight weeks before the trial date or the start of the trial period (para. 8.1(3)). The court will send copies of the questionnaire to the parties at least 14 days before the date for filing the completed questionnaires (para. 8.1(4)). Parties are encouraged (but not required) to exchange copies of the questionnaires before filing so as to avoid the court being given conflicting or incomplete information (para. 8.1(5)). **29.6.2**

On listing, the court will also give any necessary directions concerning expert evidence, a trial timetable and time estimate, the preparation of a trial bundle and similar directions (para. 9.2).

Filing costs estimates—The Practice Direction relating to Pt 43 requires parties to file with the listing questionnaire an estimate of their costs incurred and to be incurred in the proceedings. In most cases this will be the second such estimate parties will file (the first having been filed with the allocation questionnaire). Such estimates may also be required at other stages if the court so directs. As a general rule parties will not be able to recover from other parties any costs in excess of the estimate unless the court, in its discretion, otherwise orders. **29.6.3**

Pre-trial review

29.7 If, on receipt of the parties' listing questionnaires, the court decides— **29.7**

(a) to hold a pre-trial review; or

(b) to cancel a pre-trial review which has already been fixed,

it will serve notice of its decision at least 7 days before the date fixed for the hearing or, as the case may be, the cancelled hearing.

Pre-trial review—On receipt of the completed listing questionnaire the court will again consider whether to hold a pre-trial review or, if one has already been fixed, whether to cancel it. Pre-trial reviews will not be held in every case. However, they are likely to be held in all cases in which the trial is estimated to last more than 10 days. **29.7.1**

If practicable the pre-trial review will be conducted by the judge before whom the case will be listed for trial. Similarly, the trial advocates should attend as should the parties or someone authorised to settle the action (see r.29.3 and the commentary thereto).

The purpose of the pre-trial review is to provide a further opportunity for settlement before the full trial costs are incurred and, where settlement is not possible, to prepare an agenda for trial.

The judge will check that the case management directions previously given have been complied with and will explore the extent to which evidence can be agreed. The agenda for trial to be finalised at the hearing will normally comprise a list of issues to be tried and a timetable for the trial. The timetable will break down the trial into stages, allotting time at each stage to each party. Such a timetable will give the judge firm control over the progress of the trial and may focus the advocates' minds on the best method of using time.

Setting a trial timetable and fixing or confirming the trial date or week

29.8 As soon as practicable after— **29.8**

(a) each party has filed a completed listing questionnaire;

(b) the court has held a listing hearing under rule 29.6(3); or

(c) the court has held a pre-trial review under rule 29.7,

the court will—

(i) set a timetable for the trial unless a timetable has already been fixed, or the court considers that it would be inappropriate to do so;

(ii) fix the date for the trial or the week within which the trial is to begin (or, if it has already done so, confirm that date); and

(iii) notify the parties of the trial timetable (where one is fixed under this rule) and the date of trial period.

Effect of rule—Once the listing stage is complete and the pre-trial review (if appropriate) has been held the court will notify the parties of the firm date for trial and of any trial timetable which has been fixed (see further, the commentary to r.29.7). **29.8.1**

Conduct of trial

29.9 Unless the trial judge otherwise directs, the trial will be conducted in accordance with any order previously made. **29.9**

29.9.1 **Effect of rule**—This rule confirms that, despite the timetable (if any) and directions previously given, the trial judge has full power to conduct the trial in the manner he considers best to enable him to deal with the case justly. Paragraphs 10.1 to 10.6 of the Practice Direction supplementing Pt 29 (see para. 29PD–001 below) make various provisions about the trial of multi-track cases and draw attention to r.32.1 (court's power to control evidence and to restrict cross-examination) and r.32.5(2) (Statements and reports to stand as evidence in chief). For cases in the Chancery Division of the High Court, further guidance is given as to the conduct of the trial in Chapter 9 of the Chancery Guide (April 1999).

PRACTICE DIRECTION—THE MULTI-TRACK

This Practice Direction supplements CPR Part 29

1. General

29PD–001 **1.1** Attention is drawn in particular to the following Parts of the Civil Procedure Rules:

Part 1	The Overriding Objective
Part 3	The Court's Case Management Powers
Part 26	Case Management—Preliminary Stage
Part 31	Disclosure and Inspection of Documents
Parts 32–34	Evidence
Part 35	Experts and Assessors

and to the Practice Directions which relate to those Parts.

1.2 Attention is also drawn to Part 49 of the Rules (Specialist Jurisdictions) and to the Practice Directions which apply to those jurisdictions.

2. Case Management in the Royal Courts of Justice

2.1 This part of the Practice Direction applies to claims begun by claim form issued in the Central Office or Chancery Chambers in the Royal Courts of Justice.

2.2 A claim with an estimated value of less than £50,000 will generally, unless—

(a) it is required by an enactment to be tried in the High Court,
(b) it falls within a specialist list (as defined in CPR Part 49), or
(c) it falls within one of the categories specified in 2.6 below or is otherwise within the criteria of article 7(5) of the High Court and County Courts Jurisdiction Order 1991,

be transferred to a county court.

2.3 Paragraph 2.2 is without prejudice to the power of the court in accordance with Part 30 to transfer to a county court a claim with an estimated value that exceeds £50,000.

2.4 The decision to transfer may be made at any stage in the proceedings but should, subject to paragraph 2.5, be made as soon as possible and in any event not later than the date for the filing of Listing Questionnaires.

2.5 If an application is made under rule 3.4 (striking out) or under Part 24 (summary judgment) or under Part 25 (interim remedies), it will usually be convenient for the application to be dealt with before a decision to transfer is taken.

2.6 Each party should state in his Allocation Questionnaire whether he considers the claim should be managed and tried at the Royal Courts of Justice and, if so, why. Claims suitable for trial in the Royal Courts of Justice include—

(1) professional negligence claims;
(2) Fatal Accident Act claims;
(3) fraud or undue influence claims;
(4) defamation claims;
(5) claims for malicious prosecution or false imprisonment;

(6) claims against the police;
(7) contentious probate claims.
Such claims may fall within the criteria of article 7(5) of the High Court and County Courts Jurisdiction Order 1991.

2.7 Attention is drawn to the Practice Direction on Transfer (Part 30).

3. Case Management—General Provisions

3.1 (1) Case management of a claim which is proceeding at the Royal Courts of Justice will be undertaken there.

(2)(a) Case management of any other claim which has been allocated to the multi-track will normally be undertaken at a Civil Trial Centre.

(b) The Practice Direction supplementing Part 26 provides for what will happen in the case of a claim which is issued in or transferred to a court which is not a Civil Trial Centre.

3.2 The hallmarks of the multi-track are:

(1) the ability of the court to deal with cases of widely differing values and complexity, and

(2) the flexibility given to the court in the way it will manage a case in a way appropriate to its particular needs.

3.3 (1) On allocating a claim to the multi-track the court may give directions without a hearing, including fixing a trial date or a period in which the trial will take place,

(2) Alternatively, whether or not it fixes a trial date or period, it may either

(a) give directions for certain steps to be taken and fix a date for a case management conference or a pre-trial review to take place after they have been taken, or

(b) fix a date for a case management conference.

(3) Attention is drawn to rule 29.2(2) which requires the court to fix a trial date or period as soon as practicable.

3.4 The court may give or vary directions at any hearing which may take place on the application of a party or of its own initiative.

3.5 When any hearing has been fixed it is the duty of the parties to consider what directions the court should be asked to give and to make any application that may be appropriate to be dealt with then.

3.6 The court will hold a hearing to give directions whenever it appears necessary or desirable to do so, and where this happens because of the default of a party or his legal representative it will usually impose a sanction.

3.7 When the court fixes a hearing to give directions it will give the parties at least 3 days' notice of the hearing unless rule 29.7 applies (7 days notice to be given in the case of a pre-trial review).

3.8 Where a party needs to apply for a direction of a kind not included in the case management timetable which has been set (for example to amend his statement of case or for further information to be given by another party) he must do so as soon as possible so as to minimise the need to change that timetable.

3.9 Courts will make arrangements to ensure that applications and other hearings are listed promptly to avoid delay in the conduct of cases.

3.10 (1) Case management will generally be dealt with by:

(a) a Master in cases proceeding in the Royal Courts of Justice,

(b) a District Judge in cases proceeding in a District Registry of the High Court, and

(c) a District Judge or a Circuit Judge in cases proceeding in a county court.

(2) A Master or a District Judge may consult and seek the directions of a judge of a higher level about any aspect of case management.

(3) A member of the court staff who is dealing with the listing of a hearing may seek the directions of any judge about any aspect of that listing.

4. Directions on Allocation

29PD–002 **4.1** Attention is drawn to the court's duties under Rule 29.2.

4.2 The court will seek to tailor its directions to the needs of the case and the steps which the parties have already taken to prepare the case of which it is aware. In particular it will have regard to the extent to which any pre-action protocol has or (as the case may be) has not been complied with.

4.3 At this stage the court's first concern will be to ensure that the issues between the parties are identified and that the necessary evidence is prepared and disclosed.

4.4 The court may have regard to any document filed by a party with his allocation questionnaire containing further information provided that the document states either that its contents has been agreed with every other party or that it has been served on every other party, and when it was served.

4.5 On the allocation of a claim to the multi-track the court will consider whether it is desirable or necessary to hold a case management conference straight away, or whether it is appropriate instead to give directions on its own initiative.

4.6 The parties and their advisers are encouraged to try to agree directions and to take advantage of Rule 29.4 which provides that if:

(1) the parties agree proposals for the management of the proceedings (including a proposed trial date or period in which the trial is to take place); and

(2) the court considers that the proposals are suitable,

it may approve them without a hearing and give directions in the terms proposed.

4.7(1) To obtain the court's approval the agreed directions must—

(a) set out a timetable by reference to calendar dates for the taking of steps for the preparation of the case,

(b) include a date or a period (the trial period) when it is proposed that the trial will take place,

(c) include provision about disclosure of documents, and

(d) include provision about both factual and expert evidence.

(2) The court will scrutinise the timetable carefully and in particular will be concerned to see that any proposed date or period for the trial and (if provided for) for a case management conference is no later than is reasonably necessary.

(3) The provision in (1)(c) above may—

(a) limit disclosure to standard disclosure or less than that, and/or

(b) direct that disclosure will take place by the supply of copy documents without a list, but it must in that case say either that the parties must serve a disclosure statement with the copies or that they have agreed to disclose in that way without such a statement.

(4) The provision in (1)(d) about expert evidence may be to the effect that none is required.

4.8 Directions agreed by the parties should also where appropriate contain provisions about:

(1) the filing of any reply or amended statement of case that may be required,

(2) dates for the service of requests for further information under the Practice Direction supplementing Part 18 and of questions to experts under Rule 35.6 and by when they are to be dealt with,

(3) the disclosure of evidence,

(4) the use of a single joint expert, or in cases where it is not agreed, the exchange of expert evidence (including whether exchange is to be simultaneous or sequential) and without prejudice discussions between experts.

4.9 If the court does not approve the agreed directions filed by the parties but decides that it will give directions of its own initiative without fixing a case management conference, it will take them into account in deciding what directions to give.

4.10 Where the court is to give directions on its own intiative without holding a case management conference and it is not aware of any steps taken by the parties other than the exchange of statements of case, its general approach will be:

(1) to give directions for the filing and service of any further information required to clarify either party's case,

(2) to direct standard disclosure between the parties,

(3) to direct the disclosure of witness statements by way of simultaneous exchange,

(4) to give directions for a single joint expert on any appropriate issue unless there is a good reason not to do so,

(5) unless paragraph 4.11 (below) applies, to direct disclosure of experts' reports by way of simultaneous exchange on those issues where a single joint expert is not directed,

(6) if experts' reports are not agreed, to direct a discussion between experts for the purpose set out in rule 35.12(1) and the preparation of a statement under rule 35.12(3),

(7) to list a case management conference to take place after the date for compliance with those directions, and

(8) to specify a trial period.

4.11 If it appears that expert evidence will be required both on issues of liability and on the amount of damages, the court may direct that the exchange of those reports that relate to liability will be exchanged simultaneously but that those relating to the amount of damages will be exchanged sequentially.

4.12(1) If it appears to the court that it cannot properly give directions on its own initiative and no agreed directions have been filed which it can approve, the court will direct a case management conference to be listed.

(2) The conference will be listed as promptly as possible.

4.13 Where the court is proposing on its own initiative to make an order under rule 35.7 (which gives the court power to direct that evidence on a particular issue is to be given by a single expert) or under rule 35.15 (which gives the court power to appoint an assessor), the court must, unless the parties have consented in writing to the order, list a case management conference.

5. Case Management Conferences

5.1 The court will at any case management conference: 29PD–003

(1) review the steps which the parties have taken in the preparation of the case, and in particular their compliance with any directions that the court may have given,

(2) decide and give directions about the steps which are to be taken to secure the progress of the claim in accordance with the overriding objective, and

(3) ensure as far as it can that all agreements that can be reached between the parties about the matters in issue and the conduct of the claim are made and recorded.

5.2(1) Rule 29.3(2) provides that where a party has a legal representative, a representative familiar with the case and with sufficient authority to deal with any issues that are likely to arise must attend case management conferences and pre-trial reviews.

(2) That person should be someone who is personally involved in the conduct of the case, and who has the authority and information to deal with any matter which may reasonably be expected to be dealt with at such a hearing, including the fixing of the timetable, the identification of issues and matters of evidence.

(3) Where the inadequacy of the person attending or of his instructions leads to the adjournment of a hearing, the court will expect to make a wasted costs order.

5.3 The topics the court will consider at a case management conference are likely to include:

(1) Whether the claimant has made clear the claim he is bringing, in particular the amount he is claiming, so that the other party can understand the case he has to meet.

(2) Whether any amendments are required to the claim, a statement of case or any other document,

(3) What disclosure of documents, if any, is necessary,

(4) What expert evidence is reasonably required in accordance with rule 35.1 and how and when that evidence should be obtained and disclosed,

(5) What factual evidence should be disclosed,

(6) What arrangements should be made about the giving of clarification or further information and the putting of questions to experts, and

(7) Whether it will be just and will save costs to order a split trial or the trial of one or more preliminary issues.

5.4 In all cases the court will set a timetable for the steps it decides are necessary to be taken. These steps may include the holding of a case management conference or a pre-trial review, and the court will be alert to perform its duty to fix a trial date or period as soon as it can.

5.5(1) The court will not at this stage give permission to use expert evidence unless it can identify each expert by name or field in its order and say whether his evidence is to be given orally or by the use of his report.

(2) A party who obtains expert evidence before obtaining a direction about it does so at his own risk as to costs, except where he obtained the evidence in compliance with a pre-action protocol.

5.6 To assist the court, the parties and their legal advisers should:

(1) ensure that all documents that the court is likely to ask to see (including witness statements and experts' reports) are brought to the hearing,

(2) consider whether the parties should attend,

(3) consider whether a case summary will be useful, and

(4) consider what orders each wishes to be made and give notice of them to the other parties.

5.7(1) A case summary:

(a) should be designed to assist the court to understand and deal with the questions before it,

(b) should set out a brief chronology of the claim, the issues of fact which are agreed or in dispute and the evidence needed to decide them,

(c) should not normally exceed 500 words in length, and

(d) should be prepared by the claimant and agreed with the other parties if possible.

5.8(1) Where a party wishes to obtain an order not routinely made at a case management conference and believes that his application will be opposed, he should issue and serve the application in time for it to be heard at the case management conference.

(2) If the time allowed for the case management conference is likely to be insufficient for the appliation to be heard he should inform the court at once so that a fresh date can be fixed.

(3) A costs sanction may be imposed on a party who fails to comply with sub-paragraph (1) or (2).

5.9 At a case management conference the court may also consider whether the case ought to be tried by a High Court Judge or by a judge who specialises in that type of claim and how that question will be decided. In that case the claim may need to be transferred to another court.

6. Variation of Directions

6.1 This paragraph deals with the procedure to be adopted— 29PD–004

(1) where a party is dissatisfied with a direction given by the court,

(2) where the parties have agreed about changes they wish made to the directions given, or

(3) where a party wishes to apply to vary a direction.

6.2(1) It is essential that any party who wishes to have a direction varied takes steps to do so as soon as possible.

(2) The court will assume for the purposes of any later application that a party who did not appeal and who made no application to vary within 14 days of service of the order containing the directions was content that they were correct in the circumstances then existing.

6.3(1) Where a party is dissatisfied with a direction given or other order made by the court he may appeal or apply to the court for it to reconsider its decision.

(2) Unless paragaph 6.4 applies, a party should appeal if the direction was given or the order was made at a hearing at which he was present, or of which he had due notice.

(3) In any other case he should apply to the court to reconsider its decision.

(4) If an application is made for the court to reconsider its decision:

(a) it will usually be heard by the judge who gave the directions or another judge of the same level,

(b) the court will give all parties at least 3 days notice of the hearing, and

(c) the court may confirm its directions or make a different order.

6.4 Where there has been a change in the circumstances since the order was made the court may set aside or vary a direction it has given. It may do so on application or on its own initiative.

6.5 Where the parties agree about changes they wish made to the directions given:

(1) If rule 2.11 (variation by agreement of a date set by the court for doing any act other than those stated in the note to that rule) or rule 31.5, 31.10(8) or 31.13 (agreements about disclosure) applies the parties need not file the written agreement.

(2)(a) In any other case the parties must apply for an order by consent.

(b) The parties must file a draft of the order sought and an agreed statement of the reasons why the variation is sought.

(c) The court may make an order in the agreed terms or in other terms without a hearing, but it may direct that a hearing is to be listed.

7. Failure to Comply with Case Management Directions

7.1 Where a party fails to comply with a direction given by the court any other party may apply for an order that he must do so or for a sanction to be imposed or both of these.

7.2 The party entitled to apply for such an order must do so without delay but should first warn the other party of his intention to do so.

7.3 The court may take any such delay into account when it decides whether to make an order imposing a sanction or to grant relief from a sanction imposed by the rules or any other practice direction.

7.4(1) The court will not allow a failure to comply with directions to lead to the postponement of the trial unless the circumstances are exceptional.

(2) If it is practical to do so the court will exercise its powers in a manner that enables the case to come on for trial on the date or within the period previously set.

(3) In particular the court will assess what steps each party should take to prepare the case for trial, direct that those steps are taken in the shortest possible time and imose a sanction for non-compliance. Such a sanction may, for example, deprive a party of the right to raise or contest an issue or to rely on evidence to which the direction relates.

(4) Where it appears that one or more issues are or can be made ready for trial at the time fixed while others cannot, the court may direct that the trial will proceed on the issues which are then ready, and direct that no costs will be allowed for any later trial of the remaining issues or that those costs will be paid by the party in default.

(5) Where the court has no option but to postpone the trial it will do so for the shortest possible time and will give directions for the taking of the necessary steps in the meantime as rapidly as possible.

(6) Litigants and lawyers must be in no doubt that the court will regard the postponement of a trial as an order of last resort. Where it appears inevitable the court may exercise its power to require a party as well as his legal representative to attend court at the hearing where such an order is to be sought.

(7) The court will not postpone any other hearing without a very good reason, and for that purpose the failure of a party to comply on time with directions previously given will not be treated as a good reason.

8. Listing Questionnaires and Listing

29PD–005 **8.1**(1) The Listing Questionnaire will be in Form N170.

(2) Unless it dispenses with Listing Questionnaires and orders an early trial on a fixed date, the court will specify the date for filing completed listing questionnaires when it fixes the trial date or trial period under rule 29.2(2).

(3) The date for filing the completed Listing Questionnaires will be not later than 8 weeks before the trial date or the start of the trial period.

(4) The court will serve the Listing Questionnaires on the parties at least 14 days before that date.

(5) Although the rules do not require the parties to exchange copies of the Questionnaires before they are filed they are encouraged to do so to avoid the court being given conflicting or incomplete information.

(6) The file will be placed before a judge for his directions when all the Questionnaires have been filed or when the time for filing them has expired.

8.2 The court's general approach will be as set out in the following paragraphs. The court may however decide to make other orders, and in particular the court will take into account the steps, if any, of which it is aware which the parties have taken to prepare the case for trial.

8.3(1) Where no party files a Listing Questionnaire the court will normally make an order that if no Listing Questionnaire is filed by any party within 3 days from service of the order, the claim and any counterclaim will be struck out.

(2) Where a party files a Listing Questionnaire but another party (the defaulting party) does not do so, the court will fix a Listing Hearing. Whether or not the defaulting party attends the hearing, the court will normally fix or confirm the trial date and make other orders about the steps to be taken to prepare the case for trial.

8.4 Where the court decides to hold a listing hearing the court will fix a date which is as early as possible and the parties will be given at least 3 days notice of the date.

8.5 Where the court decides to hold a pre-trial review (whether or not this is in addition to a listing hearing) the court will give the parties at least 7 days notice of the date.

9. Directions the court will give on Listing

9.1 Directions the court must give.

The court must fix the trial date or week, give a time estimate and fix the place of trial.

9.2 Other directions

(1) The parties should seek to agree directions and may file an agreed

order. The court may make an order in those terms or it may make a different order.

(2) Agreed directions should include provision about:
(a) Evidence especially expert evidence,
(b) A trial timetable and time estimate,
(c) The preparation of a trial bundle,
(d) Any other matter needed to prepare the case for trial.

(3) The court will include such of these provisions as are appropriate in any order that it may make, whether or not the parties have filed agreed directions.

(4) Unless a direction doing so has been given before, a direction giving permission to use expert evidence will say whether it gives permission to use oral evidence or reports or both and will name the experts concerned.

9.3 The principles set out in paragraph 6 of this Practice Direction about variation of directions applies equally to directions given at this stage.

10. The Trial

10.1 The trial will normally take place at a Civil Trial Centre but it may be at another court if it is appropriate having regard to the needs of the parties and the availability of court resources.

10.2 The judge will generally have read the papers in the trial bundle and may dispense with an opening address.

10.3 The judge may confirm or vary any timetable given previously, or if none has been given set his own.

10.4 Attention is drawn to the provisions in Part 32 and the following parts of the Rules about evidence, and in particular

(1) to rule 32.1 (court's power to control evidence and to restrict cross-examination), and

(2) to rule 32.5(2) statements and reports to stand as evidence in chief.

10.5 In an appropriate case the judge may summarily assess costs in accordance with rule 44.7. Attention is drawn to the Practice Directions about costs and the steps the parties are required to take.

10.6 Once the trial of a multi-track claim has begun, the judge will normally sit on consecutive court days until it has been concluded.

PART 30

TRANSFER

30.0.1 **Contents**

Editorial Introduction

30.0.2 Like CCR, O 16 and RSC, O.4, this Part contains rules relating to transfer: (i) between county courts; (ii) within the High Court; (iii) from High Court to county court; and (iv) from county court to High Court.

Related sources

30.0.3
- Practice Direction to Pt 30.
- Supreme Court Act 1981, ss.61–65 and Sched. 1 (SCP 1999, Vol. 2, Section 20A, paras 20A–426 to 20A–441).
- County Courts Act 1984, ss.40–45 (SCP 1999, Vol. 2, Section 20A, paras 20A–702 to 20A–718).
- High Court and County Court Jurisdiction Order 1991 (S.I. 1991 No. 724) (SCP 1999, Vol. 2, Section 20B, paras 20B–241 to 20B–265).
- Insolvency Rules 1986, r.7.15.
- CPR r.26.2 (automatic transfer to defendant's home court (see r.2.3) when defence filed in claim for specified amount of money), r.13.4 (automatic transfer to defendant's home court when application to set aside) and r.14.12 (automatic transfer to defendant's home court when admission—determination of rate of payment by judge).
- CCR, O.25, r.2 (transfer of proceedings for enforcement)
- CCR, O.30, r.10 (transfer of garnishee proceedings)

Scope of this Part

30.1 **30.1** This Part deals with the transfer of proceedings between county courts, between the High Court and the county courts and within the High Court.

(Rule 26.2 provides for automatic transfer in certain cases.)

Transfer between county courts and within the High Court

30.2 **30.2**—(1) A county court may order proceedings before that court, or any part of them (such as a counterclaim or an application made in the proceedings), to be transferred to another county court if it is satisfied that—
- (a) an order should be made having regard to the criteria in rule 30.3; or
- (b) proceedings for—
  - (i) the detailed assessment of costs; or
  - (ii) the enforcement of a judgment or order,

could be more conveniently or fairly taken in that other county court.

(2) If proceedings have been started in the wrong county court, a judge of the county court may order that the proceedings—
- (a) be transferred to the county court in which they ought to have been started;
- (b) continue in the county court in which they have been started; or

(c) be struck out.

(3) An application for an order under paragraph (1) or (2) must be made to the county court where the claim is proceeding.

(4) The High Court may, having regard to the criteria in rule 30.3, order proceedings in the Royal Courts of Justice or a district registry, or any part of such proceedings (such as a counterclaim or an application made in the proceedings) to be transferred—

(a) from the Royal Courts of Justice to a district registry; or

(b) from a district registry to the Royal Courts of Justice or to another district registry.

(5) A district registry may order proceedings before it for the detailed assessment of costs to be transferred to another district registry if it is satisfied that the proceedings could be more conveniently or fairly taken in that other district registry.

(6) An application for an order under paragraph (4) or (5) must, if the claim is proceeding in a district registry, be made to that registry.

(7) Where some enactment, other than these rules, requires proceedings to be started in a particular county court, neither paragraphs (1) nor (2) give the court power to order proceedings to be transferred to a county court which is not the court in which they should have been started or to order them to continue in the wrong court.

(8) Probate proceedings may only be transferred under paragraph (4) to Chancery Division at the Royal Courts of Justice or to one of the Chancery district registries.

"a county court" (r.30.2(1))—The power may be exercised by a judge or district judge—CPR r.2.4. **30.2.1**

"counterclaim" (r.30.2(1))—See Pt 20. **30.2.2**

"application" (r.30.2(1), 2(3), 5 and 6)—See Pt 23. **30.2.3**

"detailed assessment of costs" (r.30.2(1)(b) and 2(5))—See Pt 47. **30.2.4**

"enforcement" (r.30.2(1)(b))—See the provisions of the rules of the Supreme Court retained in Schedule 1 and the County Court Rules retained in Schedule 2. **30.2.5**

"more conveniently and fairly" (r.30.2(1)(b))—This is the same phrase as was used in the former CCR, O.16, r.1. If an application is made by one party for transfer, the burden lies upon that party to show that transfer should take place. For the criteria for transfer see r.30.3(2). **30.2.6**

Note that the power to transfer may be exercised by judges of their own initiative (r.3.3).

"If proceedings have been commenced in the wrong court..." (r.30.2(2))—See r.7.1 and the Practice Direction to Pt 7 and Pt 8, especially paras B6 and B7. Rule 30.2(2) replaces CCR, O.16, r.2. This rule will always be answer to an objection raised on appeal that proceedings have been commenced in the wrong court—see *R v. Judge Lailey, ex p Koffman* [1932] 1 K.B. 568 at 577, CA, and *Thomas Allen Ltd v. Hagger (No. 3)* (1931) 24 B.W.C.C. 513, CA. **30.2.7**

Although r.30.2(c) gives the court power to strike out an action commenced in the wrong court, in view of the overriding objective (r.1.1(1) and (2)(b)) the power to strike out is only likely to be exercised in extreme cases.

"the county court where the claim is proceeding" (r.30.2(3))—See too r.23.2(1)–(3). **30.2.8**

"The High Court may..." (r.30.2(4))—This replaces RSC, O.4, r.5. For the criteria for transfer **30.2.9**

see r.30.3(2). Note that r.30.2 does not provide for transfer from the High Court to the county court and vice versa—jurisdiction to make such transfers is given by County Courts Act 1984, s.40, as amended (SCP 1999, Vol. 2, Section 20A, para. 20A–702). The jurisdiction may be exercised by any judge, Master or district judge—see r.2.4.

30.2.10 **"Probate proceedings. . ." (r.30.2(8))**—See SCP 1999, Vol. 1, para. 4/5/4.

Criteria for a transfer order

30.3 **30.3**—(1) Paragraph (2) sets out the matters to which the court must have regard when considering whether to make an order under—

(a) section 40(2), 41(1) or 42(2) of the County Courts Act 1984[1] (transfer between the High Court and a county court);

(b) rule 30.2(1) (transfer between county courts); or

(c) rule 30.2(4) (transfer between the Royal Courts of Justice and the district registries).

(2) The matters to which the court must have regard include—

(a) the financial value of the claim and the amount in dispute, if different;

(b) whether it would be more convenient or fair for hearings (including the trial) to be held in some other court;

(c) the availability of a judge specialising in the type of claim in question;

(d) whether the facts, legal issues, remedies or procedures involved are simple or complex;

(e) the importance of the outcome of the claim to the public in general;

(f) the facilities available at the court where the claim is being dealt with and whether they may be inadequate because of any disabilities of a party or potential witness.

30.3.1 **"transfer between the High Court and a county court" (r.30.3(1)(a))**—See High Court and County Court Jurisdiction Order 1991 (S.I. 1991 No. 724) (SCP 1999, Vol. 2, Section 20B, paras 20B–241 to 20B–265). If proceedings are commenced in the High Court when they should have been commenced in a county court, the High Court must transfer to a county court, but if the person bringing the proceedings knew, or ought to have known, that they should have been brought in the county court, there is a residual jurisdiction to strike out—see *Restick v. Crickmore* [1994] 1 W.L.R. 420, CA. However, in view of the overriding objective (r.1.1(1) and (2)(b)) the power to strike out is only likely to be exercised in extreme cases.

30.3.2 **"The matters to which the court must have regard include . . ." (r.30.3(2))**—The list is not exhaustive. In addition regard should be had to r.1.1 (The overriding objective) and r.1.4 (Court's duty to manage cases). Note that the r.30.3 criteria do not apply to a transfer under r.30.2(1)(b).

30.3.3 **"the financial value" (r.30.3(2)(a))**—See High Court and County Court Jurisdiction Order 1991 (S.I. 1991 No. 724) (SCP 1999, Vol. 2, Section 20B, paras 20B–241 to 20B–265) and Pt 29 (The Multi-Track). See too r.16.3.

30.3.4 **"the availability of a judge specialising" (r.30.3(2)(c))**—Practitioners should ensure that they are aware not only of county courts with specialist lists (see r.2.3(2)) but also of individual judges with specialist knowledge.

30.3.5 **"Transfer between Divisions and to and from a specialist list" (r.30.5)**—This rule replaces RSC, O.4, r.3. See SCP 1999, Vol. 1, paras 4/3/1 to 4/3/7.

30.3.6 **"the place" (r.30.6)**—Note that the venue of hearings is not limited to court buildings—see r.2.7.

30.3.6A **"child or patient" (r.30.7)**—See r.21.1(2).

[1] 1984 c. 28. Section 40 was substituted by section 2(1) of the Courts and Legal Services Act 1990 (c. 41). Section 41 was amended by the Matrimonial and Family Proceedings Act 1984 (c. 42), Schedule 1, paragraph 31 and by section 2(2) of the Courts and Legal Services Act 1990. Section 42 was substituted by section 2(3) of the Courts and Legal Services Act 1990.

Certiorari or prohibition (r.30.8)—See RSC, O.53. Permission to apply for judicial review is normally obtained without notice being given—see former RSC, O.53, r.3(2). As to certiorari or prohibition, see too County Courts Act 1984, ss.83 and 84, SCP 1999, Vol. 2, paras 20A–759 to 20A–760. 30.3.7

The date of transfer—See the Practice Direction. Transfer takes effect from the date that the order is made. This is in contrast to the former position referred to in RSC, O.107 (see SCP 1999, Vol. 1, para. 107/2/7B). 30.3.8

Notice of Transfer—The court making the transfer should send notice of the transfer to the receiving court and to all parties. 30.3.9

Appeals against transfer—See the Practice Direction supplementing Pt 23, para. 5 which sets out the appropriate court in which to make an appeal depending on where and by when the order of transfer was made (para. 23PD–001), and the former RSC, O.59. See too County Courts Act 1984, s.40(5) (SCP 1999, Vol. 2, Section 20A, para. 20A–702). 30.3.10

Applications to set aside transfers—See the Practice Direction, para. 6, and rr.3.3(5) and 23.10. Applications to set aside should be made to the court where the order for transfer was made. 30.3.11

Procedure

30.4—(1) Where the court orders proceedings to be transferred, the court from which they are to be transferred must give notice of the transfer to all the parties. 30.4

(2) An order made before the transfer of the proceedings shall not be affected by the order to transfer.

Transfer between Divisions and to and from a specialist list

30.5—(1) The High Court may order proceedings in any Division of the High Court to be transferred to another Division. 30.5

(2) The court may order proceedings to be transferred to or from a specialist list.

(3) An application for the transfer of proceedings to or from a specialist list must be made to a judge dealing with claims in that list.

Specialist list—See r.49. 30.5.1

Power to specify place where hearings are to be held

30.6 The court may specify the place (for instance, a particular county court) where the trial or some other hearing in any proceedings is to be held and may do so without ordering the proceedings to be transferred. 30.6

Transfer of control of money in court

30.7 The court may order that control of any money held by it under rule 21.11 (control of money recovered by or on behalf of a child or patient) be transferred to another court if that court would be more convenient. 30.7

Certiorari or prohibition

30.8 A party obtaining from the High Court, on an application made without notice, an order giving permission to make an application for— 30.8

(a) an order of certiorari to remove proceedings from a county court; or

(b) an order of prohibition to any county court,

must immediately serve a copy of the order on the other parties and on the court officer of the county court.

(Other rules about transfer can be found in Schedule 2 in the following CCR—O.25(transfer of proceedings for enforcement); O.30(transfer of garnishee proceedings).)

PRACTICE DIRECTION—TRANSFER

This Practice Direction supplements CPR Part 30

Value of a case and transfer

30PD–001 **1.** In addition to the criteria set out in Rule 30.3(2) attention is drawn to the financial limits set out in the High Court and County Courts Jurisdiction Order 1991, as amended.

2. Attention is also drawn to paragraph 2 of the Practice Direction on Part 29 (the multi-track).

Date of Transfer

3. Where the court orders proceedings to be transferred, the order will take effect from the date it is made by the court.

Procedure on Transfer

4.1 Where an order for transfer has been made the transferring court will immediately send notice of the transfer to the receving court. The notice will contain;

(1) the name of the case, and

(2) the number of the case.

4.2 At the same time as the transferring court notifies the receiving court it will also notify the parties of the transfer under rule 30.4(1).

Procedure for an appeal against order of transfer

5.1 An appeal against an order that proceedings be transferred:

(1) where either the transferring court or the receiving court is the High Court, and the order was made by a Master or District Judge, should be made in the High Court,

(2) where the order was made in proceedings in the High Court by a High Court Judge, should be made in the Court of Appeal,

(3) where both the transferring and receiving courts are county courts, and the order was made by a District Judge, should be made in the receiving court,

(4) where the order was made in county court proceeedings by a Circuit Judge, should be made in the Court of Appeal.

5.2 Where paragraph 5.1(3) applies, the receiving court may, if it is convenient to the parties, remit the appeal to the transferring court to be dealt with there.

5.3 An appeal made under 5.1(1) or 5.1(3) above must be begun by the issue of an application notice in accordance with Part 23 of the Rules and the practice direction which supplements Part 23.

5.4 An appeal made under 5.1(2) or 5.1(4) above must be begun by the issue of a notice of appeal in accordance with the provisions of RSC Order 59 (see Part 50 and Schedule 1 to the Rules).

Applications to set aside

6.1 Where a party may apply to set aside an order for transfer (e.g. under Rule 23.10) the application should be made to the court which made the order.

6.2 Such application should be made in accordance with Part 23 of the Rules and the practice direction which supplements it.

PART 31

Disclosure and Inspection of Documents

Contents 31.0.1

Editorial Introduction

This part concerns disclosure (defined as "stating that a document exists or has existed": see r.31.2) and inspection of documents. There is no provision under the rules for automatic disclosure. The duty to disclose will arise if and when and to the extent that the court orders disclosure. This will generally be at the first case management hearing or upon an application by a party, but parties are reminded that consistent with the parties' duty to help the court further the overriding objective of the rules the parties can proceed with disclosure and inspection on a consensual basis, albeit subject to review by the Court. Part 31 applies to all claims except claims on the small claims track (see r.31.1(2)). 31.0.2

There is a right to inspect a disclosed document save where it is no longer in the control of the disclosing party, or that party has a right to withhold inspection or it would be disproportionate to the issues in the case to permit inspection (see r.31.3).

Central to the rules on disclosure is the concept of standard disclosure. This is defined in terms of:

(a) documents upon which a party relies;
(b) documents which adversely affect his own case, or adversely affect another party's case or which support another party's case; and
(c) documents of which disclosure is required by a relevant practice direction (see r.31.6).

The rules also require that only a reasonable search be made in respect of the documents referred to under (b) and (c) above (see r.31.7) and specify factors relevant to the reasonableness of a search. Such rules on disclosure define and delimit the extent and nature of disclosure and are intended to avoid excesses of effort, resources and costs in relation to disclosure and consequent inspection. They replace the *Peruvian Guano* test which should be discarded.

There is provision for specific disclosure and inspection (see r.31.12). It is considered that the concept of "proportionality" is implicit in the granting of an order for specific disclosure or inspection.

Under the rules there is power in the court to dispense with or limit standard disclosure and the parties may do likewise by agreement (see r.31.5(2) and (3)). However, in many cases disclosure and inspection will still form a fundamental part of the litigation process assisting an evaluation and if called for determination of the respective parties contentions.

Disclosure may now be obtained:

(a) Between parties to proceedings (see this Part);

(b) Where an Act permits disclosure before proceedings (see r.31.16). Such is permitted by s.33 of the SCA 1981 and s.52 of the CCA 1984 between likely parties to subsequent proceedings in all types of claim. The former restriction to personal injuries claims was removed by The Civil Procedure (Modification of Enactments) Order 1998 (S.I. 1998 No. 2940) paras 5 and 6;

(c) Where an Act permits disclosure against a non-party during proceedings (see r.31.17). Such is permitted by s.34 of the SCA 1981 and s.53 of the CCA 1984 in all types of claim. The former restriction to personal injuries claim was removed by S.I. 1998 No. 2940 mentioned under (b) above;

(d) In certain other well-established situations such as under the principles of the *Norwich Pharmacal* case, *Anton Piller* and *Mareva* cases and see r.31.18. and the commentary thereunder.

Part 31 is to be read in conjunction with the Civil Procedure Practice Direction PT31PD(F). Disclosure and Inspection: see para. 31PD–001.

Related Sources

31.0.3
- Practice Direction (Disclosure and Inspection) (see para. 31PD–001)
- Supreme Court Act 1981, ss.33 and 34 (SCP 1999, Vol. 2, Section 20A, paras 20A–215 to 20A–219)
- County Court Act 1981, ss.52 and 53 (SCP 1999, Vol. 2, Section 20A, paras 20A–725 to 20A 726/2)
- The Civil Procedure (Modification of Enactments) Order 1998 (S.I. 1998 No. 2940)
- Part 23 Applications for Court Orders.
- Part 35, r.35.10(4) Restrictions on disclosure of instructions to expert
- Chancery Guide, Section 3.4.11 (Discovery and Interogatories) (SCP 1999, Vol. 2, Section 2B, paras 2B–212 *et seq.*)
- Guide to Commercial Court Practice, Part E, Sections E1 to E5.

Forms

31.0.4
- N265—List of Documents (see para. C75–001)
- PD Pt 31 PDF Annex A Disclosure Statement (see r.31.10)
- Practice Direction (Disclosure and Inspection) Annex A: Disclosure Statement (para. 31PD–002)

Synopsis of Rules

31.0.5 Disclosure means stating that a document exists or has existed (r.31.2). There is a right to inspect a disclosed document save where it is no longer in the control (see r.31.8) of the party, that party has a right to withhold it (see further r.31.19) or it would be disproportionate to the issues in the case to permit inspection (r.31.3). The meaning of a document and of a copy is set out in r.31.4 in terms wide enough to embrace modern forms of electronic recording.

Unless the court otherwise orders, disclosure means "standard disclosure" (r.31.5). This may be dispensed with or limited by the court and the parties may do likewise by agreement (r.31.5(2) and (3)). By r.31.6 standard disclosure is defined in terms of:

(a) the documents on which a party relies;

(b) documents which:

(i) adversely affect his own case;

(ii) adversely affect another party's case;

(iii) support another party's case.

(c) documents a party is required to disclose by a relevant practice direction.

As to the documents referred to under (b) and (c) above, r.31.7 requires a reasonable search to be made and where the absence of search is asserted and justified on the basis of unreasonableness that a statement to such effect appear in the disclosure statement.

There is no requirement to disclose more than one copy of a document unless a copy contains a modification obliteration or other marking or feature upon which a party intends to rely or which falls within (b) above (r.31.9).

Standard disclosure is by list in the relevant practice direction form (Form N265): see r.31.10. The documents must be identified in "a convenient order and manner and, as concisely as possible". The list must state those documents in respect of which a right to withhold from inspection is claimed and those documents which are no longer in the disclosing party's control and what has happened to the same. The list must include a disclosure statement (see r.31.10(5), (6) and (7)).

The duty to disclose continues throughout the proceedings (r.31.11).

Rule 31.12 provides for specific disclosure and inspection to be ordered. Such may include an order to carry out a search to an extent specified in the order.

Under r.31.13 disclosure and/or inspection may be ordered to take place in stages.

Inspection of documents referred to in a statement of case, a witness statement, a witness summary, an affidavit or an experts' report (subject to the court's powers not to order disclosure of documents of instruction where substance thereof is accurately and completely stated in the report (see r.35.10(4)) is provided by r.31.14.

The formalities of inspection are contained in r.31.15.

Rule 31.16 deals with disclosure sought pursuant to any Act which provides for disclosure before proceedings as is permitted under s.33 of the SCA 1981 and s.52 of the CCA 1984. The respondent must be likely to be a party to subsequent proceedings and who would have to disclose the documents therein as part of his duty to make standard disclosure therein.

Disclosure against a non-party during the proceedings where an Act permits such disclosure as under s.34 of the SCA 1981 and s.53 of the CCA 1984 is provided by r.31.17.

Rule 31.18 expressly states that r.31.16 and r.31.17 do not limit any other power the court may have to order disclosure before proceedings have started or against a non party to proceeedings.

A person may apply without notice for an order to withhold disclosure of a document on the basis that disclosure would damage the public interest: see r.31.19(1). Unless the court otherwise orders an order made under this provision must not be served on any other person, nor be open to inspection by any person r.31.19(2). This rule also deals with a claim of a right to withhold inspection of a document. The claim must be asserted together with the grounds relied upon in the party's list of documents or, if there is no list, to the person wishing to inspect. An application can be made to the court to challenge such a claim (see r.31.19(5), (6) and (7)).

Rule 31.20 provides that where a party inadvertently allows a privileged document to be inspected, the inspecting party may only make use of it or its contents with court permission.

A party in breach of the duty to disclose or allow inspection of a document will not be allowed to rely upon such document unless the court allows: see r.31.21 This rule is far less draconian than the former RSC, O.24, r.16.

Rule 31.22 concerns the subsequent use of disclosed documents. This is allowed only where the document has been read to or by the court or referred to a hearing in public unless the court restricts or prohibits the use of such a document, where the court gives permission and where the disclosing party and the person to whom the document belongs agree.

Scope of this Part

31.1—(1) This Part sets out rules about the disclosure and inspection of documents. **31.1**

(2) This Part applies to all claims except a claim on the small claims track.

Meaning of disclosure

31.2 A party discloses a document by stating that the document exists or has existed. **31.2**

Right of inspection of a disclosed document

31.3—(1) A party to whom a document has been disclosed has a right to inspect that document except where— **31.3**

- (a) the document is no longer in the control of the party who disclosed it;
- (b) the party disclosing the document has a right or a duty to withhold inspection of it; or
- (c) paragraph (2) applies.

(Rule 31.8 sets out when a document is in the control of a party)

(Rule 31.19 sets out the procedure for claiming a right or duty to withhold inspection)

(2) Where a party considers that it would be disproportionate to the issues in the case to permit inspection of documents within a category or class of document disclosed under rule 31.6(b)—

- (a) he is not required to permit inspection of documents within that category or class; but
- (b) he must state in his disclosure statement that inspection of those documents will not be permitted on the grounds that to do so would be disproportionate.

(Rule 31.6 provides for standard disclosure)

(Rule 31.10 makes provision for a disclosure statement)

(Rule 31.12 provides for a party to apply for an order for specific inspection of documents)

31.3.1 **"... control of the party who disclosed it"**—The concept of control is defined in r.36.8(2) below.

31.3.2 **"... right or duty to withhold inspection of it"**—For instance:

(a) Legal professional privilege:
   (i) Communications privileged although no litigation was contemplated.
   (ii) Communications privileged only when litigation is contemplated or pending.

See paras 31.3.5 to 31.3.19 inclusive below. See too the consequences of fraud or illegality, see paras 31.3.22 below and of waiver/loss of privilege, see paras 31.3.27 to 31.3.29 inclusive below.

(b) Documents tending to criminate or expose to a penalty. See para. 31.3.31 below.
(c) Documents privileged on the ground that inspection would be injurious to the public interest. See paras 31.3.32 to 31.3.33 inclusvie below.
(d) Other grounds of privilege such as without prejudice communications: see para 31.3.42 below.

31.3.3 **Procedure for claiming a right or duty to withhold inspection**—See under r.36.19 below.

31.3.4 **"Disproportionate"**—The parties should bear in mind the overriding principle of proportionality (see r.1.1(2)(c)) and the matters set out in r.31.7(2) below, and see PT31PD(F)2.

31.3.5 **Legal professional privilege**—It is necessary to divide into two classes the documents that are protected on this ground, namely (a) those that are privileged whether or not litigation was contemplated or pending, and (b) those that are only privileged if litigation was contemplated or pending when they were made or came into existence. Where legal professional privilege exists and is not waived or abrogated it is paramount and absolute and not subject to the balancing exercise of weighing competing public interests against each other as in the field of public interest immunity, see *R. v. Derby Magistrates' Court, Ex p. B* [1996] A.C. 487; [1995] 4 All E.R. 526, HL. In this case Lord Taylor C.J. said:

> "The principle which runs through all these cases, and many other cases which were cited, is that a man must be able to consult his lawyer in confidence, since otherwise he might hold back half the truth. The client must be sure that what he tells his lawyers in confidence will never be revealed without his consent. Legal professional privilege is thus much more than an ordinary rule of evidence, limited in its application to the facts of a particular case. It is a fundamental condition on which the administration of justice as a whole rests. ... Nobody doubts that legal professional privilege could be modified, or even abrogated, by statute, subject always to the objection that legal professional privilege is a fundamental human right protected by the European Convention for the Protection of Human Rights and Fundamental Freedoms, as to which we did not hear any argument ... (But) whatever inroads may have been made by Parliament in other areas, legal professional privilege is a field which Parliament has so far left untouched."

(a) Communications privileged although no litigation was contemplated or pending

31.3.6 **Solicitor and client**—Letters and other communications passing between a party, or his predecessors in title, and his, or their solicitors are privileged from production, provided they are, and are sworn to be, confidential, and written to, or by, the solicitor in his professional capacity, and for the purpose of getting legal advice or assistance for the client (*O'Shea v. Wood* [1891] P. 286, CA; *Gardner v. Irvin* (1878) 4 Ex.D. 49 at 53, CA; *Kennedy v. Lyell* (1883) 23 Ch.D. 387 at 404, CA; *Wheeler v. Le Marchant* (1881) 17 Ch.D. 675 at 682, CA; *cf. More v. Weaver* [1928] 2 K.B. 520; *Minter v. Priest* (1930) 46 T.L.R. 301, HL; *Re Duncan*, (decd.), *Garfield v. Fay* [1968] P. 306; [1968] 2 W.L.R. 1479—foreign legal advisers); but not otherwise (*ibid.*, *Original Hartlepool Collieries v. Moon* (1874) 30 L.T. 193 at 585; *Moseley v. Victoria Co.* (1886) 55 L.T. 482.

Although originally confined to advice about litigation, legal professional privilege has long been extended to non-litigious business. The test is whether the communication or other document is made confidentially for the purposes of legal advice. Those purposes have to be construed broadly. Privilege obviously attaches to a document conveying legal advice from solicitor to client and to a specific request from the client for such advice. It does not follow, however, that all other communications between solicitor and client lack privilege. Where information is passed by the solicitor or client to the other as part of a process aimed at keeping both informed, so that advice may be sought and given, privilege will attach. Moreover legal advice is not confined to telling the client the law; it may include advice about what should prudently and sensibly be done in the relevant legal context. Privilege does not extend without limit, however, to all solicitor and client communications upon matters within the ordinary business of a solicitor. The range of assistance given by solicitors to their clients and of activities carried out by solicitors on behalf of their clients has greatly broadened in recent times, and is still developing. The scope of legal professional privilege has to be kept within reasonable bounds (*Balabel v. Air India* [1988] 2 W.L.R. 1036; [1988] 2 All E.R. 246, CA; *Smith-Bird v. Blower* [1939] 2 All E.R. 406).

The reasons for this privilege are fully stated by Lord Brougham in *Greenough v. Gaskell* (1833) 1 My. & K. 98; by Lord Cottenham in *Reid v. Langlois* (1849) 1 Mac. & G. 627; by Jessel M.R. in *Anderson v. Bank of British Columbia* (1876) 2 Ch.D. 644 at 649; by Cotton L.J. in *Southwark Water Co. v. Quick* (1878) 3 Q.B.D. 315 at 321, and by Stirling J. in *Ainsworth v. Wilding* [1900] 2 Ch. 315 at 321; see Bray at 350 and more recently by Lord Taylor C.J. in *R. v. Derby Magistrates Court* (see above). It precludes an action for libel in respect of statements contained in such communications (*More v. Weaver* [1928] 2 K.B. 520, CA; but in *Minter v. Priest* (1930) 46 T.L.R. 301, HL, the question whether the privilege was absolute or qualified was expressly reserved).

This privilege extends to documents otherwise within it, although they contain statements of fact as to matters in the public domain, such as statements as to proceedings in private in the presence of the other party (*Ainsworth v. Wilding*). It extends to bills of costs relating to litigation actual or in contemplation (*Chant v. Brown* (1852) 9 Ha. 790; *Turton v. Barber* (1874) L.R. 17 Eq. 329) but it does not extend to a communication which took place in the presence of the opposite party, or with the opposite party (but see *Feuerheerd v. L. G. O. Co.*) or which are wholly in the public domain (*Ainsworth v. Wilding*). The privilege is not affected by the fact that the action in which disclosure is sought is founded on a policy insuring the plaintiff against damages and costs incurred in an claim to which the disclosure relates (*Daily Express (1908) Ltd v. Mountain* (1916) 32 T.L.R. 592, CA).

The privilege extends to information which the solicitor receives in a professional capacity from a third party and which he conveys to his client (*Re Sarah C. Getty Trust, Getty v. Getty* [1985] 3 W.L.R. 302; [1985] 2 All E.R. 809).

The principle that a client should be able to obtain legal advice in confidence requires that, where professional privilege applies to lawyer-client communications, internally circulated documents or parts of documents revealing such communications are also privileged, whatever the purpose, other than fraud, for which such documents are brought into existence (*Bank of Nova Scotia v. Hellenic Mutual War Risk Assn. (Bermuda) Ltd; The Good Luck* [1992] 1 A.C. 233; [1991] 2 W.L.R. 1279; [1991] 3 All E.R. 1; [1991] 2 Lloyd's Rep. 191; *The Independent*, October 31, 1988, HL), noted at [1992] 2 Lloyd's Rep. 540). See too *British & Commonwealth Holdings plc v. Quadrex Holdings Inc. (No. 2)*, *The Times*, December 8, 1988.

Third party as medium of communications—So confidential letters or communications between a party and his solicitor, in his professional capacity, made through a clerk or agent employed by the solicitor (*Wheeler v. Le Marchant* (1881) 17 Ch.D. 675 at 682, CA) or, and by the client in order to convey information to or from the solicitor (*Reid v. Langlois* (1849) 1 Mac. & G. 627; *Hooper v. Gumm* (1862) 2 Johns. & H. 602; *MacFarlan v. Rolt* (1872) L.R. 14 Eq. 580; *Anderson v. Bank of British Columbia* (1876) 2 Ch.D. 644 at 649; *Wheeler v. Le Marchant* (1881) 17 Ch.D. 675 at 682, 684) are privileged. **31.3.7**

Solicitors and partners as professional agents—So, too, letters and communications between a solicitor and his partner (*Mostyn v. West Mostyn Coal Co.* (1876) 34 L.T. 531), or professional agent (*Hughes v. Biddulph* (1827) 4 Russ. 190; *Bolton v. Liverpool Corp.* (1833) 1 My. & K. 88 at 96; *Catt v. Tourle* (1870) 23 L.T. 485 at 486; *Goodall v. Little* (1851) 1 Sim.(N.S.) 155; *MacFarlan v. Rolt* (1872)) are equally privileged. This does not apply to correspondence between the solicitors for opposite parties (*Gore v. Harris* (1851) 21 L.J.Ch.10). **31.3.8**

Legal advisers in the service of a party—The same privilege attaches to communications with a solicitor in the whole-time service of a party (*e.g.* a solicitor to a government department or a commercial enterprise) as to communications with a solicitor practising independently, provided that such communication relates to legal as distinct from administrative matters (*Alfred Crompton Amusement Machines Ltd v. Commrs. of Customs and Excise (No. 2)* [1974] A.C. 405; [1973] 2 All E.R. 1169, HL). An applicant has no right to inspect communications between in-house lawyers where there is an application for judicial review pending, as such documents are subject to legal professional privilege once litigation has started (*R. v. Law Society, ex p. Rosen*, *The Independent*, February 19, 1990). **31.3.9**

Counsel—Instructions and briefs to counsel and cases for counsel's opinion and counsel's opinions thereon, and counsel's drafts and notes, are privileged (*Mostyn v. West Mostyn Coal and Iron Co.*; *Bristol Corp. v. Cox* (1884) 26 Ch.D. 678; *Curtis v. Beaney* [1911] P. 181; *Lowden v. Blakey* (1889) 23 Q.B.D. 332, draft advertisements settled by counsel; *Pearse v. Pearse* (1846) 1 De G. & S. 12; *Bolton v. Liverpool Corp.* (1833) 1 My. & K. 88, 93; *Manser v. Dix* (1855) 1 K. & J. 451; *In the Estate of Copper* (1911) 27 T.L.R. 462; *Vigneron-Dahl, Ltd v. Pettit* [1925] W.N. 177, drafts of documents in support of application for leave of Att.-Gen.) but the indorsement on a brief of the result of the trial or the order made is not (*Walsham v. Stainton* (1863) 2 H. & M. 1; *Nicholl v. Jones* (1865) 2 H. & M. 588). **31.3.10**

All the above are privileged, although no litigation was pending or contemplated at the time when the communication took place (*Minet v. Morgan* (1873) L.R. 8 Ch. 361; *O'Shea v. Wood* [1891] P. 286 at 289, 290; *Mostyn v. West Mostyn Coal and Iron Co.* (1876) 34 L.T. 531; *Wheeler v. Le Marchant* (1881) 17 Ch.D. 675 at 682; *Turton v. Barber* (1874) L.R. 17 Eq. 329; *Lowden v. Blakey* (1889) 23 Q.B.D. 332; *Collins v. London General Omnibus Co.* (1893) 68 L.T. 831; *Greenough v. Gaskell* (1833) 1 My. & K. 98 at 102).

31.3.11 **Patent and trade mark agents**—By virtue of the provisions of s.280 of the Copyright, Designs and Patents Act 1988, communications between a client and his patent agent relating to the protection of any invention, design, technical information or trade mark or any matter involving passing off are privileged in the same way as such communications would be protected if they were between the client and his solicitor. Similarly, by virtue of s.87 of the Trade Marks Act 1994, communications between a client and his trade mark agent in relation to the protection of any design or trade mark or as to any matter involving passing off are also privileged.

(b) Communications privileged only when litigation was contemplated or pending

31.3.12 **Solicitors and non-professional agent or third party**—Communications between a solicitor and a non-professional agent or a third party, directly, or through an agent (*Anderson v. Bank of British Columbia* (1876) 2 Ch.D. 644 at 650) which come into existence after litigation is contemplated or commenced and made with a view to such litigation, either for the purpose of obtaining or giving advice in regard to it, or of obtaining or collecting evidence to be used in it, or obtaining information which may lead to the obtaining of such evidence, are privileged (*Anderson v. Bank of British Columbia* (1876) 2 Ch.D. 644 at 649; *Wheeler v. Le Marchant* (1881) 17 Ch.D. 675 at 681, CA; *Steele v. Stewart* (1843) 13 Sim. 533, affirmed 1 Ph. 471; *Walsham v. Stainton* (1863) 2 H. & M. 1; *Simpson v. Brown* (1864) 33 Beav. 482; *Wilson v. Northampton Rail* (1872) L.R. 14 Eq. 477; *Re Duncan (decd), Garfield v. Fay* [1968] P. 306; [1968] 2 All E.R. 395—litigation in a foreign Court). Except in the case where the non-professional agent is acting merely as the medium of communication between the solicitor and his client (*ibid.*, at 681, and see *Reid v. Langlois* and cases cited) such communications between a solicitor and a non-professional agent are not privileged, unless made with a view to litigation contemplated or existing (*Wheeler v. Le Marchant* (1881) 17 Ch.D. 675 at 682, CA). This applies to information such as a surveyor's report obtained by a solicitor with a view to giving his client legal advice, and such information is not privileged unless obtained with a view to contemplated or existing litigation (*ibid., per* Brett L.J. at 683). As to the extent of this principle, see *per* Cotton L.J. *Kennedy v. Lyell* (1883) 23 Ch.D. 387 at 407; *per* Stirling J. *Learoyd v. Halifax Banking Co.* [1893] 1 Ch. 686 at 691; *per* Denman J. *Lowden v. Blakey* (1889) 23 Q.B.D. 332 at 334; *per* Lindley M.R. *Calcraft v. Guest* [1898] 1 Q.B. 759 at 762. It is not open to a licensee to claim the privilege to which his licensor is entitled if the licensor is not a party to the claim and has not claimed privilege (*Reeves Bros. Inc. v. Lewis Reed & Co. Ltd* [1971] R.P.C. 355, refusing to extend the basis of the reasoning in *Calcraft v. Guest*).

Documents obtained by a solicitor with a view to enabling him to prosecute or defend a claim, or give advice with reference to existing or contemplated litigation, are privileged (*Learoyd v. Halifax Banking Co.* [1893] 1 Ch. 686 at 690; *cf, North Australian Co. v. Goldsborough* [1893] 2 Ch. 381); so are documents which come into existence merely as materials for the brief (*Southwark Water Co. v. Quick* (1878) 3 Q.B.D. 315 at 320; *The Palermo* (1883) 9 P.D. 6); but this does not extend to copies of unprivileged documents, such as letters, although obtained by the solicitor (*Chadwick v. Bowman* (1886) 16 Q.B.D. 561. See *Lyell v. Kennedy* (1884) 27 Ch.D. 1). When depositions of the crew of the R. in regard to a collision with the P. were taken by the Receiver of Wrecks, and in a claim arising out of the collision the Board of Trade refused to give copies of the depositions to the owners of the P., it was held that copies of the depositions obtained for the purpose of the claim by the solicitors to the owners of the R. were privileged (*The Palermo* (1883)).

Documents which come into existence for some purpose other than to instruct a lawyer or to form part of his brief are not privileged, and do not subsequently become privileged simply because they are sent to a lawyer as part of his instructions. Privilege cannot be claimed in respect of a copy of an affidavit taken for the purposes of legal advice when the original affidavit is not privileged (*Dubai Bank Ltd v. Galadari* [1989] 3 All E.R. 769, CA, not following *R. v. Board of Inland Revenue, ex p. Goldberg* [1989] Q.B. 267; [1988] 3 All E.R. 248).

Documents prepared confidentially after a dispute has arisen between the claimant and the defendant, and for the purpose of obtaining information, evidence or legal advice with reference to litigation existing or contemplated between the parties to a claim, are privileged (*per* Cotton L.J.; *Wheeler v. Le Marchant* (1881) 17 Ch.D. 675 at 685). So where an examination under s.27 of the B.A. 1883 was held with a view to enable the solicitor of the trustee to advise him whether a claim should be brought, the transcript of notes of the proceedings at the examination was held to be privileged (*Learoyd v. Halifax Joint Stock Banking Co.* (1893)). So where during a claim, anonymous letters relating to the matters in dispute were sent to the claimant, to her solicitor, and to her counsel, the two latter were held privileged, but not the letter to the claimant (*Re Holloway* (1887) 12 P.D. 167, CA).

Communications between an advising lawyer and the client's trade mark agent when litigation is contemplated are privileged (*McGregor Clothing Co. Ltd's T.M.* [1978] F.S.R. 353).

31.3.13 **Client and non-professional agent or third party**—The general principle is that documents embodying communications with (including reports to or from) a non-professional servant, agent or third party are privileged if, and only if, coming into existence for the purpose of obtaining legal advice in existing or anticipated proceedings (see the cases summarised in the judgment of Havers J. in *Seabrook v. British Transport Commission* [1959] 1 W.L.R. 509, [1959] 2 All E.R. 15).

The application of this test is easy enough in straightforward cases; privilege will clearly extend to communications for such purposes made to a solicitor through an agent, and to information obtained from a third party at the request of a solicitor to enable him to enforce or resist a claim by legal proceedings. Difficulties arise, however, (a) in determining the status of documents coming into existence for more than one purpose, and (b) in deciding at what stage it can fairly be said any such purpose is obtaining advice in anticipated litigation, as contrasted with obtaining information as to an occurrence which may lead to litigation.

As to (a) a document which is produced or brought into existence where the *dominant* purpose of its author, or of the person or authority under whose direction (whether particular or general) it is produced or brought into existence, is the use of the document or its contents in order to obtain legal advice, or to conduct or aid in the conduct of litigation in reasonable prospect at the time of its production, is privileged and excluded from inspection (*Waugh v. British Railways Board* [1980] A.C. 521, [1979] 2 All E.R. 1169, HL).

The dominant purpose of a document does not necessarily fall to be ascertained by reference to the intention of its actual composer (*Guinness Peat Properties Ltd v. Fitzroy Robinson Partnership* [1987] 1 W.L.R. 1027; [1987] 2 All E.R. 716, CA). The person or authority under whose direction a document is produced or brought into existence is in many cases the employer of the author; in such cases reference must be made to the intentions of the employer rather than to the intention of the author alone (*Waugh v. British Railways Board* (above); *McAvan v. London Transport Executive* [1982] CA Transcript 498). In other cases a document may be brought into existence at the direction of insurers (either as a condition of the insurance policy of a party to the claim or otherwise). In such cases reference must be made to the intention of the insurers. Where the dominant purpose of the insurers in procuring the document is its submission to legal advisers for advice on whether the claim should be paid or resisted, *e.g.* because fraud is suspected (*Re Highgrade Traders Ltd* [1984] B.C.L.C. 151, CA), or because the claim is in a complicated area of indemnity involving large sums of money (*Guinness Peat Properties Ltd v. Fitzroy Robinson Partnership* [1987] 1 W.L.R. 1027; [1987] 2 All E.R. 716, CA), the document will be held to be privileged. Such privilege can be claimed by a party to a claim notwithstanding that it is the insurers rather than that party who seek to use the document to obtain legal advice (*Guinness Peat Properties Ltd v. Fitzroy Robinson Partnership* (above)). The document will not be held to be privileged, however, where the insurance claim is simple and straightforward, and where the dominant purpose of the insurers in procuring the document is the assessment of the quantum of the claim rather than obtaining of legal advice on liability.

As to (b) the question, which is often closely connected with that raised in (a), is whether it is sufficient that the documents were made against the more or less likely contingency of it becoming necessary to obtain legal advice to make or resist a claim by litigation, or whether there must be an actual, present intention to obtain such advice at the time that the documents are made. In answer to this question the Court of Appeal has held that, if litigation is reasonably in prospect, documents brought into existence for the purpose of enabling solicitors to advise whether a claim shall be made or resisted are protected by privilege, whether or not a decision to instruct solicitors has been made at the time the documents are brought into being, subject only to establishing that such purpose is the dominant purpose of their creation (*Re Highgrade Traders Ltd* [1984] B.C.L.C. 151, CA; *Guinness Peat Properties Ltd v. Fitzroy Robinson Partnership* [1987] 1 W.L.R. 1027; [1987] 2 All E.R. 716, CA).

It must always be remembered that the time at which the dominant purpose of the author of a document, or of the person or authority under whose direction it is made, is to be judged, is the time when the document is brought into being. Such judgment ought not to be coloured by the subsequent use of the document or the subsequent intentions of the author, or of the person or authority under whose direction it is made, about how the document may best be used. Thus in *Jones v. Great Central Railway Co.* [1910] A.C. 4, HL, the dominant purpose of the making of a report by a trade union member to his trade union was, at the time the document was made, to allow the trade union to consider whether or not it should give financial assistance to the member to enable him to bring proceedings against his employer for wrongful dismissal. In *Alfred Crompton Amusement Machines Ltd v. Commrs. of Customs and Excise (No. 2)* [1974] A.C. 405; [1973] 2 All E.R. 1169, HL, the dominant purpose of the commissioners in procuring certain documents from the third parties was, at the time the documents were brought into being, the valuation of the appellants' goods for purchase tax. In neither case were the documents held to be privileged, notwithstanding that in both cases litigation was reasonably in prospect at the time the documents were brought into being and that in both cases the documents were subsequently used to obtain legal advice and to conduct the litigation.

Accident reports to employers or insurers may fall on either side of the line. In several cases such reports have been held to be privileged on the grounds that, at the time they were made or procured, the dominant purpose of those who made or procured them was the obtaining of legal advice whether to resist a claim for damages (*Ogden v. London Electric Ry. Co.* (1933) 49 T.L.R. 542; *Westminster Airways v. Kuwait Oil Co.* [1951] 1 K.B. 134; *Seabrook v. British Transport Commission* [1959] 1 W.L.R. 509; [1959] 2 All E.R. 15). On the other hand an accident report, the preparation of which is required by National Health Service circulars is not subject to legal professional privilege where the dominant purpose of its preparation is not submission to solicitors in anticipation of litigation, even although one of the purposes of such reports, mentioned in the circulars, is use by solicitors if litigation should be commenced in respect of the accident (*Lask v. Gloucester Health Authority* [1991] 2 Med LR, 379, CA). Thus where the dominant purpose in the preparation of an accident report is the avoidance of similar accidents in the future, the report will not be privileged, even although a subsidiary purpose in its preparation is its use in the conduct of anticipated litigation.

Where a document produced under a statutory duty (*e.g.* s.7(3) of the Company Directors Disqualification Act 1986) did not threaten the inviolability of communication between a party and his lawyer, that party could not claim legal professional privilege for it by asserting that the document's dominant purpose was for use in litigation, see *Secretary of State for Trade and Industry v. Baker* [1998] Ch. 356; [1998] 2 W.L.R. 667; [1998] 1 All E.R. 673. The court stated that there was no general privilege that attached to documents brought into existence for the purposes of litigation independent of the need to keep inviolate communications between client and legal adviser. If documents for which professional privilege was sought did not relate in some fashion to communications between client and legal adviser, there was no element of public interest that could override the ordinary rights of disclosure and inspection.

31.3.14 **Pre-existing documents or copies of or extracts therefrom**—Documents do not become privileged by the mere fact that they have at some time been submitted to a solicitor (*Graham v. Bogle* [1924] 1 Ir.R. 68); and copies, obtained by a party from third persons, of unprivileged documents which he had lost, do not necessarily become privileged (*Chadwick v. Bowman* (1886) 16 Q.B.D. 561). Thus legal professional privilege does not extend to cover an original document, even if obtained by a party to litigation or his legal adviser for purposes of the litigation, if the document has not come into existence for the purposes of the litigation, but is already in existence before the litigation is contemplated or commenced. A pre-existing document not entitled to privilege does not become privileged merely because it is handed to a solicitor for the purposes of litigation (*Ventouris v. Mountain, The Italia Express* [1991] 3 All E.R. 472, CA). But original or copy documents obtained or prepared by the party for the purpose of obtaining his solicitor's advice in view of pending or anticipated litigation, or by his solicitor for the purposes of pending or anticipated litigation, are privileged (*The Palermo* (1883) 9 P.D. 6; *Lyell v. Kennedy* (1884) 27 Ch.D. 1; *Pearce v. Foster* (1885) 15 Q.B.D. 114; *Watson v. Cammell Laird & Co. Ltd* [1959] 1 W.L.R. 702; [1959] 2 All E.R. 757). However the notion that there may be a privileged copy of an un-privileged document is now discounted; *Lubrizol v. Esso Petroleum Co. (No. 4)* [1993] F.S.R. 64. Legal professional privilege does not attach to documents which are in the possession of both parties unless the documents would tend to indicate either the advice that might be sought or the advice that was given (*ibid.*, at 70).

31.3.15 **Confidential documents**—No communication made by or on behalf of the opposite party can be confidential; *per* Cotton L.J. *Kennedy v. Lyell* (1883) 23 Ch.D. 387, p.405; *Ainsworth v. Wilding* [1900] 2 Ch.321; *Spenceley v. Schulenburgh* (1806) 7 East 357; *Desborough v. Rawlins* (1838) 3 My. & Cr. 515; *Baker v. L. & S. W. Ry. Co.* (1867) L.R. 3 Q.B. 91; *Gore v. Bowser* (1851) 5 De G. & S. 30; *Ford v. Tennant* (1863) 32 Beav. 162. In *Feuerheerd v. L. G. O. Co.* [1918] 2 K.B. 565, however (where the above cases were not cited and the point apparently not even raised) the CA is reported to have held that a statement made and signed by the claimant, and obtained from her by the defendants' claims inspector for the purpose of being laid before the defendants' solicitor was privileged. It is submitted that this decision is wrong, and that *Tobakin v. Dublin Southern Trams Co.* [1905] 2 I.R. 58, which the CA refused to follow, was right. The previous sentence was cited with approval by the Court of Appeal in Northern Ireland (see *McKay v. McKay* [1988] N.I.L.R. 79 at 92–93).

31.3.16 **Other legal advisers**—The above principles are not confined to solicitors, but extend to confidential communications with any legal adviser, as for instance, a Scots (*Wheeler v. Le Marchant* (1881) 17 Ch.D. 675, p.679; *Lawrence v. Campbell* (1859) 4 Drew 485) or French (*MacFarlan v. Rolt* (1872) L.R. 14 Eq. 580) or Dutch (*Bunbury v. Bunbury* (1839) 2 Beav. 173) legal adviser.

31.3.17 **Co-plaintiffs or co-defendants**—Communications between co-claimants (*Hutt v. Haileybury College* (1888) 4 T.L.R. 277, CA) or co-defendants (*Hamilton v. Nott* (1873) L.R. 16 Eq. 112; *Jenkyns v. Bushby* (1866) L.R. 2 Eq. 547; *Betts v. Menzies* (1857) 26 L.J.Ch.528; *Goodall v. Little* (1851) 1 Sim.(N.S.) 155) stand on the same footing as communications with non-professional agents, and are only privileged under the same circumstances. But where one of several trustees is a solicitor, communications between him and his co-trustees which would be privileged if he were not a co-trustee, are privileged (*Re Whitworth* [1919] 1 Ch.320, CA; affirmed, *sub nom. O'Rourke v. Darbishire* [1920] A.C. 581, HL).

31.3.18 **Common interest legal privilege**—A privilege in aid of anticipated litigation in which several persons have a common interest although all such persons have not been made parties to the claim; see *Buttes Gas and Oil Co. v. Hammer (No. 3)* [1981] 1 Q.B. 223 at 243, 267. Such common interest did not come to an end simply because a dispute arises as to who should conduct the proceedings but documents brought into existence in respect of such dispute did not attract common interest legal privilege though they might attract some other form of privilege; see *Leif Hoegh & Co. A/S v. Petrolsea Inc. (The World Era) (No. 2)* [1993] 1 Lloyd's Rep. 363. See too *Formica Ltd v. Export Credits Guarantee Department* [1995] 1 Lloyd's Rep. 692; held that where a guarantor of losses incurred by a company had been contractually entitled to view documents which had come into existence in the company's pursuit of its potential losses, the guarantor was entitled to specific discovery of the documents as the guarantor had a common interest with the company in the recovery of the company's debts.

Other advisers—Communications between a party and his medical adviser (*Wheeler v. Le Marchant* (1881) 17 Ch.D. 675 at 681) or his spiritual adviser (*ibid.*) or a non-professional friend or adviser (*ibid.*; *Smith v. Daniel* (1874) L.R. 18 Eq. 649) are not privileged although of the most confidential kind (*ibid.*); nor are communications with a pursuivant of the Herald's College (*Slade v. Tucker* (1880) 14 Ch.D. 824). For position in relation to patent and trade mark agents, see para. 31.3.11, above. 31.3.19

Reports prepared by bank accountants in course of investigating problem loans were not protected as (a) such were not communications between bank and its legal advisers and (b) were not documents produced in contemplation of litigation (*Price Waterhouse (A Firm) v. B.C.C.I. Holdings Luxembourg SA* (1992) B.C.L.C. 583).

Where proceedings had been conducted initially by a party receiving advice from a firm of personnel consultants, that advice was not privileged from discovery as it was not covered by legal professional privilege (*New Victoria Hospital v. Ryan* [1993] I.C.R. 201, E.A.T.).

The public interest in making confidential documents relating to an alleged fraud of an international bank available to parties to private foreign litigation directed towards exposing such fraud outweighed the public interest in preserving the confidentiality in those documents, *Pharaon and Others v. Bank of Credit and Commerce International SA*, Price Waterhouse intervening, (application for permission to comply with a *subpoena* to produce documents), [1998] 4 All E.R. 455.

Subsequent litigation—The general principle is, that a document once privileged is always privileged (*Calcraft v. Guest* [1898] 1 Q.B. 759, *per* Lindley M.R. at 761; *Goldstone v. Williams* [1899] 1 Ch. 47 at 52) and the privilege applies both in the existing or contemplated and any other litigation (*ibid.*; *Pearce v. Foster* (1885) 15 Q.B.D. 114; *Bullock v. Corrie* (1878) 3 Q.B.D. 356; *Curtis v. Beaney* [1911] P.181). If documents for which privilege can be claimed are brought into existence for the purpose of a claim which ultimately is not proceeded with, the privilege does not cease, but can be claimed in a subsequent claim other than that for which they were originally brought into existence (*Pearce v. Foster* (1885) and see *Ainsworth v. Wilding* [1900] 2 Ch.315); and "the mere fact that documents used in a previous litigation are held and have not been destroyed, does not amount to waiver of the privilege" (*Calcraft v. Guest* [1898] 1 Q.B. 759). But the privilege can be claimed only by a party to the original litigation or his successor in title (*Reeves Bros. Inc. v. Lewis Reed & Co. Ltd* [1971] F.S.R. 17); a licensing arrangement with such a party is not equivalent to a succession in title (*ibid.*). 31.3.20

If the privilege which prevailed in the original claim is properly claimed in a subsequent claim by the person originally entitled to it, or his successor, there is no additional requirement that the subsequent claim should be between the same parties or involve the same subject-matter; provided there is sufficient connection for the document to be relevant, the party entitled to privilege is able to assert it in the subsequent claim (*The Aegis Blaze* [1986] 1 Lloyd's Rep. 203; (1986) 130 S.J. 15, CA). The same rule prevails even where the original and subsequent claim are in different jurisdictions. A litigant's privilege arising in proceedings in a foreign court is an answer to a claim in subsequent proceedings in England for production of a document the subject of such privilege (*Minnesota Mining & Manufacturing Co. v. Rennicks (UK) Ltd* [1991] F.S.R. 97). Nor does the use of the documents in the foreign proceedings constitute a waiver of the privilege where the documents were called into existence for the purpose of such litigation: *ibid.*

A document adduced or evidence given by a party in a private arbitration, however, is not privileged from disclosure in subsequent litigation between such party and others who are not parties to the arbitration (*Shearson Lehman Hutton Inc. v. Maclaine Watson & Co. Ltd (No. 3)* [1988] 1 W.L.R. 946; [1989] 1 All E.R. 1056). But see restriction on use without leave in Hassneh Insurance case, para. 31.22.1 below.

Legal professional privilege generally

Documents in the public domain—Documents which are in the public domain are not privileged (*Nicholl v. Jones* (1865) 2 H. & M. 588; *Goldstone v. Williams* [1899] 1 Ch. 47, p. 52). This applies to shorthand or other notes of proceedings in open Court (*ibid.*; *Re Worswick* (1888) 38 Ch.D. 370; *Lambert v. Home* [1914] 3 K.B. 86, CA, overruling *Nordon v. Defries* (1882) Q.B.D. 508) or in a private hearing (*Ainsworth v. Wilding* [1900] 2 Ch.315) or before an arbitrator (*Rawstone v. Preston Corp.* (1885) 30 Ch.D. 116) and to the indorsements on counsel's brief of the result of the trial or the order of the Court (*Nicholl v. Jones*) or depositions filed in the course of a claim (*Goldstone v. Williams*) or office copies thereof (*ibid.*). But this does not apply to privileged documents merely because they are exhibited to depositions which are entered and read in an order of compromise (*ibid.*). Nor does it apply to a collection of copies or extracts of public records or documents made by a solicitor for the purposes of a defence, or the result of his research and skill (*Lyell v. Kennedy (No. 3)* (1884) 27 Ch.D. 1, CA, see *Lambert v. Home* [1914] 3 K.B. 86, at 90, 92) and see Bray, p. 490). 31.3.21

Fraud or illegality—This professional privilege does not extend to cases where the document came into existence as a step in a criminal or illegal proceeding, as, *e.g.* if a solicitor is consulted on how to do an illegal act (*Bullivant v. Att.-Gen. for Victoria* [1901] A.C. 196 at 201, *per* Lord Halsbury and at 206, *per* Lord Lindley; see also *R. v. Cox* (1884) 14 Q.B.D. 153). In a claim against 31.3.22

ex-employees for conspiracy to injure, breach of the duty of fidelity and breach of confidence, disclosure was ordered of documents passing between the defendants and their solicitors relating to the setting up of the companies within which the defendants proposed to operate (*Gamlen Chemical Co. (U.K.) Ltd v. Rochem Ltd* [1983] R.P.C.1.). But privilege is not lost if the purpose of the document was to ask, or give, advice as to how (lawfully) "to keep out of an Act of Parliament" (*Bullivant v. Att.-Gen. for Victoria*, above, at 207) or to warn against the results of contemplated acts (*Butler v. Board of Trade* [1971] Ch.680; [1970] 3 All E.R. 593). To bring a case within this exception there must be a definite charge of fraud or illegality and a prima facie case must be made out (*Re Whitworth* [1919] 1 Ch. 320 at 336, 349, CA; affirmed [1920] A.C. 581; 89 L.J.Ch.162, *sub nom. O'Rourke v. Darbishire*, HL). The Court will be slow to displace the privilege and would not do so on mere suspicion as opposed to the establishment of a prima facie case of fraud or illegality (*Royscott Spa Leasing Ltd v. Lovett* (1995) *The Independent*, January 23). Notwithstanding that the word "fraud" has not been used in the statement of case, privilege can be displaced if the facts alleged enable the Court to recognise fraud (*Gamlen* case, above). It is immaterial whether the solicitor is party to the alleged fraud or not (*Williams v. Quebrada Railway, Land & Copper Co.* [1895] 2 Ch. 751). Where communications which would otherwise be within the protection of legal professional privilege have been made in furtherance of a fraudulent design, a party is not entitled to assert legal professional privilege as a ground for refusing to disclose such communications in circumstances where the party seeking disclosure is able to establish a strong prima facie case of fraud; the court, however, will be very slow to deprive a party of the important protection of legal professional privilege on an interlocutory application, and will judge each case on its facts, striking a balance between the important considerations on which legal professional privilege is founded and the gravity of the charge of fraud that is made (*Derby & Co. Ltd v. Weldon (No. 7)* [1990] 1 W.L.R. 1156; [1990] 3 All E.R. 161). See also *Nationwide B.S. v. Various Solicitors* (1998) *The Times*, February 5.

Fraud is here used in a relatively wide sense. It embraces the effecting of iniquity. Advice sought for the purpose of effecting iniquity is not privileged. Thus in *Barclays Bank plc v. Eustace* [1995] 1 W.L.R. 1238; [1995] 4 All E.R. 511, CA, court held that where on a prima facie view the client was seeking to enter into transactions at an under value the purpose of which was to prejudice the bank, such purpose was sufficiently iniquitous for public policy to require removal of legal professional privilege from communications between client and solicitor in relation to setting up such transactions.

The existence or absence of privilege cannot be affected by whether the fraud concerns an earlier transaction or the conduct of the proceedings in which disclosure is sought. See too *Dubai Aluminium Co. Ltd v. Al Alauri* [1999] 1 All E.R. 703 where there was found a strong prima facie case of criminal or fraudulent conduct in the obtaining of information relating to the defendent's accounts during a Mareva process and the court held that documents generated by or reporting on such conduct fell outside the legitimate area of legal professional privilege. Disclosure at an interlocutory stage, however, based on prima facie evidence of fraud in the conduct of the proceedings, carries a far greater risk of injustice to the party against whom disclosure is sought than disclosure in relation to earlier transactions. The risk of injustice to such party if he is compelled to disclose what he has told his solicitors to enable them to defend him against allegations of fraud, together with the damage to the public interest which would be caused by requiring the disclosure of such confidences, outweighs the risk of the other party being deprived of the information (*Chandler v. Church* (1987) 137 N.L.J. 451).

It is not the law that legal professional privilege is defeated whenever there is a fraud. A fraudulent party should not be protected by privilege, but the victim of fraud should not lose the privilege in respect of his innocent correspondence through the fraud of another (*Banque Keyser Ullman S.A. v. Skandia (U.K.) Insurance Co. Ltd* [1986] 1 Lloyd's Rep. 336, CA).

In order to determine whether a communication between a solicitor and his client is not privileged because its purpose is the furtherance of crime, the Court is entitled to look at the document in question without requiring the party who objects to the claim for privilege to prove by evidence outside the document that it came into existence for that purpose (*R. v. Cox* (1884) 14 Q.B.D. 153; *R. v. Governor of Pentonville Prison, ex p. Osman (No. 2)* [1989] 3 All E.R. 701. Communications in furtherance of fraud are not protected by legal professional privilege regardless of whether the claimant's case is founded on that particular fraud. Where a defendant, having committed a fraud, subsequently attempts to further the fraud through the deception of his solicitor, the relevant communication between the defendant and his solicitor is deprived of the element of professional confidence and privilege in respect thereof is displaced (*Dubai Bank Ltd v. Galadari (No. 6)* (1991) *The Times*, April 22).

31.3.23 **Trustee and cestui que trust**—Privilege cannot be claimed by a trustee against his *cestui que* trust (*Re Mason* (1883) 22 Ch.D. 609; *Wynne v. Humberston* (1858) 27 Beav. 421; *Devaynes v. Robinson* (1855) 20 Beav. 42; *Re Postlethwaite, Re Rickman, Postlethwaite v. Rickman* (1887) 35 Ch.D. 722); nor against persons in an analogous position (*Gouraud v. Edison Co.* (1888) 57 L.J.Ch.498; *cf. Bristol Corp. v. Cox* (1884) 26 Ch.D. 678 at 683. See also Re Whitworth [1919] 1 Ch. 320 affirmed [1920] A.C. 581 (solicitor trustee)).

31.3.24 **Proprietary right**—The privilege would not cover documents in which the party seeking disclosure has a proprietary right, but he must establish the existence of the right (*Re Whitworth* above).

Company and shareholder—See *Woodhouse & Co. v. Woodhouse* (1914) 30 T.L.R. 559. **31.3.25**

Parties employing same solicitor—Where two parties employ the same solicitor in the course of, for example, a conveyancing transaction, communications between either of them and the solicitor in his joint capacity have to be disclosed in favour of the other; where one of the parties is subsequently adjudicated bankrupt the other party cannot assert legal professional privilege as a ground for refusing to disclose such communications to the trustee in bankruptcy, who is to be treated for such purpose as being in the same position as the bankrupt and not as a third party (*Re Konigsberg (a bankrupt), ex p. The Trustee v. Konigsberg* [1989] 3 All E.R. 289). **31.3.26**

Waiver or loss of privilege—The privilege is in all cases the privilege of the client and not of the solicitor or legal adviser (*Anderson v. Bank of British Columbia* (1876) 2 Ch.D. 644 at 649; *Procter v. Smiles* (1886) 55 L.J.Q.B. 467 at 527, 528, CA) and may be waived by the client (*Calcraft v. Guest* [1898] 1 Q.B. 759 at 761, CA) but not by the solicitor or legal adviser (*Procter v. Smiles*; *Greenough v. Gaskell* (1833) 1 My. & K. 98 at 102). But it is not waived by reason of the documents being put to the defendant in examination before an examiner and exhibited to his depositions, or by being put before a judge in a private hearing in order that he may decide whether a compromise of the claim is a proper one (*Goldstone v. Williams* [1899] 1 Ch. 47). Nor is it waived merely by referring to the documents in a statement of case (*Roberts v. Oppenheim* (1884) 26 Ch.D. 724, CA) or in an affidavit (*Infields Ltd v. Rosen & Son* [1938] 3 All E.R. 591, CA). Waiver as to some of several documents does not involve a waiver as to the others (*Lyell v. Kennedy* (1884) 27 Ch.D. 1, CA). If part of a document is put in evidence, or read to the Court, privilege will be waived for the whole document, unless the remaining part deals with an entirely different subject-matter (*Great Atlantic Insurance Co. v. Home Insurance Co.* [1981] 1 W.L.R. 529; [1981] 2 All E.R. 485, CA). Similarly, if part of a letter is disclosed, the disclosing party is deemed to be waiving privilege in relation to the whole letter, unless it can be shown that the other parts of the letter are so distinct as to amount to different documents (*Pozzi v. Eli Lilly & Co.* (1986) *The Times*, December 3). Likewise disclosure of part of contents of a report waives privilege as to the whole, *Chandris Lines v. Wilson & Horton Ltd* [1981] 2 N.Z.L.R. 600. See also *Bank of Nova Scotia v. Hellenic Mutual War Risks Assn. (Bermuda) Ltd*; *The Good Luck* (1988) *The Independent*, October 31, 1988. Noted at [1992] 2 Lloyd's Rep. 540. The rule that the reading in open court of part of a privileged document resulted in waiver of privilege in the whole does not apply where the non-waiving party had already seen the whole document (*Def American Inc. v. Phonogram Ltd* (1994) *The Times*, August 16). **31.3.27**

By CPR r.35.10(3) an expert's report must state the substance of all material instructions, whether written or oral, on the basis of which the report was written. Sub-section (4) of r.35.10 provides that the "instructions referred to in paragraph (3) shall not be privileged against disclosure but the court will not, in relation to those instructions—

(a) order disclosure of any specific document; or

(b) permit any questioning in court, other than by the party who instructed the expert, unless it is satisfied that there are reasonable grounds to consider the statement of instructions given under paragraph (3) to be inaccurate or incomplete."

But the use of a document for the purpose of cross-examination does not itself make it part of the evidence so as to entitle the other party to investigate other privileged documents on all the topics mentioned in it; the use of a document for cross-examination waives privilege for the transaction actually described in the document but not for matters merely mentioned in it (*General Accident Fire & Life Assurance Corp. Ltd v. Tanter, The Zephyr* [1984] 1 W.L.R. 100; [1984] 1 All E.R. 35).

The mere fact that a party may have waived the professional privilege which exists between solicitor and client does not result in the waiver of the further privilege which protects documents brought into existence for the purpose of litigation, pending or contemplated; consequently the opposite party is entitled to the discovery of documents relating to the matters as to which professional privilege has been waived up to the date that litigation was contemplated but not thereafter (*George Doland Ltd v. Blackburn Robson Coates & Co.* [1972] 1 W.L.R. 1338; [1973] 2 All E.R. 959).

The institution of civil proceedings against a solicitor by his client constituted an implied waiver of professional privilege in relation to all relevant documents concerned with the suit to the extent necessary to enable the court to adjudicate the dispute fully and fairly. Where an issue was one of causation of loss and the defendants alleged that the claimants would have gone ahead with the transaction involved irrespectively of the advice received and sought to establish such by reference to earlier transactions in which they had acted for the claimants, the claimants' implied waiver extended to the documents in the other transactions (*Lillicrap v. Nalder & Son (a firm)* [1993] 1 W.L.R. 94; [1993] 1 All E.R. 724, CA). But such a waiver is limited. Thus where a client brought proceedings against his former solicitors for negligence in handling a commercial transaction between the client and a third party, the client's waiver of legal privilege implied from his bringing the proceedings did not extend to confidential communications between himself and different solicitors instructed to pursue and settle his claim against the third party, see *Paragon Finance plc and Others v. Freshfields (a firm)* [1999] 1 W.L.R. 1183, CA.

A reference in an affidavit to a legal document or to a conversation with solicitors does not amount to a waiver of legal professional privilege in respect of the communication (*Tate & Lyle International Ltd v. Government Trading Corp.* (1984) 87 L.S.Gaz. 3341, CA).

The mere service of a witness statement under an order of the court does not waive privilege in connected documents. There is no waiver unless and until statement is deployed in court (*Balkanbank v. Taher* (1994) *The Times*, February 19). Contrast *Clough v. Tameside and Glossop Health Authority* [1998] 1 W.L.R. 1478; [1998] 2 All E.R. 971.

Where a party deploys material in court on an interlocutory application, privilege that can otherwise be claimed in relation to that and associated material will be treated as waived altogether, with the result that the party cannot then assert privilege for the same material at the subsequent trial. Where, however, the party merely refers in interlocutory proceedings to the fact that he has obtained legal advice, and states the effect of that advice without disclosing the substance of it or the extent of the instructions given to the legal adviser, he does not thereby waive the right to claim privilege at the trial in respect of the legal advice itself (*Derby & Co. Ltd v. Weldon (No. 10)* [1991] 1 W.L.R. 660; [1991] 2 All E.R. 908). Affidavit evidence in without notice proceedings exhibiting opinions from counsel and solicitors was not in the public domain and neither party to the claim waived any rights they had to assert against third parties a claim for privilege in respect of such documents; see *Leif Hoegh & Co. A/S v. Petrolsea Inc. (The World Era) (No. 2)* [1993] 1 Lloyd's Rep. 363. The question whether, if privilege has been waived in relation to part of a document or evidence by production of a tape recording or transcript of part of a conversation, fairness requires that the other party should be entitled to adduce in evidence the whole of the document or evidence of the whole of the conversation to ensure that the court is not misled by seeing or hearing part out of context, is a question that can only be answered by the judge after he has read the whole of the document or transcript or heard the tape recording in full (*ibid.*). Although the fact that a party may have waived the privilege which protects documents brought into existence for the purpose of litigation does not automatically result in a waiver of the privilege for the same documents which exists between solicitor and client, the court will not sever the two privileges in circumstances where both the privileges attach to a single communication, and say that one has been waived but the other not (*ibid.*).

There is a statutory requirement for a claimant for costs to disclose privileged documents to the Court on taxation, and, when this is done, part of the privilege attaching to such documents is temporarily relaxed. The taxing officer, however, has a duty to be fair to both parties and to ensure that privilege is maintained as far as possible without preventing the other party from having an opportunity to challenge the taxation. In rare circumstances the taxing officer may have to disclose privileged documents in order to strike an appropriate balance, but any disclosure will only be for the purposes of the taxation; the privilege can subsequently be reasserted (*Goldman v. Hesper* [1988] 1 W.L.R. 1238; [1988] 3 All E.R. 197, CA; see also *Hobbs v. Hobbs* [1960] P. 112; [1959] 3 All E.R. 827, and *Pamplin v. Express Newspapers Ltd* [1985] 2 All E.R. 185).

Where documents which are clearly privileged when made are disclosed by a party to the police in accordance with his public duty to assist in a criminal investigation, and where such disclosure is for the limited purpose of such investigation and any subsequent criminal trial, no waiver of privilege in relation to civil proceedings is made or implied. It is contrary to public policy that assistance with a criminal investigation should lead to loss of legal professional privilege in a civil action (*British Coal Corp. v. Dennis Rye Ltd (No. 2)* [1988] 3 All E.R. 816, CA).

In Children Act 1989 and wardship matters where the interests of the child were paramount, the legal professional privilege attaching to medical reports yielded to such overriding principle (*Essex County Council v. R.* [1994] 2 W.L.R. 407 and noted at [1994] Fam. 167; *Oxfordshire County Council v. M* [1994] Fam. 151; [1994] 2 W.L.R. 393; [1994] 2 All E.R. 269).

Legal privilege may also give way to a contractual obligation to disclose (*Brown v. G.R.E.* [1994] 2 Lloyd's Rep. 325, CA).

In *Director General of Fair Trading v. Reid*, December 20, 1994, Buckley J., Restrictive Practices Court, held that civil contempt proceedings should be approached more by analogy with the criminal than the civil practice and ordered discovery of prior drafts of witness statements just as a criminal prosecutor would have to in order to comply with his duty to disclose unused material.

31.3.28 **Death of client**—Privilege is not lost by reason of the death of the client (*Bullivant v. Att.-Gen. for Victoria*, above).

31.3.29 **Successor in title to party**—Legal professional privilege of a party to a claim enures for the benefit of the successor in title to that party, at any rate, where the relevant interest subsists (*Cresent Farm (Sidcup) Sports Ltd v. Sterling Offices Ltd* [1972] Ch. 553; [1971] 3 All E.R. 1192, applying *Minet v. Morgan* (1873) 8 Ch.App. 361; *Schneider v. Leigh* [1955] 2 Q.B. 195, CA, and doubting *Greenlaw v. King* (1838) 1 Beav. 137).

31.3.30 **Secondary evidence or copies of privileged document**—Secondary evidence as to the contents of a privileged document is admissible as against the party resisting its production (*Calcraft v. Guest* [1898] 1 Q.B. 759, CA). Thus if a party has an opportunity of taking or getting a copy of such a document he can use it as secondary evidence (*ibid.*), though use of an improperly acquired document will be restrained.

If, however, he has possession of such a copy document but has not yet used it in his litigation, the mere fact that he intends so to use it in the future is no answer to a claim against him by the person in whom the privilege is vested for delivery up of the copy, or to restrain him from disclosing or making use of its contents (*Goddard v. Nationwide Building Society* [1987] Q.B. 670; [1986] 3 W.L.R. 734; [1986] 3 All E.R. 264, CA). Moreover public policy requires that a litigant should not be permitted to make use of a copy of a privileged document as evidence, where he has obtained it by stealth or a trick, or by otherwise acting improperly (*I.T.C. Film Distributors Ltd v. Video Exchange Ltd* [1982] Ch. 431; [1982] 2 All E.R. 241).

Where counsel's papers are accidentally sent to the other side an injunction may be granted against a stranger who has innocently come by confidential information to which he is not entitled, but so as to be capable of being policed the order should be directed towards outward acts rather than inwards thoughts, though without sanctioning deliberate covert action (*English and American Insurance Co. Ltd v. Herbert Smith* [1988] F.S.R. 232). See too *Ablitt v. Mills & Reeve (a firm), The Times,* October 25, 1995; injunction granted restraining the first defendants, solicitors to the seond defendant, from continuing to act on the second defendants' behalf in the main claim in addition to the undertaking they had given not to make use of information gained from files mistakenly sent to them. It does not follow, however, that an injunction will be granted in every case following the unauthorised disclosure of a privileged and confidential document to prevent its future use. The Court must exercise discretion by balancing the legitimate interests of the party to whom the document belongs in seeking to keep its contents suppressed and the legitimate interests of the other party in seeking to make use of it. In carrying out such a balancing exercise, the circumstances in which the document comes into the hands of the latter party, the issues in the claim, the relevance of the document and whether it would in one way or another have to be disclosed, together with the nature of the privilege, are all matters which have to be taken into account (*Webster v. James Chapman & Co.* [1989] 3 All E.R. 939).

In general, however, and except where it is too late to restore the status quo, the law will not encourage parties to litigation or their solicitors to take advantage of obvious mistakes made in the course of the process of disclosure; where a party seeks to take advantage of an obvious mistake made by his opponent, copies of privileged documents of the other party which may have come into the possession of the party seeking such advantage, or his solicitors, will be ordered to be handed back to the other party, and an injunction will be granted restraining the party seeking such advantage from using information contained in or derived from the documents (*Derby & Co. Ltd v. Weldon (No. 8)* [1991] 1 W.L.R. 73; [1990] 3 All E.R. 762, CA). See too *Breeze v. John Stacey & Sons Ltd, The Times,* July 8, 1999, CA to effect that the former rules applicable to cases of inadvertent disclosure of privileged documents had not been affected by the introduction of the present new rules.

Documents tending to criminate or expose to a penalty—A party is not compelled to give disclosure which will tend to criminate or expose to proceedings for a penalty him or his spouse under the law of any part of the U.K. (Civil Evidence Act 1968, s.14). It is sufficient if he claims that he believes that the disclosure "will," "would," "may," or "might," tend to incriminate him or so expose him: the difference in phraseology is immaterial, provided the risk is apparent to the Court (*Lamb v. Munster* (1882) 10 Q.B.D. 110; *Triplex Safety Glass Co. Ltd v. Lancegaye Safety Glass (1934) Ltd* [1939] 2 K.B. 395, CA; *Spokes v. Grosvenor Hotel Co.* [1897] 2 Q.B. 124, CA; *National Association of Operative Plasterers v. Smithies* [1906] A.C. 434; *Waterhouse v. Barker* [1924] 2 K.B. 759; *Sitwell v. Sun Engraving Co.* [1937] 4 All E.R. 366, CA). In *Den Norske Bank ASA v. Antonatos* [1999] Q.B. 271, CA, where this head of privilege was asserted in the context of cross-examination it was held that the ambit of the privilege is not confined simply to the risk of prosecution but that a witness was entitled to claim the privilege against self-incrimination not merely on the ground that an answer might increase the risk of prosecution, but in respect of any piece of information or evidence on which a prosecuting authority might wish to rely in establishing guilt or in determining whether to prosecute, and that the court should uphold the privilege even if he was acting from mixed motives or mala fide as a result of not fully appreciating the risk. The risk of exposure must be real, see *Renworth v. Stephanson* [1996] 3 All E.R. 244, CA, a case where in addition to the protection of s.31 of the Theft Act 1968, the chances of a charge separate and distinct from a Theft Act Offence was remote and the claim to privilege failed. 31.3.31

The prohibition with criminal sanctions against disclosing information relating to the business affairs of any party under s.82(1) of the Banking Act 1987 cannot be overridden by any party's obligation to give disclosure, *BCCI (Overseas) Ltd (in liquidation) v. Price Waterhouse* [1998] Ch. 84; [1997] 4 All E.R. 781. See too *C. v. S.* [1999] 2 All E.R. 343, CA, a case involving potential offences under the tipping-off provisions of s.93D of the Criminal Justice Act 1988 in which the Court laid down the procedure to be adopted to give protection to the financial institution involved and the party seeking disclosure without prejudicing the investigations of the Economic Crimes Unit of the National Criminal Intelligence Services (NCIS).

Proceedings for civil contempt are proceedings for the "recovery of a penalty" within section 14(1) of the Civil Evidence Act 1968 in respect of which there is a privilege against self-incrimination, though for the purposes of civil proceedings pertaining to infringement of intellectual property or passing off such privilege has been withdrawn by section 72 of the Supreme Court Act 1981, see *Cobra Golf Inc. v. Rata* [1998] Ch. 109; 1997 2 W.L.R. 629; [1997] 2 All E.R. 150.

Claims to withhold from inspection on this ground can be made in the party's list see CPR, r.31.10(4)(a) and by the procedure set out in r.31.19(3) *et seq.*

The privilege no longer extends to a liability to penal proceedings abroad (Civil Evidence Act 1968, s.14) but for the purposes of this section liability to a penalty under EEC legislation forming part of the law of the U.K. by virtue of the European Communities Act 1972 is a penalty under the law of the U.K., and privilege may be claimed. It does not extend to a penalty which is no longer recoverable, nor an offence which has been pardoned (see, *e.g. Att.-Gen. v. Cunard Co.* (1877) 4 T.L.R. 177). Some statutes provide that the liability to criminal prosecution shall afford no objection to discovery in civil suits (*Ramsden v. Brearley* (1875) 33 L.T. 322; *Lefroy v. Burnside* (1879) 41 L.T. 199) and by s.14(3) of the Civil Evidence Act 1968, this equally applies to such liability of a spouse.

Where a claim to privilege against self-incrimination is made in a case involving allegations of breaches of the Rome Treaty, the Court may order a stay (subject to appropriate conditions) pending investigation by the Commission (*British Leyland Motor Corp. v. Wyatt* [1979] F.S.R. 583).

By the SCA. 1981, s.72, the privilege against compliance with orders for disclosure or the answering of questions on the grounds that compliance might involve penalties or criminal proceedings relating to infringement of industrial property rights, has been withdrawn. The section is not limited to a case where criminal proceedings have not yet been commenced (*Charles of the Ritz Group Ltd v. Jory* [1986] F.S.R. 14).

Privilege under this heading will prevail unless the person claiming it can be adequately protected by some other means. In *A.T. & T. Istel Ltd v. Tully* [1993] A.C. 45; [1992] 3 W.L.R. 344; [1992] 3 All E.R. 523, the House of Lords stated that although the privilege against self-incrimination existed and could only be removed or altered by Parliament, there was no reason to allow a defendant in civil proceedings to rely upon it thus depriving the claimant of his rights where the defendant's own protection was adequately covered by other means. In this case the C.P.S. had stated by letter that the order for disclosure in its terms restricted them to utilising material already collected or independently gathered and para. 33 of the original order of Buckley J. prohibited use of material so disclosed in the prosecution of either defendant and accordingly compliance with the order for disclosure would not create any real danger for the defendants of prejudice in criminal proceedings. See too *United Norwest Co-operatives Ltd v. Johnstone* (1993) *The Times*, February 24, CA. In civil proceedings under the Drug Trafficking Act 1980, however, where disclosure is sought by the prosecutor in related criminal proceedings, an undertaking by the prosecutor not to use information obtained on disclosure in or in connection with criminal proceedings against the defendant may adequately protect the defendant, and accordingly disclosure may be ordered notwithstanding the plea of privilege (*Re A Defendant* (1987) *The Independent*, April 2).

The privilege against self-incrimination may be overridden where Parliament has expressly or by necessary implication, so provided (see *R. v. Harz; R. v. Power* [1967] 1 A.C. 760 (demand for information under s.24(6) of the Purchase Tax Act 1963); applied in *Bank of England v. Riley* [1992] Ch. 475; [1992] 2 W.L.R. 840, CA (demand for information under s.42 of the Banking Act 1987)).

Disclosure to police authority of a report obtained voluntarily and filed without objection did not infringe privilege against self-incrimination, see *Re L (Minors) (Police Investigation: Privilege)* [1995] 1 F.L.R. 999, CA (affirmed by the House of Lords) [1997] A.C. 16; [1996] 2 W.L.R. 395; [1996] 2 All E.R. 78, HL(E).

31.3.32 **Documents privileged on the ground that production would be injurious to the public interest**—A special procedure for asserting this head of privilege is provided by CPR, r.31.19.1 (see below). This provides for an application to be made to the Court without notice. Such privilege may also be claimed in the same way as other heads of privilege see r.31.19.3 *et seq.*

The law defining this ground of privilege or, more properly, immunity from production and the conditions of its exercise are mainly to be found in the decisions of the House of Lords in *Burmah Oil Co. Ltd v. Governor and Co. of the Bank of England* [1980] A.C. 1090; [1979] 3 All E.R. 700 and *Conway v. Rimmer* [1968] A.C. 910; [1968] 1 All E.R. 874. This privilege does not depend on the objection of a party; the rule is one on which a Judge should if necessary insist, even though no objection is taken. The test is not whether the documents are "State documents" or marked "confidential" or whether their production might invoke public discussion or criticism of a government department, or the attendance of officials needed elsewhere, but whether production would be injurious to the public interest—or, in other words, whether the withholding of the documents is necessary for the proper functioning of the public service. The public interest in concealment should be balanced against the public interest that the administration of justice should not be frustrated. The applicable principles are comprehensively re-stated in *Evans v. Chief Constable of Surrey* [1989] 2 All E.R. 594, and are also usefully and succinctly summarised in *Barrett v. Ministry of Defence* (1989) *The Independent*, January 23. See further *R. v. Bromell, Re Coventry Evening Newspapers Ltd* [1993] Q.B. 278; [1992] 3 W.L.R. 916, [1993] 1 All E.R. 86, CA—held, re-affirming the requirement to balance the two public interests referred to in the text above, that it would be repugnant to justice to withhold documents which appeared to point to corruption on part of named police officers in a libel claim brought by those officers who had already recovered substantial libel damages from other sections of the media.

For the application of these principles, see:

Alfred Crompton Amusement Machines v. Commissioners of Customs and Excise [1974] A.C. 405; [1973] 2 All E.R. 1169, HL (information obtained confidentially by the Crown for the valuing of goods for tax purposes; not protected).

R. v. Lewes Justices, ex p. the Gaming Board of Great Britain [1973] A.C. 388; [1972] 2 All E.R. 1057, HL, affirming D.C. (confidential inquiries by the Gaming Board from the police as to applicants for certificates of consent; protected);

Norwich Pharmacal Co. v. Customs and Excise Commrs. [1974] A.C. 133; [1973] 2 All E.R. 943 (names of persons likely to have violated the claimant's patent rights not protected);

D. v. N.S.P.C.C. [1978] A.C. 171; [1977] 1 All E.R. 589, HL (information as to ill treatment of children given to a charitable body having statutory authority to bring proceedings protected, though the body was not an organ of the government);

Re M. (A Minor) (1989) *The Times*, December 29, CA (local authority social work records);

Lonrho Ltd v. Shell Petroleum Ltd [1980] 1 W.L.R. 627 HL (material furnished in confidence to an inspector inquiring into breaches of sanctions-protected);

Arias v. Metropolitan Police Commr. (1984) 128 S.J. 784; CA (documents of finance corporation seized by police investigating offences involving fraud);

Hasselblad (G.B.) Ltd v. Orbinson [1985] Q.B. 475; [1985] 1 All E.R. 173, CA (public interest requires that a letter written to the European Community Commission, in the course of proceedings begun by the Commission against the claimant alleging breach of Art. 85 of the EEC Treaty, could not be used as the basis of a libel claim);

Continental Re-insurance Corp. (U.K.) Ltd v. Pine Top Insurance Ltd [1986] 1 Lloyd's Rep. 8, CA (documents brought into being in circumstances of confidentiality protected);

R. v. Bournemouth Justices, ex p. Grey, [1986] 150 J.P., 392; [1987] 1 F.L.R. 36 (records of adoption agency, containing admission of paternity by the putative father not protected);

Re M. (Minors) (Confidential Documents) [1987] F.L.R. 46 (probation service records, protected unless disclosure requried in the public interest).

Barrett v. Ministry of Defence, The Independent, January 23, 1989 (report of Ministry of Defence Board to Inquiry into death of airman).

Bookbinder v. Tebbitt (No. 2) [1992] 1 W.L.R. 217 (information obtained during investigations carried out by Audit Commission into local authority spending protected).

Gill and Goodwin v. Chief Constable of Lancashire (1992) *The Guardian*, October 27, (Police Public-Order Manual protected but disclosure could be ordered if otherwise impossible to present case).

Re Barlow Clowes Gilt Managers Ltd [1992] Ch. 208 (transcripts of interviews conducted on behalf of joint liquidators in compulsory winding up prima facie protected. Court also applied *Marcel v. Commissioner of Police for the Metropolis* [1992] 2 W.L.R. 50, CA, in directing liquidators not to make voluntary disclosure of transcripts but to restore application (made originally by liquidators for directions in respect of disclosure to Companies Court) in the Crown Court to set aside witness summonses on ground of public interest immunity). In any event there should be no disclosure without notice to witnesses concerned, see *Soden v. Burns, R. v. Secretary of State for Trade and Industry, ex p. Soden* [1996] 1 W.L.R. 1512.

DPP v. Morrow, The Independent, April 14, 1993, documents maintained in an abortion clinic relating to abortions carried out under the Abortion Act 1967 protected.

Lonhro plc v. Fayed (No. 4) [1994] Q.B. 775; [1994] 2 W.L.R. 209; [1994] 1 All E.R. 870 CA, documents which related to a person's tax affairs and which came into existence with specific reference to his tax liability did not attract public interest immunity where they were held by the taxpayer and he refused consent to their disclosure.

Kelly v. Commissioner of Police of the Metropolis (1997) *The Times*, August 20, (Forms MG3A, 6, 6A, 6D, 6E and 20 of the forms sent to the Crown Prosecution Service by police forces following an investigation into a suspected criminal offence covered by class public interest immunity).

The confidentiality of the records of a local education authority is insufficient ground for protection from disclosure (*Thompson v. Inner London Education Authority* (1977) 74 L.S.Gaz. 66). The Court would not protect information from disclosure just because it was "exempt information" within s.100 of the Local Government Act 1972, but the information could be protected if the necessary elements of breach of confidence could nevertheless be made out (*West Midlands Police Authority v. Walsall Metropolitan Borough Council* (1992) *The Independent*, February 26).

In *R. v. Chief Constable of West Midlands Police, ex p. Wiley*; *R. v. Chief Constable of Nottinghamshire Police, ex p. Sunderland* [1995] 1 A.C. 274; [1994] 3 All E.R. 420, the House of Lords held that there was no general public interest immunity in respect of documents coming into existence during an investigation into a complaint against the police under Part IX of the Police and Criminal Evidence Act 1984 though there might be reasons why because of the contents of a particular document it would be appropriate to extend such immunity to that document. The House of Lords also sought to discourage the use of collateral proceedings rather than the proceedings in which the document/s were relevant to determine the status of the document/s. The *Neilson* case and the cases in which it was subsequently applied should therefore be regarded as wrongly decided. *Quaere* to what extent class immunity in other areas as opposed to individual document immunity is still available.

See too *Kaufmann v. Credit Lyonnais Bank, The Times*, February 1, 1995; no class immunity for confidential bank report sent to SFA (the regulatory body of which the bank was a member) unless it could be clearly demonstrated there was a need to withhold such information from investors. In *Taylor v. Chief Constable of Greater Manchester* [1995] 1 W.L.R. 447; [1995] 2 All E.R. 420, CA the Court of Appeal held that reports prepared by investigating officers on the conduct of proceedings under Part IX of the Criminal Evidence Act 1984 formed a class which was entitled to public interest immunity and that their disclosure would only be ordered where the public interest in production outweighed that in preserving their confidentiality.

Alfred Crompton Amusement Machines Ltd v. Commissioners of Customs and Excise (No. 2) [1974] A.C. 405; [1973] 2 All E.R. 1169, HL, prevents the conclusion that confidential information obtained by public authorities from the citizen under compulsion remains inviolate and incommunicable to anyone. Moreover, the police may produce documents in their hands to the court for use in civil proceedings in obedience to an order to produce documents to the court if the owner of the documents could have been required to produce them under such an order if they had still been in his possession (*Marcel v. Commissioner of Police* [1992] 2 W.L.R. 50, CA).

Although public interest immunity cannot be waived, it may evaporate if those involved in the giving and receiving of the information concerned consent to its disclosure; in deciding whether the administration of justice should prevail over public interest immunity, the fact that partial disclosure has already eroded the immunity is a relevant consideration (*Multi Guarantee Co. Ltd v. Cavalier Insurance Co. Ltd* (1986) *The Times*, June 24).

The objection on ground of public interest immunity may be made either on an application for disclosure under this Order—as when inspection is asked of documents referred to in a party's list of documents—or at the trial when, by witness summons or other means, the production of the documents is called for. Where the objection is taken before trial, the decision to object should be taken by the Minister who is the political head of the department, and he should have seen and considered their contents and himself have formed the view that it would be contrary to the public interest to produce them—either because of their actual contents or because of the class of documents to which they belong. And if the objection is that they belong to a class of documents which it would be contrary to the public interest to produce, the class to which they belong must be specified (*Re Grosvenor Hotel, London* [1964] Ch. 464; [1964] 1 All E.R. 92, CA; *Merricks v. Nott-Bower* [1965] 1 Q.B. 57; [1964] 1 All E.R. 717). But the decision remains that of the Judge, and if, in spite of the Minister's affidavit, in the view of the Court the objection was not taken bona fide, or there are no reasonable grounds for apprehending danger to the public interest, the Court has a residual power to override the objection. It is generally best that the Judge should see the documents before ordering production, and if he thinks that the Minister's reasons for refusing production are not clearly expressed he will have to see them before ordering production. He can see them without their being shown to the parties and the Minister has a right to appeal before they are produced. However although a court was obliged to be vigilant to see that a claim of public interest immunity was raised only in appropriate circumstances where an appropriate certificate signed by a Secretary of State claiming immunity from disclosure of material on the ground of national security was before the court, the court should not exercise its right to inspect that material (*Balfour v. Foreign and Commonwealth Office*, [1994] 1 W.L.R. 681; [1994] 2 All E.R. 588, CA).

The objection should be made by affidavit or certified statement of the political head. But where it is not convenient or practicable for the Minister to act, either because he is ill or out of reach or because the effective head of the department is a permanent official, it would be reasonable for the permanent head to take the objection, as, *e.g.* the Chairman of the Board of Customs and Excise (*Alfred Crompton Amusement Machines v. Commissioners of Customs etc.* [1971] 2 All E.R. 843, *per* Eveleigh J.). There is, however, no rule of law or practice that precludes the claim being raised in other ways. Thus, where there was clear authority to support the assertion that class immunity applied, it was sufficient for the claim to be raised by a responsible official within the organisation involved; see *O'Sullivan v. Commissioner of Police of the Metropolis* (1995) *The Times*, July 3, a case concerning Form 151 the initial report sent by police to Crown Prosecution Service following an investigation into a suspected criminal offence where claim made by barrister employed in commissioner's solicitor's department. If the objection to production arises at the trial, it may in the first instance be conveyed to the Court by an official of the department, producing a certificate signed by the Minister, stating what is necessary. If the Court is not satisfied, it can request the Minister's personal attendance (see, on the question whether the Minister can be cross-examined, *Re Grosvenor Hotel* [1964] Ch. 464, CA). The same principles apply to the exclusion of oral as of documentary evidence (*Duncan v. Cammell Laird & Co.* [1942] A.C. 624 and cases there cited). So, a witness may not look at those documents to refresh his memory and then give oral evidence (*Gain v. Gain* [1961] 1 W.L.R. 1469; [1962] 1 All E.R. 63). Once a Court has decided that documents are covered by this privilege, that position continues though they have passed into the possession of another person (*Auten v. Rayner (No. 2)* [1960] 1 Q.B. 669; [1958] 3 All E.R. 566). The contents of a certificate given by a Secretary of State are evidence in the claim and may be challenged by other parties. Even where such a certificate leads to a consent order whereby other parties agree not to challenge the certificate (*i.e.* that the documents to which it refers should not be disclosed); it does not prevent them from denying the contents (*Sethia v. Stern* (1987) *The Times*, November 4, CA).

See further, as to the circumstances in which the objection to disclosure should and will be taken, *Ellis v. Home Office* [1953] 2 Q.B. 135, CA.

In *Bennett v. Commissioner of Police for the Metropolis* [1995] 1 W.L.R. 488; [1995] 2 All E.R. 1 it was held that it is at least arguable that the Secretary of State concerned is under a duty to consider, before objecting to disclosure, whether the public interest in non-disclosure is outweighed by the public interest in the documents being available in the interests of the administration of justice.

Discovery against the Crown—At the time of the decision of *Duncan v. Cammell Laird & Co.* [1942] A.C. 624 disclosure could not be ordered against the Crown. Now, however, by s.28(1) of the Crown Proceedings Act 1947, the Crown, when a party to civil proceedings, may be required to make disclosure of documents or give further information, subject to Crown privilege, and the principles in regard to that privilege and its exercise are the same as in a claim to which the Crown is not a party. See RSC, O.77, r.12(2). 31.3.33

Other grounds of privilege

Communications between husband and wife—This ground of privilege, which arose from s.3 of the Evidence (Amendment) Act 1853, was abrogated by section 16(3) of the Civil Evidence Act 1968 (see *Shenton v. Tyler* [1939] Ch.620). 31.3.34

Legal aid—Information obtained by the Law Society and associated bodies on an application for a civil aid certificate was privileged from disclosure under what is now section 38 of the Legal Aid Act 1988 (*Whipman v. Whipman* [1951] 2 T.L.R. 518). 31.3.35

Privileged communication under the law of defamation—In a claim of slander a defendant questioned as to whether he spoke the words may object to answer on the ground that, if spoken, they were spoken on an occasion absolutely privileged (*Barratt v. Kearns* [1905] 1 K.B. 504; *cf. Webb v. East* (1880) 5 Ex.D. 108, CA). 31.3.36

Documents relating solely to the case of the party giving discovery—This ground of privilege was abolished by section 16(2) of the Civil Evidence Act 1968. 31.3.37

Confidential communications—A litigant is not entitled to claim privilege for documents and information merely because they were supplied to him in confidence by a third party (*Alfred Crompton Amusement Machines Ltd v. Commrs. of Customs and Excise (No. 2)* reversing, on this point, the Court of Appeal); but the confidentiality of the communication may be relevant to other heads of privilege, *e.g.* public interest (*ibid.*). See also *Norwich Pharmacal Co. v. Commrs. of Customs and Excise* [1974] A.C. 133 and *Science Research Council v. Nassé* [1980] A.C. 1028; [1979] 3 All E.R. 673, HL). 31.3.38

Technical secrets—Where a party claims secrecy in relevant material (*e.g.* a defendant in a patent infringement claim asserts that his process is secret) the governing principle is that the Court should order a controlled measure of disclosure to select individuals upon terms ensuring that there should be neither use nor further disclosure of the confidential information to the prejudice of the party concerned and yet so that the other party may have full free disclosure as is consistent with adequate protection of the trade secrets concerned. There is no form of universal order, nor is it the case that at later stages in a claim wider disclosure cannot be ordered. In each case the Court must decide what measure of disclosure is appropriate, to whom it should be made and upon what terms (*Warner-Lambert Co. v. Glaxo Laboratories Ltd* [1975] R.P.C. 354, CA). See also *Centri-Spray Corp. v. Cera International Ltd* [1979] F.S.R. 175, where disclosure to independent expert of secret drawings is unlikely to be useful, controlled disclosure to the plaintiff's employees may be permitted subject to express undertakings to keep the disclosed material confidential). See further *Format Communications Mfg. Ltd v. I.T.T. (United Kingdom) Ltd* [1983] F.S.R. 473, CA, disclosure and inspection of secret computer source code ordered, subject to suitable safeguards and notwithstanding claimant's offer of inspection by independent expert. 31.3.39

In *Atari Inc. v. Philips Electronics & Associated Industries Ltd* [1988] F.S.R. 416, disclosure of the claimants' secret computer source code was ordered without limitation on the terms of disclosure upon the defendants and their expert giving strict undertakings as to confidentiality.

Admiralty—A report made by a master to his owners for which privilege is claimed should be identified in the appropriate part of the list of documents and privilege there claimed. Such a document is not one which can be considered covered by the words "letters sent by the claimant (defendant) to his agents or solicitors for the purposes of the claim" (Direction of the Admiralty Registrar, March 8, 1955). 31.3.40

Disclosed documents—Once a document such as a witness statement has been disclosed (by being exchanged or otherwise) no question of privilege can arise but only one of admissibility, and such statements once disclosed can be used as the basis for an application for disclosure (*Black & Decker Inc. v. Flymo Ltd* [1991] 3 All E.R. 158; [1991] F.S.R. 93). 31.3.41

Without prejudice communications—The "without prejudice" rule governs the admissibility of evidence and is founded upon the public policy of encouraging litigants to settle their differences rather than litigate them to a finish (*Cutts v. Head* [1984] Ch. 290; [1984] 1 All E.R. 597, CA). The rule applies to exclude all negotiations genuinely aimed at a settlement, whether 31.3.42

oral or in writing, from being given in evidence. The purpose of the rule is to protect a litigant from being embarrassed by any admission made purely in an attempt to achieve a settlement. "Without prejudice" material will be admissible if the issue is whether or not negotiations resulted in an agreed settlement (*Walker v. Wilsher* (1889) 23 Q.B.D. 335), but in relation to any other issue an admission made in order to achieve a compromise should not be held against the maker of the admission or received in evidence; moreover an admission made to reach a settlement with a party is not admissible in proceedings between the maker of the admission and a different party, even if such proceedings are within the same litigation (*Rush & Tompkins Ltd v. Greater London Council* [1988] 3 W.L.R. 939; [1988] 3 All E.R. 737, HL). The right to disclosure and production of documents does not necessarily depend upon the admissibility of documents in evidence (*O'Rourke v. Darbishire* [1920] A.C. 581, HL), but the general public policy that applies to protect genuine negotiations from being admissible in evidence is also extended by the Courts to protect those negotiations from being discloseable to third parties (*Rush & Tompkins Ltd v. Greater London Council* (*above*)). Any discussions between the parties for the purpose of resolving the dispute between them are not admissible, even if the words "without prejudice" or their equivalent are not expressly used (*Chocoladefabriken Lindt & Sprungli A.G. v. Nestle Co. Ltd* [1978] R.P.C. 287). It follows that documents containing such material are themselves privileged from production. This head of privilege is not confined to admissions but applies to all bona fide without prejudice statements which touched upon the strengths or weaknesses of the parties' cases or which placed a valuation on a party's rights forming a part of the attempt to compromise the litigation, see *Unilever v. Procter & Gamble*, [1999] 2 All E.R. 691.

Without prejudice correspondence before settlement of a claim for damages by first named claimant against his former employers not privileged in claimant's subsequent claim for negligence against solicitors who had advised the claimant before his former employer had dismissed him where the statement of case in the subsequent claim asserted that the settlement was an attempt to mitigate loss caused by the negligence and the defendants did not seek to show that admissions made in the course of such correspondence were true. The claimants had put their own conduct in issue and had thereby waived any privilege in such correspondence (*Muller v. Linsley & Mortimer (a firm)* (1994) *The Times*, December 8; [1995] Gazette No. 3, p.38, CA).

If one party to negotiations on a without prejudice basis wishes to change the basis thenceforth to an open one, the burden is on that party to bring the change to the attention of the other party and to establish on an objective basis that the recipient would have realised that a change in the basis of negotiation was being made (see *Cheddar Valley Ltd v. Chaddlewood Ltd* [1992] 1 W.L.R. 820).

Conversely the heading "without prejudice" does not conclusively or automatically render privileged a document so marked. If privilege is claimed, but challenged, the Court has to examine the document in question and determine its nature (*South Shropshire District Council v. Amos* [1986] 1 W.L.R. 1271; [1987] 1 All E.R. 340, CA). The rule which confers privilege on "without prejudice" communications is not limited to documents which constitute offers; privilege may also attach to "without prejudice" documents written in the opening stages of negotiations (*ibid.*).

A letter, stated by a party to be written without prejudice, which amounts not to an offer to negotiate, but merely to an assertion of that party's rights, or an attempt to argue that his case is well founded, is not privileged (*Buckinghamshire County Council v. Moran* [1989] 2 All E.R. 225, CA).

Transcripts of tape recordings of conversations between the parties, made by one party without the knowledge of the other, where there is a bona fide and reasonably tenable charge of crime or fraud, and where there is a prima facie case that the communications in question are made in preparation for, or in furtherance or as part of it, are not covered by "without prejudice" privilege (*Hawick Jersey International Ltd v. Caplan* (1988) *The Times*, March 11). But an unambiguous admission of impropriety during a conversation is required to render admissible in evidence a tape recording of a negotiation aimed at settling the dispute (*Alizadeh v. Nikbin* (1993) *The Times*, March 19, CA). See further *Forster v. Friedland*, November 10, 1992, CA Transcript 92/1052.

A note made by a claimant's solicitor of a telephone conversation between him and the defendant's solicitor, which merely records the substance of the conversation and contains nothing in the nature of a communication to the claimant, is not a document privileged from disclosure as between claimant and defendant even if the subject matter of the conversation is "without prejudice"; hence, where such a note has been properly disclosed by the claimant, the defendant is not entitled, on the principle that waiver of a privileged document requires the release from privilege of all material relevant to the matter as to which professional privilege has been waived (for which see para. 31.3.27, above), to disclosure of all memoranda passing between the claimant and his solicitor relating to the conversation, because there has been no waiver of a privileged document (*Parry v. News Group Newspapers Ltd* (1990) New L.J. 1719, CA).

A letter containing an offer to settle may be written as an open letter and used by the party writing it during the trial, providing it has relevance and does not form part of continuing without prejudice negotiations (*Dixons Stores Group Ltd v. Thomas Television Plc* [1993] 1 All E.R. 349).

When a solicitor writes "threats" letters on behalf of a client, he has no confidence or legal professional privilege therein, whatever the position as regards his client himself. If such a "threats" letter is inaccurate the solicitor has a duty to put that right, though there may be difficulties when the solicitor has ceased to act for that client or when questions arise as to whether he should write such a correcting letter of his own accord (*CHC Software Care Ltd v. Hopkins and Wood* [1993] F.S.R. 241).

Meaning of document

31.4 In this Part— 31.4

"document" means anything in which information of any description is recorded; and

"copy", in relation to a document, means anything onto which information recorded in the document has been copied, by whatever means and whether directly or indirectly.

"Document"—The meaning of "documents" is not restricted to paper writings, but extends to anything upon which evidence or information is recorded in a manner intellgible to the senses or capable of being made intelligible by the use of equipment. Thus tape recordings of evidence or information are documents (*Grant v. Southwestern and County Properties Ltd* [1975] Ch. 185; [1974] 2 All E.R. 465). 31.4.1

A computer database which forms part of the business records of a company is, in so far as it contains information capable of being retrieved and converted into readable form, a "document" for the purposes of 31.4 and therefore susceptible to discovery (*Derby & Co. Ltd v. Weldon (No. 9)* [1991] 1 W.L.R. 652; [1991] 2 All E.R. 901) And see *Alliance & Leicester Building Society v. Ghahremani* [1992] 32 R.V.R. 198; word processing file of computer within the definition of document for purpose of an order preserving documents in connection with proceedings.

Microfilms used to keep records are "documents" falling within the definition of this provision.

Disclosure limited to standard disclosure

31.5—(1) An order to give disclosure is an order to give standard disclosure unless the court directs otherwise. 31.5

(2) The court may dispense with or limit standard disclosure.

(3) The parties may agree in writing to dispense with or to limit standard disclosure.

(The court may make an order requiring standard disclosure under rule 28.3 which deals with directions in relation to cases on the fast track and under rule 29.2 which deals with case management in relation to cases on the multi-track)

Standard disclosure—This is the degree of disclosure required unless the court otherwise directs. It is defined in r.31.6 (see below). The *Peruvian Guano* test has gone. 31.5.1

Foreign sovereign or state—Once disclosure has been ordered a foreign sovereign or state suing in this country must give disclosure (*South African Co. v. Compagnie Franco-Belge* [1898] 1 Ch. 190; *U.S.A. v. Wagner* (1867) L.R. 2 Ch. 582) and the Court will stay proceedings until the claimant has named a proper person to give diclosure (*Costa Rica Republic v. Erlanger* (1875) 1 Ch.D. 171; *Peru (Republic) v. Weguelin* (1875) L.R. 20 Eq. 140). 31.5.2

Standard disclosure—what documents are to be disclosed

31.6 Standard disclosure requires a party to disclose only— 31.6

(a) the documents on which he relies; and

(b) the documents which—

(i) adversely affect his own case;

(ii) adversely affect another party's case; or

(iii) support another party's case; and

(c) the documents which he is required to disclose by a relevant practice direction.

"... required to disclose by a relevant practice direction"—*e.g.* as under Practice Direction—Protocols and the Personsal Injury Protocol Annex B and the Clinical Negligence Protocol referred to therein. 31.6.1

Disclosure not confined to existence of issue—In an appropriate case for good reason shown a party may be obliged to give disclosure to another in the same matter even though it related to a matter that was not an issue between them, see *Manatee Towing Co. v. Oceanbulk Maritime S.A.* [1999] 1 Lloyd's Rep. 876. (A case under the former RSC, O.24.) 31.6.2

Duty of search

31.7—(1) When giving standard disclosure, a party is required to make a reasonable search for documents falling within rule 31.6(b) or (c). 31.7

(2) The factors relevant in deciding the reasonableness of a search include the following—

(a) the number of documents involved;
(b) the nature and complexity of the proceedings;
(c) the ease and expense of retrieval of any particular document; and
(d) the significance of any document which is likely to be located during the search.

(3) Where a party has not searched for a category or class of document on the grounds that to do so would be unreasonable, he must state this in his disclosure statement and identify the category or class of document.

(Rule 31.10 makes provision for a disclosure statement)

31.7.1 **"... a reasonable search ..."**—See too PT31PD(F) Disclosure and Inspection 2 (see para. 31PD–001).

Duty of disclosure limited to documents which are or have been in a party's control

31.8 **31.8**—(1) A party's duty to disclose documents is limited to documents which are or have been in his control.

(2) For this purpose a party has or has had a document in his control if—

(a) it is or was in his physical possession;
(b) he has or has had a right to possession of it; or
(c) he has or has had a right to inspect or take copies of it.

Disclosure of copies

31.9 **31.9**—(1) A party need not disclose more than one copy of a document.

(2) A copy of a document that contains a modification, obliteration or other marking or feature—

(a) on which a party intends to rely; or
(b) which adversely affects his own case or another party's case or support another party's case;

shall be treated as a separate document.

(Rule 31.4 sets out the meaning of a copy of a document)

Procedure for standard disclosure

31.10 **31.10**—(1) The procedure for standard disclosure is as follows.

(2) Each party must make, and serve on every other party, a list of documents in the relevant practice form.

(3) The list must identify the documents in a convenient order and manner and as concisely as possible.

(4) The list must indicate—

(a) those documents in respect of which the party claims a right or duty to withhold inspection; and
(b) (i) those documents which are no longer in the party's control; and
(ii) what has happened to those documents.

(Rule 31.19(3) and (4) require a statement in the list of documents relating to any documents inspection of which a person claims he has a right or duty to withhold)

(5) The list must include a disclosure statement.

(6) A disclosure statement is a statement made by the party disclosing the documents—

(a) setting out the extent of the search that has been made to locate documents which he is required to disclose;
(b) certifying that he understands the duty to disclose documents; and
(c) certifying that to the best of his knowledge he has carried out that duty.

(7) Where the party making the disclosure statement is a company, firm, association or other organisation, the statement must also—

(a) identify the person making the statement; and

(b) explain why he is considered an appropriate person to make the statement.

(8) The parties may agree in writing—

(a) to disclose documents without making a list; and

(b) to disclose documents without the disclosing party making a disclosure statement.

(9) A disclosure statement may be made by a person who is not a party where this is permitted by a relevant practice direction.

"... a list of documents in the relevant practice form"—The form is PF N265. The list must *inter alia* identify documents in respect of which privilege is claimed and state those documents which are no longer in the control of the disclosing party and what has happened to such documents (r.31.10(4)). Where privilege is claimed, the grounds on which it is claimed must be stated: see PT31PD(F) 4.5. **31.10.1**

"... in a convenient order and manner and as concisely as possible"—By PT31PD(F) 3.2 (see para. 31PD–001) it is provided: **31.10.2**

> "In order to comply with rule 31.10(3) it will normally be necessary to list the documents in date order, to number them consecutively and to give each a concise description (*e.g.* letter to defendant). Where there is a large number of documents all falling into a particular category the disclosing party may list those documents as a category rather than individually, *e.g.* 50 bank statements relating to account number at Bank, 19 to 19 ; or, 35 letters passing between and between 19 and 19 "

Description-Privileged Documents—So far as describing such is concerned there is a certain difference between documents for which privilege from production is claimed and other documents. As regards privileged documents the description is not for the purpose of enabling the other party to learn the contents of the document or to test the truth of the plea of privilege. Nor is it for the purpose of causing the party giving disclosure to furnish evidence against himself (*Gardner v. Irvin* (1878) 4 Ex.D. 49 at 53, CA). It is not required that the dates of the documents should be specified nor the names of the makers (*ibid.*). "Correspondence between the (defendant) and his solicitors for the purpose of obtaining legal advice" is sufficient (*ibid.*). **31.10.3**

Where privilege is claimed for professional communications of a confidential character obtained for the purpose of getting legal advice, the claim for privilege is to be treated as itself a sufficient description of the communications, irrespective of the scale of disclosure or the complexity of the issues involved, and consequently the party seeking disclosure is not entitled to satisfy himself by means of fuller description of the communications for which privilege is claimed that it is not claimed for documents outside its proper scope; moreover the court will not order the party claiming privilege to disclose all communications with his legal advisers, or to provide fuller particulars of such communications, even where it has been shown in relation to one transaction that the advice was sought in furtherance of a fraudulent design, since to order such disclosure would be contrary to the public policy on which legal professional privilege is founded (*Derby & Co. Ltd v. Weldon (No. 7)* [1990] 1 W.L.R. 1156; [1990] 3 All E.R. 161).

"... the party claims a right or duty to withhold inspection"—See commentary "... right or duty to withhold inspection" and "Procedure for claiming a right or duty to withhold inspection" at paras 31.3.2 and 31.3.3 above. **31.10.4**

Disclosure statement—The form is set out in Practice Direction (Disclosure and Inspection) Annex A , para. 31PD–002. **31.10.5**

Obligations of solicitors in respect of disclosure and of production by their clients—It is necessary for solicitors to take positive steps to ensure that their clients appreciate at an early stage of the litigation, promptly after the claim form is issued, not only the duty of disclosure and to produce for inspection which will arise if disclosure is agreed or ordered by the Court and of the extent of such duty but also the importance of not destroying documents which might possibly have to be disclosed (*per* Megarry J. in *Rockwell Machine Tool Co. Ltd v. E.P. Barrus (Concessionaires) Ltd* [1968] 2 All E.R. 98). Moreover it is not enough simply to give instructions that documents be preserved. Steps should be taken to ensure that documents are preserved (*Infabrics Ltd v. Jaytex Ltd* [1985] F.S.R. 75 where, because a defendant had not preserved documents affecting the quantum of damage, the maxim *omnia praesummuntur contra spoliatorem* was applied against him). **31.10.6**

"It cannot be too clearly understood that solicitors owe a duty to the court, as officers of the court, carefully to go through the documents disclosed by their client to make sure, as far as possible, that no relevant documents have been omitted from their clients' [list]" *per* Salmon J. (as he then was) in *Woods v. Martins Bank Ltd* [1959] 1 Q.B. 55 at 60.

See too comments on duty to notify court and/or to withdraw in the event of client not complying with proper advice in respect of disclosure in *Myers v. Elman* [1940] A.C. 282 at 293–4, 300–301 and 322–3.

See also para. 31.11—Duty of disclosure continues during proceedings.

31.10.7 **Consequences of failure to disclose documents or permit inspection**—See r.31.21 below.

Duty of disclosure continues during proceedings

31.11 **31.11**—(1) Any duty of disclosure continues until the proceedings are concluded.

(2) If documents to which that duty extends come to a party's notice at any time during the proceedings, he must immediately notify every other party.

31.11.1 **Supplemental list**—If documents falling within a party's duty to give standard disclosure come to a party's notice after service of his list of documents, a supplemental list must be prepared and served. An obvious example is where a claimant who is claiming damages for prospective loss of earnings, obtains new lucrative employment during the course of the case, this fact must be communicated to the defendant and further disclosure must be made.

In *Vernon v. Bosley (No. 2)* [1999] Q.B. 18; [1997] 1 All E.R. 614 it was held that where a document was disclosed to a party after he had closed his case, or the evidence as a whole was concluded, he should apply to the court to reopen the case in the light of the disclosure if the document was of real significance and there was otherwise a risk of injustice.

Specific disclosure or inspection

31.12 **31.12**—(1) The court may make an order for specific disclosure or specific inspection.

(2) An order for specific disclosure is an order that a party must do one or more of the following things—

(a) disclose documents or classes of documents specified in the order;

(b) carry out a search to the extent stated in the order;

(c) disclose any documents located as a result of that search.

(3) An order for specific inspection is an order that a party permit inspection of a document referred to in rule 31.3(2).

(Rule 31.3(2) allows a party to state in his disclosure statement that he will not permit inspection of a document on the grounds that it would be disproportionate to do so)

31.12.1 **Application for specific disclosure or inspection**—The application should be made in accordance with Pt 23. The application should state what order is sought and must be supported by evidence: see r.31.12(2) and PT31PD(F) 6.2.

31.12.2 **The court may make an order for specific disclosure or specific inspection**—The court will take into account all the circumstances of the case and in particular the overriding objective in Pt 1 (see PT31PD(F) 6.4 (para. 31PD–001) and the concept of proportionality).

Disclosure in stages

31.13 **31.13** The parties may agree in writing, or the court may direct, that disclosure or inspection or both shall take place in stages.

31.13.1 **Disclosure in stages**—For example in relation to and restricted to a split trial of a particular issue or issues. Where a split trial had been ordered so that the issue of liability was to be determined separately from the issue of quantum discovery on the issue of quantum would not normally be ordered, and only special circumstances going beyond a plaintiff's or defendant's interest in learning the amount in issue for the purpose of making informed decisions on whether to negotiate a compromise or to proceed with the action or defence would justify making such an order. *Baldock v. Addison* [1995] 1 W.L.R. 158; [1995] 3 All E.R. 437; [1994] F.S.R. 665. Compare *Kapur v. J.W. Francis & Co., The Times*, March 4, 1998.

Documents referred to in statements of case etc.

31.14 A party may inspect a document mentioned in— 31.14

(a) a statement of case;
(b) a witness statement;
(c) a witness summary;
(d) an affidavit(GL); or
(e) subject to rule 35.10(4), an expert's report.

(Rule 35.10(4) makes provision in relation to instructions referred to in an expert's report)

"(e) subject to rule 35.10(4), an expert's report"—Whilst instructions to an expert are not privileged, a court will not order disclosure of any specific document unless it is satisfied that there are reasonable grounds for considering that the statement of instructions contained in the report is inaccurate or incomplete. 31.14.1

Inspection and copying of documents

31.15 Where a party has a right to inspect a document— 31.15

(a) that party must give the party who disclosed the document written notice of his wish to inspect it;
(b) the party who disclosed the document must permit inspection not more than 7 days after the date on which he received the notice; and
(c) that party may request a copy of the document and, if he also undertakes to pay reasonable copying costs, the party who disclosed the document must supply him with a copy not more than 7 days after the date on which he received the request.

(Rules 31.3 and 31.14 deal with the right of a party to inspect a document)

Document in a foreign language—There is no obligation on a party giving disclosure/inspection of a document in a foreign language to provide a translation (*Bayer A.G. v. Harris Pharmaceuticals Ltd* [1991] F.S.R. 170). 31.15.1

Meaning of "inspection"—"Inspection" extends to examining electronic, audio or visual recordings or other documents with appropriate equipment. 31.15.2

Place of inspection—In the case of an action proceeding in the Central Office, the appropriate place is the office of the solicitor or agent in London; but if circumstances warrant, the production may be ordered elsewhere, or partly in London and partly elsewhere (*Prestney v. Corporation of Colchester* (1883) 24 Ch.D. 376, CA) and even abroad (*Whyte & Co. v. Ahrens & Co.* (1884) 50 L.T. 344). It should never be necessary to bring to the Court a dispute as to the appropriate place of inspection, but the Court has a complete discretion in the matter. It may still order that the documents be deposited in Court to be inspected there in accordance with the old Chancery practice (*Leslie v. Cave* [1886] W.N. 162). Otherwise the usual and proper place for inspection is the office of his solicitors, or in the case of bankers' books or other books of account or books in constant use for the purpose of any trade or business their usual place of custody. 31.15.3

Disclosure before proceedings start

31.16—(1) This rule applies where an application is made to the court under any Act for disclosure before proceedings have started.[1] 31.16

(2) The application must be supported by evidence.

(3) The court may make an order under this rule only where—

(a) the respondent is likely to be a party to subsequent proceedings;
(b) the applicant is also likely to be a party to those proceedings;
(c) if proceedings had started, the respondent's duty by way of standard disclosure, set out in rule 31.6, would extend to the documents or classes of documents of which the applicant seeks disclosure; and
(d) disclosure before proceedings have started is desirable in order to—
  (i) dispose fairly of the anticipated proceedings;

[1] An application for disclosure before proceedings have started is permitted under section 33 of the Supreme Court Act 1981 (c. 54) or section 52 of the County Courts Act 1984 (c. 28).

(ii) assist the dispute to be resolved without proceedings; or
(iii) save costs.

(4) An order under this rule must—
(a) specify the documents or the classes of documents which the responent must disclose; and
(b) require him, when making disclosure, to specify any of those documents—
(i) which are no longer in his control; or
(ii) in respect of which he claims a right or duty to withhold inspection.

(5) Such an order may—
(a) require the respondent to indicate what has happened to any document which are no longer in his control; and
(b) specify the time and place for disclosure and inspection.

31.16.1 **"... under any Act for disclosure before proceedings have started"**—For instance under the Supreme Court Act 1981, s.33 and the County Courts Act 1984, s.52. See too under 31.0.2 above.

31.16.2 **"The application must be supported by evidence"**—The application should be made in accordance with Pt 23. The contents of an application notice may be used as evidence provided those contents have been verified by a statement of truth under Pt 22, see PT31PD(F) 9.7 (see para. 31PD–001). Otherwise the evidence in support will usually be in writing. Supporting evidence can be in the form of an affidavit but the additional costs of making it may not be allowed unless the court orders otherwise.

Orders for disclosure against a person not a party

31.17 **31.17**—(1) This rule applies where an application is made to the court under any Act for disclosure by a person who is not a party to the proceedings.[2]

(2) The application must be supported by evidence.

(3) The court may make an order under this rule only where—
(a) the documents of which disclosure is sought are likely to support the case of the applicant or adversely affect the case of one of the other parties to the proceedings; and
(b) disclosure is necessary in order to dispose fairly of the claim or to save costs.

(4) An order under this rule must—
(a) specify the documents or the classes of documents which the respondent must disclose; and
(b) require the respondent, when making disclosure, to specify any of those documents—
(i) which are no longer in his control; or
(ii) in respect of which he claims a right or duty to withhold inspection.

(5) Such an order may—
(a) require the respondent to indicate what has happened to any documents which are no longer in his control; and
(b) specify the time and place for disclosure and inspection.

31.17.1 **"... under any Act for disclosure by a person who is not a party to the proceedings"**—

[2] An application for disclosure against a person who is not a party to proceedings is permitted under section 34 of the Supreme Court Act 1981 or section 53 of the County Courts Act 1984.

For instance under the Supreme Court Act 1981, s.34 and the County Courts Act 1984, s.53. See too under 31.0.2.

"The application must be supplied by evidence"—See commentary at para. 31.16.2 above. **31.17.2**

Rules not to limit other powers of the court to order disclosure

31.18 Rules 31.16 and 31.17 do not limit any other power which the court may have to order— **31.18**

(a) disclosure before proceedings have started; and

(b) disclosure against a person who is not a party to proceedings.

"... do not limit any other power which the court may have, etc, ..."—For other powers in such respect see "Disclosing identity of wrongdoer (the Norwich Pharmacal principal)" and other extensions thereof (see below), the "Claim for disclosure and Production" (see below). *Anton Piller* and *Mareva* relief (q.v.) and disclosure in aid of execution of judgment under RSC, O.48. **31.18.1**

Disclosing identity of wrongdoer (Norwich Pharmacal principal)—In *Upmann v. Elkan* (1871) L.R. 12 Eq. 140, Lord Romilly M.R. said: "if through no fault of his own a person gets mixed up in the tortious acts of others so as to facilitate their wrongdoing he may incur no personal liability but he comes under a duty to assist the person who has been wronged by giving him full information and disclosing the identity of wrongdoers". This principle was endorsed by the House of Lords in *Norwich Pharmacal v. Customs and Excise Commissioners* [1974] A.C. 133; [1973] 2 All E.R. 943, HL. It has been relied on and developed in a number of subsequent cases, for instance *P. v. T. Ltd* [1997] 1 W.L.R. 1309; [1997] 4 All E.R. 200. For both the Norwich case and P. v. T., see further under "Claim for disclosure and Production". **31.18.2**

Claim for disclosure and production (The former action for discovery)—This form of claim will be unnecessary where the Court's powers to order disclosure and production against a non-party during proceedings under section 34 of the Supreme Court Act 1981 and section 53 of the County Court Act 1984 can be invoked but will retain its usefulness where such powers cannot be invoked. A claim solely for disclosure and production does not lie against a defendant who is not himself a wrongdoer and has no connection with the wrong-doing. A claim for disclosure and production will therefore not lie against a person who knows the identity of the alleged tortfeasor, but who himself has neither committed nor facilitated the committal of the tort (*Ricci v. Chow* [1987] 1 W.L.R. 1658; [1987] 3 All E.R. 534, CA). But where a defendant through no fault of his own (and whether voluntarily or not) "has got mixed up in the tortious acts of others so as to facilitate their wrong-doing he may incur no person liability but he comes under a duty to assist the person who had been wronged by giving him full information and disclosing the identity of the wrongdoers" (*per* Lord Reid in *Norwich Pharmacal Co. v. Commrs. of Customs and Excise* [1974] A.C. 133; [1973] 2 All E.R. 943, HL). See also *British Steel Corp. v. Granada Television Ltd* [1981] A.C. 1096; [1981] 1 All E.R. 417, HL; *Harrington v. North London Polytechnic* [1984] 1 W.L.R. 1293; [1984] 3 All E.R. 666, CA; and *Re Goodwin* [1990] 1 All E.R. 608. In *CHC Software Care Ltd v. Hopkins and Wood* [1993] F.S.R. 24, the Court followed and extended *Norwich Pharmacol Co. v. Commissioners of Customs & Excise*, above, and held that the jurisdiction to order such disclosure was not limited to cases of identifying wrongdoers. Thus disclosure was ordered against the defendant solicitors of the names and addresses of the persons to whom similar threat letters had been sent together with the text thereof even though the recipients were not wrongdoers since the copies of the letter and any distribution list of names and addresses of recipients, were documents relevant to the issues pleaded in the claim (slander of title, malicious falsehood and trade libel). See too *P. v. T. Ltd* [1997] 1 W.L.R. 1309; [1997] 4 All E.R. 200, where the Court extended *Norwich Pharmacal* and granted disclosure against the defendant to enable the claimant to use the fruits of disclosure to bring proceedings against a third party even though it could not be ascertained whether the third party had committed a tort against the claimant without the information sought. **31.18.3**

In the absence of evidence of an intention to sue the wrongdoer, it cannot be asserted that it is necessary in the interests of justice to have his name disclosed. The test is necessity not expediency or desirability (*Handmade v. Express Newspapers* [1986] F.S.R. 463). If there are facts which will require investigation at trial, it is not proper to make a Norwich Pharmacal order on a pre-trial application (*ibid.*).

The claimant seeking the name of the wrongdoer will have to pay a blameless defendant's expenses in providing the information; and if the defendant has any doubts then he may properly require the matter to be submitted to the Court before supplying the information and the claimant will nevertheless be obliged to pay the costs of these proceedings (*ibid.*). Where a claimant obtains the name of a wrongdoer by a claim for disclosure and production in which he has to pay the costs, and where the wrongdoer can or ought to foresee that steps by way of investigation and disclosure are likely to result from his wrong, the claimant may recover such costs as damages in subsequent proceedings against the wrongdoer (*Morton-Norwcih Products Inc. v. Intercon (No. 2)* [1981] F.S.R. 337).

A claim for disclosure and production alone, like the making of an order under the Bankers' Books Evidence Act 1879 requires the exercise of the Crown's Sovereign authority to assist in the administration of justice, and therefore the Court will not, save in exceptional circumstances, impose on a foreigner, in particular a foreign bank, who or which is not a party to the principal proceedings, any requirement to produce documents which are outside the jurisdiction and which concern business transacted outside the jurisdiction (*Mackinnon v. Donaldson Lufkin & Jenrette Securities Corp.* [1986] Ch. 482; [1986] 1 All E.R. 653).

Diclosure of the identities of infringers and other wrongdoers may also be obtained by an interlocutory order in proceedings for other relief in relation to the same subject-matter (*R.C.A. Corp v. Reddingtons Rare Records* [1974] 1 W.L.R. 1445; [1975] 1 All E.R. 38). See *Loose v. Williamson* [1978] 1 W.L.R. 639; [1978] 3 All E.R. 89 (disclosure of identity of parties removing shellfish from the claimant's sole and several fishery and seaground). But disclosure of customers' names in a copyright infringement action will not be ordered, because until those persons have notice of the claim they are not wrongdoers (*Roberts v. Jump Knitwear Ltd* [1981] F.S.R. 527).

Where a party is properly sued as defendant to a claim for a *quia timet* injunction restraining him from publishing information imparted to him in breach of confidence, he is amenable to the full scope of the court's wide power to order disclosure between parties, the fact that the claimant's primary purpose in seeking disclosure and production is to identify the source of the information does not inhibit or restrict the court's power to order such for the purposes of the *quia timet* litigation (*X. Ltd v. Morgan-Grampian (Publishers) Ltd* [1990] 2 All E.R. 1, HL).

Claim to withhold inspection or disclosure of a document

31.19 **31.19**—(1) A person may apply, without notice, for an order permitting him to withhold disclosure of a document on the ground that disclosure would damage the public interest.

(2) Unless the court orders otherwise, an order of the court under paragraph (1)—

(a) must not be served on any other person; and

(b) must not be open to inspection by any person.

(3) A person who wishes to claim that he has a right or a duty to withhold inspection of a document, or part of a document must state in writing—

(a) that he has such a right or duty; and

(b) the grounds on which he claims that right or duty.

(4) The statement referred to in paragraph (3) must be made—

(a) in the list in which the document is disclosed; or

(b) if there is no list, to the person wishing to inspect the document.

(5) A party may apply to the court to decide whether a claim made under paragraph (3) should be upheld.

(6) For the purpose of deciding an application under paragraph (1) (application to withhold disclosure) or paragraph (3) (claim to withhold inspection) the court may—

(a) require the person seeking to withhold disclosure or inspection of a document to produce that document to the court; and

(b) invite any person, whether or not a party, to make representations.

(7) An application under paragraph (1) or paragraph (5) must be supported by evidence.

(8) This Part does not affect any rule of law which permits or requires a document to be withheld from disclosure or inspection on the ground that its disclosure or inspection would damage the public interest.

31.19.1 **"... would damage the public interest" and "... a right or duty to withhold inspection"**— See note on public interest and other examples of a right or duty to withhold inspection under r.31.3 above. The application in respect of a public interest claim can be for an order permitting the withholding of disclosure. The other approach envisaged under this rule is a claim to withhold inspection. This claim can be challenged by application to the court.

An application under paragraph (1) or paragraph (5) must be supported by evidence—See commentary at para. 31.16.2 above. Rule 23.4(2) allows the making of an application under Pt 23 without notice as is envisaged in respect of a claim based on damage to the public interest under para. (1). 31.19.2

Inherent jurisdiction of court—The Court has inherent jurisdiction to take precautions against the possibility that disclosure and inspection may be abused, or cause unjustifiable hardship and may, to that end, impose restrictions upon inspection or permit it subject to undertakings. (*Church of Scientology v. D.H.S.S.* [1979] 1 W.L.R. 723; [1979] 3 All E.R. 97); for an example of undertakings against discloure of material obtained on discovery see *Halcon International Inc. v. Shell Transport & Trading Co.* [1979] R.P.C. 97, CA (leave to make use of material obtained on disclosure for some purpose other than the claim refused). 31.19.3

Restriction on use of a privileged document inspection of which has been inadvertently allowed

31.20 Where a party inadvertently allows a privileged(GL) document to be inspected, the party who has inspected the document may use it or its contents only with the permission of the court. 31.20

Consequence of failure to disclose documents or permit inspection

31.21 A party may not rely on any document which he fails to disclose or in respect of which he fails to permit inspection unless the court gives permission. 31.21

Subsequent use of disclosed documents

31.22—(1) A party to whom a document has been disclosed may use the document only for the purpose of the proceedings in which it is disclosed, except where— 31.22

(a) the document has been read to or by the court, or referred to, at a hearing which has been held in public;
(b) the court gives permission; or
(c) the party who disclosed the document and the person to whom the document belongs agree.

(2) The court may make an order restricting or prohibiting the use of a document which has been disclosed, even where the document has been read to or by the court, or referred to, at a hearing which has been held in public.

(3) An application for such an order may be made—

(a) by a party; or
(b) by any person to whom the document belongs.

Subsequent use of disclosed documents—This rule now specifies clear exceptions to the general rule that a document disclosed in the proceedings may only be used for the purpose of the proceedings in which it is disclosed. It avoids concepts of implied or express undertakings. The rule is the statutory enactment so far as civil court proceedings are concerned of the common-law implied undertaking not to use documents disclosed in the course of civil court proceedings save for the purpose of the proceedings in which disclosed without court permission or the consent of the document owner. The rule is concise and avoids the intricacies of the concepts of implied and express undertakings. 31.22.1

Documents read by the judge out of court before the hearing on which the judge based his decision and to which he made compendious reference in his judgment were documents referred to at a hearing held in public, see *Smith Kline Beecham Biologicals S.A. v. Connaught Laboratories Inc.*, *The Times*, July 13, 1999, CA (a case under the former RSC, O.24, r.14A).

As regards arbitration proceedings it has been held that an implied undertaking not to use disclosed documents for purposes other than the arbitration in which they are disclosed arises in respect of documents disclosed during arbitration proceedings (*Hassneh Insurance Co. of Israel v. Steuart J. Mew* [1993] 2 Lloyd's Rep. 243). The qualification to such implied undertaking namely that an award and reasons might be disclosed as of right if it was reasonably necessary for one party to disclose them for the purpose of the establishment of that party's rights against a third party either in order to found a defence or as the basis for a cause of action (see *Hassneh* above) was further considered in *Insurance Company v. Lloyd's Syndicate*, [1995] 1 Lloyd's Rep. 272, where the court held that "reasonably necessary" covered only the case where the right in question could not be enforced or protected unless the award and reasons are disclosed to a stranger to the arbitration. The making of the award must be a necessary element in the establishment of the party's legal rights aganst the stranger. See too in relation to the implied undertaking *Ali Shipping Corp. v. Shipyard Trogir* [1999] 1 W.L.R. 314, CA.

As regards documents disclosed during criminal proceedings the position is not so clear. Despite *Mahon v. Rahn* [1998] Q.B. 424; [1997] 3 All E.R. 687 in which a Court of Appeal held that there was no implied undertaking restricting the use of such documents to the proceedings in which they were disclosed analogous to the undertaking which existed in civil proceedings, it is considered that it is open to argue that such an implied undertaking of general applicability to documents disclosed in criminal proceedings exists since in *Taylor v. Director of the Serious Fraud Office* [1998] 3 W.L.R. 1040; [1998] 4 All E.R. 801, HL(E), the case of *Mahon v. Rahn* was disapproved of, the House of Lords holding in particular in the case that in order to ensure that the privacy and confidentiality of those who made, and those who were mentioned in, statements contained in unused material which had come into existence as a result of a criminal investigation were not invaded more than was absolutely necessary for the purposes of justice, compliance by the prosecution with its obligation to disclose all such material to the defence generated an implied undertaking not to use the material for any purpose other than the conduct of the defence; and that, accordingly, documents disclosed to solicitors for one of the accused could not be used for the purposes of the claim for defamation by the claimants. The court further held that the absolute immunity from suit which applied to judges, advocates and witnesses in respect of statements made in court extended also to out of court statements which could fairly be said to be part of the process of investigating a crime or a possible crime with a view to a prosecution; and that, accordingly, the statements made in the letter and the file note was subject to absolute immunity from suit in respect of a claim for defamation.

At the conclusion of a case the Court will not order one party to return to another photocopies of documents obtained on disclosure, where the party who has obtained the copies has paid photocopying charges and where the title to the paper on which the copies are made is thereby vested in him, and where there is no real cause to believe that he will disregard the obligation not to use the copies for any purpose outside the case (*Brue Ltd. v. Solly*, *The Times*, February 9, 1988).

Documents disclosed during the process of taxation fall within this provision, see *Bourns Inc. v. Raychem Corp.* [1999] 1 All E.R. 908 (a pre CPR case); affirmed [1999] 3 All E.R. 154, CA.

Permission has been granted to use material obtained on disclosure under the Anton Piller jurisdiction to bring proceedings against other parties shown by that material to be involved in misuse of the claimant's name or commercial property (*Sony Corp. v. Anand*; *Seiko Time Ltd v. Domicrest (Fancy Goods) Ltd* [1981] F.S.R. 398).

In *Omar v. Omar* [1995] 1 W.L.R. 1428; [1995] 3 All E.R. 571 it was held that the documents disclosed, or to be disclosed, by the bank could be used by the claimant both at the trial of the claim and in foreign proceedings aimed at following and tracing the shares, and to establish ultimate liability in those foreign proceedings; that the use of the documents for a personal claim, being within the broad purpose of the original disclosure, was an entirely legitimate purpose, so that leave to amend the claimant's claim and to use the documents in relation to *Mareva* relief would be granted. In *Miller v. Scorey* [1996] 1 W.L.R. 1122; [1996] 3 All E.R. 18, the court held *per curiam* that while it may be that the court has jurisdiction to grant retrospective leave to use disclosed documents for a purpose outside the claim in which they were disclosed, the circumstances in which it would be proper to exercise it would be rare. In this case leave was refused as such would have constituted a *de facto* validation of the issue of the proceedings obviating the need to issue fresh proceedings, thereby depriving the defendants of a limitation defence and permitting the claimants to take unfair advantage of their own wrong.

Documents of a confidential nature, read out in camera in English proceedings may nevertheless be ordered to be available in proceedings before the E.C. Commission: *Apple Corps. Ltd v. Apple Computer Inc.* [1992] F.S.R. 389; [1992] 1 C.M.L.R. 969.

In *Bank of Crete SA v. Koskotas (No. 2)* [1992] 1 W.L.R. 919; [1993] 1 All E.R. 748, it was held that the Court should not prevent a party to claim disclosing documents to another person pursuant to a legal obligation in a foreign jurisdiction.

In *Attorney-General for Gibraltar v. May*, [1999] 1 W.L.R. 998, CA is was held that although the Attorney-General was bound by an implied undertaking not to use in criminal proceedings against the defendant taking place in Gibraltar the contents of an affidavit sworn by the defendant under a court order ancillary to an application for a *Mareva* injunction to freeze the defendant's assets, the court would exercise is discretion to release the Attorney-General from the implied undertaking.

A claim based on a misused document will, ordinarily, be dismissed as an abuse of the process of the Court (*Riddick v. Thames Board Mills Ltd* [1977] Q.B. 881; [1977] 3 All E.R. 677, CA). See also *Home Office v. Harman* [1983] A.C. 280; [1982] 1 All E.R. 532, HL; and *Wilden Pump & Engineering Co. v. Fusfield* [1985] F.S.R. 581.

PRACTICE DIRECTION—DISCLOSURE AND INSPECTION

This Practice Direction supplements CPR Part 31

General

1.1 The normal order for disclosure will be an order that the parties give standard disclosure 31PD–001

1.2 In order to give standard disclosure the disclosing party must make a reasonable search for documents falling within the paragraphs of rule 31.6.

1.3 Having made the search the disclosing party must (unless rule 31.10(8) applies) make a list of the documents of whose existence the party is aware that fall within those paragraphs and which are or have been in the party's control (see rule 31.8).

1.4 The obligations imposed by an order for standard disclosure may be dispensed with or limited either by the court or by written agreement between the parties. Any such written agreement should be lodged with the court.

The Search

2. The extent of the search which must be made will depend upon the circumstances of the case including, in particular, the factors referred to in rule 31.7(2). The parties should bear in mind the overriding principle of proportionality (see rule 1.1(2)(c)). It may, for example, be reasonable to decide not to search for documents coming into existence before some particular date, or to limit the search to documents in some particular place or places, or to documents falling into particular categories.

The List

3.1 The list should be in practice form N265.

3.2 In order to comply with rule 31.10(3) it will normally be necessary to list the documents in date order, to number them consecutively and to give each a concise description (e.g. letter, claimant to defendant). Where there is a large number of documents all falling into a particular category the disclosing party may list those documents as a category rather than individually e.g. 50 bank statements relating to account number at Bank, 19 to 19 ; or, 35 letters passing between and between 19 and 19 .

3.3 The obligations imposed by an order for disclosure will continue until the proceedings come to an end. If, after a list of documents has been prepared and served, the existence of further documents to which the order applies comes to the attention of the disclosing party, the party must prepare and serve a supplemental list.

Disclosure Statement

4.1 A list of documents must (unless rule 31.10.(8)(b) applies) contain a disclosure statement complying with rule 31.10. The form of disclosure statement is set out in the Annex to this practice direction.

4.2 The disclosure statement should:

(1) expressly state that the disclosing party believes the extent of the search to have been reasonable in all the circumstances, and

(2) in setting out the extent of the search (see rule 31.10(6)) draw attention to any particular limitations on the extent of the search which were adopted for proportionality reasons and give the reasons why the limitations were adopted e.g. the difficulty or expense that a search not subject to those limitations would have entailed or the marginal relevance of categories of documents omitted from the search.

4.3 Where rule 31.10(7) applies, the details given in the disclosure statement about the person making the statement must include his name and address and the office or position he holds in the disclosing party.

4.4 If the disclosing party has a legal representative acting for him, the legal representative must endeavour to ensure that the person making the disclosure statement (whether the disclosing party or, in a case to which rule 31.10(7) applies, some other person) understands the duty of disclosure under rule 31.

4.5 If the disclosing party wishes to claim that he has a right or duty to withhold a document, or part of a document, in his list of documents from inspection (see rule 31.19(3)), he must state in writing:

(1) that he has such a right or duty, and

(2) the grounds on which he claims that right or duty.

4.6 The statement referred to in paragraph 4.5 above should normally be included in the disclosure statement and must identify the document, or part of a document, to which the claim relates.

4.7 An insurer or the Motor Insurers' Bureau may sign a disclosure statement on behalf of a party where the insurer or the Motor Insurers' Bureau has a financial interest in the result of proceedings brought wholly or partially by or against that party. Rule 31.10(7) and paragraph 4.3 above shall apply to the insurer or the Motor Insurers' Bureau making such a statement.

Specific Disclosure

31PD–002 **5.1** If a party believes that the disclosure of documents given by a disclosing party is inadequate he may make an application for an order for specific disclosure (see rule 31.12).

5.2 The application notice must specify the order that the applicant intends to ask the court to make and must be supported by evidence (see rule 31.12(2) which describes the orders the court may make).

5.3 The grounds on which the order is sought may be set out in the application notice itself but if not there set out must be set out in evidence filed in support of the application.

5.4 In deciding whether or not to make an order for specific disclosure the court will take into account all the circumstances of the case and, in particular, the overriding objective described in Part 1. But if the court concludes that the party from whom specific disclosure is sought has failed adequately to comply with the obligations imposed by an order for disclosure (whether by failing to make a sufficient search for documents or otherwise) the court will usually make such order as is necessary to ensure that those obligations are properly complied with.

Claims to withhold disclosure or inspection of a document

6.1 A claim to withhold inspection of a document, or part of a document, disclosed in a list of documents does not require an application to the court. Where such a claim has been made, a party who wishes to challenge it must apply to the court (see rule 31.19(5)).

6.2 Rule 31.19(1) and (6) provide a procedure enabling a party to apply for an order permitting disclosure of the existence of a document to be withheld.

Inspection of documents mentioned in expert's report (rule 31.14(e))

7 Reference should be made to the practice direction supplementing Part 35 (Experts and Assessors) for provisions dealing with applications to inspect these documents.

Annex

Disclosure statement

I, the above named claimant [or defendant] [if party making disclosure is a company, firm or other organisation identify here who the person making the disclosure statement is and why he is the appropriate person to make it] state that I have carried out a reasonable and proportionate search to locate all the documents which I am required to disclose under the order made by the court on day of . I did not search;

(1) for documents predating ,

(2) for documents located elsewhere than ,

(3) for documents in categories other than .

I certify that I understand the duty of disclosure and to the best of my knowledge I have carried out that duty. I certify that the list above is a complete list of all documents which are or have been in my control and which I am obliged under the said order to disclose."

PART 32

EVIDENCE

32.0.1 **Contents**

Editorial Introduction

32.0.2 This Part contains provisions formerly found in the RSC and CCR modified in some respects for the purpose of implementing particular recommendations made in the Access to Justice Reports. The provenance of many of the rules may be traced to RSC, O.38 and O.41 and CCR, O.20, Pt II.

The power to make rules of court relating to evidence is derived from various sources (*e.g.* Courts and Legal Services Act 1990, s.5 (witness statements), Civil Evidence Act 1995, s.12(hearsay evidence)). In the Civil Procedure Act 1997, the extent of the power to make Civil Procedure Rules is stated as including the power to "modify the rules of evidence as they apply to proceedings in any court within the scope of the rules" (s.1(2) and Sched. 1, para. 4) (see SCP 1999, Vol. 2, paras 20A–5 and 20A–15). Neither the Supreme Court Act 1981, s. 85 nor the County Courts Act 1984, s. 75 contained such a broad rule-making power. The law of evidence covers a wide diversity of topics and is based on a large corpus of case law and legislation. It has been said (*Cross and Tapper on Evidence* (8th ed., 1995), p. 5) that it is to be expected that "the fullest range of the rules of evidence will apply to proceedings in courts [as distinct from other tribunals], but there are still important variations in the precise mixture of rules which apply to different types of jurisdiction, to different types of court, and at different stages in the proceedings". Traditionally, rules of court have been confined to a narrow aspect of the law of evidence and have concentrated on matters falling on the border between rules of evidence and rules of procedure (the best example being rules relating to the manner in which evidence may be given). Further, they have provided very good illustrations of the ways in which the "mixture of rules" may be varied at "different stages in the proceedings". But the lines that divide these two bodies of legal rules (evidence and procedure) and which separate them from substantive legal rules are not clear cut. The question as to the extent to which power to make court rules relating to practice and procedure permits the making of rules on evidentiary matters has been much debated (even in the days when rule-making was the province of judges and judges alone). Generally, the suggestion that, what could be called, the substantive law of evidence could be altered by court rules has been resisted. The rule-making power now given by section 1(2) and Schedule 1, para. 4 of the 1997 Act changes the position significantly (see SCP 1999, Vol. 2, para. 20A–5/4).

However, most of the rules found in Pt 32, whilst altering the law in some important respects, are confined to matters traditionally thought to be the legitimate concern of rule-making authorities.

Related Sources 32.0.3

- Practice Direction (Written Evidence) (see para. 32PD–001, below).
- Interim Report, pp. 175–180.
- Final Report, pp. 128–130.
- Courts and Legal Services Act 1990, s.5 (witness statements) (see SCP 1999, Vol. 2, para. 20B–202).
- Civil Evidence Act 1995 (admissible hearsay) (see SCP 1999, Vol. 2, para. 21I–1).
- Part 8 (Alternative procedure for claims) rr.8.5 (Filing and serving witness statements) and 8.6 (Evidence—general).
- Part 22 (Statements of truth).
- Part 33 (Miscellaneous rules about evidence).
- Part 34 (Depositions and court attendance by witnesses).
- Part 35 (Experts and assessors).

Forms 32.0.4

- N20—Witness Summons (see para. C11–001).
- N21—Order for examination of deponent (before hearing) (see para. C13–001).

Power of court to control evidence

32.1—(1) The court may control the evidence by giving directions as to— 32.1

(a) the issues on which it requires evidence;

(b) the nature of the evidence which it requires to decide those issues; and

(c) the way in which the evidence is to be placed before the court.

(2) The court may use its power under this rule to exclude evidence that would otherwise be admissible.

(3) The court may limit cross-examination[GL].

Effect of rule—Under the CPR and related Practice Directions the court has extensive powers to manage cases and these powers may be used flexibly. The nature of court management may vary, depending on whether a case is allocated to the fast track or is proceeding on the multi-track, and, in the latter event, on whether the case is straightforward or less simple (Final Report, pp. 60–61). Rule 32.1applies to cases proceeding on the small claims track but the other rules in Pt 32 do not apply to such cases (r.27.2(1)(c)). Directions may be given at any time and may include directions as to evidence. Questionnaires to be filed by the parties to assist case management are designed in part to alert the court to the possibility that directions as to evidence may be helpful (Final Report, p. 61). 32.1.1

The general power to "control the evidence" is a far-reaching one to which some of the rules which follow in this part are subject.

This rule does not exhaust the court's powers to restrict evidence (either to fact or opinion) and to regulate the manner in which it is given (see, *e.g.* Pt 35 (Experts and Assessors)).

Directions as to issues on which evidence required—Courts decide issues of fact on the basis of evidence. Where no evidence is forthcoming, issues have to be determined in accordance with rules as to the incidence of the burden of proof. It may be necessary for the court to determine issues in the light of evidence available, not only at a trial, but also at the pre-trial stage. The powers given by r.32.1(a) may be exercised at any time in relation to any hearing but is likely to be principally used in preparing for trial. The basic proposition stated in this rule would appear to be that the court can direct that, in preparing for the determination of a particular issue at a particular time, it requires evidence on certain issues only and not on others (or at least no evidence yet or no further evidence on others). Doubtless, the circumstances in which the court would choose to do that are many and various and cannot be stated in a short compass. Having identified the particular issues to which the court does not wish to shut its ears (perhaps only temporarily), the court can then further stipulate the nature of the evidence to be given and the way in which the evidence is to be placed before the court. It should be noted that, in terms, r.32.1 is not restricted to evidence as to fact. 32.1.2

The court must further the overriding objective (r.1.1) by actively managing cases (r.1.4(1)) and must give effect to it when exercising any power under the CPR (r.1.2(a)). Active management includes "identifying the issues at an early stage" (r.1.4(2)(b)). The court's case management powers include the power to direct a separate trial of any issue, to decide the order in which issues are to be tried, and to exclude an issue from consideration (r.3.1(2)(i), (j), (k)). In certain circumstances the court may determine cases without an oral hearing (see rr.1.4(2)(j) and 23.8) (Final Report, p. 68).

The court is encouraged (in appropriate cases proceeding on the multi-track particularly) to resolve issues that have been identified at the pre-trial stage by "rolling adjudication" instead of leaving all issues alive until trial (Interim Report, p. 50 and Final Report, p. 63). The discharge of all of these powers is facilitated by the specific power given to the court by r.32.1.

32.1.3 **Nature of the evidence**—It should be noted that, under the CPR, evidence may consist, not only of the *viva voce* testimony of witnesses, or their witness statements and affidavits, but also of the statements of case and notices of application (which are to be verified a "statement of truth").

32.1.4 **Exclusion of evidence otherwise admissible (r.32.1(2))**—Hitherto, the extent to which a judge in civil proceedings (whether sitting with a jury or not) has a discretion to exclude evidence which is relevant and admissible has not been entirely clear (see *Cross and Tapper on Evidence* (8th ed., 1995), pp. 5 and 215). Certainly, a court has no general power to exclude relevant and admissible evidence. Where a court exercises its power under r.32.1(1)(a) and directs that evidence should be given on particular issues only and not on others (having perhaps excluded the other issues in exercise of the power given by r.3.1(2)(k)) the effect of the direction will be (almost inevitably) to exclude admissible evidence. Further, the same result may ensue when the court gives a direction under r.32.1(1)(b) limiting the evidence to be given on a particular issue to evidence of a particular "nature". Rule 32.1(2) rightly assumes that the court has no general power to exclude admissible evidence but provides that the court may exercise its powers under r.32.1(1) even though the effect of doing so will be the exclusion of admissible evidence.

32.1.5 **Limiting cross-examination (r.32.1(3))**—The court may limit cross-examination (r.32.1(3)). Conceivably, cross-examination may be limited in two ways. First, the court may limit the issues to be explored on cross-examination. The power to control evidence referred to in r.32.1(1) would provide authority for this. Secondly, the court may limit the trial time to be devoted to cross-examination of a particular witness. In the Chancery Guide it was said (para. 6.10) that the court may at any time, before or during the cross-examination of a witness, impose a time limit within which the cross-examination is to be completed (see SCP 1999, Vol. 2, para. 2B–265). If there was any doubt as to the basis of the power to limit cross-examination in this way it is cleared up by the express terms of r.32.1(3).

Evidence of witness—general rule

32.2 **32.2**—(1) The general rule is that any fact which needs to be proved by the evidence of witness is to be proved—

(a) at trial, by their oral evidence given in public; and

(b) at any other hearing, by their evidence in writing.

(2) This is subject—

(a) to any provision to the contrary contained in these Rules or elsewhere; or

(b) to any order of the court.

32.2.1 **Proof by oral evidence at trial**—Traditionally, English law has placed greatest weight to evidence given by witnesses in open court on oath or affirmation under examination by the parties. Rule 32.2(1)(a) follows the former RSC, O.38, r.1 and former CCR, O.20, r.4 and restates the general principle in relation to the most important part of the civil process, the trial. See SCP 1999, Vol. 1, para. 38/1/2. The rule applies only to evidence as to matters of fact.

In the former rules, a distinction was drawn between evidence given by witnesses *viva voce* and by other means, principally by affidavit (but also by witness statements). In r.32.2, the distinction drawn is between oral evidence and "evidence in writing". The rule that evidence at trial should be given *viva voce* is a "general rule". The court has power to order otherwise (as it did heretofore, see, *e.g.* RSC, O.38, r.2(1) and CCR, O.20, r.6). (Former RSC, O.38, r.1 was confined to actions commenced by writ and did not apply to proceedings coming before the court on originating summons or motion, see RSC, O.8, r.2(3).)

A statement of case may be used as evidence in an interim application provided it is verified by a statement of truth. For form of statement of truth in this context, see Practice Direction (Written Evidence), para. 26.2 (see para. 32PD–006, below).

In hearings under the Pt 8 procedure (Alternative procedure for claims), see r.8.6(1) for rules as to written evidence and r.8.6(2) for oral evidence.

As to hearings in public, see r.39.2.

32.2.2 **Proof by evidence in writing at any other hearing**—Rule 32(1)(b) states that, as a general rule, any fact which needs to be proved by the evidence of witnesses at a hearing other than the trial is to be proved by their evidence in writing. Former rules permitting evidence by affidavit were not confined to evidence tending to prove facts (*e.g.* RSC, O.38, r.2 and CCR, O.20, rr.5 and 6). Rule 32(1)(b) should be read with r.32.6 which states, as a further general rule, that evidence at "hearings other than the trial" is to be by witness statement (but may be given by affidavit, see r.32.15(1) and (2), and, in some circumstances, reliance may be placed on a statement of case or notice of application). (Rule 32.6 is not confined to evidence as to facts.)

The general rules stated in paras (a) and (b) of r.32.2 are subject to "any order of the court" (see r.32.1(1)). This restates in rather broader terms previous court rules (*e.g.* RSC, O.38, r.3 and CCR, O.20, r.6). The general rules are also subject "to any provision to the contrary contained in these Rules or elsewhere". Previous court rules were made subject to special rules and to provisions made in or under other enactments. Presumably, by making the general rules subject to contrary provisions "contained ... elsewhere" it is not intended to make them subject to practice directions.

Examples of specific powers in the hands of the court to order otherwise are found in Practice Direction (Contentious Probate Proceedings) para. 6.5 (see 49PD–001), Practice Direction (Miscellaneous Provisions Relating to Hearings) para. 1.15 (hearing of possession claim in private) (see 39PD–001).

For provisions as to written evidence in committal applications, see Practice Direction (Committal Applications) paras 3.1 to 3.4, and for Interim Injunctions, see Practice Direction (Interim Injunctions) paras 3.1 to 3.4 (see 25CPD–001).

Evidence by video link or other means

32.3 The court may allow a witness to give evidence through a video link or by other means. 32.3

Effect of rule—This rule is consistent with r.1.4(2)(k) which states that, in furthering the overriding objective stated in r.1.1, the court may make use of appropriate technology. The use of video links was approved under earlier rules (see SCP 1999, Vol. 1, para. 38/3/2). The court may allow a witness to give evidence either through a video link "or by other means"; presumably this means other forms of communications technology. 32.3.1

Requirement to serve witness statements for use at trial

32.4—(1) A witness statement is a written statement signed by a person which contains the evidence, and only that evidence, which that person would be allowed to give orally. 32.4

(2) The court will order a party to serve on the other parties any witness statement of the oral evidence which the party serving the statement intends to rely on in relation to any issues of fact to be decided at the trial.

(3) The court may give directions as to—

(a) the order in which witness statements are to be served; and

(b) whether or not the witness statements are to be filed.

Effect of rule—This rule builds on the general power of the court to give directions controlling evidence stated in r.32.1. 32.4.1

Formerly, rules of court as to the service before trial (by one party on another) of the "written statements of oral evidence which the party intends to adduce on any issues of facts to be decided at the trial" were found in RSC, O.38, r.2A (Exchange of witness statements) (see SCP 1999, Vol. 1, para. 38/2A) and in CCR, O.20, r.12A.

Rule 32.4 requires the court (as did its predecessors) to direct any party at any stage of the proceedings to serve witness statements.

For objectives of these provisions, see SCP 1999, Vol. 1, para. 38/2A/3.

Evidence of experts—See Pt 35 (Experts and Assessors) 32.4.2

Witness "statements" and witness "summaries"—The CPR draw a clearer distinction than heretofore between witness "statements" and witness "summaries" (see rr.32.8 and 32.9). This is a response to perceived weaknesses in the former exchange of witness statements procedure explained in the Interim Report, pp. 176 *et seq.* (see also Final Report, p. 128 *et seq.*). In particular, witness statements had ceased to be an authentic account of the evidence which the witness could give and had become "an elaborate, costly branch of legal drafting" (Final Report, p. 129). 32.4.3

A witness "statement" is, in effect, a full proof of evidence. However, the court may order that initially a witness statement should be limited to certain issues (see r.32.1). It could be said, therefore, that a distinction can be drawn between "full" and "limited" witness statements.

A witness "summary", on the other hand, merely identifies the witness and indicates the issues with which his evidence will deal; see r.32.9(3) below. (Under the former RSC, O.38, r.2A(5) and CCR, O.20, r.12A(5) a witness summary could be exchanged instead of a witness statement.) In the Interim Report it was recommended (p. 43) that in cases proceeding on the fast track oral evidence of witnesses as to fact would be limited, supplemented as necessary by written submissions and written evidence. It was said that, for this purpose, witness summaries would suffice (see also p. 178). However, in the Final Report (p. 38) it was said that the evidence of witnesses in fast track cases should be handled, not by way of witness summaries, but by way of "brief" witness statements.

32.4.4 **Form of witness statement**—Witness statements are to be in the form stipulated by r.32.8. They must be signed (r.32.4(1)) and verified by a "statement of truth" (r.22.1(1)); see further notes following r.32.8.

For form of witness summaries, see r.32.9. See further, Final Report, p. 130.

32.4.5 **Content of witness statements**—In the Final Report it was said (at p. 130) that witness statements should, so far as possible, be in the witness's own words, should not discuss legal propositions, and should not comment on documents.

Rule 32.4(1) provides that a witness statement should contain admissible evidence only (see comments on former RSC, O.38, r.2A(8) in SCP 1999, Vol. 1, para. 38/2A/13).

32.4.6 **Hearsay evidence in witness statements**—With the coming into effect of the Civil Evidence Act 1995, hearsay evidence became generally admissible in civil proceedings, thus relieving lawyers of the task of editing witness statements to remove hearsay. Under s. 2(1) of the 1995 Act, a party proposing to adduce hearsay evidence in civil proceedings is obliged to give notice of his intention to do so in accordance with the rules of court found in Pt 33. Where the hearsay evidence is to be given by a witness called to give oral evidence, notice is given by serving the witness's witness statement as directed by the court. Where the intention is not to call the witness and the evidence is contained in a witness statement, again notice is given by serving the witness statement as directed (r.33.2).

32.4.7 **Court's directions**—When a case is allocated to the fast track the court will give directions under r.28.3 and it is specifically provided in the rules that the matters dealt with will include the service of witness statements (r.28.3(1)(b)); see Appendix to Practice Direction (The Fast Track) (see 28PD–005). When a case is allocated to the multi-track the court will give directions for the management of the case under r.29.2(1) and it is obvious that this would include directions as to witness statements (see also r.32.4(2)); see Practice Direction (The Multi-track) para. 4.7(1)(d) (see 29PD–002). It is the intention that, normally, in fast track cases directions will be confined to the service of witness summaries, at least in the first instance.

The court may direct that parties should exchange witness statements simultaneously or sequentially; *cf.* RSC, O.38, r.2A(4)(c) and CCR, O.20, r.12A(4)(c) (see SCP 1999, Vol. 1, para. 38/2A/4).

32.4.8 **Circumstances in which service of witness statements ordered**—In terms, r.32.4 does not stipulate the circumstances in which, and the time at which, the court should order the service of witness statements. It simply says the court should so order. The power is not limited to particular proceedings or to the evidence of the witnesses of particular parties within proceedings. Orders to serve witness statements will be given in accordance with the court's case management powers as stated elsewhere in the CPR and in accordance with relevant Practice Directions. (The pre-action protocols should have the effect of encouraging the exchange of certain witness statements before proceedings are started.)

The powers given by this rule should be exercised in a manner which furthers the overriding objective (r.1.1) including the objective of ensuring that cases are dealt with "expeditiously and fairly" (former RSC, O.38, r.2A(1) imposed a similar requirement).

A party ordered to serve a witness statement may apply to serve a witness summary instead (r.32.9(1)).

32.4.9 **Time limits**—Rule 32.4 does not stipulate a period within which witness statements should be served. However, it is to be expected that time limits may be imposed by practice directions and orders made in individual cases (see too r.32.9(4) (Witness summaries to be served within period within which witness statement would have to be served)).

32.4.10 **Service of witness statement**—The witness statement is to be served by the party on such other parties as the order may stipulate. A witness statement is a "document" within Pt 6 (Service of Documents) and the provisions in Pt 1 of that Part will apply to such service except where a practice direction makes a different provision or the court orders otherwise. Where a witness chooses to give evidence by affidavit instead of a witness statement, the rules relating to service of a witness statement apply to the affidavit (r.32.15(3)).

For rules as to filing and service of witness statements for use at hearing "other than at trial", see r.23.7(2)(3).

In a number of procedural contexts, special rules obtain as to the service of witness statements; *e.g.* r.24.5 (Evidence for the purposes of a summary judgment hearing).

32.4.11 **Order in which witness statements are to be served**—Former RSC, O.38, r.2A(4)(c) and

CCR, O.20, r.12A(4)(c) stated that, where witness statements were to be served by more than one party, they were to be "exchanged simultaneously". However, the court could direct otherwise. Now it is stated in r.32.4(3)(a) that the court may give directions as to the order in which witness statements are to be served. In the past it was thought that sequential exchange of statements of lay witnesses should be ordered only in exceptional cases (see SCP 1999, Vol. 1, para. 38/2A/4). (In *Rayment v. Ministry of Defence, The Times*, July 6, 1998, a Master's order in a medical negligence case requiring that parties' expert's reports as to liability should be exchanged simultaneously but those as to quantum should be exchanged sequentially was upheld.) Under the system of case management now being introduced, circumstances in which sequential exchange is appropriate may arise with greater frequency.

Filing of witness statements—The court may give directions as to whether or not the witness statements are to be filed. In a number of procedural contexts, special rules requiring the filing of witness statements apply, *e.g.* r.24.5 (Evidence for the purposes of a summary judgment hearing); see further Practice Direction (Written Evidence), para. 23 (see para. 32PD–005, below). **32.4.12**

Alteration of witness statement—As is explained in SCP 1999, Vol. 1, para. 38/2A/9, a witness statement was a "document" which could be amended under former RSC, O.20, r.8(1). The former provision is not reproduced in the CPR. Nevertheless, presumably the court retains power to amend a witness statement in circumstances similar to those stated in former r.8(1). As to practice relating to alteration of witness statements, see Practice Direction (Written Evidence), para. 22 (see para. 32PD–005, below). **32.4.13**

Supplementary witness statements—Although there is no express provision to this effect, the court has power to direct that a further written statement of a witness be served supplementary to that already served (see S.C.P 1999, Vol. 1, para. 38/2A/10). **32.4.14**

Costs for preparation of witness statements—The costs allowed for witness statements (and summaries) should reflect the fact that they are not intended to be elaborate documents (Interim Report, pp. 179–180). This is reinforced by the rule that where an affidavit is used where a witness statement would suffice there may be a costs penalty (r.32.15(2)). **32.4.15**

Consequences of failure to serve witness statement—See r.32.10. **32.4.16**

Written evidence in claim under Pt 8 procedure—If the claimant is intending to use the Pt 8 procedure (Alternative procedure for claims), he must when filing his claim form also file any "written evidence" on which he intends to rely (r.8.5(1)) and the claimant's evidence must be served on the defendant with the claim form (r.8.5(2)). Thereafter, in the Pt 8 procedure r.8.5(3)–(6) deals with the filing and serving of written evidence by the defendant and, if appropriate, by the claimant in reply. **32.4.17**

Defects in written statements—Where a written statement or an exhibit to a witness statement is defective, in the sense that it does not conform with the provisions of Pt 32 or the supplementary practice direction, the consequences referred to in Practice Direction (Written Evidence), paras 25.1 and 25.2, follow (see para. 32PD–005, below). **32.4.18**

References to written evidence in practice forms—The High Court and county court forms in use before April 26, 1999, and remaining in use after that date are listed, respectively, in Practice Direction (Forms) Tables 2 and 3 (see 4PD–002). Where a rule permits, a party intending to use a witness statement as an alternative to an affidavit should amend any form in Table 2 or 3 to be used in connection with that rule so that "witness statement" replaces "affidavit" wherever it appears in the form (*ibid.* paras 4.3 and 5.2). **32.4.19**

Use at trial of witness statements which have been served

32.5—(1) If— **32.5**

(a) a party has served a witness statement; and
(b) he wishes to rely at trial on the evidence of the witness who made the statement,

he must call the witness to give oral evidence unless the court orders otherwise or he puts in the statement as hearsay evidence.

(Part 33 contains provisions about hearsay evidence.)

(2) Where a witness is called to give oral evidence under paragraph (1), his witness statement shall stand as his evidence in chief[GL] unless the court orders otherwise.

(3) A witness giving oral evidence at trial may with the permission of the court—

(a) amplify his witness statement; and

(b) give evidence in relation to new matters which have arisen since the witness statement was served on the other parties.

(4) The court will give permission under paragraph (3) only if it considers that there is good reason not to confine the evidence of the witness to the contents of his witness statement.

(5) If a party who has served a witness statement does not—

(a) call the witness to give evidence at trial; or

(b) put in the witness statement as hearsay evidence,

any other party may put in the witness statement as hearsay evidence.

32.5.1 **"witness statement ... as ... evidence in chief" (r.32.5(2))**—This sub-rule builds on r.32.1(c) (court's power to give directions as to way in which evidence is to be placed before the court). Parties are required to serve their witness statements on other parties in advance of trial (for the purposes of promoting settlement and avoiding surprise). Further, in the event of the witness being called at trial, his witness statement should normally stand as his evidence-in-chief (for the purpose of reducing trial time). Formerly, the latter practice was stated in Practice Direction (Case Management) [1995] 1 W.L.R. 262, para. 3 (SCP 1999, Vol. 2, para. 2C–22), Guide to Commercial Court Practice paras 14.4 and 19.4 (SCP 1999, Vol. 2, paras 72–A17 and 72–A22) and the Chancery Guide, para. 3.7 (SCP 1999, Vol. 2, para. 2B–231); it is now put in rule form (former RSC, O.38, r.2A(7) and CCR, O.20, r.12A(7) gave the court power to direct that a witness's statement or part of it should stand as evidence-in-chief). The court retains a discretion and may order that the witness's evidence or part of it should be given *viva voce* (*Cole v. Kivells, The Times*, May 2, 1997, CA (conflict of evidence on crucial issue); see also *Anonima Petroli Italiana SpA v. Marlucidez Armadora S.A.* (*The Filiatra Legacy*), *The Times*, April 10, 1991, CA) (SCP 1999, Vol. 1, para. 38/2A/11).

32.5.2 **Amplification of evidence (r.32.5(3) and (4))**—Former RSC, O.38, r.2A(7) and CCR, O.20, r.12A(7) restricted the evidence which could be adduced from a party other than that disclosed in his witness statement. Paragraphs (3) and (4) adopt and implement generally the Chancery approach to what was called "supplementary examination in chief" (Chancery Guide para. 6.9 (SCP 1999, Vol. 2, para. 2B–264). For explanation, see Interim Report, pp. 177–178.

If amplification of witness statements at trial is too strictly limited there is a risk that statements will become over-elaborate and that costs of the preparation will be accordingly increased. If, on the other hand, amplification is too readily allowed there is a risk that statements will fail to deal with important issues. Where a party's witness is allowed to amplify, prejudice to the opponent should not be regarded routinely as remediable simply by an order for costs. A late, unjustified change of tack may be regarded as an injustice to the opponent which, in the light of the overriding objective (r.1.1) should not be permitted (Final Report, p. 129).

32.5.3 **Witness not called**—The general rule under r.32.2(1)(a) is that any fact which needs to be proved by the evidence of witnesses is to be proved at trial, by their oral evidence given in public.

Where a party serves a witness statement of one of his witnesses and wishes to rely on it, he must call the witness to give oral evidence, unless the court orders otherwise, or put the statement in as a hearsay statement in accordance with the Pt 33 procedure. (See "Hearsay evidence in witness statements" in notes following r.32.4.)

The significance of the phrase "unless the court orders otherwise" in r.32.5(1) is not immediately apparent. In early drafts of the CPR, what is now r.32.5 was subject to a further rule dealing specifically with witness statements as evidence where the witness is not called and the meaning of the phrase was clear.

Rule 32.5(5) states that if the party does not wish to have the benefit of the evidence by either calling the witness to give evidence at trial or by putting in the witness statement as hearsay any other party may put in the witness statement as hearsay evidence. The effect of this provision is to overcome the difficulty encountered in (*Husbands v. Commissioners of Police for the Metropolis*, unrep. July 7, 1994, CA).

Note "Witness called or not called" SCP 1999, Vol. 1, para. 38/2A/11.

Evidence in proceedings other than at trial

32.6 **32.6**—(1) Subject to paragraph (2), the general rule is that evidence at hearings other than the trial is to be by witness statement unless the court, a practice direction or any other enactment requires otherwise.

(2) At hearings other than the trial, a party may, in support of his application, rely on the matters set out in—

(a) his statement of case; or
(b) his application,
if the statement of case or application is verified by, a statement of truth.

Effect of rule—This rule should be read with r.32.2(1)(b) which states the general rule that any fact which needs to be proved by the evidence of witnesses is to be proved, at any hearing other than the trial, by their evidence in writing. Rule 32.6(1) adds to this by stating that, as a general rule, evidence in writing in hearings other than the trial should be in the form of witness statements. A statement of case (*e.g.* a claim form, or a defence) carries a statement of truth and constitutes "evidence in writing". Presumably, in proceedings other than at trial, a party may rely on his statement of case or just the application in support of his application in addition to any witness statements. In any event, r.32.6 provides that he may rely solely on his statement of case (provided it is verified by a statement of truth). **32.6.1**

For claims under the Pt 8 procedure (Alternative procedure for claims), see also r.8.5(7) which reflects r.32.6 by stating that a Pt 8 claimant may rely on matters set out in his claim form as evidence if the claim form is verified by a statement of truth.

Note Pt 22 (Statement of truth).

Note "Proof by evidence in writing at any other hearing", following r.32.2.

Note "Written evidence in claim under Pt 8 procedure", following r.32.4.

"enactment requires otherwise"—Under many different enactments, applications may be made to the court giving rise to proceedings which are not trials. The provisions in r.32.6 are subject to any provisions as to evidence in such enactments. **32.6.2**

Order for cross-examination

32.7—(1) Where, at a hearing other than the trial, evidence is given in writing, any party may apply to the court for permission to cross-examine the person giving the evidence. **32.7**

(2) If the court gives permission under paragraph (1) but the person in question does not attend as required by the order, his evidence may not be used unless the court gives permission.

Effect of rule—Evidence in writing may consist of matters set out in a statement of case, an affidavit, a witness statement, a witness summary, or an application notice. In some instances the evidence either may be or must necessarily be the evidence of a party. **32.7.1**

Under former RSC, O.38, r.2 and CCR, O.20, rr.5 and 6, the court could order that the affidavit of any witness could be read at trial or in chambers. Where such an order was made, the general rule was that the deponent should not be subject to cross-examination and need not attend trial for that purpose. However, the court had power to order otherwise (see "Cross-examination upon affidavit" SCP 1999, Vol. 1, paras 38/2/6, 38/2/7 and 38/2/10). It would seem that r.32.7 attempts to carry the former rules into the CPR and to apply them to evidence in writing generally.

Under the Pt 8 procedure (Alternative procedure for claims), directions may be given for the attendance for cross-examination of a witness who has given written evidence (r.8.6(3)).

Form of witness statement

32.8 A witness statement must comply with the requirements set out in the relevant practice direction. **32.8**

(Part 22 requires a witness statement to be verified by a statement of truth.)

Effect of rule—Practice Direction (Written Evidence), paras 17 to 22 and Annex 2 contain provisions dealing with the form of witness statements and their verification by statements of truth (see para. 32PD–004, below). The requirements as to form, etc., formerly found in RSC, O.38, r.2A(4) and CCR, O.20, r.12A(4) are not repeated in r.32.8 ; instead such matters are now dealt with by Practice Direction (see further SCP 1999, Vol. 1, para. 38/2A/8). **32.8.1**

A witness statement must be verified by a statement of truth (r.22.1(1)(b) and r.32.4(1)) stating that the maker of the statement believes the facts stated in the document are true (r.22.1(4)). (See Pt 22 further for provisions regarding the statement of truth.) This requirement follows from RSC, O.38, r.2A(4)(a). If the witness statement is not verified by a statement of truth the court may direct that it shall not be admissible as evidence (r.22.3).

Solicitors and witnesses alike have an obligation to take the greatest care to ensure that statements contain the truth (*ZYX Music GmbH v. King* [1995] 3 All E.R.1). Proceedings for contempt of court may be brought against a witness who makes a false statement without an honest belief in its truth (r.32.14(2)).

Witness summaries

32.9 **32.9**—(1) A party who—

(a) is required to serve a witness statement for use at trial; but

(b) is unable to obtain one,

may apply, without notice, for permission to serve a witness summary instead.

(2) A witness summary is a summary of—

(a) the evidence, if known, which would otherwise be included in a witness statement; or

(b) if the evidence is not known, the matters about which the party serving the witness summary proposes to question the witness.

(3) Unless the court orders otherwise, a witness summary must include the name and address of the intended witness.

(4) Unless the court orders otherwise, a witness summary must be served within the period in which a witness statement would have had to be served.

(5) Where a party serves a witness summary, so far as practicable, rules 32.4 (requirement to serve witness statement for use at trial), 32.5(3) (amplifying witness statements), and 32.8 (form of witness statement) shall apply to the summary.

32.9.1 **Effect of rule**—For distinction between "witness statements" and "witness summaries" see "Witness statements" and "witness summaries" following r.32.4 above.

Under former RSC, O.38, r.2A(5) and CCR, O.20, r.12A(5), where a party was unable to obtain a witness statement from an intended witness he could apply to the court for a direction permitting him to exchange a witness summary instead. Similar provision is now made in r.32.9. Under the CPR, service of witness summaries may be directed by the court in a broader range of circumstances. The contents of a witness summary should accord with this rule. Otherwise, the rules applicable to witness statements apply to witness summaries as far as may be. However, a witness summary does not include a certificate by its maker as to truth. The court may order that the witness summary should not include the witness's name and address.

Consequence of failure to serve witness statement or summary

32.10 **32.10** If a witness statement or a witness summary for use at trial is not served in respect of an intended witness within the time specified by the court, then the witness may not be called to give oral evidence unless the court gives permission.

32.10.1 **Effect of rule**—This rule indicates the consequences that may follow where a witness statement or summary for use at trial is not served. As to consequences of failure to serve written evidence in a claim under the Pt 8 procedure (Alternative procedure for claim), see r.8.6. Presumably, where a party fails to serve a written statement for a hearing other than a trial the court could refuse to admit it if directions for exchange had been given.

32.10.2 **"witness may not be called ... unless the court gives permission"**—Former RSC, O.38, r.2A(10) provided that, where a party failed to comply with a direction for the exchange of witness statements, the sanction was that he would "not be entitled to adduce evidence to which the direction related" without the leave of the court (see also former CCR, O.20, r.12A(10)). The same rule was expressly applied in actions proceeding under automatic directions (former RSC, O.25, r.8(2), but no express provision was made in the former CCR, O.17, r.11(3)(b)).

Whereas the former sanction was that the party would "not be entitled to adduce evidence to which the direction related", in r.32.10 the sanction is that the witness "may not be called to give oral evidence". The latter formulation is broader than the former and this may be significant.

Previously, the nature of the factors to be taken into account by the court in the exercise of its discretion to dis-apply the sanction was the subject of case law (*e.g. Beachley Property Ltd. v. Edgar The Times*, July 18, 1996, CA, and *B.V. Tapijtfabriek van den Brink v. Shierson*, unrep., May 12, 1997, CA). Presumably, the rule stated in r.32.10 will be regarded as a "sanction" within r.3.8 (Sanctions having effect unless defaulting party obtains relief) and, therefore, the factors to be taken into account by the court in determining whether to permit a witness to give oral evidence despite the failure to serve a witness statement should include those listed in r.3.9 (Relief from sanctions).

32.10.3 **"within the time specified by the court"**—See "Time limits" in note following r.32.4.

Cross-examination on a witness statement

32.11 **32.11** Where a witness is called to give evidence at trial, he may be cross-examined on his witness statement, whether or not the statement or any part of it was referred to during the witness's evidence in chief[GL].

Effect of rule—Under the previous rules, the effect of the service of a witness statement was a matter for some doubt, and some doubts remain (see SCP 1999, Vol. 1, para. 38/2A/11). Former RSC, O.38, r.2A(6) and CCR, O.20, r.12A(6) stated the general proposition that, "where the party serving a statement ... does not call the witness to whose evidence it relates, no other party may put the statement in evidence at the trial". A witness statement does not become evidence by service. It becomes evidence by being adopted by the witness in the witness box as his evidence in chief (see SCP 1999, Vol. 1, para. 38/2A/4). **32.11.1**

Where a witness is called to give evidence, his witness statement shall stand as his evidence in chief, unless the court orders otherwise (r.32.5(2)). Normally, therefore, it would follow that a witness could be cross-examined on his witness statement as a matter of course. This rule provides that where the witness's statement (or part of it) does not stand as his evidence in chief he may be cross-examined on it (or on that part of it). In the former rules, this rule was stated as an exception to the general proposition mentioned above (RSC, O.38, r.2A(7)(c) and CCR, O.20, r.12A(7)(c)).

Use of witness statements for other purposes

32.12—(1) Except as provided by this rule, a witness statement may be used only for the purpose of the proceedings in which it is served. **32.12**

(2) Paragraph (1) does not apply if and to the extent that—

(a) the witness gives consent in writing to some other use of it;

(b) the court gives permission for some other use; or

(c) the witness statement has been put in evidence at a hearing held in public.

Effect of rule—This rule follows from RSC, O.38, r.2A(11) and CCR, O.20, r.12A(11). The procedure for requiring parties to serve witness statements has the principal effect of alerting each party to what their opponent's witnesses are going to say at trial, in the event of there being a trial. (This has the advantages of promoting settlements and avoiding unfair surprise at trial.) If there is a trial and the evidence contained in a particular witness's statement is given in court, the evidence is in the public domain and certain legal consequences follow from that (*e.g.* any privilege is waived). However, if the case is settled without trial, or if there is a trial but the witness is not called (or his statement adduced in evidence under the hearsay provisions) the general rule is that no other party may make use of that statement subsequently. The difficulty which arises is whether a party upon whom a witness statement has been served may make any use of it before trial (or settlement), during the interlocutory stages of the proceedings. Rule 32.12(1) says a witness statement "may be used only for the purpose of the proceedings in which it is served". The exceptions in paras (a) and (b) of r.32.2 are obvious enough and follow the former rules. Paragraph (c) is new and may go some way towards clarifying problems that have arisen in the past as to the status of witness statements before they are deployed at trial (see further, r.39.2 (General rule—hearing to be in public)). **32.12.1**

Availability of witness statements for inspection

32.13—(1) A witness statement which stands as evidence in chief[GL] is open to inspection unless the court otherwise directs during the course of the trial. **32.13**

(2) Any person may ask for a direction that a witness statement is not open to inspection.

(3) The court will not make a direction under Paragraph (2) unless it is satisfied that a witness statement should not be open to inspection because of—

(a) the interests of justice;

(b) the public interest;

(c) the nature of any expert medical evidence in the statement;

(d) the nature of any confidential information (including information relating to personal financial matters) in the statement; or

(e) the need to protect the interests of any child or patient.

(4) The court may exclude from inspection words or passages in the statement.

Effect of rule—There is a general presumption that the business of the courts is to be done in **32.13.1**

public unless this is likely to lead to a denial of justice. In the Report of the Review Body on Civil Justice, Cm. 394 (1988) greater use of witness statements was recommended. The Review Body recognised that this recommendation, together with other proposed changes, would lead to less evidence being given orally and in open court with the result that evidence would be "less open to public scrutiny". Consequently, the Review Body further recommended that in cases where written evidence is relied on in court but is not read out public access should be provided for a period after the conclusion of the case (*ibid.* para. 298). This recommendation was carried into effect by provisions formerly found in RSC, O.38, r.2A(12) to (16) and CCR, O.20, r.12A(12) to (16) and supporting Practice Directions (see SCP 1999, Vol. 1, para. 38/2A/15). The former rules are recast and in some respects altered in r.32.13.

For inspection by parties or by any other person of documents from the records of the court generally see r.5.4.

For certification by court officer of material excluded from inspection under r.32.13(2) or r.32.13(4), see Practice Direction (Written Evidence), para. 24.1 (see para. 32PD–005, below).

False statements

32.14 **32.14**—(1) Proceedings for contempt of court may be brought against a person if he makes, or causes to be made, a false statement in a document verified by a statement of truth without an honest belief in its truth.

(Part 22 makes provision for a statement of truth.)

(2) Proceedings under this rule may be brought only—

(a) by the Attorney General; or

(b) with the permission of the court.

32.14.1 **Effect of rule**—Various documents may or must be verified by a statement of truth (see Pt 22 and notes thereto). Generally, the person who is required to complete the statement of truth is the person making or putting forward the document. However, in certain circumstances, verification may be given by a party's legal representative or by a litigation friend (former "next friend" or guardian ad litem).

Pleadings are now called "statements of case" (r.2.3(1)) and include the claim form, the particulars of claim, the defence, the reply and any Pt 18 response. Statements of case are to carry "statements of truth" (see. r.22.1) signed by the parties (or their litigation friend) or their legal representatives to the effect that it is believed that the facts stated in the document being verified are true. In certain circumstances, statements of case may stand as evidence in the course of the proceedings (see, *e.g.* r.32.6(2)(a)). Further, an application notice for a court order made under Pt 23 may contain a statement, by the applicant or his legal representative, that the applicant believes any facts stated in the application are true (r.22.1(3)). If the application contains a statement of truth, the applicant may rely on the matters set out in the application in support of his application (r.32.6(2)(b)). Furthermore, as was explained above, r.22.1(1)(b) states that the maker of a witness statement must certify that he believes the statements of fact in it are true.

This rule provides that proceedings for contempt of court may be brought against a person who makes or causes to be made a false statement without an honest belief in its truth in a document verified by a statement of truth. Rule 22.1(6) provides that in the case of documents in the form of a statement of case, an application notice, or a response complying with an order under r.18.1 to provide further information, the statement of truth may be signed by a legal representative "on behalf of the party". Where a legal representative signs the statement of truth and it turns out that the document to which it relates contains a false statement a question may arise as to whether the legal representative may be exposed to liability for contempt under r.32.14. (Drafts of r.32.14 said that proceedings for contempt of court could be brought against "a party" who made or caused to be made a false statement in a document in relation to which a legal representative was permitted by the rules to sign the statement of truth on his behalf. In the final version it is said that proceedings may be brought against "a person" who makes or causes to be made a false statement.)

In the case of a witness statement, the statement of truth must be signed by the maker of the statement. Conceivably, a legal representative who caused the maker of a witness statement to make a false statement in the witness statement could be liable.

The persons who may or must sign the statement of truth are stipulated by the rules, and by Practice Direction (Statements of Truth) para. 3.1 (see 22PD–002) and Practice Direction (Experts and Assessors) para. 1.3 (see 35PD–001). Presumably, where a false statement is made in a document verified by a statement of truth signed by a person who (in the event) was not permitted by the rules to sign, contempt liability under r.32.14 does not arise.

The contempt consists, not of the breach of a court order or of an undertaking to the court, but in the making of a false statement in a document verified by a statement of truth. It would seem that the maximum penalty is as stated in the Contempt of Court Act 1981, s.14(1) (a fixed term not exceeding on any occasion two years). If proceedings are to be brought by a person other than the Attorney General, the permission of the court is required.

As to bringing of proceedings for contempt, see Sched. 1, RSC, O.52 (paras R52.1 *et seq.* below).

Affidavit evidence

32.15—(1) Evidence must be given by affidavit[GL], instead of or in addition to a witness statement if this is required by the court, a provision contained in any other rule, a practice direction or any other enactment. **32.15**

(2) Nothing in these Rules prevents a witness giving evidence by affidavit[GL], at a hearing other than the trial, if he chooses to do so in a case where paragraph (1) does not apply, but the party putting forward the affidavit[GL] may not recover the additional cost of making it from any other party unless the court orders otherwise.

Effect of rule—An affidavit is defined in the Glossary as "a written, sworn statement of evidence". **32.15.1**

The expectation is that there will be greater reliance on evidence in writing other than affidavits and that the circumstances in which parties are obliged to prepare and file affidavits in the course of civil proceedings will be reduced. Where possible, evidence in writing should be given in witness statement form. Although the voluntary use of affidavit evidence is permitted at hearings other than the trial the potential costs penalty is explicit (r.32.15(2)). However, affidavits may be required by order of the court or by Practice Direction. Further, affidavits should be used where any enactments relating specifically to the proceedings in hand require them to be used. See further Practice Direction (Written Evidence), paras 1.4 *et seq.* (see para. 32PD–001, below). The court may give a direction that the evidence shall be given by affidavit of its own initiative or on the application of a party (*ibid.*, para. 1.6).

Former RSC, O.41 contained detailed rules as to affidavits and these were adopted with modifications in county court proceedings by CCR, O.20, r.10. Much of what used to be expressed in rule form is now reduced to practice directions.

Service of affidavit—Where appropriate the procedures relating to witness statements apply to affidavits used in lieu of witness statements. In particular, the rules as to the service of witness statements contained in r.32.4 apply where evidence is to be given by affidavit instead of by witness statement. See "Service of witness statement" in notes following r.32.4. In a number of procedural contexts, special rules obtain as to the service of witness statements where particular applications are made, *e.g.* r.24.5 (Evidence for the purposes of a summary judgment hearing). By operation of r.32.15(3), such special rules apply to the service of affidavits where a witness chooses to give evidence by affidavit instead of a witness statement. **32.15.2**

Filing of affidavit—Formerly, provisions as to the filing of affidavits were found in RSC, O.41, r.9 and CCR, O.20, r.10(2) and elsewhere. Under the CPR, the court may give directions as to whether or not affidavits are to be filed (r.32.4(3)(b)). For practice as to filing of affidavits, see Practice Direction (Written Evidence), para. 10 (see para. 32PD–003, below). **32.15.3**

Form of affidavits

32.16 An affidavit[GL] must comply with the requirements set out in the relevant practice direction. **32.16**

Effect of rule—Previously, provisions as to the form of affidavits were contained in RSC, O.45, r.1 and CCR, O.29, r.10. For form and swearing of affidavits, see further Practice Direction (Written Evidence), paras 2 *et seq.* and Annex 1 (see paras 32PD–002 and 32PD–006, below). **32.16.1**

Defects in affidavits—Where an affidavit or an exhibit to an affidavit is defective, in the sense that it does not conform with the provisions of Pt 32 or the supplementary practice direction, the consequences referred to in Practice Direction (Written Evidence), paras 25.1 and 25.2 follow (see para. 32PD–005, below). **32.16.2**

Alterations to affidavits—For practice, see Practice Direction (Written Evidence), para. 8 (see para. 32PD–002, below). **32.16.3**

Affidavit made outside the jurisdiction

32.17 A person may make an affidavit[GL] outside the jurisdiction in accordance with— **32.17**

(a) this Part; or
(b) the law of the place where he makes the affidavit[GL].

32.17.1 **Effect of rule**—The former rules as to the swearing of affidavits outside the jurisdiction contained in RSC, O.41, r.12 and elsewhere were unnecessarily complicated (see SCP 1999, Vol. 1, para. 41/12/1). In a given case, ascertaining the place where the affidavit was made should not prove too difficult; where it is necessary to do so, ascertaining whether an affidavit conforms with the law of the place where made may require proof of the relevant foreign law.

Notice to admit facts

32.18 **32.18**—(1) A party may serve notice on another party requiring him to admit the facts, or the part of the case of the serving party, specified in the notice.

(2) A notice to admit facts must be served no later than 21 days before the trial.

(3) Where the other party makes any admission in response to the notice the admission may be used against him only—

(a) in the proceedings in which the notice to admit is served; and

(b) by the party who served the notice.

(4) The court may allow a party to amend or withdraw any admission made by him on such terms as it thinks just.

32.18.1 **Effect of rule**—Formerly, notices to admit facts were dealt with in RSC, O.27, r.2 and CCR, O.20, r.2 . Under the former rules the time limits for service differed; it is now fixed at 21 days. For effect of admission in response to notice to admit, see SCP 1999, Vol. 1, para. 27/2/2.

32.18.2 **Costs where failure to admit facts**—Provisions as to the costs implications for a party who failed to admit facts where he ought to have done were found in RSC, O.62, r.6(7) and CCR, O.20, r.2(2). See now CPR, r.44.3 (Court's discretion and circumstances to be taken into account when exercising discretion as to costs) and r.44.4. (Factors to be taken into account in deciding the amount of costs.)

Notice to admit or produce documents

32.19 **32.19**—(1) A party shall be deemed to admit the authenticity of a document disclosed to him under Part 31 (disclosure and inspection of documents) unless he serves notice that he wishes the document to be proved at trial.

(2) A notice to prove a document must be served—

(a) by the latest date for serving witness statements; or

(b) within 7 days of disclosure of the document,

whichever is later.

32.19.1 **Effect of rule**—The former rules as to notices to admit documents were RSC, O.27, r.5 and CCR, O.20, r.3. Formerly, these rules also dealt with notices requiring production of documents at trial. Rule 32.19 is confined to notices to admit the authenticity of documents, and so the heading to the rule is misleading.

This rule differs from its predecessors in that now a party will be deemed to admit the authenticity of documents disclosed to him unless he serves notice that he wishes the document to be proved at trial. (It is not incumbent on the disclosing party to seek an admission of authenticity.)

PRACTICE DIRECTION—WRITTEN EVIDENCE

This Practice Direction supplements CPR Part 32

Evidence in General

32PD–001 **1.1** Rule 32.2 sets out how evidence is to be given and facts are to be proved.

1.2 Evidence at a hearing other than the trial should normally be given by witness statement[1] (see paragraph 17 onwards). However a witness may give evidence by affidavit if he wishes to do so[2] (and see paragraph 1.4 below).

[1] See rule 32.6(1).
[2] See rule 32.15(2).

1.3 Statements of case (see paragraph 26 onwards) and application notices[3] may also be used as evidence provided that their contents have been verified by a statement of truth.[4]

(For information regarding evidence by deposition see Part 34 and the practice direction which supplements it.)

1.4 Affidavits must be used as evidence in the following instances—

(1) where sworn evidence is required by an enactment,[5] Statutory Instrument, rule,[6] order or practice direction,

(2) in any application for a search order, a freezing injunction, or an order requiring an occupier to permit another to enter his land, and

(3) in any application for an order against anyone for alleged contempt of court.

1.5 If a party believes that sworn evidence is required by a court in another jurisdiction for any purpose connected with the proceedings, he may apply to the court for a direction that evidence shall be given only by affidavit on any pre-trial applications.

1.6 The court may give a direction under rule 32.15 that evidence shall be given by affidavit instead of or in addition to a witness statement or/statement of case—

(1) on its own initiative, or

(2) after any party has applied to the court for such a direction.

1.7 An affidavit, where referred to in the Civil Procedure Rules or a practice direction, also means an affirmation unless the context requires otherwise.

Affidavits

Deponent

2. A deponent is a person who gives evidence by affidavit or affirmation. **32PD–002**

Heading

3.1 The affidavit should be headed with the title of the proceedings (see paragraph 4 of the practice direction supplementing Part 7 and paragraph 7 of the practice direction supplementing Part 20); where the proceedings are between several parties with the same status it is sufficient to identify the parties as follows:

	Number:
A.B. (and others)	Claimants/Applicants
C.D. (and others)	Defendants/Respondents (as appropriate)

3.2 At the top right hand corner of the first page (and on the backsheet) there should be clearly written—

(1) the party on whose behalf it is made,

(2) the initials and surname of the deponent,

(3) the number of the affidavit in relation to that deponent,

(4) the identifying initials and number of each exhibit referred to, and

(5) the date sworn.

Body of Affidavit

4.1 The affidavit must, if practicable, be in the deponent's own words, the affidavit should be expressed in the first person and the deponent should—

(1) commence "I (*full name*) of (*address*) state on oath ...",

[3] See Part 23 for information about making an application.

[4] Rule 32.6(2) and see Part 22 for information about the statement of truth.

[5] See, e.g., sec. 3(5)(a) of the Protection from Harassment Act 1997.

[6] See, e.g., RSC, O.115, rr.(2B), (14) and others (Confiscation and Forfeiture in Connection with Criminal Proceedings) and RSC, O.110, r.(3) (Environmental Control Proceedings—injunctions "in rem" against unknown Defendant).

(2) if giving evidence in his professional, business or other occupational capacity, give the address at which he works in (1) above, the position he holds and the name of this firm or employer,

(3) give his occupation or, if he has none, his description, and

(4) state if he is a party to the proceedings or employed by a party to the proceedings, if it be the case.

4.2 An affidavit must indicate—

(1) which of the statements in it are made from the deponent's own knowledge and which are matters of information or belief, and

(2) the source for any matters of information or belief.

4.3 Where a deponent—

(1) refers to an exhibit or exhibits, he should state "there is now shown to me marked "..." the (*description of exhibit*)", and

(2) makes more than one affidavit (to which there are exhibits) in the same proceedings, the numbering of the exhibits should run consecutively throughout and not start again with each affidavit.

Jurat

5.1 The jurat of an affidavit is a statement set out at the end of the document which authenticates the affidavit.

5.2 It must—

(1) be signed by all deponents,

(2) be completed and signed by the person before whom the affidavit was sworn whose name and qualification must be printed beneath his signature,

(3) contain the full address of the person before whom the affidavit was sworn, and

(4) follow immediately on from the text and not to be put on a separate page.

Format of Affidavits

6.1 An affidavit should—

(1) be produced on durable quality A.4 paper with a 3.5 cm margin,

(2) be fully legible and should normally be typed on one side of the paper only,

(3) where possible, be bound securely in a manner which would not hamper filing, or otherwise each page should be endorsed with the case number and should bear the initials of the deponent and of the person before whom it was sworn,

(4) have the pages numbered consecutively as a separate document (or as one of several documents contained in a file),

(5) be divided into numbered paragraphs,

(6) have all numbers, including dates, expressed in figures, and

(7) give in the margin the reference to any document or documents mentioned.

6.2 It is usually convenient for an affidavit to follow the chronological sequence of events or matters dealt with; each paragraph of an affidavit should as far as possible be confined to a distinct portion of the subject.

Inability of Deponent to read or sign Affidavit

7.1 Where an affidavit is sworn by a person who is unable to read or sign it, the person before whom the affidavit is sworn must certify in the jurat that—

(1) he read the affidavit to the deponent,

(2) the deponent appeared to understand it, and

(3) the deponent signed or made his mark, in is presence.

7.2 If that certificate is not included in the jurat, the affidavit may not be used in evidence unless the court is satisfied that it was read to the deponent and that he appeared to understand it. Two versions of the form of jurat with the certificate are set out in Annex 1 to this practice direction.

Alterations to Affidavits

8.1 Any alteration to an affidavit must be initialled by both the deponent and the person before whom the affidavit was sworn.

8.2 An affidavit which contains an alteration that has not been initialled may be filed or used in evidence only with the permission of the court.

Who may administer oaths and take Affidavits

9.1 Only the following may administer oaths and take affidavits; **32PD–003**

(1) Commissioners for oaths[7];

(2) Practising Solicitors,[8]

(3) other persons specified by Statute,[9]

(4) certain officials of the Supreme Court,[10]

(5) a Circuit Judge or District Judge,[11]

(6) any justice of the peace,[12] and

(7) certain officials of any County Court appointed by the Judge of that court for the purpose.[13]

9.2 An affidavit must be sworn before a person independent of the parties or their representatives.

Filing of Affidavits

10.1 If the court directs that an affidavit is to be filed,[14] it must be filed in the Court or Division, or Office or Registry of the Court or Division where the action in which it was or is to be used, is proceeding or will proceed.

10.2 Where an affidavit is in a foreign language;

(1) the party wishing to rely on it

(a) must have it translated, and

(b) must file the foreign language affidavit with the court, and

(2) the translator must make and file with the court an affidavit verifying the translation and exhibiting both the translation and a copy of the foreign language affidavit.

Exhibits

Manner of Exhibiting Documents

11.1 A document used in conjunction with an affidavit should be—

(1) produced to and verified by the deponent, and remain separate from the affidavit, and

(2) identified by a declaration of the person before whom the affidavit was sworn.

11.2 The declaration should be headed with the name of the proceedings in the same way as the affidavit.

[7] Commissioner for Oaths Act 1889 and 1891.
[8] S.81 of the Solicitors Act 1974.
[9] S.65 of the Administration of Justice Act 1985 s.113 of the Courts and Legal Services Act 1990 and the Commissioners for Oaths (Prescribed Bodies) Regulations 1994 and 1995 .
[10] S.2 of the Commissioners for Oaths Act 1889.
[11] S.58 of the County Courts Act 1984.
[12] S.58 as above.
[13] S.58 as above.
[14] Rules 32.1(3) and 32.4(3)(b).

11.3 The first page of each exhibit should be marked—
(1) as in paragraph 3.2 above, and
(2) with the exhibit mark referred to in the affidavit.

Letters

12.1 Copies of individual letters should be collected together and exhibited in a bundle or bundles. They should be arranged in chronological order with the earliest at the top, and firmly secured.

12.2 When a bundle of correspondence is exhibited, the exhibit should have a front page attached stating that the bundle consists of original letters and copies. They should be arranged and secured as above and numbered consecutively.

Other documents

13.1 Photocopies instead of original documents may be exhibited provided the originals are made available for inspection by the other parties before the hearing and by the judge at the hearing.

13.2 Court documents must not be exhibited (official copies of such documents prove themselves).

13.3 Where an exhibit contains more than one document, a front page should be attached setting out a list of the documents contained in the exhibit; the list should contain the dates of the documents.

Exhibits other than documents

14.1 Items other than documents should be clearly marked with an exhibit number or letter in such a manner that the mark cannot become detached from the exhibit.

14.2 Small items may be placed in a container and the container appropriately marked.

General provisions

15.1 Where an exhibit contains more than one document—
(1) the bundle should not be stapled but should be securely fastened in a way that does not hinder the reading of the documents, and
(2) the pages should be numbered consecutively at bottom centre.

15.2 Every page of an exhibit should be clearly legible; typed copies of illegible documents should be included, paginated with "a" numbers.

15.3 Where affidavits and exhibits have become numerous, they should be put into separate bundles and the pages numbered consecutively throughout.

15.4 Where on account of their bulk the service of exhibits or copies of exhibits on the other parties would be difficult or impracticable, the directions of the court should be sought as to arrangements for bringing the exhibits to the attention of the other parties and as to their custody pending trial.

Affirmations

16. All provisions in this or any other practice direction relating to affidavits apply to affirmations with the following exceptions—
(1) the deponent should commence "I (*name*) of (*address*) do solemnly and sincerely affirm . . .", and
(2) in the Jurat the word "sworn" is replaced by the word "affirmed".

Witness Statements

Heading

32PD–004 **17.1** The witness statement should be headed with the title of the proceedings (see paragraph 4 of the practice direction supplementing Part 7 and paragraph 7 of the practice direction supplementing Part 20); where the proceedings are between several parties with the same status it is sufficient to identify the parties as follows:

	Number:
A.B. (and others)	Claimants/Applicants
C.D. (and others)	Defendants/Respondents (as appropriate)

17.2 At the top right hand corner of the first page there should be clearly written—

(1) the party on whose behalf it is made,
(2) the initials and surname of the witness,
(3) the number of the statement in relation to that witness,
(4) the identifying initials and number of each exhibit referred to, and
(5) the date the statement was made.

Body of Witness Statement

18.1 The witness statement must, if practicable, be in the intended witness's own words, the statement should be expressed in the first person and should also state—

(1) the full name of the witness,
(2) his place of residence or, if he is making the statement in his professional, business or other occupational capacity, the address at which he works, the position he holds and the name of his firm or employer,
(3) his occupation, or if he has none, his description, and
(4) the fact that he is a party to the proceedings or is the employee of such a party if it be the case.

18.2 A witness statement must indicate—

(1) which of the statements in it are made from the witness's own knowledge and which are matters of information or belief, and
(2) the source for any matters of information or belief.

18.3 An exhibit used in conjunction with a witness statement should be verified and identified by the witness and remain separate from the witness statement.

18.4 Where a witness refers to an exhibit or exhibits, he should state "I refer to the (*description of exhibit*) marked "..." ".

18.5 The provisions of paragraphs 11.3 to 15.4 (exhibits) apply similarly to witness statements as they do to affidavits.

18.6 Where a witness makes more than one witness statement to which there are exhibits, in the same proceedings, the numbering of the exhibits should run consecutively throughout and not start again with each witness statement.

Format of Witness Statement

19.1 A witness statement should—

(1) be produced on durable quality A.4 paper with a 3.5 cm margin,
(2) be fully legible and should normally be typed on one side of the paper only,
(3) where possible, be bound securely in a manner which would not hamper filing, or otherwise each page should be endorsed with the case number and should bear the initials of the witness,
(4) have the pages numbered consecutively as a separate statement (or as one of several statements contained in a file),
(5) be divided into numbered paragraphs,
(6) have all numbers, including dates, expressed in figures, and
(7) give in the margin the reference to any document or documents mentioned.

19.2 It is usually convenient for a witness statement to follow the chronological sequence of the events or matters dealt with, each paragraph of a witness statement should as far as possible be confined to a distinct portion of the subject.

Statement of Truth

20.1 A witness statement is the equivalent of the oral evidence which that witness would, if called, give in evidence; it must include a statement by the intended witness that he believes the facts in it are true.[15]

20.2 To verify a witness statement the statement of truth is as follows:

"I believe that the facts stated in this witness statement are true."

20.3 Attention is drawn to rule 32.14 which sets out the consequences of verifying a witness statement containing a false statement without an honest belief in its truth.

Inability of Witness to read or sign Statement

32PD–005 **21.1** Where a witness statement is made by a person who is unable to read or sign the witness statement, it must contain a certificate made by an authorised person.

21.2 An authorised person is a person able to administer oaths and take affidavits but need not be independent of the parties or their representatives.

21.3 The authorised person must certify—

(1) that the witness statement has been read to the witness,

(2) that the witness appeared to understand it and approved its content as accurate,

(3) that the declaration of truth has been read to the witness,

(4) that the witness appeared to understand the declaration and the consequences of making a false witness statement, and

(5) that the witness signed or made his mark in the presence of the authorised person.

21.4 The form of the certificate is set ouf at Annex 2 to this Practice Direction.

Alterations to Witness Statements

22.1 Any alteration to a witness statement must be initialled by the person making the statement or by the authorised person where appropriate (see paragraph 21).

22.2 A witness statement which contains an alteration that has not been initialled may be used in evidence only with the permission of the court.

Filing of Witness Statements

23.1 If the court directs that a witness statement is to be filed,[16] it must be filed in the Court or Division, or Office or Registry of the Court or Division where the action in which it was or is to be used, is proceeding or will proceed.

23.2 Where the court has directed that a witness statement in a foreign language is to be filed—

(1) the party wishing to rely on it must:

(a) have it translated and

(b) file the foreign language witness statement with the court, and

(2) the translator must make and file with the court an affidavit verifying the translation and exhibiting both the translation and a copy of the foreign language witness statement.

Certificate of court officer

24.1 Where the court has ordered that a witness statement is not to be open to inspection by the public[17] or that words or passages in the statement are not

[15] See Part 22 for information about the statement of truth.
[16] Rule 32.4(3)(b) .
[17] Rule 32.13(2) .

to be open to inspection[18] the court officer will so certify on the statement and make any deletions directed by the court under rule 32.13(4).

Defects in affidavits, witness statements and exhibits

25.1 Where—
(1) an affidavit
(2) a witness statement, or
(3) an exhibit to either an affidavit or a witness statement
does not comply with Part 32 or this practice direction in relation to its form, the court may refuse to admit it as evidence and may refuse to allow the costs arising from its preparation.

25.2 Permission to file a defective affidavit or witness statement or to use a defective exhibit may be obtained from a Judge[19] in the court where the case is proceeding.

Statement of Case

26.1 A statement of case may be used as evidence in an interim application provided it is verified by a statement of truth.[20] **32PD–006**

26.2 To verify a statement of case the statement of truth should be set out as follows:

> "[I believe] [the (party on whose behalf the statement of case is being signed) believes] that the facts stated in the statement of case are true."

26.3 Attention is drawn to rule 32.14 which sets out the consequences of verifying a witness statement containing a false statement without an honest belief in its truth.

(For information regarding statements of truth see Part 22 and the practice direction which supplements it.)

(Practice directions supplementing Parts 7, 9 and 17 provide further information concerning statements of case.)

Annex 1

Certificate to be used where a deponent to an affidavit is unable to read or sign it

Sworn at . . . this . . . day of . . . Before me, I having first read over the contents of this affidavit to the deponent [*if there are exhibits, add* "and explained the nature and effect of the exhibits referred to in it"] who appeared to understand it and approved its content as accurate, and made his mark on the affidavit in my presence.

Or, (after, *Before me*) the witness to the mark of the deponent having been first sworn that he had read over etc. (*as above*) and that he saw him make his mark on the affidavit. (*Witness must sign.*)

Certificate to be used where a deponent to an affirmation is unable to read or sign it

Affirmed at . . . this . . . day of . . . Before me, I having first read over the contents of this affirmation to the deponent [*if there are exhibits, add* "and explained the nature and effect of the exhibits referred to in it"] who appeared to understand it and approved its content as accurate, and made his mark on the affirmation in my presence.

Or, (after, *Before me*) the witness to the mark of the deponent having been first sworn that he had read over etc. (*as above*) and that he saw him make his mark on the affirmation. (*Witness must sign.*)

[18] Rule 32.13(4).
[19] Rule 2.3(1); definition of Judge.
[20] See rule 32.6(2)(a).

Annex 2

Certificate to be used where a witness is unable to read or sign a witness statement

I certify that I [*name and address of authorised person*] have read over the contents of this witness statement and the declaration of truth to the witness [*if there are exhibits, add* "and explained the nature and effect of the exhibits referred to in it"] who appeared to understand (a) the statement and approved its content as accurate and (b) the declaration of truth and the consequences of making a false witness statement, and made his mark in my presence.

PART 33

Miscellaneous Rules About Evidence

Contents 33.0.1

Editorial Introduction

The rules in this Part replace with modifications those formerly found in RSC, O.38, rr.5, 7 and 11 and rr.20 to 23, and in CCR, O.20, rr.14 to 17 and r.25. Rules 33.1 to 33.5 deal with the adducing of hearsay evidence. The remaining three rules deal with matters which, though not unimportant, may be regarded as "miscellaneous". 33.0.2

The law as to hearsay in civil proceedings was reformed by the Civil Evidence Act 1995. This Act implemented proposals made by the Law Commission (see "The Hearsay Rule in Civil Proceedings" Law Com. No. 216, Cm 2321, 1993). As a result of this reform, rules of court in the RSC and the CCR as to the adducing of hearsay were substantially simplified.

The rules in this Part do not apply to cases allocated to the small claims track (r.27.2(1)(d)).

The Civil Evidence Act 1995, s.1(1) states that, in civil proceedings, evidence shall not be excluded on the ground that it is "hearsay" in the sense that hearsay is defined in s.1(2) of the Act. Subsequent sections in the Act constitute a legislative scheme stipulating the circumstances in which, and the conditions under which, hearsay evidence may be received in evidence. This scheme is complemented by the rules of court found in this Part. The power to make rules of court given by the Civil Procedure Act 1997, s.1(2) and Sched. 1 includes the power to make "such provision as may be necessary or expedient for carrying into effect" the provisions of the 1995 Act. Further, the rule-making power in the 1997 Act includes the power to "modify the rules of evidence as they apply to proceedings in any court within scope of the rules" (s.1(2) and Sched. 1, see SCP 1999, Vol. 2, paras 20A–5 and 20A–15).

The legislative scheme laid down by the 1995 Act and the rules in this Part apply in relation to hearsay evidence made admissible by the 1995 Act. The scheme does not apply to hearsay evidence made admissible otherwise, notwithstanding that it may also be admissible under the Act (s.1(4)).

Rules of court consequential upon the 1995 Act were introduced in the RSC and CCR in 1996. It was held that the 1995 Act applies to cases begun on or after Janaury 31, 1997 (*Bairstow v. Queen's Moat, The Times*, October 23, 1997, CA) and that the previous law, including the rules of court in effect before 1996, continued to govern cases begun before that date (for earlier rules, see SCP 1997, paras 38/20 *et seq.*).

Related Sources 33.0.3

- Civil Evidence Act 1995 (see SCP 1999, Vol. 2, para. 21I–1A)
- Rule 27.2(1)(d) (Part 33 not to apply to small claims)
- Part 6 (Service of documents)
- Part 32 (Evidence)
- Part 34 (Depositions and court attendance by witnesses)

Introductory

33.1 In this Part— 33.1

(a) "hearsay" means a statement made otherwise than by a person while giving oral evidence in proceedings which is tendered as evidence of the matters stated; and

(b) references to hearsay include hearsay of whatever degree.

33.1.1 **Definition of "hearsay"**—This rule repeats the definition of "hearsay" given in the Civil Evidence Act 1995, s.1(2) (see SCP 1999, Vol. 2, para. 2I1–18). Under the Civil Evidence Act 1968, the precursor to the 1995 Act, a distinction was drawn between "first-hand" and "second-hand" (or "multiple") hearsay and the circumstances in which hearsay of the latter variety was admissible were more limited than the former. Under the 1995 Act and the rules in this Part "hearsay" includes hearsay "of whatever degree" and therefore includes hearsay of both varieties. (Whether hearsay evidence is "first-hand" or "second-hand" may effect the weight to be given to it, see s.4 of the 1995 Act.)

Notice of intention to rely on hearsay evidence

33.2 **33.2**—(1) Where a party intends to rely on hearsay evidence at trial and either—

(a) that evidence is to be given by a witness giving oral evidence; or
(b) that evidence is contained in a witness statement of a person who is not being called to give oral evidence;

that party complies with section 2(1)(a) of the Civil Evidence Act 1995[1] by serving a witness statement on the other parties in accordance with the court's order.

(2) Where paragraph (1)(b) applies, the party intending to rely on the hearsay evidence must, when he serves the witness statement—

(a) inform the other parties that the witness is not being called to give oral evidence; and
(b) give the reasons why the witness will not be called.

(3) In all other cases where a party intends to rely on hearsay evidence at trial, that party complies with section 2(1)(a) of the Civil Evidence Act 1995 by serving a notice on the other parties which—

(a) identifies the hearsay evidence; and
(b) states that the party serving the notice proposes to rely on the hearsay evidence at trial; and
(c) give the reasons why the witness will not be called.

(4) The party proposing to rely on the hearsay evidence must—

(a) serve the notice no later than the latest date for serving witness statements; and
(b) if the hearsay evidence is to be in a document, supply a copy to any party who requests him to do so.

33.2.1 **Effect of rule**—See former RSC, O.38, r.21 and CCR, O.20, r.15.

The Civil Evidence Act 1995, s.2(1)(a) states that a party proposing to adduce hearsay evidence "in civil proceedings" must notify any other party of that fact. The duty to give notice may be excluded by agreement of the parties and may be waived by the person to whom notice is required to be given (s.2(3)).

Section 2(2)(a) states that provision may be made by rules of court as to the manner in which (including the time within which) the duty to give notice is to be complied with. The provisions in r.33.2 are in exercise of that power and are largely self-explanatory.

Section 2(2)(a) also states that provision may be made by rules of court specifying classes of proceedings or evidence in relation to which the duty to give notice does not apply. The provisions in r.33.3 were made in exercise of this power. By that rule civil proceedings in the form of trials are not excluded. The rules as to notice in r.33.2 are confined to the situation where "a party intends to rely on hearsay evidence at trial". (Under the former rules the requirement to give notice did not apply to evidence which was authorised to be given by or in an affidavit.)

33.2.2 **Giving notice**—Rule 33.2(1) deals with the situation where the hearsay evidence is to be given by a witness called to give oral evidence or in a witness statement of a person who is not being called. In both events, notice is given by serving the witness statement (no separate notice of hearsay is required) and, in the latter event, by, in addition, informing the other parties that the witness will not be called. The witness statements are to be served on the other parties "in accordance with the court's order" (see r.32.4). In terms, there is no duty on the party required to give notice to identify the hearsay, or to indicate the part of the witness statement in which the hearsay is set out; however, where it is not proposed to call the witness, there is a requirement to say why (see former RSC, O.38, r.21(1) and CCR, O.20, r.15(1)).

[1] 1995 c. 38. Section 2 provides that a party proposing to bring hearsay evidence must notify any other party of that fact and, on request give particulars of or relating to the evidence.

Rule 33.2(3) deals with "all other cases". In these cases the party required to give notice must, in doing so, identify the hearsay and state that he proposes to rely on the hearsay evidence at trial. He must give such notice to all other parties and, if the evidence is to be in a document, supply a copy to any party who requests him to do so (r.33.2(4)(b)). (As to proof of statements contained in documents, see Civil Evidence Act 1995, s.8, SCP 1999, Vol. 2, para. 21I–15.)

Whether the case falls under r.33.2(1) or r.33.2(3) notice must be served no later than the latest date for serving witness statements. That date will be fixed by court order.

Failure to give notice of hearsay—A failure to give notice in accordance with s.2 of the 1995 Act and rules of court made thereunder (specifically r.33.2) does not affect the admissibility of the evidence but may be taken into account by the court (a) in considering "the exercise of its powers with respect to the course of proceedings and costs", and (b) as a matter affecting the weight to be given to the evidence in accordance with s.4 (s.2(4)). **33.2.3**

Particulars of hearsay evidence—The Civil Evidence Act 1995, s.2(1)(b) states that, in addition to giving notice, a party proposing to adduce hearsay evidence must give to other parties on request "such particulars of or relating to the evidence as is reasonable and practicable in the circumstances for the purpose of enabling them to deal with matters arising from its being hearsay". Section 2(2)(b) states that provision may be made by rules of court as to the manner in which the duty to give particulars is to be complied with. It may be noted that r.33.2 does not deal expressly with the duty to give particulars upon request. Doubtless, in the ordinary case, if the party proposing to adduce hearsay evidence at trial gives notice in the manner stipulated by the rule, then, not only will that party have complied with the duty to give notice, but also he will have provided particulars to satisfy any request that may be forthcoming from any other party. (Historically speaking, the duty to provide particulars on request pre-dates the mandatory disclosure of witness statements.) However, that will not always be so; where it is not the party upon whom notice of hearsay is served may rely on section 2(1)(b) of the 1995 Act. **33.2.4**

Circumstances in which notice of intention to rely on hearsay evidence is not required

33.3 Section 2(1) of the Civil Evidence Act 1995 (duty to give notice of intention to rely on hearsay evidence) does not apply— **33.3**

(a) to evidence at hearings other than trials;

(aa) to an affadavit or witness statement which is to be used at trial but which does not contain hearsay evidence;

(b) to a statement which a party to a probate action wishes to put in evidence and which is alleged to have been made by the person whose estate is the subject of the proceedings; or

(c) where the requirement is excluded by a practice direction.

Effect of rule—The Civil Procedure Act 1995, s.2(2) states that provision may be made by rules of court specifying classes of proceedings or evidence in relation to which the duty to give notice imposed by s.2(1) on a party proposing to adduce hearsay evidence does not apply. The provisions in r.33.3 are in exercise of this power. **33.3.1**

The duty to give notice does not apply where a party proposes to adduce hearsay evidence at "hearings other than trials"; consequently, no duty arises in relation to interlocutory proceedings.

Power to call witness for cross-examination on hearsay evidence

33.4—(1) Where a party— **33.4**

(a) proposes to rely on hearsay evidence; and

(b) does not propose to call the person who made the original statement to give oral evidence,

the court may, on the application of any other party, permit that party to call the maker of the statement to be cross-examined on the contents of the statement.

(2) An application for permission to cross-examine under this rule must be made not more than 14 days after the day on which a notice of intention to rely on the hearsay evidence was served on the applicant.

Effect of rule—See former RSC, O.38, r.22 and CCR, O.20, r.16. **33.4.1**

Rule 32.5 states that, if a party has served a witness statement and he wishes to rely at trial on the evidence of the witness who made the statement, he must call the witness to give oral evidence unless the court orders otherwise "or he puts in the statement as hearsay evidence". If the party is to put in the statement as hearsay evidence he must comply with the rules in Pt 33.

Rule 33.2 states that, where a party proposes to rely on hearsay evidence at trial he must give notice to all other parties either by serving the witness statement (where the hearsay is contained in a witness statement) (r.33.2(1)) or by hearsay notice (in all other cases) (r.33.2(3)). Where notice is given by service of a witness statement and the party serving the statement does not propose to call the witness at trial he must inform all other parties of his intention in that respect. Where notice is given, not by service of a witness statement but by service of a hearsay notice it will be obvious to the other parties that it is not the intention to call the maker of the statement.

The Civil Evidence Act 1995, s.3 states that rules of court may provide that where a party adduces hearsay evidence of a statement made by a person and does not call that person as a witness, any other party may, with the leave of the court, call that person as a witness and cross-examine him on the statement as if he had been called by the first-mentioned party and as if the hearsay statement were his evidence in chief (see SCP 1999, Vol. 2, para. 21I–10). The provisions in r.33.4 are made in exercise in this rule-making power. The main significance of these provisons is that they enable the party against whom the evidence is adduced to obtain the permission of the court to call the maker of the statement for cross-examination. It should be noted that cross-examination is confined to "the contents of the statement". Application for permission must be made within 14 days after the day on which notice of intention to rely on the hearsay evidence was served.

Former RSC, O.38, r.22(2) and CCR, O.20, r.16(2) said an application to call a witness for cross-examination on hearsay evidence had to be made "on notice to all other parties". Presumably, where permission to cross-examine is sought under r.33.4 copies of the application notice should be served, not just on the party proposing to rely on the hearsay, but on all other parties.

It may be noted that r.32.7(1) provides that, at a hearing other than a trial, where evidence is given in writing (whether hearsay or not), any party may apply to the court for permission to cross-examine the person giving the evidence. If permission is granted but the person in question does not attend for cross-examination his evidence may not be used unless the court gives permission (r.32.7(2)). Presumably, if the evidence of the person who fails to attend is hearsay the court is less likely to give permission for the evidence to be used.

Credibility

33.5 **33.5**—(1) Where a party—

(a) proposes to rely on hearsay evidence; but
(b) does not propose to call the person who made the original statement to give oral evidence; and
(c) another party wishes to call evidence to attack the credibility of the person who made the statement,

the party who so wishes must give notice of his intention to the party who proposes to give the hearsay statement in evidence.

(2) A party must give notice under paragraph (1) not more than 14 days after the day on which a hearsay notice relating to the hearsay evidence was served on him.

33.5.1 **Effect of rule**—See former RSC, O.38, r.23 and CCR, O.20, r.17.

The Civil Evidence Act 1995, s.5(2) (see SCP 1999, Vol. 2, para. 21I–12) states that, where hearsay evidence is adduced and the maker of the original statement, or of any statement relied upon to prove another statement, is not called as a witness, evidence attacking the maker's credibility is admissible. This rule provides that a party who wishes to introduce such evidence must give notice of his intention to the party who proposes to give the hearsay statement in evidence within the time specified. The genesis of s.5(2) and of this rule pre-dates the introduction of rules requiring the mandatory exchange of witness statements. If a party wishes to introduce evidence attacking the credibility of the maker of a hearsay statement he will have to have served on other parties the witness statement of the witness who is going to provide such impeaching evidence.

Evidence tending to prove that the maker of the statement made any other statement inconsistent with it is also admissible for the purpose of showing that he had contradicted himself (s.5(2)). Rule 33.5 does not say that a party who wishes to introduce such evidence must give notice of his intention to the party who proposes to give the hearsay statement in evidence. If a party wishes to introduce evidence of an inconsistent statement he will have to have served on other parties the witness statement of the witness who is going to provide evidence of the inconsistent statement, thereby alerting the party relying on the hearsay of his intentions in this respect.

Use of plans, photographs and models as evidence

33.6 **33.6**—(1) This rule applies to evidence (such as a plan, photograph or model) which is not—

(a) contained in a witness statement, affidavit[GL] or expert's report;
(b) to be given orally at trial; or
(c) evidence of which prior notice must be given under rule 33.2.

(2) This rule includes documents which may be received in evidence without further proof under section 9 of the Civil Evidence Act 1995.[2]

(3) Unless the court orders otherwise the evidence shall not be receivable at a trial unless the party intending to put it in evidence has given notice to the other parties in accordance with this rule.

(4) Where the party intends to use the evidence as evidence of any fact then, except where paragraph (6) applies, he must give notice not later than the latest date for serving witness statements.

(5) He must give notice at least 21 days before the hearing at which he proposes to put in the evidence, if—
(a) there are not to be witness statements; or
(b) he intends to put in the evidence solely in order to disprove an allegation made in a witness statement.

(6) Where the evidence forms part of expert evidence, he must give notice when the expert's report is served on the other party.

(7) Where the evidence is being produced to the court for any reason other than as part of factual or expert evidence, he must give notice at least 21 days before the hearing at which he proposes to put in the evidence.

(8) Where a party has given notice that he intends to put in the evidence, he must give every other party an opportunity to inspect it and to agree to its admission without further proof.

Effect of rule—See former RSC, O.38, r.5. 33.6.1
Unless the court orders otherwise, no plan, photograph or model is receivable at trial unless the party intending to use such material "as evidence of any fact" has given notice to other parties as required by the rule and given them an opportuntiy to inspect it and to agree its admission without further proof. The rule is designed to facilitate the proving of the fact that the plan, photograph or model is what it purports to be and to enable evidence as to this to be dispensed with at trial.

Proof of records of business or public authority—Rule 33.6(2) refers to the Civil Evidence Act 1995, s.9. That section simplifies the manner in which a party may prove that a document is part of the records of a business or public authority (see SCP 1999, Vol. 2, para. 21I–16). A document shall be taken to form part of such a record if there is produced to the court a certificate to that effect signed by an officer of the business or authority to which the records belong. Upon production to the court of such a certificate, no further proof that the document is what it purports to be is required. (The section also provides a simple means for proving the absence of an entry in the records of a business or public authority, s.9(3).) 33.6.2

The section is not concerned with the proof of any facts stated in a document forming part of the records of a business or public authority. Normally, proof of such facts will involve the adducing of documentary hearsay made admissible in evidence by the Civil Evidence Act 1995, s.1. A party wishing to adduce such evidence must give prior notice under r.33.2. The notice and inspection provisions in r.33.6 do not apply to evidence of which prior notice must be given under r.33.3 (r.33.6(c)) but yet the rule "includes a document which may be received in evidence without further proof" under s.9 (r.33.6(2)). The implications of this are not entirely clear. Where a party wishes to adduce documentary hearsay, and the document forms part of the records of a business or public authority, the question arises whether he is required to comply, not only with the notice requirements in r.33.2 but also with the notice and inspection requirements in r.33.6. This may be important because the consequences of failure to give notice are different. The consequence of a failure to give notice under r.33.2 is not that the evidence is inadmissible but that the court may take the failure into account (a) in considering "the exercise of its powers with respect to the course of proceedings and costs", and (b) as a matter affecting the weight to be given to the evidence in accordance with s.4 (s.2(4)). However, a failure to give notice under r.33.6 is that "the evidence shall not be receivable" unless the court orders otherwise (r.33.6(3)). It should also be noted that the court may, having regard to the circumstances of the case, direct that any of the provisions in s.9 do not apply to particular records (s.9(5)). This power might be used, for example, where the court has real doubt as to the genuineness of the certificate

[2] Section 9 of the Civil Evidence Act 1995 provides that documents that form part of the records of a business or public authority, as defined in that section, may be received in evidence without further proof.

produced to the court and decides that further evidence to prove that the document is what it purports to be is required.

Evidence of finding on question of foreign law

33.7 **33.7**—(1) This rule sets out the procedure which must be followed by a party who intends to put in evidence a finding on a question of foreign law by virtue of section 4(2) of the Civil Evidence Act 1972.[3]

(2) He must give any other party notice of his intention.

(3) He must give the notice—

(a) if there are to be witness statements, not later than the latest date for serving them; or

(b) otherwise, not less than 21 days before the hearing at which he proposes to put the finding in evidence.

(4) The notice must—

(a) specify the question on which the finding was made; and

(b) enclose a copy of a document where it is reported or recorded.

33.7.1 **Effect of rule**—See former RSC, O.38, r.7 and CCR, O.20, r.25, and note SCP 1999, para. 38/7/2. For Civil Evidence Act 1972, s.4(2), see SCP 1999, Vol. 2, para. 21H–9.

Evidence of consent of trustee to act

33.8 **33.8** A document purporting to contain the written consent of a person to act as trustee and to bear his signature verified by some other person is evidence of such consent.

33.8.1 **Effect of rule**—See former RSC, O.33, r.11, and note SCP 1999, paras 38/11/1, *et seq.*

PRACTICE DIRECTION—CIVIL EVIDENCE ACT 1995

This Practice Direction Supplements CPR Part 33

33PD–001 **1.** Section 16(3A) of the Civil Evidence Act 1995 (c. 38) (as amended) provides that transitional provisions for the application of the provisions of the Civil Evidence Act 1995 to proceedings begun before 31 January 1997 may be made by practice direction.

2. Except as provided for by paragraph 3, the provisions of the Civil Evidence Act 1995 apply to claims commenced before 31 January 1997.

3. The provisions of the Civil Evidence Act 1995 do not apply to claims—

(a) in which directions have been given, or orders have been made, as to the evidence to be given at the trial or hearing; or

(b) where the trial or hearing began before 26 April 1999.

[3] 1972 c. 30.

PART 34

Depositions and Court Attendance by Witnesses

Contents 34.0.1

Editorial Introduction

Part 34 deals with two separate and distinct topics which would perhaps have been better in two separate Parts as they were under the RSC. One (the attendance of witnesses) is common, important and of relevance to both High Court and county court cases. The other (depositions) is rare and likely to be of practical significance only in substantial cases in the High Court. This editorial introduction deals with both separately. **34.0.2**

Attendance of witnesses—Part 34, rr.34.1 to 34.7, deals with topics formerly covered by RSC, O.38, Pt II and CCR, O.20, Pt III. It was inevitable that the modern jargon of the CPR would abandon the term "subpoena", in use in the High Court and its predecessors since 1467, in favour of the term "witness summons" already in use in the county courts and the Crown Court. A witness summons is used to secure the attendance of the witness at the trial or at a hearing prior to trial; or to require the witness to produce documents to the court at the trial or at a hearing prior to trial (*e.g.* a "*Khanna* hearing", where the witness summons is used merely to obtain documents and prove their authenticity, the witness producing them not being relied on to give any other evidence. The practice is to specify a date for production of the documents which is earlier than the date fixed for the rest of the trial, see *Khanna v. Lovell White Durrant* [1995] 1 W.L.R. 121; [1994] 4 All E.R. 267). **34.0.3**

Part 34 does not deal with penalties for non-compliance with a witness summons. In the High Court disobedience of a *subpoena* (Latin: *sub*, under; *poena*, penalty), and now a witness summons is a contempt of court under RSC, O.52 (which is re-enacted in Schedule 1 to the CPR). In the county courts the penalty is a fine (see section 55 of the County Courts Act 1984; and CCR, O.34 which is re-enacted in Schedule 2 to the CPR).

A witness summons is used not just to secure the attendance of a witness who is reluctant to come to court but also, for example, to enable the witness to produce evidence (*e.g.* to an employer) of the requirement to attend court or to secure priority so that the witness is not summonsed to appear elsewhere on the same day.

Depositions—Before applying for the evidence of a witness to be taken on deposition, consider whether there is a cheaper or better way: there usually is. **34.0.4**

At an examination (see rr.34.8 and 34.9) the evidence of the witness is taken before an "examiner" in the same way as if the witness were giving evidence at the trial. The deposition is then admitted in evidence at the trial. This procedure is necessarily expensive, especially if the witness is abroad. (The CCR contained no provision for depositions of witnesses outside England and Wales. The law was, and is, in s.56 of the County Courts Act 1984: but the former procedural provision, RSC, O.107, r.3 has been repealed; see now r.34.13(3).)

In practice, the taking of depositions outside England and Wales is restricted to substantial High Court cases. Even in such cases consider (as the court will—see the overriding objective in Pt 1) if there is a cheaper way. Three options are:

(1) If a witness statement has been obtained, rely on the statement itself without calling the witness at all (see Pt 33 and Civil Evidence Act 1995, especially r.33.2). If no witness statement has been obtained can an agent be employed to obtain one?

(2) Pay the witness his expenses to attend the trial. With the frequency and availability of modern air travel the cost of the journey and associated expenses is commonly less than that of an examination abroad.

(3) Obtain an order that the witness gives evidence by video link (see r.32.3).

One option, formerly available under the RSC is no longer relevant, namely seeking an order to put the evidence in by affidavit (RSC, O.38, r.2 and CCR, O.20, rr.6 and 7). It used to be said that affidavits, though not cross-examinable, were sworn and had some advantage over a witness statement. If that ever was true it is no longer relevant now that all witness statements must be verified by a statement of truth (see r.22.1).

In addition to depositions taken abroad for use in proceedings in the High Court and (in theory) county courts, Pt 34 also deals with depositions taken in England and Wales for use in the courts of England and Wales. Depositions taken in England and Wales for use in courts abroad pursuant to a letter of request (though mentioned in the Practice Direction which supplements Pt 34) are still governed by RSC, O.70 which is re-enacted in Sched. 1 to the CPR).

Related Sources

34.0.5
- Practice Direction (Depositions and Court Attendance by Witnesses) (see para. 34PD–001)
- Civil Evidence Act 1995
- County Courts Act 1984, ss.55 and 56.
- RSC, O.52 (see Sched. 1 to CPR)
- RSC, O.70 (see Sched. 1 to CPR)
- Part 1 (the Overriding Objective)
- Part 22 (Statement of Truth)
- Part 32 (Evidence)
- Part 33 (Miscellaneous Rules about Evidence)

Forms

34.0.6
- N20—Witness summons (see para. C11–001)
- N21—Order for examination of deponent (see para. C13–001)

Scope of this Part

34.1 **34.1**—(1) This Part provides—

(a) for the circumstances in which a person may be required to attend court to give evidence or to produce a document; and

(b) for a party to obtain evidence before a hearing to be used at the hearing.

(2) In this Part, reference to a hearing includes a reference to the trial.

34.1.1 **Scope of Part 34**—The rule provides for witness summonses and depositions. See "Editorial Introduction" at para. 34.0.2 above.

Witness summonses

34.2 **34.2**—(1) A witness summons is a document issued by the court requiring a witness to—

(a) attend court to give evidence; or

(b) produce documents to the court.

(2) A witness summons must be in the relevant practice form.

(3) There must be a separate witness summons for each witness.

(4) A witness summons may require a witness to produce documents to the court either—

(a) on the date fixed for a hearing; or

(b) on such date as the court may direct.

(5) The only documents that a summons under this rule can require a person to produce before a hearing are documents which that person could be required to produce at the hearing.

"witness summons"—This term, already in use in county courts, has replaced the former term "*subpoena*" in the High Court. Rule 34.2 is clear and is based on CCR, O.20, r.12. A separate witness summons is required for each witness and can require the witness to attend court to give evidence or produce documents to the court or both. 34.2.1

"On such date as the court may direct"—It is clear from r.34.2(4) that a witness can be required to attend not only the trial itself but any other pre-trial hearing. However, permission is required to issue the witness summons if the hearing is not the trial itself (see r.34.3). 34.2.2

Issue of a witness summons

34.3—(1) A witness summons is issued on the date entered on the summons by the court. 34.3

(2) A party must obtain permission from the court where he wishes to—

(a) have a summons issued less than 7 days before the date of the trial;

(b) have a summons issued for a witness to attend court to give evidence or to produce documents on any date except the date fixed for the trial; or

(c) have a summons issued for a witness to attend court to give evidence or to produce documents at any hearing except the trial.

(3) A witness summons must be issued by—

(a) the court where the case is proceeding; or

(b) the court where the hearing in question will be held.

(4) The court may set aside[GL] or vary a witness summons issued under this rule.

"issue of a witness summons"—A separate summons is required for each witness (see r.34.2(3)). Two copies of the witness summons are required; one is for sealing prior to service, the other is retained on the court file. 34.3.1

permission not required—Permission to issue a witness summons is not required provided that the summons is to attend, or produce documents at, the trial itself and the summons is issued 7 days or more before the trial. 34.3.2

permission required—Permission to issue a witness summons is required in the three situations mentioned in r.34.3(2): this includes, for example, a pre-trial hearing whether in private or not. Where r.34.3(2)(a) applies (less than 7 days before trial) see also r.34.5(2). 34.3.3

pre-trial production of non-party's documents—Rule 34.3(2)(b) recognises and gives statutory effect to "*Khanna* hearings" (see *Khanna v. Lovell White Durrant* [1995] 1 W.L.R. 121 referred to in the "Editorial Introduction", at para. 34.0.2 above). A party who wishes to have sight of the documents of a non-party before the trial of the substantive issues can do so by obtaining an order for a witness summons to be served on that party and an order that the witness do then produce the documents at a hearing which is confined to receiving the documents, the subject of the witness summons, the remainder of the trial being adjourned to a date to be fixed. This practice is useful where the witness has no evidence to give other than proving the authenticity of the documents concerned. 34.3.4

"the court may set aside or vary a witness summons"—Applications to set aside a witness summons are made to the district judge or, if the case is in the High Court in London, to the master (*R. v. Investors' Review* [1928] 2 K.B. 644; *Macbryan v. Brooke* [1946] 2 All E.R. 688). On such an application the court is concerned to see that parties do not abuse their privilege of summoning witnesses (*Raymond v. Tapson* (1882) 22 Ch.D. 430, CA, at 435). A witness served with a witness summons cannot have it set aside merely by swearing that he can give no material evidence; but if the court is satisfied that the witness summons has not been issued in good faith for the purpose of obtaining relevant evidence and that the witness named is in fact unable to give relevant evidence, it will set it aside. Such an order does not prejudice the power of the trial judge to order the witness to attend if he thinks his presence is necessary (*R. v. Baines* [1909] 1 K.B. 258). The court will also set aside a witness summons which is oppressive, for example which relates to documents disclosure of which has been refused by the court (*Steele v. Savory* [1891] W.N. 195; 8 T.L.R. 84), or which relates to documents protected by public interest immunity (*Bookbinder v. Tebbit (No. 2)* [1992] 1 W.L.R. 217). 34.3.5

A witness summons (or an application in the nature of such, *e.g.* to produce and show a film) may be set aside (or refused) where it appears that the request is irrelevant, fishing, speculative or oppressive: see *Senior v. Holdsworth ex p. Independent Television News Ltd* [1976] Q.B. 23; [1975] 2 All E.R. 1009, CA.

Witness summons in aid of inferior court or of tribunal

34.4 **34.4**—(1) The court may issue a witness summons in aid of an inferior court or of a tribunal.

(2) The court which issued the witness summons under this rule may set it aside.

(3) In this rule, "inferior court or tribunal" means any court or tribunal that does not have power to issue a witness summons in relation to proceedings before it.

34.4.1 **"inferior court or tribunal"**—This term is defined in r.34.4(3). For a list of the various tribunals which do not have power to issue a witness summons see SCP 1999, Vol. 1, paras 38/19/4 *et seq*. Previously application was to the High Court but, as r.34.4(1) draws no distinction, either the High Court or a county court can issue the witness summons. An application to set aside (see commentary, para. 34.3.5) must be to the court which issued the summons (r.34.4(2)).

Time for serving a witness summons

34.5 **34.5**—(1) The general rule is that a witness summons is binding if it is served at least 7 days before the date on which the witness is required to attend before the court or tribunal.

(2) The court may direct that a witness summons shall be binding although it will be served less than 7 days before the date on which the witness is required to attend before the court or tribunal.

(3) A witness summons which is—

(a) served in accordance with this rule; and

(b) requires the witness to attend court to give evidence;

is binding until the conclusion of the hearing at which the attendance of the witness is required.

34.5.1 **Effect of rule**—Rule 34.5(1) is clear and requires the witness summons to be served at least 7 days before the date on which the witness must attend (RSC, O.38, r.17 and CCR, O.20, r.12 both required service "not less than four days" before trial so the new rule has deliberately extended that period in both the High Court and county courts). For who is to serve, see r.34.6.

Permission is required to issue a witness summons less than 7 days before the date of trial (see r.34.3(2)(a)) and a direction that the witness summons shall be binding pursuant to r.34.5(2) should be obtained at the same time.

34.5.2 **"shall be binding" ... "will be served"**—The use of the future tense in r.34.5(2) clearly envisages that a direction pursuant to that rule should be sought before the witnes summons is served and not retrospectively.

34.5.3 **Duration of witness summons**—Rule 34.5(3), like its predecessor RSC, O.38, r.18, makes it clear that the witness summons continues to have effect until the conclusion of the trial or hearing at which the attendance is required. Thus, a new witness summons is not required if the hearing is adjourned, even if the adjournment is not to the next day. Of course, the trial judge can release the witness at some convenient point after the witness has given evidence. If for any reason the trial is abortive rather than adjourned, for example where a jury disagrees, a fresh witness summons would be required for a new trial.

Who is to serve a witness summons

34.6 **34.6**—(1) A witness summons is to be served by the court unless the party on whose behalf it is issued indicates in writing, when he asks the court to issue the summons, that he wishes to serve it himself.

(2) Where the court is to serve the witness summons, the party on whose behalf it is issued must deposit, in the court office, the money to be paid or offered to the witness under rule 34.7.

34.6.1 **"a witness summons is to be served by the court..."**—Rule 34.6(1) creates a presumption that the court will serve the summons on the witness. Accordingly, r.6.3(2) applies and the court will decide which of the methods of service specified in r.6.2 is to be used. Having regard to the provisions of r.34.5(1) (witness summons to be served at least 7 days before the hearing) it is clearly necessary to issue in sufficient time for the court to effect service. See also r.34.7 and note that where the court is to effect service the money to be paid to the witness must be deposited in court pursuant to r.34.6(2).

How will the court effect service? The Practice Direction supplementing Pt 34 (see para. 34PD–001) says "normally" by first class post. Whether or not service by post is appropriate for a witness summons must depend on the circumstances of the case. If the witness summons is being served for a "non-hostile" reason (*e.g.* to enable a willing witness to obtain time off work or to enable an expert witness to break other commitments—see further "Editorial Introduction" to Pt 34, para. 34.0.2) then service by post is likely to be sufficient. On the other hand, if the witness is refusing to attend and the witness summons is being issued to compel attendance, service by post is likely to be insufficient to impress the importance of his attendance on the witness. Personal service is not only more likely to create the appropriate impression but also more likely, as a consequence, to secure the attendance of the witness.

Thus, although personal service of a witness summons is no longer a prerequisite of the rule (unlike RSC, O.38, r.17) in practice it is likely to be necessary to secure the attendance of a witness who has indicated his reluctance to attend or failed to confirm that he will attend and accordingly the extra cost of personal service is justified and likely to be allowed upon assessment of costs.

Personal service—Unlike RSC, O.38, r.17, personal service is not a prerequisite of r.34.6. But **34.6.2**
see further commentary above.

"indicates in writing ... that he wishes to serve it himself"—The general rule is that the **34.6.3**
court will serve the witness summons. Often there will be good reason for the party issuing the witness summons to arrange personal service through a process server who will explain the summons and tender the necessary money to the witness (see Commentary above and r.34.7).

If the witness summons is being issued (as of right or after permission) through the post it is a simple matter for the letter requesting issue to also request return of the witness summons for personal service. But r.34.6(1) goes further than this. Even a party attending in person at the court office to issue a witness summons must indicate "in writing, when he asks the court to issue the summons, that he wishes to serve it himself".

"money to be paid to the witness"—See r.34.7. **34.6.4**

Right of witness to travelling expenses and compensation for loss of time

34.7 At the time of service of a witness summons the witness must be offered **34.7**
or paid—

(a) a sum reasonably sufficient to cover his expenses in travelling to and from the court; and

(b) such sum by way of compensation for loss of time as may be specified in the relevant practice direction.

Conduct money—The term "conduct money" does not appear in Pt 34 but nor did it appear **34.7.1**
in RSC, O.38 or CCR, O.20. Conduct money is money given to a witness to defray his expenses of coming to, staying at, and returning from the place of trial. A witness was entitled to decline to attend or be sworn until his expenses were paid to him and the court would not entertain an application to commit or fine a witness for non-attendance unless it was proved that conduct money had been paid or tendered to that witness (*Testes qui postulat debet dare eis sumptus competentes*: he who requires witnesses must find their expenses to a sufficient extent). The CCR were explicit: "at the time of service of the summons there shall be paid or tendered to the witness the sum of £6 for a police officer and £8.50 for any other person and, in addition, a sum reasonably sufficient to cover his expenses in travelling to and from the court" (CCR, O.20, r.12(7)). In addition to conduct money the witness was entitled to be paid later for his loss of income incurred in attending court.

Rule 34.7 effects an important change in practice. In addition to "conduct money" (provided for by r.34.7(a)) at the time of service the witness must be offered or paid "such sum by way of compensation for loss of time as may be specified in the relevant practice direction" (r.34.7(b)). (The relevant practice direction is at para. 34PD–001.) Paragraph 3.2 thereof provides for "a sum in respect of the period during which earnings or benefit are lost, or such lesser sum as it may be proved that the witness will lose as a result of his attendance at court in answer to the witness summons" and para. 3.3 of the Practice Direction provides that the sum "is to be based on the sums payable to witnesses attending the Crown Court".

The new rule thus at least has the merit of introducing some consistency between the Crown Court, the High Court and County Courts. The actual amounts payable are prescribed by the Lord Chancellor pursuant to s.19(3) of the Prosecution of Offences Act 1985 and regs 18, 19, 20 and 25 of the Costs in Criminal Cases (General) Regulations 1986. The figures are reviewed annually, usually in April (though there was no change in April 1999). As from May 1, 1998 the maximum amount payable to an "ordinary witness" for financial loss not exceeding 4 hours is

£26.05 and if exceeding 4 hours, £52.10. The subsistence allowance is £2.10 (not exceeding 5 hours); £4.25 (exceeding 5 hours but not exceeding 10 hours) or £9.30 (over 10 hours). The overnight allowance is £63.15 (£68.50 if within a five mile radius of Charing Cross). No one could accuse the regulations of generosity.

See further para. 3 of Practice Direction, at para. 34PD–001.

Evidence by deposition

34.8 **34.8**—(1) A party may apply for an order for a person to be examined before the hearing takes place.

(2) A person from whom evidence is to be obtained following an order under this rule is referred to as a "deponent" and the evidence is referred to as a "deposition".

(3) An order under this rule shall be for a deponent to be examined on oath before—

(a) a judge;

(b) an examiner of the court; or

(c) such other person as the court appoints.

(Rule 34.15 makes provision for the appointment of examiners by the court.)

(4) The order may require the production of any document which the court considers is necessary for the purposes of the examination.

(5) The order must state the date, time and place of the examination.

(6) At the time of service of the order the deponent must be offered or paid—

(a) a sum reasonably sufficient to cover his expenses in travelling to and from the place of examination; and

(b) such sum by way of compensation for loss of time as may be specified in the relevant practice direction.

(7) Where the court makes an order for a deposition to be taken, it may also order the party who obtained the order to serve a witness statement or witness summary in relation to the evidence to be given by the person to be examined.

(Part 32 contains the general rules about witness statements and witness summaries.)

34.8.1 **Purpose of rule**—If a witness cannot attend trial it may be possible to obtain an order under this rule for the examination of the witness. The witness gives evidence before the examiner as if the examination were the trial itself. Thus there is full opportunity for cross-examination. The evidence is reduced to writing and the resulting document (the "deposition") is then received into evidence at the trial.

There are three distinct situations—

(1) Depositions taken in England and Wales for use as evidence in proceedings in courts in England and Wales (see para. 4 of Practice Direction, at para. 34PD–001).

(2) Depositions taken abroad for use as evidence in proceedings before courts in England and Wales (see para. 5 of Practice Direction, at para. 34PD–001).

(3) Depositions taken in England and Wales for use as evidence in proceedings abroad (see para. 6 of Practice Direction, at para. 34PD–001).

34.8.2 **"before a judge; an examiner of the court; or such other person as the court appoints"**—In England and Wales examination is usually before an examiner of the court appointed as such by the Lord Chancellor pursuant to r.34.15. Should there be no suitable examiner in the locality where the examination is to take place, a suitable person (formerly known as a "local special examiner") should be appointed pursuant to r.34.8(3)(c). An examination before a judge will only be ordered in the most exceptional cases and then only with the approval of the judge. Where an examination is sought before a master, the advice of the Senior Master should be sought either directly or through the Master's Secretary.

A party who wishes the examination to take place before a judge rather than an examiner has the substantial burden of making out a sufficient case. Such an order will only rarely be made, for example where the greater authority of the judge is required as the witness is known to be recalcitrant or unruly: see further *Re Brickman's Settlement, Brickman v. Goddard Trustees (Jersey) Ltd (Note)* [1982] 1 All E.R. 336, *sub nom.: Practice Direction (Chancery: Deposition)* [1981] 1 W.L.R. 1560.

34.8.3 **"date, time and place of the examination"**—Anywhere suitable may be used, for example the residence of a witness too ill to attend elsewhere (*Re Bradbrook* (1889) 23 Q.B.D. 226, CA). Rule 34.8(5) requires the order for examination to state the date, time and place of it.

conduct money—Note the requirement of r.34.8(6) to tender travelling expenses and a sum "by way of compensation for loss of time ...". The Practice Direction referred to is at para. 34PD–001; but it does not differentiate between witness summonses and depositions. See further Commentary at para. 34.7.1. **34.8.4**

"witness statement or witness summary"—Note the provisions of r.34.8(7) which replicates normal trial practice by requiring advance service of a witness statement or witness summary of the evidence to be given by the person to be examined: see rr.32.8 and 32.9. **34.8.5**

Evidence by video link—See r.32.3. As an alternative to obtaining a deposition, evidence by video link will be preferable (and probably cheaper) in some cases and has the further advantage that the trial judge will hear the evidence first hand. **34.8.6**

Conduct of examination

34.9—(1) Subject to any directions contained in the order for examination, the examination must be conducted in the same way as if the witness were giving evidence at a trial. **34.9**

(2) If all the parties are present, the examiner may conduct the examination of a person not named in the order for examination if all the parties and the person to be examined consent.

(3) The examiner may conduct the examination in private if he considers it appropriate to do so.

(4) The examiner must ensure that the evidence given by the witness is recorded in full.

(5) The examiner must send a copy of the deposition—

(a) to the person who obtained the order for the examination of the witness; and

(b) to the court where the case is proceeding.

(6) The party who obtained the order must send each of the other parties a copy of the deposition which he receives from the examiner.

"in the same way as if the witness were giving evidence at trial"—The main purpose of taking evidence on examination is to obtain the evidence of the witness as if the witness were giving evidence at trial. The examination takes place in the presence of the examiner, the parties and their counsel and solicitors. Modern trial practice is for a witness statement (if there is one) to stand as evidence in chief and the examiner will follow this practice if it is appropriate to do so. Cross-examination and re-examination follow. The examiner may allow a hostile witness to be treated as such by the party calling him (*Ohlsen v. Terrero* (1875) L.R. 10 Ch. 127). **34.9.1**

"a person not named in the order"—Note the useful provision in r.34.9(2). **34.9.2**

"may conduct the examination in private"—The general rule is that all hearings are in public (r.39.2(1)) but this rule obviously requires exceptions in the case of depositions, for example if examination is taking place at the witness's home or at a nursing home. See further r.39.2(3). Examiners have always had a discretion (*Wright v. Wilkin* (1858) 6 W.R. 643). **34.9.3**

"evidence ... is recorded"—Rule 34.9(4) imposes a duty on the examiner to record the evidence. By arrangement, a shorthand writer may be and usually is employed. Alternatively, an audio recording can be made. Ordinarily the deposition will take the form of a verbatim transcript of question and answer this being the more accurate and convenient way of recording the evidence (see *per* Pennycuick V.-C. in *Lloyds Bank Ltd v. Marcan* [1973] 1 W.L.R. 339 at 348; [1973] 2 All E.R. 359 at 371). The former practice of the deposition being taken down in narrative form, rather than in question and answer form, is no longer followed. **34.9.4**

"In some cases video recordings have been used to record evidence ... for use in English courts" (*per* Evans J. in *J. Barber & Sons v. Lloyds Underwriters* [1987] Q.B. 103) and this practice is likely to grow in popularity (*cf.*, r.32.3—evidence by video link). Para. 43 of the Practice Direction (see para. 34PD–001) requires a written record as well as an audiotape or videotape recording.

Filing and serving of deposition—The examiner has the duty of filing the deposition with the court (r.34.9(5)(b)) and serving a copy on the person who obtained the order for examination (r.34.9(5)(a)): that party must serve other parties (r.34.9(6)). **34.9.5**

Enforcing attendance of witness

34.10 **34.10**—(1) If a person served with an order to attend before an examiner—
(a) fails to attend; or
(b) refuses to be sworn for the purpose of the examination or to answer any lawful question or produce any document at the examination,

a certificate of his failure or refusal, signed by the examiner, must be filed by the party requiring the deposition.

(2) On the certificate being filed, the party requiring the deposition may apply to the court for an order requiring that person to attend, or to be sworn or to answer any question or produce any document, as the case may be.

(3) An application for an order under this rule may be made without notice.

(4) The court may order the person against whom an order is made under this rule to pay any costs resulting from his failure or refusal.

34.10.1 **Effect of rule**—The title to r.34.10 is too wide: it is concerned solely with the failure of a witness to attend for examination and not with failure of a witness to attend in answer to a witness summons (as to which see Editorial Introduction to Part 34 at para. 34.0.2).

An order for the examination of a witness under r.34.8 is not an order on the witness to attend for examination (*Stuart v. Balkis* (1884) 50 L.T. 479). Usually the witness is willing to attend and does attend his examination voluntarily. If he does not attend—or does attend but refuses to be sworn, answer a lawful question or produce any document—the examiner signs a certificate pursuant to r.34.10(1). Thereupon, the party seeking the deposition can apply without giving notice (r.34.10(3)) for an order "requiring that person to attend or be sworn ..., etc." (see r.34.10(2)). If the witness then fails to attend he is in contempt of court: an order for committal can be sought (see RSC, O.52, re-enacted in Sched. 1 to the CPR). Note r.34.10(4) regarding costs.

Use of deposition at a hearing

34.11 **34.11**—(1) A deposition ordered under rule 34.8 may be given in evidence at a hearing unless the court orders otherwise.

(2) A party intending to put in evidence a deposition at a hearing must serve notice of his intention to do so on every other party.

(3) He must serve the notice at least 21 days before the day fixed for the hearing.

(4) The court may require a deponent to attend the hearing and give evidence orally.

(5) Where a deposition is given in evidence at trial, it shall be treated as if it were a witness statement for the purposes of rule 32.13 (availability of witness statements for inspection).

34.11.1 **Effect of rule**—Having obtained a deposition a party is not obliged to use it as evidence. Indeed notice is required (see r.34.11(2) and (3)). There is nothing to prevent any party putting the deposition in evidence ("a party ...", r.34.11(2)) subject to the requirement of notice. A deposition given in evidence is available for inspection in the same way as a witness statement (see r.32.13 applied by r.34.11(5)).

An order pursuant to r.34.11(4) requiring the deponent to attend would be highly unusual. Even if a witness not expected to be available (hence the deposition) is now available, ordinarily the deposition will suffice.

Restrictions on subsequent use of deposition taken for the purpose of any hearing except the trial

34.12 **34.12**—(1) Where the court orders a party to be examined about his or any other assets for the purpose of any hearing except the trial, the deposition may be used only for the purpose of the proceedings in which the order was made.

(2) However, it may be used for some other purpose—
(a) by the party who was examined;
(b) if the party who was examined agrees; or
(c) if the court gives permission.

Effect of rule—The title which has been given to r.34.12 is misleadingly wide. Rule 34.12(1) applies only to a deposition which resulted from an order requiring "a party to be examined about his or any other assets for the purpose of any hearing except the trial". **34.12.1**

Where a person to be examined is out of the jurisdiction—letter of request

34.13—(1) Where a party wishes to take a deposition from a person outside the jurisdiction, the High Court may order the issue of a letter of request to the judicial authorities of the country in which the proposed deponent is. **34.13**

(2) A letter of request is a request to a judicial authority to take the evidence of that person, or arrange for it to be taken.

(3) The High Court may make an order under this rule in relation to county court proceedings.

(4) If the government of a country allows a person appointed by the High Court to examine a person in that country, the High Court may make an order appointing a special examiner for that purpose.

(5) A person may be examined under this rule on oath or affirmation or in accordance with any procedure permitted in the country in which the examination is to take place.

(6) If the High Court makes an order for the issue of a letter of request, the party who sought the order must file—

(a) the following documents and, except where paragraph (7) applies, a translation of them—

(i) a draft letter of request;

(ii) a statement of the issues relevant to the proceedings;

(iii) a list of questions or the subject matter of questions to be put to the person to be examined; and

(b) an undertaking to be responsible for the Secretary of State's expenses.

(7) There is no need to file a translation if—

(a) English is one of the official languages of the country where the examination is to take place; or

(b) a practice direction has specified that country as a country where no translation is necessary.

Effect of rule—Rule 34.13 is based upon former RSC, O.39, r.3. A "letter of request" issues only in the High Court but the High Court can make an order in a county court case (r.34.13(3)) though, in practice the cost is likely to be disportionate in a county court case (see r.1.1(2)(c)). "Letter of request" is defined in r.34.13(2). See further, SCP 1999, Vol. 1, para. 39/3/2. For the procedure to be followed when applying to the Foreign Process section of the Masters' Secretary's Department at the Royal Courts of Justice see SCP 1999, Vol. 1, para. 39/3/10. **34.13.1**

Non-convention countries—See SCP 1999, Vol. 1, paras 39/3/3 and 39/3/7. **34.13.2**

Bilateral Convention countries—See SCP 1999, Vol. 1, para. 39/3/5. **34.13.3**

Hague Convention countries—See SCP 1999, Vol. 1, paras 39/3/6 and 39/3/13. **34.13.4**

Practice Direction—See para. 5 at para. 34PD–001. **34.13.5**

Obtaining evidence for foreign courts, etc.—This topic is not governed by Pt 34 but by RSC, O.70 which is re-enacted in Sched. 1 to the CPR. But see also para. 6 of the Practice Direction at para. 34PD–001. **34.13.6**

Fees and expenses of examiner of the court

34.14—(1) An examiner of the court may charge a fee for the examination. **34.14**

(2) He need not send the deposition to the court unless the fee is paid.

(3) The examiner's fees and expenses must be paid by the party who obtained the order for examination.

(4) If the fees and expenses due to an examiner are not paid within a reasonable time, he may report that fact to the court.

(5) The court may order the party who obtained the order for examination to deposit in the court office a specified sum in respect of the examiner's fees and, where it does so, the examiner will not be asked to act until the sum has been deposited.

(6) An order under this rule does not affect any decision as to the party who is ultimately to bear the costs of the examination.

34.14.1 **Practice Direction**—See Practice Direction—Fees for Examiners of the Court (para. 34BPD–001).

34.14.2 **Effect of rule**—Ultimately the costs of an examination will be dealt with in the same way as other costs of the litigation (r.34.14(6)). But the examiner is entitled to be paid and need not file the deposition with the court under r.34.9(5) unless his fee is paid (r.34.14(2)).

See the Practice Direction at para. 34BPD–001 which sets out how to calculate the fees an examiner may charge.

Examiners of the court

34.15 **34.15**—(1) The Lord Chancellor shall appoint persons to be examiners of the court.

(2) The persons appointed shall be barristers or solicitor-advocates who have been practising for a period of not less than three years.

(3) The Lord Chancellor may revoke an appointment at any time.

(Other relevant rules can be found in Schedule 1, in the following RSC—O.70 (obtaining evidence for foreign court); O.79 (issue of witness summons in relation to criminal proceedings in the High Court).)

34.15.1 **Effect of rule**—Rule 34.15 is self-explanatory. The former RSC, O.39, r.16 enabled the Lord Chancellor to appoint persons as examiners "for a period not exceeding five years at a time" but there is now no statutory period.

Examiners are used on a rota basis. In London the order for examination should be taken to the Rota Clerk, Room E217, Royal Courts of Justice, and will be indorsed with the name of the examiner.

PRACTICE DIRECTION—DEPOSITIONS AND COURT ATTENDANCE BY WITNESSES

This Practice Direction supplements CPR Part 34

Witness Summonses

Issue of Witness Summons

34PD–001 **1.1** A witness summons may require a witness to:

(1) attend court to give evidence,

(2) produce documents to the court, or

(3) both,

on either a date fixed for the hearing or such date as the court may direct.[1]

1.2 Two copies of the witness summons[2] should be filed with the court for sealing, one of which will be retained on the court file.

1.3 A mistake in the name or address of a person named in a witness summons may be corrected if the summons has not been served.

1.4 The corrected summons must be re-sealed by the court and marked "Amended and Re-Sealed".

[1] Rule 34.2(4).

[2] In Practice form N20.

Witness Summons issued in aid of an inferior court or tribunal

2.1 A witness summons may be issued in the High Court or a county court in aid of a court or tribunal which does not have the power to issue a witness summons in relation to the proceedings before it.[3]

2.2 A witness summons referred to in paragraph 2.1 may be set aside by the court which issued it.[4]

2.3 An application to set aside a witness summons referred to in paragraph 2.1 will be heard—

(1) in the High Court by a Master at the Royal Courts of Justice or by a District Judge in a District Registry, and

(2) in a county court by a District Judge.

2.4 Unless the court otherwise directs, the applicant must give at least 2 days notice to the party who issued the witness summons of the application, which will normally be dealt with at a hearing.

Travelling expenses and compensation for loss of time

3.1 When a witness is served with a witness summons he must be offered a sum to cover his travelling expenses to and from the court and compensation for his loss of time.[5]

3.2 If the witness summons is to be served by the court, the party issuing the summons must deposit with the court—

(1) a sum sufficient to pay for the witness's expenses in travelling to the court and in returning to his home or place of work, and

(2) a sum in respect of the period during which earnings or benefit are lost, or such lesser sum as it may be proved that the witness will lose as a result of his attendance at court in answer to the witness summons.

3.3 The sum referred to in 3.2(2) is to be based on the sums payable to witnesses attending the Crown Court.[6]

3.4 Where the party issuing the witness summons wishes to serve it himself,[7] he must—

(1) notify the court in writing that he wishes to do so, and

(2) at the time of service offer the witness the sums mentioned in paragraph 3.2 above.

Depositions

To be taken in England and Wales for use as evidence in proceedings in Courts in England and Wales

4.1 A party may apply for an order for a person to be examined on oath before— **34PD–002**

(1) a judge,

(2) an examiner of the court, or

(3) such other person as the court may appoint.[8]

4.2 The party who obtains an order for the examination of a deponent[9] before an examiner of the court[10] must;

(1) apply to the Foreign Process Section of the Masters' Secretary's Department at the Royal Courts of Justice for the allocation of an examiner,

(2) when allocated, provide the examiner with copies of all documents in the proceedings necessary to inform the examiner of the issues, and

[3] Rule 34.4(1).
[4] Rule 34.4(2).
[5] Rule 34.7.
[6] Fixed pursuant to the Prosecution of Offences Act 1985 and the Costs in Criminal Cases (General) Regulations 1986.
[7] Rule 34.6(1).
[8] Rule 34.8(3).
[9] See rule 34.8(2) for explanation of "deponent" and "deposition".
[10] For the appointment of examiners of the court see rule 34.15.

(3) pay the deponent a sum to cover his travelling expenses to and from the examination and compensation for his loss of time.[11]

4.3 In ensuring that the deponent's evidence is recorded in full, the court or the examiner may permit it to be recorded on audiotape or videotape, but the deposition[12] must always be recorded in writing by him or by a competent shorthand writer or stenographer.

4.4 If the deposition is not recorded word for word, it must contain, as nearly as may be, the statement of the deponent; the examiner may record word for word any particular questions and answers which appear to him to have special importance.

4.5 If a deponent objects to answering any question or where any objection is taken to any question, the examiner must—

(1) record in the deposition or a document attached to it:

(a) the question,

(b) the nature of and grounds for the objection, and

(c) any answer given, and

(2) give his opinion as to the validity of the objection and must record it in the deposition or a document attached to it.

The court will decide as to the validity of the objection and any question of costs arising from it.

4.6 Documents and exhibits must—

(1) have an identifying number or letter marked on them by the examiner, and

(2) be preserved by the party or his legal representative[13] who obtained the order for the examination, or as the court or the examiner may direct.

4.7 The examiner may put any question to the deponent as to—

(1) the meaning of any of his answers or

(2) any matter arising in the course of the examination.

4.8 Where a deponent—

(1) fails to attend the examination, or

(2) refuses to:

(a) be sworn, or

(b) answer any lawful question, or

(c) produce any document,

the examiner will sign a certificate[14] of such failure or refusal and may include in his certificate any comment as to the conduct of the deponent or of any person attending the examination.

4.9 The party who obtained the order for the examination must file the certificate with the court and may apply for an order that the deponent attend for examination or as may be.[15] The application may be made without notice.[16]

4.10 The court will make such order on the application as it thinks fit including an order for the deponent to pay any costs resulting from his failure or refusal.[17]

4.11 A deponent who wilfully refuses to obey an order made against him under Part 34 may be proceeded against for contempt of court.

4.12 A deposition must—

(1) be signed by the examiner,

(2) have any amendments to it initialled by the examiner and the deponent,

[11] Rule 34.8(6).
[12] See rule 34.8(2) for explanation of "deponent" and "deposition".
[13] For the definition of legal representative see rule 2.3.
[14] Rule 34.10.
[15] Rule 34.10(2) and (3).
[16] Rule 34.10(3).
[17] Rule 34.10(4).

(3) be endorsed by the examiner with:
(a) a statement of the time occupied by the examination and
(b) a record of any refusal by the deponent to sign the deposition and of his reasons for not doing so, and
(4) be sent by the examiner to the court where the proceedings are taking place for filing on the court file.

4.13 Rule 34.14 deals with the fees and expenses of an examiner.

Depositions to be taken abroad for use as evidence in proceedings before Courts in England and Wales

5.1 Where a party wishes to take a deposition from a person outside the jurisdiction, the High Court may order the issue of a letter of request to the judicial authorities of the country in which the proposed deponent is.[18]

5.2 An application for an order referred to in paragraph 5.1 should be made by application notice in accordance with Part 23.

5.3 The documents which a party applying for an order for the issue of a letter of request must file with his application notice are set out in rule 34.13(6). They are as follows—
(1) a draft letter of request in the form set out in Annex A to this practice direction,
(2) a statement of the issues relevant to the proceedings,
(3) a list of questions or the subject matter of questions to be put to the proposed deponent,
(4) a translation of the documents in (1), (2) and (3) above unless the proposed deponent is in a country:
(a) of which English is one of the official languages, or
(b) listed at Annex B to this practice direction, unless the particular circumstances of the case require a translation,
(5) an undertaking to be responsible for the expenses of the Secretary of State, and
(6) a draft order.

5.4 The above documents should be filed with the Masters' Secretary in Room E214, Royal Courts of Justice, Strand, London WC2A 2LL.

5.5 The application will be dealt with by the Senior Master of the Queen's Bench Division of the High Court who will, if appropriate, sign the letter of request.

5.6 Attention is drawn to the provisions of rule 23.10 (application to vary or discharge an order made without notice).

5.7 If parties are in doubt as to whether a translation under paragraph 5.3(4) above is required, they should seek guidance from the Foreign Process Section of the Masters' Secretary's Department.

5.8 A special examiner appointed under rule 34.13(4) may be the British Consul or the Consul-General or his deputy in the country where the evidence is to be taken if;
(1) there is in respect of that country a Civil Procedure Convention providing for the taking of evidence in that country for the assistance of proceedings in the High Court or other court in this country, or
(2) with the consent of the Secretary of State.

5.9 The provisions of paragraphs 4.1 to 4.12 above apply to the depositions referred to in this paragraph.

Depositions to be taken in England and Wales for use as evidence in proceedings before courts abroad pursuant to letters of request

6.1 Schedule 1 to Part 50 (RSC Order 70) relating to obtaining evidence for

[18] Rule 34.13(1).

foreign courts applies to letters of request and should be read in conjunction with this part of the practice direction.

6.2 The Evidence (Proceedings in Other Jurisdictions) Act 1975 applies to these depositions.

6.3 Where a foreign court sends a letter of request under which it is proposed that an application to give effect to the request be made by an agent in England or Wales of a party to the foreign proceedings, the application should be made by an application notice (see CPR Part 23) and should be supported by a witness statement or affidavit exhibiting:

(1) the letter of request;

(2) a statement of the issues relevant to the proceedings;

(3) a list of questions or the subject matter of questions to be put to the proposed deponent;

(4) a translation of the documents in (1), (2) and (3) above if necessary; and

(5) a draft order.

6.4 Where the application to give effect to the request is made by the Treasury Solicitor (see RSC Order 70 rule 3), he must provide to the court:

(1) a statement of the issues relevant to the proceedings;

(2) a list of questions or the subject matter of questions to be put to the proposed deponent;

(3) a translation of

(a) the documents in (1) and (2) above and

(b) the letter of request, if necessary; and

(4) a draft order.

6.5 The order for the deponent to attend and be examined together with the evidence upon which the order was made must be served on the deponent.

6.6 Attention is drawn to the provisions of rule 23.10 (application to vary or discharge an order made without notice).

6.7 Arrangements for the examination to take place at a specified time and place before an examiner of the court or such other person as the court may appoint shall be made by the applicant for the order (*i.e.* the agent referred to in paragraph 6.3 or the Treasury Solicitor) and approved by the Senior Master.

6.8 The provisions of paragraph 4.2 to 4.12 apply to the depositions referred to in this paragraph, except that the examiner must send the deposition to the Senior Master.

(For further information about evidence see Part 32 and the practice direction which supplements it.)

Annex A

Draft Letter of Request

34PD–003 To the Competent Judicial Authority of
in the of

I [*name*] Senior Master of the Queen's Bench Division of the Supreme Court of England and Wales respectfully request the assistance of your court with regard to the following matters.

1. A claim is now pending in the Division of the High Court of Justice in England and Wales entitled as follows
[*set out full title and claim number*]
in which [*name*] of [*address*] is the claimant and [*name*] of [*address*] is the defendant.

2. The names and addresses of the representatives or agents of [*set out names and addresses of representatives of the parties*].
3. The claim by the claimant is for:
   (a) [*set out the nature of the claim*]
   (b) [*the relief sought, and*]
   (c) [*a summary of the facts.*]
4. It is necessary for the purposes of justice and for the due determination of the matters in dispute between the parties that you cause the following witnesses, who are resident within your jurisdiction, to be examined. The names and addresses of the witnesses are as follows:

5. The witnesses should be examined on oath or if that is not possible within your laws or is impossible of performance by reason of the internal practice and procedure of your court or by reason of practical difficulties, they should be examined in accordance with whatever procedure your laws provide for in these matters.
6. Either/
   The witnesses should be examined in accordance with the list of questions annexed hereto.
   Or/
   The witnesses should be examined regarding [*set out full details of evidence sought*]
   N.B. Where the witness is required to produce documents, these should be clearly identified.
7. I would ask that you cause me, or the agents of the parties (if appointed), to be informed of the date and place where the examination is to take place.
8. Finally, I request that you will cause the evidence of the said witnesses to be reduced into writing and all documents produced on such examinations to be duly marked for identification and that you will further be pleased to authenticate such examinations by the seal of your court or in such other way as is in accordance with your procedure and return the written evidence and documents produced to me addressed as follows:

   Senior Master of the Queen's Bench Division
   Royal Courts of Justice
   Strand
   London WC2A 2LL
   England

Annex B

Countries where the translation referred to in paragraph 5.3(4) above should not be required:

Australia
Canada (other than Quebec)
Holland
New Zealand
The United States of America

PRACTICE DIRECTION—FEES FOR EXAMINERS OF THE COURT

This Practice Direction supplements CPR Part 34

Scope

34BPD–001 **1.1** This practice direction sets out—

(1) how to calculate the fees an examiner of the court ("an examiner") may charge; and

(2) the expenses he may recover.

(CPR Rule 34.8(3)(b) provides that the court may make an order for evidence to be obtained by the examination of a witness before an examiner of the court.)

1.2 The party who obtained the order for the examination must pay the fees and expenses of the examiner.

(CPR rule 34.14 permits an examiner to charge a fee for the examination and contains other provisions about his fees and expenses, and rule 34.15 provides who may be appointed as an examiner of the court.)

The examination fee

2.1 An examiner may charge an hourly rate for each hour (or part of an hour) that he is engaged in examining the witness.

2.2 The hourly rate is to be calculated by reference to the formula set out in paragraph 3.

2.3 The examination fee will be the hourly rate multiplied by the number of hours the examination has taken. For example—

Examination fee = hourly rate × number of hours.

How to calculate the hourly rate—the formula

3.1 Divide the amount of the minimum annual salary of a post within Group 7 of the judicial salary structure as designated by the Review Body on Senior Salaries,[19] by 220 to give "x"; and then divide "x" by 6 to give the hourly rate.

For example—

$$\frac{\text{minimum annual salary}}{220} = x$$

$$\frac{x}{6} = \text{hourly rate}$$

Single fee chargeable on making the appointment for examination

4.1 An examiner of court is also entitled to charge a single fee of twice the hourly rate (calculated in accordance with paragraph 3 above) as "the appointment fee" when the appointment for the examination is made.

4.2 The examiner is entitled to retain the appointment fee where the witness fails to attend on the date and time arranged.

4.3 Where the examiner fails to attend on the date and time arranged he may not charge a further appointment fee for arranging a subsequent appointment.

(The examiner need not send the deposition to the court until his fees are paid—see CPR rule 34.14(2).)

[19] The Report of the Review Body on Senior Salaries is published annually by the Stationery Office.

Examiners' expenses

5.1 The examiner of court is also entitled to recover the following expenses—

(1) all reasonable travelling expenses;

(2) any other expenses reasonably incurred; and

(3) subject to paragraph 5.2, any reasonable charge for the room where the examination takes place.

5.2 No expenses may be recovered under sub-paragraph (3) above if the examination takes place at the examiner's usual business address.

(If the examiner's fees and expenses are not paid within a reasonable time he may report the fact to the court, see CPR Rule 34.14(4) and (5).)

PART 35

EXPERTS AND ASSESSORS

35.0.1 **Contents**

Editorial Introduction

35.0.2 The provisions in Pt 35 cover much the same ground as those formerly found in RSC, O.38, Pt IV.

In the Access to Justice Reports, expert evidence was identified as a major source of problems in the civil justice system (see Interim Report Chap. 23 and Final Report Chap. 13). It was said that the need to engage experts was a source of excessive expense, delay and, in some cases, increased complexity through the excessive or inappropriate use of experts. Concern was also expressed as to the failure of experts to maintain their independence from the parties by whom, they had been instructed. The principal recommendation made in the Access to Justice Reports was that the calling of expert evidence should be subject to the complete control of the court through the exercise of the court's case management powers. This recommendation is carried into effect by the rules relating to the pre-trial directions which the court may give in cases proceeding on the fast track or the multi-track (see Pts 28 and 29 and the Practice Directions supplementing those Pts (see paras 28PD–001 and 29PD–001)). It should be noted that, in addition, under r.32.1 the court has power to control the evidence given by directions as to (a) the issues on which it requires evidence, and (b) the nature of the evidence which it requires to decide those issues, and (c) the way in which the evidence is to be placed before the court.

In small claims the strict rules of evidence do not apply (r.27.8(3)). Further, generally, the provisions in Pt 35 dealing with expert evidence do not apply to small claims (r.27.2(1)(e)). The exceptions are: r.35.1 (Duty to restrict expert evidence), r.35.3 (Experts—overriding duty to the court) and r.35.8 (Instructions to a single joint expert). In small claims, the court has complete control over expert evidence. In such cases, no expert may give evidence, whether written or oral, without the permission of the court (r.27.5).

In the Access to Justice Reports it was recommended that the courts should have a wider power to make use of assessors and that impediments to this should be removed (see Interim Report p. 187 and Final Report p. 151). This recommendation is implemented by r.35.15 (replacing former RSC, O.33, rr.2 and 6 and CCR, O.13, r.11).

Related Sources

35.0.3
- Part 18 (Further Information)
- Part 23 (General Rules About Applications for Court Orders)
- Part 25 (Interim Remedies)
- Part 32 (Evidence)
- Part 33(Miscellaneous Rules About Evidence)
- Part 34 (Depositions and Court Attendance by Witnesses)

- Practice Direction (Experts and Assessors) (see para. 35PD–001)
- Civil Evidence Act 1972 s.2 (Rules of court with respect to expert reports and oral expert evidence) (see SCP 1999, Vol. 2, para. 21H–5)
- Civil Evidence Act 1972, s.3 (Admissibility of expert opinion) (see SCP 1999, Vol. 2, para. 21H–8)
- Supreme Court Act 1981, s.70 (see SCP 1999, Vol. 2, para. 20A–457)
- County Courts Act 1984, s.63 (see SCP 1999, Vol. 2, para. 20A–736)

Duty to restrict expert evidence

35.1 Expert evidence should be restricted to that which is reasonably required to resolve the proceedings. 35.1

Effect of rule—The court may control the evidence by giving directions as to (a) the issues on which it requires evidence, (b) the nature of the evidence which it requires to decide those issues, and (c) the way in which the evidence is to be placed before the court (see r.32.1 and notes thereto). The general power to control evidence may be exercised to exclude evidence that would otherwise be admissible (*ibid*). Rule 35.1 speaks to the parties as well as to the court. It indicates that parties and court alike should seek to restrict the excessive or inappropriate use of expert evidence (see Interim Report p. 185). Other rules seek to enforce this policy (*e.g.* r.35.4 (Court's power to restrict expert evidence)). 35.1.1

The overriding objective of the CPR is to enable the court to deal with cases justly (r.1.1(1)) and this includes, so far as is practicable, accomplishing the objectives listed in r.1.1(2). Some of these objectives are particularly apposite to the regulation of the use made of expert evidence in civil proceedings (*e.g.* saving expense and applying the principle of proportionality). The court must further the overriding objective by "actively managing cases" (r.1.4(1)) and this includes, amongst other things, "considering whether the likely benefits of taking a particular step justifies the cost of taking it" (r.1.4(2)(h)). This, too, is relevant to the use of expert evidence. The particular policy objective underlying r.35.1 is that of reducing the incidence of inappropriate use of experts to bolster cases.

Interpretation

35.2 A reference to an "expert" in this Part is a reference to an expert who has been instructed to give or prepare evidence for the purpose of court proceedings. 35.2

Effect of rule—This recognises a practical distinction between an "expert" and an "expert witness". The relevant consideration is when the expert's duty to the court arises. This is clearly when he is instructed to prepare a report which might be used in the case. Where an expert who has prepared a report other than as evidence and is later asked to be an expert witness the first report is not governed by the same considerations but nevertheless may be a discoverable document. 35.2.1

Expert witnesses—The Civil Evidence Act 1972, s.3 states that, subject to rules of court made in pursuance of that Act, where a person is called as a witness in any civil proceedings, his opinion on any relevant matter on which he is qualified to give expert evidence shall be admissible in evidence. A statement of opinion by him on any relevant matter on which he is not qualified to give expert evidence, if made as a way of conveying relevant facts personally perceived by him is admissible as evidence of what he perceived. In this context, "relevant matter" includes an issue in the proceedings in question (see SCP 1999, Vol. 2, para. 21H–8). 35.2.2

The function of an expert witness is (*inter alia*) to explain words, or terms of science or art appearing on the documents which have to be construed by the court, to give expert assistance to the court (*e.g.* as to the laws of science, or the working of a technical process or system) or to inform the court as to the state of public knowledge with regard to the matters before it (*British Celanese Ltd v. Courtaulds Ltd* (1935) 152 L.T. 537, HL. "The opinion of scientific men upon proven facts may be given by men of science within their own science" (*United States Shipping Board v. Ship St. Albans* [1931] A.C. 632, P.C. In no case is it competent for them to express their opinion upon any of the issues, whether of law or fact, which the court or a jury has to determine (*Crosfield & Sons v. Techno-Chemical Laboratories Ltd* (1913) 29 T.L.R. 378, *per* Neville J.). "However expert evidence may be admissible on the issue of whether the legal test has been breached (except in solicitors' negligence cases), even if that question is the ultimate question in issue or to establish the primary factual matrix on which the court makes its decision as to the legal test to be applied" *per* Jacob J. in *Routestone Ltd v. Minories Finance Ltd* [1997] B.C.C. 180; (1977) 1 E.G.L.R. 123, *per* Jacob J.).

Under former RSC, O.40, r.1 (appointment of court expert) "expert", in relation to any question arising in a court or matter, meant "any person who has such knowledge or experience of or in connection with that question that his opinion on it would be admissible in evidence".

The court has the discretion whether to compel the appearance of expert witness having regard to his connection with the case, where he had other important work which might be disrupted where evidence could be gained from another source of equal authority (*Society of Lloyds v. Clementson (No. 2), The Times,* February 29, 1996). See further Pt 34 (Depositions and court attendance by witnesses).

Experts—overriding duty to the court

35.3 **35.3**—(1) It is the duty of an expert to help the court on the matters within his expertise.

(2) This duty overrides any obligation to the person from whom he has received instructions or by whom he is paid.

35.3.1 **Effect of rule**—In the Interim Report it was said (p. 182) that most of the problems with expert evidence arise because the expert is initially recruited as part of the team which investigates and advances a party's contentions and then has to change roles and seek to provide the independent expert evidence which the court is entitled to expect. In the Final Report it was said (p. 243) that a new approach was required which emphasises the expert's impartiality. Accordingly, it was recommended that rules of court should provide that where an expert is preparing evidence for court proceedings, or is giving evidence in court, his responsibility is to the court impartially on the matters within his expertise. This recommendation is implemented by r.35.3.

It should be remembered that "expert" in this context means an expert who has been instructed to give or prepare evidence for the purpose of court proceedings (r.35.2).

The expert's overriding duty is reinforced by the requirement that his report should be addressed to the court (see "Form and contents of expert's reports" at para. 35.10.2 below).

For duties and responsibilities of expert witnesses, see SCP 1999, Vol. 1, para. 38/4/3.

The case law as to the duties and responsibilities of experts, in relation to the court and to the party was considered by Cresswell J. in *National Justice Compania Naviera S.A. v. Prudential Assurance Co. Ltd (The "Ikarian Reefer")* [1993] 2 Lloyd's Rep. 68. His lordship said (at pp. 81–82) they included the following:

1. Expert evidence presented to the Court should be, and should be seen to be, the independent product of the expert uninfluenced as to the form or content by the exigencies of litigation (*Whitehouse v. Jordan* [1981] 1 W.L.R. 246, HL, at 256 *per* Lord Wilberforce).
2. An expert witness should provide independent assistance to the court by way of objective unbiased opinion in relation to matters within his expertise (see *Pollivitte Ltd v. Commercial Union Assurance Company Plc* [1987] 1 Lloyd's Rep. 379 at 386 *per* Garland J., and *Re J* (1990) F.C.R. 193 *per* Cazalet J. An expert witness in the High Court should never assume the role of an advocate.
3. An expert witness should state the facts or assumption on which his opinion is based. He should not omit to consider material facts which could detract from his concluded opinion (*Re J. supra*).
4. An expert witness should make it clear when a particular question or issue falls outside his expertise.
5. If an expert's opinion is not properly researched because he considers that insufficient data are available then this must be stated with an indication that the opinion is no more than a provisional one (*Re J. supra*). In cases where an expert witness who has prepared a report could not assert that the report contained the truth, the whole truth and nothing but the truth without some qualification that qualification should be stated in the report (*Derby and Co. Ltd v. Weldon (No. 9), The Times,* November 9, 1990, CA *per* Staughton L.J.
6. If, after exchange of reports, an expert witness changes his view on the material having read the other side's expert report or for any other reason, such change of view should be communicated (though legal representative) to the other side without delay and when appropriate to the court.
7. Where expert evidence refers to photographs, plans, calculations, analyses, measurements survey reports or other similar documents, these must be provided to the opposite party at the same time as the exchange of reports.

The requirements of this rule emphasise that it is to the court, that the overriding duty is owed irrespective of who instructed or called the expert. The other duties and responsibilities (*supra*) remain to be fulfilled. See also the requirements as to the contents of an expert's report (r.32.11).

See also *Stanton v. Callaghan*, see para. 35.12.2.

Court's power to restrict expert evidence

35.4 **35.4**—(1) No party may call an expert or put in evidence an expert's report without the court's permission.

(2) When a party applies for permission under this rule he must identify—

(a) the field in which he wishes to rely on expert evidence; and

(b) where practicable the expert in that field on whose evidence he wishes to rely.

(3) If permission is granted under this rule it shall be in relation only to the expert named or the field identified under paragraph (2).

(4) The court may limit the amount of the expert's fees and expenses that the party who wishes to rely on the expert may recover from any other party.

Effect of rule—Under former RSC, O.38, r.4 the court had power to limit the number of expert witnesses who could be called at trial. The court's powers in this respect are now strengthened. 35.4.1

The court has total control over the use of evidence (r.32.1), including expert evidence. The court must restrict it to that which is necessary to resolve the proceedings justly and the court may direct the manner in which the evidence is given (see r.35.5). There should be no expert evidence at all unless it will help the court, and no more than one expert in any one speciality unless this is necessary for some real purpose (Final Report, p. 139).

The options available to the court in giving directions as to expert evidence include the following (see Final Report, p. 140):

(a) directing that no expert evidence is to be adduced at all, or no expert evidence of a particular type or relating to a particular issue;
(b) limiting the number of expert witnesses which each party may call, either generally or in a given speciality;
(c) directing that evidence is to be given by one or more experts chosen by agreement between the parties or, where they cannot agree, chosen by a method stated in r.35.7(3).

The uses which parties are permitted to make of expert evidence may vary depending on the nature of the case management track to which proceedings are allocated. The fact that expert evidence is to be relied on in a case, and the extent of that evidence, may affect the question whether a case is allocated to the fast track or to the multi-track. In small claims, no expert may give evidence, whether written or oral, without the permission of the court (r.27.5). See, further, the provisions as to allocation of a case to an appropriate case management track in Pts 26 to 30 and the Practice Directions supplementing those Parts (see paras 26PD–001 *et seq.*); note also "Court's permission" below.

In certain circumstances, the court may transfer proceedings from the High Court to a county court, or vice versa, from one county court to another, and from a district registry to the Royal Courts of Justice or vice versa. The criteria to be taken into account are stated in r.30.3. In relation to certain of those criteria, the existence of issues requiring expert evidence may be relevant.

Court's permission—Permission to call an expert to testify or to put in evidence an expert's report may be given in the court's own case management directions or in response to an application to the court by a party. It may be anticipated that the court will prompt the parties to give consideration to their intentions regarding the use of expert evidence at an early stage. In the allocation questionnaire the court may request information from the parties on such matters as (1) whether any party will be seeking to adduce expert evidence, if so (2) the name and other details of the expert whom the party wishes to use, and (3) whether any progress has been made towards the preparation of a single report by several experts (r.35.12) or the instruction of a single joint expert (r.35.7). 35.4.2

In cases proceeding on the multi-track, the purpose of the case management conference is to set an agenda for the further progress of the case at the earliest possible stage and to ensure that procedures are followed and costs incurred that are proportionate to the case. This is likely to include exploring with the parties the extent to which the evidence of experts will be needed, the prospects for limiting the number of experts (perhaps to a single or joint expert), and whether it will be necessary for experts to give oral evidence at trial.

In fast track cases, the matters to be dealt with by directions under r.28.2(1) include expert evidence (r.28.3(1)(c)). In such cases, the principle of proportionality dictates that expert evidence should be particularly limited, generally restricting each party to two experts (r.26.6(6)(b)), with single joint experts being used wherever possible (see r.35.7) (Final Report, p. 140).

Identification of expert and field of expertise—The parties are required to help the court in furthering the overriding objective (r.1.3) and this includes helping the court to deal with cases justly and swiftly. It is in the spirit of this requirement that parties at the earliest stage of proceedings should be candid and open and should be prepared to provide their opponents with information as to the identity of experts likely to be relied upon and their disciplines as and when this information is known. 35.4.3

Costs of expert evidence—Rule 35.4(4) states that the court may limit the amount of the expert's fees and expenses that the party who wishes to rely on the expert may recover from any other party. Thus, where the costs of an expert are payable by one party to another, the amount recovered by the receiving party may be less than full costs reasonably incurred. 35.4.4

When exercising its discretion as to costs, the court must have regard to all the circumstances, including the conduct of all the parties (r.44.3(4)(a)). In this context, the "conduct of the parties" would include the unreasonable raising and pursuing of issues requiring expert evidence and any failure to comply with any pre-action protocol relating to such evidence (r.44.3(5)). (Note also r.43.6 (factors to be taken into account in deciding amount of costs).)

In cases proceeding on the fast track, the court's power to award trial costs is limited in accordance with Pt 45 (r.28.2(5)).

In small claims cases, the court may order a party to pay all or part of an expert's fee. Such sum must not exceed the amount specified in the relevant practice direction (r.27.14(3)(d)).

General requirement for expert evidence to be given in a written report

35.5 **35.5**—(1) Expert evidence is to be given in a written report unless the court directs otherwise.

(2) If a claim is on the fast track, the court will not direct an expert to attend a hearing unless it is necessary to do so in the interests of justice.

35.5.1 **Effect of rule**—For form and contents of expert's reports, see Practice Direction (Experts and Assessors), paras 1.1 to 1.6 (see para. 35PD–001); see further notes following r.35.10, below. The general rule is that expert evidence, insofar as it is permitted, is to be given in a written report. The court may order that the expert should give evidence orally. The lifting of the limitation will be considered (and reconsidered) by the court on a case management occasion. The court will have to be satisfied that there is no scope for further minimising the matters in issue between the experts by discussions (r.35.12), written questions (r.35.6) etc., before lifting that limitation.

It is also the general rule that, where a party wishes to use an expert's report at trial, or, having obtained the court's permission, wishes to call the expert to give evidence orally, he must disclose the report to other parties (r.35.13).

The court has wide powers under its general powers of case management to make orders as to the exchange of experts' statements. This may be mutual or sequential. Such order may prescribe the time and date of such exchange and may spell out the consequences of non-compliance (rr.5.1(2) and 5.3). It is to be expected that a court will impose a sensibly rigorous timetable for such matters as may include the exchange of experts' reports and for experts' discussions or meetings as often as may be necessary (having regard to the complexity of a case) as may be necessary in order to agree such matters as may be agreed, and identify matters that cannot be agreed however in that case giving a summary of reasons why not (see r.35.12).

As to the contents of an expert's report, see r.35.10. Rule 35.6 states that a party may put to an expert instructed by another party, or to a single joint expert appointed under r.35.7, written questions about his report.

35.5.2 **Fast track claims**—In the Final Report it was recommended (p. 38) that in fast track cases expert evidence should be in writing and expert witnesses should not be called to give oral evidence. Subsequently, it was appreciated that there is a risk that a blanket exclusion of oral expert evidence may lead to a large number of cases otherwise suitable for the fast track procedure being transferred to the multi-track, simply because the court believed oral evidence and cross-examination thereon was necessary. Further, it was acknowledged that in some fast track cases evidence by oral testimony may be the cheapest, quickest and most effective method for providing the court and the parties with the necessary expert information. In fast track cases, as well as in multi-track cases, the general rule is that expert evidence is to be given in a written report prepared by the expert and not, unless the court so directs, by the expert's oral testimony. However, in fast track cases the court will not give a direction "unless it is necessary to do so in the interests of justice" (r.35.5(2)).

35.5.3 **Use of plans, photographs and models as evidence**—Where evidence of this type forms part of expert evidence but is not contained in the expert's report, the party proposing to adduce such evidence must give notice to the other party when serving the expert's report (r.33.6(6)).

35.5.4 **Expert evidence as to foreign law**—See r.33.7.

35.5.5 **Witness summonses**—A witness may be required to attend court to give evidence or produce documents by process now universally known as a "witness summons"; see provisions in Pt 34 (Depositions and court attendance by witnesses. See also *Society of Lloyds v. Clementson (No. 2), The Times*, February 29, 1996, referred to in notes following r.35.2.

35.5.6 **Inspection of written evidence**—Where an expert witness is called to give evidence, generally his report will stand as his evidence in chief. Rule 32.13 provides that a witness statement which stands as evidence in chief is open to inspection unless the court otherwise directs during the course of the trial. Any person may ask the court to direct that such a witness statement should not be open for inspection. The court should not make a direction preventing inspection except on specific grounds, for example because of the nature of any expert medical evidence in the statement (r.32.13). Where the expert is not called to give oral evidence and his report is put in evidence it would be open to inspection.

Written questions to experts

35.6—(1) A party may put to— 35.6

(a) an expert instructed by another party; or

(b) a single joint expert appointed under rule 35.7,

written questions about his report.

(2) Written questions under paragraph (1)—

(a) may be put once only;

(b) must be put within 28 days of service of the expert's report; and

(c) must be for the purpose only of clarification of the report;

unless in any case—

(i) the court gives permission; or

(ii) the other party agrees.

(3) An expert's answers to questions put in accordance with paragraph (1) shall be treated as part of the expert's report.

(4) Where—

(a) a party has put a written question to an expert instructed by another party in accordance with this rule; and

(b) the expert does not answer that question,

the court may make one or both of the following orders in relation to the party who instructed the expert—

(i) that the party may not rely on the evidence of that expert; or

(ii) that the party may not recover the fees and expenses of that expert from any other party.

Effect of rule—It should be remembered that "expert" in this context means an expert who has been instructed to give or prepare evidence for the purpose of court proceedings (r.35.2). 35.6.1

The general rule is that, where expert evidence is permitted, it is to be given by written report without the maker of the report being called to testify. An expert's report must be disclosed to the other side (r.35.13), whether or not the expert is to give oral evidence. Under r.35.6 a party may put to an expert instructed by another party written questions about his report in accordance with the terms of the rule. (As to putting questions about a report prepared by a single joint expert see notes following r.35.7.) The answers form part of the report (r.35.6(3)). Where an expert does not answer a question put, r.35.6(4) comes into play.

This is a useful provision, perhaps particularly so in fast track cases (see r.35.5(2)). It enables a party to obtain clarification of a report prepared by an expert instructed by his opponent or to arrange for a point not covered in the report (but within his expertise) to be dealt with. In a given case, were it not possible to achieve such clarification or extension of a report, the court, for that reason alone, may feel obliged to direct that the expert witness should testify at trial.

Written questions may be put once only and must be put within 28 days of service of the expert's report. Service of the report will be at the time and on the date prescribed in the relevant court order or direction. Practice Direction (Experts and Assessors) para. 4.2 (see para. 35PD–001) states that, where a party sends a written question or questions direct to an expert and the other party is represented by solicitors, a copy of the questions should, at the same time, be sent to those solicitors.

Court's power to direct that evidence is to be given by a single joint expert

35.7—(1) Where two or more parties wish to submit expert evidence on a particular issue, the court may direct that the evidence on that issue is to be given by one expert only. 35.7

(2) The parties wishing to submit the expert evidence are called "the instructing parties".

(3) Where the instructing parties cannot agree who should be the expert, the court may—

(a) select the expert from a list prepared or identified by the instructing parties; or

(b) direct that the expert be selected in such other manner as the court may direct.

35.7.1 **Effect of rule**—Former RSC, O.40 gave the court power to appoint an expert. This could be done only on the application of a party. The power was rarely used, and was unlikely to be used where one party was opposed. Rule 35.7 introduces the concept of the "single joint expert". Strictly speaking, the single joint expert is not a "court expert".

Rule 35.7 provides that where several parties wish to submit expert evidence on "a particular issue" the court may direct that, instead of permitting each party to submit the evidence of an expert, the court may direct that the evidence "on that issue" should be given by one expert only. Such a direction may be given by the court on its own initiative (see r.3.3). This is yet another way in which the court may exercise its power to control expert evidence for the purpose of reducing costs and delay.

This discretionary power may be exercised at any time. It may be anticipated that the court is likely to direct that the evidence on a particular issue is to be given by a single joint expert where it appears to the court, on the information then available, that the issue falls within a substantially established area of knowledge and where it is not necessary for the court to sample a range of opinion. There is no presumption in favour of the appointment of a single joint expert. The object is to do away with the calling of multiple experts where, given the nature of the issue over which the parties are at odds, that is not justified. This has the advantages of reducing costs and delays and of strengthening the impartial role of experts.

Obviously, if a direction for a single joint expert is to be given a mechanism has to be available for the selection of the single joint expert. If the parties can agree on whom the expert should be the matter is resolved. (It is open to the parties to agree that the expert should be a person already instructed by one party.) The parties who are to agree are not necessarily all the parties but only those wishing to submit the expert evidence. In the event of the parties being unable to agree, the default machinery for appointment by the court stated in r.35.7(3) comes into play. That machinery has been specifically designed for the purpose of ensuring that the disadvantages associated with "court experts" are avoided (see Interim Report pp. 186–187). The court will not retain a list of its own "approved" experts. Even where the parties cannot agree on a list from which the court should select an expert the court does not have an entirely free hand but must direct that the expert be selected in some "other manner"; for example, by requesting one of the experts' professional bodies to make an appointment.

The single joint expert, however selected, is instructed by the parties concerned (see r.35.8). In the light of his report, the parties may agree that the evidence of a single joint expert should not be given at the trial. If the evidence is to be used at trial it may be submitted as a written report without the expert being called. In such a case the instructing parties may examine him in chief; the other parties may cross-examine.

A direction that the evidence on a particular issue should be given by one expert only may be given by the court on its own initiative or on application. (Where the court proposes to make an order of its own initiative, it may give *any person* likely to be affected by it an opportunity to make representations.) An application may be made, not only by one or other of the two or more parties wishing to submit expert evidence on the issue, but also by any other party.

Rule 3.1(7) states that where the court has power to make "an order" under the CPR that power "includes a power to vary or revoke the order" (see former RSC, O.38, r.44). Presumably, r.3.1(7) may be relied on by the court whenever it is thought necessary to vary or revoke a direction given under r.35.7(1), for example, where it subsequently transpires that the issue upon which evidence by a single joint expert was directed turns out not to lie within an established field of expert knowledge.

Practice Direction (Experts and Assessors) para. 5 (see para. 35PD–001) states that, where the court has directed that the evidence on a particular issue is to be given by one expert only but there are a number of disciplines relevant to that issue, a leading expert in the dominant discipline should be identified as the single expert. He should prepare the general part of the report and be responsible for annexing or incorporating the contents of any reports from experts in other disciplines.

For provenance of r.35.7, see Interim Report pp. 186–187, and Final Report pp. 140–142. Rule 35.6 states that a party may put to a single joint expert appointed under r.35.7 written questions about his report.

Instructions to a single joint expert

35.8 **35.8**—(1) Where the court gives a direction under rule 35.7 for a single joint expert to be used, each instructing party may give instructions to the expert.

(2) When an instructing party gives instructions to the expert he must, at the same time, send a copy of the instructions to the other instructing parties.

(3) The court may give directions about—

(a) the payment of the expert's fees and expenses; and

(b) any inspection, examination or experiments which the expert wishes to carry out.

(4) The court may, before an expert is instructed—

(a) limit the amount that can be paid by way of fees and expenses to the expert; and
(b) direct that the instructing parties pay that amount into court.

(5) Unless the court otherwise directs, the instructing parties are jointly and severally liable[GL] for the payment of the expert's fees and expenses.

Effect of rule—The provisions of this rule are supplementary to the court's power to appoint a single joint expert given in r.35.7. The first two paragraphs in r.35.8 deal with the manner in which the single joint expert is to be instructed. The remaining paragraphs deal with the matter of the expert's fees and expenses and solve the problems which existed in this respect under former RSC, O.40. **35.8.1**

Instructions to single joint expert—It is conceivable that the several parties may be able to agree on joint instructions to be given to the single joint expert. However, it has to be expected that they may not be able to agree. Rule 35.8 does not give the court the power in that event to order that joint instructions should be settled. Instead it is provided that each instructing party may give instructions to the expert provided that, when he does so, those instructions are revealed to the other instructing parties. **35.8.2**

An expert's report, including the report of a single joint expert, must state the substance of all material instructions, whether written or oral, on the basis of which the report was written (r.35.10(3)).

Single joint expert's fees and expenses—Compare former RSC, O.40, r.5. **35.8.3**

Under r.35.8, the parties are liable (jointly and severally) for the costs of the single joint expert's fees but the extent of their liability will depend on any order as to costs. Obviously, particularly where the parties have not been able to agree on the appointment of a single joint expert, it is important that they should be clear at the outset of the extent of their potential liability as to costs. Consequently, it is provided that the court may give directions about the payment of the expert's fees and expenses and may, before an expert is instructed, limit the amount that can be paid by way of fees and expenses to the expert. (Further, this is consistent with the other powers which the court has to limit fees payable to experts.) The court may secure the payments of the expert's fees and expenses by instructing the parties to make a payment into court.

Directions as to inspection, etc.—In appointing a single joint expert, the court may give directions about any inspection, examination or experiments which the expert wishes to carry out (r.35.8(3)(b)). The powers of the court in this respect are similar to those granted in former RSC, O.40, r.3. **35.8.4**

Note also, r.33.6(8) (inspection of plans, models, photographs, etc.).

Power of court to direct a party to provide information

35.9 Where a party has access to information which is not reasonably available to the other party, the court may direct the party who has access to the information to— **35.9**

(a) prepare and file a document recording the information; and
(b) serve a copy of that document on the other party.

Effect of rule—In the Final Report it was said (p. 146) that there should be, so far as possible, a level playing field between litigants of unequal financial or other resources. A particular problem arises when one party, often the defendant (*e.g.* a hospital or a large company), has an easily available source of expertise to which the other party does not have access (see also p. 138). In the Final Report it was suggested that a new procedure should be introduced enabling claimants to apply to the court (either before or after proceedings have started) for an order requiring a defendant with access to expertise to provide the claimant with an expert's report on a particular situation. **35.9.1**

Rule 35.9 carries that recommendation into effect, but with modifications. The rule is careful to say that what is provided is not an expert's "report" but merely "information" but, presumably, information derived from a source of expertise.

In terms, r.35.9 contrasts with the proposed provisions of draft versions of the rule whereby a court could order a party to arrange for an expert to prepare a report on any matter and if appropriate to arrange for an examination in relation to the matter to be carried out. Rule 35.9 makes no express reference to examination, experiment or tests in relation to the matter in issue. The omission must be deliberate. A situation may arise wherein one party has researched and developed a technical process over a long period of time and is therefore possessed with the greatest expertise in that area. It might thus be reasonable for the court to require that party to share information as to those matters which might reasonably assist the opposing party's expert without the necessity of time-consuming and expensive research before he can form a view. Any direction under r.35.9 would have to take into account such matters as commercial confidentiality in the use of such information in connection with the proceedings. It is hard to conceive of circumstances whereby such information could be sought by a party before proceedings have commenced. There seems to be no basis upon which a court could order an examination, experiment or tests on the matter in issue before preparing and filing the document recording the information. An application on notice in writing would be made to the court stating what order the applicant is seeking and the reasons relied upon by the applicant. Such an application may be supported by evidence from the applicant's expert setting out his particular difficulties in the absence of such information and the advantage that such information would have as to the just and expeditious resolution of the case. On the face of it there is nothing to prevent a court of its own motion making such an order under this rule. If it was satisfied upon evidence before it that it was necessary to make such an order to enable the court to deal with the case justly considering its overriding objectives of ensuring so far as is practical that the parties are on equal footing expense could be saved and that the matter could be dealt with expeditiously.

Practice Direction (Expert and Assessors) para. 3 (see para 35PD–001) states that where the court makes an order under this rule, the document to be prepared recording the information should set out sufficient details of any facts, tests or experiments which constitute the information to enable an assessment and understanding of the significance of the information to me made and obtained.

Contents of report

35.10 **35.10**—(1) An expert's report must comply with the requirements set out in the relevant practice direction.

(2) At the end of an expert's report there must be a statement that—

(a) the expert understands his duty to the court; and

(b) he has complied with that duty.

(3) The expert's report must state the substance of all material instructions, whether written or oral, on the basis of which the report was written.

(4) The instructions referred to in paragraph (3) shall not be privileged[GL] against disclosure but the court will not, in relation to those instructions—

(a) order disclosure of any specific document; or

(b) permit any questioning in court, other than by the party who instructed the expert,

unless it is satisfied that there are reasonable grounds to consider the statement of instructions given under paragraph (3) to be inaccurate or incomplete.

35.10.1 **Effect of rule**—An expert's report must comply with the provisions of this rule and the requirements set out in the relevant practice direction (see para. 35PD–001). The purpose of the requirement in r.35.10(2) is to remind the expert preparing a report that his duty to "help the court" overrides any obligation to the person from whom he has received instructions or by whom, he is paid (r.35.3(2)). Full compliance with this duty would include ensuring that the report includes everything which the expert regards as being relevant to the opinion which he has expressed, and that any matter which would affect the validity of that opinion has been drawn to the attention of the court.

An expert's report which is to be adduced in evidence should carry a statement of truth (see Practice Direction (Expert and Assessors), paras 1.3 and 1.4 (see para. 35PD–001)) (see also Pt 22 (Statements of Truth)).

35.10.2 **Form and content of expert's report**—Practice Direction (Experts and Assessors), para. 1.1 states that an expert's report should be addressed to the court and not to the party from whom the expert has received his instructions. The report must deal with the matters itemised in para. 1.2 of that Practice Direction. In addition it should comply with the requirements of any approved expert's protocol. (See further "Material instructions" below.)

35.10.3 **Material instructions**—The requirement that the expert's report must state the substance of all material instructions, whether written or oral, on the basis of which the report was written (r.35.10(3)) is an important innovation (see Practice Direction (Experts and Assessors) para. 1.2(8), see para. 35PD–001). From, the court's perspective, knowledge of the instructions adds considerably to the value to the court of the expert's report received. Further, the discipline of reciting instructions should serve to reinforce the expert's overriding duty to the court (r.35.3)). In this respect, the objective of the rules is to prevent the suppression of relevant opinions or factual material which does not support the case put forward by the party instructing the expert (Final Report, p. 144).

In a given case, the drawing of a distinction between material and non-material instructions may be difficult.

Approved experts' protocol—An experts' report should comply with the requirements of any approved experts' protocol (Practice Direction (Experts and Assessors), para 1.6 (see para. 35PD–001 below)). 35.10.4A

Privilege—See Interim Report p. 188 and Final Report p. 144. 35.10.4

In the Interim Report it was stated (p. 144) that, once an expert has been instructed to prepare a report for use by the court, any communications between the expert and the client and the client or his advisers should no longer be privileged. In the Final Report (p. 144) it was conceded that this was too sweeping and could lead to additional delay and expense. Consequently, under r.35.10(4) the withdrawal of privilege against disclosure is restricted to the material instructions on which the report is based (r.35.10(3)) (for guidance as to meaning of "privilege", see Glossary). The expert's report must recite the "substance" of those instructions. The significance of the withdrawal of privilege in relation to material instructions is that it opens up the possibility that the opposing party may be able to apply for disclosure of the actual instructions themselves and, perhaps, of related documents, and, further, that it exposes the expert to cross-examination at trial about his instructions. The objective is to ensure that the instructions are transparent and, normally, that should be achieved without disclosure of documents or cross-examination being required. Consequently, r.35.10(4) provides that the court will not, in relation to material instructions (a) order disclosure of any specific document, or (b) permit any questioning in court, other than by the party who instructed the expert, unless it is satisfied that there are reasonable grounds to consider that the statement of the substance of all material instructions given in the expert's report is inaccurate or incomplete. Practice Direction (Experts and Assessors) para. 3 (see para. 35PD–001) adds that, if the court is so satisfied, it will allow cross-examination "where it appears to be in the interests of justice to do so".

Rule 35.10(3) requires that the substance of all material instructions whether written or oral and the basis on which the report was written must be stated. This can only relate to instructions given in relation to the reports prepared for the use of the court on which the evidence would be based. It cannot relate to reports prepared by an expert for a party before leave was granted by a court and thus the expert's status changed from that of expert, advising a party to that of expert witness both advising a party and with an overriding duty to the court under the rules. To remove legal professional privilege completely would lead to all reports being disclosed in all cases. Such a proposal would be outside the terms of the Access to Justice Report and there had been no consultation on it as was required under the Civil Procedure Act. The provision is drafted in allowing the cross-examination of the substance of material instructions implicitly overrides privilege. In this connection it should be remembered that "expert", in r.35.10 and elsewhere in Pt 35, means an expert who has been instructed "to give or prepare evidence for the purpose of court proceedings" (r.35.2).

Use by one party of expert's report disclosed by another

35.11 Where a party has disclosed an expert's report, any party may use that expert's report as evidence at the trial. 35.11

Effect of rule—A party who fails to disclose an expert's report may not use the report at the trial or call the expert to give evidence orally unless the court gives permission (r.35.13). Rule 35.11 states that a party to whom an expert's report is disclosed may use that report as evidence at the trial. (In terms, the rule does not apply to "information" disclosed following a direction made under r.35.9.) 35.11.1

Rule 35.11 follows former RSC, O.38, r.42 (applied in county courts by CCR, O.20, r.28). That rule did not apply to an expert's report disclosed voluntarily by one party to another, unless the parties agreed to put the report in evidence.

Discussions between experts

35.12—(1) The court may, at any stage, direct a discussion between experts for the purpose of requiring the experts to— 35.12

(a) identify the issues in the proceedings; and

(b) where possible, reach agreement on an issue.

(2) The court may specify the issues which the experts must discuss.

(3) The court may direct that following a discussion between the experts they must prepare a statement for the court showing—

(a) those issues on which they agree; and

(b) those issues on which they disagree and a summary of their reasons for disagreeing.

(4) The content of the discussion between the experts shall not be referred to at the trial unless the parties agree.

(5) Where experts reach agreement on an issue during their discussions, the agreement shall not bind the parties unless the parties expressly agree to be bound by the agreement.

35.12.1 **Effect of rule**—Former RSC, O.38, r.38 (applied in county courts by CCR, O.20, r.27) gave the court power to direct that there should be a meeting without prejudice of the parties' expert witnesses for the purpose of identifying those parts of their evidence which are in issue (see SCP 1999, para. 38/39/7). This procedural device was designed to assist parties to reach agreement on outstanding issues requiring evidence. The procedure worked well enough in certain circumstances but was criticised in the Access to Justice Reports (see Interim Report pp. 183 and 188, and Final Report pp. 147–149). The recommendations made in those reports proved controversial in certain respects and were significantly modified subsequently.

The expectation is that this rule, together with the assertion of the rule that the expert's overriding duty is to the court (r.35.3), should increase the effectiveness of the procedure. Rule 35.12 does not stipulate that there should be a "meeting" between experts, but rather that there should be a "discussion". This indicates that, in the interest of saving costs, experts might use telephone conferencing and video conferencing techniques. The important point is that they should communicate effectively (Final Report p. 148).

It is likely that the power given to the court by r.35.12 will be used extensively. According to r.1.4(2)(a), active case management includes encouraging the parties to co-operate in the conduct of the proceedings. (The use of the power granted by r.35.12 could be seen as an aspect of such encouragement.) Obviously, discussions between experts may be held voluntarily and without any direction from the court under this rule. Conceivably, the discussion may be concluded at a single meeting or may stretch over a longer time. The court may direct a timetable for the completing of the discussions. The Court must further the overriding objective to enable the court to deal with cases justly by actively managing cases, this will include, under r.1.4(2)(g) the fixing of timetables to control the progress of the case. It has been common practice in the specialist tribunals such as the Commercial Court and the Technology and Construction Court to order parties' expert witnesses to meet to identify those parts of their evidence which are in issue. It is usually profitable if such meetings take place as often as may be necessary before the exchange of the experts' reports, otherwise positions are taken too early to the detriment of proper discussions at such without prejudice meetings.

In terms, r.35.12 differs in significant respects from former RSC, O.38, r.38. The rules require the experts, not simply to identify those parts of their evidence which are in issue, but to identify the issues in the proceedings and, where possible, to "reach agreement on an issue". Further, the court may specify the issues which the experts must discuss. Narrowing, at an early stage, the issues to be put before the court, including issues of expert opinion, is one of the fundamental purposes of case management (r.1.4(2)(b)). The procedural judge conducting a case management conference should not only direct an experts' meeting but define, with the help of the parties and their legal representatives, the subject matter to be covered (Final Report p. 148).

The former rule said, rather lamely, that, where a meeting of experts took place, the experts may prepare a joint statement indicating those parts of their evidence on which they are, and those on which they are not, in agreement. Rule 35.12 is much more prescriptive in this respect. The court may direct that the expert must prepare a statement for the court, not only showing areas of agreement and disagreement, but also giving a summary of their reasons for disagreeing. The meeting should cover only matters within the expert's professional competence; it is for the parties and their legal representatives to consider the effect of any agreement or disagreement on the future conduct of the case (Final Report p. 148).

Where a direction is given under para. 35.12.3 compliance with those directions (and any later variation of them) is a condition of evidence being admitted at trial. To achieve compliance through those directions, it is necessary for the party wishing to call expert evidence to instruct the expert to meet and make the joint statement as required by the court. Any interference with the order of the court is likely to result in non-compliance with condition laid down by the court with the result that there is no leave for the evidence of the expert to be produced at trial. The purpose of the meeting is not to achieve a settlement of the proceeding or produce agreements binding on the parties unless they express agreement to be bound (see para. 35.12.5). The purpose is stated in para. 35.12.3. Before the court will allow the evidence to be adduced it is refined by the experts so far as possible. It is not for the party to tell experts what opinions they are allowed to hold. The duty owed by the experts to the court is to express in their joint statement and in their report to the court the views which they themselves honestly hold. It is well understood that after giving his initial privileged advice to the party to the litigation an expert may honestly change his opinion either as a result of further research and thought or as a result of discussions with other experts. The freedom and duty of the expert to record freely such changes of opinion is most clear when the expert is to give evidence on opinion as to scientific or engineering theory and practice. The party to the litigation cannot properly tell the expert what evidence he is to give under oath in court nor can he tell the expert what opinion to express in documents produced by him as a condition of the party being allowed to produce that evidence.

See *Robin Ellis Ltd* and *Malwright Ltd*, QBD Technology and Construction Court, judgment of His Honour Judge Bowsher Q.C. of February 1, 1999.

Discussions between experts may be directed at any stage and either before or after the disclosure of their reports. It is important that experts should communicate at the earliest possible stage in the case to establish that they are answering the same questions or addressing the same issues.

A discussion may be most effective if it is chaired by one expert and there is an agenda agreed in advance. It may also be of value for experts to exchange key criteria which they wish to discuss, for example, standards or codes of practice or methods of valuation. It is appropriate for the parties' solicitors in conjunction with their experts to identify matters in issue in order to determine items for the agenda. It is often desirable that lawyers and clients should not be present at the without prejudice meeting of experts. It is important that the meeting of experts addresses the matters that expert evidence that relate to the matters in issue at the proceedings. Normally experts of like discipline will meet together. Sometimes it may be appropriate to have meetings of experts in more than one discipline following an initial meeting. The experts in conjunction with the other experts of like discipline should prepare a written note signed by each of them as to matters of opinion on which they are agreed. Whilst all experts may not agree particular point limited agreement should be explored.

Rule 34.12(5) acknowledges that, where in the course of their discussions experts reach agreement on an issue, that agreement should not bind the parties unless they expressly agree to be bound by the agreement. As a practical matter, the rule could hardly state otherwise (see SCP 1999, Vol. 1, para. 38/39/7). The parties may give their consent either prospectively or retrospectively.

A party who refused to ratify an agreement on particular issues reached by experts when it subsequently turned out that that was quite unreasonable and added thereby to the length of proceedings and the cost of a trial might find himself impugned in costs.

The former rule said that the meeting directed by the court should be "without prejudice". Rule 34.12.(4) provides that the contents of the discussion between the experts should be privileged in the sense that no part of their discussion should be referred to at trial unless the parties agree. The expert does not normally have authority to bind the client, but an expert should be aware of the extent of his authority and that matters which the expert agrees in a note of the meeting may be binding on him.

Expert witness immunity—An expert witness who gives evidence at trial is immune from suite in respect of anything he says in court and that immunity will extend to the contents of his report which adopts or incorporates his evidence. Where an expert gives evidence at the trial the immunity which he would enjoy in respect of that evidence is not to be circumvented by a suite based on the report itself. In *Stanton v. Callaghan*, 62 Con.L.R. 1. At page 28 Chadwick L.J. considered the position arising under former RSC, O.38, Rule 38 which substantially corresponds with the provisions in para. 35.12.3 holding that where under O.30, r.38 a joint statement is agreed and no evidence is given in the court "public interest in facilitating full and frank discussions between experts before trial does require that each should be free to make proper concessions without fear that any departure from advice previously given to the party who has retained him will be seen as evidence of negligence. That, as it seems to me, is an area in which public policy justifies immunity. The immunity is needed in order to avoid the tension between a desire to assist the court and a fear of the consequences of a departure from previous advice." 35.12.2

Consequence of failure to disclose expert's report

35.13 A party who fails to disclose an expert's report may not use the report at the trial or call the expert to give evidence orally unless the court gives permission. 35.13

Effect of rule—Former RSC, O.38, r.36 stated that, except with the leave of the court or where all parties agreed, no expert evidence could be adduced at the trial or hearing unless the parties seeking to adduce the evidence had applied to the court for a direction in relation to that evidence. On such application, where the expert was to be called as a witness the court was required to direct that the substance of the evidence should be disclosed in the form of a written report to such other parties and within such period as the court might specify unless the court considered that there were special reasons for not doing so (rr.37 and 41, see SCP 1999, para. 38/39/2) and "automatic directions" were to similar effect (see RSC, O.25, r.8(1)(b)). Any direction could, on sufficient cause being shown, be revoked or varied by a subsequent direction given at or before trial (RSC, O.38, r.44). No express sanction was attached to the former rule. Where a party failed to comply with a direction that a written report should be disclosed, the court could stay or dismiss the action, or strike out the defence, as appropriate (see SCP 1999, para. 38/36/2). 35.13.1

Expert evidence is to be restricted to that which is reasonably required to resolve the proceedings (r.35.1). Rule 35.4 states that no party may call an expert or put in evidence an expert's report without the court's permission. The general rule is that expert evidence is to be given in a written report. In terms, none of the rules in Pt 35 imposes on a party who has obtained the court's permission to call an expert or put in evidence an expert's report a duty to disclose that report, or to disclose it to particular persons within a particular time but, clearly, the court may impose directions to that effect and may vary or revoke them subsequently. Rule 35.13 assumes that a party has been directed to disclose an expert's report and has failed to do so. The rule imposes a sanction: that party may not use the report at trial or call the expert to give evidence orally unless the court gives permission. (The rule is in similar terms to former RSC, O.38, r.2A(10) (failure to comply with direction to exchange witness statements).)

Expert's right to ask court for directions

35.14 **35.14**—(1) An expert may file a written request for directions to assist him in carrying out his function as an expert.

(2) An expert may request directions under paragraph (1) without giving notice to any party.

(3) The court, when it gives directions, may also direct that a party be served with—

(a) a copy of the directions; and

(b) a copy of the request for directions.

35.14.1 **Effect of rule**—An expert, in carrying out his function, operates within a framework stipulated by the instructions he has received, by the directions, if any, given by the court, and by the rules in this Part. When, upon a party's application the court grants permission to adduce expert evidence, the court may attach directions (r.35.14). They may also be attached when the court gives a direction for a discussion between experts (r.35.12) and where it gives a direction under r.35.7 for a single joint expert to be used. Within this framework, it is the duty of the expert to help the court; this duty overrides his obligations to others (r.35.3).

The position of the expert is an onerous one. It is conceivable that, in a given case, an expert may reasonably believe that his compliance with his duty, with his instructions, with his professional responsibilities and with directions given by the court (if any) cannot readily be reconciled without clarification or amplification. Or he may believe that his instructions or directions are inappropriate, inadequate or inapt in some respect. Rule 35.14 recognises that for these or other reasons the expert may wish to seek directions from the court to assist him in carrying out his function. As an expert's first duty is to the court it is right that he should have direct access to it. Such access reinforces the expert's impartiality. The need for directions may become apparent at any time, possibly after discussions between experts (either voluntary or directed under r.35.12).

It should be noted that the expert's request for directions is made without notice.

On receipt of the request the court may before giving directions to the expert either deal with the matter forthwith or decide whether or not to notify or hear the instructing party before a decision is made as to whether to give directions to assist the expert in carrying out his function. If it decides to proceed then when it gives directions it has a discretion whether or not to direct that a party may be served with a copy of the directions and of the request. The power under r.35.14(3) is not confined to directing that the instructing party only be served. Any direction to the expert presumably should be recited in his report.

Assessors

35.15 **35.15**—(1) This rule applies where the court appoints one or more persons (an "assessor") under section 70 of the Supreme Court Act 1981[1] or section 63 of the County Courts Act 1984.[2]

(2) The assessor shall assist the court in dealing with a matter in which the assessor has skill and experience.

(3) An assessor shall take such part in the proceedings as the court may direct and in particular the court may—

(a) direct the assessor to prepare a report for the court on any matter at issue in the proceedings; and

(b) direct the assessor to attend the whole or any part of the trial to advise the court on any such matter.

(4) If the assessor prepares a report for the court before the trial has begun—

(a) the court will send a copy to each of the parties; and

(b) the parties may use it at trial.

[1] 1981 c. 54.

[2] 1984 c. 28 Section 63 was amended by S.I. 1998/2940.

(5) The remuneration to be paid to the assessor for his services shall be determined by the court and shall form part of the costs of the proceedings.

(6) The court may order any party to deposit in the court office a specified sum in respect of the assessor's fees and, where it does so, the assessor will not be asked to act until the sum has been deposited.

(7) Paragraphs (5) and (6) shall not apply where the remuneration of the assessor is to be paid out of money provided by Parliament.

Effect of rule—See Interim Report p. 187 and Final Report p. 151. 35.15.1

The Supreme Court Act 1981, s.70(1), states that the High Court may, if it thinks it expedient to do so, call in the aid of one or more assessors specially qualified "and hear and dispose of the cause or matter wholly or partially with their assistance" (see SCP 1999, Vol. 2, para. 20A–457). Paras (2) and (4) of s.70 deal with the remuneration of assessors. Former RSC, O.33, r.6 said that such trial should take place "in such manner and on such terms as the court may direct" (note also RSC, O.33, r.2). The County Courts Act 1984, s.63(1) is to similar effect and enables a county court judge to sit with assessors on an application of a party (see SCP 1999, Vol. 2, para. 20A–736). Rules of court relevant to s.63(1) were found in former CCR, O.13, r.11. For the purpose of implementing r.35.15 (and other provisions in the CPR), section 63 of the 1984 Act has been amended by the Modification of Enactments Order (S.I. 1998 No. 2940) art. 6(d).

Under r.35.15, an assessor may be appointed by the court of its own initiative and the assessor's remuneration shall form part of the costs of the proceedings. The court may appoint several assessors, for example, where a case raises several matters calling for different skills and experiences.

Paragraphs (5) and (6) of r.35.15 deal with the assessor's remuneration (*cf.* r.35.8(4)(5) (remuneration of single joint expert)); not also para. (7).

Formerly, the appointment of assessors in Admiralty cases, and also in patent cases, was common. It is to be expected that the practice will be extended to other cases in the future under r.35.15.

The court may vary or revoke an order or direction made under this rule (r.3.1(7)).

Appointment of assessor—Practice Direction (Experts and Assessors) para. 6.1 (see para. 35PD–001) states that, not less than 21 days before appointing an assessor, the court will notify each party in writing of the name of the proposed assessor, of the matter in respect of which the assistance of the assessor will be sought, and of the qualifications of the assessor to give that assistance. Paragraph 6.2 states that objection to a proposed appointment of an assessor, either personally or in respect of his qualifications, may be taken by any party (County Courts Act 1984, s.63(5)). Objection must be made in writing and filed with the court within seven days of receipt of the notification from the court. The objection will be taken into account by the court in deciding whether or not to make the appointment. 35.15.2

Assessor advising court at trial (r.35.15(3)(b))—The court may direct the assessor to attend the trial to advise the court on any matter at issue in the proceedings. This is consistent with s.70(1) of the 1981 Act and s.63(1) of the 1984 Act. Both of these provisions envisage the assessor sitting with the judge at the trial or hearing. 35.15.3

Assessor preparing report for court (r.35.15(3)(a))—The court may direct the assessor to prepare a report for the court on any matter at issue in the proceedings. It would seem that this provision anticipates that the assessor may assist the judge without actually participating in the trial or hearing itself. (Conceivably, the assessor may prepare a report for the court and attend the trial to advise.) It is important that a clear distinction should be drawn between the expert witness and the assessor. The assessor has a judicial role, he is not an expert witness appointed by the court. He cannot be cross-examined. 35.15.4

The assessor assists the judge in discharging his judicial role. His function is to "educate" the judge and to enable him to reach a properly informed decision. An assessor is likely to be of particular assistance in a case raising complex technical issues. However, normally the use of an assessor in addition to the parties' expert witnesses would not be cost effective except in the heaviest of cases. Even in smaller cases, where technical issues are not agreed, the assistance of an assessor may provide the most economical way of disposing of the case and, in addition, may provide the parties with a decision no less satisfactory than that of a judge lacking the assessor's expertise.

Expense is incurred in the engaging of an assessor. In this respect, as in others, the court has to bear in mind the overriding objective, and especially the matter of cost to the parties (see r.1.1(2)(b) and (c)(i)). In a given case, the appointment of an assessor may result in substantial savings in the length of the hearing.

Rule 35.15(3) speaks of the assessor taking such part "in the proceedings as the court may direct". This seems wider than the former provisions and with the statutory provisions. Section 70(1) of the 1981 Act says the court "may hear and dispose" of the case "with their assistance" and s.63(1) of the 1984 Act says the judge may "sit with the judge".

Practice Direction (Experts and Assessors) para. 6.4 (see para. 35PD–001) states that copies of any report prepared by the assessor will be sent to each of the parties but the assessor will not give oral evidence or be open to cross-examination or questioning.

PRACTICE DIRECTION—EXPERTS AND ASSESSORS

This Practice Direction supplements CPR Part 35

35PD–001 *Part 35 is intended to limit the use of oral expert evidence to that which is reasonably required. In addition, where possible, matters requiring expert evidence should be dealt with by a single expert. Permission of the court is always required either to call an expert or to put an expert's report in evidence.*

Form and Content of expert's reports

1.1 An expert's report should be addressed to the court and not to the party from whom the expert has received his instructions.

1.2 An expert's report must:

(1) give details of the expert's qualifications,

(2) give details of any literature or other material which the expert has relied on in making the report,

(3) say who carried out any test or experiment which the expert has used for the report and whether or not the test or experiment has been carried out under the expert's supervision,

(4) give the qualifications of the person who carried out any such test or experiment, and

(5) where there is a range of opinion on the matters dealt with in the report—

(i) summarise the range of opinion, and

(ii) give reasons for his own opinion,

(6) contain a summary of the conclusions reached,

(7) contain a statement that the expert understands his duty to the court and has complied with that duty (rule 35.10(2)), and

(8) contain a statement setting out the substance of all material instructions (whether written or oral). The statement should summarise the facts and instructions given to the expert which are material to the opinions expressed in the report or upon which those opinions are based (rule 35.10(3)).

1.3 An expert's report must be verified by a statement of truth as well as containing the statements required in paragraph 1.2(7) and (8) above.

1.4 The form of the statement of truth is as follows:

"I believe that the facts I have stated in this report are true and that the opinions I have expressed are correct."

1.5 Attention is drawn to rule 32.14 which sets out the consequences of verifying a document containing a false statement without an honest belief in its truth.

(For information about statements of truth see Part 22 and the practice direction which supplements it.)

1.6 In addition, an expert's report should comply with the requirements of any approved expert's protocol.

Information

2. Under Part 35.9 the court may direct a party with access to information which is not reasonably available to another party to serve on that other party a document which records the information. The document served must include sufficient details of all the fact, tests, experiments and assumptions which underlie any part of the information to enable the party on whom it is served to make, or to obtain, a proper interpretation of the information and an assessment of its significance.

Instructions

3. The instructions referred to in paragraph 1.2(8) will not be protected by privilege (see rule 35.10(4)). But cross-examination of the expert on the contents of his instructions will not be allowed unless the court permits it (or unless the party who gave the instructions consents to it). Before it gives permission the court must be satisfied that there are reasonable grounds to consider that the statement in the report of the substance of the instructions is inaccurate or incomplete. If the court is so satisfied, it will allow the cross-examination where it appears to be in the interests of justice to do so.

Questions to experts

4.1 Questions asked for the purpose of clarifying the expert's report (see rule 35.6) should be put, in writing, to the expert not later than 28 days after receipt of the expert's report (see paragraphs 1.2 to 1.5 above as to verification).

4.2 Where a party sends a written question or questions direct to an expert and the other party is represented by solicitors, a copy of the questions should, at the same time, be sent to those solicitors.

4.3 The party or parties instructing the expert must pay any fees charged by that expert for answering questions put under rule 35.6. This does not affect any decision of the court as to the party who is ultimately to bear the experts costs.

Single expert

5. Where the court has directed that the evidence on a particular issue is to be given by one expert only (rule 35.7) but there are a number of disciplines relevant to that issue, a leading expert in the dominant discipline should be identified as the single expert. He should prepare the general part of the report and be responsible for annexing or incorporating the contents of any reports from experts in other disciplines.

Assessors

6.1 An assessor may be appointed to assist the court under rule 35.15. Not less than 21 days before making any such appointment, the court will notify each party in writing of the name of the proposed assessor, of the matter in respect of which the assistance of the assessor will be sought and of the qualifications of the assessor to give that assistance.

6.2 Where any person has been proposed for appointment as an assessor, objection to him, either personally or in respect of his qualification, may be taken by any party.

6.3 Any such objection must be made in writing and filed with the court within 7 days of receipt of the notification referred to in paragraph 6.1 and will be taken into account by the court in deciding whether or not to make the appointment (section 63(5) of the County Courts Act 1984).

6.4 Copies of any report prepared by the assessor will be sent to each of the parties but the assessor will not give oral evidence or be open to cross-examination or questioning.

PART 36

Offers to Settle and Payments into Court

36.0.1 **Contents**

Editorial Introduction

36.0.2 Part 36 concerns offers to settle and payments into court made in accordance with its provisions (called respectively a Pt 36 offer and a Pt 36 payment), and the consequences which follow if such offers and payments do so comply. There is no prohibition against a party making an offer to settle in any way he chooses, but if the offer made does not comply with the provisions of this Part, the consequences specified will not follow unless the court so orders (see r.36.2). Part 36 applies not only to claims but also to counterclaims and other additional claims within Pt 20 (see r.20.3). In the case of a claim being dealt with on the small claims track, the specified consequences do not follow even where a Pt 36 offer or Pt 36 payment is made unless the court orders otherwise (see r.36.2(5)).

Part 36 offers and payments may be made once proceedings have started and may be made in appeal proceedings (see r.36.2(4)). Whilst this Part makes provision for settling money claims and non-money claims, for an offer to settle a money claim to have the specified consequences, it must be made by way of a Pt 36 payment (see r.36.3(1)).

The formalities of a Pt 36 offer and of a Pt 36 payment are set out in r.36.5 and r.36.6 respectively. Such formalities include in each case a statement whether it relates to the whole of the claim or to a part of it or to an issue that arises and if so which part or issue, a statement whether it takes into account any counterclaim, and if not expressed to be inclusive of interest, the details relating to interest set out in r.36.22(2).

Where both money and non-monetary claims are made and it is desired to make an offer to settle the whole claim which will have the specified consequences, a Pt 36 payment must be made in respect of the money claims and a Pt 36 offer in respect of the non-money claims (see r.36.4). Further the Pt 36 notice must identify the document setting out the Pt 36 offer and state that acceptance of the Pt 36 payment will be treated as acceptance of the Pt 36 offer. Acceptance in such a case of the Pt 36 payment will be treated as acceptance of the Pt 36 offer.

Rule 36.10 provides that where a party makes an offer to settle before proceedings are begun, the court will take that offer into account when making any order as to costs so long as the provisions of r.10 are complied with. Such include in respect of a money claim a Pt 36 payment being made within 14 days of the service of the claim form in an amount not less than that offered before proceedings began.

The specified consequences as to costs upon acceptance of a Pt 36 offer or Pt 36 payment by the sole or all of the defendants are set out in r.36.13. It provides *inter alia* that where such is accepted without needing the permission of the court, the claimant will be entitled to his costs of the proceedings up to the date of serving the notice of acceptance and where the Pt 36 offer or payment relates to part only of the claim and the claimant abandons the balance, he will again be entitled to such costs unless the court orders otherwise. Costs will be on the standard basis if not agreed.

Rule 36.15 sets out the effect of acceptance of a Pt 36 offer or payment. If the Pt 36 offer or Pt 36 payment relates to the whole claim, the claim will be stayed. If it relates to part only, the stay will be limited to such part and the court will decide the liability for costs unless the parties agree costs.

Rule 44.3(4)(c) provides that the court must have regard to any payment into court or admissible offer to settle made by a party which is drawn to its attention, whether or not it is made in accordance with Pt 36.

The consequences of acceptance of a Pt 36 offer or a Pt 36 payment made by one or more but not all defendants are set out in r.36.17. Such depend upon and vary according to whether the defendants are "sued jointly or in the alternative" on the one hand, and on the other are alleged to have a "several liability" to the claimant.

Whilst these rules provide in large measure for consequences to follow without court involvement, including payment out on request made in the appropriate practice form (r.36.16), there are some circumstances where court involvement to enable acceptance is mandatory, as under r.36.18 which concerns claims by or on behalf of a child or patient, acceptance after trial has begun and the defence of tender made before claim.

Rule 36.19 contains restrictions on disclosure of a Pt 36 offer or payment to the trial judge until all questions of liability and the amount to be awarded has been decided. Such restriction does not apply where the defence of tender has been raised, a stay under r.36.15 is in place, or where the issue of liability has been determined before any assessment of the money claimed and the payment may be relevant to the question of costs of the issue of liability (see further, para. 36.15.1 below).

The consequences which follow where a claimant fails to do better than the Pt 36 offer or Pt 36 payment are set out in r.36.20. These are that the court will order the claimant to pay the defendant's costs after the latest date upon which the payment or offer could have been accepted without needing the permission of the court unless the court considers it unjust to do so. Rule 36.21 sets out the consequences as to costs and otherwise where the claimant does better than he proposed in his Pt 36 offer. These include a new provision to award interest to the claimant at a rate not exceeding 10 per cent above base rate for some or all of the period starting with the latest date on which the defendant could have accepted the offer without needing the permission of the court.

Rule 36.22 deals with interest. Unless a Pt 36 payment notice of a claimant's Pt 36 offer which offers to accept a sum of money indicates to the contrary, it will be deemed to be inclusive of interest. Where it indicates to the contrary the details set out in r.36.22(2) must be given.

The deduction of statutory benefits is dealt with in r.36.23. In such a case the Pt 36 payment notice must give the details set out in r.36.23(3).

By making a Pt 36 offer or a Pt 36 payment a party defending a claim takes steps to minimise his exposure to liability for his opponent's costs under the ordinary costs rules.

Related Sources

- Practice Direction—Offers to Settle and Payments into Court PT 36 PD(F) (see para. 36PD–001) **36.0.3**
- CPR, r.20.3 (Pt 20 claim to be treated as a claim for purposes *inter alia* of Pt 36)
- CPR, r.21.10 (Compromise by or on behalf of a child or patient)
- CPR, r.44.3(4)(c) (Court to take into account any payment into Court or admissible offer whether or not made in accordance with Pt 36)
- CPR, Schedule 1, RSC, O.45, r.15(4) (Signing judgment for costs under deemed order)
- CPR, Schedule 1, RSC, O.82, r.4 (Provisions as to payment into court in defamation actions)
- Court Funds Rules 1987 as amended by Court Funds (Amendment) Rules 1999 (S.I. 1999 No. 1021)

Forms

36.0.4
- N242A—Part 36 Payment to Notice
- N243—Request for Payment Out
- Court Funds Office Forms: Form 100 Request for Lodgment (SCP 1999, Vol. 2, para. 5C–116) Form 201 Request for a Payment (SCP 1999, Vol. 2, para. 5C–124).

Scope of this Part

36.1 **36.1**—(1) This Part contains rules about—

(a) offers to settle and payments into court; and

(b) the consequences where an offer to settle or payment into court is made in accordance with this Part.

(2) Nothing in this Part prevents a party making an offer to settle in whatever way he chooses, but if that offer is not made in accordance with this Part, it will only have the consequences specified in this Part if the court so orders.

(Part 36 applies to Part 20 claims by virtue of Rule 20.3.)

36.1.1 **General Note**—Under the provisions of Pt 36 the same status and effect is given both to a Pt 36 offer and a Pt 36 payment. The need, therefore, to resort to a *Calderbank* letter (see *Calderbank v. Calderbank* [1976] Fam. 93; [1975] 3 All E.R. 333, CA has been largely obviated. However, the concept of a *Calderbank* letter which does not in its terms comply with the provisions of Pt 36 and other non-complying offers has been preserved though the consequences specified in this Part will not follow unless the court so orders. Such a non-conforming offer is one made by letter written "without prejudice save as to costs" or "without prejudice" but subject to an express reservation of the right to refer to the letter on the issue of costs should the claim proceed to judgment. However, it is to be noted that although the existence of a *Calderbank* letter may be a very important consideration in the exercise of the Court's discretion with regard to costs, it should not be equated precisely to a payment or Pt 36 offer. The Court retains its discretion and the existence of a *Calderbank* letter should influence but not govern the exercise of the discretion (see *McDonnell v. McDonnell* [1977] 1 W.L.R. 34; [1977] 1 All E.R. 766, CA). Moreover the discretion of the trial judge as to costs, and as to what weight should be given to a *Calderbank* letter, cannot be usurped. Hence the Court will not, in advance of a trial, make an Order that an offer contained in a *Calderbank* letter should be treated for all purposes as though it were a complying Pt 36 payment or Pt 36 offer (see *Corby District Council v. Holst & Co. Ltd* [1985] 1 W.L.R. 427; [1985] 1 All E.R. 321, CA a case under the former RSC O.22, r.1. Part 36 is supplemented by the Practice Direction—Offers to Settle and Payments into court Pt 36 PD(F) which must be read in conjunction with Pt 36 (see para. 36PD–001).

Part 36 offers and Part 36 payments—general provisions

36.2 **36.2**—(1) An offer made in accordance with the requirements of this Part is called—

(a) if made by way of a payment into court, "a Part 36 payment";

(b) otherwise "a Part 36 offer".

(Rule 36.3 sets out when an offer has to be made by way of a payment into court.)

(2) The party who makes an offer is the "offeror".

(3) The party to whom an offer is made is the "offeree".

(4) A Part 36 offer or a Part 36 payment—

(a) may be made at any time after proceedings have started; and

(b) may be made in appeal proceedings.

(5) A Part 36 offer or a Part 36 payment shall not have the consequences set out in this Part while the claim is being dealt with on the small claims track unless the court orders otherwise.

(Part 26 deals with allocation to the small claims track.)

(Rule 27.2 provides that Part 36 does not apply to small claims.)

36.2.1 **Nature of a Part 36 offer and a Part 36 payment**—Of a payment into court under the former RSC, O.22 it was said: "A payment into court is simply an offer to dispose of the claim on terms" (*per* Devlin L.J. in *A. Martin French v. Kingswood Hill Ltd* [1961] 1 Q.B. 96 at 103; [1960] 2 All E.R. 251 at 252). When a claimant accepts the amount paid in in respect of a claim what happens is that that claim is settled, as if by a payment under a compromise; but the conclusion of a claim in this way is something quite different from its conclusion by a judgment. "The payment in implies no admission about the merits of the claim; there has been no adjudication on it, and therefore no estoppel is created" (*ibid.*). It was also held that: "There is, however, nothing contractual about payment into Court; it is wholly a procedural matter and has no true analogy to a settlement arranged between the parties out of court" (*per* Goddard L.J. in *Cumper v. Pothecary* [1941] 2 K.B. 58 at 67).

In *Toprak Enerji Sanayi A.S. v. Sale Tilney Technology Plc* [1994] 1 W.L.R. 840; [1994] 3 All E.R. 483; [1994] 1 Lloyd's Rep. 303; the court held that there was nothing in the former RSC, O.22, r.1 to suggest that a payment into court was of its nature so personal to the claimant that in no circumstances could the payment be treated as available to an assignee, transferee or successor of the claimant. The whole structure of the rule is directed to matching payments to claims, not to identifying a payment as an offer made to the claimant personally. Further, it was held that a defendant who made a payment into court was not estopped from asserting that the claim form had not bee duly served (*Towers v. Morley* [1992] 1 W.L.R. 511, CA).

It is considered that a Pt 36 payment and a Pt 36 offer will be similarly treated by the courts.

Time for making a Part 36 offer or a Part 36 payment—Though a Pt 36 offer or a Pt 36 payment can not be made until after proceedings have started, it is to be noted that the court will take into account an offer made before the commencement of proceedings when making any order as to costs so long as the provisions of r.36.10 (*q.v.*) are complied with. **36.2.2**

A defendant's offer to settle a money claim requires a Part 36 payment

36.3—(1) Subject to rules 36.5(5) and 36.23, an offer by a defendant to settle a money claim will not have the consequences set out in this Part unless it is made by way of a Part 36 payment. **36.3**

(2) A Part 36 payment may only be made after proceedings have started.

(Rule 36.5(5) permits a Part 36 offer to be made by reference to an interim payment.)

(Rule 36.10 makes provision for an offer to settle a money claim before the commencement of proceedings.)

(Rule 36.23 makes provision for where benefit is recoverable under the Social Security (Recovery of Benefit) Act 1997[1].)

Defendant's offer to settle the whole of a claim which includes both a money claim and a non-money claim

36.4—(1) This rule applies where a defendant to a claim which includes both a money claim and a non-money claim wishes— **36.4**

(a) to make an offer to settle the whole claim which will have the consequences set out in this Part; and

(b) to make a money offer in respect of the money claim and a non-money offer in respect of the non-money claim.

(2) The defendant must—

(a) make a Part 36 payment in relation to the money claim; and

(b) make a Part 36 offer in relation to the non-money claim.

(3) The Part 36 payment notice must—

(a) identify the document which sets out the terms of the Part 36 offer; and

(b) state that if the claimant gives notice of acceptance of the Part 36 payment he will be treated as also accepting the Part 36 offer.

(Rule 36.6 makes provision for a Part 36 payment notice.)

(4) If the claimant gives notice of acceptance of the Part 36 payment, he shall also be taken as giving notice of acceptance of the Part 36 offer in relation to the non-money claim.

Note—Where a claim includes both a money claim and a non-money claim, it is essential for the defendant to make a Pt 36 payment in relation to the money claim and a Pt 36 offer in relation to the non-money claim. Furthermore, the Pt 36 payment notice must comply with the provisions of r.36.4(3). **36.4.1**

[1] 1997 c. 27.

Form and content of a Part 36 offer

36.5 **36.5**—(1) A Part 36 offer must be in writing.

(2) A Part 36 offer may relate to the whole claim or to part of it or to any issue that arises in it.

(3) A Part 36 offer must—

(a) state whether it relates to the whole of the claim or to part of it or to an issue that arises in it and if so to which part or issue;
(b) state whether it takes into account any counterclaim; and
(c) if it is expressed not to be inclusive of interest, give the details relating to interest set out in rule 36.22(2).

(4) A defendant may make a Part 36 offer limited to accepting liability up to a specified proportion.

(5) A Part 36 offer may be made by reference to an interim payment.

(Part 25 contains provisions relating to interim payments.)

(6) A Part 36 offer made not less than 21 days before the start of the trial must—

(a) be expressed to remain open for acceptance for 21 days from the date it is made; and
(b) provide that after 21 days the offeree may only accept it if—
  (i) the parties agree the liability for costs; or
  (ii) the court gives permission.

(7) A Part 36 offer made less than 21 days before the start of the trial must state that the offeree may only accept it if—

(a) the parties agree the liability for costs; or
(b) the court gives permission.

(Rule 36.8 makes provision for when a Part 36 offer is treated as being made.)

(8) If a Part 36 offer is withdrawn it will not have the consequences set out in this Part.

36.5.1 **Note**—The Pt 36 offer must comply with the provisions of r.36.5(3) above. See Pt 36 PD(F) 6 (para. 36PD–001). Clarity is required in the information given and if given will avoid the need for an application for clarification under r.36.9 below. See PT36 PD(F) 5.1 for documents which must be filed when making a Pt 36 payment (para. 36PD–001).

The general rule is that such an offer should be made 21 days before the start of the trial and be expressed to remain open for 21 days. It must also provide for a subsequent acceptance on the terms set out in r.36.5(6)(b).

A Part 36 offer can also be made less than 21 days before trial but must state that it may be accepted only on the terms set out in r.36.5(7).

It may be withdrawn, but if it is it will not have the consequences set out in Pt 36: see r.36(8).

Notice of a Part 36 payment

36.6 **36.6**—(1) A Part 36 payment may relate to the whole claim or part of it or to an issue that arises in it.

(2) A defendant who makes a Part 36 payment must file with the court a notice ("Part 36 payment notice") which—

(a) states the amount of the payment;
(b) states whether the payment relates to the whole claim or to part of it or to any issue that arises in it and if so to which part or issue;
(c) states whether it takes into account any counterclaim;
(d) if an interim payment has been made, states that the defendant has taken into account the interim payment; and
(e) if it is expressed not to be inclusive of interest, gives the details relating to interest set out in rule 36.22(2).

(Rule 25.6 makes provision for an interim payment.)

(Rule 36.4 provides for further information to be included where a defendant wishes to settle the whole of a claim which includes a money claim and a non-money claim.)

(Rule 36.23 makes provision for extra information to be included in the payment notice in a case where benefit is recoverable under the Social Security (Recovery of Benefit) Act 1997.)

(3) The court will serve the Part 36 payment notice on the offeree unless the offeror informs the court, when the money is paid into court, that the offeror will serve the notice.

(4) Where the offeror serves the Part 36 payment notice he must file a certificate of service.

(Rule 6.10 specifies what must be contained in a certificate of service.)

(5) A Part 36 payment may be withdrawn only with the permission of the court.

Note—The notice of a Pt 36 payment must contain the details set out in r.36.6(2)(a)–(e). Note too the requirement to include the further information referred to in r.36.4 where the defendant wishes to settle the whole of a claim which includes a money and non-money claim and the further detail required in a case where benefit is recoverable under the Social Security (Recovery of Benefit) Act 1997. Note too r.36.7 which requires specific information in a Pt 36 notice in a claim for provisional damages. See too Pt 36 PD(F) 5 and 6 for the requirements of a Pt 36 payment notice (para. 36PD–001). **36.6.1**

Withdrawal—A Pt 36 payment can only be withdrawn with the permission of the court (see r.36.6(5)). The application should be made in accordance with Pt 23. See Pt 36PD(F) 3.5 (para. 36PD–001). **36.6.2**

See below for the considerations which the court took into account in exercising its discretion in applications to withdraw a payment in under the former RSC, O.22, r.1. A similar approach is likely under the CPR 36.6(5).

If the defendant can show good reason, *e.g.* the discovery of further evidence which puts a wholly different complexion on the case, or a change in legal outlook brought about by a new judicial decision, the court may grant leave for the payment out to him of the whole or part of the money paid in (*Cumper v. Pothecary* [1941] 2 All E.R. 516 at 522, CA). Money paid into Court by mistake (see *Spurr v. Hall* (1877) 2 Q.B.D. 615 at 624) or on a mistaken meaning of the statement of case (*Kaprow & Co. v. Maclelland & Co.* [1948] 1 K.B. 618, CA) may be ordered to be withdrawn by the defendant.

The Court has a complete discretion, to be exercised judicially, whether to allow a payment into Court to be paid out back to the defendant, and if so, on what terms, and it will do so where since the date of the notice of payment in the character of the litigation has entirely changed (*Peal Furniture Co. Ltd v. Adrian Share (Interiors) Ltd* [1977] 1 W.L.R. 464; [1977] 2 All E.R. 211, CA).

Where the defendant has made a payment into Court *before* an order for interim payment is made under r.25.7, the former RSC, O.29, r.11, the Court may well entertain an application by him for leave to withdraw a sum equivalent to the whole or part of the amount which he has paid by way of interim payment.

In *Williams v. Boag* [1940] 4 All E.R. 248, it was stated that where by an amendment to the statement of case an insuperable obstacle is raised to any possible success by the claimant, there is inherent power in the Court to order payment out of the money in Court to the defendant. In that case the claimant had taken £100 out of Court, but he was ordered to repay it to the defendant.

On the other hand where the claimant paid money into Court to cover a counterclaim set up in the case by affidavit, and afterwards discontinued the case, the Court refused to order payment out to the claimant (*Bildt v. Foy* (1892) 9 T.L.R. 34, affirmed *ibid.*, p. 83).

The Court may grant leave to withdraw money paid in, even where, at the date of the application for leave, it is still open to the claimant to accept the money; acceptance of the money by the claimant between the date of the application for leave and its hearing will not necessarily serve to defeat the application, although it may be an important consideration in deciding whether or not leave to withdraw should be granted (*Manku v. Seehra* [1985] C.I.L.L. 224; (1985) New L.J. 236). A revaluation of the claimant's claim by a fresh expert retained by the defendant, acting on the same material as an earlier expert, is not a sufficient reason or change of circumstances to justify withdrawal of money paid into Court (*ibid.*).

Where the defendant withdraws the money paid into Court with the leave of the Court, more than 21 days after payment in, but before the commencement of the trial of the claim, he thereby basically nullifies his own payment in and the successful claimant at the trial is entitled to the costs of the claim, though the Court has a discretion to order him to pay the costs in respect of the period between the expiry of the 21 days after the payment in and the date when he could no longer have taken the money out of Court on the ground of a change in circumstances (*Garner v. Cleggs* [1983] 1 W.L.R. 862; [1983] 2 All E.R. 398, CA).

For cases on the exercise of discretion to grant leave to withdraw a payment in where the defendant becomes bankrupt or goes into liquidation after the payment in, see para. 36.6.6 below.

36.6.3 **Reduction**—This requires court permission on application made in accordance with Pt 23. See Pt 36 PD(F) 3.5 (para 36PD–001).

36.6.4 **Payment Into Court of foreign currency**—See Pt 36 PD(F) 10.1 to 4 (para. 36PD–003). An application to the Court is necessary. This should be made in accordance with Pt 23 and state the matters set out in r.10.4.

36.6.5 **Death of defendant or claimant**—Where the defendant dies after payment in, his personal representative (if an order to carry on is made under RSC, O.15, r.7) may apply for the withdrawal of the money paid in (see *Brown v. Feeney* [1906] 1 K.B. 562, CA); and where the claimant dies after payment in, and the action abates on his death, the Court may order the money to be repaid to the defendant, or possibly to the claimant's personal representative (see *Maxwell v. Wolseley* [1907] 1 K.B. 274, CA).

36.6.6 **Bankruptcy of defendant after payment into court**—In such a case it was held that the payment in, notwithstanding a denial of liability, was a conditional payment to the creditor suing, who became a secured creditor to the extent to which his claim in the action was admitted by the trustee (*Re Gordon* [1897] 2 Q.B. 516). After annulment of bankruptcy while the money paid in with denial of liability remained in Court, an issue was directed to determine what sum, if any, was due from defendant to claimant, and to order accordingly (*Dessau v. Rowley* [1916] W.N. 238, CA).

Money paid into Court does not remain an asset of the defendant which, on his bankruptcy, forms part of his property available for distribution; a defendant paying into Court under Pt 36 parts outright with his money. The claimant is therefore a secured creditor to the extent of the money in Court and the defendant's bankruptcy or liquidation does not by itself constitute a change of circumstances which would justify the Court in exercising discretion to order repayment *Sherratt (W. A.) Ltd v. Bromley (John) (Church Stretton) Ltd* [1985] Q.B. 1038; [1985] 1 All E.R. 216, CA, applying *Re Gordon* (above), *Re Ford* [1900] 2 Q.B. 211 and *Dessau v. Rowley* (above), and not following in this respect *Peal Furniture Co. Ltd v. Adrian Share (Interiors) Ltd* [1977] 1 W.L.R. 464; [1977] 2 All E.R. 211, CA).

36.6.7 **Bankruptcy: payment in after petition**—Where a petition is stayed pending the trial of the validity of the debt claimed by the petitioning creditor, and the debtor admits the debt and pays the amount thereof and a sum for costs into Court, the petitioning creditor is not bound to accept such payment and take the money out at the risk of having to pay it back, but may proceed with the bankruptcy petition, and a receiving order may be made on it (*Re Gentry* [1910] 1 K.B. 825, CA).

Offer to settle a claim for provisional damages

36.7 **36.7**—(1) A defendant may make a Part 36 payment in respect of a claim which includes a claim for provisional damages.

(2) Where he does so, the Part 36 payment notice must specify whether or not the defendant is offering to agree to the making of an award of provisional damages.

(3) Where the defendant is offering to agree to the making of an award of provisional damages the payment notice must also state—

(a) the sum paid into court is in satisfaction of the claim for damages on the assumption that the injured person will not develop the disease or suffer the type of deterioration specified in the notice;

(b) that the offer is subject to the condition that the claimant must make any claim for further damages within a limited period; and

(c) what that period is.

(4) Where a Part 36 payment is—

(a) made in accordance with paragraph (3); and

(b) accepted within the relevant period in rule 36.11,

the Part 36 payment will have the consequences set out in rule 36.13, unless the court orders otherwise.

(5) If the claimant accepts the Part 36 payment he must, within 7 days of doing so, apply to the court for an order for an award of provisional damages under rule 41.2.

(Rule 41.2 provides for an order for an award of provisional damages.)

(6) The money in court may not be paid out until the court has disposed of the application made in accordance with paragraph (5).

Time when a Part 36 offer or a Part 36 payment is made and accepted

36.8—(1) A Part 36 offer is made when received by the offeree. **36.8**

(2) A Part 36 payment is made when written notice of the payment into court is served on the offeree.

(3) An improvement to a Part 36 offer will be effective when its details are received by the offeree.

(4) An increase in a Part 36 payment will be effective when notice of the increase is served on the offeree.

(5) A Part 36 offer or Part 36 payment is accepted when notice of its acceptance is received by the offeror.

Note—Times run from receipt or service of the relevant document. In the event of a clarification order being made under r.36.9 the court must specify the date when the Pt 36 offer or Pt 36 payment is to be treated as having been made (see r.36.9(3)). **36.8.1**

Clarification of a Part 36 offer or a Part 36 payment notice

36.9—(1) The offeree may, within 7 days of a Part 36 offer or payment being made, request the offeror to clarify the offer or payment notice. **36.9**

(2) If the offeror does not give the clarification requested under paragraph (1) within 7 days of receiving the request, the offeree may, unless the trial has started, apply for an order that he does so.

(3) If the court makes an order under paragraph (2), it must specify the date when the Part 36 offer or Part 36 payment is to be treated as having been made.

Application for clarification—This should be made in accordance with Pt 23. See Pt 36 PD(F) 7.2 (para. 36PD–001). **36.9.1**

Court to take into account offer to settle made before commencement of proceedings

36.10—(1) If a person makes an offer to settle before proceedings are begun which complies with the provisions of this rule, the court will take that offer into account when making any order as to costs. **36.10**

(2) The offer must—

(a) be expressed to be open for at least 21 days after the date it was made;

(b) if made by a person who would be a defendant were proceedings commenced, include an offer to pay the costs of the offeree incurred up to the date 21 days after the date it was made; and

(c) otherwise comply with this Part.

(3) If the offeror is a defendant to a money claim—

(a) he must make a Part 36 payment within 14 days of service of the claim form; and

(b) the amount of the payment must be not less than the sum offered before proceedings began.

(4) An offeree may not, after proceedings have begun, accept—

(a) an offer made under paragraph (2); or

(b) a Part 36 payment made under paragraph (3),

without the permission of the court.

(5) An offer under this rule is made when it is received by the offeree.

Time for acceptance of a defendant's Part 36 offer or Part 36 payment

36.11—(1) A claimant may accept a Part 36 offer or a Part 36 payment made not less than 21 days before the start of the trial without needing the court's permission if he gives the defendant written notice of acceptance not later than 21 days after the offer or payment was made. **36.11**

(Rule 36.13 sets out the costs consequences of accepting a defendant's offer or payment without needing the permission of the court.)

(2) If—

(a) a defendant's Part 36 offer or Part 36 payment is made less than 21 days before the start of the trial; or

(b) the claimant does not accept it within the period specified in paragraph (1)—

(i) if the parties agree the liability for costs, the claimant may accept the offer or payment without needing the permission of the court;

(ii) if the parties do not agree the liability for costs the claimant may only accept the offer or payment with the permission of the court.

(3) Where the permission of the court is needed under paragraph (2) the court will, if it gives permission, make an order as to costs.

36.11.1 **Transfer of money paid in to deposit account**—Money paid into court under r.36.6 (or appropriated under r.37.2 in satisfaction of a claim which is not accepted within the time specified under r.36.11 will be placed on deposit 21 days after the effective date of lodgment or appropriation, though where the claimant is a minor or a patient the money will be so placed, whether or not he has accepted it (Court Fund Rules 1987, r.31(1)). Such a transfer to the deposit account will be effected without the need for any application or request by the defendant.

On the other hand where the money paid into court is accepted within the time specified in r.3(1) no interest will be payable in respect of the period between lodgment or appropriation or where there has been more than one payment in between the latest lodgment or appropriation and the date of payment out of court (Court Funds Rules 1987, r.32(4)).

36.11.2 **Formalities of acceptance including the notice of acceptance**—See Pt 36 PD(F) 8.1 to 8.11 (para. 36PD–001).

Time for acceptance of a claimant's Part 36 offer

36.12 **36.12**—(1) A defendant may accept a Part 36 offer made not less than 21 days before the start of the trial without needing the court's permission if he gives the claimant written notice of acceptance not later than 21 days after the offer was made.

(Rule 36.14 sets out the costs consequences of accepting a claimant's offer without needing the permission of the court.)

(2) If—

(a) a claimant's Part 36 offer is made less than 21 days before the start of the trial; or

(b) the defendant does not accept it within the period specified in paragraph (1)—

(i) if the parties agree the liability for costs, the defendant may accept the offer without needing the permission of the court;

(ii) if the parties do not agree the liability for costs the defendant may only accept the offer with the permission of the court.

(3) Where the permission of the court is needed under paragraph (2) the court will, if it gives permission, make an order as to costs.

Costs consequences of acceptance of a defendant's Part 36 offer or Part 36 payment

36.13 **36.13**—(1) Where a Part 36 offer or a Part 36 payment is accepted without needing the permission of the court the claimant will be entitled to his costs of the proceedings up to the date of serving notice of acceptance.

(2) Where—

(a) a Part 36 or a Part 36 payment relates to part only of the claim; and

(b) at the time of serving notice of acceptance the claimant abandons the balance of the claim, the claimant will be entitled to his costs of the proceedings up to the date of serving notice of acceptance, unless the court orders otherwise.

(3) The claimant's costs include any costs attributable to the defendant's counterclaim if the Part 36 offer or the Part 36 payment notice states that it takes into account the counterclaim.

(4) Costs under this rule will be payable on the standard basis if not agreed.

Costs under r.36.13 and r.36.14—Part 44.12 provides that where a right to costs arises under r.36.13(1) (claimant's right to costs where he accepts defendant's Pt 36 offer or Pt 36 payment); or r.36.14 (claimant's right to costs where defendant accepts the claimant's Pt 36 offer), a costs order will be deemed to have been made on the standard basis. 36.13.1

Interest on costs—A party accepting money in court and entitled under rules to costs is entitled to interest on costs under section 17 of the Judgments Acts 1838, and section 74 of the County Courts Act 1984. 36.13.2

Interest payable pursuant to s.17 of the Judgments Act 1838 or s.74 of the County Courts Act 1984 on the costs deemed to have been ordered begins to run from the date on which the event which gave rise to the entitlement to costs occurred, see CPR 44.12, para. 44.12 below.

Costs consequences of acceptance of a claimant's Part 36 offer

36.14 Where a claimant's Part 36 offer is accepted without needing the permission of the court the claimant will be entitled to his costs of the proceedings up to the date upon which the defendant serves notice of acceptance. 36.14

The effect of acceptance of a Part 36 offer or Part 36 payment

36.15—(1) If a Part 36 offer or Part 36 payment relates to the whole claim and is accepted, the claim will be stayed.[GL]. 36.15

(2) In the case of acceptance of a Part 36 offer which relates to the whole claim—

(a) the stay[GL] will be upon the terms of the offer; and

(b) either party may apply to enforce those terms without the need for a new claim.

(3) If a Part 36 offer or a Part 36 payment which relates to part only of the claim is accepted—

(a) the claim will be stayed[GL] as to that part; and

(b) unless the parties have agreed costs, the liability for costs shall be decided by the court.

(4) If the approval of the court is required before a settlement can be binding, any stay[GL] which would otherwise arise on the acceptance of a Part 36 offer or a Part 36 payment will take effect only when that approval has been given.

(5) Any stay[GL] arising under this rule will not affect the power of the court—

(a) to enforce the terms of a Part 36 offer;

(b) to deal with any question of costs (including interest on costs) relating to the proceedings;

(c) to order payment out of court of any sum paid into court.

(6) Where—

(a) a Part 36 offer has been accepted; and

(b) a party alleges that—

(i) the other party has not honoured the terms of the offer; and

(ii) he is therefore entitled to a remedy for breach of contract,

the party may claim the remedy by applying to the court without the need to start a new claim unless the court orders otherwise.

Note—Where the approval of the court is required before a settlement can be binding (as in the case of a claim involving a child or patient) any stay hereunder will take effect only when that approval has been given (r.36.15(4)). Furthermore, the stay under this rule will not effect the powers of the court listed in r.36.15(5)(a)–(c). 36.15.1

Payment out of a sum in court on the acceptance of a Part 36 payment

36.16 **36.16** Where a Part 36 payment is accepted the claimant obtains payment out of the sum in court by making a request for payment in the practice form.

36.16.1 **Formalities of acceptance**—See Pt 36 PD(F) 8.6 and 8.7 and 9.1 to 9.5 (para. 36PD–001). The restrictions specified in r.36.18 are to be noted.

Acceptance of a Part 36 offer or a Part 36 payment made by one or more, but not all, defendants

36.17 **36.17**—(1) This rule applies where the claimant wishes to accept a Part 36 offer or a Part 36 payment made by one or more, but not all, of a number of defendants.

(2) If the defendants are sued jointly or in the alternative, the claimant may accept the offer or payment without needing the permission of the court in accordance with rule 36.11(1) if—

(a) he discontinues his claim against those defendants who have not made the offer or payment; and

(b) those defendants give written consent to the acceptance of the offer or payment.

(3) If the claimant alleges that the defendants have a several liability[GL] to him the claimant may—

(a) accept the offer or payment in accordance with rule 36.11(1); and

(b) continue with his claims against the other defendants if he is entitled to do so.

(4) In all other cases the claimant must apply to the court for—

(a) an order permitting a payment out to him of any sum in court; and

(b) such order as to costs as the court considers appropriate.

36.17.1 **Note**—Whether defendants are sued jointly or in the alternative on the one hand, or as being severally liable, depends not upon the manner in which they are sued but upon the nature and quality of the liability alleged. See further *Townsend v. Stone Toms and Partners* [1981] 1 W.L.R. 1153; [1981] 2 All E.R. 690, CA, a case under the former RSC and which contains examples of joint and of alternative liability.

36.17.2 **Discretion to costs**—SCA 1981, s.51 gives the court complete discretion as to costs. Rule 44.3(4)(c) provides that the court, when exercising its discretion as to costs, must have regard to any payment into court or admissible offer to settle made by a party which is drawn to its attention, whether or not it is made in accordance with Pt 36.

Other cases where a court order is required to enable acceptance of a Part 36 offer or a Part 36 payment

36.18 **36.18**—(1) Where a Part 36 offer or a Part 36 payment is made in proceedings to which rule 21.10 applies—

(a) the offer or payment may be accepted only with the permission of the court; and

(b) no payment out of any sum in court shall be made without a court order.

(Rule 21.10 deals with compromise etc. on behalf of a child or patient.)

(2) Where the court gives a claimant permission to accept a Part 36 offer or payment after the trial has started—

(a) any money in court may be paid out only with a court order; and

(b) the court must, in the order, deal with the whole costs of the proceedings.

(3) Where a claimant accepts a Part 36 payment after a defence of tender before claim[GL] has been put forward by the defendant, the money in court may be paid out only after an order of the court.

(Rule 37.3 requires a defendant who wishes to rely on a defence of tender before claim[GL] to make a payment into court.)

Application for court approval—The application should be made in accordance with Pt 23: see Pt 36 PD(F) 8.8 (see para. 36PD–001). **36.18.1**

Restriction on disclosure of a Part 36 offer or a Part 36 payment

36.19—(1) A Part 36 offer will be treated as "without prejudice[GL] except as to costs". **36.19**

(2) The fact that a Part 36 payment has been made shall not be communicated to the trial judge until all questions of liability and the amount of money to be awarded have been decided.

(3) Paragraph (2) does not apply—

(a) where the defence of tender before claim[GL] has been raised;

(b) where the proceedings have been stayed[GL] under rule 36.15 following acceptance of a Part 36 offer or Part 36 payment; or

(c) where—

(i) the issue of liability has been determined before any assessment of the money claimed; and

(ii) the fact that there has or has not been a Part 36 payment may be relevant to the question of the costs of the issue of liability.

Interlocutory proceedings and a Part 36 payment (r.36.19(2))—The restriction on communication under paragraph (2) as formulated under the forerunner of this rule was held to have no application to interlocutory proceedings in the course of which it is often both necessary and desirable that the Court should know of a payment into Court (*Williams v. Boag* (1941) 57 T.L.R. 70, *per* Goddard L.J. at 71). The rule has been applied equally to the Court of Appeal (see RSC, O.59, r.12A) and on an appeal as to the quantum of damage the Court of Appeal was not told the amount paid into Court (see the former practice in *Mason v. Mason* [1966] 1 W.L.R. 767; [1965] 3 All E.R. 492). **36.19.1**

It was further held that the rule contemplates communications of the fact of payment into Court and the amount thereof before the judgment is perfected by entry, for it assumes that the trial Judge will be told about such payment in, for the purposes of the order as to costs (*Millensted v. Grosvenor House (Park Lane) Ltd* [1937] 1 K.B. 717, *per* Scott L.J.).

It is considered that the same principles apply to the present rule.

Costs consequences where claimant fails to do better than a Part 36 offer or a Part 36 payment

36.20—(1) This rule applies where at trial a claimant— **36.20**

(a) fails to better a Part 36 payment; or

(b) fails to obtain a judgment which is more advantageous than a defendant's Part 36 offer.

(2) Unless it considers it unjust to do so, the court will order the claimant to pay any costs incurred by the defendant after the latest date on which the payment or offer could have been accepted without needing the permission of the court.

(Rule 36.11 sets out the time for acceptance of a defendant's Part 36 offer or Part 36 payment.)

Unless it considers it injust (r.36.20(2))—The court will doubtless take into account all the circumstances of the case inlcuding those specified under r.36.21(5). **36.20.1**

Costs and other consequences where claimant does better than he proposed in his Part 36 offer

36.21—(1) This rule applies where at trial— **36.21**

(a) a defendant is held liable for more; or

(b) the judgment against a defendant is more advantageous to the claimant,

than the proposals contained in a claimant's Part 36 offer.

(2) The court may order interest on the whole or part of any sum of money (excluding interest) awarded to the claimant at a rate not exceeding 10% above base rate[GL] for some or all of the period starting with the latest date on

which the defendant could have accepted the offer without needing the permission of the court.

(3) The court may also order that the claimant is entitled to—

(a) his costs on the indemnity basis from the latest date when the defendant could have accepted the offer without needing the permission of the court; and

(b) interest on those costs at a rate not exceeding 10% above base rate[GL].

(4) Where this rule applies, the court will make the orders referred to in paragraphs (2) and (3) unless it considers it unjust to do so.

(Rule 36.12 sets out the latest date when the defendant could have accepted the offer.)

(5) In considering whether it would be unjust to make the orders referred to in (2) and (3) above, the court will take into account all the circumstances of the case including—

(a) the terms of any Part 36 offer;

(b) the stage in the proceedings when any Part 36 offer or Part 36 payment was made;

(c) the information available to the parties at the time when the Part 36 offer or Part 36 payment was made; and

(d) the conduct of the parties with regard to the giving or refusing to give information for the purposes of enabling the offer or payment into court to be made or evaluated.

(6) The power of the court under this rule is in addition to any other power it may have to award interest.

36.21.1 **"... order interest ... at a rate not exceeding 10% above base rate ..."**—The court will make in the circumstances specified in this rule such an order unless it considers it unjust to do. This is a new provision. The matters which the court is to consider are set out in paragraph (5).

36.21.2 **Note**—The amendments to section 17 of the Judgments Act 1838 enable the court to order interest to run on costs from a date earlier than the judgment (see r.44.3(6)(g)). That power may well be exercised where this Part applies to penalise further the refusal of a reasonable offer.

Interest

36.22 **36.22**—(1) Unless—

(a) a claimant's Part 36 offer which offers to accept a sum of money; or

(b) a Part 36 payment notice,

indicates to the contrary, any such offer or payment will be treated as inclusive of all interest until the last date on which it could be accepted without needing the permission of the court.

(2) Where a claimant's Part 36 offer or a Part 36 payment is expressed not to be inclusive of interest, the offer or notice must state—

(a) whether interest is offered; and

(b) if so, the amount offered, the rate or rates offered and the period or periods for which it is offered.

36.22.1 **Interest accrued on money paid into court**—Pt 36 PD(F) 8.10 (see para. 36PD–001) provides that unless the parties agree otherwise interest accruing up to the date of acceptance will be paid to the offeror and interest accuring as from date of acceptance until payment out will be paid to the offeree.

Deduction of benefits

36.23 **36.23**—(1) This rule applies where a payment to a claimant following acceptance of a Part 36 offer or Part 36 payment into court would be a compensation payment as defined in section 1 of the Social Security (Recovery of Benefits) Act 1997.[2]

[2] 1997 c. 27.

(2) A defendant to a money claim may make an offer to settle the claim which will have the consequences set out in this Part, without making a Part 36 payment if—

(a) at the time he makes the offer he has applied for, but not received, a certificate of recoverable benefit; and

(b) he makes a Part 36 payment not more than 7 days after he receives the certificate.

(Section 1 of the 1997 Act defines "recoverable benefit".)

(3) A Part 36 payment notice must state—

(a) the amount of gross compensation;

(b) the name and amount of any benefit by which that gross amount is reduced in accordance with section 8 and Schedule 2 to the 1997 Act; and

(c) that the sum paid in is the net amount after deduction of the amount of benefit.

(4) For the purposes of rule 36.20, a claimant fails to better a Part 36 payment if he fails to obtain judgment for more than the gross sum specified in the Part 36 payment notice.

(5) Where—

(a) a Part 36 payment has been made; and

(b) application is made for the money remaining in court to be paid out,

the court may treat the money in court as being reduced by a sum equivalent to any further recoverable benefits paid to the claimant since the date of payment into court and may direct payment out accordingly.

"**... but has not received a certificate of recoverable benefit**"—This is a new provision allowing a defendant to make an offer to settle at a time when he has applied for but not received a certificate which will have the consequences set out in Pt 36. The conditions specified must be complied with to achieve such consequences. **36.23.1**

PRACTICE DIRECTION—OFFERS TO SETTLE AND PAYMENTS INTO COURT

This Practice Direction supplements CPR Part 36

Part 36 Offers and Part 36 Payments

1.1 A written offer to settle a claim[3] or part of a claim or any issue that arises in it made in accordance with the provisions of Part 36 is called; **36PD–001**

(1) if made by way of a payment into court, a Part 36 payment,[4] or

(2) if made otherwise, a Part 36 offer.[5]

1.2 A Part 36 offer or Part 36 payment has the costs and other consequences set out in rules 36.13, 36.14, 36.20 and 36.21.

1.3 An offer to settle which is not made in accordance with Part 36 will only have the consequences specified in that Part if the court so orders and will be given such weight on any issue as to costs as the court thinks appropriate.[6]

Parties and Part 36 offers

2.1 A Part 36 offer, subject to paragraph 3 below, may be made by any party.

2.2 The party making an offer is the "offeror" and the party to whom it is made is the "offeree".

2.3 A Part 36 offer may consist of a proposal to settle for a specified sum or for some other remedy.

[3] Includes Part 20 claims.
[4] See rule 36.2(1)(a).
[5] See rule 36.2(1)(b).
[6] See rule 36.1(2).

2.4 A Part 36 offer is made when received by the offeree.[7]

2.5 An improvement to a Part 36 offer is effective when its details are received by the offeree.[8]

Parties and Part 36 payments

3.1 An offer to settle for a specified sum made by a defendant[9] must, in order to comply with Part 36, be made by way of a Part 36 payment into court[10].

3.2 A Part 36 payment is made when the Part 36 payment notice is served on the claimant.[11]

3.3 An increase to a Part 36 payment will be effective when notice of the increase is served on the claimant.[12]

(For service of the Part 36 payment notice see rule 36.6(3) and (4).)

3.4 A defendant who wishes to withdraw or reduce a Part 36 payment must obtain the court's permission to do so.

3.5 Permission may be obtained by making an application in accordance with Part 23 stating the reasons giving rise to the wish to withdraw or reduce the Part 36 payment.

Making a Part 36 payment

4.1 To make a Part 36 payment the defendant must file the following documents:

(1) where that court is a county court or a district registry—

(a) the Part 36 payment notice, and

(b) the payment, usually a cheque made payable to Her Majesty's Paymaster General,

with the court, and

(2) where that court is the Royal Courts of Justice—

(a) the Part 36 payment notice with the court, and

(b) the payment, usually a cheque made payable to the Accountant General of the Supreme Court, and

(c) a sealed copy of the Claim Form,

(d) the Court Funds Office form 100 with the Court Funds Office.

Part 36 offers and Part 36 payments—general provisions

5.1 A Part 36 offer or a Part 36 payment notice must;

(1) state that it is a Part 36 offer or that the payment into court is a Part 36 payment, and

(2) be signed by the offeror or his legal representative.[13]

5.2 The contents of a Part 36 offer must also comply with the requirements of rule 36.5(3), (5) and (6).

5.3 The contents of a Part 36 payment notice must comply with rule 36.6(2) and, if rule 36.23 applies, with rule 36.23(3).

5.4 A Part 36 offer or Part 36 payment will be taken to include interest unless it is expressly stated in the offer or the payment notice that interest is not included, in which case the details set out in rule 36.22(2) must be given.

5.5 Where a Part 36 offer is made by a company or other corporation, a person holding a senior position in the company or corporation may sign the offer on the offeror's behalf, but must state the position he holds.

[7] See rule 36.8(1).
[8] See rule 36.8(3).
[9] Includes a respondent to a claim or issue.
[10] See rule 36.3(1).
[11] See rule 36.8(2).
[12] See rule 36.8(4).
[13] For the definition of legal representative see rule 2.3.

5.6 Each of the following persons is a person holding a senior position:

(1) in respect of a registered company or corporation, a director, the treasurer, secretary, chief executive, manager or other officer of the company or corporation, and

(2) in respect of a corporation which is not a registered company, in addition to those persons set out in (1), the major, chairman, president, town clerk or similar officer of the corporation.

Clarification of Part 36 offer or payment

6.1 An offeree may apply to the court for an order requiring the offeror to clarify the terms of a Part 36 offer or Part 36 payment notice (a clarification order) where the offeror has failed to comply within 7 days with a request for clarification.[14] 36PD–002

6.2 An application for a clarification order should be made in accordance with Part 23.

6.3 The application notice should state the respects in which the terms of the Part 36 offer or Part 36 payment notice, as the case may be, are said to need clarification.

Acceptance of a Part 36 offer or payment

7.1 The times for accepting a Part 36 offer or a Part 36 payment are set out in rules 36.11 and 36.12.

7.2 The general rule is that a Part 36 offer or Part 36 payment made more than 21 days before the start of the trial may be accepted within 21 days after it was made without the permission of the court. The costs consequences set out in rules 36.13 and 36.14 will then come into effect.

7.3 A Part 36 offer or Part 36 payment made less than 21 days before the start of the trial cannot be accepted without the permission of the court unless the parties agree what the costs consequences of acceptance will be.

7.4 The permission of the court may be sought:

(1) before the start of the trial, by making an application in accordance with Part 23, and

(2) after the start of the trial, by making an application to the trial judge.

7.5 If the court gives permission it will make an order dealing with costs and may order that, in the circumstances, the costs consequences set out in rules 36.13 and 36.14 will apply.

7.6 Where a Part 36 offer or Part 36 payment is accepted in accordance with rule 36.11(1) or rule 36.12(1) the notice of acceptance must be sent to the offeror and filed with the court.

7.7 The notice of acceptance:

(1) must set out—
- (a) the claim number, and
- (b) the title of the proceedings,

(2) must identify the Part 36 offer or Part 36 payment notice to which it relates, and

(3) must be signed by the offeree or his legal representative (see paragraphs 6.5 and 6.6 above).

7.8 Where:

(1) the court's approval, or

(2) an order for payment of money out of court, or

(3) an order apportioning money in court
- (a) between the Fatal Accidents Act 1976 and the Law Reform (Miscellaneous Provisions) Act 1934, or
- (b) between the persons entitled to it under the Fatal Accidents Act 1976,

[14] See rule 36.9(1) and (2).

is required for acceptance of a Part 36 offer or Part 36 payment, application for the approval or the order should be made in accordance with Part 23.

7.9 The court will include in any order made under paragraph 7.8 above a direction for:

(1) the payment out of the money in court, and

(2) the payment of interest.

7.10 Unless the parties have agreed otherwise:

(1) interest accruing up to the date of acceptance will be paid to the offeror, and

(2) interest accruing as from the date of acceptance until payment out will be paid to the offeree.

7.11 A claimant may not accept a Part 36 payment which is part of a defendant's offer to settle the whole of a claim consisting of both a money and a non-money claim unless at the same time he accepts the offer to settle the whole of the claim. Therefore:

(1) if a claimant accepts a Part 36 payment which is part of a defendant's offer to settle the whole of the claim, or

(2) if a claimant accepts a Part 36 offer which is part of a defendant's offer to settle the whole of the claim,

the claimant will be deemed to have accepted the offer to settle the whole of the claim.[15]

(See paragraph 8 below for the method of obtaining money out of court.)

Payment out of court

8.1 To obtain money out of court following acceptance of a Part 36 payment, the claimant should file a request for payment with the court.[16]

8.2 The request for payment should contain the following details:

(1) where the party receiving the payment—
  - (a) is legally represented—
    - (i) the name, business address and reference of the legal representative, and
    - (ii) the name of the bank and the sort code number, the title of the account and the account number where the payment is to be transmitted, and

(2) where the party is acting in person—
  - (a) his name and address, and
  - (b) his bank account details as in (ii) above.

8.3 Where the request for payment is made to the Royal Courts of Justice, the claimant should also complete Court Funds Office form 201 and file it in the Court Funds Office.

8.4 Subject to paragraph 9.5(1) and (2), if a party does not wish the payment to be transmitted into his bank account or if he does not have a bank account, he may send a written request to the Accountant General for the payment to be made to him by cheque.

8.5 Where a party seeking payment out of court has provided the necessary information, the payment:

(1) where a party is legally represented, must be made to the legal representative,

(2) if the party is not legally represented but is, or has been, in receipt of legal aid in respect of the proceedings and a notice to that effect has been filed, should be made to the Legal Aid Board by direction of the court,

(3) where a person entitled to money in court dies without having made a will and the court is satisfied—

[15] See rule 36.4.
[16] In practice form N243.

(a) that no grant of administration of his estate has been made and
(b) that the assets of his estate, including the money in court, do not exceed in value the amount specified in any order in force under section 6 of the Administration of Estates (Small Payments) Act 1965,

may be ordered to be made to the person appearing to have the prior right to a grant of administration of the estate of the deceased, *e.g.* a widower, widow, child, father, mother, brother or sister of the deceased.

Foreign currency

9.1 Money may be paid into court in a foreign currency: 36PD–003

(1) where it is a Part 36 payment and the claim is in a foreign currency; or
(2) under a court order.

9.2 The court may direct that the money be placed in an interest bearing account in the curency of the claim or any other currency.

9.3 Where a Part 36 payment is made in a foreign currency and has not been accepted within 21 days, the defendant may apply for an order that the money be placed in an interest bearing account.

9.4 The application should be made in accordance with Part 23 and should state:

(1) that the payment has not been accepted in accordance with rule 36.11, and

(2) the type of currency on which interest is to accrue.

Compensation recovery

10.1 Where a defendant makes a Part 36 payment in respect of a claim for a sum or part of a sum:

(1) which falls under the heads of damage set out in column 1 of Schedule 2 of the Social Security (Recovery of Benefits) Act 1997 in respect of recoverable benefits received by the claimant as set out in column 2 of that Schedule, and

(2) where the defendant is liable to pay recoverable benefits to the Secretary of State,

the defendant should obtain from the Secretary of State a certificate of recoverable benefits and file the certificate with the Part 36 payment notice.

10.2 If a defendant wishes to offer to settle a claim where he has applied for but not yet received a certificate of recoverable benefits, he may, provided that he makes a Part 36 payment not more than 7 days after he has received the certificate, make a Part 36 offer which will have the costs and other consequences set out in rules 36.13 and 36.20.

10.3 The Part 36 payment notice should state in addition to the requirements set out in rule 36.6(2):

(1) the total amount represented by the Part 36 payment (the gross compensation),

(2) that the defendant has reduced this sum by £   , in accordance with section 8 of and Schedule 2 to the Social Security (Recovery of Benefits) Act 1997, which was calculated as follows:

Name of benefit   Amount

and

(3) that the amount paid in, being the sum of £   is the net amount after the deduction of the amount of benefit.

10.4 On acceptance of a Part 36 payment to which this paragraph relates, a claimant will receive the sum in court which will be net of the recoverable benefits.

10.5 In establishing at trial whether a claimant has bettered or obtained a judgment more advantageous than a Part 36 payment to which this paragraph relates, the court will base its decision on the gross sum specified in the Part 36 payment notice.

General

11.1 Where a party on whom a Part 36 offer, a Part 36 payment notice or a notice of acceptance is to be served is legally represented, the Part 36 offer, Part 36 payment notice and notice of acceptance must be served on the legal representative.

11.2 In a claim arising out of an accident involving a motor vehicle on a road or in a public place:

(1) where the damages claimed include a sum for hospital expenses, and

(2) the defendant or his insurer pays that sum to the hospital under section 157 of the Road Traffic Act 1988,

the defendant must give notice of that payment to the court and all the other parties to the proceedings.

11.3 Money paid into court:

(1) as a Part 36 payment which is not accepted by the claimant, or

(2) under a court order,

will be placed after 21 days in a basic account[17] (subject to paragraph 11.4 below) for interest to accrue.

11.4 Where money referred to in paragraph 11.3 above is paid in in respect of a child or patient it will be placed in a special investment account[18] for interest to accrue.

(A practice direction supplementing Part 21 contains information about the investment of money in court in respect of a child or patient.)

(Practice directions supplementing Part 40 contain information about adjustment of the judgment sum in respect of recoverable benefits, and about structured settlements.)

(A practice direction supplementing Part 41 contains information about provisional damages awards.)

[17] See rule 26 of the Court Funds Office Rules 1987.
[18] See rule 26 as above.

PART 37

MISCELLANEOUS PROVISIONS ABOUT PAYMENTS INTO COURT

Contents 37.0.1

Editorial Introduction

If money is paid into court under a court order notice of such payment will be given to every other party and such money may not be paid out without court order save where the defendant elects to treat the money or part thereof as a Pt 36 payment and the claimant accepts the Pt 36 payment without needing the permission of the court (see r.37.1(1) and (2)). Rule 37.2 provides the facility to so treat the whole or part of the sum paid into court under order and requires a Pt 36 payment notice to be filed. 37.0.2

If a defendant wishes to rely upon the defence of tender before claim he must make a payment into court of the amount he says was tendered (see r.37.3(1)) where he does so he may elect to treat the whole or part thereof as a Pt 36 payment so long as he files a Pt 36 payment notice (see r.37.3(3)).

Where a claim includes claims under the Fatal Accidents Act 1976 and the Law Reform (Miscellaneous Provisions) Act 1934 and a single sum is paid into court which is accepted, the court must apportion the money between the different claims (see r.37.4(1)).

Similarly where a claim is made under the Fatal Accidents Act 1976 by or on behalf of more than one person, again the court must apportion the sum paid in and accepted between those entitled to it unless it has already been apportioned by the court, a jury or agreement between the parties (see r.37.4(3)). Note too the courts control over money received by a child or patient under r.20.11.

Related Sources

- Practice Direction (Offers to Settle and Payments Into Court) (see para. 36PD–001). 37.0.3
- Practice Direction (Miscellaneous Provisions about Payments Into Court) (see para. 37PD–001).

Forms

- Court Funds Office Forms—Form 100 and Form 101. 37.0.4

Money paid into court under a court order—general

37.1—(1) When a party makes a payment into court under a court order, the court will give notice of the payment to every other party. 37.1

(2) Money paid into court under a court order may not be paid out without the court's permission except where—

(a) the defendant treats the money as a Part 36 payment under rule 37.2; and

(b) the claimant accepts the Part 36 payment without needing the permission of the court.

(Rule 36.11 sets out when the claimant can accept a Part 36 payment without needing the permission of the court.)

Formalities of payment into court under order—See Pt 37 PD(F) 1.1 to 1.3 (see para. 37PD–001). 37.1.1

Money paid into court may be treated as a Part 36 payment

37.2—(1) Where a defendant makes a payment into court following an 37.2

order made under rule 3.1(3) or 3.1(5) he may choose to treat the whole or any part of the money paid into court as a Part 36 payment.

(Rule 36.2 defines a Part 36 payment.)

(2) To do this he must file a Part 36 payment notice.

(Rule 36.6 sets out what a Part 36 payment notice must contain and provides for the court to serve it on the other parties.)

(3) If he does so this Part applies to the money as if he had paid it into court as a Part 36 payment.

37.2.1 **Formalities of payment into court where defence of tender before claim**—See Pt 37 PD(F) 2.1 and 2.2 (see para. 37PD–001).

Money paid into court where defendant wishes to rely on defence of tender before claim

37.3 **37.3**—(1) Where a defendant wishes to rely on a defence of tender before claim[GL] he must make a payment into court of the amount he says was tendered.

(2) If the defendant does not make a payment in accordance with paragraph (1) the defence of tender before claim[GL] will not be available to him until he does so.

(3) Where the defendant makes such payment into court—

(a) he may choose to treat the whole or any part of the money paid into court as a Part 36 payment; and if so

(b) if he does so, he must file a Part 36 payment notice.

Proceedings under Fatal Accidents Act 1976 and Law Reform (Miscellaneous Provisions) Act 1934—apportionment by court

37.4 **37.4**—(1) Where—

(a) a claim includes claims arising under—

(i) the Fatal Accidents Act 1976[1]; and

(ii) the Law Reform (Miscellaneous Provisions) Act 1934[2];

(b) a single sum of money is paid into court in satisfaction of those claims; and

(c) the money is accepted,

the court shall apportion the money between the different claims.

(2) The court shall apportion money under paragraph (1)—

(a) when it gives directions under rule 21.11 (control of money received by a child or patient); or

(b) if rule 21.11 does not apply, when it gives permission for the money to be paid out of court.

(3) Where, in an action in which a claim under the Fatal Accidents Act 1976 is made by or on behalf of more than one person—

(a) a sum in respect of damages is ordered or agreed to be paid in satisfaction of the claim; or

(b) a sum of money is accepted in satisfaction of the claim,

the court shall apportion it between the persons entitled to it unless it has already been apportioned by the court, a jury, or agreement between the parties.

(Other rules about payment into court can be found—

(a) in Schedule 1, in the following RSC—O.49 (garnishee proceed-

[1] 1976, c. 30.
[2] 1934, c. 41.

ings); O.50 (stop orders in funds in court); O.82 (defamation claims); O.92 (payments into court in particular circumstances); and

(b) in Schedule 2, in the following CCR—O.30 (garnishee proceedings); O.49 (payment in under various statutes)).

Obtaining of courts permission for payment out—Application may be made in accordance with Pt 23. 37.4.1

PRACTICE DIRECTION—MISCELLANEOUS PROVISIONS ABOUT PAYMENTS INTO COURT

This Practice Direction supplements CPR Part 37

For information about payments into and out of court in relation to offers to settle see Part 36 and the practice direction which supplements it. 37PD–001

Payments into court under an order

1.1 Where money is paid into court under an order, the party making the payment should:

(1) lodge his payment, and

(2) file a copy of the order directing payment into court.

1.2 Where the order is made in a county court or district registry the payment will usually be made by cheque payable to Her Majesty's Paymaster General.

1.3 Where the order is made in the Royal Courts of Justice, the payment will usually be made by cheque payable to the Accountant General of the Supreme Court, and should be;

(1) accompanied by

(a) a completed Court Funds Office forms 100 or 101, and

(b) a sealed copy of the order, and

(2) lodged in the Court Fund Office.

A copy of the Court Funds Office receipt should be filed in the appropriate court office in the Royal Courts of Justice.

Defence of tender

2.1 A defendant paying a sum of money into court in support of a defence of tender[3] should do so when filing his defence and should at the same time complete and file:

(1) a notice of payment into court, and

(2) where the defence is filed in the Royal Courts of Justice, Court Funds Office form 100.

2.2 A defence of tender will not be available to a defendant until he has complied with paragraph 2.1.

General

3.1 Where money is paid into court:

(1) under an order permitting a defendant to defend or to continue to defend under rule 37.2(1), or

(2) in support of a defence of tender under rule 37.3,

the party making the payment may, if a defendant, choose to treat the whole or any part of the money as a Part 36 payment.[4]

3.2 In order to do so the defendant must file a Part 36 payment notice in

[3] Rule 37.3.

[4] Rules 37.2(2) and 37.3(3).

accordance with rule 36.6 (see also paragraph 6 of the practice direction which supplements Part 36).

3.3 Rule 37.4 deals with the apportionment of money paid into court in respect of claims arising under:

(1) the Fatal Accidents Act 1976, and

(2) the Law Reform (Miscellaneous Provisions) Act 1934.

(See also paragraph 8.8 of the practice direction supplementing Part 36.)

Payment out of court

4.1 Except where money which has been paid into court is treated as a Part 36 payment and can be accepted by the claimant without needing the court's permission, the court's permission is required to take the money out of court.

4.2 Permission may be obtained by making an application in accordance with Part 23. The application notice must state the grounds on which the order for payment out is sought. Evidence of any facts on which the applicant relies may also be necessary.

4.3 To obtain the money out of court the applicant must comply with the provisions of paragraph 9 of the practice direction supplementing Part 36 where they apply.

Foreign currency

5. For information on payments into court made in a foreign currency, see paragraph 9 of the practice direction supplementing Part 36.

PART 38

DISCONTINUANCE

Contents **38.0.1**

Editorial Introduction

The former High Court and County Court procedures differed fundamentally in one important respect. In the High Court, leave to discontinue was required once 14 days had elapsed after service of the defence: in the county court, leave to discontinue was never required. Part 38 does not (as a general rule) require the claimant to obtain permission to discontinue and to that extent Pt 38 is derived from former CCR, O.18 rather than RSC, O.21. However, Pt 38 is far more thorough than CCR, O.18. **38.0.2**

The former High Court requirement to obtain leave was imposed to prevent a discontinuance which would unfairly prejudice the defendant. The High Court could grant leave on terms or refuse leave and force the plaintiff to trial (*Fox v. Star Newspapers* [1898] 1 Q.B. 636; [1900] A.C. 19). The new procedure caters for this situation by enabling a defendant to apply to have the notice of discontinuance set aside (see r.38.4(1)).

Discontinuance by the claimant terminates his action in whole or in part (see r.38.2(1)).

Permission to discontinue is required by the claimant only in the three situations prescribed by r.38.2(2).

A claimant who discontinues is liable for the defendant's costs unless the court orders otherwise (r.38.6).

Practice Direction

Part 38 is not supplemented by a Practice Direction. **38.0.3**

Related sources

Pt 17 (amendment) PD to Part 39, para. 4. **38.0.4**

Scope of this Part

38.1—(1) The rules in this Part set out the procedure by which a claimant may discontinue all or part of a claim. **38.1**

(2) A claimant who—

(a) claims more than one remedy; and

(b) subsequently abandons his claim to one or more of the remedies but continues with his claim for the other remedies,

is not treated as discontinuing all or part of a claim for the purposes of this Part.

(The procedure for amending a statement of case, set out in Part 17, applies where a claimant abandons a claim for a particular remedy but wishes to continue with his claim for other remedies.)

Effect of rule—The word "claim" in RSC, O.21 was used in the sense of "cause of action" rather **38.1.1**

than a form of relief. Part 38 is clearly to like effect. Thus a claimant may discontinue all or part of a claim but a claimant who merely abandons one or more of the remedies sought is not treated as discontinuing for the purposes of Pt 38. (*cf.* the power to amend in Pt 17 which may result in the withdrawal of part of a claim.)

Right to discontinue claim

38.2 **38.2**—(1) A claimant may discontinue all or part of a claim at any time.

(2) However—

(a) a claimant must obtain the permission of the court if he wishes to discontinue all or part of a claim in relation to which—

(i) the court has granted an interim injunction[GL]; or

(ii) any party has given an undertaking to the court;

(b) where the claimant has received an interim payment in relation to a claim (whether voluntarily or pursuant to an order under Part 25), he may discontinue that claim only if—

(i) the defendant who made the interim payment consents in writing; or

(ii) the court gives permission;

(c) where there is more than one claimant, a claimant may not discontinue unless—

(i) every other claimant consents in writing; or

(ii) the court gives permission.

(3) Where there is more than one defendant, the claimant may discontinue all or part of a claim against all or any of the defendants.

38.2.1 **Effect of rule**—Rule 38.2 is clear. As a general rule it gives the claimant, a right to discontinue all or part of a claim at any time without having to first seek the permission of the court. Permission is required only in the special situations provided for by r.38.2(2). The claimant may discontinue all or part of a claim against all or any of the defendants.

For the procedure to discontinue see r.38.3 and for the costs consequences see r.38.6.

Procedure for discontinuing

38.3 **38.3**—(1) To discontinue a claim or part of a claim, a claimant must—

(a) file a notice of discontinuance; and

(b) serve a copy of it on every other party to the proceedings.

(2) The claimant must state in the notice of discontinuance which he files that he has served notice of discontinuance on every other party to the proceedings.

(3) Where the claimant needs the consent of some other party, a copy of the necessary consent must be attached to the notice of discontinuance.

(4) Where there is more than one defendant, the notice of discontinuance must specify against which defendants the claim is discontinued.

38.3.1 **Notice of discontinuance**—All that is required to discontinue is for the claimant to file notice of discontinuance with the court and serve a copy of it on every other party to the proceedings. A notice of discontinuance must comply with r.38.3(2), (3) and (4) and must be in Form N279 (See Pt 4(1)).

38.3.2 **Discontinuance after the trial date is fixed**—PD to Part 39, para. 4.1 provides that the listing officer must be informed immediately if a claim is discontinued after a date or "window" has been fixed for trial.

Right to apply to have notice of discontinuance set aside

38.4 **38.4**—(1) Where the claimant discontinues under rule 38.2(1) the defendant may apply to have the notice of discontinuance set aside[GL].

(2) The defendant may not make an application under this rule more than 28 days after the date when the notice of discontinuance was served on him.

38.4.1 **Effect of rule**—The rule provides a procedure and time limit for a defendant to apply to have a notice of discontinuance set aside.

A court may set aside a notice of discontinuance as an abuse of the process of the court (*Ernst and Young v. Butte Mining plc* [1996] 1 W.L.R. 1605; *Fakih Bros v. Moller (Copenhagen)* [1994] 1 Lloyd's Rep. 103).

The former requirement to obtain leave to discontinue in RSC, O.21, r.3 is not repeated in the CPR. Consequently, a defendant who would have opposed an application for leave must now invoke r.38.4 and apply to have the notice of discontinuance set aside within 28 days of service of the notice upon him.

Application—Such an application should be made with notice and be supported by evidence (see Pt 23, PD to Pt 23, para. 9 and r.32.2). **38.4.2**

When discontinuance takes effect where permission of the court is not needed

38.5—(1) Discontinuance against any defendant takes effect on the date when notice of discontinuance is served on him under rule 38.3(1). **38.5**

(2) Subject to rule 38.4, the proceedings are brought to an end as against him on that date.

(3) However, this does not affect proceedings to deal with any question of costs.

"Where permission of the court is not needed"—Permission to discontinue is not required as a general rule. However, permission is required in the three special situations set out in r.38.2(2). **38.5.1**

Effect of rule—Discontinuance takes effect on the date when notice of discontinuance is served. In a case where permission to discontinue is required pursuant to r.38.2(2) the order granting permission will provide for the date when discontinuance takes effect. **38.5.2**

"question of costs"—See r.38.6. **38.5.3**

Liability for costs

38.6—(1) Unless the court orders otherwise, a claimant who discontinues is liable for the costs which a defendant against whom he discontinues incurred on or before the date on which notice of discontinuance was served on him. **38.6**

(2) If proceedings are only partly discontinued—

(a) the claimant is liable under paragraph (1) for costs relating only to the part of the proceedings which he is discontinuing; and

(b) unless the court orders otherwise, the costs which the claimant is liable to pay must not be assessed until the conclusion of the rest of the proceedings.

(3) This rule does not apply to claims allocated to the small claims track.

(Rule 44.12 provides for the basis of assessment where right to costs arises on discontinuance.)

Effect of rule—A claimant who discontinues his claim is, as a general rule, conceding that he has lost or cannot win the case. Accordingly, the general rule is that the discontinuing claimant must pay the defendant's costs. An order is deemed to have been made in the defendant's favour on the standard basis (see r.44.12(1)). For the procedure for assessing costs see r.44.7. Statutory interest on costs will run from the date of service of the notice—see r.44.12(2). **38.6.1**

A claimant who, for good reason, wishes to avoid the costs penalty must apply for an order under r.38.6(1). This could include, for example, a case where the dispute has since become academic and therefore discontinuance is not a defeat or an acknowledgment of likely defeat (see e.g. *Barretts and Baird (Wholesale) Ltd v. Institution of Professional Civil Servants* [1987] 1 F.T.L.R. 121; [1987] I.R.L.R. 3) or a case where the claimant having obtained an injunction does not now wish to pursue a claim for damages.

Note that the normal rule as to costs does not apply if a claimant in a case allocated to the small claims track serves a notice of discontinuance (r.38.6(3)) although it might be contended that costs should be awarded if a party has behaved unreasonably (r.27.14(2)(d)).

Discontinuance and subsequent proceedings

38.7 A claimant who discontinues a claim needs the permission of the court to make another claim against the same defendant if— **38.7**

(a) he discontinued the claim after the defendant filed a defence; and
(b) the other claim arises out of facts which are the same or substantially the same as those relating to the discontinued claim.

38.7.1 **Effect of rule**—As a matter of common sense a claimant who has brought and then abandoned a claim ought not, as a general rule, to be allowed to start another claim arising out of the same facts.

A claimant who wishes to do so is first required to seek permission. The court is likely to give permission, for example, where the claimant was misled or tricked by the defendant, where important new evidence has come to light or where there has been a retrospective change in the law (*e.g.* a House of Lords case overruling a Court of Appeal decision which had led the claimant to discontinue). All these examples are, of course, exceptional cases and assume that the limitation period has still not expired.

Under the former practice of former RSC, O.21, r.3 where leave to discontinue was required, the court would often impose terms as a condition of granting leave including a term that no new action be brought. Such an order is no longer required as r.38.7 puts the onus on the claimant to seek permission before making another claim against the same defendant arising out of the same facts.

The rule is silent as to how the claimant seeks permission. Therefore the general rules in Pt 23 apply. The application will be on notice.

Permission for another claim is not required if the claimant discontinues the first claim before the defendant filed a defence.

Stay of remainder of partly discontinued proceedings where costs not paid

38.8 **38.8**—(1) This rule applies where—
(a) proceedings are partly discontinued;
(b) a claimant is liable to pay costs under rule 38.6; and
(c) the claimant fails to pay those costs within 21 days of—
(i) the date on which the parties agreed the sum payable by the claimant; or
(ii) the date on which the court ordered the costs to be paid.

(2) Where this rule applies, the court may stay[GL] the remainder of the proceedings until the claimant pays the whole of the costs which he is liable to pay under rule 38.6.

38.8.1 **Effect of rule**—Rule 38.8 needs to be read in conjunction with r.38.6. Under r.38.6, if proceedings are only partly discontinued, the claimant is liable for the defendant's costs relating to the part of the proceedings which are discontinued, but, unless the court orders otherwise, the costs which the claimant is liable to pay must not be assessed until the conclusion of the rest of the proceedings. Rule 38.8 can only come into play, therefore, where the court has ordered otherwise under r.38.6(2)(b). If the court has ordered otherwise the claimant must pay the defendant's costs within 21 days (r.38.8(1)(c)) and if he fails to do so the court may stay the remainder of the proceedings until the costs have been paid. Rule 38.8(2) provides that the court "may stay" the remainder of the proceedings. Thus a stay is not automatic and an application to the court is required.

PART 39

Miscellaneous Provisions Relating to Hearings

Contents **39.0.1**

Editorial Introduction

As its title suggests this Part sweeps up various remaining provisions concerning hearings, in particular setting out which hearings should be in public and which should be in private. Significantly the Practice Direction (see para. 39PD–001) deals with a number of subjects not dealt with in the Rules themselves, namely settlement or discontinuance after the fixing of a trial date, recording of proceedings and exhibits. **39.0.2**

Related sources

- Practice Directions to Pt 39 (see paras 39PD–001 and 39BPD–001). **39.0.3**
- Human Rights Act 1998, Sched. 1, Art. 6.

Interpretation

39.1 In this Part, reference to a hearing includes a reference to the trial. **39.1**

"hearing" (r.39.1, r.39.2)—Apart from expressly providing that "hearing" includes trial, there is no further definition. It is clear that it includes interlocutory hearings (*e.g.* under Pt 23—see, *e.g.* the reference in r.39.2(3)(e)) and hearings of cases on the Small Claims Track (see *e.g.* r.27.6(4) and r.27.8) as well as fast track and multi-track trials. **39.1.1**

General rule—hearing to be in public

39.2—(1) The general rule is that a hearing is to be in public. **39.2**

(2) The requirement for a hearing to be in public does not require the court to make special arrangements for accommodating members of the public.

(3) A hearing, or any part of it, may be in private if—

(a) publicity would defeat the object of the hearing;

(b) it involves matters relating to national security;

(c) it involves confidential information (including information relating to personal financial matters) and publicity would damage that confidentiality;

(d) a private hearing is necessary to protect the interests of any child or patient;

(e) it is a hearing of an application made without notice and it would be unjust to any respondent for there to be a public hearing;

(f) it involves uncontentious matters arising in the administration of trusts or in the administration of a deceased person's estate; or

(g) the court considers this to be necessary, in the interests of justice.

(2) The court may order that the identity of any party or witness must not be disclosed if it considers non-disclosure necessary in order to protect the interests of that party or witness.

(RSC, O.52, in Schedule 1, provides that a committal hearing may be in private.)

39.2.1 **"hearing to be in public" (r.39.2)**—See Human Rights Act 1998, Sched. 1 (incorporating the European Convention on Human Rights) where Art. 6 states:

> "In the determination of his civil rights and obligation ... everyone is entitled to a fair and public hearing within a reasonable time by an independent and impartial tribunal established by law. Judgment shall be pronounced publicly but the press and public may be excluded from all or part of the trial in the interest of morals, public order or national security in a democratic society, where the interests of juveniles or the protection of the private life of the parties so require, or to the extent strictly necessary in the opinion of the court in special circumstances where publicity would prejudice the interests of justice."

The exceptions are set out in r.39.2 and fleshed out in the Practice Direction (see para. 39PD–001).

Note that one consequence of hearings in public is an automatic right to a transcript, subject to payment of the appropriate fee (Practice Direction, para. 1.11, see 39PD–001) whereas if the hearing is in private, a member of the public who is not a party to the proceedings must seek the permission of the judge before obtaining a transcript of the judgment (Practice Direction, para. 1.12, see 39PD–001).

Note that the venue of a hearing and whether it is in public or private does not affect existing rights of audience (Practice Direction, para. 1.14, see 39PD–001).

39.2.2 **"A hearing, or any part of it, may be in private" (r.39.2(3))**—See too the Practice Direction (39PD–001). Paragraph 1.4 states that the decision as to whether to hold a hearing in public or in private must be made by the judge conducting the hearing having regard to any representations which may have been made to him. Paragraph 1.5 of the Practice Direction sets out types of hearings which shall in the first instance be listed in private.

39.2.3 **"Publicity would defeat the object of the hearing" (r.39.2(3)(a))**—For example, an application for a freezing injunction or a search order. See SCP 1999, Vol. 1, paras 29/L/35A–29/L/97.

39.2.4 **"personal financial matters" (r.39.2(3)(c))**—Practice Direction, para. 1.5 (see 39PD–001) provides that the following hearings shall in the first instance be listed in private, namely mortgage possession proceedings against individuals, landlord and tenant possession proceedings based on non-payment of rent, applications to suspend warrants where the ability to make payments is an issue, redetermination under r.14.13, applications to vary or suspend payment of judgment debts, applications for charging orders, garnishee orders, attachment of earnings orders, administration orders or the appointment of a receiver, oral examinations, determination of an assisted person's liability for costs under reg. 127 of the Civil Legal Aid (General) Regulations 1989; applications for security for costs under Companies Act 1985, s.726(1), proceedings brought under Consumer Credit Act 1974, Inheritance (Provision for Family and Dependents) Act 1975 or Protection from Harassment Act 1997 and applications under the Variation of Trusts Act 1958 where no facts are in dispute. See too Practice Direction, para. 1.7 (see 39PD–001) and para. 5.1 of the Practice Direction which supplements Pt 27 (see para. 27PD–001) (hearing of claims in the small claims track). Note that a hearing of a small claim in premises other than a court is not a hearing in public (Practice Direction, para. 1.7, see 39PD–001).

39.2.5 **"child or patient" (39.2(3)(d))**—See r.21.1(2). Practice Direction, para. 1.6 (see 39PD–001) states that this includes the approval of a compromise or settlement on behalf of a child or patient or an application for the payment of money out of court to such a person—see CCR, O.10, rr.10, and 11, RSC, O.80, rr.10–12, SCP 1999, Vol. 1, paras 80/10–80/12/23 and Vol. 2, para. 2C–214.

39.2.6 **"an application made without notice and it would be unjust to any respondent" (r.39.2(3)(e))**—See r.23.4(2).

39.2.7 **"necessary in the interests of justice" (r.39.2(3)(g))**—Clearly this gives the judge a wide discretion. See too r.1.1 (the overriding objective) and Practice Direction, para. 1.8 (see para. 39PD–001).

Transcripts—See Practice Direction, paras 1.11 and 1.12 (para. 39PD–001). 39.2.8

Failure to attend the trial

39.3—(1) The court may proceed with a trial in the absence of a party but— 39.3

(a) if no party attends the trial, it may strike out[GL] the whole of the proceedings;

(b) if the claimant does not attend, it may strike out his claim and any defence to counterclaim; and

(c) if a defendant does not attend, it may strike out his defence or counterclaim (or both).

(2) Where the court strikes out proceedings, or any part of them, under this rule, it may subsequently restore the proceedings, or that part.

(3) Where a party does not attend and the court gives judgment or makes an order against him, the party who failed to attend may apply for the judgment or order to be set aside[GL].

(4) An application under paragraph (2) or paragraph (3) for an order to restore proceedings must be supported by evidence.

(5) Where an application is made under paragraph (2) or (3) by a party who failed to attend the trial, the court may grant the application only if the applicant—

(a) acted promptly when he found out that the court had exercised its power to strike out[GL] or to enter judgment or make an order against him;

(b) had a good reason for not attending the trial; and

(c) has a reasonable prospect of success at the trial.

"Failure to attend the trial" (r.39.3)—This must be read in conjunction with Practice Direction, paras 2.1–2.4 (see 39PD–001) (*cf.* RSC, O.35, r.1 and CCR, O.21). 39.3.1

"The court may . . . strike out the whole of the proceedings" (r.39.3(1))—Note the power to restore: r.39.3(2). Any application to restore should be made in accordance with Pt 23: see Practice Direction, para. 2.3 (see para. 39PD–001). 39.3.2

"counterclaim" (r.39.3(1))—See Pt 20. 39.3.3

"If the claimant does not attend" (r.39.3(1)(b))—The Practice Direction, para. 2.2 (see 39PD–001) envisages that even though a defence to counterclaim may be struck out, the defendant will still have to prove his or her counterclaim, although this will normally only entail tendering witness statements: see Pt 32. 39.3.4

"If the defendant does not attend" (r.39.3(1)(c))—The Practice Direction, para. 2.2 (see 39PD–001) envisages that even though a defence may be struck out, the claimant will still have to prove his or her claim, although this will normally only entail referring to the statement of case: see r.32.6(2) and r.22.1(1)(a). 39.3.5

"the party who failed to attend may apply for the judgment or order to be set aside"—See Pt 23. Any application should be made on notice and be supported by evidence (r.39.3(4)) giving reasons for the failure to attend court and stating when the applicant found out about the order against him: see Practice Direction, para. 2.4 (see para. 39PD–001). Unlike CCR, O.37, r.2, r.39.3(3) does not specify the judge who should hear the application (see too the reference to "court" in r.2.4). Although the aim of the rules is to provide maximum flexibility, as a matter of practice, if all other things are equal, it would be wise for any such application to be heard by the same judge or same level of judge as the one who made the original order. 39.3.6

"the court may grant the application only if . . ." (r.39.3(5))—Note that the wording of r.39.3(5) provides more stringent requirements than CCR, O.37, r.2 which it replaces. The court no longer has a broad discretion. There is only jurisdiction to set aside a regular judgment if the party seeking to have the order set aside can satisfy all three requirements in r.39.3(5). In view of this, cases such as *Hayman v. Rowlands* [1957] 1 W.L.R. 317, CA and *Grimshaw v. Dunbar* [1953] 1 Q.B. 408, CA, no longer apply. The test is more similar to that set out in *Alpine Bulk Transport v. Saudi Eagle Shipping* [1986] Lloyd's Rep. 721, CA, and *Shocked v. Golschmidt* [1998] 1 All E.R. 372, 39.3.7

CA. Note that if the judgment is a nullity (*e.g.* because no notification of the hearing was sent to a party) he or she is entitled to have any order set aside as of right (*ex debito justitiae*)—*White v. Weston* [1968] 2 Q.B. 647, CA.

Timetable for trial

39.4 **39.4** When the court sets a timetable for a trial in accordance with rule 28.6 (fixing or confirming the trial date and giving directions—fast track) or rule 29.8 (setting a trial timetable and fixing or confirming the trial date or week—multi-track) it will do so in consultation with the parties.

Trial bundles

39.5 **39.5**—(1) Unless the court orders otherwise, the claimant must file a trial bundle containing documents required by—

(a) a relevant practice direction; and
(b) any court order.

(2) The claimant must file the trial bundle not more than 7 days and not less than 3 days before the start of the trial.

39.5.1 **Trial bundles (r.39.5)**—This rule replaces CCR, O.17, r.12 and RSC, O.37, r.10. Note that unlike the former rules, responsibility lies solely on the plaintiff. Although the rules no longer state that defendants have an obligation to notify plaintiffs of the documents that they want to have included in bundles, the parties should attempt to agree the contents of trial bundles where possible (Practice Direction, para. 3.9, see para. 39PD–002).

39.5.2 **"file" (r.39.5(1))**—See r.2.3.

39.5.3 **"a relevant practice direction" (r.39.5(1)(a))**—See Practice Direction, para. 3.2 (see para. 39PD–001) which sets out in detail the documents to be included unless the court orders otherwise. The originals of any documents contained in the trial bundles should be available at trial (Practice Direction, para. 3.3, see para. 39PD–002).

The preparation and production of the trial bundle, even where delegated to another person, is the responsibility of the legal representative who has conduct of the claim on behalf of the claimant (Practice Direction, para. 3.4, see para. 39PD–002).

Trial bundles should be paginated continuously throughout and indexed. Where the total number of pages is more than 100, numbered dividers should be placed at intervals between groups of documents (Practice Direction, para. 3.5, see para. 39PD–002). Bundles should normally be contained in ring binders or lever arch files. If there are numerous bundles, a core bundle should be prepared (Practice Direction, para. 3.6, see para. 39PD–002).

If a copy of a document is illegible a typed copy should be included in the bundle next to it (Practice Direction, para. 3.8, see para. 39PD–002).

The party filing the trial bundle should supply identical bundles to all parties to the proceedings and for the use of witnesses (Practice Direction, para. 3.10). Note that there is no provision for payment.

39.5.4 **"not more than 7 days and not less than 3 days" (r.39.5(2))**—See r.2.8. Days means clear days.

Representation at trial of companies or other corporations

39.6 **39.6** A company or other corporation may be represented at trial by an employee if—

(a) the employee has been authorised by the company or corporation to appear at trial on its behalf; and
(b) the court gives permission.

39.6.1 **"Representation at trial of companies or other corporations" (r.39.6)**—See *Charles P Kinnell & Co. Ltd v. Harding Wace & Co.* [1918] 1 K.B. 405 at 413 where Swinfen Eady L.J. said: "As from its nature a company cannot appear in person, not having as a legal entity any visible person, it must appear by counsel or solicitor, or by leave of the judge some other person may be allowed to appear instead of the company to address the court which includes the examination of witnesses and generally conducting the case." In "Access to Justice", Final Report, Lord Woolf MR stated:

"The court should normally exercise its discretion in favour of allowing an employee of a company to take any steps on behalf of the company which a litigant in person could take in High Court or county court proceedings." (Recommendation 153.)

Notwithstanding Recommendation 155, there is no practice direction indicating considerations relevant to the exercise of the court's discretion.

Note PD to Pt 39, para. 5.2 which sets out additional information to be included in the written statement giving details about representation at hearings where a company appears without solicitor or barrister.

Representation—See also Practice Direction supplementing Pt 5 (see para. 5PD–001) which provides that at any hearing a written statement with the name and address of each advocate, his qualification or entitlement to act as an advocate and the party for whom he acts should be provided for the court. **39.6.2**

Impounded documents

39.7—(1) Documents impounded by order of the court must not be released from the custody of the court except in compliance— **39.7**

(a) with a court order; or

(b) with a written request made by a Law Officer or the Director of Public Prosecutions.

(2) A document released from the custody of the court under paragraph (1)(b) must be released into the custody of the person who requested it.

(3) Documents impounded by order of the court, while in the custody of the court, may not be inspected except by a person authorised to do so by a court order.

Impounded documents (r.39.7)—See RSC, O.35, r.13, SCP 1999, Vol. 1, para. 35/13/1 and CCR, O.50, r.11. **39.7.1**

Exhibits at trial—See Practice Direction, para. 7 (see para. 39PD–002). Exhibits handed in during a trial should be recorded on an exhibit list. They should be kept in the custody of the court until the conclusion of the trial unless the judge directs otherwise. At the conclusion of the trial it is the parties' responsibility to obtain their return. **39.7.2**

Settlement or discontinuance after the trial date is fixed—See Practice Direction, para. 4.1 (see para. 39PD–002). In such circumstances the parties must ensure that the listing officer for the trial court is notified immediately. **39.7.3**

Recording of proceedings—See Practice Direction, para. 6.1 (see para. 39PD–002). Judgments will be recorded unless judges direct otherwise. Oral evidence will normally be recorded also. No party or member of the public may use unofficial recording equipment without the permission of the court—*i.e.* the judge, master or district judge (see r.2.4). To do so without permission constitutes contempt of court. **39.7.4**

Note PD to Pt 39, paras 6.3 to 6.5 which deal with transcripts.

PRACTICE DIRECTION—MISCELLANEOUS PROVISIONS RELATING TO HEARINGS

This Practice Direction supplements CPR Part 39

Hearings

1.1 In Part 39, reference to a hearing includes reference to the trial.[1] **39PD–001**

1.2 The general rule is that a hearing is to be in public.[2]

1.3 Rule 39.2(3) sets out the type of proceedings which may be dealt with in private.

1.4 The decisions as to whether to hold a hearing in public or in private must be made by the judge conducting the hearing having regard to any representations which may have been made to him.

[1] Rule 39.1.
[2] Rule 39.2(1).

1.5 The hearings set out below shall in the first instance be listed by the court as hearings in private under rule 39.2(3)(c), namely:

(1) a claim by a mortgagee against one or more individuals for an order for possession of land,

(2) a claim by a landlord against one or more tenants or former tenants for the repossession of a dwelling house based on the non-payment of rent,

(3) an application to suspend a warrant of execution or a warrant of possession or to stay execution where the court is being invited to consider the ability of a party to make payments to another party,

(4) a redetermination under rule 14.13 or an application to vary or suspend the payment of a judgment debt by instalments,

(5) an application for a charging order (including an application to enforce a charging order), garnishee order, attachment of earnings order, administration order, or the appointment of a receiver,

(6) an oral examination,

(7) the determination of an assisted person's liability for costs under regulation 127 of the Civil Legal Aid (General) Regulations 1989,

(8) an application for security for costs under section 726(1) of the Companies Act 1985, and

(9) proceedings brought under the Consumer Credit Act 1974, the Inheritance (Provision for Family and Dependants) Act 1975 or the Protection from Harassment Act 1997,

(10) an application by a trustee or personal representative for directions as to bringing or defending legal proceedings.

(11) an application under the Variation of Trusts Act 1958 where there are no facts in dispute.

1.6 Rule 39.2(3)(d) states that a hearing may be in private where it involves the interests of a child or patient. This includes the approval of a compromise or settlement on behalf of a child or patient or an application for the payment of money out of court to such a person.

1.7 Attention is drawn to paragraph 5.1 of the practice direction which supplements Part 27 (relating to the hearing of claims in the small claims track), which provides that the judge may decide to hold a small claim hearing in private if the parties agree or if a ground mentioned in rule 39.2(3) applies. A hearing of a small claim in premises other than the court will not be a hearing in public.

1.8 Nothing in this practice direction prevents a judge ordering that a hearing taking place in public shall continue in private, or vice-versa.

1.9 If the court or judge's room in which the proceedings are taking place has a sign on the door indicating that the proceedings are private, members of the public who are not parties to the proceedings will not be admitted unless the court permits.

1.10 Where there is no such sign on the door of the court or judge's room, members of the public will be admitted where practicable. The judge may, if he thinks it appropriate, adjourn the proceedings to a larger room or court.

1.11 When a hearing takes place in public, members of the public may obtain a transcript of any judgment given or a copy of any order made, subject to payment of the appropriate fee.

1.12 When a judgment is given or an order is made in private, if any member of the public who is not a party to the proceedings seeks a transcript of the judgment or a copy of the order, he must seek the leave of the judge who gave the judgment or made the order.

1.13 A judgment or order given or made in private, when drawn up, must have clearly marked in the title:

"Before [*title and name of judge*] sitting in Private"

1.14 References to hearings being in public or private or in a judge's room contained in the Civil Procedure Rules (including the Rules of the Supreme

Court and the County Court Rules scheduled to Part 50) and the practice directions which supplement them do not restrict any existing rights of audience or confer any new rights of audience in respect of applications or proceedings which under the rules previously in force would have been heard in court or in chambers respectively.

Failure to attend the trial

2.1 Rule 39.3 sets out the consequences of a party's failure to attend the trial.

2.2 The court may proceed with a trial in the absence of a party.[3] In the absence of:

(1) the defendant, the claimant may—

(a) prove his claim at trial and obtain judgment on his claim and for costs, and

(b) seek the striking out of any counterclaim,

(2) the claimant, the defendant may—

(a) prove any counterclaim at trial and obtain judgment on his counterclaim and for costs, and

(b) seek the striking out of the claim, or

(3) both parties, the court may strike out the whole of the proceedings.

2.3 Where the court has struck out proceedings, or any part of them, on the failure of a party to attend, that party may apply in accordance with Part 23 for the proceedings, or that part of them, to be restored and for any judgment given against that party to be set aside.[4]

2.4 The application referred to in paragraph 2.3 above must be supported by evidence giving reasons for the failure to attend court and stating when the applicant found out about the order against him.

Bundles of documents for hearings or trial

3.1 Unless the court orders otherwise, the claimant must file the trial bundle not more than 7 days and not less than 3 days before the start of the trial. 39PD–002

3.2 Unless the court orders otherwise, the trial bundle should include a copy of:

(1) the claim form and all statements of case,

(2) a case summary and/or chronology where appropriate,

(3) requests for further information and responses to the requests,

(4) all witness statements to be relied on as evidence,

(5) any witness summaries,

(6) any notices of intention to rely on hearsay evidence under rule 32.2,

(7) any notices of intention to rely on evidence (such as a plan, photograph etc.) under rule 33.6 which is not—

(a) contained in a witness statement, affidavit or experts report,

(b) being given orally at trial,

(c) hearsay evidence under rule 33.2,

(8) any medical reports and responses to them,

(9) any experts' reports and responses to them,

(10) any order giving directions as to the conduct of the trial, and

(11) any other necessary documents.

3.3 The originals of the documents contained in the trial bundle, together with copies of any other court orders should be available at the trial.

3.4 The preparation and production of the trial bundle, even where it is delegated to another person, is the responsibility of the legal representative[5] who has conduct of the claim on behalf of the claimant.

[3] Rule 39.3(1).
[4] Rule 39.3(2) and (3).
[5] For the definition of legal representative see rule 2.3.

3.5 The trial bundle should be paginated (continuously) throughout, and indexed with a description of each document and the page number. Where the total number of pages is more than 100, numbered dividers should be placed at intervals between groups of documents.

3.6 The bundle should normally be contained in a ring binder or lever arch file. Where more than one bundle is supplied, they should be clearly distinguishable, for example, by different colours or letters. If there are numerous bundles, a core bundle should be prepared containing the core documents essential to the proceedings, with references to the supplementary documents in the other bundles.

3.7 For convenience, experts' reports may be contained in a separate bundle and cross referenced in the main bundle.

3.8 If a document to be included in the trial bundle is illegible, a typed copy should be included in the bundle next to it, suitably cross-referenced.

3.9 The contents of the trial bundle should be agreed where possible. The parties should also agree where possible:

(1) that the documents contained in the bundle are authentic even if not disclosed under Part 31, and

(2) that documents in the bundle may be treated as evidence of the facts stated in them even if a notice under the Civil Evidence Act 1995 has not been served.

Where it is not possible to agree the contents of the bundle, a summary of the points on which the parties are unable to agree should be included.

3.10 The party filing the trial bundle should supply identical bundles to all the parties to the proceedings and for the use of the witnesses.

Settlement or discontinuance after the trial date is fixed

4.1 Where:

(1) an offer to settle a claim is accepted,

(2) or a settlement is reached, or

(3) a claim is discontinued,

which disposes of the whole of a claim for which a date or "window" has been fixed for the trial, the parties must ensure that the listing officer for the trial court is notified immediately.

4.2 If an order is drawn up giving effect to the settlement or discontinuance, a copy of the sealed order should be filed with the listing officer.

Representation at hearings

5.1 At any hearing, a written statement containing the following information should be provided for the court:

(1) the name and address of each advocate,

(2) his qualification or entitlement to act as an advocate, and

(3) the party for whom he so acts.

5.2 Where a party is a company or other corporation and is to be represented at a hearing by an employee the written statement should contain the following additional information:

(1) The full name of the company or corporation as stated in its certificate of registration.

(2) The registered number of the company or corporation.

(3) The position or office in the company or corporation held by the representative.

(4) The date on which and manner in which the representative was authorised to act for the company or corporation, e.g. ______ 19 ______: written authority from managing director; or ______ 19 ______: Board resolution dated ______ 19 ______ .

5.3 Rule 39.6 is intended to enable a company or other corporation to represent itself as a litigant in person. Permission under rule 39.6(b) should therefore be given by the court unless there is some particular and sufficient reason why it should be withheld.

5.4 Permission under rule 39.6(b) should be obtained in advance of the hearing from, preferably, the judge who is to hear the case, but may, if it is for any reason impracticable or inconvenient to do so, be obtained from any judge by whom the case could be heard.

5.5 The permission may be obtained informally and without notice to the other parties. The judge who gives the permission should record in writing that he has done so and supply a copy to the company or corporation in question and to any other party who asks for one.

Recording of proceedings

6.1 At any hearing, whether in the High Court or a county court, the judgment (and any summing up given by the judge) will be recorded unless the judge directs otherwise. Oral evidence will normally be recorded also.

6.2 No party or member of the public may use unofficial recording equipment in any court or judge's room without the permission of the court. To do so without permission constitutes a contempt of court.[6]

6.3 Any party or person may require a transcript or transcripts of the recording of any trial or hearing to be supplied to him, upon payment of the charges authorised by any scheme in force for the making of the recording or the transcript.

6.4 Where the person requiring the transcript or transcripts is not a party to the proceedings and the trial or hearing or any part of it was held in private under CPR rule 39.2, paragraph 6.3 does not apply unless the court so orders.

6.5 Attention is drawn to paragraph 7.9 of the Court of Appeal (Civil Division) Practice Direction which deals with the provision of transcripts for use in the Court of Appeal at public expense.

Exhibits at trial

7. Exhibits which are handed in and proved during the course of the trial should be recorded on an exhibit list and kept in the custody of the court until the conclusion of the trial, unless the judge directs otherwise. At the conclusion of the trial it is the parties' responsibility to obtain the return of those exhibits which they handed in and to preserve them for the period in which any appeal may take place.

PRACTICE DIRECTION—COURT SITTINGS

This Practice Direction Supplements CPR Part 39

Court Sittings

1.1 (1) The sittings of the Court of Appeal and of the High Court shall be four in every year, that is to say **39BPD–001**

(a) the Michaelmas sittings which shall begin on 1st October and end on 21st December;
(b) the Hilary sittings which shall begin on 11th January and end on the Wednesday before Easter Sunday;
(c) the Easter sittings which shall begin on the second Tuesday after Easter Sunday and end on the Friday before the spring holiday; and
(d) the Trinity sittings which shall begin on the second Tuesday after the spring holiday and end on 31st July.

(2) In the above paragraph "spring holiday" means the bank holiday falling

[6] Section 9 of the Contempt of Court Act 1981.

on the last Monday in May or any day appointed instead of that day under section 1(2) of the Banking and Financial Dealings Act 1971.

Vacations

The Court of Appeal

2 Attention is drawn to paragraph 11.2 of the Court of Appeal (Civil Division) Practice Direction which deals with the sittings of the Court of Appeal during vacations.

The High Court

3.1(1) One or more judges of each Division of the High Court shall sit in vacation on such days as the senior judge of that Division may from time to time direct, to hear such cases, claims, matters or applications as require to be immediately or promptly heard and to hear other cases, claims, matters or applications if the senior judge of that Division determines that sittings are necessary for that purpose.

(2) Any party to a claim or matter may at any time apply to the Court for an order that such claim or matter be heard in vacation and, if the Court is satisfied that the claim or matter requires to be immediately or promptly heard, it may make an order accordingly and fix a date for the hearing.

(3) Any judge of the High Court may hear such other cases, claims, matters or applications in vacation as the Court may direct.

3.2 The directions in paragraph 3.1 shall not apply in relation to the trial or hearing of cases, claims, matters or applications outside the Royal Courts of Justice but the senior Presiding Judge of each Circuit, with the concurrence of the Senior Presiding Judge, and the Vice-Chancellor of the County Palatine of Lancaster and the Chancery Supervising Judge for Birmingham, Bristol and Cardiff, with the concurrence of the Vice-Chancellor, may make such arrangements for vacation sittings in the courts for which they are respectively responsible as they think desirable.

3.3(1) Subject to the discretion of the Judge, any appeal and any application normally made to a Judge may be made in the month of September.

(2) In the month of August, save with the permission of a Judge or under arrangements for vacation sittings in courts outside the Royal Courts of Justice, appeals to a Judge will be limited to the matters set out in paragraph 3.5 below, and only applications or real urgency will be dealt with, for example urgent appliations in respect of injunctions or for possession under RSC Order 113 (Schedule 1 to the CPR).

(3) It is desirable, where this is practical, that applications or appeals are submitted to a Master, District Judge or Judge prior to the hearing of the application or appeal so that they can be marked "fit for August" or "fit for vacation." If they are so marked, then normally the Judge will be prepared to hear the application or appeal in August, if marked "fit for August" or in September if marked "fit for vacation". A request to have the papers so marked should normally be made in writing, shortly setting out the nature of the application or appeal and the reasons why it should be dealt with in August or in September, as the case may be.

Chancery Masters

3.4 There is no distinction between term time and vacation so far as business before the Chancery Masters is concerned. The Masters will deal with all types of business throughout the year, and when a Master is on holiday his list will normally be taken by a Deputy Master.

Queen's Bench Masters

3.5(1) An application notice may, without permission, be issued returnable before a Master in the month of August for any of the following purposes:

to set aside a claim form or particulars of claim, or service of a claim form or particulars of claim;
to set aside judgment; for stay of execution;
for any order by consent;
for judgment or permission to enter judgment;
for approval of settlements or for interim payment;
for relief from forfeiture; for charging order; for garnishee order;
for appointment or discharge of a receiver;
for relief by way of sheriff's interpleader;
for transfer to a county court or for trial by Master;
for time where time is running in the month of August;

(2) In any case of urgency any other type of application notice (that is other than those for the purposes in (1) above), may, with the permission of a Master be issued returnable before a Master during the month of August.

PART 40

Judgments and Orders

40.0.1 **Contents**

Editorial Introduction

40.0.2 The differences between the new CPR rules and the former RSC and CCR are mainly in form rather than in substance, but there are a few changes which are significant and practitioners should check the wording of the new rule very carefully and not assume that the former practices of the High Court or county courts have necessarily been continued.

Related Sources

40.0.3
- RSC, O.42
- CCR, O.22
- Part 12 (Default judgments)
- Part 13 (Setting aside default judgments)
- Part 16 (Statements of case—r.16.4(1)(b) and r.16.4(2)—Interest)
- Practice Direction to Pt 16—para. 12.1 (see para. 16PD–001)

Practice Direction

40.0.4 Part 40 is supplemented by Practice Directions:
- Accounts and Inquiries
- Structured Settlements
- Judgment and Orders

Scope of this Part

40.1 **40.1** This Part sets out rules about judgments and orders which apply except where any other of these Rules makes a different provision in relation to the judgment or order in question.

Standard requirements

40.2 **40.2**—(1) Every judgment or order must state the name and judicial title of the person who made it, unless it is—

(a) default judgment entered under rule 12.4(1) (entry of default judgment where judgment is entered by a court officer) or a default costs certificate obtained under rule 47.11;

(b) judgment entered under rules 14.4, 14.5, 14.6, 14.7 and 14.9 (entry of judgment on admission where judgment is entered by a court officer); or

(c) a consent order under rule 40.6(2) (consent orders made by court officers).

(2) Every judgment or order must—

(a) bear the date on which it is made; and

(b) be sealed[GL] by the court.

Effect of judgment before entry—A judgment takes effect from the time when the judge pronounces it, and the subsequent entry of it is in obedience to the rules of court (*Holtby v. Hodgson* (1889) 24 Q.B.D. 103). But it is within the powers of a judge to alter his judgment at any time before it is entered and perfected (*Re St Nazaire Co.* (1879) 12 Ch.D. 88; *Re Suffield and Wattsex p. Brown* (1888) 20 Q.B.D. 693); and the disclosure to him of a payment into court does not affect this right (*Millensted v. Grosvenor House Ltd* [1937] 1 K.B. 717, CA). See also under r.40.12(1), the "slip rule". 40.2.1

Entry of judgment in foreign currency—The English court has power to give judgment for a sum of money expressed in a foreign currency (*Miliangos v. George Frank (Textiles) Ltd* [1976] A.C. 443; [1975] 3 All E.R. 801, HL). This power may be exercised even where the foreign currency is payable under a contract the proper law of which is English law (*Barclays Bank International Ltd v. Levin Brothers (Bradford) Ltd* [1977] Q.B. 270; [1976] 3 All E.R. 900 (dishonoured bills of exchange accepted payable in England but expressed in foreign currency)). The court has further power to award damages for breach of contract in foreign currency (*Kraut (Jean) A.G. v. Albany Fabrics Ltd* [1977] Q.B. 182; [1977] 1 All E.R. 116) and to award damages for tort in a foreign currency (*Owner of the M.V. Eleftherotria v. Owner of the M.V. Despina R., The Despina R.* [1978] Q.B. 396; [1979] 1 All E.R. 421; and in both cases to award damages in the currency that best expresses the plaintiff's loss (see *Services Europe Atlantique Sud SEAS v. Stockholms Rederiaktiebolag SVEA, The Folias* [1979] A.C. 685; [1979] 1 All E.R. 421, HL). It does not not matter whether the foreign currency is that of a Member State of the European Community (see *Schorsch Meier GmbH v. Hennin* [1975] Q.B. 416; [1975] 1 All E.R. 152, CA) or the currency of any other State (*Miliangos v. George Frank (Textiles) Ltd*). The judgment will be for payment of the amount of the foreign currency or its sterling equivalent (*ibid.*) converted for the purposes of the enforcement of the judgment at the time of payment, *i.e.* the date on which enforcement process is taken or authorised in terms of sterling (*ibid.*). 40.2.2

Where a charterparty provides that demurrage is to be calculated in U.S. dollars and does not provide for it to be paid in sterling the reasonable inference is that the money of payment as well as the money of account, is U.S. dollars, even though the freight is payable in sterling and the contract is to be governed by English law, the rate of exchange for demurrage is that prevailing at the date of the payment of the demurrage and not at the date of the bill of lading, and therefore the owners are entitled to the difference between the amount of sterling actually paid at the date of the bill of lading and the sum required to be paid at the rate of exchange ruling at the date of payment and to have the balance awarded in U.S. dollars (*George Veflings Rederi A/S v. President of India* [1979] 1 W.L.R. 59; [1979] 1 All E.R. 380, CA).

In the case of liquidation of a company, the practice of converting a foreign currency judgment into sterling as at the date of its enforcement does not apply, but instead the foreign currency debt must not be proved according to its sterling value at the date of the commencement of the winding-up (*Re Lines Bros Ltd (In Liquidation)* [1982] Ch. 1; [1982] 2 All E.R. 183, CA), though in a wholly solvent liquidation, the liquidator should make good a shortfall in the full contractual foreign currency debt before he pays anything to the shareholders (*ibid., per* Brightman L.J.).

Where there is more than one eligible foreign currency in which the judgment may be given, the applicable principles are those stated by Lord Wilberforce in *Services Europe Atlantique Sud (SEAS) v. Stockholms Rederiaktiebolag SVEA, The Folias* [1979] A.C. 685; [1979] 1 All E.R. 421, and in the absence of an agreed currency of account and payment, the judgment would be expressed in the currency in which the plaintiff's loss was felt or which most expressed his loss (*Société Française Bunge SA v. Belcan N.V.; The Federal Huron* [1985] 2 All E.R. 378).

In an action by a foreign national for damages for personal injuries suffered during a visit to England, the damages will be assessed in the currency of his country, since his loss is most closely linked with that currency, except that the damages for pain, suffering and loss of amenities will be assessed in sterling (*Hoffman v. Sofaer* [1982] 1 W.L.R. 1350).

If the court does express its judgment for the payment of money in a foreign currency, the judgment will be entered in that currency or its sterling equivalent at the time of payment.

It is not clear whether the plaintiff has the *right* to elect that the judgment should be expressed in sterling or in a foreign currency. It would seem that the court retains a residual discretion to determine whether the judgment should be expressed in sterling or in a foreign currency and that it will exercise this discretion having regard to all the circumstances including the position of the parties and the fluctuations in the rates of exchange between the currency of the contract and sterling during the period between the date when the cause of action whether in contract or tort arose and the date of judgment. There may well be cases in which although the plaintiff may elect that the judgment should be expressed in sterling, yet the defendant may wish, or it might otherwise be just, that the judgment should be expressed in a foreign currency of the contract and *vice versa.*

40.2.3 **Orders enforceable like judgments**—By virtue of the provisions of this Part and RSC, O.45, (Sched. 1), an order may be enforced in the same manner as a judgment, and therefore the express provision to this effect contained in the former O.42, r.24, has been omitted as being unnecessary. It is doubtful whether there is still any distinction between a "judgment" and an "order" (see, *per* Lord Esher M.R. in *Onslow v. Commissioners of Inland Revenue* (1890) 25 Q.B.D. 465: "A judgment is a decision obtained in an action, and every other decision is an order"; *Ex p. Chinery* (1884) 12 Q.B.D. 342; *Ex p. Moore* (1885) 14 Q.B.D. 627; *cf. Shaw v. Hertford C.C.* [1899] 2 Q.B. 282 .

The term "order" includes, *e.g.* an order made by the Disciplinary Committee of the Law Society, pursuant to the Solicitors Act 1974, s.47(2).

An action will lie on an order against a solicitor to pay the costs of proceedings to strike him off the rolls, notwithstanding that an attempt to enforce the order by attachment has failed (*Godfrey v. George* [1896] 1 Q.B. 48). And an action will lie on a garnishee order against garnishees, where payment cannot be obtained by execution (*Pritchett v. English and Colonial Syndicate* [1899] 2 Q.B. 428).

A balance order can be enforced by execution as a judgment against a party within the jurisdiction. Where the contributory was out of the jurisdiction it was held that the company could bring an action for the recovery of the amount due, and leave was given to serve the writ in such action out of the jurisdiction (*Westmoreland, etc., Slate Co. v. Fielden* [1891] 3 Ch. 15). An award under a submission can (by order) be enforced as a judgment. See Arbitration Act 1950, s.26(1) (SCP 1999, Vol. 2, Section 21A, paras 21A–245 to 21A–261).

40.2.4 **Irish Court**—In the Republic of Ireland, the Courts will act on a Master's certificate of an English judgment, but the practice is not reciprocal.

40.2.5 **Judgment of House of Lords**—The jurisdiction to ante-date a judgment of the House of Lords can only be derived from the order itself; if this is silent the judgment can only speak from its date (*Nitrate Producers S.S. Co. Ltd v. Short Bros. Ltd* (1922) 127 L.T. 727; 91 L.J.K.B. 871).

Where on appeal to the House of Lords a judgment is reversed with the result that a sum of money then *for the first time* becomes payable, interest runs from the date of the judgment in the House of Lords. But if the effect of an appeal to the tribunal to restore a judgment of a court of first instance under which money was payable, interest runs from the date of that judgment.

Drawing up and filing of judgments and orders

40.3 **40.3**—(1) Every judgment or order will be drawn up by the court unless—

(a) the court orders a party to draw it up; or
(b) a party, with the permission of the court, agrees to draw it up;
(c) the court dispenses with the need to draw it up;
(d) it is a consent order under rule 40.6.

(2) The court may direct that—

(a) a judgment or an order drawn up by a party must be checked by the court before it is sealed[GL]; or
(b) before a judgment or an order is drawn up by the court, the parties must file an agreed statement of its terms.

(3) Where a judgment or an order is to be drawn up by a party—

(a) he must file it no later than 7 days after the date on which the court ordered or permitted him to draw it up so that it can be sealed[GL] by the court; and
(b) if he fails to file it within that period, any other party may draw it up and file it.

Service of judgments and orders

40.4 **40.4**—(1) Where a judgment or an order has been drawn up by a party and is to be served by the court—

(a) the party who drew it up must file a copy to be retained at court and sufficient copies for service on him and on the other parties; and

(b) once it has been sealed[GL], the court must serve a copy of it on each party to the proceedings.

(2) Unless the court directs otherwise, any order made otherwise than at trial must be served on—

(a) the applicant and the respondent; and

(b) any other person on whom the court orders it to be served.

(Rule 6.3 specifies who must serve judgments and orders.)

(RSC, O.44, in Schedule 1 contains rules about the service of notice of certain judgments.)

Effect of rule—Whereas there was no requirement in the former RSC to serve orders, this is now compulsory if the judgment or order is drawn by a party and filed with the court. The party doing so must provide sufficient copies for service on all the other parties. **40.4.1**

Power to require judgment or order to be served on a party as well as his solicitor

40.5 Where the party on whom a judgment or order is to be served is acting by a solicitor, the court may order the judgment or order to be served on the party as well as on his solicitor. **40.5**

Effect of rule—Normally it is sufficient to serve the solicitor "on the record" as acting for a party, but this provision enables orders, likely to be "unless" orders, to be served on the party personally where such a party has to do some particular act. **40.5.1**

Consent judgments and orders

40.6—(1) This rule applies where all the parties agree the terms in which a judgment should be given or an order should be made. **40.6**

(2) A court officer may enter and seal[GL] an agreed judgment or order if—

(a) the judgment or order is listed in paragraph (3);

(b) none of the parties is a litigant in person; and

(c) the approval of the court is not required by these Rules, a practice direction or any enactment before an agreed order can be made.

(3) The judgments and orders referred to in paragraph (2) are—

(a) a judgment or order for—

(i) the payment of an amount of money (including a judgment or order for damages or the value of goods to be decided by the court); or

(ii) the delivery up of goods with or without the option of paying the value of the goods or the agreed value.

(b) an order for—

(i) the dismissal of any proceedings, wholly or in part;

(ii) the stay[GL] of proceedings on agreed terms, disposing of the proceedings, whether those terms are recorded in a schedule to the order or elsewhere;

(iii) the stay[GL] of enforcement of a judgment, either unconditionally or on condition that the money due under the judgment is paid by instalments specified in the order;

(iv) the setting aside under Part 13 of a default judgment which has not been satisfied;

(v) the payment out of money which has been paid into court;

(vi) the discharge from liability of any party;

(vii) the payment, assessment or waiver of costs, or such other provision for costs as may be agreed.

(4) Rule 40.3 (drawing up and filing judgments and orders) applies to judgments and orders entered and sealed[GL] by a court officer under paragraph (2) as it applies to other judgments and orders.

(5) Where paragraph (2) does not apply, any party may apply for a judgment or order in the terms agreed.

(6) The court may deal with an application under paragraph (5) without a hearing.

(7) Where this rule applies—

(a) the order which is agreed by the parties must be drawn up in the terms agreed;

(b) it must be expressed as being "By Consent";

(c) it must be signed by the legal representative acting for each of the parties to whom the order relates or, where paragraph (5) applies, by the party if he is a litigant in person.

40.6.1 **Effect of rule**—This rule continues the useful provisions of RSC, O.42, r.5A but not all the former classes of judgments or orders have been repeated in this rule, namely possession of land where the claim does not relate to a dwelling-house.

The former rule did not apply to proceedings where any of the parties were under a disability but the consent of the court was and is still required in such cases (see Pt 21).

When judgment or order takes effect

40.7 **40.7**—(1) A judgment or order takes effect from the day when it is given or made, or such later date as the court may specify.

(2) This rule applies to all judgments and orders except those to which rule 40.10 (judgment against a State) applies.

Time from which interest begins to run

40.8 **40.8**—(1) Where interest is payable on a judgment pursuant to section 17 of the Judgments Act 1838[1] or section 74 of the County Courts Act 1984,[2] the interest shall begin to run from the date that judgment is given unless—

(a) a rule in another Part or a practice direction makes different provision; or

(b) the court orders otherwise.

(2) The court may order that interest shall begin to run from a date before the date that judgment is given.

40.8.1 **Interest on judgment debts**—Every judgment debt carries interest at the statutory rate from the time of entering up the judgment and such interest may be levied under a writ of execution (Judgments Act 1838, s.17). The statutory rate of interest on a judgment debt has been increased from time to time, as appears from the following table, by reference to the date on which the judgment is entered up:

Date judgment entered up	statutory rate of interest (per annum)	authority
before April 20, 1971 since April 20, 1971	4 per cent 7½ per cent	Judgments Act 1838, s.17 Judgment Debts (Rate of Interest) Order 1971 (S.I. 1971 No. 491)

[1] 1838 c. 110. Section 17 was amended by S.I. 1998/2940.

[2] 1984 c.28. Section 74 was amended by section (2) of the Private International Law (Miscellaneous Provisions) Act 1995 (c. 42).

since March 1, 1977	10 per cent	Judgment Debts (Rate of Interest) Order 1977 (S.I. 1977 No. 141). This increase was made under s.44 of A.J.A. 1970 which implemented the recommendations of the Report of the Committee on the Enforcement of Judgment Debts 1969 (Cmnd. 3909, para. 1168).
since December 3, 1979	12½ per cent	Judgment Debts (Rate of Interest) Order 1979 (S.I. 1979 No. 1382)
since June 9, 1980	15 per cent	Judgment Debts (Rate of Interest) Order 1980 (S.I. 1980 No. 672)
since June 8, 1982	14 per cent	Judgment Debts (Rate of Interest) Order 1982 (S.I. 1982 No. 696)
since November 10, 1982	12 per cent	Judgment Debts (Rate of Interest) (No. 2) Order 1982 (S.I. 1982 No. 1427)
since April 16, 1985	15 per cent	Judgment Debts (Rate of Interest) Order 1985 (S.I. 1985 No. 437)
since April 1, 1993	8 per cent	Judgment Debts (Rate of Interest) Order 1993 (S.I. 1993 No. 564)

The court has no power either under the AJA 1970, s.44 or under its inherent jurisdiction to vary the rate of interest prevailing at the date of entry up of the judgment during the currency of that judgment, whether the rate during that period is increased or decreased under a fresh Statutory Instrument made under s.44 (*Rocco Guiseppe & Figli v. Tradex Export SA* [1984] 1 W.L.R. 742; [1983] 3 All E.R. 598; [1983] 2 Lloyd's Rep. 434). See also *Thomas v. Bunn* [1991] 1 A.C. 362; [1991] 1 All E.R. 193, HL.

The entitlement to the statutory rate of interest on a judgment applies of course to a default judgment for the payment of a debt or liquidated demand; to an order to pay a sum of money; to money payable under an arbitration award from the date of the award (see Arbitration Act 1950, s.20 and Arbitration Act 1996, s.49, and *London & Overseas Freighters Ltd v. Timber Shipping Co. SA* [1971] 1 Q.B. 268; [1970] 3 All E.R. 756, CA; [1972] A.C. 1; [1972] 2 All E.R. 599, HL); and to judgment debts due to or from the Crown (see Crown Proceedings Act 1947, s.24(1), SCP 1999, Vol. 2, Pt 18). It also applies to an interlocutory order directing the payment of costs (*Taylor v. Roe* [1894] 1 Ch. 413; *Alexander v. Curragh* [1915] 1 Ir.R. 273); to a salvage award (*The Jones Brothers* (1877) 46 L.J.P. 75); to a judgment to secure an annuity (*Knight v. Bowyer* (1899) 4 De G. & J. 619); and to a judgment in a representative action (*Zachariassin v. London General Insurance Co. Ltd* (1925) 135 L.T. 604, CA). On the other hand, the statutory interest is not payable on the instalments due under a consent order for payment of the judgment debts by instalments which have been regularly paid (*Caudrey v. Finnerty* (1892) 66 L.T. 684). Nor, where a judgment debt has ceased to exist by reason of an intervening order that the debt be paid by instalments, is the judgment creditor entitled to interest on the amount outstanding pending completion of payment by instalments (*Morse v. Muir* [1939] 2 K.B. 106). See also *Woodham Smith v. Edwards* [1908] 2 K.B. 899, CA; *Aman v. Southern Railway* [1926] 1 K.B. 59, CA.

The statutory interest runs from the date of the pronouncement of the judgment in court, as that is the date from which the plaintiff becomes entitled to the judgment debt, and not from the date on which the judgment is finally entered, since the words "the time of entering up judgment" in s.17 of the Judgments Act 1838 mean the date of the pronouncement of the judgment in court and not the formal entry of judgment (*Parsons v. Mather & Platt Ltd* [1977] 1 W.L.R. 855; [1977] 2 All E.R. 715, approved in *Erven Warnink B.V. v. Townend (J.) & Sons (Hull) Ltd (No. 2)* [1982] 3 All E.R. 312, CA) (see Judgments Act 1838, s.17, *Omnium Insurance Corporation Ltd v. United London, etc. Insurance Co. Ltd* (1920) 36 T.L.R. 386).

The statutory interest on a judgment or order for the payment of costs runs from the date of the judgment or order, not from the date of the certificate of taxation quantifying the same or such other date as may be ordered as the date on which payment is to be made (*Hunt v. R.M. Douglas (Roofing) Ltd* [1990] 1 A.C. 398; [1988] 3 All E.R. 823, HL, overruling *K v. K* [1977] Fam. 39, CA). Costs directed by a judgment or order to be charged on land bear interest from the date on which they became a charge (*Re Macdermott's Estate* [1912] 1 Ir.R. 166).

In an administration action, where it is found that arrears of annuity have occurred since judgment, the statutory interest is payable from the date when such arrears accrued (*Re Salvin Worseley v. Marshall* [1912] 1 Ch. 332).

Where interlocutory judgment is entered for damages to be assessed by a Master or district judge or other tribunal, and where no further order of the court is required to make the judgment final save the certificate of the Master or district judge or other tribunal, certifying the amount of the damages, interest under section 17 of the Judgments Act 1838, runs from the date of the assessment (*Borthwick v. The Elderslie Steamship Co. Ltd (No. 2)* [1905] 2 K.B. 516, CA; *Ashover Fluor Spar Mines Ltd v. Jackson* [1911] 2 Ch. 355 and *Hunt v. R.M. Douglas (Roofing) Ltd* (above), *per* Lock Ackner at 988 and 833). *Aliter* where the interlocutory judgment is for an inquiry as to damages, and some further order of the court is needed after the amount of the damages has been ascertained in order to make the judgment final, interest under section 17 of the 1838 Act begins, and interest under s.35A of the Supreme Court Act 1981 stops at the date of the final judgment (*Ashover Fluor Spar Mines Ltd v. Jackson* [1911] 2 Ch. 355).

Equally, it would seem that, under the former form of "Tomlin Order," where an action is stayed upon terms agreed between the parties and one of the terms provides for the payment of a sum of money by one party to the other, the statutory interest on such sum does not become payable unless and until a judgment or order for the payment of such sum is entered pursuant to a further order made under the liberty to apply.

Where the plaintiff fails at the trial, but on appeal obtains judgment for damages, interest runs from the date of the judgment of the CA, unless that court makes an order r.40.8(2) ante-dating its judgment (*Borthwick v. Elderslie S.S. Co.* [1905] 2 K.B. 516, CA).

The statutory interest is payable as part of the judgment debt (*Re Clagett, ex p. Lewis* (1888) 36 W.R. 653); and in a bankruptcy notice issued on the judgment, the interest accrued since the judgment can be added to the amount of the judgment debt (*Re Lehman* (1890) 62 L.T. 941).

Income tax is not deductible from the statutory interest on the judgment (*Re Cooper* [1911] 2 K.B. 550, CA) though if the judgment is for a sum including taxable interest, income tax on that interest is deductible on paying the judgment debt (*Riches v. Westminster Bank Ltd* [1947] A.C. 390).

40.8.2 **Interest on claims in foreign currency**—By section 1 of the Private International Law (Miscellaneous Provisions) Act 1995 there has been added a new s.44A to the Administration of Justice Act 1970 (the new section is printed in SCP 1999, Vol. 2, paras 20B–87 to 20B–89). This has the effect of giving the court a discretion to apply a different rate of interest to the one prescribed under section 17 of the Judgments Act 1838 when a judgment is given in a foreign currency.

40.8.3 *(1) Money claims*—Where the claim is for a specified amount of money a default judgment may include the amount of interest claimed to the date of judgment if the requirements of r.12.6 are satisfied.

40.8.4 *(2) Default judgments*—In the case of a foreign currency claim if the claimant requires a rate of interest on the judgment different from the statutory rate this must also be specified in particulars of claim. It is likely that he will specify the same rate both before and after judgment. If it is less than the statutory rate this will be awarded automatically. If it is more than the statutory rate the claimant will have to apply for the rate to be assessed. It is anticipated that in the absence of special circumstances the court would award interest at the rate that the court of the country of the currency of claim would award. This will have to be proved.

A defendant who disputes the rate of interest claimed where it is the statutory rate or less but is otherwise content for a default judgment to enter should enter an appearance stating that he does not contest the claim "save as to the amount of interest claimed" and issue an application for interest to be assessed specifying the lower rate of interest for which he contends. This will also have to be proved.

It will obviously be prudent for claimants in foreign currency claims where the foreign rate of interest is lower than the domestic rate to confine their claim for interest to the foreign rate and so avoid successful applications by defendants.

40.8.5 *(3) Other judgments*—Where interest falls to be assessed by the court (as under summary judgment or after trial) the parties must make out their case in those proceedings if they are seeking a judgment rate of interest different from the statutory rate.

40.8.6 **Interest on damages assessed by Master or district judge**—Interest cannot be awarded on the same sum in respect of the same period under both section 35A of the Supreme Court Act 1981 and section 17 of the Judgments Act 1838. Interest on damages may be awarded under section 35A(1)(b) of the 1981 Act until "the date of judgment," while under s.17 of the 1838 Act interest runs from "the time of entering up judgment." In cases where an interlocutory judgment for damages to be assessed is followed by a final judgment there has been much debate as to what is the relevant date. The House of Lords has now held that interest payable on an award of damages under section 17 of the 1838 Act begins to run from the date when damages are finally assessed or agreed and judgment is entered for that sum (*i.e.* the date of final judgment), and not from the earlier date when, liability having been determined or agreed, a judgment or order is made for damages to be assessed (*i.e.* the date of interlocutory judgment); hence interest on damages under section 35A of the 1981 Act may be awarded up to the date of final judgment (*Thomas v. Bunn* [1991] 1 A.C. 362; [1991] 1 All E.R. 193, HL, disapproving dicta to the contrary in *Hunt v. R. M. Douglas (Roofing) Ltd* [1990] 1 A.C. 398; [1988] 3 All E.R. at 833, HL).

40.8.7 **Rate of interest**—A contract to pay the debt with interest at, *e.g.* 15 per cent, does not entitle a claimant to levy under his execution more than the current statutory interest. The contract (or a subsequent agreement) must state specifically that any judgment obtained for recovery of the debt shall carry interest at a specified rate per cent. and the higher rate until payment of interest should form part of the judgment (see *Re European Central Ry.* (1877) 4 Ch.D. 33; *Ex p. Fewings* (1883) 25 Ch.D. 338; *Arbuthnot v. Bunsilall* (1890) 62 L.T. 234; and see *Economic Life Assurance Society v. Usborne* [1902] A.C. 152).

Who may apply to set aside or vary a judgment or order

40.9 A person who is not a party but who is directly affected by a judgment or order may apply to have the judgment or order set aside or varied. **40.9**

Judgment against a State in default of acknowledgment of service

40.10—(1) Where the claimant obtains default judgment under Part 12 on a claim against a State where the defendant has failed to file an acknowledgment of service, the judgment does not take effect until 2 months after service on the State of— **40.10**

(a) a copy of the judgment; and

(b) a copy of the evidence in support of the application for permission to enter default judgment (unless the evidence has already been served on the State in accordance with an order made under Part 12).

(2) In this rule, "State" has the meaning given by section 14 of the State Immunity Act 1978.[3]

Effect of rule—This rule gives effect to the provisions of section 12(5) of the State Immunity Act 1978 that the time for an application by the defendant state to set aside a default judgment entered against it with leave of the court shall begin to run two months after the date on which the copy of the judgment is served on the state. It would be contrary to international comity and indeed perhaps injurious to international relations to allow a foreign state to have a default judgment entered against it and *enforced* without prior warning. This rule therefore provides expressly that during such period of two months the default judgment will not take effect, *i.e.* it will not be enforceable and during that period it will be open to the state to apply to set aside the default judgment. **40.10.1**

If, however, the claimant has duly served on the state a copy of the default judgment and a copy of any supporting affidavit to obtain leave to enter such judgment and two further months have expired, he will be entitled to proceed to enforce the judgment. Before doing so, it will be necessary for him to satisfy the court that such due service has been effected and that such two months has expired from the date of service so that the judgment has taken effect.

As to the extent to which a judgment or an award against a foreign state can be enforced, see section 13 of the State Immunity Act 1978.

Judgment of overseas country against a state—A judgment given by a court of an overseas country against a state other than the United Kingdom or the state to which that court belongs must be recognised and enforced in the United Kingdom if, and only if, (a) it would be so recognised and enforced if it had not been given against a state, and (b) that court would have had jurisdiction in the matter if it had applied rules corresponding to those applicable to such matters in the United Kingdom in accordance with sections 2 to 11 of the State Immunity Act 1978 (see Civil Jurisdiction and Judgments Act 1982, s.31(1)). For this purpose a judgment given against a state includes references to (a) judgments against the government, or a department of the government, of the state but not judgments against an entity which is distinct from the executive organs of government, unless such judgment is given in proceedings relating to anything done by that entity in the exercise of the sovereign authority of the state, and (b) judgments against the sovereign or head of state in his public capacity (*ibid.*, s.32(2)). The provisions of sections 12, 13 and 14(3) and (4) of the State Immunity Act, relating to the service of process and procedural privileges apply to proceedings for the recognition or enforcement in the United Kingdom of a judgment given by a court of an overseas country (*ibid.*, s.31(4)). In the case of a federal state, the term "state" includes any of its constituent territories (*ibid.*, s.31(5)). The **40.10.2**

[3] 1978 c. 33.

recognition or enforcement of judgments given by a court of an overseas country is not affected by a judgment to which Part I of the Foreign Judgments (Reciprocal Enforcement) Act 1933 applies by virtue of the relevant provisions of specified statutes (*ibid.*, s.31(3)).

Time for complying with a judgment or order

40.11 **40.11** A party must comply with a judgment or order for the payment of an amount of money (including costs) within 14 days of the date of the judgment or order, unless—

(a) the judgment or order specifies a different date for compliance (including specifying payment by instalments);
(b) any of these Rules specifies a different date for compliance; or
(c) the court has stayed the proceedings or judgment.

(Parts 12 and 14 specify different dates for complying with certain default judgments and judgments on admissions.)

Correction of errors in judgments and orders

40.12 **40.12**—(1) The court may at any time correct an accidental slip or omission in a judgment or order.

(2) A party may apply for a correction without notice.

Cases where court gives judgment both on claim and counterclaim

40.13 **40.13**—(1) This rule applies where the court gives judgment for specified amounts both for the claimant on his claim and against the claimant on a counterclaim.

(2) If there is a balance in favour of one of the parties, it may order the party whose judgment is for the lesser amount to pay the balance.

(3) In a case to which this rule applies, the court may make a separate order as to costs against each party.

Judgment in favour of certain part owners relating to the detention of goods

40.14 **40.14**—(1) In this rule "part owner" means one of two or more persons who have an interest in the same goods.

(2) Where—

(a) a part owner makes a claim relating to the detention of the goods; and
(b) the claim is not based on a right to possession,

any judgment or order given or made in respect of the claim is to be for the payment of damages only, unless the claimant had the written authority of every other part owner of the goods to make the claim on his behalf as well as for himself.

(3) This rule applies notwithstanding anything in subsection (3) of section 3 of the Torts (Interference with Goods) Act 1977,[4] but does not affect the remedies and jurisdiction mentioned in subsection (8) of that section.

40.14.1 **Effect of rule**—This rule gives effect to the current rule of law that a person without an immediate right to the possession of goods cannot sue for wrongful detention for specific delivery or in conversion, but is confined to his remedy in damages limited to his "reversionary" interest in

[4] 1977 c. 32.

the goods. One of two or more co-owners of goods cannot therefore obtain an order for specific delivery of the goods or even their assessed value, unless he can show that he has the written authority of every other owner to sue on his or their behalf.

PRACTICE DIRECTION—ACCOUNTS, INQUIRIES ETC.

This Practice Direction Supplements CPR Part 40

Section 1 contains provisions as to taking accounts and conducting inquiries under a judgment or order. Section 2 contains provisions formerly in CCR Order 23. **40PD–001**

As to obtaining an interim or summary order for accounts or inquiries, attention is drawn to the Accounts & Inquiries Practice Direction that supplements CPR Part 25 and to paragraph 6 of the Summary Judgment Practice Direction that supplements CPR Part 24.

Section 1

Accounts and inquiries: general

1.1 Where the court orders any account to be taken or any inquiry to be made, it may, by the same or a subsequent order, give directions as to the manner in which the account is to be taken and verified or the inquiry is to be conducted.

1.2 In particular, the court may direct that in taking an account, the relevant books of account shall be evidence of their contents but that any party may take such objections to the contents as he may think fit.

1.3 Any party may apply to the court in accordance with CPR Part 23 for directions as to the taking of an account or the conduct of an inquiry or for the variation of directions already made.

1.4 Every direction for the taking of an account or the making of an inquiry shall be numbered in the order so that, as far as possible, each distinct account and inquiry is given its own separate number.

Verifying the account

2. Subject to any order to the contrary:

(1) the accounting party must make out his account and verify it by an affidavit or witness statement to which the account is exhibited,

(2) the accounting party must file the account with the court and at the same time notify the other parties that he has done so and of the filing of any affidavit or witness statement verifying or supporting the account.

Objections

3.1 Any party who wishes to contend:

(a) that an accounting party has received more than the amount shown by the account to have been received, or

(b) that the accounting party should be treated as having received more than he has actually received, or

(c) that any item in the account is erroneous in respect of amount, or

(d) that in any other respect the account is inaccurate,

must, unless the court directs otherwise, give written notice to the accounting party of his objections.

3.2 The written notice referred to in paragraph 3.1 must, so far as the objecting party is able to do so:

(a) state the amount by which it is contended that the account understates the amount received by the accounting party,

(b) state the amount which it is contended that the accounting party should be treated as having received in addition to the amount he actually received,

(c) specify the respects in which it is contended that the account is inaccurate, and

(d) in each case, give the ground on which the contention is made.

3.3 The contents of the written notice must, unless the notice contains a statement of truth, be verified by either an affidavit or a witness statement to which the notice is an exhibit.

(Part 22 and the Practice Direction that supplements it contain provisions about statements of truth).

Allowances

4. In taking any account all just allowances shall be made without any express direction to that effect.

Management of proceedings

5. The court may at any stage in the taking of an account or in the course of an inquiry direct a hearing in order to resolve an issue that has arisen and for that purpose may order that points of claim and points of defence be served and give any necessary directions.

Delay

6.1 If it appears to the court that there is undue delay in the taking of any account or the progress of any inquiry the court may require the accounting party or the party with the conduct of the inquiry, as the case may be, to explain the delay and may then make such order of the management of the proceedings (including a stay) and for costs as the circumstances may require.

6.2 The directions the court may give under paragraph 6.1 include a direction that the Official Solicitor take over the conduct of the proceedings and directions providing for the payment of the Official Solicitor's costs.

Distribution

7. Where some of the persons entitled to share in a fund are known but there is, or is likely to be, difficulty or delay in ascertaining other persons so entitled, the court may direct, or allow, immediate payment of their shares to the known persons without reserving any part of those shares to meet the subsequent costs of ascertaining the other persons.

Guardian's accounts

40PD–002 **8.** The accounts of a person appointed guardian of the property of a child (defined in CPR 21.1(2)) must be verified and approved in such manner as the court may direct.

Section 2

Application of RSC Order 44 to county court proceedings

9.1 The provision of rules 1 to 10 of RSC 44 (see Part 50 and Schedule 1 to the CPR) relating to proceedings under a judgment or order in the Chancery Division shall apply to proceedings under a judgment or order made in a County Court—

(a) in proceedings for:

(i) the administration of the estate of a deceased person; or

(ii) the execution of a trust; or

(iii) the sale of any property; or

(b) in any other proceedings in the exercise of its equity jurisdiction.

9.2 Where a judgment or order directs an account to be taken or an inquiry to be made and does not otherwise provide, the account shall be taken or the inquiry made by a Master or district judge (if the proceedings are in the High Court) or a district judge (if the proceedings are in the county court).

10. The court shall give to every creditor or other person whose claim or any part of whose claim has been allowed or disallowed, and who did not attend when the claim was disposed of, a notice informing him of that fact.

11. Rule 11 of RSC 44 (Schedule 1 to the CPR) shall apply to proceedings in a county court as if references to "the Master" were references to a district judge.

12. An appeal shall lie to the judge from any order made by a district judge under rules 1 to 10 of RSC Order 44 (including an order giving directions as to the further conduct of the proceedings) and the provisions about an appeal in rule 12 of RSC 44 shall apply.

PRACTICE DIRECTION—JUDGMENTS AND ORDERS

This Practice Direction supplements CPR Part 40

Drawing up and filing of judgments and orders

1.1 Rule 40.2 sets out the standard requirements for judgments and orders and rule 40.3 deals with how judgments and orders should be drawn up. **40BPD–001**

1.2 A party who has been ordered or given permission to draw up an order must file it for sealing within 7 days of being ordered or permitted to do so.[5] If he fails to do so, any other party may draw it up and file it.[6]

1.3 If the court directs that a judgment or order which is being drawn up by a party must be checked by the court before it is sealed, the party responsible must file the draft within 7 days of the date the order was made with a request that the draft be checked before it is sealed.

1.4 If the court directs the parties to file an agreed statement of terms of an order which the court is to draw up[7], the parties must do so no later than 7 days from the date the order was made, unless the court directs otherwise.

1.5 If the court requires the terms of an order which is being drawn up by the court to be agreed by the parties the court may direct;

(1) a copy of the draft order to be sent to all parties for their agreement to be endorsed on it and returned to the court before the order is sealed, or

(2) a copy of the draft order together with notice of an appointment to attend before the court to agree the terms of the order.

Preparation of deeds or documents under an order

2.1 Where a judgment or order directs any deed or document to be prepared, executed or signed, the order will state:

(1) the person who is to prepare the deed or document, and

(2) if the deed or document is to be approved, the person who is to approve it.

2.2 If the parties are unable to agree the form of the deed or document, any party may apply in accordance with Part 23 for the form of the deed or document to be settled.

2.3 In such case the judge may:

[5] Rule 40.3(3)(a).
[6] Rule 40.3(3)(b).
[7] Rule 40.3(2(b).

(1) settled the deed or document himself, or
(2) refer it to
(a) a maste, or
(b) a district judge, or
(c) a conveyancing counsel of the Supreme Court to settle.
(See also the Sale of Land practice direction supplementing RSC Order 31 scheduled to the CPR at Part 50)

Consent orders

3.1 Rule 40.6(3) sets out the types of consent judgments and orders which may be entered and sealed by a court officer. The court officer may do so in those cases provided that:
(1) none of the parties is a litigant in person, and
(2) the approval of the court is not required by the Rules, a practice direction or any enactment.[8]
3.2 If a consent order filed for sealing appears to be unclear or incorrect the court officer may refer it to a judge for consideration.[9]
3.3 Where a consent judgment or order does not come within the provisions of rule 40.6(2):
(1) an application notice requesting a judgment or order in the agreed terms should be filed with the draft judgment or order to be entered or sealed, and
(2) the draft judgment or order must be drawn so that the judge's name and judicial title can be inserted.
3.4 A consent judgment or order must:
(1) be drawn up in the terms agreed,
(2) bear on it the words "By Consent", and
(3) be signed by
(a) solicitors or counsel acting for each of the parties to the order, or
(b) where a party is a litigant in person, the litigant.[10]
3.5 Where the parties draw up a consent order in the form of a stay of proceedings on agreed terms, disposing of the proceedings[11], and where the terms are recorded in a schedule to the order, any direction for:
(1) payment of money out of court, or
(2) payment and assessment of costs
should be contained in the body of the order and not in the schedule.

Correction of errors in judgments and orders

4.1 Where a judgment or order contains an accidental slip or omission a party may apply for it to be corrected.[12]
4.2 The application notice (which may be an informal document such as a letter) should describe the error and set out the correction required. An application may be dealt with without a hearing:
(1) where the applicant so requests,
(2) with the consent of the parties, or
(3) where the court does not consider that a hearing would be appropriate.
4.3 The judge may deal with the application without notice if the slip or omission is obvious or may direct notice of the application to be given to the other party or parties.
4.4 If the application is opposed it should, if practicable, be listed for hearing before the judge who gave the judgment or made the order.

[8] Rule 40.6(2).
[9] Rule 3.2.
[10] Rule 40.6(7).
[11] Rule 40.6(3)(b)(ii)
[12] Rule 40.10.

4.5 The court has an inherent power to vary its own orders to make the meaning and intention of the court clear.

Adjustment of final judgment figure in respect of compensation recovery payments

5.1 In a final judgment[13] where some or all of the damages awarded: 40BPD–002

(1) fall under the heads of damage set out in column 1 of Schedule 2 to the Social Security (Recovery of Benefits) Act 1997 in respect of recoverable benefits received by the claimant set out in column 2 of that Schedule and

(2) where the defendant has paid to the Secretary of State the recoverable benefits in accordance with the certificate of recoverable benefits,

there should be stated in a preamble to the judgment or order the amount awarded under each head of damage and the amount by which it has been reduced in accordance with section 8 and Schedule 2 to the Social Security (Recovery of Benefits) Act 1997.

5.2 The judgment or order should then provide for entry of judgment and payment of the balance.

Adjustment of final judgment figure in respect of an interim payment

6.1 In a final judgment[14] where an interim payment has previously been made which is less than the total amount awarded by the judge, the judgment or order should set out in a preamble:

(1) the total amount awarded by the judge, and

(2) the amount and date of the interim payment(s).

6.2 The total amount awarded by the judge should then be reduced by the total amount of any interim payments, and the judgment or order should then provide for entry of judgment and payment of the balance.

6.3 In a final judgment where an interim payment has previously been made which is more than the total amount awarded by the judge, the judgment or order should set out in a preamble;

(1) the total amount awarded by the judge, and

(2) the amount and date of the interim payment(s).

6.4 An order should then be made for repayment, reimbursement, variation or discharge under rule 25.8(2) and for interest on an overpayment under rule 25.8(5).

Statement as to service of a claim form

7.1 Where a party to proceedings which have gone to trial requires a statement to be included in the judgment as to where, and by what means the claim form issued in those proceedings was served, application should be made to the trial judge when judgment is given.

7.2 If the judge so orders, the statement will be included in a preamble to the judgment as entered.

Orders requiring an act to be done

8.1 An order which requires an act to be done (other than a judgment or order for the payment of an amount of money) must specify the time within which the act should be done.

8.2 The consequences of failure to do an act within the time specified may be set out in the order. In this case the wording of the following examples suitably adapted must be used:

[13] In this paragraph final "judgment" includes any order to pay a sum of money, a final award of damages and an assessment of damages.

[14] As in Note 9 above.

(1) Unless the [claimant][defendant] serves his list of documents by 4.00pm on Friday, January 22, 1999 his [claim][defence] will be struck out and judgment entered for the [defendent][claimant]., or

(2) Unless the [claimant][defendant] serves his list of documents within 14 days of service of this order his [claim][defence] will be struck out and judgment entered for the [defendant][claimant].

Example (1) should be used wherever possible.

Non-compliance with a judgment or order

9.1 An order which restrains a party from doing an act or requires an act to be done should, if disobedience is to be dealt with by an application to bring contempt of court proceedings, have the penal notice endorsed on it as follows:

"If you the within-named [   ] do not comply with this order you may be held to be in contempt of court and imprisoned or fined, or [in the case of a company or corporation] your assets may be seized."

9.2 The provisions of paragraph 9.1 above also apply to an order which contains an undertaking by a party to do or not do an act, subject to paragraph 9.3 below.

9.3 The court has the power to decline to:

(1) accept an undertaking, and

(2) deal with disobedience in respect of an undertaking by contempt of court proceedings,

unless the party giving the undertaking has made a signed statement to the effect that he understands the terms of his undertaking and the consequences of failure to comply with it.

9.4 The statement may be endorsed on the [court copy of the] order containing the undertaking or may be filed in a separate document such as a letter.

Foreign currency

10. Where judgment is ordered to be entered in a foreign currency, the order should be in the following form:

"It is ordered that the defendant pay the claimant (*state the sum in the foreign currency*) or the Sterling equivalent at the time of payment."

Costs

40BPD–003 **11.1** Attention is drawn to the costs practice direction and, in particular, to the court's power to make a summary assessment of costs.

11.2 Attention is also drawn to costs rule 43.5(5) which provides that if an order makes no mention of costs, none are payable in respect of the proceedings to which it relates.

Judgments paid by instalments

12. Where a judgment is to be paid by instalments, the judgment should set out:

(1) the total amount of the judgment,

(2) the amount of each instalment,

(3) the number of instalments and the date on which each is to be paid, and

(4) to whom the instalments should be paid.

Order to make an order of the house of lords an order of the High Court

13.1 Application may be made in accordance with Part 23 for an order to make an order of the House of Lords an order of the High Court. The application should be made to the procedural judge of the Division, District Registry or court in which the proceedings are taking place and may be made without notice unless the court directs otherwise.

13.2 The application must be supported by the following evidence:

(1) details of the order which was the subject of the appeal to the House of Lords,

(2) details of the order of the House of Lords, with a copy annexed, and

(3) a copy annexed of the certificate of the Clerk of Parliaments of the assessment of the costs of the appeal to the House of Lords in the sum of £.........

13.3 The order to make an order of the House of Lors an order of the High Court should be in form no. PF68.

Examples of forms of trial judgment

14.1 The following general forms may be used;

(1) judgment after trial before judge without jury—form no. 45,

(2) judgment after trial before judge with jury—form no. 46,

(3) judgment after trial before a Master or district judge—form no. 47,

(4) judgment after trial before a judge of the Technology and Construction court—form no. 47 but with any necessary modifications.

14.2 A trial judgment should, in addition to the matters set out in paragraphs 5, 6 and 7 above, have the following matters set out in a preamble:

(1) the questions put to a jury and their answers to those questions,

(2) the findings of a jury and whether unanimous or by a majority,

(3) any order made during the course of the trial concerning the use of evidence,

(4) any matters that were agreed between the parties prior to or during the course of the trial in respect of

(a) liability,

(b) contribution,

(c) the amount of the damages or part of the damages, and

(5) the findings of the judge in respect of each head of damage in a personal injury case.

14.3 Form no. 49 should be used for trial judgment against an Estate.

The forms referred to in this practice direction are listed in the practice direction which supplements Part 4 (Forms).

For information about

(1) Orders for provisional damages: see Part 41 and the practice direction which supplements it.

(2) Orders in respect of children and patients: see Part 22 and the practice direction which supplements it.

(3) Orders containing directions for payment of money out of court: see Parts 36 and 37 and the practice directions which supplement them.

(4) Structure settlement orders: see the separate practice direction supplementing Part 40.

(5) Taking accounts and conducting inquiries under a judgment or order: see the separate practice direction supplementing Part 40.

PRACTICE DIRECTION—STRUCTURED SETTLEMENTS

This Practice Direction Supplements CPR Part 40

Structured Settlements:

40CPD–001 **1.1** A structured settlement is a means of paying a sum awarded to or accepted by a claimant by way of instalments for the remainder of the claimant's life. The payments are either funded by an annuity from an insurance company or, where the party paying is a government body, by payments direct from that body.

1.2 The agreed sum which purchases the annuity or provides for payments (including any sum to be retained as capital for contingencies) is based on the sum offered or awarded on a conventional basis, less an amount representing the tax benefits obtained by the structure.

1.3 This type of order may be used both on settlement of a claim and after trial where the judge has found in favour of the claimant. In the latter case the claimant or his legal representative should ask the judge:

(1) not to provide for entry of judgment,

(2) to state the total amount to which the judge has found the claimant to be entitled, and

(3) for an adjournment to enable advice to be sought as to the formulation of a structured settlement based on that amount.

1.4 Where a claim settles before trial, an application should be made in accordance with CPR Part 23 for the consent order embodying the structured settlement to be made, and for the approval of the structured settlement where the claimant is a child or patient.[15]

1.5 If the claimant is not a child or patient, the consent order may be made without a hearing.

1.6 Where a hearing is required and as the annuity rate applicable to the structure may only remain available for a short time, the claimant's legal representative on issue of his application notice, should immediately seek an early date for the hearing.

1.7 At such a hearing the court will require the following documents and evidence to be filed not later than midday on the day before the hearing is to take place:

(1) Counsel's or the legal representative's opinion of the value of the claim on the basis of a conventional award (unless approval on that basis has already been given or the judge has stated the amount as in paragraph 1.3(2) above),

(2) a report of forensic accountants setting out the effect of a structured settlement bearing in mind the claimant's life expectancy and the anticipated cost of future care,

(3) a draft of the proposed structure agreement,

(4) sufficient information to satisfy the court that—

(a) enough of the agreed sum is retained as a contingency fund for anticipated future needs, and

(b) the structured settlement is secure and the annuities are payable by established insurers,

(5) details of any assets available to the claimant other than the agreed sum which is the subject of the application, and

(6) where the claimant is a patient, the approval or consent of the Court of Protection

1.8 To obtain the approval of the Court of Protection the claimant's legal representative should lodge the documents and information set out in

[15] For the definition of child or patient see Part 21.

paragraph 1.7(1) to (5) above together with a copy of the claim form and any statements of case filed in the proceedings in the Enquiries and Acceptances Branch of the Public Trust Office, Stewart House, 24 Kingsway, London WC2B 6JH by midday on the fourth day before the hearing.

1.9 If an application for the appointment of a receiver by the Court of Protection has not already been made:

(1) two copies of the application seeking his appointment (form CP1),

(2) a certificate of family and property (form CP5), and

(3) a medical certificate (form CP3)

should be lodged at the same time as the documents and information mentioned in paragraph 1.8 above. Forms CP1, 3 and 5 may be obtained from the address set out in paragraph 1.8.

1.10 Wherever possible a draft order should also be filed at the same time as the documents in paragraph 1.7 above.

1.11 Examples of structured settlement orders are set out in an Annex to this practice direction which may be adapted for use after trial or as the individual circumstances require. It should be noted that the reference in the second paragraph of the Part 2—structured settlement order to the "defendant's insurers" means the Life Insurer providing the annuity on behalf of the defendant.

1.12 Where it is necessary to obtain immediate payment out of money in court upon the order being made, the claimant's legal representatives should:

(1) contact the officer in charge of funds in court at the Court Funds Office at least 2 days before the hearing, and arrange for a cheque for the appropriate sum made payable to the insurers or government body to be ready for collection,

(2) notify the court office the day before the hearing so that the court is aware of the urgency, and

(3) bring to the hearing a completed Court Funds Office form 200 for authentication by the court upon the order being made.

Annex

Part 1—Structured settlement order

(Order to settle for conventional sum and for an adjournment to seek advice on the formulation of a structured settlement) **40CPD—002**

Title of Claim

UPON HEARING (Counsel/solicitor) for the claimant and (Counsel/ solicitor) for the defendant

AND UPON the defendant by (Counsel/solicitor) having undertaken to keep open an offer of £................. in full and final settlement of the claim and the claimant having undertaken to limit the claim to £.................

AND UPON the claimant's solicitors undertaking to instruct appropriate advisers to advise upon a structured settlement and to use their best endeavours promptly to make proposals to the defendant's solicitors as to the most equitable formulation of a structured settlement and after to seek (further directions/approval) from the court if necessary

IT IS ORDERED that this claim is adjourned with permission to both parties to apply in respect of the further hearing relating to further directions providing for a structured settlement as undertaken by the claimant's solicitors and that these proceedings be reserved to the (trial judge) unless otherwise ordered

AND IT IS ORDERED that the costs of these proceedings together with the costs relating to any proposal for a structured settlement be (*as ordered*).

Part 2—Structured settlement order

(Order giving effect to and approval of a structured settlement)

Title of Claim

UPON HEARING (Counsel/solicitor) for the claimant and (Counsel/solicitor) for the defendant

AND the claimant and defendant having agreed to the terms set forth in the Schedule to this order in which the claimant accepts the sum of £................ (*overall sum*) in satisfaction of the claim of which the sum of £................ is to be used by the [defendant's insurers for the purchase of an annuity] [defendant for the provision of the appropriate payments]

AND UPON the Judge having approved the terms of the draft minute of order, the agreement and the schedule to this order

AND UPON the claimant and the insurer (*name*) undertaking to execute the agreement this day

BY CONSENT

IT IS ORDERED

(1) that of the sum of £................ (*total sum in court*) now in court standing to the credit of this claim the sum of £................ be paid out to (*insurers/payee*) on behalf of the defendant for the purchase of an annuity as specified in the payment schedule to this order.

(2) (*other relevant orders*)

() that all further proceedings in this claim be stayed except for the purpose of carrying the terms into effect

() that the parties have permission to apply to carry the terms into effect

Schedule

(*Attach draft agreement and set out any other terms of the settlement*)

PART 41

PROVISIONAL DAMAGES

Contents 41.0.1

Editorial Introduction

Provisional damages may be awarded in a claim for personal injuries where it is proved or admitted that there is a chance that at some time in the future the injured person will, as a result of the act or omission which gave rise to the cause of action, develop some serious disease or suffer some serious deterioration in his physical or mental condition. See Supreme Court Act 1981, s.32A and County Courts Act 1984, s.51 and *Wilson v. Ministry of Defence* [1991] 1 All E.R. 638. 41.0.2

Part 41 largely follows the format of RSC, O.37, rr.7–10 which was also incorporated into the County Court Rules by CCR, O.22, r.6A. See SCP 1999, Vol. 1, paras 37/7–37/10/4. Note though that the period of notice of intention to apply for further damages in r.41.3(3) is 28 days, as opposed to three months in RSC, O.37, r.2(3).

Related sources 41.0.3

- Supreme Court Act 1981, s.32A (see SCP 1999, Vol. 2, para. 20A–213)
- County Courts Act 1984, s.51
- Practice Direction (Provisional Damages, Procedure) [1985] 1 W.L.R. 961, as amended by the Lord Chief Justice, March 23, 1995 (see SCP 1999, Vol. 2, paras 2C–217 to 2C–222)
- Part 25
- Rule 16.4(1)(d)
- Practice Direction to Pt 41

Application and definitions

41.1—(1) This Part applies to proceedings to which SCA, s.32A or CCA, s.51 applies. 41.1

(2) In this Part—

(a) "SCA, s.32A" means section 32A of the Supreme Court Act 1981[1];

(b) "CCA, s.51" means section 51 of the County Courts Act 1984[2]; and

(c) "award of provisional damages" means an award of damages for personal injuries under which—

(i) damages are assessed on the assumption referred to in SCA, s.32A or CCA, s.51 that the injured person will not develop the disease or suffer the deterioration; and

(ii) the injured person is entitled to apply for further damages at a future date if he develops the disease or suffers the deterioration.

Information included in Particulars of claim—Pt 16 and PD to Pt 16 set out the information that must be included in particulars of claim if a claim for provisional damages is to be made. In particular see r.16.4(1)(d) and PD to Pt 16, para 4.4 which provide that the particulars of claim must state that the claimant is claiming provisional damages, that there is a chance that at some future time the claimant will develop a serious disease or deterioration in his physical or mental condition, what that disease or deterioration will be and the grounds for claiming provisional damages. 41.1.1

Order for an award of provisional damages

41.2—(1) The court may make an order for an award of provisional damages if— 41.2

[1] 1981 c. 54. Section 32A was inserted by section 6(1) of the Administration of Justice Act 1982 (c. 53).

[2] 1984 c. 28.

(a) the particulars of claim include a claim for provisional damages; and
(b) the court is satisfied that SCA, s.32A or CCA, s.51 applies.

(Rule 16.4(1)(d) sets out what must be included in the particulars of claim where the claimant is claiming provisional damages.)

(2) An order for an award of provisional damages—
(a) must specify the disease or type of deterioration in respect of which an application may be made at a future date;
(b) must specify the period within which such an application may be made; and
(c) may be made in respect of more than one disease or type of deterioration and may, in respect of each disease or type of deterioration, specify a different period within which a subsequent application may be made.

(3) The claimant may make more than one application to extend the period specified under paragraph (2)(b) or (2)(c).

41.2.1 **An order for an award for provisional damages**—See the form for a provisional damages judgment in the Annex to the PD to Pt 41.

Note that when giving judgment the judge should:
(1) specify the disease or type of deterioration which for the award of immediate damages it has been assumed will not occur and will entitle the claimant to further damages if they do occur;
(2) give an award of immediate damages;
(3) specify the period within which an application for further damages may be made (an application may be made to extend the period. The period may be expressed as being for the duration of the life of the claimant); and
(4) direct what documents are to be filed and preserved. (See PD to Pt 41, paras 2.1 to 2.4).

41.2.2 **The case file**—See PD to Part 41, paras 3.1 to 3.6.

41.2.3 **Consent orders**—See PD to Pt 41, paras 4.1 to 4.3.

41.2.4 **Default judgment**—See PD to Pt 41, paras 5.1 to 5.3.

41.2.5 **"particulars of claim"**—(r.41.2)—See rr.7.4 and 16.4.

Application for further damages

41.3 **41.3**—(1) The claimant may not make an application for further damages after the end of the period specified under rule 41.2(2), or such period as extended by the court.

(2) Only one application for further damages may be made in respect of each disease or type of deterioration specified in the award of provisional damages.

(3) The claimant must give at least 28 days' written notice to the defendant of his intention to apply for further damages.

(4) If the claimant knows—
(a) that the defendant is insured in respect of the claim; and
(b) the identity of the defendant's insurers,

he must also give at least 28 days' written notice to the insurers.

(5) Within 21 days after the end of the 28 day notice period referred to in paragraphs (3) and (4), the claimant must apply for directions.

(6) The rules in Part 25 about the making of an interim payment apply where an application is made under this rule.

41.3.1 **"application"**—(rr.41.2 and 41.3)—See Pt 23.

"28 days"—(r.41.3(3)–(5))—See r.28. 41.3.2

PRACTICE DIRECTION—PROVISIONAL DAMAGES

This Practice Direction Supplements CPR Part 41

Claims for provisional damages

1.1 CPR Part 16 and the practice direction which supplements it set out information which must be included in the particulars of claim if a claim for provisional damages is made. 41PD–001

Judgment for an award of provisional damages

2.1 When giving judgment at trial the judge will:

(1) specify the disease or type of deterioration, or diseases or types of deterioration, which

(a) for the purpose of the award of immediate damages it has been assumed will not occur, and

(b) will entitle the claimant to further damages if it or they do occur at a future date,

(2) give an award of immediate damages,

(3) specify the period or periods within which an application for further damages may be made in respect of each disease or type of deterioration, and

(4) direct what documents are to be filed and preserved as the case file in support of any application for further damages.

2.2 The claimant may make an application or applications to extend the periods referred to in paragraph 2.1(3) above.[3]

2.3 A period specified under paragraph 2.1(3) may be expressed as being for the duration of the life of the claimant.

2.4 The documents to be preserved as the case file ("the case file documents") referred to in paragraph 2.1(4) will be set out in a schedule to the judgment as entered.

2.5 Causation of any further damages within the scope of the order shall be determined when any application for further damages is made.

2.6 A form for a provisional damages judgment is set out in the Annex to this practice direction.

The case file

3.1 The case file documents must be preserved until the expiry of the period or periods specified or of any extension of them.

3.2 The case file documents will normally include:

(1) the judgment as entered,

(2) the statements of case,

(3) a transcript of the judge's oral judgment,

(4) all medical reports relied on, and

(5) a transcript of any parts of the claimant's own evidence which the judge considers necessary.

3.3 The associate/court clerk will:

(1) ensure that the case file documents are provided by the parties where necessary and filed on the court file,

[3] See CPR rule 41.2(3).

(2) endorse the court file
(a) to the effect that it contains the case file documents, and
(b) with the period during which the case file documents must be preserved, and
(3) preserve the case file documents in the court office where the proceedings took place.

3.4 Any subsequent order:
(1) extending the period within which an application for further damages may be made, or
(2) of the Court of Appeal discharging or varying the provisions of the original judgment or of any subsequent order under sub-paragraph (1) above,
will become one of the case file documents and must be preserved accordingly and any variation of the period within which an application for further damages may be made should be endorsed on the court file containing the case file documents.

3.5 On an application to extend the periods referred to in paragraph 2.1(3) above a current medical report should be filed.

3.6 Legal representatives are reminded that it is their duty to preserve their own case file.

Consent orders

4.1 An application to give effect to a consent order for provisional damages should be made in accordance with CPR Part 23. If the claimant is a child or patient[4] the approval of the court must also be sought and the application for approval will normally be dealt with at a hearing.

4.2 The order should be in the form of a consent judgment and should contain;
(1) the matters set out in paragraph 2.1(1) to (3) above, and
(2) a direction as to the documents to be preserved as the case file documents, which will normally be
(a) the consent judgment,
(b) any statements of case,
(c) an agreed statement of facts, and
(d) any agreed medical report(s).

4.3 The claimant or his legal representative must lodge the case file documents in the court office where the proceedings are taking place for inclusion in the court file. The court file should be endorsed as in paragraph 3.3(2) above, and the case file documents preserved as in paragraph 3.3(3) above.

Default Judgment

41PD–002 **5.1** Where a defendant:
(1) fails to file an acknowledgment of service in accordance with CPR Part 10, and
(2) fails to file a defence in accordance with CPR Part 15,
within the time specified for doing so, the claimant may not, unless he abandons his claim for provisional damages, enter judgment in default but should make an application in accordance with CPR Part 23 for directions.

5.2 The Master or district judge will normally direct the following issues to be decided:
(1) whether the claim is an appropriate one for an award of provisional damages and if so, on what terms, and

[4] See CPR Part 21 for the definitions of a child and patient.

(2) the amount of immediate damages.
5.3 If the judge makes an award of provisional damages, the provisions of paragraph 3 above apply.

Annex

(Example of an Award of Provisional Damages after Trial)

(*Title of proceedings*) **Annex**

THIS CLAIM having been tried before [*title and name of judge*] without a jury at [the Royal Courts of Justice *or as may be*] and [*title and name of judge*] having ordered that judgment as set out below be entered for the claimant

IT IS ORDERED—

(1) that the defendant pay the claimant by way of immediate damages the sum of £................ (being (i) £................ for special damages and £................. [agreed interest] [interest at the rate of .... from .... to ....] (ii) £................ for general damages and £................ [agreed interest] [interest at the rate of 2% from .... to ....] and (iii) £................ for loss of future earnings and/or earning capacity) on the assumption that the claimant would not at a future date as a result of the act or omission giving rise to the claim develop the following disease/type of deterioration namely [*set out disease or type of deterioration*]
(2) that if the claimant at a further date does develop that [disease] [type of deterioration] he should be entitled to apply for further damages provided that the application is made on or before [*set out period*]
(3) that the documents set out in the schedule to this order be filed on the court file and preserved as the case file until the expiry of the period set out in paragraph (2) above or of any extension of that period which has been ordered
(4) (costs)

Schedule

(*list documents referred to in paragraph (3)*)

PART 42

Change of Solicitor

42.0.1 **Contents**

Editorial Introduction

42.0.2 In the time-honoured expression, a solicitor acting for a party is said to be "on the record". A solicitor who ceases to act for a party is removed "from the record". These expressions pre-date the RSC (Rev.) 1962 and are not used in RSC, O.67 (Change of Solicitor) save in the title to RSC, O.67, r.5. No doubt the expressions will continue even though not found in the CPR.

To an opponent, the consequences of a party acting by solicitor are twofold: first, the solicitor's business address will be that party's address for service (see r.6.5(5) and r.6.13(2)); secondly, the signing by the solicitor of the claim form (which has replaced the High Court writ and County Court summons), acknowledgment of service or statement of case (the term which has replaced "pleadings": see r.2.3) notifies the opponent that the party will be claiming solicitor's costs. Part 42 deals with four distinct situations frequently arising in practice and one rare situation.

The common situations are:

(1) a new solicitor appointed to act instead of a previous solicitor;
(2) a solicitor being appointed by a party who has hitherto acted in person;
(3) a party who has previously employed a solicitor now deciding to act in person;
(4) a solicitor applying to the court for an order that he has ceased to act.

The first three do not require an order (merely a notice), the fourth does.

The rare situation is removal of a solicitor on application of another party.

Related Sources

42.0.3
- Solicitors Act 1974 (SCP 1999, Vol. 2, paras 15A–1 *et seq.*)
- Civil Legal Aid (General) Regulations 1989, reg. 83 (SCP 1999, Vol. 2, Section 16D, para. 160–14g)
- Rule 6.5(5) (Address for service)
- Rule 6.13(2) (Service of claim form—defendant's address for service)
- Part 48, pt II (Costs relating to solicitors)
- Part 44 (General rules about costs)
- Practice Direction to Pt 42
- Part 23 (applications)

Forms

42.0.4 **N434 Notice of change of solicitor**—r.42.2. Note also the Queen's Bench Masters Practice forms relevant to RSC, O.67 (Change of Solicitor) in SCP 1999, Vol. 2, Section 1B can be adapted for use under Pt 42. These forms are listed in SCP 1999, Vol. 1 at para. 67/0/4.

Solicitor acting for a party

42.1 **42.1** Where the address for service of a party is the business address of his solicitor, the solicitor will be considered to be acting for that party until the provisions of this Part have been complied with.

(Part 6 contains provisions about the address for service.)

42.1.1 **Effect of rule**—Every party to proceedings in the High Court or County Court must have an address for service (see Pt 6—Service of Documents, especially r.6.5(5) (address for service) and r.6.13(2) (service of claim form)). Where a party employs a solicitor, the solicitor's business address will be the address for service. All documents served at that address by the Court or another party are properly served. Rule 42.1 emphasises that the solicitor will be considered to be acting for that party until he filed the notice of change with the court and served it upon every other party, including the former client (PD to Pt 42, para. 12).

Change of solicitor—duty to give notice

42.2—(1) This rule applies where— 42.2

(a) a party for whom a solicitor is acting wants to change his solicitor;

(b) a party, after having conducted the claim in person, appoints a solicitor to act on his behalf (except where the solicitor is appointed only to act as an advocate for a hearing); or

(c) a party, after having conducted the claim by a solicitor, intends to act in person.

(2) Where this rule applies, the party or his solicitor (where one is acting) must—

(a) file notice of the change; and

(b) serve notice of the change on every other party and, where paragraph (1)(a) or (c) applies, on the former solicitor.

(3) The notice must state the party's new address for service.

(4) The notice filed at court must state that notice has been served as required by paragraph (2)(b).

(5) Subject to paragraph (6), where a party has changed his solicitor or intends to act in person, the former solicitor will be considered to be the party's solicitor unless and until—

(a) notice is served in accordance with (1); or

(b) the court makes an order under rule 42.3 and the order is served as required by paragraph (3) of that rule.

(6) Where the certificate of an assisted person within the meaning of the Civil Legal Aid (General) Regulations 1989[1] is revoked or discharged—

(a) the solicitor who acted for the assisted person shall cease to be the solicitor acting in the case as soon as his retainer is determined under regulation 83 of those Regulations; and

(b) if the assisted person wishes to continue—

(i) where he appoints a solicitor to act on his behalf paragraph (2) will apply as if he had previously conducted the claim in person; and

(ii) where he wants to act in person he must give an address for service.

(Rule 6.5 deals with a party's address for service.)

"duty to give notice"—Rule 42.2, where it applies, imposes a duty to give notice. This is emphasised by the use of the word "must" in r.42.2(2), 4.42.2(3) and 4.42.2(4). 42.2.1

"change of solicitor"—Rule 42.2 applies to three distinct situations set about in 4.42.2(1), namely a party changing his solicitor; a party who has acted in person now appointing a solicitor; and a party having employed a solicitor who now intends to act in person. The rule is derived from CCR, O.50, r.5 rather than RSC, O.67, rr.1, 3 and 4. Like CCR, O.50, r.5(2), CPR, r.42.2(1)(b) does not require notice where a party who has acted in person appoints a solicitor only to act as an advocate. Further, like CCR, O.50, r.5 (and unlike RSC, O.67, r.2), CPR, r.42.2 does not apply to a solicitor acting as agent for another solicitor. 42.2.2

"notice of the change"—In the case of the three situations to which r.42.2(1) applies, no order of the court is required. All that is required is that a notice of the appropriate change which complies with r.42.2(3) and (4) must be filed with the court and served on every other party and the former solicitor: r.42.2(2). 42.2.3

Rule 42.2(5) is not really necessary having regard to r.42.1, but suffices to emphasise the mandatory requirements of the rule and that once a solicitor is appointed to act, that solicitor is considered to be the party's solicitor unless and until the requirements of Pt 42 are complied with.

Revocation or discharge of legal aid certificate—Rule 42.2(6) is a reminder that under reg. 83 of the Civil Legal Aid (General) Regulations 1989 a solicitor's retainer is determined upon revocation or discharge of his client's legal aid certificate. In accordance with the Regulations the solicitor must serve notice of the revocation/discharge on all other parties and file a copy with the 42.2.4

[1] S.I. 1989/339 to which there are amendments not relevant to these Rules.

court. This is sufficient to remove the solicitor from the record without further notice or order. The issue which then arises is whether the previously legally aided party has abandoned the proceedings or whether he wishes to continue the case either by acting in person or appointing a solicitor as a private client. Hence r.42.2(6) which requires the "assisted person" (strictly, of course, the formerly assisted person) to give an address for service if he now intends to act in person and requires a new solicitor to give notice pursuant to r.42.2(2). Failure to do this may result in his statement of case being struck out—see r.34(2)(c). See too PD to Pt 42, paras 2.1 to 22.

42.2.5 **Effect of change on lien**—The CPR have not changed the law on a solicitor's lien for costs. The law is discussed in SCP 1999, Vol. 1 at paras 67/1/11 and 67/6/5.

Order that a solicitor has ceased to act

42.3 **42.3**—(1) A solicitor may apply for an order declaring that he has ceased to be the solicitor acting for a party.

(2) Where an application is made under this rule—

(a) notice of the application must be given to the party for whom the solicitor is acting, unless the court directs otherwise; and

(b) the application must be supported by evidence.

(3) Where the court makes an order that a solicitor has ceased to act—

(a) a copy of the order must be served on every party to the proceedings; and

(b) if it is served by a party or the solicitor, the party or the solicitor (as the case may be) must file a certificate of service.

42.3.1 **Effect of rule**—Strictly, no order under r.42.3 should ever be necessary. Where a party has determined his solicitor's retainer, or the solicitor has notified the former client that the solicitor has determined the retainer, the party or the party's new solicitor should simply give notice of change pursuant to r.42.2. It has been common for that party to fail to do so. No doubt r.42.3 will be as commonly utilised as the rules from which it is derived (RSC, O.67, r.6 and CCR, O.50, r.5(4)).

Where the solicitor's retainer has been determined but no notice has been given in accordance with r.42.2, the solicitor can apply for a an order under r.42.3 declaring that he has ceased to act. Having regard to the provisions of r.42.1and r.42.2(5), the solicitor should do so promptly upon determination of the retainer.

42.3.2 **Determination of solicitor's retainer**—Pursuant to s.65(2) of the Solicitors Act 1974, a solicitor has good cause to determine his retainer if the client, on being requested, fails within a reasonable time to make a payment of a reasonable sum on account of past or future costs generally. See also SCP 1999, Vol. 1, para. 67/6/5.

42.3.3 **Purpose of rule**—The concern of the rule is with the record of the cost and the service of court documents. it comes into play when, rightly or wrongly, a solicitor has ceased to act and the party has not given notice of change of solicitor or notice of intention to act in person. The court has a discretion whether or not to make the order, but unless there are special circumstances which render it expedient to retain the solicitor on the record, the order will generally be made as a matter of course upon proof that the solicitor has in fact ceased to act for the party and that no steps have been taken by that party to remove the solicitor's name from the record. An order under the rule does not affect the rights or liabilities of a solicitor and the party as between themselves (*Plenty v. Gladwin* (1986) 67 A.L.R.26, High Court of Australia).

42.3.4 **"order declaring that he has ceased to be the solicitor acting for a party"**—Unlike r.42.2 where notice suffices, an order is required where r.42.3 applies.

42.3.5 **"notice of the application"**—Notice of the application must, pursuant to r.42.3(2), be served on the former client by the solicitor. Note that there is no requirement to serve any other party. Indeed other parties should not be served, for to do so might injure the client (*Re Creehouse Ltd* [1983] 1 W.L.R. 77; [1982] 3 All E.R. 659, CA). Proof of service on the client will be required if he does not attend the hearing of the application. This should be proved by filing a certificate of service—see r.6.10 and Form N215.

42.3.6 **"supported by evidence"**—Rule 42.3(2)(b) makes it clear that the application by the solicitor must be supported by evidence. Although the former practice was for the solicitor to file an affidavit, this is no longer necessary. Evidence may be contained on the notice of application itself, if the statement of truth is completed, or may be given in the form of a separate witness statement (see rr.22.1, 32.2 and 32.15). Copies should be served on the solicitor's client, but not on other parties—para. 42.3.5 above.

"a copy of the order must be served on every party . . ."—If a solicitor obtains an order declaring that he has ceased to be the solicitor acting for a party, pursuant to r.42.3(3) a copy of that order must be served "on every party to the proceedings". This does, of course, include the solicitors' former client who is still a "party to the proceedings". A certificate of service of the order must then be filed with the court if service is effected by the solicitor (as it usually will be) rather than by the court (see r.6.10 and Form N215). As to where to file the certificate see PD to Pt 42, paras 2.5 to 2.7. **42.3.7**

Address for service of party whose solicitor is removed—RSC, O.67, r.7 contained an express rule dealing with the address for service of a party whose solicitor was removed from the record. Part 42 contains no such express provision that, note, is necessary having regard to the omnibus provisions of Pt 6 and in particular the table set out in r.6.5(6). Nevertheless, it is a useful practice for the order declaring that a solicitor has ceased to act to also declare the address for service of the party concerned. **42.3.8**

Removal of solicitor who has ceased to act on application of another party

42.4—(1) Where— **42.4**

(a) a solicitor who has acted for a party—
  (i) has died;
  (ii) has become bankrupt;
  (iii) has ceased to practice; or
  (iv) cannot be found; and

(b) the party has not given notice of a change of solicitor or notice of intention to act in person as required by rule 42.2(2),

any other party may apply for an order declaring that the solicitor has ceased to be the solicitor acting for the other party in the case.

(2) Where an application is made under this rule, notice of the application must be given to the party to whose solicitor the application relates unless the court directs otherwise.

(3) Where the court makes an order made under this rule—

(a) a copy of the order must be served on every other party to the proceedings; and

(b) where it is served by a party, that party must file a certificate of service.

Effect of r.42.4—Rule 42.4 is derived from RSC, O.67, r.5 and no doubt will be as rarely used in practice as was its predecessor. Nevertheless it is a necessary rule to deal with the four situations set out in r.42.4(1)(a) where no notice has been given in accordance with r.42.2(2). The rule itself is clear and self-explanatory. **42.4.1**

Address for service of party whose solicitor is removed—See note under this heading in Commentary at para. 42.3.8. **42.4.2**

PRACTICE DIRECTION—CHANGE OF SOLICITOR

This Practice Direction Supplements Part 42 of the Civil Procedure Rules

Solicitor acting for a party

1.1 Rule 42.1 states that where the address for service of a party is the business address[2] of his solicitor, the solicitor will be considered to be acting for that party until the provisions of Part 42 have been complied with. **42PD–001**

[2] Rule 6.5 and the Practice Direction supplementing Part 6 contain information about the business address.

1.2 Subject to rule 42.2(6) (where the certificate of an assisted person within the meaning of the Civil Legal Aid (General) Regulations 1989 is revoked or discharged), where a party has changed his solicitor or intends to act in person, the former solicitor will be considered to be the party's solicitor unless or until;

(1) a notice of the change is

(a) filed with the court,[3] and

(b) served on every other party,[4] or

(2) the court makes an order under rule 42.3 and the order is served on every other party.[5]

The notice should not be filed until every other party has been served.

1.3 A solicitor appointed to represent a party only as an advocate at a hearing will not be considered to be acting for that party within the meaning of Part 42.

Notice of change of solicitor

2.1 Rule 42.2(1) sets out the circumstances following which a notice of the change must be filed and served.

2.2 A notice of the change giving the last known address of the former assisted person must also be filed and served on every party where, under rule 42.2(6):

(1) the certificate of an assisted person within the meaning of the Civil Legal Aid (General) Regulations 1989 is revoked or discharged,

(2) the solicitor who acted for the assisted person has ceased to act on determination of his retainer under regulation 83 of those Regulations, and

(3) the assisted person wishes either to act in person or appoint another solicitor to act on his behalf.

2.3 In addition, where a party or solicitor changes his address for service, a notice of that change should be filed and served on every party.

2.4 A party who, having conducted a claim by a solicitor, intends to act in person must give in his notice an address for service that is within the jurisdiction.[6]

2.5 Practice form N434 should be used to give notice of any change. The notice should be filed in the court office in which the claim is proceeding.

2.6 Where the claim is proceeding in the High Court the notice should be filed either in the appropriate District Registry or if the claim is proceeding in the Royal Courts of Justice, as follows;

(1) a claim proceeding in the Queen's Bench Division—in the Action Department of the Central Office,

(2) a claim proceeding in the Chancery Division—in Chancery Chambers,

(3) a claim proceeding in the Crown Office—in the Crown Office,

(4) a claim proceeding in the Admiralty and Commercial Registry—in the Admiralty and Commercial Registry, and

(5) a claim proceeding in the Technology and Construction Court—in the Registry of the Technology and Construction Court.

2.7 Where the claim is the subject of an appeal to the Court of Appeal, the notice should also be filed in the Civil Appeals Office.

Application for an order that a solicitor has ceased to act

3.1 A solicitor may apply under rule 42.3 for an order declaring that he has ceased to be the solicitor acting for a party.

3.2 The application should be made in accordance with part 23[7] and must

[3] Rule 42.2(2)(a)
[4] Rule 42.2(2)(b).
[5] Rule 42.2(5).
[6] See rule 6.5(3).
[7] See Part 23 and the Practice Direction which supplements it.

be supported by evidence.[8] Unless the court directs otherwise the application notice must be served on the party.[9]

3.3 An order made under rule 42.3 must be served on every party and takes effect when it is served. Where the order is not served by the court, the person serving must file a certificate of service in practice form N215.

Application by another party to remove a solicitor

4.1 Rule 42.4 sets out circumstances in which any other party may apply for an order declaring that a solicitor has ceased to be the solicitor acting for another party in the proceedings.

4.2 The application should be made in accordance with Part 23 and must be supported by evidence. Unless the court directs otherwise the application notice must be served on the party to whose solicitor the application relates.

4.3 An order made under rule 42.4 must be served on every other party to the proceedings. Where the order is not served by the court, the person serving must file a certificate of service in practice form N215.

[8] See Part 32 and the Practice Direction which supplements it for information about evidence.
[9] Rule 42.3(2).

PART 43

Scope of Cost Rules and Definitions

43.0.1 **Contents**

Editorial Introduction

43.0.2 The rules relating to costs in Pts 43 to 48 deal with the main provisions as to costs and the way in which the court will award and assess costs. These parts do not however provide a complete self contained code and other provisions relating to costs may be found under related sources.

Transitional Provisions

43.0.3 Paragraph 18 of the Practice Direction supplemental to Pt 51 (see para. 51PD–001) deals with the extent to which the Civil Procedure Rules apply to proceedings issued before April 26, 1999.

So far as costs are concerned all the provisions in the new costs rules apply from April 26, 1999, both as to the procedure to be adopted and also the way in which costs are to be assessed. It is recognised that litigation may well have been in progress for some considerable time before April 26, 1999 without the parties or their lawyers being aware that the new rules might alter the way in which the steps which they were undertaking would be viewed by the court at the time of assessment of costs. The Vice-Chancellor, as Head of Civil Justice, decided that when the court is assessing costs of work done prior to April 26, 1999 the new rules will apply, but the judge dealing with the costs (whether by summary or detailed assessment) will not disallow anything in respect of that work which would not have been disallowed under the rules in force prior to April 26, 1999. The Costs Practice Direction (see para. 48PD–001) deals with the detailed provisions in respect of proceedings for taxation commenced prior to April 26, 1999 (see paras 3.1–3.7 of the Directions relating to Pt 48).

Costs officers have all the powers of the court under the CPR and accordingly the overriding objective set out in Pt 1 and the court's general powers of management set out in Pt 3 apply equally to all questions of costs. Authorised court officers have all the powers of the court when making a detailed assessment except certain penal powers (see r.47.3).

Related Sources

43.0.4 Other provisions relating to costs include:

- Rule 3.1 (The courts general powers of management)
- Rule 3.4 (Power to strike out a statement of case)
- Rule 3.5 (Judgment without trial after striking out)
- Rule 3.7 (Sanctions for non payment of certain fees)
- Rule 3.8 (Sanctions have effect unless defaulting party obtains relief)
- Rule 12.5 (Nature of judgment where default judgment obtained by filing a request)
- Rule 12.9 (Procedure for obtaining a default judgment for costs only)
- Rule 14.4 (Admission of whole of claim for specified amount of money)
- Rule 14.5 (Admission of part of a claim for a specified amount of money)
- Rule 14.6 (Admission of liability to pay whole of claim for unspecified amount of money)
- Rule 14.7 (Admission of liability to pay for unspecified amount of money where defendant offers a sum in satisfaction of the claim)
- Rule 14.9 (Request for time to pay)
- Rule 14.11 (Determination of rate of payment by court officer)
- Rule 21.9 (Procedure where appointment of litigation friend ceases)
- Rule 27.14 (Costs on the small claims track)
- Rule 27.15 (Claims re-allocated from the small claims track to another track)
- Rule 28.2 (Fast track general provisions)
- Rule 30.2 (Transfer between county courts and within the High Court)
- Rule 34.4 (The court's power to restrict expert evidence)
- Rule 34.10 (Enforcing attendance of witness)
- Rule 34.14 (Fees and expenses of examiner)

- Rule 35.6 (Written questions to experts)
- Rule 35.8 (Instructions to a single joint expert)
- Rule 35.15 (Assessors)
- Part 36 (Offers to settle and payments into court) (the whole of this part has costs consequences and accordingly individual rules are not identified within Pt 36)
- Rule 38.5 (When discontinuance takes effect where permission of a court is not needed)
- Rule 38.6 (Liability for costs (on discontinuance))
- Rule 38.8 (Stay of remainder of partly discontinued proceedings where costs not paid)
- Rule 40.6 (Consent judgments or orders)
- Rule 40.11 (Time for complying with a judgment or order)
- Rule 40.13 (Cases where court gives judgment both on claim and counterclaim)

There are also discreet provisions relating to interest as follows:

- Rule 12.6 (Interest (on default judgment))
- Rule 12.7 (Procedure for deciding an amount or value)
- Rule 14.14 (Interest (on judgment under r.14.4 (admission of whole of claim for specified amount of money)))
- Rule 25.8 (Powers of court where it has made an order for interim payment)
- Rule 40.8 (Time from which interest begins to run)

Other Sources

- Solicitors Act 1974 (SCP 1999, Vol. 2, Section 15A): 43.0.5
  - —Pt I: ss.19–27
  - —Pt II: ss.33, 37A, 41–44 and 50–53
  - —Pt III
  - —Pt IV: s.87
  - —Sched. 1A
- Litigants in Person (Costs and Expenses) Act 1975 (SCP 1999, Vol. 2, Section 21R)
- Charging Orders Act 1979, ss.1 and 2 (SCP 1999, Vol. 2, Section 21F)
- Supreme Court Act 1981, ss.51, 130 and 131 (SCP 1999, Vol. 2, Section 20A)
- County Courts Act 1984, ss.45 and 76 (SCP 1999, Vol. 2, Section 20A)
- Legal Aid Act 1988 (SCP 1999, Vol. 2, Section 16A)
  - —Pt I
  - —Pt IV
  - —Pt VI
  - —Pt VII
  - —Sched. 2
- Courts and Legal Services Act 1990 (SCP 1999, Vol. 2, Section 20B)
- Arbitration Act 1996, ss.59–65 (SCP 1999, Vol. 2, Section 21D)
- Matrimonial Causes (Costs) Rules 1988
- Civil Legal Aid (General) Regulations 1989 (SCP 1999, Vol. 2, Section 16D)
- Civil Legal Aid (Matrimonial Proceedings) Regulations 1989
- Legal Aid (Disclosure of Information) Regulations 1991 (SCP 1999, Vol. 2, Section 16B)
- Legal Aid in Family Proceedings (Remuneration) Regulations 1991
- Court of Protection Rules 1994 (SCP 1999, Vol. 2, Section 10C)
  - —Pt XVIII
  - —Pt XIX
- Legal Aid in Civil Proceedings (Remuneration) Regulations 1994 (SCP 1999, Vol. 2, Section 16F)
- Solicitors (Non-Contentious Business) Remuneration Order 1994 (SCP 1999, Vol. 2, Section 15D)
- Conditional Fee Agreements Order 1998
- Conditional Fee Agreements Regulations 1995 (SCP 1999, Vol. 2, Section 15F)
- Judgment Debts (Rate of Interest) Order 1995
- Legal Aid in Contempt Proceedings (Remuneration) Regulations 1995 (SCP 1999, Vol. 2, Section 16C)
- RSC, O.17, r.8
- RSC, O.23
- RSC, O.30
- RSC, O.49
- RSC, O.62, Appendix 3
- RSC, O.106
- CCR, O.38, r.18 and Appendix BCCR, O.1, r.6

Scope of this Part

43.1 This Part contains definitions and interpretation of certain matters set out in the rules about costs contained in Parts 44 to 48. 43.1

(Part 44 contains general rules about costs; Part 45 deals with fixed costs; Part 46 deals with fast track trial costs; Part 47 deals with the detailed assessment of costs and related appeals and Part 48 deals with costs payable in special cases.)

Definitions and application

43.2 **43.2**—(1) In Parts 44 to 48, unless the context otherwise requires—

(a) "costs" includes fees, charges, disbursements, expenses, remuneration, reimbursement allowed to a litigant in person under rule 48.6 and any fee or reward charged by a lay representative for acting on behalf of a party in proceedings allocated to the small claims track;

(b) "costs judge" means a taxing master of the Supreme Court;

(c) "costs officer" means—

(i) a costs judge;

(ii) a district judge; and

(iii) an authorised court officer;

(d) "authorised court officer" means any officer of—

(i) a county court;

(ii) a district registry;

(iii) the Principal Registry of the Family Division; or

(iv) the Supreme Court Costs Office;

whom the Lord Chancellor has authorised to assess costs;

(e) "fund" includes any estate or property held for the benefit of any person or class of person and any fund to which a trustee or personal representative is entitled in his capacity as such;

(f) "receiving party" means a party entitled to be paid costs;

(g) "paying party" means a party liable to pay costs;

(h) "assisted person" means an assisted person within the statutory provisions relating to legal aid; and

(i) "fixed costs" means the amounts which are to be allowed in respect of solicitors' charges in the circumstances set out in Part 45.

(2) The costs to which the rules in Parts 44 to 48 apply include—

(a) the following costs where those costs may be assessed by the court;

(i) costs of proceedings before an arbitrator or umpire;

(ii) costs of proceedings before a tribunal or other statutory body; and

(iii) costs payable by a client to his solicitor; and

(b) costs which are payable by one party to another party under the terms of a contract, where the court makes an order for an assessment of those costs.

43.2.1 **Comment**—The word "taxation" has been dropped and in its place "assessment" has been adopted. Assessment is the process by which the court decides the amount of any costs payable.

As to summary assessment see r.43.3 and as to detailed assessment r.43.4. For the purpose of these rules a Taxing Master of the Supreme Court is referred to as a "Costs Judge".

Rule 43.2(2) Application of CPR

43.2.2 **Arbitration**—As to costs in regard to arbitrations, see Arbitration Act 1996, ss.59–65 (Vol. 2, Section 21A, para. 21A–268). The Costs Judge is merely the delegate of the arbitrator or other tribunal assessing the amount (*Perkins (H.G.) Ltd v. Best-Shaw* [1973] 1 W.L.R. 975; [1973] 2 All E.R. 924).

43.2.3 **Family proceedings**—The Family Proceedings Rules 1991 have been amended to provide that Parts 43, 44 (except Rules 44.9 to 44.12), 47 and 48 of the CPR shall apply. Rule 44.3(2) (costs follow the event) shall not apply. Family Proceedings (Miscellaneous Amendments) Rules 1999, S.I. 1999 No. 1012.

The Family Proceedings (Costs) Rules 1991 are revoked.

43.2.4 **Insolvency proceedings**—The Insolvency Rules 1986 are modified by the Insolvency (Amendment) (No. 2) Rules 1999 S.I. 1999 No. 1022. Subject to any inconsistent provisions CPR,

Pt 43, Pt 44, Pt 45, Pt 47 and Pt 48 shall apply to insolvency proceedings with any necessary modifications.

Meaning of summary assessment

43.3 "Summary assessment" means the procedure by which the court, when making an order about costs, orders payment of a sum of money instead of fixed costs or "detailed assessment". **43.3**

Comment—Judges are required to assess the costs of a case if practicable and in cases lasting up to one day the parties are under an obligation to provide the court and their opponents with details of the costs which may be sought in the event of success (see paras 4.3–4.11 of the Directions relating to Pt 44). **43.3.1**

Appeal—Appeals from summary assessment are dealt with under the ordinary rules relating to appeals (see RSC, O.58 and O.59, CCR, O.37). See also Practice Direction for the Court of Appeal (Civil Division) para. PD–001 (after RSC, O.52), [1992] 2 All E.R. 638. **43.3.2**

Meaning of detailed assessment

43.4 "Detailed assessment" means the procedure by which the amount of costs is decided by a cost officer in accordance with Part 47. **43.4**

Comment—"Detailed assessment" is the name given to the procedure formerly known as taxation. (See paras 1.4–1.8 of the Directions relating to Pt 43.) **43.4.1**

PRACTICE DIRECTION ABOUT COSTS

Supplementing Parts 43 to 48 of the Civil Procedure Rules **43PD–001**

Introduction

1. This Practice Direction supplements Parts 43 to 48 of the Civil Procedure Rules. It applies to all proceedings to which those Parts apply.

2. Section III of the Directions Relating to Part 48 deals with transitional provisions affecting proceedings about costs which were pending before 26 April 1999.

3. Attention is drawn to the powers to make orders about costs conferred on the Supreme Court and any county court by Section 51 of the Supreme Court Act 1981.

4. In these Directions:

"counsel" means a barrister or other person with a right of audience in relation to all proceedings in the High Court or in the County Courts in which he is instructed to act.

"solicitor" means a solicitor of the Supreme Court or other person with a right of audience in relation to proceedings, who is conducting the claim or defence (as the case may be) on behalf of a party to the proceedings and, where the context admits, includes a patent agent.

5. In respect of any document which is required by these Directions to be signed by a party or his legal representative the Practice Direction supplementing Part 22 will apply as if the document in question was a statement of truth. (The Practice Direction supplementing Part 22 makes provision for cases in which a party is a child, a patient or a company or other corporation and cases in which a document is signed on behalf of a partnership).

DIRECTIONS RELATING TO PART 43

Scope of Costs Rules and Definitions

Section 1 Model Forms for Claims for Costs

Rule 43.3 Meaning of Summary Assessment

1.1 Rule 43.3 defines summary assessment. **43BPD–001**

1.2 Form 1 of the Schedule of Costs Forms annexed to this Direction is a model form of Statement of Costs to be used for summary assessments.

1.3 Further details about Statements of Costs are given in paragraph 4 of the Directions Relating to Part 44 (Procedure for assessing costs).

Rule 43.4 Meaning of Detailed Assessment

1.4 Rule 43.4 defines detailed assessment.

1.5 Form 2 of the Schedule of Costs Forms annexed to this Practice Direction is a model form of bill of costs to be used for detailed assessments.

1.6 Further details about bills of costs are given in the next section of these Directions and in paragraph 2.7 of the Directions Relating to Part 47 (Procedure for detailed assessment of costs and default provisions).

1.7 Form 2 of the Schedule of Costs Forms and the next section of this Practice Direction both refer to the ideal form of bills of costs. A party wishing to rely upon a bill which departs from the ideal form should include in the background information of the bill an explanation justifying the departure.

1.8 In any order of the court (whether made before or after 26 April 1999) the word "taxation" will be taken to mean "detailed assessment" and the words "to be taxed" will be taken to mean "to be decided by detailed assessment" unless in either case the context otherwise requires.

Section 2 Form and Contents of Bills of Costs

43BPD–002 **2.1** A bill of costs may consist of such of the following sections as may be appropriate:

(1) title page;
(2) background information;
(3) items of costs claimed under the headings specified in paragraph 2.5;
(4) summary showing the total costs claimed on each page of the bill;
(5) schedules of time spent on non-routine attendances; and
(6) the certificates referred to in paragraph 2.14.

2.2 Where it is necessary or convenient to do so, a bill of costs may be divided into two or more parts, each part containing sections (2), (3) and (4) above. A division into parts will be necessary or convenient in the following circumstances:

(1) Where the receiving party acted in person during the course of the proceedings (whether or not he also had a legal representative at that time) the bill should be divided into different parts so as to distinguish between;
  (a) the costs claimed for work done by the legal representative; and
  (b) the costs claimed for work done by the receiving party in person.

(2) Where the receiving party was represented by different solicitors during the course of the proceedings, the bill should be divided into different parts so as to distinguish between the costs payable in respect of each solicitor.

(3) Where the receiving party obtained legal aid in respect of all or part of the proceedings the bill should be divided into separate parts so as to distinguish between;
  (a) costs claimed before legal aid was granted;
  (b) costs claimed against the Legal Aid Board only; and
  (c) any costs claimed after legal aid ceased.

(4) Where value added tax (VAT) is claimed and there was a change in the rate of VAT during the course of the proceedings, the bill should be divided into separate parts so as to distinguish between;
  (a) costs claimed at the old rate of VAT; and
  (b) costs claimed at the new rate of VAT.

(5) Where the bill covers costs payable under two or more orders under which there are different paying parties the bill should be divided into parts so as to deal separately with the costs payable by each paying party.

2.3 The title page of the bill of costs must set out:

(1) the full title of the proceedings;

(2) the name of the party whose bill it is and a description of the document showing the right to assessment (as to which see paragraph 4.5 of the Directions Relating to Part 47);

(3) if VAT is included as part of the claim for costs, the VAT number of the legal representative or other person in respect of whom VAT is claimed;

(4) details of all legal aid certificates and legal aid amendment certificates in respect of which claims for costs are included in the bill.

2.4 The background information included in the bill of costs should set out:

(1) a brief description of the proceedings up to the date of the notice of commencement;

(2) a statement of the status of the solicitor or solicitor's employee in respect of whom costs are claimed and (if those costs are calculated on the baiss of hourly rates) the hourly rates claimed for each such person;

(3) a brief explanation of any agreement or arrangement between the receiving party and his solicitors which affects the costs claimed in the bill.

2.5 The bill of costs may consist of items under such of the following heads as may be appropriate:

(1) attendances on the court and counsel up to the date of the notice of commencement;

(2) attendances on and communications with the receiving party;

(3) attendances on and communications with witnesses incuding any expert witness;

(4) attendances to inspect any property or place for the purposes of the proceedings;

(5) searches and enquiries made at offices of public records, the Companies Registry and similar searches and enquiries;

(6) attendances on and communications with other persons;

(7) communications with the court and with counsel;

(8) work done in connection with arithmetical calculations of compensation and/or interest;

(9) work done on documents: preparing and considering documentation which was of and incidental to the proceedings, including time spent on pre-action protocols where appropriate and time spent collating documents;

(10) work done in connection with mediation, alternative dispute resolution and negotiations with a view to settlement if not already covered in the heads listed above;

(11) attendances on and communications with London and other agents and work done by them;

(12) other work done which was of or incidential to the proceedings and which is not already covered in the heads listed above.

2.6 In respect of each of the heads of costs:

(1) "communications" means letters out and telephone calls;

(2) communications which are not routine communications must be set out in chronological order;

(3) routine communications should be set out as a single item at the end of each head;

2.7 Routine communications are letters out and telephone calls which by reason of their simplicity should not be regarded as letters of substance or telephone calls which properly amount to an attendance.

2.8 Each item claimed in the bill of costs must be consecutively numbered.

2.9 In each part of the bill of costs which claims items under head (1) (attendances on court and counsel) a note should be made of:

(1) all relevant events, including events which do not constitute chargeable items;

(2) any orders for costs which the court made (whether or not a claim is made in respect of those costs in this bill of costs).

2.10 The numbered items of costs must be set out on paper divided into five columns, of which the last two columns should be left blank. The five columns should be headed as follows: Item, Amount claimed, VAT, Amount allowed, VAT.

2.11 In respect of heads (2) to (12) in paragraph 2.5 above, if the number of attendances and communications other than routine communications is five or more, the claim for the costs of those items in that section of the bill of costs should be for the total only and should refer to a schedule in which the full record of dates and details is set out. If the bill of costs contains more than one schedule each schedule should be numbered consecutively.

2.12 The bill of costs must not contain any claims in respect of costs or court fees which relate soley to the detailed assessment proceedings other than costs claimed for preparing and checking the bill.

2.13 The summary must show the total profit costs and disbursements claimed separately from the total VAT claimed. Where the bill of costs is divided into parts the summary must also give totals for each part. If each page of the bill gives a page total the summary must also set out the page totals for each page.

2.14 The bill of costs must contain such of the certificates, the texts of which are set out in Form 4 of the Schedule of Costs Forms annexed to this Practice Direction, as are appropriate.

2.15 The following provisions relate to work done by solicitors:

(1) Routine letters out and routine telephone calls will in general be allowed on a unit basis of 6 minutes each, the charge being calculated by reference to the appropriate hourly rate. The unit charge for letters out will include perusing and considering the relevant letters in and no separate charge should be made for in-coming letters.

(2) E-mails received or sent by solicitors will not normally be allowed but the court may, in its discretion, allow an actual time charge for preparation of e-mails sent by solicitors which properly amount to attendances provided that the time taken has been recorded. The court may also, in its discretion, allow a sum in respect of e-mails sent to the client or others where it is satisfied that, had e-mails not been sent, the number of communications which it would have been reasonable to allow would have been substantially greater than the number actually claimed.

(3) Local travelling expenses incurred by solicitors will not be allowed. The definition of "local" is a matter for the discretion of the court. While no absolute rule can be laid down, as a matter of guidance, "local" will, in general, be taken to mean within a radius of 10 miles from the court dealing with the case at the relevant time.

(4) The cost of postage, couriers, out-going telephone calls, fax and telex messages will in general not be allowed but the court may exceptionally in its discretion allow such expenses in unusual circumstances or where the cost is unusually heavy.

(5) The cost of making copies of documents will not in general be allowed but the court may exceptionally in its discretion make an allowance for copying in unusual circumstances or where the documents copied are unusually numerous in relation to the nature of the case. Where this discretion is invoked the number of copies made, their purpose and the costs claimed for them must be set out in the bill.

(6) Agency charges as between a principal solicitor and his agent will be dealt with on the principle that such charges, where appropriate, form part of the principal solicitor's charges. Where these charges relate to head (1) in paragraph 2.5 (attendances at court and on counsel) they should be included in their chronological order in that head. In other cases they should be included in head (11) (attendances on London and other agents).

Costs of preparing the bill

2.16 In head (12) in paragraph 2.5 (other work done) a claim may be made for the reasonable costs of preparing and checking the bill of costs.

Section 3 Special Provisions Relating to VAT

3.1 This section deals with claims for value added tax (VAT) which are made in respect of costs being dealt with by way of summary assessment or detailed assessment. **43BPD–003**

VAT Registration Number

3.2 The number allocated by HM Customs and Excise to every person registered under the Value Added Tax Act 1983 (except a Government Department) must appear in a prominent place at the head of every statement, bill of costs, fee sheet, account or voucher on which VAT is being included as part of a claim for costs.

Entitlement to VAT on Costs

3.3 VAT should not be included in a claim for costs if the receiving party is able to recover the VAT as input tax. Where the receiving party is able to obtain credit from HM Customs and Excise for a proportion of the VAT as input tax, only that proportion which is not eligible for credit should be included in the claim for costs.

3.4 The receiving party has responsibility for ensuring that VAT is claimed only when the receiving party is unable to recover the VAT or a proportion thereof as input tax.

3.5 Where there is a dispute as to whether VAT is properly claimed the receiving party must provide a certificate signed by the solicitors or the auditors of the receiving party in the form in the Schedule of Certificates annexed to this Practice Direction. Where the receiving party is a litigant in person who is claiming VAT, reference should be made by him to HM Customs and Excise and wherever possible a Statement to similar effect produced at the hearing at which the costs are assessed.

3.6 Where there is a dispute as to whether any service in respect of which a charge is proposed to be made in the bill is zero rated or exempt, reference should be made to HM Customs and Excise and wherever possible the view of HM Customs and Excise obtained and made known at the hearing at which the costs are assessed. Such application should be made by the receiving party. In the case of a bill from a solicitor to his own client such application should be made by the client.

Form of bill of costs where VAT rate changes

3.7 Where there is a change in the rate of VAT, suppliers of goods and services are entitled by ss.88(1) and 88(2) of the VAT Act 1994 in most circumstances to elect whether the new or the old rate of VAT should apply to a supply where the basic and actual tax points span a period during which there has been a change in VAT rates.

3.8 It will be assumed, unless a contrary indication is given in writing, that an election to take advantage of the provisions mentioned in paragraph 3.7 above and to charge VAT at the lower rate has been made. In any case in which an election to charge at the lower rate is not made, such a decision must be justified to the court assessing the costs.

Apportionment

3.9 All bills of costs, fees and disbursements on which VAT is included must be divided into separate parts so as to show work done before, on and after the date or dates from which any change in the rate of VAT takes effect. Where, however, a lump sum charge is made for work which spans a period during which there has been a change in VAT rates, and paragraphs 3.7 and 3.8 above do not apply, reference should be made to paragraphs 8 and 9 of Appendix F of Customs' Notice 700 (or any revised edition of that notice), a copy of which should be in the possession of every registered trader. If necessary, the lump sum should be apportioned. The totals of profit costs and disbursements in each part must be carried separately to the summary.

3.10 Should there be a change in the rate between the conclusion of a detailed assessment and the issue of the final costs certificate, any interested party may apply for the detailed assessment to be varied so as to take account of any increase or reduction in the amount of tax payable. Once the final costs certificate has been issued, no variation under this paragraph will be permitted.

Disbursements

3.11 Petty (or general) disbursements such as postage, fares etc which are normally treated as part of a solicitor's overheads and included in his profit costs should be charged with VAT even though they bear no tax when the solicitor incurs them. The cost of travel by public transport on a specific journey for a particular client where it forms part of the service rendered by a solicitor to his client and is charged in his bill of costs, attracts VAT.

3.12 Reference is made to the criteria set out in the VAT Guide (Customs and Excise Notice 700—1st August 1991 edition paragraph 83, or any revised edition of that Notice), as to expenses which are not subject to VAT. Charges for the cost of travel by public transport, postage, telephone calls and telegraphic transfers where these form part of the service rendered by the solicitor to his client are examples of charges which do not satisfy these criteria and are thus liable to VAT at the standard rate.

Legal Aid

3.13 VAT will be payable in respect of every supply made pursuant to a Legal Aid Certificate provided only that the person making the supply is a taxable person and that the assisted person is not resident outside the European Union. Where the assisted person is registered for VAT and the legal services paid for by the Legal Aid Board are in connection with the assisted person's business, the VAT on those services will be payable by the Legal Aid Board only.

3.14 In Legal Aid cases the legal aid summary must be drawn so as to show the total VAT on Counsel's fees as a separate item from the VAT on other disbursements and the VAT on profit costs.

Tax invoice

3.15 A bill of costs filed for detailed assessment is always retained by the Court. Accordingly if a solicitor waives his solicitor and client costs and accepts the costs certified by the court as payable by the unsuccessful party in settlement, it will be necessary for a short statement as to the amount of the certified costs and the VAT thereon to be prepared for use as the tax invoice.

Vouchers

3.16 Where receipted accounts for disbursements made by the solicitor or his client are retained as tax invoices a photostat copy of any such receipted account may be produced and will be accepted as sufficient evidence of payment when disbursements are vouched.

Certificates

3.17 In non legal aid cases the total VAT allowed will be shown in the final costs certificate as a separate item. In legal aid cases the VAT on Counsel's fees will be shown separately from the remaining VAT.

Litigants acting in person

3.18 Where a litigant acts in litigation on his own behalf he is not treated for the purposes of VAT as having supplied services and therefore no VAT is chargeable on that litigant's costs (even where, for example, that litigant is a solicitor or other legal representative).

3.19 Consequently in the circumstances described in the preceding paragraph, a bill of costs presented for agreement or assessment should not claim any VAT which will not be allowed on assessment.

Government Departments

3.20 On an assessment between parties, where costs are being paid to a Government Department in respect of services rendered by its legal staff, VAT should not be added.

Section 4 Estimates of Costs

4.1 This section sets out certain steps which parties must take in order to keep the other parties informed about their potential liability in respect of costs and in order to assist the court to decide what, if any, order to make about costs and about case management. **43BPD–004**

4.2 In this section an estimate of costs means an estimate of those costs already incurred and, if appropriate, to be incurred by the party who gives it which he intends, if he is successful in the case, to seek to recover from any other party under an order for costs.

4.3 The court may at any stage in a case order any party to file an estimate of costs and to serve copies of the estimate on all other parties. The court may direct that the estimate be prepared in such a way as to demonstrate the likely effects of giving or not giving a particular case management direction which the court is considering, for example a direction for a split trial or for the trial of a preliminary issue. The court may specify a time limit for filing and serving the estimate. However, if no time limit is specified the estimate should be filed and served within 28 days of the date of the order.

4.4 An estimate of costs should be substantially in the form of a Statement of Costs as illustrated in Form 1 of the Schedule of Costs Forms annexed to this Practice Direction.

4.5(1) When a party to a claim which is outside the financial scope of the small claims track files an allocation questionnaire, he must also file an estimate of costs and serve a copy of it on every other party unless the court otherwise directs.

(2) When a party to a claim which is being dealt with on the fast track or the multi-track or under Part 8 files a listing questionnaire, he must also file an estimate of costs and serve a copy of it on every other party, unless the court otherwise directs.

(3) An estimate of costs filed with a listing questionnaire must be divided into parts to show the costs already incurred by the party separately from those which will be incurred by him if the case proceeds to trial.

(4) This paragraph does not apply to litigants in person.

PART 44

General Rules about Costs

44.0.1 **Contents**

Scope of this Part

44.1 **44.1** This Part contains general rules about costs, and entitlement to costs. (The definitions contained in Part 43 are relevant to this Part.)

Solicitor's duty to notify client

44.2 **44.2**—(1) Where—

(a) the court makes a costs order against a legally represented party; and

(b) the party is not present when the order is made,

the party's solicitor must notify his client in writing of the costs order no later than 7 days after the solicitor receives notice of the order.

44.2.1 **Comment**—This rule is the result of Lord Woolf's view that one of the reasons for the expense of litigation was that the client was not aware of the costs being incurred in his name by his legal representatives. The original requirement that the client should attend every case management conference has been dropped but the solicitor is under a duty to inform the client whenever an adverse costs order is made. Although the court is not given specific penal powers in relation to failure to notify the client, such failure, if deliberate, might amount to professional misconduct. See also the similar provision in relation to costs orders for misconduct, r.44.14. The court may require the solicitor to produce evidence showing that he took reasonable steps to comply with the rule. (See paras 1.1–1.3 of the Directions relating to Pt 44.)

Court's discretion and circumstances to be taken into account when exercising its discretion as to costs

44.3 **44.3**—(1) The court has discretion as to—

(a) whether costs are payable by one party to another;

(b) the amount of those costs; and
(c) when they are to be paid.

(2) If the court decides to make an order about costs—
(a) the general rule is that the unsuccessful party will be ordered to pay the costs of the successful party; but
(b) the court may make a different order.

(3) The general rule does not apply to the following proceedings—
(a) proceedings in the Court of Appeal on an application or appeal made in connection with proceedings in the Family Division; or
(b) proceedings in the Court of Appeal from a judgment, direction, decision or order given or made in probate proceedings or family proceedings.

(4) In deciding what order (if any) to make about costs, the court must have regard to all the circumstances, including—
(a) the conduct of all the parties;
(b) whether a party has succeeded on part of his case, even if he has not been wholly successful; and
(c) any payment into court or admissible offer to settle made by a party which is drawn to the court's attention (whether or not made in accordance with Part 36).

(Part 36 contains further provisions about how the court's discretion is to be exercised where a payment into court or an offer to settle is made under that Part.)

(5) The conduct of the parties includes—
(a) conduct before, as well as during, the proceedings, and in particular the extent to which the parties followed any relevant pre-action protocol;
(b) whether it was reasonable for a party to raise, pursue or contest a particular allegation or issue;
(c) the manner in which a party has pursued or defended his case or a particular allegation or issue;
(d) whether a claimant who has succeeded in his claim, in whole or in part, exaggerated his claim.

(6) The orders which the court may make under this rule include an order that a party must pay—
(a) a proportion of another party's costs;
(b) a stated amount in respect of another party's costs;
(c) costs from or until a certain date only;
(d) costs incurred before proceedings have begun;
(e) costs relating to particular steps taken in the proceedings;
(f) costs relating only to a distinct part of the proceedings; and
(g) interest on costs from or until a certain date, including a date before judgment.

(7) Where the court would otherwise consider making an order under paragraph (6)(f), it must instead, if practicable, make an order under paragraph (6)(a) or (c).

(8) Where the court has ordered a party to pay costs, it may order an amount to be paid on account before the costs are assessed.

(9) Where a party entitled to costs is also liable to pay costs the court may assess the costs which that party is liable to pay and either;
(a) set off the amount assessed against the amount the party is entitled to be paid and direct him to pay any balance; or
(b) delay the issue of a certificate for the costs to which the party is entitled until he has paid the amount which he is liable to pay.

Comment—Although this rule preserves the general rule that the unsuccessful party will be ordered to pay the costs of the successful party, Lord Woolf M.R. was anxious to move away from 44.3.1

the position that any success is sufficient to obtain an order for costs. He therefore envisaged far more partial orders for costs which more accurately reflect the level of success achieved by the receiving party.

Costs in proceedings before trial

44.3.2 **Orders for costs**—The court has the powers contained in section 51 of the Supreme Court Act 1981 in relation to costs. See paras 2.1–2.7 of the Directions relating to Part 44 for the effect of some common orders for costs; in respect of the fees of counsel (note definition of "counsel" at para. 5 of the Introduction); and the fees of conveyancing counsel. The general rule is that the unsuccessful party will be ordered to pay the costs of the successful party usually on the standard basis. The rule and the Practice Direction set out the correct approach. (See Directions relating to Rule 44.3 paras 2.1–2.5.) The Practice Direction contains the table of commonly made orders for costs and this effect.

44.3.3 **Counsels' fees**—Unless a rule specifically requires the court to give a certificate for Counel, there is no longer any need for such a certificate. The Directions relating to Rule 44.3 state that a costs officer conducting a detailed assessment will take into account any opinion expressed by the court (see paras 2.6 to 2.7).

44.3.4 **Summary assessment**—As to summary assessment see note at para. 44.7.1 and Directions relating to Pt 44 paras 4.1–4.11.

44.3.5 **Discretion as to costs**—In *Aiden Shipping Ltd v. Interbulk Ltd* [1986] A.C. 965; [1986] 2 All E.R. 409; the House of Lords (overruling the Court of Appeal) held that the discretionary power to award costs contained in S.C.A. 1981, s.51 (1) was expressed in wide terms leaving the rule-making authority to control its exercise by rules of Court, if it saw fit to do so, and the appellate Courts to establish principles for its exercise; and there was no justification for implying a limitation to the effect that costs could only be ordered to be paid by parties to the proceedings.

Lord Goff of Chieveley in *Aiden Shipping v. Interbulk Ltd* [1986] A.C. 965 at 981, said that he did not, for his part, foresee any injustice flowing from the abandonment of the implied limitation and expressed the view that "Courts of first instance are ... well capable of exercising their discretion under the statute in accordance with reason and justice."

See *Re Gibson's Settlement Trusts* [1981] Ch. 179; [1981] 1 All E.R. 233, in which Sir Robert Megarry V.-C. considered the circumstances in which costs incurred prior to the commencement of proceedings could be allowed. Disputes antecedent to the proceedings which bear no real relation to the subject of the litigation could not be regarded as part of the costs of the proceedings but disputes which are in some degree relevant to the proceedings as ultimately constituted and the other parties' attitude made it reasonable to apprehend that the litigation would include them could be allowed.

There is no logical basis for saying that the claimant must have identified the precise claim that is in the event made, before costs can be potentially recoverable. Lord Harnworth in speaking of costs "ultimately proving of use and service in the action" and Megarry V.-C. talking of "a kind of legitimation by subsequent litigation" make clear that the matter is one of hindsight rather than foresight, *per* Kay J. in *Rentall Ltd v. D. S. Willcock Ltd Review of Taxation*, July 30, 1997 (unrep.—decision given in Open Court).

Neither a costs judge nor the Court on Appeal can properly refuse to carry out an order for detailed assessment because it is considered to be wrong or *ultra vires*; the only remedy if the order be wrong, is an appeal from the order to the Judge in Chambers, *per* Megaw J. in *Cope v. United Dairies (London) Ltd* [1963] 2 Q.B. 33. A defendant who consented to judgment with costs could not appeal on grounds of mistake as to the terms of the claimants solicitor's retainer, a separate action was necessary (*Skinner v. Thames Valley & Aldershot Co. Ltd*, July 7, 1995, CA (unrep.)).

Costs between parties are awarded as an indemnity to the party incurring them and a successful party cannot therefore recover a sum in excess of his liability to his own solicitor (*Gundry v. Sainsbury* [1910] 1 K.B. 645). For the circumstances when costs can still be recovered even though it was never realistically expected that the successful party would pay his own solicitor, see *R. v. Miller & Glennie* [1983] 1 W.L.R. 1056; [1983] 3 All E.R. 186 (following *Adams v. London Improved Motor Coach Builders Ltd* [1921] 1 K.B. 495); and *Commissioners of Customs and Excise v. Valerian Raz and Portcullis (VAT Consultancy) Limited*, 1995 S.T.C. 14, Macpherson of Cluny J.

It is now appropriate for a trial judge to award costs on the indemnity basis in situations where in the past it might not have been appropriate: *Constable v. Streets* December 10, 1998, Alliott J. (unrep.).

44.3.6 **Rule 44.3(4)**—The rule introduces new factors to which the court must have regard to when considering what order to make about costs. These factors include the conduct of all the parties which is further analysed at r.44.3(5). See the Directions relating to Pt 36 (see para. 36PD–001) in respect of offers and payments under that Part.

Rule 44.3(6)—The rule sets out a list (which is not exhaustive) of orders which the court may make and r.44.3(7) provides that if the court is minded to make an order for costs relating to a distinct part of the proceedings the court should, if practicable, make an order for a proportion (*i.e.* a percentage) of another party's costs or costs from or until a certain date. **44.3.7**

Rule 44.3(8)—The court has power to order an amount to be paid on account of costs even though the costs have not been assessed. **44.3.8**

The discretion to make *pre-emptive costs orders*, even in cases involving public interest challenges, should be exercised only in the most exceptional circumstances. Necessary conditions were that the issues raised were truly ones of general public importance and that the Court had sufficient appreciation of the merits of the claim that it could conclude that it was in the public interest to make the order. The Court also had to have regard to the financial resources of the applicant and the respondent and the amount of costs likely to be in issue: *R. v. Lord Chancellor, ex p. Child Poverty Action Group*; *R. v. DPP, ex p. Bull* [1999] 1 W.L.R. 347, Dyson J.

Legal Aid—Where the Court makes an order for costs against a legally aided person, which is not to be enforced without leave, the Court is exercising a power to suspend payments of a costs order. The Court of Appeal has suggested that instead of asking for a suspended order the successful party should invite the Court to exercise its powers under reg. 127 of the Civil Legal Aid (General) Regulations 1989 (see SCP 1999, Vol. 2, Section 16D, paras 16D–245 and 16D–246) and make an order for costs in his favour with the determination of the assisted person's liability postponed for such time as the Court thinks fit. If such an order is made there is then no "determination" to which the limitations in reg. 130 may attach (*Parr v. Smith* [1995] All E.R. 1031, CA; see also SCP 1999, Vol. 2, Section 16D, paras 16D–250 and 16D–251). **44.3.9**

Basis of assessment

44.4—(1) Where the court is to assess the amounts of costs (whether by summary or detailed assessment) it will assess those costs— **44.4**

(a) on the standard basis; or

(b) on the indemnity basis,

but the court will not in either case allow costs which have been unreasonably incurred or are unreasonable in amount.

(Rule 48.3 sets out how the court decides the amount of costs payable under a contract.)

(2) Where the amount of costs is to be assessed on the standard basis, the court will—

(a) only allow costs which are proportionate to the matters in issue; and

(b) resolve any doubt which it may have as to whether costs were reasonably incurred or reasonable and proportionate in amount in favour of the paying party.

(Factors which the court may take into account are set out in rule 44.5.)

(3) Where the amount of costs is to be assessed on the indemnity basis, the court will resolve any doubt which it may have as to whether costs were reasonably incurred or were reasonable in amount in favour of the receiving party.

(4) Where—

(a) the court makes an order about costs without indicating the basis on which the costs are to be assessed; or

(b) the court makes an order for costs to be assessed on a basis other than the standard basis or the indemnity basis,

the costs will be assessed on the standard basis.

(5) This rule and Part 47 (detailed assessment of costs by a costs officer) do not apply to the extent that regulations made under the Legal Aid Act 1988[1] determine the amount payable.

(6) Where the amount of a solicitor's remuneration in respect of

[1] 1988 c. 34.

non-contentious business is regulated by any general orders made under the Solicitors Act 1974,[2] the amount of the costs to be allowed in respect of any such business which falls to be assessed by the court will be decided in accordance with those general orders rather than this rule and rule 44.5.

44.4.1 **Comment**—Although the new rules retain familiar names for the standard basis and the indemnity basis the meaning of those terms is entirely different. The test to be applied under each basis is whether or not the costs have been reasonably incurred or are reasonable in amount. On the standard basis the additional test of proportionality is imposed and the court will only allow costs which are proportionate to the matters in issue. Rule 44.5 sets out the factors which the court must take into account in deciding the amount of costs.

Where the assessment is on the indemnity basis the test of proportionality does not apply.

As to proportionality see Directions relating to Pt 44, paras 3.1–3.3.

44.4.2 **Costs on the Indemnity Basis**—It is not possible to define the exact circumstances in which indemnity costs might be ordered. It is a matter, in each case of the judge exercising his discretion on the facts before him (*Munkenbeck and Marshall v. McAlpine* 44 Con. L.R. 30, CA). Where the Court found that the conduct of the litigation was deserving of moral condemnation an order for costs on the indemnity basis was appropriate (*Glyne Investments Ltd v. Hill Samuel Life Assurance Ltd,* June 17, 1997 (unrep.), Moses J.)

In group litigation where the defendants mounted a full frontal attack on medical evidence underpinning field research programmes which they themselves had helped to set up, the judge found that the defendants' experts, whose evidence was effectively rebutted by two of the claimants' experts, had, by attempting to hold the basis of their written thoughts, lost intellectual and professional credibility. The Court found that the decision to continue the challenge through the defendants' experts after the claimant's experts had completed their evidence amounted to unreasonable conduct of the litigation. Therefore on the generic medical issues it was directed that the defendants should pay the costs on the indemnity basis, whereas in respect of all other issues, in the cases where the claimants succeeded, costs should be on the standard basis: *Re The British Coal Respiratory Disease Litigation,* January 23, 1998, Turner J., unrep. Where cross-examination of a claimant took the form of a totally uncalled for personal attack, the Court made an order for costs on the indemnity basis in favour of the claimant for that portion of the trial, *Clark v. Associated Newspapers Ltd, The Times,* January 28, 1998, Lightman J.

Where a party to litigation acted in a way that could be described as disgraceful or deserving of moral condemnation an order for costs on the indemnity basis could be made: *Wailes v. Stapleton Construction & Commercial Services Ltd*; *Wailes v. Unum Ltd* [1997] 2 Lloyds' Rep. 112, Newman J. and see *Cooper v. P. & O. Stena Line Ltd, The Times,* February 5, 1999.

A judge was wrong to award costs on the indemnity basis against a claimant who had not acted improperly in availing himself of the opportunity presented by statute to apply to the court. The claimant had made an application under the provisions of section 263 of the Insolvency Act 1986. The application had failed on the basis that the claimant had no sufficient interest to make the application. The Court of Appeal found the claimant had not acted improperly and that the costs should be on the standard basis; *Raja v. Rubin, The Times,* April 14, 1999, CA.

Factors to be taken into account in deciding the amount of costs

44.5 **44.5**—(1) The court is to have regard to all the circumstances in deciding whether costs were—

(a) if it is assessing costs on the standard basis—
 (i) proportionately and reasonably incurred; or
 (ii) were proportionate and reasonable in amount, or
(b) if it is assessing costs on the indemnity basis—
 (i) unreasonably incurred; or
 (ii) unreasonable in amount.

(2) In particular the court must give effect to any orders which have already been made.

(3) The court must also have regard to—

(a) the conduct of all the parties, including in particular—
 (i) conduct before, as well as during, the proceedings; and

[2] 1974 c. 47.

(ii) the efforts made, if any, before and during the proceedings in order to try to resolve the dispute;

(b) the amount or value of any money or property involved;

(c) the importance of the matter to all the parties;

(d) the particular complexity of the matter or the difficulty or novelty of the questions raised;

(e) the skill, effort, specialised knowledge and responsibility involved;

(f) the time spent on the case; and

(g) the place where and the circumstances in which work or any part of it was done.

(Rule 35.4(4) gives the court power to limit the amount that a party may recover with regard to the fees and expenses of an expert.)

Comment—Rule 44.3 sets out the circumstances which the court must take into account when exercising its discretion as to costs. Rule 44.5 sets out the factors to be taken into account when deciding the amount of costs whether on a summary or detailed assessment. The conduct of all the parties is again relevant to the amount to be allowed and that conduct may be before as well as during the proceedings and includes the efforts made before and during the proceedings to try to resolve the dispute. It follows that failure without good reason to utilise ADR may result in a reduction of costs. As to proportionality see Directions relating to Pt 44, paras 3.1–3.3 (see para. 44PD–001). **44.5.1**

In *Francis v. Francis and Dickerson* [1956] P. 87; [1953] 3 All E.R. 836, it was held that the correct viewpoint to be taken by a taxing officer in considering whether any step was reasonable is that of a sensible solicitor considering what, in the light of his then knowledge, was reasonable in the interest of his client. It was further held that any step taken on the advice of a properly instructed counsel should rarely be disallowed, but the Court of Appeal in *Davy-Chiesman v. Davy-Chiesman* [1984] 2 W.L.R. 291; [1984] 1 All E.R. 321 held that a solicitor did not abdicate his own responsibility by instructing counsel, and where counsel's advice was "glaringly wrong" the solicitor should have expressed his own views.

Fixed costs

44.6 A party may recover the fixed costs specified in Part 45 in accordance with that Part. **44.6**

Comment—Part 45 sets out the amounts to be allowed as fixed costs. **44.6.1**

Procedure for assessing costs

44.7 Where the court orders a party to pay costs to another party (other than fixed costs) it may either— **44.7**

(a) make a summary assessment of the costs; or

(b) order detailed assessment of the costs by a costs officer,

unless any rule, practice direction or other enactment provides otherwise.

(The costs practice direction sets out the factors which will affect the court's decision under this rule.)

Comment—Attention is drawn to paras 4.1–4.11 of the Directions relating to Pt 44 dealing with the procedure for assessment and the summary assessment of costs. The court will make a summary assessment of costs unless it is not practicable to do so. At the conclusion of a trial of a case which has been dealt with on the fast track or at the conclusion of any other hearing which has lasted less than one day the parties are required to prepare and serve upon each other a statement of costs in the form of a schedule. The statement must be filed at the court and served on the other parties as early as possible and in any event not less than 24 hours before the hearing at which the assessment will take place. **44.7.1**

Estimates of costs—On completing the allocation questionnaire the party must set out an **44.7.2**

estimate of costs incurred to date and an estimate of likely future costs, paras 4.1–4.5 of the Directions relating to Pt 43 deal with this. Considerable care and precision is required in the preparation of such estimates since the estimates of opposing parties are likely to be compared one with another. An over generous estimate may result in an opponent recovering a similar amount, while an under-generous estimate may result in a recovery on behalf of the client which does not reflect the actual costs involved.

44.7.3 **Signing the Bill of Costs**—In signing the bill or statement of costs the solicitor certifies that the contents of the bill are correct: "that signature is no empty formality, the bill specifies the hourly rates applied [...]. If an agreement between the receiving solicitor and his client [...] restricted (say) the hourly rate payable by the client, that hourly rate is the most that can be claimed or recovered on [assessment] [...]. The signature of the bill of costs under the rules is effectively the certificate of an officer of the Court that the receiving party's solicitors are not seeking to recover in relation to any item more than they have agreed to charge their client". *Per* Henry L.J., in *Bailey v. IBC Vehicles Ltd* [1998] 3 All E.R. 570, CA.

"[...] in view of the increasing interest taken in (the indemnity principle) by unsuccessful parties to litigation coupled with the developing practice in relation to conditional fees, the extension of the client care letter and contentious business agreements under section 60(3) (of the Solicitors Act 1974), in future a short written explanation [...] should normally be attached to the bill of costs. This will avoid skirmishes which add unnecessarily to the costs of litigation." *Per* Judge L.J., in *Bailey v. IBC Vehicles Ltd* [1998] 3 All E.R. 570, CA.

See Directions relating to Pt 43, paras 2.1(6) and 2.14.

44.7.4 **Summary Assessment**—Judges are required to assess the costs of a case if practicable, and in cases lasting up to one day, the parties are under an obligation to provide the court and their opponents with details of the costs which may be sought in the event of success (see paras 4.3–4.11 of the Directions relating to Pt 44).

44.7.5 **Appeals relating to Summary Assessment**—Such appeals are dealt with under the ordinary rules relating to appeals. (See RSC, O.58 and O.59, CCR, O.37.) See also Practice Direction for the Court of Appeal (Civil Division) para. PD–001 (after RSC, O.52), [1999] 2 All E.R. 638.

44.7.6 **Detailed Assessment**—For the practice and procedure of detailed assessment see Pt 47 (para. 47.0.1) and the Directions relating to Pt 47 (para. 47PD–001).

Time for complying with an order for costs

44.8 **44.8** A party must comply with an order for the payment of costs within 14 days of—

(a) the date of the judgment or order if it states the amount of those costs; or

(b) if the amount of those costs (or part of them) is decided later in accordance with Part 47, the date of the certificate which states the amount.

(Part 47 sets out the procedure for detailed assessment of costs.)

44.8.1 **Comment**—The imposition of a 14 day period for payment of costs is new to the High Court. It should be borne in mind that all certificates (default costs certificates, interim certificates and final certificates) contain an order to pay.

Costs on the small claims track and fast track

44.9 **44.9**—(1) Part 27 (small claims) and Part 46 (Fast track trial costs) contain special rules about—

(a) liability for costs;

(b) the amount of costs which the court may award; and

(c) the procedure for assessing costs.

(2) Once a claim is allocated to a particular track, those special rules shall apply to the period before, as well as after, allocation except where the court or a practice direction provides otherwise.

44.9.1 **Comment**—The rules relating to small claims and fast track trial costs do not apply until a claim is allocated to a particular track. With regard to costs prior to the allocation (see para. 5.1 of

the Directions relating to Pt 44 as to the way in which costs are dealt with). Rule 44.11(1) provides that any costs orders made before a claim is allocated will not be affected by the allocation.
Amended by S.I. 1999 No. 1008.

Limitation on amount court may allow where a claim allocated to the fast track settles before trial

44.10—(1) Where the court— 44.10
(a) assesses costs in relation to a claim which—
(i) has been allocated to the fast track; and
(ii) settles before the start of the trial; and
(b) is considering the amount of costs to be allowed in respect of a party's advocate for preparing for the trial,
it may not allow, in respect of those advocate's costs, an amount that exceeds the amount of fast track trial costs which would have been payable in relation to the claim had the trial taken place.
(2) When deciding the amount to be allowed in respect of the advocate's costs, the court shall have regard to—
(a) when the claim was settled; and
(b) when the court was notified that the claim had settled.
(3) In this rule, "advocate" and "fast track trial costs" have the meanings given to them by Part 46.
(Part 46 sets out the amount of fast track trial costs which may be awarded.)

Comment—Although Lord Woolf's original intention was that fast track costs should be fixed or capped there are no provisions to this effect in the CPR, save that fast track trial costs are fixed and this is dealt with at Pt 46. "Fast track trial costs" means the costs of a party's advocate for preparing for and appearing at the trial (see r.46.1(2)(b)). Rule 44.10 deals only with the amount of costs to be allowed in respect of a party's advocate for preparing for a fast track trial which settles before the start of the trial. The costs which may be allowed in respect of that work may not exceed the amount which would have been payable in accordance with Pt 46 had the trial taken place. 44.10.1

Costs following allocation and reallocation

44.11—(1) Any costs orders made before a claim is allocated will not be affected by allocation. 44.11
(2) Where—
(a) a claim is allocated to a track; and
(b) the court subsequently re-allocates that claim to a different track,
then unless the court orders otherwise, any special rules about costs applying—
(i) to the first track, will apply to the claim up to the date of reallocation; and
(ii) to the second track, will apply from the date of reallocation.
(Part 26 deals with the allocation and reallocation of claims between tracks.)

Comment—The special rules which apply to small claims and fast track trial costs do not apply until the claim is allocated to a particular track (see r.44.9(2)). Any costs orders which are made before the claim is allocated to a track are not affected by subsequent allocation. Where the claim is re-allocated to a different track the special rules apply, according to track, up to and after the re-allocation unless the court makes a different order. See paras 6.1–6.3 of Directions relating to Pt 44. 44.11.1

Cases where costs orders deemed to have been made

44.12—(1) Where a right to costs arises under— 44.12
(a) rule 3.7 (defendant's right to costs where claim struck out for non-payment of fees);
(b) rule 36.13(1) (claimant's right to costs where he accepts defendant's Part 36 offer or Part 36 payment);

(c) rule 36.14 (claimant's right to costs where defendant accepts the claimant's Part 36 offer); or

(d) rule 38.6 (defendant's right to costs where claimant discontinues),

a costs order will be deemed to have been made on the standard basis.

(2) Interest payable pursuant to section 17 of the Judgments Act 1838[3] or section 74 of the County Courts Act 1984[4] on the costs deemed to have been ordered under paragraph (1) shall begin to run from the date on which the event which gave rise to the entitlement to costs occurred.

44.12.1 **Comment**—In certain cases costs orders are deemed to have been made. Rule 3.7 introduces an automatic strike-out for non payment of fees which gives the defendant the right to costs. Paragraph 4.5 of the Directions relating to Pt 47 deals with the way in which a defendant may seek assessment of those costs.

Paragraphs 7.1–7.11 of the Practice Direction supplementing Pt 36 deal with acceptance by a claimant of a defendant's Pt 36 offer or payment, or a defendant's acceptance of the claimant's Pt 36 offer. Rule 38.6 deals with a claimant's liability for costs where a claimant has discontinued wholly or in part.

44.12.2 **Interest**—Interest under the Judgments Act 1838, s.17 or County Courts Act 1984, s.74 runs from the date on which the event giving rise to the entitlement to costs occurred or from such date as the court may order. Section 17(1) of the Judgments Act 1838 has been amended by the Civil Procedure (Modification of Enactments) Order 1998 (S.I. 1998 No. 2940) to provide that interest will run from such time as is prescribed by rules of court. See r.44.3(6)(g).

Special situations

44.13 **44.13**—(1) Where the court makes an order which does not mention costs no party is entitled to costs in relation to that order.

(2) The court hearing an appeal may, unless it dismisses the appeal, make orders about the costs of the proceedings giving rise to the appeal as well as the costs of the appeal.

(3) Where proceedings are transferred from one court to another, the court to which they are transferred may deal with all the costs, including the costs before the transfer.

(4) Paragraph (3) is subject to any order of the court which ordered the transfer.

44.13.1 **Comment**—Rule 44.13(1) makes it clear that where an order is silent as to costs no party is entitled to the costs in relation to that order.

See chart at para. 2.4 of the Directions relating to Pt 48, see para. 48PD–001, as to meaning of "Costs here and below" and the exception for the Divisional Court.

Court's powers in relation to misconduct

44.14 **44.14**—(1) The court may make an order under this rule where—

(a) a party or his legal representative fails to conduct detailed assessment proceedings in accordance with Part 47 or any direction of the court; or

(b) it appears to the court that the conduct of a party or his legal representative, before or during the proceedings which gave rise to the assessment proceedings, was unreasonable or improper.

(2) Where paragraph (1) applies, the court may—

[3] 1838 c. 110. Section 17 was amended by S.I. 1998/2940.

[4] 1984 c. 28. Section 74 was amended by section (2) of the Private International Law (Miscellaneous Provisions) Act 1995 (c. 42).

(a) disallow all or part of the costs which are being assessed; or
(b) order the party at fault or his legal representative to pay costs which he has caused any other party to incur.

(3) Where—
(a) the court makes an order under paragraph (2) against a legally represented party; and
(b) the party is not present when the order is made,

the party's solicitor must notify his client in writing of the order no later than 7 days after the solicitor receives notice of the order.

(Other rules about costs can be found—
(a) in Schedule 1, in the following RSC—Order 45 (court may order act to be done at the expense of disobedient party); Order 47 (writ of fieri facias to enforce payment of costs); and
(b) in Schedule 2, the following CCR—Order 27 (attachment of earnings—judgment creditor's entitlement to costs); Order 28 (costs on judgment summons); Order 30 (garnishee proceedings—judgment creditor's entitlement to costs); Order 49 (costs incurred in making a payment in under section 63 of the Trustee Act 1925 to be assessed by the detailed procedure)).

Comment—The provisions relating to misconduct now extend to the legal representative of a party as well as to the party personally. The provisions relate both to unreasonable or improper conduct before or during the proceedings giving rise to the assessment proceedings, and during the detailed assessment proceedings themselves. The effect of this is that a costs officer may of his or her own initiative, or at the request of a party, investigate and make orders in respect of unreasonable or improper conduct by a party or a legal representative. This means that a legal representative who has been found to have acted unreasonably or improperly may be ordered personally to pay costs which another party has been caused to incur. This power is in addition to the power to make wasted costs orders in accordance with section 51(6) of the Supreme Court Act 1981 (see r.48.7). 44.14.1

Where the court makes an order against a party who is legally represented (whether the order is against the party personally or against the legal representative personally) the party's solicitor must notify the client in writing within 7 days of receipt of notice of the order if the party was not present when the order was made. This provision is in terms similar to r.44.2 which refers to "a costs order" made against a legally represented party.

As to wasted costs orders see r.48.7.

The solicitor and counsel relationship—In *Davy-Chiesman v. Davy-Chiesman* [1984] Fam. 48; [1984] 1 All E.R. 311, the Court of Appeal held that where the relief sought as advised by counsel was glaringly wrong, the solicitor had a duty to inform the legal aid authorities of the change of circumstances, and to express his own views, and did not abdicate his own responsibility by instructing counsel. He was ordered to pay the costs of both sides personally. 44.14.2

In *Re A (A Minor)* (1988) 18 Fam. Law. 339, CA, solicitors were held personally responsible for the costs of four abortive hearings, in a case where it was apparent that counsel was not competent and the solicitors should have withdrawn the instructions. (A wasted costs order might now have been made against counsel.)

Although solicitors cannot automatically shelter behind counsel, if the circumstances warrant it they may be justified in relying upon counsel's advice (*Swedac Ltd v. Magnet & Southern plc* [1990] F.S.R. 89). In circumstances where there was no evidence that a solicitor had expertise in the field of judicial review, the proposition that a solicitor who acted on counsel's advice had to bear responsibility for that advice in all circumstances could not be supported: *R. v. Luton Family Proceedings Court Justices, ex p. R.* (1998) 4 C.L. 51, CA.

Counsel is under a duty to reassess any advice in the light of further information. Failure to do so may lead to a wasted costs order (*C v. C (Wasted Costs Order)* [1994] 2 F.L.R. 34, Ewbank J.).

It was unreasonable for a barrister in sole practice to rely wholly on instructing solicitors to notify him of the dates and times of his cases. It was counsel's responsibility to adopt a system which enabled him to keep abreast of the listing arrangements for his cases (*Re A Barrister (Wasted Costs Order) (No. 4 of 1992) The Times,* March 15, 1994, CA (Criminal Division) and see *Re A Barrister (Wasted Costs Order) (No. 4 of 1993), The Times,* April 21, 1993, CA (Criminal Division)).

Where the conduct of both the barrister and the solicitor in a case are the subject of criticism, any investigation of their professional conduct should be conducted by a joint tribunal (*Vowles v. Vowles, The Times,* October 4, 1990, CA).

Legal Aid Act 1988—The court has power under its inherent jurisdiction to order a solicitor to repay personally to the legal aid fund, costs which have been incurred by a legally aided client 44.14.3

as the result of a serious dereliction of duty on the part of the solicitor, but the court will not exercise that power if the Legal Aid Board is dilatory in seeking an order that the solicitor pay the costs personally (*Clark v. Clark (No. 2)* [1991] 1 F.L.R. 179). Booth J. felt that where an issue is to be taken as to costs of any proceedings, it is essential that it should follow swiftly upon the event. Notice should be given of an application as soon as possible and in the normal course of events that should be at the conclusion of any substantive hearing or very shortly afterwards. There may be exceptional circumstances where for good reason notice of an application in relation to costs is not or cannot be made at the end of a hearing and some delay is inevitable (*Clark v. Clark* (above)).

The Court of Appeal has set out the procedure to be adopted where an assisted party has been unsuccesful and the unassisted party seeks to recover costs against the Legal Aid Board or under the wasted costs jurisdiction (*Re O (A Minor) (Costs: Liability of Legal Aid Board)* [1997] 1 F.L.R. 465, CA see also Vol. 2, Section 16A, para. 16A–73).

Slow action by the Legal Aid Authorities and delay in obtaining counsel's written opinion that contributed to the tardy prosecution of the case, entitled solicitors to have set aside an order that they were personally liable for wasted costs (*Trill v. Sacher (No. 2)* (1992) *The Times*, November 14, CA).

For the additional power to disallow solicitors' costs or counsels' fees wasted by failure to conduct legally aided proceedings with reasonable competence and expedition see reg. 109(1) CLA(G) R1989.

A solicitor's failure to warn either the Court or his opponent in sufficient time, that because of his difficulties with the Legal Aid Board he might have to seek at a late stage an adjournment of the hearing was an error of judgment on his part, but did not warrant the making of a wasted costs order against him personally (*Re A Solicitor (Wasted Costs Order)* [1993] 2 FLR 959, CA).

See also *R. & T. Thew Ltd v. Reeves* [1981] 3 W.L.R. 190; [1981] 2 All E.R. 964, and in the Court of Appeal [1982] Q.B. 1283; [1982] 3 All E.R. 1068 (Vol. 2, Section 16D, paras 16D–213 and 16D–214) *Davy-Chiesman v. Davy-Chiesman* [1984] Fam. 48; [1984] 1 All E.R. 321.

DIRECTIONS RELATING TO PART 44—GENERAL RULES ABOUT COSTS

Rule 44.2 Solicitor's Duty to Notify Client

44PD–001 **1.1** For the purposes of rule 44.2 "client" includes a party for whom a solicitor is acting and any other reason (for example an insurer or a trade union) who has instructed the solicitor to act or who is liable to pay his fees.

1.2 Where a solicitor notifies a client of an order under that rule, he must also explain why the order came to be made.

1.3 Although rule 44.2 does not specify any sanction for breach of the rule the court may, either in the order for costs itself or in a subsequent order, require the solicitor to produce to the court evidence showing that he took reasonable steps to comply with the rule.

Rule 44.3 Court's Discretion and Circumstances to be taken into Account when Exercising its Discretion as to Costs

44PD–002 **2.1** Attention is drawn to the factors set out in this rule which may lead the court to depart from the general rule stated in rule 44.3(2) and to make a different order about costs.

2.2 In a probate claim where a defendant has in his defence given notice that he requires the will to be proved in solemn form (see paragraph 8.3 of the Contentious Probate Practice Direction Supplementing Part 49), the court will not make an order for costs against the defendant unless it appears that there was no reasonable ground for opposing the will. The term "probate claim" is defined in paragraph 1.2 of the Contentious Probate Practice Direction.

2.3(1) The court may make an order about costs at any stage in a case.

(2) In particular the court may make an order about costs when it deals with any application, makes any order or holds any hearing and that order about costs may relate to the costs of that application, order or hearing.

2.4 There are certain costs orders which the court will commonly make in proceedings before trial. The following table sets out the general effect of these orders. The table is not an exhaustive list of the orders which the court may make.

Term	Effect
• Costs • Costs in any event	The party in whose favour the order is made is entitled to the costs in respect of the part of the proceedings to which the order relates, whatever other costs orders are made in the proceedings.
• Costs in the case • Costs in the application	The party in whose favour the court makes an order for costs at the end of the proceedings is entitled to his costs of the part of the proceedings to which the order relates.
• Costs reserved	The decision about costs is deferred to a later occasion, but if no later order is made the costs will be costs in the case.
• Claimant's/ Defendant's costs in the case/ application	If the party in whose favour the costs order is made is awarded costs at the end of the proceedings, that party is entitled to his costs of the part of the proceedings to which the order relates. If any other party is awarded costs at the end of the proceedings, the party in whose favour the final costs order is made is not liable to pay the costs of any other party in respect of the part of the proceedings to which the order relates.
• Costs thrown away	Where, for example, a judgment or order is set aside, the party in whose favour the costs order is made is entitled to the costs which have been incurred as a consequence. This includes the costs of— (a) preparing for and attending any hearing at which the judgment or order which has been set aside was made; (b) preparing for and attending any hearing to set aside the judgment or order in question; (c) preparing for and attending any hearing at which the court orders the proceedings or the part in question to be adjourned; (d) any steps taken to enforce a judgment or order which has subsequently been set aside.
• Costs of and caused by	Where, for example, the court makes this order on an application to amend a statement of case, the party in whose favour the costs order is made is entitled to the costs of preparing for and attending the application and the costs of any consequential amendment to his own statement of case.

• Costs here and below	The party in whose favour the costs order is made is entitled not only to his costs in respect of the proceedings in which the court makes the order but also to his costs of the proceedings in any lower court. In the case of an appeal from a Divisional Court the party is not entitled to any costs incurred in any court below the Divisional Court.
• No order as to costs • Each party to pay his own costs	Each party is to bear his own costs of the part of the proceedings to which the order relates whatever costs order the court makes at the end of the proceedings.

2.5 Where, under rule 44.3(8), the court orders an amount to be paid before costs are assessed—

(1) the order will state that amount, and

(2) if no other date for payment is specified in the order rule 44.8 (Time for complying with an order for costs) will apply.

Fees of counsel

2.6(1) This paragraph applies where the court orders the detailed assessment of the costs of a hearing at which one or more counsel appeared for a party.

(2) Where an order for costs states the opinion of the court as to whether or not the hearing was fit for the attendance of one or more counsel, a costs officer conducting a detailed assessment of costs to which that order relates will have regard to the opinion stated.

Fees payable to conveyancing counsel appointed by the court to assist it

2.7(1) Where the court refers any matter to the conveyancing counsel of the court the fees payable to counsel in respect of the work done or to be done will be assessed by the court in accordance with rule 44.3.

(2) An appeal from a decision of the court in respect of the fees of such counsel will be dealt with under the general rules as to appeals unless the appeal is against the decision of a costs officer when the appeal will be dealt with in accordance with Part 47 Section VIII. In either case the decision of the appellate court is final.

Rule 44.5 Factors to be Taken into Account in Deciding the Amount of Costs

44PD–003 **3.1** In applying the test of proportionality the court will have regard to rule 1.1(2)(c). The relationship between the total of the costs incurred and the financial value of the claim may not be a reliable guide. A fixed percentage cannot be applied in all cases to the value of the claim in order to ascertain whether or not the costs are proportionate.

3.2 In any proceedings there will be costs which will inevitably be incurred and which are necessary for the successful conduct of the case. Solicitors are not required to conduct litigation at rates which are uneconomic. Thus in a modest claim the proportion of costs is likely to be higher than in a large claim, and may even equal or possibly exceed the amount in dispute.

3.3 Where a trial takes place, the time taken by the court in dealing with a particular issue may not be an accurate guide to the amount of time properly spent by the legal or other representatives in preparation for the trial of that issue.

Rule 44.7 Procedure for Assessing Costs

4.1 Where the court does not order fixed costs (or no fixed costs are provided for) the amount of costs payable will be assessed by the court. This rule allows the court making an order about costs either. 44PD–004

(a) to make a summary assessment of the amount of the costs, or
(b) to order the amount to be decided in accordance with Part 47 (a detailed assessment).

4.2 An order for costs will be treated as an order for the amount of costs to be decided by a detailed assessment unless the order otherwise provides.

Summary Assessment

4.3 Whenever a court makes an order about costs which does not provide for fixed costs to be paid the court should consider whether to make a summary assessment of costs.

4.4(1) The general rule is that the court will make a summary assessment of the costs:

(a) at the conclusion of the trial of a case which has been dealt with on the fast track, in which case the order will deal with the costs of the whole claim, and
(b) at the conclusion of any other hearing which has lasted less than one day, in which case the order will deal with the costs of the application or matter to which the hearing related;

unless there is good reason not to do so *e.g.* where the paying party shows substantial grounds for disputing the sum claimed for costs that cannot be dealt with summarily or there is insufficient time to carry out a summary assessment.

(2) The general rule in paragraph 1 does not apply to a mortgagee's costs incurred in mortgage possession proceedings or other proceedings relating to a mortgage unless the mortgagee asks the court to make an order for his costs to be paid by another party. Section 1 of the Practice Direction relating to Part 48 also deals with a mortgagee's costs.

(3) The general rule is that no summary assessment of costs will be made if the court has ordered that the costs in question will be treated as costs in the case (as to which see paragraph 2.4 above).

(4) Where an application has been made and the parties to the application agree an order by consent without any party attending, the parties should agree a figure for costs to be inserted in the consent order or agree that there should be no order for costs. If the parties cannot agree the costs position attendance on the appointment will be necessary but unless good reason can be shown for the failure to deal with costs as set out above no costs will be allowed for that attendance.

4.5(1) It is the duty of the parties and their legal representatives to assist the judge in making a summary assessment of costs in any case to which paragraph 4.4 above applies, in accordance with the following paragraphs.

(2) Each party who intends to claim costs must prepare a written statement of the costs he intends to claim showing separately in the form of a schedule:

(a) the number of hours to be claimed,
(b) the hourly rate to be claimed,
(c) the grade of fee earner,

(d) the amount and nature of any disbursement to be claimed, other than counsel's fee for appearing at the hearing,
(e) the amount of solicitor's costs to be claimed for attending or appearing at the hearing,
(f) the fees of counsel to be claimed in respect of the hearing, and
(g) any Value Added Tax to be claimed on these amounts.

(3) The statement of costs should follow as closely as possible Form 1 of the Schedule of Costs Forms annexed to this practice direction and must be signed by the party or his legal representative.

(4) The statement of costs must be filed at court and copies of it must be served on any party against whom an order for payment of those costs is intended to be sought. The statement of costs should be filed and the copies of it should be served as soon as possible and in any event not less than 24 hours before the date fixed for the hearing.

4.6 The failure by a party, without reasonable excuse, to comply with the foregoing paragraphs will be taken into account by the court in deciding what order to make about the costs of the claim, hearing or application, and about the costs of any further hearing or detailed assessment hearing that may be necessary as a result of that failure.

4.7 If the court makes a summary assessment of the costs the court will specify the amount payable as a single figure which will include

(a) all sums in respect of profit costs, disbursements and VAT which is allowed, and

(b) the amount which is awarded under Part 46 (Fast Track Trial Costs).

4.8 The court awarding costs cannot make an order for a summary assessment of costs by a costs officer. If a summary assessment of costs is appropriate but the court awarding costs is unable to do so on the day, the court must give directions as to a further hearing.

4.9(1) The court must not make a summary assessment of the costs of a receiving party who is an assisted person within the meaning of the Legal Aid Act 1988.

(2) A summary assessment of costs payable by an assisted person is not by itself a determination of the assisted person's liability to pay those costs (as to which see Section 17 of the Legal Aid Act 1988). Accordingly the court may make a summary assessment of costs payable by an assisted person.

(3) The court may not make a summary assessment of the costs of a receiving party who is a child or patient within Part 21 unless the solicitor acting for the child or patient has waived the right to further costs (see paragraph 1.2(c) of the Directions Relating to Part 48).

(4) The court may make a summary assessment of costs payable by a child or patient.

4.10 Paragraphs 4.4 and 4.5 do not apply where the parties have agreed the amount of costs.

Payments on account of costs

4.11 Whenever the court awards costs to be assessed by way of detailed assessment it should consider whether to exercise the power in rule 44.3(8) (Courts Discretion as to Costs) to order the paying party to pay such sum of money as it thinks just on account of those costs.

Rule 44.9 Costs on the Small Claims Track and Fast Track

44PD–005 **5.1**(1) Before a claim is allocated to one of those tracks the court is not restricted by any of the special rules that apply to that track.

(2) Where a claim has been allocated to one of those tracks, the special rules which relate to that track will apply to work done before as well as after allocation save to the extent (if any) that an order for costs in respect of that work was made before allocation.

(3)(i) This paragraph applies where a claim issued for a sum in excess of the normal financial scope of the small claims track is allocated to that track only because an admission of part of the claim by the defendant reduces the amount in dispute to a sum within the normal scope of that track.

(See also paragraph 7.4 of the practice direction supplementing CPR Part 26)

(ii) On entering judgment for the admitted part before allocation of the balance of the claim the court may allow costs in respect of the proceedings down to that date.

Rule 44.11 Costs Following Allocation and Re-allocation

6.1 This paragraph applies where the court is about to make an order to re-allocate a claim from the small claims track to another track. **44PD–006**

6.2 Before making the order to re-allocate the claim, the court must decide whether any party is to pay costs to any other party down to the date of the order to re-allocate in accordance with the rules about costs contained in Part 27 (The Small Claims Track).

6.3 If it decides to make such an order about costs, the court will make a summary assessment of those costs in accordance with that Part.

Rule 44.14 Court's Powers in Relation to Misconduct

7.1 Before making an order under rule 44.14 the court must give the paty or legal representative in question a reasonable opportunity to attend a hearing to give reasons why it should not make such an order. **44PD–007**

7.2 Conduct before or during the proceedings which gave rise to the assessment which is unreasonable or improper includes steps which are calculated to prevent or inhibit the court from furthering the overriding objective.

7.3 Although rule 44.14(3) does not specify any sanction for breach of the obligation imposed by the rule the court may, either in the order under paragraph (2) or in a subsequent order, require the solicitor to produce to the court evidence that he took reasonable steps to comply with the obligation.

PART 45

FIXED COSTS

45.0.1 **Contents**

Editorial Introduction

45.0.2 Schedule 1 to the CPR contains RSC, O.62, Appendix 3, Pts II and III. Schedule 2 to the CPR contains CCR, O.38, r.18(1) and (2) and Appendix B, Pts I, II and III. These provisions are retained in order to deal with cases where default judgment is obtained in accordance with the previous rules (see Practice Direction Transitional Arrangements supplementing Pt 51 (see para. 51PD–001)).

Scope of this Part

45.1 **45.1**—(1) This Part sets out the amounts which, unless the court orders otherwise, are to be allowed in respect of solicitors' charges in the cases to which this Part applies.

(The definitions contained in Part 43 are relevant to this Part.)

(2) This Part applies where—

(a) the only claim is a claim for a specified sum of money and—

(i) judgment in default is obtained under rule 12.4(1);

(ii) judgment on admission is obtained under rule 14.4(3);

(iii) judgment on admission on part of the claim is obtained under rule 14.5(6);

(iv) summary judgment is given under Part 24;

(v) the court has made an order to strike out[GL] a defence under rule 3.4(2)(a)as disclosing no reasonable grounds for defending the claim; or

(vi) rule 45.3 applies; or

(b) the only claim is a claim where the court gave a fixed date for the hearing when it issued the claim and judgment is given for the delivery of goods;

and in either case the value of the claim exceeds £25.

(The practice direction supplementing rule 7.9 sets out the types of case where a court may give a fixed date for a hearing when it issues a claim.)

(3) The rules in this Part do not apply to the extent that regulations under the Legal Aid Act 1988[1] determine the amount of costs payable to legal representatives.

(4) Any appropriate court fee will be allowed in addition to the costs set out in this Part.

45.1.1 **Comment**—Part 45 is specifically applied to judgment in default (r.12.4(1)); judgment on admission in whole (r.14.4(3)) or in part (r.14.56(6)); summary judgment under Pt 24 strike out (r.3.4(2)(a)); or when the defendant is only liable for fixed commencement costs (r.45.3). Part 45 also applies to judgment for delivery of goods on a fixed date hearing. If the value of a claim does not exceed £25, Pt 45 does not apply.

In relation to a claim on the small claims track the court may not order a party to pay a sum to another party in respect of costs except the fixed costs payable under Pt 45 attributable to issuing the claim (see r.27.14(2)(a)). See Directions relating to Pt 45, paras 1.1–1.2. The Directions also

[1] 1988 c. 34.

provide for fixed costs to be paid on the issue of a default costs certificate. See Directions relating to Pt 45, paras 2.1–2.2.

Amount of fixed commencement costs

45.2—(1) The claim form may include a claim for fixed commencement costs. 45.2

(2) The amount of fixed commencement costs which the claim form may include shall be calculated by reference to the following table (Table 1).

(3) Additional costs may also be claimed in the circumstances specified in Table 3.

(4) The amount claimed, or the value of the goods claimed if specified, in the claim form is to be used for determining the band in the table that applies to the claim.

TABLE 1

FIXED COSTS ON COMMENCEMENT OF A CLAIM

Relevant Band	**Where the claim form is served by the court or by any method other than personal service by the claimant**	**Where • the claim form is served personally by the claimant; and • there is only one defendant**	**Where there is more than one defendant, for each additional defendant personally served at separate addresses by the claimant**
Where— • the value of the claim exceeds £25 but does not exceed £500	£50	£60	£15
Where— • the value of the claim exceeds £500 but does not exceed £1000	£70	£80	£15
Where— • the value of the claim exceeds £1000 but does not exceed £5000; or • the only claim is for delivery of goods and no value is specified or stated on the claim form	£80	£90	£15

Where— • the value of the claim exceeds £5000	£100	£110	£15

45.2.1 **Comment**—The table provides different levels of fees depending upon the value of the claim, the method of service and the number of defendants. The relevant band is ascertained by reference to the amount claimed and the value of the goods in the claim form.

When defendant only liable for fixed commencement costs

45.3 **45.3**—(1) Where—

(a) the only claim is for a specified sum of money; and

(b) the defendant pays the money claimed within 14 days after service of particulars of claim on him, together with the fixed commencement costs stated in the claim form,

the defendant is not liable for any further costs unless the court orders otherwise.

(2) Where—

(a) the claimant gives notice of acceptance of a payment into court in satisfaction of the whole claim;

(b) the only claim is for a specified sum of money; and

(c) the defendant made the payment into court within 14 days after service of the particulars of claim on him, together with the fixed costs stated in the claim form,

the defendant is not liable for any further costs unless the court orders otherwise.

Costs on entry of judgment

45.4 **45.4** Where—

(a) the claimant has claimed fixed commencement costs under rule 45.2; and

(b) judgment is entered in the circumstances specified in the table in this rule (Table 2),

the amount to be included in the judgment in respect of the claimant's solicitor's charges is the aggregate of—

(i) the fixed commencement costs; and

(ii) the relevant amount shown in Table 2.

TABLE 2

FIXED COSTS ON ENTRY OF JUDGMENT

	Where the amount of the judgment exceeds £25 but does not exceed £5000	**Where the amount of the judgment exceeds £5000**
Where judgment in default of an acknowledgment of service is entered under rule 12.4(1) (entry of judgment by request on claim for money only)	£22	£30

Where judgment in default of a defence is entered under rule 12.4(1) (entry of judgment by request on claim for money only)	£25	£35
Where judgment is entered under rule 14.4 (judgment on admission), or rule 14.5 (judgment on admission of part of claim), and claimant accepts the defendant's proposal as to the manner of payment.	£40	£55
Where judgment is entered under rule 14.4 (judgment on admission), or rule 14.5 (judgment on admission on part of claim) and court decides the date or times of payment	£55	£70
Where summary judgment is given under Part 24 or the court strikes out a defence under rule 3.4(2)(a), in either case, on application by a party	£175	£210
Where judgment is given on a claim for delivery of goods under a regulated agreement within the meaning of the Consumer Credit Act 1974[2] and no other entry in this table applies	£60	£85

Comment—The table sets out the fixed costs on entry of judgment. Different costs are payable in respect of cases above and below £5,000 and in different circumstances. The amount which is included in the judgment is the aggregate of the fixed commencement costs (see Table 1, r.45.2) and the relevant figure in Table 2. **45.4.1**

Miscellaneous fixed costs

45.5 The table in this rule (Table 3) shows the amount to be allowed in respect of solicitor's charges in the circumstances mentioned. **45.5**

[2] 1974 c. 39.

TABLE 3

MISCELLANEOUS FIXED COSTS

For service by a party of any document required to be served personally including preparing and copying a certificate of service for each individual served	£15
Where service by an alternative method is permitted by an order under rule 6.8 for each individual served	£25
Where a document is served out of the jurisdiction—	
(a) in Scotland, Northern Ireland, the Isle of Man or the Channel Islands	£65
(b) in any other place	£75

(Other rules which provide for situations where fixed costs may be allowed can be found in Schedule 1 in RSC Order 62 and in Schedule 2 in CCR Order 38, Appendix B.)

45.5.1 **Comment**—As to fixed costs on the issue of a Default Costs Certificate see Directions relating to Pt 45, paras 2.1–2.2 (see para. 45PD–001).

DIRECTIONS RELATING TO PART 45

Fixed Costs

Fixed costs in small claims

45PD–001 **1.1** Under Rule 27.14 the costs which can be awarded to a claimant in a small claims track case include the fixed costs payable under Part 45 attributable to issuing the claim.

1.2 Those fixed costs shall be the sum of

(a) the fixed commencement costs calculated in accordance with Table 1 of Rule 45.2 and;

(b) the appropriate court fee or fees paid by the claimant.

Fixed costs on the issue of a default costs certificate

2.1 Unless paragraph 2.2 applies or unless the court orders otherwise, the fixed costs to be included in a default costs certificate are £80 plus a sum equal to any appropriate court fee payable on the issue of the certificate.

2.2 The fixed costs included in a certificate must not exceed the maximum sum specified for costs and court fee in the notice of commencement.

PART 46

FAST TRACK TRIAL COSTS

Contents 46.0.1

Editorial Introduction

This Part contains the limited Fast Track costs regime. At the moment it covers only trial costs but the intention is that a limited costs regime will govern the whole Fast Track procedure. The LCD is presently collecting data. 46.0.2

Scope of this Part

46.1—(1) This Part deals with the amount of costs which the court may award as the costs of an advocate for preparing for and appearing at the trial of a claim in the fast track (referred to in this rule as "fast track trial costs"). 46.1

(2) For the purposes of this Part—

(a) "advocate" means a person exercising a right of audience as a representative of, or on behalf of, a party;

(b) "fast track trial costs" means the costs of a party's advocate for preparing for and appearing at the trial, but does not include—

(i) any other disbursements; or

(ii) any value added tax payable on the fees of a party's advocate; and

(c) "trial" includes a hearing where the court decides an amount of money or the value of goods following a judgment under Part 12 (default judgment) or Part 14 (admissions) but does not include—

(i) the hearing of an application for summary judgment under Part 24; or

(ii) the court's approval of a settlement or other compromise under rule 21.10.

(Part 21 deals with claims made by or on behalf of, or against, children and patients.)

Comment—All rules relating to the fast track are new. Lord Woolf's original intention was for fast track costs to be fixed or capped but the CPR make no provision for fast track costs, except for fast track trial costs. Fast track trial costs are the costs of a party's advocate for preparing for and appearing at the trial. Trial is defined at r.46.1(2)(c) but does not include the hearing of an application for summary judgment under Pt 24, or approval of a settlement or compromise under r.21.10 (children and patients), see Directions relating to Pt 46, paras 1.1–1.4 (see para. 46PD–001). 46.1.1

Amount of fast track trial costs

46.2—(1) The following table shows the amount of fast track trial costs which the court may award (whether by summary or detailed assessment). 46.2

Value of the claim	Amount of fast track trial costs which the court may award
Up to £3,000	£350
More than £3,000 but not more than £10,000	£500
More than £10,000	£750

(2) The court may not award more or less than the amount shown in the table except where—

(a) it decides not to award any fast track trial costs; or

(b) rule 46.3 applies;

but the court may apportion the amount awarded between the parties to reflect their respective degrees of success on the issues at trial.

(3) Where the only claim is for the payment of money—

(a) for the purpose of quantifying fast track trial costs awarded to a claimant, the value of the claim is the total amount of the judgment excluding—

(i) interest and costs; and

(ii) any reduction made for contributory negligence;

(b) for the purpose of the quantifying fast track trial costs awarded to a defendant, the value of the claim is—

(i) the amount specified in the claim form (excluding interest and costs);

(ii) if no amount is specified, the maximum amount which the claimant reasonably expected to recover according to the statement of value included in the claim form under rule 16.3; or

(iii) more than £10,000, if the claim form states that the claimant cannot reasonably say how much he expects to recover.

(4) Where the claim is only for a remedy other than the payment of money the value of the claim is deemed to be more than £3,000 but not more than £10,000, unless the court orders otherwise.

(5) Where the claim includes both a claim for the payment of money and for a remedy other than the payment of money, the value of the claim is deemed to be the higher of—

(a) the value of the money claim decided in accordance with paragraph (3); or

(b) the deemed value of the other remedy decided in accordance with paragraph (4),

unless the court orders otherwise.

(6) Where—

(a) a defendant has made a counterclaim against the claimant;

(b) the counterclaim has a higher value than the claim; and

(c) the claimant succeeds at trial both on his claim and the counterclaim,

for the purpose of quantifying fast track trial costs awarded to the claimant, the value of the claim is the value of the defendant's counterclaim calculated in accordance with this rule.

(Rule 20.4 sets out how a defendant may make a counterclaim.)

46.2.1 **Comment**—The amount of fast track trial costs may not be exceeded or reduced except where the court decides not to award any fast track trial costs or the provisions of r.46.3 apply. This includes where the court considers it necessary for a legal representative to attend to assist the advocate when a further £250 may be awarded in accordance with r.46.3. In addition the court may apportion the amount between the parties to reflect their respective degrees of success on the issues at the trial but even where this is done the total amount of fast track trial costs may not be exceeded.

Power to award more or less than the amount of fast track trial costs

46.3—(1) This rule sets out when a court may award— 46.3

(a) an additional amount to the amount of fast track trial costs shown in the table in rule 46.2(1); and

(b) less than those amounts.

(2) If—

(a) in addition to the advocate, a party's legal representative attends the trial;

(b) the court considers that it was necessary for a legal representative to attend to assist the advocate; and

(c) the court awards fast track trial costs to that party,

the court may award an additional £250 in respect of the legal representative's attendance at the trial.

(Legal representative is defined in rule 2.3.)

(3) If the court considers that it is necessary to direct a separate trial of an issue then the court may award an additional amount in respect of the separate trial but that amount is limited in accordance with paragraph (4) of this rule.

(4) The additional amount the court may award under paragraph 3 must not exceed two-thirds of the amount payable for that claim, subject to a minimum award of £350.

(5) Where the party to whom fast track trial costs are to be awarded is a litigant in person, the court will award—

(a) if the litigant in person can prove financial loss, two thirds of the amount that would otherwise be awarded; or

(b) if the litigant in person fails to prove financial loss, an amount in respect of the time spent reasonably doing the work at the rate specified in the costs practice direction.

(6) Where a defendant has made a counterclaim against the claimant, and—

(a) the claimant has succeeded on his claim; and

(b) the defendant has succeeded on his counterclaim,

the court will quantify the amount of the award of fast track trial costs to which—

(i) but for the counterclaim, the claimant would be entitled for succeeding on his claim; and

(ii) but for the claim, the defendant would be entitled for succeeding on his counterclaim,

and make one award of the difference, if any, to the party entitled to the higher award of costs.

(7) Where the court considers that the party to whom fast track trial costs are to be awarded has behaved unreasonably or improperly during the trial, it may award that party an amount less than would otherwise be payable for that claim, as it considers appropriate.

(8) Where the court considers that the party who is to pay the fast track trial costs has behaved improperly during the trial the court may award such additional amount to the other party as it considers appropriate.

Comment—If the court is considering the award of an additional amount in respect of a 46.3.1

party's legal representative it should be noted that the test is one of necessity rather than reasonableness.

Where a separate trial is directed an additional amount may be allowed but will not exceed two thirds of the amount payable in respect of the claim but will not be less than £350.

Travelling time does not fall within the exceptions to r.46.2(2) and is not separately recoverable.

Litigant in Person

46.3.2 **Rule 46.3(5)**—Where the litigant in person proves financial loss, two thirds of the amount which would otherwise be awarded is payable irrespective of the amount of time involved. If financial loss is not proved the court must decide an amount in respect of the time reasonably spent doing the work at the rate specified at para. 1.6 of the Directions relating to Part 48 (see para. 48PD–001)—see r.48.6. Although the rule is not specific it would seem that a litigant in person who fails to prove financial loss cannot recover more than two thirds of the amount which would otherwise be awarded.

Misconduct

46.3.3 **Rule 46.3(7) and (8)**—The court has powers in addition to those at r.44.14 (powers in relation to misconduct) and may allow less than it would otherwise have done, where the party has behaved unreasonably or improperly during the trial, or may award an additional amount where it considers that the party who is to pay fast track trial costs has behaved improperly during the trial. Note that the powers under these sub-rules are in respect of the party only and not in respect of the legal representative.

Fast track trial costs where there is more than one claimant or defendant

46.4 **46.4**—(1) Where the same advocate is acting for more than one party—

(a) the court may make only one award in respect of fast track trial costs payable to that advocate; and

(b) the parties for whom the advocate is acting are jointly entitled to any fast track trial costs awarded by the court.

(2) Where—

(a) the same advocate is acting for more than one claimant; and

(b) each claimant has a separate claim against the defendant,

the value of the claim, for the purpose of quantifying the award in respect of fast track trial costs is to be ascertained in accordance with paragraph (3).

(3) The value of the claim in the circumstances mentioned in paragraph (2) is—

(a) where the only claim of each claimant is for the payment of money—

(i) if the award of fast track trial costs is in favour of the claimants, the total amount of the judgment made in favour of all the claimants jointly represented; or

(ii) if the award is in favour of the defendant, the total amount claimed by the claimants;

and in either case, quantified in accordance with rule 46.2(3);

(b) where the only claim of each claimant is for a remedy other than the payment of money, deemed to be more than £3,000 but not more than £10,000; and

(c) where claims of the claimants include both a claim for the payment of money and for a remedy other than the payment of money, deemed to be—

(i) more than £3,000 but not more than £10,000; or

(ii) if greater, the value of the money claims calculated in accordance with sub-paragraph (a) above.

(4) Where—

(a) there is more than one defendant; and

(b) any or all of the defendants are separately represented,

the court may award fast track trial costs to each party who is separately represented.

(5) Where—

(a) there is more than one claimant; and

(b) a single defendant,

the court may make only one award to the defendant of fast track trial costs, for which the claimants are jointly and severally liable[GL].

(6) For the purpose of quantifying the fast track trial costs awarded to the single defendant under paragraph (5), the value of the claim is to be calculated in accordance with paragraph (3) of this rule.

Comment—Where the same advocate acts for more than one party, there will be only one award in respect of fast track trial costs. Normally one advocate will represent all claimants but where defendants are represented separately the court may award fast track trial costs to each party who is separately represented. Rule 46.4(3) sets out how the value of the claim is to be calculated where the same advocate is acting for more than one claimant and each claimant has a separate claim against the defendant. The same method of calculation is also used for quantifying the fast track trial costs awarded to a single defendant against more than one claimant. **46.4.1**

DIRECTIONS RELATING TO PART 46

Fast Track Trial Costs

Rule 46.1 Scope of Part 46

1.1 Part 46 applies to the costs of an advocate for preparing for and appearing at the trial of a claim in the fast track. **46PD–001**

1.2 It applies only where, at the date of the trial, the claim is allocated to the fast track. It does not apply in any other case, irrespective of the financial value of the claim.

1.3 In particular it does not apply to:

(a) the hearing of a claim which is allocated to the small claims track with the consent of the parties given under rule 26.7(3); or

(b) a disposal hearing at which the amount to be paid under a judgment or order is decided by the court (see paragraph 12.8 of the Practice Direction which supplements Part 26 (Case Management—Preliminary Stage)).

Cases which settle before trial

1.4 Attention is drawn to rule 44.10 (limitation on amount court may award where a claim allocated to the fast track settles before trial).

PART 47

Procedure for Detailed Assessment of Costs and Default Provisions

47.0.1 Contents

I. General Rules About Detailed Assessment

II. Costs Payable by One Party to Another—Commencement of Detailed Assessment Proceedings

III. Costs Payable by One Party to Another—Default Provisions

IV. Costs Payable by One Party to Another—Procedure Where Points of Dispute are Served

V. Interim Costs Certificate and Final Costs Certificate

VI. Detailed Assessment Procedure Where Costs Are Payable Out of the Legal Aid Fund

VII. Costs of Detailed Assessment Proceedings

VIII. Appeals in Detailed Proceedings

Editorial Introduction

Proceedings for detailed assessment are commenced by serving the bill and supporting documents on other interested parties. The court does not come into contact with the detailed assessment proceedings until either the receiving party seeks a default costs certificate, where the paying party has failed to serve points of dispute, or where the receiving party requests a detailed assessment hearing. **47.0.2**

The procedure for carrying in objections is no longer available. Instead the procedure is by way of appeal to a judge of the next tier. Appeals from authorised court officers are to the costs judge or district judge.

The court has power to order a party to make a payment on account before assessment takes place in accordance with r.44.3(8).

The court may also issue an interim certificate in accordance with r.47.15 at any time after the receiving party has filed a request for a detailed assessment hearing for such sum as it considers appropriate. There is no requirement that the amount of the interim certificate should relate to an amount agreed between the parties or decided by detailed assessment.

All certificates (default, interim and final) include an order to pay the costs within 14 days (see r.44.8) and are therefore enforceable unless the court orders otherwise.

Costs officers have all the powers of the court except that authorised court officers are not permitted to exercise penal powers (see r.47.3(1)), see also r.2.4.

(The definitions contained in Part 43 are relevant to this Part.)

I. GENERAL RULES ABOUT DETAILED ASSESSMENT

Time when detailed assessment may be carried out

47.1 The general rule is that the costs of any proceedings or any part of the proceedings are not to be assessed by the detailed procedure until the conclusion of the proceedings but the court may order them to be assessed immediately. **47.1**

(The costs practice direction gives further guidance about when proceedings are concluded for the purpose of this rule.) p 612

Comment—See paragraph 1.1 of the Directions relating to Pt 47 (para. 48PD–008) in relation to deciding when proceedings are concluded. **47.1.1**

No stay of detailed assessment where there is an appeal

47.2 Detailed assessment is not stayed pending an appeal unless the court so orders. **47.2**

Comment—See Directions relating to Pt 47, para. 1.2 (at para. 47PD–008) as to application to stay. **47.2.1**

Powers of an authorised court officer

47.3—(1) An authorised court officer has all the powers of the court when making a detailed assessment, except— **47.3**

(a) power to make a wasted costs order as defined in rule 48.7;

(b) power to make an order under—

(i) rule 44.14 (powers in relation to misconduct)

(ii) rule 47.8 (sanction for delay in commencing detailed assessment proceedings)

(iii) paragraph (2) (objection to detailed assessment by authorised court officer); and

(c) power to make a detailed assessment of costs payable to a solicitor by his client, unless the costs are being assessed under rule 48.5 (costs where money is payable to a child or patient).

(2) Where a party objects to the detailed assessment of costs being made by an authorised court officer, the court may order it to be made by a costs judge or a district judge.

(The costs practice direction sets out the relevant procedure.)

47.3.1 **Comment**—An authorised court officer has all the powers of the court except for the penal powers listed in the rule. Rule 2.4 confirms the position.

If a party wishes the detailed assessment to be conducted by somebody other than an authorised court officer an application must be made in accordance with Pt 23 (see para. 1.3 of the Directions relating to Pt 47 (para. 47PD–008)).

In the Supreme Court Costs Office authorised court officers are permitted to conduct detailed assessments up to £35,000 in the case of grade 7 officers, and up to £17,500 in the case of SEO officers.

At the time of writing there are no authorised court officers outside the SCCO except in the Principal Registry of the Family Division where authorised court officers are permitted to conduct detailed assessments up to £17,500.

Venue for detailed assessment proceedings

47.4 **47.4**—(1) All applications and requests in detailed assessment proceedings must be made to or filed at the appropriate office.

(The costs practice direction sets out the meaning of "appropriate office" in any particular case.)

(2) The court may direct that the appropriate office for any detailed assessment proceedings is to be the Supreme Court Costs Office.

(3) Any county court may direct that another county court is to be the appropriate office.

(4) A direction under paragraph (3) may be made without proceedings being transferred to that court.

(Rule 30.2 makes provision for any county court to transfer the proceedings to another county court for detailed assessment of costs.)

47.4.1 **Comment**—See paras 1.4–1.5 of the Direction relating to Pt 47 as to the appropriate office in any particular case.

The court (including a County Court) may direct that the appropriate office is to be the Supreme Court Costs Office, in addition one County Court may direct another to be the appropriate office.

II. Costs Payable By One Party to Another—Commencement of Detailed Assessment Proceedings

Application of this Section

47.5 **47.5** This section of Part 47 applies where a costs officer is to make a detailed assessment of costs which are payable by one party to another.

47.5.1 **Comment**—For the practice where costs are payable by one party to another and also out of the legal aid fund at prescribed rates see Directions relating to Pt 47, paras 9.1–9.7 (para. 47PD–008).

Commencement of detailed assessment proceedings

47.6 **47.6**—(1) Detailed assessment proceedings are commenced by the receiving party serving on the paying party—

(a) notice of commencement in the relevant practice form; and
(b) a copy of the bill of costs.

(Rule 47.7 sets out the period for commencing detailed assessment proceedings.)

(2) The receiving party must also serve a copy of the notice of commencement and the bill on any other relevant persons, specified in the costs practice direction.

(3) A person on whom a copy of the notice of commencement is served under paragraph (2) is a party to the detailed assessment proceedings (in addition to the paying party and the receiving party).

(The costs practice direction deals with—

- other documents which the party must file when he requests detailed assessment;
- the court's powers where it considers that a hearing may be necessary;
- the form of a bill; and
- the length of notice which will be given if a hearing date is fixed.)

Comment—The procedure for commencing detailed assessment is entirely new and does not at that stage involve the court. The receiving party must serve on the paying party, and any other relevant persons, notice of commencement (see Form 5 at para. C66–001) and a copy of the bill of costs. (See Form 2 at para. 48PD–007.) **47.6.1**

See paras 2.1–2.6 of the Directions relating to Pt 47 (para. 47PD–002) as to the procedure, and paras 2.1–2.16 of the Directions relating to Pt 43 (para. 43PD–001) as to the form and contents of the bill of costs.

Period for commencing detailed assessment proceedings

47.7 The following table shows the period for commencing detailed assessment proceedings. **47.7**

Source of right to detailed assessment	Time by which detailed assessment proceedings must be commenced
Judgment, direction, order, award or other determination	3 months after the date of the judgment, etc. Where detailed assessment is stayed pending an appeal, 3 months after the date of the order lifting the stay.
Discontinuance under Part 38	3 months after the date of service of notice of discontinuance under rule 38.3; or 3 months after the date of the dismissal of application to set the notice of discontinuance aside under rule 38.4
Acceptance of an offer to settle or a payment into court under Part 36	3 months after the date when the right to costs arose.

Comment—The table sets out the time by which detailed assessment proceedings must be **47.7.1**

commenced. The time is essentially three months after the event giving rise to the right to detailed assessment. See Directions relating to Pt 47, paras 2.7–2.10 (para. 48PD–008).

Sanction for failure to commence in time

47.8 **47.8**—(1) Where the receiving party fails to commence detailed assessment proceedings within the period specified—

(a) in rule 47.7; or

(b) by the direction of the court,

the paying party may apply for an order requiring the receiving party to commence detailed assessment proceedings within such time as the court may specify.

(2) On an application under paragraph (1), the court may direct that, unless the receiving party commences detailed assessment proceedings within the time specified by the court, all or part of the costs to which the receiving party would otherwise be entitled will be disallowed.

(3) If—

(a) the paying party has not made an application in accordance with paragraph (1); and

(b) the receiving party commences the proceedings later than the period specified in 47.7,

the court may disallow all or part of the interest otherwise payable to the receiving party under—

(a) section 17 of the Judgments Act 1838[1]; or

(b) section 74 of the County Courts Act 1984[2];

but must not impose any other sanction except in accordance with rule 44.14 (powers in relation to misconduct).

(4) Where the costs to be assessed in a detailed assessment are payable out of the Legal Aid Fund, this rule applies as if the receiving party were the solicitor to whom the costs are payable and the paying party were the Legal Aid Board.

47.8.1 **Comment**—It is not necessary to obtain permission to commence detailed assessment proceedings out of time, but r.47.8 provides a sanction for delay in commencing detailed assessment proceedings. If the time for commencing detailed assessment proceedings has expired, the paying party may apply for an order under r.47.8(1) and if the receiving party does not comply with this, all or part of the costs may be disallowed. See Directions relating to Pt 47, para. 2.11 (para. 47PD–002) as to such applications. If the receiving party commences proceedings for detailed assessment out of time but before the paying party has made an application, the only sanction which the court may impose is to disallow all or part of the interest which would otherwise be payable. Section 17(1) of the Judgments Act 1838, as amended, provides that interest will run from the time prescribed by rules of court (see r.44.12(2)). The court may exercise its powers in relation to misconduct under r.44.14 if the circumstances warrant it.

47.8.2 **Rule 47.8(4)**—Where costs are payable out of the legal aid fund and there has been a delay in commencing detailed assessment proceedings, such delay is not infrequent and can cause difficulties for counsel who remain unpaid and cannot themselves commence detailed assessment proceedings. The rule enables the Legal Aid Board to make an application under r.47.8(1).

Points of dispute and consequence of not serving

47.9 **47.9**—(1) The paying party and any other party to the detailed assessment proceedings may dispute any item in the bill of costs by serving points of dispute on—

(a) the receiving party; and

(b) every other party to the detailed assessment proceedings.

[1] 1838 c. 110. Section 17 was amended by S.I. 1998/2940.

[2] 1984 c. 28. Section 74 was amended by section (2) of the Private International Law (Miscellaneous Provisions) Act 1995 (c. 42).

(2) The period for serving points of dispute is 21 days after the date of service of the notice of commencement.

(3) If a party serves points of dispute after the period set out in paragraph (2) he may not be heard further in the detailed assessment proceedings, unless the court gives permission.

(The costs practice direction sets out requirements about the form of points of dispute.)

(4) The receiving party may file a request for a default costs certificate if—

(a) the period set out in rule 47.9(2) for serving points of dispute has expired; and

(b) he has not been served with any points of dispute.

(5) If any party (including the paying party) serves points of dispute before the issue of a default costs certificate the court may not issue the default costs certificate.

(Section IV of this Part sets out the procedure to be followed after points of dispute have been filed.)

Comment—Any person served with a copy of the bill and notice of commencement may serve points of dispute within 21 days after the date of service. If points of dispute are served after the time laid down in the rule that party may not be heard further unless the court gives permission. **47.9.1**

See paras 2.12–2.17 of the Directions relating to Pt 47 (para. 47PD–002) as to time limits, the form and contents of points of dispute.

Failure to serve points of dispute entitles the receiving party to request a default costs certificate in accordance with r.47.11. Even if points of dispute are served out of time the court may not subsequently issue a default costs certificate (see r.47.9(5)).

Procedure where costs are agreed

47.10—(1) If the paying party and the receiving party agree the amount of costs, either party may apply for a costs certificate (either interim or final) in the amount agreed. **47.10**

(Rule 47.15 and Rule 47.16 contain further provisions about interim and final costs certificates respectively.)

(2) An application for an order under paragraph (1) must be made—

(a) where the right to detailed assessment arises from a judgment or court order—

(i) to the court where the judgment or order was given or made, if the proceedings have not been transferred since then; or

(ii) to the court to which the proceedings have been transferred; and

(b) in any other case, to the court which would be the venue for assessment proceedings under rule 47.4.

Comment—It is open to the parties to agree all or part of the costs being claimed. Either party may apply for an appropriate certificate from the court; *i.e.* an interim certificate, if part of the costs are agreed or a final certificate, if all the costs are agreed (see rr.47.15 and 47.16). **47.10.1**

If agreement is reached before the court has become involved in the detailed assessment proceedings, the application for a certificate is made to the court which gave the judgment or made the order giving the right to the detailed assessment proceedings, or if the proceedings have been transferred to another court to that court. In any other case the court will be the "appropriate office" ascertained in accordance with r.47.4. See Directions relating to Pt 47, paras 2.18–2.22 (para. 47PD–002) as to procedure where costs are agreed.

III. COSTS PAYABLE BY ONE PARTY TO ANOTHER—DEFAULT PROVISIONS

Default costs certificate

47.11—(1) Where the receiving party is permitted by rule 47.9 to obtain a **47.11**

default costs certificate, he does so by filing a request in the relevant practice form.

(The costs practice direction deals with the procedure by which the receiving party may obtain a default costs certificate.)

(2) A default costs certificate will include an order to pay the costs to which it relates.

(3) Where a receiving party obtains a default costs certificate, the costs payable to him for the commencement of detailed assessment proceedings shall be the sum set out in the costs practice direction.

47.11.1 **Comment**—As to the procedure for obtaining a default costs certificate see paras 3.1–3.7 of the Directions relating to Pt 47 (para. 47PD–003). A default costs certificate, like all certificates, includes an order to pay the costs to which it relates. A party must comply with an order for payment within 14 days of the date of the certificate in accordance with r.44.8.

This will normally be the first occasion when the court has come into contact with the detailed assessment proceedings.

Amended by S.I. 1999 No. 1008.

Setting aside default costs certificate

47.12 **47.12**—(1) The court must set aside a default costs certificate if the receiving party was not entitled to it.

(2) In any other case, the court may set aside or vary a default costs certificate if it appears to the court that there is some good reason why the detailed assessment proceedings should continue.

(3) Where—

(a) the receiving party has purported to serve the notice of commencement on the paying party;

(b) a default costs certificate has been issued; and

(c) the receiving party subsequently discovers that the notice of commencement did not reach the paying party at least 21 days before the default costs certificate was issued;

the receiving party must—

(i) file a request for the default costs certificate to be set aside; or

(ii) apply to the court for directions.

(4) Where paragraph (3) applies, the receiving party may take no further step in

(a) the detailed assessment proceedings; or

(b) the enforcement of the default costs certificate,

until the certificate has been set aside or the court has given directions.

(The costs practice direction contains further details about the procedure for setting aside a default costs certificate and the matters which the court must take into account.)

47.12.1 **Comment**—The onus is on the receiving party to request that a default costs certificate be set aside, or to apply for directions where the notice of commencement did not reach the paying party at least 21 days before the default costs certificate was issued.

Either party may apply to the court to set aside or vary a default costs certificate for good reason. See paras 3.8–3.11 of the Directions relating to Pt 47 for the procedure for setting aside a default costs certificate and the matters which the court will take into account.

The court issuing the default costs certificate has, among its other powers, the power to stay enforcement of the certificate.

IV. COSTS PAYABLE BY ONE PARTY TO ANOTHER—PROCEDURE WHERE POINTS OF DISPUTE ARE SERVED

Optional reply

47.13 **47.13**—(1) Where any party to the detailed assessment proceedings serves points of dispute, the receiving party may serve a reply on the other parties to the assessment proceedings.

(2) He may do so within 21 days after service on him of the points of dispute to which his reply relates.

Comment—There is no obligation upon the receiving party to serve a reply but, if the receiving party fails to do so, this may be a factor taken into account under r.47.18(2) when the court is considering what order to make in respect of the costs of the detailed assessment proceedings. See Directions relating to Pt 47, para. 4.1 (para. 47PD–004). **47.13.1**

Detailed assessment hearing

47.14—(1) Where points of dispute are served in accordance with this Part, the receiving party may file a request for a detailed assessment hearing. **47.14**

(2) He must file a request within 3 months of the expiry of the period for commencing detailed assessment proceedings as specified—

(a) in rule 47.7; or

(b) by any direction of the court.

(3) Where the receiving party fails to file a request in accordance with paragraph (2), the paying party may apply for an order requiring the receiving party to file the request within such time as the court may specify.

(4) On an application under paragraph (3), the court may direct that, unless the receiving party requests a detailed assessment hearing within the time specified by the court, all or part of the costs to which the receiving party would otherwise be entitled will be disallowed.

(5) If—

(a) the paying party has not made an application in accordance with paragraph (3); and

(b) the receiving party files a request for a detailed assessment hearing later than the period specified in paragraph (2)

the court may disallow all or part of the interest otherwise payable to the receiving party under—

(i) section 17 of the Judgments Act 1838[3]; or

(ii) section 74 of the County Courts Act 1984,[4]

but must not impose any other sanction except in accordance with rule 44.14 (powers in relation to misconduct).

(6) No person other than—

(a) the receiving party;

(b) the paying party; and

(c) any party who has served points of dispute under rule 47.9,

may be heard at the detailed assessment hearing unless the court gives permission.

(7) Only items specified in the points of dispute may be raised at the hearing, unless the court gives permission.

(The costs practice direction specifies other documents which must be filed with the request for hearing and the length of notice which the court will give when it fixes a hearing date.)

Comment—If no application is made for a default costs certificate, the request for a detailed assessment hearing is likely to be the first occasion on which the court has come into contact with the detailed assessment proceedings. **47.14.1**

If the receiving party does not apply for a detailed assessment hearing within the time specified, the paying party may make an application under r.47.14(3). Such an application enables the court to make an order which could result in the receiving party having disallowed all or part of the costs.

Where the receiving party files the request for a detailed assessment hearing out of time, but

[3] 1838 c. 110. Section 17 was amended by S.I. 1998/2940.

[4] Section 74 was amended by section (2) of the Private International Law (Miscellaneous Provisions) Act 1995 (c. 42).

before any application by the paying party, the court may disallow interest for the period of the delay but may not impose any other sanction. The court's powers in relation to misconduct under r.44.14 are unaffected.

Amended by S.I. 1999 No. 1008.

47.14.2 **Rule 47.14(5) and (6)**—The rule limits the number of parties who may be heard at the detailed assessment hearing and the matters which may be raised at the hearing unless the court gives permission.

See paras 4.2–4.14 of the Directions relating to Pt 47 (para. 47PD–004) as to the documents which must be filed with request for hearing, the document giving the right to detailed assessment and procedure, including agreement, adjournment and amendment.

The court will give at least 14 days notice of the date of hearing.

47.14.3 **Power to order disclosure**—"The Costs Officer is exercising a judicial function with substantial financial consequences for the parties if some feature of the case alerts him to the need to make further investigation he may seek further information. No doubt he would begin by asking for a letter or some form of written confirmation or reassurance as appropriate. If this were to prove inadequate he might then make orders for discovery or require evidence." *Per* Judge L.J. in *Bailey v. IBC Vehicles Ltd,* [1998] 3 All E.R. 570, CA.

"When a party lodges a privileged document for detailed assessment in order to claim the costs of it; if the other party wishes to see it to dispute that claim for costs the claimant must be given the right to elect to withdraw it and not claim costs or he must disclose it." *Per* Drake J., *Skuse v. Granada Television Ltd* [1994] 1 W.L.R. 1156, Drake J. see also *Pamplin v. Express Newspapers Limited* [1985] 1 W.L.R. 689; *Goldman v. Hesper* [1998] 1 W.L.R. 1238, CA and *Derby & Co. v. Weldon (No. 7)* [1990] 1 W.L.R. 1156. The Judge stated "Had I ordered disclosure . . . of any part of the bundle I would have ordered that the document should be edited so as to remove the irrelevant material". It is permissible to blank out parts of documents disclosed on discovery on the ground that they are irrelevant to the issues in the action. See *G.E. Corporate Finance Group v. Bankers Trust Co., The Times,* August 3, 1994, CA.

47.14.4 **Privilege**—Where documents were disclosed in the course of assessment proceedings, and the party to whom they were disclosed wished to use them in proceedings in the USA, the Court of Appeal decided that the documents were privileged and were disclosed for the purpose of assessment only. They were relevant to an issue and should have been disclosed in the interests of justice and an order for disclosure would have been made if sought. The privilege in them was waived only for the purposes of detailed assessment. The court rejected an argument that enforcing privilege amounted to interference with the U.S. proceedings. It was for the U.S. court to decide whether there had been a breach of U.S. law and what to do about it. The documents were subject to an implied undertaking (*Prudential Insurance Co. v. Fountain Page Ltd* [1991] 1 W.L.R. 756) even though they were disclosed without an order. Special circumstances were required if the undertaking was to be released and this depended on all the facts (*Crest Homes Plc v. Marks* [1997] 1 A.C. 829), *Bourns Inc v. Raychem Corp,* March 30, 1999, CA, (unrep.).

47.14.5 **Acceptance of briefs and instructions and application of the "Cab-rank rule"**—A practising barrister must not accept any brief or instructions if to do so would cause him to be professionally embarrassed and for this purpose a barrister will be professionally embarrassed:

(a) if he lacks sufficient experience or competence to handle the matter;

(b) if having regard to his other professional commitments he will be unable to do or will not have adequate time and opportunity to prepare that which he is required to do;

(c) if the brief or instructions seek to limit the ordinary authority or discretion of a barrister in the conduct of proceedings in Court or to impose on a barrister an obligation to do any excepted work (except as permitted by the International Practice Rules or in the case of an employed barrister by para. 406) or to act otherwise than in conformity with the provisions of this Code;

(d) if the matter is one in which he has reason to believe that he is likely to be a witness or in which whether by reason of any connection of his with the client or with the Court or a member of it or otherwise it will be difficult for him to maintain professional independence or the administration of justice might be or appear to be prejudiced;

(e) if there is or appears to be some conflict or a significant risk of some conflict either between the interests of the barrister and some other person or between the interests of any one or more of his clients;

(f) if the matter is one in which there is a risk of a breach of confidences entrusted to him by another client or where the knowledge which he possesses of the affairs of another client would give an undue advantage to the new client;

(g) if he is a barrister in independent practice in a privately funded matter if the brief or instructions are delivered by a solicitor or firm of solicitors in respect of whom a Withdrawal of Credit Direction has been issued by the Chairman of the Bar pursuant to the Terms of Work on which Barristers Offer their Services to Solicitors and the Withdrawal of Credit Scheme 1988 (reproduced in Annex B) unless the brief or instructions are accompanied by payment of an agreed fee or the barrister agrees in advance to accept no fee for such work or has obtained the consent of the Chairman of the Bar;

(h) if he is a barrister in independent practice in a Direct Professional Access matter or an International matter unless he has previously informed BMIF that he intends to accept Direct Professional Access work or International work (as the case may be) and has paid the appropriate insurance premium.

A barrister in independent practice is not obliged to accept a brief or instructions:

(a) requiring him to do anything other than during the course of his ordinary working year;
(b) other than at a fee which is proper having regard to the complexity length and difficulty of the case and to his ability experience and seniority and any brief or instructions in a legally aided matter shall for this purpose unless the Bar Council or the Bar in general meeting otherwise determines (either in a particular case or in any class or classes of case or generally) be deemed to be at a proper professional fee;
(c) if the expenses which will be incurred are likely to be unreasonably high in relation to the fee likely to be paid and are not to be paid additionally to such fee;
(d) save in the case of legal aid work:
   (i) unless and until his fees are agreed;
   (ii) if having required his fees to be paid before he accepts the brief or instructions to which the fees relate those fees are not paid;
(e) in a Direct Professional Access matter unless he has previously notified BMIF that he intends to accept Direct Professional Access work and has paid the appropriate insurance premium;
(f) in an International matter.

A Queen's Counsel in independent practice is not obliged to accept a brief or instructions:

(a) to settle alone any document of a kind generally settled only by or in conjunction with a junior;
(b) to act without a junior if he considers that the interests of the lay client require that a junior should also be instructed.

A practising barrister (whether he is instructed on his own or with another advocate) must in the case of each brief and if he is a barrister in independent practice also in the case of all instructions consider whether consistently with the proper and efficient administration of justice and having regard to:

(i) the circumstances (including in particular the gravity complexity and likely cost) of the case;
(ii) the nature of his practice;
(iii) his ability experience and seniority; and
(iv) his relationship with his client;

the best interests of the client would be served by instructing or continuing to instruct him in that matter.

Where more than one advocate is instructed in any matter each barrister must in particular consider whether the best interests of the client would be served by:

(a) his representing the client together with the other advocate or advocates; or
(b) his representing the client without the other advocate or advocates; or
(c) the client instructing only the other advocate or advocates; or
(d) the client instructing some other advocate.

Unless he considers that the best interests of the client would be served by his continuing to represent the client (together with any other advocate instructed with him) a barrister must immediately advise the client accordingly.

In cases involving several parties, a practising barrister must in the case of each brief and, if he is a barrister in independent practice, also in the case of all instructions, consider, on receipt of the brief or instructions and further in the event of any change of circumstances, whether, consistently with the proper and efficient administration of justice and having regard to all the circumstances and any actual or potential conflict of interest, his client needs to be separately represented or advised or whether he could properly be jointly represented or advised with another party or, where there is more than one client, whether it is in all their interests to be jointly represented or advised.

(a) If the barrister considers that the client could properly be jointly represented or advised with another party, he must immediately advise the client accordingly.
(b) If the barrister considers that it is not in the interests of all his clients that they should be jointly represented or advised, he must immediately advise the clients accordingly.

Not used pending approval.

Withdrawal from a case and return of brief or instructions—A practising barrister must cease to act and if he is a barrister in independent practice must return any brief or instructions: 47.14.6

(a) if continuing to act would cause him to be professionally embarrassed within the meaning of para. 501 provided that if he would be professionally embarrassed only because it appears to him that he is likely to be a witness on a material question of fact he may retire or withdraw only if he can do so without jeopardising his client's interests;

(b) if having accepted a brief or instructions on behalf of more than one client there is or appears to be:
  (i) a conflict or a significant risk of a conflict between the interests of any one or more of such clients; or
  (ii) a risk of a breach of confidence;

and the clients do not all consent to him continuing to act;

(c) if in any legally aided case (whether civil or criminal) it has become apparent to him that legal aid has been wrongly obtained by false or inaccurate information and action to remedy the situation is not immediately taken by his client;

(d) if the circumstances set out in Regulation 67 of the Civil Legal Aid (General) Regulations 1989 arise at a time when it is impracticable for the Area Committee to meet in time to prevent an abuse of the Legal Aid Fund;

(e) if the client refuses to authorise him to make some disclosure to the court which his duty to the court requires him to make;

(f) if having become aware during the course of a case of the existence of a document which should have been but has not been disclosed on discovery the client fails forthwith to disclose it;

(g) if having come into possession of a document belonging to another party by some means other than the normal and proper channels and having read it before he realises that it ought to have been returned unread to the person entitled to possession of it he would thereby be embarrassed in the discharge of his duties by his knowledge of the contents of the document provided that he may retire or withdraw only if he can do so without jeopardising his client's interests.

Subject to para. 508 a practising barrister may withdraw from a case where he is satisfied that:

(a) his brief or instructions have been withdrawn;
(b) his professional conduct is being impugned; or
(c) there is some other substantial reason for so doing.

A practising barrister must not:

(a) cease to act or return a brief or instructions without having first explained to his professional client his reasons for doing so;
(b) return a brief or instructions to another barrister without the consent of his professional client or his representative;
(c) if he is a barrister in independent practice return a brief which he has accepted and for which a fixed date has been obtained or (except with the consent of his lay client and where appropriate the Court) break any other professional engagement so as to enable him to attend a social or non-professional engagement;
(d) except as provided in para. 506 return any brief or instructions or withdraw from a case in such a way or in such circumstances that his client may be unable to find other legal assistance in time to prevent prejudice being suffered by the client.

47.14.7 **Leading Counsel and the Two Counsel rule**—For the purpose of implementing the recommendation of the Monopolies and Mergers Commission (1975–76: House of Commons Paper 512: para. 208) that the "Two Counsel" rule should be abrogated, new rules were introduced by The Bar Council with effect from October 1, 1977. The rules for the acceptance of instructions by Queen's Counsel were subsequently incorporated into The Code of Conduct and now appear at para. 503 of The Code (see above).

Evans J. sitting with assessors in open court on reviews of taxation examined the question of two counsel in some depth in *Juby v. London Fire and Civil Defence Authority* and *Saunders v. Essex County Council*, April 24, 1990 (unrep.). Evans J. first listed the most likely factors affecting the decision whether or not to instruct a leader; they include:

(a) the nature of the case, including in accident cases;
  (i) the nature and severity of the plaintiff's injury;
  (ii) the likely duration of the trial;
  (iii) difficult questions regarding the quantum of damages, including medical evidence and questions of law;
  (iv) difficult questions of fact, including expert engineering evidence, or issues as to causation;
(b) its importance for the client;
(c) the amount of damages likely to be recovered;
(d) the general importance of the case, *e.g.* as affecting other cases;
(e) any particular requirements of the case, *e.g.* the need for legal advice, or for special expertise, *e.g.* examining or cross examining witnesses; and
(f) other reasons why an experienced and senior advocate may be required.

The learned judge felt that the fact that the other party has instructed leading counsel or intends to do so cannot and should not be disregarded as a factor to be taken into account when deciding the question whether or not it is reasonable to have instructed leading counsel. It was treated as relevant though not conclusive in *British Metal Corp. Ltd v. Ludlow Brothers (1913) Ltd* [1938] Ch. 987.

With regard to the question of whether or not a junior should be instructed in addition to leading counsel, it must be answered by reference to the test of reasonableness. The test must be applied by the taxing officer in the particular circumstances of each case. The correct approach is exemplified by The Code of Conduct (para. 503): reasonableness of the decision to instruct junior counsel in addition to a leader must be judged from the point of view of the (lay) client's interests, which are paramount even on a taxation when it is the losing party (or the legal aid fund) who is required to pay.

Particular reasons why a junior may be necessary for the proper conduct of the case, in the interests of the client include:

(a) to assist with the court proceedings either by taking an active part or by keeping a full note of the evidence, editing transcripts etc.;
(b) dealing with documents generally, particularly when the same junior counsel has taken part in discovery;
(c) to carry out legal or other research, *e.g.*. on matters on which expert evidence is given;
(d) to assist leading counsel in negotiations with the other party, particularly when, as in many accident cases, junior counsel has already advised the injured person and has become known to him. The lay client might well fail to understand why the junior who has dealt with his case up to trial should no longer be present when his claim is settled by negotiation or dealt with by judgment.

The fact that the solicitors are experienced in the type of litigation and able to present comprehensive and competent instructions to counsel is not relevant to the question whether it is reasonable to instruct junior counsel.

A balance has to be struck between the advantages of the more efficient presentation of the client's case and the extra expense involved in instructing leading counsel, or two counsel rather than one. The test laid down in *Francis v. Francis and Dickenson* [1956] P. 87, has equal relevance to the assessment of standard basis costs today.

With regard to the instruction of leading counsel the correct question is not whether the case was well within the capabilities of junior counsel but rather whether or not it was reasonable to instruct leading counsel (following *R. v. Dudley Magistrates' Court, ex p. Power City Stores Ltd* [1990] 140 New L.J. 361).

Legal aid—An authority issued by an area committee under reg. 15(6) (now reg. 59(1)) "to brief leading counsel" will cover the brief and any necessary consultation in connection with it, including consultation on quantum. Written advice on evidence, a written advice on quantum or a consultation or advice on discovery or other interlocutory matters must be specially authorised. See *Din (Taj) v. Wandsworth London Borough Council* [1983] 1 W.L.R. 1171; [1983] 2 All E.R. 841. See also Vol. 2, Section 16D. As to the scope and quantum of brief fee (see *Loveday v. Renton (No. 2)* para. 62/A2/15). **47.14.8**

Brief fee—quantum—In *Simpsons Motor Sales (London) Ltd v. Hendon Borough Council* [1965] 1 W.L.R. 112; [1964] 3 All E.R. 833, Pennycuick J., stated a proper measure for counsel's fees was to estimate what fee a hypothetical counsel, capable of conducting the case effectively, but unable or unwilling to insist on the high fees sometimes demanded by counsel of pre-eminent reputation, would be content to take on the brief: but there was no precise standard of measurement, and the taxing master or the Judge must, using their knowledge and experience, determine what was the proper figure. **47.14.9**

In assessing counsel's brief fee it is always relevant to take into account what work that fee together with any refreshers has to cover. The brief fee covers all the work done by way of preparation for representation at the trial and attendance on the first day of the trial. But in heavy litigation particularly where there is a team of barristers and experts additional work is involved in ensuring that the client is properly represented and his case fully developed beyond simply appearing in court, such as counsel having to meet to consider strategy and tactics and prepare material and to meet experts prior to their going into the witness box to give evidence. Counsel is only entitled to charge for the work he has been instructed to do and where the work is done on legal aid, which has been authorised by the legal aid certificate. Where legal aid authorisation is for representation at the trial, counsel will have to base his claim for remuneration on the delivery of the brief and what is required for the representation of the assisted party in court; in such cases, therefore, the remuneration should be the brief fee and daily refreshers calculated by reference to the time during which the trial is proceeding but not for days on which the court is not sitting. Counsel is not normally entitled to be remunerated separately for necessary work which is an incident of the proper representation of the client; rather, in a privately funded case a barrister must negotiate a brief fee sufficient to cover such work while in legal aid work the barrister may, on the legal aid taxation, require that the brief fee and the refresher rate properly reflect the amount of work that actually had to be done. On a legal aid taxation the brief fee should be assessed and allowed having regard to the full history of the trial as known at the date of taxation or of any subsequent review. Although it should take into account any need for counsel to have meetings with each other and with experts out of court hours and to prepare final submissions, it should also take account of the fact that all heavy trials include such a need to a greater or lesser extent. Preparation by counsel of his examinations-in-chief and cross-examinations and of his final submissions is an ordinary part of his conduct of a trial on behalf of his client being all part of the work which counsel accepts an obligation to perform by accepting the brief and for which he is remunerated by the brief fee and the refreshers. *Per* Hobhouse J. *Loveday v. Renton (No. 2)* [1992] 3 All E.R. 184.

47.14.10 **Written submissions**—The court made observations on the subject of written closing submissions at the end of a lengthy review of taxation.

"In the hearing of the preliminary issue in this review of taxation the court was occupied for nine hearing days, a daily transcript was obtained and there were in excess of 5,000 documents including original documents before the court. The issues were complex and at the conclusion of the evidence the matter was adjourned so that written submissions could be prepared. These were detailed and of assistance to the court. As Mr Justice Hobhouse, as he then was, said in *Loveday v. Renton (No. 2)* [1992] 3 All E.R. at 191 final submissions are an ordinary part of the conduct of a trial by a barrister on behalf of his client as part of the work which he accepts an obligation to perform in accepting the brief fee and for which he is remunerated by the brief fee and the agreed refreshers. Thus the preparation of final submissions, whether or not reduced into the form of a written document, is all work that has to be done in any event by counsel.

There may however be circumstances where the case is properly regarded as sufficiently complex or exceptional not to have been covered by the brief fee, and hence for a separate fee to have been specifically agreed for the preparation of written submissions by counsel.

Where such an agreement is made it would in my judgment be perfectly proper for the costs judge to consider it allowable in principle subject to detailed assessment of the amount when assessing the bill of costs."

Per Nelson J. *Chohan v. Times Newspapers Ltd*, September 7, 1998 (unreported).

47.14.11 **House of Lords—Brief fee—quantum**—For a discussion of the appropriate quantum of counsel's brief fee in the House of Lords, see *A. T. and T. Istel Ltd v. Tully (No. 2), R. v. Reid (No. 2)* [1994] 1 W.L.R. 279, HL.

47.14.12 **Leave to Appeal and Skeleton Arguments**—The Practice Direction of the Court of Appeal dated November 17, 1998 [1999] 1 W.L.R. 2 is reproduced at paragraph PD–001. Since January 1, 1999 permission has been required to appeal in almost all types of civil and family cases. The general test for permission is that it will be given unless an appeal would have no realistic prospect of success. Skeleton arguments from represented applicants are now mandatory in the case of applications for leave which are to be considered on paper as well as those which proceed to an oral hearing. Under the previous Practice Direction Lord Donaldson M.R. had directed Taxing Masters to allow separate fees for the skeleton argument and the brief. The current Practice Direction contains no such direction but it may be assumed that any Judge assessing costs by either summary or detailed assessment will allow a reasonable amount in respect of all work actually, reasonably and proportionately undertaken.

47.14.13 **Expert witnesses**—See Part 35 for the courts powers in respect of experts.

The duties and responsibilities of expert witnesses in civil cases include:

1. Evidence should be and should be seen to be the independent product of the expert uninfluenced as to form or content by the exigencies litigation. See *Whitehouse v. Jordan* [1981] 1 All E.R. 276.

2. Independent assistance should be provided to the Court by way of objective unbiased opinion regarding matters within the expertise of the expert. See *Polivitte Limited v. Commercial Union Assurance Co. PLC* [1987] 1 Lloyd's Rep. 379, 386, *per* Garland J. and *Re J* [1990] F.C.R. 193, *per* Cazalet J. An expert witness in the High Court should never assume the role of advocate.

3. Facts or assumptions upon which the opinion is based should be stated together with material facts which could detract from the concluded opinion.

4. The witness should make it clear when a question or issue falls outside his experience.

5. If the opinion is not properly researched because it is considered that insufficient data was available that must be stated with an indication that the opinion is provisional (see *Re J.*) if the witness cannot assert that the report contains the truth the whole truth and nothing but the truth that qualification should be stated on the report. See *Derby and Co. Limited v. Weldon (No. 9)* [1991] 1 W.L.R. 652; [1991] 2 All E.R. 901, *per* Staughton L.J.

6. If after exchange of reports an expert changes his mind on a material matter the change of view should be communicated to the other side through legal representatives without delay and when appropriate to the Court.

7. Photographs, plans, survey reports and other documents referred to in the expert evidence must be provided to the other side at the same time as the exchange of reports *per* Cresswell J. in *National Justice Compania Naviera SA v. Prudential Assurance Company Limited (Ikarian Reefer)* [1993] 2 Lloyd's Rep. 68.

47.14.14 **Witness expenses**—Where a Merchant bank, retained to advise a defendant, was the subject of a witness summons served by the claimant, the witness was entitled to the costs incurred in complying with the summons and was not limited to conduct money only. The costs could include taking legal advice, where it was reasonable to have done so. The court could decide whether the costs were payable on the standard or on the indemnity basis, any dispute being resolved by a Costs judge (*J. H. Shannon v. Country Casuals Holdings Plc* (1997) *The Times*, June 16, *per* Garland J.).

The Indemnity Principle—"Costs as between party and party are given by the law as an indemnity to the person entitled to them; they are not imposed as a punishment on the party who pays them, or given as a bonus to the party who receives them." (*Harold v. Smith* [1860] 5 H. & N. 381, Bramwell B.). "It is of great importance to litigants who are unsuccessful, that they should not be oppressed into having to pay an excessive amount of costs ... the costs chargeable as between party and party are all that are necessary to enable the adverse party to conduct the litigation and no more. Any charges merely for conducting litigation more conveniently may be called luxuries and must be paid by the party incurring them." (*Smith v. Buller* [1875] L.R. 19 Eq. 473, Sir Richard Malins V.-C.). The test is now one of reasonableness and proportionality rather than necessity. The purpose of assessment is to ascertain the amount payable to the party recovering costs not to fix the remuneration of solicitors. The order for costs may not be more than an indemnity, *i.e.* the amount which the successful party has to pay to his own solicitor (*Gundry v. Sainsbury* [1910] 1 K.B. 99). 47.14.15

The indemnity principle is to be applied on an item by item basis rather than on a global basis "where applicable the figures in a contentious business agreement provide both a measure and a ceiling for each recoverable item of costs", *per* Sir Brian Neill, *The General of Berne Insurance Co. v. Jardine Reinsurance Management* [1998] 2 All E.R. 301, CA. That judgment related to a contentious business agreement where the hourly rate was agreed. The principle applies even where there is no contentous business agreement: "In my judgment there should be no distinction between those cases where a formal contentious business agreement is in place and which are governed by section 60(3) of the Solicitors Act 1974 and other cases where there is an agreement partly evidenced in writing, an unwritten agreement or no agreement at all, but merely an understanding arising perhaps from a long established relationship ..."; *Nederlandse Reassurantie Groep Holding NV v. Bacon & Woodrow*, April 21, 1998, Tucker, J., unrep.

"In my judgment there is nothing unlawful in a solicitor acting for a party to litigation agreeing to forego all or part of his fee if he loses provided that he does not seek to recover more than his ordinary profit costs and disbursements if he wins." *Per* Millett L.J. in *Thaw Trading Co. v. Taylor* [1998] Q.B. 781, CA.

The difficulty identified by the Divisional Court in *Hughes v. Kingston upon Hull City Council* [1999] 2 All E.R. 49 has been overcome by the amendment of r.8 of the Solicitors Practice Rules 1990. The decision in Thai Trading is therefore correct in respect of such agreements entered into after the Rule was amended.

Conditional fee agreements are permitted by section 58 of the Courts and Legal Services Act 1990 (see Part 15(E) and 15(F) for Conditional Fee Agreements Order 1998 and Regulations 1995). A conditional fee agreement relating to a claim to be determined by arbitration was held not to be void for champerty. The Court held that the effect of the Courts and Legal Services Act 1990 and the 1995 Conditional Fee Agreements Order and Regulations which had been substantially complied with was not champertous. (*Bevan Ashford v. Geoff Yeandle (Contractors) Ltd (in liquidation)*, [1998] 3 W.L.R. 172, Sir Richard Scott V.-C.).

The hourly rate—Evans J. sitting with assessors examined the question of solicitors' hourly rates and gave judgment in open court in *Johnson v. Reed Corrugated Cases Ltd* [1992] 1 All E.R. 169. The judge quoted with approval the decisions in *Re Eastwood (dec'd.)* [1975] Ch. 112; *Leopold Lazarus Ltd v. Secretary of State for Trade and Industry* (1976) 120 S.J. 268; *Stubbs v. Royal National Orthopaedic Hospital*, December 21, 1988 (unrep.); *Finlay v. Glaxo Laboratories Ltd*, October 9, 1989 (unrep.) and *R. v. Wilkinson* [1980] 1 All E.R. 597. The solicitors had submitted evidence as to their expense rate calculated in accordance with the Law Society's book, *The Expense of Time*, and the judge expressed the view that presenting such figures, requiring non-expert analysis, *i.e.* by persons who are not accountants, is misconceived as a means of assisting the court in a particular case. Assessing costs is not an exact science; neither is accountancy. Treating the latter as if it were, so that the results of an accountancy exercise can be used as a basis for the former, seemed to the judge to achieve the worst of both worlds. The costs officer's general knowledge and experience of local conditions and circumstances remains the only firm basis for reliable and consistent assessment. 47.14.16

Evans J. did not support any idea that part of the court's functions on an assessment is to discipline solicitors into charging less than they have done, or to regulate the amount of their charges to their clients. The court is not concerned with charges, only with costs; it is not concerned with any market, except indirectly, certainly not to influence any market. Its function is to assess the reasonable amount of costs for work reasonably done; that, and nothing else.

Where a salaried solicitor is employed see *Re Eastwood (dec'd.)* and *Leopold Lazarus Ltd v. Secretary of State for Trade and Industry* (above). See also *Loveday v. Renton (No. 2)* [1992] 3 All E.R. 184.

"If as the solicitors argue, the proper guide is that of the average solicitor employed by the average firm in the area concerned, then the Central London Law Societies' Survey, whilst not necessarily a perfect indication of that average, is, on the evidence in this case, the closest approach we have to that average", *per* Mr. Justice Lindsay in *Re A Company* 1989, C. No. 4081;

[1995] 2 All E.R. 155. Approach of Lindsay J. followed in *KPMG Peat Marwick McLintock v. HLT Group Ltd*, Auld J. [1995] 2 All E.R. 180.

Where a claimant was injured in Sheffield and the union to which he belonged instructed solicitors in London, the trial being in Sheffield, it was submitted by the defendants that only the Sheffield rate should be allowed, and not the London solicitors' rate. It was decided, that given the undoubted expertise of the union's solicitors, it was reasonable to instruct them, the costs had therefore been reasonably incurred and were of a reasonable amount. The London rate was allowed (*Wraith v. Sheffield Forgemasters Ltd* [1996] 1 W.L.R. 617, Potter J.). But on appeal, on the issue whether the liability of an unsuccessful party ordered to pay costs should be restricted to what a reasonable competent solicitor, practising in the area of the court (or in the area where the successful party lived) might have been expected to charge or whether the successful party should be entitled to recover the sums claimed by the solicitor who was in fact instructed on his behalf, the Court of Appeal, whilst upholding Potter J. in principle, took issue with the way the principle was applied to the facts of the case because the Trade Union knew or ought to have known what sort of legal fees it would have to expend to obtain competent services for the claimant who lived in Sheffield who had sustained a serious accident there. "It is the duty of Unions and Insurers in each individual case to keep down the costs of litigation, this means that if they instruct London solicitors who charge London rates for a case which has no obvious connection with London and which does not require expertise only to be found there, they will, even if successful, recover less than the solicitors have charged" (*Wraith v. Sheffield Forgemasters Ltd* [1998] 1 W.L.R. 132, CA). In another case heard at the same time as *Wraith*, solicitors acting for a wife in Family Proceedings wrongly applied for a Charging Order in Brighton County Court, they persisted with this application, having been told it was incorrect and ultimately the husband, having changed solicitors from a firm in East Grinstead, with whom he had become dissatisfied, to a firm in London was successful in having the order for sale struck out and obtaining a wasted costs order against the wife's solicitors. It was argued that the husband should have obtained the services of solicitors in Brighton or in Tunbridge Wells, where he lived. The Court found that there were certain matters which were relevant when considering the reasonableness of the husband instructing the London firm:

"(1) The importance of the matter to him, it was obviously of great importance, it threatened his home.

(2) The legal and factual complexities insofar as he might reasonably be expected to understand them. Due to the incompetence of the wife's solicitors the matter had taken on an appearance of some complexity.

(3) The location of his home, his place of work and the location of the court in which the relevant proceedings had been commenced.

(4) The husband's possibly well-founded dissatisfaction with the solicitors he had originally instructed, which may well have resulted in a natural desire to instruct solicitors further afield who would not be inhibited in representing his interests.

(5) The fact that he has sought advice as to who to consult and had been recommended to consult the London firm.

(6) The location of the London firm, including their accessibility to him and their readiness to attend at the relevant court.

(7) What, if anything he might reasonably be expected to know of the fees likely to be charged by the London firm as compared with the fees of other solicitors whom he might reasonably be expected to have considered."

Having applied those considerations to the facts, the Court allowed the London rate for the solicitors (*Truscott v. Truscott*, July 31, 1997, reported as *Wraith v. Sheffield Forgemasters Ltd* [1998] 1 W.L.R. 132, CA). Where a firm outside London dealt only with specialised commercial cases for selected clients and was thus clearly outside the range of local solicitors, it was possible to allow a rate more than the broad average direct cost for that area. This would not be appropriate if the firm had engaged in a case which could reasonably have been handled by other local firms since the cost would not then have been reasonably incurred, *i.e.* it must have been reasonable to instruct a firm for the particular case (*Jones v. Secretary of State for Wales and Vale of Glamorgan B.C.* [1997] 1 W.L.R. 1008, *per* Buckley J.).

If a party chooses a particular status or type of solicitor or counsel or one located in a particular area then the costs will have been reasonably incurred if, having regard to the circumstances, a reasonable choice has been made. The question to be asked is whether the solicitor chosen is the sort of solicitor that a person would have instructed with a view to the proper conduct of his case in minimising the costs of litigation. *Per* Hooper J. review of detailed assessment, *A v. F Co. Ltd; S v F Co. Ltd*, (1996) SCTO Digest No. 13.

In a case where a claimant was injured in an accident in the Manchester area and the union instructed London solicitors the Court of Appeal decided that the question to be determined was whether objectively the claimant acted reasonably in instructing London solicitors. The fact that a trade union habitually used a particular firm of solicitors was of only limited relevance. On the particular facts of the case there was no obvious connection to London and this factor became increasingly important when the case did not require expertise that could only be found there. The availability of expert medical witnesses in London could not give the case a connection with London. On the facts the case was pre-eminently a Manchester one that required no expertise that could be found only in London, *Sullivan v. Co-Operative Insurance Society*, *The Times*, May 19, 1999, CA (unrep.).

In cases involving vast amounts of documents, a party may sometimes reduce a document into an electronic form to ease management. The cost of the equipment necessary to undertake this work is not normally recoverable, although the actual work required to analyse the documents may be regarded as fee earners work. The party contemplating reducing documents into electronic form may apply to the court in advance for an order regulating the matter, including the basis of charge for electronic copies. The Court has power to give directions as to whether inspection should be by electronic means or hard copy (*Grupo Torrassa v. Al Sabah, Jafter v. Grupo Torrassa, The Times*, October 13, 1997, Mance J.). On the particular facts of that case the Court directed that inspection shold be by means of CD, which could be produced at a relatively modest cost, as against production of photostat copies of the documents themselves, which would have cost a very great deal of money. The actual work of assembling the database was a matter to be left to the outcome of the trial and subsequent assessment.

Rights of Audience on Detailed Assessment—In detailed assessment proceedings, rights of audience may be exercised by any counsel properly instructed by solicitors, any solicitor or employee of a solicitor representing one of the parties to the proceedings. If the party is legally represented costs consultants, costs draftsmen and the like can only be heard on the basis that they are temporarily, and for the purpose of those detailed assessment proceeding, employees of the solicitors representing the party. The solicitors are responsible for the conduct of the detailed assessment proceedings and cannot avoid that responsibility merely by instructing a costs draftsman. 47.14.17

> "A costs draftsman can appear on behalf of a party only as the duly authorised representative of the solicitor who has instructed him to be there. The scope of his apparent authority would be the same . . . as any costs draftsman employed by the firm." *per* Evans L.J., *Waterson Hicks v. Eliopoulos*, November 14, 1995, CA, (unrep.).

Where a party is a litigant in person the party may appear in person or may be assisted by an expert in accordance with rule 48.6(3)(c). Expert assistance in those circumstances may be given by a barrister, solicitor, Fellow of the Institute of Legal Executives, Fellow of the Association of Law Costs Draftsmen, a law costs draftsman who is a member of the Academy of Experts or a law costs draftsman who is a member of the Expert Witness Institute (see 47PD–001, para. 1.3).

V. INTERIM COSTS CERTIFICATE AND FINAL COSTS CERTIFICATE

Power to issue an interim certificate

47.15—(1) The court may at any time after the receiving party has filed a request for a detailed assessment hearing— 47.15

(a) issue an interim costs certificate for such sum as it considers appropriate;

(b) amend or cancel an interim certificate.

(2) An interim certificate will include an order to pay the costs to which it relates, unless the court orders otherwise.

(3) The court may order the costs certified in an interim certificate, to be paid into the court.

Comment—There is no requirement that any of the costs be assessed or agreed prior to the issue of an interim costs certificate. The court is given complete discretion once a request for a detailed assessment hearing has been filed to issue an interim certificate for such sum as it considers appropriate. 47.15.1

As with default costs certificates and final costs certificates the interim costs certificate includes an order to pay. Rule 44.8 provides that payment must be made within 14 days of the date of the certificate. The court issuing the certificate has the power to stay enforcement of it. See Directions relating to Pt 47, para. 5.1 (para. 47PD–005).

The court may order that, instead of the certified amount being paid to the receiving party, it should be paid into court. This may be appropriate where the paying party is proving dilatory but where there is also an order for costs in favour of the paying party.

Final costs certificate

47.16—(1) In this rule a completed bill means a bill calculated to show the amount due following the detailed assessment of the costs. 47.16

(2) The period for filing the completed bill is 14 days after the end of the detailed assessment hearing.

(3) When a completed bill is filed the court will issue a final costs certificate and serve it on the parties to the detailed assessment proceedings.

(4) Paragraph (3) is subject to any order made by the court that a certificate is not to be issued until other costs have been paid.

(5) A final costs certificate will include an order to pay the costs to which it relates, unless the court orders otherwise.

(The costs practice direction deals with the form of a final costs certificate.)

47.16.1 **Comment**—Once the detailed assessment hearing has finished the receiving party is required to complete the bill by calculating the amounts due and to file it with the court within 14 days after the end of the detailed assessment hearing.

See paras 5.2–5.13 of the Directions relating to Pt 47 (para. 47PD–005) as to completion of the bill and the form of the final costs certificate.

As with a default costs certificate and interim costs certificate, the final costs certificate will include an order to pay the costs. The time for payment, in accordance with r.44.8, is within 14 days of the date of the certificate. The court issuing the certificate has the power to stay enforcement of the certificate.

Amended by S.I. 1999 No. 1008.

VI. DETAILED ASSESSMENT PROCEDURE FOR COSTS OF AN ASSISTED PERSON WHERE COSTS ARE PAYABLE OUT OF THE LEGAL AID FUND

Detailed assessment procedure for costs of an assisted person where costs are payable out of the legal aid fund

47.17 **47.17**—(1) Where the court is to assess costs of an assisted person which are payable out of the legal aid fund, the assisted person's solicitor may commence detailed assessment proceedings by filing a request in the relevant practice form.

(2) A request under paragraph (1) must be filed within 3 months after the date when the right to detailed assessment arose.

(3) The solicitor must also serve a copy of the request for detailed assessment on the assisted person, if notice of the assisted person's interest has been given to the court in accordance with legal aid regulations.

(4) Where the solicitor has certified that the assisted person wishes to attend an assessment hearing, the court will on receipt of the request for assessment, fix a date for the assessment hearing.

(5) Where paragraph (3) does not apply, the court will on receipt of the request for assessment provisionally assess the costs without the attendance of the solicitor, unless it considers that a hearing is necessary.

(6) After the court has provisionally assessed the bill, it will return the bill to the solicitor.

(7) The court will fix a date for an assessment hearing if the solicitor informs the court, within 14 days after he receives the provisionally assessed bill, that he wants the court to hold such a hearing.

47.17.1 **Comment**—This section of the rules deals with costs payable only out of the legal aid fund. It is the only situation in which there may be a provisional taxation. (For the practice where costs are payable by one party to another and also out of the legal aid fund at prescribed rates see Costs Practice Direction supplementing Pt 47, paras 9.1–9.7.)

The detailed assessment proceedings are commenced by filing a request for detailed assessment (in Form 8, para. C74–001). The time for filing the request is within 3 months after the date when the right to detailed assessment arose. A copy of the request must be served on the assisted person if the assisted person has a financial interest and wishes to attend the assessment hearing (see Civil Legal Aid (General) Regulations 1989, reg. 119).

The court will give a date for the detailed assessment hearing in every case where the assisted person wishes to attend and may do so if it considers that a hearing is necessary. Otherwise the court will provisionally assess the costs without the attendance of the solicitor but, if the solicitor does not accept the provisional assessment the court will fix a date for a detailed assessment hearing, if the solicitor informs the court within 14 days that that is what is wanted. See Directions relating to Pt 47, paras 6.1–6.8 (para. 47PD–006) for these procedures.

VII. COSTS OF DETAILED ASSESSMENT PROCEEDINGS

Liability for costs of detailed assessment proceedings

47.18—(1) The receiving party is entitled to his costs of the detailed assessment proceedings except where— **47.18**

(a) the provisions of any Act, any of these Rules or any relevant practice direction provide otherwise; or

(b) the court makes some other order in relation to all or part of the costs of the detailed assessment proceedings.

(2) In deciding whether to make some other order, the court must have regard to all the circumstances, including—

(a) the conduct of all the parties;

(b) the amount, if any, by which the bill of costs has been reduced; and

(c) whether it was reasonable for a party to claim the costs of a particular item or to dispute that item.

Comment—There is a presumption that the receiving party is entitled to the costs of the detailed assessment proceedings unless some provision to the contrary is in existence, or the court makes a different order in relation to all or part of the costs. **47.18.1**

In deciding what order to make the court is required to have regard to: all the circumstances, including the conduct of all the parties (presumably this means conduct in relation to the detailed assessment proceedings rather than in the substantive proceedings); the amount of any reduction; and whether it was reasonable for a party to claim or dispute a particular item. The last two categories overlap to a certain extent and are aimed at unreasonable demands and/or unreasonable objections. See Directions relating to Pt 47, paras 7.1–7.3 (para. 47PD–007).

See also r.44.14 as to Misconduct in assessment proceedings.

Offers to settle without prejudice save as to costs of the detailed assessment proceedings

47.19—(1) Where— **47.19**

(a) a party (whether the paying party or the receiving party) makes a written offer to settle the costs of the proceedings which gave rise to the assessment proceedings; and

(b) the offer is expressed to be without prejudice[GL] save as to the costs of the detailed assessment proceedings,

the court will take the offer into account in deciding who should pay the costs of those proceedings.

(2) The fact of the offer must not be communicated to the costs officer until the question of costs of the detailed assessment proceedings falls to be decided.

(The costs practice direction provides that rule 47.19 does not apply where the receiving party is an assisted person.)

Comment—The *Calderbank* procedure is retained in respect of the costs of detailed assessment proceedings. Either party may make a written offer and the court will take that offer into account in deciding who should pay the costs of the detailed assessment proceedings. **47.19.1**

See paras 7.4–7.6 of the Directions relating to Pt 47 (para. 47PD–007) in relation to such offers.

The rule does not apply where the receiving party is an assisted person, unless the court orders otherwise.

VIII. APPEAL AGAINST DECISIONS IN DETAILED ASSESSMENT PROCEEDINGS

Right to appeal

47.20—(1) Any party to the detailed assessment proceedings may appeal **47.20**

against any decision of the court in those proceedings, subject to the requirements of rule 47.21.

(2) For the purposes of this Section, an assisted person is not a party to the detailed assessment proceedings.

47.20.1 **Comment**—The rule makes it clear that an assisted person is not a party to the detailed assessment proceedings and therefore does not have a personal right to appeal. The Civil Legal Aid (General) Regulations 1989, regs 113 to 117 refer to the previous procedures of objections and review but reg. 113 makes it clear that it is for the assisted person's solicitor (not the assisted person) to make whatever application is appropriate.

Because the requirement to serve points of dispute is now contained in the rule, and the issues are therefore identified before the start of the detailed assessment hearing, the objections procedure is no longer available and all appeals are to the judge of the next tier (see r.47.22 below).

Where a detailed assessment has been carried out by an authorised court officer there is a right of appeal to the costs judge or district judge without the need to obtain permission, reasons may however be required (see r.47.25).

Preliminary requirements for bringing an appeal

47.21 **47.21**—(1) A party may not appeal against a decision in detailed assessment proceedings until he has—

(a) sought written reasons for the decision in accordance with rule 47.23; and

(b) obtained the court's permission where necessary in accordance with rule 47.24,

unless the court orders otherwise.

(2) Where a party has complied with the requirements under paragraph (1) he may file a notice of appeal in accordance with rule 47.25.

47.21.1 **Comment**—Before a party may file a notice of appeal, written reasons must be sought and the court's permission must be obtained. The court may dispense with written reasons if the decision to be appealed against is one which does not require reasons, for example if the reasons are sufficiently endorsed on the face of the bill or if the decision is a case management decision. See paras 8.1–8.9 of the Directions relating to Pt 47 (para. 47PD–008) as to written reasons. The rule states that the court may order otherwise, both in respect of the need to seek written reasons and in respect of the need to obtain permission. It is difficult to envisage any circumstances in which the court would dispense with the permission requirement since it would be simpler for the court to grant the permission there and then.

Court to hear appeal

47.22 **47.22**—(1) Where an appeal is made against a decision of an authorised court officer the appeal is—

(a) if the detailed assessment proceedings were in the High Court, to a costs judge or district judge of that court; or

(b) if they were in a county court, to a district judge.

(2) Where an appeal is made to a costs judge or a district judge against a decision of an authorised court officer, a further appeal lies—

(a) if the detailed assessment proceedings were in the High Court, to a judge of that court;

(b) if they were in a county court, to a circuit judge.

(3) Where an appeal against a decision of a costs judge or a district judge hearing the detailed assessment is made the appeal lies—

(a) if the detailed assessment proceedings were in the High Court, to a judge of that court;

(b) if they were in a county court, to a circuit judge.

47.22.1 **Comment**—All appeals are to a judge of the next tier. Appeals from an authorised court officer go to a costs judge or district judge. At the time of writing (April 1999) authorised court officers only exist in the Supreme Court Costs Office and the Principal Registry of the Family Division. The Lord Chancellor has the power to appoint authorised court officers in any court.

In discussions concerning the rules for appeals in respect of costs Lord Woolf made it clear that he expected appeals from district judges in District Registries to go to a circuit judge rather than to a High Court Judge. This would mean that the circuit judge would have to sit under section 9 of the Supreme Court Act 1981.

Duty to seek reasons

47.23—(1) A party may seek reasons for a decision in detailed assessment proceedings by filing a request with the court that gave the decision. **47.23**

(2) Where the party seeking reasons is the receiving party, he must file his request for reasons when he files the completed bill of costs.

(Rule 47.16 deals with completed bills of costs.)

(3) Where the party seeking reasons is the paying party, he must file his request for reasons within 7 days after the end of the detailed assessment hearing.

Comment—Reasons must be requested in writing and the request filed within 7 days after the end of the detailed assessment hearing by the paying party, or when the completed bill of costs is filed (*i.e.* within 14 days after the detailed assessment hearing in accordance with r.47.16(2)), if the request is by the receiving party. See Directions relating to Pt 47, paras 8.1–8.9 (para. 47PD–008). **47.23.1**

Obtaining the court's permission to appeal

47.24—(1) Permission is not required to appeal against— **47.24**

(a) decision of an authorised court officer; or
(b) a decision of a costs judge or a district judge to impose a sanction on a legal representative under—
   (i) rule 44.14 (powers in relation to misconduct); or
   (ii) rule 48.7 (wasted costs order).

(2) Subject to paragraph (1)(b), permission is required to appeal against a decision of a costs judge or a district judge.

(3) Permission to appeal may be given by—

(a) the costs judge or district judge who made the decision in question; or
(b) a High Court judge or a circuit judge, as the case may be.

(4) A party may seek permission to appeal—

(a) within 14 days after receiving written reasons under rule 47.23; or
(b) if the court directs that reasons do not need to be obtained, within 7 days after the date of the direction.

Comment—Permission is generally required if any party wishes to appeal. No permission is required to appeal against a decision of an authorised court officer or a decision to impose a penal sanction. See Directions relating to Pt 47, paras 8.10–8.14 (para. 47PD–008) as to obtaining permission to appeal. **47.24.1**

Permission may be granted by the judge who made the decision to be appealed against or by a judge of the next tier (see commentary at para. 47.22.1 above).

The time for seeking permission is within 14 days after receiving the written reasons, or, if there are no reasons, within 7 days after notification of the decision of the court directing that they were not required.

Amended by S.I. 1999 No. 1008.

Appeal procedure

47.25—(1) A party who has a right to appeal may do so by filing a notice of appeal. **47.25**

(2) Where the appeal is against a decision of an authorised court officer, he must file the notice—

(a) within 14 days after service of the court officer's reasons on him; or
(b) if the court has directed that reasons need not be obtained, within 7 days after the date of the direction.

(3) Where the appeal is against a decision of a costs judge or a district judge, he may must do so within 14 days after the date of the court's decision to give permission to appeal.

(4) On receipt of a notice of appeal, the court will—

(a) serve a copy of the notice on the other parties to the detailed assessment proceedings; and

(b) give notice of the appeal hearing to those parties.

47.25.1 **Comment**—Having obtained the reasons and permission, the party wishing to appeal must file notice of appeal (see paras 8.15–8.18 of the Directions relating to Pt 47 (para. 47PD–008) and Form 16 para. 48PD–012).

Attention is drawn to the time limits. If the appeal is against the decision of an authorised court officer where no permission is required the notice of appeal must be filed within 14 days after service of the reasons, or if no reasons are required, within 7 days after the notification of the court's decision to that effect. Where permission is required, the notice of appeal must be filed within 14 days after the court's decision to give permission.

Amended by S.I. 1999 No. 1008.

Powers of the court on appeal

47.26 **47.26**—(1) On an appeal from an authorised court officer the court will—

(a) re-hear the proceedings which gave rise to the decision appealed against; and

(b) make any order and give such directions as it considers appropriate.

(2) On an appeal from a costs judge or district judge, if the court is satisfied that the appeal should be allowed, it may make any order and give such directions as it considers appropriate.

(3) If on an appeal the court exercises the power to appoint assessors conferred—

(a) by section 70 of the Supreme Court Act 1981[5]; or

(b) by section 63 of the County Courts Act 1984,[6]

it must appoint at least two assessors.

(Rule 32.15 contains further provisions about the appointment of assessors.)

(4) One assessor must be a district judge or costs judge and one must be a practising barrister or solicitor.

47.26.1 **Comment**—An appeal from an authorised court officer is a re-hearing and the court may make any order and give such directions as it considers appropriate. An appeal from a costs judge or district judge is an appeal proper and the court will only make a different order if it is satisfied that the appeal should be allowed.

47.26.2 **Rule 47.26(3)—Assessors**—It is a matter for the judge hearing the appeal whether or not to appoint assessors. If assessors are appointed one must be a district judge or costs judge and one must be a practising barrister or solicitor. The subject matter of the appeal will assist in determining whether a barrister or solicitor assessor is the more appropriate. Rule 35.15 deals with assessors. Rule 35.15(5) provides that the remuneration of an assessor will be determined by the court and forms part of the costs of the proceedings. Rule 35.15(6) gives the court power to order any party to deposit an amount in respect of assessor's fees in advance.

PRACTICE DIRECTIONS RELATING TO PART 47

Procedure for Detailed Assessment of Costs and Default Provisions

Section I—General rules about detailed assessment

Rule 47.1 Time when assessment may be carried out

47PD–001 **1.1** (1) For the purposes of this rule, proceedings are concluded when the

[5] 1981 c. 54.

[6] 1984 c. 28. Section 63 was amended by S.I. 1998/ No. 2940.

court has finally determined the matters in issue in the claim, whether or not there is an appeal.

(2) For the purposes of this rule, the making of an award of provisional damages under Part 41 will be treated as a final determination of the matters in issue.

(3)(a) A party who is served with a notice of commencement (see paragraph 2.3 below) may apply to a costs judge or a district judge to determine whether the party who served it is entitled to commence detailed assessment proceedings.

(b) On hearing such an application the orders which the court may make include: an order allowing the detailed assessment proceedings to continue, or an order setting aside the notice of commencement.

(4) A costs judge or a district judge may make an order allowing detailed assessment proceedings to be commenced where there is no realistic prospect of the claim continuing.

Rule 47.2 No stay of detailed assessment where there is an appeal

1.2(1) Rule 47.2 provides that detailed assessment is not stayed pending an appeal unless the court so orders.

(2) An application to stay the detailed assessment of costs pending an appeal may be made to the court whose order is being appealed or to the court who will hear the appeal.

Rule 47.3 Powers of an authorised court officer

1.3(1) The court officers authorised by the Lord Chancellor to assess costs in the Supreme Court Costs Office and the Principal Registry of the Family Division are authorised to deal with claims for costs not exceeding £17,500 (excluding VAT) in the case of senior executive officers and £35,000 (excluding VAT) in the case of principal officers.

(2) Where the receiving party, paying party and any other party to the detailed assessment proceedings who has served points of dispute are agreed that the assessment should not be made by an authorised court officer, the receiving party should so inform the court when requesting a hearing date. The court will then list the hearing before a costs judge or a district judge.

(3) In any other case a party who objects to the assessment being made by an authorised court officer must make an application to the costs judge or district judge under Part 23 (General Rules about Applications for Court Orders) setting out the reasons for the objection and if sufficient reason is shown the court will direct that the bill be assessed by a costs judge or district judge.

Rule 47.4 Venue for detailed assessment proceedings

1.4 For the purposes of rule 47.4(1) the "appropriate office" means

(1) the district registry or county court in which the case was being dealt with when the judgment or order was made or the event occurred which gave rise to the right to assessment, or to which it has subsequently been transferred; or

(2) the Principal Registry of the Family Division if the costs in question are the costs of any proceedings which were being dealt with in that registry when the judgment or order was made or when the event occurred which gave rise to the right to assessment, or which have subsequently been transferred to that registry; or

(3) in all other cases, the Supreme Court Costs Office.

1.5(1) A direction under rule 47.4(2) or (3) specifying a particular court, registry or office as the appropriate office may be given on application or on the court's own initiative.

(2) Before making such a direction on its own initiative the court will give the parties the opportunity to make representations.

(3) Unless the Supreme Court Costs Office is the appropriate office for the purposes of Rule 47.4(1) an order directing that an assessment is to take place at the Supreme Court Costs office will be made only if it is appropriate to do so having regard to the size of the bill of costs, the difficulty of the issues involved, the likely length of the hearing, the cost to the parties and any other relevant matter.

Section II—Costs payable by one party to another— commencement of detailed assessment proceedings

Rule 47.6 Commencement of detailed assessment proceedings

47PD–002 **2.1** Form 2 of the Schedule of Costs Forms annexed to this Practice Direction is a model form bill of costs for detailed assessment. Further information about bills of costs is set out in Sections 2 and 3 of the Directions Relating to Part 43.

Not here

2.2 The receiving party must serve on the paying party and all other relevant persons the following documents:

(1) a notice of commencement;

(2) a copy of the bill of costs;

(3) copies of the fee notes of counsel and of any expert in respect of fees claimed in the bill;

(4) written evidence as to any other disbursement which is claimed and which exceeds £250;

(5) a statement giving the name and address for service of any person upon whom the receiving party intends to serve the notice of commencement.

2.3(1) The notice of commencement must be in Form 5 of the Schedule of Costs Forms annexed to this Practice Direction.

Not here

(2) Before it is served it must be completed to show as separate items

(a) the total amount of the bill of costs as drawn;

(b) the additional amounts which will be payable by way of fixed costs and court fees if a default costs certificate is obtained.

(3) The fixed costs payable in respect of solicitors' charges on the issue of a default costs certificate are £80.

2.4(1) This paragraph applies where the notice of commencement is to be served outside England and Wales.

(2) The date to be inserted in the notice of commencement for the paying party to send points of dispute is a date (not less than 21 days from the date of service of the notice) which must be calculated by reference to the Practice Direction supplementing RSC Order 11 as if the notice were a claim form and as if the date to be inserted was the date for the filing of a defence.

2.5(1) For the purposes of rule 47.6(2) a "relevant person" means:

(a) any person who has taken part in the proceedings which gave rise to the assessment and who is directly liable under an order for costs made against him;

(b) any person who has given to the receiving party notice in writing that he has a financial interest in the outcome of the assessment and wishes to be a party accordingly;

(c) any other person whom the court orders to be treated as such.

(2) Where a party is unsure whether a person is or is not a relevant person, that party may apply to the appropriate office for directions.

(3) The court will generally not make an order that the person in respect of whom the application is made will be treated as a relevant person, unless within a specified time he applies to the court to be joined as a party to the assessment proceedings in accordance with Part 19 (Addition and Substitution of Parties).

2.6(1) This paragraph applies in cases in which the bill of costs is capable of being copied onto a computer disk.

(2) If, before the detailed assessment hearing, a paying party requests a disk copy of a bill to which this paragraph applies, the receiving party must supply him with a copy free of charge not more than 7 days after the date on which he received the request.

Rule 47.7 Period for commencing detailed assessment proceedings

2.7 The parties may agree under rule 2.11 (Time limits may be varied by parties) to extend or shorten the time specified by rule 47.7 for commencing the detailed assessment proceedings.

2.8 A party may apply to the appropriate office for an order under rule 3.1(2)(a) to extend or shorten that time.

2.9 Attention is drawn to rule 47.6(1). The detailed assessment proceedings are commenced by service of the documents referred to.

2.10 Permission to commence assessment proceedings out of time is not required.

Rule 47.8 Sanction for delay in commencing detailed assessment proceedings

2.11(1) An application for an order under rule 47.8 must be made in writing and be issued in the appropriate office.

(2) The application notice must be served at least 7 days before the hearing.

Rule 47.9 Points of dispute and consequences of not serving

2.12 The parties may agree under rule 2.11 (Time limits may be varied by parties) to extend or shorten the time specified by rule 47.9 for service of points of dispute. A party may apply to the appropriate office for an order under rule 3.1(2)(a) to extend or shorten that time.

2.13 Points of dispute should be short and to the point and should follow as closely as possible Form 6 of the Schedule of Costs Forms annexed to this Practice Direction.

2.14 Points of dispute must—

(1) identify each item in the bill of costs which is disputed,

(2) in each case state concisely the nature and grounds of dispute,

(3) where practicable suggest a figure to be allowed for each item in respect of which a reduction is sought, and

(4) be signed by the party serving them or his solicitor.

2.15(1) The normal period for serving points of dispute is 21 days after the date of service of the notice of commencement.

(2) Where a notice of commencement is served on a party outside England and Wales the period within which that party should serve points of dispute is to be calculated by reference to the Practice Direction supplementing RSC Order 11 as if the notice of commencement was a claim form and as if the period for serving points of dispute were the period for filing a defence.

2.16 A party who serves points of dispute on the receiving party must at the same time serve a copy on every other party to the detailed assessment proceedings, whose name and address for service appears on the statement served by the receiving party in accordance with paragraph 2.2(5) above.

2.17(1) This paragraph applies in cases in which Points of Dispute are capable of being copied onto a computer disk.

(2) If, within 14 days of the receipt of the Points of Dispute, the receiving party requests a disk copy of them, the paying party must supply him with a copy free of charge not more than 7 days after the date on which he received the request.

Rule 47.10 Procedure where costs are agreed

2.18 Where the parties have agreed terms as to the issue of a costs certificate (either interim or final) they should apply under rule 40.6 (Consent judgments and orders) for an order that a certificate be issued in terms set out in the application. Such an application may be dealt with by a court officer, who may issue the certificate.

2.19 Where the receiving party claims that the paying party has agreed to pay costs but that he will neither pay those costs nor join in a consent application under paragraph 2.18, the receiving party may apply under part 23 (General Rules about Applications for Court Orders) for a certificate either intrim or final to be issued.

2.20 An application under paragraph 2.19 must be supported by evidence and will be heard by a costs judge or a district judge. The respondent to the application must file and serve any evidence he relies on at least two days before the hearing date.

2.21 Nothing in rule 47.10 prevents parties who seek a judgment or order by consent from including in the draft a term that a party shall pay to another party a specified sum in respect of costs.

2.22(1) The receiving party may discontinue the detailed assessment proceedings in accordance with Part 38 (Discontinuance).

(2) Where the receiving party discontinues the detailed assessment proceedings before a detailed assessment hearing has been requested, the paying party may apply to the appropriate office for an order about the costs of the detailed assessment proceedings.

(3) Where a detailed assessment hearing has been requested the receiving party may not discontinue unless the court gives permission.

(4) A bill of costs may be withdrawn by consent whether or not a detailed assessment hearing has been requested.

Section III—Costs payable by one party to another—default provisions

Rule 47.11 Default costs certificate

47PD–003 **3.1** A request for the issue of a default costs certificate must be made in Form 7 of the Schedule of Costs Forms annexed to this Practice Direction and must be signed by the receiving party or his solicitor.

3.2 The request must be filed at the appropriate office.

3.3 A default costs certificate will be in Form 9 or Form 10 of the Schedule of Costs Forms annexed to this Practice Direction.

3.4 Attention is drawn to Rules 40.3 (Dawing up and Filing of Judgments and Orders) and 40.4 (Services of Judgments and Orders) which apply to the preparation and service of a default costs certificate. The receiving party will be treated as having permission to draw up a default costs certificate by virtue of this Practice Direction.

3.5 The issue of a default costs certificate does not prohibit, govern or affect any detailed assessment of the same costs which is made pursuant to the Legal Aid Act 1988.

3.6 An application for an order staying enforcement of a default costs certificate may be made either—

(1) to a costs judge or district judge of the court office which issued the certificate; or

(2) to the court (if different) which has general jurisdiction to enforce the certificate.

3.7 Proceedings for enforcement of default costs certificates may not be issued in the Supreme Court Costs Office.

Rule 47.12 Setting aside default costs certificate

3.8(1) A court officer may set aside a default costs certificate at the request of the receiving party under rule 47.12(3).

(2) A costs judge or a district judge will make any other order or give any directions under this rule.

3.9(1) An application for an order under rule 47.12(2) to set aside or vary a default costs certificate must be supported by evidence.

(2) In deciding whether to set aside or vary a certificate under rule 47.12(2) the matters to which the court must have regard include whether the party seeking the order made the application promptly.

(3) As a general rule a default costs certificate will be set aside under rule 47.12(2) only if the applicant shows a good reason for the court to do so and if he files with his application a draft of the points of dispute he proposes to serve if his application is granted.

3.10(1) Attention is drawn to rule 3.1(3) (which enables the court when making an order to make it subject to conditions) and to rule 44.3(8) (which enables the court to order a party whom it has ordered to pay costs to pay an amount on account before the costs are assessed).

(2) A costs judge or a district judge may exercise the power of the court to make an order under rule 44.3(8) although he did not make the order about costs which led to the issue of the default costs certificate.

3.11 If a default costs certificate is set aside the court will give directions for the management of the detailed assessment proceedings.

Section IV—Costs payable by one party to another—procedure where points of dispute are served

Rule 47.13 Optional reply

4.1 Where the receiving party wishes to serve a reply he must also serve a copy on every party to the detailed assessment proceedings. The time for doing so is within 21 days after service of the points of dispute. **47PD–004**

Rule 47.14 Detailed assessment hearing

4.2 The time for requesting a detailed assessment hearing is within 3 months of the expiry of the period for commencing detailed assessment proceedings.

4.3 The request for a detailed assessment hearing must be in form 8 of the Schedule of Costs Forms annexed to this Practice Direction. The request must be accompanied by: Not there

(a) a copy of the notice of commencement of detailed assessment proceedings;

(b) a copy of the bill of costs;

(c) the document giving the right to detailed assessment (see paragraph 4.5 below);

(d) a copy of the points of dispute, annotated as necessary in order to show which items have been agreed and their value and to show which items remain in dispute and their value;

(e) as many copies of the points of dispute so annotated as there are persons who have served points of dispute;

(f) a copy of any replies served;

(g) a copy of all orders made by the court relating to the costs which are to be assessed;

(h) copies of the fee notes and other written evidence as served on the paying party in accordance with paragraph (2.2) above;

(i) where there is a dispute as to the receiving party's liability to pay costs to the solicitors who acted for the receiving party, any letter or other written information provided by the solicitor to his client explaining how the solicitor's charges are to be calculated;

(j) a statement signed by the receiving party or his solicitor giving the name, address for service, reference and telephone number and fax number, if any, of—

(i) the receiving party
(ii) the paying party;
(iii) any other person who has served points of dispute or who has given notice to the receiving party under paragraph 2.5 above;

and giving an estimate of the length of time the detailed assessment hearing will take;

(k) where the application for a detailed assessment hearing is made by a party other than the receiving party, such of the documents set out in this parargraph as are in the possession of that party;

(l) where the court is to assess the costs of an assisted person—
(i) the legal aid certificate, any amendment certificates, any authorities and any certificates of discharge or revocation of legal aid;
(ii) a certificate, in Form 4(2) of the Schedule of Costs Forms annexed to this Practice Direction;
(iii) if the assisted person has a financial interest in the detailed assessment hearing and wishes to attend, the postal address of that person to which the court will send notice of any hearing;
(iv) if the rates payable out of the legal aid fund are prescribed rates, a schedule to the bill of costs setting out all the items in the bill which are claimed against other parties calculated at the legal aid prescribed rates with or without any claim for enhancement: (further information as to this schedule is set out in Section IX (Legal aid costs at prescribed rates below));
(v) a copy of any default costs certificate in respect of costs claimed in the bill of costs.

4.4(1) This paragraph applies to any document described in paragraph 4.3(i) above which the receiving party has filed in the appropriate office. The document must be the latest relevant version and in any event have been filed not more than 2 years before filing the request for a detailed assessment hearing.

(2) In respect of any documents to which this paragraph applies, the receiving party may, instead of filing a copy of it, specify in the request for a detailed assessment hearing the case number under which a copy of the document was previously filed.

4.5 "The document giving the right to detailed assessment" means such one or more of the following documents as are appropriate to the detailed assessment proceedings:

(a) a copy of the judgment or order of the court giving the right to detailed assessment;

(b) a copy of the notice served under rule 3.7 (sanctions for non-payment of certain fees) where a claim is struck out under that rule;

(c) a copy of the notice of acceptance where an offer to settle is accepted under Part 36 (Offers to settle and payments into court);

(d) a copy of the notice of discontinuance in a case which is discontinued under Part 38 (Discontinuance);

(e) a copy of the award made on an arbitration under any Act or pursuant to an agreement, where no court has made an order for the enforcement of the award;

(f) a copy of the order, award or determination of a statutorily constituted tribunal or body;

(g) in a case under the Sheriffs Act 1887, the sheriff's bill of fees and charges, unless a court order giving the right to detailed assessment has been made;

(h) a notice of revocation or discharge under Regulation 82 of the Civil Legal Aid (General) Regulations 1989.

4.6 On receipt of the request for a detailed assessment hearing the court will fix a date for the hearing, or, if the costs officer so decides, will give directions or fix a date for a preliminary appointment.

4.7(1) The court will give at least 14 days notice of the time and place of the detailed assessment hearing to every person named in the statement referred to in paragraph 4.3(j) above.

(2) The court will when giving notice, give each person who has served points of dispute a copy of the points of dispute annoted by the receiving party in compliance with paragraph 4.3(d) above.

(3) Attention is drawn to rule 47.14(6)&(7): apart from the receiving party, only those who have served points of dispute may be heard on the detailed assessment unless the court gives permission, and only items specified in the points of dispute may be raised unless the court gives permission.

4.8(1) If the receiving party does not file a request for a detailed assessment hearing within the prescribed time, the paying party may apply to the court to fix a time within which the receiving party must do so. The sanction, for failure to request a detailed assessment hearing within the time specified by the court, is that all or part of the costs may be disallowed (see rule 47.8(2)).

(2) Where the receiving party requests a detailed assessment hearing after the time specified in the rules but before the paying party has made an application to the court to specify a time, the only sanction which the court may impose is to disallow all or part of the interest which would otherwise be payable for the period of delay, unless the court exercises its powers under rule 44.14 (court's powers in relation to misconduct).

4.9 If either party wishes to make an application in the detailed assessment proceedings the provisions of Part 23 (General Rules about Applications for Court Orders) apply.

4.10(1) This paragraph deals with the procedure to be adopted where a date has been given by the court for a detailed assessment hearing and

- (a) the detailed assessment proceedings are settled; or
- (b) a party to the detailed assessment proceedings wishes to apply to vary the date which the court has fixed; or
- (c) the parties to the detailed assessment proceedings agree about changes they wish to make to any direction given for the management of the detailed assessment proceedings.

(2) If detailed assessment proceedings are settled, the receiving party must give notice of that fact to the court immediately, preferably by fax.

(3) A party who wishes to apply to vary a direction must do so in accordance with Part 23 (General Rules about Applications for Court Orders).

(4) If the parties agree about changes they wish to make to any direction given for the management of the detailed assessment proceedings:—

- (a) they must apply to the court for an order by consent; and
- (b) they must file a draft of the directions sought and an agreed statement of the reasons why the variation is sought; and
- (c) the court may make an order in the agreed terms or in other terms without a hearing, but it may direct that a hearing is to be listed.

4.11(1) If a party wishes to vary his bill of costs, points of dispute or a reply, an amended or supplementary document must be filed with the court and copies of it must be served on all other relevant parties.

(2) Permission is not required to vary a bill of costs, points of dispute or a reply but the court may disallow the variation or permit it only upon conditions, including conditions as to the payment of any costs caused or wasted by the variation.

4.12 Unless the court directs otherwise the receiving party must file with the court the papers in support of the bill not less than 7 days before the date for the detailed assessment hearing and not more than 14 days before that date.

4.13 The papers to be filed in support of the bill and the order in which they are to be arranged, are as follows:

(i) instructions and briefs to counsel arranged in chronological order together with all advices, opinions and drafts received in response to such instructions;

(ii) reports and opinions of medical and other experts arranged in chronological order;
(iii) correspondence files and attendance notes;
(iv) any other relevant papers;
(v) in detailed assessment proceedings to which rule 48.9 (Conditional Fees) applies, a copy of the conditional fee agreements;
(vi) in detailed assessment proceedings in proceedings which commenced before 26 April 1999, a full set of any relevant pleadings which have been served by the parties but not filed at court.

4.14 Once the detailed assessment hearing has ended it is the responsibility of the legal representative appearing for the receiving party or, as the case may be, the receiving party in person to remove the papers filed in support of the bill.

Section V—Interim costs certificate and final costs certificate

Rule 47.15 Power to issue an interim certificate

47PD–005 **5.1**(1) A party wishing to apply for an interim certificate may do so by making an application in accordance with Part 23 (General Rules about Applications for Court Orders).

(2) Attention is drawn to the fact that the court's power to issue an interim certificate arises only after the receiving party has filed a request for a detailed assessment hearing.

Rule 47.16 Final costs certificate

5.2 At the detailed assessment hearing the court will indicate any disallowance or reduction in the sums claimed in the bill of costs by making an appropriate note on the bill.

5.3 Where the bill of costs is in the form illustrated in Form 2 of the Schedule of Costs Forms annexed to this Practice Direction, the receiving party must, in order to complete the bill after the detailed assessment hearing, enter in the fourth and fifth columns of the bill, the correct figures agreed or allowed in respect of each item and must re-calculate the summary of the bill appropriately.

5.4 The completed bill of costs must be filed with the court no later than 14 days after the detailed assessment hearing.

5.5 At the same time as filing the completed bill of costs, the party whose bill it is must also produce receipted free notes and receipted accounts in respect of all disbursements except those covered by a certificate in Form 4(4) in the Schedule of Costs Forms annexed to this Practice Direction.

5.6 No final costs certificate will be issued until all relevant court fees payable on the assessment of costs have been paid.

5.7 If the receiving party fails to file a completed bill in accordance with rule 47.16 the paying party may make an application under Part 23 (General Rules about Applications for Court Orders) seeking an appropriate order under rule 3.1 (The court's general powers of management).

5.8 A final costs certificate will show:
(a) the amount of any costs which have been agreed between the parties or which have been allowed on detailed assessment;
(b) where applicable the amount agreed or allowed in respect of VAT on the costs agreed or allowed.

This provision is subject to any contrary provision made by the statutory provisions relating to legal aid.

5.9 A final costs certificate will include disbursements in respect of the fees of counsel only if receipted fee notes or accounts in respect of those disbursements have been produced to the court and only to the extent indicated by those receipts.

5.10 Where the certificate relates to costs payable between parties a separate certificate will be issued for each party entitled to costs.

5.11 Model forms of an interim costs certificate (Form 11) and final costs certificates (Forms 12 and 13) are included in the Schedule of Costs Forms annexed to this Practice Direction.

5.12 An application for an order staying enforcement of a interim costs certificate or final costs certificate may be made either:

(1) to a costs judge or district judge of the court office which issued the certificate; or

(2) to the court (if different) which has general jurisdiction to enforce the certificate.

5.13 Proceedings for enforcement of interim costs certificates or final costs certificates may not be issued in the Supreme Court Costs Office.

Section VI—Detailed assessment procedure for costs of an assisted person payable out of the legal aid fund

Rule 47.17 Detailed assessment procedure where costs are payable out of the legal aid fund

6.1 The provisions of this section apply where the court is to assess costs which are payable only out of the legal aid fund. Sections IV and IX apply in cases involving costs by another person as well as costs payable only out of the legal aid fund. 47PD–006

6.2 The time for requesting a detailed assessment of legal aid costs is within 3 months after the date when the right to detailed assessment arose.

6.3 The request for a detailed assessment of legal aid costs must be in Form 8 of the Schedule of Costs forms annexed to this Practice Direction. The request must be accompanied by:

(a) a copy of the bill of costs;

(b) the document giving the right to detailed assessment (for further information as to this document, see paragraph 4.5 above);

(c) a copy of all orders made by the court relating to the costs which are to be assessed;

(d) copies of any fee notes of counsel and any expert in respect of fees claimed in the bill;

(e) written evidence as to any other disbursement which is claimed and which exceeds £250;

(f) the legal aid certificates, any amendment certificates, any authorities and any certificates of discharge or revocation of legal aid;

(g) the relevant papers in support of the bill as described in paragraph 4.13, above;

(h) a statement signed by the solicitor giving his name, address for service reference, telephone number and fax number if any and, if the assisted person has a financial interest in the detailed assessment and wishes to attend, giving the postal address of that person, to which the court will send notice of any hearing:

6.4 Rule 47.17 provides that the court will hold a detailed assessment hearing if the assisted person has a financial interest in the detailed assessment and wishes to attend. The court may also hold a detailed assessment hearing in any other case, instead of provisionally asssessing a bill of costs, where it considers that a hearing is necessary. Before deciding whether a hearing is necessary under this rule, the court may require the solicitor whose bill it is, to provide further information relating to the bill.

6.5 Where the court has provisionally assessed a bill of costs, it will send to the solicitor a notice in Form 14 in the Schedule of Costs Forms annexed to this Practice Direction the amount of costs which the court proposes to allow together with the bill itself.

6.6 The court will fix a date for a detailed assessment hearing if the solicitor informs the court within 14 days after he receives the notice of amount allowed on provisional assessment that he wants the court to hold such a hearing.

6.7 The court will give at least 14 days notice of the time and place of the detailed assessment hearing to the solicitor and, if the assisted person has a financial interest in the detailed assessment and wishes to attend, to the assisted person.

6.8 If the solicitor whose bill it is, or any other party wishes to make an application in the detailed assessment proceedings, the provisions of Part 23 (General Rules about Applications for Court Orders) applies.

Section VII—Costs of detailed assessment proceedings

Rule 47.18 Liability for costs of detailed assessment proceedings

47PD–007 **7.1** As a general rule the court will assess the receiving party's costs of the detailed assessment proceedings and add them to the bill of costs.

7.2 If the costs of the detailed assessment proceedings are awarded to the paying party, the court will either assess those costs by summary assessment or make an order for them to be decided by detailed assessment.

7.3 Attention is drawn to the fact that in deciding what order to make about the costs of detailed assessment proceedings the court must have regard to the conduct of all parties, the amount by which the bill of costs has been reduced and whether it was reasonable for a party to claim the costs of a particular item or to dispute that item.

Rule 47.19 Offers to settle without prejudice save as to the costs of the detailed assessment proceedings

7.4 Rule 47.19 allows the court to take into account offers to settle, without prejudice save as to the costs of detailed assessment proceedings, when deciding who is liable for the costs of those proceedings. The rule does not specify a time within which such an offer should be made. An offer made by the paying party should usually be made within 14 days after service of the notice of commencement on that party. If the offer is made by the receiving party it should normally be made within 14 days after the service of points of dispute by the paying party. Offers made after these periods are likely to be given less weight by the court in deciding what order as to costs to make unless there is good reason for the offer not being made until the later time.

7.5 Where an offer to settle is accepted, an application may be made for a certificate in agreed terms, or the bill of costs may be withdrawn, in accordance with rule 47.10 (Procedure where costs are agreed).

7.6 Where the receiving party is an assisted person, an offer to settle without prejudice save as to the costs of the detailed assessment proceedings will not have the consequences specified under rule 47.19 unless the court so orders.

Section VIII—Appeal against decisions in detailed assessment proceedings

Rule 47.23 Duty to seek reasons

47PD–008 **8.1** A party wishing to appeal must request written reasons for the decision in accordance in rule 47.23 and obtain the court's permission in accordance with rule 47.24 unless the court orders otherwise. The request must be made in writing and filed at the end of the detailed assessment hearing or subsequently in accordance with rule 47.23(2) and (3). A request for written reasons made by one party will be treated as a request made by all parties.

8.2 Attention is drawn to the time limits for requesting written reasons. In the case of the receiving party this is 14 days after the detailed assessment hearing (i.e. when the completed bill of costs is filed). In the case of the paying party it is within 7 days after the detailed assessment hearing.

8.3 A request for written reasons must clearly identify the particular parts of the decision for which reasons are requested.

8.4 Before it gives written reasons the court may require the party seeking reasons to file a note of the decision in question and of the reasons which the court gave for it at the hearing.

8.5 Where a party requests written reasons the court may refuse the request. Such a refusal will usually be made only where the reasons underlying the decision are sufficiently recorded on the bill itself or in a note of the hearing which has been approved by the court.

8.6 The court will usually direct that written reasons are not necessary where the decision to be appealed against was a case management decision rather than a decision on the substance of the assessment proceedings.

8.7 A case management decision is one which does not decide the merits of the assessment proceedings. Examples are a decision to allow or refuse an extension of time, to adjourn proceedings or to add a party to the proceedings.

8.8 Where the court exercises any of its general case management powers under Part 3 the decision will generally be a case management decision.

8.9 Where written reasons are given the court will serve a copy of them on every party to the detailed assessment proceedings.

Rule 47.24 Obtaining the court's permission to appeal

8.10 A party may request permission to appeal by letter delivered to the court and copied to the other parties. The letter must correctly set out the title of the action and the court reference. It must also set out the basis upon which permission is sought.

8.11 As a general rule the court will not rule upon a request for permission to appeal without first providing written reasons for the decision to which the request relates or without first dispensing with the need for written reasons.

8.12 Attention is drawn to the time limits for seeking permission to appeal i.e. 14 days after receiving written reasons; or, if the court directs that no written reasons are required, within 7 days after service of that direction.

8.13 The time limit for appeal will be calculated without taking into account the day upon which the letter requesting permission was delivered to the court, the day upon which the party wishing to appeal received the court's reply to that letter or any day in between those days. (See rule 2.8 (Time).)

8.14 In considering an application for permission to appeal the court will take into account:

(1) whether the ground of appeal has a reasonable prospect of success;

(2) whether the costs of the appeal are likely to be disproportionate; this factor is particularly relevant where the appeal is as to quantum only;

(3) if the appeal is against a case management decision, whether an appeal at that stage in the proceedings is appropriate.

Rule 47.25 Appeal procedure

8.15 The time for filing notice of appeal is set out at rule 47.25. Attention is drawn to the fact that permission is not required to appeal against the decision of an authorised court officer or in respect of a decision of a Costs Judge or District Judge against a legal representative in relation to misconduct or in respect of wasted costs.

8.16 A notice of appeal against the decision of a Costs Officer must be in Form 16 of the Schedule of Costs Forms annexed to this Practice Direction. The Notice must set out the grounds of appeal.

8.17(1) If it is necessary to obtain the court's permission to appeal and the Costs Officer refuses to give permission, the party wishing to appeal must, before filing a notice of appeal, apply to the High Court Judge or Circuit Judge, as the case may be, on notice requesting permission.

(2) A copy of that notice must be served on all other parties who may be affected by the appeal.

(3) If the Judge who deals with the application grants permission to appeal, the order made will extend the time for appealing.

(4) The extended period will be as stated in the order, or, if no period is stated will be the period up to 7 days after the date of the Judge's decision to give permission to appeal.

8.18 Where a decision of a costs judge or district judge on an appeal from an authorised court officer is taken on further appeal to a High Court Judge or a Circuit Judge, the appellant must, before the hearing of the further appeal, file a note of the decision given by the costs judge or district judge. The note filed must be agreed (if possible) with the other parties to the appeal and must be approved by the costs judge or district judge.

Section IX—Legal aid costs at prescribed rates

47PD–009 **9.1** This section applies to a bill of costs of an assisted person which is payable by another person where the costs which can be claimed out of the legal aid fund are restricted to legal aid prescribed rates (with or without enhancement).

9.2 Where this section applies, the solicitor of the assisted person must file a legal aid schedule in accordance with Paragraph 4.3(1) above. The schedule should follow as closely as possible Form 3 of the Schedule of Costs Forms annexed to this Practice Direction.

9.3 The schedule must set out by reference to the item numbers in the bill of costs, all the costs claimed as payable by another person, but the arithmetic in the schedule should claim those items at prescribed rates only (with or without any claim for enhancement).

9.4 Where there has been a change in the prescribed rates during the period covered by the bill of costs, the schedule (as opposed to the bill) should be divided into separate parts, so as to deal separately with each change of rate. The schedule must also be divided so as to correspond with any divisions in the bill of costs.

9.5 Costs which are claimed as payable only out of the legal aid fund should be set out in a separate part or parts of the schedule.

9.6 The detailed assessment of the legal aid schedule will take place immediately after the detailed assessment of the bill of costs.

9.7 Attention is drawn to the possibility that, on occasions, the court may decide to conduct the detailed assessment of the legal aid schedule separately from any detailed assessment of the bill of costs. This will occur, for example, where a default costs certificate is obtained as between the parties but that certificate is not set aside at the time of the detailed assessment pursuant to the Legal Aid Act 1988.

PART 48

Costs—Special Cases

Contents 48.0.1

(The definitions contained in Part 43 are relevant to this Part.)

I. Costs Payable by or to Particular Persons

Pre-commencement disclosure and orders for disclosure against a person who is not a party

48.1—(1) This paragraph applies where a person applies— 48.1

(a) for an order under—

(i) section 33 of the Supreme Court Act 1981[1]; or

(ii) section 52 of the County Courts Act 1984,[2]

(which give the court powers exercisable before commencement of proceedings); or

(b) for an order under—

(i) section 34 of the Supreme Court Act 1981[3]; or

(ii) section 53 of the County Cours Act 1984,[4]

(which give the court power to make an order against a non-party for disclosure of documents, inspection of property, etc.).

(2) The general rule is that the court will award the person against whom the order is sought his costs—

(a) of the application; and

[1] 1981 c. 54. Section 33 was amended by S.I. 1998/2940.

[2] 1984 c. 28. Section 52 was amended by the Courts and Legal Services Act 1990 (c. 41), Schedule 18, paragraph 43 and by S.I. 1998/2940.

[3] 1981 c. 54. Section 34 was amended by S.I. 1998/2940.

[4] 1984 c. 28. Section 53 was amended by the Courts and Legal Services Act 1990 (c. 41), Schedule 18, paragraph 44 and S.I. 1998/2940.

(b) of complying with any order made on the application.

(3) The court may however make a different order, having regard to all the circumstances, including—

(a) the extent to which it was reasonable for the person against whom the order was sought to oppose the application; and

(b) whether the parties to the application have complied with any relevant pre-action protocols.

48.1.1 **Comment**—In relation to pre-commencement disclosure the court will normally award the costs of the application and the costs of complying with any order for disclosure, inspection, etc., in favour of the party against whom the order is sought. If, however, that party has unreasonably opposed the application or failed to comply with any relevant pre-action protocol, the court may well make a different order.

Costs orders in favour of or against non-parties

48.2 **48.2**—(1) Where the court is considering whether to exercise its power under section 51 of the Supreme Court Act 1981[5] (costs are in the discretion of the court) to make a costs order in favour of or against a person who is not a party to proceedings—

(a) that person must be added as a party to the proceedings for the purposes of costs only; and

(b) he must be given a reasonable opportunity to attend a hearing at which the court will consider the matter further.

(2) This rule does not apply—

(a) where the court is considering whether to—

(i) make an order against the Legal Aid Board;

(ii) make a wasted costs order (as defined in 48.7); and

(b) in proceedings to which 48.1 applies (pre-commencement disclosure and orders for disclosure against a person who is not a party).

48.2.1 **Comment**—Section 51 of the Supreme Court Act 1981 (see SCP 1999, Vol. 2, para. 20A–401) gives the court full power to determine by whom and to what extent costs are to be paid. The Court of Appeal has laid down guidelines for the exercise of this power, see *Symphony Group Plc v. Hodgson* 1993 4 All E.R. 143, CA. The following are material considerations.

(1) An order for the payment of costs by a non-party would always be exceptional. The judge should treat any application for such an order with considerable caution.

(2) It would be even more exceptional for an order for the payment of costs to be made against a non-party where the applicant had a cause of action against the non-party, and could have joined him as a party to the original proceedings.

(3) Even if the applicant could provide a good reason for not joining the non-party against whom he had a valid cause of action, he should warn the non-party at the earliest opportunity of the possibility that he might seek to apply for costs against him.

(4) An application for payment of costs by a non-party should normally be determined by the trial judge (see *Bahai v. Rashidian* [1985] 1 W.L.R. 1337).

(5) The fact that the trial judge in the course of his judgment had expressed views on the conduct of the non-party, neither consistuted bias nor the appearance of bias.

(6) The procedure for the determination of costs is a summary procedure, not necessarily subject to all the rules that would apply in an action. Thus, subject to any relevant statutory exceptions, judicial findings are inadmissible as evidence of the facts upon which they were based in proceedings between one of the parties to the original proceedings and a stranger. Yet in the summary procedure for the determination of the liability of a solicitor to pay the costs of an action to which he was not a party, the judge's findings of fact may be admissible. This departure from basic principles can only be justified if the connection of the non-party with the original proceedings was so close that he will not suffer any injustice by allowing this exception to the general rule.

(7) In so far as the evidence of a witness in proceedings might lead to an application for the costs of those proceedings against him or his company, it introduced yet another exception to a valuable general principle.

(8) The fact that an employee of a company gave evidence in an action did not normally mean that the company was taking part in that action, in so far as that was an allegation relied upon by the party who applied for an order for costs against a non-party.

[5] 1981 c. 54. Section 51 was substituted by section 4(1) of the Courts and Legal Services Act 1990 (c. 41).

(9) The judge should be alert to the possibility that an application for costs against a non-party was motivated by a resentment of an inability to obtain an effective order for costs against a legally aided litigant.

Per Balcombe L.J. *Symphony Group Plc v. Hodgson* [1993] 4 All E.R. 143 (the above is necessarily much reduced and reference should be made to the full judgment).

The discretion to award costs under section 51 of the Supreme Court Act 1981, did not confer jurisdiction on the Court to award costs other than those incurred in the proceedings before it (*Zanussi v. Anglo Venezuelan Real Estate and Agricultural Development Ltd* (1966) *The Times*, April 18).

In circumstances where the judge at first instance had stayed an action because the claimant appeared to be funded by a non-party who would not or could not satisfactorily accept liability to pay the successful opponent's costs, the proper course was to allow the action to proceed to trial, and then, if the need arose, for the defendant to make an application for costs under section 51 of the Supreme Court Act 1981 (*Abraham v. Thompson* [1997] 4 All E.R. 362, CA).

The Court refused to make an order for costs against a legal expenses insurance company since the insurers had not instigated or controlled the litigation and the circumstances did not make it reasonable and just that they should pay the defendants costs (*Murphy v. Young & Co.'s Brewery Plc* [1997] 1 W.L.R. 159, CA).

Where legal expenses insurers took over the defence of an action in circumstances where the defendant, a limited company, was in liquidation, the Court ordered the costs to be paid by the insurers. The decisive factor being, that the insurers took over the defence of the action and conducted it for their own benefit. The defendant took no further part. It could properly be said that the real defendants were the insurers. That factor outweighed any other factors pointing against the making of a costs order (*Pendennis Shipyard Ltd v. Margrathea (Pendennis) Ltd (In liquidation), The Times*, August 27, 1997, DC). In a case where insurers of a negligent and impecunious defendant were found liable to indemnify the defendant and to pay the claimants' costs of the action, the liability for *inter partes* costs was independent of the policy limit and unrestricted, it flowed from the insurers' decision that the action should be defended (*T.G.A. Chapman Ltd. v. Christopher* [1998] 1 W.L.R. 12, CA).

Guidelines may be deduced from *Symphony Group Plc v. Hodgson*; *Murphy v. Young & Co's Brewery Plc* and *TGA Chapman Ltd v. Christopher* (above): two issues need to be considered, first whether there were exceptional circumstances to justify an order against a non party and second to what extent the conduct of that party caused loss to the applicant in the sense of occasioning or increasing the costs, *Bristol & West Plc v. Bhadresa (No. 2), The Times*, November 23, 1998, Lightman J. See also *Globe Equities Ltd v. Globe Legal Services Ltd., The Times*, April 14, 1999, CA. Where the power is to be exercised, the person in respect of whom the order is comtemplated must be made a party to the proceedings and must be given a reasonable opportunity to attend the hearing at which the matter is considered.

The rule does not apply where the court is making an order against the Legal Aid Board (this is dealt with by section 18 of the Legal Aid Act 1988: see SCP 1999, Vol. 2, para. 16A–71); making a wasted costs order (this is governed by r.48.7); or in relation to orders for pre-commencement disclosure against a person who is not a party (see r.48.1 above).

Group litigation—The courts are entitled to devise new procedures adapted to the circumstances of particular group litigation (*Horrocks v. Ford Motor Company Ltd, The Times*, February 15, 1990, CA). There is nothing in the guidance given by appellate courts which precludes a costs sharing order, accordingly an order could be made that any cost incurred or ordered to be paid by any claimant should be paid equally by all claimants (*Chrzanowska v. Glass Laboratories Ltd, The Times*, March 16, 1990). See *Davies (Joseph Owen) v. Eli Lilley* [1987] 1 W.L.R. 1136; [1987] 3 All E.R. 94, for the procedure to be followed in cases where large numbers of claimants, including some who are legally aided, make related claims against the same defendants. (In essence, no difference should be drawn between parties who are legally aided and those who are funding the litigation on a private basis). In group proceedings in which common issues were raised, in lead actions chosen for trial of principal issues, costs sharing orders were made against other defendants (*Re Interest Rate Swap Litigation, The Times*, December 19, 1991). **48.2.2**

Legal Aid—The Court has jurisdiction under s.51 of the Supreme Court Act 1981, to make a costs order against the Board as a non-party, the power is not restricted to the circumstances set out in section 18 of the Legal Aid Act 1988. The Court held that s.18 of the 1988 Act was not a complete code and did not deal with the situation where the Board was at fault. In the exceptional circumstances of the particular case, where both the Board and claimant's solicitors had been at fault, an order was made to protect the claimant who might otherwise have lost a substantial part of her damages by way of set-off against costs thrown away by an adjournment (*Kelly v. South Manchester Health Authority* [1997] 3 All E.R. 274, Thomas J.). **48.2.3**

Amount of costs where costs are payable pursuant to a contract

48.3—(1) Where the court assesses (whether by the summary or detailed **48.3**

procedure) costs which are payable by the paying party to the receiving party under the terms of a contract, the costs payable under those terms are, unless the contract expressly provides otherwise, to be presumed to be costs which—

(a) have been reasonably incurred; and

(b) are reasonable in amount;

and the court will assess them accordingly.

(The costs practice direction sets out circumstances where the court may make order otherwise.)

(2) This rule does not apply where the contract is between a solicitor and his client.

48.3.1 **Comment**—In respect of costs payable under a contract there is a presumption that the costs have been reasonably incurred and were reasonable in amount. However if the terms of the contract are manifestly unreasonable the presumption will be rebutted. In such a case the court may make a special order, for example, reducing or disallowing some or all of the costs recovered, see para 1.1 of the Directions relating to Pt 48 para. 48PD–001). A mortgagee is allowed to reimbruse himself out of the mortgaged property for all costs, charges and expenses reasonably and properly incurred in enforcing or preserving his security. Often the process of enforcement or preservation makes it necessary for him to take or defend proceedings. In regard to such proceedings three propositions may be stated:

(i) The mortgagee's costs, reasonably and properly incurred, of proceedings between himself and the mortgagor or his surety are allowable.

(ii) Allowable also are the mortgagee's costs, reasonably and properly incurred, of proceedings between himself and a third party where what is impugned is the title to the estate.

(iii) But where a third party impugns the title to a mortgage, or the enforcement or exercise of some right or power accruing to the mortgagee thereunder, the mortgagee's costs of the proceedings, even though they be reasonable and properly incurred, are not allowable.

Per Nourse L.J. in *Parker-Tweedale v. Dunbar Bank plc (No. 2)* [1990] 2 All E.R. 588 at 591.

Propositions (i) and (ii) form the general rule (iii) is the exception to it. The general rule is to be found in *Detillin v. Gale* [1802] 7 Ves. 583, 32 E.R. 234; *Dryden v. Frost* [1838] 3 My. & Cr. 670, [1835–42] All E.R. Rep. 390; and *National Provincial Bank of England v. Games* [1886] 31 Ch.D. 582.

The exception is to be found in *Owen v. Crouch* [1857] 5 W.R. 545; *Parker v. Watkins* [1859] John 133, 70 E.R. 369; and *Re Smith's Mortgage, Harrison v. Edwards* [1931] 2 Ch. 168, All E.R. Rep. 698. The decision of the Court of Appeal in *Re Leighton's Conveyance* [1936] 3 All E.R. 1033, [1937] Ch. 149, supports both propositions.

A mortgagee is entitled to recover, under the terms of the mortage deed, the actual costs, charges and expenses incurred, except for any costs that have not been reasonably incurred or were unreasonable in amount. But litigation and non-litigation costs may be referred to a Costs Judge for quantification and the mortgagee is contractually entitled to payment on the indemnity basis. The court's discretion as to the basis of assessment of a mortgagee's costs will normally be exercised so as to correspond with the contractual entitlement. It follows that the judge has power to order that the contractual costs, charges and expenses and the costs incurred in the litigation be assessed on the indemnity basis (*Gomba Holdings (U.K.) Limited v. Minories Finance Limited (No. 2)* [1992] 3 W.L.R. 723).

The Court of Appeal reviewed the law and set out principles which emerge:

(i) An order for the payment of costs of proceedings by one party to another party is always a discretionary order: section 51 of the Supreme Court Act 1981.

(ii) Where there is a contractual right to the costs the discretion should ordinarily be exercised, so as to reflect that contractual right.

(iii) The power of the Court to disallow a mortagee's costs sought to be added to the mortgage security is a power that does not derive from s.51, but from the power of the Courts of Equity to fix the terms on which redemption will be allowed.

(iv) A decision by a Court to refuse costs in whole or in part to a mortgage litigant may be a decision in the exercise of the s.51 discretion; or a decision in the exercise of the power to fix the terms on which redemption will be allowed, or a decision as to the extent of a mortgagee's contractual right to add his costs to the security of a combination of two or more of these things. The pleadings in the case and the submissions made to the Judge may indicate which of the decisions has been made.

(v) A mortgagee is not to be deprived of a contractual or equitable right to add costs to the security, merely by reason of an order for payment of costs made without reference to the mortagee's contractual or equitable rights, and without any adjudication as to whether or not the mortgagee should be deprived of those costs (*Gomba Holdings U.K. Ltd v. Minories Finance Ltd (No. 2)* [1992] 3 W.L.R. 723).

If the mortgagees seek to deduct an excessive sum, the remedy of the defendant mortagor is to ask for an account and to challenge the figure which the claimant mortagees seek to charge for their costs. At that stage the Court would not be bound by the contractual provisions and would be entitled to say that the costs sought to be charged were excessive and could make the appropriate order at that point. This would however depend on the mortagees having behaved unreasonably. *Per* Balcombe L.J. in *Mortgage Funding Corporation plc v. Kashef-Hamadani*, April 26, 1993, CA, unrep.

This rule does not apply to a contract between a solicitor and his client since this is governed by the Solicitors Act, Pt III, ss.56 to 75.

Limitations on court's power to award costs in favour of trustee or personal representative

48.4—(1) This rule applies where— **48.4**

(a) a person is or has been a party to any proceedings in the capacity of trustee or personal representative; and

(b) rule 48.3 does not apply.

(2) The general rule is that where he is entitled to be paid his costs of the proceedings, out of any fund held by him as trustee or personal representative, those costs shall be assessed on the indemnity basis.

(3) The court may order otherwise if a trustee or personal representative has acted for a benefit other than that of the fund.

Comment—As a general rule a trustee or personal representative is entitled to the costs of any proceedings brought in that capacity on the indemnity basis. Frequently the court orders that such costs are payable out of the trust fund, see *Re Beddoe* [1893] 1 Ch. 547. **48.4.1**

Amended by S.I. 1999 No. 1008.

Costs where money is payable by or to a child or patient

48.5—(1) This rule applies to any proceedings where the claimant is a child or patient and— **48.5**

(a) money is ordered or agreed to be paid to, or for the benefit of, that party; or

(b) money is ordered to be paid by him or on his behalf.

("Child" and "patient" are defined in rule 2.3.)

(2) The general rule is that—

(a) the court must order a detailed assessment of the costs payable by any party who is a child or patient to his solicitor; and

(b) on an assessment under paragraph (a), the court must also assess any costs payable to that party in the proceedings, unless the court has issued a default costs certificate in relation to those costs under rule 47.11.

(3) The court need not order detailed assessment of costs in the circumstances set out in the costs practice direction.

(4) Where—

(a) a claimant is a child or patient; and

(b) a detailed assessment has taken place under paragraph (2)(a),

the only amount payable by the child or patient to his solicitor is the amount which the court certifies as payable.

(This rule applies to a counterclaim by or on behalf of a child or patient by virtue of rule 20.3.)

Comment—This rule is designed to protect money belonging to a child or patient, and the court must therefore order detailed assessment of the costs payable by a child or patient to his or her solicitor, and must also carry out an assessment of the costs payable to the child or patient in the proceedings, unless a default costs certificate has been issued in respect of those costs. Where costs are recovered from a paying party on behalf of the child or patient, solicitors frequently waive any further claim for costs, in which case there is no need for a detailed assessment of the solicitor and client costs. **48.5.1**

See para. 1.2 of the Directions relating to Pt 48, see 48PD–001, as to the circumstances in which detailed assessment need not be ordered.

The rule applies equally to a counterclaim by or on behalf of the child or patient; see r.20.3.

Litigants in person

48.6 **48.6**—(1) This rule applies where the court orders (whether by summary assessment or detailed assessment) that the costs of a litigant in person are to be paid by any other person.

(2) The costs allowed under this rule must not exceed, except in the case of a disbursement, two-thirds of the amount which would have been allowed if the litigant in person had been represented by a legal representative.

(3) Costs allowed to the litigant in person shall be—

(a) such costs which would have been allowed if the work had been done or the disbursements made by a legal representative on the litigant in person's behalf;

(b) the payments reasonably made by him for legal services relating to the conduct of the proceedings; and

(c) the costs of obtaining expert assistance in connection with assessing the claim for costs.

(The costs practice direction deals with who may be an expert for the purpose of paragraph (3)(c).)

(4) Subject to paragraph (2), the amount of costs to be allowed to the litigant in person for any item of work to which the costs relate shall, if he fails to prove financial loss, be an amount in respect of the time spent reasonably doing the work at the rate specified in the costs practice direction.

(5) A litigant who is allowed costs for attending at court to conduct his case is not entitled to a witness allowance in respect of such attendance in addition to those costs.

(6) For the purposes of this rule, a litigant in person includes—

(a) a company or other corporation which is acting without a legal representative; and

(b) a barrister, solicitor, solicitor's employee or other authorised litigator (as defined in the Courts and Legal Services Act 1990[6] who is acting for himself.

48.6.1 **Comment**—There is an absolute cap on the amount recoverable by a litigant in person, namely two thirds of the amount which would have been allowed if the litigant in person had been represented by a legal representative. Disbursements, if reasonable, may be recoved in full. Those disbursements may include payment by the litigant in person for legal services relating to the conduct of the proceedings. Lord Woolf envisaged a move towards the supply of partial legal services. A litigant in person may also recover the reasonable costs of obtaining expert assistance in connection with assessing the claim for costs, see para. 1.3 of the Directions relating to Pt 48 (para. 48PD–001) as to who may be an expert for these purposes.

The onus is on the litigant in person to prove financial loss in respect of any item of work and if he fails to do so the amount recoverable is that fixed periodically by statutory instrument (at April 1999, £9.25 per hour). See paras 1.4–1.7 of the Directions relating to Pt 48 (para. 48PD–001) as to the amount payable.

Attention is drawn to the fact that a litigant in person may now include a company or other corporation acting without a legal representative and a barrister, solicitor, solicitor's employee or other authorised litigator acting for himself. The previous exemption for a solicitor acting on his own behalf has been removed although para. 1.7 of the Directions provides a way out of the difficulty. A company acting through an in-house legal representative who is in possession of a practising certificate or equivalent authorisation will not be treated as a litigant in person but the legal representative will be able to recover costs in the normal way on behalf of the company.

48.6.2 **Effect of Rule Prior to the Litigants in Person (Costs and Expenses) Act 1975**—A litigant in person could only recover out of pocket expenses (*Buckland v. Watts* [1970] 1 Q.B. 27; [1969] 2 All E.R. 985, CA. See also Litigants in Person (Costs and Expenses) Act 1975 (Vol. 2, Section 21R, paras 21R–1 to 21R–5). The Litigants in Person (Costs and Expenses) Order 1980 (S.I. 1980 No. 1159) extended the scope to the Employment Appeal Tribunal.

In *Parikh v. Midland Bank Ltd.*, 1982 (unrep.) the Court of Appeal held that a payment made by a doctor litigant to a locum was not a disbursement of the purpose of costs. In *McLeod-Johnson-Hart*

[6] 1900 c. 41.

v. Aga Khan Foundation (U.K.) [1984] 1 All E.R. 239 Lloyd J. held that a litigant was not entitled to a notional disbursement in respect of a brief fee in quantifying two-thirds of the daily attendance fee and also the claim must distinguish between leisure and pecuniary loss time. This decision was upheld by the Court of Appeal [1984] 1 W.L.R. 994; [1984] 2 All E.R. 439).

Although a litigant in person cannot be allowed a notional disbursement in respect of counsel who is not employed that does not mean the costs judge is required to disallow a disbursement actually incurred so as to avoid the necessity of employing not only a solicitor but also counsel; thus a successful defendant is entitled to travelling expenses (from South Africa) to conduct the case in person and to the reasonable costs of travelling in connection with the case (*Law Society v. Persaud, The Times,* May 10, 1990).

Interest on money borrowed by a successful claimant to finance litigation is not costs, and cannot properly be included in an order for costs (*Mann v. Eccott,* June 27, CA (unrep.)).

Calculating the costs of a litigant in person—The exercise is as follows. Find out, in respect of the item, what, at the litigant in person charging rate, the total is. Compare that with two thirds of the notional solicitor rate, give the lower of the two items. That does mean that the bill of costs drawn by the litigant in person must be gone through in some detail item by item. *Per* Jacob J. in *Morris v. Wiltshire & Woodspring District Council,* January 16, 1998, unrep. **48.6.3**

VAT Tribunal—A successful party in proceedings before a VAT tribunal is only entitled to out-of-pocket expenses, with no allowance for time spent, as there is no provision of this in rule 29(1)(a) of the Value Added Tax Tribunals Rules 1986 (S.I. 1986 No. 590) (*Commissioners of Customs & Excise v. Ross* [1990] 2 All E.R. 65): Approved: *Nader v. H.M. Customs & Excise* [1993] S.T.C. 806, CA. **48.6.4**

Official Receiver—In a case in which the Official Receiver obtained disqualification orders in the High Court against three respondents, together with an order for the Official Receiver's costs, the issue arose, in respect of work done by the Official Receiver himself, whether he was entitled to be treated as a litigant in person or whether recovery was limited to out of pocket expenses. The court of Appeal found that the Official Receiver, if unrepresented in the conduct of an application to disqualify a director, was himself a litigant in person for the purpose of assessing and recovering costs. The court also considered whether or not the Official Receiver had suffered financial loss. The court referred with approval to Re: Eastwood (deceased) *Lloyds Bank Ltd v. Eastwood & Ors* [1973] 3 All E.R. 603. The court found that the Official Receiver worked upon the case like the Treasury Solicitor and an employed solicitor. The costs, like the costs of the Treasury Solicitor in *Re Eastwood* were pecuniary in nature and therefore the amount recoverable should be that provided for by the rules. *Re Minotaur Data Systems Ltd* and *The Official Receiver v. Brunt & Ors, The Times,* March 18, 1999, CA. **48.6.5**

II. COSTS RELATING TO SOLICITORS AND OTHER LEGAL REPRESENTATIVES

Personal liability of legal representative for costs—wasted costs orders

48.7—(1) This rule applies where the court is considering whether to make an order under section 51(6) of the Supreme Court Act 1981[7] (court's power to disallow or (as the case may be) order a legal representative to meet, "wasted costs"). **48.7**

(2) The court must give the legal representative a reasonable opportunity to attend a hearing to give reasons why it should not make such an order.

(3) For the purposes of this rule, the court may direct that privileged[GL] documents are to be disclosed to the court and, if the court so directs, to the other party to the application for an order.

(4) When the court makes a wasted costs order, it must specify the amount to be disallowed or paid.

(5) The court may direct that notice shall be given to the legal representative's client, in such manner as the court may direct—

(a) of any proceedings under this rule; or

(b) of any order made under it against his legal representative.

(6) Before making a wasted costs order, the court may direct a costs judge or a district judge to inquire into the matter and report to the court.

[7] 1981 c. 54. Section 51 was substituted by section 4(1) of the Courts and Legal Services Act 1990 (c. 41).

(7) The court may refer the question of wasted costs to a costs judge or a district judge, instead of making a wasted costs order.

48.7.1 **Comment**—The wasted costs provisions are set out in s.51(6) of the Supreme Court Act 1981 and have not been altered. See paras 2.1–2.8 of the Directions relating to Pt 48 (para. 48PD–001) as to the way in which the court will deal with wasted costs applications.

The Rule gives the court power to order that privileged documents be disclosed to the court and, if the court thinks it appropriate, to the other party to the application. Such disclosure would be solely for the purpose of the wasted costs application. The Rule Committee included this provision to overcome difficulties caused by privilege where the court was, in the past, effectively prevented from exercising proper control because the legal representatives were not in a position to rely on documents which might either exonerate or incriminate them. Rule 48.7(3) was held to be *ultra vires* and of no effect by Mr Justice Toulson in *General Mediterranean Holdings S.A. v. Patel*, July 19, 1999, unrep.

The court has power to order that the client be informed of any application for wasted costs and of any order made against the legal representative. Even if the court does not make such an order, r.44.2 has the effect of requiring the legal representative to notify the client of any adverse order made if the client was not present when it was made.

The court may refer the matter to a Costs Judge or District Judge for enquiry and report, or may leave it to the Costs Judge or District Judge to deal with the matter.

48.7.2 **Supreme Court Act 1981, s.51**—Section 4 of the Courts and Legal Services Act 1996 substitutes a new section 51 in the Supreme Court Act 1981. The new section provides *inter alia*, that the court may disallow, or order the legal or other representative to meet, the whole or part of any wasted costs. "Wasted costs" means any costs incurred by a party—

(a) as a result of any improper, unreasonable or negligent act or omission on the part of any legal or other representative or any employee of such a representative; or
(b) which, in the light of any such act or omission occurring after they were incurred, the court considers it unreasonable to expect that party to pay.

48.7.3 **Wasted costs orders**—The Court of Appeal has considered in detail the wasted costs jurisdiction introduced by the Courts and Legal Services Act 1990 (*Ridehalgh v. Horsefield*; *Allen v. Unigate Dairies Ltd*; *Roberts v. Coverite (Asphalters) Ltd*; *Philex plc v. Golban*; *Watson v. Watson Antonelli v. Wide Gery Farr (A Firm)*, *The Times*, January 28, 1994, CA). The Court held that while litigants should not be financially prejudiced by the unjustifiable conduct of litigation by their or their opponent's lawyers, the courts in the exercise of the wasted costs jurisdiction, should be astute to control the threat of a new and costly form of satellite litigation. When a wasted costs order was contemplated a three state test should be applied:

(a) Had the legal representative of whom complaint was made acted improperly, unreasonably or negligently?
(b) If so, did such conduct cause the applicant to incur unnecessary costs?
(c) If so, was it, in all the circumstances, just to order the legal representative to compensate the applicant for the whole or part of the relevant costs?

Improper, unreasonable or negligent—"Improper" covered, but not confined to, conduct which would ordinarily be held to justify disbarment, striking off, suspension from practice or other serious professional penalty.

"Unreasonable" aptly described conduct which was was vexatious, designed to harass the other side, rather than advance the resolution of the case, and it made no difference that the conduct was the product of excessive zeal and not impropoer motive.

"Negligence" should be understood in an untechnical way to denote failure to act with the competence reasonably expected of ordinary members of the profession. In adopting that approach the court firmly discountenanced any suggestion that an application for a wasted costs order needed to prove, under the negligence head, anything less than he would had to prove in an action for negligence. See *Saif Ali v. Sydney Mitchell & Co.* [1980] A.C. 198 at 218, 220 (see also *Sampson v. John Boddy Timber Ltd* [1995] 145 New L.J. 851, CA); and *D. Walter & Co. Ltd v. Neville Eckley & Co.* (1997) B.C.C. 331 *per* Sir Richard Scott, V.-C.,).

Pursuing a hopeless case—A personal representative was not to be held to have acted improperly and unreasonably or negligently simply because, he acted for a party who pursued a claim or defence which was plainly doomed to fail. The legal representatives would advise their clients of the perceived weakness of their case and of the risk of failure, but the clients were free to reject advice and insist that cases be litigated.

It was rarely if ever safe for a court to assume that a hopeless case was being litigated on the advice of the lawyers involved. They were there to present the case and it was for the Judge and not the lawyers to judge it.

It was not entirely easy to distinguish by definition between the hopeless case; and the case which amounted to an abuse of the process, but in practice it was not hard to say which was which, and if there was doubt the legal representative was entitled to the benefit of it. (See also *Re O (A*

Minor) (Wasted Costs Application) [1994] 2 F.L.R. 842, Connell J.). (Where at a hearing counsel accepted that an application to suspend a warrant of possession was hopeless, and counsel, with a senior partner of the solicitors behind him, made no application for an adjournment nor gave an explanation of the conduct of the solicitors, it was held that the solicitors had had a reasonable opportunity to show cause why the order should not be made and, whilst the original application was doomed to failure, that did not of itself justify a wasted costs order but the absence of explanation suggested playing for time and the commonplace nature of the original application rendered it unnecessary for the Judge to insist on a full investigation of the solicitors' motivation. *Woolwich Building Society v. Finberg* [1998] P.N.L.R. 216, CA.)

Legal Aid—It was incumbent on the courts to which wasted costs applications were made to bear prominently in mind the peculiar vulnerability of legal representatives acting for assisted persons. *Symphony Group plc v. Hodgson* [1993] 3 W.L.R. 830, 842. It would subvert the benevolent purposes of the legal aid legislation if such representatives were subject to any unusual personal risk, and they should bear prominently in mind that their advice and conduct was no to be tempered by the knowledge that their client was not their paymaster, and so no, in all probability, liable for the costs of the other side (This view was endorsed by Otton L.J. in *Wall v. Lefever* (1997) *The Times*, August 1, CA).

The Court of Appeal has set out the procedure to be adopted where an assisted party has been unsuccessful, and the unassisted party seeks to recover costs against the Legal Aid Board or under the wasted costs jurisdiction: *Re O (A Minor) (Costs: Liability of the Legal Aid Board)* [1997] 1 F.L.R. 465, CA.

Where a party is legally aided the solicitor is under a duty (see Civil Legal Aid (General) Regulations 1989, reg. 82(2)) to serve notice of revocation or discharge of legal aid on all other parties to the proceedings and also on counsel and on the Court hearing the matter. Failure to do so could amount to unreasonable behaviour and costs suffered by other parties as a result of the failure should not be borne by the Legal Aid Board: *Banks v. Woodhall Duckham Ltd; Bank v. British Steel Corporation; Banks v. Brown Tawse Ltd; Banks v. Humphrey & Glasgow, sub nom. Re Stathams (Wasted Costs Order)* [1997] P.I.Q.R. P464, CA.

Where the Legal and Certificates of both parties in a partnership dispute, were discharged, and a wasted costs order was made against the plaintiff's representatives for passing the action pending appeal against discharge, the Court of Appeal held that the court should be slow to supplement stationary or supplementary duties by placing a higher standard on the parties. No order as to costs was substituted. *Tate v. Hart*, March 1, 1999, CA (unrep.).

Immunity—A barrister and a solicitor acting as advocate was immune from action for negligence at the suit of a client in respect of his conduct and management of a case in court, and the pre-trial work immediately connected with it (*Rondel v. Worsley* [1969] 1 A.C. 191, and *Saif Ali v. Sydney Mitchell*, above).

If an advocate's conduct in court was improper, unreasonable or negligent he was liable to a wasted costs order, subject to the qualification that, although the court was satisfied that the legislation intended to encroach on the traditional immunity of the advocate, by subjecting him to the wasted costs jurisdiction, it did not follow that the public interest considerations on which the immunity was founded were to be regarded as irrelevant or lacking in weight.

A judge must make full allowance for the fact that an advocate in court often had to make decisions quickly and under pressure. Mistakes would inevitably be made, things done which the outcome showed to have been unwise. Advocacy was more an art than a science and it could not be conducted according to formulae. It was only when, with all allowances made, an advocate's conduct of court proceedings was quite plainly unjustifiable that it would be appropriate to make a wasted costs order against him.

Privilege—If the applicant's privileged communications were germane to the application he could waive privilege, and if he declined to do so, adverse inferences could be drawn. The respondent's lawyers were in a different position. The privilege was not theirs to waive. Judges invited to make such orders should make full allowance for the inability of the respondent lawyers to tell the whole story. Where there was room for doubt the respondent lawyers were entitled to the benefit of it. It was only when, with all allowances made, a lawyer's conduct of proceedings was quite plainly unjustifiable, that it could be appropriate to make the order.

Causation—Demonstration of the causal link between the improper, unreasonable, or negligent conduct and the waste of costs was essential. Where conduct was proved but no waste of costs shown to have resulted the case might be referred to the appropriate disciplinary body or the legal aid authorities. It was not a matter for the exercise of the wasted costs jurisdiction.

Reliance on counsel—A solicitor did not abdicate his professional responsibility when he sought the advice of counsel. He had to apply his mind to the advice received. The more specialist the nature of the advice, the more reasonable it was likely to be for him to accept it (*Locke v. Camberwell H.A.* [1991] 2 Med. L.R. 249) (and see *Reaveley v. Safeway Stores plc* [1998] P.N.L.R. 526, CA).

Threats to apply for wasted costs orders—Such threats should not be made as a means of intimidation. If one side considered that the conduct of the other was improper, unreasonable or negligent, and was likely to cause a waste of costs it was not objectionale to alert the other side to that view.

Timing of the application—In general wasted costs application were best left until after the end of the trial (*Film Lab Systems International Ltd v. Pennington* [1994] 4 All E.R. 673, DC).

The applicant—The court itself might initiate the enquiry, but save in the most obvious case courts should be slow to initiate the enquiry. The courts would usually be well advised to leave an aggrieved party to make the application. The costs would then in the ordinary way follow the event between the parties.

Procedure—The procedure to be followed was to be laid down by courts so as to the meet the requirements of the individual case before them. The overriding requirements were that any procedure had to be fair and as simple and summary as fairness permitted. The respondent lawyer was to be very clearly told what he was said to have done wrong and what was claimed. The requirements of simplicity and summariness meant that elaborate pleadings should in general be avoided. No formal process of discovery would be appropriate. The court could not imagine any circumstances in which the applicant should be permitted to interrogate the respondent lawyer or vice versa. Hearings should be measured in hours not days or weeks.

When an application for a wasted costs order has been settled, the Court should be provided with a succinct written statement giving information as to matters relevant to the reputations of the lawyers which would otherwise not be brought to the Court's attention (*Manzanilla Ltd v. Corton Property & Investments Ltd* (1997) *The Times*, August 4, CA).

Fairness requires that any respondent legal representative must be told very clearly what is alleged to have been done wrong and what is claimed. There should be no pleadings and discovery is not appropriate. The applicant will not be permitted to interrogate the respondent lawyer or vice versa. *Per* Pumfrey J. in *S. v. M. (Wasted Costs Order), The Times*, March 26, 1998.

An application for a wasted costs order was held to be inappropriate where complicated proceedings requiring detailed investigation into the facts would ensue as the procedure was a summary one to be applied in uninvolved and clear cases where unnecessary costs were incurred. *Manzanilla Ltd v. Corton Property* (above) followed. The summary procedure might also be inappropriate in circumstances where a solicitor was alleged to be in breach of his professional duty to his client. *Turner Page Music v. Torres Design Associates Ltd, The Times*, August 3, 1998, CA.

In deciding whether or not to make a wasted costs order on the basis of negligent non disclosure on an application without notice the court held that section 51(7) of the Supreme Court Act 1981 did not require knowing complicity of a legal representative. A solicitor did not have to know he was failing to make a disclosure which he ought to make, it was sufficient if he knew of a material fact which was not disclosed but negligently or unreasonably believed it was not material or negligently failed to make enquiries which would have revealed material matters; *Lowline (PSV) Ltd v. Direct Aviation Ltd*, April 15, 1999, Rix J. (unrep.).

Rule 48.9(2) provides that the court must give the legal representative opportunity to show cause why an order should not be made. That should not be understood to mean that the burden was on the legal representative to exculpate himself.

An order should not be made unless the applicants satisfied the court, or the court was itself satisfied that an order should be made. The rule clearly envisaged that the representative would not be called on to reply unless an apparently strong prima facie case had been made against him, and the language of the rule recognised a shift in the evidential burden.

Discretion—The jurisdiction to make a wasted costs order depended at two stages on the court's discretion:

(a) At the stage of initial application when the court was invited to give the representative an opportunity to show cause. That was not something to be done automatically. The costs of the enquiries compared with the cost claimed would always be a relevant consideration. The discretion, like any other, was to be exercised judicially, but judges might not infrequently decide that further proceedings were not likely to be justified (and see *Re Freudiana Holdings Ltd, The Times*, December 4, 1995, CA).

(b) The final stage: even if the court were satisfied that legal representatives had acted improperly, unreasonably or negligently so as to waste costs, it was not bound to make an order, but would have to give sustainable reasons for the exercise of its discretion in that way.

Although a legal representative might not be liable for wasted costs under the Supreme Court Act 1981, s.51(6) if he is not acting for a party to the proceedings the Court nevertheless has a general power to order costs under s.51(3) even against someone not representing a party to the proceedings where the legal representative has acted improperly and unreasonably (*Kleinwort Benson v. De Montenegro* [1994] NPC 46, Aldous J.)

General principles—Save in exceptional circumstances, no application for a wasted costs order should in civil litigation be sought against a party's legal representative until after trial. The test to be applied on such an application has to be the same whether the legal representative was acting for a legally aided or for a paying client. No lawyer who acts in the public interest by accepting legally aided clients should stand any greater risk of being ordered to pay costs, than if he acts for a paying client, *per* Aldous J. (*Filmlab Systems International Ltd v. Pennington* [1994] 4 All E.R. 673, DC).

The Court of Appeal summarised the principles derived from *Ridehalgh v. Horsefield* [1994] Ch. 205; *Tolstoy-Miloslavsky v. Aldington* [1996] 1 W.L.R. 736 and *Wall v. Lefever, The Times*, August 1, 1997. The power to make a wasted costs order is to be found in section 51 of the Supreme Court Act 1981, the principles to be applied include:

(a) Improper conduct is that which would be so regarded "according to the consensus of professional (including judicial) opinion". Unreasonable conduct "aptly describes conduct which is vexatious, designed to harass the other side rather than advance the resolution of the case and it makes no difference that the conduct is the product of excessive zeal and not improper motive . . . the acid test is whether the conduct permits of a reasonable explanation". Negligent conduct was to be understood "in an untechnical way to denote failure to act with the competence reasonably to be expected of ordinary members of the profession". (*Ridehalgh.*)

(b) "Legal representatives will . . . whether barristers or solicitors, advise clients of the perceived weakness of their case and of the risk of failure. But clients are free to reject their advice and insist that cases be litigated. It is rarely if ever safe for a Court to assume that a hopeless case is being litigated on the advice of the lawyers involved . . . it is however one thing for a legal representative to present on instructions a case which he regards as bound to fail, it is quite another to lend his assistance to proceedings which are an abuse of the process of the Court . . . it is not entirely easy to distinguish by definition between the hopeless case and the case which amounts to an abuse of the process, but in practice it is not hard to say which is which and if there is doubt the legal representative is entitled to the benefit of it." (*Ridehalgh.*)

(c) "A solicitor does not abdicate his professional responsibility when he seeks the advice of counsel." (*Ridehalgh.*) Where leading and junior counsel have put their signatures to a statement of claim this "did not exonerate the solicitors from their obligations to exercise their own independent judgment to consider whether the claim could properly be pursued, they were not entitled to follow counsel blindly". (*Tolstoy.*)

(d) "The jurisdiction to make a wasted costs order must be exercised with care and only in clear cases." (*Tolstoy.*) "It should not be used to create satellite litigation which is as expensive and as complicated as the original litigation. It must be used as a remedy in cases where the need for a wasted costs order is reasonably obvious. It is a summary remedy which is to be used in circumstances where there is a clear picture which indicates that a professional adviser has been negligent." (*Wall v. Lefever.*): *Fletamentos Maritimos SA v. Effjohn International BV*, December 10, 1997, CA (unrep.).

Basis of detailed assessment of solicitor and client costs

48.8—(1) This rule applies to every assessment of a solicitor's bill to his client except— **48.8**

(a) a bill which is to be paid out of the legal aid fund under the Legal Aid Act 1988[8]; or

(b) where the solicitor and his client have entered into a conditional fee agreement as defined by section 58 of the Courts and Legal Services Act 1990.[9]

(1A) Section 74(3) of the Solicitors Act 1974(a) applies unless the solicitor and client have entered into a written agreement which expressly permits payment to the solicitor of an amount of costs greater than that which the client could have recovered from another party to the proceedings.

(2) Subject to paragraph (1A), costs are to be assessed on the indemnity basis but are to be presumed—

(a) to have been reasonably incurred if they were incurred with the express or implied approval of the client;

(b) to be reasonable in amount if their amount was expressly or impliedly approved by the client;

(c) to have been unreasonably incurred if—

(i) they are of an unusual nature or amount; and

[8] 1988 c. 34.

[9] 1990 c. 41. Section 58 was amended by the Family Law Act 1996 (c. 27), Schedule 8, Part III, paragraph 61.

(ii) the solicitor did not tell his client that as a result he might not recover all of them from the other party.

48.8.1 **Comment**—Since a detailed assessment of a solicitor and client bill is on the indemnity basis, no question of proportionality arises but the presumptions set out at r.48.8(2) apply. See Directions relating to Pt 48, paras 2.9–2.12 (para. 48PD–002).

Costs payable out of the legal aid fund and costs payable under a conditional fee agreement are not dealt with under this rule.

This rule preserves the freedom of the client and the solicitor to make whatever agreement they may desire for the supply of the solicitors services subject to the provisions of the Solicitors Act 1974, ss.59 *et seq.*, regarding contentious business agreements, and to the requirement in (2)(c) of the rule.

A client who retains a solicitor whose practice is carried on in a high cost area or in a manner which is plainly luxurious is generally presumed to have impliedly approved of the additional costs necessarily incurred in maintaining that type of practice.

Unusual expense includes special fees for counsel which are unusual or extraordinary or generous fees (*Canvendish v. Strutt* [1904] 1 Ch. 524). On the other hand a party is entitled to be allowed a brief fee to Counsel which is the normal and reasonable fee for such a case, heard out of London, even if it is heard in a town where there are a few local members of the bar who are prepared to do the work for less: and this whether the party is legally aided or not (*Self v. Self* [1954] P. 480; [1954] 2 All E.R. 550; *Young v. Kohler* [1955] 1 W.L.R. 395; [1955] 1 All E.R. 796); and whether Counsel has another brief in the same Court on the same day (*Isaac v. Isaac* [1955] P. 333; [1955] 2 All E.R. 811).

48.8.2 **Rule 48.8(2)**—Where a client had been provided with an estimate of costs on the basis of an hourly rate shortly prior to trial, it was held to be unreasonable that the client should then be charged a higher hourly rate than he was led to believe would be charged. The estimate of costs up to and including trial did not constitute a binding agreement but the correspondence amounted to a clear and considered indication of the client's maximum liability to the solicitors upon which the client was likely to and did rely. The Law Society's Guide to Professional Conduct of Solicitors indicates that the final amount payable should not vary substantially from an estimate given unless the client has been informed of the changed circumstances in writing. *Wong v. Vizards* (1997) 2 Costs L.R. 46, Toulson J.

48.8.3 **Family Division**—Although district judges of the Principal Registry have power to assess bills of costs as between solicitor and client, it has been agreed with the Senior Costs Judge of the Supreme Court Costs Office that assessment to which Rule 48.8 applies shall be dealt with in the Supreme Court Costs Office. If a solicitor or his client presents a solicitor and own client bill for assessment under the Solicitors Act 1974 at the Principal Registry, he should be invited to lodge it at the Supreme Court Costs Office (*Senior District Judge's Direction,* June 21, 1993).

Amended by S.I. 1999 No. 1008.

Conditional fees

48.9 **48.9**—(1) This rule applies to every assessment (whether by the summary or detailed procedure) of a solicitor's bill to his client where the solicitor and the client have entered into a conditional fee agreement as defined in section 58 of the Courts and Legal Services Act 1990.

(2) In this rule—

"the base costs" means the costs other than a percentage increase;

"percentage increase" means a percentage increase pursuant to a conditional fee agreement entered into between the solicitor and his client or between counsel and the solicitor, or counsel and the client; and

"costs" includes all fees, charges, disbursements and other expenses charged by the solicitor or counsel under the conditional fee agreement in question.

(3) On assessment to which this rule applies, the client may apply for assessment of the base costs or of a percentage increase or of both.

(4) Where the client applies for assessment of the base costs, the base costs are to be assessed in accordance with rule 48.8(2) as if the solicitor and his client had not entered into a conditional fee agreement.

(5) Where the client applies for assessment of a percentage increase, the court may reduce percentage increase where it considers it to be disproportionate having regard to all relevant factors as they reasonably appeared to the solicitor or counsel when the conditional fee agreement was entered into.

(6) The court will not vary a percentage increase where the client is a child or patient, except in accordance with paragraph (5).

(The costs practice direction specifies some of the relevant factors.)

Comment—See paras 2.13–2.16 of the Directions relating to Pt 48 (para. 48PD–002) as to the way in which the court will approach detailed assessment of a conditional fee agreement. **48.9.1**

The base costs will be assessed in accordance with r.48.8(2) (*i.e.* the presumptions apply), whilst in respect of the percentage increase, the test of proportionality comes into play. In considering all the factors the court may not use hindsight and must consider the factors as they reasonably appeared to the solicitor or counsel when the conditional fee agreement was entered into.

The position of legal representatives acting under conditional fee agreements—The existence of a conditional fee agreement does not alter the relationship between the legal adviser and the client. Legal representatives owe the client exactly the same duties and remain under the same duty to the client to disregard their own interests as if there were no conditional fee agreement. The legal representative also owes the same duties to the Court. There is no reason why the circumstances in which a legal representative acting under a conditional fee agreement can be made personally liable for the costs of a party other than his client should differ from those in which a legal representative who is not acting under a conditional fee agreement would be liable. The existence of a conditional fee agreement should make the legal representative's position as a matter of law no worse, so far as being ordered to pay costs is concerned, than it would be if there were no conditional fee agreement. Legal representatives acting under conditional fee agreements are under no more risk of paying costs personally than they would be if they were not so acting. In addition whether or not conditional fee agreements are properly the subject of professional privilege they are not normally required to be disclosed. *Per* Lord Woolf M.R. in *Hodgson v. Imperial Tobacco Ltd, The Times,* February 13, 1998, CA. **48.9.2**

For a note as to the Indemnity Principle and Conditional Fee Agreements in arbitration cases see 47.14.15and *Bevan Ashford v. Geoff Yeandle (Contractors) Ltd (in liquidation), The Times,* April 23, 1998, Sir Richard Scott V.-C.

Assessment procedure

48.10—(1) This rule sets out the procedure to be followed where the court has made an order under Part III of the Solicitors Act 1974[10] for the assessment of costs payable to a solicitor by his client. **48.10**

(2) The solicitor must serve a breakdown of costs within 28 days of the order for costs to be assessed.

(3) The client must serve points of dispute within 14 days after service on him of the breakdown of costs.

(4) If the solicitor wishes to serve a reply, he must do so within 14 days of service on him of the points of dispute.

(5) Either party may file a request for a hearing date—

(a) after points of dispute have been served; but

(b) no later than 3 months after the date of the order for the costs to be assessed.

(6) This procedure applies subject to any contrary order made by the court.

(Other rules about costs payable in special cases can be found in Schedule 1, in the following RSC—O.30 (remuneration of receivers); O.49 (costs of garnishee).)

Comment—RSC, O.106 is contained in Sched. 1 of the CPR and governs all applications made under Pt III of the Solicitors Act 1974, see paras 2.17–2.19 of the Directions relating to Pt 48 (para. 48PD–003) in relation to this type of application (see also Pt 8—alternative procedure for claims). **48.10.1**

The present rule sets out the procedure where the court has made an order for the detailed assessment of costs payable to a solicitor by his client.

Where the court makes an order for detailed assessment the solicitor is required to serve a breakdown of the costs within 28 days of the order. This breakdown is not a detailed bill for the

[10] 1974 c. 47.

purposes of section 64(2) of the Solicitors Act 1974. If the client does not serve points of dispute no default costs certificate may be issued. In the case of default by either party the other party may make an appropriate Pt 23 application.

The procedure set out in Pt 47 applies subject to the provisions of this rule and to any contrary order made by the court. (See paras 2.20–2.36 of the Directions relating to Pt 48 (para. 48PD–003) as to the procedure to be adopted.)

Amended by S.I. 1999 No. 1008.

48.10.2 **VAT**—For the provisions relating to VAT in relation to bills being dealt with by way of summary or detailed assessment see Directions relating to Pt 43, paras 3.1–3.20 (para. 43BPD–003).

48PD–001

DIRECTIONS RELATING TO PART 48—COSTS—SPECIAL CASES

Section I. Costs Payable by or to Particular Persons

Rule 48.3 Amount of costs where costs are payable pursuant to contract

48PD–001 **1.1** Where the court is assessing costs payable under a contract, the court may make an order that all or part of the costs payable under the contract shall be disallowed if the court is satisfied by the paying party that costs have been unreasonably incurred or are unreasonable in amount.

1.2 Rule 48.3 only applies if the court is assessing costs payable under a contract. It does not—

(1) require the court to make an assessment of such costs; or

(2) require a mortgagee to apply for an order for those costs that he has a contractual right to recover out of the mortgage funds.

1.3 The following principles apply to costs relating to a mortgage—

(1) An order for the payment of costs of proceedings by one party to another is always a discretionary order: section 51 of the Supreme Court Act 1981.

(2) Where there is a contractual right to the costs the discretion should ordinarily be exercised so as to reflect that contractual right.

(3) The power of the court to disallow a mortgagee's costs sought to be added to the mortgage security is a power that does not derive from section 51, but from the power of the courts of equity to fix the terms on which redemption will be allowed.

(4) A decision by a court to refuse costs in whole or in part to a mortgagee litigant may be—

- (a) a decision in the exercise of the section 51 discretion;
- (b) a decision in the exercise of the power to fix the terms on which redemption will be allowed;
- (c) a decision as to the extent of a mortgagee's contractual right to add his costs to the security;

  or
- (d) a combination of two or more of these things.

The statements of case in the proceedings or the submissions made to the court may indicate which of the decisions has been made.

(5) A mortgagee is not to be deprived of a contractual or equitable right to add costs to the security merely be reason of an order for payment of costs made without reference to the mortgagee's contractual or equitable rights, and without any adjudication as to whether or not the mortgagee should be deprived of these costs.

1.4(1) Where the contract entitles a mortgagee to—

- (a) add the costs of litigation relating to the mortgage to the sum secured by it;
- (b) require a mortgagor to pay those costs, or
- (c) both,

[11] [1993] Ch 171

the mortgagor may make an application for the court to direct that an account of the mortgagee's costs be taken.

(Rule 25.(1)(n) provides that the court may direct that a party file an account)

(2) The mortgagor may then dispute an amount in the mortgagee's account on the basis that is has been unreasonably incurred or is unreasonable in amount.

(3) Where a mortgagor disputes an amount, the court may make an order that the disputed costs are assessed under rule 48.3.

Rule 48.5 Costs where money is payable by or to a child or patient

1.5 The circumstances in which the court need not order the assessment of costs under rule 48.5(3) are as follows:

(a) where there is no need to do so to protect the interests of the child or patient or his estate;
(b) where another party has agreed to pay a specified sum in respect of the costs of the child or patient and the solicitor acting for the child or patient has waived the right to claim further costs;
(c) where the court has decided the costs payable to the child or patient by way of summary assessment and the solicitor acting for the child or patient has waived the right to claim further costs;
(d) where an insurer or other person is liable to discharge the costs which the child or patient would otherwise be liable to pay to his solicitor and the court is satisfied that the insurer or other person is financially able to discharge those costs.

Rule 48.6 Litigants in person

1.6 In order to qualify as an expert for the purpose of rule 48.6(3)(c) (expert assistance in connection with assessing the claim for costs), the person in question must be a

(1) barrister,
(2) solicitor,
(3) Fellow of the Institute of Legal Executives,
(4) Fellow of the Association of Law Costs Draftsmen,
(5) law costs draftsman who is a member of the Academy of Experts,
(6) law costs draftsman who is a member of the Expert Witness Institute.

1.7 Where a litigant in person wishes to prove that he has suffered financial loss he should produce to the court any written evidence he relies on to support that claim, and serve a copy of that evidence on any party against whom he seeks costs at least 24 hours before the hearing at which the question may be decided.

1.8 Where a litigant in person commences detailed assessment proceedings under rule 47.6 he should serve copies of that written evidence with the notice of commencement.

1.9 The amount which may be allowed to a litigant in person under rule 46.3(5)(b) and rule 48.6(4) is £9.25 per hour.

1.10 Attention is drawn to rule 48.6(6)(b). A solicitor who, instead of acting for himself, is represented in the proceedings by his firm or by himself in his firm's name, is not, for the purpose of the Civil Procedure Rules, a litigant in person.

Section II. Costs Relating to Solicitors and Other Legal Representatives

Rule 48.7 Personal liability of legal representative for costs—wasted costs orders

2.1 Rule 48.7 deals with wasted costs orders against legal representatives. Such orders can be made at any stage in the proceedings up to and including the proceedings relating to the detailed assessment of costs. In general, applications for wasted costs are best left until after the end of the trial.

2.2 The court may make a wasted costs order against a legal representative on an application under Part 23 or of its own initiative.

2.3 A party who wishes to apply for a wasted costs order must first give to the legal representative against whom the order is sought notice in writing

(a) of what the legal representative is alleged to have done or failed to do, and

(b) of the costs that he may be ordered to pay or which are sought against him.

The notice must be given at least 3 days before the hearing.

2.4 It is appropriate for the court to make a wasted costs order against a legal representative only if—

(a) he has acted improperly, unreasonably or negligently,

(b) his conduct has caused another party to incur unnecessary costs, and

(c) it is just in all the circumstances to order him to compensate that party for the whole or part of those costs.

2.5 The court will give directions about the procedure that will be followed in each case in order to ensure that the issues are dealt with in a way that is fair and as simple and summary as the circumstances permit.

2.6 As a general rule the court will consider whether to make a wasted costs order in two stages:

(a) in the first stage, the court must be satisfied—

(i) that it has before it evidence or other material which, if unanswered, would be likely to lead to a wasted costs order being made, and

(ii) the wasted costs proceedings are justified notwithstanding the likely costs involved.

(b) At the second stage (even if the court is satisfied under (a) above) the court will consider, after giving the legal representative an opportunity to put forward his case, whether it is appropriate to make a wasted costs order in accordance with paragraph 2.4 above.

2.7 A wasted costs order is an order that the legal representative pay a specified sum in respect of costs to another party or that costs relating to a specified sum or items of work be disallowed.

Rule 48.8 Basis of Detailed Assessment of Solicitor and Client Costs

48PD–002 **2.9** A client and his solicitor may agree whatever terms they consider appropriate about the payment of the solicitor's charges for his services. If, however, the costs are of an unusual nature (either in amount or in the type of costs incurred) those costs will be presumed to have been unreasonably incurred unless the solicitor satisfies the court that he informed the client that they were unusual and, where the costs relate to litigation, that he informed the client they might not be allowed on an assessment of costs between the parties. That information must have been given to the client before the costs were incurred.

2.10(1) Costs as between a solicitor and client are assessed on the indemnity basis, as defined by rule 44.4; proportionality is therefore not relevant.

(2) Attention is drawn to the presumptions set out in rule 48.8(2). These presumptions may be rebutted by evidence to the contrary.

2.11 Rule 48.10 and paragraphs 2.17 to 2.36 of this Practice Direction deal with the procedure to be followed for obtaining assessment of a solicitor's bill pursuant to an order under Part III of The Solicitors Act 1974.

2.12 If a party fails to comply with the requirements of rule 48.10 concerning the service of a breakdown of costs or points of dispute, any other party may apply to the court in which the detailed assessment hearing should take place for an order requiring compliance with rule 48.10. If the court makes such an order, it may:

(a) make it subject to conditions including a condition to pay a sum of money into court; and

(b) specify the consequence of failure to comply with the order or a condition.

Rule 48.9 Conditional Fees

2.13(1) A client who has entered into a conditional fee agreement with a solicitor may apply for assessment of the base cost (which is carried out in accordance with rule 48.8(2) as if there were no conditional fee agreement) or for assessment of the percentage increase (success fee) or both.

(2) Where the court is to assess the percentage increase, proportionality is relevant and the court will have regard to all the relevant factors as they appeared to the solicitor or counsel when the conditional fee agreement was entered into.

2.14 Where the client applies to the court to reduce the percentage increase which the solicitor has charged the client under the conditional fee agreement, the client must set out in his application notice:

(a) the reasons why the percentage increase should be reduced; and
(b) what the percentage increase should be.

2.15 The factors relevant to assessing the percentage increase include:

(a) the risk that the circumstances in which the fees or expenses would be payable might not occur;
(b) the disadvantages relating to the absence of payment on account;
(c) whether the amount which might be payable under the conditional fee agreement is limited to a certain proportion of any damages recovered by the client;
(d) whether there is a conditional fee agreement between the solicitor and counsel;
(e) the solicitor's liability for any disbursements.

2.16 When the court is considering the factors to be taken into account, it will have regard to the circumstances as they reasonably appeared to the solicitor or counsel when the conditional fee agreement was entered into or at the time of any variation of the agreement.

Rule 48.10 Assessment procedure

2.17 Paragraphs 2.18 to 2.36 apply to orders made under Part III of the Solicitors Act 1974 for the assessment of costs. **48PD–003**

2.18 The procedure for obtaining an order under Part III of the Solicitors Act 1974 is by the alternative procedure for claims under Part 8. The provisions of RSC, O.106 appear, appropriately amended, in Schedule 1 to the CPR.

2.19 Model forms of order which the court may make are set out in Forms 17, 18 and 19 of the Schedule of Costs Forms annexed to this Practice Direction.

2.20 Attention is drawn to the time limits within which the required steps must be taken: *i.e.* the solicitor must serve a breakdown of cost within 28 days of the order for costs to be assessed, the client must serve points of dispute within 14 days after service on him of the breakdown; and any reply must be served within 14 days of service of the points of dispute.

2.21 The breakdown of costs referred to in rule 48.10 is a document which contains the following information:

(a) details of the work done under each of the bills sent for assessment; and
(b) in applications under Section 70 of the Solicitors Act 1974, an account showing money received by the solicitor to the credit of the client and sums paid out of that money on behalf of the client but not payments out which were made in satisfaction of the bill or of any items which are claimed in the bill.

2.22 Form 20 of the Schedule of Costs Forms annexed to this Practice Direction is a model form of breakdown of costs. A party who is required to serve a breakdown of costs must also serve—

(1) copies of the fee notes of counsel and of any expert in respect of fees claimed in the breakdown, and

(2) written evidence as to any other disbursement which is claimed in the breakdown and which exceeds £250.

2.23 The provisions relating to default costs certificates (rule 47.11) do not apply to cases to which rule 48.10 applies.

2.24 Points of dispute should as far as practicable be in the form complying with paragraphs 2.12 and 2.13 of the Directions relating to Part 47.

2.25 The time for requesting a detailed assessment hearing is within 3 months after the date of the order of the costs to be assessed.

2.26 The form of request for a hearing date must be in Form 21 of the Schedule of Costs Forms annexed to this Practice Direction. The request must be accompanied by copies of—

(a) the order sending the bill or bills for assessment;
(b) the bill or bills sent for assessment;
(c) the solicitor's breakdown of costs and any invoices or accounts served with that breakdown;
(d) a copy of the points of dispute, annotated as necessary in order to show which items have been agreed and their value and to show which items remain in dispute;
(e) as many copies of the points of dispute so annotated as there are other parties to the proceedings to whom the court should give details of the assessment hearing requested;
(f) a copy of any replies served;
(g) a statement signed by the party filing the request or his legal representative giving the names and addresses for service of all parties to the proceedings.

2.27 The request must include an estimate of the length of time the detailed assessment hearing will take.

2.28 On receipt of the request for a detailed assessment hearing the court will fix a date for the hearing or if the Costs Judge or District Judge so decides, will give directions or fix a date for a preliminary appointment.

2.29(1) The court will give at least 14 days notice of the time and place of the detailed assessment hearing to every person named in the statement referred to in paragraph 2.26(g) above.

(2) The court will when giving notice, give all parties other than the party who requested the hearing a copy of the points of dispute annotated by the party requesting the hearing in compliance with paragraph 2.26(e) above.

(3) Attention is drawn to rule 47.15(6) and (7): apart from the solicitor whose bill it is, only those parties who have served points of dispute may be heard on the detailed assessment unless the court gives permission, and only items specified in the points of dispute may be raised unless the court gives permission.

2.30(1) If a party wishes to vary his breakdown of costs, points of dispute or reply, an amended or supplementary document must be filed with the court and copies of it must be served on all other relevant parties.

(2) Permission is not required to vary a breakdown of costs, points of dispute or a reply but the court may disallow the variation or permit it only upon conditions, including conditions as to the payment of any costs caused or wasted by the variation.

2.31 Unless the court directs otherwise the solicitor must file with the court the papers in support of the bill not less than 7 days before the date for the detailed assessment hearing and not more than 14 days before that date.

2.32 Once the detailed assessment hearing has ended it is the responsibility of the legal representative appearing for the solicitor or, as the case may be, the solicitor in person to remove the papers filed in support of the bill.

2.33(1) Attention is drawn to rule 47.15 (power to issue an interim certificate).

(2) If, in the course of a detailed assessment hearing of a solicitor's bill to his client, it appears to the costs judge or district judge that in any event the solicitor will be liable in connection with that bill to pay money to the client, he may issue an interim certificate specifying an amount which in his opinion is payable by the solicitor to his client. Such a certificate will include an order to pay the sum it certifies unless the court orders otherwise.

2.34(1) Attention is drawn to rule 47.16 which requires the solicitor to file a completed bill within 14 days after the end of the detailed assessment hearing. The court may dispense with the requirement to file a completed bill. If it does so the time for a request by the solicitor for written reasons under rule 47.23 is 7 days after the date of the order dispensing with the requirement for a completed bill.

(2) After the detailed assessment hearing is concluded the court will—

(a) complete the court copy of the bill so as to show the amount allowed;
(b) determine the result of the cash account;
(c) award the costs of the detailed assessment hearing in accordance with Section 70(8) of the Solicitors Act 1974; and
(d) issue a final costs certificate showing the amount due following the detailed assessment hearing.

2.35 A final costs certificate will include an order to pay the sum it certifies unless the court orders otherwise.

2.36 Attention is drawn to Section VIII of Part 47 (appeal against decisions in detailed assessment proceedings).

Section III. Transitional Arrangements

3.1(1) This section deals with the application of the Civil Procedure Rules ("CPR") to taxation proceedings commenced before 26th April 1999. **48PD–004**

(2) In this section "the previous rules" means the Rules of the Supreme Court ("RSC") or County Court Rules 1981 ("CCR"), as appropriate.

General Scheme of Transitional Arrangements concerning Costs Proceedings

3.2(1) Paragraph 18 of the Practice Direction which supplements Part 51 (Transitional Arrangements) provides that the CPR govern any assessments of costs which take place after 26th April 1999 and states a presumption to be applied in respect of costs for work undertaken before 26th April 1999.

(2) The following paragraphs provide four further transitional arrangements:

(a) to provide an additional presumption to be applied when assessing costs which were awarded by an order made in a county court before 26th April 1999 which allowed costs "on Scale 1" to be determined in accordance with CCR Appendix A or "on the lower scale" to be determined in accordance with CCR Appendix C;
(b) to preserve the effect of CCR, Appendix B, Part III, paragraph 2;
(c) to clarify the approach to be taken where a bill of costs was provisionally taxed before 26th April 1999 and the receiving party is unwilling to accept the result of the provisional taxation;
(d) to preserve the right to carry in objections or apply for a reconsideration in all taxation proceedings commenced before 26th April 1999.

Scale 1 or lower scale costs

3.3 Where an order was made in county court proceedings before 26th April 1999 under which the costs were allowed on Scale 1 or the lower scale, the general presumption is that no costs will be allowed under that order which would not have been allowed in a taxation before 26th April 1999.

Fixed costs on the lower scale

3.4 The amount to be allowed as fixed costs for making or opposing an application for a rehearing to set aside a judgment given before 26th April 1999 where the costs are on lower scale is £11.25.

Bills provisionally taxed before 26th April 1999

3.5 In respect of bills of costs provisionally taxed before 26th April 1999:

(1) The previous rules apply on the question who can request a hearing and the time limits for doing so; and

(2) the CPR govern any subsequent hearing in that case.

Bills taxed before 26th April 1999

3.6 Where a bill of costs was taxed before 26th April 1999, the previous rules govern the steps which can be taken to challenge that taxation.

Other taxation proceedings

3.7(1) This paragraph applies to taxation proceedings which were commenced before 26th April 1999, were assigned for taxation to a Taxing Master or District Judge, and which were still pending on 26th April 1999.

(2) Any assessment of costs that takes place in cases to which this paragraph applies which is conducted on or after 26th April 1999, will be conducted in accordance with the CPR.

(3) In addition to the possibility of appeal under rules 47.20 to 47.26 any party to a detailed assessment who is dissatisfied with any decision on a detailed assessment made by a costs judge or district judge may apply to that costs judge or district judge for a review of the decision. The review shall, for procedural purposes, be treated as if it were an appeal from an authorised court officer.

(4) The right of review provided by paragraph (3) above, will not apply in cases in which, at least 28 days before the date of the assessment hearing, all parties to that hearing were served with notice that the rights of appeal in respect of that hearing would be governed only by Part 47 Section VIII (Appeal against Decisions in Detailed Assessment Proceedings).

(5) An order for the service of notice under sub-paragraph (4) above may be made on the application of any party to the detailed assessment proceedings or may be made by the court of its own initiative.

Schedule of Costs Forms

48PD–005
1. Statement of Costs (summary assessment)
2. Bill of Costs (detailed assessment)
3. Legal Aid Schedule of Costs
4. Certificates for inclusion in bills
5. Notice of Commencement of Assessment of Bill of Costs—N252
6. Points of Dispute
7. Request for Default Costs Certificate—N254
8. Request for a Detailed Assessment Hearing—N258
9. Default Costs Certificate (CC)—N255
10. Default Costs Certificate (HC)—N255HC
11. Interim Costs Certificate—N257
12. Final Costs Certificate (CC)—N256
13. Final Costs Certificate (HC)—N256HC
14. Notice of Amount Allowed on Provisional Assessment (Legal Aid only)—N253
15. Legal Aid Assessment Certificate
16. Notice of Appeal
17. Solicitors Act: order delivery of bill
18. Solicitors Act: order for detailed assessment (client)
19. Solicitors Act: order for detailed assessment (solicitors)
20. Solicitors Act: breakdown of costs
21. Solicitors Act: request for a hearing date

48PD–006

SCHEDULE OF COSTS FORMS: FORM 1

COURT CASE REFERENCE
JUDGE/MASTER
CASE TITLE

[Party]'s Statement of Costs for the hearing on [date]

Description of fee earners*
(1) [name] [grade] [hourly rate claimed]
(2) [name] [grade] [hourly rate claimed]

Attendances on [Party]
[number] hours at £ £

Attendances on opponents
[number] hours at £ £

Attendances on others
(1) [number] hours at £ £
(2) [number] hours at £ £

Work done on documents
[number] hours at £ £

Attendance at hearing
[number] hours at £ £
[number] hours travel and waiting at £ £

Counsel's fees [name] [year of call]
Fee for [advice/conference/documents] £
Fee for hearing £

Other expenses
[court fees] £
Others [give brief description] £

TOTAL
Amount of VAT claimed
on solicitor's and counsel's fees £
on other expenses £

GRAND TOTAL £

The costs estimated above do not exceed the costs which the [party] is liable to pay in respect of the work which this estimate covers.

Dated

Signed
Name of firm of solicitors
[partner] for the [party]

* 3 grades of fee earner are suggested: (1) solicitors with over 4 years PQE (2) other solicitors and legal executives and fee earners of equivalent experience and (3) trainee solicitors and fee earners of equivalent experience. In respect of each fee earner communications should be treated as attendances and routine communications should be claimed at one tenth of the hourly rate.

48PD–007

SCHEDULE OF COSTS FORMS: FORM 2

IN THE HIGH COURT OF JUSTICE 1997-B-9999

QUEEN'S BENCH DIVISION

BRIGHTON DISTRICT REGISTRY

B E T W E E N

AB

Claimant

– and –

CD

Defendant

CLAIMANT'S BILL OF COSTS TO BE ASSESSED PURSUANT TO THE ORDER DATED 26 FEBRUARY 1999 AND IN ACCORDANCE WITH REGULATION 107A OF THE CIVIL LEGAL AID (GENERAL) REGULATIONS 1989

Legal Aid Certificate No. 01.01.96.32552X issued on 9 September 1997.

VAT NO. 33 4404 90

In these proceedings the claimant sought compensation for personal injuries and other losses suffered in a road accident which occurred on Wednesday 1 January 1997 near the junction between Bolingbroke Lane and Regency Road, Brighton, East Sussex. The claimant had been travelling as a front seat passenger in a car driven by the defendant. The claimant suffered severe injuries when, because of the defendant's negligence, the car left the road and collided with a brick wall.

The defendant was later convicted of various offences arising out of the accident including careless driving and driving under the influence of drink or drugs.

In the civil action the defendant alleged that immediately before the car journey began the claimant had known that the defendant was under the influence of alcohol and therefore consented to the risk of injury or was contributorily negligent as to it. It was also alleged that, immediately before the accident occurred, the claimant wrongfully took control of the steering wheel so causing the accident to occur.

The claimant first instructed solicitors, E F & Co, in this matter in July 1997. The writ was issued in October 1997 and in February 1998 the claimant successfully applied for an interim payment. In July 1998 the proceedings were listed for a two day trial commencing 25 February 1999. At that trial the defendant was found liable but the compensation payable was reduced by 25% in order to take account of contributory negligence by the claimant. The claimant was awarded a total of £78,256.83 plus £1,207.16 interest plus costs.

The proceedings were conducted on behalf of the claimant by an assistant solicitor, admitted November 1996. The bill is divided into four parts.

Part 1 Costs payable by the defendant

This covers the period from 8 July 1997 to 8 September 1997 which was financed under the Legal Aid Green Form scheme. In this part the solicitor's time is charged at £120 per hour, letters out and telephone calls at £12 each and travel and waiting at £60 per hour. However, the claim for costs is limited to the sum payable under the Green Form scheme, £95 plus VAT of £16.62.

Part 2 Costs payable by the defendant

This part covers the period from 9 September 1997 to 19 May 1998 which was financed under the legal aid scheme. In this part the solicitor's time has been charged as in Part 1.

Part 3 Costs payable only out of the legal aid fund

This part covers the same period as Part 2. In this part the solicitor's time is charged at the prescribed hourly rates plus enhancement of 50%.

Preparation: £74.00
Attending counsel in conference or at court: £36.40
Travelling and waiting: £32.70
Routine letters out: £7.40
Routine telephone calls: £4.10

Part 4 Costs payable by the defendant

This part covers the period from 19 May 1998 to the present time. Once the claimant had become financially ineligible for legal aid, E F & Co agreed to continue acting for him on payment of disbursements and profit costs for E F & Co at the following hourly rates.

Assistant solicitor: £120.00
Costs draftsman: £80.00
Trainee solicitor: £60.00

Item	Amount Claimed	VAT	Amount Allowed	VAT
Part 1: COSTS PAYABLE BY THE DEFENDANT				
Claimant				
(1) 8th July 1997 – First instructions – 0.75 hours 90.00	*	*		
(2) Routine letters out – 3 36.00	*	*		
Witnesses of fact				
(3) Routine letters out – 2 24.00	*	*		
The Defendant				
(4) 8th July 1997 – Timed letter sent – 0.5 hours 60.00	*	*		
(Total claim for Part 1 is limited to £95 plus VAT of £16.62)*				
To Summary	95.00	16.62		
PART 2: COSTS PAYABLE BY THE DEFENDANT				
Attendances on Court and counsel				
9th September 1997 – legal aid certificate issued				
11th September 1997 – Conference with counsel Engaged 2.5 hours 300.00 Travel & waiting 2.25 hours 135.00				
(5) Total solicitor's fee for conference	435.00	76.12		
(6) Counsel's fee for conference	250.00	43.75		
7th October 1997 – Issue of writ				
(7) Writ fee	500.00			
21st October 1997 – Writ and Statement of Claim served				
25th November 1997 – Time for service of defence extended by agreement to 15th January 1998				
25th November 1997 – Summons for interim payment issued				
(8) Court fee for summons	50.00			
28th November 1998 – Affidavit of AB sworn				
(9) Paid oath fee	14.00			
15th January 1998 – Defence served				
16th January 1998 – Instructions to Counsel to advise on evidence and settle 2 witness statements				
29th January 1998 – Advice on evidence received				
(10th) Counsel's fee for advice on evidence (Miss GH)	400.00	70.00		
(11) Counsel's fee for settling 2 witness statements	120.00	21.00		
6th February 1998: Claimant's application for an interim payment (interim payment of £10,873.67 ordered with claimant's costs in the case: certificate for counsel) Engaged 0.33 hours 40.00 Travel & waiting 2.00 hours 120.00				
(12) Total solicitor's fee for attending	160.00	28.00		
(13) Counsel's brief fee (Miss GH)	120.00	21.00		
20th March 1998: Exchange of witness statements				
15th April 1998: Payment into court of £25,126.33 – in addition to the interim payment and a further payment to the Compensation Recovery Unit				

Item	Amount Claimed	VAT	Amount Allowed	VAT
20th April 1998: Telephone conference with counsel Engaged 0.5 hours 60.00 (14) Total solicitor's fee for conference	60.00	10.50		
(15) Counsel's fee for conference (Miss GH)	216.00	37.80		
Claimant				
Timed attendances in person and by telephone – see Schedule 1				
(16) Total fees for Schedule 1 – 6.5 hours	780.00	136.50		
(17) Routine letters out and telephone calls – 18 (10 + 8)	216.00	37.80		
Witnesses of fact				
Timed attendances in person, by letter out and by telephone – see Schedule 2				
(18) Total fees for Schedule 2 – 3.9 hours	468.00	81.90		
(19) Paid travelling on 9th October 1997	22.96	4.01		
Medical expert (Dr. IJ)				
(20) 11th September 1997 – long letter out – 0.33 hours	40.00	7.00		
(21) 30th January 1998 – long letter out – 0.25 hours	30.00	5.25		
(22) 23rd April 1998 – telephone call – 0.2 hours	24.00	4.20		
(23) Routine letters out and telephone calls – 6	72.00	12.60		
(24) Dr IJ's fee for report	350.00			
Solicitors for defendant				
(25) Routine letters out and telephone calls – 12 and 4	192.00	33.60		
Communications with the Court				
(26) Routine letters out to court – 6	72.00	12.60		
Communications with Counsel				
(27) Routine letters out and telephone calls to counsel – 11 (7 + 4)	132.00	23.10		
Work done on arithmetic				
(28) 18th September 1997: 1 hour	120.00	21.00		
(29) 3rd November 1997: 0.75 hours	90.00	15.75		
(30) 23rd February 1998: 0.5 hours	60.00	10.50		
Work done on documents				
Timed attendances: see Schedule 3				
(31) Total fees for Schedule 3 – 39 hours	4680.00	819.00		
Work done on negotiations				
23rd March 1998: meeting at offices of solicitors for defence Engaged 1.5 hours 180.00 Travel & waiting 1.25 hours 75.00 (32) Total solicitor's fee for meeting	255.00	44.63		
To Summary	9928.96	1577.61		
PART 3: COSTS PAYABLE ONLY OUT OF THE LEGAL AID FUND				
Claimant				
(33) 11th September 1997 telephone call				

Item		Amount Claimed	VAT	Amount Allowed	VAT
Engaged 0.25 hours	18.50				
Enhancement 50%	9.25	27.75	4.85		
(34) 18th April 1998: telephone call					
Engaged 0.1 hours	4.10				
Enhancement 50%	2.05	6.15	1.08		
Legal Aid Board					
(35) 12th May 1998: report on case					
Engaged 0.5 hours	37.00				
Enhancement 50%	18.50	55.50	9.71		
(36) Routine letters out and telephone calls					
Letters out 2	14.80				
Telephone calls 4	16.40				
Enhancement 50%	15.60	46.80	8.19		
Other work done					
(37) Preparing and checking bill – (part: 2 hours)		200.00	35.00		
To Summary		336.20	58.83		
PART 4: COSTS PAYABLE BY THE DEFENDANT					
Attendances on Court and counsel					
19th May 1998: Discharge of legal aid certificate					
16th July 1998: Set down for trial (date fixed, 2 days – starting 25th February 1999)					
(38) 4th December 1998: Setting down fee		150.00			
25th February 1999: attending first day of trial: adjourned part heard					
Engaged in court: 5 hours	600.00				
Engaged in conference: 0.75 hours	90.00				
Travel and waiting: 1.5 hours	90.00				
(39) Total solicitor's fee for attending		780.00	136.50		
(40) Counsel's brief fee (Miss GH)		1750.00	306.25		
(41) Fee of expert witness (Dr. IJ)		850.00			
(42) Expenses of witnesses of fact		84.00			
26th February 1999: attending second day of trial when judgment was given for the claimant in the sum of £78,256.83 plus £1207.16 interest plus costs					
Engaged in court: 3 hours	360.00				
Engaged in confeernce: 1.5 hours	180.00				
Travel and waiting: 1.5 hours	90.00				
(43) Total solicitor's fee for attending		630.00	110.25		
(44) Counsel's fee for second day (Miss GH)		650.00	113.75		
Claimant					
(45) 20th May 1998: telephone call 0.2 hours		24.00	4.20		
(46) 20th February 1999: telephone call 0.33 hours		40.00	7.00		
(47) 22nd February 1999: telephone call 0.25 hours		30.00	5.25		
(48) Routine letters out and telephone calls – 8(4 + 4)		96.00	16.80		
Witnesses of fact					
(49) Routine letters out and telephone calls – 6(4 + 2)		72.00	12.60		

Item		Amount Claimed	VAT	Amount Allowed	VAT
Medical expert (Dr. IJ)					
(50) Routine letters out and telephone calls – 4 (2 + 2)		48.00	8.40		
Solicitors for defendant					
(51) 19th February 1998: telephone call – 0.25 hours		30.00	5.25		
(52) Routine letters out and telephone calls – 8 (6 + 2)		90.00	15.75		
Communications with the Court					
(53) Routine letters out and telephone calls – 3 (2 + 1)		36.00	6.30		
Communications with counsel					
(54) Routine letters out and telephone calls – 8 (4 + 4)		96.00	16.80		
Work done on documents					
(55) Timed and estimated attendances: see Schedule 4		1200.00	210.00		
4 hours at £120	480				
12 hours at £60	720.00				
Other work done					
Preparing and checking bill					
Engaged: assistant solicitor – 1 hour	120.00				
Engaged: costs draftsman – 6 hours	480.00				
(56) Total fees for preparing and checking bill		600.00	105.00		
To Summary		7256.00	1080.10		
Summary					
Costs payable by the Defendant					
Part 1		95.00	16.62		
Part 2		9928.96	1577.61		
Part 4		7256.00	1080.10		
Total Costs payable by the Defendant		17279.96	2674.33		
Costs payable out of the Legal Aid Fund					
Part 3		336.20	58.83		
Total costs payable out of the Legal Aid Fund		336.20	58.83		
Grand Totals					
Costs payable by the Defendant		17279.96	2674.33		
Costs payable out of the Legal Aid Fund		336.20	58.83		
Grand Total		17616.16	2733.16		

48PD–008

SCHEDULE OF COSTS FORMS: FORM 3

IN THE HIGH COURT OF JUSTICE 1997 –B– 9999

QUEEN'S BENCH DIVISION

BRIGHTON DISTRICT REGISTRY

B E T W E E N

AB

Claimant

– and –

CD

Defendant

CLAIMANT'S BILL OF COSTS: LEGAL AID SCHEDULE

Item	Amount Claimed	VAT	Amount Allowed	VAT
PART 2: COSTS PAYABLE BY THE DEFENDANT				
(5) Solicitor's fee for conference	164.58	28.80		
(6) Counsel's fee	250.00	43.75		
(7) Writ fee	500.00			
(8) Summons fee	50.00			
(9) Oath fee	14.00			
(10) Counsel's fee	400.00	70.00		
(11) Counsel's fee	120.00	21.00		
(12) Solicitor's fee for hearing	77.52	13.57		
(13) Counsel's fee	120.00	21.00		
(14) Solicitor's fee for conference	18.20	3.18		
(15) Counsel's fee	216.00	37.80		
(16) Timed attendances on claimant 6.5 hours £481.00 Enhancement 240.50	721.50	126.27		
(17) Routine attendances on claimant Letters out 10 74.00 Telephone calls 8 32.80	106.80	18.69		
(18) Timed attendances on witnesses of fact 3.9 hours £288.60 Enhancement 50% 144.30	432.90	75.76		
(19) Paid travelling	22.96	4.01		
(20) Timed attendance on medical expert 0.33 hours 24.64 Enhancement 50% 12.32	36.96	6.47		
(21) Timed attendance on medical expert 0.25 hours 19.50 Enhancement 50% 9.25	27.75	4.85		

Item		Amount Claimed	VAT	Amount Allowed	VAT
(22) Timed attendance on medical expert 0.2 hours Enhancement 50%	 14.80 7.40	22.20	3.88		
(23) Routine attendances on medical expert Letters out 4 Telephone calls 2	 29.60 8.20	37.80	6.62		
(24) Medical expert's fee		350.00			
(25) Routine attendances on solicitors for defendant Letters out 12 Telephone calls 4	 88.80 16.40	105.20	18.41		
(26) Routine attendances on court Letters out 6	 44.40	44.40	7.77		
(27) Routine attendances on counsel Letters out 7 Telephone calls 4	 68.20 16.40	68.20	11.94		
(28) Work done on arithmetic 1 hour Enhancement 50%	 74.00 37.00	111.00	19.42		
(29) Work done on arithmetic 0.75 hours Enhancement 50%	 55.50 27.75	83.25	14.57		
(30) Work done on arithmetic 0.5 hours Enhancement	 37.00 18.50	55.50	9.71		
(31) Attendances on documents 39 hours Enhancement 50%	 2,886.00 1,443.00	4,329.00	757.58		
TOTALS FOR PART 2		8,485.72	1,325.05		
PART 4: COSTS PAYABLE BY THE DEFENDANT					
(38) Court fee		150.00			
(39) Solicitors fee for hearing 5.75 hours Travel & waiting	 209.30 41.05	258.35	45.21		
(40) Counsel's fee		1,750.00	306.25		
(41) Expert's fee		850.00			
(42) Witnesses expenses		84.00			
(43) Solicitors fee for hearing 4.5 hours Travel and waiting	 163.80 49.05	212.85	37.25		
(44) Counsel's fee		650.00	113.75		
(45) Timed attendances on claimant 0.2 hours Enhancement 50%	 14.80 7.40	22.20	3.88		
(46) Timed attendance on claimant 0.33 hours Enhancement 50%	 24.64 12.32	36.96	6.47		
(47) Timed attendance on claimant 0.25 hours Enhancement 50%	 18.50 9.25	27.75	4.85		

Item			Amount Claimed	VAT	Amount Allowed	VAT
(48) Routine attendances on claimant						
	Letters out 4	29.60				
	Telephones 4	16.40	46.00	8.05		
(49) Routine attendances on witnesses						
	Letters out 4	29.60				
	Telephones 2	8.20	37.80	6.62		
(50) Routine attendances on medical expert						
	Letters out 2	14.80				
	Telephones 2	8.20	23.00	4.02		
(51) Timed attendance on solicitors for defendant						
	0.25 hours	18.50				
	Enhancement 50%	9.75	27.75	4.86		
(52) Routine attendances on solicitors for defendant						
	Letters out 6	44.40				
	Telephones 2	8.20	52.50	9.21		
(52) Routine attendances on court						
	Letters out 2	14.80				
	Telephones 1	4.10	18.90	3.31		
(54) Routine attendances on counsel						
	Letters out 4	29.60				
	Telephones 4	16.40	46.00			
(55) Attendances on documents						
	16 hours	1,184.00				
	Enhancement 50%	592.00	1,776.00	310.80		
(56) Preparing and checking bill			600.00	105.00		
TOTALS FOR PART 4			6,670.16	977.58		
GRAND TOTAL FOR PARTS 2 AND 4			15,155.88	2,302.63		

48PD–009

SCHEDULE OF COSTS FORMS: FORM 4

An appropriate certificate under heading (1) is required in all cases. The appropriate certificate under (2) is required in all cases in which the receiving party is an assisted person. Certificates (3), (4) and (5) are optional. Certificate (5) may be included in the bill, or, if the dispute as to VAT recoverability arises after service of the bill, may be filed and served as a supplementary document amending the bill under paragraph 4.11 of the Directions relating to Part 47.

All certificates must be signed by the receiving party or by his solicitor. Where the bill claims costs in respect of work done by more than one firm of solicitors a certificate in the form of the final paragraph of certificate (1), appropriately completed, should be signed on behalf of each firm of solicitors.

(1) GENERAL CERTIFICATE AS TO INTEREST, PAYMENTS AND ACCURACY

I certify that:

☐ No rulings have been made in this case which affects my entitlement (if any) to interest on costs.

or

☐ The only rulings made in this case as to interest on costs are as follows:

[give brief details as to the date of each ruling, the name of the Judge who made it and the text of the ruling]

and

☐ No payments have been made by any paying party on account of costs included in this bill of costs.

or

☐ The following payments have been made on account of costs included in this bill of costs:

[give brief details of the amounts, the dates of payment and the name of the person by or on whose behalf they were paid]

and *(where costs are claimed for work done by a solicitor)*

☐ This bill is both accurate and complete and that in relation to each and every item included in Part(s) ...... of the bill the costs claimed herein do not exceed the costs which the receiving party/parties is/are required to pay me/my firm.

(2) CERTIFICATE AS TO INTEREST OF ASSISTED PERSON PURSUANT TO REGULATION 119 OF THE CIVIL LEGAL AID (GENERAL) REGULATIONS 1989

I certify that the assisted person has no financial interest in the detailed assessment.

or

I certify that a copy of this bill has been sent to the assisted person pursuant to Regulation 119 of the Civil Legal Aid General Regulations 1989 with an explanation of his/her interest in the detailed assessment and the steps which can be taken to safeguard that interest in the assessment. He/she has/has not requested that the costs officer be informed of his/her interest and has/has not requested that notice of the detailed assessment hearing be sent to him/her.

(3) CONSENT TO THE SIGNING OF THE CERTIFICATE WITHIN 21 DAYS OF DETAILED ASSESSMENT PURSUANT TO REGULATION 112 AND 121 OF THE CIVIL LEGAL AID (GENERAL) REGULATIONS 1989

I certify that notice of the fees reduced or disallowed on detailed assessement has been given in writing to counsel on [date].

or

I certify that: there having been no reduction or disallowance of counsel's fees it is not necessary to give notice to counsel.

I/we consent to the signing forthwith of the costs officer's certificate.

(4) CERTIFICATE IN RESPECT OF DISBURSEMENTS NOT EXCEEDING £500

I hereby certify that all disbursements listed in this bill which individually do not exceed £500 (other than those relating to counsel's fees) have been duly discharged.

(5) CERTIFICATE AS TO RECOVERY OF VAT

With reference to the pending assessment of the [claimant's/defendant's] costs and disbursements herein which are payable by the [claimant/defendant] we the undersigned [solicitors to] [auditors of] the [claimant/defendant] hereby certify that the [claimant/defendant] on the basis of its last completed VAT return [would/would not be entitled to recover would/be entitled to recover only   per cent of the] Value Added Tax on such costs and disbursements, as input tax pursuant to section 14 of the Value Added Tax Act 1983.

48PD–010

SCHEDULE OF COSTS FORMS: FORM 6

IN THE HIGH COURT OF JUSTICE 1997-B-9999

QUEEN'S BENCH DIVISION

BRIGHTON DISTRICT REGISTRY

B E T W E E N

AB

Claimant

– and –

CD

Defendant

POINTS OF DISPUTE SERVED BY THE DEFENDANT

Item	Dispute	Claimant's Comments
General point	Hourly rates claimed for the solicitor and trainee are excessive. Reduce to £100 and £50 respectively plus VAT. These items should be recalculated at the reduced rates.	
(5)	The duration of the conference is excessive. Reduce to one hour *i.e.* £212.50 at reduced rates.	
(11)	The total fees for items (10) and (11) are excessive. Reduce item (11) to £50.	
(12)	Allow at reduced rates only.	
(14)	Telephone conference not justified. Disallow.	
(15)	Telephone conference not justified. Disallow.	
(16)	6.5 hours is excessive. Reduce to 3 hours *i.e.* £300 at reduced rates.	
(17) (18) (20) (21) (22) (23) (25) (26)	Allow at reduced rates only.	
(27)	The claim for routine attendances on counsel is excessive. Reduce to 6 units *i.e.* £60 at reduced rates.	
(28) (29) (30)	Allow at reduced rates only.	

Item	Dispute	Claimant's Comments
(31)	The total claim for documents in this part is excessive. A reasonable allowance in respect of documents concerning court and counsel is 8 hours, for documents concerning witnesses and the expert witness, 6.5 hours for other documents, 5.5 hours. Reduce to 20 hours *i.e.* £2,000 at reduced rates.	
(32) (39) (43) (45)	Allow at reduced rates only.	
(46)	Telephone call not justified. Disallow.	
(47)	Telephone call not justified. Disallow.	
(48) (49) (50) (51) (52) (53)	Allowed at reduced rates only.	
(54)	The claim for routine attendances on counsel is excessive. Reduce to 4 units *i.e.* £40 at reduced rates.	
(55)	Allow at reduced rates only.	
(56)	The time claimed is excessive. Reduce solicitors time to 0.5 hours *i.e.* to £50 at reduced rates and reduce the costs draftsman's time to three hours *i.e.* £240 (£290 in total).	

Served on [date] by [name] [solicitors for] the Defendant.

48PD–011

SCHEDULE OF COSTS FORMS: FORM 15

Legal Aid Assessment Certificate

In the	
Claim No.	
Legal Aid Certificate No.	
Solicitors Ref.	

Claimant

Defendant

The costs in this matter have been assessed as set out in boxes A, B and C below and are claimed from the Legal Aid Fund.

The costs are those of the ☐ Claimant ☐ Defendant ☐ Other

They were taxed in the ☐ High Court ☐ County Court *(please tick appropriate boxes)*

Total pre-certificate costs, which are not being claimed were (Include disbursements, profit costs and VAT) £

Date ______________ Signed ______________

A. Costs payable by another party as allowed or as in legal aid schedule if appropriate
(Do not include any pre-certificate costs, or the costs of assessment)

Profit Costs	
VAT	
Counsel's Fees	
VAT	
Disbursements	
VAT (Where appropriate)	
Total	£

B. Legal aid only costs
(Do not include the costs of assessment)

Profit Costs	
VAT	
Counsel's Fees	
VAT	
Disbursements	
VAT (Where appropriate)	
Total	£

C. Costs of assessment
(Allowed in respect of A and B above)

For Part A	
VAT	
Court Fees (Where appropriate)	
For Part B	
VAT	
Court fee (Where appropriate)	
Total	£

C. Total claimed
(Add totals A, B and C)

Total part A	
Total part B	
Total part C	
Total	£

Sealed by the court on ______________________

48PD–012

**SCHEDULE OF COSTS FORMS:
FORM 16**

In the	
Claim No.	
Claimant (including ref.)	
Defendant (including ref.)	
Date	

NOTICE OF APPEAL

[The *party wishes*] [I] [wish] to appeal against [some of] the decision(s) made by the costs officer at the hearing on [date] concerning the detailed assessment of [the *party's*] bill of costs. The grounds of appeal are:

[Each ground must be numbered. Grounds which relate to decisions on items in the bill of costs must also state the number of the item, a short description of the item, the amount claimed and the amount allowed. Some illustrations are given below.]

Ground 1

Decision to refuse permission to amend the Points of Dispute.

[Here state the grounds upon which the appellant intends to rely]

Ground 2

Bill item 6, counsel's fee, £250 plus VAT claimed £250 plus VAT allowed.

[Here state the grounds upon which the appellant intends to rely]

Ground 3

Bill item 28, attendances on expert witnesses, £480 plus VAT claimed, £420 plus VAT allowed.

[Here state the grounds upon which the appellant intends to rely]

I now enclose copies of *(tick as appropriate)*

☐ The Costs Certificate or other order being appealed

☐ Costs Officer's written reasons (or other dispensing with written reasons)

☐ Bill of Costs

☐ Points of Dispute lodged with request for detailed assessment hearing

☐ Points in Reply (if any)

☐ The authority for the detailed assessment

To *[Costs Officer whose decision is being appealed]* and to *[the intended respondents to the appeal]*

Signed   Date

[Party]   [Party's Solicitor]

48PD–013

SCHEDULE OF COSTS FORMS: FORM 17

DATED the [DATE]

IN THE HIGH COURT OF JUSTICE [Case No]

[DIVISION]

[JUDGE TYPE] [JUDGE NAME]

BETWEEN:

[CLAIMANT]

Claimant

– and –

[DEFENDANT]

Defendant

UPON THE APPLICATION OF THE [PARTY]

AND UPON HEARING [ATTEND]

AND UPON READING the documents on the Court File

IT IS ORDERED THAT

1 The [PARTY 1] must within [NUMBER OF DAYS] deliver to the [PARTY 2], or to his solicitor, a bill of costs in all causes and matters in which he has been concerned for the [PARTY 2]

2 The [PARTY 1] must give credit in that bill for all money received by him from or on account of the [PARTY 2]

48PD–014

SCHEDULE OF COSTS FORMS: FORM 18

ORDER ON CLIENT'S APPLICATION FOR DETAILED ASSESSMENT OF SOLICITOR'S BILL

Upon hearing . . upon reading . .

IT IS ORDERED

(1) A detailed assessment must be made of the bill dated [ ] delivered to the claimant by the defendant.

(2) On making the detailed assessment, the court must also assess the costs of these proceedings and certify what is due to or from either party in respect of the bill and the costs of these proceedings.

(3) Until these proceedings are concluded the defendant must not commence or continue any proceedings against the claimant in respect of the bill mentioned above.

(4) Upon payment by the claimant of any sum certified as due to the defendant in these proceedings the defendant must deliver to the claimant all the documentation in the defendant's possession or control which belong to the claimant.

48PD–015

SCHEDULE OF COSTS FORMS: FORM 19

ORDER ON SOLICITOR'S APPLICATION FOR ASSESSMENT UNDER THE SOLICITORS ACT 1974 PART III

Upon hearing . . upon reading . .

IT IS ORDERED

(1) A detailed assessment must be made of the bill dated [ ] delivered to the defendant by the claimant.

(2) If the defendant attends the detailed assessment the court making that assessment must also assess the costs of these proceedings and certify what is due to or from either party in respect of the bill and the costs of these proceedings.

(3) Until these proceedings are concluded the claimant must not commence or continue any proceedings against the defendant in respect of the bill mentioned above.

(4) Upon payment by the defendant of any sum certified as due to the claimant in these proceedings the claimant must deliver to the defendant all the documentation in the defendant's possession or control which belong to the defendant.

48PD–016

SCHEDULE OF COSTS FORMS: FORM 20

IN THE HIGH COURT OF JUSTICE — Case Number

QUEEN'S BENCH DIVISION

SUPREME COURT COSTS OFFICE

B E T W E E N

EF

Claimant

– and –

GH & Co

Defendants

BREAKDOWN OF DEFENDANT'S BILL OF COSTS DATED 26 FEBRUARY 1999 TO BE ASSESSED PURSUANT TO THE ORDER DATED 27 APRIL 1999

The claimant instructed the defendants in connection with a summons for careless or inconsiderate driving which had been served upon him. By letter dated 21 October 1998 the defendants wrote to the claimant setting out their terms of business including the hourly rates of fee earners who would act on his instructions. On 23 October 1998 the claimant dated and signed a copy of that letter and returned it to the defendants so indicating his acceptance of the terms set out.

The proceedings were of the highest importance to the claimant who feared losing his licence and who wished to defend any civil proceedings that might be taken against him as a result of the prosecution. The defendants entered into correspondence with the CPS and eventually obtained their witness statements and invited them to consent to an adjournment because of the absence overseas of an important witness for the claim (Mr LM). Eventually the defendants successfully applied to the court for an adjournment, and also applied for and obtained a witness summons. At the trial the claimant was found guilty and was fined £300 and 4 points were endorsed on his driving licence.

Proceedings were conducted by an assistant solicitor admitted in 1990 whose time is charged at an agreed rate of £150 per hour with routine letters out and telephone calls at an agreed rate of £15 each. At the trial a trainee attended with counsel. The trainee's time is charged at an agreed rate of £75 per hour.

Cash account for client: EF

Received		Paid	
From client on account generally: 22 October 1998	1,500.00	Refund to client: 26 February 1999	385.00
From client on account generally: 12 February 1998	1,000.00	Balancing item	2,115.00
	2,500.00		2,500,00

Balance due to client EF: £2,115

Item		Amount Claimed	VAT	Amount Allowed	VAT
Attendances on Court and Counsel					
5th November 1998—application made for an adjournment for the convenience of a witness					
13th November 1998—contested hearing of the application	Engaged 10 minutes	25.00			
Travel and waiting 30 minutes	75.00				
(1) Total solicitor's fee for hearing		100.00	17.50		
17th November 1998—conference with counsel					
Engaged 45 minutes	112.50				
Travel and waiting 1 hour	150.00				
(2) Total solicitor's fee for conference		262.50	45.94		
(3) Counsel's fee for conference (paid: Miss JK)		75.00	13.13		
15th February 1999—brief to counsel—4 pages A4					
23rd February 1999—attending the trial					
Trainee engaged in court 1 hour	75.00				
Engaged in conference 30 minutes	37.50				
Travel and waiting (apportioned) 45 minutes	56.25				
(4) Total trainee solicitor's fee for trial		168.75	29.53		
(5) Counsel's brief fee (paid: Miss JK)		100.00	17.50		
Claimant					
(6) 21st October 1998—first instructions 1 hour		150.00	26.25		
(7) 16th November 1998—finalising proof of evidence 45 minutes		112.50	19.69		
(8) Routine letters out and telephone calls—12 (9 + 3)		180.00	31.50		
Witness (Mr LM)					
Personal attendance by trainee solicitor					
Engaged 45 minutes	56.25				
Travel and waiting 1 hour	75.00				
(9) Total trainee solicitor's fee for attendance		131.25	22.97		
(10) Routine letters out—6		90.00	15.75		
Other persons					
(11) Routine letters out and telephone calls to the CPS—8 (6 + 2)		120.00	21.00		
Communications with the Court					
(12) Routine letters out—6		90.00	15.75		
Communications with counsel					
(13) Routine letters out and telephone calls—8 (4 + 4)		120.00	21.00		
Work done on documents					
(14) Instructions to counsel—30 minutes		75.00	13.13		
(15) Attendance note of conference 15 minutes		37.50	6.56		
(16) Brief to counsel—30 minutes		75.00	13.13		
(17) Attendance note of trial (trainee)—45 minutes		56.25	9.84		
Summary					
Summary costs claimed in breakdown (Total costs billed £1,800 + £315.00 VAT)		1,943.75	340.17		

48PD–017

SCHEDULE OF COSTS FORMS: FORM 21

In the	
Claim No.	
Claimant (including ref.)	
Defendant (including ref.)	

Request for Detailed Assessment Hearing Pursuant to an Order under Part III of the Solicitors Act 1974

I certify that the [*party*] has served a breakdown of costs in this case and the [*party*] has served points of dispute thereon.

I now ask the court to arrange an assessment hearing. The names, addresses and references of the parties upon whom the court should give notice of the hearing are as follows:

I enclose copies of (*tick as appropriate*)

- ☐ the order made under Part III of the Solicitors Act 1974 in this case
- ☐ Bills of Costs to be assessed
- ☐ breakdown of costs
- ☐ any fee notes of counsel and receipts or accounts for other disbursements served with the breakdown of costs
- ☐ the [party's] points of dispute plus copies to be sent to the other parties to these proceedings details of whom are given above
- ☐ points in reply (if any)

I believe the hearing will take .... (*give estimate of time court should allow*).

I enclose my fee of £ ....

Signed .... Date ....
(Claimant) (Defendant) (Solicitor)

48PD–018

SUMMARY ASSESSMENT OF COSTS GUIDELINE FIGURES

The recent publication of the Guide to the Summary Assessment of Costs and its associated guideline hourly rates for solicitors has led to a considerable amount of discussion as to the status of the guideline figures. The purpose of this letter is to make it clear that the figures are guidelines only, the first paragraph of Appendix 4 to the explanatory notes makes this clear:

> "The guideline rates for solicitors are broad approximations only. In any particular area the Designated Civil Judge may after consultation between District Judges and local Law Societies supply more exact guidelines for rates in that area. Also the costs estimate provided by the paying party may give further guidance if the solicitors for both parties are based in the same locality."

There is anecdotal evidence that practitioners have been told that the rates set out in the guidelines supersede those which have been agreed locally and that Judges have no discretion to allow anything other than the guideline figures. If that approach has been adopted it is erroneous.

Rates arrived at by local agreement are likely to be much more reliable than those suggested centrally by the Costs Office and the guideline figures are not intended to replace figures used by those with accurate local knowledge. They are intended to provide a starting point for those faced with summary assessment who do not have that local knowledge.

The figures, like any guidance figures, reflect the levels at which rates were being allowed at the time when the guidelines were drawn up. In addition it should be borne in mind that these guidelines were prepared in support of the Practice Direction of 1 February 1999 which relates only to interlocutory applications in respect of which it is normal to allow a lower level of uplift than in respect of the substantive preparation for trial.

Following a meeting with representatives of the Law Society discussion should now take place at local levels between the Profession and District Judges with a view to arriving at appropriate rates for the particular area. The Law Society intends to suggest revised categories of fee earners but until those details are to hand and have been approved it will be necessary for rates to be agreed in accordance with the categories mentioned in the Guide. The local rates, once agreed, should be reported to the Senior Costs Judge at the Supreme Court Costs Office in London. Once rates have been received for each of the areas covered by the Designated Civil Judges it will be possible for revised guideline figures for the area in question to be circulated.

The hope is that this exercise will produce a measure of consistency across the country. Even when rates have been agreed locally these will be no more than a starting point and Judges faced with assessment of costs may adjust the rates up or down depending on the circumstances of any particular case.

On a related topic, where either party has entered into a conditional fee agreement the Judge needs to be aware of the existence of the agreement because the Judge should consider staying payment of any costs which have been assessed until the end of the action; otherwise Rule 44.8 requires the order for payment of costs to be complied with within 14 days. If a Judge decides not to carry out a summary assessment it may not be appropriate to order a party to pay an amount on account before the end of the action in accordance with Rule 44.3(8) if there is a conditional fee agreement in existence.

SIR RICHARD SCOTT

VICE-CHANCELLOR
HEAD OF CIVIL JUSTICE

48PD–019

COURT OF APPEAL (CIVIL DIVISION)
PRACTICE NOTE ON THE ASSESSMENT OF COSTS

Introduction

Part 44 of the Civil Procedure Rules (General rules about costs), and its accompanying Practice Direction do not explicitly set out the extent to which the provisions on the summary assessment of costs apply to the Court of Appeal (Civil Division). This Practice Note therefore outlines the approach that the Court of Appeal will be taking with regard to the summary assessment of costs from 26 April.

Summary assessment of costs

The Practice Direction to Part 44 explains (paragraph 4.3) that, in first instance courts, whenever a court makes an order about costs which does not provide for fixed costs to be paid, the court should consider whether to make a summary assessment of costs. The Court of Appeal fully supports this approach as an appropriate means of disposing of costs issues quickly and openly. However, the practice is less straightforward in the Court of Appeal. The Court of Appeal is therefore concerned to ensure that it operates a system which avoids putting parties to the unnecessary expense of preparing statements of costs in cases which are unsuitable for a summary assessment.

To achieve this aim, the Court of Appeal itself will identify those cases which appear to be suitable for summary assessment of costs and will notify the relevant parties accordingly. Parties to appeals will not therefore need to file statements of costs unless they are informed by the Court of Appeal that this is required.

Where the Court of Appeal informs the parties that it is minded to assess costs summarily, each party must: prepare, file and exchange statements of costs; and identify any items of the other party's statement which are in dispute, giving reasons for the dispute, not less than 7 calendar days before the hearing.

It should be noted, however, that the fact that the Court of Appeal may have requested statements of costs does not place an obligation on the Court to assess costs summarily. This can be determined only when the parties' statements of costs are available and the extent to which any items are in dispute is known. In addition, the fact that the Court of Appeal has not invited parties to file statements of costs does not prevent parties who agree on this proposing by letter to the Court that a summary assessment might be suitable. If the Court agrees, it will ask for statements of costs to be filed.

Partial orders for costs

Although the Court of Appeal does not propose to make a summary assessment of costs, the Court of Appeal may nonetheless make orders for costs which reflect the fact that a party to the application, while successful in general on the appeal, has been unsuccessful in relation to certain issues. After 26 April, the Court of Appeal will be more likely than hitherto to make orders for costs which reflect the outcome in relation to different issues.

Future review
These practices will be monitored over the coming months and will be looked at again as part of the review of RSC Order 59. It is hoped that new Civil Procedure Rules and accompanying Practice Directions on civil appeals will be implemented early in the New Year.

The Rt Hon the Lord Woolf
Master of the Rolls

20 April 1999

GENERAL PRINCIPLES AND CASE LAW RELATING TO COSTS AND THEIR ASSESSMENT

Introductory note—This section is not intended to be a definitive work on the general principles of assessment, but a compilation of decisions and commentary which may from time to time need to be referred to. 48.11.1

Contents

General Principles and Case relating to Costs and their Assessment

1. COSTS IN SPECIFIC COURTS AND OTHER TRIBUNALS

ARBITRATION

Costs of the Reference—The "costs of the reference" are those "which are incidental to the reference and incurred in bringing it about—costs of the arrangements, meetings, discussions, consultations, conferences and all that are necessary to bring the parties *ad idem* to a point on which they agree, but up to which there must be preliminary steps". *Per* Huddleston B. in *Autothreptic Steam Boiler Co. Ltd v. Townsend Hook and Co.* (1888) 21 Q.B.D. 182. 48.12.1

An agreement which has the effect that a party is to pay the whole or part of the costs of the arbitration in any event is only valid if made after the dispute in question has arisen (s.60 of the Arbitration Act 1996). *Everglade Maritime Inc. v. Schiffahrtsgesellschaft Detlaf Von Appen mbH. The Maria* [1993] 3 All E.R. 748, CA).

Where an arbitrator made a final award in which he ruled in favour of the applicants on some issues and in favour of the respondent on others and ordered the applicants to pay the respondents costs, and in giving reasons for the decision the arbitrator relied on two matters which the parties had not raised, the Court found that the arbitrator had not acted in accordance with the general duty, under section 33 of the Act, to act fairly and impartially between the parties. His failure to raise these matters with the parties amounted to a serious irregularity within the meaning of section 63(2) of the Arbitration Act 1996. *Gbangbola v. Smith & Sherriff Ltd* [1998] 3 All E.R. 730 Judge Lloyd, Q.C. (Technology and Construction Court).

It is not improper for an arbitrator to propose to both parties an arrangement for payment of fees, including a commitment fee payable in advance of the hearing. It would probably constitute misconduct for an arbitrator to conclude an agreement as to fees with one party when the other refused to join in the agreement (*Norjar A/S v. Hyundai Heavy Industries Co. Ltd* [1991] 3 All E.R. 211). See also section 60(1) of the Arbitration Act 1996.

The parties are free to argue what costs of the arbitration are recoverable (section 63 of the Arbitration Act 1996). As to the recoverable fee and expenses of arbitrators, see *ibid.*, s.64.

Where a whole cause is referred to an arbitrator, and he awards "the costs of the action and of this my award," the costs of the reference are included in "the costs of the action" (*Patten v. West of England Iron, etc., Co.* [1894] 2 Q.B. 159). See also section 61 of the Arbitration Act 1996.

It is not competent for an arbitrator to deal with costs which might be incurred before the Divisional Court (*Higham v. Havant and Waterloo U.D.C.* [1951] 2 K.B. 527, CA; (1951) 2 T.L.R. 87).

For the statutory provisions relating to the costs of arbitration see Arbitration Act 1996, ss.59–65 at SCP 1999, Vol. 2, Section 21D, paras 21D–128 to 21D–138.

48.12.2 **Costs of claims consultants**—In *Piper Double Glazing Ltd v. D.C. Contracts* [1994] 1 All E.R. 117, Potter J. answered in the affirmative the preliminary issue "where in an arbitration conducted in England or Wales in accordance with English law:

(i) a party is represented by a person who is neither a qualified solicitor, nor a barrister ('the unqualified person'), but who provides services and performs functions similar to those provided or performed by a solicitor or barrister, and;

(ii) an award is made by the Arbitrator in favour of that party which includes a direction that another party should pay the first party's costs of the arbitration; and

(iii) the award provides such for such costs to be [assessed] in the High Court, if not agreed [...] and

(iv) the arbitration agreement or reference to arbitration contains no provision excluding the recovery of such costs;

in proceedings for the [assessment] of costs pursuant to the award, does the Court on a proper construction of [Rules of Court] and or sections 20–25 of the Solicitors Act 1974, have power to allow any amount for the costs incurred by the unqualified person in relation to the conduct of the arbitration?"

The learned Judge refused to answer the second issue: "If the Court does have power to allow amounts for the costs so incurred by the unqualified person in relation to the conduct of the arbitration, are those costs to be allowed or to be assessed on the basis set out by Master Hurst in *William Tarr & Co. Ltd v. Royal Insurance plc*, April 8, 1989 (unrep.), that being that the costs recovered cannot [...] be more than the amount recoverable had the arbitration been conducted by solicitor and counsel, and if not upon what basis should they be assessed or allowed?"

COPYRIGHT TRIBUNAL

48.12.3 The Copyright Tribunal may at its discretion at any stage in the proceedings make an order in relation to the payment of costs by one party to another in respect of the whole or part of the proceedings. The Tribunal may direct payment of a lump sum by way of costs, or such a proportion of the costs as may be just, in which case the Tribunal may assess the sum to be paid or direct it to be assessed by the Chairman or by a Costs Judge of the Supreme Court (or the Supreme Court of Northern Ireland or the Auditor of the Court of Session) (Copyright Tribunal Rules 1989, r.48(1)(2)). Neither the Copyright, Design and Patents Act 1988 nor the 1989 Rules provide that costs should follow the event. The Tribunal has a very wide discretion as to costs under section 151 of the 1988 Act: *AEI Redifusion Music Ltd v. Phonographic Performance Ltd (Costs), The Times*, March 3, 1999, CA.

The Court of Appeal has jurisdiction over the costs of the proceedings below (SCA 1981, s.51) and may vary the order as to costs made in the Court below and make such order as it thinks fit. The general rule applies equally in a salvage suit, where the appellant succeeds in reducing substantially the amount of the salvage awarded, and in collision cases in admiralty (*The Toscana* [1905] P. 148; *The London* [1905] P. 152). The Court of Appeal, like any other Court, has jurisdiction over the costs of the proceedings, even though it may have no jurisdiction over their subject-matter (*Ecclesiastical Commissioners for England v. National Provincial Bank Ltd* [1935] 1 K.B. 566 at 575, CA; *Diss Urban Sanitary Authority v. Aldrich* (1877) 2 Q.B.D. 179; *Crowther v. Boult* (1884) 13 Q.B.D. 680).

The Court of Appeal has no power following a Civil Appeal to order that a successful appellant's costs be awarded out of central funds (*Holden & Co. v. Crown Prosecution Service (No. 2)* [1993] 2 W.L.R. 934, HL).

DIVISIONAL COURT

48.12.4 The Divisional Court has no jurisdiction on an application for judicial review to award costs out of central funds to the successful applicant. Section 51 of the Contempt of Court Act 1981 gave the court a general and wide discretion to make such orders as to payments of costs as it thought fit. This power does not include the power to make an award out of central funds even where there is "no other possible source of costs" in an application for judicial review (*Holden & Co. v. CPS (No. 2)* [1993] 2 W.L.R. 934, HL, reversing *R. v. Bow Street Metropolitan Stipendiary Magistrate, ex p. Mirror Group Newspapers*; *R. v. same, ex p. B.B.C.* [1992] 1 W.L.R. 412, DC).

An applicant for judicial review who abandons his application because he no longer requires relief from the court is not entitled to recover his costs. Under s.51(1) of the Supreme Court Act

1981 costs are only recoverable when there are proceedings before the court: an application for leave to move for judicial review cannot constitute proceedings (*R. v. Test Valley Borough Council, ex p. Goodman* [1992] C.O.D. 101).

EMPLOYMENT APPEAL TRIBUNAL

Costs ordered to be paid under the Employment Appeal Tribunal Rules 1980 and 1993 (S.I. 1980 No. 2035; S.I. 1993 No. 2854), are in practice assessed in the Supreme Court Costs Office. The costs of an assisted party in EAT proceedings are assessed in accordance with the Civil Legal Aid (General) Regulations 1989 (S.I. 1989 No. 339), reg. 105 (SCP 1999, Vol. 2, Section 16D, para. 16D–196) or assessed on the standard basis (*ibid.*, reg. 149(7)) (SCP 1999, Vol. 2, Section 16D, para. 16D–272). **48.12.5**

The Litigants in Person (Costs and Expenses) Act 1975 has been applied to the Employment Appeal Tribunal with effect from September 1, 1980 by the Litigants in Person (Costs and Expenses) Order 1980 (S.I. 1980 No. 1159) and see SCP 1999, Vol. 2, Section 21R, paras 21R–1 to 21R–5. Bristow J. in *Johnson v. Baxter* [1984] I.C.R. 675, EAT, said that a party who expected to be successful and thought he had grounds for applying for costs under r.11 of Sched. I to the Industrial Tribunals (Rules of Procedure) Regulations (S.I. 1985 No. 16) should make his application at the conclusion of the hearing even if the decision was to be reserved.

LANDS TRIBUNAL

Where a claim for pre-reference costs is not quantified by the claimant, it will be sufficient for the sealed offer to agree to the payment of those costs in general terms. If they are later quantified for the claimant a revised sealed offer may be substituted. This is relevant for the purpose of deciding whether the award of costs of the proceedings before the Tribunal are controlled by section 4 of the Land Compensation Act 1961 or whether they are in the unfettered discretion of the Tribunal (*Day v. Greater London Council* (1972) 122 New L.J. 23). Where the Lands Tribunal made an award of compensation in 1988 which was subsequently set aside and the matter remitted for redetermination, the Tribunal redetermining the compensation in 1991, interest on costs ran from the date of the 1991 award which was the only effective award on the reference: *Barclays Bank plc v. Kent County Council* [1998] R.V.R. 74, CA. **48.12.6**

2. COSTS RELATING TO SPECIFIC STATUTES

Consumer Credit Act 1974—On an appeal to the Secretary of State under Pt III of the Act he may under s.41(3) direct any party to pay costs. Where such directions are made an order of the High Court under s.41(4) they are assessed by a Costs Judge. **48.13.1**

Local Government Act 1972, s.250—power to make orders for costs in planning cases—In deciding whether to make an order for costs against a planning authority which had raised objections to a planning application there is an evidential threshold which, if reached, is likely to put a planning authority beyond the risk of a finding that it has been guilty of unreasonable conduct (*R. v. Secretary of State for the Environment, ex p. North Norfolk D.C.* [1994] 2 P.L.R. 78; and *R. v. Secretary of State for the Environment, ex p. Chichester D.C.* [1993] 2 P.L.R. 1). "Sufficient evidential basis" means evidence not lacking real substance capable of belief and which, if accepted, would be capable of making good the plaintiff authority's objection (*R. v. Secretary of State for the Environment, ex p. Wakefield Metropolitan B.C.* (1996) *The Times*, October 29). **48.13.2**

3. COSTS RELATING TO PARTICULAR TYPES OF ACTION OR PROCEEDINGS

Multiple representation in planning appeals.—The practice of awarding two sets of costs in certain types of planning appeal, notably where a decision of the Secretary of State in favour of the developer is challenged by the local authority, and the Secretary of State successfully defends his decision (in such cases the developer has usually been regarded as having a separate interest which he is entitled to protect at the local authority's expense), is recognised by the Court: *Waverley Borough Council v. Secretary of State for the Environemnt* (1988) 55 P. & C.R. 111; [1987] J.P.L. 202, Simon Brown J. The House of Lords has reviewed the practice: As in all questions to do with costs the fundamental rule is that there are no rules. Costs are always in the discretion of the Court, and a practice however widespread and long standing must never be allowed to harden into a rule. The following propositions may be supported: **48.14.1**

(1) The Secretary of State when successful in defending his decision will normally be entitled to the whole of his costs. He should not be required to share his award of costs by apportionment whether by agreement with other parties or by further Order of the Court. In so far as the Court of Appeal in *Wychavon District Council v. Secretary of State for the Environment* [1994] C.O.D. 205; *The Times*, January 7, 1994, may have encouraged or sanctioned such a course, their Lordships disagreed.

(2) The developer will not normally be entitled to his costs, unless he can show that there was likely to be a separate issue on which he was entitled to be heard. That is to say, unless an issue not covered by Counsel for the Secretary of State; or unless he has an

interest which requires separate representation. The mere fact that he is a developer will not of itself justify a second set of costs in every case.

(3) A second set of costs is more likely to be awarded at first instance, than in the Court of Appeal or House of Lords by which time the issues should have crystallised, and the extent to which they are indeed separate interests should have been clarified.

(4) An award of a third set of costs will rarely be justified even if there are in theory three or more separate interests; *per* Lord Lloyd of Berwick, *Bolton MDC v. Secretary of State for the Environment* [1995] 1 W.L.R. 1176, HL.

An order of a government department as to costs on an enquiry will not be assessed in the High Court unless it is made a rule of Court under section 250(4) of the Local Government Act 1972.

The Court has jurisdiction to make an anticipatory costs order so that where lead cases were selected the purpose should not be vitiated by having regard to the means and willingness of claimants to accept a high degree of risk as to costs rather than the issues in the particular actions (*Ward v. Guiness Mahon & Co. Ltd* [1996] 1 W.L.R. 894, CA).

4. COSTS RELATING TO PARTICULAR TYPES OF PARTIES AND MISCELLANEOUS

48.15.1 **Bankrupt**—A creditor who serves a statutory demand, without judgment having already been given in his favour, does so at his own risk on costs. The service of a statutory demand is a step in the bankruptcy proceedings and a cause of action in its own right. In *Re A Debtor (No. 620 of 1997), The Times*, June 18, 1998, Hart J.

When, following service of the petition, the debt is paid, the appropriate order for costs must reflect the ultimate success of the creditors but must also reflect any avoidable defects in the creditor's proceedings. Where substantial additional costs were incurred, quite unnecessarily by the debtor, because of *e.g.* adjournments, the proper order should be no order as to costs. In *Re A Debtor (No. 510 of 1997), The Times*, June 18, 1998, Mr Stanley Burnton, Q.C.

A costs order made against a discharged bankrupt in proceedings commenced prior to the bankruptcy was not a bankruptcy debt pursuant to section 382(1)(a) of the Insolvency Act 1986. The costs order was not a contingent liability at the date of the commencement of the bankruptcy. Until an order was made there could be no obligation to pay costs: *Glenister v. Rowe, The Times* April 28, 1999, CA.

48.15.2 **Counterclaim**—Where claim and counterclaim are both dismissed with costs, upon assessment the rule is that the claim should be treated as if it stood alone and the counterclaim should bear only the amount by which the costs of the proceedings have been increased by it. No costs not incurred by reason of the counterclaim can be costs of the counterclaim. In the absence of special directions by the Court, there should be no apportionment. The same principle applies where both the claim and the counterclaim have succeeded (*Medway Oil and Storage Co. v. Continental Contractors* [1929] A.C. 88, HL). But see *Millican v. Tucker* [1980] 1 W.L.R. 640; [1980] 1 All E.R. 1083, where the Court of Appeal held it was well within the Judge's discretion *inter partes* to order the apportionment of the costs of claim and counterclaim equally.

48.15.3 **Receiver**—As to remuneration of a receiver see R30.3. Receivers are personally bound by their contract with their solicitors and must pay the proper charges, but they should give close scrutiny to the solicitors' bills and whether such charges should be recovered from the estate would depend on whether they had acted properly in employing them for the tasks in question. Office holders such as Receivers were not normally expected to act voluntarily, but office holders who sought remuneration at a particular level had to justify their claim as one aspect of their duty to account. They had to give full particulars and they ought to be remunerated on the basis of time spent. They had to do significantly more than giving the total number of hours spent by them or their staff and multiplying it by the charging rate of the individual whose time was spent. They should explain the nature of each task undertaken and why it was undertaken. The charging rate should be proved by evidence, they should keep records, the test being whether a reasonably prudent man, faced with the same circumstances in relation to his own affairs, would have done the same things (*Mirror Group Newspapers Plc v. Maxwell, The Times*, July 15, 1997, Ferris J.).

Trustees, personal representatives

48.15.4 *Powers of the court as to costs*—The court has jurisdiction to make an order as to the ultimate incidence of costs in the proceedings ahead of the trial of the action (*Re Wedstock Realizations Ltd* [1988] B.C.L.C. 354 at 358, 359). There is a discretion to make an order in terms which ensure that, win or lose, a litigant would be entitled to costs out of the property in dispute, before the facts have been fully explored and before the relevant law has been fully argued. That discretion is most frequently exercised in favour of trustees and executors (*Re Beddoe* [1893] 1 Ch. 547 at 557, 561 at 562).

A trustee who defends proceedings brought against him in a representative capacity without obtaining a Beddoe order will be at risk as to costs. If the court would not have given authority to defend the proceedings in accordance with the principles set out in *Re Beddoe* it would not allow the costs to be paid out of the trust funds either even if the trustee was advised by counsel that he had a good defence to the claim: *Singh v. Bhasin, The Times* August 21, 1998, Mr Alan Boyle, Q.C.

The discretion has also been exercised in favour of an executor who, on application to the court, has been authorised to bring or defend proceedings so that, even if unsuccessful, he would be entitled to be indemnified out of the estate for all the costs for which he might be liable (*Re Dallaway (dec'd.)* [1982] 1 W.L.R. 756).

The court is much influenced by the fact that it is the duty of trustees and executors to protect the estate, that they are entitled to be indemnified for costs properly incurred for the benefit of the estate and Rules of Court expressly provide that executors and trustees are entitled to their costs out of the fund held by them in that capacity (*National Anti-Vivisection Society Ltd v. Duddington* (1989) *The Times*, November 23, *per* Mummery J.). Thus in *Re Wedstock* (above) an order was made that the costs of liquidation should be paid from the fund held by the receiver; but in *Re Charge Card Services Ltd* [1986] B.C.L.C. 136, Hoffmann J. declined to make an order ahead of the final hearing of a liquidator's summons for directions.

The court may also exercise its discretion to make pre-emptive costs orders in the case of an action by a minority shareholder in a similar way to a trustee on a *Beddoe* application (*Wallersteiner v. Moir* [1975] Q.B. 373 at 389 at 391–392, 403–405; *Smith v. Croft* [1986] 1 W.L.R. 580).

The essence of the discretion depends on the facts of each case (*Re Evans (dec'd.)* [1986] 1 W.L.R. 101). However it is not necessarily limited to categories of case which have arisen to date (*e.g.* trustee, executor, liquidator, receiver, minority shareholder) but must be exercised judiciously having regard only to the relevant factors (*National Anti-Vivisection Society Ltd* (above)). The following factors have featured in decided cases as relevant to the court's jurisdiction to make pre-emptive costs orders:

(i) The merits.
(ii) The likely order for costs at trial.
(iii) The justice of the case.
(iv) Special factors.

(i) The merits.—The prospects of success of a claim or a defence is the most important question to be taken into account in considering whether the action or defence should be financed out of the estate or fund in dispute (*Re Evans (dec'd.)* (above)). The fund in dispute should not be used to support contentions which were not made in good faith or on reasonable grounds.

(ii) The likely order for costs at trial.—Unless the court is satisfied that it is likely that an order would be made after trial, that the costs in question be paid out of the fund, it is not in general right to make such an order before trial (*Re Wedstock* (above)). In the case of a trustee the court at trial will in general give effect to the trustee's right to indemnity out of the trust fund if he has acted properly for the benefit of the fund in the pursuit or defence of proceedings even if he is ultimately unsuccessful.

(iii) The justice of the case.—A pre-emptive order should not be made if there is a real possibility of it acting unjustly. It might be unjust in a particular case for the successful claimant to the property in dispute to be placed in a position where even if he wins, property held to be his is burdened with payment of the unsuccessful parties' costs. That is a powerful consideration where the persons who would benefit from the pre-emptive order are all adult and *sui juris* (*Re Evans (dec'd).*

(iv) Special factors.—Examples of other special factors which might make a pre-trial order appropriate include the following: Where it is essential for the due administration of justice for a liquidator or administrator to obtain the court's decision because there are large classes of persons, *e.g.* creditors, who might be affected by the decision (*Re Exchange Securities Ltd (No. 2)* [1985] B.C.L.C. 392 at 395). Again the application might be a test case in which a decision is necessary on a point in order to resolve a number of pending cases (*Re Wedstock* (above) at 360–361).

In a case which depends on the resolution of the question whether property is held in trust by the defendants for the claimant, the very existence of the trustee/beneficiary relationship is in issue in the action. Since that involves hostile litigation between two rival claimants it is wrong for the court to fetter the discretion of the trial judge by making a pre-emptive interlocutory order for costs in favour of the defendants, to be paid out of the property in dispute, which might operate unjustly against the claimant (*National Anti-Vivisection Society Ltd* (above)).

A pre-emptive costs order could be made in favour of employees who were representative claimants in an action against their employers and the trustees of relevant pension funds, where they had not the resources to pursue major litigation, and their claims were so strong that it was inconceivable that if an independent trustee were appointed he would not apply for and obtain such an order (*McDonald v. Horn* (1993) *The Times*, October 12, Vinelott J.

The Court of Appeal upheld the Judgment of Mr Justice Vinelott, stating that the point was one of considerable practical importance. Reference should be made to the full judgment for an analysis of the law. *Statutory Costs Jurisdiction*: The Court's jurisdiction to deal with litigation costs is based upon section 51 of the Supreme Court Act 1981, this discretion must be exercised in accordance with the Rules of Court and established principles: *McDonald v. Horn* [1995] 1 All E.R. 961 and see *Machin v. National Power (No. 2)*, July 31, 1998 (unrep.), Carnwath J.

48.15.5 **Counsel's Fees**—Prior to the introduction of the CPR, figures for run of the mill personal injury cases were agreed with the Bar. Reproduced below are the most recently agreed figures. It is unlikely that similar figures will be published in future.

PRACTICE DIRECTION NO. 2 OF 1998—QUEEN'S BENCH DIVISION—PERSONAL INJURY CASES

Interlocutory Fees 48BPD–001

Revised Scales from August 1, 1998

This list of scale fees, which was last increased in March 1996, has been the subject of discussion between the Chief Master and the General Council of the Bar. A list of new fees relating to such cases, which will come into operation in respect of instructions and briefs delivered on or after August 1, 1998, is set out below.

The fees in the list are the basic amounts proper to be allowed upon taxation in the normal run of personal injury claims where the item has been dealt with fully, on the assumption that the value of the action exceeds £50,000. Save in the case of conference fees, each fee is intended to cover any necessary perusal of papers in connection with the item. A lower fee may be appropriate where the item has not been dealt with comprehensively, was exceptionally simple or if the value of the action when commenced was below £50,000. If a higher fee has been agreed it will need to be justified on taxation.

The fees of Queen's Counsel have been omitted on the basis that they will not ordinarily be instructed in the normal run of personal injury cases.

Practice Direction Dated July 31, 1998

48BPD–002

Item	Basic fees to be allowed in the normal run of personal injury cases
Statement of claim	£90.00
Defence without counterclaim	£80.00
Defence (plain submission)	£26.50
Particulars—request answers	£42.50 £53.00
Reply with or without defence to counterclaim	£53.00
Third party notice (not to stand as statement of claim)	£53.00
Interrogatories and answers	£80.00
Advice on evidence	£106.00
Opinion (including opinion on appeal)	£90.00
Opinion on liability	£95.00
Opinion on quantum	£106.00
Opinion on liability and quantum	£160.00
Opinion on liability, quantum and evidence	£212.00
Notice of appeal to Court of Appeal and counternotice	£80.00

Brief on summons before master (short summons)	£132.50
Conference fees (junior counsel) first half hour each succeeding half hour	 £64.00 £37.00

PART 49

SPECIALIST PROCEEDINGS

Contents **49.0.1**

Editorial Introduction

The CPR apply to all proceedings in county courts, the High Court and the Court of Appeal (Civil Division) (r.2.1(1)). They cover what could be called general county court and High Court business, and, to an extent, make separate provision for specialist jurisdictions or procedures in either court (see paras 2.1.1 and 2.1.2, above, and para. 50.1.1, below). **49.0.2**

Rule 49 states that "These Rules", by which must be meant the provisions in Pts 1 to 48 and in Pt 50 (which brings into effect certain surviving provisions in the RSC and the CCR), apply to the "specialist proceedings" as listed in r.49(2) "subject to the provisions of the relevant practice direction which applies to those proceedings". No "relevant practice direction" was available in final form at the time when this volume went to press. Clearly, from a practice point of view, any practice directions dealing with the "specialist proceedings" listed in r.49(2) are very important as they may modify the effect of the provisions of the CPR.

"Specialist proceedings" shall be distinguished from "specialist lists" (see para. 2.3.12, above).

49—(1) These Rules shall apply to the proceedings listed in paragraph (2) subject to the provisions of the relevant practice direction which applies to those proceedings. **49.1**

(2) The proceedings referred to in paragraph (1) are—

(a) admiralty proceedings;

(b) arbitration proceedings;

(c) commercial and mercantile actions;

(d) Patents Court business (as defined by the relevant practice direction) and proceedings under—

(i) the Copyright, Designs and Patents Act 1988[1];

(ii) the Trade Marks Act 1994[2]; and

(iii) the Olympic Symbol etc. Protection Act 1995[3] and Olympics Association Right (Infringement Proceeding) Regulations 1995[4];

(e) Technology and Construction Court Business (as defined by the relevant practice direction);

(f) proceedings under the Companies Act 1985[5] and the Companies Act 1989[6]; and

(g) contentious probate proceedings.

[1] 1988 c. 48.
[2] 1994 c. 26.
[3] 1995 c. 32.
[4] S.I. 1995/3325.
[5] 1985 c. 6.
[6] 1989 c. 40.

PRACTICE DIRECTION—CONTENTIOUS PROBATE PROCEEDINGS

49PD–001 *This Practice Direction supplements Part 49 of the CPR and replaces RSC, Order 76 and CCR, Order 41*

Editorial Introduction

This Practice Direction in essence reproduces the rules formerly contained in RSC, O.76 together with some of the editorial notes to those rules set out in *The Supreme Court Practice* 1999. RSC, O.76 has not been retained as a schedule to the new Civil Procedure Rules, and so the procedure for contentious probate is now to be found only in this Practice Direction. It is understood, however, that this Practice Direction will itself in due course be superceded by a new contentious probate rule which will then take its place within the Civil Procedure Rules.

It is important to note that a defendant to a contentious probabe claim must file an acknowledgment of service. This does not sound unusual because until now every defendant in every action had to file an acknowledgment of service. But under the new Civil Procedure Rules in a normal case a defendant will only need to file an acknowledgment of service if he wishes to challenge jurisdiction or to obtain more time for filing his defence, but not otherwise. That is why it is important to note that in a contentious probate action this will not be so, and that a defendant will always have to file an acknowledgment of service.

One difference between the older RSC, O.76 and this new Practice Direction is the period for serving particulars of claim. Under O.76, r.7 if a statement of claim was not specially indorsed on the writ a plaintiff had to serve the statement of claim within *six* weeks after acknowledgment of service (or eight days after the defendant filed his affidavit of scripts, whichever was the later). Under this Practice Direction, para. 7.1, if particulars of claim are not contained in or served with the claim form they must be served within *twenty eight days* after acknowledgment of service (or eight days after the defendant has filed his affidavit or witness statement of scripts, whichever is the later).

In practice this difference is hardly likely to be of much significance. This is because in the past the statement of claim in a contentious probate action was always short and laconic, and was therefore almost invariably specially indorsed on the writ. Accordingly O.76, r.7 was hardly ever invoked. It is likely that in future particulars of claim will be similarly short and laconic and therefore contained in the claim form itself, thus making it unnecessary to invoke para. 7.1.

The Practice Direction, at para. 2.5, says that every person who may be affected by a probate claim either as a beneficiary under a will in issue or on an intestacy should either be joined as a party or given notice of proceedings. This reproduces an editorial note in *The Supreme Court Practice* 1999. The important words are "who may be affected". Thus if under an earlier uncontested will and a later contested will the identity of the specific legatees and the amounts of their legacies are the same, and it is only the identity of the residuary legatees or the amounts of their shares that differ, it would be necessary to join or give notice to the residuary legatees but not the specific legatees. If there is a doubt whether a particular beneficiary should be joined or given notice of proceedings it would be sensible to raise the question with the Master at the case management conference.

Summary judgment. There is a conflict between Practice Direction, para. 11 (which contemplates the possibility of a summary judgment application under CPR Part 24 in contentious probate proceedings) and CPR Part 24 itself (which—at 24.3(2)(c)—states that summary judgment is not available in contentious probate proceedings). As the Rules presumably take precedence over the Practice Directions it is best to assume that summary judgment is not available in contentious probate proceedings.

The text of the Practice Direction on Contentious Probate Proceedings is as follows:

General

49PD–002 **1.1** This Practice Direction applies to contentious probate proceedings and to applciations for the rectification of a will both in the High Court and in the county court.

(For the rules and procedure relating to non-contentious probate proceedings, see the Non-Contentious Probate Rules 1987 as amended. The Non-Contentious Probate Rules deal, among things, with the procedure for entering a caveat, for warning-off a caveat and for entering an appearance to a warning. If an application for the rectification of a will is not contentius, the application may be made to the Family Division: see Non-Contentious probate Rules 1987, rule 55.)

(For the jurisdiction of a county court in respect of contentious probate proceedings and proceedings for the rectification of a will, see s.32 County Courts Act 1984.)

1.2 In this Practice Direction:—

(i) "probate claim" means a claim in respect of any contentious matter arising in connection with an application for the grant or revocation of probate or letters of administration and includes a claim for an order pronouncing for or against the validity of an alleged will, "claim form" means a claim form by which a probate claim is begun and "probate proceedings" means the proceedings in which a probate claim is brought.

(ii) "relevant office" means:

(a) in the case of High Court proceedings in a Chancery district registry, that registry,

(b) in the case of any other High Court proceedings, Chancery Chambers at the Royal Courts of Justice, Strand, London, WC2A 2LL; and

(c) in the case of county court proceedings, the office of the county court in question.

(iii) "testamentary script" means a will or draft thereof, written instructions for a will made by or at the request, or under the instructions, of the testator and any document purporting to be evidence of the contents, or to be a copy, of a will which is alleged to have been lost or destroyed.

Commencement of proceedings

2.1 If a probate claim is to be commenced in the High Court, the claim form must be issued out of Chancery Chambers or one of the Chancery district registries.

(There are Chancery district registries at Birmingham, Bristol, Cardiff, Leeds, Liverpool, Manchester, Newcastle upon Tyne and Preston).

2.2(i) If a claim form is wrongly issued out of a district registry other than a Chancery district registry, an application for the transfer of the claim to the Royal Courts of Justice or to a Chancery district registry should be made forthwith.

(ii) The court may, in a case to which paragraph 2.2(i) applies, order the transfer on its own initiative.

2.3 On the issue of a claim form the relevant office will send a notice to Leeds District Probate Registry, Coronet House, Queen Street, Leeds, LS1 2BA, DX 26451 Leeds (Park Square), Telephone 0113 243 1505, requesting that all testamentary scripts and other relevant documents in any probate registry be sent to the relevant office.

2.4 A claim form must, before it is issued, contain a statement of the nature of the interest of the claimant and of the defendant in the estate of the deceased to which the claim relates.

2.5 Every person who may be affected by a probate claim, either as a beneficiary under a will in issue or on an intestacy, and who is not joined as a party to the probate claim, should be given notice of the proceedings. It may in some cases be appropriate for a representation order to be sought under RSC, Order 15, rule 13 (Schedule 1 to the CPR) or CCR, Order 5, rule 6 (Schedule 2 to the CPR).

2.6 The court may direct that notice of the probate claim be served on any such person as is mentioned in paragraph 2.5 and, for that purpose, rule 13A of RSC, Order 15 (Schedule 1 to the CPR) applies to probate claims in the county court as well as to probate claims in the High Court.

2.7 Every person who is entitled, or claims to be entitled, to administer the estate of a deceased person under an unrevoked grant of probate or letters of administration must be made a party to any probate claim seeking revocation of a grant.

2.8 The commencement of a probate claim will, unless a court otherwise directs, prevent any grant of probate or letters of administration being made until the probate claim has been disposed of (see rule 45 of the Non-Contentious Probate Rules 1987: but see also s.117, Supreme Court Act, 1981 and paragraph 14 below).

Lodgment of grant in action for revocation

3.1 Where, on the issue of a claim form seeking revocation of a grant of probate or letters of administration, the probate or letters of administration, as the case may be, have not been lodged in court, then—

(a) if a person to whom the grant was made is a claimant, he must lodge the probate or letters of administration in the relevant office within 7 days after the issue of the claim form;

(b) if a defendant to the action has the probate or letters of administration in his possession or under his control, he must lodge it or them in the relevant office within 14 days after the service of the claim form on him.

In this paragraph "court" includes the principle registry of the Family Division or a district probate registry.

3.2 Any person who fails to comply with paragraph 3.1 may, on the application of any party to the probate claim, or by the court on its own initiative, be ordered to lodge the probate or letters of administration in the relevant office within a specified time.

3.3 Any person against whom an order is made under paragraph 3.2 shall not be entitled to take any step in the probate proceedings without the permission of the court until he has complied with the order.

Acknowledgment of service

4. A defendant on whom a claim form is served must, subject to CPR rule 10.3(2), file an acknowledgment of service within 14 days after service of the claim form on him.

Testamentary scripts

49PD–003 **5.1** Unless the court otherwise directs, the claimant and every defendant who has acknowledged service of the claim form must by affidavit or witness statement:

(a) describe any testamentary script of the deceased person, whose estate is the subject of the action, of which he has any knowledge or, if such be the case, state that he knows of no such script, and

(b) if any such script of which he has knowledge is not in his possession or under his control, give the name and address of the person in whose possession or under whose control it is or, if such be the case, state that he does not know the name or address of that person.

5.2 Any affidavit or witness statement required by paragraph 5.1 must be filed, and any testamentary script referred to therein which is in the possession or under the control of the deponent must be lodged in the relevant office within 14 days after the acknowledgment of service by a defendant to the claim or, if no defendant acknowledges service and the court does not otherwise direct, before an order is made for the trial of the claim.

5.3 Where any testamentary script required by paragraph 5.2 to be lodged in the relevant office or any part thereof is written in pencil, then, unless the court otherwise directs, a facsimile copy of that script, or of the page or pages thereof containing the part written in pencil, must also be lodged in the relevant office and the words which appear in pencil in the original must be underlined in red ink in the copy.

5.4 Except with the permission of the court, a party to a probate claim shall not be allowed to inspect an affidavit or witness statement filed under paragraph 5.2 or any testamentary script lodged under paragraph 5.3 unless and until an affidavit or witness statement sworn or made by him containing the information referred to in paragraph 5.1 has been filed.

5.5 Copies of testamentary scripts lodged under paragraph 5.2 should be filed with the originals. The testamentary scripts will remain in the relevant office until the probate claim has been disposed of.

5.6 It is important that testamentary scripts should not be marked in any way; nor should they be stapled or folded.

5.7(i) Any party desiring to have any testamentary script subjected to examination by an expert should make an application in accordance with CPR Part 23.

(ii) The application notice or the written evidence in support should explain the nature and purpose of the examination and the points to which the examination should be directed.

(iii) The court may order such an examination on its own initiative.

Failure to acknowledge service

6.1 A default judgment cannot be obtained on a probate claim and CPR rule 10.2 and Part 12 do not apply to probate claims.

6.2 Where any of several defendants to a probate claim fails to acknowledge service of the claim form, the claimant may, after the time for acknowledging service has expired and upon filing an affidavit or witness statement proving due service of the claim form on that defendant proceed with the probate claim as if that defendant had acknowledged service.

6.3 Where the defendant, or all the defendants, to a probate claim, fails or fail to acknowledge service of the claim form then, unless on the application of the claimant the Court orders the claim to be discontinued, the claimant may after the time for acknowledging service has expired apply to the court for an order for trial of the claim.

6.4 Before applying for an order under paragraph 6.3 the claimant must file an affidavit or witness statement proving due service of the claim form on the defendant or defendants and, if no particulars of claim were contained in or served with the claim form, he must file particulars of claim in the relevant office.

6.5 Where the court makes an order under paragrpah 6.3, it may direct the claim to be tried on written evidence. (See also paragraph 10.3 below).

(For rules about written evidence, see Part 32 and the Practice Direction supplementing that Part.)

Service of particulars of claim and defence

7.1 The claimant in a probate claim must, unless the court gives permission to the contrary or particulars of claim were contained in or served with the claim form, serve particulars of claim on every defendant who acknowledges service of the claim form and must do so before the expiration of 28 days after acknowledgment of service by that defendant or of 8 days after the filing by that defendant of an affidavit or witness statement under paragraph 5.1, whichever is the later.

7.2 If particulars of claim were contained in or served with the claim form or are served before the claimant has complied with paragraphs 5.1 and 5.2 above, the time for filing a defence shall, subject to CPR 15.4(2), be 28 days after the affidavit or witness statement required by paragraph 5.1 has been filed and the testamentary scripts have been lodged.

Defence and counterclaim

8.1 A defendant to a probate claim who alleges that he has any claim or is entitled to any remedy relating to the grant of probate of the will, or letters of administration of the estate, of the deceased person must add to his defence a counterclaim in respect of that matter. **49PD–004**

8.2 If the claimant fails to serve particulars of claim, any such defendant may, with the permission of the Court, serve a counterclaim and the probate proceedings shall then continue as if the counterclaim were the particulars of claim and the counterclaiming defendant were the claimant.

8.3 A defendant may in his defence give notice that he will raise no positive case but will insist on the will being proved in solemn form of law and, for that purpose, will cross-examine the witnesses who attested the will.

(Attention is drawn to paragraph 2.2 of the Costs Practice Direction Relating to CPR Part 44 and supplementing CPR 44.3.)

Contents of statements of case

9.1 Where the claimant in a probate claim disputes the interest of a defendant, he must state in his particulars of claim that he denies the interest of that defendant.

9.2 In a probate claim in which the interest by virtue of which a party claims to be entitled to a grant of letters of adminsitration is disputed, the party disputing that interest must show in his statement of case that if the allegations he makes in it are proved he would be entitled to an interest in the estate.

9.3 Any party who wants to contend that at the time when a will, the subject of the probate claim, was alleged to have been executed the testator did not know and approve of its contents must specify in his statement of case the nature of the case on which he intends to rely, and no allegation in support of that contention which would be relevant in support of any of the following other contentions, that is to say:

(a) that the will was not duly executed,

(b) that at the time of the execution of the will the testator was not of sound mind, memory and understanding, and

(c) that the execution of the will was obtained by undue influence or fraud,

shall be made by that party unless that other contention also is made in his statement of case.

Default of pleadings

10.1 A default judgment cannot be obtained on a probate claim (see paragraph 6.1 above).

10.2 Where any party to a probate claim fails to serve on any other party a pleading which he is required by the CPR or this Practice Direction to serve on that other party, then, unless the court orders the claim to be discontinued or dismissed, that other party may, after the expiration of the period fixed by the CPR or this Practice Direction for service of the pleading in question, apply to the court for an order for trial of the probate claim; and if an order is made the court may direct the probate claim to be tried on written evidence.

10.3 If a trial is ordered under paragraph 10.2 (or under paragraph 6.2), the hearing may lead to an order pronouncing for the will in solemn form.

Summary judgment

11. Where an order pronouncing for a will in solemn form is sought on an application for summary judgment, the evidence in support of the application must include an affidavit or a witness statement proving due execution of the will. (CPR Part 24 and the practice direction supplementing Part 24 deal with summary judgment applications).

Discontinuance and dismissal

12.1 CPR Part 38 does not apply to a probate claim.

12.2 At any stage of probate proceedings the court may, on the application of the claimant, or of any party to the probate claim who has acknowledged service of the claim form, order the claim to be discontinued or dismissed on such terms as to costs or otherwise as it thinks just, and may further order that a grant of probate of the will, or letters of administration of the estate, of the deceased person, as the case may be, which is the subject of the claim, be made to the person entitled thereto.

12.3 An application for an order under this rule may be made by application notice in accordance with CPR Part 23.

12.4 An order for the discontinuance or dismissal of a probate claim under paragraph 11.2 will normally lead to a grant of probate or of letter of administration in a common form.

Compromise of action

13.1 Where, whether before or after the service of the defence in a probate claim, the parties to the claim agree to a compromise, the Court may order the trial of the claim on written evidence.

(For a form of order which is also applicable to discontinuance and which may be adapted as appropriate, see Practice Form No. CH38.)

13.2 Section 49 of the Administration of Justice Act 1985 permits a probate claim to be compromised without a trial if every "relevant beneficiary" has consented to the proposed order.

13.3 Applications under section 49 may be heard by a master or district judge and should be supported by affidavit or witness statement identifying the "relevant beneficiaries" and exhibiting their respective consents. Affidavits or witness statements of testamentary scripts (see paragraph 5 above) will still be necessary.

Application for order to bring in will, etc.

14.1 Any application in a probate claim for an order under section 122 of the Supreme Court Act 1981 shall be for an order requiring a person to bring a will or other testamentary paper into the relevant office or to attend in court for examination. **49PD–005**

14.2 An application under paragraph 13.1 shall be made by application notice in accordance with CPR Part 23. The application notice must be served on the person against whom the order is sought.

14.3 Any application in a probate claim for the issue of a witness summons under section 123 of the Act shall be for the issue of a witness summons requiring a person to bring into the relevant office a will or other testamentary paper.

14.4 An application under paragraph 13.3 may be made without notice and must be supported by an affidavit or witness statement setting out the grounds of the application.

14.5 An application under section 122 or 123 of the 1981 Act should be made to a master or district judge.

14.6 Any person against whom a witness summons is issued under section 123 of the 1981 Act and who denies that the will or other testamentary paper referred to in the witness summons is in his possession or under his control may file an affidavit or witness statement to that effect.

14.7 Section 32 of the County Courts Act 1984 enables orders under section 122 and 123 of the 1981 Act to be made in county court proceedings.

Administration pending the determination of a probate claim

15.1 An application under section 117 of the Supreme Court Act 1981 for an order for the grant of administration may be made by application notice in the probate proceedings in question.

15.2 Where an order for a grant of administration is made under the said section 117, RSC, Order 30 (Receivers), rules 2, 4 and 6 and (subject to subsection (3) of the said section), rule 3 (Schedule 1 to the CPR), shall apply as if the administrator were a receiver appointed by the court; and every application relating to the conduct of the administration shall be made by application notice in the probate proceedings in question.

15.3 An order under section 117 may be made by a master or district judge.

15.4 If an order is made under section 117 an application for the grant of letters of administration should be made at the principal probate registry of the Family Division.

15.5 The appointment of an administrator to whom letters of administration are granted following an order under section 117 will cease automatically when a final order in the probate proceedings is made but will continue pending any appeal.

Probate counterclaim in other proceedings

16.1 In these paragraphs "probate counterclaim" means a counterclaim by which the defendants makes a probate claim in any proceedings other than probate proceedings.

16.2 Subject to the following paragraphs, this Practice Direction shall apply with the necessary modifications to a probate counterclaim as it applies to a probate claim begun by a probate claim form.

16.3 A probate counterclaim must contain a statement of the nature of the interest of the defendant and of the claimant in the estate of the deceased to which the counterclaim relates.

16.4 Unless within seven days after the service of a probate counterclaim in High Court proceedings an application is made for an order under CPR 3.2(e) or 3.4 for the probate counterclaim to be struck out or dealt with in separate proceedings and the application is granted, the court shall, if necessary on its own initiative, order the transfer of the proceedings to the Chancery Division (if it is not already assigned to that Division) and to either the Royal Courts of Justice or a Chancery district registry (if it is not already proceeding in one of those places).

16.5 If an order is made that a probate counterclaim be dealt with in separate proceedings, the order shall (if the proceedings are in the High Court) order the transfer of the probate counterclaim as required under paragraph 15.4.

Rectification of wills

17.1 Where an application is made for the rectification of a will and the grant has not been lodged in court, paragraph 5 of this Practice Direction shall apply, with the necessary modifications, as if the proceedings were probate proceedings.

17.2 A copy of every order made for the rectification of a will shall be sent to the principal registry of the Family Division for filing, and a memorandum of the order shall be endorsed on, or permanently annexed to, the grant under which the estate is administred.

PRACTICE DIRECTION—APPLICATIONS UNDER THE COMPANIES ACT 1985 AND THE INSURANCE COMPANIES ACT 1982

This Practice Direction supplements CPR, Part 49 and replaces, with modifications, RCS, Order 102 and CCR, Order 49, Rule 3

General

49BPD–001 **1.**(1) In this practice direction—

"the Act" means the Companies Act 1985.

"the companies court registrar" means any officer of the High Court who is a registrar within the meaning of any rules for the time being in force relating to the winding-up of companies;

"the court" includes the companies court registrar;

"the ICA" means the Insurance Companies Act 1982;

"the Rules" means the Civil Procedure Rules 1998.

(2) Applications under the Act may be made in the county court if the

county court would have jurisdiction to wind up the company in question (see the definition of "the court" in section 744 of the Act). A company can be wound up in the county court if its paid-up capital is not more than £120,000 (s.117(2) Insolvency Act 1986).

(3) Every claim form or petition by which an application under the Act or the ICA is begun and all affidavits, witness statements, notices and other documents in those proceedings must be entitled in the matter of the company in question and in the matter of the Act, or the ICA as the case may be.

Commencement of proceedings

2.(1) Except in the case of the applications mentioned in sub-paragraph (4) below, every application under the Act, whether made in the High Court or in the county court, must be made by the issue of a claim form and the use of the procedure set out in CPR Part 8, subject to any modification of that procedure under this practice direction or any other practice direction relating to applications under the Act.

(2) Notice of an application under section 721 of the Act need not be given to the respondent and the claim form need not be served on him.

(3) A claim form issued under this paragraph must, in the High Court, be issued out of the office of the companies court registrar or a chancery district registry, or in the county court, out of a county court office.

(4) This paragraph does not apply to applications under sections 459 or 460 of the Act or to applications under the ICA or to any of the applications specified in paragraph 4(1) of this practice direction.

3. All High Court applications under the Act shall be assigned to the Chancery Division.

Applications made by petition

4.(1) The following applications under the Act in addition to applications under sections 459 and 460 of the Act and applications under the ICA must be made by petition, namely, applications:

(a) under section 5 to cancel the alteration of a company's objects,

(b) under section 17 to cancel the alteration of a condition contained in a company's memorandum,

(c) under section 130 to confirm a reduction of the share premium account of a company,

(d) under section 136 to confirm a reduction of the share capital of a company,

(e) under section 127 to cancel any variation or abrogation of the rights attached to any class of shares in a company,

(f) under section 425 to sanction a compromise or arrangement between a company and its creditors or any class of them or between a company and its members or any class of them,

(g) under section 653 for an order restoring the name of a company to the register, where the application is made in conjunction with an application for the winding up of the company,

(h) under section 690 to cancel the alteration of the form of a company's constitution,

(i) under section 727 for relief from liability of an officer of a company or a person employed by a company as auditor,

(j) under section 54(1) to cancel resolution to which that section applies,

(k) under sections 157(2) or 176(1) to cancel a special resolution to which either of those sections applies, and

(l) under section 170 in relation to the reduction of capital redemption reserve.

(2) Paragraphs 5 to 14 of this practice direction apply to the applications specified in sub-paragraph (1).

49BPD–002 **5.**(1) After the presentation of a petition by which any application mentioned in paragraph 4 is made, the petitioner, except where his application is one of those mentioned in sub-paragraph (2), must apply for directions by filing an application notice.

(2) The exceptions referred to in sub-paragraph (1) are:

(a) an application under section 425 of the Act to sanction a compromise or arrangement unless there is included in the petition for such sanction an application for an order under section 427 of the Act,

(b) an application under section 653 of the Act for an order restoring the name of a company to the register,

(c) an application under section 54(1) of the Act for an order cancelling a special resolution to which that section applies, and

(d) an application under section 157(2) or 176(1) of the Act for an order cancelling a special resolution to which those sections apply.

(3) At the directions hearing the court may by order give such directions for the hearing of the application as it thinks fit including, in particular, directions for the publication of notices and the making of any inquiry.

(4) Where the application made by the petition is to confirm a reduction of the share capital, the share premium account, or the capital redemption reserve, of a company the Court may give directions:

(a) for an inquiry to be made as to the debts of, and claims against, the company or as to any class or classes of such debts or claims,

(b) as to the proceedings to be taken for settling the list of creditors entitled to object to the reduction and fixing the date by reference to which the list is to be made,

and the power of the court under section 136(6) of the Act to direct that section 136(3) to (5) thereof shall not apply as regards any class of creditors may be exercised at any directions hearing.

Reduction of capital and schemes of arrangement

6.(1) The consent of a creditor to such reduction as is mentioned in paragraph 5(4) may be proved in such manner as the Court thinks sufficient.

(2) The evidence in support of a petition to confirm a reduction of capital need not show as regards any issue of shares made since 1900 for a consideration other than cash that the statutory requirements as to registration were complied with. It is sufficient to state in the petition the extent to which any issued shares (other than shares issued otherwise than for cash before 1901) are or are deemed to be paid up.

(3) The existing practice will remain unaltered in respect of issues of shares otherwise than for cash made before 1901 whilst s.25 of the Companies Act 1867 remained in operation.

7.(1) This paragraph applies to:

(a) schemes of arrangement under sections 425 to 427A of the Companies Act 1985, whether made with creditors or members,

(b) schemes for the transfer of the whole or part of the long-term business of an insurance company to which schedule 2C to the ICA applies, and

(c) reductions of capital, share premium account or capital redemption reserve.

References in this and subsequent paragraphs to "schemes" are to schemes falling within (a) or (b) above, and references to "reductions" are to reductions falling within (c) above.

(2) Petitions to sanction schemes will be heard by the Companies Court Judge.

(3) Petitions to confirm reductions will be heard by the Companies Court

Registrar unless otherwise ordered. The Registrar will hear petitions to confirm reductions in open court on a Wednesday each week after completion of the list of winding up petitions.

Schemes and reductions in the long vacation

8. (1) The following requirements must be satisfied for a hearing to be fixed to sanction a scheme and/or confirm a reduction in the Long Vacation: **49BPD–003**

(a) The application is one in which for financial, commercial or economic reasons a hearing before the end of the Long Vacation is desirable. This category will include cases of mergers and takeovers which arise in the summer and are likely to be affected by market fluctuations.

(b) The application is one which could not with reasonable diligence have been made and prosecuted in time to be heard before the Long Vacation begins.

(2) An informal application in chambers, to the Court Manager, accompanied by an advocate's certificate that requiremens (a) and (b) are satisfied, must be made as soon as possible so that a suitable timetable may be settled, including a date for hearing.

(3) In the case of reductions to be heard by the Registrar, certain applications which do not fall within the above categories will be heard provided (i) that there is an urgent need for a hearing or (ii) that there is sufficient time available after the Registrar has disposed of the urgent applications.

(4) Applications to the Registrar in chambers for orders convening meetings to consider schemes and for directions on reduction applications will continue to be heard during the Long Vacation. Provided notice is given to the court before the Long Vacation begins, a timetable will be fixed which will enable any necessary documents to be settled in chambers and enable the Registrar to hear the application.

(5) The Vacation Judge will be available to hear petitions to sanction schemes and any petitions to confirm reductions which require to be heard by a judge on one Wednesday in August and two Wednesdays in September on dates to be arranged and subsequently notified in the Long Vacation Notice which is printed in the Daily Cause List.

(6) The Vacation Judge may also hear petitions to sanction schemes or confirm reductions on other days if he thinks fit.

9. (1) Attention is drawn to the undesirability of asking as a matter of course for a winding up order as an alternative to an order under s.459 Companies Act 1985. The petition should not ask for a winding up order unless that is the relief which the petitioner prefers or it is thought that it may be the only relief to which the petitioner is entitled.

(2) Whenever a winding up order is asked for in a contributory's petition, the petition must state whether the petitioner consents or objects to an order under s.127 of the Act in the standard form. If he objects, the written evidence in support must contain a short statement of his reasons.

(3) If the petitioner objects to a s.127 order in the standard form but consents to such an order in a modified form, the petition must set out the form of order to which he consents, and the written evidence in support must contain a short statement of his reasons for seeking the modification.

(4) If the petition contains a statement that the petitioner consents to a s.127 order, whether in the standard or a modified form, but the petitioner changes his mind before the first hearing of the petition, he must notify the respondents and may apply on notice to a Judge for an order directing that no. s.127 order or a modified order only (as the case may be) shall be made by the Registrar, but validating dispositions made without notice of the order made by the Judge.

(5) If the petitition contains a statement that the petitioner consents to a s.127 order, whether in the standard or a modified form, the Registrar shall without further enquiry make an order in such form at the first hearing unless an order to the contrary has been made by the Judge in the meantime.

(6) If the petition contains a statement that the petitioner objects to a s.127 order in the standard form, the company may apply (in the case of urgency, without notice) to the Judge for an order.

(7) Section 127 Order—Standard Form:

(Title, etc.)

ORDER that notwithstanding the presentation of the said Petition

(1) payments made into or out of the bank accounts of the Company in the ordinary course of the business of the Company and

(2) dispositions of the property of the Company made in the ordinary course of its business for proper value between the date of presentation of the Petition and the date of judgment on the Petition or further order in the meantime

shall not be void by virtue of the provisions of section 127 of the Insolvency Act 1986 in the event of an Order for the winding up of the Company being made on the said Petition Provided that (the relevant bank) shall be under no obligation to verify for itself whether any transaction through the company's bank accounts is in the ordinary course of business, or that it represents full market value for the relevant transaction.

This form of Order may be departed from where the circumstances of the case require.

Case management

49BPD–004 **10.** Every application under the Act shall be allocated to the multi-track and the CPR relating to allocation questionnaires and track allocation will not apply.

Service

11. Service of documents in proceedings in the High Court to which this practice direction applies will be the responsibility of the parties and will not be undertaken by the court. Subject to that CPR Part 6 applies.

Filing of documents

12.(1) Where an application to which this practice direction relates is proceeding in any Chancery district registry, all affidavits and witness statements made in connection with the application must be filed in that registry.

(2) Where an application to which this practice direction relates in proceeding in any county court, all affidavits and witness statements made in connection with the application must be filed in the office of that county court.

Drawing up of orders

13. The court will draw up all orders with the following exceptions:

(a) orders by the Registrar on the application of the Official Receiver or for which the Treasury Solicitor is responsible under the existing practice,

(b) orders by the court in relation to reductions or schemes.

PRACTICE DIRECTION—TECHNOLOGY AND CONSTRUCTION COURT

This Practice Direction supplements CPR, Part 49 and replaces, with modifications, Order 36 of the Rules of the Supreme Court 49CPD–001

The Technology and Construction Court

This court is the successor in title to the Official Referees Courts. The first Official Referees of the Supreme Court of Justice were appointed in 1876 under the Judicature Acts 1873–75. Any question could be referred for trial with or without consent of the parties if it involved the prolonged investigation of documents or accounts or of any scientific or local investigation. The report of an Official Referee on a trial had to be accepted as if it were the verdict of a jury but he could not give judgment or make any order as to costs. By the Judicature Act of 1884 power was given for an Official Referee to give a judgment, make orders for costs and exercise the powers of a High Court Judge in a case referred to him. The Arbitration Act of 1889 enabled parties to an arbitration agreement to require an Official Referee to sit as an arbitrator. From the outset much of the Official Referee's work was concerned with the construction industry in all its aspects. The Courts Act 1971 provided that in future "Official Referees business" should be dealt with by such Circuit Judges as the Lord Chancellor should determine. Although the title "Official Referee" was not legally preserved it continued to be used universally. By 1998 references were a rarity and most of the work tried in the court was commenced in the Official Referees Registry or transferred from the Chancery Division or the Queens Bench Division. The description of the court was considered to be inaccurate and anachronistic and in October of 1998 the Lord Chancellor with the concurrence of the Lord Chief Justice directed that the court should be renamed the Technology and Construction Court of the High Court of Justice. The Technology and Construction Court (TCC) was opened by the Lord Chancellor on October 9, 1998. From that date the presiding High Court Judge has regularly sat in the Technology and Construction Court trying TCC cases, and from that time the mode of address of all judges has been "my Lord". On April 26, 1999 the Civil Procedure Rules came into force incorporating many of the case management practices pioneered by the Official Referees during the 1980s and 1990s and reflecting the interventionist ethos of the court.

The Technology and Construction Courts—There are nine large and two small courts situated on the 2nd to 6th floors of St Dunstans House, 133–137 Fetter Lane, London EC4A 1HD. The Registry is on the third floor. There are presently eight London TCC judges who undertake only TCC work. They are assisted by Circuit TCC judges provided by the circuits normally for 10–15 days at a time and by a number of Recorders authorised to take TCC work who sit when they are available and required but not normally for more than 10 days at a time. In practice "over 10 days cases" are taken by the London TCC judges.

The court is presided over by a High Court Judge who spends up to half of each term sitting in the TCC, and who supervises the administration in conjunction with the Court Manager. Each TCC judge has a clerk who acts as his personal clerk, also as Court Clerk and Listing Officer and maintains a file of each case and records orders and judgments. The registry manager is also the rota clerk and the registry staff assign new work to the judges in rotation. From October of 1998 the assignment of cases to individual judges has continued to be by way of the rota, however the individual trial lists of the judges have not been maintained. There is now a common trial list to ensure that in every category of case the earliest trial date is made available but, where possible, the trials are undertaken by the assigned judge who has had the management of the case. Cases of public importance or particular difficulty may be listed for trial before the Presiding Judge. The following Practice Direction supplements CPR, Pt 49 and replaces, with modifications Order 36 of the Rules of the Supreme Court.

General

1.1 This practice direction applies to cases allocated to the Technology and Construction Court ("the TCC"). 49CPD–002

1.2 A TCC claim is a claim which involves issues or questions which are technically complex or for which a trial by a judge of the TCC is for any other reason desirable.

1.3 TCC claims may be dealt with either in the High Court or, subject to paragraph 2.3 below, in a county court but cases allocated to the TCC will, unless and until a judge of the TCC otherwise directs, be dealt with by a judge of the TCC.

1.4 A judge will be appointed to be the judge in charge of the TCC (currently Mr Justice Dyson).

Commentary—Technology and Construction Court business in 1.2 is defined as a TCC claim which involves issues or questions which are technically complex or for which a trial by a judge of a TCC is for any other reason desirable. The effect of the rule is that a TCC judge may try any case within the business of the Chancery and Queens Bench divisions. The new rule is widely framed because the court has historically adapted itself to deal with new problems arising out of technical advances and customarily deals with cases involving multi-parties and cases which may occupy a great deal of time. The definition is wider than the inclusive definition in RSC, O.36, r.1 which provided that Official Referees business includes ... any cause or matter commenced in the Chancery Division or Queens Bench Division being a cause or matter (a) which involves a prolonged examination of documents or accounts, or a technical, scientific or local investigation such as could more conveniently be conducted by an official Referee: or (b) for which trial by Official Referee is desirable in the interests of one or more of the parties on grounds of expedition, economy or convenience or otherwise. Classes of action normally tried by judges of the TCC concern:

(a) Civil or mechanical engineering;
(b) Building and other construction work generally;
(c) Claims by and against engineers, architects, surveyors accountants and other such specialised persons or bodies;
(d) Claims by and against local authorities relating to their statutory duties concerning the development of land or the construction of buildings;
(e) Claims between neighbours owners and occupiers of land and trespass nuisance and liability under *Rylands v Fletcher* (1868) L.R. 3 H.L. 330;
(f) Claims between landlord and tenant for breaches of repairing covenants;
(g) Claims relating to the quality of goods sold or hired;
(h) Claims relating to work done and the materials supplied or services rendered;
(i) Claims involving taking of accounts especially when these are complicated;
(j) Claims arising out of fires;
(k) Claims relating to computers;
(l) Claims relating to the environment.

In 1984 the Commercial Court which had previously from time to time referred application for leave to appeal from appeals from arbitrators in construction cases to the Official Referees (now a TCC) began to do so as a matter of course. In *Tate and Lyle Industries v. Davy McKee* [1990] 1 All E.R. 157 the Court of Appeal upheld the legality of such references.

Paragraph 1.3 provides that TCC claims may be dealt with either in the High Court or subject to paragraph 2.3 in a County Court. Hitherto TCC business (formally O.R. business) fell only within the jurisdiction of the High Court. A claim with a value below the County Court limit can be issued in a County Court Office where there is a High Court District Registry or in the Office of the Central London County Court. A case of complexity or involving matters of public importance may be considered appropriate will transfer to the London Technology and Construction Court by way of example where a point on a contract is involved which may effect similar contracts commonly used in the construction industry. Otherwise such a case would proceed to trial in the appropriate County Court.

The present judge in charge of the TCC is a High Court Judge. Since 1991 a High Court Judge has been appointed to be in charge of what was then Official Referee business in England and Wales. Under the new rules it is envisaged that the judge in charge, the presiding judge will sit for half of his sitting time trying TCC cases.

Commencement of proceedings

2.1 Before the issue of a claim form relating to a TCC claim, the claim form, whether to be issued in the High Court or in a county court, should, if it is intended that the case be allocated to the TCC, be marked in the top right hand corner "Technology and Construction Court". The case will then be allocted to the TCC. The words "Technology and Construction Court" should follow the reference to "The ______ County Court" or "The High Court, Queen's Bench Division", as the case may be.

2.2 The TCC is a specialist list for the purposes of CPR Part 30 (Transfer) but no order for the transfer of proceedings from or to the TCC shall be made unless the parties have either:

(1) had an opportunity of being heard on the issue, or
(2) consented to the order.

2.3 A claim form marked as mentioned in paragraph 2.1 may not be issued in a county court office other than:

(1) a County Court ofice where there is also a High Court District Registry; or
(2) the office of the Central London County Court.

2.4 Where a claim form marked as mentioned in paragraph 2.1 is issued in the Royal Courts of Justice, the case will be assigned to a named TCC judge (the "assigned judge") who will have the primary responsibility for the case management of that case. All documents relating to that case should be marked, under the words "Technology and Construction Court" in the title, with the name of the assigned judge.

Comment—See note supra (the first note relating to the assignment by rota)

Applications

3.1 Where a claim form is to be marked as mentioned in paragraph 2.1, any application before issue of the claim form should be made to a judge of the TCC. **49CPD–003**

3.2 If an application is made before the use of the claim form, the written evidence in support of the application must state, in addition to any other necessary matters, that the claimant intends to mark the claim form in accordance with paragraph 2.1.

3.3 Any application in a case which has been allocated to the TCC must be made to a judge of the TCC.

3.4 Where there is an assigned judge of a TCC case, any application in that case should be made to the assigned judge but, if the judge in charge of the TCC so authorises or if the assigned judge is not available, may be made to another judge of the TCC.

3.5 If an application is urgent and no TCC judge is available to deal with it, the application may be made to any judge who, if the case were not allocated to the TCC, would be authorised to deal with the application.

Comment—Paragraph 3.4 reflects the established practice of the court whereby continuity of case management is ensured by the same judge but provision is made for an application to another TCC judge where there could be unacceptable delay (see Pt 1.1(1)(d)).

In the long and short vacations a TCC judge sits as vacation TCC judge on Wednesdays to deal with interlocutory matters of all kinds, and at other times by arrangement with his clerk or the registry to deal with applications for injunctions charging matters and other urgent matters.

Case management

4.1 Every claim allocated to the TCC will be allocated to the multi-track and the CPR relating to track allocation will not apply.

4.2 Where a claim has been allocated to the TCC either on issue (*i.e.* in every case in which the claim form has been marked "Technology and Construction Court") or by transfer to the TCC, an application for directions (including an application for a fixed date of hearing) must be made by the claimant within 14 days of the filing by the defendant of an acknowledgment of service or of a defence (whichever is the earlier) or, as the case may be, within 14 days of the date of the order of transfer.

4.3 If the claimant does not make an application in accordance with paragraph 4.2—

(1) any other party may do so or may apply for the claim of the claimant in default to be struck out or dismissed; or

(2) a TCC judge may on his own initiative fix a directions hearing.

4.4 The provisions of CPR Part 29 and the practice direction supplementing that Part apply to the case management of TCC cases except where inconsistent with this or any other TCC practice direction. But reference in those provisions to a listing questionnaire shall be read as references to a pre-trial review questionnaire and paragraphs 8 and 9 of the practice direction do not apply. Attention is drawn, in particular, to the following provisions of CPR Part 29 and the supplementing practice direction:

CPR Part 29

rule 29.3(2) (attendance of legal representatives)

rule 29.4 (agreed proposals)
rule 29.5 (variation of case management timetable)
rule 29.6 (pre-trial review (listing) questionnaire)

Practice Direction supplementing CPR Part 29

paragraphs 3.4 to 3.9 (general provisions)
paragraphs 5.1 to 5.8 (case management conferences)
paragraphs 6.1 to 6.5 (variation of directions)
paragraphs 7.1 to 7.4 (failure to comply with case management directions)
paragraphs 10.1 to 10.6 (the trial)

Comment—Paragraph 4.3 provides that a TCC judge may on his own initiative fix a direction hearing in default of a claimant making an application for directions within 14 days of the filing by the defendant of an acknowledgment of service or defence (whichever is the earlier) or as the case may be within 14 days of the date of the order of transfer part of the general scheme in the rules to enable a judge to intervene and prevent slippage which is an essential part of case management.

Note the reminder in 4.4 the reference within the provisions of CPR, Pt 29 and the Practice Direction supplementing that a part which applied to the Case Management of TCC cases except where inconsistent with the Practice Direction the listing questionnaire referred to in those provisions. In relation to the TCC procedure reference in those provisions to a listing questionnaire should be read as references to a pre-trial review questionnaire. Specific references to CPR, Pt 29 and the Practice Direction emphasise the importance of the parties consulting with each other and endeavouring to agree proposals for the case management conference and having legal representatives familiar with the case and with authority to deal with the issues likely to arise.

Case management conference

49CPD–004 **5.1** The first case management conference will take place at the directions hearing referred to in paragraphs 4.2 and 4.3 above.

5.2 When the court notifies the parties of the time and date of the hearing of the first case management conference it will also send them a case management questionnaire and a case management directions form. These documents will be in the forms annexed to this practice direction, and marked respectively Appendix 1 and 2.

5.3 The parties shall complete, exchange and return both forms by no later than 4pm two days before the date on which the case management conference is to take place. The parties are encouraged to try to agree directions by reference to the case management directions form.

5.4 If a party fails to exchange or return the forms by the date specified, the court may make an order which leads to the claim or defence being struck out, or impose such other sanction as it sees fit, or may hold a case management conference without the forms.

5.5 At the first case management conference, the court will usually fix the date for trial of the case and of any preliminary issue that it orders to be tried. It will also give case management directions. The directions will usually include the fixing of a date for a pre-trial review.

5.6 Whenever possible, the trial of a case will be heard by the assigned judge of that case.

Comment—Note that 5.3 gives a minimum time for exchange and return of the case management questionnaire and case management directions form. In substantial and complex cases it is desirable to exchange and serve at least four clear days before the hearing to assist the judge. An early exchange and return also gives the parties further opportunity to consider each other's proposals and agree matters before the hearing. 5.4 provides for sanctions and underlines the philosophy behind the rules and reflected in 4.3 (*supra*) there should be no slippage and the time and resource of the court should not be wasted.

Paragraph 5.5—The Agenda for the first case conference will be based upon the form as Appendix 2 of the Practice Direction. Each case coming before the TCC varies as to its length, complexity and parties, and tailor made directions may be given or agreed to suit the case. For example, where a view is appropriate the timing of the view having regard to the changing state of the matter in dispute as when remedial work is being carried out. Directions may be given that a building or structure must not be altered before experts have had the proper opportunity to examine it fully; for the joint making of trial pits, bore holes, laboratory tests, or analyses; where a Scott schedule has been ordered, that the parties should select representative items for trial; arrangements for video displays, demonstrations and the like. It is at this stage that the Court may consider whether an ADR direction may be given (see Part 1.4(2)(E)) and whether it is necessary to extend time compliance requirements of the CPR to enable the parties to investigate ADR. Consideration may also be given at this stage as to whether an early neutral evaluation (ENE) would be appropriate by a judge of the court. In relation to resolution by trial, consideration will be given to the trial of an issue, or split trials of liability/damages.

Paragraph 5.5 contains provision that at the first case management conference, the court will usually fix the date for the trial of the case. This is so, but the direction will normally be in the following form:

Trial: Week beginning ...	*For fees' purposes only this is not notice by the court of the trial date.*
Estimated length ... days	(see Supreme Court Fees Order 1999, para. 2.2, Schedule 1, column 2).

Paragraph 5.6—The Rota arrangement for definement of cases the London Technology & Construction Court is retained. A claimant is not able to choose the list of the TCC judge in which his case will appear. All cases are assigned to the TCC judge in rotation by the rota clerk, or by members of the Registry on his behalf. If possible, the trial of a case will be heard by the assigned judge of that case. There may however be times when this is inappropriate, for example, because a prior fixed case has substantially overrun, or for other reasons. These may include the desirability of a case of exceptional difficulty or public importance being heard by the presiding judge.

Pre-trial review

6.1 When the court fixes the date for a pre-trial review it will also provide the parties with a pre-trial review questionnaire and a pre-trial review directions form. These documents will be in the forms annexed to this practice direction marked respectively as Appendix 3 and 4.

6.2 The parties shall complete, exchange and return both forms no later than 4pm two days before the date on which the pre-trial review is to take place. The parties are encouraged to try to agree directions by reference to the pre-trial review directions form.

6.3 If a party fails to exchange or return the pre-trial review questionnaire or pre-trial review directions form by the date specified, the court may make an order which leads to the claim or defence and any counterclaim being struck out, or it may impose such other sanction as it sees fit, or it may hold a pre-trial review without the forms.

6.4 At the pre-trial review, the court will give such directions for the conduct of the trial as it sees fit.

Comment—The parties will be reminded by a letter from the court of the date and time of the pre-trial review. That letter will contain the following text.

"For the purposes of the fees order notice is now given that the trial has been fixed for (date) accordingly a fee of £400 must be paid within 14 days of the date of this notice, *i.e.* by (date 14 days from the date of dispatch of the letter) by the claimant or claimants, if the action is proceeding on the counter claim alone by the defendant. Payment is to be made (preferably by cheque) at the Registry of this Court or to the Fees Room in the Main Building (*i.e.* at the Royal Courts of Justice). The PTR questionnaire (see below) must be presented when payment is made as the receipt of payment of the fee is stamped on it.

If the fee is not paid by the date specified Rule 3.7(4) states that the claim (or counterclaim) will be struck out automatically and that the claimant (or the defendant, as the case may be) will be liable for the costs incurred by the other party(ies) unless the Court orders otherwise.

You are reminded that as well as the completed Pre-Trial Reviews Questionnaires all proposed directions (which should be agreed wherever possible) be lodged by all parties with me not later than two clear days before the date of the PTR. Copies of the Questionnaire and the PTR Direction Form are obtainable from the Registry. Any questions relating to the fee should be addressed to the Registry but all other questions about the PTR must be addressed to me. Signed Clerk to the Judge."

Paragraph 6.2—See note to 5.3 supra.

Paragraph 6.4—The court will take stock and ensure that there has been no unjustifiable slippage of the timetable. Where there has, directions will be given to ensure timely compliance. Since witness statements and experts may well have been exchanged this may be an appropriate time for parties to further consider ADR. In relation to conduct of the trial, further directions may be given to ensure that the proper issues are tried. The parties in the light of the pleadings, expert reports exchanged and witness statements served, may well have been required to provide a list of issues for trial to be considered at the PTR. If not already given, leave to call expert witnesses may be considered in the light of the exchange of expert reports and the identification of issues on which they are or are not agreed (see Pt 35.12(3)). Consideration will be given as to the necessity of supplemental witness/expert reports, and leave may be given. A trial timetable will be ordered to be agreed by the parties and, failing such agreement, to be determined by the trial judge. Consideration will be given to such matters as the order of witnesses, *e.g.* the hearing of all witnesses' fact on both sides followed by the expert evidence, and to the organisation of trial bundles, *i.e.* indexing, time and service of index and proposed bundles, and the preparation of a core bundle(s) with cross references to the full trial bundles, where appropriate. Directions may be given at this as to whether on the pleadings the claimant or defendant will open the trial and as to the service of written openings for the court/opposing party(ies) and written responses, if appropriate, and the provision of a chronology and cast list. A direction may be given as to the filing of disks (if obtainable) of the statements of case, witness statements, experts' reports, trial bundles and opening notes.

The Civil Procedure Rules

49CPD–005 **7.1** The Civil Procedure Rules and the practice directions supplementing them apply to TCC cases subject to the provisions of this practice direction and any other TCC practice direction.

Comment—A guide to the TCC is currently in course of preparation.

49CPD–005

First Case Management Conference Questionnaire

In the County Court/High Court Queen's Bench Division Technology and Construction Court	
Claim No.	
Last date for filing with court office	

To

Please read the notes on page five before completing the questionnaire.

Please note the date by which it must be returned and the name of the court it should be returned to since this may be different from the court where proceedings were issued.

If you have settled this case (or if you settle it on a future date) and do not need to have it heard or tried, you must let the court know immediately.

A Settlement

Do you wish there to be a stay to attempt to settle the case by negotiations or by any other form of alternative dispute resolution? ☐ Yes ☐ No

If yes, at what stage and for how long?
If no, please give reasons.

B Transfer

If you think your case is suitable for a transfer to another court or track, say which:

Court: Chancery Division/Queen's Bench Division/another TCC Court/ Commercial Court/County Court Track: Small claims/fast track

Please give brief reasons for your choice:

C Pre-Action protocols

Have you complied with any pre-action protocol applicable to your claim? ☐ None applicable to this claim ☐ Yes ☐ No

If Yes, please say which protocol:

If No, please explain to what extent and for what reason it has not been complied with:

D Applications

If you have not already sent the court an application for summary judgment, do you intend to do so? ☐ Yes ☐ No

If you have not already issued a claim in the case against someone not yet a party, do you intend to apply for the court's permission to do so? ☐ Yes ☐ No

Have you any other applications to make? ☐ Yes ☐ No

In any such case, if Yes, please give details:

E Witnesses of fact

So far a you know at this stage, what witnesses of fact do you intend to call at the hearing?

Witness name	Witness to which facts

F Experts' evidence

Do you wish to use expert evidence at the hearing? ☐ Yes ☐ No

Have you already copied any experts' report(s) to the other party(ies)? ☐ None obtained as yet ☐ Yes ☐ No

Please list the experts whose evidence you think you will use:

Expert's name	Field of expertise (eg. architect, mechanical engineer)

Will you and the other party use the same expert(s)? ☐ Yes ☐ No

If No, please explain why not:

Should any, and if so what, inspections, samples, experiments or calculations by experts be directed? ☐ Yes ☐ No

Do you want your expert(s) to give evidence orally at the hearing or trial? ☐ Yes ☐ No

If Yes, give the reasons why you think oral evidence is necessary:

G Location of trial

Is there any reason why your case needs to be heard at a particular court? ☐ Yes ☐ No

If Yes, give reasons (eg. particular facilities required, convenience of witnesses, etc.)

and specify the court:

H Representation and estimate of hearing/trial time

Do you expect to be represented by a solicitor or counsel at the hearing/trial? ☐ No ☐ Solicitor ☐ Counsel

How long do you estimate it will take to put your case to the court at the hearing/trial? days hours minutes

How long do you estimate for the whole of the trial, excluding judgment? days hours minutes

If there are days when you, your representative, expert or an essential witness will not be able to attend court, give details:

Name	Dates not available

I Costs (only relates to costs incurred by legal representatives)

What is your estimate of costs incurred to date, excluding disbursements, VAT and court fees? £

What do you estimate your overall costs are likely to be, excluding disbursements, VAT and court fees? £

J Other Information

Have you attached documents you wish the judge to take into account when considering what directions to make? ☐ Yes ☐ No

Have they been served on the other parties? ☐ Yes ☐ No

If Yes, say when

Have the other parties agreed their content? ☐ Yes ☐ No

Have you attached a list of the directions you think appropriate for the management of your case on the case management directions form? ☐ Yes ☐ No

Are they agreed with the other parties? ☐ Yes ☐ No

Are there any other facts which might affect the timetable the court will set? If so, please state

Signed Date

[Counsel][Solicitor][for the][Claimant][Defendant]

49CPD–006

Notes for completing this Questionnaire

- If the case is not settled, a judge must give directions for its management. To help the judge give the most just and cost-effective directions, you must now complete the attached questionnaire.
- If you fail to return the questionnaire by the date given, the judge may make an order which leads to your claim or defence being struck out, or hold a case management conference without it. If there is a case management conference the judge may order any party who has not filed their questionnaire to pay, immediately, the costs of that hearing.
- If you wish to make an application, for example, for special directions, for summary judgment on the grounds that the other party has no reasonable chance of success in their claim or defence, or for permission to add another party to the claim, you should send it and any required fee with the completed questionnaire. If a hearing is fixed for your application, it may also be used as a case management conference.
- Any other documents you wish the judge to take into account should be filed with the questionnaire. But you must confirm that the documents have been sent to the other party, or parties, saying when they would have received them and whether they agreed their contents.
- Use a separate sheet if you need more space for your answers marking clearly which section the information refers to. Write the case number on it, sign and date it and attach it securely to the questionnaire.
- The letters below refer to the sections of the questionnaire and tell you what information is needed.

A Settlement
If you think that you and the other party may be able to negotiate a settlement you should tick the 'Yes' box. The court may order a stay, whether or not all the other parties to the case agree. Where a stay is granted it will be for an initial period which the judge will specify.

B Transfer

C Pre-action protocols
For certain kinds of claim, there are protocols which set out what ought to be done before court proceedings are issued. As at April 1999 there are protocols for clinical negligence and personal injury claims.

D Applications
If you intend to apply for summary judgment or for permission to add another party to the claim or make any application you should, if you have not already done so, file an application with your completed questionnaire.

E Witnesses of fact
Remember to include yourself, if you will be giving evidence; but not experts, who should be included in section E.

F Experts' evidence
Oral or written expert evidence will only be allowed at the trial with the court's permission. The judge will decide what permission it seems appropriate to give.

G Location of trial

H Representation and estimate of hearing time

Appendix 2

Technology and Construction Court

49CPD–007 **CASE MANAGEMENT CONFERENCE DIRECTIONS FORM**

CLAIM 199 TCC No . ORDER ON CASE MANAGEMENT CONFERENCE HELD 1999

( ) Trial: Week beginning .Estimated length days. [Directions, if appropriate, for separate trials of issues or for parties to serve and file proposals for such directions.]

( ) This claim to be [consolidated] [managed and tried] with 19 TCC No . [This] [19 TCC No] to be lead claim. [All directions in lead claim to apply to both claims unless otherwise directed.]

( ) Permission to amend [see below].

( ) Defence and any counterclaim to be served by am/pm on 1999/20 .

( ) Reply to defence, if desired, and defence to any counterclaim, to be served by am/pm on 1999/20 .

( ) Disclosure of documents by am/pm on 1999/20 .[Standard disclosure dispensed with/limited/varied as follows:]

.]

( ) Claimant/defendant to serve a Scott Schedule [of defects and damages] [under paragraph of the particulars of claim/defence] by am/pm on 1999/20 . Column headings to be as follows: [see below].

( ) Defendant/claimant to respond to the Scott Schedule by am/pm on 1999/20 .

( ) Signed statements of witnesses of fact to be served [and filed] by am/pm on 1999/20 . [Directions, if appropriate, for control of evidence of fact under rule 32.1.]

( ) [No expert evidence without further order.] [Permission for expert evidence on the following terms: (see below).]

( ) [Inspections to be made/samples to be obtained/experiments to be conducted/calculations to be carried out as follows:

].

( ) Experts in like fields to hold discussions in accordance with rule 35.12 by am/pm on 1999/20 on [all the issues arising in their common fields] [the following issues:

].

Statements under rule 35.2(3) to be prepared and filed by am/pm on 1999/20 .

( ) The parties are to consult with each other and the court with a view to arranging service and (where required) filing of statements of case, witness statements, experts' reports, disclosure lists and other documents in computer readable form as well as in hard copy. Format for court disks:

( ) [Time under paragraphs above not to be extended with permission.]

( )

( ) Pre-trial Review: . Time allowed: . Parties to complete, file and serve pre-trial questionnaire, after consultation, by am/pm on 1999/20.

( ) Liberty to restore. Costs in cause.

Permission to amend

The [Part 20] claimant/defendant to have permission to [re-]amend the [Part 20] particulars of claim/defence [and counterclaim]/reply to defence [and defence to counterclaim] in accordance with the draft initialled by the Judge. Re-service [to be effected by am/pm on 1999/20] [deemed to have been effected today]. The [Part 20] defendant/claimant to have permission to [re-]amend the defence/reply to defence [and defence to counterclaim] by am/pm on 1999/20, limited to amendments consequential upon the amendment for which permission is first given above. The [Part 20] claimant/defendant to pay in any event the costs of and consequential upon that amendment, or thrown away thereby [and of this application].

Scott Schedule

Column headings:	1.	Serial number.
	2.	
	3.	
	4.	
	5.	
	6.	
	7.	
	8.	
	9.	
	10.	
	11.	
	12.	

Expert Evidence

Party (or state "Joint")	Field	Name	Date of exchange	Whether leave for oral evidence

Reports to be exchanged [and filed] by am/pm on the dates specified.

49CPD–008

Pre-trial review Questionnaire

In the County Court/High Court Queen's Bench Division Technology and Construction Court	
Claim No.	
Last date for filing with court office	

To

- The judge will use the information which you and the other party(ies) provide to conduct a pre-trial review.
- If you do not complete and return the questionnaire the judge may
  - make an order which leads to your statement of case (claim or defence) being struck out.
  - conduct the pre-trial review without it. You may be ordered to pay (immediately) the other parties' costs of attending.

A Directions complied with

1. Have you complied with all the previous directions given by the court? ☐ Yes ☐ No
2. If no, please explain which directions are outstanding and why.

Directions outstanding	Reasons directions outstanding

3. Are any further directions required to prepare the case for trial? ☐ Yes ☐ No

If no, go to Section B

4. If yes, please explain directions required and give reasons.

Directions required	Reasons required

B Experts

1. Has the court already given permission for you to use written expert evidence? ☐ Yes ☐ No *If no, go to Section C*

2. If yes, please give name and field of expertise.

Name of expert	Whether joint expert *(please tick, if appropriate)*	Field of expertise

3. Have the experts held discussions as directed? ☐ Yes ☐ No

4. Have they filed statements as directed following those discussions? ☐ Yes ☐ No

5. Have the expert(s') report(s) been served and filed as ordered? ☐ Yes ☐ No

6. Has the court already given permission for the expert(s) to give oral evidence at the trial? *(If yes go to section C)* ☐ Yes ☐ No

7. If no, are you seeking that permission? ☐ Yes ☐ No *(If no go to section C)*

8. If yes, give your reasons for seeking permission.

9. If yes, what are the names, addresses and fields of expertise of your experts?

Expert 1	Expert 2	Expert 3	Expert 4

10. Please give details of any dates within the trial period when your expert(s) will not be available.

Name of expert	Dates not available

49CPD–009

C Other witnesses

(If you are not calling other witnesses, go to section D)

1. How many other witnesses (including yourself) will be giving evidence on your behalf at the trial? *(do not include experts—see Section B above)* ☐ *(Give number)*

2. What are the names and addresses of your witnesses?

Witness 1	Witness 2	Witness 3	Witness 4

3. Please give details of any dates within the trial period when you or your witnesses will not be available?

Name of witness	Dates not available

4. Are any of the witness statements agreed? ☐ Yes ☐ No *(If no go to question C6)*

3. If yes, give the name of the witness and the date of his or her statement

Name of witness	Date of statement

6. Do you or any of your witnesses need any special facilities ☐ Yes ☐ No *(If no go to question C8)*

7. If yes, what are they?

8. Will any of your witnesses be provided with an interpreter? ☐ Yes ☐ No *(If no go to section D)*

9. If yes, say what type of interpreter e.g. language (stating which), deaf/blind etc.

D Legal representation

1. Who will be presenting your case at the hearing or trial? ☐ You ☐ Solicitor ☐ Counsel
2. Please give details of any dates within the trial period when the person presenting your case will not be available.

Name	Dates not available

E Other matters

1. How long do you estimate the whole of the trial will take, excluding judgment?

Minutes	Hours	Days

2. What is the estimated number of pages of evidence to be included in the trial bundle?

(please give number)

3. Please provide a case summary and proposals (agreed if possible) for directions to be given, by reference to the pre-trial review directions form.

Signed

Claimant/defendant or Counsel/Solicitor for the claimant/defendant

Date

Appendix 4

Technology and Construction Court

PRE-TRIAL REVIEW DIRECTIONS FORM 49CPD–010

( ) [Directions in relation to orders not yet complied with]

( ) Trial bundle to include [all admissible disclosed documents required by either party] [documents in the following categories only:

.]

Claimant/defendant to serve proposed index of trial bundle by am/pm on 1999/20.

Defendant/claimant to rspond by am/pm on 1999/20 . Trial bundle to be agreed by am/pm on 1999/20 and filed by am/pm on 1999/20 with any witness statements and experts' reports not already filed.

( ) Claimant/defendant to open trial and to serve and file chronology, cast list and note of opening by am/pm on 1999/20 . [Defendant/claimant to make an opening response and to serve and file a note of it by am/pm 1999/20 .]

( ) Disks (if obtainable) of statements of case, witness statements, experts' reports, trial bundle and opening notes, so far as not already filed, to be filed in format by am/pm on 1999/20 .

( ) [Adjourned hearing of pre-trial review, if required.]

( ) Costs in cause.

PRACTICE DIRECTION—COMMERCIAL COURT

This Practice Direction supplements CPR, Part 49 and replaces, with modifications, Order 72 of the Rules of the Supreme Court

General

1.1 This practice direction applies to commercial claims in the Commercial Court of the Queen's Bench Division. 49DPD–001

1.2(1) In this practice direction "commercial claim" includes any case arising out of trade and commerce in general, including any case relating to—

(i) a business document or contract,
(ii) the export or import of goods,
(iii) the carriage of goods by land, sea, air or pipeline,
(iv) the exploitation of oil and gas reserves,
(v) insurance and re-insurance,
(vi) banking and financial services,
(vii) the operation of markets and exchanges,
(viii) business agency, and
(ix) arbitration

and "commercial proceedings" has a corresponding meaning.

(2) "Judge" means Judge of the Commercial Court.

1.3 The rules relating to arbitration are set out in the Arbitration Practice Direction that supplements CPR Part 49.

1.4 The Civil Procedure Rules (the "CPR") apply to commercial proceedings in the Commercial Court subject to the provisions of this practice direction and any Commercial Court practice direction.

The commercial list

2.1 There shall be a list called "the commercial list" in which commercial claims in the Queen's Bench Division may be entered for trial in the Commercial Court, and one of the Commercial Court judges shall be in charge of that list.

2.2 All proceedings in the Commercial Court, including all pre-trial applications and any appeal from any judgment, order or decision of a master or district judge prior to the transfer of any case to the commercial list, shall be heard or otherwise dealt with by a Judge, except that:

(i) if an application is urgent and no Judge is available to deal with it, the application may be made to some other judge of the Queen's Bench Division authorised to hear applications in the Commercial Court; and

(ii) unless a Judge otherwise orders, all proceedings for the enforcement of any judgment or order for the payment of money given or made in the Commercial Court shall be referred to a master of the Queen's Bench Division.

2.3 The commercial list is a specialist list for the purposes of the CPR (see *e.g.* Rules 16.3(5) and 30.5 of the CPR).

Entry of case in commercial list

3.1 The claim form by which a commercial claim intended to be entered in the commercial list is begun should be issued out of the Admiralty and Commercial Registry at the Royal Courts of Justice.

3.2 The claim form should, before it is issued, be marked with the words "Queen's Bench Division, Commercial Court" and on the issue of the claim form out of the said Registry the case will be entered in the commercial list.

3.3 Where a claim form is to be marked as mentioned in paragraph 3.2, any application before issue of the claim form should be made to a Judge.

3.4 If an application is made before issue of the claim form, the written evidence in support of the application must state, in addition to any other necessary matters, that the claimant intends to mark the claim form in accordance with paragraph 3.2.

3.5 If the Judge hearing an application made before the issue of the claim form is of the opinion that the case in question should not be entered in the commercial list, he may adjourn the application to be heard by a master or by a judge of the Queen's Bench Division who is not a judge of the Commercial Court.

4.1 At any stage of the proceedings of commercial proceedings not entered in the commercial list any party:

(1) may apply to a Judge for an order transferring the proceedings to the commercial list; or

(2) may apply to the court where the proceedings are being dealt with for an order that they be transferred to the commercial list.

4.2 On an application under paragraph 4.1(2) the court may not itself make the order for transfer, but, if it considers the proceedings might be suitable to be entered in the commercial list, may adjourn the application for hearing by a Judge.

4.3 Where the Judge orders commercial proceedings to be transferred to the commercial list he may also order the proceedings to be transferred to the Royal Courts of Justice and at the same time may give directions for the management of the case.

4.4 A Judge may, on his own initiative, (but not unless the parties have had an opportunity of being heard or have consented) or on the application of any party, order proceedings in the commercial list to be removed from that list.

4.5 Where a commercial claim has been entered in the commercial list by virtue of paragraph 3.2, an application by a defendant, including a Part 20 defendant, to remove it from that list must be made within 7 days after the defendant has filed an acknowledgment of service or a defence, whichever is the later.

Dispensing with particulars of claim or defence

5. The Judge may at any time, before or after the issue of the claim form, order that proceedings in the commercial list be tried without the filing or service of particulars of claim or of a defence or of any other statement of case. 49DPD–002

Directions and case management

6.1 All proceedings in the commercial list will be allocated to the multi-track and the CPR relating to allocation questionnaires and track allocation will not apply.

6.2(1) If proceedings are transferred to the commercial list following an application under paragraph 4, then, unless the Judge who made the order for transfer gave directions for the management of the case, an application to the Judge for such directions shall be made within 14 days of the date of the order of transfer.

(2) If the claimant does not make an application in accordance with paragraph 6.2(1), any other party may do so, or may apply for the claim of the claimant in default to be struck out or dismissed.

Ship's papers

7.1 Where in proceedings in the commercial list relating to a marine insurance policy an application for specific disclosure under Rule 31.12 of the CPR is made by the insurer, the Judge, if it appears to him to be necessary or expedient to do so, may make an order in such form as he thinks fit for the production of the documents specified in the order.

7.2 An order under this rule may be made at the stage of the proceedings and on such terms, if any, as to staying the proceedings or otherwise, as the Judge thinks fit.

Admiralty and commercial registry

8.1 All administrative acts which under the Civil Procedure Rules or any Practice Direction are to be carried out by the Court office shall in relation to cases in the commercial list be carried out by or through the Admiralty and Commercial Registry.

8.2 All documents which under the Civil Procedure Rules are to be filed with the Court office shall in cases in the commercial list be filed with the Admiralty and Commercial Registry.

8.3 All claim forms, arbitration forms (see the Arbitration practice direction supplementing CPR Part 49) issued in and other documents filed with the Admiralty and Commercial Registry are (if they need to be served) to be served by the parties, not by the Admiralty and Commercial Registry.

The commercial court guide

9.1 The first edition of the Guide to Commercial Court Practice was published in 1986. The most recent edition has been the Fourth Edition published in 1997.

9.2 With the approval of the Judges of the Commercial Court a Fifth Edition has been prepared and adopted by the Commercial Court Committee. The Fifth Edition (now entitled "The Commercial Court Guide") is designed to be introduced at the same time as the new Civil Procedure Rules and the practice directions that supplement them.

9.3 The Fifth Edition incorporates and adapts into one text provisions of the Fourth Edition and of the many Practice Directions and Statements appended to it. The revision also incorporates a number of new provisions.

9.4 The combined result is intended to be a Guide that will, in the specialist context of commercial cases, serve the "overriding objective" defined in CPR Part 1. The Guide will be kept under review by the Judges of the Commercial Court and by the Commercial Court Committee.

9.5 The practice of the Commercial Court set out in this revised edition should be followed from 26 April 1999, subject to the provisions of this or any other Commercial Court practice direction and to any order that may be made in an individual case.

10. This practice direction supersedes all practice directions and Practice Statements in the Commercial Court.

PRACTICE DIRECTION—PATENTS ETC.

This Practice Direction supplements CPR, Part 49 and replaces, with modifications, RSC, Order 104, Order 100 and Order 93, Rule 24, and CCR, Order 48A and Order 49, Rule 4A

Editorial Introduction

49EPD–001 This Practice Direction—Patents, etc., supplements CPR, Pt 49. It replaces, with modifications, RSC, O.104 (proceedings relating to patents, registered designs and under the Defence Contracts Act 1958), O.100 (trade marks) and O.93 (applications under ss.114, 204 or 231 of the Copyright, Designs and Patents Act 1988) and the equivalent rules for the Patents County Court and CCR, O.48A and O.49A. Most of the changes are designed to ensure that the same terminology applies to these specialist proceedings as apply to all others. Furthermore, some minor changes have to be made to ensure that case management in these areas is consistent with the new system.

As before, all claims made under the Patent Acts, the Registered Design Acts and under the Defence Contracts Act are assigned either to the Patents Court, a part of the Chancery Division of the High Court, or the Patents County Court (2(a)). There is a possibility of transfer from one to the other. Every claim allocated to the Patents Court will be allocated to the multi-track. As a consequence the rules relating to track allocation do not apply (2(d)). It should be noted that claims and appeals arising under the Trade Marks Acts 1938 and 1994, and the Olympic Symbol, etc., Act 1995 are assigned to the Chancery Division, not the Patents Court (para. 21). In practice, actions for passing off and under the Copyright, etc., Act are also dealt with by the Chancery Division. All these types of cases are treated as any other form of litigation and the track allocation rules apply. With very few exceptions, all applications in patent and registered design matters are made direct to the Patents Court. Paragraph 4 contains detailed provisions relating to applications in the Patents Court for the amendment of patent specifications.

The Practice Direction requires the parties to take various steps to limit the scope of the dispute between them and to reduce the amount of material relied on at the trial. To this end, para. 6 stipulates that the claimant in a patent action must identify not only what the acts of infringement relied on are but also the particular claims which are said to be infringed. Similarly, in those cases where the defendant intends to attack the validity of a patent, para. 7 contains detailed provisions requiring him to specify the nature of the attack and any prior art he intends to rely upon. Similar directions exist for proceedings in which the validity of a trade mark is being put in issue (para. 23). Paragraph 9 limits the scope of disclosure in patent actions, particularly by exempting old documentation from disclosure and providing any claimant who is relying on commercial success to support the validity of his patent with a means of avoiding disclosure of the extensive documentation which might otherwise be relevant to that issue. Any part wishing to rely on experiments has to comply with para. 10 which specifies, amongst other things, the date on which a notice of experiments must be served. In fact, the order for directions made in patent actions frequently includes more detailed provisions for the timing and content of a notice of experiments. A standard form notice of experiments is annexed to the *Patents Court Guide.* (The latest issue of that document can be obtained from the Patents Court website at www.courtservice.gov.uk/highhome.htm.) Paragraph 12 prevents a party from relying on any evidence of which the other party has had inadequate notice.

Paragraph 13 sets a time limit of 28 days within which applications must be made to the Court in cases where the Comptroller General of Patents has either declined to deal with a question or application made to him under the 1977 Act or where he certifies under s.72(7)(b) that it is a matter which would be more properly determined by the Court.

The procedure to be adoped when an employee applies for compensation under s.40 of the 1977 Act is set out in para. 14, while para. 15 sets out the procedure to be adopted for appeals to the Court from decisions of the Comptroller where such an appeal lies.

General

1.1 This practice directions applies to the business of the Patents Court and proceedings under the Copyright, Designs and Patents Act 1988, the Trade Marks Acts 1938 and 1994 and the Olympic Symbol, etc. Protection Act 1995 and Olympic Association Right (Infringement Proceedings) Regulations 1995. **49EPD–002**

1.2 The Civil Procedure Rules apply to Patents Court business and proceedings under the Copyright, Designs and Patents Act 1988, the Trade Marks Acts 1938 and 1994 and the Olympic Symbol, etc. Protection Act 1995 and Olympic Association Right (Infringement Proceedings) Regulations 1995 subject to the provisions of this and any other Patents Court practice direction.

1.3 Definitions

In this Practice Direction—

"the 1949 Act" means the Patents Act 1949;

"the 1977 Act" means the Patents Act 1977;

"the Comptroller" means the Comptroller-General of Patents, Designs and Trade Marks;

"the Court" means the Patents Court;

"existing patent" means a patent mentioned in section 127(2)(a) or (c) of the 1977 Act;

"the journal" means the journal published pursuant to rules made under section 123(6) of the 1977 Act;

"1977 Act patent" means a patent under the 1977 Act;

"patent" means an existing patent or a 1977 Act patent and includes any application for a patent, supplementary protection certificate granted pursuant to the Patents (Supplementary Protection Certificates) Rules 1997, the Patents (Supplementary Protection Certificate for Medicinal Products) Regulations 1992 and the Patents (Supplementary Protection Certificate for Plant Protection Products) Regulations 1996.

"Patents Court" includes the Patents Court of the High Court and the Patents County Court.

"Patents Court business" includes:

(a) any claim under the Patents Acts 1949 to 1961 and 1977;

(b) any claim under the Registered Designs Acts 1949 to 1961;

(c) any claim under the Defence Contracts Act 1958, and

(d) all proceedings for the determination of a question or the making of a declaration relating to a patent (or an application for a patent) under the inherent jurisdiction of the High Court.

"the CPR" means the Civil Procedure Rules.

Allocation of patents court business

2.1 Patents Court business may be dealt with either in the High Court or the Patents county court.

2.2 Before the issue of a claim form relating to Patents Court business, the claim form, whether it is to be issued in the High Court or the county court, should be marked in the top right hand corner "Patents Court" and the claim will then be allocated to the Patents Court.

2.3 The Patents Court is a specialist list for the purposes of Part 30 of the CPR but no order for the transfer of proceedings to or from the Patents Court shall be made unless the parties have either:

(a) had an opportunity of being heard on the issue, or

(b) consented to the order.

2.4 Every claim in the Patents Court will be allocated to the Multi-track and the CPR relating to allocation questionnaires and track allocation will not apply.

2.5(1) Where a claim has been allocated to the Patents Court either on issue (*i.e.* in every case in which the claim form has been marked Patents Court) or by transfer to the Patents Court, an application for directions (including an application for a fixed date of hearing) shall be made by the claimant within 14 days of the filing by the defendant of an acknowledgment of service or of a defence (whichever is the earlier) or, as the case may be, within 14 days of the date of the order of transfer.

(2) If the claimant does not make an application in accordance with paragraph 2.5, any other party may do so or may apply for the claim of the claimant in default to be struck out or dismissed.

(3) Any application under this paragraph must be made to a judge of the Patents Court unless a judge of the Patents Court otherwise directs.

(4) On the hearing of the application for directions under paragraph 2.5(1) the judge shall give directions for any further directions hearing and direct the time by which the hearing of any further application for directions is to take place.

2.6 Except where inconsistent with the provisions of this Practice Direction, CPR Part 29 and the Multi-track Practice Direction apply to Patents Court business.

2.7 This practice direction shall apply with any necessary modifications to proceedings in respect of Registered Designs.

Service of documents

3.1 This rule applies to the service of any document on a party until such time as that party has provided an address for service in accordance with CPR rule 6.5.

3.2 Subject to sub-paragraph (3) below, for the purposes of any proceedings relating to a patent or a registered design (including proceedings for revocation, declaration as to non-infringement or groundless threats of infringement proceedings or any other proceedings of a kind mentioned in this Practice Direction) where any document is served in the manner authorised by CPR Part 6 at an address for service given in the register kept under section 32 of the 1977 Act or, as the case may be, section 17 of the Registered Designs Act 1949.

(1) service shall be deemed to have been effected on the registered proprietor of the patent or registered design on the date on which the document was served at the said address;

(2) the party on whom service is deemed to have been effected under sub-paragraph (a) shall be treated, for the purposes of any provision of these rules which specifies a time-limit for responding to the document so served (whether by filing or serving an admission, filing a defence, acknowledging service, or otherwise), as having been served on the seventh day after the date on which the document was served at the said address.

3.3 Nothing in paragraph 3.2 shall prevent service being effected on the proprietor in accordance with the provisions of Part 6 of the CPR.

Application in proceedings before the court for permission to amend a patent specification under s.30 of the 1949 act or s.75 of the 1977 act

49EPD–003 **4.1** A patentee or the proprietor of a patent intending to apply in proceedings before the Court under section 30 of the 1949 Act or under section 75 of the 1977 Act for permission to amend his specification must give notice of his intention to the Comptroller accompanied by a copy of an advertisement—

(1) identifying the proceedings pending before the Court in which it is intended to apply for such permission;

(2) giving particulars of the amendment sought;

(3) stating the applicant's address for service within the United Kingdom;

(4) stating that a Statement of Reasons is available from that address; and

(5) stating that any person intending to oppose the amendment must within 28 days after the appearance of the advertisement give written notice of his intention to the applicant; such notice to be accompanied by a Statement of Opposition

and the Comptroller shall insert the advertisement once in the journal. A person who gives notice in accordance with the advertisement shall be entitled to be heard on the application subject to any direction of the Court as to costs.

4.2 The applicant must at the same time as giving notice to the Comptroller serve a copy of the Statement of Reasons together with a copy of the patent as proposed to be amended on all parties to the proceedings.

4.3 The Statement of Reasons referred to in paragraph 4.1(4) shall contain full particulars of the amendment sought, of the reasons therefor and of the reasons why the applicant contends that in the exercise of discretion the amendment should be allowed. In particular the Statement should contain:

(1) A statement whether the amendment is by way of deletion of claims or re-writing of claims.

(2) In so far as it involves re-writing claims, details as to why the proposed amendment is in accordance with the statutory requirements of an amendment.

(3) In so far as the amendment is sought to distinguish (more clearly) over prior art, an indication of the prior art.

4.4 The Statement of Opposition shall contain full particulars of all grounds of opposition to the application to amend.

4.5 As soon as may be after the expiration of 35 days from the appearance of the advertisement the applicant must make his application under the said section 30 or 75, as the case may be, by an application notice in the proceedings before the Court; and the application notice, together with a copy of the specification certified by the Comptroller and showing in coloured ink the amendment sought, must be served on the Comptroller, the parties to the proceedings and any person who has given notice of his intention to oppose the amendment.

4.6 Not less than two days before the date fixed for the hearing of the application, the applicant, the Comptroller, the parties to the proceedings and any other opponent should serve on all other parties and on the Court a Statement of Directions being the directions which that party seeks for the further conduct of the proceedings. Any of the foregoing not serving a Statement of Directions shall take no further part in the proceedings without permission of the Court and shall not be liable for the costs thereof.

4.7 On the hearing of the amendment application the Court shall give such directions for its further conduct as it thinks necessary or expedient and, in particular, directions—

(1) determining whether the application shall be heard forthwith or with the other proceedings relating to the patent in question or separately and, if separately, fixing the date of hearing thereof;

(2) as to whether any evidence is necessary, and, if so, as to the manner in which that evidence shall be given and, if written evidence is to be given, fixing the times within which the affidavits or witness statements must be filed;

(3) as to whether any disclosure is necessary, and, if so, as to the extent of disclosure and the manner and time within which the same is to be given.

4.8 Where the Court allows a specification to be amended, the applicant must forthwith file with the Comptroller an office copy of the order made in the Court and, if so required by the Court or Comptroller, leave at the Patent Office a new specification and drawings as amended, prepared in compliance with the 1949 or 1977 Act, whichever is applicable, and the rules made under those Acts respectively.

4.9 The Comptroller shall cause a copy of the order to be inserted at least once in the journal.

Application for revocation

5.1 An application under section 72 of the 1977 Act for the revocation of a patent shall be commenced by the issue of a claim form. This direction does not apply to an application made in existing proceedings. An application in existing proceedings shall be made by way of a counterclaim or other Part 20 claim (as defined in CPR rule 20.2(1)).

Claim for infringement

6.1 The claimant in a claim for infringement must serve with his claim form particulars of the infringement relied on, showing which of the claims in the specification of the patent are alleged to be infringed and giving at least one instance of each type of infringement alleged.

6.2 If a defendant in such a claim alleges, as a defence to the claim, that at the time of the infringement there was in force a contract or licence relating to the patent made by or with the consent of the claimant and containing a condition or term void by virtue of section 44 of the 1977 Act, he must serve on the claimant particulars of the date of, and parties to, each such contract or licence and particulars of each such condition or term.

Objections to validity

7.1 A person who presents a claim for the revocation of a patent must serve with his claim form particulars of the objections to the validity of the patent on which he relies.

7.2 A party to a claim concerning a patent who either challenges the validity of the patent or applies by counterclaim or other Part 20 claim for revocation of the patent must, serve his defence, counterclaim or other Part 20 claim (as the case may be), together with particulars of the objections to the validity of the patent on which he relies, within 42 days after service upon him of the claim form.

7.3 Particulars given pursuant to paragraph 7.1 or 7.2 must state every ground on which the validity of the patent is challenged and must include such particulars as will clearly define every issue (including any challenge to any claimed priority date) which it is intended to raise.

7.4 If the grounds stated in the particulars of objections include want of novelty or want of any inventive step, the particulars must state the manner, time and place of every prior publication or user relied upon and, if prior user is alleged, must:

(1) specify the name of every person alleged to have made such user,

(2) state whether such user is alleged to have continued until the priority date of the claim in question or of the invention, as may be appropriate, and, if not, the earliest and latest date on which such user is alleged to have taken place,

(3) contain a description accompanied by drawings, if necessary, sufficient to identify such user, and

(4) if such user relates to machinery or apparatus, state whether the machinery or apparatus is in existence and where it can be inspected.

7.5 If either (a) in the case of an existing patent one of the grounds stated in the particulars of objections is that the invention, so far as claimed in any claim of the complete specification, is not useful, or, (b) in the case of a patent one of the grounds stated in the particulars of objections is that the specification of the patent does not disclose the invention clearly enough and comletely enough for the invention to be performed and it is intended, in connection with either of such grounds, to rely on the fact that an example of the invention which is the subject of any claim cannot be made to work, either at all or as described in the specification, the particulars must state that fact and identify each such claim and must include particulars of each such example, specifying the respects in which it is alleged that it does not work or does not work as described.

7.6 In any proceedings relating to a patent in which the validity of the patent has been put in issue on the ground of obviousness a party who wishes to rely on the commercial success of the patent must state in his pleadings the grounds upon which he so relies.

Admissions

8.1 Where a party desires any other party to admit any facts, he shall, within 21 days after service of a reply or after the expiration of the period fixed for the service thereof, serve on that other party a notice requiring him to admit for the purpose of the claim the facts specified in the notice. **49EPD–004**

8.2 A party upon whom a notice under paragraph 8.1 is served shall within 21 days after service thereof serve upon the party making the request a notice stating in respect of each fact specified in the notice whether or not he admits it.

Disclosure and inspection

9.1 CPR Part 31 shall apply in a claim for infringement of a patent or a declaration of non-infringement of a patent or any proceedings where the validity of a patent is in issue.

9.2 Standard disclosure does not require the disclosure of documents in the following exempt classes:

(1) documents relating to the infringement of a patent by a product or process if, before serving a list of documents, the party against whom the allegation of infringement is made has served on the other parties full particulars of the product or process alleged to infringe, including if necessary drawings or other illustrations;

(2) documents relating to any ground on which the validity of a patent is put in issue, except documents which came into existence within the period beginning two years before the earliest claimed priority date and ending two years after that date; and

(3) documents relating to the issue of commercial success.

9.3 Where the issue of commercial success arises in any proceedings specified in paragraph 9.1, the patentee shall, within such time limit as the Court may direct, serve a schedule containing the following details—

(1) where the commercial success relates to an article or product—

- (a) an identifcation of the article or product (for example by product code number) which the patentee asserts has been made in accordance with the claims of the patent;
- (b) a summary by convenient periods of sales of any such article or product;
- (c) a summary for the equivalent periods of sales, if any, of any equivalent prior article or product marketed before the article or product mentioned in sub-paragraph (a); and
- (d) a summary by convenient periods of any expenditure on advertising and promotion which supported the marketing of the articles or products mentioned in sub-paragraph (a) and (c),

(2) where the commercial success relates to the use of a process—

- (a) an identification of the process the patentee asserts has been used in accordance with the claims of the patent;
- (b) a summary by convenient periods of the revenues received from the use of such process;

(c) a summary for the equivalent periods of the revenues, if any, received from the use of any equivalent prior art process; and

(d) a summary by convenient periods of any expenditure which supported the use of the process mentioned in sub-paragraphs (a) and (c).

Experiments

10.1 Where a party desires to establish any fact by experimental proof he must, at least 21 days before the service of the application notice for directions under paragraph 10.3 or within such other time as the Court may direct at a hearing for further directions pursuant to paragraph 2.5(4), serve on the other party a notice stating the facts which he desires to establish and giving full particulars of the experiments proposed to establish them.

10.2 A party upon whom a notice under paragraph 10.1 is served shall, within 21 days after service thereof, serve upon the other party a notice stating in respect of each fact whether or not he admits it.

10.3 Where any fact which a party desires to establish by experimental proof is not admitted he shall apply to the Court for directions in respect of such experiments.

Application for further directions

11.1(1) The parties must comply with any directions given by the judge pursuant to paragrpah 2.5(4) in respect of any hearing for further directions.

(2) If the claimant does not serve an application notice for further directions in accordance with this paragraph, the defendant may do so.

(3) The application notice must be accompanied by minutes of the order proposed, and such other documents as will be necessary for the hearing of the application.

11.2 At a further directions hearing under this paragraph the judge may give such directions relating to:

(1) the service of further pleadings or of further information pursuant to Part 18 of the CPR;

(2) disclosure and inspection of documents;

(3) requests for or the making of admissions pursuant to paragraphs 8.1 and 8.2 above and Part 14 of the CPR;

(4) the obtaining of written evidence relating to matters requiring expert knowledge, and for the filing of affidavits or witness statements and the service of copies thereof on the other parties,

(5) the holding of a meeting of such experts as the judge may specify, for the purpose of producing a joint report on the state of the relevant art;

(6) the exchanging of experts' reports, in respect of those matters on which they are not agreed;

(7) the making of experiments, tests, inspections or reports;

(8) the determination, as a preliminary issue, of any question that may arise (including any questions as to the construction of the specification or other documents)

and otherwise as the judge thinks necessary or expedient for the purpose of giving effect to the overriding objective. Where evidence is directed to be given by affidavit or witness statement, the witnesses must attend at the trial for cross-examination unless, with the concurrence of the Court, the parties otherwise agree.

11.3 On the hearing of an application under this paragraph the judge shall consider, if necessary of his own initiative, whether:

(a) the parties' advisers should be required to meet for the purpose of agreeing which documents will be required at the trial and of paginating such documents;

(b) an independent scientific adviser should be appointed to assist the Court, whether as an assessor under CPR rule 35.15 or otherwise.

Restrictions on admission of evidence

12.1 Except with the permission of the judge hearing any claim or other proceedings relating to a patent, no evidence shall be admissible in proof of any alleged infringement, or of any objection to the validity, of the patent, if the infringement or objection was not raised in the particulars of infringements or objections, as the case may be. **49EPD–005**

12.2 In any claim or other proceedings relating to a patent, evidence which is not in accordance with a statement contained in particulars of objections to the validity of the patent shall not be admissible in support of such an objection unless the judge hearing the proceeding allows the evidence to be admitted.

12.3 If any machinery or apparatus alleged to have been used before the priority date mentioned in paragraph 7.4(2) is n existence at the date of service of the particulars of objections, no evidence of its user before that date shall be admissible unless it is proved that the party relying on such user offered, where the machinery or apparatus is in his possesion, inspection of it to the other parties to the proceedings or, where it is not, used all reasonable endeavours to obtain inspection of it for those parties.

Determination of question or application where comptroller declines to deal with it

13 Where the Comptroller—

(1) declines to deal with a question under section 8(7), 12(2), 37(8) or 61(5) of the 1977 Act;

(2) declines to deal with an application under section 40(5) of that Act, or

(3) certifies under section 72(7)(b) of that Act that the question whether a patent should be revoked is one which would more properly be determined by the court,

any person entitled to do so may, within 28 days after the Comptroller's decision apply to the Court to determine the question or application.

Application by employee for compensation under section 40 of the 1977 Act

14.1 An application by an employee for compensation under section 40(1) or (2) of the 1977 Act shall be begun by the issue of a claim form within the period which begins when the relevant patent is granted and which expires one year after it has ceased to have effect.

Provided that, where a patent has ceased to have effect by reason of a failure to pay any renewal fee within the period prescribed for the payment thereof and an application for restoration is made to the Comptroller under section 28 of the said Act, the said period shall—

(1) if restoration is ordered, continue as if the patent had remained continuously in effect, or

(2) if restoration is refused, be treated as expiring one year after the patent ceased to have effect or six months after the refusal, whichever is the later.

14.2 Either at the hearing of an application for directions under paragraph 2.5(1) or at a hearing of an application for further directions under paragraphs 11.1–11.3, the Court must give directions as to the manner in which the evidence (including any accounts of expenditure and receipts relating to the claim) shall be given at the hearing of the claim and, if written evidence is to be given, specify the period within which witness statements or affidavits must be filed.

14.3 The Court must also give directions as to the provision by the defendant to the claimant, or a person deputed by him for the purpose, of reasonable facilities for inspecting and taking extracts from the books of account by which the defendant proposes to verify the accounts mentioned in paragraph 14.2 or from which those accounts have been derived.

Procedure for the determination of certain disputes

15.1 The following proceedings must be begun by the issue of a claim form, that is to say—

(1) proceedings for the determination of any dispute referred to the court under—

(a) section 48 of the 1949 Act or section 58 of the 1977 Act;
(b) paragraph 3 of Schedule 1 to the Registered Designs Act 1949;
(c) section 4 of the Defence Contracts Act 1958; or
(d) section 252 of the Copyright, Designs and Patent Act 1988;

(2) any application under section 45(3) of the 1977 Act.

Appeals from the comprtoller

16.1 In this paragraph "the Court" means the Patents Court of the High Court.

16.2 An appeal to the Court from a decision of the Comptroller in any case in which a right of appeal is given by the 1949 or 1977 Act must be brought by issuing a Notice of Appeal. The parties are, in this paragraph, referred to as "appellant" and "respondent" respectively.

16.3 The Notice of Appeal shall be issued:

(1) in the case of a decision on a matter of procedure, within 14 days after the date of the decision; and

(2) in any other case, within six weeks after the date of the decision.

16.4 The Comptroller may determine whether any decision is on a matter of procedure and any such determination shall itself be a decision on a matter of procedure.

16.5 Except with permission of the Court, no appeal shall be entertained unless the Notice of Appeal has been issued within the period specified in paragraph 16.3 or within such further time as the Comptroller may allow upon request made to him prior to the expiry of that period.

16.6 The Notice of Appeal may be given in respect of the whole or any specific part of the decision of the Comptroller and must specify the grounds of the appeal and the relief which the appellant seeks.

16.7 Except with the permission of the Court the appellant shall not be entitled on the hearing of the appeal to rely on any ground of appeal or to apply for any relief not specified in the Notice of Appeal.

16.8 The appellant shall, within 21 days of issuing the Notice of Appeal, serve a copy thereof on the Comptroller and any other party to the proceedings before the Comptroller.

16.9 After receiving the Notice of Appeal the Comptroller shall lodge with the Clerk or other person in charge of the Patents Court list all papers relating to the matter which is subject of the appeal.

16.10 A respondent who, not having appealed from the decision of the Comptroller, desires to contend on the appeal that the decision should be varied, either in any event or in the event of the appeal being allowed in whole or in part, must give notice to that effect, specifying the grounds of that contention and the relief which he seeks from the Court.

16.11 A respondent who desires to contend on the appeal that the decision of the Comptroller should be affirmed on grounds other than those set out in the decision must give notice to that effect, specifying the grounds of that contention.

16.12 A respondent's notice shall be served on the Comptroller and on the appellant and every other party to the proceedings before the Comptroller within 14 days after service of the Notice of Appeal by the respondent, or within such further time as the Court may direct.

16.13 A party by whom a respondent's notice is given must within 5 days after service of the notice on the appellant, furnish 2 copies of the notice to the Clerk or other person in charge of the Patents List.

16.14 The Clerk or other person in charge of the Patents list shall give to the Comptroller and to the appellant and every other party to the proceedings before the Comptroller not less than seven days' notice of the date appointed for the hearing of the appeal, unless the Court directs shorter notice to be given.

16.15 An appeal shall be by way of rehearing and the evidence used on appeal shall be the same as that used before the Comptroller and, except with the permission of the Court, no further evidence shall be given.

16.16 Any notice given in proceedings under this rule may be signed by or served on any patent agent, or member of the Bar of England and Wales not in actual practice, who is acting for the person giving the notice or, as the case may be, the person on whom the notice is to be served, as if the patent agent or member of the Bar were a solicitor.

16.17 The Notice of Appeal shall be in the form annexed hereto or in such other form as may be approved by the Court.

Communication of information to the European Patent Office

17.1 The Court may authorise the communication to the European Patent Office or the competent authority of any country which is a party to the European Patent Convention of any such information in the files of the court as the Court thinks fit. **49EPD–006**

17.2 Before complying with a request for the disclosure of information under paragraph 17.1 the Court shall afford to any party appearing to be affected by the request the opportunity of making representations, in writing or otherwise, on the question whether the information should be disclosed.

Claim for rectification of register of patents or designs

18.1 Where a claim is made for the rectification of the register of patents, the claimant shall at the same time as serving the other party serve a copy of the claim form and the accompanying documents on the Comptroller, who shall be entitled to appear and to be heard on the application.

Other intellectual property matters included in this practice direction

A. Copyright matters

Additional damages under Section 97(2) of the Copyright, Designs and Patents Act 1988

19.1 Where a claimant seeks to recover additional damages under section 97(2) of the Copyright, Designs and Patents Act 1988, he must so state in his claim form and the particulars of claim must set out the grounds relied upon in support.

Applications for delivery up and forfeiture under Sections 99, 114, 195, 204, 230 or 231 of the Copyright Designs and Patents Act 1988

20.1 An application under Sections 99, 114, 195, 204, 230 or 231 of the Copyright, Designs and Patents Act 1988 ("CDPA") shall be made by the issue of a claim form or, if made in existing proceedings, an application notice in those proceedings.

20.2 Where such an application is made the applicant shall serve the claim form or application notice on all persons having an interest in the goods, material or articles within the meaning of sections 114, 204 or 231 of the CDPA in so far as such persons are reasonably ascertainable.

B. Trademark matters

Definitions

21.1 In this section of this practice direction—

"the 1938 Act" means the Trade Marks Act 1938 as amended by the Trade Marks (Amendment) Act 1984 and the Patents, Designs and Marks Act 1986;

"the 1994 Act" means the Trade Marks Act 1994;

"the Olympic Symbol Act" means the Olympic Symbol etc. (Protection) Act 1995;

"the Olympic Symbol Regulations" means the Olympic Association Right (Infringement Proceedings) Regulations 1995;

"the Registrar" means the Comptroller-General of Patents, Designs and Trade Marks;

"the register" means the register of trade marks maintained by the Registrar pursuant to section 63 of the 1994 Act;

"appointed person" means a person appointed by the Lord Chancellor to hear and decide appeals under the 1994 Act.

Assignment to the Chancery Division

49EPD–007 **22.1** Proceedings in the High Court under the 1938 Act, the 1994 Act or the Olympic Symbol Act and Regulations shall be dealt with in the Chancery Division.

Appeals and applications under the 1938 Act, the 1994 Act and the Olympic Symbol Act and the Olympic Symbol Regulations

23.1 Every appeal to the High Court under the 1938 Act or the 1994 Act shall be heard and determined by a single judge.

23.2 Such appeals shall be brought by a Notice of Appeal in such form as may be approved by the court.

23.3 The Notice of Appeal must be issued within 28 days of the decision appealed from.

23.4 Within 21 days of issue the Notice of Appeal must be served on the Registrar and any Respondents and lodged with the Clerk or other person in charge of the Chancery List.

23.5 Every other application to the High Court under the said Acts and the Olympic Symbol Regulations must be begun by the issue of a claim form under CPR Part 8 or, if made in existing proceedings, an application notice in those proceedings.

23.6 Notices of Appeal, claim forms or application notices by which any such application is begun must be served on the Registrar.

23.7 Where—

(1) the Registrar refers to the High Court an application made to him under the 1938 Act or the 1994 Act;

(2) the Board of Trade under the 1938 Act or an appointed person under section 76 of the 1994 Act refers to that Court an appeal,

then unless within one month after receiving notification of the decision to refer, the applicant or the appellant, as the case may be, makes to that Court the application or appeal referred, he shall be deemed to have abandoned it.

23.8 The period prescribed above in relation to an appeal to which paragraph 23.1 applies or the period prescribed by paragraph 23.7 in relation to an application or appeal to which that paragraph applies, may be extended by the Registrar on the application of any party interested and may be so extended although the application is not made until after the expiration of that period, but the foregoing provision shall not be taken to affect the power of the Court to extend that period.

23.9 Where under subsection (6) of section 17 or subsection (9) of section

18 of the 1938 Act an appellant becomes entitled and intends to withdraw the application which is the subject-matter of the appeal, he must give notice of his intention to the Registrar and to any other party to the appeal within one month after the Court has given permission under the said subsection (6) or the said subsection (9), as the case may be, for further grounds of objection to be taken.

23.10 Where an application is made under section 19 of the 1994 Act or under Regulation 5 of the Olympic Symbol Regulations the applicant shall serve the claim form or application notice on all persons having an interest in the goods, material or articles within the meaning of section 19 of the 1994 Act or Regulation 5 of the Olympic Symbol Regulations as the case may be insofar as such persons are reasonably ascertainable.

Proceedings for infringement of registered trade mark; validity of registration disputed or revocation or rectification sought

24.1 Where in any proceedings a claim is made for relief for infringement of the rights conferred on the proprietor of a registered trade mark by section 9 of the 1994 Act, the party against whom the claim is made may in his defence put in issue the validity of the registration of that trade mark or may apply by counterclaim or other Part 20 claim for an order for revocation of the registration or for a declaration of invalidity of the registration or for rectification of the register, or may do any or all of those things.

24.2 A party to any such proceedings who in his pleading (whether a defence or counterclaim or other Part 20 claim) disputes the validity of the registration of a registered trade mark or seeks a declaration of invalidity or an order for revocation of the registration, or rectification of the register, must serve with his pleading particulars of the objections to the validity of the registration or of any grounds for revocation or rectification, on which he relies.

24.3 A party to any such proceedings who applies for an order for revocation of the registration or for a declaration of invalidity of the registration or for rectification of the register must serve on the Registrar a copy of his counterclaim or other Part 20 claim together with a copy of the particulars mentioned in paragraph 24.2 and the Registrar shall be entitled to take such part in the proceedings as he may think fit but need not serve a defence or other statement of case unless ordered to do so by the Court.

Service of documents

25.1 This rule applies to the service of any document on a party until such time as that party has provided an address for service in accordance CPR rule 6.5.

25.2 Subject to paragraph 25.3 for the purposes of any proceedings relating to a registered trade mark (including proceedings for revocation, declaration of invalidity or non-infringement or groundless threats of infringement proceedings or any other proceedings under the 1938 Act or the 1994 Act), where any document is served in the manner authorised by Part 6 of the CPR at an address for service given in the register kept under section 63 of the 1994 Act—

(1) service shall be deemed to have been effected on the registered proprietor of the trade mark on the date on which the document was served at the said address;

(2) the party on whom service is deemed to have been effected under sub-paragraph (1), shall be treated, for the purposes of any provision which specifies a time-limit for responding to the document so served (whether by acknowledging service, giving notice of intention to defend or otherwise), as having been served on the seventh day after the date on which the document was served at the said address.

25.3 Nothing in paragraph 25.2 shall prevent service being effected on the proprietor in accordance with the provisions of CPR Part 6.

Service of orders on the Registrar

Where an order is made by the Court in any case under the 1938 Act or the 1994 Act, the person in whose favour the order is made (if there is more than one, such one of them as the Court shall direct) shall serve an office copy of the order on the Registrar.

In the High Court of Justice Chancery Division Patents Court

NOTICE OF APPEAL 49EPD–008

(a) Here insert the nature of the application or proceedings, the name of the Patentee or Applicant, the number of the Patent or Application for Letters Patent followed by the name of the Opponent (if any)
(b) Patent Agent or Applicant in person
(c) Here insert name(s) and full address(es) of Appellant(s)
(d) Here insert "the decision 'or' that part of the decision" as the case may be
(e) Here insert "Comptroller General" or "Officer acting for the Comptroller General" as the case may be
(f) Summarise the decision appealed against
(g) Here set out the grounds of appeal
(h) Here set out the relief which the Appellant seeks
(i) To be signed by the Appellant personally or by his duly authorised representative
(j) To be addressed to the other side and to their authorised representative and to the Comptroller-General at the Patent Office.

IN THE MATTER(a)

(e.g. of an Application by ....
and
an Opposition by ....)

TAKE NOTICE that the HIGH COURT OF JUSTICE, CHANCERY DIVISION, PATENTS COURT, will be moved before a Judge of the Patents Court at a time to be set by the Patents Court not less than twenty-four days after service of this notice, or so soon thereafter as Counsel(b) can be heard by Counsel(b), on behalf of(c)

....
by the way of appeal from(d) ....
of the(e) ....
dated the .... day of .... 19 ....
whereby he(f) ....
....
....
....

The grounds of appeal are as follows:—(g)

I/WE ask the Patents Court to grant the relief set out below:—(h)

DATE ....
SIGNATURE .... (i)
ADDRESS ....
....
....
TO .... (j)
....
....

NOTE: Two copies of this Notice of Appeal must be sent to the Chancery Chambers (Room 307), Thomas More Building, Royal Courts of Justice, Strand, London WC2A 2LL. They must be accompanied with the remittance for the prescribed fee. The remittance must if sent by post be paid by Bankers Draft or ***postal order made payable to H.M. Paymaster General and crossed.*** *A copy of the notice must be sent to the Comptroller-General at the Patent Office, Room GR15, Concept House, Cardiff Road, Gwent NP10 1RH and to any party entitled to appear before the Patents Court within the period prescribed by paragraph 16 of* ***the Patents Practice Direction***

PRACTICE DIRECTION—ADMIRALTY

This Practice Direction supplements CPR Part 49 and replaces, with modifications, Order 75 of the Rules of the Supreme Court

Editorial Introduction

49FPD–001 This Practice Direction does not provide a complete code for these proceedings but has to be read in conjunction with the other Civil Procedure Rules. The application of the Civil Procedure Rules and the Practice Directions which supplement them is in Admiralty proceedings subject to the provisions of this Practice Direction. This Practice Direction also assigns certain claims to the QBD and provides that they are to be taken by the Admiralty court. It also replaces and incorporates most of the Admiralty Practice Directions set out in SCP 1999, Vol. 2, Section 6B at para 6B–1 *et seq.*

The following points are of importance:

There is now no jurisdiction in the County Court in Admiralty matters (see Civil Courts (Amendment) (No. 2) Order 1999 (S.I. 1999 No. 1011).

All Admiralty claims *in rem* or *in personam* must be commenced in the Admiralty and Commercial Registry at the RCJ or in a High Court district registry. If commenced in a district registry a copy of the claim form and any original file relating thereto will be sent to the Admiralty and Commercial Registry for consideration by the Admiralty Registrar.

All arrests will be dealt with by the Admiralty Marshal at the Admiralty and Commercial Registry in London.

As a general rule in cases where there is an arrest, the file and matter will be retained in the Admiralty and Commercial Registry for all purposes save as may be otherwise specifically ordered.

All arrests are to be supported by a Solicitor's undertaking to pay the Marshal's arrest expenses or disbursements or by a payment in in respect thereof.

The caveat system is preserved.

An acknowledgment of service must be filed in every Admiralty claim *in rem* and in every Admiralty claim *in personam* unless liability is admitted on ADM16 in a limitation claim. Such acknowledgment must be filed within 14 days of service of the claim form irrespective of whether or not particulars of claim are served with it.

An Admiralty claim *in personam* form is subject to the same rules as an ordinary claim form *in personam* where service is to be affected out of the jurisdiction save for the special rules set out in para. 3.1(2) and as regards a limitation claim form only in para. 9.1(6) and a collision claim form in para. 4.4.

There are special rules as to times for service

(a) The validity for service of an *in rem* claim form is 12 months, see para. 2.1(6).

(b) The time for service of particulars of claim in an *in rem* claim if not served with the *in rem* claim form is 75 days after service of the *in rem* claim form, see para. 2.1(2). A similar time limit applies to service of particulars of claim in an admiralty claim *in personam*, see para. 3.2(4).

Collision and limitation claims have their own special procedures see paras 4 and 9 respectively. The Preliminary Act procedure still applies in collision claims.

Related Sources

- Hovercraft Act 1968, ss.2–4 (see SCP 1999, Vol. 2, Section 6D, para. 6D–102)
- Supreme Court Act 1981, ss.20–24 and s.27 (see SCP 1999, Vol. 2, Section 6D at paras 6D–1 *et seq.*)
- Merchant Shipping Act 1995, ss.185–189, ss.92–93, ss.190, 192, 224 and 229–230 (see SCP 1999, Vol. 2, Part 6D, paras 6D–202 *et seq.*)

Forms

The text of the forms will be printed in full in the next publication of SCP 1999, Vol. 2, Section 6A—Special Admiralty Forms. Meanwhile see Supplement No. 3.

The forms are:

ADM 1	Claim Form (Admiralty claim IN REM)
ADM 1A	Claim Form (Admiralty claim IN PERSONAM)
ADM 1B	Notes for Claimant on completing an IN REM claim form
ADM 1C	Notes for Defendant on replying to an IN REM claim form
ADM 2	Acknowledgment of Service/Response Pack (Admiralty claim IN REM)
ADM 3	Preliminary Act
ADM 4	Application and Undertaking for Arrest & Custody
ADM 5	Outline form of Declaration (Affidavit) in support of application for Warrant of Arrest
ADM 6	Notice to Consular Officer of intention to apply for Warrant of Arrest
ADM 7	Request for Caveat against Arrest
ADM 8	Request for Caveat against Arrest after constitution of a Limitation Fund
ADM 9	Warrant of Arrest

ADM 10	Standard Directions to the Admiralty Marshal
ADM 11	Request for Caveat against Release
ADM 12	Application and Undertaking for Release
ADM 13	Application for Judgment in default of filing an Acknowledgment of Service and/or Defence or Preliminary Act
ADM 14	Order for sale of a ship
ADM 15	Claim Form (Admiralty LIMITATION CLAIM)
ADM 15A	Notes for Claimant on completing a Claim Form in an Admiralty Limitation Claim
ADM 15B	Notes for Defendant (Admiralty Limitation Claim)
ADM 16	Notice of admission of right of Claimant to limit liability
ADM 16A	Defence to admiralty limitation claim
ADM 16B	Acknowledgment of Service/Response Pack (Admiralty Limitation Claim)
ADM 17	Application for restricted Decree of Limitation
ADM 18	Restricted decree of Limitation
ADM 19	Decree of Limitation
ADM 20	Defendant's Claim in a Limitation Claim
ADM 21	Outline form of Declaration (Affidavit) as to inability of a Defendant to file and serve Statement of Case under a Decree of Limitation
ADM 22	Notice of Appeal against Registrar's decision on a Reference

General

1.1 This practice direction applies to all Admiralty proceedings. 49FPD–002

1.2 The provisions of the Civil Procedure Rules and the Practice Directions that supplement them apply to Admiralty proceedings subject to the provisions of this practice direction, any other Admiralty practice direction and, where applicable, the Commercial Court Guide (see paragraph 16 below).

1.3 "Admiralty proceedings" means proceedings in the Admiralty Court of the Queen's Bench Division of the High Court of Justice and in any other court exercising Admiralty jurisdiction.

1.4 In this Practice Direction:

(a) "the Admiralty Court" includes:
  (i) the Admiralty Court of the Queen's Bench Division of the High Court of Justice; and
  (ii) any other court exercising Admiralty jurisdiction.

(b) "claim *in rem*" means an Admiralty claim *in rem*;

(c) "claim *in personam*" means an Admiralty claim *in personam*;

(d) a "collision claim" means a claim falling within section 20(3)(b) of the Supreme Court Act 1981, namely any action to enforce a claim for damage, loss of life or personal injury arising out of—
  (i) a collision between ships; or
  (ii) the carrying out or omission to carry out any manoeuvre in the case of one or more of two or more ships; or
  (iii) non-compliance, on the part of one or more of two or more ships, with the collision regulations;

(e) a "salvage claim" includes any claim in the nature of salvage, any claim for special compensation under Article 14 of Schedule 11 to the Merchant Shipping Act 1995, any claim for the apportionment of salvage and any claim arising out of or connected with any contract for salvage services;

(f) "caveat against arrest" means a caveat entered in the caveat book under paragraph 6.3(1);

(g) "caveat against release" means a caveat entered in the caveat book under paragraph 6.5(2);

(h) "caveat book" means the book kept in the Admiralty and Commercial Registry in which caveats under this practice direction are entered;

(i) "limitation claim" means a claim by shipowners or other persons under the Merchant Shipping Act 1995 for the limitation of the amount of their liability in connection with a ship or other property;

(j) "Marshal" means the Admiralty Marshal;
(k) "ship" includes any description of vessel used in navigation.
(l) "The Admiralty Registrar" means the Queen's Bench master with responsibility for Admiralty proceedings;
(m) "*in rem* claim form" means a claim form by which an *in rem* claim is brought.
(n) Any references to the Merchant Shipping Act 1995 include any re-enactment thereof.
(o) "the CPR" means the Civil Procedure Rules.

1.5 The following claims must be commenced in the Admiralty Court.
(a) Any claim *in rem*;
(b) Any collision claim;
(c) Any limitation claim;
(d) Any application to the court under the Merchant Shipping Act 1995;
(e) Any salvage claim.

1.6 Any other claim within the admiralty jurisdiction of the High Court may be commenced either in the Admiralty Court or in the Commercial Court.

1.7 Any claim may be transferred to the Admiralty Court with the consent of the Admiralty Court.

1.8 A claim within paragraph 1.5 wrongly commenced in any other court will be transferred automatically to the Admiralty Court.

1.9 A claim form by which a claim within paragraphs 1.5 or 1.6 is begun may be issued out of the Admiralty and Commercial Court Registry or the registry of any Admiralty Court.

1.10 If a claim form referred to in paragraph 1.9 is issued out of a registry other than the Admiralty and Commercial Registry that other registry will immediately after issue send a copy of the claim by facsimile to the Admiralty and Commercial Registry, and will also send the original file to the Admiralty and Commercial Registry.

1.11 Subject to paragraph 1.13, the Admiralty Registrar shall, after the issue of a claim form referred to in paragraph 1.9 issue a direction in writing stating:
(a) whether the claim should remain in the Admiralty Court or should be transferred to another court; and
(b) if the claim is to remain in the Admiralty Court, whether it should be in the Admiralty Judge's list or should be placed in the Admiralty Registrar's list for trial in London or elsewhere.

In issuing these directions the Admiralty Registrar will have regard to the nature of the issues in dispute and the criteria set out in Rule CPR rule 26.8 in so far as they are applicable.

1.12 Where the Admiralty Registrar directs that the claim should be placed in the Judge's list, case management directions will be given and any case management conference or pre-trial review will be heard by the Admiralty Judge.

1.13 All matters concerning the arrest, detention, sale of property and the determination of priorities in a claim *in rem*, all proceedings concerning the ownership or the mortgage of a vessel registered under the Merchant Shipping Act 1995, all proceedings in a limitation claim and proceedings against the International Oil Pollution Compensation Fund under s.175 of the Merchant Shipping Act 1995 shall be dealt with only by the Admiralty Court of the High Court.

1.14 All Admiralty proceedings will be allocated to the multi-track and the CPR relating to allocation questionnaires and track allocation will not apply.

49FPD–003 **Admiralty jurisdiction**—As to the Admiralty jurisdiction of the High Court see SCA 1981, ss.20 to 24 (SCP 1999, Vol. 2, Section 6D, paras 6D–2 *et seq.*), the Hovercraft Act 1968 as amended by SCA 1981 (SCP 1999, Vol. 2, Section 6D, paras 6D–101 to 6D–105), the Merchant Shipping Act 1995, s.166.

The Court is seised of a claim *in rem* from the moment of service of the claim form or of arrest of a ship (whichever is the earlier). Where, however, proceedings are brought against a ship already under arrest in High Court proceedings, the Court will be seised of jurisdiction from the moment the claim form is issued. The Court cannot have jurisdiction over a ship which does not come within the jurisdiction (*The Freccia del Nord* [1989] 1 Lloyd's Rep. 388). The Court is seised of a claim *in personam* when the defendant is served with the claim form (*Neste Chemicals SA v. D.K. Line SA The Sargasso* [1993] 1 Lloyd's Rep. 424, affirmed [1994] 3 All E.R. 180; [1994] 2 Lloyd's Rep. 6, CA). This is so whether service is to be effected within or without the jurisdiction and in the latter case may have first involved an application for permission to serve out of the jurisdiction. This is a matter of importance when considering Arts 21 and 22 of the Convention on Jurisdiction and the Enforcement of Judgments in Civil and Commercial Matters 1968.

Article 2 of the 1968 Convention on Jurisdiction and the Enforcement of Judgments in Civil and Commercial Matters covers all forms of proceedings in civil and commercial matters whether *in rem* or *in personam* and the word "sued" in Arts 2 and 3 of the Convention should be construed accordingly (*The Deichland* [1989] 2 Lloyd's Rep. 113, CA). Where an arrest within Art. 1(2) of the 1952 Arrest Convention is effected, the claimant is entitled to rely upon Art. 57 of the 1968 Convention as excluding the exclusive jurisdiction of another convention country which would otherwise apply under Art. 2 of the 1968 convention in the absence of some exempting factor under Art. 5 of the 1968 Convention, see *The Anna H* [1994] 1 Lloyd's Rep. 287. Affirmed CA [1995] 1 Lloyd's Rep. 11. The Court of Appeal further held that the Arrest Convention required only that the legal consequences of judicial detention of the ship should be that it became security for a maritime claim not that the claimant's commercial motive must be to obtain security.

Admiralty Court—This is part of the QBD. It has jurisdiction in all causes and matters assigned by SCA 1981 to that division which involve the exercise of the High Court's Admiralty jurisdiction or its jurisdiction as a prize court. See SCA 1981, ss.5, 6, 61 and 62 and Sched. 1.

Claim in rem—Admiralty claims may be either *in rem* or *in personam*.

An Admiralty claim *in rem* is in effect a claim against a res. (*The Longford* (1888) 14 PD. 34, *per* Lord Esher M.R. at 37; *The City of Mecca* (1879) 5 P.D. 28 at 33; 6 P.D. 106; *The Burns* [1907] P.137; SCA 1981, s.21 (SCP 1999, Vol. 2, Section 6D, para. 6D–53)). A *res* is usually a ship but may in some cases be cargo or freight, an aircraft or hovercraft. In such a claim the claimant may cause the *res* to be arrested if it is within the jurisdiction (see paras 6.1 *et seq.*). If the *res* is arrested and the claimant's claim is successful then unless the *res* has been released (as to which see paras 6.1(1) *et seq.*) judgment may be given against the *res* and an order made for its appraisement and sale. The proceeds of sale will be paid into Court and will, after deduction of the fees and expenses of the Admiralty Marshal in connection with the arrest, custody, appraisement and the sale of the *res*, be available in or towards satisfaction of the claimant's judgment. If, as is frequently the case, there is more than one claim against the *res*, payment out of the proceeds of sale will be ordered in accordance with the Admiralty rules as to the priorities of claims, claims of the same priority ranking *pari passu*. As to proceedings for the determination of priority of claims (see para. 6.9).

A claim *in rem* may also be instituted against the proceeds of sale by the Court of a *res*.

If in a claim *in rem* issue or service of the claim form has been acknowledged and the claim form is not set aside, the personal liability of the defendant who has appeared is added and judgment may be given against him as well as against the *res*. See *The Gemma* [1899] P.285, CA and *The August 8* [1983] 2 A.C. 450; [1983] 1 Lloyd's Rep. 351, P.C.

In *Republic of India v. India Steamship Co. Ltd* [1977] 3 W.L.R. 818; [1998] 1 Lloyd's Rep. 1 H.L.(E)) it was held that for the purposes of section 34 of the Civil Jurisdiction and Judgments Act 1982, "a [claim] *in rem* is an action against the owners from the moment that the Admiralty Court is seised with jurisdiction. The jurisdiction of the Admiralty Court is invoked by the service of a [claim form], or, where a [claim form] is deemed to be served, as a result of the acknowledgment of the issue of the [claim form] by the defendant before service (*The Banco* [1971] P.137). From that moment the owners are parties *in rem*". Dicta of Lord Brandon in *The August 8* [1983] A.C. 450 at 456, PC, and *The Deichland* [1990] 1 Q.B. 361, CA, applied and *The Nordglimt* [1988] Q.B. 183 overruled. The case reviews claims *in rem* generally and states that the idea that a ship can be a defendant in legal proceedings was always a legal fiction which can now be discarded holding that in reality a claim *in rem* is an action against the owners. *Quaere* the extent and effect of the reasoning in this case in claims *in rem* generally. The position in respect of cases involving a maritime lien was expressly reserved as requiring separate consideration.

A defendant who has acknowledged issue or service of the claim form may provide security in order to avoid the arrest of the *res* or to obtain its release if it has been arrested.

Sale by the Court in a claim *in rem* is a sale of the whole property and it is sold free of all claims, encumbrances, liens, etc., with a clean title (see, *e.g. The Acrux* [1962] 1 Lloyd's Rep. 405) all existing claims, etc., being transferred to the proceeds of sale, against which claims begun after the sale must be brought. See also *The Blitz* [1992] 2 Lloyd's Rep. 441—sale of vessel by a local authority pursuant to its powers under section 44 of the Harbours, Docks and Piers Clauses Act 1847 is a sale free from mortgages. The position regarding maritime liens is unclear.

In *The Cerro Colorado* [1993] 1 Lloyd's Rep. 58, the Court declared that any conduct which impedes or is likely to impede the ability of the Admiralty Marshal to achieve a fair market value upon the sale of the vessel (including but not limited to published statements that the vessel will, after sale by the Admiralty Marshal, remain encumbered with existing claims) is an interference with the administration of justice. Such conduct may expose anyone responsible to proceedings for contempt of court.

The following are the main matters of procedure peculiar to a claim *in rem*:

(a) a special form of claim form is used. See para. 2.1(1);

(b) service of the claim form must be in a manner prescribed by paragraph 2.2;

(c) judgment in default of acknowledgment of service, defence, defence to counterclaim or the filing of a preliminary act must be applied for by application under paragraph 7;

(d) a claim form *in rem* cannot be served outside the jursidiction;

(e) an order for substituted service is inappropriate to a claim form *in rem*. (*The Good Herald* [1987] 1 Lloyd's Rep. 236).

Claims against two or more "sister" ships—When the A.J.A. 1956 came into force it became possible in many cases for a claimant to proceed *in rem* against any one of a number of ships in the same beneficial ownership, see s.3(4). The practice soon became established in such cases of issuing one claim form against some or all of the ships against which the claimant was entitled to proceed and later amending the claim form by striking out the names of all ships save the one in respect of which the claim form had been served or against which a warrant of arrest had been issued. The claim form should be amended immediately after service by deleting all but one of the ship's names upon it (*The Freccia del Nord* [1989] 1 Lloyd's Rep. 388, at 391).

In *The Banco* [1971] P. 137; [1971] 1 Lloyd's Rep. 49, CA, in which it was held that only one ship could be served with a claim form *in rem* or arrested in respect of one cause of action, the practice described above was, by a majority, approved. See now SCA 1981, s.21(8) (SCP 1999, Vol. 2, Section 6D, para. 6D–66).

Claims in personam—An Admiralty action *in personam* is like an action in tort or contract in the QBD. It differs from such an action however in that it is subject to the rules of this order which modify those applicable to an ordinary Q.B. action, *e.g.* para. 4.2 (Preliminary acts).

Claims in rem and in personam—If it is desired to commence proceedings both *in rem* and *in personam* separate claim forms must be issued. See *Practice Direction (Admiralty: 3)* (SCP 1999, Vol. 2, Section 6B, para. 6B–3).

Caveats—See para. 6.3(1), (2) and (3), para. 6.5(2) and para. 6.7(1).

Limitation Claim—See para. 1.4, *British Shipping Laws*, Vols 1, and 11 (but note the change of onus of proof introduced since last publication of volumes 1 and 11). Limitation actions must be assigned to the Queen's Bench Division and taken by the Admiralty Court (para. 1.5). For special rules relating to limitation actions see para. 9 below.

Ship—Compare the definition of ship in SCA 1981, s.24 and see note "Ship" at SCP 1999, Vol. 2, Section 6D, para. 6D–9.

A ship is equipment within the meaning of s.1 of the Employers' Liability (Defective Equipment) Act 1969 (*The Derbyshire* [1988] A.C. 276; [1988] 1 Lloyd's Rep. 109, HL).

Limitation of claims—There are special periods, subject to Court's discretion, in collision and salvage: Merchant Shipping Act 1995, ss.190 and 195.

Restrictions on Admiralty jurisdiction

(1) Collision and similar actions if in personam—See SCA 1981, s.22 (SCP 1999, Vol. 2, Section 6D, para. 6D–67).

(2) Wages actions—Section 4 of the Consular Relations Act 1968, provides that Orders in Council may be made to exclude or limit the jurisdiction to entertain proceedings relating to the pay or conditions of service of the master or crew of any ship or aircraft belonging to a state specified in the Order unless the Consul has first been notifed of the intention to invoke the jurisdiction of the Court and has not objected. Orders have been made in respect of Austria, Belgium, Bulgaria, Denmark, Federal Republic of Germany, Greece, Hungary, Italy, Japan, Mexico, Norway, Poland, Romania, Spain, Sweden, USSR and Yugoslavia. (See Statutory Instruments 1970 Nos. 1903–1905, 1907–1914, 1916–1920, 1971 No. 1846, 1978 No. 275 [1970 No. 1919 revoked by 1978 No. 275]). Each of these orders provides for a period of two weeks for objection. Following the dissolution of the USSR and Yugoslavia the position in respect of the individual former constituent member states is uncertain. It is suggested that the Consul of the individual state concerned is notified.

The above-mentioned Orders in Council additionally require a statement to the effect that the consular officer of the state concerned has been notified of the intention to invoke the jurisdiction of the court and has not objected within a period of two weeks from the date of such notification to be included among the details on which the claim is based at the time when the proceedings are commenced.

Further Orders in Council may be issued from time to time.

In *The Andrea Ursula* [1971] Fo. 61 and 81, it was held that proceedings were a nullity for non-compliance with the above mentioned statutory requirements.

(3) Crown—No claim *in rem* lies against the Crown, but in certain circumstances such a claim may be allowed to continue as if *in personam*: Crown Proceedings Act 1947, s.29 (Vol. 2, Section 21L, para. 21L–78).

(4) Foreign sovereign states, etc.—As to claims against foreign sovereigns, foreign sovereign states, ambassadors and diplomatic agents, members of their suites and certain international organisations generally, see Vol. 2, Section 17B, paras 17B–7 and 17B–23 *et seq.* As to claims *in rem* against state owned ships and cargoes see also the State Immunity Act 1978, ss.10, 12 and 13.

A ship, belonging to private owners, requisitioned by the Crown, cannot be arrested while in Government service though if a maritime lien attaches it may be enforced after derequisitioning (*The Broadmayne* [1916] P. 64) and though a claims lies against the owners of the ship if the crew remain their servants (*The Messicano* (1916) 32 T.L.R. 519; *The Crindon* (1918) 35 T.L.R. 81; *The Eolo* [1918] 2 Ir.R. 78).

(5) Rhine Navigation Convention 1868—No Court in England or Wales has jurisdiction in cases falling to be determined in accordance with the provisions of this convention. See SCA 1981, s.23 (Vol. 2, Section 6D, para. 6D–71).

(6) Nuclear Installations Act 1965—This Act consolidates and repeals the Nuclear Installations (Licensing and Insurance) Act 1959, and (with one exception relating to the Electricity (Amendment) Act 1961) the Nuclear Installations (Amendment) Act 1965. In the event of an occurence involving nuclear matter, reference should be made to the Act; in particular, s.14 (protection for ships and aircraft) makes claims *in rem* against ships or aircraft and limitation of liability under the Merchant Shipping Act 1995 unavailable: the Act substitutes a new approach. This Act was amended by the Nuclear Installations Act 1969.

(7) Liquidation and bankruptcy—As to liquidation see the Insolvency Act 1986, s.130. See also *The Constellation* [1966] 1 W.L.R. 272: [1965] 2 Lloyd's Rep. 538: *Re Aro Co. Ltd* [1980] Ch. 196; [1980] 1 All E.R. 1067, CA.

Admiralty and Commercial Registry—RCJ Room E200A (Tel. 0171 936 6112). Hours: 10.00–16.30 except during August, when 10.00–14.30. See O.64, r.7.

Inquiries as to practice may be made in person or by telephone. The Admiralty and Commercial Registry was initially established by Practice Question [1987] 3 All E.R. 616 issued by the Lord Chief Justice with the concurrence of the Admiralty Judge and the Judge in charge of the Commercial List. In relation to Admiralty and Commercial matters it replaces and carries out all the functions of the Central Office including the issuing of processes. Fees are paid to the Supreme Court Accounts Office.

Application to Judge and to Admiralty Registrar—Any party wishing to make an application to an Admiralty Judge should apply to the Admiralty and Commercial Registry (Listing Office) where all necessary arrangements will be made. Applications to the Admiralty Registrar should be applied for in the Admiralty and Commercial Registry (General Office).

Claims in rem

2.1 (1) A claim *in rem* is begun by issuing an *in rem* claim form in Admiralty Form No. ADM1. 49FPD–003

(2) Subject to paragraph 4, the particulars of an *in rem* claim must

(a) be contained in or served with the *in rem* claim form; or

(b) be served on the Defendant by the Claimant within 75 days after service of the *in rem* claim form.

(3) The Claimant to a claim *in rem* may be named or may be described, but if not named in the *in rem* claim form shall upon the request of any other party, identify himself by name.

(4) The Defendant must be described in the claim form.

(5) An acknowledgment of service must be filed in every *in rem* claim. The period for filing the acknowledgment of service is 14 days after service of the claim form irrespective of whether the claim form contains particulars of

claim. The acknowledgment must be in Admiralty Form No. ADM2. The person who acknowledges services must identify himself by name therein.

(6) The period within which an *in rem* claim form must be served is, subject to CPR rule 7.6, 12 months from the date of issue.

2.2 Service of an *in rem* claim form must be made in one of the following ways:

(a) Upon the property against which the claim *in rem* is brought by fixing the *in rem* claim form, or a copy of it, on the outside of the property proceeded against in a position which may reasonably be expected to be seen.

Where the property is freight, service may be made either on the cargo in respect of which the freight was earned or on the ship upon which that cargo was carried.

(b) If the property to be served is in the custody of a person who will not permit access to it, by leaving a copy of the *in rem* claim form with that person.

(c) Where the property has been sold by the Marshal, by filing the *in rem* claim form in the Admiralty and Commercial Registry.

(d) Where there is a caveat against arrest, on the person named in the caveat as being authorised to accept service.

(e) On any solicitor who has authority to accept service.

(f) On such person and in such manner as is stated to constitute effective service in any agreement providing for service of the proceedings;

(g) In any other manner directed under CPR rule 6.8 provided that the *res* or part thereof is within the jurisdiction of the Court; or

(h) In such other manner as may be provided by rule or by practice directions.

2.3 In cases where the property is to be arrested, or in cases where the property is already under arrest in current proceedings, the Marshal will effect service of the *in rem* claim form if the Claimant requests the Court to do so. In all other cases Admiralty *in rem* claim forms are to be served by the claimant, not the Registry.

2.4 Where an *in rem* claim form has been issued, any person who wishes to defend the claim may file an acknowledgment of service notwithstanding that the *in rem* claim form has not been served.

2.5 Except as otherwise provided in this practice direction, after acknowledgment of service has been filed, the procedure relating to the claim shall be the procedure applicable to a claim *in personam*, but the claim also continues to be a claim *in rem*.

2.6 Where the defendants are described and not named on the claim form, for example as "The Owners of the Ship X", any acknowledgment of service in addition to stating the description appearing on the claim form shall also state the full names of the persons acknowledging service and the nature of their ownership. In the event of there being insufficient space on the acknowledgment of service form itself, such additional information shall appear on a separate document to accompany and be lodged with the acknowledgment of service form.

2.7 A Defendant who files an acknowledgment of service to an *in rem* claim form does not by doing so lose any right that he may have to dispute the Court's jurisdiction. (see CPR10.1(3)(b) and Part 11).

Issue of claim form by fax—See Commercial Court Guide

Claim in rem—A claim *in rem* may properly be issued only when the jurisdiction can be invoked by proceedings *in rem* under section 21(2), (3), (4) or (5) of SCA, 1981 (SCP 1999, Vol. 2, Section 6D, paras 6D–67 and 6D–70). See too note "Claim in rem" under paragraph 1 above.

Amendment of claim form—Where after the issue of a claim in an action *in rem* the defendants' vessel is sold, the title of the defendants should be amended to read "The Owners of the ship X, now named Y." (*The Mawan* [1988] 2 Lloyd's Rep. 459 at 460.)

Renewal of claim form—As to renewal of a claim form *in rem* on grounds of impossibility of service on the ship see *The Berny* [1979] Q.B. 80; [1978] 1 All E.R. 1065; [1977] 2 Lloyd's Rep. 533. As to renewal of claim form generally see CPR, r.7.6 and notes thereto.

Acknowledgment of service before actual service—In a claim *in rem* or limitation claim *issue* of the claim form should be acknowledged, see para. 2.4 above.

Substituted service—An order for substituted service is inappropriate to a claim form *in rem* (*The Good Herald* [1987] 1 Lloyd's Rep. 236).

Para. (2)(c)—The property must have been sold by the Court and part of the proceeds of sale must still be in Court. Where property has been sold by an agent who retains the proceeds, a claim form cannot be served on those proceeds (*The Optima* (1905) 74 L.T.P. 94; *The Fornjot* (1907) 24 T.L.R. 26). In *The Eva* (1950) 84 Ll.L.R. 20 wartime compensation money was held not to be a *res* or represent a *res*.

Claims in personam

3.1 (1) A claim form by which a claim *in personam* is brought (an *in personam* claim form in Admiralty Form ADM1A) may be served within the jurisdiction as provided in CPR Part 6 and, except in the case of a collision claim, may be served out of the jurisdiction as provided RSC Order 11 (Schedule 1 to the CPR). **49FPD–004**

(2) An *in personam* claim form may also be served out of the jurisdiction where:

- (a) the Defendant has agreed to submit the claim to the jurisdiction of the court; or
- (b) the claim is in the nature of salvage and any part of the services took place within the jurisdiction; or
- (c) the claim is to enforce a claim under sections 153 and/or 154 and/or 175 of the Merchant Shipping Act 1995 and the Court grants permission to serve the claim out of the jurisdiction.

(3) *In personam* claim forms are to be served by the claimants, not by the Registry.

3.2 (1) An *in personam* claim form may seek judgment on liability alone and request that the amount of the claim be referred to the Admiralty Registrar, or be dealt with as the Admiralty Registrar may direct.

(2) The Claimant in a claim *in personam* may be named or may be described in the claim form, but if not named, shall, upon the request of any other party, identify himself by name.

(3) The Defendant in a claim *in personam* must be named in the claim form.

(4) Subject to paragraph 4, the particulars of an *in personam* claim must

- (a) be contained in or served with the claim form; or
- (b) be served on the Defendant by the Claimant within 75 days after service of the claim form.

(5) The person who files a defence must identify himself by name in the defence.

3.3 An acknowledgment of service must be filed in every *in personam* claim. Subject to paragraph B7.4 of the Commercial Court Guide, the period for filing the acknowledgment of service is 14 days after service of the claim form irrespective of whether the claim form contains particulars of claim.

Duration of Admiralty Writ in personam for service out of the jurisdiction—The period of validity of a claim form *in personam* in admiralty proceedings for service out of the jurisdiction is six months.

Special provisions relating to collision claims

4.1 (1) A collision claim is begun by issuing a claim form. The claim form need not contain or be followed by particulars of claim and CPR rule 7.4 will not apply.

(2) An acknowledgment of service must be filed in every collision claim.

4.2(1) In any collision claim each party shall, within 2 months after the filing by the Defendant of the acknowledgment of service or, in the event that the Defendant makes an application under CPR Part 11 (disputing the jurisdiction or the exercise by the court of its jurisdiction), within 2 months of the determination of the Defendant's application, file in the Registry a completed Admiralty Form No. ADM3 ("a Preliminary Act").

(2) A Preliminary Act shall contain—
- (a) in Part One of the Form, answers to the questions set out in that Part; and
- (b) in Part Two of the Form, a statement—
  - (i) that the information in Part One is incorporated in Part Two;
  - (ii) of any other facts and matters upon which the party filing the Preliminary Act relies;
  - (iii) of all allegations of negligence or other fault which the party filing the Preliminary Act makes;
  - (iv) of the relief or remedy which the party filing the Preliminary Act claims.

(3) Each party must verify his Preliminary Act by a statement of truth.

(4) Upon filing their Preliminary Act each party must give notice that he has done so to each other party. Within 14 days after the last Preliminary Act is filed each party must serve on every other party a copy of his Preliminary Act.

(5) After each party has filed his Preliminary Act, the claim shall proceed as any other Admiralty claim.

4.3 In any collision claim an application under CPR Part 11 disputing the Court's jurisdiction must be made within 2 months of the filing of the acknowledgment of service.

4.4 A claim form in a collision claim may not be served out of the jurisdiction unless the case falls within section 22(2)(a) to (c) of the Supreme Court Act 1981 or the Defendant has submitted to or agreed to submit to the jurisdiction of the court.

4.5 Where, in a collision claim *in rem*, ("the original claim")—
- (a) (i) a Part 20 claim; or
  - (ii) a cross claim *in rem*

  arising out of the same collision or occurrence is made; and
- (b) (i) the party bringing the original claim has caused the arrest of a ship or has obtained security in order to prevent such arrest; and
  - (ii) the party bringing the Part 20 claim or cross claim is unable to arrest a ship or otherwise to obtain security,

then the party bringing the Part 20 claim or cross claim may apply to the Admiralty Court to stay the original claim until sufficient security is given to satisfy any judgment that may be given in favour of that party.

4.6 In collision claims the skeleton argument of each party should be accompanied by a plot or plots of that party's case or alternative cases as to the navigation of vessels during and leading to the collision. All plots must contain a sufficient indication of the assumptions used in the preparation of the plot.

4.7 Where the authenticity of any document or entry in any document is challenged or where it will be suggested at trial that a document or entry in a document was not made at the time or by the person stated or is in any other way challenged in a manner which may require a witness to be produced at trial to support the document or entry in the document, such challenge must be raised in good time in advance of the trial to enable any such witness to be produced. In addition, the skeleton argument should make it plain what challenges to documents or entries in documents will be made.

Preliminary act—"The object of the preliminary act is to obtain from the parties statements of the facts at a time when they are fresh in their recollection" (*per* Sir Robert Phillimore, in *The Frankland* (1872) L.R. 3 A. & E. 511). The other main purpose is to force the parties to "plead blind" (*The Vortigern* (1859) Sw. 518). A statement of fact in a preliminary act is a formal admission, binding the party making it, and can only be departed from by special permission (*per* Fletcher Moulton L.J. in *The Seacombe, The Devonshire* [1912] P. 21, 59; see *The Ladybell* (1933) 49 T.L.R. 595; 46 Ll.L.Rep. 342). As a rule, therefore, the Court will not allow either party subsequently to alter anything in his preliminary act, not even to correct a clerical error (*The Miranda* (1882) 7 P.D. 185). But in *The Esso Brussels* (1968) Fo. 373 (unrep.) on this point, permission was given during the trial to amend Articles xii and xiv. Permission, however, is sometimes asked for and given to lead evidence not in accordance with the party's preliminary act; if witnesses give evidence not in accordance with the preliminary act and no leave is asked for, the Court may hold the party to what is in the preliminary act (see *The Semiramis* [1952] 2 Lloyd's Rep. 86 at 93). The Court is not bound by the admissions in any preliminary act (see *e.g. The Vanessa* [1960] 1 Lloyd's Rep. 82; *The Geo. W. McKnight* (1947) 80 Ll.L.R. 419, HL) (*The Geo. W. McKnight* above). A party who has filed a defective preliminary act, which does not give the information required by the rule, may be ordered on application by the other party to amend it (*The Godiva* (1886) 11 P.D. 20) or to give particulars.

Note that the present and previous rules are wider than the rule which they replaced. The old rule referred to "actions for damage by collision between vessels . . ."; *The El Oso* (1925) 21 Ll.L.Rep. 340; *Armstrong v. Gaselee* (1889) 22 Q.B.D. 250; *Secretary of State for India v. Hewitt & Co.* (1888) 6 Asp. 384; *The John Boyne* (1877) 36 L.T. 29; 3 Asp. M.L.C. 346, are cases decided under that rule. Each party is required in his preliminary act to state the material facts upon which he founds his case and the Court may order the costs of a preliminary act which differs widely from the facts proved at the trial to be disallowed on taxation (*The Pelican I* (1926) 25 Ll.L.Rep. 150). The information must be given fully; any concealment will be viewed by the Court with suspicion and, as stated, on the application of the other party, the Court may order amendment (*The Godiva,* above) or particulars so that all the questions are answered properly. When a ship in a river is on a fixed course as opposed to a course which is constantly changed, either the magnetic or the true course should be stated (*The Rievaulx Abbey* (1910) 11 Asp. 437). In a collision case in which one ship is, or both ships are, at anchor, the preliminary act or acts filed on behalf of the owners of the anchored ship or both anchored ships should state in Art. vii the heading of the ship at anchor (*The Macroom* (1927) 17 Asp. 288 (one ship at anchor, the other under way): *The Erna* (1927) 27 Ll.L.Rep. 170 (a dragging case; both ships at anchor)). In *The Judith M.* (1968) 112 S.J. 859, a statement in the claimant's preliminary act (Art. (ix) (b)) and elsewhere that the defendants' ship was heading "across the bows" of the claimant's ship "from port to starboard" was criticised by Brandon J.; it was desirable to state such heading with greater particularity. A defendant is not entitled to demand of another defendant whom he blames in his defence that he shall file a preliminary act, unless he issues a claim form against him (*The Carlston and the Balcombe* [1926] P. 82).

Section 20(3)(b)(i) SCA 1981 ". . . collision between ships . . ."—A floating landing stage is not a ship, therefore no preliminary acts are required in an action arising from a collision between a steamship and it (*The Craighall* [1910] P. 207). On the other hand, where claimants whose ship, A, was in collision with another, B, blamed the owners of B and also the dock authority which had some measure of control over B it was held that all three parties must file preliminary acts; the dock authority were obliged to do the best they could to answer the questions in the preliminary act (*The Beaverford* [1961] 1 W.L.R. 793; [1960] 3 All E.R. 612; [1960] 2 Lloyd's Rep. 216). This case was followed in *British Oil & Cake Mills Ltd v. John H. Whitaker (Tankers) Ltd (The Grainger's No. 4)* [1964] 1 W.L.R. 1474; [1964] 3 All E.R. 705; [1964] 2 Lloyd's Rep. 415. A preliminary act is required of a widow whose husband has been killed in a collision (see *Webster v. M. S. & L. Ry.* [1884] W.N. 1). This is so even where the ship has been sunk in the collision with the loss of all hands. See as to further information concerning information contained in preliminary acts: (*The Isle of Cyprus* (1890) 15 P.D. 134; *The Bernard* [1905] W.N. 73; *The Biola* (1876) 34 L.T. 185; *The Radnorshire* (1880) 5 P.D. 172).

Dispensing with or limiting Preliminary Act—It is considered that the Court retains power to order dispensing with or limiting the requirement under this paragraph of Preliminary Acts under its general CPR powers or inherent jurisdiction in approximate though rare cases. An order to dispense with a limit the filing of preliminary acts will not be made on a consent application or under para. 12; the Court will always require the parties to attend and explain the reasons for the application. Application is made by application notice before the Registrar.

Proceedings against or concerning the International Oil Pollution Compensation Fund*

49FPD–005 **5.1** [7]For the purposes of section 177 of the Merchant Shipping Act 1995 and the corresponding provision of Schedule 4 to the Act, any party to proceedings against an owner or guarantor in respect of liability under section 153 and/or section 154 of the said Act or the corresponding provisions of Schedule 4 to the Act may give the Fund notice of the proceedings by serving a notice in writing on the Fund together with a copy of the claim form and copies of the statements of case (if any) served in the proceedings.

5.2 The court will, on application by the Fund made without notice, grant permission to the Fund to intervene in any proceedings to which paragraph 5.1 applies, whether notice of the proceedings has been served on the Fund or not.

5.3 Where a judgment is given against the Fund in any proceedings under section 175 of the Merchant Shipping Act 1995 or the corresponding provision of Schedule 4 to the Act, the Admiralty Registrar will arrange for a stamped copy of the judgment to be sent to the Fund by post.

5.4 Notice by the Fund to the Admiralty Registrar of the matters set out in section 176(3)(b) of the Merchant Shipping Act 1995 and the corresponding section of Schedule 4 to the Act shall be in writing sent by post to, or delivered at, the Registry.

Arrest, release, interveners etc.

6.1 Except as provided in this Practice Direction, the Claimant in a claim *in rem* and a judgment creditor in a claim *in rem* is entitled to have the property proceeded against arrested by the Admiralty Court by filing an application to arrest in Admiralty Form No. ADM4 (which shall also contain an undertaking) accompanied by a declaration in Admiralty Form No. ADM5 upon which the Admiralty Court will issue an arrest warrant.

6.2(1) An application for arrest may be made by filing the application notice in the Admiralty and Commercial Registry or the registry of any Admiralty Court.

(2) When the relevant registry is closed an application for arrest shall be dealt with in such manner (if any) as may be provided in Admiralty practice directions.

(3) Any party making an application for arrest must (i) request a search to be made in the caveat book before the warrant is issued in order to ascertain whether there is a caveat in force with respect to that property and (ii) file a declaration in Admiralty Form No. ADM5 containing the particulars required in paragraph 6.2(4). However the Admiralty Court may, if it thinks fit, give permission for the issue of the arrest warrant notwithstanding that the declaration does not contain all those particulars.

(4) The declaration required by paragraph 6.2(3) must state—

(a) in every case:

(i) the nature of the claim or counterclaim and that it has not been satisfied and if it arises in connection with a ship, the name of that ship; and

(ii) the nature of the property to be arrested and, if the property is a ship, the name of the ship and her port of registry; and

(iii) the amount of the security sought, if any.

(b) in the case of a claim against a ship by virtue of section 21(4) of the Supreme Court Act 1981:

(i) the name of the person who would be liable on the claim if it were commenced *in personam* ("the relevant person"); and

[7] *See Chapter IV, Merchant Shipping Act 1995.

(ii) that the relevant person was when the cause of action arose the owner or charterer of, or in possession or in control of, the ship in connection with which the claim arose, specifying which; and
(iii) that at the time when the claim form was issued the relevant person was either the beneficial owner of all the shares in the ship in respect of which the warrant is required or (where appropriate) the charterer of it under a charter by demise, as the case may be; and
(c) in the cases set out in paragraphs 6.2(6) and 6.2(7) that the relevant notice has been sent or served, as appropriate; and
(d) in the case of a claim in respect of liability incurred under section 153 of the Merchant Shipping Act 1995, the facts relied on as establishing that the Court is not prevented from entertaining the claim by reason of section 166(2) of that Act,

and must be sworn as an affidavit.

(5) No registry other than the Admiralty and Commercial Registry will issue an arrest warrant and where an application for arrest is made to any registry other than the Admiralty and Commercial Registry that registry will use its best endeavours to cause the application form and declaration and a copy of the form to be transmitted immediately to the Admiralty and Commercial Registry for consideration of the application and, if appropriate, the issue of the warrant. Thereafter the arrest shall be administered by the Marshal and all applications in respect thereof and in respect of the property under arrest other than an order for sale before judgment shall be made to and considered by the Admiralty Registrar himself or as he may direct.

(6) A warrant of arrest may not be issued as of right in the case of property in respect of which the beneficial ownership, as a result of a sale or disposal by any court exercising Admiralty jurisdiction, has changed since the claim form was issued.

(7) No warrant of arrest will be issued against a ship owned by a State where, by any convention or treaty, the United Kingdom has undertaken to minimise the possibility of arrest of ships of that State until notice in Admiralty Form No. ADM6 has been served on a consular officer at the consular office of that State in London or the port at which it is intended to cause the ship to be arrested and a copy of the notice is exhibited to the declaration filed under paragraph 6.2(3).

6.3(1) Any person may file in the Admiralty and Commercial Registry a notice requesting a caveat against arrest in Admiralty Form No. ADM7, undertaking to file an acknowledgment of service and to give sufficient security to satisfy the claim with interest and costs. Upon filing the notice of request a caveat shall be entered in the caveat book. The record of such caveats shall be open for inspection as provided in the Admiralty practice directions. Caveats shall be valid for a period of 12 months but may be renewed for a similar period or periods. The entry of a caveat against arrest shall not be treated as a submission to the jurisdiction of the English Court.

(2) Where a Claimant in a limitation claim constituted a limitation fund in accordance with Article 11 of the Convention on Limitation of Liability for Maritime Claims 1976 and desires to prevent the arrest of property for a claim which may be or has been made against the fund, he must file in the Admiralty and Commercial Registry a notice requesting a caveat, in Admiralty Form No. ADM8, signed by him or his solicitor—
(a) stating that a limitation fund in respect of the damage arising from the relevant incident has been constituted; and
(b) undertaking to acknowledge service of the claim form by which any claim may be begun against the property described in the notice;

and on the filing of the notice a caveat against the issue of a warrant to arrest the property described in the notice shall be entered in the caveat book.

(3) Property may be arrested notwithstanding that a caveat against arrest has been filed, but in such a case the Admiralty Court may if it considers that it is appropriate to do so, order that the arrest be discharged and that the party procuring the arrest do pay compensation to the owner of or other persons interested in the property arrested.

6.4(1) The arrest of property may only be effected by the Marshal or his substitute.

(2) Arrest is effected by service on the property of an arrest warrant in Admiralty Form No. ADM9 in the manner set out in paragraph 2.2(a) or, where it is not reasonably practicable to serve the warrant, by service of a notice of the issue of the warrant in that manner upon the property or by giving notice to those in charge of the property.

(3) Property under arrest may not be moved without an order of the Admiralty Court and the property may be immobilised or otherwise prevented from sailing in such manner as the Marshal or his substitute may decide is appropriate.

(4) Upon arrest, standard directions will be issued by the Admiralty Registrar in Admiralty Form No. ADM10.

6.5(1) Where property is under arrest an *in rem* claim form may be served upon it and, in addition, it may be arrested by any other person claiming to have an *in rem* claim against it.

(2) Any person claiming to have an *in rem* right against any property under arrest who wishes to be given notice of any application to the court in respect of that property or its proceeds of sale may file in the Admiralty and Commercial Registry a notice requesting a caveat against release in Admiralty Form No. ADM11. Upon the filing of the notice of request, a caveat shall be entered in the caveat book. The record of such caveats shall be open for inspection as provided in the Admiralty practice directions.

6.6(1) Property will be released from arrest if:

(a) it is sold by the Admiralty Court; or
(b) the Admiralty Court orders release upon application made by any party; or
(c) the arresting party and all caveators, if any, file in the Registry a request for release in Admiralty Form No. ADM12, or
(d) any party files in the Registry a request for release in Admiralty Form No. ADM12 (which shall also contain an undertaking) together with a consent to the release of the arresting party and all caveators, if any.

(2) Any application for release made when the Registry is closed shall be made in any manner as may be provided in Admiralty practice directions.

6.7(1) Where the release of any property under arrest is delayed by the entry of a caveat under this rule, any person having an interest in the property may apply to the Admiralty Court for an order requiring the person who procured the entry of the caveat to pay damages to the applicant in respect of losses suffered by the applicant by reason of the delay and the Court may make such an order unless it is satisfied that the person procuring the entry of the caveat had a good and sufficient reason for doing so and for maintaining the caveat.

(2) Where an *in rem* claim form has been issued and security sought, any person who has filed an acknowledgment of service may apply to the Admiralty Court for an order specifying the amount and form of security to be provided.

(3) Where in relation to a claim *in rem* security has been provided to obtain the release of property under arrest or to prevent the arrest of property the Admiralty Court may at any stage:

(a) order that the amount of security be reduced, and may stay the claim pending compliance with such order;

(b) order that the Claimant be permitted to arrest or re-arrest the property proceeded against for the purposes of obtaining further security, provided that the total security provided shall not exceed the value of the property at the time of the original arrest or at the time security was first given if the property was not arrested.

6.8 Any person interested in property under arrest or in the proceeds of sale of property sold by the Admiralty Court or whose interests are affected by any order sought or made may be made a party to any claim *in rem* against the property or proceeds of sale where the Court considers it would be just and convenient and upon such terms as the Court may think fit.

6.9 Any application to the Admiralty Court concerning the sale of the property under arrest or the proceeds of sale of property sold by the Court shall be heard in public and the application notice served on all parties to the claim and caveators against the property or the proceeds of sale.

6.10(1) Where a ship is not under arrest but cargo on board her is, and those interested in the ship wish to discharge the cargo which is under arrest, they may, without intervening in the action, request the Marshal to take the appropriate steps. If the Marshal considers the request reasonable and if the applicant gives an undertaking in writing satisfactory to the Marshal to pay on demand the fees of the Marshal and all expenses to be incurred by him or on his behalf in taking the desired steps, the Marshal will apply to the court for the appropriate order.

(2) Where those interested are unable or unwilling to arrange for such an undertaking to be given they may intervene in the action in which the cargo is under arrest and apply to the Admiralty Registrar for an order for discharge of the cargo and for directions as to the fees and expenses of the Marshal in and about the discharge and storage of the cargo pursuant to such order.

6.11 Where a ship is under arrest but cargo on board her is not, and those interested in the cargo wish to secure its discharge, one or other of the procedures outlined in paragraph 6.10(1) and 6.10(2) may be followed.

General note—Where the Admiralty jurisdiction of the High Court may be and is invoked by a claim *in rem* the *res* proceeded against may be arrested if it is within the territorial jurisdiction of the Court. For the circumstances in which the jurisdiction *in rem* may be invoked see SCA 1981, s.21 (Vol. 2, Section 6D, paras 6D–53 *et seq.*). It will be observed that in some cases only the property concerned may be proceeded against *in rem* (s.21(2) *ibid.*) and that if a maritime lien has attached, a claim *in rem* may be brought against the ship or property in question regardless of any change of ownership since the cause of action arose other than by a judicial sale. In all other cases it is necessary to look at the person, if any, who was liable *in personam* at the time the cause of action arose; a claim *in rem* may be brought against ships of which he is the beneficial owner or demise charterer at the time of the issue of the claim provided he was the owner or charterer or in possession or control of the ship in connection with which the claim arose at the time when the claim arose. The expression "claim is brought" means "when the claim form is issued" (*The Carmania II* [1963] 2 Lloyd's Rep. 152). Once a claim is brought against a ship by issue of a claim form a sale of the ship by her owner will not deprive the plaintiff of any rights he may have (*The Monica S* [1968] P. 741; [1967] 3 All E.R. 740; [1967] 2 Lloyd's Rep. 113). But *quaere* the effect of *The Blitz* [1992] 2 Lloyd's Rep. 441. As to the requirements regarding personal liability in actions *in rem* generally and where there is a maritime lien in particular, see *The Father Thames* [1979] 2 Lloyd's Rep. 364.

Until the Civil Jurisdiction and Judgments Act 1982 the sole purpose of an action *in rem* was to obtain security in respect of a judgment of the Court (or a sum due under a settlement) in that claim, the Court had no jurisdiction to arrest ships or to keep ships under arrest for other purposes, see *The Cap Bon* [1967] 1 Lloyd's Rep. 543. Now section 26 of the 1982 Act enables the Admiralty Court to retain the security of the *res* or the security for the purpose of arbitration or other proceedings in a United Kingdom or overseas Court. See also *The Jalamatsyr* [1987] 2 Lloyd's Rep. 164.

The issue of a warrant of arrest is not a discretionary remedy. If the statutory requirements set out in para. 6.2(4) are complied with the claimant is entitled to issue the warrant of arrest and if there is such compliance there is no further scope for the application of any duty of full and frank disclosure, *The Varna* [1993] 2 Lloyd's Rep. 253.

A vessel cannot remain in the custody of the Admiralty Marshal and yet be allowed to trade outside the jurisdiction (*The Bazias 3, The Bazias 4* [1993] Q.B. 673; [1993] 2 W.L.R. 854; [1993] 2 All E.R. 964; [1993] 1 Lloyd's Rep. 101, CA).

Merchant Shipping Act 1995—Where a state has enacted legislation giving effect to the provisions of the International Convention Relating to the Limitation of the Liability of Owners of Sea-Going Ships 1957, but not the International Convention on Limitation of Liability for Maritime Claims 1976, the setting up of a limitation fund in such a state will not prevent the arrest of a ship in another state which has enacted legislation giving effect to the 1976 Convention.

Crown: foreign sovereign states, etc.—See notes under para. 1 of this Practice Direction above.

Delay in prosecution of claim—The Marshal is not a shipkeeper and parties should not delay in prosecuting an action in which a vessel is under arrest (*The Italy II* [1987] 2 Lloyd's Rep. 162).

Insurance premiums—Premiums paid by claimants to insure their interest in arrested property were held in *The Fairport* [1965] 2 Lloyd's Rep. 183 at 186, to be recoverable as costs but not to constitute a head of claim under A.J.A. 1956, s.1 (see now SCA 1981, s.20).

Insurance of arrested property—In 1970 the President gave his approval to the following practice which is still followed by the Marshal:

INSURANCE OF ARRESTED PROPERTY

(1) As from May 1, 1970, the Marshal will cease to insure any arrested property for the benefit of parties at any time during the period of arrest (whether before or after the lodging of a Commission for Appraisement and Sale, if any).

(2) The Marshal will use his best endeavours (but without any legal liability for failure to do so) to advise all parties known to him as being on the record in [claims] *in rem* against the arrested property, including caveators against release of that property, before any such property moves or is moved beyond the area covered by the usual port risks policy.

In these circumstances, practitioners' attention is drawn to the necessity of considering the questions of insuring against port risks for the amount of their clients' interest in any property arrested in an Admiralty [claim] and the inclusion in any policy of a "Held Covered" clause in case the ship moves or is moved outside the area covered by the usual port risks policy. The usual port risks policy provides, *inter alia*, for a ship to be moved or towed from one berth to another up to a distance of five miles within the port where she is lying.

Para. 6.2(3) "... caveat book ..."—There is only one book in which all caveats in Admiralty are entered; it is kept in the Admiralty and Commercial Registry at the Royal Courts of Justice in London where all caveats must be entered. As to caveats against arrest see para. 6.3(1) and against release see para. 6.5(2). As to searches see paras 6.2(3) and 6.5(2).

Para. 6.2(4) Affidavits—An affidavit filed pursuant to this paragraph may contain statements of information and belief with the sources and grounds thereof, see CPR 32.16, and PD32 para. 4.2(2). The sources and grounds should be stated with precision and particularity. A general statement such as from documents and information supplied to me by the claimants will not suffice. In connection with the ownership of ships the grounds usually relied upon are the information contained in Lloyd's Register of Ships and its supplements and the result of inquiry of Lloyd's Intelligence as to whether they know of any change of ownership since the last edition or supplement. Sea Data information is also used. As to the contents of these affidavits see para. 6.2(4).

Para. 6.2(4)(a)(ii) "... her port of registry ..."—The object of this requirement is to minimise the risk of the arrest of a different ship bearing the same name as the ship intended to be arrested. If the port of registry is not known this should be stated in the affidavit.

Practice—The affidavit, warrant and a copy of it are taken to or transmitted to the Admiralty and Commercial Registry and a search of the caveat book requested. A clerk in the Registry will search the caveat book and inform the applicant whether a caveat against arrest of the property is in force. If there is no caveat against arrest in force or if it is desired to issue a warrant despite the existence of a caveat, the affidavit is filed and the warrant and copy lodged. The proper officer, if he is satisfied that the affidavit complies with the requirements of this rule (or if permission to issue despite non-compliance has been given) will issue the warrant. The warrant and copy are retained in the Registry.

False or inaccurate statement in affidavit to lead warrant of arrest—If the statutory requirements set out in 6.2(4) are complied with then there is no further scope for the application of any duty of full and frank disclosure see *The Varna* [1993] 2 Lloyd's Rep. 253 but as to such statutory requirements it is the duty of a deponent to correct promptly and frankly any false or inaccurate statement that he finds he has made in his affidavit (*The Nordglimt* [1988] Q.B. 183; [1987] 2 Lloyd's Rep. 470).

"... the amount of the security sought, if any".—This is a new requirement.

Practice—Applications under para. 6.2(5) include applications to move a vessel under arrest or to sell the same below the appraised value. Such applications are made to the Admiralty Registrar or as he may direct.

As to the practice to be followed by the Marshal when a ship is under arrest and a harbour or dock authority claims or purports to exercise a statutory power of detention or sale in respect of unpaid dock dues, see *The Queen of the South* [1968] P. 449; [1968] 1 All E.R. 1163; [1968] 1 Lloyd's Rep. 182 and *The Freightline One* [1986] 1 Lloyd's Rep. 266. In *The Girl Irene* [1991] Fo. 774; (unrep.), the Court directed that the Marshal was to follow the same practice in respect of a claim by Trinity House for unpaid light dues. Where some doubt arises as to the right of a harbour or dock authority to detain a ship, that authority should seek a declaration from the Court (*The Baltico* (1982) H. No. 140. Hartlepool District Registry).

Mooring charges do not constitute "ship dues" within the meaning of section 26(3) of the Harbours Act 1964 and as defined by section 57(1) of the 1964 Act. Accordingly there is no power to distain for non-payment of mooring charges under section 44 of the Harbours, Docks and Piers Clauses Act 1847: see *R. v. Carrick District Council, ex p. Prankerd,* (*The Winnie Rigg*) [1998] 2 Lloyd's Rep. 675.

As to applications to discharge cargo where ship or cargo is under arrest, see paras 6.10 and 11.

Applications under paras 6.2(3) and 6.2(6) are made without notice to the Admiralty Registrar.

Para. 6.3(1)—Caveat against arrest—The entry of a caveat does not in fact prevent the issue or execution of a warrant of arrest but a person who causes property to be arrested despite the existence of a caveat and without good and sufficient reason may be ordered to pay damages. See para. 6.3(3).

Wrongful arrest—Whether a caveat has been entered or not, if property is arrested by reason of *mala fides* or *crassa negligentia,* damages may be recovered in Admiralty or, indeed, at common law (*The Walter D. Wallett* [1893] P. 202; *The Evangelismos* (1858) 12 Moo. P.C. 352; Swa. 378; *The Strathnaver* (1875) 1 App. Cas. 58; *The Cathcart* (1867) L.R. 1 A. & E. 314; *The Eudora* (1879) 4 P.D. 208). Damages may also be recovered where an arrest has been unduly continued (*The Cheshire Witch* (1858) Br. & Lush. 362; *The Margaret and Jane* (1869) L.R. 2 A. & E. 345). As to claims for damages where release has been delayed owing to a caveat against release and payment having been entered without good and sufficient reason, see para. 6.7(1). See also para. 6.3(3).

Para. 6.3(2).—The 1976 Convention is now to be found in Sched. 7 to the Merchant Shipping Act 1995.

Para. 6.4(1) "... effected by the marshal ..."—The warrant may only be executed by being served by the Marshal or his substitute upon the ship or property concerned in accordance with paras 2.2(a) and 6.4(2). The Marshal's officer acts as his substitute in London; elsewhere Customs officers do so. See too *The Burney* [1977] 2 Lloyd's Rep. 533 at 548:

> "The Court has to bear in mind that the duty of arresting a ship, and often at the time of serving a [claim form] on her, falls on the Admiralty Marshal or his deputies, and it should not adopt an approach to the matter which would or might expose these persons to unreasonable difficulties or dangers."

The claim form and warrant are frequently served at approximately the same time, but either may be served first. As to effect of failure to comply with the requirements as to service, see *The Prins Bernhard* [1964] P. 117; [1963] 3 All E.R. 735; [1963] 2 Lloyd's Rep. 236. As to the non-fatal character of a minor failure, see *The Sullivar* [1965] 2 Lloyd's Rep. 350.

Freight, being incorporeal, cannot be arrested nor can a claim form be served upon it, but where a claim is brought against freight, or cargo and freight, or ship, cargo and freight, the claim form can as against freight, be served on the cargo concerned or the ship in which it was carried, see para. 2.2(a) and a warrant can be executed against the cargo or ship or both (para. 6.4(2)) in the manner prescribed.

To move a ship from where she is lying with knowledge of the fact that a warrant has been issued, is contempt of Court (*The Seraglio* (1885) 10 P.D. 120) and *a fortiori* after the warrant has been served. As to various acts amounting to contempt see *The Petrel* (1836) 3 Hagg. 299; *The Bure* (1850) 14 Jur. Pt 1, 1123; *The Armenian* (Sh.Gaz. March 1874); *The Rhenania* (Sh.Gaz. November 1909); *The Selina Stanford* (1908) *The Times,* November 17. For modern examples see *The Jarlinn* [1965] 1 W.L.R. 1098; [1965] 2 All E.R. 886; [1965] 2 Lloyd's Rep. 191; *The Jarvis Brake* [1976] 2 All E.R. 886; [1976] 2 Lloyd's Rep. 320; *The Merdeka* [1982] 1 Lloyd's Rep. 401.

It is contempt to attempt to sell a ship in respect of which an order for sale by the Court is in force (*The Jarvis Brake,* above). See also *Cerro Colorado* [1993] 1 Lloyd's Rep. 58.

Paragraph 6.5(2)—Caveat against release—General note—A caveat under this paragraph may be entered by any person, whether he has begun a claim against the property under arrest (or the proceeds of sale) or not. A caveator whose claim carries no maritime lien should consider the desirability of issuing a claim *in rem* in addition, to entering a caveat because, if the *res* is sold by the owner while under arrest, the claimant's remedy against that *res* will be lost, though he may in some circumstances be able to proceed in a claim against a "sister ship". See SCA 1981, s.21(4). The effect of entering a caveat is to prevent the release of the property or payment out of the proceeds of sale without the consent of the caveator or order of the Court. See paras 6.5(2) and 6.6(1). A party applying for an order for release or payment out notwithstanding the existence of a caveat, should serve the application notice on any caveators. The principle now is "no caveat, no notice". Co-arrestors should consider advisability of entering caveat.

Use of the caveat procedure normally makes it unnecessary for a claimant in a claim *in rem* against property which is under arrest in another claim to issue a warrant for the arrest of that property. A claimant who has issued a claim *in rem* against a ship which is under arrest and has entered a caveat under this paragraph will be considered as a secured creditor for the purpose of deciding whether or not the discretion of the court should be exercised in his favour under section 231 of the Companies Act 1948 (now Insolvency Act 1986, s.130) (*Re Aro Co. Ltd* [1980] Ch. 196; [1980] 1 All E.R. 1067, CA). An order for appraisement and sale however can only be made in a claim in which the property is under arrest. Therefore, if the arresting claimant is dilatory or does not proceed with his claim it will become necessary for the claimant in a second or subsequent claim to issue a warrant and procure its execution so as to be in a position when he moves for judgment to apply for an order for appraisement and sale. The costs of a second or subsequent arrest are not normally allowed except in such circumstances.

Use of fax when registry is closed—As regards such use for a caveat against release when registry is closed see para. 17.3 *et seq.* below.

Release of property in usual case—The owner may obtain the consent of the arresting party to the release by giving security to his satisfaction. There are many forms of security accepted but in almost all cases the arresting party is satisfied with a guarantee or undertaking given out of court by, *e.g.* by the Defendant's P & I Club or by a bank or insurance company. Payment into court is sometimes used. Bail by bond is now a rarity.

The arresting party is "entitled to sufficient security to cover the amount of his claim with interest and costs on the basis of his reasonably arguable best case". (*The Moschanthy* [1971] 1 Lloyd's Rep. 37 at 44). Where the right to limit liability under the Merchant Shipping Acts is not disputed it seems that the proper amount is the limitation figure with interest and costs. It seems also that in no case can the amount exceed the value of the *res.* See *The Charlotte* [1920] P. 78. Where there is a dispute as to the amount of security to be provided, an application can be made to the court to determine the amount. See, for example, *The Moscanthy*, above. The application should normally be made to the Admiralty Registrar by application notice in the claim asking for the release of the property upon provision of security for a stated amount. Where security has been provided in an excessive amount, *e.g.* in order to obtain the prompt release of the property, an application may be made to the court for reduction of the amount of security.

It is, of course, always open to a party not to provide security and to allow his property to remain under arrest.

A party demanding excessive security may have to pay (1) the costs of a successful application to reduce the amount of that security and (2) the expense of providing the excess. Further as to security and release see *British Shipping Laws*, Vol. 1. The power to exact security must not be used oppressively; where there is a genuine dispute or discussion about the appropriate amount, the party seeking security ought to put his cards on the table and explain to the other party or his solicitors the grounds on which he claims to exercise this strong power: (*The Moscanthy* [1971] 1 Lloyd's Rep. 37 at 46–47).

Release when claim stayed—In *The Bazias 3, The Bazias 4* [1993] Q.B. 673; [1993] 2 W.L.R. 854; [1993] 1 Lloyd's Rep. 101, the Court of Appeal held that the effect of section 26 of the Civil Jurisdiction and Judgments Act 1982 was to assimilate *in rem* proceedings in the Admiralty Court with arbitration claims so that the discretion to release an arrested vessel was the same in both cases. Accordingly on an application to release a vessel held as security for a claim in arbitration the court would in accordance with the usual practice only exercise its discretion to release on provision of sufficient security to cover the claim, plus interest and costs on the basis of the claimant's reasonably arguable best case. Inconvenience and difficulty in finding sufficient liquid financial resources were not sufficient grounds for departing from the usual practice. There would be no cross-undertaking as to damages under s.26(2). The court granted a stay of action under s.1 of the Arbitration Act 1975 and ordered both vessels to remain under arrest pending further order.

Release by setting aside warrant of arrest—*e.g.* where the affidavit leading to warrant of arrest contains material inaccuracies relating to the statutory requirements set out in para. 6.4 and arrest cannot be validly maintained: in *The Varna* [1993] 2 Lloyd's Rep. 253, CA, the Court held that beyond the establishment of the facts then required by O.75, r.5(9) and now by para. 6.4 there was no further scope for an attack upon the issue not being a discretionary remedy. The

Court of Appeal, however, stated that a warrant might be set aside as a result of the claim *in rem* being struck out or the proceedings stayed and that there might be a general discretionary power on a with notice application to set aside the warrant on the basis that its continuance was in all the circumstances unjust.

Summons to secure release—In cases where an applicant wishes to secure release of his property whether held at the instance of the arrestor or any caveator, the procedure in the Admiralty and Commercial Registry will be as set out below. The purpose of this procedure is to arrange that such an application is dealt with by the tribunal likely to be able to dispose of it most expeditiously and cheaply.

(1) The application notice should be issued nominally before the Registrar with the date left blank.

(2) The applicant should attend at the Admiralty and Commercial Registry upon the issue of the application notice for the purpose of obtaining a direction by the Registrar as to whether the application will be heard before the Registrar or before the Judge. Unless there is attendance at the Registry the application will be issued before the Registrar.

(3) The applicant attending upon the issue of the application notice should, if it is desired that the application be heard initially by the Judge, be prepared to indicate orally why the application is more suitable for the Judge than the Registrar (*e.g.* substantial savings in costs or time would normally be reasons militating in favour of initial hearing by the Judge).

(4) A direction as to the hearing will normally be given forthwith and date and time set for the hearing.

Release pursuant to Merchant Shipping Act 1995—Section 185 and Sched. 7 provide that the Court may, and in certain circumstances must, order the release of a ship or other property which has been arrested, or the security given to prevent, or obtain release from, arrest. See also *The Putbus* [1969] P. 136; [1969] 2 All E.R. 676; [1969] 1 Lloyd's Rep. 253, CA).

Withdrawal of caveats—A caveat may be withdrawn by lodging a written request in Form ADM12 in RSC App. B set out at Vol. 2, Section 6A, para. 6A–16. Where a solicitor acts for more than one caveator and wishes to withdraw some or all of their caveats, this may be done by a single request, adapted as necessary.

Para. 6.7(1).—For cases see *The Corner* (1863) Br. & L. 161; *The Don Ricardo* (1880) 5 P.D. 121; 4 Asp. M.L.C. 225.

Para. 6.7(2) and (3).—When security has been given the property cannot be arrested or re-arrested after judgment if the security proves to be insufficient (*The Point Breeze* [1928] P. 135). See also *The Alletta* [1974] 1 Lloyd's Rep. 40. As to arrest or re-arrest before judgment see *The Hero* (1865) Br. & Lush. 447; *The Flora* (1866) L.R. 1 A. & E. 45. And see *The Prinsengracht* [1993] 1 Lloyd's Rep. 41, applying *The Arctic Star* (1985), *The Times*, February 5; arrest or re-arrest after security is given and before judgment is to be viewed in the light of whether the arrest or re-arrest is oppressive and vexatious in the circumstances of the particular case.

Para. 6.8.—The object of this provision is to enable a person who has a substantial interest in the *res* to intervene, if this interest may be injuriously affected by the claim against the *res* and to protect his interests (*The Dowthorpe* (1843) 2 W.Rob. 73, 77). The rights of an intervener are limited to the protection of his interest in the *res*, and he has not *locus standi* to raise issues which are not material to his purpose (*The Lord Strathcona* [1925] P. 143; see also *The Byzantion* (1922) 127 L.T. 756; 16 Asp. M.L.C. 19, as to defences which an intervener may and those which he may not set up).

Inherent jurisdiction—The Court has inherent jurisdiction to allow a person who has no interest in the property under arrest to intervene, if the effect of the arrest is to cause him serious hardship, difficulty or danger (*The Mardina Merchant* [1975] 1 W.L.R. 147; [1974] 3 All E.R. 749; [1974] 2 Lloyd's Rep. 424, in which the interests of a harbour authority were adversely affected by the presence of the arrested ship at one of their quays).

As to intervention for the purpose of applying to be added as a defendant or for other purposes see CPR, r. 19.

Practice for intervening—Application is to the Admiralty Registrar.

Property not under arrest—If a ship under arrest is being adversely affected by property on board (*e.g.* perishables) which is not under arrest, an order, if granted, may include an order for sale of that property.

Default

7.1 If no acknowledgment of service and/or defence to a claim *in rem* 49FPD–006 (other than one to which paragraph 4 applies) is filed within the time required by this practice direction a Claimant may apply for judgment in default by filing an application in Admiralty Form No. ADM13, a certificate proving proper service of the claim form and evidence proving the claim to the satisfaction of the Admiralty Court. Where the claim form has been served by the Court it shall be presumed to have been properly served unless it is proved not to have been.

7.2 In the case of a claim to which paragraph 4 applies, where any party fails to file a Preliminary Act within the time specified any other party who has filed a Preliminary Act may apply for judgment in default:

(a) in a claim *in rem*, by filing an application in Admiralty Form No. ADM13, a certificate proving proper service of the claim form and evidence proving the claim to the satisfaction of the Admiralty Court. Where the claim form has been served by the Court it shall be presumed to have been properly served unless it is proved not to have been.

(b) in a claim *in personam*, in accordance with the rules in CPR Part 12 so far as applicable.

7.3 In the case of any other claim *in personam*, the rules as to judgment in default in CPR Part 12 will apply so far as applicable.

7.4 The Admiralty Court may, on such terms as it thinks just, set aside or vary any judgment entered in pursuance of paragraphs 7.1 or 7.2

7.5 Where a claim form has been served upon a party at whose instance a caveat against arrest was issued the Claimant may, after filing evidence to the satisfaction of the Admiralty Court verifying the facts on which the claim is based, apply to the Court for judgment in default provided that:

(a) the sum claimed in the claim form does not exceed the amount specified in the undertaking given by that party or his solicitor to procure the entry of the caveat, and

(b) that party or his solicitor does not within 14 days after service of the claim form fulfil the undertaking given by him as aforesaid.

Arrest of the res—The rule does not require the arrest of the *res* as a condition precedent to judgment in default (*The Nautik* [1895] P. 121).

Practice—It should be noted that before judgment in default can be obtained under this provision there must be adduced "evidence proving the claim to the satisfaction of the Admiralty Court". See para. 7(1). It is therefore necessary for the claimant's case to be properly proved.

The usual practice is for evidence to be given by affidavit or in appropriate cases certified statements and the Court usually refuses to allow oral evidence to be adduced. See *The Nettuno, Lloyd's List and Shipping Gazette*, Janury 30, 1969.

The application notice and any affidavits and exhibits or other evidence should be filed in the registry in good time in order that figures, etc. may be checked there before the hearing. If this is done it may be possible to obtain judgment for a specified sum and so avoid the expense of a reference. Any document in a foreign language must be accompanied by a translation which must itself be proved. If an order for appraisement and sale (para. 8 below) is desired this should be stated in the application notice.

Priorities—If caveats have been entered under para. 6.5(2) any decree made on the hearing of the application for judgment will usually reserve all questions of priorities. As to the determination of priorities and orders that may be made in connection therewith on an application for a judgment under this rule, see para. 8.

Payment out of proceeds of sale—See para. 8.3 below.

Setting aside judgment—It is not necessary for the defendant to have acknowledged service of the claim form when applying to set aside a judgment given in default (*The Ruben Martinez Villena* [1987] 1 Lloyd's Rep. 621).

Sale by the court, priorities and payment out

8.1 (1) An order for the survey, appraisement, or sale of a ship may be made in a claim *in rem* at any stage of the proceedings on the application of any party.

(2) An order for sale before judgment may only be made by the Admiralty Judge.

(3) Unless the Admiralty Court otherwise orders, an order for sale will be in Admiralty Form No. ADM14.

(4) In giving directions for sale the Admiralty Court may fix a time within which notice of claims against the proceeds of sale must be filed, and the time and manner in which notice of that time must be advertised.

8.2(1) Any party with a judgment against the property or proceeds of sale may at any time after the time referred to in paragraph 8.1(4) apply to the Admiralty Court for the determination of priorities. The application notice must be served on all persons who have filed a claim against the property.

(2) Unless otherwise ordered by the Admiralty Judge, a determination of priorities may only be made by the Admiralty Judge.

8.3 Payment out of the proceeds of sale will be made only to judgment creditors and in accordance with the detemination of priorities or as the Admiralty Court may otherwise order.

8.4(1) When proceeds of sale are paid into court by the Marshal and such payment is in a foreign currency, the funds will be placed on one day call interest bearing account unless otherwise ordered by the court.

(2) An application to place foreign currency on longer term deposit unless made at the same time as the application for sale, or other prior application, may be made to the Admiralty Registrar. Notice of the placement of foreign currency in an interest bearing account shall be given to all parties interested in the fund by the party at whose instance the foreign currency is invested.

(3) Any interested party who wishes to object to the mode of investment of foreign currency paid into court may apply to the Admiralty Registrar for directions.

Res must be under arrest—The *res* must be in the hands of the Court before an order for sale will be made (*The Wexford* (1888) 13 P.D. 10) but in special circumstances an order for arrest, appraisement and sale may be made where it is not (*The Berriz* 1905 Fo. 497). In *The Ricuna* 1974 Fo. 380 (unrep.) the practice of requiring that the *res* be under arrest in the claim in which an order for appraisement and sale is sought was approved. The power of the court in an Admiralty claim to order a court sale cannot be invoked in a claim *in personam* (*The Lady Tahilla* [1967] 1 Lloyd's Rep. 591 at 601). Appraisement and sale may be ordered *pendente lite*. As to the circumstances in which such an order will be made see *The Myrto* [1977] 2 Lloyd's Rep. 243 at 259. Such a sale was ordered on the *defendant's* application in *The Westport (No. 1)* [1965] 1 W.L.R. 796.

The Court may order a sale by the Admiralty Marshal without Appraisement to a specific buyer for a specific price.

Sale in foreign currency—The Admiralty Marshal may if he thinks fit in order to obtain the best price in any particular case, invite offers and sell the property for a price in a foreign currency. (*The Halcyon the Great* [1975] 1 W.L.R. 515; [1975] 1 All E.R. 882; [1975] 1 Lloyd's Rep. 518).

Para. 8.2(1)—An application under this paragraph should be made in the claim brought by the applicant. Notice of application must be served on all persons who have obtained judgment against the ship and on all caveators. The names and addresses for service of these persons can be obtained from the Admiralty and Commercial Registry.

Note—As to priorities, see *British Shipping Laws, McGuffie: Admiralty Practice* and Halsbury's *Laws of England*; and Meeson, *Admiralty Jurisdiction and Practice*. See also as to variation of order determining priorities, *The Fairport (No. 4)* [1967] 1 W.L.R. 964; [1967] 2 All E.R. 914n; [1967] 1 Lloyd's Rep. 602. For examples of subrogation of mortgagees to the rights and priorities of master and crew upon payment, *with permission of the court*, by the mortgagees of the master's and crew's wages, see *The Berostar* [1970] 2 Lloyd's Rep. 403 and *The Vasilia* [1972] 1 Lloyd's Rep. 51.

Payment out from proceeds of sale under para. 8.3—The Court has no jurisdiction to order payment out from the proceeds of a sale by order of the Court, to persons other than judgment holders or, in the case of the residue after all claims have been satisfied, the defendant

(*The Saxon King*, 1975 Fo. 253 (unrep.)). Exceptionally, payment out may be ordered to any person where the defendants and all other parties interested in the proceeds of sale (judgment holders, interveners and caveators) consent (*The Valiant* 1977 Fo. 446 (unrep.)). A payment out on account may be ordered where all parties consent, or where the priorities are such that it is clear the claimant will ultimately be entitled to at least the amount ordered. See *The Reina (No. 2)* [1963] 2 Lloyd's Rep. 513.

Charging and stop orders—Payment out from proceeds of sale may be affected by a charging order or stop order pursuant to RSC, O.50 or an application or order under RSC, O.49, r.9.

Note—As to apportionment of a payment in a salvage action, see *The Talamba and the Troll* [1965] P. 433; [1965] 2 All E.R. 775; [1965] 2 Lloyd's Rep. 128.

In particular, note the observations of Sheen J. in *The Vasili Shelgunov* [1988] 2 Lloyd's Rep. 34, at 38 in relation to Admiralty claims *in personam*. Approved by Court of Appeal [1989] 1 Lloyd's Rep. 542, CA.

Limitation claims

49FPD–007 **9.1** (1) Limitation may be relied upon by way of defence to any claim.

(2) A limitation claim may be brought by counterclaim with the permission of the Admiralty Court.

(3) A limitation claim is begun by the issue of a claim form in Admiralty Form No. ADM15 ("a limitation claim form"). The limitation claim form must be accompanied by a declaration:

- (a) proving the facts upon which the Claimant relies
- (b) stating the names and addresses (if known) of all persons who to the knowledge of the Claimant have claims against him in respect of the occurrence to which the claim relates, other than named defendants,

and sworn as an affidavit.

(4) The Claimant and at least one of the Defendants must be named in the limitation claim form, but all other Defendants may be described.

(5) The limitation claim form must be served on all named Defendants.

(6) The limitation claim form may not be served out of the jurisdiction unless:

- (a) the case falls within section 22(2)(a) to (c) of the Supreme Court Act 1981;
- (b) the Defendant has submitted to or agreed to submit to the jurisdiction of the court; or
- (c) the Admiralty Court has jurisdiction over the claim under any applicable Convention.

(7) Every Defendant upon whom a limitation claim form is served must either:

- (a) within 28 days of service file a defence to the limitation claim in Admiralty Form No. ADM16A or file a notice in Admiralty Form No. ADM16 that he admits the right of the claimant to limit liability; or
- (b) if he wishes to dispute the jurisdiction of the court or to argue that the court should not exercise its jurisdiction file within 14 days of service or, if the limitation claim form is served out of the jurisdiction, within the time specified in RSC, Order 11, rule 1A (Schedule 1 to the CPR), an acknowledgment of service in Admiralty Form No. ADM16B.

(8) In the event that the Defendant files an acknowledgment of service pursuant to paragraph 9.1(7)(b) he will be treated as having accepted that the court has jurisdiction to hear the limitation claim unless he makes an application under CPR Part 11 within 14 days of filing his acknowledgment of service.

9.2 (1) Where one or more named Defendants admits the right to limit, the

Claimant may file in the registry an application for a restricted limitation decree in Admiralty Form No. ADM17 and the Court will issue a decree in Admiralty Form No. ADM18 limiting liability only against such named Defendants as have admitted the Claimant's right to limit liability.

(2) A restricted limitation decree may be obtained against any named Defendant failing to file a defence within the time specified for doing so.

(3) A restricted decree need not be advertised, but a copy must be served on the Defendants to whom it applies.

(4) Where the right to limit is not admitted or the Claimant seeks a general limitation decree in Admiralty Form No. ADM19, he must within 7 days of the date of the filing of the defence of the named Defendant last served or the expiry of the time for doing so, apply for an appointment before the Admiralty Registrar for a case management conference at which directions will be given for the further conduct of the proceedings.

9.3(1) When a limitation decree is granted the Admiralty Court:

(a) may order that any proceedings relating to any claim arising out of the occurrence be stayed;

(b) may order the Claimant to establish a limitation fund if one has not been established or make such other arrangements for payment of claims against which liability is limited as the Court considers appropriate;

(c) may, if the decree is a restricted limitation decree, distribute the limitation fund;

(d) shall, if the decree is a general limitation decree, give directions as to advertisement of the decree and fix a time within which notice of claims against the fund must be filed or an application made to set aside the decree.

(2) When the Admiralty Court grants a general limitation decree the Claimant must:

(a) advertise it in such manner and within such time as the Court shall direct;

(b) file in the registry a declaration that the decree has been advertised in accordance with (a) and copies of the advertisements.

9.4 Any person other than a named Defendant may apply to the Admiralty Registrar within the time fixed in the decree to have a general limitation decree set aside. Any such application must be supported by a declaration proving that the person has a good faith claim against the Claimant arising out of the occurrence and sufficient grounds for contending that the Claimant is not entitled to the decree obtained, either in the amount of limitation or at all.

9.5(1) A limitation fund may be established before or after a limitation claim has been commenced.

(2) If a limitation claim is not commenced within 75 days of the date the fund was established, the fund will lapse and all monies in court, including any interest accrued therein, will be repaid to the person making the payment into court. The lapsing of a limitation fund shall not prevent the establishment of a new fund.

9.6(1) The Claimant may constitute a limitation fund by paying into court the sterling equivalent of the number of special drawing rights to which he claims to be entitled to limit his liability under the Merchant Shipping Act 1995 together with interest thereon from the date of the occurrence giving rise to his liability to the date of payment into court.

(2) Where the Claimant does not know the sterling equivalent of the said number of special drawing rights on the date of payment into court he may calculate the same on the basis of the latest available published sterling equivalent of a special drawing right as fixed by the International Monetary Fund, and in the event of the sterling equivalent of a special drawing right on

the date of payment into court under paragraph (1) being different from that used for calculating the amount of that payment into court the Claimant may—

(a) make up any deficiency by making a further payment into court which, if made within 14 days after the payment into court under paragraph (1), shall be treated, except for the purposes of the rules relating to the accrual of interest on money paid into court, as if it has been made on the date of that payment into court, or

(b) apply to the Admiralty Court for payment out of any excess amount (together with any interest accrued thereon) paid into court under paragraph (1).

(3) An application under paragraph 9.6(2)(b) may be made without notice to any party and must be supported by evidence to the satisfaction of the Court proving the sterling equivalent of the appropriate number of special drawing rights on the date of payment into court.

(4) On making any payment into court under this rule, the Claimant shall give notice thereof in writing to every named Defendant, specifying the date of payment in, the amount paid in, the amount of interest included therein, the rate of such interest, and the period to which it relates.

The Claimant shall also give notice in writing to every Defendant of any excess amount (and any interest thereon) paid out to him under paragraph 9.6(2)(b).

(5) Money paid into court under this paragraph shall not be paid out except under an order of the court.

9.7(1) A claim against the fund must be in Admiralty Form No. DM20.

(2) No later than the time fixed in the decree for filing claims, each of the Defendants must file and serve his statement of case on the limiting party and on all other Defendants. The statement of case must contain the particulars of the Defendant's claim. Any Defendant unable to do so must file a declaration in Admiralty Form No. ADM21 stating the reason for his inability. The declaration must be sworn as an affidavit.

(3) Within 7 days of the time for filing claims or declarations, the Admiralty Registrar will fix a date for a case management conference at which directions will be given for the further conduct of the proceedings.

Limitation Claim—For definition see para. 1.4(3). These claims are assigned to the Queen's Bench Division and taken by the Admiralty Court, see para. 1.5(c). See also SCA 1981, s.20(1)(b) and (3)(c). Limitation of liability may be relied on by way of defence to a claim or counterclaim.

A limitation decree or declaration can be granted before liability is established. The establishment of liability either by trial or agreement is not a pre-condition to the seeking and granting of a limitation decree or declaration, see *Bouygues Offshore S.A. v. Caspian Shipping Co. and Others* [1998] 2 Lloyd's Rep. 461.

In *Herceg Novi (Owners) v. Ming Galaxy (Owners)* [1998] 4 All E.R. 238; [1998] 2 Lloyd's Rep. 454, CA, the Court held that the 1976 Convention was not an internationally sanctioned and objective view of where substantial justice was viewed as lying, but was simply the view of some 30 states. Moreover, the preference for the 1976 Convention had no greater justification than for the 1957 regime and, in terms of abstract justice, neither convention was objectively more just than the other. Accordingly, since substantial justice would be done in Singapore, the appeal would be allowed and an unconditional stay of the English action would be granted.

Claim Form—See SCP 1999, Vol. 2, Pt 6A—Special Admiralty Forms and Supplement No. 3.

Service—The claim form must be served on at least one defendant named in the claim form and not merely described. As to service out of the jurisdiction see para. 3.1(1).

Limitation fund and interest—Any person wishing to constitute a limitation fund must pay into Court a fund constituted in accordance with section 185 and Schedule 7 of the Merchant Shipping Act 1995, together with interest thereon from the date of the occurrence giving rise to his liability until the date of the constitution of the limitation fund pursuant to para. 8(1) of Pt II of Sched. 7 to the Act. The rate of interest is now fixed by the Merchant Shipping (Liability of Shipowners and Others) (Rate of Interest) Order 1999 (S.I. 1999 No. 1922), effective September 1, 1999.

The rate of interest is;

(a) where the occurrence takes place before September 1, 1999 but the fund is constituted on or after that date:

(i) 12 per cent from the date of the occurrence until December 31, 1994;

(ii) 6.75 per cent on and after January 1, 1995 until August 31, 1998;

(iii) 8.5 per cent on and after September 1, 1998 until August 31, 1999, and

(iv) the prescribed rate on and after September 1, 1999, or

(b) where the occurrence takes place on or after September 1, 1999, the prescribed rate.

The prescribed rate is defined as one per cent more than the base rate quoted from time to time by the Committee of London Clearing Bankers or, where there is for the time being more than one such rate, the lowest of them.

Tonnage—The limitation tonnage is usually proved in the case of a British registered ship by a certified copy of the Tonnage Certificate. As to the tonnage of ships of a foreign country which has adopted the British tonnage regulations, see Merchant Shipping Act 1995, s.12. For a list of these countries see *British Shipping Laws*, Vol. 11, under section 84 of the Merchant Shipping Act 1894, now section 12 of the 1995 Act. See too the Merchant Shipping (Liability of Shipowners and Others) (Calculation of Tonnage) Order 1986. (S.I. 1986 No. 1040) and the Merchant Shipping (Tonnage) Regulations 1997 (S.I. 1997 No. 1510).

Restricted decree—When a claimant in a limitation claim is satisfied that there will be no claims upon the fund other than the claims of the defendants who have acknolwedged issue or service of the claim form the claimant may not want a decree which is good against the world. The claimant may apply to the Admiralty Registrar to amend the claim form by deleting reference to any defendants other than those named. The application should be accompanied by a letter signed by all consenting parties stating that in their view it is not anticipated that any further claims will emerge. The Registrar may then order payment out of the limitation fund in Court.

If further claimants do emerge after payment out the claimant will be obliged to constitute a new fund should they wish to limit their liability against the new claimants. This practice arises from a decision of Sheen J. in an unreported case (*The Rena* [1979] Fo. 138).

Owner-master—As to the right of an owner-master to limit his liability, see *The Annie Hay* [1968] P. 341; [1968] 1 All E.R. 657; [1968] 1 Lloyd's Rep. 141.

Charterers—Charterers cannot limit their liability under the 1976 Convention in respect of claims brought by owners against them: see *Aegean Sea Traders Corporation v. Repsol Petroleo SA and Another* [1998] 2 Lloyd's Rep. 39.

Sterling equivalents—For ascertainment of sterling equivalents see Sched. 7, Pt II, para. 7 to the Merchant Shipping Act 1995.

Para. 9.2(4) "... directions ..."—An order will usually be made providing for statements of case, disclosure, and any other directions deemed necessary and the imposition of a set timetable for expeditious disposal of the matter.

Para. 9.3(1)—It seems that in a distribution pursuant to this paragraph, the Court would order interest accrued on the limitation fund in Court to be apportioned *pro rata* to the distribution.

Costs of application—The costs of an application for a decree of limitation under the former section 17 of the Merchant Shipping Act 1979, now section 185 of the Merchant Shipping Act 1995, should normally follow the event, see *The Capitan San Luis* [1994] Q.B. 465; [1994] 2 W.L.R. 465; [1994] 2 W.L.R. 299; [1994] 1 All E.R. 1016; [1993] 2 Lloyd's Rep. 573. In this case it was held that the shipowners should pay the costs of proving the matters which he had to establish in order to obtain the decree and that the claimant should pay the costs of investigating and determining the facts which the Convention provided he must prove, if at the end of the day he failed to establish those facts.

References to the Admiralty Registrar

10(1) The Admiralty Court may at any stage in the claim refer any question or issue for determination by the Admiralty Registrar (a "reference").

(2) Unless otherwise ordered, where a reference has been ordered:

(a) The Claimant must file and serve particulars of claim on all other parties within 14 days of the date of the order.

(b) Any party opposing the claim must file a defence to the claim within 14 days of service of the particulars of claim upon him.

(3) Within 7 days of the filing of the defence, the Claimant must apply for an appointment before the Admiralty Registrar for a case management conference at which directions will be given for the further conduct of the proceedings.

(4) Any decision of the Admiralty Registrar on the hearing of the reference may be appealed to the Admiralty Judge, by Notice in Admiralty Form No. ADM25 filed within 75 days of the decision on the reference appealed against.

General note—It is the long-established practice of the Admiralty Court after liability has been determined, to refer to the Admiralty Registrar the matter of the assessment of the amount of the claimant's claim and of the counterclaim if there be one. There is, however, no rule that the assessment of damages must be referred (*The Fremantle* [1954] 2 Lloyd's Rep. 20) and in personal injury and Fatal Accidents Acts cases it is not unusual for the Judge to assess damages. See, *e.g. Connell v. Hellyer Brothers Ltd* [1963] 2 Lloyd's Rep. 249; *The St Chad (No. 2)* [1965] 2 Lloyd's Rep. 347.

Questions of amount have occasionally been referred before trial. (See, *e.g. The Happy Return* (1828) 2 Hagg. 198 at 207) but this has not been done for many years. In *The Lathara* (1930) 37 Ll.L.Rep. 160, it seems that all issues in the claim were referred to the Registrar.

Where the assessment of damages involves a question of causation this is in some cases decided by the Judge at the trial or thereafter. See, *e.g. The Maid of Kent* (1881) 6 P.D. 178, *The Guildford* [1956] 2 Lloyd's Rep. 74; *The Lucile Bloomfield* [1967] 2 Lloyd's Rep. 308. If it is desired to have such questions decided by the Judge at the trial this matter should be raised on the case management conference. In exercising its discretion the Court will be guided by the consideration whether the matter is one which can better be dealt with by the Court at the trial, or later at the reference (*The Maid of Kent, ibid.*).

Assessors—In modern practice the Registrar decides questions without the assistance of merchants. Nautical and other assessors, however, are sometimes appointed. If the parties agree in desiring the Registrar to sit with a merchant (the full title is "merchant assessor") or other assessor, they should apply by letter to the Admiralty and Commercial Registry. In the event of disagreement between the parties an application should be made on notice.

How references may rise—A reference may arise out of the judgment or decree made on the trial or the hearing of an application; out of the decree in a limitation claim made on the hearing of an application under para. 9; out of an agreement filed under para. 12, or an order on a consent application.

Where in an action *in personam* judgment in default is entered "for an amount of money to be decided by the Court" there can be no reference and the assessment is governed by CPR 12.7.

Claim in reference—The claim referred to in this provision should in the first place state in a few words how the claim arises; thus in a collision claim it would begin with a short statement giving the date of the collision, the voyage on which the vessel was engaged, and, if she was repaired, the place and date and duration of such repair. In every case the several heads of claim should then be set out and numbered consecutively. It is not correct and is confusing, to call the claim a statement of case. It is a claim in a reference. For content and format of forms of claim see British Shipping Laws, *Forms and Precedents 1993*, and *Atkin's Encyclopaedia of Court Forms in Civil Proceedings*, Vol. 3, Form 155 (1994 issue), adapted as necessary.

Limitation references—In references in limitation claim a claimant need not serve a copy of his claim on any other party. Any claimant may, however, on the payment of the proper fee, inspect and obtain a copy of the claim and any other documents filed by any other claimant against the fund. See CPR 5.4(1). In practice copies of these documents are supplied on request by the solicitors concerned on payment of the usual copying charges.

If any claimant wishes to dispute the claim of another he should so inform the Admiralty and Commercial Registry by letter in order that he can be given notice of the appointment fixed for the hearing of that other's claim.

In a claim arising out of a collision between ships A and B if there are cross claims and both ships have been held to blame (or the matter has been settled on a both to blame basis) and the owners of A obtain a limitation decree it may be necessary to assess their claim in order to arrive at the amount which the owners of B are entitled to claim against the fund. It will be necessary to do this if there are other claimants against the fund. See *The Stoom vart Maatschappf Nederland v. The Peninsular and Oriental Steam Navigation Co.* (1882) 7 App. Cas. 795. In this event the practice is for the owners of B to put forward in their claim a deduction in respect of the appropriate proportion of the damages of the owners of A as agreed or, failing agreement, estimated. This figure may be disputed by any other claimant.

Filing amended claims—A claimant should not amend his filed claim but should file another claim in amended form. No leave is required. If, however, the alterations are of such a character and are made at such a late stage as to embarrass the paying party at the reference, the Registrar may, in his discretion, adjourn the reference or take some other course as he thinks fit.

Evidence—The ordinary rules of evidence apply on the hearing of a reference but are, by agreement between the parties, frequently relaxed in order to save time and expense.

Proved recoverable amount—The convention of awarding one per cent of proved recoverable amount to compensate for disruption to business and expenditure of management available to shipowners does not extend to cargo owners (*Owners of the Ship Kumanova v. Owners of the Ship Massira* [1998] 2 Lloyd's Rep. 301.

Hearing; general note—A party to a reference may be represented by counsel, solicitor, legal executive or solicitor's clerk.

If a sum has been paid into Court and the award is less than the amount paid in, the party who made the payment in is entitled to an order enabling him to take the balance out of Court (*The Mona* [1894] P. 265).

Inquiry regarding a shorthand record at references may be made of the Registry.

Delay; interest—See *The Nassau* [1965] 1 Lloyd's Rep. 236 and cases cited.

Interest: date for addition—On compromising an Admiralty claim for collision damages interest should be added to each claim before striking the balance, such balance to be struck on the date of assessment or of agreement of claims; see *The Lu Shan* [1993] 2 Lloyd's Rep. 259.

Interest in personal injury and fatal accident cases—See SCA 1981, s.35A (SCP 1999, Vol. 2, Section 20A, paras 20A–224 to 20A–226).

Costs of reference—The costs of the reference are in the Registrar's discretion. Where two vessels are held to blame in a collision claim the costs in the reference of each claimant are dealt with on the basis of the reference being a separate proceeding from the claim (*The Consett* (1880) 5 P.D. 77). As to the effect of failure to give notice of survey, see *The Solace (No. 2)* (1936) 55 Ll.L.Rep. 201. Usually where the claimant recovers a substantial proportion of the sum claimed he is given the costs of the reference, and where an offer has been made and the amount awarded in the reference is less, the offeror will usually be entitled to the costs after the offer was made (see *The Norseman* [1957] 1 Lloyd's Rep. 503; *The Reading* [1908] P. 162). If one claimant in a reference in a limitation claim puts forward a claim which is contested successfully by another, the former may be condemned to pay the costs of the successful claimant in contesting the claim, *i.e.* the costs over and above those of proving his own claim (*The Clan Canning*, 1906, Fo. 206 (unrep.)).

Appeal to Admiralty Judge—No objection can be taken to an item which was uncontested at the reference (*The Princess Helena* (1861) Lush. 190). Fresh evidence will not be allowed on the hearing of the application in objection unless the Judge is satisfied that the evidence could not reasonably, by proper diligence and application, have been produced at the reference (*The Flying Fish* (1866) Br. & Lush. 436; *The Thuringia* (1871) 1 Asp. 166). A further appeal lies to the Court of Appeal and thence to the House of Lords. The appeal to the Court of Appeal lies only with leave, see RSC, O.59, r.1B as amended with effect from October 1, 1995.

Inspection of ship etc.

11. The Admiralty Court may, on the application of any interested persons or on its own initiative, make an order for the inspection by any person of any ship or other property, whether real or personal, the inspection of which may be necessary or desirable for the purpose of obtaining full information or evidence in connection with any issue in a claim or proposed claim whether *in rem* or *in personam.*

Effect of rule—The power conferred by this paragraph and its predecessors is now commonly exercised. For examples of its exercise see *The Magnet* (1874) L.R. 4 A. & E. 417; *The Cumberland Queen* (1921) 6 H.L.Rep. 280; *The Olympic and H.M.S. Hawke* [1913] P. 214. It has been held that an order will not be made when the applicant has an opportunity of proving the facts by evidence in the ordinary way (*The Victor Covacevich* (1885) 10 P.D. 40).

As to orders for inspection under general rules, see CPR 25.1(c)(ii). As to inspection before the commencement of proceedings or of property not belonging to or in the possession of a party to the proceedings under general rules see CPR 25.4 and 5.

As to taking samples from the bunkers of a ship where there is a claim for short delivery of an oil cargo, see note on two unreported cases in Lloyd's Maritime and Commercial Law Quarterly, February 1985, p. 10 and [1985] 3 C.L. 338a.

An order made pursuant to CPR 25 aforesaid and this paragraph permitting a party's surveyor to inspect a ship and her documents and to take samples from a vessel, although mandatory in form, is not an injunction. Claimants seeking such an order must produce evidence to show:

(1) That they have a good arguable case on the merits.
(2) That there was more than *de minimis* shortage of cargo on delivery.
(3) That such inspection and/or taking of samples and/or analysis is likely to assist the trial judge.

To protect the shipowners from unnecessary interference and any third party adversely affected by the order, the claimant will be required to give an undertaking in damages against any loss suffered as a result of the order (*The Mare del Nord* [1990] 1 Lloyd's Rep. 40).

In *The Cienvik* [1996] 2 Lloyd's Rep. 395, the Admiralty Court expressed the view that the forerunner of this paragraph cannot have been intended to give the court power to make an order for the inspection of a ship or other property out of the jurisdiction which was not in the ownership, possession, custody or power of a person over whom the court had jurisdiction either because he was personally within the jurisdiction or because permission to serve process upon him out of the jurisdiction could be granted under rules of court then in force. It is considered that such is also the position under this paragraph.

Agreement of solicitors to be made an order of the Court

49FPD–008 **12.** Subject to any restrictions contained in other Rules, any agreement in writing between the solicitors of the parties to any Admiralty claim dated and signed by those solicitors may, if the Admiralty Register thinks it reasonable, be filed in the Admiralty and Commercial Registry and the agreement shall then become an order of the Admiralty Court.

General note—An order of the Court may be enforced in the same ways as a judgment and this paragraph therefore provides a convenient method of settling an Admiralty claim. An agreement filed under this paragraph binds only the parties to it. Thus where the owners of two ships filed in agreement that both ships were to blame, it was held that this did not affect the owners of cargo carried in one of the ships (*The Karo* (1888) 13 P.D. 24).

Practice—The signed agreement is left at the Admiralty and Commercial Registry. If the Admiralty Registrar approves the same, it will be filed and become an order of Court. No order is drawn up. An office copy of the approved agreement may be obtained by any party upon payment of the proper fee. If the Registrar refuses to approve the agreement the Registry will so inform the party filing it. Appeal against the refusal to approve lies to an Admiralty Judge in private.

Interest—Where the agreement amounts to an admission of full liability and consent to a reference, the matter of interest may be left to be dealt with on the reference. Where the agreement provides for the payment by one party of a proportion of another's claim (*i.e.* damages) it is usual to provide "together with interest" leaving the rate and period to be agreed or dealt with on the reference. This is sound practice as it removes any doubt as to whether the word "claim" means damages plus interest thereon or damages only. See *The Virtsu* [1982] 2 Lloyd's Rep. 33, CA. Where the agreement provides for the payment of a specified sum together with interest, the rate and period must be specified. In such a case, the agreement should also state a time within which payment is to be made.

It seems that a sum payable under an agreement filed in pursuance of this paragraph is a judgment debt and carries interest at the statutory rate from the time when it became due until payment is made. As to interest on judgment debts generally and the rate of interest see CPR 40.8 also.

Undertakings

13(1) Where in this practice direction any undertaking to the Marshal is required it shall be given in writing and to his satisfaction or in accordance with such other arrangements as he may require.

(2) Where any party is dissatisfied with a direction given by the Marshal in this respect he may apply to the Admiralty Registrar for a ruling.

Note—The personal undertaking of the party's solicitor is normally given. Where the expenses of effecting or maintaining the arrest are more than minimal, successive demands are likely to be made by the Marshal beginning soon after the arrest.

As to recovery from the proceeds of sale of sums paid to the Marshal by an arresting party, see *The Falcon* [1981] 1 Lloyd's Rep. 13. The Marshal's expenses of maintaining the arrest from the time of the order for appraisement and sale and the expenses of the sale are payable in the first instance by the party applying therefor. *The Falcon*, above at 17. As to liability for the expenses of a second and subsequent arrests see *ibid.* As to recovery from the proceeds of sale of sums paid to the Marshal, insurance premiums, solicitors' costs of arrest, etc., crew's wages, interveners' costs and interest, see *The World Star* [1987] 1 Lloyd's Rep. 452.

For priorities and the method of determining the same see *British Shipping Laws*, Vol. 1 para. 1574, *The Falcon*, above. *The World Star*, above, and *The Rubi Sea* [1992] 1 Lloyd's Rep. 634.

The fees and commission paid by the Marshal to Brokers in addition to their reasonable expenses for carrying out a Judicial sale of a vessel are as follows:

Scale of valuation Fees as from May 25, 1998

Not exceeding £20,000: £200

Exceeding £20,000: £400

Where the condition of the ship and/or the state of the market make it advisable that there should be a dual valuation for both trading and demolition purposes the full fee will apply in respect of the valuation for trading and in addition a fee at half the above rates will apply in respect of the valuation for demolition.

Scale of Commission as from May 25, 1998

6 per cent on the first £5,000

5 per cent on the next £10,000 up to £15,000

3 per cent on the next £15,000 up to £30,000

1 per cent on the balance over £30,000.

Stay of proceedings

14. Where the Admiralty Court orders a stay of any claim *in rem*, any property under arrest in the action shall remain under arrest and any security representing the *res* shall remain in force unless the Court otherwise orders.

Provisions for the appointment of examiners in Admiralty etc.

15(1) The Admiralty Court may make an order with the consent of the parties for a deposition to be taken as if before an examiner but without the examiner actually being appointed or being present.

(2) Where an order is made under paragraph 15(1) provision may be made for any consequential matters, but in the absence of such provision the following provisions shall apply:

(a) the party whose witness is to be examined shall provide a shorthand writer to take down the evidence of the witness;

(b) any representative, being counsel or solicitor, of either of the parties shall have authority to administer the oath to the witness;

(c) the shorthand writer need not be sworn but shall certify in writing as correct a transcript of his notes of the evidence and deliver it to the solicitor for the party whose witness was examined, and that solicitor must file it in the Registry;

(d) unless the parties otherwise agree or the court otherwise orders, the transcript or a copy of it, shall be made available to the persons who acted as advocates at the examination before it is filed, and if any of those persons is of the opinion that the transcript does not accurately record the evidence he shall make a certificate specifying the corrections which in his opinion should be made and that certificate must be filed with the transcript.

(3) In a collision claim no order shall be made under CPR Part 34 authorising the examination of a witness before the Preliminary Acts have been filed, unless the Admiralty Court considers that there are special reasons for doing so.

(4) The Lord Chief Justice may appoint such number of barristers or solicitors as he thinks fit to act as examiners of the Admiralty Court in connection with Admiralty claims, and may revoke any such appointment.

List of examiners—See *The Solicitors Directory*.

The Commercial Court Guide

16.1 The practice of the Commercial Court set out in the Commercial Court Guide should, except where inapplicable, be followed in Admiralty 49FPD–009 proceedings subject to the provisions of this or any other Admiralty practice direction and to any order that may be made in an individual case.

16.2 Part D of the Commercial Court Guide shall be modified as follows:

(a) D3 shall not apply;

(b) In the Admiralty Court the Case Management Information Sheet should be in the form of Appendix 6 to the Commercial Court Guide but also include the following additional question:

(20)a. Do any of the issues contained in the List of Issues involve questions of navigation or other particular matters of an essentially Admiralty nature which require the trial to be before the Admiralty Judge or is there any other reason why you consider trial before the Admiralty Judge to be necessary?

b. Are you prepared to have the case tried before a deputy nominated by the Admiralty Judge who has experience of such questions or matters?

c. Do you consider that the court should sit with nautical or other Assessors? Are you intending to ask that the court sit with one or more Assessors who is not a Trinity Master? If so please state the reasons for such application.

16.3 One significant area of difference between practice in the Commercial Court and practice in the Admiralty Court is that in the Admiralty Court many interlocutory applications are normally heard by the Admiralty Registrar and this practice will continue, save as specifically mentioned elsewhere in this practice direction.

Gyro-compass and other records—An order is sometimes made for an expert's interpretation of the record to be admissible in evidence. In *The Statue of Liberty* [1968] 1 W.L.R. 739; [1968] 2 All E.R. 195; [1968] 1 Lloyd's Rep. 429, it was held that automatically recorded film strip of radar echoes was admissible in evidence; it had nothing to do with the heresay rule and did not depend upon the Evidence Act 1938, but was in the nature of real evidence.

Use of fax when Registry is closed

17.1 When the Registry is closed (and only when it is closed) and Admiralty claim form may be issued on the following designated fax machine: 0171-936 6667 and only on that machine.

17.2 The procedure to be followed is set out in paragraph B3.11 and Appendix 3 of the Commercial Court Guide.

17.3(1) When the Registry is closed (and only when it is closed) a notice requesting a caveat against release may be filed on the following designated fax machine: 0171-936 6056 and only on that machine. This machine is manned 24 hours a day by court security staff (telephone 0171-936 6000). The notice requesting the caveat should be transmitted with a note in the following form for ease of identification by security staff:

"CAVEAT AGAINST RELEASE

Please find notice requesting caveat against release of the . . . (name ship/identify cargo) . . . for filing in the Admiralty Court and Commercial Registry."

(2) The notice must be in Admiralty Form No. ADM11 and signed by a solicitor acting on behalf of the intending caveator.

17.4(1) Subject to the provisions of paragraph 17.4(3) below, the filing of the notice takes place when the fax is recorded as having been received.

(2) When the Registry is next open to the public, the filing solicitor or his agent shall attend and deliver to the Registry the document which was transmitted by fax together with the transmission report. Upon satisfying himself that the document delivered fully accords with the document received by the Registry, the court officer shall stamp the document delivered with the time and date at which the notice was received, enter the same in the caveat book and retain the same with the faxed copy.

(3) Unless otherwise ordered by the court, the stamped notice shall be conclusive proof that the notice was filed at the time and on the date stated.

(4) If the filing solicitor does not comply with the foregoing procedure, or if the notice is not stamped, the notice shall be deemed never to have been filed.

Use of postal facilities in the Registry

18.1 Applications together with the requisite documents may be posted to:
The Admiralty and Commercial Registry
Room E200
Royal Courts of Justice
Strand
London
WC2A 2LL

18.2 In addition to the classes of business for which the use of postal facilities is permitted by the CPR or the Commercial Court Guide, the filing of the following classes of documents shall also be permitted in Admiralty matters:

(1) Requests for notices of caveats

(2) Preliminary Acts

(3) Claims in References

(4) Agreements between solicitors under paragraph 12 of this practice direction.

18.3 Documents sent by post for filing must be accompanied by two copies of a list of the documents sent and an envelope properly addressed to the sender.

18.4 On receipt of the documents in the Registry, the court officer will, if the circumstances are such that had the documents been presented personally they would have been filed, cause them to be filed and will, by post, notify the sender that this has been done. If the documents would not have been accepted if presented personally the court officer will not file them but will retain them in the Registry for collection by the sender and will, by post, so inform the sender.

18.5 When documents received through the post are filed by the court officer they will be sealed and entered as filed on the date on which they were received in the Registry.

Drawing up of orders

19. All orders made in Admiralty proceedings will be drawn up by the parties unless otherwise ordered by the court.

Assessors

20.1 The usual practice in the Admiralty Court is to sit with Assessors when hearing collision claims or other cases involving issues of navigation or seamanship and the parties will not normally be permitted to call expert witnesses on matters of navigation or seamanship where the court sits with Assessors. The Assessors will usually be Trinity Masters. Parties should indicate at the Case Management Conference whether they consider that the case is suitable for Assessors and whether Assessors other than Trinity Masters would be appropriate. **49FPD–010**

20.2 Provision is made in CPR 35.15 for assessor's remuneration. The usual practice is for the court to seek an undertaking from the claimant (or appellant) to pay the remuneration on demand after the case has concluded.

Assessors—In Admiralty cases, nautical assessors usually advise the Court of Appeal and the Judge of the Admiralty Court upon questions of navigation and seamanship if such questions arise. In some cases only one nautical assessor is called in and occasionally their attendance is dispensed with altogether. In the Admiralty Court, the assessors are usually two of the Elder Brethren of Trinity House neither of whom should have been in the service of any party to the claim (*The Bremen* (1931) 47 T.L.R. 505) save where an Elder Brother is a retired officer of the Royal Navy and one of H.M. ships is involved. If Trinity House is a party, one or two of such Court of Appeal assessors as are not Elder Brethren may be called on. Where nautical assessors are present, evidence in the nature of expert opinion on matters of nautical skill and practice, and as to the deductions to be drawn from nautical facts, is usually inadmissible (*The Gazelle* (1842) 1 W.Rob. 471). In *The St Chad* [1965] 2 Lloyd's Rep. 1, affirming; [1965] 1 Lloyd's Rep. 107, however, an order made provided for a fishery assessor to assist the Court and also for each side to be at liberty to call an experienced trawler skipper to give general evidence on the system of work in trawlers of the relevant type, as the system was said to have changed so recently that the new developments might be outside the practical experience of a fishery assessor. A comparable order was made in *The Bedford Earl* 1954 RSC Fo. 218 (unrep.), but this case never came to trial. As to the Court of Appeal, see n. to RSC, O.59, r. 10, and the Practice Note issued by Lord Denning M.R. on April 29, 1965 ([1965] 1 W.L.R. 853; [1965] 1 Lloyd's Rep. 564).

Assessors may be called in to assist the Registrar at a reference, see para. 10.3. The function of nautical assessors is to advise the court upon nautical matters (*The City of Berlin* [1908] P. 110; see *The New Pelton* [1891] P. 258; *The River Derwent* (1891) 7 Asp. 467). There is no right of cross-examination. (Contrast the position of a single expert: see CPR 35.) The decision of the case rests entirely with the Judge (*The Gannet* [1900] A.C. 234; *Owners of SS. Australia v. Owners of SS. Nautilus* [1927] A.C. 145; *Owners of S.S. Melanie v. Owners of SS. San Onofre (No. 1)* [1927] A.C. 162n; *Owners of SS. Artemisia v. Owners of S.S. Douglas* [1927] A.C. 164n.); this equally applies in the Court of Appeal (*The Llanelly* (1926) 25 Ll.L.Rep. 37, p.39, HL) and House of Lords (*The Marinegra* [1960] 2 Lloyd's Rep. 1). Even in purely nautical matters the Judge is not bound to follow the advice of his assessors, if it does not agree with his own opinion (see *The Magna Charta* (1872) 1 Asp. 153; *The Aid* (1881) 6 P.D. 84; *The Beryl* (1884) 9 P.D. 137, 141; *The Swanland* (1855) 2 Sp. 107; *The Fred* (1895) 7 Asp. 550; *Owners of SS. Melanie v. Owners of SS. San Onofre (No. 1)*; *Owners of SS. Australia v. Owners of Cargo of SS. Nautilus*, above; *The Spero* (1948) 81 Ll.L.Rep. 350 at 354 see *The British Resource* (1941) 70 Ll.L.Rep. 93 at 102, *per* du Parcq L.J., and *The Carrick Coast* (1948) 81 Ll.L.Rep. 447 at 451, *per* Willmer J.) as to judging ordinary navigating officers by the exceptionally high standard of knowledge and experience of the Elder Brethren. The assessors should not be asked any question that is tantamount to asking them whether they would find for the claimant or the defendant (see *The Ausonia* (1920) 2 L.L.Rep. 123 at 124, HL). The assessors in an appeal Court are not substituted for those previously consulted. They are additional but not to be preferred to them unless the advice given is such as in itself is more acceptable to the appellate Court (*The Sobieski* (1949) 82 Ll.L.Rep. 370 at 379). There is no question of appeal from one set of assessors to another set (*Owners of SS. Australia v. Owners of Cargo of SS. Nautilus*. See also *The Fina Canada* [1962] 2 Lloyd's Rep. 445). In *The St Chad* [1965] 2 Lloyd's Rep. 1, CA, Willmer L.J. pointed out that nautical assessors in the Court of Appeal and the Court below were of equal standing. He also said that it was their function to advise on nautical questions put to them by the Court whether or not such question had been canvassed by counsel. If there is a difference of opinion between assessors and a Judge cannot decide which advice is sound he must regard the point as not proven (see *The Dageld* (1947) 80 Ll.L.Rep. 517, reversing (1947) 80 Ll.L.Rep. 225 at 230; *Owners of S.S. Australia v. Owners of Cargo of SS. Nautilus*) but he may reach a decision by rejecting the advice of one assessor and accepting that of the other (see *The Taiwan* (1947) 80 Ll.L.Rep. 580, p. 586).

The Court of Appeal has been known to adopt the advice of Elder Brethren in the lower Court, rejecting that of their own assessors (*The Sobieski*, above; see also *The Miraflores and The Abadesa* [1966] P. 18; [1966] 1 All E.R. 553; [1966] 1 Lloyd's Rep. 97 at 108, *per* Willmer L.J. A Judge will not infrequently state in his judgment that he has sought advice on certain points, giving the results of having done so without detail, and saying whether he accepts or rejects the advice tendered (contrast *The Aurelian* [1957] 2 Lloyd's Rep. 417 at 422, where Willmer J. set out verbatim in his judgment the questions put to the Elder Brother). Questions and answers are in writing in the Court of Appeal.

As to assessors' fees, see SCP 1999, Vol. 2, Section 6, para. 6C–1; *mutatis mutandis* the fees in the High Court and CA are the same.

49FPD–011

Claim Form (Admiralty claim in rem)

In the High Court of Justice Queen's Bench Division Admiralty Court	
Claim No.	
Issue date	

Admiralty claim in rem against

SEAL

of the Port of

Claimant

Defendant(s)

Brief details of claim

The Admiralty Registry within the Royal Courts of Justice, Strand, London WC2A 2LC is open between 10am and 4.30pm Monday to Friday. District Registries with Admiralty jurisdiction are open between 10am and 4pm.
Please address all correspondence to the admiralty registry and quote the claim number.

ADM1 Claim form (Admiralty action in rem) **(4.99)** *Printed on behalf of The Court Service*

Claim No.	

Particulars of Claim (attached) (to follow)

Statement of Truth

* (I believe) (The Claimant believes) that the facts stated in these particulars of claim are true.

* I am duly authorised by the claimant to sign this statement

Full name ____________________

Name of claimant's solicitor's firm ____________________

signed ____________________

* (Claimant) (Litigation friend) (Claimant's solicitor)

position or office held ____________________

(if signing on behalf of firm or company)

* delete as appropriate

Claimant's or claimant's solicitor's address to which documents or payments should be sent if different from overleaf including (if appropriate) details of DX, fax or e-mail.

49FPD–012

Notes for Claimant on completing an IN REM claim form

Further information may be obtained from the Admiralty & Commercial Registry, room E200 Royal Courts of Justice, London, WC2A 2LL. Tel. 0171 936 6112 Fax. 0171 936 6245.

Please read all these guidance notes before you begin completing the claim form. The notes follow the order in which information is required on the form.

You may only issue an IN REM claim form in the Admiralty Court of the High Court (The High Court means either a District Registry attached to a County Court or the Royal Courts of Justice in London).

Staff can help you fill in the claim form and give information about procedure once it has been issued. But they cannot give legal advice. If you need legal advice, for example, about the likely success of your claim or the evidence you need to prove it, you should contact a solicitor or a Citizens Advice Bureau.

If you are filling in the claim form by hand, please use black ink and write in block capitals.

Copy the completed claim form and the defendant's notes for guidance so that you have one copy for yourself, one copy for the court and one copy for each Defendant. **You will need an additional copy of the claim form if you are seeking to arrest a vessel.** Send or take the forms to the court office with the appropriate fee. The court will tell you how much this is.

N.B. The time for filing an Acknowledgment of Service in an IN REM claim is within 14 days of service of the CLAIM FORM irrespective of whether or not the PARTICULARS OF CLAIM are served with it. The CLAIM FORM must therefore be served with the forms on which the defendant may reply to your claim.

Notes on completing the claim form

Heading

You should add to the heading the name of the court in which you are issuing:
either 'Royal Courts of Justice' or
'......................... District Registry'
(inserting name of the District Registry)

Ship and port details

You should supply the name of the vessel or vessels you are proceeding against and the **Port of Registry** (**not** the Port where the vessel may be berthed). If you do not know the Port of Registry you should insert 'port of registry unknown'. If you are proceeding in addition or separately against other property, e.g. cargo, you should describe it.

Claimant details

As the person issuing the claim, you are called the 'claimant'. The person you are suing is called the 'defendant'. Claimants who are under 18 years old (unless otherwise permitted by the court) or patients within the meaning of the Mental Health Act 1983, must have a litigation friend to issue and conduct court proceedings on their behalf. Court staff will tell you more about what you need to do if this applies to you.

The Claimant in an in rem claim, whether or not an individual, may be named or described. If not named, you must provide a name upon the request of any other party. If described rather than named you must still give an address. See below as to the appropriate address.

Descriptions that may be used are 'The owners of the ship 'X' or 'The owners of cargo lately laden on board the vessel 'Y'. Court staff can advise you of other acceptable descriptions.

You must provide the following information about yourself according to the capacity in which you are suing. When suing as:—

an individual by name:
All known forenames and surname, (whether Mr, Mrs, Miss, Ms or Other e.g. Dr) and residential address (including postcode and telephone number) in England and Wales.

an individual by name who is under 18 write '(a child by Mr John Smith his litigation friend)' after the child's name

a patient within the meaning of the Mental Health Act 1983
write "(by Mr John Smith his litigation friend)" after the patient's name.

as an individual trading under another name
you must add the words "trading as" and the trading name e.g. "Mr John Smith trading as Smith's Groceries".

in a representative capacity
you must say what that capacity is e.g. "Mr John Smith as the representative of Mrs Mary Smith (deceased)".

in the name of a club or other unincorporated association
add the words "suing on behalf of" followed by the name of the club or other unincorporated association.

a firm
Enter the name of the firm followed by the words "a firm" e.g. "Bandbox – a firm" and an address for service which is either a partner's residential address or the principal or last known place of business.

ADMIB Notes for claimant IN REM (4.99) *Printed on behalf of The Court Service*

a corporation (other than a company)
Enter the full name of the corporation and the address which is either its principal office or any other place where the corporation carries on activities and which has a real connection with the claim

a company registered in England and Wales:
Enter the name of the company and an address which is either the company's registered office or any place of business that has a real, or the most, connection with the claim.

an overseas company (defined by s744 of the Companies Act 1985):
Enter the name of the company and either the address registered under s691 of the Act or the address of the place of business having a real or the most, connection with the claim.

Defendant details

The defendant **must** be described and not named.

'The owners and/or demise charterers of the ship Z', unless it is known that the ship either is, or is not, under demise charter when the claim can be issued simply against 'the owners of the ship Z' or 'the demise charterers of the ship Z'.

In ownership and/or possession actions, the defendant may be described as 'all other persons claiming ownership and/or possession of the ship A'.

When action is taken against cargo and/or freight the defendant may be described as 'owners of cargo now or lately laden on board the ship X' together with the freight earned thereon.

The defendant in an action against the proceeds of a Judicial sale by the Admiralty Marshal should be described as 'the owners of the proceeds of sale of the vessel Y'

Permutations of the above can be used as appropriate. The Court staff will advise you as necessary.

Brief details of claim

Note: the facts and full details about your claim should be set out in the 'particulars of claim' (see note under 'Particular of Claim')

You must set out under **this** heading:

- a concise statement of the nature of your claim in rem
- the remedy you are seeking
- if your claim is for money, the amount you are claiming
- the amount of any interest you are claiming.

If your claim is in foreign currency you should endorse the claim form with a certificate as to the sterling equivalent. Court staff will inform you of the appropriate certificate.

Particulars of claim

You may include your particulars of claim on the claim form in the space provided or in a separate document which you should head 'Particulars of Claim'. It should include the names and/or descriptions of the parties, the court, the claim number and your address for service and also contain a statement of truth. You should keep a copy for yourself, provide one for the court and one for each defendant.

Separate particulars of claim can either be served

- with the claim form **or**
- within 75 days after the date on which the claim form was served, provided that the service of the particulars of claim is not later than 12 months from the date of issue of the claim form.

Note: If the particulars of claim are not contained or served with the claim form you must include the following statement 'Particulars of claim will follow if an acknowledgment of service is filed indicating an intention to defend the claim'.

Your particulars of claim must include

- a concise statement of the facts on which you rely
- a statement (if applicable) to the effect that you are seeking aggravated damages or exemplary damages
- details of any interest which you are claiming
- any other matters required for your type of claim as set out in the relevant practice directions

Note: You are not required to complete and serve particulars of claim if your claim is in respect of a collision between ships.

Address for documents

Insert in this box the address at which you wish to receive documents and/or payments, if different from the address you have already given under the heading 'Claimant'. The address must be in England or Wales. If you are willing to accept service by DX, fax or e-mail, add details.

Statement of truth

This must be signed by you, by your solicitor or your litigation friend, as appropriate.

Where the claimant is a registered company or a corporation the claim must be signed by either the director, treasurer, secretary, chief executive, manager or other officer of the company or (in the case of a corporation) the mayor, chairman, president or town clerk.

49FPD–013

Notes for defendant on replying to an in REM claim form

Please read these notes carefully—they may help you decide what to do about this claim. Further information can be obained from the Admiralty & Commercial Registry, Royal Courts of Justice, Strand, London, WC2A 2LL.

You must file an acknowledgement of service within 14 days of the date of service of the Claim Form on your property (or a Solicitor acting on your behalf) irrespective of whether or not particulars of claim are served with it.

If you do not file an acknowledgment of service, judgment may be given against you and if the property described on the claim form is under arrest of this court, it may be sold by order of the court.

You may either:

- pay the amount claimed
- provide security for the claim in a form acceptable to the Claimant
- admit that you owe all or part of the claim and ask for time to pay or
- dispute the claim.

The notes below tell you what to do.

The response pack, which should accompany the claim form, will tell you which forms to use for your reply.

Court staff can help you complete the forms of reply and tell you about court procedures. But they cannot give legal advice. If you need legal advice, for example about the likely success of disputing the claim, you should contact a solicitor or a Citizens Advice Bureau immediately.

Costs and Interest: Additional costs and interest may be added to the amount claimed on the front of the claim form if judgment is given against you.

Once your completed acknowledgment of service is received by the court, the claimant will send you the particulars of claim, unless previously sent to you.

Your response and what happens next

How to pay

Do not bring any payments to the court—they will not be accepted.

When making payments to the claimant, quote the claimant's reference (if any) and the claim number.

Make sure that you keep records and can account for any payments made. Proof may be required if there is any disagreement. It is not safe to send cash unless you use registered post.

Admitting the Claim

Claim for specified amount

If you admit all the claim, take or send the money, including any interest and costs, to the claimant at the address given for payment on the claim form within 14 days of receipt of the particulars of claim.

If you admit all the claim and you are asking for time to pay, complete Form N9A and send it to the claimant at the address given for payment on the claim form, within 14 days of receipt of the particulars of claim. The claimant will decide whether to accept your proposal for payment. If it accepted, the claimant may request a judge to give judgment against you and you will be sent an order to pay. If your offer is not accepted, the judge will decide how you should pay or, if your vessel is under arrest, may order that your vessel be sold in order to satisfy the judgment.

If you admit only part of the claim, complete Form N9A and Form N9B (see "Disputing the Claim" overleaf) send them to the court within 14 days of receipt of the particulars of claim. At the same time send copies of the completed Forms N9A and N9B to the claimant who will decide whether to accept your part admission. If it is accepted, the claimant may request a judge to give judgment against you and the court will send you an order to pay or, if your vessel is under arrest, order that your vessel be sold in order to satisfy the judgment. If your part admission is not accepted, the case will proceed as a defended claim.

Claim for unspecified amount

If you admit liability for the whole claim but do not make an offer to satisfy the claim, complete Form N9C and send it to the court within 14 days of receipt of the particulars of claim. At the same time send a copy of the completed Form N9C to the claimant within the same period. The claimant may request a Judge to give judgment against you for an amount to be decided by the court, and costs. If your vessel is under arrest, the Judge may at the same time order that your vessel be sold.

If you admit liability for the claim and offer an amount of money to satisfy the claim, of receipt of the particulars of claim. At the same time send a copy of the completed Form N9C to the claimant. The claimant must indicate within 14 days if the offer is acceptable.

ADMIC Defendants notes (4,99) *Printed on behalf of The Court Service* and send you a copy. If a reply is not received, the claim will be stayed. If the amount you have offered is **accepted**, the claimant may request a Judge to give judgment against you for that amount.

If you have requested time to pay which is not accepted by the claimant, the rate of payment will be decided by the court, or, if your vessel is under arrest the court may order the vessel to be sold by the court.

If your offer in satisfaction is not accepted.

The claimant may apply to the court for judgment against you for an amount to be decided by the court, and costs.

If your vessel is under arrest, order that your vessel be sold. You and the claimant will be sent a copy of the court's order.

Disputing the Claim

If you are being sued as an individual for a specified amount of money and you dispute the claim, the claim may be transferred to your home court i.e. the one nearest your home or your solicitor's business address if different from the court where the claim was issued.

If you need longer than 14 days to prepare your defence or to contest the court's jurisdiction to try the claim, completion of the acknowledgement of service form will allow you 28 days from the date of service of the particulars of claim to serve your defence or make an application to contest the court's jurisdiction. The court will tell the claimant that your acknowledgment of service has been received.

If the case proceeds as a defended claim, the action will be allocated to the multi-track and the claimant will apply for a date to be fixed for a Case Management Conference before a Judge. You and the claimant will be required to file a completed case management information sheet at least 7 days before the Conference.

Further details are available from the Admiralty & Commercial Registry.

If your vessel is under the arrest of the court and you are disputing the claim you may nevertheless obtain the release of the vessel is you are able to offer security for the claim in a form acceptable by the claimant.

Claim for specified amount

If you wish to dispute the full amount claimed or wish to claim against the claimant (a counterclaim), complete Form N9B and send it to the court within 14 days of receipt of the particulars of claim. Send a copy of the completed Form N9B to the claimant within the same period.

If you admit part of the claim, complete the defence Form N9B and the Admission Form N9A and send them to the court within 14 days of receipt of the particulars of claim. At the same time send copies of the completed Forms N9B and N9A to the claimant within the same period.

If you dispute the claim because you have already paid it, complete Form N9B and send it to the court within 14 days of receipt of the particulars of claim. At the same time send a copy of the completed Form N9B to the claimant within the same period. The claimant will decide whether to proceed with the claim or withdraw it and notify the court and you within 28 days. If the claimant wishes to proceed, the case will proceed as a defended claim.

Claim for unspecified amount/non-money claims

If you dispute the claim or wish to claim against the claimant (counterclaim), complete Form N9D and send it to the court within 14 days of receipt of the particulars of claim. At the same time send a copy of the completed Form N9D to the claimant.

Personal injuries claims:

If the claim is for personal injuries and the claimant has attached a medical report to the particulars of claim, in your defence you should state whether you:

agree with the report **or**

dispute all or part of the report **and** give

your reasons for doing so **or**

neither agree nor dispute the report **or**

have no knowledge of the report

Where you have obtained your own medical report you should attach it to your defence.

If the claim is for personal injuries and the claimant has attached a schedule of past and future expenses and losses, in your defence you must state which of the items you:

agree **or**

dispute **and** supply alternative figures where appropriate **or**

neither agree nor dispute or have no knowledge of

Statement of truth

This must be signed by you, by your solicitor or your litigation friend, as appropriate.

Where the defendant is **a registered company or a corporation** the response must be signed by either the director, treasurer, secretary, chief executive, manager or other officer of the company **or** (in the case of a corporation) the mayor, chairman, president or town clerk.

49FPD–014

Response Pack
Admiralty claim in rem

You should read the 'notes for defendant' attached to the claim form which will tell you when and where to send the forms

Included in this pack are:

- either **Admission Form N9A** (if the claim is for a specified amount) or **Admission Form N9C** (if the claim for an unspecified amount or is not a claim for money)
- either **Defence and Counterclaim Form N9B** (if the claim is for a specified amount) or **Defence and Counterclaim Form N9D** (if the claim is for an unspecified amount or is not a claim for money)
- **Acknowledgment of service** (see below)

You are required to complete an Acknowledgement of Service form within 14 days from service of the Claim Form on you whether or not Particulars of claim are served with the Claim Form.

	Complete
If you admit the claim or the amount claimed and/or you want time to pay	the admission form
If you admit part of the claim	the admission form and the defence form
If you dispute the whole claim or wish to make a claim (a counterclaim) against the claimant	the defence form
If you need longer than 14 days to prepare your defence or to contest the court's jurisdiction to try the claim, completion of the acknowledgment of service form will allow you 28 days from service of particulars of claim to do so	the acknowledgment of service
If you do nothing, judgment may be entered against you	

Acknowledgment of Service
Admiralty claim in rem

In the High Court of Justice **Queen's Bench Division** **Admiralty Court**	
Claim No.	
Claimant(s) (including ref.)	
Defendant(s)	

Description of defendant(s):—

Full name of person described above:—

Nature of ownership of property

The court office at

is open between 10 am and 4.30 pm Monday to Friday. Please address forms or letters to the Court Manager and quote the claim number.

ADM2 Acknowledgment of Service (4.99) *Printed on behalf of The Court Service*

Address to which documents about this claim should be sent (including reference if appropriate)

			if applicable	
			fax no.	
			DX no.	
Tel. no.	Postcode		e-mail	

If you do not file an acknowledgment of service within 14 days of the claim form on you, whether or not particulars of claim are served with it, judgment may be given against you.

Tick the appropriate box

1. I intend to defend all of this claim ☐
2. I intend to defend part of this claim ☐
3. I intend to contest jurisdiction ☐

If you file an acknowledgment of service but do not file a defence within 28 days of the date of service of the particulars of claim, judgment may be given against you.

If you do not file an application within 28 days of the date of service of the particulars of claim it will be assumed that you accept the court's jurisdiction and judgment may be given against you.

Signed		**Position or office held** (if signing on behalf of firm or company)		
	(Defendant) (Defendant's Solicitor) (Litigation friend)			**Date**

49FPD–014

Warrant of Arrest

In the High Court of Justice Queen's Bench Division Admiralty Court	
Claim No.	

Admiralty action in rem against:

Claimant(s)

Defendant(s)

ELIZABETH THE SECOND, by the Grace of God, of the United Kingdom of Great Britain and Northern Ireland and of Our other realms and territories Queen, Head of the Commonwealth, Defender of the Faith:

To the Admiralty Marshal of Our High Court of Justice, and to all singular his substitutes, Greeting.

We hereby command you to arrest the ship

of the port of and to keep same under arrest until you should receive further orders from Us.

WITNESS , Lord High Chancellor of Great Britain,

the day of

The Claimant's claim is for [copy from Claim Form]

Take out by

Solicitors for the

ADM9 Warrant of arrest **(4.99)** *Printed on behalf of The Court Service*

Certificate as to Service

On the day of

the within-named ship

lying at

was arrested by virtue of

for a short time on*

of the said ship, and on taking off the process, by leaving a copy thereof fixed in its place.

Signed ______________________ Date______________________

*State on which parts of the outside of the ship's superstructure

49FPD–015

Claim Form (Admiralty limitation claim)

In the High Court of Justice Queen's Bench Division Admiralty Court	
Claim No.	
Issue date	

Claimant(s)

SEAL

Defendant(s)

Details of limitation claim *(see also overleaf)*

Named defendant's name and address

The Admiralty Registry within the Royal Courts of Justice, Strand, London WC2A 2LC is open between 10am and 4.30pm Monday to Friday.
District Registries with Admiralty jurisdiction are open between 10am and 4pm.
Please address all correspondence to the admiralty registry and quote the claim number.

ADM15 Claim form Admiralty limitation claim (4.99) *Printed on behalf of The Court Service*

Claim No.	

Details of limitation claim *(continued)*

Full name ______________________________

Name of claimant's solicitor's firm ______________________________

signed ______________________ position or office held ______________________

*(Claimant) (Litigation friend) (Claimant's solicitor) (if signing on behalf of firm or company)

*delete as appropriate

Claimant's or claimant's solicitor's address to which documents or payments should be sent if different from overleaf including (if appropriate) details of DX, fax or e-mail.

49FPD–016

Notes for claimant on completing a claim form in an admiralty limitation claim

Further information may be obtained from the Admiralty and Commercial Registry, room E200 Royal Courts of Justice, London, WC2A 2LL. Tel. 0171 936 6112 Fax. 0171 936 6245.

Please read all these guidance notes before you begin completing the claim form. The notes generally follow the order in which information is required on the form.

You may only issue an Admiralty Limitation Claim Form in the Admiralty Court of the High Court (The High Court means either a District Registry (attached to a County Court) or the Royal Courts of Justice in London).

Staff can help you fill in the claim form and give information about the procedure once it has been issued. But they cannot give legal advice. If you need legal advice, for example, about the likely success of your claim or the evidence you need to prove it, you should contact a solicitor or a Citizens Advice Bureau.

If you are filling in the claim form by hand, please use black ink and write in block capitals.

You should file a sworn declaration at the court with your completed claim form:

- proving the facts you rely on in your claim; and
- stating the names and addresses (if known) of all persons who to your knowledge have claims against you in respect of the occurrence to which the claim relates (other than named defendants)

Copy the completed claim form, the defendant's notes for guidance and your sworn declaration so that you have one copy for yourself, one for the court and one for each 'named' defendant (see defendant details below). Send or take the forms to the court office with the appropriate fee. The court will tell you how much this is.

Each named defendant must be served with copies of the claim form, notes for guidance, your declaration and a response pack (ADM Form Nos 15, 15A, 15B, 16 and 16A)

Notes on completing the claim form

Heading

You should add to the heading the name of the court in which you are issuing:

either 'Royal Courts of Justice' or

'......................... District Registry'

(inserting name of the District Registry)

Defendant details

At least one of the defendants in a limitation claim **must** be named.

All other defendants may be described e.g. 'and all other persons claiming or being entitled to claim damages by reason of, or rising out of the collision between the ship "Alpha" and the ship "Omega" which occurred in the English Channel on or about the 6th October, 1999'.

Claimant and named defendant details

The Claimant must be named not described.

As the person issuing the claim, you are called the 'claimant'; the person you are suing is called the 'defendant'. Claimants who are under 18 years old (unless otherwise permitted by the court) and patients within the meaning of the Mental Health Act 1983 must have a litigation friend to issue and conduct court proceedings on their behalf. Court staff will tell you more about what you need to do if this applies to you.

You must provide the following information about yourself **and** the named defendants according to the capacity in which you are suing and in which the defendant is being sued.

When suing or being sued as:—

an individual: All known forenames and surname, (whether Mr, Mrs, Miss, Ms or Other e.g. Dr) and residential address (**including** postcode and telephone no. and any fax or e-mail number) in England and Wales. Where the defendant is a proprietor of a business, a partner in a firm or an individual sued in the name of a club or other unincorporated association, the address for service should be the usual or last known place of residence **or** principal place of business of the company, firm or club or other unincorporated association.

Where the individual is: under 18 write '(a child by Mr John Smith his litigation friend)' after the child's name.

If the child is conducting proceedings on their own behalf write '(a child)' after the child's name.

a patient within the meaning of the Mental Health Act 1983 write '(by Mr John Smith his litigation friend)' after the patient's name.

trading under another name you must add the words 'trading as' and the trading name e.g. 'Mr John Smith trading as Smith's Groceries'.

ADMI5A Notes for defendant (4.99) *Printed on behalf of The Court Service*

suing or being sued in a representative capacity you must say what that capacity is e.g. 'Mr John Smith as the representative of Mrs Mary Smith (deceased)'.

suing or being sued in the name of a club or other unincorporated association add the words 'suing/sued on behalf of' followed by the name of the club or other unincorporated association.

a firm enter the name of the firm followed by the words 'a firm' e.g. 'Bandbox—a firm' and an address for service which is either a partner's residential address or the principal or last known place of business.

a corporation (other than a company) enter the full name of the corporation and the address which is either its principal office **or** any other place where the corporation carries on activities and which has a real connection with the claim.

a company registered in England and Wales enter the name of the company and an address which is either the company's registered office **or** any place of business that has a real, or the most, connection with the claim.

an overseas company (defined by s744 of the Companies Act 1985) enter the name of the company and either the address registered under s691 of the Act **or** the address of the place of business having a real, or the most, connection with the claim.

Details of claim

Under this heading you must set out:

- a brief description of the incident for which you are claiming to have your liability limited, including the date and place of the incident
- that your claim is limited to the provisions of the Merchant Shipping Act 1995
- that you are seeking all necessary and proper directions for the purposes of ascertaining and distributing the amount of your liability between the parties who are entitled to receive it.

Named defendant's name and address

Enter in this box the full name and address of the named defendant(s) to be served with the claim form (i.e. one claim form for each defendant)

An Admiralty Limitation Claim form may NOT be served outside of England & Wales unless:

(a) the case falls within section 22(2)(a) to (c) of the Supreme Court Act 1981; or

(b) the defendant has submitted to or agreed to submit to the jurisdiction of the Admiralty Court; or

(c) the Admiralty Court has jurisdiction over such claim under any applicable Convention.

Address for documents

Insert in this box the address at which you wish to receive documents, if different from the address you have already given under the heading 'Claimant'. The address you give must be either that of your solicitors or your residential or business address and must be in England and Wales. If you live or carry on business outside of England and Wales, you can give some other address within England and Wales. If you are willing to accept service by DX, fax or e-mail, add details.

49FPD–017

Notes for defendant (admiralty limitation claim)

Please read these notes carefully—they will help you decide what to do about this claim.

Further information may be obtained from the Admiralty and Commercial Registry, Room E200, Royal Courts of Justice, Strand, London WC2A 2LL. Tel: 0171 936 6112. Fax: 0171 936 6245.

You have only a limited time to reply to this claim—the notes below tell you what to do.

You may either:

dispute the court's jurisdiction or contend that the court should not exercise it

admit the claimant's right to limit liability

dispute the claim

The response pack, which should accompany the claim form, will tell you which forms to use for your reply

If you **do not** respond in any way the court may grant the claimant a Limitation Decree in your absence.

Court staff can tell you about procedures but they cannot give legal advice. If you need legal advice, you should contact a solicitor or Citizens Advice Bureau immediately.

Responding to this claim

Time for responding

You have from the date the claim form was served on you: 14 days to file an acknowledgment of service disputing the court's jurisdiction.

or

28 days to file a completed defence or admission of the claimant's right to limit liability

(or, if the claim form was served outside of England and Wales, within the time specified by RSC Order 11 r.1A.)

If the claim form was:

- sent by post, the date of service is taken as the second day after posting (see date of postmark on the envelope)
- delivered or left at your address, the date of service will be the day after it was delivered.
- handed to you personally, the date of service will be the day it was given to you.

Completing the acknowledgment of service

You should tick either

- Box A—if you dispute the court's jurisdiction **or**
- Box B—if you contend that the court should not exercise its jurisdiction

and complete all the other details on the form.

You should send the completed form to the court and at the same time send a copy to the claimant.

You should file also an application at the court within 14 days of filing of your acknowledgment of service. The court will arrange a hearing date for the application. If you do not file the application you will be treated as having accepted that the court has jurisdiction to hear the claim.

Completing the admission

You should complete admission form ADM16 and send it to the court and at the same time send a copy to the claimant. The claimant may file an application for the court to issue a restricted limitation decree limiting liability against any of the named defendants in the claim form who have filed an admission.

Completing the defence

You should file defence form ADM16A at the court and at the same time send a copy to the claimant. Within 7 days of filing of your defence (or filing of defence of other named defendants or expiry of the time for doing so) the claimant must apply for an appointment before the Admiralty Registrar for a case management conference. The court will give directions at this appointment for the future conduct of the case.

Statement of truth

This must be signed by you, by your solicitor or your litigation friend, as appropriate.

If you do nothing

The claimant may apply for a limitation decree against you.

ADM15B Notes for Defendant (4.99) *Printed on behalf of The Court Service*

49FPD–018

Notice of admission of right of claimant to limit liability

In the High Court of Justice Queen's Bench Division Admiralty Court	
Claim No.	

Claimant(s)

Defendant(s)

TAKE NOTICE THAT pursuant to Part Y, rule 8.1(7) Admiralty Proceedings, the following defendant(s) *(name them)*

admit the right of the claimant in this actioin to limit their liability in accordance with the provisions of *(give details of the relevant Act)*

Signed

Date

ADM16 Notice of admission of right of claimant to limit liability (4.99) *Printed on behalf of The Court Service*

49FPD–019

Defence to admiralty limitation claim

In the High Court of Justice
Queen's Bench Division
Admiralty Court

Claim No.	

Claimant(s)

Defendant(s)

You have a limited number of days to file and serve this form. See notes for guidance attached to the claim form.

Signed
(To be signed by you or by your solicitor or litigation friend)

*(I believe)(The defendant believes) that the facts stated in this form are true. *I am duly authorised by the defendant to sign this statement

**delete as appropriate*

Position or office held
(if signing on behalf of firm or company)

Date

Give an address to which notices about this case can be sent to you

Postcode

Tel. no.

if applicable	
fax no.	
DX no.	
e-mail	

ADM16A Defence to admiralty limitation claim (4.99)

Printed on behalf of The Court Service

49FPD–020

Response Pack
(Admiralty Limitation claim)
Included in this pack are:

You should read the 'notes for defendant' attached to the claim form which will tell you when and where to send the forms

Admission Form ADM16	Defence Form ADM16A	**Acknowledgment of service** *(see below)*

	Complete
If you wish to dispute the court's jurisdiction or argue that the court should not exercise its jurisdiction	**the acknowledgment of service**
If you admit the right of the claimant to limit liability	**the admission form**
If you dispute the claim	**the defence form**
If you do nothing, the claimant may apply for a restricted limitation decree against you	

Acknowledgment of Service
(Admiralty limitation claim)

Defendant's full name if different from the name given on the claim form

. . . .

. . . .

In the High Court of Justice Queen's Bench Division Admiralty Court	
Claim No.	
Claimant (including ref.)	
Defendant	

Address to which documents about this claim should be sent (including reference if appropriate)

		if applicable
	fax no.	
	DX no.	
Tel. no. Postcode	e-mail	

Tick the appropriate box

A I intend to dispute jurisdiction ☐

B I intend to argue that the court should not exercise its jurisdiction ☐

You should file an application at the court within 14 days of service of this acknowledgment of service or you will be treated as having accepted the court's jurisdiction.

Signed		**Position or office held** (if signing on behalf of firm or company)		**Date**
	(Defendant) (Defendant's solicitor) (Litigation friend)			

The Admiralty Registry within the Royal Courts of Justice, Strand, London WC2A 2LC is open between 10am and 4.30pm Monday to Friday. District Registries with Admiralty jurisdiction are open between 10am and 4pm.
Please address all correspondence to the admiralty registry and quote the claim number.

ADM16B Response Pack (4.99)

Printed on behalf of The Court Service

PRACTICE DIRECTION—ARBITRATIONS

This Practice Direction supplements CPR, Part 49 and replaces, with modifications, Order 73 of the Rules of the Supreme Court

Editorial Introduction

Part I of the Practice Direction is concerned with applications to which the Arbitration Act 1996 applies, Pt II is concerned with matters to which the old law applies, and Pt III with common enforcement procedures. **49GPD–001**

"The old law" means the enactments specified in section 107 of the Arbitration Act 1996 as they stood before their amendment or repeal by the Act, namely the Arbitration Act 1950 (see SCP 1999, Vol. 2, Section 21A, paras 21A–1 *et seq.*); the Arbitration Act 1975 (see SCP 1999, Vol. 2, Section 21B, paras 21B–1 *et seq.*) and the Arbitration Act 1979 (see SCP 1999, Vol. 2, Section 21C, paras 21C–1 *et seq.*).

The old law is preserved as a result of the provisions of section 109(2) of the Arbitration Act 1996 which provided that any order bringing the Act into force might contain any transitional provisions as might appear necessary and the provisions of the Arbitration Act 1996 (Commencement No. 1) Order 1996, made on December 16, 1996, by way of transitional provision, provide that:

2. The old law shall continue to apply to:
   (a) arbitral proceedings commenced before the appointed day [January 31, 1997];
   (b) arbitration applications commenced or made before the appointed day;
   (c) arbitration applications commenced or made on or after the appointed day relating to arbitral proceedings commenced before the appointed day;

and the provisions of the Act which would otherwise be applicable shall not apply.

General note—Arbitration procedure—Commercial court guide—Section M of the Commercial Court Guide (5th ed.) provides:

M1 *Applications relating to arbitrations*

M1.1 The Arbitration Practice Direction continues the procedure existing before the introduction of the CPR (*i.e.* the procedure under RSC, O. 73), save for minor changes necessitated by the new forms of originating and subsidiary process.

M1.2 The additional applicable practice for applications relating to arbitrations (adapted from that previously set out in the Fourth Edition of the Guide) is set out at Appendix 19 [see below]

M2 *Orders for transfer*

M2.1 Orders for transfer to lists other than the Commercial List will normally be made, if no significant point of arbitration law or practice is raised:
   (a) in rent-review arbitrations to a Judge of the Chancery Division;
   (b) in building and civil engineering arbitrations to a Judge of the Technology and Construction Court.

Salvage arbitrations will normally be transferred to the Admiralty Judge.

M2.2 Applications relating to arbitration which are not required by the CPR to be heard by a Commercial Judge should not normally be issued in the Commercial List unless they concern:
   (a) a commercial arbitration; or
   (b) a significant point of arbitration law or practice.

M3 *Service of arbitration forms*

M3.1 In accordance with paragraph 8.3 of the Commercial Court Practice Direction, arbitration forms in the Commercial List are to be served by the parties, not by the Registry.

M4 *Appointment of a Commercial Judge as sole arbitrator or umpire*

M4.1 Provision allowing the appointment of a Commercial Judge as sole arbitrator or as umpire is made under section 93 of the Arbitration Act 1996. The Act limits the circumstances in which a Judge may accept such an appointment.

M4.2 Enquiries in this regard should be directed to the Judge in charge of the Commercial List or the Clerk to the Commercial Court.

Appendix 19 to the Commercial Court Guide (5th ed.) is entitled "Arbitration Matters: Related Practice" and provides as follows:

Generally—The procedure to be used in arbitration matters differs according to whether or not the Arbitration Act 1996 applies to the arbitration matter to be raised. The 1996 Act applies in general to all arbitrations commenced on or after January 31, 1997 and to applications to the court made on or after that date in respect of arbitrations yet to be commenced.

Part I of the Arbitration Practice Direction applies to arbitration matters covered by the 1996 Act, whereas Pt II of the Arbitration Practice Direction applies to matters covered by the Arbitration Acts 1950, 1975 and 1979. Part III of the Arbitration Practice Direction relates to enforcement of arbitration awards and contains a procedural regime of universal application regardless of the date when the arbitration was commenced.

The Commercial Court will continue to have primary responsibility for the administration and monitoring of the supervisory jurisdiction over arbitration and awards under the 1996 Act. Although such applications can be made not only in the Commercial Court but also in the Mercantile Courts, and the Business Lists at the Central London County Court or elsewhere, the decision whether to retain the application in a Mercantile List or Business List or to transfer it to the Commercial Court or to some other court is to be taken by the Mercantile Judge or Business List Judge, but in consultation with the Judge in charge of the Commercial List.

In giving effect to the 1996 Act and to the Arbitration Practice Direction the Judges of the Commercial Court will endeavour as far as possible to achieve consistency in matters of construction both of the Act and of the Arbitration Practice Direction. In order to facilitate consistency of approach, arrangements have been made for decisions on matters of construction and application to be circulated between the Judges immediately they are given. Members of the profession who identify particular problems in the working of the Arbitration Practice Direction are strongly encouraged to bring them to the attention of the Judge in charge of the Commercial List to enable the Judges to carry out their function of monitoring the effective working of the 1996 Act and the Arbitration Practice Direction.

Commencement—In respect of arbitrations to which the 1996 Act does not apply arbitration matters are normally raised in proceedings commenced by an arbitration claim form under CPR, Pt 8 (paragraphs 24–25 of the Arbitration Practice Direction), or in some cases by an application notice (paragraph 25(3) of the Arbitration Practice Direction).

In respect of arbitrations to which the 1996 Act does apply arbitration matters are raised in proceedings commenced by an arbitration claim form in the required practice form. The same practice form is used as the application notice for applications under section 9 of the 1996 Act to stay legal proceedings (paragraph 6 of the Arbitration Practice Direction).

The required practice form is to be used for all applications in respect of arbitration to which the 1996 Act applies except enforcement and including applications to stay judicial proceedings, to determine issues as to jurisdiction, to enforce peremptory orders, to make orders in support of arbitral proceedings, to challenge awards on the grounds of want of jurisdiction or serious irregularity and including appeals on a question of law arising out of an award. The form is also to be used at the permission to appeal stage under section 69 of the 1996 Act.

Applications for permission to enforce an award (whether under the 1996 Act or not) are made by an arbitration claim form in the required practice form: paragraph 31 of the Arbitration Practice Direction.

Progress—In arbitation matters it is the particular duty of the Court to see that court proceedings are not a cause of delay.

A hearing date must (where applicable) be applied for promptly after the issue of the required practice form (whether serving as an arbitration claim form or an application notice) or after obtaining permission to appeal under the Arbitration Acts 1979 and 1996.

The duty to apply promptly for a date for hearing exists even if the case may be transferred to the Chancery Division or to the Technology and Construction Court or to a Mercantile Court or Business List. The duty to act promptly persists after transfer.

A failure to act with all deliberate speed founds the Court's discretion to strike out. When it comes to the attention of the Court that delay is occurring, the Court may itself direct that the matter be listed for hearing.

Directions under Part I of the Arbitration Practice Direction—Paragraph 13 of the Arbitration Practice Direction contains a comprehensive series of directions relating to arbitration applications under Part I of the Arbitration Practice Direction. These directions will apply automatically unless the Court otherwise orders. The Judges of the Commercial Court will require strict compliance with these directions except with the permission of the Court. Parties who do not comply will risk the dates for hearings being vacated and/or adverse costs orders.

49GPD–002 **Requirements on applications by way of appeal under section 1(2) of the 1979 Act**—For applications by way of appeal under section 1(2) of the 1979 Act please see paragraph 27 of the Arbitration Practice Direction, in particular, at (6) to (9). Paragraphs 15 to 18 below amplify the practice.

Every arbitration application form used to appeal against an arbitration award under section 1(2) of the 1979 Act shall contain a succinct statement in numbered paragraphs of each ground upon which it is sought to contend that the arbitral tribunal erred in law. Reference shall be made to the paragraph or passage of the award and reasons where each alleged error is to be found. A copy of the award and reasons forming part of the award and any documents expressly incorporated in the award or such reasons shall accompany the arbitration application form when the same is issued unless the appeal arises from a minor part only of the award and reasons in which case the relevant extracts shall accompany the arbitration claim form.

Any respondent to an application by way of appeal under section 1(2) of the 1979 Act who contends that the award should be upheld on grounds not or not fully expressed in the award and reasons should provide to the applicant and to the Court not later than two clear days before the application for permission to appeal is listed for argument a succinct statement of such grounds in numbered paragraphs, with reference where appropriate to any relevant paragraphs or passage of the award and reasons.

Any statement provided under paragraphs 15 and 16 should contain specific reference to any authority relied on. A copy should be provided with the statement of any authority not contained in the Law Reports, the Weekly Law Reports, the All England Law Reports, Lloyd's Law Reports or the English Reports.

Where the applicant contends that any question of law arising out of an award concerns a term of contract or an event which is not a one-off clause or event, he shall serve on the respondent with his application and lodge with the Court an affidavit or witness statement setting out the facts relied on in support of his contention. A respondent who challenges that contention shall provide to the application and to the Court, not later than two days before the application is listed for argument, an affidavit or witness statement setting out the facts upon which he relies.

Evidence on applications for permission to enforce an award—Applications for permission to enforce an award must be supported by affidavit or witness statement (see paragraph 31 of the Arbitration Practice Direction) and two copies of a draft order must be provided. Care must be taken to see that the affidavit or witness statement and the draft order meet the requirements of the rule.

Determination of applications—For applications for permission to appeal under the 1979 Act there will not be a hearing but it will be expected to last more than half an hour. Any permission to appeal may be given on terms; these may restrict the points on which permssion to appeal is given or require the provision of security, etc. For the hearing of the substantive appeal the parties are expected to lodge skeleton arguments in the same way as for other contested hearings.

For applications for permission to appeal under the 1996 Act there will normally be no oral hearing of the application, unless the Court considers that one is required as provided by section 69(5) of the 1996 Act.

Substantive appeals and preliminary points of law are heard in public unless otherwise ordered.

All other arbitration applications are heard in private unless the Court orders that the hearing be in public.

Service on overseas parties and service out of the jurisdiction—For arbitration applications under Part I of the Arbitration Practice Direction, where an overseas party has been represented by an English solicitor who was authorised to accept service of notices or documents in the arbitration and has not determined that solicitor's authority to act in the arbitration, the arbitration claim form can, with the Court's authorisation, be served on that solicitor and it will be unnecessary to obtain permission to serve the party outside the jurisdiction (see paragraph 7(2) of the Arbitration Practice Direction).

Service out of the jurisdiction is covered by paragraph 8 of the Arbitration Practice Direction (1996 Act arbitrations) and paragraph 29 of the Arbitration Practice Direction (1950–1979 Act arbitrations).

Security for costs—The matters stated in Appendix 18 to the Commercial Court Guide are applicable to applications under section 12(6) of the Arbitration Act 1950 for the Court to exercise its power, for the purpose of and in relation to a reference, to make an order that a claimant give security for costs.

Multiple applications—Where applications are being made to set aside or remit under the 1950 Act and for permission to appeal under the 1979 Act the Court may direct that one application be heard before the other or that they may be heard together if that is appropriate. Multiple relief applications under the 1996 Act will be similarly dealt with.

Related Sources

- Arbitration Act 1950, Pt II (see SCP 1999, Vol. 2, Section 21A, paras 21A–288 to 21A–320).
- Arbitration Act 1996 (see SCP 1999, Vol. 2, Section 21D, paras 21D–1 *et seq.*).
- The preserved "old law"
  —Arbitration Act 1950, Pt I (see SCP 1999, Vol. 2, Section 21A).
  —Arbitration Acts 1975 and 1979 (see SCP 1999, Vol. 2, Sections 21B and 21C).
- High Court and County Court (Allocation of Arbitration Proceedings) Order 1996 (S.I. 1996 No. 3215), as amended.
- CPR 6.
- CPR 7.
- CPR 9, 10 and 11.
- RSC, O.11.

- RSC, O.12.
- The Commercial Court Guide (5th ed.) and in particular Section M and Appendix 19 (see above).

Forms—The following Prescribed Forms in Appendix A are relevant to the Arbitration Practice Direction.

- PF N8A—Arbitration application (para. 4(1)).
- PF N15A—Acknowledgment of Service of Arbitration Application (para. 11(1)).
- Part 8 Claim Form CPR, r. 8.6.

Part I

The overriding objective

49GPD–003 **1.** This Part of this practice direction is founded on the general principles in section 1 of the Arbitration Act and shall be construed accordingly.

Meaning of arbitration application

2.1 Subject to paragraph 22.2, "arbitration application" means the following—

(1) an application to the court under the Arbitration Act;

(2) proceedings to determine—

(a) whether there is a valid arbitration agreement;

(b) whether an arbitration tribunal is properly constituted;

(c) what matters have been submitted to arbitration in accordance with an arbitration agreement;

(3) proceedings to declare that an award made by an arbitral tribunal is not binding on a party;

(4) any other application affecting arbitration proceedings (whether instituted or anticipated) or to construe or affecting an arbitration agreement.

2.2 In this Part, an arbitration application does not include proceedings to enforce an award—

(1) to which Part III applies; or

(2) by a claim on the award.

Interpretation

3. In this Part—

"applicant" means the party making an arbitration application and references to respondent shall be construed accordingly;

"the Arbitration Act" means the Arbitration Act 1996 and any expressions used in this Part and in Part I of the Arbitration Act have the same meanings in this Part as they have in that Part of the Arbitration Act.

"arbitration claim form" means the arbitration claim form by the issue of which an arbitration application is begun.

Form and content of arbitration claim form

4.1 An arbitration claim form must be in the practice form No. 8A.

4.2 Every arbitration claim form must—

(1) include a concise statement of

(a) the remedy claimed, and

(b) (where appropriate) the questions on which the applicant seeks the determination or direction of the Court;

(2) give details of any arbitration award that is challenged by the applicant, showing the grounds for any such challenge;

(3) where the applicant caims an order for costs, identify the respondent against whom the claim is made,

(4) (where appropriate) specify the section of the Arbitration Act under which the application is brought; and

(5) show that any statutory requirements have been satisfied including those set out, by way of example, in the table below.

Application made	**Statutory requirements**
section 9 (stay of legal proceedings)	see section 9(3)
section 12 (extensions of time for beginning arbitral proceedings	see section 12(2)
section 18 (failure of appointment procedure)	see section 18(2)
section 21 (umpires)	see section 21(5)
section 24 (removal of arbitrators)	see section 24(2)
section 32 (preliminary point of jurisdiction)	see section 32(3)
section 42 (enforcement of peremptory orders)	see section 42(3)
section 44 (powers in support of arbitral proceedings)	see section 44(4), (5)
section 45 (preliminary point of law)	see section 45(3)
section 50 (extension of time for making award)	see section 50(2)
section 56 (power to withhold award)	see section 56(4)
sections 67, 68 (challenging the award)	see section 70(2), (3)
section 69 (appeal on point of law)	see sections 69(2), (4), 70(2), (3)
section 77 (service of documents)	see section 77(3)

4.3 The arbitration claim form must also state

(1) whether it is made on notice or without notice and, if made on notice, must give the names and addresses of the persons on whom it is to be served, stating their role in the arbitration and whether they are made respondents to the application;

(2) whether (having regard to paragraph 15) the application will be heard by a judge sitting in public or in private; and

(3) the date and time when the application will be heard or that such date has not yet been fixed.

4.4 Every arbitration claim form shall be indorsed with the applicant's address for service in accordance with CPR Rule 6.5(2).

Note—Form No. 8A is printed in Vol. 2 at Section 1A, para. 1A–4 and may be adapted as necessary.

Issue of arbitration claim form

5.1 These paragraphs (5.1 to 5.7) are to be read with the provisions of the High Court and County Courts (Allocation of Arbitration Proceedings) Order 1996 which allocates proceedings under the Arbitration Act to the High Court and the county courts and specifies proceedings which may be commenced or taken only in the High Court or in a county court.

5.2 These paragraphs (5.1 to 5.7) do not apply to applications under section 9 of the Arbitration Act to stay legal proceedings.

5.3 Subject to paragraphs 5.1 and 5.2 above, an arbitration claim form by which proceedings are commenced may be issued:

(1) out of the Admiralty and Commercial Registry in the Royal Courts of Justice, in which case the arbitration application will be entered into the commercial list;

(2) out of a district registry where a Mercantile Court has been established, in which case the arbitration application will be entered into the list of that Mercantile Court; or

(3) out of the office of the Central London County Court, in which case the arbitration application will be entered into the Business List of that court. (Attention is drawn to the provisions relating to the commencement of proceedings contained in the Commercial Court Practice Direction and the Mercantile Court and Business Lists Practice Direction which supplement CPR Part 49).

5.4 Except where an arbitration claim form is issued out of the Admiralty and Commercial Registry, the Judge in charge of the list into which the arbitration application has been entered shall

(1) as soon as practicable after the issue of the arbitration claim form, and

(2) in consultation with the Judge in charge of the commercial list,

consider whether the application should be transferred to the Commercial Court or to any another list.

5.5 Where an arbitration claim form is issued out of the Admiralty and Commercial Registry, the Judge in charge of the commercial list may at any time after the issue of the arbitration claim form transfer the application to another list, court or Division of the High Court to which he has power to transfer proceedings.

5.6 In considering whether to transfer an arbitration application, the Judges referred to in paragraphs 5.4 and 5.5 shall have regard to the criteria specified in article 5(4) of the High Court and County Courts (Allocation of Arbitration Proceedings) Order 1996 and the application shall be transferred if those Judges so decide.

5.7 In this practice direction "Judge in charge of the list" means:

(a) in relation to the commercial list, a judge of the Commercial Court;

(b) in relation to the list of a Mercantile Court, a Circuit mercantile judge of that court; and

(c) in relation to the Business List in the Central London County Court, a Circuit Judge authorised to deal with cases in that list,

but nothing in this paragraph shall be construed as preventing the powers of a judge of the Commercial Court from being exercised by any judge of the High Court.

Note—". . . the High Court and County Courts (Allocation of Arbitration Proceedings) Order 1996" is S.I. 1996 No. 3215 in force on January 31, 1997, and has been amended by S.I. 1999 No. 1010.

Fees—See the Supreme Court Fees Order 1999 (S.I. 1999 No. 687) and, in particular, items 1.2: 2.4 and 2.5: 3.5: 4.4 and 4.5.

Stay of legal proceedings

49GPD–004 **6.1** An application notice by which an application under section 9 of the Arbitration Act to stay legal proceedings is made shall be served—

(1) in accordance with CPR Rule 6.5 on the party bringing the relevant legal proceedings and on any other party to those proceedings who has given an address for service; and

(2) on any party to those legal proceedings who has not given an address for service, by sending to him (whether or not he is within the jurisdiction) at his last known address or at a place where it is likely to come to his attention, a copy of the application notice for his information.

6.2 Where a question arises as to whether an arbitration agreement has been concluded or as to whether the dispute which is the subject-matter of the proceedings falls within the terms of such an agreement, the Court may determine that question or give directions for its determination, in which case it may order the proceedings to be stayed pending the determination of that question.

Service of arbitration claim form

7.1 Subject to paragraphs 7.2 and 7.4 below and to paragraphs 6.1 and 8.1 to 8.4, an arbitration claim form shall be served in accordance with CPR Part 6.

7.2 Where the Court is satisfied on an application made without notice that

(1) arbitral proceedings are taking place, or an arbitration award has been made, within the jurisdiction; and

(2) an arbitration application is being made in connection with those arbitral proceedings or being brought to challenge the award or to appeal on a question of law arising out of the award; and

(3) the respondent to the arbitration application (not being an individual residing or carrying on business within the jurisdiction or a body corporate having a registered office or a place of business within the jurisdiction)

- (a) is or was represented in the arbitral proceedings by a solicitor or other agent within the jurisdiction who was authorised to receive service of any notice or other document served for the purposes of those proceedings; and
- (b) has not (at the time when the arbitration application is made) determined the authority of that solicitor or agent,

the Court may authorise service of the arbitration claim form to be effected on the solicitor or agent instead of the respondent.

7.3 An order made under paragraph 7.2 must limit a time within which the respondent must acknowledge service and a copy of the order and of the arbitration claim form must be sent by post to the respondent at his address out of the jurisdiction.

7.4 Where an applicant has made an arbitration application (the first arbitration application) and a subsequent arbitration application arising out of the same arbitration or arbitration agreement is made by a party to the first arbitration application (other than the applicant), that party's arbitration claim form may be served in accordance with CPR rule 6.5 or may be served on the applicant at his address for service given in this arbitration claim form, and on any other party to the first arbitration application at the address for service given in that party's acknowledgment of service in the first arbitration application, and on any further arbitration application the same provisions as to service will apply.

7.5 For the purposes of service, an arbitration claim form is valid in the first instance—

(1) where service is to be effected out of the jurisdiction, for such period as the Court may fix;

(2) in any other case, for one month, beginning with the date of its issue.

Service out of the jurisdiction

8.1 The Court may give permission to serve an arbitration claim form out of 49GPD–005 the jurisdiction if the arbitration application falls into one of the categories mentioned in the following table and satisfies the conditions specified.

Nature of application	Conditions to be satisfied
1. The applicant seeks to challenge, or to appeal to the Court on a question of law arising out of, an arbitration award.	Award must have been made in England & Wales. Section 53 of the Arbitration Act shall apply for determining the place where award is treated as made.
2. The application is for an order under section 44 of the Arbitration Act (Court powers exercisable in support of arbitral proceedings). Where the application is for an interim remedy in support of arbitral proceedings which are taking (or will take) place outside England and Wales, the Court may give permission for service out of the jurisdiction notwithstanding that no other remedy is sought.	None.
3. The applicant seeks some other remedy or requires a question to be determined by the court, affecting an arbitration (whether pending or anticipated), an arbitration agreement or an arbitration award.	The seat of the arbitration is or will be in England & Wales or the conditions in Section 2(4) of the Arbitration Act are satisfied.

8.2 An application for the grant of permission under paragraph 8.1 must be supported by an affidavit or witness statement—

(1) stating, or, if the grounds were set out in the application notice, confirming the grounds on which the application is made; and

(2) showing in what place or country the person to be served is, or probably may be found, and no such permission shall be granted unless it shall be made sufficiently to appear to the Court that the case is a proper one for service out of the jurisdiction under this paragraph.

8.3 RSC Order 11, rules 5 to 8 (Schedule 1 to the CPR) shall apply to the service of an arbitration claim form under this paragraph as they apply to the service of other claim forms.

8.4 Any order made on an arbitration application may be served out of the jurisdiction with the permission of the court.

Evidence in support of arbitration application

9.1 The applicant shall file an affidavit or witness statement in support of the arbitration application which sets out the evidence on which he intends to rely and a copy of every affidavit or witness statement so filed must be served with the arbitration claim form.

9.2 Where an arbitration application is made with the written agreement of all the other parties to the arbitral proceedings or with the permission of the arbitral tribunal, the affidavit or witness statement in support must

(1) give details of the agreement or, as the case may be, permission; and

(2) exhibit copies of any document which evidences that agreement or permission.

Requirements as to notice

10.1 Where the Artbitration Act requires that an application to the Court is to be made upon notice to other parties notice shall be given by making those parties respondents to the application and serving on them the arbitration claim form and any affidavit or witness statement in support.

10.2 Where an arbitration application is made under section 24, 28 or 56 of the Arbitration Act, the arbitrators or, in the case of an application under section 24, the arbitrator concerned shall be made respondents to the application and notice shall be given by serving on them the arbitration claim form and any affidavit or witness statement in support.

10.3 In cases where paragraph 10.2 does not apply, an applicant shall be taken as having complied with any requirement to give notice to the arbitrator if he sends a copy of the arbitration claim form to the arbitrator for his information at his last known address with a copy of any affidavit or witness statement in support.

10.4 This paragraph does not apply to applications under section 9 of the Arbitration Act to stay legal proceedings.

Acknowledgment of service

11.1 Service of an arbitration claim form may be acknowledged by completing an acknowledgment of service in Form No. N15A in accordance with CPR Rule 8.3.

11.2 A respondent who—

(1) fails to acknowledge service within the time limited for so doing; or

(2) having indicated on his acknowledgment of service that he does not intend to contest the arbitration application, then wishes to do so, shall not be entitled to contest the application without the permission of the Court.

11.3 The Court will not give notice of the date on which an arbitration application will be heard to a respondent who has failed to acknowledge service.

11.4 The failure of a respondent to give notice of intention to contest the arbitration application or to acknowledge service shall not affect the applicant's duty to satisfy the Court that the order applied for should be made.

11.5 This paragraph does not apply to—

(1) applications under section 9 of the Arbitration Act to stay legal proceedings; or

(2) subsequent arbitration applications.

Acknowledgment of service, etc., by arbitrator

12.1 An arbitrator who is sent a copy of an arbitration claim form for his information may make

(1) a request (without notice to any party) to be made a respondent; or

(2) representations to the Court under this rule,

and, where an arbitrator is ordered to be made a respondent, he shall acknowledge service within 14 days of the making of that order.

12.2 An arbitrator who wishes to make representations to the Court under this rule may file an affidavit or witness statement or make representations in writing to the Court.

12.3 The arbitrator shall as soon as is practicable send a copy of any document filed or made under paragraph 12.2 to all the parties to the arbitration application.

12.4 Nothing in this paragraph shall require the Court to admit a document filed or made under sub-paragraph (2) and the weight to be given to any such document shall be a matter for the Court.

Automatic directions

49GPD–006 **13.1** Unless the Court otherwise directs, the following directions shall take effect automatically.

13.2 A respondent who wishes to put evidence before the Court in response to any affidavit or witness statement filed in support of an arbitration application shall serve his affidavit or witness statement on the applicant before the expiration of 21 days after the time limited for acknowledging service or, in a case where a respondent is not required to file an acknowledgment of service, within 21 days after service of the arbitration claim form.

13.3 An application who wishes to put evidence before the court in response to an affidavit or witness statement filed under paragraph 13.2 shall serve his affidavit or witness statement on the respondent within 7 days after service of the respondent's evidence.

13.4 Where a date has not been fixed for the hearing of the arbitration application, the applicant shall, and the respondent may, not later than 14 days after the expiration of the time limit specified in paragraph 13.2, apply to the Court for such a date to be fixed.

13.5 Agreed indexed and paginated bundles of all the evidence and other documents to be used at the hearing shall be prepared by the applicant (with the co-operation of the respondent).

13.6 Not later than 5 clear days before the hearing date estimates for the length of the hearing shall be lodged with the Court together with a complete set of the documents to be used.

13.7 Not later than 2 days before the hearing date the applicant shall lodge with the Court—

(1) a chronology of the relevant events cross-referenced to the bundle of documents;

(2) (where necessary) a list of the persons involved;

(3) a skeleton argument which lists succinctly—

(a) the issues which arise for decision,

(b) the grounds of relief (or opposing relief) to be relied upon,

(c) the submissions of fact to be made with the references to the evidence, and

(d) the submissions of law with references to the relevant authorities,

and shall send copies to the respondent.

13.8 Not later than the day before the hearing date the respondent shall lodge with the Court a skeleton argument which lists succinctly—

(1) the issues which arise for decision,

(2) the grounds of relief (or opposing relief) to be relied upon,

(3) the submissions of fact to be made with the references to the evidence, and

(4) the submissions of law with references to the relevant authorities, and shall send a copy to the applicant.

Directions by the court

14.1 The rules of the CPR relating to allocation questionnaires and track allocation do not apply to arbitration applications, and the Court may give such directions as to the conduct of the arbitration application as it thinks best adapted to secure the just, expeditious and economical disposal thereof.

14.2 Where the Court considers that there is or may be a dispute as to fact and that the just, expeditious and economical disposal of the application can best be secured by hearing the application on oral evidence or mainly on oral evidence, it may, if it thinks fit, order that no further evidence shall be filed and that the application shall be heard on oral evidence or partly on oral evidence and partly on written evidence, with or without cross-examination of any of the witnesses, as it may direct.

14.3 The Court may give directions as to the filing of evidence and as to the attendance of witnesses for cross-examination and any other directions which it could give in proceedings begun by claim form.

14.4 If the applicant makes default in complying with these provisions or with any order or direction of the Court as to the conduct of the application, or if the Court is satisfied that the applicant is not prosecuting the application with due despatch, the Court may order the application to be dismissed or may make such other order as may be just.

14.5 If the respondent fails to comply with these provisions or with any order or direction given by the Court in relation to the evidence to be relied on, or the submission to be made by that respondent, the Court may, if it thinks fit, hear and determine the application without having regard to that evidence or those submissions.

14.6 Unless the Court orders otherwise, affidavits and witness statements may contain hearsay.

Hearing of applications: public or private

15.1 The Court may order that any arbitration application be heard either in public or in private.

15.2 Subject to any order made under paragraph 15.1 and paragraph 15.3, all arbitration applications shall be heard in private.

15.3 Subject to any order made under paragraph 15.1, the determination of a perliminary point of law under section 45 of the Arbitration Act, or an appeal under section 69 on a question of law arising out of an award shall be heard in public.

15.4 Paragraph 15.3 shall not apply to—

(1) the preliminary question whether the Court is satisfied of the matters set out in section 45(2)(b); or

(2) an application for permission to appeal under section 69(2)(b).

Securing the attendance of witnesses

16.1 A party to arbitral proceedings being conducted in England and Wales who wishes to rely on section 43 of the Arbitration Act to secure the attendance of a witness may apply for a witness summons in accordance with Part 34 of the CPR to the Admiralty and Commercial Registry or, if the attendance of the witness is required within the district of a district registry, at that registry at the option of the party. **49GPD–007**

16.2 A witness summons shall not be issued until the applicant files an affidavit or witness statement which shows that the application is made with the permission of the tribunal or the agreement of the other parties.

Securing for costs

17.1 Subject to section 70(6) of the Arbitration Act, the Court may order any applicant (including an applicant who has been granted permission to appeal) to provide security for costs of any arbitration application.

Powers exercisable in support of arbitral proceedings

18.1 Where the case is one of urgency, an application for an order under section 44 of the Arbitration Act (Court powers exercisable in support of arbitral proceedings) may be made without notice on affidavit or witness statement (before the issue of an arbitration claim form) and the affidavit or witness statement shall (in addition to dealing with the matters required to be dealt with by paragraphs 9.1 & 9.2) state the reasons—

(1) why the application is made without notice; and

(2) (where the application is made without the permission of the arbitral tribunal or the agreement of the other parties to the arbitral proceedings) why it was not practicable to obtain that permission or agreement; and

(3) why the witness believes that the condition in section 44(5) is satisfied.

18.2 Where the case is not one of urgency, an application for an order under section 44 of the Arbitration Act shall be made on notice and the affidavit or witness statement in support shall (in addition to dealing with the matters required to be dealt with by paragraph 9 and paragraph 18.1(3) above) state that the application is made with the permission of the tribunal or the written agreement of the other parties to the arbitral proceedings.

18.3 Where an application for an order under section 44 of the Arbitration Act is made before the issue of an arbitration claim form, any order made by the Court may be granted on terms providing for the issue of an arbitration calim form and such other terms, if any, as the court thinks fit.

Applications under sections 32 and 45 of the Arbitration Act

19.1 This paragraph applies to the following arbitration applications:

(1) applications for the determination of a question as to the substantive jurisdiction of the arbitral tribunal under section 32 of the Arbitration Act; and

(2) applications for the determination of a preliminary point of law under section 45 of the Arbitration Act.

19.2 Where an application is made without the agreement in writing of all the other parties to the arbitral proceedings but with the permission of the arbitral tribunal, the affidavits or witness statements filed by the parties shall set out any evidence relied on by the parties in support of their contention that the Court should, or should not, consider the application.

19.3 As soon as practicable after the written evidence is filed, the Court shall decide whether or not it should consider the application and, unless the Court otherwise directs, shall so decide without a hearing.

Applications for permission to appeal

20.1 Where the applicant seeks permission to appeal to the Court on a question of law arising out of an arbitration award, the arbitration claim form shall identify the question of law and state the grounds on which the applicant alleges that permission should be granted.

20.2 The affidavit or witness statement in support of the application shall set out any evidence relied on by the applicant for the purpose of satisfying the Court of the matters mentioned in section 69(3) of the Arbitration Act and for satisfying the Court that permission should be granted.

20.3 The affidavit or witness statement filed by the respondent to the application shall—

(1) state the grounds on which the respondent opposes the grant of permission;

(2) set out any evidence relied on by him relating to the matters mentioned in section 69(3) of the Arbitration Act, and

(3) specify whether the respondent wishes to contend that the award should be upheld for reasons not expressed (or not fully expressed) in the award and, if so, state those reasons.

20.4 As soon as practicable after the filing of the affidavits and witness statements, the Court shall determine the application for permission in accordance with section 69(5) of the Arbitration Act.

20.5 Where permission is granted, a date shall be fixed for the hearing of the appeal.

Extension of time: applications under section 12

21.1 An application for an order under section 12 of the Arbitration Act may include as an alternative an application for a declaration that such an order is not needed.

Time limit for challenges to or appeals from awards

22.1 An applicant shall not be taken as having complied with the time limit of 28 days referred to in section 70(3) of the Arbitration Act unless the arbitration claim form has been issued, and all the affidavits or witness statements in support have been filed, by the expiry of that time limit.

22.2 An application who wishes—

(1) to challenge an award under section 67 or 68 of the Arbitration Act; or

(2) to appeal under section 69 on a question of law arising out of an award, may, where the time limit of 28 days has not yet expired, apply without notice on affidavit or witness statement for an order extending that time limit.

22.3 In any case where an applicant seeks to challenge an award under section 67 or 68 of the Arbitration Act or to appeal under section 69 after the time limit of 28 days has already expired, the following provisions shall apply:

(1) the applicant must state in his arbitration claim form the grounds why an order extending time should be made and his affidavit or witness statement in support shall set out the evidence on which he relies;

(2) a respondent who wishes to oppose the making of an order extending time shall file an affidavit or witness statement within 7 days after service of the applicant's evidence, and

(3) the Court shall decide whether or not to extend time without a hearing unless it appears to the Court that a hearing is required, and, where the Court makes an order extending the time limit, the respondent shall file his affidavit or witness statement in response to the arbitration application 21 days after the making of the order.

Part II

Application of this Part

23.1 This Part of this practice direction applies to any application to the Court to which the old law applies and, in this rule, "the old law" means the enactments specified in section 107 of the Arbitration Act 1996 as they stood before their amendment or repeal by that Act.

23.2 This Part does not apply to proceedings to enforce an award—

(1) to which Part III of this practice direction applies; or

(2) by a claim based on the award.

23.3 Reference should be made to the other provisions of the CPR (except Parts I and III of this Part) for the procedure for any application not expressly provided for in this Part.

Note—"The old law" namely the Arbitration Act 1950; the Arbitration Act 1975; and the Arbitration Act 1979, the texts of which are set out in SCP 1999, Vol. 2, Section 21 at paras 21A–1 *et seq.*; 21B–1 *et seq.*; and 21C–1 *et seq.* respectively.

Matters for a judge in court

24.1 Every application to the Court— 49GPD–008

(1) to remit an award under section 22 of the Arbitration Act 1950; or
(2) to remove an arbitrator or umpire under section 23(1) of that Act; or
(3) to set aside an award under section 23(2) of that Act, or
(4) to determine, under section 2(1) of the Arbitration Act 1979, any question of law arising in the course of a reference,

must be made by the issue of an arbitration claim form under CPR rule 8.6 (a Part 8 claim form).

24.2 Any appeal to the High Court under section 1(2) of the Arbitration Act 1979 shall be made by the issue of a Part 8 claim form.

24.3 An application for a declaration that an award made by an arbitrator or umpire is not binding on a party to the award on the ground that it was made without jurisdiction may be made by the issue of a Part 8 claim form, but the foregoing provision shall not be taken as affecting the judge's power to refuse to make such a declaration in proceedings begun otherwise.

Note—"The old law" namely the Arbitration Act 1950, the Arbitration Act 1975; and the Arbitration Act 1979, the text of which is set out in SCP 1999, Vol. 2 at Section 21.

Effect of rule—This paragraph specifies four separate matters under the Arbitration Act 1950 and the Arbitration Act 1979 and regulates the mode of proceedings in these matters. These matters are,

(1) applications to remit an award under section 22 of the 1950 Act,
(2) to remove an arbitrator or umpire under section 23(1) of the 1950 Act,
(3) to set aside an award under section 23(2) of the 1950 Act,
(4) application to determine under section 2(1) of the 1979 Act any question of law arising in the course of a reference.

Such applications must be made by issuing an arbitration claim form under CPR, r. 8.6 (a Part 8 claim form) and will be heard by a judge of the Commercial Court unless such judge otherwise directs and in court, see paras 24 and 28.

Where permission to appeal is required, it should be applied for to a Judge in private by an application in existing proceedings or by a Part 8 claim if no existing proceedings issued in the Admiralty and Commercial Registry (para. 25.2, below). Such permission is required under section 1(3) of the Act of 1979, unless all the parties to the reference consent.

It should be emphasised that applications under this paragraph are required to be heard by a Judge and must be heard by a Commercial Judge, unless any such Judge otherwise directs (see para. 28.1) but of course this provision will not by itself prevent the powers of a Commercial Judge from being exercised by any Judge of the High Court (see para. 28.2) as, for example, during any vacation or where a Commercial Judge is not available or it is impractical to bring the application for hearing by a Commercial Judge.

In *Hiscox v. Outhwaite (No. 2)* [1991] 1 W.L.R. 545, CA, where an appeal was pending in the House of Lords on the question whether leave to appeal under section 1(2) of the 1979 Act should have been given, the Court of Appeal ordered that the Judge should be at liberty to go ahead with hearing the appeal and that he should give judgment in writing which should be signed by him and placed in a sealed envelope to be opened only in the event of the decision of the House of Lords being that there was jurisdiction to hear that appeal.

Para. 24.3 enables an application for a declaration that an award made by an arbitrator or umpire is not binding on the ground it was made without jurisdiction to be made by the issue of a Part 8 claim form. If the Judge thinks that the matter cannot properly be dealt with in such manner but should be decided in a claim, this paragraph makes it clear that he is not bound to decide it on the application so made.

For sections 22 and 23 of the Arbitration Act 1959 and sections 1 and 2 of the Arbitration Act 1979, see Vol. 2, Section 21.

Appeal under section 1(2) of the Arbitration Act 1979—practice—The practice is regulated by the provisions of para. 27, and, in particular, by paras (6) to (9) thereof inclusive (see para. 27 below). Paragraphs 15 to 18 of Appendix 19 (see above) amplify the practice and provide as follows—

Every arbitration application form used to appeal against an arbitration award under s.1(2) of the 1979 Act shall contain a succinct statement in numbered paragraphs of each ground upon which it is sought to contend that the arbitratl tribunal erred in law. Reference shall be made to the paragraph or passage of the award and reasons where each alleged error is to be found. A copy of the award and reasons forming part of the award and any documents expressly incorporated in the award or such reasons shall accompany the arbitration application form when the same is issued unless the appeal arises from a minor part only of the award and reasons in which case the relevant extracts shall accompany the arbitration claim form.

Any respondent to an application by way of appeal under s.1(2) of the 1979 Act who contends that the award should be upheld on grounds not or not fully expressed in the award and reasons should provide to the applicant and to the Court not later than two clear days before the application for permission to appeal is listed for argument a succinct statement of such grounds in numbered paragraphs, with reference where appropriate to any relevant paragraphs or passage of the award and reasons.

Any statement provided under paragraphs 15 and 16 should contain specific reference to any authority relied on. A copy should be provided with the statement of any authority not contained in the Law Reports, the Weekly Law Reports, the All England Law Reports, Lloyd's Law Reports or the English Reports.

Where the applicant contends that any question of law arising out of an award concerns a term of contract or an event which is not a one-off clause or event, he shall serve on the respondent with his application and lodge with the Court an affidavit or witness statement setting out the facts relied on in support of his contention. A respondent who challenges that contention shall provide to the applicant and to the Court, not later than two days before the application is listed for argument, an affidavit or witness statement setting out the facts upon which he relies.

Matters for judge in chambers or master

25.1 Subject to the foregoing provisions of this Order and the provisions of this rule, the jurisdiction of the High Court or a judge thereof under the Arbitration Act 1950 and the jurisdiction of the High Court under the Arbitration Act 1975 and the Arbitration Act 1979 may be exercised by a judge in chambers, a master or the Admiralty Registrar.

25.2 Any application

(1) for permission to appeal under section 1(2) of the Arbitration Act 1979, or

(2) under section 1(5) of that Act (including any application for permission), or

(3) under section 5 of that Act,

shall be made to a judge in chambers.

25.3 Any application to which this rule applies shall, where there are existing court proceedings be made by the issue of an application notice in those proceedings, and in any other case a Part 8 claim form.

25.4 Where an application is made under section 1(5) of the Arbitration Act 1979 (including any application for permission), the Part 8 claim form or the application notice as the case may be, must be served on the arbitrator or umpire and on any other party to the reference.

Effect of paragraph—This paragraph makes it clear that, save for three important exceptions, applications under the 1979 Act may be heard in chambers by a Judge, Master or the Admiralty Registrar.

The first exception is that application under section 1(5) of the 1979 Act must be made to a Judge, and *not* to a Master or the Admiralty Registrar (see para. 25.2). These are applications to order the arbitrator or umpire concerned to state the reasons for his award in sufficient detail to enable the court, should an appeal be brought under section 1 of the 1979 Act, to consider any questions of law arising out of the award. The reason for this requirement is because of the likely complexity and importance of the questions which will probably arise in considering whether the award does or does not sufficiently set out the reasons for the award. An application under section 1(5) of the 1979 Act, including any application for permission is made by a Part 8 claim form, which must be served on the arbitrator or umpire, as the case may be, and on all the parties to the reference (see para. 25.4). Where an application is made to the Court of Appeal under section 1(5) of the 1979 Act, including an application for permission with regard to proceedings before a Judge-arbitrator or a Judge-umpire, notice thereof must be served on the Judge-arbitrator or Judge-umpire and on all the parties to the reference (see RSC, O.59, r.14(6)).

The second exception is that applications under section 5 of the 1979 Act must be made to a judge, and *not* to a master or the Admiralty Registrar (see para. 25.2). These are applications to empower the arbitrator or umpire to continue with the reference in default of acknowledgment of service by any party or of non-compliance by a party with an order made by the arbitrator or umpire in the same manner as a Judge of the High Court might continue with proceedings where a party fails to comply with an order of the court or a requirement of the rules of court.

The third exception is that applications for permission to appeal to the Court under section 1(2) of the 1979 Act must be made to a Judge and *not* to a Master or the Admiralty Registrar (see para. 25.2). Section 1(2) provides that an appeal shall lie to the Court on any question of law arising out of an award made on an arbitration agreement and in s.1(3) it is stated that an appeal may be brought by any of the parties to the reference (a) with the consent of all the other parties or (b) with the permission of the court.

Applications under this rule must be made, where a claim is pending by application notice in the claim, and in any other case by a Part 8 claim form (see para. 25.3).

It should further be noted that applications under this rule which are required to be heard by a judge must be heard by a Commercial Judge, unless he directs otherwise, although any Judge of the High Court may of course exercise his powers (see para. 28).

Apart from the matters specified in sub-para. 2, all other applications arising under the Arbitration Act 1950, may be made in chambers and heard by the Judge, Master or Admiralty Registrar. They include applications to stay proceedings under s.4, to appoint an arbitrator or umpire under s.10, for the issue of a witness summons, and all other matters included in s.12(6) of the Arbitration Act 1950. The effect of this rule is to negative the decisions in *Raymond and Reid v. Granger* [1952] 2 All E.R. 1952, and *Kruger Townwear Ltd v. Northern Assurance Co.* [1953] 1 W.L.R. 1049; [1953] 2 All E.R. 727n.

In the QBD, such applications are made by application notice returnable in the first instance before the Master, unless of course the application is for an injunction in reference to the arbitration proceedings. Where there is no pending claim, the application is made by a Part 8 claim form (see para. 25.3); but where there is a pending claim, the application is made by application notice in the claim.

Ex parte applications for injunctions—Paragraph 25.3 has to be read in conjunction with CPR, r. 25.2, which permits applications for injunctive relief in cases in urgency, before the issue of a Part 7 claim form or a Part 8 claim form. Where injunctive relief is granted in such circumstances, however, the claim form should be issued promptly thereafter. It is unacceptable that a *Mareva* injunction, for example, granted in aid of an arbitration, should remain in force for two months after its grant without any originating process to sustain it; accordingly such an injunction will be discharged (*Siporex Trade SA v. Comdel Commodities Ltd* [1986] 2 Lloyd's Rep. 428; (1986) 136 N.L.J. 538).

Applications in district registries

26.1 An application under section 12(4) of the Arbitration Act 1950 for an order that a witness summons shall issue to compel the attendance before an arbitrator or umpire of a witness may, if the attendance of the witness is required within the district of a district registry, be made at that registry, instead of at the Admiralty and Commercial Registry, at the option of the applicant.

Time limits and other special provisions as to appeals and applications under the Arbitration Acts

49GPD–009 **27.1** An application to the Court—

(1) to remit an award under section 22 of the Arbitration Act 1950; or
(2) to set aside an award under section 23(2) of that Act or otherwise, or
(3) to direct an arbitrator or umpire to state the reasons for an award under section 1(5) of the Arbitration Act 1979,

must be made, and the Part 8 claim form or application notice, as the case may be, must be served, within 21 days after the award has been made and published to the parties.

27.2 In the case of an appeal to the Court under section 1(2) of the Arbitration Act 1979, the application for permission to appeal, where permission is required, and the Part 8 claim form must be served and the appeal entered, within 21 days after the award has been made and published to the parties. Provided that, where reasons material to the appeal are given on a date subsequent to the publication of the award, the period of 21 days shall run from the date on which the reasons are given.

27.3 An application, under section 2(1) of the Arbitration Act 1979, to determine any question of law arising in the course of a reference, must be made, and the Part 8 claim from served, within 14 days after the arbitrator or umpire has consented to the application being made, or the other parties have so consented.

27.4 For the purpose of paragraph 27.3 the consent must be given in writing.

27.5 In the case of every appeal or application to which this paragraph applies, the Part 8 claim form or the application notice, as the case may be, must state the grounds of the appeal or application and, where the appeal or application is founded on evidence by affidavit or witness statement, or is made with the consent of the arbitrator or umpire or of the other parties, a copy of every affidavit or witness intended to be used, or, as the case may be, of every consent given in writing, must be served with the Part 8 claim form or application notice.

27.6 Without prejudice to sub-paragraph (5), in an appeal under section 1(2) of the Arbitration Act 1979 the statement of the grounds of the appeal shall specify the relevant parts of the award and reasons, or the relevant parts thereof, shall be lodged with the court and served with the Part 8 claim form.

27.7 In an application for permission to appeal under section 1(2) of the Arbitration Act 1979, any affidavit or witness statement verifying the facts in support of a contention that the question of law concerns a term of a contract or an event which is not a one-off term or event must be filed with the court and served with the Part 8 claim form.

27.8 Any affidavit or witness statement in reply to written evidence under sub-paragraph (7) shall be filed with the court and served on the applicant not less than two clear days before the hearing of the application.

27.9 A respondent to an application for permission to appeal under section 1(2) of the Arbitration Act 1979 who desires to contend that the award should be upheld on grounds not expressed or fully expressed in the award and reasons shall not less than two clear days before the hearing of the application file with the court and serve on the applicant a notice specifying the grounds of his contention.

Time for applying—Para. 27.2 applies the same time limit to an application for permission to appeal as applies to a Pt 8 claim form of appeal. It is the practice to enter the appeal subject to any necessary leave being obtained; it is therefore, logical that the same limit apply to all these steps. The 21 days time limit imposed by para. 27.1 applies both to an application to set aside an award under section 23(2) of the Arbitration Act 1950 and to an application at common law for a declaration that an award is void on the grounds of the arbitrator's conduct. The time limit cannot be circumvented simply by avoiding the use of the term "misconduct" in the application (*Cook International Inc. v. B.V. Handelsmaatschappij Jean Delvaux* [1985] 2 Lloyd's Rep. 225 at 233).

"Made and published"—An award is made and published when the arbitrator gives notice to the parties that it is ready. Delay in taking up the award does not extend the time for appealing or applying (*The Archipelagos* [1979] Lloyd's Rep. 289; *Selous Street Properites Ltd v. Oronel Fabrics Ltd* (1984) 270 E.G. 643).

Applications and appeals to be heard by commercial judges

28.1 Any matter which is required, by paragraph 24 or 25, to be heard by a judge, shall be heard by a judge of the Commercial Court unless any such judge otherwise directs.

28.2 Nothing in the foregoing sub-paragraph shall be construed as preventing the powers of a judge of the Commercial Court from being exercised by any judge of the High Court.

Effect of paragraph—This rule has the effect of channelling all applications under sub-paras 2 and 3, in the first instance to the Commercial Court. The rule thus recognises that in practice the subject of arbitration is substantially a commercial matter and should be dealt with by a Commercial Judge both as a matter of convenience and the proper distribution of business in the High Court and also to enable uniformity of practice and procedure to be fostered and encouraged.

On the other hand, of course, there is a great volume of important arbitrations which may be described as "non-commercial" in the sense that the subject matter does not fall within the definition of a "commercial claim" (see Practice Direction—Commercial Court para. 1.2) and applications relating to such arbitrations which require to be heard by a judge under sub-paras 2 and 3, will no doubt be directed by a Commercial Judge to be heard by another judge of the High Court.

The normal practice should be that all applications for permission to appeal to the High Court are to be heard by a Commercial Judge unless any such Judge otherwise directs, and if permission is granted, consideration could then be given to whether there should be a direction that the appeal itself should be heard by a Judge who is not a Commercial Judge (*per* Donaldson L.J. in *F. G. Whitley & Sons Co. Ltd v. Clwyd County Council, The Times*, August 6, 1982).

In Ashbank Property Co. Ltd v. Department of Transport (1994) *The Times*, July 25; (1994) *The Independent*, October 3; held that where a notice of application to set aside an arbitration award had been incorrectly issued in the Chancery Division it was inappropriate to transfer the same to the Commercial Court as that would be to grant an inappropriate extension of time for an appeal.

It is the practice in the Commercial Court for one Judge to hear the application for permission to appeal under s.1(2) of the 1979 Act (see para. 25.2.1) and for another Judge to hear the appeal itself but there are exceptional cases where it would be quite right that the same Judge should hear the appeal; ultimately, it must be a matter for the judge's discretion (*Hiscox v. Outhwaite (No. 2)* [1991] 1 W.L.R. 545, CA).

Service out of the jurisdiction

29.1 Subject to paragraph 29.2,

(1) any Part 8 claim form whereby any application under the Arbitration Act 1950 or the Arbitration Act 1979, is made, or

(2) any order made on such an application,

may be served out of the jurisdiction with the permission of the Court provided that the arbitration to which the application relates is governed by English law or has been, is being or is to be held within the jurisdiction.

29.2 A Part 8 claim form whereby permission to enforce an award is sought may be served out of the jurisdiction with the permission of the Court whether or not the arbitration is governed by English law.

29.3 An application for the grant of permission under this paragraph must be supported by an affidavit or witness statement stating the grounds on which the application is made and showing in what place or country the person to be served is, or probably may be found; and no such permission shall be granted unless it shall be made to appear to the Court that the case is a proper one for service out of the jurisdiction under this paragraph.

29.4 RSC, Order 11, rules 5 to 8, (Schedule 1 to the CPR) shall apply in relation to any such Part 8 claim form or order as is referred to in sub-paragraph (1) as they apply in relation to any other claim form.

Note—This rule is really an extension of RSC, O.11, and an additional case in which service out of the jurisdiction is permissible with the leave of the Court. For observations on the differences between service out of jurisdiction under RSC, O.11 and under this rule, see *Mayer Newman Co. Ltd v. Al Ferro Commodities Corporation SA* [1990] 2 Lloyd's Rep. 290 at 293, CA, *per* Bingham L.J. The basis of the jurisdiction under this rule is that the "arbitration is to be or has been held within the jurisdiction". The practice under this rule is the same in all respects as under RSC, O.11. Including the requirement under RSC, O.11, r.7 that translations be provided of documents for service on a foreign state in arbitration proceedings unless the official language or an official language of that State is English.

Civil Jurisdiction and Judgments Acts 1982—Art. 1 of the Brussels Convention, which forms the first Schedule to the Act, provides that the convention shall not apply to arbitration. The word "arbitration" in Art. 1 covers all matters connected with arbitration, including the question whether there is a valid arbitration agreement (*Marc Rich & Co. AG v. Societa Italiana Impianti PA. The Atlantic Emperor* (1988) *The Independent*, November 21). Thus where a claimant issues a Part 8 claim form seeking the appointment of an arbitrator under section 10(3) of the Arbitration Act 1950, the Italian defendant having denied the existence of the alleged arbitration agreement, the claimant may properly seek permission to serve the Part 8 claim form out of the jurisdiction under paragraph 29, and should not attempt to serve without leave in Italy under the convention (*ibid.*).

Application—Paragraph 29 is concerned only with applications by and against parties to an arbitration which relate to the arbitration to which they are parties. Thus the natural meaning of the para. is that the application must be against the other party to the reference and not a non-party (as case under the pre 1997 RSC, O.73, r. 7 being *The Cienvik* [1996] 2 Lloyd's Rep. 395). The reasoning of the court in *The Cienvik* was adopted by the Court of Appeal in *Tate and Lyle Industries Ltd v. CIA Usina Bulhoes and Cargill Inc.* [1997] 1 Lloyd's Rep. 355, when holding that there is no jurisdiction to issue a without notice injunction against a proposed defendant not a party to the arbitration under section 12 of the 1950 Act.

Part III

Application of this part

49GPD–010 **30.1** This Part of this practice direction applies to all enforcement proceedings (other than by an action or claim on the award) regardless of when they are commenced and when the arbitral proceedings took place.

Enforcement of awards

31.1 This rule applies to applications to enforce awards which are brought in the High Court and such an application may be made in the Royal Courts of Justice or in any district registry.

31.2 An application for permission under—

(1) section 66 of the Arbitration Act 1996;

(2) section 101 of the Arbitration Act 1996;

(3) section 26 of the Arbitration Act 1950; or

(4) section 3(1)(a) of the Arbitration Act 1975;

to enforce an award in the same manner as a judgment or order may be made without notice by use of the practice form referred to in paragraph 4.1.

31.3 The Court hearing an application under paragraph 31.2 may direct that the form (in this Part of this practice direction called "the enforcement form") is to be served on such parties to the arbitration as it may specify and the enforcement form may with the permission of the court be served out of the jurisdiction irrespective of where the award is, or is treated as, made.

31.4 Where a direction is given under paragraph 31.3, paragraphs 11.1 to 11.5 and 13.1 to 17.1 shall apply with the necessary modifications as they apply to applications under Part 1 of this practice direction.

31.5 Where the applicant applies to enforce an agreed award within the meaning of section 51(2) of the Arbitration Act 1996, the enforcement form must state that the award is an agreed award and any order made by the Court shall also contain such a statement.

31.6 An application for permission must be supported by affidavit or witness statement—

(1) exhibiting

(a) where the application is made under section 66 of the Arbitration Act 1996 or under section 26 of the Arbitration Act 1950, the arbitration agreement and the original award or, in either case, a copy thereof;

(b) where the application is under section 101 of the Arbitration Act 1996, the documents required to be produced by section 102 of that Act;

(c) where the application is under section 3(1)(a) of the Arbitration Act 1975, the documents required to be produced by section 4 of that Act;

(2) stating the name and the usual or last known place of residence or business of the applicant and of the person against whom it is sought to enforce the award respectively,

(3) stating, as the case may require, either that the award has not been complied with or the extent to which it has not been complied with at the date of the application.

31.7 An order giving permission must be drawn up by or on behalf of the applicant and must be served on the respondent by delivering a copy to him personally or by sending a copy to him at his usual or last known place of residence or business or in such other manner as the Court may direct.

31.8 The order may be served out of the jurisdiction without permission, and RSC, Order 11, rules 5 to 8, (Schedule 1 to the CPR) shall apply in relation to such an order as they apply in relation to a claim form.

31.9 Within 14 days after service of the order or, if the order is to be served out of the jurisdiction, within such other period as the Court may fix, the respondent may apply to set aside the order and the award shall not be enforced until after the expiration of that period or, if the respondent applies within that period to set aside the order, until after the application is finally disposed of.

31.10 The copy of the order served on the respondent shall state the effect of paragraph 31.9.

31.11 In relation to a body corporate paragraphs 31.1–31.10 shall have effect as if for any reference to the place of residence or business of the applicant or the respondent there were substituted a reference to the registered or principal address of the body corporate.

Nothing in paragraphs 31.1–31.10 shall affect any enactment which provides for the manner in which a document may be served on a body corporate.

Affidavit in support of application—As to the importance of full and frank disclosure in affidavit and by like token in any witness statement in support of application which in the first instance is made without notice, and the relevant considerations where non-disclosure is established (see *Curacao Trading Co. B.V. v. Harkisandas & Co.* [1992] 21 Lloyd's Rep. 186).

Copies of draft order/Contents of affidavit/Witness statement in support—In addition to an affidavit or witness statement Appendix 19 item 19 (see above requires two copies of a draft order to be provided and requires that care be taken to see that the affidavit or witness statement and the draft order meet the requirements of this provision.

Interest on awards

32.1 Where an applicant seeks to enforce an award of interest, the whole or any part of which relates to a period after the date of the award, he shall file a certificate giving the following particulars

(1) whether simple or compound interest was awarded;

(2) the date from which interest was awarded;

(3) whether rests were provided for, specifying them;

(4) the rate of interest awarded, and

(5) a calculation showing the total amount claimed up to the date of the certificate and any sum which will become due thereafter on a per diem basis.

32.2 The certificate under paragraph 32.1 must be filed whenever the amount of interest has to be quantified for the purpose of obtaining a judgment or order under section 66 of the Arbitration Act (enforcement of the award) or for the purposes of enforcing such a judgment or order by one of the means mentioned in RSC, Order 45, rule 1 (Schedule 1 to the CPR).

Registration in High Court of foreign awards

33.1 Where an award is made in proceedings on an arbitration in any part of Her Majesty's dominions or other territory to which Part I of the Foreign Judgments (Reciprocal Enforcement) Act 1933 extends, being a part to which Part II of the Administration of Justice Act 1920 extended immediately before the said Part I was extended thereto, then, if the award has, in pursuance of the law in force in the place where it was made, become enforceable in the same manner as a judgment given by a court in that place, RSC Order 71 (Schedule 1 to the CPR) shall apply in relation to the award as it applies in relation to a judgment given by that court, subject, however, to the following modifications:

(1) for references to the country of the original court there shall be substituted references to the place where the award was made; and

(2) the affidavit required by rule 3 of the said Order must state (in addition to the other matters required by that rule) that to the best of the information or belief of the deponent the award has, in pursuance of the law in force in the place where it was made, become enforceable in the same manner as a judgment given by a court in that place.

Foreign award expressed in a foreign currency—A foreign award expressed in a foreign currency must not be converted into sterling for the purposes of registration (see "Rate of Exchange", SCP 1999, Vol. 1, para. 71/3/2).

Registration of awards under the Arbitration (International Investment Disputes) Act 1966

34.1 In paragraphs 34.1–34.7 and in any provision of this practice direction as applied by this paragraph—

"the Act of 1996" means the Arbitration (International Investment Disputes) Act 1966.

"award" means an award rendered pursuant to the Convention;

"the Convention" means the Convention referred to in section 1(1) of the Act of 1966;

"judgment creditor" and "judgment debtor" mean respectively the person seeking recognition or enforcement of an award and the other party to the award.

34.2 Subject to the provisions of paragraphs 34.1–34.7, the following provisions of RSC, Order 71, namely, rules 1, 3(1) (except sub-paragraphs (c)(iv) and (d) thereof), 7 (except paragraph (3)(c) and (d) thereof), and 10(3) shall apply with the necessary modifications in relation to an award as they apply in relation to a judgment to which Part II of the Foreign Judgments (Reciprocal Enforcement) Act 1933 applies.

34.3 An application to have an award registered in the High Court under section 1 of the Act of 1966 shall be made by claim form under CPR rule 8.6.

34.4 The witness statement or affidavit required by Order 71, rule 3, in support of an application for registration shall—

(1) in lieu of exhibiting the judgment or a copy thereof, exhibit a copy of the award certified pursuant to the Convention; and

(2) in addition to stating the matters mentioned in paragraph 3(1)(c)(i) and (ii) of the said rule 3, state whether at the date of the application the enforcement of the award has been stayed (provisionally or otherwise) pursuant to the Convention and whether any, and if so what, application has been made pursuant to the Convention, which, if granted, might result in a stay of the enforcement of the award.

34.5 There shall be kept in the Admiralty and Commercial Registry under the direction of the Senior Master a register of the awards ordered to be registered under the Act of 1966 and particulars shall be entered in the register of any execution issued on such an award.

34.6 Where it appears to the court on granting permission to register an award or an application made by the judgment debtor after an award has been registered—

(1) that the enforcement of the award has been stayed (whether provisionally or otherwise) pursuant to the Convention; or

(2) that an application has been made pursuant to the Convention, which, if granted, might result in a stay of the enforcement of the award,

the Court shall, or in the case referred to in sub-paragraph (2) may, stay execution of the award for such time as it considers appropriate in the circumstances.

34.7 An application by the judgment debtor under paragraph 34.6 shall be made by application notice and supported by affidavit.

Scope of paragraph—This paragraph provides the machinery for the registration of an award rendered pursuant to the Convention set out in the Schedule to the Arbitration (International Investment Disputes) Act 1966. The procedure follows, in large measure, but with the necessary modifications, the provisions of RSC, O.71, since this Act is in many respects similar to the Foreign Judgments (Reciprocal Enforcement) Act 1933.

Paragraph 34.2 makes it unnecessary to convert an award under this Act expressed in foreign currency into sterling for the purposes of its registration.

PRACTICE DIRECTION—MERCANTILE COURTS AND BUSINESS LISTS

49HPD–001 *This Practice Direction supplements Part 49 of the CPR and replaces, with modifications, Order 48C of the County Court Rules 1981 and the Practice Directions establishing Mercantile Courts in Manchester, Liverpool, Birmingham, Bristol, Leeds and Newcastle upon Tyne. The Lord Chancellor has given his approval to a Mercantile Court being established in Cardiff. This Practice Direction complements the Commercial Court Practice Direction, also supplemental to Part 49.*

General

1.1 In this practice direction:—

(1) "mercantile claim" means a claim relating to a commercial or business transaction and includes (but is not limited to) any claim relating to—

(i) a business document or contract;
(ii) the export or import of goods or the sale of goods;
(iii) the carriage of goods by land, sea, air or pipeline;
(iv) the exploitation of oil and gas reserves;
(v) insurance and re-insurance;
(vi) banking and financial services;
(vii) the operation of markets and exchanges;
(viii) business agency;
(ix) the customs and practices of particular trades, businesses or commercial organisations;
(x) commercial fraud;
(xi) professional negligence in a commercial context;
(xii) arbitration applications (paragraph 6 below)

but does not include—

(i) any claim concerning the sale of goods by or against an individual comsumer; or
(ii) any claim to which CPR Part 49 (other than rule 49(2)(c)) applies;

and "mercantile proceedings" has a corresponding meaning.

(2) "Mercantile Court" means one of the Mercantile Courts established to deal with mercantile claims in the High Court but does not include the Commercial Court of the Queen's Bench Division.

(3) "Authorised county court" means the Central London County Court and any other county court authorised by the Lord Chancellor to operate a Business list for the purposes of dealing with mercantile proceedings.

(4) "Mercantile judge" means, in relation to proceedings in the High Court, a judge, or a person authorised to sit as a judge, of a Mercantile Court and, in relation to proceedings in a county court, the judge or judges authorised to deal with cases in the Business list of an authorised county court.

1.2 Mercantile proceedings may be dealt with in the High Court subject to the restrictions on claims that can be commenced in the High Court (see CPR rule 16.3(5) and paragraph 2.1 to 2.4 of the Practice Direction that supplements CPR Part 7), or may be dealt with in an authorised county court.

1.3 The Civil Procedure Rules (the CPR) and the practice directions supplementing them apply to mercantile claims subject to the provisions of this practice direction.

1.4 For the purposes of the CPR the list of a Mercantile Court and the Business list of an authorised county court is a specialist list (see *e.g.* CPR rules 2.3(2) and 16.3(5)(d)).

Commencement of Proceedings:

High Court

2.1 A mercantile claim intended to be entered in the commercial list of the

Commercial Court Queen's Bench Division should be begun by a claim form issued out of the Admiralty and Commercial Registry at the Royal Courts of Justice. (For further information reference should be made to the Commercial Court Practice Direction supplemental to CPR Part 49 and to the Commercial Court Guide).

2.2(1) If a claimant wants a mercantile claim to be entered in the list of a Mercantile Court the claim should be begun by a claim form issued out of the district registry of the Mercantile Court in question and marked with the words "Queen's Bench Division, ____ District Registry, Mercantile Court".

(2) On the issue out of the said registry of a claim form so marked, the claim will be entered in the list of that Mercantile Court.

(3) Where a claim form is to be marked as mentioned in sub-paragraph (2), any application before the issue of the claim form should be made to a judge of that Mercantile Court.

Transfer

3.1 Where mercantile proceedings are entered in the list of a Mercantile Court or in the Business list of an authorised county court, the provisions of CPR rule 26.2 (automatic transfer) do not apply. **49HPD–002**

3.2 At any stage in the course of mercantile proceedings not entered in the list of a Mercantile Court or the Business list of an authorised county court, any party may apply for an order transferring the case to a Mercantile Court or to the Business list of an authorised county court.

3.3 An application under paragraph 3.2—

(1) may be made to a mercantile judge of the court to which it is proposed the case should be transferred; or

(2) may be made to the court where the mercantile proceedings are being dealt with.

3.4 The court where the mercantile proceedings are being dealt with may not itself make an order for transfer but, if it considers the case might be suitable to be dealt with by a Mercantile Court or in the Business list of an authorised county court, it may

(1) on an application under paragraph 3.3(2) adjourn the application for hearing by a mercantile judge of the court to which it is proposed the case should be transferred; or

(2) on its own initiative refer the case to a mercantile judge of that court for a decision as to whether an order for transfer should be made.

3.5 Where all parties consent to the transfer, an application for transfer should be made by letter addressed to the listing officer of the Mercantile Court or the authorised county court, as the case may be, enclosing the written consents of the other parties and the claim form and statements of case. The letter should state why the case is suitable for the Mercantile Court or, as the case may be, for the Business list of the authorised county court.

3.6 Where a mercantile judge orders mercantile proceedings to be transferred to the list of a Mercantile Court, or to the Business list of an authorised county court, he may at the same time give directions for the management of the case.

3.7 A mercantile judge may, on his own initiative (but not unless the parties have had an opportunity of making submissions), or on the application of any party, order a case in the list of a Mercantile Court or in the Business list of an authorised county court to be removed from that list and may at the same time give case management directions.

3.8 Where a case is in the list of a Mercantile Court by virtue of paragraph 2.2(2) or in a Business list by virtue of paragraph 2.3(4), an application by a defendant, including a Part 20 defendant, to remove it from that list must be made within 7 days after the defendant has filed an acknowledgment of service or a defence, whichever is the later.

3.9 Where proceedings in the Business list of an authorised county court are removed from that list, the mercantile judge may at the same time:

(1) make an order allocating the proceedings to a track in accordance with CPR Part 26; or

(2) give directions for the purposes of allocation; and

(3) give case management directions.

Dispensing with Particulars of Claim or Defence

4. A mercantile judge may at any time, before or after the issue of the claim form, order that a case in the list of a Mercantile Court or in the Business list of an authorised county court be tried without the filing or service of particulars of claim or of a defence or of any other statement of case, but if such an order is made without any other party having had an opportunity to be heard that party may apply for it to be revoked.

Directions and Case Management

5.1 All cases in the list of a Mercantile Court or in the Business list of an authorised county court will be allocated to the multi-track. Subject to paragraph 3.9, the CPR rules relating to allocation questionnaires and to track allocation will not apply to them. They will be subject to case management by the court.

5.2(1) If mercantile proceedings are transferred to a Mercantile Court or a Business list under paragraph 3 then, unless the mercantile judge who made the order for transfer gave directions for the management of the case, an application to a mercantile judge for such directions shall be made within 14 days of the date of the order of transfer.

(2) If the claimant does not make an application in accordance with sub-paragraph (1), any other party may do so or may apply for the claim of the claimant in default to be struck out.

5.3(1) Subject to sub-paragraphs (2) and (3), interim applications in and trials of proceedings in a Mercantile Court or the Business list of an authorised county court shall be dealt with or heard, as the case may be, by a mercantile judge of the court in question.

(2) When an interim application needs to be dealt with urgently and a mercantile judge of the court in question is not available, the application may be dealt with by another judge, including a district judge.

(3) When the hearing of an application would involve the mercantile judge becoming aware of any matter which might embarrass him as the potential trial judge and there is no other mercantile judge of the court in question available to hear the application, the application may be heard by another judge, including a district judge.

(4) Matters concerning the enforcement of any judgment given in proceedings in a Mercantile Court or in the Business list of an authorised county court may be, and ordinarily will be, dealt with by a district judge.

(5) Subject to an express provision in a statute, rule or practice direction, sub-paragraphs (2), (3) and (4) above do not apply to applications for injunctions, freezing orders, search orders, committal or sequestration of assets.

(6) Nothing in this paragraph shall be construed as preventing the powers of a mercantile judge from being exercised by any judge of the High Court.

5.4 Paragraph 5 of the Practice Direction—The Multi-Track—supplementing CPR Part 29 applies to case management conferences in proceedings in a Mercantile Court or in the Business list of an authorised county court.

5.5 It is intended that a Mercantile Courts and Business Lists Guide will be prepared after consultation with the judges of the Mercantile Courts, the judges of the Central London County Court Business List and their respective Users Committees, and that the Guide will set out any special procedures to apply to the conduct of proceedings in Mercantile Courts and the Business lists of authorised county courts. In the meantime the practice set out in any "approved Guide" (see paragraph 5.6 below) should be followed subject to the provisions of this or any other Mercantile Courts and Business Lists practice direction and to any order that may be made in an individual case.

5.6(1) In relation to mercantile proceedings in any Mercantile Court or in the Business List of the Central London County Court, an "approved Guide" is a Guide that has been approved by the Head of Civil Justice for the purpose of mercantile proceedings in that court or in that list.

(2) In relation to any Mercantile Court or Business list in respect of which there is for the time being no "approved Guide", Section D of the Commercial Court Guide, 5th Edition, relating to Case management in the Commercial Court, shall be treated as the "approved Guide" for the purpose of mercantile proceedings in that court or in that list.

Arbitration Applications and Proceedings

6.1 An arbitration application (as defined in paragraph 2 of the Arbitration Practice Direction supplemental CPR Part 49) and proceedings to enforce an award under section 26 of the Arbitration Act 1950 or under sections 66 or 101(2) of the Arbitration Act 1996, shall be treated as mercantile claims for the purposes of this practice direction and may be included in the mercantile list of a Mercantile Court or the Business list of an authorised county court.

6.2 A mercantile judge may also deal with any other application under the Arbitration Act 1979 which may be commenced in or transferred to the mercantile list of a Mercantile Court or the Business list of an authorised county court.

PART 50

APPLICATION OF THE SCHEDULES

Editorial Introduction

50.0.1 A number of Orders of the former RSC and CCR remain in force, either in whole or in part. Unfortunately, they have not been re-cast in a style consistent with the provisions found in Pts 1 to 49 of the CPR but are simply re-enacted (with some amendments) in Schedules attached to the CPR.

For convenience, the several RSC and CCR provisions re-enacted in the Schedules are listed in the notes below.

50.1 **50.1**—(1) The Schedules to these Rules set out, with modifications, certain provisions previously contained in the Rules of the Supreme Court 1965[1] and the County Court Rules 1981.[2]

(2) These Rules apply in relation to the proceedings to which the Schedules apply subject to the provisions in the Schedules and the relevant practice directions.

(3) A provision previously contained in the Rules of the Supreme Court 1965—

(a) is headed "RSC";

(b) is numbered with the Order and rule numbers it bore as part of the RSC; and

(c) unless otherwise stated in the Schedules or the relevant practice direction, applies only to proceedings in the High Court.

(4) A provision previously contained in the County Court Rules 1981—

(a) is headed "CCR";

(b) is numbered with the Order and rule numbers it bore as part of the CCR; and

(c) unless otherwise stated in the Schedules or the relevant practice direction, applies only to proceedings in the county court.

(5) A reference in a Schedule to a rule by number alone is a reference to the rule so numbered in the Order in which the reference occurs.

(6) A reference in a Schedule to a rule by number prefixed by "CPR" is a reference to the rule with that number in these Rules.

(7) In the Schedules, unless otherwise stated, "the Act" means—

(a) in a provision headed "RSC", the Supreme Court Act 1981; and

(b) in a provision headed "CCR", the County Courts Act 1984.

50.1.1 **Effect of rule**—In the Report of the Review Body on Civil Justice (Cm 394, 1988) it was said that "a single set of rules, or a common core of rules ... should now be adopted covering general county court and High Court business, with separate provisions for specialist jurisdictions or procedures in either court" (p. 50). It was acknowledged that the task of creating such a set of rules would not be a simple one. It was recommended that the necessary work be put in hand. Accordingly, the terms of reference of the inquiry set-up by the Lord Chancellor in April 1994, which culminated in the publication of the Access to Justice Reports in April 1995 and July 1996, stated that the inquiry should produce "a single procedural code covering general High Court and county court business, with provisions for specialist jurisdictions and procedures in each court".

The CPR is the "single procedural code". Put broadly, it can be said that Pts 1 to 48 contain the rules "covering general High Court and county court business", complete with most of the procedural innovations recommended in the Access to Justice Reports. Consequently, the rules in these Parts are a mixture of old provisions presented more simply and clearly than heretofore and completely new provisions designed to implement the recommended innovations.

Many matters formerly dealt with in the former RSC and CCR did not fall for specific investigation in the Access to Justice Inquiry. Consequently, if there was to be "a single procedural

[1] S.I. 1965/1776.
[2] S.I. 1981/1687.

code", former rules dealing with these matters could be largely re-enacted. It might have been expected (in the spirit of the CPR) that those provisions would have been re-enacted in simpler and clearer language. However, it would seem that time did not permit that. Instead, former RSC and CCR Orders falling into this category are simply re-enacted (either in whole or in part) in, respectively, Sched. 1 and Sched. 2 of the CPR with some minor modifications to the text here and there to ensure that some of the basic procedural terminology used, in the one hand, in Pts 1 to 48 of the CPR and, on the other, in the RSC and CPR Orders and rules re-enacted in the Schedules is consistent. In addition, a few more significant modifications are made, for example, RSC, O.30 (Receivers) and O.99 (Inheritance (Provisions for Family and Dependants) Act 1975) are amended so that they apply to proceedings both in the High Court and county courts. Further, some amendments are designed to ensure that the surviving RSC and CCR provisions in future take effect in accordance with or subject to important provisions found in what could be called "the main body" of the CPR (note "Part 23" below).

The result is highly unsatisfactory and confusing, albeit, for reasons mentioned below, unavoidable.

Many of the former RSC and CCR Orders and rules re-enacted in Sched. 1 and 2 make use of prescribed forms. The former forms are to be used, subject to necessary amendments. Also, some are supplemented by practice directions.

Some of the former RSC and CCR Orders re-enacted in the Schedules contained within them cross-references to other former RSC and CCR Orders. In their re-enacted form those cross-references remain where the provision referred to itself is re-enacted. RSC, O.49 (Garnishee proceedings), r.9 (Money in Court) contains in sub-rule (4) a cross-reference to RSC, O.75, r.24. However, O.75, r.24 is not among the provisions re-enacted in Schedule 1. Also, RSC, O.77 (Proceedings by and against the Crown), r.7 (Summary judgment) contains in sub-rule (1) a cross-reference to RSC, O.86, r.1. However, again, O.86, r.1 is not among the provisions re-enacted in Schedule 1. These appear to be drafting lapses (other examples may be given).

Surviving RSC and CCR provisions—It will be noted from the list set out below of the former RSC and CCR provisions re-enacted in Scheds 1 and 2, that the bulk of the surviving provisions relate to (1) aspects of the law of parties, (2) proceedings in relation to land, (3) foreign proceedings and enforcement of foreign judgments, (4) the enforcement of domestic judgments and orders, (5) appeals of various kinds, and (6) proceedings under miscellaneous statutes. Important RSC and CCR Orders re-enacted (either in whole or in part) in the Schedules to the CPR and not falling in any of these six categories include RSC, O.53 (Applications for judicial review), O.81 (Partners) and O.82 (Defamation claims). **50.1.2**

The reform of the law relating to proceedings for possession of land remains unfinished business. Consequently, the Schedules to the CPR include (with some amendments RSC, O.88 (Mortgage claims) and O.113 (Summary provisions for possession of land) and CCR, O.24 (Summary proceedings for the recovery of land).

Parties (and "multi-party situations")—Former RSC, O.15 contained rules dealing with the joinder of causes of action, the joinder of parties and counterclaims. The work done by these provisions is now done by rules found in particular parts of the CPR. However, RSC, O.15 also contained various provisions dealing with parties, including what is sometimes called "multi-party situations". These survive in Schedule 1, at least in part, and with necessary amendments. The surviving rules include r.6A (Proceedings against estates), r.7(1) (Change of parties by reasons of death, etc.), r.9(1) (Failure to proceed after death of a party) and r.15 (Representation of deceased person interested in proceedings). The surviving RSC, O.15 provisions dealing with multi-party situations are: r.11 (Relator actions), r.12 (Representative proceedings), r.12A (Derivative claims), r.13 (Representation of interested persons who cannot be ascertained, etc.), r.13A (Notice of claim to non-parties), r.15 (Representation of beneficiaries by trustees, etc.) and r.17 (Conduct of proceedings). **50.1.2A**

Foreign proceedings and judgments—The law relating to foreign proceedings, both within and beyond the E.C., is in a state of flux and it will be some time before the provisions in RSC, O.11 (Service of process, etc., out of the jurisdiction), O.69 (Service of foreign process) and O.71 (Reciprocal enforcement of judgments, etc.) can be amended in accordance with the changes which are anticipated. **50.1.3**

Appeals—The subject of appeals was referred to in the Access to Justice Reports and appeals to the Court of Appeal was the subject of separate inquiry in recent times. As a result, RSC, O.59 (Appeals to the Court of Appeal) was amended by the Rules of the Supreme Court (Amendment No. 2) 1998 (S.I. 1998 No. 3049), brought into effect on January 1, 1999. **50.1.4**

Enforcement of judgments—The subject of the enforcement of domestic judgments is presently undergoing inquiry and, presumably, in due course some proposals will emerge which will enable many of the provisions re-enacted in the two Schedules to be represented as a single coherent code and in a style consistent with that which obtains in Pts 1 to 49. **50.1.5**

Miscellaneous statutes—Finally, there are many statutes under which proceedings in the **50.1.6**

High Court or the county courts (or both) can be taken and for which special provision was made in separate Orders found in the RSC from O.74 onwards and in the CCR in O.49 (Miscellaneous statutes). These Orders are re-enacted in the Schedules as necessary.

50.1.7 **Part 23**—Many of the former RSC and CCR rules re-enacted in the Schedules to the CPR contained, either within themselves or by cross-reference to other RSC and CCR Orders, provisions regulating the manner in which applications may be made to the court. Many of these rules incorporated by reference (sometimes with modifications) provisions found in former RSC, O.32 (Applications and proceedings in chambers) and CCR, O.13 (Applications and orders in the course of proceedings). In the CPR, RSC, O.32 and CCR, O.13 are in effect replaced by Pt 23 (General rules about applications for court orders). Consequently, references to former RSC, O.32 and CCR, O.13 in the RSC and CCR provisions re-enacted in the Schedules to the CPR have been replaced with references to Pt 23.

50.1.8 **Specialist jurisdictions and procedures in each court**—As was explained above, it was expected that the CPR would constitute "a single procedural code" making provision, not only for "general High Court and county court business", but also for "specialist jurisdictions and procedures" in each court. In Pt 49 (Specialist proceedings) it is stated in r.49(1) that the CPR shall apply to the specialist proceedings listed in r.49(2) subject to the provisions of relevant practice directions which applies to those proceedings. The former RSC contained a number of Orders dealing specifically with proceedings listed as "specialist proceedings" in r.49(2) (*e.g.* RSC, O.72 (Commercial actions) and RSC, O.73 (Applications relating to arbitration)). These Orders are not re-enacted in the Schedules to the CPR. However, much of what was found in those Orders is now covered by the practice directions relating to the specialist proceedings listed in r.49(2).

50.1.9 **Judicial review**—It is important to note that RSC, O.53 (Applications for judicial review) is re-enacted in Schedule 1. Some significant modifications are made to this Order as re-enacted.

Schedule 1—RSC provisions

50.2 Order 10, r.4 (Service of claim form in certain actions for possession of land)
Order 11 (Service of process etc., out of jurisdiction)
Order 15, rr.6A, 7(1), 9(1), 11 to 17 (Causes of action, counterclaims and parties)
Order 17 (Interpleader)
Order 23 (Security for costs)
Order 30 (Receivers)
Order 31 (Sales, etc., of land by order of court etc.)
Order 44 (Proceedings under judgments and orders: Chancery Division)
Order 45 (Enforcement of judgments and orders: general)
Order 46 (Writs of execution: general)
Order 47 (Writs of fieri facias)
Order 48 (Examination of judgment debtor, etc.)
Order 49 (Garnishee proceedings)
Order 50 (Charging orders, stop orders, etc.)
Order 51 (Receivers: equitable execution)
Order 52 (Estoppel)
Order 53 (Applications for judicial review)
Order 54 (Applications for writ of habeas corpus)
Order 55 (Appeals to High Court from court, tribunal or person: general)
Order 56 (Appeals, etc., to High Court by case stated: general)
Order 57 (Divisional Court proceedings, etc.: supplementary provisions)
Order 58 (Appeals from masters, registrars, referees and judges)
Order 59 (Appeals to the Court of Appeal)
Order 60 (Appeals to Court of Appeal from the Restrictive Practices Court)
Order 61 (Appeals from tribunals to Court of Appeal by case stated)
Order 62 (Costs) Appendix 3 Fixed costs Pts II & III (in part)
Order 64 (Sittings, vacations and office hours)
Order 69 (Services of foreign process)
Order 70 (Obtaining evidence for foreign court, etc)
Order 71 (Reciprocal enforcement of judgments, etc.)
Order 74 (Applications and appeals under the Merchant Shipping Act 1995)
Order 77 (Proceedings by and against the Crown)
Order 79 (Criminal proceedings)
Order 81 (Partners)
Order 82 (Defamation claims)
Order 85 (Administration and similar actions)
Order 87 (Debenture holders' claims: receiver's register)
Order 88 (Mortgage claims)
Order 91 (Revenue proceedings)
Order 92 (Lodgement, investment, etc., of funds in Court: Chancery Division)

Order 93 (Applications and appeals to High Court under various Acts: Chancery Division)
Order 94 (Applications and appeals to High Court under various Acts: Queen's Bench Division)
Order 95 (Bills of Sale Acts 1878 and 1882 and the Industrial and Provident Societies Act 1967)
Order 96 (The Mines (Working Facilities and Support) Act 1966, etc.)
Order 97 (The Landlord and Tenant Acts 1927, 1954 and 1987)
Order 98 (Local Government Finance Act 1982, Pt III)
Order 99 (Inheritance (Provisions for Family and Dependants) Act 1975)
Order 101 (The Pensions Appeal Tribunals Act 1943)
Order 106 (Proceedings relating to solicitors: the Solicitors Act 1974)
Order 108 (Proceedings relating to charities: the Charities Act 1993)
Order 109 (The Administration of Justice Act 1960)
Order 110 (Environmental Control Proceedings)
Order 111 (The Social Security Administration Act 1992)
Order 112 (Applications for use of blood tests in determining paternity)
Order 113 (Summary proceedings for possession of land)
Order 114 (References to the European Court)
Order 115 (Confiscation and forfeiture in connection with criminal proceedings)

Schedule 2—Surviving CCR provisions

Order 1, r.6 (Application of RSC to county court proceedings) 50.3
Order 3 (Commencement of proceedings), r.6 (Appeals to county court)
Order 4 (Venue for bringing proceedings), r.3 (Proceedings relating to land)
Order 5 (Causes of action and parties), rr.5 to 14 (excluding r.11)
Order 6 (Particulars of claim), rr.3, 5, 5A and 6
Order 7 (Service of documents), rr.15 and 15A
Order 13 (Applications and orders in the course of proceedings), r.1(10) and (11)
Order 19, r.15 (Reference to ECJ – making and transmission of order)
Order 22 (Judgments and orders), rr.8, 10, 11 and 13
Order 24 (Summary proceedings for the recovery of land)
Order 25 (Enforcement of judgments and orders: General)
Order 26 (Warrants of execution, delivery and possession)
Order 27 (Attachment of earnings)
Order 28 (Judgment summonses)
Order 29 (Committal for breach of order or undertaking)
Order 30 (Garnishee proceedings)
Order 31 (Charging orders)
Order 33 (Interpleader proceedings), excluding r.12
Order 34 (Penal and disciplinary provisions), excluding r.5
Order 35 (Enforcement of county court judgments outside England and Wales)
Order 37 (Rehearing, setting aside and appeal from district judge), rr.1, 6 and 8
Order 38 (Costs), r.18 and App. 8 (edited)
Order 39 (Administration orders)
Order 42 (Proceedings by and against the Crown), excluding rr.2 and 3
Order 43 (The Landlord and Tenants Acts 1927, 1954, 1985 and 1987)
Order 44 (The Agricultural Holdings Act 1986)
Order 45 (The Representation of the People Act 1983)
Order 46 (The Legitimacy Act 1976)
Order 47 (Domestic and matrimonial proceedings)
Order 48B (Enforcement of parking penalties under the Road Traffic Act 1991)
Order 48D (Enforcement of fixed penalties under the Road Traffic (Vehicle Emissions) (Fixed Penalty) Regulations 1997)
Order 49 (Miscellaneous statutes)

PART 51

Transitional Arrangements

Part 51

Transitional Arrangements

51.1 **51.1** A practice direction shall make provision for the extent to which these Rules shall apply to proceedings issued before 26 April 1999.

51.1.1 **Editorial Introduction**—The general scheme of the transitional arrangements is to apply the CPR to defended cases. When a new step has to be taken it is to be taken under the CPR. The overriding objective (see Pt 1) applies. In particular, when existing proceedings come before a judge for the first time (whether at a hearing or on paper) after April 26, 1999 he is to direct how the CPR will apply to the proceedings from then on. These principles are simple to state but have proved to be very difficult and time consuming to apply in practice. It is never easy to change horses in mid-stream. Every case requires an individualised order according to the type of case, the steps taken so far and the steps now needed to get the case ready for trial. In many cases insufficient time has been allowed to enable the master/district judge to consider how to apply the CPR to the pending case.

Solicitors should ensure that a sufficient time estimate is given to allow the court to deal with the matter which has caused the application and then additionally to give directions pursuant to the Practice Direction which supplements Part 51 and, of course, the assessment of costs. Wherever possible the necessary directions should be agreed with the other side and submitted for the court's approval. It is suggested that, for cases commenced prior to April 26, 1999, the following matters need to be addressed:

(1) Allocation to track (consider Pt 26)
(2) Statements of Case (consider Pts 7, 8, 15, 16, 17 and 18)
(3) Disclosure and Inspection of Documents (consider Pt 31)
(4) Expert Evidence (consider Pt 35)
(5) Exchange of witness statements (consider Pt 32)
(6) Other outstanding matters
(7) Likely length of trial and proposed trial "window".

It may be helpful to complete Listing Questionnaires.

All cases pending as at April 26, 1999 should be brought before a judge, at a hearing or on paper, by April 25, 2000. If this is not done the proceedings are automatically stayed: (see 51PD–001, para. 19).

PRACTICE DIRECTION—TRANSITIONAL ARRANGEMENTS

This Practice Direction supplements CPR Part 51

Contents of this Practice Direction

51PD–001 **1**(1) This Practice Direction deals with the application of the Civil Procedure Rules ("CPR") to proceedings issued before 26 April 1999 ("existing proceedings").

(2) In this Practice Direction "the previous rules" means as appropriate the Rules of the Supreme Court 1965 ("RSC") or County Court Rules 1981 ("CCR"), in force immediately before 26 April 1999.

General scheme of transitional arrangements

2 The general scheme is—

(a) to apply the previous rules to undefended cases, allowing them to progress to their disposal; but
(b) to apply the CPR to defended cases so far as is practicable.

Where the previous rules will normally apply

3 General principle—Where an initiating step has been taken in a case before 26 April 1999, in particular one that uses forms or other documentation required by the previous rules, the case will proceed in the first instance under the previous rules. Any step which a party must take in response to something done by another party in accordance with the previous rules must also be in accordance with those rules.

4 Responding to old process—A party who is served with an old type of originating process (writ, summons etc.) on or after 26 April 1999 is required to respond in accordance with the previous rules and the instructions on any forms received with the originating process.

5 Filing and service of pleadings where old process served—Where a case has been begun by an old type of originating process (whether served before or after 26 April 1999), filing and service of pleadings will continue according to the previous rules.

6 Automatic directions/discovery

High Court

(1) Where the timetable for automatic directions under RSC, Order 25, rule 8 or automatic discovery under RSC, Order 24 has begun to apply to proceedings before 26 April 1999, those directions will continue to have effect on or after 26 April 1999.

County Court

(2) Where automatic directions under CCR, Order 17, rule 11 have begun to apply to existing proceedings before 26 April 1999 or the court has sent out notice that automatic directions under CCR, Order 17, rule 11 (Form N.450) will apply (even if the timetable will not begin until 26 April 1999 or after), those directions will continue to have effect on or after 26 April 1999.

(3) However CCR, Order 17, rule 11(9) will not apply and therefore proceedings will not be struck out where there has been no request for a hearing to be fixed within 15 months of the date when pleadings were deemed to close. (But see paragraph 19.)

High Court and County Court

(4) However, if the case comes before the court on or after 26 April 1999, the new rules may apply. (See paragraph 15.)

7 Default judgment—(1) If a party wishes default judgment to be entered in existing proceedings, he must do so in accordance with the previous rules.

(2) Where default judgment has been entered and there are outstanding issues to be resolved (e.g. damages to be assessed), the court officer may refer the proceedings to the judge, so that case management decisions about the proceedings and the conduct of the hearing can be made in accordance with the practice set out in paragraph 15.

(3) If a party needs to apply for permission to enter default judgment, he must make that application under CPR Part 23 (general rules about applications for court orders).

(4) An application to set aside judgment entered in default must be made under CPR Part 23 (general rules about applications for court orders) and CPR Part 13 (setting aside or varying default judgment) will apply to the proceedings as it would apply to default judgment entered under the CPR.

(5) CPR rule 15.11 (claims stayed if it is not defended or admitted) applies to these proceedings.

8 Judgment on admission in the county court—(1) If a party to existing proceedings in the county court wishes to request judgment to be entered on an admission, he must do so in accordance with the previous rules.

(2) Where judgment has been entered and there are outstanding issues to be resolved (e.g. damages to be assessed), the court officer may refer the proceedings to the judge, so that case management decisions about the proceedings and the conduct of the hearing can be made in accordance with the practice set out in paragraph 15.

(3) If a party needs to apply for permission to enter judgment, he must make that application under CPR Part 23 (general rules about applications for court orders).

9 Order inconsistent with CPR—Where a court order has been made before 26 April 1999, that order must still be complied with on or after 26 April 1999.

10 Steps taken before 26 April 1999—(1) Where a party has taken any step in the proceedings in accordance with the previous rules that step will remain valid on or after 26 April 1999.

(2) A party will not normally be required to take any action that would amount to taking that step again under the CPR. For example if discovery has been given, a party will not normally be required to provide disclosure under CPR Part 31.

Where the CPR will normally apply

11 General principle—Where a new step is to be taken in any existing proceedings on or after 26 April 1999, it is to be taken under the CPR.

12 Part 1 (Overriding objective) to apply—Part 1 (Overriding objective) will apply to all existing proceedings from 26 April 1999 onwards.

13 Originating process—(1) Only claim forms under the CPR will be issued by the court on or after 26 April 1999.

(2) If a request to issue an old type of originating process (writ, summons etc.) is received at the court on or after 26 April 1999 it will be returned unissued.

(3) An application made on or after 26 April 1999 to extend the validity of originating process issued before 26 April 1999 must be made in accordance with CPR Part 23 (general rules about applications for court orders), but the court will decide whether to allow the application in accordance with the previous law.

14 Application to the court—(1) Any application to the court made on or after 26 April 1999 must be made in accordance with CPR Part 23(General rules about applications for court orders).

(2) Any other relevant CPR will apply to the substance of the application, unless this practice direction provides otherwise. (See paragraphs 13(3) (application to extend the validity of originating process)and 18(2) (costs)).

(3) For example, a party wishing to apply for summary judgment must do so

having regard to the test in CPR Part 24. A party wishing to apply for an interim remedy must do so under CPR Part 25 etc.

(4) Any other CPR will apply as necessary. For example, CPR Part 4 will apply as to forms and CPR Part 6 will apply to service of documents.

(5) If the pleadings have not been filed at court, the applicant must file all pleadings served when he files his application notice.

15 First time before a judge on or after 26 April 1999—(1) When proceedings come before a judge (whether at a hearing or on paper) for the first time on or after 26 April 1999, he may direct how the CPR are to apply to the proceedings and may disapply certain provisions of the CPR. He may also give case management directions (which may include allocating the proceedings to a case management track).

(2) The general presumption will be that the CPR will apply to the proceedings from then on unless the judge directs or this practice direction provides otherwise. (See paragraphs 13(3) (application to extend the validity of originating process) and 18(2) (costs)).

(3) If an application has been issed before 26 April 1999 and the hearing of the application has been set for a date on or after 26 April 1999, the general presumption is that the application will be decided having regard to the CPR. (For example an application for summary judgment issued before 26 April 1999, with a hearing date set for 1 May 1999, will be decided having regard to the test in CPR Part 24 (summary judgment).)

(4) When the first occasion on which existing proceedings are before a judge on or after 26 April 1999 is a trial or hearing of a substantive issue, the general presumption is that the trial or hearing will be conducted having regard to the CPR.

16 Where pleadings deemed to close on or after 26 April 1999—(1) This paragraph applies to existing proceedings where pleadings are deemed to close on or after 26 April 1999. However this paragraph does not apply to those county court proceedings where notice that automatic directions apply (Form N.450) has been sent (in which case the automatic directions will apply—see paragraph 6).

(2) CPR Part 26 (case management—preliminary stage) applies to these proceedings.

(3) If a defence is filed at court on or after 26 April 1999, the court will serve an allocation questionnaire where CPR rule 26.3 would apply, unless it dispenses with the need for one.

(4) If pleadings have not been filed at court (this will normally be the case in the Queen's Bench Division) the claimant must file copies of all the pleadings served within 14 days of the date that pleadings are deemed to close.

(5) Unless it dispenses with the need for one, the court will then serve an allocation questionnaire.

(6) In the previous rules pleadings are deemed to close:

(a) High Court—

(i) 14 days after service of any reply, or

(ii) if there is no reply, 14 days after service of the defence to counterclaim, or

(iii) if there is no reply or defence to counterclaim, 14 days after the service of the defence.

(b) County Court—

14 days after the delivery of a defence or, where a counterclaim is served with the defence, 28 days after the delivery of the defence.

(7) Where there are 2 or more defendants the court will normally wait until the claimant has filed copies of all the pleadings before serving an allocation

questionnaire. However, the court may (in cases where there is a delay) serve allocation questionnaires despite the fact that pleadings have not closed in respect of any other defendant.

(8) The court will then allocate the proceedings in accordance with CPR rule 26.5.

(9) The CPR will then apply generally to the proceedings.

17 Agreement to apply the CPR—The parties may agree in writing that the CPR will apply to any proceedings from the date of the agreement. When they do so:

(a) all those who are parties at that time must agree,
(b) the CPR must apply in their entirety,
(c) the agreement is irrevocable,
(d) the claimant must file a copy of the agreement at court.

18 Costs—(1) Any assessment of costs that takes place on or after 26 April 1999 will be in accordance with CPR Parts 43 to 48.

(2) However, the general presumption is that no costs for work undertaken before 26 April 1999 will be disallowed if those costs would have been allowed in a costs taxation before 26 April 1999.

(3) The decision as to whether to allow costs for work undertaken on or after 26 April will generally be taken in accordance with CPR Parts 43 to 48.

(The costs practice direction contains more information on the operation of the transitional arrangements in relation to costs.)

19 Existing proceedings after one year—(1) If any existing proceedings have not come before a judge, at a hearing or on paper, between 26 April 1999 and 25 April 2000, those proceedings shall be stayed.

(2) Any party to those proceedings may apply for the stay to be lifted.

(3) Proceedings of the following types will not be stayed as a result of this provision:

(a) where the case has been given a fixed trial date which is after 25 April 2000,
(b) personal injury cases where there is no issue on liability but the proceedings have been adjourned by court order to determine the prognosis,
(c) where the court is dealing with the continuing administration of an estate or a trust or a receivership.
(d) applications relating to funds in court.

SCHEDULE 1

Rule 50(3)

RSC ORDER 10

SERVICE OF ORIGINATING PROCESS: GENERAL PROVISIONS

Service of claim form in certain actions for possession of land

4. Where a claim form contains a claim for the possession of land, the court may— **R10.4**

(a) if satisfied on an application without notice being served on any other person that no person appears to be in possession of the land and that service cannot be otherwise effected on any defendant, authorise service on that defendant to be effected by affixing a copy of the claim form to some conspicuous part of the land;

(b) if satisfied on such an application that no person appears to be in possession of the land and that service could not otherwise have been effected on any defendant, order that service already effected by affixing a copy of the claim form to some conspicuous part of the land shall be treated as good service on that defendant.

Editorial Note—See also Sched. 2, CCR, O.7, r.5(4) for comparable provisions relating to service of claim form in county court proceedings. **R10.4.1**

RSC ORDER 11

SERVICE OF PROCESS, ETC., OUT OF THE JURISDICTION

Contents **R11.0.1**

Editorial Introduction

Rules 2 and 3 long revoked. **R11.0.2**
Rules 1A and 1B added with CPR.

Order to apply to county court r.10.

Before the CPR came into force, service out of the jurisdiction in High Court proceedings was dealt with by the provisions in RSC, O.11 and in county court proceedings by CCR, O.8. Order 11, with some modifications, has been re-enacted in Sched. 1 of the CPR and made applicable to the county court proceedings at both levels of court (therefore, CCR, O.8 does not appear in Sched. 2). Rules 1A and 1B are new and did not appear in O.11 before the CPR came into force. They reflect provisions as to the filing of an acknowledgement of service or defence now found in Pt. 10 and Pt. 14, and as to the filing and serving of an admission now found in Pt. 15. As these provisions are not the same as the ones they replace, some changes to O.11 were necessary and are found mainly in rr.1A and 1B.

R11.0.3 **Jurisdiction and service**—Service is a procedural mechanism which is normally a precondition to the exercise of jurisdiction. Service does not create jurisdiction, but except for limited situations, such as where applications are made without notice before proceedings are started, the court's jurisdiction cannot be exercised against an individual unless either he has been served or the court has dispensed with service. In this context the expression "jurisdiction" refers to the subject matter of the proceedings whether with regard to the nature of the claim or the person against whom the claim is brought. The courts also have a general jurisdiction to decide whether they have jurisdiction to try any case or part of a case having regard to the subject-matter of the claim, the nature of the defendant and whether adequate procedural steps have been taken against the defendant in question to make him a party to the proceedings *Canada Trust Co. v. Stolzenberg* [1997] 1 W.L.R. 1582. In appropriate circumstances the courts also have a discretion to decide whether to exercise jurisdiction where there is a more suitable jurisdiction for the trial of a case.

R11.0.4 **Service within the jurisdiction**—The application of the principle stated in the previous paragraph is less apparent in respect of proceedings started by service upon a party within the territorial jurisdiction than where service is to be effected elsewhere; but it is nevertheless relevant. Most such situations arise under the Civil Jurisdiction and Judgments Act 1982 as amended by that of 1991. This Act gives effect to the Brussels and Lugano Conventions which regulate the places where proceedings are to be held in respect of the subject matter and persons to whom they relate. The Act also regulates where within the territories that comprise the United Kingdom such proceedings should be heard. The effect of the Act is that, even where service has been properly made upon a person within the territorial jurisdiction, the courts may not have jurisdiction to retain the proceedings. Apart from the operation of the Act the constraints upon the courts' jurisdiction usually arise from a combination of the nature of the subject matter of the proceedings and the person against whom they are brought, as for instance a claim covered by section 2(5) of the Crown Proceedings Act 1947 or proceedings against a diplomatic agent where there is immunity under the Diplomatic Immunities and Privileges Act 1964.

R11.0.5 **Service outside the territorial jurisdiction**—The ability to exercise civil jurisdiciton *in personam* in this country is founded upon the concept of personal service. The rigour of the concept has been modified both in respect of corporations and natural persons situated within the jurisdiction by provisions such as the ability to serve by post; but the position remains that where a defendant is outside the jurisdiction he can only be made a party to proceedings within the jurisdiction either by service or where service has been expressly dispensed with. Since the Common Law Procedure Act 1852, statutory powers have been used to list situations in which service may be made upon persons who are out of the jurisdiction, subject to permission being given by the court. The grant of permission is discretionary. More recently the Civil Jurisdiction and Judgments Act 1982, as amended by the Act of 1991, has conferred power to serve proceedings without the permission of the court in a wide variety of civil and commercial matters upon persons within territories of the Contracting States. The Isle of Man and the Channel Islands are not subject to the provisions of the Act.

R11.0.6 **Service under the Brussels and Lugano Conventions**—The Civil Jurisdiction and Judgments Act 1982 introduced the Brussels Convention on Jurisdiction and the Enforcement of Judgment in Civil and Commercial matters into the law of the three jurisdictions that make up the United Kingdom. The Convention applies to civil and commercial matters as defined; certain matters (*e.g.* revenue matters) are excluded. The text of the Convention is contained in Sched. 1 (for further notes and text of this Act, see SCP 1999, Vol. 2, Section 7). The Contracting States are those states that comprise the European Community. The Civil Jurisdiction and Judgments Act 1991 introduced the Lugano Convention. This Convention enables EFTA countries, subject to minor modifications, to join the Brussels Convention regime. The Convention has its own rules for allocating jurisdiction among the courts of the several Contracting States and they are quite complicated in certain respects. The general rule is that persons domiciled in a Contracting State should, whatever their nationality, be sued in the courts of that State. However, a person domiciled in a Contracting State may be sued in the courts of another Contracting State insofar as that is permitted by the Convention. By agreement, parties may confer jurisdiction on the courts of a particular Contracting State (Art. 17). The result is that cases can arise under the Convention where a claimant can bring proceedings in the High Court by serving his claim form on a defendant elsewhere within the E.C. In these circumstances, the jurisdiction of the High Court under the Convention is not based on service of the claim form on the defendant within the jurisdiction or on the extended jurisdiction rules provided by CPR, Sched. 1, RSC, O.11, r.1(1). Service elsewhere within the Community will be effective service and no leave of the Court to make such service is required. This state of affairs is acknowledged by CPR, Sched. 1, RSC, O.11, r.1(2)(a).

Service in Scotland or Northern Ireland—The United Kingdom consists of, in addition to England and Wales, two other legal systems. They are Scotland and Northern Ireland. In certain circumstances, a claim form may be served on a defendant in either of those jurisdictions. The matter is mainly regulated, not by the extended jurisdiction rules found in CPR, Sched. 1, RSC, O.11, r.1(1), but by a modified version of the Brussels Convention set out in Sched. 4 to the Civil Jurisdiction and Judgments Act 1982. The general rule is that persons domiciled in a part of the United Kingdom shall be sued in the courts of that part. However, a person domiciled in a part of the United Kingdom may be sued in the courts of another part insofar as that is permitted by the modified Convention. By agreement, parties may confer jurisdiction on the courts of a particular part (Art. 17). The result is that cases can arise under this Convention where a claimant can bring proceedings in the High Court by serving his claim form on a defendant in Scotland and Northern Ireland. In these circumstances, the jurisdiction of the High Court is not based on service of the claim form on the defendant within the jurisdiction or on the extended jurisdiction rules provided by O.11, r.1(1). Service in Scotland and Northern Ireland will be effective service and no leave of the Court to make such service is required. This state of affairs is acknowledged by O.11, r.1(2)(a). However where the Act does not apply permission to serve out of the jurisdiction will be required. R11.0.7

Summary of service regimes:—Where permission is not required. R11.0.8

(a) Cases where the Court has jurisdiction given by the Brussels or Lugano Convention and the defendant is not domiciled in Scotland or Northern Ireland (O.11, r.1(2)(a)). The relevant Convention provisions are summarised in paras R11.4.52–R11.4.56

(b) Similar cases where the defendant is domiciled in Scotland or Northern Ireland (O.11, r.1(2)(a)). The modified Convention provisions are found in Sched. 4 to the 1982 Act.

(c) Cases where the Court has been given jurisdiction by statute to entertain a claim notwithstanding that the defendant is not within the jurisdiction (O.11, r.1(2)(b)).

Where permission is required.

(d) Cases where permission may be given under O.11, r.1(1). As this rule does not apply to any case coming within O.11, r.1(2), that is to say, within (a) to (c) above, the provisions of r.1(1) will apply (i) where the defendant is neither domiciled in a Contracting State nor has agreed to give to a court in England and Wales jurisdiction under a valid agreement made under Art. 17 of the Brussels Convention or the modified Convention; (ii) where, though the defendant is so domiciled, the claim itself is not a civil or commercial matter within the Convention (*e.g.* revenue claims). The Conventions do not apply either to the Isle of Man or to the Channel Islands.

In the annotations following r.4 of this Order the subject of service where permission is required is dealt with first and the subject of service without permission follows (paras R11.4.52 *et seq.*).

Related Sources

- Civil Jurisdiction and Judgments Act 1982 R11.0.9
- SCP Mainwork 1999 Vol. 2, Section 7
- Practice Direction—Service out of the Jurisdiction
- Practice Direction—Admiralty
- Practice Direction—Arbitrations
- Commercial Court Guide (5th ed.)

Principal cases in which service of claim form out of jurisdiction is permissible

1.—(1) Provided that the claim form is not a claim form to which paragraph (2) of this rule applies, a claim form may be served out of the jurisdiction with the permission of the court if— R11.1

(a) a remedy is sought against a person domiciled within the jurisdiction;

(b) an injunction is sought ordering the defendant to do or refrain from doing anything within the jurisdiction (whether or not damages are also claimed in respect of a failure to do or the doing of that thing);

(c) the claim is brought against a person duly served within or out of the jurisdiction and a person out of the jurisdiction is a necessary or proper party thereto;

(d) the claim is brought to enforce, rescind, dissolve, annul or otherwise affect a contract, or to recover damages or obtain other remedy in

respect of the breach of a contract, being (in either case) a contract which—
- (i) was made within the jurisdiction, or
- (ii) was made by or through an agent trading or residing within the jurisdiction on behalf of a principal trading or residing out of the jurisdiction, or
- (iii) is by its terms, or by implication, governed by English law, or
- (iv) contains a term to the effect that the High Court shall have jurisdiction to hear and determine any claim in respect of the contract;

(e) the claim is brought in respect of a breach committed within the jurisdiction of a contract made within or out of the jurisdiction, and irrespective of the fact, if such be the case, that the breach was preceded or accompanied by a breach committed out of the jurisdiction that rendered impossible the performance of so much of the contract as ought to have been performed within the jurisdiction;

(f) the claim is founded on a tort and the damage was sustained, or resulted from an act committed, within the jurisdiction;

(g) the whole subject-matter of the proceedings is land situate within the jurisdiction (with or without rents or profits) or the perpetuation of testimony relating to land so situate;

(h) the claim is brought to construe, rectify, set aside or enforce an act, deed, will, contract, obligation or liability affecting land situate within the jurisdiction;

(i) the claim is made for a debt secured on immovable property or is made to assert, declare or determine proprietary or possessory rights, or rights of security, in or over movable property, or to obtain authority to dispose of movable property, situate within the jurisdiction;

(j) the claim is brought to execute the trusts of a written instrument being trusts that ought to be executed according to English law and of which the person to be served with the claim form is a trustee, or for any remedy which might be obtained in any such action;

(k) the claim is made for the administration of the estate of a person who died domiciled within the jurisdiction or for any remedy which might be obtained in any such action;

(l) the claim is brought in a probate action;

(m) the claim is brought to enforce any judgment or arbitral award;

(n) the claim is brought against a defendant not domiciled in Scotland or Northern Ireland in respect of a claim by the Commissioners of Inland Revenue for or in relation to any of the duties or taxes which have been, or are for the time being, placed under their care and management;

(o) the claim is brought under the Nuclear Installations Act 1965 or in respect of contributions under the Social Security Contributions and Benefits Act 1992;

(p) the claim is made for a sum to which the Directive of the Council of the European Communities dated 15th March 1976 No. 76/308/EEC applies, and service is to be effected in a country which is a member State of the European Economic Community;

(q) the claim is made under the Drug Trafficking Offences Act 1994;

(r) the claim is made under the Financial Services Act 1986 or the Banking Act 1987;

(s) the claim is made under Part VI of the Criminal Justice Act 1988;

(t) the claim is brought for money had and received or for an account or other remedy against the defendant as constructive trustee, and the defendant's alleged liability arises out of acts committed, whether by him or otherwise, within the jurisdiction;

(u) the claim is made under the Immigration (Carriers' Liability) Act 1987.

(2) A claim form may be served out of the jurisdiction on a defendant without the permission of the court provided that each claim against that defendant is either—

(a) a claim which by virtue of the Civil Jurisdiction and Judgments Act 1982 the court has power to hear and determine, made in proceedings to which the following conditions apply—

(i) no proceedings between the parties concerning the same cause of action are pending in the courts of any other part of the United Kingdom or of any other Convention territory; and

(ii) either the defendant is domiciled in any part of the United Kingdom or in any other Convention territory, or the proceedings begun by the claim form are proceedings to which Article 16 of Schedule 1, 3C or 4 refers, or the defendant is a party to an agreement conferring jurisdiction to which Article 17 of Schedule 1, 3C or 4 to that Act applies; or

(b) a claim which by virtue of any other enactment the High Court has power to hear and determine notwithstanding that the person against whom the claim is made is not within the jurisdiction of the Court or that the wrongful act, neglect or default giving rise to the claim did not take place within its jurisdiction.

(4) For the purposes of this rule, and of rule 9 of this Order, domicile is to be determined in accordance with the provisions of sections 41 to 46 of the Civil Jurisdictions and Judgments Act 1982 and "Convention territory" means the territory or territories of any Contracting State, as defined by section 1(3) of that Act, to which, as defined in section 1(1) of that Act, the Brussels or the Lugano Convention apply.

Effect of rule—Slightly re-phrased, *e.g.* at start of (1) and (2) sub-para (a) "remedy" instead of "relief", sub-para (1) "within the meaning of Order 76" dropped from end; para. (3) has gone but taken care of by new rr.1A and 1B. **R11.1.1**

O.75, r.2(1) has gone: see now the Practice Directions—Admiralty (see para. 49FPD–001).

The period for filing an acknowledgment of service or filing or serving an admission where the claim form is served under rule 1(2)

1A.—(1) This rule sets out the period for filing an acknowledgment of service under CPR Part 10 or filing or serving an admission under CPR Part 14 where a claim form has been served out of the jurisdiction under rule 1(2). **R11.1A**

(2) If the claim form is to be served under rule 1(2)(a) in Scotland, Northern Ireland or in the European territory of another contracting state the period is—

(a) Where the defendant is served with a claim form which states that particulars of claim are to follow, 21 days after the service of the particulars of claim; and

(b) in any other case, 21 days after service of the claim form

(3) If the claim form is to be served under rule 1(2)(a) in any other territory of a Contracting State the period is—

(a) where the defendant is served with a claim form which states that particulars of claim are to follow, 31 days after the service of the particulars of claim; and

(b) in any other case, 31 days after service of the claim form.

(4) If the claim form is to be served under—

(a) rule 1(2)(a) in a country not referred to in paragraphs (2) or (3); or

(b) rule 1(2)(b).

the period is set out in the relevant practice direction.

R11.1A.1 **Effect of rule**—This rule and its accompanying practice directions set out the period for filing an acknowledgement of service or filing or serving an admission where the claim form has been served without the need for permission. It should be noted that where the proceedings are in the Commercial Court the defendant's time starts to run when the claim form is served but elsewhere time only starts to run when the particulars of claim have been served.

The period for filing a defence where the claim form is served under rule 1(2)

R11.1B **1B.**—(1) This rule sets out the period for filing a defence under CPR Part 15 where a claim form has been served out of the jurisdiction under rule 1(2).

(2) If the claim form is to be served under rule 1(2)(a) in Scotland, Northern Ireland or in the European territory of another contracting state the period is—

(a) 21 days after service of the particulars of claim; or

(b) if the defendant files an acknowledgment of service under CPR Part 10, 35 days after service of the particulars of claim.

(3) If the claim form is to be served under rule 1(2)(a) in any other territory of a Contracting State the period is—

(a) 31 days after service of the particulars of claim; or

(b) if the defendant files an acknowledgement of service under CPR Part 10, 45 days after service of the particulars of claim.

(4) If the claim form is to be served under—

(a) rule 1(2)(a) in a country not referred to in paragraphs (2) or (3); or

(b) rule 1(2)(b),

the period is set out in the relevant practice direction.

R11.1B.1 **Effect of rule**—This rule and its accompanying practice direction set out the period for filing an ackowledgement of service or filing or serving an admission where the claim form has been served without the need for permission. It should be noted that where the proceedings are in the Commercial Court the defendant's time starts to run when the claim form is served but, elsewhere, time only starts to run when the particulars of claim have been served.

Application for, and grant of, leave to serve claim form out of jurisdiction

R11.4 **4.**—(1) An application for the grant of permission under rule 1(1) must be supported by written evidence stating—

(a) the grounds on which the application is made;

(b) that in the belief of the witness the claimant has a good cause of action;

(c) in what place or country the defendant is, or probably may be found; and

(d) where the application is made under rule 1(1)(c), the grounds for the belief of the witness that there is between the claimant and the person on whom a claim form has been served a real issue which the claimant may reasonably ask the court to try.

(2) No such permission shall be granted unless it shall be made sufficiently to appear to the court that the case is a proper one for service out of the jurisdiction under this Order.

(3) Where the application is for the grant of permission under rule 1 to serve a claim form in Scotland or Northern Ireland, if it appears to the court that there may be a concurrent remedy there, the court, in deciding whether to grant permission shall have regard to the comparative cost and convenience of proceeding there or in England, and (where that is relevant) to the powers and jurisdiction of the sheriff court in Scotland or the county courts or courts of summary jurisdiction in Northern Ireland.

(4) An order granting under rule 1 permission to serve a claim form, out of the jurisdiction must specify the periods within which the defendant may—

(a) file an acknowledgement of service in accordance with CPR Part 10;

(b) file or serve an admission in accordance with CPR Part 14; and

(c) file a defence in accordance with CPR Part 15.

Effect of rule—"written evidence" formerly "affidavit". R11.4.1
"permission" not "leave".

History of Rule—Derived from RSC 1883, O.11, r.1, subsequently and frequently amended; R11.4.2
the most important amendment was by S.I. 1983 No. 1181 which recast the rule. Also amended by S.I. 1990 No. 1689; S.I. 1990 No. 2599; S.I. 1992 No. 1907; S.I. 1993 No. 2760; S.I. 1996 No. 2892 and S.I. 1998 No. 3132.

WHERE PERMISSION IS REQUIRED (R.1(1) AND (R.4))

Service "out of the jurisdiction" (r.1(1)) R11.4.3

General—In circumstances where an English court has no means of enforcing its order and reliance must be placed upon the courts of the country in which the order is, in practice, to have effect, special regard must be had to the likely attitude of those courts and principles of comity, especially within the European Unions (*Phillip Alexander Securities and Futures Ltd. v. Bamberger and Others* [1997] I.L.Pr. 73, CA)

The expression "jurisdiction" in this context denotes the area of the territorial jurisdictions of the High Court and the county courts, as the case may be; see further SCP Mainwork 1999, Vol. 1, para. 11.1.5.

Practice in obtaining permission (r.4)—Applications for permission to serve out are made R11.4.4
under Pt 23 except that applications in the Commercial Court made under section 25 of the Civil Jurisdiction and Judgments Act 1982 are made under Pt 8.

The application for permission R11.4.5

QBD—The application is made without notice to a master. The documents should be left in the Master's Secretary's Department (Room E214) and collected when the master's decision has been placed upon it. Applications in the Commercial Court are similarly made without notice to a judge of that Court.

Applications may also be made to a relevant Mercantile Judge or to a district registrar.

Chancery Division—The relevant documents should be delivered to the Masters' Appoint- R11.4.6
ments Clerk in Room TM7.09. In a clear case the master himself gives permission (Memo. of the Chancery Judges, March 30, 1955). Otherwise the master refers to the judge who, if satisfied, gives permission which is indorsed on the claim form.

The practice direction sets out the documents that are to be served and the requirements for translations.

The written evidence—The written evidence may be given by any person with knowledge of the R11.4.7
facts but it is more usually made by the claimant's solicitor upon knowledge, information and belief. The contents of the written evidence are set out in r.4 but the following points should be borne in mind:

(a) The evidence should be sufficiently full to show that the claimant has established his right to permission to the standards of proof that govern the different elements of the application.
(b) The evidence must make clear which sub rule of r.1(1) is relied on.
(c) The evidence must set out sufficient facts to show that England and Wales constitute the *forum conveniens*.
(d) The evidence must be frank. If any material fact is omitted this would itself justify the court in discharging the order, even though the party might be in a position to apply again (*The Hagen* [1908] P.189 at 201, CA). Whilst an applicant must disclose anything which casts doubt upon his case, it is unreasonable to expect him to anticipate all the arguments or points which might be raised against his case (*Electric Furance Co. v. Selar Corp. of America* [1987] R.P.C. 23).
(e) Permission is usually given for service in a particular country. If it turns out that the defendant is in a country other than that named in the order, application to amend the order should be made without notice supported by written evidence to the Practice Master or other relevant judge.

The same practice (as outlined above) is, with any necessary modifications applied where it is necessary to make an application to the court for permission to serve out of the jurisdiction any application made in the course of proceedings (see r.9) and para. 5 of the practice directions.

The matters to be taken into consideration by the court in exercising its discretion to grant permission to serve out of the jurisdiction and the standard of proof to be applied are the subject of the decision by the House of Lords in *Seaconsar Far East Ltd v. Bank Markazi Jomhouri Islam Iran* [1994] 1 A.C. 43; [1993] 4 All E.R. 456. There is no presumption in favour of granting permission in a case falling within O.11, r.1(1)(c) but as the forum is already chosen the only questions that may remain are (1) is the foreign defendant (or Pt 20 defendant) a necessary or proper party and (2) is it right to bring him here as a party? (*Eras Eil Actions* [1992] 2 All E.R. 82; [1992] 1 Lloyd's Rep. 570.)

R11.4.8 **Application for permission under r.1 to serve in Scotland or Northern Ireland**

Effect of rule 4(3)—This is often misunderstood. It is not an additional ground for giving permission to serve out of the jurisdiction; it is an additional obstacle that the applicant has to surmount (see *Williams v. Cartwright* [1895] 1 Q.B. Lord Esher M.R at 146). But the Civil Jurisdiction and Judgments Act 1982 will make it rare for permission to be required to serve in Scotland or Northern Ireland.

R11.4.9 *"Comparative cost and convenience"*—*i.e.* of all parties to the action, not of the claimant alone (*Williams v. Cartwright* [1895] 1 Q.B. 142 at 147, 149; *Kinahan v. Kinahan* (1890) 45 Ch.D.78; *Logan v. Bank of Scotland (No.2)* [1906] 1 K.B. 141 at 147; *Watson v. Daily Record* [1907] 1 K.B. 853 at 860; *Egbert v. Short* [1907] 2 Ch.205; *Re Norton's Settlement* [1908] 1 Ch.471; *The Hagen* [1908] P.189). The chief considerations of convenience are the residence of the parties and witnesses, the inconvenience of double litigation and the fact of one of the courts having already acquired seisin of the case, the situation of documents for convenience of disclosure, probability of despatch or delay, and enforcement of the remedy sought in the action (see the above cases and also *Tozier v. Hawkins* (1885) 15 Q.B.D. 680, CA; *Speckhart v. Campbell* (1884) Bittlestone C.C. 248; *Washburn v. Cunard Co.* (1889) 5 T.L.R. 592; *Re Burland* (1889) 41 Ch.D. 542; *Re De Penny* [1891] 2 Ch.63).

R11.4.10 **Admiralty actions**—Formerly, RSC, O.75, r.4 dealt with the service out of the jurisdiction with the leave of the court of writs containing claims for the principal Admiralty actions (as defined in RSC, O.75, r.2). Consequently, r.1(1) was expressed in terms which indicated that its provisions did not apply to such writs (see also CCR, O.8, r.2(1) and r.3). Admiralty proceedings now constitute one of the "specialist proceedings" referred to in Pt 49. The CPR apply to such proceedings subject to the provisions of "the relevant practice direction" (r.49.1). The relevant practice direction is Practice Direction—Admiralty (see para. 49FPD–001) (replacing with modifications RSC, O.75 and CCR, O.40). As re-enacted in Sched. 1, RSC, O.11, r.1(1) in terms excludes "any claim mentioned in O.75, r.2(1)."

R11.4.11 **"An order ... must limit a time within which the defendant must acknowledge service"**—See the practice direction.

R11.4.12 **Adding in the claim form or particulars of claim, a cause of action other than that for which permission was given to serve**—This is not permissible where the added cause of action is not one of those in respect of which there is power to service out of the jurisdiction (*Waterhouse v. Reid* [1938] 1 K.B. 743, CA). Subject to this, the rules as to the amendment of claim forms and particulars of claim apply in regard to claim forms for service out of the jurisdiction as in other actions (*Holland v. Leslie* [1894] 2 Q.B. 346 at 450, CA; *Dickson v. Law* [1895] 2 Ch.62; *N. v. Kwik Hoo Tong v. Finlay* [1927] A.C. 604; see *Indigo Co. v. Ogilvy* [1891] 2 Ch.31, CA). These authorities concern whether amendments should be allowed with permission after the unamended claim form has been served. The situation is different where the claimant seeks permission to amend a claim form after permission has been given to serve out of the jurisdiction, but before service has been effected. In such a case the claimant may not serve under the original permission but must return to the court to seek permission to serve the claim form in its amended form (*Trafalgar Tours Ltd. v. Henry* [1990] 2 Lloyd's Rep. 298).

There is nothing in Pt 11 which expressly excludes power to make amendments while there is a jurisdictional challenge under Pt 11; no such implied limitation exists; and there is no incongruity in recognising that the Court might by its rules or by permission allow ancillary amendments to statements of case which did not introduce a new cause of action (*Gruppo Toras S.A. v. Al-Sabah* [1995] Lloyd's Rep. 298).

R11.4.13 **Counterclaim**—Permission is not needed to serve a counterclaim on a foreign claimant: by suing in England he submits to the jurisdiction in regard to any counterclaim (*Derby & Co. v. Larsson* [1976] 1 W.L.R. 202 at 205; [1976] All E.R. 401, at 414, HL).

R11.4.14 **Service of claim form**—See the subsequent rules of this Order.

R11.4.15 **Application to set aside the order or service**—See the notes to Pt 11.

R11.4.16 **Appeal**—Appeal from the refusal of the Master to give permission to serve the claim form lies from the Master to the Judge, and from him with permission to the CA (O.58, rr.1.7; O.59, r.14(3); SCA 1981, s.18). The discretion of the Judge is not lightly interfered with by the CA (*Reynolds v. Coleman* (1887) 36 Ch.D. 453; *Harvey v. Dougherty* 56 L.T. 322; contrast *The Hagen* [1908] P.189, CA; *Williams v. Cartwright* [1895] 1 Q.B. 142 at 148).

Principles upon which permission to serve outside the jurisdiction is granted—The principles upon which permission to serve outside the jurisdiction is granted are set out in r.1(1) and r.4 as explained in the case law of which the two most important authorities are *Seaconsar Far East Ltd. v. Bank Markazi Jomhouri Islam Iran* [1994] 1 A.C. 43; [1993] 4 All E.R. 456 and *Spiliada Maritime Corp. v. Consulex Ltd, The Spiliada* [1987] A.C. 460; [1986] 3 All E.R. 843, HL. Further authorities and consideration of the principles may be found in Dicey & Morris, *Conflict of Laws* (12th ed., 1993), Rule 24 and commentary thereon. The principles can be summarised as follows. **R11.4.17**

(1) rule 1(1)

The applicant must show that each claim made by him has the attributes set out in at least one of the sub-paragraphs listed under r.1(1); each such paragraph being read, generally speaking, disjunctively (*Matthews v. Kuwait Bechtel Corp.* [1959] 2 Q.B. 57);

The burden is upon the applicant to show in respect of each claim that he has a good arguable case that it falls within a relevant sub-paragraph of r.1(1). This burden applies regardless of whether the relevant attribute is one which goes to the merits, such as breach of a contract within the jurisdiction, or has no such connection, such as a remedy against a person domiciled within the jurisdiction. This standard of proof is that which governs r.4(2) which contains the requirement that it should be made sufficiently to appear to the court that the case is a proper one for service out of the jurisdiction under the Order (*Seaconsar v. Bank Markazi*, above).

The court must decide upon the application on the basis of the cause or causes of action expressly mentioned in the claim form and the particulars of claim if they accompany the form. The claimant will not be allowed to rely upon an alternative cause of action which he seeks to spell out of the facts pleaded, if such cause of action has not been so mentioned (*Metall und Rohstoff AG v. Donaldson Lufkin & Jenrette Inc.* [1990] 1 Q.B. 391; [1989] 3 W.L.R. 563, CA, *DSQ Property Co. Ltd v. Lotus Cars Ltd, The Times,* June 28, 1990, CA).

(2) The Merits

The applicant must show a serious issue to be tried in respect of each cause or cause of action in respect of which he asks for permission (*Seaconsar v. Bank Markazi*, above.).

(3) Discretion

The court has a general discretion to decide whether or not the case is a proper one for service out of the jurisdiction. In particular it must consider the question of *forum conveniens* namely, in which forum the case could most suitably be tried for the interests of all the parties and for the ends of justice (*Spiliada* above). Pt 1 governs the exercise of the discretion.

(4) *Forum Conveniens*

Subject to the differences set out below, the criteria that govern the application of the principle of *forum conveniens* where permission is sought to serve out of the jurisdiction are the same as those that govern the application of the principle of *forum non conveniens* where a stay is sought in respect of proceedings started within the jurisdiction. Those criteria are set out in *Spiliada* above:

(i) The burden is upon the claimant to persuade the court that England is clearly the appropriate forum for the trial of the action.

(ii) The appropriate forum is that forum where the case may most suitably be tried for the interests of all the parties and the ends of justice.

(iii) One must consider first what is the "natural forum"; namely that with which the action has the most real and susbstantial connection. Connecting factors will include not only factors concerning convenience and expense (such as the availability of witnesses), but also factors such as the law governing the relevant transaction and the places where the parties reside and respectively carry on business.

(iv) In considering where the case can be tried most "suitably for the interests of all the parties and for the ends of justice" ordinary English procedural advantages such as a power to award interest, are normally irrelevant as are more generous English limitation periods where the claimant has failed to act prudently in respect of a shorter limitation period elsewhere.

(v) If the court concludes at that stage that there is another forum which is apparently as suitable or more suitable than England, it will normally refuse permission unless there are circumstances by reason of which justice requires that permission should nevertheless be granted. In this inquiry the court will consider all the circumstances of the case, including circumstances which go beyond those taken into account when considering connecting factors with other jurisdictions. One such factor can be the fact, if established objectively by cogent evidence, that the claimant will not obtain justice in the foreign jurisdiction.

(vi) Where a party seeks to establish the existence of a matter that will assist him in persuading the court to exercise its discretion in his favour, the evidential burden in respect of that matter will rest upon the party asserting it.

R11.4.18 **Criteria governing the grant of a stay of proceedings started within the jurisdiction on the grounds of forum non conveniens**—The criteria that govern the stay on the grounds of *forum non conveniens* of proceedings started within the jurisdiction are the converse of those set out in respect of the *forum conveniens* element of permission to serve out of the jurisdiction; subject to the fact that where a defendant is served as of right within the jurisdiction it would appear that the court will place more weight in favour of the claimant where he has the benefit of a limitation period within the jurisdiction that would be lost in competing forum (*Spiliada Maritime Corp. v. Cansulex Ltd, The Spiliada* [1987] A.C. 460 at 484; [1986] 3 All E.R. 843 at pages 860 and 861).

R11.4.19 **Relevant factors**—Special considerations apply where proceedings are already on foot in another jurisdiction (see *The Hagen* [1908] P. 189 at 202, and the *GAF Corp. v. Amahen Products Inc.* [1975] 1 Lloyd's Rep. 601). The fact that foreign proceedings have been under way for a substantial time, have involved the parties in substantial costs and are ready for trial, will be a strong factor in favour of the grant of a stay of English proceedings (*Cleveland Museum of Art v. Capricorn Art International SA* [1990] B.C.L.C. 546; [1990] 2 Lloyd's Rep. A claimant who initiates proceedings against the same defendant in two separate jurisdictions in respect of the same subject matter is required to elect which set of proceedings he wishes to pursue, and, if he elects to pursue the proceedings abroad, the English action will be dismissed, not merely stayed (*Australian Commercial Research and Development Ltd v. ANZ McCaughan Merchant Bank Ltd* [1989] 3 All E.R. 65, see also *Re Harrods (Buenos Aires) Ltd (No. 2)* [1991] 4 All E.R. 348).

Where a claimant who has sued the defendant in a foreign jurisdiction, had abandoned those proceedings so as to sue the defendant (whose domicil and place of business was England) in England, the claimant should not be permitted to apply to the English court to stay the English proceedings so that he might revive the proceedings in the foreign jurisdiction. In such circumstances the English court would not only refuse the claimant a stay of his own proceedings but following the reasoning in *Societe Nationale Industrielle Aerospatiale v. Lee Jui Jak (SNIA)* [1987] A.C. 871, would grant the defendant an injunction restraining the foreign proceedings as it would be oppressive to force the defendant to fight the case in two jurisdictions (*Advanced Portfolio Technologies Inc. v. Ainsworth), The Times*, November 15, 1995. In SNIA, the Privy Council held that the court would not restrain proceedings in a jurisdiction other than the *forum conveniens* unless it could be shown that such proceedings were oppressive or vexatious.

Special considerations also apply where the parties have agreed that a particular court shall have exclusive jurisdiction over the dispute. In such an event the court will ordinarily enforce the agreement, if asked, and, if the chosen court is foreign, will refuse leave to serve proceedings out of the jurisdiction under O.11, r.1(1) (*Mackender v. Feldia A.G.* [1967] 2 Q.B. 590; [1966] 3 All E.R. 847, CA); *Re Jogia* [1988] 2 All E.R. 328).

The court retains a discretion under r.11(1) when allowing service out of the jurisdiction not to give effect to a foreign jurisdiction clause. The discretion might still be exercised in a claimant's favour even where the claimaint has allowed his claim to become time-barred in the chosen jurisdiction provided he has acted reasonably in so doing. This might be the case where the probable result, had proceedings been issued in time in the chosen jurisdiction, was that there would have been proceedings in England as well with the risk of conflicting decisions. However, to override a foreign jurisdiction clause strong cause has to be shown (*Citi-March Ltd v. Neptune Orient* [1996] 2 All E.R. 545, *per* Colman J).

If, however, the legal and political systems of the foreign country have changed since the contract was made, different considerations may apply, both as a matter of construction and of discretion (*Carvalho v. Hull Blyth Ltd* [1979] 1 W.L.R. 1228, [1979] 3 All E.R. 280, CA). A non-exclusive jurisdiction clause raises a strong prima facie case that such jurisdiction is the *forum conveniens* (*E.D.X.F. Manship Ltd v. Kuaemer Gibraltar Ltd* [1996] 2 Lloyd's Rep. 206.

Where a stay of an action for breach of contract is sought on the grounds of *forum non conveniens*, however, the proper law of the contract has to be identified. It would not be conducive to justice to require a claimant with an arguable claim under what the English court is likely to hold to be the proper law to litigate in another jurisdiction where his claim will be summarily rejected; in such circumstances the application to stay the English action will be dismissed (*Banco Atlantico SA v. The British Bank of the Middle East* [1990] 2 Lloyd's Rep. 504, CA).

The court may refuse to stay proceedings on the grounds of *forum non conveniens*, even if satisfied that a foreign country is a more appropriate than England, if the party opposing the stay has been convicted and sentenced in his absence to a term of imprisonment in that country (*Purcell v. Khayat, The Times*, November 23, 1987, CA).

In deciding whether the appropriate forum for trying an action is England or a specified foreign forum, the court may take into account the different rules as to costs in that forum and in England; where costs in the foreign forum do not follow the event, and where the damages awarded to a successful claimant will effectively be diminished by such costs, the court may properly conclude that justice will not be done, and that, not withstanding that the foreign forum is otherwise appropriate, the forum should be England (*Roneleigh Ltd v. MII Exports Inc.* [1989] 1

W.L.R. 619). Furthermore if it can be shown that in the foreign forum, costs are not awarded on a realistic basis, or if there is substantial evidence indicating that trial in the foreign forum may be delayed for many years, the court may refuse to stay the English proceedings (*The Vishva Ajay* [1989] 2 Lloyd's Rep. 558).

A difference between English rules as to the conflict of laws and the equivalent rules applicable in the foreign forum, where such difference favours the claimant, is a juridical advantage which may be prayed in aid by the claimant and which may be taken into account by the court in exercising discretion to refuse a stay of English proceedings (*Irish Shipping Ltd v. Commercial Union Assurance Co. plc, The Irish Rowan* [1989] 3 All E.R. 853, CA).

The court has no discretion to stay proceedings on the ground of *forum non conveniens* or *lis alibi pendens* if the proceedings fall within the Conventions embodied in the Civil Jurisdiction and Judgments Act 1982 (*S & W Berisford plc v. New Hampshire Insurance Co. Ltd* [1990] 3 W.L.R. 705; [1990] 2 All E.R. 321, *Arkwight Mutual Insurance Co. v. Bryanston Insurance Co. Ltd* [1990] 3 W.L.R. 705; [1990] 2 All E.R. 335).

Notwithstanding section 33(1)(b) of the Legal Aid Act 1988 which provides that the receipts of legal aid "shall not affect ... the principles on which the discretion of any court or tribunal is normally exercised" the court may take into account the fact that a claimant is legally aided in considering whether to stay proceedings on the grounds of *forum conveniens*. So, where a defendant had made out a prima facie case that the action had the closest connection with the foreign jurisdiction, the fact that legal aid was available in this country but not in the foreign jurisdiction was the decisive consideration which influenced the majority of the House of Lords in overruling the Court of Appeal which had granted a stay (*Connelly v. RTZ Corp. plc* [1998] A.C. 854.

The more important of the reported cases in which the *Spiliada* principles have been considered are as follows:

Appl'd—*E.I. Du Pont de Nemours & Co. v. Agnew* [1987] 2 Lloyd's Rep. 585, CA. **R11.4.20**
Mitsubishi Corporation v. Alfaforzos [1988] 1 Lloyd's Rep. 191
de Dampierre v. de Dampierre [1988] A.C. 92, HL, [1987] 2 W.L.R. 1006, HL.
Virgo Steamship Co. S.A. v. Skaarup Shipping Corp. [1988] Lloyd's Rep. 352
Roneleigh Ltd v. MII Exports Inc. [1989] 1 W.L.R. 619, CA.
Irish Shipping Ltd v. Commercial Union Assurance Co. Plc., The Irish Rowan [1991] 2 Q.B. 206, CA, [1990] 2 W.L.R. 117, CA, [1989] 3 All E.R. 853, CA, [1989] 2 Lloyd's Rep. 144, CA.
Cleveland Museum of Art v. Capricorn Art International S.A. [1990] 2 Lloyd's Rep. 166
Marc Rich & Co. A.G. v. Societa Italiana Impianti P.A., The Atlantic Emperor [1989] 1 Lloyd's Rep. 548, CA, affd. European Court of Justice, *The Independent*, September 23, 1991.
Re Harrods (Buenos Aires) Ltd [1992] Ch. 72, [1991] 3 W.L.R. 397, CA.
The Varna [1994] 2 Lloyd's Rep. 41
Bank of Credit and Commerce Hong Kong Ltd v. Sonali Bank [1995] 1 Lloyd's Rep. 227
Connelly v. R.T.Z. Corp. [1996] Q.B. 361, [1996] 2 W.L.R. 251, CA, [1997] 3 W.L.R. 373, HL, [1998] A.C. 854, HL.
Mohammed v. Bank of Kuwait and the Middle East K.S.C. [1996] 1 W.L.R. 1483, CA
Citi-March Ltd v. Neptune Orient Lines Ltd [1996] 1 W.L.R. 1367
The Bergen (No. 2) [1997] 2 Lloyd's Rep. 710

Cons'd—*Sapiem S.p.A. v. Dredging VO2 B.V.* [1988] 2 Lloyd's Rep. 361, CA. **R11.4.21**
Meadows Indemnity Co. Ltd v. Insurance Corp. of Ireland Ltd [1989] 1 Lloyd's Rep. 181
British Aerospace Plc. v. Dee Howard Co. [1993] 1 Lloyd's Rep. 368
Butler v. Butler [1998] 1 W.L.R. 1208, CA.
Egon Oldendorff v. Liberia Corp. [1995] 2 Lloyd's Rep. 64

Discretion and delay—Inordinate delay in seeking permission to serve the writ may be a ground for refusing permission (*Schothorst and Schuitema v. Franz Dauter G.m.b.H. (The Nimrod)* [1973] 2 Lloyd's Rep. 91 (two-and-a-half years' delay between issuing writ and seeking permission to serve, during which the limitation period expired)). **R11.4.22**

Libel—An alleged libel published in more than one country could give rise to a cause of action in each country in which the victim was known and in which he claimed to have suffered injury. A multi-jurisdictional libel should not be treated as giving rise to a single cause of action in respect of which the court had to ascertain where the global cause of action arose. The principles applied in the Convention case of *Shevill v. Presse Alliance* followed in a non-convention case therefore allowing Russian nationals with a demonstrated connection with this country to sue in England the publisher of an American magazine with a circulation in England: *Berezovsky v. Forbes Inc., The Times*, November 27, 1988, CA. **R11.4.23**

Actions against foreign states—The State Immunity Act 1978 came into force on November 22, 1978. It gives statutory force to the doctrine of restrictive immunity, by which the immunity of a foreign state from action is not absolute but is restricted to acts of a governmental nature, *jure imperii*, and not of a commercial nature *jure gestionis*. The conflict between the theories of absolute **R11.4.24**

and restrictive immunity is explained in the judgment of Lord Denning M.R. in *Trendtex Trading v. Central Bank of Nigeria* [1977] Q.B. 529. See also *Kuwait Airways Corp. v. Iraqi Airways Co.* [1995] 1 W.L.R. 1147, [1995] 3 All E.R. 694.

Under the Act activities which could equally well be performed by a trading corporation or private individual will not generally enjoy immunity from the jurisdiction of the U.K. courts merely because they are carried on by a state or by a "separate entity" under the control of a state and on its behalf. The Act is complex and presents many problems.

The practitioner should note that:

(i) The Act restricts immunity; it does not directly confer jurisdiction. If, in order to institute proceedings, it is necessary to serve the claim form or other process outside the jurisdiction, permission must be obtained under O.11, r.1 or 9.

(ii) Although the circumstances which will restrict immunity will, in most cases, bring the case within one of the headings of O.11, r.1; the Act and O.11 do not precisely correspond. An application for permission under O.11 must show distinctly: (a) why the prospective defendant is not absolutely immune from suit; (b) under which heading O.11 the action falls.

(iii) The consideration, referred to in para. R11.4.17, that it is undesirable to subject the jurisdiction of the English court a foreigner who owes no allegiance here, applies with peculiar force to a suit against a foreign state. Dubious or borderline applications ought not to be made and it should be made clearly to appear that the case is proper for the English courts.

(iv) It will also be relevant to consider whether a judgment of the English court is likely to be effective. For the service of process against a foreign state see section 12 of the Act.

Restraint of foreign proceedings

R11.4.25 1. In considering whether an injunction should be granted to restrain a claimant beginning or pursuing an action in another jurisdiction the court does not proceed on the same principles as those applied when granting a stay of proceedings on the grounds of *forum non conveniens.*

First, the jurisdiction is to be exercised when the "ends of justice" require it.

Secondly, where the court decides to grant an injunction restraining proceedings in a foreign court, its order is directed not against the foreign court but against the parties so proceeding or threatening to proceed.

Thirdly, it follows that an injunction will only be issued restraining a party who is amenable to the jurisdiction of the court, against whom an injunction will be an effective remedy.

Fourthly, since such an order indirectly effects the foreign court, the jurisdiction is one which must be exercised with caution.

In a case where a remedy for a particular wrong is available both in the English court and in a foreign court, the English court will, generally speaking, only restrain the claimant from pursuing proceedings in the foreign court if such pursuit would be vexatious or oppressive. This presupposes that, as a general rule, the English court must conclude that it provides the natural forum for the trial of the actions; and further, since the court is concerned with the ends of justice, that account must be taken not only of injustice to the defendant if the claimant is allowed to pursue the foreign proceedings, but also of injustice to the claimant if he is not allowed to do so. So the court will not grant an injunction if, by doing so, it will deprive the claimant of advantages in the foreign forum of which it would be unjust to deprive him. That problem can often be overcome by appropriate undertakings given by the defendant, or by granting an injunction upon appropriate terms; just as, in cases of stay of proceedings, the parallel problem of advantages to the plaintiff in the domestic forum which is prima facie, inappropriate, can likewise often be solved by granting a stay upon terms.

See: *Societe Nationale Indistrielle Aerospatiale v. Lee Kui Jak* [1987] A.C. 871; [1987] 3 All E.R. 510 (P.C.); *DVA v. Voest Alpine* [1997] 2 Lloyd's Rep. 279; and *Airbus Industrie G.I.E. v. Patel* [1999] 1 A.C. 119.

2. The English court has a discretionary power to restrain by injunction a breach of contract and that power can be used to restrain foreign proceedings where, for example, there is an agreement to arbitrate the dispute (*Taepfer v. Societe Cargill* [1998] 1 Lloyd's Rep. 379, CA).

Cases in which service out permissible with court's permission

R11.4.26 *Rule 1(1)(a): "domiciled within the jurisdiction*—A claim form may be served out of the jurisdiction with the permission of the court "if a remedy is sought" (formerly "if relief is sought") against a person domiciled within the jurisdiction. In this context, by virtue of r.1(4) "domicile" is to be determined in accordance with, not the common law, but with the Civil Jurisdiction and Judgments Act 1982, ss. 41 to 46 (see S.C.P. 1999, Vol. 2, paras 8–045 to 8–051).

R11.4.27 *Rule 1(1)(b): Injunction*—A claim form may be served out of the jurisdiction with the permission of the court if an injunction is sought. (Formerly, r.1(1)(b) stated that the injunction had to be sought "in the action begun by the writ"; now it would seem to be a matter of necessary inference that the injunction must be sought in the claim form.) The discretion to grant permission under this provision will not be exercised unless: (i) an injunction is a genuine part of the substantive relief sought and has not been claimed merely to bring the case within the rule (*Rosler v. Hilbery* [1925] 1 Ch. 250, pp. 261 *et seq.*, CA) and (ii) there is a reasonable prospect of an injunction (itself a discretionary remedy) being granted (*Watson v. Daily Record* [1907] 1 K.B. 853, CA.).

Interim injunctions—Where there are no substantive proceedings, following the full implementation of section 25 of the Civil Jurisdiction and Judgments Act 1982 and the introduction of O.11, r.8A applications may now be made with permission for interim injunctions in support of overseas proceedings. In the Commercial Court applications for permission are made under CPR, Part 8; elsewhere they are made under Part 23. **R11.4.28**

Rule 1(1)(c): "necessary or proper party" to proceedings already duly served on a defendant—"person duly served"—The original defendant (the person already "duly served") need not have been served within the jurisdiction. Where the original defendant, though served out of the jurisdiction, was not properly served he is not a person already "duly served" for the purposes of this rule, even though he has waived the non-compliance by submitting to the jurisdiction (*Amanuel v. Alexandros Shipping Co.* [1986] Q.B. 464). However, whilst refusing to sanction such service, the court might cure the defect by granting retrospective permission under CPR, r.3.10 (*Kuwait Oil Tanker SAK v. Al Bader* [1997] 2 All E.R. 858. **R11.4.29**

The proceedings against the original defendant must have been brought bona fide and not merely to provide a basis upon which to make an application under this rule for service on a person out of the jurisdiction (*Witted v. Galbraith* [1893] 1 Q.B. 577, *Deutsche National Bank v. Paul* [1898] 1 Ch. 283, *Bloomfield v. Serenyi* [1945] 2 All E.R. 646, *Derby & Co. Ltd v. Larsson* [1976] 1 All E.R. 401). However, such proceedings, though bona fide, are not properly brought against the original defendant where the law is plain or the facts are uncontradicted and it is clear that the claimant could not succeed against the defendant (*Tyne Improvement Commissioners v. Armement Anversois S.A. (The Brabo)* [1949] A.C. 326, [1949] 1 All E.R. 294, *Multinational Gas and Petrochemical Co. v. Multinational Gas and Petrochemical Services Ltd* [1983] 2 All E.R. 563. As a safeguard against a specious claim against the original defendant being used as a device to found jurisdiction to serve another party outside the jurisdiction, r.4(1)(d) requires that the written evidence supporting the application for permission must state that there is a real issue between the claimaint and the original defendant, which the claimant may reasonably ask the court to try.

"necessary or proper party"—The terms are alternative. Generally, a person who may be joined in proceedings in accordance with the rules as to joinder of parties is a "proper" party (*Massey v. Heynes* [1881] 21 Q.B.D. 330, CA). **R11.4.30**

A person may be a proper party when the liability of several persons whether cumulative or alternative depends upon one investigation (*Massey v. Heynes* [1881] 21 Q.B.D. 330, CA.). For the joinder of a party being necessary for justice to be done, see *Electric Furance Co. v. Selas Corp. of America* [1987] R.P.C. 23. Where the proposed joinder would confer no real additional advantage on the claimant, e.g. where the proposed defendant outside the jurisdiction has merely induced the tort of the internal defendant and the total damages will not be increased by the joinder, leave may not be given; but where the plaintiff has a cause of action for damages against two possible defendants, and where it may be valuable to have the ability to choose against which of them to enforce judgment, or, a fortiori, where the relief claimed is an account of profits, leave will be granted (*ibid.*). A person out of the jurisdiction not shown to be arguably liable is not a "proper party", and permission under r.1(1)(c) should not be granted merely for the purpose of making him a party to proceedings to enable the claimant to obtain disclosure of documents from him (see *Unilever Plc v. Chefaro Proprietaries Ltd* [1994] F.S.R. 135; *The Times* March 29, 1993, CA, where the question arose in the context of the Brussels Convention art. 6).

Counterclaims and other additional claims—Part 20 contains provisions dealing with counterclaims and certain other claims (being claims other than a claim by a claimant against a defendant), including, what used to be called, "third party notices", all of which are now known, collectively as "Part 20 claims". Permission is not needed to serve a Part 20 claim in the form of a counterclaim on a foreign claimant because, by suing in England, he submits to the jurisdiction in regard to any counterclaim (*Derby & Co. v. Larsson* [1976] 1 W.L.R. 202, at 205; [1976] 1 All E.R. 401, at 414, HL). **R11.4.31**

Former RSC, O.16, r.3(4) stated that, for the purposes of RSC, O.11, a defendant bringing third party proceedings should be treated as a claimant issuing a writ and specifically provided that, in the application of O.11, r.1(1)(c), "leave may be granted to serve a third party notice out of the jurisdiction on any necessary and proper party to the proceedings brought against the defendant". No such express provision appears in the CPR. However, it would seem that the same result is achieved by operation of r.20.3(1) which provides that, generally, a Part 20 claim "shall be treated as if it were a claim for the purposes of these Rules". It is not necessarily the case that a person who could be brought into proceedings by a Part 20 claim as a third party would be a "necessary or proper" party under r.1(1)(c) (*Speller & Co. v. Bristol Steam Navigation Co.* (1884) 13 Q.B.D. 96).

R11.4.32 *Disclosure*—Where relevant documents in a case between domestic parties are in the possession of the overseas holding company of one of them, it is not a good arguable case against the overseas holding company under O.11, r.1(c) if the only purpose of joining the overseas company to the proceedings is to obtain disclosure. The same principles would apply to prevent joinder of a party for that purpose under the Brussels Convention (Art. 6): *Unilever plc v. Chefaro Proprietaries Ltd* [1994] F.S.R. 135.

R11.4.33 *Rule 1(1)(d): Claim brought to enforce etc. a contract*—A claim form may be served out of the jurisdiction with the permission of the court if the claim is brought (1) to enforce etc. or "otherwise affect" a contract", or (2) to recover damages or obtain other remedy in respect of the breach of a contract, being in either case a contract which satisfies one or other of the conditions stated in sub-paras. (i) to (iv).

R11.4.34 *"a contract"*—The connecting thread is the existence of a contract. In order to bring a claim within the scope of O.11, r.1(1)(d) or (e) the claimant must show that there is a good arguable case that there exists a contract between himself and the defendant and that there is a good arguable case that the claim affects such contract.

For a case of an implied contract, see *Bowling v. Cox* [1926] A.C. 751.

A claim upon a dishonoured cheque drawn abroad by a foreigner on a foreign bank may properly be said to be a claim brought to affect a contract made within the jurisdiction or governed by English law, and hence may be the subject of leave to serve out of the jurisdiction, if the cheque is given as security for the performance of such a contract, because the cheque, if honoured, serves to reduce the contractual debt and its dishonour constitutes a breach of the contract (*E. F. Hutton & Co. (London) Ltd v. Moffarij* [1989] 1 W.L.R. 488; [1989] 2 All E.R. 633; [1989] 2 Lloyd's Rep. 348, CA).

An action on an award is an action on the contract contained in the submission to arbitration, but the award itself may also, it seems, be treated as the contract, in that it contains an implied agreement to perform it (*Bremer Oeltransport v. Drewry* [1933] 1 K.B. 753, CA and cases there cited). An action on a judgment is also an action on the implied contract, contained in the judgment, to perform it (*Grant v. Easton* (1883) 13 Q.B.D. 302, CA).

An action for a declaration that a contract has been discharged by frustration or repudiation or otherwise is one brought to affect the contract and is within this sub-rule (*B.P. Exploration (Libya) Ltd v. Hunt* [1976] 1 W.L.R. 788; [1976] 1 Lloyd's Rep. 471; [1976] 3 All E.R. 879, CA).

It is insufficient for the claimant to rely upon a contract made between himself and a third party. Accordingly where a claimant denies the existence of any contract between himself and the defendant, and seeks a declaration to that effect, his claim does not fall within O.11, r.1(d) or (e) (*Finnish Marine Insurance Co. Ltd v. Protective National Insurance Co.* [1990] 2 W.L.R. 914; [1989] 2 All E.R. 929).

Rule 1(1)(d) does not extend to cover a claim against the company director based upon his appointment as director without a specific contract of employment (*New Therapeutics Ltd v. Katz* [1990] 3 W.L.R. 1183; [1991] 2 All E.R. 151).

A claim for negative declaratory relief can fall within r.1(1)(d) (*HIB v. Guardian Insce.* [1997] 1 Lloyd's Rep. 412).

If a claimant has a remedy in contract or tort upon the same facts, he can choose his remedy and if choosing tort may seek permission to serve out of the jurisdiction under r.1(1)(f) (*Matthews v. Kuwait Bechtel Corp.* [1959] 2 Q.B. 57; [1959] 2 All E.R. 345).

R11.4.35 *Made within the jurisdiction (para. (d)(i))*—The jurisdiction is the territorial jurisdiction.

Where a contract is concluded by cable or letter passing between one country and another, prima facie the contract is made where the offer is accepted, by posting the letter or dispatching the cable of acceptance or sending off the goods ordered (*per* du Parcq J., in chambers, June 22, 1934 (unrep.); following *Cowan v. O'Connor* (1888) 20 Q.B.D. 640). On the other hand, in the case of telex or telephone communications, the contract is made at the place where the offeror receives the notification of the acceptance by the offeree (*Entores v. Miles Far East Corp.* [1955] 2 Q.B. 327]. By parity of reasoning communication by facsimile and email is governed by the principles set out in *Entores v. Miles Far East.*

A quasi-contract or other similar obligation comes within the meaning of "contract" in this rule, and in such a case the word "made" in this rule should be read as "arising" (*Rousou's (A Bankrupt) Trustee v. Rousou* [1955] 3 All E.R. 486 affirming [1955] 1 W.L.R. 545; [1955] 2 All E.R. 169).

If a contract which was made within the jurisdiction is subsequently amended by an agreement made outside the jurisdiction, it seems that the amended contract will still be taken as made within the jurisdiction unless the amendment has the effect of substituting a new agreement (*B.P. Exploration (Libya) Ltd v. Hunt* [1976] 1 W.L.R. 788; [1976] 1 Lloyd's Rep. 471; [1976] 3 All E.R. 879). Presumably the question is one of degree.

Made through an agent etc. (para. (d)(ii))—"Contract made by or through an agent trading or residing within the jurisdiction—"Through" denotes the case of a contract negotiated by an agent in this country but concluded by the principal abroad (*National Mortgage Co. v. Gosselin* (1922) 38 T.L.R. 832, CA). See also O.10, r.2(1)(a) [see now CPR, r.6.16(2)(a)]; and the *Metamorphosis* [1953] 1 W.L.R. 543; [1954] 1 All E.R. 723.

O.11, r.1(1)(d)(ii) applies where the principal of the agent in question is the defendant, and not where the principal is the claimant (*Union International Insurance Co. Ltd v. Jubilee Insurance Co. Ltd* [1991] 1 All E.R. 740).

Governed by English law (para. (d)(iii))—For the rules for ascertaining which is the law of the contract, see Dicey & Morris, *The Conflict of Laws* (12th ed., 1993), Chaps 28, *et seq.* Typical cases are where the contract provides for arbitration in England and enforcement of an award in England (*N.V. Kwik Hoo Tong, etc. v. Finlay Ltd* [1927] A.C. 604) or that disputes shall be determined by the English courts or contains a clause such as the "follow London" clause in an insurance contract, showing an intention that claims should be negotiated and settled by Lloyd's underwriters in London (*Armadora Occidental S.A. v. Horace Mann Insurance Co.* [1977] 1 W.L.R. 1098; [1978] 1 All E.R. 407, CA). But in the absence of express agreement as to the proper law, no one factor is necessarily decisive. The ultimate test appears to be: what is the system of law with which the transaction has the closest and most real connection? (*Compagnie Tunisienne de Navigation S.A. v. Compagnie d'Armement Maritime S.A.* [1971] A.C. 572; [1970] 3 All E.R. 71 HL (E.); *Coast Lines Ltd v. Hudig Chartering* [1972] 2 Q.B. 39; [1972] 1 All E.R. 451, CA, *per* Lord Denning M.R.: *DVA v. Voest Alpine* [1997] 2 Lloyd's Rep. 279, CA).

Where parties have had a course of dealing in a market where their contracts have contained a number of express terms including one that the governing law is English, when they enter a new market under a contract that is silent on the governing law and other terms the court may infer that the parties intended to contract on the same terms, including the governing law, unless such terms were inapplicable in the new market or clearly and indisputably inconsistent with its practice: *Banque Paribas v. Cargill International S.A.* [1992] 1 Lloyd's Rep. 96. Webster J. affirmed CA [1992] 2 Lloyd's Rep. 19.

For a discussion of the proper law of a contract of agency for a foreign principal, see *Mauroux v. Soc. Com. Pereira*, etc. [1972] 1 W.L.R. 962; [1972] 2 All E.R. 1085, not following Dicey.

"Contract or tort"—If a plaintiff has a remedy in contract or tort upon the same facts, he can choose his remedy (*Matthews v. Kuwait Bechtel Corp.* [1959] 2 Q.B. 57; [1959] 2 All E.R. 345). **R11.4.36**

Para. (1)(e): Breach within the jurisdiction of a contract wherever made.

Application of the para—A good arguable case of breach of contract must be made out (*Seaconsar Far East Ltd v. Bank Markazi Jomhouri Islam Iran* [1994] 1 A.C. 43). Where no place of payment is provided by the terms of the contract (including such as are to be implied from the course of dealing between the parties) it is the duty of the debtor to seek out his creditor at his residence or place of business, and therefore a failure to pay money due to a claimant who resides or carries on business within the jurisdiction falls within this sub-rule (*Robey v. Snaefell Co.* (1887) 20 Q.B.D. 152; *The Eider* [1893] P.119, CA; *Thompson v. Palmer* [1893] 2 Q.B. 80, CA; *Chas. Duval & Co. v. Gans* [1904] 2 K.B. 685; *Drexel v. Drexel* [1916] 1 Ch. 251; *Bremer Oeltransport v. Drewry* [1933] 1 K.B. 753, CA.). As to a breach of contract to deliver goods, see *Nathan v. Seitz* (1888) 4 T.L.R. 570; *Wancke v. Wingren* (1889) 58 L.J.Q.B. 519; *Crozier, Stephens & Co. v. Auerbach* [1908] 2 K.B. 161, CA.; *Johnson v. Taylor* [1920] A.C. 144, HL. On the other hand, if there is no obligation which had to be performed within the jurisdiction, no breach can be committed within the jurisdiction within this sub-paragraph (*Cuban Atlantic Sugar Sales Corp. v. Compania de Vapores, etc.* [1960] 1 Q.B. 187; [1960] 1 All E.R. 141, CA). Where a contract is made by a defendant in country A to employ the claimant as his representative in country B, and the defendant wrongfully dismisses the claimant by a letter posted in country A, the breach takes place there (*Holland v. Bennett* [1902] 1 K.B. 867; *Martin v. Stout* [1925] A.C. 359) and if by a letter posted in country B, the breach takes place there (*Mutzenbacher v. La Asseguradora Espanola* [1906] 1 K.B. 254; Oppenheimer v. Rosenthal [1937] 1 All E.R. 23). **R11.4.37**

"Breach preceded . . . by a breach out of the jurisdiction," etc.—These words were added in view of *Johnson v. Taylor* [1920] A.C. 144, HL, where it was decided, under the previous form of the sub-paragraph, that where there was a breach of contract abroad to ship goods C. I. F. England, and a breach of contract within the jurisdiction to deliver shipping documents to the buyer, leave would not be given in respect of the latter breach of contract to serve the writ out of the jurisdiction. **R11.4.38**

R11.4.39 *Para. (1)(f): Tort*—This sub-paragraph amends the law. Leave may be given if either the act causing damage was committed in the jurisdiction or if damage was suffered within the jurisdiction, wherever the act was done. A similar rule prevails under Article 5(3) of the Convention as interpreted by the European Court of Justice in *Bier v. Mines de Potasse D'Alsace* [1976] E.C.R. 1735. The cases on the former r.1(1)(h) are unlikely to be helpful. Under O.11, r.1(1)(f) the claimant must show that (a) his claim is founded on a tort, and either (b) damage has been sustained within the jurisdiction or (c) damage has resulted from an act committed within the jurisdiction. In deciding, for the purposes of requirement (a), whether a tort has been committed in this or another country, the court should look back over the series of events constituting the tort and ask where in substance the cause of action arises. In answering that question the court must apply English law. If the court finds that the tort has in substance been committed in this country, the fact that some of the relevant events have happened abroad is irrelevant, as is the law of the foreign country where such events may have happened. If, on the other hand, the tort has in substance been committed in a foreign country, the court must apply the rule in *Boys v. Chaplin* [1971] A.C. 356; [1969] 2 All E.R. 1085, HL, as developed by *Red Sea Insurance Co. Ltd v. Bouygues S.A.* [1995] 1 A.C. 190, PC; [1994] 3 All E.R. 749, PC in respect of torts committed before the coming into force of Part III of the Private International Law (Miscellaneous Provisions) Act 1995 on May 1, 1996. Torts committed after that date are governed by Part III of the Act. Under requirement (b) it is enough that some significant damage has been sustained in England. Requirement (c) obliges the court to look at the tort alleged in a common sense way, and to ask whether damage has resulted from substantial and efficacious acts committed within the jurisdiction, regardless of whether or not such acts have been committed elsewhere (*Metall und Rohstoff AG v. Donaldson Lufkin & Jenrette Inc.* [1990] 1 Q.B. 391, CA).

Infringement of copyright is not tortious but only a breach of statutory rights; acts done outside the U.K. are not unlawful by the Act; nor, not being tortious, do they fall within the rule. See further Dicey and Morris Conflict of Laws (12th ed., 1993) Accordingly service out of the jurisdiction was set aside (*Def Lepp Music v. Stuart-Browne* [1986] R.P.C. 273).

The decision in *PSM International v. Specialised Fastener Products (Southern) Ltd* [1993] F.S.R. 113 (where Def Lepp Music was not cited) must be taken to be wrong on this point, unless it can be argued that infringement of copyright can be a tort for one purpose but not for another.

R11.4.40 *Para. (1)(g): Land within the jurisdiction (with or without rents or profits)*—These words include a claim to possession as well as title (see *Agnew v. Usher* [1884] L.J.Q.B. 371. *per* Coleridge C.J.).

Para. (1)(h): Liability affecting land situate with the jurisdiction

R11.4.41 *"An act, deed etc., affecting land . . . within the jurisdiction"*—Notwithstanding the decision of the Divisional Court in *Agnew v. Usher* [1885] 14 Q.B.D. 78 (doubted in the same case in the CA, 51 L.T. 752 and see *Iveagh v. Harris* [1929] 2 Ch. 142) these words include, semble, a mere action for rent; as also for possession and breach of covenant to repair (*Tassell v. Hallen* [1892] 1 Q.B. 321); for a declaration that the defendants are trustees of the land and for breach of trust in selling it (*Att.Gen. v. Drapers Co* [1894] 1 I.R. 185, CA); to claim the proceeds of the sale of land held under a trust or similar deed, even though all the land has been sold and the proceeds are no longer within the jurisdiction (*Official Solicitor v. Stype Investments (Jersey) Ltd* [1983] 1 W.L.R. 214; [1983] 1 All E.R. 629; and semble, proceedings to enforce a changing order obtained on land (*per* North J., in *Mority v. Stephan* [1885] 58 L.T. 850; *cf. Kolchmann v. Meurice* [1903] 1 K.B. 5534, CA); but not a claim in the nature of slander of title to land (*Casey v. Arnott* (1876) 2 C.P.D. 24; *Bree v. Narescaux* (1881) 7 Q.B.D. 434).

R11.4.42 *Para. (1)(i): Debts secured on immovable property in the jurisdiction, rights over movable property in the jurisdiction*—This paragraph is deliberately wider than the rule which it replaces (the former r.1(1)(k)).

R11.4.43 *Para. (1)(j): Trusts*—It is not necessary that the trust property should be within the jurisdiction; an absconding trustee will not now be able to rely on his success in removing the assets. If he is in a Convention country the English courts will probably have jurisdiction under Art. 5(6) of the convention, read with section 45 of the 1982 Act. Even though the question of legal entitlement to a European patent application by a non resident cannot (by virtue of the Patents Act 1977, s.82) be tried by an English court, the question whether the patent is held in trust by a non-resident for an English resident is not within the scope of *ibid.*, s.82(3) and can be dealt with by an English Court (*Kakkar v. Szelke* [1988] F.S.R. 97).

R11.4.44 *Para. (1)(k): Administration of the estate of a person who died domiciled within the jurisdiction*—For the meaning of domiciled in this context see r.1(4).

R11.4.45 *"probate action" (r.1(1)(l))*—Formerly, this paragraph said that service out of the jurisdiction was permissible with the leave of the court where the claim was brought "in a probate action within the meaning of Order 76" (see also CCR, O.8, r.2(1)(k) where O.41 was referred to) and "probate action" was defined accordingly in RSC, O.1, r.4(1)). Contentious probate proceedings now constitute one of the "specialist proceedings" referred to in Pt 49. The CPR apply to such proceedings subject to the provisions of "the relevant practice direction" (r.49.1). The relevant practice direction is Practice Direction—Contentious Probate Proceedings (see para. 49PD–001) (replacing RSC, O.76 and CCR, O.41). That Practice Direction makes no reference to a "probate action" but in para. 1.2 refers to and defines a "probate claim". Presumably, "probate action" in r.1(1)(1) has the same meaning as "probate claim" in para. 1.2.

Para. (1)(m): Judgment or award—The presence of assets within the jurisdiction does not in itself give the English courts jurisdiction over a person outside the jurisdiction. Accordingly a foreign judgment could not be enforced against English assets in cases not falling within the provisions for the reciprocal enforcement of judgments legislation unless the debtor could be served in England or was "domiciled or ordinarily resident with the jurisdiction." Now the foreign judgment or award is itself a sufficient ground for the grant of leave. An interim order freezing assets in pending litigation in a foreign jurisdiction is not a judgment within the meaning of this paragraph: (*Mercedes-Benz A.G. v. Leiduck* [1995] 2 All E.R. 929, PC. **R11.4.46**

Para. (1)(n): Duties and taxes—This paragraph has been reworded for technical reasons and in order to avoid having to list a number of statutes. **R11.4.47**

Para. 1(o):—The Social Securities Act 1975 and other statutes have been repealed by the Social Security (Consequential Provisions) Act 1992 and replaced by consolidating legislation which includes the Social Security Contributions and Benefits Act 1992 under which contributions are now payable. The continuity of the law has been preserved by section 2 of the Social Security (Consequential Provisions) Act 1992 and the reference to the 1975 Act will be construed as a reference to the corresponding provisions of the consolidating Acts. **R11.4.48**

Para. (1)(p):—This is subject to a lower limit of 1,500 ECU (E.C. Directive 86/489/EEC). **R11.4.49**

Para. (1)(t): Constructive trustees—The words "constructive trustee" should be construed as referring to a constructive trustee against whom a personal claim could be made as well as against one against whom a proprietary claim could be made (*Ghana Commercial Bank v. C., The Times*, March 3, 1997). **R11.4.50**

Omissions—The rule no longer contains references to the Carriage by Air Act 1961, the Carriage by Air (Supplementary Provisions) Act 1962, the Carriage of Goods by Road Act 1965, nor the Protection of Trading Interests Act 1980: leave to serve outside the jurisdiction will seldom if ever be required in these cases. **R11.4.51**

SERVICE WITHOUT THE NEED FOR PERMISSION (R.1(2))

Rule 1(2)(a):—Rule 1(2)(a) states that a claim form may be served out of the jurisdiction on a defendant without the permission of the Court provided that each claim against that defendant is a claim which by virtue of the Civil Jurisdiction and Judgments Act 1982 the Court has power to hear and determine. A claimant may take advantage of this rule and serve the defendant out of the jurisdiction without first obtaining the court's permission provided the proceedings in which such claim or claims are made satisfy the conditions stated in r.1(2)(a). Under the 1982 Act, jurisdiction arising under various Conventions is conferred on the English courts (see "Service under the Brussels and Lugano Conventions" para. and cross-references to S.C.P. 1999 found there). **R11.4.52**

The conditions stated in r.1(2)(a) are:

(i) no proceedings between the parties concerning the same cause of action are pending in the courts of any other part of the United Kingdom or of any other Convention territory; and

(ii) either the defendant is domiciled in any part of the United Kingdom or in any other Convention territory, or the proceedings begun by the claim form are proceedings to which Article 16 of Schedule 1, 3C or 4 refers, or the defendant is a party to an agreement conferring jurisdiction to which Article 17 of Schedule 1, 3C or 4 to that Act applies.

Note the requirement under paragraph 1.4 of the Practice Direction—Service Out of the Jurisdiction for the relevant certificate of jurisdiction.

It is important to note that r.1.(2)(a) cannot be understood on its own. It must be read with the Act and Conventions. See Vol. 2, Section 7 for text and also see, e.g. Halsbury's Statutes, Vol. 22, pp. 381 *et seq.* The Conventions are drafted differently from English statutes: by s.3 of the Act the Jenard and Schlosser reports are made official guides to their interpretation (see Halsbury above for the references).

Rule 1(2)(b):—Rule 1(2)(b) states that a claim form may be served out of the jurisdiction on a **R11.4.53** defendant without the permission of the Court provided that each claim against that defendant is a claim which by virtue of any enactment other than the Civil Jurisdiction and Judgments Act 1982 (as to which see r.1(2)(a)) the Court has power to hear and determine notwithstanding that the person against whom the claim is made is not within the jurisdiction of the Court or that the wrongful act, neglect or default giving rise to the claim did not take place within its jurisdiction. In the case of *Re Harrods (Buenos Aires) Ltd* [1992] Ch. 72, CA, the background to this rule was explained and it was said (at p. 116 per Dillon L.J.) that, to be within r.1(2)(b) an enactment must, if it does not use the precise wording of the rule, at least indicate on its face that it is expressly contemplating proceedings against persons who are not within the jurisdiction of the court or where the wrongful act, neglect or default giving rise to the claim did not take place within the jurisdiction. (In the *Harrods* case it was held that r.1(2)(b) did not permit the service out of the jurisdiction without leave of a petition under the Companies Act 1985, s.459).

Note the requirement under paragraph 1.4 of the Practice Direction—Service Out of the Jurisdiction for the relevant certificate of jurisdiction.

The following overview is intended to make the rules intelligible: and not as a detailed commentary.

The Civil Jurisdiction and Judgments Act 1991 incorporates the Lugano Convention into the 1982 Act. This enables the E.F.T.A. countries (Austria, Finland, Iceland, Norway, Sweden and Switzerland), subject to minor modifications to join the Brussels Convention regime. It came into force in relation to Switzerland on May 1, 1992; Sweden on January 1, 1993; Norway on April 1, 1993 and Finland on July 1, 1993. (Sweden and Finland are now E.C. countries.) The Brussels Convention applies between E.C. Member States. For full details see the current edition of the International Litigation Procedure Reports.

For detailed commentaries on the rules see the leading textbooks, *e.g.* Dicey & Morris, *Conflict of Laws* (12th ed.) and Briggs & Rees, *Civil Jurisdiction and Judgments* (2nd ed.)

The 1982 Act now applies to all E.C. countries. Gibraltar is included: S.I. 1997 No. 2602.

The Brussels Convention has been amended to bring it into line with the Lugano Convention and the decision of *Ivenel*, below (Civil Jurisdiction and Judgments Act 1982 (Amendment) Order 1990 (S.I. 1990 No. 2591)).

It should be noted that where the claim form makes several claims against the defendant, each claim must fall within these categories. It is conceivable that a claim form may make claims against two (or more) defendants out of the jurisdiction and that the claim or claims made against one defendant will all fall within the categories mentioned above, with the result that leave to serve the writ on him will not be required, but that the claim or claims made against the other defendant will not all fall within the categories, with the result that leave to serve the claim form on him will be required.

The object of the Convention is not to unify the rules of substantive law and of procedure of different Contracting States, but to determine which courts had jurisdiction in disputes relating to civil and commercial matters in relations between Contracting States and to facilitate the enforcement of judgments (see *Shevill v. Presse Alliance* [1996] A.C. 959).

R11.4.54 **Subject matter of the proceedings**—The Conventions and the Act apply to all civil matters (except revenue, customs, administrative matters, legal status, rights in matrimonial property, wills and succession, insolvency, social security and arbitration) (Sched. 1, Art. 1). The word "arbitration" in Art. 1 covers all matters connected with arbitration, including the question whether there is a valid arbitration agreement (*Marc Rich & Co. A.G. v. Societa Italiana Impianti PA, The Atlantic Emperor* [1989] 1 Lloyd's Rep. 548, CA affd. Europeean Court of Justice (1991) *The Independent*, September 23.

However in *Partenreederei M/S Heidberg v. Grosvenor Grain and Feed Co. Ltd ("The Heidberg")* [1994] 2 Lloyd's Rep. 287, H.H. Judge Diamond Q.C. held that where an issue as to the existence or otherwise of an arbitration clause arose as a subsidiary rather than a primary point at issue, the Brussels Convention would still apply. In *Firswood v. Petra Bank*, CA December 13, 1995, (following *Gourdain v. Nadler* [1979] E.C.R. 733) a claim against a guarantor arising on the winding up of the company was held to come within the insolvency exception in Article 1(2).

Where the Convention does not apply by reason of the exceptions contained in Article 1, judgments of other Contracting States may be enforced in the United Kingdom under the Foreign Judgments (Reciprocal Enforcement) Act 1933 or at common law as the case may be.

R11.4.55 **Basic jurisdiction: domicile of the defendant**—By Sched. 1, Art. 2 to the Act a defendant must be sued in the courts of the state in which he is domiciled if that state has adhered to the Conventions unless one of the alternative grounds of jurisdiction specified in Arts 5–18 are available. Note that: (a) "domicle" for the purposes of the Act and of O.11 generally is defined in sections 41–46 of the Act; it has a different meaning to that borne in other branches of English law, and, in the case of an individual, approximates to genuine residence. Jurisdiction will no longer be obtainable by serving a defendant domiciled in France while he is on a short visit to Ascot (see Art. 3).

In *Canada Trust v. Stolzenberg (No. 2)* [1998] 1 All E.R. 318, CA it was held that domicile should be ascertained for this purpose as at the date of issue rather than service of the writ. See note below.

(b) "Convention territory" is used in the rules and in this note in place of "Contracting State" to get over the difficulty that not all the territories of the Member States of the E.C. are within the Convention; generally speaking all the European territories of the E.C. are "Convention territory" but see section 1.(3) of the Act and r.1(4), for the exact definition of the phrase.

Service in Scotland or Northern Ireland without permission

Civil Jurisdiction and Judgments Act 1982—The Act of 1982 was not only intended to render the Brussels Convention applicable in the United Kingdom but also by Schedule 4 provided for the allocation of civil jurisdiction between the three separate jurisdictions within the United Kingdom. These provisions are modelled on the Convention and by s.16(3) in determining any question as to the meaning of any provision in Schedule 4. **R11.4.56**

> "regard shall be had to any relevant principles laid down by the European Court in connection with title II of the 1968 Convention and to any relevant decision of that court as to the meaning or effect of any provisions of that Title."

Where in a case where there was a question on the interpretation and inter-relation of Arts 5(1) and 5(3) and, depending upon the answer, whether the English or Scottish courts had jurisdiction and the question had been referred to the European Court by the Court of Appeal, the European Court held that the interpretation of Sched. 4 was a matter for the United Kingdom national courts and that it did not have any jurisdiction to rule on the matter (*Kleinwort Benson Ltd v. City of Glasgow District Council* (1995) *The Times*, April 17 (E.C. Case No. C–346/93).

In all cases that fall within Article 5 of Schedule 4 jurisdiction will depend on the terms of the Article and service must be effected if permitted without permission. In cases covered by O.11, r.1(1) which fall outside the Convention it may still be possible to obtain permission to serve in Scotland or Northern Ireland applying the principles set out in notes.

The Court has power to stay an English libel action on the grounds of *forum non conveniens* where an action based on the same libel is proceeding in Scotland rejecting the submission that it had no jurisdiction to do so under the Civil Jurisdiction and Judgments Act (*Cumming v. Scottish Daily Mail* (1995) *The Times*, June 8; [1995] EMLR 538). In this case *Drake J.* declined to follow an earlier decision of his *Foxen v. Scotsman Publications* (1994) *The Times*, February 17; [1995] E.M.L.R. 145.

This case should be contrasted with the Convention cases of *S & W Berisford v. New Hampshire Ins. Co.* and *Arkwright Mutual Ins. Co. v. Bryanston Inc. Co.* noted at in both of which there was only one set of proceedings and it should also be noted that Article 21 of the Convention (giving jurisdiction to the court "first seised") is not included in Schedule 4.

Service of claim form abroad: general

5.—(1) Subject to paragraphs (2) to (8) of this rule— **R11.5**

(a) a claim form must be served personally on each defendant by the claimant or his agent;

(b) where a defendant's solicitor indorses on the claim form a statement that he accepts service of the claim form on behalf of that defendant, the claim form shall be deemed to have been duly served on that defendant and to have been so served on the date on which the indorsement was made;

(c) where a claim form is not duly served on a defendant but he acknowledges service of it, the claim form shall be deemed, unless the contrary is shown, to have been duly served on him and to have been so served on the date on which he acknowledges service;

(d) CPR rule 6.8 (service by an alternative method) shall apply in relation to the claim form.

(2) Nothing in this rule or in any order or direction of the court made by virtue of it shall authorise or require the doing of anything in a country in which service is to be effected which is contrary to the law of that country.

(3) A claim form which is to be served out of the jurisdiction—

(a) need not be served personally on the person required to be served so long as it is served on him in accordance with the law of the country in which service is effected; and

(b) need not be served by the claimant or his agent if it is served by a method provided for by rule 6 or rule 7.

(5) An official certificate stating that a claim form as regards which rule 6 has been complied with has been served on a person personally or in accordance with the law of the country in which service was effected, on a specified date, being a certificate—

(a) by a British consular authority in that country;
(b) by the government or judicial authorities of that country; or
(c) by any other authority designated in respect of that country under the Hague Convention,

shall be evidence of the facts so stated.

(6) An official certificate by the Secretary of State stating that a claim form has been duly served on a specified date in accordance with a request made under rule 7 shall be evidence of that fact.

(7) A document purporting to be such a certificate as is mentioned in paragraph (5) or (6) shall, until the contrary is proved, be deemed to be such a certificate.

(8) In this rule and rule 6 "the Hague Convention" means the Convention on the service abroad of judicial and extra-judicial documents in civil or commercial matters signed at the Hague on November 15, 1965.

R11.5.1 **History of Rule**—Taken from O.11, r.5, 1962, as amended in 1963, 1968 and 1979.

Service abroad—General note

R11.5.2 **Effect of rule**—The rule consists of two parts: Paras (1) to (3) are mainly concerned with the method of service out of the jurisdiction generally, where there is no special provision for alternative methods, and proof of such service. Paras (5) to (8) set out the method of proof of service of Pt 6 where the service is by one of the methods allowed by rr.6 and 7 in the circumstances there mentioned. Most of the provisions are excluded and postal service of a claim form or other originating process is not authorised except in pursuance of a convention or an order for an alternative method of service or a contractually agreed method of service (see rule 6.15(2)).

By virtue of O.11, r.5(2) no order of the English court can be taken to authorise or direct the doing of anything contrary to the law of the state where service is to be effected. Thus where service of a claim form is purportedly made in a foreign country by a private person instructed by the claimant, and where the law of that country stipulates that service should be through official channels, the English court will not, except in a very strong and unusual case, exercise discretion to allow the purported service to stand (*Ferrarini S.p.A. v. Magnol Shipping Co. Inc., the Sky One* [1988] 1 Lloyd's Rep. 238).

R11.5.3 **Service on foreign companies abroad**—May be either in accordance with rule 6.4(4), or in accordance with the law of the country where the service is to be effected. If, however, the company has established a branch of a place of business in England, no question need arise of service out of the jurisdiction (see r.6.2.2).

R11.5.4 **Service on foreign firms**—Pt 6 applies to partners, or an individual, carrying on a business under a firm name within the jurisdiction. A firm that trades only abroad presents difficulties; if such a firm has no legal existence apart from its individual members, those members ought to be named and served (*Von Hellfeld v. Rechnityer* [1914] 1 Ch. 748 at 755). It is, however, difficult to ascertain the legal status of foreign firms, particularly in continental countries, where there are bodies of a status not found in England. As a working rule it is often fairly safe to sue a firm in the style in which it enjoys legal rights and liabilities in its country of domicile.

R11.5.5 **Service on a foreign state**—See section 12 of the State Immunity Act 1978 and r.7 and note at para. R11.7.2.

R11.5.6 **Hague Convention**—Printed HMSO, Cmnd. 3986 (1969). This Convention came into effect on February 10, 1969, after ratification by three States (Art. 27). It provides (*inter alia*) that each contracting state shall designate a Central Authority to receive requests for service coming from other contracting states and execute them. Documents for service must be lodged with the Masters' Secretary's Foreign Process Office, Room E02, Royal Courts of Justice, Strand, London WC2A 2LL, for onward transmission. The contracting states are at liberty to impose restrictions under certain articles of the Convention and information as to these can be obtained from the above-named Department. This multilateral Convention does not invalidate the bilateral Conventions already in force and listed under para. R11.6.3.

Anguilla
Antigua
Aruba
Associate States of St Kitts & Nevis
Israel
Italy
Japan
Luxembourg

Barbados
Belgium
Bermuda
Botswana
Canada
Cayman Islands
China
Cyprus (South only)
Denmark
Egypt
Estonia
Falkland Islands
France
Germany
Gibraltar
Greece
Malawi
Montserrat
Netherlands
Norway
Pakistan
Portugal
St Helena and dependencies
Seychelles
Spain
Sweden
Turkey
Turks and Caicos Islands
United Kingdom (including the Channel Islands and the Isle of Man)
United States of America

Service abroad without permission—Rules 5 and 6 apply to claim forms which it is proposed to serve out of the jurisdiction without the permission of the court, pursuant to rule 1(2) and the Civil Jurisdiction and Judgments Act 1982. R11.5.7

The Hague Convention permits the sending of "judicial documents by postal channels directly to persons abroad" provided "the state of destination does not object" to such method of service (see Arts 10 and 19). Provided therefore that service by post is permitted by and effected in accordance with the law of the country in which service is effected, there is nothing in the Hague Convention or in the Brussels Convention which cuts down the scope of this permission (*Noirhomme v. Walklate, The Times*, August 2, 1991).

Service under Hague Convention and Brussels and Lugano Conventions—Article 27(2) of the Brussels Convention denies recognition to a judgment given in default if the defendant "was not duly served with the document which instituted the proceedings in sufficient time for him to arrange his defence". In *Minalmet GmbH v. Brandeis Ltd* [1993] 4 I.L.Pr. 132 (Case C–123/91), the European Court held that lack of due service precluded the enforcement of a default judgment even though the defendant had become aware of it and had taken no steps to set aside the judgment. The steps taken in the action were as follows: R11.5.8

(1) English proceedings sent under Art. 5(a) of the Hague Convention to the Amtsgericht which certified that service had been duly effected;
(2) Default judgment entered in the High Court;
(3) Enforcement of the judgment authorised by the Landgericht;
(4) The defendant appealed this order to the Oberlandesgericht which dismissed the appeal;
(5) The defendant further appealed this order to the Bundesgerichthof which decided that service did not accord with the provisions of German Civil Law (*lex loci executionis*) but that the defendants had become aware of the judgment and had taken no steps to set it aside in England (*lex loci decisionis*) and referred the question of whether the default judgment should nevertheless be recognised to the European Court.

A certificate of due service sent from a foreign authority under The Hague Convention to the court issuing a writ cannot of itself validate an invalid form of service where service did not in fact comply with the rules of service in the state of destination (*Re Postal Service Abroad* [1995] I.L.Pr. 523 (Bundesgerichthof)).

These cases underline problems that may face the holder of a default judgment and should be borne in mind when choosing to use the exceptional jurisdiction under Art. 5 rather than proceeding under Art. 2.

Service of claim form abroad through foreign governments, judicial authorities and British consuls

6.—(1) Save where a claim form is to be served pursuant to paragraph (2A) this rule does not apply to service in— R11.6

(a) Scotland, Northern Ireland, the Isle of Man or the Channel Islands;
(b) any independent Commonwealth country;
(c) any associated state;
(d) any colony;
(e) the Republic of Ireland.

(2) Where in accordance with these rules a claim form is to be served on a defendant in any country with respect to which there subsists a Civil Procedure Convention (other than the Hague Convention) providing for service in that country of process of the High Court, the claim form may be served—

(a) through the judicial authorities of that country; or
(b) through a British consular authority in that country (subject to any provision of the convention as to the nationality of persons who may be so served).

(2A) Where in accordance with these rules a claim form is to be served on a defendant in any country which is a party to the Hague Convention, the claim form may be served—

(a) through the authority designated under the Convention in respect of that country; or
(b) if the law of that country permits—
  (i) through the judicial authorities of that country, or
  (ii) through a British consular authority in that country.

(3) Where in accordance with these rules a claim form is to be served on a defendant in any country with respect to which there does not subsist a Civil Procedure Convention providing for service in that country of process of the High Court, the claim form may be served—

(a) through the government of that country, where that government is willing to effect service; or
(b) through a British consular authority in that country, except where service through such an authority is contrary to the law of that country.

(4) A person who wishes to serve a claim form by a method specified in paragraph (2), (2A) or (3) must file in the Central Office of the Supreme Court a request for service of the claim form by that method, together with a copy of the claim form and an additional copy thereof for each person to be served.

(5) Every copy of a claim form filed under paragraph (4) must be accompanied by a translation of the claim form in the official language of the country in which service is to be effected or, if there is more than one official language of that country, in any one of those languages which is appropriate to the place in that country where service is to be effected: provided that this paragraph shall not apply in relation to a copy of a claim form which is to be served in a country the official language of which is, or the official languages of which include, English, or is to be served in any country by a British consular authority on a British subject, unless the service is to be effected under paragraph (2) and the Civil Procedure Convention with respect to that country expressly requires the copy to be accompanied by a translation.

(6) Every translation lodged under paragraph (5) must be certified by the person making it to be a correct translation; and the certificate must contain a statement of that person's full name, of his address and of his qualifications for making the translation.

(7) Documents duly filed under paragraph (4) shall be sent by the Senior Master to the Parliamentary Under-Secretary of State to the Foreign Office with a request that he arrange the claim form to be served by the method indicated in the request lodged under paragraph (4) or, where alternative methods are so indicated, by such one of those methods as is most convenient.

R11.6.1 **History of Rule**—Taken from O.11, r.6, of 1962, as amended in 1963, 1968 and by S.I. 1976 No. 337 and S.I. 1980 No. 2000.

R11.6.2 **Para. (1)—Independent Commonwealth countries, etc. and the Republic of Ireland**—This paragraph in effect excepts from the ambit of r.6 countries which are British colonies, independent Commonwealth countries, the Republic of Ireland and any remaining protectorates. In these countries service cannot be effected through official channels (that is, through the government or judicial authorities or a British consular authority) and is therefore made by the plaintiff or agent direct (see r.5(3)(b)).

For the list of Independent Commonwealth Countries, past and present, inquire of the Masters' Secretary's Foreign Process Office, Room E02, Royal Courts of Justice, Strand, London.

Para. (2)—Convention countries—This paragraph concerns service in "convention countries". Conventions providing for service of process of the High Court have been made with the following countries: R11.6.3

Austria	Germany	*Latvia*	Romania
Belgium	Greece	Lebanon*	Spain
Czechoslovakia	Hungary	*Lithuania*	Sweden
Denmark	Iraq	Netherlands	Syria*
Estonia	Israel	Norway	Turkey
Finland	Italy	Poland	Yugoslavia†
France	Laos*	Portugal	

*The French Convention of 1922 included Laos, Lebanon and Syria, and these countries have stated that they accept its terms as applicable to them. There is no separate convention with these countries.

†Position now unclear.

Conventions with the countries printed in italics are at present ineffective, but in the case of the German Federal Republic the German Convention has been re-applied. The conventions with Estonia, Latvia and Lithuania have never formally lapsed, but have ceased to operate owing to the *de facto* incorporation of these states in the former Soviet Union and have not yet been re-applied. It should be noted that some of the conventions have been extended to colonies of the countries concerned.

There is some variety in the methods of service permitted and prohibited by the various conventions, but two methods are permitted by each of them, namely (1) service through the judicial authorities of the country where the service is to take place, and (2) service through a British consular authority in that country. In regard to method (2) however, there is some variety in the provisions of the conventions as to the nationality of the persons who may be so served. In Denmark, Germany and Hungary, subjects of the country of service may not be served in this way. In Portugal, Portuguese nationals may not be so served without their consent. In Turkey service may only be made in this way upon British subjects. The other important method of service is through an agent appointed by the claimant but this is not permitted in some countries, and in others it is not permitted on subjects of those countries. Therefore, for simplicity, r.6(2) expressly permits service in convention countries by one of the above two numbered methods, and subject to the qualification in sub-para. (b) though it does not exclude other methods which may be available. A doubt arises, however, in regard to orders made in England by post as an alternative method of service upon defendants in certain convention countries. The conventions with France, Iraq and Italy do not permit service by post, and that with Turkey does not permit such service except upon British nationals. Though, therefore, the Court here has probably jurisdiction to make an order for service by post as an alternative method of service in such cases, the claimant is likely to find that a default judgment based upon such service would not be recognised in those countries.

Of the two methods of service allowed by para. (2), that through the British consular authority is generally to be preferred, for the consuls are familiar with the local and English requirements, and the certificate of service is received in the approved form and without prejudicing enforcement of the judgment in the foreign court. In some cases, such as divorce suits, where identification of the party served is of special importance (see Family Proceedings Rules 1991, r.2.9) service through the consular authority is desirable. But serious delay sometimes results from the fact that the consular staff is busily engaged or unable for some other reason to effect prompt service. This can be avoided if applicants in the form of request ask that the process be served through the British consul or by the local judicial authorities as may be most convenient (see para. (7)).

If the third method of service mentioned above (namely that through an agent appointed by the claimant) is employed in the cases where the convention permits, r.6 does not apply. The claimant makes his own arrangements, but he should see that the affidavit of service is sworn before a qualified person.

For fuller information as to the provisions of the conventions, apply to the Masters' Secretary's Foreign Process Office, Room E02, Royal Courts of Justice, WC2A 2LL, by which service out of the jurisdiction is handled in any Division of the High Court, including cases proceeding in a District Registry.

Para. (3)—Non-Convention countries other than British Dominions, etc.—This paragraph concerns service abroad in countries other than convention countries and countries specified in para. (1). It takes the place of the former r.8, which only allowed service through the government of the country in which the writ was to be served, though the service was always in fact executed by the judicial authority. Now the two methods allowed are: R11.6.4

(1) through the government of the country (where that government is willing to effect service); and

(2) through the British consular authority (except where service through that authority is contrary to the law of the country).

The paragraph does not exclude any other method which may be available.

In the USA District Courts may order service, and service may also be effected through private agents or the British consular authority. There are no facilities for service of foreign process in the Sheikhdom of Muscat and Oman.

It is understood that there is no objection under the local law to the service of process through the British consular authority in Andorra, Argentine, Brazil, Burma, Chile, Colombia, Costa Rica, Cuba, Dominican Republic, Ecuador, Ethiopia, Guatemala, Haiti, Honduras, Iceland, Indonesia, Japan, Mexico, Monaco, Morocco, Nicaragua, Panama, Paraguay, Peru, Salvador, South Africa, Tunisia, USA, Uruguay and Vietnam. Service, however, by this method is only permitted upon British subjects in the case of Brazil, Honduras, Monaco, and Tunisia; and in Burma and Vietnam it is not permitted upon local nationals. It is understood, however, that Argentine, Ecuador, Guatemala, and Panama do not regard a judgment based on such service as valid. In all cases where this method is not available or considered valid, service through the foreign government (which is a method permitted in most countries) should be attempted, or through agents. It is understood that there is no objection to service by the party's agent in Argentine, Chile, Cuba, Ethiopia, Japan, Mexico, Nicaragua, Sudan, USA, and Uruguay, though a judgment based on such service may not be enforceable in Argentine.

R11.6.5 **Paras. (4)–(7)—practice**—The practice concerning the documents to be served is set out in the Practice Direction—Service Out of the Jurisdiction. The document to be served is lodged in duplicate and sealed in the office with the seal of the Supreme Court. One copy is served and the other copy is eventually returned through the Foreign Office to the Masters' Secretary's Foreign Process Office, with the official certificate of service (r.5) or inability to effect service, and is sent in Probate and Divorce matters to the Principal Probate Registry, Somerset House, in Admiralty matters to the Admiralty Registry, in Queen's Bench and Chancery matters to the Filing Department or the Chancery Registry, Royal Courts of Justice, and in District Registry cases to the appropriate District Registry. The Masters' Secretary notifies the applicant's solicitor of the receipt of the certificate and of the amount of expenses incurred. These are payable to the Finance Officer of the Diplomatic Service. If the certificate is sent for filing in the Filing Department a filing fee is payable.

In cases where there is no acknowledgment of service and the claimant wishes to sign judgment, production of the certificate of service is required. If this certificate is in a foreign language, the solicitor should attend at the Filing Department with a translator for the purpose of having the certificate translated, and the translation is verified by an affidavit. The translation is then accepted by the court.

R11.6.6 **Service abroad without leave**—See the note and Practice Direction under this heading at para. R11.5.7 above.

Service of claim form in certain actions under certain Acts

R11.7 **7.**—(1) Subject to paragraph (4) where a person to whom permission has been granted under rule 1 to serve a claim form on a State, as defined in section 14 of the State Immunity Act 1978, wishes to have the claim form served on that State, he must file in the Central Office—

(a) a request for service to be arranged by the Secretary of State; and

(b) a copy of the claim form; and

(c) except where the official language of the State is, or the official languages of the State include, English, a translation of the claim form in the official language or one of the official languages of that State.

(2) Rule 6(6) shall apply in relation to a translation filed under paragraph (1) of this rule as it applies in relation to a translation filed under paragraph (5) of that rule.

(3) Documents duly filed under this rule shall be sent by the Senior Master to the Secretary of State with a request that the Secretary of State arrange for the claim form to be served.

(4) Where section 12(6) of the State Immunity Act 1978 applies and the State has agreed to a method of service other than that provided by the preceding paragraphs, the claim form may be served either by the method agreed or in accordance with the preceding paragraphs of this rule.

R11.7.1 **History of Rule**—Amended by S.I. 1980 No. 629 and S.I. 1980 No. 2000.

R11.7.2 **State Immunity Act 1978**—for an explanatory note and summary of its provisions, see SCP 1999 Vol. 2, Section 17B, paras 17B–24 to 17B–31.

R11.7.3 **Effective Service**—Service on a diplomatic mission is not service on the state of that mission for the purposes of section 12(1) of the 1978 Act. The express terms of s.12(1) required service at, not merely on, the Foreign Ministry of the state and service was not effected until there was transmission of the document to the ministry and the document was received at the ministry (*Kuwait Airways Corpn. v. Iraqi Airways Co.* [1995] 1 W.L.R. 1147; [1995] 3 All E.R. 691).

Undertaking to pay expenses of service by Secretary of State

8. Every request lodged under rule 6(4) or rule 7 must contain an undertaking by the person making the request to be responsible personally for all expenses incurred by the Secretary of State in respect of the service requested and, on receiving due notification of the amount of those expenses, to pay that amount to the Finance Officer of the office of the Secretary of State and to produce a receipt for the payment to the proper officer of the High Court. **R11.8**

Applications for interim remedy under section 25(1) of the Civil Jurisdiction and Judgments Act 1982

8A.—(1) A claim form for an interim remedy under section 25(1) of the Civil Jurisdiction and Judgments Act 1982 [1] (as extended by Order in Council made under section 25(3)) may be served out of the jurisdiction with the permission of the court. **R11.8A**

(2) An application for the grant of permission under paragraph (1) must be supported by written evidence stating—

(a) the grounds on which the application is made;

(b) that in the belief of the witness the claimant has a good claim to an interim remedy;

(c) in what place or country the defendant is, or probably may be, found.

(3) The following provisions of this order shall apply, with the necessary modifications, where service is to be effected under this rule as they apply where service is effected under rule 1—

Rule 1(A) (period for acknowledging service or filing or serving admission);

Rule 1B (period for filing defence);

Rule 4(2), (3) and (4) (grant of permission);

Rule 5 (service of claim form abroad: general);

Rule 6 (service of claim form abroad through foreign governments, etc.); and

Rule 8 (undertaking to pay expenses of service).

Effect of rule—This provision confers on the court jurisdiction to allow service out of the jurisdiction of a claim for interim relief against a person resident whether in a Convention or a non-Convention country even though no substantive relief is claimed in the English proceedings. **R11.8A.1**

Where interim relief only is claimed the proceedings must be by Pt 23 where not in the Commercial Court and Pt 8 where in the Commercial Court.

The application for leave will follow the practice set out in the notes to O.11, r.4 with the modification in the contents of the written evidence required by sub-rule (2). In urgent cases application may be made direct to a Master or Judge.

Service of petition and order etc.

9.—(1) Rule 1 of this Order shall apply to the service out of the jurisdiction of a petition or an application notice issued before proceedings have started as it applies to service of a claim form. **R11.9**

(4) Any application notice issued or order made in any proceedings may be served out of the jurisdiction with the permission of the court but permission shall not be required for such service in any proceedings in which the claim form may by these rules or under any Act be served out of the jurisdiction without permission.

(5) Rule 4(1), (2) and (3) shall, so far as applicable, apply in relation to an application for the grant of permission under this rule as they apply in relation to an application for the grant of permission under rule 1.

[1] 1982 c.27. Section 25 was amended by the Civil Jurisdiction and Judgments Act 1991 (c. 12), s.3, Sched. 2, paragraph 12.

(7) Rules 5, 6 and 8 shall apply in relation to any document for the service of which out of the jurisdiction permission has been granted under this rule as they apply in relation to a claim form.

R11.9.1 **History of Rule**—Taken from O.11, r.9 of 1962. Amended by S.I. 1979 No. 1716; S.I. 1980 No. 629; S.I. 1980 No. 2000; S.I. 1983 No. 1181; S.I. 1996 No. 3219 and S.I. 1999 No. 1008.

R11.9.2 **Service of a notice (para. 4)**—This paragraph has no reference to cases where, for mere grounds of convenience or interest, it is desirable or proper to give a person abroad notice by way of information of proceedings pending in this country—as, for example, where a person abroad is thought to have an interest in a fund which it is desired to distribute, or where it is intended to place him on the list of contributories of a company in liquidation (*Re Nathan, Newman & Co.* (1887) 35 Ch.D. 1; *Re King & Co's Trade Mark* [1892] 2 Ch. 462; *Re Cliff* [1895] 2 Ch. 21 at 28; *Re La Compagnie Générale de'Eaux Minerales* [1891] 3 Ch. 451 at 456). Notice in such a case can be given without an order. The present rule relates to service of process, originating or interim, on persons who are necessary respondents to proceedings or on which further proceedings are to be based, or on which to found jurisdiction over persons abroad (see the two cases last cited).

R11.9.3 **Service out of the jurisdiction of extra-judicial documents**—On May 18, 1931, the following notice with regard to extra-judicial documents was published by order of the Lord Chancellor:

1. The procedure prescribed by O.11, r.11(1) and (2) [now O.11, rr.5, 6 and 8] of the rules of the Supreme Court with regard to the transmission of judicial documents from England for service in a foreign country with which a Civil Procedure Convention has been made may be adopted, and, if the assistance of a British Consul is desired, must be adopted, for the transmission from England to the foreign country of any extra-judicial documents to which the Convention applies, subject to the modifications in this Notice.

2. Subject to the provisions of the Convention, the expression "extra-judicial documents" includes any formal notice given by one person to another under a contract between them or concerning their relations under contract, as, for example, a notice by a landlord determining a tenancy, a notice of dishonour of a bill of exchange, or a notice of the assignment of a debt.

3. Any question whether a document is an extra-judicial document within the meaning of the Convention may be decided by the Senior Master of the Supreme Court "Queen's Bench Division," whose decision for the purpose of this procedure shall be final.

4. Service by this procedure will be no evidence of the validity of the document served.

Service of part 20 claim form

R11.9A **9A.**—(1) This rule applies to any Part 20 claim, except

(a) a counterclaim; and

(b) a claim for a contribution of indemnity made in accordance with CPR rule 20.6

(2) Permission may be granted to serve a Part 20 claim form on any necessary or proper party to the proceedings brought against the defendants in accordance with rule 1(1)(c).

R11.9A.1 **Editorial Note**—Rule 9A was added by S.I. 1999 No. 1008. For definition of Pt 20 claim, see CPR, r.20.2(1).

Order to apply to county court

R11.10 **10.** This order applies to proceedings in any county court in addition to proceedings in the High Court.

PRACTICE DIRECTION—SERVICE OUT OF THE JURISDICTION

R11PD–001 *This Practice Direction Supplements RSC Order 11 (Schedule 1 to the CPR)*

Matters to be included in claim forms:

1.1 CPR Part 7 provides that when particulars of claim are served on a defendant they must be accompanied by—

(a) a form for defending the claim;
(b) a form for admitting the claim; and
(c) a form for acknowledging service.

1.2 In addition, the particulars of claim must be accompanied by the complete Response Pack. The Response Pack must clearly state the appropriate period for responding to the claim form, as specified in this Practice Direction, and accordingly both Form N9 and Form N1C and other relevant forms must be amended.

1.3 Where the claim form is to be served in a place or country listed in the table below in accordance with paragraph 6.4, the particulars of claim, if not included in it, must accompany the claim form.

1.4 Where a claim form is served out of the jurisdiction without permission under Schedule 1, RSC O11, r.1(2), it must include a certificate that the court has power under the Civil Jurisdiction and Judgments Act 1982 to hear the claim, and that no proceedings involving the same issues are pending between the parties in the courts of any part of the United Kingdom or any other Convention territory as specified in RSC O.11, r.1(2)(a)(i).

1.5 The usual form of words of the certificate will be:

> "We certify that the High Court of England and Wales has power under the Civil Jurisdiction and Judgments Act 1982 to hear this claim and that no proceedings are pending between the parties in Scotland, Northern Ireland or another Convention territory of any contracting state as defined by section 1(3) of the Act."

1.6 The usual form of words of the certificate where the proceedings begun by the claim form are proceedings to which Article 16 of Schedule 1, 3C or 4 to that Act refers will be:

> "We certify that the High Court of England and Wales has power under the Civil Jurisdiction and Judgments Act 1982, the claim having as its object rights in rem in immovable property or tenancies in immovable property (or otherwise in accordance with the provisions of Article 16 of Schedule 1, 3C or 4 to that Act) to which Article 16 of Schedule 1, 3C or 4 to that Act applies, to hear the claim and that no proceedings are pending between the parties in Scotland, Northern Ireland or another Convention territory of any contracting state as defined by Section 1(3) of the Act."

1.7 The usual form of words of the certificate where the defendant is a party to an agreement conferring jurisdiction to which Article 17 of Schedule 1, 3C or 4 to that Act applies will be:

> "We certify that the High Court of England and Wales has power under the Civil Jurisdiction and Judgments Act 1982, the defendant being a [party to an agreement conferring jurisdiction to which Article 17 of Schedule 1, 3C or 4 of that Act applies, to hear the claim and that no proceedings are pending between the parties in Scotland, Northern Ireland or another Convention territory of any contracting state as defined by Section 1(3) of the Act."

1.8 If a certificate under paragraph 1.4 is omitted, the issued claim form will be marked, "Not for service out of the jurisdiction."

Documents to be filed

2.1 The claimant must file the following documents for each person to be served—

(1) a request for service of the claim form by one of the methods under O.11, rr.5 and 6 or for service—
- (a) under any order for service by an alternative method,
- (b) in accordance with the law of the country in which service is to be effected,

(c) in a country which is a party to the Hague Convention of 1965 on the Service Abroad of Judicial and Extrajudicial Documents in Civil and Commercial Matters[2] in accordance with the provisions of that Convention;

(d) in a country in respect of which there subsists a civil procedure convention (other than the Hague Convention) in accordance with the provisions of such a convention,

(2) a sealed original of the claim form and accompanying documents,

(3) a duplicate copy of the claim form and accompanying documents,

(4) copies of the particulars of claim (see paragraph 1.3 above),

(5) the response pack amended as necessary (see paragraph 1.2 above),

(6) any translation required under RSC O.11, r.6(5) and paragraph 3.3, in duplicate; and

(7) a statement by the person making any translation that it is a correct translation, as required by RSC O.11, r.6(6), in duplicate.

2.2(1) Care should be taken to ensure that the method of service requested under paragraph 2.1(1) is a method recognised in the country in which service is to be effected.

(2) Service in the countries listed in RSC O.11, r.6(1) should be effected by the claimant or his agent direct.

2.3 The request for service must include an undertaking under RSC O.11, r.8 by the person making the request—

(1) to be responsible for all expenses incurred by the Foreign and Commonwealth Office, and

(2) to pay those expenses to the Foreign and Commonwealth Office on being informed of the amount.

2.4 RSC O.11, r.7(1) sets out the documents to be filed where a claimant wishes to serve the claim form on a State. The additional documents listed in paragraph 2.1 must also be filed in such cases.

2.5 Where the claimant files the documents specified, he must obtain a sealed copy and an ordinary copy and take them to the Foreign Process Office.

2.6 In certain countries the documents filed will require legalisation. The Foreign Process Office (Rm E219, The Royal Courts of Justice) will advise as to particular cases.

Translations:

R11PD–002 **3.1** RSC O.11, r.6(5) provides that, except in certain specified instances (see paragraph 3.4 below), every copy of the claim form filed under RSC O.11, r.6 (service through judicial authorities, foreign governments and British Consular authorities) or RSC O.11, r.7 (service of claim form on a State), must be accompanied by a translation of the claim form.

3.2 RSC O.11, r.6(5) and (6) apply to particulars of claim where they are not included in the claim form.

3.3 Where a translation of the claim form is required under RSC O.11, r.6(5), the claimant must also file a translation of the forms in the Response Pack.

3.4 Unless made necessary by the particular circumstances of the case, translations are not required where the claim form is to be served—

(1) in a country where English is an official language (r.6(5));

(2) by a British consular authority on a British subject, unless a Civil Procedure Convention expressly requires a translation (r.6(5));

(3) on a State in which English is an official language (r.7(1)(c)).

(It should be noted that English is not an official language in the Province of Quebec.)

[2] November 15, 1965; TS50 (1969); Cmnd. 3986

Service with the permission of the court under certain Acts

4.1 RSC Order, rule 1 provides that a claim form may be served out of the jurisdiction with the court's permission if the claim is made under certain specified enactments.

4.2 These are:

(1) claims under the Nuclear Installations Act 1965,[3]

(2) claims in respect of contributions under the Social Security Contributions and Benefits Act 1992,[4]

(3) claims for a sum to which the Directive of the Council of the European Communities dated 15 March 1976 No. 76/308/EEC applies, where service is to be effected in a Member State of the European Economic Community,

(4) claims under the Drug Trafficking Offences Act 1994,[5]

(5) claims under the Financial Services Act 1986,[6]

(6) claims under the Banking Act 1987,[7]

(7) claims under Part VI of the Criminal Justice Act 1988,[8] and

(8) claims under the Immigration (Carriers' Liability) Act 1987.[9]

Service of other documents:

5.1 RSC O.11, r.1(2) (service without the court's permission) and RSC O.11, r.1(1) (service with the court's permission) apply to service out of the jurisdiction of a petition, application notice or order as they apply to service of a claim form. R11PD–003

5.2 Applications to which this paragraph applies include applications made under CPR r.23.2(4) before a claim has been started; for example

(1) applications made under CPR r.25.4(1)(b) for order for disclosure, inspection etc, before a claim has been made, or

(2) orders for disclosure under CPR r.31.16 before proceedings have started.

5.3 RSC O.11, r.4 applies where appropriate to an application for permission to serve documents under this paragraph.

5.4 RSC O.11, rr.5–9 apply to any document for which permission has been granted under this paragraph as they apply to a claim form.

5.5 Paragraphs 6, 7 and 8 of this Practice Direction apply as appropriate to response to service of any other document as they apply to response to service of a claim form.

Period for responding to a claim form

6.1 Where the permission of the court is required, under RSC O.11, r.4, for a claim form to be served out of the jurisdiction, r.4(4) requires the order granting permission to specify the period within which the defendant may respond to the claim form.

6.2 RSC O.11, r.1A sets out period for filing an acknowledgment of service or filing or serving an admission where a claim form has been served out of the jurisdiction without permission under r.1(2).

6.3 RSC O.11, r.1B sets out the period for filing a defence where a claim form has been served out of the jurisdiction without permission under r.1(2).

6.4 The table below specifies the periods for responding to a claim form which has been served out of the jurisdiction without permission—

[3] 1965 c.57
[4] 1992 c.4
[5] 1994 c.37
[6] 1986 c.60
[7] 1987 c.22
[8] 1988 c.33
[9] 1987 c.24

(1) under RSC O.11, r.1(2) in a country not covered by r.1A(2) or (3); or
(2) under r.1(2)(a).

6.5 Where an order grants permission to serve a claim form out of the jurisdiction under RSC O.11, r.1(1), the periods within which the defendant may—

(1) file an acknowledgment of service in accordance with CPR Part 10,
(2) file or serve an admission in accordance with CPR Part 14, and
(3) file a defence in accordance with CPR Part 15,

which, in accordance with RSC O.11, r.4(4), are required to be specified in the order will be calculated having regard to the table below.

Period for filing acknowledgment of service or filing or serving an admission

R11PD–004 **7.1** This paragraph sets out the period for filing an ackowledgment of service under CPR Part 10 or filing or serving an admission under CPR Part 14 where a claim form has been served in a place or country listed in the table.

7.2 The period for filing an acknowledgment of service or filing or serving an admission is the number of days listed in the table after service of the claim form.

7.3 For example, where a defendant has been served with a claim form in the Bahamas, the period for acknowledging service or admitting the claim is 22 days after service.

Period for filing a defence

8.1 This paragraph sets out the period for filing a defence under CPR Part 15 where a claim form has been served in a place or country listed in the table.

8.2 The period for filing a defence is—

(1) the number of days listed in the table after service of the claim form, or
(2) where the defendant has filed an acknowledgment of service, the number of days listed in the table plus an additional 14 days after service of the claim form.

8.3 For example, where a defendant has been served with a claim form in Gibraltar and has acknowledged service, the period for filing a defence is 45 days after service of the claim form.

Address for service

R11PD–005 **9.** CPR r.6.5(2) provides that a party must give an address for service within the jurisdiction.

Service of application notice

10.1 Where an application notice or order needs to be served out of the Jurisdiction, the period for responding to service is 7 days less than the number of days listed in the table.

10.2 When applying for a date for a hearing adequate time must be allowed for service of the response to the application notice or order.

Further information

11.1 For further information concerning service out of the jurisdiction contact the Foreign Process Office (Rm. E219, The Royal Courts of Justice).

Table

R11PD–006

Place or country	number of days	Place or country	number of days
Abu Dhabi	22	Bhutan	28
Afghanistan	23	Bolivia	23
Albania	25	Bosnia-Hercegovina	21
Algeria	22	Botswana	23
Angola	22	Brazil	22
Anguilla	31	Brunei	25
Antigua	23	Bulgaria	23
Antilles (Netherlands)	31	Burkina Faso	23
Argentina	22	Burma	23
Armenia	21	Burundi	22
Ascension	31	Cameroon	22
Australia	25	Canada	22
Austria	21	Canary Islands	22
Azores	23	Cape Verde Islands	25
Bahamas	22	Caroline Islands	31
Bahrain	22	Cayman Islands	31
Balearic Islands	22	Central African Republic	25
Bangladesh	23	Chad	25
Barbados	23	Chile	22
Belarus	21	China	24
Belgium	21	Christmas Island	27
Belize	23	Cocos (Keeling) Islands	41
Benin	25	Colombia	22
Bermuda	31	Comoros	23

Place or country	number of days
Congo (People's Republic)	25
Corsica	21
Costa Rica	23
Croatia	21
Cuba	24
Cyprus	31
Cyrenaica (see Libya)	21
Czech Republic	21
Denmark	21
Djibouti	22
Dominica	23
Domonican Republic	23
Dubai	22
Ecuador	22
Egypt (Arab Republic)	22
El Salvador (Republic of)	25
Equatorial Guinea	23
Estonia	21
Ethiopia	22
Falkland Islands and Dependencies	31
Faroe Islands	31
Fiji	23
Finland	24

Place or country	number of days
France	21
French Guiana	31
French Polynesia	31
French West Indies	31
Gabon	25
Gambia	22
Georgia	21
Germany	21
Ghana	22
Gibraltar	31
Greece	21
Greenland	31
Grenada	24
Guatemala	24
Guernsey	18
Guyana	22
Haiti	23
Holland (Netherlands)	21
Honduras	24
Hong Kong	31
Hungary	22
Iceland	22
India	23
Indonesia	22

SCHEDULE 1

Place or country	number of days	Place or country	number of days
Iran	22	Libya	21
Iraq	22	Liechtenstein	21
Ireland (Republic of)	21	Lithuania	21
Ireland (Northern)	21	Luxembourg	21
Isle of Man	18	Macau	31
Israel	22	Macedonia	21
Italy	21	Madagascar	23
Ivory Coast	22	Madeira	31
Jamaica	22	Malawi	23
Japan	23	Malaya	24
Jersey	18	Maldive Islands	26
Jordan	23	Mali	25
Kampuchea	38	Malta	21
Kazakhstan	21	Mariana Islands	26
Kenya	22	Marshall Islands	32
Kirgizstan	21	Mauritania	23
Korea (North)	28	Mauritius	22
Korea (South)	24	Mexico	23
Kuwait	22	Moldova	21
Laos	30	Monaco	21
Latvia	21	Montserrat	31
Lebanon	22	Morocco	22
Lesotho	23	Mozambique	23
Liberia	22	Nauru Island	36

Place or country	number of days
Nepal	23
Netherlands	21
Nevis	24
New Caledonia	31
New Hebrides (now Vanuatu)	29
New Zealand	26
New Zealand Island Territories	50
Nicaragua	24
Niger (Republic of)	25
Nigeria	22
Norfolk Island	31
Norway	21
Oman (Sultanate of)	22
Pakistan	23
Panama (Republic of)	26
Papua New Guinea	26
Paraguay	22
Peru	22
Philippines	23
Pitcairn Islands	31
Poland	21
Portugal	21
Portuguese Timor	31

Place or country	number of days
Puerto Rico	23
Qatar	23
Reunion	31
Romania	22
Russia	21
Rwanda	23
Sabah	23
St. Helena	31
St. Kitts–Nevis	24
St. Lucia	24
St. Pierre and Miquelon	31
St. Vincent and the Grenadines	24
Samoa (U.S.A. Territory) (See also Western Samoa)	30
Sarawak	28
Saudi Arabia	24
Scotland	21
Senegal	22
Seychelles	22
Sharjah	24
Sierra Leone	22
Singapore	22
Slovakia	21
Slovenia	21

SCHEDULE 1

Place or country	number of days
Society Islands (French Polynesia)	31
Solomon Islands	29
Somali Democratic Republic	22
South Africa (Republic of)	22
South Georgia (Falkland Island Dependencies)	31
South Orkneys	21
South Shetlands	21
Spain	21
Spanish Territories of North Africa	31
Sri Lanka	23
Sudan	22
Suriname	22
Swaziland	22
Sweden	21
Switzerland	21
Syria	23
Taiwan	23
Tajikistan	21
Tanzania	22
Thailand	23
Tibet	34
Tobago	23

Place or country	number of days
Togo	22
Tonga	30
Tortola	31
Trinidad & Tobago	23
Tristan Da Cunha	31
Tunisia	22
Turkey	21
Turkmenistan	21
Turks & Caicos Islands	31
Uganda	22
Ukraine	21
United States of America	22
Uruguay	22
Uzbekistan	21
Vanuatu	29
Vatican City State	21
Venezuela	22
Vietnam	28
Virgin Islands–British (Tortola)	31
Virgin Islands–U.S.A.	24
Wake Island	25
Western Samoa	34
Yemen (Republic of)	30

Place or country	number of days	Place or country	number of days
Yugoslavia (except for Bosnia-Hercegovina, Croatia, Macedonia and Slovenia)	21	Zambia	23
		Zimbabwe	22
Zaire	25		

RSC ORDER 15
CAUSES OF ACTION, COUNTERCLAIMS AND PARTIES

R15.0.1 **Contents**

Proceedings against estates

R15.6A **6A.**—(1) Where any person against whom a claim would have lain has died but the cause of action survives, the claim may, if no grant of probate or administration has been made, be brought against the estate of the deceased.

(2) Without prejudice to the generality of paragraph (1), a claim brought against "the personal representatives of A.B. deceased" shall be treated, for the purposes of that paragraph, as having been brought against his estate.

(3) A claim purporting to have been commenced against a person shall be treated, if he was dead at its commencement, as having been commenced against his estate in accordance with paragraph (1), whether or not a grant of probate or administration was made before its commencement.

(4) In any such claim as is referred to in paragraph (1) or (3)—

(a) the claimant shall, during the period of validity for service of the claim form, apply to the court for an order appointing a person to represent the deceased's estate for the purpose of the proceedings or, if a grant of probate or administration has been made for an order that the personal representative of the deceased be made a party to the proceedings, and in either case for an order that the proceedings be carried on against the person appointed or, as the case may be, against the personal representative, as if he had been substituted for the estate;

(b) the court may, at any stage of the proceedings and on such terms as it thinks just and either of its own motion or on application, make any such order as is mentioned in paragraph (a) and allow such amendments (if any) to be made and make such other order as the court thinks necessary in order to ensure that all matters in dispute in the proceedings may be effectually and completely determined and adjudicated upon.

(5) Before making an order under paragraph (4) the court may require notice to be given to any insurer of the deceased who has an interest in the proceedings and to such (if any) of the persons having an interest in the estate as it thinks fit.

(5A) Where an order is made under paragraph (4) appointing the Official Solicitor to represent the deceased's estate, the appointment shall be limited to his accepting service of the claim form by which the proceedings were begun unless, either on making such an order or on a subsequent application, the court, with the consent of the Official Solicitor, directs that the appointment shall extend to taking further steps in the proceedings.

(6) Where an order is made under paragraph (4), rules 7(4) and 8(3) and (4) shall apply as if the order had been made under rule 7 on the application of the claimant.

(7) Where no grant of probate or administration has been made, any judgment or order given or made in the proceedings shall bind the estate to the same extent as it would have been bound if a grant had been made and a personal representative of the deceased had been a party to the proceedings.

Change of parties by reason of death, etc.

7.—(1) Where a party to a claim dies or becomes bankrupt but the cause of action survives, the claim shall not abate by reason of the death or bankruptcy. **R15.7**

Failure to proceed after death of party

9.—(1) If after the death of a claimant or defendant in any claim the cause of action survives, but no order under rule 7 is made substituting as claimant any person in whom the cause of claim vests or, as the case may be, the personal representatives of the deceased defendant, the defendant or, as the case may be, those representatives may apply to the court for an order that unless the claim is proceeded with within such time as may be specified in the order the claim shall be struck out as against the claimant or defendant, as the case may be, who has died; but where it is the claimant who has died, the court shall not make an order under this rule unless satisfied that due notice of the application has been given to the personal representatives (if any) of the deceased claimant and to any other interested persons who, in the opinion of the court, should be notified. **R15.9**

Relator actions

11. Before the name of any person is used in any claim as a relator, that person must give a written authorisation so to use his name to his solicitor and the authorisation must be filed in the Central Office of the Supreme Court or Chancery Chambers, or, if the claim form is to issue out of a district registry, in that registry. **R15.11**

Representative proceedings

12.—(1) Where numerous persons have the same interest in any proceedings, not being such proceedings as are mentioned in rule 13, the proceedings may be begun, and, unless the court otherwise orders, continued, by or against any one or more of them as representing all or as representing all except one or more of them. **R15.12**

(2) At any stage of proceedings under this rule the court may, on the application of the claimant, and on such terms, if any, as it thinks fit, appoint any one or more of the defendants or other persons as representing whom the defendants are sued to represent all, or all except one or more, of those persons in the proceedings; and where, in exercise of the power conferred by

this paragraph, the court appoints a person not named as a defendant, it shall make an order adding that person as a defendant.

(3) A judgment or order given in proceedings under this rule shall be binding on all the persons as representing whom the claimants sue or, as the case may be, the defendants are sued, but shall not be enforced against any person not a party to the proceedings except with the permission of the court.

(4) An application for the grant of permission under paragraph (3) must be made in accordance with CPR Part 23 (general rules about applications for court orders) and the application notice must be served personally on the person against whom it is sought to enforce the judgment or order.

(5) Notwithstanding that a judgment or order to which any such application relates is binding on the person against whom the application is made, that person may dispute liability to have the judgment or order enforced against him on the ground that by reason of facts and matters particular to his case he is entitled to be exempted from such liability.

(6) The court hearing an application for the grant of permission under paragraph (3) may order the question whether the judgment or order is enforceable against the person against whom the application is made to be tried and determined in any manner in which any issue or question in claim may be tried and determined.

Derivative claims

R15.12A **12A.**—(1) This rule applies to every claim by one or more shareholders of a company where the cause of action is vested in the company and relief is accordingly sought on its behalf (referred to in this rule as a "derivative claim").

(2) Where a defendant in a derivative claim has responded to the particulars of claim, the claimant must apply to the court for permission to continue the claim.

(3) The application must be supported by witness statement or affidavit verifying the facts on which the claim and the entitlement to sue on behalf of the company are based.

(4) Unless the court otherwise orders, the application must be issued within 21 days after the relevant date, and must be served, together with the witness statement or affidavit in support and any exhibits to the witness statement or affidavit, not less than 10 clear days before the return day on all defendants who have responded to the particulars of claim; any defendant so served may show cause against the application by witness statement or affidavit or otherwise.

(5) In paragraph (4), "the relevant date" means the later of—

(a) the date of service of the particulars of claim; and

(b) the date when the defendant responded to the particulars of claim (provided that, where there is more than one defendant, that date shall be the earliest date when any of them respond).

(6) Nothing in this rule shall prevent the claimant from applying for interim relief pending the determination of an application for permission to continue the claim.

(7) In a derivative claim, CPR rule 15.4 (period for filing a defence) shall not have effect unless the court grants permission to continue the claim and, in that case, shall have effect as if it required the defendant to serve a defence within 14 days after the order giving permission to continue, or within such other period as the court may specify.

(8) On the hearing of the application under paragraph (2), the court may—

(a) grant permission to continue the claim, for such period and upon such terms as the court may think fit;

(b) subject to paragraph (11), dismiss the claim;

(c) adjourn the application and give such directions as to joinder of parties, the filing of further evidence, disclosure, cross examination of witnesses and otherwise as it may consider expedient.

(9) If the claimant does not apply for permission to continue the claim as required by paragraph (2) within the time laid down in paragraph (4), any defendant who has responded to the particulars of claim may apply for an order to dismiss the proceedings or any claim made in them by way of derivative claim.

(10) On the hearing of such an application for dismissal, the court may—

(a) subject to paragraph (11), dismiss the claim;

(b) if the claimant so requests, grant the claimant (on such terms as to costs or otherwise as the Court may think fit) an extension of time to apply for permission to continue the claim; or

(c) make such other order as may in the circumstances be appropriate.

(11) Where only part of the relief claimed is sought on behalf of the company, the court may dismiss the claim for that part of the relief under paragraphs (8) and (10), without prejudice to the claimant's right to continue the claim as to the remainder of the relief and CPR rule 15.4 (period for filing a defence) shall apply as modified by paragraph (7).

(12) If there is a material change in circumstances after the court has given permission to the claimant to continue the claim in pursuance of an application under paragraph (2), any defendant who has responded to the particulars of claim may make an application supported by witness statement or affidavit requiring the claimant to show cause why the court should not dismiss the proceedings or any claim made in them by way of derivative claim. On such application the court shall have the same powers as it would have had upon an application under paragraph (2).

(13) The claimant may include in an application under paragraph (2) an application for an indemnity out of the assets of the company in respect of costs incurred or to be incurred in the claim and the court may grant such indemnity upon such terms as may in the circumstances be appropriate.

(14) So far as possible, any application under paragraph (13) and any application by the claimant under CPR Part 24 shall be made so as to be heard at the same time as the application under paragraph (2).

Representation of interested persons who cannot be ascertained, etc.

13.—(1) In any proceedings concerning— R15.13

(a) the estate of a deceased person, or

(b) property subject to a trust, or

(c) the construction of a written instrument, including a statute,

the court, if satisfied that it is expedient so to do, and that one or more of the conditions specified in paragraph (2) are satisfied, may appoint one or more persons to represent any person (including an unborn person) or class who is or may be interested (whether presently or for any future, contingent or unascertained interest) in or affected by the proceedings.

(2) The conditions for the exercise of the power conferred by paragraph (1) are as follows:—

(a) that the person, the class or some member of the class, cannot be ascertained or cannot readily be ascertained;

(b) that the person, class or some member of the class, though ascertained, cannot be found;

(c) that, though the person or the class and the members thereof can be ascertained and found, it appears to the court expedient (regard being had to all the circumstances, including the amount at stake and the degree of difficulty of the point to be determined) to exercise the power for the purposes of saving expense.

(3) Where, in any proceedings to which paragraph (1) applies, the court exercises the power conferred by that paragraph, a judgment or order of the court given or made when the person or persons appointed in exercise of that power are before the court shall be binding on the person or class represented by the person or persons so appointed.

(4) Where, in any such proceedings, a compromise is proposed and some of the persons who are interested in, or who may be affected by, the compromise are not parties to the proceedings (including unborn or unascertained persons) but—

(a) there is some other person in the same interest before the court who assents to the compromise or on whose behalf the court sanctions the compromise, or

(b) the absent persons are represented by a person appointed under paragraph (1) who so assents,

the court, if satisfied that the compromise will be for the benefit of the absent persons and that is expedient to exercise this power, may approve the compromise and order that it shall be binding on the absent persons, and they shall be bound accordingly except where the order has been obtained by fraud or non-disclosure of material facts.

Notice of claim to non-parties

R15.13A **13A.**—(1) At any stage in a claim to which this rule applies, the court may, on the application of any party or of its own motion, direct that notice of the claim be served on any person who is not a party thereto but who will or may be affected by any judgment given therein.

(2) An application under this rule may be made without notice being served on any other party and shall be supported by witness statement or affidavit stating the grounds of the application.

(3) Every notice of a claim under this rule shall be in Form No. 52 in the relevant practice direction and shall be issued out of the appropriate office, and the copy to be served shall be a sealed copy accompanied by a copy of the claim form and of all other statements of case served in the claim, and by a form of acknowledgment of service with such modifications as may be appropriate.

(4) A person may, within 14 days of service on him of a notice under this rule, acknowledge service of the claim form and shall thereupon become a party to the claim, but in default of such acknowledgment and subject to paragraph (5) he shall be bound by any judgment given in the claim as if he was a party thereto.

(5) If at any time after service of such notice on any person the claim form is amended so as substantially to alter the relief claimed, the court may direct that the judgment shall not bind such person unless a further notice together with a copy of the amended claim form is issued and served upon him under this rule.

(6) This rule applies to any claim relating to—

(a) the estate of a deceased person; or

(b) property subject to a trust.

(7) CPR rule 7.2(2) shall apply in relation to a notice of a claim under this rule as if the notice were a claim form and the person by whom the notice is issued were the claimant.

Representation of beneficiaries by trustees, etc.

R15.14 **14.**—(1) Any proceedings, including proceedings to enforce a security by foreclosure or otherwise, may be brought by or against trustees, executors or administrators in their capacity as such without joining any of the persons having a beneficial interest in the trust or estate, as the case may be; and any judgment or order given or made in those proceedings shall be binding on those persons unless the court in the same or other proceedings otherwise orders on the ground that the trustees, executors or administrators, as the case may be, could not or did not in fact represent the interests of those persons in the first-mentioned proceedings.

(2) Paragraph (1) is without prejudice to the power of the court to order any person having such an interest as aforesaid to be made a party to the proceedings or to make an order under rule 13.

Representation of deceased person interested in proceedings

15.—(1) Where in any proceedings it appears to the court that a deceased person was interested in the matter in question in the proceedings and that he has no personal representative, the court may, on the application of any party to the proceedings, proceed in the absence of a person representing the estate of the deceased person or may by order appoint a person to represent that estate for the purposes of the proceedings; and any such order, and any judgment or order subsequently given or made in the proceedings, shall bind the estate of the deceased person to the same extent as it would have been bound had a personal representative of that person been a party to the proceedings. **R15.15**

(2) Before making an order under this rule, the court may require notice of the application for the order to be given to such (if any) of the persons having an interest in the estate as it thinks fit.

Declaratory judgment

16. No claim or other proceeding shall be open to objection on the ground that a merely declaratory judgment or order is sought thereby, and the court may make binding declarations of right whether or not any consequential relief is or could be claimed. **R15.16**

Conduct of proceedings

17. The court may give the conduct of any claim, inquiry or other proceeding to such person as it thinks fit. **R15.17**

RSC ORDER 17

INTERPLEADER

Contents **R17.0.1**

Editorial Introduction

Interpleader is a process by which a person from whom two or more persons claim the same property or debt, and who does not himself claim the property or dispute the debt, can protect himself from legal proceedings by calling upon the rival claimants to interplead i.e. claim against one another so that the title to the property or debt can be determined by the Court. Before the Interpleader Act 1831 (now repealed and replaced by RSC, O.17) he would have had to defend both actions or file a bill in equity (called a bill of interpleader). There are two distinct types of **R17.0.2** interpleader usually called "stakeholder's interpleader" and "sheriff's interpleader". Examples of the former would be a solicitor or estate agent holding a deposit which is now claimed by both the seller and the buyer or a carrier holding goods which he wishes to deliver but which are claimed by two or more persons alleging title. A sheriff's interpleader arises where the sheriff seeks to levy execution on goods in the possession of the judgment debtor but which are claimed by another. The sheriff will notify the execution creditor of the claim and, unless the execution creditor admits it, will start interpleader proceedings. Some of the rules in RSC, O.17 apply only to sheriff's interpleaders (rr.2, 4 and 6).

Application is made by claim form unless made in existing proceedings when it is made by application under Part 23 (see r.3). In interpleader proceedings the rival claimants have always been called "claimant" in O.17 but that term has now replaced "plaintiff" in the CPR. Hence the amended version of RSC, O.17 in Sched. 2 now refers to "interpleader claimant". The Court still has power to direct which of the interpleader claimants is to be claimant and which defendant (see r.5(1)(b)).

Of particular practical importance is the Court's power to determine the interpleader issue summarily (r.5(2)).

Related Sources

R17.0.3
- Part 7 CPR—How to start proceedings—the Claim Form
- Part 23 CPR—General Rules about applications for Court Orders
- Part 31 CPR—Disclosure and Inspection of Documents
- RSC, O.23—Security for Costs
- CCR, O.33—Interpleader Proceedings
- Crown Proceedings Act 1947, s.16 (SCP 1999, Vol 2, Section 21L)

Forms

R17.0.4
- PF 23 QB Notice of claim to goods taken in execution
- PF 24 QB Notice by claimant of admission of dispute of title of interpleader claimant
- PF 25 QB Interpleader application by defendant
- PF 26 QB Interpleader application by sheriff
- PF 27 QB Evidence in support at interpleader application
- PF 28 QB Interpleader order (1) claim barred where sheriff interpleads
- PF 29 QB Interpleader order (1a) sheriff to withdraw
- PF 30 QB Interpleader order (2) interpleader claimant substitutes as defendant
- PF 31 QB Interpleader order (3) trial at issue
- PF 32 QB Interpleader order (4) conditional order for sheriff to withdraw and trial of issue
- PF 34 QB Interpleader order (6) summary disposal

Entitlement to relief by way of interpleader

R17.1 1.—(1) Where—

(a) a person is under a liability in respect of a debt or in respect of any money, goods or chattels and he is, or expects to be, sued for or in respect of that debt or money or those goods or chattels by two or more persons making adverse claims thereto, or

(b) claim is made to any money, goods or chattels taken or intended to be taken by a sheriff in execution under any process, or to the proceeds or value of any such goods or chattels, by a person other than the person against whom the process is issued,

the person under liability as mentioned in sub-paragraph (a) or (subject to rule 2) the sheriff, may apply to the court for relief by way of interpleader.

(2) References in this Order to a sheriff shall be construed as including references to any other officer charged with the execution of process by or under the authority of the High Court.

R17.1.1 **"Relief by way of interpleader"**—Interpleaders may be divided into two types: the first is where a sheriff seizes or intends to seize goods by way of execution and a person (other than the judgment debtor) claims them. Here the sheriff initiates the proceedings to determine whether the property belongs to the judgment debtor (and therefore can be seized) or to the claimant. Para. 1(b) of this rule applies, and the proceeding is known as a sheriff's interpleader. The second type compromises all other interpleader proceedings. Para. 1(a) of this rule applies to them and they are generally known as stakeholder's interpleaders. The same general principles apply to both types.

R17.1.2 **"where a person is under a liability in respect of a debt"**—The applicant may interplead as to so much of a debt as he admits, the dispute as to the residue being settled separately (*Reading v.*

London School Board (1886) 16 Q.B.D. 686). A liability to unliquidated damages is not a "debt" for this purpose (*Walter v. Nicholson* (1838) 6 Dowl. 517; *Ingham v. Walker* (1887) 3 T.L.R. 448, CA. *cf. Attenborough v. London and St. Katharine's Dock Co.* (1878) 3 C.P.D. 450, CA, where a separate claim for damages was reserved, and *cf. Ex p. Mersey Docks* [1899] 1 Q.B. 546, CA). A debt due but not yet payable is presumably within the words of the rule (*Reading v. London School Board*). The Court will not entertain proceedings to determine the right to winnings under a gaming contract (*Shoolbred v. Roberts* [1900] 2 Q.B. 497 at 501 and 502; and see *Applegarth v. Colley* (1842) 2 Dowl. 223; *Dowson v. Macfarlane* (1899) 81 L.T. 67; *Hill v. William Hill (Park Lane Ltd)* [1949] A.C. 530).

"goods, or chattels"—Chattels is "one of the widest words known to the law in its relation to personal property" (*per* Fry L.J. in *Robinson v. Jenkins* (1890) 24 Q.B.D. 275, at 279). It includes shares in a company (*ibid.*) and, *semble,* title deeds to property (*Roberts v. Bell* (1857) 7 E. & B. 323). "Liability in respect of any goods or chattels" includes a claim by a claimant to a mere lien over or a right to possession of goods (*Jennings v. Mather* [1902] 1 K.B. 1, CA). **R17.1.3**

"expects to be sued . . . by two or more persons"—There must be a real foundation for the expectation (*Harrison v. Payne* (1836) 2 Hodges 107; *Diplock v. Hammond* (1854) 23 L.J.Ch. 550; *Watson v. Park Royal Caterers* [1961] 1 W.L.R. 727). A person cannot protect himself by interpleader proceedings against a claim on which the claimant has obtained judgment (*Stevenson & Son, Ltd v. Brownell* [1912] 2 Ch. 344 (a judgment by consent); *Randall v. Lithgow* (1884) 12 Q.B.D. 525 (a garnishee order absolute)). The fact, however, that the applicant may be legally liable to both defendants may be a ground for refusing him relief (*Farr v. Ward* (1837) 2 M. & W. 244; *Crawford v. Fisher* (1842) 1 Hare 436, at 441; *Victor Söhne v. British, etc., Steam Navigation* [1888] W.N. 84; *Sablicich v. Russell* (1866) L.R. 2 Eq. 441. Compare *Ex p. Mersey Docks* [1899] 1 Q.B. 546 where relief was given, the question of an estoppel in favour of one claimant being reserved). **R17.1.4**

"making adverse claims thereto"—There must be adverse claims to the same property or debt (*Greatorex v. Shackle* [1895] 2 Q.B. 249, where two auctioneers were each claiming a commission under a separate contract on the same sale of the same house, and relief was refused; *Smith v. Saunders* (1877) 37 L.T. 359; *Wright v. Freeman* (1879) 48 L.J.C.P. 276; *Sun Insurance Office v. Galinsky* [1914] K.B. 545). **R17.1.5**

"claim is made to any money, goods, or chattels"—The claim must be actual and not merely anticipated (*Isaac v. Spilsbury* (1833) 2 Dowl. 211; *Bentley v. Hook* (1834) 2 Dowl. 339; *Salmon v. James* (1832) 1 Dowl. 369; *Day v. Waldock* (1833) 1 Dowl. 523). A claim to a lien or right of possession over the goods, and not to the absolute property, is within these words (see *Ford v. Baynton* (1832) 1 Dowl. 357; *Green v. Stevens* (1857) 2 H. & N. 146)—for example, a claim by the hirer under a hiring or hire-purchase agreement. **R17.1.6**

"taken or intended to be taken . . . in execution under any process"—There must have been either an actual seizure or an intention of the sheriff to seize (*Day v. Carr* (1852) 7 Ex. 883; *Lea v. Rossi* (1855) 11 Ex. 13). The fact that the goods are seized in the possession of the claimant or a third person and not in that of the judgment debtor does not, of course, affect the sheriff's right to interplead (*Allen v. Gibbon* (1833) 2 Dowl. 292; *Aylwin v. Evans* (1883) 52 L.J. Ch. 105). But if the sheriff, after seizure, has withdrawn from possession (*Moore v. Hawkins* (1894) 43 W.R. 235) or delivered up the goods seized to the claimant (*Braine v. Hunt* (1834) 2 Dowl. 391) or sold them and paid the proceeds to the execution creditor (*Anderson v. Calloway* (1833) 1 Dowl. 636; *Inland v. Bushell* (1836) 5 Dowl. 147) the Court will not grant him relief (except under r.2(3)). **R17.1.7**

"or to the proceeds or value of any such goods or chattels"—Where a claimant pays the sheriff out under protest, the amount paid is "the proceeds or value of" the goods within this rule (*Smith v. Critchfield* (1885) 14 Q.B.D. 873, CA) but the claimant cannot succeed unless he was entitled to the goods (*Plant v. Collins* [1913] 1 K.B. 242). **R17.1.8**

"by a person other than the person against whom the process is issued"—The claim may be by the execution debtor if he claims not in his own right but as executor or trustee (*Fenwick v. Laycock* (1841) 6 Jur. 341). A beneficiary under a trust may claim without joining trustees (*Schroeder v. Hanrott* (1873) 28 LT 704). **R17.1.9**

"may apply to the Court for relief"—The applicaiton is usually heard and determined by the Master or district judge in the High Court. See also rr.3 and 5. **R17.1.10**

Crown—These rules apply to the Crown: section 16 Crown Proceedings Act 1947 (SCP 1999, Vol. 2, Section 21L). **R17.1.11**

Equitable rights—Equitable claims and rights can be asserted and protected by interpleader: see *Jennings v. Mather* [1901] 1 K.B. 108 at 115 and cases there cited. **R17.1.12**

R17.1.13 **Landlords**—If the rent is owing to the landlord of the premises upon which goods are seized in execution, the sheriff is prohibited by the Landlord and Tenant Act 1709 from removing the goods after having notice of rent being due, until the rent owing (up to one year's arrears) has been paid. Should he remove or sell them before such rent has been paid, he would be liable to an action founded on the statute. Though the execution creditor could not compel him to sell, it became the practice for the sheriff to sell and pay the landlord out of the proceeds; but a sheriff is entitled to withdraw and return *nulla bona,* when it becomes clear that neither the execution creditor nor the tenant will pay the landlord. (See Lindley L.J., at pp. 573–576 in *Re Mackenzie* [1899] 2 Q.B. 566, CA). A sheriff, therefore, upon the landlord claiming, cannot interplead (*Clarke v. Lord* (1833) 2 Dowl. 55, 227; *cf. Bateman v. Farnsworth* (1860) 29 L.J.Exch. 365).

R17.1.14 **Claim by co-owner or partner**—If goods are the property of A and B, who hold them jointly or as tenants in common, the sheriff can seize and sell them on a judgment against A and B or a judgment against either of them (subject to the question of the distribution of the proceeds)—see *Farrar v. Beswick* (1836) 1 M. & W. 682, *per* Parke, B. p. 685; *Mayhew v. Herrick* (1849) 7 C.B. 229 at 240, 248 and 250. The same applied to partnership property, but now, on a judgment against one partner, execution will not issue against partnership property (Partnership Act 1890, s.23) and instead a charging order can be obtained on the partner's interest (*ibid.*). If, on execution being levied on a judgment against one partner, another partner sets up the partnership, and the execution creditor disputes the partnership or denies that the goods seized are property of the partnership, the dispute is proper subject-matter for interpleader (see *Peake v. Carter*[1916] 1 K.B. 652 , *per* Swinfen Eady L.J. at 655–656). If the goods are admitted to be partnership property, the sheriff will be ordered to withdraw.

R17.1.15 **Claim by debenture-holders**—A debenture usually creates a floating charge on a company's assets, and only where the charge has been crystallised—*e.g.* by appointment of a receiver—before the completion of an execution by seizure and sale do the rights of the debenture holders have priority over those of the execution creditor (*Re Standard Manufacturing Co.* [1891] 1 Ch. 627, CA; *Re Opera* [1891] 3 Ch. 260, CA; and see *Taunton v. Sheriff of Warwickshire* [1895] 2 Ch. 319, CA; *Evans v. Rival Granite Quarries* [1910] 2 K.B. 979, CA; *Robinson v. Burnell's Bakery* [1904] 2 K.B. 624; *Heaton & Dugard v. Cutting Bros.* [1925] 1 K.B. 655).

Claim to goods, etc., taken in execution

R17.2 **2.**—(1) Any person making a claim to or in respect of any money, goods or chattels taken or intended to be taken in execution under process of the court, or to the proceeds or value of any such goods or chattels, must give notice of his claim to the sheriff charged with the execution of the process and must include in his notice a statement of his address, and that address shall be his address for service.

(2) On receipt of a claim made under this rule the sheriff must forthwith give notice thereof to the execution creditor and the execution creditor must, within seven days after receiving the notice, give notice to the sheriff informing him whether he admits or disputes the claim.

An execution creditor who gives notice in accordance with this paragraph admitting a claim shall only be liable to the sheriff for any fees and expenses incurred by the sheriff before receipt of that notice.

(3) Where—

(a) the sheriff receives a notice from an execution creditor under paragraph (2) disputing a claim, or the execution creditor fails, within the period mentioned in that paragraph, to give the required notice, and

(b) the claim made under this rule is not withdrawn,

the sheriff may apply to the court for relief under this order.

(4) A sheriff who receives a notice from an execution creditor under paragraph (2) admitting a claim made under this rule shall withdraw from possession of the money, goods or chattels claimed and may apply to the court for relief under this Order of the following kind, that is to say, an order restraining the bringing of a claim against him for or in respect of his having taken possession of that money or those goods or chattels.

R17.2.1 **"address for service"**—see r.6.5 of CPR 1998.

Claim in respect of goods protected from seizure

2A.—(1) Where a judgment debtor whose goods have been seized, or are intended to be seized, by a sheriff under a writ of execution claims that such goods are not liable to execution by virtue of section 138(3A) of the Act, he must within 5 days of the seizure give notice in writing to the sheriff identifying all those goods in respect of which he makes such a claim and the grounds of such claim in respect of each item. R17.2A

(2) Upon receipt of a notice of claim under paragraph (1), the sheriff must forthwith give notice thereof to the execution creditor and to any person who has made a claim to, or in respect of, the goods under rule 2(1) and the execution creditor and any person who has made claim must, within 7 days of receipt of such notice, inform the sheriff in writing whether he admits or disputes the judgment debtor's claim in respect of each item.

(3) The sheriff shall withdraw from possession of any goods in respect of which the judgment debtor's claim is admitted or if the execution creditor or any person claiming under rule 2(1) fails to notify him in accordance with paragraph (2) and the sheriff shall so inform the parties in writing.

(4) Where the sheriff receives notice from—

(a) the execution creditor; or

(b) any such person to whom notice was given under paragraph (2),

that the claim or any part thereof is disputed, he must forthwith seek the directions of the court and may include therein an application for an order restraining the bringing of any claim against him for, or in respect of, his having seized any of those goods or his having failed so to do.

(5) The sheriff's application for directions under paragraph (4) shall be made by an application in accordance with CPR Part 23 and, on the hearing of the application, the court may

(a) determine the judgment debtor's claim summarily; or

(b) give such directions for the determination of any issue raised by such claim as may be just.

(6) A Master and a district judge of a district registry shall have power to make an order of the kind referred to in paragraph (4) and the reference to Master shall be construed in accordance with rule 4.

"Section 138(3A) of the Act"—see SCP 1999, Vol. 2 para. 20A–539. R17.2A.1

Mode of application

3.—(1) An application for relief under this order must be made by claim form unless made in an existing claim, in which case it must be made in accordance with CPR Part 23. R17.3

(2) Where the applicant is a sheriff who has withdrawn from possession of money, goods or chattels taken in execution and who is applying for relief under rule 2(4) the claim form must be served on any person who made a claim under that rule to or in respect of that money or those goods or chattels, and that person may attend the hearing of the application.

(4) Subject to paragraph (5) a claim form or application notice under this rule must be supported by evidence that the applicant—

(a) claims no interest in the subject-matter in dispute other than for charges or costs,

(b) does not collude with any of the claimants to that subject-matter; and

(c) is willing to pay or transfer that subject-matter into court or to dispose of it as the court may direct.

(5) Where the applicant is a sheriff, he shall not provide such evidence as is referred to in paragraph (4) unless directed by the court to do so.

(6) Any person who makes a claim under rule 2 and who is served with a claim form under this rule shall within 14 days serve on the execution creditor and the sheriff a witness statement or affidavit specifying any money and

describing any goods and chattels claimed and setting out the grounds upon which such claim is based.

(7) Where the applicant is a sheriff a claim form under this rule must give notice of the requirement in paragraph (6).

R17.3.1 **"claim form"**—see Part 7 of CPR 1998.

R17.3.2 **"in accordance with Part 23"**—Part 23, and its supplementing Practice Direction (para. 23 PD–001) contain general rules about applications for court orders in existing proceedings. The application notice can be in Form N244 (see para. 2.1 of the Practice Direction). Note the requirement for an application notice to be verified by a statement of truth—see Part 22.

R17.3.3 **"must be served"**—see generally, Part 6. Service by the Court is the general rule and service by post the general method (rr.6.2 and 6.3). The claim form or application notice must be served on each interpleader claimant otherwise no order can be made affecting him (*Lambert v. Townsend* (1832) 1 L.J. ex. 113) and only interpleader claimants who are parties as claimant or defendant (claim form) or applicant or respondent (application notice under Part 23) will be heard (*Clarke v. Lord* (1833) 2 Dowl. 53). For service out at the jurisdiction see RSC, O.11, r.9 and *Attenborough v. London and St. Katherine's Dock Co.* (1878) 3 C.P.D. 455.

R17.3.4 **Authority of solicitor**—A solicitor, retained in the case, has no implied authority to conduct interpleader proceedings (*James v. Ricknell* (1888) 20 Q.B.D. 64).

R17.3.5 **"must be supported by evidence"**—The evidence is best reduced to writing and given in the form of a witness statement of affidavit. Interpleader proceedings are unique in that the person seeking relief must be a truly disinterested party: hence the need for such evidence as required by O.17, r.3(4). In a sheriff's interpleader the sheriff is assumed to be disinterested and is thus not required to provide evidence in the first instance (O.17, r.3(5)).

R17.3.6 **"other than for charges or costs"**—A lien over goods for charges for storage, or over the proceeds of sale for commission on the sale, does not disentitle the applicant to relief (*Cotter v. Bank of England* (1833) 2 Dowl. 728; *Best v. Hayes* (1863) 1 H. & C. 718; *De Rothschild Frères v. Morrison, Kekewich & Co.* (1890) 24 Q.B.D. 750, CA).

R17.3.7 **"that the applicant does not collude"**—"Collusion" does not here necessarily entail anything morally wrong, but means "playing the same game" as one of the claimants (*Murietta v. South American Co.*; *Tucker v. Morris* (1832) 1 C. & M. 73; 2 L.J.Ex. 1; and see, as to sheriffs, *Duddin v. Long* (1834) 3 Dowl. 139); *Fredericks and Pelhams Timber Buildings v. Wilkins, Read (Claimant)* [1971] 1 W.L.R. 1197 at 1204; [1971] 3 All E.R. 545 at 550–551, CA) and where the applicant has agreed to do so, or has taken an indemnity from that claimant (*Murietta v. South America Co.*; *Thopson v. Wright* (1884) 13 Q.B.D. 632) though that claimant cannot complain, there is collusion (*ibid.*). Similarly where the applicant has placed himself in the position of being sued at the request and in the interests of one claimant (*Belcher v. Smith* (1832) 9 Bing. 82).

R17.3.8 **"any person who makes a claim"**—Any person who claims the property or debt is required to serve a witness statement or affidavit within 14 days of service. O.17, r.3(6), in its present form imposes this requirement on such a person "who is served with a claim form". This should read (as does r.3(4)) "claim form or applicaiton notice": see r.3(1)—the application must be by application notice in accordance with Part 23 if made in existing proceedings.

The witness statement or affidavit should be by the person who makes the claim and who will give evidence in support of the claim and not, *e.g.*, by his solicitor (*Wood v. Lyne* (1850) 4 DeG & Sm 16; *Nelson v. Barter* (1864) 2 H. & M. 334). The person who makes the claim cannot call on the sheriff for particulars of the goods seized so as to assist him to make out his claim (*Bauly v. Crook* (1891) 65 L.T. 377). Particulars of the claim must be stated with such precision as to enable the opposing claimant or the execution creditor to decide whether to oppose it, and the Court to make an appropriate order (*Powell v. Lock* (1835) 3 A. & E. 315; *Webster v. Delafield* (1849) 7 C.B. 187).

To whom Sheriff may apply for relief

R17.4 **4.** An application to the court for relief under this order may, if the applicant is a sheriff, be made—

(a) where the claim in question is proceeding in the Royal Courts of Justice, to a Master or, if the execution to which the application relates has been or is to be levied in the district of a District Registry, either to a Master or to the district judge of that Registry;

(b) where the claim in question is proceeding in a District Registry, to the district judge of that Registry or, if such execution has been or is to be levied in the district of some other District Registry or outside the district of any District Registry, either to the said district judge or to the district judge of that other Registry or to a Master as the case may be.

Where the claim in question is proceeding in the Admiralty Court or the Family Division, references in this rule to a Master shall be construed as references to the Admiralty Registrar or to a Registrar of that Division.

Powers of Court hearing claim

5.—(1) Where on the hearing of a claim under this order all the persons by whom adverse claims to the subject-matter in dispute (hereafter in this order referred to as "the interpleader claimants") appear, the court may order— R17.5

(a) that any interpleader claimant be made a defendant in any claim pending with respect to the subject-matter in dispute in substitution for or in addition to the applicant for relief under this order, or

(b) that an issue between the interpleader claimants be stated and tried and may direct which of the interpleader claimants is to be claimant and which defendant.

(2) Where—

(a) the applicant under this order is a sheriff; or

(b) all the interpleader claimants consent or any of them so requests; or

(c) the question at issue between the interpleader claimants is a question of law and the facts are not in dispute,

the court may summarily determine the question at issue between the interpleader claimants and make an order accordingly on such terms as may be just.

(3) Where an interpleader claimant, having been duly served with a claim form under this order, does not appear at the hearing or, having appeared, fails or refuses to comply with an order made in the proceedings, the court may make an order declaring the interpleader claimant, and all persons claiming under him, for ever barred from prosecuting his claim against the applicant for such relief and all persons claiming under him, but such an order shall not affect the rights of the interpleader claimants as between themselves.

"the court may order"—On the hearing of the application the Master or district Judge may make one of the following orders:— R17.5.1

1. Dismiss the application—*e.g.* on the ground that the conditions of rr.1 and 3 are not satisfied. R17.5.2

2. Decide the issue summarily—Summary disposal is the most usual and consent to a summary disposal is not required where the applicant is the sheriff (r.5(2)(a)). Summary disposal contrasts with ordering an issue to be stated and tried (see 3 below). Summary disposal is the course usually taken in straightforward cases and in sheriff's interpleaders. However, if the goods are of considerable value and difficult questions of law may arise, summary disposal is not appropriate even if the parties consent (*Fredericks and Pelhams Timber Buildings v. Wilkins, Read (Claimant)* [1971] 1 W.L.R. 1197; [1971] 3 All E.R. 545, CA). R17.5.3

If the Master or district judge is to decide the case summarily it is usually necessary to adjourn to a fixed date giving all necessary case-management directions—*e.g.* as to evidence, disclosure or other interim steps. If the value of the goods justifies it, he may order the sheriff to prepare, file and serve an inventory (*Fredericks and Pelhams Timber Buildings v. Wilkins, Read (Claimant)*). At the hearing the modern practice is for witness statements (or affidavits) to stand as evidence-in-chief upon which rival claimants can cross-examine. If supporting witnesses are to be called directions should be sought at the initial hearing as for filing and service of witness statements.

3. Order that an issue be stated and tried.—Even if the issue is not tried summarily it is usual for the parties to consent to trial by the Master or district judge to save delay and costs. The order defines the issue which is to be tried, *e.g.* "whether the goods are the property of A (the claimant in the issue) as against B (the defendant in the issue)". The court can direct which of the rival R17.5.4

interpleader claimants is to be claimant and which defendant (r.5(1)(b)). In a sheriff's interpleader the execution creditor is usually made defendant but will be made claimant if the goods were in the possession of the interpleader-claimant at the time of seizure.

The burden of proof is on the party made claimant to prove title to the goods. If he proves merely that they belonged to a third person, the defendant is entitled to succeed (*Richards v. Jenkins* (1887) 18 Q.B.D. 451 CA; *Re Bordon v. Westminster Bank* (1933) 49 T.L.R. 414, CA).

Where the applicant for relief is not the sheriff similar considerations apply. Where a bailee holds goods in the name of one of the interpleader claimants, that person will generally be made defendant (*De la Rue v. Hernu, Peron and Stockwell Ltd* [1936] 2 K.B. 164 CA).

R17.5.5 *4. Transfer the issue/proceedings to the county court.*—The whole proceedings, or the issue, can be transferred to the county court for trial by a circuit judge. This was not commonly done in the past but is more likely under the unified CPR. In the High Court a sheriff's interpleader is usually summarily determined by the Master/district judge (see 2 above) but a bailiff's interpleader (the county court equivalent) must be heard by a circuit judge as—anomalously—the county court district judge (as successor to the high bailiff) is in the same position as the sheriff and is therefore, technically, the applicant for relief. In practice, interpleader proceedings are rarely before a High Court judge and are suitable for release to a circuit judge under s.9 of the SCA 1981. Transfer to the county court is thus a sensible alternative.

R17.5.6 *5. Refer the dispute to arbitration.*—If all interpleader claimants are parties to an arbitration agreement, the Court may order the issue between them to be determined under that agreement (see s.5 of the Arbitration Act 1950; Arbitration Act 1996; *Re Phoenix Timber Co. Ltd's Application* [1958] 2 Q.B. 1; [1958] 1 All E.R. 815). In any event the court must further the overring objective by "encouraging the parties to use an alternative dispute resolution procedure . . ."; r.1.4(2)(e) of the CPR 1998.

R17.5.7 **Payment into court**—The court will wish to release the applicant for relief—the "stakeholder"—from the interpleader proceedings as soon as possible. Where the dispute concerns a debt or a sum of money the applicant can be released by ordering him to pay the sum into court having deducted his assessed (or agreed) costs of the application: these costs will ultimately be paid by the unsuccessful interpleader claimant.

R17.5.8 **Sale or deposit of goods**—For the purpose of saving costs and sheriff's charges, and especially where the goods are perishable, an order may be made for the sale of the goods under r.6 (*Paquin v. Robinson* (1901) 85 L.T. 5, CA) or under r.8. Alternatively the court can order sale unless a payment into court is made or security given by the interpleader claimant (see Form PF 32 QB).

Where it is not appropriate for the goods to be sold (*e.g.* the dispute concerns a specific chattel) the court can order the property to be deposited in the joint names of the solicitors for the parties. Alternatively, it may release the property to one of the interpleader claimants on his giving security or paying into court a sum representing the value of the goods.

Power to order sale of goods taken in execution

R17.6 **6.** Where an application for relief under this order is made by a sheriff who has taken possession of any goods or chattels in execution under any process, and an interpleader claimant alleges that he is entitled, under a bill of sale or otherwise, to the goods or chattels by way of security for debt, the court may order those goods or chattels or any part thereof to be sold and may direct that the proceeds of sale be applied in such manner and on such terms as may be just and as may be specified in the order.

R17.6.1 **Effect of rule**—See "sale or deposit of goods" in Commentary to r.5.

R17.6.2 **Seizure of mortgaged goods**—The sheriff is not bound to seize under a writ of *fi. fa.* goods in which the judgment debtor's interest is only an equitable one, but can, on ascertaining this, withdraw and make a return of *nulla bona* (*Scarlett v. Hanson* (1884) 12 Q.B.D. 213, CA). He can, however, on claim being made to such goods so seized by him, interplead, and if he does so, the jurisdiction to make an order for sale under this rule arises. The object of the rule is, whilst protecting the rights of the secured creditor, to render any surplus realised, after due protection of such rights, available to satisfy the claim of the execution creditor (see *per* Lindley M.R. in *Stern v. Tegner* [1989] 1 Q.B. 37 at 41). If the security is plainly enough to leave a surplus for the execution creditor, the bill of sale holder will not be allowed to defeat him: a sale will be ordered. If the security is plainly deficient, the sheriff will be ordered to withdraw. But if it is doubtful whether the security is or is not sufficient to pay off the secured creditor, the Court will refuse to order a sale unless the execution creditor guarantees the secured creditor against loss by sale (*ibid.*).

Power to stay proceedings

7. Where a defendant to a claim applies for relief under this Order in the claim, the court may by order stay all further proceedings in the claim. R17.7

Effect of rule—The rule gives express power to stay. If the applicant for relief (the "stakeholder") is already being sued and is therefore defendant in an existing case, and the claimant in that case and a third person (the interpleader claimant) both claim from him the same money or goods, the simplest course may be to substitute the interpleader claimant as defendant in the existing case: see Form PF 30 QB. R17.7.1

Other powers

8.—(1) Subject to the foregoing rules of this Order, the court may in or for the purposes of any interpleader proceedings make such order as to costs or any other matter as it thinks just. R17.8

(2) Where the interpleader claimant fails to appear at the hearing, the Court may direct that the sheriff's and execution creditor's costs shall be assessed by a master or, where the hearing was heard in a district registry, by a district judge of that registry and the following CPR rules shall apply—

(a) 44.4 (basis of assessment);
(b) 44.5 (factors to be taken into account in deciding the amount of costs);
(c) 48.4 (limitations on court's power to award costs in favour of trustee or personal representative); and
(d) 48.6 (litigants in persons).

(3) Where the claim in question is proceeding in the Admiralty Court or the Family Division, references in this rule to a Master shall be construed as references to the Admiralty Register or to a Registrar of that Division.

"order as to costs"—In a sheriff's interpleader, where the interpleader claimant fails the sheriff is entitled to his costs (including possession money) from the time of notice of the claim or from sale, whichever is earlier. Where the interpleader claimant succeeds, the sheriff is entitled to his costs as against the execution creditor from the time when the creditor made it necessary for the sheriff to interplead. However, in either case, as a general rule, the sheriff recovers his costs from the execution creditor who, if successful, has a remedy over against the interpleader claimant. A successful interpleader claimant will generally be awarded costs against the execution creditor. R17.8.1

In a stakeholders interpleader, the applicant is usually required to pay the disputed sum into court (see **payment into court** in commentary to r.5) having deducted his assessed costs to date leaving open the issue (now to be determined) which of the interpleader claimants will ultimately bear those costs (*Searle v. Matthews* (1887) 19 Q.B.D. 79; *Smith v. Darlow* (1884) 26 Ch.D. 605, CA). Costs are discretionary and in an appropriate case the stakeholder can be refused costs (*Elder Dempster Lines v. Ishag, The Lycaon* [1983] 2 Lloyd's Rep. 538).

The amount of costs will generally be assessed by summary assessment (see Part 43 CPR and Practice Direction About Costs, see para. 48PD–001).

"order as to . . . any other matter"—"Other matters" include the charges (referred to in r.8) of a stakeholder, *e.g.* a warehouseman with whom the goods have been stored; and the unsuccessful claimant who stored them may be ordered to pay his charges (*De Rothschild Frères v. Morrison, Kekewich & Co.* (1890) 24 Q.B.D. 750). If the execution creditor fails in the issue, the sheriff will not be allowed to retain the amount of his charges out of the proceeds of sale. The powers of the Court are wide and may be exercised notwithstanding that the order may interfere with property rights (*B.P. Benzin und Petroleum A.G. v. European-American Banking Corp.* [1978] 1 Lloyd's Rep. 364). R17.8.2

"Other matters" also include the sale of the goods pending the decision of the interpleader (*Paguin v. Robinson* (1901) 85 L.T. 5, CA). In *P. B. J. Davis Manufacturing Co. v. Fahn, Fahn (Claimant)* [1967] 1 W.L.R. 1059; [1967] 2 All E.R. 1274, CA, the claim had been allowed by the Master and the CA ordered a new trial and directed that the sheriff do retake posession and his possession be deemed to have continued without interruption, and that he was not to be liable for any dealings with the goods in the meantime.

Orders barring future actions—Power is given under r.2(4) or under this rule to order that no action may be brought against a sheriff who has interpleaded and such an order—"no action"—is ordinarily made. It may be refused if the Court thinks that it would be unjust to deprive an injured party of a right of action, as, for instance if the sheriff has acted oppressively or R17.8.3

if the claimant has a substantial grievance against the sheriff. The principles have been explained by the Court of Appeal in *Neumann v. Bakeway Ltd* [1983] 1 W.L.R. 1016; [1983] 2 All E.R. 935, and by Glidewell J. in *The Observer Ltd v. Gordon* [1983] 1 W.L.R. 1008; [1983] 2 All E.R. 945.

A sheriff who acts in good faith will be protected by s.138B of the Supreme Court Act 1981, accordingly the claimant must show an arguable claim which would override the Sheriff's defences (*ibid.*).

There may also be power to bar an action against the execution creditor (*Carpenter v. Pearce* (1858) 27 L.J.Exch. 143), but there has been no such order for very many years; generally speaking the execution creditor is not liable for the sheriff's acts (*Barclays Bank Ltd v. Roberts* [1954] 1 W.L.R. 1212; [1954] 3 All E.R. 107, following *Williams v. Williams & Nathan* [1937] 2 All E.R. 559).

One order in several proceedings

R17.9 **9.** Where the court considers it necessary or expedient to make an order in any interpleader proceedings in several proceedings pending in several Divisions, or before different Judges of the same Division, the court may make such an order; and the order shall be entitled in all those causes or matters and shall be binding on all the parties to them.

Disclosure

R17.10 **10.** CPR Parts 31 and 18 shall, with the necessary modifications, apply in relation to an interpleader issue as they apply in relation to any other proceedings.

Trial of interpleader issue

R17.11 **11.**—(1) CPR Part 39 shall, with the necessary modifications, apply to the trial of an interpleader issue as it applies to the trial of a claim.

(2) The court by whom an interpleader issue is tried may give such judgment or make such order as finally to dispose of all questions arising in the interpleader proceedings.

RSC ORDER 23

SECURITY FOR COSTS

R23.0.1 **Contents**

Editorial Introduction

R23.0.2 Rule 44.3(2) states that, if the court decides to make an order about costs

(a) the general rule is that the unsuccessful party will be ordered to pay the costs of the successful party; but

(b) the court may make a different order.

English law takes the view that it is up to a claimant to decide whether or not to sue a party who may not be good for costs in such an event. Whether he runs the risk is a matter for him. A defendant has no comparable choice. Consequently, the law regards him more favourably, but only slightly. The court has a discretionary power, at any stage of the proceedings, to order a person the position of claimant to give security for his opponent's costs. The purpose of the order is to endeavour to ensure that, if he defeats the claim brought against him, the defendant will have a fund available within England and Wales against which he can enforce any award of costs he may obtain. The discretion to order security for costs is not at large. There are four principal sources of law, O.23, the Companies Act 1985, s.726(1), O.59, r.10(5), and r.3.1(5).

Rule 1(1) states that if, having regard to all the circumstances of the case, the court thinks it just to do so, it may order security for costs in any one of four situations. The first mentioned (and, from a practical point of view, the most important) is that the claimant is ordinarily resident out of the jurisdiction (r.1(1)(a)). In modern times, the court's exercise of discretion under this head has been affected by E.C. treaty considerations (see para. R23.3.6).

Section 726(1) of the Companies Act 1985 gives the court power to order security where there is reason to believe that a claimant limited company may be unable to pay the defendant's costs in the event of his being successful in the claim (see para. R23.3.19).

The bulk of the notes in this Order relate to r.1(1)(a) and to s.726(1) of the 1985 Act (see para. R23.3.19). For information on r.1(1)(b) (nominal claimant) (see para. R23.3.14), or r.1(1)(c) (mis-description of claimant's address) see para. R23.3.16, on r.1(1)(d) (change of claimant's address), see para. R23.3.17. For information on O.59, r.10(5) (security for costs on appeal) see para. R59.10 and the commentary thereto. For information on r.3.1(5) (sanction for failure to comply with a rule, practice direction or relevant pre-action protocol), see para. 3.1.2.

Related sources

- CPR, 3.1(5) (sanction for failure to comply with a rule, practice direction or relevant pre-action protocol) **R23.0.3**
- RSC, O.59, r.10(5) (security for costs on appeal)
- RSC, O.71 (reciprocal enforcement of judgments), r.4 (security for costs)
- CCR, O.49, r.2(4) (security for costs in proceedings under the Chancel Repairs Act 1932)
- Commercial Court Guide (5th edition)
- Legal Aid Act 1988, s.34(5)(b) (regulations as to security for costs) (SCP 1999, Vol. 2, para. 26A–97)
- Civil Legal Aid (General) Regulations 1989, r.123 (restriction on security for costs given by an assisted person; SCP 1999, Vol. 2, para. 16D–239)
- Companies Act 1985, s.726(1) (security for costs where claimant is an impecunious limited company; see para. R23.3.19)
- Arbitration Act 1996, s.38(3) (security for costs for arbitration; see SCP 1999, Vol. 2, para. 21D–84)
- County Courts Act 1984, s.49 (security for costs where claimant's trustee in bankruptcy elects to continue the claim; SCP 1999, Vol. 2, para. 20A–722)

Forms

The following Queen's Bench Masters Practice Forms are relevant to O.23 (see Practice Direction supplementing Pt 4; see para. 4PD–001). **R23.0.4**

- PF43—Application for security for costs
- PF44—Order for security for costs

Order to apply to High Court and County Court

A1. This Order applies to proceedings both in the High Court and the county court. **R23.A1**

"High court and . . . County Court"—This Order replaces the former RSC, O.23 (upon which it is closely based) and CCR, O.13, r.8. This Order does not apply to cases in the Court of Appeal as to which see RSC, O.59, r.10(5) at para. R59.10 below. **R23.A1.1**

Security for costs of proceedings, etc.

1.—(1) Where, on the application of a defendant, it appears to the court— **R23.1**

(a) that the claimant is ordinarily resident out of the jurisdiction; or

(b) that the claimant (not being a claimant who is suing in a representative capacity) is a nominal claimant who is suing for the benefit of some other person and that there is reason to believe that he will be unable to pay the costs of the defendant if ordered to do so, or

(c) subject to paragraph (2) that the claimant's address is not stated in the claim form or other originating process or is incorrectly stated therein; or

(d) that the claimant has changed his address during the course of the proceedings with a view to evading the consequences of the litigation,

then if, having regard to all the circumstances of the case, the court thinks it just to do so, it may order the claimant to give such security for the defendant's costs of the proceedings as it thinks just.

(2) The court shall not require a claimant to give security by reason only of paragraph (1)(c) if he satisfies the court that the failure to state his address or the mis-statement thereof was made innocently and without intention to deceive.

(3) The references in the foregoing paragraphs to a claimant and a defendant shall be construed as references to the person (howsoever described on the record) who is in the position of claimant or defendant, as the case may be, in the proceeding in question, including a proceeding on a counterclaim.

Manner of giving security

R23.2 **2.** Where an order is made requiring any party to give security for costs, the security shall be given in such manner, at such time, and on such terms (if any) as the court may direct.

Saving for enactments

R23.3 **3.** This order is without prejudice to the provisions of any enactment which empowers the court to require security to be given for the costs of any proceedings.

R23.3.1 **Scope of Order (rr.1–3)**—This Order must be read subject to the powers of the Court to order security for costs conferred by any enactment, see r.3; for a list of the relevant enactments see "Related sources" above.

As to International Conventions affecting security for costs, see this note para. 23.3.21. Though the power to grant security for costs is derived from the inherent jurisdiction of the court, the categories set out in r.1 should not be extended (*C.T. Bowring & Co. (Insurance Ltd) v. Corsi & Partners Ltd* [1994] 2 Lloyd's Rep. 567) and are indeed exhaustive (*Condliffe v. Hislop* [1996] 1 W.L.R. 753).

R23.3.2 **"On the application of a defendant"**—Rule 2.3(1) defines "defendant" as a person against whom a claim is made. The word "claim" is not defined. When used as a noun in other rules it usually refers to the whole of the case in question (see, for example, r.8.1 and r.26.2) or to a separate cause of action raised in proceedings (see, for example, r.7.3). Rule 1(3) widens the meaning of the word "defendant" in this Order to include a person (howsoever described on the record) who is in the position of ... defendant ... in the proceeding in question, including a proceeding on a counterclaim. It therefore appears that, under this Order, as under the previous Order 23 which was worded slightly differently on this point, a party to proceedings whose stance in relation to any claims made in those proceedings is merely defensive, is not in the position of a claimant for the purposes of Rule 1 even if he initiates some interlocutory application, for example an application under Pt 17 to amend his defence or under Pt 18 for further information as to the particulars of claim and therefore cannot be ordered to give security for the party's costs of resisting the application (for a case authority on the previous Order 23, see (*Re B. (Infants)* [1965] 1 W.L.R. 946; [1965] 2 All E.R. 651n). Similarly there is no jurisdiction to order a claimant to give security for a third party's costs of defending interlocutory applications directly against the third party. The third party is in the position of a defendant in relation to the third party proceedings brought against him by the original defendant, but not in relation to the interlocutory proceedings brought against him by the claimant (*Taly N.D.C. International N.V. v. Terra Nova Insurance Co. Ltd* [1985] 1 W.L.R. 1359; [1986] 1 All E.R. 69, CA).

R23.3.3 **Discretionary power to order security for costs (rr.1–3)**—Rule 1(1) provides that the Court *may* order security for costs "if, having regard to all the circumstances of the case, the Court thinks it just to do so". These words have the effect of conferring upon the Court a real discretion, and indeed the Court is bound, by virtue thereof, to consider the circumstances of each case, and in the light thereof to determine whether and to what extent or for what amount a claimant (or the defendant as the case may be) may be ordered to provide security for costs.

In exercising its discretion under r.1(1) the Court will have regard to all the circumstances of the case. Security cannot now be ordered as of course from a foreign claimant, but only if the Court thinks it just to order such security in the circumstances of the case. For the circumstances which the Court might take into account whether to order security for costs, see *per* Lord Denning M.R. in *Sir Lindsay Parkinson & Co. Ltd v. Triplan Ltd* [1973] Q.B. 609 at 626–627; [1973] 2 All E.R. 273 at 285–86, and see "Claimant a limited company", para. R23.3.19. A major matter for consideration is the likelihood of the claimant succeeding. This is not to say that every application for security for costs should be made the occasion for a detailed examination of the merits of the case. Parties should not attempt to go into the merits of the case unless it can be clearly demonstrated one way or another that there is a high degree of probability of success or failure (*Porzelack KG v. Porzelack (U.K.) Ltd* [1987] 1 All E.R. 1074).

In considering an application for security for costs the Court must take account of the claimant's prospects of success, admissions by the defendant, open offers and payments into Court; but a defendant should not be adversely affected in seeking security merely because he has attempted to reach a settlement. Evidence of negotiations conducted "without prejudice" should not be admitted without his consent (*Simaan Contracting Co. v. Pilkington Glass Ltd* [1987] 1 W.L.R. 516; [1987] 1 All E.R. 345).

For the effect of delay in applying for security on the exercise of discretion, see "Time for making application for security", para. R23.3.35.

R23.3.4 **Claimant resident abroad (rr.1–3)**—A claimant who is ordinarily resident abroad *may* be ordered to give security for costs. The onus is on the defendant to prove that the claimant is "ordinarily resident" out of the jurisdiction. The question is one of fact and of degree; it does not depend upon the duration of the residence, but upon the way in which a man's life is usually ordered, and it contrasts with occasional or temporary residence (see *Levene v. I.R.C.* [1928] A.C. 217 and *Lysaght v. I.R.C.* [1928] A.C. 234, both decided under the Income Tax Acts).

In *R. v. London Borough of Barnet, ex p. Shah* [1983] 2 A.C. 309; [1983] 1 All E.R. 226, HL, it was held that, in the context of the Education Acts, the phrase "ordinarily resident" should be construed according to its ordinary and natural meaning, and that a person is ordinarily resident in a place if he habitually and normally resides lawfully in such place from choice and for a settled purpose, apart from temporary or occasional absences, even if his permanent residence or "real home" is elsewhere. The relevant dicta in *Levene v. I.R.C.* [1928] A.C. 217, HL, *Lysaght v. I.R.C.* [1928] A.C. 234, HL, and *R. v. London Borough of Barnet, ex p. Shah* [1983] A.C. 309; [1983] 1 All E.R. 226, HL, were applied by the Court of Appeal to an application under O.23, r.1 in *Parkinson v. Myer Wolff & Manley*, April 23, 1985, CA (unrep.). A claimant who makes a provisional decision to go and live abroad is not "ordinarily resident" out of the jurisdiction, at any rate so long as he has not left the country (*Appah v. Monseu* [1967] 1 W.L.R. 893; [1967] 2 All E.R. 583).

There is no longer any inflexible rule or practice that a claimant resident abroad will be ordered to give security for costs; the power to make such order is entirely discretionary under rule 1(1) (see *Aeronave S.P.A. v. Westland Charters Ltd* [1971] 1 W.L.R. 1445; [1971] 3 All E.R. 531, CA, and see *Corfu Navigation Co. v. Mobil Shipping Co. Ltd* [1991] 2 Lloyd's Rep. 52. On the other hand, as a matter of discretion, it is the usual ordinary or general rule of practice of the Court to require the foreign claimant to give security for costs, because it is ordinarily just to do, and this is so, even though by the contract between the parties, the foreign claimant is required to bring the action in England (*Aeronave S.P.A. v. Westland Charters Ltd* [1971] 1 W.L.R. 1445; [1971] 3 All E.R. 531, CA). There is, moreover, no rule or practice that a claimant resident abroad suing on a dishonoured bill of exchange should not be ordered to give security (*Banque du Rhone S.A. v. Fuerst Day Lawson Ltd* [1968] 2 Lloyd's Rep. 153, CA).

A foreign claimant in an English arbitration who is ordinarily resident out of the jurisdiction is within r.1(1) and may be ordered to give security for the respondent's costs in the arbitration (*Hudson Strumpffabrik G.m.b.H. v. Bentley Engineering Co. Ltd* [1962] 2 Q.B. 587; *Mavani v. Ralli Bros. Ltd* [1973] 1 W.L.R. 468; [1973] 1 All E.R. 555).

To find whether a claimant corporation was ordinarily resident out of the jurisdiction the court had to locate its central management and control (*Re Little Olympian Eachways Ltd* (1994) *The Times*, July 29, applying the test propounded in *De Beers Consolidated Mines Ltd v. Howes* [1906] A.C. 455 at 458, and *Unit Construction Co. Ltd v. Bullock* [1960] AC 351 at 363, 365).

Foreign and English co-claimants (rr.1–3)—The ordinary rule of practice is that no order for security for costs will be made if there is a co-claimant resident within the jurisdiction (*Winthorp v. Royal Exchange Assurance Co.* (1755) 1 Dick. 282; *D'Hormusgee v. Gray* (1882) 10 Q.B.D. 13). The ordinary rule, however, is subject to the general discretion of the Court; it is not an unvarying rule. Its application is appropriate where the foreign and English co-claimants rely on the same cause of action, where each of the claimants is bound to be held liable for all of such costs as may be ordered to be paid by any of the claimants to the defendants at the conclusion of the trial, and where one or more of the claimants has funds within the jurisdiction to meet such liability. Its application is inappropriate where there is a possibility that each of the claimants may be ordered to pay an *aliquot* share of the defendant's costs (*Slazengers Ltd v. Seaspeed Ferries Ltd; The Seaspeed Dora* [1988] 1 W.L.R. 221; [1987] 2 All E.R. 905, CA). Where the claimants do not rely on identical causes of action, or, even where they do, the outcome as to costs is unpredictable, security may be ordered against the foreign claimant (*ibid.*). Security may also be ordered where the English co-claimant is not a genuine co-claimant, but is merely joined to defeat an application for security for costs (*Jones v. Gurney* [1913] W.N. 72). R23.3.5

In general the practice may be summarised as follows: there is a well settled rule that orders for security for costs will not be made against a foreign claimant if there are one or more co-claimants resident in England; but the court has a wide discretion and the principles on which it is exercised are more important than the semantic analysis of particular cases; arguments for and against security have to focus on the circumstances and justice of the particular case, viewed in the light of the wording of O.23, r.1 and the principle that it is prima facie unjust to allow a foreign claimant to proceed without making funds available in England to cover any order for costs made against him (*Corfu Navigation Co. v. Mobil Shipping Co.* [1991] 2 Lloyd's Rep. 52; (1991) *The Times*, February 28, CA).

For an example of a case where a second claimant (being a foreign company with insufficient funds) was ordered to give security for costs see *Okotcha v. Voest Alpine Intertrading GmbH* [1993] B.C.L.C. 474.

Brussels Convention (rr.1–3)—The line of cases including *Porzelack KG v. Porzelack (U.K.) Ltd* [1987] 1 W.L.R. 420, *De Bry v. Fitzgerald* [1990] 1 W.L.R. 552, and *Berkeley Administration Inc. v. McLelland* [1990] 2 Q.B. 407 that concluded that ordering security for costs against individual claimants resident in other E.C. countries did not discriminate against them on the ground of nationality (and thus impugning Art. 6 of the E.C. Treaty) were reviewed by the Court of Appeal in *Fitzgerald v. Williams* [1996] 2 All E.R. 171 in the light of the European Court decision of Case C–398/92, *Mund and Fester v. Hatrex International Transport* [1994] E.C.R. I–467. R23.3.6

The Court of Appeal held that O.23, r.1(1)(a), whilst not overtly discriminatory, was covertly discriminatory on grounds of nationality as most claimants ordinarily resident outside the jurisdiction would not be British. Consequently, the English Court should never exercise its discretion to order security of costs against an individual claimant who was a national of and resident in another Member State. The court affirmed that this decision had no application to the case of a foreign insolvent company whether resident in the E.C. or not or to a claimant resident in a country not a member of the Community.

The Court conceded, without deciding whether or not it was sound in Community law, that a possible exception might exist if there was cogent evidence of substantial difficulty in enforcing a judgment in the claimant's country or residence.

The reasoning in this case was followed in *Cheque Point SARL v. McLelland* (1996) *The Times*, June 18, where security was ordered against an insolvent French company. The court emphasised that O.23, r.1(a) was not of itself void as contrary to Community law, merely that it was now subject to a proviso that it would not be exercised in a manner contrary to Community law. The anomaly whereby a company incorporated in a Member State but resident in England was exempt from applications for security for costs was discussed.

A provision in Swedish Law which allows the Swedish Courts to order a foreign claimant, whether individual or corporate, to furnish security for costs has been held by the European Court to contravene Article 6 of the E.C. Treaty and to constitute direct discrimination on the grounds of nationality (*Data Delecta Aktiebolag v. MSL Dynamics Ltd* [1997] I.L.P. 738; E.C. Case No. C43/95).

R23.3.7 **Foreign claimant with property in England (rr.1–3)**—Security will not be required from a person permanently residing out of the jurisdiction, if he has substantial property, whether real or personal, within it (*Redondo v. Chaytor* (1879) 4 Q.B.D. 453 at 457; *Hamburgher v. Poetting* (1882) 47 L.T. 249; *Clarke v. Barber* (1890) 6 T.L.R. 256; *Redfern v. Redfern* (1890) 63 L.T. 780); and the same rule applies to a foreign company (*Re Apollinaris Co.'s Trade Marks* [1891] 1 Ch. 1); but *semble*, the property must be of a fixed and permanent nature, which can certainly be available for costs (*Ebrard v. Gassier* (1884) 28 Ch.D. 232); or at any rate such as common sense would consider to be so (*Re Appollinaris Co.'s Trade Marks* (1891)); and such person must show that it is so available (*Sacker v. Bessler & Co.* (1887) 4 T.L.R. 17). Where the subject-matter of an action for breach of warranty was a Greek statue, it being alleged that the statue was spurious, application was made that the claimant should give security for costs. The Court had already made an order that the statue, which was deposited within the jurisdiction, should not be removed without the consent of the defendants or an order of Court. Held that as in the event of the claimant being unsuccessful in the action the value of the statue must be more than any order for costs that could be made against him, there ought to be no order for security (*Kevorkian v. Burney* [1937] 4 All E.R. 468). *A fortiori* where the statue the subject matter of the dispute is said to be by Michelangelo (*De Bry v. Fitzgerald* [1990] 1 W.L.R. 552; [1990] 1 All E.R. 560, CA).

Claimant resident in Scotland or Northern Ireland (rr.1–3)

R23.3.8 *1. Claimant a natural person resident in Scotland or Northern Ireland*—Where the claimant is a natural person resident in Scotland or Northern Ireland, security for costs will not be required from him, because, by reason of the statutory procedure for the enforcement of judgments within the United Kingdom (formerly contained in the Judgments Extension Act 1868; see now Civil Jurisdiction and Judgments Act 1982, s.18 and Sch. 6) a judgment in any division of the High Court is enforceable in Scotland or Ireland (*Raeburn v. Andrews* (1874) L.R. 9 Q.B. 118; *Re Howe Machine Co.* (1889) 41 Ch.D. 118; *Wilson Vehicle Distribution Ltd v. Colt Car Co. Ltd* [1984] B.C.L.C. 93). The Civil Jurisdiction and Judgments Act 1982 is set out in Vol. 2, Section 7B.

R23.3.9 *2. Claimant a solvent company resident in Scotland or Northern Ireland*—The same reasoning applies to a claimant which is a solvent limited company resident in Scotland or Northern Ireland, and which is able to pay the defendant's costs of action. Security will not be required from such a company.

R23.3.10 *3. Claimant an insolvent company resident in Scotland*—The Companies Act 1985 applies to Scotland. Hence a company incorporated in Scotland is a company within the meaning of that Act (see Companies Act 1985, s.735). A claimant which is such a company and which is insolvent or otherwise unable to pay the defendant's costs of action, may therefore be required to give security by virtue of Companies Act 1985, s.726(1) (see para. R23.3.19 below) (*Wilson Vehicle Distribution Ltd v. Colt Car Co. Ltd* [1984] B.C.L.C. 93).

R23.3.11 *4. Claimant an insolvent company resident in Northern Ireland*—The Companies Act 1985 does not apply generally to Northern Ireland (see s.745); it follows that a company incorporated in Northern Ireland is not within the scope of s.726(1). The equivalent Northern Irish legislation does not affect proceedings in England or Wales. In *Wilson Vehicle Distribution Ltd v. Colt Car Co. Ltd* [1984] B.C.L.C. 93, Bingham J. held that the reasoning of the Divisional Court in *Raeburn v. Andrews* (1874) L.R. 9 Q.B. 118, applied to an application for security against a claimant company incorporated and resident in Northern Ireland which was unable to pay the defendant's costs of action, and that he was thereby bound to refuse the application. In *D.S.Q. Property Co. Ltd v. Lotus Cars Ltd* [1987] 1 W.L.R. 127, however, Millett J. held that the true *ratio* of *Raeburn v. Andrews* (above) was that irrelevant circumstances should be ignored, and that where a claimant was an individual, with or without means, his residence in Scotland or Northern Ireland was irrelevant because he was within reach of the Court's process, and security should not be ordered against him any more than it would be against an individual claimant resident in England. This reasoning, said Millett J., had no application to a claimant which was an insolvent company, and accordingly there was no reason in principle why an order for security order O.23, r.1 should not be made against such a company resident and incorporated in Northern Ireland.

In *Dynaspan (UK) Ltd v. H. Katzenberger Baukonstructionen GmbH & KG, The Times*, February 21, 1995, Robert Walker J. followed *DSQ Property Company v. Lotus Cars Ltd* and held, notwithstanding the fact that s.726 of the Companies Act 1985 did not apply to Northern Ireland, that the court under its inherent jurisdiction could order security against a Northern Ireland Company and that though its lack of funds was a factor to be taken into account, it would carry less weight than on an application under s.726.

Claimant resident abroad (other than in Scotland or Northern Ireland) (rr.1–3)—On the other hand, the procedure for enforcing judgments under Pt II of the A.J.A. 1920, and the Foreign Judgments (Reciprocal Enforcement) Act 1933, is different and claimants residing in countries to which those Acts apply, and to which the 1968 Convention does not apply, may be ordered to give security (*Kohn v. Rindon & Stafford (Brod.) Ltd* [1948] 1 K.B. 327). See also O.71, r.4. **R23.3.12**

The position of claimants residing in E.C. and EEA countries, however, is affected by the Civil Jurisdiction and Judgments Act 1982, the relevant sections of which came into force on January 1, 1987, and which implements the provisions of the 1968 Convention on the enforcement of judgments within the E.C. The convention procedure is an important, but not necessarily decisive factor to be considered by the Court in exercising discretion under O.23, r.1 (*Porzelack KG v. Porzelack (U.K.) Ltd* [1987] 1 W.L.R. 420; [1987] 1 All E.R. 1074).

Counterclaiming defendant resident abroad (rr.1–3)—The mere making of a counterclaim does not put the defendant in the position of claimant under r.1(3); the question is whether, in the particular case, the counterclaim is a cross-action or operates as a defence. **R23.3.13**

Where a claim and counterclaim arise out of different matters, so that the counterclaim is really in the nature of a cross-action, the defendant, if resident out of the jurisdiction, may be ordered to give security (*Sykes v. Sacerdoti* (1885) 15 Q.B.D. 423; and see *Lake v. Haseltine* (1885) 55 L.J. Q.B. 205; *The Julia Fisher* (1877) 2 P.D. 115; but where the counterclaim arises out of the same matter, and is in fact the defence to the action, the Court will ordinarily refuse to order the defendant, resident out of the jurisdiction, to give security for costs (*Neck v. Taylor* [1893] 1 Q.B. 560). Thus, where a counterclaim arises out of the same subject matter as the claim and can properly be relied upon as a set-off, the counterclaiming defendant ought not to be required to give security for costs of the counterclaim unless there are exceptional circumstances (*Ashworth v. Berkeley-Walbrook Ltd* (1989) *The Independent*, October 9, CA). In *Mapleson v. Masini* (1879) 5 Q.B.D. 144, where a plaintiff sued for breach of contract, and the defendant, a foreigner resident abroad, counterclaimed in respect of breaches of the same contract, it was held the defendant could not be compelled to give security. But each case must be judged on its own merits, and security for costs of a cross-action may be ordered where the claims therein set up are quite independent of the matters in question in the original action (*New Fenix, etc., Co. v. General Accident, etc., Corp.* [1911] 2 K.B. 619).

Where the claimant obtains a freezing injunction (formerly a *Mareva* injunction) against defendants resident abroad for a sum exceeding the amount of the costs of the counterclaim by the defendants, the defendants are in the same position as a claimant resident abroad who has substantial assets in this country, and therefore the Court will refuse to make an order for security for costs in favour of the claimant against the defendants in respect of such counterclaim (*Hitachi Shipbuilding & Engineering Co. Ltd v. Viafiel Compania Naviera S.A.* [1981] 2 Lloyd's Rep. 498, CA).

Where both the claimant and the counterclaiming defendant reside out of the jurisdiction, and the counterclaim arises out of the same transaction and raises the same basic issues as the claim, both parties should be treated alike in relation to security for costs, since it would be mere chance which party would be claimant and which defendant, and therefore the Court should order the claimant to give security for costs in respect of the claim, and also order the counterclaiming defendant to give security for costs in a similar amount in respect of the counterclaim (*The Silver Fir* [1980] 1 Lloyd's Rep. 371, CA).

Nominal claimant (r.1(1)(b))—Rule 1(1)(b) empowers the Court to order a nominal claimant who may be unable to pay the costs of the defendant to give security for costs. A trustee in bankruptcy suing as such is not a nominal claimant (*Cowell v Taylor* (1885) 31 Ch.D. 34). However a trustee in bankruptcy who elects to continue a claim in the county court commenced by the bankrupt may be ordered to give security under CCA 1984, s.49 (see SCP 1999, Vol. 2, para. 20A-722). **R23.3.14**

The trustee of a bankrupt claimant is not a necessary party to proceedings relating to matters which occurred after the bankruptcy, and in such case the bankrupt will not be treated as a nominal claimant, nor ordered to give security for costs (*Buchan v. Hill* [1888] W.N. 233; *Cook v. Whellock* (1890) 24 Q.B.D. 658). A claimant who has assigned the benefit of the action may be a nominal claimant (*Semler v. Murphy* [1968] Ch. 183). So, an insolvent claimant who assigns to a trustee for the benefit of his creditors all his estate, and covenants to prosecute the action, is merely a nominal claimant, and must give security (*Lloyd v. Hathern Station Brick Co.* (1901) 85 L.T. 158). And an insolvent claimant, who sues as trustee of a deed executed by a debtor for the benefit of his creditors, and who is not beneficially interested in the subject-matter, must give security (*Greener v. Kahn & Co.* [1906] 2 K.B. 374). *Aliter*, in the case of trustees of a separation deed (*White v. Butt* [1909] 1 K.B. 50, CA). But a person clothed with a representative capacity by a Court of competent jurisdiction, *e.g.* an administrator, will not be ordered to give security for costs of an action brought by him though merely a nominee of a person resident abroad (*Rainbow v. Kittoe* [1916] 1 Ch. 313).

A bankrupt, to whom the trustee in bankruptcy has assigned the right to claim damages for negligence against his former accountants, who undertook to receive only 65 per cent of the net proceeds of the action and to pay to the trustee the remaining 35 per cent is not a "nominal" claimant against whom an order for security for costs would be made and in any event as a matter of discretion on the ground that the negligence of the defendants had itself led or contributed to his bankruptcy it would be manifestly unjust to order the claimant to give security for costs (*Ramsey v. Hartley* [1977] 1 W.L.R. 686; [1977] 2 All E.R. 673, CA).

R23.3.15 **Litigation friend**—The litigation friend (formerly next friend) of a child or patient (formerly a person under disability) is unlikely to be regarded as a nominal claimant and therefore is unlikely to be ordered to give security even if impecunious and a stranger (*Jones v. Evans* [1886] 31 S.J. 11) but if he appeals and is insolvent, he may have to give security (see O.59, r.10(5) and the commentary thereto). If a litigation friend is ordered to give security for costs and does not do so and the claim is dismissed, proceedings in another claim by another litigation friend are unlikely to be stayed even though the claim is against the same defendant for the same purpose (*per* Cotton L.J., *Re Payne* (1883) 23 Ch.D. 288 at 289, CA).

R23.3.16 **Misdescription of claimant's residence (r.1(1)(c))**—Rule 1(1)(c) empowers the Court to order a claimant whose address is not stated in the claim form or other originating process or is incorrectly stated there to give security for costs.

If, however, the claimant fails to state his address or he mis-states his address innocently and without intention to deceive, he will not be ordered to give security for costs (see *Chellew v. Brown* [1923] 2 K.B. 844, CA, where a master mariner with no permanent home gave his sister's address).

An American company suing under an English address, at which it could not be found, was ordered to give security for costs (*Pittsburgh Crushed Steel Co. v. Jacob Marx & Co.* [1897] W.N. 36).

R23.3.17 **Change of address by claimant (r.1(1)(d))**—Rule 1(1)(d) empowers the Court to order a claimant who has changed his address during the course of the proceedings with a view to evading the consequences of the litigation to give security for costs. However, security will not be ordered from a claimant who has indorsed a sufficient address on his claim form or other originating process, and has afterwards removed from that address, and is prevented by poverty and adversity from acquiring a fresh permanent address (*Knight v. Ponsonby* [1925] 1 K.B. 545, CA).

R23.3.18 **Insolvency or poverty no ground for security (rr.1–3)**—The insolvency or poverty of a claimant is no ground for requiring him to give security for costs (*Cowell v. Taylor* (1885) 31 Ch.D. 34, and cases there cited; *Le Mesurier v. Ferguson* (1903) 20 T.L.R. 32); even though he is an undischarged bankrupt (*Cook v. Whellock* (1890) 24 Q.B.D. 658); nor is possible or probable bankruptcy any ground (*Rhodes v. Dawson* (1886) 16 Q.B.D. 548). The fact that a corporation (other than a limited company) is insolvent, and that a receiver of the profits of its undertaking has been appointed, is no ground for requiring it to give security (*Dartmouth Harbour Commissioners v. Mayor of Dartmouth* (1886) 55 L.J.Q.B. 483).

There are, however, certain exceptions to the rule that insolvency or poverty is no ground for requiring security for costs, *e.g.* in the case of an appellant (see O.59, r.10(5), at para. R59.10) and of a nominal claimant (see "Nominal claimant", para. R23.3.14).

R23.3.19 **Claimant a limited company (rr.1–3)**—Section 726(1) of the Companies Act 1985 provides:

> "Where in England and Wales a limited company is plaintiff in an action or other legal proceeding, the Court having jurisdiction in the matter may, if it appears by credible testimony that there is reason to believe that the company will be unable to pay the defendant's costs if successful in his defence, require sufficient security to be given for those costs, and may stay all proceedings until the security is given."

The fact that a company is in liquidation is prima facie evidence that it is unable to pay the costs, unless evidence to the contrary is given (*Northampton Coal, Iron & Waggon Co. v. Midland Waggon Co.* (1878) 7 Ch.D. 500, CA; *Pure Spirit Co. v. Fowler* (1890) 25 Q.B.D. 235). Apart from such a case, the application for security must be supported by evidence which credibly and reasonably shows the inability of the company to pay the costs of the successful defendant. Thus, security was ordered where a banking company in voluntary liquidation had before bringing the action sold its business to another bank (*National Bank of Wales v. Atkins* (1894) 38 S.J. 186) and where a small company was suing for an infringement of patent which was its substratum (*Diamond Steel Manufacturing Co. v. Harrison* (1910) 27 R.P.C. 451). But the mere fact that a company has issued a debenture charging all its assets to secure the repayment of all moneys then or at any time owing to a particular person was not considered to be a sufficient reason for ordering security (*Universal Aircraft Ltd v. Hickey*, May 4, 1943, Morton J. (unrep.)). The court is not entitled to ignore the unchallenged evidence of an accountant as to a company's present ability to pay the costs of an action (*Kim Barker v. Aegon Insurance Co. (U.K.) Ltd*, *The Times*, October 9, 1989, CA).

An applicant for security for costs has to show that the company would not (as opposed to may not) be able to meet its debts when an order for costs was made against it. This question had to be answered at the time of the application though the court could take into account evidence of what was to be expected in the future before any order would be made (*Re Unisoft Group (No. 2)* [1993] B.C.L.C. 532).

"Sufficient security" within the above section ought not to be either illusory or oppressive (*Dominion Brewery v. Foster* (1897) 77 L.T. 507; *Imperial Bank of China and Japan v. Bank of Hindustan* (1866) L.R. 1 Ch. 437). It should be for the probable amount of costs taking into account the chance of the case collapsing, but of course the amount of security is in the discretion of the Court.

The Court has a discretion under s.726(1) of the Companies Act 1985, just as under r.1, whether to order security for costs having regard to all the circumstances of the case (*Sir Lindsay Parkinson & Co. Ltd v. Triplan Ltd* [1973] Q.B. 609; [1973] 2 All E.R. 273, CA). Among the circumstances which the Court might take into account are the following: (1) whether the claimant's claim is bona fide and not a sham; (2) whether the claimant has a reasonably good prospect of success; (3) whether there is an admission by the defendants in their defence or elsewhere that money is due; (4) whether there is a substantial payment into Court or an "open offer" of a substantial amount; (5) whether the application for security was being used oppressively, *e.g.* so as to stifle a genuine claim; (6) whether the claimant's want of means has been brought about by any conduct by the defendants, such as delay in payment or in doing their part of the work; (7) whether the application for security is made at a late stage of the proceedings (*ibid. per* Lord Denning M.R.). The Court may order a claimant company in liquidation to give security for costs, even though it is one of two or more claimants, especially where there is a comparatively small overlap between its own claims and those of the other claimants (*John Bishop (Caterers) Ltd v. National Union Bank Ltd* [1973] 1 All E.R. 707). In the case of a limited company s.726(1) applies to all companies irrespective of whether or not it happens to be suing as claimant with a natural person as co-claimant, and the inability of the claimant company to pay the defendants' costs is a substantial factor in the Court's decision whether to order security for costs; and while the Court must not allow s.726(1) to be used as an instrument of oppression, it must equally not allow an impecunious company to put unfair pressure on a prosperous company (*Pearson v. Naydler* [1977] 1 W.L.R. 899; [1977] 3 All E.R. 531). Where an order for security for costs against a claimant company might result in oppression in that the claimant company would be forced to abandon a claim which has a reasonable prospect of success, the Court is entitled to refuse to make that order, notwithstanding that the claimant company, if unsuccessful, will be unable to pay the defendant's costs (*Aquila Design (GRB) Products Ltd v. Cornhill Insurance plc* [1988] B.C.L.C. 134, CA). In this respect it is sufficient for the claimant to show that there is a probability that it will be unable to pursue the action if the order is granted; it need not show with certainty that it will be unable to do so (*Trident International Freight Services Ltd v. Manchester Ship Canal Co.* [1990] B.C.L.C. 263, CA).

Section 726(1) of the Companies Act 1985 applies only to limited companies and cannot found an application for security against other corporate bodies or unincorporated associations against whom an application cannot be made under the general provisions of r.1.

Security may be ordered if the claimant company goes into liquidation after the trial has actually commenced (*Lydney and Wigpool Iron Co. v. Bird* (1883) 23 Ch.D. 358).

In considering whether to exercise its discretion under s.726(1) to order security for costs in a case where there may be a risk of stifling a genuine claim the court has to perform a balancing exercise by weighing the injustice to the claimant if prevented from pursuing a proper claim against the injustice to the defendant if no security is ordered and, on the claimant's claim failing, being unable to recover the costs incurred in defending its claim.

Factors to be taken into account include:

(1) whether the claimant company is using its impecuniosity to put pressure on the defendant;
(2) the claimant's prospects of success (without going into the merits in detail: *Porzelack KG v. Porzelack UK Ltd* above, para. R23.3.3);
(3) whether the claimant's claim would in fact be stifled by considering whether the claimant can raise funds outside its own resources to conduct the litigation, the onus being upon the claimant to satisfy the court that no such resources are available;
(4) Lateness of the application; whether this factor weighs against the claimant or defendant depends upon whether blame for the delay rests with the claimant or defendant.

If the court does order security it can order any amount up to full security. It need not be substantial provided it is more than nominal (applying *Roburn Construction Ltd v. William Irwin*

(*South*) *& Co. Ltd* [1991] B.C.C. 726): *Keary Developments Ltd v. Tarmac Construction Ltd* [1995] 3 All E.R. 534. *Keary Developments* was followed in *Danemark Ltd v. BAA* [1996] 12 C.L., CA, where in a late application for additional security the court in allowing the appeal carried out the balancing exercise in favour of the claimant where the potential loss to the claimant if the claim was stifled was £300,000 whereas the extra exposure of the defendants was only £60,000. Other factors taken into account were that the defendants had not made out a strong prima facie case on the merits and that expert evidence had been introduced into the case at a late stage.

R23.3.20 **No security for costs against defendant (rr.1–3)**—Security for costs cannot be required from a defendant who is exercising his right to defend himself against attack, though resident out of the jurisdiction (*Naamlooze, etc. v. Bank of England* [1948] 1 All E.R. 465, CA), nor from a person seeking to intervene as defendant (*Maatschappij Voor Fondsenbezit v. Shell Transport and Trading Co.* [1923] 2 K.B. 166, CA), nor from a defendant sued on a dishonoured bill who raises a defence under the Bills of Exchange Act 1882 (*Banque du Rhone SA v. Fuerst Day Lawson Ltd* [1968] 2 Lloyd's Rep. 153, CA). Security for costs cannot be required from a defendant who raises the issue of domicile as part of his defence, even though he is made the claimant on the trial of a preliminary issue (*Visco v. Minter* [1969] P. 82; [1969] 2 All E.R. 714). But a defendant setting up a counterclaim may be required to give security, see "Counterclaiming defendant resident abroad", para. R23.3.13.

R23.3.21 **International Conventions affecting security for costs (rr.1–3)**—The following Conventions expressly forbid any requirement of security for costs, namely Carriage of Goods by Rail (Berne) 1952, Art. 55(4); Carriage of Passengers by Rail (Berne) 1961, Art. 56(4); Carriage of Goods by Road (Geneva) 1956, Art. 31(5); Carriage of Passengers by Road Convention, Art. 41(6). It should be noted, however, that these Conventions, although ratified, have not yet been brought into force in England. The 1968 Convention on the enforcement of foreign judgments, brought into force by the Civil Jurisdiction and Judgments Act 1982, provided by Art. 45 that security for costs shall not be required from a person seeking to enforce a foreign judgment given in a Convention (*i.e.* E.C.) country.

International carriage by rail is now governed by the Convention concerning International Carriage by Rail 1980 (Cmd. 8335) given force of law in the U.K. by International Transport Conventions Act 1983 and brought into force in 1985 by S.I. 1985 No. 612.

The following Conventions impliedly exclude requests for security for costs by non-discrimination clauses, *i.e.* Third Party Liability in the Field of Nuclear Energy (Paris) 1960, Art. 14(a) as amended by the additional Protocol of 1964; Civil Liability for Nuclear Damage (Vienna) 1963, Art. 13; Convention for Liability in Nuclear Ships (Brussels) 1962, Art. 12(3) (not yet ratified).

On the other hand, the Warsaw Convention on Carriage by Air 1929, Art. 28, impliedly permits a requirement of security for costs by providing that the procedure is to be governed by the *lex fori*.

Conventions with the following countries contain Articles relevant to security for costs:

Austria	Cmd. 4007 (1932) Art. 11
Belgium	Cmd. 2069 (1924) Art. 2
Belgium (supplementary)	Cmd. 4639 (1934) Art. 2
Czechoslovakia	Cmd. 2637 (1926)
Czechoslovakia (supplementary)	Cmd. 4980 (1935) Art. 3
Denmark	Cmd. 4334 (1933) Art. 12
Finland	Cmd. 4507 (1934) Art. 11
France	Cmd. 1661 (1922)
France (supplementary)	Cmd. 6206 (1940) Art. 3
Germany	Cmd. 3286 (1929) Art. 14
Greece	Cmd. 5643 (1938) Art. 11
Hungary	Cmd. 5190 (1936) Art. 12
Iraq	Cmd. 5369 (1937) Art. 12
Israel	Cmd. 3513 (1968) Art. 13
Italy	Cmd. 4105 (1932)
Netherlands	Cmd. 4381 (1933)
Netherlands (supplementary)	Cmd. 4278 (1970) Art. 3
Norway	Cmd. 3934 (1931) Art. 11
Poland	Cmd. 4104 (1932) Art. 12
Portugal	Cmd. 4070 (1932) Art. 11
Spain	Cmd. 3544 (1930) Art. 13
Sweden	Cmd. 3777 (1931) Art. 11
Switzerland	Cmd. 5973 (1939) Art. 3
Turkey	Cmd. 4318 (1933) Art. 12
Yugoslavia	Cmd. 5542 (1937) Art. 12

It would appear that the provisions of these Conventions do not involve any departure from the rules and practice of the High Court. Further information regarding these Conventions can be obtained from the Queen's Bench Masters' Secretary's Department, Room E113, Royal Courts of Justice, Strand, London WC2A 2LL.

The application of these Conventions is effectively superseded in relation to countries which are party to the Brussels or Lugano conventions.

Security for costs of appeal (rr.1–3)—See O.59, r.10(5), para. R59.10. R23.3.22

Mode of application for security (rr.1–3)—The provisions in Pt 23 (General rules about applications for court orders) apply to an application under O.23, r.1. For a form of application see PF43 (see Practice Direction supplementing Pt 4; para. PD4–001). Evidence in support is generally necessary. An applicant cannot rely upon oral evidence unless the court so permits (r.32.6). Instead he may rely upon written evidence set out in his statement of case, or application notice, or in a witness statement. Each item of written evidence relied on must contain a statement of truth (as to which see further the Practice Direction supplementing Pt 22) (see para. 22PD–001) and the Practice Direction supplementing Pt 8, para. 5.2 (see para. 8PD–001). An applicant may also rely upon affidavit evidence if he so wishes. However if he does so, he may not recover any additional costs thereby incurred unless the court orders otherwise (r.32.15 and as to affidavits generally, r.32.16, r.32.17 and the Practice Direction which supplements Pt 32 at para. 32PD–001, below). R23.3.23

Evidence relied on which is not set out in the application notice itself must be served with the application notice (unless already served) and must also be filed (Practice Direction supplementing Pt 23, paras 9.3 and 9.6 respectively; see para. 23PD–001, below).

If the application is intended to be made to a Judge other than a Master or District Judge the application notice should so state (para. 2.6 of the Practice Directions supplementing Pt 23 at para. 23PD–001, below). The hearing of the application will normally take place before a Master or District Judge. Applications under section 726(1) of the Companies Act 1985 are, in the first instance, listed by the court as hearings in private under r.39.2(3)(c) (Practice Direction supplementing Pt 39, para. 1.5(8); para. 39PD–001).

Order for security for costs (rr.1–3)—An order for security for costs should specify the time limit within which security is to be provided, should stay the proceedings until security is given and provide for automatic dismissal of the proceedings if security is not provided "without further order". Provision for automatic dismissal should be omitted if the court wishes to give further consideration to the matter before the proceedings are dismissed: *Clive Brooks & Co. Ltd v. Baynard, The Times* April 30, 1998. The Practice Directions supplementing Pt 4 provides a model form of order; PF44. R23.3.24

Subsequent applications for security (rr.1–3)—If the court refuses to order security, and that refusal is not reversed on appeal, the applicant may reapply only if he is able to put before the court fresh material which was not before the court at the original application. It is otherwise if security is ordered: the amount of security may later be increased or reduced on proof of a material change of circumstances (*Gordano Building Contractors Ltd v. Burgess* [1988] 1 W.L.R. 890). R23.3.25

Arbitration proceedings (rr.1–3)—Unless otherwise agreed by the parties, an arbitral tribunal has power to order a claimant to provide security for the costs of the arbitration (Arbitration Act 1996, s.38(3)). Where an international arbitration is of a type regularly conducted in London for many years and not a one-off arbitration, security for costs should generally be ordered, the more so if the litigation costs are very high (*K/S A/S Bani v. Korea Shipbuilding and Engineering Corp., The Times*, July 15, 1987, CA, applying *Bank Mellat v. Helleniki Techniki SA* [1984] Q.B. 291; [1983] 3 All E.R. 428, CA). R23.3.26

Where a foreigner residing out of the jurisdiction applied for the appointment of an arbitrator under Arbitration Act 1889, s.5 the Court made the giving of security for costs a condition of assisting him (*Re Bjornstad and Ouse Shipbuilding Co. Ltd* [1924] 2 K.B. 673, CA).

In an exceptional case the Court can order security for costs in respect of an arbitration being held within the jurisdiction under the *ICC Rules of Conciliation and Arbitration* (*SA Coppee Lavalin NV v. Ken-Ren Chemicals and Fertilisers (in liquidation in Kenya)* [1994] 2 All E.R. 449, HL).

Miscellaneous proceedings (rr.1–3)—The Prize Court Rules 1939, O.18, enables security for costs applications to be made against any claimant; but in ordering security the Judge must not increase the difficulty of enforcing bona fide rights: he may consider the type of case which usually proves fraudulent, but must remember that costs are not usually ordered against a bona fide claimant, though he may fail (*The Stanton* [1917] A.C. 380). The CPR do not apply to proceedings in the High Court when acting as a Prize Court except to the extent that they are applied by another enactment (Rule 2.1(2) and see further para. 2.1.7). R23.3.27

The claimant in condemnation proceedings instituted in the High Court must give security for costs (Customs and Excise Management Act 1979, Sched. 3, para. 10(2)).

A caveator cannot as such be ordered to give security for costs (*In the Goods of Emery* [1923] P. 184); he cannot be regarded as being in the position of a claimant and his position cannot be altered by the election of a beneficiary under the will to be joined as a co-defendant (*Rose v. Epstein* [1974] 1 W.L.R. 1565; [1974] 3 All E.R. 745, CA).

A relator bringing an action at the suit of the Att.-Gen. may be required to give security for costs (*Att.-Gen. v. Allman* [1906] 1 Ir.R. 473).

Claimants whose persons are privileged from arrest, such as ambassadors' servants, may be required to give security (*Goodwin v. Archer* (1727) 2 P.W. 452). See 10 Morg. 542; but an ambassador will not be required to give security (*Duke de Montellano v. Christin* (1816) 5 M. & S. 503).

When one of two partners had instituted an action expressly against his partner's wishes he was ordered to give his partner (who disclaimed any interest in the subject-matter) a full and complete indemnity coupled with security against all costs, expenses, charges, and liabilities in respect thereof and the action was stayed till this was done (*Davey v. Alby United Carbide Factories Ltd*, March 19, 1914, Coleridge J. at Chambers).

R23.3.28 **Security for costs on application under Part III of the Solicitors Act 1974 (rr.1–3)**—A party resident out of the jurisdiction who applies for a detailed assessment of his former solicitor's bill of costs may be ordered to give security, unless the solicitor already holds sufficient security, for the costs which the former client may be ordered to pay on the assessment including the costs of the assessment (*Re Pasmore* (1839) 1 Beav. 94, *Anon.* (1841) 12 Sim. 262).

R23.3.29 **Bankruptcy (rr.1–3)**—Bankruptcy is not, as such, a ground for ordering a plaintiff to give security for costs (*Rhodes v. Dawson* (1886) 16 Q.B.D. 548; *Cook v. Whellock* (1890) 24 Q.B.D. 658) but an insolvent trustee under a deed of assignment must give security (*Greener v. Kahn & Co. Ltd* [1906] 2 K.B. 374). Also, in the county court, if the claimant becomes bankrupt and his trustee elects to continue to the proceedings, the court may order the trustee to give security for costs (County Courts Act 1984, s.49; see SCP 1999, Vol. 2, para. 20A–722).

R23.3.30 **Legal aid (rr.1–3)**—The fact that the claimant is an assisted person is not a sufficient reason why security should not be ordered, although (since the object of such an order is to give the defendant security against such costs as are likely to be awarded him, if successful, at the trial) the amount of security ordered may be smaller than usual (see further Civil Legal Aid (General) Regulations 1989, reg. 123; see SCP 1999, Vol. 2, para. 16D–239). In a claim for damages for personal injuries an order for security was made against an assisted person who was ordinarily resident abroad (*Jackson v. John Dickinson & Co. (Bolton) Ltd* [1952] W.N. 9; [1952] 1 All E.R. 104, CA; *Friedmann v. Austay (London) Ltd* [1954] 1 W.L.R. 466; [1954] 1 All E.R. 594; *Williams v. Williams* [1953] 1 W.L.R. 905; [1953] 2 All E.R. 474).

R23.3.31 **Security by undertaking to pay costs (rr.1–3)**—Where the undertaking of a party or his solicitor to pay the whole or a specified proportion of the costs or a specified sum in lieu of security for costs is accepted by the other party, there is no need for any application to the Court.

Where such an undertaking is given and is accepted in lieu of security for costs, it lasts as long as there is no final judgment from which an appeal lies (*Hawkins Hill Co. v. Want* (1893) 69 L.T. 297). It will be limited to the amount of the security so given.

R23.3.32 **Security agreed without an order (rr.1–3)**—Where the defendant demands security from a foreign claimant who is willing to give the required security for an agreed amount without any application for an order being made, the plaintiff's solicitor should obtain and complete Court Funds Office Form 100 (SCP 1999, Vol. 2, Section 5C, para. 5C–115).

This form should be signed by a master or district judge. After signing the form should be taken to the Court Office for sealing (the Action Department in Central Office actions) and then produced at the Court Funds Office.

R23.3.33 **Security by payment into court (rr.1–3)**—The more usual and convenient mode in which to order security for costs is to require a specified sum to be paid into Court within a specified period. This mode saves a great deal of costs and trouble, as compared with requiring security by bond, and is much to be preferred.

Where a party has been compelled to pay money into Court as security for costs, such fund cannot be looked upon as property recovered or preserved, so as to enable the Court to give the solicitor of the party paying in a charging order upon it for the amount of his costs (*Re Wadsworth* (1885) 29 Ch.D. 517).

R23.3.34 **Security by bond (rr.1–3)**—Security for costs may in special cases be ordered to be given by bond and is usually given by bond with two sureties, though one obligor is sufficient. The bond has usually to be approved by the Master or District Judge but is given to the person requiring the security.

The proposed sureties on the bond must be solvent (*Cliffe v. Wilkinson* (1830) 4 Sim. 122); and the claimant's solicitor cannot be surety (*Panton v. Labertouche* (1843) 1 Ph. 265, where the reason is stated) nor is the solicitor's undertaking sufficient (*Re Norman* (1849) 11 Beav. 401). If the surety becomes bankrupt, the claimant must find a new one, and proceedings may be stayed in the meantime (*Lautour v. Holcombe* (1843) 1 Ph. 262; *Veitch v. Irving* (1840) 11 Sim. 122). Where there are several defendants separately represented, each may have a separate security, though only one penalty is recoverable (*Lowndes v. Robertson* (1819) 4 Mad. 465).

Security may be given by the bond of a guarantee society, which is made out to the party entitled to the security and is lodged with their solicitors.

There is no general rule that the bond of a foreign company will not be accepted as security (*Aldrich v. Griffin, etc., Co.* [1904] 2 K.B. 850, CA).

A solicitor who takes a guarantee in lieu of an order for security for costs may be liable to his client in negligence if he fails to ensure that the guarantee is properly secured (*Boston v. Roberts* (1995) *The Times*, March 17).

Time for making application for security (rr.1–3)—The right to security is not waived by service of the defence, and an order for security may be made at any stage of the proceedings (*Re Smith* (1896) 75 L.T. 46, CA; and see *Arkwright v. Newbold* [1880] W.N. 59; *Martano v. Mann* (1880) 14 Ch.D. 419, CA; *Lydney, etc. Iron Ore Co. v. Bird* (1883) 23 Ch.D. 358). R23.3.35

An application for security may be made after judgment for the costs of further proceedings directed by the judgment as, *e.g.* the taking of an account (*Brown v. Haig* [1905] 2 Ch. 379).

Delay in making an application for security for costs, however, may be relevant to the exercise of the Court's discretion to order security. Although in most cases delay is not a decisive factor, it may be treated as important, especially where it has led, or may have led the claimant to act his detriment, or may cause him hardship in the future conduct of the action (*Jenred Properties Ltd v. Ente Nazionale Italiano per il Turismo, Financial Times*, October 29, 1985, CA).

The circumstances in which a court would order security for costs during the course of a trial would be rare. There would at least have to be a substantial change of circumstances upon which the party applying had acted promptly as soon as the facts were known (*Cheffick v. J. D. M. Associates (No. 3)* (1989) 22 Con L.R. 36).

Amount of security (rr.1–3)—The amount of security awarded is in the discretion of the Court, which will fix such sum as it thinks just, having regard to all the circumstances of the case. It is not always the practice to order security on a full indemnity basis. If security is sought, as it often is, at an early stage in the proceedings, the Court will be faced with an estimate made by a solicitor or his clerk of the costs likely in the future to be incurred; and probably the costs already incurred or paid will be only a fraction of the security sought by the applicant. At that stage one of the factors for the court to consider is the possibility that the proceedings may soon settle. In such a situation it may well be sensible to make an arbitrary discount of the costs estimated as probable future costs, but there is no hard and fast rule. On the contrary each case has to be decided on its own circumstances, and it may not always be appropriate to make such a discount (*Procon (Great Britain) Ltd v. Provincial Building Co. Ltd* [1984] 1 W.L.R. 557; [1984] 2 All E.R. 368, CA). It is a great convenience to the Court to be informed what are the estimated costs, and for this purpose a skeleton bill of costs usually affords a ready guide (cited with approval by Lane J. in *T. Sloyan & Sons (Builders) Ltd v. Brothers of Christian Instruction* [1974] 3 All E.R. 715 at 720). R23.3.36

Where the claim of the claimant, who may be required to give security for costs, whether under r.1 or under the Companies Act 1985, s.726(1), is countered by a cross-claim put forward by the defendant, the amount by which such cross-claim exceeds the claimant's claim has to be treated as a counter-claim in relation to which the claimant is in the position of a defendant and in respect of which therefore he cannot be ordered to give security for costs, and accordingly, in such case the appropriate amount of security must be determined by having regard to the fact that the defence goes to the whole of the plaintiff's claim while disregarding the excess of the defendant's claim over the claimant's claim (*T. Sloyan & Sons (Builders) Ltd v. Brothers of Christian Instruction* [1974] 3 All E.R. 715).

Security for costs is not necessarily confined to future costs, but may, when applied for promptly, be extended to costs already incurred in the suit (*Brocklebank v. King's Lynn Steamship Co.* (1878) 3 C.P.D. 365); *Massey v. Allen* (1879) 12 Ch.D. 807; *Procon (Great Britain) Ltd v. Provincial Building Co. Ltd* [1984] 1 W.L.R. 557; [1984] 2 All E.R. 368, CA).

The amount of security awarded may be increased, see *Sturla v. Freccia* [1877] W.N. 166, 188; [1878] W.N. 161; *Republic of Costa Rica v. Erlanger* (1876) 3 Ch.D. 62; *Northampton Coal, etc., Co. v. Midland Waggon Co.* (1878) 7 Ch.D. 500; *Massey v. Allen* (1879) 12 Ch.D. 807.

"Sufficient security" or "security that in all the circumstances ... [is] just" does not mean complete security. Where a defendant was seeking £147,000 by way of security and the judge ordered £10,000 the Court of Appeal declined to interfere as the judge had correctly taken into account that the delay by the defendant in making the application had deprived the plaintiff of time to collect the security and that the plaintiff's strong and genuine claim would be stifled by ordering a larger sum (*Innovare Displays v. Corporate Booking Services* [1991] B.C.C. 174, CA).

Default in giving security (rr.1–3)—If the claimant makes default in giving security the court may strike out his claim or statement of case unless he remedies the default within a specified time (rr.3.1(3) and 3.4(2)(c)). R23.3.37

Return of security (rr.1–3)—A claimant against whom an order for security had been made R23.3.38

on account of his residence out of the jurisdiction was in Chancery allowed to get the order discharged at his own expense on coming to reside within the jurisdiction (*Mathews v. Chichester* (1861) 30 Beav. 135) but at common law the case was otherwise (*Badnall v. Haylay* (1838) 4 M. & W. 535) at any rate where security had actually been given, though not otherwise (*Place v. Campbell* (1848) 6 D. & L. 113). In *Tottenham v. Cove*, April 15, 1918, (unrep.). Astbury J. at Chambers adopted the common law practice and declined to order payment out of the deposit to a plaintiff who had returned from abroad. The order being good when made must stand in spite of subsequent circumstances (*Westenberg v. Mortimore* (1875) L.R. 10 C.P. 438). It may be doubted whether this practice would be followed today at any rate where the claimant's return from abroad is bona fide and permanent.

The conclusion expressed in the previous sentence of this note was approved by the Court of Appeal in *Parkinson v. Myer Wolff & Manley*, April 23, 1985, CA (unrep.). Just as a defendant may from time to time make further applications for security in the light of changed circumstances, so a claimant may be entitled to apply for variation or discharge of an order previously made if his circumstances have changed; whether the Court will accede to such an application will depend on the circumstances, the nature of the order previously made and any other material considerations (*ibid.*). A claimant cannot seek to have an order against him for security for costs varied or set aside by producing fresh evidence about his affairs at the date of the order. If however, he can show a material change of circumstances since the date of the order, he may apply for variation or discharge of the order. Whether such an application will be allowed depends on the circumstances and is a matter of discretion to be exercised by the Court (*Gordano Building Contractors Ltd v. Burgess* [1988] 1 W.L.R. 890, CA).

R23.3.39 **Payment out (rr.1–3)**—Successful claimants are entitled to have money paid in by them as security for costs paid out to them notwithstanding a stay of execution pending appeal (*The Bernisse* [1920] P. 1; *Comitato Portuario, etc. v. Instone* [1922] W.N. 260, CA). However, where money is ordered to be paid into court by way of security for costs it is the defendant's costs of trial that are secured. In the event of an appeal by an unsuccessful defendant against the order made at trial, an order requiring the sum lodged by way of security to remain in court pending the outcome of the appeal is within the legitimate scope of the jurisdictional basis on which an order for security is made under O.23 or under the Companies Act 1985, s.726 (*Stabilad Ltd v. Stephens & Carter Ltd* [1998] 4 All E.R. 129).

RSC ORDER 30

RECEIVERS

R30.0.1 **Contents**

Editorial Introduction

R30.0.2 This order deals with receivers appointed by the Court. It does not apply to receivers appointed out of Court by mortgagees or debenture holders (whether or not they are administrative receivers as defined in section 29(2) of the Insolvency Act 1986), nor does it apply to appointments of receivers under section 99 of the Mental Health Act 1983; these are governed by the Court of Protection Rules 1984 (S.I. 1984 No. 2035). RSC, O.30 will be replaced by Pt 37A CPR and a Pt 37A Practice Direction.

Related sources

R30.0.3
- Supreme Court Act 1981, s.37
- County Courts Act 1984, ss.38, 107
- Sched. 1, RSC, O.77, r.16 (para. R77.16)
- Sched. 1, RSC, O.115, r.8 (para. R115.8)
- Sched. 2, CCR, O.42, r.14 (para. C42.14)

Forms

R30.0.4 The following Chancery Masters' former Practice Form is relevant to RSC, O.30.
- PF30CH.

Order to apply to High Court and County Court

A1. This order applies to proceedings both in the High Court and the county court. R30.A1

Application of Order—O.30 applies to the High Court and county courts as part of the dovetailing exercise of the CPR. Before April 26, 1999 CCR, O.32, r.1 dealt with applications for the appointment of a receiver in the county courts and r.2 applies RSC, O.30, rr.3–8. R30.A1.1

Application for receiver and injunction

1.—(1) An application for the appointment of a receiver made in existing proceedings must be made in accordance with CPRPart 23 and the practice direction supplementing that Part. R30.1

(2) An application for an injunction ancillary or incidental to an order appointing a receiver may be joined with the application for such order.

(3) The relevant practice direction will apply to an application for the immediate grant of such an injunction.

Power to appoint receiver: generally—SCA 1981, s.37 enables the Court to appoint a receiver by interlocutory or final order when it appears just and convenient. R30.1.1

Application—The application to appoint a receiver will be made by application notice and such application can be combined with an application for an injunction if such injunction is ancillary or incidental to it. The application will usually be made to the Master or district judge. However, the Master or district judge will not make an injunction unless in connection with or ancillary to an Order appointing a receiver by way of equitable execution (PD Pt 2, para. 2.3(c)). R30.1.2

Form of Order—The Order should specify in respect of what property the receiver is appointed and the application will be supported by an affidavit or witness statement. Example of special cases of appointment of receivers are receivers appointed in the course of partnership proceedings and in probate claims. R30.1.3

Effect of appointment and powers of receiver—The appointment of the receiver is an equitable remedy. It vests no property in him, but operates as an injunction restraining other parties from getting in assets which the receiver has been appointed to receive. His duties are to collect the property over which he is appointed, and to pay it into Court, or as the Court directs. The receiver is an officer of the Court, and interference with his possession of property is punishable as a contempt of Court. R30.1.4

Cross-undertaking in damages—he Court has jurisdiction to require a party to give a cross-undertaking in damages for the benefit of third parties on appointing a receiver by way of equitable execution, just as it has when a Freezing (Mareva) injunction is ordered (*Allied Irish Bank v. Ashford Hotels Ltd* [1997] 3 All E.R. 309, CA, where, however, on the facts the Court in its discretion refused to require such a cross-undertaking). R30.1.5

Giving of security by receiver

2.—(1) A judgment or order directing the appointment of a receiver may include such directions as the court thinks fit as to the giving of security by the person appointed. R30.2

(2) Where by virtue of any judgment or order appointing a person named therein to be receiver a person is required to give security in accordance with this rule he must give security approved by the court duly to account for what he receives as receiver and to deal with it as the court directs.

(3) Unless the court otherwise directs, the security shall be by guarantee.

(4) The guarantee must be filed in the office or registry of the court in which the claim is proceeding and it shall be kept as of record until duly vacated.

Security—RSC, O.30, r.2 gives the court discretion whether or not to require security to be given and the Order will be made either without requiring security or subject to security or to security being given at some later stage but with permission to act at once on an undertaking to be answerable for what he shall receive or become liable to pay. The Order will provide that if security is not given within the time ordered the appointment will forthwith determine. In either R30.2.1

case the security is fixed by the Master or district judge and an application notice should be issued to proceed and fix the security as soon as possible after the Order appointing the receiver. The application should also deal with the receivers' remuneration and with directions as to receivers' accounts security is given by guarantees which is filed in court. A draft order should be submitted to the court with the application notice.

Remuneration of receiver

R30.3 **3.**—(1) A person appointed receiver shall be allowed such proper remuneration, if any, as may be authorised by the court.

(2) The court may direct that such remuneration shall be—

(a) fixed by reference to such scales or rates of professional charges as it thinks fit; or

(b) assessed by a costs judge or a district judge.

(3) Where remuneration is assessed by a costs judge or district judge following a direction under paragraph 2(b), CPR rules 44.4(1) and (2) and 44.5(1) will apply as though the remuneration were costs directed to be assessed on the standard basis.

(4) An appeal shall lie from the assessment in accordance with section 8 of CPR Part 47 (CPR rules 47.21 to 47.27).

R30.3.1 **Remuneration of receivers**—In practice the amount of remuneration is determined by reference to fixed scales of rates of professional charges and it will be a rare case where the Master or district judge fixes the rate of remuneration. However, assessment as opposed to fixing of remuneration can be ordered and this will be either by Costs judge or District judge.

R30.3.2 **Interim Orders and receivers lien**—The Court can in a suitable case make an interim Order requiring one of the parties to pay in receiver's remuneration and expenses. The receiver has a lien for his remuneration and expenses over all the assets subject to the receivership.

Service of order and notice

R30.4 **4.** A copy of the judgment or order appointing a receiver shall be served by the party having conduct of the proceedings on the receiver and all other parties to the proceedings in which the receiver has been appointed.

Receiver's accounts

R30.5 **5.**—(1) A receiver shall submit such accounts to such parties at such intervals or on such dates as the court may direct.

(2) Any party to whom a receiver is required to submit accounts may, on giving reasonable notice to the receiver, inspect, either personally or by an agent, the books and other papers relating to such accounts.

(3) Any party who is dissatisfied with the accounts of the receiver may give notice specifying the item or items to which objection is taken and requiring the receiver within not less than 14 days to file his accounts with the court and a copy of such notice shall be filed in the office or registry of the court dealing with the proceedings.

(4) Following an examination by or on behalf of the court of an item or items in an account to which objection is taken the result of such examination must be certified by a Master, the Admiralty Registrar, a district judge of the Family Division or a district judge, as the case may be, and an order may thereupon be made as to the incidence of any costs or expenses incurred.

R30.5.1 **Receiver's accounts**—Previously, the receiver's accounts had to be passed by the Court, and this procedure is still available in appropriate cases. However, the Court now normally, in the order appointing the receiver, or on the application to proceed, directs him to serve his accounts on the interested parties, and it is only if objection is taken by a party to any item or items in the accounts that the Court will become involved.

Payment into court by receiver

6. The court may fix the amounts and frequency of payments into court to be made by a receiver. **R30.6**

Default by receiver

7.—(1) Where a receiver fails to attend for the examination of any account of his, or fails to submit any account, provide access to any books or papers or do any other thing which he is required to submit, provide or do, he and any or all of the parties to the cause or matter in which he was appointed may be required to attend the court to show cause for the failure, and the court may give such directions as it thinks proper including, if necessary, directions for the discharge of the receiver and the appointment of another and the payment of costs. **R30.7**

(2) Without prejudice to paragraph (1) where a receiver fails to attend for the examination of any account of his or fails to submit any account or fails to pay into court on the date fixed by the court any sum required to be so paid, the court may disallow any remuneration claimed by the receiver and may, where he has failed to pay any such sum into court, charge him with interest at the rate currently payable in respect of judgment debts in the High Court on that sum while in his possession as receiver.

Receiver's default—It is the duty of the parties, primarily of the claimant, to bring to the attention of the Court any delay or other default on the part of a receiver and to apply for an appropriate remedy. **R30.7.1**

In cases of delay the Master or District judge may, without application by the parties, restore the matter to the list for a report.

Directions to receivers

8. A receiver may at any time request the court to give him directions and such request shall state in writing the matters with regard to which directions are required. **R30.8**

Application—This will often be by letter to the Court. In simple or non-contentious cases the Master or District judge will direct an answer by letter but may direct an application notice be issued and served on the parties. **R30.8.1**

Upon completion of the receivers duties an application should be made seeking an order for discharge and the vacation of any security. Such application should be made in the form of a draft order dealing with all directions sought and dealing with the payment out of all monies remaining in the hands of the receiver.

RSC ORDER 31

SALES, ETC. OF LAND BY ORDER OF COURT: CONVEYANCING COUNSEL OF THE COURT

Contents **R31.0.1**

Editorial Introduction

R31.0.2 The rules in Pt I of this Order apply where the Court orders that land should be sold and stipulates the manner in which a sale should be carried out and the certification of the result of a sale. The rules in Pt 2 are concerned with references by the Court to conveyancing counsel for investigation as to title etc. RSC, O.31 will be replaced by Pt 25A and a Pt 25A Practice Direction.

Practice Direction

R31.0.3 Practice Direction supplementing RSC, O.31 (see para. R31PD–001).

Order to apply to High Court and County Court

A1. This order applies to proceedings both in the High Court and the
R31.A1 county court.

I. SALES, ETC. OF LAND BY ORDER OF COURT

Power to order sale of land

R31.1 **1.** Where in any proceedings relating to any land it appears necessary or expedient for the purposes of the proceedings that the land or any part thereof should be sold, the court may order that land or part to be sold, and any party bound by the order and in possession of that land or part, or in receipt of the rents and profits thereof, may be compelled to deliver up such possession or receipt to the purchaser or to such other person as the court may direct.

In this order "land" includes any interest in, or right over, land.

R31.1.1 **Effect of Order**—Pt I of this Order which is scheduled to CPR Pt 50 deals with the making of Orders in respect of the sale of land. The Court is empowered to give such directions as are necessary r.2(2). It applies to both the Chancery Division of the High Court and the County Court. Often the Court will direct a sale "in such manner as the parties may agree or the court may direct in default of agreement". The application is made by application notice PD para. 2.

Pt II of the Order is concerned with reports or opinions of conveyancing counsel to the court.

R31.1.2 **Sale by personal representatives of real estate**—See O.85, r.2(3)(d).

R31.1.3 **Discharge of incumbrances on sale**—The L.P.A. 1925, s.50, provides for the payment into Court and invetment of a sum sufficient to answer any incumbrances on land sold by order of the Court, or out of Court, and also a sum to answer the contingency of further costs, etc., and for sale of land free from the incumbrance. This is expressly provided for in para. 3 of the PD to RSC, O.31. The application, if made in existing proceedings, is to be made in accordance with Pt 23.

Except under statutory provision, a sale of land by order of the Court must necessarily take place subject to the incumbrances who do not consent to the sale.

Manner of carrying out sale

R31.2 **2.**—(1) Where an order is made directing any land to be sold, the court may permit the party or person having the conduct of the sale to sell the land in such manner as he thinks fit, or may direct that the land be sold in such manner as the court may either by the order or subsequently direct for the best price that can be obtained, and all proper parties shall join in the sale and conveyance as the court shall direct.

(2) The court may give such directions as it thinks fit for the purpose of effecting the sale, including, without prejudice to the generality of the foregoing words, directions—

(a) appointing the party or person who is to have the conduct of the sale;

(b) fixing the manner of sale, whether by contract conditional on the

approval of the court, private treaty, public auction, tender or some other manner;
(c) fixing a reserve or minimum price;
(d) requiring payment of the purchase money into court or to trustees or other persons;
(e) for settling the particulars and conditions of sale;
(f) for obtaining evidence of the value of the property;
(g) fixing the security (if any) to be given by the auctioneer, if the sale is to be by public auction, and the remuneration to be allowed him;
(h) requiring an abstract of the title to be referred to conveyancing counsel of the court or some other conveyancing counsel for his opinion thereon and to settle the particulars and conditions of sale.

Directions—In the absence of agreement the Court will give directions in connection with in particular the reserve or minimum sale price and, if necessary, an auctioneer's or estate agent's remuneration. If a sale is by private treaty, the estate agent's remuneration is from his or her commission as agent, r.2(2) lists examples of directions that may be given. The Court will wish to ensure that the sale is completed and will make any necessary vesting order under section 47 of the Trustee Act 1925 or if appropriate appoint a person to convey pursuant to section 50 of the Trustee Act 1925. **R31.2.1**

Leave to bid—Under a sale directed by the Court any party to the claim, or his solicitor, desiring to purchase, should obtain leave to bid before the sale; but the sale will not necessarily be set aside because such leave has not been obtained. **R31.2.2**

If all parties are given leave to bid, the conduct of the sale may be given to an independent solicitor. As to the effect of leave to bid given to persons previously in a fiduciary position, see *Lewin on Trusts* (16th ed.), pp. 699–700.

Certifying result of sale

3.—(1) If either the court has directed payment of the purchase money into court or the court so directs, the result of a sale by order of the court must be certified— **R31.3**
(a) in the case of a sale by public auction, by the auctioneer who conducted the sale; and
(b) in any other case, by the solicitor of the party or person having the conduct of the sale,

and the court may require the certificate to be verified by the witness statement or affidavit of the auctioneer or solicitor, as the case may be.

(2) The solicitor of the party or person having the conduct of the sale must file the certificate and any witness statement or affidavit in the office of the court dealing with the proceedings.

Certifying result of sale—Such an order is rare but may be sought as protection of a party against future claims. **R31.3.1**

Mortgage, exchange or partition under order of the court

4. Rules 2 and 3 shall, so far as applicable and with the necessary modifications, apply in relation to the mortgage, exchange or partition of any land under an order of the court as they apply in relation to the sale of any land under such an order. **R31.4**

Partition—Trustees for sale have power to partition with the consent of the beneficiaries (s.7 of the Trusts of Land and Appointment of Trustees Act 1996, replacing section 28(3) of the LPA 1925, *Re Brooker* [1934] Ch. 610). The power of the Court to direct a partition is rarely exercised. **R31.4.1**

II. CONVEYANCING COUNSEL OF THE COURT

Reference of matters to conveyancing counsel of court

5. The court may refer to the conveyancing counsel of the court— **R31.5**
(a) any matter relating to the investigation of the title to any property

with a view to an investment of money in the purchase or on mortgage thereof, or with a view to the sale thereof;

(b) any matter relating to the settlement of a draft of a conveyance, mortgage, settlement or other instrument; and

(c) any other matter it thinks fit,

and may act upon his opinion in the matter referred.

R31.5.1 **Jurisdiction**—Both the High Court and the County Court can refer any matter of title to conveyancing counsel. The Practice Direction supplementing Pt 31 at paras 6 and 7 outline the procedure

Objection to conveyancing counsel's opinion

R31.6 **6.** Any party may object to the opinion given by any conveyancing counsel on a reference under rule 5, and if he does so the point in dispute shall be determined by the judge.

Obtaining counsel's opinion on reference

R31.8 **8.** The order referring any matter to conveyancing counsel of the court shall be recorded in the books of the court and a copy of such order shall be sent by the court to counsel and shall constitute sufficient authority for him to proceed with the reference.

PRACTICE DIRECTION—SALE, ETC. OF LAND BY ORDER OF COURT: CONVEYANCING COUNSEL OF THE COURT

R31PD–001 *This Practice Direction supplements RSC, Order 31 in Schedule 1 to the Civil Procedure Rules*

Sales, etc. of land by order of court

1. It should be noted that Order 31 now applies not only to proceedings in the High Court but also to county court proceedings.

2. An application under rule 1 of Order 31 should be made by issuing an application notice in the proceedings in question.

(Part 23 and the practice direction that supplements Part 23 contain rules about applications.)

3. If the land to be sold is subject to any incumbrance, the court may, on an application under section 50 of the Law of Property Act 1925, direct that a sum sufficient to provide for the incumbrance and for further costs and expenses to be paid into court. The land may then be sold free from the incumbrance (s.50(2) ibid.).

4. Any application under section 50 should, if made in existing proceedings, be made in accordance with CPR Part 23.

Manner of carrying out sale

5. Where a sale has been directed by the court, any party who wishes to bid should, before the sale, apply to the court for permission to do so. If all parties are given permission to bid, the conduct of the sale may be given to an independent person, usually a solicitor.

Conveyancing counsel to the court

R31PD–002 **6.** Not only the High Court but also a county court may refer a matter to conveyancing counsel of the court under Order 31 rule 5.

7.1 Notice of every reference under Order 31 rule 5 should be given to the Chief Chancery Master.

7.2 Unless the reference was to a particular conveyancing counsel, matters referred to conveyancing counsel of the court will be distributed among them in rotation in accordance with arrangements made by the Chief Chancery Master.

7.3 The proper officer of the court that has referred the matter must supply the conveyancing counsel to whom the matter has been allocated with a copy of the order of the court referring the matter and all other necessary documents.

7.4 The fees of conveyancing counsel will be fixed by a costs judge, subject to an appeal to the judge whose decision will be final (see the Costs Practice Direction relating to Part 44, paragraph 2.7).

RSC ORDER 44

PROCEEDINGS UNDER JUDGMENTS AND ORDERS: CHANCERY DIVISION

Contents R44.0.1

Editorial Introduction

This Order deals with the procedure under Chancery judgments and orders which require to be implemented, particularly orders for accounts and inquiries. It provides a machinery for the adjudication of claims and appeals from the Master's Order. The provisions of rr.1 to 10 of this Order apply to proceedings under a judgment or Order made in a county court: (a) in proceedings for, (i) the administration of the estate of a deceased person, (ii) the execution of a trust, or (iii) the sale of any property; or (b) in any other proceedings in the exercise of its equity jurisdiction (Practice Direction (Accounts, Inquiries, etc) para. 9.1, see 40PD–001). R44.0.2

Related sources

- CPR Part 10 R44.0.3
- Chancery Guide, Section 9, Proceedings after judgment (SCP 1999, Vol. 2, Section 2B, para. 2B–273)

Forms

The following Chancery Masters' former Practice Forms are relevant to RSC, O.44 R44.0.4

- PF 12—Advertisement for creditors (O.44, r.5)
- PF 13—Advertisement for claimants other than creditors (O.44, r.5)
- PF 14—Affidavit verifying list of creditors' claims (O.44, r.6)
- PF 15—List of claims sent in pursuant to advertisement by persons claiming to be creditors (O.44, r.6)
- PF 16—List of claims by persons claiming to be creditors other than those sent in pursuant to advertisement (O.44, r.6)
- PF 17—List of sums of money which may be due but in respect of which no claim has been received (O.44, r.6)
- PF 18—Notice to creditor to prove claim (O.44, r.7)
- PF 19—Notice to creditor or other claimant to produce documents (O.44, r.7(b))
- PF 20—Notice to creditor of allowance of claim (O.44, r.8)
- PF 21—Notice to creditor of disallowance of claim (O.44, r.8)
- PF 22—Order for administration: beneficiaries' action reconstituted as creditors' claim (Van Oppen Order)
- PF 23—Affidavit verifying list of claims other than creditors' claims (O.44, r.6(2)(c))
- PF 24—List of claims sent in pursuant to advertisement not being creditors' claims (O.44, r.6(2)(c))
- PF 25—List of claims not being creditors' claims other than those sent in pursuant to advertisement (O.44, r.6(2)(c))
- PF 26—Notice to claimant other than a creditor to prove a claim
- PF 29—Master's order stating the results of proceedings before him on the usual accounts and inquiries in an administration action (O.44, r.11)

Application to Orders

R44.1 **1.** In this order references to a judgment include references to an order.

Service of notice of judgment on person not a party

R44.2 **2.**—(1) Where in a claim for—

(a) the administration of the estate of a deceased person; or
(b) the execution of a trust; or
(c) the sale of any property,

the court gives a judgment or makes a direction which affects persons not parties to the claim, the court may when giving the judgment or at any stage of the proceedings under the judgment direct notice of the judgment to be served on any such person and any person so served shall, subject to paragraph (4), be bound by the judgment as if he had originally been a party to the claim.

(2) If it appears that it is not practicable to serve notice of a judgment on a person directed to be served the court may dispense with service and may also order that such person be bound by the judgment.

(3) Every notice of a judgment for service under this rule must be indorsed with a memorandum in Form No. 52A in the relevant practice direction and accompanied by a form of acknowledgment of service with such modifications as may be appropriate and the copy of the notice to be served shall be a sealed copy.

(4) A person served with notice of a judgment may, within one month after service of the notice on him, and after acknowledging service apply to the court to discharge, vary or add to the judgment.

(5) A person served with notice of a judgment may, after acknowledging service of the notice, attend the proceedings under the judgment.

(6) CPR Part 10 except for CPR rule 10.2 shall apply in relation to the acknowledgment of service of a notice of judgment as if the judgment were a claim form, the person by whom the notice is served were the claimant and the person on whom it is served were a defendant.

R44.2.1 **Effect of rule**—In the proceedings to which it applies, which includes certain county court proceedings (see para. R44.0.2 above), this rule provides for the giving on notice of judgment to persons who are not parties to the proceedings. The Court may "direct notice of the judgment to be served". A notice must be in the prescribed form and accompanied by an acknowledgment of service. The notice of a judgment must be endorsed with a memorandum in Form No. 52A accompanied by a form of acknowledgment of service.

Directions by the court

R44.3 **3.**—(1) Where a judgment given in a proceedings in the Chancery Division contains directions which make it necessary to proceed in private under the judgment the court may, when giving the judgment or at any time during proceedings under the judgment, give further directions for the conduct of those proceedings, including, in particular, directions with respect to—

(a) the manner in which any account or inquiry is to be prosecuted;
(b) the evidence to be adduced in support thereof;
(c) the preparation and service on the parties to be bound thereby of the draft of any deed or other instrument which is directed by the judgment to be settled by the court and the service of any objections to the draft;
(d) the parties required to attend all or any part of the proceedings;
(e) the representation by the same solicitors of parties who constitute a class and by different solicitors of parties who ought to be separately represented; and
(f) the time within which each proceeding is to be taken, and may fix a day or days for the further attendance of the parties.

(2) The court may revoke or vary any directions given under this rule.

Application of rules 5 to 8

4. Rules 5 to 8 apply— R44.4

(a) where in proceedings for the administration under the direction of the court of the estate of a deceased person the judgment directs any account of debts or other liabilities of the deceased's estate to be taken or any inquiry for next of kin or other ascertained claimants to be made; and

(b) where in proceedings for the execution under the direction of the court of a trust the judgment directs any such inquiry to be made,

and those rules shall, with the necessary modifications, apply where in any other proceedings the judgment directs an account of debts or other liabilities to be taken or any inquiry to be made.

Advertisements for creditors and other claimants

5. The court may, when giving a judgment or at any stage of proceedings under a judgment, give directions for the issue of advertisements for creditors or other claimants and may fix the time within which creditors and claimants may respond. R44.5

Examination of claims

6.—(1) Where an account of debts or other liabilities of the estate of a deceased person has been directed, such party as the court may direct must— R44.6

(a) examine the claims of persons claiming to be creditors of the estate;

(b) determine, so far as he is able, to which of such claims the estate is liable; and

(c) at least seven clear days before the time appointed for adjudicating on claims, make a witness statement or affidavit stating his findings and his reasons for them and listing all the other debts of the deceased which are or may still be due.

(2) Where an inquiry for next of kin or other unascertained claimants has been directed, such party as the court may direct must—

(a) examine the claims;

(b) determine, so far as he is able, which of them are valid; and

(c) at least seven clear days before the time appointed for adjudicating on claims, make witness statement or affidavit stating his findings and his reasons for them.

(3) If the personal representatives or trustees concerned are not the parties directed by the court to examine claims, they must join with the party directed to examine them in making the witness statement or affidavit required by this rule.

Adjudication on claims

7. For the purpose of adjudicating on claims the court may— R44.7

(a) direct any claim to be investigated in such manner as it thinks fit;

(b) require any claimant to attend and prove his claim or to furnish further particulars or evidence of it; or

(c) allow any claim after or without proof thereof.

Notice of adjudication

8. The court shall give directions that there be served on every creditor whose claim or any part thereof has been allowed or disallowed, and who did not attend when the claim was disposed of, a notice informing him of that fact. R44.8

Interest on debts

9.—(1) Where an account of the debts of a deceased person is directed by any judgment, then, unless the deceased's estate is insolvent or the court otherwise orders, interest shall be allowed— R44.9

(a) on any such debt as carries interest, at the rate it carries; and
(b) on any other debt, from the date of the judgment at the rate payable on judgment debts at that date.

(2) A creditor who has established his debt in proceedings under the judgment and whose debt does not carry interest shall be entitled to interest on his debt in accordance with paragraph (1)(b) out of any assets which may remain after satisfying the costs of the proceedings, the debts which have been established and the interest on such of those debts as by law carry interest.

(3) For the purpose of this rule "debt" includes funeral, testamentary or administration expenses and, in relation to expenses incurred after the judgment, for the reference in paragraph (1)(b) to the date of the judgment there shall be substituted a reference to the date when the expenses became payable.

Interest on legacies

R44.10 **10.** Where an account of legacies is directed by any judgment, then, subject to any directions contained in the will or codicil in question and to any order made by the court, interest shall be allowed on each legacy at the rate of 6 per cent per annum beginning at the expiration of one year after the testator's death.

Master's order

R44.11 **11.**—(1) The result of proceedings before a Master under a judgment shall be stated in the form of an order.

(2) Subject to any direction of the Master under paragraph (3) or otherwise an order under this rule shall have effect as a final order disposing of the proceedings in which it is made.

(3) An order under this rule shall contain such directions as the Master thinks fit as to the further consideration of the proceedings in which it is made.

(4) Every order made under this rule shall have immediate binding effect on the parties to the proceedings in which it is made and copies of the order shall be served on such of the parties as the Master may direct.

Appeal against Master's order

R44.12 **12.** Subject to Order 58, rule 2, rule 1 of that order shall apply to an order made pursuant to rule 11 above, save that—

(a) except where paragraph (e) below applies, the notice referred to in Order 58, rule 1(2) shall state the grounds of the appeal, and must be issued within 14 days after the order is made;

(b) [omitted by S.I. 1999 No. 1008];

(c) no fresh evidence (other than evidence as to matters which have occurred after the date of the Master's order) shall be admitted except on special grounds;

(d) the judge hearing the appeal shall have the same power to draw inferences of fact as has the Court of Appeal under Order 59, rule 10(3);

(e) if the order is to be acted on by the Accountant-General or is an order passing a receiver's account, notice of appeal must be issued not later than two clear days after the making of the order and, where the order is to be acted on by the Accountant-General, a copy of it must be served on the Accountant-General as soon as practicable after it is made.

RSC ORDER 45

ENFORCEMENT OF JUDGMENTS AND ORDERS: GENERAL

Contents R45.0.1

Editorial Introduction

Although the term "writ" has been abolished for the purpose of issuing proceedings (see Part 7) it survives for the purpose of enforcement. R45.0.2

It can be forcibly argued that the "Access to Justice" reforms have started at the wrong end. "Access to the Court" is not the same as "access to justice" and it is hardly justice if the successful party is unable to enforce the judgment which the court has granted. The law on enforcement must now be regarded as unsatisfactory and in urgent need of reform.

The series of orders, formerly contained in the RSC and now in Schedule 1 to the CPR, comprising Orders 45 to 52 inclusive together contain the methods of enforcement of the judgments and orders of the High Court. They should be read together as they deal with the various ways in which the successful party can employ the machinery of the High Court towards obtaining satisfaction of his judgment or compelling compliance therewith or obedience thereto.

It is still a feature of the civil justice system that judgments are not enforced automatically by the court. It is for the successful party to decide when and how to enforce the judgment.

Orders 45–52 do not apply in respect of any Order against the Crown (O.77, r.15(1) and see *Franklin v. The Queen (No. 2)* [1974] Q.B. 205; [1973] 3 All E.R. 861, CA).

These Orders apply to a judgment or order of the Court of Appeal as they apply to the High Court (SCA 1981, s.15(4)).

Order 45 itself deals in a general way with the methods of enforcement of certain judgments and orders, namely:

(a) for the payment of money (rr.1 and 2)
(b) for possession of land (r.3)
(c) for delivery of goods (r.4); and
(d) to do or abstain from doing any act (rr.5, 6 and 7).

Related sources R45.0.3

- RSC, O.17—Interpleader
- RSC, O.46—Writs of Execution: General
- RSC, O.47—Writs of Fieri Facias
- RSC, O.48—Examination of Judgment Debtor, etc.
- RSC, O.49—Garnishee Proceedings
- RSC, O.50—Charging Orders, Stop Orders, etc.
- RSC, O.51—Receivers: Equitable Execution
- RSC, O.52—Committal
- CCR, O.25—Enforcement of Judgments and Orders: General

Forms

The following forms (formerly included amongst the Prescribed Forms in Appendix A to the RSC) are relevant to O.45. These forms are included in Table 2 (Practice Forms) attached to Practice Direction (Forms) and may be found in SCP 1999, Vol. 2, Section 1A, paras 1A–49 to 1A–50, 1A–53 to 1A–59 and 1A–65 to 1A–68: R45.0.4

- PF No 50—Judgment for defendant's costs on discontinuance (r.15)
- PF No 51—Judgment for costs after acceptance of money paid into court (r.15)
- PF No 53—Writ of fieri facias (r.12)
- PF No 54—Writ of fieri facias on order for costs (r.12)
- PF No 55—Notice of Seizure (r.2)
- PF No 56—Writ of fieri facias after levy of part (r.12)
- PF No 57—Writ of fieri facias against personal representative (r.12)
- PF No 58—Writ of fieri facias de bonis ecclesiastics (r.12)
- PF No 59—Writ of sequestrari de bonis ecclesiasticis (r.12)
- PF No 64—Writ of delivery: delivery of goods, damages and costs (r.12)
- PF No 65—Writ of delivery: delivery of goods or value, damages, costs (r.12)
- PF No 66—Writ of possession (r.12)
- PF No 66A—Writ of possession under Order 113 (r.12)
- PF No 67—Writ of sequestration (r.12)

The following Queen's Bench Masters' Practice Forms are relevant to O.45. These forms are included in Table 2 (Practice Forms) attached to Practice Direction (Forms) and may be found in SCP 1999, Vol. 2, Section 1B, paras 1B–65 to 1B–69 and 1B–104:

- PF 87—Praecipe for writ of sequestration (O.45)
- PF 88—Praecipe for writ of possession (O.45)
- PF 89—Praecipe for writ of possession and fieri facias combined (O.45)
- PF 90—Praecipe for writ of delivery (O.45)
- PF 91—Form of affidavit in support of application to enforce judgment for possession (O.45, r.3)
- PF 141—Affidavit of personal service of judgment or order (O.45, r.7)

Enforcement of judgment, etc., for payment of money

R45.1 **1.**—(1) Subject to the provisions of these rules, a judgment or order for the payment of money, not being a judgment or order for the payment of money into court, may be enforced by one or more of the following means, that is to say—

(a) writ of fieri facias;
(b) garnishee proceedings;
(c) a charging order;
(d) the appointment of a receiver;
(e) in a case in which rule 5 applies, an order of committal;
(f) in such a case, writ of sequestration.

(2) Subject to the provisions of these rules, a judgment or order for the payment of money into court may be enforced by one or more of the following means, that is to say—

(a) the appointment of a receiver;
(b) in a case in which rule 5 applies, an order of committal;
(c) in such a case, writ of sequestration.

(3) Paragraphs (1) and (2) are without prejudice to any other remedy available to enforce such a judgment or order as is therein mentioned or to the power of a court under the Debtors Acts 1869 and 1878, to commit to prison a person who makes default in paying money adjudged or ordered to be paid by him, or to the right of a person prosecuting a judgment or order for the payment of money to a person to apply under section 105(1) of the County Courts Act 1984, to have the judgment or order enforced in a county court, or to the enactments relating to bankruptcy or the winding up of companies.

(4) In this order references to any writ shall be construed as including references to any further writ in aid of the first mentioned writ.

R45.1.1 **Effect of rule**—This rule deals with the enforcement of money judgments. See also rule 13. The term "judgment" includes "decree" (SCA 1981, s.151(1) (SCP 1999, Vol. 2, Section 20A, para. 20A–555)).

An order made under the Inheritance (Provision for Family and Dependants) Act 1975, is not an order for the payment of money and the proper course to enforce such an order is by proceedings for administration of the estate (*Re Jennery (dec'd.)* [1967] Ch. 280; [1967] 2 W.L.R. 201; [1967] 1 All E.R. 691).

Rule 1 distinguishes sharply between a judgment or order (a) for the payment of money to a person (para. (1)) and (b) for the payment of money into Court (para. (2)) for which limited modes of enforcement are provided see *Re Greer* [1895] 2 Ch. 217).

The judgment or order must be for payment to a person and not to an account in a bank (*Re Leeds Banking Co.* (1866) L.R. 1 Ch. 150).

Rule 1 applies to a judgment or order for the payment of costs. Execution for costs cannot issue until the sum payable has been ascertained following assessment (the term "assessment" has replaced the former term "taxation"). Production of the judgment or order for payment of costs together with the certificate of the costs judge certifying the sum due is required before execution can issue.

Rule 1 applies to a judgment or order for the payment of costs as it applies to the payment of money. The ordinary form of order to tax on a client's application provides that the solicitor do "refund" what, if anything, he is found to have been overpaid. This expression constitutes an order to pay within this rule, and execution issues as of course (*Re Newson*, Pickford J. in Chambers, July 11, 1907 (unrep.)).

Execution for costs cannot issue on any judgment for "costs to be taxed", until the certificate for costs has been filed and the costs duly entered up (*Re Crump, ex p. Crump* (1891) 64 L.T. 799). Both in ChD and in QBD a judgment or order for costs to be taxed is enforceable by execution on production of the judgment or order and taxing-officer's certificate. Unless specially directed by the judgment or order, service thereof is not required. Where service is required an affidavit of service must be filed before execution can issue.

Rule 1 applies to an undertaking by a solicitor to pay money or costs. If such an undertaking given by a solicitor is not performed, an order may be made for payment (*Re Woodfin & Wray* (1882) 30 W.R. 422; *Swyny v. Harland* [1894] 1 Q.B. 707). Such an undertaking will be enforced though not given in legal proceedings nor to a client, and though no discreditable conduct is alleged (*United Mining and Finance Corp. Ltd v. Becher* [1910] 2 K.B. 296).

Modes of enforcing judgment or order for payment of money to a person—A judgment or order for the payment of money to a person may be enforced by any of the six methods listed in para. (1) which are not alternative, but cumulative remedies. On the other hand, if the judgment or order does not and as a general rule it will not, specify a time for the payment of the money to a person, the method of enforcement by way of an order of committal or writ of sequestration will not be available (subparas (e) and (f)). R45.1.2

For writ of *fieri facias*, see nn. under this rule, paras R45.1.6 *et seq.* and O.47.

For garnishee proceedings, see O.49.

For charging order, see O.50, r.(1) (charging order on land) O.50, rr.2–7 (charging order on securities) O.50, r.8 (charging order on fund in Court).

For appointment of receiver, see O.51.

For order of committal, see O.52.

For writ of sequestration, see O.46, r.5.

In addition to the above methods of enforcement, a judgment or order for the payment of money to a person may be enforced:

(a) under the Debtors Acts 1869 and 1878, see notes under this rule, but subject to section 11 of the AJA 1970 (see SCP 1999, Vol. 2, Section 20B, para. 20B–77).
(b) by the bankruptcy of a person or partnership or the winding up of companies.
(c) by enforcement under section 105(1) of the County Courts Act 1984, which provides that a judgment or order of the High Court for the payment of money to a person shall, on an application being made to the county court by the party prosecuting the judgment, be enforceable under s.85 of the Act as if it were a judgment of that Court.

It will be noted that a judgment for the recovery of money from a person cannot be enforced by an order of committal or writ of sequestration, nor can a supplemental order be made fixing a time for payment by a certain day or limiting the time within which it is to be made, so as to found a right to sequestration or committal in default of payment (*Re Oddy* [1906] 1 Ch. 93; *Hulbert v. Cathcart* [1894] 1 Q.B. 244).

Modes of enforcing judgment or order for payment of money into Court—Note the methods of enforcement prescribed by O.45, r.1(2). Such a judgment may be enforced, not only by an order of committal or writ of sequestration under r.5, but also by the appointment of a receiver (*Stanger-Leathes v. Stanger-Leathes* [1882] W.N. 71; *Re Coney* (1885) 29 Ch.D. 993; *Re Whiteley* (1887) 56 L.T. 846; *Re Pemberton* [1907] W.N. 118). R45.1.3

In *Lady de la Pole v. Dick* (1885) 29 Ch.D. 351, an order for payment into Court was varied on appeal by directing payment to the plaintiff in order that it might be better enforced.

The evidence required on issuing execution for non-payment of money into Court is a certificate of the Accountant General that the money is not in Court. A certificate of non-lodgment of money in Court, under the Direction of May 18, 1946, will certify that no lodgment has been made up to and including the day it is dated. In the Ch D the certificate will be available on the second day after that on which it was requested, but in the QBD it will be available at the date agreed at the time that the request is lodged at the Court Funds Office. The want of such evidence is cured by the acknowledgment of service of the opposite party, and his not disputing the facts (*Treherne v. Dale* (1884) 27 Ch.D. 66).

The reality is, however, that it will rarely be necessary to enforce an order for payment of money into court. If a party so ordered does not comply the court will invariably use its case management powers (see Part 3) to stay or dismiss the claim or defence (as the case may be) of the defaulting party.

Enforcement of money judgments by writ of fi. fa.

R45.1.4 **Time for issue of writ of fi. fa.**—The writ of *fi. fa.* may issue to enforce a judgment or order for the payment to, or for the recovery by, any person, of money or costs. The practice is clear, that a writ of *fi. fa.* may issue immediately upon payment becoming due and as a matter of course without leave and without the necessity for prior notice to, or for prior service of the judgment or order, upon the debtor (see *Land Credit Company of Ireland v. Fermoy* (1870) L.R. 5 Ch. 323; *Hopton v. Robertson* (1884) W.N. 77; 23 Q.B.D. 126n.; *Re A Solicitor* (1884) 33 W.R. 131). Accordingly, a judgment in the ordinary form of requiring the defendant to pay money to a person, is enforceable by writ of *fi. fa.*, immediately it is entered, even though no time is specified for the payment to be made and even though notice of the judgment, still less the judgment itself, has not been served on the debtor. On the other hand, where the judgment or order directs payment within a specified time, the writ will issue immediately after, but not before, such time has expired; and where the judgment or order directs payment within a certain time after service on the debtor, the writ will issue immediately after, but not before, due service has been effected upon the debtor and proof of such service duly lodged with the Court. Similarly, if the judgment or order is conditional, the writ will issue immediately after, but not before, there has been default in complying with the condition.

Where the judgment or order is for the payment (or recovery) of money and costs to be assessed, separate writs of *fi. fa.* may issue to enforce payment of the judgment debt and the costs after they have been assessed (see O.47, r.3).

It is wrongful to issue a writ of *fi. fa.* after payment, and therefore a person (including the solicitor for a party) who issues execution after payment (*Clissold v. Cratchley* [1910] 2 K.B. 244) or after a valid tender (*Cubitt v. Gamble* (1919) 35 T.L.R. 223) is liable to trespass. Ignorance of the payment is no defence. Similarly, it is submitted that it is wrongful to issue a writ of *fi. fa.* for a sum greater than the amount actually due at the time for its issue.

If neither the judgment creditor nor a person authorised by him is in England to receive the money, a stay of execution will be granted on payment into Court (*Re A Debtor*) [1912] 1 K.B. 53).

There is now a "Sheriff Lodgment Centre" based at 2 Sargeant's Inn, Fleet Street, London EC4 to which a judgment credit need only fax the details of a county court judgment over £600 or any High Court judgment and the Centre will

(a) bring up from the county court by N293A the judgment
(b) obtain a Writ of Fieri Facis from the RCJ
(c) send it to the correct sheriff nationwide
(d) and obtain a return.

R45.1.5 **Nature of writ of fi. fa.**—The writ of *fi. fa.* is the mode for the enforcement of a money judgment by the seizure and sale of the debtor's goods and chattels sufficient to satisfy the judgment debt and costs of the execution. The writ is expressed in the general form of a royal direction to the sheriff of the county in which the goods of the debtor are situate to seize in execution such of the goods of the debtor within that county as may be sufficient to satisfy the amount of the judgment debt together with the current rate of interest thereon until payment and the costs of the execution including the sheriff's costs and charges. The writ further directs the sheriff to pay the judgment creditor the amount levied (other than his own costs and charges) and to indorse on the writ a statement of how he has executed it, sending a copy of such statement to the judgment creditor.

For forms of writs of *fi. fa.* see Practice Direction (Forms) Table 2, Forms 53–63 (SCP 1999, Vol. 2, Section 1A, paras 1A–53 to 1A–63).

The prescribed forms must be used wherever applicable with such variations as the circumstances of the particular case require (O.1, r.9(1)), *i.e.* having regard to the directions contained in the judgment or order itself (*Boswell v. Coaks* (1887) 36 W.R. 65). Variation will be required in the case of a judgment expressed in foreign currency.

The writ must correspond with the judgment in the names of the parties and to the subject-matter of the judgment, and should be directed to the proper person.

The writ of *fi. fa.* should be delivered to the sheriff for execution and not to the sheriff's officer, for he is not the person liable if the writ is not properly executed (*Triminger v. Keene* [1882] W.N. 106).

For a list of the sheriffs to whom the writ may be directed, see *Chitty and Jacob*, Form 952 and para. R45.1.4 "Sheriff Lodgment Centre".

At the request of the person delivering a writ to him for execution, the sheriff must give a receipt for it (Sheriffs Act 1887, s.10).

The writ must bear the date of the day and the hour of its issue.

The writ must be indorsed with the name and address of the solicitor actually issuing it out, and if he is acting as agent for another solicitor, the name and address of such other solicitor. Where there has been a change of solicitor, the new solicitor must place his name on the record before he can issue execution in the action. (See Pt 42.)

The writ must also be indorsed with the place of residence or business of the judgment creditor, whether he is acting in person or not.

Although not so prescribed by the forms the address of the person against whom it is issued should also be indorsed on the writ. This is desirable for the assistance of the sheriff and his officers for the purpose of enforcement.

Enforcement of judgment debt in foreign currency by writ of fi. fa.—Where the judgment creditor desires to proceed to enforce a judgment expressed in a foreign currency by the issue of a writ of *fi. fa.* the *praecipe* for the issue of the writ must first be indorsed and signed by or on behalf of the solicitor for the judgment creditor or by the judgment creditor if he is acting in person with the requisite certificate (see para. 11(a) of the Practice Direction (Judgment: Foreign Currency) [1976] 1 W.L.R. 83; [1976] 1 All E.R. 669 (SCP 1999, Vol. 2, Section 2A, para. 2A–47)). The amount so certified will then be entered in the writ of *fi. fa.* by adapting Form 53 to meet the circumstances of the case but substituting the requisite recital (see *ibid.*, para. 11(b)). **R45.1.6**

Effect of writ of fi. fa.—The SCA 1981, s.138 (replacing the Sale of Goods Act 1893, s.26) provides that a writ of *fi. fa.* or other writ of execution against the goods shall bind the property in the hands of the execution debtor as from the time when the writ is delivered to the sheriff to be executed, and that, for the better manifestation of such time, it shall be the duty of the sheriff, without fee, upon the receipt of any such writ to indorse upon the back thereof the hour, day, month, and year when he received the same. Equally, in the county court, the bailiff must indorse on the back of the warrant of execution the hour, day, month and year when he received the application for it (County Courts Act 1984, s.99(3)). **R45.1.7**

Such a writ will not prejudice the title to such goods acquired by any person in good faith and for valuable consideration, unless such person has at the time when he acquired his title notice that such writ or any other writ, by virtue of which the goods of the execution debtor might be seized or attached, had been delivered to and remained unexecuted in the hands of the sheriff.

In the county court, the time at which the application for a warrant is made, and not the time at which it was delivered to the bailiff for execution, is the time to be regarded under s.138 (*Murgatroyd v. Wright* [1907] 2 K.B. 333).

The question whether there is an effective seizure of the goods by the sheriff's officer under the writ of execution is a question of fact and there may be such a seizure even though the debtor refuses to sign a possession agreement, and even though the sheriff's officer leaves the premises in which the goods are, and although the debtor may pass a good title to a purchaser who buys in good faith and for valuable consideration without notice of the writ or seizure under s.138(2) of the Act, the goods remain subject to the sheriff's rights, and therefore any sale by such purchaser, though it may pass a good title, will be in breach of the implied warranties as to quiet possession and freedom from encumbrances for which he will be liable in damages (*Lloyds and Scottish Finance Ltd v. Modern Cars and Caravans (Kingston)* [1966] 1 Q.B. 764; [1964] 2 All E.R. 732).

The term of this section "shall bind the property in the goods of the execution debtor" simply means that on delivery of the goods to him, the sheriff acquires a legal right to seize sufficient of the debtor's goods to satisfy the account specified in the writ but from such delivery the goods become, as it were, impressed with the superimposed right of the sheriff (see *Samuel v. Duke* (1838) 3 M & W. 622). Thereafter, the debtor cannot deal with his goods except by sale to a bona fide purchaser for value and without notice of the delivery of the writ.

It has been held that notice to the judgment debtor of the delivery of the writ of execution to the sheriff was notice to the trustees of a deed of assignment for the benefit of his creditors, subsequently resolved upon and executed by the judgment debtors (*Ehlers v. Kauffman* (1883) 49 L.T. 806).

If a deed of assignment to a trustee for creditors is revocable, as not having been communicated to any of them, at the time when the writ of execution is delivered to the sheriff the execution creditors are entitled to the goods (*Ellis & Co. v. Cross* [1915] 2 K.B. 654).

The property in the goods remains in the debtor until sale (*Giles v. Grover* (1832) 1 Cl. & Fin. 72).

Priority of writs of fi. fa.—The priority as between writs of *fi. fa.* depends upon the time each is delivered to the sheriff for execution (see SCA 1981, s.138, and above). **R45.1.8**

As between writs issued out of the High Court and warrants of execution issued from a county court against the same party, the priority to the goods seized is determined by the priority of the time of the delivery of the writ to the sheriff to be executed, which will be found indorsed on the back of the writ or the time at which the warrant is received by the bailiff of the enforcing county court, which will be found indorsed on the back of the warrant, see section 138 of SCA 1981, replacing section 26 of the Sale of Goods Act 1893 which as to warrants issued out of different county courts negatived *Bistall Candle Co v. Daniels* [1908] 2 K.B. 254.

R45.1.9 **Duties of sheriff**—As a rule, a sheriff in executing a writ must have regard to the interests and instructions of the execution creditor as far as compatible with his duty (*Re Crook* (1894) 63 L.J.Q.B. 756).

The truth is that the sheriff though for some purposes is an agent of the party who puts the writ in his hands, is not a mere agent. He is a public functionary having indeed duties to perform towards those who set him in motion analogous, in many respects, to those of an agent towards his principal; but he also has duties towards others and particularly towards those against whom the writs in his hands are directed (see *per* Lord Cranworth L.C. in *Hooper v. Lane* (1857) 6 HLCas. 443, 549–550, cited in *Re A Debtor (No. 2 of 1977), ex p. the Debtor v. Goacher* [1979] 1 W.L.R. 956; [1979] 1 All E.R. 870).

Where the writ has been withdrawn, the sheriff cannot re-enter without further instructions from the execution creditor, and, if a second execution creditor subsequently issues a writ against the same debtor the sheriff is justified in executing it without notice to the former execution creditor (*Shaw v. Kirby* (1888) 52 J.P. 182).

Although an execution creditor or his solicitor, after delivery of the writ to the sheriff, may withdraw the execution or postpone the sale of chattels seized under it, there is no implied power in the managing clerk of the solicitor to do so (*Whyte v. Nutting* [1897] 2 Ir.R. 241).

As to the position of the under-sheriff on the death of the sheriff, see *Gloucestershire Banking Co. v. Edwards* (1887) 20 Q.B.D. 107; Sheriffs Act 1887, s.25.

As to the liability of the sheriff under s.29 of the Sheriffs Act 1887, for neglect of his officer, see *Bagge v. Whitehead* [1892] 2 Q.B. 355.

R45.1.10 **Sale by sheriff without notice of claim**—Where the sheriff sells goods in the possession of the judgment debtor which he has seized under an execution without any claim having been made to such goods, the sheriff is protected from any liability by the Supreme Court Act 1981, s.138B(1) which re-enacted the Bankruptcy and Deeds of Arrangement Act 1913, s.15 unless it is proved that he had notice or ought by making reasonable inquiry have ascertained that the goods were not the property of the judgment debtor (*The Observer Ltd v. Gordon* [1983] 1 W.L.R. 1008; [1983] 2 All E.R. 945).

Moreover, where the claimant has a "substantial grievance" on the ground that the sheriff has wrongfully, but without misconduct, seized his goods under a writ of *fi.fa.* and sold them at auction at a price greatly under their value, the onus is on him to show that there was a substantial difference between the value of the goods at the date of the sale and the price in fact realised, and in the absence of such proof, the sheriff is entitled to an order protecting him from proceedings by the claimant (*Neumann v. Bakeaway Ltd* [1983] 1 W.L.R. 1016, CA).

R45.1.11 **Forcible entry**—The sheriff is not entitled to break open the outer door in order to levy execution (*Semayne's Case* (1604) 5 Co. 91) nor to force his way in for the purpose of gaining entry (*Vaughan v. McKenzie* [1969] 1 Q.B. 557; [1968] 1 All E.R. 1154, DC). But he may break open the outer door of the judgment debtor's workshop or other building not being his dwelling-house, nor connected with the dwelling-house (*Hodder v. Williams* [1895] 2 Q.B. 663). This applies as well to distress for rent as to execution (*American Concentrated Must Corp. v. Hendry* [1893] W.N. 67, 82).

A Sheriff already with walking possession of goods may lawfully break the lock to gain access to a house to seize the goods (*McLeod v. Butterwick, The Times*, March 12, 1996).

R45.1.12 **Landlord**—As to the rights of a landlord to payment of arrears of rent by a judgment creditor, see Insolvency Act 1986, s.347(6). Sections 6 and 7 of Landlord and Tenant Act 1709 did not apply as against execution creditors in favour of persons entitled to distrain (*Lewis v. Davies* [1914] 2 K.B. 469, CA). As to the effect of petition for winding up, see *Re British Salicylates Ltd* [1919] 2 Ch. 155.

R45.1.13 **Possession, abandonment of**—Where a sheriff, who has seized goods under a writ of *fi. fa.* goes out of possession, the question whether in so doing he has abandoned possession or not is always a question of fact (*Bagshawes v. Deacon* [1898] 2 Q.B. 173; *National Commercial Bank of Scotland v. Arcam Demolition, etc.* [1966] 2 Q.B. 593; [1966] 3 All E.R. 113, CA). See also *Lloyds and Scottish Finance Ltd v. Modern Cars and Caravans (Kingston)* [1966] 1 Q.B. 764; [1964] 2 All E.R. 732.

R45.1.14 **Wrongful seizure by sheriff**—Where a sheriff, being misled by an indorsement put upon a writ of *fi. fa.* by the solicitor of the execution creditor, seized goods of the wrong person, it was held that the execution creditor was liable in an action of trespass (*Morris v. Salberg* (1889) 22 Q.B.D. 614; see, too, *Jarmain v. Hooper* (1843) 6 M. & G. 827; *Smith v. Keal* (1882) 9 Q.B.D. 340; *Lee v. Rumilly* (1891) 7 T.L.R. 303; *Hewitt v. Spiers & Pond* (1897) 13 T.L.R. 64). But where there is nothing untrue in the directions in the indorsement so as to mislead the sheriff, the action is not maintainable against the judgment creditor (*Condy v. Blaiberg* (1891) 7 T.L.R. 424, where the sheriff seized the goods of a third person). As to the exemption of a sheriff from penalties for an innocent mistake, see *Lee v. Dangar* [1892] 2 Q.B. 337; and as to exemption from liability for the wrongful act of his own officer, see *Bagge v. Whitehead* [1892] 2 Q.B. 355.

Where neither the premises on which the goods are seized, nor the goods, belong to the execution debtor, the sheriff may, upon interpleader proceedings, be protected against an action for trespass as well as for wrongful seizure, if no substantial grievance has been done to the person whose premises are wrongfully entered (*Smith v. Critchfield* (1885) 14 Q.B.D. 873) and the evidence shows that the sheriff has made all necessary and proper inquiries (*Salberg v. Morris* (1888) 4 T.L.R. 47). But the sheriff was held not to be entitled to protection against an action of trespass where a substantial grievance had been done (*De Coppett v. Barnett* (1901) 17 T.L.R. 273).

As to the protection of a sheriff selling goods of a third party in the possession of a judgment debtor see the Supreme Court Act 1981, s.138B(1)(b) which re-enacted the Bankruptcy Act 1913, s.15.

Receiver, interference with possession of—The Court will not protect a sheriff who executes process after notice from a receiver that he is in possession (*Try v. Try* (1851) 13 Beav. 422; *Rock v. Cook* (1848) 2 Ph. 691). A sheriff who seizes goods in the possession of a receiver is guilty of a contempt of Court (*Lane v. Sterne* (1862) 3 Giff. 629) and may be committed though the act is really that of the under-sheriff, and there is no reason to infer that it is the personal act of the sheriff (*Russell v. East Anglian Ry.* (1850) 3 Mac. & G. 112). **R45.1.15**

Reserve and Auxiliary Forces (Protection of Civil Interests) Act 1951—A judgment or order for the payment or recovery of a sum of money may not (except in certain specified cases) without the leave of the Court be enforced by execution or otherwise against a person protected by this Act (s.2(1)). **R45.1.16**

Crown—Save as provided by section 25(1)–(3) of the Crown Proceedings Act 1947, no execution or attachment or process in the nature of execution or attachment can issue for enforcing payment by the Crown of money or costs, and no person can be made individually liable under any order for payment by the Crown, or any government department, or any officer of the Crown as such, for any such money or costs (*ibid.*, subs. (4) (SCP 1999, Vol. 2, Section 21L)). But see RSC, O.77, r.16. **R45.1.17**

Foreign sovereign—A sovereign state does not by initiating proceedings in this country render its property within the jurisdiction liable to execution to enforce an order for payment of costs (*Duff Dev. Co. v. Kelantan* [1923] 1 Ch. 385). See also State Immunity Act 1978, s.20. **R45.1.18**

Goods liable to seizure under writ of fi. fa.—At common law, only the goods and chattels of the judgment debtor could be taken in execution under a writ of *fi. fa.* By the Judgments Act 1838, s.12, money and banknotes, and other specified choses in action may also be seized, but they cannot be seized in execution after the death of the judgment debtor (*Johnson v. Pickering* [1908] 1 K.B. 1, CA). A pawnbroker's interest in redeemable pledges is the subject of execution under a writ of *fi. fa.* (*Re Rollason* (1887) 34 Ch.D. 495). **R45.1.19**

An agreement that the wearing apparel of the wife provided by the husband is to remain his property is valid against execution creditors of the wife (*Rondeau v. Marks* [1918] 1 K.B. 75).

Goods exempt from seizure—Every Sheriff or Officer executing any writ of execution issued from the High Court against the goods of any person may by virtue of it seize: **R45.1.20**

(a) any of that person's goods except
  (i) such tools, books, vehicles and other items of equipment as are necessary to that person for use personally by him in his employment, business or vocation
  (ii) such clothing, bedding, furniture, household equipment and provisions as are necessary for satisfying the basic domestic needs of that person and his family

(Supreme Court Act 1981, s.138(3A)).

What were "tools" or "implements" of trade within the Bankruptcy Act 1883, s.44(2) was a question of fact in each case. The hired cab of a cab driver was held as exempt within County Courts Act 1888, s.147 (*Lavell v. Ritching* [1906] 1 K.B. 480). "The general principle is that prima facie all the judgment debtor's goods are liable to seizure under a writ of fieri facias. If a judgment debtor claims the benefit of a statutory exemption, the burden of showing that the exemption applies rests squarely on him" (*per* Steyn L.J. in *Toseland Building Supplies Ltd v. Bishop (t/a Bishop Groundworks)*, October 28, 1993, CA (unrep.)). See also *Brookes v. Harris* [1995] 1 W.L.R. 918 where a disc jockey's records were held to be "tools of his trade".

Equitable interest in chattels—The general rule is that a judgment creditor cannot under a *fi. fa.* seize chattels in which the judgment debtor has only an equitable interest; but this rule does not extend to cases where the whole beneficial interest is vested in the judgment debtors, *e.g.* where furniture has been assigned to trustees upon trust to allow one of two judgment debtors to use it during the joint lives of himself and his wife (the other judgment debtor) and after the death of either upon trust for the survivor (*Stevens v. Hince* [1914] W.N. 148). **R45.1.21**

Where the goods seized are held by the defendant under another name—The common form of *fi. fa.* relates to "the goods and chattels of C.D. in your bailiwick". Cases have been known where a defendant has been sued as "John Brown", and the sheriff, when about to execute a writ **R45.1.22**

of *fi. fa.*, finds that all the goods are claimed by "Smith & Co.", under which name J. Brown carries on business. In such a case the judgment creditor should issue an application (see Part 23) supported by evidence seeking permission to enforce against "Smith & Co.". Enforcing judgment or order against a firm see O.8, r.5.

R45.1.23 **Goods of third persons**—A sheriff may be restrained by injunction from remaining in possession of, and from selling goods, which do not belong to the judgment debtor; but the execution creditor should either be made a party to the action, or at least notice of it should be served upon him before the injunction is granted (*Hilliard v. Hanson* (1882) 21 Ch.D. 69). In the usual case of the Sheriff receiving a third party claim which is disputed by the execution creditor, he will issue interpleader proceedings under RSC, O.17 for the issue as to ownership to be decided by the Court.

Where goods belonging to a builder were seized in execution, and such goods were subject to an agreement under which the building owner would have a lien on them on giving a notice in writing to the builder, but such notice was not given until seizure by the sheriff, it was held that the intervening seizure prevented the building owner's rights of lien from being effectual (*Byford v. Russell* [1907] 2 K.B. 522). Where execution is sought to be levied against certain classes of goods, which experience may have taught that they might belong to third persons or be subject to a hire purchase agreement, *e.g.* motor cars, caravans, motor boats, it may be advisable, where other enquiries have failed to make enquiry of H.P. Information Ltd.

R45.1.24 **Goods owned by debtor and third person**—Where two persons own chattels as co-owners (whether joint tenants or tenants in common) each is entitled to possession and to sell without the consent of the other. Accordingly the sheriff acting under a *fi. fa.* upon a judgment against one co-owner is in no worse position and so can seize and sell the whole of the property (see *Farrar v. Beswick* (1836) 1 M. & W. 682; *Mayhew v. Herrick* (1849) 7 C.B. 229). In such a case, upon the sheriff interpleading, the Court or a Judge would order the sheriff to divide the proceeds of the sale accordingly between the judgment debtor and the co-owner claimant (*cf. The James W. Elwell* [1921] P.351.

The position is different in garnishee proceedings: an action upon a debt owing to two creditors jointly must be brought in their joint names, and therefore such a debt could not be attached under a judgment against one only of the joint creditors (*Macdonald v. Tacquah Gold Mines* (1884) 13 Q.B.D. 535, *per* Bowen L.J., at 539; *Beasley v. Roney* [1891] 1 Q.B. 509, *per* Pollock, B., at 512; *Hirschorn v. Evans* [1938] 2 K.B. 801).

When two persons have separate and different interests in a chattel (*e.g.* one is owner subject to another's charge or lien) the sheriff may seize if the judgment debtor is entitled to possession, but may only sell the debtor's interest.

R45.1.25 **Goods of a company**—As to seizure of property of a company comprised in debentures issued by such company, see *Re Opera Ltd* [1891] 3 Ch. 260; *Taunton v. Sheriff of Warwickshire* [1895] 1 Ch. 734; 2 Ch. 319.

A seizure of goods comprised in debentures constituting a floating charge on the property of a company is not a dealing with them in the ordinary course of business, and the fact that the moneys secured by the debentures have not become payable, does not debar the holders of them from intervening to protect their security as against an execution creditor (*Davey v. Williamson* [1898] 2 Q.B. 194). But they must intervene in such a way as to cause the whole security to crystallise; they cannot claim a specific asset against the execution creditor while allowing the security to remain a floating charge *qua* the other assets (*Evans v. Rival Granite Quarries Ltd* [1910] 2 K.B. 979, CA).

Under the Companies Act 1985, s.621 (which is analogous to the Insolvency Act 1986, s.346) where execution has issued against a company, and the company is subsequently wound up, the creditor cannot retain the benefit of the execution against the liquidator unless he has completed the execution before the commencement of the winding up, but the section gives the Court a discretion to defeat the rights conferred on the liquidator, either wholly or partially, according to what is right and fair in the circumstances of the case (*Re Grosvenor Metal Co. Ltd* [1950] Ch. 63). As to completion by the appointment of a receiver, see AJA 1956, s.36(4).

By the C.A. 1985, s.622, where any goods of a company are taken in execution, and before sale or completion of the execution, notice is served on the sheriff that a provisional liquidator has been appointed or a winding-up order made, etc., the sheriff, on being required, is to deliver up the goods or money seized to the liquidator, but the costs of the execution are a first charge on the goods or money so delivered, and the liquidator may sell the goods or a sufficient part of them to satisfy that charge. The "costs" referred to in this section only include costs incurred by the sheriff himself. They do not include any costs of the execution creditor (*Re Woods (Bristol) Ltd* (1931) 75 S.J. 458), *cf.* Insolvency Act 1986, s.346 and "Bankruptcy of debtor", para. R45.1.28.

Where a company contracts to issue debentures charging its property under such circumstances that equity would decree specific performance of the contract, and before the debentures are actually issued goods intended to be comprised therein are seized in execution, the intended debenture-holder stands practically in the same position, for the purpose of asserting his priority over the execution, as if the debentures had actually been issued; for an execution creditor takes subject to all equities (*Simultaneous Colour Printing Syndicate v. Foweraker* [1901] 1 K.B. 771; and see

Re Standard Manufacturing Co. [1891] 1 Ch. 627; *Duck v. Tower Galvanising Co.* [1901] 2 K.B. 314; *Re London Pressed Hinge Co.* [1905] 1 Ch. 576). But, where goods of a company were seized under a *fi. fa.*, and, in order to avoid a sale, the company, with the assent of the execution creditor, agreed that in consideration of his not selling they would pay a sum to the sheriff out of the daily takings, it was held that the judgment creditor was entitled to retain the moneys against the debenture holders of the company (*Robinson v. Burnell's Vienna Bakery Co.* [1904] 2 K.B. 624).

So where, in order to get rid of a man in possession, the managing director of a company paid out the sheriff who had seized goods to satisfy a judgment in respect of an ordinary trade debt but before the sheriff paid over to the execution creditors debenture-holders, who had a floating charge, had secured the appointment of a receiver, it was held that as the company had an implied licence from the debenture-holders to pay trade debts, the execution creditors were entitled to the money in the hands of the sheriff (*Heaton and Dugard, Ltd v. Cutting Bros Ltd* [1925] 1 K.B. 655).

Ship—Where the debtor owns some only of the shares in a foreign ship the sheriff is entitled to seize the ship as a whole and sell the shares (*The James W. Elwell* [1921] P. 351); *quaere* whether this procedure is applicable to an English ship, the shares in which are transferable by bill of sale (*ibid.*, at 368). The possession of the sheriff does not deprive the marshall of his power to arrest in actions *in rem.* The maritime lien of the Master for wages even after seizure has priority to the claims of the execution creditor, but where the sheriff has seized before arrest by the marshal, the execution creditors have priority over necessaries men (*ibid.*); and the Master's lien has priority over the claim of the sheriff in respect of his costs of execution (*The Ile de Ceylan* [1922] P. 256). As to priority of a claim under a French *hypothèque* to a claim by necessaries men, see *Hills, etc., Co. Ltd v. Owners of Colorado* (1923) 39 T.L.R. 216. R45.1.26

Though judgment creditors cannot proceed *in rem* in respect of a judgment for an amount exceeding the bail given for release of the vessel, they may proceed by *fi. fa.* (*The Joannis Vatis* [1922] P. 213).

Goods of a patient in control of Court of Protection—When the property of a patient has become subject to the control of the Court of Protection by the appointment of a receiver, it cannot be seized under a writ of *fi. fa.* by an execution creditor of the patient (*Re Winkle* [1894] 2 Ch. 519, distinguished in *Davies v. Thomas* [1900] 2 Ch. 462). But where, before the appointment of a receiver, the goods of a debtor who is a mental patient are taken in execution under a *fi. fa.*, there is no jurisdiction to order a sale of the goods for maintenance of the debtor in priority to the claims of the execution creditor (*Re Clarke* [1898] 1 Ch. 336; see now Mental Health Act 1983, s.96). R45.1.27

Bankruptcy of debtor—In order to entitle an execution creditor to retain the benefit of his execution against the trustee in bankruptcy of the debtor, he must have completed the execution by seizure and sale before the commencement of the bankruptcy (see Insolvency Act 1986, s.346). R45.1.28

A payment made by the debtor to the sheriff even if made before a bankruptcy order is made against him, operates in satisfaction of a judgment creditor's debt only when the judgment creditor is in a position to maintain an action against the sheriff for money had and received (*Re A Debtor (No. 2 of 1977), ex p. the Debtor v. Goacher* [1979] 1 W.L.R. 956; [1979] 1 All E.R. 870).

The effect of the provisions of the Insolvency Act 1986, s.346, is that the title of the trustee will prevail over that of the execution creditor unless (1) the execution has been completed by seizure and sale or receipt of the full amount of the levy in the case of goods (*Figg v. Moore* [1894] 2 Q.B. 690) or by a return of *nulla bona* as in *Re Fairley, ex p. Low and Bonar Ltd* [1922] 2 Ch. 791, or in the case of land by seizure or appointment of a receiver or payment; (2) the completion has taken place before the commencement of the bankruptcy (see *Burns v. Brown* [1895] 1 Q.B. 324). The execution is completed by seizure and sale where, after execution, the sheriff has sold under authority given on an interpleader issue and paid the money into Court (*Re Chiandetti* (1921) 91 L.J.K.B. 70).

For the purposes of section 346 of the Insolvency Act 1986, and section 621 of the CA 1985, an execution against goods is completed by seizure and sale or by the making of a charging order under s.1 of the Charging Orders Act 1979 (see Charging Orders Act 1979, s.4; and O.50, r.1).

The execution is not "completed" within section 346 of the Insolvency Act 1986, unless payment has been made direct to the sheriff: payment of the amount of the levy to the creditor direct does not amount to such completion (*Re Godding* [1914] 2 K.B. 70; *Re Pollock* (1902) 87 L.T. 238). Where by arrangement certain goods supposed to be the property of the debtor's wife were withdrawn and sold before notice of the act of bankruptcy and the proceeds were paid after such notice, it was held that execution was not completed within the section (*Re Evans* [1916] H.B.R. 111).

A sheriff failed to execute a writ of *fi. fa.* if he did no more than call at the debtor's house and report his inability to gain access and such failure was not "a formal defect or irregularity" in insolvency proceedings capable of remedy under r.7.55 of the Insolvency Rules (*Re A Debtor (No. 340 of 1992) The Times,* July 19, 1993).

If a debtor pays money in order to avoid a sale of goods taken in execution by the sheriff under a writ of *fi. fa.* it will be treated as "money in order to avoid sale" under s.346 of the Insolvency Act 1986, and not for "money received in part satisfaction of the execution" under s.346 of the Act, and accordingly such money becomes vested in the execution creditor and his title to it is subject to defeasance only if within 14 days of its receipt the sheriff receives notice of the debtor's bankruptcy (*Marley Tile Co. Ltd v. Burrows* [1978] Q.B. 241; [1978] 1 All E.R. 657, CA).

R45.1.29 **Debtors Act 1869, s.4**—Decrees and orders for payment or recovery of a sum of money were formerly enforced in the first place by attachment of the debtor, and then by sequestration of his effects (O.29, r.3) but they cannot as a rule be now enforced by committal, by reason of the Debtors Act 1869, s.4 of which provides as follows:

"Abolition of imprisonment for debt, with exceptions

R45.1.30 4.—With the exceptions hereinafter-mentioned, no person shall, after the commencement of this Act, be arrested or imprisoned for making default in payment of a sum of money.

There shall be excepted from the operation of the above enactment:

1. Default in payment of a penalty, or sum in the nature of a penalty other than a penalty in respect of any contract:

2. Default in payment of any sum recoverable summarily before a justice or justices of the peace:

3. Default by a trustee or person acting in a fiduciary capacity and ordered to pay by a Court of Equity [High Court of Justice] any sum in his possession or under his control:

4. Default by an attorney or solicitor in payment of costs when ordered to pay costs for misconduct as such, or in payment of a sum of money when ordered to pay the same in his character of an officer of the Court making the order:

5. Default in payment for the benefit of creditors of any portion of a salary or other income in respect of the payment of which any Court having jurisdiction in bankruptcy is authorised to make an order:

6. Default in payment of sums in respect of the payment of which orders are in this Act authorised to be made:

Provided, first, that no person shall be imprisoned in any case excepted from the operation of this section for a longer period than one year; and, secondly, that nothing in this section shall alter the effect of any judgment or order of any Court for payment of money except as regards the arrest and imprisonment of the person making default in paying such money."

The order of committal must accurately specify under which exception the default is included (*Re Wilde* [1910] W.N. 128, CA).

An order to pay money creates a debt. And a person ordered to pay money to another person will not be committed to prison for disobedience to such order without proof of ability to pay (*Buckley v. Crawford* [1893] 1 Q.B. 105).

R45.1.31 **Crown debts**—This section applies to sums of money payable and debts due to the Crown, including such sums payable in respect of any of the taxes, contributions or liabilities specified in Sched. 4 to AJA 1970, see s.11(b)(ii) of that Act (SCP 1999, Vol. 2, Section 20B, para. 20B–77), and Crown Proceedings Act 1947, s.26(2) (Vol. 2, Section 21L, para. 21L–63).

R45.1.32 **Party in default**—Though default in payment of a sum ordered to be paid cannot be punished by committal, the default remains a contempt, and the court has a discretion whether or not to allow the party in default to take any further proceeding in the action in which payment was ordered (*Leavis v. Leavis* [1921] P. 299).

R45.1.33 **"Penalty"**—includes penal interest ordered to be paid by a trustee in bankruptcy under a financial provision under Sched. 9, para. 21 to the Insolvency Act 1986, but not the costs of the order (*Re Nicholson* (1890) 63 L.T. 322) and see, *per* Morton L.J. in *Att.-Gen. v. Randall* [1944] K.B. 709; (1944) 60 T.L.R. 523 at 524.

R45.1.34 **"Sum recoverable before a justice"**—Costs which have been awarded by a Crown Court against one of the parties to an appeal, or which by the Magistrates' Courts Act 1980, s.110 (previously 1952 Act, s.86) may be enforced before a justice by warrant of distress, and in default of distress by warrant of commitment, are within the second exception (*R. v. Pratt* (1870) L.R. 5 Q.B. 176).

A committal to prison by a magistrate under the Distress for Rates Act 1849, s.2, is punitive in character and the Court cannot, under s.285 of the Insolvency Act 1986, order the debtor's release when proceedings as a bankruptcy petition are pending or an individual has been adjudged bankrupt (*Re Edgcome* [1902] 2 K.B. 403, CA).

R45.1.35 **"Trustee or person acting in a fiduciary capacity"**—The words "person acting in a fiduciary capacity" in the third exception include any person who stands in a fiduciary relation towards any other person who may be entitled to call on him to pay, whether such other person is or is not a plaintiff in the action (*per* Jessel M.R. in *Marris v. Ingram* (1880) 13 Ch.D. 338); and have been applied to an agent who received bills that he might discount them and hand the proceeds to the owner (*Hutchinson v. Hartmont* [1877] W.N. 29); to a London agent making default in payment of a balance found due to the country solicitor (*Litchfield v. Jones* (1887) 36 Ch.D. 530); to an auctioneer in respect of proceeds of goods intrusted to him for sale (*Crowther v. Elgood* (1887) 34 Ch.D. 691); to a receiver who had made default in payment of a sum found to be due from him, even where he had been discharged before the order for payment (*Re Gent* (1889) 40 Ch.D. 190); to an executor indebted to his testator's estate, who having means to pay the debt due from him had persistently evaded payment (*Re Bourne* [1906] 1 Ch. 697, CA); and to a trustee who has received money in connection with the sale of heirlooms (*Re Berwick (Lord), Re Lord Berwick* (1900) 81 L.T. 797); but they have been held, under the circumstances, not to include a director or promoter of a company (*Metcalfe's Case* (1880) 13 Ch.D. 815; *Phosphate, etc. Co. v. Hartmont* (1887) 25 W.R. 743); nor a creditor ordered to repay money received by way of fraudulent preference (*Ex p. Hooson* (1873) L.R. 8 Ch. 231; *Re Bishop* (1891) 7 T.L.R. 610). They do not apply to the case of a partner who has received moneys on behalf of his firm (*Piddocke v. Burt* [1894] 1 Ch. 343) even if he has given an undertaking (*Carter v. Roberts* [1903] 2 Ch. 312, at 321).

The remedy is only intended to be given as between trustee and *cestuis que trust*, and is not a remedy for a mere creditor for whom the person against whom he seeks to assert the remedy is not a trustee (*per* Kay J., *Re Firmin* (1887) 57 L.T. 45); but a debtor who has admitted that a sum is due from him and submitted to an order directing him to hold it upon certain trusts is within the exception (*Preston v. Etherington* (1887) 37 Ch.D. 104; and see *Taaffe v. Fitzsimmons* [1894] 1 Ir.R.63).

Where a sole creditor in an administration action takes an order against an executor for personal payment of his certified debt the fiduciary relationship between them is at an end, and the creditor cannot bring the executor within the third exception in s.4 of the Debtors Act 1869 (*Re Thomas* [1912] 2 Ch. 348, CA).

"Possession or control"—A trustee who has without moral delinquency lost the trust moneys (*Middleton v. Chichester* (1871) L.R. 6 Ch. 152) or has innocently suffered his co-trustee to appropriate and misapply them (*Evans v. Bear* (1875) L.R. 10 Ch. 76) is within the third exception (see s.4, Debtors Act 1869 above); but not a trustee who has omitted to get in the trust moneys (*Ferguson v. Ferguson* (1875) L.R. 10 Ch. 661) or is not proved to have ever had them in his possession (*Re Hincks, ex p. Cuddeford* (1878) 45 L.J. Bk. 127; *Re Hickey* (1866) 35 W.R. 53; *Re Fewster* [1901] 1 Ch. 447; and see *Phosphate, etc., Co. v. Hartmont* (1887) 25 W.R. 743; *Re Hind* (1878) 37 L.T. 168; *Harper v. McIntyre* (1908) 99 L.T. 191). R45.1.36

An order on a defendant to pay into Court the alleged value of bonds previously directed to be deposited in Court cannot be enforced by committal, as there is no breach of an order to pay money in defendant's possession or under his control (*Cronin v. Twinberrow* [1887] W.N. 201); nor can a judgment directing a trustee to make good the difference between the value of bonds at the date when he improperly sold them and their value at the date of judgment (*Re Walker* (1891) 60 L.J.Ch. 25).

An executor may be attached for default in payment of a debt due from him to the testator in his lifetime, but not for default in payment of such a debt and interest (not distinguished) because the interest could not be "in his possession or under his control" (*Re Hickey* (1886) 35 W.R. 53).

The exception applies only where there has been actual receipt of the money by the person sought to be imprisoned (*Re Fewster* [1901] 1 Ch. 447; *Re Wilkins* [1901] W.N. 202; and see *Re Underwood* (1903) 51 W.R. 335).

Privilege of Parliament—Privilege of parliament cannot be claimed by a person liable to imprisonment, as having acted in a fiduciary capacity (*Re Gent* (1889) 40 Ch.D. 190). Whether privilege of parliament can be set up where the trustee has been guilty of no moral culpability, *quaere* (*Aylesford v. Poulett* [1892] 2 Ch. 60). R45.1.37

Bankruptcy Order—Where a "receiving order" under the Bankruptcy Act 1914 (now replaced by a "bankruptcy order" under the Insolvency Act 1986) was made against a person within the exceptions to s.4, Debtors Act 1869 (see above) he was held not to be protected from committal under that section (see *Re Smith* [1893] 2 Ch. 1; *Re Edye* (1891) 63 L.T. 762 not following *Re Simes* (1890) 62 L.T. 721 and *Cobham v. Dalton* (1875) L.R. 10 ChD 655. See also above note "Bankruptcy of debtor". R45.1.38

Service, where necessary—Where the order is for payment within a certain time after service, the trustee is not in default until the order has been served on him, and cannot be restrained by writ *ne exeat regno* from going out of the jurisdiction (*Colverson v. Bloomfield* (1885) 29 Ch.D. 341). R45.1.39

Terms of order—It need not be stated in the order required to be enforced that the person ordered to pay is a trustee or person in a fiduciary capacity, and that the money is in his possession or under his control, but such matters may be proved *aliunde* (*Brewster v. Prior* (1887) 3 T.L.R. 590). R45.1.40

The amount to be paid must be specified in the order for payment (*Re Spicer* [1881] W.N. 85).

R45.1.41 **"Default by an attorney or solicitor", etc.**—As to an order of committal of a solicitor for non-payment of costs under the fourth exception in s.4, Debtors Act 1869 (see above), see *Tilney v. Stansfeld* (1880) 28 W.R. 582. A committal may issue for default in payment of a balance found due following a detailed assessment (formerly "taxation") of costs (*Re Rush* (1870) L.R. 9 Eq. 147; *Re White* (1871) 19 W.R. 39) including the costs of the detailed assessment *Re A Solicitor* [1895] 2 Ch. 66; *Re N., A Solicitor* [1917] W.N. 138); but not where the solicitor is liable to pay costs as an ordinary litigant (*Re Hope* (1872) L.R. 7 Ch. 523; see *Jenkins v. Fereday* (1872) L.R. 7 C.P. 358). The order must distinguish between the sum due for costs and the sum due from the solicitor as money in his hands (*Re Wilde* [1910] W.N. 128, CA).

The sum ordered to be paid must be accurately defined (see *Re Weatherley* (1918) 88 L.J.K.B. 482, CA).

An order enforceable by committal for payment of money received by a solicitor for his client may be made, notwithstanding judgment has been obtained against him for the amount (*Re Grey* [1892] 2 Q.B. 440).

As to committal of a solicitor ordered to pay a sum of money belonging to a client and improperly dealt with by him, see *Re Dudley* (1883) 12 Q.B.D. 44.

Quaere, whether a London agent making default in payment of a balance found due on taking account between him and his principals is within the fourth exception, though he is certainly within the third exception *per* North J., *Litchfield v. Jones* (1887) 36 Ch.D. 530). See *Re Farman* (1897) 14 T.L.R. 20.

After an order striking a solicitor off the roll has been made he may be attached for disobedience to a direction in the same order for payment of money due from him (*Re Strong* (1886) 32 Ch.D. 342).

R45.1.42 **Service**—It is not necessary to serve on the solicitor the order to tax along with the certificate of the result of taxation before an order for attachment can issue against him for the balance found due, provided that the order to tax has been previously duly served on him (*Re Wilde* [1910] W.N. 105, 128, CA). (The term "taxation" has now been replaced by "detailed assessment".)

R45.1.43 **Waiver**—Giving time and accepting part payment was held not to amount to a waiver of the right of attachment (*Re Fereday* [1895] 2 Ch. 437).

R45.1.44 **"For a longer period than one year"**—In case of re-arrest, the period of imprisonment must end with the twelve months from date of the original imprisonment, inclusive of the time the debtor has been at liberty (*Church's Trustee v. Hibbard* [1902] 2 Ch. 784, CA).

R45.1.45 **Discretion in cases within exceptions 3 and 4**—The Debtors Act 1878 provides that in any case coming within the third and fourth exceptions in section 4 of the Debtors Act 1869, the Court may inquire into the case, and "may grant or refuse, either absolutely or upon terms, any application for a writ of attachment, or other process or order of arrest or imprisonment, and any application to stay the operation of any such writ, process or order, or for discharge from arrest or imprisonment thereunder."

R45.1.46 **Policy of Debtors Act**—In *Barrett v. Hammond* (1879) 10 Ch.D. 285, it was held by Bacon V.-C. (following *Street v. Hope* (1879) 10 Ch.D. 287n., *per* Malins V.-C.) that the policy of the Debtors Act 1869, s.4, was not vindictive, and that the Court, in the exercise of its discretion under the Debtors Act 1878, would not order the imprisonment of a defaulting trustee, unless it was likely to be productive of payment; but Jessel M.R. in *Marris v. Ingram* (1880) 13 Ch.D. 338, held that the Act of 1869 was intended for the punishment of fraudulent or dishonest debtors and declined to exercise the discretion given him by the Act of 1878, as he was not satisfied that defendant was unable to pay; and see *Re Knowles* (1883) 52 L.J.Ch. 685, *per* Kay J.; *Re Dudley* (1883) 12 Q.B.D. 44; *Re Freston* (1883) 11 Q.B.D. 545; *Re Gent* (1889) 40 Ch.D. 190; *Church's Trustee v. Hibbard* [1902] 2 Ch. 784, CA; *Re Edgcome* [1902] 2 K.B. 403; *Re Wray* (1887) 36 Ch.D. 138 (where it was held that a receiving order against a defaulting solicitor did not prevent an order of committal issuing) followed in *Re Edye* (1891) 63 L.T. 762.

It is not necessary, in order to commit a defaulting trustee, to show that he has been guilty of fraud (*Preston v. Etherington* (1888) 37 Ch.D. 104 at 110); but where there is no fraud the Court may decline to make an order of committal where the defaulting trustee executes a charge upon his property (*cf. Holroyde v. Garnett* (1882) 20 Ch.D. 532).

Where there was no moral culpability involved in the misapplication of trust funds, the Court exercised its discretion in favour of the debtor (*Aylesford v. Poulett* [1892] 2 Ch. 60).

R45.1.47 **Discretion of Judge**—The CA will not readily interfere with the conclusion of the Court below as to the debtor's ability or inability to pay (*Esdaile v. Visser* (1880) 13 Ch.D. 421; but on this case see *Chard v. Jervis* (1882) 9 Q.B.D. 178); or generally with the discretion of the Court below under the above section in refusing or granting an order of committal (*Re Wray* (1887) 36 Ch.D.

138 at 145; *Preston v. Etherington* (1888) 37 Ch.D. 104; and see *Crowther v. Elgood* (1887) 34 Ch.D. 691); unless the discretion is shown to have been exercised on an erroneous ground (*Re Smith* [1893] 2 Ch. 1 at 18).

Debtors Act 1869, s.5—The jurisdiction given by s.5 to commit to prison a person who makes default in payment of a debt or instalment of a debt due from him in pursuance of an order or judgment is exercisable by the High Court only in respect of a High Court maintenance order A.J.A. 1970, s.11(a). This jurisdiction will therefore only be exercised by the Family Division of the High Court; see Family Proceedings Rules 1991, rr.7.4–7.6. **R45.1.48**

Debtors Act 1869, s.6—Its material parts provide as follows: **R45.1.49**

"Where the plaintiff in any action in any of Her Majesty's superior Courts of law at Westminster in which, if brought before the commencement of this Act, the defendant would have been liable to arrest, proves at any time before final judgment by evidence on oath, to the satisfaction of a judge of one of those Courts, that the plaintiff has good cause of action against the defendant to the amount of £50 or upwards, and that there is probable cause for believing that the defendant is about to quit England unless he be apprehended, and that the absence of the defendant from England will materially prejudice the plaintiff in the prosecution of his action, such judge may in the prescribed manner order such defendant to be arrested and imprisoned for a period not exceeding six months, unless and until he has sooner given the prescribed security, not exceeding the amount claimed in the action, that he will not go out of England without the leave of the Court ..."

The application for an order under this section is made to the Judge in Chambers; it may be made *ex parte*, at any time after the issue of the writ and before final judgment; and it must be supported by affidavit evidence establishing the existence of the necessary conditions to the satisfaction of the Judge according to the high standard of proof required.

An order can be made under this section only if the following four conditions are satisfied, namely:

(1) the action is one in which the defendant would formerly, *i.e.* before the Debtors Act 1869 have been liable to arrest at law;
(2) a good cause of action for at least £50 is established;
(3) there is "probable cause" for believing that the defendant is about to quit England unless he is arrested; and
(4) "the absence of the defendant from England will materially prejudice the plaintiff in the prosecution of the action."

The making of an order under this section is discretionary (*Re Lehman, ex p. Hasluck* (1890) 6 T.L.R. 435).

It should be noted that an order under this section is available before judgment, and not after; it is designed to assist in obtaining a judgment, and it is not a form of process of execution. For an examination of the history and the relevant authorities, see *per* Megarry J. in *Felton v. Callis* [1969] 1 Q.B. 200; [1968] 3 All E.R. 673.

Writ ne exeat regno—This writ, which is in the nature of equitable bail, is still extant but by analogy can issue only if the requirements of s.6 of the Debtors Act 1869 are satisfied (*Felton v. Callis* [1969] 1 Q.B. 200; [1968] 3 All E.R. 673 where the authorities are fully examined by Megarry J.). **R45.1.50**

This writ, which has the effect of restraining the defendant from departing out of the jurisdiction, is ordered to issue to assist the plaintiff in obtaining judgment and not in executing it, and therefore it may properly issue in an action to recover a large sum of money belonging to clients of the plaintiff firm which the defendant had wrongfully converted to his own use and to secure full disclosure from the defendant as to what happened to such monies and a full inquiry into his monetary accounts (*Lipkin Gorman (a firm) v. Cass* (1985) *The Times*, May 29, 1985). In practical terms the writ will require the passport of the defendant to be impounded (*ibid.*).

The writ may be issued in support of a Mareva injunction and should be directed to the Tipstaff rather than to the Sheriff with the direction to bring the arrested defendant before the Judge forthwith or as soon as possible (*Al Nahkel for Contracting and Trading Ltd v. Lowe* [1986] Q.B. 235; [1986] 1 All E.R. 729).

Even where the conditions for the issue of the writ *ne exeat regno* are not or cannot be fulfilled, the Court has power, sitting *in camera*, to grant an *ex parte* injunction to restrain the defendant from leaving England and Wales and forthwith to deliver his passport to the person serving the order on him, where it appears just and convenient to do so, or when it is necessary to protect the plaintiff's rights pending the hearing of the action and to obtain information ordered to be disclosed in the Anton Piller and Mareva forms, but such injunction should run only for so long as it is necessary to give effect to such orders (*Bayer A.G. v. Winter* [1986] 1 W.L.R. 497; [1986] 1 All E.R. 733, CA). It will not be allowed to issue if its true purpose is to facilitate execution in the event of the plaintiff's action succeeding, and not to prevent the defendant leaving the country and thereby prejudicing the plaintiff in prosecuting his claim (*Allied Arab Bank v. Hajjar* [1988] Q.B. 787).

In the interest of the ward of Court to know his or her true identity if that can be established by the blood test "DNA fingerprinting," the Court will grant an injunction to restrain the mother from leaving the jurisdiction until the completion of the tests (*Re I. (A Minor)* (1987) *The Times*, May 22).

The application for the writ *ne exeat regno* is by motion *ex parte* at any time before final judgment. See *Annual Practice 1966*, pp.1858–1859.

R45.1.51 **County court judgments**—By virtue of section 42 of the County Courts Act 1984 (as amended by the Courts and Legal Services Act 1990), provision is made for specific judgments of the county court to be transferred to the High Court for enforcement, see SCP 1999, Vol. 2, Section 20A, paras 20A–601 *et seq.* for County Courts Act 1984. A judgment so transferred may be enforced in the High Court as if it were a judgment or order of High Court and must be treated as a judgment or order of the High Court for all purposes, except the power to set aside, correct, vary or quash the judgment or order or to appeal again it shall continue as if it were a county court judgment or order and not a High Court judgment or order.

By virtue of article 8 of the High Court and County Court Jurisdiction Order 1991 (S.I. 1991 No. 724), a judgment or order of a county court for the payment of a sum of money which it is sought to enforce wholly or partially by execution against goods:

(a) shall be enforced only in the High Court where the sum which it is sought to enforce is £5,000 or more and the proceedings in which the judgment or order was obtained did not arise out of an agreement regulated by the Consumer Credit Act 1974;
(b) shall be enforced only in the county court where the sum which it is sought to enforce is less than £600;
(c) in any other case may be enforced in either the High Court or in a county court.

R45.1.52 **Magistrates' courts**—The Magistrates' Courts Act 1980, s.87, provides that payment of a sum adjudged to be paid by a conviction of a magistrates' court may be enforced by the High Court or a county court (otherwise than by issue of a writ of *fi. fa.* or other process against goods or by imprisonment or attachment of earnings) as if the sum were due to the clerk of the magistrates' court in pursuance of a judgment or order of the High Court or county court, as the case may be.

So far as the Central Office is concerned, the Senior Master issued a Practice Direction dated November 22, 1967, setting out the following procedure to be followed for this purpose:

1. The applicant will bring an affidavit, framed for the purpose of the particular type of execution desired and exhibiting the authority of the magistrates' court to take the proceedings (M.C. Forms Rules 1981, Form 63). The authority will recite the conviction, the amount outstanding and the nature of the proceedings authorised to be taken. *An extra copy of the exhibit* will be required for filing in the Central Office.

2. Attendance will be made in the first place in the alphabetical section of the judgment department appropriate to the surname of the applicant. The copy of the exhibit will be lodged there and a reference number will be assigned to the matter, which will later be entered by the judgment clerk in a special register.

3. If the application is for an *ex parte* order (*e.g.* a charging order nisi or garnishee order *nisi*) the affidavit and original exhibit will then be taken to the Masters' Secretary's Office (Room E214) and lodged in the usual way.

4. Any other application by way of summons or otherwise will be initiated in the usual way after a reference number has been assigned.

R45.1.53 **Sheriff Lodgment Centre**—see para. R45.1.4.

Notice of seizure

R45.2 **2.** When first executing a writ of fieri facias, the Sheriff or his officer shall deliver to the debtor or leave at each place where execution is levied a notice in Form No. 55 in the relevant Practice Direction informing the debtor of the execution.

Enforcement of judgment for possession of land

R45.3 **3.**—(1) Subject to the provisions of these rules, a judgment or order for the giving of possession of land may be enforced by one or more of the following means, that is to say—

(a) writ of possession;
(b) in a case in which rule 5 applies, an order of committal;
(c) in such a case, writ of sequestration.

(2) A writ of possession to enforce a judgment or order for the giving of possession of any land shall not be issued without the permission of the court except where the judgment or order was given or made in mortgage proceedings to which Order 88 applies.

(3) Such permission shall not be granted unless it is shown—

(a) that every person in actual possession of the whole or any part of the land has received such notice of the proceedings as appears to the court sufficient to enable him to apply to the court for any relief to which he may be entitled, and

(b) if the operation of the judgment or order is suspended by subsection (2) of section 16 of the Landlord and Tenant Act, 1954, that the applicant has not received notice in writing from the tenant that he desires that the provisions of paragraphs (a) and (b) of that subsection shall have effect.

(4) A writ of possession may include provision for enforcing the payment of any money adjudged or ordered to be paid by the judgment or order which is to be enforced by the writ.

Effect of rule—Under this rule, leave is required in all cases to enforce a judgment or order for the giving of possession of land, except in a mortgage action to which O.88, applies or an order for possession made under O.113. **R45.3.1**

A writ of possession may be issued without the leave of the Court to enforce an order for possession made in summary proceedings for possession of land (see O.113, r.7) and in such case the writ of possession must be in Form No. 66A (see SCP 1999, Vol. 2, Section 1A, para. 1A–67).

Leave to issue a writ of possession cannot be given on an interlocutory motion or summons but only to enforce a final judgment or order for possession (*Manchester Corp. v. Connolly* [1970] Ch. 420; [1970] 1 All E.R. 961, CA).

A judgment or order to give possession of land will not be enforceable by an order of committal or by writ of sequestration unless it specifies the time within which this act is required to be done, and the defendant refuses or neglects to do it within that time (see r.5(1)). Accordingly, as a judgment or order to give possession of land will not in practice specify the time within which this act is required to be done (see O.42, r.2(2)) it will not ordinarily be enforceable by an order of committal or by writ of sequestration, but only by a writ of possession, which will normally be sufficient to enforce the judgment. If, however, in an extreme case, it is desired to enforce the judgment against a recalcitrant defendant by an order of committal or writ of sequestration, it will be necessary first to apply to the Court under r.6, for an order to fix the time within which the defendant is required to give possession of the land, and to serve that order upon the defendant under r.7, and then to apply under r.5, for the order of committal (see O.52) or writ of sequestration.

Writ of possession—For form of writ of possession, see Form No. 66 (SCP 1999, Vol. 2, Section 1A, para. 1A–66). The writ of possession may be combined with the writ of *fi. fa.* (para. (4) and see Form No. 53 (Vol. 2, Section 1A, para. 1A–53)). **R45.3.2**

The writ of possession contains a recital of the judgment or order that the defendant "do give" to plaintiff possession of the land. It must therefore contain a description of the property of which possession is to be given. General words will not do, and if necessary the writ of possession may have to be altered by inserting a sufficient description (*Thynne v. Sarl* [1891] 2 Ch. 79).

The writ of possession will issue upon a judgment entered before October 1, 1966, for the "recovery" of possession (see r.13) but in that case, the recital of the writ may have to be altered so as to correspond with the form of the judgment entered.

The writ of possession does not require the sheriff to make a "return," but he is directed to indorse it immediately after execution with a statement of the name in which he has executed it, and to send a copy of such statement to the plaintiff. This, however, is a mere formal matter of procedure and is not necessary in order to complete a seizure under the writ (*Re Hobson* (1886) 33 Ch.D. 493).

A second writ of possession for the giving of the same property cannot be issued until the first writ has been duly indorsed by the sheriff, showing that possession has not been given to the plaintiff of the whole property of which possession has been given under the judgment.

Housing Acts 1988/1996—All tenancies created on or after January 29, 1989 in respect of dwellings are governed by the Housing Act 1988. Consequently there are now relatively few tenancies governed by the Rent Act 1977 or its predecessors. See generally SCP 1999, Vol 2, 8H1–8H150—Recovery of Land actions. **R45.3.3**

The granting of a possession order always requires the exercise of a judicial discretion. Consequently, in relation to a dwelling a writ of possession will not issue to enforce a default judgment or order for possession (*Peachey Property Corp. Ltd. v. Robinson* [1967] 2 Q.B. 543; [1966] 2 All E.R. 981, CA, applying *Smith v. Poulter* [1947] K.B. 339). Nor will such a writ issue to enforce a judgment or order obtained by consent, since in such cases the question whether "it is reasonable to make such an order" has not been considered by a Court. (Such a consent order should not, of course, be made.)

In relation to premises let as a dwelling on a lease which is subject to a right of re-entry or forfeiture, that right cannot be enforced otherwise than by proceedings in the Court while any person is lawfully residing in the premises or part of them (Protection from Eviction Act 1977, s.2) and equally where any premises have been let as a dwelling under a tenancy to which the Rent Act/Housing Act does not apply the owner is not entitled to recover possession of the premises or part of them, at the termination of the former tenancy, otherwise than by proceedings in the Court (Protection from Eviction Act 1977, s.3). For these purposes, the Court is the county court where it has jurisdiction in respect of the recovery of these premises, otherwise it is the High Court (see Protection from Eviction Act 1977, s.9(1)). Where the right of forfeiture is being enforced by proceedings, the Court can make an order so limited as to produce only a forfeiture and not procure delivery of the premises to the landlord (see *Wolmer Securities Ltd v. Corne* [1966] 2 Q.B. 243; [1966] 2 W.L.R. 1381; [1966] 2 All E.R. 691, CA).

In relation to a dwelling-house to which Pt I or Pt II of the Landlord and Tenant Act 1954 applies, or which is held under a tenancy of an agricultural holding, the right to recover possession, otherwise than by virtue of the right of re-entry or forfeiture under the lease, must be enforced in the county court, and therefore in such a case also, the writ of possession will not issue (see Protection from Eviction Act 1977, ss.3(1), 9(1)).

In relation to a dwelling-house, whether it is a protected tenancy or not, the plaintiff may not enter into possession himself, even peaceably, and he can only enter into possession under a writ of possession (Protection from Eviction Act 1977, s.3) negativing to this extent *Aglionby v. Cohen* [1955] 1 Q.B. 558; [1955] 1 All E.R. 785.

On the other hand, in relation to land or premises which did not come within the Rent Act 1968 or Pt I or Pt II of the Landlord and Tenant Act 1954, or were not let as a dwelling under a tenancy of an agricultural holding, the plaintiff may obtain a writ of possession to enforce his judgment or order for possession; and he may, having such a judgment for possession, enter at his own risk without issuing out a writ of possession, if he can do so without force (*Aglionby v. Cohen*).

R45.3.4 **Reserve and Auxiliary Forces (Protection of Civil Interests) Act 1951**—In the cases covered by this Act no judgment or order for recovery of possession of land in default of payment of rent may be enforced without the leave of the Court (s. 2(3)).

R45.3.5 **Leave to issue writ of possession**—Leave to issue a writ of possession is necessary, except in a mortgage action under O.88, for in that case the position of every person in occupation is known before an order for possession is made (see *Leicester Permanent Building Society v. Shearley* [1951] Ch. 90; [1950] 2 All E.R. 738).

In the Queen's Bench Division the application for leave to issue the writ of possession is made *ex parte* upon affidavit, which must comply with the requirement of para. (3). For forms of affidavit, see PF. No. 91 (Vol. 2, Section 1B, para. 1B–69); Chitty and Jacob, Form 979.

Where (as often happens) the property consists of a house of which various parts are sublet to, or in the occupation of, different persons, the affidavit should show the nature and length of the notice which has been given to the various occupiers. Where the defendant or any other person is in actual possession of the premises the affidavit must contain, *inter alia*, the following information:—(a) whether the premises or any part thereof is a dwelling-house; (b) if so (i) what is the rateable value of the dwelling-house; (ii) whether it is let furnished or unfurnished and, if furnished, what is the amount of furniture therein; (c) any other matters which will assist the Master in determining whether any occupier is protected by the Rent Acts (*Practice Direction* [1955] 1 W.L.R. 1314; [1955] 3 All E.R. 646).

In the Chancery Division it is not necessary to file and bespeak an office copy of any affidavit unless in any particular case the Court or Judge so directs, but the original affidavit properly stamped must be left in Chambers (*Practice Direction* [1955] 1 W.L.R. 36; [1955] 1 All E.R. 30).

Leave is required to issue execution on suspended order for possession, see para. 46/4/1.

R45.3.6 **Stay of writ of possession**—The Court has no power to grant a stay of a writ of possession as against a trespasser and a stay against a former tenant or service occupier would normally be limited to between four and six weeks (*McPhail v. Persons' Names Unknown* [1973] Ch. 447, CA) However in a serious and substantial dispute between parties of commercial strength a period of three months or even longer may be granted (*Bain & Co. v. Church Commissioners for England* [1989] 1 W.L.R. 24).

R45.3.7 **Notice of the proceedings**—Where the defendant is the only person in possession of the premises the plaintiff must give the defendant notice of the judgment or order, and call upon him to give up possession under the judgment or order. Where there are other persons (not parties to the proceedings) in actual possession it is also necessary to serve them with such written notice as will give them a reasonable opportunity of applying to the Court.

The combined effect of O.45 and O.46 is that notice of an application for a warrant of possession must be given to a tenant and the writ of execution should not be issued without the tenant having an opportunity to apply to the court for relief (*Leicester City Council v. Aldwinkle, The Times*, April 5, 1991, CA).

It should be observed that the rule does not confer any *new* rights on a tenant or other occupier. Its only effect is to give those who may apply for relief an opportunity of doing so.

In the course of winding-up proceedings, the Companies Court has jurisdiction to make an order for possession against the company where there is no defence to the claim for the forfeiture of the lease, but the Companies Court has no jurisdiction to entertain an application by a sub-tenant or mortgagee for relief from forfeiture under s.146 of the Law of Property Act 1925, since a winding-up proceeding is not "an action" and therefore relief from forfeiture has to be applied for by a separate proceeding (*Re Blue Jeans Sales Ltd* [1979] 1 W.L.R. 362; [1979] 1 All E.R. 641).

Landlord and Tenant Act 1954—In order to obtain the benefit of the provisions of s.16 a tenant, against whom an order for possession has been made, has not only to give notice in writing to the immediate landlord that he desires that the provisions of paras (a) and (b) of s.16(2) shall have effect, but also to lodge a copy of the notice in Court. In such a case the order will not have effect except if and so far as it provides for the payment of costs. **R45.3.8**

Wrongful or irregular execution of writ of possession—A sheriff and his officers executing a judgment (*e.g.* by causing an eviction) however wrong the judgment, or however they may be mistaken as to its effect, are not liable in an action for damages. Nor is the landlord rendered liable by his mere presence at the time of the eviction (*Williams v. Williams & Nathan* [1937] 2 All E.R. 559, CA). Nor is the character and quality of the actions of the sheriff and his officers altered because they have acted on the advice of the landlord's solicitors, unless at the very least they have made it plain that their subsequent actions were undertaken only on the basis of the landlord assuming responsibility therefor (*Barclays Bank Ltd v. Roberts* [1954] 1 W.L.R. 1212; [1954] 3 All E.R. 107, CA). **R45.3.9**

Costs—See O.62, App. 3, "Fixed Costs" (see para. R62.A3 below). No costs of application are given where no costs are allowed on the judgment. **R45.3.10**

Writ of restitution—This writ is a writ of execution in aid of the writ of possession. See O.46, r.3. **R45.3.11**

Enforcement of judgment for delivery of goods

4.—(1) Subject to the provisions of these rules, a judgment or order for the delivery of any goods which does not give a person against whom the judgment is given or order made the alternative of paying the assessed value of the goods may be enforced by one or more of the following means, that is to say— **R45.4**

(a) writ of delivery to recover the goods without alternative provision for recovery of the assessed value thereof (hereafter in this rule referred to as a "writ of specific delivery");
(b) in a case in which rule 5 applies, an order of committal;
(c) in such a case, writ of sequestration.

(2) Subject to the provisions of these rules, a judgment or order for the delivery of any goods or payment of their assessed value may be enforced by one or more of the following means, that is to say—

(a) writ of delivery to recover the goods or their assessed value;
(b) by order of the court, writ of specific delivery;
(c) in a case in which rule 5 applies, writ of sequestration.

An application for an order under sub-paragraph (b) shall be made in accordance with CPR Part 23, which must be served on the defendant against whom the judgment or order sought to be enforced was given or made.

(3) A writ of specific delivery, and a writ of delivery to recover any goods or their assessed value, may include provision for enforcing the payment of any money adjudged or ordered to be paid by the judgment or order which is to be enforced by the writ.

(4) A judgment or order for the payment of the assessed value of any goods may be enforced by the same means as any other judgment or order for the payment of money.

Effect of rule—This rule makes a sharp distinction between a judgment or order for delivery of goods (1) which does *not* give the defendant the option of retaining them by paying their assessed value and (2) which *does* give the defendant such an option. In the case of a judgment or order in the first form, the method of enforcement is by writ of specific delivery, for the issue of which no leave of the Court is required. In the case of a judgment or order in the second form, the method of enforcement is by a writ of delivery to recover the goods or their assessed value, for which again **R45.4.1**

no leave is required, but in the case of such a judgment, if it is desired to enforce it by a writ of specific delivery, *i.e.* by depriving the defendant of the option of paying the assessed value of the goods, then the leave of the Court must first be obtained (see para. 2(b)).

A judgment or order to deliver goods which does not give the defendant the option of retaining them by paying their assessed value will not be enforceable by an order of committal or by writ of sequestration unless it specifies the time within which this act is required to be done and the defendant refuses or neglects to do it within that time (see r.5(1); and a judgment order to deliver goods or to pay their assessed value will not be enforceable by writ of sequestration unless it specifies the time within which the delivery of the goods or the payment of the assessed value is required to be done and the defendant refuses or neglects to do either such act within that time (see r.5(1)). Accordingly, as a judgment or order to deliver goods, whether or not it gives the defendant the option of paying their assessed value, will not in practice specify the time within which the act is required to be done it will not ordinarily be enforceable by an order of committal or by writ of sequestration, but only by a writ of specific delivery or a writ of delivery. If, however, in an extreme case, it is desired to enforce the judgment or order by an order of committal or writ of sequestration, as the case may be, it will be necessary first to apply to the Court under r.6, or in the case of a judgment or order for the delivery of goods or payment of their assessed value under r.5(3) for an order for a writ of specific delivery under r.4(2)(b) which will fix the time within which the defendant is required to deliver the goods and to serve such order upon the defendant with the requisite penal notice indorsed thereon under r.7, and then to apply under r.5, for order of committal (see O.52) or under this rule for a writ of sequestration, as the case may be.

R45.4.2 **Writ of delivery**—For forms of writs of delivery, see Forms Nos 64 and 65 (SCP 1999, Vol. 2, Section 1A, paras 1A–64 and 1A–65). It should be observed that there is no writ named as "a writ of specific delivery", but Form No. 64, is the form of a writ of delivery of goods which does not give the defendant the option of paying their assessed value and it is referred to in this rule as a "writ of specific delivery."

It is important to note that the power of distress until delivery, which was contained in the former prescribed writ of delivery for the return of chattels alone, has been omitted from the new form of the writ of specific delivery, but this is not a material change in the practice.

The writ of delivery may be combined with a writ of *fi. fa.* (para. (3) and see Forms 64 and 65).

The writ of delivery contains a recital of the judgment or order that the defendant "do deliver" the goods to the plaintiff. It must therefore contain sufficient description of the goods which are to be so delivered.

The writ of delivery will issue upon a judgment or order entered before October 1, 1966, in the form that the plaintiff "do have a return of the chattels" (see r.13) but in such a case the recital of the writ may have to be altered so as to correspond to the judgment entered.

Where a writ of delivery is issued for the delivery up of goods which are not in the custody of the defendant or for payment of their value, it is the duty of the defendant to take proper steps to make effective the delivery of the goods wherever they are to the plaintiff and for this purpose at least inform the plaintiff and any other persons concerned that the goods, being the property of the plaintiff, were at his disposal, otherwise the plaintiff is entitled to issue a writ of *fi. fa.* for the assessed value of the goods (*Metals and Ropes Co. Ltd v. Tattersall* [1966] 1 W.L.R. 1500; [1966] 3 All E.R. 401, CA).

R45.4.3 **Leave to issue writ of delivery**—Where the judgment creditor has obtained a judgment or order under O.14 (see O.14, r.9) or at trial for the delivery of the goods which does not give to the judgment debtor the option of paying their assessed value, he is entitled to issue a writ of specific delivery (Form No. 64) without the leave of the court, and without the previous assessment of their value (see *per* Collins M.R. in *Hymas v. Ogden* [1905] 1 K.B. 246, CA).

For the actual delivery a writ of assistance may issue with leave (see O.46, r.3).

Where the judgment creditor has obtained a judgment or order for the delivery of the goods or the payment of their assessed value, he must first proceed to the assessment of the value, and then he may issue the writ of delivery (Form No. 65) for the delivery of the goods or their assessed value, and he is entitled to do so without leave.

On the other hand, where the judgment creditor has obtained a judgment or order for the delivery of the goods, or the payment of their assessed value, and he desires to proceed to recover the goods without giving the judgment debtor the option of paying their value, he must apply for an order of the Court to issue a writ of specific delivery under r.4(2)(b). The Court has a discretion whether to grant such leave to issue a writ for specific delivery (see *Whiteley Ltd v. Hilt* [1918] 2 K.B. 808, CA; *Cohen v. Roche* [1927] 1 K.B. 169).

R45.4.4 **Reserve and Auxiliary Forces (Protection of Civil Interests) Act 1951**—In the cases covered by this Act no judgment or order for delivery of any property other than mortgaged property by reason of a default in payment of money may be enforced without the leave of the Court (s.2(3)).

R45.4.5 **Costs**—See O.62, App.3, "Fixed costs" in Sched. 1 (see para. R62.A3 below).

Enforcement of judgment to do or abstain from doing any act

5.—(1) Where— R45.5

(a) a person required by a judgment or order to do an act within a time specified in the judgment or order refuses or neglects to do it within that time or, as the case may be, within that time as extended or abridged under a court order or CPR rule 2.11; or

(b) a person disobeys a judgment or order requiring him to abstain from doing an act,

then, subject to the provisions of these rules, the judgment or order may be enforced by one or more of the following means, that is to say—

(i) with the permission of the court, a writ of sequestration against the property of that person;

(ii) where that person is a body corporate, with the permission of the court, a writ of sequestration against the property of any director or other officer of the body;

(iii) subject to the provisions of the Debtors Act 1869 and 1878, an order of committal against that person or, where that person is a body corporate, against any such officer.

(2) Where a judgment or order requires a person to do an act within a time therein specified and an order is subsequently made under rule 6 requiring the act to be done within some other time, references in paragraph (1) of this rule to a judgment or order shall be construed as references to the order made under rule 6.

(3) Where under any judgment or order requiring the delivery of any goods the person liable to execution has the alternative of paying the assessed value of the goods, the judgment or order shall not be enforceable by order of committal under paragraph (1), but the court may, on the application of the person entitled to enforce the judgment or order, make an order requiring the first mentioned person to deliver the goods to the applicant within a time specified in the order, and that order may be so enforced.

Effect of rule—This rule governs the methods for the enforcement by the Court of its judgments or orders in circumstances amounting to a contempt of Court. It applies to both positive and negative judgments or orders, *i.e.* those which require a party to do an act as well as those which require a party to abstain from doing an act, subject, however, to this important qualification that the coercive methods of enforcement under this rule cannot be employed to enforce a judgment or order to do an act unless that act is required to be done, but is not done, within a specified time which has been fixed either by the original judgment or order, or by a subsequent order extending or abridging such time under CPR, r.3.1(2)(a) or fixing such time under r.6. R45.5.1

An order made by a Court of unlimited jurisdiction, even though irregular, must be obeyed unless and until it is set aside, and therefore disobedience to an interlocutory injunction which is irregular amounts to a contempt of Court (*Isaacs v. Robertson* [1985] A.C. 97); [1984] 3 W.L.R. 705; [1984] 3 All E.R. 140, PC).

The effect of the qualification is, that a judgment or order to pay money to some other person or to give possession of land or to deliver goods which need not, and will not as a general rule, specify the time within which such act is required to be done will not come within this rule, and so will not be enforceable by writ of sequestration or order of committal, unless and until time is specified for the doing of that Act (see para. (2) and r.6).

The methods of enforcement under the rule are

(i) by writ of sequestration, see O.46, r.5, and

(ii) by order of committal, see O.52, which is additional to the powers of the court under the Debtors Acts 1869 and 1878, under r.1, which, however, are curtailed by section 11 of AJA 1970 (see SCP 1999, Vol. 2, Section 20B, para. 20B–77).

This rule must be read together with r.7, under which as a general rule, enforcement under this rule cannot be obtained unless a copy of the order is served personally on the person in default with the requisite penal notice indorsed thereon.

Enforcing judgment requiring act to be done—A judgment or order requiring any act to be done must state the time within which the act is to be done before it can be enforced by the methods provided by this rule. Such time may be specified either by the original judgment or R45.5.2

order (see Practice Direction (Judgments and Orders) para. 8.1 (40BPD–002)) as extended or abridged under CPR, r.3.1(2)(a), or by agreement of the parties under CPR. r.2.11, or by a supplemental order made subsequently under r.6 (see para. (2)).

A further requirement for the enforcement under this rule of a judgment or order requiring an act to be done is due compliance with r.7.

An act required to be done may be directed to be done by the party by whom the judgment or order was obtained or by some other person appointed by the Court, and at the expense of the disobedience party (see r.8).

A person practising as a solicitor but not duly qualified, who has been ordered to deliver up documents and to pay money, may be committed for breach of the order under this rule (*Re Hulm & Lewis* [1892] 2 Q.B. 261).

A declaratory order is not a coercive order, and refusal of a party to comply with its terms does not amount to a contempt of Court (*Webster v. Southwark London Borough Council* [1983] Q.B. 698).

R45.5.3 **Breach of an undertaking**—An undertaking given to the Court is equivalent to an injunction, and its breach may be punished in the same way as the breach of an injunction (*L. & Birm. Ry. v. Grand Junction Canal Co.* (1835) 1 Ry. Ca. 224; *Neath Canal Co. v. Ynisarwed Resolven Coll. Co.* (1875) L.R. 10 Ch. 450; *Milburn v. Newton Colliery Ltd* (1908) 52 S.J. 317); *Northern Counties Securities Ltd v. Jackson and Steeple Ltd* [1974] 1 W.L.R. 1133, p. 1143; [1974] 2 All E.R. 625 at 634; *Re British Concrete Pipe Association's Agreement (Note)* [1983] I.C.R. 215, CA, affirming [1982] I.C.R. 182, RPCt).

Although an undertaking given to the Court in lieu of an injunction is recorded in a formal order, nevertheless it is the undertaking itself and not the order which requires the person giving it to comply with its terms and therefore failure to do so does not constitute disobedience to the order; and moreover, although such an undertaking is as binding and effective as an order, it differs from it in a fundamental way in that an undertaking is voluntary rather than imposed, and the person giving it is presumed to know of it. For these reasons the procedural requirements for the enforcement of an undertaking are not as strict as those applying to the enforcement of a judgment or order, and where the Court is satisfied that the person giving it knew and understood its effect, it is not necessary for a copy of the order recording the undertaking to be served on him or to be indorsed with a penal notice (*Hussain v. Hussain* [1986] Fam. 134; [1986] 2 W.L.R. 801; [1986] 1 All E.R. 961, CA; see also *Camden London Borough Council v. Alpenoak* (1985) 135 New L.J. 1209. The general practice to be adopted, however, in enforcing an undertaking given in lieu of an injunction is (1) that it should be included as a recital or preamble to an order of the Court; (2) that the order incorporating the undertaking should be issued and served on the person who gave it; and (3) that the order should be indorsed with a suitably worded notice explaining the consequences of a breach of the undertaking (*per* Neill L.J. in *Hussain v. Hussain*, above).

The Court has jurisdiction, on the application by a person to whom a solicitor gives an undertaking in his capacity as a solicitor, to exercise its summary procedure to compel the solicitor to carry out the undertaking, even though the applicant is not the client of the solicitor, and the undertaking was not given in the course of legal proceedings, and there is no suggestion of dishonourable or discreditable conduct on the part of the solicitor (*United Mining and Finance Corp. Ltd v. Becher* [1910] 2 K.B. 296; as to enforcing undertaking after action has come to an end through death, see *Coleman v. Coleman* [1920] P. 71). As to whether a director who has neither aided nor abetted the contempt can be liable under the rule for breach by the company of its undertaking, an undertaking to abstain, given to the Court and embodied in a written order, is equivalent to an injunction (*Biba Ltd v. Stratford Investments Ltd* [1973] 1 Ch. 281).

Where a defendant has voluntarily given an undertaking it is not necessary to serve on him the order containing the undertaking (*D. v. A. & Co.* [1900] 1 Ch. 484). See also *Re Launder* (1908) 98 L.T. 554.

An undertaking to give bail to avoid arrest of a vessel cannot be withdrawn by substituting the vessel for the bail (*The Borre* [1921] P. 390).

The Court will not vary an undertaking given by a party to a suit, but may release him if sufficient reason is shown (*Cutler v. Wandsworth Stadium Ltd* (1945) 172 L.T. 207, CA).

R45.5.4 **Enforcement against body corporate**—The remedies under this rule for enforcement of a judgment or order against a body corporate are (1) by writ of sequestration against the corporate property of that body; (2) by writ of sequestration against the personal property of any director or other officer of the body; and (3) by an order of committal against any director or other officer of that body. For position of directors on an undertaking, see *Biba Ltd v. Stratford Investments* [1973] 1 Ch. 281.

Where a company disobeys an injunction, a director or other officer of the company will not be liable in contempt to be committed or have his property sequestrated merely by virtue of his office or his knowledge of the order but will only be liable if he can be shewn to be in contempt under the general law of contempt and accordingly, in the absence of *mens rea* or an *actus reus*, such a director or other officer will not be liable in contempt (*Director General of Fair Trading v. Buckland* [1990] 1 W.L.R. 920; [1990] 1 All E.R. 545).

R45.5.5 **"Refuses or neglects or disobeys"**—The remedies under this rule may be applied where the person "refuses or neglects" to do an act within the time specified by the judgment or order, or where he "disobeys" a judgment or order requiring him to abstain from doing an act. Such refusal, neglect or disobedience must, however, be of a character or quality to constitute a contempt of Court, and to this extent the omission of the word "wilful" as qualifying the word "disobedience" (contained in the former O.42, r.31, but not in the former O.43, r.6, as respects refusal or neglect) has not changed the practice. See *per* Lord Wilberforce in *Heatons Transport (St Helens) Ltd v. Transport and General Workers' Union* [1973] A.C. 15 at 109; [1972] 3 All E.R. 101 at 117.

A person or corporation commits a breach of the injunction requiring him to abstain from doing an act, and is liable for process of contempt, if he or it does the act, and it is no answer to say that the act was not contumacious in the sense that, in doing it, there was no direct intention to disobey the order, and only those acts will be excluded from constituting a breach of the injunction which are casual or accidental and unintentional (*Heatons Transport (St. Helens) Ltd v. Transport and General Workers' Union*, above. Lack of intention to disobey, may however affect the penalty (*Chelsea Man plc v. Chelsea Girl Ltd (No. 2)* [1988] F.S.R. 217).

It is not a defence that the plaintiff's application is stale, though delay in bringing proceedings may affect any penalty (*Chanel Ltd v. F.G.M. Cosmetics* [1981] F.S.R. 471). A question of contempt must be decided even if it is virtually a decision of the matter in question in the action between the parties (*ibid.*). Whilst there may be jurisdiction to dismiss a contempt motion for want of prosecution, such an application failed in *Japan Capsule Computers (UK) Ltd v. Sonic Games Sales* [1988] F.S.R. 256. See also *Spectravest Inc. v. Aperknit Ltd* [1988] F.S.R. 161. However, when the breach alleged is of an interlocutory order, subsistence and ownership of the rights claimed must be assumed (*ibid.*).

Disobedience means refusal by the corporation or its servants (*Att.-Gen. v. Walthamstow U.D.C.* (1895) 11 T.L.R. 533) or neglect by its servants (*Stancomb v. Trowbridge U.D.C.* [1910] 2 Ch. 190) to do the things which the corporation has been ordered to do. In the two cases cited the writ of sequestration was ordered to lie in the office for a period of nine and six months respectively; and see *Lee v. Aylesbury Urban District Council* (1902) 19 T.L.R. 106. A man is deemed to do a relevant act "by his servants or agents" if (a) the persons who did the acts were his servants or agents (b) the acts were done in the course of the service or agency and (c) he either (i) authorised the acts or (ii) could reasonably have foreseen the possibility of such acts and failed to take all reasonable steps to prevent them (*Hone v. Page* [1980] F.S.R. 500). Accidental and unintentional results of an act may be sufficient to cause that act to constitute disobedience if repeated (*Davis v. Rhayader Granite Quarries Ltd* (1911) 131 L.T.J. 79). Moreover, the failure to carry out an undertaking for no excuse whatever cannot be regarded as casual, accidental or unintentional, but will amount to a refusal or neglect or even disobedience under this rule, and will constitute a contempt of court, for which sequestration may issue, though if the disregard of the order is not obstinate a fine may be imposed in lieu of sequestration (*Steiner Products Ltd v. Willy Steiner Ltd* [1966] 1 W.L.R. 986; [1966] 2 All E.R. 387).

As to the enforcement of a declaratory order by the process of sequestration, see *Webster v. Southwark London Borough Council* [1983] Q.B. 698.

Costs may be awarded on the indemnity basis (*Att.-Gen. v. Walthamstow U.D.C.* (1895) 11 T.L.R. 533; *Lee v. Aylesbury U.D.C.* (1902) 19 T.L.R. 106; and *Stancomb v. Trowbridge U.D.C.* [1910] 2 Ch. 190. This may be a sufficient punishment where there have been minor breaches of the order because the defendants did not take sufficient care to comply with its terms (*G.C.T. (Management) Ltd v. The Laurie Marsh Group Ltd* [1973] R.P.C. 432, distinguishing *Plating Co. v. Farquharson* (1881) 17 Ch.D. 49).

Judgment or order requiring delivery of goods—Where the judgment or order for the delivery of goods gives the defendant the option either to deliver the goods or to pay their assessed value, it cannot be enforced by an order of committal (para. (3) and r.4(2)). In such a case, however, an order may be obtained under para. (3) for the delivery of the goods to the plaintiff within a specified time, and upon the making of such order, enforcement may be obtained by order of committal. Such order, however, can only be obtained by application to the Master, which should be served upon the defendant. If, however, it is desired to proceed by writ of sequestration, the proper course is to apply for an order for the issue of a writ of specific delivery, see r.4(2)(b) and (c). It is a question of construction of the order whether the defendants are required to deliver up only articles which were in their possession at the time of the order and not articles coming into their possession subsequently; (*Spectravest Inc. v. Aperknit Ltd* [1988] F.S.R. 161). **R45.5.6**

Judgment or order referring to legal basis of order—Where an order refers to the legal right involved (*e.g.* passing-off) as well as the acts not to be done these words are not otiose, and there is no breach of the order unless the acts relied on are in fact breaches of the legal right; but though no question of *res judicata* is involved, the matter being purely one of construction of the order, the terms of the order may presuppose a wide range of the acts now complained of as constituting an invasion of the legal right (*Chelsea Man plc v. Chelsea Girl Ltd (No. 2)* [1988] F.S.R. 217 following *Calor Gas (Distributing) Co. Ltd v. G. Cooper* [1962] R.P.C. 16). And it is only the defendant's acts that must be proved beyond reasonable doubt; it may be a question for the impression of the Court whether the facts amount in law to a breach of the court order (*Chelsea Man plc v. Chelsea Girl Ltd (No. 2)* [1988] F.S.R. 217). **R45.5.7**

Judgment, etc. requiring act to be done: order fixing time for doing it

R45.6 **6.**—(1) Notwithstanding that a judgment or order requiring a person to do an act specifies a time within which the act is to be done, the court shall, have power to make an order requiring the act to be done within another time, being such time after service of that order, or such other time, as may be specified therein.

(2) Where a judgment or order requiring a person to do an act does not specify a time within which the act is to be done, the court shall have power subsequently to make an order requiring the act to be done within such time after service of that order, or such other time, as may be specified therein.

(3) An application for an order under this rule must be made in accordance with CPR Part 23 and the application notice must, be served on the person required to do the act in question.

R45.6.1 **Effect of rule**—This rule logically follows through the scheme under which judgments for the payment of money to a person or for giving possession of land or for delivery of goods are expressed in the form of requiring the defendant to do an act and while such judgments will not as a general rule in the first instance specify the time within which the required act is to be done, this rule provides that the Court may specify such a time subsequently by a supplemental order made upon an application issued for this purpose. (See generally SCP 1999, Vol. 2, paras 1A–45 to 1A–64).

This rule only applies to a judgment or order which requires an act to be done. It does not apply to merely prohibitive orders (*Selous v. Croydon Rural Sanitary Authority* (1885) 53 L.T. 209). Nor does this Rule apply to an order made under the Inheritance (Family Provision) Act 1938 (now the Inheritance (Provision) for Family and Dependants) Act 1975 (Re Jennery (dec'd.) [1967] Ch. 280; [1967] 1 All E.R. 691, CA).

Para.(1) of the rule states the present practice, under which a judgment or order which specifies the time within which an act is required to be done may, by supplemental order of the Court made subsequently, fix another time for the required act to be done. The practice extends to an order containing a positive undertaking to do a certain act within a specified time (*D. v. A. & Co.* [1900] 1 Ch. 484; *Re Launder* (1908) 98 L.T. 554). Thus where the undertaking was to do an act forthwith (*Halford v. Hardy* (1900) 81 L.T. 721) or where no time was fixed (*Carter v. Roberts* [1903] 2 Ch. 312) orders were made fixing a time. In *Cotton v. Heyl* [1930] 1 Ch. 510, where the undertaking was to "pay out of the first moneys received", the Court made a similar order.

Para.(2) of the rule empowers the Court to make an order specifying the time within which the required act is to be done in two cases, namely (1) where the judgment or order does not itself specify such a time whether by omission or inadvertence or otherwise: and (2) where the judgment or order is to pay money to some other person, or to give possession of land or to deliver goods, and the time within which such act is to be done is not as it generally would not be, specified by the judgment or order. This para. accordingly negatives the former practice, under which in the case of a judgment for the recovery of money, the Court had no jurisdiction to add a limitation of time within which payment was to be made and so formed a right to sequestration in default of payment (*Hulbert v. Cathcart* [1894] 1 Q.B. 244) nor subsequently to make a supplemental order to fix a time for payment by a certain day (*Re Oddy* [1906] 1 Ch. 93; *cf. Drewett v. Edwards* (1878) 37 L.T. 622).

The time within which the Court may under the rule specify that the required act is to be done may be fixed by reference to the sense of the order, or it may be such other time as the Court may think fit. It is, however, desirable that the time should be stated in the order with precision, *e.g.* "on or before (*or* not later than) the 31st May, 1999," *or* "before noon (*or* 4 p.m. *or as may be*) on —— day, the —— day of ——, 2000."

Service of copy of judgment, etc., prerequisite to enforcement under rule 5

R45.7 **7.**—(1) In this rule references to an order shall be construed as including references to a judgment.

(2) Subject to paragraphs (6) and (7) of this rule, an order shall not be enforced under rule 5 unless—

(a) a copy of the order has been served personally on the person required to do or abstain from doing the act in question; and
(b) in the case of an order requiring a person to do an act, the copy has been so served before the expiration of the time within which he was required to do the act.

(3) Subject as aforesaid, an order requiring a body corporate to do or

abstain from doing an act shall not be enforced as mentioned in rule 5(1)(b)(ii) or (iii) unless—

(a) a copy of the order has also been served personally on the officer against whose property permission is sought to issue a writ of sequestration or against whom an order of committal is sought; and

(b) in the case of an order requiring the body corporate to do an act, the copy has been so served before the expiration of the time within which the body was required to do the act.

(4) There must be prominently displayed on the front of the copy of an order served under this rule a warning to the person on whom the copy is served that disobedience to the order would be a contempt of court punishable by imprisonment, or (in the case of an order requiring a body corporate to do or abstain from doing an act) punishable by sequestration of the assets of the body corporate and by imprisonment of any individual responsible.

(5) With the copy of an order required to be served under this rule, being an order requiring a person to do an act, there must also be served a copy of any order or agreement under CPR rule 2.11 extending or abridging the time for doing the act and, where the first-mentioned order was made under rule 5(3) or 6 of this order, a copy of the previous order requiring the act to be done.

(6) An order requiring a person to abstain from doing an act may be enforced under rule 5 notwithstanding that service of a copy of the order has not been effected in accordance with this rule if the court is satisfied that pending such service, the person against whom or against whose property is sought to enforce the order has had notice thereof either—

(a) by being present when the order was made, or

(b) by being notified of the terms of the order, whether by telephone, telegram or otherwise.

(7) The court may dispense with service of a copy of an order under this rule if it thinks it just to do so.

Effect of rule—The rule makes explicit the conditions precedent to the enforcement of a judgment or order by writ of sequestration or by order of committal under rule by specifying (1) the requisite document(s) to be served; (2) the time within which such document(s) must be served; (3) the person on whom such document(s) must be served; and (4) the terms of the penal notice to be indorsed. The rule also recognises the present practice under which the Court may dispense with service of the requisite document(s). R45.7.1

Paragraph (6) the Court has the power to proceed to the enforcement of a negative order by writ of sequestration or by order of committal even though the original order has not yet been served in accordance with the requirements of this rule, provided however that the Court is satisfied that the person or party in question has had notice of it either by being present when the order was made or by being notified of its terms by telephone, telegram or in such other manner as the Court may deem sufficient. A negative order is often made without notice in circumstances of great urgency to preserve the status quo, and it would be highly inconvenient if it could not be enforced until it was first served as required by this rule. Paragraph (6) is designed to enable the Court, if necessary before service, to prevent disobedience or further disobedience or to compel obedience to a negative order.

Documents required to be served—The document or documents which are required by this rule to be served as a condition precedent to enforcement by writ of sequestration or order of committal under r.5 are: R45.7.2

(a) in the case of a judgment or order to abstain from doing an act, a copy of that judgment or order;

(b) in the case of a judgment or order to do an act

 (i) a copy of that judgment, whether or not it specifies the time within which the required act is to be done; and

 (ii) a copy of any order extending or shortening time under CPR 3.1(2)(a) or of any written agreement to extend a time limit made under CPR, r.2.11; and

 (iii) if an order is subsequently made, whether or not the original judgment or order specified the time within which the required act was to be done, specifying the time within which such required act is to be done under r.6, or r.5(3) a copy of that order also (see para. (5) and *Re Seal* [1903] 1 Ch. 87).

R45.7.3 **Method of service**—In every case the requisite document or documents must be served personally on the person required to do or abstain from doing the act in question, or on the officer of the body corporate against whom it is sought to enforce an order requiring that body to do or abstain from doing the act in question. The Court, however, has power to order service of the requisite documents "by an alternative method" (see CPR, r.6.8).

R45.7.4 **Time for service of documents**—Where a specified time is limited for doing the act required, the order must be served within that time (para. 2(b) and para. 3(b): *Iberian Trust Ltd v. Founders Trust and Investment Co. Ltd* [1932] 2 K.B. 87); or else a supplemental order extending the time fixed must be obtained (*Treherne v. Dale* (1884) 27 Ch.D. 66; *Re Seal* [1903] 1 Ch. 87).

R45.7.5 **Person on whom documents to be served**—In the case of a judgment or order requiring an individual to do or abstain from doing an act, the requisite documents must be served on that person personally.

Where an order is made against parties jointly and severally liable (as *e.g.* trustees) and one of them cannot be served with the requisite documents, service against the other is sufficient to found committal against him (*Re Ellis* (1906) 54 W.R. 526).

In the case of a judgment or order requiring a body corporate to do or abstain from doing an act, the requisite documents must be served on the body corporate in order to found an application for a writ of sequestration against the corporate property, and if it is sought to proceed by way of a writ of sequestration against the property of any director or other officer of that body or by way of committal against the person of such director or other officer, the requisite documents must be served personally on that director or officer.

R45.7.6 **Indorsement of penal notice or order**—It is a necessary condition for the enforcement of a judgment or order under r.5 by way of sequestration or committal, that the copy of the judgment or order served under this rule should have the requisite penal notice prominently indorsed thereon.

This must be indorsed on the copy for service of all orders which are required to be served, whether personally or not, (*Hampden v. Wallis* (1884) 26 Ch.D. 746) and this rule applies, even where the "defendant" is a limited liability company (*Benabo v. William Jay & Partners Ltd* [1941] Ch. 52; [1940] W.N. 330). A similar memorandum has to be indorsed on orders in divorce proceedings requiring a person to do an act under O.45, r.7(4) (High Court Cases) or CCR 1981, O. 29, r.1 (county court cases).

Although it was doubted in *Evans v. Evans* (1893) 67 L.T. 719, whether a citation to bring in a grant in Probate proceedings was within this rule, it is the practice for it to be indorsed hereunder. It is also the practice to indorse a witness summons to bring in scripts (*Re Bristow* (1892) 66 L.T. 60).

The indorsement on the front of the order should be in the following words or in words to the following effect:—

In the case of a judgment or order requiring a person to do an act within a specified time or to abstain from doing an act:

> "If you, the within named A.B. neglect to obey this judgment (*or* order) by the time stated (*or in the case of an order to abstain from doing an act,* "If you, the within named A.B. disobey this judgment (*or* order)), you may be held to be in contempt of Court and liable to imprisonment."

In the case of a judgment (*or* order) requiring a body corporate to do within a specified time or to abstain from doing an act:

> "If you, the within named A.B., Ltd neglect to obey this judgment (*or* order) by the time stated (*or in the case of an order to abstain from doing an act,* "If you, the within named A.B., Ltd disobey this judgment (*or* order)), you may be held to be in contempt of Court and liable to sequestration of your assets."

In the case of a judgment (*or* order) requiring a body corporate to do or to abstain from doing an act, but it is sought to take enforcement proceedings against a director or other officer of that body:—

> "If A.B., Ltd neglect to obey this judgment (*or* order) by the time stated (*or in the case of an order to abstain from doing an act,* "If A.B., Ltd disobey this judgment (*or* order)), you, X.Y. (a director or officer of the said A.B., Ltd) may be held to be in contempt of Court and liable to imprisonment."

The Court has a discretion under O.45, r.7(6) to dispense with the failure to incorporate a penal notice in a judgment or order requiring a person to abstain from doing an act but it has no such discretion to dispense with the penal notice where the judgment or order requires the person to do an act (*Dempster v. Dempster The Independent,* November 9, 1990, CA).

The Court had no discretion to dispense with the requirement for the display on the front of the copy order in a prominent manner of the warning that disobedience would be a contempt of court punishable with imprisonment (*Moerman-Lenglet v. Henshaw The Times,* November 23, 1992).

R45.7.7 **Dispensing with service of documents**—Para. (7) embodies the former practice under which the Court has power to dispense with the service of the requisite documents in order to found an order for sequestration or committal.

An order to sign judgment unless a sum is paid before a day named need not be served on the defendant before judgment is signed upon it (*Hopton v. Robertson* (1884) W.N. 77; 23 Q.B.D. 126(n)).

An order of committal of a person for disobedience to an order requiring him to do a given act within a given time will not be directed unless a copy of the order, with a proper indorsement, has been personally served upon him in due time, or unless he has had notice of the order and is evading service thereof. The fact that the person was present in Court when the order was made is not sufficient to dispense with service of the order (*Re Tuck; Century Insurance Co. v. Larkin* [1910] 1 Ir.R. 91); but in *Haydon v. Haydon* [1911] 2 K.B. 191, CA, on an application under the Debtors Acts, an order for committal was made although the debtor had not been personally served with the order disobeyed, but he was in Court when it was made and was present when the order was made for his committal.

Effect of notice of injunction—Where the injunction is to restrain the doing of an act, the person restrained, or a person who chooses to step into his place to do the act enjoined against (*Avory v. Andrews* (1882) 51 L.J.Ch. 414) may be committed for breach of the injunction if he has in fact had notice of the granting of the injunction, either by his presence in Court at the time of granting the injunction (*Hearn v. Tennant* (1807) 14 Ves. 136; *Husson v. Husson* [1962] 1 W.L.R. 1434; [1962] 3 All E.R. 1056); or by telegram (*Anon.*, cited by Malins, V.-C., in *Heywood v. Wait* (1869) 18 W.R. 205; *Re Bryant* (1877) 4 Ch.D. 98) which should be sent by the solicitor to the party obtaining the order to a solicitor at the place where the defendant is, instructing him to give notice to the defendant of the order (*Ex p. Langley* (1879) 13 Ch.D. 110 at 122; see *The Seraglio* (1885) 10 P.D. 120); or in any other way (*Avory v. Andrews* (1882) 51 L.J.Ch. 414; but if the person charged with breach of the injunction swears positively that he did not believe the injunction had been granted, and is not cross-examined on that point, he will not be committed for contempt (*Kimpton v. Eve* (1813) 2 V. & B. 349; *Ex p. Langley* (1879) 13 Ch.D. 110). He will not escape, after entry of the order, on the ground that it has not been served, unless there is something to show that the party obtaining it did not intend to enforce it (*United Telephone Co. v. Dale* (1884) 25 Ch.D. 778). R45.7.8

Where notice of an injunction had been obtained from the Press Association by newspapers subscribing to the Association, they were shown to have sufficient notice of the injunction and could be in contempt of court if they published material subject to an injunction since personal service could be dispensed with if unpracticable (*Cleveland County Council v. W.* (1988) *The Independent*, May 5).

Receipt by a person who has been restrained by injunction from receiving it, of money from the Crown, which is not bound by the injunction, is a contempt (*Eastern Trust Co. v. McKenzie, Mann & Co.* [1915] A.C. 750).

Court may order act to be done at expense of disobedient party

8. If an order of mandamus, a mandatory order, an injunction or a judgment or order for the specific performance of a contract is not complied with, then, without prejudice to its powers under section 39 of the Act and its powers to punish the disobedient party for contempt, the court may direct that the act required to be done may, so far as practicable, be done by the party by whom the order or judgment was obtained or some other person appointed by the court, at the cost of the disobedient party, and upon the act being done the expenses incurred may be ascertained in such manner as the court may direct and execution may issue against the disobedient party for the amount so ascertained and for costs. R45.8

Effect of rule—Under the S.C.A. 1981, s.39 the Court has power to order a conveyance, contract or other document to be executed or a negotiable instrument to be indorsed by a person nominated by the Court in place of the party who has neglected or refused to comply with a judgment or order directing him to do so, and such conveyance, contract, document or instruments executed and indorsed will operate and be available for all purposes as if it had been executed or indorsed by the party directed to do so. For the practice under this section, see Vol. 2, Section 20A, paras 20A–240 to 20A–247. R45.8.1

Where a party fails to carry out an undertaking this rule does not apply, but leave may be given to the other party to the work and apply for an order for payment of his expenses (*Mortimer v. Wilson* (1885) 33 W.R. 927).

Upon a motion to rectify the register of a company, where it appeared that there was no one having authority to carry out the order of the Court, Kekewich J., refused to make an order under this rule in the first instance, but made a mandatory order on the company to rectify, leaving the parties to make a subsequent application in case of non-compliance (*Re L.L.Syndicate* (1901) 17 T.L.R. 711; *cf. Manihot Plantations* (1919) 63 S.J. 827).

Execution by or against person not being a party

R45.9 **9.**—(1) Any person, not being a party to proceedings, who obtains any order or in whose favour any order is made, shall be entitled to enforce obedience to the order by the same process as if he were a party.

(2) Any person, not being a party to proceedings, against whom obedience to any judgment or order may be enforced, shall be liable to the same process for enforcing obedience to the judgment or order as if he were a party.

R45.9.1 **Effect of rule**—By its very nature, this rule is of limited application. It has been used to enforce payment by trustees of maintenance for a child; see *Blackett v. Blackett* (1884) 51 L.T. 427 and *Oliver v. Lowther* (1880) 28 W.R. 381.

See also RSC, O.15, r.12 as to enforcing an order in representative proceedings.

Conditional judgment: waiver

R45.10 **10.** A party entitled under any judgment or order to any relief subject to the fulfilment of any condition who fails to fulfil that condition is deemed to have abandoned the benefit of the judgment or order, and, unless the court otherwise directs, any other person interested may take any proceedings which either are warranted by the judgment or order or might have been taken if the judgment or order had not been given or made.

R45.10.1 **Effect of rule**—This rule makes the fulfilment of a condition subject to which a party is entitled to relief of the essence of the judgment or order. Thus, where an order was made for relief from forfeiture conditional on the performance by defendants of certain conditions some of which they declined to carry out, it was held that the order fell to the ground, and that the position was the same as if the application for relief had been refused (*Tabot v. Blindell* [1908] 2 K.B. 114).

After the grant of an injunction for infringement of patent, the European Court of Justice changed the law so as to forbid the granting of an injunction in like circumstances on the happening of a certain event (the endorsement of a patent "licences of right"). The injunction was stayed in advance of the happening of that event in the exercise of the Court's discretion (*E.I. Du Pont de Nemours & Co. v. Enka B.V. (No.2)* [1988] F.S.R. 69; [1988] R.P.C. 497).

Matters occurring after judgment: stay of execution, etc.

R45.11 **11.** Without prejudice to Order 47, rule 1, a party against whom a judgment has been given or an order made may apply to the court for a stay of execution of the judgment or order or other relief on the ground of matters which have occurred since the date of the judgment or order, and the court may by order grant such relief, and on such terms, as it thinks just.

Forms of writs

R45.12 **12.**—(1) A writ of fieri facias must be in such of the Forms Nos. 53 to 63 in the relevant practice direction as is appropriate in the particular case.

(2) A writ of delivery must be in Form No. 64 or 65 in the relevant practice direction, whichever is appropriate.

(3) A writ of possession must be in Form No. 66 or 66A in the relevant practice direction, whichever is appropriate.

(4) A writ of sequestration must be in Form No. 67 in the relevant Practice Direction.

R45.12.1 **Forms of writs**—The forms of writs of execution have not changed and are those contained in (see SCP 1999, Vol. 2, Section 1A). These forms must be used where applicable and appropriate in the particular case, but of course with such variations as the circumstances of the particular case require. The form must be followed, having regard to the directions contained in the judgment or order itself (*Boswell v. Coaks* (1887) 36 W.R. 65).

The more important forms of writs of *fi. fa.* are: the writ of *fi. fa.*, employed to enforce a judgment or order for the payment of money to a person (Form No. 53, see Vol. 2, Section 1A, para. 1A–53); the writ of *fi. fa.* on an order for costs (Form No. 54, see Vol. 2, Section 1A, para. 1A–54); the writ of *fi. fa.* after levy of part (Form No. 56, see Vol. 2, Section 1A, para. 1A–56); and the writ of *fi. fa.* against personal representative (Form No. 57, see Vol. 2, Section 1A, para. 1A–57).

Form No. 64 (Vol. 2, Section 1A, para. 1A–64) is the writ of specific delivery and is the appropriate writ to enforce a judgment or order for the specific delivery of goods without the alternative of paying the assessed the value (see r.4(1)): whereas the writ of delivery in Form No. 65 (Vol. 2, Section 1A, para. 1A–65) is appropriate to enforce a judgment or order for the delivery of goods or the payment of their value.

Form No. 66 (Vol. 2, Section 1A, para. 1A–66) is the general writ of possession of land, and Form No. 66A (Vol. 2, Section 1A, para. 1A–67) is the writ of possession for the recovery of land which will issue only under an order for possession made under O.113.

In addition to the writs of execution mentioned in the rule, contains the prescribed form of the writ of restitution (Form No. 68, see Vol. 2, Section 1A, para. 1A–69) and the writ of assistance (Form No. 69, see Vol. 2, Section 1A, para. 1A–70) see O.46, r.3.

Enforcement of judgments and orders for recovery of money, etc.

13.—(1) Rule 1(1) of this order, with the omission of sub-paragraphs (e) and (f) thereof, and Orders 46 to 51 shall apply in relation to a judgment or order for the recovery of money as they apply in relation to a judgment or order for the payment of money. R45.13

(2) Rule 3 of this order, with the omission of paragraphs (1)(b) and (c) thereof, and Order 47, rule 3(2) shall apply in relation to a judgment or order for the recovery of possession of land as they apply in relation to a judgment or order for the giving or delivery of possession of land.

(3) Rule 4 of this order, with the omission of paragraph 1(b) and (c) and (2)(c) thereof, and Order 47, rule 3(2) shall apply in relation to a judgment or order that a person do have a return of any goods and to a judgment or order that a person do have a return of any goods or do recover the assessed value thereof as they apply in relation to a judgment or order for the delivery of any goods and a judgment or order for the delivery of any goods or payment of the assessed value thereof respectively.

Effect of rule—It is a surprise to find RSC, O.45, r.13 preserved in Sched 1 of the CPR given that its purpose is to make provision for the enforcement of certain judgments entered in the old forms before October 1, 1966. R45.13.1

The judgments to which this rule applies are (1) a judgment or order for the recovery of money (para. (1)); (2) a judgment or order for the recovery of possession of land (para. (2)); and (3) a judgment or order for the return of goods (para. (3)). The rule, however, expressly excludes a means of enforcing such judgments an order of committal or a writ of sequestration, thus preserving the law as it applied to such judgments before October 1, 1966 (see *Hulbert v. Cathcart* [1894] 1 Q.B. 244; *Re Oddy* [1906] 1 Ch. 93). Moreover, r.6, does not apply to such judgments, and therefore the Court has no jurisdiction to make an order specifying the time within which the judgment or order is to be performed (*Re Oddy*) so that such judgments cannot be transformed into judgments which will become enforceable by writ of sequestration or committal order in the High Court.

Notwithstanding that it is not expressly mentioned in this rule, it seems that r.11 will apply to such judgments.

Enforcement of decisions of Value Added Tax Tribunals

14.—(1) An application under section 29 of the Finance Act 1985 for registration of a decision of a Value Added Tax Tribunal on an appeal under section 83 of the Value Added Tax Act 1994 shall be made by a request in writing to the head clerk of the Crown Office— R45.14

(a) exhibiting the decision or a duly authenticated copy thereof;

(b) stating, so far as is known to the witness, the name and occupation and the usual or last known address or place of business of the person against whom it is sought to enforce the decision; and

(c) stating, to the best of the information and belief of the witness, the amount which as a result of the decision is, or is recoverable as, tax from such person at the date of the application and the amount then remaining unpaid of any costs awarded to the Commissioners of Customs and Excise by the decision.

(2) Notice of the registration of a decision must be served on the person

against whom it is sought to enforce the decision by delivering it to him personally or by sending it to him at his usual or last known address or place of business or in such manner as the court may direct.

(3) There shall be kept in the Central Office under the direction of the Senior Master a register of the decisions registered under section 29 of the Finance Act 1985, and there shall be included in the register particulars of any execution issued on a decision so registered.

RSC ORDER 46

WRITS OF EXECUTION: GENERAL

R46.0.1 **Contents**

Editorial Introduction

R46.0.2 A writ of execution is the most commonly used method of enforcement in the High Court. For enforcement purposes the term "writ" survives the "Access to Justice" reforms (see also editorial introduction to RSC, O.45).

In addition to the writs of execution mentioned in r.1, the Order applies to the writs of execution in aid of those mentioned, namely, the writ of assistance, the writ of restitution, the writ of *venditioni exponas*, and the writ of *distringas nuper vicecomitem* (see r.3). The Order probably also applies to the writ of *fieri facias de bonis ecclesiasticis*, and the writ of *sequestrari de bonis ecclesiasticis* (see O.47, r.5). It would not appear to apply to a writ of attachment, since the power to punish for contempt of court is now to be exercised by an order of committal (see O.52, r.1(1)). The Order does not apply to the appointment of a receiver (*Norburn v. Norburn* [1894] 1 Q.B. 448).

Related sources

R46.0.3
- Supreme Court Act 1981, s.138 (SCP 1999, Vol. 2, Section 20A, paras 20A–539 to 20A–541)
- County Courts Act 1984, s.89 (Vol. 2, Section 20A, para. 20A–765)
- CCR, O.26 (Warrants of execution, delivery and possession)
- The following *Queen's Bench Practice Directions* are relevant to this Order (Vol. 2, Section 2C, paras 2C–210 to 2C–212). These Directions continue to apply for the time being (see *Practice Direction (Civil: Litigation: Procedure)* [1999] 1 W.L.R. 1124).
  —No. 36—Leave to issue writ of possession
  —No. 37—Execution against property of foreign or Commonwealth states
  —No. 38—Enforcement of magistrates' courts order
- Chancery and Queen's Bench Division Fixed Costs (Writ of Possession) (para. 62/A3/6)
- *Queen's Bench Masters' Practice Direction No. 47—Recovery of enforcement costs* (Vol. 2, Section 2A, paras 2A–119 to 2A–121)
- *Chancery Division Practice Direction No. 18—Suspended possession orders* (Vol. 2, Section 2B, para. 2B–161)

Forms

R46.0.4 The following forms (formerly included amongst the Prescribed Forms in Appendix A to the RSC) are relevant to O.46. These forms are included in Table 2 (Practice Forms) attached to Practice Direction (Forms) and may be found in SCP 1999, Vol. 2, Section 1A, paras 1A–68 to 1A–70 and 1A–72):

- PF No. 67—Writ of sequestration (r.5)
- PF No. 68—Writ of restitution (r.1)
- PF No. 69—Writ of assistance (r.1)
- PF No. 71—Notice of renewal of writ of execution (r.8)

The following Queen's Bench Masters' Practice Forms are relevant to O.46 (Vol. 2, Section 1B, para. 1B–64):

- PF 86—Praecipe for writ of *fieri facias* (r.6)

The following Chancery Masters Practice Forms are relevant to O.46 (Vol. 2, Section 1B, para. 1B–207).

- Form No. 6—Certificate on application for leave to issue execution on suspended order for possession where defendant in default of acknowledgment of service (rr.2 and 4)

Definition

1. In this order, unless the context otherwise requires, "writ of execution" includes a writ of *fieri facias*, a writ of possession, a writ of delivery, a writ of sequestration and any further writ in aid of any of the aforementioned writs. **R46.1**

When permission to issue any writ of execution is necessary

2.—(1) A writ of execution to enforce a judgment or order may not issue without the permission of the court in the following cases, that is to say:— **R46.2**

(a) where 6 years or more have elapsed since the date of the judgment or order;

(b) where any change has taken place, whether by death or otherwise, in the parties entitled or liable to execution under the judgment or order;

(c) where the judgment or order is against the assets of a deceased person coming to the hands of his executors or administrators after the date of the judgment or order, and it is sought to issue execution against such assets;

(d) where under the judgment or order any person is entitled to a remedy subject to the fulfilment of any condition which it is alleged has been fulfilled;

(e) where any goods sought to be seized under a writ of execution are in the hands of a receiver appointed by the court or a sequestrator.

(2) Paragraph (1) is without prejudice to section 2 of the Reserve and Auxiliary Forces (Protection of Civil Interests) Act 1951, or any other enactment or rule by virtue of which a person is required to obtain the permission of the court for the issue of a writ of execution or to proceed to execution on or otherwise to the enforcement of a judgment or order.

(3) Where the court grants permission, whether under this rule or otherwise, for the issue of a writ of execution and the writ is not issued within one year after the date of the order granting such permission, the order shall cease to have effect, without prejudice, however, to the making of a fresh order.

Effect of rule—The requirement of leave to issue execution under this rule applies to all writs of execution and is additional to the requirement of leave to issue particular writs of execution under other rules, *e.g.* O.45, r.3 (writ of possession); O.45, r.4(2) (writ of specific delivery of goods); O.46, r.3 (writs of execution in aid of other writs); O.46, r.5 (writ of sequestration); O.81, r.5(2) (execution against a person as a partner upon a judgment against a firm); O.81, r.6 (execution in actions between partners). **46.2.1**

The rule is also without prejudice to any other enactment or rule requiring leave to issue execution, *e.g.*, leave to enforce an award under the Arbitration Act 1950, s.26 (see SCP 1999, Vol. 2, Section 21A, paras 21A–245 to 21A–261) under which leave is only given in a clear case (*Grech v. Board of Trade* [1923] W.N. 235).

The order granting leave to issue execution shall be operative for one year after which it will cease to have effect, though a new order may be made.

Judgment over six years old—practice—Application for permission to issue execution on a judgment more than six years old should be made without notice supported by evidence (usually an affidavit of facts by the applicant or his solicitor). The evidence should state (1) the date of the judgment (2) the amount of the original judgment debt (3) the amount remaining due (4) the causes of delay (5) that the applicant is entitled to execution, *i.e.* that there has been no change of parties or devolution of interest (or, if there has been the precise nature of it). The master/district judge may decline to deal with the application without notice to the judgment debtor and require the application for permission to be served and heard on notice. **R46.2.2**

An application to issue or to extend the time for execution under a judgment was not an "action" within the meaning of s.38(1) of the Limitation Act 1980, hence to do so did not come within the provisions of s.24(1) prohibiting the bringing of an action on a judgment after the expiration of six years (*National Westminster Bank v. Powney* [1991] Ch. 339; [1990] 2 All E.R. 416, CA).

A garnishee order absolute is effective although more than six years have elapsed since the judgment (*Fellows v. Thornton* (1885) 14 Q.B.D. 335).

Dismissal of an application under this rule does not make a second application impossible, but the later application should not be granted unless it is founded on material which was not before the Court on the first application (*W. T. Lamb & Sons v. Rider* [1948] 2 K.B. 331).

R46.2.3 **Change of parties**—(1) Where the judgment creditor has died the application should be without notice (see *Mercer v. Lawrence* (1878) 26 W.R. 506, for form of order). In an Irish case (*Meehan v. Tynan* [1915] 2 Ir.R. 52) where notice was given to the debtor, no costs were allowed.

(2) Where the judgment debtor has died, notice of the application must be served on the personal representative (see *Re Shephard* (1890) 43 Ch.D. 131 at 137; commented on in *Thompson v. Gill* [1903] 1 K.B. 760, CA).

(3) Where there has been an assignment of the judgment debt it appears that the application must be properly made without notice as was the case in *Re Bagley* [1911] 1 K.B. 317, CA; the Irish practice is otherwise (see *Meehan v. Tynan*, above); *Donohoe v. Flavelle* [1916] 2 Ir.R. 192).

(4) Where a surety is seeking to enforce a judgment which he has obtained on assignment, permission to issue execution must be obtained under this rule (*Kayley v. Hothersall* [1925] 1 K.B. 607). The master/district judge will often direct an application to be made on notice (see Part 23).

R46.2.4 **Death of judgment debtor**—The rule does not apply to an executor *de son tort* (*Lord Westmeath v. Coyne* [1896] 2 Ir.R. 436).

Leave given under this rule to issue execution against the executor of a deceased debtor does not operate as a judgment against the executor. It dispenses with the necessity of recovering judgment against him (*Stewart v. Rhodes* [1900] 1 Ch. 386). A charging order *nisi* against the interest of a deceased judgment debtor is not valid as against his executor (see *Scott v. Scott* [1952] W.N. 522; [1952] 2 All E.R. 890).

R46.2.5 **Death of judgment creditor**—Until the executors have obtained permission under this rule, they cannot issue a statutory demand under the Insolvency Act 1986 (see *Ex p Woodall* (1884) 13 Q.B.D. 479, a case involving a "bankruptcy notice" which has now been superceded by the "statutory demand"). Executors can obtain permission and issue the demand without being added as parties: RSC, O.15, r.7: *Re Bagley* [1911] 1 K.B. 317.

On the death of one of several partners, the survivors are entitled to an order hereunder for execution (*Davis v. Andrews* [1884] W.N. 94).

Asking for appointment of a receiver and injunction is not asking for leave to issue execution within this rule (see *Morgan v. Hart* [1914] 2 K.B. 183, CA, and *Re A Company* [1915] 1 Ch. 520 at 527). The executors of a deceased creditor are therefore not entitled to obtain an order for appointment of a receiver of the judgment debtor's property under this rule (*Norburn v. Norburn* [1894] 1 Q.B. 448). *Semble*, the proper course in such a case is for the party becoming entitled to enforce the judgment to apply first to be added as a party to the proceedings under O.15, r.7, see *Re Shephard* (1890) 43 Ch.D. 131 at 135; *Salt v. Cooper* (1880) 16 Ch.D. 544 at 552, 553.

Presentation of a winding-up petition by a judgment creditor is not execution on a judgment (*Re A Company*, above).

R46.2.6 **Bankruptcy of judgment creditor**—The trustee in bankruptcy of a judgment creditor cannot petition for a bankruptcy order to be made until he has obtained an order under this rule; for, until that is done, he is not a petitioning creditor to whom the debt is owed (Insolvency Act 1986, s.120(1) *Re Clements* [1901] 1 K.B. 260); but the trustee can obtain an order under this rule without being added as a party under O.15, r.7 and when he had done so he is a person entitled to sign judgment (*Re Bagley* [1911] 1 K.B. 317).

R46.2.7 **Assignment**—The assignment of part of judgment does not effect such a change of parties to enable the assignee to issue execution. Execution can only be levied in respect of the whole judgment (*Forster v. Baker* [1910] 2 K.B. 636, CA; see *Rothschild v. Fisher* [1920] 2 K.B. 243, CA; *Chung Kwok Hotel Co. v. Field* [1960] 1 W.L.R. 1112 at 1115; [1960] 3 All E.R. 143 at 145).

An assignee of a judgment debt must apply for leave to issue execution under this rule; he need not obtain an order adding him as a party under O.15, r.7 (*Re Bagley* [1911] 1 K.B. 317, CA). It is submitted that an application to be so added would be improper.

Where a surety has paid a judgment debt and has obtained an assignment of the judgment under the Mercantile Law Amendment Act 1856, s.5, he must obtain the leave of the Court before he can issue execution against his co-surety to enforce contribution (*Kayley v. Hothersall* [1925] 1 K.B. 607, CA, following a *dictum* of Parker J. in *Dale v. Powell* (1911) 105 L.T. 291 at 292).

R46.2.8 **Conditional judgment or order**—An application for permission to issue execution upon the fulfilment of any condition subject to which the judgment or order was made should be made without notice supported by evidence (usually an affidavit sworn by the applicant). The master/district judge may direct that the application be made on notice.

R46.2.9 **Partner, retirement of**—Where judgment is recovered by a firm, the retirement of a partner does not amount to a change in the parties entitled to execution within this rule (*Re Frank Hill* [1921] 2 K.B. 831).

Goods in hands of receiver appointed by Court of sequestrator—Paragraph (1)(e) requires that leave must first be obtained to issue execution against goods in the hands of a receiver appointed by the Court or a sequestrator. This provision is necessary because otherwise a sheriff who seizes goods in the possession of a receiver appointed by the Court is guilty of contempt (see *Lane v. Sterne* (1862) 3 Giff. 629; *Edwards v. Edwards* (1876) 2 Ch.D. 291; and see also *Angel v. Smith* (1804) 9 Ves. 335 (sequestrator) and *Russell v. E. Anglian Ry.* (1850) 3 Mac. & G. 104). **R46.2.10**

Reserve and Auxiliary Forces (Protection of Civil Interests) Act 1951—A judgment or order for the payment or recovery of a sum of money may not (except in certain specified cases) without the leave of the Court be enforced against a person protected by this Act (s.2(1)). **R46.2.11**

Remedy barred by Limitation Act 1980—By virtue of the 1980 Act, s.24(1) which applies to judgments generally, not merely those which operate as charges on land (*Jay v. Johnstone* [1893] 1 Q.B. 25, 189, CA; see also *Watson v. Birch* (1847) 15 Sim. 523; *Hebblethwaite v. Peever* [1892] 1 Q.B. 124) no action may be brought upon any judgment after the expiration of six years from the date on which the judgment became enforceable. An action on any judgment can be an abuse of the process of the Court where there is an effective alternative method of obtaining satisfaction (*Pritchett v. English & Colonial Syndicate* [1899] 2 Q.B. 428). It was held in *Brew v. Brew* [1899] 2 Ir.R. 163, that where a judgment was obtained against A and B, and two years later execution was issued against A, and part of the debt levied, such execution kept the judgment debt alive against both A and B for a further period of six years, and the judgment creditor was entitled under the corresponding Irish rule to an order to issue execution, though more than twelve years had elapsed since the date of the judgment. See *Taylor v. Hollard* [1902] 1 K.B. 676, as to when a payment of part is sufficient to take the case out of the statute. But the right to sue on a judgment is quite distinct from the right to levy execution under it and the above-mentioned section does not enable execution to be issued without the leave of the Court at any time within six years of the judgment (*W. T. Lamb & Sons v. Rider* [1948] 2 K.B. 331, CA) and see *Berliner Industrie-bank A.G. v. Jost* [1971] 2 Q.B. 463; [1971] 2 All E.R. 1513, CA. **R46.2.12**

An application for leave to issue execution on a judgment or to extend the process of execution was not an action within the Limitation Act 1980, s.38(1) (*National Westminster Bank plc v. Powney* [1990] 2 W.L.R. 1084; [1990] 2 All E.R. 416, CA following *W. T. Lamb & Sons v. Rider* [1948] 2 K.B. 331, CA and not following *Lougher v. Donovan* [1948] 2 All E.R. 11, CA).

Duration of order—Paragraph (3) adopts the current practice under which, where leave to issue execution has been given, it was considered to endure for one year only. This was by analogy to a practice of long standing (approved by Stirling J., in *Kemp v. Abraham*, July 1888) under which the Masters required an affidavit explaining the delay before the issue of a writ of attachment upon an order which was more than a year old. **R46.2.13**

If the Master gives leave he may impose terms, *e.g.* that the writ of execution be issued within a specified time.

Execution against property of foreign or commonwealth states—In cases where judgment has been obtained against a foreign or Commonwealth state and it is sought to execute the judgment by writ of *fieri facias*, charging order or garnishee order, the provisions of *Queen's Bench Practice Direction No. 37* apply (SCP 1999, Vol. 2, Section 2C, para. 2C–211). This *Practice Direction* applies also in the Chancery Division. **R46.2.14**

Permission required for issue of writ in aid of other writ

3. A writ of execution in aid of any other writ of execution shall not issue without the permission of the court. **R46.3**

Effect of rule—In practice the writ of restitution (warrant of restitution in the county court) is the most commonly used writ "in aid of any other writ of execution". Permission to issue a writ "in aid of" another should be sought without notice supported by evidence usually in the form of an affidavit sworn by someone with knowledge of the relevant facts. **R46.3.1**

Writ of assistance—The Court still has power to order a writ of assistance to issue, and will do so in certain cases where the writ of delivery has proved or will probably prove to be fruitless. The permission of the Court must first be obtained by application made without notice supported by an affidavit, which must prove that the order for the specific delivery of goods has been served and not complied with (*Webster v. Taylor* (1854) 18 Jur. 869). **R46.3.2**

Writ of restitution—Where, after entry of the sheriff under a writ of possession, or after the **R46.3.3**

claimant has been put in possession by the sheriff, the defendant forcibly or by stratagem resumes possession of the property, the claimant may have a writ of restitution (*Pitcher v. Roe* (1841) 9 Dowl. 971). This is the normal procedure and not an application to commit for contempt (*Alliance Building Society v. Austen* [1951] 2 All E.R. 1068). Application for the writ should be made without notice to a Master on an affidavit of facts, and an order will be made for the writ to issue.

Similarly, where a claimant has entered under a judgment for possession and a writ of possession issued thereunder and where the judgment is subsequently set aside and the application nevertheless fails to restore possession to the defendant: the defendant should apply by summons to a Master for an order setting aside the writ of possession and ordering possession to be given by the claimant to the defendant and giving leave then (or subsequently on without notice application) to issue a writ of restitution. Similarly, where possession has been obtained under an irregular writ of possession, or of more land than is properly covered by the writ of possession (*ibid.*).

Where an order for possession has been made under O.113, the Court has power, on the claimant's application to order the issue of a writ of restitution, even if not all the people then in possession of the land were in such possession when the order for possession under O.113 was obtained provided that there is a plain and sufficient nexus between the original recovery of possession and the need to effect recovery of the same land (*Wiltshire County Council v. Frazer (No. 2)* [1986] 1 W.L.R. 109; [1986] 1 All E.R. 65).

R46.3.4 **Writ of venditioni exponas**—This is a writ in aid of execution by writ of *fi. fa.* It can only be issued after the sheriff has made a return that he has seized goods under the writ of *fi. fa.* which he has not sold or has been unable to sell "for want of buyers." There is now no need to file such return but the affidavit in support of the without notice application for the writ should exhibit such return.

R46.3.5 **Writ of caplas ad satisfaciendum**—This writ is abolished (see SCA 1981, s.141).

Application for permission to issue writ

R46.4 **4.**—(1) An application for permission to issue a writ of execution may be made in accordance with CPR Part 23 but the application notice need not be served on the respondent unless the court directs.

(2) Such an application must be supported by a witness statement or affidavit—

(a) identifying the judgment or order to which the application relates and, if the judgment or order is for the payment of money, stating the amount originally due thereunder and the amount due thereunder at the date the application notice is filed;

(b) stating, where the case falls within rule 2(1)(a) the reasons for the delay in enforcing the judgment or order;

(c) stating, where the case falls within rule 2(1)(b), the change which has taken place in the parties entitled or liable to execution since the date of the judgment or order;

(d) stating, where the case falls within rule 2(1)(c) or (d), that a demand to satisfy the judgment or order was made on the person liable to satisfy it and that he has refused or failed to do so;

(e) giving such other information as is necessary to satisfy the court that the applicant is entitled to proceed to execution on the judgment or order in question and that the person against whom it is sought to issue execution is liable to execution on it.

(3) The court hearing such application may grant permission in accordance with the application or may order that any issue or question, a decision on which is necessary to determine the rights of the parties, be tried in any manner in which any question of fact or law arising in proceedings may be tried and, in either case, may impose such terms as to costs or otherwise as it thinks just.

R46.4.1 **Permission for leave to issue execution on suspended orders of possession**—There is still a significant (but surely unnecessary) distinction between enforcing suspended orders for possession in the High Court and the county courts (in the county courts see CCR, O.26 in Sched. 2). In the High Court a suspended possession order is an order under which a person is entitled to relief subject to the fulfilment of a condition for the purposes of r.1.2(1)(d) and accordingly r.4 applies. Therefore an application on notice supported by evidence is required. Permission to issue execution must not be given without first allowing the defendant an opportunity of being heard. (*Fleet Mortgage and Investment Co. Ltd v. Lower Maisonette, 46 Eaton Place Ltd* [1972] 1 W.L.R. 765; [1972] 2 All E.R. 737).

Although permission is not required to issue in the county court the defendant can apply to suspend the warrant.

Application for permission to issue writ of sequestration

5.—(1) Notwithstanding anything in rules 2 and 4, an application for permission to issue a writ of sequestration must be made in accordance with CPR Part 23 and be heard by a Judge. R46.5

(2) Subject to paragraph (3) the application notice, stating the grounds of the application and accompanied by a copy of the witness statement or affidavit in support of the application, must be served personally on the person against whose property it is sought to issue the writ.

(3) The court may dispense with service of the application notice under this rule if it thinks it just to do so.

(4) The judge hearing an application for permission to issue a writ of sequestration may sit in private in any case in which, if the application were for an order of committal, he would be entitled to do so by virtue of Order 52, rule 6 but, except in such a case, the application shall be heard in public.

Sequestration—is a form of contempt proceedings available in both the High Court and the county court. It can be used only in respect of orders in the nature of an injunction and therefore only raely concerns money judgments. R46.5.1

Effect of rule—As sequestration is a form of contempt (*Pratt v. Inman* (1890) 43 Ch.D. 175) the rule requires that a writ of sequestration can issue only with permission of the court granted by a judge on an application duly served and supported by evidence. R46.5.2

Where the disobedience to the order of the Court is not obstinate and the breaches have been remedied, the Court may impose a fine in lieu of the sequestration of the assets of a company or other corporate body, especially where such sequestration would adversely affect the livelihood of innocent parties (*Steiner Products Ltd v. Willy Steiner Ltd* [1966] 1 W.L.R. 986; [1966] 2 All E.R. 387).

Judgments enforceable by sequestration—The judgments or orders that may be enforced by writ of sequestration are (1) those that require a person "to do an act" within a specified time, extended if necessary, and (2) those that require a person to abstain from "doing an act" (see O.45, r.5(1)). Negative orders are now therefore enforceable by sequestration by virtue of express provision of O.45, r.5(1)(b). R46.5.3

The overriding condition subject to which a positive judgment or order may be enforced by sequestration is that it must specify the time within which the required act must be done. In the usual case, no such time will be specified in a judgment or order to pay money to some other person, or to give possession of land, or to deliver goods, and such time will not generally be specified unless the person required to such an act is shown to be wilfully refusing or neglecting to do it. It is therefore likely to be as rare in the future as it has been in the past for the writ of sequestration to be available to issue or to issue in the case of the ordinary common law judgments for the payment of money to another person or for delivery of possession of land or goods.

Similarly it is not the practice to limit the time for payment of costs and therefore sequestration is unlikely to be used as a method of enforcing an order for the payment of costs.

Nevertheless, although O.45, r.5 refers to the power of the Court to grant permission to issue a writ of sequestration where a party refuses or neglects to comply with or disobeys a coercive order of the Court, the Court nevertheless has inherent power to ensure that its orders are carried out where the interests of justice demand that they be complied with, and therefore, in the case of a declaratory order, where a party knowingly adopts and continues a policy of refusing, neglecting or disobeying to comply with its terms, the Court has power under its inherent jurisdiction to give permission to issue a writ of sequestration (*Webster v. Southwark London Borough Council* [1983] Q.B. 698).

For instances where an order to pay money or costs has been enforced by sequestration see *Knill v. Dumergue* [1911] 2 Ch. 199 (where the facts are inaccurately stated) a vendor's action for specific performance; *Re Slade* (1881) 18 Ch.D. 653 (damages and costs); *Willcock v. Terrell* (1878) 3 Ex. D. 323 (an order to pay by instalments); *Capron v. Capron* [1927] W.N. 178 (alimony).

On the other hand, sequestration may be issued to enforce a judgment or order for the payment of money into court, which must specify the time within which such act is to be done.

Sequestration may be issued against a child (see Pt 21); or against a defendant who has become a patient since the date of the order (*Robinson v. Galland* [1889] W.N. 108).

Sequestration of course does not lie to enforce a judgment against the Crown (O.77, r.15(1));

nor against third persons who are not parties to the suit (*per* Gorell Barnes J. in *Craig v. Craig* [1896] P. 171 at 174).

R46.5.4 **Form of writ**—See Form No. 67 (SCP 1999, Vol. 2, Section 1A, para. 1A–68). The writ is addressed to four persons named in it and chosen by the person presenting the judgment or order. They need not be professional persons and are not required to give security for what they may receive.

R46.5.5 **Effect of writ**—The writ binds real property (*Re Lush* (1870) L.R. 10 Eq. 442) and personal property in possession from the time it is issued (*Burdett v. Rockley* (1682) 1 Vern. 58; *Dixon v. Rowe* (1876) 35 L.T. 548) but creates no charge on land unless it is registered (Land Charges Act 1972, s.6); in case of a chose in action the mere issue of the writ, and the service of it on the party indebted to the judgment debtor, is not enough to create a charge on the chose in action (*Ex p. Nelson* (1880) 14 Ch.D. 41; *Re Pollard* (1903) 87 L.T. 61); an order for payment must be obtained. See too, as to the effect and operation of a sequestration, the judgment of Romer L.J. in *Re Pollard* [1903] 2 K.B.41 at 47, 48, CA.

The issue of the writ, coupled with the receipt of the money of the debtor by the sequestrator, does not in itself make the creditor a secured creditor within the meaning of the Bankruptcy Act 1914 (*Re Hastings* (1892) 67 L.T. 234; *Re Pollard* [1903] 2 K.B. 41, CA) or the Insolvency Act 1986.

The title of a sequestrator will prevail over that of a mortgagee under a mortgage made with notice, and in order to avoid the effect, of a writ of a sequestration (*Ward v. Booth* (1872) L.R. 14 Eq. 195).

As to the effect of writ upon the death of the person whose estate has been sequestrated, see *Pratt v. Inman* (1890) 43 Ch.D. 175.

In relation to a writ of sequestration, the position of a third party is analogous to that of a third party in relation to an injunction, *i.e.* that he is subject to a duty not knowingly to take any action which will obstruct compliance with the terms of the writ of sequestration which requires the sequestrators to take possession of the assets of the contemnor (*Eckman v. Midland Bank Ltd* [1973] Q.B. 519; [1973] 1 All E.R. 609, N.I.R.C., not following *Re Pollard*, above).

Where sequestration of a contemnor's assets has been ordered, anyone who knowingly takes any action which prevents the sequestrators from carrying out their duty will be treated as obstructing a Court order and therefore technically in contempt of Court. Any proper and necessary request addressed by the sequestrators to the contemnor's accountants to give information concerning details of the contemnor's assets must be answered, and the accountants must divulge the information asked for, even in the absence of the contemnor's consent which is irrelevant (*Messenger Newspaper Group Ltd v. National Graphical Association* [1984] 1 All E.R. 293, CA).

R46.5.6 **Land**—The writ should be registered, so far as it affects land under the Land Charges Act 1972, s.6(1)(a).

R46.5.7 **Property liable to sequestration**—The writ includes the rents and profits of real estate and all personal estate (see Form No. 67, see SCP 1999, Vol. 2, Section 1A, para. 1A–68). The pension of a retired naval officer (*Dent v. Dent* (1867) L.R. 1 P.& D. 366); of a Judge (*Willcock v. Terrell* (1878) 3 Ex.D. 323); and of a civil servant (*Sansom v. Sansom* (1879) 4 P.D. 69); money received in commutation of a pension (*Crowe v. Price* (1889) 22 Q.B.D. 429); a deposit on appeal, ordered to be returned (*Conn v. Garland* (1874) L.R. 9 Ch. 101); a rentcharge (*Wilson v. Metcalfe* (1839) 1 Beav. 263); a pension under the East India Annuity Funds Act 1874 (*Knill v. Dumergue* [1911] 2 Ch. 199, CA); and a balance in a bank (*Miller v. Huddlestone* (1883) 22 Ch.D. 233; *Guerrine v. Guerrine* [1959] 1 W.L.R. 760; [1959] 2 All E.R. 594) have been held liable to sequestration; but not the pension of an officer in the army (*Birch v. Birch* (1883) 8 P.D. 163; *Lucas v. Lucas* (1887) 18 Q.B.D. 127; *Crowe v. Price* (1889) 22 Q.B.D. 429). The liability of property to sequestration may be determined by application under Part 23 (*Knill v. Dumergue* [1911] 2 Ch. 199).

The expression "personal estate" in the writ of sequestration includes both legal and equitable choses in action, *e.g.* surplus of proceeds of sale held on trust (*Bucknell v. Bucknell* [1969] 1 W.L.R. 1204; [1969] 2 All E.R. 998).

In a clear and simple case, a third party from whom the sequestrators claim a chose in action belonging to the contemnor does not need a specific order of the Court to give him protection to make such payment and if he unreasonably compels the sequestrators to seek such an order, he may himself be liable for the costs of such proceedings (*ibid.*, and see *Eckman v. Midland Bank Ltd* [1973] Q.B. 519; [1973] 1 All E.R. 609, N.I.R.C.).

R46.5.8 **Enforcement of order**—Bankers holding a balance belonging to the person against whom sequestration has been issued may be ordered, upon application in the original action, to verify the amount by affidavit and pay it into Court (*Miller v. Huddlestone* (1883) 22 Ch.D. 233 *q.v.*, for form of order).

Discovery in aid of sequestration—See *Re Suarez (No. 3)* (1918) 88 L.J.Ch. 10. R46.5.9

Injunction in aid of sequestration—The judgment debtor may be restrained from receiving the fund, if necessary to make the sequestration effectual (*Willcock v. Terrell* (1878) 3 Ex.D. 323). R46.5.10

Injunction in lieu of sequestration—Where an undertaking had been broken, an injunction was granted in lieu of sequestration, the defendants being ordered to pay costs as between solicitor and client (*Marsden & Sons Ltd v. Old Silkstone Collieries Ltd* (1915) 13 L.G.R. 642). R46.5.11

Application of proceeds—The property sequestered may be applied to meet the demand of the party prosecuting the writ, but an application to the Court for the sale thereof is necessary. R46.5.12

Where there is a fund in Court representing proceeds of a sequestration, the Court has jurisdiction to order payment out of the fund to the judgment creditor of costs which the judgment debtor has been ordered to pay to him (*Etherington v. Big Blow Gold Mines* [1897] W.N. 21).

Costs of unsuccessful claim—Though sequestrators act under an order of the Court, they are liable for the costs of an issue to determine their claim to property, if they fail on such issue (*Wiebalck v. Told* (1913) 29 T.L.R.741). R46.5.13

Forms—See Form No. 67 (SCP 1999, Vol. 2, Section 1A, para. 1A–68). R46.5.14

Discharge of sequestration—Where the person whose property has been sequestered has purged his contempt, an order may be obtained on application for the discharge of the sequestration, and directing the sequestrators to withdraw from possession, and to pass their final accounts, and, after retaining their costs, charges and expenses, and any payments properly made by them, to pay the balance to him, and for the discharge therefrom of the sequestrators from all liability in respect of their office. R46.5.15

Where after a writ of sequestration had been issued the person whose property had been sequestered committed an act of bankruptcy but had not purged his contempt, it was held that the trustee in bankruptcy was not entitled to have the writ discharged (*Coles v. Coles* [1957] P. 68; [1956] 3 All E.R. 542).

Issue of writ of execution

6.—(1) Issue of a writ of execution takes place on its being sealed by a court officer of the appropriate office. R46.6

(2) Before such a writ is issued, a praecipe for its issue must be filed.

(3) The praecipe must be signed by or on behalf of the solicitor of the person entitled to execution or, if that person is acting in person, by him.

(4) No such writ shall be sealed unless at the time of the tender thereof for sealing—

- (a) the person tendering it produces—
  - (i) the judgment or order on which the writ is to issue, or an office copy thereof;
  - (ii) where the writ may not issue without the permission of the court, the order granting such permission or evidence of the granting of it;
  - (iii) where judgment on failure to acknowledge service has been entered against a State, as defined in section 14 of the State Immunity Act 1978, evidence that the State has been served in accordance with CPR rule 40.10 and that the judgment has taken effect; and
- (b) the court officer authorised to seal it is satisfied that the period, if any, specified in the judgment or order for the payment of any money or the doing of any other act thereunder has expired.

(5) Every writ of execution shall bear the date of the day on which it is issued.

(6) In this rule "the appropriate office" means—

- (a) where the proceedings in which execution is to issue are in a District Registry, that Registry;
- (b) where the proceedings are in the Principal Registry of the Family Division, that Registry;

(c) where the proceedings are Admiralty proceedings or commercial proceedings which are not in a District Registry, the Admiralty and Commercial Registry;

(ca) where the proceedings are in the Chancery Division, Chancery Chambers;

(d) in any other case, the Central Office of the Supreme Court.

Duration and renewal of writ of execution

R46.8 **8.**—(1) For the purpose of execution, a writ of execution is valid in the first instance for 12 months beginning with the date of its issue.

(2) Where a writ has not been wholly executed the court may by order extend the validity of the writ from time to time for a period of 12 months at any one time beginning with the day on which the order is made, if an application for extension is made to the court before the day next following that on which the writ would otherwise expire or such later day, if any, as the court may allow.

(3) Before a writ the validity of which had been extended under paragraph (2) is executed either the writ must be sealed with the seal of the office out of which it was issued showing the date on which the order extending its validity was made or the applicant for the order must serve a notice (in Form No. 71 in the relevant practice direction) sealed as aforesaid, on the sheriff to whom the writ is directed informing him of the making of the order and the date thereof.

(4) The priority of a writ, the validity of which has been extended under this rule, shall be determined by reference to the date on which it was originally delivered to the sheriff.

(5) The production of a writ of execution, or of such a notice as is mentioned in paragraph (3) purporting in either case to be sealed as mentioned in that paragraph, shall be evidence that the validity of that writ, or, as the case may be, of the writ referred to in that notice, has been extended under paragraph (2).

(6) If, during the validity of a writ of execution, an interpleader summons is issued in relation to an execution under that writ, the validity of the writ shall be extended until the expiry of 12 months from the conclusion of the interpleader proceedings.

R46.8.1 **Effect of rule**—This rule provides for extending the validity of the writ of execution which is to be valid for 12 months from the date of its issue. This change in terminology makes no material change in practice.

R46.8.2 **Practice on extending validity of writ of execution**—The application is made without notice supported by an affidavit stating the reason why the writ has not been executed.

It is not the usual practice to extend the validity of a writ of execution under this rule, except in cases where priority of date is important. After the year has expired the ordinary course is to issue a new writ on the certificate of a solicitor that nothing has been levied under the first writ.

In a cause or matter proceeding in a District Registry, the application to extend the validity of a writ of execution is to be made there to the District Judge.

The renewal of a writ of execution under para. (2) should not be granted as a matter of course, and especially after the year has expired, good cause should be shown for such renewal. This is all the more important where questions of priority may arise as between two or more judgment creditors. On an application for renewal of a writ of execution the Court should be informed as to whether there are any other judgment creditors who have delivered writs of execution to the sheriff, and the next subsequent judgment creditor or creditors ought to be heard and if necessary he or they ought to be allowed to intervene for this purpose on the question whether he or they will suffer any, and if so what prejudice if the writ of execution is renewed, which would deprive him or them of priority in the execution process.

R46.8.3 **Extension of writ of fi. fa.**—Rule 8(6) was added to ensure that interpleader proceedings were not frustrated by the inadvertence of the execution creditor to renew the relevant writ of *fi. fa.*; Hence if an interpleader summons is issued in relation to an execution under a writ of execution, then the validity of the writ is automatically extended for 12 months from the conclusion of the interpleader proceedings by virtue of r.8(6).

Lost writ of fi. fa.—There is no provision in these rules for the issue of a duplicate writ of *fi. fa.* should the original be lost or destroyed before coming into the hands of the sheriff and which is within a year of issue. In such a case an application made without notice supported by evidence (usually an affidavit sworn by the judgment creditor's solicitor) setting out the circumstances under which the loss or destruction occurred should be made to the master/district judge for the issue of a duplicate writ. A statement from the under-sheriff that the original writ has not been delivered to him for execution should also be submitted. A solicitor should undertake to return the original for cancellation in the event of it being found. R46.8.4

Return to writ of execution

9.—(1) Any party at whose instance or against whom a writ of execution was issued may serve a notice on the sheriff to whom the writ was directed requiring him, within such time as may be specified in the notice, to indorse on the writ a statement of the manner in which he has executed it and to send to that party a copy of the statement. R46.9

(2) If a sheriff on whom such a notice is served fails to comply with it the party by whom it was served may apply to the court for an order directing the sheriff to comply with the notice.

Effect of rule—A sheriff was formerly required to make a "return" to a writ. This is no longer required and accordingly r.9 makes provision for the execution creditor to serve notice requiring the sheriff "to indorse on the writ a statement of the manner in which he has executed it . . .". In practice such notice is not usually required as the sheriff will inform the execution creditor of the action he has taken. R46.9.1

A sheriff is responsible for the acts and defaults of the under-sheriff and sheriff's officers. Should a sheriff fail to comply with a notice served pursuant to r.9(1) an application for an order directing compliance is made to a master/district judge pursuant to r.9(2).

An execution creditor has no right to a return whilst interpleader is pending (*Angell v. Baddeley* (1877) 3 Ex.D. 49, CA).

RSC ORDER 47

WRITS OF FIERI FACIAS

Contents R47.0.1

Editorial Introduction

This Order contains special rules relating to execution by writ of *fieri facias.* For more general information as to the issue, etc., of writs of *fieri facias,* see O.45, r.1 and notes thereto. Rule 1 confers express power on the Court to stay execution by writ of *fieri facias.* (The bulk of the notes in this Order are concerned with this matter.) Rule 2 enables a judgment creditor to issue two or more writs to enforce a single judgment and r.3 states that separate writs may be issued for the judgment debt and for costs. R47.0.2

Previously, unlike the CCR, the RSC contained no provision for the court itself to order payment by instalments at the time when the judgment or order was pronounced. Thus, to achieve payment by instalments in the High Court it was necessary for the judgment debtor to apply to the court under RSC, O.47 for a stay of execution on terms. By contrast the county court could order payment by instalments on pronouncing judgment or at any time thereafter. See now Pt 40. By r.40.11 both the High Court and county court have power to order payment by instalments and accordingly one of the most common reasons for seeking a story of execution under RSC, O.47 has gone.

Related sources R47.0.3

- Supreme Court Act 1981, s.138A (SCP 1999, Vol. 2, Section 20A)
- RSC, O.45—Enforcement of Judgments and Orders: General
- RSC, O.46—Writs of Execution: General
- CCR, O.25—Enforcement of Judgments and Orders: General
- CCR, O.26—Warrants of Execution, Delivery and Possession
- CPR, Part 40—Judgments and Orders

Forms

R47.0.4 The following Queen's Bench Masters' Practice Forms (now listed in Table 2 (Practice Forms) attached to Practice Direction (Forms)) are relevant to O.47 (SCP 1999, Vol. 2, Section 1B, paras 1B–64 and 1B–70):

- PF 86—Praecipe for writ of *fieri facias* (r.6)
- PF 97—Order for sale by sheriff by private contract (r.6)

Power to stay execution by writ of fieri facias

R47.1 **1.**—(1) Where a judgment is given or an order made for the payment by any person of money, and the court is satisfied, on an application made at the time of the judgment or order, or at any time thereafter, by the judgment debtor or other party liable to execution—

(a) that there are special circumstances which render it inexpedient to enforce the judgment or order, or

(b) that the applicant is unable from any cause to pay the money,

then, notwithstanding anything in rule 2 or 3, the court may by order stay the execution of the judgment or order by writ of fieri facias either absolutely or for such period and subject to such conditions as the court thinks fit.

(2) An application under this rule, if not made at the time the judgment is given or order made, must be made in accordance with CPR Part 23 and may be so made notwithstanding that the party liable to execution did not acknowledge service of the claim form or serve a defence or take any previous part in the proceedings.

(3) The grounds on which an application under this rule is made must be set out in the application notice and be supported by a witness statement or affidavit made by or on behalf of the applicant substantiating the said grounds and, in particular, where such application is made on the grounds of the applicant's inability to pay, disclosing his income, the nature and value of any property of his and the amount of any other liabilities of his.

(4) The application notice and a copy of the supporting witness statement or affidavit must, not less than 4 clear days before the hearing, be served on the party entitled to enforce the judgment or order.

(5) An order staying execution under this rule may be varied or revoked by a subsequent order.

R47.1.1 **Effect of rule**—This rule confers express power on the Court to stay execution by writ of *fi. fa.* either absolutely or for such period and subject to such conditions as the Court thinks fit, provided that the applicant can satisfy either (a) or (b) in r.1(1). Previously applications were very common as the High Court, unlike the county court, had no power to order payment by instalments but see now CPR, r.40.11. If execution has been issued clearly a judgment debtor may need to apply for a stay pursuant to O.47, r.1. If, however, execution has not yet been issued it may be preferable to apply to vary the judgment to provide for payment by instalments (or lower instalments) see, *e.g.* CPR, r.40.11 and CPR, r.13.4.

The usual form of order granting a stay of execution under this rule is as follows: "stay of execution (under O.47, r.1) so long as the defendant pays the judgment debt and costs by instalments at the rate of £—— per month on the —— day of each month, the first instalment to commence on the —— day of ——, 20—, provided that if he should make default in the payment of the said instalments or any part thereof on the due date, the stay be forthwith removed in respect of the whole outstanding balance at the time of such default and the plaintiff be then at liberty forthwith to issue execution by writ of *fi. fa.* on the said judgment and costs" (see *Chitty and Jacob's Queen's Bench Forms*, Form 1124).

Para. (2) makes it clear that the judgment debtor is entitled to apply for a stay of execution by *fi. fa.*, notwithstanding that he has not acknowledged the service of the claim form or taken part in the proceedings.

It should perhaps be emphasised that the Court has power to order a stay of execution by writ of *fi. fa.* either absolutely or for such period and subject to such conditions as the Court thinks fit. If the debtor is the owner of premises the Court has power there and then to impose a charging order absolute on the premises provided the judgment debtor agrees, so that the judgment creditor need not go through the elaborate machinery of obtaining such a charging order absolute under O.50, and in the absence of such agreement the Court should endeavour as far as possible to maintain a fair and proper balance between the needs of the judgment debtor to be granted a stay of execution and the needs of the judgment creditor to obtain due and prompt satisfaction of his judgment debt.

The terms of this rule give the Court sufficiently wide discretion, if the circumstances of the case warrant it, for the Court to pierce the corporate veil, and to look behind the incorporated companies involved in the dispute so as to ascertain the identity of the persons who controlled the companies and in a proper case, the Court will grant a stay of execution (*Canada Enterprises Corp. v. MacNab Distilleries Ltd* [1987] 1 W.L.R. 813; [1981] Com.L.R. 167, CA). The court has jurisdiction to order a stay of execution under this rule, where as a result of a particular transaction a judgment debt is owed by a subsidiary company to a third party and that subsidiary's parent company has a claim against the same third party which also arises from that transaction. In such circumstances, it is right for the court to look behind the fact that there are companies concerned and to consider the parties who are controlling those companies (*Burnet v. Francis Industries plc* [1987] 1 W.L.R. 802; [1987] 2 All E.R. 323, CA). The factors to be considered in deciding special circumstances are set out in the judgment of Bingham L.J. (*ibid.*).

The power to stay execution under this rule is separate and distinct from the power to stay execution pending an appeal under O.59, r.13 (*Ellis v. Scott (Practice Note)* [1964] 1 W.L.R. 976; [1964] 2 All E.R. 987).

A stay of execution of a judgment, including a foreign judgment duly registered in England, will not ordinarily be granted simply because the judgment debtor brings a cross-claim in another action against the judgment creditor, or at any rate in the absence of special circumstances rendering it inexpedient to enforce the judgment (*Wagner v. Laubscher Brothers & Co.* [1970] 2 Q.B. 313, CA).

It is open to the Court to grant a stay of execution by a judgment creditor against a statutory body (*Marine, etc., Ass. Soc. v. Feltwell* [1945] K.B. 394 at 398).

Practice under this rule—The application must be made in accordance with Pt 23. R47.1.2

Setting aside execution—If execution has been improperly issued it may be set aside even after execution has been levied. If the Court sets aside a default judgment pursuant to Pt 13 it will be necessary for the order to deal with payment of the costs of execution. These will have to be paid by the judgment debtor if the judgment was regular. R47.1.3

Creditor out of jurisdiction—It is the duty of the judgment debtor to find the creditor if the latter is within the jurisdiction; but if neither the creditor nor anyone authorised to receive payment is within the jurisdiction a stay of execution may be obtained (*Re A Debtor (1838 of 1911)* [1912] 1 K.B. 53 at 62, CA). R47.1.4

Bankruptcy of debtor—The Insolvency Act 1986, s.285(3), provides that after the making of a bankruptcy order, no creditor to whom the debtor is indebted in respect of any debt provable in bankruptcy shall have any remedy against the property or person of the debtor in respect of the debt, or shall commence any action or other legal proceedings unless with the leave of the Court and on such terms as the Court may impose. R47.1.5

This includes a judgment debt due to a creditor where a proof has been rejected in bankruptcy; execution cannot be levied after the bankruptcy has been annulled (*Brandon v. McHenry* [1891] 1 Q.B. 538).

A covenant to pay money out of the estate of the covenantor after his birth is a debt provable in bankruptcy within this section (*Barnett v. King* [1891] 1 Ch. 4).

Under Insolvency Act 1986, s.285(1) "at any time when proceedings on a bankruptcy petition are pending or an individual has been adjudged bankrupt, the Court may stay any action, execution or other legal process against the property or person of the debtor or as the case may be, the bankrupt."

The presentation of a petition for a bankruptcy order protects a debtor from arrest as soon as it is "made" (Insolvency Act 1986, s.285(1) and (2)), *i.e.* pronounced (*Re Manning* (1885) 30 Ch.D. 480); but it does not protect a debtor who is within the exceptions to section 4 of Debtors Act 1869, and the Court will not, without a good reason, interfere to prevent committal of a person who has filed a petition to avoid consequences of an order to pay into Court money in his hands in a fiduciary capacity (*Re Mackintosh, ex p. Mackintosh* (1884) 13 Q.B.D. 235).

Where a sheriff had been unable to gain access to a debtor's house and the creditors had countermanded the execution and the sheriff had returned the writ marked "unsatisfied in whole", the execution had not been "returned unsatisfied in whole or in part" within the meaning of s.368(1)(b) of the Insolvency Act 1986 as to entitle the creditors to present a bankruptcy petition (*Re A Debtor (No. 340 of 1992) The Times*, March 6, 1995).

Stays of execution and bankruptcy petitions—(1) A stay of execution by writ of *fi. fa.* under O.47, r.1 will not prevent a creditor's petition being presented because, although execution by this particular means would be stayed, the judgment debt would in theory remain "payable" and would be enforceable by other means (as listed in O.45, r.1). R47.1.6

(2) In practice the High Court Bankruptcy Registrars will not normally make a bankruptcy order while an O.47, r.1 stay is in force but will adjourn the petition (if necessary from time to time) so long as the stay persists.

(3) If a general stay of execution (*e.g.* pending appeal of under O.45, r.11) is in existence *at the date* of the presentation of the petition, this will be regarded as an obstacle to the acceptance of the petition or as grounds for immediate dismissal of the petition because there would not then be any debt payable in existence at the date of the petition. If a general stay comes into existence *after* the presentation of the petition it could provide grounds for dismissal of the petition or (more likely) for adjournment during the operation of the stay.

(4) Once a bankruptcy order has been made, the Insolvency Act 1986, s.285(3) provides that after the making of a bankruptcy order, no creditor to whom the debtor is indebted in respect of any debt provable in bankruptcy, shall have any remedy against the property or person of the debtor in respect of the debt or shall commence any action or other legal proceedings unless with the leave of the Court and upon such terms as the Court may impose.

(5) An interim order made by a bankruptcy court under section 252 of the Insolvency Act operates as a general stay of all proceedings and execution in any other court.

(6) Under the Insolvency Act 1986, s.285(1), "At any time when proceedings on a bankruptcy petition are pending or an individual has been adjudged bankrupt, the [Bankruptcy] Court may stay any action, execution or other legal process against property or person of the debtor or, as the case may be, of the bankrupt."

Further under section 254(1) of the Act, the Bankruptcy Court has jurisdiction to stay any particular proceedings or execution while an application for an interim order is pending, similar to the jurisdiction under s.285(1) while a bankruptcy petition is pending.

R47.1.7 **Winding up of defendant company**—The Court may, at any time after the presentation of a petition for winding up a company under the C.A. 1948, and before making an order for winding up the company, restrain further proceedings in any action, suit or proceeding against the company, and in the case of a company registered in pursuance of s.680 of the C.A. 1985, of an unregistered company, against any contributory of the company, upon such terms as the Court thinks fit (C.A. 1985, ss.521(1), (2) and 672). A stay will, in ordinary circumstances be ordered although a winding up is not in immediate prospect, *e.g.* pending approval of a scheme of arrangement (*Bowkett v. Fuller's United Electric Works Ltd* [1923] 1 K.B. 160, CA) but after execution levied a stay may be refused (*Booth v. Walkden Spinning Co.* [1909] 2 K.B. 368). However where the primary form of relief sought by a claimant is injunctive, a stay will not generally be ordered (*Landi Den Hartog B.V. v. Stopps* [1976] F.S.R. 497).

Where an order has been made for winding up a company under the C.A. 1985, no suit, action, or other proceeding shall be proceeded with or commenced against the company, and in the case of a company registered under s.680 of the C.A. 1985, or of an unregistered company, against any contributory of the company in respect of any debt of the company except with the leave of the Court, and subject to such terms as the Court may impose (Insolvency Act 1986, s.130).

Where any company is being wound up by the Court, or subject to the supervision of the Court, any attachment, sequestration, distress, or execution put in force against the estate or effects of the company after the commencement of the winding-up shall be void to all intents and purposes (Insolvency Act 1986, s.128).

As to the effect of these sections, see *Re Zoedone Co.* (1884) 32 W.R. 312; *Re The Opera Ltd* [1891] 3 Ch. 260. The rule under which the Court gives effect to the rights of an execution creditor when the sheriff is in possession at the date of the commencement of the winding-up applies in favour of other execution creditors, who prior to such commencement, have lodged their writs with the sheriff in possession (*Re Hille India Rubber Co.* [1897] W.N. 20).

Where the sheriff is in possession at the date of a winding up order under an execution to recover a sum due under a judgment of the QBD, application to stay a sale by him should be made to the QBD not in the winding-up (*Re Twentieth Century Equitable Friendly Society* [1910] W.N. 236).

R47.1.8 **Voluntary liquidation**—The Court has the same jurisdiction to stay execution in the case of a voluntary as of a compulsory winding-up (*Westbury v. Twigg & Co.* [1892] 1 Q.B. 77); a stay will in some cases be refused (*Currie v. Consolidated Kent Collieries Corp. Ltd* [1906] 1 K.B. 134, CA).

Where the creditors had been induced to postpone issuing execution by a trick on the part of the defendant company, the CA refused to prevent the creditors from proceeding with their execution after a resolution for voluntary winding-up had been passed (*Armorduct Manufacturing Co. Ltd v. General Incandescent Co. Ltd* [1911] 2 K.B. 143, CA) but this will be done only in exceptional circumstances. The fact that the only right of the company to recover the money claimed from certain garnishees was based upon the company's liability to the judgment creditors is not such an exceptional circumstance as to take the case out of the general rule (*Anglo-Baltic Bank v. Barber* [1924] 2 K.B. 410 at 418, CA).

R47.1.9 **Matters occurring after judgment**—See O.45, r.11.

Two or more writs of fieri facias

R47.2 **2.**—(1) A party entitled to enforce a judgment or order by writ of fieri facias may issue two or more such writs, directed to the sheriffs of different counties, at either the same time or different times, to enforce that judgment or order, but no more shall be levied under all those writs together than is authorised to be levied under one of them.

(2) Where a party issues two or more writs of fieri facias directed to the sheriffs of different counties to enforce the same judgment or order he must inform each sheriff of the issue of the other writ or writs.

Effect of rule—The general rule of practice is summed up in the maxim "One judgment, one execution," *i.e.* judgment creditor cannot issue a series of small executions upon his judgment, making in the aggregate the amount of the judgment debt; upon one judgment he can issue only one execution (*Forster v. Baker* [1910] 2 K.B. 636, CA, *per* Vaughan Williams L.J. at 641; *Rothschild v. Fisher* [1920] 2 K.B. 243, CA). For this reason assignees of part of a judgment debt cannot issue execution. **R47.2.1**

If however, the judgment or order is for the recovery or payment of money, and at the same time for the recovery of property other than money, the appropriate writs for the enforcement of the two parts of the judgment or order may issue simultaneously or successively.

The order in which writs of execution may be issued is in no way affected by the RSC.

A judgment creditor may issue writs of *fi. fa.* simultaneously directed to sheriffs of different counties, and he may, after issuing out a writ directed to a sheriff of one county, issue out another directed to a sheriff of another county without requiring or waiting for a return to the first writ; in either case he must be careful not to levy more than the whole of the money and costs that are due (the principle laid down in *Lee v. Dangar* [1892] 1 Q.B. 231; [1892] 2 Q.B. 337 at 343, is no longer applicable).

The general rule as to suing out more than one writ of *fi. fa.* to the same sheriff is that it cannot be done until a return has been made to the first writ, if, under the first writ, any of the following conditions are present:

(1) If any part of the amount recoverable has been levied under the first writ (*Hodgkinson v. Whalley* (1831) 2 Cr. & J. 86; *Chapman v. Bowlby* (1841) 8 M. & W. 249, where the sheriff received a payment of part of the amount leviable with leave to re-enter) or

(2) If there had been any seizure, even though subsequently abandoned (*Miller v. Parnell* (1815) 5 Taunt. 370; *Andrews v. Saunderson* (1857) 1 H. & N. 725); or

(3) If the existence of the first writ is necessary for the protection of the sheriff (*Andrews v. Saunderson*; see also *Re A Debtor* [1902] 2 K.B. 260, CA; *Foster v. Jackson* (1613) Hob. 58; *Coppendale v. Debonaire* (1757) Barnes 213; *Wilson v. Kingston* (1816) 2 Chit. Rep. 203; *Lawes v. Codrington* (1831) 1 Dowl. P.C. 31; *R. v. Sheriff of Essex* (1839) 8 Dowl. P.C. 3).

There are, however, two exceptions to this general rule. The first is under r.3, which provides that upon any judgment or order for the recovery or payment of a sum of money and costs there may be, at the election of the party entitled thereto, either one writ or separate writs of execution for the recovery of the sum and for the recovery of the costs, but a second writ shall only be for costs, and shall be issued not less than eight days after the first writ.

The judgment creditor need not wait until after taxation to issue execution, but may have one writ for the debt, and when taxation is completed, a second for the costs (*Harris v. Jewell* [1883] W.N. 216). The writ of execution for costs is issuable on production of the judgment and the Taxing Master's certificate, but not before the giving of the latter (*Re Crump, ex p. Crump* (1891) 64 L.T. 799). (Taxation is now known as "detailed assessment".)

The second exception is where the writ is more than a year old, and there has been a partial levy, but a return cannot be obtained from the sheriff owing to his having been out of office six months (Sheriffs Act 1887, s.28(3)). In such a case a second writ, to levy the balance only, may issue by leave of the Practice Master on a certificate by the solicitor seeking leave to issue to the effect that the sheriff has been out of office for six months or more and that under the first writ he made a partial levy, or on such other evidence as the Master may require.

It follows that no return of the first writ is necessary before the issue of a second writ, where the first writ has not been delivered to the sheriff, or has been withdrawn before any seizure or levy is made under it; as, for instance, where the sheriff entered the judgment debtor's premises, but made no seizure because the goods there were either (1) already in the possession of a bailiff under a distress for rent (*Edmund v. Ross* (1821) 9 Price 5) or (2) assigned under a bill of sale and in *custodia legis* (*Drear v. Warren* (1833) 10 Bing. 341). In all such cases the writ should be brought back to the writ room and filed by the solicitor for the judgment creditor with a certificate indorsed that it has not been executed, and also (if it is more than a year old) that it has not been renewed, and that nothing has been levied under it. A return is also unnecessary where there has been no seizure of any goods of the judgment debtor, and where, therefore, the writ is not necessary for the justification of the sheriff (*Re A Debtor* [1902] 2 K.B. 260 at 267, 268, CA).

In all cases where a return has been made to the first writ (*i.e.* an indorsement on the writ of the manner in which it has been executed, see O.46, r.9) the second writ must recite the first and the return to it (*Chapman v. Bowlby* (1841) 8 M. & W. 249, *per* Parke B. at p.251; *Re Ford, ex p. Ford* (1886) 18 Q.B.D. 369, *per* Cave J. at p.371). This also applies where the writ is issued to a different sheriff.

No second writ is necessary where, under a *fi. fa.* in the ordinary form returnable immediately after the execution, a portion of the amount for which it was issued has been realised by levy, for a *fi. fa.* in that form remains in force till it has been completely executed; and, therefore, without any return having been made to the first writ, a second levy can be made under it for the balance (*Jordan v. Binckes* (1849) 13 Q.B. 757; *R. v. Sheriff of Essex* (1839) 8 Dowl.P.C. 3 at 7).

Where writs of *fi. fa.* are issued against the same property by more than one judgment creditor, separate seizures are not necessary, one seizure enuring for the benefit of all (*Re Henderson* [1884] W.N. 60; and *Re Hille, etc., Co.* [1897] W.N. 20).

In *Hunt v. Passmore* (1833) 2 Dowl. 414, a plaintiff, who had by mistake indorsed a *fi. fa.* for too little, applied for a rule for a second writ to levy the residue, and was allowed to take a rule to show cause why the defendant should not pay over the money or, in default thereof, why a new writ should not be issued. The present practice in such a case is to make an application on notice under Pt 23 for permission to issue a second writ of *fi. fa.*

Separate writs to enforce payment of costs, etc.

R47.3 **3.**—(1) Where only the payment of money, together with costs to be assessed in accordance with CPR Part 47 (detailed costs assessment) is adjudged or ordered, then, if when the money becomes payable under the judgment or order the costs have not been assessed, the party entitled to enforce that judgment or order may issue a writ of fieri facias to enforce payment of the sum (other than for costs) adjudged or ordered and, not less than 8 days after the issue of that writ, he may issue a second writ to enforce payment of the assessed costs.

(2) A party entitled to enforce a judgment or order for the delivery of possession of any property (other than money) may, if he so elects, issue a separate writ of fieri facias to enforce payment of any damages or costs awarded to him by that judgment or order.

R47.3.1 **Effect of rule**—This rule entitles a judgment creditor to enforce a judgment immediately without waiting for a detailed assessment of his costs under Pt 47. Once costs have been assessed he can issue a second writ to enforce payment of the costs—see r.3(1).

The costs referred to in para. (2) are of course the costs of the action. In the case of the writ of delivery of goods (see Form Nos 64 and 65, see SCP 1999, Vol. 2, Section 1A, paras 1A–64 and 1A–65) the costs of execution are included. On the other hand, in the case of the writ of delivery of possession of land (see Form No. 66, see Vol. 2, Section 1A, para. 1A–66) notwithstanding the form of the writ, the costs of the execution relating to the possession of the land are not included in the writ; and normally such costs are not recoverable by the writ of possession, which relates only to land. Such costs may, however, be awarded on application to the Master (see *Dartford Brewery Co. v. Moseley* [1906] 1 K.B. 462, CA).

An order for payment of costs to be taxed (now called assessment) was a judgment debt within the Judgments Act 1838, s.17, and the principle established since the enactment of the Rules of the Supreme Court 1883, following the common law rule, that interest on costs ran from the date of the judgment had not been altered by the revision of the Rules in 1965, notwithstanding that the footnote to that effect had been omitted from the prescribed form of the writ of *fieri facias*; accordingly a party who had been awarded costs in an action was entitled to interest on the amount of the costs from the date upon which judgment was pronounced (*Hunt v. R. M. Douglas (Roofing) Ltd* [1990] 1 A.C. 398; [1988] 3 All E.R. 823, HL). See further CPR, r.40.8 and para. 40.8.1.

No expenses of execution in certain cases

R47.4 **4.** Where a judgment or order is for less than £600 and does not entitle the claimant to costs against the person against whom the writ of fieri facias to enforce the judgment or order is issued, the writ may not authorise the sheriff to whom it is directed to levy any fees, poundage or other costs of execution.

R47.4.1 **Effect of rule**—This rule will rarely apply in practice. A claim form can only be issued in the High Court for more than £15,000. A claim which results in a judgment of order "for less than £600" is unlikely to be tried in the High Court. The "no costs of execution" rule only applies where the judgment is far "less than £600" *and* does not entitle the claimant to costs. If the judgment did award costs the execution creditor is entitled to costs of execution.

R47.4.2 **Entitlement of sheriff to his fees and poundage**—The provision entitling the judgment creditor to "levy the poundage, fees and expenses of execution over and above the sum recovered" is contained in the prescribed forms of writs of *fi. fa.* (see Forms Nos 38/53, see SCP 1999, Vol. 2, Section 1A, paras 1A–36 and 1A–53).

In the execution of a writ of *fi. fa.*, where the money has been obtained by the seizure of the goods, although there has been no sale, the sheriff has a right to his poundage (*Mortimore v. Cragg* (1878) 3 C.P.D. 216) but there must be an actual seizure (*Bissicks v. Bath Colliery Co.* (1878) 3 Ex.D. 174). When after seizure the execution creditor becomes disentitled to recover the judgment debt, the sheriff cannot sell the goods for the purpose of realising his possession money, fees and expenses (*Sneary v. Abdy* (1876) 1 Ex.D. 299); but the debtor's bankruptcy and an injunction restraining a sale do not affect the sheriff's right to payment by the trustee in bankruptcy of the necessary expenses of possession (*Re Craycraft* (1878) 8 Ch.D. 596).

The sheriff is not entitled to poundage unless he has actually obtained the money by compulsion from the judgment debtor, and has it ready to hand over to the judgment creditor (*per* Cave J., *Re Ludmore* (1884) 13 Q.B.D. 415 at 417). So, where two seizures were made under different writs in different counties, poundage was disallowed under one of the writs because the whole debt was realised under the other writ (*Lee v. Dangar* [1892] 1 Q.B. 231; 2 Q.B. 337). The sheriff is not entitled to charge for more than one seizure in one place (*Re Wells, ex p. Sheriff of Kent* (1893) 68 L.T. 231). Nor is he entitled to poundage where, after seizure, a receiving order is made against the execution debtor, and the goods are delivered to the Official Receiver under s.41(1) of the B.A. 1914 (*Re Thomas* [1899] 1 Q.B. 460). See also Sheriffs Act 1887, s.20.

If the execution is stayed before the sale, the execution creditor is liable to pay the sheriff his fees, unless the order staying the execution provides, otherwise or unless the sale is stopped at the instance of the trustee in bankruptcy or the Official Receiver, who are in such cases liable for the fees; the order as to fees made under the Sheriffs Act 1887, does not alter the former law on the subject (*Montague v. Davies, Benachi & Co.* [1911] 2 K.B. 595).

Where, by a bona fide accident, the sheriff levied too much for poundage, he was held not liable to the penalty under s.29 of the Sheriffs Act 1887 (*Shoppee v. Nathan* [1892] 1 Q.B. 245).

The right of the sheriff to charge poundage where no sale took place was recognised in *Re Thomas, ex p. Sheriff of Middlesex* [1899] 1 Q.B. 460, *per* Lindley M.R. at p.462, "the Sheriff has seized no doubt but he has not sold. It has been by law settled for years that he is not entitled to poundage. I am aware there has been a qualification on that where the Sheriff has seized but has not sold in consequence of a compromise between the parties; there the law regards him as having secured the money for the creditor and gives him poundage".

Possession money—several writs—The sheriff can recover possession money from one creditor only. Where he is in under several writs he is not entitled to charge possession money in respect of each writ (*Glasbrook v. David* [1905] 1 K.B. 615). **R47.4.3**

Sheriff's fees, etc.—As to sheriff's fees and poundages on execution of writ of *fi. fa.* see Order as to Sheriff's Fees July 8, 1920; Sheriffs' Fees (Amendment) Order 1971 (S.I. 1971 No. 808) and Sheriffs' Fees (Amendment) Order 1982 (S.I. 1982 No. 89) (SCP 1999, Vol. 2, Section 4F). **R47.4.4**

Writ of fieri facias de bonis ecclesiasticis, etc.

5.—(1) Where it appears upon the return of any writ of fieri facias that the person against whom the writ was issued has no goods or chattels in the county of the sheriffs to whom the writ was directed but that he is the incumbent of a benefice named in the return, then, after the writ and return have been filed, the party by whom the writ of fieri facias was issued may issue a writ of fieri facias de bonis ecclesiasticis or a writ of sequestrari de bonis ecclesiasticis directed to the bishop of the diocese within which that benefice is. **R47.5**

(2) Any such writ must be delivered to the bishop to be executed by him.

(3) Only such fees for the execution of any such writ shall be taken by or allowed to the bishop or any diocesan officer as are for the time being authorised by or under any enactment, including any measure of the General Synod.

Practice—These writs cannot be obtained until there has been an actual return of *nulla bona* under the former writ (*Rabbitts v. Woodward* (1869) 20 L.T. 693, 778); and the sheriff must certify that the person against whom execution is issued is a beneficed clerk, and has no lay fee. For requirement on issuing, see Execution Table, Nos 29, 30 (SCP 1999, Vol. 2, Section 3C, para. 3C–21). **R47.5.1**

Forms—For forms, see Forms Nos 58, 59 (SCP 1999, Vol. 2, Section 1A, paras 1A–58 and 1A–59). **R47.5.2**

Order for sale otherwise than by auction

6.—(1) An order of the court under section 145 of the Bankruptcy Act 1883, that a sale under an execution may be made otherwise than by public auction may be made on the application of the person at whose instance the **R47.6**

writ of execution under which the sale is to be made was issued or the person against whom that writ was issued (in this rule referred to as "the judgment debtor") or the sheriff to whom it was issued.

(2) Such an application must be made in accordance with CPR Part 23 and the application notice must contain a short statement of the grounds of the application.

(3) Where the applicant for an order under this rule is not the sheriff, the sheriff must, on the demand of the applicant, send to the applicant a list containing the name and address of every person at whose instance any other writ of execution against the goods of the judgment debtor was issued and delivered to the sheriff (in this rule referred to as "the sheriff's list"); and where the sheriff is the applicant, he must prepare such a list.

(4) Not less than 4 clear days before the hearing the applicant must serve the application notice on each of the other persons by whom the application might have been made and on every person named in the sheriff's list.

(5) Service of the application notice on a person named in the sheriff's list is notice to him for the purpose of section 12 of the Bankruptcy Act 1890 (which provides that the court shall not consider an application for leave to sell privately goods taken in execution until notice directed by rules of court has been given to any other execution creditor).

(6) The applicant must produce the sheriff's list to the court on the hearing of the application.

(7) Every person on whom the summons was served may attend and be heard on the hearing of the application.

R47.6.1 **Effect of rule**—This rule enables the sheriff himself to apply for an order for sale otherwise than by auction; it is his duty to get the best price he can for the goods, and he is the person who may be likely to know whether and when this can be achieved by a private sale.

R47.6.2 **Sale of goods by sheriff**—The Supreme Court Act 1981, s.138A(1) enacts that "where any goods seized under a Writ of Execution issued from the High Court are to be sold for a sum exceeding £20 (including legal incidental expenses) the sale shall unless the Court otherwise orders, be made by public auction, and not by bill of sale or private contract, and shall be publicly advertised by the Sheriff on, and during three days preceeding, the day of sale."

An application for permission to sell the debtor's goods by private contract is made by application notice as prescribed by O.47, r.6.

R47.6.3 **Supreme Court Act 1981, s.138A(2)**—This section provides: "Where any goods of a debtor are taken in execution and the sheriff has notice of another execution or other executions, the Court shall not consider an application for leave to sell privately until the notice directed by Rules of Court has been given to the other execution creditor or creditors, who may appear before the Court and be heard upon the application."

R47.6.4 **Protection of sheriff—Supreme Court Act 1981, s.138B**—Where the sheriff or other officer charged with enforcement of a process of execution sells goods in the possession of the debtor at the time of seizure, the purchaser of such goods acquires a good title and no person can recover against such sheriff or officer except as provided by the Bankruptcy Acts for any sale or payment of proceeds prior to the receipt of claim for the same, unless it is proved that the person against whom recovery is sought had notice or might by making reasonable inquiry have ascertained that the goods were not the property of the judgment debtor. As to the object and effect of this section see *Curtis v. Maloney* [1951] 1 K.B. 736; [1950] 2 All E.R. 982, CA.

See *Newmann v. Bakesway Ltd* [1983] 1 W.L.R. 1016 and *Observer Ltd v. Gordon* [1983] 1 W.L.R. 1008; [1983] 2 All E.R. 945, for consideration of grounds under which the sheriff may by order be protected from action under similar provisions in Bankruptcy Act 1913, s.15.

RSC ORDER 48

EXAMINATION OF JUDGMENT DEBTOR, ETC.

R48.0.1 **Contents**

Editorial Introduction

As noted in the Introduction to RSC, O.45 it is for the judgment creditor, not the court, to enforce a judgment. Enforcement can be expensive and abortive enforcement is just throwing good money after bad. The purpose of RSC, O.48 is to enable the judgment creditor to obtain an order for the oral examination of the judgment debtor as to his means (there must be a judgment: the procedure is not available pre-action). **R48.0.2**

The examination "is not only intended to be an examination, but a cross-examination, and that of the severest kind" (*Republic of Costa Rica v. Stronsberg* (1880) 16 Ch.D. 8).

The relevant wording of RSC, O.48, r.1 is now the same as CCR, O.25, r.3: "... the court may, on an application made without notice being served on any other party ...". Although the High Court and county court have made orders *ex parte* (now called "without notice") there was an important difference of practice in that the application was made on affidavit in the High Court and by prescribed form in the county court. Such a difference of practice ought not to survive under the CPR and as RSC, O.48 does not expressly require an affidavit it is submitted that High Court practice should no longer insist upon one as a prerequisite to the making of the order.

Related sources

- CCR, O.25, rr.3 and 4 (examination of judgment debtors) **R48.0.3**
- *Queen's Bench Masters' Practice Direction No. 37—Examination of judgment debtor* (SCP 1999, Vol. 2, Section 2A, para. 2A–105) (applies also in Chancery Division, see Vol. 2, Section 2B, para. 2B–179).

Forms

The following Queen's Bench Masters' Practice Forms (formerly included amongst the Prescribed Forms in Appendix A to the RSC) are relevant to O.48. These forms are included in Table 2 (Practice Forms) attached to Practice Direction (Forms) and may be found in SCP 1999, Vol. 2, Section 1B, paras 1B–71 and 1B–72): **R48.0.4**

- PF No. 98—Affidavit in support of application of order for examination of judgment debtor or officer (O.48)
- PF 99—Order for examination of judgment debtor or officer (O.48, r.1)

Order for examination of judgment debtor

1.—(1) Where a person has obtained a judgment or order for the payment by some other person (hereinafter referred to as "the judgment debtor") of money, the court may, on an application made without notice being served on any other party by the person entitled to enforce the judgment or order, order the judgment debtor or, if the judgment debtor is a body corporate, an officer thereof, to attend before such Master, Registrar, district judge or nominated officer as the court may appoint and be orally examined on the questions— **R48.1**

(a) whether any and, if so, what debts are owing to the judgment debtor; and

(b) whether the judgment debtor has any and, if so, what other property or means of satisfying the judgment or order;

and the court may also order the judgment debtor or officer to produce any books or documents in the possession of the judgment debtor relevant to the questions aforesaid at the time and place appointed for the examination.

In this paragraph "district judge" includes the district judge of a district registry or county court, and where the court appoints such a district judge without specifying him personally, the examination may, if he thinks fit, be conducted on his behalf by a nominated officer of that registry or county court.

(2) An order under this rule must be served personally on the judgment debtor and on any officer of a body corporate ordered to attend for examination.

(3) Any difficulty arising in the course of an examination under this rule before a nominated officer, including any dispute with respect to the obligation of the person being examined to answer any question put to him, may be referred to the Senior Master or Practice Master (or, in the case of an examination at the Principal Registry of the Family Division, a district registry or a county court, a district judge of that registry, district registry or county

court respectively) and he may determine it or give such directions for determining it as he thinks fit.

(4) In this rule "nominated officer" in relation to an examination which is to take place at the Central Office of the Supreme Court, the Principal Registry of the Family Division, a district registry or a county court means such of the officers of that office, registry or county court as may be nominated for the purposes of this rule by the Senior Master, the Senior District Judge of the Family Division or the district judge of that district registry or county court respectively.

R48.1.1 **History of Rule**—Amended by Civil Procedure (Amendment) Rules 1999 (S.I. 1999 No. 1008)).

Examination of party liable to satisfy other judgment

R48.2 **2.** Where any difficulty arises in or in connection with the enforcement of any judgment or order, other than such a judgment or order as is mentioned in rule 1, the court may make an order under that rule for the attendance of the party liable to satisfy the judgment or order and for his examination on such questions as may be specified in the order, and that rule shall apply accordingly with the necessary modifications.

Examiner to make record of debtor's statement

R48.3 **3.** The officer conducting the examination shall take down, or cause to be taken down, in writing the statement made by the judgment debtor or other person at the examination, read it to him and ask him to sign it; and if he refuses the officer shall sign the statement.

R48.3.1 **Practice**—It has always been High Court practice for an application for an order to be made *ex parte* (now "without notice") on affidavit. The rule does not expressly require an affidavit and in the county court (where CCR, O.25, r.3 is identical in relevant wording) no affidavit has ever been required. Such a diffeence in practice cannot be justified under the CPR and it is submitted that an affidavit should no longer be insisted upon. Clearly the court needs to be satisfied that the applicant is entitled to enforce a judgment which remains unpaid in whole or in part. This information could be given by witness statement (including that of a solicitor) or letter which in either case, contains a "statement of truth" (see Practice Direction Supplementing Part 22 at para. 22PD–001). The examination will normally be ordered to take place at the court where the least expense will be incurred and this will usually be the county court for the area where the judgment debtor resides. Accordingly, the relevant address of the debtor and court should be provided

If for any reason the examinaiton is sought before a Master of the Queen's Bench Division, the advice of the Senior Master should be sought either directly or through the Master's secretary (Room E218).

Once an order for oral examination has been obtained it should (following transfer to another court if appropriate) be served on the debtor or on the particular officer of the body corporate who has been ordered to attend for examination. In the first instance the court will effect service but if there is no attendance personal service is required before an order for committal can be obtained.

R48.3.2 **District Registry (rr.1–3)**—In a cause or matter proceeding in a District Registry, the examination will be taken there; but if desired, the examination may be taken before an officer of the Court in London, in which case the order should read "before an officer of the High Court of Justice in London." The costs of the application and examination will be dealt with by the District Judge making the order.

R48.3.3 **Right to concurrent remedies (rr.1–3)**—Where a writ of *fi. fa.* has been issued it is not necessary to wait for a return to the writ to be made before applying for an examination under this rule.

R48.3.4 **Examination to enforce judgment other than payment of money (rr.1–3)**—Rule 2 is taken from the former O.42, r.33. Its purpose is to enable the judgment creditor to obtain necessary information from the judgment debtor in order to enforce a judgment other than the payment of money, *e.g.* the whereabouts of a motor-car ordered to be delivered up to him. The practice is the same as in the case of an examination under r.1.

Persons within the order (rr.1–3)—Under r.1 "an officer" may be examined: this includes former officers (*Société Générale, etc. v. J. M. Farina & Co.* [1904] 1 K.B. 794, CA). As to whether, if a director of a limited company be ordered to attend and produce documents, the documents of the company are in the custody or power of the director, *quaere* (see *Re Maville Hose Ltd* [1939] 1 Ch. 32). R48.3.5

Rule 1 extends only to the judgment debtor and to the past and present officers of a corporation (*Irwell v. Eden* (1887) 18 QBD 588; *Jeffris v. Tomlinson* (1887) 3 T.L.R. 193; *Hood-Barrs v. Heriot* [1896] 2 Q.B. 338). But a garnishee, against whom an order absolute has been made, can be examined under this rule (*Cowan v. Carlill* (1885) 33 W.R. 583).

If a judgment creditor obtains an order under section 5 of the Debtors Act 1869, in respect of a High Court maintenance order for payment by instalments he can, before default in payment, apply to commit the judgment debtor for disobedience to an order previously obtained for examination under this Rule (*Hayter v. Beall* (1881) 44 L.T. 131, reversing 29 W.R. 333; but *cf. Montgomery v. de Bulmes* [1898] 2 Q.B. 420).

The Court has no power to order an officer of a non-corporate body such as the International Tin Council to attend to be orally examined as to the nature, value and location of its assets within the U.K., but nevertheless the Court has an inherent jurisdiction to order that body to disclose such full particulars respecting its assets and to require such disclosure to be verified by affidavit by its proper office (*Maclaine Watson & Co. Ltd v. International Tin Council (No. 2)* [1988] 3 W.L.R. 1190, CA).

Where a judgment debtor is being orally examined pursuant to r.1 regarding any debts owing to him and his assets, he is required to answer questions relating to assets outside the jurisdiction, although of course the English Court has no jurisdiction in relation to enforcement proceedings in any other country in which those assets may be situated (*Interpool Ltd v. Galani* [1988] Q.B. 738).

The Court will grant an injunction to restrain a judgment debtor from dealing with his assets outside the jurisdiction in order to prevent him frustrating the purposes of an oral examination. (*Babanaft International Co. SA v. Bassatrie* (1988) 138 New L.J. 203, CA.)

Service of order (rr.1–3)—When the appointment has been obtained a copy of the order, indorsed with the appointment and the notice provided for by O.45, r.7(4)(a) must be served upon the judgment debtor or other person ordered to attend. Personal service is generally necessary as a preliminary to proceedings for committal in case of disobedience to the order (*Mason v. Muggeridge* (1856) 18 C.B. 642) but where it can be proved that the existence of the order has come to the debtor's knowledge, and he is evading service, it may be enforced by committal (*Kistler v. Tettmar* [1905] 1 K.B. 39; *R. v. Wigand* [1913] 2 K.B. 419). But personal service will not be dispensed with merely on the ground that the debtor knows of the existence of the order even in the case where he was in Court when the order was made. See *Re Tuck, Murch v. Loosemore* [1906] 1 Ch. 692, CA. R48.3.6

Where the examination of the judgment debtor is adjourned to a further appointed date he must be personally served with an amended order indorsed with the new or adjourned date for his examination and with a fresh penal notice, otherwise his failure to attend at such new and adjourned date will not constitute a contempt of Court, even though the original order was indorsed with a penal notice and even if his legal representatives are themselves aware of the adjourned date and know the consequence of the debtor's non-attendance (*Beeston Shipping Ltd v. Babanaft International SA, The Eastern Venture* [1985] 1 All E.R. 923, CA, distinguishing *Rendell v. Grundy* [1895] 1 Q.B. 16, CA, and see *Chiltern District Council v. Keane* [1985] 1 W.L.R. 619; [1985] 2 All E.R. 118, CA).

Conduct money (rr.1–3)—A debtor before examination under this rule is entitled to his expenses for coming and attending to give evidence, and if it is not shown that such expenses were tendered to him, and that there is good reason for not examining him at his place of residence he will not be liable to committal for non-compliance with an order for his examination elsewhere (*Protector Endowment Co. v. Whitlam* (1877) 36 L.T. 467). But he is entitled to conduct money merely, not witness's expenses. The Master is the proper person to judge whether sufficient conduct money has been tendered (*Rendell v. Grundy* [1895] 1 Q.B. 16). R48.3.7

"Has any and what other property" (rr.1–3)—*Semble*, before a receiver by way of equitable execution will be appointed by the Court, the property to be received by him must first be ascertained, if necessary, by examination of the judgment debtor, under this rule (*Hamilton v. Brogden* [1891] W.N. 14). See *per* Phillimore L.J. in *Morgan v. Hart* [1914] 2 K.B. 183 at 191. R48.3.8

Although the Court has express powers in specified circumstances to give leave for service of process out of the jurisdiction (see, *e.g.* O.11, rr.1 and 9), it has no general power to do so, and where a defendant had submitted to the jurisdiction of the English court by a contract which included an English jurisdiction clause, the defendant, against whom a default judgment had been entered, had submitted to both the adjudicative and enforcement jurisdictions of the English court and accordingly an order might be served out of the jurisdiction requiring him to attend for examination (*Union Bank of Finland v. LeLakis* [1997] 1 W.L.R. 590; [1996] 4 All E.R. 314, CA).

R48.3.9 **"Nominated officer" (rr.1–3)**—Every Order directs examination before an officer of the Court. The names of the officers nominated by the Senior Master for the purpose of r.1 may be ascertained by enquiry from the Masters' Secretary's Department (Room E214).

The amendments of r.1 considerably extend the classes of persons before whom the oral examination of a judgment debtor may take place. For this purpose a "nominated officer" means an officer of a grade not lower than that of a Higher Executive Officer. Such an examination may accordingly be conducted as follows:

(a) In the Central Office, by officers of that Office nominated for the purpose by the Senior Master.

(b) In the Principal Registry of the Family Division, by officers of that registry nominated for the purpose by the Senior District Judge of that Division.

(c) In district registries, by the District Judge or by an officer of that registry nominated by him to conduct the examination on his behalf, unless the District Judge is personally specified in the order.

(d) In county courts, by the District Judge, or by an officer of that county court nominated for the purpose by the District Judge. Under the rule as amended, the High Court has power to order the oral examination of a debtor to take place in a county court, and this power can usefully be employed in cases where the debtor resides in Outer London and other places which are some distance from a District Registry.

The form of the order should be to order the judgment debtor to be examined "in accordance with the provisions of O.48, r.1(1)". This form of order leaves the master with the widest possible discretion as to the forum and person before whom the examination takes place.

R48.3.10 **Nature of examination (rr.1–3)**—An examination under this rule "is not only intended to be an examination, but to be a cross-examination and that of the severest kind," and is not confined to answering the simple question "what debts are owing," but the debtor must answer all questions "fairly pertinent and properly asked" with a view of ascertaining what debts are owing to him, and from whom they are due and must give "all necessary particulars to enable the creditor to recover under a garnishee order" (*Republic of Costa Rica v. Strousberg* (1880) 16 Ch.D. 8, see judgments of James L.J. and Jessel M.R. at 12).

If the debtor refuses to answer questions or any other difficulty arises before the nominated officer, *e.g.* an application for an adjournment, the matter must be referred to the Senior Master or Practice Master who will determine it and give such direction as he thinks fit. If the debtor should still refuse to answer the question, then the judgment creditor may apply to the Court for his committal under O.52.

Upon an objection being made by a judgment debtor under O.48 that his answers would amount to self-incrimination, it was held that the risk of prosecution whether by leak or by unintended disclosure was very slight and that there was no reason to think that by answering the questions, directed at ascertaining the whereabouts of his assets, he would open himself to any significant risk of prosecution. (*Boden v. Inca Gemstone*, January 20, 1994, CA, unrep.).

R48.3.11 **Further examination (rr.1–3)**—Where an examination of the judgment debtor has been held pursuant to an order under r.1 or 2, a further examination may be ordered in special circumstances. See *Sturges v. Countess of Warwick* (1914) 30 T.L.R. 112.

R48.3.12 **Costs (rr.1–3)**—In the QBD the order for examination usually provides that the costs shall be in the discretion of the Master or District Judge in whose Court the examination has taken place. Application should be made to him after the examination is concluded. The amount allowed by the Master or District Judge is then indorsed upon the order with a direction that it be added to the judgment debt. Costs are not usually allowed unless the judgment creditor can show that the examination was justified in the sense that it produced some fruitful information or the disclosure of some income, property or assets on which enforcement process could usefully be issued. If the examination proves abortive or does not yield any useful information or material, the general practice, by analogy with an abortive execution, no costs will be awarded. An appeal from a refusal to order costs or as to the amount ordered will lie only by leave of the Court, and will fail except when the Judge or Master has exercised no discretion. See *Adlington v. Conyngham* [1898] 2 Q.B. 492, CA.

The costs of an application to commit a defendant for disobedience to an order to attend for examination under an order declaring the plaintiff had a charge on his property were added to the charge (*Tottenham U.D.C. v. Nielson & Co.* [1915] W.N. 275).

RSC ORDER 49

GARNISHEE PROCEEDINGS

Contents R49.0.1

Editorial Introduction

If a judgment debtor is owed money by another, the judgment creditor can obtain an order that that other (referred to in O.49 as "the garnishee") should discharge the debt by payment direct to the judgment creditor. This is known as a garnishee order and is obtained in two stages. R49.0.2

A bank account in credit is a debt due by the bank to the customer. Consequently judgment creditors who have details of the judgment debtor's bank (possibly as a result of an oral examination—see RSC, O.48) frequently attempt to enforce the judgment by garnishee proceedings against a bank.

The procedure is in rr.1 to 4. The rules take account of the fact that the garnishee may wish to dispute that he is indebted (see r.5) or that a third person may wish to assert a claim (r.6).

The powers under this Order are exercised by the Master or District Judge.

Related sources

- Supreme Court Act 1981, ss.40 and 139 (SCP 1999, Vol. 2, Section 20A, paras 20A–245 and 20A–546) R49.0.3
- RSC, O.45, r.1 (Enforcement of judgment, etc., for payment of money)
- CCR, O.27 (Attachment of earnings)
- CCR, O.30 (Garnishee proceedings)
- *Queen's Bench Masters' Practice Direction No. 11—Claims, judgments and enforcement of judgments in foreign currency*, paras 12 & 13 (judgment debt or debt to be garnished in foreign currency) (Vol. 2, Section 2A, paras 2A–48 and 2A–49) (also applies in Chancery Division, see Vol. 2, Section 2B, para. 2B–179).
- Chancery and Queen's Bench Division Fixed Costs (Garnishee Proceedings) (para. 62/A3/6)

Forms

The following Prescribed Forms (formerly included amongst the Prescribed Forms in Appendix A to the RSC) are relevant to O.49. These forms are included in Table 2 (Practice Forms) attached to Practice Direction (Forms) and may be found in SCP 1999, Vol. 2, Section 1A, paras 1A–73 to 1A–75): R49.0.4

- PF No. 72—Garnishee order to show cause (O.49, r.1)
- PF No. 73—Garnishee order absolute where garnishee owes more than judgment debt (O.49, rr.1, 4)
- PF No. 74—Garnishee order absolute where garnishee owes less than judgment debt (O.49, rr.1, 4)

The following Queen's Bench Masters' Practice Form is relevant to O.49 (Vol. 2, Section 1B, para. 1B–73):

- PF 100—Affidavit in support of garnishee order (O.49, r.2)

Attachment of debt due to judgment debtor

1.—(1) Where a person (in this order referred to as "the judgment creditor") has obtained a judgment or order for the payment by some other person (in this order referred to as "the judgment debtor") of a sum of money amounting in value to at least £50, not being a judgment or order for the payment of money into court, and any other person within the jurisdiction (in R49.1

this order referred to as "the garnishee") is indebted to the judgment debtor, the court may, subject to the provisions of this order and of any enactment, order the garnishee to pay the judgment creditor the amount of any debt due or accruing due to the judgment debtor from the garnishee, or so much thereof as is sufficient to satisfy that judgment or order and the costs of the garnishee proceedings.

(2) An order under this rule shall in the first instance be an order to show cause, specifying the time and place for further consideration of the matter, and in the meantime attaching such debt as is mentioned in paragraph (1) or so much thereof as may be specified in the order, to answer the judgment or order mentioned in that paragraph and the costs of the garnishee proceedings.

(3) Among the conditions mentioned in section 40 of the Supreme Court Act 1981 (which enables any sum standing to the credit of a person in certain types of account to be attached notwithstanding that certain conditions applicable to the account in question have not been satisfied) there shall be included any condition that a receipt for money deposited in the account must be produced before any money is withdrawn.

(4) An order under this rule shall not require a payment which would reduce below £1 the amount standing in the name of the judgment debtor in an account with a building society or a credit union.

R49.1.1 **Supreme Court Act 1981, ss.40 & 139**—These sections extended the range of debts which may be attached in garnishee proceedings (SCP Mainwork 1999, Vol. 2, Section 20A, paras 20A–245 and 20A–546). Under s.40, subject to any orders made by the Lord Chancellor, garnishee proceedings will apply to the following accounts, namely (a) any deposit account with a bank or other deposit-taking institution and (b) any withdrawable share account with any deposit-taking institution. Such an institution is defined as meaning any person carrying on a business which is a deposit-taking business for the purposes of the Banking Act 1987, and this would seem to include all forms of banks, building societies and finance houses. Under s.139(1) of the 1981 Act, the provision in the Crown Proceedings Act 1947 (see s.27(1)(c)) which precluded the making of garnishee orders in respect of money payable on account of a deposit in the National Savings Bank, were repealed.

The Order does not apply to a judgment or order for the payment of money into court (para. (1); and see *Re Greer* [1895] 2 Ch. 217).

R49.1.2 **Limitation**—It is open to obtain a garnishee order by way of procedural machinery to enforce a judgment even though the statutory period of limitation under section 24(1) of the Limitation Act 1980 for bringing an action on the judgment has expired (*Lowsley v. Forbes*, *The Times*, April 5, 1996, CA, applying *National Westminster Bank Plc v. Powney* [1991] Ch.339, CA; and see *Fellows v. Thornton* at para. R49.1.8, below).

R49.1.3 **Crown**—This Order does not apply in respect of any order against the Crown (O.77, r.15); and no order for the attachment of debts under this Order can be made or have any effect in respect of money due or accruing due from the Crown (O.77, r.16). Instead, an application can be made under s.27(1) of the Crown Proceedings Act 1947 (see O.77, r.16(2)) and on such an application rr.5 and 6 of the present Order apply, except that the Court has no power to order execution to issue against the Crown (*ibid.*, para. (3)).

R49.1.4 **Debts owed by partnership firm**—O.81, r.7, prescribes what is to be done to attach a debt owing by a firm.

R49.1.5 **Executors of person indebted**—Where a testator was indebted to the judgment debtor a garnishee order can be made against the executors; but it must show upon its face that it is made against them *qua* executors, and not personally (*Stevens v. Phelips* (1875) L.R. 10 Ch. 417, and remarks of Mellish L.J. at 423).

R49.1.6 **Object of the process**—It should always be borne in mind that the object and intention of the process is to render "debts" as a form of property available in execution. This marks both the nature of the process and its limitations. For the history and scope of the order, see *Annual Practice* 1945, p.842.

R49.1.7 **"The Court may"**—The word "may" imports a discretion, though of course a judicial one, and the order will be refused where it would be inequitable—*e.g.* where the garnishee would still be liable in a foreign court (*Martin v. Nadel* [1906] 2 K.B. 26, CA). A garnishee order should not be made if, as a result of proceedings in a foreign jurisdiction for the recovery of the same debt, the garnishee faces a risk of having to pay the same debt twice; such risk outweighs the fact that the foreign judgment of which the garnishee stands in peril is one which has been irregularly obtained as the result of the exercise of an exorbitant jurisdiction (*Deutsche Schachtbau-und Tiefbohr G.m.b.H. v. Shell International Petroleum Co. Ltd* [1988] 3 W.L.R. 230; [1988] 2 All E.R. 833, HL). A statement in an affidavit that an order to pay the debt would leave the garnishee "liable to an action to recover the same debt brought in a competent court in a foreign place", which specified neither the "competent court" nor the "foreign place", was held to be too vague to establish a risk of double payment (*Swiss Bank Corp. v. Boehmische Industrial Bank* [1923] 1 K.B. 673, CA; distinguishing *Martin v. Nadel*, above).

A garnishee order which is basically an equitable remedy will not generally be granted if the effect will be to prefer one creditor over another, *e.g.* where an estate is insolvent (*Prichard v. Westminster Bank Ltd* [1969] 1 W.L.R. 547; [1969] 1 All E.R. 999, CA) and therefore, if there is doubt whether the estate of the deceased is insolvent, the money in the hands of the garnishee should be ordered to be paid into court, pending an enquiry whether or not the estate is insolvent (*George Lee & Sons (Builders) Ltd v. Olink* [1972] 1 W.L.R. 214; [1972] 1 All E.R. 359, CA). Equally, the order will not be made if the money is due to the judgment debtor as trustee for another (*Roberts v. Death* (1881) 8 Q.B.D. 319).

In considering whether or not to exercise its discretion to make absolute a garnishee order, the Court must bear in mind not only the position of the judgment creditor, the judgment debtor and the garnishee, but also the position of the other creditors of the judgment debtor and must have regard to the fact that proceedings are on foot for ensuring the distribution of the available assets of the judgment debtor among the creditors *pari passu* (*D. Wilson (Birmingham) Ltd v. Metropolitan Property Developments Ltd* [1975] 2 All E.R. 814, CA cited in *Rainbow v. Moorgate Properties Ltd* [1975] 2 All E.R. 821, CA, a case in relation to charging orders in which identical considerations were held to apply.

"A person who has obtained a judgment"—If the whole of a judgment debt is assigned, these words include the assignee (*Goodman v. Robinson* (1887) 18 Q.B.D. 332; *Re Freshwater, etc., Ry.* [1913] W.N. 184) if he has obtained leave under O.46, r.2(1)(b) to issue execution. They do not, however, include the assignee of a part only of a judgment debt (*Forster v. Baker* [1910] K.B. 636, CA). They also include a party added under O.15, r.7, owing to death, marriage, bankruptcy, or other event (*cf. Baynard v. Simmons* (1855) 5 E. & B. 59). A garnishee order can be obtained though six years have elapsed since the judgment (*Fellows v. Thornton* (1885) 14 Q.B.D. 335) but whether in such a case it is necessary to get leave under O.46, r.2(1)(a) is uncertain, in view of the conflicting views of Lord Coleridge C.J. and Stephen J. on this point (*ibid.*). The safer course is to seek leave. R49.1.8

Where the defendant gives an undertaking to the Court which is embodied in a written order to pay a sum of money, which the claimant would otherwise be liable to pay, the Court will treat the undertaking as the equivalent of a judgment or order obtained by the claimant, *e.g.* an undertaking by the husband to pay the school fees of the child of the marriage, and accordingly, the Court has jurisdiction to make a garnishee order against the defendant's bank for the payment of such sum (*Gandolfo v. Gandolfo (Standard Chartered Bank Ltd Garnishee)* [1981] Q.B. 359; [1980] 1 All E.R. 833, CA).

The judgment dates from the time when it is pronounced, not when it is entered or signed (*Holtby v. Hodgson* (1889) 24 Q.B.D. 103, CA).

Extension of U.K. judgment—Garnishee proceedings might formerly have been founded upon a judgment extended from one part of the United Kingdom to another, under the Judgments Extension Act 1868, repealed by the Civil Jurisdiction and Judgments Act 1982 (*Galbraith v. Grinshaw* [1910] A.C. 508. See, too, *Johnstone v. Bucknall* [1898] 2 Ir.R. 499). Now, a judgment for money given in one part of the U.K. may be enforced in another part pursuant to s.18 of and Sched. 6 to the Act of 1982. For the procedure for obtaining an order for enforcement, see O.71, r.37. R49.1.9

Right to concurrent remedies—In *Hayter v. Beall* (1881) 44 L.T. 131, CA, a judgment creditor, after obtaining an order upon a judgment summons for payment by instalments, was held to be entitled to examine the judgment debtor as to debts owing to him, Bramwell L.J., observing that he could see no reason why these remedies should not be concurrent, and every reason why they should be. But in *Montgomery v. De Bulmes* [1898] 2 Q.B. 420, CA, where a judgment creditor had got an order under s.5 of the Debtors Act 1869 made by a county court for payment by instalments of a debt due under a High Court judgment, the CA held that he could not issue execution in the High Court, and approved the principle of *Jones v. Jenner* (1856) 25 L.J. Exch. 319, which decided that a judgment creditor could not return to the High Court for a garnishee order after getting an order from an inferior Court for payment by instalments. Where the Judge in bankruptcy had ordered payment by instalments a garnishee order was granted in respect of instalments overdue (*Woodham Smith v. Edwards* [1908] 2 K.B. 899, CA). A judgment creditor, who has obtained a garnishee order absolute attaching a debt owing to the judgment R49.1.10

debtor, is not thereby precluded from serving a bankruptcy notice upon such judgment debtor, as the obtaining of such order does not amount to a stay of execution (*Re Renison, ex p. Greaves* [1913] 2 K.B. 300); and, *a fortiori*, the obtaining of a garnishee order *nisi* in such a case would not amount to such a stay (*Re H. B.* [1904] 1 K.B. 94 at 97, CA).

Where a writ of *fi. fa.* has been issued it is not necessary to wait for a return (*i.e.* a statement indorsed on the writ of the manner in which it was executed, O.46, r.9) to be made before applying for a garnishee order.

R49.1.11 **Payment not immediately enforceable**—"Attachment is applicable where a *fi. fa.* would be open to the judgment creditor" (*Bramwell B. in Jones v. Jenner* (1856) 25 L.J.Exch. 319). A garnishee proceeding being a species of execution, a judgment creditor never ought to be allowed to take out a garnishee summons or get an order thereon if he could not issue a *fi. fa.* (*White, Son & Pill v. Stennings* [1911] 2 K.B. 418, CA); so, to entitle a judgment creditor to a garnishee order, the judgment debtor must be bound to pay at the moment (*Kennett v. Westminster Improvement Commissioners* (1856) 25 L.J.Exch. 97; 11 Exch. 349; *White, Son & Pill v. Stennings*).

R49.1.12 **Garnishee "within the jurisdiction"**—The garnishee must be within the jurisdiction. If the garnishee is outside the jurisdiction there is no power under the rule to make an order. Temporary physical presence within the jurisdiction at the time of the making of the order *nisi* may suffice; and, if the garnishee has agreed to submit to the jurisdiction for the purposes of the garnishee proceedings, that will suffice even though he has left the jurisdiction before order *nisi* made (*S.C.F. Finance Co. Ltd v. Masri (No. 3)* [1987] 1 Q.B. 1028, CA). There is no limitation that the garnished debt must be properly recoverable within the jurisdiction. As a matter of discretion, however, the court will not garnish a debt where, although the garnishee is within the jurisdiction, the debt is recoverable outside the jurisdiction, if to do so may expose the garnishee to the risk of having to pay the debt, or part of it, twice over (*Martin v. Nadel* [1906] 2 K.B. 26, CA; *S.C.F. Finance Co. Ltd v. Masri (No. 3)* [1987] Q.B. 1028; [1987] 1 All E.R. 194, CA; *Interpool Ltd v. Galani* [1988] Q.B. 738; [1987] 2 All E.R. 981, CA). To resist an order the garnishee must show that such risk is real or substantial; the reality of the risk will be more readily assumed where the *situs* of the debt is outside the jurisdiction (*Swiss Bank Corp. v. Boehmische Industrial Bank* [1923] 1 K.B. 673, CA). In so far as *Richardson v. Richardson* [1927] P. 228 goes further, and decides that there is no power to garnish a debt situate outside the jurisdiction, it must be taken to be wrongly decided in the light of the Court of Appeal's reasoning in *S.C.F. Finance Co. Ltd v. Masri (No. 3)* [1987] Q.B. 1028; [1987] 1 All E.R. 194, CA, and *Interpool Ltd v. Galani* [1988] Q.B. 738; [1987] 2 All E.R. 981, CA). As to the exercise of discretion, see para. R49.1.7.

R49.1.13 **Any debt due or accruing due**—It is essential that the relation of creditor and debtor should exist between the judgment debtor and the garnishee. If the judgment debtor could sue the garnishee for the amount and recover it, it is plain that there would be an attachable debt; but this is not an infallible test.

There must be money *due* to the judgment debtor. In the case, for example, of a building contract in the R.I.B.A. form, where the builder is paid on the certificate of the architect, it is plain that money in the hands of the building owner cannot be attached until a certificate is issued, and then only for the amount mentioned in that certificate (*Dunlop & Ranken Ltd v. Hendall Steel Structures, Ltd, Pitchers Ltd (Garnishees)* [1957] 1 W.L.R. 1102 at 1105; [1957] 3 All E.R. 344 at 347).

Of course a garnishee order cannot accelerate the time for payment of a debt. Where the debt is not due there is nothing to be attached (*Webb v. Stenton* (1883) 11 Q.B.D. 518, CA; *Re Greenwood* [1901] 1 Ch. 887).

A judgment creditor cannot, by means of attachment, stand in a better position as regards the garnishee than the judgment debtor did; "he can only obtain what the judgment debtor could honestly give him" (Chitty J., at 516, *Re General Horticultural Co., ex p. Whitehouse* (1886) 32 Ch.D. 512; *cf. Glegg v. Bromley* [1912] 3 K.B. 474; and *Sinnott v. Bowden* (1912) 2 Ch. 414).

R49.1.14 **Deposit accounts with a bank or other deposit-taking institution**—Section 40 of the Supreme Court Act 1981 has greatly extended the earlier, restricted, position in relation to attachment of deposit accounts. Subject to any order made by the Lord Chancellor by way of amendment, S.C.A. 1981, s.40 applies to the following accounts, namely:

(a) any deposit account with a bank or other deposit-taking institution; and
(b) any withdrawable share account with any deposit-taking institution (s.40(1)).

In determining whether, for the purposes of the jurisdiction of the High Court to attach debts under this Order, a sum standing to the credit of a person in an account to which s.40 applies is a sum due or accruing due to that person and, as such, attachable in accordance with the rules of this Order, any of the following conditions which apply to the account must be disregarded (see s.40(2)), namely:

(a) any condition that notice is required before any money or share is withdrawn;
(b) any condition that a personal application must be made before any money is withdrawn;
(c) any condition that a deposit book or share-account book must be produced before any money or share is withdrawn; or
(d) any other prescribed condition (s.40(3)).

Deposit-taking institutions—For the purposes of section 40 of the S.C.A. 1981, a "deposit-taking institution" means any person carrying on a business which is a deposit-taking business for the purposes of the Banking Act 1987 (see section 40(6) of the 1981 Act). For the meaning of "deposit-taking business", see s.6 of the Banking Act 1987 which, subject to the provisions of that section, describes such a business as one where (a) in the course of the business money received by way of deposit is lent to others; or (b) any other activity of the business is financed, wholly or to any material extent, out of the capital of or the interest on money received by way of deposit. For the meaning of "deposit", see section 5 of the Act; and for an examination whether, in the particular circumstances of that case, there was a deposit-taking business see *S.C.F. Finance Co. Ltd v. Masri (No. 2)* [1987] Q.B. 1002, CA. **R49.1.15**

Section 3 of the Banking Act 1987 imposes restrictions on the acceptance of deposits in the course of carrying on a deposit-taking business unless the person accepting the deposit is an institution authorised by the Bank of England. Such authorisation extends to authorised banks. Furthermore, by s.4 there are exempted from the provisions of s.3 the Bank of England itself, and other institutions which may be regarded as deposit-taking institutions, as specified in Sched. 2 to the Act. The terms of Sched. 2 as amended are as follows:

Exempted Persons

1. The central bank of a member State other than the United Kingdom. **R49.1.16**
2. The National Savings Bank.
3. A penny savings Bank.
4. A municipal bank.
5. A building society incorporated (or deemed to be incorporated) under the Building Societies Act 1986.
6.—(1) A friendly society within the meaning of section 7(1)(a) of the Friendly Societies Act 1974.
(2) This paragraph applies only to the acceptance of deposits in the course of carrying out transactions permitted by the rules of the society.
7. A society registered under either of the Acts mentioned in paragraph 6 above other than such a society as is there mentioned.
8.—(1) Any institution which is for the time being authorised under section 3 or 4 of the Insurance Companies Act 1982 to carry on insurance business of a class specified in Schedule 1 or 2 to that Act.
(2) This paragraph applies only to the acceptance of deposits in the course of carrying on the authorised insurance business.
9. A loan society whose rules are certified, deposited and enrolled in accordance with the Loan Societies Act 1840.
10. A credit union within the meaning of the Credit Unions Act 1979 or the Credit Unions (Northern Ireland) Order 1985.
10A.—(1) Keesler Federal Credit Union.
(2) [This sub-para. limits the application of the paragraph to classes of persons specifically described and by reference to the Visiting Forces Act 1952.]
11. A body of persons certified as a school bank by the National Savings Bank or an authorised institution.
12. A local authority.
13. Any other body which by virtue of any enactment has power to issue a precept to a local authority in England or Wales or a requisition to a local authority in Scotland.
14. The Crown Agents for Oversea Governments and Administrations.
14A. Crown Agents Financial Services Limited.
15. The European Atomic Energy Community.
16. The European Coal and Steel Community.
17. The European Economic Community.
18. The European Investment Bank.
19. The International Bank for Reconstruction and Development.
20. The International Finance Corporation.
21. The International Monetary Fund.
22. The African Development Bank.
23. The Asian Development Bank.
24. The Caribbean Development Bank.
25. The Inter-American Development Bank.
26. The European Bank for Reconstruction and Development.
27. The Council of Europe Resettlement Fund.

The scope of para. 8 above has been extended to include E.C. insurance companies (see S.I. 1994 No. 1696).

Cases where there is an attachable debt

1. Rent—Rent due can be attached (*Mitchell v. Lee* (1867) L.R. 2 Q.B. 259). But though it **R49.1.17**

accrues due *de die in diem* under the Apportionment Act 1870, it is not attachable until it becomes payable by the tenant (*Barnett v. Eastman* (1898) 67 L.J.Q.B. 517).

R49.1.18 **2. Joint judgment against two or more persons**—A judgment creditor who has got a joint judgment against two or more persons can attach a debt owing to any of his judgment debtors (*Miller v. Mynn* (1859) 28 L.J.Q.B. 324) by a third person. In *Chapman v. Callis* (1862) 6 L.T. 282, a doubt was expressed whether a judgment creditor could attach a debt owing by one judgment debtor to another, but this has been regarded as *obiter dictum*, and is not followed.

R49.1.19 **3. Debt of unascertained amount**—The fact that the amount of the debt due or accruing due is not ascertained does not prevent a garnishee order *nisi* being made (*Lucy v. Wood* [1884] W.N. 58; *De Pass v. Capital & Industries Corp.* [1891] 1 Q.B. 216).

Money payable to a "panel doctor" by an Insurance Committee under the National Insurance Acts, after receipt by the Committee of funds received by them to enable them to pay such doctor was held to be attachable, although the precise sum payable to him had not yet been ascertained (*O'Driscoll v. Manchester Insurance Committee* [1915] 3 K.B. 499, CA). Note that it was of the essence of the decision in that case that the garnishees were found *as a fact* to be indebted in a specified sum at the date of the inquiry by the Court. While this did not represent the entire indebtedness, it was the actual amount ascertained and proved to be due at the date of the inquiry. In *Olds Discount Co. Ltd v. Alldred* in Chambers in March, 1952 (unrep.) where moneys belonging to a judgment debtor were alleged to be in the hands of the Law Society under the Legal Aid and Advice Act 1949 (now 1988 Act), and it was denied that anything was owing to the debtor, an order was made directing an inquiry whether in respect of the debt owing by the garnishees to the judgment debtor any and what amount had been ascertained and determined to have become payable pursuant to regulation 16 of the Legal Aid (General) Regulations 1950 (see now reg. 18 of the Civil Legal Aid (General) Regulations 1989), the amount to which the garnishees were indebted to the judgment debtor to be certified, and ordering the garnishees to pay to the judgment creditor the amount so certified. This order was based upon the old Form No.PF 101. See *Dawson v. Preston (Law Society, Garnishees)* [1955] 1 W.L.R. 1219; [1955] 3 All E.R. 314.

"Rateable deductions" of unascertained amount from the pay of a police officer (being contributions to a pension fund) have been held to be attachable on his leaving the force without pension or gratuity (*Devlin v. County Court Judge of Fermanagh* [1938] 2 N.I.R. 50).

R49.1.20 **4. Debt already paid by cheque**—Where the judgment debtor has been paid by cheque, which is stopped by the garnishee upon his being served with a garnishee order *nisi*, there is an attachable debt (*Cohen v. Hale* (1878) 3 Q.B.D. 371); but not if the garnishee does not stop the cheque, nor is he bound so to do (*Elwell v. Jackson* (1885) 1 T.L.R. 454; CA; *cf. Ex p. Richdale* (1882) 19 Ch.D. 409, CA).

R49.1.21 **5. Debt due to judgment debtor in a representative capacity**—After judgment obtained against him *qua* executor, a debt due to an executor can be attached, although a decree for the administration of the testator's estate has been made since the attachment order (*Burton v. Roberts* (1860) 29 L.J.Exch. 484; 6 H. & N. 93; *Fowler v. Roberts* (1860) 2 L.T. 368).

R49.1.22 **6. Annuity payable by trustees**—Annuities payable by trustees are attachable (*Nash v. Pease* (1878) 47 L.J.Q.B.D. 766) but the money must have reached their hands and be also payable (*Webb v. Stenton* (1883) 11 Q.B. 518, CA, and judgments of Lindley and Fry L.JJ., *ibid.*).

R49.1.23 **7. Money payable in winding up a company**—An order has been made attaching money in the hands of the official manager of a company in its winding up (*Ex p. Turner* (1861) 30 L.J.Ch.92; 2 De G.F. & J. 354); but in that case the garnishee order was made against the company (Stirling L.J., p. 207, in *Spence v. Coleman* [1901] 2 K.B. 199, CA) and the circumstances were peculiar (Bovill, C.J., in *Re Greensill* (1872) L.R. 8 C.P. 24 at 28). Dividends due from a company in voluntary liquidation have been attached in the liquidator's hands (*Klauber v. Weill* (1901) 17 T.L.R. 344, CA); but that case was argued solely on the point as to the garnishee order not having been appealed against (see Collins L.J.'s comment at the end of *Spence v. Coleman*) and A. L. Smith M.R. thought that the liquidator might have successfully objected; moreover the CA thought it desirable to make the order against the company itself, even if there was power to make it against the liquidator (*cf. Dawson v. Malley* (1867) 15 W.R. 791). But see *Gerard v. Worth of Paris Ltd* [1936] 2 All E.R. 905; (1936) 82 L.J. Newsp. 101. See also n. "Cases where there is no attachable debt—14. money paid into companies liquidation account and 15. Money in the hands of a liquidator," paras R49.1.55 *et seq.*

R49.1.24 **8. Money held by a receiver in administration action**—This was held to be attachable by a judgment creditor of a beneficiary (*Re Cowan's Estate* (1880) 14 Ch.D. 638): but that case is only applicable now to money already in the receiver's hands (*Webb v. Stenton* (1883) 11 Q.B.D. 518, CA).

R49.1.25 **9. Proceeds of execution in hands of sheriff**—The proceeds of an execution in the hands of the sheriff are attachable; but he should not pay them over until fourteen days have elapsed, in case the garnishor should be divested of his right to the money by Insolvency Act 1986, s.346 through the judgment debtor becoming bankrupt.

10. Representatives of deceased third person—Where the third person, who was indebted to the judgment debtor, has died, a garnishee order can be served upon his executors; but must be directed to them as such and not personally (*Stevens v. Phelips* (1875) L.R. 10 Ch. 417). **R49.1.26**

11. Sums payable as interest to stockholders in a company—Sums payable under a statutory agreement by A. Co. to B. Co., to be applied by B. Co. in paying interest to the holders of their preference stock, were held attachable (*Bouch v. Sevenoaks, etc., Ry*, (1879) 4 Ex.D. 133). **R49.1.27**

12. Money deposited with third party for purpose which fails—Money deposited with A by the judgment debtor for a special purpose which fails is attachable in A's hands (*Stumore v. Campbell* [1892] 1 Q.B. 314, CA). **R49.1.28**

13. Judgment debtor's bank balance—Money standing to the credit of the judgment debtor at his bank is attachable (*cf. Rogers v. Whiteley* [1892] A.C. 118); but not money paid in after the garnishee summons is served (*Heppenstall v. Jackson and Barclays Bank Ltd (Garnishees)* [1939] 1 K.B. 585, CA) nor the money of other people, which the judgment debtor has no right to dispose of (*Hancock v. Smith* (1889) 41 Ch.D. 456, CA). Where a debtor requested his bank to transfer the money in his current account to the account of another customer, and the necessary entries were made by the bank a garnishee order *nisi* served upon the bank an hour later was made absolute, it being held that the mere entry in the bank books of the transaction gave no title to the other customer in the absence of knowledge of and assent to the transfer by them (*Rekstin v. Severo, etc., and Bank for Russian Trade Ltd* [1933] 1 K.B. 47). **R49.1.29**

A demand for payment is necessary to render a credit balance on current account attachable, but service of a garnishee order *nisi* on the bank constitutes such a demand (see *Joachimson v. Swiss Bank Corp.* [1921] 3 K.B. 110, CA; *Rekstin v. Severo, etc., and Bank for Russian Trade Ltd*, above, pp.70–71; *Bagley v. Winsome and National Provincial Bank, Ltd* [1952] 2 Q.B. 236 at 240–1, 245, CA; *Arab Bank Ltd v. Barclays Bank* [1954] A.C. 495; [1954] 2 All E.R. 226).

By the S.C.A. 1981, s.40 amounts standing to the credit of the debtor in deposit and many similar accounts may be attached; see above commentary.

14. Bill of exchange before maturity—Money which will become payable by the garnishee when a bill of exchange matures is attachable, the order suspending execution until maturity and restraining the judgment debtor by injunction from dealing with the bill in the interval (*Hyam v. Freeman* (1890) 35 S.J. 87; *cf.* Crompton J. in *Jones v. Thompson* (1858) 27 L.J.Q.B. 234 at 235). **R49.1.30**

15. Pension for past services—A pension solely for past services as distinguished from half-pay is attachable (*Dent v. Dent* (1867) L.R. 1 P. & D. 366; *Willcock v. Terrell* (1878) 3 Ex.D. 323, CA). But a pension which by statute cannot be voluntarily alienated by the pensioner is unattachable, even though payable solely for past services (*Lucas v. Harris* (1887) 18 Q.B.D. 127, CA) unless it has lost its character as pension, *e.g.* by being received by the pensioner's bankers (*Jones & Co. v. Coventry* [1909] 2 K.B. 1029; *cf. Crowe v. Price* (1889) 22 Q.B.D. 429, CA). **R49.1.31**

16. Unvouched fees payable after vouching—The fees of a public vaccinator, not payable until the work is done and vouched, were held to be attachable when the work is done, though it has not yet been vouched (*Edmunds v. Edmunds* [1904] P. 362). **R49.1.32**

17. Estoppel by garnishee order absolute—If the garnishee allows an order absolute to be made against him, he cannot evade payment although no attachable debt existed when the order was made (*Randall v. Lithgow* (1884) 12 Q.B.D. 525). But an order absolute may be set aside (*O'Brien v. Killeen* [1914] 2 Ir.R. 63; and see r.4 n. "Setting aside garnishee orders", paras R49.4.5 to R49.4.7). **R49.1.33**

18. Debitum in praesenti solvendum in futuro—(*Tapp v. Jones* (1875) L.R. 10 Q.B. 591; *Ex p. Joselyn, Re Watt* (1878) 8 Ch.D. 327, CA). As where, for example, there is an existing debt, payable by instalments. In such a case an order may be made in respect of the future instalments "as and when they become due". But the distinction must be borne in mind between the case where there is an existing debt, payment whereof is deferred, and the case where both the debt and its payment rest in the future. In the former case there is an attachable debt, in the latter case there is not. (This passage, which has appeared in many editions of the *Annual Practice* before 1966, was cited with approval by Bankes L.J., in *O.'Driscoll v. Manchester Insurance Committee* [1915] 3 K.B. 499 at 516.) **R49.1.34**

19. Debt situate within the jurisdiction—Where a foreign defendant submits to the **R49.1.35**

jurisdiction a debt that is properly recoverable within the jurisdiction is attachable, since payment under the garnishee order extinguishes the debt (*Swiss Bank Corp. v. Boehmische Industrial Bank* [1923] 1 K.B. 673); for the position where the debt is situate in a foreign country, see *Martin v. Nadel* [1906] 2 K.B. 26 and para. R49.1.12, above).

R49.1.36 **20. Judgment debt**—A judgment debt may be attached in the hands of the judgment debtor (*Holtby v. Hodgson* (1889) 24 Q.B.D. 103) and this although the judgment was not entered until after the application for the order *nisi*. The question whether a judgment upon which there is a stay of execution can be attached has never been decided. It is submitted, however, that until the stay is removed there can be no attachment. As Lopes L.J. said in *Holtby v. Hodgson,* (1889) 24 Q.B.D. 103 at 108: "What is the test whether a debt is attachable? That it is owing by the garnishee, and that it is a debt of which the judgment debtor can enforce payment if he desire to do so."

R49.1.37 **21. Judgment of inferior court**—A garnishee application may be made on a judgment of an inferior court after removal into the High Court, and the costs of removal may be included in the amount of the debt attached, but not the costs of execution. The removal must be proved by the affidavit in support of the application.

R49.1.38 **22. Foreign currency**—A judgment creditor whose judgment is expressed in sterling can attach a sum owing to the judgment debtor in foreign currency so as to make it available to meet the judgment debt (*Choice Investments Ltd v. Jeromnimon; Midland Bank Ltd (garnishee)* [1981] Q.B. 149; [1981] 1 All E.R. 225, CA). The machinery which should be followed to attach a sum payable in foreign currency to satisfy a sterling judgment debt is as follows. First, as soon as practicable after the service of the order *nisi,* the bank should ascertain at its normal buying rate of exchange against sterling that amount of the foreign currency balance of the judgment debtor as would if converted at that date, produce an amount equal to the sterling debt and costs, and the amount of foreign currency so ascertained should be attached.

Secondly, so soon as reasonably practicable after service of the order absolute, the bank should purchase at its then normal buying rate of exchange against sterling the attached amount of foreign currency or so much as would by the application of that rate produce the sterling judgment debt and costs, and pay the same into Court or to the judgment creditor.

Thirdly, the bank should inform the court of the amount of foreign currency attached and the rate of exchange used, so that when the Court makes the garnishee order absolute, it should order the bank to pay the sterling equivalent of the foreign currency or the amount of the judgment debt and costs whichever is the lesser (*ibid.*).

For other instances where there is a foreign currency element in garnishee proceedings see para. R49.2.3, *e.g.* where the judgment debt is expressed in foreign currency and attachment is sought of a debt due to the judgment debtor in sterling or where the judgment debt is expressed in foreign currency and attachment is sought of a debt due to the judgment debtor in that currency (see *Queen's Bench Masters' Practice Direction No. 11* at SCP 1999, Vol. 2, Section 2A, paras 2A–37 *et seq.*).

R49.1.39 **23. Funds derived under international treaty**—In *Philipp Brothers Ltd v. Republic of Sierra Leone* [1995] 1 Lloyd's Rep. 289, CA, the judgment debtor held monies in a bank account representing funds provided by the E.C. under a programme of financial aid. It was held by the CA, affirming Saville J. at [1994] 1 Lloyd's Rep. 111, that the transactions under which the judgment debtor received the funds were governed not by municipal law but by an international treaty. Obligations arising thereunder were not justiciable in an English court, and no trust or other equitable right under English law attached. The account was a debt due from the bank and a garnishee order absolute was upheld.

Cases where there is no attachable debt

R49.1.40 **1. Verdict for damages before judgment pronounced**—A mere verdict for damages does not constitute an attachable debt (*Jones v. Thompson* (1858) 27 L.J.Q.B. 234); but if the Judge pronounces judgment in conformity with the verdict, there is an attachable debt as from the time when he so pronounces it (*Holtby v. Hodgson* (1889) 24 Q.B.D. 103, CA).

R49.1.41 **2. Allowance to retired servant**—An allowance granted by the directors to a retired clerk of a company was held unattachable, because it was not under a seal, and was a gratuity instead of a debt (*Innes v. East India Co.* (1856) 25 L.J.C.P. 154; *cf. Ex p. Hawker* (1872) L.R. 7 Ch. 214).

R49.1.42 **3. Costs not yet assessed**—It seems that a garnishee order cannot be made in respect of untaxed costs (*Widgery v. Tepper* (1877) 6 Ch.D. 364, *per* James L.J. at p.369). ("Taxation" is now called "detailed assessment".)

R49.1.43 **4. Pay of officer on active list**—(*Apthorpe v. Apthorpe* (1887) 12 P.D. 192, CA). See Attachment of Earnings Act 1971, s.24(2)(b) for exclusion of forces pay and allowances.

5. Unassignable pension—A pension cannot be attached if the pensioner could not assign it (*Birch v. Birch* (1883) 8 P.D. 163; *Lucas v. Harris* (1887) 18 Q.B.D. 127, CA). See nn. "15. Pension for past services", paras R49.1.31 and R49.1.32, and 34. "Statutes forbidding attachment of debts", para. R49.1.73. **R49.1.44**

6. Debts already assigned—A bona fide assignment of the debt before the judgment (*Hirsch v. Coates* (1856) 25 L.J.C.P. 315) or after it, but before service of the order *nisi* upon the garnishee (*Wise v. Birkenshaw* (1860) 29 L.J.Exch. 240) defeats attachment, even though the garnishee has no notice of such assignment (*Pickering v. Ilfracombe Ry.* (1868) L.R. 3 C.P. 235; *Robinson v. Nesbitt* (1868) L.R. 3 C.P. 264; *Glegg v. Bromley* [1912] 3 K.B. 474, CA; and see *Curran v. Newpark Cinemas* [1951] 1 All E.R. 295, CA). **R49.1.45**

7. Legacy—Unless there has been an account stated such as to entitle the party to maintain an action, a legacy is unattachable in the hands of the executor, though he is ready to pay the judgment creditor (*MacDowell v. Hollister* (1855) 25 L.T. (o.s.) 185; 3 W.R. 522; *cf. Ballard v. Marsden* (1880) 14 Ch.D. 374). **R49.1.46**

8. Salary not yet payable—(*Hall v. Pritchett* (1878) 3 Q.B.D. 215; *cf. Holmes v. Millage* [1893] 1 Q.B. 551, CA). Where the judgment debtor had contracted to give performances for a week at a fee of £180, it was held that the judgment creditor could not attach any portion of such sum until the whole of the performances had been given (*Mapleson v. Sears* (1911) 105 L.T. 639). **R49.1.47**

9. Surplus of a bankrupt's estate—Not being a debt, the surplus in the hands of an official assignee or trustee in bankruptcy is not attachable (*Re Greensill* (1873) L.R. 8 C.P. 24). **R49.1.48**

10. Money in hands of receiver appointed by the Court—(*De Winton v. Brecon Corp. (No. 2)* (1860) 28 Beav. 200). See, however, *Re Cowan's Estate* (1880) 14 Ch.D. 638, and *Webb v. Stenton* (1883) 11 Q.B.D. 518, CA, from which it would appear that this case can only be supported on the ground that the Receiver had already been ordered by the Court to pay the money to the judgment debtor. **R49.1.49**

11. Money paid into Court by executors in administration action—This was held unattachable, though the order *nisi* was served before payment into Court, since the whole personalty passed by the administration action into the Court's possession (*Stevens v. Phelips* (1875) L.R. 10 Ch. 417, CA). **R49.1.50**

12. Money paid into Court—The proper method nowadays of getting money standing in Court to the credit of the judgment debtor is by a charging order (*Brereton v. Edwards* (1888) 21 Q.B.D. 488, CA). **R49.1.51**

13. Money held by officer of county court—Where the judgment debtor has got a judgment against A, who has paid the amount to the county court District Judge, the latter cannot be subjected to garnishee proceedings (*Dolphin v. Layton* (1879) 4 C.P.D. 131). But see CCR 1981, O.30, r.12 and see further Insolvency Act 1986, ss. 324, 421, for the modern equivalent. **R49.1.52**

14. Dividend payable by Official Receiver—A dividend, payable in the administration of the estate of a deceased insolvent under ss.62, 130 of the Bankruptcy Act 1914, to the judgment debtor as a creditor of the deceased, is not a debt due from the Official Receiver, who is responsible to the Court only (*Prout v. Gregory* (1890) 24 Q.B.D. 281). **R49.1.53**

15. Money paid into "companies liquidation account"—When a liquidator has paid into the "Companies liquidation account" at the Bank of England, under s.642 of the Companies Act 1985, assets payable to the judgment debtor (whom he could not find) attachment cannot be had against any officer of the Board of Trade (*Spence v. Coleman* [1901] 2 K.B. 199, CA) and see n. "Cases where there is an attachable debt—7. Money payable in winding up a company", paras R49.1.23 and R49.1.24. **R49.1.54**

16. Money in the hands of a liquidator—A company in liquidation took unsuccessful proceedings against the appellants and was ordered to pay the costs. The appellants sought to recover the costs by garnishee proceedings in respect of money in a bank, the account being in the name of the liquidator. The bank paid the money into Court. It was held that the money in the hands of the bank was not owing to the company, but to the liquidator, and the judgment creditors were not entitled to attach it (*Lancaster Motor Co. (London) Ltd v. Bremith Ltd* [1941] 1 K.B. 675, CA). **R49.1.55**

17. Maintenance or lump sum payments—Money ordered by the Family Division to be paid **R49.1.56**

either as maintenance or lump sum payments (*Re Robinson* (1884) 27 Ch.D. 160, CA) or maintenance (*Watkins v. Watkins* [1896] P. 222, CA) is unassignable and inalienable. Equally, maintenance orders made by magistrates' courts are not attachable (*cf. Lucas v. Harris* (1887) 18 Q.B.D. 127, CA).

R49.1.57 **18. Notice to treat for compulsory purchase**—This does not constitute a debt which is attachable, as the judgment debtor may prove to have no right to the compensation (*Richardson v. Elmit* (1877) 2 C.P.D. 9).

R49.1.58 **19. Purchase price of land sold compulsorily**—Until the conveyance is executed or tendered, the price fixed by a jury upon land purchased under statutory powers is not attachable (*Howell v. Metropolitan District Ry.* (1882) 19 Ch.D. 508; *cf. Guardians of the East London Union v. Metropolitan Ry. Co.* (1869) L.R. 4 Exch. 309).

R49.1.59 **20. Contract to indemnify judgment debtor**—Where D induced C to sue the judgment creditor, giving C a bond binding D to pay to the judgment creditor all costs for which C might become liable to him, the amount of such costs was held unattachable in D's hands, as no attachable debt was due from D to C (*Johnson v. Diamond* (1855) 24 L.J.Exch. 217). "The Legislature never intended to attach causes of action" (Parke B. at 219, *ibid.*).

R49.1.60 **21. Where attachment would work injustice**—Where the judgment debtor had issued bonds, whereby all bondholders were to be paid *pari passu*, a bondholder who had got a judgment upon his bond was not allowed to attach a debt owing to the defendants, and thereby get priority over the other bondholders (*Kennett v. Westminster Improvement Commissioners* (1856) 25 L.J.Exch. 97; 11 Exch. 349). Similarly, where the debt is properly recoverable in a foreign country, and the garnishee would therefore be liable to an action in such country in respect of the same debt (*Martin v. Nadel* [1906] 2 K.B. 26, CA; distinguished and explained in *Swiss Bank Corporation v. Boehmische Industrial Bank* [1923] 1 K.B. 673, CA).

R49.1.61 **22. Income of trust funds before time for payment**—A trustee is not a debtor to his *cestui que trust* until he holds money which he ought to pay over, or until he has by some breach of trust or default made himself personally liable to pay (*Webb v. Stenton* (1883) 11 Q.B.D. 518; CA; *cf. Re Greenwood* [1901] 1 Ch. 887).

R49.1.62 **23. Debt due to judgment debtor jointly with another person**—(*Macdonald v. Tacquah Gold Mines Co.* (1884) 13 Q.B.D. 535, CA; *Hirschorn v. Evans* [1938] 2 K.B. 801, CA; *cf. Beasley v. Roney* [1891] 1 Q.B. 509). The principle was applied by Henn Collins J. in Chambers, where the judgment debtor was a partner in a firm (*Fox v. Mainwaring*, June 13, 1891).

R49.1.63 **24. Money of arrested persons held by police**—Money is not attachable in the hands of the police, which was found upon a judgment debtor when arrested, who is subsequently convicted (*Jervis v. Peel* (1885) 1 T.L.R. 306).

R49.1.64 **25. "Cover" deposited with stockbrokers**—"Cover" deposited with stockbrokers cannot be attached while the share transactions remain open (*Hutt v. Shaw* (1887) 3 T.L.R. 354, CA).

R49.1.65 **26. Money payable under a garnishee order absolute**—(*Cooper v. Lawson* (1890) 6 T.L.R. 34).

R49.1.66 **27. Money held on trust created by judgment debtor**—A trustee, who holds money settled by the judgment debtor upon trust to pay it to A, is not a debtor in respect of such money, even if the judgment creditor gets the settlement set aside as void, and the trustee directed to pay over to him the money settled (*Vyse v. Brown* (1884) 13 Q.B.D. 199).

Where a judgment debtor paid £400 to a trustee for his creditor as though a deed of arrangement existed, the deed, in fact, having become a nullity, as the circumstances precluded its registration, it was held that a trust was created and the £400 was unattachable (*Runtz v. Longbourne* (1892) 8 T.L.R. 568; *cf. Roberts v. Jones* (1892) 61 L.J.Q.B. 523).

R49.1.67 **28. Counsel's fees**—Unpaid fees due to a counsel, though received from the client by the solicitor, cannot be attached by a garnishee order against the solicitor, as the counsel could not sue the solicitor for them (*Wells v. Wells* [1914] P. 157, CA).

R49.1.68 **29. Debts from the Crown**—No order for the attachment of debts under O.49 shall be made or have effect in respect of any money due or accruing due from the Crown: see O.77, r.16(1). However, where money is due to a judgment debtor from the Crown, the Court may, subject to the provisions of the Crown Proceedings Act 1947, and in accordance with rules of Court, make an order restraining a person who would normally be in the position of a judgment debtor in garnishee proceedings from receiving the money, and directing payment thereof to the judgment creditor. But no such order can be made in respect of (a) wages or salary due to an officer of the Crown, or (b) money which cannot (by statute) be assigned, charged or taken in execution (see section 27(1) and (2) of the Crown Proceedings Act 1947). And, for the procedure for making an order under the Act in an appropriate case, see O.77, r.16(2) and (2A).

30. Insurance company—Where an insurance company agreed to indemnify the owner of a motor car against "third party" claims, and a third party obtained judgment against the owner of the car, it was held that there was no "debt" due from the insurers which could be attached (*Israelson v. Dawson, Port of Manchester Insurance Co., Garnishees* [1933] 1 K.B. 301, CA). **R49.1.69**

31. Banking account—An order *nisi* does not attach the balance of an account at a bank unless it correctly sets forth the name of the account as it stands in the books of the bank. Where the debtor has and operates an account in a name other than his own, that name must be inserted in the order *nisi* (see *Koch v. Mineral Ore Syndicate* (1910) 54 S.J. 600). **R49.1.70**

As to attachment of money on current account and on deposit account, see n. "Cases where there is an attachable debt—13. Judgment debtor's bank balance" see para. R49.1.29 above.

Where two persons have a joint account on which either can draw, the account is not attachable in respect of a debt owed by one of them (*Hirschorn v. Evans* [1938] 2 K.B. 801, CA).

32. Judgment on which execution stayed—See n. "Cases where there is an attachable debt—20. Judgment debt" see para. R49.1.36 above. **R49.1.71**

33. Building society deferred shares—These are shares issued by a building society in accordance with the Building Societies (Authorisation) Regulations 1981. They are issued subject to the condition that the building society will not give effect to or recognise any transfer of such shares by the person to whom they were issued. As this is *not* one of the conditions which is required to be disregarded under section 40(3) of SCA 1981 (see para. R49.1.14) such shares are not sums due or accruing due to the judgment debtor and are therefore *not* attachable. **R49.1.72**

34. Statutes forbidding attachment of debts—There were formerly a number of statutes which had forbidden the attachment of specified debts (see, *e.g.* Wages Attachment Abolition Act 1870, s.1 repealed by the S.L.(R.)A. 1976). These debts have largely been dealt with either by allowing or forbidding their attachment by the Attachment of Earnings Act 1971. For the attachment of any forces pay or pensions, see Attachment of Earnings Act 1971, s.24(1) and s.24(2)(b); the Army Act 1955, s.203; and the Army and Air Force Act 1961, s.128G. See also the Police Pensions Act 1976, s.9. As to the attachment of wages due or accruing due to seamen, see Merchant Shipping Act 1995, s.34 and Attachment of Earnings Act 1971, s.24(2)(e). **R49.1.73**

The restriction imposed by proviso (c) to s.27(1) of the Crown Proceedings Act on the making of an order under that section, and under O.77, r.16(2), in respect of deposits held by the National Savings Bank has been repealed by s.139(1) of the S.C.A. 1981 (see SCP 1999, Vol. 2, Section 20A, para. 20A–546). But, by s.139(2), the Lord Chancellor may by order re-impose the restriction in relation to any such deposits, or any deposits in that Bank of any description specified in the order.

In cases covered by the Reserve and Auxiliary Forces (Protection of Civil Interests) Act 1951, unless leave to proceed to execution has been obtained from the Court, garnishee proceedings cannot be instituted.

35. Foreign public law—The court will not, by way of garnishee order, enforce the penal, revenue or other public law of a foreign state, as where funds are bound, under exchange control regulations of that state imposing criminal sanctions, to be remitted to the judgment debtor (*Camdex International Ltd v. Bank of Zambia (No. 3), The Times,* January 28, 1997, CA). **R49.1.74**

Application for order

2.—(1) An application for an order under rule 1 must be made in accordance with CPR Part 23 but the application notice need not be served on the judgment debtor. **R49.2**

(2) An application must be supported by a witness statement or affidavit—

(a) stating the name and last known address of the judgment debtor,

(b) identifying the judgment or order to be enforced and stating the amount of such judgment or order and the amount remaining unpaid under it at the time of the application,

(c) stating that to the best of the information or belief of the witness the garnishee (naming him) is within the jurisdiction and is indebted to the judgment debtor and stating the sources of the witness's information or the grounds for his belief; and

(d) stating, where the garnishee is a deposit-taking institution having more than one place of business, the name and address of the branch at which the judgment debtor's account is believed to be held and the number of that account or, if it be the case, that all or part of this information is not known to the witness.

R49.2.1 **Practice under rule**—The application for a garnishee order *nisi* is made without notice, and must be supported by a witness statement or affidavit which complies with this rule.

In the QBD the application is left with the Masters' Secretary (Room E214) and the applicant calls later on to learn the decision of the Master, and draw up the order if made.

In the Ch D the application is made *without notice* in Chambers.

In the Fam Div the application is made to a District Judge; the order *nisi* is drawn up in the Registry and a time inserted therein for making the order absolute.

In a cause or matter proceeding in a District Registry, the application must be made to the District Judge.

R49.2.2 **Affidavit to support garnishee order nisi**—For form, see PF 100 (SCP 1999, Vol. 2, Section 1B, para. 1B–73).

This rule has changed the former practice so that the affidavit need no longer be made by the judgment creditor or his solicitor. It can, for example, be made by a legal executive or other clerk in the employ of the plaintiff's solicitors, or any other person who can properly depose to the required facts according to his information or belief. It may be made by a director or secretary or manager of a company, or of the liquidator of a company in liquidation. In every case, the sources of the deponent's information or the grounds of his belief must be stated; and of course, the deponent, if not the judgment creditor himself, should also state that he is duly authorised to make the affidavit. A witness statement, permitted as an alternative to an affidavit, must contain a statement of truth (see CPR, Part 22).

The amount of the debt sought to be attached should be stated in the affidavit, if it is known; but even if it is not stated in the affidavit a garnishee order *nisi* will be made (*Lucy v. Wood* [1884] W.N. 58, and see *De Pass v. Capital Industries Corp.* [1891] 1 Q.B. 216, and *Vinall v. De Pass* [1892] A.C. 90).

An affidavit that the deponent is informed and believes that the garnishee is indebted to the judgment debtor is sufficient, provided it shows the ground of belief, but not otherwise (r.2(b)).

It is not necessary that the debt should be specifically described, but even where this has been done it is not sufficient for the garnishee in an affidavit opposing the application to deny that he owes the specific debt, he must deny that he owes anything to the judgment debtor (*De Pass v. Capital and Industries Corp.* [1891] 1 Q.B. 216; *Vinall v. De Pass* [1892] A.C. 90).

Where the judgment creditor desires to proceed to enforce a judgment expressed in foreign currency by garnishee proceedings the affidavit made in support of an application for an order under RSC, O.49, r.1 must contain words to the following effect: "The rate current in London for the purchase of (*state the amount of the judgment in foreign currency*) at the close of business on the .... day of .... 20.... (*being the date nearest to or most nearly preceding the swearing of the affidavit*) was .... to the £ sterling, and at this rate the said sum of .... amounts to £.... sterling. I have ascertained the above information (*state the source of the information*) and believe the same to be true." See *Queen's Bench Masters' Practice Direction No. 11*, paras 12 and 13 (SCP 1999, Vol. 2, Section 2A, paras 2A–48 and 2A–49). The Master will then make an order *nisi* for the sterling equivalent of the judgment debt as so verified.

Where the judgment creditor desires to attach a debt due or accruing due to the defendant within the jurisdiction in the unit of foreign currency in which the judgment debt is itself expressed, the affidavit made in support of an application for an order under RSC, O.49, r.1 must state all the relevant facts relied on and in such event the Master may make the order to attach such debt due or accruing due in that foreign currency (*ibid.*, para. 12(b)).

R49.2.3 **Garnishee order on bank**—Where it is sought to attach a banking account, and the garnishee bank has more than one place of business, the affidavit in support must state the name and address of the branch at which the judgment debtor's account is believed to be held, unless this information is not known to the deponent, in which case the affidavit must state that fact (r.2(d)).

Where the supporting affidavit has named the branch of the garnishee bank at which the debtor's account is believed to be held, such name and address of the branch must be stated in the garnishee order itself (see SCP 1999, Vol. 2, Section 1A, para. 1A–73, App. A, Form

No. 72) which must be served at the registered office, usually the Head Office, of the bank (see Companies Act 1985, s.725 and *Addis Ltd v. Berkeley Supplies Ltd* [1964] 1 W.L.R. 943; [1964] 2 All E.R. 753). The order should not be served on the named branch office of the bank, for that would not be effective service on the bank and this would give rise to the risk that the debtor might withdraw his funds from his account at the branch office, before service of the order is duly effected on the garnishee bank at its registered office, and so defeat the proceedings.

The amendment of the rules imposing a positive requirement that the supporting affidavit must state, if this information is known to the deponent, the name and address of the branch of the bank at which the judgment debtor's account is believed to be held and further requiring such name and address to be stated on the garnishee order itself should be of great administrative convenience to banks having several branches throughout the country, and should also at the same time be of great value to the judgment creditor, by making the operation of the garnishee order *nisi* more speedy and effective by guarding against the debtor drawing on his account. On the other hand, the rules do not alter the substantive law relating to the liability of the garnishee bank, though they are intended to improve the practice relating to garnishee orders on banks which have several branches. (As to the liability of the bank to repay its customer at the branch where the account is kept, see *Joachimson v. Swiss Bank Corp.* [1921] 3 K.B. 110, *per* Atkin L.J. at pp. 127–129; *Richardson v. Richardson* [1927] P. 228; and as to the entitlement of the bank to consolidate the accounts of its customer held at more than one branch, see *Garnett v. McKewan* (1872) L.R. 8 Ex. 10).

Order nisi—Only one order is drawn up, attaching the debt and ordering the garnishee to appear, but a separate order must be drawn up for each garnishee, if there be more than one (although they may all be included in one affidavit on making the application) except where the garnishees are partners in a firm, when one order will suffice. If the judgment creditor applies for orders against more than one garnishee the title of each order should be distinct and should refer only to the garnishee against whom it is sought or made. **R49.2.4**

In the QBD the practice is to limit the order *nisi* to such sums as, with reasonable costs of the garnishee proceedings, will be sufficient to cover the amount outstanding in respect of the judgment debt and costs. This has the effect of preventing any residue of the debtor's banking account being bound by the order.

For terms of order and affidavit in support, see Form No. 72 (SCP 1999, Vol. 2, Section 1A, para. 1A–72), and PF 100 (Vol. 2, Section 1B, para. 1B–73).

Service and effect of order to show cause

3.—(1) Unless the court otherwise directs, an order under rule 1 to show cause must be served— **R49.3**

(a) on the garnishee personally, at least 15 days before the time appointed thereby for the further consideration of the matter; and

(b) on the judgment debtor, at least 7 days after the order has been served on the garnishee and at least 7 days before the time appointed by the order for the further consideration of the matter.

(2) Such an order shall bind in the hands of the garnishee as from the service of the order on him any debt specified in the order or so much thereof as may be so specified.

Effect of rule—The order "to show cause" (still often referred to as an "order *nisi*") is only binding on the garnishee as from service upon him (r.49.3(2)). It is clearly a matter of some urgency to serve the garnishee as otherwise the proceedings might be defeated. **R49.3.1**

It is necessary to serve both the garnishee (r.3(1)(c)) and the judgment debtor (r.3(1)(b)). Note the differing periods of notice (15 and 7 days respectively): the rule sensibly anticipates servie of the garnishee first so as, *e.g.* to prevent the debtor assigning the debt.

The requirement of personal service in r.3(1)(a) applies to the garnishee not the judgment debtor. It is still possible to obtain an order under the CPR for "service by an alternative method": see r.6.8.

Where the garnishee is a bank or similar institution service must be at the head office, even though the garnishee's account is at a branch office. However, in addition, a copy of the order could be sent to the relevant branch.

Service on the judgment debtor will usually be by post (see Part 6).

Effect of service of order on the garnishee—Until service no charge is created (*Re Stanhope Silkstone Collieries Co.* (1879) 11 Ch.D. 160, CA); if before service the garnishee bona fide pays the debt to the judgment debtor the attachment is inoperative, as there is no debt to be attached (*Cooper v. Brayne* (1858) 27 L.J.Ex. 446). **R49.3.2**

"Service of a garnishee order *nisi* does not operate as a transfer of the property in the debt, but it is an equitable charge on it, and the garnishee cannot pay the debt to anybody but the garnishor without incurring the risk of having to pay it over again" (Farwell L.J. at 343, in *Galbraith v.*

Grimshaw [1910] 1 K.B. 339, CA; affirmed [1910] A.C. 508). When the order is made absolute, the garnishor is entitled to give a valid receipt and discharge for the money, and to obtain execution if the money is not paid, but he is not created a creditor (*Re Combined Weighing Co.* (1890) 43 Ch.D. 99, CA). Thus a garnishee order against a mortgagor of land obtained by a judgment creditor of a second mortgagee does not entitle the judgment creditor to the surplus proceeds after a sale of the land by the first mortgagee, as it does not transfer the security to the judgment creditor (*Chatterton v. Watney* (1881) 17 Ch.D. 259, CA).

Where money is paid by a solicitor into a "clients account" kept in the name of the solicitor, the service on the bank by a creditor of the solicitor of a garnishee order *nisi* attaching all debts owing or accruing due from the banker to the solicitor creates an equitable charge on the debts in favour of that creditor and binds the debts in the banker's hands even where the banker knows that the solicitor is a trustee (*Plunkett v. Barclays Bank Ltd* [1936] 1 All E.R. 653). The bank will be under a duty in such case to inform the court of the nature of the account. And judgment creditors applying for garnishee orders in such circumstances may incur costs unnecessarily if the order is drawn so as to affect a client account. It is always open to the creditor to ask the court to restrict the terms of the order *nisi* so that such account will not be affected by it: *ibid.*, at 658–659.

Judgment debtors instructed their bank to transfer their current account to another body, to whom they owed nothing, and to close their account. The transaction was duly entered in the bank's books but before notice had been given to the proposed transferees or the transfer accepted by them, a garnishee order *nisi* was served by the judgment creditor on the bank. It was held that at the time of service the relation of banker and customer still existed between the bank and the judgment debtors and that a debt from the bank to the judgment debtors was due upon which the order *nisi* could operate. The instruction given by the judgment debtor to the bank was still revocable at the time when the garnishee order *nisi* was served, and that order operated in law as a revocation (*Rekstin v. Severo Sibirsko, etc., and the Bank for Russian Trade Ltd* [1933] 1 K.B. 47, CA).

Where judgment debtors directed and authorised the garnishees to pay to a bank all moneys payable by them to the judgment debtors but no notice of an assignment to the bank had been given by the bank to the garnishees, it was held that the direction and authority, although not in point of form an assignment to the bank, constituted prima facie evidence of an assignment (*Curran v. Newpark Cinemas* [1951] 1 All E.R. 295, CA).

R49.3.3 **Effect of garnishee order on an assigned debt**—It seems that where a judgment debt has been assigned before the date of an order *nisi* attaching the debt, the title of the assignee prevails over that of the garnishee although there was no consideration for the assignment and notice of assignment was not given until after the service of the order *nisi* (*Holt v. Heatherfield* [1942] 2 K.B. 1).

Position of judgment creditor (garnishor)

R49.3.4 **Right to fresh execution**—See "Right to concurrent remedies," in commentary to RSC, O.49, r.1.

R49.3.5 **Right to petition in bankruptcy or present a winding-up petition on a garnishee order absolute**—In *Re Chinery, ex p. Chinery* (1884) 12 Q.B.D. 342, it was held that a garnishee order absolute was not a "final judgment" within section 4 of B.A. 1883, but was a final order. But a winding-up petition cannot be based upon a garnishee order absolute, as it is said not to make the garnishor a creditor of the garnishee (*Re Combined Weighing, etc., Co.* (1890) 43 Ch.D. 99, CA; *Re Steel Wing Co.* [1921] 1 Ch. 349 at 355). Nevertheless an action can be brought and judgment obtained on the order absolute if, and only if, execution cannot be got, and a winding-up order can be based on the judgment (*Pritchett v. English & Colonial Syndicate* [1899] 2 Q.B. 428, CA).

R49.3.6 **Where a judgment debt is attached**—Where the judgment debtor had got a judgment against A, an order absolute attaching the judgment debt was held to entitle the garnishor to be added as a co-plaintiff with the judgment debtor in the action against A (*Wallis v. Smith* (1882) 51 L.J.Ch. 577).

R49.3.7 **Where judgment debtor becomes bankrupt**—Section 346 of the Insolvency Act 1986 contains provisions which deprive a judgment creditor of the right to retain a debt which he has attached unless he has completed the attachment by receipt of the debt before the commencement of the bankruptcy.

R49.3.8 **Where a company is wound up**—Section 183 of the Insolvency Act 1986 contains provisions which deprive a judgment creditor of the benefit of the attachment of a debt as against the liquidator unless the attachment has been completed by receipt of the debt before the commencement of the winding up.

R49.3.9 **Where garnishee becomes bankrupt**—A deed of composition made by a garnishee under

B.A. 1861, was held to defeat an order for execution against him (*Kent v. Tomkinson* (1867) L.R. 2 C.P. 502).

Debentures and floating charges—A debenture-holder, who has not got a receiver appointed nor taken any steps to enforce his security, has no right to prevent an order *nisi* attaching debts due to the company being made absolute, although the debenture gives him the usual floating charge upon such debts (*Evans v. Rival Granite Quarry Co.* [1910] 2 K.B. 979, CA); and if a garnishee in fact pays the garnishor pursuant to an order absolute he obtains a valid discharge for the debt and cannot be made to pay the debt again to the debenture-holders (*Robson v. Smith* [1895] 2 Ch. 118; and see in this connection the terms of r.8). Until, however, the judgment creditor obtains actual payment, a receiver for debenture holders, even though appointed subsequently to the garnishee order absolute, will obtain priority over him (*Norton v. Yates* [1906] 1 K.B. 112; *Cairney v. Back* [1906] 2 K.B. 746). See and compare *Vacuum Oil Co. v. Ellis* [1914] 1 K.B. 693, CA, a case of struggle for priority as to rent between a garnishor and second mortgagee; see also *Pennington v. Cave* (1917) 144 L.T.Jo. 112. **R49.3.10**

Garnishor represents judgment debtor—A garnishee order places the garnishor in the position of an assignee of the judgment debtor and makes him subject to any equities which exist against the judgment debtor (*Levene v. Maton* (1907) 51 S.J. 532). **R49.3.11**

Attachment of money liable to forfeiture—An annuity liable to forfeiture, "if aliened, charged or anticipated" by the beneficiary, is not forfeited upon a garnishee order being made against the trustees (*Re Greenwood* [1901] 1 Ch. 887, where *Bates v. Bates* [1884] W.N. 129, was not followed). **R49.3.12**

Solicitor's lien upon judgment debt—An attachment of a judgment debt overrides any lien of the judgment debtor's solicitor upon the judgment for his general costs (*Hough v. Edwards* (1857) 1 H. & N. 171) but not for his particular costs of the action, which resulted in the judgment in question (*Sympson v. Prothero* (1857) 26 L.J.Ch. 672). But see *James Bibby Ltd v. Woods* [1949] 2 K.B. 449, where it was held that a solicitor who had not obtained a charging order had no lien. If a garnishor, who knows of the lien's existence, is paid by the garnishee, he must refund to the solicitor (*Eisdell v. Coningham* (1859) 28 L.J.Exch. 213). **R49.3.13**

A solicitor's lien for his client's unpaid fees entitles him to retain money held in the client's account and has priority over a claim by the client's judgment creditor (*Plovidba v. LNT Lines Srl, The Independent*, July 1, 1988).

Solicitor obtaining charging order—A charging order under section 73 of the Solicitors Act 1974, SCP 1999, Vol.2, Pt 8, upon the property recovered or preserved by the judgment, gets priority over a garnishee order *nisi* (*Birchall v. Pugin* (1875) L.R. 10 C.P. 397) though the latter preceded the charging order (*Shippey v. Grey* (1880) 49 L.J.Q.B. 524, CA; *Faithfull v. Ewen* (1878) 7 Ch.D. 495, CA) and though the solicitor has not acted promptly (*Dallow v. Garrold* (1884) 14 Q.B.D. 543, CA). There seems no reason why the same principle is not applicable where a garnishee order absolute exists (see judgment of Brett L.J. in *Shippey v. Grey*, and n., "Solicitors' lien upon judgment debt", para. R49.3.13 above) especially as the solicitors' right to a lien must be known to the garnishor of a judgment debt; and in *Cole v. Eley* [1894] 2 Q.B. 350, CA, a solicitor was held entitled to a charging order after the judgment debt had been assigned, on the ground that the assignee (who knew of the action and the solicitor having conducted it) was not a bona fide purchaser for value without notice within section 28 of the Solicitors Act 1860, as those words meant "without notice of the solicitor's right to a lien" and not "without notice of a charging order". But the solicitor can only preserve his rights by obtaining a charging order before a garnishee order absolute is made (*James Bibby Ltd v. Woods* [1949] 2 K.B. 449). **R49.3.14**

Position of garnishee when served with garnishee order—The order must so name the judgment debtor as to establish his identity with the garnishee's creditor, or it will not bind the garnishee (*Koch v. Mineral Ore Syndicate* (1910) 54 S.J. 600, CA). A garnishee should not pay the garnishor upon a mere order *nisi* (*Re Webster* [1907] 1 K.B. 623) and without compulsion by process of the Court (*Turner v. Jones* (1858) 26 L.J.Exch. 262; 1 H. & N. 878. He must inform the Court of any claim to, or lien upon, the debt; and if, having knowledge thereof, he pays the garnishor, then he will have to pay the person entitled to such claim or lien (*The Leader* (1868) L.R. 2 A. & E. 314; and see r.6). As "All debts due or accruing" are attached, the garnishee must not appropriate any part of his debt to any other purpose, even though he owes more to the judgment debtor than the latter's liability to the garnishor: thus a banker served with a garnishee order may dishonour any cheque drawn upon him by the judgment debtor (*Rogers v. Whiteley* [1892] A.C. 118). When a garnishee receives notice that the judgment debtor has assigned the surplus of the debt, which will remain after satisfying the garnishee order, he may not appropriate such surplus in satisfaction of another garnishee order which is served after notice of such assignment (*Yates v. Terry* [1902] 1 K.B. 527, CA). If the garnishee order attaches proceeds of an execution in the hands of a sheriff, the latter should allow 14 days to pass before payment, in case bankruptcy should supervene (*Re Greer* [1895] 2 Ch. 217). **R49.3.15**

R49.3.16 **Debt paid by cheque before service**—A garnishee who has paid the debt by cheque before service of the order *nisi* need not stop the cheque (*Elwell v. Jackson* (1885) 1 T.L.R. 454, CA) but if he does the attachment operates (*Cohen v. Hale* (1878) 3 Q.B.D. 371).

R49.3.17 **Subsequent mortgage by garnishee**—Where a garnishee company after an order absolute, acting bona fide, issued debentures charging all its property in consideration of a loan, and execution was subsequently levied upon such property by the garnishor, it was held that the garnishee order did not make such honest issue of debentures a breach of duty on the part of the company, and that the garnishor had no right to the property in priority to the debenture-holders (*Geisse v. Taylor* [1905] 2 K.B. 658, but see comments of Kennedy L.J. in *Galbraith v. Grimshaw* [1910] 1 K.B. 339, at 345, CA; affirmed [1910] A.C. 508).

R49.3.18 **Execution issued by judgment debtor**—Where the garnished debt is due under a judgment obtained by the judgment debtor, it has been held that the latter could issue execution against the garnishee notwithstanding the attachment, until an order was made under rr.5 or 6 (*Cronmire v. MacColla* (1893) 9 T.L.R. 549, CA).

R49.3.19 **Bankruptcy notice by judgment debtor**—It was held in *Re Connan, ex p. Hyde* (1888) 20 Q.B.D. 690, CA, that, where a garnishee order absolute for payment of the garnished (a *judgment*) debt has been made, the judgment debtor was thereby precluded from issuing a bankruptcy notice against the garnishee in respect of the garnished debt, as such order amounted to a stay of execution. *Re Connan* was apparently not cited in *Cronmire v. MacColla* (1893) 9 T.L.R. 549, CA, and the two decisions seem difficult to reconcile.

R49.3.20 **Set-off or counterclaim**—A garnishee cannot set off against the debt attached a debt owing to him from the judgment creditor (the garnishor) (*Sampson v. Seaton Ry* (1875) L.T. 10 Q.B. 28); but he can avail himself of a set-off against the judgment debtor, which existed when the order *nisi* was made (*Nathan v. Giles* (1814) 5 Taunt. 558; *Sampson v. Seaton Ry*; *Tapp v. Jones* (1875) L.R. 10 Q.B. 591 at 593).

The garnishee can also avail himself of a counterclaim which exceeds the amount of the debt (*Hale v. Victoria Plumbing Co. and En Tout Cas Co.* [1966] 2 Q.B. 746; CA; distinguishing *Stumore v. Campbell* [1892] 1 Q.B. 314, CA).

No appearance or dispute of liability by garnishee

R49.4 4.—(1) Where on the further consideration of the matter the garnishee does not attend or does not dispute the debt due or claimed to be due from him to the judgment debtor, the court may make an order absolute under rule 1 against the garnishee.

(2) An order absolute under rule 1 against the garnishee may be enforced in the same manner as any other order for the payment of money.

R49.4.1 **Effect of rule**—The order absolute which the Court makes is an order upon the garnishee forthwith to pay the amount specified in the order to the judgment creditor (see the forms of order, Forms No. 73 and 74, see Vol. 2, Section 1A, paras 1A–74 and 1A–75); and of course such an order can be enforced against the garnishee in the same way as any other order for the payment of money. Execution may therefore issue upon a garnishee order absolute in the same way as upon a judgment.

R49.4.2 **"Does not dispute"**—If the garnishee upon receipt of an order *nisi* pays the judgment creditor, and the judgment debtor becomes bankrupt, he may have to pay the trustee in bankruptcy as well (*Re Webster* [1907] 1 K.B. 623; and see r.3 n. "Position of garnishee" para. R49.3.15 above). If he disputes the debt r.5 applies.

As to what constitutes a payment which discharges the garnishee, see r.8, and commentary thereto.

R49.4.3 **"The amount due from him to such debtor"**—See r.3 n. "Position of garnishee" para. R49.3.15 above and *Cane v. Seloceve Co. Ltd* (1941) 57 T.L.R. 601.

R49.4.4 **Effect of acquiescence**—Where a garnishee remained inert and an order absolute was therefore made, he became bound to pay the garnishor although no attachable debt existed at the time of the order (*Randall v. Lithgow* (1884) 12 Q.B.D. 525). There is, however, jurisdiction to set aside an order absolute obtained under such circumstances (*O'Brien v. Killeen* [1914] 2 Ir.R. 63).

R49.4.5 **Setting aside garnishee orders**—There is power to set aside a garnishee order. Application should be made under Part 23 supported by evidence. See *e.g. Moore v. Peachey* (1892) 66 L.T. 198; *Burrell & Sons v. Read* (1895) 11 T.L.R. 36; *Marshall v. Jones* [1905] 1 Ch. 430; *O'Brien v. Killeen* [1914] 2 Ir.R 63. There is also a right of appeal, see below.

Suggestion that judgment debtor is not beneficially interested—When the suggestion is made on reasonable grounds that the judgment debtor's interest in the debt attached by the order *nisi* is not a personal one, *e.g.* that it is due to him as trustee, the Court should exercise its equitable powers and refuse to make the order absolute till after an inquiry (*Roberts v. Death* (1882) 8 Q.B.D. 319, CA); and see r.6, and nn. thereto. **R49.4.6**

Appeal, right of—Appeal from any judgment, order or decision of a Master or District Judge in garnishee proceedings lies to the Judge in Chambers (see O.58, r.1(1)). **R49.4.7**

Dispute of liability by garnishee

5. Where on the further consideration of the matter the garnishee disputes liability to pay the debt due or claimed to be due from him to the judgment debtor, the court may summarily determine the question at issue or order that any question necessary for determining the liability of the garnishee be tried in any manner in which any question or issue in proceedings may be tried, without, if it orders trial before a Master, the need for any consent by the parties. **R49.5**

Effect of rule—If the garnishee disputes liability (that is to say, does not merely deny a particular debt, but denies indebtedness, *Vinall v. De Pass* [1892] A.C. 90) the Master may take any of the following courses in the QBD: **R49.5.1**

1. Determine the issue as to the garnishee's liability summarily, without the consent of the parties, and whether the issue is one of fact or of law;
2. Direct an issue to be tried by a Judge or a Master, and give directions.
3. Transfer the matter to a county court (County Courts Act 1984, s.40).

"May order"—The words indicate that there is discretionary power; and in *Newman v. Rook* (1858) 4 C.B. (N.S.) 434, similar words in s.64 of the Common Law Procedure Act 1854, were held to mean that the garnishee must set up a prima facie case before he could get an issue ordered; so, too, where the garnishee satisfies the Master that there is no attachable debt, an issue will not be ordered (*Wise v. Birkenshaw* (1860) 29 L.J.Exch. 240). If there is any reasonable doubt the matter should be tried (*ibid.*, and *Employers Liab. Assurance Corp. v. Sedgwick, Collins & Co.* [1927] A.C. 95; (1926) 42 T.L.R. 749). A higher Court will be reluctant to question the exercise of such discretionary power (*ibid.*, and *Seymour v. Brecon Corporation* (1860) 29 L.J.Exch. 243). **R49.5.2**

Judgment creditor refusing issue—If the judgment creditor declines to contest the issue the attachment will be discharged, and he will have to pay the costs thereby occasioned (*Wintle v. Williams* (1858) 3 H. & N. 288; 27 L.J.Exch. 311). **R49.5.3**

Claims of third persons

6.—(1) If in garnishee proceedings it is brought to the notice of the court that some other person than the judgment debtor is or claims to be entitled to the debt sought to be attached or has or claims to have a charge or lien upon it, the court may order that person to attend before the court and state the nature of his claim with particulars thereof. **R49.6**

(2) After hearing any person who attends before the court in compliance with an order under paragraph (1) the court may summarily determine the questions at issue between the claimants or make such other order as it thinks just, including an order that any question or issue necessary for determining the validity of the claim of such other person as is mentioned in paragraph (1) be tried in such manner as is mentioned in rule 5.

Effect of rule—The rule applies where another person makes claim to the debt which the judgment creditor seeks to attach by garnishee. The rule empowers the court to summarily determine the issue. **R49.6.1**

If the court directs trial of an issue pursuant to r.6(2) it will direct who is to be claimant and who is to be defendant and give all necessary directions.

It is the garnishee's duty to acquaint the Court with any claim or lien known to him (*The Leader* (1868) L.R. 2 A. & E. 314) and see r.3 n. "Position of garnishee", para. R49.3.15.

Where the garnishee suggests not that the debt is due to a third person, but that the debtor is not entitled to the money for his own use—*e.g.* that it is payable to him *qua* trustee—this rule apparently applies (*Roberts v. Death* (1882) 8 Q.B.D. 319, CA). But though the garnishee does not make the suggestion, if it, in fact, comes to the Master's notice and is not unreasonable, he ought not to make the order absolute, but order the money to be paid into Court to abide the result of an inquiry, being empowered so to order under his equitable jurisdiction, and not under these rules (*ibid*).

For a case where the provider of funds intervened on the ground that the funds were subject to obligations arising under international treaty, see *Philipp Brothers Ltd v. Republic of Sierra Leone* [1995] 1 Lloyd's Rep. 289, CA; and see paras R49.1.38 and R49.1.39, above.

Discharge of garnishee

R49.8 **8.** Any payment made by a garnishee in compliance with an order absolute under this order, and any execution levied against him in pursuance of such an order, shall be a valid discharge of his liability to the judgment debtor to the extent of the amount paid or levied notwithstanding that the garnishee proceedings are subsequently set aside or the judgment or order from which they arose reversed.

R49.8.1 **Effect of rule**—The object of the rule is to discharge the garnishee from his liability to his own creditor, *i.e.* the judgment debtor in the proceedings, if but only if, he makes his payment or suffers execution in compliance with or in pursuance of the garnishee order absolute. Thus, if the garnishee makes payment, not under the garnishee proceedings, but by way of private arrangement, he will not get a valid discharge (see *Turner v. Jones* (1858) 26 L.T.Exch. 262; 1 H. & N. 878). Similarly, a payment made voluntarily without legal compulsion, *e.g.*, a payment made upon the order *nisi*, before the order absolute, will not discharge the garnishee (*Re Webster* [1907] 1 K.B. 623).

On the other hand, where the garnishee pays the money into Court pursuant to the order, he will get a valid discharge (*Culverhouse v. Wickens* (1868) L.R. 3 C.P. 295).

Where a garnishee, being in danger of having execution levied upon him, pays the debt owing to such pressure, he gets a good discharge, even though he has notice of the judgment debtor having become bankrupt (*Wood v. Dunn* (1867) L.R. 2 Q.B. 73, Ex. Ch.). If a garnishee in such a case is not in immediate danger of an execution, he probably ought to apply to get the order absolute set aside (*cf.* Channell B., *ibid.* p.84). And where a debt owing by the garnishee under a judgment has been attached by an order *nisi*, the garnishee is entitled to pay such debt to the sheriff upon a *fi. fa.* being levied under the judgment debtor's judgment, and is not bound to apply to the Court for protection (*cf. Turnbull v. Robertson* (1878) 47 L.J.C.P. 296). As to payment of a debt due to a foreign debtor resident outside the jurisdiction, see *Swiss Bank Corp. v. Boehmische Industrial Bank* [1923] 1 K.B. 673, and n. "Garnishee within the jurisdiction", in commentary to O.49, r.1.

Payment made by a garnishee under an order absolute may be a good discharge to him, though the judgment creditor may have to return the money, *e.g.* to the trustee in bankruptcy of the judgment debtor (*Re Smith, ex p. Brown* (1888) 20 Q.B.D. 321, CA).

Money in Court

R49.9 **9.**—(1) Where money is standing to the credit of the judgment debtor in court, the judgment creditor shall not be entitled to take garnishee proceedings in respect of that money but may apply to the court in accordance with CPR Part 23 for an order that the money or so much thereof as is sufficient to satisfy the judgment or order sought to be enforced and the costs of the application be paid to the judgment creditor.

(2) On filing an application notice under this rule the applicant must produce the application notice at the office of the Accountant General and leave a copy at that office, and the money to which the application relates shall not be paid out of court until after the determination of the application.

If the application is dismissed, the applicant must give notice of that fact to the Accountant General.

(3) Unless the court otherwise directs, the application notice must be served on the judgment debtor at least 7 days before the hearing.

(4) Subject to Order 75, rule 24, the court hearing an application under this rule may make such order with respect to the money in court as it thinks just.

R49.9.1 **Effect of rule**—It is not possible to garnishee money in court. This rule, however, provides a simpler and cheaper alternative procedure where money is standing to the credit of the judgment debtor in court.

Costs

10. The costs of any application for an order under rule 1 or 9, and of any proceedings arising therefrom or incidental thereto, shall, unless the court otherwise directs, be retained by the judgment creditor out of the money recovered by him under the order and in priority to the judgment debt. **R49.10**

Effect of rule—If the garnishee appears and admits the debt, it is the practice to allow him to deduct his costs from the amount he has to pay over. See O.62, App. 3 para R62.A3 below. **R49.10.1**

Under this Rule, the judgment creditor is entitled to deduct his costs of the proceedings out of the money received by him and in priority to the judgment debt. See O.62, App. 3 para. R62.A3 below.

If the garnishee proceedings are unsuccessful the Court has a wide discretion as to the costs incurred (see SCA 1981, s.51, see SCP 1999, Vol. 2, Section 20A, para. 20A–401) and in a proper case, may order the judgment debtor who remains a party even though he does not attend the garnishee proceedings, to pay the costs of both the judgment creditor and the garnishee (*T. Wright & Son (Hull) Ltd v. Westoby (Saffman & Co., garnishees)* [1972] 3 All E.R. 1078, CA).

On the other hand, the judgment creditor proceeds at his own risk as to costs where he takes garnishee proceedings without being led into them by the judgment debtor or where the judgment debtor has no interest in the result of the proceedings and has in no way done anything to affect their conduct or where the judgment creditor proceeds with the full facts of a plain case put before him in the knowledge of what will happen if he goes on and fails (see *ibid., per* Sachs L.J.).

Banks' expenses—Deposit-taking institutions may, independently of any award of costs, deduct a sum for administrative expenses from the balance in their hands when complying with a garnishee order in accordance with section 40A(1) of the SCA 1981, and section 109(1) of the CCA 1984. The sum is £55 (see Attachment of Debts (Expenses) Order 1996 (S.I. 1996 No. 3098)). The order absolute should be for the amount the bank, etc., is actually to pay after allowing for the bank's expenses, if the bank wishes to deduct these from the balance in its hands. **R49.10.2**

RSC ORDER 50

CHARGING ORDERS, STOP ORDERS, ETC.

Contents **R50.0.1**

Editorial Introduction

RSC, O.50 contains the necessary procedural rules to give effect to the Charging Orders Act 1979. This Act is in SCP 1999, Vol. 2 at Section 21F. **R50.0.2**

A charging order on land provides the judgment creditor with the equivalent of a mortgage over the land specified in the order. Thus, subject to any prior mortgages and charges affecting that land, the judgment creditor becomes a secured creditor. The charging order does not affect the accrual of interest payable on the judgment.

For enforcement of a charging order by sale see RSC, O.88, r.5A.

In addition to a charging order on land a judgment creditor can also obtain a charging order on a judgment debtors' beneficial interest in securities of the kind listed in Charging Orders Act 1979, s.2.

Furthermore, stop orders are available to the judgment creditor of a person having funds in court; and to the mortgagee or assignee of such a person (see r.10 and commentary thereto). A stop notice is available to persons claiming to be beneficially entitled to other securities defined in the Act (see rr.11 to 14 and commentary thereto).

Related sources

R50.0.3
- Charging Orders Act 1979
- RSC, O.45, r.1 (Enforcement of judgment, etc., for payment of money)
- CCR, O.31 (Charging orders)
- Chancery and Queen's Bench Division Fixed Costs (Charging Orders) (para. R62.A3)
- *Queen's Bench Masters' Practice Direction No. 38—Charging orders nisi* (SCP Mainwork 1999, Vol. 2, Section 2A, para. 2A–106) (applies also in Chancery Division, see Vol. 2, Section 2B, para. 2B–179).

Forms

R50.0.4 The following Prescribed Forms (formerly included amongst the Prescribed Forms in Appendix A to the RSC) are relevant to O.50. These forms are included in Table 2 (Practice Forms) attached to Practice Direction (Forms) and may be found in SCP 1999, Vol. 2, Section 1A, paras 1A–76 and 1A–77, 1A–80 to 1A–82:
- PF No. 75—Charging order: notice to show cause (O.50, r.1)
- PF No. 76—Charging order absolute (O.50, r.3)
- PF No. 79—Stop order on capital and income of funds in court (O.50, r.10)
- PF No. 80—Affidavit and notice under O.50, r.11 (O.50, r.11)
- PF No. 81—Order on originating motion restraining transfer of stock, etc. (O.50, r.15)
- Chancery Masters' Practice Form No. 34 (Order in inquiry as to title in proceedings to enforce charging order where the defendant's title is not disclosed) (SCP 1999, Vol. 2, Section 1B, para. 1B–235).

Order imposing a charge on a beneficial interest

R50.1 **1.**—(1) The power to make a charging order under section 1 of the Charging Orders Act 1979 (referred to in this order as "the Act") shall be exercisable by the court.

(2) An application by a judgment creditor for a charging order in respect of a judgment debtor's beneficial interest must be in accordance with CPR Part 23, but the application notice need not be served on the judgment debtor, and any order made on such an application shall in the first instance be an order, made in Form No. 75 in the relevant Practice Direction, to show cause, specifying the time and place for further consideration of the matter and imposing the charge in any event until that time.

(3) The application shall be supported by a witness statement or affidavit—

(a) identifying the judgment or order to be enforced and stating the amount unpaid at the date of the application:

(b) stating the name of the judgment debtor and of any creditor of his whom the applicant can identify;

(c) giving full particulars of the subject matter of the intended charge, including, in the case of securities other than securities in court, the full title of the securities, their amount and the name in which they stand and, in the case of funds in court, the number of the account; and

(d) verifying that the interest to be charged is owned beneficially by the judgment debtor.

(4) Unless the court otherwise directs, a witness statement or affidavit for the purposes of this rule may contain statements of information or belief with the sources and grounds thereof.

(5) An application may be made for a single charging order in respect of more than one judgment or order against the debtor.

R50.1.1 **Effect of rule**—The rule gives procedural effect to the Charging Orders Act 1979 (section numbers in this commentary refer to that Act).

Application is made without notice but supported by evidence.

The Act and rules can be summarised as follows:

(1) Power of Court to impose charging orders—The appropriate Court is empowered to impose a charge, called a charging order, on specified property of the judgment debtor who by the judgment or order of the Court is required to pay a sum of money to another person to secure the payment of such money due or to become due under the judgment or order (s.1(1)). **R50.1.2**

(2) Jurisdiction of the High Court—The High Court has, by virtue of s.1(2)(a)(b) and (c), jurisdiction to make a charging order only: **R50.1.3**

(a) where the property to be charged is a fund in Court which is lodged in the High Court; or
(b) where the order to be enforced is a maintenance order of the High Court; or
(c) where the judgment or order to be enforced is a judgment or order of the High Court and exceeds £5,000 in amount, this being the county court limit, for the purposes of the Charging Orders Act 1979, specified by the County Courts Jurisdiction Order 1981 (S.I. 1981 No. 1123). It should be noted however that under art.8(1) of the High Court and County Courts Jurisdiction Order 1991 (S.I. 1991 No. 724) a judgment or order of the county court for the payment of a sum of money which it is sought to enforce wholly or partially by execution against goods *shall* be enforced only in the High Court where it exceeds £5,000 in amount (unless arising out of a regulated agreement under the Consumer Credit Act 1974). Thus, where such a judgment is transferred for enforcement to the High Court, it becomes a judgment of the High Court and will be treated as such for the purposes of enforcement by charging order. For the procedure on transfer, see the *Practice Direction (County Court Order: Enforcement)* [1991] 1 W.L.R. 695; [1991] 3 All E.R. 438.

In all other cases the application for a charging order must be made in the county court.

(3) Discretion of the Court to impose charging order—The existing discretion of the Court to impose a charging order has been statutorily recognised (s.1(5)). **R50.1.4**

(4) Property or assets which may be charged—The classes or kinds of property or assets on which a charging order may be imposed have been extensively enlarged (s.2). **R50.1.5**

(5) Bankruptcy or liquidation of judgment debtor—The completion of an execution for the purposes of ss.346(5) and 183(3) of the Insolvency Act 1986 will take effect on the making of the charging order *nisi*. **R50.1.6**

(6) Charge on beneficial interest of judgment debtor—The Court has power to impose a charge on any interest held by the judgment debtor beneficially in any asset of the kinds specified in section 2(2) of the 1979 Act (s.2(1)(a)(i)) and of course this will ordinarily be the kind of charging order which will be made. **R50.1.7**

(7) Charge on interest held under a trust—The Court has power to impose a charge on any interest held by the debtor beneficially under any trust: see (s.2(1)(a)(ii)). Such power extends to a beneficial interest in the proceeds of sale of land held under a trust for sale (*National Westminster Bank Ltd v. Stockman* [1981] 1 W.L.R. 67; [1981] 1 All E.R. 800, and therefore so far as concerns a trust of land has the effect of statutorily negativing *Irani Finance Ltd v. Singh* [1971] Ch. 59, CA). **R50.1.8**

(8) Charging an interest held by a person as a trustee—Furthermore the Court has power to impose a charging order on any interest held by a person as a trustee, if the interest is in one of the assets mentioned in s.2(2), or is an interest under another trust, and if one of the conditions set forth in s.2(1)(b)(i), (ii) or (iii) is satisfied. **R50.1.9**

(9) Charging order on securities out of court—The Court has power to impose a charging order on securities out of Court of the kinds specified in s.2(2)(b); and see r.5. **R50.1.10**

(10) Charging order on funds in court—The Court has power to impose a charging order on funds in court (s.2(2)(c) and r.6). **R50.1.11**

(11) Procedure for obtaining charging order—The existing procedure for obtaining charging orders has been retained namely by the two-stage process of obtaining a charging order *nisi* on an application made without notice supported by evidence (usually an affidavit, r.1(2)) and the making of an order absolute on the further consideration of the matter (r.3). **R50.1.12**

(12) Power to grant injunction—The power of the Master to grant an injunction which is ancillary or incidental to the grant of a charging order *nisi* has been retained (r.9, as amended). **R50.1.13**

(13) Discharge of charging order—The power of the Court to discharge or vary a charging **R50.1.14**

order has been statutorily recognised (s.3(5)) and at the same time the Court may direct, where a charging order is discharged, that any entry registered under the Land Charges Act 1972 or the Land Registration Act 1925 should be cancelled (s.3(6)).

R50.1.15 *(14) Limitation*—It is open to obtain a charging order by way of procedural machinery to enforce a judgment even though the statutory period of limitation under section 24(1) of the Limitation Act 1980 for bringing an action on the judgment has expired (*Lowsley v. Forbes* (1996) *The Times,* April 5, CA, applying *National Westminster Bank Plc v. Powney* [1991] Ch.339, CA). It has also been held that the right under a charging order to include interest on the judgment debt over a period of more than six years is not affected by section 20(5) of the Limitation Act 1980 (see *Ezekiel v. Orakpo* [1996] 10 C.L. 46, CA).

R50.1.16 **Enforcement of judgments or orders by charging orders on property of judgment debtor (rr.1–9A)**—By virtue of s.1(1) of the Charging Orders Act 1979, the High Court may, for the purpose of enforcing a judgment or order of that Court under which a person, called "the debtor" is required to pay a sum of money to another person, called "the creditor", make an order imposing on any such property of the debtor as may be specified in the order, a charge for securing the payment of any money due or to become due under the judgment or order. The Court may make a charging order either absolutely or subject to conditions as to notifying the debtor or as to the time when the charge is to become enforceable, or as to other matters (s.3(1)).

The provisions of s.1 apply in relation to a judgment order, decree or award, however called, of any Court or arbitrator, including any foreign Court or arbitrator which is or has become enforceable whether wholly or to a limited extent as if it were a judgment or order of the High Court (s.6(2)).

R50.1.17 **Nature and effect of charging order (rr.1–9A)**—A charging order on the property or assets of the debtor is one of the modes of enforcement of a judgment or order for the payment of money to the creditor. It is, however, not a direct mode of enforcement in the sense that the creditor can immediately proceed to recover the fruits of his judgment, but is rather an indirect mode of enforcement in the sense that it provides the creditor with security, in whole or in part, over the property of the debtor. It makes the creditor a secured creditor, who having obtained his charging order must proceed, as may be necessary according to the nature of the property charged, to enforce his charge in order to obtain the actual proceeds of his charge to satisfy his judgment, in whole or in part. Subject to the provisions of the Act of 1979, a charge imposed by a charging order will have effect and will be enforceable in the same Courts and in the same manner as an equitable charge created by the debtor by writing under his hand (s.3(4)).

"The judgment creditor cannot by his charging order get any more than the debtor could honestly give him" (*per* Bramwell B., *Gill v. Continental Gas Co.* (1872) L.R. 7 Ext. 332, 338) by an instrument of charge made by him (see *Re Onslow's Trusts* (1875) L.R. 20 Eq. 677). The beneficial interest of the debtor only is affected (*Gray v. Stone* (1893) 69 L.T. 282; *Hawks v. McArthur* [1951] 1 All E.R. 22). A charging order to enforce a judgment for a debt which is void by reason of the debtor's infancy is inoperative (*Re Onslow's Trusts* (1875) L.R. 20 Eq. 677); and will not affect property assigned by the debtor subsequently to the judgment and prior to the charging order, though the debtor's interest be equitable, and no notice has been given by the assignee to the trustees (*Scott v. Lord Hastings* (1858) 4 K. & J. 633; and see *Brearcliff v. Dorrington* (1850) 4 De G. & Sm. 122); and a judgment creditor cannot by obtaining a charging order upon a fund in Court belonging to his debtor, acquire priority over a previous mortgagee (*Re Bell* (1886) 34 W.R. 363). An order appointing a receiver by way of equitable execution has priority over a subsequent charging order (*Re Anglesey* [1903] 2 Ch. 727).

A charging order creates such an incumbrance as will determine a life interest determinable on the execution of any assignment or act whereby the same should be incumbered (*Montefiore v. Behrens* (1865) L.R. 1 Eq. 171); or when the life tenant "should do or suffer any act" whereby the dividends should become payable to another person (*Roffey v. Bent* (1867) L.R. 3 Eq. 759; *cf.* where the debtor had an ultimate reversion, *South-Western Loan and Discount Co. v. Robertson* (1882) 8 Q.B.D. 17).

A charging order of which notice has been given to the Accountant-General has priority over an order appointing a receiver by way of equitable execution over a fund in Court, not completed, even though followed by a stop order (*Fahey v. Tobin* [1901] 1 Ir.R. 511).

A charging order, when made absolute, takes effect from the date of the order *nisi,* and is not therefore defeated by an administration decree made in the interval (*Haly v. Barry* (1868) L.R. 3 Ch. 452; and see *Brereton v. Edwards* (1888) 21 Q.B.D. 488).

It does not depend upon the capacity of the debtor but upon the validity of the judgment and therefore a charging order against a mental patient is effective (*Re Leavesley* [1891] 2 Ch. 1).

Once a charging order is made absolute the Court has no jurisdiction to order a stay of proceedings on the charging order on condition that the defendant should pay the judgment debts and costs by specified instalments (*Lane v. Vmenylora* November 18, 1977, *per* Park J. in Chambers (unrep.)). This decision, however, would not preclude the Court exercising its powers under O.47, r.1, to order a stay of execution by writ of *fi. fa.* on payment of the judgment debt by instalments, and indeed, when ordering such a stay, it may often be desirable to accompany it with a charging order absolute on the property of the debtor, so as to give the creditor adequate security for his judgment.

Enforcing charging order (rr.1–9A)—The remedy under an equitable charge under hand is sale (*Tennant v. Trenchard* (1869) L.R. 4 Ch.App., p.537) but the Court may also appoint a receiver. As to the procedure for obtaining an order for sale, see O.88. **R50.1.18**

In addition, the power of the High Court to appoint a receiver by way of equitable execution has been extended so as to operate in relation to all legal estates and interests in land (AJA 1956, s.36(1). See also O.51.

The proceedings must be commenced in the Ch D (see S.C.A. 1981, s.61(3)(b), SCP 1999, Vol. 2, Section 20A); they should be commenced under Part 8, CPR.

It should be noted that proceedings under O.88, r.5A are brought to enforce a charging order by sale of "the property charged". Thus, where, as is frequently the case, the beneficial interest of one of two or more co-owners of land is charged, the sale, if ordered under that provision, will be of the beneficial interest only and may be of limited value to the creditor. But, as accepted by the Court of Appeal in *Thames Guaranty Ltd v. Campbell* [1985] Q.B. 210, at 239 *per* Slade L.J., and in *First National Securities Ltd v. Hegerty* [1985] Q.B. 850, and in *Harman v. Glencross* [1986] 1 All E.R. 545; [1986] Fam. 81, and applied in *Midland Bank plc v. Pike* [1988] 2 All E.R. 434, a person entitled to a charging order on the share of a co-owner in the proceeds of sale of land has a proprietary interest in that share and is a "person interested" who is entitled to apply for an order for sale of the land pursuant to section 30 of the Law of Property Act 1925. It was under that provision that a charging order in such circumstances is usually enforced; see now Trusts of Land and Appointment of Trustees Act 1996.

Right to charging order: general considerations (rr.1–9A)—The conditions prerequisite to the right to a charging order are (a) there must be a final judgment or order (b) under which the debtor is required to pay a sum of money (c) to another person, *i.e.* the creditor; and of course the charging order can only be imposed on the property and assets of the debtor specified in s.2 of the 1979 Act, namely land, certain specified securities and funds in Court (see para. R50.1.25). **R50.1.19**

Accordingly, the Court has no power to impose a charge on the property or assets of a judgment debtor for an unascertained sum, *e.g.* the amount of a bill of costs which has not been finally taxed: (*A. & M. Records Inc. v. Darakdjian* [1975] 1 W.L.R 1610; [1975] 3 All E.R. 883; nor presumably on a judgment or order for damages to be assessed or for the value of goods to be assessed. This principle had been expressly contained in the former O.50, r.2(1) (which had provided for a charging order on securities to be made in respect of "the payment of an ascertained sum to a person") which had adopted *Widgery v. Tepper* (1877) 6 Ch.D. 364, which had itself overruled *Burns v. Irvin* (1876) 3 Ch.D. 291).

Moreover, the Court has no power to impose a charging order under a judgment or order for the payment of money into Court (see *per* Kindersley V.-C. in *Ward v. Shakeshaft* (1860) 1 Dr. & Sm. 269).

The grant of the right of pre-emption in a conveyance of land does not confer on the grantee a present or contingent interest in the land to which the right of pre-emption relates, and presumably therefore a charging order cannot effectively be made to impose a charge on such right of pre-emption (see *Pritchard v. Briggs* [1980] Ch. 338; [1980] 1 All E.R. 294, CA) although if the grantor chooses to fulfil the conditions on which the grantee could exercise his right of pre-emption, then the grantee would have the right to call for a conveyance and thus acquire an interest in the land, on which a charging order may then be imposed (*ibid.*).

In *Bagnall v. Carlton* (1877) 6 Ch.D. 131, a charging order was made in respect of a fixed sum payable at a future time. But such an order will only be made in exceptional cases (*Robinson v. Bailey* [1942] Ch. 268).

Right to charging order where judgment debt payable by instalments (rr.1–9A)—Section 1(1) of the Charging Orders Act 1979 empowers the Court to order a charge "for securing the payment of any money due or to become due" under a judgment or order. Hence, when a judgment debt is payable by instalments, the High Court has power to make a charging order to secure the whole debt and not merely arrears of instalments, and, indeed, there is power to make an order where there are no arrears. The fact, however, that a debtor is up to date in complying with an order for payment by instalments is likely to be a relevant factor in the exercise of the Court's discretion to make or refuse a charging order (*Mercantile Credit Co. Ltd v. Ellis, The Independent*, March 17, 1987; *The Times*, April 1, 1987, CA). Moreover the effect of s.86(1) of the County Courts Act 1984 is to prevent the making of a charging order where a county court has made an order for payment of any sum by instalments until after default in payment of one or more instalments (*ibid.*). **R50.1.20**

Right to charging order: other considerations (rr.1–9A)—The Stock Exchange Rules operate to effect an assignment of a defaulting broker's assets to the official assignee of the Stock Exchange. That assignment, unless invalidated by the bankruptcy of the defaulter, is valid as against others as well as against members of the Stock Exchange. A judgment creditor of the **R50.1.21**

broker cannot therefore obtain a charging order on a sum of money recovered by the assignee (*Lomas v. Graves* [1904] 2 K.B. 557, CA).

In cases covered by the Reserve and Auxiliary Forces (Protection of Civil Interests) Act 1951, an order of the Court for leave to proceed must be obtained before a charging order *nisi* can be made.

There is no right to a charging order against the Crown since O.50 does not apply in respect of any order against the Crown (see O.77, r.15(1)).

R50.1.22 **Jurisdiction of the High Court (rr.1–9A)**—The jurisdiction to impose a charging order is conferred on the appropriate Court, and the High Court is the appropriate Court for this purpose in the following cases:

(a) where the property to be charged is a fund which is lodged in the High Court;
(b) where the order to be enforced is a maintenance order (as defined in s.2(a) of the Attachment of Earnings Act 1971) of the High Court, though in such a case the county court also has jurisdiction; and
(c) where the judgment or order to be enforced is a judgment or order of the High Court for a sum exceeding £5,000, though in such case again the county court also has jurisdiction.

In any other case, the jurisdiction to impose a charging order is vested in the county court alone (see s.1(1) and (2)).

In order to invoke the jurisdiction of the High Court, the Court will have to look at the amount of the original judgment or order disregarding any increase in the amount recoverable due to interest under the Judgments Act and any decrease due to payments on account.

It is provided that an application may be made for a single charging order in respect of more than one judgment or order against the debtor if any one or more of such judgments exceeds £5,000 (s.1(4)).

The power of the High Court to impose a charging order may be exercised by the Judge or Master, Admiralty Registrar, or District Judge (see r.1(1) and O.1, r.4(2)).

R50.1.23 **Transfer to county court (rr.1–9A)**—The High Court has power to transfer an application for a charging order absolute to the county court. Indeed, under s.1(2)(c) of the Charging Orders Act, as amended, the High Court and county court have parallel jurisdiction in cases where the judgment or order to be enforced is a judgment or order of the High Court exceeding £5,000.

R50.1.24 **Judicial discretion to make charging orders (rr.1–9A)**—By section 1(5) of the 1979 Act, it is provided that:

"in deciding whether to make a charging order the Court shall consider all the circumstances of the case, and, in particular any evidence before it as to—
(a) the personal circumstances of the debtor, and
(b) whether any other creditor of the debtor would be likely to be unduly prejudiced by the making of the order."

The judgment creditor is required by r.1(3)(b) to state the name of any creditor of the debtor whom he (the applicant) can identify. In such case, the Court has power on making the order *nisi* to direct service of copies of the order and of the affidavit in support on any other creditor of the judgment debtor or indeed on any other interested persons as may be appropriate in the circumstances. Such other creditor or other interested person is entitled to attend and to be heard on the hearing of the further consideration of the matter, when the Court will be considering whether or not to make the order absolute.

The term "any other interested person as may be appropriate in the circumstances" in r.2(2) is wide enough to include the spouse of the judgment debtor or other person with whom he or she has been cohabiting who is "in actual occupation of the land" on which a charging order is sought, but it is thought that the application to make a charging order absolute against a judgment debtor is not the appropriate time to consider whether such other person has an overriding interest in the property, within the meaning of *Williams & Glyn's Bank Ltd v. Boland* [1981] A.C. 487; [1980] 2 All E.R. 408, HL.

The Court has a discretion whether or not to make a charging order absolute and the considerations relevant to the exercise of this discretion are equally the same as those that apply to the making of garnishee orders (see para. R49.1.7). The court may therefore refuse to make the charging order absolute where to do so would give the judgment creditor priority over unsecured creditors of a defendant who is probably insolvent. The Court should not in such circumstances exercise its discretion so as to place the judgment creditor at an advantage over the other creditors: (*Rainbow v. Moorgate Properties Ltd* [1975] 1 W.L.R. 788; [1975] 2 All E.R. 821, CA).

In exercising its discretion whether to make or to refuse to make a charging order absolute, the Court is entitled to consider events which have occurred subsequent to the date of the order *nisi*, and indeed the Court should exercise its discretion in the light of all relevant circumstances shown in evidence, including events occurring both before and after the order *nisi*. It is not just to make a charging order absolute on registered property for a debt, where the purchaser of the property is not liable for the debt, and where he has purchased the property after making of the order *nisi* but without notice of the charge imposed by such order (*Howell v. Montey* (1990) 61 P. & C.R. 18; *The Times*, March 17, 1990, CA).

If there is an appeal to the Judge in Chambers against the order of the Master making a charging order absolute, and the debtor company goes into liquidation by a creditor's voluntary winding-up before the hearing of such appeal, the Judge, exercising a completely fresh discretion (see *Evans v. Bartlam* [1937] A.C. 473, HL), will discharge the charging order both *nisi* and absolute (*Weldtite Engineering Ltd v. Beverley Engineering Ltd*, April 25, 1986 (unrep.), *per* Hirst J.).

The general principles governing the exercise of the discretion to make a charging order may be summarised as follows:

1. The question whether a charging order *nisi* should be made absolute is one for the discretion of the Court.

2. The burden of showing cause why a charging order *nisi* should not be made absolute is on the judgment debtor.

3. For the purpose of the exercise of the Court's discretion there is, in general, no material difference between the making absolute of a charging order *nisi* on the one hand and a garnishee order *nisi* on the other.

4. In exercising its discretion the Court has both the right and the duty to take into account all the circumstances of a particular case, whether such circumstances arose before or after the making of the order *nisi*.

5. The Court should so exercise its discretion as to do equity, so far as possible, to all the various parties involved, that is to say, the judgment creditor, the judgment debtor and all other unsecured creditors.

(The above principles which were stated by Lord Brandon in *Roberts Petroleum Ltd v. Bernard Kenny Ltd* [1982] 1 W.L.R. 301, 307; [1982] 1 All E.R. 685 at 690, CA are not affected by the reversal of that case by the House of Lords [1983] A.C. 192; [1983] 1 All E.R. 564.)

6. The liquidation of a company, whether by a resolution for voluntary winding up or by a compulsory order for winding up brings into operation a statutory scheme for dealing with the company's assets, and accordingly if such liquidation occurs after the making of the charging order *nisi* and before such order is made absolute, the Court in its discretion will decline to make the charging order absolute (*Roberts Petroleum Ltd v. Bernard Kenny Ltd* [1983] A.C. 192; [1983] 1 All E.R. 564, HL, reversing [1982] 1 W.L.R. 301; [1982] 1 All E.R. 685, CA on this last point.

It would seem that the same principle will apply to the bankruptcy of an individual which occurs between the charging order *nisi* and the hearing of the application to make it absolute.

It would not be a proper exercise of discretion to make a charging order on an asset of considerable or substantial value in respect of a relatively small debt payable by the debtor: see *per* Simmonds J. in *Robinson v. Bailey* [1942] Ch. 268, 271.

The Court has a discretion which will not be interfered with by the CA unless exercised on a wrong principle (*Wicks v. Shanks* (1893) 67 L.T. 109).

Where execution of a judgment by *fi. fa.* has been stayed on terms that the defendant satisfies the judgment debt by payment of instalments, and where the defendant complies with such terms and is not in arrears, the Court may properly exercise discretion not to make a charging order (*Mercantile Credit Co. Ltd v. Ellis, The Independent*, March 17, 1987; *The Times*, April 1, 1987, CA).

For the considerations which may arise upon an application to *discharge* a charging order absolute upon supervening bankruptcy, see *Jelle Zwemstra v. Walton and Stuart* [1997] 6 C.L. 347.

Property which may be charged (rr.1–9A)—The property and assets of the judgment debtor on which a charge may be imposed by a charging order are specified by s.2 of the Act of 1979 which provides as follows: **R50.1.25**

"2.—(1) Subject to subsection (3) below, a charge may be imposed by a charging order only on—

(a) any interest held by the debtor beneficially—
   (i) in any asset of a kind mentioned in subsection (2) below, or
   (ii) under any trust; or
(b) any interest held by a person as trustee of a trust ("the trust") if the interest is in such an asset or is an interest under another trust and—
   (i) the judgment or order in respect of which a charge is to be imposed was made against that person as trustee of the trust, or
   (ii) the whole beneficial interest under the trust is held by the debtor unencumbered and for his own benefit, or
   (iii) in a case where there are two or more debtors all of whom are liable to the creditor for the same debt, they together hold the whole beneficial interest under the trust unencumbered and for their own benefit.

(2) The assets referred to in subsection (1) above are—

(a) land,
(b) securities of any of the following kinds—
   (i) government stock,
   (ii) stock of any body (other than a building society) incorporated within England and Wales,
   (iii) stock of any body incorporated outside England and Wales or of any state or territory outside the United Kingdom, being stock registered in a register kept at any place within England and Wales,
   (iv) units of any unit trust in respect of which a register of the unit holders is kept at any place within England and Wales, or

(c) funds in Court.

(3) In any case where a charge is imposed by a charging order on any interest in an asset of a kind mentioned in paragraph (b) or (c) of subsection (2) above, the Court making the order may provide for the charge to extend to any interest or dividend payable in respect of the asset."

It should be noted that power is conferred on the Lord Chancellor to amend s.2(2) by statutory instrument by adding to, or removing from, the kinds of asset for the time being referred to there, any asset of a kind which in his opinion ought to be added or removed (s.3(7) and (8)).

R50.1.26 **Effect of charging order on bankruptcy or liquidation of judgment debtor (rr.1–9A)**—By ss.346 and 183 of the Insolvency Act 1986 a judgment creditor may retain the benefit of a charging order provided that the order absolute was made before the commencement of the bankruptcy or winding up. For the position where the bankruptcy or liquidation occurs before the making of an application for a charging order *nisi*, or between the making of an order *nisi* and the hearing of the application to make such order absolute, see "Judicial discretion to make charging orders", above.

A charging order obtained on the after-acquired property of a bankrupt is not an acquisition for value within the meaning of s.307(4) of the Insolvency Act 1986; *cf. Hosack v. Robins* [1918] 2 Ch. 389, CA; *Re Pascoe* [1944] Ch. 219.

R50.1.27 **Charging orders on land (rr.1–9A)**—Under the provisions of section 2 of the 1979 Act (see para. R50.1.25) the Court has power to impose a charging order in respect of the beneficial interest of the debtor under a trust for sale of land including a trust in the proceeds of the sale of the land (see s.2(1)(a)(ii) and s.2(2)(a)). Accordingly if a judgment debtor owns any interest in land, whether a freehold or leasehold interest jointly with another person, a charging order can be made to charge *his* beneficial interest under such trust for sale. The power of the Court extends to making a charging order in respect of the beneficial interest in the proceeds of sale of land held under a trust for sale (*National Westminster Bank Ltd v. Stockman* [1981] 1 W.L.R. 67; [1981] 3 All E.R. 800). The effect of these provisions is therefore statutorily to negative *Irani Finance Ltd v. Singh* [1971] Ch. 59; [1970] 3 All E.R. 199, CA and this accords with the express recommendations of the Law Commission in its Report on Charging Orders (see Cmnd. 6412 (1976), para. 104(6), p.33).

Under the provisions of section 2 of the Act of 1979 (see para. R50.1.25) the Court also has power to make a charging order in respect of a legal estate or lesser interest in land held by the debtor as trustee of a trust, if:

(i) the judgment or order is against the debtor as trustee of the trust; or

(ii) the whole beneficial interest under the trust is held by the debtor unencumbered and for his own benefit; or

(iii) in a case where there are two or more debtors all of whom are liable to the creditor for the same debt, they together hold the whole beneficial interest under the trust unencumbered and for their own benefit.

This last provision, under the principle of the "unity of the debt," has the effect of statutorily affirming *National Westminster Bank Ltd v. Allen* [1971] 2 Q.B. 718; [1971] 3 All E.R. 201.

In a case where there is a trust, including a statutory trust of the kind which exists when land is vested in joint proprietors, the court has no jurisdiction to grant a charging order over the trust property under s.2(1)(a)(i). If the relevant conditions are satisfied, it has jurisdiction to grant a charging order over the trust property under s.2(1)(b). If the relevant conditions are not satisfied, the only charging order that can be made is one over the beneficial interest of a debtor pursuant to s.2(1)(a)(ii) (*Clark v. Chief Land Registrar* [1993] 2 W.L.R. 141, *per* Ferris J.).

The Land Charges Act 1972 and the Land Registration Act 1925 will apply in relation to charging orders as they apply in relation to other orders or writs issued or made for the purpose of enforcing judgments (see section 3(2) of the 1979 Act). As to writs and orders affecting land, see section 6 of the Land Charges Act 1972 and s.59 of the Land Registration Act 1925; and see Wolstenholme and Cherry's *Conveyancing Statutes* (13th ed.) Vol. 6, at pp. 53–55. For the extension of section 49 of the Land Registration Act 1925 to charging orders, see section 3(3) of the 1979 Act.

Although a charging order can be made against an interest held by a debtor beneficially, including an undivided share of land, such a charging order is not registrable under the Land Charges Act 1972 as being an interest in land (*Perry v. Phoenix Assurance plc* [1988] 1 W.L.R. 940; [1988] 2 All E.R. 60).

R50.1.28 **Production of title to registered land (rr.1–9A)**—Following the bringing into force of the Land Registration Act 1988 on December 3, 1990 by the Land Registration Act 1988 (Commencement) Order 1990 (S.I. 1990 No. 1359), leave to inspect the register is no longer necessary.

R50.1.29 **Charging orders on beneficial interest of judgment debtor (rr.1–9A)**—A charge may be imposed by a charging order on "any interest held by the debtor beneficially" in any asset of a kind mentioned in s.2(2) of the 1979 Act (see para. R50.1.25). These assets are, broadly speaking, of three kinds, namely (a) land (see *National Westminster Bank Ltd v. Stockman* [1981] 1 W.L.R. 67;

[1981] 1 All E.R. 800), (b) certain specified securities (other than stock of a building society) and (c) funds in Court.

Accordingly, stock standing in the name of a trustee in trust for the judgment debtor and others may be the subject of a charging order (*South-Western Loan and Discount Co. v. Robertson* (1882) 8 Q.B.D. 17). A debtor's contingent interest can be charged (*Cragg v. Taylor* (1866) L.R. 2 Ex. 131) also a surplus in bankruptcy *Re Wars* [1942] Ch. 294). And where stock was held upon trust to pay the income to the defendant for life, or until he should alien or encumber, with trusts in case or forfeiture for his wife and children, and an ultimate reversion in his favour and a dividend had accrued due, it was held that a charging order on the stock to the extent of the defendant's interest therein was rightly made (*South-Western Loan and Discount Co. v. Robertson* (1882) 8 Q.B.D. 17). See too, *Bolland v. Young* [1904] 2 K.B. 824, CA; *Ideal Bedding Co. v. Holland* [1907] 2 Ch. 157.

Moreover, under the provisions of s.2(2), it would seem that a judgment debtor interested in the proceeds of a trust estate is a person beneficially interested in the stocks and shares of which the estate in part consists, so as to make them chargeable (negativing *Dixon v. Wrench* (1869) L.R. 4 Ex. 154).

There is jurisdiction to charge an interest under a foreign trust, but it may not be easy to determine whether an interest under such a trust is enforceable under English law, and, as a matter of discretion, the Court will not exercise the jurisdiction where it could expose the trustee to a risk of double jeopardy here and in a foreign jurisdiction (*Interpool Ltd v. Galani* [1988] Q.B. 738; [1987] 2 All E.R. 981, CA).

Charging orders on interest held by a trustee (rr.1–9A)—A charge may be imposed by a charging order on any interest held by a person as trustee of a trust, if the interest is in such an asset of a kind mentioned in s.2(2) or is an interest under another trust, and one of the conditions mentioned in section 2(1)(b) of the Act is satisfied (see para. R50.1.25). This provision would have the effect, in the specified circumstances, that stock standing in the name of the debtor in a public company (other than a building society) would be subject to a charging order even if it were shown that the debtor is merely a trustee. Such cases as *Re Blakeley Ordnance Co.* (1877) 25 W.R. 111; *Cooper v. Griffen* [1892] 1 Q.B. 740; *Howard v. Sadler* [1893] 1 Q.B. 1; and *cf. Pulbrook v. Richmond Consolidated Mining Co.* (1878) 9 Ch.D. 610 and the observations of Buckley J. in *Sutton v. English and Colonial Produce Co.* [1902] 2 Ch. 502, if not in fact negatived by, would at least have to be re-examined in the light of, the above position. R50.1.30

The practice relating to a charging order imposing a charge on an interest held by trustee is substantially the same as in the case of a charging order on a beneficial interest of the judgment debtor (see r.4(1)). However, instead of verifying the judgment debtor's beneficial ownership of the interest to be charged, the supporting affidavit must state the ground on which the application is based and must verify the material facts (see r.4(2)); and on making the order to show cause the Court must give directions for copies of the order, and the supporting affidavit, to be served on such of the trustees and beneficiaries, if any, as may be appropriate (see r.4(3)). The relevant forms, *i.e.* Forms 75 and 76 in Appendix A must be modified (see Vol. 2, Section 1A, paras 1A–76 and 1A–77) so as to indicate that the interest to be charged is held by the debtor as trustee or, as the case may be, that it is held by a trustee (who must be named in the order) on trust for the debtor beneficially (see r.4(5)).

Charging order on legal estate—or on beneficial interest (rr.1–9A)—A charging order over the beneficial interests of two joint owners does not take effect as a charge over the legal estate and can gain no priority over a legal charge of the legal estate subsequently made and registered: *Clark v. Chief Land Registrar* [1993] 2 W.L.R. 141. A charging order made under section 2(1)(a)(i) of the Act creates a charge on the beneficial interests of the proprietors only. There is no jurisdiction under para. (a)(i) to make an order over the trust property itself. That jurisdiction arises only under para. (1)(b) and then only if the conditions of that para. are satisfied. If the conditions are not satisfied the Court may make an order only over the beneficial interest of the debtor under the trust pursuant to para. (a)(ii): (*ibid.*). This case illustrates the importance to be attached to the precise nature of the interest sought to be charged in any application being made; and the precise nature of the interest which is the subject of any order when made. R50.1.31

Clark v. Chief Land Registrar was approved in the Court of Appeal [1994] 3 W.L.R. 593; [1994] 4 All E.R. 96, where it was held as a matter of construction that the charging order in question referred to the debtors' legal and beneficial interest and was effective to create a charge over the legal estate in the land and not merely their interest in the proceeds of sale. Neither s.2(1) of the Charging Orders Act 1979 nor O.50, rr.1–4 (which detailed the procedure for obtaining a charging order) nor any technical breach of the rules of Court could alter the clear effect of the order.

It should be noted that by *Practice Direction (Queen's Bench: 38)* set out at SCP Mainwork 1999, Vol. 2, Section 2A, para. 2A–106, a charging order *nisi* on land shall be drawn charging the debtor's interest in the land and not the land itself, unless the Court otherwise directs.

Charging orders on funds in Court (rr.1–9A)—Under s.2(1)(a)(i) and 2(2)(c) of the 1979 Act, a charging order may be imposed on funds in Court. This provision substantially repeats the former O.50, r.8 (which incidentally has been revoked and not replaced as being unnecessary) R50.1.32

which itself was new in the RSC 1965 but had reflected the practice of the Court as laid down in *Brereton v. Edwards* [1888] 21 Q.B.D. 488, which decided that under its jurisdiction to order equitable execution, the Court may make a charging order against money in Court standing to the credit of a judgment debtor (see also, *Re Prior* [1921] 3 K.B. 333; and *London County Council v. Manks* [1959] Ch. 239 at 243; and see also O.49, r.9, as to proceedings in the nature of garnishee in respect of money in Court standing to the credit of the judgment debtor).

Where a charging order *nisi* has been made in relation to funds in Court including securities in Court, and a copy thereof has been served on the Accountant-General, no disposition by the judgment debtor of any interest to which the order relates, made after the making of that order, shall be valid as against the judgment creditor, so long as the order remains in force (see r.6(1)) and if the order *nisi* is made absolute a copy of it must be served on the Accountant-General at the Court Funds Office (see r.6(2)).

Where a charging order has been obtained on a fund in Court, the Accountant General must take notice of it, and a stop order in addition is necessary (O.50, r.6).

The practice to obtain a charging order on funds in Court is substantially the same as in the case of a charging order on the beneficial interest of the debtor. Prima facie, the application should be made to the Court under whose control the fund is, *e.g.* if the fund is with the Official Receiver the application is made in bankruptcy and the order may be made by the Registrar (*Re Prior* [1921] 3 K.B. 333, CA).

The basis of the cases cited above, however, is that where the Court has a fund under its own control, as in the case of a fund in Court held in an account of the Accountant General, the Accountant General being an officer of the High Court (see Court Funds Rules 1987 (S.I. 1987, No. 821), r.2(2) (SCP 1999, Vol. 2, Section 5C) and all the Judges of any division of the High Court being Judges of that Court, the Judges will enforce a High Court judgment by directing their officer to pay out the money or make a charging order on the fund in question (*London County Council v. Manks* [1959] Ch. 239; [1958] 3 All E.R. 670).

R50.1.33 **Practice in application to obtain charging order (rr.1–9A)**—The application by the judgment creditor for a charging order in respect of a beneficial interest of the judgment debtor is made without notice (r.1(2)) and it must be supported by a witness statement or an affidavit which must comply with the requirements of r.1(3).

In the QBD the application is made to the Practice Master. The supporting affidavit deposing to the matters mentioned in para. (3) is left in the Masters' Secretary's Department (Room E214) and obtained later from that Department with the Master's decision indorsed thereon. If an order *nisi* is made, the order on being drawn up will have a date upon it when the matter is again to come before the Master for the "further consideration" mentioned in para. (2).

In the Ch D the application in pending proceedings is made by lodging the supporting affidavit at the appropriate Master's Chambers.

In proceedings in a District Registry, the application is made, in the same way, to the District Judge.

In the Family Division, the application comes before a District Judge upon a like affidavit.

Any order made on such application must in the first instance be an order made in Form No. 75 in Appendix A, to show cause, and it must specify the time and place for further consideration of this matter but it will impose the charging order in any event until that time (see r.1(2)).

The order *nisi* must be drawn and notice of the order must be served as required by r.2, unless the Court directs otherwise.

R50.1.34 **Contents of supporting witness statement or affidavit (rr.1–9A)**—Great care should be taken in preparing the supporting affidavit, so that it will fully and accurately comply with the requirements of r.1(3). The witness statement or affidavit must accordingly:

(1) identify the judgment or order to be enforced;
(2) state the amount unpaid at the date of the application;
(3) state the name of the judgment debtor;
(4) state the name of any creditor of the debtor whom the applicant can identify;
(5) give full particulars of the subject matter of the intended charge, including (a) in the case of securities other than securities in Court, the full title of the securities, their amount and the name in which they stand; and (b) the case of funds in Court, the number of the account; and (c) verify that the interest to be charged is owned beneficially by the judgment debtor.

It should perhaps be emphasised that the amount unpaid at the date of the application includes any interest accrued on the judgment since the date of its entry.

For the purposes of this rule, the supporting witness statement or affidavit may contain statements of information or belief with the sources and grounds thereof, unless the Court otherwise directs (see r.1(4)).

Requirement (4) above is important. If the applicant is unable to identify any creditor of the debtor other than the judgment creditor himself, the affidavit should say so. "The applicant", in this context, means the judgment creditor, and not the solicitor or other person making the affidavit on his behalf. Thus, if the solicitor swears the affidavit, he may upon information and belief state that the applicant cannot identify any other creditor, but he must state the sources of such information and grounds of such belief.

A witness statement containing a statement of truth can be used instead of an affidavit (see r.1(3)).

Charging order nisi with injunction (rr.1–9A)—It is sometimes necessary for the charging order *nisi* to contain an injunction to prevent the property or asset charged being dealt with before the hearing of the application for the order to be made absolute. In such cases, the supporting affidavit should set out the relevant facts and circumstances to show that there is a risk or danger that the debtor will or might deal with the property or assets to be charged between the making of the charging order *nisi* and the order absolute. There must be clear and adequate evidence to support the making of such an injunction, just as in the case of any other injunction, and the creditor should give the usual undertaking as to damages as in the case of any other interlocutory injunction. **R50.1.35**

The application for the injunction may be joined with the substantive application for the charging order *nisi* (see r.9) and if after the making of the charging order *nisi*, fresh material should come to the knowledge of the creditor, he may then apply for an injunction, even though it may be subsequent to the order *nisi*.

Express power is conferred on the Master and District Judge in the QBD, the Admiralty Registrar and a District Judge of the Family Division to grant such an injunction but only if and so far as it is ancillary or incidental to the making of a charging order *nisi* or absolute (see r.9).

Making charging order absolute (rr.1–9A)—On the further consideration of the matter, the Court must either make absolute the order *nisi*, with or without modifications or discharge it. A charging order *nisi* ought not to be left in a state of uncertainty or ambiguity; it must either be made absolute or discharged. If the Court is minded, for good reasons, to adjourn the further consideration of the matter, it should not adjourn the matter generally to a date to be fixed, but it should adjourn the matter to a fixed time and place as in the case of the original order *nisi*. **R50.1.36**

Effect of death of judgment debtor (rr.1–9A)—The order will not be made absolute where it appears that the judgment debtor was dead when the order *nisi* was obtained (*Finney v. Hinde* (1879) 4 Q.B.D. 102; *Stewart v. Rhodes* [1900] 1 Ch. 386). There must be a judgment against the executors. See also *Scott v. Scott* [1952] 2 All E.R. 890. **R50.1.37**

Issue directed (rr.1–9A)—If the title to the stock or shares is disputed, an issue may be directed to be tried, in which case the practice is to adjourn the application to make the charging order absolute until after the decision of the issue. **R50.1.38**

This note was expressly approved by the Court of Appeal in *Rosseel NV v. Oriental Commercial and Shipping (UK) Ltd* [1991] E.G.C.S. 94, CA. What is said applies equally where the dispute is over the beneficial ownership of land; where the dispute is one of fact the normal course will be for the court to exercise its discretion to direct an issue to be tried (*ibid.*).

Extent of the order—interest and costs (rr.1–9A)—It has been held that though a charging order did not expressly provide for the payment of interest or costs, it did extend to both. Reference was made to the purpose of the words in square brackets as to interest in PF 76 (*Ezekiel v. Orakpo* [1994] N.P.C. 140, upheld at [1996] C.L.Y. 684, CA). It was further held in the CA, allowing the judgment creditor's appeal on this point, that interest falling due more than six years before the commencement of the instant proceedings was recoverable under the charge. The right to include interest over a period of more than six years was not affected by s.20(5) of the Limitation Act 1980. **R50.1.39**

Costs (rr.1–9A)—In QBD, on making the charging order absolute, the fixed costs prescribed by O.62, App. 3, Pt III (see para. R62 below) will be added to the judgment. If there are significant disbursements in addition to the court and oath fees the practice is for these to be allowed in addition. **R50.1.40**

Discharge of charging order (rr.1–9A)—The Court by which a charging order was made may at any time, on the application of the debtor or of any person interested in any property to which the order relates, make an order discharging or varying the charging order (section 3(5) of the 1979 Act); and in such case where the charging order has been protected by an entry registered under the Land Charges Act 1972 or the Land Registration Act 1925, the order discharging the charging order may direct that such entry be cancelled (s.3(6) of the Act of 1979). **R50.1.41**

An application to discharge or vary a charging order may be made by the judgment debtor or any other person interested in subject matter of the charge, and the Court may, at any time, whether before or after the charging order is made absolute, discharge or vary the order on such terms, if any, as to costs or otherwise as it thinks just (see r.7(1)). The phrase "any other person interested in the subject-matter of the charge" is very wide and of course includes the creditor. Notice of such an application, however, must be served on such interested parties as the Court may direct (see r.7(3)). It would seem therefore that if such application is made by the creditor, and there are no other interested parties, it may be made *ex parte* to the Practice Master, who may direct that notice of the discharge of the charging order should be served on the debtor.

Where an order is made for the discharge or variation of a charging order in respect of funds in Court, a copy thereof must be served on the Accountant-General at the Court Funds Office (see r.7(4)); and where such an order is made in respect of securities other than securities in Court, a copy of the order must be served on the Bank of England or on such other person or body specified in r.2(1)(b) as may be appropriate, and such service shall discharge or vary any stop notice in respect of such securities which may be in force pursuant to the original order (see r.7(5)).

If the application for the discharge of a charging order in respect of the judgment debtor's land is made on the ground that the judgment debt has been satisfied, the applicant must state in his application and the Court must specify in its order, the title number of the land in case of registered land, and the entry number of any relevant land charge in the case of unregistered land (see r.7(2)).

Supervening bankruptcy of the judgment debtor may be a ground to discharge a charging order absolute. Whilst s.346 of the Insolvency Act 1986 allows a creditor to obtain the benefit of a charging order absolute, the Court has a discretion to discharge it. Assistance can be gained from *Roberts Ltd v. Bernard Kenny Ltd* [1983] A.C. 192; [1983] 1 All E.R. 564, HL. Regard must be had to the position of all the creditors, although the grounds for discharging a valid charging order absolute must be more compelling than the grounds to discharge a charging order *nisi.* In the instant case the order should stand (*Jelle Zwemstra Ltd v. Walton and Stuart* [1997] 6 C.L. 347).

Service of notice of order to show cause

R50.2 **2.**—(1) On the making of an order to show cause, notice of the order shall, unless the court otherwise directs, be served as follows—

(a) a copy of the order, together with a copy of the witness statement or affidavit in support, shall be served on the judgment debtor;

(b) where the order relates to securities other than securities in court, copies of the order shall also be served—

(i) in the case of government stock for which the Bank of England keeps the Register, on the Bank of England;

(ii) in the case of government stock to which (i) does not apply, on the keeper of the register;

(iii) in the case of stock of any body incorporated within England and Wales, on that body, or, where the register is kept by the Bank of England, on the Bank of England;

(iv) in the case of stock of any body incorporated outside England and Wales or of any state or territory outside the United Kingdom, being stock registered in a register kept in England and Wales, on the keeper of the register;

(v) in the case of units of any unit trust in respect of which a register of the unit holders is kept in England and Wales, on the keeper of the register;

(c) where the order relates to a fund in court, a copy of the order shall be served on the Accountant General at the Court Funds Office; and

(d) where the order relates to an interest under a trust, copies of the order shall be served on such of the trustees as the court may direct.

(2) Without prejudice to the provisions of paragraph (1), the court may, on making the order to show cause, direct the service of copies of the order, and of the witness statement or affidavit in support, on any other creditor of the judgment debtor or on any other interested person as may be appropriate in the circumstances.

(3) Documents to be served under this rule must be served at least seven days before the time appointed for the further consideration of the matter.

R50.2.1 **Effect of rule**—On the making of the order to show cause notice of the order must, unless the Court otherwise directs, be served as required by r.2(1) and the documents to be served under this rule must be served at least seven days before the time appointed for the further consideration of the matter (see r.2(3)).

The most important requirement is that a copy of the order *nisi*, together with a copy of the supporting affidavit must be served on the judgment debtor (see r.2(1)(a)). These documents need not, however be served personally on the judgment debtor, but the service of such documents must comply with the requirements of CPR, r.6.2, *i.e.* they must be left or posted to his proper address or served in such other manner as the Court may direct.

Where the judgment debtor is out of the jurisdiction, unless the Master, being satisfied that the order *nisi* has come to the judgment debtor's knowledge, is prepared to make the order absolute, the practice is to apply to the Master for leave under O.11, r.9, to serve him with notice of the order *nisi* out of the jurisdiction.

Where the order *nisi* relates to securities other than securities in Court copies of the order *nisi* must also be served according to the nature of the securities in question on the Bank of England, the keeper of the register, or the company whose stick is sought to be charged (see r.2(1)(b)); and where the order *nisi* relates to a fund in Court a copy of the order must also be served on the Accountant-General at the Court Funds Office (see r.291)(c)). Where the order *nisi* relates to an interest under a trust, copies of the order must also be served on such of the trustees as the Court may direct (see r.2(1)(d)).

The Bank, company of Accountant-General should not attend unless special circumstances warrant their attendance, and in the absence of such circumstances the costs of attendance will not be allowed.

In any event, the Court may, on making the order to show cause, direct that copies of the order and of the supporting affidavit should also be served on any creditor of the debtor or any interested person as may be appropriate in the circumstances (see r.2(2)).

Order made on further considerations

3.—(1) On the further consideration of the matter the court shall either make the order absolute, with or without modifications, or discharge it. **R50.3**

(2) Where the order is made absolute, it shall be made in Form No. 76 in the relevant practice direction, and where it is discharged, the provisions of rule 7, regarding the service of copies of the order of discharge, shall apply.

Effect of rule—The essence of the procedure is that an order *nisi* is obtained by an application without notice supported by evidence. The issue of whether the order *nisi* should then be made absolute or discharged is listed for consideration by the Master or District Judge. **R50.3.1**

See generally detailed commentary to r.1.

Order imposing a charge on an interest held by a trustee

4.—(1) Save as provided by this rule, the provisions of rules 1, 2 and 3 shall apply to an order charging an interest held by a trustee as they apply to an order charging the judgment debtor's beneficial interest. **R50.4**

(2) Instead of verifying the judgment debtor's beneficial ownership of the interest to be charged, the witness statement or affidavit required by rule 1(3) shall state the ground on which the application is based and shall verify the material facts.

(3) On making the order to show cause, the court shall give directions for copies of the order, and of the witness statement or affidavit in support, to be served on such of the trustees and beneficiaries, if any, as may be appropriate.

(4) Rules 5, 6 and 7 shall apply to an order charging an interest held by a trustee as they apply to an order charging the judgment debtor's beneficial interest, except that, where the order is made under sub-section (ii) or (iii) of section 2(1)(b) of the Act references in those rules to "the judgment debtor" shall be references to the trustee.

(5) Forms No. 75 and 76 in the relevant practice direction shall be modified so as to indicate that the interest to be charged is held by the debtor as trustee or, as the case may be, that it is held by a trustee (to be named in the order) on trust for the debtor beneficially.

Effect of rule—See commentary to r.1. **R50.4.1**

Effect of order in relation to securities out of court

5.—(1) No disposition by the judgment debtor of his interest in any securities to which an order to show cause relates made after the making of that order shall, so long as that order remains in force, be valid as against the judgment creditor. **R50.5**

(2) Until such order is discharged or made absolute, the Bank of England (or other person or body served in accordance with rule 2(1)(b)), shall not permit any transfer of any of the securities specified in the order, or pay any dividend, interest or redemption payment in relation thereto, except with the

authority of the court, and, if it does so, shall be liable to pay the judgment creditor the value of the securities transferred or, as the case may be, the amount of the payment made or, if that value or amount is more than sufficient to satisfy the judgment or order to which such order relates, so much thereof as is sufficient to satisfy it.

(3) If the court makes the order absolute, a copy of the order, including a stop notice as provided in Form No. 76 in the relevant practice direction, shall be served on the Bank of England, or on such other person or body specified in rule 2(1)(b) as may be appropriate and, save as provided in rule 7(5), rules 11 to 14 shall apply to such a notice as they apply to a stop notice made and served under rule 11.

(4) this rule does not apply to orders in respect of securities in court.

R50.5.1 **Effect of rule**—See generally commentary to r.1.

R50.5.2 **Form No. 76**—The form has not changed: it is based on Form 76 (see SCP 1999, Vol. 2).

Effect of order in relation to funds in court

R50.6 **6.**—(1) Where an order to show cause has been made in relation to funds in court (including securities in court) and a copy thereof has been served on the Accountant General in accordance with rule 2, no disposition by the judgment debtor of any interest to which the order relates, made after the making of that order, shall, so long as the order remains in force, be valid as against the judgment creditor.

(2) If the court makes the order absolute, a copy of the order shall be served on the Accountant General at the Court Funds Office.

R50.6.1 **Effect of rule**—Funds in court can be the subject of a charging order but consider also O.49, r.9 and see O.50, r.10, and commentary to O.50, r.1.

Discharge, etc., of charging order

R50.7 **7.**—(1) Subject to paragraph (2), on the application of the judgment debtor or any other person interested in the subject matter of the charge, the court may, at any time, whether before or after the order is made absolute, discharge or vary the order on such terms (if any) as to costs or otherwise as it thinks just.

(2) Where an application is made for the discharge of a charging order in respect of the judgment debtor's land on the ground that the judgment debt has been satisfied, the applicant shall state in his application, and the court shall specify in its order, the title number of the land in the case of registered land, and the entry number of any relevant land charge in the case of unregistered land.

(3) The application notice seeking the discharge or variation of the order shall be served on such interested parties as the court may direct.

(4) Where an order is made for the discharge or variation of a charging order in respect of funds in court, a copy thereof shall be served on the Accountant General at the Court Funds Office.

(5) Where an order is made for the discharge or variation of a charging order in respect of securities other than securities in court, a copy thereof shall be served on the Bank of England or on such other person or body specified in rule 2(1)(b) as may be appropriate, and the service thereof shall discharge, or, as the case may be, vary, any stop notice in respect of such securities which may be in force pursuant to the original order.

R50.7.1 **Effect of rule**—A charging order as such does not result in the satisfaction of the judgment debt but rather gives the judgment creditor security. It frequently happens that the judgment debtor, after order absolute, arranges to pay the debt so as to prevent an application for an order for sale. The order can then be discharged and r.7 specifies the procedure.

Jurisdiction of Master, etc., to grant injunction

9. A Master and the Admiralty Registrar and a district judge of the Family Division shall have power to grant an injunction if, and only so far as, it is ancillary or incidental to an order under rule 1, 3 or 4 and an application for an injunction under this rule may be joined with the application for the order under rule 1, 3 or 4 to which it relates. R50.9

Effect of rule—An injunction may be necessary to protect the judgment creditor's interest ancillary to an order under rr.1, 3 or 4. Rule 9 gives express power to grant it to a Master. See further, commentary to r.1 expecially para "charging order nisi with injunction". R50.9.1

Enforcement of charging order by sale

9A.—(1) Proceedings for the enforcement of a charging order by sale of the property charged must be begun by claim form issued out of Chancery Chambers or out of one of the Chancery District Registries. R50.9A

(2) The provisions of Order 88 shall apply to all such proceedings.

Effect of rule—A charging order merely gives security to the judgment creditor and does not, of itself, result in payment of the judgment debt. Having obtained the order absolute the judgment creditor will usually negotiate an arrangement for payment by the debtor. The security obtained by the creditor is, of course, subject to prior incumbrances. R50.9A.1

As provided by r.9A, if the creditor wishes to enforce the charging order by sale, separate proceedings in the Chancery Division are required pursuant to RSC, O.88.

Funds in court: stop order

10.—(1) The court, on the application of any person— R50.10

(a) who has a mortgage or charge on the interest of any person in funds in court; or

(b) to whom that interest has been assigned, or

(c) who is a judgment creditor of the person entitled to that interest,

may make an order prohibiting the transfer, sale, delivery out, payment or other dealing with such funds, or any part thereof, or the income thereon, without notice to the applicant.

(2) An application for an order under this rule must, if there are existing proceedings, be made in accordance with CPR Part 23 by filing an application notice relating to the funds in court, or, if there are no such proceedings, by a claim.

(3) The application notice or claim form must be served on every person whose interest may be affected by the order applied for and on the Accountant-General but shall not be served on any other person.

(4) Without prejudice to the court's powers and discretion as to costs, the court may order the applicant for an order under this rule to pay the costs of any party to the proceedings relating to the funds in question, or of any person interested in those funds, occasioned by the application.

Effect of rule—A judgment creditor may obtain a stop order on a fund in court in the Ch D without first obtaining a charging order in the Division in which judgment was recovered (*Hopwell v. Barnes* (1879) 48 L.J.Ch. 689; *Hopwell v. Barnes* (1876) 1 Ch. 630). R50.10.1

A stop order may be obtained on a fund ordered to be paid into court, though it has not actually been paid in (*Shaw v. Hudson*); but not where there is no fund in court, and no order for bringing in any fund (*Wellesley v. Mornington* (1863) 11 W.R. 17).

Application—The application must be made under CPR Part 23 in pending proceedings see (r.10(2)) or by claim form, if there are no pending proceedings (para. (2)). R50.10.2

Stop orders should distinguish between capital and income affected by them (*Mack v. Postle* [1894] 2 Ch. 449).

A certificate of funds issued by the Accountant General must state particulars of any charges or restraints on the fund of which the Accountant General is aware: Court Funds Rules 1987, r.63(1) (SCP 1999, Vol. 2, Section 5C).

Parties—Unless the assignor joins in the application, he must be served with the summons, whether the assignment is absolute or by way of mortgage (*Parsons v. Groome* (1842) 4 Beav. 521). R50.10.3

R50.10.4 **Evidence**—It is necessary on an application for a stop order to give evidence of the title of the assignor generally (which, however, will usually appear from the proceedings in the cause) and of the assignment, unless the assignor appears and admits the execution (*Wood v. Vincent* (1842) 4 Beav. 419; *Quarman v. Williams* (1842) 5 Beav. 133); a certificate of the fund being in court should also be produced.

R50.10.5 **Effect of stop order**—By granting a stop order nothing is decided as to the rights of the parties (*Lucas v. Peacock* (1846) 9 Beav. 177). As to effect on priorities, see n. "Priority acquired by stop order", para. R50.10.8 below.

The effect of a stop order, however general in its terms, is confined to the specific portion of the fund in respect of a dealing with which the order is made (*Macleod v. Buchanan* (1864) 33 Beav. 234).

R50.10.6 **Fund carried to separate account**—The effect of an order carrying a fund to a separate account is to release it from the general questions in the cause, and incumbrancers advancing money on the faith of such an order are entitled to priority over a claim made in respect of a breach of trust against the person to whose account such fund is carried (*Re Eyton* (1887) 45 Ch.D. 458).

R50.10.7 **Funds improperly paid out of court**—Unless a stop order has been obtained on a fund in court the Accountant General is not guilty of default so as to give rise to a claim against public funds if the money has been paid out in disregard of the creditor's possible rights (*Bath v. Bath* [1901] 1 Ch. 460).

R50.10.8 **Priority acquired by stop order**—The priorities on a fund in court are generally determined by the priorities of the respective stop orders, rather than by the date or nature of the charge (*Greening v. Beckford* (1832) 5 Sim. 195; *Swayne v. Swayne* (1849) 11 Beav. 463). Therefore, a mortgagee obtaining a stop order after the bankruptcy of the mortgagor has priority over the trustees in bankruptcy who have not obtained one (*Stuart v. Cockerell* (1869) L.R. 8 Eq. 607; *Palmer v. Locke* (1882) 18 Ch.D. 381). But one incumbrancer, by obtaining a stop order on a fund after it has been carried to the account of the mortgagor and his incumbrancers, does not obtain priority over a stop order obtained before the fund was carried over (*Lister v. Tidd* (1867) L.R. 4 Eq. 462). When money has been paid into court, an incumbrance upon it can afterwards be perfected only by obtaining a stop order, the date of which governs priority.

This is the case where part only of the fund is in court. A subsequent incumbrancer does not lose his priority by reason of his having had notice of the previous incumbrance when he obtained the stop order, provided he had no notice of it when he took his security (*Mutual Life Ass. Soc. v. Langley* (1886) 32 Ch.D. 460). But see *Stephens v. Green* [1895] 2 Ch. 148.

But if proper notice has been given before the fund is in court, the priority is not lost by a stop order obtained after transfer of the fund into court (*Livesey v. Harding* (1857) 23 Beav. 141; *Re Anglesey* [1903] 2 Ch. 727 at 732).

Where the mortgage to a subsequent mortgagee, who obtained a stop order, recited a prior mortgage, it was held that the priority of the prior mortgagee was not affected by the stop order (*Re Holmes* (1885) 29 Ch.D. 786).

But an order appointing a receiver by way of equitable execution has priority over a subsequent stop order (*Re Anglesey* [1903] 2 Ch. 727).

R50.10.9 **No personal representative**—Where the person who obtained the stop order is dead and has no English personal representative, the Court may proceed in the absence of any representative of his estate where the proposed transaction does not affect his interest: *e.g.* payment out of another share in the fund: or may appoint someone to represent his estate (see RSC, O.15, r.15).

R50.10.10 **Equitable assignment—stop order**—See *Montefiore v. Guedalla* [1903] 2 Ch. 26, CA.

R50.10.11 **Contingent interest**—A petition for payment of a fund out of court need not be served on the mortgagee of a person having a contingent interest who has died before the interest vested, even though such mortgagee has obtained a stop order (*Vernon v. Croft* (1888) 36 W.R. 778).

R50.10.12 **Construction of stop order**—In ascertaining the effect of a stop order the Court is not bound to confine its attention to the language of the order itself (*Mack v. Postle* [1894] 2 Ch. 449).

Securities not in court: stop notice

R50.11 **11.**—(1) Any person claiming to be beneficially entitled to an interest in any securities of the kinds set out in section 2(2)(b) of the Act, other than securities in court, who wishes to be notified of any proposed transfer or payment of those securities may avail himself of the provisions of this rule.

(2) A person claiming to be so entitled must file in Chancery Chambers or in a District Registry—

(a) a witness statement or affidavit identifying the securities in question and describing his interest therein by reference to the document under which it arises; and

(b) a notice in Form No. 80 in the relevant practice direction (a stop notice) signed by the witness who made the witness statement or affidavit, and annexed to it, addressed to the Bank of England or, as the case may be, the body, state, territory or unit trust concerned,

and must serve an office copy of the witness statement or affidavit, and a copy of the notice sealed with the seal of Chancery Chambers or the District Registry, on the Bank or other person or body, as provided in rule 2(1)(b).

(3) There must be indorsed on the witness statement or affidavit filed under this rule a note stating the address to which any such notice as is referred to in rule 12 is to be sent and, subject to paragraph (4), that address shall for the purpose of that rule be the address for service of the person on whose behalf the witness statement or affidavit is filed.

(4) A person on whose behalf a witness statement or affidavit under this rule is filed may change his address for service for the purpose of rule 12 by serving on the Bank of England, or other person or body, a notice to that effect, and, as from the date of service of such a notice the address stated therein shall for the purpose of that rule be the address for service of that person.

Effect of rule—See commentary following r.14. R50.11.1

Effect of stop notice

12. Where a stop notice has been served in accordance with rule 11, then, so long as the stop notice is in force, the Bank of England or other person or body on which it is served shall not register a transfer of the securities or take any other step restrained by the stop notice until 14 days after sending notice thereof, by ordinary first class post, to the person on whose behalf the stop notice was filed, but shall not by reason only of that notice refuse to register a transfer, or to take any other step, after the expiry of that period. R50.12

Effect of rule—See commentary following r.14. R50.12.1

Amendment of stop notice

13. If any securities are incorrectly described in a stop notice which has been filed and of which a sealed copy has been served in accordance with rule 11, an amended stop notice may be filed and served in accordance with the same procedure and shall take effect as a stop notice on the day on which the sealed copy of the amended notice is served. R50.13

Effect of rule—See commentary following r.14. R50.13.1

Withdrawal etc. of stop notice

14.—(1) The person on whose behalf a stop notice was filed may withdraw it by serving a request for its withdrawal on the Bank of England or other person or body on whom the notice was served. R50.14

(2) Such request must be signed by the person on whose behalf the notice was filed and his signature must be witnessed by a practising solicitor.

(3) The court, on the application of any person claiming to be beneficially entitled to an interest in the securities to which a stop notice relates, may by order discharge the notice.

(4) An application for an order under paragraph (3) must be made in the Chancery Division by a claim form, and the claim form must be served on the person on whose behalf a stop notice was filed.

R50.14.1 **Effect of rr.11–14.**—These rules provide the procedure for a stop notice in respect of securities which are not in court. The "stop notice" replaced the old writ of *distringas* (and is sometimes referred to in older cases as "a notice in lieu of *distringas*").

The applicant must be a person who claims to be beneficially interested in such securities. See Form No. 80 (SCP 1999, Vol. 2, Section 1A, para. 1A–81) which requires the deponent to prove the party's beneficial interest "in the stock comprised in the (*settlement, will,* etc.) above mentioned." There must therefore be a beneficial interest in the stock sought to be affected, comprised in some document or legal instrument in writing. A beneficial interest is created by deposit of a certificate of shares as security for a debt and interest, without a transfer or memorandum (*Harrold v. Plenty* [1901] 2 Ch. 314).

A judgment creditor who has obtained a charging order absolute upon the contingent equitable interest of a judgment debtor in Government and Bank of England Stock standing in the name of a trustee, can issue a stop notice under these rules. In *Adam v. Bank of England* (1908) 52 S.J. 682, it was held that the Bank was bound to transfer stock on the direction of the legal owner, notwithstanding a charging order obtained against a person equitably entitled (following *Churchill v. Bank of England* (1843) 11 M. & W. 323). Subsequently to this decision Joyce J. (November 9, 1908) authorised the issue in a Chancery action of a *distringas* notice based upon a charging order absolute.

R50.14.2 **Official requirements (rr.11–14)**—The witness statement or affidavit and notice are filed in the filing department. The original notice and the duplicate must be signed. If the deponent is a partner in a firm, he is not entitled to sign the notice or duplicate in the firm's name. The duplicate is sealed by the filing department without fee. Where the party interested is child or patient, the witness statement or affidavit must so state, and that the child or patient is interested *by A. B. his or her next friend,* and that the said A. B. has no interest in the matters adverse to that of the child or patient.

A separate notice and witness statement or affidavit must be filed for each company or corporation to be served, but any number of different kinds of stock standing in the books of a company or corporation may be included in one affidavit and notice. The witness statement or affidavit must be in the form No. 80 (SCP 1999, Vol. 2, Section 1A, para. 1A–81).

A judgment is not an instrument under which a stop notice and affidavit can be filed; the process in that case being under r.1.

R50.14.3 **Accountant General's holding (rr.11–14)**—A stop notice placed upon a holding of the Accountant General of the Supreme Court at a bank or in a company is ineffective, and will not prevent the transfer of the fund. An order must be obtained and lodged at the Court Funds Office, if it is desired to stop the transfer; see nn. to r.15.

R50.14.4 **Failure to give notice (rr.11–14)**—See *Peat v. Clayton* [1906] 1 Ch. 659.

R50.14.5 **Effect of stop notice (rr.11–14)**—The effect of the stop notice is to prevent a fund being dealt with without the person who issues it having an opportunity of asserting his claim. "Where there is a *distringas* on stock, the Bank of England gives notice (after application to deal with the stock) to the issuer that unless he takes proceedings in a short time to assert his right the *distringas* will be disregarded, but a trustee has no such right" (*per* V.-C. Stuart, *Wilkins v. Sibley* (1863) 4 Giff. 442, 446–7). The effect of the writ of *distringas,* therefore, was, and by these rules the effect of a notice under the new procedure is, merely temporary, and the person issuing it must proceed to obtain a restraining order under r.15, or an injunction in a suit against a person in whose name the stock stands; as to which modes of procedure see *Re Blakeley's Trusts* (1883) 23 Ch.D. 549; *Re Prynne* (1885) 53 L.T. 465; *Société Générale de Paris v. Tramways Union Co.* (1885) 14 Q.B.D. 424 at 453, *per* Lindley L.J.; *Hobbs v. Wayet* (1887) 36 Ch.D. 256, *per* Kekewich J.

Failure to give notice under r.11, does not affect priorities, for it will not postpone an assignee of shares, who has given notice (apart from r.11) to the company of an assignment to him as against a subsequent assignee, nor prevent the company from registering a transfer to such prior assignee (*Peat v. Clayton* [1906] 1 Ch. 659).

Service of notice and affidavit as to stock comprised in legacy by legatee does not prevent a subsequent disclaimer of the legacy (*Hobbs v. Wayet* (1887) 36 Ch.D. 256).

Where the bank gave notice that an application had been made to allow the transfer of stock and to pay the dividends thereon, and an *ex parte* motion was made to restrain the bank from dealing with the stock, the Court granted an interim injunction over the next motion day, and required notice of the order to be served on the legal owner or stock (*Re Blakeley's Trusts* (1883) 23 Ch.D. 549).

An application to restrain a transfer of funds belonging to the estate of a testator should be entitled in the matter of the trusts of the will (*Re Pike* [1902] W.N. 42).

Presumptive next of kin contingently entitled and those claiming under them have no sufficient interest to enable them to apply for an injunction to restrain the transfer of stock standing in the names of trustees (*Re Ashton* [1900] W.N. 109).

R50.14.6 **Withdrawal or discharge of stop notice (rr.11–14)**—At the Bank of England the notice withdrawing a stop notice must be signed by the person claiming to be beneficially interested, and his signature must be witnessed by a practising solicitor. This would appear to be the proper practice in all cases.

The notice of withdrawal by the party who put on the *distringas* notice operates immediately.

Order prohibiting transfer, etc. of securities

15.—(1) The court, on the application of any person claiming to be beneficially entitled to an interest in any securities of the kinds set out in section 2(2)(b) of the Act may by order prohibit the Bank of England or other person or body concerned from registering any transfer of the securities or taking any other step to which section 5(5) of the Act applies. **R50.15**

The order shall specify the securities to which the prohibition relates, the name in which they stand and the steps which may not be taken, and shall state whether the prohibition applies to the securities only or to the dividends or interest as well.

(2) An application for an order under this rule must be made by claim form or if made in existing proceedings, in accordance with CPR Part 23 in the Chancery Division.

(3) The court, on the application of any person claiming to be entitled to an interest in any securities to which an order under this rule relates, may vary or discharge the order on such terms (if any) as to costs or otherwise as it thinks fit.

Effect of rule—Under this rule, the Bank of England or other company may be restrained at the instance of a person claiming to be beneficially entitled to an interest in part of their stock from registering any transfer of such stock or paying any dividend or interest in respect thereof, so that it is not necessary to make the Bank of England or other company a party to an action in which an injunction to this effect is sought. **R50.15.1**

The practice is set out in r.15(2) and is by claim form or, if in existing proceedings, by application under CPR Part 23, in either case in the Chancery Division. In an urgent case the injunction can be obtained without notice.

It should be observed that the reference in the Rule to securities of the kinds set out in section 2(2)(b) of the 1979 Act has the effect of enabling stop orders being made on stock "of any state or territory outside the United Kingdom" but it is thought that such an order would be sought only in exceptional circumstances, and in any event such an order may not be made if it would contravene section 13(2) of the State Immunity Act 1978.

RSC ORDER 51

RECEIVERS: EQUITABLE EXECUTION

Contents **R51.0.1**

Editorial Introduction

This Order provides for the appointment of a receiver "by way of equitable execution" and incorporates the provisions of O.30 (Receivers) to that end. For the reasons explained in the notes following r.3, such appointments are rarely necessary nowadays. **R51.0.2**

Related sources

- Supreme Court Act 1981, s.37 (SCP 1999, Vol. 2, Section 20A, para. 20A–231) **R51.0.3**
- RSC, O.30 (Receivers)
- RSC, O.45, r.1 (Enforcement of judgment, etc., for payment of money)
- CCR, O.32 (Receivers)

Forms

The following Prescribed Forms (formerly included amongst the Prescribed Forms in Appendix A to the RSC) are relevant to O.51. These forms are included in Table 2 (Practice Forms) attached to Practice Direction (Forms) and may be found in SCP 1999, Vol. 2, Section 1A, paras 1A–83 *et seq.*: **R51.0.4**

- PF No. 82—Summons for appointment of receiver (r.3)

- PF No. 83—Order directing summons for appointment of receiver and granting injunction meanwhile (r.3)
- PF No. 84—Order appointing receiver by way of equitable execution.

Appointment of receiver by way of equitable execution

R51.1 **1.** Where an application is made for the appointment of a receiver by way of equitable execution, the court in determining whether it is just or convenient that the appointment should be made shall have regard to the amount claimed by the judgment creditor, to the amount likely to be obtained by the receiver and to the probable costs of his appointment and may direct an inquiry on any of these matters or any other matter before making the appointment.

Masters etc. may appoint receiver

R51.2 **2.** A Master and the Admiralty Registrar and a district judge of the Family Division shall have power to make an order for the appointment of a receiver by way of equitable execution and to grant an injunction if, and only so far as, the injunction is ancillary or incidental to such an order.

Application of rules as to appointment of receiver, etc.

R51.3 **3.** An application for the appointment of a receiver by way of equitable execution may be made in accordance with Order 30, rule 1, and rules 2 to 6 of that order shall apply in relation to a receiver appointed by way of equitable execution as they apply in relation to a receiver appointed for any other purpose.

R51.3.1 **When receiver by way of equitable execution necessary**—Because of the greatly increased scope of charging orders the appointment of a receiver by way of equitable execution is rarely necessary nowadays. Before 1925 it was the only means of reaching land in mortgage; and even after 1925 it was the only means of reaching the beneficial interest in land of a joint tenant or tenant in common. But since the Charging Orders Act 1979 a charging order may be imposed on the beneficial interest of a judgment debtor in land, securities or funds in court or under any trust. In the case of an ordinary joint tenant or tenant in common it will nearly always be more just and convenient (and cheaper) to impose a charging order than to appoint a receiver by way of equitable execution. The charging order can then be enforced by an order for sale. However, execution against life interests in trust funds or in land is still more conveniently by way of the appointment of a receiver than the making of a charging order. Likewise for legacies payable under wills. Periodic payments under insurance policies and the like may also be reached by this means. A receiver by way of equitable execution is sometimes appointed of the fittings and furniture of an old persons' home or similar properties where the judgment creditor has a charge over the building but not over the contents to enable the building and its contents to be sold together.

Equitable execution

R51.3.2 **Definition**—There are various interests in property to which a judgment debtor may be entitled, yet which cannot be taken in execution under any of the processes specified in these rules. Such interests may generally be reached by the appointment of a receiver; supplemented, if necessary, by an injunction restraining the judgment debtor from dealing with the property. This subparagraph was cited with approval by Balcombe J. in *Levermore v. Levermore* [1979] 1 W.L.R. 1277; [1980] 1 All E.R. 1 (a case decided before the Charging Orders Act 1979 came into force).

"Equitable execution is a process which the Court allows for the purpose of enabling a judgment creditor to obtain payment of his debt, when the position of the real estate is such that ordinary execution will not reach it" (*per* Chitty, J., *Wills v. Luff* (1888) 38 Ch.D. 197, 200).

The appointment of a receiver of the interest of a judgment debtor in real estate, though sometimes termed "equitable execution", is not a mere form of execution, but it is relief producing the same benefit as execution properly so called, but obtainable only by means of an order of the Court in that behalf, based on the fact that execution so called cannot be had (*Re Shephard* (1890) 43 Ch.D. 131; "Equitable execution is not like legal execution: it is equitable relief, which the Court gives because execution at law cannot be had. It is not execution, but a substitute for execution" (*ibid. per* Bowen L.J., 137) though it has been held to come within the term "execution by process of law". See *Blackman v. Fysh* [1892] 3 Ch. 209.

A receiver ought not to be appointed where there are no impediments to legal execution, and no special circumstances making the appointment "just or convenient" within SCA 1981, s.37, nor where it is shown that there is property which can be taken in legal execution (*Manchester, etc.,*

District Bank v. Parkinson (1888) 22 Q.B.D. 173; and see judgment of Cotton L.J. in *Re Shephard* (1890) 43 Ch.D. 131, 136; and *Harris v. Beauchamp* [1894] 1 Q.B. 801; *Morgan v. Hart* [1914] 2 K.B. 183, CA; *cf. Re Bueb* [1927] W.N. 297). It is "just and convenient" to enforce a claimant's judgment by giving him equitable execution where he cannot get legal execution (*per* Cotton L.J., *Smith v. Cowell* (1881) 6 Q.B.D. 75, 78). And so where impediments exist to ordinary execution, as *e.g.* where the judgment debtor is out of the jurisdiction, and the judgment creditor is unable to take the necessary steps to found garnishee proceedings (*Goldschmidt v. Oberrheinische Metallwerke* [1906] 1 K.B. 373, CA); but not where legal execution is only impeded by a mixture of chattels with those of other persons (*Morgan v. Hart* [1914] 2 K.B. 183). The Court has no jurisdiction to appoint a receiver merely because under the circumstances of the case it would be a more convenient mode of obtaining satisfaction of a judgment than the usual modes of execution (*Harris v. Beauchamp* [1894] 1 Q.B. 801). (The authority of these two decisions is doubtful after *Soinco Saci v. Novokuznetsk Aluminium* [1998] 2 W.L.R. 234, where the judge was prepared to treat the jurisdiction to appoint a receiver by way of equitable execution as a flexible and developing jurisdiction, analogous to the jurisdiction to grant *Mareva* injunctions, which was not to be trammelled by old authorities.) The Court will protect a fund out of which costs have been ordered to be paid by the appointment of a receiver (*Cummins v. Perkins* [1899] 1 Ch. 16); but will not grant equitable execution in respect of untaxed costs.

For jurisdiction-attachable debt see *Bourne v. Colodense* [1985] I.C.R. 291; *Maclaine Watson & Co. Ltd v. International Tin Council* [1989] Ch. 253; [1988] 3 All E.R. 257, CA (no receiver where no cause of action and no assets capable of being taken over by receiver).

Bankruptcy of judgment debtor—See Insolvency Act 1986, ss.285, 286 and n. "Effect of appointment of receiver," below. R51.3.3

Reserve and Auxiliary Forces (Protection of Civil Interests) Act 1951—In the cases covered by this Act no judgment or order for the payment or recovery of a sum of money may be enforced by execution or otherwise without the leave of the Court (s.2(1)). R51.3.4

Effect of appointment of receiver—See Charging Orders Act 1979, s.4, execution against land completed by seizure, by appointment of a receiver, or making of a charging order. See also Insolvency Act 1986, s.346. As to the effect of a foreign insolvency, see *Levasseur v. Mason* [1891] 2 Q.B. 73, CA and as to the effect of a Scottish bankruptcy, see *Singer v. Fry* (1916) 113 L.T. 552; nor does notice of the order create a charge; it has been held not to prevent a bank with notice of the order from paying money on deposit to the credit of the defendant to him (*Giles v. Kruyer* [1921] 3 K.B. 23), but in that case there was a considerable interval in which no step had been taken by the creditor. *Semble* the order ought not to have been made in the first instance over a legal chose in action. The receipt by a person to whom money is due after notice of an order appointing a receiver is punishable as a contempt. R51.3.5

The order operates as an injunction to prevent the judgment debtor receiving the money (*Tyrrell v. Painton* [1895] 1 Q.B. 206) and prevents him from dealing with the money to the prejudice of the judgment creditor, *e.g.* from utilising a debt by way of set-off or counterclaim against a third person (*Ex p. Peak Hill Goldfield* [1909] 1 K.B. 430 at 437, 437; *Ideal Bedding Co. v. Holland* [1907] 2 Ch. 157). It gives priority over stop and charging orders subsequently obtained (*Re Marquis of Anglesey* [1903] 2 Ch. 727).

An assignee for value of a debt has priority over a person who subsequently obtains an order for a receiver by way of equitable execution over such debt, although such order was obtained before notice given to the debtor (*Re Bristow* [1906] 2 Ir.R. 215).

Injunction in aid of equitable execution—In *Archer v. Archer* [1866] W.N. 66, an injunction was granted on the issue of a writ by a wife to recover arrears of maintenance payable under a magistrate's order, to restrain payment of a legacy to the husband. In the Fam D an injunction of this kind is sometimes granted in lieu of equitable execution (*Bullus v. Bullus* (1910) 102 L.T. 399, where an injunction was granted to restrain payment of a legacy to a husband who had not paid his wife's costs). See also *Gillet v. Gillet* (1890) 14 P.D. 158; *Brewis v. Brewis* [1893] W.N. 6; *Dooley v. Dooley* (1911) 56 S.J. 207. See also *Oliver v. Lowther* (1880) 28 W.R. 381, where a divorced husband who had been ordered to pay alimony was restrained from advancing a settlement fund in favour of children. R51.3.6

Procedure generally (rr.1–3)—The procedure for appointment of a receiver by way of equitable execution is the same as that for the appointment of receivers generally. Application is made in accordance with CPR Part 23 (see RSC, O.30). Forms in SCP 1999, Vol. 2 can be adapted to the needs of the case, see Forms Nos 82, 83, and 84. R51.3.7

An order can be made "without notice" or, in cases where there is a danger of the property being dissipated pending the hearing, an injunction may be granted to restrain dealing.

A Master can make an order for the appointment of a receiver by way of equitable execution and for an injunction ancillary or incidental to equitable execution (r.2).

If the applicant seeks an interim injunction he applies without notice but the application must be supported by evidence in the form of a witness statement containing a statement of truth or an affidavit. The statement/affidavit should state:

(1) Date and particulars of the judgment, stating that it remains wholly unsatisfied, or to what extent it remains unsatisfied.
(2) Particulars and result of any execution which has been issued, stating the nature of the sheriff's return (if any).
(3) That the defendant has no property which can be taken by the ordinary process of execution. If he has, give reasons showing that legal execution would be futile.
(4) Particulars of the property as to which it is proposed to appoint a receiver.
(5) The name and address of the receiver proposed to be appointed, and stating that in the deponent's judgment he is a fit and proper person to be appointed receiver.
(6) That the defendant is in pecuniary difficulties [that the immediate appointment of a receiver without the delay of giving security is of great importance] and that the deponent verily believes that the defendant may assign or dispose of his estate or interest in the said [*description of property*] unless restrained from doing so by the order and injunction of the Court.

In London the affidavit is left at Room E16 and the applicant should call for it the next day when the Master's decision will be indorsed.

If the affidavit is sufficient it is discretionary for the Master to give permission to issue an application for the appointment of a receiver returnable in about a week, and to grant an injunction (to be embodied in the application) restraining the defendant from assigning, charging, or otherwise dealing with the property in question until after the hearing of the application. The injunction is not granted as a matter of course in all cases; and will not be granted in the absence of anything to show that there was danger of the property being made away with before the hearing of the application (*Lloyds Bank v. Medway, etc., Co.* [1905] 2 K.B. 359, CA).

It is not always necessary that legal execution should be exhausted before the appointment of a receiver, which will be made if there are special circumstances. For example, if it is shown that legal execution would be futile, but that there is property which could be reached by equitable execution, a receiver may be appointed without legal execution being issued (*Hills v. Webber* (1901) 17 T.L.R. 513, CA).

In a case where no injunction is required (this would be unusual) no permission is needed and the application can be issued pursuant to CPR Pt 23.

R51.3.8 **Security (rr.1–3)**—The giving of security is governed by RSC, O.30, r.2 which provides by para. (1) that the order appointing a receiver may include such directions as the Court thinks fit for the giving of security, by para. (2) for the giving of security when required, by para. (3) that unless otherwise directed, the security shall be by guarantee and by para. (4) for the filing of the guarantee.

The order directing security should be taken to the Masters' Secretary's Department, Room E214, for an appointment to be given before the Master to settle the form of security and the amount thereof. Notice of this appointment must be given to the judgment debtor, who is entitled to have an opportunity of objecting to the sureties and amount of security. The guarantee or undertaking of all recognised guarantee companies will be accepted. A bond might still be required (SCA 1981, s.135). When it is required, it should be given to two Masters, for no Rules were ever published, as they might have been, to indicate any special officer to whom it should be given.

The penalty or amount of security is generally fixed at twice the amount of the gross annual income of the property, or at the amount of the capital money, if any, likely to be paid to the Receiver. On the appointment before the Master the applicant's solicitors must be prepared with the draft guarantee or undertaking for approval, which will be indicated by the Initials of the Master on the draft. For forms, see Ch.M.P.F. No. 30 (guarantee) the appropriate form being adapted when used in QBD; see SCP 1999, Vol. 2, Section 1B, para. 1B–231. When the guarantee has been executed it does not have to be taken to the Inland Revenue for any revenue stamp to be impressed (see Finance Act 1971, s.64). It should be taken to the Masters' Secretary's Department together with the approved draft with the Master's formal approval endorsed upon the document.

If the surety is not one of the usually accepted societies the usual affidavit of justification will have to be made to satisfy the Master that the society is one that should properly be treated as responsible for the purpose. If the surety is a person the Master may require a certificate by the solicitors for the judgment creditor to the effect that the surety is a responsible person. It is not the practice in QBD to issue a formal certificate of completion of security, but if required for good reason an endorsement will be made upon the Order appointing the receiver, as follows: "I certify that the security directed by the within Order has been completed ... Master." For this endorsement application should be made to the Masters' Secretary.

R51.3.9 **Receiver's accounts (rr.1–3)**—These are governed by RSC, O.30, r.5. This provides by para. (1) for a receiver to submit such accounts to such parties at such intervals or dates as the Court may direct, by para. (2) for any party to whom a receiver is required to submit accounts to be able to inspect the receiver's books and papers, by para. (3) for any party who is dissatisfied with the accounts to give a notice of objection and require the receiver to lodge his accounts in Court and by para. (4) for the examination by the Court of any items to which objection is taken.

If an order in the old form requiring the receiver to pass his accounts is made, a simple form of account is accepted provided the items of receipts and payments are dated and numbered and show clearly from or to whom received or paid and for what purpose. As to fees payable see Supreme Court Fees Order 1980, No. 13. The account when impressed with the appropriate judicature fee should be taken, together with the affidavit verifying (for form of affidavit, see Ch.M.P.F. No. 27) to the Masters' Secretary's Department (Room E214) where a form of appointment is stamped on the account. The account is then taken to the Master who will fill in the date of the appointment, notice of which must be given to the other side. By a direction of the Masters (June, 1929) receivers' accounts, together with vouchers, are to be lodged with the Masters' Secretary (Room E214) at least four clear days prior to the appointment before the Master to pass the same, in order that queries may be disposed of before the formal appointment. After the account has been passed by the Master a certificate of such passing is prepared in the Masters' Secretary's Department, and is available, in that department, after signature by the Master. No fee is payable on the certificate. The account and affidavit are sent officially to the Filing Department.

Receiver's remuneration (rr.1–3)—This is governed by RSC, O.30, r.3 which provides that a receiver shall be allowed such proper remuneration as the Court authorises, and empowers the remuneration to be fixed by reference to a scale fee or rate of professional charges. The following memorandum was approved by the King's Bench Masters in June, 1929: **R51.3.10**

> "Where a receiver is appointed by way of equitable execution, unless the Court or a Judge otherwise orders, the total amount to be allowed for costs of the receiver (including his remuneration, the costs of obtaining his appointment, of completing his security (if any) of passing his accounts, and of obtaining his discharge) should not exceed 10 per cent of the amount due under the judgment or the amount recovered by the receiver whichever may be the lesser sum; provided that not less than £5 be allowed unless otherwise ordered, and that where the amount due under the judgment does not exceed £50 the plaintiff or party applying shall be made answerable and the usual security be dispensed with. The amount allowed shall, when required, be apportioned by the Master as between costs and remuneration respectively."

For the form or order limiting the costs, etc., of the receiver, see Form No. 84, SCP 1999, Vol. 2, Section 1A, para. 1A–85.

Where the receiver's remuneration is not limited as above but is required to be fixed, the practice is as follows:

(1) In the case of rent a percentage varying from, say, 2 to 10 per cent is allowed on the gross rents collected varying according to the amount of the rent and circumstances as follows:

- (a) If the rents are large and are payable yearly or half yearly and no undue trouble arises owing to the state of repair or otherwise 2 per cent or slightly over would be allowed.
- (b) If the rents are collected monthly or quarterly, 3 to 5 per cent would be allowed.
- (c) If collected weekly, from 7 to 10 per cent would be allowed.

In each of the above cases the difficulties, trouble and labour involved would be taken into consideration, and although the percentage as above is taken as a guide, it is not slavishly followed, and is only used as means to arrive at a *quantum meruit* or proper remuneration. Moreover, the above figures and percentages would have to be adjusted to accord with modern financial conditions.

(2) In the case of dividends a percentage of 1 to 3 per cent on the gross sums collected would be allowed according to whether the dividends were numerous, or large or small, and in exceptional cases the percentage might be reduced or increased—the percentage being only used to assist in arriving at the proper remuneration.

(3) In other cases a *quantum meruit* allowance is made according to time and trouble involved.

Instances of equitable execution (rr.1–3) **R51.3.11**

Maintenance—A receiver cannot be obtained over sums ordered to be paid as periodical payments and a voluntary allowance by the husband taken into account in fixing the amount of maintenance within this rule (*Walls Ltd v. Legge* [1923] 2 K.B. 240). **R51.3.12**

A receiver by way of equitable execution cannot be appointed of a weekly sum payable under the Domestic Proceedings and Magistrates' Courts Act 1978 (*Paquine v. Snary* [1909] 1 K.B. 688, applying *Watkins v. Watkins* [1896] P. 222).

Debt—The proper form of execution against debts due to the judgment debtor is by attachment of the debt under RSC, O.49. **R51.3.13**

Where a debt was due to a judgment debtor by a party out of the jurisdiction, which could not therefore be attached, Phillimore J. in Chambers made an order for equitable execution, on evidence that the money was about to be sent over to the judgment debtor (*Grahame v. Van Biene*, November 3, 1906 (unrep.); and see *Goldschmidt v. Oberrheinische Metallwerke* [1906] 1 K.B. 373, CA; cited in n. "Definition", para. R51).

Where the judgment creditor had obtained an inquiry as to damages, a receiver was appointed of the sum awarded to the defendant in an arbitration (*Duncan v. Scaife* (1888) 4 T.L.R. 716).

R51.3.14 **Future debts**—A receiver may be appointed of future debts and other after-acquired assets, just as such assets are within the scope of a *Mareva* injunction: *Soinco Saci v. Novokuznetsk Aluminium* [1998] 2 W.L.R. 234. However, future *earnings* are now the subject of statutory regulations by the Attachment of Earnings Act 1971 which must be intended to be a complete code and to exclude any power to appoint a receiver of future earning.

R51.3.15 **Director's fees**—Directors' fees not yet earned are not the subject of equitable execution (*Hamilton v. Brogden* [1891] W.N. 36).

R51.3.16 **Earnings**—See Attachment of Earnings Act 1971.

A receiver appointed at the instance of a judgment creditor of a theatre is not entitled to receive the money paid by the public for entrance fees, though he is entitled to receive the rents and profits of the company's lands and possession of the lands (*Cadogan v. Lyric Theatre* [1894] 3 Ch. 338).

The above cases were followed in *Re Johnson* [1898] 2 Ir.R. 551.

R51.3.17 **Fund in Court**—A receiver may be appointed of a fund in Court, payable to the judgment debtor (*Westhead v. Riley* (1884) 25 Ch.D. 413). In that case the fund was in the Chancery Court of the County Palatine of Lancaster. Only the Division in which the action is pending to the credit of which the fund stands in Court, can make an order dealing with the fund. A receiver, therefore, appointed in the QBD of a fund in Court in the Ch D would have to apply in the latter Division for an order to pay the income to him as receiver, which application would be made in the action to the credit of which the fund stands.

R51.3.18 **Furniture**—It has been held that where legal execution is impracticable only because the debtor's furniture is mixed with that of other persons in a repository there is no jurisdiction to appoint a receiver (*Morgan v. Hart* [1914] 2 K.B. 183, CA, although this should be queried since the *Soinco Saci case* ([1998] 2 W.L.R. 234)). But where furniture of the judgment debtor had been leased with a house which was in mortgage the rent was apportioned (*C. Hoare & Co. v. Hove Bungalows* (1912) 56 S.J. 686, CA).

R51.3.19 **Legacy, etc.**—A receiver can be appointed of a reversionary interest under a will (*Fuggle v. Bland* (1883) 11 Q.B.D. 711; *Tyrrell v. Painton* [1895] 1 Q.B. 202; *Ideal Bedding Co. v. Holland* [1907] 2 Ch. 157); and of a sufficient portion of a legacy, expectant on the death of a tenant for life, to satisfy the judgment debt (*Macnicoll v. Parnell* (1887) 35 W.R. 773; and of the income of a trust fund (*Webb v. Stenton* (1883) 11 Q.B.D. 518 at 530).

R51.3.20 **Partnership**—See RSC, O.81, r.10.

R51.3.21 **Salaries and pensions**—Pay and pensions of officers and other ranks, being rendered inalienable by the Army Act 1881, cannot be taken in execution by the appointment of a receiver or in any other way (*Lucas v. Harris* (1887) Q.B.D. 127); even where the pension has been intercepted by the officer's trustee in bankruptcy, and remains in his hands on the annulment of the bankruptcy (*Crowe v. Price* (1889) 22 Q.B.D. 429); but *secus*, as to money awarded in commutation of a pension (*ibid.*). See Army Act 1955, s.203 and the Attachment of Earnings Act 1971, s.24(2)(b).

Quaere, as to remuneration of a member of Parliament (see *Hollinshead v. Hazleton* [1916] 1 A.C. 428).

R51.3.22 **Value**—It has been held that a receiver will not be appointed over property in which the interest of the debtor is of nominal or very small value (*Walls Ltd v. Legge* [1923] 2 K.B. 240, 245, CA).

R51.3.23 **Vendor and purchaser**—A purchaser who has merely paid a deposit has not such an interest in land as can be reached by a receivership order obtained by his judgment creditor (*Ridout v. Fowler* [1904] 1 Ch. 658; 2 Ch. 93, CA).

R51.3.24 **Priorities**—A judgment creditor who has obtained equitable execution subject to existing incumbrances, obtains no priority by giving notice to the trustees of the debtor (*Arden v. Arden* (1885) 29 Ch.D. 702).

An order granting equitable execution over a fund in Court if not completed, even though followed by a stop order, gives no priority over a subsequent charging order of which notice has been given to the Accountant General (*Fahey v. Tobin* [1901] 1 Ir.R. 511).

Relief against receiver—It has been held that if a receiver appointed by way of equitable execution exceeds his powers or acts improperly, any person prejudiced thereby should apply for relief in the action in which the receiver was appointed, and should not commence an independent action for an injunction to restrain the receiver (*Searle v. Choat* (1884) 25 Ch.D. 723). Nevertheless, it is submitted that a person damnified, if a stranger to the action, is not limited to that remedy. R51.3.25

RSC ORDER 52

COMMITTAL

Contents R52.0.1

Editorial Introduction

The Court's power to punish for contempt of court may be exercised by an order for committal to prison (r.1) or by other means such as a fine (r.9). However, in punishing a contempt the court's powers are limited and the full range of sentencing options available to a criminal court are not available: for example, there is no power to impose a community penalty. The common law power to commit for an indefinite term has been abolished and committal must be for a fixed term which cannot exceed two years (Contempt of Court Act 1981, s.14). R52.0.2

Contempt can be either a civil contempt (*e.g.* disobedience of a court order) or a criminal contempt (*e.g.* disrupting court proceedings) and can take a multiplicity of different forms—see further Summary of types of contempt in commentary to O.52, r.1.

The rules in O.52 provide that in certain circumstances a committal order may be made only by a Divisional Court (rr.2 and 3) but in others may be made by a single judge (rr.1 and 4). In certain cases the application may be heard in private (r.6). Execution of an order may be suspended (r.7): this means, for example, that a sentence of imprisonment can be suspended and the restrictions which govern such sentences in the criminal courts do not apply. The court may summarily commit for contempt "in the face of the court" (r.5).

The court has power to discharge a contemnor prior to completion of sentence (r.8). There is a right of appeal which, in the case of civil contempt, is available to both applicant and contemnor (see section 13 of the AJA 1960 and RSC, O.59 r.20). Order 52 is supplemented by a Practice Direction—Committal Applications; see post. It applies to any application for an order for committal of a person to prison for contempt of court (a "committal application" where an alleged contempt concerns the county court the application may be made to the county court in question but otherwise to the High Court—see Practice Direction paras 1.1 to 1.3 post.

Related sources R52.0.3

- Contempt of Court Act 1981 (SCP 1999, Vol. 2, section 13A)
- Criminal Justice Act 1991, s.45
- Administration of Justice Act 1960, s.13
- RSC, O.45, r.5 (Enforcement of judgment to do or abstain from doing any act)
- RSC, O.57 (Divisional Court proceedings, etc: supplementary provisions)
- RSC, O.59, r.20 (Appeals in cases of Contempt of Court)
- CCR, O.29 (Committal for Breach of order of Undertaking)
- Practice Direction (Committal Applications) (see para. R52PD–001)

Forms

The following Prescribed Form (formerly included amongst the Prescribed Forms in Appendix A to the RSC) are relevant to O.52. These forms are included in Table 2 (Practice Forms) attached to Practice Direction (Forms) and may be found in SCP 1999, Vol. 2, Section 1A, para. 1A–86): R52.0.4

- PF No. 85—Order of committal (O.52).

The following Queen's Bench Masters' Practice Forms (now listed in Table 2 (Practice Forms) attached to Practice Direction (Forms)) are relevant to O.52 (Vol. 2, Section 1B, paras 1B–74 to 1B–76):

- PF103—Warrant of committal (general) (O.52)

- PF104—Warrant of committal (in face of court) (O.52)
- PF105—Warrant for committal (failure of witness to attend) (O.52)

Committal for contempt of court

R52.1 **1.**—(1) The power of the High Court or Court of Appeal to punish for contempt of court may be exercised by an order of committal.

(2) Where contempt of court—

(a) is committed in connection with—

(i) any proceedings before a Divisional Court of the Queen's Bench Division; or

(ii) criminal proceedings, except where the contempt is committed in the face of the court or consists of disobedience to an order of the court or a breach of an undertaking to the court; or

(iii) proceedings in an inferior court; or

(b) is committed otherwise than in connection with any proceedings, then, subject to paragraph (4), an order of committal may be made only by a Divisional Court of the Queen's Bench Division.

This paragraph shall not apply in relation to contempt of the Court of Appeal.

(3) Where contempt of Court is committed in connection with any proceedings in the High Court, then, subject to paragraph (2), an order of committal may be made by a single judge of the Queen's Bench Division except where the proceedings were assigned or subsequently transferred to some other Division, in which case the order may be made only by a single judge of that other Division.

The reference in this paragraph to a single judge of the Queen's Bench Division shall, in relation to proceedings in any court the judge or judges of which are, when exercising the jurisdiction of that court, deemed by virtue of any enactment to constitute a court of the High Court, be construed as a reference to a judge of that court.

(4) Where by virtue of any enactment the High Court has power to punish or take steps for the punishment of any person charged with having done any thing in relation to a court, tribunal or person which would, if it had been done in relation to the High Court, have been a contempt of that court, an order of committal may be made by a single judge of the Queen's Bench Division.

R52.1.1 **"The power ... to punish for contempt of court"**—The term "contempt of court" is of ancient origin having been used in England certainly since the thirteenth century and probably earlier. It is based not on any exaggerated notion of the dignity of individuals be they judges, witnesses or others but on the duty of preventing any attempt to interfere with the administration of justice (see *Attorney General v. Times Newspapers Ltd* [1991] 2 W.L.R. 994, HL).

Although a finding of contempt cannot be made against the Crown directly it may be made against a government department or against a minister of the Crown both in his official and personal capacity (*Re M* [1993] 3 W.L.R. 433).

R52.1.2 **Civil and criminal contempts**—In *Att-Gen v. Newspaper Publishing plc* [1988] Ch. 333, Sir John Donaldson M.R. said:

> "Despite its protean nature, contempt has been classified under two heads, 'civil contempt' and 'criminal contempt'. Whatever the value of this classification in earlier times, I venture to think that it now tends to mislead rather than assist, because the standard of proof is the same, namely the criminal standard and there are now common rights of appeal. Of greater assistance is a reclassification as (a) conduct which involves a breach, or assisting in the breach, of a court order and (b) any other "conduct which involves an interference with the due administration of justice, either in a particular case, or more generally, as a continuing process, the first category being a special form of the latter, such interference being a characteristic common to all contempts; per Lord Diplock in *Att-Gen v. Leveller Magazine Ltd* [1979] AC 440 at 449. What distinguishes the two categories is that in general conduct which involves a breach, or assisting in the breach, of a court order is treated as a matter for the

parties to raise by complaint to the court, whereas other forms of contempt are in general considered to be a matter for the Attorney-General to raise. In doing so he acts not as a government minister or legal adviser, but as the guardian of the public interest in the due administration of justice."

Civil contempt is not a criminal offence (*Cobra Golf Ltd v. Rata* [1998] Ch. 109) but the standard of proof in all forms of contempt is the criminal standard i.e. proof beyond a reasonable doubt (*Dean v. Dean* [1987] 1 F.L.R. 517; *Att-Gen v. Newspaper Publishing plc*, above). The chief instance of civil contempt (or "contempt in procedure") is disobedience to an order of the Court by a party to the proceedings; the chief instances of criminal contempt are contempt *in facie curiae* by any person (*e.g.* by hurling abuse or an object at the Court) and conduct obstructing or calculated to prejudice the due administration of justice (see the cases as to this distinction collected in *Re Bahama Islands* [1893] A.C. 138 at 146; and *Seldon v. Wilde* [1911] 1 K.B. 701, CA; *Miller v. Knox* (1838) 4 Bing. N.C. 574, at 587 *et seq*). The distinction remains in force (a) in regard to privilege from arrest (as to which see para. R52.7.5); (b) in regard to the principle (rarely heard of) that the prerogative of the Crown extends to remission of a sentence for criminal, not civil contempt: and (c) in regard to the principle that a civil contempt can be waived, for if the party for whose benefit an order was made is content that it should not be performed, the Court has generally no interest to interfere (see *Roberts v. Albert Bridge Co.* (1873) L.R. 8 Ch. 753; *Anon.* (1809) 15 Ves. 174; *Woodward v. Twinaine* (1840) 8 Sim. 301; and *R. v. Newton* (1903) 19 T.L.R. 627, a criminal contempt).

Order of committal—This is a process under which the contemnor is seized, under order of the Court, by a Court official (normally the tipstaff or his deputy, or, if a tipstaff is not available, an usher) or by a police officer acting as his assistant, and taken to prison. For the Form of Warrant, which is signed by the judge making the order, see SCP 1999, Vol. 2, Section 1B, paras 1B–74 *et seq.* **R52.1.3**

Form of order of committal—The form required to be used for a committal order for contempt of court (see SCP 1999, Vol. 2, Section 1A, Form No. 85, para. 1A–86) requires that the contempt be stated. That requirement must be strictly complied with by setting out in detail the acts constituting the contempt (*Chiltern District Council v. Keane* [1985] 1 W.L.R. 619; [1985] 2 All E.R. 118, CA). The period of imprisonment must be stated in the order. **R52.1.4**

In particular the following points should be noted: the order must state the contempt and must make clear to whom the order is directed and what that person must do to comply with it (*Re C (A Minor)* (1985) *The Times*, November 15); the contemnor must be able to see from the face of the order what it is that he is being committed for (*Parra v. Rones* (1986) 16 Fam. Law 262, CA); the particulars of the contempt set out in the order must not contain references to matters not comprised in the affidavits in support of the application for committal, since the contemnor has had no notice of those matters (*Tabone v. Seguna* [1986] 1 F.L.R. 591, CA) and must conform with the oral judgment given by the Court making the order (*Re C (A Minor)* (above)). An order for committal which fails to specify the contempt for which it has been made is fundamentally defective and the Court of Appeal may decline to cure the defect by exercising its powers under RSC O. 59, r. 10(3): *Linkleter v Linkleter* (1988) 18 Fam Law 93 but see further per Lord Woolf MR in *Nicholls v. Nicholls* [1997] 1 W.L.R. 314. If the contemnor was present at the committal proceedings the Court of Appeal may decide to rectify the order; if he was not it is likely to order a re-trial.

A committal order based on contempts proved by the judge which are not set out in the committal notice is invalid (*Javadi-Babreh v. Javadi Babreh, The Independent*, November 16, 1992 (Stuart-Smith, Simon Brown L.JJ.)).

Recent authorities make clear that O.59, r.10(3) and s.13(3) of the Administration of Justice Act 1960 give a court the power to rectify procedural defects both in the procedure leading up to the making of the order and after it has been made. That discretion must be exercised so as to best reflect the requirements of justice. The court must not only take into account the interests of the contemnor but also the interests of the other parties and the interest of upholding the reputation of civil justice in general. It is no longer appropriate to regard an order for committal as being no more than a form of execution available to another party. The court itself has a very substantial interest in seeing that its orders are upheld. If orders are set aside on purely technical grounds this will undermine the system of justice and the credibility of court orders. As long as the order made by the judge is valid the approach of the court will be to uphold the order in the absence of any prejudice or injustice to the contemnor (*Nicholls v. Nicholls* [1997] 1 W.L.R. 314 (Lord Woolf M.R.; Auld & Ward L.JJ.)).

Other remedies for contempt of court—See r.9, *post.* Apart from the power to imprison for contempt, there is jurisdiction to fine or to take security for good behaviour. For the latter power, see *Skipworth and the Defendant's Case* (1873) L.R. 9 Q.B. 230 at 241. Information or indictment is also applicable in a case of criminal contempt (*Schreiber v. Lateward* (1781) 2 Dickens 592; *R. v. Gray* [1900] 2 Q.B. 36; *R. v. Ribbits* [1902] 1 K.B. 77 at 87; *Att.-Gen. v. Butterworth* [1963] 1 Q.B. 696 at 728; [1962] 3 All E.R. 326 at 334, CA; but see *R. v. Parke* [1903] 2 K.B. 442 at 443; *R. v. Davies* [1906] 1 K.B. 32 at 41); and the Court, instead of committing, may take the more lenient course of granting an injunction against repetition of the act of contempt (*Kitcat v. Sharp* (1882) 52 L.J.Ch. 134; *Coats v. Chadwick* [1894] 1 Ch. 347 at 349; *Cronmire v. Daily Bourse* (1892) 9 T.L.R. 101); and **R52.1.5**

the injunction may be granted against a person not a party to the action (*Lewis v. James* (1887) 3 T.L.R. 527). It has been held that the remedy against a stranger to the action, for aiding and abetting a breach of an injunction or undertaking, is to apply for committal or sequestration and not an injunction, even though the Court may take the more lenient course of granting an injunction instead. All that is required is that the aiders and abettors should be given notice of the terms of the injunction or undertaking (*Elliott v. Klinger* [1967] 1 W.L.R. 1165; [1967] 3 All E.R. 141). The assets of a company may be sequestrated. A witness damnified by contemptuous conduct may even have a civil claim for damages (*Att.-Gen. v. Butterworth*, above, 696 at 719; but see *Chapman v. Honig* [1963] 2 Q.B. 502; [1963] 2 All E.R. 513, CA). But a breach of an undertaking given by a party to the Court does not necessarily give rise to a cause of action by the other party against him (see *Re Hudson* [1966] Ch. 207; [1966] 1 All E.R. 110).

It is a general principle that process by way of contempt should not be lightly employed, and not in aid of a civil remedy where some other method of achieving justice is available (*Re Clement* (1877) 46 L.J.Ch. 375; *Danchevsky v. Danchevksy* [1975] Fam. 17; [1974] 3 All E.R. 9334, CA).

R52.1.6 **Contempt proceedings and criminal proceedings arising from same facts**—It is a well-established principle that the jurisdiction of the Court in contempt proceedings arises out of its inherent jurisdiction to enforce its own orders and is quite separate from any criminal proceedings, notwithstanding that they arise out of the same set of facts, and therefore, since contempt proceedings should be dealt with swiftly and decisively, the Court should not generally adjourn the contempt proceedings until any pending criminal proceedings arising out of the same circumstances have been completed (*Szczepanski v. Szczepanski* [1985] F.L.R. 468, CA; *Caprice v. Boswell* (1986) 16 Fam. Law 52, CA). In particular contempt proceedings for breach of a non molestation order should be dealt with swiftly and decisively and should not be adjourned pending the outcome of the criminal proceedings where no real risk of prejudice has been established *Keeber v. Keeber* (*The Times*, July 14, 1995 (Butler-Sloss & Otton L.JJ.)). However, the need to deal promptly with contempt proceedings does not remove a Judge's discretion to decide whether serious prejudice would be caused by proceeding with the hearing of contempt proceedings before the conclusion of criminal proceedings arising out of the same incident (*Harris v. Crisp* (1992) *The Times*, August 12 (Neill, Butler-Sloss and Mann L.JJ.)).

R52.1.7 **Summary of types of contempt**—For a modern summary of contempt, see *Att-Gen v. Times Newspapers Ltd* [1992] 1 A.C. 191. For criminal contempt see further Archbold: *Criminal Pleading Evidence and Practice 1999* para 20–30 *et seq.* In the following summary those lettered A to H inc. are civil; the remainder are criminal (note letter I, contempt pursuant to r. 32.14 CPR).

R52.1.8 *A. Failure to carry out an undertaking given to the Court*—Service of the order containing the undertaking is not necessary in order to enforce the undertaking by committal; it is sufficient that the defendant has notice of the order (*D. v. A. & Co.* [1900] 1 Ch. 484). The fact that a party who is in breach of an undertaking has acted on legal advice may be regarded as a mitigating circumstance, but cannot be relied upon as a matter of course as complete mitigation (*Re Mileage Conference Group of the Tyre Manufacturers' Conference Ltd's Agreement* [1966] 1 W.L.R. 1137; [1966] 2 All E.R. 849, RPC). In order to establish a contempt of court by a party it is sufficient to prove that his conduct is intentional and that he knows all the facts which make it a breach of the undertaking or order; it is not necessary to prove that he appreciates that his conduct is in fact a breach of the undertaking or order (*Spectravest Inc. v. Aperknit Ltd* [1988] F.S.R. 161). Where, by an undertaking or interlocutory order, a defendant is required to refrain from "infringing the plaintiff's copyright," this means the copyright which the plaintiff claims to have, and requires the subsistence and ownership of the copyright to be assumed; it is not open to the defendant to argue questions relating to the subsistence and ownership of the copyright in committal proceedings (*ibid.*).

In order to enforce a negative undertaking it is not necessary that the order containing the undertaking should be drawn, indorsed with a penal notice and served personally in accordance with O.45. Such an undertaking is a promise to the Court, as a result of which the Court has taken a particular course, whether by judgment or order or otherwise, and the Court has the same power to punish a breach of the undertaking as a contempt as it has to punish a breach of an injunction. Therefore the Court can enforce a negative undertaking by using the appropriate remedies for contempt, provided only that the alleged contemnor knows of the undertaking given on his behalf (*Camden Borough Council v. Alpenoak Ltd* (1985) 135 New L.J. 1209). As to procedure on an application to commit for breach of an undertaking, see para. R52.4.3 below, "Service of notice".

Where an undertaking is unqualified in its terms, and it is proved that the party giving the undertaking has not complied with it, it is no answer to a contempt charge to prove that the non-compliance was casual, inadvertent or accidental, rather than deliberate; such features go only to the question of what, if any, penalty should be imposed (*West Oxfordshire District Council v. Beratec Ltd, The Times*, October 30, 1986).

A fine imposed jointly and severally on a company and one of its directors for contempt for breaches of undertakings, is wrong in principle. Each defendant should be considered separately (*McMillan Graham Printers Ltd v. RR (UK) Ltd, The Times*, March 19, 1993 (Nourse, Stuart-Smith and Waite L.JJ.)).

Great care should be taken in drawing up orders to ensure that undertakings are drafted in clear and precise terms so as to avoid long arguments about whether breaches have occurred (*O'Neill v. Murray, The Times,* October 15, 1990, CA).

A breach of an undertaking to the court may constitute a contempt and an abuse of its process, irrespective of the contemnor's intentions (*Miller v. Scorey* [1996] 1 W.L.R. 1122; [1996] 3 All E.R. 18) even where, for example, a client is in ignorance of the effect of an implied undertaking given by his solicitor (*Watkins v. A. J. Wright (Electrical) Ltd, The Times,* July 15, 1996, *per* Blackburn J.).

B. Failure of a solicitor to carry out an undertaking given by him in his capacity as solicitor—even if not given to or in the presence of the Court or to a party to the suit or to his own client (see SCP 1999, Vol. 2, Section 15, Solicitors, "Jurisdiction to enforce undertakings given by solicitors", para. 15G–6). **R52.1.9**

For the purpose of an application to commit a solicitor for contempt for breach of an order restraining him from destroying or altering any document, the word "document" includes information stored in the hard disk of a computer and the word "page" includes "screen". (*Alliance and Leicester Building Society v. Ghahramani* [1992] RVR 198; (1992) *The Independent,* March 9 (Hoffmann J.).

C. Disobedience to a judgment or order for the payment of money (other than for the payment of money into court) within a time specified—subject to the provisions of the Debtors Acts 1869 and 1878 (RSC, O.45, rr.1(1) and 5(1)(a)). **R52.1.10**

D. Disobedience to a judgment or order for the payment of money into court within a time specified—(subject as in C.) (RSC, O.45, rr.1(2) and 5(1)(a)). **R52.1.11**

E. Disobedience to a judgment or order to do any act within a time specified (RSC, O.45, r.5(1)(a)).—Such order would include an order of mandamus (see, *e.g. R. v. Leicester Guardians* (1899) 81 L.T. 559; *R. v. Worcester Corporation* (1903) 98 J.P. 130) or an order to attend for cross-examination if, but only if, conduct money has been tendered (*In the estate of Harvey* [1907] P. 239). Casual or unintentional disobedience to an order will not usually justify an order of committal; it must be contumacious (*Fairclough v. Manchester Ship Canal Co.* [1897] W.N. 7, CA, CA; *Steiner Products Ltd v. Willy Steiner, Ltd* [1966] 1 W.L.R. 986; [1966] 2 All E.R. 387). Thus an applicant who seeks to commit a person for breach of an injunction must establish a deliberate or wilful breach of a Court order beyond reasonable doubt (*Deborah Building Equipment v. Scaffco, The Times,* November 5, 1986). The High Court also has however a discretionary power to commit a contemnor to prison for negligently failing to comply with an injunction. It is not therefore automatically available at the demand of the claimant whose rights have been infringed. Thus it had been rightly refused to evict gypsies from green belt land where no other site was available because of the County Council's failure to perform its statutory duty to provide suitable caravan sites for gypsies (*Guildford Borough Council v. Valler, The Times,* October 15, 1993 (Russell, Staighton and Steyn L.JJ.)). **R52.1.12**

Where the judgment or order is against a body corporate, a director or other officer of the body may be committed (r.5(1)(iii)). The company itself cannot be committed but it can be fined (*R. v. Hammond & Co. Ltd* [1914] 2 K.B. 866). Since a company is not a physical person it can only act by its agents and falls to be judged by its actions and not simply by its words. A company can be held to be in contempt where an order is disobeyed as a result of a deliberate act by one of its employees (*Director General of Fair Trading v. Pioneer Concrete (U.K.) Ltd & Another* [1994] 3 W.L.R. 1249).

Failure to comply with certain orders, etc., peculiar to probate matters is punishable by committal—*e.g.* a citation to take a grant when the citee (an executor) has intermeddled in the estate (*Mordaunt v. Clarke* (1869) 1 P. & D. 592; *Re Lister* (1894) 70 L.T. 812; *Re Coates* (1898) 78 L.T. 820); a subpoena to bring in a will (*Simmons v. Deane* (1858) 27 L.J.P. 103; *Parkinson v. Thornton* (1868) 37 L.J.P. 3); a citation to bring in a grant (*Evans v. Evans* (1893) 67 L.T. 719); and an order to file an inventory (*Baker v. Baker* (1860) 2 S. & T. 380; *Marsham v. Brookes* (1863) 32 L.J.P. 95).

F. Disobedience to a judgment or order to abstain from doing an act (RSC, O.45, r.5(1)(b)).—Where the judgment or order is against a body corporate, a director or other officer may be committed (O.45, r.5(1)(iii)). **R52.1.13**

G. Disobedience to a judgment or order for the giving of possession of land within a time specified (RSC, O.45, r.3)—subject to the requirement of the leave of the Court to issue a writ of possession, except in a mortgage action to which O.88 applies. **R52.1.14**

H. Disobedience to a judgment or order for the delivery of any goods within a time specified which does not give the alternative of paying the assessed value (O.45, r.4(1)).—Where there is a breach of an order to do an act by a certain date, such as the delivery of goods, and non-compliance has been visited with imprisonment for contempt, a continuing breach cannot **R52.1.15** thereafter be the subject matter of a further committal under the same order. If the failure by the alleged contemnor has continued it is necessary to return to court and obtain a new order (*Kumari v. Jalal* [1997] 1 W.L.R. 97, CA; [1996] 4 All E.R. 65).

R52.1.16 *I. Making a false statement in a document verified by a statement of truth*—(see CPR, r.32.14).

R52.1.17 *J. Contempt in the face of the court.*—The summary procedure to deal with contempt in the face of the court is unique in English law (see Mustill LJ in *R. v. Griffin* 88 Cr.App R 63 at 67). The nature of the jurisdiction was reviewed in *Balogh v. St Albans Crown Court* [1975] Q.B. 73; [1974] 3 All E.R. 283, CA. Examples of this type of contempt are: assaulting (*Re Cosgrave* (1887)) or insulting (*R. v. Jordan* (1888) 36 W.R. 797, CA) the presiding Judge; seizing a document in the hands of the Court during the hearing and carrying it away in defiance of the Court (*Watt v. Ligertwood* (1874) L.R. 2 HL(Sc.) 361); a barrister becoming a party to a fraud and conducting his case so as intentionally to deceive the Court (*Linwool v. Andrews* (1888) 58 L.T. 612); a solicitor deceiving the Court (*R. v. Weisz, ex p. Macdonald (Hectar)* [1951] 2 K.B. 661; [1951] 2 All E.R. 408); assault on a solicitor within the precincts of the Court (*Re Johnson* (1887) 20 Q.B.D. 68); and see *Apted v. Apted and Bliss* [1930] P. 246; *Kirk v. Kirk and Gundy* (1934) 150 L.T. 514, and rr.1(1) and 5. Service of process within the precincts of the Court is not necessarily contempt (*R. v. Jones, ex p. McVittie* [1931] 1 K.B. 664).

The provisions of s.12 of the Contempt of Court Act 1981 give a good indication of the type of behaviour which may amount to contempt in the face of the court at common law. Thus a wolf whistle directed at a juror returning into court was potentially insulting, offensive and a serious interference with the administration of justice. Jurors did not come to courts in order to have comments made about their personal appearance. The appropriate penalty was a moderate fine or detention until the end of the day or over the luncheon adjournment (*R. v. Powell* (1993) *The Times*, June 3 (Staughton L.J., Popplewell and Laws JJ.)).

Contempt committed before a Judge in Chambers, Master or District Judge is punishable by a Judge in Court.

R52.1.18 *K. Words, written or spoken, scandalising the Court*—"Personal scurrilous abuse of a Judge as Judge"—very rare in fact—is contempt (*R. v. Gray* [1900] 2 Q.B. 36; *McLeod v. St Aubyn* [1899] A.C. 549 at 551). Statements to the effect that the accused in a criminal case will not get a fair trial are a contempt (*Skipworth's Case* (1873) L.R. 9 Q.B. 230) but libellous or misleading criticisms on the conduct of a Judge, after the trial, are not necessarily contempt (*Re Bahama Islands* [1893] A.C. 138; *Dunn v. Bevan* [1922] 1 Ch. 276). Criticism of the Court or its decisions, in the course of the exercise of the right of free speech, even if it is inaccurate is not a contempt of Court (*R. v. Commissioners of Police of the Metropolis, ex p. Blackburn (No. 2)* [1968] 2 Q.B. 150; [1968] 1 All E.R. 763, CA). See also *R. v. Lefroy* (1873) L.R.Q.B. 134; *Re Sarbadhicary* (1906) 23 T.L.R. 180, P.C.; *R. v. Editor of New Statesman* (1928) 44 T.L.R. 301). Communications by letter to a Judge or officer of the Court intended to influence a decision are a contempt (*Lechmere Charlton's Case* (1837) 2 My. & Cr. 316; and see *Martin's Case* (1747) 2 Russ. & M. 674; *Re Dyce Sombre* (1844) 1 Mac. & G. 116, 122).

R52.1.19 *L. Words written or spoken, calculated to interfere with the course of justice*—This branch of the subject has given rise to some controversy as it involves restriction upon freedom of speech. The law has been discussed and explained in *Att.-Gen. v. Times Newspapers Ltd* [1974] A.C. 273; [1973] 3 All E.R. 54, HL and *F. (orse A.) (A Minor)* [1977] Fam. 58; [1976] 3 All E.R. 74, CA.

Two distinct types of contempt are involved:

(a) Publications which create a substantial risk that the course of justice in proceedings that are active will be impeded or prejudiced. This type of contempt is now dealt with by the Contempt of Court Act 1981 (see SCP 1999, Vol. 2, Section 13A) which should be consulted. To impede is to retard, slow down, delay, hinder or obstruct. To prejudice is to say or do that which is detrimental or injurious to the interests of that thing or person (see *Attorney General v. British Broadcasting Corporation* [1992] C.O.D. 264). The consent of the Attorney-General is required for proceedings to punish contempt of this kind (s.7 *ibid.*). For the defence of bona fide discussion of public affairs, see s.5, *ibid.*, and *Att.-Gen. v. English* [1983] A.C. 116; [1982] 2 All E.R. 903, HL. Such prejudice may be by influencing the tribunal, or potential jurors for or against a party, or by putting pressure on parties or witnesses or by other means. Examples are: (i) publication by a newspaper before the trial of the result of its own investigation into a crime (*R. v. Evening Standard* (1924) 40 T.L.R. 833); (ii) inciting public opinion against a party so as to affect his conduct of the case or the assertion of his rights (*Att.-Gen. v. Times Newspapers Ltd*, above; publications of the amount paid into Court by a defendant (*R. v. Wealdstone News and Harrow News* [1925] W.N. 154); (iii) publishing, during the course of a criminal trial before a jury, information revealing that the accused had committed other offences besides those for which he was being tried (*R. v. Border Television Ltd, ex p. Att.-Gen.* (1978) 122 S.J. 162). The mischief is the risk of prejudice to a fair trial; the Court requires to be satisfied that the proceedings are genuine (*R. v. Editor of the Daily Mail, ex p. Factor* (1928) 44 T.L.R. 303) and that risk of prejudice is real (*R. v. Ingrams, ex p. Goldsmith* [1976] 10 C.L. 309a; (1976) 120 S.J. 835). It is a defence, by section 3 of the Contempt of Court Act 1981, to show that the publisher of offending material, having taken all reasonable care, did not know and had no reason to believe that proceedings were active.

(b) Publication of matters which the law or the Court has decided should be kept confidential in the interests of justice. Even when sitting in open court the Court may direct, in the interests of justice, that some matter should not be published; knowingly to frustrate a clear direction, properly given, will be a contempt (*Att.-Gen. v. Leveller Magazine Ltd* [1979] A.C. 440; [1979] 1 All E.R. 745, HL). The mischief is the unauthorised disclosure of confidential matter, irrespective of whether it will prejudice the fair trial of proceedings. It is necessary to establish that the offender had guilty knowledge, that is, knew, or must be taken to have known, that publication was not permitted (*F. (orse A.) (A Minor)*, above). The Court has a discretion to permit disclosure of evidence given in camera (*Re R. (M. J.)* [1975] Fam. 89; [1975] 2 All E.R. 749).

The Contempt of Court Act 1981 has given to courts express power to order the postponement of publication of their proceedings of such publication and might create a substantial risk of prejudice to the administration of justice in those proceedings (s.4(2)); a Court may also prohibit publication of any matter (such as a name) which it allowed to be withheld from the public during the proceedings (s.14). It appears reasonably clear from the judgments of Shaw and Ackner L.JJ. in *R. v. Horsham JJ., ex p. Farquharson* [1982] Q.B. 762; [1982] 2 All E.R. 269 that a disregard of any such order or prohibition would be a contempt of court.

Where the court is contemplating the making or continuance of an order under s.4(2) of the 1981 Act, prohibiting the publication of any matter, it has a discretionary power to hear representations from the press, and should ordinarily do so when the press ask to be heard (*R. v. Clerkenwell Magistrates' Court, ex p. The Telegraph Plc* [1993] 2 W.L.R. 233 (Mann L.J. and Leonard J.)).

In an application under s.4(2) of the Contempt of Court Act 1981, the Court must first consider whether there is a substantial risk of prejudice and then, secondly, whether it was necessary to make an order for avoiding such a risk. In determining whether publication of matter would cause a substantial risk of prejudice to a future trial, a court should credit the jury with the will and ability to abide by the judge's direction to decide the case only on the evidence before them. The court should also bear in mind that the staying power and detail of publicity, even in cases of notoriety, are limited and that the nature of a trial is to focus the jury's minds on the evidence put before them, rather than on matters outside the courtroom. The Court of Appeal's function on an appeal under s.159 of the Criminal Justice Act 1988 was to form its own view on the material before it (*Ex p. The Telegraph Plc* [1993] 1 W.L.R. 980 (Lord Taylor of Gosforth C.J.; Auld and Curtiss JJ.)).

In cases where no active steps had been taken in any prosecution against a plaintiff (so that the strict liability rule under sections 1 and 2 of the Contempt of Court Act 1981 did not apply), but it was sought to restrain publication of material on the ground of contempt of court at common law, it is necessary for the court to be sure that (a) publication would create a risk of real prejudice if and when the prosecution proceeded and (b) the material would be published with the specific intention of causing that risk (*Coe v. Central Television, Cook and Thorne* (1993), *The Independent*, August 11 (Glidewell, Butler-Sloss and Kennedy L.JJ.)).

M. Acts calculated to prejudice the due course of justice—may constitute contempt, whether committed before, during or after the proceedings (*Att.-Gen. v. Butterworth* [1963] 1 Q.B. 696; [1962] 3 All E.R. 326). So, interference with solicitors (*Re Johnson* (1887) 20 Q.B.D. 68, CA); parties (*Smith v. Lakeman* (1856) 2 Jur.(N.S.) 1202); *Att.-Gen. v. Times Newspapers Ltd* [1974] A.C. 273; witnesses (*Bromilow v. Phillips* (1891) 40 W.R. 220)—for example, by victimising persons who have given evidence (*Att.-Gen. v. Butterworth*; *Chapman v. Honig* [1963] 2 Q.B. 502; [1963] 2 All E.R. 513, CA)—or are likely to give evidence, or by publishing the name of a witness in a blackmail case contrary to the order of the judge (*R. v. Socialist Worker Printers, etc. Ltd* [1975] Q.B. 637; [1975] 1 All E.R. 142). Interference with jurors or the impersonation of a juror may be contempt and the principles set out in *A.G. v. Butterworth* apply equally to jurors. *H.M. Attorney General v. Jackson* [1994] C.O.D. 169 (Mann L.J. and Holland J.); *H.M. Attorney General v. Judd* [1995] C.O.D. 15 (Steyn L.J. and Kay J.). An offer of money to a bankrupt to suppress evidence at his public examination is a contempt (*Re Hooley, Rucker's Case* (1899) 79 L.T. 306). A third person aiding a party to flout an injunction may be guilty of contempt (*Seaward v. Paterson* [1897] 1 Ch. 545, CA; *Hubbard v. Woodfield* (1913) 57 S.J. 529). R52.1.20

A person seeking by threats to induce a prosecutor to withdraw a private prosecution may be guilty of contempt (*R. v. Martin, The Times*, April 23, 1986).

The Contempt of Court Act 1981, s.8 has made it a contempt of court to violate, or to attempt to violate, the confidentiality of a jury's deliberations. It has also, by s.9, made it a contempt of court to bring into Court, or to use in Court, a tape recorder, except with the leave of the Court, or to publish to the public any recordings made in Court or to use any recordings in contravention of any conditions imposed by the Court in granting such leave.

Intimidation of jurors in or immediately outside the Court also constitutes contempt and may be dealt with by the judge summarily and of his own motion (*R. v. Gough* (1982) *The Times*, November 15).

Disclosure of the deliberations of a jury amounts to a contempt under s.8(1) of the Contempt of Court Act 1981, notwithstanding that the information has been obtained indirectly, since the section is aimed at keeping the secrets of the jury room inviolate in the interests of justice (*Attorney-General v. Associated Newspapers Ltd* [1993] 2 All E.R. 535 (Beldam L.J. and Tudor Evans J.)).

A fear of reprisal may amount to a defence in proceedings for contempt where the contempt consists of a refusal to give evidence against a defendant by whom the alleged contemnor claimed to have been attacked (*R. v. Lewis* (1993) 96 Cr.App.R. 412 (Beldam L.J., Ian Kennedy and Morland JJ.)). For guidance on sentencing in such circumstances see *R. v. Montgomery* [1995] 2 All E.R. 28.

Where a shorthand writer used a tape recorder in court without leave, contrary to s.9(1) of the Contempt of Court Act 1981, it had to be shown that her conduct contained some element of defiance or was otherwise intolerable before she could be punished under s.12 of the Act. Moreover a court should be very slow to act in a contempt matter without giving reasonable thought to the problem and without giving the alleged contemnor an opportunity to take advice and to apologise (*Re Hooker* [1993] C.O.D. 190 (Kennedy L.J. and Waterhouse J.)).

A threat to an officer of the court, such as a solicitor, can amount to a contempt of court in the same way as a threat to a witness (*R. v. Osbourne, The Independent,* September 28, 1992). The prohibition on interfering with witnesses extends also to interference with proper and reasonable attempts by a party's legal adviser to identify and interview potential witnesses (*Connolly v. Dale* (1995) *The Times,* July 13.

The invasion of the papers of counsel or solicitors when they are in court acting for a party, may constitute a contempt (*Re Griffin (Paul), The Times,* November 6, 1996).

A juror's contumacious refusal to reach a verdict because of a reluctance to judge another may establish the actus reus of contempt but the *mens rea,* namely an intention to impede or create a real risk of prejudicing the administration of justice, must also be proved. When a judge has already expressed a view about a juror's conduct in relation to an alleged contempt it may be appropriate to refer the matter to another judge at the Crown Court or to invite the Attorney-General to bring proceedings under RSC, O.52 (*R. v. Schot & Barclay, The Times,* May 14, 1997 (Rose L.J.; Forbes & Keene JJ.)).

In the case of an allegation of interference with a prosecution witness the Crown Court has no power to remand an alleged contemnor in custody. If a judge wishes to ensure that an alleged contemnor is not at liberty he must either adjourn the trial, so as to deal with the matter himself, or refer the matter to another judge. He may not remand the alleged contemnor in custody pending the decision of the Attorney-General (*Re Stevens and Holness, The Independent,* June 9, 1997).

A physical assault on a court official, engaged in official business in the administration of justice, is a contempt, *Re de Court, The Times,* November 27, 1997 (Sir Richard Scott V.-C.).

R52.1.21 *N. Interference with receivers may be contempt*—(see *Helmore v. Smith* (1887) 35 Ch.D. 449; *Dixon v. Dixon* [1904] 1 Ch. 161; *Re New Gold Coast Exploration Co.* [1901] 1 Ch. 860; *King v. Dopson* (1911) 56 S.J. 51; *Re Seaton* [1928] W.N. 307). Interference with other officers of the Court may also be contempt.

R52.1.22 *O. Interference with property under arrest in an admiralty action in rem*—*The Petrel* (1836) 3 Hagg. 299; *The Harmonie* (1841) 1 Wm. Rob. 179, as, *e.g.* by removing the ship from the jurisdiction (breaking arrest) *The Seraglio* (1885) 10 P.D. 120; *The Jarlinn* [1965] 1 W.L.R. 1098; [1965] 3 All E.R. 36. In *The Rhenania, The Times,* November 12, 1909, the motion for committal, for failure to bring the ship into port after service within the three-mile limit, was made by the Official Solicitor, as it was in *The Selina Stanford, The Times,* November 17, 1908.

R52.1.23 *P. Impeding the service of process may be contempt*—(*Price v. Hutchison* (1870) L.R. 9 Eq. 534; *Lewis v. Owen* [1894] 1 Q.B. 102). Preventing the execution of a writ of possession may be contempt (*Lacon v. De Groat* (1894) 10 T.L.R. 24; *Alliance Building Society v. Austen* [1951] 2 All E.R. 1068).

R52.1.24 *Q. Forging or altering the process of the Court*—is contempt (2 Hawk. P.C. 8th ed., pp.207, 212; *Re Jacobs, The Times,* June 13, 1874).

R52.1.25 *R. Neglect of duty by sheriffs and other officers of the Court may be contempt*—See 2 Hawk. P.C. (8th ed.) pp.207, 212; Sheriffs Act 1887, s.29; *Bagge v. Whitehead* [1892] 2 Q.B. 355, CA. As to receivers see notes to RSC, O.30, rr.5 and 6. A liquidator or a trustee under a deed of arrangement, who fails to deliver accounts pursuant to orders of the Board of Trade, is punishable for contempt (*Re Allen* [1935] Ch. 74; *Re Grantham Wholesale Fruit, etc., Merchants Ltd* [1972] 1 W.L.R. 559).

R52.1.26 *S. Disobedience to a writ of habeas corpus by the person to whom it is directed*—is a contempt punishable by committal, if the original writ is personally served (*R. v. Rowe* (1895) 71 L.T. 578).

R52.1.27 *T. Disobedience to a subpoena ad testificandum or duces tecum though not wilful*—(*R. v. Daye* [1908] 2 K.B. 333) or refusal of a witness to answer a question (*Ex p. Fernandez* (1861) 30 L.J.C.P. 321; and see *Att.-Gen. v. Clough* [1963] 1 Q.B. 773; [1963] 1 All E.R. 420) may be contempt. Parties and witnesses summoned to attend before a Master are liable to process of contempt in case of default (O.32, r.15).

Section 3(1) of the Criminal Procedure (Attendance of Witnesses) Act 1965 provides that it is a contempt to disobey a witness order, without just excuse. The disobedience need not be wilful or deliberate since the offence is absolute, save for the qualification as to the just excuse, and culpable forgetfulness of the order could therefore amount to a contempt (*R. v. Lennock* (1993) 97 Cr.App.R. 228).

U. Acting as solicitor, though unqualified—is contempt under the Solicitors Act 1974, s.20. See *Abercrombie v. Jordan* (1881) 8 Q.B.D. 187; *Re Simmons* (1885) 15 Q.B.D. 348; *Re Panton* [1901] P. 239; *Re Ainsworth* [1905] 2 K.B. 103; *Davies v. Davies* (1913) 29 T.L.R. 513. The sanction is committal, indictment or action for penalties. Committal may issue for breach of an order directing a person who professed to be a solicitor, but was not qualified, to deliver up documents and pay money (*Re Hulm & Lewis* [1892] 2 Q.B. 261). R52.1.28

Ministers and civil servants—are amenable to the court's contempt jurisdiction when acting in discharge or purported discharge of their official duties, provided the factual basis and the necessary intention are proved beyond all reasonable doubt (*M. v. Home Office* [1993] 3 W.L.R. 433). R52.1.29

Effect of party being in contempt—The court has a discretion whether to hear a contemnor who has not purged his contempt. However where a contemnor not only fails to comply with an order of the court but, for example, makes it clear that he will continue to defy the court's authority whatever the outcome of an appeal, the court is entitled to exercise its discretion to decline to entertain his appeal (*X. Ltd v. Morgan-Grampian (Publishers) Ltd* [1990] 2 W.L.R. 1000; [1990] 2 All E.R. 1, HL). A court's power to refuse to hear an alleged contemnor in support of an appeal against the order in respect of which he is said to be in contempt, should be exercised only exceptionally. The proper approach is first to decide whether he has an arguable case and, if so, to decide whether the judgment should be set aside or the contempt proceedings should be adjourned until the appeal has been heard (*Atlantic Capital Corporation v. Johnson* (1994) *The Independent*, September 26, CA (Glidewell & Legatt L.JJ. & Sir Michael Kerr)). The court will exercise discretion to hear contemnors who have not purged their contempt where the contemnors are trustees, and it is in the interest of the beneficiaries under the trust that the application should be heard (*Clarke v. Heathfield* [1985] I.C.R. 203, CA). Moreover, a contemnor who appeals against an order committing him for contempt on the ground of lack of jurisdiction in the court to make the original order, has, of course, a right to be heard (*Gordon v. Gordon* [1904] P. 163, CA). R52.1.30

For the origins of the learning on this branch of the law see *Chuck v. Cremer* (1846) Coop. *temp.* Cott. 205 and 338, and *Hodkinson v. Hodkinson* [1952] P. 285, CA and the old authorities therein cited.

Para. (2)—orders of committal by a Divisional Court of the QBD—This paragraph in effect restates the practice which has existed for many years (see Short & Mellor, *Crown Practice*, 2nd ed., pp. 341 *et seq.* and the former O.59) except for the change instituted by para. (3) *q.v.* R52.1.31

(a)(i) "contempt ... in connection with any proceedings before a Divisional Court of the QBD"—For example, disobedience to a writ of habeas corpus, or to an order of mandamus (*R. v. Poplar Borough Council (No. 2)* [1922] 1 K.B. 95) prohibition or certiorari (*Mungean v. Wheatley* (1851) 6 Ex. 88). In these cases the Court is punishing as contempt the disobedience to its own order. R52.1.32

(ii) "contempt ... in connection with criminal proceedings"—If the contempt is *in facie curiae*, or consists of disobedience to an order of the Court or a breach of an undertaking to the Court, that Court will usually punish the contempt itself. In such cases a single Judge has jurisdiction, and in cases of disobedience to a Master's order on the application is made by motion to a Judge. There remains the wide and important jurisdiction of the QBD, exercised by the Divisional Court, to punish by committal or fine conduct calculated (*R. v. Odhams Press Ltd* [1957] 1 Q.B. 73; [1956] 3 All E.R. 494; *R. v. Griffiths* [1957] 2 Q.B. 192; [1957] 2 All E.R. 379; A.J.A. 1960, s.11) to interfere with the due administration of justice in criminal proceedings; though the Crown Court has power to commit for contempt, the QBD has residual jurisdiction and is the appropriate Court in respect of contempt of Magistrates' Courts and Courts-martial (see *R. v. Davies*; *R. v. Evening Standard Co.*; *R. v. Daily Mail, ex p. Farnsworth* [1921] 2 K.B. 733). Disobedience of a witness summons issued by a Magistrates' Court cannot be punished as a contempt by a Divisional Court of the QBD, whereas disobedience to a Crown Office subpoena, issued in connection with the same proceedings, would be so punishable under para. 2(a) (*R. v. Judge* [1931] 2 K.B. 442). R52.1.33

An application to commit a person for breach of restraint and charging orders made under the Drug Trafficking Offences Act 1986, ss.8 and 9, and RSC, O.115, r.3, relates to breach of an order made in civil proceedings, albeit closely connected to criminal proceedings; hence such application must be made to a single judge and not to the Divisional Court (*Re H* (1988) *The Times*, April 1, CA). Where both the Crown Court and the Divisional Court have power to punish for contempt see the guidance provided by the Divisional Court in relation to O.52, r.1 in *DPP v.*

Channel 4 Television Co. Ltd [1993] C.O.D. 6 and *Attorney General v. Martonia* [1993] C.O.D. 9 (Woolf L.J. and Pill J.).

R52.1.34 *(iii) "contempt ... in connection with proceedings in an inferior Court"*—Thirdly, just as the QBD has inherent power to supervise the proceedings of inferior Courts, so it has power to protect them from acts calculated to interfere with the administration of justice by them, as for example, by punishing as a contempt any publication in a newspaper calculated to have that effect (*R. v. Davies* [1906] 1 K.B. 32; *R. v. Daily Herald* [1932] 2 K.B. 402 (proceedings in a Consistory Court); *R. v. Evening Standard Co. Ltd* [1954] 1 Q.B. 578; [1954] 1 All E.R. 1026) or any act obstructing process issued by order of such a Court (*R. v. Edwards* (1933) 49 T.L.R. 383). Where an inferior Court is scandalised, the appropriate proceeding is by committal under the present rule, although it may also be dealt with on summary process for committal (*R. v. Bairstow, ex p. DPP* [1941] W.N. 104).

When a contempt of court is committed in respect of proceedings in a county court, and the contempt is of a kind which the county court has no statutory power to punish, only a Divisional Court of the Queen's Bench Division has jurisdiction to make a committal order; the county court Judge has no jurisdiction to deal with the matter and the appropriate course is for him to contact the Attorney-General, who should consider whether the matter needs to be raised in the Divisional Court (*Bush v. Green* [1985] 1 W.L.R. 1143; 3 All E.R. 721, CA). The powers of a county court to punish for contempt are limited. A county court has power under s.118 of the County Courts Act 1984 to commit for contempt committed in the face of the Court or closely related to events occurring in and about the Court (*ibid.*). A county court also has power, derived from s.38 of the same Act, to order sequestration of a company's assets to compel obedience to an order of the Court (*Rose v. Laskington Ltd* [1989] 3 W.L.R. 873; [1989] 3 All E.R. 306). Where a county court has statutory power to punish the contempt the Queen's Bench Divisional Court, although having jurisdiction by virtue of O.52, r.1(2)(a)(iii), may decline to exercise it if the matter can more conveniently be dealt with in the county court (*ibid.*). See also *R. v. Bloomsbury County Court, ex p. Brady, The Independent*, December 14, 1987; *The Times*, December 16, 1987, DC.

"Court" for this purpose means a Court of law; a Court dealing with matters of administration, such as local valuation Courts, and not within the scope of O.52, r.1 (*Att.-Gen. v. BBC* [1981] A.C. 303; [1980] 3 All E.R. 161, HL). An industrial tribunal is an inferior court for the purposes of r.1(2)(a)(iii) and the Divisional Court therefore has jurisdiction to punish for contempt of that tribunal (*Peach Grey & Co. (A Firm) v. Sommers* [1995] 2 All E.R. 513 (Rose L.J. & Tuckey J.)).

The power of a county court judge to punish for contempt under s.118 of the County Courts Act 1984 is not limited to dealing with contempts committed in the face of the court but extends to situations where a witness is wilfully insulted on his way to or from court, *Manchester City Council v. McCann and Another, The Times*, November 28, 1998 (Lord Woolf M.R., Henry and Clarke L.JJ.).

The Professional Conduct Committee of the General Medical Council is not part of the judicial system of the state and does not therefore fall within the definition of a "court" for the purposes of contempt proceedings: *General Medical Council v. British Broadcasting Corporation* [1998]3 All E.R. 426 (Stuart-Smith, Aldous and Robert Walker L.JJ.).

R52.1.35 **(b) "contempt ... committed otherwise than in connection with any proceedings"**—For example, the offence of scandalising the High Court or a Judge thereof, or any particularly outrageous conduct amounting to a contempt of that Court, without reference to any particular proceedings (see *M'Leod v. St Aubyn* [1899] A.C. 549 at 551; *R. v. Gray* [1900] 2 Q.B. 36).

R52.1.36 **Para.(3)—orders of committal by a single judge of the QBD**—This paragraph was introduced by RSC 1965.

The first sentence enables a single judge of the QBD to punish contempt of Court committed in connection with any civil proceedings in that Division (not being proceedings before a Divisional Court) even though the contempt is not in face of the Court and does not consist of disobedience to an order of the Court. The practice, therefore, of the QBD and the other divisions is the same in this respect.

R52.1.37 **Para.(4)—contempt of other tribunals**—See the Tribunals of Enquiry (Evidence) Act 1921, s.1(2); the Army Act 1955, s.101; the Air Force Act 1955, s.101; the Naval Discipline Act 1957, s.65; the Nuclear Installations (Licensing and Insurance) Act 1959, Sched. 1, para. 7; and the Pipe Lines Act 1962, Sched. 5, para. 7. Under each of these Acts, if any person does anything which, if the tribunal were a court of law having power to commit for contempt, would have been a contempt of court, his offence may be certified to the High Court, which may punish in like manner as for a contempt of the High Court (see as to the Tribunals of Enquiry (Evidence) Act 1921, *Att.-Gen. v. Clough* [1963] 1 Q.B. 773; [1963] 1 All E.R. 420; *Att.-Gen. v. Mullholland & Foster* [1963] 2 Q.B. 477; [1963] 1 All E.R. 767, CA). By virtue of Orders in Council made under s.8 of the Visiting Forces Act 1952, the above service enactments apply to service courts of certain visiting forces.

R52.1.38 **Appeal**—An appeal lies from an order punishing an offender for contempt of court. If the Court making the order is the Crown Court, the appeal lies to the criminal division of the Court of

Appeal; in all other cases it lies to the civil division of that Court (A.J.A. 1960, s.13; S.C.A. 1981, s.53).

Where there has been no unfairness or material irregularity in the committal proceedings, and where there has been nothing more than an irregularity in the drawing up of the committal order, the irregularity can be corrected on appeal by virtue of A.J.A. 1960, s.13(3), and the sentence varied to make it a just sentence (*Linnett v. Coles* [1987] Q.B. 555; [1986] 3 All E.R. 652, CA; *Wright v. Jess* [1987] 1 W.L.R. 1076; [1987] 2 All E.R. 1067, CA). See further *per* Lord Woolf MR in *Nicholls v. Nicholls* [1997] 1 W.L.R. 314.

Where there is a defect in the committal application rather than in the committal order, the Court should be cautious before exercising its power under s.13(3) of the A.J.A. 1960 to substitute a new order, since a defect in the application can affect materially the fairness of the proceedings and render it unjust for the Court to use such power (*Harmsworth v. Harmsworth* [1987] 1 W.L.R. 1676; [1987] 3 All E.R. 816, CA).

Section 13(3) of the A.J.A. 1960 enables the Court of Appeal to correct errors in orders made by lower courts, but in cases of contempt this power will be used only in exceptional circumstances; while the court will not permit a technical infringement of the rules to prevent justice being done, it will not use the power to correct orders where requirements affecting important rights of contemnors have not been complied with (*Clarke v. Clarke* [1990] 2 F.L.R. 115, CA). Thus where a committal order is not served on a contemnor until after he has been imprisoned for the contempt, and does not set out the lower court's findings so as to enable the contemnor to challenge them, the Court of Appeal will not intervene to correct the errors (*ibid.*).

On appeal from a committal order for a civil contempt, leave to adduce fresh evidence will be given if it is necessary or expedient in the interests of justice by analogy with s.23 of the Criminal Appeal Act 1968 (see for example *R. v. Lattimore* (1975) 62 Cr.App.R. 53). There is no obligation on the appellant to fulfil the requirements set out in *Ladd v. Marshall* [1954] 1 W.L.R. 1489 (*Irtelli v. Squatriti* [1992] 3 W.L.R. 218 (Sir Donald Nicholls V.-C., Taylor and Farquharson L.JJ.)). There is no jurisdictional bar to prevent an *applicant* in committal proceedings from applying to the Court of Appeal under section 13(2) of the AJA 1960 for a redetermination of the sentence passed on a contemnor by a county court, where it is said that the sentence failed properly to reflect the seriousness of the contempt. However the Court of Appeal will only interfere in exceptional circumstances and where the decision of the court below was plainly wrong: *Wilson v. Webster* [1998] 1 F.L.R. 1097 (Sir Stephen Brown P. and Sir Patrick Russell).

Application to Divisional Court

2.—(1) No application to a Divisional Court for an order of committal against any person may be made unless permission to make such an application has been granted in accordance with this rule. R52.2

(2) An application for such permission must be made without notice to a Divisional Court, except in vacation when it may be made to a judge in chambers, and must be supported by a statement setting out the name and description of the applicant, the name, description and address of the person sought to be committed and the grounds on which his committal is sought, and by an affidavit, to be filed before the application is made, verifying the facts relied on.

(3) The applicant must give notice of the application for permission not later than the preceding day to the Crown Office and must at the same time lodge in that office copies of the statement and affidavit.

(4) Where an application for permission under this rule is refused by a judge in chambers, the applicant may make a fresh application for such permission to a Divisional Court.

(5) An application made to a Divisional Court by virtue of paragraph (4) must be made within 8 days after the judge's refusal to give permission or, if a Divisional Court does not sit within that period, on the first day on which it sits thereafter.

Effect of rule—The rule requires permission to be obtained by application made without notice (see Practice Direction, para. 2.4 see para. R52PD–001 and CPR, r.23.2(4)) supported by affidavit before an order of commital is sought from the Divisional Court. See further commentary to O.52, r.4. R52.2.1

Application for order after leave to apply granted

3.—(1) When permission has been granted under rule 2 to apply for an order of committal, the application for the order must be made to a Divisional Court and, unless the court or judge granting permission has otherwise R52.3

directed, there must be at least 14 clear days between the service of the claim form and the day named therein for the hearing.

(2) Unless within 14 days after such permission was granted, the claim form is issued the permission shall lapse.

(3) Subject to paragraph 4, the claim form, accompanied by a copy of the statement and affidavit in support of the application for permission, must be served personally on the person sought to be committed.

(4) Without prejudice to the powers of the court or judge under Part 6 of the CPR, the court or judge may dispense with service under this rule if it or he thinks it just to do so.

R52.3.1 **General**—The date on which and the name of the judge by whom the requisite permission was granted must be stated on the claim form or application notice by which the commital application is commenced: See Practice Direction, para. 2.4, para. R52PD–001.

R52.3.2 **Personal service**—No order will be issued for the committal of a person unless he is aware of the order, disobedience to which is said to constitute the contempt, and usually this requires proof that he has been personally served with it. If the order is directed to a group of persons or a corporation, some appropriate person must be personally served. An applicant must give each person sought to be committed the fullest notice that an application is being made for his committal (*R. v. Poplar Borough Council (No. 2)* [1992] 1 K.B. 95)—*e.g.* by inserting his name in the claim form and personally serving him with it and the affidavit in support. O.52, r.3(4) gives express power to dispense with service, *e.g.* where the alleged contemnor is evading service. Service may be dispensed with only where there is no other course available to uphold the authority of the Court and protect the applicant: the dispensation should be recorded in the committal order (*Wright v. Jess* [1987] 1 W.L.R. 1076; [1987] 2 All E.R. 1067, CA).

Failure to comply with a proper procedure, such as personal service, is not necessarily fatal to the lawfulness of a contempt order. The court has complete discretion, under s.13(3) of A.J.A. 1960 to perfect an invalid committal order in a contempt case, but that power should only be used in exceptional cases and should be dictated by the need to do justice having regard to the interests of the contemnor, the victim of the contempt and other court users. Where a contemnor has not suffered any injustice by the failure to follow the proper procedures (such as service) the committal order could stand subject to variation to take account of any technical or procedural defects (*M v. P (Contempt of Court: Committal Order, Butler v. Butler)* [1992] 3 W.L.R. 813; [1992] 4 All E.R. 833 (Lord Donaldson of Lymington M.R. Nolan and Scott L.JJ.) *Nichoils v. Nichoils* [1997] 1 W.L.R. 314.

Where a new or adjourned date is fixed for the hearing of the notice of motion, personal service ought also to be affected of notification of the date (*Phonographic Performance Ltd v. Tsang* (1985) 82 L.S. Gaz. 2331, CA).

R52.3.3 **"14 clear days"**—Both r.3(1) and r.3(2) refer to "14 days". Prior to its incorporation into Sched. 1 to the CPR, r.3(1) used to provide for eight clear days.

R52.3.4 **"claim form"**—Rule 3(3) now requires service of a claim form rather than a notice of motion. The application for permission is made in accordance with R52.2 (see above).

Application to court other than Divisional Court

R52.4 **4.**—(1) Where an application for an order of committal may be made to a court other than a Divisional Court, the application must be made by claim form or application notice and be supported by an affidavit.

(2) Subject to paragraph (3) the claim form or application notice, stating the grounds of the application and accompanied by a copy of the affidavit in support of the application, must be served personally on the person sought to be committed.

(3) Without prejudice to its powers under Part 6 of the CPR, the court may dispense with service under this rule if it thinks it just to do so.

(4) this rule does not apply to committal applications which under rules 1(2) and 3(1) should be made to a Divisional Court but which, in vacation, have been properly made to a single judge in accordance with RSC Order 64, rule 4.

R52.4.1 **Claim form on application notice**—Generally a committal application must be commenced by the issue of a Part 8 claim form (see Practice Direction, para. 2.1, see para. R52PD–001) but if the committal application is made in existing proceedings it may be commenced by filing an application notice in those proceedings. The application notice must state that it is made in those existing proceedings and include the title and reference number of those proceedings (see Practice Direction, para. 2.2).

A claim form, together with copies of all written evidence in support must, unless the court otherwise directs, be served personally on the respondent (see Practice Direction, para. 2.5(1)). It must set out in full the grounds on which the committal application is made and should identify, separately and numerically, each alleged act of contempt (see Practice Direction, para. 2.5(2)). An amendment may be made only with the permission of the court (see Practice Direction, para. 2.5(3)).

If the committal application is commenced by the filing of an application notice CPR Pt 23 applies as amended by the Practice Direction. There is a similar requirement as to service and as to the provision of particulars and amendment (see Practice Direction, para. 2.6).

There is no requirement to make the application to the judge who made the original order which is alleged to have been breached but it is preferable to do so if this can be done conveniently and without delay. If the contempt is of an Order of the Court of Appeal made on appeal, the application should be made to the Court below (*Fortescue v. McKeown* [1914] 1 IrR30; *Pott v. Stuteley* [1935] W.N. 140); otherwise to the Court of Appeal.

The application must specify the breaches of the injunction or undertaking which are relied on (*Chanel Ltd v. FGM Cosmetics Ltd* [1981] F.S.R. 471).

Service of the order—If the order requires a positive act to be done, the evidence must prove service of the order alleged to have been disobeyed. The order must be indorsed with a penal notice under O.45, r.7. In the case of a company, the penal notice must be directed to the company even though it may be desired to enforce it against the directors; the order may be served on the company as provided in s.725 of the CA 1985 but must be served personally on any director against whom it is intended to proceed (*Iberian Trust v. Founder's Trust* [1932] 2 K.B. 87; *Bernabo v. William Jay & Partners Ltd* [1941] Ch. 52). If the order is to abstain from doing an act, it is sufficient to prove that the person against whom it is desired to proceed for contempt had notice of, and disregarded, the prohibition (*Ronson Products Ltd v. Ronson Furniture Ltd* [1966] R.P.C. 497 (enforcement against a director) not following *Redwing Ltd v. Redwing Forest Products Ltd* (1947) 177 L.T. 387). Service of the order is, of course, the best way of giving notice of it, and must be effected if possible (see O.45, r.7). R52.4.2

Service of application to commit—The claim form/application notice must be served personally on the alleged contemnor (even if he has an address for service) unless the Court dispenses with such service (see r.4(2) and (3) and Practice Direction (Committal Applications) paras 2.5 and 2.6 see para. R52PD–001.) In *Mander v. Falcke* [1891] 3 Ch. 488 it was held that the attendance of the contemnor at the hearing did not waive the necessity for service but it is submitted that this decision is not consistent with the modern procedure having regard to RSC, O.52, r.4(3) and Part I CPR. Service is not an end in itself but a means of bringing to the attention of persons concerned notice that a hearing is to take place. Personal service is always preferable but the Court will dispense with it in appropriate cases, eg upon evidence that the contemnor is evading service. The Court can not only dispense with service but can dispense with service altogether see Practice Direction (Committal Applications), paras 2.5(1) and 2.6(1) at para. R52PD–001. In *O'Donovan v. O'Donovan* [1955] 1 W.L.R. 1086 a committal order was made against a person out of the jurisdiction who had not been served with notice. Similarly in *Favard v. Favard* (1896) 75 LT 664 where a respondent, in flagrant disobedience to an order, removed a child from the jurisdiction. R52.4.3

The general rule, however, is that an alleged contemnor is entitled to know, before the hearing of the committal application, of what he is accused and the supporting evidence. Thus where he had not been served with the application to commit him, and did not know until the day of the hearing (save indirectly) what was alleged against him, the judge erred in law in refusing an adjournment for the service of the relevant documents. Even where an alleged contemnor is legally represented he must nevertheless be given the opportunity to mitigate the proposed penalty, where the judge has the intention of imposing a term of imprisonment (*Taylor v. Persico* (1992) *The Times*, February 12, CA (Parker, Stocker L.JJ. and Sir David Croom-Johnson)).

Undertakings—An undertaking given to the Court, although as binding and effective as an order, differs from an order in that it is volunteered rather than imposed; hence the person giving the undertaking is presumed to know of it, and proof of service of the order reciting the undertaking is not required prior to enforcement (*Hussain v. Hussain* [1986] 2 W.L.R. 805; [1986] 1 All E.R. 961, CA). R52.4.4

Grounds of the application—Where committal is sought for breach of an injunction, it must be made clear what the defendant is alleged to have done and that it is a breach. So, if the injunction is in general terms, restraining the defendant from disclosing or making use of any confidential information acquired by him in the course of his employment with the claimant, the latter must show what information is alleged to have been disclosed or used, and that it was confidential (*P. A. Thomas & Co. v. Mould* [1968] 2 Q.B. 913; [1968] 1 All E.R. 963). An alleged R52.4.5

contemnor is not a compellable witness, even in proceedings for civil contempt, but he may be cross-examined upon an affidavit (*Comet Products U.K. Ltd v. Hawker Plastics Ltd* [1971] 2 Q.B. 67; [1971] 1 All E.R. 1141).

The application notice must state exactly what the alleged contemnor has done or omitted to do which constitutes a contempt of court with sufficient particularity to enable him to meet the charge (*Chiltern District Council v. Keane* [1985] 1 W.L.R. 619; [1985] 2 All E.R. 118, CA). The necessary information must be given in the application itself; if lengthy particulars are required it is permissible to include them in a schedule or addendum to the application, provided that they form part of the application itself; it is not permissible to refer in the application to an affidavit or other separate document for particulars which ought to be in the application (*Harmsworth v. Harmsworth* [1987] 1 W.L.R. 1676; [1987] 3 All E.R. 816, CA).

R52.4.6 **Evidence**—The standard of proof required at committal proceedings is the criminal standard (*Dean v. Dean* [1987] F.L.R. 517). Proceedings for committal for contempt of court for breach of an injunction or undertaking are however, civil proceedings. Evidence is governed by Part 32 CPR and its Supplementing Practice Direction. For affidavits see CPR, r.32.15 and para. 2, *et seq* of the Practice Direction at para. 32PD-002. The Court will require the best available evidence of the alleged breach and the applicant must bear in mind that the burden of proof is on him.

The rule of practice in criminal cases that no comment may be made by the prosecution on the defendant's failure to give evidence does not apply, however, to an application for committal for contempt for refusal to comply with an Anton Piller order, and the judge is entitled to draw appropriate inferences from the absence of any explanation by the person served with the order as to the non-production of documents within its scope (*Bhimji v. Chatwani* [1991] 1 All E.R. 705). The Court has power to direct a respondent to a committal summons to swear affidavits or produce statements of witnesses of fact upon which he might wish to rely and to file and serve such evidence in convenient time before the hearing in order to permit proper presentation of evidence in reply. Although the respondent nevertheless retains the right not to have such evidence adduced at the hearing the wise course, generally speaking, is either to make a full and frank admission of the contempt or, if it is denied, to set out his case clearly and in detail (*Re B (A Minor) (Contempt Evidence), The Times*, November 15, 1995 (Wall J.)).

As to the relationship generally between the rules of criminal procedure and the procedure applicable to civil proceedings to commit for contempt, see *Barclays De Zoete Wedd Securities Ltd v. Nadir, The Times*, March 25, 1992 (Knox J.).

A finding of contempt in summary proceedings should not be based upon hearsay evidence given by a police officer concerning what he had been told by someone who was not a witness before the court (*R. v. Shokoya* (1992), *The Times*, June 10, 1992 (Russel L.J., Schiemann and Ebsworth JJ.)).

Re B (a Minor) (Contempt Evidence) [1996] 1 W.L.R. 627, contains an extensive review of the authorities.

Proceedings for a civil contempt are proceedings for the "recovery of a penalty" within s.14(1) of the Civil Evidence Act 1968 in respect of which the privilege against self incrimination applies. However, section 72 of the Supreme Court Act 1981 has the effect of withdrawing that privilege in relation to proceedings for infringement of intellectual property rights or passing off (*Cobra Golf Ltd v. Rata* [1997] 2 All E.R. 150, Rimer J.).

Saving for power to commit without application for purpose

R52.5 **5.** Nothing in the foregoing provisions of this order shall be taken as affecting the power of the High Court or Court of Appeal to make an order of committal of its own initiative against a person guilty of contempt of court.

R52.5.1 **Effect of rule**—The rule enables the court to commit without any formal application to do so. In its original form the rule was confined to a contempt "in the face of the court" and although no longer so confined that is still the best example of when the court is likely to act of its own initiative. Another example would be disobedience of an order made in wardship proceedings (*R. v. Gray* [1900] 2 Q.B. 36; *Bernstein v. Bernstein* [1960] Ch. 120; *Hipgrave v. Hipgrave* [1962] P.91; *Warwick Corporation v. Russell* [1964] 1 W.L.R. 613. The summary power to deal with contempt is unique in English law; see Mustill LJ in *R. v. Griffin*, 88 Cr.AppR.63 at 67.

The Court also has power to issue a witness summons of its own initiative in order to ascertain the facts (*Yianni v. Yianni* [1966] 1 W.L.R. 120).

Provisions as to hearing

R52.6 **6.**—(1) Subject to paragraph (2), the court hearing an application for an order of committal may sit in private in the following cases, that is to say—

(a) where the application arises out of proceedings relating to the wardship or adoption of an infant or wholly or mainly to the guardianship, custody, maintenance or upbringing of an infant, or rights of access to an infant;

(b) where the application arises out of proceedings relating to a person suffering or appearing to be suffering from mental disorder within the meaning of the Mental Health Act 1983;

(c) where the application arises out of proceedings in which a secret process, discovery or invention was in issue;

(d) where it appears to the court that in the interests of the administration of justice or for reasons of national security the application should be heard in private;

but, except as aforesaid, the application shall be heard in public.

(2) If the court hearing an application in private by virtue of paragraph (1) decides to make an order of committal against the person sought to be committed, it shall in public state—

(a) the name of that person;

(b) in general terms the nature of the contempt of court in respect of which the order of committal is being made; and

(c) the length of the period for which he is being committed.

(3) Except with the permission of the court hearing an application for an order of committal, no grounds shall be relied upon at the hearing except the grounds set out in the statement under rule 2 or, as the case may be, in the claim form or application notice under rule 4.

(4) If on the hearing of the application the person sought to be committed expresses a wish to give oral evidence on his own behalf, he shall be entitled to do so.

History of Rule—Amended by Civil Procedure (Amendment) Rules 1999 (S.I. 1999 No. 1008) R52.6.1

Effect of rule—The applicant for the committal order must obtain a hearing date from the Court when he files his application—see Practice Direction, para. 4.1, para. R52PD–003. Unless the Court otherwise directs there must be 14 clear days between service and hearing—see Practice Direction, para. 4.2. The Court may however at any time give case management directions. The general rule is that all hearings are to be in public (CPR, r.39.2). Order 52.6 provides the limited exceptions where application for an order of committal may be in private (r.6(1)). If the court, having heard an application in private finds the respondent guilty of contempt of court, the judge must state in public (1) the name of the respondent, (2) the nature of the contempt and (3) the penalty, if any, imposed: see r.6(2) and Practice Direction, para. 9, R52PD–003. An order of committal is for a fixed term (section 14 of the Contempt of Court Act 1981). R52.6.2

Power to suspend execution of committal order

7.—(1) The court by whom an order of committal is made may by order direct that the execution of the order of committal shall be suspended for such period or on such terms or conditions as it may specify. R52.7

(2) Where execution of an order of committal is suspended by an order under paragraph (1), the applicant for the order of committal must, unless the court otherwise directs, serve on the person against whom it was made a notice informing him of the making and terms of the order under that paragraph.

Suspended committal order—The courts power to suspend an order of committal to prison for contempt of court derives from this rule (and is not affected by the need for "exceptional circumstances" before a suspended sentence can be passed in a criminal case: s.22 of the Powers of Criminal Courts Act 1973 as amended). If a committal order is made for a fixed period but the sentence is suspended subject to the contemnor's compliance with a condition, and it is subsequently found that he has not complied with it, the power of the Court is not limited to declaring that the committal order is now operative: it retains a discretion to do whatever is just in the circumstances (*Re W (B) (An Infant)* [1969] 2 Ch. 50; [1969] 1 All E.R. 594, CA). If committal is suspended and the contemnor is then found guilty of another breach the court can activate the suspended sentence and impose another sentence to be served consecutively. However, the maximum sentence is still subject to the overall limit of two years prescribed by s.14 of the Contempt of Court Act 1981 (*Villiers v. Villiers* [1994] 2 All ER 149). R52.7.1

R52.7.2 **Committal order**—The practice of issuing to the tipstaff an order of the Lord Chancellor (an historical survival from the time when the Lord Chancellor was the Judge of the Court of Chancery) has been discontinued (*Practice Direction*, January 30, 1961) and the committal order is now executed by the tipstaff or, if there is none, by the usher or some other official to whom the order of the Court is addressed, on the authority of a warrant signed by the Judge, or one of the Judges of the Court, making the order (*ibid.*, and see SCP 1999, Vol. 2, Section 1B, paras 1B–74 *et seq.* for forms of warrant).

If the contemnor is present the tipstaff takes him to prison. If the contemnor is absent but has a settled, known address, the tipstaff travels thither with the order and arrests him; if not, or if the contemnor moves or is likely to move, the tipstaff communicates with the local police who hold him and put him in the cells at the police station till the tipstaff arrives and conveys him to the gaol specified in the warrant (in London, Pentonville or Holloway, according to sex).

R52.7.3 **Appeal**—See O.59, r.20 and commentary thereto.

R52.7.4 **Arrest**—In all cases where an order is made for the committal of any person by reason of his contempt of court, it is the duty of the officer charged with the execution of such order, if necessary, and after the notice, to break open the outer door of the house of the party to be arrested (see *Burdett v. Abbot* (1811) 14 East 1; *Re Freston* (1883) 11 Q.B.D. 545; *Harvey v. Harvey* (1884) 26 Ch.D. 644).

R52.7.5 **Privilege from arrest**—There is no privilege from arrest where a committal is granted for a contempt of Court which is of a criminal nature (*Re Freston*; *Stourton v. Stourton* [1963] P. 302; [1963] 1 All E.R. 606); *e.g.* for disobedience by a solicitor to an order of the Court made against him as an officer of the Court (*Re Freston*; *Re Dudley* (1883) 12 Q.B.D. 44; *Re Grey* [1892] 2 Q.B. 440); or for disobedience by a receiver, even though a member of Parliament, to an order against him to pay his balance into Court (*Re Gent* (1889) 40 Ch.D. 190) or for disobedience by any person to an order of the Court for his attendance before an examiner (*Re Hunt* [1959] 2 Q.B. 69; [1959] 2 All E.R. 252).

Where, however, a committal is granted merely for the purpose of enforcing judgments in civil disputes, and where the breach of the order to do or not to do something cannot be said to be in the nature of an offence, then privilege may be successfully claimed (*Re Freston*, *per* Brett M.R.; *Stourton v. Stourton*, above); *e.g.* by Members of Parliament (see *Onslow and Whalley's Case* (1874) L.R. 9 Q.B. 219, 228; *cf.* also *Ex p. Lindsay* [1892] 1 Q.B. 327) even until the expiration of 40 days after the prorogation and dissolution of Parliament, although the member claiming privilege has not been re-elected (*Re Anglo-French Co-operative Soc.* (1880) 14 Ch.D. 533); and, *semble*, by peers of the realm whether Parliament is sitting or not (*Stourton v. Stourton*, above). But the jurisdiction of the Court was held not to be ousted where the act constituting the breach had occurred in the precincts of the House of Commons but was not connected with any proceedings in Parliament (*Rivlin v. Bilainkin* [1953] 1 Q.B. 485; [1953] 1 All E.R. 534). See also *Re Gent* (1889) 40 Ch.D. 190, p. 196. Privilege may also be claimed by barristers and solicitors going to or returning from professional attendance at Court, including a Magistrates' Court (*Re Freston*, above).

Although C. O. 42, r.1, providing that officers and attendants upon the Court, suitors, and witnesses, were to have privilege *eundo, redeundo, et morando* for their necessary attendance, and making it a contempt of Court to arrest them at such times, was repealed, and not re-enacted, still, it is conceived, the privilege of such persons remains unaffected according to the rules at common law (see Bac. Abr. Courts (E.); *Meekins v. Smith* (1791) 1 H.Bl. 636). A witness in a suit arrested under a warrant of commitment for non-payment of poor rates immediately after leaving Court, was discharged from custody (*Hobern v. Fowler* (1893) 62 L.J.Q.B. 49). See *Young v. Young* (1896) 12 T.L.R. 503. But in the case of ordinary contempt the only privilege from arrest is the privilege of the Court to ensure that justice is done; and therefore arrest in Court is not wrongful (*Re Hunt* [1959] 2 Q.B. 69; [1959] 2 All E.R. 252, CA).

R52.7.6 **Restrictive Practices Court**—For instances of contempt by way of breach of an undertaking given to this Court, see *Re Galvanized Tank Manufacturers' Association's Agreement* [1965] 1 W.L.R. 1074; [1965] 2 All E.R. 1003 and *Re Mileage Conference Group of the Tyre Manufacturers' Conference Ltd's Agreement* [1966] 1 W.L.R. 1137; [1966] 2 All E.R. 849. A committal order made in this Court may be executed on the authority of a warrant signed by the presiding Judge, or one of the Judges sitting as a member of the Court making the order (*Queen's Bench Practice Direction No. 46*, SCP 1999, Vol. 2, Section 2C, para. 2C–239).

Discharge of person committed

R52.8 **8.**—(1) The court may, on the application of any person committed to prison for any contempt of court, discharge him.

(2) Where a person has been committed for failing to comply with a judgment or order requiring him to deliver any thing to some other person or to deposit it in court or elsewhere, and a writ of sequestration has also been issued to enforce that judgment or order, then, if the thing is in the custody or

power of the person committed, the commissioners appointed by the writ of sequestration may take possession of it as if it were the property of that person and, without prejudice to the generality of paragraph (1), the court may discharge the person committed and may give such directions for dealing with the thing taken by the commissioners as it thinks fit.

(RSC Order 46, rule 5 contains rules relating to writs of sequestration.)

Effect of rule—The rule permitting the court to discharge a person committed for contempt used to be very important in the days when a person could be committed sine die (i.e. indefinitely or until he had purged his contempt). The rule survives even though committal must be for a fixed period not exceeding two years (which in any event is subject to early release—see below) including activation of any suspended sentence (*Villiers v. Villiers* [1994] 2 All E.R. 149). R52.8.1

In practice a contempt prisoner is told of his right to "purge his contempt" and apply for early discharge by the prison authorities. The Official Solicitor is also notified of all committals.

Early release—Persons committed to prison for contempt are subject to the early release provisions at the Criminal Justice Act 1991. Section 33(1), as substituted by s.45, provides "As soon as a person committed ... has served the appropriate proportion of his term, that is to say (a) one-half, in the case of a person committed for a term of less than twelve months; (b) two-thirds, in the case of a person committed for a term of twelve months or more, it shall be the duty of the Secretary of State to release him unconditionally". Note that release is unconditional and not a licence: there is no power to recall to prison. R52.8.2

Mode of application—The application for discharge should, if possible, be made to the tribunal which made the order for an order of committal, but such applications are now dealt with by any Judge of the Division in which the order was made, if the particular Judge who made it is not available. Application should now be by application notice. The Judge hearing the application for discharge has a complete discretion. The application can be granted resulting in immediate release: refused resting in the original release date remaining unchanged: or the Judge can order release on a future date (*Yager v. Musa* [1961] 2 Q.B. 214. R52.8.3

Release by mistake—There is no jurisdiction to make a second order for committal for the same default, though the release has been made by mistake, but *semble* an order for re-arrest may be made under the original order (*Church's Trustee v. Hibbard* [1902] 2 Ch. 784, CA). R52.8.4

Saving for other powers

9. Nothing in the foregoing provisions of this order shall be taken as affecting the power of the court to make an order requiring a person guilty of contempt of court, or a person punishable by virtue of any enactment in like manner as if he had been guilty of contempt of the High Court, to pay a fine or to give security for his good behaviour, and those provisions, so far as applicable, and with the necessary modifications, shall apply in relation to an application for such an order as they apply in relation to an application for an order of committal. R52.9

Effect of rule—The rule preserves the power to fine or give security for good behaviour. In many cases a fine will be more effective than imprisonment. The court does not have the full range of sentencing options available to a criminal court. In fixing the amount of a fine the judge can take judicial notice of previous breaches of undertakings given in similar cases (*Mullen v. Hackney London Borough Council* [1997] 2 All E.R. 906). R52.9.1

Striking out—The Court may, on the application of the respondent or on its own initiative, strike out a committal application if no reasonable grounds are disclosed, or if it is an abuse of process or likely to obstruct the just disposal of proceedings—or if there has been a failure to comply with a rule, practice direction or court order—see Practice Direction (Committal Applications) para. 5 at R52PD–003. R52.9.2

Miscellaneous—Some provisions of the CPR regime are disapplied including CPR, 35.7 (power to direct that evidence be given by a single joint expert) 35.8 (instructions to a single joint expert), 35.9 (power to direct the provision of information) and 18.1 (order for a party to give additional information) see Practice Direction (Committal Applications) paras 6 and 7, para. R52PD–003. R52.9.3

A committal application may not be discontinued without the permission of the court, see Practice Direction (Committal Applications) para. 8, para. R52PD–003.

Any procedural defect in the commencement or conduct of a committal application may be waived by the court if it is satisfied that no injustice has been caused to the respondent by the defect: PD para 10.

Except where under any enactment a Master or district judge has power to make a committal order such an order can only be made (1) in High Court proceedings by a High Court Judge or a person authorised to act as such and (2) in county court proceedings by a circuit judge or a person authorised to act or capable by virtue of his office of acting as such: Practice Direction (Committal Application) para 11, para. R52PD–001.

PRACTICE DIRECTION—COMMITTAL APPLICATIONS

R52PD–001 *This Practice Direction is supplemental to RSC Order 52 (Schedule 1 to the CPR) and CCR Order 29 (Schedule 2 to the CPR)*

General

1.1 This practice direction applies to any application for an order for committal of a person to prison for contempt of court (a "committal application").

1.2 Where the alleged contempt of court consists of or is based upon disobedience to an order made in a county court or breach of an undertaking given to a county court or consists of an act done in the course of proceedings in a county court, or where in any other way the alleged contempt is contempt of a county court, the committal application may be made in the county court in question.

1.3 In every other case, a committal application must be made in the High Court.

Commencement of committal proceedings

2.1 A committal application must, subject to paragraph 2.2, be commenced by the issue of a claim form. The Part 8 claim form must be used (see paragraph 2.5).

2.2(1) If the committal application is made in existing proceedings it may be commenced by the filing of an application notice in those proceedings

(2) An application to commit for breach of an undertaking or order may be commenced by the filing of an application notice in the proceedings in which the undertaking was given or the order was made.

(3) The application notice must state that the application is made in the proceedings in question and its title and reference number must correspond with the title and reference number of those proceedings.

2.3 If the committal application is one which cannot be made without permission, the claim form or application notice, as the case may be, may not be issued or filed until the requisite permission has been granted.

2.4 If the permission of the court is needed in order to make a committal application:

(1) the permission must be applied for by filing an application notice (see CPR rule 23.2(4));

(2) the application notice need not be served on the respondent;

(3) the date on which and the name of the judge by whom the requisite permission was granted must be stated on the claim form or application notice by which the committal application is commenced;

(4) the permission may only be granted by a judge who, under paragraph 11, would have power to hear the committal application if permission were granted; and

(5) CPR rules 23.9 and 23.10 do not apply.

2.5 If the committal application is commenced by the issue of a claim form, CPR Part 8 shall, subject to the provisions of this practice direction, apply as though references to "claimant" were references to the person making the committal application and references to "defendant" were references to the person against whom the committal application is made (in this practice direction referred to as "the respondent") but:

(1) the claim form together with copies of all written evidence in support must, unless the court otherwise directs, be served personally on the respondent,

(2) the claim form must set out in full the grounds on which the committal application is made and should identify, separately and numerically, each alleged act of contempt,

(3) an amendment to the claim form can be made with the permission of the court but not otherwise, and

(4) CPR rule 8.4 does not apply.

2.6 If a committal application is commenced by the filing of an application notice, CPR Part 23 shall, subject to the provisions of this practice direction, apply, but:

(1) the application notice together with copies of all written evidence in support must, unless the court otherwise directs, be served personally on the respondent,

(2) the application notice must set out in full the grounds on which the committal application is made and should identify, separately and numerically, each alleged act of contempt,

(3) an amendment to the application notice can be made with the permission of the court but not otherwise, and

(4) the court may not dispose of the committal application without a hearing.

Written evidence

3.1 Written evidence in support of or in opposition to a committal application must be given by affidavit. R52PD–002

3.2 Written evidence served in support of or in opposition to a committal application must, unless the court otherwise directs, be filed.

3.3 A respondent, notwithstanding that he has not filed or served any written evidence, may give oral evidence at the hearing if he expresses a wish to do so. If he does so, he may be cross-examined.

3.4 A respondent may, with the permission of the court, call a witness to give oral evidence at the hearing notwithstanding that the witness has not sworn an affidavit.

Case management and date of hearing

4.1 The applicant for the committal order must, when lodging the claim form or application notice with the court for issuing or filing, as the case may be, obtain from the court a date for the hearing of the committal application. R52PD–003

4.2 Unless the court otherwise directs, the hearing date of a committal application shall be not less than 14 clear days after service of the claim form or of the application notice, as the case may be, on the respondent. The hearing date must be specified in the claim form or application notice or in a Notice of Hearing or Application attached to and served with the claim form or application notice.

4.3 The court may, however, at any time give management decisions, including directions for the service of written evidence by the respondent and written evidence in reply by the applicant, or may convene and hold a directions hearing.

4.4 The court may on the hearing date:

(1) give case management directions with a view to a hearing of the committal application on a future date, or

(2) if the committal application is ready to be heard, proceed forthwith to hear it.

Striking out

5. The court may, on application by the respondent or on its own initiative, strike out a committal applicatiaon if it appears to the court:

(1) that the committal application and the evidence served in support of it disclose no reasonable ground for alleging that the respondent is guilty of a contempt of court,

(2) that the committal application is an abuse of the court's process or, if made in existing proceedings, is otherwise likely to obstruct the just disposal of those proceedings, or

(3) that there has been a failure to comply with a rule, practice direction or court order.

Miscellaneous

6. CPR Rules 35.7 (Court's power to direct that evidence is to be given by a single joint expert), 35.8 (Instructions to single joint expert) and 35.9 (Power of court to direct a party to provide information) do not apply to committal applications.

7. An order under CPR rule 18.1 (order for a party to give additional information) may not be made against a respondent to a committal application.

8. A committal application may not be discontinued without the permission of the court.

9. A committal application should normally be heard in public (see CPR rule 39.2), but if it is heard in private and the court finds the respondent guilty of contempt of court, the judge shall state in public:

(1) the name of the respondent,

(2) in general terms the nature of the contempt or contempts found proved, and

(3) the penalty (if any) imposed.

10. Any procedural defect in the commencement or conduct by the applicant of a committal application may be waived by the court if satisfied that no injustice has been caused to the respondent by the defect.

11. Except where under an enactment a Master or district judge has power to make a committal order[1] a committal order can only be made:

(1) in High Court proceedings, by a High Court Judge or a person authorised to act as such,[2]

(2) in county court proceedings by a Circuit Judge or a person authorised to act or capable by virtue of his office of acting as such.[3]

RSC ORDER 53

APPLICATIONS FOR JUDICIAL REVIEW

R53.0.1 **Contents**

Editorial Introduction

The Supreme Court Act 1981, s.37 provides that an application to the High Court for (a) an order for mandamus, prohibition or certiorari, (b) a declaration or injunction (under s.31(2)), or (c) an injunction under s.30 restraining a person not entitled to do so from acting in an office to which that section applies, shall be made in accordance with rules of court by a procedure to be known as "an application for judicial review" (SCP 1999, Vol. 2, Section 2A, paras 2A–101 *et seq.*). The rules in this order were introduced in 1977 and constitute a uniform, flexible and comprehensive procedural code for the exercise by the Court of its supervisory jurisdiction by way of judicial review over the proceedings and decisions of inferior courts, tribunals, or other persons or bodies which perform public duties or functions. R53.0.2

An application for judicial review is a two-stage process. The applicant must first apply for permission to apply for judicial review (see paras *et seq.*). Then, if such leave is granted, the applicant can proceed with a substantive application for judicial review (see paras R53.14.66 *et seq.*).

The rules governing applications for judicial review—Order 53 has not yet been the subject of full-scale revision, and in the interim the Civil Procedure Rules 1998 (CPR) (S.I. 1998 No. 3132) have re-enacted O.53 in Sched. 1 to the CPR, subject to a few modifications. The provisions of Order 53, as so re-enacted, have been slightly amended by the Civil Procedure (Amendment) Rules 1999 (S.I. 1999 No. 1008). Both the CPR and those amendments came into effect on April 26, 1999. R53.0.3

New Practice Direction—There is a Practice Direction which supplements O.53 (in its CPR, Sched. 1 form) and which also came into effect on April 26, 1999 (the Order 53 Practice Direction). R53.0.4

Related sources

- Supreme Court Act 1981, s.31 (SCP 1999, Vol. 2, Section 20A, para. 20A–208) R53.0.5
- O.57 (Divisional Court proceedings, etc.: supplementary provisions)

The following *Queen's Bench Practice Directions* are relevant to this Order (Vol. 2, Section 2C, paras 2C–169 *et seq.*). These Directions continue to apply for the time being (see Practice Direction (Civil: Litigation: Procedure) [1999] 1 W.L.R. 1124).

- No. 24—The Crown Office List listing arrangements
- No. 25—Crown Office List: striking out for want of prosecution, withdrawal of solicitors and applications for leave
- No. 30—Hearing of substantive judicial review application
- No. 45—Judicial review—respondent's affidavits.

Forms

The following Prescribed Forms (formerly included amongst the Prescribed Forms in Appendix A to the RSC) are relevant to O.53. These forms are included in Table 2 (Practice Forms) attached to Practice Direction (Forms) and may be found in SCP 1999, Vol. 2, Section 1A, paras 1A–87 to 1A–89): R53.0.6

- PF No. 86A—Application notice for permission to apply for judicial review (O.53, r.3)
- PF No. 86B—Notice of renewal of application for permission to apply for judicial review (O.53, r.3(5)).
- PF No. 86—Claim form for judicial review (O.53, r.5)

Cases appropriate for application for judicial review

1.—(1) An application for— R53.1

(a) an order of mandamus, prohibition or certiorari; or

(b) an injunction under section 30 of the Act restraining a person from acting in any office in which he is not entitled to act,

shall be made by way of an application for judicial review in accordance with the provisions of this Order.

(2) An application for a declaration or an injunction (not being an injunction mentioned in paragraph (1)(b)) may be made by way of an application for judicial review, and on such an application the court may grant the declaration or injunction claimed if it considers that, having regard to—

(a) the nature of the matters in respect of which a remedy may be granted by way of an order of mandamus, prohibition or certiorari;
(b) the nature of the persons and bodies against whom a remedy may be granted by way of such an order; and
(c) all the circumstances of the case,

it would be just and convenient for the declaration or injunction to be granted on an application for judicial review.

Joinder of claims for relief

R53.2 **2.** On an application for judicial review any remedy mentioned in rule 1(1) or (2) may be claimed as an alternative or in addition to any other remedy so mentioned if it arises out of or relates to or is connected with the same matter.

Grant of permission to apply for judicial review

R53.3 **3.**—(1) No application for judicial review shall be made unless the permission of the court has been obtained in accordance with this rule.

(2) An application for permission must be made to a judge by filing in the Crown Office—

(a) an application notice in Form No. 86A containing a statement of—
(i) the name and description of the applicant;
(ii) the relief sought and the grounds upon which it is sought;
(iii) the name and address of the applicant's solicitors (if any); and
(iv) the applicant's address for service; and
(b) written evidence verifying the facts relied on.

(2A) The documents referred to in paragraphs 2(a) and (b) need not be served on any other person.

(3) The judge may determine the application without a hearing, unless a hearing is requested in the notice of application, in any case, the Crown Office shall serve a copy of the judge's order on the applicant.

(4) Where the application for permission is refused by the judge, or is granted on terms, the applicant may renew it by applying—

(a) in any criminal cause or matter, to a Divisional Court of the Queen's Bench Division;
(b) in any other case, to a single judge or, if the court so directs, to a Divisional Court of the Queen's Bench Division:

Provided that no application for permission may be renewed in any non-criminal cause or matter in which the judge has refused permission under paragraph (3) after a hearing.

(5) In order to renew his application for permission the applicant must, within 10 days of being served with notice of the judge's refusal, lodge in the Crown Office notice of his intention in Form No. 86B.

(6) The court hearing an application for permission may allow the applicant's statement to be amended, whether by specifying different or additional grounds or relief or otherwise, on such terms, if any, as it thinks fit.

(7) The court shall not grant permission unless it considers that the applicant has a sufficient interest in the matter to which the application relates.

(8) Where permission is sought to apply for an order of certiorari to remove for the purpose of its being quashed any judgment, order, conviction or other proceeding which is subject to appeal and a time is limited for the bringing of the appeal, the court may adjourn the application for permission until the appeal is determined or the time for appealing has expired.

(9) If the court grants permission, it may impose such terms as to costs and as to giving security as it thinks fit.

(10) Where permission to apply for judicial review is granted, then—

(a) if the relief sought is an order of prohibition or certiorari and the court so directs, the grant shall operate as a stay of the proceedings to which the application relates until the determination of the application or until the court otherwise orders;

(b) if any other relief is sought, the court may at any time grant in the proceedings interim remedies in accordance with CPR Part 25.

History of rule—Amended by S.I. 1999 No. 1008. R53.3.1

Delay in applying for relief

4.—(1) An application for permission to apply for judicial review shall be made promptly and in any event within three months from the date when grounds for the application first arose unless the court considers that there is good reason for extending the period within which the application shall be made. R53.4

(2) Where an order of certiorari is sought in respect of any judgment, order, conviction or other proceeding, the date when grounds for the application first arose shall be taken to be the date of that judgment, order, conviction or proceeding.

(3) Paragraph (1) is without prejudice to any statutory provision which has the effect of limiting the time within which an application for judicial review may be made.

Mode of applying for judicial review

5.—(1) In any criminal cause or matter, where permission has been granted to make an application for judicial review, the application shall be made to a Divisional Court of the Queen's Bench Division. R53.5

(2) In any other such cause or matter, the application shall be made to a judge unless the court directs that it shall be made to a Divisional Court of the Queen's Bench Division.

(2A) An application for judicial review shall be made by claim form.

(3) The claim form must be served on all persons directly affected and where it relates to any proceedings in or before a court and the object of the application is either to compel the court or an officer of the court to do any act in relation to the proceedings or to quash them or any order made therein, the claim form must also be served on the Clerk or Registrar of the Court and, where any objection to the conduct of the judge is to be made, on the judge.

(4) Unless the court granting permission has otherwise directed, there must be at least 10 days between the service of the claim form and the hearing.

(5) The application must be entered for hearing within 14 days after the grant of permission.

(6) Written evidence giving the names and addresses of, and the places and dates of service on, all persons who have been served with the claim form must be filed before the application is entered for hearing and, if any person who ought to be served under this rule has not been served, the written evidence must state that fact and the reason for it; and shall be before the court on the hearing of the application.

(7) If on the hearing of the application the court is of opinion that any person who ought, whether under this rule or otherwise, to have been served has not been served, the court may adjourn the hearing on such terms (if any) as it may direct in order that the claim form may be served on that person.

Statements and evidence

6.—(1) Copies of the statement in support of an application for permission under rule 3 must be served with the claim form and, subject to paragraph (2), no grounds shall be relied upon or any remedy sought at the hearing except the grounds and remedies set out in the statement. R53.6

(2) The court may on hearing of the application for judicial review allow the applicant to amend his statement, whether by specifying different or

additional grounds or otherwise, on such terms, if any, as it thinks fit and may allow further written evidence to be relied on by him.

(3) Where the applicant intends to ask to be allowed to amend his statement or to rely on further written evidence he shall give notice of his intention and of any proposed amendment to every other party.

(4) Any respondent who intends to use written evidence at the hearing shall file it in the Crown Office and give notice thereof to the applicant as soon as practicable and in any event, unless the court otherwise directs, within 56 days after service upon him of the documents required to be served by paragraph (1).

(5) Each party to the application must supply to every other party on demand and on payment of the proper charges copies of any written evidence which he proposes to rely on at the hearing, including, in the case of the applicant, the written evidence in support of the application for permission under rule 3.

Claim for damages

R53.7 7.—(1) On an application for judicial review the court may, subject to paragraph (2) award damages to the applicant if—

(a) he has included in the statement in support of his application for permission under rule 3 a claim for damages arising from any matter to which the application relates; and

(b) the court is satisfied that, if the claim had been made in proceedings for damages begun by the applicant at the time of making his application for judicial review, he could have been awarded damages.

(2) CPR Part 16 shall apply to a statement relating to a claim for damages as it applies to a statement of case.

Application for disclosure, further information, cross-examination, etc.

R53.8 8.—(1) Unless the court otherwise directs, any interlocutory application in proceedings on an application for judicial review may be made to any judge or a Master of the Queen's Bench Division, notwithstanding that the application for judicial review has been made to and is to be heard by a Divisional Court.

In this paragraph "interlocutory application" includes an application for an order under CPR Part 31 or CPR Part 18 or for an order for permission to cross-examine any person who has given written evidence or for an order dismissing the proceedings by consent of the parties.

(2) In relation to an order made by a Master pursuant to paragraph (1) Order 58, rule 1, shall, where the application for judicial review is to be heard by a Divisional Court, have effect as if a reference to that court were substituted for the reference to a judge in Chambers.

(3) this rule is without prejudice to any statutory provision or rule of law restricting the making of an order against the Crown.

Hearing of application for judicial review

R53.9 9.—(1) On the hearing of any application for judicial review under rule 5, any person who desires to be heard in opposition to the application, and appears to the court to be a proper person to be heard, shall be heard, notwithstanding that he has not been served with the claim form.

(2) Where the remedy sought is or includes an order of certiorari to remove any proceedings for the purpose of quashing them, the applicant may not question the validity of any order, warrant, commitment, conviction, inquisition or record unless before the hearing of the application he has filed in the

Crown Office a copy thereof verified by witness statement or affidavit or accounts for his failure to do so to the satisfaction of the court hearing the application.

(3) Where an order of certiorari is made in any such case as is referred to in paragraph (2) the order shall, subject to paragraph (4) direct that the proceedings shall be quashed forthwith on their removal into the Queen's Bench Division.

(4) Where an order of certiorari is sought and the court is satisfied that there are grounds for quashing the decision to which the application relates, the court may, in addition to quashing it, remit the matter to the court, tribunal or authority concerned with a direction to reconsider it and reach a decision in accordance with the findings of the court.

(5) Where the remedy sought is a declaration, an injunction or damages and the court considers that it should not be granted on an application for judicial review but might have been granted if it had been sought in a claim begun by the applicant at the time of making his application for judicial review, the court may, instead of refusing the application, order the judicial review proceedings to continue as proceedings brought under CPR Part 7 and if it does so may give any directions it considers appropriate.

Saving for person acting in obedience to mandamus

10. No action or proceeding shall be begun or prosecuted against any person in respect of anything done in obedience to an order of mandamus. R53.10

Proceedings for disqualification of member of local authority

11.—(1) Proceedings under section 92 of the Local Government Act 1972 must be begun by the issue of a claim form and brought before a Divisional Court of the Queen's Bench Division. R53.11

(1A) Unless otherwise directed, there must be at least 10 days between the service of the claim form and the hearing.

(2) The claim form must set out the name and description of the applicant, the remedy sought and the grounds on which it is sought, and must be supported by written evidence verifying the facts relied on.

(3) Copies of any written evidence must be filed in the Crown Office before the proceedings are entered for hearing and must be supplied to any other party on demand and on payment of the proper charges.

(4) The provisions of rules 5, 6 and 9(1) as to the persons on whom the claim form is to be served and as to the hearing shall apply, with the necessary modifications, to proceedings under the said section 92 as they apply to an application for judicial review.

Consolidation of applications

12. Where there is more than one application pending under section 30 of the Act, or section 92 of the Local Government Act 1972, against several persons in respect of the same office, and on the same grounds, the court may order the applications to be consolidated. R53.12

Appeal from judge's order

13. No appeal shall lie from an order made under paragraph (3) of rule 3 on an application for leave which may be renewed under paragraph (4) of that rule. R53.13

Meaning of "Court"

14. In relation to the hearing by a judge of an application for leave under rule 3 or of an application for judicial review, any reference in this order to "the Court" shall, unless the context otherwise requires, be construed as a reference to the judge. R53.14

R53.14.1 **Introduction**—In 1977 the former prerogative remedies of certiorari, prohibition and mandamus were replaced by the new and comprehensive public law remedy of "judicial review". In consequence this Order (which was substituted by S.I. 1977 No. 1955), entirely replaced the former O.53. It created a uniform, flexible and comprehensive code of procedure for the exercise by the High Court of its supervisory jurisdiction over the proceedings and decisions of inferior courts, tribunals or other persons or bodies which perform public duties or functions. At the same time, it eliminated procedural technicalities relating to the machinery of administrative law, mainly by removing procedural differences between the remedies which an applicant was formerly required to select as the most appropriate to his case. (The second and third sentences of this paragraph were cited with approval by Ackner L.J. in *R. v. Inland Revenue Commissioners, ex p. National Federation of Self-Employed and Small Businesses Ltd* [1980] Q.B. 407; [1980] 2 All E.R. 378, CA).

This Order was based largely on the recommendations of the Law Commission made in their Report on Remedies in Administrative Law (Law Com. No. 73; Cmnd. 6407 (1976)). Their main recommendation was that a new form of procedure should be introduced to be known as an "application for judicial review" which would enable a person seeking to challenge an administrative act or omission to apply to the High Court either for one of the prerogative orders of mandamus, certiorari, or prohibition, or, in appropriate circumstances, a declaration, an injunction, or damages. The Law Commission had envisaged that their recommendations would be implemented by Act of Parliament. Instead, the changes were originally effected by the substitution in 1977 of this new version of O.53. Subsequently, in 1981, statutory backing was given to the new O.53 by section 31 of S.C.A. 1981. Thus, unusually, the rules preceded the statutory provisions; however, there do not appear to be any provisions in s.31 which conflict with anything contained in O.53, and accordingly there was no reason to think that s.31 would significantly alter the practice and procedure concerning judicial review.

Stages in the progress of an application for judicial review

R53.14.2 *1. Application for permission to apply (r.3)*—In all cases (whether civil or criminal) the applicant must first make an application for permission. The application for permission must be made in the prescribed form, Form 86A (which includes a statement of the relief sought and the grounds), and there must be written evidence verifying the facts relied on. The application for permission and evidence in support need not be served on any other person (O.53, r.3(2A)). Accordingly, the application for permission will be determined without notice to any other party, unless the Court otherwise directs. Where the documents in support of an application for permission exceed 10 pages, a paginated, indexed bundle must be lodged (see further paras R53.14.55 to R53.14.57 below). All applications at first instance for and relating to judicial review are dealt with by the Crown Office: for further information see para. R53.14.18. The application for permission will normally be dealt with initially by a single Judge without a hearing, and a copy of the order made by the single Judge will be sent to the applicant by the Crown Office (r.3(3)). If leave is granted, the applicant then institutes a substantive judicial review application by serving a claim form (see further sub-para. 4, below).

R53.14.3 *2. Renewal of application for permission (r.3(4))*—Where permission has been refused by the single Judge, the applicant can renew his application, in a criminal case, to a Divisional Court of the Queen's Bench Division, and, in a civil case to a single Judge of the Queen's Bench Division (unless the court directs that it be heard by a Div. Court): see O.59, r.3(4) and para. R53.14.61. Unless the court otherwise directs, the hearing of that renewed application will be without notice to any other party. If permission is granted, following the hearing in open court, then again the applicant institutes a substantive judicial review application by serving a claim form (see further sub-para. 4, below).

If the renewed application is refused, then the applicant can, in a civil case (but not in the case of a "criminal cause or matter") renew the application for leave to move for judicial review before the Court of Appeal (Civil Division) by an application lodged with the Civil Appeals Office within seven days (see O.59, r.14(3) and paras R53.14.22 and R53.14.65). If the Court of Appeal grants leave, then (unless the Court of Appeal otherwise directs) the substantive application must be made to the QBD.

R53.14.4 *3. Discharge of permission*—Where (as will normally be the case) the application for permission to apply for judicial review has not been served on any other party and permission has been granted either on paper or at a hearing which the respondent did not attend, it is open to the respondent to apply for the grant of permission to be rescinded see paras R53.14.62 to 64); but such applications are discouraged and should only be made where the respondent can show that the substantive judicial review application will clearly fail.

R53.14.5 *4. Instituting the substantive judicial review application (r.5)*—Where permission to apply for judicial review has been granted, either in the QBD or by the CA, the next stage is for the applicant to institute a substantive application for judicial review. The substantive application is made by a claim form. The applicant must then take the following steps in the following order within 14 days of the date of the grant of leave:

(1) *Service*—He must serve the claim form (together with a copy of the statement which he filed in support of the application for permission) on all persons directly affected (O.53, r.5(3) & 6(1)). As a matter of good practice, the applicant should also include with those documents a copy of the written evidence he has filed in support of his application. (For further details about service, see paras R53.14.69 to R53.14.71.)

(2) *Entry for hearing*—This is the process whereby the substantive application is entered in the records of the Crown Office. In order to enter an application for hearing the applicant must:—
   (a) file in the Crown Office written evidence giving details of all those who have been served with the claim form and, if anyone has not been served who should have been, the reasons for that (O.53, r.5(6) and see further paras R53.14.69 to R53.14.71).
   (b) enter the application for hearing (see O.53, r.5(5) and see further para. R.53.14.72).

5. Respondent's evidence (r.6(4))—If any respondent wishes to rely on any evidence, he must file it in the Crown Office within 56 days after service on him of the applicant's claim form and accompanying documents, (O.53, r.6(4) (as amended)); that 56-day time limit is strictly enforced (see further paras R53.14.74 and R53.14.75). **R53.14.6**

6. Interim remedies/interlocutory orders (rr.3(10) and 8))—It is possible to apply for an interim injunction, interim declaration or other form of interim remedy under CPR Part 25 (O.53, r.1(10)), and to apply for other orders of an interlocutory nature, such as disclosure of documents and further information (O.53, r.8). (For further commentary on interim remedies and interlocutory relief see paras R53.14.47 to R.53.14.53.) **R53.14.7**

7. Listing—All judicial review proceedings (both permission and substantive applications) are assigned to the Crown Office List and are dealt with by Judges nominated by the Lord Chief Justice to hear cases in that List. Listing of judicial review cases is dealt with by the Crown Office. The List is divided into five parts: Part A (cases not yet ready to be heard); Part B (cases ready to be heard); Part C (cases stood out); Part D (expedited cases); and Part E (cases with hearing dates). Applications for expedition or for a case to be stood out of the List, and other applications relating to listing are made on summons to the Master of the Crown Office with an appeal without leave to a nominated Judge or a Divisional Court. (For further information relating to listing, see paras R53.14.77 to R53.14.79.) **R53.14.8**

8. Time estimates—For all cases in Part B or Part D of the List counsel must provide an estimate of the likely length of the hearing. **R53.14.9**

9. The "warned list letter"—As a case reaches the top of Part B of the Crown Office List, the applicant's solicitors will be informed by a letter from the Crown Office that the case is likely to be listed, at short notice, with effect from a date specified in that letter (the "warned date"). It is the responsibility of the applicant's solicitor to inform the respondent of the "warned date", or, if the case has been given a fixture, of the fixed date (see further para. R53.14.80). **R53.14.10**

10. Lodging of bundles—Not less than five clear working days before the "warned date", (or where a fixture has been given, the fixed date) the applicant's solicitors must lodge with the Crown Office a paginated indexed bundle for the use of the court (see paras R53.14.81 and R53.14.82). **R53.14.11**

11. Skeleton arguments—Skeleton arguments are now required in judicial review cases. The applicant's advocate must lodge a skeleton argument with the Crown Office, at least *five* clear working days before the warned date, or the fixed date, as the case may be. Advocates for the respondent, or any other party wishing to be heard, must lodge their skeleton arguments with the Crown Office at least *three* clear working days before the warned (or fixed) date (see further para. R53.14.83). **R53.14.12**

12. Hearing—Judicial review proceedings are heard in public. If it is a criminal cause or matter, it will always be heard by a Divisional Court of the Queen's Bench Division. Civil cases are listed before a single nominated Judge, unless the court has directed that the case be heard by a Divisional Court, or a Judge in Chambers. **R53.14.13**

13. Order—All orders in judicial review proceedings (whether relating to permission or a substantive application) are drawn and issued by the Crown Office, not by the parties. **R53.14.14**

14. Appeals—In civil cases the avenue of appeal is to the Court of Appeal (Civil Division) (see paras R53.14.22 and R53.14.92). Where it is a criminal cause or matter, appeal lies from the **R53.14.15**

Divisional Court directly to the House of Lords, but only with leave and a certificate of a point of law of general public importance (see paras R53.14.22 and R53.14.92).

Guide to commentary on judicial review

TABLE 1

R53.14.16

Subject	*Para.*	*RSC*
Procedure Information and enquiries	R53.14.18	
Permission to apply for judicial review	R53.14.21, 54, 55 & 60	O.53, r.3
Delay—extensions of time	R53.14.58 & 59	O.53, r.4
Renewal of application for permission	R53.14.61 & 65	O.53, r.3 O.59, r.14 (3)
Discharge of permission	R53.14.62–64	
Instituting substantive judicial review application	R53.14.67	O.53, r.5
Claim form	R53.14.67 & 68	O.53, r.5(2) & (2A)
Service	R53.14.69–71	O.53, r.5(3) (4) & (6), & r.6(1)
Entry for hearing	R53.14.72	O.53, r.5(5)
Written evidence	R53.14.66 & 71	O.53, r.6
Amendment of grounds	R53.14.73	O.53, r.6(2) & (3)
Further evidence	R53.14.73	O.53, r.6(2) & (3)
Respondents' evidence	R53.14.74 & 75	O.53, r.6(4)
Lodging bundles	R53.14.81	
Estimates	R53.14.78 & 83	
Expedition	R53.14.66	
Listing	R53.14.77	
Skeleton arguments	R53.14.83	
Hearing	R53.14.84	
Who can apply for judicial review?	R53.14.24	O.53, r.3(7)
Against whom does judicial review lie?	R53.14.25 & 26	
Who may oppose the application?	R53.14.76	O.53, r.9(1)

Subject	*Para.*	*RSC*
On what grounds can judicial review be granted?	R53.14.28–32	
Judicial review discretionary	R53.14.32	
Distinction between public and private law	R53.14.33	
Fresh evidence	R53.14.85	
Estoppel	R53.14.37 & 38	
Powers of court	R53.14.20 & R53.14.39 *et seq.*	O.53, r.1
Certiorari	R53.14.39	O.53, r.1(1)(a)
Prohibition	R53.14.40 & 41	O.53, r.1(1)(a)
Mandamus	R53.14.42	O.53, r.1(1)(a)
Declaration	R53.14.43	O.53, r.1(2)
Injunctions	R53.14.43 & 44, R53.14.49 & 50	O.53, r.1(2)
Damages	R53.14.45	O.53, r.7
Joinder	R53.14.46	O.53, r.2
Order to continue proceedings as if begun by an ordinary civil claim	R53.14.87	O.53, r.9(5)
Remitting matter for review	R53.14.86	O.53, r.9(4)
Costs	R53.14.88	
Interlocutory orders/interim remedies Procedure on applications for interlocutory orders/interim remedies	R53.14.47 & 48	O.53, rr.3(10(b) & 8
Disclosure	R53.14.47	O.53, r.8
Further information	R53.14.47	O.53, r.8
Evidence	R53.14.55–57, 71, 73–75, 85	O.53, rr.3(2), 5, 6 & 8
Interim injunctions	R53.14.49 & 50	O.53, rr.3(10)(b) & 8
Stay	R53.14.51	O.53, r.3(10)(a)
Bail	R53.14.52 & 53	

Subject	*Para.*	*RSC*
Appeals		
Civil cases	R53.14.22 R53.14.92 (Second Table)	
Criminal cases	R53.14.92 (First Table)	

R53.14.17 **Judicial review in a criminal cause or matter**—Any detailed treatise on judicial review in criminal proceedings is outside the scope of this work, but some reference will be made in the course of the commentary to O.53 to criminal cases. For discussion on what constitutes a "criminal cause or matter", see para. R53.14.46, below. The following is a brief summary of the procedure applicable to judicial review proceedings in a criminal cause or matter.

In general the procedure regulating applications for leave, and substantive judicial review applications, in civil cases also applies to applications in a criminal cause or matter; but the following are the main differences:—

(i) In criminal cases an application for permission can be renewed to a Divisional Court wherever a single Judge has refused permission (or granted it on terms) whether "on paper" or after a hearing (O.53, r.3(4)(a)). But in civil cases, an application for permission cannot be renewed in the QBD if the single Judge has refused permission (or granted it on terms) after a hearing (see the proviso to O.53, r.3(4)(b)). (It can, however, be renewed to the Court of Appeal.)

(ii) Where an application for permission to apply for judicial review in a criminal cause or matter has been refused by a single Judge (whether on paper or after a hearing), any renewed application has to be heard by a Divisional Court of the Queen's Bench Division (O.53, r.3(4)(a)).

(iii) Where permission has been granted, the substantive application must, in a criminal case, be made to a Divisional Court of the QBD; it cannot be heard by a single Judge (O.53, r.5(1)).

(iv) No appeal lies to the Court of Appeal against a decision in a criminal cause or matter (whether given on an application for permission to apply for judicial review or in substantive judicial review proceedings). Insofar as there is any appeal at all, it will be to the House of Lords (see para. R53.14.22, the tables in para. R53.14.92).

R53.14.18 **Information and enquiries**—All applications at first instance for, or relating to, judicial review should be lodged with the Crown Office which is responsible for administration and listing of judicial review cases and all other matters assigned to the Crown Office List. The relevant direct lines are as follows:—

Lodging of judicial review applications and other general enquiries (Room C315) 0171–936–6205.

Listing (Room C317) 0171–936–6013 and 0171–936–6297.

All enquiries relating to the renewal to the Court of Appeal of applications for permission to apply to move for judicial review in civil cases, or appeals to the Court of Appeal in judicial review proceedings in civil cases, should be made to the Civil Appeals Office (not the Crown Office) and all application notices or notices of appeal relating to such cases must be lodged with the Civil Appeals Office. (For the relevant telephone numbers in the Civil Appeals Office, see para. R59.1.34.)

Scope of Judicial Review

R53.14.19 **Nature and scope of judicial review**—The remedy of judicial review is concerned with reviewing, not the merits of the decision in respect of which the application for judicial review is made, but the decision-making process itself. "It is important to remember in every case that the purpose of [the remedy of judicial review] is to ensure that the individual is given fair treatment by the authority to which he has been subjected and that it is no part of that purpose to substitute the opinion of the judiciary or of individual judges for that of the authority constituted by law to decide the matters in question" (*Chief Constable of North Wales Police v. Evans* [1982] 1 W.L.R. 1155 at 1160; [1982] 3 All E.R. 141 at 143, *per* Lord Hailsham L.C.). Thus, a decision of an inferior court or a public authority may be quashed (by an order of certiorari made on an application for judicial review) where that court or authority acted without jurisdiction, or exceeded its jurisdiction, or failed to comply with the rules of natural justice in a case where those rules are applicable, or where there is an error of law on the face of the record, or the decision is unreasonable in the *Wednesbury* sense (see para. R53.14.31). The court will not, however, on a judicial review application act as a "court of appeal" from the body concerned; nor will the court interfere in any way with the exercise of any power or discretion which has been conferred on that body, unless it has been exercised in a way which is not within that body's jurisdiction, or the decision is *Wednesbury* unreasonable. The function of the court is to see that lawful authority is not abused by unfair treatment. If the court were to attempt itself the task entrusted to that authority by the law, the court would, under the guise of preventing the abuse of power, be guilty itself of usurping power (*Chief Constable of North Wales Police v. Evans* [1982] 1 W.L.R. 1155 at 1173; [1982] 3 All E.R. 141 at 154, *per* Lord Brightman). That applies, whether or not there is some avenue of appeal against the decision on the merits. If there is no avenue of appeal on the merits, it follows that the decision of the body concerned is meant to be final, provided that the decision-making process was properly carried out. If, on the other hand, an appeal on the merits does lie, that avenue of appeal should be pursued, and resort should only be had to an application for judicial review if the decision-making process itself was improperly carried out. Normally, even where there are grounds for judicial review, the court will not allow an applicant to proceed by way of judicial review until he has availed himself of any alternative remedy. There may, however, be exceptional cases where the court would grant relief by way of judicial review without requiring the applicant to pursue the alternative remedy available to him (see *R. v. Chief Constable of Merseyside Police, ex p. Calveley* [1986] Q.B. 424; [1986] 1 All E.R. 257, CA and para. R53.14.27).

Normally the proper and convenient way to mount an appeal from the Crown Court to the Divisional Court is by way of case stated, rather than judicial review (see *R. v. Crown Court at Ipswich, ex p. Baldwin* (*Note*) [1981] 1 All E.R. 596, DC). On the other hand, where a tribunal has misunderstood its functions and as a result its functions are not exercised, or are not exercised in a proper manner, the appropriate remedy is by way of judicial review (*R. v. Chief Commons Commissioner, ex p. Winnington, The Times,* November 26, 1982; *R. v. Windsor Licensing Justices, ex p. Hodes* [1983] 1 W.L.R. 685; [1983] 2 All E.R. 551, CA).

Neither s.31 nor O.53 has extended the circumstances in which judicial review is available so as to permit the enforcement of private rights, such as rights of particular employees *vis-à-vis* their employer; only activities of a public nature can be the subject of judicial review (*R. v. BBC, ex p. Lavelle* [1983] 1 W.L.R. 23; [1983] 1 All E.R. 241, approved and applied by the Court of Appeal in *Law v. National Greyhound Racing Club Limited* [1983] 1 W.L.R. 1302; [1983] 3 All E.R. 300). In the *BBC* case it was held that judicial review was not the appropriate procedure to challenge the decision of domestic tribunals, such as the disciplinary tribunals of the BBC; in such cases the appropriate remedy is by an action for a declaration and an injunction (see further paras R53.14.25, 26 and 33).

For a discussion of the distinction between infringement of public law rights (where judicial review is the appropriate remedy) and infringement of private rights (where an ordinary action should be brought) see para. R53.14.33.

In *R. v. Panel on Take-Overs and Mergers, ex p. Datafin Ltd* [1987] Q.B. 815 the Court of Appeal held that judicial review would lie against the Take-over Panel notwithstanding the fact that it is not a creature of statute or a product of the exercise of the prerogative (see para. R53.14.33).

Types of order which can be made in judicial review proceedings (r.1)—In judicial review proceedings the court can grant orders of mandamus, prohibition, and certiorari (r.1). S.C.A. 1981, s.29 provides that the High Court shall have jurisdiction to make orders of mandamus, prohibition and certiorari in those classes of cases in which it had power to do so immediately before the passing of that Act (see paras R53.14.39 to R53.14.42). The court also has power in judicial review proceedings to grant declarations and injunctions, and to award damages (rr.1 and 7; and see paras R53.14.43 to 45). **R53.14.20**

Under SCA 1981, s.31 and O.53, r.1(1)(a) an application for mandamus, prohibition or certiorari *must* be made by way of an application for judicial review. A declaration, injunction or damages *may* be obtained in proceedings for judicial review (*ibid.*, s.31(2) and (4) and O.53, r.1(2) and r.7), but such remedies may also be sought in ordinary civil proceedings commenced by claim form. The claimant does not have a free choice; for a discussion of the authorities on the question whether judicial review or a civil claim is the appropriate procedure see para. R53.14.33. Broadly, if the proceedings are directed to challenging the decision of a public law nature, and are not for enforcement of private rights, an application for judicial review is the only permissible course; the court will not permit a claim for a declaration to be used as a means of circumventing the procedural restrictions on the availability of judicial review, in particular the rule that leave to apply for judicial review must be obtained and the requirement that the application for judicial review must be made promptly, and in any event within three months (*O'Reilly v. Mackman* [1983] 2 A.C. 237; [1983] 3 All E.R. 1124, HL).

Permission to apply for judicial review (r.3)—No application for judicial review can be made (whether in a civil or criminal matter) unless permission to apply for judicial review has been obtained (S.C.A. 1981, s.31(3) and O.53, r.3). Applications for permission are normally determined without notice to any other parties by a single Judge, in the first instance without a hearing. (For further details see paras R53.14.60 *et seq.*) The purpose of the requirement of permission is: **R53.14.21**

(a) to eliminate frivolous, vexatious or hopeless applications for judicial review without the need for a substantive judicial review hearing; and
(b) to ensure that an applicant is only allowed to proceed to a substantive hearing if the court is satisfied that there is a case fit for further investigation at a full hearing.

R53.14.22 **Avenues of appeal in judicial review proceedings**—In civil cases the avenues of appeal are as follows. If the single Judge refuses permission without a hearing, the application can be renewed before a single Judge sitting in court (or, if the court so directs, a Divisional Court of the Queen's Bench Division) (r.3(4)(b)). If permission is refused after a hearing, the application for permission can be renewed before the Court of Appeal within seven days under O.59, r.14(3). If the Court of Appeal grants permission, the substantive application will (unless the Court of Appeal otherwise directs) be sent back to be heard in the QBD (see para. R53.14.65). If the Court of Appeal refuses permission to apply for judicial review that decision is final; there is no appeal to the House of Lords (*Re Poh* [1983] 1 W.L.R. 2; [1983] 1 All E.R. 287, HL). Where permission has been granted and the substantive application for judicial review has been heard by the single Judge or a Divisional Court, there is an appeal to the Court of Appeal under s.16 of S.C.A. 1981. Under O.59, r.1B(1) permission to appeal is now required. Permission may be granted either by the court below or the Court of Appeal.

In criminal cases, where the single Judge has refused permission to apply for judicial review, the application for permission can be renewed before a Divisional Court (r.3(1)(a)). No appeal lies to the Court of Appeal in criminal judicial review proceedings (S.C.A. 1981, s.18(1)(a)). Appeal against a decision of the Divisional Court in a criminal cause or matter lies to the House of Lords under s.1 of A.J.A. 1960, but only with the requisite certificate and leave (see also the first table in para. R53.14.92).

When Does Judicial Review Lie?

R53.14.23 **Grounds on which judicial review can be granted**—This is a vast topic and in a commentary of this kind it is not practicable to give more than a very brief outline (for a detailed analysis of the principles and the authorities see: de Smith, *Judicial Review of Administrative Action*; Wade, *Administrative Law*; and Gordon, *Judicial Review and Crown Office Practice*). The principal questions which have to be considered are:

(1) Who can apply for judicial review?
(2) Against what persons or bodies of persons does judicial review lie?
(3) On what grounds can the decisions of such persons or bodies be impugned? and
(4) Does the cause involve matters of public, as opposed to private, law?

R53.14.24 **Who can apply for judicial review? — "Sufficient interest" (r.3(7))**—The overriding rule governing the standing of the applicant to apply for judicial review is that the court must consider that he "has a sufficient interest in the matter to which the application relates" (S.C.A. 1981, s.31(3) and O.53, r.3(7)). If the applicant has a direct personal interest in the relief which he is seeking, he will very likely be considered as having a sufficient interest in the matter to which the application relates. If, however, his interest in the matter is not direct or personal, but is a general or public interest, it will be for the court to determine whether he has the requisite standing to apply for judicial relief. Clearly, the formula "sufficient interest" is not intended to create a class of person, popularly referred to as a "private attorney-general", who seeks to champion public interests, in which he is not himself directly or personally concerned, under the guise of applying for judicial review.

The question of what is a "sufficient interest in the matter to which the application relates" appears to be a mixed question of fact and law; a question of fact and degree and the relationship between the applicant and the matter to which the application relates, having regard to all the circumstances of the case (cited with approval by Lord Roskill in *R. v. Inland Revenue Commissioners, ex p. National Federation of Self-Employed and Small Businesses Ltd* [1982] A.C. 617, 659; [1981] 2 All E.R. 93 at 107). The term "interest" should perhaps not be given a narrow construction, but should be regarded as including any connection, association or interrelation between the applicant and the matter to which the application relates.

It should also be remembered that the requirement to establish a "sufficient interest" must be shown at the stage of the application for permission to apply for judicial review. At this stage, the only question before the court is whether a sufficient interest has been shown to justify granting permission. Except in simple cases where it is appropriate at the earliest stage to find that the applicant for judicial review has no interest at all or no sufficient interest to support his application, it is undesirable that the court should delve into the question of whether the applicant has a sufficient interest or *locus standi* as a preliminary issue, since the question of sufficient interest must be taken together with the legal and factual context of the application and whether there has been a breach or failure to carry out statutory or public duties (*R. v. Commissioners of Inland Revenue, ex p. National Federation of Self-Employed and Small Businesses Ltd* [1982] A.C. 617; [1981] 2 All E.R. 93, HL). If permission is granted, neither the court itself nor the opposing party will be precluded from considering afresh or contending as the case may be, that the applicant has no sufficient interest to maintain his substantive application for judicial review (*ibid.*). In other words, if permission is granted this will not act as a fetter on the court's power to grant or refuse the substantial relief sought in the application for judicial review.

One taxpayer or a group of taxpayers has no sufficient interest to found an application for judicial review seeking an investigation into the tax affairs of another taxpayer or group of taxpayers or raising the complaint that the other taxpayer or group have been under-assessed to tax (*R. v. Inland Revenue Commissioners, ex p. National Federation of Self-Employed and Small Businesses*

Ltd [1982] A.C. 617; [1981] 2 All E.R. 93, HL); but this does not preclude the possibility that decisions of the Inland Revenue may be brought before the court on judicial review, nor that, in a case of sufficient gravity, the court might hold that another taxpayer or group of taxpayers could challenge them (*ibid.*). On the *locus standi* of a citizen in his capacity as a taxpayer see also *R. v. H.M. Treasury, ex p. Smedley* [1985] Q.B. 657; [1985] 1 All E.R. 589, CA.

A newspaper reporter and the National Union of Journalists have *locus standi* to apply for judicial review to quash the order of magistrates made under the Contempt of Court Act 1981, s.4(2) prohibiting the publication of any report of committal proceedings until the commencement of any subsequent trial (*R. v. Horsham Justices, ex p. Farquharson* [1982] Q.B. 762; [1982] 2 All E.R. 269, CA).

Against whom does judicial review lie?—At various stages (particularly between the 1920s and the 1960s) it was thought that what were then the prerogative orders of certiorari, prohibition and mandamus lay only against persons or bodies with judicial or quasi-judicial functions, and did not apply to an authority exercising administrative powers. The distinction between judicial and administrative activities was swept away by the decision of the House of Lords in *Ridge v. Baldwin* [1964] A.C. 40; [1963] 2 All E.R. 66. Judicial review now lies against an interior court or tribunal, and against any persons or bodies who perform public duties or functions. In *R. v. Panel on Take-Overs and Mergers, ex p. Datafin Ltd* [1987] Q.B. 815; [1987] 1 All E.R. 564, the Court of Appeal held that the judicial review would lie against the Take-over Panel notwithstanding the fact that it is part of the "self-regulatory" system in the City, and does not derive its authority or powers from statute or the exercise of the prerogative; but see further para. R53.14.33. R53.14.25

In *R. v. Secretary of State for Foreign and Commonwealth Affairs, ex p. Everett* [1989] Q.B. 811; [1989] 1 All E.R. 655 the Court of Appeal held that a decision of the Foreign Secretary to refuse to issue the applicant with a passport was susceptible of judicial review, notwithstanding the fact that the decision involved the exercise by the minister of a prerogative power, and held that reasons should be given for the decision to refuse the issue of a passport. (Judicial review was, however, refused on the facts on the grounds that the applicant knew by the time of the hearing of the reasons for the refusal and he had not suffered any injustice.)

In *R. v. Civil Service Board, ex p. Bruce* [1989] 2 All E.R. 907 the Court of Appeal left open the question whether a decision of the Civil Service Board that the applicant had not been unfairly dismissed from his position as a civil servant was susceptible of judicial review on the grounds that (as the Divisional Court had stated *obiter*) he had no contract of employment and there was a sufficient public law element involved to make the decision amenable to judicial review, or whether a civil servant has a contract of employment which takes the case outside the scope of judicial review. (The CA confined itself to affirming the Div. Court's decision refusing judicial review, in the exercise of the court's discretion, on the grounds that the applicant had already brought proceedings before an industrial tribunal for unfair dismissal and was in the process of litigating in the High Court the issue whether those proceedings had been settled by a contract of compromise.)

Judicial review will not lie against a person or body carrying out private law and not public law functions. Thus, the following have been held not to be susceptible to judicial review: an employer's domestic tribunal (*R. v. BBC, ex p. Lavelle* [1983] 1 W.L.R. 23; [1983] 1 All E.R. 241, QBD); the stewards of the National Greyhound Racing Club (*Law v. National Greyhound Racing Club Limited* [1983] 1 W.L.R. 1302; [1983] 3 All E.R. 300, CA); the Jockey Club (*R. v. Disciplinary Committee of the Jockey Club, ex p. The Aga Khan* [1993] 1 W.L.R. 909; [1993] 2 All E.R. 853, CA) and the Football Association (*R. v. Football Association Ltd, ex p. Football League Ltd* [1992] C.O.D. 52, QBD). In such cases the appropriate remedy is by way of a claim for a declaration and, where appropriate, an injunction.

Examples of cases where judicial review would lie against persons and bodies carrying out public law functions are: *Pyx Granite Co. v. Ministry of Housing and Local Government* [1960] A.C. 260; [1959] 2 All E.R. 1, HL (minister); *Secretary of State for Education and Science v. Tameside Metropolitan Borough Council* [1977] A.C. 1014; [1976] 3 All E.R. 665, HL (local authority); *Ridge v. Baldwin* [1964] A.C. 40; [1963] 3 All E.R. 66, HL (police authority); *Leech v. Deputy Governor of Parkhurst Prison* [1988] A.C. 533; [1988] 1 All E.R. 485, HL (prison governor's disciplinary decision); *R. v. Chief Immigration Officer Lympne Airport, ex p. Amrit Singh* [1968] 1 Q.B. 333; [1968] 3 All E.R. 163, DC and *R. v. Secretary of State for the Home Department, ex p. Khawaja* [1984] A.C. 74; [1983] 1 All E.R. 765, HL (immigration officials); *R. v. Criminal Injuries Compensation Board, ex p. Ince* [1973] 1 W.L.R. 1334; [1973] 3 All E.R. 808, CA (Criminal Injuries Compensation Board); *R. v. Commissioners of Inland Revenue, ex p. Preston* [1985] A.C. 835; [1985] 2 All E.R. 327, HL (Inland Revenue Commissioners); *R. v. Harrow London Borough Council, ex p. D* [1990] Fam. 133, CA (decision by a local authority to put a child's name on their "Abuse Register"); *R. v. Panel on Take-overs and Mergers, ex p. Datafin Ltd* [1987] Q.B. 815; [1987] 1 All E.R. 564, CA (the City Take-over Panel); *R. v. Advertising Standards Authority Ltd, ex p. The Insurance Service plc* [1990] C.O.D. 42; *The Times*, July 14, 1989, DC (the Advertising Standards Authority).

Judicial review against courts and tribunals—As far as courts are concerned, judicial review does not lie against the High Court or the Court of Appeal, but only against decisions of R53.14.26

inferior courts (*e.g.* The Crown Court and county courts) and tribunals (*e.g.* The Immigration Appeals Tribunal, and the General and Special Commissioners of Income Tax). It should be noted, however, that even in the case of inferior courts and tribunals against whom judicial review does lie, an applicant will not normally be permitted to proceed by way of judicial review if there is another avenue of appeal against the decision concerned. Thus, for example, an applicant will not be allowed to use judicial review to challenge a decision of a county court judge when he could, and should, have proceeded by way of an appeal (or on application for permission to appeal) to the Court of Appeal. Furthermore, if he has already unsuccessfully sought to appeal to the Court of Appeal, he will not then be allowed to re-litigate the matter by way of judicial review (see further para. R53.14.27).

R53.14.27 **Alternative avenue of challenge to decision sought to be reviewed**—The courts will not normally grant judicial review where there is another avenue of appeal. "It is a cardinal principle that, save in the most exceptional circumstances [the jurisdiction to grant judicial review] will not be exercised where other remedies were available and have not been used" (*R. v. Epping and Harlow General Commissioners, ex p. Goldstraw* [1983] 3 All E.R. 257, 262, *per* Sir John Donaldson M.R.). Although the court, in the exercise of its discretion, would rarely allow the applicant to proceed by way of judicial review where there is an alternative remedy available to him, there may be exceptional cases where the circumstances are such that the court would grant relief by way of judicial review without requiring the applicant to pursue the alternative remedy available to him (*R. v. Chief Constable of Merseyside Police, ex p. Calveley* [1986] Q.B. 424; [1986] 1 All E.R. 257, where the Court of Appeal held, reversing the Divisional Court, that the delay in instituting the disciplinary charges against the applicant police officers was such a serious breach of the relevant Police Regulation that judicial review, quashing the Chief Constable's decision, should be granted immediately without requiring the applicants to exercise the right of appeal to the Secretary of State against the Chief Constable's decision). Not only will an applicant normally be precluded from proceeding by way of judicial review where there is an alternative avenue of appeal which he has not yet pursued, but, even where he has already pursued it (certainly if it is an appeal to a superior court), he will not be permitted to re-litigate the matter by means of judicial review (see below).

The normal avenues of appeal in Crown Court cases are as follows. Where the Crown Court was hearing an appeal from a magistrates' court in a criminal cause of matter, appeal lies by way of case stated to the Division Court. Appeal lies to the Criminal Division of the Court of Appeal against conviction or sentence where there was a trial on indictment before the Crown Court. For discussion of the circumstances in which a party to summary criminal proceedings before magistrates' court may be permitted to proceed by way of judicial review (notwithstanding any right of appeal to the Crown Court) see *R. v. Hereford Magistrates' Court, ex p. Rowlands* [1998] Q.B. 110, DC. In *R. v. Reading Crown Court, ex p. Hutchinson* [1988] Q.B. 384; [1988] 1 All E.R. 333 the Divisional Court held that where a defendant in summary criminal proceedings wishes to challenge the validity of a byelaw under which he is charged or a decision of a local authority which is an essential element in proving the criminal offence alleged, that challenge can be mounted before the magistrates' court and the matter can then be appealed to the Crown Court, or by way of stated case, to a Divisional Court. The Divisional Court rejected the argument put forward by the prosecution that the summary proceedings should be adjourned and the validity of the bye-law or decision concerned determined by way of judicial review. The normal avenue of appeal against decisions of the county court is to the Court of Appeal under the County Courts Act 1984, s.77.

Where there is an avenue of appeal from an inferior court or tribunal to the Court of Appeal (*e.g.* from a county court, or a tribunal such as the I.A.T. or the S.S.C.) or to the High Court (*e.g.* county court bankruptcy cases) and the applicant has already followed that avenue, but his appeal has been dismissed or he has been refused leave to appeal, he will not be permitted to re-litigate the matter by way of an application for judicial review because that would be an abuse of the process of the court. *Aliter*, if the point is one which he *could not* (rather than merely *did not*) take on the appeal.

Where, however, an inferior court or tribunal has acted outside its jurisdiction or there has been a denial of natural justice, judicial review may be the appropriate remedy. Judicial review cannot be used to appeal against the decisions of the General or Special Commissioners of Income Tax on the merits of tax cases. Appeal lies from those bodies to the High Court by way of case stated, but on points of law only: section 46(2) of the Taxes Management Act 1970 precludes any other method of appealing against tax assessments. *Aliter* if the General or Special Commissioners exceed their jurisdiction, or fail to observe the rules of natural justice (in a way which cannot be dealt with on an appeal by way of case stated: *cf. R. v. Special Commissioner, ex p. Napier* [1988] 3 All E.R. 166, CA), or refuse to state a case where they are obliged to do so; then judicial review would normally be the appropriate remedy.

R53.14.28 **On what grounds can judicial review be granted?**—The grounds on which judicial review can be granted fall under the following main headings:

R53.14.28A *1. Want or excess of jurisdiction*—Clearly if an inferior court or tribunal or a public authority charged with a public duty acts without jurisdiction or exceeds its jurisdiction judicial review will lie. A particularly vexed question is whether every error of law amounts to an excess of jurisdiction. One school of thought is that if the decision is founded upon an erroneous proposition of law, it follows that the body must have asked itself the wrong question and no such body has jurisdiction to base its decision on the wrong question. The other school of thought, which prevailed in this country for a long time, is that a distinction must be drawn between errors of law which go to jurisdiction and errors of law which do not. Following the decision of the House of Lords in *Anisminic Ltd v. Foreign Compensation Commission* [1969] 2 A.C. 147; [1969] 1 All E.R. 208 the first school of thought now obtains in English law, except possibly in relation to inferior courts. In *Anisminic* it was held that where the decision of an administrative authority or tribunal is founded, wholly or partly, on an error of law, the authority or tribunal has acted outside its jurisdiction and accordingly its decision is liable to be quashed. It may be that *Anisminic* does not apply to inferior courts, such as county courts; there is much to be said for the view that, where an inferior court has jurisdiction to adjudicate upon a particular type of case, it has jurisdiction to decide incorrectly as well as correctly the questions of law which go to the merits and do not go to jurisdiction (see *Racal Communications Limited* [1981] A.C. 374; [1980] 2 All E.R. 634, HL; and *South East Asia Fire Bricks SDN. BHD. v. Non-Metallic Mineral Products Manufacturing Employees Union* [1981] A.C. 363; [1980] 2 All E.R. 689, PC).

2. Where there is an error of law on the face of the record—Judicial review will lie where there is an error of law on the face of the record (*R. v. Northumberland Compensation Appeal Tribunal* [1952] 1 K.B. 338; *Baldwin and Francis Limited v. Patents Appeal Tribunal* [1959] A.C. 663; [1959] 2 All E.R. 433, HL). Recently what constitutes the "record" has been widely interpreted: it is not confined to the formal order, but extends to the reasoned decision given by the Judge in his written or oral judgment (*R. v. Crown Court at Knightsbridge, ex p. International Sporting Club (London) Ltd* [1982] Q.B. 304; [1981] 3 All E.R. 417, DC, applying *R. v. Northumberland Compensation Appeal Tribunal* [1952] 1 All E.R. 122). **R53.14.29**

3. Failure to comply with the rules of natural justice—Where the rules of natural justice apply and the decision has been reached in breach of those rules judicial review will lie (see, *e.g. Ridge v. Baldwin* [1964] A.C. 40; [1963] 2 All E.R. 66, HL). In that case a chief constable was dismissed by the police authority. The first decision to dismiss him was taken without giving him a hearing at all, which was held to be a breach of the rules of natural justice. Although the matter was reconsidered by the police authority on a later occasion after he had been given a hearing, the second decision to dismiss him was also found to have been reached in breach of the rules of natural justice because he was not informed of the allegations made against him or the reasons why it was proposed to dismiss him. **R53.14.30**

Broadly the rules of natural justice embody a duty to act fairly. Whether those rules apply and the extent of the duty depend upon the particular type of case concerned. "The rules of natural justice—or of fairness—are not cut and dried. They vary infinitely" (*R. v. Home Secretary, ex p. Santillo* [1981] Q.B. 778; [1981] 2 All E.R. 897, *per* Lord Denning M.R.). The rules of natural justice will normally apply where the decision concerned affects a person's rights, for example where his property is taken by compulsory purchase or he is dismissed from a public office (as in *Ridge v. Baldwin* [1964] A.C. 40; [1963] 2 All E.R. 66). The rules of natural justice can also apply where the applicant for judicial review does not have a right, for example where he is applying for some requisite statutory licence; in such cases, although he has no right to a licence unless and until it is granted, there is a duty to comply with the rules of natural justice and to act fairly because a legal power which affects his interests is being exercised. (For example see *R. v. Liverpool Corporation, ex p. Liverpool Taxi Operators' Association* [1972] 2 Q.B. 299; [1972] 2 All E.R. 589 and *R. v. Gaming Board for Great Britain, ex p. Benaim and Khaida* [1970] 2 Q.B. 417; [1970] 2 All E.R. 528).

Where a tribunal desires to proceed on the basis of some point which has not been advanced before it by any party, the person whose case is being considered by the tribunal and any other persons represented at the hearing or enquiry should be altered to the possibility of the tribunal taking the point concerned into account, so that all those affected by the decision have the opportunity to put forward any material which might persuade the tribunal differently on the point (*R. v. Mental Health Review Tribunal, ex p. Clatworthy* [1985] 3 All E.R. 699, *per* Mann J. at 704, following the observations of Lord Diplock in *Mahon v. Air New Zealand Ltd.* [1984] A.C. 808, at 821; [1984] 3 All E.R. 201 at 210).

In *R. v. General Medical Council, ex p. Gee* [1987] 1 W.L.R. 564; [1987] 2 All E.R. 193 the HL held (affirming the decision of the CA) that the criminal law doctrine that a count which is duplicitous is bad does not apply to charges of professional misconduct which are being brought before a professional disciplinary body; the CA had upheld Mann J's decision that the General Medical Council must furnish certain particulars of the professional misconduct alleged, and there was no appeal to the HL on that issue.

4. The Wednesbury principle—Decisions of persons or bodies which perform public duties or functions will be liable to be quashed or otherwise dealt with by an appropriate order in judicial **R53.14.31** review proceedings where the court concludes that the decision is such that no such person or body properly directing itself on the relevant law and acting reasonably could have reached that decision (*Associated Provincial Picture Houses Limited v. Wednesbury Corporation* [1948] 1 K.B. 223; [1947] 2 All E.R. 680, *per* Lord Green M.R.).

In *R. v. Hillingdon London B.C. ex p. Puhlhofer* [1986] A.C. 484; [1986] 1 All E.R. 467 the HL held that a local authority was entitled to decide that an applicant and his family were not homeless because they had one room at a bed and breakfast guest house available for their occupation; the room was "accommodation" within the meaning of sections 1 and 4 of the Housing (Homeless Persons) Act 1977 and the word "accommodation" was not to be qualified by importing such words as "appropriate" or "reasonable". What can properly be regarded as "accommodation" is a question of fact to be decided by the local authority.

Lord Brightman (with whose speech the other members of the House of Lords agreed) said (at 518/474):

"My Lords, I am troubled at the prolific use of judicial review for the purpose of challenging the performance by local authorities of their functions under the 1977 Act. Parliament intended the local authority to be the judge of fact. The Act abounds with the formula when, or if, the housing authority are satisfied as to this, or that, or have reason to believe this, or that. Although the action or inaction of a local authority is clearly susceptible to judicial review where they have misconstrued the Act, or abused their powers or otherwise acted perversely, I think that great restraint should be exercised in giving leave to proceed by judicial review ... [It] is not, in my opinion, appropriate that the remedy of judicial review, which is a discretionary remedy, should be made use of to monitor the actions of local authorities under the Act save in the exceptional case. The ground on which the courts will review the exercise of an administrative discretion is abuse of power, *e.g.* bad faith, a mistake in construing the limits of the power, a procedural irregularity or unreasonableness in the *Wednesbury* sense ... *i.e.* unreasonableness verging on an absurdity: see the speech of Lord Scarman in *Nottinghamshire C.C. v. Secretary of State for the Environment* [1986] A.C. 240 at 248; [1986] 1 All E.R. 199, at 202. Where the existence or non-existence of a fact is left to the judgment and discretion of a public body and that fact involves a broad spectrum ranging from the obvious to the debateable to the just conceivable, it is the duty of the court to leave the decision of that fact to the public body to whom Parliament has entrusted the decision-making power save in a case where it is obvious that the public body, consciously or unconsciously, are acting perversely."

It remains to be seen to what extent this doctrine will be applied to other statutory functions or to other bodies (compare: *R. v. Secretary of State for the Home Department, ex p. Khawaja*, paras R53.14.34 to R53.14.36).

R53.14.32 **Court's discretion**—Even if a case falls into one of the categories where judicial review will lie, the court is not bound to grant it; the jurisdiction to make any of the various orders available in judicial review proceedings is discretionary. What order or orders the court will make depends upon the circumstances of the particular case. For instance, if an inferior court or tribunal is about to adjudicate upon some matter which is outside its jurisdiction an order of prohibition will be appropriate; if the decision has already been made and there are grounds for setting it aside under one of the above heads, the usual form of order would be certiorari. (For an account of the function of the various forms of order available see paras R53.14.39 to 42 (certiorari, prohibition and mandamus) and paras R53.14.43 to 45 (declaration, injunction and damages)).

R53.14.33 **Distinction between public and private law**—Where a person seeks to establish that a decision of a person or body infringes rights which are entitled to protection under public law he must, as a general rule, proceed by way of judicial review and not by way of ordinary civil proceedings whether for a declaration or an injunction or otherwise (*O'Reilly v. Mackman* [1983] 2 A.C. 237; [1982] 3 All E.R. 1124, HL). If a person commences ordinary civil proceedings where he should have applied for judicial review, the claim will be struck out by summary process (*ibid.*). "... it would ... as a general rule be contrary to public policy, and as such an abuse of the process of the court, to permit a person seeking to establish that a decision of a public authority infringed rights to which he was entitled to protection under public law to proceed by way of an ordinary action and by this means to evade the provisions of O.53 for the protection of such authorities" (*ibid., per* Lord Diplock at 285/1134). Thus proceedings by action have been struck out where the plaintiffs sought declarations that the findings of the Board of Visitors of a prison were void on the grounds of failure to comply with the Prison Rules and the rules of natural justice (*O'Reilly v. Mackman*, above), and where the plaintiff commenced an action for a declaration, a mandatory injunction and damages in respect of an alleged breach by local authority of its duties under the Housing (Homeless Persons) Act 1977 (*Cocks v. Thanet District Council* [1983] 2 A.C. 286; [1982] 3 All E.R. 1135, HL); in both cases it was held that the plaintiffs should have made an application for judicial review. In *Waverley Borough Council v. Hilden* [1988] 1 W.L.R. 246; [1988] 1 All E.R. 807 Scott J. held that a challenge by the defendants, who were gypsies, to the reasonableness of the council's decision to take proceedings against them seeking an injunction restraining breaches of enforcement notices could be mounted only by way of proceedings for judicial review and not by way of defence to the action.

There are, however, cases where it is permissible to litigate public law issues in private law proceedings, for instance where the invalidity of the decision of the public authority arises as a collateral issue in a claim for infringement of a right of the plaintiff arising under private law, or where none of the parties objects to the proceedings being continued by way or ordinary action (*O'Reilly v. Mackman*, above *per* Lord Diplock). The question whether there are other exceptions was left to be decided on a case-by-case basis (*ibid.*). In *Davy v. Spelthorne Borough Council* [1984] A.C. 262; [1983] 3 All E.R. 278, HL the plaintiff commenced proceedings against the defendant council alleging that it had negligently advised him as to his rights under the Town and Country Planning Act 1971 and he claimed (1) an injunction restraining the council from implementing an enforcement notice which it had served, (2) damages and (3) an order that the enforcement notice be set aside. The Court of Appeal held that (1) and (3) (but not (2)) should be struck out applying the rule in *O'Reilly v. Mackman.* The House of Lords upheld the decision of the Court of Appeal that (2) should not be struck out because it was an ordinary common law action in tort concerning his private rights and not rights protected under public law. In *London Borough of Wandsworth v. Winder* [1985] A.C. 461; [1984] 3 All E.R. 976, the defendant pleaded by way of defence to a claim for possession based on rent arrears that the rent increases made by the council were invalid. The council applied for that defence to be struck out in reliance on *O'Reilly v. Mackman.* The HL held that the defence was not an abuse of the process of the court within the meaning of the rule in *O'Reilly v. Mackman* and refused the application to strike out.

The scope of the rule in *O'Reilly v. Mackman* is still a matter of debate. There are two main approaches which have been canvassed. The broad approach is that the rule does not apply to actions brought to vindicate private law rights even though involving a challenge to a public law act or decision. If the broad approach is adopted, the aggrieved person will be forced to proceed by way of judicial review only in a case where private law rights are not at stake. The narrower approach is that the rule in *O'Reilly v. Mackman* generally applies to all cases where it is sought to challenge a public law act or decision, subject to some exceptions when private rights are being invoked. In *Roy v. Kensington and Chelsea and Westminster Family Practitioner Committee* [1992] 1 A.C. 624; [1992] 1 All E.R. 705, the House of Lords left open the question which of these approaches should be adopted, but indicated a preference for the broad approach; in *Mercury Ltd v. Telecommunications Director* [1996] 1 W.L.R. 48, the HL adopted a broad flexible approach (see further below).

A claim in connection with the dismissal of an employee from an employment with a public authority, where the conditions of employment are governed by a statutory instrument, is nevertheless a matter of private, not public, law (*R. v. East Berkshire Health Authority, ex p. Walsh* [1985] Q.B. 152; [1984] 3 All E.R. 425, CA (senior nursing officer)). *Aliter* where the employment is one which is the subject of a code of discipline deriving its authority from statute: *R. v. Secretary of State for the Home Department, ex p. Benwell* [1985] Q.B. 554; [1984] 3 All E.R. 854 (prison officer). In *R. v. Civil Service Board, ex p. Bruce* [1989] 2 All E.R. 907 the Court of Appeal left open the question whether a decision upholding the dismissal of a civil servant was susceptible of judicial review (see para. R53.14.25).

In *R. v. Panel on Take-overs and Mergers, ex p. Datafin Ltd* [1987] Q.B. 815; [1987] 1 All E.R. 564, CA, it was held that a challenge to a decision of the Take-over Panel was a matter of public law and within the scope of judicial review, notwithstanding the fact that the Panel was not a creature of statute or the product of the exercise of the prerogative. The Court of Appeal considered that, although the Take-over Panel was part of a self-regulatory system with no statutory or other legal foundation, nevertheless its activities were of a public law character and susceptible to judicial review, whilst making it clear that only rarely would leave to apply for judicial review of the Panel's decisions be likely to be granted. But, in another case involving a non-statutory regulatory system (*R. v. Disciplinary Committee of the Jockey Club, ex p. The Aga Khan* [1993] 1 W.L.R. 909; [1993] 2 All E.R. 853) the Court of Appeal held that judicial review did not lie against a decision of the Jockey Club's Disciplinary Committee because the applicant was someone who had entered into a contract with the Club and therefore the case was within the province of private law, not public law. (The Court left open the question whether a person who did not have a contract with the Jockey Club could ever obtain judicial review of one of its decisions.) That approach was also adopted and applied by the Divisional Court in *R. v. Insurance Ombudsman Bureau, ex p. Aegon Life Insurance Ltd, The Times,* January 7, 1994, where the Court held that judicial review would not lie against such voluntary bodies unless they were "public bodies". A body whose birth and constitution owed nothing to any exercise of governmental power could be classed as a public body only if it had been woven into the fabric of public regulation, or into a system of governmental control, or was integrated into a system of statutory regulation, or, but for its existence, a governmental body would assume control. Judicial review should not lie against a body whose powers derived from agreement of the parties and when private law remedies were available against the body concerned. The Insurance Ombudsman Bureau fell into the latter category because it was a body whose jurisdiction was dependent on the contractual consent of its members and its decisions were of a private law arbitrative nature.

In *Roy v. Kensington and Chelsea and Westminster Family Practitioner Committee* [1992] 1 A.C. 624; [1992] 1 All E.R. 705, the House of Lords held that a claim by a general medical practitioner that the Family Practitioner Committee had acted wrongly in deciding to reduce the amount he was to be paid by way of "practice allowance" under the NHS Regulations was a matter which could be litigated in an ordinary action, notwithstanding the fact that the claim involved challenging a public law decision. The House of Lords said that, even on the narrower approach (*i.e.* that the rule in *O'Reilly v. Mackman* generally requires all challenges to public laws acts or decisions to be made by way of judicial review, subject only to certain exceptions) this case was not within, or was excepted from, the rule because Dr Roy's claim was based on either a contractual or statutory private law right to be paid his remuneration in accordance with his terms of service, private law rights dominated the proceedings, and the order sought (namely for payment of the full "practice allowance") was one which could not be made in judicial review proceedings. In *Mercury Ltd v. Telecommunications Director* [1996] 1 W.L.R. 48 the HL said that it was important to retain some flexibility, that the precise limits of what is called "private law" and "public law" are by no means worked out, and that private law proceedings should be struck out only if they constitute an abuse of the process of the court.

For further discussion of the distinction between public and private law see: *Gillick v. West Norfolk & Wisbech Area Health Authority* [1986] A.C. 112; [1985] 3 All E.R. 402, HL and *Bourgoin S.A. v. Ministry of Agriculture Fisheries and Food* [1986] Q.B. 716; [1985] 3 All E.R. 585, CA.

Where the relief sought in judicial review proceedings is a declaration, injunction or damages, and the court considers that it should not be granted on an application for judicial review, but might have been granted if it had been sought in ordinary civil proceedings begun by claim form the Court may, instead of refusing the application, order the proceedings to continue as proceedings brought under CPR, Part 7 (see para. R53.14.87 below). There is, however, no converse power under RSC to permit an ordinary claim to continue as if it were an application for judicial review (*O'Reilly v. Mackman* [1983] 2 A.C. 237 at 284; [1982] 3 All E.R. 1124 at 1133, *per* Lord Diplock). The proceedings must be commenced afresh by an application for judicial review. But, in many cases, by that stage, the three-month time limit for applying for leave to move for judicial review will have expired and, in consequence, any judicial review application is likely to fail on the grounds of delay (see paras R53.14.58 and 59 below).

R53.14.34 **Immigration cases**—Decisions in immigration matters are capable of challenge by way of judicial review (*R. v. Chief Immigration Officer Lympne Airport, ex p. Amrit Singh* [1968] 1 Q.B. 333; [1968] 3 All E.R. 163, DC; and *R. v. Secretary of State for the Home Department, ex p. Khawaja* [1984] A.C. 74; [1983] 1 All E.R. 765, HL); but now that there is a statutory appeal to the Court of Appeal under the Asylum and Immigration Appeals Act 1993, s.9 against decisions of the Immigration Appeals Tribunal, it will not be permissible to use judicial review in cases where the decision concerned can be challenged by an appeal from an adjudicator (or special adjudicator) to the I.A.T. and thence to the Court of Appeal (see para. R53.14.27).

R53.14.35 *Illegal entrants*—Where a decision that someone is an illegal entrant is susceptible to challenge by way of judicial review the court investigates whether the evidence justifies that decision. Where an official's decision is one which would restrict or take away a person's liberty and the exercise of the power to make that decision depends upon the existence of certain facts, the court is not limited to inquiry whether the official had reasonable grounds for believing that those facts existed. The court has to be satisfied on the civil standard of proof to the appropriate degree of probability that those facts did exist at the time when the power was exercised (*R. v. Secretary of State for the Home Department, ex p. Khawaja* [1984] A.C. 74; [1983] 1 All E.R. 765, HL). Thus where an immigration officer concludes that a person who has obtained leave to enter the U.K. is an illegal entrant on the grounds that he has obtained leave to enter by fraud or deception and detains him pending removal from the U.K., the court will in judicial review proceedings scrutinise the evidence to see whether it has been proved that leave to enter was obtained by fraud or deception (*ibid.*, and *R. v. Secretary of State for the Home Department, ex p. Momin Ali* [1984] 1 All E.R. 1009, CA). (For the position concerning bail see paras R53.14.52 and 53.)

Where, however, any such decision is challenged by way of appeal to an adjudicator and thence to the I.A.T., the I.A.T. (and not the Court) will be the final arbiter of all such issues of fact, because appeal lies from the I.A.T. to the Court of Appeal only on questions of law.

R53.14.36 *Habeas corpus in immigration cases*—Where a person is being lawfully detained under the immigration legislation pending removal from the U.K. and he wishes to challenge the validity of the underlying decision upon which the decision to remove him and detain him pending removal is based, habeas corpus cannot be used as a means of challenging that underlying decision or his detention. Even though there may be grounds, even strong grounds, for challenging such decision (*e.g.* error of law, want of natural justice, or "*Wednesbury*") the underlying decision is valid until set aside by the court in judicial review proceedings, or by way of an appeal to an adjudicator or the I.A.T. Unless and until that decision is set aside, his detention is lawful and there are no grounds for granting habeas corpus (see *R. v. Secretary of State for the Home Department, ex p. Muboyayi* [1992] 1 Q.B. 244; [1991] 4 All E.R. 72, CA and *R. v. Secretary of State for the Home Department and Governor of H.M. Prison Hindley, ex p. Ali*, CA, August 31, 1993 (unrep.)).

R53.14.37 **No issue estoppel in judicial review proceedings**—The doctrine of issue estoppel cannot be relied on in proceedings for judicial review because in such proceedings there are no formal pleadings and it would frequently be difficult, if not impossible, to identify a particular issue as having been decided in the earlier application; furthermore in such proceedings there is no "*lis*" between the Crown, in whose name the proceedings are brought, and the respondent, or between the applicant and the respondent, nor is the decision a final determination (*R. v. Secretary of State for the Environment, ex p. Hackney London Borough Council* [1983] 1 W.L.R. 524; [1983] 3 All E.R. 358, DC).

R53.14.38 **No estoppel against the Crown**—The Crown cannot put itself in a position where it is prevented from performing its public duty, and cannot, by entering into an agreement or arrangement estop itself from exercising in the future a power or discretion which it is its duty to exercise; but officers of the Crown (for instance officials of the Inland Revenue) are amenable to judicial review if they exceed or abuse their powers: *R. v. Inland Revenue Commissioners, ex p. Preston* [1985] A.C. 835; [1985] 2 All E.R. 327, where the HL held that the Commissioners of Inland Revenue were amenable to judicial review, but upheld the decision of the CA that, on the facts of that case, the application for judicial review failed because the Commissioners had acted *intra vires* and had not in any way abused their powers. "Counsel for the taxpayer submitted that if, as Lord Scarman announced in the *Self-Employed* case, the commissioners owe a duty of fairness to the general body of taxpayers the commissioners must equally owe a duty of fairness to each individual taxpayer. I agree, but a taxpayer cannot complain of unfairness merely because the commissioners decide to perform their statutory duties ... and to enforce a liability to tax. The commissioners may decide to abstain from exercising their powers and performing their duties on grounds of unfairness, but the commissioners themselves must bear in mind that their primary duty is to collect, not to forgive, taxes. And, if the commissioners decide to proceed, the court cannot in the absence of exceptional circumstances decide to be unfair that which the commissioners by taking action against the taxpayer have determined to be fair.... The court can only intervene by judicial review to direct the commissioners to abstain from performing their statutory duties or from exercising their statutory powers if the court is satisfied that 'the unfairness' of which the applicant complains renders the insistence by the commissioners on performing their duties or exercising their powers an abuse of power by the commissioners" (*per* Lord Templeman at 864/339).

Types of Relief Available in Judicial Review Proceedings

Certiorari (rr.1(1) and 9(4))—Certiorari is an order which brings up into the High Court a decision of an inferior court or tribunal or of a public authority for it to be quashed. Thus, where in judicial review proceedings the court concludes that a decision which has been made by an inferior court or tribunal or a public authority should be set aside, certiorari would normally be the appropriate form of order. Where the court quashes a decision, it has power to remit the matter to the court, tribunal or authority concerned with a direction to reconsider it and to reach a decision in accordance with the judgment given by the court in the judicial review proceedings (see S.C.A. 1981, s.31(5) and O.53, r.9(4) and para. R53.14.86). **R53.14.39**

Prohibition (rr.1(1))—Prohibition is an order restraining an inferior court or tribunal or a public authority from acting outside its jurisdiction. Thus where, for example, a tribunal is proposing to adjudicate upon some matter which is not within its jurisdiction judicial review will lie and the court can make an order of prohibition. If the inferior court has no jurisdiction, the fact that an appeal lies to some court from its decision does not prevent an order of the prohibition being made (*Turner v. Kingsbury Collieries Ltd* [1921] 3 K.B. 169; *R. v. North, ex p. Oakey* [1927] 1 K.B. 491 at 503; *R. v. Comptroller-General of Patents and Designs* [1953] 2 Q.B. 48; [1953] 1 All E.R. 862). Prohibition may be invoked before the court, tribunal or authority has made any decision (*R. v. Electricity Commissioners* [1924] K.B. 171, *R. v. Minister of Health* (1929) 45 T.L.R. 176). The granting of an order of prohibition is discretionary (*Parochial Church Council of St. Magnus-the-Martyr v. Chancellor of London* [1923] P. 38); and although it will normally be made to prevent an excess of jurisdiction (*Worthington v. Jeffries* (1875) L.R. 10 C.P. 379), it ought not to be made lightly (*Governors of Queen Anne's Bounty v. Pitt-Rivers* [1936] 2 K.B. 419 at 431), and may be refused in a case of laches or misconduct of the applicant (*Parochial Church Council of St. Magnus-the-Martyr v. Chancellor of London*, above). **R53.14.40**

Prohibition in county court cases—Section 84 of the County Courts Act 1984 provides that the county court judge is not to be served with notice of an application for prohibition, nor (except by order of a Judge of the High Court) is he required to appear or be heard, or liable for costs. The application is to proceed and be heard in the same manner as an appeal from a decision of the judge (*ibid.*). **R53.14.41**

Mandamus (r.1(1))—Mandamus is an order requiring an inferior court or tribunal or a person or body of persons charged with a public duty to carry out its judicial or other public duty. An order of mandamus cannot be made against the Crown (Crown Proceedings Act 1947, s.40), but it will lie against an officer of the Crown who is obliged by statute to do some ministerial or administrative act which affects the rights or interests of the applicant. An order of mandamus may be made against an inferior court or tribunal to set it in motion, *e.g.* where it refuses to record its adjudication (*R. v. Essex Justices, ex p. Final* [1963] 2 Q.B. 816; [1962] 3 All E.R. 924). **R53.14.42**

It can be granted where an inferior court or tribunal is obliged to state a case and is refusing to do so. In addition there are statutory provisions under which an order for mandamus, requiring a case to be stated, may be directed to the Crown Court (S.C.A. 1981, s.29(3)) or a magistrates' court (Magistrates' Courts Act 1980, s.111(6)). Where a party to an appeal from a tribunal by way of case stated wishes to have particular material included in the stated case, *e.g.* a statement of the evidence upon which particular findings of fact are based, and the tribunal refuses to include it, it is unclear whether an application in judicial review proceedings for mandamus is the appropriate remedy. On principle it should be, but there are dicta in *R. v. Special Commissioners of Income Tax, ex p. Emery* [1980] S.T.C. 549, DC that, where the court which will hear the appeal by way of case stated has power to amend the case, that court should deal with the question of the content of the case. *Sed quaere* the tribunal will not be a party to that appeal and will therefore not put in any evidence or be represented; and yet it is the members of the tribunal who will be in the best position to say on what evidence their findings are based.

R53.14.43 **Claims for declaration or injunction (r.1)**—For the principles relating to declaratory judgments see RSC, O.15, r.16 (re-enacted in CPR Sched. 1) (para. R15). Under CPR, r.25(1)(b) there is now power to grant an interim declaration.

As to claims for an injunction, see S.C.A. 1981, s.37.

An application for an injunction under S.C.A. 1981, s.30 restraining a person from acting in any office in which he is not entitled to act *must* be brought by application for judicial review (O.53, r.1(1)(b) and see further para. R53.14.91 below).

An application for a declaration or injunction (other than an injunction under s.30) *may* be made by way of an application for judicial review. On such an application the court is given a wide discretion subject to certain specified factors. Under O.53, r.1(2), the court must have regard to the following specified factors, namely.

(a) the nature of the matters in respect of which relief may be granted by way of a prerogative order,
(b) the nature of the persons and bodies against whom relief may be granted by way of such an order, and
(c) all the circumstances of the case.

Those factors suggest that, if the court should conclude that the grant of an appropriate prerogative order will effectively give the applicant the relief he seeks or should have, it would lean against the grant of a declaration or injunction, and simply grant the appropriate prerogative order.

Until recently it was thought to be a well established rule (based on s.21(2) of the Crown Proceedings Act 1947) that injunctions could not be granted against a minister or Crown servant in his official capacity (see *R. v. Secretary of State for Transport, ex p. Factortame Ltd (No. 1)* [1990] 2 A.C. 95). In *M. v. Home Office* [1993] 3 W.L.R. 433; [1993] 3 All E.R. 537, however, the House of Lords held that injunctions (whether final or interlocutory) can be granted against ministers and Crown servants in their official, as well as their private capacities.

R53.14.44 **Injunctions to give effect to European Community Law**—In *R. v. Secretary of State for Transport, ex p. Factortame Ltd (No. 2)* [1991] A.C. 603; [1991] 1 All E.R. 70, C.J.E.C. and HL (which was decided at a time when it was thought that injunctions could not be granted against the Crown or its servants) it was held that an injunction could be granted against the Crown, or an officer of the Crown, were it necessary to do so in order to give a remedy in favour of a party invoking rights derived from directly applicable Community Law. (That case concerned an interim injunction, but it is submitted that the reasoning and ruling of the CJEC would apply equally to a perpetual injunction where it was necessary to grant such an injunction against the Crown or an officer of the Crown in order to ensure that full effect is given to directly applicable Community Law.)

R53.14.45 **Claim for damages (r.7)**—On an application for judicial review, the court has power to award damages to the applicant, provided (1) he has included in his statement in support of the application for leave, a claim for damages, and (2) the court is satisfied that, if the claim had been made in an ordinary civil claim by the applicant he could have been awarded damages (r.7(1)). For these purposes CPR, Part 16 (which contains the new rules relating to statements of case) applies to a claim for damages in judicial review proceedings.

The claim to damages in an application for judicial review is not the creation of a new substantive right, but must be one which could have been made in proceedings begun by claim form.

R53.14.46 **Joinder of claims for relief (r.2)**—Rule 2 makes it clear that a claim for one form of relief, whether it be any of the prerogative orders or a declaration, injunction or damages may be joined, either alternatively or in addition to, a claim for another form of relief. The only condition for such joinder is that both heads of relief must arise out of or relate to or be connected with the same matter. If the two forms of relief are not related as provided by the rule, the court will no doubt put the applicant to his election as to which form of relief he wishes to proceed on.

Moreover, each head of claim must be separately set out in the statement in support of the application for judicial review (Form 86A), and it must be made clear whether each claim is additional or alternative to any other.

R53.14.47 **Applications for interlocutory orders (r.8)**—A useful development in applications for judicial review is the introduction of applications for interlocutory relief (see r.8). It is specifically provided (in r.8(1)) that "interlocutory application" includes applications for disclosure and inspection of documents (under CPR, Part 31), for further information (under CPR, Part 18), and for permission to cross-examine any person on his written evidence; but r.8(1) also covers any other form of interlocutory application and it would follow, therefore, that a party in judicial review proceedings (whether applicant or respondent) could apply for any type of procedural order, remedy or direction which could be sought under the CPR in ordinary civil proceedings. Under r.8(1) an application can be made for an order dismissing the proceedings by consent of the parties.

An application for such interlocutory orders may be made to any Judge or to a Master of the Queen's Bench Division (r.8(1)) though in the latter case where the application for judicial review is to be heard by a Divisional Court, any appeal will lie not to a Judge, but to the Divisional Court itself (r.8(2)). In practice, contested applications for interlocutory relief are normally heard by a Judge nominated to hear Crown Office List cases.

This rule is, however, subject to the limitation that it is without prejudice to any statutory provision or rule of law restricting the making of an order against the Crown (r.8(3)).

Interim remedies—At any time in the course of judicial review proceedings the Court may grant any interim remedy in accordance with CPR, Part 25, in particular interim injunctions (CPR, r.25.1(a)) and an interim declaration (CPR, r.25.1(b)). In addition the Court has power to grant certain forms of interim relief in the exercise of its inherent jurisdiction (e.g. bail (see para. R53.14.52) and a stay (see para. R53.14.51). R53.14.48

The power to grant an interim injunction or other interim remedy in judicial review proceedings is ancillary to an application for permission to apply for judicial review, and to the substantive application for judicial review. Thus the judge can grant an interim remedy on granting permission to apply for judicial review, or, subsequent to the grant of permission, at any stage during the course of the substantive judicial review proceedings. Where the case is so urgent as to justify it, the Judge can grant an interim injunction or other interim remedy pending the hearing of the application for permission. But, if the judge has refused permission to apply for judicial review, he is *functus officio* and has no jurisdiction to grant any form of interim remedy. The application for an interim remedy can, however, be renewed before the Court of Appeal along with the renewal of the application for permission to apply for judicial review. (This passage was cited with approval by Lord Woolf in *M. v. Home Office* [1994] 1 A.C. 377, 423; [1993] 3 All E.R. 537, 565.) If the Judge grants permission, but refuses interim relief, the applicant can appeal to the Court of Appeal against that refusal, subject to obtaining permission to appeal: (see further discussion of the case of *Turkoglu* in para. R53.14.52).

For guidance on the practice and procedure relating to applications for interim relief see *R. v. Kensington & Chelsea Royal L.B., ex p. Hammell* [1989] Q.B. 518; [1989] 1 All E.R. 1202 where the Court of Appeal held:

(1) The jurisdiction to grant an interim remedy in judicial review proceedings arises on the grant of permission to apply for judicial review. An application for an interim injunction or other interim remedy can be made without notice to any other party at the same time as the application for permission. In deciding whether to grant the interim remedy at that stage, the judge should consider whether the urgency and other circumstances of the case warrant its being granted without the other party(ies) being heard. Unless the judge is satisfied that the urgency and other circumstances do justify it, he should adjourn the application for the interim remedy for hearing on notice.

(2) With a view to avoiding two hearings, the applicant should give notice to the respondent(s) of any application for an interim remedy so that the respondent(s) can consider whether to attend the initial hearing of the application for permission in order to make representations.

(3) Applying *De Falco v. Crawley Borough Council* [1980] 1 Q.B. 460; [1980] 1 All E.R. 913, interim relief by way of mandatory injunction should be granted only where a strong prima facie case of breach of duty has been made out at the interim stage. *Cf. R. v. Cardiff City Council, ex p. Barry*, CA November 6, 1988 (unrep.) where the Court of Appeal granted an injunction when granting leave at an *ex parte* hearing.

Interim injunctions in judicial review proceedings—An interim injunction can be obtained in judicial review proceedings pending the determination of the substantive judicial review application, or, if the urgency of the case justifies it, pending the hearing of the application for permission. The approach to applications for interim injunctions in judicial review proceedings is similar to that adopted in the case of such applications in ordinary civil proceedings (see *R. v. Kensington and Chelsea Royal London Borough Council, ex p. Hammell* [1989] Q.B. 518; [1989] 1 All E.R. 1202, above). R53.14.49

In *M. v. Home Office* [1993] 3 W.L.R. 433; [1993] 3 All E.R. 537, HL, it was held that injunctions, including interlocutory injunctions, can be granted against ministers and Crown servants, see further para. R53.14.43.

Interim relief to give effect to European Community Law—In *R. v. Secretary of State for Transport, ex p. Factortame Ltd (No. 2)* [1991] A.C. 603; [1991] 1 All E.R. 70, ECJ and HL (which was decided at a time when it was thought that injunctions could not be granted against the Crown or its servants) it was held that an interlocutory injunction could be granted preventing a minister of R53.14.50

the Crown from implementing legislation alleged to be a contrary to Community Law, pending final determination of that issue. The Court of Justice of the European Communities ruled that where a national court is seised of a case involving issues of Community Law and it is necessary to grant interim relief in order to ensure the full effectiveness of rights claimed under directly applicable Community Law, any rule of national law preventing the grant of such interim relief must be set aside. Accordingly s.21(2) of the Crown Proceedings Act 1947 did not prevent the English courts from granting an interim injunction against the Crown, pending the final determination of the issues to Community Law arising in the case. The question whether interim relief should be granted is a matter for the national court. The case therefore came back before the House of Lords for decision on whether an injunction should be granted and, if so, in what terms. The House of Lords held:

(1) that the balance of convenience was likely to be the determining factor, because it was unlikely, in such cases, there would be an adequate remedy in damages available to either side;
(2) that generally, the court should not restrain a public authority from enforcing an apparently authentic law unless the court is satisfied, having regard to all the circumstances, that the challenge to the validity of that law is, prima facie, so firmly based as to justify so exceptional a course being taken; but it is always a matter of discretion; and
(3) that, on the facts of the instant case, the applicants' challenge was, prima facie, a strong one, and the balance of convenience came down in favour of the grant of the interim injunction sought.

R53.14.51 **Stay in judicial review proceedings (r.3(10))**—By virtue of O.53, r.3(10)(a), where permission to apply for judicial review has been granted and the relief sought is an order of prohibition or certiorari, then, if the court so directs, the grant of permission to apply for judicial review operates as a stay of the proceedings to which the judicial review application relates until the determination of that application or further order. In *R. v. Secretary of State for Education and Science, ex p. Avon County Council* [1991] 1 Q.B. 558; [1991] 2 All E.R. 282 the Court of Appeal held:

(1) that r.3(10)(a) is not, as counsel for the Secretary of State had contended, confined to cases where the judicial review application relates to judicial or quasi judicial proceedings, but enables the court to impose a stay on "the process by which the decision challenged has been reached, including the decision itself."
(2) That the stay sought was not in the nature of an injunction and therefore the court is not precluded by s.21(2) of the Crown Proceedings Act 1947 from granting a stay against a minister or officer of the Crown.

Thus, on the grant of permission to apply for judicial review, the court has jurisdiction, where appropriate, to stay the decision making process (if it has not yet been completed), the decision itself and its implementation.

There is no authority, as yet, on the question whether the court has power to grant a stay pending the hearing of the application for permission to apply for judicial review, if the circumstances of the case warrant it. O.53, r.3(1)(a) does not confer such a power because that sub-rule only applies "where permission to apply for judicial review is granted"; but it is arguable that the court has inherent jurisdiction to grant a stay. It would be very strange, and most unsatisfactory, if the person or body whose decision is sought to be reviewed could pre-empt the matter by implementing the decision before a leave application could be heard.

Often the problem is overcome by the government department, local authority or other body concerned agreeing to defer the implementation of the decision to enable the applicant to make an expedited application for permission to apply for judicial review, and, if permission is refused at first instance, to renew it before the Court of Appeal. In most, if not all, cases where such an agreement is not forthcoming, the solution will be for the court to grant an appropriate form of interlocutory injunction: such an injunction can now be granted against a government department or Crown official (see para. R53.14.43).

There may, however, come a time when the question of the court's jurisdiction to grant a stay pending the hearing of the application for permission has to be resolved. If such a case arises, it is submitted that, just as the court has inherent jurisdiction to grant bail pending an application for leave to move for judicial review (see *R. v. Secretary of State for the Home Department, ex p. Turkoglu* [1988] Q.B. 398; [1987] 2 All E.R. 283), so should it have inherent jurisdiction to grant a stay where that is necessary to ensure that the application for judicial review is not pre-empted or the interests of justice defeated. There is no reason why an inherent jurisdiction to grant a stay should not co-exist with the more limited power to grant a stay conferred by O.53, r.3(1)(a).

R53.14.52 **Bail in judicial review cases**—In *R. v. Secretary of State for the Home Department, ex p. Turkoglu* [1988] Q.B. 398; [1987] 2 All E.R. 283, the Court of Appeal reviewed the position regarding bail in judicial review cases and held as follows:

(i) The High Court Judge has inherent jurisdiction to grant bail where there is pending before the High Court either an application for permission to apply for judicial review or a substantive judicial review application.
(ii) Where the High Court Judge refuses bail in any case within (i), appeal lies to the CA

against that decision under s.16 of S.C.A. 1981 (*Re Dhillon, The Times,* January 28, 1987, not followed).

(iii) Where the High Court Judge has refused permission to apply for judicial review, the High Court has no jurisdiction to grant bail because the High Court Judge is *functus officio*; bail has to be ancillary to some other proceeding: it cannot be granted *in vacuo.*

(iv) But, in a case where permission to apply for judicial review has been refused by the High Court, the applicant can renew that application to the CA (see para. R53.14.65) and the CA has inherent jurisdiction to grant bail; the bail application to the CA would be ancillary to the renewed application for permission to apply for judicial review.

Bail in immigration cases—In *Re Vilvarajah's application for bail, The Times,* October 31, 1987 the Court of Appeal considered the approach to be adopted in the case of applications for bail in immigration cases. (The court only has jurisdiction to grant bail where the application for bail is incidental to some other proceedings: see *R. v. Secretary of State for the Home Department, ex p. Turkoglu,* above.) The Court of Appeal said that, in deciding whether it is appropriate to grant bail, it is necessary to distinguish between two categories of case: R53.14.53

(1) Cases where the applicant is being detained pending a decision to grant or refuse him leave to enter the U.K.; and

(2) Cases where an applicant who has been refused admission and is therefore required to leave the U.K., is in custody pending implementation of that decision.

In the first type of case the adjudicator has jurisdiction, in an appropriate case, to grant bail (Immigration Act 1971, Sched. 2, para. 22) and therefore an application for bail should be made by that route. The adjudicator has power to grant bail subject to conditions requiring provision of sureties.

In the second type of case the Secretary of State can grant what is, in effect, bail by granting temporary leave to enter the U.K., pending determination of the applicant's judicial review proceedings. The Secretary of State has no power, however, to impose a requirement of sureties in connection with the grant of temporary leave to enter. Where the Secretary of State has refused temporary leave to enter, the position is as follows. There are some cases where the Secretary of State has refused temporary admission, but would not oppose the grant of bail by the court subject to conditions requiring provision of suitable sureties. In such cases the court would normally grant conditional bail. Where, however, the Secretary of State has refused temporary admission and opposes the application to the court for bail, the court will not grant bail unless the Secretary of State has committed some error of principle in refusing temporary admission, or his decision is unreasonable in the *Wednesbury* sense.

Procedure for Applying for Judicial Review in Civil Cases

Two-stage process for judicial review—The recommendation of the Law Commission (see para. 59(c) of their Report) that an application for judicial review must be made in two stages, has been adopted and applied. Thus it is first necessary to apply for, and obtain, permission to apply for judicial review, and only if and to the extent that such permission is granted will the court proceed to hear the substantive application for judicial review (r.3(1)). The applicant for permission must: R53.14.54

(a) have a "sufficient interest" (see para. R53.14.24 above);

(b) have a case sufficiently arguable to merit investigation at a substantive hearing (see paras R53.14.58 to R53.14.60 below); and

(c) must apply for permission promptly (see paras R53.14.58 and 59).

Application for Permission to Apply for Judicial Review

Permission to apply for judicial review (r.3)—The application for permission to apply for judicial review is made to a single Judge, whether in term time or vacation (see r.3(2)). R53.14.55

The purpose of the requirement of permission is: (a) to eliminate at an early stage any applications which are either frivolous, vexatious or hopeless, and (b) to ensure that an applicant is only allowed to proceed to a substantive hearing if the court is satisfied that there is a case fit for further consideration (see below). The requirement that permission must be obtained is designed to "prevent the time of the court being wasted by busybodies with misguided or trivial complaints of administrative error, and to remove the uncertainty in which public officers and authorities might be left as to whether they could safely proceed with administrative action while proceedings for judicial review of it were actually pending even though misconceived" (*R. v. Inland Revenue Commissioners, ex p. National Federation of Self-Employed and Small Businesses Ltd* [1982] A.C. 617 at 642; [1981] 2 All E.R. 93 at 105, *per* Lord Diplock). Permission should be granted, if on the material then available the court thinks, without going into the matter in depth, that there is an arguable case for granting the relief claimed by the applicant (*ibid.*, at 644/106). In *R. v. Secretary of State for the Home Department, ex p. Rukshanda Begum* [1990] C.O.D. 107, the Court of Appeal held that the test to be applied in deciding whether to grant permission to apply for judicial review is whether the judge is satisfied that there is a case fit for further investigation at a full hearing of a substantive application for judicial review (see para. R53.14.62). If, on considering the papers, the Judge cannot tell whether there is, or is not, an arguable case, he should invite the putative respondent to attend the hearing of the application for permission and make representations on the question whether permission should be granted (*ibid.*).

An application for permission to apply for judicial review is made by filing in the Crown Office

(a) an application notice in Form 86A (see SCP 1999, Vol. 2, para. 1A–88) containing a statement of
  (i) the name and description of the applicant;
  (ii) the relief sought and the grounds upon which it is sought;
  (iii) the name and address of the applicant's solicitor, if any; and
  (iv) the applicant's address for service; and

(b) written evidence verifying the facts relied on (see r.3(2)).

The statement contained in the application notice is not the equivalent of a statement of case or particulars of claim in ordinary civil proceedings, but is analogous to the part of a claim form specifying the remedies which the claimant seeks.

The written evidence can be either an affidavit or a witness statement (see the O.53 Practice Direction, para. 5.1, see R53PD–002). The requirements relating to affidavits are set out in paras 2 to 16 of the Practice Direction which supplements Part 32 of the CPR (see para. 32PD-001). The requirements relating to witness statements are set out in paras 17 to 23 of the Practice Direction which supplements Part 32 of the CPR (see para. 32PD-001) and all witness statements must be verified by a statement of truth (CPR, r.22.1(c)).

The written evidence filed in support of the application for permission must set out and verify all the facts relied on and exhibit any relevant documentary material.

The Court has power to permit the statement to be amended either when granting permission (r.3(6)) or at the substantive hearing (r.6(2)).

If more than one form of relief is sought, each form must be claimed in the statement, and it must be made clear whether the second or further form of relief is alternative or additional to any other form of relief claimed.

If damages are sought they must be claimed in the statement (r.7(1)(a)), and Part 16 of the CPR (dealing with statements of case) applies to a claim for damages in judicial review proceedings (r.7(2)).

Where permission is sought to apply for an order of certiorari to remove for the purpose of its being quashed, any judgment, order, conviction or other proceeding which is subject to appeal and a time is limited for the bringing of the appeal, the court may adjourn the application for leave until the appeal is determined or the time for appealing has expired (r.3(6)) (see *R. v. Barnes, ex p. Vernon* (1910) 102 L.T. 860; *R. v. Brompton West JJ., ex p. Storey* (1949) July 5, 1949).

R53.14.56 *Bundles of documents*—Where the documents in support of an application for permission to apply for judicial review exceed 10 pages, the applicant's solicitor (or the applicant, if in person) must lodge with the Crown Office an indexed and paginated bundle comprising those documents (see *Practice Direction (Crown Office List: Preparation for Hearings)* [1994] 1 W.L.R. 1551; [1994] 4 All E.R. 671).

R53.14.57 *Duty on applicant to make full and frank disclosure*—The applicant for permission must show *uberrima fides*, and if permission is obtained on false statements or a suppression of material facts in the affidavit, the court may refuse an order on this ground alone (*R. v. Kensington Commissioners, ex p. Polignac* [1917] 1 K.B. 486, CA; *R. v. Barnes, ex p. Vernon* (1910) 102 L.T. 860). In *R. v. Jockey Club Licensing Committee, ex p. Wright* [1991] C.O.D. 306, QBD the grant of leave to move for judicial review was set aside on the grounds of material non-disclosure on the part of the applicant (see para. R53.14.60 below).

R53.14.58 **Delay in applying for relief and extensions of time (r.4)**—Application for permission to apply for judicial review must be made promptly, which in this context means as soon as practicable or as soon as the circumstances of the case will allow, and in any event such application must be made within three months from the date when grounds for the application first arose (see r.4(1); see also S.C.A. 1981, s.31(6)). For this purpose time starts to run from the date when the grounds for the application first arose. In the particular case of an application for an order of certiorari in respect of any judgment, order, conviction or other proceeding, the date when grounds for the application first arose will be taken to be the date of that judgment, order, conviction or proceedings (r.4(2)). It is sometimes thought that an applicant for judicial review is always allowed three months in which to make his application for permission, and provided that he lodges it within that period permission cannot be refused on the grounds of delay. That is not so. The primary requirement laid down by the rules (r.4(1)) is that the application must be made "promptly", followed by the secondary provision "... and in any event within three months ..." Thus, there can be cases where, even though the application for permission was made within the three-month period, permission might be refused because, on the facts, the application had not been made promptly (for an example of such a case see: *R. v. Independent Television Commission, ex p. TV NI Ltd, The Times,* December 30, 1991, CA).

On the other hand, the court has power to extend time for applying for permission, but only if it considers that there is "good reason" for doing so (see r.4(1)). Where an application to extend the time is made under r.4 notice thereof must be given to the person who will be respondent to the motion (*R. v. Ashford, Kent JJ., ex p. Rickley* [1955] 1 W.L.R. 562; [1955] 2 All E.R. 327n). The court will consider whether the grant of an extension of time for applying for judicial review will be likely to cause substantial hardship or prejudice, not only to the instant parties, but to a wider public or may be detrimental to good administration.

Section 31(6) of S.C.A. 1981 provides that:

> "Where the High Court considers that there has been undue delay in making an application for judicial review, the court may refuse to grant (a) leave for the making of the application; or (b) any relief sought on the application, if it considers that the granting of the relief sought would be likely to cause substantial hardship to, or substantially prejudice the rights of, any person or would be detrimental to good administration."

The provisions of s.31(6) and r.4(1) and (2) are without prejudice to any other statutory provision which has the effect of limiting the time within which an application for judicial review must be made (see r.4(3)).

In *R. v. Stratford-on-Avon District Council, ex p. Jackson* [1985] 1 W.L.R. 1319; [1985] 3 All E.R. 769, the Court of Appeal considered the construction and effect of O.53, r.4 and s.31(6) of S.C.A. 1981 and held as follows—

(i) The "application" referred to in r.4 means the application for [permission to apply] for judicial review. Accordingly the question is whether [permission] was applied for promptly and, in any event, within the three month period. (This point was put beyond doubt by an amendment to the rule made by S.I. 1987 No. 1423.)

(ii) The fact that an application for [permission] has been made within the three month period does not necessarily mean that it has been made promptly. There could be cases where, even though the application for [permission] was made within the three month period, the applicant would nevertheless have to seek an extension of time because, on the facts, he had not acted promptly (for an example see: *R. v. Independent Television Commission, ex p. TV NI Ltd, The Times*, December 30, 1991, CA).

(iii) The cases concerning renewal of writs are of no assistance in deciding whether to grant an extension of time for applying for [permission to apply] for judicial review, because judicial review proceedings involve public law and there is no true *lis inter partes*. The question is whether, on the facts, there is a reasonable excuse for the delay and there are good reasons for extending time. The time taken to obtain legal aid may constitute a reasonable excuse provided that the application for legal aid has been expeditiously pursued on the part of the applicant.

(iv) Whether there has been "undue delay" within the meaning of s.31(6) has to be determined objectively. Thus, wherever there is a failure to comply with r.4(1) (*i.e.* a failure to apply for leave promptly or within the three month period, as the case may be) there is "undue delay" for the purposes of s.31(6), even though the court is satisfied that there are good grounds for extending time under r.4. In such cases the court retains a discretion under s.31(6) to refuse to grant [permission], or to refuse the relief sought at the hearing of the substantive application for judicial review, if it considers that the granting of the relief sought would be likely to cause substantial hardship to, or substantially prejudice the rights of, any person or would be detrimental to good administration. Whether the s.31(6) issue should be determined at the [permission] stage, or whether [permission] should be given and the s.31(6) issue dealt within the substantive judicial review proceedings depends on the circumstances. If the s.31(6) issue involves going substantially into the merits, the latter is likely to be the more appropriate course.

In *R. v. Dairy Produce Quota Tribunal for England and Wales, ex p. Caswell* [1989] 1 W.L.R. 1089; [1989] 3 All E.R. 205 the Court of Appeal held that, where an applicant has failed to apply for [permission] promptly, or within three months at the latest, but the Judge at the [permission] stage grants the applicant an extension of time, good reason for the delay having been shown, it is not open to the applicant to argue at the substantive hearing that there has not been undue delay. The fact that the application for leave was not made promptly, or within three months at the latest, carries with it the inevitable consequence of undue delay, even where the applicant has shown good reason for it and extension has been granted; and it is open to the court hearing the substantive application for judicial review to refuse relief on the grounds of "substantial hardship" or "detriment to good administration" within the meaning of s.31(6).

"Detrimental to good administration"—In *R. v. Dairy Produce Quota for Tribunal for England and Wales, ex p. Caswell* [1989] 1 W.L.R. 1089; [1989] 3 All E.R. 205 the Court of Appeal declined to attempt to define the expression "detrimental to good administration" or to give examples, but put forward the following guidelines:— **R53.14.59**

(i) The subsection requires proof of detriment to good administration; anything else, such as inconvenience, will not suffice. To constitute such detriment the foreseen consequences of granting the relief sought must be positive harm to good administration.

(ii) In considering whether the consequences would be harmful to good administration, the court can take into account not only the particular case, but also the effect on other potential applicants and the consequences if their applications were successful.

(iii) There must be affirmative evidence of such detriment, or at least evidence from which it can properly be inferred.

R53.14.60 **Determination of application for permission to apply for judicial review (r.3)**—The application for permission may be determined by the Judge without a hearing (unless a hearing is requested in the notice of application). This procedure enables the court to deal with such applications more conveniently and expeditiously and saves costs. Although the applicant is entitled to request a hearing, this would not necessarily be to his advantage since the application may be granted without a hearing, thus saving the applicant the expense of briefing counsel to apply for permission, and if permission is refused, the applicant still has the right to renew his application with the added advantage of knowing the Judge's preliminary reaction and his observations, if any, concerning the application.

On the other hand, since the court has power to determine the application without a hearing, it behoves the applicant to prepare the statement which must be contained in his notice of application and the supporting affidavit which must verify the facts relied upon fully, clearly and carefully, so that the Judge reading these documents will have before him all the relevant material relied upon to support the application. Great care and circumspection will therefore be necessary in the preparation of these documents. In *R. v. Jockey Club Licensing Committee, ex p. Wright* [1991] C.O.D. 306, QBD, on the application of the respondent, the grant of leave to move for judicial review was set aside on the grounds of material non-disclosure on the part of the applicant. Potts J. cited with approval the above passage, and emphasised that, particularly as the application for [permission] is made on paper, the applicant must take the greatest care to ensure that the court is acquainted with all material matters.

A copy of the Judge's order whether he grants permission or refuses it on terms will be sent from the Crown Office to the applicant (see r.3(3)).

R53.14.61 **Renewal of application for permission to apply for judicial review (r.3(4))**—If the Judge determines the application for permission without a hearing and either refuses permission or grants it on terms, the applicant is entitled to renew it. He must do so by lodging in the Crown Office a notice of renewal of the application for permission to apply for judicial review in the prescribed Form No. 86B, and he must do so within 10 days of being served with notice of the Judge's refusal or his grant of permission on terms (see r.3(5)).

In a criminal cause or matter, the application for renewal is made by applying to a Divisional Court of the QBD (see r.3(4)(a)) but in a civil case, such an application is made to a single judge, or if the court so directs to a Divisional Court of the QBD (see r.3(4)(b)).

Where an application for permission has been refused or granted on terms without a hearing in the case of non-criminal cause or matter, so that the applicant has the right to renew the application in court before a Crown Office Judge, he cannot appeal against such order (see r.13) and he must therefore proceed to apply for renewal if he desires to pursue the matter. If, however, there has been no decision on paper and the application for permission has proceeded straight to an oral hearing (either on the request of the applicant in his application notice, or by the direction of the Judge), then, in a civil case, if permission has been refused or granted on terms, the application cannot be renewed to a Crown Office Judge (see r.3(4)); but it can be renewed to the Court of Appeal (see below). In a criminal cause or matter, the application can be renewed to a Divisional Court of the QBD whether the single Judge's decision refusing permission, or granting it on terms, was given on paper or in court (r.3(4)(a)).

Where permission has been refused (or granted on terms) after a hearing in a civil matter (whether at an initial hearing or a hearing on a renewed application), the application for permission may be renewed before the Court of Appeal within seven days (see para. R.53.14.65).

Applications by respondents for the discharge of permission to apply for judicial review and appeals against orders made on such applications

R53.14.62 **Application by a respondent seeking discharge of the grant of permission to apply for judicial review**—In *R. v. Secretary of State for the Home Department, ex p. Rukshanda Begum* [1990] C.O.D. 107, CA, the Court of Appeal dealt with two cases where permission to apply for judicial review had initially been granted by the High Court Judge, and then, on the application of the respondent at a hearing without notice to any other party the grant of permission was set aside. The Court of Appeal held—

(1) The applicants could bring their cases before the CA and there were arguably two possible routes: either by way of an appeal (with permission to appeal) against the order discharging the grant of permission to apply for judicial review, or by way of a renewed application to the CA for permission to apply for judicial review. The court granted permission to appeal, and it was therefore unnecessary to decide between those procedural routes, but the CA inclined to the view that either route could be adopted.

(2) The High Court Judge should adopt the following approach to applications for permission to apply for judicial review:

(i) The Judge should grant permission if it is clear that there is a point fit for further investigation at a full substantive hearing with all such evidence as is necessary on the facts and all such argument as is necessary on law.

(ii) If the Judge is satisfied that there is no arguable case he should dismiss the application for permission to apply for judicial review.

(iii) If, on considering the papers, the Judge comes to the conclusion that he really does not know whether there is or is not an arguable case, the right course is for the Judge to invite the putative respondent to attend and make representations as to whether or not permission should be granted. That hearing should not be anywhere near so extensive as a full substantive judicial review hearing; the test to be applied by the Judge should be analogous to the approach adopted in deciding whether to grant leave to appeal against an arbitrator's award (see *Antaios Compania Naviera SA v. Salen Rederierna AB* [1985] A.C. 191 at 207) namely: if, taking account of a brief argument on either side, the Judge is satisfied that there is a case fit for further consideration, then he should grant leave.

In this case the CA granted permission in one of the cases, but affirmed the refusal of permission in the other. The implication of this decision of the Court of Appeal appears to be that, once the recommended approach is put into practice, there should be relatively few applications by respondents to set aside the grant of permission.

Appeal/application to the Court of Appeal by an applicant where permission to apply for judicial review has been set aside—Where a respondent has successfully applied for the discharge of permission to apply for judicial review, the applicant can take the matter to the Court of Appeal (see *R. v. Secretary of State for the Home Department, ex p. Rukshanda Begum* [1990] C.O.D. 107, CA, but in that case the Court of Appeal left open the question whether that should be by way of a renewed application to the CA for permission to apply for judicial review, or whether it should be by way of appeal (subject to obtaining permission to appeal). It is submitted that the former is the more appropriate procedure. This view was approved by the Court of Appeal *obiter* in *R. v. Secretary of State for the Home Department, ex p. Ryoo* [1992] C.O.D. 134. In *Ryoo* the Court of Appeal said that the judge, having discharged the grant of permission to apply for judicial review on the grounds that there was no arguable case, should not have granted [permission] to appeal to the Court of Appeal against that decision because the two were mutually inconsistent. The reason why the applicant in *Ryoo* had chosen the appeal route, rather than a renewed application, was to keep open the possibility of an appeal to the House of Lords; there is no appeal to the House of Lords against the decision of the Court of Appeal on a renewed application for permission to apply for judicial review (see *Re Poh* [1983] 1 W.L.R. 2; [1983] 1 All E.R. 287, HL and para. R53.14.65 below). That issue should not arise in future. If the judge discharges the grant of permission to apply for judicial review, he will, following the decision in *Ryoo*, refuse permission to appeal to the Court of Appeal against that decision. If the Court of Appeal agrees with the judge that the judicial review application is unarguable, the Court of Appeal would, in the event of the appeal route being taken, almost certainly refuse permission to appeal against the judge's decision; the refusal by the Court of Appeal of permission to appeal could not be appealed to the House of Lords (see *Lane v. Esdaile* [1981] A.C. 10 and para. R59.14.37 below). R53.14.63

Appeal to the Court of Appeal by a respondent against the refusal to set aside the grant of permission to apply for judicial review—Where a respondent has applied to the QBD for the discharge of the grant of permission to apply for judicial review and that application has been refused, it is open to the respondent to appeal to the Court of Appeal (subject to obtaining permission to appeal). Given that the Q.B. Judge will have reached the conclusion, after hearing argument from all parties, that he is "satisfied that there is a case for further consideration" (see *R. v. Secretary of State for the Home Department, ex p. Rukshanda Begum* [1990] C.O.D. 109, CA), only rarely would an appeal against his decision be likely to succeed. It would be necessary to be able to show that the judge's decision that the case was fit for further consideration at a substantive judicial review hearing was plainly wrong. R53.14.64

Refusal of permission in a non-criminal matter—renewal of application before the Court of Appeal—Where permission to apply for judicial review is refused in a non-criminal case either by a single Judge or by the Divisional Court, the application can be renewed before the Court of Appeal within seven days (O.59, r.14(3)). The former practice under which, if the Court of Appeal granted permission, it would proceed to hear the substantive application (see *R. v. Industrial Injuries Commission, ex p. Amalgamated Engineering Union* [1966] 2 Q.B. 21; [1966] 2 All E.R. 97, CA) has been abandoned, subject to very limited exceptions. The practice now is that, if the Court of Appeal grants permission, the matter will be remitted to be heard by a single nominated Judge in the QBD, unless it is one of the exceptional cases where the Court of Appeal reserves the substantive application to itself. The Court of Appeal will not normally deal with the substantive judicial review proceedings itself unless the court below is bound by authority or for some other reason an appeal to the Court of Appeal is inevitable (*Practice Directions (Judicial Review: Appeals)* issued by Lord Lane, L.C.J. and Lord Donaldson, M.R. on November 2, 1982 [1982] 1 W.L.R. 1375; [1982] 3 All E.R. 800) and December 15, 1989, [1990] 1 All E.R. 128. R53.14.65

No appeal lies to the House of Lords against a refusal by the Court of Appeal of permission to apply for judicial review (*Re Poh* [1983] 1 W.L.R. 2; [1983] 1 All E.R. 287, HL).

Expedited hearing—The Divisional Court or a single Judge may, when giving leave to move R53.14.66

for judicial review, direct that the case be considered for expedition. (The Crown Office List is divided into parts and Part D is the expedited list: see para. R.53.14.77.) In a case other than one where the Court has assigned it to Part D, a party to judicial review proceedings who wishes to apply for expedition should make his application in the first instance to the Master of the Crown Office; but if he declines to direct that the case be included in Part D, an application may be made to a Divisional Court or a single Judge by notice of motion (see the *Practice Direction* at para. R53.14.77).

Substantive Judicial Review Application

R53.14.67 **Mode of applying for judicial review—the substantive application (r.5)**—Having obtained permission to apply for judicial review (whether from the QBD or the CA) the next stage is for the applicant to institute a substantive application for judicial review. Under the amended rules which came into force on April 26, 1999, substantive applications for judicial review (whether civil or criminal) are now made by a claim form (r.5(2A)). The claim form to be used is Form 86, modified in accordance with the CPR Practice Direction (Forms) (Order 53 Practice Direction, para. 3.1, see para. R53PD–001). To institute such a substantive application the applicant must within 14 days of the date of the grant of permission:

(i) serve a claim form (together with the statement in Form 86A and the written evidence in support): see paras R53.14.68 to 71.
(ii) enter the application for hearing: see para. R53.14.72.

R53.14.68 **Service of the claim form (r.5(3))**—The claim form must be served (r.5(3)) and a copy of the Form 86A (the application notice and statement filed on the application for permission) must be attached to the claim form and served with it (r.6(1) and para. 4.1 of the Order 53 Practice Direction). Although not expressly required by the rules or any practice direction, it is advisable also to serve with the claim form copies of the written evidence filed in support of the judicial review application (see further para. R53.14.71).

R53.14.69 **Persons required to be served (r.5(3))**—The claim form (and accompanying documents) must be served on all persons "directly affected" (O.53, r.5(3)). Where the application relates to any proceedings in or before a court and the object of the application is either to compel the court or an officer of the court to do any act in relation to the proceedings or to quash them or any order made therein, the claim form (plus a copy of the statements) must also be served on the clerk or registrar of the court and, where any objection to the conduct of the Judge is to be made, on the Judge also (r.5(3)).

R53.14.70 **Timetable for service (r.5(4))**—The service must be effected so that there must be at least 10 days between the date of service and the hearing (unless of course the court otherwise directs (r.5(4)). This 10-day time limit will not normally give rise to any problem because, in most cases, unless there is a direction for expedition, the substantive judicial review application will not come on for hearing for some months. Where, however, the case is one which is subject to a direction giving it a very high degree of expedition, it may be necessary for the applicant to apply for this 10-day time limit, and for other time limits (*e.g.* the 56-day time limit allowed to respondents for filing their evidence in reply) to be abridged.

In all cases service must be effected very promptly after the grant of leave, because the case has to be entered for hearing in the Crown Office within 14 days of the grant of leave (see r.5(5) and para. R53.14.72), and it cannot be entered for hearing unless service has been effected and an affidavit of service lodged with the Crown Office (r.5(6)).

R53.14.71 **Service of the written evidence in support (r.6)**—Although the rules do not stipulate that a copy of the written evidence in support be served with the claim form it is advisable to do so, because a copy of any written evidence must be supplied to any party on demand (r.6(5)), and a respondent who receives a claim form plus the statement in support of the application for permission, but no copy of the written evidence in support, is almost certain to ask for it.

A party will not be allowed to rely upon any grounds or seek any relief at the hearing except the grounds and relief set out in the statement (r.6(1)); but the court may allow the applicant to amend his statement whether by specifying different or additional grounds or relief, or otherwise, on such terms, if any, as it thinks fit, and may allow further the affidavits to be used (r.6(2)). A party must, however, give notice of his intention to amend the statement or rely on further written evidence, and he must also give notice to every other party (r.6(3); see further para. R53.14.73).

Each party must supply to every other party on demand and on payment of the proper charges, copies of any written evidence on which he proposes to rely on at the hearing, including copies of any additional written evidence (r.6(5)).

Leave to cross-examine deponents upon their written evidence in judicial review proceedings should be granted where the interests of justice so require (*O'Reilly v. Mackman* [1983] 2 A.C. 237; [1982] 3 All E.R. 1124, *per* Lord Diplock); only rarely will it be essential in the interests of justice to require the attendance for cross-examination of a witness from overseas (*R. v. Secretary of State for the Home Department, ex p. Khawaja* [1984] A.C. 74; [1983] 1 All E.R. 765, HL).

Entry for hearing (r.5(5) and (6))—This is the process whereby the substantive application for judicial review is entered in the records of the Crown Office. In order to enter the application for hearing the applicant must, within 14 days of the grant of permission to apply for judicial review, file with the Crown Office: R53.14.72

(i) A copy of the claim form, and
(ii) Written evidence of service (which can be either an affidavit or a witness summons: see para. R53.14.55). The written evidence must: (a) give the names and addresses of, and places and dates of service on, all persons who have been served with the claim form, and (b) if any person who ought to have been served under r.5(3) has not been served, state that fact and the reason for it (r.5(6)).

Amendment of grounds and further evidence (r.6(2))—The Court has power to grant an applicant leave to amend his statement or to allow him to rely on further written evidence (O.53, r.6(2); the applicant must give notice of any such request (r.6(3)). If an applicant intends to seek to amend the grounds for applying for judicial review, or the relief sought, or to rely on further evidence, notice of such intention must be given to the other party(ies) and to the Crown Office no later than *five* clear working days before the warned date (or fixed date) together with copies of the proposed amendments and/or additional evidence (see *Practice Direction (Crown Office List: Preparation for Hearings)* [1994] 1 W.L.R. 1551; [1994] 4 All E.R. 671). R53.14.73

Respondent's written evidence (r.6(4))—Any respondent to an application for judicial review who wishes to rely on any evidence in opposition to the application must file written evidence in reply. Any such affidavit must be filed with the Crown Office within 56 days after the service on the respondent concerned of the applicant's notice of motion (or summons) applying for judicial review (r.6(4)). R53.14.74

The time limit for filing affidavit evidence in reply by respondents was formerly 21 days. That period was increased to 56 days with effect from March 7, 1989. The new time limit of 56 days is considered to be realistic and adequate and it will be strictly enforced (see the *Practice Note* of March 7, 1989, the text of which is set out below). The rules do not stipulate that copies of the respondent's written evidence should be served on the applicant, but the respondent would be well advised to send a copy to the applicant's solicitor (or the applicant, if in person) because the applicant is entitled to call for a copy (r.6(5)) and, if he only learns of the existence of the respondent's written evidence at a late stage, he may seek an adjournment on the grounds that he needs time to deal with it.

Practice Note

With effect from March 7, 1989 and by virtue of S.I. 1989 No. 177 the period allowed to a respondent in judicial review proceedings for filing an affidavit in reply under O.53, r.6(4) [was] increased from 21 days to 56 days. R53.14.75

This follows a general acceptance that the period of 21 days was unrealistically short and therefore, in many cases, unenforceable. The period substituted cannot be so characterised. It has been set realistically, having regard to the interests of both applicants and respondents, and as such must be strictly adhered to. Although there is provision for extending this period (see [CPR, r.3.1(2)(a)]) it must be clearly understood that extensions of time will be granted only in circumstances which are wholly exceptional and for the most compelling reasons. For all practical purposes respondents would be well advised to treat the period of 56 days as absolute.

Thus, in any case in which the notice of motion and other documents referred to in RSC, O.53, r.6(1) are served upon a respondent on or after March 7, that respondent has 56 days in which to file in the Crown Office any affidavit in reply.

The Crown Office will not accept respondents' [written evidence] outside the 56 day period unless an extension of time has first been obtained.

Applications for extensions of time will be considered in the first instance by the Master of the Crown Office. An appeal against his decision will lie to a Judge hearing cases in the Crown Office List.

Where a Judge directs an expedited hearing by entering a case in Part D of the Crown Office List (see the Lord Chief Justice's *Practice Direction* [1987] 1 W.L.R. 232) applicants should have in mind the need to invite the Judge to abridge the 56-day period where the circumstances of the case so require.

Delays in lodging respondents' affidavits have hitherto caused severe prejudice to applicants and consequent damage to the administration of justice. The amendment to Order 53 rule 6(4) and the procedure set out in this Practice Note will prevent the continuance of this difficulty.

Lord Justice Watkins, D.C.J. *Practice Note* [1989] 1 W.L.R. 358; [1989] 1 All E.R. 1024.

Opposition to application for judicial review (r.9(1))—On the hearing of any application, for judicial review, if it appears to the court that "a proper person" desires to be heard in opposition and that he is such a proper person, that person will be heard notwithstanding that he has not been served with notice of the claim form (r.9(1)). R53.14.76

Thus, justices may show cause by affidavit though they may also show cause either by counsel or in person (*R. v. Field* (1895) 11 T.L.R. 240). On appeals from justices the justices ought not to appear by counsel unless their character or bona fides is questioned or other special circumstances are present (*R. v. Thornton* (1898) 67 L.J.Q.B. 249, 251; *R. v. Cambourne JJ., ex p. Pearce* [1954] 2 All E.R. 850). No fee is payable on filing the affidavit, which should be sent direct to the Crown Office by the clerk to the justices. The court may allow the justices the costs of showing cause by affidavit (*R. v. Spurling*, February 26, 1923; *R. v. Lawrence*, October 23, 1924). It is not usual to give costs against justices unless they have acted perversely, oppressively or mala fide (*R. v. Goodall* (1874) L.R. 9 Q.B. 559; *R. v. Bell* (1899) 15 T.L.R. 487; *R. v. Meyer* (1875) 1 Q.B.D. 173).

R53.14.77 **Listing of judicial review and other proceedings in the Crown Office List**—On February 3, 1987 the Lord Chief Justice handed down the following Practice Direction concerning listing of Crown Office cases:—

This *Practice Direction* applies to the Crown Office List, the elements of which are described in the Directions for London given on July 31, 1981 and reported at [1981] 1 W.L.R. 1296 and [1981] 3 All E.R. 61.

1. As from March 2, 1987 the following arrangements will apply to the listing of cases included in the Crown Office List.
2. The Head Clerk, under the direction of the Master of the Crown Office, will arrange the Crown Office List into the following parts.
3. *Part A: Cases not ready to be heard*
   Cases where leave has yet to be obtained, or the time limits for the filing or lodging of notices, affidavits or other documents have not expired and where, in consequence, a case is not yet ready to be heard.
4. *Part B: Cases ready to be heard*
   In cases where the time limits mentioned in Part A have expired it will be assumed that all parties are ready to be heard. When a case enters Part B the applicant or his solicitors will be informed by letter. It will be the responsibility of the applicant or his solicitors to forward a copy of that letter to (i) the clerk to counsel instructed by the applicant and (ii) any respondent to the case or his solicitor who should inform the clerk to counsel instructed by him. It will be the responsibility of counsel's clerk to inform the Head Clerk, *in writing*, of counsel's time estimate for the case and any alteration thereto.
5. The Head Clerk will make arrangements for hearing dates to be fixed, drawing cases from Part B in order of entry so far as is practicable. While the Head Clerk will give as much notice as possible of the date fixed for hearing he cannot undertake to accommodate the wishes of applicants, respondents, their solicitors or counsel. The occasional need to list cases at short notice may mean that parties are unable to be represented by the counsel of their first choice. In particular it should be remembered that the cases listed in the Crown Office List take precedence, so far as the attendance of counsel is concerned, over cases listed for hearing in the Crown Court unless a Divisional Court or a Judge otherwise directs.
6. *Part C: Cases stood out*
   Where a case appears in Part B, or Part E (see *post*), and any party to the case is of the opinion that he is not ready to be heard he may apply to the Master of the Crown Office to have the matter stood out into Part C. Where the Master of the Crown Office accedes to such an application he may do so on such terms as he thinks fit. Where he declines to direct that the matter be stood out into Part C application may be made to a Divisional Court or a Judge, as the case may be, by way of notice of motion.
7. *Part D: The expedited list*
   Cases entered in this list will be listed for hearing as soon as practicable. In cases other than those where a Divisional Court or a Judge has directed that a case be considered for expedition, application for inclusion in Part D should be made in the first instance to the Master of the Crown Office but where he declines to direct its inclusion in Part D, application may be made to a Divisional Court or a Judge, as the case may be, by way of notice of motion.
8. *Part E: Cases listed for hearing*
   This part of the list will contain those cases where a date for hearing has been fixed.
9. As from March 2, 1987 the Daily Cause List will, in relation to the Crown Office List, contain only such cases as are to be heard on the next sitting day.
10. A copy of Parts B, C, D and E of the Crown Office List may be inspected in the Crown Office.
11. In this Practice Direction the expression "applicant" includes "appellant" where the context so requires and the expression "Judge" means a Judge hearing cases in the Crown Office List.

Lord Lane, L.C.J. February 3, 1987, *Practice Direction (Crown Office List)* [1987] 1 W.L.R. 232; [1987] 1 All E.R. 368.

R53.14.78 **Counsel's estimates**—In respect of all cases in Part B and Part D a written estimate from counsel of the likely length of the hearing must be lodged with the Crown Office by counsel's clerks. In *Practice Note (Crown Office List: Estimated Length of Hearing)* [1987] 1 All E.R. 1184 Mann J. emphasised the importance of counsel providing estimates which are as realistic as possible. The pressure on both those lists is great, and Mann J. pointed out that problems have been caused in a number of cases by ill-judged and unrealistic under-estimates. He emphasised that under-estimation does not secure an earlier hearing.

Applications for permission to apply for judicial review—length of hearing—With effect from April 9, 1991, applications for leave to move for judicial review will be listed on the footing that the application will take no more than 20 minutes, and that any reply by a respondent who attends will take no more than 10 minutes. If, in any particular case, counsel considers that the application will require more time than that, he or she must put in a written estimate and a special fixture will have to be arranged (see *Practice Direction: (Crown Office List) (No. 2)* [1991] 1 W.L.R. 280; [1991] 1 All E.R. 1055, DC). **R53.14.79**

The "warned list letter"—As a case reaches the top of Part B of the Crown Office List, the applicant's solicitors will be informed by a letter from the Crown Office that the case is likely to be listed, at short notice, with effect from a date specified in that letter (the "warned date"). It is the responsibility of the applicant's solicitors to inform the respondent's side and all interested parties of the likelihood of the case being so listed. Likewise where an application is given a fixed date, it is the responsibility of the applicant's solicitors to inform the respondent's side and all interested parties of that fixed date (see *Practice Direction (Crown Office List: Preparation for Hearings)* [1994] 1 W.L.R. 1551; [1994] 4 All E.R. 671). **R53.14.80**

Bundles and other documents for the use of the Court

Bundles—Not less than five clear working days before the "warned date", (or where a fixture has been given, the fixed date) the applicant's solicitors must lodge with the Crown Office a paginated indexed bundle for the use of the court (see *Practice Direction (Crown Office List: Preparation for Hearings)* [1994] 1 W.L.R. 1551; [1994] 4 All E.R. 671). If the obligation to lodge a proper bundle is not complied with, applications for judicial review are liable to be struck out and the costs visited on the applicants or their solicitors (*R. v. Home Secretary, ex p. Meyer-Wulff, The Times*, May 9, 1986, DC). **R53.14.81**

Citation of Hansard—Any party intending to refer to any extract from Hansard, where such citation is permitted, must unless the court otherwise directs, serve on all parties and on the court copies of any such extract together with a brief summary of the argument to be based upon it. Unless the court otherwise directs, copies of that material must be served on the other parties (using any method of service permitted by O.65, r.5) and two copies must be lodged with the Head of the Crown Office (Room C312) in each case not less than five clear working days before the hearing (see *Practice Direction (Hansard extracts)* [1995] 1 W.L.R. 192; [1995] 1 All E.R. 234). **R53.14.82**

Skeleton arguments—Skeleton arguments are now mandatory in all cases in the Crown Office List. Within a minimum *five* clear working days of the warned date, or fixed date, as the case may be, the applicant's advocate must lodge a skeleton argument with the Crown Office and serve a copy of it on the respondent's side and on all other interested parties. Within *three* clear working days of the warned date (or fixed date) the advocates for the respondent, and any other parties wishing to be heard, must lodge their skeleton arguments with the Crown Office and serve copies on the applicant's side and other interested parties. Advocates may supplement their skeleton arguments up to one working day before the hearing. **R53.14.83**

Each skeleton argument must quote the Crown Office reference number and the warned date (or fixed date), and must compromise:

(a) an estimate of how long the hearing will take, including delivery of judgment (whether or not an estimate has already been provided);
(b) a list of issues;
(c) a list of the propositions of law which are going to be advanced, together with the authorities relied on in support of them (with page references to the passages relied upon);
(d) a chronology of events, cross-referenced to the pages in the bundle lodged for the use of the Court;
(e) a list of the documents which the Court will need to pre-read, with the page references to the relevant passages; and
(f) a list of the *dramatis personae* where the number of people who feature in the case warrants it.

(See generally *Practice Direction (Crown Office List: Preparation for Hearings)* [1994] 1 W.L.R. 1551; [1994] 4 All E.R. 671.)

Hearing of substantive judicial application—The substantive application for judicial review in civil cases is normally heard by a single judge sitting in open court. A direction of the court that the substantive application in a civil case should be heard by the Divisional Court is made only in exceptional circumstances, where the application raises questions of difficulty, complexity or **R53.14.84**

importance. The application may be moved by a litigant in person (*Practice Note* [1947] W.N. 218; and, as regards proceedings in the Court of Appeal, *Practice Note* [1956] 1 W.L.R. 430).

Where the relief sought is or includes an order of certiorari to remove any proceedings for the purpose of quashing them, the applicant may not question the validity of any order, warrant, commitment, conviction, inquisition or record unless before the hearing of the notice or summons, as the case may be, he has lodged in the Crown Office a copy thereof verified by witness statement or affidavit accounts for his failure to do so to the satisfaction of the court (r.9(2)). If in such a case an order of certiorari is made, the order will ordinarily direct that the proceedings shall be quashed forthwith on their removal into the Queen's Bench Division (r.9(3)).

Where a conviction imposing a sentence of imprisonment is quashed, and the applicant is serving the sentence, the order of the court must direct that he be forthwith discharged from custody in respect of that conviction and the commitment thereunder, and notification of the order must be given forthwith to the Under-Secretary of State, Home Office, by the Crown Office (Direction of Lord Goddard, L.C.J., February 5, 1947).

R53.14.85 **Fresh evidence in judicial review proceedings**—The principles on which fresh evidence can be admitted before the Divisional Court, or the single Judge, in judicial review proceedings are: (1) the court can receive evidence to show what material was before the minister or inferior tribunal; (2) where the jurisdiction of the minister or inferior tribunal depends on a question of fact or where the question is whether essential procedural requirements were observed, the court may receive and consider additional evidence to determine the jurisdictional fact or procedural error; and (3) where the proceedings are tainted by misconduct on the part of the minister or member of the inferior tribunal or one of the parties before it, fresh evidence is admissible to prove the particular misconduct alleged. Examples of such misconduct are bias by the decision making body, or fraud or perjury by a party. Where a party deliberately suppressed material facts with the intention of misleading the minister, it would be for the court to consider whether the conduct of that party could be described as fraudulent so as to permit the admission of fresh evidence (*R. v. Secretary of State for the Environment, ex p. Powis* [1981] 1 W.L.R. 584; [1981] 1 All E.R. 788, CA).

Where it is sought to adduce fresh evidence before the Court of Appeal which was not adduced before the Divisional Court or the single Judge in the judicial review proceedings below, the position is as follows. Normally in the case of appeals against a decision after a trial on the merits fresh evidence cannot be admitted before the Court of Appeal unless the three conditions laid down in *Ladd v. Marshall* [1954] 1 W.L.R. 1489 are satisfied (see para. R59.10.13). In judicial review proceedings, however, the decision in *Ladd v. Marshall* does not, as such, apply (*Momin Ali v. Secretary of State for the Home Department* [1984] 1 W.L.R. 663; [1984] 1 All E.R. 1009, CA). The Court of Appeal has a wider discretion to admit fresh evidence in judicial review cases than exists in ordinary civil litigation. Nevertheless, in the interests of achieving finality in litigation, the Court of Appeal applies in judicial review proceedings a similar approach to that in *Ladd v. Marshall*, subject to the court's discretion to depart from it if the wider interests of justice so require.

R53.14.86 **Remitting matter for review (r.9(4))**—Where the relief sought is an order of certiorari and the court is satisfied that there are grounds for quashing the decision to which the application relates, the court has power, in addition to quashing the decision, to remit the matter to the court, tribunal or authority concerned with a direction to reconsider it and reach a decision in accordance with the findings of the court (r.9(4)).

Thus the court's powers are not limited simply to finding whether the decision should be upheld or reversed, but it can remit the case to the proper authority to do what is right in the light of its findings (see *R. v. Northumberland Compensation Appeal Tribunal* [1952] 1 K.B. 338, *per* Denning L.J. at p. 347).

R53.14.87 **Order to contine proceedings as if begun as an ordinary civil claim (r.9(5))**—Order to continue proceedings as if begun as an ordinary civil claim (r.9(5))—Where the application for judicial review seeks relief in the form of a declaration, an injunction or damages, the court has power, if it considers that such relief should not be granted in an application for judicial review, but might have been granted if it had been sought in ordinary civil proceedings to order that the proceedings, instead of being refused, should continue as proceedings brought under CPR, Part 7, and, if the court does so, it can give any directions it considers appropriate (r.9(5)).

If, however, a claim is brought by ordinary civil proceedings, there is no power to convert it into an application for judicial review; otherwise, if there were, that would bypass the requirement that permission to apply for judicial review must first be obtained on an application made promptly and, in any event, within three months, as a condition precedent to making the substantive application of judicial review (*Heywood v. Board of Visitors of Hull Prison* [1980] 1 W.L.R. 1386; [1980] 3 All E.R. 594).

R53.14.88 **Costs**—The court has discretion in regard to costs generally (*R. v. Woodhouse* [1906] 2 K.B. 501 and S.C.A. 1981, s.51). Costs will not usually be granted to a party who has appeared although not served. Two sets of costs will not usually be granted, namely to the other party to the dispute and also the court, person, or body whose decision is under review (*R. v. Industrial Disputes Tribunal,* *ex p. American Express Co.* [1954] 1 W.L.R. 1118; [1954] 2 All E.R. 764). Where two or more parties appear in the same interest (whether as applicants or as respondents) on an application for judicial review, they will generally be allowed only one set of costs between them. But there is no inflexible rule to that effect; in exceptional circumstances the court will award more than one set of costs (*R. v. Registrar of Companies, ex p. Central Bank of India* [1986] Q.B. 1114 at 1162; [1986] 1 All E.R. 105, 112), (*e.g.* the court may award two sets of costs where the interests of the two applicants or respondents are to some extent divergent, or where the issues are very complex and important, *ibid.*, and see also *R. v. Monopolies & Mergers Commission, ex p. Matthew Brown plc, Macpherson J.*, July 17, 1986, and *R. v. Panel on Take-overs & Mergers, ex p. Datafin Ltd*, December 5, 1986, CA both unreported on this issue.)

When, after permission has been obtained to apply for judicial review, but before service of the claim form, the respondent performs the act for which an order is sought, the costs of the application for leave may be obtained on a two clear days' notice of motion supported by affidavit.

Special Categories

Coroners—There is power at common law, by order of certiorari addressed to a coroner, to remove into the QBD and quash an inquisition irregular on its face (*R. v. Directors of G.W. Ry.* (1888) 20 Q.B.D. 410; *R. v. Clerk of Assize of Oxford Circuit* [1897] 1 Q.B. 370). See s.20 of Coroners Act 1887, for powers of amendment of formal defects). There is also power at common law to quash an inquisition for misconduct of coroner or jury. The Divisional Court has power at common law to review the decision of a coroner's inquest, whether or not the decision is bad or irregular on its face (*R. v. Greater Manchester Coroner, ex p. Tal* [1985] Q.B. 67; [1984] 3 All E.R. 240, DC not following *R. v. Surrey Coroner, ex p. Campbell* [1982] 2 Q.B. 661, DC). The application must be made by the Crown or a party interested, and there must be written evidence verifying a copy of the inquisition of accounting for its absence. The Divisional Court also has power at common law, when quashing an inquisition, to order the same or another coroner to hold a fresh inquest with another jury. It also has statutory power, on an application by or under authority of the Attorney-General, to quash an inquisition and order a fresh inquest to be held (see Coroners Act 1887, ss.6, 35; Coroners (Amendment) Act 1926, s.19). The coroner may be ordered to pay such costs as the court thinks fit (see generally as to the jurisdiction of the court in regard to coroners, Short and Mellor, *Crown Practice* (2nd ed., 1908) p. 28f). A coroner is obliged to hold an inquest where the body of a deceased person lies within his territorial jurisdiction and he has reason to believe that the deceased has died a violent or unnatural death, even though the cause of death and the death itself occurred out of the jurisdiction of the English courts (*R. v. West Yorkshire Coroner, ex p. Smith* [1983] Q.B. 335; [1982] 3 All E.R. 1098, CA). **R53.14.89**

Disqualification of members of local authorities (r.11)—Proceedings for such disqualifications are taken under section 92 of the Local Government Act 1972 (see also s.272(2) of that Act). Proceedings may be taken in the High Court, by a local government elector for the area of the local authority concerned, against any person acting as a member of a local authority or mayor of a borough, or claiming to be entitled to act as such, on the ground of his being disqualified within the meaning of the section, and the court is empowered to make a declaration that he has acted as such while disqualified, and to declare the office vacant, grant an injunction and impose a fine not exceeding £50 for each occasion on which he has so acted. **R53.14.90**

Since these proceedings are criminal or penal in character, they are required to be brought before a Divisional Court of the QBD, even during the vacation (see r.11).

Claim to restrain persons from acting in an office in which he is not entitled to act (r.1(1))—*Quo warranto* proceedings have been abolished and replaced by statutory provisions, now re-enacted in S.C.A. 1981, s.30, which provides that in any case where any person acts in an office in which he is not entitled to act, and an information in the nature of *quo warranto* would have lain against him, the High Court may grant an injunction restraining him from so acting and may declare the office to be vacant, provided that the proceedings are brought by a person who would have been entitled to apply for such information. An application under s.30 has to be made by way of an application for judicial review (r.1(1)(b)). For the former practice in *quo warranto* see Short and Mellor, *Crown Practice* (2nd ed., 1908), pp. 172 *et seq.* The order is not issued as of course, and the conduct and motives of the applicant may be enquired into (*Everett v. Griffiths* [1924] 1 K.B. 941 at 958). **R53.14.91**

Appeals

Appeals in judicial review cases—The following tables indicate the avenues of appeal at the various stages. **R53.14.92**

Judicial review in a criminal cause or matter		
Decision to be appealed against	*Mode of Appeal*	*para.*
Refusal of permission without a hearing	Renew the application for permission before a Div Court	R53.14.61
Decision of a Div Court on a substantive application for judicial review	Appeal to the HL but only with the necessary leave and certificate required by AJA 1960, s.1	R53.14.22
Judicial review in a civil matter		
Decision to be appealed against	*Mode of appeal*	*para.*
Refusal of permission without a hearing	Renew the application before a single judge in open court (or Div Court if the court so directs)	R53.14.61
Refusal of permission by single Judge or Div Court after a hearing	Renew the application for permission before the CA within 7 days (O.59, r.14(3))	R53.14.65
Refusal of permission by the CA	No appeal—CA decision final	R53.14.65
Decision on a substantive application for judicial review (either of single Judge or Div Court)	Appeal to the CA permission to appeal is required	R53.14.22 R53.1B.13
Decision of the CA on a substantive application for judicial review	Appeal to the House of Lords with the leave of the CA or the HL	R53.1.152

PRACTICE DIRECTION—SCHEDULE 1, ORDER 53 (APPLICATION FOR JUDICIAL REVIEW)

R53PD–001 *This Practice Direction supplements CPR Part 50, and Schedule 1 to the CPR*

Terminology

1.1 In this practice direction—

(1) "Order 53" means those provisions contained in Schedule 1, RSC Order 53, which were previously contained in the Rules of the Supreme Court (1965);

(2) a reference to a rule or Part prefixed with CPR is a reference to a rule or Part contained in the CPR rules; and

(3) a reference to a rule number alone is a reference to the rule so numbered in Order 53.

Scope

2.1 This practice direction supplements Order 53 (which sets out the procedure for applying for judicial review) by providing further detail about the application.

2.2 This practice direction must be read together with Order 53.

2.3 It also lists at paragraph 8 other practice directions which governed procedure relating to Order 53 before 26 April 1999 and which will continue to do so.

Claim form

3.1 Rule 5. (2A) specifies that an application for judicial review must be made by claim form. The claim form to be used if Form 86, modified in accordance with the guidance contained in the Forms practice direction.

3.2 The claimant must also use a modified Form 86 where he is making an application under rule 11(1) (Proceedings for disqualification of a member of a local authority).

Application for judicial review

4.1 In order to comply with the requirement in rule 6(1) (copy of the statement in support of the application for permission to be served), Form 86A must be attached to Form 86 (the claim form) and served with it.

Meaning of written evidence

5.1 The written evidence required by— R53PD–002

(1) rule 5.6 (written evidence to be filed before the application is entered for hearing);

(2) rule 6 (statements and evidence); and

(3) rule 11 (proceedings for disqualification of member of a local authority, may be either an affidavit or a witness statement.)

(CPR rule 32.16 provides for the form of an affidavit, CPR rule 32.8 provides for the form of a witness statement, and CPR rule 22.1 requires a witness statement to be verified by a statement of truth.)

Service

6.1 The Crown Office will prepare and serve all orders of the court.

(CPR rule 6.3 provides that the court will normally serve a document which it has issued or prepared).

6.2 All other documents (and copies) must be prepared and served by the parties.

Cases entered in the Crown Office List

7.1 When an application is entered in accordance with rule 5(5)— R53PD-003

(a) for judicial review; or

(b) under rule 11(1) (Proceedings for disqualification of member of local authority),

the application must be entered in the Crown Office List in accordance with Practice Direction (Crown Office List) 1987 1 WLR 232 [1987] 1 All ER 368.

(In Schedule 1, RSC Order 57 rule 2 provides for the entry of claims in the appropriate office and for the filing of copy documents for the use of the court.)

Practice Directions etc., which apply to proceedings under Order 53

8. The Practice directions, Statements and Practice Notes set out in Table 1 continue to apply to proceedings under Order 53 on and after 26 April 1999.

TABLE 1

R53PD–004

Practice Direction etc.	Content
Practice Note [1983] 2 All E.R. 1020	Urgent matters outside London—consultation of Crown Office and continuation in London; Delay in applying for permission to apply for judicial review
Practice Note (Crown Office List) [1987] 1 All E.R. 1184	Need for accuracy in time estimates
Practice Direction (Crown Office List) [1987] 1 WLR 232 [1987] 1 All E.R. 368	Parts of the List
Practice Note [1991] 1 All E.R. 1055	Permission to apply for judicial review and time allowed for such applications
Practice Direction (Crown Office List: Preparation for hearings) [1994] 4 All E.R. 671, [1994] 1 WLR 1551 (18th November 1994)	Preparation for hearings; Documentation; Time limits; Skeleton arguments: amendment of grounds
Practice Direction (Crown Office List: Consent Orders) [1997] 1 WLR 825	Consent orders
Practice Note [1997] 1 All E.R. 128 (6th December 1997)	Permission to apply for judicial review—Documents to be lodged; relevant legislative provisions and statutory instruments
Practice Statement (Supreme Court: Judgments) [1998] 1 WLR 825, [1998] 2 All E.R. 638	Judgments

R54PD–005 **Editorial Note**—The proper citations and dates of the practice directions listed in Table 1 above are as shown immediately below. These practice directions are printed in the Mainwork at the places indicated.

- Practice Direction (Crown Office List: Criminal Proceedings) [1983] 1 W.L.R. 925; *sub nom.* Practice Note (Crown Office List: Uncontested Proceedings: Applications Outside London: Delay) [1983] 2 All E.R. 1020 (July 21, 1983) (see Queen's Bench Practice Direction No. 23 (part), SCP 1999, Vol. 2, paras 2C–164 to 2C–167)
- Practice Direction (Crown Office List) [1987] 1 W.L.R. 232; *sub nom.* Practice Note (Crown Office List: Arrangement) [1987] 1 All E.R. 368 (February 3, 1987) (see Queen's Bench Practice Direction No. 24, SCP 1999, Vol. 2, para. 2C–168)
- Practice Note (Crown Office List: Estimated Length of Hearing) [1987] 1 All E.R. 1184 (April 3, 1987) (see para. R53.14.78 above)
- Practice Direction (Crown Office List) (No. 2) [1991] 1 W.L.R. 280; *sub nom.* Practice Note (Crown Office List: Striking Out for Want of Prosecution) [1991] 1 All E.R. 1055 (March 18, 1991) (see Queen's Bench Practice Direction No. 25, at para. R53.14.79 above and SCP 1999, Vol. 2, para. 2C–172)
- Practice Direction (Crown Office List: Preparation for Hearings) [1994] 1 W.L.R. 1551; *sub nom.* Practice Note (Crown Office List: Penalties for Late Papers) [1994] 4 All E.R.

671 (October 25, 1994) (see Queen's Bench Practice Direction No. 26, at paras R53.14.56, R53.14.73, R53.14.80 and R53.14.81 above, and SCP 1999, Vol. 2, paras 2C–173 to 2C–175)

- Practice Direction (Crown Office List: Consent Orders) [1997] 1 W.L.R. 825; *sub nom.* Practice Note (Crown Office List: Uncontested Proceedings) [1997] 2 All E.R. 799 (May 12, 1997) (see Queen's Bench Practice Direction No. 27, SCP 1999, Vol. 2, paras 2C–176 to 2C–179)
- Practice Direction (Crown Office List: Legislation Bundle) [1997] 1 W.L.R. 52; *sub nom.* Practice Note (Judicial Review: Documents to be Lodged) [1997] 1 All E.R. 128 (December 6, 1996)
- Practice Statement (Supreme Court: Judgments) [1998] 1 W.L.R. 825; *sub nom.* Practice Statement (Royal Courts of Justice: Judgments) [1998] 2 All E.R. 667 (April 22, 1998); as modified by Practice Statement (Supreme Court: Judgments) (No. 2) [1999] 1 W.L.R. 1; *sub nom.* Practice Note (Royal Courts of Justice: Judgments) [1999] 1 All E.R. 125 November 25, 1998)

RSC ORDER 54

APPLICATIONS FOR WRIT OF HABEAS CORPUS

Contents R54.0.1

Editorial Introduction

The writ of habeas corpus may take various forms (see, generally, Gordon, *Judicial Review and Crown Office Proceedings*). The writ of habeas corpus *ad subjiciendum*, which is used to test the validity in the commitment of a prisoner, or want of jurisdiction to hold him, is the most important of all of the writs of this denomination. These rules provide the procedure for the granting of this writ. Two further forms of the writ of habeas corpus consist of habeas corpus *ad testificandum* (to bring up a prisoner to give evidence), and habeas corpus *ad respondendum* (to bring up a prisoner to answer a criminal charge). They are referred to in r.9. Forms for these three varieties of the writ are found in Appendix A and must be used as appropriate (r.10). The Court may direct that a claim form shall be used, being a modified form 87. These and other matters are covered by a Practice Direction, *post*. R54.0.2

Related Sources

R.57 (Divisional Court proceedings, etc.: supplementary provisions) R54.0.3

Forms

The following Prescribed Forms (formerly included amongst the Prescribed Forms in Appendix A to the RSC) are relevant to O.54. These forms are included in Table 2 (Practice Forms) attached to Practice Direction (Forms) and may be found in SCP 1999, Vol. 2, Section 1A, paras 1A–90 to 1A–95): R54.0.4

- PF No. 87—Notice of motion for writ of habeas corpus *ad subjiciendum* (O.54, r.2)
- PF No. 88—Notice directed by Court of adjourned application for writ of habeas corpus (O.54, r.2)

- PF No. 89—Writ of habeas corpus *ad subjiciendum* (O.54, r.10)
- PF No. 90—Notice to be served with writ of habeas corpus *ad subjiciendum* (O.54, r.6)
- PF No. 91—Writ of habeas corpus *ad testificandum* (O.54, r.10)
- PF No. 92—Writ of habeas corpus *ad respondendum* (O.54, r.10)

Application for writ of habeas corpus ad subjiciendum

R54.1 **1.**—(1) Subject to rule 11, an application for a writ of habeas corpus ad subjiciendum shall be made to a judge in court, except that—

(a) it shall be made to a Divisional Court of the Queen's Bench Division if the court so directs;

(b) it may be made to a judge otherwise than in court at any time when no judge is sitting in court; and

(c) any application on behalf of a child must be made in the first instance to a judge otherwise than in court.

(2) An application for such writ may be made without notice being served on any other party and, subject to paragraph (3) must be supported by a witness statement or affidavit by the person restrained showing that it is made at his instance and setting out the nature of the restraint.

(3) Where the person restrained is unable for any reason to make the witness statement or affidavit required by paragraph (2) the witness statement or affidavit may be made by some other person on his behalf and that witness statement or affidavit must state that the person restrained is unable to make the witness statement or affidavit himself and for what reason.

R54.1.1 **History of Rule**—Replaces the former O.59, rr.14 and 15. Amended by S.I. 1971 No. 1269 and S.I. 1980 No. 2000.

R54.1.2 **Haebus corpus**—The writ of habeas corpus *ad subjiciendum* (commonly known as habeas corpus) remains of the highest constitutional importance, for by it the liberty of the subject is vindicated and his release from any manner of unjustifiable detention assured. It is a prerogative writ familiar to the common law at least as long ago as the thirteenth century, and its efficiency has been furthered by a number of statutes (the Habeas Corpus Acts of 1640, 1679 and 1816). It is a writ of right and granted *ex debito justitiae,* but not as of course (see *e.g. Re Corke* [1954] 1 W.L.R. 899; [1954] 2 All E.R. 440) and may be refused where another remedy lies whereby the validity of the restraint can be effectively questioned.

Formerly the writ might be issued to any part of the Dominions of the Crown, but now by the Habeas Corpus Act 1862, it is enacted that no writ of habeas corpus shall issue out of England by authority or any Judge or Court of justice therein into any colony or foreign dominion of the Crown where Her Majesty has a lawfully established Court of Justice having authority to grant and issue the writ and to ensure its due execution throughout such colony or dominion. The writ will not issue to Scotland (*R. v. Cowle* (1759) 2 Burr. 856) nor to Northern Ireland (*Re Keenan* [1972] 1 Q.B. 533; [1971] 3 All E.R. 884) but it will to the Isle of Man (being a "dominion" but not a "foreign dominion" *Ex p. Brown* (1864) 33 L.J.Q.B. 193). As regards Jersey it appears that before 1862 a writ of habeas corpus could be enforced there if so ordered by the Privy Council (*Re Belson* (1850) 7 Moore P.C. 114). But this is probably no longer so, since Jersey is, historically a "foreign dominion". It may issue to a protectorate which is not a dominion of the Crown if the authority in fact exercised by the Crown makes this just and convenient (*R. v. Crewe (Earl), ex p. Sekgome* [1910] 2 K.B. 576; *Re Ning Yi-Ching,* 56 T.L.R. 3; *Re Mwenya* [1960] 1 Q.B. 241; [1959] 3 All E.R. 525 CA). It will not issue against any person who is abroad and out of the jurisdiction (*R. v. Pinckney* [1904] 2 K.B. 84) or who is upon a public vessel of a foreign State, nor will it issue in respect of an alien detained in this country in the embassy or legation of the State of which he is a subject (*Re Sun Yat* (1896), cited in Short and Mellor, *Crown Office Practice* (1908).

The purpose of the writ is that the body may be produced before the Court, so that release from restraint may be secured—and not that someone who has unlawfully detained or unlawfully parted with the custody may be punished; and therefore the writ is not granted after the release of the person detained (*Bernardo v. Ford, Gossage's Case* [1892] A.C. 326, disagreeing with the contrary view expressed in *R. v. Barnardo, Tye's Case* [1889] 23 Q.B.D. 305 ; see also *R. v. Secretary of State for Home Affairs, ex p. O'Brien* [1923] 2 K.B. 361; [1923] A.C. 603). The writ is used to test any alleged invalidity in the commitment of a prisoner, or want of jurisdiction to hold him in custody—as, for example, where he is held under military arrest without being brought to trial, or is detained under order of a naval, military or ecclesiastical Court. In *Re Maychell, The Independent,* February 26, 1993 (Kennedy L.J. and Clark J.) a person's detention by military authorities for 75 days was held to be lawful in circumstances where there had to be proper investigation of serious allegations. *R. v. Royal Army Service Corp., Colchester, ex p. Elliott* [1949] 1 All E.R. 373 is authority for the proposition that the Divisional Court's powers extend to a person held in military custody, even where the military authorities are satisfied that the custody was lawful. It is used on behalf of a person committed without jurisdiction under the Extradition Acts (see section 11 of the 1870 Act, and *R. v. Governor of Brixton Prison* [1924] 1 K.B. 455; *Re Kolczynski* [1955] 1 Q.B. 540; [1955] 1 All E.R. 31; *R. v. Governor of Brixton Prison, ex p. Schtraks* [1964] A.C. 556; [1962] 3 All E.R 529, HL) or under the Fugitive Offenders Act 1881, (see ss.5, 7, and *R. v. Governor of Brixton Prison, ex p. Mourat Mehmet* [1962] 2 Q.B. 1; [1962] 1 All E.R. 463). In all these cases the writ is equally available on behalf of a British subject or friendly or enemy alien, provided he is within the realm and under the protection of the Crown (contrast *R. v. Bottrill* [1947] K.B. 41, the case of an alien enemy interned by order of the Crown, and *Re Ning Yi-Ching*). On the other hand, the writ does not in general lie in respect of a person who is in execution on a criminal charge, or committed by a Court of record for a contempt or by Parliament for a contempt or breach of privilege. In the former case, the right to be discharged must be tested by appeal (see *Ex p. Corke; Re Featherstone* (1953) 37 Cr.App.R. 146; *Re Wring* [1960] 1 W.L.R. 138; [1960] 1 All E.R. 536n.; *Re Philpot* [1960] 1 W.L.R. 115; [1960] 1 All E.R. 165, 166) or certiorari, and in the other cases, the Court is the proper Judge of what is contempt of itself (see *Re Hunt of Middlesex Case* (1840) 11 A. & E. 273). Applications by parents or guardians as to the custody or care of infants are made to the Family Division (S.C.A. 1981, s.61, Sched. 1, para. 3). Applications to the High Court for bail are made by summons before a Judge in Chambers to show cause why the defendant should not be admitted to bail.

Whether a person is detained is a question of objective fact which does not depend on the presence or absence of consent or knowledge. A person is detained in law if those who have control over the premises in which he is have the intention that he shall not be permitted to leave those premises and have the ability to prevent him from leaving: *R. v. Bournewood Community and Mental Health NHS Trust, ex p.* [1998] 1 All E.R. 635 (Lord Woolf M.R., Phillips and Chadwick L.JJ.).

Application for the writ—Under the present procedure the application is made without notice in the first instance (to this extent a return to the practice in force till about 1780). Except in applications on behalf of a child, upon the hearing, if the Court gives leave, the application is usually adjourned for notice to be served on such persons as the Court directs; and upon the adjourned hearing, if the application succeeds, the writ is ordered to issue. **R54.1.3**

The applications for a writ of habeas corpus must, subject to r.11, be made to a Judge in Court (r.1) except that if the Court so directs it must be made to a Divisional Court of the QBD (r.1(a)) and it may be made to a Judge otherwise than in Court at any time when no Judge is sitting in Court (r.1(b)).

On a criminal application for habeas corpus an order for the release of the person restrained can be refused only by a Divisional Court of the QBD (see s.14(1) of A.J.A. 1960) so that in such a case, a single Judge has no power to refuse an application for habeas corpus.

Applications on behalf of a minor must be made to a Judge in Chambers whether in term time or in vacation (see r.1(c)) who, if he thinks fit, directs a summons to issue, and if the applicant is successful the issue of the writ is ordered. For Forms, see Vol. 2, Section 1A.

However it is not open to the court to issue a writ of habeas corpus, at the instance of a third person, when the subject of the application is *sui juris* and had plainly stated in an affidavit that he was not being unlawfully detained (*In the matter of M* [1995] C.O.D. 64 (Sir Stephen Brown P.)).

So far does the law lean in favour of the liberty of the subject that the application is entitled to precedence over virtually all other court business (*R. v. Home Secretary, ex p. Cheblak* [1991] 1 W.L.R. 890 at 894). The Court of Appeal (which is not part of the High Court) has no original jurisdiction in the matter, nor has any judge of the High Court sitting in the Court of Appeal (*Stoneham v. Woods* [1914] W.N. 202; *Re Carroll* [1931] 1 K.B. 104; *Ex p. Chapple* (1950) 66 T.L.R. (Pt 2) 932).

When an application for habeas corpus has once been made in a civil or criminal matter no such application may be made on the same grounds in respect of the same person to any other court or judge unless fresh evidence is adduced in support of the application (A.J.A. 1960, s.14(2)). The Lord Chancellor has no original or appellate jurisdiction to grant habeas corpus (see A.J.A. 1960, s.14(2) and *Re Kray* [1965] Ch. 736).

Section 14(2) does no more than allow successive applications for habeas corpus on the same grounds provided fresh evidence is adduced in support of each application. The court retains jurisdiction to control its own procedures so as to prevent them being used vexatiously or in abuse of process and may thus strike out proceedings in an appropriate case (*R. v. Governor of Brixton Prison, ex p. Osman (No. 4)* [1992] 1 All E.R. 579).

When the Home Secretary considers that an application for a writ of habeas corpus by a person awaiting extradition does not comply with the requirements of s.14(2) of the A.J.A. 1960 he may proceed with arrangements for that applicant's return to the requesting state. Where there is argument as to whether s.14(2) has been complied with no doubt the Secretary of State will consider it prudent to await the decision of the court. Where the applicant is fearful that the Secretary of State might not do so application can be made to the court for the sort of interim relief envisaged in *R. v. Secretary of State for the Home Department, ex p. Muboyayi* [1992] Q.B. 244; *R. v. Governor of Brixton Prison, ex p. Osman (No. 5), The Times,* November 26, 1992 (Kennedy L.J. and Waterhouse J.). The approach adopted by the court in relation to detention by order of the Secretary of State under the Immigration Act 1971 is exemplified in *Re Mahmod* [1994] C.O.D. 404 where Laws J., ordering the writ to issue forthwith, observed: "while, of course, Parliament is entitled to confer powers of administrative detention without trial, the courts will see to it that where such a power is conferred the statute that confers it will be strictly and narrowly construed and its operation and effect will be supervised by the court according to high standards".

In general, on an application for a writ of habeas corpus, fresh evidence will not be admitted. Therefore, where the applicant did not raise any issue or call any evidence before the magistrates that he would, if sent back to Ireland, be prosecuted or detained for an offence of a political character, he is precluded from raising this issue or adducing evidence on the matter before a higher Court (*Re Nobbs* [1978] 1 W.L.R. 1302; [1978] 3 All E.R. 390, DC).

Where the order for detention and removal of a person as an illegal entrant is completely in order, it is prima facie good, and the burden is on the applicant for habeas corpus to challenge its validity and to show that he is being unlawfully detained, *e.g.* by proving that his passport had been stamped with lawful authority (*R. v. Secretary of State for the Home Department ex p. Choudhary* [1978] 1 W.L.R. 1177; [1978] 2 All E.R. 790, CA).

In an application for habeas corpus the court will adopt the sort of "special responsibility" and "most anxious scrutiny" as was proposed for asylum cases in *Bugdaycay v. Home Secretary* [1987] 1 A.C. 514; *R. v. Secretary of State for, ex p. Osman* [1993] C.O.D. 39 (Woolf L.J. and Pill J.).

In considering an application for habeas corpus in a deportation case the court may see all the evidence available to the Secretary of State, even if it is hearsay, but it will be for the court to decide what weight to attach to it. Generally in such cases the remedies in proceedings for judicial review will be more appropriate (*Re Saidur Rahman* [1996] C.O.D. 465, *per* Collins J.; and in the Court of Appeal, *The Times*, December 24, 1996).

Where an applicant persists in making hopelessly misconceived applications for habeas corpus, in respect of a particular conviction, constituting a plain abuse of process, the court may direct that no further such applications are to be accepted or processed by the Crown Office in respect of that conviction: *Re Leachman* [1998] C.O.D. 466 (Simon Brown L.J. and Mance J.).

R54.1.4 **Application for discharge from committal order**—The High Court has power, without prejudice to any other jurisdiction of the Court, to order the person committed to stand charges abroad to be discharged from custody if it appears to the Court that it would, having regard to all the circumstances be unjust or oppressive to return him to the country seeking his return either (a) by reason of the trivial nature of the offence of which he is accused, or (b) by reason of the passage of time since he is alleged to have committed it or (c) because the accusation against him is not made in good faith in the interests of justice (see the Extradition Act 1989, s.11(3)). In ordering discharge under this provision the Court is not exercising a separate and distinct statutory power to mitigate what is in fact a lawful detention, but on the contrary is granting relief by way of habeas corpus and is dealing with the application as a true habeas corpus application, *i.e.* discharge from unlawful detention (*R. v. Governor of Pentonville Prison, ex p. Tarling* [1979] 1 W.L.R. 1417; [1979] 2 All E.R. 1103, DC, distinguishing *R. v. Governor of Brixton Prison, ex p. Savarkan* [1910] 2 K.B. 1056). The date of "the passage of time" is to be considered on a second application for the writ as the date of that application, but the passage of time resulting from bona fide appeals even to the House of Lords affords no ground for holding that it would be unjust or oppressive or make it unfair to return the applicant to face the charge on which he has been committed (*ibid.*).

R54.1.5 **Habeas corpus or judicial review**—See generally *R. v. Secretary of State for the Home Department, ex p. Khawaja* [1984] A.C. 74. Where the power to detain is dependent upon the existence of a precedent fact, and the existence of that fact is challenged by or on behalf of the person detained, a challenge to the detention may be mounted by means of an application for a writ of habeas corpus even if there are alternative procedures available.

"A writ of habeas corpus will issue where someone is detained without any authority or the purported authority is beyond the powers of the person authorising the detention and so is unlawful. The remedy of judicial review is available where the decision or action sought to be impugned is within the powers of the person taking it but, due to procedural error, a misappreciation of the law, a failure to take account of relevant matters, or taking account of irrelevant matters or the fundamental unreasonableness of the decision or action, it should never have been taken", *per* Lord Donaldson of Lymington M.R. in *R. v. Home Secretary, ex p. Cheblak* [1991] 1 W.L.R. 890 at 894.

In certain circumstances habeas corpus may serve to prevent the removal of an applicant from the jurisdiction. Thus the Court will not permit a would-be immigrant to be compulsorily removed from its jurisdiction if he has sought the protection and assistance of the Court. Since any compulsory removal necessarily involves some deprivation of liberty a writ of habeas corpus is an alternative remedy to a "stay" under O.53, r.3(10)(a). The effect of service of such a writ is to make the "gaoler" responsible to the Court in place of the authority which ordered the detention, leaving it to the Court to determine on the return of the writ whether the detention should continue.

"If it be objected, and shown, that the use of a writ of *habeas corpus quia timet* is a novelty, so be it. Thus, the greatest and oldest of all prerogative writs, is quite capable of adapting itself to the circumstances of the times. An alternative might be to adapt the writ of *ne exeat regno* which was designed to prevent debtors fleeing the country, to suit a situation in which far from wishing to leave the jurisdiction someone is being compulsorily removed therefrom," *per* Lord Donaldson of

Lymington M.R. in *R. v. Secretary of State for the Home Department, ex p. Muboyayi* [1991] 3 W.L.R. 442. Glidewell L.J. expressed no concluded view on this point but Taylor L.J. agreed with the Master of the Rolls. See also *M. v. Home Office and Kenneth Baker* [1992] 2 W.L.R. 73.

It is usually a sufficient response to an application for habeas corpus to satisfy the court that there is, *ex facie*, a statutory authority for the detention. If the legal or factual merits of the underlying processes which had led to the detention could be entertained, there would be no distinction between habeas corpus and judicial review: *Re Mulcahy (Eleanor)* [1993] C.O.D. 223 (Laws J.).

Where a defendant has been invalidly arraigned but judicial review may not be available by reason of section 29(3) of the Supreme Court Act 1981 (matters relating to trial on indictment) habeas corpus may issue (*R. v. Maidstone Crown Court, ex p. Clark* [1995] 1 W.L.R. 831 (Glidewell L.J. and Curtis J.)).

Where a person is committed to custody by justices by means of a defective warrant for failing to pay a fine, the appropriate remedy is judicial review rather than habeas corpus. In judicial review proceedings the court has wider powers of disposal and the challenge is properly directed at the justices, rather than at the prison governor whose involvement is, in truth, immaterial. (*Re Crawley, The Times*, December 7, 1995 (Simon Brown L.J., Scott Baker & Latham JJ.)).

Where the object is to show that there was no jurisdiction to detain a patient under the Mental Health Act 1983, because the relevant procedures had not been properly complied with, rather than to overturn an administrative decision, the appropriate remedy is habeas corpus, and not judicial review (*Re S-C (Mental patient: Habeas Corpus), The Times*, December 4, 1995 (Sir Thomas Bingham M.R., Neill & Hirst L.JJ.)). In relation to the Mental Health Act 1983, where many requirements are so precise, the court will be cautious in implying a need for procedural precision in relation to detention under the Act, where none has been specifically expressed (*Re Whitbread (Mental patient: Habeas Corpus)* (1997) *The Times*, July 14; and *Re A W* [1997] C.O.D. 269 at first instance).

Where a challenge is made to an allegedly defective warrant of commitment the appropriate procedure is by way of an application for judicial review and not an application for habeaus corpus. In judicial review the court has wider powers of disposal. And see also, generally, on the question whether habeas corpus or judicial review, and for an extensive examination of the authorities (*R. v. Oldham Justices, ex p. Cawley* [1996] 2 W.L.R. 681).

Where an application is made by way of habeas corpus, in circumstances which would have been best dealt with by an application for judicial review, the court will not simply reject it out of hand if the matter can be put into decent procedural shape so as to enable the issue to be resolved: *Re John (Julie)* [1998] C.O.D. 306 (Latham J.).

It was sometimes thought that habeas corpus had advantages over judicial review because of the difference in the burden of proof but in practice that had no practical consequences. Judicial review had advantages over habeas corpus because of the range of remedies available. If a person wrongly detained was released prior to an order for habeas corpus there was no relief which the court could grant, whereas in the case of judicial review it could grant an injunction and, in appropriate cases, damages. In *Re S-C (Mental Patient: Habeas Corpus)* [1996] Q.B. 599, an application for judicial review would have been equally appropriate and would even have had advantages over habeas corpus. Applications for habeas corpus were to be discouraged unless it was clear that no other relief would be required. If both applications were lodged every effort should be made to harmonise the proceedings and the same affidavits should be used. At any interlocutory and final hearing both set of proceedings should be before the court, and in the event of an appeal the same notice of appeal would suffice: *Re Barker, R. v. BHB Community Healthcare NHS Trust and Another, ex p. Barker, The Times*, October 14, 1998 (Lord Woolf M.R., Hobhouse and Thorpe L.JJ.).

Bail—An immigrant on whom a deportation order had been served was not to be granted bail pending determination of an application for habeas corpus. Even if the Court hearing a civil application for habeas corpus had jurisdiction to grant bail the fear that he would remain out of sight justified his being kept in custody (*R. v. Governor of Haslar Prison, ex p. Egbe, The Times*, June 4, 1991 (Parker and Taylor L.JJ. and Sir Roualeyn Cumming-Bruce). **R54.1.6**

Appeals—The applicant may, however, go to the CA by way of appeal, unless it is in a criminal cause or matter, that is to say, unless the direct outcome of the proceedings may be the trial of the applicant and his possible punishment for an alleged offence by an (English or foreign) Court claiming jurisdiction (*Amand v. Home Secretary and Minister of Defence of Royal Netherlands Government* [1943] A.C. 147, *per* Viscount Simon at p. 156; *Ex p. Woodhall* (1888) 20 Q.B.D. 832; *Ex p. Savarkar* [1910] 2 K.B. 1036) or unless the question is whether the sentence for a criminal offence is being duly carried out (*R. v. Governor of Maidstone Prison, ex p. Maguire* (1925) 41 T.L.R. 554; *Re Hastings (No. 3)* [1959] Ch. 368; [1959] 1 All E.R. 698), or the person in respect of whom the application is made is restrained as a person liable, or treated under an enactment as liable, to be detained under certain provisions of the Mental Health Act 1983 (see A.J.A. 1960, s.14(3)). From an order of a single Judge in a criminal matter there is no appeal (S.C.A. 1981, s.18(1)(a) and A.J.A. 1960, s.15(2)); but from a decision of a Divisional Court in such a matter appeal now lies to the House of Lords under the provisions of sections 1 and 15 of the 1960 Act, subject to **R54.1.7**

leave being obtained from the Divisional Court or the House of Lords. The conditions contained in s.1(2) restricting the grant of such leave by the Divisional Court or the House of Lords, are not applicable to appeals in habeas corpus proceedings (s.15(3)) or proceedings under s.10 of the Fugitive Offenders Act 1881 (*Zacharia v. Republic of Cyprus* [1963] A.C. 634; [1962] 2 All E.R. 438, HL). An application to the Divisional Court for leave to appeal to the House of Lords must be made within fourteen days after its decision (A.J.A. 1960, s.2(1)) but the time may be extended in all cases on application by the defendant (ss.2(3) and 15(3)). In criminal or civil matters appeal now lies in all cases (subject to what is stated above) from an order for the release of the person restrained as well as against the refusal of such an order (s.15(1)) and from an order in proceedings on behalf of a child (*Barnado v. McHugh* [1891] A.C. 388) as well as in other cases. In civil matters, from any decision of a Judge appeal lies to the CA; and from a Divisional Court to the CA; in each case without leave.

The effect of s.15(4) of the Administration of Justice Act 1960 is to provide that once a judge at first instance has granted a writ of habeas corpus, a successful appeal by the person having had custody of the applicant cannot render the applicant liable to detention, unless an interim order for detention or release on bail was made, by the Divisional Court under s.5 of the Act (*R. v. Secretary of State for the Home Department, ex p. Vink, Taggar, Vink and Singh* [1996] C.O.D. 134).

Extradition proceedings under the Extradition Act 1989 are criminal proceedings for the purposes of an application for habeas corpus (*Re Levin* [1997] 3 W.L.R. 117, HL), and an order relating to the obtaining of evidence under the Criminal Justice (International Co-operation) Act 1990 for the purposes of such proceedings is likewise a criminal cause or matter and the Court of Appeal, Civil Division therefore has no jurisdiction (*Cuoghi v. Governor of Brixton Prison* (1997) *The Times*, July 24).

R54.1.8 **Costs**—In the discretion of the Court (*R. v. Mansell-Jones or Jones* [1894] 2 Q.B. 382); either the applicant or the respondent may be ordered to pay the costs.

R54.1.9 **Forms generally**—See Forms Nos 87–92 (SCP 1999, Vol. 2, Section 1A, paras 1A–90 to 1A–95).

R54.1.10 **The application**—The application should, as a rule, be made by counsel, but litigants may for sufficient reason be allowed to apply in person for this and the other prerogative writs (*Re Newton* (1855) 16 C.B. 97; *Cobbett v. Hudson* (1855) 15 Q.B. 988; *Re Greene* (1941) 57 T.L.R. 533; *Practice Note* [1947] W.N. 218; *Re Wring* [1960] 1 W.L.R. 138; [1960] 1 All E.R. 536). In *Pharoah* (unrep.) CO/1279/87 (Schiemann J.), the applicant was a patient under section 3 of the Mental Health Act 1983. He submitted an application for habeas corpus challenging the psychiatric diagnosis. The Health Authority declined to produce him for the purpose of the hearing of his application unless directed to do so by the Court. The Court refused to order his production but invited the Official Solicitor to produce a report which disclosed that in 1985 the applicant had been made subject to an order of the Court of Protection. In refusing his application, Schiemann J. expressed himself satisfied that the applicant was lawfully detained, but in any event the applicant was not entitled to apply for habeas corpus because (i) he was a patient of the Court of Protection and thus, by operation of O.80, r.2, he could only bring proceedings by his next friend and (ii) he was not represented by counsel. See also more generally *R. v. Secretary of State for the Home Department, ex p. Wynne* [1992] C.O.D. 74, *The Times*, December 27, 1991.

The application need not be in the name of a person detained, but may be made by any other person at his instance, or by a person entitled to his custody, or, where no communication has been possible, by a relative or friend on his behalf (contrast *Ex p. Child* (1854) 15 C.B. 238); and the witness statement or affidavit in support of the application should depose to the facts on this head, as well as to the facts on which the intervention of the Court is sought. Three copies of the witness statement or affidavit are required for the use of the Court, to be lodged, if possible, the day before the application. An application can be initiated after an extradition warrant has been signed only in the most exceptional circumstances (see *R. v. Governor of Pentonville Prison, ex p. Tarling* [1979] 1 W.L.R. 1417, and *Re Hagan and Croft* [1993] C.O.D. 215). It is to be noted that Rule 54 now allows for the provision of a witness statement or affidavit.

R54.1.11 **Northern Ireland**—The writ does not run to Northern Ireland (*Re Keenan* [1972] 1 Q.B. 523; [1971] 3 All E.R. 883, CA).

Power of Court to whom application made without notice being served on any other party

R54.2 2.—(1) The court or judge to whom an application under rule 1 is made without notice being served on any other party may make an order forthwith for the writ to issue, or may—

(a) where the application is made to a judge otherwise than in court, direct the issue of a claim form seeking the writ, or that an application therefor be made by claim form to a Divisional Court or to a judge in court;

(b) where the application is made to a judge in court, adjourn the application so that notice thereof may be given, or direct that an application be made by claim form to a Divisional Court;
(c) where the application is made to a Divisional Court, adjourn the application so that notice thereof may be given.

(2) The claim form must be served on the person against whom the issue of the writ is sought and on such other persons as the court or judge may direct, and, unless the court or judge otherwise directs, there must be at least 8 clear days between the service of the claim form and the date named therein for the hearing of the application.

History of Rule—Reproduces the former O.59, rr.16 and 17. R54.2.1

Practice—Where the court directs that a claim form is to be used it must be in Form 87 modified in accordance with the guidance set out in the forms Practice Direction—see Practice Direction, para. 3.1, para. R54PD–001. Where an application is adjourned for service of the notice of the application a suitably modified Form 88 must be used. As to the former practice directions which still apply, see the Practice Direction which supplements O.54, para. 7.1, see para. R54PD–003. Although there is power by this rule to make an order forthwith for the issue of the writ on the without notice application, it is only exercised where there is a likelihood that delay may defeat justice, or where the facts and law are clear. In other cases the Court or the Judge makes one of the other orders mentioned in the rule, in which event the person detained must not be ordered to be released meanwhile. He may, however, be admitted to bail, in which case the jurisdiction of the Court is unaffected (*Re Amand* [1941] 2 K.B. 239 at 249). R54.2.2

The summons is issued at the Crown Office, and the motion entered for hearing in that department (O.57, r.2). Three copies of the notice, affidavits and exhibits must be lodged for use of the Divisional Court.

Persons to be served—The notice of adjourned hearing and the claim form should as a rule be directed to the person having control of the body (for example, the prison governor, not the Secretary of State); but (*semble*) it may be addressed to a person who has such control that he can order the gaoler to release the prisoner (*R. v. Crewe (Earl), ex p. Sekgome* [1910] 2 K.B. 576 at 592, 604, CA). Further, the Court may direct service on any other person whom it considers interested or desires to hear, or may hear him without such direction (*e.g.* in extradition proceedings, the requisitioning government (*R. v. Governor of Brixton Prison, ex p. Minervini* [1959] 1 Q.B. 155; [1958] 3 All E.R. 318). The notice may be directed to a corporation (see *Re Carroll* [1931] 1 K.B. 104) but it is better directed to an officer thereof. See Practice Direction, para. 5.1 see para. R54PD–002 as to service. The claim form must be served, together with the writ and notice—Form 90 as modified. R54.2.3

Copies of witness statements or affidavits to be supplied

3. Every party to an application under rule 1 must supply to every other party on demand and on payment of the proper charges copies of the witness statements or affidavits which he proposes to use at the hearing of the application. R54.3

History of Rule—Reproduces the former O.59, r.18. R54.3.1

Power to order release of person restrained

4.—(1) Without prejudice to rule 2(1), the court or judge hearing an application for a writ of habeas corpus ad subjiciendum may in its or his discretion order that the person restrained be released, and such order shall be a sufficient warrant to any governor of a prison, constable or other person for the release of the person under restraint. R54.4

(2) Where such an application in a criminal proceedings is heard by a judge and the judge does not order the release of the person restrained, he shall direct that the application be made by claim form to a Divisional Court of the Queen's Bench Division.

History of Rule—Reproduces in substance the former O.59, r.19. R54.4.1

Practice—The prisoner will not be brought up on the adjourned application or hearing of the R54.4.2

motion unless the Court or Judge, who heard the application in the first instance, has so directed, or the Court so orders in the course of the hearing. At the hearing an order may be made for the writ to issue in accordance with r.5, but a modern practice has grown up of making an order for release as provided by r.4 (see *Chitty and Jacobs Queen's Bench Forms*, Form 1756) in which case the writ is not formally issued: the Master of the Crown Office writes to the prison governor directing the discharge of the prisoner, and the return to the writ need not show the cause of detainer but merely the fact of release.

Directions as to return to writ

R54.5 **5.** Where a writ of habeas corpus ad subjiciendum is ordered to issue, the court or judge by whom the order is made shall give directions as to the court or judge before whom, and the date on which, the writ is returnable.

R54.5.1 **History of Rule**—Reproduces in substance the previous O.59, r.20, but omits to provide that "every such writ shall be returnable immediately".

R54.5.2 **Form of order**—This is made by a Judge in Chambers.

Service of writ and notice

R54.6 **6.**—(1) Subject to paragraphs (2) and (3), a writ of habeas corpus ad subjiciendum must be served personally on the person to whom it is directed.

(2) If it is not possible to serve such writ personally, or if it is directed to a governor of a prison or other public official, it must be served by leaving it with a servant or agent of the person to whom the writ is directed at the place where the person restrained is confined or restrained.

(3) If the writ is directed to more than one person, the writ must be served in manner provided by this rule on the person first named in the writ, and copies must be served on each of the other persons in the same manner as the writ.

(4) There must be served with the writ a notice (in Form No. 90 of the relevant practice direction) stating the court or judge before whom and the date on which the person restrained is to be brought and that in default of obedience proceedings for committal of the party disobeying will be taken.

R54.6.1 **History of Rule**—Reproduces the previous O.59, r.21.

Return to the writ

R54.7 **7.**—(1) The return to a writ of habeas corpus ad subjiciendum must be indorsed on or annexed to the writ and must state all the causes of the detainer of the person restrained.

(2) The return may be amended, or another return substituted therefor, by permission of the court or judge before whom the writ is returnable.

R54.7.1 **Form of return**—This is indorsed on the writ, and if it is too long for indorsement a schedule should be attached as follows—

"The return to (or execution of) this writ appears by the Schedule annexed hereto (or, by affidavit of X. Y. filed herein).

The Schedule

R54.7.2 I, X. Y. (the person ordered to produce the body) in obedience to the writ herewith do certify and return that A. B. is detained in my custody under and by virtue of a (warrant of commitment, order, etc.) as follows. (Set out verbatim its terms.)

It appears to be doubtful whether a return to an applicant for habeas corpus which merely specifies that the applicant is being detained under a particular section of the Immigration Act 1971 is sufficient, since the rule requires that the return "must state all the causes of the detainer of the person restrained" see *R. v. Secretary of State for the Home Department, ex p. Iqbal* [1978] Q.B. 264; [1979] 1 All E.R. 675.

R54.7.3 **"The causes of the prisoner's detainer"**—The Court has power to examine by affidavit evidence the truth of the facts alleged in the return, but does not act as a Court of appeal. If the detainer is under an order or conviction of a judicial authority, it will enquire if there was any evidence to justify it; if there was, it cannot be disturbed; if there was not, the Court can release on habeas corpus or quash on certiorari (*R. v. Board of Control, ex p. Rutty* [1956] 2 Q.B. 109; [1956] 1 All E.R. 769).

Onus of proof—If the return to the writ on its face shows a valid authority for the detention, it is for the applicant to show, that the detention is, prima facie, *illegal* (*R. v. Governor of Risley Remand Centre, ex p. Hassan* [1976] 1 W.L.R. 971; [1976] 2 All E.R. 123, DC). **R54.7.4**

Where the return to an applicant for habeas corpus appears valid on its face but is subsequently found to contain some material error, the Court is entitled, as part of its inquiry under section 3 of the Habeas Corpus Act 1816 into the truth of the facts stated in the return, to go behind the wording on the face of the return and see whether there were in fact good grounds for the detention of the applicant and is not restricted to merely examine the reasons for the detention given in the return (*R. v. Secretary of State for the Home Department, ex p. Iqbal* [1978] Q.B. 264; [1979] 1 All E.R. 675).

Where applicants had established, prima facie, that they were the beneficiaries of a valid pardon which would render their detention relating to offences covered by that pardon unlawful, it is for the prosecution to justify their detention and the applicants were entitled to a writ of habeas corpus as of right so that the lawfulness of their imprisonment could be determined (*Phillip v. DPP of Trinidad and Tobago* [1992] 2 W.L.R. 211; [1992] All E.R. 665).

Procedure at hearing of writ

8. When a return to a writ of habeas corpus ad subjiciendum is made, the return shall first be read, and motion then made for discharging or remanding the person restrained or amending or quashing the return, and where that person is brought up in accordance with the writ, his counsel shall be heard first, then the counsel for the Crown, and then one counsel for the person restrained in reply. **R54.8**

History of Rule—Reproduces r.23 of the former O.59. **R54.8.1**

Form of order of discharge—If the respondent does not appear, and the body is not produced, application may be made to the Court, supported by affidavit of service and disobedience, for committal for contempt, or to a Judge for the issue of a bench warrant. **R54.8.2**

Bringing up prisoner to give evidence, etc.

9.—(1) An application for a writ of habeas corpus ad testificandum or of habeas corpus ad respondendum must be made on witness statement or affidavit to a judge. **R54.9**

(2) An application for an order to bring up a prisoner, otherwise than by writ of habeas corpus, to give evidence in any proceedings, civil or criminal, before any court, tribunal or justice, must be made on witness statement or affidavit to a judge.

History of Rule—Reproduces the former O.36, r.35, and O.59, rr.24, 25. **R54.9.1**

Habeas corpus ad testificandum and ad respondendum—The writ of habeas corpus *ad testificandum* is granted by a Judge of the High Court under common law powers, and, for the purposes of trials in the High Court, under the Habeas Corpus Act 1804. It is issued for bringing up a prisoner to give evidence before a Court. See Short and Mellor's, *Crown Office Practice* (2nd ed.), pp.332–334 for the relevant decisions. Under s.12(5) of The Arbitration Act 1950, the High Court or a Judge (and a Master under R.73, r.3(1)) may order the issue of the writ to bring up a prisoner for examination before an arbitrator or umpire. A similar case is provided for by Sched. 11, para. 13 to the Agricultural Holdings Act 1986. The writ of habeas corpus *ad respondendum* is granted at common law, and, in regard to Courts-martial and proceedings before commissioners in bankruptcy, under the Habeas Corpus Act 1803. It issues to bring up a prisoner for trial or to be examined (see Short & Mellor (2nd ed.), p. 334). **R54.9.2**

By the Criminal Procedure Act 1853, s.9, power is given to the Judge to compel the attendance of a prisoner under sentence or commitment (*except under civil process*) by warrant or order.

In QBD the attendance of a prisoner in custody on civil process is enforced by issue of a writ of habeas corpus *ad testificandum* at the Action Department, Central Office, on the order of a Judge at Chambers under the Habeas Corpus Act 1804. The order for the writ to issue is obtained without notice on affidavit.

In Ch D, in a case of *Jenks v. Ditton* (1897) 76 L.T. 591, on an application for a habeas corpus to bring up a prisoner detained under civil process Stirling, J., declined to order a habeas corpus to issue, and made an order on the governor of the prison to bring up the prisoner.

In QBD, applications under the Criminal Procedure Act 1853, for an order for attendance of a prisoner detained under criminal process are made without notice to a Judge on an affidavit stating whether the prisoner is confined under sentence, or under commitment for trial, or otherwise, and giving the name of the prison in which he is confined, and stating that his evidence is necessary, and when and where required. The order is drawn up at the Crown Office (Short and Mellor's *Crown Office Practice*, p. 335).

A party requiring the attendance of a prisoner to give evidence in a civil suit must tender the reasonable expenses of the prisoner and his escort (*Becker v. Home Office* [1972] 2 Q.B. 407; [1972] 2 All E.R. 676, CA). The Court cannot grant a habeas corpus to a party to a suit, who is in custody, to enable him to appear in Court merely for the purpose of arguing his case in person (*Weldon v. Neal* (1887) 15 Q.B.D. 471; *R. v. Secretary of State for the Home Department, ex p. Wynne* [1992] C.O.D. 74).

R54.9.3 **Obtaining attendance of prisoner in custody**—Section 29 of the Criminal Justice Act 1961 provides that the Secretary of State, if satisfied that the attendance at any place in the United Kingdom of a person detained in any part of the United Kingdom in a prison, youth custody centre, remand centre, detention centre or remand home, is desirable in the interests of justice, may direct that person to be taken to that place. The threshold is not what is *necessary* in the interests of justice but what is *desirable*—that being a lower threshold, see *Ex p. Wynne*, above.

Applications under this section for attendance at a civil Court are normally made by the solicitor acting for the party at whose instance the prisoner is required. Owing to the increasing number of litigants acting in person, it is likely that a Court will occasionally find it necessary to give some guidance to such a person.

An application for the production of a prisoner should be made in the first instance to the prison governor but in case of difficulty enquiry may be made of the Home Office's Tactical Management and Planning Unit, telephone 0121–455–9855.

In some instances the Home Office may require confirmation from the Court that the attendance of the prisoner is essential. It is suggested that in those instances the applicant attend before the District Judge to give his reason for the request. If the District Judge is satisfied that the request ought to be granted, the Court should then communicate direct with the Home Office to this effect (Direction issued by the Lord Chancellor's Department, March 3, 1978).

Form of writ

R54.10 **10.** A writ of habeas corpus must be in Form No. 89, 91 or 92 in the relevant practice direction, whichever is appropriate.

Applications relative to the custody, etc., of child

R54.11 **11.** An application by a parent or guardian of a child for a writ of habeas corpus ad subjiciendum relative to the custody, care or control of the child must be made in the Family Division, and this order shall accordingly apply to such applications with the appropriate modifications.

R54.11.1 **History of Rule**—Added by S.I. 1971 No. 1269.

R54.11.2 **Effect of rule**—This rule gives effect to the provisions of s.1(2) and Schedule 1 to A.J.A. 1970 (now replaced by S.C.A. 1981, s.61, Sched. 1, para. 3) under which there are assigned to the Family Division, "proceedings in which a parent or guardian of a minor applies for a writ of habeas corpus *ad subjiciendum* relative to the custody, care or conduct of the minor". The effect of this rule, together with the amendment of r.1, which makes it subject to this rule, is to apply O.54 to such applications with the appropriate modifications.

PRACTICE DIRECTION—SCHEDULE 1, ORDER 54 (APPLICATION FOR WRIT OF HABEAS CORPUS)

R54PD-001 *This Practice Direction supplements CPR part 50, and Schedule 1 to the CPR*

Terminology

1.1 In this practice direction—

(1) "Order 54" means those provisions contained in Schedule 1, RSC Order 54 which were previously contained in the Rules of the Supreme Court (1965);

(2) a reference to a rule or Part prefixed with CPR is a reference to a rule or Part contained in the CPR rules; and

(3) a reference to a rule number alone is a reference to the rule so numbered in Order 54.

Scope

2.1 This practice direction supplements Order 54 (which sets out how to apply for a writ of habeas corpus) by providing further detail about the application.

2.2 This practice direction must be read together with Order 54.

2.3 It also lists at paragraph 7 other practice directions which governed procedure relating to Order 54 before 26 April 1999 and which will continue to do so.

Form to be used where court directs claim form to be used

3.1 Where the court directs that an application be made by claim form, under—

(1) rule 2 (on hearing application under rule 1); or

(2) rule 4(2) (application in criminal proceedings ordered to be made to Divisional Court of the Queen's Bench Division),

the claimant must use Form 87 modified in accordance with the guidance set out in the Forms practice direction.

Form to be used for Notice of adjourned application directed by court

4.1 Where the court directs under rule 2(1)(c) that an application made under rule 1 is adjourned to allow for service of notice of the application, such notice must be given in modified Form 88. R54PD–002

Service

5.1 The party seeking the writ must serve—

(1) the claim form in accordance with rule 2.2; and

(2) the writ of habeas corpus ad subjiciendum and notice in Form 90, as modified, in accordance with rule 6.

(CPR rule 6.3 provides that the court will normally serve a document which it has issued or prepared).

The Crown Office List

6.1 When the court directs that an application is to be made by claim form under—

(1) rule 2(1) (powers of court to whom application made under rule 1); or

(2) rule 4(2) (power of court in where application made in criminal proceedings)

the application must be entered in the Crown Office List in accordance with Practice Direction (Crown Office List) 1987 1 WLR 232 [1987] 1 All ER 368.

(In Schedule 1, RSC Order 57 rule 2 provides for the entry of claims in the appropriate office and for the filing of copy documents for the use of the court)

Practice Directions etc., which apply to Order 54

7.1 On and after 26 April 1999, the Practice Directions, Statements and Practice Notes set out in Table 1 continue to apply to proceedings under Order 54.

R54PD–003

TABLE 1

Practice Direction etc.	Content
Practice Note [1983] 2 All ER 1020	Urgent matters outside London—consultation of Crown Office and continuation in London;
Practice Note (Crown Office List) [1987] 1 All ER 1184	Need for accuracy in time estimates
Practice Direction (Crown Office List) [1987] 1 WLR 232; [1987] 1 All ER 368.	Parts of the List.
Practice Direction (Crown Office List: Preparation for hearings) [1994] 4 All ER 671, [1994] 1 WLR 1551 (18th November 1994).	Preparation for hearings; Documentation; Time limits; Skeleton arguments; amendment of grounds.
Practice Direction (Crown Office List; Consent Orders) [1997] 1 WLR 825	Consent orders
Practice Statement (Supreme Court; Judgments) [1998] 1 WLR 825, [1998] 2 All ER 638.	Judgments

R54PD–004 **Editorial Note**—The proper citations and dates of the practice directions listed in Table 1 above are as shown immediately below. These practice directions are printed in the Mainwork at the places indicated.

- Practice Direction (Crown Office List: Criminal Proceedings) [1983] 1 W.L.R. 925; *sub nom.* Practice Note (Crown Office List: Uncontested Proceedings: Applications Outside London: Delay) [1983] 2 All E.R. 1020 (July 21, 1983) (see Queen's Bench Practice Direction No. 23 (part), SCP 1999, Vol. 2, paras 2C–164 to 2C–167)
- Practice Note (Crown Office List: Estimated Length of Hearing) [1987] 1 All E.R. 1184 (April 3, 1987)
- Practice Direction (Crown Office List) [1987] 1 W.L.R. 232; *sub nom.* Practice Note (Crown Office List: Arrangement) [1987] 1 All E.R. 368 (February 3, 1987) (see Queen's Bench Practice Direction No. 24, SCP 1999, Vol. 2, para. 2C–168)
- Practice Direction (Crown Office List: Preparation for Hearings) [1994] 1 W.L.R. 1551; *sub nom.* Practice Note (Crown Office List: Penalties for Late Papers) [1994] 4 All E.R. 671 (October 25, 1994) (see Queen's Bench Practice Direction No. 26, SCP 1999, Vol. 2, paras 2C–173 to 2C–175)
- Practice Direction (Crown Office List: Consent Orders) [1997] 1 W.L.R. 825; *sub nom.* Practice Note (Crown Office List: Uncontested Proceedings) [1997] 2 All E.R. 799 (May 12, 1997) (see Queen's Bench Practice Direction No. 27, SCP 1999, Vol. 2, paras 2C–176 to 2C–179)
- Practice Statement (Supreme Court: Judgments) [1998] 1 W.L.R. 825; *sub nom.* Practice Statement (Royal Courts of Justice: Judgments) [1998] 2 All E.R. 667 (April 22, 1998); as modified by Practice Statement (Supreme Court: Judgments) (No. 2) [1999] 1 W.L.R. 1; *sub nom.* Practice Note (Royal Courts of Justice: Judgments) [1999] 1 All E.R. 125 November 25, 1998)

R55.0.1

RSC ORDER 55

APPEALS TO HIGH COURT FROM COURT, TRIBUNAL OR PERSON: GENERAL

Contents R55.0.1

Editorial Introduction

The provisions of this Rule govern the procedure to be followed in "every appeal which by or under any enactment lies to the High Court from any court, tribunal or person". An appeal shall be by way of re-hearing and must be brought by notice of appeal (r.3). In r.1 it is specifically stated that the Order shall not apply to certain appeals, for example, appeals by case stated and appeals in arbitration proceedings. Further, in r.1(4) it is stated that, in relation to any appeals to which this Order applies, the rules in the Order shall have effect subject to any provision made in relation to that appeal by any other provision of the CPR or by or under any enactent (see also r.2). Many such other provisions exist (see further, para. 55.1.2). R55.0.2

Application

1.—(1) Subject to paragraphs (2), (3) and (4), this order shall apply to every appeal which by or under any enactment lies to the High Court from any court, tribunal or person. R55.1

(2) This order shall not apply to an appeal by case stated or to any appeal to which the arbitration practice direction applies.

(3) The following rules of this order shall not apply to an appeal from a county court to a single judge under section 375 of the Insolvency Act 1986, but subject to the Insolvency Rules 1986, as amended, Order 59 shall, with the necessary modifications, apply to such an appeal as it applies to an appeal from a county court to the Court of Appeal.

(4) The following rules of this order shall, in relation to an appeal to which this order applies, have effect subject to any provision made in relation to that appeal by any other provision of these rules or by or under any enactment.

(5) In this order references to a tribunal shall be construed as references to any tribunal constituted by or under any enactment other than any of the ordinary courts of law.

History of Rule—Amended by S.I. 1968 No. 1244, S.I. 1986 No. 2001 and S.I. 1989 No. 1307. R55.1.1

General effect of rules—Care must be taken to examine the statutory basis of the appeal, and any relevant provisions of the CPR. Appeals from the VAT Tribunal, which are affected by O.91, r.6, and appeals against decisions of auditors under the Local Government Finance Act 1982 are affected by O.98. In many instances appeals may be limited by the statutory provision creating the right appeal to points of law and thus the provisions of this Order concerning a rehearing will have no application (*Green v. The Minister of Housing and Local Government* [1967] 2 Q.B. 606). Tribunals whose decisions may be the subject of an appeal under this order by way of a rehearing include the Statutory Committee of the Council of the Royal Pharmaceutical Society of Great Britain, the Professional Conduct Committee of the United Kingdom Central Council for Nursing, Midwifery and Health Visiting, The Solicitors Disciplinary Tribunal and the Licensed Conveyancers Discipline and Appeals Committee. R55.1.2

Rule (1) expressly applies O.55 to every statutory appeal. Thus in an appeal under section 20 of the Local Government Finance Act 1982, against an auditor's findings, O.98 must be read together with O.55 since the latter provides the requirement for grounds to be stated, for the appeal to be by way of re-hearing and for the admission of evidence (*Phillips v. Maghill* [1997] C.O.D. 354).

Statutory Appeal or Judicial Review—It should be noted that the court's powers under this Order are wider than those conferred on the Court under O.53. Thus r.3(1) provides that an appeal shall be by way of rehearing, r.7(2) provides for the reception of further evidence and for directions to be given as to the manner of its receipt and r.7(5) for any order to be made by the court which should have been made by the tribunal. A challenge to a decision of a Special Educational Needs Tribunal should be made by way of an appeal under O.55 and not by way of an application for judicial review (*R. v. Special Educational Needs Tribunal, ex p. South Glamorgan County Council* (1995) *The Times*, December 12). Only a parent and not a child may bring such an appeal *S. v. Special Educational Needs Tribunal, The Times*, December 18, 1995). The appropriate respondent to such an appeal is the Education Authority and not the Tribunal since, on a proper construction of O.55 r.8, the Tribunal cannot be heard as of right (*R. v. Special Educational Needs Tribunal, ex p. Fairpo* [1996] C.O.D. 179).

R55.2 The ordinary route for an appeal against a final decision of the Special Educational Needs Tribunal is by an appeal under O.55 and not by way of an appeal by case stated (*Allton-Evans and others v. Leicester Local Education Authority* [1997] C.O.D. 113, Carnwath J.)

No appeal lies under O.55 against an order for costs made in disciplinary proceedings under the Hearing Aid Council Act 1968 and accordingly any challenge can only be made by judicial review (*R. v. Hearing Aid Council, ex p. Holden* [1997] C.O.D. 377).

Court to hear appeal

R55.2.1 **2.** Except where it is otherwise provided by these rules or by or under any enactment, an appeal to which this order applies shall be assigned to the Queen's Bench Division and shall be heard and determined—

R55.2.2 (a) where the decision of the High Court on the appeal is final, by a Divisional Court, and

(b) in any other case, by a single judge.

History of Rule—Substituted by S.I. 1977 No. 1955.

R55.3 **Effect of rule**—The generality of this provision may be subject to exceptions provided elsewhere in the CPR, for example in appeals under section 289 or 290 of the Town and Country Planning Act 1990 governed by O.94, r.13 which provides that any such appeal shall be "heard and determined by a single judge unless the court directs that the matter shall be heard and determined by a Divisional Court."

Bringing of appeal

3.—(1) An appeal to which this order applies shall be by way of rehearing and must be brought by notice of appeal.

(2) Every notice by which such an appeal is brought must state the grounds of the appeal and, if the appeal is against a judgment, order or other decision of a court, must state whether the appeal is against the whole or a part of that decision and, if against a part only, must specify the part.

R55.3.1 (3) The bringing of such an appeal shall not operate as a stay of proceedings on the judgment, determination or other decisions against which the appeal is brought unless the court by which the appeal is to be heard or the court, tribunal or person by which or by whom the decision was given so orders.

R55.4 **Procedure**—The grounds of appeal should state the reasons why it is contended that the decision impugned is wrong and it is not sufficient merely to set out the conclusions which the Court will be invited to reach. It is to be noted that only where the appeal is against the judgment, order or other decision of a Court, need the notice of motion state whether the appeal is against the whole or part of the decision. If a stay is sought under r.3(3) application should be made by motion on two days notice.

Service of notice of appeal and entry of appeal

4.—(1) The persons to be served with the notice of appeal are the following—

(a) if the appeal is against a judgment, order or other decision of a court, the registrar or clerk of the court and any party to the proceedings in which the decision was given who is directly affected by the appeal;

(b) if the appeal is against an order, determination, award or other decision of a tribunal, Minister of the Crown, government department or other person, the chairman of the tribunal, Minister, government department or person, as the case may be, and every party to the proceedings (other than the appellant) in which the decision appealed against was given.

(2) The notice must be served, and the appeal entered, within 28 days after the date of the judgment, order, determination or other decision against which the appeal is brought.

(3) In the case of an appeal against a judgment, order or decision of a court, the period specified in paragraph (2) shall be calculated from the date of the judgment or order or the date on which the decision was given.

(4) In the case of an appeal against an order, determination, award or other decision of a tribunal, Minister, government department or other person, the period specified in paragraph (2) shall be calculated from the date on which notice of the decision, or, in a case where a statement of the reasons for a decision was given later than such notice, on which such a statement was given to the appellant by the person who made the decision or by a person authorised in that behalf to do so.

History of Rule—Amended by S.I. 1982 No. 1111. R55.4.1

Procedure—It appears to be uncertain whether a decision or reasons are "given" to an appellant within the meaning of r.4(4) when sent to him or when received by him—See *Ringroad Investment Ltd v. Secretary of State for the Environment* 1979 40 P. & C.R. 99 and the judgment of the Court of Appeal in *Griffiths v. Secretary of State for the Environment, The Times*, January 28, 1982. It seems likely, however, that in calculating the period regard should be had to the date on which the decision letter was received—see *Smith v. Secretary of State for the Environment, The Times*, July 6, 1987 considered in *Ynys Mon Borough Council v. Secretary of State for Wales* [1992] C.O.D. 410 (Rose J.). In this latter case the court emphasised that it was the duty of legal advisers either to know or to discover the law and it should not follow that their ignorance of relevant time limits should attract judicial dispensation. Moreover when there would be prejudice to the respondent and there was no substantive and valid reason for exercising the discretion conferred by CPR, r.3.1(2)(a), an application for extension of time will be refused. R55.4.2

In the absence of agreement, the court will normally need to be satisfied that there is an acceptable explanation for the delay before extending time. Even where such an explanation is forthcoming the court might still refuse to extend time if the delay is substantial or when to do so would cause significant prejudice to the respondent. In the interests of good administration public law challenges to decisions of tribunals have to be made within limited time scales (a consideration which is absent in ordinary *inter partes* litigation) and the courts will always be reluctant to extend time in such situations: (*Realbourne Ltd v. East Lindsey District Council* [1993] C.O.D. 297 (Sir Thomas Bingham M.R., Kennedy and Evans L.JJ. dismissing an appeal from the decision of Potts J. [1992] C.O.D. 493)). An application under O.3, r.5 to extend the period of 28 days must be made by summons supported by affidavit.

A notice of motion, by which the appeal is brought is entered in the Crown Office, Royal Courts of Justice, Strand, London WC2A 2LL, together with two copies and a fee of £70. Cheques should be made payable to H.M. Paymaster General. For the hearing of the appeal, the Court will require three paginated bundles comprising copies of:

(a) an index;
(b) the notice of motion;
(c) the decision appealed;
(d) any affidavits filed; and
(e) any other relevant documents.

As to extension of time see also *Van der Velde v. Special Educational Needs Tribunal* [1996] C.O.D. 121–122; and *R. v. Special Educational Needs Tribunal, ex p. Fairpo* [1996] C.O.D. 179.

For an extension of time to be granted under CPR, r.3.1(2)(a) there must be an acceptable explanation for the delay. Without such an explanation the question of prejudice will not arise. A series of derelictions of duty by the applicant's advisers will not be sufficient (*Phillips v. Derbyshire County Council* [1997] C.O.D. 130, Sedley J.).

As to extension of time under CPR, r.3.1(2)(a) of the 28 day period prescribed by r.4(4), where in the case of the Special Educational Needs Tribunal, the tribunal itself had suggested the possibility that it might review its own decision under reg. 31 of its regulations, and the applicant was thus deflected from seeking legal advice, and no prejudice arose, an extension of time would be granted: *Sage v. South Gloucestershire County Council and Another* [1998] C.O.D. 384 (Hidden J.).

Date of hearing of appeal

5. Unless the court having jurisdiction to determine the appeal otherwise directs, an appeal to which this order applies shall not be heard sooner than 21 days after service of notice of the motion by which the appeal is brought. R55.5

R55.5.1 **Uncontested appeals**—Where the parties are agreed as to the terms on which an appeal can be disposed of and require an order of the Court to put them into effect the practice described in Queen's Bench Practice Direction No. 27 (SCP 1999, Vol. 2, Section 2C, para. 2C–176) should be followed.

Amendment of grounds of appeal, etc.

R55.6 **6.**—(1) The notice by which an appeal to which this order applies is brought may be amended by the appellant, without permission, by supplementary notice served not less than 7 days before the day appointed for the hearing of the appeal, on each of the persons on whom the notice to be amended was served.

(2) Within 2 days after service of a supplementary notice under paragraph (1) the appellant must file two copies of the notice in the office in which the appeal is entered.

(3) Except with the permission of the court hearing any such appeal, no grounds other than those stated in the notice by which the appeal is brought or any supplementary notice under paragraph (1) may be relied upon by the appellant at the hearing; but that court may amend the grounds so stated or make any other order, on such terms as it thinks just, to ensure the determination on the merits of the real question in controversy between the parties.

R55.6.1 **Amendment of grounds**—In considering an application for leave to amend under r.6(3) the court will have regard to all the circumstances of the case, including the manner in which the litigation has been conducted (*Steinberg v. McLeod Russel Holdings PLC* and *London Rent Assessment Panel* [1996] C.O.D. 23).

Interlocutory applications

R55.6A **6A.**—(1) Unless the court otherwise directs, any interlocutory application in proceedings to which this order applies may be made to any judge or a Master of the Queen's Bench Division or, as the case may be, any judge or a district judge of the Family Division, notwithstanding that the appeal is to be heard by a Divisional Court.

In this paragraph "interlocutory application" includes an application for the extension of time for the service of the notice of appeal or the entry of the appeal or for the amendment of the notice of appeal.

(2) In relation to an order made by a Master or district judge pursuant to paragraph (1), Order 58, rule 1 shall, where the appeal is to be heard by a Divisional Court, have effect as if a reference to that court were substituted for the reference to a judge.

(3) this rule is without prejudice to any statutory provision or rule of law restricting the making of an order against the Crown.

R55.6A.1 **History of Rule**—Added by S.I. 1987 No. 1423.

Powers of Court hearing appeal

R55.7 **7.**—(1) In addition to the power conferred by rule 6(3) the court hearing an appeal to which this order applies shall have the powers conferred by the following provisions of this rule.

(2) The court shall have power to receive further evidence on questions of fact, and the evidence may be given in such manner as the court may direct either by oral examination in court, by witness statement or affidavit, by deposition taken before an examiner or in some other manner.

(3) The court shall have power to draw any inferences of fact which might have been drawn in the proceedings out of which the appeal arose.

(4) It shall be the duty of the appellant to apply to the judge or other person presiding at the proceedings in which the decision appealed against was given for a signed copy of any note made by him of the proceedings and to furnish that copy for the use of the court; and in default of production of such a note,

or if such note is incomplete, in addition to such note, the court may hear and determine the appeal on any other evidence or statement of what occurred in those proceedings as appears to the court to be sufficient.

Except where the court otherwise directs, a witness statement or affidavit or note by a person present at the proceedings shall not be used in evidence under this paragraph unless it was previously submitted to the person presiding at the proceedings for his comments.

(5) The court may give any judgment or decision or make any order which ought to have been given or made by the court, tribunal or person and make such further or other order as the case may require or may remit the matter with the opinion of the court for rehearing and determination by it or him.

(6) The court may, in special circumstances, order that such security shall be given for the costs of the appeal as may be just.

(7) The court shall not be bound to allow the appeal on the ground merely of misdirection, or of the improper admission or rejection of evidence, unless in the opinion of the court substantial wrong or miscarriage has been thereby occasioned.

History of Rule—Amended by S.I. 1968 No. 1244. R55.7.1

Power of Court to receive further evidence r.7(2)—In *Smith v. Pharmaceutical Society of Great Britain* C.O. 1066/85, December 10, 1986; (unrep.), the Divisional Court declined to receive evidence as to the conduct of the appellant *since* the hearing before the Statutory Committee because it could not be relevant to the decision of the Committee which was made in the light of the evidence before it. However, in *Hefferon v. Committee of the United Kingdom Central Council for Nursing, Midwifery and Health Visiting, The Independent,* March 11, 1988, the Divisional Court applying *Stock v. Central Midwives Board* [1915] 3 K.B. 756 received further evidence from an expert witness as to the effect which an inoculation administered in error might have since that had been an issue at the hearing. "Where there has been an opinion expressed or an assertion of relevant fact made in the course of that hearing, as revealed in the transcript of evidence given, in my judgment, it is competent for this Court to receive in its discretion fresh evidence going to that expression of opinion or that assertion of fact." *per* Watkins L.J. R55.7.2

The power to receive further evidence may be disapplied by operation of some other rule, see for example O.101, r.4(6), which governs appeals under the Pensions Appeal Tribunals Act 1943, and which was considered by Drake J. in *Rivett v. Secretary of State for Social Security* [1990] C.O.D. 479.

In relation to an appeal under s.289 of the Town and Planning Act 1990, which is on a point of law, the High Court should not receive evidence unless it is argued that the inspector had not properly summarised, or had disregarded, some material evidence (*Clarke v. Secretary of State for the Home Environment* [1993] C.O.D. 80 (Fox, Glidewell L.JJ. and Boreham J.), CA).

Other powers of Court—Where a respondent concedes a material and relevant ground of appeal r.7(5) does not impose any obligation on the court to deal with every other ground of appeal. The court has a discretion to limit the scope of argument in the wider interests of the proper administration of justice. It will however be astute to prevent a respondent from avoiding the determination of an issue which should be determined by making a tactical concession (*Northumberland and Durham Property Trust Ltd v. London Rent Assessment Committee* [1997] C.O.D. 428 (Latham J.)). R55.7.3

The principles to be applied, in considering whether to make an order for security for costs under r.7(6), are different from those applicable where there has been no hearing at first instance but are rather the same as those applicable to appeals to the Court of Appeal from decisions of the High Court (*R. v. Royal Pharmaceutical Society for Great Britain, ex p. Kansal* [1997] C.O.D. 321 (Tuckey J.)).

In considering the provisions of O.55, r.7(7), in a case involving an allegation of dishonesty, it was appropriate to apply the test for deciding whether to invoke the proviso to s.2 of the Criminal Appeal Act 1968, namely whether the disciplinary committee must inevitably have found the dishonesty proved; *per* Simon Brown J. in *Crabtree v. United Kingdom Central Council for Nursing, Midwifery and Health Visiting* [1990] C.O.D. 277.

As to the exercise of the Court's discretion under r.7(7) see *Botton v. Secretary of State for the Environment and the London Borough of Bromley* [1992] C.O.D. 249 (Roch J.) and *P.G. Vallance Ltd v. Secretary of State for the Environment* (1992) *The Independent,* November 19 (Henry J.). Where the Court concludes that a tribunal has misdirected itself in point of law, but would have reached the same decision had it not done so, the court may dismiss the appeal, under r.7(7), if satisfied that no substantial wrong or miscarriage has been occasioned (*Knight v. Dorset County Council* [1997] C.O.D. 256 (Tucker J.)).

In an appeal against a decision of the Statutory Committee of the Royal Pharmaceutical Society, the function of the Court was not to impose its own view in substitution for the

Committee's view unless it concluded that the Committee's decision was plainly wrong or that the Committee had misdirected itself in reaching its conclusion (*Thobani v. Pharmaceutical Society of Great Britain* [1990] C.O.D. 279 (Watkins L.J. and Nolan J.)).

Before the High Court can remit a case to a VAT Tribunal for a re-hearing under O.55, r.7(5) it must first consider the merits of the case and quash the decision under appeal (*Commissioners of Customs and Excise v. Ferrero U.K. Ltd* (1997) *The Times*, May 19, Lord Woolf, M.R.; Hutchison and Mummery L.JJ., CA).

An order for the production of notes or a transcript under r.7(4) will only be made in exceptional and rare circumstances and where it is necessary in order to dispose properly of an issue raised in the appeal: *Joyce v. Dorset County Council* [1997] E.L.R. 26. An order will not be made if its purpose is to conduct a fishing expedition or to add to grounds or to seek to discover grounds on which an appeal could be pursued: *Fisher v. Hughes and Another* [1998] C.O.D. 281 (Keene J.).

Right of Minister, etc., to appear and be heard

R55.8 **8.** Where an appeal to which this order applies is against an order, determination or other decision of a Minister of the Crown or government department, the Minister or department, as the case may be, shall be entitled to appear and be heard in the proceedings on the appeal.

RSC ORDER 56

APPEALS, ETC., TO HIGH COURT BY CASE STATED: GENERAL

R56.0.1 **Contents**

Editorial Introduction

R56.0.2 The High Court has jurisdiction (sometimes to be exercised only by a Divisional Court) to entertain appeals by way of case stated in various circumstances. The rules in this Order govern the procedure for appeals from the Crown Court (rr.1, 4 and 4A) and from a magistrates' court (rr.5 & 6). Also, under various enactments the Court has jurisdiction to hear and determine a case stated by a Minister, government department, tribunal, or other person (rr.7 to 12). Special provision is made for case stated appeals in extradition proceedings (r.12A). Interlocutory applications in case stated appeals (however arising) are dealt with in accordance with r.13. The provisions of O.57 also apply to appeals by way of case stated. In some instances, appeals by case stated may go from a tribunal, not to the High Court, but to the Court of Appeal (O.61).

Related sources

R56.0.3
- Supreme Court Act 1981, ss.28 and 28A (SCP 1999, Vol. 2, Section 20A, paras 20A–198 to 20A–202)
- RSC, O.57 (Divisional Court proceedings, etc.; supplementary provisions)
- RSC, O.61 (Appeals from tribunals to Court of Appeal by case stated)
- RSC, O.79 (Criminal proceedings)
- RSC, O.93, r.10 (Determination of appeal or case stated under various Acts)

The following *Queen's Bench Practice Directions* are relevant to this Order (Vol. 2, Section 2C, paras 2C–168, 2C–169 and 2C–176). These Directions continue to apply for the time being (see Practice Direction (Civil: Litigation: Procedure) [1999] 1 W.L.R. 1124).

- No. 24 Crown Office list listing arrangements
- No. 25 Crown Office list—striking out, etc.
- No. 27 Disposal of uncontested proceedings in Crown Office list.

Chancery Division Practice Direction No. 1, (Appeals) see Chancery Guide, p. 70 (see paras D1–312 *et seq.*

Appeals from the Crown Court by case stated

1.—(1) Except where they relate to affiliation proceedings or to care proceedings under the Children and Young Persons Act 1969 all appeals from the Crown Court by case stated shall be heard and determined— R56.1

(a) in any criminal proceedings, by a Divisional Court of the Queen's Bench Division;

(b) in any other proceedings, by a single judge, or if the court so directs, by a Divisional Court of the Queen's Bench Division.

[(2) Revoked by RSC (Amendment No. 5) 1971 (S.I. 1971 No. 1955).]

(3) An appeal from the Crown Court by case stated shall not be entered for hearing unless and until the case and a copy of the judgment, order or decision in respect of which the case has been stated and, if that judgment, order or decision was given or made on an appeal to the Crown Court, a copy of the judgment, order or decision appealed from, have been filed in the Crown Office.

(4) No such appeal shall be entered after the expiration of 10 days from the receipt by the appellant of the case unless the delay is accounted for to the satisfaction of the Divisional Court.

Notice of intention to apply for an extension of time for entry of the appeal must be served on the respondent at least 2 clear days before the day named in the notice for the hearing of the application.

(5) Where any such appeal has not been entered by reason of a default in complying with the provisions of this rule, the Crown Court may proceed as if no case had been stated.

History of Rule—Replaces the previous O.59, rr.29(1) and 30. Amended by S.I. 1971 No. 1269; S.I. 1971 No. 1955; S.I. 1980 No. 1908; S.I. 1980 No. 2000 and S.I. 1982 No. 1786. R56.1.1

Appeals from the Crown Court by case stated—The provisions governing appeal by case stated from the Crown Court are to be found in this order, s.28 of the Supreme Court Act 1981 and r.26 of the Crown Court Rules 1982. Section 28 of the Supreme Court Act 1981 provides: R56.1.2

"(1) Subject to subs. (2), any order, judgment or other decision of the Crown Court may be questioned by any party to the proceedings, on the ground that it is wrong in law or is in excess of jurisdiction, by applying to the Crown Court to have a case stated by that Court for the opinion of the High Court.

(2) Subsection (1) shall not apply to—

(a) a judgment or other decision of the Crown Court relating to trial on indictment; or

(b) any decision of that Court under the Betting, Gaming and Lotteries Act 1963, the Licensing Act 1964, the Gaming Act 1968 or the Local Government (Miscellaneous Provisions) Act 1982 which, by any provision of any of those Act, is to be final.

(3) Subject to the provisions of this Act and to rules of Court, the High Court shall, in accordance with s.19(2), have jurisdiction to hear and determine—

(a) any application, or any appeal (whether by way of case stated or otherwise), which it has power to hear and determine under or by virtue of this or any other Act; and

(b) all such other appeals as it had jurisdiction to hear and determine immediately before the commencement of this Act."

In *Loade v. Director of Public Prosecutions* [1989] 3 W.L.R. 1281, the Divisional Court held that "any order, judgment or other decision" in s.28(1) precluded the Crown Court from stating a case, at least in a criminal cause or matter, where the proceedings in the Crown Court had not yet been finally concluded. On appeal to the Crown Court against a conviction by a Magistrates' Court under s.4 of the Public Order Act 1986, it was submitted that the offence of which the appellants had been convicted was unknown to law. The Crown Court rejected that submission but proceeded to state a case before hearing any evidence. The Divisional Court was satisfied that "decision" in this context meant "final decision". As to civil proceedings the Divisional Court would approach with the caution expressed in *R. v. Secretary of State for the Environment ex p. Kensington and Chelsea Royal Borough Council* (1987) 19 H.L.R. 161, the question whether it should hear an appeal by way of case stated when the proceedings in the Crown Court have not yet been concluded.

It is to be noted that the expression "any party to the proceedings" in s.28(1) appears to be somewhat narrower than "any person aggrieved" in s.111 of the Magistrates' Courts Act 1980 (see para. R56.5.2). The expression "relating to trial on indictment", which also appears in s.29(3) of the Supreme Court Act 1981 in connection with applications for mandamus, prohibition or certiorari, has been considered by the Courts, in relation to that section, on a number of occasions in recent years, most notably by the House of Lords in *Re Smalley* [1985] 1 A.C. 622, *Re Sampson* [1981] W.L.R 194 and *DPP v. Crown Court at Manchester and Ashton* [1993] 2 All E.R. 663. See also *R. v. Leicester Crown Court, ex p. S* [1991] C.O.D. 231, reporting restrictions; *R. v. Liverpool Crown Court, ex p. Mende* [1991] C.O.D. 483, fixing of a trial date.

It is the duty of the Crown Court when hearing an appeal from a Magistrates' Court to make proper findings of fact. If a necessary fact is proved the court should clearly say so in the case stated. Equally if a necessary fact is not proved to the required standard again the court should say so. If a two-member court irreconcilably disagrees as to whether a necessary fact has been established it should in the last resort abandon the hearing and cause the case to be relisted before another court. The problem cannot be overcome by the chairman regarding himself as having a casting vote (*DPP v. Szarzynski* (1992) *The Times*, November 14 (Kennedy L.J. and Waterhouse J.)).

Where the Crown Court has failed to give adequate reasons for dismissing an appeal from a conviction by Magistrates it may be required to state a case. However, where the events had occurred some time before, and the offence was not the most serious, it was preferable to take the course adopted in *R. v. Leeds Crown Court, ex p. Barlow* [1989] R.T.R. 246, and simply quash the decision of the Crown Court, thus leaving the conviction in the Magistrates' Court outstanding and the appellant free to apply to have his appeal reheard in the Crown Court (*R. v. Winchester Crown Court, ex p. Morris* [1996] C.O.D. 104).

Where there has been a refusal to state a case it may be conventional and technically correct to apply by way of judicial review for an order of mandamus to compel the Crown Court to state a case, but where the facts are not in dispute it is far better for the true issue to be placed before the court by way of a straightforward judicial review challenge to the correctness of the Crown Court's adjudication in point of law: *R. v. Knightsbridge Crown Court, ex p. Foot* [1998] C.O.D. 165 (Simon Brown L.J. and Mance J.).

R56.1.3 **Case stated or judicial review**—In *R. v. Crown Court of Ipswich, ex p. Baldwin* [1981] 1 All E.R. 596, the Divisional Court, gave guidance as to when it might be appropriate to appeal by way of case stated "... in a case such as this which bristles with factual difficulties the only convenient and proper way to get it before the Divisional Court is by case stated and not by way of application for judicial review." In general case stated is preferable to judicial review as a means of examining justices' decisions since, as a general rule, judicial review is reserved for cases where legislation has provided no alternative remedy (*Benham v. Poole Borough Council* (1991) 135 S.J. (L.B.) 173). It is also generally better suited where it is necessary to enquire into the Crown Court's process of reasoning (*R. v. Southwark Crown Court, ex p. Mitchell* [1994] C.O.D. 15 (Kennedy L.J. and Bell J.)).

Parliament has prescribed case stated as the appropriate route from the magistrates' court to the Divisional Court and judicial review should be sought only when case stated was inapposite or clearly inappropriate. Had the justices stated a case the court would have known what were their findings of fact and what were the relevant points of law for the court's decision (*R. v. Morpeth Justices, ex p. Joseland, The Times*, March 4, 1992). See also *R. v. Brent Justices, ex p. Liles* [1992] C.O.D. 269 (Woolf L.J. and Pill J.).

Issues of the sort which arise in a case concerning special reasons for not disqualifying a driver depend very much as to the precise facts found and the most satisfactory way of putting them before the court is by way of case stated (*DPP v. Connors* [1992] C.O.D. 81 (Woolf L.J. and Leonard J.)). In a situation where judicial review is appropriate it is irrelevant that, had the challenge proceeded by way of case stated, a right of appeal to the House of Lords might have been subsequently conferred (*R. v. Metropolitan Stipendiary Magistrate, ex p. Director of the Serious Fraud Office* [1994] C.O.D. 509 (Butler-Sloss L.J. & Macpherson J.)).

For a general consideration of rights of appeal and the appropriateness of judicial review, see *R. v. Hereford Magistrates Court, ex p. Rowlands* [1997] C.O.D. 236, Lord Bingham of Cornhill C.J. & Moses J.

R56.1.4 **Sentence**—A sentence alleged to be "wrong in law or in excess of jurisdiction" may be impugned by case stated, although in recent times most such challenges have been made by the way of judicial review. See *R. v. St Albans Crown Court, ex p. Cinnamond* [1981] Q.B. 480 but, as importantly, the words of caution uttered by Watkins L.J. in *R. v. Crown Court of Croydon, ex p. Miller* (1987) 85 Cr.App.R. 152, DC. In *Tucker v. DPP* [1992] 4 All E.R. 901; [1992] C.O.D. 231 (Woolf L.J. and Pill J.), the court observed that *ex p. Cinamond* should be regarded with circumspection as having only a narrow application. Anyone seeking to have a severe sentence reviewed should be warned accordingly. In all but the most exceptional circumstances the appropriate course is to appeal to the Crown Court (*R. v. Ealing Justices, ex p. Scrafield* (1993) *The Times*, March 29 (Evans L.J. and Morland J.)). For some such exceptional cases where the Divisional Court has quashed sentences see *R. v. Chelmsford Crown Court, ex p. Birchall* (1989) 11 Cr.App.R.(S.) 510 [1990] C.O.D. 200; *R. v. Southwark Crown Court, ex p. Ager* (1990) 91 Cr.App.R.(S.) 322 [1990] C.O.D. 311 and *R. v. Burnley Magistrates' Court, ex p. Halstead* (1991) 155 J.P. 288 [1991] C.O.D. 156.

As to the test to be applied in determining whether a sentence is such as to enable the Divisional Court to interfere, Lord Bingham of Cornhill C.J. observed: "The court has on previous occasions suggested a test of whether the sentence in question is regarded by any acceptable standard as truly astonishing. I would, for my part, question whether that is an ideal test since some people are more readily astonished than others and it would appear to be a somewhat subjective approach. It would perhaps seem more helpful to ask the question whether the sentence or order in question falls clearly outside the broad area of the lower court's sentencing discretion." (*R. v. Truro Crown Court, ex p. Adair* [1997] C.O.D. 296.)

Time in which case to be entered—Where an extension of the 10 day period is sought the delay must be accounted for to the satisfaction of the court. The phrase "pressure of work" was not, of itself, a sufficient explanation (*Reid v. DPP* [1993] C.O.D. 111 (Mann L.J. and Leonard J.)). **R56.1.5**

Bail—Section 81(1) of the Supreme Court Act 1981 provides that the Crown Court may grant bail to any person "—(d) who, after the decision of his case by the Crown Court, has applied to that Court for the statement of a case for the High Court on that decision...." If bail is refused, there is a right to apply to a High Court Judge; see section 22 of the Criminal Justice Act 1967, section 5(6) of the Bail Act 1976 and O.79. **R56.1.6**

Practice—Three copies of all the documents specified in O.56, r.1(3) must be lodged in the Crown Office, Royal Court of Justice, Strand, London WC2A 2LL, together with a fee of £20. Cheques must be made payable to H.M. Paymaster General. Note also the requirement in O.56, r.1(3), concerning copy judgments and orders. **R56.1.7**

Delay—The short period of time, 10 days, prescribed by O.56, r.1(4) should be noted. An application for an extension of time, under CPR, r.3.1(2)(a), in which to enter an appeal by case stated should be made by summons, on at least two days notice to the respondent, to the Master of the Crown Office—see O.56, r.13. On such a summons a fee of £20 is payable. A solicitor's negligence may be sufficient to explain the delay but each case will depend on its own facts, see *Collyer v. Dring* [1952] 2 All E.R. 1004. **R56.1.8**

Procedure for obtaining a case stated—The provisions governing an application for a case stated by the Crown Court are to be found in r.26 of the Crown Court Rules 1982 (S.I. 1982 No. 1109) which are summarised in tabular form below. The rules refer to "the appropriate officer of the Crown Court" who will generally be the chief clerk at the relevant location of that Court. **R56.1.9**

Paragraph		
1 & 2	Within 21 days after the date of the decision impugned.	Application is made in writing to the chief clerk stating the ground on which the decision is questioned.
3	Forthwith after making the application.	A copy is sent to the parties to the proceedings in the Crown Court.
4	Forthwith on receipt.	The chief clerk sends copy to the Judge who presided at the proceedings at which the decision was made.
5	On receipt of application.	The Judge informs the chief clerk whether or not he has decided to state a case and the chief clerk then gives the applicant notice in writing of the Judge's decision.
6		If the Judge considers that the application is frivolous he may refuse to state a case and, if the applicant so requires, cause a certificate stating the reasons for the refusal to be given to him.
7		If the Judge decides to state a case the procedures described in Paras 8 to 12 are adopted unless the Judge, in a particular case, otherwise directs.
8	Within 21 days of the receipt of the notice referred to in Para. 5.	The applicant drafts a case and sends it to the chief clerk and to the parties to the proceedings in the Crown Court.

Paragraph		
9	Within 21 days of receipt of the draft case.	Each party either (a) gives notice in writing to the chief clerk that he does not intend to take part in the proceeding before the High Court, or (b) indicates in writing on his copy of the draft that he agrees with it and sends the copy to the chief clerk, or (c) drafts an alternative case and sends it with a copy of the applicant's draft to the chief clerk.
10		The Judge considers the applicant's draft and any alternative drafts.
11		If the Crown Court so orders the applicant must, before the case is stated and delivered to him, enter before an officer of the Crown Court into a recognisance, with or without sureties, and in such sum as the Crown Court considers proper, having regard to the means of the applicant, conditioned to prosecute the appeal without delay.
12	Within 14 days after entry of (a) the receipt of all the documents in Para. 9 or (b) the 21 days referred to in Para. 9 whichever is the sooner.	The Judge states and signs the case.
13		A case stated by the Crown Court shall state the facts found by the Crown Court, the submissions of the party (including any authorities relied on by the parties during the course of those submissions), the decision of the Crown Court in respect of which the application is made and the question on which the opinion of the High Court is sought.
14		Any time limit may be extended either before or after it expires, by the Crown Court.
15		Where a Judge declines to state a case but is subsequently required to do so by order of mandamus, Paras 7 to 14 shall apply save that in Para. 7 the words "if the Judge decides to state a case" shall be omitted and, in Para. 8, the date on which the order of mandamus is made, is substituted for the receipt of the application to state a case.

It had been hoped that the procedure for stating a case in the Crown Court would conform with that for stating a case in the magistrates' court. To that end Lord Widgery C.J. made the following Practice Direction (unrep.) on December 4, 1978:

"It is desirable that there should be uniformity in Cases Stated by the Crown Court.

Pending any amendment of the relevant Rules, the content of any such Case should comply with rule 68 of the Magistrates' Courts Rules 1968 and the form with Form 148 of the Magistrates' Courts (Forms) Rules 1968, with necessary amendments only.

What that means, in a sentence, is that as regards appeals by Case Stated from the Crown Court the same form and content is required of the Cases as is already prescribed for Magistrates' Cases."

A letter from the Crown Court stating that the Judge refuses to state a case "on the grounds that your application is frivolous in accordance with the Rules" may be a sufficient statement of the reasons for refusal (*R. v. Carlisle Crown Court, ex p. Jackson, Watson and McDonagh* [1991] C.O.D. 273 (Mann L.J. and Simon Brown J.).

"[Frivolous] is not a word which is used in the ordinary meaning attached to it by people in everyday life. What it means is that . . . there was no possible prospect of a case stated succeeding, because there was no substance in the request that this case should be stated, and no particular ground on which the matter should be put before the Divisional Court." (*R. v. Betting Licensing Committee, Cardiff Petty Sessions, ex p. Les Croupiers Casino Ltd*, April 13, 1992, CO/1965/91 (unrep.) (Macpherson J.).) There is a duty to state a case where the point is arguable, albeit devoid of merit (*R. v. Newcastle under Lyme Magistrates' Court, ex p. Mark Coupe Ltd* [1993] C.O.D. 330).

Where magistrates refused to state a case on the ground that the application was frivolous, and persisted in that refusal notwithstanding the grant of leave to move for judicial review to challenge that decision, an order for costs was made against them (*R. v. Huntingdon Magistrates Court, ex p. Percy* [1994] C.O.D. 323 (Balcombe L.J. & Schiemann J.)).

The fact that an offence is not serious and that an offender, with previous convictions, is only conditionally discharged does not of itself render an application "frivolous": he is fully entitled to have his point of law considered by way of case stated. There may well be cases in which it will be useful to have a statement from the judge setting out further reasons for his refusal to state a case. It will be a matter for the Divisional Court to decide whether to consider such a statement, which should simply be signed by the judge and not in the form of an affidavit (*R. v. Crown Court at Portsmouth, ex p. Thomas* [1994] C.O.D. 373 (McCowan L.J. & Curtis J.)).

The question of the admissibility of evidence is always a matter of law. While there are cases where that question is of such minimal importance to the real issues as to justify a refusal to state a case that was not the position where there was a substantial point affecting the conduct of the defendant's case (*R. v. West Midlands Magistrates, ex p. PMS International Group plc* [1993] C.O.D. 455).

As to a refusal to state case persisted in after the grant of leave to move for judicial review to challenge that refusal, see also *R. v. Aldershot Justices, ex p. Rushmoor Borough Council* [1996] C.O.D. 21.

After the introductory paragraphs, a case stated should next set out the facts found, the submissions made on each side, followed by the court's opinion about those submissions and the basis upon which it reached its overall conclusion. Finally, there should be set out the questions of law upon which the opinion of the court was sought. Only if a question arose as to whether the Crown Court should reasonably have found any facts on the basis of the evidence it had heard should it include a statement or summary of the evidence. It was appropriate to remind the Crown Court that the responsibility for the production of a properly stated case rested with it. Its duty was not simply to sign a draft case but to scrutinise it so as to ensure that it contained only that which would be required by the High Court (*R. v. Crown Court at Croydon, ex p. Sutton* [1996] C.O.D. 11). As to the difficulties which may arise where a Recorder in the Crown Court decides that paras 8 to 12 of r.26 of the Crown Court Rules 1982 shall not apply and himself states the case under para. 7, see *Colfox v. Dorset County Court* [1996] C.O.D. 275.

The word "frivolous" as used in section 111(5) of the Magistrates' Courts Act 1980 is a term of art. It means that the matter does not brook any substantial argument, or that it is so clear that the matter should not be investigated (*R. v. Lowestoft Magistrates, ex p. Adamson* [1996] C.O.D. 276, MacPherson J.).

It was unfortunate that the expression "frivolous" had ever entered the lexicon of procedural jargon. To the man or woman in the street "frivolous" was suggestive of light-heartedness or a propensity to humour and those were not qualities associated with most actual or prospective appellants. It meant rather that the court considered the application to be futile, misconceived, hopeless or academic. That was not a conclusion that would be often or lightly reached. However, where Magistrates reached that conclusion it would be helpful if they were to indicate, however briefly, why they did so (*R. v. Mildenhall Magistrates Court, ex p. Forest Heath District Council* [1997] C.O.D. 352, Lord Bingham of Cornhill C.J.; Millett and Potter L.JJ.).

Absent want of jurisdiction on application to the State cannot be refused on any ground other than that it is "frivolous" (*R. v. Manchester Crown Court, ex p. Wallwork* [1997] C.O.D. 417, Simon Brown L.J. and Owen J.).

The power to extend time provided for by r.26(14) of the Crown Court Rules 1982 may be exercised by a judge of the Crown Court alone and there is no requirement that the justices should also participate in that decision. Where an application for an extension of time is made by the prosecution the Crown Court must afford the acquitted defendant an opportunity to be heard in opposition to such an application. Such extensions should not be routinely granted and cogent reasons for doing so will be required from the prosecution. *DPP v. Coleman* [1998] 1 All E.R. 912 (Pill L.J. and Garland J.).

Where the Crown Court refuses to state a case it should give its reasons for refusal with some particularity: *R. v. Preston Crown Court, ex p. Chief Constable of the Lancashire Constabulary* [1998] C.O.D. 272 (Moses J.). And the same requirement applies where the challenge might be either by way of judicial review or case stated: *R. v. Gloucester Crown Court, ex p. Chester* [1998] C.O.D. 365 (Lord Bingham of Cornhill C.J. and Thomas J.).

Amendment of the case—There are no specific provisions either under the Supreme Court Act or under this Order for the amendment by the High Court of a case stated by the Crown Court (*cf.* the position in the magistrates' court under section 28A(2) of the Supreme Court Act 1981). However, a Divisional Court may remit a case to the Crown Court for it to be re-stated (see *Vyner v. Wirral Rural District Council* [1909] 73 J.P. 242 and *R. v. Bloxham* [1834] 1 Ad. & El. 386). **R56.1.10**

Costs—Where the Court allowed a prosecutor's appeal by case stated from the Crown Court **R56.1.11**

and the point taken on appeal had (a) been raised by the Crown Court itself, (b) had not been of the defendant's making, (c) the defendant had not completed giving evidence in the Crown Court, and (d) the defendant had not been asked whether she would consent to the appeal being allowed in her absence, it was grotesquely unjust to require that she should pay the costs in the High Court. However, as a matter of principle, what was or was not just in the circumstances was in the last resort a matter of impression. The court would set aside an order for costs made against her by the Divisional Court on March 5, 1992 (*Canterbury City Council v. Cook* (1992) *The Times*, December 23 (Mann L.J. and Leonard J.)).

R56.1.12 **Appeal**—An appeal from the decision of the High Court lies as follows:

(i) in a criminal cause or matter with a certificate and leave to the House of Lords (s.1 of the Administration of Justice Act 1960);

(ii) in a civil cause or matter the decision of the High Court is final, sections 18(1)(c) and 28A(1) of the S.C.A. 1981 (*Maile v. Manchester City Council* [1998] C.O.D. 19, Nourse, Hutchison and Thorpe L.JJ.).

Notice of entry of appeal

R56.4 **4.** Within 4 days after an appeal from the Crown Court by case stated is entered for hearing, the appellant must serve notice of the entry of the appeal on the respondent.

R56.4.1 **Delay**—The practice to be followed in relation to an application or an extension of time in which to serve notice of the entry is the same as that to be followed for an extension of time in which to enter the appeal: see the note *delay* in para. 56.1.8. Where extension of time is sought both for entry and service, it is the usual practice to include both applications in the same summons.

Appeals relating to affiliation proceedings and care proceedings

R56.4A **4A.** Appeals from the Crown Court by case stated which relate to affiliation proceedings or to care proceedings under the Children and Young Persons Act 1969 shall be heard and determined by a single judge, or if the court so directs, a Divisional Court of the Family Division, and the foregoing provisions of this order shall accordingly apply to such appeals with the substitution of references to the principal registry of the Family Division for references to the Crown Office and such other modifications as may be appropriate.

R56.4A.1 **History of Rule**—Added by S.I. 1971 No. 1269. Amended by S.I. 1971 No. 1955; S.I. 1980 No. 1908 and S.I. 1980 No. 2000.

R56.4A.2 **Effect of rule**—This rule gives effect to S.C.A. 1981, s.61 and Sched. 1, para. 3 (as amended by the High Court (Distribution of Business) Order 1991 (S.I. 1991 No. 1210)), under which business is assigned to the Family Division. Rules 1–4 will apply to such proceedings with the necessary modifications.

R56.4A.3 **Appeals relating to affiliation proceedings**—The following *Practice Direction* [1981] 1 W.L.R. 138; [1981] 1 All E.R. 400, has been issued by the President with the concurrence of the Lord Chancellor.

"With effect from January 12, 1981, RSC, O.56, rr.4A and 5 are amended so that appeals by case stated in any of the types of proceedings therein set out are taken by a single Judge as a general rule and only by a Divisional Court of the Family Division if the Court so directs (see RSC (Amendment No. 4) 1980 (S.I. 1980 No. 2000), r.9(2)).

The rules require that all relevant papers be lodged in the Principal Registry of the Family Division, but there is no requirement in the rules that the single Judge must be a single Judge sitting in London. Accordingly, any party wishing the appeal to be heard and determined by a single Judge outside London should apply to the President for a direction to this effect. The application should be made by letter addressed to the Clerk of the Rules. Where such a direction is given, the Clerk of the Rules will inform the appellant of the relevant divorce town and will refer the papers to the listing officer of the appropriate circuit office for a date of hearing to be fixed and notified to the appellant."

Appeal from Magistrates' Court by case stated

R56.5 **5.**—(1) Except as provided by paragraph (2) all appeals from a Magistrates' Court by case stated shall be heard and determined—

(a) in any criminal proceedings, by a Divisional Court of the Queen's Bench Division;

(b) in any other proceedings, by a single judge or, if the court so directs, by a Divisional Court of the Queen's Bench Division.

(2) An appeal by way of case stated against an order or determination of a Magistrates' Court shall be heard and determined by a single judge or, if the court so directs, a Divisional Court of the Family Division if the order or determination appealed against was made or given in family proceedings.

History of Rule—Substituted by S.I. 1971 No. 1269. Amended by S.I. 1976 No. 337; S.I. 1980 No. 1010; S.I. 1980 No. 1908; S.I. 1980 No. 2000; S.I. 1983 No. 1181 and S.I. 1988 No. 1340. **R56.5.1**

Appeals from a magistrates' court by case stated—The provisions governing appeals by case stated from the magistrates' court are to be found in this Order, s.111 of the Magistrates' Courts Act 1980 and the Magistrates' Rules 1981. Magistrates' Courts Act 1980, s.111, provides: **R56.5.2**

"(1) Any person who was a party to any proceeding before a Magistrates' Court or is aggrieved by the conviction order, determination or other proceeding of the Court may question the proceeding on the ground that it is wrong in law or is in excess of jurisdiction by applying to the justices composing the Court to state a case for the opinion of the High Court on the question of law or jurisdiction involved; but a person shall not make an application under this section in respect of a decision against which he has a right of appeal to the High Court or which by virtue of any enactment passed after December 31, 1879 is final.

(2) An application under subsection (1) above shall be made within 21 days after the day on which the decision of the Magistrates' Court was given.

(3) For the purpose of subsection (2) above, the day on which the decision of the Magistrates' Court is given shall, where the Court has adjourned the trial of an information after conviction, be the day on which the Court sentences or otherwise deals with the offender.

(4) On the making of an application under this section in respect of a decision any right of the applicant to appeal against the decision to the Crown Court shall cease.

(5) If the justices are of opinion that an application under this section is frivolous, they may refuse to state a case, and, if the application so requires, shall give him a certificate stating that the application has been refused; but the justices shall not refuse to state a case if the application is made by or under the direction of the Attorney General.

(6) Where justices refuse to state a case, the High Court may, on the application of the person who applied for the case to be stated, make an order of mandamus requiring the justices to state a case."

Power to state a case—In *Card v. Salmon* [1953] 1 Q.B. 392, it was held that magistrates sitting as examining justices had no power to state a case; and see also *Atkinson v. United States Government* [1971] A.C. 197. It is however for consideration whether this still applies in view of the terms of s.111 of the Magistrates' Courts Act 1980 and the definition of "magistrates' Court" in s.148 namely "... any justice or justices of the peace acting under any enactment or by virtue or under the Common Law". It is to be observed however, that licensing justices may state a case (see *R. v. East Riding Quarter Sessions, ex p. Newton* [1968] 1 Q.B. 32). When hearing an information under their summary jurisdiction, justices have no power to state a case until they have reached a final determination of the matter before them (*Streames v. Copping* [1985] Q.B. 920; see also *R. v. Greater Manchester Justices, ex p. Aldi GmbH & Co. KG* (1994) *The Times*, December 28 (Butler-Sloss L.J. and Latham J.) where judicial review was held to be the appropriate remedy). **R56.5.3**

In civil proceedings magistrates have a discretion to state a case before the final determination of those proceedings but it is to be exercised sparingly and only in exceptional circumstances (*R. v. Chesterfield Justices, ex p. Kovacs and Fawbert* [1990] C.O.D. 367 (Roch J.)). In *Wilkinson v. Crown Prosecution Service* [1998] C.O.D. 387 (Lord Bingham of Cornhill C.J. and Cresswell J.) the Divisional Court found it unnecessary to resolve the question whether case stated lies from a decision of examining justices but Cresswell J. observed "In the light of [*Atkinson v. Government of the United States of America* [1971] A.C. 197] it is doubtful whether the matters sought to be raised in this case were properly ventilated by way of case stated. The appropriate procedure was probably an application for judicial review". Moreover, the court noted that the latter procedure had been followed in *Williams v. Bedwellty Justices* [1996] 3 All E.R. 737, HL.

Time limits—There is no power either in the Magistrates' Court or in the High Court to extend the period of 21 days provided by s.111(2) (*R. v. Clerkenwell Metropolitan Stipendiary Magistrates, ex p. DPP* [1984] Q.B. 821 and *Bristol and West Building Society v. Hickmot* [1980] 144 J.P. 443). An application under section 111(2) of the Magistrates' Courts Act 1980 for a case to be stated is completed when the application is sent, if made in such circumstances as, in the normal course of events, will ensure that the application will arrive within the period of 21 days prescribed by that section (*P. & M. Supplies (Essex) Ltd v. Hackney Borough Council* (1990) 154 J.P. 814; [1990] C.O.D. 228 (Woolf L.J. and Pill J.)). **R56.5.4**

R56.5.5 **Choice of forum**—It is to be noted that s.111(4) applies even if the appeal by case stated is subsequently abandoned (see *R. v. Winchester Crown Court, ex p. Lewington* [1982] 1 W.L.R. 1277).

Where an appeal to the Crown Court has been lodged, but an appellant subsequently applies for a case to be stated, the effect of that application is that the right of appeal to the Crown Court is lost. There is, therefore, no requirement to abandon the appeal to the Crown Court before the Magistrates' Court can consider the application for a case stated (*R. v. Fyle & Wyre Justices, ex p. Gornall* [1996] C.O.D. 434).

R56.5.6 **Bail**—Where an application has been made to the Magistrates' Court to state a case, that Court may grant bail—see s.113 of the Magistrates' Courts Act 1980. If bail is not granted there is a right to apply to a High Court Judge, section 22 of the Criminal Justice Act 1967, section 5(6) of the Bail Act 1976 and O.79. In a civil case an application for bail cannot be made until the case has been stated and lodged in the Crown Office. Thus it will be necessary to apply also for judicial review so as to create an immediate substantive High Court procedure to which a bail application can attach (*Benham v. Poole Borough Council* (1991) 135 S.J. (L.B.) 173; [1992] C.O.D. 148. See also *R. v. Margate Justices, ex p. Haddow, The Times,* July 30, 1992 (Watkins L.J., Tucker and Buckley JJ.).

There is a power both in the Magistrates' Court and in the High Court to suspend a driving disqualification pending the hearing of the appeal by case stated (s.94 of the Road Traffic Act 1972 as amended.) In relation to the High Court, the application is made by a notice of motion on two days notice.

R56.5.7 **Recognisances**—Justices shall not be required to state a case until the applicant has entered into a recognisance with or without sureties, conditioned to prosecute the appeal, see s.114 of the Magistrates' Courts Act 1980. It is by no means clear that *R. v. Newcastle upon Tyne Justices, ex p. Skinner* [1987] 1 W.L.R. 312; [1987] 1 All E.R. 349, was authority for the proposition that justices could in some circumstances be required to state a case notwithstanding that no recognisance had been entered into (*R. v. Loughborough Justices, ex p. Smith (Steven)* [1992] C.O.D. 299 (Nolan L.J. and Jowitt J.)).

A clerk's refusal to provide a *draft* of a case stated until a recognisance has been entered into, conditioned to prosecute the appeal, does not constitute a refusal to state a case and conforms to the practice provided for by s.114 of the Magistrates' Courts Act 1980 and r.77 of the Magistrates' Court Rules 1981 (*R. v. Warrington Magistrates, ex p. Worsley, R. v. Cheshire Magistrates, ex p. Henshaw* [1996] C.O.D. 346).

Section 114 of the 1980 Act does not prevent justices from stating a case without obtaining a recognisance but relieves them of any requirement to do so. The applicant's means must be taken into account but the justices can only act on material which they have heard. It is to be noted that the entering into of a recognisance does not require the appellant to produce any money unless and until the recognisance is forfeit by reason of a failure to pursue the appeal with due diligence. Furthermore, s.120(3) of the 1980 Act then allows the justices to remit all or part of the sum (*R. v. Croydon Magistrates Court, ex p. Morgan* [1997] C.O.D. 176 Schiemann L.J. and Butterfield J.).

R56.5.8 **Enforcement**—A decision of a Magistrates' Court varied by the High Court on an appeal by case stated and any judgment or order of the High Court on such an appeal may be enforced as if it were a decision of the Magistrates' Court from which the appeal was brought, see s.112 of the Magistrates' Courts Act 1980.

R56.5.9 **Procedure for obtaining a case stated by Magistrates**—The provisions governing an application for a case stated by a Magistrates' Court are to be found in rr.76 to 81 of the Magistrates' Courts' Rules 1981 (S.I. 1981 No. 552). Rule 76(1) provides:

> "An application under section 111(1) of the Act of 1980 shall be made in writing and signed by or on behalf of the applicant and shall identify the question or questions of law or jurisdiction on which the opinion of the High Court is sought.
>
> (2) Where one of the questions on which the opinion of the High Court is sought is whether there was evidence on which the Magistrates' Court would come to its decision, the particular finding of fact made by the Magistrates' Court which it is claimed cannot be supported by the evidence before the Magistrates' Court shall be specified in such application.
>
> (3) Any such application shall be sent to the clerk of the Magistrates' Court whose decision is questioned."

The procedure then to be followed is set out in tabular form below; the Rules are mandatory and not directory (see *R. v. Croydon Justices, ex p. Lefore Holdings Ltd* [1980] 1 W.L.R. 1465; [1981] 1 All E.R. 520.

Rule		
77(1)	Within 21 days after receipt of the application.	The clerk of the magistrates' court sends a draft case to the applicant or his solicitor with a copy to the respondent or his solicitor.

Rule		
77(2)	Within 21 days after receipt.	Each party may make representations in writing, on the draft, to the clerk.
77(3)		Where the magistrates refuse to state a case under s.111(5) of the Magistrates' Courts Act 1980 and mandamus issues the period given above begins on the day the order of mandamus is made.
78(1)	Within 21 days of the expiry of the period above.	Justices make any adjustments to the draft in the light of any representations made and state and sign the case.
78(2)		Any two Justices may sign the case or, if magistrates so direct, it may be signed by their clerk.
78(3)	Forthwith after the case is stated and signed.	Clerk sends case stated to the appellant or his solicitor together with any statement required by r.79.
79(1)		If the clerk is unable to comply with the 21 day time provided by r.77(1) he shall do so as soon as practicable thereafter and shall attach to the draft, and to the final case, a statement of the delay and the reasons therefor.
79(2)		If the clerk receives representations in writing in support of an extension of time in which to make representations under r.77(2) he may extend the time by notice in writing but shall then attach to the final case a statement of the extension and the reasons therefor.
79(3)		If the Justices are unable to state a case within the time prescribed by r.78(1) they shall do so as soon as practicable, and the clerk shall attach a statement of the delay, and the reasons therefor, to the final case.
80		Documents required to be sent by these rules shall either be delivered or sent by registered post or recorded delivery to the last known or usual place of abode.

Where an application to state a case fails properly to identify the point of law on which the opinion of the High Court is sought, magistrates have a discretion to allow the initial application to be supplemented, within a reasonable time, by a notice identifying the questions of law in issue (*R. v. Bideford Justices, ex p. South West Water Authority* [1990] C.O.D. 369, L.A. (Mann L.J. and Brooke J.)).

Content of case—Rule 81 provides—"(1) A case stated by the Magistrates' Court shall state the facts found by the Court and the question or questions of law or jurisdiction on which the opinion of the High Court is sought. R56.5.10

(2) Where one of the questions on which the opinion of the High Court is sought is whether there was evidence on which the Magistrates' Court could come to its decision, the particular finding of fact which is claimed cannot be supported by the evidence before the Magistrates' Court shall be specified in the case.

(3) Unless one of the questions on which the opinion of the High Court is sought is whether there was evidence on which the Magistrates' Court could come to its decision, the case shall not contain a statement of evidence."

It is the duty of a lower court to prepare a case stated in the appropriate form having regard to the clear directions to be found in the Supreme Court Practice (*Cartwright v. DPP* [1995] C.O.D. 36 (Kennedy L.J. and Alliott J.)).

It is entirely inappropriate to seek to sustain an appeal by case stated by inviting the Court to consider a draft of the case stated so as to contrast a passage in the draft with an analogous passage in the case as finally signed. "It is fundamental, as we conceive the position, that the matter on which the decision of this Court is given is the case finally agreed and signed by the Justices. . . . The purpose of the procedure is that all those concerned, the Justices in particular and the parties through their power to make representations, should have an opportunity to contribute to what will ultimately be the document upon which the decision of this Court is to be obtained *per* Hutchison J. in *Tesco Stores Limited v. Seabridge, The Times*, April 29, 1988, DC.

A case stated should contain the facts found by the Justices and not a summary of the evidence. ". . . The case has been stated in a very unusual and wrong form. What the Justices have done is to set out the evidence or part of the evidence. What we need to be informed from a stated case are the facts which the Justices have found from the evidence which they have heard, and not a recital, albeit in summary form of the evidence which came before them. There is also attached to the stated case what appear to be notes taken by the Clerk to the Justices of the evidence. That too is an appendage to a stated case which ought not to be there." *per* Watkins L.J. in *Laird (Inspector of Factories) v. Simms (Gomersal) Ltd, The Times* and *The Independent*, March 7, 1988, CO 1378/87, March 1, 1988. It is essential that the Court state its findings of fact rather than the evidence it has heard (*DPP v. Kellet* [1995] C.O.D. 32 (McCowan L.J. and Buxton J.)).

In *Riley v. DPP* (1990) 91 Cr.App.R. 14 (Watkins L.J. and Garland J.), the Divisional Court gave further guidance as to the form in which a case should be stated. "Justices must endeavour to ensure in stating a case that (1) the whole of their findings of fact are contained in one and of course an early paragraph of the case; (2) their reasons for rejecting a submission of no case to answer are shortly and succinctly stated; and (3) they are not drawn . . . to amending a draft case so as to burden it with an over-elaborate discussion upon the law."

A case stated which fails to separate the justices' findings of fact from their opinions and from the question which it purported to pose for the opinion of the High Court is wholly unsatisfactory. The function of that Court is not to decide whether the justices were correct but only whether they were entitled to make the findings which they did (*Schulmans Incorporated Ltd v. National Rivers Authority, The Independent*, January 20, 1992 (Leggatt L.J. and Owen J.)).

The justices should set out the facts found by them in an as explicit a way as possible and the question asked of the court should directly relevant to those facts and to the conclusions they had reached (*DPP v. Price, The Independent*, June 15, 1992 (Watkins L.J., May J.)).

A case stated should indicate whether the magistrates received submissions based on any authority. It is important for the proper evaluation of appeals by case stated that the case, as drafted, should contain the argument which the magistrates had heard (*DPP v. Kirk* [1993] C.O.D. 99 (Watkins L.J. and Laws J.)).

Although the Divisional Court is loath to have original material or affidavits appended to a case stated, an affidavit exhibiting a computer disc could be appended in an appeal following proceedings before justices under the Video Recordings Act 1984 to ensure that the original material before the justices could be viewed by the Divisional Court (*Kent County Council v. Multi Media Marketing (Canterbury) Ltd, The Times*, December 7, 1994 (Rose L.J. and Potts J.)).

Where an appellant has put a properly framed question to the justices, but in response to representations by the prosecution the question is then fundamentally altered, the appellant must be given the opportunity of commenting on the altered question before the case is finally stated (*Waldie v. DPP, The Times*, April 18, 1995 (Pill L.J. and Keene J.)).

R56.5.11 **Amendment of the case**—Section 28A(2) of the Supreme Court Act 1981 (replacing s.7 of the Summary Jurisdiction Act 1857) confers on the Court a power to remit a case stated to the justices for amendment. This power may be exercised either at or before the hearing of the case. If an applicant or respondent is of the opinion that the case is deficient he should apply by notice of motion supported by affidavit, on two days notice, for the case to be sent back to the justices for restatement (*Practice Note (Case Stated)* [1953] 1 W.L.R. 334). Where all parties consent, the Court may itself direct the amendment of a case, without remitting it, where there is a mere slip corrected by a letter from the justice (*Rylands v. Marchant*, October 3, 1952 (unrep.)) or an ambiguity is resolved by an affidavit from their clerk (*Avon and Dorset River Board v. Bridport Rural District Council* (1953) 52 L.G.R. 19, DC), but usually the Court will not amend a case even with consent.

Where the justices' findings of fact do not coincide with the notes of evidence taken by the Crown Prosecutor who appeared at trial, the principle to be followed is as set out by Lord Goddard C.J. in *Spicer v. Warbey* [1953] 1 All E.R. 284. The court is not concerned with the evidence given in the case but with facts found by the justices and unless the justices found, or must have found, certain facts which they had not included in the case it will not be remitted for amendment. Only where relevant material findings of fact had been omitted can the case be remitted for amendment. The court is not concerned with whether the notes of either the justices, the clerk or the Crown Prosecutor are accurate but only with the findings upon which the justices have reached their decision (*DPP v. Clarke* (1991) 135 S.J. 135; *DPP v. Fidler and Moran* [1991] C.O.D. 235 (Taylor L.J. and Morland J.)).

It is important that where a draft case has been stated those involved should co-operate, if necessary by informal discussion, in an attempt to avoid the need for, and costs of, an application for amendment (*Ramage v. DPP* [1995] C.O.D. 315 (Pill L.J. and Keene J.)).

Once the final version of the case stated has been signed it must be lodged in the Crown Office within the 10 day period stipulated by r.6(1)(a). It is then too late to seek to persuade the justices to alter the case and the matter falls exclusively within the province of the High Court. If a party continues to seek modification of the case the appropriate procedure is to apply to the High

Court, on notice, to have the case remitted for amendment pursuant to s.28A(2) of the Supreme Court Act 1981 (*Basingstoke and Dean Borough Council v. Houlton and Webb* [1995] C.O.D. 96 (Dyson J.)).

Powers of Court—The findings of fact by the justices cannot be questioned except on the ground that there is no evidence to support them, or that they were findings to which no reasonable bench of justices could come (*Bracegirdle v. Oxley* [1947] K.B. 349). No agreement or other fact can be inferred unless it appears to have been found by the Justices (*Northern Theatres Co. v. Shillito* [1925] K.B. 100). **R56.5.12**

Decision of High Court on case stated to be final—Section 28A of the Supreme Court Act 1981, as introduced by para. 9 of Pt I of Sched. 2 to the Statute Law (Repeals) Act 1993, (replacing section 6 of the Summary Jurisdiction Act 1857) provides: **R56.5.13**

(1) The following provisions apply where a case is stated for the opinion of the High Court under section 111 of the Magistrates' Courts Act 1980 (case stated on question of law or jurisdiction).

(2) The High Court may, if it thinks fit, cause the case to be sent back for amendment, whereupon it shall be amended accordingly.

(3) The High Court shall hear and determine the question arising on the case (or the case as amended) and shall—

(a) reverse, affirm or amend the determination in respect of which the case has been stated, or

(b) remit the matter to the justice or justices with the opinion of the court, and may make such other order in relation to the matter (including as to costs) as it thinks fit.

(4) Except as provided by the Administration of Justice Act 1960 (right of appeal to House of Lords in criminal cases), a decision of the High Court under this section is final and conclusive on all parties.

In *Griffith v. Jenkins* [1992] A.C. 76, HL, the House of Lords considered s.6 of the 1857 Act. That section had conferred a power on the court hearing an appeal by case stated to order a rehearing before the same or a different bench when that appeared, in the Court's discretion, to be an appropriate course. Although a rehearing can only be ordered where a fair trial is still possible, when errors of law by justices have led to an acquittal, and matters can only be put right by a rehearing, a court should normally exercise its discretion in favour of that course. Different considerations might apply following a defendant's successful appeal against a conviction. In some such cases a rehearing might appear inappropriate or oppressive but all will depend on the circumstances of the case.

Section 6 did not require the Divisional Court, where it allowed a prosecutor's appeal by way of case stated, to remit the matter to the justices. Where there were a number of arguments as to the facts and the law which the justices had not yet considered, and there was a real possibility that if the case were remitted it would result in acquittal, no order remitting the case should be made (*Forestry Commission v. Frost* [1990] C.O.D. 1 (Glidewell L.J. and Rose J.)).

In a criminal case there is no power to vary a sentence. However, where the Court allows a prosecutor's appeal it may proceed to impose what it considers to be the only available penalty (see *Coote v. Winfield* [1980] R.T.R. 42, DC).

Case stated by Magistrates' Court: filing case, etc.

6.—(1) Where a case has been stated by a magistrates' court the appellant must— **R56.6**

(a) within 10 days after receiving the case, file it in the Crown Office or, if the appeal falls to be heard by a Divisional Court of the Family Division, the principal registry of the Family Division; and

(b) within 4 days after filing the case as aforesaid serve on the respondent a notice of the entry of appeal together with a copy of the case.

(2) Unless the court having jurisdiction to determine the appeal otherwise directs, the appeal shall not be heard sooner than 8 clear days after service of notice of the entry of the appeal.

Practice—Three copies of all the documents specified in O.56, r.6(1) must be lodged in the Crown Office, Royal Courts of Justice, London WC2A 2LL, together with a fee of £20. Cheques must be made payable to H.M. Paymaster General. **R56.6.1**

Delay—The short period of time, 10 days, for lodging the relevant documents, subsequent period of four days for service, should be noted. An application for an extension of time in which to lodge the case stated, or serve a notice of entry and copy of the case, under CPR, r.3.1(2)(a) **R56.6.2**

should be made by summons, on at least two days notice to the respondent, to the Master of the Crown Office—see O.56, r.13. On such a summons a fee or £20 is payable.

R56.6.3 **Costs**—The award of costs is governed by section 28A of the Supreme Court Act 1981, see para. R56.5.13 and CPR, r.44.3. Where both parties appear, costs usually follow the event but they will not generally be awarded against a party who is not represented unless some conduct of the respondent has contributed to the necessity for the appeal, see, *e.g. Robinson v. Gregory* [1905] 1 K.B. 534. Where costs are awarded against a respondent, they may include if the Court so orders, the cost of the hearing before the justices (*Mills and Rockley Ltd v. Leicester City Council* [1946] K.B. 315; *Turner & Sons Ltd v. Owen* [1956] 1 Q.B. 48).

Where justices act unreasonably in refusing to agree to a consent order, in accordance with *Queen's Bench Practice Direction No. 27* (SCP 1999, Vol. 2, Section 2C, paras 2C–176 to 2C–179), and an otherwise unnecessary hearing takes place before the Divisional Court only for the purpose of allowing the appeal, the court may in its discretion make an order against the justices for the costs of that hearing pursuant to s.28A of the Supreme Court Act 1981 (*R. v. Newcastle under Lyme Magistrates Court, ex p. Massey* [1994] 1 W.L.R. 1684 (Rose L.J. & Smith J.)).

R56.6.4 **Appeal**—The same provisions apply as in a case stated by the Crown Court, see note at para. R56.1.12.

R56.6.5 **Withdrawal**—An appeal by way of case stated may be withdrawn without the necessity of obtaining the leave of the High Court. Thus the appellant was at liberty to withdraw his appeal, with a view to seeking to reopen his case before the magistrates under s.142 of the Magistrates' Courts Act 1980 (*Collet v. Bromsgrove District Council, The Times*, July 15, 1996).

Case stated by Ministers, tribunal, etc.

R56.7 **7.**—(1) The jurisdiction of the High Court under any enactment to hear and determine a case stated by a Minister of the Crown, government department, tribunal or other person, or a question of law referred to that court by such a Minister or department or a tribunal or other person by way of case stated, shall be exercised by a single judge of the Queen's Bench Division, except where it is otherwise provided by these rules or by or under any enactment.

(2) The jurisdiction of the High Court under any enactment to hear and determine an application for an order directing such a Minister or department or a tribunal or other person to state a case for determination by the High Court, or to refer a question of law to that court by way of case stated, shall be exercised by the court or judge having jurisdiction to hear and determine that case or question except where by some other provision of these rules or by or under any enactment it is otherwise provided.

(3) this rule and rules 8 to 12 of this order shall apply to proceedings for the determination of such a case, question or application and, in relation to any such proceedings, shall have effect subject to any provision made in relation to those proceedings by any other provision of these rules or by or under any enactment.

(4) In this order references to a tribunal shall be construed as references to any tribunal constituted by or under any enactment other than any of the ordinary courts of law.

(5) In the following rules references to a Minister shall be construed as including references to a government department, and in those rules and this rule "case" includes a special case.

R56.7.1 **History of Rule**—Amended by S.I. 1987 No. 1423.

R56.7.2 **Effect of rule**—Rules 7–12 of this Order set out a general code of procedure for applications under enactments for orders requiring Ministers, Government Departments, tribunals or other persons to state a case or refer a question of law for the opinion of the Court. These enactments include the Tribunals and Inquiries Act 1992, s.11; Caravan Sites and Control of Development Act 1960, s.34 and Sched. 3, para. 4; Control of Pollution Act 1974; Public Health Act 1961, s.66; Agriculture (Miscellaneous Provisions) Act 1954, s.6(1) and (2); Mental Health Act 1983, s.78; Copyright Act 1956, s.30; they were amended by RSC (Amendment No. 3) 1977 (S.I. 1977 No. 1955) to provide for hearings by a single Judge instead of by the Divisional Court, except in special cases.

The Lands Tribunal cannot be required to state a case on an interlocutory point, such as discovery, but only on a final award or decision (*Watneys of London v. City of London Corp.* (1982) 126 S.J. 626; (1982) 261 E.G. 1089, CA).

In respect of case stated by certain tribunals further provisions are to be found elsewhere and in particular, but not exclusively, in O.94, *e.g.*

(i) The Agricultural Land Tribunal—O.94, r.7;
(ii) Tribunals mentioned in s.11(1) of the Tribunals and Enquiries Act 1992—O.94, r.9.
(iii) Mental Health Review Tribunal—O.94, r.11.
(iv) The Social Securities Act 1975 to 1986—O.111.

Application for order to state a case

8.—(1) An application to the court for an order directing a Minister, tribunal or other person to state a case for determination by the court or to refer a question of law to the court by way of case stated must be made by claim form; and the persons to be served with the claim form are the Minister, secretary of the tribunal or other person, as the case may be, and every party (other than the applicant) to the proceedings to which the application relates. **R56.8**

(2) The claim form must state the grounds of the application, the question of law on which it is sought to have the case stated and any reasons given by the Minister, tribunal or other person for his or its refusal to state a case.

(3) The claim must be entered for hearing, and the claim form served, within 14 days after receipt by the applicant of notice of the refusal of his request to state a case.

Signing and service of case

9.—(1) A case stated by a tribunal must be signed by the chairman or president of the tribunal, and a case stated by any other person must be signed by him or by a person authorised in that behalf to do so. **R56.9**

(2) The case must be served on the party at whose request, or as a result of whose application to the court, the case was stated; and if a Minister, tribunal, arbitrator or other person is entitled by virtue of any enactment to state a case, or to refer a question of law by way of case stated, for determination by the High Court without request being made by any party to the proceedings before that person, the case must be served on such party to those proceedings as the Minister, tribunal, arbitrator or other person, as the case may be, thinks appropriate.

(3) When a case is served on any party under paragraph (2) notice must be given to every other party to the proceedings in question that the case has been served on the party named, and on the date specified, in the notice.

Proceedings for determination of case

10.—(1) Proceedings for the determination by the High Court of a case stated, or a question of law referred by way of case stated, by a Minister, tribunal, arbitrator or other person must be begun by claim form by the person on whom the case was served in accordance with rule 9(2) or, where the case is stated without a request being made, by the Minister, secretary of the tribunal, arbitrator or other person by whom the case is stated. **R56.10**

(2) The applicant shall serve the claim form under paragraph (1), together with a copy of the case, on—

(a) the Minister, secretary of the tribunal, arbitrator or other person by whom the case was stated, unless that Minister, tribunal, arbitrator or other person is the applicant;
(b) every party (other than the applicant) to the proceedings in which the question of law to which the case relates arose; and
(c) any other person (other than the applicant) served with the case under rule 9(2).

(3) The claim form must set out the applicant's contentions on the question of law to which the case stated relates.

(4) The claim must be entered for hearing, and the claim form served, within 14 days after the case stated was served on the applicant.

(5) If the applicant fails to enter the claim within the period specified in paragraph (4) then, after obtaining a copy of the case from the Minister, tribunal, arbitrator or other person by whom the case was stated, any other party to the proceedings in which the question of law to which the case relates arose may, within 14 days after the expiration of the period so specified, begin proceedings for the determination of the case, and paragraphs (1) to (4) shall have effect accordingly with the necessary modifications.

The references in this paragraph to the period specified in paragraph (4) shall be construed as including references to that period as extended by any order of the court.

(6) The documents required to be filed in accordance with Order 57, rule 2, before entry of the claim include a copy of the case stated.

(7) Unless the court having jurisdiction to determine the case otherwise directs, the claim form shall not be heard sooner than 7 days after service of notice of the claim form.

R56.10.1 **History of Rule**—Amended by S.I. 1990 No. 2599.

R56.10.2 **Proceedings for determination of a case**—Under some enactments a Minister, tribunal, arbitrator or other person may be entitled to state a case, or to refer a question of law by way of case stated for determination by the High Court, without a request being made by any party to the proceedings. The purpose of the amendments effected by RSC (Amendment No. 3) 1990 (S.I. 1990 No. 2599) is to provide also for this situation where the case is stated for the Minister's tribunal's, etc., own motion. Thus the persons who stated the case may now issue the originating claim.

Amendment of case

R56.11 **11.** The court hearing a case stated by a Minister, tribunal, arbitrator or other person may amend the case or order it to be returned to that person for amendment, and may draw inferences of fact from the facts stated in the case.

Right of Minister to appear and be heard

R56.12 **12.** In proceedings for the determination of a case stated, or of a question of law referred by way of case stated, the Minister, chairman or president of the tribunal, arbitrator or other person by whom the case was stated shall be entitled to appear and be heard.

R56.12.1 **History of Rule**—Amended by S.I. 1990 No. 2599.

R56.12.2 **Effect of rule**—The amendment effected by RSC (Amendment No. 3) 1990 (S.I. 1990 No. 2599) extends the pre-existing provision, which permitted a Minister to appear and be heard in the proceedings for the determination of the case, to encompass also any person who stated a case, including the chairman or president of a tribunal.

Extradition

R56.12A **12A.**—(1) Rules 5 and 6 of this order shall apply to appeals by case stated under—

(a) section 7 of the Criminal Justice Act 1988; and

(b) section 7A of the Fugitive Offenders Act 1967,

as they apply to appeals by case stated from a Magistrates' Court and references in those rules to appellant and respondent shall be construed as references to the requesting state and the person whose surrender is sought respectively.

(2) An application for an order under either of the sections mentioned in paragraph (1) or under section 2A of the Backing of Warrants (Republic of Ireland) Act 1965 requiring a court to state a case shall be made in accordance with rule 8 of this order the references in that rule to a tribunal and the

secretary of a tribunal being construed for this purpose as references to the court and the clerk of the court respectively.

History of Rule—Added by S.I. 1989 No. 1307. R56.12A.1

Effect of rule—Criminal Justice Act 1988, s.7, provides that, in extradition proceedings, where a court of committal refuses to make an order of committal in respect of an offence to which an authority to proceed relates, the state seeking the surrender may question the proceeding, on the ground that it is wrong in law, by applying to the Court to state a case for the opinion of the High Court. Backing of Warrants (Republic of Ireland) Act 1965, s.2A, as amended by Pt 2 of Sched. 1 of the Criminal Justice Act 1988, makes similar provisions. Rule 12A seeks to adapt rr.5, 6 and 8 of this Order for the purpose of appeals under these provisions. As to bail, see O.79, r.9(14). R56.12A.2

Interlocutory applications

13.—(1) Unless the court otherwise directs, any interlocutory application in proceedings to which this order applies may be made to any judge or a Master of the Queen's Bench Division or, as the case may be, any judge or a district judge of the Family Division, notwithstanding that the appeal has been brought by case stated and is to be heard by a Divisional Court. R56.13

In this paragraph "interlocutory application" includes an application for an order extending the time for entry of the appeal or for service of notice of entry of the appeal.

(2) In relation to an order made by a Master or district judge pursuant to paragraph (1), Order 58, rule 1 shall, where the application is to be heard by a Divisional Court, have effect as if a reference to that court were substituted for the reference to a judge.

(3) this rule is without prejudice to any statutory provision or rule of law restricting the making of an order against the Crown.

History of Rule—Added by S.I. 1987 No. 1423. The office of registrar is now the office of district judge further to Courts and Legal Services Act 1990, s.74. R56.13.1

The Crown Office List—The provisions of *Queen's Bench Practice Directions Nos 24 & 25* (SCP 1999, Vol. 2, Section 2C, paras 2C–168 and 2C–169 to 2C–172), which govern, among other things, applications for expedited hearings, apply in relation to all cases stated which are required by this order to be entered in the Crown Office List, as they apply to other proceedings in that list. R56.13.2

RSC ORDER 57

DIVISIONAL COURT PROCEEDINGS, ETC.: SUPPLEMENTARY PROVISIONS

Contents R57.0.1

Editorial Introduction

The provisions of this Order apply to proceedings before a Divisional Court and certain proceedings before a single judge. The rules are concerned with process in such proceedings (issuing of writs and originating summonses and entry of motions) and the filing of affidavits and the drawing up of orders. R57.0.2

Related sources

- RSC, O.56 (Appeals, etc., to High Court by case stated: general) R57.0.3
- RSC, O.64, r.4 (Divisional Court business during vacation)

The following *Queen's Bench Practice Directions* are relevant to this Order. These Directions continue to apply for the time being (see Practice Direction (Civil: Litigation: Procedure) [1999] 1 W.L.R. 1124).

- *Practice Direction (Crown Office List: Uncontested Proceedings)* [1982] 1 W.L.R. 979 (replaced by [1997] 1 W.L.R. 825, see below)
- *Practice Direction (Crown Office List: Criminal Proceedings)* [1983] 1 W.L.R. 925 (replaced in part by [1997] 1 W.L.R. 825, see below) (see *Queen's Bench Practice Direction Nos 23 & 27*, SCP 1999, Vol. 2, Section 2C, paras 2C–163 and 2C–176 to 2C–179)
- *Practice Direction (Crown Office List)* [1987] 1 W.L.R. 232 (extended by [1991] 1 W.L.R. 280, see below) (see *Queen's Bench Practice Direction No. 24*, SCP 1999, Vol. 2, Section 2C, para. 2C–168)
- *Practice Direction (Crown Office List: Estimated Length of Hearing)* [1987] 1 All E.R. 1184
- *Practice Direction (Crown Office List) (No. 2)* [1991] 1 W.L.R. 280 (see *Queen's Bench Practice Direction No. 25*, SCP 1999, Vol. 2, Section 2C, paras 2C–169 to 2C–172)
- *Practice Direction (Crown Office List: Preparation for Hearings)* [1994] 1 W.L.R. 1551 (see *Queen's Bench Practice Direction No. 26*, SCP 1999, Vol. 2, Section 2C, paras 2C–173 to 2C–175)
- *Practice Direction (Crown Office List: Legislation Bundle)* [1997] 1 W.L.R. 52 (see *Queen's Bench Practice Direction No. 27*, SCP 1999, Vol. 2, Section 2C, paras 2C–176 to 2C–179)
- *Practice Direction (Crown Office List: Consent Proceedings)* [1997] 1 W.L.R. 825 (see *Queen's Bench Practice Direction No. 27*, SCP 1999, Vol. 2, Section 2C, paras 2C–176 to 2C–179).

Application

R57.1 **1.**—(1) Subject to paragraph (2) this order shall apply to—

(a) any proceedings before a Divisional Court;

(b) any proceedings before a single judge under Order 52, rule 2, Order 53, Order 54, or Order 79;

(c) any proceedings before a single judge, being proceedings which consist of or relate to an appeal to the High Court from any court, tribunal or person including an appeal by case stated and the reference of a question of law by way of case stated.

(2) The following rules of this order shall not apply to an appeal from a county court to a single judge under section 375 of the Insolvency Act 1986.

R57.1.1 **History of Rule**—Amended by S.I. 1986 No. 2001 and S.I. 1991 No. 1329.

R57.1.2 **Divisional Courts, generally**—As to the constitution of Divisional Courts see S.C.A. 1981, s.66. For the Divisional Courts of the Chancery Division, their constitution and functions, see also O.93, r.10(1). For the Divisional Courts of the Family Division, see O.56, r.5.

Whether the Divisional Court is to be regarded as a court of first instance may depend on the nature of the proceedings in question and the status of the decision under review. Where the decision is that of an individual or a body other than a court or tribunal, the court of first instance is the single Judge or Divisional Court charged with the judicial review. Thus, where the decision impugned was that of a local authority and the issue was the limitation under s.18 of the Legal Aid Act 1988 on the power of a court of first instance to make an order for the payment of costs by the Legal Aid Board, that limitation applied to the Divisional Court. The Divisional Court which had reached a contrary conclusion in *R. v. Leeds County Court, ex p. Morris* [1990] 1 Q.B. 523, had not been referred to *R. v. Greater Manchester Coroner, ex p. Tal* [1985] Q.B. 67, see on this point *R. v. London Borough of Greenwich, ex p. Lovelace* [1992] C.O.D. 18; [1992] 1 All E.R. 679 (Neill, Staughton and Stocker L.JJ.).

R57.1.3 **Constitution and powers of Divisional Courts of QBD**—In the QBD all cases for hearing before a Divisional Court are entered in the Crown Office List. The Court is usually constituted of two Judges but exceptionally three Judges will sit in cases of unusual difficulty and where the Court so directs. For appeals under the Solicitors Act 1974, s.49, not less than three Judges are necessary unless the L.C.J. otherwise directs (O.106, r.11) and usually the L.C.J. himself presides.

The extent to which the Divisional Court is bound by its own previous decisions was considered by the Divisional Court in *R. v. Greater Manchester Coroner, ex p. Tal* [1985] 1 Q.B. 67. With regard to applications for Judicial Review the Court observed "Having regard to the nature of this jurisdiction, we do not consider that there is any authority which decides that a Divisional Court in such a case is not free to depart from a previous decision of another Divisional Court. The only case which might be thought so to decide is *Huddersfield Police Authority v. Watson* [1947] K.B. 842. The foundation of the decision in that case was, however, that the Divisional Court in question was there sitting as a final Court of Appeal. There must be some doubt whether, in the light of the change of policy in the House of Lords, evinced in the *Practice Statement (Judicial Precedent)* [1966] 1 W.L.R. 1234, the basis of the opinion expressed by Lord Goddard C.J. in the *Watson* case can still be regarded as valid. But, even if it were, it can in our judgment have no application with regard to applications for judicial review.

... We have no doubt that it will be only in rare cases that a Divisional Court will think it fit to depart from a decision of another Divisional Court exercising this jurisdiction. Furthermore, we find it difficult to imagine that a single Judge exercising this jurisdiction would ever depart from a decision of a Divisional Court. If any question of such a departure should arise before a single Judge, a direction can be made under RSC, O.53, r.5(2), that the relevant application should be made before a Divisional Court."

As to the Divisional Court's power to depart from its own earlier decisions, when determining an appeal by case stated, see *C (A Minor) v. D.P.P.* [1995] 2 W.L.R. 383, HL.

The jurisdictions of the Divisional Court and the Visitors to the Inns of Court are in the alternative and the judges of the Divisional Court are unable to sit simultaneously as Visitors. One reason to sit as a Divisional Court is the availability of legal aid and another the more extensive powers of appeal from its decisions (*R. v. Council of Legal Education, ex p. Halstead* (1994) *The Times*, August 11 (Henry L.J., Popplewell and Rougier JJ.)).

The Divisional Court has no jurisdiction to judicially review the issue or execution of a warrant issued in Scotland because article XIX of the Union with Scotland Act 1706 does not permit it (*R. v. Metropolitan Police Commissioner and Chief Constable of Grampian Police, ex p. Bennett* [1995] 2 W.L.R. 598).

As to the powers of the Court of Appeal on an application for judicial review see *R. v. Parole Board, ex p. Wilson* [1992] 1 Q.B. 740 (Nourse, Taylor and Scott L.JJ.), following *R. v. Spencer* [1985] 1 Q.B. 771. In a case involving the liberty of the subject the court is not bound by an earlier decision if injustice might thereby result.

Court divided in opinion—Where there is a difference of opinion between two Judges on an appeal from an inferior Court, the view of the Judge who agrees with the Judge below will prevail and the appeal will be dismissed with costs (*Poulton v. Morris* [1913] W.N. 360; *Johnson v. Rees* (1915) 84 L.J.K.B. 1276; *Cheater v. Cater* (1918) 61 S.J. 547; *Derry v. Sanders* (1918) 62 S.J. 549; *Flannagan v. Shaw* [1920] 2 K.B. 107, 108; and see *Ellis v. Banyard* (1911) 104 L.T. 460). The former practice was otherwise, the junior Judge withdrawing his judgment, see *Poulton v. Moore* [1915] 1 K.B. 400, 405; and see comments of Phillimore L.J. at p. 415. *Semble*, a decision of an equally divided Divisional Court or CA, given on the hearing of an appeal (with the result that the decision of the Court below stands) does not bind the Divisional Court or CA (the *Vera Cruz* (1884) 9 P.D. 96, CA but see, *per* Scrutton L.J. to the contrary effect in *Hart v. Riversdale Mill Co.* [1928] 1 K.B. 176, 188–189). The position is otherwise with the HL, see the *Vera Cruz*, at 98; *Usher's Wiltshire Brewery Ltd v. Bruce* [1915] A.C. 433; *Hart v. Riversdale Mill Co.*, above. R57.1.4

Power of a single Judge—See SCA 1981, s.67. Certain applications normally required to be made to a Divisional Court may, in vacation, be made to a single Judge by virtue of RSC, O.64, r.4, as added by RSC (Amendment No. 2) 1991 (S.I. 1991 No. 1329), with effect from July 1, 1991 as follows: R57.1.5

(a) O.52, rr.1(2) and 3(1)—committal for contempt.
(b) O.53, rr.3(4)(a) and 5(1)—judicial review, renewal of an application for leave in a criminal cause or matter and the hearing of the substantive application itself.
(c) O.55, r.2(a)—appeal to High Court where the decision of the court is final.
(d) O.56, r.1(1)(a)—appeals from the Crown Court by case stated in a criminal cause or matter.

Costs—The Divisional Court of the Queen's Bench Division may make a defendant's costs order on determining proceedings in a criminal cause or matter (*Practice Direction (Crime: Costs in Criminal Proceedings)* [1991] 1 W.L.R. 498; [1991] 2 All E.R. 924). R57.1.6

Appeal from a Divisional Court to the Court of Appeal—Leave must be obtained from the Divisional Court or the Court of Appeal to appeal from the determination by the Divisional Court of any *appeal* to the High Court (SCA 1981, s.18(1)(e)). See more generally, as to leave to appeal, paras R59.1.92 *et seq.* R57.1.7

Where leave to move for judicial review has been refused, that application may be renewed to the Court of Appeal within seven days (see O.59, r.14(3)). As to a criminal cause or matter, SCA 1981, s.18, provides:

"(1) no appeal shall lie to the Court of Appeal—
(a) except as provided by the Administration of Justice Act 1960, from any judgment of the High Court in any criminal cause or matter."

As to the meaning of "criminal cause or matter" see *Carr v. Atkins* [1987] Q.B. 963, which was in turn considered and approved in *Re O. (Disclosure Order)* [1991] 2 W.L.R. 475; [1991] 1 All E.R. 330 (Lord Donaldson of Lymington M.R., Glidewell and Ralph Gibson L.JJ.) where the authorities are further considered. Essentially the issue in each case is whether the order sought to be appealed is a judgment in a criminal cause or matter or merely a judgment collateral to a criminal cause or matter. See also *R. v. Blandford Justices, ex p. Pamment* [1990] 1 W.L.R. 1490 (Lord Donaldson of Lymington M.R., Balcombe and Taylor L.JJ.).

Appeal from a Divisional Court to the House of Lords—Lies in certain cases under the A.J.A. 1960. R57.1.8

By section 1 of the Act an appeal lies to the House of Lords, at the instance of the defendant or prosecutor, from any decision of a Divisional Court of the QBD in a criminal cause or matter. No such appeal lies without the leave of the Divisional Court or House of Lords, and (except in proceedings for habeas corpus or contempt) leave cannot be granted unless the Divisional Court certifies that a point of law of general public importance is involved in the decision (see *Gelberg v. Miller* [1961] 1 W.L.R. 459; [1961] 1 All E.R. 291, HL) and it appears to the Divisional Court or House of Lords that the point is one which ought to be considered by that House (*Att.-Gen. for Northern Ireland v. Gallagher* [1963] A.C. 349; [1961] 3 All E.R. 299). See O.109, rr.1 and 3.

By s.13 of the Act an appeal lies to the House of Lords from an order or decision of a Divisional Court in the exercise of jurisdiction to punish for contempt of Court (including criminal contempt). The appeal lies in any case at the instance of the defendant, and, in the case of an application for committal at the instance of the applicant. By s.15 appeal lies from a decision of a Divisional Court on a criminal application for habeas corpus. Leave of the Divisional Court or of the House of Lords is required under either section. See those sections for the conditions of grant of leave, and also O.109, r.3.

The respondent to an application to the House of Lords for leave to appeal under s.1 or s.15 must be served with a copy of the petition, and he may appear by counsel before the Appeal Committee.

On an application under s.15 for leave to appeal against the refusal by a Divisional Court of a writ of habeas corpus in the criminal cause or matter the applicant will not be heard in person unless some exceptional ground is shown for doing so. The application must be made by counsel or solicitor or the applicants' wife or other relative, or some other person who is prepared to apply on his behalf. If the applicant has no means to instruct counsel or solicitor, and no other person is able or willing to apply on his behalf, the Committee will consider a letter from the applicant to see if it discloses an arguable point. If it does, the Committee will arrange for the Official Solicitor to represent him (*Practice Direction of the Committee,* February 13, 1962). See also "House of Lords Appeals" (SCP 1999, Vol. 2, Section 19).

Entry of claims

R57.2 **2.**—(1) Every claim in proceedings to which this order applies must be entered for hearing in the appropriate office; and entry shall be made when a copy of the claim form, and any other documents required to be lodged before entry, have been filed in that office.

(2) The party entering the claim for hearing must file in the appropriate office copies of the proceedings for the use of the judges.

(3) Except where it relates to proceedings in the Admiralty Court every claim entered for hearing by a Divisional Court of the Queen's Bench Division shall be entered in the Divisional Court list.

(4) In this rule "the appropriate office" means—

(a) in relation to proceedings in the Queen's Bench Division (including the Admiralty Court) the Crown Office or the Admiralty and Commercial Registry, as the circumstances of the case require;

(b) in relation to proceedings in the Chancery Division, Chancery Chambers;

(c) in relation to proceedings in the Family Division, the principal registry of the Family Division.

R57.2.1 **History of Rule**—Amended by S.I. 1971 No. 1269; S.I. 1982 No. 1111 and S.I. 1987 No. 1423.

R57.2.2 **The Crown Office List**—The majority of claims in Divisional Court proceedings are entered in the Crown Office for hearing in the Crown Office List. The constituent parts of that list are set out in the *Practice Direction (Trials in London)* [1981] 1 W.L.R. 1296. New arrangements for the listing of cases in the Crown Office List, whether to be heard by a single Judge nominated by the Lord Chief Justice to try cases in that list or by a Divisional Court, were made in a Practice Direction given by the Lord Chief Justice on February 3, 1987, *Practice Direction (Crown Office List)* [1987] 1 W.L.R. 232, as follows:

1. As from March 2, 1987 the following arrangements will apply to the listing of cases included in the Crown Office list.
2. The head clerk, under the direction of the Master of the Crown Office, will arrange the Crown Office list into the following parts.
3. *Part A: cases not ready to be heard*

   Cases where leave has yet to be obtained, or the time limits for the filing or lodging of notices, affidavits or other documents have not expired and where, in consequence, a case is not yet ready to be heard.
4. *Part B: cases ready to be heard*

   In cases where the time limits mentioned in Part A have expired it will be assumed that all parties are ready to be heard. When a case enters Part B the applicant or his solicitors will be informed by letter. It will be the responsibility of the applicant or his solicitors to forward a copy of that letter to (i) the clerk to counsel instructed by the applicant and (ii) any respondent to the case or his solicitor who should inform the clerk to counsel instructed by him. It will be the responsibility of counsel's clerks to inform the head clerk, *in writing*, of counsel's time estimate for the case and of any alteration thereto.

5. The head clerk will make arrangements for hearing dates to be fixed, drawing cases from Part B in order of entry so far as is practicable. While the head clerk will give as much notice as possible of the date fixed for hearing he cannot undertake to accommodate the wishes of applicants, respondents, their solicitors or counsel. The occasional need to list cases at short notice may mean that parties are unable to be represented by the counsel of their first choice. In particular it should be remembered that the cases listed in the Crown Office list take precedence, so far as the attendance of counsel is concerned, over cases listed for hearing in the Crown Court unless a Divisional Court or a Judge otherwise directs.

6. *Part C: cases stood out*

Where a case appears in Part B, or Part E, and any party to the case is of the opinion that he is not ready to be heard he may apply to the Master of the Crown Office to have the matter stood out into Part C. Where the Master of the Crown Office accedes to such an application he may do so on such terms as he thinks fit. Where he declines to direct that the matter be stood out into Part C application may be made to a Divisional Court or a Judge, as the case may be, by way of notice of motion.

7. *Part D: the expedited list*

Cases entered in this list will be listed for hearing as soon as practicable. In cases other than those where a Divisional Court or a Judge has directed that a case be considered for expedition, application for inclusion in Part D should be made in the first instance to the Master of the Crown Office but where he declines to direct its inclusion in Part D, application may be made to a Divisional Court or a Judge, as the case may be, by way of notice of motion.

8. *Part E: cases listed for hearing*

This part of the list will contain those cases where a date for hearing has been fixed.

9. As from March 2, 1987 the Daily Cause List will, in relation to the Crown Office list, contain only such cases as are to be heard on the next sitting day.

10. A copy of Parts B, C, D and E of the Crown Office List may be inspected in the Crown Office.

11. In this practice direction the expression "applicant" includes "appellant" where the context so requires and the expression "Judge" means a Judge hearing cases in the Crown Office list.

These provisions have now been supplemented by *Practice Direction (Crown Office List) (No. 2)* [1991] 1 W.L.R. 280; [1991] 1 All E.R. 1055 issued by Watkins L.J., Alliott and Cresswell JJ. on March 18, 1991, as follows:

Striking out for want of prosecution—1. Further to the *Practice Direction (Crown Office List)* [1987] 1 W.L.R. 232 cases which are approaching the top of Part B of the Crown Office List must be confirmed as active by the applicant, or the appellant, as the case may be. The Crown Office will seek written confirmation that the case is active and if such confirmation is not received within two weeks of the request from the Crown Office the matter will be listed before the court to show cause as to why it should not be struck out for want of prosecution. **R57.2.3**

Withdrawal of solicitors—2. Where a solicitor ceases to act for a party and the party has not given notice of change of solicitors in accordance with RSC, O.67, r.1 the solicitor may apply to the court, by way of summons to the Master of the Crown Office, for an order declaring that the solicitor has ceased to act for the party: RSC, O.67, r.6. **R57.2.4**

3. If no such order is obtained, the solicitor must be regarded as continuing to act and notice of listing dates, etc. will be given to the solicitor, whose responsibility it will be to brief counsel to appear before the court.

Ex parte applications for leave to apply for judicial review—4. With effect from April 9, 1991 applications for leave to apply for judicial review will be listed on the footing that the application will take no more than 20 minutes, and any reply by a respondent who attends such an application will take no more than 10 minutes. Where counsel considers that the hearing of the application will require more than the time allowed he should provide a written estimate and a special fixture must be arranged. **R57.2.4A**

On October 25, 1994 a further practice direction, dealing with preparation for hearings in the Crown Office List, was issued by Lord Taylor of Gosforth C.J. as follows:

Practice Direction (Crown Office List: Preparation for hearings) [1994] 1 W.L.R. 1551; [1994] 4 All E.R. 671. The following arrangements will take effect immediately.

Applications for leave to apply for judicial review and for leave to appeal under section 289 of the Town and Country Planning Act 1990—Where the documents in support of an application for leave exceed 10 pages, they must be paginated and indexed in a convenient bundle. In addition, a list must be provided of the pages essential for reading by the court. Where only part of **R57.2.5** a page needs to be read, that part should be indicated, by side lining or in some other way, but not by highlighting.

R57.2.6 *Substantive hearings*—As a case reaches the top of Part B of the Crown office List the applicant/appellant's solicitors will be informed by letter that the case is likely to be listed, at short notice, with effect from a date specified in the letter (the "warned date"). It is the responsibility of the applicant/appellant's solicitors to inform the respondent and all interested parties of the likelihood of the case being listed at short notice.

In cases where a fixed date is given, it is the responsibility of the applicant/appellant's solicitors to inform the resondent and all interested parties of the fixed date.

The applicant/appellant's solicitors are also responsible for providing a paginated, indexed, bundle for the use of the court. The bundle must be lodged with the Crown Office at least *five* clear working dates before the warned date or, where a fixed date has been given, at least *five* clear working days before the fixed date.

Advocates are required to lodge skeleton arguments in the Crown Office. Advocates for the applicant must lodge, and serve, their skeleton arguments at least *five* clear working days before the warned date or the fixed date, as appropriate. Advocates for the respondent or other party wishing to be heard must lodge, and serve, their skeleton arguments at least *three* clear working days before the warned date or the fixed date, as appropriate. The skeleton argument must quote the Crown Office reference number and the warned date or the fixed date, as appropriate and contain (a) the time estimate for the complete hearing, including delivery of judgment (whether or not an estimate has been given earlier); (b) a list of issues; (c) a list of propositions of law to be advanced (together with the authorities relied upon in support, with page references to passages relied upon); (d) a chronology of events (with reference to the paginated bundle prepared for the court); (e) a list of the essential documents for advance reading by the court, with page references to passages relied upon; (f) a list of dramatis personae where the number of people who feature in the documents warrants it.

The above time limits must be strictly observed. Failure to do so may result in adjournment and may be penalised in costs. Advocates may however supplement their skeleton arguments up to one working day before the hearing.

Where a case is due to be listed for hearing before a Divisional Court two copies of the skeleton argument and paginated bundle are required. Where the case is due to be listed for hearing before a single judge only one copy of each is required.

R57.2.7 *Amendment of grounds and further written statements or affidavits*—Any notice of intention to seek leave to amend the grounds or relief or to rely upon further written statements or affidavits must be given to the other party or parties and the Crown Office, together with the proposed amendments or affidavits, no later than *five* clear working days before the warned date or the fixed date, as appropriate. If notice is not given at that time, the court will be reluctant to exercise its powers to allow amendment or the use of further affidavits, save in exceptional circumstances.

On December 6, 1996, *Practice Direction (Crown Office List: Legislation Bundle)* [1997] 1 W.L.R. 52; [1997] 1 All E.R. 128, dealing with the provision of copies of relevant legislative material, was issued by the Lord Chief Justice as follows:

On lodging an application for leave to apply for judicial review the applicant's solicitor must lodge, in addition to the material required to be lodged by *Practice Direction (Crown Office List: Preparation for Hearings)* [1994] 1 W.L.R. 1551; a paginated, indexed bundle of the *relevant* legislative provisions and statutory instruments required for the proper consideration of the application.

An applicant who acts in person should comply with the present direction so far as he or she is able. In any event, an applicant acting in person should list the legislative provisions and statutory instruments on which he or she relies.

As from January 2, 1997 applications which do not comply with the requirements of *Practice Direction* [1994] 1 W.L.R. 1551 (the provision of a paginated, indexed bundle of documents with a list of essential reading) and *Practice Direction* [1997] 1 W.L.R. 52, [1997] 1 All E.R. 128 (the provision of copies of relevant legislative material) will not be accepted, even with undertakings, save in exceptional circumstances such as urgency where a decision is required from the court within 14 days of the lodging of the application. If the only reason given in support of urgency is the imminent expiry of the three month time limit for lodging an application the papers will nonetheless be returned for compliance with the *Practice Direction(s)* and if necessary the applicant must seek an extension of time and provide reasons for the delay in lodging the papers in proper form (*Lynne Knapmann, Head of the Crown Office*, January 1997).

R57.2.8 **Office Copies**—The expression "appropriate office copies of the proceedings for the use of the Judges" in r.2(2) means three copies where the matter is to be heard by a Divisional Court and one copy in cases where the matter is to be heard by a single Judge. In *either* case the copy should be included in an indexed and paginated bundle which conforms with the terms of the *Practice Direction* given by the Lord Chief Justice on July 27, 1983—*Practice Direction (Evidence: Documents)* [1983] 1 W.L.R. 922. Failure to comply with that *Practice Direction* may result in the matter being struck out.

Withdrawal of proceedings—Where proceedings before the Divisional Court concern the liberty of the subject, *i.e.* for habeas corpus or committal, they cannot be withdrawn by consent of the parties but must be the subject of an application to withdraw made in open Court. Other proceedings may be withdrawn by consent by lodging in the Crown Office the written consent of the parties which includes where appropriate provision as to costs. An order of the Master of the Crown Office will be drawn up providing for the respondent's costs where such provision has been agreed. Where parties are agreed as to the terms on which proceedings entered in the Crown Office List can be disposed of, but require an order of the Court to put them into effect, they should follow the procedure set out in the Practice Directions given by the Lord Chief Justice (*Practice Direction (Crown Office List: Uncontested Proceedings)* [1982] 1 W.L.R. 979 in relation to civil proceedings and *Practice Direction (Crown Office List: Criminal Proceedings)* [1983] 1 W.L.R. 925, in relation to criminal proceedings.) **R57.2.9**

Uncontested Applications—On May 12, 1997 Lord Bingham of Cornhill C.J., Hirst and Millett L.JJ. issued the following *Practice Direction* ([1997] 2 All E.R. 799): **R57.2.10**

Practice Direction (Crown Office List: Consent Orders)—Uncontested applications in civil and criminal causes or matters will be dealt with under a procedure which replaces that set out, in respect of civil matters, in *Practice Direction (Crown Office List: Uncontested Proceedings)* [1982] 1 W.L.R. 979) and in so far as relevant to criminal matters, in *Practice Direction (Crown Office List: Criminal Proceedings)* [1983] 1 W.L.R. 925). **R57.2.11**

(1) *Determination of proceedings:* Where the parties are agreed as to the terms on which proceedings entered in the Crown Office List can be disposed of and required an order of the court to put those terms into effect, they should lodge with the Crown Office a document, with two copies thereof, signed by the parties setting out the terms of the proposed agreed order and a short statement of the matters relied on as justifying the making of the order, authorities and statutory provisions relied on being quoted.

The Crown Office will then submit the document to the court, in a civil cause or matter to a single judge and in a criminal cause or matter to a Divisional Court, and if the court is satisfied that the order should be made, the proceedings will be listed for pronouncement of the order in open court without the need for attendance by the parties of their representatives.

If the court is not satisfied on the information originally provided or subsequently provided at the court's request, that the order can properly be made, the proceedings will be listed for hearing in the normal way.

(2) *Interlocutory orders:* Where the parties seek an interlocutory order and were agreed as to the terms of that proposed order they should lodge with the Crown Office a document, with two copies thereof, signed by the parties setting out the terms of the proposed agreed order and a short statement of the matters relied on as justifying the making of the order and where appropriate, citing authorities and statutory provisions relied on.

The Crown Office will then submit the document to a judge and, if he is satisfied that the order should be made, the order will be drawn and sent to the parties without the need for the proceedings to be listed.

(3) *Withdrawal of proceedings including habeas corpus*

(a) Where leave of the court is not necessary for proceedings to be withdrawn, the applicant or appellant, as the case might be, must lodge a notice of withdrawal with the Crown Office and serve a copy of that notice on all other parties to the proceedings. The court file will then be closed.

(b) Where the parties are agreed that the proceedings should be withdrawn but required the leave of the court to do so, or seek an order for costs in relation to those proceedings, they should lodge with the Crown Office a document, with two copies thereof, signed by the parties setting out the terms of the proposed withdrawal.

The Crown Office will then submit the document to the Master of the Crown Office and, if he is satisfied that the proceedings should be withdrawn on the terms proposed, any order necessary will be drawn and sent to the parties without the need for the proceedings to be listed in open court. The court file will then be closed.

Issue, etc., of claim form

3. A claim form by which any proceedings to which this order applies are begun must be issued— **R57.3**

(a) in the case of proceedings in the Family Division, out of the principal registry of the Family Division; and

(b) in the case of any other proceedings, out of the Crown Office, Chancery Chambers or the Admiralty and Commercial Registry, as the circumstances of the case require.

History of Rule—Amended by S.I. 1971 No. 1269; S.I. 1979 No. 1716; S.I. 1982 No. 1111 and S.I. 1987 No. 1434. **R57.3.1**

Filing of witness statements or affidavits and drawing up of orders

R57.4 **4.**—(1) Every witness statement or affidavit used in proceedings to which this order applies must be filed in the Crown Office, Chancery Chambers or the Admiralty and Commercial Registry, as the circumstances of the case require.

(2) Every order made in proceedings to which this order applies in the Queen's Bench Division shall be drawn up in the Crown Office or the Admiralty and Commercial Registry, as the circumstances of the case require, and a copy of any order made by a judge sitting in private in any such proceedings must be filed in that office.

R57.4.1 **History of Rule**—Amended by S.I. 1971 No. 1269; S.I. 1982 No. 1111 and S.I. 1987 No. 1423.

R57.4.2 **Affidavits**—A respondent may file affidavits in opposition to a motion, but these should be filed, and included in the indexed and paginated bundles, before the hearing. Additional affidavits may be filed by any party if leave is obtained at the hearing. Leave may be given to a party to read additional affidavits upon any new matter arising out of the affidavits of the opposite party. Cross-examination on affidavits used in proceedings under this Order is very rarely allowed (see *R. v. Kent JJ.* [1928] W.N. 137; *R. v. Stokesley JJ.* [1956] 1 W.L.R. 254; [1956] 1 All E.R. 563).

In applications for judicial review a respondent's affidavit must be filed within 56 days (see O.53, r.6(4) (as amended)). As to the principles governing application for an extension of time of that period, see *Practice Note (QBD) (Judicial Review: Affidavit in Reply)* [1989] 1 W.L.R. 358; [1989] 1 All E.R. 1024, issued by Watkins L.J., Deputy Chief Justice, on March 7, 1989.

Filing a claim form

R57.5 **5.** Every claim form must be filed in the Crown Office, Chancery Chambers or the principal registry of the Family Division as the circumstances of the case require together with the return thereto and a copy of any order made thereon.

R57.5.1 **History of Rule**—Amended by S.I. 1971 No. 1269 and S.I. 1982 No. 1111.

R57.5.2 **"Filing of claim form" in proceedings to which this order applies**—*e.g.* habeas corpus and committal and also a *fi.fa.* on an order for payment of costs made by a Divisional Court of the QBD or by the CA on appeal. The claim form is issued on production of the sealed copy order and taxing master's certificate. Writs in habeas corpus proceedings must be issued out of and filed in the Crown Office, save that where such writs affect minors they must be issued out of and filed in the principal registry of the Family Division; see O.59, r.11.

R57.5.3 **Writs of subpoena**—See Form No. 28, SCP 1999, Vol. 2, Section 1A, para. 1A–26), and O.38, r.19. Subpoenas *ad testificandum* or *duces tecum* are issued from the Crown Office in all causes pending on the Crown side of the QBD, and in Crown Courts. They are not, however, issued to summon witnesses before a Judge in Chambers, Divisional Court or CA without leave of the Court or a Judge. They are issued to compel attendance of witnesses at coroners' inquests, and before any inferior tribunal which lacks the means of enforcing such attendance, unless some statute has impliedly taken away this power of the QBD (*R. v. Hurle-Hobbs, ex p. Simmons* [1945] K.B. 165). Subpoenas *duces tecum* are, for example, issued in proceedings before the Income Tax Commissioners (*Soul v. I.R.C.* [1963] 1 W.L.R. 112; [1963] 1 All E.R. 68n.).

On a subpoena *duces tecum* the police are liable to produce to the court in a civil action, documents seized by them under the Police and Criminal Evidence Act 1984, subject to the right of the owner of the documents to challenge the subpoena; *Marcel v. Commissioner of the Police of the Metropolis, The Independent,* July 24, 1991 (Dillon, Nolan L.JJ. and Sir Christopher Slade) allowing an appeal from the injunction granted by Sir Nicolas Browne-Wilkinson, V.-C. (reported at [1991] 1 All E.R. 845, 855).

Where a *Subpoena duces tecum* is served on a bank requiring it to produce a customer's bank statement it is under a duty to do so and it does not therefore act in breach of the duty of confidentiality owed to its customer (*Maurice Robertson v. Canadian Imperial Bank of Commerce* [1994] 1 W.L.R. 1493, PC).

They will not issue against an ambassador or other person entitled to diplomatic privilege. They will not issue to compel production of any document kept by the Registrar of Companies, without leave of the Master of the Crown Office, and if issued must record that they are issued with leave of the Court (C.A. 1985, ss.709, 710). Crown Office subpoenas may be addressed to and served upon any person in any part of the United Kingdom (which term includes Northern Ireland but not the Isle of Man nor the Channel Islands (see the Writ of Subpoena Act 1805, s.3; Attendance of Witnesses Act 1854, and S.C.A. 1981, s.36).

R57.5.4 **Duration of subpoena**—Crown Office subpoenas issued for the attendance of witnesses before inferior Courts remain in force until the disposal of the proceedings before such Courts (see CPR, r.34.4). As to the procedure to be adopted for setting aside a *subpoena duces tecum* see generally *Khanna v. Lovell White Durrant* [1995] 1 W.L.R. 121 (Sir Donald Nicholls V.-C.).

Practice—The party requiring the subpoena must attend at the Crown Office either in person or by solicitor: business is not transacted through the post. For a form of subpoena see Form No. 28 (SCP 1999, Vol. 2, Section 1A, para. 1A–26). They must be completed before issue, with all details including the name and address of the witness; but a list specifying any documents to be produced may be inserted. If they are required for proceedings in the Divisional Court, leave must be obtained from the Court by motion: if for service in Scotland or Northern Ireland, an order must be obtained *ex parte* from the Master of the Crown Office on affidavit, and at the foot of the writ must be added:—"Notice. Take Notice that this writ was ordered to be issued by an order of Her Majesty's High Court of Justice dated ... pursuant to the Attendance of Witnesses Act 1854." R57.5.5

Expenses of witnesses—in criminal cases need not be tendered unless required by a statute (as, for example, Writs of Subpoena Act 1805, s.3, in regard, to prosecutions in another part of the United Kingdom) for it is a public duty to give evidence. R57.5.6

In general a witness upon whom a *subpoena duces tecum* has been served is entitled to his costs in complying and is not restricted merely to receiving conduct money. Thus such costs may include the taking of legal advice where it is reasonable to do so (*J. H. Shannon v. Country Casuals Holdings plc, The Times*, June 16, 1997 (Garland J.)).

Disobedience to a Crown Office subpoena—is punishable in the QBD by committal (*R. v. Daye* [1908] 2 K.B. 333) in whatever Court the witness is summoned to appear, though disobedience to a *subpoena* issued by an inferior Court is not so punishable (*R. v. Judge, ex p. Justice of Ely* [1931] 2 K.B. 442). Where a person knowingly fails to comply with a *subpoena duces tecum* issued in support of a disciplinary enquiry he commits a serious contempt. The applicant had, however, made an abject apology and, having regard to the alarming figure mentioned in relation to costs, a fine of only £100 would be imposed (*United Kingdom Central Council for Nursing Midwifery and Health Visiting v. Gifford* [1991] C.O.D. 436 (Russell L.J. and Hodgson J.). R57.5.7

Criminal Procedure (Attendance of Witnesses) Act 1965—For the convenient procedure of issuing witness summons under this Act for the purpose of criminal proceedings in the Crown Court see s.2 and O.79, r.10, and Form Nos 101–103 (SCP 1999, Vol. 2, paras 1A–106—1A–108). R57.5.8

Custody of records

6. The master of the Crown Office or the Admiralty and Commercial Registry, as the circumstances of the case require shall have the custody of the records of or relating to proceedings in the Queen's Bench Division to which this order applies. R57.5.9

RSC ORDER 58

APPEALS FROM MASTERS, REGISTRARS, REFEREES AND JUDGES

Contents R58.0.1

Editorial Introduction

This Order contains seven rules dealing with (1) appeals to a judge from certain decisions by R58.0.2

masters, etc. (rr.1 and 3), (2) appeals to the Court of Appeal from certain other decisions by masters, etc. (r.2), and (3) subject to some legislative restrictions, appeals to the Court of Appeal from decisions of Judges of the Technology and Construction Court.

R58.0.3 **Rules**—Order 58 has not yet been the subject of full-scale revision; in the interim the Civil Procedure Rules 1998 (CPR) (S.I. 1998 No. 3132) have re-enacted O.58, rr.1 to 4 in Sched. 1 to the CPR, subject to a few modifications. Those rules, as so re-enacted, have been slightly amended by the Civil Procedure (Amendment) Rules 1999 (S.I. 1999 No. 1008). Both the CPR and those amendments came into effect on April 26, 1999. O.58, rr.5, 6 & 7 have not been re-enacted in Sched. 1 and therefore they stand repealed.

Related sources

R58.0.4
- RSC, O.59 (Appeals to the Court of Appeal)
- CCR, O.13, r.10 (Appeal to Judge from District Judge)
- *Practice Direction (Judge in Chambers: Revised Procedure)* [1996] 1 W.L.R. 1432

The following *Queen's Bench Practice Directions* are relevant to this Order. These Directions continue to apply for the time being (see Practice Direction (Civil: Litigation: Procedure) [1999] 1 W.L.R. 1124).

- No. 17—Sitting of Queen's Bench judge in chambers out of London (SCP 1999, Vol. 2, Section 2C, para. 2C–155)
- No. 18—Practice on appeals to Queen's Bench judge in chambers from district judge (SCP 1999, Vol. 2, Section 2C, para. 2C–156)
- No. 39—Appeals from district judges (SCP 1999, Vol. 2, Section 2A, para. 2A–107)
- *Chancery Division Practice Direction No. 1—see* Chancery Guide, p. 70 at paras D1–312 *et seq.*

Forms

R58.0.5 The following Queen's Bench Masters' Practice Form (now listed in Table 2 (Practice Forms) attached to Practice Direction (Forms)) is relevant to O.58 (SCP 1999, Vol. 2, Section 1B, para. 1B–77):

- PF110—Notice of appeal to judge in chambers (O.58)

Appeals from certain decisions of Masters, etc. to judge sitting in private

R58.1 **1.**—(1) Except as provided by rule 2, an appeal shall lie to a judge from any judgment, order or decision of a Master, the Admiralty Registrar or a district judge of the Family Division.

(2) The appeal shall be brought by serving on every other party to the proceedings in which the judgment, order or decision was given or made a notice of appeal.

(3) Unless the court otherwise orders, the notice must be issued within 5 days after the judgment, order or decision appealed against was given or made and must be served within five days after issue and an appeal to which this rule applies shall not be heard sooner than two clear days after such service.

(3A) When it issues the notice of appeal, the court will fix a date for the hearing.

(4) Except so far as the court may otherwise direct, an appeal under this rule shall not operate as a stay of the proceedings in which the appeal is brought.

R58.1.1 **History of Rule**—Amended by S.I. 1971 No. 1269, S.I. 1982 No. 1111 and S.I. 1987 No. 1423. By s.74 of the Courts and Legal Services Act 1990 the office of registrar is now the office of district judge.

R58.1.2 **Effect of rule**—Rules 1 and 2 are the counterparts of each other, r.1 dealing with appeals to the Judge in Chambers and r.2 dealing with appeals to the Court of Appeal, from a Master of the QBD or Ch D or a District Judge of the Family Division.

For the avoidance of doubt, the Admiralty Registrar is expressly added, so as to reserve the practice of appeals to go from him to the Admiralty Judge.

R58.1.3 **Nature of appeal from Master or District Judge to Judge**—An appeal from the Master or District Judge to the Judge in Chambers is dealt with by way of an actual rehearing of the application which led to the order under appeal, and the Judge treats the matter as though it came before him for the first time, save that the party appealing, even though the original application was not by him but against him, has the right as well as the obligation to open the appeal. The Judge "will of course give the weight it deserves to the previous decision of the Master;

but he is in no way bound by it" (*per* Lord Atkin in *Evans v. Bartlam* [1937] A.C. 473 at 478). The Judge in Chambers is in no way fettered by the previous exercise of the Master's discretion, and on appeal from the Judge in Chambers, the Court of Appeal will treat the substantial discretion as that of the Judge, and not of the Master (*Evans v. Bartlam*, above; *Cooper v. Cooper* [1936] W.N. 205; and *Cremin v. Barjack Properties Ltd* (1985) 273 Est. Gaz. 299, CA).

A Judge hearing an appeal from a Master or District Judge, however, is entitled, if he thinks fit, to adopt the Master's or District Judge's reasoning in his own judgment without setting out the reasoning himself; by so doing the Judge does not fail to exercise the discretion conferred on him (*Rae v. Yorkshire Bank plc* (1989) *The Times*, October 16, CA).

It is common practice for the Judge in Chambers, subject of course to the question of costs, to admit further or additional evidence by affidavit to that which was before the Master or District Judge; but if a party has taken his stand on the evidence as it stood before the Master or District Judge, the Judge in Chambers may in his discretion, by analogy with the practice in the Court of Appeal, refuse to allow him to adduce further evidence (see *Krakauer v. Katz* [1954] 1 W.L.R. 278; [1954] 1 All E.R. 244, CA).

Where leave to defend is given under O.14 upon the terms of the defendant giving security to the satisfaction of the Master no appeal lies from the Master's decision as to the sufficiency of the security (*Hoare v. Morshead* [1903] 2 K.B. 359, CA).

Although O.58 contains no provision for a formal notice of cross-appeal, the judge's discretion on hearing an appeal from a Master is in no way hindered by the previous exercise of the Master's discretion; hence where a defendant appeals against a Master's order under O.14 giving conditional leave to defend, and the Judge is satisfied that there is no defence to the action, he may properly give summary judgment for the plaintiff notwithstanding that no formal notice of cross-appeal has been given by the plaintiff (*Europa Property & Finance Services Ltd v. Stubbert* (1991) *The Times*, November 25, CA).

An appeal from the refusal of a Master to make an *ex parte* order lies to the Judge in Chambers. On the other hand, where the Master has granted an order *ex parte*, the proper course is not to appeal, but to apply to him or another Master to set aside such order (see O.32, r.6).

In general a judge in chambers will not allow an appeal from a master's costs order unless it is unreasonable or the master erred in law: *Hoddle v. CCF Construction* [1992] 2 All E.R. 550, Morland J.

Practice on appeal from a Queen's Bench Master or District Judge—The appeal is brought by way of a notice to attend before the Judge on a day specified in the notice. If the appeal is to be heard in London, the notice is issued out of the Judge in Chambers Listing Office, and it must be issued, unless the time is enlarged, within five days from the decision complained of, and served on the opposite party within five days of issue and not less than two clear days before the day fixed for hearing the appeal. See O.54, r.1. **R58.1.4**

If the appeal is to be heard out of London, the notice is issued in the District Registry at the trial centre at which the appeal is to be heard (see para. R58.1.8).

It is not necessary, for the purpose of an appeal to the Judge in Chambers, to draw up the order appealed from.

Where the Judge in Chambers himself gives directions, he may add to his order that all further interlocutory applications are to be made to a Master (*Practice Note* [1932] W.N. 182).

As to the form of Notice of Appeal, see PF 110, SCP 1999, Vol. 2, Section 1B, para. 1B–77.

Practice on appeal from a Chancery master—In Ch D the notice of appeal is issued in Room TM8.13 (fee £15). See *Practice Direction No. 1* see Chancery Guide, p. 70 at paras D1–312 *et seq.* The notice in form PF110 is issued for a date and time to be fixed and is listed in the non-witness list. It must be served within five days after issue. **R58.1.5**

Withdrawal of appeal—In the Chancery Division application for withdrawal of an appeal against a decision of a Chancery Master must be made to the Judge. If an appeal from a Chancery Master is to be dismissed by consent, a request for dismissal by consent can be signed by all parties and lodged with the Chancery Judges Listing General Office, Room W.11/W.12 (*Buckbod Investments Ltd v. Nana-Otchere* [1985] 1 W.L.R. 342; [1985] 1 All E.R.). Where, however, the appeal is simply to be dismissed with costs to be taxed, an application signed by the appellants' solicitor, alone (or by the applicant if he is in person) will suffice.

Enlargement of time—This rule must be read with O.3, r.5, so that the time limited for appeal may be extended by the Master, and the time limited by the Master may be extended by the Judge in Chambers after such time has expired or the five days for appealing have elapsed (see *Burke v. Rooney* (1879) 4 C.P.D. 226). Where no explanation, excuse or reason is given for the delay in issuing the notice of appeal, the Judge may refuse to extend the time (*Revici v. Prentice Hall Inc.* [1969] 1 W.L.R. 157; [1969] 1 All E.R. 772, CA). **R58.1.6**

The time for appealing against an order dismissing an action for want of prosecution may be enlarged after the order has taken effect (*Carter v. Stubbs* (1880) 6 Q.B.D. 116; *Burke v. Rooney*). The time may be enlarged by the Judge, on the hearing of the appeal, without a summons being taken out at Chambers for that purpose (*Gibbons v. London Financial Association* (1879) 4 C.P.D. 263).

R58.1.7 **Practice before the Q.B. Judge in Chambers in London**—*Practice Direction (Judge in Chambers: Revised Procedure)* [1996] 1 W.L.R. 1432 states as follows:

1. All *inter partes* applications and appeals to the Queen's Bench Judge in Chambers would initially be entered in a general list. They would be listed for hearing in Room E101 or some other room at the Royal Courts of Justice on Tuesdays or Thursdays.

Whenever it appeared or was agreed that any application or appeal was likely to last more than 30 minutes, it would be transferred to the Chambers Warned List. If the parties agreed that it was likely to last more than 30 minutes, the applicant/appellant must as soon as practicable, and in any event not later than 12 noon on the working day before the date given, transfer the case to the Chambers Warned List.

If the parties did not so agree, or agreed less than 4 hours before the date given, the parties must attend on the date given.

2. Cases in the Chambers Warned List would be listed in *The Daily Cause List.* That would be done by the Clerk of the Lists when he prepared the following day's list at 2.15 p.m.

The Clerk of the Lists would, where it was possible, accept "offers" in the week in which the matter appeared in the Warned List.

Fixtures would only be given in exceptional circumstances.

3. In order to ensure that a complete set of papers in proper order was available for the judge before hearing such applications and appeals, the parties must in advance of the hearing lodge in Room W.11/W.13 a bundle properly paged and indexed in date order containing copies of the following documents:

(i) the notice of appeal, or, as the case might be, the summons;
(ii) the pleadings, if any;
(iii) copies of all affidavits, together with copy exhibits thereto, upon which any party intended to rely; and
(iv) any relevant order made in the action

The bundle should be agreed. The originals of all affidavits intended to be relied on should be bespoken or produced at the hearing and all exhibits should be available. A skeleton argument and, where that would be helpful, a chronology should be lodged.

The bundle had to be lodged not later than 48 hours after the parties had been notified that the case was to appear in the Warned List.

For cases to be heard in the General List, the bundle had to be lodged at least 48 hours before the hearing. Skeleton arguments, with chronology, had to be lodged not later than 24 hours before the hearing.

4. Except with leave of the judge, no document could be adduced in evidence or relied on unless a copy of it had been lodged and original produced.

R58.1.8 **Sittings of Q.B. Judge in Chambers out of London**—*Queen's Bench Practice Direction No. 17* (SCP 1999, Vol. 2, Section 2C, para. 2C–155) states as follows:

1. To the extent that the business of the Courts permit, and subject to the provisions of this direction, Judges of the Queen's Bench Division will sit in chambers at any place where sittings of the High Court are held, as well as in London, to deal with any business which may be dealt with by a Judge of the Queen's Bench Division in Chambers except any business which may from time to time be notified.

2. Where a party desires that a matter be heard before a Judge in Chambers outside London the notice of an appeal or summons shall bear the title of the District Registry in which the action is proceeding but shall be issued in the District Registry at the place at which it is to be heard.

3. Before a party issues a Judge's summons or a notice of appeal in a District Registry, he should inquire at the Registry whether the state of business will permit the matter to be heard there, and it is proper to be so heard.

4. A Judge's summons or notice of appeal issued in a District Registry may be transferred for hearing to a Judge in Chambers sitting in London or at another place outside London on the application of a party made to the Judge or by the Court of its own motion, and such a summons or notice issued in the Central Office may similarly be transferred for hearing to a place outside London. Before a transfer to a place outside London is ordered, the Court will require to be informed, from inquiries made by the parties or the Court officers, whether the matter can conveniently be taken there.

5. In cases not specifically provided for, the practice of the Central Office as to district registry appeals shall be followed as nearly as circumstances permit.

6. Applications for bail under RSC, O.79 to a Judge in chambers may, and should wherever possible, be made to a Judge of the Queen's Bench Division at any place where sittings of the High Court or of the Crown Court are held, being the place nearest to the Court where the applicant has appeared: provided that such applications made through the Official Solicitor may in any case be made in London. Outside London the summons should be issued in the District Registry at the place where the application can be heard, and the order drawn up and perfected in that Registry.

R58.1.9 **Practice on appeals to Q.B. Judge in Chambers from District Judge**—*Queen's Bench Practice Direction No. 18* (SCP 1999, Vol. 2, Section 2C, para. 2C–156) applies to the hearing of appeals in the Queen's Bench Division from District Judges on all circuits and states as follows:

1. In order to ensure that a complete set of papers in proper order is available for perusal by the Judge before hearing such appeals, the parties must in advance of the hearing lodge in the civil listing office of the trial centre concerned a bundle properly paged in order of date and indexed, containing copies of the following documents:

(i) the notice of appeal
(ii) the pleadings (if any);
(iii) copies of all affidavits (together with exhibits thereto) upon which any party intends to rely;
(iv) any relevant order made in the action;
(v) notes (if any) of reasons given by the District Judge, prepared by the District Judge, counsel or solicitors.

The bundle should be agreed. The original of all affidavits intended to be relied on should be bespoken or produced at the hearing and all exhibits thereto should be available.

2. Where a date for hearing has been fixed, the bundle must be lodged not later than three clear days before the fixed date. For appeals where there is no fixed date for hearing, the bundle must be lodged not later than 24 hours after the parties have been notified that the case is to appear in the warned list or, if that is not possible, it must be lodged as soon as practicable thereafter.

3. Except with the leave of the Judge, no document may be adduced in evidence or relied on unless a copy of it has been lodged and the original bespoken as aforesaid.

4. In cases of complexity a skeleton argument or, where that would be helpful, a chronology should be lodged at the same time as the bundle.

Appeals from certain decisions of Masters, etc., to Court of Appeal

2.—(1) An appeal shall lie to the Court of Appeal from any judgment, order or decision of a Master given or made at trial— R58.2

(a) on the hearing or determination of any cause, matter, question or issue tried before him; or
(b) on an assessment of damages or of the value of goods, or an assessment of interest,

and where a judgment, order or decision of a kind referred to in paragraph (b) includes or involves a determination of any other matter, an appeal shall lie to the Court of Appeal in relation to such other matter.

(An appeal from the decision of a Master made other than at trial shall be made to the judge in accordance with rule 1.)

Effect of rule—Where a Master tries a claim or conducts a trial of an assessment of damages or the value of goods, or an assessment of interest, appeal lies directly to the Court of Appeal against the Master's judgment or order (subject to obtaining permission to appeal, see para. R58.2.2). Where, during the course of such a trial, the Master makes a decision on any other matter (such as permission to amend or a ruling on evidence) appeal will also lie to the Court of Appeal against that decision (subject to obtaining permission to appeal). Where, however, a Master gives any judgment, order or other decision otherwise than at such a trial, any appeal will lie to a Judge under r.1, and not to the Court of Appeal. Thus, if a Master deals with a request for permission to amend at such a trial the avenue of appeal is to the Court of Appeal (subject to obtaining permission to appeal.) Where, however, a Master deals with an application for permission to amend in any other circumstances (whether in proceedings which will be tried by a Judge or antecedent to a trial by Master) the appeal must be brought to a Judge and not to the Court of Appeal. R58.2.1

The same rules apply to appeals from a District Judge acting in his/her High Court capacity (O.58, r.3 and see para. R58.3.1).

Permission to appeal—In any case where appeal lies directly to the Court of Appeal against a judgment, order or other decision of a Master (whether procedural or final) permission to appeal is required under RSC, O.59, r.1B. R58.2.2

Procedure where appeal lies from a Master to the Court of Appeal—In those cases where appeal lies against a judgment or order of a Master directly to the Court of Appeal the time limits and procedure are those laid down by O.59 for appeals to the Court of Appeal. R58.2.3

Appeals from district judges

3.—(1) An appeal shall lie from any judgment, order or decision of a district judge in any proceedings in any Division in the same circumstances and, except as provided by paragraph (2) subject to the same conditions as if the judgment, order or decision were given or made by a Master or Registrar R58.3

in those proceedings in that Division, and the provisions of these rules with respect to appeals shall apply accordingly.

(2) In relation to an appeal from a judgment, order or decision of a district judge, rule 1 shall have effect subject to the modification that for the first reference therein to 5 days and the reference therein to 2 clear days there shall be substituted references to 7 days and 3 clear days respectively.

R58.3.1 **Effect of rule**—The effect of this rule is to equate in all respects appeals from District Judges in any cause or matter in any Division with appeals from a Master, except that in the case of an appeal from a District Judge the notice of appeal must be issued within seven days after the decision appealed against, then (as in the case of an appeal from a Master) it must be served five days after issue, and there must be not less than three clear days between the date of such service and the hearing of the appeal.

Appeal lies directly to the Court of Appeal against any order made by a District Judge in his/her High Court capacity on an assessment of damages or at a trial conducted by the District Judge as in the case of any such order made by a Master (see further para. R58.2.1 above). Permission to appeal will be required (see O.59, r.1B(1)).

R58.3.2 **Practice on Appeal, QBD**—The ordinary course is to give notice of appeal. The notice must be issued within the seven days after the judgment, order or decision is given or made, unless extended. It must be entered at the Action Department and served as soon as possible after the District Judge's decision, and at least three clear days before the day named for hearing. If the Judge's list is full, or the Judge is not sitting in Chambers, the appeal may be heard later without extension of time.

The notice of appeal may be signed by the country solicitor (*Mayor, etc., of Rotherham v. Peace* [1883] W.N. 216).

For the practice regulating appeals from District Judges to Q.B. Judges out of London, see para. R58.1.8.

R58.3.3 **Papers for the Judge in London**—In the QBD the usual practice is for the District Judge, on request, to forward to the Chief Clerk to the Judge in Chambers, Central Office, Royal Courts of Justice, Strand, London WC2A 2LL, the file of proceedings in the District Registry for the Judge hearing the appeal—including all the original affidavits used before the District Judge. After the appeal is heard the papers, together with any additional affidavits, will be returned to the District Judge.

In Chancery matters, where there is an appeal from the District Judge to the Judge, the papers must be sent to Chancery Chambers (Room 307, Thomas More Building, Royal Courts of Justice, Strand, London WC2A 2LL). The papers should include the District Judge's note of the point for decision (*Queen's Bench Masters' Practice Direction No. 39*), SCP 1999, Vol. 2, Section 2A, para. 2A–107).

Appeals from judge of the Technology and Construction Court

R58.4 **4.** Subject to section 18 of the Act (which shall apply in relation to a decision of a judge of the Technology and Construction Court as if he were a judge of the High Court), an appeal shall lie to the Court of Appeal from a decision of a judge of the Technology and Construction Court as if he were a judge of the High Court.

R58.4.1 **Effect of the rule**—Appeal lies to the Court of Appeal against a decision of a judge of the Technology and Construction Court as if he were a Judge of the High Court. Under SCA 1981, s.16 appeal lies to the Court of Appeal against a decision of a High Court Judge. Save where it is an appeal against a committal order, permission to appeal will be required (RSC, O.59, r.1B). For the practice and procedure governing appeals to the Court of Appeal see O.59 and the commentary thereon.

R58.4.2 **Question of Fact**—An Appeal lies to the Court of Appeal with the leave of the judge of the TCC or the Court of Appeal on any question of fact. The test to be applied is whether the ground of appeal identified has a reasonable prospect of success. It will be difficult to satisfy the test where it is sought to challenge:

(i) a primary fact based upon the evaluation of oral evidence;
(ii) findings of fact fall within a TCC judge's specialised expertise and where he has had the benefit of inspecting the site, or the subject matter of the dispute; or
(iii) the fine detail of the TCC judge's factual investigation.

Where, however, the facts are based upon a secondary inference from the primary facts or closely bound up with a ground of appeal in law, then the test may be more readily discharged. That is not to say that leave to appeal a question of fact should be given merely because an appeal on legal grounds is being pursued. See *Virgin Management Ltd v. de Morgan Group* (1994) 68 B.L.R. 26, CA.

PRACTICE DIRECTION—RSC ORDER 58—APPEALS FROM MASTERS ETC.

This Practice Direction Supplements RSC Order 58, Rule 2 R58PD–001

1.1 RSC Order 58, rule 2 (Schedule 1 to the Civil Procedure Rules) provides for an appeal from certain decisions of Masters or District Judges (High Court) to the Court of Appeal. This provision is not intended to alter the route of appeal from a decision of a Master or District Judge.

1.2 Where, before 26 April 1999, an appeal would have lain from a decision of a Master or District Judge to a judge under RSC Order 58, rule 1, it shall continue to do so under the Civil Procedure Rules.

1.3 RSC Order 58, rule 2(1)(a) provides that an appeal lies to the Court of Appeal from a decision of a Master or District Judge made "at trial ... on the hearing or determination of any cause, matter, question or issue tried before him". This provision only applies where the parties have given their consent for the Master or District Judge to try a case which has been allocated to the multi-track under Part 26 (see paragraph 4.1 of the Practice Direction on Allocation of Cases to Levels of Judiciary—Part 2B).

RSC ORDER 59

APPEALS TO THE COURT OF APPEAL

Contents R59.0.1

Editorial Introduction

R59.0.2 The constitution, jurisdiction and powers of the Court of Appeal are governed by the Supreme Court Act 1981, ss.1–3, 15–17, and 53–58 (see also paras R59.1.18 *et seq.*, R59.1.62 and R59.1.140 *et seq.* and SCP 1999, Vol. 2, Section 20A, paras 20A–130 to 20A–138; 20A–170 to 20A–176; 20A–404 to 20A–423). The creation of a right of appeal is an act which requires legislative authority. Neither the inferior nor the superior tribunal nor both combined can create such a right (*Att.-Gen. v. Sillem* (1864) 10 HLCas. 704; and see *R. v. Hanson* (1821) 4 B. & Ald. 519; *R. v. Cashiobury, JJ.* (1823) 3 D. & R. 35; *National Telephone Co. v. Postmaster-General* [1913] 2 K.B. 614; [1913] A.C. 546). But "when a question is stated to be referred to an established court without more, it imports that the ordinary incidents of the procedure of that court are to attach, and also that any general right of appeal from the decision likewise attaches" (*per* Viscount Haldane L.C., *National Telephone Co. v. Postmaster-General* [1913] A.C. 546 at 552). Where the statute provides no procedure for the appeal it is the duty of the appeal court to do so, so that the appeal may be heard (*Smith v. Williams* [1922] 1 K.B. 158, p. 165, *cf. Hoser v. Ministry of Housing* [1963] Ch. 428).

The jurisdiction of the former Court of Criminal Appeal is now vested in the Criminal Division of the Court of Appeal (see S.C.A. 1981, s.53). O.59 and this commentary on it deal only with appeals to the Civil Division. For a list of the principal courts and tribunals from which appeal lies directly to the Court of Appeal (Civil Division) see paras R59.1.8 *et seq.*

The Court of Appeal has, generally speaking, no original jurisdiction. But it can make orders (*e.g.* by way of injunctions or the appointment of a receiver and manager) for the protection of property or person pending the determination of an appeal to it or from it to the House of Lords even though no application for such order was made in the court below (*Hyde v. Warden* (1876) 1 Ex.D. 309; *Wilson v. Church* (1879) 11 Ch.D. 576; *Polini v. Gray, Sturla v. Freccia* (1879) 12 Ch.D. 438). There are a few statutory provisions giving the Court of Appeal original jurisdiction. It has original (but not appellate) jurisdiction under ss.10 and 35 of the Fugitive Offenders Act 1881, as a "superior court" (*R. v. Governor of Brixton Prison, ex p. Savarkar* [1910] 2 K.B. 1056; *De Demko v. Home Secretary* [1959] A.C. 654; [1959] 1 All E.R. 341, HL).

Some of the practice and procedure of the Court of Appeal (Civil Division) is not based on statutory provisions or rules of court, but derives from the exercise of the Court's inherent jurisdiction or is enshrined in Practice Directions or established practices of the Court. For that reason some of the parts of the ensuing text are not commentary on any rule within O.59, but are an account of practices and procedures not founded on the rules. Such material has been interspersed in the commentary in appropriate places; much of it (because it relates to the general practices of the Court of Appeal) has been placed with the commentary on r.1. To assist in locating the relevant material there is a table (in para. R59.1.2) which provides a guide to the commentary relating to appeals and applications to the Court of Appeal.

R59.0.3 **The rules governing appeals to the Court of Appeal**—The rules relating to appeals to the Court of Appeal have not yet been the subject of full-scale revision, and in the interim the Civil Procedure Rules 1998 (CPR) (S.I. 1998 No. 3132) have re-enacted the relevant Rules of the Supreme Court (including O.59) in Sched. 1 to the CPR, subject to a few relatively minor modifications. The provisions of O.59, as so re-enacted, have been slightly amended by the Civil Procedure (Amendment) Rules 1999 (S.I. 1999 No. 1008). Both the CPR and those amendments came into effect on April 26, 1999.

R59.0.4 **The new consolidated Court of Appeal Practice Direction**—On April 19, 1999 Lord Woolf, the Master of the Rolls handed down a comprehensive consolidated Practice Direction ("the 1999 Practice Direction") which replaces a large number of previous individual practice directions relating to the Court of Appeal (which are listed in Annex D to the 1999 Practice Direction). The 1999 Practice Direction came into effect on April 26, 1999.

R59.0.5 **The Head of the Civil Appeals Office and the Master**—The administration of the Civil Appeals Office is under the direction of the Head of the Civil Appeals Office (a new post recently created). He has judicial jurisdiction and when acting in his judicial capacity he is known as the Master (see the 1999 Practice Direction, para. 1.3.1). There are two Deputy Masters who also exercise judicial as well as administrative functions within the Civil Appeals Office. (References in this commentary to "the Master" include the Deputy Masters.)

Related Sources

R.59.0.6
- Supreme Court Act 1981, ss.1–3, 15–18, 53, 54 and 58 (SCP 1999, Vol. 2, Section 20A, paras 20A–130 to 20A–138; 20A–170 to 20A–179; 20A–404; 20A–406; and 20A–422)
- Courts and Legal Services Act 1990, ss.7 and 8 (SCP 1999, Vol. 2, Section 20B, para. 20B–204)
- Practice Direction (Court of Appeal) Civil Division [1999] 1 W.L.R. 1027 (see para. PD–001)

Forms

R59.0.7 There are no Prescribed Forms for the Court of Appeal, but the following are forms which are customarily used in practice:
- Notice of appeal (para. R59.3.13)

- Certificate of service (para. R59.5.13)
- Application notice (para. R59.14)
- Application notice (permission to appeal) (para. R59.14)

Requests for a dismissal by consent order:

- Appeals (para. R59.1.65)
- Applications (para. R59.1.66)
- Applications (not served) (para. R59.1.67)

Application of Order to appeals

1. This order applies, subject to the provisions of these Rules with respect to particular appeals, to every appeal to the Court of Appeal (including so far as it is applicable thereto, any appeal to that court from a judge of the Technology and Construction Court, master or other officer of the Supreme Court or from any tribunal from which an appeal lies to that court under or by virtue of any enactment) not being an appeal for which other provision is made by these Rules, and references to "the court below" apply to any court, tribunal or person from which such an appeal lies. **R59.1**

History of Rule—Amended by S.I. 1981 No. 1731. **R59.1.1**

Guide to commentary on appeals and applications to the Court of Appeal **R59.1.2**

Subject	*Para.*	*RSC*
Instituting an appeal Information and Enquiries	R.59.1.33	
Stages in the progress of an appeal	R.59.4 59.1.5	
Courts and tribunals from which appeal lies to CA	R.59.1.18	
Cases where applications should be made to the court below rather than appealing to the CA	R.59.1.3 and 30	
Other restrictions on appealing	R.59.1.74 to 91	
Notice of appeal	R.59.1.3 *et seq.*	O.59, r.3
Form of notice of appeal	R.59.1.13	
Service of notice of appeal	R.59.3.14 and R59.4.2 *et seq.*	O.59, r.3(5) & r.4
Parties to appeal	R.59.3.3 & 15; R59.8.2	O.59, r.3(5) & r.8
Setting down appeal and entry in the records of the Court	R.59.5.2 *et seq.*	O.59, r.5
Respondent's notice	R.59.6.2 *et seq.*	O.59, r.6
Amendment of notices of appeal and respondent's notices	R.59.7.2	O.59, r.7
Appeals in cases of contempt of court	R.59.1.76 & 98; R59.20.2 *et seq.*	O.59, r.20
Stated case/tribunal appeals	R.60.4.2 & R61.1.2 *et seq.*	O.59, r.22, O.60 & O.61
Documents Appeal bundles	R.59.9.2 *et seq.*	O.59, r.9

Subject	*Para.*	*RSC*
Skeleton Arguments	R.59.9	
Applications Instituting application	R.59.14.2 R.59.14.5 to 14	O.59, r.14(1) & (2)
Forms of application notice	R.59.14.43 to 47	
Application bundles	R.59.14.43 to 14 and R59.14.29	
Extension of time for serving notice of appeal	R.59.4.15	O.3, r.5
Extension of time for setting down	R.59.5.8	O.3, r.5
Stay of execution	R.59.13.2 *et seq.*	O.59, r.13
Injunction pending appeal	R.59.10.44	O.59, r.10(1) & (9)
Renewal of application without notice refused by court below	R.59.14.39	O.59, r.14(3)
Judicial review	R.59.14.2 to 16	O.53
Permission to amend	R.59.7.2	O.59, r.7
Permission to adduce further evidence	R.59.10.11 to 23	O.59, r.10(2)
Permission to appeal	R.59.14.15 to 35	O.59, r.14(2), (2A) & (2B)
Security for costs	R.59.10.32 to 41	O.59, r.10(5)
Expedition	R.59.1.45	
Directions	R.59.9.21 & 59.14.4	O.59, r.9(3) & (4) and r.14(1A)
Bail	R.59.20.5	O.59, r.20
Appeal against decision of the Master	R.59.14.10	O.59, r.14(11)
Appeal against decision of single Lord Justice	R.59.14.41	O.59, r.14(12)
Application for an order that a solicitor has ceased to act	R.59.1.99	CPR, r.42.3
Listing Time estimates	R.59.1.47	
Constitution of court	R.59.1.62	
Listing arrangements in CA	R.59.1.45 *et seq.*	
Lists of authorities	R.59.1.54	
Very urgent appeals/applications	R.59.1.57 & 59	
Hearing Powers of CA	R.59.1.100 & 59.10.2 *et seq.*	O.59, r.10
CA Orders	R.59.1.16 and 59.10.27	

Subject	*Para.*	*RSC*
Rehearings	R.59.1.105 to 109	
Settlements in CA Dismissal by consent of appeals or applications	R.59.1.63 to 69	
Tomlin orders in CA	R.59.1.69	
Withdrawal of appeals or applications	R.59.1.70	
Allowing appeals by consent	R.59.1.71	
Appeal to House of Lords Leave to appeal to HL	R.59.1.110	
Stay of execution pending appeal to HL	R.59.13.13	

Appeal to CA contrasted with application back to court below—An appeal is an application to set aside or vary the decision of the court below on the ground that it was wrongly made, or the appellant may seek a new trial. An appeal to the Court of Appeal must be distinguished from: **R59.1.3**

(1) An application at first instance for the variation or discharge of the order under "a liberty to apply", or based on a change of circumstances since the original order was made. So where an order has been made giving the custody of an infant "until further order", an application to vary the order by reason of subsequent circumstances should be made to the court of first instance, not by way of appeal (*Re Holt* (1880) 16 Ch.D. 115).

(2) An application to discharge or vary an order made *ex parte*. Where an order has been made *ex parte* in the court below the appropriate procedure, if the other party wishes to contest it, is to apply to the court below to set it aside, or vary its terms. Although the Court of Appeal has jurisdiction to hear an appeal against an *ex parte* order, it will not normally do so (*WEA Records v. Visions Channel 4 Ltd* [1983] 1 W.L.R. 721; [1983] 2 All E.R. 589). The same applies even where the intending appellant attended the hearing of the *ex parte* application; for the practice of the Court of Appeal in relation to appeals against orders made at "opposed *ex parte*" hearings see *Hunter & Partners v. Welling & Partners* ((1987) 131 S.J. 75; *The Times*, October 16, 1986, CA). Where an order, such as an injunction, is made by the Court of Appeal on an *ex parte* application renewed before the Court of Appeal (see O.59, r.14(3) below) and the other side wishes to apply to discharge or vary that *ex parte* order that application must be made to the court below and not to the Court of Appeal (*Ocean Software Ltd v. Kay* [1992] 1 Q.B. 583; [1992] 2 W.L.R. 633, CA).

(3) An application for an order to be set aside on the grounds that it was made in the absence of the party concerned (see further para. 59/1/147, below). Where a party was not present at the trial or hearing in the court below the proper course is for him to apply to the court below for the order to be set aside (under O.35, r.2, or, in county court cases, under CCR, O.37, r.2), not to appeal to the Court of Appeal (*Re Edwards' Will Trusts* [1982] Ch. 30; [1981] 2 All E.R. 941, CA). Although the Court of Appeal has jurisdiction to entertain an appeal in such circumstances without requiring the appellant to apply back to the court below for a re-hearing, the Court will not normally exercise that jurisdiction; it is more appropriate that the application for a rehearing should be dealt with by the court below, particularly if the matter turns on disputed issues of fact.

(4) An application to the court below for a rehearing where the rules make provision for such a rehearing (*e.g.* CCR, O.35, r.1: see further para. R59.1.147, below).

? see R 59.1.105 to 108 (p. 1101)

[THE NEXT PARAGRAPH IS R59.1.5.]

Stages in the progress of an appeal

1. Service of notice of appeal—This is the process whereby the other parties are notified that an appeal is being made. The time limit for appealing is (subject to a few exceptions) four weeks (r.4). In county court cases the notice of appeal has to be served on the district judge of the county court as well as on the party or parties affected by the appeal (see para. R59.19.8, below). A notice of appeal does not have to be stamped, sealed or otherwise authenticated by the Court prior to **R59.1.5** service; there is no such process as "issue" of a notice of appeal (or summons or application) to the Court of Appeal (see para. R59.3.5, below). Where permission to appeal is required, it must be obtained before service of a notice of appeal. Where permission to appeal is required a valid notice of appeal can only be served after leave has been granted (*Cumbes v. Robinson* [1951] 2 K.B. 83; [1951] 1 All E.R. 661, CA). It is not possible to stop time running by serving a purported notice of appeal which includes an application for permission to appeal. For the requirements relating to the content and service of notices of appeal, see O.59, rr.3 and 4 and paras R59.3.2 *et seq.* and R59.4.2 *et seq.*

R59.1.6 *2. Setting down of the appeal*—Setting down an appeal does not mean the same as "setting down an action for trial." Setting down is the process whereby the appeal is lodged with the office of the Court of Appeal. In order to set down an appeal, the appellant's solicitor (or the appellant, if in person) must pay the requisite appeal fee (currently £200) and lodge with the Civil Appeals Registry (Room E330) the documents required by O.59, r.5(1). The time limit for setting down is seven days from the date on which the notice of appeal was served or (except in county court cases), if later, seven days from the date on which the order appealed against was sealed or otherwise perfected (see O.59, r.5(1)). For the procedure relating to setting down an appeal, see O.59, r.5 and paras R59.5.2 *et seq.*

[THE NEXT PARAGRAPH IS R59.1.8.]

R59.1.8 *3. Entry in the records of the Court*—If the notice of appeal has been served and set down within the prescribed time limits and appears to be in order, it will then be entered in the computerised records of the Court and assigned to the appropriate List of Appeals (see para. R59.5.19, below). After the appeal has been entered in the records of the Court, a letter (generated by the computer) will be sent to the appellant's solicitor (or the appellant, if in person) informing him/her that the appeal has been so entered, giving the Court of Appeal Reference allocated to it (see para. R59.1.43, below), and outlining the steps which need to be taken by the appellant's side thereafter.

R59.1.9 *4. Notification to respondents of entry*—The appellant's solicitor (or the appellant, if acting in person) must, within four days of receipt of that letter, give notice in writing to all persons on whom the notice of appeal was served that the appeal has been entered in the records of the Court, specifying the Court of Appeal Reference allocated to it (see para. R59.5.22, below).

R59.1.10 *5. Requisitioning and vetting of documents*—The requisite number of bundles of documents for the use of the Lords Justices who will hear the appeal must be lodged within 14 days of the date on which the appeal first appears in the Document List; see r.9. It is the normal practice for an appeal to be added to the Document List well before the anticipated hearing date. This is to ensure that the bundles are lodged well in advance of the hearing and that there is sufficient time for them to be checked. The letter sent to the appellant's solicitor (or the appellant, if in person) notifying him that the appeal has been entered in the records of the Court will inform him of the date on which the appeal will be added to the Document List. If the requisite bundles of documents are not lodged in time or there is a failure to remedy defects in the bundles, the Court will list the appeal for dismissal. (See generally paras R59.9.2 *et seq.*).

R59.1.11 *6. Listing*—Listing is dealt with by the Civil Appeals Office, Listing Office (Room E329). For a full account of the Court of Appeal listing system see para. R59.1.45 below.
Applications for an expedited hearing should be made to the Master (*ibid.*).

R59.1.12 *7. Skeleton arguments*—With the exception of appeals heard as a matter of great urgency or any individual case where the Court otherwise directs, advocates must provide skeleton arguments (and, in the case of the appellant's advocate, also a chronology) for all appeals all applications for permission to appeal and all Full Court applications. For details of the requirements concerning skeleton arguments see paras R59.9.23 *et seq.*

R59.1.13 *8. Applications*—There may be incidental applications in connection with an appeal. Some incidental applications are heard either by a single Lord Justice or the Master (see r.14 and paras R59.14.1 *et seq.*). A fee (currently £100) is payable in respect of an application.

R59.1.14 *9. Settling appeals and applications*—Appeals can be dismissed by consent on paper without a hearing, by lodging with the Civil Appeals Office a request for dismissal by consent in the appropriate form (see paras R59.1.63 to 66). Appeals can also be settled by a Tomlin order (see para. R59.1.68). In appropriate circumstances the Court of Appeal will allow an appeal by consent (see para. R59.1.70). Applications to the Court of Appeal can be dismissed by consent or otherwise settled in the same ways as appeals.

10. Hearing—All appeals are heard by the Court of Appeal sitting in the Royal Courts of Justice **R59.1.15**
in London. Appeals are heard in open court before a Full Court consisting either of two or three Lords Justices; (for the provisions dealing with the jurisdiction of two and three Judge Courts see para. R59.1.62, below). Unless otherwise directed, hearings are in public.

11. Order—Court of Appeal Orders are drawn by the Court Associate, and not by the parties. **R59.1.16**
When the order has been drawn, the Associate will seal it and send copies to all parties to the appeal/application.

12. Appeal to House of Lords—Appeal lies to the House of Lords only with the leave of the **R59.1.17**
Court of Appeal or the House of Lords. In certain instances appeal to the House of Lords is precluded altogether (see, S.C.A. 1981, s.54(6)).

Courts and tribunals from which appeal lies to the Court of Appeal—The courts and **R59.1.18**
tribunals from which the appeal lies to the Court of Appeal include the following:

1. *High Court*—Appeal lies to the Court of Appeal from all divisions of the High Court **R59.1.19**
(S.C.A. 1981, s.16).
2. *Technology Construction Court*—Appeal lies to the Court of Appeal from a decision of **R59.1.20**
a Judge of the Technology and Construction Court (O.58, r.4).
3. *County court*—Appeal lies to the Court of Appeal against any determination of a judge **R59.1.21**
or jury in any county court proceedings (County Courts Act 1984, s.77).
4. *Employment Appeal Tribunal*—Appeal lies to the Court of Appeal from decisions of the **R59.1.22**
Employment Appeal Tribunal on questions of law only (Industrial Tribunals Act 1996, s.37(1) and (2)(a)).
5. *Patents Court*—Appeal lies to the Court of Appeal from decisions of the Patents Court **R59.1.23**
(Patents Act 1977, ss.96 and 97).
6. *Masters and District Judges*—In most cases appeal lies from a decision of a master or **R59.1.24**
district judge in High Court proceedings to a judge of the division of the High Court concerned (see O.58, rr.1 & 3 and paras R58.1.2 *et seq.* and R58.3.2 *et seq.* above); but, in certain cases, appeal lies against a master's or district judge's decision directly to the Court of Appeal, namely appeals against any decision of a master or district judge on an assessment of damages and on the trial of any cause or issue tried before or referred to him (see O.58, r.2 above). Except possibly in the case of a committal order made by a district judge, appeal never lies directly to the Court of Appeal against a decision of a district judge given in county court proceedings; any appeal lies to a county court judge (CCR, O.13, r.1(10) and O.37, r.6).
7. *Immigration Appeals Tribunal*—With effect from July 26, 1993 appeal lies to the Court **R59.1.25**
of Appeal from decisions of the Immigration Appeals Tribunal on questions of law, with the leave of the Tribunal or the Court of Appeal (Asylum and Immigration Appeals Act 1993, s.9). (See further O.59, r.24).
8. *Lands Tribunal*—Appeal lies to the Court of Appeal on points of law against decisions of **R59.1.26**
the Lands Tribunal. The appeal is by way of case stated (Lands Tribunal Act 1949, s.3(4)).
9. *Social Security Commissioners*—Appeal lies to the Court of Appeal on points of law **R59.1.27**
against decisions of the Social Security Commissioners (Social Security Act 1980, s.14).
10. *Restrictive Practices Court*—Appeal lies to the Court of Appeal against decisions of the **R59.1.28**
Restrictive Practices Court (Restrictive Practices Court Act 1976, s.10).
11. *Miscellaneous tribunals*—A right of appeal to the Court of Appeal is conferred by **R59.1.29**
particular statutes in respect of the decisions of certain other tribunals. (*e.g.* the Transport Tribunal (Transport Act 1985, s.117 and Sched. 4, para. 14), the Commons Commissioners (Commons Registration Act 1965, s.18(2)), and the Foreign Compensation Commission (Foreign Compensation Act 1969, s.3(2)(8)). In certain circumstances, and with the consent of the parties and the leave of the Court of Appeal, there can be a "leap frog" appeal directly to the Court of Appeal from a decision of the VAT Tribunal or the Special Commissioners of Income Tax (see O.59, r.22 and r.25).

Alternatives to appeal to Court of Appeal—In certain cases the matter should be dealt with by **R59.1.30**
way of a further application to the court below rather than an appeal to the Court of Appeal, *e.g.*:

(i) where the order of the court below was made *ex parte* (see para. R59.1.3, above);
(ii) an application to the court below for the order to be varied or discharged where there has been a change of circumstances since the original order was made (*ibid.*);
(iii) an application to the court below for the order to be set aside on the grounds that it was made in the absence of the party concerned; (ibid)
(iv) an application to the court below for a rehearing where the rules provide for such a rehearing (*ibid.*).

Judicial review—For the avenues of appeal in judicial review proceedings see paras R53.14.22 **R59.1.31**
and R53.14.92, above.

R59.1.31A **Appeals are against orders, not reasoned judgments**—Appeal lies against the order made by the Judge, not against the reasons he gave for his decision (*Lake v. Lake* [1955] P.336; [1955] 2 All E.R. 538, CA). Thus a party who has succeeded in obtaining, or, as the case may be, resisting, all relief sought cannot appeal even though he disagrees with the reasons which the Judge has given for deciding all points in his favour. On the other hand, if a party has succeeded in obtaining, or resisting, only part of the relief sought, he can, of course, appeal against the order to the extent that he was unsuccessful.

R59.1.32 **Restrictions on appealing**—There are numerous provisions which restrict the right to appeal. Restrictions may be absolute (*e.g.* there is no appeal at all against the grant by the court below of an extension of time for appealing to the court below: see para. R59.1.73, below. There are other restrictions on appealing. In almost all cases where an appeal lies to the Court of Appeal permission to appeal is now required (see O.59, r.1B and paras R59.1B.1 *et seq.*). In some cases an appeal is confined to questions of law (see para. R59.1.90 below).

R59.1.33 **Enquiries and information**—Enquiries relating to setting down of appeals or applications, or about other matters of Court of Appeal procedure should be made to the Civil Appeals Registry (Room E330). Bundles of documents for the use of the Lords Justices, and skeleton arguments, should be lodged in the Civil Appeals Documents Room (Room E307).

All enquiries about appeal and application bundles should be made to the relevant Case Management Section (see further para. R59.1.37, below).

Listing of appeals and applications is dealt with by the Listing Office (Room E306).

The Royal Courts of Justice telephone exchange has direct dialling facilities for outside callers.

R59.1.34 **Direct-dial enquiry numbers**—The direct-dial enquiry numbers for the various offices are:

- *Registry*: 0171–936–6409 or 6916
- *Case Management Sections*: 0171–936–6184 (that number is only for general enquiries; if the caller has received a letter from the Civil Appeals Office with a direct line number shown on it, that number should be dialled instead, because it will give direct access to the administrative assistant in the Case Management Section assigned to the case).
- *Documents Room*: 0171–936–6533
- *Listing Office*: 0171–936–6195 or 6917

[THE NEXT PARAGRAPH IS R59.1.37.]

R59.1.37 **Civil Appeals Office**—The Civil Appeals Office is divided into a number of sections; the areas of responsibility of each are as follows:

R59.1.38 *Registry*—The Civil Appeals Registry (Room E330) deals with the receipt of notices of appeal, summonses and notices of *ex parte* application. They may be lodged by personal attendance, by post or by DX. On receipt the administrative staff will carry out a *preliminary* check on such matters as whether the relevant time limits have been complied with, whether a copy of the order sought to be appealed has been lodged, and whether the correct fee has been paid. If the appeal or application appears to be in order, they will then enter it on the computer and a letter (generated by the computer) will be sent to the solicitor for the appellant or applicant (or to the appellant or applicant, if acting in person) acknowledging that the case has been entered in the records of the Court and giving information about what further steps need to be taken. The file will then be passed to the relevant Case Management Section.

R59.1.39 *Case Management Sections*—Under new arrangements, which came into effect in February 1998, four new Case Management Sections were set up within the Civil Appeals office. Each Section is headed by a Civil Appeals Office Lawyer who works to one or more of the Supervising Lords Justices (see para. R59.1.44, below); because Section 2 (county court and family cases) has a very large caseload, there are two Office Lawyers assigned to that Section. Subject to the oversight of the Supervising Lords Justices and any directions given by the Registrar, each Case Management Section is responsible for dealing with the appeals and applications assigned to that Section from the point of time when they have been passed to it from the Registrar following entry on the computer until they have been heard or otherwise determined (save for listing which is still dealt with centrally by the Civil Appeals Listing Office).

The allocation of cases to the Case Management Sections is designed to reflect, so far as practicable, the division of appeals between the Supervising Lords Justices (see para. R59.1.44).

Cases (*i.e.* appeals and applications) are allocated to the Case Management Sections as follows:

Case Section 1	All Queen's Bench cases (other than Commercial and Crown Office) and applications and appeals from Social Security and Child Support Commissioners
Case Section 2	All county court cases and all family cases (both High Court and county court)
Case Section 3	All Chancery, Patent, Commercial, Admiralty and Bankruptcy cases and applications and appeals from all Tribunals (except the Immigration Appeals Tribunal and the Social Security and Child Support Commissioners)
Case Section 4	Crown Office and all other public law cases (including applications and appeals from the Immigration Appeals Tribunal)

Case management support—Documents Room—There is a Case Management Support section which includes within its scope the Civil Appeals Documents Room, and also deals (*inter alia*) with the administration of the Dismissal List. **R59.1.40**

Listing Office—Listing of all appeals and applications to the Court of Appeal (Civil Division) is dealt with centrally by the Civil Appeals Listing Office (Room E306). For a detailed account of the listing system see para. R59.1.45, below. **R59.1.41**

Associates' Office—All court of Appeal orders are drawn by the Court's Associates, and not by the parties. When the order has been drawn, the Associate will seal it and send copies to all solicitors who are on the record and to any party acting in person. **R59.1.42**

Court of Appeal records—computerisation—The Court of Appeal records are kept on a computer and cause books are no longer used. Appeals and applications are entered on the computer after they have been set down and alphabetical lists of appeals and applications in the form of computer print-outs are available in the Civil Appeals Registry (Room E330) for inspection by the public, in the same way as the cause books were previously publicly available. **R59.1.43**

The CA reference comprises four elements: a List Code, a two-digit year indicator, the appeal/application number, and a Progress Group reference.

In the case of appeals, the first element, the List Code, will consist of five alphabetical characters, the first four of which denote the List in which the appeal has been set down, with the fifth being either an F (appeal against a final order) or an I (appeal against an interlocutory order).

In the case of applications (as opposed to appeals) the List Code consists of three characters indicating whether it will be heard by the full Court, a single Lord Justice, or the Master. The application List Codes are:

FC3 (an application to be heard by a three-Judge Court),

FC2 (an application to be heard by a two-Judge Court),

LTA (an application for leave to appeal which is to be listed for oral hearing before a two- or three-Judge Court),

SLJ (an application to a single Lord Justice),

REG (an application to the Master).

The second element in the Court of Appeal reference number consists of two digits denoting the year in which the appeal or application was set down (*i.e.* lodged with the Civil Appeals Office).

The third element is the four-digit appeal or application number. Appeals are numbered 0001 onwards, and applications are numbered 5001 onwards.

The final element in the reference is /CMS followed by a single digit denoting which Case Management Section is responsible for the case. (The Case Management Sections and the types of case allocated to each are listed in para. R59.1.39.)

Supervising Lords Justices—In November 1997 Lord Woolf, the Master of the Rolls, established a team of Lords Justices (known as Supervising Lords Justices) to oversee groups of appeals (see the 1999 Practice Direction, para. 4.1). The membership of the team will change from time to time; the names of the current Supervising Lords Justices and their areas of responsibility are set out in Annex D to the 1999 Practice Direction. **R59.1.44**

The Supervising Lords Justices will normally deal with applications for expedition and they will also give directions concerning the progress and future conduct of appeals, both of their own motion and on the application of any party (1999 Practice Direction, para. 4.2.2). In the interests of saving costs directions will be given on paper wherever possible (*ibid.*, para. 4.2.3). Where a hearing does prove to be necessary, it will normally be before the Supervising Lord Justice in chambers and it will be kept as short and informal as possible (*ibid.*, para 4.2.4).

In order to ensure that all requests for directions are centrally monitored and correctly allocated, all requests for directions or rulings (whether relating to listing or any other matters) must be addressed and sent to the Senior Listing Officer, Civil Appeals Listing Office (Room E306). Those seeking directions or rulings must not in any circumstances attempt to communicate with the Supervising Lord Justice (or any other Lord Justice) either directly or via his or her clerk (*ibid.*, para. 4.2.5). When directions have been given on paper they will be transmitted to the relevant parties' advisers via the Listing Office. Any queries should be made to the Senior Listing Officer and not to the Lord Justice or the Lord Justice's clerk.

R59.1.45 **Court of Appeal Listing**—Listing for the Court of Appeal (Civil Division) is dealt with centrally by the Civil Appeals Listing office (Room E329; for telephone numbers see para. R59.1.33, above). The listing arrangements are as follows:

R59.1.46 **Appeals**—Except in the case of appeals in the priority categories (*e.g.* child cases, appeals against certain interlocutory orders, contempt appeals, expedited appeals, and any other cases where the Court has otherwise directed) a hearing date will not normally be arranged until: (i) the appeal bundles have been lodged and any defects remedied; (ii) counsel's certified time estimate has been lodged; and (iii) the Civil Appeals Office has been supplied with details of the counsel who are to be briefed on the appeal.

R59.1.47 *Certified estimates*—Not later than 14 days after the appeal was entered in the records of the Court, the appellant's advocate is required:

(a) to lodge with the Civil Appeals Office his/her certified estimate (on a form which is supplied to the appellant's solicitors as Annex B enclosed with the letter from the Civil Appeals Office notifying them that the appeal has been so entered); and

(b) to forward a photocopy of his/her estimate to the respondent's advocate. The respondent's advocate is required to consider the appellant's advocate's estimate immediately on receiving it, and if the respondent's advocate's own estimate differs he/she must notify the Civil Appeals Office in writing (on the photocopy of the estimate form) of his/her own estimate forthwith. In the absence of such notification the respondent's advocate is deemed to accept the appellant's counsel estimate as his/her own (see the 1999 Practice Direction, para. 5.12.1).

A copy of the time estimate must be placed and kept with each advocate's papers. Each time the advocate for any party is asked to give any advice or to deal with anything in connection with the appeal, he/she must look at the time estimate and see whether it is still correct (*ibid.* para. 5.12.3). Any revised time estimate must be lodged with the Civil Appeals Office *in writing* signed by the advocate concerned. No account will be taken of revised time estimates given by any other means; in particular no notice will be taken of revised time estimates given over the telephone.

The Listing Officers place considerable reliance on advocates' time estimates for the purposes of arranging hearing dates and managing the list. It is therefore essential that realistic estimates be given. If a time estimate is increased after the hearing has been arranged it is likely that the appeal (or application) may have to be adjourned to a much later date, particularly if the estimate has been revised at a late stage.

Where appropriate, the Court will form its own view of how long the hearing should be allowed to take and will impose time limits on oral argument accordingly (*ibid.*, para. 5.12.3).

R59.1.48 *"Hear-by" Dates*—In order to ensure, so far as possible, that appeals are heard in order in the List to which they have been assigned each appeal is given a "hear-by" date when it is initially entered in the records of the Court. In the absence of a direction from the Court for expedition or deferment, the aim is that each appeal should be heard not significantly earlier nor significantly later than its "hear-by" date (see the 1999 Practice Direction, para 6.1.1). The table in para. R59.1.61, below sets out the current "hear-by" dates (measured in months from the date on which the appeal was entered in the Court's records) for each species of appeal. That system does not, however, apply to cases assigned to the Short Warned List; cases in that List may be called on considerably earlier than their "hear-by" dates or, in some cases later. When an SWL case will be called on depends upon when and where gaps occur in the Court of Appeal list (see below).

R59.1.49 *Arranging hearing dates*—Court of Appeal hearing dates are arranged with counsel's clerks. It is the responsibility of the clerk to each counsel concerned to inform his/her instructing solicitors of the hearing date. Where a solicitor holding a Higher Courts Advocacy Qualification is appearing the hearing date will be arranged with that solicitor's office. Appellants or respondents acting in person will be informed of the hearing date by letter from the Listing Officer. (Respondents in person should, at the earliest possible stage, inform the Civil Appeals Office in writing of the address to which they wish notification of the hearing date to be given. See the form of notice to respondents in person annexed to the end of the standard form of notice of appeal.

Apart from very urgent appeals (see below) and other cases where special directions are given, appeals are divided into three categories for listing purposes: (1) those which are given fixed dates ("fixtures"); (2) those which are given fixed dates, but double-booked ("second fixtures") and (3) those which are assigned to the Short Warned List ("SWL cases"). The majority of cases are given one or other type of fixture. The remainder are assigned to the Short Warned List. SWL cases are put "on call" from a specified date and are then called on for hearing at short notice as and when spaces occur in the Court of Appeal list.

Fixtures—Fixtures are advance bookings of hearing dates arranged with counsel's clerks, usually several months ahead. In the case of fixtures, the hearing is due to commence on the specified date, or the next following sitting day, *at the option of the Court.* All hearing dates, including fixtures, are, however, subject to any overrun of a preceding case, the interposition of a very urgent expedited matter, judicial illness, or other exigencies. If, by reason of an overrun or some other problem, it does not prove to be possible for the Court concerned to take the appeal on the specified date or on the next following sitting day, and the Listing Officer is unable to transfer the appeal to another court, a fresh date will be fixed with counsel's clerks. (See the 1999 Practice Direction, para 6.2). **R59.1.50**

Second Fixtures—Some appeals (and applications) are designated by the Court as "second fixtures". A second fixture is an advanced booking arranged with counsel's clerks, but on the express basis that the list is already fully booked for the period in question and the case will be heard on the date(s) booked only if a suitable gap occurs in the list. Any second fixture for which space does not become available will be given a first fixture on the earliest convenient date (see the 1999 Practice Direction, para. 6.3). **R59.1.51**

SWL Cases—The cases assigned to the Short Warned List are the shorter less complicated appeals and Full Court applications. The system applicable to SWL cases is as follows: **R59.1.52**

(1) The parties' solicitors are notified (by letter from the Civil Appeals Office) that the case has been assigned to the Short Warned List.
(2) Skeleton arguments must be lodged with the Civil Appeals Office within 14 days of the receipt by the solicitors of that letter.
(3) It is the duty of the solicitors to all parties (whether appellants or respondents) on receipt of that letter from the Civil Appeals Office to inform their advocates forthwith of the fact that the case has been assigned to the Short Warned List, and of the date on which the skeleton arguments are due, and to provide their advocates with all necessary instructions and papers to enable them to lodge their skeleton arguments timeously.
(4) When the skeleton arguments have been lodged, the Listing Office will notify counsel's clerks by telephone of the date from which the SWL case will be "on call" and it will remain in the Short Warned List liable to be called on either on half a day's notice or (if the Master has so directed) on 48 hours' notice. The Listing Officers will put SWL cases "on call" in such numbers and from such dates as the state of the List requires.
(5) When a case has been assigned to the Short Warned List, it is the duty of solicitors to inform their lay clients of that fact and of the consequences of assignment of the case to that list. It is important that this is done so that the clients are not taken by surprise if, as is quite likely to be the case, they have to be represented by a different advocate. (See paras. 6.4.1 to 6.5.7 of the 1999 Practice Direction.)

How long it will be before an SWL case is called on for hearing will depend on what gaps occur in the Court of Appeal list; an appeal may remain in the Short Warned List for some time. Experience has shown that there are certain cases which are appropriate for assignment to the Short Warned List, but where substitute counsel would require rather more than half a day's notice to prepare; the Master designates such cases as SWL cases to be called on for hearing on 48 hours' notice.

The Short Warned List does not proceed on the assumption (which would be quite unrealistic) that the parties' counsel of first choice can guarantee to be available for a Court of Appeal hearing on half a day's notice over a period which may be as much as 12 weeks or more. SWL cases are selected on the basis that they are appeals which can reasonably be prepared by substitute counsel at about half a day's notice (or 48 hours' notice, as the case may be). If any party's advocate is, *for whatever reason,* not available to appear on the date for which and SWL case is called on, then a substitute advocate must be instructed immediately; time should not be spent asking that the case should not be called on for that particular date because the advocate is unavailable, nor should the transfer of instructions to a substitute advocate be delayed in the hope that something will occur which will enable the original advocate to appear (see the 1999 Practice Direction, paras 6.5.3 to 6.5.7).

SWL cases are not called on in chronological order of setting down or assignment to the Short Warned List; which SWL case will be called on will depend on the length of the gap, the subject matter of the case and the constitution of the court. Because the number of CA cases which settle at the last minute, or go short, varies enormously, it is not possible to predict when any particular SWL case will be called on for hearing (see para. 6.4.1 of the 1999 Practice Direction).

Any application to take a case out of the Short Warned List must be made by letter addressed to the Master as soon as the parties' solicitors have been notified that the case has been assigned to the Short Warned List (*i.e.* at stage (1) above); it is not acceptable to wait until counsel's clerks have been notified of the "on call" date. *A fortiori*, it is far too late to apply for a fixed date at the stage when the SWL case is actually called on for hearing. It is not a valid ground for taking a case out of the Short Warned List that the parties' advocates of first choice may not be available to represent them at the Court of Appeal hearing (see the 1999 Practice Direction, para. 6.5.5). An SWL case will only be taken out of that list if it is, viewed objectively, one which cannot be properly presented save by a particular advocate (*ibid.* para. 6.5.2). Applications to remove cases from the SWL will be dealt with either by a supervising Lord Justice or the Master (*ibid.*). Generally such applications are decided with on paper without a hearing.

It is important that all concerned should appreciate that SWL cases remain on call, on half a day's notice, or 48 hours' notice, as the case may be, until they are called on for hearing. The Listing Officers have no authority to take cases out of the Short Warned List. It follows that there is no point in solicitors or counsel's clerks, on learning that a case has been assigned to the Short Warned List, making requests to the Listing Officers that it be given a fixed date, or contending that it is not suitable to be an SWL case. The question whether a case should be taken out of the Short Warned List and any directions relating to SWL cases are matters to be determined judicially by a supervising Lord Justice or the Master, not decided by the Listing Officers. The Listing Officers have standing instructions from the Master not to give any direction or assurance that an SWL will not be called on for hearing on any particular date, or to give any indication as to when it is likely to be called on. In most cases they will not know until a late stage what gaps will occur in the list. It is therefore pointless for counsel's clerks to ask the Listing Officers when an SWL case is likely to be called on for hearing, or to put in pleas that it should not be listed on certain dates because counsel will not be available on those dates.

R59.1.53 *Skeleton arguments*—The provision of skeleton arguments for all appeals, applications for permission to appeal, and Full Court applications is mandatory, except where the case is heard as a matter of great urgency, or where the Court otherwise directs.

R59.1.54 *Lists of authorities*—Lists of authorities must still be lodged with the Head Usher's office for Court of Appeal cases, notwithstanding the fact that the authorities and references thereto will be set out in the skeleton arguments (see the 1999 Practice Direction, para. 10.1.4). Lists of authorities are still required because the skeleton arguments are sent straight to the Lords Justices and the ushers do not have access to them (*ibid.*). Advocates must ensure that the lists of authorities are delivered to the Head Usher's office not later than 5.30 p.m. on the working day before the hearing is due to commence. It is important that this deadline should be adhered to, so that the ushers are able to assemble the requisite number of the law reports, statutes and other books in time for the hearing to start promptly. The list of authorities must include an accurate description of the law report, statute or other book, together with the page(s) to be referred to, so that the ushers can flag the relevant page(s). Advocates should also seek confirmation that an adequate number of copies are available for the use of the Court and, if this is not the case, should themselves provide an appropriate number of photocopies (*ibid.*).

R59.1.55 *Citation of authorities*—In the Court of Appeal (as in the House of Lords) the practice is that, if a case is reported on the official Law Reports published by the Incorporated Council of Law Reporting, that report should be cited.

R59.1.56 *Expedition*—Applications for expedition are normally dealt with by the relevant Supervising Lord Justice or the Master; (for the procedure to be adopted where the appeal requires exceptional expedition, *i.e.* needs to be heard within days or hours of the decision in the court below, see the sub-heading "Very urgent appeals" below). In the interests of saving time and costs, the Court deals with as many requests for expedition as possible on paper without a hearing. Requests for expedition should be made initially by a letter (or fax) from the applicant's solicitor or counsel, addressed to the Master, stating why the case is considered fit for expedition and what degree of expedition is sought. A copy of that letter, or fax, *MUST* be sent to the solicitors (or counsel) to any other parties to the appeal, so that they know at the earliest possible stage that an expedited hearing is being applied for and why (see para. 6.6.1 of the 1999 Practice Direction). The letter requesting expedition should be accompanied by a transcript or note of the judgment being appealed, draft grounds of appeal (if the appeal has not already been set down) and a *realistic* advocate's time estimate. Where, however, a very urgent hearing is sought (see further below) the letter or fax should be sent to the Master (with a copy to the other side) without waiting for the transcript or note of judgment and the draft grounds of appeal, so that the Court has the maximum possible notice that such a high degree of expedition is sought (*ibid.* para. 6.6.2).

For guidance on the criteria which the Court takes into account in deciding whether or not to grant expedition see paras 6.6.3 to 6.7.6 of the 1999 Practice Direction.

R59.1.57 *Very urgent appeals*—Where an appeal needs to be heard exceptionally expeditiously—within days or hours of the matter being determined in the court below—the solicitors concerned or the clerks to their counsel should contact the Listing Office at the earliest possible moment, particularly if it is a case where it is sought to have the appeal heard on the same day as the hearing in the court below. In such cases it is a considerable help to the Listing Officers if someone alerts them to the possibility of an appeal even before the case has been concluded in the court below.

Where a case is thought to require a very urgent hearing the solicitors, or counsel's chambers, should telephone the Civil Appeals Listing Office at the earliest possible stage. The caller must have available as much as possible of the following information:

(1) the name of the matter;
(2) details of the court below;
(3) the terms of the order appealed against and the nature of the proceedings in the court below;
(4) the names and telephone numbers of all solicitors and counsel involved in the case;
(5) the reasons why an urgent hearing is sought and how soon the appeal needs to be heard; in particular whether there is any relevant specific deadline;
(6) whether any "holding order" pending appeal has been applied for in the court below and what the result of that application was; and
(7) a *realistic* estimate of the likely length of the Court of Appeal hearing.

In all cases where a very urgent hearing is sought, counsel's (or solicitor's) note of judgment must be typed up as soon as any decision to appeal is contemplated, because that is the most important document for any urgent appeal or application. The note of judgment must be typed up *before* any draft notice or grounds of appeal are prepared.

It is most important, in any case where a very urgent Court of Appeal hearing is being sought, that the other party(ies) are informed of this either before or immediately after the appellant's side have made the initial contact with the Civil Appeals Listing Office. The purpose of that requirement is so that the respondent(s) have the maximum possible time to instruct counsel and prepare themselves for a Court of Appeal hearing at such short notice. It is most unfair if a respondent's legal advisers have less time to prepare for the urgent hearing than the appellant's side.

Once the Civil Appeals Listing Officer has the requisite information, a decision will then be taken whether the case is sufficiently urgent to merit the degree of expedition sought. Unless the case is self-evidently urgent, the request for an urgent hearing will be referred to a Supervising Lord Justice, or the Master, for judicial determination.

The court, may well need further information about the case and the reasons for urgency. Such information must be provided as soon as possible. Either counsel, or the solicitor who has conduct of the case, must be prepared to speak to the Listing Officer or the Master if requested to do so, particularly if the case is complicated. That way the matter will be explained to the office correctly and any queries raised will be accurately answered (see the observations of Lord Donaldson M.R. in *Normid Housing Association v. Mansell, The Times*, May 27, 1988).

Where a case is so exceptionally urgent that it needs a hearing out of normal court hours, either solicitors or counsel's chambers should telephone the Royal Courts of Justice Security Desk (0171–936–6260).

Applications—Listing of full Court applications is dealt with in the same way as listing of appeals (see above). **R59.1.58**

In the case of applications to a single Lord Justice or the Master, the application notice should state that the application will be heard "on a date and at a time to be notified by the Civil Appeals Office", and, when the documents are in order, the Listing Office will notify the applicant (and, if the application is *inter partes*, the respondent(s)) by letter of the hearing date. Applications for permission to appeal (with or without an application for an extension of time for appealing and/or a stay of execution) are normally referred to by a single Lord Justice for consideration on paper without a hearing.

Expedition and very urgent applications—What is said above about expedition and arrangements for very urgent appeals applies equally to applications. **R59.1.59**

Unless the Court otherwise directs, all applications which merit exceptionally expeditious treatment are listed for oral hearing with all parties invited to attend. That is so even if the application is of a type which would, in the absence of a direction for exceptional expedition, be dealt with on paper, or at a hearing without notice (*e.g.* an application for leave to appeal and a stay of execution). The reason is that where an application needs to be heard within a very short timescale it is not satisfactory to deal with the matter at a hearing without notice because the other side would be entitled to apply to have the order discharged or varied and that would necessitate arranging a second very urgent hearing when there was even less time to spare. The Listing Officers have no power to vary the Court's directions and therefore lawyers and their clerks should not take up precious time pleading for, still less demanding, a hearing without notice, or a decision on paper.

Adjournments—An application to postpone the hearing of an appeal or application will not be granted as a matter of course, even if made by consent, but some good and sufficient reason must be shown (*Bird v. Andrew* (1887) 4 T.L.R. 7; *Unilever Computer Services Ltd v. Tiger Leasing SA* **R59.1.60**

[1983] 1 W.L.R. 856; [1983] 2 All E.R. 139, CA). An application for adjournment of any appeal or application should be made to the Senior Listing Officer.

R59.1.61 **"Hear-by" dates**—The current Hear-by Dates are set out in the table below. They apply to all cases entered in the Court's records on or after December 1, 1998.

TYPE OF CASE		"Hear-by" Date
Family	Child cases	3 months
	Financial and other	6 months
Crown Office Cases and Immigration appeals	Immigration Appeals and Crown Officer Interlocutory	3 months
	Other Crown Office final Orders	9 months
High Court	Order 14	3 months
	Other interlocutory orders*	5 months
	Bankruptcy and Directors' Disqualification cases	5 months
	Limitation as a preliminary issue in personal injury cases	5 months
	All other preliminary issues	8 months
	Personal injury final orders	12 months
	Other final orders	15 months
County Court	Interlocutory orders	4 months
	Possession	4 months
	All preliminary issues	4 months
	Personal injury final orders	8 months
	Other final orders	12 months
Tribunals (other than immigration appeals)		12 months

* includes appeals confined to RSC O.14A. For appeals referring to O.14A and another issue, the Hear-by Date will be determined by the other issue.

R59.1.61A **September Sittings in the Court of Appeal**—The Court of Appeal sets in vacations as the Master of the Rolls may direct and hears such appeals and applications in vacation as the Court may direct (see the 1999 Practice Direction, para. 10.8.1). An appeal or application can be listed before the Civil Division in August or September without any order or direction that it is "vacation business", although most cases listed in those months will, in practice, be urgent matters.

R59.1.62 **Constitution of Court**—Except where the legislation otherwise provides, a Court must consist of an uneven number of judges not less than three (SCA 1981, s.54(2)). Two-judge Courts are, however, empowered to hear certain types of appeal, including the following: appeals against interlocutory orders or interlocutory judgments, county courts appeals (whether final or interlocutory), applications for leave to appeal, appeals against any decision of a single Lord Justice exercising the incidental jurisdiction of the Court of Appeal by virtue of s.58(1), and appeals where all the parties have, prior to the appeal hearing, consented in writing to the appeal being heard by two judges (*ibid.*, s.54(4)). (See further SCP 1999, Vol. 2, Section 20A, paras 20A–404 *et seq.*) Where the members of a two-judge court disagree either party has the right to a re-hearing before a three-judge court (*ibid.*, s.54(5)).

Unless the full Court, a single Lord Justice, or the Master otherwise directs, an appeal which two Lords Justices would have jurisdiction to hear will be listed before a two-judge Court.

Where any party to an appeal considers that the appeal involves points of such difficulty or such importance to the general law as to require a hearing before three Lords Justices, the party concerned should apply to the Master for the appeal to be heard by a three-judge court. That application should be made by a letter from counsel or the solicitors acting for the party concerned. (It is not sufficient for counsel's clerks to tell the Listing Office that a three-judge court is requested.) The letter to the Master from counsel or the solicitors should set out the reasons why it is thought that a three-judge court is required. Normally the Master will deal with that application on paper, without a hearing. The Master may make a direction for a three-judge court of his own motion (see the 1999 Practice Direction, para. 5.9.1).

In any case where points of real difficulty arise, counsel should consider whether an application for a three-judge court should be made (*Coldunell Ltd v. Gallon* [1986] Q.B. 1184 at 1202; [1986] 1 All E.R. 429 at 441). Consideration should be given to that question as soon as the notice of appeal has been served, and, if it is concluded that the appeal does merit hearing before three Lords Justices, the application should be made to the Master as soon as the appeal has been set down. If an application for a three-judge court is made and granted after a hearing date has been fixed, it is highly likely that the date will have to be vacated; and a fresh date in a three-judge court will be unlikely to be available until some months later. Once a direction for hearing before a three-judge court has been made, the court will not rescind that direction in order to preserve an existing hearing date before a two-judge court.

Dismissal of appeals by consent—compromise of appeals

Straightforward dismissals by consent—Where an appellant does not wish to continue with his appeal, it can be dismissed by consent on paper without a hearing. The procedure is as follows. A form of request for dismissal by consent ("a DBC") must be signed and sent to the Registrar of Civil Appeals. After setting out the appeal number and the names of the parties; the DBC must contain the following words: **R59.1.63**

> "We, the solicitors for the above-named Appellant [and Respondent], who [is] [are] *sui juris*, hereby request the dismissal of the appeal in the above matter with [costs] [no order as to costs] or [specify what other order for costs is required]."

Applications to the CA (whether to the full Court, a single Lord Justice, or the Registrar) can be dismissed by consent using the above form of words, substituting "application" and "Applicant" for "appeal" and "Appellant".

For the current forms of DBC see paras R59.1.65 to 66, below and the 1999 Practice Direction, Annex I.

If the appeal is being dismissed with costs, only the appellant's solicitors need sign the DBC. If there is an agreement either that there be no order as to costs, or that costs should be less than the full taxed costs, the solicitors to all parties must sign. Where any party is legally aided, the DBC should request legal aid taxation of his costs. Where a party has no solicitors on the record, the DBC must be signed by that party personally and the form of words should be appropriately altered. When the DBC has been lodged with the Master he, or a Lord Justice, will, if it is in order, initial it. The effect of that is that the appeal is thereby dismissed, and it will be removed from the list (see the 1999 Practice Direction, para. 10.4.). An order will be drawn and issued by the CA Associates. For the position relating to DBC's and other consent orders where an infant or a mental patient is a party, see paras R59.1.71 and R59.1.73A, below.

Effect of dismissal by consent on a cross-appeal or respondent's notice—The dismissal of an appeal does not affect a respondent's notice under r.6 if it asks that the decision of the court below should be varied in any event: or if it is a respondent's notice by way of cross-appeal. The respondent has a right to elect whether to proceed with it as a cross-appeal or to withdraw it (*Re Cavander's Trusts* (1881) 16 Ch.D. 1270, CA). If he proceeds, the former appellant may serve a respondent's notice saying that he intends to bring forward the subject-matter of his original notice of appeal (*The Beeswing* (1885) 10 P.D. 18). **R59.1.64**

R59.1.65 **Form of DBC—Appeals**

PLEASE NOTE SECTION A IS TO BE COMPLETED WHERE THERE IS NO RESPONDENT'S NOTICE AND THE APPEAL IS BEING DISMISSED WITH COSTS. WHERE SECTION A IS APPLICABLE, ONLY THE APPELLANT'S SOLICITOR (OR THE APPELLANT, IF ACTING IN PERSON) NEED SIGN.

IN ALL OTHER CASES SECTION B MUST BE COMPLETED AND IT MUST BE SIGNED BY THE SOLICITORS FOR ALL PARTIES (AND BY ANY PARTY ACTING IN PERSON).

IN THE COURT OF APPEAL
ON APPEAL FROM

Appeal No. ....

BETWEEN:

Claimant (Plaintiff)/Appellant
Petitioner/Respondent

and

Defendant/Appellant
Respondent/Respondent

Section A

WE, the solicitors* for the above-named Appellant, who is of full legal capacity, HEREBY REQUEST the dismissal of the appeal in the above matter with costs.

DATED this day of 19

(Signed) ....
*(Solicitor for Appellant)

Section B

WE, the solicitors* for the above-named Respondent and Appellant, who are of full legal capacity, HEREBY REQUEST the dismissal of the appeal [*and respondent's notice*]† in the above matter with no order as to costs [*or specify other costs order required*].

DATED this day of 19

(Signed) ....
*(Solicitor for Appellant)

(Signed) ....
*(Solicitor for Respondent)

**If any party is acting in person, please modify the wording as appropriate.*
†*Delete where not applicable*

Form of DBC—Applications R59.1.66

PLEASE NOTE SECTION A IS TO BE COMPLETED WHERE THE APPLICATION IS BEING DISMISSED WITH COSTS. WHERE SECTION A IS APPLICABLE, ONLY THE APPLICANT'S SOLICITOR (OR THE APPLICANT, IF ACTING IN PERSON) NEED SIGN.

IN ALL OTHER CASES SECTION B MUST BE COMPLETED AND IT MUST BE SIGNED BY THE SOLICITORS FOR ALL PARTIES (AND BY ANY PARTY ACTING IN PERSON).

IN THE COURT OF APPEAL Application No. ....
ON APPEAL FROM

BETWEEN:

Claimant (Plaintiff)/Appellant
Petitioner/Respondent

and

Defendant/Appellant
Respondent/Respondent

Section A

WE, the solicitors* for the above-named Applicant, who is of full legal capacity, HEREBY REQUEST the dismissal of the appeal in the above matter with costs.

DATED this day of 19

(Signed) ....
*(Solicitor for Applicant)

Section B

WE, the solicitors* for the above-named Respondent and Applicant, who are of full legal capacity, HEREBY REQUEST the dismissal of the application in the above matter with no order as to costs [*or specify other costs order required*].

DATED this day of 19

(Signed) ....
*(Solicitor for Applicant)

(Signed) ....
*(Solicitor for Respondent)

**If any party is acting in person, please modify the wording as appropriate.*

R59.1.67 **Form of DBC—Applications (*without notice*)**

THIS FORM IS FOR USE ONLY FOR AN APPLICATION WHICH HAS NOT BEEN SERVED ON ANY OTHER PARTY.

IN THE COURT OF APPEAL
ON APPEAL FROM

Application No. ....

BETWEEN:

Claimant (Plaintiff)/Applicant
Petitioner/Respondent

and

Defendant/Applicant
Respondent/Respondent

WE, the solicitors* for the above-named Applicant, who is of full legal capacity,
(1) CERTIFY that that application in the above matter has not been served on any other party and

(2) REQUEST the dismissal of the said application with no order for costs.

DATED this day of 19

(Signed) ....
*(Solicitor for Applicant)

**If any party is acting in person, please modify the wording as appropriate.*

Can an appellant resile from a request for dismissal by consent?—The initialling by a Lord Justice of the Master Registrar of the request for dismissal by consent has the same effect as the making of an order in open court: unless and until the order has been drawn up and entered the Court has a discretion to alter the order and to allow the appeal to proceed (*Re Samuel* [1945] Ch. 364; [1945] 2 All E.R. 39, CA, and *James Lamont & Co. Limited v. Hyland Limited* [1950] 1 K.B. 585; [1950] 1 All E.R. 341, CA). In those circumstances, subject to questions of costs, the appeal may be allowed to proceed unless the respondent has altered his position or would be embarrassed (*ibid.*), or the appellant has agreed for good consideration to abandon his appeal (*National Benzole Co. Limited v. Gooch* [1961] 1 W.L.R. 1489; [1961] 3 All E.R. 1097). Whether there has been a contact not to proceed with the appeal will depend upon the facts of the particular case. Where a request for the appeal to be dismissed with costs has been signed that will not, by itself, amount to a contract, even if the respondent's side has signed; since the appellant can unilaterally request the dismissal of the appeal with costs, the signing by the respondent's side does not constitute consideration (*Re Samuel*, above). R59.1.68

Where, however, a request for dismissal by consent has been lodged and initialled and the order giving effect to it has been sealed, the appeal cannot be proceeded with either under the original notice of appeal or by a fresh notice of appeal: see *Ogwr Borough Council v. Knight, The Times*, January 13, 1994, where the Court of Appeal held that the appellant could not go behind a sealed order issued in response to a request for dismissal by consent. The Court of Appeal was *functus officio* and it was not open to the appellant to seek to revive the original appeal which had been dismissed at its request or to commence a new appeal by applying for an extension of time.

Settlement of appeals on terms—Where the parties have compromised the appeal on terms, those terms cannot be included in an order obtained by DBC. There is one exception to that: terms as to the costs of the appeal should be included in the DBC and in any resultant order. R59.1.69

The question then arises: What is the procedure for dealing with settlement of an appeal on terms? There are a number of possibilities:

(1) The terms can be included in a contract of compromise and a plain DBC lodged. In that event the order will simply record that the appeal has been dismissed by consent and set out the agreed costs order. If it becomes necessary to enforce the terms of the settlement, that will have to be done by bringing an action on the contract of compromise.

If any party wishes to have reference made in the consent order to the fact that the appeal has been compromised (rather than simply abandoned), the words "The parties having agreed terms . . ." can be added to the beginning of the DBC immediately before the words "We, the solicitors for the above-named . . ." Or, the terms of the settlement can be set out in the DBC (see para. 10.4.1 of the 1999 Practice Direction); but, if the agreed terms involve any variation of the order of the court below, that cannot be done by a DBC (see below).

(2) The parties can ask the Court of Appeal to make an order in the agreed terms. That may have the disadvantage of causing the parties to incur the costs of a hearing for mention. It should also be borne in mind that there are limits to the circumstances in which the Court of Appeal will allow an appeal by consent (see para. R59.1.71, below).

(3) The parties can ask the Court of Appeal to make a Tomlin order (*i.e.* that the appeal be stayed save for the purposes of enforcing the terms of the compromise (which will be set out in a schedule to the order) with liberty to apply for the purposes of enforcing those terms). If the Court of Appeal is persuaded that it is appropriate to make such an order, it will normally direct that the liberty to apply for the purpose of enforcing the terms be liberty to apply to the court below. Tomlin orders were made in *Lees v. Motor Insurers' Bureau* [1953] 1 W.L.R. 620, CA and in *Goulston Discount Co. Ltd v. Campbell* [1962] 1 W.L.R. 1425; [1962] 2 All E.R. 956, CA.

Not infrequently parties lodge DBCs which take the form of requesting that the appeal be dismissed by consent but also asking for terms to be inserted in the consent order which involve varying the judgment or order of the court below. *E.g.* on an appeal by a plaintiff who lost in the court below, the parties compromise the appeal by agreeing that the defendant will pay a specified amount by way of partial damages, and the solicitors lodge a DBC which asks for an order that the appeal be dismissed by consent, and that the defendant pay £x damages. The Court of Appeal cannot, and will not, make an order in that form, because it is a contradiction in terms. The Court of Appeal cannot make an order providing for payment of a sum by way of damages and at the same time dismiss the appeal against the judge's decision that the defendant is not liable to pay anything. The same applies to DBCs which purport to increase or decrease the amount of damages awarded by the judge, or to vary the costs order made by the court below. Such negotiated settlements must either be dealt with by a contract of compromise, followed by the lodging of a plain DBC (see above), or, where appropriate, by a request that the appeal be allowed by consent in whole or in part (but see para. R59.1.71 below).

Withdrawal of appeals—An appeal cannot be withdrawn without the leave of the Court (*Tod-Heatley v. Barnard* [1890] W.N. 130, CA). If an appeal is withdrawn, as opposed to being dismissed, it would appear that, subject to obtaining the necessary permission and/or extension of time, the appellant could proceed with an appeal by serving a fresh notice of appeal. For this and other reasons it is now the usual practice of the Court of Appeal to insist that appeals are either heard or disposed of by means of a dismissal by consent or other consent order. Only in rare circumstances will the Court of Appeal permit an appeal to be withdrawn. R59.1.70

R59.1.71 **Allowing appeals by consent**—The Court of Appeal has jurisdiction to allow an appeal by consent, but it does not exercise that jurisdiction unless the Court considers it appropriate to do so. If the consent order sought does no more than alter the relief granted, *e.g.* altering the quantum of damages, the percentages of contributory negligence or contribution, the terms of an injunction, or the incidence of costs, the Court of Appeal probably will make the consent order. The Court is also prepared to allow appeals by consent against orders of a procedural nature *e.g.* orders made on applications for summary judgment or for a default judgment to be set aside, interim injunctions and orders relating to disclosure. If, however, the consent order sought involves reversing the judge's decision on a point of law given at a final trial or hearing, the Court of Appeal will only make the order if special reasons are shown. The Court of Appeal will not declare that the judge's view of the law is wrong merely because the parties consent to an order which has that effect. Examples of cases where the Court of Appeal has allowed an appeal on points of law by consent are: where it was accepted by all parties that the legal submission on which the judgment was founded was wrong by reason of other statutory provisions which were not cited to the Judge (see *Nabi v. Heaton* [1983] 1 W.L.R. 626; [1983] S.T.C. 344), where the order made by the judge was one which neither party had asked for, and were the order made in the court below was contrary to Court of Appeal authority.

In order to save costs the Court of Appeal will generally make the an order on paper without a hearing in those cases where it is willing to allow an appeal by consent. Where such an order is sought, a draft of the proposed order signed by the solicitors to all parties (and stating that the parties are of full legal capacity), together with a document setting out the relevant background and the matters relied on as justifying the proposed order, should be sent to the Master so the that Court can consider whether it is appropriate to allow the appeal by consent and, if so, whether the order can be made on paper or whether the case needs to be listed for mention (see the 1999 Practice Direction, para. 10.5.1).

R59.1.72 **Consent orders where a party is an infant**—Where a party to an appeal (or application) is an infant, any settlement (whether taking the form of a dismissal by consent, or allowing the appeal or application by consent, or any other type of disposal by consent) must be approved by the Court of Appeal (*Walsh v. Geo. Kemp Ltd* [1938] W.N. 120; [1938] 2 All E.R. 266, CA); but, in order to save unnecessary expense to the parties, the question whether the consent order or settlement should be approved is now usually dealt with in court without the attendance of the parties or their advocates. The solicitors acting on behalf of the infant should lodge with the Master a copy of the proposed consent order signed by the solicitors to all parties together with an opinion from the advocate acting on behalf of the child stating why approval of the proposed settlement or consent order is recommended. In most cases the Court of Appeal will then dispose of the matter by listing the case for mention and dealing with the request for approval without any attendance (see *Hadfield v. Knowles* [1996] 1 W.L.R. 1004, CA and the 1999 Practice Direction, para. 10.7.1). Normally the parties' advocates will be asked to attend that hearing only if the Court has doubts about whether the proposed settlement or consent order should be approved or where there are other special reasons for having a hearing at which the parties are represented (*ibid.*, para. 10.7.2).

R59.1.73 **Structured settlements**—Where a structured settlement has been negotiated in a case which is under appeal, the above procedure should be adopted, but the documents filed should also include those which would be required for a structured settlement as first instance (see para. 10.7.1(c) of the 1999 Practice Direction).

R59.1.73A **Consent orders where a party is a mental patient**—Order 59, r.23 makes provision for a DBC to be signed on behalf of an appellant who is a patient within the meaning of the Mental Health Act by the receiver or other person authorised under that Act to conduct legal proceedings in the name of or on behalf of the patient. But, if the patient is a respondent, or the consent order takes some form other than a DBC, the consent order or other settlement must be approved by the Court of Appeal. In order to save costs the Court adopts the same procedure as it now does in the case of infants. In such cases the documents filed should also include any relevant reports prepared by the Court of Protection and a document evidencing formal approval by that court, where required (see para. 10.7.1(b) of the 1999 Practice Direction).

Restrictions on Appealing

Appeals prohibited by statute or by the RSC

R59.1.74 **In a criminal cause or matter**—Except as provided by A.J.A. 1960, s.13 no appeal lies to the

Court of Appeal from any judgment of the High Court in any criminal cause or matter. (S.C.A. 1981, s.18(1)(a)).

Meaning of "criminal cause or matter"—The intention was that no appeal to the Court of Appeal [Civil Division] should lie in any "criminal matter" in the widest sense of the term, the Court of Appeal being constituted for the purposes of hearing appeals in civil causes and matters. "The clause [*i.e.* what is now s.18(1)(a)] applies to a decision by way of judicial determination of any question raised in or with regard to proceedings, the subject matter of which is criminal, at whatever stage of the proceedings the question arises." (*Ex p. Woodhall* (1888) 20 Q.B.D. 835 at 836, *per* Lord Esher, CA). A matter may be criminal although no breach of the criminal law of England is charged. A matter will be a "criminal cause or matter" if it arises in any proceedings "the direct outcome of which may be trial of the applicant and his possible punishment for an alleged offence by a court claiming jurisdiction to do so". (*Amand v. Home Secretary* [1943] A.C. 147 at 156 (*per* Viscount Simon L.C.); *Re Clifford and O'Sullivan* [1921] 2 A.C. 570 at 580 (*per* Viscount Cave).) R59.1.75

Thus an appeal against conviction or sentence in respect of a criminal offence under English law, whether the trial was summary or on indictment, is a criminal cause or matter; and extradition proceedings and proceedings under the Fugitive Offenders Act are also criminal matters (*Ex p. Woodhall*, above; *R. v. Governor of Brixton Prison* [1910] 2 K.B. 1056; and *Cuoghi v. Governor of Brixton Prison* [1997] 1 W.L.R. 1346, CA). Proceedings concerned with mechanisms for obtaining evidence for the purposes of a prosecution or possible prosecution are criminal causes or matters (see *Day v. Grant* [1987] Q.B. 972; *Bonalumi v. Home Secretary* [1985] Q.B. 675; [1985] 1 All E.R. 797, CA; and *Carr v. Atkins* [1987] Q.B. 963; [1987] 3 All E.R. 684, below). On the other hand offences against the Prison Rules are not criminal causes or matters because those Rules are a code of private law applicable to a limited class of persons and not offences against public law triable before a criminal tribunal (*R. v. Board of Visitors of Hull Prison, ex p. St. Germain* [1979] Q.B. 425; [1979] 1 All E.R. 701, CA).

In *R. v. Secretary of State for the Home Department, ex p. G, The Times*, June 26, 1990 the Court of Appeal held that an application for judicial review of a decision by the Home Secretary refusing a request to refer a conviction or sentence to the Court of Appeal (Criminal Division) under s.17 of the Criminal Appeal Act 1968 was a "criminal cause or matter" and therefore the Court of Appeal had no jurisdiction to entertain an application for judicial review in respect of such a decision.

The Civil Division of the Court of Appeal thus has no jurisdiction to entertain an appeal in respect of a criminal cause or matter whether in judicial review proceedings or otherwise (see below). The avenues of appeal in the case of a criminal cause or matter are: in the case of trial on indictment appeal lies to the Criminal Division of the Court of Appeal; in the case of summary trial appeal lies from the magistrates' court either directly to the QBD Div. Ct by way of case stated, or to the Crown Court and thence to the QBD Div. Ct. Under A.J.A. 1960, s.1 appeal lies from the Div. Ct in a criminal cause or matter to the HL but only with the requisite certificate and leave prescribed by that section. Substantive applications for judicial review in the case of a criminal cause or matter are heard by the QBD Div. Ct. with the possibility of appeal to the HL under A.J.A. 1960, s.1 if the necessary certificate and leave have been granted.

A recommendation for deportation made by a magistrates' court or the Crown Court in respect of a convicted offender is a criminal cause or matter, but the implementation of that recommendation by the Home Office is a civil matter; thus, if judicial review proceedings are brought against the Home Secretary on the grounds of alleged irregularity in the implementation of the recommendation, the Civil Division of the Court of Appeal has jurisdiction to entertain an appeal or application in those judicial review proceedings and can quash the deportation order (if grounds for doing so are established), but it has no power to set aside or vary the recommendation for deportation (*R. v. Governor of Holloway Prison, ex p. Giambi* [1982] 1 W.L.R. 535; [1982] 1 All E.R. 434; *R. v. Secretary of State for the Home Department, ex p. Dannenberg* [1984] Q.B. 766; [1984] 2 All E.R. 481, CA). An application for mandamus to the Army Council in respect of a petition to mitigate, remit or commute a sentence imposed by a Court Martial is a criminal cause or matter (*R. v. Army Council, Ex p. Sandford* [1940] 1 K.B. 719, CA; *cf. Re Clifford and O'Sullivan*, above). An order of the court directing that a solicitor be struck off for misconduct is not made in a criminal cause or matter; it is the court exercising its disciplinary jurisdiction over its own officers (*Re Hardwick* (1883) 12 Q.B.D. 148, CA; *Re Eede* (1890) 25 Q.B.D. 228). A fine imposed on a convicted offender is a criminal matter, but where a statute provides for imposition of a monetary penalty as a civil debt that is not a criminal cause or matter (*R. v. Kerswill* [1895] 1 Q.B. 1 at p. 7). (For other cases on what is a criminal cause or matter see: *R. v. Commissioner of Metropolitan Police, ex p. Blackburn* [1968] 2 Q.B. 118; [1968] 1 All E.R. 763; *R. v. Southampton Justices, ex p. Green* [1976] Q.B. 11; [1975] 2 All E.R. 1073; (but see *Carr v. Atkins* [1987] Q.B. 963; [1987] 3 All E.R. 684, below. *L.B. of Camden v. Herwald* [1978] Q.B. 626; [1978] 2 All E.R. 880; *R. v. Sheffield Crown Court, ex p. Brownlow* [1980] Q.B. 530; [1980] 2 All E.R. 444; and *R. v. D.P.P., ex p. Raymond* (1980) 70 Cr.App.R. 233).

In *Day v. Grant* (above) and *R. v. Manchester Crown Court, ex p. Williams* [1987] Q.B. 972 (note); [1985] R.T.R. 299, CA it was held that appeals relating to the issue of witness summonses in criminal proceedings were criminal matters and the Civil Division of the CA had no jurisdiction to entertain them. The CA reviewed some of the previous authorities on what is a "criminal cause or matter" and distinguished the CA decisions in *R. v. Southampton JJ., ex p. Green* (above); *R. v. Sheffield Crown Court, ex p. Brownlow* (above), and *R. v. Lambeth Stipendiary Magistrate, ex p. McComb*

[1983] Q.B. 551; [1983] 1 All E.R. 321 on the grounds that the questions at issue in those cases were extrinsic to the criminal proceedings, whereas the question whether a witness should be required to attend or evidence should be produced in criminal proceedings was an intrinsic part of those proceedings.

In *Bonalumi v. Home Secretary* (above), CA, a High Court Judge made an order under section 7 of the Bankers' Books Evidence Act 1879 at the request of the Home Secretary for inspection of the applicant's bank accounts. The purpose of that order was to obtain evidence for use in criminal proceedings pending against the applicant in Sweden. The CA held that it has no jurisdiction to entertain an appeal against that Bankers' Books Evidence Act order because this was a criminal cause or matter. (The CA held that *R. v. Grossman* (1981) 73 Crim.App.R. 302 was decided *per incuriam* and declined to follow it.)

In *R. v. Bolton Magistrates' Court, ex p. Graeme, The Times*, March 14, 1986, the CA expressed the view that it had no jurisdiction to entertain an application for leave to move for judicial review in connection with a summons to bind over because that was a criminal cause or matter. In *R. v. Tottenham Justices, ex p. Ewing* (July 30, 1986, unrep.) the CA held that it has no jurisdiction to entertain any application for leave to move for judicial review in a criminal cause or matter. *A fortiori* it has no jurisdiction to entertain an appeal against a decision of the High Court given on a substantive judicial review application in a criminal cause or matter.

In *Carr v. Atkins* (above) the applicants sought judicial review by way of certiorari to quash orders made by a judge of the Crown Court under Sched. 1 of the Police and Criminal Evidence Act 1984. Those orders, which had been made on the application of the respondent detective chief inspector, required the applicants to produce documents to the police for the purposes of a criminal investigation. The substantive application for judicial review was heard and refused by the Q.B. Divisional Court. The applicants sought to appeal, and the Divisional Court ruled that it was a "criminal cause or matter" within the meaning of S.C.A. 1981, s.18(1)(a). (If it was rightly characterised as a criminal cause or matter, any appeal against the Divisional Court's decision would lie to the House of Lords, but only with leave and a certificate of a point of law of general public importance.)

The applicants sought to appeal to the Court of Appeal (Civil Division). On the preliminary issue of jurisdiction the Court of Appeal held:

(1) In deciding whether s.18(1)(a) applied in judicial review proceedings, what has to be considered is not the nature of the order granting or refusing judicial review, but the nature of the order or decision which is sought to be reviewed in the judicial review proceedings.

(2) Although the result in *R. v. Southampton Justices, ex p. Green* (above) had been upheld by the House of Lords in *Re Smalley* [1985] A.C. 622; [1985] 1 All E.R. 769, the reasoning in *Green's* case is no longer tenable, in the light of the decision in *Smalley*. (In *Green's* case the CA had held that an appeal by a surety against an order estreating her recognisance was not a criminal cause or matter because there was no "trial" of the surety, and the outcome of the proceedings would not be punishment of the surety for an offence.)

(3) Accordingly, the CA was free to depart from the reasoning in *Green's* case (and the reasoning in *R. v. Sheffield Crown Court, ex p. Brownlow* (above) and *R. v. Lambeth Stipendiary Magistrate, ex p. McComb* (above)) and look at the matter afresh. Looking at it afresh, these orders under P.A.C.E. were orders made in a criminal cause or matter because they were made for the purposes of a criminal investigation and possible prosecution. The CA therefore had no jurisdiction to entertain the applicants' proposed appeal against the Divisional Court's decision. The result in *Green's* case was justified on the grounds that questions of estreatment were so collateral to a criminal trial that they did not constitute a criminal cause of matter. S.18(1)(a) does not apply to an appeal against a garnishee order made by way of enforcement of compensation and costs orders made on conviction of an accused person, and therefore such an appeal can be entertained by the Civil Division of the Court of Appeal (*Gooch v. Ewing* [1986] Q.B. 791; [1985] 3 All E.R. 654, CA). In *Re O.* [1991] 2 Q.B. 520 the Court of Appeal held that a disclosure order in support of a restraint order made under the Drug Trafficking Offences Act 1986 was not a "criminal cause or matter", and therefore such an order could be appealed to the Civil Division of the Court of Appeal.

No appeal lies against the refusal by a Judge in Chambers to grant bail in criminal proceedings (appeal to the CA (Civil Div.) is precluded by S.C.A. 1981, s.18(1)(a) and there is no statute or rule which allows any other avenue of appeal; furthermore the applicant who has been refused bail cannot make a fresh application either to another Judge or a Div. Ct, see O.79, r.9(12)). No appeal lies from an order made by a single Judge of the High Court on a criminal application for habeas corpus (A.J.A. 1960, s.15(2)), but in relation to a decision of a Div. Ct on a criminal application for habeas corpus appeal lies to the HL with leave (*ibid.*, s.15(3)).

R59.1.76 *Contempt*—It is necessary to distinguish between civil contempt and criminal contempt. Civil contempt is committed where a person disobeys an order made in civil proceedings; process for civil contempt is designed to enforce obedience to the order and punish the disobedience. Failure to obey an order made in civil proceedings is not a crime and an appeal from the order punishing the civil contempt is not a "criminal cause or matter". Criminal contempt consists of acts done outside the suit which interfere with the course of justice, such as contumacious behaviour in the face of the court, the scandalising of a judge, or prejudicing the proper and fair conduct of the proceedings. Since 1960 there has been provision for appeals against decisions and orders made in respect of criminal contempt (see A.J.A. 1960, s.13). In the case of decisions and orders made in respect of criminal contempt committed in civil proceedings in the High Court or a county court appeal lies to the Civil Division of the Court of Appeal (S.C.A. 1981, s.53). In the case of criminal contempt in the Crown Court the appeal is to the Criminal Division of the Court of Appeal (*ibid.*). Appeal against orders made by magistrates' courts in respect of criminal contempt in criminal proceedings lies to the Crown Court (Magistrates' Courts Act 1980, s.108); and to the Div. Ct in respect of criminal contempt committed in civil proceedings before magistrates (AJA 1960, s.13(2)(a)).

From an order extending time for appealing—No appeal lies from an order allowing an extension of time for appealing from a judgment or order (S.C.A. 1981, s.18(1)(b)). But, in *Rickards v. Rickards* [1990] Fam. 194; [1989] 3 All E.R. 193, CA, it was held that the Court of Appeal does have jurisdiction (subject to the requirement of leave to appeal) to entertain an appeal against a refusal of an extension of time for appealing to the court below. The rule in *Lane v. Esdaile* [1981] A.C. 210 (see para. 59/14/38, below) applies only to decisions granting or refusing leave to appeal to the court below where such leave is required. The Court held that the decisions of the Court of Appeal in *Podberry v. Peak* [1981] 1 Ch. 344 and *Bokhari v. Mahmoud* (1988) *The Independent*, April 19; *The Times*, April 26, 1988, were wrongly decided and fell within the scope of the *per incuriam* rule; they were therefore not binding and should not be followed. R59.1.77

From a final decision—No appeal lies from a decision of the High Court or any Judge thereof where it is provided by any Act that the decision is to be final (*ibid.*, s.18(1)(c)). See, for example, O.94, r.6: Companies Act 1985, s.127(4); Patents Act 1949, s.87(2) (continued in Patents Act 1977, s.127, Sched. 1, para. 1). R59.1.78

Vexatious litigants—No appeal lies against the refusal by a High Court Judge of an application for leave to institute or continue any legal proceedings made by a person who is the subject of a vexatious litigant order and (S.C.A. 1981, s.42(4)). R59.1.79

Arbitration—No appeal lies against the refusal by the High Court to grant a certificate under s.1(7)(b) of the Arbitration Act 1979; *National Westminster Bank plc v. Arthur Young McClelland Moores & Co.* [1985] 1 W.L.R. 1123; [1985] 2 All E.R. 817; and no appeal lies against a refusal by the High Court to grant leave under s.1(6A) of that Act to appeal to the CA: *Aden Refinery Co. Ltd v. Ugland Management Co. Ltd* [1987] Q.B. 650; [1986] 3 All E.R. 737, CA). (In the *Aden Refinery* case the CA held that the principle in *Scherer v. Counting Instruments Ltd* [1986] 1 W.L.R. 615 (which permitted the CA, in certain circumstances, to entertain appeals against costs orders notwithstanding S.C.A. 1981, s.18(1)(f) does not apply to arbitration cases.) R59.1.80

From a Prize Court—No appeal lies to the Court of Appeal from a judgment or order of the High Court when acting as a Prize Court (S.C.A. 1981, s.16(2) which provides that an appeal lies to H.M. in Council in accordance with the Naval Prize Acts 1864–1916). R59.1.81

From an order made by a Judge without a hearing on an application under O.53, r.(3) for to apply for judicial review—See O.53, r.13 and para. R53.14.60. R59.1.82

Other cases where appeal does not lie

Hypothetical cases—Where the question which the Court of Appeal is asked to decide does not arise, either because the facts are hypothetical (*Glasgow Navigation Co. v. Iron Ore Co.* [1910] A.C. 293; *Sutch v. Burns* [1944] K.B. 406; *Stephenson, Blake & Co. v. Grant, Legros & Co.* [1917] W.N. 47; 33 T.L.R. 174) or because the parties have no interest in the result of the appeal, having agreed that, whichever way it is decided it should not affect their proprietary position (*Sun Life Assurance Co. of Canada v. Jervis* [1944] A.C. 111) or for any other reason (see *Tindall v. Wright* [1922] W.N. 124). On the question of the attitude of the appellate courts to "academic" appeals see also: *Ainsbury v. Millington* [1987] 1 W.L.R. 379, HL; *R. v. Secretary of State for the Home Department, ex p. Wynne* [1993] 1 W.L.R. 115; [1993] 1 All E.R. 574, HL; *National Coal Board v. Ridgeway* [1987] 3 All E.R. 582, CA; and *Star Cinemas (London) Ltd v. Barnett* (1987) *The Times*, December 9, CA). R59.1.83

Where decision is not given in a judicial capacity—Where, at the request of the parties, a judge decides a question outside the regular course of judicial proceedings (*extra cursum curiae*) no appeal lies (*Burgess v. Morton* [1896] A.C. 136); nor does an appeal lie from an administrative decision (*Hoare & Co. v. Moreshead* [1903] 2 K.B. 359), but the remedy of judicial review may be available (see O.53). R59.1.84

Where Judge acted as arbitrator—Similarly, if a Judge acts as an arbitrator, not as a judge, his award is not subject to appeal to the Court of Appeal under legislation governing that Court's general appellate jurisdiction (*Re Durham County Permanent Benefit Building Society, ex p. Wilson* R59.1.85

(1871) L.R. 7 Ch.App. 45). If a Judge of the Commercial Court sits as an arbitrator under A.J.A. 1970, s.4, his award may be reviewed by the Court of Appeal under the Arbitration Act 1950 as modified by Sched. 3 to A.J.A. 1970.

R59.1.86 **Agreement not to appeal**—No appeal lies where there has been an agreement, embodied in an order, not to appeal (*Jones v. Victoria Graving Dock Co.* (1877) 2 Q.B.D. 314, CA; *Re Hull & County Bank, Trotter's claim* (1880) 13 Ch.D. 261, CA; *Re West Devon Great Consols Mine* (1888) 38 Ch.D. 51, CA). See also O.25, r.4, which empowers the court or judge, on the hearing of a summons for directions, to record an agreement of the parties to exclude or limit any right of appeal. An agreement not to appeal, made on behalf of a minor by his next friend, is not binding on the minor if it is not for his benefit (*Rhodes v. Swithenbank* (1889) 22 Q.B.D. 577, CA). An appeal will not lie from the decision of a county court judge if, before the decision is given, the parties agree, in writing signed by themselves or their solicitors or agents, that it shall be final (County Courts Act 1984, s.79).

R59.1.87 **Loss of right of appeal by reason of the appellant's conduct since judgment**—"The receipt of a remedy" under the judgment appealed from may in some circumstances preclude an appeal—as, for example, where the appellant's conduct since the judgment is such as to render impossible or inequitable the restitution claimed (*per* Lord Atkin in *Lissenden v. CAV. Bosch Ltd* [1940] A.C. 412 at 429, 430) and the same result may follow where "he is by his conduct estopped from appealing, or has in equity or at law released his right of appeal" (*per* Lord Maugham, *ibid.* at 420).

R59.1.88 **De minimis non curat lex**—Upon this maxim courts have sometimes refused to entertain appeals where the amount at stake was trifling (see *Re National Assurance and Investment Association, Re Cross* (1872) L.R. 7 Ch. 221).

R59.1.89 **Where a party has obtained all relief sought, or has successfully resisted all relief sought by the other side**—See para. R59.1.31.

Right of appeal limited by statute

R59.1.90 **Appeal confined to questions of law in certain cases**—Generally where an appeal lies to the Court of Appeal the appellant can appeal on questions of fact as well as issues of law. It should be borne in mind, however, that the Court of Appeal does not generally interfere with the judge's findings of fact, particularly where they turn on which witnesses are to be believed or the weight to be attached to particular evidence.

In certain cases appeal is confined to questions of law, *e.g.* appeals by way of case stated (such as tax appeals and appeals from the Lands Tribunal), appeals from decisions of the Employment Appeal Tribunal, the Immigration Appeals Tribunal, or the Social Security Commissioners, and certain county court possession cases (see County Courts Act 1984, s.77(6)).

R59.1.91 **Appeals against decrees absolute of divorce or nullity**—No appeal lies to the Court of Appeal against a decree absolute of divorce or nullity by a party who had time and opportunity to appeal from the decree nisi on which the decree absolute is founded and who did not appeal against that decree nisi (S.C.A. 1981, s.18(1)(d), SCP 1999, Vol. 2, Section 20A, para. 20A–177). A party who wishes to appeal against a decree absolute must first make an application *to the court below* under r.2.42(8) of the Family Proceedings Rules 1991 and prove that he or she did not have time and opportunity to appeal against the decree nisi.

R59.1.92 **Permission to appeal**—With effect from January 1, 1999 permission to appeal is required in the case of all appeals to the Court of Appeal, save for three very limited exceptions (see paras R59.1B.1 *et seq.* below).

R59.1.93 **Permission to appeal must be obtained before a notice of appeal can be served**—Where permission to appeal is required, a valid notice of appeal cannot be served unless and until permission to appeal has been obtained (*Cumbes v. Robinson* [1951] 2 K.B. 83; [1951] 1 All E.R. 661, CA; see also para. R59.1).

R59.1.94 **Respondents requiring permission to appeal**—Where a respondent wishes to serve a respondent's notice to vary (see O.59, r.6) in a case where leave to appeal is required he must himself make application for leave to appeal (O.59, r.1B(2)); the grant of permission to appeal to an appellant does not carry with it the grant of permission to appeal to any respondent. The reasoning in *Cumbes v. Robinson* (above) applies *mutatis mutandis* to a respondent and therefore, in a case where a respondent requires permission to cross-appeal, any such notice served without permission having been obtained will be invalid.

R59.1.95 **Failure to obtain permission**—As the Court of Appeal has no jurisdiction to entertain an appeal, where permission to appeal is required, unless permission has been obtained, the Court will raise any question of permission to appeal of its own motion (*White v. Brunton* [1984] 2 All E.R. 606, CA). It has been held that failure to obtain permission before setting down an appeal is an irregularity only and does not render the notice of appeal a nullity: *Knighthood Assurance Consultants Ltd v. Meacher* (1976) 120 S.J. 117, CA, where it was held that a respondent who had applied for security of costs had thereby waived the irregularity of failure on the part of the appellant to obtain permission to appeal. It is submitted that the decision in that case is *per incuriam* because the requirement of permission to appeal goes to the jurisdiction of the Court of Appeal (see *White v. Brunton* [1984] 2 All E.R. 606, CA); since jurisdiction cannot conferred by the express consent of all parties, *a fortiori* it cannot be conferred in consequence of an implied waiver by one party.

Miscellaneous Matters

Meaning of interlocutory order—The distinction between final and interlocutory orders is no longer relevant for the purposes of deciding whether permission to appeal is required, because leave is now almost universal (see O.59, r.1B). The distinction is, however, still relevant for the purposes of appeals in two other respects: (1) an appeal in a High Court case can only be heard by a two-judge court if the order being appealed is interlocutory; and (2) it is necessary to decide whether an order is interlocutory for the purposes of allocating it to the correct List of Appeals. R59.1.96

From 1986 until April 26, 1999 there was a lengthy rule (O.59, r.1A) defining which orders were interlocutory and which were final for the purposes of appeals to the Court of Appeal, but r.1A has not been re-enacted in the CPR. It is uncertain whether the question will therefore be determined by applying the test laid down in the pre-1986 authorities (in particular *White v. Brunton* [1984] Q.B. 570; [1984] 2 All E.R. 606) or whether the description of an interlocutory order in para. 2.12.1 of the 1999 Practice Direction is the test to be applied for the purposes of deciding whether a two-judge court has jurisdiction in High Court cases and of allocating appeals to Lists. (In some respects the two differ: *e.g.* an order striking out a claim and an order refusing to set aside a default judgment would be interlocutory according to the *White v. Brunton* test, but would appear to be final applying what is said in para. 2.12.1.)

Bankruptcy appeals—An appeal against a decision given in bankruptcy proceedings by a bankruptcy registrar, a district judge or a circuit judge, lies initially to a High Court Judge of the Chancery Division (Insolvency Act 1986, s.375). The decision of the High Court Judge can then be appealed to the Court of Appeal, but permission to appeal will be required (under O.59, r.1B). R59.1.97

Appeals against a committal order made by a district judge in county court proceedings—In county court cases a district judge has jurisdiction to make a committal order or to impose a fine for contempt in the face of the court (County Courts Act 1984, s.118(3)), and for an assault on an officer of the court in the execution of his duty (*ibid.*, s.14(3)). An appeal against such a committal order lies to a Judge of that county court (under CCR, O.37, r.6) or directly to the Court of Appeal (under the Administration of Justice Act 1960, s.13(2)(b)); but normally the appeal should initially be made to a circuit judge at the local county court. R59.1.98

[THE NEXT PARAGRAPH IS R59.1.100.]

Powers of Court

Powers of Court of Appeal—On an appeal the Court of Appeal can: R59.1.100

(1) Affirm, vary or discharge the order of the court or tribunal below, and can make any order which that court or tribunal could have made (S.C.A. 1981, s.15(3) and O.59, r.10(1)).
(2) Order a new trial (S.C.A. 1981, s.17 and O.59, rr.2 and 11).
(3) Draw any inferences of fact and give any judgment or make any order which ought to have been made, and make such further or other order as the case may require (O.59, r.10(3) below).
(4) Make any order, on such terms as the Court thinks just, to ensure the determination on the merits of the real question in controversy between the parties, notwithstanding that no notice of appeal or respondent's notice has been given in respect of any particular part of the decision of the court or tribunal below, or that any ground for allowing the appeal or affirming that decision is not specified in the notice of appeal or respondent's notice (O.59, r.10(4)).

Principles upon which the Court of Appeal Acts

Appeals against decisions of questions of fact—On an appeal in an action tried by a judge R59.1.101

alone, the burden of showing that the trial judge was wrong in his decision as to the facts lies on the appellant (as it lay in the Court of Appeal in Chancery) and if the Court of Appeal is not satisfied that he was wrong the appeal will be dismissed (*Savage v. Adams* [1895] W.N. 109, *per* Lopes L.J.; *Colonial Securities Trust Co. v. Massey* [1896] 1 Q.B. 38, *per* Lord Esher M.R. at 39; and, in an appeal from a county court, *Norman v. King* [1946] 1 All E.R. 339). But, as was said by Lindley M.R. in *Coghlan v. Cumberland* [1898] 1 Ch. 704: "Even where . . . the appeal turns on a question of fact, the Court has to bear in mind that its duty is to rehear the case, and the Court must reconsider the materials before the Judge, with such other materials as it may have decided to admit. The Court must then make up its own mind, not disregarding the judgment appealed from but carefully weighing and considering it, and not shrinking from overruling it if on full consideration it comes to the conclusion that it is wrong." "Great weight is due to the decision of a judge of first instance whenever, in a conflict of testimony, the demeanour and manner of witnesses who have been seen and heard by him are material elements in the consideration of the truthfulness of these statements. But the parties to the cause are nevertheless entitled as well on questions of fact as on questions of law to demand the decision of the Court of Appeal, and that Court cannot excuse itself from the task of weighing conflicting evidence, and drawing its own conclusions, though it should always bear in mind that it has neither seen nor heard the witnesses and should make due allowance in this respect." (*The Glannibanta* (1876) 1 P.D. 283 at 287; and see *Bigsby v. Dickinson* (1876) 4 Ch.D. 24, *per* James L.J. at 28). A distinction must be drawn between the judge's view of conflicting testimony, and the inferences to be drawn from facts not in controversy (*per* Lord Denedin in *Dominion Trust Co. v. New York Life Insurance Co.* [1919] A.C. 254 at 255, PC) or between facts deposed to by witnesses and found by the court, and inferences of fact drawn therefrom (see *Benmax v. Austin Motor Co. Ltd* [1955] 1 All E.R. 326, *per* Viscount Simonds at 327). "The judge sees the demeanour of the witnesses and can estimate their intelligence, position and character in a way not open to the courts who deal with later stages of the case" (*Khoo Sit Hoh v. Lim Thean Tong* [1912] A.C. 323 at 325, PC). Not to have seen the witnesses puts appellate judges in a permanent position of disadvantage against the trial judge, and unless it can be shown that he has failed to use or has palpably misused his advantage—for example has failed to observe inconsistencies or indisputable fact or material probabilities (*ibid.* and *Yuill v. Yuill* [1945] P.15; *Watt v. Thomas* [1947] A.C. 484)—the higher court ought not to take the responsibility of reversing conclusions so arrived at merely as the result of their own comparisons and criticisms of the witnesses, and of their own view of the probabilities of the case (*per* Lord Sumner in *S. S. Hontestroom v. S. S. Sagaporack* [1927] A.C. 37 at 47). Where a defendant has been acquitted of fraud, the decision should not be displaced on appeal except on the clearest grounds (*Akerhielm v. De Mare* [1959] A.C. 789; [1959] 3 All E.R. 485, PC). If the trial judge's estimate of the man forms any substantial part of his reasons for his judgment his conclusions of fact should be let alone (*ibid.* and see *Powell v. Streatham Manor Nursing Home* [1935] A.C. 243). But while the Court of Appeal is always reluctant to reject a finding by a judge of the specific or primary facts deposed to by the witnesses, especially when the finding is based on the credibility or bearing of a witness, it is willing to form an independent opinion upon the proper inferences to be drawn from it (*Benmax v. Austin Motor Co. Ltd* above; and see *Montgomerie & Co. v. Wallace-Jones* [1904] A.C. 73, *per* Lord Halsbury L.C. at 75; *Mersey Docks & Harbour Board v. Procter* [1923] A.C. 253, *per* Viscount Cave L.C. at 258).

R59.1.102 **Appeals against exercise of discretion**—There are many authorities for the proposition that an appeal will not be entertained from an order which it was within the discretion of the judge to make, unless it be shown that he exercised his discretion under a mistake of law (*Evans v. Bartlam* [1937] A.C. 473) or in disregard of principle (*Young v. Thomas* [1892] 2 Ch. 134) or under a misapprehension as to the facts (*ibid.*); or that he took into account irrelevant matters (*Egerton v. Jones* [1939] 3 All E.R. 889 at 892, CA) or failed to exercise his discretion (*Crowther v. Elgood* (1887) 34 Ch.D. 691 at 697) or the conclusion which the judge reached in the exercise of his discretion was "outside the generous ambit within which a reasonable disagreement is possible" (*G. v. G.* [1985] 1 W.L.R. 647; [1985] 2 All E.R. 225, HL). Many of the cases in this area are decisions refusing to interfere with a judge's discretion in making some interlocutory order. Examples are: striking out or refusing to strike out a pleading as being embarrassing (*Golding v. Wharton Saltworks Co.* (1876) 1 Q.B.D. 374; *Watson v. Rodwell* (1876) 3 Ch.D. 380) or transferring an action to the county court (*Coulver v. Beard* [1937] 1 All E.R. 301) or giving directions for trial (*Mangan v. Metropolitan Electric Supply Co.* [1891] 2 Ch. 551) or granting or refusing an adjournment of the trial (compare *Maxwell v. Keun* [1928] 1 K.B. 645, with *Re Yates's Settlement Trusts, Yates v. Yates* [1954] 1 W.L.R. 564; [1954] 1 All E.R. 619, where the appeal was allowed), or the grant or refusal of an interlocutory injunction (*Hadmore Productions Ltd v. Hamilton* [1983] 1 A.C. 191; [1982] 1 All E.R. 1042, HL); or where the judge expressed an opinion or conclusion as to the minutes of his judgment (*James v. Jones* (1892) 67 L.T. 584, CA) or refused to issue an attachment for contempt (*Re Wray* (1887) 36 Ch.D. 138). The principle is general: it applies to the exercise of any judicial discretion—that is, a discretion which the holder of the judicial office exercises either because it has been conferred upon him by some statute or rule of law, or because it is something which is inherent in the judicial office itself (*per* Greene M.R. in *Bradford Third Equitable Benefit Building Society v. Borders (No. 2)* [1939] 3 All E.R. 29 at 33). The discretion in all these cases is that of the judge; if he reverses the decision of a master, district judge or registrar, still the disrcretion is his for the purposes of an appeal to the Court of Appeal (*Cooper v. Cooper* [1936] 2 All E.R. 542; *Evans v. Bartlam*, above).

The limitations on the power of the Court of Appeal to interfere with the exercise of a discretion conferred on the judge in the court below apply to residence or contact orders in child cases or any other decisions concerning the welfare of children: *G. v. G.* [1985] 1 W.L.R. 647; [1985] 2 All E.R. 225, HL.

Subject to well-established exceptions, a judge exercising a judicial discretion must give reasons for his decision; but the particularity with which he is required to set out his reasons will depend on the circumstances of the case and the nature of the decision concerned (*Eagil Trust Co. Ltd v. Pigott-Brown* [1985] 3 All E.R. 119, CA). The most common of the well-established exceptions are: where the judge is exercising a discretion on costs and he is not making an unusual award of costs; and when a judge refuses leave to appeal to the Court of Appeal against his refusal of leave to appeal to the High Court from the award of an arbitrator (*ibid.*).

Appeal from order giving leave to defend—If a judge has given unconditional leave to defend under O.14, because he thinks that there is a triable issue of fact, the Court of Appeal will rarely differ; but if there is no defence in law, the Court of Appeal will interfere (*European Asian Bank v. Punjab Sind Bank (No. 2)* [1983] 1 W.L.R. 642; [1983] 2 All E.R. 508). It should be noted that since the passing of S.C.A. 1981 a plaintiff can appeal against an order of a judge refusing an application for summary judgment, or granting unconditional leave to defend; but leave to appeal will be required. (Previously such an appeal was prohibited by J.A. 1925, s.31(1)(c) but that provision was not re-enacted in S.C.A. 1981.) **R59.1.103**

Previous decisions of the Court of Appeal—The Court "is one Court, though it usually sits in two or three divisions; each division has co-ordinate jurisdiction, but the full Court has no greater powers of jurisdiction than any division of the Court, . . . and conversely what cannot be done by a division of the court cannot be done by the full Court." Except in the following cases (and of course in the Criminal Division of the CA; see *R. v. Gould* [1968] 2 Q.B. 65; [1968] 1 All E.R. 849) the Court of Appeal is bound to follow previous decisions of its own as well as those of courts of co-ordinate jurisdiction (see *Gallie v. Lee* [1969] 2 Ch. 17, CA). Where there are conflicting previous decisions of the Court of Appeal, it is not bound by either; and the same applies where the only previous decision or decisions of the Court cannot stand with a decision of the House of Lords. The Court is also not bound to follow a decision of its own in the rare case where it is satisfied that the decision was given *per incuriam*—for example, in ignorance of the inconsistent terms of a statute, or rule having the force of a statute, or of a previous decision of its own or of a court of co-ordinate jurisdiction or of the House of Lords, which covers the point (*Young v. Bristol Aeroplane Co.* [1944] K.B. 718, CA, *per* Lord Greene M.R.; *Morelle Ltd v. Wakeling* [1955] 2 Q.B. 379; [1955] 1 All E.R. 708, CA), or, in extremely rare circumstances where the Court of Appeal is satisfied that the previous decision involved a manifest slip or error (*Rickards v. Rickards* [1990] Fam 194; [1989] 3 All E.R. 193, CA). **R59.1.104**

Rehearings

Rehearing by court of first instance—Before an order has been sealed, or otherwise perfected, there is jurisdiction in the court that made it to rehear the matter and withdraw or modify it (*Re Harrison's Settlement* [1955] Ch. 260; [1955] 1 All E.R. 185, CA). But after an order has been sealed, or otherwise perfected, then, unless it is an *ex parte* order (which can be discharged: *Boyle v. Sacker* (1888) 39 Ch.D. 249), or an order which does not embody the intention of the court (which can be corrected under O.20, r.11) the court making the order has no jurisdiction to review it, and the remedy is to appeal to the Court of Appeal (*Re St. Nazaire Co.* (1879) 12 Ch.D. 88; *Preston Banking Co. v. Allsup* [1895] 1 Ch. 141, CA; *Chas. Bright & Co. Ltd v. Sellar* [1904] 1 K.B. 6; *Hession v. Jones* [1914] 2 K.B. 421, *per* Bankes J. at 427). In certain circumstances, the court which made an interlocutory order may vary or discharge it on the grounds of change of circumstances (*Preston Banking v. Allsup*, above; *Re Scowby, Scowby v. Scowby* [1897] 1 Ch. 741, CA; *Re May* (1883) 25 Ch.D. 237; *Scott v. Alvarez* [1895] 1 Ch. 596). (See generally paras R20.11.6 to 8). In some cases the court may have power to conduct a rehearing (see below). An action may be brought to set aside a judgment obtained by fraud. **R59.1.105**

In *Hyde & South Bank Housing Association v. Kain, The Times*, August 30, 1989; (1989) 133 S.J. 1578, the Court of Appeal held that the rule that a judge can alter his decision at any time prior to the order being perfected applies in county court cases in the same way as it does in High Court cases.

Rehearing where one party did not appear—Where a party did not appear, and the proceedings were struck out and not heard, the same court has a discretion to reinstate and hear them (*Walker v. Budden* (1879) 5 Q.B.D. 267; *Allum v. Dickinson* (1882) 9 Q.B.D. 662; *Vint v. Hudspith* (1885) 29 Ch.D. 322, CA; *Rackham v. Tabrum* (1923) 39 T.L.R. 380; *cf. Hession v. Jones* [1914] 2 K.B. 421, 427. **R59.1.106**

In *Craig v. Kanssen* [1943] K.B. 256 there had been no service of process on the defendant with the result that he had no notice of the hearing. On appeal by the defendant, the CA set aside the order made in his absence, but the CA held that it was not necessary to appeal, because an order made in such circumstances was a nullity and the court below had jurisdiction to set it aside *ex debito justiciae.* See also *Walker v. Walker* below where the CA held that in such circumstances the order could be set aside either by the court below or by the CA, but went on to say that it is better for the application to be made to the court below because that would be quicker and cheaper. It is submitted that it is *a fortiori* where the matter turns on issues of fact (*e.g.* whether or not a defendant did receive due notice of the hearing date) because the court below is a more appropriate forum for resolving disputed issues of fact: (see also para. R59.1.3).

In addition there are rules enabling a party who did not appear to apply to have the order set aside (see CPR, r.39.3(2) 4(3)).

R59.1.107 *Rehearing of a matrimonial cause*—For the jurisdiction of the Family Division to rehear a cause where no error of the court at the hearing is alleged, see Family Proceedings Rules 1991, r.2.42. See also *Walker v. Walker*, May 21, 1986, CA (unrep.) where the Court of Appeal held that the court below had inherent jurisdiction to set aside a decree nisi of divorce where the respondent to the suit had not been given notice of the hearing at which the decree was pronounced.

R59.1.108 *Application for a rehearing in the county court by a party who did appear*—Even where a party did appear at the trial in the county court, he can apply, within 14 days thereafter, for a re-hearing, provided that "no error of the court at the hearing is alleged" (CCR, O.37, r.1). Thus, for example, the county court would have jurisdiction to entertain an application for a re-hearing under CCR, O.37, r.1 on the grounds that fresh evidence has come to light, but not an application based on a contention that the first county court judge's decision was wrong on the material before him (otherwise the second county court judge would, in effect, be hearing an appeal against the first county court judge's decision).

R59.1.109 **Rehearing of appeal or application by Court of Appeal**—The Court of Appeal has power to alter its decision before its order has been perfected, but it has no power to rehear an appeal after its order has been passed and entered (*Hession v. Jones* [1914] 2 K.B. 421) see also the observations of the CA in *Wood v. Gahlings, The Times*, November 29, 1996; and *Zincroft Civil Engineering Ltd v. Sphere Drake Insurance plc., The Times*, December 13, 1996).

Where, however, the appeal has been struck out or dismissed for non-appearance of the appellant, the Court of Appeal has inherent jurisdiction to reinstate the appeal and hear it (*Brooksbank v. Rawsthorne & Co.* [1951] 2 All E.R. 413). Such an application to re-instate the appeal must be made on summons to the Full Court, supported by an affidavit which must give a full explanation for the applicant's failure to attend the first Court of Appeal hearing. The principal factors which the Court of Appeal takes into account in deciding whether, in the exercise of its discretion, to re-instate the appeal are: (1) whether the applicant had a reasonable excuse for failing to attend the first hearing; (2) any relevant prejudice to the respondent; and (3) whether there is sufficient merit in the appeal to justify re-instating it. The jurisdiction to re-instate applies equally to applicatons to the Court of Appeal which have been heard in the absence of the applicant.

In *Hession v. Jones* [1914] 2 K.B. 421 the respondent failed to attend the hearing of the appeal (which was an appeal to the K.B. Div. Ct, not to the CA); the appeal was heard on its merits and allowed. On a subsequent application by the respondent, the KB Div. Ct held that it had no jurisdiction to re-open the matter, because the appeal had been heard on its merits, not merely struck out or no order made. It is submitted that *Hession v. Jones* (which is not binding on the CA) is wrongly decided. Given that the Court of Appeal has inherent jurisdiction to re-instate an appeal which has been struck out or dismissed for non-appearance of an appellant, it should surely have a similar jurisdiction, *ex debito justitiae*, to re-instate an appeal where the respondent is able to show that there are good grounds for re-opening the matter. A respondent who has a reasonable excuse for his failure to attend the first hearing should not be treated differently from an appellant who has a reasonable excuse for non-appearance. Futhermore, it is surely irrelevant whether, at the first hearing, the court summarily disposed of the appeal or whether it reached a decision based on the merits. The point is that the decision at the first hearing was reached without hearing argument from an absent party who wished to be heard and the question should be whether, having regard to all the circumstances of the case, the interests of justice require that the order be set aside and the matter re-heard, so that the party who was, for some good reason, not present, has the opportunity to put his case.

Appeal to House of Lords

R59.1.110 **Appeal from Court of Appeal to House of Lords**—Appeal lies only with leave of the Court of Appeal or the House of Lords (Administration of Justice (Appeals) Act 1934, s.1, SCP 1999, Vol. 2, Section 20B, para. 20B–1); but that section does not enable an appeal to be brought if otherwise it would not lie. By virtue of the County Courts Act 1984, s.82, no appeal lies from the decision of the Court of Appeal on any appeal from a county court in any probate proceedings. No appeal lies from a decision of the Court of Appeal on appeal from the decision of the High Court on a question of law under Part III of the Representation of the People Act 1983 (*ibid.*, s.157(1)). From the decision of the CA on appeal from an order or decision of a court in the exercise of jurisdiction to punish for contempt of court (including criminal contempt) appeal lies to the House of Lords, but subject to the restrictions specified in section 1(2) of A.J.A. 1960; see *ibid.*, s.13. No appeal lies to the House of Lords against the refusal of leave to appeal to the Court of Appeal, or the refusal by the Court of Appeal of leave to apply for judicial review.

The application to the Court of Appeal for leave to appeal to the House of Lords should normally be made at the hearing of the appeal immediately after judgment has been given. But, if that was not done, an application may be made in writing and dealt with by the Court on paper, without a hearing. Such written application should be lodged with the Registrar of Civil Appeals. It should include the title of action, the name of the applicant, date of order of the Court of Appeal, and a brief statement of the grounds on which leave to appeal to the House of Lords is sought. The written application will be referred to the Lords Justices who heard the appeal and an order will be drawn up. If, on considering the application, the Court desires to hear oral argument, directions will be given for the matter to be dealt with *inter partes* in open court.

For the directions as to procedure and the standing orders regulating appeal to the House of Lords, see SCP 1999, Vol. 2, Section 19A, paras 19A–1 *et seq.*

Classes of case where permission to appeal is required

1B.—(1) Permission is required for every appeal except an appeal against— R59.1B

(a) the making of a committal order;

(b) the refusal to grant habeas corpus; or

(c) an order made under section 25 of the Children Act 1989 (secure accommodation orders).

(2) A respondent who wishes to serve a respondent's notice to which rule 6(1)(a) applies must first obtain permission to cross-appeal unless the case is one to which sub-paragraphs (a), (b) or (c) of paragraph (1) applies.

(3) Permission to appeal or cross-appeal to the Court of Appeal may be given by the court below or by the Court of Appeal.

Application of Order to applications for new trial

2. This order (except so much of rule 3(1) as provides that an appeal shall be by way of rehearing and except rule 11(1)) applies to an application to the Court of Appeal for a new trial or to set aside a verdict, finding or judgment after trial with or without a jury, as it applies to an appeal to that court, and references in this order to an appeal and to an appellant shall be construed accordingly. R59.2

Interpretation

2A. In this order "a single judge" means a single judge of the Court of Appeal and "the registrar" tmeans he registrar of civil appeals. R59.2A

GENERAL PROVISIONS AS TO APPEALS

Who may exercise the powers of the Court of Appeal

2B. Subject to section 58(1) of the Act the functions of the Court of Appeal may be performed by— R59.2B

(a) that court;

(b) a single judge; or

(c) the registrar.

Variation of time

2C. Any date set by the court or this order for doing any act may not be varied by the parties. R59.2C

(CPR Rule 2.11 allows the parties to vary a date by written agreement except where these Rules provide otherwise or the court orders otherwise.)

Notice of appeal

3.—(1) An appeal to the Court of Appeal shall be by way of rehearing and must be brought by notice of appeal. R59.3

(2) Notice of appeal may be given either in respect of the whole or in

respect of any specified part of the judgment or order of the court below; and every such notice must specify the grounds of the appeal and the precise form of the order which the appellant proposes to ask the Court of Appeal to make.

(3) Except with the permission of the Court of Appeal, a single judge or the registrar, the appellant shall not be entitled on the hearing of an appeal to rely on any grounds of appeal, or to apply for any relief, not specified in the notice of appeal.

(4) Every notice of appeal must specify the list of appeals to which the appellant proposes that the appeal should be assigned.

(5) A notice of appeal must be served on all parties to the proceedings in the court below who are directly affected by the appeal; and, subject to rule 8, it shall not be necessary to serve the notice on parties not so affected.

(6) No notice of appeal shall be given by a respondent in a case to which rule 6(1) relates.

Time for appealing

R59.4 **4.**—(1) Except as otherwise provided by this order, every notice of appeal must be served under rule 3(5) not later than 4 weeks after the date on which the judgment or order of the court below was sealed or otherwise perfected.

(2) In the case of an appeal from a decision in respect of which a certificate has been granted under section 12 of the Administration of Justice Act 1969 the period referred to in paragraph (1) shall be calculated from the end of the time during which, in accordance with section 13(5) of that Act, no appeal lies to the Court of Appeal.

(3) Where permission to appeal is granted by the Court of Appeal or the court below upon an application made within the time limited for serving notice of appeal under paragraph (1), a notice of appeal may, instead of being served within that time, be served within 7 days after the date when permission is granted.

Setting down appeal

R59.5 **5.**—(1) Within 7 days after the later of (i) the date on which service of the notice of appeal was effected, or (ii) the date on which the judgment or order of the court below was sealed or otherwise perfected, the appellant must set down his appeal by filing with the court—

- (a) a copy of the said judgment or order; and
- (b) two copies of the notice of appeal, one of which shall be indorsed with the amount of the fee paid, and the other indorsed with a certificate of the date of service of the notice.

(2) Upon the said documents being so filed, the court shall enter the appeal in the records of the court and assign it to the appropriate list of appeals.

(3) The appropriate list of appeals for the purpose of paragraph (2) shall be decided by the registrar, without prejudice, however, to any decision of the Court of Appeal on the question whether the judgment or order appealed against is interlocutory or final.

(4) Within 4 days of receipt of notification from the office of the registrar that the appeal has been entered in the records of the court, the appellant must give notice to that effect to all parties on whom the notice of appeal was served, specifying the Court of Appeal reference allocated to that appeal.

Respondent's notice

R59.6 **6.**—(1) A respondent who, having been served with a notice of appeal, desires—

- (a) to contend on the appeal that the decision of the court below should be varied, either in any event or in the event of the appeal being allowed in whole or in part; or

(b) to contend that the decision of the court below should be affirmed on grounds other than those relied upon by that court;

must give notice to that effect, specifying the grounds of his contention and, in a case to which paragraph (a) relates, the precise form of the order which he proposes to ask the court to make.

(2) Except with the permission of the Court of Appeal or a single judge or the registrar, a respondent shall not be entitled on the hearing of the appeal to apply for any remedy not specified in a notice under paragraph (1) or to rely, in support of any contention, upon any ground which has not been specified in such a notice or relied upon by the court below.

(3) Any notice given by a respondent under this rule (in this order referred to as a "respondent's notice") must be served on the appellant, and on all parties to the proceedings in the court below who are directly affected by the contentions of the respondent, and must be served within 21 days after the service of the notice of appeal on the respondent.

(4) A party by whom a respondent's notice is given must, within 4 days after the later of (i) the date on which the service of the respondent's notice was effected or (ii) the date on which he was notified under rule 5(4) that the appeal had been entered in the records of the court, file with the court two copies of the respondent's notice, one of which shall be indorsed with the amount of the fee paid, and the other indorsed with a certificate of the date of service of such respondent's notice.

Amendment of notice of appeal and respondent's notice

7.—(1) A notice of appeal or respondent's notice may be amended— **R59.7**

(a) with the permission of the Court of Appeal, a single judge or the registrar, at any time;

(b) without such permission, by supplementary notice served, before the date on which the appeal first appears in the Document List referred to in rule 9(1) on each of the parties on whom the notice to be amended was served.

(2) A party by whom a supplementary notice is served under this rule must, within 2 days after service of the notice, file two copies of the notice at the Court.

Directions of the Court as to service

8.—(1) The Court of Appeal or a single judge or the registrar may in any case direct that a notice of appeal or respondent's notice be served on any party to the proceedings in the court below on whom it has not been served, or on any person not party to those proceedings. **R59.8**

(2) Where a direction is given under paragraph (1) the hearing of the appeal may be postponed or adjourned for such period and on such terms as may be just and such judgment may be given and such order made on the appeal as might have been given or made if the persons served in pursuance of the direction had originally been parties.

Documents to be filed by appellant

9. Not more than 14 days after an appeal or application first appears in a list to be called "the Document List" the appellant must file documents with the court in accordance with the relevant practice direction. **R59.9**

General powers of the Court

10.—(1) In relation to an appeal the Court of Appeal shall have all the powers and duties of the court below. **R59.10**

(2) The Court of Appeal shall have power to receive further evidence on questions of fact, either by oral examination in court, by witness statement or affidavit, or by deposition taken before an examiner, but, in the case of an

appeal from a judgment after trial or hearing of any proceedings on the merits, no such further evidence (other than evidence as to matters which have occurred after the date of the trial or hearing) shall be admitted except on special grounds.

(3) The Court of Appeal shall have power to draw inferences of fact and to give any judgment and make any order which ought to have been given or made, and to make such further or other order as the case may require.

(4) The powers of the Court of Appeal under the foregoing provisions of this rule may be exercised notwithstanding that no notice of appeal or respondent's notice has been given in respect of any particular part of the decision of the court below or by any particular party to the proceedings in that court, or that any ground for allowing the appeal or for affirming or varying the decision of that court is not specified in such a notice; and the Court of Appeal may make any order, on such terms as the court thinks just, to ensure the determination on the merits of the real question in controversy between the parties.

(5) The Court of Appeal may, in special circumstances, order that such security shall be given for the costs of an appeal as may be just.

(6) The powers of the Court of Appeal in respect of an appeal shall not be restricted by reason of any interlocutory order from which there has been no appeal.

(7) Documents impounded by order of the Court of Appeal shall not be delivered out of the custody of that court except in compliance with an order of that court:

Provided that where a Law Officer or the Director of Public Prosecutions makes a written request in that behalf, documents so impounded shall be delivered into his custody.

(8) Documents impounded by order of the Court of Appeal, while in the custody of that court, shall not be inspected except by a person authorised to do so by an order of that court.

(9) In any proceedings incidental to any cause or matter pending before the Court of Appeal, the powers conferred by this rule on the court shall be exercisable in relation to—

(a) the grant, variation, discharge or enforcement of an injunction, or an undertaking given in lieu of an injunction; and

(b) the grant or lifting of a stay of execution or proceedings,

only by the court or a single judge.

Powers of the Court as to new trials

R59.11 **11.**—(1) On the hearing of any appeal the Court of Appeal may, if it thinks fit, make any such order as could be made in pursuance of an application for a new trial or to set aside a verdict, finding or judgment of the court below.

(2) The Court of Appeal shall not be bound to order a new trial on the ground of misdirection, or of the improper admission or rejection of evidence, or because the verdict of the jury was not taken upon a question which the judge at the trial was not asked to leave to them, unless in the opinion of the Court of Appeal some substantial wrong or miscarriage has been thereby occasioned.

(3) A new trial may be ordered on any question without interfering with the finding or decision on any other question; and if it appears to the Court of Appeal that any such wrong or miscarriage as is mentioned in paragraph (2) affects part only of the matter in controversy, or one or some only of the parties, the court may order a new trial as to that part only, or as to that party or those parties only, and give final judgment as to the remainder.

(4) In any case where the Court of Appeal has power to order a new trial on the ground that damages awarded by a jury are excessive or inadequate, the court may, instead of ordering a new trial, substitute for the sum awarded by

the jury such sum as appears to the court to be proper; but except as aforesaid the Court of Appeal shall not have power to reduce or increase the damages awarded by a jury.

Evidence on appeal

12. Where any question of fact is involved in an appeal, the evidence taken in the court below bearing on the question shall, subject to any direction of the Court of Appeal, or a single judge or the registrar, be brought before that Court as follows:— R59.12

(a) in the case of evidence taken by affidavit or witness statement, by the production of a true copy of such affidavit or witness statement;
(b) in the case of evidence given orally, by a copy of so much of the transcript of the official shorthand note as is relevant or by a copy of the judge's note, where he has intimated that in the event of an appeal his note will be sufficient, or by such other means as the Court of Appeal, or a single judge or the registrar, may direct.

Non-disclosure of payment into Court

12A.—(1) Where— R59.12A

(a) any question on an appeal in a claim for a debt, damages or salvage relates to liability for the debt, damages or salvage or to the amount thereof; and
(b) money was paid into court under CPR Part 36 or CPR rule 37.3 in the proceedings in the court below before judgment,

neither the fact of the payment nor the amount thereof shall be stated in the notice of appeal or the respondent's notice or in any supplementary notice or be communicated to the Court of Appeal until all such questions have been decided.
this rule shall not apply in the case of an appeal as to costs only or an appeal in a claim to which a defence of tender before claim was made.

(2) To comply with this rule the appellant must cause to be omitted from the copies of the documents filed by him under rule 9 every part thereof which states that money was paid into court in the proceedings in that court before judgment.

Stay of execution, etc.

13.—(1) Except so far as the court below or the Court of Appeal or a single judge may otherwise direct— R59.13

(a) an appeal shall not operate as a stay of execution or of proceedings under the decision of the court below;
(b) no intermediate act or proceeding shall be invalidated by an appeal.

(2) On an appeal from the High Court, interest for such time as execution has been delayed by the appeal shall be allowed unless the Court of Appeal otherwise orders.

Applications to Court of Appeal

14.—(1) Unless otherwise directed, every application to the Court of Appeal, a single judge or the registrar must be made by application notice in accordance with CPR Part 23. R59.14

(2) An application to the Court of Appeal for permission to appeal shall—

(a) include, where necessary, any application to extend the time for appealing; and
(b) be made in writing without notice being served on any other party setting out the reasons why permission should be granted and, if the time for appealing has expired, the reasons why the application was not made within that time unless the court otherwise directs,

and the court may grant or refuse the application or direct that the application be renewed at a hearing either with or without notice being served on any other party.

(2A) If an application under paragraph (2) is refused otherwise than after a hearing, the applicant shall be entitled, within 7 days after he has been given notice of the refusal, to renew his application; and such renewed application shall be heard without notice being served on any other party unless the court otherwise directs.

(2B) If an application under paragraph (2) is granted otherwise than after a hearing with notice, notice of the order shall be served on the party or parties affected by the appeal and any such party shall be entitled, within 7 days after service of the notice, to apply with notice to have the grant of permission reconsidered unless the court otherwise directs.

(3) Where an application without notice being served on any other party has been refused by the court below, an application for a similar purpose may be made to the Court of Appeal without notice being served on any other party within 7 days after the date of the refusal.

(4) Wherever under these rules an application may be made either to the court below or to the Court of Appeal, it shall not be made in the first instance to the Court of Appeal, except where there are special circumstances which make it impossible or impracticable to apply to the court below or unless the court otherwise directs.

(5) Where an application is made to the Court of Appeal with regard to arbitration proceedings before a judge-arbitrator or judge-umpire, which would, in the case of an ordinary arbitrator or umpire, be made to the High Court, the provisions of the Arbitration Practice Direction relating to such applications shall apply as appropriate.

(6) Where an application is made to the Court of Appeal under section 1(5) of the Arbitration Act 1979 (including any application for permission) notice thereof must be served on the judge-arbitrator or judge-umpire and on any other party to the reference.

(7) The registrar may refer to a single judge any matter which he thinks should properly be decided by a single judge, and, following such reference, the judge may either dispose of the matter or refer it back to the registrar with such direction as the single judge thinks fit.

(8) A single judge may refer to the Court of Appeal any matter which he thinks should properly be decided by that court, and, following such reference, that court may either dispose of the matter or refer it back to a single judge or the registrar, with such directions as that court thinks fit.

(9) An appeal shall lie to a single judge from any determination made by the registrar and shall be brought by way of fresh application made within 10 days of the determination appealed against.

(10) An appeal shall lie to the Court of Appeal from any determination by a single judge, not being the determination of an application for permission to appeal, and shall be brought by way of fresh application made within 10 days of the determination appealed against.

Provided that an appeal shall not lie to the Court of Appeal without the permission of that court in respect of a determination of the registrar which has been reviewed by a single judge.

Extension of time

R59.15 **15.**—(1) The period for serving notice of appeal under rule 4 or for making application without notice being served on any other party under rule 14(3) may be extended or abridged by the court below on application made before the expiration of that period.

SPECIAL PROVISIONS AS TO PARTICULAR APPEALS

Appeal against decree nisi

16.—(1) The following provisions of this rule shall apply to any appeal to the Court of Appeal in a matrimonial cause against a decree nisi of divorce or nullity of marriage. R59.16

(2) The period of 4 weeks specified in rule 4 shall be calculated from the date on which the decree was pronounced and rule 15 shall not apply in relation to that period.

(2A) The notice of appeal shall be served on the appropriate district judge as well as on the party or parties required to be served under rule 3.

(3) The appellant must, within the period mentioned in paragraph (2) and after service of the notice of appeal, file with the court a copy of that decree and two copies of the notice of appeal (one of which shall be indorsed with the amount of the fee paid and the other indorsed with a certificate of the date of service of the notice); and the appeal shall not be competent unless this paragraph has been complied with.

(4) For the purposes of rule 5 the leaving of the said copies shall be sufficient for the setting down of the appeal and rule 5(1) shall not apply.

(5) A party who intends to apply without notice being served on any other party to the Court of Appeal to extend the period referred to in paragraphs (2) and (3) must give notice of his intention to the appropriate district judge before the application is made; and where any order is made by the Court of Appeal extending the said period, it shall be the duty of the registrar of civil appeals forthwith to give notice of the making of the order and of the terms thereof to the appropriate district judge.

(6) In this rule "the appropriate district judge" means—

(a) in relation to a cause pending in a county court, the district judge of that court;

(b) in relation to a cause proceeding in the principal registry of the Family Division, the senior district judge of that Division; and

(c) in relation to a cause proceeding in a district registry, the district judge of that registry.

Appeal against order for revocation of patent

17.—(1) The following provisions of this rule shall apply to any appeal to the Court of Appeal from an order for the revocation of a patent. R59.17

(2) The notice of appeal must be served on the Comptroller-General of Patents, Designs and Trade Marks (in this rule referred to as "the Comptroller") as well as on the party or parties required to be served under rule 3.

(3) If, at any time before the appeal comes on for hearing, the respondent decides not to appear on the appeal or not to oppose it, he must forthwith serve notice of his decision on the Comptroller and the appellant, and any such notice served on the Comptroller must be accompanied by a copy of the petition or of the statements of case in the claim and the written evidence filed therein.

(4) The Comptroller must, within 14 days after receiving notice of the respondent's decision, serve on the appellant a notice stating whether or not he intends to appear on the appeal.

(5) The Comptroller may appear and be heard in opposition to the appeal—

(a) in any case where he has given notice under paragraph (4) of his intention to appear; and

(b) in any other case (including, in particular, a case where the respondent withdraws his opposition to the appeal during the hearing) if the Court of Appeal so directs or allows.

(6) The Court of Appeal may make such orders for the postponement or adjournment of the hearing of the appeal as may appear to the court necessary for the purpose of giving effect to the foregoing provisions of this rule.

Appeal from Patents Court on appeal from Comptroller

R59.18 **18.** In the case of an appeal to the Court of Appeal from a decision of the Patents Court on an appeal from a decision of the Comptroller-General of Patents, Designs and Trade Marks the notice of appeal must be served on the Comptroller-General as well as on the party or parties required to be served under rule 3.

Appeal from county court

R59.19 **19.**—(1) The following provisions of this rule shall apply to any appeal to the Court of Appeal from a county court other than an appeal against a decree nisi of divorce or nullity of marriage.

(2) The appellant must, within the time specified in rule 4, serve the notice of appeal on the district judge of the county court as well as on the party or parties required to be served under rule 3.

(3) In relation to the appeal rule 4(1) and rule 5(1) shall have effect as if for the words "the date on which the judgment or order of the court below was sealed or otherwise perfected" there were substituted the words "the date on which the court below gave its decision."

(5) Rule 13(1)(a) shall not apply, but the appeal shall not operate as a stay of execution or of proceedings in the county court unless the judge of that court or the Court of Appeal so orders or unless, within 10 days after the date of the judgment or order appealed against, the appellant deposits a sum fixed by the judge not exceeding the amount of the money or the value of the property affected by the judgment or order, or gives such security for the said sum as the judge may direct.

(6) In the case of an appeal to the Court of Appeal from the decision of a county court on the hearing of an appeal from a registration officer under section 56 of the Representation of the People Act 1983, notice of the decision of the Court of Appeal shall be given by the registrar of civil appeals to the registration officer, specifying every alteration to be made in pursuance of the decision in the register or list concerned, and a copy of every such notice shall be sent to the district judge of the county court.

(7) In relation to any proceedings in the principal registry of the Family Division which by virtue of any statutory provision are treated as pending in a county court, paragraphs (1) to (5) shall have effect with the necessary modifications as if the principal registry were a county court.

Appeals in cases of contempt of court

R59.20 **20.**—(1) In the case of an appeal to the Court of Appeal under section 13 of the Administration of Justice Act 1960, the notice of appeal must be served on the court from whose order or decision the appeal is brought as well as on the party or parties required to be served under rule 3.

This paragraph shall not apply in relation to an appeal to which rule 19 applies.

(2) Where, in the case of an appeal under the said section 13 to the Court of Appeal or to the House of Lords from the Court of Appeal, the appellant is in custody, the Court of Appeal may order his release on his giving security (whether by recognisance, with or without sureties, or otherwise and for such reasonable sum as that court may fix) for his appearance within 10 days after the judgment of the Court of Appeal or, as the case may be, of the House of

Lords on the appeal shall have been given, before the court from whose order or decision the appeal is brought unless the order or decision is reversed by that judgment.

(3) An application for the release of a person under paragraph (2) pending an appeal to the Court of Appeal or House of Lords under the said section 13 must be made in accordance with CPR Part 23, and the application notice must, at least 24 hours before the day named therein for the hearing, be served on the court from whose order or decision the appeal is brought and on all parties to the proceedings in that court who are directly affected by the appeal.

(4) Order 79, rule 9(6), (6A), (6B) and (8) shall apply in relation to the grant of bail under this rule by the Court of Appeal in a case of criminal contempt of court as they apply in relation to the grant of bail in criminal proceedings by the High Court, but with the substitution for references to a judge of references to the Court of Appeal and for references to the defendant of references to the appellant.

(5) When granting bail under this rule in a case of civil contempt of court, the Court of Appeal may order that the recognisance or other security to be given by the appellant or the recognisance of any surety shall be given before any person authorised by virtue of section 119(1) of the Magistrates' Courts Act 1980 to take a recognisance where a magistrates' court having power to take it has, instead of taking it, fixed the amount in which the principal and his sureties, if any, are to be bound. An order by the Court of Appeal granting bail as aforesaid must be in Form 98 in the relevant practice direction with the necessary adaptations.

(6) Where in pursuance of an order of the Court of Appeal under paragraph (5) of this rule a recognisance is entered into or other security given before any person, it shall be the duty of that person to cause the recognisance of the appellant or any surety or, as the case may be, a statement of the other security given, to be transmitted forthwith to the clerk of the court which committed the appellant; and a copy of such recognisance or statement shall at the same time be sent to the governor or keeper of the prison or other place of detention in which the appellant is detained, unless the recognisance or security was given before such governor or keeper.

(8) The powers conferred on the Court of Appeal by paragraphs (2), (4), (5) and (6) of this rule may be exercised by a single judge.

Appeals from Social Security Commissioners

21.—(1) this rule shall apply to any appeal to the Court of Appeal under section 14 of the Social Security Act 1980 (appeal from the decision of a Commissioner on a question of law, with the permission of the Commissioner or of the Court of Appeal). **R59.21**

(2) The notice of appeal must be served within 6 weeks from the date on which notice of the Commissioner's grant or refusal of permission was given in writing to the appellant and must be served on the Secretary of State and any person appointed by him to proceed with a claim as well as on the party or parties required to be served under rule 3.

(3) The provisions of rule 4(3) apply to this rule, with the substitution for the reference in rule 4(3) to paragraph (1) of a reference to paragraph (2).

Appeals from Value Added Tax Tribunals

22.—(1) An application to the Court of Appeal for permission to appeal from a value added tax tribunal direct to that court under section 26 of the Finance Act 1985 shall be made within 28 days from the date on which the tribunal certifies that its decision involves a point of law relating wholly or mainly to the construction of an enactment or of a statutory instrument, or of **R59.22**

any of the Community Treaties or any Community Instrument, which has been fully argued before it and fully considered by it.

(2) Such an application shall be made by the parties jointly by filing a copy of the decision, endorsed with the certificate of the tribunal and a statement of the grounds of the application, with the court, and shall be determined by a single judge of the Court of Appeal, who may do so without a hearing.

(3) In the case of all applications, the court shall notify the parties of the determination of the single judge, and

(a) where permission to appeal to the Court of Appeal is granted, the appellant shall within 14 days after such notification serve the notice of appeal on the chairman of the tribunal as well as on the party or parties required to be served by rule 3;

(b) where permission to appeal to the Court of Appeal is refused, the period specified in Order 55, rule 4(2) for appealing to the High Court shall be calculated from the date of notification of the refusal.

Dismissal of patient's appeal by consent

R59.23 **23.** Where the receiver or other person authorised under Part VII of the Mental Health Act 1983 to conduct legal proceedings in the name of the patient or on his behalf has also been authorised by the Court of Protection under its seal to consent to the dismissal of an appeal to the Court of Appeal by that patient, the appeal may be dismissed by consent without a hearing.

Appeals from Immigration Appeals Tribunal

R59.24 **24.**—(1) this rule shall apply to any appeal to the Court of Appeal under section 9 of the Asylum and Immigration Appeals Act 1993 (appeal on a question of law from a final determination of an Immigration Appeals Tribunal, with the permission of the Immigration Appeals Tribunal or the Court of Appeal).

(2) Rule 4(1) shall have effect as if for the words "the date on which the judgment or order of the court below was sealed or otherwise perfected" there were substituted the words "the date of the tribunal's written decision to grant or refuse permission to appeal".

(3) The notice of appeal must be served on the other party or parties to the proceedings before the tribunal, and on the chairman.

(5) Rule 13 shall not apply.

Appeals from Special Commissioners

R59.25 **25.**—(1) An application to the Court of Appeal for permission to appeal from the Special Commissioners direct to that court under section 56A of the Taxes Management Act 1970 shall be made within 28 days from the date on which the Special Commissioners certify that their decision involves a point of law relating wholly or mainly to the construction of an enactment which was fully argued before them and fully considered by them.

(2) Such an application shall be made by the parties jointly filing a copy of the decision, endorsed with the certificate of the Special Commissioners, and a statement of the grounds of the application with the court. The application shall be determined by a single judge of the Court of Appeal, who may make his determination without a hearing.

(3) The court shall notify the parties of the determination of the single judge, and—

(a) where permission to appeal to the Court of Appeal is granted, the applicant shall within 14 days after such notification serve the notice of appeal on the Clerk to the Special Commissioners as well as on all parties directly affected by the proceedings before the Special Commissioners;

(b) where permission to appeal to the Court of Appeal is refused, the period specified in Order 55, rule 4(2) for appealing to the High Court shall be calculated from the date of notification of the refusal.

RSC ORDER 60

APPEALS TO COURT OF APPEAL FROM THE RESTRICTIVE PRACTICES COURT

Appeal to be brought by notice of appeal

1. An appeal to the Court of Appeal from the Restrictive Practices Court under the Restrictive Practices Court Act 1976 must be brought by notice of appeal, and the notice of appeal must state any question of law and, in the case of proceedings under Part III of the Fair Trading Act 1973, any question of fact on which the appeal is brought together in each case with the appellant's contentions thereon. **R60.1**

Service of notice of appeal

2.—(1) Within 28 days after the appellant receives a copy of the judgment constituting the case stated by the Restrictive Practices Court or within 28 days of the date on which permission to appeal to the Court of Appeal was granted, he must serve the notice of appeal and a copy of the judgment on every other party to the proceedings before that court and must serve the notice of appeal on that court. **R60.2**

(2) Where the appellant applies to the said court for the court's judgment to be amplified or amended—

(a) he shall be deemed for the purpose of paragraph (1) to have received a copy of the judgment on the date on which he receives a copy of the order made on his application; and

(b) the judgment constituting the case stated shall be the judgment with such amplifications or amendments, if any, as may be specified in that order.

Entry, etc. of appeal

3.—(1) Within 7 days after service of the notice of appeal, the appellant must file the judgment constituting the case and two copies of the notice with the Court of Appeal and Order 59, rule 5 shall apply subject to any necessary modifications. **R60.3**

(2) The office of the Court of Appeal shall notify the Restrictive Practices Court of the decision of the Court of Appeal on the appeal and of any directions given by the Court of Appeal thereon.

Powers of Court of Appeal

4. The Court of Appeal shall have power to draw inferences of fact from the facts set forth in the judgment of the Restrictive Practices Court constituting the case. **R60.4**

RSC ORDER 61

APPEALS FROM TRIBUNALS TO COURT OF APPEAL BY CASE STATED

Statement of case by Lands Tribunal

1.—(1) The time within which a person aggrieved by a decision of the Lands Tribunal as being erroneous in point of law may under section 3(4) of the Lands Tribunal Act 1949, or any other enactment require the Tribunal to state a case for the decision of the Court of Appeal shall be 4 weeks from the **R61.1**

date of the decision, and the application for the statement of the case must be made to the registrar of the tribunal in writing.

(2) A case stated by the tribunal must state the facts on which the decision was based and the decision of the tribunal and must be signed by the member or members of the tribunal by whom it was given.

(3) The case must be stated as soon as may be after the application therefor is made and must be sent by post to the applicant.

(4) Where the decision of the Lands Tribunal in respect of which a case is stated states all the relevant facts found by the tribunal and indicates the questions of law on which the decision the Court of Appeal is sought, a copy of the decision signed by the person who presided at the hearing shall be annexed to the case, and the facts so found and the questions of law to be decided shall be sufficiently stated in the case by referring to the statement thereof in the decision.

Statement of case by other tribunals

R61.2 **2.**—(1) Where any tribunal is empowered or may be required to state a case on a question of law for determination by the Court of Appeal, any party to the proceedings who is aggrieved by the tribunal's refusal to state a case may apply to the Court of Appeal or a single judge of that court for an order requiring the tribunal to state a case.

(2) An application under this rule must be made in accordance with CPR Part 23 and the application notice, stating in general terms the grounds of the application, together with the question of law on which it is desired that a case shall be stated and any reasons given by the tribunal for its refusal, must within 28 days after the refusal, be served on the clerk or registrar of the tribunal and on every other party to the proceedings before the tribunal.

(3) Within 7 days after service of the application notice, the applicant must file two copies of the application notice with the Court of Appeal.

(4) Where a tribunal is ordered under this rule to state a case, the tribunal must, within such period as may be specified in the order, state a case, stating the facts on which the decision of the tribunal was based and the decision, sign it and cause it to be sent by post to the applicant.

(5) Rule 1(4) shall apply in relation to a case stated by a tribunal other than the Lands Tribunal as it applies in relation to a case stated by that tribunal.

(6) In this rule, references to a tribunal other than the Lands Tribunal include references to a judge of the Commercial Court acting as an arbitrator or umpire under section 4 of the Administration of Justice Act 1970.

Proceedings on case stated

R61.3 **3.**—(A1) An application for permission to appeal to the Court of Appeal from any tribunal to which this order applies may be combined with an application to the tribunal to state a case.

(A2) An application for permission to appeal may not be made to the Court of Appeal until the tribunal has stated a case.

(1) The party at whose instance a case has been stated by any tribunal to which this order applies must, within 21 days after the date on which permission to appeal to the Court of Appeal was granted—

(a) serve on every other party to the proceedings before the tribunal a copy of the case, together with a notice of appeal setting out his contentions on the question of law; and

(b) serve a copy of the notice on the clerk or registrar of the tribunal.

(2) Within 7 days after service of the notice of appeal, the said party must file the case, and two copies of the notice with the Court of Appeal and Order 59, rule 5 shall apply subject to any necessary modifications.

(3) Where any enactment under which the case is stated provides that a Minister or government department shall have a right to be heard in the

proceedings on the case, a copy of the case and of the notice of appeal served under paragraph (1) must be served on that Minister or department.

(4) On the hearing of the case, the Court of Appeal may amend the case or order it to be sent back to the tribunal for amendment.

(5) Order 59 shall, so far as applicable, apply, in relation to a case stated by a tribunal to which this order applies.

(6) The office of the Court of Appeal shall notify the clerk or registrar of the tribunal of the decision of the Court of Appeal on the case and of any directions given by that court thereon.

RSC ORDER 62

COSTS

APPENDIX 3

FIXED COSTS

The scale of costs set out in this Appendix shall apply in the cases to which the Appendix refers. R62.A3

PART II

Costs on judgment without trial for possession of land

1.—(1) Where the claim is for the possession of land, and the claimant obtains judgment— R62.A3.3

(a) under CPR Part 12 (default judgment); or

(c) under CPR Part 24 (summary judgment)

for possession of the land and costs, then, subject to sub-paragraph (2), there shall be allowed the costs prescribed by paragraph 2 of this Part of this Appendix.

(2) Where the claimant is also entitled under the judgment to damages to be assessed, or where the plaintiff claims any remedy of the nature specified in Order 88, rule 1 (mortgage claims), this Part of this Appendix shall not apply.

2. The costs to be allowed under this Part of this Appendix shall be £143.75, together with any court fee, and additional costs where appropriate set out in the Table below.

B ADDITIONAL COSTS

R62.A3.1C

Amount to be allowed	£
(1) Where there is more than one defendant, in respect of each additional defendant served	£13.75
(2) Where service by an alternative method is ordered and effected, in respect of each defendant served	£53.25
(3) Where service out of the jurisdiction is ordered and effected, in the case of service—	
(a) in Scotland, Northern Ireland, the Isle of Man or the Channel Islands	£68.25
(b) in any other place out of the jurisdiction	£77.00
(4) In the case of default judgment under CPR Part 12 or summary judgment under CPR Part 24 the claimant makes an affidavit of service for the purpose of a judgment where the defendant failed to respond to the claim form (the allowance to include the search fee)	£20.50
(5) In the case of summary judgment under CPR Part 24 where an affidavit of service of the Part 23 application is required	£20.50
(6) In the case of summary judgment under CPR Part 24 for each adjournment of the application	£20.50

PART III

R62.A3.4 This part shows the amount to be allowed in respect of enforcement costs.

Miscellaneous

2. Where a certificate in respect of money provisions contained in a judgment is registered in the High Court in the Register of United Kingdom judgments under Schedule 6 to the Civil Jurisdiction and Judgments Act 1982, there shall be allowed—

Costs of registration £39.00

2A. Where costs are allowed under the following paragraphs of this Part, the appropriate court fees shall be allowed in addition.

3. Where, upon the application of any person who has obtained a judgment or order against a debtor for the recovery or payment of money, a garnishee order is made under Order 49, rule 1, against a garnishee attaching debts due or accruing due from the debtor, the following costs shall be allowed—

(a) to the garnishee to be deducted by him from any debt due by him as aforesaid before payment to the applicant £23.00

(b) to the applicant, to be retained, unless the court otherwise orders, out of the money recovered by him under the garnishee order and in priority to the amount of the debt owing to him under the judgment or order—

(i) *Basic costs* If the amount recovered by the applicant from the garnishee is—

less than £150.............................one half of the amount recovered

not less than £150 ....£98.50

(ii) *Additional costs* Where the garnishee fails to attend the hearing of the application and an affidavit of service is required £18.00

4. Where a charging order is granted and made absolute there shall be allowed—

Basic costs...£110.00

Additional costs where an affidavit of service is required £18.00

together with such reasonable disbursements in respect of search fees and the registration of the order as the court may allow.

5. Where leave is given under Order 45, rule 3, to enforce a judgment or order for the giving of possession of land by writ of possession, if the costs are allowed on the judgment or order there shall be allowed the following costs, which shall be added to the judgment or order—

Basic costs...£42.50

Where notice of the proceedings has been given to more than one person, in respect of each additional person £2.75

6. Where a writ of execution within the meaning of Order 46, rule 1, is issued against any party, there shall be allowed—

Costs of issuing execution..£51.75

RSC ORDER 64

SITTINGS, VACATIONS AND OFFICE HOURS

Divisional Court business during vacation

R64.4 **4.** Proceedings which require to be immediately or promptly heard and which by virtue of the following provisions must be brought in a Divisional Court may, in vacation, be brought before a single judge:

(a) Order 52, rules 1(2) and 3(1);
(b) Order 53, rules 3(4)(a) and 5(1);
(c) Order 55, rule 2(a);
(d) Order 56, rule 1(1)(a).

RSC ORDER 69

SERVICE OF FOREIGN PROCESS

Contents R69.0.1

Editorial Introduction

The rules in this regulate the practice for the service within England and Wales of foreign process. The rules were substantially reformed in 1980. For the effect of the rules, see commentary following r.4. The intention of the CPR is to make no substantive changes. R69.0.2

Related sources

- RSC, O.11, rr.5 and 6(1) R69.0.3

Definitions

1. In this Order— R69.1

"a convention country" means a foreign country in relation to which there subsists a civil procedure convention providing for service in that country of process of the High Court, and includes a country which is a party to the Convention on the Service Abroad of Judicial and Extra-Judicial Documents in Civil or Commercial Matters signed at the Hague on 15 November 1965;

"officer of the county court" means any clerk or bailiff in the service of a county court;

"process" includes a citation;

"process server" means the process server appointed under rule 4 or his authorised agent;

History of rule—Amended by S.I. 1980 No. 629. R69.1.1

Applications

2. This order applies to the service on a person in England or Wales of any process in connection with civil or commercial proceedings in a foreign court or tribunal where the Senior Master receives a written request for service— R69.2

(a) from Her Majesty's Principal Secretary of State for Foreign and Commonwealth Affairs, with a recommendation by him that service should be effected; or
(b) where the foreign court or tribunal is in a convention country, from a consular or other authority of that country.

History of rule—Substituted by RSC (Amendment) 1980 (S.I. 1980 No. 629). R69.2.1

Service of process

3.—(1) The request shall be accompanied by a translation thereof in English, two copies of the process and, unless the foreign court or tribunal certifies that the person to be served understands the language of the process, two copies of a translation thereof. R69.3

(2) Subject to paragraphs (3) and (5) and to any enactment providing for the manner of service of documents on corporate bodies, the process shall be

served by the process server's leaving a copy of the process and a copy of the translation or certificate, as the case may be, with the person to be served.

(3) The provisions of CPR rule 6.2(1)(c) and CPR rule 6.7 regarding service by leaving at a place specified in CPR rule 6.5, shall apply to the service of foreign process as they apply to the service of claim form, except that service may be proved by a witness statement or affidavit or by a certificate or report in such form as the Senior Master may direct.

(4) The process server shall send to the Senior Master a copy of the process and a witness statement or affidavit, certificate or report proving due service of process or stating the reason why service could not be effected, as the case may be, and shall, if the court so directs, specify the costs incurred in effecting or attempting to effect service.

(5) CPR rule 6.8 (service by an alternative method) shall apply to the service of foreign process as it applies to the service of claim forms, except that the Senior Master may make an order for alternative service of foreign process on the basis of the process server's witness statement or affidavit, certificate or report, without an application being made to him in that behalf.

(6) The Senior Master shall send a certificate, together with a copy of the process, to the consular or other authority or the Secretary of State, as the case may be, stating—

(i) when and how service was effected or the reason why service could not be effected, as the case may be;

(ii) where appropriate, the amount certified by the costs judge to be the costs of effecting or attempting to effect service.

(7) The certificate under paragraph (6) shall be sealed with the seal of the Supreme Court for use out of the jurisdiction.

R69.3.1 **History of rule**—Substituted by S.I. 1980 No. 629.

Appointment of process server

R69.4 **4.** The Lord Chancellor may appoint a process server for the purposes of this order.

R69.4.1 **History of rule**—Substituted by S.I. 1980 No. 629.

R69.4.2 **Effect and operation of Order (rr.1–4)**—The Order:

(1) Equates the method of service of foreign process for requests received by the Senior Master for such service emanating from a non-convention country through the Secretary of State for Foreign and Commonwealth Affairs and from a consular or other authority of a convention country, whether it be a country with whom a bilaterial convention or the multi-lateral convention, known as "the Hague Convention", exists.

(2) Enables the foreign process to be served through the machinery of the county court by the employment of county court clerks or bailiffs, and in this way, it gives effect to the policy that, in general, no fee should be charged for the service of foreign process in England.

(3) Eliminates the need to seek the recovery of the actual cost of serving process from the litigant in the foreign Court of tribunal, which anyway was often difficult, delayed and expensive, save for two exceptions, namely (a) that the United Kingdom retains a discretion to charge a fee in exceptional circumstances, *e.g.* where a disproportionate number of requests is received from one country, and (b) where the country requesting service is not prepared to offer reciprocal free service.

(4) Enables the foreign Court or tribunal to certify that the person to be served understands the language of the process and in such case, to eliminate the need for the process to be translated, thus saving the considerable expense involved in obtaining such a translation and making two copies thereof.

(5) While retaining the method of personal service, authorises, as an alternative method of service, service by leaving the foreign process at a place specified in CPR, r.6.5 in accordance with CPR, r.6.2(1)(c) and CPR, r.6.5 except that service may be proved by a witness statement or affidavit, or by a certificate or report in such forms as the Senior Master may direct.

(6) The Senior Master may make an order for service by an alternative method of the foreign process on the basis of the process server's witness statement or affidavit certificate or report, without an application being made to him in that behalf.

(7) Relating the power of the Court, in appropriate cases, such as those mentioned above, to request the costs of effecting or attempting to effect service, as specified.

Foreign Country (rr.1–4)—This has the same meaning as in O.11, r.6(1), and accordingly this rules does not apply to the countries or territories described therein. Service of process from such countries or territories should therefore be effected by the party or his agent direct. R69.4.3

RSC ORDER 70

OBTAINING EVIDENCE FOR FOREIGN COURTS, ETC.

Contents R70.0.1

Editorial Introduction

The rules in this Order were amended following the enactment of the Evidence (Proceedings in Other Jurisdictions) Act 1975 (SCP 1999, Vol. 2, Section 21M, para. 21M–1). That Act set out a comprehensive code for the taking of evidence in the U.K. on behalf of other courts. It re-enacted the existing law on the taking of evidence by courts in England, Scotland and Northern Ireland for the purposes of civil proceedings in a case in another part of the U.K. It contained new provisions to enable the U.K. to ratify the Hague Convention on the Taking of Evidence Abroad in Civil or Commercial Matters (Cmnd. 3991, 1969) (see further para. R70.6.2). A power to make rules of court necessary or expedient to facilitate the purposes of the Act in the High Court and the Court of Appeal was contained in s.7. The 1975 Act and the rules in this Order should be read together. R70.0.2

Related sources

- Evidence (Proceedings in Other Jurisdictions) Act 1975 (SCP 1999, Vol. 2, Section 21M, para. 21M–1). R70.0.3
- CPR, Part 34.
- Practice Direction (Depositions and Court Attendances by Witnesses) para. 4.2 and following (see para. 34PD–002)

Forms

See Pt 4: Practice Directions, Table 2 for the general approach. R70.0.4

The following Prescribed Form (formerly included amongst the Prescribed Forms in Appendix A to the RSC) are relevant to O.70. These forms are included in Table 2 (Practice Forms) attached to Practice Direction (Forms) and may be found in SCP 1999, Vol. 2, Section 1A, para. 1A–96):

- PF No. 93—Order under the Evidence (Proceedings in Other Jurisdictions) Act 1975 (O.70, r.1)

The following Queen's Bench Masters' Practice Forms (now listed in Table 2 (Practice Forms) attached to Practice Direction (Forms)) are relevant to O.70 (SCP 1999, Vol. 2, Section 1B, paras 1B–113 and 1B–114);

- PF152 1QB—Affidavit appying for examination of a witness under Evidence (Proceedings in other Jurisdictions) Act 1975 (O.70, r.2).
- PF153 1QB—Certificate under the Evidence (Proceedings in Other Jurisdictions) Act 1975 (O.70, r.5).

Interpretation and exercise of jurisdiction

1.—(1) In this Order "the Act of 1975" means the Evidence (Proceedings in Other Jurisdictions) Act 1975 and expressions used in this order which are used in that Act shall have the same meaning as in that Act. R70.1

(2) The power of the High Court to make an order under section 2 of the Act of 1975 may be exercised by a Master of the Queen's Bench Division.

History of rule—Amended by S.I. 1976 No. 337. R70.1.1

Application for order

2.—(1) Subject to paragraph (3) and rule 3 an application for an order under the Act of 1975 must be made without notice being served on any other party and must be supported by witness statement or affidavit. R70.2

(2) There shall be exhibited to the witness statement or affidavit the request in pursuance of which the application is made, and if the request is not in the English language, a translation thereof in that language.

(3) Where on an application under section 1 of the Act of 1975 as applied by section 92 of the Patents Act 1977 an order is made for the examination of witnesses the court may allow an officer of the European Patent Office to attend the examination and examine the witnesses or request the court or the examiner before whom the examination takes place to put specified questions to them.

R70.2.1 **History of rule**—Amended by S.I. 1976 No. 337 and S.I. 1978 No. 579.

Application by Treasury Solicitor in certain cases

R70.3 **3.** Where a request—

(a) is received by the Secretary of State and sent by him to the Senior Master with an intimation that effect should be given to the request without requiring an application for that purpose to be made by the agent in England of any party to the matter pending or contemplated before the foreign court or tribunal; or

(b) is received by the Senior Master in pursuance of a Civil Procedure Convention providing for the taking of the evidence of any person in England or Wales for the assistance of a court or tribunal in the foreign country, and no person is named in the document as the person who will make the necessary application on behalf of such party,

the Senior Master shall send the document to the Treasury Solicitor and the Treasury Solicitor may, with the consent of the Treasury, make an application for an order under the Act of 1975, and take such other steps as may be necessary, to give effect to the request.

R70.3.1 **History of rule**—Amended by S.I. 1976 No. 337.

Person to take and manner of taking examination

R70.4 **4.**—(1) Any order made in pursuance of this order for the examination of a witness may order the examination to be taken before any fit and proper person nominated by the person applying for the order or before an examiner of the court or before such other qualified person as to the court seems fit.

(2) Subject to rule 6 and to any special directions contained in any order made in pursuance of this order for the examination of any witness, the examination shall be taken in manner provided by CPR rules 34.9 and 34.10 and an order may be made under CPR rule 34.14, for payment of the fees and expenses due to the examiner, and those rules shall apply accordingly with any necessary modifications.

R70.4.1 **History of rule**—Amended by S.I. 1976 No. 337.

Dealing with deposition

R70.5 **5.** Unless any order made in pursuance of this Order for the examination of any witness otherwise directs, the examiner before whom the examination was taken must send the deposition of that witness to the Senior Master, and the Senior Master shall—

(a) give a certificate sealed with the seal of the Supreme Court for use out of the jurisdiction identifying the documents annexed thereto, that is to say, the request, the order of the court for examination and the deposition taken in pursuance of the order; and

(b) send the certificate with the documents annexed thereto to the

Secretary of State, or, where the request was sent to the Senior Master by some other person in accordance with a Civil Procedure Convention to that other person, for transmission to the court or tribunal out of the jurisdiction requesting the examination.

History of rule—Amended by S.I. 1976 No. 337 and S.I. No. 1987 No. 1423. R70.5.1

Claim to privilege

6.—(1) The provisions of this rule shall have effect where a claim by a witness to be exempt from giving any evidence on the ground specified in section 3(1)(b) of the Act of 1975 is not supported or conceded as mentioned in subsection (2) of that section. R70.6

(2) The examiner may, if he thinks fit, require the witness to give the evidence to which the claim relates and, if the examiner does not do so, the court may do so, on the application without notice being served on any other party of the person who obtained the order under section 2.

(3) If such evidence is taken—

(a) it must be contained in a document separate from the remainder of the deposition of the witness;

(b) the examiner shall send to the Senior Master with the deposition a statement signed by the examiner setting out the claim and the ground on which it was made;

(c) on receipt of the statement the Senior Master shall, notwithstanding anything in rule 5, retain the document containing the part of the witness's evidence to which the claim relates and shall send the statement and a request to determine the claim to the foreign court or tribunal with the documents mentioned in rule 5;

(d) if the claim is rejected by the foreign court or tribunal, the Senior Master shall send to that court or tribunal the document containing that part of the witness's evidence to which the claim relates, but if the claim is upheld he shall send the document to the witness, and shall in either case notify the witness and the person who obtained the order under section 2 of the court or tribunal's determination.

History of rule—Added by S.I. 1976 No. 337. R70.6.1

Effect of 1975 Act and Order (rr.1–6)—The 1975 Act and this Order should be read and applied in close conjunction, for together they provide a comprehensive, self-contained code for obtaining evidence in England for use in proceedings in foreign Courts in those cases in which the help of the High Court is invoked. The jurisdiction of the English courts to order persons within its jurisdiction to provide oral or documentary evidence in aid of proceedings in foreign Courts has always been exclusively statutory (*Rio Tinto Zinc Corporation v. Westinghouse Electric Corporation* [1978] A.C. 547; [1978] 1 All E.R. 434, HL at 633 and 461, *per* Lord Diplock); and this jurisdiction and the powers of the High Court to make such orders are now contained in the 1975 Act, as supplemented by this Order. The Act is clear in its terms, so that references in aid of interpretation to the previous statutes which have been repealed is not required nor is any assistance to be gained from previous decisions of English Courts under the former statutes, though in practice it is almost inevitable that references will be so made; and presumably it would also not be helpful in aid of interpretation to refer to the Hague Convention itself. R70.6.2

The Act of 1975 applies to civil proceedings which are either pending or contemplated (s.1(b)). The application of the 1975 Act is not confined to countries which are parties to the Hague Convention; nor is the Act limited in its application to courts of law, but extends to tribunals as well (see, *per* Lord Diplock in *Rio Tinto Zinc Corporation v. Westinghouse Electric Corporation,* above). On the other hand, the 1975 Act does not affect any of the bilateral Civil Procedure Conventions which the U.K. has with a number of foreign countries for the taking of evidence of a person within the jurisdiction for the assistance of courts or tribunals within those foreign countries (see r.3(b)).

It should perhaps be further noted that the 1975 Act does not affect the taking of evidence given *voluntarily* to foreign diplomatic or consular officers or other persons appointed by foreign courts to take evidence or to legal representatives taking evidence in this country for the purpose of proceedings abroad. There is in England no legal objection to the taking of evidence in this country for use outside the jurisdiction without the intervention of the High Court. A foreign

Court is at liberty to appoint the consul in England of its own country, or any other person it desires, as an examiner to take evidence. So long as the witnesses are willing to attend to give evidence, the examination may be completed and the depositions returned to the foreign Court without the intervention of the Court in England. Thus American Courts often appoint some person in this country to take the evidence. On the other hand, the rules of this Order concern the power of the High Court to order such evidence to be taken, and they lay down the procedure.

R70.6.3 **General principles for compliance with foreign request for evidence (rr.1–6)**—The general principle which is followed in England in relation to a request from a foreign Court for assistance in obtaining evidence for the purpose of proceedings in that Court is that the English Court will ordinarily give effect to such a request so far as is proper and practicable and to the extent that is permissible under English law. This principle reflects judicial and international comity (see, *per* Cooke J. in *Seyfang v. G. D. Searle & Co.* [1973] Q.B. 148 at 151; [1973] 1 All ER. 290 at 293) and it conforms with the spirit of the Hague Convention and the 1975 Act as it conformed with the spirit of the former statutes. "We ought to afford foreign Courts the fullest benefit we can" (*per* Cockburn C.J. in *Desilla v. Fells* (1879) 40 LT. 423 at 424). It is the duty and the pleasure of the English Court to do all it can to assist the foreign Court, just as the English Court would expect the foreign Court to help it in like circumstances (see, *per* Lord Denning M.R. in *Rio Tinto Zinc Corporation v. Westinghouse Electric Corporation* [1978] A.C. 547 at 560; [1977] 3 All E.R. 703 at 708).

In dealing with a request for evidence from a foreign Court, the English Court has first to decide whether it has jurisdiction to make an order to give effect to the request, and secondly, if it has, whether as a matter of discretion it ought to make or refuse to make such an order. As a matter of jurisdiction, in the ordinary way and in the absence of evidence to the contrary the English Court should be prepared to accept the statement of the foreign Court in its request that the evidence is required for the purposes of civil proceedings in that Court (see, *per* Lord Diplock in *Rio Tinto Zinc Corporation v. Westinghouse Electric Corporation*, above). On the other hand, the form of the letter of request is not conclusive; the Court must examine the request objectively by the nature of the testimony sought (see, *per* Lord Wilberforce in *Rio Tinto Zinc Corporation v. Westinghouse Electric Corporation*, above) and it has to look at the substance of the matter (see, *per* Lord Goddard in *Radio Corporation of America v. Rauland Corporation* [1956] 1 Q.B. 618 at 641) but it may have regard to what was said in the foreign Court when the request for evidence was issued. If there is any doubt about the matter, the English Court may allow the parties to refer back to the foreign Court or Judge who issued the request for evidence (see *American Express Warehousing Ltd v. Doe* [1967] 1 Lloyd's Rep. 222).

As a matter of discretion, again in the ordinary way, the English Court should exercise its discretion to make the order asked for unless it is satisfied that the application would be regarded as falling within the description of frivolous, vexatious or an abuse of the process of the Court (*per* Lord Diplock in *Rio Tinto Zinc Corporation v. Westinghouse Electric Corporation*, above). Thus, the English Court will in its discretion refuse to order an expert to give evidence against his wishes in a case where he has had no connection with the facts or history of the matter in issue and still less to produce his working papers from which he had prepared published articles (*Seyfang v. G. D. Searle & Co.* [1973] Q.B. 148; [1973] 1 All E.R. 290).

The English Court has power to accept or reject the foreign request in whole or in part, whether as to oral or documentary evidence; and it can and should delete from the foreign request any parts that are excessive either as regards witnesses or as regards documents. The English Court will act on the principle that it should salve what it can, but should decline to comply with the foreign request in so far as it is not proper or permissible or practicable under English law to give effect to it. The English Court, moreover, ought not to embark on the process of re-structuring or re-casting or re-phrasing the foreign request so that it becomes different in substance from the original request. The Court has no power so to modify the original foreign request as to substitute a different category of documents for the category which had been requested by the foreign Court (see, *per* Lord Diplock in *Rio Tinto Zinc Corporation v. Westinghouse Electric Corporation*, above).

A request could not be denied on the ground of "fishing" if there was sufficient reason to believe that the witness could give relevant evidence to issues in the action and the issue of relevance fell to be determined by the foreign court. It was necessary however to protect witnesses from oppressive requirements such as submitting them to wide ranging examination while at the same time they were under threat of being added as defendants. The test of whether to disallows the request was similar to that applied in setting aside a domestic witness summons: *First American Corp. v. Al-Nahyan* [1998] 4 All E.R. 439, CA.

R70.6.4 **Evidence for civil proceedings (rr.1–6)**—Under section 1 of the 1975 Act, the High Court has the powers conferred on it by the Act to render assistance to a foreign Court to obtain evidence in England and Wales for civil proceedings in that Court. Three conditions precedent must be fulfilled before the English Court can exercise the jurisdiction conferred upon it to make any order under the 1975 Act, namely:

(1) there must be an application to the Court for an order for evidence to be obtained in England and Wales;

(2) the Court must be satisfied that such application is made in pursuance of a request by or on behalf of a Court or tribunal described as "the requesting Court" exercising jurisdiction outside England and Wales (s.1(a)); and
(3) the Court must be satisfied that the evidence to which the application relates is to be obtained for the purposes of civil proceedings which either have been instituted before the requesting Court or where institution before that Court is contemplated (s.1(b)).

For this purpose, civil proceedings means proceedings in any civil or commercial matter, and request includes any commission, order or other process issued by or on behalf of the requesting Court, sometimes called "letters rogatory" (see s.9(1)).

The term "civil or commercial matter" is a wide general term, covering all kinds of suits, petitions, summonses, applications for orders and so forth, of which Courts are competent to take cognisance (*per* Chapman J. in *Re Extradition Act 1870, ex p. Treasury Solicitor* [1969] 1 W.L.R. 12; *sub nom. Re Gross* [1968] 3 All E.R. 804).

Affiliation proceedings are a "civil matter" (*S. v. E.* [1967] 1 Q.B. 367; [1967] 1 All E.R. 593).

For the purposes of civil proceedings, the English Court must be satisfied that the requesting Court is requiring the evidence for the purposes of proceedings which have been begun or are contemplated in that Court. It is an unusual concept that evidence should be required, not for proceedings which are actually pending but are merely "contemplated." It would seem that "contemplated" in this context means, not simply that the institution of proceedings is possible or even probable but that it is imminent or impending, that the institution of proceedings has reached the stage not merely of being considered or examined but is almost about to happen. The English Court should, it is thought, be somewhat more hesitant about being satisfied that proceedings in the requesting Court are contemplated unless there are substantial and cogent grounds for supporting the foreign request made on this ground.

The English court will extend its assistance in obtaining evidence to be used for the enforcement of the revenue law of a foreign state in that state itself, since this will not breach the rule that the English courts will not assist in the direct or indirect enforcement in England of the revenue law of that foreign state (*Re State of Norway's Applications (Nos 1 & 2)* [1989] 2 W.L.R. 458, HL reversing [1988] 3 W.L.R. 603; [1989] 1 All E.R. 745, HL).

Powers of the Court (rr.1–6)—Under section 2 of the 1975 Act, the High Court is given extensive powers on an application under s.1 to make an order for obtaining the requested evidence in England or Wales. The Court may by its order make such provision for obtaining the requested evidence "as may appear to the Court appropriate for the purposes of giving effect to the request in pursuance of which the application is made" (s.2(1)) and the order may require a person specified therein to take such steps as the Court may consider appropriate for that purpose (*ibid.*). **R70.6.5**

In particular, the order of the Court may make provision for the examination of witnesses, either orally or in writing; the production of documents; the inspection, photographing, preservation, custody or detention of any property; the taking of samples of any property and the carrying out of any experiments on or with any property; the medical examination of any person, and the taking and testing of samples of blood from any person (s.2(2)).

Nevertheless, there are important limitations upon the powers of the English Court imposed by subss.(3) and (4) in making an order for obtaining evidence at the request of a foreign Court and by the common law. These limitations include:

(1) "evidence" required for pre-trial purposes;
(2) no order for general disclosure of documents;
(3) production only of particular documents specified in the foreign request; and
(4) breach of U.K. sovereignty.

In addition, of course, the Act of 1975 preserves the grounds of privilege of a witness from giving evidence or producing documents recognised under the law of England or of the requesting Court (s.3).

These limitations and the preservation of the recognised grounds of privilege are intended to protect and safeguard the position of a person, not a party to the foreign litigation, from giving evidence in aid of foreign proceedings, which according to the policy of English procedural law he ought not to be compelled to give.

Distinction between evidence for trial or for pre-trial purposes (rr.1–6)—Unlike s.2(3), the English Court is prohibited from making an order requiring any particular steps to be taken unless they are steps which can be required to be taken by way of obtaining evidence for the purposes of civil proceedings in the English Court, whether or not they are proceedings of the same description as those to which the application for the order relates. This provision, which applies both to oral and documentary evidence recognises and gives effect to the distinction between evidence in the nature of proof to be used for the purposes of the trial and evidence in the nature of pre-trial disclosure to be used for the purposes of leading to a train of inquiry which might produce direct evidence for the trial. This distinction was in the mind of the draftsman of the Act of 1975 and was made the subject of an express declaration by Her Majesty's Government when ratifying the Hague Convention that the United Kingdom would "not execute letters of request issued for the purpose of obtaining pre-trial discovery of documents" (see Cmnd. 6727 (1976)). **R70.6.6**

Accordingly, the English Court will refuse to make an order in aid of a foreign request for evidence if it appears or to the extent to which it appears that that evidence is required, not for the purpose of proof at the foreign trial, where it is admissible and relevant to the issues in those proceedings, but for the purpose of disclosure, something in the nature of a roving inquiry in which a party is seeking to "fish out" some material which might lead to obtaining admissible evidence at the trial, even though the procedure of the foreign Court permits such a practice, as does, for example, r.26 of the U.S. Federal Rules of Civil Procedure and as do the rules of many State Courts in the U.S.A., and Rule 18 of the Nova Scotia Civil Procedure Rules (see *Radio Corporation of America v. Rauland Corp.* [1956] 1 Q.B. 214; [1956] 1 All E.R. 549; DC; *Burchard v. Macfarlane* [1891] 2 Q.B. 241; *Penn-Texas Corporation v. Murat Anstalt* [1964] 1 Q.B. 40; [1963] 1 All E.R. 258). On the other hand, if the foreign request is for evidence in the nature of proof to be adduced to the trial, the English Court will give effect to such request and it may do so subject to modifications as to the disallowances of certain witnesses or documents (*Rio Tinto Zinc Corporation v. Westinghouse Electric Corporation* [1978] A.C. 547; [1978] 1 All ER. 434, HL, upholding the CA [1977] 3 W.L.R. 430; [1977] 3 All E.R. 703, though reversing the decision on other grounds; and see *American Express Warehousing Ltd v. Doe* [1967] 1 Lloyd's Rep. 222, CA).

The Second Division of the Inner House of the Court of Session amended a letter of request from the Superior Court of the State of California which had the dual purpose of discovery and obtaining evidence for the use at trial by adding the words "for the purpose of his trial testimony only". The Court also directed that a legal representative of the witness should be allowed to be present at the examination with power to object to questions which appeared to be objectionable. It would then be for the examiner (in this case the Sheriff Principal of North Strathclyde) to rule upon these objections (*Lord Advocate v. Murdoch* (1993) *The Times*, December 3).

In relation to legal systems which do not recognise the distinction between the stages of pre-trial and trial, as in the case of many European Continental systems, it seems that the English Court may have to give effect to the request of the foreign Court, since all the material which such a Court gathers in the way of evidence forms part of the material on which that Court makes its final adjudication, so that the evidence is the equivalent of testimony at the trial. It remains to be seen how the more restrictive approach of the English courts to disclosure (PC 31) is likely to effect the position given the extensive discretionary powers that remain.

R70.6.7 **No order for general disclosure of documents (rr.1–6)**—Under section 2(4)(a) of the 1975 Act, the English Court is prohibited from making an order against a stranger to the proceedings requiring him to make general disclosure of documents, *i.e.* to state whether documents relevant to the proceedings to which the application for the order relates are or have been in his possession, custody or power. Such an order would be in the nature of a "fishing" expedition which is never allowed in the English Court (see, *per* Lord Goddard C.J. in *Radio Corporation of America v. Rauland Corporation* [1956] 1 Q.B. 618, at 649; see also *Buchard v. Macfarlane* [1891] 2 Q.B. 241). This provision was made pursuant to the express declaration of H.M. Government when modifying the Hague Convention (see Cmnd. 6727 (1976)). The words "possession, custody or power are set out in the Act. CPR r.31.8 refers to "control".

R70.6.8 **Production of particular documents specified (rr.1–6)**—Under section 2(4)(b) of the Act of 1975, the English court is prohibited from making an order against a stranger to the proceedings requiring him to produce any documents other than particular documents specified in the order as being documents appearing to the Court making the order to be, or be likely to be, in his possession, custody or power.

In making an order for the production of documents, the Court must first be satisfied that they are likely to be, in the control of the person against whom the order is made CPR, r.31.8. The burden of proving this fact is upon the applicant, and there must be sufficient evidence supporting this ground.

Moreover, in applying this provision of the Act, the Court is limited to ordering the production of "particular documents specified," *i.e.* individual documents separately described, together with replies to letters where replies must have been sent (*per* Lord Diplock and *per* Lord Wilberforce respectively in *Rio Tinto Zinc Corporation v. Westinghouse Electric Corporation*, above). General words like a request for "any memoranda, correspondence or other documents relevant thereto" or "any memoranda, correspondence or other documents referred to therein" are far too wide and will be struck out (*Rio Tinto Zinc Corporation v. Westinghouse Electric Corporation*, above, negating to this extent *American Express Warehousing Ltd v. Doe* [1967] 1 Lloyd's Rep. 222, CA). The analogy to be followed is, not what description of documents would be sufficient for the purposes of a witness summons to produce documents but what particular documents would fall within CPR, r.31.12, for the production of "particular documents." Indeed, the Act of 1975 has not dealt more liberally than its predecessor with pre-trial discovery but it has taken a stricter line (see, *per* Lord Wilberforce in *Rio Tinto Zinc Corporation v. Westinghouse Electric Corporation*, above).

The House of Lords has explained in *Re Asbestos Insurance Coverage Cases* [1985] 1 W.L.R. 331; [1985] 1 All ER. 716 that (1) "particular documents" means individual documents separately described; a compendious description of several documents (*e.g.* "monthly bank statements for August to December") may be used provided that the exact document in each case is clearly indicated. (2) A second test of "particular documents" is that they must be actual documents shown by evidence to exist or to have existed. Conjectural documents which may or may not exist, or have existed, do not satisfy this test (*per* Lord Fraser at 720–722).

On the other hand, documents to be produced under letters rogatory need not be ancillary to the oral evidence of witnesses (*Rio Tinto Zinc Corporation v. Westinghouse Electric Corporation* [1978] A.C. 547).

In *Panayiotou v. Sony Music* [1994] 1 All E.R. 755, 763, 764 a case concerning an outgoing letter of request under O.39, r.2, Nicholls V.-C. after discussing *Rio Tinto Zinc Corporation v. Westinghouse Electric Corporation* and *Re Asbestos Insurance Coverage Cases*, above, considered that letters of request for the production of documents whether outgoing or incoming should be governed by a uniform standard and that standard was the standard applicable to a domestic summons to produce documents.

Breach of U.K. sovereignty (rr.1–6)—Quite apart from the provisions of the 1975 Act, where it appears to the Court that the Ministry or Department of another state, *e.g.* the USA has intervened in the letters rogatory proceedings with a view to the exercise by that State of extra-territorial jurisdiction in penal matters which in the view of Her Majesty's Government is prejudicial to the sovereignty of the U.K., the Court will refuse to give effect to the letters rogatory; and in any event, such letters rogatory will have changed their character from being a request for evidence in proceedings for the foreign Court and converted into a request for evidence for the purpose of penal or grand jury investigation, *e.g.* under breaches of the U.S. anti-trust legislation (*Rio Tinto Zinc Corporation v. Westinghouse Electric Corporation*, above). **R70.6.9**

Privilege of witnesses (rr.1–6)—Under section 3(1) of the 1975 Act, a witness is entitled to claim privilege from giving any evidence which he could not be compelled to give on any ground recognised under the law of England or under the law of the requesting Court. The claim to privilege against giving evidence extends not only to giving answers to any questions, whether oral or in writing but to producing any document (s.3(4)). Ordinarily, the English Court will make the order to give effect to the foreign request for evidence (see *Re Westinghouse Uranium Litigation* [1977] 3 W.L.R. 430; [1977] 3 All E.R. 703) and the claim to privilege must be properly taken by the witness at the time of his examination under the order or at the stage at which the relevant document is required to be produced (see *Re Westinghouse Uranium Litigation (No. 2)* [1977] 3 W.L.R. 492; [1977] 3 All E.R. 717, CA). **R70.6.10**

The Court will give effect to the claim for privilege on any ground recognised by English law, even though it be a ground which is not recognised or known in the courts or territory of the requesting Court. Thus, in relation to letters rogatory from a U.S. Federal Court, an English company was entitled to claim privilege against self-incrimination under section 14(1) of the Civil Evidence Act 1968 in respect of documents required to be produced, since such production would have exposed the company to fines imposed by the Commission of the European Communities under Art. 17 of reg. 17 for intentionally or negligently acting in breach of Art. 85 of the Treaty of Rome, which formed part of the law of England, and such fines imposed by the Commission under this regulation constituted a "penalty" for the purposes of section 14 of the Civil Evidence Act 1968 and were recoverable by proceedings in England (*Rio Tinto Zinc Corporation v. Westinghouse Electric Corporation* [1978] A.C. 547; [1978] 1 All E.R. 434, affirming [1977] 3 W.L.R. 492; [1977] 3 All E.R. 717, CA).

The Act provides a further ground entitling a witness who has been ordered to give evidence in aid of foreign proceedings to refuse to do so. By s.3(3), such a person will not be compelled to give any evidence, whether in answering any question or producing any document, if his doing so would be prejudicial to the security of the United Kingdom, and a certificate signed by or on behalf of the Secretary of State to this effect will be conclusive evidence of that fact. This provision is additional to the claim for privilege on the ground that disclosure of the document would be injurious to the public interest (see CPR, r.31.19).

Privilege claimed under foreign law (rr.1–6)—Where the ground of privilege claimed is one not recognised by the law of England, but is recognised by the law of the country or territory of the requesting Court, the claim to privilege must either be supported by a statement contained in the request, whether unconditionally or subject to conditions which are fulfilled or it is conceded by the applicant for the order (s.3(2)(a) and (b)). If it is not so supported or conceded the witness may be required to give the evidence to which the claim relates but that evidence must not be transmitted to the requesting Court if that Court, on the matter being referred to it, upholds the claim (s.3(2) of the Act of 1975). **R70.6.11**

An example of such a claim for privilege would be the privilege afforded by the Fifth Amendment of the U.S. Constitution, which is available only to individuals and not to companies (see *Rio Tinto Zinc Corporation v. Westinghouse Electric Corporation* [1978] A.C. 547).

When such a claim is made, the practice is that the examiner may, if he thinks fit, require the witness to give the evidence to which the claim relates and if the examiner does not do so the Court may do so, on the application without notice of the person who obtained the order (see r.6(2)). If such evidence is taken then it must be contained in a document separate from the remainder of the deposition of the witness; the examiner must send to the Senior Master with the deposition a statement signed by the examiner setting out the claim and the ground on which it was made. On receipt of the statement the Senior Master must *retain* the document containing the part of the witness's evidence to which the claim relates, and he must send the statement and a request to determine the claim to the requesting Court with the rest of the deposition; and if the claim is rejected by the requesting Court, the Senior Master must send that Court the documents containing that part of the witness's evidence to which the claim relates, but if the claim is upheld, he must send the documents to the witness himself, and he must in either case notify the witness and the person who obtained the order for the examination of the Court's determination (see r.6(3)).

R70.6.12 **Evidence for criminal proceedings (rr.1–6)**—Section 5 of the 1975 Act which enabled the High Court to make an order in pursuance of a foreign request for the evidence of a witness to be obtained for the purpose of criminal proceedings has been repealed with effect from July 1, 1991 by the Criminal Justice (International Co-operation) Act 1990 and see para. R70.6.17.

R70.6.13 **Evidence for United Kingdom Court (rr.1–6)**—Section 4 of the 1975 Act extends the powers of the High Court under SCA 1981, s.36 (previously s.49 of J.A. 1925) to order the issue of a summons in special form, enforceable throughout the United Kingdom, for the attendance of a witness at a trial, so as to enable the witness's attendance to be required before an examiner or commissioner appointed by the Court or Judge in any cause or matter in that Court, including an examiner or commissioner appointed to take evidence outside the jurisdiction of the Court.

R70.6.14 **Evidence for proceedings in the European Court of Justice (rr.1–6)**—The 1975 Act has been made to apply to the Court of Justice of the European Communities with the modification that the person by whom a certificate may be given is the Registrar of that Court (see S.I. 1976 No. 428). This enables evidence for proceedings before the European Court of Justice to be taken at the request of that Court in the United Kingdom.

R70.6.15 **Evidence for international proceedings (rr.1–6)**—Section 6 of the 1975 Act enables the provisions of ss.1–3 of the Act to be extended by Order in Council to international proceedings of any description specified in the order including the International Court of Justice, or any other Court, tribunal, commission, body or authority referred to in s.6(3).

Application for order by party (rr.1–6)

R70.6.16 *(a) Civil Proceedings*—the application for an order under s.2 of the Act of 1975 to give effect to a foreign request for evidence to be obtained in England and Wales for the purpose of civil proceedings in the foreign court is made to a Master of the Queen's Bench Division (see r.1(2)).

The application for an order in Civil Proceedings must be made without notice being served on every other party and must be supported by witness statement or affidavit (r.2(1)) to which there must be exhibited in the request in pursuance of which the application is made, and if the request is not in the English language a translation must accompany the request and must be exhibited. As to sufficiency of letters of requests etc., see *Simpson v. Hazard* [1887] W.N. 115.

Letters of request for evidence in foreign civil proceedings are dealt with in the office of the Q.B. Masters' Secretary, Room E214, Royal Courts of Justice, Strand, London WC2A 2LL.

Forms of affidavit, see PF 152, Vol. 2, Section 1B, para. 1B–113; for form of Order see App.A, No. 93 (Vol. 2, Section 1A, para. 1A–96).

R70.6.17 *(b) Criminal Proceedings*—Subject to consequential amendment the following remains relevant—The Criminal Justice (International Co-operation) Act 1990 provides the procedure whereunder an application is made to the Secretary of State for him to nominate a court to hear the evidence. This procedure is not governed by O.70.

R70.6.18 **Application for order by Treasury Solicitor (rr.1–6)**—Where a letter of request is received by the Senior Master from the Foreign Office or from a consul of a country with which a Civil Procedure Convention has been concluded, and no solicitors in this country have been instructed to act, the Senior Master calls upon the Treasury solicitor to act and will then take the steps necessary to give effect to the letter of request (see r.3).

It is unlikely that any legal representative of any of the parties to the proceedings will attend the examination. If, however, representatives (who may include counsel as well as solicitors) do attend, the Treasury Solicitor will conduct the examination-in-chief of the witness. Thereafter the witness may be cross-examined by the legal representative of the other party and re-examined by the representative of the party on whose behalf the examination has been sought. Finally, with the approval of the examiner the Treasury Solicitor may put further questions to the witness to elucidate any points remaining obscure. Care must be taken to see that all the questions asked of the witness are within the ambit of the letter of request.

R70.6.19 **Convention countries (rr.1–6)**—A list of the countries with which conventions have been concluded is given under O.39, r.3 (see SCP 1999). The letter of request is sent by the consul in

England of the foreign country direct to the Senior Master instead of through the Foreign Office, but otherwise the general practice as to the Senior Master calling upon the Treasury Solicitor to act applies, subject to any specific provisions in the particular convention.

Application to discharge order (rr.1–6)—As the order is made without notice being served on any other party, application may be made to discharge. Such application must be made by Pt 23 application and should be supported by written evidence stating the grounds on which the order is sought to be discharged. A party in proceedings abroad has the right to be heard to challenge an order made under the Evidence (Proceedings in Other Jurisdictions) Act 1975, obtained in this country by the other party to the foreign proceedings and directed to a third party requiring the production of documents (*Boeing Co. v. P.P.G. Industries Inc.* [1988] 3 All E.R. 839). **R70.6.20**

Persons to take examination (rr.1–6)—The examination may be ordered to be taken before any fit and proper person nominated by the person applying for the order or before an examiner of the court or before such other qualified person as to the court seems fit (r.4(1)). The witness statement or affidavit should therefore name the examiner where it is decided to appoint or ask for an examiner of the court to be appointed. If the examiner is named, the witness statement or affidavit should state that he is, in the dependant's opinion, a fit and proper person. A consular officer of the foreign country may be the examiner **R70.6.21**

The court may make an order under CPR, r.34.14, for the payment of the fees and expenses due to the examiner (see r.4(2)).

Because the 1975 Act sets limits on the extent of examination permitted (summarised in para. R70.6.5) which may give rise to the sort of difficulties discussed in subsequent paragraphs of the note it is generally desirable that an English lawyer be appointed to conduct the examination. The wide discretion given to the Court under rule 4 either to nominate or approve the nomination of the examiner does not preclude the nomination and approval of a foreign lawyer, but in many cases, particularly those of a complex nature, it is better practice that the examiner be a person familiar with English law and procedure. The court in the exercise of its discretion may require that such a person be nominated. It is open to the court to require that the examination is conducted by an examiner of the court.

Enforcing attendance of witnesses (rr.1–6)—Failure of a witness to attend is addressed in CPR, r.34.10. **R70.6.22**

The witness is entitled both to conduct money and payment of expenses and loss of time as on attendance as a witness in civil proceedings before the court making the order (see s.2(5) of the 1975 Act).

Manner of taking examination (rr.1–6)—Subject to r.6, and to any special directions contained in the order for the examination of a witness, the examination must be taken in the manner provided by CPR r.34.9 and 34.10. **R70.6.23**

Where a request is made by the foreign court as to the particular manner for taking depositions, that manner should be employed unless the manner proposed is so contrary to English established procedures that it should not be permitted and subject to the exercise of judicial discretion to permit it, and, therefore where the request is for tape or video recording of the depositions, which would be admissible in English courts if taken outside the court, the court will accede to that request and make such order accordingly (*J. Barber & Sons (a firm) v. Lloyds Underwriters* [1986] 3 W.L.R. 515; [1986] 2 All E.R. 845).

The arrangements for the examination are made by the solicitor having conduct of the matter. Correspondence or oral communications passing between him and the witness will show whether it will be necessary to have an interpreter present at the examination. It will also be the duty of the solicitor to decide whether the evidence is likely to be of such length as will make it desirable to arrange for the evidence to be noted by shorthand. If a shorthand note is thought necessary the solicitor must arrange for the presence of a shorthand writer, but should first of all consult the examiner and any solicitors who he knows are going to attend.

The evidence can only be taken "in the English mode," but that does not mean that it is to be limited to what is admissible in English courts. The foreign Court should be afforded the fullest help it is possible to give. If its rules of evidence are known, effect should be given to them; if not, any questions should be admitted which may be expected to throw light on the matters in issue (*per* Cockburn C.J. in *Desilla v. Fells* (1879) 40 L.T. 423–424). As the examination should be conducted in the English mode, a company cannot be ordered to attend for examination on oath (*Penn-Texas Corp. v. Murat Anstalt* [1964] 1 Q.B. 40; [1963] 1 All E.R. 258, CA) but a company or body corporate can be ordered to attend and produce specified documents by its proper officer (*Penn-Texas Corp. v. Murat Anstalt (No. 2)* [1964] 2 Q.B. 647; [1964] 2 All E.R. 594, CA; *Panthalu v. Ramnord Research Laboratories Ltd* [1966] 2 Q.B. 173; [1965] 2 All E.R. 921, CA).

At the examination the witness is questioned by the solicitor or counsel if he is instructed. If the other party to the proceedings attends or is represented, he or his representatives may cross-examine. The order of the Court may provide that the person required to give testimony, either orally or in writing, may do so otherwise than on oath where this is asked for by the requesting court (see s.2(3) of the Act of 1975).

The witness giving evidence before an examiner has to give his own answers without the intervention of legal advice and is therefore not entitled to receive legal advice while being examined, but the examiner can, if he considers that the witness is not capable of an informed judgment, permit an independent adviser to object and formulate the grounds of objection to the questions put to the applicant (*R. v. Rathbone, ex p. Dikko* [1985] Q.B. 630).

If the witness refuses to answer any question, that fact should be formally noted in the depositions, showing the ground of refusal, *i.e.* that he is not liable to answer. A witness willing to answer, notwithstanding his right to refuse, is entitled to do so and to have his answer recorded. Where a witness refuses to answer any question which he is liable to answer, a certificate of his refusal signed by the examiner must be filed and application may then be made to the court requiring the witness to answer (see para. 34PD–002). The examination should, however, be completed in all other respects and adjourned generally.

An order for committal ought not to be made in the case of a witness examined under this Act, who refuses to produce material documents of which he has possession or control only in the character of servant to a master who is not a party to the proceedings and who had not forbidden him to produce the documents (*Eccles & Co. v. Louisville and Nashville Ry.* [1912] 1 K.B. 135, CA).

R70.6.24 **Dealing with depositions (rr.1–6)**—When the examination is concluded the depositions are signed by the witness and are then transmitted by the examiner to the Senior Master for certification and transmission through diplomatic consular channels to the foreign court or tribunal.

Where the foreign tribunal so desires, the depositions are sent direct by the Senior Master to the consul or other official of the foreign government in England for transmission to the foreign court (r.5).

RSC ORDER 71

RECIPROCAL ENFORCEMENT OF JUDGMENTS AND ENFORCEMENT OF EUROPEAN COMMUNITY JUDGMENTS AND RECOMMENDATIONS ETC. UNDER THE MERCHANT SHIPPING (LINER CONFERENCES) ACT 1982

R71.0.1 **Contents**

I. Reciprocal Enforcement: The Administration of Justice Act 1920 and the Foreign Judgments (Reciprocal Enforcement) Act 1933

II. Enforcement of European Community Judgments

III. Reciprocal Enforcement: The Civil Jurisdiction and Judgments Act 1982

IV. Enforcement of Recommendations under the Merchant Shipping (Liner Conferences) Act 1982

Editorial Introduction

In the RSC, this Order and Orders 69 and 70 were grouped under the heading "Provisions as to Foreign Proceedings". Order 71 is now divided into four Parts. When the RSC were re-published in their substantially revised form in 1965, O.71 contained the rules under which the Court exercised the powers conferred on it by the Administration of Justice Act 1920, Pt II, and the Foreign Judgments (Reciprocal Enforcement) Act 1933, Pt I. The Order also contained a rule dealing with the registration of certificates under the Judgments Extension Act 1868 (r.14). At common law, a foreign judgment, though creating an obligation that is actionable in England, cannot be enforced here except by the institution of fresh legal proceedings in which the foreign judgment is, in effect, the cause of action. The Act of 1920 and the Act of 1933, both of which remain in force, and other legislation constitute important statutory exceptions to the common law doctrine and enable a judgment creditor to register a foreign judgment here and then to proceed to enforce the judgment as if it were an English judgment. **R71.0.2**

In the years since 1965, O.71 has been considerably expanded by the addition of 30 individual rules marshalled in three further Parts to the Order. Part II, now entitled Enforcement of European Community Judgments (rr.15–24), was added in 1972 following the accession of the United Kingdom to the European Communities. Part III, entitled Reciprocal Enforcement: The Civil Jurisdiction and Judgments Act 1982 (rr.25–39), was added in 1983 to make provision for the recognition and enforcement of judgments under the 1982 Act. Part IV, entitled Enforcement of Recommendations etc. under the Merchant Shipping (Liner Conferences) Act 1982 (rr.40–44), was added in 1986 when that Act came into force. Although the language of the rules has been adapted to reflect that of the new CPR no substantive changes have been made.

O.71, Pt I—The rules found in Pt I of O.71 (*i.e.* rr.1–13) relating to the Administration of Justice Act 1920 and the Foreign Judgments (Reciprocal Enforcement) Act 1933 are, subject to a few subsequent amendments, the same as those that made up the whole of the Order in 1965. (The Act of 1868 was repealed by the Civil Jurisdiction and Judgments Act 1982 with the result that r.14 was revoked.) The Act of 1920 makes provision, by a system of registration, for the enforcement within the United Kingdom of judgments obtained in a superior court of any part of the Commonwealth. The Act of 1933 extended the principle of registration to foreign countries generally. The provisions of both Acts are extended, as the case may be, to Commonwealth and foreign jurisdictions, by Orders in Council. Given the similarities between the registration **R71.0.3**

schemes in the two statutes, it is not surprising to find that the necessary rules of court facilitating the exercise of the powers of the Court found in them constitute a single code in Pt I of O.71. The rules are, of course, purely procedural and do not deal with substantive issues, such as the circumstances upon which the Court should or should not register the foreign judgment.

R71.0.4 **O.71, Pt II**—The rules in this Part of the Order prescribe the procedure for giving effect to Community judgments enforceable in the High Court in accordance with the functions assigned to the Court by the European Communities (Enforcement of Community Judgments) Order 1972 (S.I. 1972 No. 1590). Any Community judgment to which the Secretary of State has appended an order for enforcement shall be registered by the Court if application is made by the person entitled to enforce it. The judgments to which the 1972 Order applies are not those of the national courts of the Member States of the European Community but rather the judgments of the courts and institutions of the Community itself. That is to say, judgments by the European Court of Justice, and decisions of the Arbitration Committee of the European Atomic Energy Committee, of the High Authority of the European Coal & Steel Community which impose a pecuniary obligation, and of the Council of the Commission of the European Economic Community which impose a pecuniary obligation on persons other than States. Provision is made in this Part for the registration of such judgments, for notification to persons against whom they are given, and for applications to vary or cancel registration by reason of the judgment being satisfied and to register an order of the European Court of Justice suspending execution of a registered judgment. Part II also provides for the registration and enforcement of Euratom inspection orders.

The judgments, etc., of the three Community institutions referred to above have validity in the U.K. by virtue of the Treaties by which the institutions were established. The necessary ancillary legislation required to ensure that the judgments, etc., could be enforced in the U.K. was contained in the European Communities (Enforcement of Community Judgments) Order 1972. The rules in Pt II of O.71 are supplementary to that statutory instrument and the expressions used in the rules have the same meanings as in that instrument, unless the context otherwise requires (see r.15).

R71.0.5 **O.71, Pt III**—The rules in this Part (rr.25–39) should be read together with the Civil Jurisdiction and Judgments Act 1982 and Title Iii Brussels Convention and of the Lugano Convention (see SCP 1999, Vol. 2, Section 7B, paras 7B–1 *et seq.*). The Conventions seek to simplify enforcement, but, at the same time, provide safeguards for both parties. These rules provide the machinery whereby judgments entered in other contracting states may be registered and enforced in England. Again the rules are purely procedural and do not deal with the substantive issues that may arise in a given application for registration of a judgment. (It may be noted, that under the Conventions, registration is automatic in the sense that none of the usual conditions traditionally imposed by English law in cases of recognition and enforcement at common law or under the Administration of Justice Act 1920 or the Foreign Judgments (Reciprocal Enforcement) Act 1933 have to be satisfied before recognition can take place.)

It has to be remembered that, in so far as it applies to the registration and enforcement of judgments, the 1982 Act is not confined to judgments of courts of states affected by the Brussels Convention and the Lugano Convention. Section 18 and Scheds 6 and 7 of the 1982 Act deal with the enforcement of judgments of courts of one part of the United Kingdom in the courts of another part. The necessary rules of court for registration in the High Court are also found in Pt III of O.71. The fact that rules found in Pt III deal with enforcement through the High Court (1) of judgments of courts in Convention countries and, also, (2) of judgments of certain courts in other parts of the United Kingdom can cause confusion.

For incoming judgments from outside the United Kingdom to be enforceable in the United Kingdom they have to be registered in the appropriate jurisdiction (Art. 32(1)) which in England and Wales is the Central Office of the High Court where the register is kept for all judgments except maintenance judgments. The application is made to a master without notice, application to set aside registration is made by appeal to the judge (r.33).

Incoming judgments from other parts of the United Kingdom are registered in the Central Office under r.37(1) and (2) (money judgments) and under r.38(1) and (2) (non-money judgments). The former are registered ministerially on production of the prescribed documents to the proper officer; the latter can only be registered with leave.

Outgoing judgments to be enforced in other contracting states require a certificate obtained under the procedure set out in r.36. Such a certificate is obtained by application to the Central Office or the District Registry where the judgment was obtained (r.36(3)).

Outgoing judgments to be enforced in other parts of the U.K. require a certificate under r.37(3) for a money judgment and under r.38(5) for a non-money judgment. (And see notes to P.F. 165 (SCP 1999, Vol. 2, Section 1B, para. 1B–126). *N.B.* the "United Kingdom" includes only England and Wales, Scotland and Northern Ireland. It does not include other parts of "Great Britain" such as the Channel Islands and the Isle of Man.

The exercise of the powers under Title III for the registration of judgments is limited to those cases where the defendant has been served with proceedings in the original jurisdiction and has had time to arrange his defence (see *E.M.I. Records Ltd v. Modern Music Karl-Ulrich Walterbach*

GmbH [1992] Q.B. 115; [1992] 1 All E.R. 616 where Hobhouse J. set aside an order registering an injunction obtained without notice in Germany).

Interim relief—The court is empowered by section 25(1) and (2) of the 1982 Act to grant interim relief where proceedings have been or are to be commenced in a Brussels or Lugano Contracting State. (This includes interim relief in relation to an "Authentic Instrument" which under Art. 50 can be enforced without proceedings: *S & T Bautrading v. Nordling* [1997] 3 All E.R. 718.) Following the full implementation of section 25 of the 1982 Act by S.I. 1997 No. 415 the jurisdiction to grant interim relief is not confined to the territories of Contracting States. **R71.06**

O.71, Pt IV—The Merchant Shipping (Liner Conferences) Act 1982, s.1 enabled the Secretary of State to implement the Convention on a Code of Conduct for Liner Conferences negotiated in the Committee on Shipping of the United Nations Conference on Trade and Development, and signed at Geneva on April 6, 1974. A "liner conference" is a group of two or more vessel operating carriers which provides international services for the carriage of cargo on particular routes. In some respects the Code runs counter to the common policy of the European Community embodied in Council Regulation No. 954/79 of May 1979 ([1979] O.J. L121/1). This policy, which has direct effect, is directed at ensuring that there is no discrimination between shipping lines of the E.C. States or of other member countries of the O.E.C.D. which do not themselves practise discrimination. Consequently, in some respects the 1982 Act is a compromise. The Code provides for "international mandatory conciliation" for certain disputes and provision is made in s.9 of the 1982 Act for the recognition and enforcement of recommendations etc., of conciliators. The rules in this Part of O.71 deal with applications for registration of such recommendations. **R71.0.7**

Related Sources

I. Reciprocal Enforcement: The Administration of Justice Act 1920 and the Foreign Judgments (Reciprocal Enforcement) Act 1933

- *Practice Directions—Arbitrations, Pt III enforcement of arbitration awards* **R71.0.8**
- *Queen's Bench Masters' Practice Direction No. 11—Claims, judgments and enforcement of judgments in foreign currency* (SCP 1999, Vol. 2, Section 2A, paras 2A–37 to 2A–52)

Forms

See Pt 4 Practice Direction (Forms)—Table 2 for the general approach (see para. 4.1 *et seq.* at para. 4PD–003) **R71.0.9**

I. Reciprocal Enforcement: The Administration of Justice Act 1920 and the Foreign Judgments (Reciprocal Enforcement) Act 1933

The following Prescribed Forms (formerly included amongst the Prescribed Forms in Appendix A to the RSC) are relevant to Pt I of O.71. These forms are included in Table 2 (Practice Forms) attached to Practice Direction (Forms) and may be found in SCP 1999, Vol. 2, Section 1A, para. 1A–63): **R71.0.10**

- PF No. 63—Writ of *fieri facias* to enforce foreign registered judgment (O.71)

The following Queen's Bench Masters' Practice Forms (now listed in Table 2 (Practice Forms) attached to Practice Direction (Forms)) are relevant to Pt I of O.71 (SCP 1999, Vol. 2, Section 1B, paras 1B–115 and 1B–116):

- PF154QB Order for registration of foreign judgment under the Foreign Judgments (Reciprocal Enforcement) Act 1933 (O.71, r.5)
- PF155QB Certificates under section 10 of the Foreign Judgments (Reciprocal Enforcement) Act 1933 (O.71, r.13(5))

II. Enforcement of European Community Judgments

The following Queen's Bench Masters' Practice Forms (now listed in Table 2 (Practice Forms) attached to Practice Direction (Forms)) are relevant to Pt II of O.71 (Vol. 2, Section 1B, paras 1B–117 to 1B–119): **R71.0.11**

- PF156QB—Affidavit seeking registration of a community judgment (O.71, r.18)
- PF157QB—Order for registration of a community judgment (O.71, r.18)
- PF158QB—Notice of registration of community judgment (O.71, r.20)

III. Reciprocal Enforcement: The Civil Jurisdiction and Judgments Act 1982

The following Prescribed Forms (formerly included amongst the Prescribed Forms in Appendix A to the RSC) are relevant to Pt III of O.71. These forms are including in Table 2 (Practice Forms) attached to Practice Direction (Forms) and may be found in SCP 1999, Vol. 2, Section 1A, paras 1A–62 and 1A–63): **R71.0.12**

- PF No. 62—Write of *fieri facias* to enforce Northern Irish or Scottish judgment (O.71)
- PF No. 63—Writ of *fieri facias* to enforce foreign registered judgment (O.71)

The following Queen's Bench Masters' Practice Forms (now listed in Table 2 (Practice Forms) attached to Practice Direction (Forms)) are relevant to O.71 (SCP 1999, Vol. 2, Section 1B, paras 1B–120 to 1B–126):

- PF159QB Evidence in support of application for registration of a judgment of another contracting state (O.71, r.28)
- PF160QB Order for registration of a judgment of another contracting state under section 4 of the Civil Jurisdiction and Judgments Act 1982 (O.71, r.30)
- PF161QB Notice of registration of a judgment of another contracting state (O.71, r.32)
- PF163QB Evidenced in support of application for certified copy of a judgment in another Contracting State (O.71, r.36)
- PF164QB Evidence in support of application for certificate as to money provisions of a judgment in the High Court for registration elsewhere in the United Kingdom (O.71, r.37(3)
- PF165QB Evidence in support of application for registration of a judgment of a court in another part of the United Kingdom containing non-money provisions (O.71, r.38)

I. Reciprocal Enforcement: the Administration of Justice Act 1920 and the Foreign Judgments (Reciprocal Enforcement) Act 1933

Powers under relevant Acts exercisable by judge or master

R71.1 **1.** The powers conferred on the High Court by Part II of the Administration of Justice Act 1920 (in this Part of this Order referred to as the "Act of 1920") or Part I of the Foreign Judgments (Reciprocal Enforcement) Act 1933 (in this Part of this order referred to as the "Act of 1933") may be exercised by a judge in chambers and a Master of the Queen's Bench Division.

R71.1.1 **Methods of enforcement of judgments obtained outside the jurisdiction**—The methods of enforcement in this country of judgments obtained outside the jurisdiction are as follows:

(i) Judgments obtained in the superior Courts in many parts of H.M. Dominions outside the U.K., by registration under Part II of A.J.A. 1920;

(ii) Judgments obtained in the superior Courts of any foreign country to which the Foreign Judgments (Reciprocal Enforcement) Act 1933 has been applied, by registration under Pt I of that Act;

(iii) By action on the judgment, but subject to section 6 of the Foreign Judgments (Reciprocal Enforcement) Act 1933 which restricts the method of enforcement of judgments to which the Act applies to proceedings by way of registration only (see *Yukon Gold, Ltd v. Clark* [1938] 2 K.B. 241, CA).

The court may include interest when giving summary judgment for the enforcement of a foreign judgment even though the foreign law under which the judgment was obtained makes no provision for interest (*Midland International Services Ltd v. Sudairy, The Financial Times*, May 2, 1990).

R71.1.2 **Administration of Justice Act 1920**—Part II of AJA 1920, enabled certain judgments of superior Courts in any part of Her Majesty's Dominions outside the United Kingdom to be registered in the High Court (or High Court of Northern Ireland or Court of Session in Scotland) and such judgment has the same effect so far as it relates to execution as a judgment of the registering Court. The Act, however, did not operate until an Order in Council applied it to (a) any part of the British Dominions, and such Order could only be made when reciprocal provisions had been made by the Legislature of that part for registration of English, Scottish and Irish judgments; or (b) to any territory under British protection or being administered under mandate.

Section 9(2) specified certain limitations on the judgments to be registered. Thus no judgment could be registered if (a) the original Court acted without jurisdiction; or (b) the judgment debtor, being a person who was neither carrying on business nor ordinarily resident within the jurisdiction of the original Court, did not voluntarily appear or otherwise submit or agree to submit to the jurisdiction of that Court; or (c) the judgment debtor, being the defendant in the proceedings, was not duly served with the process of the original Court, and did not appear, notwithstanding that he was ordinarily resident or was carrying on business within the jurisdiction of that Court or agreed to submit to the jurisdiction of that Court; or (d) the judgment was obtained by fraud; or (e) the judgment debtor satisfied the registering Court either that an appeal was pending, or that he was entitled and intended to appeal against the judgment; or (f) the judgment was in respect of a cause of action which for reasons of public policy or for some other similar rule could not have been entertained by the registering Court. Leave of the Court was required in all cases and had to be applied for within 12 months, though this limit might be extended. For the purposes of the Act "judgment" meant any judgment or order in any civil proceedings before or after the Act whereby any sum of money was made payable, and included an award in proceedings on an arbitration if the award was enforceable as a judgment in the place where it was made. The powers of the Act might be exercised by a Judge.

Section 7 of the Foreign Judgments (Reciprocal Enforcement) Act 1933, provided that Pt II of

AJA 1920, shall cease to have effect *except in relation to the Dominions to which it extended at the date of the Order in Council applying the 1933 Act to H.M. Dominions.*

Section 10 of the Act provides for the issue to a judgment creditor under a judgment obtained in the United Kingdom of a certified copy of the judgment on proof that the judgment debtor resides in some part of the British Dominions to which the Act applies.

Extension of Act of 1920 by Orders in Council—The provisions of Pt II of AJA 1920, have been extended by Orders in Council. R71.1.3

No further extensions of Pt II have been permissible since 1933, see section 7 of the 1933 Act.

These Orders in Council may, however, be consolidated if they are in force when the consolidating Order is made (Civil Jurisdiction and Judgments Act 1982, s.35(3), see SCP 1999, Vol. 2, Pt 8 on European Jurisdiction). This consolidation took place by S.I. 1984 No. 129 and Pt II of AJA 1920 extends to the countries specified in Sched. I to that Order which has been amended by Judgments (Administration of Justice Act 1920, Pt II) (Amendment) Order 1985 (S.I. 1985 No. 1994) and now reads as follows:

Anguilla
Antigua and Barbuda
Bahamas
Barbados
Belize
Bermuda
Botswana
British Indian Ocean Territory
British Virgin Islands
Cayman Islands
Christmas Island
Cocos (Keeling) Islands
Republic of Cyprus
Dominica
Falkland Islands
Fiji
The Gambia
Ghana
Grenada
Guyana
Jamaica
Kenya
Kiribati
Lesotho
Malawi
Malaysia
Malta
Mauritius
Montserrat
New Zealand
Nigeria
Territory of Norfolk Island
Papua New Guinea
St Christopher and Nevis
St Helena
St Lucia
St Vincent and the Grenadines
Seychelles
Sierra Leone
Singapore
Solomon Islands
Sovereign Base Area of Akrotiri and Dhekelia in Cyprus
Sri Lanka
Swaziland
Tanzania
Tasmania
Trinidad and Tobago
Turks and Caicos Islands
Tuvalu
Uganda
Zambia
Zimbabwe

The 1920 Act no longer applies to Hong Kong and there is no provision for registration of Hong Kong judgments in England or English judgments in Hong Kong. Enforcement of such judgments is by action on the judgment.

Gibraltar is now subject to Pt III (S.I. 1997 No. 2602).

Foreign Judgments (Reciprocal Enforcement) Act 1933—The following is a brief summary of the provisions of this Act. By s.1 the Queen may, by Order in Council, direct that (subject to the terms of the Order) the provisions of the Act which relate to the registration of foreign judgments may extend to any foreign country which is prepared to give reciprocity of treatment to judgments given in the Courts of the United Kingdom. A "judgment" of a "Court" of a foreign country—both terms are defined in the Act and the particular Order—may be registered provided it is final and conclusive, and there is payable thereunder a sum of money not being in respect of taxes, fines or penalties (s.1(2) and s.11(1) of the Act). Application to register may (by virtue of s.2) be made within six years of the date of the judgment, but not if it has been wholly satisfied or if it could not be enforced by the execution in the country of the original Court. R71.1.4

Broadly speaking, a foreign judgment when registered can be treated as if it were the judgment of an English Court (s.2(1)). If expressed in the currency of a foreign country it will be registered in that currency or its sterling equivalent at the time of payment (see para. R71.3.2, "Rate of exchange"). Interest and the reasonable cost of registration may be added to the judgment when registered (*ibid.*, (6)). This addition will depend upon the direction in the Master's order which may be for a sum fixed or for taxation. Section 3 of the Act confers power to make rules for registration.

The cases in which the registration of a judgment may be set aside are specified in s.4 of the Act (see note to r.9).

The circumstances in which the court of the country of origin are deemed to have had jurisdiction are set out in s.4(2) and (3). If an appeal is pending when application is made to set aside registration, the Court may either set aside the registration or adjourn the application (s.5(1)). Section 8 of the Act defines the circumstances in which a judgment of that foreign Court is to be recognised as conclusive in the English courts whether registered or not. By virtue of s.8, a foreign judgment is conclusive between the parties in English proceedings as to the matter thereby adjudicated upon. Moreover, by virtue of s.3 of the Foreign Limitation Periods Act 1984, the determination of the foreign court based upon the law relating to the limitation of actions whether of its own or any other country, including England and Wales, is deemed to be a determination on the merits, so that it will be treated as final and conclusive between the parties (statutorily negativing *Black-Clawson International Ltd v. Papierwerke Waldhof-Aschaffenburg A.G.* [1975] A.C. 591; [1975] 1 All E.R. 810, HL).

The 1933 Act and the Conventions under it probably do not apply to matrimonial causes affecting status (*Vervaeke v. Smith; Messina and Att.-Gen. Intervening* [1981] Fam. 77; [1981] 1 All E.R. 55, CA).

Application of Act of 1933 to Foreign Countries

R71.1.5 Austria—S.I. 1962 No. 1339.
Belgium—S.R. & O. 1936 No. 1169.
France—S. R. & O. 1936 No. 609.
Federal Republic of Germany and West Berlin—S.I. 1961 No. 1199.
The territory formerly incorporated within the German Democratic Republic and East Berlin now forms part of the German Federal Republic.
Israel—S.I. 1971 No. 1039.
Italy—S.I. 1973 No. 1894.
The Netherlands—S.I. 1969 No. 1063.
The Netherlands Antilles, where the following courts will be deemed superior courts, namely The Hoge Raad der Nederlanden; The Hof Van Justitie der Nederlandse Antillen; The Gerecht in Eerste Aanleg—S.I. 1969 No. 1063, as amended by the Reciprocal Enforcement of Foreign Judgments (The Netherlands) (Amendment) Order 1977—S.I. 1977 No. 2149.
Norway—S.I. 1962 No. 636.
Suriname—S.I. 1981 No. 735.
Tonga—S.I. 1980 No. 1523.

All the above countries except Israel, Suriname and Tonga are now parties to the Brussels or Lugano Conventions and applications in relation to Convention countries should be made under the appropriate provisions of O.71, rr.25–39A.

R71.1.6 **Application of Act of 1933 to Commonwealth Territories**—Although Pt I of the Foreign Judgments (Reciprocal Enforcement) Act 1933, was made applicable generally to H.M. Dominions, etc., by an Order in Council dated November 10, 1933 (under the provisions of s.7 of the Act) the application of the Act to any particular part of the Commonwealth Territories is dependent upon substantial reciprocity being assured by such places (s.1) when the Act may be brought into operation for such particular place by a further Order in Council (*Yukon Consolidated Gold Corp. Ltd v. Clark* [1938] 2 K.B. 241). Orders have been made applying the Act to the following places in the Commonwealth:
Australia—S.I. 1994 No. 1901.
Australian Capital Territory—S.I. 1955 No. 559.
Canada: the Federal Court of Canada and any court to the Province of British Columbia, Manitoba, New Brunswick, Nova Scotia, Ontario, Prince Edward Island, Saskatchewan or the Yukon Territory—S.I. 1987 No. 468 as amended by S.I. 1987 No. 2211, S.I. 1988 No. 1304 and S.I. 1988, No. 1853. Northwest Territories: S.I. 1989 No. 987. Newfoundland: S.I. 1991 No. 1724, in force August 1, 1991; Alberta: S.I. 1992 No. 1731, in force August 13, 1992. For amendments consequential on the accession of the United Kingdom to the Lugano Convention—S.I. 1995 No. 2708.
Island of Guernsey—S.I. 1973 No. 610.
Isle of Man—S.I. 1973 No. 611.
Jersey, Bailiwick of—S.I. 1973 No. 612.
Republic of India, the territories named in the schedule to the Order in Council—S.I. 1958 No. 425.
Pakistan: S.I. 1958 No. 141 and see Pakistan Act 1990.

Where Pt I of the Foreign Judgments (Reciprocal Enforcement) Act 1933, is extended to a part of H.M. Dominions or other territory to which Pt II of A.J.A. 1920, extends, modifications are made by A.J.A. 1956, s.51 (see SCP 1999, Vol. 2, Section 20B, paras 20B–21 and 20B–22).

Application for registration

R71.2 **2.**—(1) An application—

(a) under section 9 of the Act of 1920, in respect of a judgment obtained in a superior court in any part of Her Majesty's dominions or other territory to which Part II of that Act applies; or

(b) under section 2 of the Act of 1933, in respect of a judgment to which Part I of that Act applies,

to have the judgment registered in the High Court may be made without notice being served on any other party, but the court hearing the application may direct that a claim form be filed and served.

History of rule—Amended by S.I. 1979 No. 1716. R71.2.1

Practice—The application to register a judgment either under the 1920 Act or the 1933 Act should be made without notice supported by a witness statement or affidavit to the Master. It should be lodged in Room E214. It will then be checked in the Action Department before being submitted to a Master for him to consider the application who may, instead of dealing with the application without notice being served on any other party, direct that a claim form be filed and served. Whether this is a Pt 7 or Pt 8 claim is likely to depend upon whether there are contested issues of fact. R71.2.2

Evidence in support of application

3.—(1) An application for registration must be supported by a witness statement or affidavit— R71.3

(a) exhibiting the judgment or a verified or certified or otherwise duly authenticated copy thereof, and where the judgment is not in the English language, a translation thereof in that language certified by a notary public or authenticated by witness statement or affidavit;

(b) stating the name, trade or business and the usual or last known place of abode or business of the judgment creditor and the judgment debtor respectively, so far as known to the witness;

(c) stating to the best of the information or belief of the witness—

(i) that the judgment creditor is entitled to enforce the judgment;

(ii) as the case may require, either that at the date of the application the judgment has not been satisfied, or the amount in respect of which it remains unsatisfied;

(iii) where the application is made under the Act of 1920, that the judgment does not fall within any of the cases in which a judgment may not be ordered to be registered under section 9 of that Act;

(iv) where the application is made under the Act of 1933, that at the date of the application the judgment can be enforced by execution in the country of the original court and that, if it were registered, the registration would not be, or be liable to be, set aside under section 4 of that Act;

(d) specifying, where the application is made under the Act of 1933, the amount of the interest, if any, which under the law of the country of the original court has become due under the judgment up to the time of registration;

(e) verifying that the judgment is not a judgment to which section 5 of the Protection of Trading Interests Act 1980 applies.

(2) Where a judgment sought to be registered under the Act of 1933 is in respect of different matters, and some, but not all, of the provisions of the judgment are such that if those provisions had been contained in separate judgments, those judgments could properly have been registered, the witness statement or affidavit must state the provisions in respect of which it is sought to register the judgment.

(3) In the case of an application under the Act of 1933, the witness statement or affidavit must be accompanied by such other evidence with respect to the enforceability of the judgment by execution in the country of the original court, and of the law of that country under which any interest has

become due under the judgment, as may be required having regard to the provisions of the Order in Council extending that Act to that country.

R71.3.1 **Forms**—The title of the witness statement or affidavit should expressly state whether it is made, "In the Matter of the Administration of Justice Act 1920, Part II" or "In the Matter of the Foreign Judgments (Reciprocal Enforcement) Act 1933": and in each case, the title of the witness statement or affidavit should also identify the Judgment by reference to the Court in which it was obtained and its date.

Rate of exchange—Following the decision in *Miliangos v. George Frank (Textiles) Ltd* [1976] A.C. 443; [1975] 3 All E.R. 801, and the repeal of section 2(3) of the Foreign Judgments (Reciprocal Enforcement) Act 1933 by section 4 of A.J.A. 1977, the witness statement or affidavit in support of the application for the registration of a foreign judgment must not convert the amount of the foreign currency into United Kingdom currency at the rate of exchange prevailing at the date of that judgment. The foreign judgment will be registered in the foreign currency in which it is expressed, or its sterling equivalent at the time of payment. There is no power entitling the claimant to convert the currency of the foreign judgment at the rate of exchange prevailing at any earlier or other date except the date of payment.

This applies also to judgments under A.J.A. 1920, Pt II, to which the relevant provision of the Act of 1933 had been extended, so negativing the case of *East India Trading Co. Inc. v. Carmel Exporters and Importers Ltd* [1952] 2 Q.B. 439.

On the other hand, it should be remembered that when it comes to enforcing the foreign judgment so registered it will become necessary to convert the foreign currency at the date of enforcement according to the method of enforcement employed in accordance with the *Queen's Bench Masters' Practice Direction No. 11* (SCP 1999, Vol. 2, Section 2A, paras 2A–37 to 2A–52).

R71.3.2 **Costs**—Application may be made to enforce a judgment or order for costs given or made in any country to which the Act of 1920 or the Act of 1933 applies.

R71.3.3 **Judgment in respect of different matters under the Act of 1933**—By s.4(5) of the Act of 1933, if the judgment is in respect of different matters, and some but not all of the provisions of the judgment are such that if they had been in separate judgments they could have been registered, the judgment may be registered in respect of such provisions.

R71.3.4 **Entitlement to enforce the judgment**—A technical defect in the form of a foreign judgment, *e.g.* omission of certain words prescribed by the foreign law, does not render that judgment a nullity but only makes it voidable, and so long as it stands, it is enforceable by execution in that country, and is therefore capable of being registered in this country (*S.A. Consortium General Textiles v. Sun and Sand Agencies Ltd* [1978] Q.B. 279; [1978] 2 W.L.R. 1; [1978] 2 All E.R. 339, CA).

Moreover, the power of a foreign court, *e.g.* in France, to award an additional compensatory sum for "resistance abusive", *e.g.* for failure to comply with the obligations of a mercantile transaction is not "a fine or other penalty" within s.1(2)(b) of the Act of 1933 and it is not contrary to public policy in England under s.4(1)(a)(ii) as being the equivalent of "exemplary damages" which are not generally awardable in England, and therefore such a foreign judgment is entitled to be enforced and capable of being registered in England (*ibid.*).

R71.3.5 **No submission to foreign court by appearance**—For the purposes of determining whether a judgment given by a court of an overseas country should be recognised or enforced in England and Wales or Northern Ireland, the person against whom the judgment was given will not be regarded as having submitted to the jurisdiction of the Court by reason only of the fact that he appeared (conditionally or otherwise) in the proceedings for all or any one or more of the following purposes, namely (a) to contest the jurisdiction of the Court; (b) to ask the Court to dismiss or stay the proceedings on the ground that the dispute in question should be submitted to arbitration or to the determination of the Courts of another country; (c) to protect, or obtain the release of, property seized or threatened with seizure in the proceedings (see Civil Jurisdiction and Judgments Act 1982, s.33(1). For text of the Act see SCP 1999, Vol. 2, Section 1B, paras 1B–1 *et seq*). The effect of this provision is to negative the decisions in *Henry v. Geoprosco International Ltd* [1976] Q.B. 726, CA and in *Harris v. Taylor* [1915] 2 K.B. 580, CA (*Tracomin SA v. Sudan Oil Seeds Ltd (Nos 1 and 2)* [1983] 1 W.L.R. 1026; [1983] 3 All E.R. 137 affirming [1983] 1 W.L.R. 662; [1983] 1 All E.R. 404). It should be remembered that such a judgment may still be recognised and enforced by the Courts of the country in which it was rendered.

This provision will not affect the recognition or enforcement in England and Wales or Northern Ireland of judgment which is required to be recognised or enforced there under the

1968 Convention on Jurisdiction and the Enforcement of Judgments (see the 1982 Act, s.2(2)(c) and Sched. 1) (*ibid.*, s.33(2)).

Security for costs

4. Save as otherwise provided by any relevant Order in Council, the court may order the judgment creditor to give security for the costs of the application for registration and of any proceedings which may be brought to set aside the registration. **R71.4**

"As otherwise provided"—The Order in Council which applies the Act to France prevents any application being made for security for costs on the registration of a French judgment (see note "Application of Act of 1933 to foreign countries", para. R71.1.5). And r.29, below, considerably modifies this rule in cases of registration under the Civil Jurisdiction and Judgments Act 1982. **R71.4.1**

"To give security"—By s.3 of the Act, rules may be made under JA 1925, s.99 (now SCA 1981, s.87), for making provision with respect to the giving of security for costs to persons applying for the registration of judgments. It is presumed that if the applicant is out of the jurisdiction the general rule applicable to all persons out of the jurisdiction bringing suit in England will prevail. As to the International Conventions affecting security for costs see this n. at para. R23.3.24. **R71.4.2**

The procedure for enforcing judgments under Pt II of AJA 1920, and the Foreign Judgments (Reciprocal Enforcement) Act 1933, makes it necessary for claimants residing in those countries to which those Acts apply to give security (*Kohn v. Rinson and Stafford (Brod.) Ltd* [1948] 1 K.B. 327).

Order for registration

5.—(1) An order giving permission to register a judgment must be drawn up by, or on behalf of, the judgment creditor. **R71.5**

(2) Except where the order is made by claim form, no such order need be served on the judgment debtor.

(3) Every such order shall state the period within which an application may be made to set aside the registration and shall contain a notification that execution on the judgment will not issue until after the expiration of that period.

(4) The court may, on an application made at any time while it remains competent for any party to apply to have the registration set aside, extend the period (either as originally fixed or as subsequently extended) within which an application to have the registration set aside may be made.

Forms of orders—For forms of orders, see *Chitty and Jacob's Queen's Bench Forms*, Form 900 (order under Act of 1920) and PF 154 (SCP 1999, Vol. 2, Section 1B, para. 1B–115) and *Chitty and Jacob's Queen's Bench Forms*, Form 913 (order under Act of 1933). These forms require slight amendment if the judgment is in a foreign currency; see para. R71.3.2 above; and see *Part 4: Practice Directions*. Table 2 for current approach to revising forms. **R71.5.1**

The order should provide for the costs of the application and of the registration to be taxed and added to the judgment, unless the Master directs otherwise (see Act of 1920, s.9(3)(c) and Act of 1933, s.2(6)).

Register of judgments

6.—(1) There shall be kept in the Central Office of the Supreme Court under the direction of the Senior Master a register of the judgments ordered to be registered under the Act of 1920 and a register of the judgments ordered to be registered under the Act of 1933. **R71.6**

(2) There shall be included in each such register particulars of any execution issued on a judgment ordered to be so registered.

Effect of registration—A foreign judgment, when registered, may form the basis of a bankruptcy notice (*Re A Judgment Debtor (No. 2176 of 1938)* [1939] Ch. 601; [1939] 1 All E.R. 1). **R71.6.1**

Notice of registration

7.—(1) Notice of the registration of a judgment must be served on the judgment debtor by delivering it to him personally or by sending it to him at **R71.7**

his usual or last known place of abode or business or in such other manner as the court may direct.

(2) Permission is not required to serve such a notice out of the jurisdiction, and Order 11, rules 5, 6 and 8, shall apply in relation to such a notice as they apply in relation to a claim form.

(3) The notice of registration must state—

(a) full particulars of the judgment registered and the order for registration,

(b) the name and address of the judgment creditor or of his solicitor or agent on whom, and at which, any application notice or other document issued by the judgment debtor may be served,

(c) the right of the judgment debtor to apply to have the registration set aside, and

(d) the period within which an application to set aside the registration may be made.

R71.7.1 **History of rule**—Amended by S.I. 1979 No. 402 and S.I. 1980 No. 2000.

Application to set aside registration

R71.9 **9.**—(1) An application to set aside the registration of a judgment must be made in accordance with CPR Part 23 and be supported by witness statement or affidavit.

(2) The court hearing such application may order any issue between the judgment creditor and the judgment debtor to be tried in any manner in which an issue in a claim may be ordered to be tried.

(3) Where the court hearing an application to set aside the registration of a judgment registered under the Act of 1920 is satisfied that the judgment falls within any of the cases in which a judgment may not be ordered to be registered under section 9 of that Act or that it is not just or convenient that the judgment should be enforced in England or Wales or that there is some other sufficient reason for setting aside the registration, it may order the registration of the judgment to be set aside on such terms as it thinks fit.

R71.9.1 **Effect of rule**—The circumstances in which registration may be set aside are set forth in s.4 of the Act of 1933. By subs. (1)(a) it *shall* be set aside if the Court is satisfied:

(i) that the judgment is not a judgment to which Part I of the Act applies or was registered in contravention of the provisions of the Act; or

(ii) that the Courts of the country of the original Court had no jurisdiction in the circumstances of the case; or

(iii) that the judgment debtor, being the defendant in the proceedings in the original Court, did not (notwithstanding that process may have been duly served on him in accordance with the law of the country of the original Court) receive notice of those proceedings in sufficient time to enable him to defend the proceedings and did not appear; or

(iv) that the judgment was obtained by fraud; or

(v) that the enforcement of the judgment would be contrary to public policy in this country; or

(vi) that the rights under the judgment are not vested in the person by whom the application for registration was made:

By subs. 1(b), a judgment *may* be set aside if the registering Court is satisfied that the matter in dispute in the proceedings in the original Court had previously to those proceedings been the subject of a final and conclusive judgment by a Court having jurisdiction in the matter.

The circumstances in which the Courts of the country of the original Court shall be deemed to have had, or not to have had, jurisdiction are set forth in s.4(2) and (3) of the Act.

The Act of 1933 is based on reciprocity, and not on the comity of nations; and therefore if the defendant does not submit to the jurisdiction of the foreign court, even though he has been duly served with process of that Court under its powers to serve its process outside its own jurisdiction, the registration of the foreign judgment obtained against him in default will be set aside (*Société Coopérative Sidmetal v. Titan International Ltd* [1966] 1 Q.B. 828; [1965] 3 All E.R. 494). If, however, the defendant who does not appear in the proceedings before the foreign court and suffers a default judgment to be entered against him but then applies to that court to appeal out of time and further appeals from the refusal of the foreign court to extend his time, and his solicitors had stated that all disputes between the parties had to be before that foreign court, he will be treated as having agreed to submit to the jurisdiction of that court under s.4(2)(a)(ii) of the Act of 1933 (*SA Consortium General Textiles v. Sun and Sand Agencies Ltd* [1978] Q.B. 279; [1978] 2 W.L.R. 1;

[1978] 2 All E.R. 339). On the other hand, submission under s.4(2)(a)(iii) of the Act of 1933 to "Courts of the country of that Court" can arise only where there is an express submission to the courts of a country rather than to an individual court, though Lord Denning M.R. expressed the view that the subsection should be construed widely, so that a submission to the jurisdiction of any one of the courts of the country should be treated as the equivalent to a submission to the jurisdiction of any of the other courts of that country (*ibid.*).

It has been held that the registration of a French judgment which could have been enforced by execution in France at the time of the registration is valid, although at a later date it could not have been so enforced (*Re A Debtor (No. 11 of 1939)* [1939] 2 All E.R. 400, CA). In that case the Court emphasised the importance of applying to set aside a registration without delay.

Fraud—In an application to set aside on the ground that the judgment was obtained by fraud, it is immaterial that the facts on which the defendants relied to establish fraud were known to them and could have been raised in the original proceedings, and the defendants are entitled to have tried the issue of fraud (*Syal v. Heyward* (1948) 64 T.L.R. 476). No order for a payment into Court can be made as a condition of trial (*ibid.*). R71.9.2

The jurisdiction to set aside a foreign judgment obtained by fraud under s.9(2) of the 1920 Act and s.4(1)(a) of the 1933 Act has been considered by the House of Lords. The House ruled in favour of the long established common law principle that there was a special defence on a foreign judgment namely that it had been obtained by fraud (see *Abouloff v. Oppenheimer* (1882) 10 Q.B.D. 295 and *Vadala v. Lawes* (1890) 25 Q.B.D. 310). The rule of law that a domestic judgment could only be set aside for fraud on fresh evidence that was not available at the trial did not apply to a foreign judgment and the position had not been changed by the 1920 and 1933 Acts. International comity might require that foreign judgments should be given the same degree of finality as English judgments, but that was a matter for Parliament and not the courts (*Owens Bank Ltd v. Bracco* [1992] 2 A.C. 443.

Issue of execution

10.—(1) Execution shall not issue on a judgment registered under the Act of 1920 or the Act of 1933 until after the expiration of the period which, in accordance with rule 5(3) is specified in the order for registration as the period within which an application may be made to set aside the registration or, if that period has been extended by the court, until after the expiration of that period as so extended. R71.10

(2) If an application is made to set aside the registration of a judgment, execution on the judgment shall not issue until after such application is finally determined.

(3) Any party wishing to issue execution on a judgment registered under the Act of 1920 or the Act of 1933 must produce to the court officer a witness statement or affidavit of service of the notice of registration of the judgment and any order made by the court in relation to the judgment.

Effect of rule—A stay of execution of a foreign judgment duly registered will not be granted, simply because the defendants bring or continue another action against the claimant, at any rate in the absence of special circumstances which render it inexpedient to enforce the judgment under O.47, r.1 (*Wagner (Ferdinand) v. Laubocher Brothers & Co.* [1970] 2 Q.B. 313; [1970] 2 W.L.R. 1019, CA). R71.10.1

The English Court should give "full faith and credit" to the foreign judgment, even though there may be arguable grounds for disputing it or raising a counterclaim against it, and should not therefore in its discretion set the registration aside or adjourn the application to set it aside pending the defendants' appeal to the foreign court, still less pending the trial of an action in the foreign court of a claim by the defendant for damages for breach of contract (*SA Consortium General Textiles v. Sun and Sand Agencies Ltd* [1978] Q.B. 279; [1978] 2 W.L.R. 1; [1978] 2 All E.R. 339, CA).

Determination of certain questions

11. If, in any case under the Act of 1933, any question arises whether a foreign judgment can be enforced by execution in the country of the original court, or what interest is payable under a foreign judgment under the law of the original court, that question shall be determined in accordance with the provisions in that behalf contained in the Order in Council extending Part I of that Act to that country. R71.11

Rules to have effect subject to Orders in Council

R71.12 **12.** The foregoing rules shall, in relation to any judgment registered or sought to be registered under the Act of 1933, have effect subject to any such provisions contained in the Order in Council extending Part I of that Act to the country of the original court as are declared by the order to be necessary for giving effect to the agreement made between Her Majesty and that country in relation to matters with respect to which there is power to make those rules.

Certified copy of High Court judgment

R71.13 **13.**—(1) An application under section 10 of the Act of 1920 or section 10 of the Act of 1933 for a certified copy of a judgment entered in the High Court must be made without notice being served on any other party in witness statement or affidavit to a master or, in the case of a judgment given in proceedings in the Family Division, to a district judge of that Division.

(2) A witness statement or affidavit by which an application under section 10 of the Act of 1920 is made must give particulars of the judgment, show that the judgment creditor wishes to secure the enforcement of the judgment in a part (stating which) of Her Majesty's dominions outside the United Kingdom to which Part II of that Act extends and state the name, trade or business and the usual or last known place of abode of the judgment creditor and the judgment debtor respectively, so far as known to the witness.

(3) A witness statement or affidavit by which an application under section 10 of the Act of 1933 is made must—

- (a) give particulars of the proceedings in which the judgment was obtained;
- (b) have annexed to it a copy of the claim form by which the proceedings were begun, the evidence of service thereof on the defendant, copies of the statements of case or pleadings, if any, and a statement of the grounds on which the judgment was based;
- (c) state whether the defendant did or did not object to the jurisdiction, and, if so, on what grounds;
- (d) show that the judgment is not subject to any stay of execution;
- (e) state that the time for appealing has expired or, as the case may be, the date on which it will expire and in either case whether notice of appeal against the judgment has been entered; and
- (f) state the rate at which the judgment carries interest.

(4) The certified copy of the judgment shall be an office copy sealed with the seal of the Supreme Court and indorsed with a certificate signed by a Master or, where appropriate, a district judge or a registrar certifying that the copy is a true copy of a judgment obtained in the High Court of England and that it is issued in accordance with section 10 of the Act of 1920 or section 10 of the Act of 1933, as the case may be.

(5) Where the application is made under section 10 of the Act of 1933 there shall also be issued a certificate (signed by a Master or, where appropriate, a district judge or a registrar and sealed with the seal of the Supreme Court) having annexed to it a copy of the claim form or other process by which the proceedings were begun, and stating—

- (a) the manner in which the claim form was served on the defendant or that the defendant acknowledged service thereof;
- (b) what objections, if any, were made to the jurisdiction;
- (c) what statements of case, if any, were served;
- (d) the grounds on which the judgment was based;
- (e) that the time for appealing has expired or, as the case may be, the date on which it will expire;
- (f) whether notice of appeal against the judgment has been entered; and

(g) such other particulars as it may be necessary to give to the court in the foreign country in which it is sought to obtain execution of the judgment,

and a certificate (signed and sealed as aforesaid) stating the rate at which the judgment carries interest.

History of rule—Amended by S.I. 1977 No. 1955; S.I. 1979 No. 1716 and S.I. 1989 No. 1307. The office of registrar is now the office of district judge further to Courts and Legal Services Act 1990, s.74. **R71.13.1**

Judgment entered in the High Court—Not every judgment of the High Court can be made the subject of a certificate. The rule applies to "a judgment under which a sum of money is payable, not being a sum payable in respect of taxes or other charges of a like nature or in respect of a fine or other penalty" (1933 Act, s.10). **R71.13.2**

It applies to an order to pay costs in divorce proceedings.

The enlargement of the County Court jurisdiction following the Courts and Legal Services Act 1990 raises the question of whether judgments transferred to the High Court for enforcement and which are to be treated "for all purposes" as a judgment or order of the High Court can be granted certificates for enforcement abroad under this rule and the 1920 and 1933 Acts. As these Acts are based on reciprocity it cannot be assumed that countries with which these reciprocal arrangements exist will enforce judgments other than those of the "High Court" or "Superior Court" as defined in the Acts, however they are described in subsequent domestic legislation which includes the repeal of references to the "Superior Court" in the 1933 Act by s.54 of the Civil Jurisdiction and Judgments Act 1982. A number of countries to which the 1933 Act applies are parties to the Brussels and Lugano Conventions (incorporated into English, Scottish and Northern Irish Law by the 1982 Act) under which the certification of county court judgments raises no problems (see Sched. 2 CCR, O.35) and in such cases applications for certificates should be made to the county court. In respect of countries not party to these conventions it can only be stated with reasonable certainty that the Isle of Man will enforce under the 1933 Act county court judgments transferred to the High Court for enforcement and certified under this rule by the High Court (*Stapleford Flying Club v. Kreisky*, April 18, 1991, High Court of the Isle of Man, Deemster Corrin (unrep.)). In all cases under the 1933 Act that do not fall within Sched. 2 CCR, O.35 application for certificates should be made in the High Court on the transferred county court judgment though there is a risk, other than in the Isle of Man, that the certificate will be rejected by the receiving country. The Royal Court of Jersey has in fact rejected registration of an English County Court judgment transferred to the High Court for enforcement. The basis of rejection was the absence of reciprocity in that a judgment of the Jersey Petty Debts Court would not be amenable to registration in England. Bailiff Bailhache commented that though the English courts might be bound to regard the judgment of the county court as a judgment of the High Court for all purposes, it was not a judgment "given in a superior court" for the purposes of the Jersey legislation (*Re Hardwick* [1995] The Jersey Law Reports 245). The position under the 1920 Act remains unchanged and permits a certificate to be issued only in respect of judgments "obtained in the High Court" which leaves open the question of whether the receiving court will consider a transferred county court judgment to be such a judgment.

No orders have been made under s.32 of the Civil Jurisdiction and Judgments Act 1982 applying all or any part of that Act to the Isle of Man, Channel Islands, Gibraltar or the Cyprus sovereign bases.

"State that the time for appealing has expired"—These words are inapplicable to a judgment signed in default of acknowledgment of service or defence under Pt 12. The witness statement or affidavit in such case must show that no application has been made to set aside the judgment. The form of certificate wil then state that the defendant may apply to set the judgment aside although he has not yet done so (Practice Direction, July 17, 1962). **R71.13.2A**

Legislation for foreign public documents—See the Convention for abolishing this requirement (Cmnd. 2617) in the case of certain public documents. **R71.13.3**

Chancery Division—The application is made to the Chief Master. **R71.13.4**

District Registries—Applications for certified copies of judgments entered in District Registries should be made to the District Registry concerned where the District Judge may exercise the powers of a Master under this rule: see CPR, r.2.4. This brings the procedure under the 1933 Act into line with the procedure under the Brussels Convention regime: see RSC, O.71, r.36. **R71.13.5**

Form of certificate (para. (5))—See Queen's Bench Masters' Practice Form No. 155QB (SCP 1999, Vol. 2, Section 1B, para. 1B–116). **R71.13.6**

II. ENFORCEMENT OF EUROPEAN COMMUNITY JUDGMENTS

Interpretation

R71.15 **15.** In this Part of this order "the Order in Council" means the European Communities (Enforcement of Community Judgments) Order 1972, and expressions used in the Order in Council shall, unless the context otherwise requires, have the same meanings as in that order.

R71.15.1 **Amendment**—By the European Communities (Enforcement of Community Judgments) (Amendment) Order 1968 (S.I. 1998 No. 1259) the 1972 Order was amended to provide for the registration and enforcement as Community judgments of awards of costs made by the Office of Harmonisation in the Internal Market, the institution which administers the Community trade mark.

Functions under Order in Council exercisable by judge or master

R71.16 **16.** The functions assigned to the High Court by the Order in Council may be exercised by a judge and a Master of the Queen's Bench Division sitting in private.

Application for registration of Community judgment, etc.

R71.17 **17.** An application for the registration in the High Court of a Community judgment or Euratom inspection order may be made without notice being served on any other party.

R71.17.1 **Note**—For form of application see PF 156QB (SCP 1999, Vol. 2, Section 1B, para. 1B–117). For form of order see PF 157 (SCP 1999, Vol. 2, Section 1B, para. 1B–118).

Evidence in support of application

R71.18 **18.**—(1) An application for registration must be supported by a witness statement or affidavit exhibiting—

(a) the Community judgment and the order for its enforcement or, as the case may be, the Euratom inspection order or, in either case, a duly authenticated copy thereof; and

(b) where the Community judgment or Euratom inspection order is not in the English language, a translation into English certified by a notary public or authenticated by witness statement or affidavit.

(2) Where the application is for registration of a Community judgment under which a sum of money is payable, the witness statement or affidavit shall also state—

(a) the name and occupation and the usual or last known place of abode or business of the judgment debtor, so far as known to the witness; and

(b) to the best of the witness's information and belief that at the date of the application the European Court has not suspended enforcement of the judgment and that the judgment is unsatisfied or, as the case may be, the amount in respect of which it remains unsatisfied.

R71.18.1 **History of rule**—Amended by S.I. 1997 No. 1955.

Register of judgments and orders

R71.19 **19.**—(1) There shall be kept in the Central Office of the Supreme Court under the direction of the Senior Master a register of the Community judgments and Euratom inspection orders registered under the Order in Council.

(2) There shall be included in the register particulars of any execution issued on a judgment so registered.

Notice of registration

20.—(1) Upon registering a Community judgment or Euratom inspection order, the court shall forthwith send notice of the registration to every person against whom the judgment was given or the order was made. R71.20

(2) The notice of registration shall have annexed to it a copy of the registered Community judgment and the order for its enforcement or, as the case may be, a copy of the Euratom inspection order, and shall state the name and address of the person on whose application the judgment or order was registered or of his solicitor or agent on whom process may be served.

(3) Where the notice relates to a Community judgment under which a sum of money is payable, it shall also state that the judgment debtor may apply within 28 days of the date of the notice, or thereafter with the permission of the court, for the variation or cancellation of the registration on the ground that the judgment had been partly or wholly satisfied at the date of registration.

Note—For form of notice see Queen's Bench Masters' Practice Form No. PF 158QB in SCP 1999, Vol. 2, Section 1B, para. 1B–119. R71.20.1

Issue of execution

21. Execution shall not issue without the permission of the Court on a Community judgment under which a sum of money is payable until the expiration of 28 days after the date of notice of registration of the judgment or, as the case may be, until any application made within that period for the variation or cancellation of the registration has been determined. R71.21

Application to vary or cancel registration

22. An application for the variation or cancellation of the registration of a Community judgment on the ground that the judgment had been wholly or partly satisfied at the date of registration shall be made by claim form supported by witness statement or affidavit. R71.22

Application for registration of suspension order

23. An application for the registration in the High Court of an order of the European Court that enforcement of a registered Community judgment be suspended may be made without notice being served on any other party by lodging a copy of the order in the Central Office of the Supreme Court. R71.23

Application for enforcement of Euratom inspection order

24. An application for an order under Article 6 of the Order in Council for the purpose of ensuring that effect is given to a Euratom inspection order may, in case of urgency, be made without notice being served on any other party on witness statement or affidavit but, except as aforesaid, shall be made by claim form. R71.24

History of rule—Added by S.I. 1972 No. 1898. R71.24.1

Community judgments enforceable in the U.K.—For the purposes of the Order in Council and of this Order, "Community judgment" means any decision, judgment or order which is enforceable under or in accordance with Art. 187 or 192 of the EEC Treaty, Arts 18, 159 or 164 of the Euratom Treaty, or Arts 44 or 92 of the ECSC Treaty, and "Euratom inspection order" means an order made by or in the exercise of the functions of the President of the European Court or by the Commission of the European Communities under Art. 81 of the Euratom Treaty (see Art. 2(1) of the Order in Council). R71.24.2

The most likely Community judgments enforceable under the provisions of the Community Treaties which would require to be registered and enforced in the United Kingdom are decisions of the Commission of the European Communities imposing fines or penalties, either of lump sums expressed in "units of account" or percentages of the offending firm's turnover, *e.g.* under EEC Regulation 17/62 relating to restrictive practices and monopolies, under EEC Regulation 1017/68 applying the rules of competition to transport by rail, road and inland waterway and under EEC Regulation 11 (June 27, 1960) relating to the abolition of discrimination in transport charges and conditions: see also Art. 65(5) of the ECSC Treaty concerning competition. If the European Court upholds an appeal from the decision of the Commission to impose a fine or penalty, the judgment of the European Court becomes itself enforceable under the relevant provisions of the Treaties; and of course the European Court's orders for costs and fines for non-attendance of witnesses are also enforceable in the same way.

The party entitled to enforce a Community judgment will normally be the Commission itself, either because it imposed the fine or penalty in question or because, by virtue of the Treaties, it represents the Communities in legal proceedings.

The Order in Council provides for the automatic registration in the High Court of Community judgments to which the Secretary of State has duly appended the order for enforcement and of Euratom inspection orders (see Art. 3(1) of the Order in Council).

R71.24.3 **Order for enforcement (rr.15–24)**—By virtue of Art. 2(1) of the Order in Council, an order for enforcement means an order by or under the authority of the Secretary of State that the Community judgment to which it is appended is to be registered for enforcement in the United Kingdom. It is the function of the Secretary of State to verify the formal authenticity of any Community judgment sought to be registered, and an order will be made by him or under his authority that it be registered for enforcement in the United Kingdom.

R71.24.4 **Application for registration of Community judgment (rr.15–24)**—The application to register for enforcement of a Community judgment is made in the first instance without notice being served on any other party to the Practice Master in the QBD who may exercise the powers assigned to the High Court by the Order in Council (see rr.16 and 17).

The application must be supported by a witness statement or an affidavit which complies with the requirements of r.18. The omission of the former sub-paragraph (3) of r.18 dispenses with the requirement that the community judgment in foreign currency must be converted into sterling at the date when the judgment was originally given, as a result of the repeal of Art. 3(2) of the Order in Council by s.4 of AJA 1977. If the witness statement or the affidavit is satisfactory, the Master must make an order for the registration of the Community judgment which must forthwith be registered pursuant to Art. 3(1) of the Order in Council."

R71.24.5 **Effect of registration of Community judgment (rr.15–24)**—Upon registration, a Community judgment becomes fully enforceable pursuant to Art. 4 of the Order in Council which provides as follows: "A Community judgment registered in accordance with Art. 3 shall, for all purposes of execution, be of the same force and effect, and proceedings may be taken on the judgment and any sum payable under the judgment shall carry interest, as if the judgment had been a judgment or order given or made by the High Court on the date of registration."

R71.24.6 **Notice of registration (rr.15–24)**—Upon registration, the proper office of the High Court must forthwith send notice of the registration to every person against whom the judgment or order is enforceable (see r.20(1)). Such notice must comply with the requirements of r.20(2) and in particular that the judgment debtor may apply within 28 days, or thereafter with the leave of the Court for the variation or cancellation of the registration on the ground that the judgment had been partly or wholly satisfied at the date of registration (see r.20(3)).

An application for such variation or cancellation must be made by summons supported by affidavit (r.22).

R71.24.7 **Issue of execution (rr.15–24)**—Although a Community judgment is enforceable immediately it is registered, nevertheless execution must not issue without the leave of the Court on a pecuniary Community judgment until the expiration of 28 days after the date of the notice of registration of the judgment or the determination of any application for the variation or cancellation of the registration (see r.21).

R71.24.8 **Application for registration of suspension order (rr.15–24)**—Article 5 of the Order in Council makes the registration of an order of the European Court suspending the enforcement of a Community judgment automatic, as in the case of a Community judgment itself. An application for the registration of such suspension order must be made without notice being served on any other party to the Practice Master in the Q.B.D. by lodging a copy of the order in the Central Office (see r.23).

R71.24.9 **Application for enforcement of Euratom inspection order (rr.15–24)**—By virtue of Art. 6

of the Order in Council, upon the registration of a Euratom inspection order in accordance with Art. 3, the High Court may make such order as it thinks fit against any person for the purpose of ensuring that effect is given to that order. The mode of application for such order is provided by r.24.

III. RECIPROCAL ENFORCEMENT: THE CIVIL JURISDICTION AND JUDGMENTS ACT 1982

Interpretation R71.25

25.—(1) In this Part of this Order—

"the Act of 1982" means the Civil Jurisdiction and Judgments Act 1982:

"Convention territory" means the territory or territories of any Contracting State, as defined by section 1(3) of the Act of 1982, to which the Brussels Convention or the Lugano Convention as defined in section 1(1) of the Act of 1982 apply;

"judgment" is to be construed in accordance with the definition of "judgment" in section 50 of the Act of 1982;

"money provision" means a provision for the payment of one or more sums of money;

"non-money provision" means a provision for any relief or remedy not requiring payment of a sum of money;

"protective measures" means the protective measures referred to in Art. 39 of Schedule 1 or of Schedule 3C to the Act of 1982.

(2) For the purposes of this Part of this Order domicile is to be determined in accordance with the provisions of sections 41 to 46 of the Act of 1982.

R71.25.1

History of rule—Amended by S.I. 1992 No. 1907.

Assignment of business and exercise of powers R71.26

26. Any application to the High Court under the Act of 1982 shall be assigned to the Queen's Bench Division.

Application for registration R71.27

27. An application for registration of a judgment under section 4 of the Act of 1982 shall be made without notice being served on any other party.

Evidence in support of application R71.28

28.—(1) An application for registration under section 4 of the Act of 1982 must be supported by a witness statement or affidavit—

(a) exhibiting—

(i) the judgment or a verified or certified or otherwise duly authenticated copy thereof together with such other document or documents as may be requisite to show that, according to the law of the State in which it has been given, the judgment is enforceable and has been served;

(ii) in the case of a judgment given in default, the original or a certified true copy of the document which establishes that the party in default was served with the document instituting the proceedings or with an equivalent document;

(iii) where it is the case, a document showing that the party making the application is in receipt of legal aid in the State in which the judgment was given;

(iv) where the judgment or document is not in the English language, a translation thereof into English certified by a notary public or a person qualified for the purpose in one of the Contracting States or authenticated by witness statement or affidavit;

(b) stating—

(i) whether the judgment provides for the payment of a sum or sums of money;

(ii) whether interest is recoverable on the judgment or part thereof in accordance with the law of the State in which the judgment was given, and if such be the case, the rate of interest, the date from which interest is recoverable, and the date on which interest ceases to accrue;

(c) giving an address within the jurisdiction of the court for service of process on the party making the application and stating, so far as is known to the witness, the name and the usual or last known address or place of business of the person against whom judgment was given;

(d) stating to the best of the information or belief of the witness—

(i) the grounds on which the right to enforce the judgment is vested in the party making the application;

(ii) as the case may require, either that at the date of the application the judgment has not been satisfied, or the part or amount in respect of which it remains unsatisfied.

(2) Where the party making the application does not produce the documents referred to in paragraphs (1)(a)(ii) and (iii) of this rule, the Court may—

(a) fix a time within which the documents are to be produced; or

(b) accept equivalent documents; or

(c) dispense with production of the documents.

R71.28.1 **Form**—For form of witness statement or affidavit see PF159 QB (SCP 1999, Vol. 2, Section 1B, para. 1B–120).

R71.28.2 **Textbooks**—The purpose of the notes that follow is only to make the rule intelligible; they are not a detailed commentary. For detailed commentaries on the rules see the leading textbooks, *e.g.* Dicey & Morris, *Conflict of Laws* (12th ed.) and Briggs & Rees, *Civil Jurisdictions and Judgments* (2nd ed.).

R71.28.3 **Service**—Art. 27(2) of the Brussels Convention denies recognition to a judgment given in default if the defendant "was not duly served with the document which instituted the proceeds ... in sufficient time for him to arrange his defence". This provision is to be complied with strictly and if service does not comply with the *lex loci executionis* the judgment cannot be enforced (Case C–123/91 *Minalment GmbH v. Brandeis Ltd* [1993] I.L.Pr. 132 and see para. R11.5.8).

Belgian process served by post on a defendant in England, following which the defendant did not enter appearance and the claimant entered a default judgment. The judgment was subsequently registered in England and the defendant appealed on the ground that he had not been duly served. Held that such service complied with both Art. 27 of the Brussels Convention and Art. 15 of the Hague Convention. The Court further held that it had power to stay execution of such a judgment under O.47, r.1 (*Noirhomme v. Walklate* [1992] 1 Lloyd's Rep. 427 *per* H.H. Judge Kershaw, Q.C. and see para. R11.5.7).

R71.28.4 **Civil proceedings**—In some Convention states it is possible for a civil claim to be joined with criminal proceedings. In Case C–172/91 *Sonntag (supported by Land Wurttemburg) v. Waidmann, The Times*, May 18, 1993, the European Court considered whether a judgment so obtained could be registered for enforcement under the provisions of the Convention and whether interested third parties could intervene in the enforcement proceedings and held:

(1) "Civil Matters" within the meaning of the first indent of Art. 1 of the Convention covered an action for damages brought before a criminal court. In this case specifically against a teacher who, during a school trip, caused injury to a pupil by reason of an illegal and culpable breach of his duty of care, even where cover was provided for such liability by a scheme of social insurance under public law.

(2) The second indent of Art. 37 of the Convention was to be interpreted as excluding any action by interested third parties against a decision given in the context of proceedings brought under Art. 36, even where the domestic law of the state enabled such parties to appeal.

(3) The non-recognition of a decision for the reasons indicated in Art. 27(2) of the Convention was only possible where the defendant was in default in the original proceedings. That provision could not be relied upon where the defendant entered an appearance.

A defendant was deemed to have entered an appearance within the meaning of Art. 27(2) of the Convention where, in the context of a claim for compensation connected to criminal proceedings, pending before the Court, the defendant through the representative which he had chosen, stated his position on the criminal proceedings during the hearing of the main issue but not on the civil proceedings which were also subject to argument which the representative had attested. (This does not appear to exclude the possibility that a defendant, whilst contesting the criminal proceedings, might refuse to enter an appearance for the purpose of the civil proceedings).

For the text of the Convention, see SCP 1999, Vol. 2, Section 7B, paras 7B–45 *et seq.*

Authentic instruments and approved court settlements—Art. 50 of the Convention provides that an "Authentic Instrument" which is enforceable in one contracting state shall have an order for enforcement made in another contracting state on application being made in accordance with the procedures provided for in Art. 31 *et seq.* Art. 51 applies the same procedure to "Settlements approved by a Court in the course of proceedings and enforceable in the State in which it is concluded." Section 13(1) of the Civil Jurisdiction and Judgments Act 1982 enabled Her Majesty by Order in Council to apply the Act to authentic instruments and court settlements with "such modifications as may be specified in the Order". The Court was faced with the problem that section 2 of the 1982 Act gives the Conventions the force of law and the Conventions clearly make authentic instruments and court settlements enforceable as judgments. In the absence of an Order the Court had been allowing registration where the case that enforcement under the domestic law was permitted was clearly made out. This problem was resolved by the Civil Jurisdiction and Judgments (Authentic Instruments and Court Settlements) Order 1993 (S.I. 1993 No. 604) which came into force on April 1, 1993. R71.28.5

An authentic instrument or a court settlement is now to be treated "as if it was a judgment which had been originally given" (para. 2(2)).

In the application of section 11 of the 1982 Act to authentic instruments there shall be substituted for s.11(a) the following:

> "A document purporting to be a copy of an authenticated instrument drawn up or registered, and enforceable, in a contracting state other than the United Kingdom is duly authenticated for the purpose of this section if it purports to be certified to be a true copy of such an instrument by a person duly authorised in that Contracting State to do so" (para. 4(2)).

Judgment—The definition of judgment (which is in the widest possible terms) is to be found in Article 25 of the Conventions where it is stated "for the purposes of this Convention 'judgment' means any judgment given by a court or tribunal of a Contracting State, whatever the judgment may be called, including a decree, order, decision or writ of execution, as well as the determination of costs or expenses by an officer of the court". R71.28.6

An order for payment (*decreto ingiuntivo*) obtained under the Italian *procedimento d'ingiunzione* (a process whereby a creditor can obtain without notice being served on any other party an order for payment but which allows the debtor to apply within a limited period after service to apply to set aside the order) is duly served within Article 27(2) by serving the application and the *decreto ingiuntivo* which together become the "document commencing the proceedings" (Case No. C–474/93 *Firma Hengst Import B.V. v. Campese* [1995] I.L.Pr. 587). The similar German *Zahlungsbefehl* procedure is also enforceable (Case No. 166/80 *Klomps v. Michel* [1981] E.C.R. 1593).

An order obtained without notice to the defendant does not qualify as a judgment for the purposes of Article 25 of the Conventions (*Denilantes v. Couchet Frères* [1980] E.C.R. 1553), at least until the defendant has applied unsuccessfully for it to be set aside.

Irreconcilable judgments—The words "irreconcilable judgment" used in Art. 27(3) do not have the same meaning as the same words used in Art. 22 (Case No. 406/92 *The Maciej Rataj* [1995] I.L.Pr. 81. R71.28.7

Maintenance orders—A distinction has to be drawn between an order regulating rights of property arising out of the matrimonial relationship which is not enforceable (Art. 1) and a maintenance order which is (Art. 5). Lump sum and property transfer orders may sometimes be one and sometimes the other a problem that has to be answered by the court enforcing the order from the reasoning of the court of origin (see Case No. C–220/95 *Van den Boogard v. Laumen* [1997] I.L.Pr. 278). (Enforcement of an English Maintenance Order in the Netherlands.) If part of the order only can be construed as a maintenance order then that part can be enforced (Art. 42). R71.28.8

Denial of Recognition—Notwithstanding Article 29 that provides that "under no circumstance may a foreign judgment be reviewed as to its substance" there are a number of circumstances where the court where recognition is sought (The Receiving State) must deny recognition. These are set out in Art. 27 and may be summarised as follows: R71.28.9

1. Recognition contrary to public policy in the Receiving State.
2. Default in service of proceedings (see para. R71.28.3, above).
3. Judgment irreconcilable with a judgment given between the same parties in the Receiving State.
4. Judgment given in the state of origin deciding a preliminary question concerning status or legal capacity of natural persons, rights of property arising out of a matrimonial relationship, wills or succession that conflicts with a rule of private international law in the receiving state.

5. Judgment irreconcilable with a judgment given in a non-contracting state involving the same cause of action and between the same parties.

In a case where a lawyer appeared for the defendant but without his authority in the court of the state of origin where judgment entered the receiving state could deny recognition of the judgment on the basis that in such circumstances the defendant was in no different position from a defendant who had not been duly served and accordingly such a defendant could rely on Article 27(2) (Case No. C–78/95 *Hendrikman v. Magenta Druck & Verlag GmbH* (1996) *The Times*, October (on appeal from the Netherlands Supreme Court).

R71.28.10 **Public Policy—Article 27(1)**—a judgment obtained in a convention country in breach of an anti-suit injunction would not be enforced in England as against public policy (*Phillip Alexander Securities and Futures Ltd* [1997] I.L.Pr. 73).

The public defence does not generally allow a foreign judgment to be challenged on the grounds that it was obtained by fraud, unlike the position at common law and under the Administration of Justice Act 1920 and the Foreign Jugments (Reciprocal Enforcement) Act 1933. See *Interdesco v. Nullifire Ltd* [1992] 1 Lloyd's Rep. 180 noted at R71.33.3 below."

The Courts of some Contracting States are reluctant to recognise default judgments. For this reason it is common practice for a claim which it is ultimately intended to enforce in a Brussels/Lugano Convention Contracting State to be taken to trial where the defendant is in default (*Berliner Bank v. Karageorgis* [1996] 1 Lloyd's Rep. 426). The Court should be invited to make an express finding of the facts on which its jurisdiction is based under Article 28(2) of the Conventions. It is advisable to rely on affidavit evidence rather than witness statements.

Security for costs

R71.29 **29.** Notwithstanding the provisions of Order 23 a party making an application for registration under section 4 of the Act of 1982 shall not be required solely on the ground that he is not domiciled or resident within the jurisdiction, to give security for costs of the application.

Order for registration

R71.30 **30.**—(1) An order giving permission to register a judgment under section 4 of the Act of 1982 must be drawn up by or on behalf of the party making the application for registration.

(2) Every such order shall state the period within which an appeal may be made against the order for registration and shall contain a notification that execution on the judgment will not issue until after the expiration of that period.

(3) The notification referred to in paragraph (2) shall not prevent any application for protective measures pending final determination of any issue relating to enforcement of the judgment.

R71.30.1 **Form**—For form of order see PF 160 QB (SCP 1999, Vol. 2, Section 1B, para. 1B–121).

Register of judgments registered under s.4 of the Act of 1982

R71.31 **31.** There shall be kept in the Central Office of the Supreme Court under the direction of the Senior Master a register of the judgments ordered to be registered under section 4 of the Act of 1982.

Notice of registration

R71.32 **32.**—(1) Notice of the registration of a judgment must be served on the person against whom judgment was given by delivering it to him personally or by sending it to him at his usual or last known address or place of business or in such other manner as the court may direct.

(2) Permission is not required to serve such a notice out of the jurisdiction, and Order 11, rules 5, 6 and 8, shall apply in relation to such a notice as they apply in relation to a claim form.

(3) The notice of registration must state—

(a) full particulars of the judgment registered and the order for registration;

(b) the name of the party making the application and his address for service within the jurisdiction;

(c) the right of the person against whom judgment was given to appeal against the order for registration; and
(d) the period within which an appeal against the order for registration may be made.

Form—For form of notice see PF 161 QB (SCP 1999, Vol. 2, Section 1B, para. 1B–122). R71.32.1

Appeals

33.—(1) An appeal under article 37 or article 40 of Schedule 1 or 3C to the Act of 1982 must be made to a judge by application in accordance with CPR Part 23. R71.33

(2) A claim form in an appeal to which this rule applies must be served—
(a) in the case of an appeal under the said article 37 of Schedule 1 or 3C, within one month of service of notice of registration of the judgment, or two months of service of such notice where that notice was served on a party not domiciled within the jurisdiction;
(b) in the case of an appeal under the said article 40 of Schedule 1 or 3C, within one month of the determination of the application under rule 27.

(3) If the party against whom judgment was given is not domiciled in a Convention territory and an application is made within two months of service of notice of registration, the court may extend the period within which an appeal may be made against the order for registration.

History of rule—Amended by S.I. 1992 No. 1997. R71.33.1

Appeals—By Art. 37(2) any appeal from the judge is limited to a single appeal on a point of law. After the appeal has been lodged the appellant may apply for a stay of proceedings under Art. 38. There is however no appeal from the decision to grant or refuse a stay made in such an application (Case C–183/90 *van Dalfsen v. van Loon* [1991] E.C.R. I–4743, ECJ). R71.33.2

Where registration of a foreign judgment under the Convention is challenged on the ground that the foreign court has been fraudulently deceived, the English court should first consider whether a remedy lay in the foreign court in question. If so it would normally be appropriate to leave the defendant to pursue his remedy in that jurisdiction (*Interdesco SA v. Nullifire Ltd* [1992] 1 Lloyd's Rep. 180).

The Conventions established an enforcement procedure which constituted an autonomous and complete system independent of the legal systems of the contracting states. The provisions relating to the stay of proceedings pending appeal against registration were to be restrictively and uniformly applied so as to avoid derogation from the Conventions' object of establishing a simple and rapid machinery for the enforcement of judgments enforceable in the state of origin. So on an appeal on a point of law allowed under Art. 37(2) the Court of Appeal had no power to review the refusal by the judge to grant a stay or to lift a stay previously ordered (Case No. C–432/93 *Société d'Informatique Service Réalisation Organisation v. Ampersand Software B.V.* (1995) *The Times*, September 25, ECJ).

Issue of execution

34.—(1) Execution shall not issue on a judgment registered under section 4 of the Act of 1982 until after the expiration of the period specified in accordance with rule 30(2) or, if that period has been extended by the Court, until after the expiration of the period so extended. R71.34

(2) If an appeal is made under rule 33(1) execution on the judgment shall not issue until after such appeal is determined.

(3) Any party wishing to issue execution on a judgment registered under section 4 of the Act of 1982 must produce to the court officer a witness statement or affidavit of service of the notice of registration of the judgment and of any order made by the court in relation to the judgment.

(4) Nothing in this rule shall prevent the court from granting protective measures pending final determination of any issue relating to enforcement of the judgment.

In *Coursier v. Fortis Bank SA*, Case C–267/97, April 29, 1999, the European Court held that the R71.34.1

requirement, under Article 31 of the Conventions, that a foreign judgment be enforceable in the court of origin referred solely to the enforceability in formal terms of the judgment. The judgment had subsequently become unenforceable in the court of origin because of the insolvency of the judgment debtor there. This did not prevent the court of the state in which enforcement was sought from determining the legal effects of the judgment in accordance with its domestic law, including private international law rules.

Application for recognition

R71.35 **35.**—(1) Registration of the judgment under these rules shall serve for the purposes of the second paragraph of Article 26 of Schedule 1 or 3C to the Act of 1982 as a decision that the judgment is recognised.

(2) Where it is sought to apply for recognition of a judgment, the foregoing rules of this Order shall apply to such application as they apply to an application for registration under section 4 of the Act, with the exception that the applicant shall not be required to produce a document or documents which establish that according to the law of the State in which it has been given the judgment is enforceable and has been served, or the document referred to in rule 28(1)(a)(iii).

R71.35.1 **History of rule**—Amended by S.I. 1992 No. 1907.

R71.35.2 **Purpose of recognition**—Recognition under Art. 26 of the Conventions includes enforcement but also includes recognition for the purpose of cause of action estoppel and issue estoppel (*Berkeley Administration Inc. v. McClelland (No. 2)* [1995] I.L.Pr. 201).

Enforcement of High Court judgments in other Contracting States

R71.36 **36.**—(1) An application under section 12 of the Act of 1982 for a certified copy of a judgment entered in the High Court must be made without notice being served on any other party on witness statement or affidavit to the court.

(2) a witness statement or affidavit by which an application under section 12 of the Act of 1982 is made must—

(a) give particulars of the proceedings in which the judgment was obtained;

(b) have annexed to it a copy of the claim form, by which the proceedings were begun, the evidence of service thereof on the defendant, copies of the statements of case, if any, and a statement of the grounds on which the judgment was based together, where appropriate, with any document under which the applicant is entitled to legal aid or assistance by way of representation for the purposes of the proceedings;

(c) state whether the defendant did or did not object to the jurisdiction, and, if so, on what grounds;

(d) show that the judgment has been served in accordance with CPR Part 6 and CPR Rule 40.4 and is not subject to any stay of execution;

(e) state that the time for appealing has expired, or, as the case may be, the date on which it will expire and in either case whether notice of appeal against the judgment has been given; and

(f) state—

(i) whether the judgment provides for the payment of a sum or sums of money;

(ii) whether interest is recoverable on the judgment or part thereof and if such be the case, the rate of interest, the date from which interest is recoverable, and the date on which interest ceases to accrue.

(3) The certified copy of the judgment shall be an office copy sealed with the seal of the Supreme Court and there shall be issued with the copy of the

judgment a certificate in Form 110, signed by a High Court judge, the Admiralty Registrar, a Master or a district judge and sealed with the seal of the Supreme Court, having annexed to it a copy of the claim form by which the proceedings were begun.

Form—For form of affidavit see PF 163 (SCP 1999, Vol. 2, Section 1B, para. 1B–124). **R71.36.1**

Service—See notes to RSC, O.11 at paras R11.5.7 and R11.5.8. **R71.36.2**

Enforcement of United Kingdom judgments in other parts of the United Kingdom: money provisions

37.—(1) An application for registration in the High Court of a certificate in respect of any money provisions contained in a judgment given in another part of the United Kingdom to which section 18 of the Act of 1982 applies may be made by producing at the Central Office of the Supreme Court, within six months from the date of its issue, a certificate in the appropriate form prescribed under that Act together with a copy thereof certified by the applicant's solicitor to be a true copy. **R71.37**

(2) A certificate under paragraph (1) must be filed in the Central Office of the Supreme Court and the certified copy thereof, sealed by an officer of the office in which the certificate is filed, shall be returned to the applicant's solicitor.

(3) A certificate in respect of any money provisions contained in a judgment of the High Court to which section 18 of the Act of 1982 applies may be obtained by producing the form of certificate prescribed in Form 111 at the office in which the judgment is entered, together with a witness statement or affidavit made by the party entitled to enforce the judgment—

(a) giving particulars of the judgment, stating the sum or aggregate of the sums (including any costs or expenses) payable and unsatisfied under the money provisions contained in the judgment, the rate of interest, if any, payable thereon and the date or time from which any such interest began to accrue;

(b) verifying that the time for appealing against the judgment has expired, or that any appeal brought has been finally disposed of and that enforcement of the judgment is not stayed or suspended; and

(c) stating to the best of the information or belief of the witness the usual or last known address of the party entitled to enforce the judgment and of the party liable to execution on it.

Forms—For form of affidavit see PF 164 QB (SCP 1999, Vol. 2, Section 1B, para. 1B–125). **R71.37.1**

Application for stay of enforcement—Under para. 9 of Sched. 6 to the 1982 Act an application may be made to stay the enforcement of the certificate issued under this rule. On such an application the registering court has to be satisfied that the applicant is entitled and intends to apply to the judgment court to set aside or stay the judgment and if the registering court is so satisfied it may stay the enforcement proceedings on such terms as it thinks fit for such period as may be reasonably sufficient to enable the application in the judgment court to be disposed of. **R71.37.2**

Where the English High Court is the registering court, though there is no settled procedure, it is suggested that the best practice would be to make the application to stay execution by claim form supported by witness statement or affidavit so that the court has evidence before it on which it "may be satisfied" of the matters referred to in the paragraph. Such an application should follow the procedure under Sched. 1, RSC, O.47, r.1 and where an immediate stay is required the initial application should be without notice being served on any other party to the practice master.

Enforcement of United Kingdom judgments in other parts of the United Kingdom: non-money provisions

38.—(1) An application for registration in the High Court of a judgment which contains non-money provisions, being a judgment given in another part of the United Kingdom to which section 18 of the Act of 1982 applies, may be made without notice being served on any other party, but the court **R71.38**

hearing the application may direct a claim form to be filed and served to which rule 2 shall apply.

(2) An application under paragraph (1) must be accompanied by a certified copy of the judgment issued under Schedule 7 to the Act of 1982 and a certificate in the appropriate form prescribed for the purposes of paragraph 4(1)(b) of that Schedule issued not more than six months before the date of application.

(3) Rules 30 and 32 of this Order shall apply to judgments registered under Schedule 7 to the Act of 1982 as they apply to judgments registered under section 4 of that Act.

(4) Paragraphs (1) and (2) of rule 9 shall apply to applications to set aside registration of a judgment under Schedule 7 to the Act of 1982 as they apply to judgments registered under the Administration of Justice Act 1920 and the Foreign Judgments (Reciprocal Enforcements) Act 1933.

(5) A certified copy of a judgment of the High Court to which section 18 of the Act of 1982 applies and which contains any non-money provision may be obtained by an application on witness statement or affidavit to the court.

(5A) An application referred to in paragraph (5) need not be served on any other party.

(6) The requirements in paragraph (3) of rule 37 shall apply with the necessary modifications to a witness statement or affidavit made in an application under paragraph (5) of this rule.

(7) A certified copy of a judgment shall be an office copy sealed with the seal of the Supreme Court to which shall be annexed a certificate in Form 112.

R71.38.1 **History of rule**—Amended by S.I. 1984 No. 1051.

R71.38.2 **Form**—For form of affidavit see PF 165 (SCP 1999, Vol. 2, Section 1B, para. 1B–126).

Register of United Kingdom judgments

R71.39 **39.** There shall be kept in the Central Office of the Supreme Court under the direction of the Senior Master a register of the certificates in respect of judgments and of the judgments ordered to be registered in the Central Office of the Supreme Court under Schedule 6, or, as the case may be, Schedule 7 to the Act.

R71.39.1 **History of rule**—Added by S.I. 1993 No. 2133.

Authentic Instruments and Court Settlements

R71.39A **39A.** Rules 27 to 35 inclusive (except rule 28(1)(a)(ii)) shall apply to—

(1) an authentic instrument to which either article 50 of Schedule 1 to the Act of 1982 or article 50 of Schedule 3C to the Act applies; and

(2) a settlement to which either article 51 of Schedule 1 to the Act of 1982 or article 51 of Schedule 3C to that Act applies,

as they apply to a judgment subject to any necessary modifications.

R71.39A.1 **History of rule**—Added by S.I. 1993 No. 2133.

R71.39A.2 **Effect of rule**—See para. R71.28.4.

IV. ENFORCEMENT OF RECOMMENDATIONS, ETC. UNDER THE MERCHANT SHIPPING (LINER CONFERENCES) ACT 1982

Exercise of powers

R71.40 **40.** The powers conferred on the High Court under the Merchant Shipping (Liner Conferences) Act 1982 (in this Part of this order referred to as "the Act of 1982") may be exercised by a Commercial Judge.

Application for registration

41. An application under section 9 of the Act of 1982 for the registration of a recommendation, determination or award, shall be made by claim form. **R71.41**

Evidence in support of application

42.—(1) An application under section 9 of the Act of 1982 for the registration of a recommendation must be supported by a witness statement or affidavit— **R71.42**

(a) exhibiting a verified or certified or otherwise duly authenticated copy of the recommendation and the reasons therefor and of the record of settlement;
(b) where the recommendation and reasons or the record of settlement is not in the English language, a translation thereof into English certified by a notary public or authenticated by witness statement or affidavit;
(c) exhibiting copies of the acceptance of the recommendation by the parties upon whom it is binding, where the acceptance was in writing, or otherwise verifying the acceptance;
(d) giving particulars of the failure to implement the recommendation; and
(e) verifying that none of the grounds which would render the recommendation unenforceable under section 9(2) of the Act of 1982 is applicable.

(2) An application under section 9 of the Act of 1982 for the registration of a determination or award as to costs must be supported by a witness statement or affidavit—

(a) exhibiting a verified or certified or otherwise duly authenticated copy of the recommendation or other document containing the pronouncement on costs; and
(b) stating that such costs have not been paid.

Order for registration

43.—(1) An order giving permission to register a recommendation, determination or award under section 9 of the Act of 1982 must be drawn up by or on behalf of the party making the application for registration. **R71.43**

(2) Such an order shall contain a provision that the reasonable costs of registration be taxed.

Register of recommendations, etc.

44.—(1) There shall be kept in the Admiralty and Commercial Registry under the direction of the Senior Master a register of the recommendations, determinations and awards ordered to be registered under section 9 of the Act of 1982. **R71.44**

(2) There shall be included in such register particulars of the enforcement of a recommendation, determination or award so registered.

History of rule—Pt IV added by S.I. 1986 No. 632. Amended by S.I. 1987 No. 1423. **R71.44.1**

RSC ORDER 74

APPLICATIONS AND APPEALS UNDER THE MERCHANT SHIPPING ACT 1995

Assignment of proceedings

1.—(1) Subject to paragraph (2), proceedings by which any application is made to the High Court under the Merchant Shipping Act 1995 shall be assigned to the Queen's Bench Division and taken by the Admiralty Court. **R74.1**

Appeals and re-hearings

R74.2 **2.**—(1) An appeal to the High Court under section 28 of the Pilotage Act 1913 against a decision of a county court judge or a magistrate shall be heard and determined by a Divisional Court of the Queen's Bench Division constituted as far as practicable of Admiralty Judges.

(2) Subject to the provisions of this rule, Orders 55 and 57 shall apply in relation to an appeal to the High Court under the Merchant Shipping Act 1995 and for this purpose a re-hearing and an application under section 61 of the Merchant Shipping Act 1995 shall be treated as an appeal.

(3) In the case of an appeal to which paragraph (2) applies, the documents required to be filed before entry for the purposes of Order 57, rule 2(1) shall include the report, if any, to the Secretary of State containing the decision from which the appeal is brought.

(4) Where a re-hearing by the High Court is ordered under sections 64 or 269 of the Merchant Shipping Act 1995, the Secretary of State shall cause such reasonable notice to be given to the parties whom he considers to be affected by the re-hearing as the circumstances of the case may, in his opinion, permit.

R74.2.1 **Note**—Section 28 of the Pilotage Act has been repealed and r.2(1) of this Order has no effect or application.

RSC ORDER 77

PROCEEDINGS BY AND AGAINST THE CROWN

R77.0.1 **Contents**

Editorial Introduction

R77.0.2 Part II of the Crown Proceedings Act 1947 (SCP 1999, Vol. 2, Section 21L, paras 21L–22 to 21L–56) contains a number of provisions dealing with matters of jurisdiction and procedure related to "civil proceedings by or against the Crown". Pt III contains provisions dealing with the enforcement of judgments where the Crown has an interest. (Part I is concerned with the substantive liability of the Crown, particularly vicarious liability in tort.)

Pt II begins with s.13 which provides that, subject to the provisions of the Act, all civil proceedings by or against the Crown in the High Court shall be "instituted and proceeded with" in accordance with rules of court and not otherwise. "Civil proceedings by or against the Crown" are as defined in s.23 (see also s.38). Section 22 provides that, subject to the provisions of the Act, all enactments and rules of court relating to appeals and stay of execution shall "with any necessary modification" apply to civil proceedings by or against the Crown as they apply to proceedings between subjects.

Section 35(1) of the 1947 Act states that the power to make rules of court shall include power to make rules for the purpose of giving effect to the provisions of the Act. A number of provisions in the Act speak specifically towards procedural issues. For example, s.7(1) states that no application shall be made against the Crown for summary judgment under O.14, r.1 in any proceedings against the Crown.

Further, any such rules may contain provisions to have effect in relation to any proceedings by or against the Crown in substitution for, or by way of addition to, any of the provisions of the rules applying to proceedings between subject and subject. Section 35(2) provides that provision shall be made by rules of court with respect to a number of specific procedural matters; for example, following s.7(1), for excepting proceedings against the Crown from the operation of any rule of court providing for summary judgment without trial.

The bulk of the rules carrying s.35 into effect are found in O.77. For example, the rule excepting the Crown from summary judgment is found in O.77, r.7. The rules have remained largely in their original form since their introduction in 1948. Rule 8A was inserted in 1971.

The broad intention of the 1947 Act is that proceedings by and against the Crown should be taken in the same circumstances and in the same way as proceedings between subjects. However, procedurally speaking, in a not insignificant number of ways (and usually for obvious reasons) the Crown as a party is in a special position and enjoys advantages not extended to the ordinary party.

Related sources

In this Order, the following provisions of the RSC are referred to expressly (usually for the purpose of qualifying their application in civil proceedings involving the Crown): R77.0.3

- O.4, r.5 (Transfer between district registries and London) (r.2)
- O.6, r.2 (Indorsement of claim) (r.3)
- O.10 (Service of originating process: general provisions, in so far as they relate to service out of the jurisdiction) (r.4)
- O.11 (Service of process, etc., out of the jurisdiction) (r.4)
- O.14, rr.1 and 5 (Application by plaintiff for summary judgment and on counterclaim) (r.7(1) and (2))
- O.14A, r.1 (Disposal of case on point of law) (r.7(1))
- O.15, r.2 (Counterclaim against plaintiff) (r.6(1) and (2))
- O.15, r.6 (Joinder of parties) (r.8A)
- O.16 (Issue of third party notices) (r.10)
- O.16, r.5(1) (Failure of third party to give notice of intention to defend) (r.9(2) and (3))
- O.17, r.5(3) (Non-appearance of claimant to interpleader summons) (r.11)
- O.18, r.17 (Defence of set-off) (r.6(1)(2))
- O.18, r.18 (Counterclaim and defence to counterclaim) (r.6(1)(2))
- O.24, r.1 (Mutual discovery of documents) (r.12(1))
- O.24, r.2 (Discovery by parties without order) (r.12(1))
- O.30 (No appointment of a receiver where money due from Crown) (r.16(1))
- O.39, r.15 (Perpetuation of testimony (r.14(1))
- O.45 to O.52 (Enforcement of judgments and orders) (nothing in these Orders shall apply in respect of any order against the Crown, r.15(1))
- O.45 (No appointment of a sequestrator where money due from Crown) (r.16(1))
- O.49 (No attachment of debts where money due from Crown) (r.16(1))
- O.49, r.1 (Attachment of debt due to judgment debtor) (r.16(3))
- O.49, r.5 (Dispute of liability by garnishee) (r.16(3))
- O.49, r.6 (Claims against third persons in garnishee proceedings) (r.16(3))
- O.51 (No appointment of a receiver by way of equitable execution where money due from Crown) (r.16(1))
- O.65, r.5 (Effecting of ordinary service of documents) (r.4(3))
- O.65, r.9 (No service of documents required in certain cases) (r.4(3))
- O.65, r.7 (Effect of service of documents after certain hours) (r.4(3))
- O.86, r.1 (Application by plaintiff for summary judgment in action for specific performance) (r.7(1) and (2))

Note also:

- RSC, O.78, r.1 (removal under Crown Proceedings Act 1947, s.20 of proceedings from a county court to the High Court)
- CCR, O.42 (Proceedings by and against the Crown).

Forms

The following Prescribed Forms (formerly included amongst the Prescribed Forms in Appendix A to the RSC) are relevant to O.77. These forms are included in Table 2 (Practice Forms) attached to Practice Direction (Forms) and may be found in SCP 1999, Vol. 2, Section 1A, paras 1A–98 and 1A–99): R77.0.4

- PF No. 95—Certificate of order against Crown (r.15)
- PF No. 96—Certificate of order for costs against Crown (r.15).

Application and interpretation

R77.1 **1.**—(1) these rules apply to civil proceedings to which the Crown is a party subject to the following rules of this order.

(2) In this order—

"civil proceedings by the Crown", "civil proceedings against the Crown" and "civil proceedings by or against the Crown" have the same respective meanings as in Part II of the Crown Proceedings Act 1947, and do not include any of the proceedings specified in section 23(3) of that Act;

"civil proceedings to which the Crown is a party" has the same meaning as it has for the purposes of Part IV of the Crown Proceedings Act 1947, by virtue of section 38(4) of that Act;

"order against the Crown" means any order (including an order for costs) made in any civil proceedings by or against the Crown or in any proceedings on the Crown side of the Queen's Bench Division, or in connection with any arbitration to which the Crown is a party, in favour of any person against the Crown or against a government department or against an officer of the Crown as such;

"order" includes a judgment, decree, rule, award or declaration.

R77.1.1 **History of rule**—Amended by S.I. 1982 No. 1111.

R77.1.2 **The Crown**—For a consideration of the nature of the Crown see *Re M* [1994] 1 A.C. 377, HL, at 408–411, *per* Lord Woolf.

R77.1.3 **Crown Proceedings Act 1947**—See SCP 1999, Vol. 2, Section 21L, paras 21L–1 *et seq.*

R77.1.4 **"Civil proceedings"**—The words are apt to include third party proceedings against the Crown, notwithstanding the separate reference to such proceedings in rule 9(1). (*St. Martin's Property Investments Ltd v. Philips Electronics (U.K.) Ltd, Secretary of State for the Environment (Third Party)* [1994] 3 W.L.R. 1074, [1995] 1 All E.R. 378 (Rattee J.). An action for specific performance of a contract for the sale of land, brought by means of a writ issued out of the QBD against the defendant Secretary of State, is a civil proceeding against the Crown within ss.21 and 23(2) (a) of the C.P.A. 1947 Act (*Firglen Ltd v. Secretary of State for the Environment* (1995) *The Times*, November 16 (Harman J.). See also *Franklin v. The Queen (No. 2)* [1974] Q.B. 205; [1973] 3 All E.R. 861, CA, para. R77.15.2 below.

R77.1.5 **Admiralty**—No action *in rem* lies against the Crown. Where proceedings *in rem* have been instituted "in the reasonable belief that the ship, aircraft, cargo or other property did not belong to the Crown" the Court may order that the proceedings shall be treated as if they were *in personam* (see CPA 1947, s.29).

Transfer of proceedings

R77.2 **2.**—(1) Subject to paragraph (2) in civil proceedings by or against the Crown no order shall be made under CPR Part 30, for the transfer of the proceedings, or of any application therein, from the Royal Courts of Justice to a district registry, except with the consent of the Crown.

(2) In any civil proceedings against the Crown begun by the issue of a claim form out of a district registry the Crown may acknowledge service of the claim form either in the district registry or, at the option of the Crown, in the appropriate office of the Supreme Court at the Royal Courts of Justice, and where service is acknowledged in an office of the Supreme Court at the Royal Courts of Justice the claim shall thereafter proceed in the Royal Courts of Justice and no order shall be made under CPR Part 30 for the transfer of any proceedings before the trial from the Royal Courts of Justice to a district registry.

R77.2.1 **History of rule**—Taken from RSC (Rev.) 1962, O.77, r.2, which had been taken from the former O.12, r.7, and O.35, r.17. See Crown Proceedings Act 1947, ss.19 and 20(2). The reference to Order 4, rule 6 should be to rule 5. The reference in the rule was not amended when Order 4 was renumbered.

Amended by S.I. 1979 No. 1716 and S.I. 1982 No. 1111.

Acknowledgment of service by the Crown—This rule gives express recognition to the statutory option of the Crown under section 19(1) of the Crown Proceedings Act 1947, that where proceedings against the Crown are issued out of a district registry, the Crown may acknowledge service of the writ either in the district registry, at its option, in the Central Office or, in the case of Admiralty actions, in the Admiralty Registry, and where that acknowledgment is sent to the Central Office or the Admiralty Registry, the action will continue in London. R77.2.2

In an action against the Crown, an originating summons for the approval of a settlement or compromise of a claim by or on behalf of a minor or patient, or under the Fatal Accidents Act 1976, which must be in Form No. 10 (SCP 1999, Vol. 2, Section 1A, para. 1A–5) may be issued and heard in a district registry, if the acknowledgment of service is sent to that registry (see CPR, r.21.10).

Particulars to be included in claim form

3.—(1) In the case of a claim form which begins civil proceedings against the Crown the contents of the claim form required by CPR rule 16.2 shall include a statement of the circumstances in which the Crown's liability is alleged to have arisen and as to the government department and officers of the Crown concerned. R77.3

(2) If in civil proceedings against the Crown a defendant considers that the claim form does not contain a sufficient statement as required by this rule, he may, before the expiration of the time limited for acknowledging service of the claim form, apply to the claimant by notice for a further and better statement containing such information as may be specified in the notice.

(3) Where a defendant gives a notice under this rule, the time limited for acknowledging service of the claim form shall not expire until 4 days after the defendant has notified the claimant in writing that the defendant is satisfied with the statement supplied in compliance with the notice or 4 days after the court has, on the application of the claimant in accordance with CPR Part 23, decided that no further information as to the matters referred to in paragraph (1) is reasonably required.

(3A) An application notice under paragraph (3) shall be served on the defendant not less than 7 days before the hearing.

History of rule—Taken from RSC (Rev.) 1962, O.77, r.3, which had been taken from the former O.3, r.3A. See CPA 1947, s.35(2)(b). R77.3.1

Amended by S.I. 1979 No. 1716.

Service on the Crown

4.—(1) Order 11 and any other provision of these rules relating to service out of the jurisdiction shall not apply in relation to the service of any process by which civil proceedings against the Crown are begun. R77.4

(2) Personal service of any document required to be served on the Crown for the purpose of or in connection with any civil proceedings is not requisite; but where the proceedings are by or against the Crown service on the Crown must be effected—

(a) by leaving the document at the office of the person who is in accordance with section 18 of the Crown Proceedings Act 1947, to be served, or of any agent whom that person has nominated for the purpose, but in either case with a member of the staff of that person or agent; or

(b) by posting it in a prepaid envelope addressed to the person who is to be served as aforesaid or to any such agent as aforesaid.

(3) Any document (other than a claim form) service of which is effected under paragraph 2(a) between 12 noon on a Saturday and midnight on the following day or after 4 in the afternoon on any other weekday shall, for the purpose of computing any period of time after service of that document, be

deemed to have been served on the Monday following that Saturday or on the day following that other weekday, as the case may be.

(4) Where by virtue of these rules any document is required to be served on any person but is not required to be served personally and at the time when service is to be effected that person is in default as to acknowledgment of service or has no address for service, the document need not be served on that person unless the court otherwise directs or any of these rules otherwise provides.

(5)(a) No process shall be served or executed within the jurisdiction on a Sunday except, in case of urgency, with the permission of the court.

(b) For the purpose of this rule "process" includes a claim form, judgment, application or other notice, order, petition, or warrant.

R77.4.1 **History of rule**—Taken from RSC (Rev.) 1962, O.77, r.4, which had been taken as to para. (1) from the previous O.9, r.5A, and O.11, r.14; as to para. (2) from O.67, rr.1A, 2; and as to para. (3) from O.67, r.2.

R77.4.2 **Service on the Crown**—See section 18 of the CPA 1947 (SCP 1999, Vol. 2, Pt. 18).
For the list published by the Treasury under the CPA 1947, s.17 of the authorised Government Departments and of their respective solicitors and addresses for service, see SCP 1999, Vol. 2, Section 21L, paras 21L–36 to 21L–40.

Counterclaim and set-off

R77.6 **6.**—(1) A person may not in any proceedings by the Crown make any counterclaim or claim a set-off in his statement case if the proceedings are for the recovery of, or the counterclaim or set-off arises out of a right or claim to repayment in respect of, any taxes, duties or penalties.

(2) No counterclaim may be made, or set-off claimed in its statements of case, without the permission of the court, by the Crown in proceedings against the Crown, or by any person in proceedings by the Crown—

(a) if the Crown is sued or sues in the name of a Government department and the subject-matter of the counterclaim or set-off does not relate to that department; or

(b) if the Crown is sued or sues in the name of the Attorney-General.

(3) Any application for permission under this rule must be made in accordance with CPR Part 23.

R77.6.1 **History of rule**—Taken from RSC (Rev.) 1962, O.77, r.6, which had been taken from the former O.19, r.3A. It embodies the effect of section 35(2)(g) of the CPA 1947. "Taxes" includes interest on certain unpaid tax (Tax Management Act 1970, s.69(b)).

Summary judgment

R77.7 **7.**—(1) No application shall be made against the Crown—

(a) under CPR Part 24, in any proceedings against the Crown;

(b) for summary judgment on a counterclaim under CPR Part 24 in any proceedings by the Crown.

(2) Where an application is made by the Crown under CPR Part 24, the affidavit or witness statement required in support of the application must be made by—

(a) the solicitor acting for the Crown; or

(b) an officer duly authorised by the solicitor so acting or by the department concerned;

and the witness statement or affidavit shall be sufficient if it states that in the belief of the witness the applicant is entitled to the relief claimed and there is no defence to the claim or part of a claim to which the application relates or no defence except as to the amount of any damages claimed.

R77.7.1 **History of rule**—Taken from RSC (Rev.) 1962, O.77, r.7, which had been taken from the former O.14, r.1, and O.14A, r.1. Para. (1) embodies the effect of s.35(2)(d) of the CPA 1947. Amended by S.I. 1990 No. 2599.

Summary applications to the Court in certain revenue matters

8.—(1) this rule applies to applications under section 14 of the Crown Proceedings Act 1947. **R77.8**

(2) An application to which this rule applies shall be made by claim form.

(3) The person from whom any account or information or payment is claimed or by whom any books are required to be produced must be made a defendant to the application.

(4) A claim form under this rule—

(a) must be entitled in the matter or matters out of which the need for the application arises and in the matter of the Crown Proceedings Act 1947; and

(b) must refer to the enactment under which the account or information or payment or the production of books is claimed and, where information is claimed, must show (by appropriate questions or otherwise) what information is required.

(5) Upon any application to which this rule applies a witness statement or affidavit by a duly authorised officer of the Government department concerned setting out the state of facts upon which the application is based and stating that he has reason to think that those facts exist shall be evidence of those facts; and if evidence is filed disputing any of those facts, further evidence may be filed, and the court may either decide the matter upon the witness statements or affidavits (after any cross-examination that may have been ordered) or may direct that it be decided by oral evidence in court.

(6) An order in favour of the Crown on an application to which this rule applies shall, unless the court otherwise determines, name a time within which each of its terms is to be complied with.

(8) Nothing in this rule shall, in relation to any case in which the only remedy claimed by the Crown is the payment of money, be construed as requiring the Crown to proceed by way of an application to which this rule applies or as preventing the Crown from availing itself of any other procedure which is open to it under these rules.

History of rule—Amended by S.I. 1982 No. 1111. **R77.8.1**
Taken from RSC (Rev.) 1962, O.77, r.8, which had been taken from the former O.54.

Section 14 of the CPA 1947—Enables the Crown to make summary application in the High Court for various kinds of relief in certain matters of revenue, subject to and in accordance with Rules of Court. See s.14 (SCP 1999, Vol. 2, Section 21L, paras 21L–25 to 21L–28). **R77.8.2**

Joinder of Commissioners of Inland Revenue

8A. Nothing in CPR rule 19.3 shall be construed as enabling the Commissioners of Inland Revenue to be added as a party to any proceedings except with their consent signified in writing or in such manner as may be authorised. **R77.8A**

History of rule—Added by S.I. 1971 No. 1269. **R77.8A.1**

Effect of rule—This rule specifically excludes the Commissioners of Inland Revenue from the ambit of CPR, r.19, so that they must not be added as a party under that rule against their will but only with their consent, which must be signified in writing or in some other authorised manner. This rule thus recognises the exceptional position of the Inland Revenue (see, *e.g. Re Vandervell's Trusts* [1971] A.C. 912; [1970] 3 All E.R. 16, HL) particularly having regard to the fact that they may be in possession of confidential information relating to one party which ought not to be disclosed to the other party but which may be relevant to an issue to be determined. **R77.8A.2**

Under the rule, however, the Inland Revenue may themselves apply to be added as a party under CPR, r.19.

Judgment in default

R77.9 **9.**—(1) Except with the permission of the court, no judgment in default under CPR Part 12 shall be entered against the Crown in civil proceedings against the Crown.

(2) Except with the permission of the court, a defendant shall not enter default judgment against the Crown as a Third Party.

(3) An application for permission under this rule may be made by an application in accordance with CPR Part 23 and the application notice must be served not less than 7 days before the return day.

R77.9.1 **History of rule**—Amended by S.I. 1979 No. 1716.
Taken from RSC (Rev.) 1962, O.77, r.9, which had been taken from the former O.13, r.18, O.16A, rr.5, 6, and O.27, r.18, made in pursuance of s.35(2)(c) of the CPA 1947.

R77.9.2 **Application for leave**—In the QBD a Master has jurisdiction, exercisable on application.

Third party notices

R77.10 **10.**—(1) A Part 20 claim for service on the Crown, where the Crown is not already a party shall not be issued without the permission of the court, and the application for the grant of such permission must be made by application in accordance with CPR Part 23, and the application notice must be served on the claimant and the Crown.

(2) Permission to issue such a claim for service on the Crown shall not be granted unless the court is satisfied that the Crown is in possession of all such information as it reasonably requires as to the circumstances in which it is alleged that the liability of the Crown has arisen and as to the departments and officers of the Crown concerned.

R77.10.1 **History of rule**—Taken from RSC (Rev.) 1962, O.77, r.10, which had been taken from the former O.16A, r.1A. See the CPA 1947, s.35(2)(b).

Interpleader: application for order against Crown

R77.11 **11.** No order shall be made against the Crown under Order 17, rule 5(3) except by application, notice of which must be served not less than 7 days before the return day.

R77.11.1 **History of rule**—Taken from RSC (Rev.) 1962, O.77, r.11, which had been taken from the former O.57, r.10. See the Crown Proceedings Act 1947, s.35(2)(c).

Disclosure and further information

R77.12 **12.**—(3) Where in any proceedings an order of the court directs that a list of documents made in answer to an order for disclosure against the Crown shall be verified by witness statement or affidavit, the witness statement or affidavit shall be made by such officer of the Crown as the court may direct.

(4) Where in any such proceedings an order is made under the said section 28 for further information to be provided by the Crown, the court shall direct by what officer of the Crown the further information is to be provided.

R77.12.1 **History of rule**—Taken from RSC (Rev.) 1962, O.77, r.12, which as to para. (1) was new, as to para. (2) repealed the former O.31, r.30, as to para. (3) was taken from the former O.31, r.28A, as to para. (4) repealed the former O.31, r.5A, and as to para. (5) repealed O.31, r.5B.
Paragraph (5) of this rule was revoked by S.I. 1989 No. 2427.

R77.12.2 **Discovery against the Crown**—Is not automatic, and the Crown need not make discovery except under order of the Court. See the words of s.28(1) of the CPA 1947.

R77.12.3 **Disclosure injurious to the public interest**—See section 28(2) of the Act and nn. to O.24, r.15.

R77.12.4 **"The affidavit shall be made by such officer of the Crown as the Court shall direct"**—See the words of s.28(1) of the Act.

Para. (5)—Embodies the provisions of section 35(2)(e) of the Act. R77.12.5

Place of trial

13.—(1) Civil proceedings by or against the Crown shall not, except with the consent of the Crown, be directed to be tried elsewhere than at the Royal Courts of Justice. R77.13

(2) Nothing in any of these rules shall prejudice the right of the Crown to demand a local venue for the trial of any proceedings in which the Attorney General has waived his right to a trial at bar.

History of rule—Taken from RSC (Rev.) 1962, O.77, r.13, which had been taken from the former O.36, r.3. R77.13.1

Evidence

14.—(1) Civil proceedings against the Crown may be instituted to perpetuate any testimony in any case in which the Crown is alleged to have an interest or estate in the honour, title, dignity or office or property in question. R77.14

(2) For the avoidance of doubt it is hereby declared that any powers exercisable by the court in regard to the taking of evidence are exercisable in proceedings by or against the Crown as they are exercisable in proceedings between subjects.

History of rule—Taken from RSC (Rev.) 1962, O.77, r.14. R77.14.1

Execution and satisfaction of orders

15.—(1) Nothing in Orders 45 to 52 shall apply in respect of any order against the Crown. R77.15

(2) An application under the proviso to subsection (1) of section 25 of the Crown Proceedings Act 1947, for a direction that a separate certificate shall be issued under that subsection with respect to the costs (if any) ordered to be paid to the applicant, may be made to the court without notice being served on any other party.

(3) Any such certificate must be in Form No. 95 or 96 in the relevant practice direction, whichever is appropriate.

History of rule—Taken from RSC (Rev.) 1962, O.77, r.16, which had been taken from the former O.41c, rr.2, 3. R77.15.1

Satisfaction of orders against the Crown—No process of execution lies for enforcing payment by the Crown of any money or costs, and no person is liable under any order for payment by the Crown or any officer of the Crown of money or costs, but the proper officer of the Court, on application made after 21 days from the order for payment of the money or the taxation of the costs, issues a certificate containing particulars of the order, and, if the Court so directs, a separate certificate in respect of the costs (see the provisions of section 25 of the Act, SCP 1999, Vol. 2, Section 21L, paras 21L–60 to 21L–62) and this is served on the person named in the record as solicitor for the Crown. R77.15.2

The judgment in favour of the suppliant of a petition of right under s.20 of the Colonial Stock Act 1877 is an order against the Crown within the meaning of para. (1) and accordingly the procedure under O.48 for the examination of the "Judgment debtor" does not apply to such a judgment (*Franklin v. The Queen (No. 2)* [1974] Q.B. 205; [1973] 3 All E.R. 861, CA).

Attachment of debts, etc.

16.—(1) No order— R77.16

(a) for the attachment of debts under Order 49; or

(b) for the appointment of a sequestrator under Order 45; or

(c) for the appointment of a receiver under Order 30 or 51,

shall be made or have effect in respect of any money due or accruing due, or alleged to be due or accruing due, from the Crown.

(1A) No application shall be made under paragraph (2) unless the order of the court to be enforced is for a sum of money amounting in value to at least £50.

(2) Every application to the court for an order under section 27(1) of the Crown Proceedings Act 1947 restraining any person from receiving money payable to him by the Crown and directing payment of the money to the applicant or some other person must be made by claim form and, unless the court otherwise directs, served—

(a) on the Crown at least 15 days before the return day; and
(b) on the person to be restrained or his solicitor at least 7 days after the claim form has been served on the Crown and at least 7 days before the return day.

(2A) An application under paragraph (2) must be supported by a witness statement or affidavit—

(a) setting out the facts giving rise to the application;
(b) stating the name and last known address of the person to be restrained;
(c) identifying the order to be enforced and stating the amount of such order and the amount remaining unpaid under it at the time of the application; and
(d) identifying the particular debt from the Crown in respect of which the application is made.

(2B) Where the debt from the Crown in respect of which the application is made is money payable by the Crown to a person on account of a deposit in the National Savings Bank, the witness statement or affidavit must state the name and address of the branch of the Post Office at which the account is believed to be held and the number of that account or, if it be the case, that all or part of this information is not known to the witness.

(2C) A Master, the Admiralty Registrar and a district judge of the Family Division shall have power to hear an application under paragraph (2).

(3) Order 49, rules 5 and 6, shall apply in relation to such an application as is mentioned in paragraph (2) for an order restraining a person from receiving money payable to him by the Crown as those rules apply to an application under Order 49, rule 1, for an order for the attachment of a debt owing to any person from a garnishee, except that the Court shall not have power to order execution to issue against the Crown.

R77.16.1 **History of rule**—Taken from RSC (Rev.) 1962, O.77, r.17, which had been taken from the former O.41c, r.4, and O.50, r.22A. Amended by S.I. 1984 No. 1051 and S.I. 1994 No. 1975.

R77.16.2 **Para. (1)**—See para. R77.15.2.

R77.16.3 **Paras (2) and (3)**—In place of the procedure of garnisheeing debts due to a judgment debtor, or appointing a sequestrator or receiver to receive the money on the judgment creditor's behalf, the procedure mentioned in the rule is substituted where money is payable to the judgment debtor by the Crown (see the full terms of section 27 of the Act).

The Court has power on an application made under O.77, r.16(2) to make an order directing the Crown to pay to the judgment creditors the amount standing to the credit of the judgment debtors in an investment deposit account with the National Savings Bank, and this power may be exercised even though the bank had its principal office in Glasgow and was therefore normally out of the jurisdiction, since the Crown was always within the jurisdiction of the English Courts (*Brooks Associates Inc v. Basu* [1983] Q.B. 220; [1983] 1 All E.R. 508). This decision follows the repeal of s.27(1)(c) of the Crown Proceedings Act 1947 by SCA 1981, ss.139(1), 153(4) and Sched. 7.

Paragraph 2(C) which was introduced by S.I. 1994 No. 1975, now permits Masters of the Queen's Bench and Chancery Divisions and District Judges of the Family Division to make orders under s.27(1) of the C.P.A. 1947 to attach debts due from the Crown. Order 32, r.11 & 14 have likewise been amended accordingly.

Proceedings relating to postal packets

R77.17 **17.**—(1) An application by any person under section 30(5) of the Post Office Act 1969, for permission to bring proceedings in the name of the sender or addressee of a postal packet or his personal representatives must be made by claim form in the Queen's Bench Division.

(2) The Crown and the person in whose name the applicant seeks to bring proceedings must be made defendants to a claim under this rule.

History of rule—Taken from RSC (Rev.) 1962, O.77, r.18, which had been taken from the former O.16, r.50, and O.54, r.47(14). R77.17.1

Amended by S.I. 1979 No. 1716 and S.I. 1982 No. 1111.

Applications under sections 17 and 29 of Crown Proceedings Act

18.—(1) Every application to the Court under section 17(4) of the Crown Proceedings Act 1947, must be made by claim form. R77.18

(2) An application such as is referred to in section 29(2) of the Crown Proceedings Act 1947, may be made to the court at any time before trial in accordance with CPR Part 23, or may be made at the trial of the proceedings.

History of rule—Taken from RSC (Rev.) 1962, O.77, r.19, which had been taken from the former O.16, r.49, and O.25, r.6. R77.18.1

RSC ORDER 79

CRIMINAL PROCEEDINGS

Contents R79.0.1

Editorial Introduction

Rules 1 to 7 of this Order were revoked in 1971 when the Crown Court was established by the Courts Act 1971 as part of the Supreme Court of England and Wales and given exclusive jurisdiction to try criminal cases arising on indictment. The rules that remain support the exercise of the High Court's jurisdiction in relation to certain matters on the criminal side, particularly the granting of bail (r.9). Rules relating to the powers of the High Court to set aside witness summonses and to issue warrants to secure the attendance of witnesses are contained in rr.10 and 11. It should be noted that those powers were granted by the Criminal Procedure (Attendance of Witnesses) Act 1965, ss.2 and 4 but have been removed by the Criminal Procedure and Investigations Act 1996, ss.66 and 67. R79.0.2

Related sources

- Criminal Procedure (Attendance of Witnesses) Act 1965, ss.2 and 4 R79.0.3
- Criminal Justice Act 1967, s.22
- RSC, O.115 (Confiscation and forfeiture in connection with criminal proceedings).

Forms

The following Prescribed Forms (formerly included amongst the Prescribed Forms in Appendix A to the RSC) are relevant to O.79. These forms are included in Table 2 (Practice Forms) attached to Practice Direction (Forms) and may be found in SCP 1999, Vol. 2, Section 1A, paras 1A–100 to 1A–103, 1A–106, and 1A–108): R79.0.4

- PF No. 97—Summons to grant bail (O.79, r.9)
- PF No. 97A—Summons to vary arrangements for bail in a criminal proceeding (O.79, r.9)
- PF No. 98—Order of judge in chambers to release prisoner on bail (O.79, r.9)
- PF No. 98A—Order of judge varying arrangements for bail (O.79, r.9)
- PF No. 101—Witness summons—Crown Court (O.79, r.10)
- PF No. 103—Witness summons—Crown Court (O.79, r.10)

Estreat of recognizances

8.—(1) No recognizance acknowledged in or removed into the Queen's Bench Division shall be estreated without the order of a judge. R79.8

(2) Every application to estreat a recognizance in the Queen's Bench Division must be made by claim form by a judge and must be supported by a witness statement or affidavit showing in what manner the breach has been committed and proving that the claim form was duly served.

(2A) When it issues the claim form the court will fix a date for the hearing of the application.

(3) A claim form under this rule must be served at least 2 clear days before the day named therein for the hearing.

(4) On the hearing of the application the judge may, and if requested by any party shall, direct any issue of fact in dispute to be tried by a jury.

(5) If it appears to the judge that a default has been made in performing the conditions of the recognizance, the judge may order the recognizance to be estreated.

R79.8.1 **Enforcement of fines and forfeited recognizances**—The machinery for the enforcement of fines and forfeited recognizances is provided by SCA 1981, s.140, see SCP 1999, Vol. 2, Section 20A, para. 20A–547.

Bail

R79.9 **9.**—(1) Subject to the provisions of this rule, every application to the High Court in respect of bail in any criminal proceeding—

(a) where the defendant is in custody, must be made by claim form to a judge to show cause why the defendant should not be granted bail;

(b) where the defendant has been admitted to bail, must be made by claim form to a judge to show cause why the variation in the arrangements for bail proposed by the applicant should not be made.

(2) Subject to paragraph (5), the claim form (in Form No. 97 or 97A in the relevant practice direction) must, at least 24 hours before the day named therein for the hearing, be served—

(a) where the application was made by the defendant, on the prosecutor and on the Director of Public Prosecutions, if the prosecution is being carried on by him;

(b) where the application was made by the prosecutor or a constable under section 3(8) of the Bail Act 1976, on the defendant.

(3) Subject to paragraph (5), every application must be supported by witness statement or affidavit.

(4) Where a defendant in custody who desires to apply for bail is unable through lack of means to instruct a solicitor, he may give notice in writing to the court stating his desire to apply for bail and requesting that the Official Solicitor shall act for him in the application, and the court may assign the Official Solicitor to act for the applicant accordingly.

(5) Where the Official Solicitor has been so assigned the court may dispense with the requirements of paragraphs (1) to (3) and deal with the application in a summary manner.

(6) Where the court grants the defendant bail, the order must be in Form No. 98 in the relevant practice direction and a copy of the order shall be transmitted forthwith—

(a) where the proceedings in respect of the defendant have been transferred to the Crown Court for trial or where the defendant has been committed to the Crown Court to be sentenced or otherwise dealt with, to the appropriate officer of the Crown Court;

(b) in any other case, to the clerk of the court which committed the defendant.

(6A) The recognizance of any surety required as a condition of bail granted as aforesaid may, where the defendant is in a prison or other place of detention, be entered into before the governor or keeper of the prison or place as well as before the persons specified in section 8(4) of the Bail Act 1976.

(6B) Where under section 3(5) or (6) of the Bail Act 1976 the court imposes a requirement to be complied with before a person's release on bail, it may give directions as to the manner in which and the person or persons before whom the requirement may be complied with.

(7) A person who in pursuance of an order for the grant of bail made by the

court under this rule proposes to enter into a recognizance or give security must, unless the court otherwise directs, give notice (in Form No. 100 in the relevant practice direction) to the prosecutor at least 24 hours before he enters into the recognizance or complies with the requirements as aforesaid.

(8) Where in pursuance of such an order as aforesaid a recognizance is entered into or requirement complied with before any person, it shall be the duty of that person to cause the recognizance or, as the case may be, a statement of the requirement complied with to be transmitted forthwith—

(a) where the proceedings in respect of the defendant have been transferred to the Crown Court for trial or where the defendant has been committed to the Crown Court to be sentenced or otherwise dealt with, to the appropriate officer of the Crown Court;

(b) in any other case, to the clerk of the court which committed the defendant,

and a copy of such recognizance or statement shall at the same time be sent to the governor or keeper of the prison or other place of detention in which the defendant is detained, unless the recognizance was entered into or the requirement complied with before such governor or keeper.

(10) An order varying the arrangements under which the defendant has been granted bail shall be in Form 98A in the relevant practice direction and a copy of the order shall be transmitted forthwith—

(a) where the proceedings in respect of the defendant have been transferred to the Crown Court for trial or where the defendant has been committed to the Crown Court to be sentenced or otherwise dealt with, to the appropriate officer of the Crown Court;

(b) in any other case, to the clerk of the court which committed the defendant.

(11) Where in pursuance of an order of the High Court or the Crown Court a person is released on bail in any criminal proceeding pending the determination of an appeal to the High Court or House of Lords or an application for an order of certiorari, then, upon the abandonment of the appeal or application, or upon the decision of the High Court or House of Lords being given, any justice (being a justice acting for the same petty sessions area as the magistrates' court by which that person was convicted or sentenced) may issue process for enforcing the decision in respect of which such appeal or application was brought or, as the case may be, the decision of the High Court or House of Lords.

(12) If an applicant to the High Court in any criminal proceedings is refused bail, the applicant shall not be entitled to make a fresh application for bail to any other judge or to a Divisional Court.

(13) The record required by section 5 of the Bail Act 1976 to be made by the High Court shall be made by including in the file relating to the case in question a copy of the relevant order of the Court and shall contain the particulars set out in Form No. 98 or 98A in the relevant practice direction, whichever is appropriate, except that in the case of a decision to withhold bail the record shall be made by inserting a statement of the decision on the court's copy of the relevant claim form and including it in the file relating to the case in question.

(14) In the case of a person whose return or surrender is sought under the Extradition Act 1989, this rule shall apply as if references to the defendant were references to that person and references to the prosecutor were references to the state seeking the return or surrender of that person.

History of rule—Amended by S.I. 1967 No. 1809; S.I. 1971 No. 1955; S.I. 1978 No. 251 and S.I. R79.9.1

1989 No. 1307. Further amended by S.I. 1995 No. 2206—this amendment shall not apply where the defendant has been committed to the Crown Court for trial and the relevant provisions of Order 79 shall continue to apply to such proceedings as if this amendment had not been made.

R79.9.2 **Application for bail**—This rule provides for applications to the High Court for bail in criminal proceedings according to the circumstances, namely:

(a) where the defendant is in custody; or
(b) where the defendant has been admitted to bail by an inferior court, *i.e.*, a magistrates' court.

The application must be made to the Judge in Chambers and must be supported by a witness statement or affidavit (para. 3).

Where the defendant is in custody, the application must be made under para. 1(a) by summons as prescribed in Form 97 (see SCP 1999, Vol. 2, Section 1A, para. 1A–100) to show cause why the defendant should not be admitted to bail. The order will be in Form 98 (see SCP 1999, Vol. 2, Section 1A, para. 1A–102). If the defendant in custody is unable through lack of means to instruct a solicitor, the court may, at his request, assign the Official Solicitor to act for him, and in such event, he may dispense with the requirements that the application for bail should be by summons and supported by an affidavit (paras (4) and (5)).

Where the defendant has been admitted to bail, the application must be made under para. 1(b) by summons as prescribed in Form 97A (see SCP 1999, Vol. 2, Section 1A, para. 1A–101) to show cause why the variation in the arrangements for bail proposed by the defendant should not be made. The order will be in Form 98A (see SCP 1999, Vol. 2, Section 1A, para. 1A–103) and a copy must forthwith be sent to the appropriate court, *i.e.* the appropriate officer of the Crown Court or of the court which committed him, as the case may be (see para. (10)).

The extended powers of the High Court to grant or to vary the conditions under which a person has been admitted to bail are conferred by the Criminal Justice Act 1967, s.22, subs. (1) and (2) of which, as amended by Sched. 2 to the Bail Act 1976, provide as follows:

"(1) Where an inferior court withholds bail in criminal proceedings or imposes conditions in granting bail in criminal proceedings, the High Court may grant bail or vary the conditions.

(2) Where the High Court grants a person bail under this section it may direct him to appear at a time and place which the inferior court could have directed and the recognizance of any surety shall be conditioned accordingly."

This rule applies to bail only in criminal proceedings, and not, for example, to an application for habeas corpus in civil proceedings, as to which see O.54. The High Court does not have to give reasons for refusal of bail and the requirement to give reasons on the grant of bail is confined to cases involving the five offences listed in para. 9A(2) of Sched. 1 to the 1976 Act. These offences are murder, manslaughter, rape, attempted murder and attempted rape. When reasons have to be given they should be annexed to Form 98 in the relevant practice direction.

The effect of para. (12) is to preclude a fresh application for bail where this has been refused in criminal proceedings by the Judge in Chambers. See also *Re Kray* [1965] Ch. 736; [1965] 1 All E.R. 710, Lord Gardiner L.C.

This rule has been amended to reflect the arrangements effected by the Bail Act 1976, under which bail in criminal proceedings may be granted only in accordance with that Act. The new arrangements include the abolition of the system of taking recognizances from persons granted bail and the addition of a provision governing the requirements under s.5(1) of the Act to make a record of decisions in the prescribed manner and containing the prescribed particulars. The Bail Act 1976 was brought into force on April 17, 1978.

Section 3(8) of the Act 1976, which provides that where a court has granted bail in criminal proceedings, an application may be made to that court for variation of the bail conditions by or on behalf of the person granted bail or for variation or imposition of conditions by the prosecutor or a constable. This power supplements s.22 of the Criminal Justice Act 1967, which as amended by para. 37 of Sched. 2 to the Bail Act 1976, enables the High Court, on the application of the defendant to vary the condition imposed or to grant bail withheld by a magistrates' court.

Para. (9) of this rule was revoked, since the requirement of personal recognizances of defendants was replaced by the criminal offence of absconding created by section 6 of the Act of 1976. Para. (13) has been added to this rule so as to provide that where bail is granted or the conditions varied, the prescribed record, required by section 5 of the Act of 1976, shall be the filed copy of the court's order and shall be in Forms 98 or 98A of the relevant practice direction as appropriate.

As the conditions to be complied with by the person granted bail are set out in the Schedules in Form 98, there ought to be no room for doubt whether a particular condition, such as the surrender of a passport, is to be complied with before or after release. Where bail is withheld by the High Court, that fact will be indorsed by the appropriate officer of the court on the summons which will then be placed on the file relating to the case.

Under para. (6A) the recognizance of a surety may be entered before the governor or keeper of the prison or other place of detention.

Under para. (6B) a judge imposing a pre-release condition under section 3(5) or (6) of the 1976 Act may give directions as to manner in which, and the person or persons before whom, the requirement may be complied with, *e.g.* that a specified sum of money be deposited with the police in cash or its equivalent or that the defendant's passport be surrendered to the police. The exercise of this power should, if the judge's directions are expressed precisely, remove any doubt in a particular case about the person who is authorised to accept custody of the money or security or passport directed to be deposited.

An appeal from the refusal of bail in criminal proceedings by a Judge in Chambers or from an order varying or refusing to vary conditions of bail, is precluded by SCA 1981, s.18(1)(a), see SCP 1999, Vol. 2, Section 20A, para. 20A–177, and see also *Ex p. Pulbrook* [1892] 1 Q.B. 86.

As to the jurisdiction of the Crown Court to grant bail, see S.C.A. 1981, s.81 and C.J.A. 1982.

The jurisdiction of the High Court and the Crown Court to grant bail are separate and distinct and para. (12) relates exclusively to the High Court and therefore a prior application to the High Court does not deprive the Crown Court of its jurisdiction to grant bail under SCA 1981, s.81 (formerly section 13(4) of the Courts Act 1971) (*R. v. Reading Crown Court, ex p. Malik* [1981] Q.B. 451; [1981] 1 All E.R. 249).

RSC ORDER 81

PARTNERS

Contents **R81.0.1**

Claims by and against firms within jurisdiction

1. Subject to the provisions of any enactment, any two or more persons claiming to be entitled, or alleged to be liable, as partners in respect of a cause of action and carrying on business within the jurisdiction may sue, or be sued, in the name of the firm (if any) of which they were partners at the time when the cause of action accrued. **R81.1**

Disclosure of partners' names

2.—(1) Any defendant to an claim brought by partners in the name of a firm may serve on the claimants or their solicitor a notice requiring them or him forthwith to furnish the defendant with a written statement of the names and places of residence of all the persons who were partners in the firm at the time when the cause of action accrued; and if the notice is not complied with the court may order the claimants or their solicitor to furnish the defendant with such a statement and to verify it on oath or otherwise as may be specified in the order, or may order that further proceedings in the claim be stayed on such terms as the court may direct. **R81.2**

(2) When the names of the partners have been declared in compliance with a notice or order given or made under paragraph (1) the proceedings shall continue in the name of the firm but with the same consequences as would have ensued if the persons whose names have been so declared had been named as claimants in the claim form.

(3) Paragraph (1) shall have effect in relation to a claim brought against partners in the name of a firm as it has effect in relation to a claim brought by partners in the name of a firm but with the substitution, for references to the defendant and the claimants, of references to the claimant and the defendants respectively, and with the omission of the words "or may order" to the end.

Acknowledgment of service in a claim against firm

4.—(1) Where persons are sued as partners in the name of their firm, service may not be acknowledged in the name of the firm but only by the **R81.4**

partners thereof in their own names, but the claim shall nevertheless continue in the name of the firm.

(2) Where in a claim against a firm the claim form by which the claim is begun is served on a person as a partner, that person, if he denies that he was a partner or liable as such at any material time, may acknowledge service of the claim form and state in his acknowledgment that he does so as a person served as a partner in the defendant firm but who denies that he was a partner at any material time.

An acknowledgment of service given in accordance with this paragraph shall, unless and until it is set aside, be treated as an acknowledgment by the defendant firm.

(3) Where an acknowledgment of service has been given by a defendant in accordance with paragraph (2) then—

(a) the claimant may either apply to the court to set it aside on the ground that the defendant was a partner or liable as such at a material time or may leave that question to be determined at a later stage of the proceedings;

(b) the defendant may either apply to the court to set aside the service of the claim form on him on the ground that he was not a partner or liable as such at a material time or may at the proper time serve a defence on the claimant denying in respect of the claimant's claim either his liability as a partner or the liability of the defendant firm or both.

(4) The court may at any stage of the proceedings in a claim in which a defendant has acknowledged service in accordance with paragraph (2) on the application of the claimant or of that defendant, order that any question as to the liability of that defendant or as to the liability of the defendant firm be tried in such manner and at such time as the court directs.

R81.4.1 **Acknowledgment of service by person managing plaintiffs business**—Paragraph (5) of this rule states that, where a claim form was served on a person having the control or management of the plaintiff's business, that person could not acknowledge service unless he was a member of the firm sued. This para. was deleted from the rule by S.I. 1999 No. 1008 after the CPR were first published. The matter is now dealt with in terms by Practice Direction (Acknowledgment of Service) para. 4.4 (see para. 10PD–001).

Enforcing judgment or order against firm

R81.5 **5.**—(1) Where a judgment is given or order made against a firm, execution to enforce the judgment or order may, subject to rule 6, issue against any property of the firm within the jurisdiction.

(2) Where a judgment is given or order made against a firm, execution to enforce the judgment or order may, subject to rule 6 and to the next following paragraph, issue against any person who—

(a) acknowledged service of the claim form as a partner; or

(b) having been served as a partner with the claim form, failed to acknowledge service of it; or

(c) admitted in his statement of case that he is a partner; or

(d) was adjudged to be a partner.

(3) Execution to enforce a judgment or order given or made against a firm may not issue against a member of the firm who was out of the jurisdiction when the claim form was issued unless he—

(a) acknowledged service of the claim form as a partner; or

(b) was served within the jurisdiction with the claim form as a partner; or

(c) was, with the permission of the court given under Order 11, served out of the jurisdiction with the claim form, as a partner,

and, except as provided by paragraph (1) and by the foregoing provisions of this paragraph, a judgment or order given or made against a firm shall not render liable, release or otherwise affect a member of the firm who was out of the jurisdiction when the claim form was issued.

(4) Where a party who has obtained a judgment or order against a firm claims that a person is liable to satisfy the judgment or order as being a member of the firm, and the foregoing provisions of this rule do not apply in relation to that person, that party may apply to the court for permission to issue execution against that person, the application to be made in accordance with CPR Part 23 and the application notice must be served personally on that person.

(5) Where the person against whom an application under paragraph (4) is made does not dispute his liability, the court hearing the application may, subject to paragraph (3) give permission to issue execution against that person, and, where that person disputes his liability, the court may order that the liability of that person be tried and determined in any manner in which any issue or question in a claim may be tried and determined.

Enforcing judgment or order in actions between partners, etc.

6.—(1) Execution to enforce a judgment or order given or made in— **R81.6**

(a) a claim by or against a firm in the name of the firm against or by a member of the firm; or

(b) a claim by a firm in the name of the firm against a firm in the name of the firm where those firms have one or more members in common,

shall not issue except with the permission of the court.

(2) The court hearing an application under this rule may give such directions, including directions as to the taking of accounts and the making of inquiries, as may be just.

Attachment of debts owed by firm

7.—(1) An order may be made under Order 49, rule 1, in relation to debts **R81.7**
due or accruing due from a firm carrying on business within the jurisdiction notwithstanding that one or more members of the firm is resident out of the jurisdiction.

(2) An order to show cause under the said rule 1 relating to such debts as aforesaid must be served on a member of the firm within the jurisdiction or on some other person having the control or management of the partnership business.

(3) Where an order made under the said rule 1 requires a firm to appear before the court, an appearance by a member of the firm constitutes a sufficient compliance with the order.

Application to person carrying on business in another name

9. An individual carrying on business within the jurisdiction in a name or **R81.9**
style other than his own name, may whether or not he is within the jurisdiction be sued in that name or style as if it were the name of a firm, and rules 2 to 8 shall, so far as applicable, apply as if he were a partner and the name in which he carries on business were the name of his firm.

Applications for orders charging partner's interest in partnership property, etc.

10.—(1) Every application to the court by a judgment creditor of a partner **R81.10**
for an order under section 23 of the Partnership Act 1890 (which authorises the High Court or a judge thereof to make certain orders on the application of a judgment creditor of a partner, including an order charging the partner's interest in the partnership property) and every application to the court by a partner of the judgment debtor made in consequence of the first mentioned application must be made in accordance with CPR Part 23.

(2) A Master or the Admiralty Registrar or a district judge may exercise the powers conferred on a judge by the said section 23.

(3) Every application notice issued by a judgment creditor under this rule, and every order made on such an application, must be served on the judgment debtor and on such of his partners as are within the jurisdiction or, if the partnership is a cost book company, on the judgment debtor and the purser of the company.

(4) Every application notice issued by a partner of a judgment debtor under this rule, and every order made on such an application, must be served—

(a) on the judgment creditor; and
(b) on the judgment debtor; and
(c) on such of the other partners of the judgment debtor as do not join in the application and are within the jurisdiction or, if the partnership is a cost book company, on the purser of the company.

(5) An application notice or order served in accordance with this rule on the purser of a cost book company or, in the case of a partnership not being such a company, on some only of the partners thereof, shall be deemed to have been served on that company or on all the partners of that partnership, as the case may be.

RSC ORDER 82

DEFAMATION CLAIMS

R82.0.1 **Contents**

Application

R82.1 **1.** these rules apply to claims for libel or slander subject to the following rules of this order.

Indorsement of claim in libel claim

R82.2 **2.** Before a claim form in a claim for libel is issued it must be indorsed with a statement giving sufficient particulars of the publications in respect of which the claim is brought to enable them to be identified.

Obligation to give particulars

R82.3 **3.**—(1) Where in a claim for libel or slander the claimant alleges that the words or matters complained of were used in a defamatory sense other than their ordinary meaning, he must give particulars of the facts and matters on which he relies in support of such sense.

(2) Where in a claim for libel or slander the defendant alleges that, in so far as the words complained of consist of statements of fact, they are true in substance and in fact, and in so far as they consist of expressions of opinion, they are fair comment on a matter of public interest, or states in his statement of case to the like effect, he must give particulars stating which of the words complained of he alleges are statements of fact and of the facts and matters he relies on in support of the allegation that the words are true.

(2A) Subject to paragraph (2B), where the defendant makes an allegation as described in paragraph (2), the claimant shall serve a reply specifically admitting or denying any such allegation raised by the defendant and specifying any fact or matter upon which he relies in opposition to the defendant's allegations.

(2B) No reply shall be required under paragraph (2A) where all the facts or matters on which the claimant intends to rely in opposition to the defendant's allegations as described in paragraph (2) are already particularised elsewhere in the statements of case.

(3) Where in a claim for libel or slander the claimant alleges that the defendant maliciously published the words or matters complained of, he need not in his particulars of claim give particulars of the facts on which he relies in support of the allegation of malice, but if the defendant states in his statement of case that any of those words or matters are fair comment on a matter of public interest or were published upon a privileged occasion and the claimant intends to allege that the defendant was actuated by express malice, he must serve a reply giving particulars of the fact and matters from which the malice is to be inferred.

(3A) The claimant must give full particulars in the particulars of claim of the facts and matters on which he relies in support of his claim for damages, including details of any conduct by the defendant which it is alleged has increased the loss suffered and of any loss which is peculiar to the claimant's own circumstances.

(4) this rule shall apply in relation to a counterclaim for libel or slander as if the party making the counterclaim were the claimant and the party against whom it is made the defendant.

Ruling on meaning

3A.—(1) At any time after the service of the particulars of claim either party may apply to the court for an order determining whether or not the words complained of are capable of bearing a particular meaning or meanings attributed to them in the statements of case. **R82.3A**

(2) If it appears to the court on the hearing of an application under paragraph (1) that none of the words complained of are capable of bearing the meaning or meanings attributed to them in the statements of case, it may dismiss the claim or make such other order or give such judgment in the proceedings as may be just.

(3) Subject to paragraph (4), each party to the proceedings may make only one application under paragraph (1).

(4) Where a party has made an application under paragraph (1) and the respondent to that application subsequently amends his statements of case to allege a new meaning, the court may allow the other party to make a further application under paragraph (1) in relation to that new meaning.

(5) This rule shall apply in relation to a counterclaim for libel or slander as if the party making the counterclaim were the claimant and the party against whom it is made the defendant, and as if the counterclaim were the statement of claim.

Provisions as to payment into court

4.—(1) Where in a claim for libel or slander against several defendants sued jointly the claimant, in accordance with CPR rule 36.11(1) accepts money paid into court by any of those defendants in satisfaction of his cause of action against that defendant, then, notwithstanding anything in CPR rule 36.17, the claim shall be stayed as against that defendant only, but— **R82.4**

(a) the sum recoverable under any judgment given in the claimant's favour against any other defendant in the claim by way of damages shall not exceed the amount (if any) by which the amount of the damages exceeds the amount paid into court by the defendant as against whom the claim has been stayed; and

(b) the claimant shall not be entitled to his costs of the claim against the other defendant after the date of the payment into court unless either the amount of the damages awarded to him is greater than the amount paid into court and accepted by him or the court is of opinion that there was reasonable ground for him to proceed with the claim against the other defendant.

(2) Where in a claim for libel a party in his statement of case relies on the defence for which section 2 of the Libel Act 1843, provides, CPR rule 36.19 shall not apply in relation to that statement of case.

Statement in open court

R82.5 **5.**—(1) Where a party wishes to accept money paid into court in satisfaction of a cause of action for libel or slander, malicious prosecution or false imprisonment, that party may before or after accepting the money apply to the court in accordance with CPR Part 23 for permission to make a statement in terms approved by the judge.

(2) Where a party to a claim for libel or slander, malicious prosecution or false imprisonment which is settled before trial desires to make a statement referred to in paragraph 1, an application must be made to the court for an order that the claim be set down for trial, and before the date fixed for the trial the statement must be submitted for the approval of the judge before whom it is to be made.

(3) The court may approve a statement under paragraph (1) or (2) which refers not only to a cause of action mentioned in those paragraphs but also to any other cause of action joined thereto.

Further information not allowed in certain cases

R82.6 **6.** In a claim for libel or slander where the defendant states in his statement of case that the words or matters complained of are fair comment on a matter of public interest or were published on a privileged occasion, no further information as to the defendant's sources of information or grounds of belief shall be allowed.

Fulfilment of offer of amends under section 4 of the Defamation Act 1952

R82.8 **8.**—(1) An application to the court under section 4 of the Defamation Act, 1952, to determine any question as to the steps to be taken in fulfilment of an offer of amends made under that section must, unless the application is made in the course of proceedings for libel or slander in respect of the publication to which the offer relates, be made in private in the Queen's Bench Division, but only a judge may determine such question.

(2) Such an application is to be made by a claim form.

RSC ORDER 85

ADMINISTRATION AND SIMILAR ACTIONS

R85.0.1 **Contents**

Editorial Introduction

R85.0.2 This Order deals with actions for the administration of the estate of a deceased person, for the execution of a trust, for the determination of any question arising in the course of administration or in connection with a trust and cognate matters. The Order emphasises that the lists of questions and orders set out therein are not intended to be comprehensive. The Order does not deal with steps which follow judgment, as to which see O.44.

Related sources

- RSC, O.44 (Proceedings under Judgments and Orders: Chancery Division) R85.0.3

Forms

The following Practice Forms are relevant to this Order (SCP 1999, Vol. 2, Section 1B, paras 1B–209 to 1B–212, 1B–228 and 1B–229) (now listed in Table 2 (Practice Forms) attached to Practice Direction (Forms)). R85.0.4

- PF7CH—Inquiry for persons entitled to the property of an intestate dying on or after January 1, 1926
- PF8CH—Summons after Master's findings on kin inquiry for Re Benjamin order giving leave to distribute estate upon footing
- PF9CH—Re Benjamin order giving leave to distribute estate upon footing
- PF10 Judgment in beneficiaries' administration action where deceased died on or after January 1, 1926
- PF11CH—Judgment in creditors' administration action where deceased died on or after January 1, 1926
- PF27CH—Affidavit verifying accounts and answering usual inquiries in administration action
- PF28CH—Executors' (or administrators') account

Interpretation

1. In this order "administration claim" means a claim for the administration under the direction of the court of the estate of a deceased person or for the execution under the direction of the court of a trust. R85.1

Effect of Order—Usually cases coming within O.85 should be brought by Pt 8 claim form because before April 26, 1999 the claim or application in the High Court would have been brought by Originating Summons: CPRPD 8(B), para.A.1(3) and A.3. However, claims by beneficiaries against trustees of a contentious nature, charging the trustees with breach of trust or with default in the proper performance of their duties were not properly brought by originating summons and should therefore now be brought by Pt 7 claim form. If the application is made by Pt 8 claim form a Master or District Judge may try it: CPRPD 2B, para. 4.1, unless it comes within the list set out in para. 5.1 of that Practice Direction. R85.1.1

O.85 discourages an application for an administration order, saying twice (in rr.2 and 5) that remedies of various kinds may be granted without such an order and nowhere that an order for general administration may be made. Nevertheless, it may occasionally be found desirable to take a full administration order so that the Court is ready to deal with any situation which may emerge in the course of proceedings relating to the estate of a deceased person or a trust. The order can expressly stipulate that no account or inquiry not immediately required shall be taken or made without leave. If the purpose of the proceedings is achieved or rendered unnecessary before the full course thereof has been run, an application to stay can be made. An administration order enures for the protection of the general body of creditors as well as beneficiaries.

Determination of questions, etc., without administration

2.—(1) A claim may be issued for the determination of any question or for any remedy which could be determined or granted, as the case may be, in an administration claim and a claim need not be made for the administration or execution under the direction of the court of the estate or trust in connection with which the question arises or the remedy is sought. R85.2

(2) Without prejudice to the generality of paragraph (1), a claim may be brought for the determination of any of the following questions—

(a) any question arising in the administration of the estate of a deceased person or in the execution of a trust;

(b) any question as to the composition of any class of persons having a claim against the estate of a deceased person or a beneficial interest in the estate of such a person or in any property subject to a trust;

(c) any question as to the rights or interests of a person claiming to be a creditor of the estate of a deceased person or to be entitled under a will or on the intestacy of a deceased person or to be beneficially entitled under a trust.

(3) Without prejudice to the generality of paragraph (1), a claim may be brought for any of the following remedies—

(a) an order requiring an executor, administrator or trustee to furnish and, if necessary, verify accounts;

(b) an order requiring the payment into court of money held by a person in his capacity as executor, administrator or trustee;

(c) an order directing a person to do or abstain from doing a particular act in his capacity as executor, administrator or trustee;

(d) an order approving any sale, purchase, compromise or other transaction by a person in his capacity as executor, administrator or trustee;

(e) an order directing any act to be done in the administration of the estate of a deceased person or in the execution of a trust which the court could order to be done if the estate or trust were being administered or executed, as the case may be, under the direction of the court.

R85.2.1 **General**—Some of the more usual forms of application with notes on the procedure in each case are set out below.

R85.2.2 **Action, leave to bring or defend—Beddoe application**—Although a trustee or executor is entitled to an indemnity out of the trust fund against all charges and expenses properly incurred by him he will be deprived of his indemnity if it is held that the expenses were not properly incurred. Therefore an executor or trustee who is sued as such, or who is proposing to sue as such, is at risk of being deprived of his costs of defending or bringing a claim if he does so without either the consent of all his beneficiaries, or in default of such consent the direction of the Chancery Division. Unless there are pending proceedings for the administration of the trust estate in which the application for directions about the conduct of the proposed or actual litigation can be made, the application should be made by Part 8 claim form with the executors or trustees as claimants and the beneficaries, or the principal beneficiaries, as defendants. Such an application is known as a *Beddoe* application, after the case of *Re Beddoe*; Downes v. Cottam [1893] 1 Ch. 547. The application cannot be made in the case to which the trustees are parties, and about the conduct of which they are seeking directions, but must be made in separate proceedings. The purpose of the application is to inform the court as to the strengths and weaknesses of the trustees' case, and the views of trustees and beneficiaries regarding the prospects of success and the course to be taken in the action, for example in respect of a possible compromise. It is inappropriate for this to be revealed to the court which has to try the case or to the other parties to that case: *Alsop Wilkinson v. Neary* [1995] 1 All E.R. 431; [1996] 1 W.L.R. 120). Further the beneficiaries are necessary parties to any *Beddoe* application (*ibid.*). It is important that the trustees reveal to the court the full strengths and weaknesses of their case, since if they fail to do so the order may not protect them against personal liability for costs. It is usually necessary for the written opinion of a suitably qualified lawyer on the prospects of success to be put in evidence, and it is always helpful for the court to have a written opinion of counsel before it. A Master or District Judge may not make the order except in plain cases: Practice Direction (Allocation of Cases to Levels of Judiciary) para 5.1(e) (see para. 2BPD–002). If the case is a plain one this will usually appear from perusal of the evidence, provided this is complete, and in such a case a Master or District Judge will make the order after reading the papers, and there will be no hearing. If the evidence is complete but the Master or District Judge feels unable to make the order on the papers alone it is likely he will adjourn the application to the judge on the basis that it is not a clear case.

The position is different where the claimant in the action against the estate or trust fund is himself one of the beneficiaries and the dispute is in the nature of a family dispute. In such cases, if the beneficaries are all ascertained and of full age so that they can make up their own minds as to whether the claim should be resisted or not, it will usually be ordered that the beneficiaries be joined as defendants and left to fight the claim, if they so wish, at their own expense, rather than the claim being fought at the expense of the estate or trust fund (*Re Evans dec'd* [1986] 1 W.L.R. 101, CA).

It should be noted that the trustees of a charity should first apply to the Charity Commissioners for advice under s.29 or for an order under s.26 of the Charities Act 1993 before considering making an application to the court. A *Beddoe* application is in any case "charity proceedings" within the definition of s.33(8) of the Act, so that it cannot be brought unless it has been authorised by the Charity Commissioners under s.33(2), or, if they refuse leave, leave has been obtained from a Judge of the Chancery Division under s.33(5).

A trustee asking for directions as to whether proceedings should be taken against a beneficiary should join that beneficiary as a defendant to the summons together with the other beneficiaries but it is not the practice in the Chancery Division that such defendant should be present when the matter is debated and they should not be furnished with the evidence upon which the Court is asked to act (*Re Moritz (decd.)* [1960] Ch. 251; [1959] 3 All E.R. 767). See also *Re Eaton* [1964] 1 W.L.R. 1269; [1964] 3 All E.R. 299, where Wilberforce J. said "... I am satisfied, after having heard argument at length, that *Re Mortiz* correctly reflects the practice and correctly states the view which is followed in this division and, moreover, that this practice is correct. *Re Moritz* does, however, do no more than to state a general rule, and it seems to me that the court in dealing with these matters, acting, as it does, essentially in an administrative capacity, should, and does, endeavour to adjust its actions to the circumstances of the individual case with a view to doing justice as far as possible to all the parties." In some cases there may be an apparent conflict between *Re Moritz* and *Re Londonderry's Settlement* [1965] Ch. 918; [1964] 3 All E.R. 855 but each case must be dealt with on its own merits.

On an application of this kind, trustees are often given leave to carry on the proceedings down to disclosure or exchange of witness statements and required then to apply for further directions. A beneficiary defendant will have an opportunity of being heard at that stage, even if he has been unable to take an effective part on the first consideration of the application.

The substantive case and the application should never be before the same Master.

Pre-emptive costs orders—Exceptionally a beneficiary claimant may obtain an order in advance of the trial that his costs should be paid out of the estate irrespective of the result of the trial if the case falls within the second class of case described in *Re Buckton* [1907] 2 Ch. 406 at 414 at 414, where although the case is brought not by the trustees (who are defendants) but by some of the beneficaries, yet is made by reason of some difficulty of construction or administration which would have justified an application by the trustees, or is not made by them only because for some reason or other a different course has been deemed more convenient. But such an order should only be made if it is considered inevitable that the trial judge would order the beneficiaries costs out of the estate (*MacDonald v. Horn* [1995] 1 All E.R. 961). The one important exception to this limitation is cases brought by beneficiaries under pension funds against the trustees. The practice here is similar to that in derivative actions, firstly laid down in *Wallersteiner v. Moir (2)* [1975] Q.B. 373. The test to be applied in pension fund cases for allowing the beneficiary his costs out of the fund in advance is whether the claimants have shown a sufficient case for further investigation. Once the court is satisfied that there are matters which need to be investigated it should choose the most economical form of investigation, and generally will not authorise any legal process until it has explored the possibility of independent investigation by a person acceptable to both parties. If that does not succeed then it may authorise immediate payment out of the fund of the claimants costs down to disclosure or exchange of witness statement and review the position at that stage. It may be more appropriate then to remove the trustees and appoint judicial trustees rather than to authorise the claimant to continue the action against the existing trustees (*MacDonald v. Horn, supra*). R85.2.3

Absence of power—The sanctioning of acts being done by trustees which they themselves have no power to do are dealt with by the Trustee Act 1925, s.57, and Settled Land Act 1925, s.64, and any order under those sections must be prefaced by a statement that in the opinion of the Court or Judge the transaction in question is expedient but that the same cannot be effected by reason of the absence of any power for that purpose vested in the trustees by law or by the trust instrument. R85.2.4

Purchase by trustee—When a trustee proposes to purchase part of the trust estate, his co-trustee should make a witness statement exhibiting the instructions given to the valuer for the purpose of making his valuation and make such criticisms as occur to him on the purchase agreement and stating whether in his opinion the purchase is in all the circumstances for the benefit of the child beneficiaries and unborn children and the valuation. It is desirable that all the beneficiaries should be parties to the application. The Master will make the order. R85.2.5

"Compromise"—child—An opinion of a suitably qualified lawyer as to whether a compromise is for the benefit of the child is necessary unless the Court otherwise directs and the instructions and written opinion should be exhibited to a witness statement by the litigation friend who should also express his own views. The child should be separately represented. On the application for approving the compromise unless the interest in the fund of the person under disability is less than £100,000 (when the master may approve the compromise) the application will have to be adjourned to the judge (Practice Direction (Allocation of Cases to Levels of Judiciary) para 5.1(a) (see para. 2BPD–002). R85.2.6

Kin inquiries—These are becoming rare but they still occur. The application should be supported by evidence setting out the family so far as known. R85.2.7

Until the first directions from the Master no great expense should be incurred. The Master will direct essential inquiries, but the claimants should approach an insurance company as early as possible. The premiums are usually far less than the cost of full investigations.

R85.2.8 **Order for partial distribution**—Sometimes all except one or two lines are known. It is possible then to authorise distribution to the known beneficiaries. The inquiry, if insurance is impossible, can continue for the remainder and the costs fall on their shares alone.

R85.2.9 **Benjamin order**—It is also possible to make what is known as a *Benjamin* order authorising the distribution of the fund on the footing that a beneficiary predeceased the testator or intestate (*Re Benjamin* [1902] 1 Ch. 723).

R85.2.10 **Leave to distribute estate**—A special procedure has been introduced by a *Practice Direction* of November 21, 1997, Estates of Deceased Lloyd's Names Chancery Division Practice Direction 12G (SCP 1999, Vol. 2, Section 2B, para. 2B–178/1) for enabling the personal representatives of a deceased Lloyd's name to distribute his estate on the footing that no, or no further, provision need be made for Lloyd's creditors.

Parties

R85.3 **3.**—(1) All the executors or administrators of the estate or trustees of the trust, as the case may be, to which an administration claim or such a claim as is referred to in rule 2 relates must be parties to the proceedings, and where the proceedings is made by executors, administrators or trustees, any of them who does not consent to being joined as a claimant must be made a defendant.

(2) Notwithstanding anything in CPR Rule 19.2 and without prejudice to the powers of the court under that CPR Part, all the persons having a beneficial interest in or claim against the estate or having a beneficial interest under the trust, as the case may be, to which such a claim as is mentioned in paragraph (1) relates need not be parties to the proceedings; but the claimant may make such of those persons, whether all or any one or more of them, parties as, having regard to the nature of the remedy claimed in the proceedings, he thinks fit.

(3) Where, in proceedings under a judgment or order given or made in a claim for the administration under the direction of the court of the estate of a deceased person, a claim in respect of a debt or other liability is made against the estate by a person not a party to the proceedings, no party other than the executors or administrators of the estate shall be entitled to appear in any proceedings relating to that claim without the permission of the court, and the court may direct or allow any other party to appear either in addition to, or in substitution for, the executors or administrators on such terms as to costs or otherwise as it thinks fit.

Judgments and orders in administration claims

R85.5 **5.**—(1) A judgment or order for the administration or execution under the direction of the court of an estate or trust need not be given or made unless in the opinion of the court the questions at issue between the parties cannot properly be determined otherwise than under such a judgment or order.

(2) Where an administration claim is brought by a creditor of the estate of a deceased person or by a person claiming to be entitled under a will or on the intestacy of a deceased person or to be beneficially entitled under a trust, and the claimant alleges that no or insufficient accounts have been furnished by the executors, administrators or trustees, as the case may be, then, without prejudice to its other powers, the court may—

(a) order that proceedings be stayed for a period specified in the order and that the executors, administrators or trustees, as the case may be, shall within that period furnish the claimant with proper accounts;

(b) if necessary to prevent proceedings by other creditors or by other persons claiming to be entitled as aforesaid, give judgment or make an order for the administration of the estate to which the claim relates and include therein an order that no proceedings are to be taken under the judgment or order, or under any particular account or inquiry directed, without the permission of the judge in person.

Conduct of sale of trust property

6. Where in an administration claim an order is made for the sale of any property vested in executors, administrators or trustees, those executors, administrators or trustees, as the case may be, shall have the conduct of the sale unless the court otherwise directs. R85.6

RSC ORDER 87

DEBENTURE HOLDERS' CLAIMS: RECEIVER'S REGISTER

Contents R87.0.1

Receiver's register

1. Every receiver appointed by the court in proceedings to enforce registered debentures or registered debenture stock shall, if so directed by the court, keep a register of transfers of, and other transmissions of title to, such debentures or stock (in this order referred to as "the receiver's register"). R87.1

"If so directed"—If there are only a few debentures the Masters do not as a rule direct the receiver to keep a register. R87.1.1

It would seem that notwithstanding this Order it is necessary for a continuing company, whose assets are the subject of a debenture-holders' action, to keep a debenture register.

Registration of transfers, etc.

2.—(1) Where a receiver is required by rule 1 to keep a receiver's register, then, on the application made in accordance with CPR Part 23 of any person entitled to any debentures or debenture stock by virtue of any transfer or other transmission of title, and on production of such evidence of identity and title as the receiver may reasonably require, the receiver shall, subject to the following provisions of this rule, register the transfer or other transmission of title in that register. R87.2

(2) Before registering a transfer the receiver must, unless the due execution of the transfer is proved by witness statement or affidavit, send by post to the registered holder of the debentures or debenture stock transferred at his registered address a notice stating—

(a) that an application for the registration of the transfer has been made; and

(b) that the transfer will be registered unless within the period specified in the notice the holder informs the receiver that he objects to the registration,

and no transfer shall be registered until the period so specified has elapsed.

The period to be specified in the notice shall in no case be less than 7 days after a reply from the registered holder would in the ordinary course of post reach the receiver if the holder had replied to the notice on the day following the day when in the ordinary course of post the notice would have been delivered at the place to which it was addressed.

(3) On registering a transfer or other transmission of title under this rule the receiver must indorse a memorandum thereof on the debenture or certificate of debenture stock, as the case may be, transferred or transmitted, containing a reference to the action and to the order appointing him receiver.

Application for rectification of receiver's register

R87.3 **3.**—(1) Any person aggrieved by any thing done or omission made by a receiver under rule 2 may apply in accordance with CPR Part 23 to the court for rectification of the receiver's register, the application to be made in the proceedings in which the receiver was appointed.

(2) The copy of the application notice shall in the first instance be served only on the claimant or other party having the conduct of the proceedings but the court may direct a copy of the application notice to be served on any other person appearing to be interested.

(3) The court hearing an application under this rule may decide any question relating to the title of any person who is party to the application to have his name entered in or omitted from the receiver's register and generally may decide any question necessary or expedient to be decided for the rectification of that register.

Receiver's register evidence of transfers, etc.

R87.4 **4.** Any entry made in the receiver's register, if verified by a witness statement or affidavit made by the receiver or by such other person as the court may direct, shall in all proceedings in which the receiver was appointed be evidence of the transfer or transmission of title to which the entry relates and, in particular, shall be accepted as evidence thereof for the purpose of any distribution of assets, notwithstanding that the transfer or transmission has taken place after the making of a certificate in the proceedings certifying the holders of the debentures or debenture stock certificates.

Proof of title of holder of bearer debenture, etc.

R87.5 **5.**—(1) this rule applies in relation to proceedings to enforce bearer debentures or to enforce debenture stock in respect of which the company has issued debenture stock bearer certificates.

(2) Notwithstanding that judgment has been given in the proceedings and that a certificate has been made therein certifying the holders of such debentures or certificates as are referred to in paragraph (1), the title of any person claiming to be such a holder shall (in the absence of notice of any defect in the title) be sufficiently proved by the production of the debenture or debenture stock certificate, as the case may be, together with a certificate of identification signed by the person producing the debenture or certificate identifying the debenture or certificate produced and certifying the person (giving his name and address) who is the holder thereof.

(3) Where such a debenture or certificate as is referred to in paragraph (1) is produced in Chancery Chambers, the solicitor of the claimant in the proceedings must cause to be indorsed thereon a notice stating—

- (a) that the person whose name and address is specified in the notice (being the person named as the holder of the debenture or certificate in the certificate of identification produced under paragraph (2)) has been recorded in Chancery Chambers as the holder of the debenture or debenture stock certificate, as the case may be; and
- (b) that that person will, on producing the debenture or debenture stock certificate, as the case may be, be entitled to receive payment of any dividend in respect of that debenture or stock unless before payment a new holder proves his title in accordance with paragraph (2); and
- (c) that if a new holder neglects to prove his title as aforesaid he may incur additional delay, trouble and expense in obtaining payment.

(4) The solicitor of the claimant in the proceedings must preserve any certificates of identification produced under paragraph (2) and must keep a record of the debentures and debenture stock certificates so produced and of

the names and addresses of the persons producing them and of the holders thereof, and, if the court requires it, must verify the record by witness statement or affidavit.

Requirements in connection with payments

6.—(1) Where in proceedings to enforce any debentures or debenture stock an order is made for payment in respect of the debentures or stock, the Accountant General shall not make a payment in respect of any such debenture or stock unless either there is produced to him the certificate for which paragraph (2) provides or the court has in the case in question for special reason dispensed with the need for the certificate and directed payment to be made without it. **R87.6**

(2) For the purpose of obtaining any such payment the debenture or debenture stock certificate must be produced to the solicitor of the claimant in the proceedings or to such other person as the court may direct, and that solicitor or other person must indorse thereon a memorandum of payment and must make and sign a certificate certifying that the statement set out in the certificate has been indorsed on the debenture or debenture stock certificate, as the case may be, and send the certificate to the Accountant General.

RSC ORDER 88

MORTGAGE CLAIMS

Contents **R88.0.1**

Editorial Introduction

Rule 1 states that the provisions of this Order apply to "mortgage claims", defined as meaning claims in which any of the seven forms of remedy listed are claimed. This is misleading because the main provisions of the Order apply only to claims by mortgagees of land for two forms of remedy, they are (1) payment of moneys secured by the mortgage of land, and (2) delivery of possession. (The overwhelming majority of mortgage claims fall within this class.) By r.2, such claims are assigned to the Chancery Division. The rules in the Order are not meant to provide a complete procedural code for the claims to which they apply. Their purpose is to provide additional protection for defendants. The rules achieve this objective: **R88.0.2**

(1) By r.2 providing that all claims by mortgagees of land for payment of the mortgage monies or possession of the mortgaged property shall be assigned to the Ch D.

(2) By r.4 requiring in a mortgage claim in the Ch D for possession or payment service on a defendant in default of the notice of appointment for the hearing and the evidence.

(3) By r.5 specifying the matters which must be contained in the plaintiff's evidence in mortgage claims in the Ch D for possession or payment.

The only rule dealing with applications for sale by mortgagees is r.5A relating to applications in the Ch D to enforce charging orders.

Apart from r.5A the procedure in claims for foreclosure, redemption or sale is not dealt with in this Order at all. The general rules for sales of land under court order are contained in O.31.

There are no rules relating to redemption or foreclosure claims which are governed by the old practice of the Ch D. Such claims are now rare. The general provisions of the CPR apply to all mortgage claims.

Related sources

R88.0.3 The following *Chancery Division Practice Directions* are relevant to O.88 (SCP 1999, Vol. 2, Section 2B, paras 2B–126 and 2B–161):

- *Chancery Guide*, Chap. 21 (Mortgage Claims) (see para. D1–264 below)
- No. 7—Mortgages and Possession Orders (see *Chancery Guide*, p. 87, see para. D1–346 below)

Forms

R88.0.4 The following Chancery Masters' Practice Forms (now listed in Table 2 (Practice Forms) attached to Practice Direction (Forms)) are relevant to O.88:

- PF5—Suspended order for possession of mortgaged property
- PF34—Order in Inquiry as to Title in Proceedings to Enforce Changing Order where the Defendant's Title is not disclosed.

Application and Interpretation

R88.1 **1.**—(1) This order applies to any claim by a mortgagee or mortgagor or by any person having the right to foreclose or redeem any mortgage, being a claim in which there is a claim for any of the following remedies, namely—

(a) payment of moneys secured by the mortgage;
(b) sale of the mortgaged property;
(c) foreclosure;
(d) delivery of possession (whether before or after foreclosure or without foreclosure) to the mortgagee by the mortgagor or by any other person who is or is alleged to be in possession of the property;
(e) redemption;
(f) reconveyance of the property or its release from the security;
(g) delivery of possession by the mortgagee.

(2) In this Order "mortgage" includes a legal and an equitable mortgage and a legal and an equitable charge, and references to a mortgagor, a mortgagee and mortgaged property shall be construed accordingly.

(3) A claim to which this order applies is referred to in this order as a mortgage claim.

(4) these rules apply to mortgage claims subject to the following provisions of this order.

R88.1.1 **Jurisdiction**—In claims for possession the County Court has exclusive jurisdiction in relation to dwelling houses outside Greater London: see para. R88.1.3, below. The High Court and the County Court have concurrent jurisdiction in claims for possession of dwelling houses within Greater London and for possession of other types of property, wherever situate. In claims for payment the High Court and the county court have concurrent jurisdiction. In claims for foreclosure, redemption or sale the county court jurisdiction is limited unless extended by agreement to cases where the amount owing is under £30,000: County Courts Act 1984, s.23(c).

R88.1.2 **"payment of moneys secured by the mortgage"**—In *National Westminster Bank v. Kitch* [1996] 1 W.L.R. 1316, CA, it was held that a claim to payment of money secured by a mortgage only falls within the definition in r.1(1)(a) if the plaintiff is relying on the mortgage to make his claim.

R88.1.3 **Claims to possession**—Section 21(1) of the County Courts Act 1984 as amended by the High Court and County Courts Jurisdiction Order 1991 gives the county court unlimited jurisdiction in any action for the recovery of land. A mortgagee's possession action is such an action. By s.21(3) where a mortgage of land consists of, or includes, a dwelling house situated outside Greater London then subject to subs. (4), if the county court has jurisdiction to hear an action for possession by the mortgagee no other court shall have jurisdiction. The effect of this subsection, since the county court jurisdiction in actions for recovery of land became unlimited, is to take away the High Court's jurisdiction over claims for possession of mortgaged dwelling houses of whatever value outside Greater London. Within Greater London the High Court retains concurrent jurisdiction with the county court. In relation to mortgages of property other than dwelling houses the High Court and the county court have concurrent jurisdiction throughout the country. If possession proceedings are brought in the High Court when it has no jurisdiction then by s.40 of the County Courts Act 1984 as amended by the Courts and Legal Services Act 1990, the High Court shall (a) order the transfer of the proceedings to a county court or (b) if satisfied that the person bringing the proceedings knew, or ought to have known, that they were required to be brought in a county court, order that they be struck out. The High Court also has jurisdiction where the claim for possession is made in an action for foreclosure or sale (s.21(4)). This subsection however only applies where the plaintiff is genuinely seeking the remedy of foreclosure or sale and not where a claim to foreclosure or sale is made merely formally: *Manchester Unity Trustees v. Sadler* [1974] 1 W.L.R. 770. Because the ordinary way to enforce an equitable mortgage is by an order for sale, s.21(4) has the effect of preserving the High Court's jurisdiction in claims under equitable mortgages. Therefore any applications for sale of dwelling houses by equitable mortgagees (including holders of charging orders), can be entertained by the High Court wherever the house is situate.

Assignment of certain actions to Chancery Division

2. Without prejudice to section 61(1) of the Act (which provides for the assignment to the Chancery Division of proceedings for the purposes, among others, of the redemption or foreclosure of mortgages and the sale and distribution of the proceeds of property subject to any lien or charge) any claim in which there is a claim for— R88.2

(a) payment of moneys secured by a mortgage of any real or leasehold property; or

(b) delivery of possession (whether before or after foreclosure) to the mortgagee of any such property by the mortgagor or by any other person who is or is alleged to be in possession of the property,

shall be assigned to the Chancery Division.

Effect of rule—Claims for payment or possession of land are to be brought in the Ch D under this rule. Therefore claims by mortgagees for possession which are brought in the QBD. will in all ordinary cases be ordered to be transferred to the Ch D. Where the only claim is one for payment the action will only be a "mortgage action" and within this rule if the plaintiff is relying on the mortgage to make his claim (*National Westminster Bank v. Kitch* [1996] 1 W.L.R. 1316). Therefore, claims by banks for payment of sums due on ordinary bank accounts are outside the rule and are appropriately brought in the QBD (*ibid.*). (Presumably claims for payment of a home purchase loan, even if the charge taken to secure it is an ordinary all moneys charge, should continue to be brought in the Chancery Division.) But if an action is clearly a mortgage dispute turning on the rights of mortgagors and the remedies of mortgagees, it will, if started in the QBD be transferred to the Ch D (*Midland Bank v. Stamps* [1978] 1 W.L.R. 635). In particular a claim by a bank for possession of a dwelling house where the question for the Court is likely to be whether and if so how the discretion under the Administration of Justice Act 1970, s.23 is to be exercised is a matter appropriate only to the Ch D. R88.2.1

Commencement of claim

3.—(1) A claim form by which a mortgage claim is begun may not be issued out of a district registry, which is not a Chancery district registry, unless the mortgaged property is situated in the district of the registry. R88.3

(3) The claim form by which a mortgage claim is begun shall be indorsed with or contain a statement showing—

(a) where the mortgaged property is situated; and

(b) if the plaintiff claims possession of the mortgaged property and it is situated outside Greater London, whether the property consists of or includes a dwelling house,

and a certificate that the claim is not one to which section 141 of the Consumer Credit Act 1974 applies.

Form of claim—Claims under O.88 must be brought by Part 8 claim form: Practice Direction (Part 8) section A.3 (see para. 8PD–002). R88.3.1

Endorsement on the writ—The purpose of the endorsement is two fold. First, to show that the jurisdiction of the High Court is not excluded by s.21(4) of the County Courts Act 1984 (see R88.3.2

para. R88.1.3) or by section 141 of the Consumer Credit Act. Secondly in cases issued in a District Registry, to show that the claim is within the jurisdiction of that District Registry.

Claim for possession: failure by a defendant to acknowledge service

R88.4 **4.**—(1) Where in a mortgage claim in the Chancery Division being a claim in which the claimant is the mortgagee and claims delivery of possession or payment of moneys secured by the mortgage or both, any defendant fails to acknowledge service of the claim form, the following provisions of this rule shall apply, and references in those provisions to the defendant shall be construed as references to any such defendant.

(2) Not less than 4 clear days before the day fixed for the first hearing of the claim the claimant must serve on the defendant a copy of the notice of appointment for the hearing and a copy of the witness statement or affidavit in support of the claim.

(4) Where the hearing is adjourned, then, subject to any directions given by the court, the claimant must serve notice of the appointment for the adjourned hearing, together with a copy of any further witness statement or affidavit intended to be used at that hearing, on the defendant not less than 2 clear days before the day fixed for the hearing.

(5) Service under paragraph (2) or (4) and the manner in which it was effected, may be proved by a certificate signed by the claimant, if he sues in person, and otherwise by his solicitor.

The certificate may be indorsed on the witness statement or affidavit in support of the claim or, as the case may be, on any further witness statement or affidavit intended to be used at an adjourned hearing.

(6) A copy of any exhibit to a witness statement or affidavit need not accompany the copy of the witness statement or affidavit served under paragraph (2) or (4).

R88.4.1 **Effect of rule**—Under the rule defendants who have failed to acknowledge service must nonetheless be served with all notices of appointment or summonses and with all affidavits and witness statements.

It is to be noted that the timetable laid down by this rule applies only where the defendant is in default. If the defendant has acknowledged service the ordinary time limits in Part 8 are applicable. However, compliance with the longer time limit for service of evidence may not be insisted on, and hearings will not be adjourned because of failure to comply with that time limit if it is considered that there has been no prejudice to the defendant.

Claim in Chancery Division for possession or payment: evidence

R88.5 **5.**—(1) The witness statement or affidavit in support of the claim (other than a claim to which rule 5A applies) to which this rule applies is begun must comply with the following provisions of this rule.

this rule applies to a mortgage claim in the Chancery Division in which the claimant is the mortgagee and claims delivery of possession or payment of moneys secured by the mortgage or both.

(2) The witness statement or affidavit must exhibit a true copy of the mortgage and the original mortgage or, in the case of a registered charge, the charge certificate must be produced at the hearing of the claim.

(2A) Unless the court otherwise directs the witness statement or affidavit may contain statements of information or belief with the sources and grounds thereof.

(3) Where the claimant claims delivery of possession the witness statement or affidavit must show the circumstances under which the right to possession arises and, except where the court in any case or class of case otherwise directs, the state of the account between the mortgagor and mortgagee with particulars of—

(a) the amount of the advance;
(b) the amount of the periodic payments required to be made;
(c) the amount of any interest or instalments in arrear at the date of

issue of the claim form and at the date of the witness statement or affidavit; and

(d) the amount remaining due under the mortgage.

(4) Where the claimant claims delivery of possession the witness statement or affidavit must—

(a) give particulars of every person who to the best of the claimant's knowledge is in possession of the mortgaged property; and

(b) state, in the case of a dwelling house, whether—

(i) a land charge of Class F has been registered, or a notice or caution registered under section 2(7) of the Matrimonial Homes Act 1967 or a notice registered under section 2(8) of the Matrimonial Homes Act 1983 has been entered, and, if so, on whose behalf; and

(ii) he has served notice of the proceedings on the person on whose behalf the land charge is registered or the notice or caution entered.

(5) If the mortgage creates a tenancy other than a tenancy at will between the mortgagor and mortgagee, the witness statement or affidavit must show how and when the tenancy was determined and if by service of notice when the notice was duly served.

(6) Where the claimant claims payment of money secured by the mortgage the witness statement or affidavit must show how the claim is calculated including—

(a) The amount of the advance and the amount and dates of any periodic repayments and any interest claimed;

(b) the amount which would have to be paid (after taking into account any adjustment for early settlement) in order to redeem the mortgage at the date of commencement of the proceedings and at a stated date not more than 14 days after the date of commencement of the proceedings, specifying the amount of the solicitor's costs and administrative charges which would be payable;

(c) The dates between which a particular rate of interest applied, the number of days in that period, and the capital on which the interest was calculated.

(7) Where the claimant's claim includes a claim for interest to judgment, the witness statement or affidavit must state the amount of a day's interest.

Evidence in applications for possession—Orders for possession or payment under O.88 are final, not interlocutory orders (*Nationwide B.S. v. Bateman* [1978] 1 W.L.R. 394). However, under para. 5(2A) the evidence in support of the summons may contain statements of information or belief with the sources and grounds thereof. The purpose of the new rule is to enable the evidence in support of applications by building societies or banks to be sworn by someone in the plaintiff's solicitor's office rather than having to be sworn by an official of the building society or bank. R88.5.1

Mortgage documents—Rule 5(2) requires a true copy of the mortgage or charge to be exhibited in support of the mortgagee's application. However, if, as is commonly the case, in building society and bank mortgages, the formal mortgage document does not itself contain the full terms of the loan, the documents which do contain those terms such as a set of standard conditions and/or the offer letter must also be exhibited so that the Court has in evidence the full terms of the mortgage (see *Chancery Division Practice Direction 7A* (*Chancery Guide*, p. 87, see para. D1–346 below.) R88.5.2

State of account—The information relating to the state of account between the parties under para. (3) is required to enable the Court to exercise its discretion under s.36 of Administration of Justice Act 1970. R88.5.3

Evidence in support of applications for payment—The current para. (6) was substituted in R88.5.4

1995 for the previous one in order to require mortgagees claiming payment to give greater details than were formerly required of how the debt is calculated. Sub-para. (a) requires the amount and date of any periodic payments to be proved. In practice this means that the mortgagee will have to exhibit the statement of the mortgage account. Sub-para. (b) requires the mortgagee to calculate a redemption figure, so that the defendant can redeem the mortgage if he wishes. (Failure to give a redemption figure will usually be waived if there is no question of the borrower in fact wanting to redeem, *e.g.* by re-financing.) Sub-para. (c) requires the necessary information to be given to enable the defendant and the Court to see how the interest has been calculated, and to check the calculation.

R88.5.5 **Form or order**—The practice is to order possession 28 days after service of the order on the defendant. An order for immediate possession will not ordinarily be made. This practice is the same for dwelling houses and other premises. If the defendant is in default of acknowledgment of service the order will be for possession 28 days after personal service on him of the order. Otherwise the order will be for possession 28 days after postal service of the order. If it proves impossible to serve the order personally an order for substituted service will be made.

For the form of a suspended order for possession see Chancery Masters' Practice Form PF5 (see R88.0.4 above).

Where the claim form asks for both payment and possession but only one is ordered (usually it will be possession only which is ordered) the order should expressly adjourn the remainder of the summons.

R88.5.6 **Joint mortgagors**—In general an order for possession ought not to be made against one of two joint borrowers where it would not advantage the lender because the other joint borrower was entitled to remain in possession (*e.g.* until trial of the action), particularly where the joint borrowers are husband and wife. In those circumstances the proceedings should be adjourned against the borrower who has no defence with liberty to restore if the other borrower leaves the property or an order for possession is made against the other borrower (*Albany Home Loans Ltd v. Massey* [1997] 2 All E.R. 609, CA).

R88.5.7 **Suspending orders for possession**—The ordinary rule is that a mortgagee is entitled as of right (unless the mortgage deed provides otherwise) to possession of the mortgaged premises, and the Court has no power to adjourn an application for possession or to make a suspended order, with the exception of an adjournment for a short time to afford to the borrower a chance of paying off the mortgage in full, which should only be granted if there is a reasonable prospect of such payment occurring (*Birmingham Citizens P.B.S. v. Caunt* [1962] Ch. 883). By statute however, where the property consists of or includes a dwelling house the Court now has power (a) to adjourn the proceedings, or (b) on giving judgment for possession to stay or suspend execution or to postpone the date for delivery of possession and may make any such adjournment, etc. subject to such conditions with regard to payment or remedying any default as the Court thinks fit (A.J.A. 1970). This power may only be exercised if it appears to the Court that in the event of its exercising the power the borrower is likely to be able, within a reasonable period, to pay any sums due under the mortgage or to remedy any other breach of his obligations under the mortgage. Where the mortgage is, as in the ordinary building society mortgage, or bank house purchase mortgage, payable over a fixed term (whether repayable by combined payments of capital and interest or an endowment mortgage under which interest only is payable during the mortgage term), the mortgage will usually make the whole sum payable on default. In such a case the Court may, in exercising its discretion under s.36, treat the sum due under the mortgage as being only the arrears of instalments or interest. It may exercise its jurisdiction under the section if it appears that the borrower is likely to be able within a reasonable period to bring his payments up-to-date by paying off all arrears at the date of the order and the payments falling due after the date of the order (A.J.A. 1973, s.8). (These two sentences were approved by the CA in *Cheltenham & Gloucester B.S. v. Norgan* [1996] 1 W.L.R. 343, as succinctly summarising the effect of s.36 and s.8.) The exercise of the discretion under s.36 is by far the commonest matter which arises for decision in disputed mortgage actions. In *Cheltenham & Gloucester B.C. v. Norgan, supra,* the CA held that (contrary to the then current practice of the Courts) the "reasonable period" for the payment of the arrears is prima facie the whole remaining period of the mortgage, and that the Court should take as its starting point this period and pose the question: Would it be possible for the mortgagor to maintain payment-off of the arrears by instalments over that period. A calculation is therefore required of the instalments which the mortgagor would be required to pay if the existing arrears were to be made payable by instalments over the whole of the remaining period of the mortgage term. In *Norgan*'s case the security was amply adequate. The CA recognised that in all cases the value or future value of the security will be relevant, and that if the value of the security may be threatened if the period allowed for payment of the arrears is too long, that is a circumstance justifying a departure from treating the remaining term of the mortgage as the "reasonable period". Evans, L.J. listed the following considerations as likely to be relevant when fixing a "reasonable period":

(a) How much can the borrower reasonably expect to pay towards the arrears, apart from the agreed instalments of interest, both now and in the future?
(b) If the borrower has a temporary difficulty in meeting his obligations, how long is the difficulty likely to last?
(c) What was the reason for the arrears which have accumulated?
(d) How much remains of the original term?
(e) What are the relevant contractual terms, and what type of mortgage is it, *i.e.* when is the principal due to be repaid?
(f) Is it a case where the court should exercise its power to disregard accelerated payment provisions (s.8 of the 1973 Act)?
(g) Is it reasonable to expect the lender, in the circumstances of the particular case, to recoup the arrears of interest
  (1) over the whole of the original term, or
  (2) within a shorter period, or even
  (3) within a longer period, *i.e.* by extending the repayment period?
  Is it reasonable to expect the lender to capitalise the interest, or not?
(h) Are there any reasons affecting the security which should influence the length of the period for payment?

One way in which the borrower may show that he is likely within a reasonable period to pay off the mortgage is by showing that the house is likely to be sold and the mortgage paid off out of the proceeds of sale (*Royal Trust Co. v. Markham* [1975] 1 W.L.R. 1416). In that case it was said the requirements of s.36 would be satisfied if the borrower had signed a contract of sale or had a purchaser immediately in view. It has since been held that there is no need to have a purchaser immediately in view and that if there is a prospect of an early sale, then, if it is better in the interest of all concerned for that sale to be effected by the borrower rather than by the mortgagee, that is a solid reason for making an order deferring possession by a short period. Further, it is sound commercial sense to leave the borrower in occupation on the basis that he is in a far better position to sell the property than the mortgagee would be, because an occupied house is more likely to look attractive and command a buyer, than one which has been re-possessed by a mortgagee (*Target Home Loans v. Clothier* [1994] 1 All E.R. 439). In that case a possession order was deferred for 3 months. But there is no rule of law that the sale must be within such a short period it is a question for the court in each individual case (*National and Provincial B.S. v. Lloyd*, (1996) *The Times*, January 24). Such orders can only be made if the Court is satisfied that the proceeds of sale will be sufficient to discharge the entirety of the mortgage debt, and cannot be made where there is negative equity (*Cheltenham & Gloucester B.S. v. Krausz* [1997] 1 All E.R. 21; [1997] 1 W.L.R. 1558, CA). In exercising the discretion under s.36 the master or judge may act without formal evidence on the basis of information given informally by or on behalf of the borrower (*Cheltenham & Gloucester B.S. v. Grant, The Times*, May 9, 1994, CA).

The Court's powers under s.36 cease once a possession order has been executed: *Cheltenham & Gloucester B.S. v. Ebbage* [1994] C.L.Y. 3292.

Counterclaim—Because a mortgagee is entitled to possession of the mortgaged premises a counterclaim by the borrower for damages or a liquidated sum is no defence to the claim for possession (*National Westminster Bank v. Skelton* [1993] 1 W.L.R. 72). However if the mortgage is of a dwelling house a counterclaim by the borrower is a ground on which the Court can exercise its jurisdiction under section 36 of A.J.A. 1970 so as to suspend the possession order until after the determination of the counterclaim (*Ashley Guarantee v. Zacaria* [1993] 1 W.L.R. 62). **R88.5.8**

Enforcement of possession orders—Orders made under O.88 are excepted from the requirement in O.45, r.3 to obtain leave before a writ of possession can be issued. Therefore where a non-suspended possession order has been made the claimant can sue out a writ of possession as soon as the time for giving up possession has elapsed upon production of a certificate of service of the possession order. **R88.5.9**

A suspended possession order cannot be enforced by the claimant without the permission of the Court which will only be granted at a further hearing, notice of which has been given to the defendant. A statement to this effect is printed at the foot of every suspended possession order. Therefore to enforce the suspended order the claimant must make an application which must be served upon the defendant even if he is in default of acknowledgment of service at his last known address, so as to reach him at least two clear days before the hearing. Evidence setting out the facts relating to the non compliance with the terms of the suspended order and setting out the payments made since the date of the order is required (see *Chancery Division Practice Direction 7B* (*Chancery Guide*, p. 87, see para. D1–346)). Proof of service where the defendant is in default is by way of certificate under r.4(5). If permission is given the master usually endorses the possession order "permission to enforce" and the plaintiff may obtain a writ of execution upon production of the order so endorsed.

Costs—A mortgagee is entitled to add indemnity costs of enforcing his mortgage to his security (see *e.g. Gomba Holdings (U.K.) Ltd v. Minories Finance Ltd (No. 2)* [1993] Ch. 171). Therefore in a claim for possession the claimant does not usually ask for an order for costs, relying on his rights under the security to avoid the need for assessment. **R88.5.10**

Claim for the enforcement of charging order by sale

R88.5A **5A.**—(1) this rule applies to a mortgage claim in the Chancery Division to enforce a charging order by sale of the property charged.

(2) The witness statement or affidavit in support of the claim must—

- (a) identify the charging order sought to be enforced and the subject matter of the charge;
- (b) specify the amount in respect of which the charge was imposed and the balance outstanding at the date of the witness statement or affidavit;
- (c) verify, so far as known, the debtor's title to the property charged;
- (d) identify any prior incumbrancer on the property charged stating, so far as is known, the names and addresses of the incumbrancers and the amounts owing to them;
- (e) set out the claimant's proposals as to the manner of sale of the property charged together with estimates of the gross price which would be obtained on a sale in that manner and of the costs of such a sale; and
- (f) where the property charged consists of land in respect of which the claimant claims delivery of possession—
  - (i) give particulars of every person who to the best of the claimant's knowledge is in possession of the property charged or any part of it; and
  - (ii) state, in the case of a dwelling house, whether a land charge of Class F has been registered, or a notice or caution pursuant to section 2(7) of the Matrimonial Homes Act 1967, or a notice pursuant to section 2(8) of the Matrimonial Homes Act 1983 has been entered and, if so, on whose behalf, and whether he has served notice of the proceedings on the person on whose behalf the land charge is registered or the notice or caution entered.

R88.5A.1 **History of rule**—Added by S.I. 1984 No. 1051.

R88.5A.2 **Enforcement of charging orders**—A charging order has effect and is enforceable in the same manner as an equitable charge created by the debtor by writing under his hand: Charging Orders Act 1979, s.3(4). The usual manner of enforcement is by an order for sale. In the High Court the application for the sale is made in the case of land invariably and in the case of other property usually in the Ch D regardless of where the charging order was made. The County Court has concurrent jurisdiction under County Courts Act 1984, s.23(c) where the amount owing does not exceed £30,000. It is made by fresh proceedings begun by Part 8 claim Form and not by application in the proceedings in which the charging order was made. The purpose of r.5A is threefold. First, to enable the Court to judge whether there is sufficient equity in the property for the chargee to justify ordering a sale. Secondly, to ensure that if possible the Court will be in possession of sufficient evidence at the first appointment under the originating summons to make an immediate order for sale, without the need for further accounts or enquiries as to the defendant's interest in the property subject to the charging order as to encumbrances or as to the amount of the sum due. Thirdly, to ensure that the rights of third party occupiers are protected. Because the proceedings are a fresh action, the charging order being enforced will not be on the Court file and it should be lodged with, or exhibited to, the evidence in support. In the case of registered land up-to-date office copy entries should be obtained from the Land Registry and exhibited. Inquiries should be made of all known incumbrancers of the amount owing to them to enable para. (2)(d) to be complied with. It is the practice of mortgagees to provide such information to subsequent incumbrancers. The proposals and estimates required by para. (2)(e) should be supported by a report or letter from an estate agent which should be exhibited.

R88.5A.3 **Charging orders on beneficial shares in land**—Under the Charging Orders Act, charging orders may be, and frequently are, made on the beneficial interest in land (usually a jointly occupied home) of a beneficial joint tenant or tenant in common. Such charging orders are also enforceable by an order for sale. However, a sale of the charged beneficial interest is often not practicable. Further the realisable value of, *e.g.* the half share in a house or land is usually very much less than half the value of the entirety of the house or land. Therefore it is rare for such charging orders to be enforced by a sale of the charged beneficial share.

The judgment creditor, however, is entitled to apply under s.4 of the Trusts of Land and Appointment of Trustees Act 1996 as a person with an interest in the land subject to the trust (see *Midland Bank v. Pike* [1988] 2 All E.R. 434 and *Bank of Baroda v. Dhillon, The Times*, November 4, 1997, CA), decided under section 30 of the Law of Property Act 1925 (now repealed and replaced by section 14 of the 1996 Act). Section 15 sets out the matters to which the court is to have regard in determining the application, namely:

(a) the intentions of the person or persons who created the trust
(b) the purposes for which the property, subject to the trust, is held
(c) the welfare of any minor who occupies, or might reasonably be expected to occupy, any land subject to the trust as his home, and
(d) the interests of any secured creditor of any beneficiary.

Of this list (a), (b), (d) reflect the case law under section 30 but (c) is new and differs from the decisions under the 1925 Act. Presumably except where (c) applies the old decisions will be followed under which it was settled that save in exceptional circumstances the voice of the creditor will prevail over that of the beneficiaries in occupation and a sale will be ordered. The most recent authorities are *Zandfarid v. B.C.C.I.* [1996] 1 W.L.R. 1420 and *Bank of Baroda v. Dhillon, supra.*

Where an order for sale of the house or land is asked for it is essential for the other joint owner(s) to be made defendants. Strictly speaking such applications are not within r.5A because the action is not one to enforce the charging order by sale of the "property charged". However, the evidence in support should comply with r.5A and contain the same material as that in an application for sale against a sole owner. The order made on such application is similar to that made on application for sale of a solely owned house with the following exceptions:

(1) Instead of a vesting order under s.90 of the Law of Property Act 1925 vesting a 3,000 year term in the purchaser to enable him to make title and sell there will be an order under s.50 of the Trustee Act 1925 appointing a person (usually it will be the plaintiff's solicitor) to convey the property.
(2) The claimant must of course be paid only out of the judgment debtor's share of the proceeds of sale.
(3) If there is a dispute or uncertainty as to the respective shares in the land the proceeds of sale may have to be paid into court to await the determination of that dispute.
(4) It is not usual to order possession until the actual sale in order to protect the position of the other co-owner so far as possible.

Foreclosure in redemption claim

7. Where foreclosure has taken place by reason of the failure of the claimant in a mortgage claim for redemption to redeem, the defendant in whose favour the foreclosure has taken place may apply in accordance with CPR Part 23 for an order for delivery to him of possession of the mortgaged property, and the court may make such order thereon as it thinks fit. R88.7

RSC ORDER 91

REVENUE PROCEEDINGS

Contents R91.0.1

Editorial Introduction

Regulations which came into force on September 1, 1994 have changed the procedure in R91.0.2

respect of appeals from the General Commissioners and the Special Commissioners. In particular a substituted s.56A of the Taxes Management Act 1970 (introduced by S.I. 1994 No. 1813) allows all appeals from the Special Commissioners to be made to the High Court without a case stated. In certain circumstances appeals may be made directly to the Court of Appeal. In the rules the amendments consequent from the Regulations are as follows:

Rule	Act/Regulation	Amendment
91.1(a)	s.56, Taxes Management Act 1970 [TMA]	Replaced by reg. 22, General Commissioners (Jurisdiction and Procedure) Regulations 1994 (S.I. 1994 No. 1812). Addition: Appeals by way of case stated from decisions made by Tribunal established under s.706 of the Income and Corporation Taxes Act 1988 (s.705A Income and Corporation Taxes Act 1988 added by S.I. 1994 No. 1813).
	Reg. 10, Stamp Duty Reserve Tax Regulations 1986	Regulation has been substituted so that appeals need no longer be by case stated (S.I. 1994 No. 1813).
91.1(b)	s.53, TMA	Amended s.53 TMA substituted (S.I. 1994 No. 1813).
	s.225 and 251, Inheritance Tax Act 1984	Sections substituted to allow appeal other than by case stated (S.I. 1994 No. 1813)
91.1(c)	s.56, TMA	Substituted by s.56A TMA.

Related Sources

R91.0.3 The following Chancery Division Practice Directions are relevant to this Rule (see *Chancery Guide*, Civil Procedure paragraphs)

- CDPD 1—Appeals—paragraph B— Dismissal by Consent
- CDPD 5—Listing—Revenue Appeals
- *Chancery Guide*, Chap. 25, Revenue proceedings.

Assignment to Chancery Division, etc.

R91.1 **1.** The following proceedings, namely—

(a) any case stated for the opinion of the High Court under—
  (i) section 13 of the Stamp Act 1891, or
  (ii) section 705A of the Income and Corporation Taxes Act 1988; or
  (iii) regulation 22 of the General Commissioners (Jurisdiction and Procedure) Regulations 1994;

(b) any appeal to the High Court under—
  (i) section 53, 56A or 100C(4) of the Taxes Management Act 1970; or
  (ii) section 222(3), 225, 249(3) or 251 of the Inheritance Tax Act 1984; or
  (iii) regulation 8(3) or 10 of the Stamp Duty Reserve Tax Regulations 1986;

(c) any application for permission to appeal under the said section 222(3) or the said regulation 8(3); and

(d) proceedings to which the provisions of section 56A of the Taxes Management Act 1970 apply under any enactment or regulation,

shall be assigned to the Chancery Division and heard and determined by a single judge.

R91.1.1 **Revenue Appeals and Cases Stated**—Rule 1(a) deals with cases stated in revenue matters and Rule 1(b) with appeals. By virtue of S.I. 1994 No. 1811, S.I. 1994 No. 1812 and S.I. 1994 No. 1813 certain applications which were formerly by case stated are now by way of appeal and necessitated the substitution of the present rule effective from October 1, 1995. In particular a new s.56A of the Taxes Management Act 1970 was brought into effect, whereby a person dissatisfied with a decision of the Special Commissioners may appeal, instead of proceeding by case stated. In certain cases appeal is to that Court of Appeal (O.59, r.25); otherwise the procedure is governed by this order—see rr.5, 5A, *infra*, which also deal with the time for appealing. Cases stated are governed by rr.3 and 4.

R91.1.2 **Dismissal of appeals**—Appeals may be dismissed by consent on submission, to the Clerk of the Lists Office (Room T.M. 8.13), of a form of consent signed by the parties. The form is obtainable from the Clerk of the Lists.

Application by Part 8 claim—Where there is no statutory provision for an appeal against a demand by the Commissioners of Inland Revenue for information, the taxpayer may apply for declaratory relief by way of a Part 8 claim. See *Beecham Group Ltd v. Inland Revenue Commissioners*, [1992] S.T.C. 935; *The Times*, December 1, 1992. R91.1.3

Appeal under section 222 of the Inheritance Tax Act 1984

2.—(1) Order 55 shall not apply in relation to an appeal to the High Court under section 222(3) of the Inheritance Tax Act 1984 or regulation 8(3) of the Stamp Duty Reserve Tax Regulations 1986. R91.2

(2) Such an appeal must be brought by notice of appeal which must—

(a) state the date on which the Commissioners of Inland Revenue (in this rule referred to as the "Board") gave notice to the appellant under section 221 of the said Act or regulation 6 of the said Regulations of the determination which is the subject of the appeal;

(b) state the date on which the appellant gave to the Board notice of appeal under section 222(1) of the said Act, or regulation 8(1) of the said Regulations and, if the notice was not given within the time limited, whether the Board or the Special Commissioners have given consent to the appeal being brought out of time, and, if they have, the date on which it was given; and

(c) either state that the appellant and the Board have agreed that the appeal may be to the High Court or contain an application for permission to appeal to the High Court.

(3) At the time of issuing the notice of appeal the appellant shall file in Chancery Chambers—

(a) two copies of the notice referred to in paragraph (2)(a);

(b) two copies of the notice of appeal (under section 222(1) of the said Act, or regulation 8(1) of the said Regulations) referred to in paragraph (2)(b); and

(c) where the notice of appeal contains an application for permission to appeal, a witness statement or affidavit setting out the grounds on which it is alleged that the matters to be decided on the appeal are likely to be substantially confined to questions of law.

(4) The notice of appeal must be issued and served on the Board within 30 days of the date on which the appellant gave to the Board notice of appeal under section 222(1) of the said Act or regulation (8)(1) of the said Regulations or, if the Board or the Special Commissioners have given consent to the appeal being brought out of time, within 30 days of the date on which such consent was given.

(5) The notice of appeal, must specify a date of hearing being not less than 40 days from the issue of the notice of appeal.

(6) Where the notice of appeal contains an application for permission to appeal to the High Court, a copy of the witness statement or affidavit lodged pursuant to paragraph (3)(c) shall be served on the Board with the notice of appeal and the Board may, within 30 days after service, file in the judge's chambers a witness statement or affidavit in answer and a copy of any such witness statement or affidavit shall be served by the Board on the appellant.

(7) Except with the permission of the court, the appellant shall not be entitled on the hearing of an appeal to rely on any grounds of appeal not specified in the notice referred to in paragraph (2)(b).

Setting down case stated under Taxes Management Act 1970

3.—(1) At any time after a case stated under section 705A of the Income R91.3

and Corporation Taxes Act 1988 or regulation 22 of the General Commissioners (Jurisdiction and Procedure) Regulations 1994 has been filed in Chancery Chambers either party may set down the case for hearing.

(2) On setting down the case the party who sets it down must give notice to the other party that he has done so.

R91.3.1 **Case stated in revenue matters**—Section 13 of the Stamp Act 1891, s.56 of the Taxes Management Act 1970, the General Commissioners (Jurisdiction and Procedure) Regulations 1994 (S.I. 1994 No. 1812) and section 705A of the Income and Corporation Taxes Act 1988 (inserted by S.I. 1994 No. 1813, and dealing with appeals by case stated against notices under section 703 of that Act), contain provisions as to procedure on a case stated under any of those provisions supplementing the provisions in rr.3 and 4. A case stated under the General Commissioners (Jurisdiction and Procedure) Regulations 1994 or under s.705A must be filed in Chancery Chambers, Room T.M. 3.07, Thomas More Building, by the person requiring it within 30 days after he has received it. This time limit is mandatory and cannot be extended (*Valleybright Ltd v. Richardson* (1985) S.T.C. 70, *Brassington v. Guthrie* [1992] S.T.C. 47).

It is important to note on or before filing the case, that a copy must be sent to the other party or his legal representatives and the case stated accordingly endorsed that this has been done. However this provision is merely directory and time may be extended by the Court (*Hughes v. Viner* (1985) 129 S.J. 225; [1985] S.T.C. 235).

The case should, either at the time of filing or subsequently, be set down for hearing by either party. An additional copy of the case must be lodged at the same time and notice of setting down given to the other side. The case must be set down at the Clerk of the Lists Office at Chancery Judges Listing General Office Room W.11/W.12.

Any application to amend a case stated or any other application may be made to a judge of the Chancery Division. (See *R. v. Commissioners of Inland Revenue, ex p. Emery* [1980] S.T.C. 549.)

Although there is no time limit in which a case stated must be set down for hearing, if an appeal is not proceeded with in a reasonable time, the court will have regard to the overriding objective stated in CPR 1.1 and may call on the appeal to consider whether it should be struck out.

Similar procedure applies to a case stated under section 13 of the Stamp Act 1891, except that the case must be set down within seven days after delivery thereof by the Commissioners.

Case stated: notice to be given of certain matters

R91.4 **4.** Not less than 10 days before the hearing of such a case as is mentioned in rule 1(a) either party must give notice to the other of any point which he intends to take at the hearing and which might take the other party by surprise and leave at Chancery Chambers two copies of the notice for the use of the court.

Appeals under section 53 and 100C(4) of the Taxes Management Act 1970

R91.5 **5.**—(1) The notice of appeal by which an appeal under section 53 or 100C(4) of the Taxes Management Act 1970 or section 249(3) or 251 of the Inheritance Tax Act 1984 is brought must be issued out of Chancery Chambers.

(2) Order 55, rule 3(2), shall apply in relation to the notice of appeal as if the decision, award or determination appealed against were the decision of a court.

(3) The persons to be served with the notice are the General or Special Commissioners against whose decision, award or determination the appeal is brought and—

(a) in the case of an appeal brought under section 100C(4) of the Taxes Management Act 1970 or section 249(3) of the Inheritance Tax Act 1984 by any party other than the defendant in the proceedings before the Commissioners, that defendant;

(b) in any other case, the Commissioners of Inland Revenue.

(4) Order 55, rules 4(2) and 5, shall apply in relation to any such appeal as if for the period of 28 days and 21 days therein specified there were substituted a period of 30 days and 35 days respectively.

(5) Within 30 days after the service on them of the notice by which any such appeal is brought, the General or Special Commissioners, as the case may be, must file in Chancery Chambers two copies of a note of their findings and of

the reasons for their decision, award or determination and must serve a copy of the note on every other party to the appeal.

(6) Any document required or authorised to be served on the General or Special Commissioners in proceedings to which this rule relates may be served by delivering or sending it to their clerk.

(7) Order 57 shall not apply to proceedings to which this rule applies.

Appeals under section 56A of the Taxes Management Act 1970, section 225 of the Inheritance Tax Act 1984 and regulation 10 of the Stamp Duty Reserve Tax Regulations 1986

5A.—(1) this rule applies to appeals under section 56A of the Taxes Management Act 1970, section 225 of the Inheritance Tax Act 1984 and regulation 10 of the Stamp Duty Reserve Tax Regulations 1986. **R91.5A**

(2) The notice of appeal by which such an appeal is brought must be issued out of Chancery Chambers.

(3) Order 55, rule 3(2) shall apply in relation to the notice of appeal as if the decision or determination appealed against were the decision of a court.

(4) Order 55, rule 4(2) shall apply in relation to such an appeal as if for the period of 28 days specified in that rule there were substituted a period of 56 days, except where the appeal is made following the refusal of the Special Commissioners to issue a certificate under section 56A(2)(b) of the Taxes Management Act 1970 or the refusal of permission to appeal to the Court of Appeal under section 56A(2)(c) of that Act.

(5) Where the appeal is made following the refusal of the Special Commissioners to issue a certificate under section 56A(2)(b) of the Taxes Management Act 1970, the period of 28 days specified in Order 55, rule 4(2) shall be calculated from the date of the release of the decision of the Special Commissioners containing the refusal.

(6) Where the appeal is made following the refusal of permission to appeal to the Court of Appeal under section 56A(2)(c) of the Taxes Management Act 1970, the period of 28 days specified in Order 55, rule 4(2) shall be calculated from the date when permission is refused.

(7) Order 57 shall not apply to proceedings to which this rule applies.

Appeals from value added tax tribunals

6.—(1) A party to proceedings before a value added tax tribunal who is dissatisfied in point of law with a decision of the tribunal may appeal under section 11(1) of the Tribunals and Inquiries Act 1992 to the High Court and Order 94, rule 9 shall not apply in relation to such an appeal. **R91.6**

(2) Such an appeal shall be heard and determined by a single judge of the Chancery Division.

(3) Order 55, rule 4(2) shall apply in relation to any such appeal as if for the period of 28 days specified in that rule there were substituted a period of 56 days, except where the appeal is made following the refusal of the Value Added Tax Tribunal to grant a certificate under article 2(b) of the Value Added Tax Tribunal Appeals Order 1986.

(3A) Where the tribunal has refused to grant a certificate under article 2(b) of the Value Added Tax Tribunal Appeals Order 1986, the 28-day period mentioned in Order 55, rule 4(2) shall be calculated from the date of the release of the decision of the tribunal containing the refusal.

(4) this rule is without prejudice to the right of the parties to appeal direct to the Court of Appeal in accordance with Order 59, rule 22.

Practice—Appeals are commenced by Part 8 claim issued in the Crown Office. The clerk of the Value Added Tax Tribunal must be served with a copy of the notice of motion. **R91.6.1**

RSC ORDER 92

LODGMENT, INVESTMENT, ETC., OF FUNDS IN COURT: CHANCERY DIVISION

R92.0.1 **Contents**

Editorial Introduction

R92.0.2 This Order deals with applications for payment into and out of Court in the Chancery Division, including payments under the Life Assurance Companies (Payment into Court) Act 1896 (r.1), the Trustee Act 1925, s.63 (r.2), and under the Banking Act 1987 (r.3A). Many applications under this rule concern money lodged in Court on the compulsory purchase of land, as to which see para. 92.5.22.

The Court Funds Office is responsible for administering funds in court under the direction of the Accountant General (appointed under the Supreme Court Act 1981, s.97). The Office is at 22 Kingsway, London WC2 6LE. The Administration of Justice Act 1965 enables funds in court to be invested in accordance with a common investment scheme under the management and control of a fund manager. Further administrative changes were made by the Administration of Justice Act 1982, Pt VI and the Public Trustee and Administration of Funds Act 1986.

Related sources

R92.0.3
- Administration of Justice Act 1982, Pt VI (Funds in Court)
- Court Funds Rules 1987
- CPR Pts 21.11

Payment into court by life assurance company

R92.1 **1.**—(1) A company wishing to make a payment into court under the Life Assurance Companies (Payment into Court) Act, 1896 (hereinafter referred to as "the Act of 1896") must file a witness statement or affidavit, made by its secretary or other authorised officer, setting out—

(a) a short description of the policy in question and a statement of the persons entitled thereunder with their names and addresses so far as known to the company;

(b) a short statement of the notices received by the company claiming an interest in or title to the money assured, or withdrawing any such claim, with the dates of receipt thereof and the names and addresses of the persons by whom they were given;

(c) a statement that, in the opinion of the board of directors of the company, no sufficient discharge can be obtained otherwise than by payment into court under the Act of 1896;

(d) the submission by the company to pay into court such further sum, if any, as the court may direct and to pay any costs ordered by the court to be paid by the company;

(e) an undertaking by the company forthwith to send to the Accountant-General any notice of claim received by the company after the making of the witness statement or affidavit with a letter referring to the title of the witness statement or affidavit; and

(f) an address where the company may be served with any application, claim form, court order, or notice of any proceedings, relating to the money paid into court.

(2) The company shall not deduct from the money payable by them under the policy any costs of or incidental to the payment into court.

(3) No payment shall be made into court under the Act of 1896 where any proceedings to which the company is a party are pending in relation to the policy or moneys thereby assured except with the leave of the court to be obtained by an application made in accordance with CPR Part 23.

(4) Unless the court otherwise directs, a CPR Part 23 application by which a claim with respect to money paid into court under the Act of 1896 is made shall not, except where the application includes an application for payment of a further sum of costs by the company who made the payment, be served on that company, but it must be served on every person who appears by the witness statement or affidavit on which the payment into court was made to be entitled to, or interested in, the money in court or to have a claim upon it or who has given a notice of claim which has been sent to the Accountant-General in accordance with the undertaking referred to in rule 1(1)(e).

"Life Assurance Companies, etc., Act"—Where, in the opinion of the Board of Directors of an assurance company, no sufficient discharge can be obtained for the moneys payable by them under a policy, they can, subject to r.1(3), relieve themselves from the responsibility of deciding who is entitled to the moneys by paying them into Court under the above Act, and thereby obtain a discharge for such moneys. The company has to bear the costs of payment in, see r.1(2). R92.1.1

Payment into court under Trustee Act 1925

2.—(1) Subject to paragraph (2) any trustee wishing to make a payment into court under section 63 of the Trustee Act 1925, must make and file a witness statement or affidavit setting out— R92.2

(a) a short description of the trust and of the instrument creating it or, as the case may be, of the circumstances in which the trust arose;

(b) the names of the persons interested in or entitled to the money or securities to be paid into court with their addresses so far as known to him;

(c) his submission to answer all such inquiries relating to the application of such money or securities as the court may make or direct, and

(d) an address where he may be served with any application notice or order, or notice of any proceedings, relating to the money or securities paid into court.

(2) Where the money or securities represents a legacy, or residue or any share thereof, to which a child or a person resident outside the United Kingdom is absolutely entitled, no witness statement or affidavit need be filed under paragraph (1) and the money or securities may be paid into court in the manner prescribed by the Supreme Court Funds Rules for the time being in force.

Trustee Act 1925, s.63—This section provides that trustees, or the majority of trustees, having in their hands or under their control money or securities belonging to a trust, may pay the same into Court. Section 38 of the Administration of Justice Act 1982 provides for the management and investment of such funds. R92.2.1

To justify a trustee paying money into Court under the Act a trustee must show that he cannot get a discharge, *e.g.* a child.

Evidence—The witness statement or affidavit must have a lodgment/schedule annexed, Court Fund Rules 1987, Form 103 R92.2.2

Investment—See Court Funds Rules 1987, Pt V, SCP 1999, Vol. 2, Section 5C, paras 5C–62 to 5C–70. R92.2.3

Costs of payment in—The Act makes no special provision as to these costs. Where the costs ought not to be borne by the general estate and no dispute has arisen or is likely to arise as to their deduction, the costs are usually deducted on making the payment in, if under an affidavit or witness statement. However, if there is likely to be a dispute as to such costs the better course is to pay in the whole fund, leaving the Court to settle the amount on the application for payment out. R92.2.4

Where the payment in is made without an affidavit or witness statement, no deduction for costs can be made. If it can be shown that the costs and expenses deducted by the trustees from the fund before payment in have been improperly retained separate proceedings must be taken against them to recover the amount; repayment cannot be ordered in an application under the Act.

Notice of lodgment (see r.4) has been dispensed with where a person interested had gone abroad many years previously and had not since been heard of; and where the address of a person was unknown, the Court having treated publication of notice in newspapers as sufficient.

Where the parties are very numerous the Court will give leave to serve some only.

R92.2.5 **Costs**—On application for payment out of Court of funds lodged under the Trustee Act without an affidavit under this rule the Master usually fixes a sum for costs without taxation.

Payments into court under section 26 Banking Act 1987

R92.3A **3A.** Where the Bank of England, having sold shares in pursuance of an order under section 26 of the Banking Act 1987, pays the proceeds of sale, less the costs of the sale, into court, it shall cause a witness statement or affidavit to be made and filed setting out the names and, so far as known, the addresses of the persons beneficially entitled to the proceeds of sale and shall file a copy of the order.

R92.3A.1 This should be a reference to Financial Services Authority pursuant to section 23(2) of the Bank of England Act 1998 and S.I. 1998 No. 1129 made by the Treasury.

Notice of lodgment

R92.4 **4.** Any person who has lodged money or securities in court in accordance with rule 1, 2 or 3A must forthwith send notice of the lodgment to every person appearing from the witness statement or affidavit on which the lodgment was made to be entitled to, or to have an interest in, the money or securities lodged.

R92.4.1 **Practice**—In practice the court can dispense with notice, alternatively order that notice is given by advertisement where the address of the person interested cannot be ascertained.

Applications with respect to funds in court

R92.5 **5.**—(1) Where an application to the High Court—

(a) for the payment or transfer to any person of any funds in court standing to the credit of any cause or matter or for the transfer of any such funds to a separate account or for the payment to any person of any dividend of or interest on any securities or money comprised in such funds;

(b) for the investment, or change of investment, of any funds in court;

(c) for payment of the dividends of or interest on any funds in court representing or comprising money or securities lodged in court under any enactment; or

(d) for the payment or transfer out of court of any such funds as are mentioned in sub-paragraph (c);

is made in the Chancery Division the application may be disposed of by the court sitting in private.

(2) Subject to paragraph (3), any such application made in the Chancery Division must be made by the issue of a claim form, unless the application is made in pending proceedings or an application for the same purpose has previously been made by such a claim form.

(3) Where an application under paragraph 1 (d) is required to be made by a claim form, then, if the funds to which the application relates do not exceed £15,000 in value, and subject to paragraph (4), the application may be made to the Chief Master, or to such master as he may designate, and the master may dispose of the application or may direct it to be made by a claim form. Unless otherwise directed, an application under this paragraph shall be made by witness statement or affidavit, and need not be served on any other person.

(4) Where the application to which paragraph (3) applies relates to funds

lodged in court in a Chancery district registry, the application may be made to, and the power conferred by paragraph (3) on a master may be exercised by, the district judge of that registry.

(5) this rule does not apply to any application for an order under CPR Part 36 and CPR Part 37.

Effect of rule—The rule is general in its scope and not confined to funds paid into Court under r.1, 2 or 3. **R92.5.1**

Form of application—The application is made by the issue of a Part 8 CPR claim form unless the application is made in existing proceedings in which case appliction is made by application notice. If the funds the subject to the application do not exceed £15,000 the Chief Master and the designated Masters, all the Masters of the Chancery Division have been designated, no claim form is required for the payment out of funds described in r.5(1)(c) unless otherwise ordered. **R92.5.2**

Persons to be served—Such persons as appear from the heading of the account to be entitled to the fund, and any other potential claimants should be served or made applicants. Service may be dispensed with where the parties are numerous and the amount small (*Re Hodges* (1858) 6 W.R. 487). **R92.5.3**

Evidence—The applicant's title must be strictly proved by certificates; but a mother's affidavit or witness statements as to the birth of her child is generally sufficient without certificate of birth, as is that of the father if he were at the place of birth at the time of birth. Formerly copy certificates were not admissible, and foreign certificates were only admissible where the appropriate order in council had been made (as to which see *Atkin's Court Forms*, Vol. 2 (1994) p.54, n.7), but the strictness of this rule is now mitigated by section 8 of the Civil Evidence Act 1995. **R92.5.4**

The evidence by witness statement or affidavit should be lodged in court together with a payment schedule annexed. Usually no order will be drawn following the making of an order since the Masters will sign the payment schedule if satisfied, Court Fund Rules 1987, r.7(2). Reference should be made to the notice in Vol. 1 of the SCP 1988, pp. 1599 and 1600 for specific situations relating to RSC, O.92, r.5 and a detailed commentary.

RSC ORDER 93

APPLICATIONS AND APPEALS TO HIGH COURT UNDER VARIOUS ACTS: CHANCERY DIVISION

Contents **R93.0.1**

Editorial Introduction

R93.0.2 Under numerous pieces of legislation, express provision is made for applications and appeals to be made to the High Court. In certain instances it has been necessary to make particular provisions in rules of court for aspects of the procedure to be adopted for the handling of such applications and appeals (*e.g.* for the purpose of indicating the form of process to be used. Proceedings under the statutes referred to in this Rule should be brought in the Chancery Division. Proceedings under the statutes referred to in the next Rule should be brought in the Queen's Bench Division. This rule simply re-enacts former RSC, O.93. It is anticipated that it will be re-considered by the Civil Procedure Rules Committee with a view to re-enactment in simpler and clearer language more in keeping with the provisions of the CPR.

Related Sources

R93.0.3
- RSC, O.56 (Appeals, etc., to High Court by case stated: general)
- RSC, O.94 (Applications and appeals to High Court under various Acts: Queen's Bench Division)
- CD PD 12, Trusts, para. A (construction application under Administration of Justice Act 1985, s.48) (Civil Procedure para. 12PD–001)
- Part 8 (Alternative procedure for claims)
- Practice Direction to Part 8, para. 8 PD–001
- Part 8 claim form (N 208) (para. C41–001)
- Part 8 Notes for claimant (N 208 A) (para. C42–001)
- Part 8 Notes for defendant (N 208 C) (para. C43–001)
- Part 8 Notice of Issue (N 209) (para. C44–001)
- Part 8 Acknowledgement of service (N 210) (para. C45–001)
- Part 23 (General Rules about Applications for Court orders).

Notice of petition under section 55 of the National Debt Act 1870

R93.1 **1.** Where a petition is presented under section 55 of the National Debt Act 1870, the petitioner must, before the petition is heard, apply to a judge of the Chancery Division for directions with respect to giving notice of the claim to which the petition relates, and the judge may direct that notice thereof be given by advertisement or in such other manner as he may direct or may dispense with the giving of such notice.

Application under the Public Trustee Act 1906

R93.2 **2.** Without prejudice to sections 10(2) and 13(7) of the Public Trustee Act 1906, the jurisdiction of the High Court under that Act shall be exercised by a judge of the Chancery Division sitting in private.

R93.2.1 **Note**—Applications under the Public Trustee Act 1906 should be made by Part 8 claim in respect of new proceedings. Applications in subsisting proceedings should be made in accordance with CPR, Pt 23.

Proceedings under the Trustee Act 1925

R93.4 **4.** All proceedings brought in the High Court under the Trustee Act 1925, shall be assigned to the Chancery Division.

R93.4.1 **Note**—The SCP 1999 sets out at paragraphs 93/4/1–93/4/27 detailed information about proceedings under the Trustee Act 1925.

Whilst the references in these paragraphs to "originating summons" and "summons" should be replaced by "Part 8 claim" and "application", practitioners should note that the substantive information referred to will still be needed if the Court is to make the order sought.

Application under section 2(3) of the Public Order Act 1936

R93.5 **5.**—(1) Proceedings by which an application is made to the High Court under section 2(3) of the Public Order Act 1936, shall be assigned to the Chancery Division.

(2) Such an application shall be made by claim form and the persons to be made defendants to the claim shall be such persons as the Attorney-General may determine.

(3) In the absence of other sufficient representation the court may appoint the Official Solicitor to represent any interests which in the opinion of the court ought to be represented on any inquiry directed by the court under the said section 2(3).

Application under the Variation of Trusts Act 1958

6.—(1) Proceedings by which an application is made to the High Court under section 1 of the Variation of Trusts Act 1958, shall be assigned to the Chancery Division. **R93.6**

(2) Such an application shall be made by claim form and in addition to any other persons who are necessary and proper defendants to the claim, the settlor and any other person who provided property for the purposes of the trusts to which the application relates must, if still alive and not the claimant, be made a defendant unless the court for some special reason otherwise directs.

Right of appeal under the Law of Property Act

9. An appeal shall lie to the High Court against a decision of the Minister of Agriculture, Fisheries and Food under paragraph 16 of Schedule 15 to the Law of Property Act 1922. **R93.9**

Determination of appeal or case stated under various Acts

10.—(1) An appeal to the High Court against an order of a county court made under the Land Registration Act 1925, shall be heard and determined by a Divisional Court of the Chancery Division. **R93.10**

(2) Subject to paragraph (1) any appeal to the High Court, and any case stated or question referred for the opinion of that court, under any of the following enactments, that is to say—

(c) paragraph 16 of Schedule 15 to the Law of Property Act 1922;
(d) the Industrial Assurance Act 1923;
(f) the Land Registration Act 1925;
(g) section 205(4) of the Water Resources Act 1991;
(j) section 38(3) of the Clergy Pensions Measure 1961;
(m) the Industrial and Provident Societies Act 1965;
(n) section 173 of the Pension Schemes Act 1993;
(o) section 151 of the Pension Schemes Act 1993

shall be heard and determined by a single judge of the Chancery Division.

(3) No appeal shall lie from the decision of the court on an appeal under any of the enactments mentioned in paragraph (2)(c), (f) or (o) except with the permission of the court or the Court of Appeal.

Note—Applications should generally be made by CPR, Part 8 claim. The evidence on a s.27 application for a vesting order must include the amount of rent owing, but as the Limitation Act 1980 applies, only six years' arrears need be paid into court (*Re Howells' Application* [1972] Ch. 509; [1972] 2 W.L.R. 1346). **R93.10.1**

Appeal under section 17 of the Industrial Assurance Act 1923

11.—(1) An application to the judge for permission to appeal to the High Court against a direction of the Commissioner under section 17(3) of the Industrial Assurance Act 1923 must be made within 21 days after the date of the Commissioner's refusal or direction. **R93.11**

(2) An application for the grant of such permission must be made without notice being served on any other party by a witness statement or affidavit

stating the material facts, the effect of the Commissioner's refusal or direction, the grounds on which the application is made and that the witness is advised and believes that the applicant has good grounds for appealing.

(3) No order under this rule granting permission to appeal shall be drawn up but the court officer shall indorse on the notice of appeal by which the appeal is brought a note signed by him stating that permission to appeal was granted by the court and the date on which it was granted.

A copy of such note shall appear on any copy of such notice served on a respondent to the appeal.

(4) Order 55, rule 4(2) shall not apply in relation to an appeal with respect to which permission has been granted under this rule, but the notice of appeal by which the appeal is brought must be served, and the appeal entered, within 28 days after permission to appeal was granted.

Appeals, etc., affecting industrial and provident societies, etc.

R93.12 **12.**—(1) At any stage of the proceedings on an appeal under—

(a) the Friendly Societies Act 1896 or the Friendly Societies Act 1974;

(c) the Industrial Assurance Act 1923; or

(e) the Industrial and Provident Societies Act 1965,

the court may direct that the notice of appeal by which the appeal is brought be served on any person or may direct that notice be given by advertisement or otherwise of the bringing of the appeal, the nature thereof and the time when it will or is likely to be heard or may give such other directions as it thinks proper for enabling any person interested in the society, trade union, alleged trade union or industrial assurance company concerned or in the subject-matter of the appeal to appear and be heard on the appeal.

(2) An application for directions under paragraph (1) may be made by either party to the appeal in accordance with CPR Part 23 returnable at Chancery Chambers.

Application under section 19 or 27 of Leasehold Reform Act 1967

R93.15 **15.** Proceedings by which an application is made to the High Court under section 19 or 27 of the Leasehold Reform Act 1967 shall be assigned to the Chancery Division.

Proceedings under the Commons Registration Act 1965

R93.16 **16.**—(1) Proceedings in the High Court under section 14 or 18 of the Commons Registration Act 1965 shall be assigned to the Chancery Division.

(2) The time within which a person aggrieved by the decision of a Commons Commissioner may require the Commissioner to state a case for the opinion of the High Court pursuant to the said section 18 shall be six weeks from the date on which notice of the decision was sent to the person aggrieved.

(3) An appeal by way of case stated under the said section 18 shall be heard and determined by a single judge.

R93.16.1 **Note**—The claim should annex an affidavit or witness statement to which must be exhibited the instructions to counsel, counsel's opinion and a draft of the proposed order. If the Master is satisfied with the evidence he will send the matter to the clerk of the Lists who will pass it to a judge. If satisfied, the judge will make the order without any attendance by the applicant.

Proceedings under section 21 or 25 of the Law of Property Act 1969

R93.17 **17.** Proceedings in the High Court under section 21 or 25 of the Law of Property Act 1969 shall be assigned to the Chancery Division.

Proceedings under section 86 of the Civil Aviation Act 1982

R93.18 **18.**—(1) Proceedings in the High Court for the amendment of any register of aircraft mortgages kept pursuant to an Order in Council made under section 86 of the Civil Aviation Act 1982 shall be assigned to the Chancery Division.

(2) Such proceedings shall be brought by claim form and every person, other than the claimant, appearing in the register as mortgagee or mortgagor of the aircraft in question shall be made a defendant to the claim.

(3) A copy of the claim form shall also be sent to the Civil Aviation Authority and the Authority shall be entitled to be heard in the proceedings.

Proceedings under section 85(7) of the Fair Trading Act 1973 and the Control of Misleading Advertisements Regulations 1988

19.—(1) Proceedings to which this rule applies shall be assigned to the Chancery Division and may be begun by claim form. **R93.19**

(2) this rule applies to any application to the High Court for an order under section 85(7) of the Fair Trading Act 1973, or under any provision to which that section applies or under the Control of Misleading Advertisements Regulations 1988.

Proceedings under section 50 of the Administration of Justice Act 1985

20.—(1) Proceedings by which an application is made to the High Court under section 50 of the Administration of Justice Act 1985 for an order appointing a substituted personal representative or terminating the appointment of an existing personal representative shall be assigned to the Chancery Division. **R93.20**

(2) An application under the said section 50 shall be made by claim form or, if it is made in existing proceedings, by an application in accordance with CPR Part 23.

(3) All the existing personal representatives and, subject to any direction of the court, such of the persons having a beneficial interest in the estate as the claimant thinks fit, must be made parties to the application.

(4) Such an application must be supported by:

(a) a sealed or certified copy of the grant of probate or letters of administration; and

(b) a witness statement or affidavit containing the grounds of the application and the following particulars so far as the claimant can gain information with regard to them—

(i) short particulars of the property comprised in the estate, with an approximate estimate of its income, and capital value;

(ii) short particulars of the liabilities of the estate;

(iii) particulars of the persons who are in possession of the documents relating to the estate;

(iv) the names of the beneficiaries and short particulars of their respective interests; and

(v) the name, address and occupation of any proposed substituted personal representative;

(c) where the application is for the appointment of a substituted personal representative—

(i) a signed or (in the case of the Public Trustee or a corporation) sealed consent to act; and

(ii) a witness statement or affidavit as to the fitness of the proposed substituted personal representative, if an individual, to act.

(5) On the hearing of an application under the said section 50 the personal representative shall produce to the court the grant of representation to the deceased's estate and, if an order is made under the said section, the grant (together with a sealed copy of the order) shall be sent to and remain in the custody of the Principal Registry of the Family Division until a memorandum of the order has been endorsed on or permanently annexed to the grant.

Proceedings under section 48 of the Administration of Justice Act 1985

R93.21 **21.** Proceedings by which an application is made to the High Court under section 48 of the Administration of Justice Act 1985 shall be assigned to the Chancery Division and shall be begun by claim form but the claim need not be served on any other party.

Proceedings under the Financial Services Act 1986

R93.22 **22.**—(1) In this rule "the Act" means the Financial Services Act 1986 and a section referred to by number means the section so numbered in that Act.

(2) Proceedings in the High Court under the Act (other than application for mandamus) and actions for damages for breach of a statutory duty imposed by the Act shall be assigned to the Chancery Division.

(3) Such proceedings and actions shall be begun by claim form except for applications by petition by the Secretary of State or a designated agency under section 72.

(4) No order shall be made under sections 6, 61, 71, 91, 104, 131, 184 or paragraph 22 of Schedule 11 against any person unless he is a party to the relevant proceedings.

Where there is a question of the construction of any of the rules or regulations referred to in section 61(1)(a) of the Act, the Secretary of State, designated agency, or any person referred to in section 61(1)(a)(iv) may make representations to the court.

Proceedings under the Banking Act 1987

R93.23 **23.**—(1) In this rule "the Act" means the Banking Act 1987 and a section referred to by number means the section so numbered in the Act.

(2) Proceedings in the High Court under the following sections of the Act shall be assigned to the Chancery Division and shall be begun—

(a) as to applications under section 26(3), 71(3) and (5) and 77(3) and (5), by claim form;

(b) as to appeals under section 31(1), by notice of appeal;

(c) as to applications under sections 48(1), 49(1) and 93(1) and (2), by claim form.

(3) No order shall be made under section 48(1) against any person unless he is a party to the proceedings.

(4) Where an application has been made under section 71(3) or (5) or section 77(3) or (5) the Bank of England shall within 28 days after service on it of copies of the claimant's written statement or affidavit evidence cause a witness statement or affidavit to be made, filed and served on the claimant setting out the reasons for its objection to the claimant's name.

RSC ORDER 94

APPLICATIONS AND APPEALS TO HIGH COURT UNDER VARIOUS ACTS: QUEEN'S BENCH DIVISION

R94.0.1 **Contents**

Editorial Introduction

Under numerous pieces of legislation, express provision is made for applications and appeals to be made to the High Court. In certain instances it has been necessary to make particular provision in rules of court for aspects of the procedure to be adopted for the handling of such applications and appeals (*e.g.* for the purpose of indicating the form of proces to be used). Proceedings under the statutes referred to in this Order should be brought in the Queen's Bench Division. Proceedings under the statutes referred to in the preceding Order should be brought in the Chancery Division. **R94.0.2**

To an extent, this Order is complementary to Orders 53, 55 and 56, which deal with appeals and applications to a Divisional Court of the Queen's Bench Division. Proceedings under most of the statutes referred to in this Order are assigned to a single judge of the Queen's Bench Division; others are assigned to a Divisional Court (see rr.13 to 15). Some of the proceedings assigned to a single judge may properly be described as appeals (*e.g.* r.8) and some may not (*e.g.* r.1). It should be noted that in the case of appeals to a single judge (but not in other proceedings), the provisions of O.57 (Divisional Court proceedings, etc.: supplementary provisions) apply (see O.57, r.1(1)(c)); consequently, every claim in such proceedings must be entered for hearing in the Crown Office (O.57, r.2) and witness statements or affidavits used and orders made in such proceedings must be filed and drawn up in the Crown Office (O.57, r.4). In r.12 (as substituted in 1992), express reference is made to the role of the Crown Office.

In a number of rules in this Order, for obvious reasons, O.55, r.7(5) is disapplied.

Related sources **R94.0.3**

- RSC, O.56 (Appeals, etc., to High Court by case stated: general)
- RSC, O.57 (Divisional Court proceedings, etc.: supplementary provisions)
- RSC, O.93 (Applications and appeals to High Court under various Acts: Chancery Division)
- CCR, O.49 (Miscellaneous statutes)
- The following *Queen's Bench Practice Directions* are relevant to this Order (SCP 1999, Vol. 2, Section 2C, paras 2C–168 to 2C–175):
  - —No. 24—Crown Office listing arrangements
  - —No. 25—Crown Office list: striking out for want of prosecution, withdrawal of solicitors and applications for leave
  - —No. 26—Crown Office list: preparation for hearings

Jurisdiction of High Court to quash certain orders, schemes, etc.

1.—(1) Where by virtue of any enactment the High Court has jurisdiction, on the application of any person, to quash or prohibit any order, scheme, certificate or plan, any amendment or approval of a plan, any decision of a Minister or government department or any action on the part of a Minister or government department, the jurisdiction shall be exercisable by a single judge of the Queen's Bench Division. **R94.1**

(2) The application must be made by claim form which must state the grounds of the application.

R94.1.1 **History of rule**—Amended by S.I. 1982 No. 1111.

R94.1.2 **Crown Office List—striking out for want of prosecution**—Applications and appeals under this Order are entered in the Crown Office List, save for the following exceptions: preliminary issues, points of law, motions to commit, motions for judgment and motions under O.73 released by the Commercial Judge which continue to be administered by the Clerk of the Lists.

In relation to cases entered in the Crown Office List the applicant or his solicitor will be sent a letter, commonly known as the Active Case Letter, requesting confirmation that the case is still active, that is to say, that the proceedings are to be pursued before the Court. Where such confirmation is not received, by completing and returning within two weeks the form attached to the letter, the case will be listed before the Court to show cause as to why it should not be struck out for want of prosecution.

If there is a possibility that the case will settle, but no final agreement has been reached, application should be made, by summons, to the Master of the Crown Office to have the case stood out into Part C of the Crown Office List—see Queen's Bench Division Practice Directions Nos 24–26 (SCP 1999, Vol. 2, Section 2C, paras 2C–168 to 2C–175).

R94.1.3 **Grounds of the application**—In *Burton v. Secretary of State for Transport* [1988] 31 E.G. 50, the Court of Appeal drew attention to the need to comply with O.94, r.1(2) and O.8, r.3(2) in relation to applications under the Highways Act 1980 to quash decisions of the Secretary of State for Transport. This requirement was particularly important since there was no obligation to obtain leave, as there was in respect of an application for Judicial Review. "Grounds should identify the actual point relied on in terms which enable the Department to ascertain the case it has to meet and whether or not it has any merit. If it is not done, then the Department should consider making an application to strike out the notice of motion" *per* Woolf L.J.

Filing and service of claim form

R94.2 **2.**—(1) A claim form under rule 1 must be filed at the Crown Office, and served, within the time limited by the relevant enactment for making the application.

(2) Subject to paragraph (4) the claim form must be served on the appropriate Minister or government department, and—

(a) if the application relates to a compulsory purchase order made by an authority other than the appropriate Minister or government department, or to a clearance order under the Housing Act 1985, on the authority by whom the order was made;

(b) if the application relates to a scheme or order to which Schedule 2 to the Highways Act 1980, applies made by an authority other than the Secretary of State, on that authority;

(c) if the application relates to a structure plan, local plan or other development plan within the meaning of the Town and Country Planning Act 1990, on the local planning authority who prepared the plan;

(d) if the application relates to any decision or order, or any action on the part of a Minister of the Crown to which section 21 of the Land Compensation Act 1961, or section 288 of the Town and Country Planning Act 1990, applies, on the authority directly concerned with such decision, order or action or, if that authority is the applicant, on every person who would, if he were aggrieved by the decision, order or action, be entitled to apply to the High Court under the said section 21 or the said section 288, as the case may be;

(e) if the application relates to a scheme to which Schedule 32 to the Local Government, Planning and Land Act 1980 applies, on the body which adopted the scheme.

(3) In paragraph (2) "the appropriate Minister or government depart-

ment" means the Minister of the Crown or government department by whom the order, scheme, certificate, plan, amendment, approval or decision in question was or may be made, authorised, confirmed, approved or given or on whose part the action in question was or may be taken.

(4) Where the application relates to an order made under the Road Traffic Regulation Act 1984, the claim form must be served—

(a) if the order was made by a Minister of the Crown, on that Minister;

(b) if the order was made by a local authority with the consent, or in pursuance of a direction, of a Minister of the Crown, on that authority and also on that Minister;

(c) in any other case, on the local authority by whom the order was made.

History of rule—Amended by S.I. 1967 No. 829; S.I. 1967 No. 1809; S.I. 1969 No. 1105; S.I. 1979 No. 1542 and S.I. 1982 No. 1111. R94.2.1

Entry and service—The combined effect of rr.1(2) and 2(1) is that the application must now be made by claim form which must be entered in the Crown Office. Where the notice of motion (as the claim form was formerly called) was correctly addressed and was received in time in the Central Office, but then subsequently out of time in the Crown Office, it would be treated as having been constructively entered in the time in the Crown Office (*Low v. Secretary of State for Wales* [1993] C.O.D. 393 (Nourse, Stuart-Smith and Waite L.JJ. allowing an appeal from Simon Brown J. [1992] C.O.D. 253.)). R94.2.2

Where an Act such as the Town and Country Planning Act 1990 prescribes the time in which an application must be made (by entering a claim form), that period may not be extended but the time for service as required by r.2(1) or (2) may be extended under O.3, r.5. However where there is prejudice to a party, in consequence of a failure to serve within time, the court may well refuse such an extension (*Mendip District Council v. Secretary of State for the Environment and Castle Housing Society Limited* [1993] C.O.D. 274 (Schiemann J.)). Where, in this context, an application is made to extend time under O.3, r.5 for the service of a notice of motion the reasonable requirements of public administration have a significance which is absent in ordinary *inter partes* litigation. *Regalbourne Ltd v. East Lindsey District Council* [1993] C.O.D. 297 (Sir Thomas Bingham M.R.), and it will only be in rare circumstances, in cases involving public bodies, that the court's discretion is likely to be exercised to extend time: *R. v. Secretary of State for the Environment and Shropshire County Council, ex p. Parry* [1998] C.O.D. 17 (Scott Barker J.).

Filing of witness statement or affidavits, etc.

3.—(1) Evidence at the hearing of an application under rule 1 shall be by witness statement or affidavit. R94.3

(2) Any witness statement or affidavit in support of the application must be filed by the applicant in the Crown Office within 14 days after service of the claim form and the applicant must, at the time of filing, serve a copy of the witness statement or affidavit and of any exhibit thereto on the respondent.

(3) Any witness statement or affidavit in opposition to the application must be filed by the respondent in the Crown Office within 21 days after the service on him under paragraph (2) of the applicant's witness statement or affidavit and the respondent must, at the time of filing, serve a copy of his witness statement or affidavit and of any exhibit thereto on the applicant.

(4) When filing a witness statement or affidavit under this rule a party must leave a copy thereof and of any exhibit thereto at the Crown Office for the use of the court.

(5) Unless the court otherwise orders, an application under rule 1 shall not be heard earlier than 14 days after the time for filing a witness statement or affidavit by the respondent has expired.

Effect of rr.1–3—Rule 1 is in general terms, and may therefore apply to Acts already passed as well as to those which may hereafter be passed, and indeed applications to quash orders, schemes, etc., under any future Act could be conveniently channelled through the procedure laid down in rr.1–3. R94.3.1

Among the Acts to which rr.1–3 apply are the following:

Water Act 1945, Second Schedule, para. 8.

Coast Protection Act 1949, First Schedule, para. 7.

National Parks and Access to the Countryside Act 1949, First Schedule, Part III, para. 9.
Caravan Sites and Control of Development Act 1960.
Road Traffic and Roads Improvement Act 1960.
Land Compensation Act 1961.
Water Resources Act 1991.
Forestry Act 1967.
Town and Country Planning Act 1990.
Local Government Act 1972.
Highways Act 1980, Schedule 2.
New Towns Act 1981.
Housing Act 1985.

The application under rr.1–3 is made to a single Judge of the QBD. It is not open to the applicant to proceed by way of case stated. See *Hoser v. Ministry of Housing and Local Government* [1963] Ch. 428; [1962] 3 All E.R. 945.

The Court has power to allow an amendment of the claim form in a proper case (*Hanily v. Minister of Local Government & Planning* [1951] 2 K.B. 917; [1951] 2 All E.R. 749).

As to service, see O.65, r.6.

It should be noted that the applicant must not only file his witness statement or affidavit evidence, but also serve a copy of every witness statement or affidavit filed and any exhibit thereto on the respondent, and similarly any witness statement or affidavit in opposition must be filed as well as served together with any exhibit thereto.

R94.3.2 **Costs (rr.1–3)**—Although *Re Mason* (1934) 50 T.L.R. 392 is authority for saying that an applicant should not be ordered to pay the costs both of Minister and public authority, in the unreported case of *Henby v. Minister of Transport and Marylebone Borough Council* (1961) in which an unsuccessful applicant had alleged failure by the Minister and a Local Authority, each to comply with a different statutory duty, the Judge held that it was proper for the Minister and the Authority to be separately represented at the hearing and ordered the applicant to pay the costs of both respondents.

Rectification of register of deeds of arrangement

R94.4 **4.**—(1) Every application to the Court under section 7 of the Deeds of Arrangement Act 1914, for an order—

(a) that any omission to register a deed of arrangement within the time prescribed by that Act be rectified by extending the time for such registration; or

(b) that any omission or mis-statement of the name, residence or description of any person be rectified by the insertion in the register of his true name, residence or description,

must be made by witness statement or affidavit without notice being served on any other party to a master of the Queen's Bench Division.

(2) The witness statement or affidavit must set out particulars of the deed of arrangement and of the omission or mis-statement in question and must state the grounds on which the application is made.

R94.4.1 **Effect of rule**—This rule provides that the jurisdiction to grant applications for extension of time for the registration of deeds of arrangement shall be exercised by the Master, and not as formerly by the Judge in Chambers.

Deeds of arrangement require to be registered, and the provisions for registration are closely similar to those relating to bills of sale (see Deeds of Arrangement Act 1914, as amended by A.J.A. 1925, s.22; and see Deeds of Arrangement Rules 1925 (S. R. & O. 1925 No. 795/L.16). By s.22 of the A.J.A. 1925, the office for registration was transferred to the Department of Trade.

An application to extend the time to register a deed of arrangement or to rectify the register by the insertion of the time, name, residence or description of any person where there has been an omission or mis-statement is made by affidavit *ex parte* to a Master in the QBD.

For the registration of deeds of arrangement affecting land, see Land Charges Act 1972, ss.7, 8, the Land Charges Rules 1974 (S.I. 1974 No. 1286), and Land Charges Fees Order 1985 (S.I. 1985 No. 358).

Exercise of jurisdiction under Representation of the People Acts

R94.5 **5.**—(1) Proceedings in the High Court under the Representation of the People Acts shall be assigned to the Queen's Bench Division.

(2) Subject to paragraphs (3) and (4) the jurisdiction of the High Court under the said Acts in matters relating to parliamentary and local government elections shall be exercised by a Divisional Court.

(3) Paragraph (2) shall not be construed as taking away from a single judge or a master any jurisdiction under the said Acts which, but for that paragraph, would be exercisable by a single judge or, as the case may be, by a Master.

(4) Where the jurisdiction of the High Court under the said Acts is by a provision of any of those Acts made exercisable in matters relating to parliamentary elections by a single judge, that jurisdiction in matters relating to local government elections shall also be exercisable by a single judge.

History of rule—Amended by S.I. 1979 No. 1716. R94.5.1

Effect of rule—Paragraph (4) is intended to produce uniformity in the procedure for dealing with parliamentary and local government election proceedings (formerly, certain matters relating to local government elections were dealt with by a Divisional Court, whereas such matters relating to parliamentary elections were dealt with by one of the rota judges for the trial of parliamentary election petitions, see sections 78(4), 86, 106(2), 167, 173 of the Representation of the People Act 1983). R94.5.2

The issue of election petitions and applications for relief under these Acts are dealt with by the Clerk to the Prescribed Officer at the Election Petition Office, Royal Courts of Justice, Strand, London WC2A 2LL, which is the office of the Q.B. Masters' Secretary.

Where any matter falls to be considered by a Divisional Court, the Q.B. Masters' Secretary makes the necessary arrangements in conjunction with the Crown Office.

Appeal to High Court where Court's decision is final

6.—(1) this rule applies to an appeal to the High Court under any of the following enactments, namely— R94.6

(a) section 22 of the Architects Act 1997;
(b) section 82(3) and 83(2) of the Medicines Act 1968;
(d) section 12 of the Nurses, Midwives & Health Visitors Act 1997;
(e) section 10 of the Pharmacy Act 1954.

(2) Every appeal to which this rule applies must be supported by witness statement or affidavit and, if the court so directs, by evidence given orally.

(3) Order 55, rule 4(2) shall apply in relation to an appeal under the enactments mentioned in paragraph (1)(c) and (h) as if for the period of 28 days therein specified there were substituted a period of 21 days.

(4) In the case of an appeal under an enactment specified in column (1) of the following table, the persons to be made respondents are the persons specified in relation to that enactment in column (2) of that table and the person to be served with notice of appeal is the person so specified in column (3) thereof:

(1) *Enactment*	(2) *Respondents*	(3) *Person to be served*
Architects Act 1997, s.22	The Architects' Registration Council of the United Kingdom	The registrar of the Council
Medicines Act 1968, s.82(3) and s.83(2)	The Pharmaceutical Society of Great Britain	The registrar of the Society
Nurses, Midwives and Health Visitors Act 1979, s.12	The United Kingdom Central Council for Nursing, Midwifery and Health Visiting	The registrar of the Council
Pharmacy Act 1954, s.10	The Pharmaceutical Society of Great Britain	The registrar of the Society

History of rule—Amended by S.I. 1967 No. 829; S.I. 1968 No. 1244; S.I. 1979 No. 1542; S.I. 1980 No. 629 and S.I. 1980 No. 1908. R94.6.1

R94.6.2 **Effect of rule**—This rule was taken from the former O.59, r.38, but made two changes, namely, the period prescribed by O.55, r.4(2) and (4) will apply for the entry of an appeal under the enactments to which the rule applies, and any direction that evidence be given orally need not be given only at the hearing but may be given before the hearing.

R94.6.3 **Architects Act 1997**—Under s.22 any person aggrieved by the removal of his name from the Register (of Registered Architects) or by a determination of the Council that he be disqualified for registration during any period, may, within three months from the date on which notice of the removal or determination was served on him, appeal to the High Court and on any such appeal the Court may give such direction in the matter as they think proper, and the order of the Court shall be final.

R94.6.4 **Nurses, Midwives and Health Visitors Act 1997—section 12**—A woman who thinks herself aggrieved by a decision of the Central Midwives Board to remove her name from the roll of certified midwives may, within 3 months after the notification to her of the decision, appeal therefrom to the High Court, and the order of that Court on the appeal shall be final. The appeal is a full right of appeal and the Court has power to hear further evidence, oral or by affidavit (*Stock v. Central Midwives Board* [1915] 3 K.B. 756; previously Midwives Act 1951, s.3(6)).

Any person aggrieved by the removal of their name from the register, roll or list referred to in the Act, within three months after the date on which notice is given to him by the appropriate authority that his name has been so removed, appeal against the removal to the High Court, which may give such directions as it thinks proper, including directions as to the costs of the appeal, and the order of the High Court shall be final. See Chitty & Jacob (21st ed., 1986), p. 1450.

R94.6.5 **Practice**—Lodge original notice of motion and affidavit and three copies.

Reference of question of law by Agricultural Land Tribunal

R94.7 **7.**—(1) Any question of law referred to the High Court by an Agricultural Land Tribunal under section 6 of the Agriculture (Miscellaneous Provisions) Act 1954, shall be referred by way of case stated by the Tribunal.

(2) The claim form by which an application is made to the court for an order under the said section 6 directing such a tribunal to refer a question of law to the court, and the claim form by which an application is made to the court to determine a question of law so referred, must, where the proceedings before the tribunal arose on an application under section 11 of the Agricultural Holdings Act 1986, be served on the authority having power to enforce the statutory requirement specified in the application as well as on every other party to those proceedings and on the secretary of the tribunal.

(3) Where in accordance with the provisions of this rule a claim form is served on the authority mentioned in paragraph (2) that authority shall be entitled to appear and be heard in the proceedings.

R94.7.1 **Effect of rule**—Section 6 of the Agriculture (Miscellaneous Provisions) Act 1954, provides that any question of law arising in the course of proceedings before an Agricultural Land Tribunal may at the request of any party to the proceedings be referred to the High Court for decision, whether before or after the Tribunal have given their decision in the proceedings (subs. (1)); and if the Tribunal, after giving their decision, refuse such request, any person aggrieved by the refusal may apply to the High Court for an order directing them to do so (subs. (2)). See also, Agriculture Act 1958, Sched. 1, Part I, para. 27, amending that section.

Tribunals and Inquiries Act 1992: appeal from tribunal

R94.8 **8.**—(1) A person who was a party to proceedings before any such tribunal as is mentioned in section 11(1) of the Tribunals and Inquiries Act 1992 and is dissatisfied in point of law with the decision of the tribunal may appeal to the High Court.

(2) Order 55, rule 4(1)(b) shall apply in relation to such an appeal as if for the reference to the chairman of a tribunal there were substituted—

(a) in the case of a tribunal which has no chairman or member who acts as a chairman, a reference to the member or members of the tribunal; and

(b) in the case of any such tribunal as is specified paragraph 16 of Schedule 1 to the said Act of 1992, a reference to the secretary of the Tribunal.

(3) Where such an appeal is against the decision of—

(a) the tribunal constituted under section 46 of the National Health Service Act 1977, or

(b) a tribunal established under section 1 of the Industrial Tribunals Act 1996.

Order 55, rule 4(2) shall apply in relation to the appeal as if for the period of 28 days therein specified there were substituted, in the case of the tribunal mentioned in sub-paragraph (a) a period of 14 days and, in the case of a tribunal mentioned in sub-paragraph (b) a period of 42 days.

History of rule—Amended by S.I. 1968 No. 1244; S.I. 1979 No. 1542; S.I. 1980 No. 1908 and S.I. 1996 No. 2892. **R94.8.1**

Tribunals and Inquiries Act 1992: case stated by tribunal

9.—(1) Any such tribunal as is mentioned in section 11(1) of the Tribunals and Inquiries Act 1992 may, of its own initiative or at the request of any party to proceedings before it, state in the course of proceedings before it in the form of a special case for the decision of the High Court any question of law arising in the proceedings. **R94.9**

(2) Any party to proceedings before any such tribunal who is aggrieved by the tribunal's refusal to state such a case may apply to the High Court for an order directing the tribunal to do so.

(3) A case stated by any such tribunal which has no chairman or member who acts as a chairman must be signed by the member or members of the tribunal.

History of rule—Amended by S.I. 1979 No. 1542 and S.I. 1996 No. 2892. **R94.9.1**

Tribunals and Inquiries Act 1971: appeal from Minister of Transport

10.—(1) A person who is dissatisfied on a point of law with a decision of the Secretary of State on such an appeal as is mentioned in section 13(5) of the Tribunals and Inquiries Act 1971, and had, or if aggrieved would have had, a right to appeal to that Secretary of State, whether or not he exercised that right, may appeal to the High Court. **R94.10**

(2) The persons to be served with the Notice of Appeal by which such an appeal is brought are the Secretary of State and every person who had, or if aggrieved would have had, a right to appeal to the Secretary of State.

(3) The court hearing the appeal may remit the matter to the Secretary of State to the extent necessary to enable him to provide the court with such further information in connection with the matter as the court may direct.

(4) If the court is of the opinion that the decision appealed against was erroneous on a point of law, it shall not set aside or vary that decision but shall remit the matter to the Minister with the opinion of the court for rehearing and determination by him.

(5) Order 55, rule 7(5) shall not apply in relation to the appeal.

History of rule—Amended by S.I. 1979 No. 1542 and S.I. 1999 No. 1008. **R94.10.1**

Effect of rr.8–10—Now s.11(1) of the Tribunals and Inquiries Act 1992, provides that if any party to proceedings before certain specified tribunals is dissatisfied in point of law with a decision of the Tribunal he may according as rules of Court may provide, either appeal therefrom to the High Court or require the Tribunal to state and sign a case for the opinion of the High Court. Rules 8 and 9 provide the relevant procedures. It should be noted that these procedures, as **R94.10.2**

envisaged by the Act, are alternative, not cumulative, *either* an appeal on a point of law *or* a case stated by the Tribunal.

The mode of appeal is governed by O.55, so that the appeal will lie to the Divisional Court of the QBD, and the general code in O.55 and O.57, will apply.

The procedure by way of case stated is governed by O.56, rr.7–12, so that the case will be heard by the Divisional Court of the QBD

Section 11(3) of the Tribunals and Inquiries Act 1992, enables the Court of Appeal to hear appeals from the decision of the Divisional Court, and such appeals lie only with the leave of the Divisional Court or the CA.

Consumer Credit Act 1974: appeal from Secretary of State

R94.10A **10A.**—(1) A person who is dissatisfied in point of law with a decision of the Secretary of State on an appeal under section 41 of the Consumer Credit Act 1974 from a determination of the Director General of Fair Trading and had a right to appeal to the Secretary of State, whether or not he exercised that right, may appeal to the High Court.

(2) The persons to be served with the Notice of Appeal by which such an appeal is brought are the Secretary of State and, where the appeal is by a licensee under a group licence against compulsory variation, suspension or revocation of that licence, the original applicant, if any; but the court may in any case direct that the notice of appeal be served on any other person.

(3) The court hearing the appeal may remit the matter to the Secretary of State to the extent necessary to enable him to provide the court with such further information in connection with the matter as the court may direct.

(4) If the court is of the opinion that the decision appealed against was erroneous in point of law, it shall not set aside or vary that decision but shall remit the matter to the Secretary of State with the opinion of the court for hearing and determination by him.

(5) Order 55, rule 7(5) shall not apply in relation to the appeal.

R94.10A.1 **History of rule**—Added by S.I. 1976 No. 337 and S.I. 1999 No. 1008.

Case stated by Mental Health Review Tribunal

R94.11 **11.**—(1) In this rule "the Act" means the Mental Health Act 1983.

(2) The reference in paragraph (3) to a party to proceedings before a Mental Health Review Tribunal, and the references in Order 56, rules 8(1), 9(2) and 10 to a party to proceedings shall be construed as references to—

(a) the person who initiated the proceedings; and

(b) any person to whom, in accordance with rules made under section 78 of the Act, the Tribunal sent notice of the application or reference or a request instead of notice of reference.

(3) A party to proceedings before a Mental Health Review Tribunal shall not be entitled to apply to the High Court for an order under section 78(8) of the Act directing the Tribunal to state a case for determination by the court unless—

(a) within 21 days after the decision of the tribunal was communicated to him in accordance with rules made under section 78 of the Act he made a written request to the tribunal to state a case, and

(b) either the tribunal failed to comply with the last-mentioned request within 21 days after it was made or the tribunal refused to comply with it.

(4) The period for issuing the claim form by which an application to the court for such an order as is mentioned in paragraph (3) is made, and for service of the claim form shall be—

(a) where the tribunal refused the applicant's request to state a case, 14 days after receipt by the applicant of notice of the refusal of his request;

(b) where the tribunal failed to comply with that request within the period mentioned in paragraph (3)(b) 14 days after the expiration of that period.

(5) A Mental Health Review Tribunal by whom a case is stated shall be entitled to appear and be heard in the proceedings for the determination of the case.

(6) If the court is of opinion that any decision of such a tribunal on the question of law raised by the case was erroneous, the court may give any direction which the tribunal ought to have given under Part V of the Act.

History of rule—Substituted by S.I. 1983 No. 1181. **R94.11.1**

Effect of rule (r.11)—This rule must be read with and subject to O.56, rr.7–12, which regulate the procedure relating to a case stated by a Mental Health Review Tribunal. **R94.11.2**

Applications for permission under section 289(6) of the Town and Country Planning Act 1990 and section 65(5) of the Planning (Listed Buildings and Conservation Areas) Act 1990

12.—(1) An application for permission to appeal to the High Court under section 289 of the Town and Country Planning Act 1990 or section 65 of the Planning (Listed Buildings and Conservation Areas) Act 1990 shall be made within 28 days after the date on which notice of the decision was given to the applicant. **R94.12**

(2) An application shall—

(a) include, where necessary, any application to extend the time for applying;

(b) be in writing setting out the reasons why permission should be granted, and if the time for applying has expired, the reasons why the application was not made within that time;

(c) be made by filing it in the Crown Office together with the decision, a draft claim form, and a witness statement or affidavit verifying any facts relied on;

(d) before being filed under sub-paragraph (c), be served together with the draft claim form and a copy of the witness statement or affidavit to be filed with the application, upon the persons who are referred to in rule 13(5); and

(e) be accompanied by a witness statement or affidavit giving the names and addresses of, and the places and dates of service on, all persons who have been served with the application and, if any person who ought to be served has not been served, the witness statement or affidavit must state that fact and the reason for it.

(3) An application shall be heard—

(a) by a single judge;

(b) unless the court otherwise orders, not less than 21 days after it was filed at the Crown Office.

Any person served with the application shall be entitled to appear and be heard.

(4) If on the hearing of an application the court is of opinion that any person who ought to have been served has not been served, the court may adjourn the hearing on such terms (if any) as it may direct in order that the application may be served on that person.

(5) If the court grants permission—

(a) it may impose such terms as to costs and as to giving security as it thinks fit;

(b) it may give directions; and

(c) the claim form by which the appeal is to be brought shall be served and filed within 7 days of the grant.

(6) Any respondent who intends to use a witness statement or affidavit at the hearing shall file it in the Crown Office and serve a copy thereof on the applicant as soon as is practicable and in any event, unless the court otherwise allows, at least 2 days before the hearing.

The court may allow the applicant to use a further witness statement or affidavit.

R94.12.1 **History of rule**—Substituted by S.I. 1992 No. 638.

R94.12.2 **Effect of rule**—Section 289 of the Town and Country Planning Act 1990 and s.65(5) of the Planning (Listed Buildings and Conservation Areas) Act 1990, as amended by the Planning and Compensation Act 1991, introduce a requirement for leave to appeal and this new r.12 provides for the procedure whereby such leave may be obtained. No fee is payable on an application for leave but a fee of £15 is payable on the entry of the claim form.

Where leave to appeal has been refused under s.289(6) of the Act and r. 12, there is no power in the Court of Appeal to entertain an application for leave to appeal against that refusal. The requirement of leave in s.289(6) was intended to deter frivolous and unmeritorious appeals and that object would be frustrated if the refusal of leave was itself the subject of appeal. The power conferred on the Court of Appeal by section 16(1) of the Supreme Court Act 1981 to hear appeals from any judgment or order does not apply to a decision refusing leave to appeal to the court below. *Huggett v. Secretary of State for the Environment*, S.J., Vol. 139, No. 16, April 28, 1995 (Sir Thomas Bingham M.R., Kennedy and Millett L.JJ.).

Rule 12(2) must be read in its entirety so that the making of an application is not simply a matter of filling in a form but a process requiring several steps including service on the respondents. *Wenman v. Secretary of State for the Environment* [1994] EGCS 100.

The purpose of r.12(5) is to make it clear that the court cannot set aside or vary the decision but, where it chooses to take any positive action, can only remit it. It is, however, open to the court, in exceptional and rare cases, to decline to remit notwithstanding that there had been an error of law. Thus where the error did not relate to the merits or substance of the application, but simply to the time in which remedial work should be completed so as to comply with an enforcement notice, it was appropriate to exercise the discretion so as not to remit (*Botton v. Secretary of State for the Environment and London Borough of Bromley*; *R. v. Secretary of State for the Environment, ex p. Botton* [1992] C.O.D. 249, Roch J. On this point see also *P. G. Vallance Ltd v. Secretary of State for the Environment, The Independent*, November 19, 1992 (Henry J.)).

Where a respondent appears in opposition to an application for leave under s.289 of the Act, the general rule is that costs will follow the event so that an unsuccessful applicant will pay the costs of a respondent who is represented at the hearing for leave. Different considerations may however apply where there is more than one respondent (*Rozhon v. Secretary of State for Wales* [1994] C.O.D. 111 (Neill, Steyn and Rose L.JJ.)).

In relation to proceedings under section 287 of the Town and Country Planning Act 1990—challenge to a local plan—there is no provision, under O.94 or O.15, r.6, for interested persons who desire to be heard to be joined. The court does however have an inherent power to allow such a person to be heard, but that power will be exercised only in a most exceptional case (*Warren, Felsted Parish Council v. Uttlesford District Council* [1996] C.O.D. 262).

An application for leave to appeal under s.289 of the Town and Country Planning Act 1990, as amended, should be made on form TCP(L), which may be obtained from the Crown Office. In settling the grounds of appeal there is an obligation, in particular, to include an outline of any propositions of law, supported by any authorities.

Proceedings under sections 289 and 290 of the Town and Country Planning Act 1990 and under section 65 of the Planning (Listed Buildings and Conservation Areas) Act 1990

R94.13 **13.**—(1) In this rule a reference to "section 65" is a reference to section 65 of the Planning (Listed Buildings and Conservation Areas) Act 1990, but, save as aforesaid, a reference to a section by number is a reference to the section so numbered in the Town and Country Planning Act 1990.

(2) An appeal shall lie to the High Court on a point of law against a decision of the Secretary of State under subsection (1) or (2) of section 289 or under subsection (1) of section 65 at the instance of any person or authority entitled to appeal under any of those subsections respectively.

(3) In the case of a decision to which section 290 applies, the person who

made the application to which the decision relates, or the local planning authority, if dissatisfied with the decision in point of law, may appeal against the decision to the High Court.

(4) Any appeal under section 289(1) or (2), section 65(1) or section 290, and any case stated under section 289(3) or section 65(2), shall be heard and determined by a single judge unless the court directs that the matter shall be heard and determined by a Divisional Court.

(5) The persons to be served with a claim form by which an appeal to the High Court is brought by virtue of section 289(1) or (2), section 65(1) or section 290 are—

(a) the Secretary of State;
(b) the local planning authority who served the notice or gave the decision, as the case may be, or, where the appeal is brought by that authority, the appellant or applicant in the proceedings in which the decision appealed against was given;
(c) in the case of an appeal brought by virtue of section 289(1) or section 65(1), any other person having an interest in the land to which the notice relates, and;
(d) in the case of an appeal brought by virtue of section 289(2), any other person on whom the notice to which those proceedings related was served.

(6) The court hearing any such appeal may remit the matter to the Secretary of State to the extent necessary to enable him to provide the court with such further information in connection with the matter as the court may direct.

(7) Where the court is of opinion that the decision appealed against was erroneous in point of law, it shall not set aside or vary that decision but shall remit the matter to the Secretary of State with the opinion of the court for re-hearing and determination by him.

(8) Order 55, rule 7(5) shall not apply in relation to any such appeal.

(9) The court may give directions as to the exercise, until an appeal brought by virtue of section 289(1) is finally concluded and any re-hearing and determination by the Secretary of State has taken place, of the power to serve, and institute proceedings (including criminal proceedings) concerning—

(a) a stop notice under section 183; and
(b) a breach of condition notice under section 187A.

History of rule—Added by S.I. 1992 No. 638. R94.13.1

Generally—Rule 13(7) and (8) do not expressly disapply RSC, O.55, r.7(7). Where the case was fit for the grant of relief it had to be remitted in accordance with r.13(7). However, where the court was satisfied that no substantial wrong or miscarriage of justice had been occasioned by any misdirection then, under RSC, O.55, r.7(7) the court need not remit the case and could decline to grant relief (*P. G. Vallance Ltd v. Secretary of State for the Environment The Independent*, November 19, 1992 (Henry J.)). R94.13.2

Applications under section 13 of the Coroners Act 1988

14.—(1) Any application under section 13 of the Coroners Act 1988 shall be heard and determined by a Divisional Court. R94.14

(2) The application must be made by claim form and the claim form must state the grounds of the application and, unless the application is made by the Attorney General, shall be accompanied by his fiat.

(3) The claim form must be filed in the Crown Office and served upon all persons directly affected by the application within six weeks after the grant of the fiat.

History of rule—Added by S.I. 1988 No. 1340. R94.14.1

R94.14.2 **Effect of rule**—Section 13 of the Coroners Act 1988 (formerly section 6 of the Coroners Act 1887) empowers the High Court, on an application by or under the authority of the Attorney General, to order an inquest to be held where a coroner has refused or neglected to hold an inquest, or where it is necessary or desirable in the interests of justice that another inquest should be held. Formerly such applications had to be heard and determined by a single Judge by virtue of section 19(3) of the Supreme Court Act 1981. Such applications are often closely connected with, and accompanied by, an application for judicial review see *Re Rapier* [1986] 3 W.L.R. 830—which, as a matter of practice, are always heard by a Divisional Court. Thus this rule now enables a Divisional Court to hear both applications.

When considering whether to give his authority to make an application under s.13 of the Act, the Attorney General is entitled to have regard to the ultimate prospects of success of such an application (*R. v. HM Attorney-General, ex p. Ferrante, The Independent*, April 3, 1995 (Sir Thomas Bingham M.R., Kennedy and Millett L.JJ.)).

The provisions of s.13(1) of the Coroners Act 1988 are apt not only to comprehend an enquiry into death but also into treasure (*Re Chaddock, The Times*, November 23, 1992 (Mann L.J. and Leonard J.)).

As to the principles to which the court will have regard in considering the question of fresh evidence in relation to an application under s.13 of the Coroners Act 1988, see *Re Fletcher (Percy Lewis)* [1992] C.O.D. 342 (Beldam L.J. and Evans J.).

Applications under section 42 Supreme Court Act 1981

R94.15 **15.**—(1) Every application to the High Court by the Attorney General under section 42 of the Supreme Court Act 1981 shall be heard and determined by a Divisional Court.

(2) The application must be made by claim form, which, together with a witness statement or affidavit in support, shall be filed in the Crown Office and served on the person against whom the order is sought.

R94.15.1 **History of rule**—Added by S.I. 1988 No. 1340.

R94.15.2 **Restriction of vexatious legal proceedings**—Section 42 of the Supreme Court Act 1981 empowers the High Court, on the application of the Attorney General, to make an order preventing a person who has habitually and persistently instituted vexatious legal proceedings from instituting or continuing legal proceedings without the leave of the High Court. In *Re Fletcher* (1984) 81 L.S.Gaz. 2464; (1984) *The Times*, June 12, the Court of Appeal held that section 19(3) of the Supreme Court Act 1981 precluded such applications from being heard and determined by a Divisional Court and required that they be heard and determined by a single Judge. Because of the importance of an order limiting the freedom to litigate such applications had formerly, and as a matter of practice, always been heard by a Divisional Court. This rule restores the former position.

R94.15.3 **Applications under s.42, Supreme Court 1981, generally**—Having regard to the fundamental right under consideration, namely the right to bring proceedings before the courts, it is appropriate that a law officer should give personal consideration to any proposed application under section 42 of the 1981 Act and that evidence of such consideration should appear in the material before the court (*Att. Gen. v. Williams* [1996] C.O.D. 368). A defendant who makes a counter-claim institutes proceedings for the purpose of s.42 in the same way as a plaintiff.

The phrase "whether in the High Court or any inferior Court" in s.42(1) is ambiguous and thus regard must be had to the mischief at which the section is directed. This was that the compulsive authority of the State, vested in the courts and the judiciary, should not be invoked without reasonable cause to the detriment of other citizens and that, where someone takes that course habitually and persistently, he should be restrained from continuing to do so unless he has reasonable cause. Given that purpose, there was no reason why the section should have been intended by Parliament to exclude proceedings in the Court of Appeal, for example a renewed application for leave to move for judicial review or appeals from decisions of bodies which were not courts.

A person whose conduct was alleged to justify the making of an order under s.42 could not challenge decisions made in the underlying proceedings that his conduct in those proceedings had been vexatious. The power to make an order was no doubt a drastic restriction on his civil rights but there were at least two reasons for doing so. First, the opponents who were harassed by the worry and expense of vexatious litigation were entitled to protection and secondly, the resources of the judicial system were barely sufficient to afford justice without unreasonable delay to whose who had genuine grievances, and should not be squandered on those who do not (*Att.-Gen. v. Marcus David Jones* [1990] 1 W.L.R. 859; [1990] 2 All E.R. 636 (Lord Donaldson of Lymington MR, Stuart-Smith and Staughton L.JJ.)).

On an application for a civil proceedings order under s.42 the appropriate standard of proof is the civil standard having due regard to the seriousness of the issue at stake, and not the criminal standard (*Att.-Gen. v. Hayward, The Times*, November 20, 1995 (Staughton, Henry & Pill L.JJ.)).

The general approach to be followed by the Court is to be found in the observations of Lord Parker C.J. in *Re Vernazza* (1959) 1 W.L.R. 622 which had been approved by the Court of Appeal at (1960) 1 Q.B. 197.

Where an application for an order under s.42 has been lodged in the Crown Office on behalf of the Attorney General, but there is no prospect of an early hearing, the court has power to grant an interlocutory injunction under s.37(1) of the Supreme Court Act 1981 to prevent the allegedly vexatious litigant from instituting, taking any further step or making any application in any civil proceeding until the application for the order under s.42 has been heard (*Re Blackstone* [1995] C.O.D. 105 (Steyn L.J and Kay J.)).

The court will only grant an interlocutory injunction in proceedings under section 42 where (a) a strong case for the granting of final relief is made out, (b) there is likely to be substantial delay before the matter can be finally heard and (c) there is a probability that, unless restrained by an interlocutory injunction, the respondent will resort to further allegedly vexatious proceedings. It is always open to a litigant, where an interim injunction is granted, to apply for leave under s.42(3) to institute, continue or make any applications in such proceedings. Breach of an interlocutory injunction will lay the litigant open to severe penalties, including committal: *H.M. Attorney-General v. Campbell* [1997] C.O.D. 249 (Lord Bingham of Cornhill C.J. and Moses J.).

The making of an order under s.42 does not offend against Article 6(1) of the European Convention on Human Rights which provides for an unfettered right of access to the courts. The court may, in its discretion, make an order limited to protecting particular defendants from the respondent's litigious attentions but generally will make an order in the usual terms. The court may also make an order which is limited in time: *H.M. Attorney-General v. Price* [1997] C.O.D. 250 (Brooke L.J. and Blofeld J.).

The institution of proceedings in breach of an order under section 42 will constitute a contempt and will be likely to result in an immediate sentence of imprisonment: *H.M. Attorney-General v. Landau* [1997] C.O.D. 350 (Brooke L.J. and Blofeld J.).

Applications for leave to institute or continue proceedings—In *Re C, The Times,* November 14, 1989, Brooke J. gave guidance as to the procedure to be adopted where a vexatious litigant applies for leave to institute or continue proceedings. In exceptional cases it might be appropriate for a judge to cause notice of the application to be given to the Attorney General so that an *amicus curiae* could be instructed to assist the court (see *Becker v. Teale* [1971] 1 W.L.R. 1475 at 1476). R94.15.4

Leave to institute or continue proceedings should be granted sparingly and very carefully. Where leave was granted care should be taken to ensure that the court file contained the order granting leave but no extraneous material. In particular it was most undesirable that an opposing party should be entitled, under the provisions of O.63, r.4, to search the court file in order to obtain copies of evidence placed before the Court in respect of other applications.

Where a person had been declared a vexatious litigant before the coming into force of s.42 of The Supreme Court Act 1981, he should be treated as having the rights and restrictions granted to him or imposed on him under the order made under the Supreme Court of Judicature (Consolidation) Act 1925, as amended, there being no transitional provisions in the 1981 Act.

An application for leave to apply for judicial review under O.53, r.3 constitutes the institution of civil proceedings for the purposes of s.42(1A) of the Supreme Court Act 1981 and a vexatious litigant therefore requires leave of the High Court in order to make such an application *R. v. Highbury Corner Magistrates' Court, ex p. Ewing* [1991] 3 All E.R. 192 (Lord Donaldson of Lymington M.R., Mustill and Nicholls L.JJ.) and *R. v. Tottenham Magistrates' Court, ex p. Gleaves* [1993] C.O.D. 332 (Evans L.J. and Otton J.). A renewed application to the Court of Appeal for leave to apply for judicial review, under O.59, r.14(3), is likewise a civil proceedings within the meaning of s.42(1A), and accordingly the Court of Appeal has no jurisdiction to entertain such an application (*Re Ewing (No. 2)* [1994] 1 W.L.R. 1553 (Sir Thomas Bingham M.R., Stuart-Smith & Leggatt L.JJ.)).

An application made in civil proceedings by a member of a partnership, one of whose members has been made the subject of a civil proceedings order under s.42 of the 1981 Act, is for the purposes of the section, an application made by the person subject to that order. It could not be in the interests of justice that a person subject to such an order should be able to avoid the effect of the prohibition contained in s.42(1A) simply by forming or joining a limited partnership and using it as a device to carry on vexatious litigation. *Mephistopheles Debt Collection Service (a firm) v. Lotay* [1994] 1 W.L.R. 1064; (1994) *The Independent,* June 1 (Nourse L.J. & Wall J.).

Where a defendant in county court proceedings is subject to a civil proceedings order under s.42 of the Supreme Court Act 1981, he may not appeal to the Court of Appeal against a judgment given against him in those proceedings without first having obtained the leave of the High Court (*Henry J. Garrett & Co. v. Ewing* [1991] 1 W.L.R. 1356; [1991] 4 All E.R. 891 (Lord Donaldson of Lymington M.R., Russell and Leggatt L.JJ.)).

Where a vexatious litigant has been given leave, without giving notice, under s.42(3) of the Supreme Court Act 1981 to institute legal proceedings the defendant cannot apply to have that leave set aside. He may however seek to impugn the proceedings under O.18, r.19 (striking out pleadings and endorsements) (*Jones v. Vans Colina* [1996] 1 W.L.R. 1580).

The fact that permission to institute proceedings has been granted should not be taken as adding weight to the arguments advanced in the proceedings themselves (*R v. London Legal Aid Area Office Committee, ex p. Ewing* [1997] C.O.D. 134, Lord Woolf M.R., Aldous and Brooke L.JJ., CA).

The findings of the High Court on which a civil proceedings order has been based are capable of having a bearing on the court's evaluation of the matters which a leave application brings into play: *R. v. Dean and Chapter of St Paul's Cathedral and the Church in Wales* [1998] C.O.D. 130 (Sedley J.).

Proceedings under the Protection from Harassment Act 1997

R94.16 **16.**—(1) In this rule, "the Act" means the Protection from Harassment Act 1997.

(2) This rule shall apply to injunctions granted on or after 1st September 1998 and injunctions granted before that date shall be treated as if this rule had not come into force.

(3) Proceedings in the High Court under section 3 of the Act shall be assigned to the Queen's Bench Division.

(4) An application for the issue of a warrant for the arrest of the defendant under section 3(3) of the Act shall—

- (a) state that it is an application for the issue of a warrant for the arrest of the defendant;
- (b) set out the grounds for making the application and be supported by an affidavit or evidence on oath;
- (c) state whether the claimant has informed the police of the defendant's conduct as described in sub-paragraph (b); and
- (d) state whether, to the claimant's knowledge, criminal proceedings are being pursued.

(5) The Court before whom a person is brought following his arrest may—

- (a) determine whether the facts, and the circumstances which led to the arrest, amounted to disobedience of the injunction, or
- (b) adjourn the proceedings and, where such an order is made, the arrested person shall be released and—
  - (i) may be dealt with within 14 days of the day on which he was arrested; and
  - (ii) be given not less than 2 days' notice of the adjourned hearing.

(6) This rule applies to the proceedings under section 3 of the Act in a county court with the following modifications—

- (a) Such proceedings in a county court shall be begun—
  - (i) in the court for the district in which the claimant resides or carries on business; or
  - (ii) in the court for the district in which the defendant resides or carries on business.
- (b) Where a county court—
  - (i) grants an injunction under section 3 of the Act; or
  - (ii) issues a warrant for the arrest of the defendant,

  the injunction or warrant shall be issued in the appropriate prescribed form.

RSC ORDER 95

BILLS OF SALE ACTS 1878 AND 1882 AND THE INDUSTRIAL AND PROVIDENT SOCIETIES ACT 1967

R95.0.1 **Contents**

Editorial Introduction

The practice of transferring the title to goods while remaining in possession of them has always created a trap for creditors, who might be led to extend credit on the strength of apparent ownership of goods in reality already conveyed or charged to another. The Bills of Sale Act 1878 and the Bills of Sale Act (1878) Amendment Act 1882 do not purport to change the equitable and legal principles relating to such transfer, but instead make it necessary for written instruments of transfer (1) to conform to certain requirements and (2) to be registered. A register of bills of sale is kept by masters under statutory authority. The function of registrar may be discharged by any of the Masters of the Queen's Bench Division. The principal effect of the Bills of Sale Acts is to render void, whether wholly or in part, those bills which fail to satisfy the statutory requirements. (For short explanation of the transactions which may be crucially affected by this legislation, of the process of registration, and of the attestation of bills of sale, see paras R95.0.2, and R95.1.2 to R95.1.4.) R95.0.2

For information as to the keeping of the register and search of the register, see notes following r.4 below at para. R95.4.1.

Deeds of arrangement also require to be registered and the provisions for registration are closely similar to those relating to bills of sale. For further information, see SCP 1999, Vol. 1, para. 95/1/13.

Rules 1 to 3 of this Order deal with applications to the High Court under, respectively, sections 14, and 15 of the 1878 Act and section 7 of the 1882 Act. Rule 4 provides for searches of the register of bills of sale (kept by Masters under statutory authority). Rule 5 contains the machinery for the exercise of the Court's jurisdiction under the Industrial and Provident Societies Act 1967, s.1(5) (the jurisdiction is comparable to that under section 14 of the 1878 Act). Rule 6 is concerned with applications for registration of assignments of book debts under the Insolvency Act 1986, s.344.

Applications under rr.1, 5 and 6 are not made by claim form or in accordance with Pt 23, but may be made "by witness statement or affidavit".

In the process of being re-enacted in Schedule 1 of the CPR, all of the rules in RSC, O.95 underwent amendment. With the exception of those made to r.2, all of these amendments were minor.

Related sources

Practice Direction (CPR, Pt 8 and Schedule 1 and Schedule 2 to the CPR) Table 1. R95.0.3

Forms

The following Queen's Bench Masters' Practice Forms are relevant to RSC, O.95 and are included in Table 2 of Practice Direction (Forms) supplementing CPR Pt 4 (Forms) (see SCP 1999, Vol. 2, Section 1B, paras 1B–137 to 1B–144) (they may be modified as the circumstances require): R95.0.4

- PF179—Evidence in support of an application for registration of a bill of sale (Bills of Sale Act 1879, s.8: Sched. 1, RSC, O.95)
- PF180—Evidence in support of an application for registration of absolute bill of sale, settlement and deed of gift (Sched. 1, RSC, O.95)
- PF181—Evidence in support of an application for re-registration of bill of sale (Bills of Sale Act 1878, s.14: Sched. 1, RSC, O.95)
- PF182—Order for extension of time to register or re-register of bill of sale (Sched. 1, RSC, O.95, r.1)
- PF183—Evidence in support of an application for permission to enter memorandum of satisfaction on a bill of sale (Sched. 1, RSC, O.95, r.2)
- PF184—Claim form for entry of satisfaction on a registered bill of sale (Sched. 1, RSC, O.95, r.2)
- PF185—Order for entry of satisfaction on a registered bill of sale (Sched. 1, RSC, O.95, r.2)
- PF186—Evidence in support of application for registration of assignment of book debts (Sched. 1, RSC, O.95, r.6(2))

The following Chancery Masters' Practice Form is also relevant (see SCP 1999, Vol. 2, Section 1B, para. 1B–210) and is included in Table 2 of Practice Direction (Forms):

- PF9—Re Benjamin order giving leave to distribute estate upon footing

Rectification of register

1.—(1) Every application to the court under section 14 of the Bills of Sale Act 1878, for an order— R95.1

(a) that any omission to register a bill of sale or a witness statement or affidavit of renewal thereof within the time prescribed by that Act be rectified by extending the time for such registration; or

(b) that any omission or mis-statement of the name, residence or occupation of any person be rectified by the insertion in the register of his true name, residence or occupation,

must be made by witness statement or affidavit to a Master of the Queen's Bench Division, and a copy of the witness statement or affidavit need not be served on any other person.

(2) Every application for such an order as is described in paragraph (1) shall be supported by a witness statement or affidavit setting out particulars of the bill of sale and of the omission or mis-statement in question and stating the grounds on which the application is made.

R95.1.1 **Effect of rule**—A bill of sale should be registered within the time prescribed by the Bills of Sale Acts and must be renewed within five years (for further information, see SCP 1999, Vol. 1, paras 95/1/3 and 95/1/9). Applications may be made in accordance with this rule to register and renew where there has been a failure to observe these time limits. Further, where registration has been effected, application may be made to correct certain errors in the register.

R95.1.2 **Registration of bill of sale**—A person wishing to register a bill of sale should produce at the Filing Department (Room E07) the original bill of sale ("with every schedule or inventory thereto annexed or therein referred to"), and also a true copy (carbon copies are not accepted) of the bill and every schedule and inventory, and as many further copies as the department may deem necessary for the purpose of local registration and an affidavit of the execution and attestation of the bill of sale and of the time when it was given or made, containing also a description of the residence and occupation of the person making or giving it and of every attesting witness. The copy and affidavit are to be filed (1878 Act, s.10(2) and Administration of Justice Act 1925, s.23(2)). A Master may accept a defective affidavit but that fact will not validate a bill otherwise void (*Brown v. London & County Advance Co.* [1889] 5 T.L.R. 199). It is not the province of the Master or Filing Department to inquire whether the bill of sale and affidavit comply with the statutory provisions (*Needham v. Johnson* (1867) 8 B. & S. 190).

For forms, see PF179 (Evidence in support of an application for registration of a bill of sale (Bills of Sale Act 1879, s.8: Sched. 1, RSC, O.95)) and PF180 (Evidence in support of an application for registration of absolute bill of sale, settlement and deed of gift (Sched. 1, RSC, O.95)) (SCP 1999, Vol. 2, Section 1B, paras 137 and 138).

For fee on registration, see Supreme Court Fees Order 1999, Sched. 1, Fee No. 4.1.

By virtue of s.11 of the 1882 Act and section 23(1) of the AJA 1925, where the affidavit on registration of a bill of sale states the residence of the grantor or person against whom the process is issued to be outside the London bankruptcy district, or where the bill of sale describes the goods as being in some place outside that district, the department is required to transmit copies of the bill of sale to the local county court. Section 11 of the 1882 Act and the Bills of Sale (Local Registration) Rule 1960, prescribe the procedure of registration and search (see also Administration of Justice Act 1925, s.23). Note, however, that there is nothing in s.11 or elsewhere which requires a bill of sale to specify the place where the goods are (*Re Lane, ex p. Hill* (1886) 17 Q.B.D. 74).

R95.1.3 **Renewal of registration**—By virtue of s.11 of the 1878 Act, the registration of a bill of sale (whether absolute or not) must be renewed once at least every five years, and, if a period of five years elapses from the registration or renewed registration without a renewal or a further renewal (as the case may be), the registration becomes void. The renewal is effected by filing at the Filing Department evidence in support stating the date of the bill of sale and of the last registration, and the names, addresses and occupations of the parties as stated in the bill of sale, and that the bill of sale is still a subsisting security. Renewal is not necessary by reasonly only of a transfer of the bill of sale. For form if evidence in support, see PF181 (Evidence in support of an application for re-registration of bill of sale (Bills of Sale Act 1878, s.14: Sched. 1, RSC, O.95)) (SCP 1999, Vol. 2, Section 1B, para. 1B-139).

R95.1.4 **Extension of time for registration or renewal**—A QB Master, on being satisfied that the omission to register a bill of sale or to renew registration within the time prescribed was accidental or due to inadvertence, may in his discretion extend the time for such registration on such terms and conditions (if any) as to security, notice by advertisement or otherwise, or as to any other matter as he thinks fit to direct. Whether or not there is a discretion to do so, the Court will not make an order under the section so as to defeat the rights of third persons which have accrued in the meantime, for example, where a creditor has obtained title by a completed execution upon the goods, *Crew v. Cummings* (1888) 21 Q.B.D. 420; or they have passed to the trustee in bankruptcy of the grantor, *Ex. p. Furber, re Parsons* [1893] 2 Q.B. 122, CA; or the grantor company has gone into liquidation, see *Re Spiral Globe Ltd* [1902] 1 Ch. 396. The order is usually in the form suggested by Swinfen Eady J. in the last-mentioned case at p. 399; "This Order to be without prejudice to the rights of parties acquired prior to the time when such bill of sale shall be actually registered (or re-registered)." This proviso is for the protection of creditors to whom have accrued rights of property in the assets of the debtor between the date of the bill of sale and the date of actual registration, and does not extend to protect the inchoate or other rights of creditors as such (see *Re Kris Cruisers Ltd* [1949] Ch. 138).

Application should be made by witness statement or affidavit in accordance with r.95(2) to a QB Master, and leave with the Masters' Secretary (Room E214). An order is drawn up. Form of order, see PF182 (Order for extension of time to register or re-register of bill of sale (Sched. 1, RSC, O.95, r.1)) (SCP 1999, Vol. 2, Section 1B, para. 1B-140).

Correction of errors in registration—A QB Master, on being satisfied that the omission or misstatement of name, residence or occupation of any person was accidental or due to inadvertence may, in his discretion, order such omission or misstatement to be rectified by the insertion in the register of the true name, residence or occupation (1878 Act, s.14, para. (1)(b)). Application for rectification should be made by witness statement or affidavit in accordance with r.1(2). R95.1.5

Entry of satisfaction

2.—(1) Every application under section 15 of the Bills of Sale Act 1878, to a Master of the Queen's Bench Division for an order that a memorandum of satisfaction be written on a registered copy of a bill of sale must be made by claim form R95.2

(1A) If a consent to the satisfaction signed by the person entitled to the benefit of the bill of sale can be obtained, the claim form and the other documents set out in paragraph (2) must not be served on any other person;

(2) Where paragraph (1A) applies, the claim form must be supported by—

(a) particulars of the consent referred to in that paragraph; and

(b) a witness statement or affidavit by a witness who attested the consent verifying the signature on it.

(3) Where paragraph (1A) does not apply, must be served on the person entitled to the benefit of the bill of sale and must be supported by evidence that the debt (if any) for which the bill of sale was made has been satisfied or discharged.

Effect of rule—Section 15 of the 1878 Act states that "upon the prescribed evidence being given that the debt (if any) ... has been satisfied or discharged", the Master may order a "memorandum of satisfaction" to be written upon the registered copy of the bill of sale. The procedure is stated in this rule. A distinction is drawn between applications for the entry of a memorandum of satisfaction (1) where the consent of the person entitled to the benefit of the bill can be obtained, and (2) where such consent cannot obtained. In the form in which this rule appeared in the RSC, applications of the former type were made ex parte and applications of the latter type were made by originating summons (in the expedited form). R95.2.1

When re-enacted in Schedule 1 of the CPR, r.2 was amended and was further amended by the Civil Procedure (Amendment) Rules 1999. Before the further amendment was made, what is now para. (1) of the rule stood as r.2(1)(b) and remains listed as such in Table 1 of Practice Direction (CPR Pt 8 and Schedule 1 and Schedule 2 to the CPR). The intention is that Section A of the Practice Direction should apply to applications for the entry of a memorandum of satisfaction, whether or not consent is forthcoming. Therefore, in accordance with para. A.3 of the Practice Direction, the applicant "must use the Part 8 claim form", subject to s.15 and r.2. Whereas, previously, where consent was forthcoming application was made ex parte, now it is made on a claim form but it "must not be served on any other person" (r.2(1A)). However, it would seem that an application or an application notice would suffice.

Practice—If the application is made on the basis that the person entitled to the benefit of the bill has consented, and the written evidence is by a solicitor, described as such, and the papers are otherwise in order, the entry of satisfaction will be directed by the Master; but the Master will accept any other deponent, if satisfied that he is a proper person to attest the consent and verify the signature (*Re White & Rubery* [1894] 2 Q.B. 923). Where a corporation is the grantee of the bill of sale, the consent must be given under its seal. For form of written evidence and consent, see PF183 (Evidence in support of an application for permission to enter memorandum of satisfaction on a bill of sale (Sched. 1, RSC, O.95, r.2)) (SCP 1999, Vol. 2, Section 1B, para. R95.2.2

1B-141). Leave the evidence in support and consent at the Master's Secretary's Dept., Room E214. If satisfied, the Master indorses evidence in support with his fiat, and the applicant obtains his papers at Room E214 and takes them to the Filing Department for satisfaction to be entered. No order is drawn up. For form of order, see form PF185 (Order for entry of satisfaction on a registered bill of sale (Sched. 1, RSC, O.95, r.2)) (SCP 1999, Vol. 2, Section 1B, para. 1B-143). For claim form, see N208 (Part 8 claim form).

Where a memorandum of satisfaction has been entered upon any registered copy of a bill of sale, an abstract of which has been transmitted to a county court, a notice of such satisfaction in due form is to be transmitted to him, and he is to enter it.

Restraining removal on sale of goods seized

R95.3 **3.** An application to the court under the proviso to section 7 of the Bills of Sale Act (1878) Amendment Act 1882 must be made by the issue of a claim form.

R95.3.1 **Effect of rule**—Formerly, application was made by originating summons (in the expedited form). Rule 3 listed in Table 1 of Practice Direction (CPR, Pt 8 and Schedule 1 and Schedule 2 to the CPR). Therefore, in accordance with para. A.3 of the Practice Direction, the applicant "must use the Part 8 claim form". Application should be made to the interim applications judge.

Search of register

R95.4 **4.** Any Master of the Queen's Bench Division shall, on a request in writing giving sufficient particulars, and on payment of the prescribed fee, cause a search to be made in the register of bills of sale and issue a certificate of the result of the search.

R95.4.1 **Effect of rule**—The Filing Department is required to keep a register for the purposes of the Bills of Sale Acts, containing the particulars of registered bills of sale prescribed by s.12 of the 1882 Act, and an alphabetical index of the names of grantors. Under s.16 any person may search the register and every registered bill of sale and may have an office copy or extract of any registered bill of sale or written evidence filed or registered, paying the same fees as for office copies of High Court judgments. Office copies of registered bills of sale and written evidence are everywhere to be prima facie evidence thereof and of the fact and date of registration shown (s.16).

The searches under this rule are made at the Filing Department, Central Office (Room E07). For prescribed fee, see Supreme Court Fees Order 1999, Sched. 1, Fee No. 4.1.

Application under section 1(5) of the Industrial and Provident Societies Act 1967

R95.5 **5.** Every application to the court under section 1(5) of the Industrial and Provident Societies Act 1967 for an order—

(a) that the period for making an application for recording a charge be extended; or

(b) that any omission from or misstatement in such an application be rectified,

must be made to a Master of the Queen's Bench Division by witness statement or affidavit setting out particulars of the charge and of the omission or mis-statement in question and stating the grounds of the application, and need not be served on any other person.

R95.5.1 **Effect of rule**—This rule provides the machinery for the exercise of the jurisdiction under the Industrial and Provident Societies Act 1967, s.1(5), to extend the time for making an application for recording a charge on the assets of a registered society and to rectify any omission or mis-statement in it. This jurisdiction is comparable to that under the Bills of Sale 1878, s.14, which is exercisable under r.1, and the effect of this rule is to cause the exercise of such jurisdiction under both Acts to operate in a similar manner.

Formerly, application was made *ex parte* by affidavit. Now it is made by witness statement or affidavit which, in either event, need not be served on any other person.

For information as to the recording of a charge under the 1967 Act, see SCP 1999, Vol. 1, paras 95/5/2 and 95/5/3.

Assignment of book debts

6.—(1) There shall continue to be kept in the Central Office, under the supervision of the registrar, a register of assignments of book debts. R95.6

(2) Every application for registration of an assignment of a book debt under section 344 of the Insolvency Act 1986 shall be made by producing at the Filing and Record Department of the Central Office—

(a) a true copy of the assignment, and of every schedule thereto; and

(b) a witness statement or affidavit verifying the date and the time, and the due execution of the assignment in the presence of the witness, and setting out the particulars of the assignment and the parties thereto.

(3) On an application being made in accordance with the preceding paragraph, the documents there referred to shall be filed, and the particulars of the assignment, and of the parties to it, shall be entered in the register.

(4) In this rule, "the registrar" has the meaning given in section 13 of the Bills of Sale Act 1878.

Effect of rule—The Insolvency Act 1986, s.344 provides that, where a person engaged in trade or business assigns his book debts and is subsequently adjudicated bankrupt, the assignment is void against the trustee in bankruptcy in relation to any unpaid debts unless the assignment has been registered as if it were a bill of sale, given otherwise than by way of security for the payment of a sum of money. Further, the provisions of the Bills of Sale Act 1878 with respect to the registration of bills of sale apply, with such necessary modifications as may be made by rules under section 10 of that Act. R95.6.1

Practice on registration of assignment of book debts—A separate register of the assignment of book debts is kept at the Filing Department of the Central Office, but the rule does not prescribe the form of register. The application for registration is made by producing at the Filing Department a true copy of the assignment and of every Schedule thereto, and a witness statement or affidavit which fulfils the requirements of r.6(2)(b) (for form, see PF186 (Evidence in support of application for registration of assignment of book debts (Sched. 1, RSC, O.95, r.6(2)) (SCP 1999, Vol. 2, Pt 2, para. 1B–144). R95.6.2

The rule does not expressly require the production of the original assignment showing it to have been duly stamped, though of course this would be helpful to the Filing Department who can then check the signature on the copy assignment produced as against that on the original assignment. Nor does the rule expressly provide for the registration of the assignment to be made within seven days after its execution, since this is laid down by section 8 of the Bills of Sale Act 1878. The responsibility for duly and timeously registering an assignment of book debts lies upon the assignee, as it is he who gets the benefit of the registration under the Act of 1914, and accordingly it is in his interests to pay the proper stamp duty on the assignment and to register it as soon as possible. The Filing Department will retain for filing the copy of the assignment and every Schedule thereto produced to it, and the supporting evidence and will enter the particulars of the assignment and of the parties thereto in the register kept for this purpose.

RSC ORDER 96

THE MINES (WORKING FACILITIES AND SUPPORT) ACT 1966, ETC.

Contents R96.0.1

Assignment to Chancery Division

1. Any proceedings in which the jurisdiction conferred on the High Court by section 1 of the Railway and Canal Commission (Abolition) Act 1949 is R96.1

invoked shall be assigned to the Chancery Division and be begun by claim form which need not be served on any other party.

Reference by Secretary of State of certain applications

R96.2 **2.** Where under any provision of the Mines (Working Facilities and Support) Act 1966, the Secretary of State refers any application to the High Court, he shall—

(a) file the reference, signed by him or by an officer authorised by him for the purpose, in Chancery Chambers, together with all documents and plans deposited with him by the applicant; and

(b) within 3 days after doing so give notice to the applicant of the filing of the reference.

Issue of claim form

R96.3 **3.** Within 10 days after receipt of the notice mentioned in rule 2(b) the applicant must issue a claim form which need not be served on any other party which must state the application of the applicant under the said Act of 1966 and any other relief sought.

Appointment for directions

R96.4 **4.**—(1) Within 7 days after issue of the claim form the applicant, having applied at Chancery Chambers for the name of the Master assigned to hear the claim, must take an appointment before that Master for the hearing of the claim and must forthwith serve notice of the appointment on the Secretary of State.

(2) Not less than 2 clear days before the day appointed for the first hearing of the claim, the applicant must leave at Chancery Chambers—

- (a) a witness statement or affidavit of facts in support of the claim, giving particulars of all persons known to the applicant to be interested in or affected by the application; and
- (b) a draft of any proposed advertisement or notice of the application.

(3) On the appointment the master shall—

- (a) fix a time within which any notice of objection under rule 5 must be given;
- (b) fix a date for the further hearing of the claim; and
- (c) direct what, if any, advertisements and notices of the application and of the date fixed for the further hearing of the claim are to be inserted and given, and what persons, if any, are to be served with a copy of the application and of any other document in the proceedings.

(4) Any such advertisement or notice must include a statement of the effect of rule 5.

Objections to application

R96.5 **5.**—(1) Any person wishing to oppose the application must, within the time fixed by the master under rule 4(3), serve on the applicant a notice of objection stating—

- (a) his name and address and the name and address of his solicitor, if any;
- (b) the grounds of his objection and any alternative methods of effecting the objects of the application which he alleges may be used; and
- (c) the facts on which he relies.

(2) Any notice required to be served on a person who has given notice of objection (hereafter in this order referred to as "the objector") may be served by delivering it or sending it by prepaid post—

- (a) where the name and address of a solicitor is stated in the notice of objection, to the solicitor at that address; and

(b) in any other case, to the objector at his address stated in the notice of objection.

(3) An objector shall be entitled to appear in person or by a solicitor or counsel at the further hearing of the claim and to take such part in the proceedings as the Master or judge thinks fit; but if he does not so appear his notice of objection shall be of no effect and he shall not be entitled to take any part in the proceedings unless the Master or judge otherwise orders.

List of objectors

6. Not less than 2 clear days before the day fixed for the further hearing of the claim, the applicant must leave at Chancery Chambers any notices of objection served on the applicant together with a list arranged in 3 columns stating— **R96.6**

(a) in column 1, the names and addresses of the objectors;

(b) in column 2, the names and addresses of their respective solicitors, if any; and

(c) in column 3, short summaries of their respective grounds of objection.

Directions on further hearing

7. At the further hearing of the claim the Master shall— **R96.7**

(a) give directions as to the procedure to be followed before the claim is set down for hearing, including, if he thinks fit, a direction—

(i) that further particulars be given of any of the grounds or facts relied on in support of or in opposition to the application made by the claim;

(ii) that the applicant may serve a reply to any notice of objection;

(iii) that any particular fact be proved by witness statement or affidavit;

(iv) that statements of case or points of claim or defence be served; and

(b) adjourn the claim for hearing before the judge in such manner, as he shall think best adapted to secure the just, expeditious and economical disposal of the proceedings.

Other applications

8. Rules 2 to 7 shall, so far as applicable and with the necessary adaptations, apply in relation to any other application to the High Court falling within rule 1 as they apply in relation to an application under the Mines (Working Facilities and Support) Act 1966. **R96.8**

RSC ORDER 97

THE LANDLORD AND TENANT ACTS 1927, 1954 AND 1987

Contents **R97.0.1**

Editorial Introduction

R97.0.2 Under the Landlord and Tenant Act 1927, the Landlord and Tenant Act 1954 and the Landlord and Tenant Act 1987, in certain circumstances proceedings may be begun either in the High Court or a county court (for transfer of proceedings from a county court to the High Court, see r.11). In the High Court such proceedings are assigned to the Chancery Division (r.2). Generally, the ordinary procedural rules apply to these proceedings. However, in significant respects the rules in this Order modify provisions in other Orders which would otherwise apply and introduce additional rules of court that should be followed in particular landlord and tenant cases.

Related sources

R97.0.3
- CCR, O.43
- Practice Direction (Allocation of Cases to levels of Judiciary), para. 5.1 restricts the powers of Masters and District Judges in some cases (see para. 2BPD–002).
- Chancery Division Practice Direction No. 4 (Landlord and Tenant), *Chancery Guide* p. 80 (see para. D1–330).

Interpretation

R97.1 **1.**—(1) In this order, "the Act of 1927" means the Landlord and Tenant Act 1927, "the Act of 1954" means the Landlord and Tenant Act 1954 and "the Act of 1987" means the Landlord and Tenant Act 1987.

(2) In relation to any proceedings under Part II of the Act of 1954, any reference in this order to a landlord shall, if the interest of the landlord in question is subject to a mortgage and the mortgagee is in possession or a receiver appointed by the mortgagee or by the court is in receipt of the rents and profits, be construed as a reference to the mortgagee.

R97.1.1 **Mortgagee**—A mortgagee who has appointed a receiver of the rent and profits or who is in possession of the property is a necessary defendant to an application for a new tenancy under the Act of 1954 (see s.67 thereof). Where the mortgagee appoints such a receiver or otherwise enters into possession after an application under the Act of 1954 has been made he must be joined to the proceedings as a defendant by order to carry on (*Meah v. Mouskos* [1964] 2 Q.B. 23; [1963] 3 All E.R. 908, CA).

Assignment of proceedings to Chancery Division, etc.

R97.2 **2.** All proceedings in the High Court under Part I of the Act of 1927 or Part II of the Act of 1954 or the Act of 1987 shall be assigned to the Chancery Division and, subject to rules 9A and 12, be begun by claim form.

R97.2.1 **Claim form**—The claimant must use the Pt 8 claim form: CPRPD8(3), section A3.

R97.2.2 **Jurisdiction of Master or District Judge**—A Master or District Judge may not (without the consent of the Vice-Chancellor) make final orders under the Landlord and Tenant Acts 1927 and 1954 except (i) by consent (ii) orders for interim rents under section 24A of the 1954 Act and (iii) on applications to authorise agreements under section 38(4) of the 1954 Act.

Issue, etc., of claim form

R97.3 **3.**—(1) Any claim or application under Part I of the Act of 1927 or Part II of the Act of 1954 or the Act of 1987 may be issued out of the district registry for the district in which the premises to which the claim or application relates are situated instead of Chancery Chambers.

(3) The court will set a day for the hearing of such a claim which shall be a day which will allow an interval of at least 14 days between the date of service of the claim form and the day so fixed.

Setting a date—Where the parties are in negotiation on the grant of a new tenancy and neither side wishes to press on with the proceedings the tenant may request the court not immediately to set a day for the hearing upon issue or service of the claim form but to await a request from either party that a hearing date be set: Chancery Division Practice Direction No. 4, para. (i) *Chancery Guide*, p. 80 (see para. D1–330). **R97.3.1**

Claim for compensation in respect of improvement

4.—(1) A claim under section 1 of the Act of 1927 for compensation in respect of any improvement, and a claim by a mesne landlord under section 8 of that Act, must be a written claim, signed by the claimant or his solicitor or agent, containing— **R97.4**

(a) a statement of the name and address of the claimant and of the landlord against whom the claim is made;
(b) a description of the holding in respect of which the claim is made and of the trade or business carried on there;
(c) a concise statement of the nature of the claim;
(d) particulars of the improvement, including the date when it was completed and the cost thereof; and
(e) a statement of the amount claimed.

(2) Where any document relating to any proposed improvement, or to any claim, is sent to or served on a mesne landlord in pursuance of Part I of the Act of 1927, he must forthwith serve on his immediate superior landlord a copy of the document, together with a notice in writing stating the date on which he received the document, and if the last-mentioned landlord is himself a mesne landlord he must accordingly comply with this paragraph.

"Serve"—As to service of documents under the 1927 Act, see s.23. **R97.4.1**

Proceedings under Part I of Act of 1927

5.—(1) The claim form by which any claim or application under Part I of the Act of 1927 is made must state— **R97.5**

(a) the nature of the claim or application or the matter to be determined;
(b) the holding in respect of which the claim or application is made and the trade or business carried on there;
(c) particulars of the improvement or proposed improvement to which the claim or application relates; and
(d) if the claim is for payment of compensation, the amount claimed.

(2) The claimant's immediate landlord shall be made a defendant.

(3) No witness statement or affidavit shall be filed in the first instance in support of or in answer to any such claim form.

(4) Any certificate of the court under section 3 of the Act of 1927 that an improvement is a proper improvement or has been duly executed shall be embodied in an order.

Claim form—The claimant must use the Pt 8 claim form: Practice Direction (Part 8), Section A.3 (see para. 8BPD–002). **R97.5.1**

Evidence—Paragraph (3) relating to a summons under Pt I of the 1927 Act is in contrast to the provisions of r.7 relating to applications under section 24 of the 1954 Act. **R97.5.2**

Application for new tenancy under section 24 of Act of 1954

6.—(1) The claim form by which an application under section 24 of the Act of 1954 for a new tenancy is made must state— **R97.6**

(a) the premises to which the application relates and where a business is carried on there, the nature of such business;
(b) particulars of the claimant's current tenancy of the premises and of every notice or request given or made in respect of that tenancy under section 25 or 26 of that Act; and

(c) the claimant's proposals as to the terms of the new tenancy applied for including, in particular, terms as to the duration thereof and as to the rent payable thereunder.

(2) The person who, in relation to the claimant's current tenancy, is the landlord as defined by section 44 of the Act of 1954 shall be made a defendant.

(3) A claim form under this rule must be served within 2 months after the date of issue whether served within or out of the jurisdiction and CPR rules 7.5(2) and 7.5(3) will not apply.

R97.6.1 **Claim Form**—The claimant must use the Pt 8 claim form: Practice Direction (Part 8), Section A.3 (see para. 8BPD–002).

R97.6.2 **Section 24**—is concerned with continuation and renewal of tenancies to which Part II of the Act applies.

R97.6.3 **Claimant's proposals**—See *Morgan v. Jones* [1960] 1 W.L.R. 1220; [1960] 3 All E.R. 583, CA, wherein it was held that it is the duty of the Judge, under ss.29(1), 33 and 34 of the 1954 Act, to decide, in exercise of his judicial discretion and on proper evidence as to valuation, whether the terms proposed by a tenant are resonable in all the circumstances and this is so whether or not the landlord is present and desirous of adducing such evidence.

R97.6.4 **Time limits**—The claim must be issued not less than two nor more than four months after the landlord's s.25 notice or, as the case may be, the tenant's request for a new tenancy; s.29(3) of the 1954 Act. The Court has no power to extend these statutory time limits. However, since the timetable is merely procedural they may be waived by the parties (*Kammins Ballrooms Co. Ltd v. Zenith Investments (Torquay) Ltd* [1971] A.C. 850; [1970] 2 All E.R. 871).

R97.6.5 **Validity and renewal of claim form**—The effect of para. (3) is that the summons, whether for service within the jurisdiction or outside the jurisdiction, is only valid in the first instance for two months and therefore should be served within that period. The validity of the summons may be extended under CPR 7.6.

Application to authorise agreement

R97.6A **6A.**—(1) An application under section 38(4) of the Act of 1954 for the authorisation of an agreement shall be made without notice being served on any other party by claim form and may be heard and determined in private.

(2) Notwithstanding that the application must be made jointly by the landlord or proposed landlord and the tenant or proposed tenant and the claim form is accordingly issued by one solicitor on behalf of both of them, they may appear and be heard at any hearing by separate solicitors or counsel or, in the case of an individual applicant, in person; and where at any stage of the proceedings it appears to the court that one of the applicants is not but ought to be separately represented, the court may adjourn the proceedings until he is.

R97.6A.1 **Claim Form**—The applicant must use the Pt 8 claim form: Practice Direction (Part 8), Section A.3 (see para. 8BPD–002).

R97.6A.2 **Application to authorise agreement**—The Order will be made by the Master: Practice Direction (Allocation of Cases to Levels of Judiciary), para. 3.1(j) (see para. 2BPD–001).

The application should be supported by a witness statement explaining the facts on which the Court is asked to exercise its discretion.

The Master will usually hear such applications at 2.15 if he is hearing applications without notice on that day.

Evidence on application under section 24 of Act of 1954

R97.7 **7.**—(1) Not less than 14 days before the day fixed for the first hearing in an application under section 24 of the Act of 1954 for a new tenancy the claimant must file a witness statement or affidavit verifying the statements of fact made in the claim form.

(2) Not less than 4 days before the day fixed for the first hearing the defendant must file a witness statement or affidavit stating—

(a) whether he opposes the grant of a new tenancy and, if he does, on what grounds;

(b) whether, if a new tenancy is granted, he objects to any of the claimant's proposals as to the terms thereof and, if he does, the terms to which he objects and the terms he proposes in so far as they differ from the terms proposed by the claimant;

(c) whether he is a tenant under a lease having less than 14 years unexpired at the date of the termination of the claimant's current tenancy, and, if he is, the name and address of his immediate landlord.

Parties to certain proceedings

8.—(1) Any person affected by any proceedings under rule 5, 6, 14, 15, 16 or 17 may apply to be made a party to the proceedings and the court may give such directions on the application as appear necessary. **R97.8**

(2) An application under paragraph (1) must in the first instance be made without notice being given to any other party but the court may require notice thereof to be given to the parties to the proceedings before making any order.

(3) The foregoing provisions are without prejudice to the power of the court, either with or without an application by any party, to order notice of the proceedings to be given to any person or any person to be made a party to the proceedings, but nothing in this rule shall be construed as requiring the court to make any such order and, if it appears that any person though he is affected by the proceedings is not sufficiently affected for it to be necessary for him to be made a party to the proceedings or given notice thereof, the court may refuse to make him a party or, as the case may be, to require him to be given notice of the proceedings.

History of rule—Amended by S.I. 1988 No. 298 and S.I. 1999 No. 1008. **R97.8.1**

Order dismissing application under section 24 which is successfully opposed

9. Where the court hearing an application under section 24 of the Act of 1954 is precluded by section 31 of that Act from making an order for the grant of a new tenancy by reason of any of the grounds specified in section 30(1) of that Act, the order dismissing the application shall state all the grounds by reason of which the court is so precluded. **R97.9**

Certificate of ground for refusing a new tenancy—Where an application for such a certificate is made at the hearing it should be incorporated in the order. If not made at the hearing a separate certificate may be issued. **R97.9.1**

This rule should be read in conjunction with s.37(4) of the Act which provides that if the Court dismisses the application on one of the grounds specified in s.37(1) and not on any other ground then it shall, on the application of the tenant, certify such fact. The rule provides that the certificate should be incorporated in the order dismissing the application for a new lease. In practice the application for the certificate should be made at the trial. If not so made, the application should be made without notice under r.10(1) to the Master or District Judge.

Application to determine interim rent

9A.—(1) An application under section 24A of the Act of 1954 to determine an interim rent shall— **R97.9A**

(a) if the tenant has begun proceedings for a new tenancy under section 24 of the Act, be made by an application in accordance with CPR Part 23 in those proceedings; and

(b) in any other case, be made by claim form.

History of rule—Para. (2) omitted by S.I. 1999 No. 1008. **R97.9A.1**

Claim Form—The claimant must use the Pt 8 claim form: Practice Direction (Part 8), Section A.3 (see para. 8BPD–002). **R97.9A.2**

R97.9A.3 **Practice**—Usually these applications will be heard with the main claim and the same evidence be used on both. If the application for an interim rent is heard separately it can be heard and determined by a Master, see Practice Direction (Allocation of Cases to Levels of Judiciary), para. 5.1(j) (see para. 2BPD–001).

A claim for interim rent is not lost if the action for a new tenancy is discontinued. See *Artoc Bank & Trust Ltd v. Prudential Assurance Co. PLC* [1984] 1 W.L.R. 1181; [1984] 3 All E.R. 538.

Other applications under Part II of Act of 1954

R97.10 **10.**—(1) An application for an order under section 31(2)(b) of the Act of 1954 and, unless made at the hearing of the application under section 24 thereof, an application for a certificate under section 37(4) of that Act may be made without notice being served on any other party.

(2) The mesne landlord to whose consent an application for the determination of any question arising under paragraph 4(3) of Schedule 6 to the Act of 1954 relates shall be made defendant to the claim.

R97.10.1 **Effect of rule**—In most cases the application for a certificate under s.37(4) will be made at the conclusion of the trial and the certificate will be embodied in the order under r.9.

If the Court dismisses an application for a new lease under s.31(2) it must make a declaration that it would have been satisfied as to one or other of the grounds specified in s.30(1)(d) (e) or (f) if the date for termination specified in the landlord's notice under s.25 or the date for commencement of the new tenancy specified in the tenant's request under s.26 had been a date not later than one year after the date so specified. In such cases the tenant has the option of leaving the date for termination as so specified or of applying to the Court for an order substituting such later date. The application must be made within fourteen days of the making of the declaration (s.31(2)(b)). This is a statutory time limit and cannot be extended.

Transfer of proceedings from county court

R97.11 **11.**—(2) Any proceedings under Part I of the Act of 1927 or Part II of the Act of 1954 that have been transferred from a county court shall proceed in the High Court as if they had been begun by claim form issued out of Chancery Chambers, and within 7 days after receipt of notification of the transfer the claimant must apply in the High Court for the appointment of a day and time for the attendance of the parties before the court.

(3) If the claimant fails to apply for an appointment within the period prescribed by paragraph (2) the defendant may do so.

Application for relief under section 16, etc., of the Act of 1954

R97.12 **12.** In any such proceedings as are mentioned in section 16(1) of the Act of 1954, paragraph 9(1) of Schedule 5 to that Act or paragraph 10(1) of that Schedule, an application for relief under that section or paragraph, as the case may be, may be made—

(a) in the applicant's statement of case; or

(b) in accordance with CPR Part 23 at any time before the trial; or

(c) at the trial.

Evidence of rateable value

R97.13 **13.** Where any dispute as to the rateable value of any holding has been referred under section 37(5) of the Act of 1954 to the Commissioners of Inland Revenue for decision by a valuation officer, any document purporting to be a statement by the valuation officer of his decision shall be admissible as evidence of the matters contained in it.

Application under section 19 of the Act of 1987

R97.14 **14.** A copy of the notice served under section 19(2)(a) of the Act of 1987 shall be appended to the claim form issued under section 19(1) thereof, and an additional copy of the notice shall be filed.

Claim form—The claimant must use the Pt 8 claim form: Practice Direction (Part 8), section A.3 (see para. 8BPD–002). **R97.14.1**

Application for acquisition order under section 29 of the Act of 1987

16.—(1) An application for an acquisition order under section 29 of the Act of 1987 shall— **R97.16**

(a) identify the premises to which the application relates and give such details of them as are necessary to show that section 25 of the Act of 1987 applies thereto;
(b) give such details of the applicants as are necessary to show that they constitute the requisite majority of qualifying tenants;
(c) state the name and address of the applicants and of the landlord of the premises, or, where the landlord cannot be found or his identity ascertained, the steps taken to find him or ascertain his identity;
(d) state the name and address of the person nominated by the applicants for the purposes of Part III of the Act of 1987;
(e) state the name and address of every person known to the applicants who is likely to be affected by the application, including, but not limited to, the other tenants of flats contained in the premises (whether or not they could have made an application), any mortgagee or superior landlord of the landlord, and any tenant's association; and
(f) state the grounds of the application,

and a copy of the notice served on the landlord under section 27 of the Act of 1987 shall be appended to the claim form, unless the requirement to serve such a notice has been dispensed with, and an additional copy of the notice shall be filed.

(2) The defendants to an application for an acquisition order under section 29 of the Act of 1987 shall be the landlord of the premises and the nominated person, where he is not an applicant.

(3) A copy of the claim form shall be served on each of the persons named by the applicant under paragraph (1)(e), together with a notice stating that he may apply under rule 8 to be made a party to the proceedings.

(4) Where the nominated person pays money into court in accordance with an order under section 33(1) of the Act of 1987, he shall file a copy of the certificate of the surveyor selected under section 33(2)(a) thereof.

Claim form—The claimant must use the Pt 8 claim form: Practice Direction (Part 8), Section A.3 (see para. 8BPD–002). **R97.16.1**

Application for order under section 38 or section 40 of the Act of 1987

17.—(1) An application for an order under section 38 or section 40 of the Act of 1987 shall state— **R97.17**

(a) the name and address of the applicant and of the other current parties to the lease or leases to which the application relates;
(b) the date of and parties to the lease or leases, the premises demised thereby, the relevant terms thereof and the variation sought;
(c) the name and address of every person who the applicant knows or has reason to believe is likely to be affected by the variation, including, but not limited to, the other tenants of flats contained in the premises of which the demised premises form a part, any mortgagee or superior landlord of the landlord, any mortgagee of the applicant, and any tenants' association; and
(d) the grounds of the application.

(2) The other current parties to the lease or leases shall be made defendants to the application.

(3) A copy of the application shall be served by the applicant on each of the

persons named by the applicant under paragraph (1)(c) and by the defendant on any other person who he knows or has reason to believe is likely to be affected by the variation, together, in each case, with a notice stating that the person may apply under rule 8 to be made a party to the proceedings.

(4) Any application under section 36 of the Act of 1987 shall be contained in the defendant's witness statement or affidavit, and paragraphs (1) to (3) shall apply to such an application as if the defendant were an applicant.

Service of notices in proceedings under the Act of 1987

R97.18 **18.** Where a notice is to be served in or before proceedings under the Act of 1987, it shall be served in accordance with section 54 and, in the case of service on a landlord, it shall be served at the address furnished under section 48(1).

Tenants' associations

R97.19 **19.** In rules 15, 16 and 17 a reference to a tenants' association is a reference to a recognised tenants' association within the meaning of section 29 of the Landlord and Tenant Act 1985 which represents tenants of the flats of which the demised premises form a part.

RSC ORDER 98

LOCAL GOVERNMENT FINANCE ACT 1982, PART III

R98.0.1 **Contents**

Interpretation

R98.1 **1.** In this order "the Act" means the Local Government Finance Act 1982 and a section referred to by number means the section so numbered in that Act.

Application by auditor for declaration

R98.2 **2.**—(1) Any application for a declaration under section 19(1) of the Act that an item of account is contrary to law shall be made by claim form.

(2) The claim form shall be served on the body to whose accounts the application relates and on any person against whom an order is sought under section 19(2).

(3) Not later than 7 days after filing the claim form in the Crown Office in accordance with Order 57, rule 2, the applicant shall file in that office a witness statement or affidavit stating the facts on which he intends to rely at the hearing of the application.

(4) The claim shall be entered for hearing within 6 weeks after the claim form has been filed in the Crown Office but, unless the court otherwise directs, the application shall not be heard sooner than 28 days after service of the claim form.

Appeal against decision of auditor

R98.3 **3.**—(1) A claim form by which an appeal is brought under section 19(4) or section 20(3) against the decision of an auditor shall be served on—

(a) the auditor who for the time being has responsibility for the audit of the accounts of the body in relation to whom the appeal relates;

(b) that body; and

(c) in the case of an appeal against a decision not to certify under section 20(1) that a sum or amount is due from another person, that person.

(2) Order 55, rules 4(2) and 5, shall apply to the appeal with the modification that the period of 28 days mentioned in the said rule 4(2) shall be calculated from the day on which the appellant received the auditor's statement of the reasons for his decision pursuant to a requirement under section 19(4) or section 20(2).

(3) Not later than seven days after filing the claim form in the Crown Office in accordance with Order 57, rule 2, the appellant must file in that office a witness statement or affidavit stating—
- (a) the reasons stated by the auditor for his decision;
- (b) the date on which he received the auditor's statement;
- (c) the facts on which he intends to rely at the hearing of the appeal;
- (d) in the case of a decision not to apply for a declaration, such facts within the appellant's knowledge as will enable the court to consider whether to exercise the powers conferred on it by section 19(2).

General provisions

4.—(1) Any proceedings in which the jurisdiction conferred on the High Court by section 19 or section 20 of the Act is invoked shall be assigned to the Queen's Bench Division and be heard by a single judge, unless the court directs that the matter shall be heard by a Divisional Court; and the court may, at any stage direct that any officer or member of the body to whose accounts the application of appeal relates be joined as a respondent. **R98.4**

(2) Except in so far as the court directs that the evidence on any such application or appeal shall be given orally, it shall be given by witness statement or affidavit.

(3) The applicant or appellant must forthwith after filing any witness statement or affidavit under rule 2(3) or 3(3) serve a copy thereof on every respondent and any person intending to oppose the application or appeal must, not less than 4 days before the hearing, serve on the applicant or appellant a copy of any witness statement or affidavit filed by him in opposition.

(4) Except by permission of the court, no witness statement or affidavit may be used at the hearing unless a copy thereof was served in accordance with paragraph (3).

RSC ORDER 99

INHERITANCE (PROVISION FOR FAMILY AND DEPENDANTS) ACT 1975

Contents **R99.0.1**

Editorial Introduction

Under the 1975 Act the Court has power to make orders for the making out of the estate of a deceased person of provision for members of the deceased's family and dependants, including for a person who lived with the deceased as husband or wife. The procedural machinery for the handling of applications is found in this Order. Proceedings may be assigned to the Chancery Division or the Family Division. The rules were revised when the 1975 Act, which replaced earlier legislation, came into force. **R99.0.2**

This Order governs all applications under the Act, whether in the Ch D or Fam D. The Family Proceedings Rules 1991 do not apply to proceedings under the Act, except to the limited extent to which r.10 makes them applicable. O.99 is not a complete procedural code. In particular the provisions of Pt 8 of CPR and the PD supplementary Part 8, apply to applications under O.99 so far as O.99 does not contain express provisions dealing with the point.

Related sources

R99.0.3
- Inheritance (Provision for Family and Dependants) Act 1975 (SCP 1997, Vol. 2, para. 7–613)
- County Courts Act 1984, s.25 (SCP 1999, Vol. 2, Section 2A, paras 2A–680 and 2A–681)
- CCR, O.48 (Family provision)
- *Chancery Division Practice Direction No. 8(B)(i)* Consent orders under the Inheritance (Provision for Family and Dependants) Act 1975 in the *Chancery Guide*, p. 90 (see para. D1–359)

Order to apply to High Court and county court

R99.A1 **A1.** This order applies to proceedings both in the High Court and the county court.

Interpretation

R99.1 **1.** In this order "the Act" means the Inheritance (Provision for Family and Dependants) Act 1975 and a section referred to by number means the section so numbered in that Act.

Assignment to Chancery or Family Division if proceedings in High Court

R99.2 **2.** Proceedings in the High Court under the Act may be assigned to the Chancery Division or to the Family Division.

Application for financial provision

R99.3 **3.**—(1) An application under section 1 is made by issue of a claim form.

(3) There shall be filed lodged with the court a witness statement or affidavit by the applicant in support of the claim, exhibiting an official copy of the grant of representation to the deceased's estate and of every testamentary document admitted to proof, and a copy of the witness statement or affidavit shall be served on every defendant with the claim form.

R99.3.1 **Jurisdiction**—The county court now has unlimited jurisdiction in applications under the Act: County Courts Act 1984, s.25, as amended by the Schedule to the High Court and County Courts Jurisdiction Order 1991. Article 7 of that Order (SCP 1999, Vol. 2, Section 20B, para. 20B–249) is applicable in deciding whether proceedings, wherever started, are to be allocated for trial to the county court or the High Court. In the High Court the proceedings may be brought in either the Ch D or the Fam D at the claimant's option (r.2). The claimant must use the Pt 8 claim form: CPRPD 8(B), Section A3. The claim will therefore be treated as being allocated to the multi-track: CPR 8.9(c). A Master or District Judge may therefore try the case: CPRPD 2B, para. 4.1. Under Art. 7 (above) claims of which the value is less than £25,000 are to be tried in the county court and claims of which the value is more than £50,000 are to be tried in the High Court, unless having regard to the criteria in para. (5) of the article, the Court considers it should be tried in the High Court or the county court respectively. Actions of which the value is between £25,000 and £50,000 may be tried either in the High Court or the county court. The value of an action under the Act is the amount of money which the applicant could reasonably state to be the financial worth of the claim to him (Art. 9(1)(b)(i)). Thus it is now the value of the applicant's claim which is material, not the value of the estate as such (though they may, of course, be the same).

R99.3.2 **Title to proceedings**—In the Ch D the action will be entitled:
"In the Estate of AB, deceased
Between PQ Plaintiff
— and —
(1) RS
(2) TV
(3) XY Defendants"
and the name of the Act should not appear in the title, but only be referred to in the body of the summons: Chancery Division PD 11. In the Fam.D. it is the practice to entitle the proceedings in the matter of the Act.

R99.3.3 **Time limit for proceedings**—By s.4 of the Act an application under s.2 shall not, except with the permission of the Court, be made after the end of the period of six months from the date on which a grant of representation to the estate of the deceased is first taken out. If the application is made outside the six months period the claim form should expressly ask the Court's permission to make the application out of time (*Practice Note* [1976] 1 W.L.R. 418). It seems that an application cannot be made before a grant has been taken out and that such an application if made will be struck out (*Re McBroom* [1992] 2 F.L.R. 49 (though *Re Searle* [1949] Ch. 73 decided under the 1938 Act does not appear to have been cited to the judge)).

Relief asked—The powers of the Court to make orders are stated in section 2 of the 1975 Act. Usually the claim form will simply ask for an order that such reasonable financial provision as the Court may think fit be made out of the net estate of the deceased, or some similar wording. However, if the applicant is seeking the permission of the Court under s.4 to make an application outside the six months time limit this should be asked for in a separate paragraph (see para. R99.3.5, above). There should also be separate paragraphs if the applicant is asking (1) that nominated property is to be treated as part of the net estate, pursuant to section 8 of the Act; (2) that the deceased's severable share of joint property be treated as part of the net estate, pursuant to s.9; (3) for an order setting aside a disposition made with the intention of defeating applications for financial provision under the Act pursuant to s.10; and (4) for an order under s.11 counteracting the effect of a contract to leave property by will. It is also usual to include a separate paragraph in the summons if a representation order is asked (see para. R99.4.2, below). **R99.3.4**

Evidence in support—The claimant is required to file an affidavit or witness statement in support of the claim with the Court. The filing of the affidavit in support is not a prerequisite to the issue of the claim form so that the claim may be issued before the evidence in support has been sworn or signed. The claimant's title to sue should be strictly proved. Thus a widow or widower should exhibit an official copy of the marriage certificate; a former wife or husband should exhibit a sealed copy of the decree absolute; and a child should exhibit an official copy of a full birth certificate. The claimant's evidence should also deal, so far as the claimant is able to do so, with all the matters to which the Court is required by section 3 of the Act to have regard in exercising its powers under s.2. In particular the evidence should deal with the financial resources and financial needs which the applicant has or is likely to have in the foreseeable future. The applicant's resources, both capital and income, therefore need to be set out. In doing this the standard form of affidavit of means in use in the Divorce Registry provides a useful aide memoire for matters to be covered. **R99.3.5**

Powers of court as to parties

4.—(1) The court may at any stage of proceedings under the Act direct that any person be added as a party to the proceedings or that notice of the proceedings be served on any person. **R99.4**

(2) Order 15, rule 13, shall apply to proceedings under the Act as it applies to the proceedings mentioned in paragraph (1) of that rule.

Parties—The personal representatives are necessary parties to any proceedings under the Act. Therefore in order to bring proceedings the applicant has to get a personal representative constituted if the executors or beneficiaries have not taken a grant. The taking of a grant by the applicant is no bar to an application under the Act and the personal representative may be the claimant because an application under the Act in no way impugns the validity of the grant, or of the will (if any). Thus there is no need for, *e.g.* the widow to renounce probate or her right to letters of administration if she wishes to bring proceedings; likewise if the executor or administrator is the principal beneficiary and is seeking to attack the deceased's severable joint share of property which has accrued by survivorship to the surviving joint tenant. At least one beneficiary should always be joined at the outset. There is no purpose in making only the personal representatives defendants (where they are not themselves also the beneficiaries) because the plaintiff's attack is not upon the personal representatives but upon the beneficiaries. The personal representatives should adopt a neutral stance in the proceedings and it is not for them to attempt to defeat the applicant's claim. That is a matter for the beneficiaries. **R99.4.1**

If the residuary beneficiaries are numerous, whether under a will or an intestacy (*e.g.* where the estate goes to a large class of cousins or cousins' descendants) only one or a small selection of them need be made parties, and a representation order may be asked for under O.15, r.13. This is an order appointing a defendant to represent the absent beneficiaries. If the beneficiaries are numerous the Court will usually make a representation order under O.15, r.13(2)(c) as being expedient to exercise the power for the purposes of saving expense. A representation order can also be asked for where a person or class of persons cannot be ascertained or readily ascertained or cannot be found: r.13(2)(a) and (b). If the claimant intends to ask for a representation order under O.15, r.13, he should expressly include the claim for the order in the claim.

Witness statement or affidavit in answer

5.—(1) A defendant to an application under section 1 who is a personal **R99.5**

representative of the deceased shall and any other defendant may, within 21 days after service of the claim form on him, inclusive of the day of service, file with the court a witness statement or affidavit in answer to the application.

(2) The witness statement or affidavit filed by a personal representative pursuant to paragraph (1) shall state to the best of the witness's ability—

(a) full particulars of the value of the deceased's net estate, as defined by section 25(1);

(b) the person or classes of persons beneficially interested in the estate, giving the names and (in the case of those who are not already parties) the addresses of all living beneficiaries, and the value of their interests so far as ascertained;

(c) if such be the case, that any living beneficiary (naming him) is a child or a patient within the meaning of CPR rule 21.1(2); and

(d) any facts known to the witness which might affect the exercise of the court's powers under the Act.

(3) Every defendant who lodges a witness statement or an affidavit shall at the same time serve a copy on the claimant and on every other defendant who is not represented by the same solicitor.

R99.5.1 **Evidence by personal representative defendant**—A defendant personal representative must set out the matters specified in (a), (b) and (c) of para. (2) above. Sub-para. (d) requires only facts known to the deponent to be stated in the evidence. The personal representative is not obliged to make enquiries and investigations in order to ascertain or confirm other matters within the 21 days after service of the claim form. Nor is he required to set out facts (possibly distasteful) which are not necessarily relevant at that stage; if they become relevant later he may lodge further evidence (*Practice Note (Inheritance—Family Provision)* [1976] 1 W.L.R. 418). The personal representatives should file a further statement shortly before the case comes to trial in order to bring the financial information about the estate up-to-date and in particular to enable the judge to make a calculation of the amount of the "net estate" for the purposes of the Act.

R99.5.2 **Beneficiaries' evidence in answer**—There is no provision in the rules as to what this is to contain. Like the applicant, the defendant beneficiary should deal with the matters to which the Court is directed by s.3 of the Act to have regard when exercising its powers under s.2. There is no obligation on the defendant to disclose his assets or income, but if a beneficiary declines to do so the Court is likely to draw the inference that his financial resources are amply sufficient for his needs without recourse to the property taken by him under the estate.

Separate representation

R99.6 **6.** Where an application under section 1 is made jointly by two or more applicants and the claim form is accordingly issued by one solicitor on behalf of all of them, they may, if they have conflicting interests, appear on any hearing of the claim by separate solicitors or counsel or in person, and where at any stage of the proceedings it appears to the court that one of the applicants is not but ought to be separately represented, the court may adjourn the proceedings until he is.

R99.6.1 **Scope of rule**—This is a special provision applying only to applications under the Act, making them an exception to the general rule that co-plaintiffs cannot sever and must be represented by the same solicitors and counsel. Rule 6 makes the old practice where a conflict of interest emerged of reconstituting the action with one of the former claimants as a defendant unnecessary. Now claimants with conflicting interests can sever and instruct and appear by separate solicitors and counsel.

Endorsement of memorandum on grant

R99.7 **7.** On the hearing of an application under section 1 the personal representative shall produce to the court the grant of representation to the deceased's estate and, if an order is made under the Act, the grant shall remain in the custody of the court until a memorandum of the order has been endorsed on or permanently annexed to the grant in accordance with section 19(3).

R99.7.1 **Procedure**—Section 19(3) of the Act enacts that a copy of every order made under the Act shall be entered and filed in the Principal Registry of the Fam.D. and that a memorandum of the order shall be endorsed on or permanently annexed to the probate or letters of administration. The Court making the order sends the grant to the Principal Registry of the Fam.D., together with a copy of the order, and the endorsement is made by the Principal Registry. Section 19(3) and this rule applies equally to consent orders as to other orders. Therefore when application is made for a consent order, whether personally or by post, the original grant must be produced or sent to the Court for onward transmission to the Principal Registry. This is so notwithstanding that any particular consent order may not, strictly speaking, be an order under the Act (*e.g.* because its provisions would not be within the Court's powers under the Act) Chancery Division Practice Direction 8B(i).

Subsequent applications in proceedings under section 1

9. Where an order has been made on an application under section 1, any subsequent application under the Act, whether made by a party to the proceedings or by any other person, shall be made by the issue of an application notice in accordance with CPR Part 23. **R99.9**

Drawing up and service of orders

10. The provisions of the Family Proceedings Rules relating to the drawing up and service of orders shall apply to proceedings in the Family Division under this order as if they were proceedings under those rules. **R99.10**

In this rule "Family Proceedings Rules" means rules made under section 40 of the Matrimonial and Family Proceedings Act 1984.

Drawing up and service of orders—It is r.2.43 of the Family Proceedings Rules (see SCP 1997, Vol. 2, Pt. 7, para. 7–066) which deals with drawing up of orders, and r.10.17 which deals with service of orders. Service of the order is by the Court in the Fam. D. Where the proceedings are in the Ch D, Part 40 of the CPR applies. **R99.10.1**

RSC ORDER 101

THE PENSIONS APPEAL TRIBUNALS ACT 1943

Contents **R101.0.1**

Assignment to Queen's Bench Division

1. Proceedings in the High Court under the Pensions Appeal Tribunals Act 1943, shall be assigned to the Queen's Bench Division. **R101.1**

Construction of reference to judge

2. In this order references to the judge shall be construed as references to the judge nominated by the Lord Chancellor under section 6(2) of the Pensions Appeal Tribunals Act 1943. **R101.2**

Application for permission to appeal

3.—(1) An application to the judge for permission to appeal against the decision of a Pensions Appeal Tribunal may not be made unless an application for such permission was made to the tribunal and was refused and must be made within 28 days after the date of the tribunal's refusal. **R101.3**

(2) The application to the judge, which may be made without notice being served on any other party, must be made by filing in the Crown Office a written statement of—

(a) the name and description of the applicant;

(b) the point of law as respects which the applicant alleges that the tribunal's decision was erroneous; and

(c) the date of the tribunal's decision refusing permission to appeal.

(3) If the application is made with the consent of the other party to the proceedings before the tribunal, that fact shall be included in the statement.

(4) On the making of the application the court officer shall request the chairman of the tribunal to give the judge a written statement of the reasons for the tribunal's decision to refuse permission to appeal, and within 7 days after receiving the request the chairman shall give the judge such a statement.

(5) The judge may determine the application without a hearing or may direct that the application be set down for hearing in private.

(6) Where the application is determined without a hearing, a copy of the judge's order shall be sent from the Crown Office to the applicant and to the other party to the proceedings before the tribunal; and where the application is to be set down for hearing, notice of the day and time fixed for the hearing shall be sent from that office to the applicant.

Appeal

R101.4 **4.**—(1) Without prejudice to Order 55, rule 3(2), the Notice of Appeal by which an appeal against the decision of a Pensions Appeal Tribunal is brought must state the question of law on which the appeal is brought, the date on which permission to appeal was granted and whether such permission was granted by the judge or the tribunal.

(2) Order 55, rules 3(3) and 4(2), shall not apply in relation to such an appeal, but the notice must be served and the appeal entered within 28 days after permission to appeal was granted.

(3) Within 28 days after service of the notice of appeal on him, the chairman of the tribunal must state a case setting out the facts on which the decision appealed against was based and must file the case in the Crown Office and serve a copy thereof on the appellant and on the respondent.

(4) Order 55, rule 5, shall apply in relation to such an appeal as if for the period of 21 days therein mentioned there were substituted a period of 6 weeks.

(5) At the hearing of the appeal the judge may order the case to be returned to the chairman for amendment.

(6) Order 55, rule 7(2), shall not apply in relation to the appeal.

(7) A copy of the judge's order on the appeal must be sent by the court officer to the appellant, the respondent and the chairman of the tribunal.

R101.4.1 **Generally**—It is to be noted that all applications and appeals under this order are to be entered in the Crown Office List. No fee is payable. The nominated judge is now Alliott J.

Rule 18 of the Pensions Appeal Tribunal (England and Wales) Rules 1980 (S.I. 1980 No. 1120) imposes an obligation on the Pensions Appeal Tribunal to give adequate reasons for its decisions. The reasons must be sufficient to show that the Tribunal has considered the points at issue between the parties and to indicate on which its conclusions are based. This will be particularly important in cases where there is dispute as to the medical diagnosis (*Secretary of State for Social Security v. Richards* [1996] C.O.D. 507, *per* Alliott J.).

R101.4.2 **Application for leave (r.3)**—The requirement that an application for permission must first be made to the Tribunal applies even where the judge himself believes that there are strong reasons for granting permission and indeed for allowing an appeal (*Hankinson v. Secretary of State for Social Security* [1995] C.O.D. 184 (Drake J.)).

R101.4.3 **Extension of time (r.3)**—Where an application is made to the Tribunal out of time for permission to appeal, and the Tribunal refuses to grant an extension of time, the judge has jurisdiction to give permission to appeal and to extend the time within which to appeal (*James v. Minister of Pensions* [1947] K.B. 867). As to extension of time the judge has a discretion to be exercised on the facts of every case in order, particularly, to see that on the one hand the rules are not wantonly ignored but on the other that, overall, justice is done. In this particular jurisdiction, which deals with claims by ex-servicemen and their widows and families, the judge is very anxious to see that justice is done without having overdue regard to the precise rules laid down for procedure (*Secretary of State for Social Security v. Titmus (Doris)* [1994] C.O.D. 266, DC (Drake J.)).

Evidence (r.4)—It is to be noted that by sub-rule (6) the provisions of O.55, r.7(2) empowering the High Court to receive further evidence on questions of fact are disapplied. In *Rivett v. Secretary of State for Social Security* [1990] C.O.D. 479, the tribunal had granted leave to appeal on the basis of fresh evidence. The nominated judge, Drake J., held that he had no jurisdiction to receive further evidence or to remit the case to the tribunal (which was in any event now *functus officio*) on the basis that it might reach a different decision if the evidence which it was desired to call had been before it. R101.4.4

The court does however have the power to remit the case to the tribunal where it is satisfied that the fresh evidence is so strong that the tribunal would be unlikely to be able to disregard it (*Brown v. Secretary of State for Social Security* [1996] C.O.D. 86).

Where no medical evidence could indicate how or why the condition giving rise to the claim had developed, the presumption falls in favour of the applicant (see *Armstrong* 3 W.P.A.R. 1449 (Denning J.) and generally *Marsh v. Secretary of State for Social Services* [1992] C.O.D. 33 (Drake J.)).

Although the burden and standard of proof is very unusual under English civil law—a reasonable doubt based on reliable evidence—the judge does not act as a court of appeal in the ordinary sense. He may only consider matters of law but an absence of reliable evidence before the Tribunal is a matter of law, to which the judge may properly have regard (*Secretary of State for Social Services v. Tait* [1995] C.O.D. 440 (Macpherson of Cluny J.)).

As to military activity whose consequences may be excluded from the definition of war-injury within the meaning of the scheme, see *Secretary of State for Social Security v. Jordan* [1994] C.O.D. 396.

RSC ORDER 106

PROCEEDINGS RELATING TO SOLICITORS: THE SOLICITORS ACT, 1974

Contents R106.0.1

Editorial Introduction

The rules in this Order are concerned with the Court's exercise of jurisdiction in matters concerning solicitors under Pt III (Remuneration of solicitors) and Sched. 1 (Powers exercisable on intervention in solicitor's practice) of the 1974 Act. R106.0.2

Related sources

- Solicitors Act 1974 (SCP 1999, Vol. 2, Section 15A, para. 15A–1) R106.0.3
- CPR 48.8, 48.9, 48.10 and Related Directions

Forms

The following Queen's Bench Masters' Practice Forms are relevant to O.106 (Vol. 2, Section 1B, paras 1B–145 to 1B–150): N208 PART 8 Application N244 Application Notice (Part 23). R106.0.4

- PF187—Application for solicitor's charging order (O.106, r.2)

- PF188—Charging order, solicitor's costs (O.106, r.2)
- Costs form 17—Order for delivery of a bill of costs (Solicitors Act 1974, s.68: O.106)
- Costs form 18—Order on client's application to tax solicitor's bill of costs (O.106)
- Costs form 19—Order on solicitor's application to tax bill of costs (O.106)
- PF195—Application to assess after action brought (O.106, r.2)
- Costs form 20—Breakdown of costs
- Costs form 21—Request for hearing date

Interpretation

R106.1 **1.**—(1) In this order—

"the Act" means the Solicitors Act 1974 and a section referred to by number means the section so numbered in that Act;

"appeal" means an appeal to the High Court against an order made by the tribunal on an application or complaint under the Act.

(2) Expressions used in this Order which are used in the Act have the same meanings in this order as in the Act.

R106.1.1 **History of rule**—Substituted by S.I. 1975 No. 128 (L2) and S.I. 1979 No. 1716.

Jurisdiction under Part III of Act

R106.2 **2.**—(2) The jurisdiction of the High Court under Part III of the Act may be exercised by—

(a) A judge;
(b) A master, a taxing master or a district judge of the Family Division; or
(c) A district judge if the costs are for contentious business done in proceedings in the district registry of which he is the district judge or for non contentious business.

R106.2.1 **History of rule**—Amended by S.I. 1971 No. 1269, S.I. 1971 No. 1955, S.I. 1972 No. 1194, S.I. 1986 No. 632 and S.I. 1994 No. 1975.

R106.2.2 **Procedure for assessment of a Solicitor's bill of Costs**—Application is by the alternative procedure for Claims under Part 8. See also Practice Direction supplementing Pts 8 and 8B, Section A. See also Directions relating to Part 48, paras 2.17—2.36 (48PD–015).

Power to order solicitor to deliver cash account, etc.

R106.3 **3.**—(1) Where the relationship of solicitor and client exists or has existed the court may, on the application of the client or his personal representatives, make an order for—

(a) the delivery by the solicitor of a cash account;
(b) the payment or delivery up by the solicitor of money or securities;
(c) the delivery to the claimant of a list of the moneys or securities which the solicitor has in his possession or control on behalf of the claimant;
(d) the payment into or lodging in court of any such moneys or securities.

(2) An application for an order under this rule must be made by the issue of claim form, or if in proceedings by an application in accordance with CPR Part 23.

(3) If the defendant alleges that he has a claim for costs, the court may make such order for detailed assessment in accordance with CPR Part 47 and payment, or securing the payment, thereof and the protection of the defendant's lien, if any, as the court thinks fit.

R106.3.1 **History of rule**—Amended by S.I. 1994 No. 1975.

Certificate to be submitted with solicitor's application for detailed assessment

R106.5A **5A.** A solicitor who applies for an order under the Act for the detailed assessment in accordance with CPR Part 47 of his bill of costs shall lodge with his application a certificate that all the relevant requirements of the Act have been satisfied.

History of rule—Amended by S.I. 1986 No. 632. R106.5A.1

Applications under Schedule 1 to Act

6.—(1) Proceedings in the High Court under Schedule 1 to the Act shall be assigned to the Chancery Division. R106.6

(2) The claim form by which an application for an order under the said Schedule is made must be entitled in the matter of a solicitor, or a deceased solicitor, as the case may be (without naming him) and in the matter of the Act.

(3) Where an order has been made under paragraph 9(4), 9(5) or 10 of the said Schedule an application for an order under paragraph 9(8) or 9(10) may be made in accordance with CPR Part 23 in the proceedings in which the first mentioned order was made.

History of rule—Amended by S.I. 1975 No. 128. R106.6.1

Defendants to applications under Schedule 1 to Act

7. The defendant to a claim by which an application for an order under Schedule 1 to the Act is made shall be— R106.7

(a) if the application is for an order under paragraph 5 thereof, the solicitor or, as the case may be, every member of the firm, on whose behalf the money in respect of which the order is sought is held;

(b) if the application is for an order under paragraph 6(4) or 9(8) thereof, the Law Society;

(c) if the application is for an order under paragraph 8, 9(4) or 9(5) thereof, the person against whom the order is sought;

(d) if the application is for an order under paragraph 9(10) thereof, the person from whom the Law Society obtained possession of the documents by virtue of paragraph 9 or 10;

(e) if the application is for an order under paragraph 10 thereof for the re-direction of postal packets addressed to a solicitor or his firm, the solicitor or, as the case may be, every member of the firm;

(f) if the application is for an order under paragraph 11 thereof, the solicitor or personal representative in substitution for whom the appointment of a new trustee is sought and, if he is a co-trustee, the other trustee or trustees.

History of rule—Amended by S.I. 1975 No. 128. R106.7.1

Rule 7(a) and (e) do not apply in the case of a recognised body: Solicitors Incorporated Practices Order 1991 (S.I. 1991 No. 2684).

Interim order restricting payment out of banking account

8. At any time after the issue of a claim form by which an application for an order under paragraph 5 of Schedule 1 to the Act is made, the court may, on the application of the claimant made without notice in accordance with CPR Part 23 make an interim order under that paragraph to have effect until the hearing of the application and include therein a further order requiring the defendant to show cause at the hearing why an order under that paragraph should not be made. R106.8

History of rule—Amended by S.I. 1975 No. 128. R106.8.1

Adding parties, etc.

9. The court may, at any stage of proceedings under Schedule 1 to the Act, R106.9

order any person to be added as a party to the proceedings or to be given notice thereof.

Service of documents

R106.10 **10.**—(1) Any document required to be served on the Law Society in proceedings under this order shall be served by sending it by prepaid post to the secretary of the Law Society.

(2) Subject to paragraph (1) a claim form by which an application under Schedule 1 to the Act is made, an order under paragraph 5 of that Schedule or rule 8 and any other document not required to be served personally which is to be served on a defendant to proceedings under the said Schedule shall, unless the court otherwise directs, be deemed to be properly served by sending it by prepaid post to the defendant at his last known address.

R106.10.1 **History of rule**—Amended by S.I. 1966 No. 1514 and S.I. 1975 No. 128.

Constitution of Divisional Court to hear appeals

R106.11 **11.** Every appeal shall be heard by a Divisional Court of the Queen's Bench Division consisting, unless the Lord Chief Justice otherwise directs, of not less than three judges.

Title, service, etc., of notice of appeal

R106.12 **12.**—(1) The notice of appeal by which an appeal is brought must be entitled in the matter of a solicitor, or, as the case may be, a solicitor's clerk, without naming him, and in the matter of the Act.

(2) Unless the court otherwise orders, the persons to be served with such notice are every party to the proceedings before the tribunal and the Law Society.

(3) Order 55, rule 4(2) shall apply in relation to the appeal as if for the period of 28 days therein specified there were substituted a period of 14 days.

(4) Order 55, rule 4(4) shall not apply and the said period of 14 days shall begin with the day on which a statement of the tribunal's findings was filed pursuant to section 48(1).

R106.12.1 **History of rule**—Amended by S.I. 1975 No. 128.

Law Society to produce certain documents

R106.13 **13.**—(1) Within 7 days after being served with notice of appeal the Law Society must lodge in the Crown Office three copies of each of the following documents—

(a) the order appealed against, together with the statement of the tribunal's findings required by section 48(1) of the Act;

(b) any document lodged by a party with the tribunal which is relevant to a matter in issue on the appeal; and

(c) the transcript of the shorthand note, or, as the case may be, the note taken by the chairman of the tribunal of the evidence in the proceedings before the tribunal.

(2) At the hearing of the appeal the court shall direct by whom the costs incurred in complying with paragraph (1) are to be borne and may order them to be paid to the Law Society by one of the parties notwithstanding that the Society does not appear at the hearing.

R106.13.1 **History of rule**—Amended by S.I. 1975 No. 128.

Restriction on requiring security for costs

R106.14 **14.** No person other than an appellant who was the applicant in the proceedings before the tribunal, shall be ordered to give security for the costs of an appeal.

History of rule—Amended by S.I. 1975 No. 128. R106.14.1

Disciplinary committee's opinion may be required

15. The court may direct the tribunal to furnish the court with a written statement of their opinion on the case which is the subject-matter of an appeal or on any question arising therein, and where such a direction is given, the clerk to the tribunal must as soon as may be lodge three copies of such statement in the Crown Office and at the same time send a copy to each of the parties to the appeal. R106.15

Persons entitled to be heard on appeal

16. A person who has not been served with notice of appeal but who desires to be heard in opposition to the appeal shall, if he appears to the court to be a proper person to be so heard, be entitled to be so heard. R106.16

Discontinuance of appeal

17.—(1) An appellant may at any time discontinue his appeal by serving notice of discontinuance on the clerk to the tribunal and every other party to the appeal and, if the appeal has been entered, by lodging a copy of the notice in the Crown Office. R106.17

(2) Where an appeal has been discontinued in accordance with paragraph (1) it shall be treated as having been dismissed with an order for payment by the appellant of the costs of and incidental to the appeal, including any costs incurred by the Law Society in complying with rule 13(1).

History of rule—Amended by S.I. 1975 No. 128. R106.17.1

Solicitors Act 1974—For the general effect of the Solicitors Act 1974, and the rules concerning accounts, etc., of solicitors, see SCP 1999, Vol. 2, Section 15, "Solicitors". R106.17.2

RSC ORDER 108

PROCEEDINGS RELATING TO CHARITIES: THE CHARITIES ACT, 1993

Contents R108.0.1

Editorial Introduction

The Order encompasses "Charity Proceedings", defined in r.1 as High Court proceedings brought under the Court's jurisdiction in relation to charities and charitable trusts, and proceedings under the Charities Act, in particular appeals from orders of the Charity Commissioners made under the Act and applications to enforce such orders. R108.0.2

Interpretation

1. In this order— R108.1

"the Act" means the Charities Act 1993;

"certificate" means a certificate that a case is a proper one for an appeal;

"charity proceedings" means proceedings in the High Court under the court's jurisdiction with respect to charities or under the court's jurisdiction with respect to trusts in relation to the administration of a trust for charitable purposes;

"the Commissioners" means the Charity Commissioners for England and Wales.

Assignment to Chancery Division

R108.2 **2.** Charity proceedings and proceedings brought in the High Court by virtue of the Act shall be assigned to the Chancery Division.

Application for permission to appeal or to take charity proceedings

R108.3 **3.**—(1) An application shall not be made under section 16(13) of the Act for permission to appeal against an order of the Commissioners unless the applicant has requested the Commissioners to grant a certificate and they have refused to do so.

(2) An application under section 33(5) of the Act for permission to start charity proceedings must be made within 21 days after the refusal by the Commissioners of an order authorising proceedings.

(3) The application must be made by lodging in Chancery Chambers a statement showing—

- (a) the name, address and description of the applicant;
- (b) particulars of the order against which it is desired to appeal or of the proceedings which it is desired to take;
- (c) the date of the Commissioners' refusal to grant a certificate or an order authorising the taking of proceedings;
- (d) the grounds on which the applicant alleges that it is a proper case for an appeal or for taking proceedings.

(4) The application may be made without notice in the first instance and if it is made with the consent of any other party to the proposed appeal or proposed proceedings that fact shall be mentioned in the statement.

(5) If the judge on considering the application so directs, the Commissioners shall furnish him with a written statement of their reasons for refusing a certificate or, as the case may be, an order authorising the taking of proceedings, and a copy of any such statement shall be sent from Chancery Chambers to the applicant.

(6) Unless, after considering the applicant's statement and the statement (if any) of the Commissioners, the judge decides to give the permission applied for without a hearing, the application shall be set down for hearing, and the hearing may be in private if the judge so directs.

(7) Where the application is determined without a hearing, a copy of the judge's order shall be sent from Chancery Chambers to the applicant and the Commissioners; and where the application is to be set down for hearing, notice of the day and time fixed for the hearing shall be sent from that office to the applicant.

R108.3.1 **Effect of rule**—This rule, which expressly applies to an application under section 16(13) of the Charities Act 1993, also applies to s.16(14), *i.e.* to an order of the Commissioners establishing a scheme for the administration of a charity, and therefore an appeal against such an order can be brought only on the grant of a certificate by the Commissioners or with the leave of a Chancery Judge in accordance or with the procedure set out in this Rule (see *Childs v. Att.-Gen.* [1973] 1 W.L.R. 497; [1973] 2 All E.R. 108, CA).

R108.3.2 **Leave to commence proceedings**—Application for an order under section 33(2) of the 1993 Act authorising charity proceedings should be made in the case of a charity to the Secretary, Charity Commission, St Alban's House, 57–60 Haymarket, London SW1Y 4ZX. A draft of the proposed notice of appeal should accompany the application.

Application for enforcement of order or direction of Commissioners

R108.4 **4.** Order 52, rule 1(4), shall apply in relation to an application under section 88 of the Act as if for the reference in that rule to a single judge of the Queen's Bench Division there was substituted a reference to a single judge of the Chancery Division.

Directions by persons other than the Commissioners—Although s.88 of the 1993 Act refers only to the ability of the Charity Commissioners to apply to the High Court to punish the non-compliance of an order or direction with an order for committal, disobedience to a direction made by a person conducting an inquiry for the Commissioners pursuant to section 8 of the 1993 Act can at the instance of the Commissioners be similarly punished. R108.4.1

Appeal against order, etc., of Commissioners

5.—(1) An appeal against an order or decision of the Commissioners shall be heard and determined by a single judge. R108.5

(2) Such an appeal must be brought by a notice of appeal to which the Attorney-General, unless he is the appellant, shall be made a defendant in addition to any other person who is a proper defendant thereto.

(3) A notice of appeal under this rule must state the grounds of the appeal and, except with the permission of the judge hearing the appeal, the appellant shall not be entitled to rely on any ground not so stated.

Service on Commissioners

6. Any document required or authorised to be served on the Commissioners in proceedings to which this order relates must be served on the Treasury Solicitor in accordance with Order 77, rule 4(2). R108.6

RSC ORDER 109

THE ADMINISTRATION OF JUSTICE ACT 1960

Contents R109.0.1

Applications under Act

1.—(1) Any of the following applications, that is to say— R109.1

(a) an application under section 2 of the Administration of Justice Act 1960, or under that section as applied by section 13 of that Act, to extend the time within which an application may be made to a Divisional Court for permission to appeal to the House of Lords under section 1 of that Act, or section 13 thereof, from an order or decision of that court, and

(b) an application by a defendant under section 9(3) of that Act to a Divisional Court for permission to be present on the hearing of any proceedings preliminary or incidental to an appeal to the House of Lords under section 1 of that Act from a decision of that court

must be made to a Divisional Court except in vacation when it may be made to a judge.

(2) Any such application to a Divisional Court, if not made in the proceedings before the Divisional Court from whose order or decision the appeal in question is brought, must be made by the issue of a claim form.

(3) Any such application to a judge must, in the case of such an application as is referred to in paragraph (1)(a) be made by the issue of a claim form and, in the case of such an application as is referred to in paragraph (1)(b) need not be served on any other person unless, in the latter case, the judge otherwise directs.

(4) No application notice or copy of the claim form (as the case may be) by

which such an application as is referred to in paragraph (1)(b) is made need be given to any party affected thereby unless the Divisional Court otherwise directs.

(5) Where any application to which this rule applies is made in vacation to a single judge and the judge refuses the application, the applicant shall be entitled to have the application determined by a Divisional Court.

Appeals under section 13 of Act

R109.2 **2.**—(1) An appeal to a Divisional Court of the High Court under section 13 of the Administration of Justice Act 1960, shall be heard and determined by a Divisional Court of the Queen's Bench Division.

(3) Order 55, rules 4(2) and 5, shall not apply in relation to an appeal to a Divisional Court under the said section 13.

(4) Unless the court gives permission, there shall be not more than 4 clear days between the date on which the order or decision appealed against was made and the day named in the notice of appeal for the hearing of the appeal.

(5) The notice must be served, and the appeal entered, not less than one clear day before the day named in the notice for the hearing of the appeal.

Release of appellant on bail

R109.3 **3.**—(1) Where, in the case of an appeal under section 13 of the Administration of Justice Act 1960, to a Divisional Court or to the House of Lords from a Divisional Court, the appellant is in custody, the High Court may order his release on his giving security (whether by recognizance, with or without sureties, or otherwise and for such reasonable sum as the court may fix) for his appearance, within 10 days after the judgment of the Divisional Court or, as the case may be, of the House of Lords, on the appeal before the court from whose order or decision the appeal is brought unless the order or decision is reversed by that judgment.

(2) Order 79, rule 9(1) to (6) and (8) shall apply in relation to an application to the High Court for bail pending an appeal under the said section 13 to which this rule applies, and to the admission of a person to bail in pursuance of an order made on the application, as they apply in relation to an application to that court for bail in criminal proceedings, and to the admission of a person to bail in pursuance of an order made on the application, but with the substitution, for references to the defendant, of references to the appellant, and, for references to the prosecutor, of references to the court officer of the court from whose order or decision the appeal is brought and to the parties to the proceedings in that court who are directly affected by the appeal.

RSC ORDER 110

ENVIRONMENTAL CONTROL PROCEEDINGS

R110.0.1 **Contents**

Editorial Introduction

R110.0.2 This Order enables an authority responsible for enforcing the legislation referred to in r.1 to protect the environment from harm in the context of breaches of planning control, tree-preservation orders, works to listed buildings and hazardous substances. An authority may obtain an injunction by proceedings in the High Court against a person whose identity is unknown. Rule 1 provides the procedure to be followed. The comparable county court procedure is found in Sched. 2, CCR, O.49, r.7.

Related sources

R110.0.3
- CPR, Pt 23 (General rules about applications for court orders)
- CPR, Pt 25 (Interim remedies)
- CPR, Sched. 1, CCR, O.49, r.7

Injunctions to prevent environmental harm

1.—(1) An injunction under— R110.1

(a) section 187B or 214A of the Town and Country Planning Act 1990;
(b) section 44A of the Planning (Listed Buildings and Conservation Areas) Act 1990; or
(c) section 26AA of the Planning (Hazardous Substances) Act 1990

may be granted against a person whose identity is unknown to the applicant; and in the following provisions of this rule such an injunction against such a person is referred to as "an injunction under paragraph (1)" and the person against whom it is sought is referred to as "the defendant".

(2) An applicant for an injunction under paragraph (1) shall, in the claim form, describe the defendant by reference to—

(a) a photograph,
(b) a thing belonging to or in the possession of the defendant, or
(c) any other evidence,

with sufficient particularity to enable service to be effected.

(3) An applicant for an injunction under paragraph (1) shall file in support of the application evidence by witness statement or affidavit—

(a) verifying that he was unable to ascertain, within the time reasonably available to him, the defendant's identity,
(b) setting out the action taken to ascertain the defendant's identity, and
(c) verifying the means by which the defendant has been described in the application and that the description is the best that the applicant is able to provide.

(4) Paragraph (2) is without prejudice to the power of the Court to make an order for service by an alternative method or dispensing with service.

Effect of rule—The sections referred to in para. (1)(a) enable a local planning authority to seek an injunction to restrain either (1) a breach of planning control, or (2) and offences against sections 210 or 211 of the Town and Country Planning Act 1990, in each case whether actual or apprehended. R110.1.1

The section mentioned in para. (1)(b) enables a planning authority (which expressly includes the Historic Buildings and Monuments Commission) to seek an injunction to restrain actual or apprehended contravention of section 9(1) or (2) of the Planning (Listed Buildings and Conservation Areas) Act 1990, which prohibit demolition, alterations, etc., unless authorised.

The section mentioned in para. (1)(c) enables a hazardous substances authority to seek an injunction to restrain any actual or apprehended contravention of the provisions for hazardous substances control.

"application made in accordance wth CPR Pt 23"—Formerly, in the High Court application for an injunction was made by originating summons and it might have been expected that, under the CPR, application would be made by claim form. However, r.1(2) provides that application should be made on application notice and that the general rules as to applications for court orders found in Pt 23 should apply, subject to paras (2), (3) and (4) of this rule. R110.1.2

RSC, O.110 applies to proceedings in the High Court for the relief referred to in r.1(1). Applications for similar relief in a county court are governed by Sched. 2, CCR, O.49, r.7 (see C49.7). That rule is listed in Table 2 of Practice Direction (CPR, Pt 8 and Sched. 1 and Sched. 2 to the CPR) (see para. 8PD–001). Consequently, Section B of that Practice Direction applies and the applicant must use the Pt 8 claim form procedure as modified therein.

RSC ORDER 111

THE SOCIAL SECURITY ADMINISTRATION ACTS 1992

Contents R111.0.1

Judge by whom appeals and references to be heard

R111.1 **1.** Any appeal to the High Court against a decision of the Secretary of State on a question of law under the Social Security Administration Act 1992, and any question of law referred to the High Court by the Secretary of State under the Act, shall be heard and determined by a single judge of the Queen's Bench Division.

Appeal: preliminary statement of facts by Secretary of State

R111.2 **2.** Any person who by virtue of section 18 or 58(8) of the Social Security Administration Act 1992 is entitled and wishes to appeal against a decision of the Secretary of State on a question of law must within the prescribed period or within such further time as the Secretary of State may allow serve on the Secretary of State a notice of appeal requiring him to state a case setting out the facts on which his decision was based and his decision.

If within 28 days after receipt of notice of the decision a request is made to the Secretary of State in accordance with regulations made under the Act to furnish a statement of the grounds of the decision, the prescribed period for the purpose of this rule shall be 28 days after receipt of that statement, and if no such request is made within 28 days after receipt of notice of the decision the prescribed period for that purpose shall be 28 days after receipt of that notice.

Special provisions as to appeals

R111.3 **3.** Order 55 shall not apply in relation to an appeal under the said section 18 or 58(8) but Order 56, rules 9 to 12, shall apply in relation to the case stated by the Secretary of State for the purpose of any such appeal as they apply in relation to any other case stated by a Minister except that Order 56, rule 10(4) and (7) as so applied, shall have effect as if for the period of 14 days and 7 days therein specified there were substituted a period of 28 days.

Reference of question of law

R111.4 **4.**—(1) Where under the said section 18 or 58(8) the Secretary of State refers to the High Court for decision any question of law, he must state that question together with the facts relating thereto in a case.

(2) Order 56, rules 9(1), 10(1), 11 and 12, shall apply in relation to a case stated under paragraph (1) of this rule as they apply in relation to any other case stated by a Secretary of State.

(3) The notice of appeal by which proceedings for the determination of the question of law stated in the case are begun, together with a copy of the case, must be served by the Secretary of State on every person as between whom and the Secretary of State the question has arisen.

(4) Unless the court having jurisdiction to determine the question of law otherwise directs, the appeal or reference shall not be heard sooner than 28 days after service of notice of appeal.

Powers of Court hearing appeal or reference

R111.5 **5.**—(1) Without prejudice to Order 56, rule 11, as applied by rules 3 and 4 of this order, the court hearing an appeal or reference under the said section 18 or 58(8) may order the case stated by the Secretary of State to be returned to the Secretary of State for him to hear further evidence.

(2) The court hearing such an appeal or reference shall determine all questions arising thereon, and in the case of any such appeal may reverse,

affirm or amend the decision appealed against or make such other order as it thinks fit.

RSC ORDER 112

APPLICATIONS FOR USE OF BLOOD TESTS IN DETERMINING PATERNITY

Contents R112.0.1

Editorial Introduction

Under the Family Law Reform Act 1969, Pt III (SCP 1997, Vol. 2, para. 7–502), in any civil proceedings in which the parentage of any person falls to be determined, the Court may give a direction for the taking of blood tests. The Secretary of State may by regulations make provision as to the manner of giving effect to directions (see para. R112.6.13). The procedure to be followed in the exercise of this jurisdiction is stated in this Order. R112.0.2

Interpretation

1. In this Order— R112.1

"the Act" means Part III of the Family Law Reform Act 1969;

"blood samples" and "blood tests" have the meanings assigned to them by section 25 of the Act;

"direction" means a direction for the use of blood tests under section 20(1) of the Act;

"the court officer" means the officer of the court who draws up a direction.

Application for direction

2.—(1) Except with the permission of the court, an application in any proceedings for a direction shall be in accordance with CPR Part 23 and a copy of the application notice shall be served on every party to the proceedings (other than the applicant) and to any other person from whom the direction involves the taking of blood samples. R112.2

(3) Any notice required by this rule to be served on a person who is not a party to the proceedings shall be served on him personally.

Children Act 1989, s.89—Section 89 amends s.20 of the 1969 Act to the effect that where the person whose paternity is in dispute is under the age of 18 the application shall specify who is to carry out the tests and the order shall specify that person to do so unless it is considered to be inappropriate, in which case the court will refuse the application. R112.2.1

Applications involving children under 16 and patients

3. Where an application is made for a direction in respect of a person who is either— R112.3

(a) under 16; or

(b) suffering from a mental disorder within the meaning of the Mental Health Act 1983 and incapable of understanding the nature and purpose of blood tests,

the application notice shall state the name and address of the person having the care and control of the person under disability and shall be served on him instead of on the person under disability.

Addition as a party of person to be tested

4. Where an application is made for a direction involving the taking of R112.4

blood samples from a person who is not a party to the proceedings in which the application is made, the court may at any time direct that person to be made a party to the proceedings.

Service of direction and adjournment of proceedings

R112.5 **5.** Where the court gives a direction in any proceedings, the court officer shall send a copy to every party to the proceedings and to every other person from whom the direction involves the taking of blood samples and, unless otherwise ordered, further consideration of the proceedings shall be adjourned until the court receives a report pursuant to the direction.

Service of copy report

R112.6 **6.** On receipt by the court of a report made pursuant to a direction, the court officer shall send a copy to every party to the proceedings and to every other person from whom the direction involved the taking of blood samples.

R112.6.1 **Practice in Family Division (rr.1–6)**—The following *Practice Note* [1972] 1 W.L.R. 353; [1972] 1 All E.R. 640 was issued on February 17, 1972.

When a direction is given pursuant to Pt III of the Family Law Reform Act 1969 for the use of blood tests in proceedings in the Family Division and divorce county courts the arrangements for the taking and testing of blood samples will be made by the solicitor for the party on whose application the direction was given.

Where the application is proceeding at the Principal Registry, on receipt of a copy of the court's direction the solicitor should apply to the Registry for the necessary number of copies of the Direction Form prescribed by the Blood Tests (Evidence of Paternity) Regulations 1971; a form is required in respect of each person to be tested. He should, in consultation with the solicitors for the other parties, get in touch with a tester (a list of the authorised testers is available) and a sampler and make arrangements for the taking and testing of the samples. The solicitor should then complete Pts I and II of a Direction Form in respect of each person to be tested and attend with the forms before the District Judge by whom the direction was given, or if it was not given by a District Judge before the District Judge for the day. If the District Judge is satisfied with the arrangements he will sign the forms and return them to the solicitor with a copy of the Notes for the Guidance of Samplers.

The subsequent procedure is set out in the Regulations and in RSC, O.112 in the case of High Court proceedings and O.46, r.23 of the County Court Rules (see now CCR 1981, O.47, r.5) in the case of proceedings in the county courts.

See *R. v. R.* [1973] 1 W.L.R. 1115; [1973] 3 All E.R. 933; if an application for a blood test to be used is opposed, the District Judge should adjourn the application to a Judge.

R112.6.2 **H.I.V. Tests—children (rr.1–6)**—Applications directed at the question of whether there should be H.I.V. tests of children should come before a High Court Judge, whether the application out of which they arise is before a Family Proceedings Court or a County Court or is in the High Court. The fact that such an application is made should, of itself, lead directly to the vertical transfer of the substantive application to the High Court for hearing by a High Court Judge or that issue. It can then, if thought appropriate, be redirected down to the level at which it should be heard as a substantive issue in the light of whatever the decision is on the H.I.V. testing point. (*Re H.I.V. Tests (Note)* [1994] 3 F.L.R. 148, *per* Singer J.)

R112.6.3 **Injunction (rr.1–6)**—*Re I. (A Minor), The Times,* May 22, 1987—injunction granted under s.37(1) of Supreme Court Act 1981 to prevent a mother from leaving the jurisdiction before she could have an opportunity of providing a blood sample (as she said she was willing to do) for the purpose of DNA testing to establish the true paternity of her child. It was considered likely that if she left the country she would not return.

R112.6.4 **Principles on which Court should act in determining whether or not to direct use of blood test (rr.1–6)**—See *S. v. S. W. v. Official Solicitor* [1972] A.C. 24; [1970] 3 All E.R. 107, HL.

In considering whether to order the taking of blood tests the court is entitled to take into account the probable outcome of the proceedings in which the issue arises. The applicant's association with the mother had ceased before the birth of the child. Parental responsibility or contact orders were unlikely to be made, and an order for blood tests would achieve no more than a theoretical declaration of paternity, the benefit of which would be outweighed by the risk of disruption to the child's family unit as a result of such tests (*Re F (A Minor) (Paternity Test)* [1993] 1 F.L.R. 598, *sub nom. Re F (A Minor) (Blood Tests: Parental Rights)* at [1993] 3 W.L.R. 369 and [1993] 3 All E.R. 596, and *sub nom. Re A (A Minor) (Blood Tests)* at [1993] 1 F.C.R. 932, CA. See also *Re T (A Minor) (Blood Tests)* [1993] 1 F.L.R. 901, CA).

The Court should decline to exercise its discretion to make a direction for the use of blood tests under s.20 of the Family Law Reform Act 1969 where the mother was adamant that she would not comply with any direction given by the Court *Re CB (A Minor) (Blood Tests)* [1994] 2 F.L.R. 762, Wall J. See also *Re G (A Minor) (Blood Tests)* [1994] 1 F.L.R. 495, M. Horowitz, Q.C.

There is no jurisdiction to make a free-standing direction for the use of blood tests. *Re E (Parental Responsibility: Blood Tests)* [1995] 1 F.L.R. 392, CA.

The Court had a duty to determine what inference should be drawn from the refusal to submit to direction for blood test. A forensic inference is the proper inference (*Re G (Parentage: Blood Sample), sub nom. Re G (A Minor) (Paternity: Blood Tests)* [1997] 1 F.L.R. 360, Ward L.J., CA).

By agreement (rr.1–6)—It should be noted that the provisions of the Act do not prohibit the obtaining of blood test evidence by agreement without any direction. **R112.6.5**

Separate representation (rr.1–6)—The court has power, if it thinks separate representation of the child is desirable, to appoint the Official Solicitor (subject to his consent) or some other person as litigation friend of the child. Such appointments have almost invariably been of the Official Solicitor. This would enable the guardian to be heard on the question whether or not blood tests should be directed, but it is now usual wherever a question of paternity needs to be resolved to direct the use of blood tests and it is not necessary for the court in the first instance to make an order appointing the Official Solicitor as litigation friend of the minor unless either: (a) the minor is 10 years old or over, or (b) there are special circumstances making such appointment immediately desirable. Where no order appointing the Official Solicitor is made at the time blood tests are directed the direction for blood tests will include a provision that the proceedings be restored for further directions by the District Judge when the report by the tester has been filed. The District Judge will then decide, in the light of the position following the report, whether to order that the Official Solicitor be appointed litigation friend of the minor. Such an order will be made, for example, where in the opinion of the Court the issue as to paternity is still a live one or other aspects of the case make it desirable that the minor should be represented by the Official Solicitor (*Practice Direction* [1975] 1 W.L.R. 81; [1975] 1 All E.R. 223). It should be noted that if a direction for blood tests is given, the appointment of a guardian *ad litem* does not empower the guardian to consent or to withhold consent to the taking of a sample from a minor under the age of 16: it is the person having the care and control of a minor under the age of 16 who is given, under the Act, the power of consenting or withholding consent to the taking of the sample. **R112.6.6**

Form of direction for taking of samples (rr.1–6)—This will be as follows: **R112.6.7**

On the application of the
and upon hearing
[It is ordered that
be made a respondent in this cause [matter]]

[And] It is directed pursuant to s.20(1) of the Family Law Reform Act 1969 that blood tests be used to ascertain whether such tests show that is or is not excluded from being the father of and that for that purpose blood samples be taken on or before the day of 19 from the following persons:—

The person appearing to the Court to have the care and control of

who is under the age of 16 [or is suffering from a mental disorder within the meaning of the Mental Health Act 1983 and is incapable of understanding the nature and purpose of blood tests] is

Dated the day of 19 .

Arrangements for tests (rr.1–6)—In the High Court (and also in county courts) the solicitor for the party on whose application the direction was given will be responsible for making the arrangements for sampling and testing (*Practice Direction* [1972] 1 W.L.R. 353; [1972] 1 All E.R. 640). **R112.6.8**

List of testers (rr.1–6)—The list of persons appointed by the Lord Chancellor to test blood in cases of disputed paternity was amended with effect from April 27, 1998. **R112.6.9**

Detailed procedure (rr.1–6)—On receipt of a copy of the court's direction the solicitor should apply for the necessary number of copies of the prescribed Direction Form to be supplied by the court. One is required for each person to be tested. **R112.6.10**

The solicitor for the party obtaining the direction should agree with the solicitors for the other parties as to the tester and inform him that a direction for blood tests has been made in a particular type of proceedings, stating the number of subjects covered by the direction and the area in which they live. The tester should be asked when it will be convenient for him to receive the samples and to suggest the name (or names) of the sampler(s) who could appropriately take the samples. (Any registered medical practitioner may act as a sampler.)

If the parties are unable to agree as to the arrangements the solicitor for the applicant should refer the matter back to the court.

When the arrangements have been made, the solicitor should complete Parts I and II of a Direction Form in respect of each subject and attend before the District Judge by whom the direction was given, or otherwise before the District Judge for the day. The District Judge, if satisfied with the arrangements, will sign Part I of each form and return the forms to the solicitor together with a copy of the Notes for the Guidance of Samplers.

The solicitor should then affix to Part III of each Direction Form the photograph required by reg. 6(2) (the requirements of reg. 2(1) as to type of photograph being noted) except in those cases in which no photograph is required. Application should where necessary be made to the solicitors for the other parties for photographs of the subjects they represent. The solicitor should send the Direction Forms with the Notes for Guidance to the nominated sampler and make arrangements with him as to the attendance of the subjects. A subject who is under 16 or who is a patient must be accompanied by a person of full age who will identify him to the sampler (reg. 4). Where, in the case of a patient, no photograph can be obtained, the Direction Form should be accompanied by a medical certificate stating that the subject is suffering from a mental disorder and that a photograph of him cannot, or should not, be taken (reg. 6(2)).

Regulations 5 and 6 set out the procedure to be followed by the sampler: the main features are explained in the Notes for Guidance. The solicitor should inform the sampler immediately if any subject cannot attend as arranged.

The sampler has a discretion to alter the arrangements for sampling if those originally made are for any reason unsatisfactory. If there is reason to think that a subject may ultimately refuse to give a sample the solicitor should advise the sampler of this possibility so that samples are not taken from other subjects to no purpose. It is particularly desirable that a sample should not be taken from a child unless it will be used for tests. It should therefore be arranged, if practicable, for the child's sample to be the last to be taken.

If the sampler does not take a sample from any subject he should state on the Direction Form the reason for this, and any reason given by the subject, or the person having his care and control, for any failure to attend.

Where a Direction Form is returned to the court by a sampler (or a tester) and is not accompanied by a Report, a copy of the Direction Form must be sent by the court to each party to the proceedings.

R112.6.11 **Report by tester (rr.1–6)**—On completion of the tests the tester will send to the court a Report in the prescribed form together with the associated Direction Form (reg. 10). A copy of the Report must be sent by the court to every party to the proceedings and to every other person from whom the direction of the court involved the taking of samples (O.112, r.6; CCR 1981, O.47, r.5). The report on the blood tests often disposes of the issue or dispute. If no guardian has been appointed of the minor the order for blood tests will contain a direction that the proceedings be restored for further directions by the District Judge when the report has been filed. If the dispute remains a live one or if there are aspects of the case making it desirable the District Judge will appoint the Official Solicitor as guardian and make any further directions which seem to be desirable.

Section 20(4) of the Act enables the court to give leave for any party to obtain a supplementary report from the tester. There is also provision for a party to call the tester as a witness subject to notice being given to the other parties within 14 days of receipt of the Report (s.20(5)).

R112.6.12 **Failure to take a necessary step (rr.1–6)**—Section 23 of the Act sets out the consequences of the failure of any person to take any step required of him for the purpose of giving effect to the direction. Such steps include, *inter alia*, supplying information as to the persons having care and control of a subject who is under 16 or a patient, supplying a photograph or medical certificate in lieu thereof, and consenting to the taking of a sample either from himself or from a person in his care and control.

BLOOD TESTS (EVIDENCE OF PATERNITY) REGULATIONS 1971

R112.6.13 (S.I. 1971 No. 1861 as amended)

Citation and Commencement

1. These Regulations may be cited as the Blood Tests (Evidence of Paternity) Regulations 1971 and shall come into operation on March 1, 1972.

Interpretation

R112.6.14 **2.**— (1) In these Regulations, unless the context otherwise requires,—

"the Act" means the Family Law Reform Act 1969;

"court" means a court which gives a direction for the use of blood tests in pursuance of section 20(1) of the Act;

"direction" means a direction given as aforesaid;

"direction form" means Form 1 in Schedule 1 to these Regulations;

"photograph" means a recent photograph, taken full face without a hat, of the size required for insertion in a passport;

"sample" means blood taken for the purpose of tests;

"sampler" means a registered medical practitioner or tester nominated in a direction form to take blood samples for the purposes of the direction;

"subject" means a person from whom a court directs that blood samples shall be taken;

"tester" means a person appointed by the Secretary of State to carry out blood tests;

"tests" means blood tests carried out under Pt III of the Act and includes any test made with the object of ascertaining the inheritable characteristics of blood.

(2) A reference in these Regulations to a person who is under a disability is a reference to a person who has not attained the age of 16 years or who is suffering from a mental disorder within the meaning of the Mental Health Act 1959 and is incapable of understanding the nature and purpose of blood tests.

(3) The Interpretation Act 1889 shall apply to the interpretation of these Regulations as it applies to the interpretation of an Act of Parliament.

[*Note*: the Interpretation Act 1889 has been replaced by the Interpretation Act 1978.]

Direction form

3. A sampler shall not take a sample from a subject unless Parts I and II of the direction form have been completed and the direction form purports to be signed by the proper officer of the court or some person on his behalf. **R112.6.15**

Subjects under disability to be accompanied to sampler

4. A subject who is under a disability who attends a sampler for the taking of a sample shall be accompanied by a person of full age who shall identify him to the sampler. **R112.6.16**

Taking of samples

5.— (1) Without prejudice to the provisions of rules of court, a sampler may make arrangements for the taking of samples from the subjects or may change any arrangements already made and make other arrangements. **R112.6.17**

(2) Subject to the provisions of these Regulations, where a subject attends a sampler in accordance with arrangements made under a direction, the sampler shall take a sample from him on that occasion.

(3) A sampler shall not take a sample from a subject if—

- (i) he has reason to believe that the subject has been transfused with blood within the three months immediately preceding the day on which the sample is to be taken; or
- (ii) in his opinion, tests on a sample taken at that time from that subject could not effectively be carried out for the purposes of and in accordance with the direction; or
- (iii) in his opinion, the taking of a sample might have an adverse effect on the health of the subject.

(4) A sampler may take a sample from a subject who has been injected with a blood product or blood plasma if, in his opinion, the value of any tests done on that sample would not be thereby affected, but shall inform the tester that the subject was so injected.

(5) Where a sampler does not take a sample from a subject in accordance with arrangements made for the taking of that sample and no other arrangements are made, he shall return the direction form relating to that subject to the court, having stated on the form his reason for not taking the sample and any reason given by the subject (or the person having the care and control of the subject) for any failure to attend in accordance with those arrangements.

(6) A subject who attends a sampler for the taking of a sample may be accompanied by his legal representative.

Sampling procedure

6.— (1) A sampler shall comply with the provisions of this Regulation, all of which shall be complied with in respect of one subject before any are complied with in respect of any other subject; so however that a report made in accordance with the provisions of section 20(2) of the Act or any other evidence relating to the samples or the tests made on the samples shall not be challenged solely on the grounds that a sampler has not acted in accordance with the provisions of this Regulation. **R112.6.18**

(2) Before a sample is taken from any subject who has attained the age of 12 months by the date of the direction, the sampler shall ensure that a photograph of that subject is affixed to the direction form relating to that subject unless the direction form is accompanied by a certificate from a medical practitioner that the subject is suffering from a mental disorder and that a photograph of him cannot or should not be taken.

(3) Before a sample is taken from a subject, he, or where he is under a disability the person of full age accompanying him, shall complete the declaration in Part V of the direction form (that that subject is the subject to whom the direction form relates and, where a photograph is affixed to the direction form, that the photograph is a photograph of that subject) which shall be signed in the presence of and witnessed by the sampler.

(4) Where a subject is suffering from a mental disorder, the sampler shall not take a sample from him unless the sampler is in possession of a certificate from a medical practitioner that the taking of a blood sample from the subject will not be prejudicial to his proper care and treatment.

(5) A sample shall not be taken from any subject unless—

(a) he or, where he is under a disability, the person having the care and control of him, has signed a statement on the direction form that he consents to the sample being taken; or

(b) where he is under a disability and is not accompanied by the person having the care and control of him, the sampler is in possession of a statement in writing, purporting to be signed by that person that he consents to the sample being taken.

(6) The sampler shall affix to the direction form any statement referred to in sub-paragraph (b) of the preceding paragraph.

(7) If a subject or, where he is under a disability, the person having the care and control of him, does not consent to the taking of a sample, he may record on the direction form his reasons for withholding his consent.

(8) When the sampler has taken a sample he shall place it in a suitable container and shall affix to the container a label giving the full name, age and sex of the subject from whom it was taken and the label shall be signed by the sampler and by that subject or, if he is under a disability, the person accompanying him.

(9) The sampler shall state in Part VII of the direction form that he has taken the sample and the date on which he did so.

Despatch of samples to tester

R112.6.19 **7.**— (1) When a sampler has taken samples, he shall, where he is not himself the tester, pack the containers together with the relevant direction forms and shall despatch them forthwith to the tester by post by special delivery service or shall deliver them or cause them to be delivered to the tester by some person other than a subject or a person who has accompanied a subject to the sampler.

(2) If at any time a sampler despatches to a tester samples from some only of the subjects and has not previously despatched samples taken from the other subjects, he shall inform the tester whether he is expecting to take any samples from those other subjects and, if so, from whom and on what date.

Procedure where sampler nominated is unable to take the samples

R112.6.20 **8.**— (1) Where a sampler is unable himself to take samples from all or any of the subjects, he may nominate another medical practitioner or tester to take the samples which he is unable to take.

(2) The sampler shall record the nomination of the other sampler on the relevant direction forms and shall forward them to the sampler nominated by him.

Testing of samples

R112.6.21 **9.**— (1) Samples taken for the purpose of giving effect to a direction shall (so far as practicable) all be tested by the same tester.

(2) A tester shall not make tests on any samples for the purpose of a direction unless he will, in his opinion, be able to show from the results of those tests (whether alone or together with the results of tests on any samples which he has received and tested or expects to receive subsequently) that a subject is or is not excluded from being the father of a subject whose paternity is in dispute.

Report by tester

R112.6.22 **10.** On completion of the tests in compliance with the direction, the tester shall forward to the court a report in Form 2 in Schedule 1 to these Regulations, together with the appropriate direction forms.

Procedure where tests not made

R112.6.23 **11.** If at any time it appears to a tester that he will be unable to make tests in accordance with the direction, he shall inform the court, giving his reasons, and shall return the direction forms in his possession to the court.

Fees

R112.6.24 **12.**— (1) The charges that may be made by samplers shall be those specified in the first two columns of Part I of Schedule 2 to the Regulations.

(2) [...].

SCHEDULE 1 Regulations 2(1) and 10 R112.6.25

FORM 1

Direction Form

FAMILY LAW REFORM ACT 1969

....

v.

....

[*Insert title of proceedings.*]

Reference No. of direction ....
Full name and date of birth of person
to be tested to whom this form relates ....

PART I

Notification of direction

The .... (*name and address of court*) on .... day of .... 19 directed that blood tests be carried out in respect of the persons whose names are set out below for the purpose of ascertaining the paternity of.................... (*name of person whose paternity is in dispute*) and that blood samples be taken from the persons named below on or before the .... day of 19

The name of the person appearing to the court to have the care and control of the person to whom this form relates who is under 16/suffering from a mental disorder within the meaning of the Mental Health Act 1983 and is incapable of understanding the nature and purpose of blood tests, is ....

.... (Signed)
Proper Officer of the Court.

Name	*Address*	*Age*
....	....	....
....	....	....
....	....	....
....	....	....
....	....	....

**Delete as appropriate*

PART II R112.6.26

Request to sampler to take sample

To .... (*name and address of sampler*).

You are hereby requested to take a blood sample from .... (*name of person to whom form relates*).

You are further requested to send the sample taken to .... (*name and address of tester*) [or the tester by whom you have arranged for tests to be made]. [*Delete if sampler is also tester.*]

[*To be completed where all the samples from the parties named in Part I are not to be taken by the same sampler.*]

[Other samples will be taken as follows:—

Name of person from whom sample will be taken	*Name, address and telephone of sampler*
....	....
....	....
....	....

.... (Signed)

[*For use where sampler named above nominates another sampler.*]

[Being unable to comply with the request set out above, I have nominated .... (*name and address of nominee*) to take the sample.

.... (Signed)]

R112.6.26

R112.6.27

PART III

Photograph

Below is a photograph of the person to whom this form relates, being a person who has attained the age of twelve months.

R112.6.28

PART IV

(*To be completed by sampler*)

I have questioned * .... and it appears that he/she/the party to whom this form relates—

has/has not† been transfused with blood in the last three months;†
has not been injected with a blood product or plasma substitute;†
has been injected with a blood product/blood plasma† on or about ....
and that the value of any tests will thereby be/not be affected†

.... (Signed)
(Sampler)

*Insert name of person to whom form relates or, in the case of person under 16 or suffering from mental disability, person accompanying that person.
†Delete as appropriate.

R112.6.29

PART V

Declaration

(*To be completed where the person to whom the form relates has attained the age of sixteen years and is not suffering from a mental disability*)

I .... (*insert full name and address of persons to whom the form relates*) declare that the photograph affixed to Part III of this form is a photograph of me and that I am a person in respect of whom the above-named court gave a direction that blood tests be made.
I hereby consent/do not consent* to the taking of a blood sample from me for the purpose of such tests.

[I do not consent because ....]†

I understand that it is a serious offence punishable by imprisonment to personate another person for the purpose of providing a blood sample.

Date .... (Signed)
The above was explained to the declarant who stated that he/she understood it and signed it in my presence.

Date ....

.... (Signed)
(Sampler)

*Delete as appropriate.
†To be deleted unless the person making the declaration withholds consent and wishes to record the reason for so doing.

PART VI R112.6.30

Declaration

(*To be completed where the person to whom the form relates has not attained the age of sixteen years or is suffering from a mental disability.*)

I .... (*full name and address of person accompanying the subject*) [*being the person having the care and control of .... (*name of person to whom form relates*)] declare that the person whom I identify to (*insert name of sampler*) [†and whose photograph is affixed to Part III of this form] is to the best of my knowledge and belief ....] who is the son/daughter of .... (*insert the name of mother of person identified.*)]

*Delete if not applicable.
†Delete as appropriate.

I, being the person having the care and control of the person to whom this form relates, consent/do not consent† to the taking of a sample. [I do not consent because:—‡

I understand that it is a serious offence punishable by imprisonment to personate another person for the purpose of providing a blood sample or to proffer the wrong child for that purpose.

Date .... (Signed)
The above was explained to the declarant who stated that he/she understood it and signed it in my presence.

Date .... (Signed)
(Sampler)

‡*To be completed if the person making the declaration withholds consent and wishes to record the reason for so doing.*

PART VII R112.6.31

(*To be completed by sampler*)

I have today taken a blood sample from .... to whom this form relates, whose [apparent] age is .... years. [I identified him/her from the photograph affixed to this form.] [He/She was [also] identified to me by ....]

Date .... (Signed)
(Sampler)

[*Delete as appropriate.*]
OBSERVATIONS
(*Any observations by the sampler which may assist the tester shall be inserted here.*)

PART VIII R112.6.32

(*To be completed by sampler*)

The person to whom this form relates did not attend on the date originally arranged [or on a new date arranged by me].
[*Delete if inappropriate.*]

His/Her reasons given to me for failing to attend were as follows:—

Date .... (Signed)
(Sampler)

PART IX R112.6.33

(*To be completed by tester*)

I have today received at .... (*insert place of receipt*) the sample referred to in Part VII of this form.
[It was received by special delivery service.]
It was handed to me by ....]

[*Delete as appropriate.*]
Date .... (Signed)
(Tester)

R112.6.34

FORM 2

Report by Tester

Ref. No. of Proceedings ....

FAMILY LAW REFORM ACT 1969

To:—(High Court of Justice, Strand, London WC2A 2LL
(District Judge, ... County Court
Justices' Clerk, ... Magistrates' Court (1)
(2)

v.

R112.6.35

PART I

I, , being a blood tester appointed by the Secretary of State for the purpose of Part III of the Family Law Reform Act 1969, certify that I have carried out blood tests (the details of which are given in Part II of this Report) on samples provided by the persons named in this direction, *viz.*,

From the results obtained Mr. .... is excluded/is not excluded from the possible paternity of ....

Reason for conclusion:—

Comments on value, if any, of tests in determining whenever any person tested is the father of the person whose paternity is in dispute:—

.... Signed
.... Status
.... Address
....

(1) Complete as appropriate.
(2) Insert title of proceedings.

R112.6.36

PART II

Test Report

SCHEDULE 2

CHARGES MADE BY SAMPLERS

The charges that may be made by a sampler in respect of one direction requesting him to take samples shall be as follows:

	Charge from 1st July 1992 £	*Charge before 1st July 1992* £
For making all necessary arrangements (whether or not samples are taken)	17.40	16.50
For making further arrangements (whether or not samples are taken) to give effect to a variation by the court of a direction	17.40	16.50

For taking sample—		
from first subject	17.40	16.50
from each subject after first	8.70	8.20
For taking second or subsequent samples from one or more subjects—		
if one such sample	17.40	16.50
if two such samples	26.10	24.70
if three or more such samples	43.50	41.20

Amended by Blood Tests (Evidence of Paternity) (Amendment) Regulations 1992 (S.I. 1992 No. 1369).

RSC ORDER 113

SUMMARY PROCEEDINGS FOR POSSESSION OF LAND

Contents R113.0.1

Proceedings to be brought by claim form

1.—(1) Where a person claims possession of land which he alleges is occupied solely by a person or persons (not being a tenant or tenants holding over after the termination of the tenancy) who entered into or remained in occupation without his licence or consent or that of any predecessor in title of his, the proceedings shall be brought by claim form in accordance with the provisions of this order. R113.1

(2) Where proceedings of the type referred to in paragraph (1) are brought, the court will fix a day for the hearing when it issues the claim form.

Jurisdiction of Masters

1A. Proceedings under this order may be heard and determined by a Master, who may refer them to a judge if he thinks they should properly be decided by the judge. R113.1A

Forms of claim form

2.—(1) The claim form shall be as set out in the relevant practice direction and no acknowledgment of service of it shall be required. R113.2

(2) The claim form shall be endorsed with or contain a statement showing whether possession is claimed in respect of residential premises or in respect of other land.

Witness statement or affidavit in support

3. The claimant shall file in support of the claim form a witness statement or affidavit stating— R113.3

(a) his interest in the land;
(b) the circumstances in which the land has been occupied without licence or consent and in which his claim to possession arises; and

(c) that he does not know the name of any person occupying the land who is not named in the claim form;

and, unless the court directs, any such witness statement or affidavit may contain statements of information or belief with the sources and grounds thereof.

Service of claim form

R113.4 **4.**—(1) Where any person in occupation of the land is named in the claim form, the claim form together with a copy of the witness statement or affidavit in support shall be served on him—

(a) personally; or

(b) by leaving a copy of the claim form and of the witness statement or affidavit or sending them to him, at the premises; or

(c) in such other manner as the court may direct.

(2) Where any person not named as a defendant is in occupation of the land, the claim form shall be served (whether or not it is also required to be served in accordance with paragraph (1)), unless the court otherwise directs, by—

(a) affixing a copy of the claim form and a copy of the witness statement or affidavit to the main door or other conspicuous part of the premises and, if practicable, inserting through the letter-box at the premises a copy of the claim form and a copy of the witness statement or affidavit enclosed in a sealed transparent envelope addressed to "the occupiers"; or

(b) placing stakes in the ground at conspicuous parts of the occupied land, to each of which shall be affixed a sealed transparent envelope addressed to "the occupiers" and containing a copy of the claim form and a copy of the witness statement or affidavit.

(2A) Every copy of a claim form for service under paragraph (1) or (2) shall be sealed with the seal of the Office of the Supreme Court out of which the claim form was issued.

Application by occupier to be made a party

R113.5 **5.** Any person not named as a defendant who is in occupation of the land and wishes to be heard on the question whether an order for possession should be made may apply at any stage of the proceedings to be joined as a defendant.

Order for possession

R113.6 **6.**—(1) A final order for possession in proceedings under this order shall, except in case of emergency and by permission of the court, not be made—

(a) in the case of residential premises, less than five clear days after the date of service; and

(b) in the case of other land, less than two clear days after the date of service.

(2) An order for possession in proceedings under this order shall be in Form No. 42A.

(3) Nothing in this order shall prevent the court from ordering possession to be given on a specified date, in the exercise of any power which could have been exercised if possession had been sought otherwise than in accordance with this Order.

Writ of possession

R113.7 **7.**—(1) Order 45, rule 3(2) shall not apply in relation to an order for possession under this order but no writ of possession to enforce such an order shall be issued after the expiry of three months from the date of the order without the permission of the court.

An application for permission may be made without notice being served on any other party unless the court otherwise directs.

(2) The writ of possession shall be in Form No. 66A.

Setting aside order

8. The court may, on such terms as it thinks just, set aside or vary any order made in proceedings under this order. R113.8

RSC ORDER 114

REFERENCES TO THE EUROPEAN COURT

Contents R114.0.1

Interpretation

1. In this order— R114.1

"the court" means the court by which an order is made and includes the Court of Appeal;

"the European Court" means the Court of Justice of the European Communities; and

"order" means an order referring a question to the European Court for a preliminary ruling under article 177 of the Treaty establishing the European Community, article 150 of the Treaty establishing the European Atomic Energy Community or article 41 of the Treaty establishing the European Coal and Steel Community or for a ruling on the interpretation of any of the Brussels Conventions (within the meaning of section 1(1) of the Civil Jurisdiction and Judgments Act 1982) or any of the instruments referred to in section 1 of the Contracts (Applicable Law) Act 1990.

Making of order

2.—(1) An order may be made by the court of its own initiative at any stage in proceedings, or on application by a party before or at the trial or hearing thereof. R114.2

(2) Where an application is made before the trial or hearing, it shall be made in accordance with CPR Part 23.

(3) In the High Court no order shall be made except by a judge in person.

Schedule to order to set out request for ruling

3. An order shall set out in a schedule the request for the preliminary ruling of the European Court, and the court may give directions as to the manner and form in which the schedule is to be prepared. R114.3

Stay of proceedings pending ruling

4. The proceedings in which an order is made shall, unless the court otherwise orders, be stayed until the European Court has given a preliminary ruling on the question referred to it. R114.4

Transmission of order to the European Court

5. When an order has been made, the Senior Master shall send a copy thereof to the Registrar of the European Court; but in the case of an order R114.5

made by the High Court, he shall not do so, unless the court otherwise orders, until the time for appealing against the order has expired or, if an appeal is entered within that time, until the appeal has been determined or otherwise disposed of.

Appeals from orders made by High Court

R114.6 **6.** On an appeal to the Court of Appeal from an order made by the High Court the period within which a notice of appeal must be served under Order 59, rule 4(1) shall be 14 days.

RSC ORDER 115

CONFISCATION AND FORFEITURE IN CONNECTION WITH CRIMINAL PROCEEDINGS

R115.0.1 **Contents**

I. Drug Trafficking Offences Act 1986 and Criminal Justice (International Co-operation) Act 1990

II. Part IV of the Criminal Justice Act 1988

III. Prevention of Terrorism (Temporary Provisions) Act 1989

Editorial Introduction

In 1986, this Order was added to the RSC to provide rules necessary for the exercise by the High Court of its jurisdiction in support of certain criminal proceedings under provisions in the Drug Trafficking Offences Act 1986. The orders which the Court may make in exercise of the jurisdiction relate to the seizure and confiscation of property under the control of defendants in criminal cases. In the years since, the machinery laid down in 1986, with some additions and amendments, has been pressed into service for the purpose of providing rules for the exercise of the Court's jurisdiction in support of criminal proceedings under the Criminal Justice Act 1988, Pt VI, the Prevention of Terrorism (Temporary Provisions) Act 1989 and the Criminal Justice (International Co-operation) Act 1990. The result is that the rules in the Order (there are now 36 of them) are not readily comprehended at first read. The rules have to be read in conjunction with the statutory provisions to which they relate. **R115.0.2**

The rules governing the procedure of the Court when exercising its jurisdiction under the 1986 Act and the 1990 Act are grouped together in Pt I (rr.1 to 21A). In Pt II (rr.22 and 23) the rules in Pt I are applied *mutatis mutandis* to the exercise of the Court's jurisdiction under the 1988 Act. Rules relating to the Court's jurisdiction under the 1989 Act are found in Pt III (rr.24 to 36).

O.115, Pt I (rr.1 to 21A)—The Drug Trafficking Act 1994 is a consolidating Act, and came into force on February 3, 1995. By s.67 and Sched. 2, para. 1 of the Act, subordinate legislation for the purposes of any provision overtaken by the Act continues to have effect in relation to any corresponding provision in the Act; and the various references to subordinate legislation which follow must be read with that in mind. The Act provides that, where a person appears before the Crown Court to be sentenced for a drug trafficking offence and has benefited from such trafficking, that Court may maker a confiscation order to recover his proceeds (ss.2 to 5). The Act further provides for charging and restraint orders to be made by the High Court on the application of the prosecution in respect of property which is held by a person against whom a confiscation order may be made or has been made by the Crown Court. **R.115.0.3**

This Part of the Order, which was added by RSC (Amendment No. 3) (S.I. 1986 No. 2289), provides for the applications that may be made to the High Court for such charging and restraint orders. The provisions of the Order must be read with the relevant provisions of the 1994 Act.

The rules in Pt I of this Order are not restricted in their application to High Court proceedings arising under the 1994 Act. The explanation for this is as follows.

The Criminal Justice (International Co-operation) Act 1990, s.9 states that, by Order in Council, provision may be made for the enforcement in the United Kingdom of orders made by overseas courts for the forfeiture of property used in the commission of an offence which corresponds to, or is similar to, specified offences. For the purpose of enforcement in England and Wales, the offences specified include offences under the Misuse of Drugs Act 1971, a drug trafficking offence as defined by the Drug Trafficking Act 1994 or an offence to which the Criminal Justice Act 1988, Pt VI applies. An Order in Council under the section may authorise the making of rules of court (see s.10(3)). The Criminal Justice (International Co-operation) Act 1990 (Enforcement of Overseas Forfeiture Orders) Order 1991 (S.I. 1991 No. 1463) was made in exercise of the power in s.9.

O.115, Pt II (rr.22 and 23)—Pt VI of the Criminal Justice Act 1988 is modelled on the provisions of the Drug Trafficking Offences Act 1986 and gives the courts powers to confiscate the proceeds of other highly profitable crimes. The offences to which Pt VI applies are prescribed by s.71(9)(c) and comprise offences listed in Sched. 4 and, if not so listed, any indictable offence other than a drug trafficking offence. Under s.71, the Crown Courts and the magistrates' courts may make confiscation orders. Supporting powers, similar to those given to the High Court by what is now the 1990 Act, are given to the Court by provisions in Pt VI. Thus the jurisdiction of the Court under the 1988 Act derives from s.77 (restraint orders), s.78 (charging orders), s.80 (appointment of receivers to realise property), s.81 (application of proceeds of realisation), s.83 (variation of confiscation orders) and s.89 (compensation of defendants not convicted etc.). **R115.0.4**

O.115, Pt III (rr.24 to 36)—This Part was added to O.115 by S.I. 1989 No. 1307. Part III of the **R115.0.5**

Prevention of Terrorism (Temporary Provisions) Act 1989, which came into force on March 22, 1989, and which is temporary in so far as its provisions are required to be renewed by Parliament from year to year (see s.27), re-enacts and creates certain offences relating to the giving of financial assistance to terrorism. Section 13 provides for the forfeiture on conviction of money or property related to such offences, and, in certain cases, other money or property in the defendant's possession or control at the time of the offence which is to be used for terrorist purposes. Sched. 4, together with s.13, provides for the restraint of dealings in property in respect of which a forfeiture order has been or could be made, for the enforcement of forfeiture orders, including those made in different parts of the British Islands, and for the making of Orders in Council for the enforcement in the United Kingdom of forfeiture orders made in designated countries.

Part III of O.115, which needs to be read in the context of Pt III of and Sched. 4 to the Act, contains provisions similar to but not the same as the provisions of Pts I and II of this Order relating, respectively to the Drug Trafficking Act 1994 and Pt VI of the Criminal Justice Act 1988. The provisions of Pt III of the Order are in some respects more limited in extent and, in particular, do not provide for charging orders to be made over the property of a defendant.

The Order was subsequently amended by RSC (Amendment No. 2) 1989 (S.I. 1989 No. 386) by the addition of rules to take account of proceedings arising under the 1988 Act. Further amendments, by addition, were made by RSC (Amendment No. 3) 1989 (S.I. 1989 No. 1307) when the 1989 Act came into force. The enactment of the 1990 Act and a related Order in Council necessitated the amendments to the Order brought about by RSC (Amendment No. 3) 1991 (S.I. 1991 No. 1884); this S.I. also amended the title of O.115. See too S.I. 1995 No. 2206.

Related Sources

R115.0.6
- Pt 23 (General rules about applications for court orders)
- Rule 32.6 (Evidence in proceedings other than at trial)
- Rule 32.15 (Affidavit evidence)
- Practice Direction (CPR Pt 8 and Sched. 1 and Sched. 2 to the CPR).

I. DRUG TRAFFICKING ACT 1994 AND CRIMINAL JUSTICE (INTERNATIONAL CO-OPERATION) ACT 1990

Interpretation

R115.1 **1.**—(1) In this Part of this order, "The Act" means the Drug Trafficking Act 1994 and a section referred to by number means the section so numbered in the Act.

(2) Expressions used in this Part of this order which are used in the Act have the same meanings in this Part of this order as in the Act and include any extended meaning given by the Criminal Justice (Confiscation) (Northern Ireland) Order 1990.

Assignment of proceedings

R115.2 **2.** Subject to rule 12, the jurisdiction of the High Court under the Act shall be exercised by a judge of the Chancery Division or of the Queen's Bench Division.

R115.2.1 **"jurisdiction of the High Court"**—The jurisdiction of the High Court under the Act derives from s.26 (restraint orders), ss.27 to 28 (charging orders), s.29 (appointment of receivers to realise property), s.30 (application of proceeds of realisation), s.17 (variation of confiscation orders), ss.18, 22 (compensation for defendants, not convicted etc.), s.59 (disclosure of information held by government departments, and the provisions of the Act supplemental thereto).

R.115.2.2 **"Subject to rule 12"**—This rule is concerned with the exercise of jurisdiction under ss.37 to 40 of the Act, see para. R115.12.2 below.

R115.2.3 **Assignment**—Until further notice, applications under O.115 should in the first instance be made to a Judge of the Crown Office list (Practice Note, January 22, 1987 (Watkins L.J.)).

R115.2.4 **"judge ... sitting in private"**—Formerly, various provisions in O.115 stated that hearings were to be "in chambers". Now, the CPR provide that, as a general rule, hearings should be in public but, in certain circumstances, may be "in private"; see, generally, CPR, r.39.2. Accordingly, amendments have been made in O.115; see, in addition to r.2, r.25(1).

Title of proceedings

R115.2A **2A.** An application made in accordance with CPR Part 23, or a claim form issued in relation to proceedings under this Part of this order shall be entitled in the matter of the defendant, naming him, and in the matter of the Act, and all subsequent documents in the matter shall be so entitled.

Originating process—Formerly, proceedings under RSC, O.115 were commenced either by originating motion or by summons. Where previously the originating process was in the form of an originating motion the rules in O.115 now provide that a claim form shall be used (see rr.2B(1), 3(1), 7(2), 17(2), 26(1)(3), and 33(2)). In some instances, the Pt 8 procedure applies, subject to provisions to the contrary and with modifications (see paras R115.3.9, R115.7.4 and R115.26.3 below). **R115.2A.1**

Where, previously, the originating process was in the form of a summons the rule in O.115 now provide that an application notice should be used. Where particular proceedings are initiated by an application notice the general rules as to applications for court orders found in CPR, Pt 23 apply, subject to any express provisions (*e.g.* as to service, the giving of notice, or evidence etc.) found in the rules in O.115 relevant to the particular application. Provisions in O.115 making express reference to application notices and Pt 23 are: rr.2B(1), 5(1), 6(1), 7(1), 8(3) and (5), 9(1), 10, 11(1), 11A(1), 13, 14, 15(1), 18, 23(e), 28(1) and (3), 29, 30 and 34.

Application for confiscation order

2B.—(1) An application by the prosecutor for a confiscation order under section 19 shall be made in accordance with CPR Part 23, where there have been proceedings against the defendant in the High Court, and shall otherwise be made by the issue of a claim form. **R115.2B**

(2) The application shall be supported by a witness statement or affidavit giving full particulars of the following matters—

(a) the grounds for believing that the defendant has died or absconded;

(b) the date or approximate date on which the defendant died or absconded;

(c) where the application is made under section 19(2), the offence or offences of which the defendant was convicted, and the date and place of conviction;

(d) where the application is made under section 19(4), the proceedings which have been initiated against the defendant (including particulars of the offence and the date and place of institution of those proceedings); and

(e) where the defendant is alleged to have absconded, the steps taken to contact him.

(3) The prosecutor's statement under section 11 shall be exhibited to the witness statement or affidavit and shall include the following particulars—

(a) the name of the defendant;

(b) the name of the person by whom the statement is given;

(c) such information known to the prosecutor as is relevant to the determination whether the defendant has benefited from drug trafficking and to the assessment of the value of his proceeds of drug trafficking.

(4) Unless the court otherwise orders, a witness statement or affidavit under paragraph (2) may contain statements of information and belief, with their sources and grounds.

(5) The application and the witness statement or affidavit in support shall be served not less than 7 days before the date fixed for the hearing of the application on—

(a) the defendant (or on the personal representatives of a deceased defendant);

(b) any person who the prosecutor reasonably believes is likely to be affected by the making of a confiscation order; and

(c) the receiver, where one has been appointed in the matter.

Application for restraint order or charging order

3.—(1) An application for a restraint order under section 26 or for a charging order under section 27 (to either of which may be joined an **R115.3**

application for the appointment of a receiver) may be made by the prosecutor by the issue of a claim form notice of which need not be served on any other party.

(2) An application under paragraph (1) shall be supported by a witness statement or affidavit, which shall—

(a) give the grounds for the application; and

(b) to the best of the witness's ability, give full particulars of the realisable property in respect of which the order is sought and specify the person or persons holding such property.

(3) Unless the court otherwise directs, a witness statement or affidavit under paragraph (2) may contain statements of information or belief with the sources and grounds thereof.

R115.3.1 **"Restraint order ... charging order"**—Under s.2, where a person appears before the Crown Court to be sentenced in respect of "drug trafficking offences" (as defined by s.1 of the Act), in certain circumstances that Court may make a confiscation order confiscating from him the proceeds of his drug trafficking. The powers conferred on the High Court by s.26 and s.27 are exercisable where (a) proceedings have been instituted in England and Wales against the defendant for a drug trafficking offence, (b) the proceedings have not been concluded (see s.64), and (c) the court is satisfied that there is reasonable cause to believe that the defendant has benefited from drug trafficking. Those powers are also exercisable where the court is satisfied (a) that whether by the laying of an information or otherwise, a person is to be charged with a drug trafficking offence, and (b) that there is reasonable cause to believe that he has benefited from drug trafficking. Under s.8 the High Court may make a restraint order prohibiting any person from dealing with any realisable property, subject to such conditions and exceptions as may be specified in the order (see further para. R115.4.2 below). Under s.27, the High Court may make a charging order on realisable property for securing payment to the Crown (a) where a confiscation order has not been made, of amount equal to the value from time to time of the property charged, and (b) in any other case, of an amount not exceeding the amount payable under the confiscation order.

R115.3.2 **Appointment of a receiver**—See r.8.

R115.3.3 **Application to external confiscation orders and proceedings in designated countries**—Under s.39, by Order in Council, subject to necessary modifications, the Act may be applied to an *external confiscation order* (as defined in s.39(2)) made by a court in a designated country and to proceedings which have been or are to be instituted in a designated country and may result in such order being made there. The principal Order in Council is the Drug Trafficking 1994 (Designated Countries and Territories) Order 1996 (S.I. 1996 no. 2880), as amended (see further paras R115.12.2 and R115.13.2 below).

R115.3.4 **Application to external forfeiture orders and proceedings in designated countries**—Under r.21A, applications may be made for restraint ordes and charging orders and the appointment of receivers in support of *external forfeiture orders* made by courts of designated countries or where such order may be made in proceedings in such countries as provided for by Order in Council made under the Criminal Justice (International Co-operation) Act 1990; see para. R115.21A.1.

R115.3.5 **"The defendant"**—"The defendant" means a person against whom proceedings have been initiated for a drug trafficking offence, whether or not he has been convicted (see s.63(1) of the 1994 Act) but includes in addition a person suspected of having committed such an offence where an information is to be laid against him and there is reasonable cause to believe that he has benefited from drug trafficking (see s.25 of the 1994 Act).

R115.3.6 **Proceedings have been instituted ... and ... have not been concluded**—The events which constitute the institution and conclusion of proceedings for a drug trafficking offence are listd in s.41 of the 1994 Act.

R115.3.7 **"realisable property"**—Section 6 of the 1994 Act defines "realisable property" as meaning subject to certain exceptions set out in s.6, (a) any property held by the defendant, and (b) any property held by a person to whom the defendant has directly or indirectly made a gift caught by the Act (as to which see s.8).

For consideration of the assets that may be made subject to an order, see *R. v. Buckman* (1977) 1 Cr.App.R.(S.) 325, CA; *R. v. Clark* [1997] 1 W.L.R. 557, CA; and *R. v. Brett*, *The Times*, October 13, 1997.

Application "supported by a witness statement or affidavit"—See also paras R115.11A.2, R115.15.3, R115.26.2 and R115.31.1. Under the CPR, the general rule is that evidence at hearings other than the trial is to be by witness statement unless the court, a practice direction or any other enactment requires otherwise (CPR, r.32.6). As to form of witness statement, see CPR, r.32.8. A witness is not prevented from giving evidence by affidavit, but the extra costs involved may not be recoverable (CPR, r.32.15). Evidence must be given by affidavit, instead of or in addition to, a witness statement if this is required by the court, a provision contained in any rule, a practice direction or any other enactment (CPR, r.32.15(1)). Previously, throughout O.115 where evidence could be given in writing it was to be given the form of affidavit. The rules have been amended so as to provide that in applications may be supported by witness statements or affidavits (see rr.2B(2), 3(2), 6(2), 7(3), 11(2), 11A, 14, 15(1), 18, 26(2), 28(3), 31(1) and 34). It may be doubted whether it was intended that throughout O.115 witness statements should be regarded as an acceptable alternative form of written evidence to affidavits; footnote 6 to Practice Direction (Written Evidence) para. 1.4 (see 32PD–001) adds to the uncertainty. R115.3.8

Rule 3(3) re-states the rule that, unless the Court otherwise directs, the witness statement or affidavit may contain statements of information or belief provided the sources of information and grounds for belief are set out. The grounds for belief that a defendant has benefited from drug trafficking may, therefore, properly be stated by the deponent as being information received from police officers who are members of a drug squad that they have kept observation on the defendant's home and a description of the observations made by them. The obligation to give full and frank disclosure to the Court does not require the naming of individual police officers concerned or the precise times at which they kept observation (*Re A Defendant, The Independent*, April 2, 1987).

Practice—Applications for a restraint order under ss.25 and 26 of the 1994 Act or for a charging order under ss.25 to 27 should be made by claim form to a judge sitting in private (see rr.2 and 2B) and should normally be made without notice in the first instance by the prosecutor. Application may be made by application notice to the extent that that is permitted by r.2B(1). The application should be supported by written evidence dealing with all the matters listed in sub-paragraphs (a) to (e) of paragraph (2) of this rule. Rules 2B and 3(1) are listed in Table 2 of Practice Direction (CPR, Pt 8, Sched. 1 and Sched. 2 to CPR) (see para. 8BPD–003). Consequently, section B of that Practice Direction takes effect where claims are brought under r.2B and r.3(1) with the result that the Pt 8 procedure applies subject to any special or contrary provisions in O.115 and as modified in paras B.6 to B.15 of the Practice Direction. R115.3.9

Committal for contempt—An application to commit a person for breach of restraining and charging orders relates to breach of an order made in civil proceedings; hence such applications must be made to a single judge and not to the Divisional Court (*Re H, The Times*, April 1, 1988, CA, see further CPR, Sched. 1, O.52). R115.3.10

Restraint order and charging order

4.—(1) A restraint order may be made subject to conditions and exceptions, including but not limited to conditions relating to the indemnifying of third parties against expenses incurred in complying with the order, and exceptions relating to living expenses and legal expenses of the defendant, but the prosecutor shall not be required to give an undertaking to abide by any order as to damages sustained by the defendant as a result of the restraint order. R115.4

(2) Unless the court otherwise directs, a restraint order made where notice it has not been served on any person shall have effect until a day which shall be fixed for the hearing where all parties may attend on the application and a charging order shall be an order to show cause, imposing the charge until such day.

(3) Where a restraint order is made the prosecutor shall serve copies of the order and of the witness statement or affidavit in support on the defendant and on all other named persons restrained by the order and shall notify all other persons or bodies affected by the order of its terms.

(4) Where a charging order is made the prosecutor shall serve copies of the order and of the witness statement or affidavit in support on the defendant and, where the property to which the order relates is held by another person, on that person and shall serve a copy of the order on such of the persons or bodies specified in Order 50, rule 2(1)(b) to (d) as shall be appropriate.

Effect of rule—See para. R115.3.1 above. R115.4.1

R115.4.2 **Service of charging order nisi**—The requirements of this order are similar to those of Sched. 1, RSC, O.50, r.2. Copies of the order and supporting affidavit must be served on the defendant, and, where the property in question is governed or other stock, on the keeper of the register, or where the order relates to a fund in Court, on the Accountant General, or where the order relates to an interest under a trust, on such of the trustees as the Court may direct.

R115.4.3 **Restraint order**—Under section 8 of the 1994 Act, the Court may make a restraint order prohibiting any person from dealing with any realisable property (as defined in s.6) subject to such conditions and exceptions as may be specified in the order.

The Court's jurisdiction to make or vary restraint orders is closely analogous to its jurisdiction to make or vary "freezing injunctions" (formerly Mareva injunctions). The object in each case is to strike a balance at the interlocutory stage between keeping the defendant's assets available to satisfy any confiscation order which may be made in the event of conviction, and meeting the defendant's reasonable requirements in the meantime. Accordingly, a restraint order ought not to be varied by providing for capitalisation of maintenance and school fees to enable the defendant to make a lump sum payment to his son, pursuant to a consent order in divorce proceedings, since such a provision involves the anticipatory discharge of future liabilities, thereby reducing the assets which may become available to satisfy any confiscation order (*Re Peters* [1988] Q.B. 871; [1988] 3 All E.R. 46, CA). Similar considerations apply to a restraint order as to a freezing injunction when the Court is determining whether sums should be released for specific purposes. Thus, where a defendant appeals against conviction for drugs offences and against a confiscation order for a large sum made at the conclusion of the trial, the Court has power to vary a restraint order made against him prior to his conviction so as to enable assets to be released to fund his appeal (*Customs Excise Commissioners v. Norris* [1991] 2 Q.B. 293; [1991] 2 All E.R. 395, CA).

A restraint order, however, is not in all respects equivalent to a freezing injunction. There is no jurisdiction either under the statute or the Court's inherent jurisdiction to provide for the payment of compensation to innocent third parties. Accordingly, a landlord who has not been given notice that his tenant's assets are subject to a restraint order seeking to distrain on machinery and premises demised to the tenant in respect of rent which is due, is entitled to determine the lease but is not entitled to keep the proceeds of the realisation of any property subject to the restraint order (*Re R. (Restraint Order)* [1990] Q.B. 307; [1990] 2 All E.R. 569).

Where a restraint order is made and expressed to be subject to an exception related to the defendant's legal expenses, it is proper for the order to direct taxation of his legal costs after verdict. However, despite the close analogy to freezing injunctions, restraint orders are not required to stipulate a fixed or maximum sum for such costs (*Re P. and Re W., The Times*, April 11, 1990, CA).

Although neither the 1994 Act nor Pt VI of the Criminal Justice Act 1988 contains any express provision empowering the Court to order a defendant to make full disclosure of all his assets, there is inherent in the statutes a power to make any order necessary to make a restraint order effective, including a power to order a defendant to make such disclosure. This power, however, is discretionary and is exercisable subject to certain conditions and exceptions. The Acts do not abrogate the common law rule against self-incrimination and hence it will be appropriate to make any such disclosure under subject to the condition that any disclosure made thereunder may not be used in criminal proceedings against the defendant or his spouse (*Re O. (Disclosure Order)* [1991] 2 W.L.R. 475, CA). The provisions of the Acts which confer jurisdiction on the Court to make restraint and charging orders are civil in character and any appeal from a judge's order made thereunder lies properly to the Civil Division of the Court of Appeal (*ibid.*).

In the absence of agreement to the contrary, a bank has a common law right to combine different accounts held by the same customer in order to establish the overall indebtedness of the bank to the customer, or the customer to the bank. The exercise by the bank of this right of combination, or any contractual right of set-off, did not constitute a disposal or diminution of the assets of the customer or a breach of a restraint order (*Re K. (Restraint Order)* [1990] 2 All E.R. 562).

Satisfaction of a confiscation order made against a defendant takes priority over an unsecured debt owed by the defendant and, therefore, the Court has no power to vary, in order to permit payment of the debt out of the defendant's assets, a restraint order freezing the defendant's assets to ensure that they are available to satisfy the confiscation order (*Re W., The Times*, November 15, 1990, a case decided under the equivalent provisions of Pt VI of the Criminal Justice Act 1988 and Pt II of this Order, see para. R115.23.1 below).

R115.4.4 **Application to commit for contempt for breach of order**—See note at para. R115.3.10.

Discharge or variation of order

R115.5 **5.**—(1) Any person or body on whom a restraint order or a charging order is served or who is notified of such an order may make an application in accordance with CPR Part 23 to discharge or vary the order.

(2) The application notice and any witness statement or affidavit in support shall be lodged with the court and served on the prosecutor and, where he is

not the applicant, on the defendant, not less than two clear days before the date fixed for the hearing of the application.

(3) Upon the court being notified that proceedings for the offences have been concluded or that the amount, payment of which is secured by a charging order has been paid into court, any restraint order or charging order, as the case may be, shall be discharged.

(4) The court may also discharge a restraint order or a charging order upon receiving notice from the prosecutor that it is no longer appropriate for the restraint order or the charging order to remain in place.

Effect of rule—After its incorporation in CPR, Sched. 1, minor amendments were made to this rule by the Civil Procedure (Amendment) Rule 1999 (S.I. 1999 No. 1008), r.59(a) for the purpose of correcting mistakes in para. (2). **R115.5.1**

Further application by prosecutor

6.—(1) Where a restraint order or a charging order has been made the prosecutor may apply by an application in accordance with CPR Part 23 with notice or, where the case is one of urgency or the giving of notice would cause a reasonable apprehension of dissipation of assets, without notice— **R115.6**

(a) to vary such order; or
(b) for a restraint order or a charging order in respect of other realisable property; or
(c) for the appointment of a receiver.

(2) An application under paragraph (1) shall be supported by a witness statement or affidavit which, where the application is for a restraint order or a charging order, shall to the best of the witness's ability give full particulars of the realisable property in respect of which the order is sought and specify the person or persons holding such property.

(3) The application and witness statement or affidavit in support shall be lodged with the court and served on the defendant and, where one has been appointed in the matter, on the receiver, not less than two clear days before the date fixed for the hearing of the application.

(4) Rule 4(3) and (4) shall apply to the service of restraint orders and charging orders respectively made under this rule on persons other than the defendant.

Effect of rule—After its incorporation in CPR, Sched. 1, a minor amendment was made to this rule by the Civil Procedure (Amendment) Rule 1999 (S.I. 1999 No. 1008), r.59(b) for the purpose of correcting a mistake in para. (3). **R115.6.1**

"application ... without notice"—Formerly, this rule provided that, in case of urgency application could be made *ex parte*. Throughout the CPR, "without notice", or some other phrase to similar effect, is preferred to "*ex parte*". Other rules similarly amended in O.115 are: rr.13, 27(2), 28(1) and 30. For urgent applications without notice generally, see CPR 23 and 25. **R115.6.2**

Realisation of property

7.—(1) An application by the prosecutor under section 29 shall, where there have been proceedings against the defendant in the High Court, be made by an application in accordance with CPR Part 23 and shall otherwise be made by the issue of a claim form. **R115.7**

(2) The application notice or claim form, as the case may be, shall be served with the evidence in support not less than 7 days before the date fixed for the hearing of the application or claim on—

(a) the defendant;
(b) any person holding any interest in the realisable property to which the application relates; and
(c) the receiver, where one has been appointed in the matter.

(3) The application shall be supported by a witness statement or affidavit, which shall, to the best of the witness's ability, give full particulars of the

realisable property to which it relates and specify the person or persons holding such property, and a copy of the confiscation order, of any certificate issued by the Crown Court under section 5(2) and of any charging order made in the matter shall be exhibited to such witness statement or affidavit.

(4) The Court may, on an application under section 29—

(a) exercise the power conferred by section 30(2) to direct the making of payments by a receiver;

(b) give directions in respect of the property interests to which the application relates; and

(c) make declarations in respect of those interests.

R115.7.1 **Application ... under section 29**—Section 29 states that where (a) in proceedings instituted for a drug trafficking offence, a confiscation order is made, (b) the order is not subject to appeal, and (c) the proceedings have not been concluded, the High Court may, on an application by the prosecutor, appoint a receiver in respect of realisable property and exercise certain other powers in respect of such receivership. As para. (4) of this rule states, in addition the Court may exercise powers conferred by s.30 concerning the application of proceeds of realisation and other sums in the hands of a receiver.

R115.7.2 **Certificate issued ... under section 5(2)**—This provision states that if the Crown Court, in making a confiscation order, is satisfied as to any matter relevant for determining the amount that might be realised at the time of the order it may, and in certain circumstances shall, issue a certificate giving the Court's opinion as to those matters.

R115.7.3 **Application to external confiscation orders and proceedings in designated countries**—Section 29 is modified by the Order in Council referred to in para. R115.3.3.

R115.7.4 **Practice**—Applications under r.7 may be made, depending on the circumstances, by claim form or by application notice. The application should be supported by written evidence dealing with all the matters stated in paragraph (3) of this rule. Rule 7(1) is listed in Table 2 of Practice Direction (CPR, Pt 8, Sched. 1 and Sched. 2 to CPR) (see para. 8BPD–003). Consequently, Section B of that Practice Direction takes effect where application is made by claim form with the result that the Pt 8 procedure applies subject to any special or contrary provisions in O.115 and as modified in paras B.6 to B.15 of the Practice Direction. See also para. R115.3.9 above.

Receivers

R115.8 **8.**—(1) Subject to the provisions of this rule, the provisions of Order 30, rules 2 to 8 shall apply where a receiver is appointed in pursuance of a charging order or under sections 26 or 29.

(2) Where the receiver proposed to be appointed has been appointed receiver in other proceedings under the Act, it shall not be necessary for a witness statement or affidavit of fitness to be sworn or for the receiver to give security, unless the court otherwise orders.

(3) Where a receiver has fully paid the amount payable under the confiscation order and any sums remain in his hands, he shall make an application to the court for directions in accordance with CPR Part 23, as to the distribution of such sums.

(4) An application under paragraph (3) shall be served with any evidence in support not less than 7 days before the date fixed for the hearing of the application on—

(a) the defendant; and

(b) any other person who held property realised by the receiver.

(5) A receiver may apply for an order to discharge him from his office by making an application in accordance with CPR Part 23, which shall be served, together with any evidence in support, on all persons affected by his appointment not less than 7 days before the day fixed for the hearing of the application.

R115.8.1 **Effect of rule**—RSC, O.30 (Receivers) is re-enacted in CPR, Sched. 1. Applications under Pt 23 are made on application notice. It would seem that, in r.8(e), "summons" should read "application". Note r.23(e) (varying effect of r.8).

"where a receiver is appointed"—Section 26 states that, where the High Court has made a restraint order, the Court may at any time appoint a receiver. As to the appointment of a receiver under s.29, see para. R115.7.1 above. Para. (1) applies to the appointment of a receiver under this rule the provisions in O.30 relating to receivers generally as to the giving of security (r.2), remuneration (r.3), accounts (r.5), payment into Court (r.6), default (r.7) and directions as to receivers (r.8). R115.8.2

Where the property charged is shares in a company, but the evidence is (for example) that the company has been used by the defendant fraudulently, the Court will not hesitate to "lift the corporate veil" and treat the company's assets as subject to the receivership (*H.M. Customs & Excise v. Hare*, February 16, 1996, (unrep.)).

Where a county court interim order under the Insolvency Act 1986, s.252 had been made preventing institution of proceedings against the defendant or his property, an application for the appointment of receiver of the defendant's realisable property was not a contravention of the interim order and the applicants were under no obligation to obtain the leave of the county court before making it (*Re M. (Restraint Order)* [1992] 1 Q.B. 377; [1992] 2 W.L.R. 340).

Application to external confiscation orders and proceedings in designated countries— Sections 26 to 29 are modified by the Order in Council referred to in para. R115.3.3 above. R115.8.3

Certificate of inadequacy

9.—(1) The defendant or a receiver appointed under section 26 or 29 or in pursuance of a charging order may apply in accordance with CPR Part 23 for a certificate under section 17(1). R115.9

(2) An application under paragraph (1) shall be served with any supporting evidence not less than 7 days before the date fixed for the hearing of the application on the prosecutor and, as the case may be, on either the defendant or the receiver (where one has been appointed).

"certificate under section 17(1)"—This section states that, if on the application by the defendant in respect of a confiscation order, the High Court is satisfied that the realisable property is indequate for the payment of any amount remaining to be recovered under the order, the Court shall issue a certificate to that effect, giving the Court's reasons. R115.9.1

Certificate under section 16

9A. An application under section 16(2) (increase in realisable property) shall be served with any supporting evidence not less than 7 days before the date fixed for the hearing of the application on the defendant and, as the case may be, on either the prosecutor or (where one has been appointed in the matter) on the receiver. R115.9A

Compensation

10. An application for an order under section 18 shall be made in accordance with CPR Part 23, which shall be served, with any supporting evidence, on the person alleged to be in default and on the relevant authority under section 18(5) not less than 7 days before the date fixed for the hearing of the application. R115.10

"application ... under section 18"—This section states that, if proceedings are instituted against a person for a drug trafficking offence and he is not convicted, or if convicted his conviction is quashed or he is pardoned, the High Court may on an application by a person who held property which was realisable property, order compensation to be paid to the applicant. See also r.29. R115.10.1

"person ... in default"—See s.19(4). R.115.10.2

"the relevant authority"—The relevant authority under section 18 of the 1994 Act is, if the appropriate police force, or, if he is a member of the Crown Prosecution Service, the Director of Public Prosecutions, or, if he is an officer within the meaning of the Customs and Excise Management Act 1979, the Commissioners of Customs and Excise. R115.10.3

Disclosure of information

11.—(1) An application by the prosecutor under section 59 shall be made R115.11

in accordance with CPR Part 23 and the application notice shall state the nature of the order sought and whether material sought to be disclosed is to be disclosed to a receiver appointed under section 26 or 29 or in pursuance of a charging order or to a person mentioned in section 59(8).

(2) The application notice and witness statement or affidavit in support shall be served on the authorised Government Department in accordance with Order 77, rule 4 not less than 7 days before the date fixed for the hearing of the application.

(3) The witness statement or affidavit in support of an application under paragraph (1) shall state the grounds for believing that the conditions in section 59(4) and, if appropriate, section 59(7) are fulfilled.

Compensation for, discharge and variation of confiscation order

R115.11A **11A.**—(1) An application under section 21, 22 or 23 shall be made in accordance with CPR Part 23 which, together with any evidence in support, shall be lodged with the court and served on the prosecutor not less than 7 days before the day fixed for the hearing of the application.

(2) Notice shall also be served on any receiver appointed in pursuance of a charging order or under section 26 or 29.

(3) An application for an order under section 22 shall be supported by a witness statement or affidavit giving details of—

- (a) the confiscation order made under section 19(4);
- (b) the acquittal of the defendant;
- (c) the realisable property held by the defendant; and
- (d) the loss suffered by the applicant as a result of the confiscation order.

(4) An application for an order under section 23 shall be supported by a witness statement or affidavit giving details of—

- (a) the confiscation order made under section 19(4);
- (b) the date on which the defendant ceased to be an absconder;
- (c) the date on which proceedings against the defendant were instituted and a summary of the steps taken in the proceedings since then; and
- (d) any indication given by the prosecutor that he does not intend to proceed against the defendant.

(5) An application made under section 21 shall be supported by a witness statement or affidavit giving details of—

- (a) the confiscation order made under section 19(4);
- (b) the circumstances in which the defendant ceased to be an absconder; and
- (c) the amounts referred to in section 21(2).

(6) Where an application is made for an order under section 23(3) or 24(2)(b), the witness statement or affidavit shall also include—

- (a) details of the realisable property to which the application relates; and
- (b) details of the loss suffered by the applicant as a result of the confiscation order.

(7) Unless the court otherwise orders, a witness statement or affidavit under paragraphs (3) to (6) may contain statements of information and belief, with the sources and grounds thereof.

R115.11A.1 **"application . . . under section 59"**—This section provides a procedure which may lead to the disclosure of material held by a government department in cases where it would be possible for the High Court to make a restraint order under ss.25 to 28 or a charging order under s.6. An order requiring production to the High Court may be made without a hearing of an officer of the department holding the material being allowed. However, a further order for the disclosure of the material (*e.g.* to a receiver) may not be made unless the department concerned has been given an opportunity to make representations.

Application "supported by a witness statement or affidavit"—See para. R115.3.8 above. R115.11A.2

Exercise of powers under sections 37 and 40

12. The powers conferred on the High Court by sections 37 and 40 may be exercised by a judge or a Master of the Queen's Bench Division. R115.12

Effect of rule—Formerly, this rule stated that the powers conferred on the High Court judge were to be exercised "in chambers". When O.115 was re-enacted in CPR, Sched. 1, "in private" was substituted for "in chambers" and, subsequently, by Civil Procedure (Amendment) Rule 1999 (S.I. 1999 No. 1008), r.59(b), the substitution was excised. The result is that, in a given case, the question whether a judge or a master should sit in public or in private when exercising these powers is to be resolved according to the general rules (see CPR, r.39.2). R115.12.1

"powers conferred . . . by sections 37 and 40"—The exercise of jurisdiction provided for by r.2 is subject to this rule. R115.12.2

Section 37 enables provision to be made by Order in Council for the registration in the High Court and the enforcement in England and Wales of orders made in Scotland in connection with the confiscation of the proceeds of drug trafficking under the Criminal Justice (Scotland) Act 1987, Pt I. The relevant Order in Council is the Drug Trafficking Offences (Enforcement in England and Wales) Order 1988 (S.I. 1988 No. 593).

Section 40 states that, on an application made by or on behalf of the Government of a designated country, the High Court may register an external confiscation order made there. Such an order is an order made by a court in a country designated by Order in Council made under s.26 for the purpose of recovering payments or other rewards received in connection with drug trafficking or their value (see s.26(2)). The relevant Order in Council is the Drug Trafficking Offences Act 1986 (Designated Countries and Territories) Order 1990 (S.I. 1990 No. 1199). For the registration and enforcement of external forfeiture orders, see r.21A below.

Procedural effect of Orders in Council made under sections 37 and 40—It should be noted that r.21 says that rr.12 to 20 of this Order shall have effect subject to the provisions of the Orders in Council made under s.37 and s.40. R115.12.3

Application for registration

13. An application for registration of an order specified in an Order in Council made under section 37 or of an external confiscation order under section 40(1) may be made in accordance with CPR Part 23, and may be made without notice. R115.13

"order specified in an Order in Council"—The relevant Order in Council is the Drug Trafficking Offences (Enforcement in England and Wales) Order 1988 (S.I. 1988 No. 593). Article 4 of this Order provides, *inter alia,* that certain orders made by the Scottish Court of Session under the Criminal Justice (Scotland) Act 1987, Pt I, including for example restraint orders, shall be registered in the High Court if application for registration is made in accordance with the relevant rules of Court (including r.12 below). Article 3 provides that, upon such registration of a Scottish order, it may be enforced by the High Court as if it had originally been made in that Court, providing it is done in accordance with the provisions of the 1988 Order mentioned above and any rules of Court relating to enforcement. R115.13.1

"external confiscation order"—External confiscation orders are provided for by the Drug Trafficking Offences Act 1986 (Designated Countries and Territories) Order 1990 (S.I. 1990 No. 1199) made under s.37 of the Act, see para. R115.12.2 above. Section 40(1) of the Act says that, on an application, the High Court may register an external confiscation order made in a designated country if (a) it is satisfied that at the time of registration the order is in force and not subject to appeal (see further s.40(2)), (b) it is satisfied, where the person against whom the order is made did not appear in the proceedings, that he received notice of the proceedings in sufficient time to enable him to defend them; and (c) it is of the opinion that enforcing the order in England and Wales would not be contrary to the interests of justice. R115.13.2

External forfeiture orders—By virtue of r.21A, external forfeiture orders may also be registered, see para. R115.21A.2 below. R115.13.3

Evidence in support of application under section 37

14. An application for registration of an order specified in an Order in Council made under section 37 must be made in accordance with CPR Part 23, and be supported by a witness statement or affidavit— R115.14

(i) exhibiting the order or a certified copy thereof, and

(ii) stating, to the best of the witness's knowledge, particulars of what property the person against whom the order was made holds in England and Wales, giving the source of the witness's knowledge.

R115.14.1 **"Order in Council made under section 37"**—See para. R115.12.3 above.

Evidence in support of application under section 40(1)

R115.15 **15.**—(1) An application for registration of an external confiscation order must be made in accordance with CPR Part 23, and be supported by a witness statement or affidavit—

(a) exhibiting the order or a verified or certified or otherwise duly authenticated copy thereof and, where the order is not in the English language, a translation thereof into English certified by a notary public or authenticated by witness statement or affidavit, and

(b) stating—

(i) that the order is in force and is not subject to appeal;

(ii) where the person against whom the order was made did not appear in the proceedings, that he received notice thereof in sufficient time to enable him to defend them;

(iii) in the case of money, either that at the date of the application the sum payable under the order has not been paid or the amount which remains unpaid, as may be appropriate, or, in the case of other property, the property which has not been recovered; and

(iv) to the best of the witness's knowledge, particulars of what property the person against whom the order was made holds in England and Wales, giving the source of the witness's knowledge.

(2) Unless the court otherwise directs, a witness statement or affidavit for the purposes of this rule may contain statements of information or belief with the sources and grounds thereof.

R115.15.1 **Proof of certification**—The Drug Trafficking Offences Act 1986 (Designated Countries and Territories) Order 1990 (S.I. 1990 No. 1199) in arts 4 and 5 makes special provision for the proof of any order made or judgment given by a court in a designated country and for the certification of various matters arising in the proceedings in that country which may be relevant to registration in the High Court.

R115.15.2 **Application "supported by a witness statement or affidavit"**—See also para. R115.3.8 above.

Register of orders

R115.16 **16.**—(1) There shall be kept in the Central Office under the direction of the Master of the Crown Office a register of the orders registered under the Act.

(2) There shall be included in such register particulars of any variation or setting aside of a registration and of any execution issued on a registered order.

Notice of registration

R115.17 **17.**—(1) Notice of the registration of an order must be served on the person against whom it was obtained by delivering it to him personally or by sending it to him at his usual or last known address or place of business or in such other manner as the court may direct.

(2) Service of such a notice out of the jurisdiction is permissible without leave, and Order 11, rules 5, 6 and 8 shall apply in relation to such a notice as they apply in relation to a claim form.

Application to vary or set aside registration

18. An application made in accordance with CPR Part 23 by the person against whom an order was made to vary or set aside the registration of an order must be made to a judge and be supported by witness statement or affidavit. **R115.18**

Statutory provisions—Section 40 of the 1994 Act states that the High Court shall cancel the registration of an external confiscation order if it appears to the Court that the order has been satisfied by payment of the amount due under it or by the person against whom it was made serving imprisonment in default of payment or by other means. Criminal Justice (International Co-operation) Act 1990 (Enforcement of Overseas Forfeiture Orders) Order 1999, art. 10(3) says that the court shall cancel the registration of an external forfeiture order in similar circumstances. See also, in relation to Scottish orders, the Drug Trafficking Offences (Enforcement in England and Wales) Order 1988. **R115.18.1**

Enforcement of order

19.—(2) If an application is made under rule 18, an order shall not be enforced until after such application is determined. **R115.19**

Effect of rule—Para. (1) of this rule was omitted in 1981. **R115.19.1**

Variation, satisfaction and discharge of registered order

20. Upon the court being notified by the applicant for registration that an order which has been registered has been varied, satisfied or discharged, particulars of the variation, satisfaction or discharge, as the case may be, shall be entered in the register. **R115.20**

Rules to have effect subject to Orders in Council

21. Rules 12 to 20 shall have effect subject to the provisions of the Order in Council made under section 37 or, as the case may be, of the Order in Council made under section 39. **R115.21**

Criminal Justice (International Co-operation) Act 1990: external forfeiture orders

21A. The provisions of this Part of this order shall, with such modifications as are necessary and subject to the provisions of any Order in Council made under section 9 of the Criminal Justice (International Co-operation) Act 1990, apply to proceedings for the registration and enforcement of external forfeiture orders as they apply to such proceedings in relation to external confiscation orders. **R115.21A**

For the purposes of this rule, an external forfeiture order is an order made by a court in a country or territory outside the United Kingdom which is enforceable in the United Kingdom by virtue of any such Order in Council.

"Order in Council made under section 9"—The Criminal Justice (International Co-operation) Act 1990, s.9 provides for the enforcement of overseas court orders for the forfeiture of property used in commission of an offence which corresponds to, or is similar to, the offences specified in s.9(6). Any Order in Council made under the section may authorise the making of rules of court (see s.10). The relevant Orders in Council are the Criminal Justice (International Co-operation) Act 1990 (Enforcement of Overseas Forfeiture Orders) Order 1991 (S.I. 1991 No. 1463), as amended by S.I. 1992 No. 1721, S.I. 1993 No. 1791, S.I. 1993 No. 3148; the Criminal Justice (International Co-operation) Act 1990 (Enforcement of Overseas Forfeiture Orders) (Northern Ireland) Order 1991 (S.I. 1991 No. 1464) as amended by S.I. 1992 No. 1721, S.I. 1993 No. 1791, S.I. 1993 No. 3148, S.I. 1994 No. 1640, S.I. 1997 No. 2977; and the Criminal Justice (International Co-operation) Act 1990 (Enforcement of Overseas Forfeiture Orders) (Scotland) Order 1991 (S.I. 1991 No. 1468) as amended by S.I. 1992 No. 1734, S.I. 1993 No. 1807, S.I. 1993 No. 3155, and as otherwise amended from time to time. The relevant Order in Council is the Criminal Justice (International Co-operation) Act 1990 (Enforcement of Overseas Forfeiture Orders) Order 1991 (S.I. No. 1463). This Order provides for the enforcement in England and Wales of orders made by a court in a designated country or territory for the forfeiture and destruction or other disposal of property (referred to as external forfeiture orders) used in connection with the commission of a drug trafficking offence. The powers given apply to **R115.21A.1**

proceedings which have been or are to be instituted in a designated country or territory and may result in such an order being made there. Article 4 and Sched. 2 to the Order designated countries and territories for the purposes of enforcement of forfeiture orders of courts in those countries and territories and proceedings which may lead to such an order being made there.

R115.21A.2 **"registration of . . . external forfeiture orders"**—Article 10 of the Order in Council made under s.9 of the 1990 Act is in similar terms to s.40 of the 1994 Act and states that on an application the High Court may register an external forfeiture order made in a designated country if (a) it is satisfied that at the time of registration the order is in force and not subject to appeal (see further art. 10(2)), (b) it is satisfied, where the person against whom the order is made did not appear in the proceedings, that he received notice of the proceedings in sufficient time to enable him to defend them; and (c) it is of the opinion that enforcing the order in England and Wales would not be contrary to the interests of justice.

R115.21A.3 **"The provisions of this Part shall . . . apply"**—The rule states that the provisions of this Part shall apply to proceedings for the registration and enforcement of external forfeiture orders as they apply to such proceedings in relation to external confiscation orders. For the manner in which the rules of this Part apply to external confiscation orders, see paras R115.12.2 and R115.13.2 above. The rules of this Part provide, not only for the registration of orders, but also for applications for restraint orders, charging orders and the appointment of receivers. It should be noted, in relation to external forfeiture orders, that the Order in Council made under section 9 of the 1990 Act contains important provisions concerning these applications to which the rules of this Part, by the clear terms of r.21A, are subject; for example, arts. 5 and 6 (restraint orders). It should also be noted that the Order of Council in arts 11 and 12 makes special provision for the proof of any order made or judgment given by a court in a designated country and for the certification of various matters arising in the proceedings in that country which may be relevant to registration and other proceedings in the High Court.

II. Part VI of the Criminal Justice Act 1988

Interpretation

R115.22 **22.**—(1) In this Part of this order, "the 1988 Act" means the Criminal Justice Act 1988 and a section referred to by number means the section so numbered in that Act.

(2) Expressions which are used in this Part of this order which are used in the 1988 Act have the same meanings in this Part of this order as in the 1988 Act and include any extended meaning given by the Criminal Justice (Confiscation) (Northern Ireland) Order 1990.

R115.22.1 **Effect of rule**—See para. R115.0.4 above.

Application of Part I of Order 115

R115.23 **23.** Part I of Order 115 (except rule 11) shall apply for the purposes of proceedings under Part VI of the 1988 Act with the necessary modifications and, in particular—

(a) references to drug trafficking offences and to drug trafficking shall be construed as references to offences to which Part VI of the 1988 Act applies and to committing such an offence;

(b) references to the Drug Trafficking Act 1994 shall be construed as references to the 1988 Act and references to sections 5(2), 26, 27, 29, 30(2), 17(1), 18, 18(5), 39 and 40 of the 1994 Act shall be construed as references to sections 73(6), 77, 78, 80, 81, 81(1), 83(1), 89, 89(5), 96 and 97 of the 1988 Act respectively;

(c) rule 3(2) shall have effect as if the following sub-paragraphs were substituted for sub-paragraphs (a) and (b)—

"(a) state, as the case may be, either that proceedings have been instituted against the defendant for an offence to which Part VI of the 1988 Act applies (giving particulars of the offence) and that they have not been concluded or that, whether by the laying of an information or otherwise, a person is to be charged with such an offence;

(b) state, as the case may be, either that a confiscation order has been made or the grounds for believing that such an order may be made;"

(d) rule 7(3) shall have effect as if the words "certificate issued by a magistrates' court or the Crown Court" were substituted for the words "certificate issued by the Crown Court";

(e) rule 8 shall have effect as if the following paragraph were added at the end—

"(6) Where a receiver applies in accordance with CPR Part 23 for the variation of a confiscation order, the application notice shall be served, with any supporting evidence, on the defendant and any other person who may be affected by the making of an order under section 83 of the 1988 Act, not less than 7 days before the date fixed for the hearing of the application.";

(f) rule 11 shall apply with the necessary modifications where an application is made under section 93J of the 1988 Act for disclosure of information held by government departments.

"Part I . . . shall apply"—This rule applies the provisions of Pt I of this Order (other than r.11) to High Court proceedings under Pt VI of the 1988 Act. Thus, these provisions need to be read in conjunction with ss.76 and 97 of the 1988 Act and in accordance with the particular modifications referred to in this rule. R115.23.1

"Sections 96 and 97 of the 1988 Act"—In the 1988 Act, these sections correspond with sections 39 and 40 of the 1994 Act (see paras R115.12.2 and R115.13.2 above). They deal with the registration and enforcement of external confiscation orders made by courts of designated countries and with the making of orders where confiscation orders may be made in proceedings in designated countries. These matters may be provided for by Order in Council made under s.96. The relevant Order in Council is the Criminal Justice Act 1988 (Designated Countries and Territories) Order 1991 (S.I. No. 2873), as amended. This Order in Council, for the purpose of applying the provisions of Pt VI to orders and proceedings in designated countires, makes certain modifications to those provisions. Some of these modifications relate to sections in Pt VI giving jurisdiction to the High Court (*e.g.* the Order modifies the court's powers under s.77 (restraint orders) and s.78 (charging orders)) and others alter the effect of rules in Pt I of O.115 (*e.g.* the Order inserts s.79A which modifies r.3(2) as applied by r.23 and r.23(c) to Pt VI applications). Thus, where the jurisdiction of the High Court is being invoked in these circumstances, the provisions of Pt VI of the 1988 Act and the rules in Pt I of O.115 have to be read in conjunction with the Order in Council made under s.96. R115.23.2

III. PREVENTION OF TERRORISM (TEMPORARY PROVISIONS) ACT 1989

Interpretation

24. In this Part of this order— R115.24

(a) "the Act" means the Prevention of Terrorism (Temporary Provisions) Act 1989;

(b) "Schedule 4" means Schedule 4 to the Act; and

(c) expressions used have the same meanings as they have in Part III of, and Schedule 4 to, the Act.

Effect of rule—See para. R115.0.5 above. R115.24.1

Assignment of proceedings

25.—(1) Subject to paragraph (2), the jurisdiction of the High Court under the Act shall be exercised by a judge of the Queen's Bench Division or of the Chancery Division. R115.25

(2) The jurisdiction conferred on the High Court by paragraph 9 of Schedule 4 may also be exercised by a Master of the Queen's Bench Division.

"paragraph 9 of Schedule 4"—This paragraph relates to the enforcement in England and Wales of orders under the Act made elsewhere in the British Islands. See para. R115.15.1. R115.25.1

"judge . . . sitting in private"—See further para. R115.2.4 above. R115.25.2

Application for restraint order

R115.26 **26.**—(1) An application for a restraint order under paragraphs 3 and 4 of Schedule 4 may be made by the prosecutor by a claim form, which need not be served on any person.

(2) An application under paragraph (1) shall be supported by a witness statement or affidavit, which shall—

(a) state, as the case may be, either that proceedings have been instituted against a person for an offence under Part III of the Act and that they have not been concluded or that, whether by the laying of an information or otherwise, a person is to be charged with such an offence; and, in either case, give particulars of the offence;

(b) state, as the case may be, that a forfeiture order has been made in the proceedings or the grounds for believing that such an order may be made;

(c) to the best of the witness's ability, give full particulars of the property in respect of which the order is sought and specify the person or persons holding such property and any other persons having an interest in it;

(d) where proceedings have not been instituted, verify that the prosecutor is to have the conduct of the proposed proceedings;

(e) where proceedings have not been instituted, indicate when it is intended that they should be instituted.

(3) A claim form under paragraph (1) shall be entitled in the matter of the defendant, naming him, and in the matter of the Act, and all subsequent documents in the matter shall be so entitled.

(4) Unless the court otherwise directs, a witness statement or affidavit under paragraph (2) may contain statements of information or belief with the sources and grounds thereof.

R115.26.1 **Restraint order**—See paras R115.3.1 and R115.4.3. See para. R115.15.1.

R115.26.2 **Application "supported by a witness statement or affidavit"**—See para. R115.3.8 above.

R115.26.3 **Practice**—Applications under r.26 should be made by claim form or by application notice. The application should be supported by written evidence dealing with all the matters stated in paragraph (2) of this rule. Rule 26(1) is listed in Table 2 of Practice Direction (CPR, Pt 8, Sched. 1 and Sched. 2 to CPR) (see para. 8BPD–003). Consequently, Section B of that Practice Direction takes effect where application is made by claim form with the result that the Pt 8 procedure applies subject to any special or contrary provisions in O.115 and as modified in paras B.6 to B.15 of the Practice Direction. See also para. R115.3.9 above.

Restraint order

R115.27 **27.**—(1) A restraint order may be made subject to conditions and exceptions, including but not limited to conditions relating to the indemnifying of third parties against expenses incurred in complying with the order, and exceptions relating to living expenses and legal expenses of the defendant, but the prosecutor shall not be required to give an undertaking to abide by any order as to damages sustained by the defendant as a result of the restraint order.

(2) Unless the court otherwise directs, a restraint order made without notice of it being served on any person shall have effect until a day which shall be fixed for the hearing where all parties may attend on the application.

(3) Where a restraint order is made the prosecutor shall serve copies of the order and of the witness statement or affidavit in support on the defendant and on all other persons affected by the order.

R115.27.1 **Restraint order**—See paras R115.3.1 and R115.4.3. See R115.15.1.

R115.27.2 **Legal expenses**—A defendant against whom a restraint order has been made may be permitted to draw on the fund which is subject to the order so as to enable him to meet the costs of legal representation, Those costs being taxed on the indemnity basis (*Re L.*, *The Times*, July 10, 1996).

Discharge or variation of order

28.—(1) Subject to paragraph (2), an application to discharge or vary a restraint order shall be made in accordance with CPR Part 23. **R115.28**

(2) Where the case is one of urgency, an application under this rule by the prosecutor may be made without notice.

(3) The application and any witness statement or affidavit in support shall be lodged with the court and, where the application is made in accordance with CPR Part 23 the application notice, shall be served on the following persons (other than the applicant)—

(a) the prosecutor;
(b) the defendant; and
(c) all other persons restrained or otherwise affected by the order;

not less than two clear days before the date fixed for the hearing of the application.

(4) Where a restraint order has been made and has not been discharged, the prosecutor shall notify the court when proceedings for the offence have been concluded, and the court shall thereupon discharge the restraint order.

(5) Where an order is made discharging or varying a restraint order, the applicant shall serve copies of the order of discharge or variation on all persons restrained by the earlier order and shall notify all other persons affected of the terms of the order of discharge or variation.

Compensation

29. An application for an order under paragraph 7 of Schedule 4 shall be made in accordance with CPR Part 23, and the application notice, shall be served, with any supporting evidence, on the person alleged to be in default and on the relevant authority under paragraph 7(5) not less than 7 days before the date fixed for the hearing of the application. **R115.29**

"Application ... under paragraph 7 of Schedule 4"—The Prevention of Terrorism (Temporary Provisions) Act 1989, Sched. 4, para. 7 states that, if proceedings are instituted against a person under Pt III of the Act and he is not convicted, or if convicted his conviction is quashed or he is pardoned, the High Court may on an application by a person who held property which was realisable property, order compensation to be paid to the applicant. See also r.10. See para. R115.15.1. **R115.29.1**

Application for registration

30. An application for registration of a Scottish order, a Northern Ireland order or an Islands order must be made in accordance with CPR Part 23 and may be made without notice. **R115.30**

Evidence in support of application

31.—(1) An application for registration of any such order as is mentioned in rule 30 must be supported by a witness statement or affidavit— **R115.31**

(a) exhibiting the order or a certified copy thereof; and
(b) which shall, to the best of the witness's ability, give particulars of such property in respect of which the order was made as is in England and Wales, and specify the person or persons holding such property.

(2) Unless the court otherwise directs, a witness statement or affidavit for the purposes of this rule may contain statements of information or belief with the sources and grounds thereof.

Application "supported by a witness statement or affidavit"—See also para. R115.3.8 above. **R115.31.1**

Register of orders

R115.32 **32.**—(1) There shall be kept in the Central Office under the direction of the Master of the Crown Office a register of the orders registered under the Act.

(2) There shall be included in such register particulars of any variation or setting aside of a registration, and of any execution issued on a registered order.

Notice of registration

R115.33 **33.**—(1) Notice of the registration of an order must be served on the person or persons holding the property referred to in rule 31(1)(b) and any other persons appearing to have an interest in that property.

(2) Service of such a notice out of the jurisdiction is permissible without permission, and Order 11, rules 5, 6 and 8 shall apply in relation to such a notice as they apply in relation to a claim form.

Application to vary or set aside registration

R115.34 **34.** An application to vary or set aside the registration of an order must be made to a judge in accordance with CPR Part 23 and be supported by a witness statement or affidavit.

This rule does not apply to a variation or cancellation under rule 36.

R115.34.1 **Statutory provision**—The Prevention of Terrorism (Temporary Provisions) Act 1989, Sched. 4, para. 4(3) states that an application for the discharge or variation of a restraint order may be made by any person affected by it. See para. R115.15.1.

Enforcement of order

R115.35 **35.**—(2) If an application is made under rule 34, an order shall not be enforced until after such application is determined.

(3) this rule does not apply to the taking of steps under paragraph 5 or 6 of Schedule 4, as applied by paragraph 9(6) of that Schedule.

R115.35.1 **Effect of rule**—Para. (1) of this rule was omitted in 1991.

Variation and cancellation of registration

R115.36 **36.** If effect has been given (whether in England or Wales or elsewhere) to a Scottish, Northern Ireland or Islands order, or if the order has been varied or discharged by the court by which it was made, the applicant for registration shall inform the court and—

(a) if such effect has been given in respect of all the money or other property to which the order applies, or if the order has been discharged by the court by which it was made, registration of the order shall be cancelled;

(b) if such effect has been given in respect of only part of the money or other property, or if the order has been varied by the court by which it was made, registration of the order shall be varied accordingly.

RSC ORDER 116

THE CRIMINAL PROCEDURE AND INVESTIGATIONS ACT 1996

R116.0.1 **Contents**

Editorial Introduction

This Order was contained in Appendix 1 to the Civil Procedure (Amendment) Rules 1999 and was inserted after CPR, Sched. 1, O.115 by r.60 of those Rules. The Order came into force on April 26, 1999. **R116.0.2**

The Order stipulates in considerable detail the procedure to be followed where an application is made to the High Court under section 54 of the Criminal Procedure and Investigations Act 1996; in effect, it is a self-contained procedural code as to matters of notice, service and evidence. Under that section, the High Court may make an order quashing the acquittal of a person acquitted by a criminal court (so-called "tainted acquittals").

The section applies where (a) a person has been acquitted of an offence (whether before or after the appointed day), and (b) a person has been convicted of "an administration of justice offence" involving interference with or intimidation of a juror or a witness (or potential witness) in any proceedings which led to the acquittal (s.54(1)). For these purposes, the administration of justice offenders are: (1) perverting the course of justice, (2) initimidation etc., of witnesses, jurors and others (Criminal Justice and Public Order Act 1994, s.51(1)), and (3) aiding, abetting etc., another person to commit an offence under the Perjury Act 1911, s.1 (s.54(6)).

Where it appears to the court before which the person was convicted that there is a real possibility that, but for the interference or intimidation, the acquitted person would not have been acquitted, "the court shall certify that it so appears" (s.54(2)), but the court should not so certify if, because of lapse of time or for any other reason, it would be contrary to the interests of justice to take proceedings against the acquitted person for the offence of which he was acquitted (s.54(5)).

Where a court makes an order under s.54(2) certifying that an acquittal was tainted, an application may be made to the High Court for an order quashing the acquittal (s.54(3)). The provisions of RSC, O.116 govern the procedure to be followed on such an application. Rule 5(1) states that an application shall be made by claim form which shall be issued out of the Crown Office by the prosecutor; that is to say, by the individual or body which acted as prosecutor in the proceedings which led to the acquittal (r.2). Rule 5(1) is listed in Table 2 of Practice Direction (CPR Part 8 and Sched. 1 and Sched. 2 to the CPR) (see para. 8BPD–001). Consequently, Section B of that Practice Direction applies and the applicant must use the Pt 8 claim form procedure as modified therein.

On an application being made the Court shall make an order quashing the acquittal if (but shall not do so unless) the four conditions in s.55 are satisfied (s.54(3)).

The four conditions stated in s.55 are as follows:

(1) that it appears to the High Court likely that, but for the interference or intimidation, the acquitted person would not have been acquitted;
(2) that it does not appear to the Court that, because of lapse of time or for any other reason, it would be contrary to the interests of justice to take proceedings against the acquitted person for the offence of which he was acquitted;
(3) that it appears to the court that the acquitted person has been given a reasonable opportunity to make written representations to the Court;
(4) that it appears to the Court that the conviction of the person convicted for the administration of justice offence will stand.

In applying the fourth condition the Court shall take into account all the information before it, but ignore the possibility of new factors coming to light (s.55(5)). Accordingly, the fourth condition has the effect that the Court shall not make an order under s.54(3) if (for instance) it appears to the Court that any time allowed for giving notice of appeal has not expired or that an appeal is pending (s.55(6)).

Related Sources

- Criminal Procedure and Investigations Act 1996, ss.54 to 57 **R116.0.3**
- CPR, Pt 8 (Alternative procedure for claims)
  Practice Direction (CPR, Pt 8 and Sched. 1 and Sched. 2 to the CPR)

Application

1. This Order shall apply in relation to acquittals in respect of offences alleged to be committed on or after 15th April 1997. **R116.1**

Interpretation

2. In this Order, unless the context otherwise requires— **R116.2**

"the Act" means the Criminal Procedure and Investigations Act 1996;
"acquitted person" means a person whose acquittal of an offence is the

subject of a certification under section 54(2) of the Act, and "acquittal" means the acquittal of that person of that offence;

"magistrates' court" has the same meaning as in section 148 of the Magistrates' Courts Act 1980;

"prosecutor" means the individual or body which acted as prosecutor in the proceedings which led to the acquittal.

"record of court proceedings" means—

(a) (where the proceedings took place in the Crown Court) a transcript of the evidence, or

(b) a note of the evidence made by the justices' clerk,

in the proceedings which led to the conviction for the administration of justice offence referred to in section 54(1)(b) of the Act or, as the case may be, the proceedings which led to the acquittal.

"single judge" means a judge of the Queen's Bench Division.

"witness" means a witness whose evidence is contained in a witness statement or affidavit filed under rule 5, 7, 8 or 9;

Assignment of proceedings

R116.3 **3.** The jurisdiction of the High Court under section 54(3) of the Act shall be exercised by a single judge.

Time limit for making application

R116.4 **4.** An application under section 54(3) of the Act shall be made not later than 28 days after—

(a) the expiry of the period allowed for appealing (whether by case stated or otherwise), or making an application for leave to appeal, against the conviction referred to i nsection 54(1)(b) of the Act; or

(b) where notice of appeal or application for leave to appeal against the conviction is given, the determination of the appeal or application for leave to appeal and, for this purpose, "determination" includes abandonment (within the meaning of rule 10 of the Criminal Appeal Rules 1968 or, as the case may be, rule 11 of the Crown Court Rules 1982).

Application

R116.5 **5.**—(1) An application under section 54(3) of the Act shall be made by claim form which shall be issued out of the Crown Office by the prosecutor.

(2) The application shall be accompanied by—

(a) a witness statement or affidavit which deals with the conditions in section 55(1), (2), and (4) of the Act and which exhibits any relevant documents (which may include a copy of any record of court proceedings);

(b) a copy of the certification under section 54(2) of the Act.

Notice to the acquitted person

R116.6 **6.**—(1) The prosecutor shall, within 4 days of the issue of the application, serve written notice on the acquitted person that the application has been issued.

(2) The notice given under paragraph (1) shall—

(a) specify the date on which the application was issued;

(b) be accompanied by a copy of the application and of the documents which accompanied it;

(c) inform the acquitted person that—

(i) the result of the application may be the making of an order by the High Court quashing the acquittal, and

(ii) if he wishes to respond to the application, he must, within 28 days of the date of service on him of the notice, file in the Crown

Office any witness statement or affidavit on which he intends to rely.

Witness statement or Affidavit of Service on Acquitted Person

7. The prosecutor shall, as soon as practicable after service of the notice under rule 6, file at the Crown Office a witness statement or affidavit of service which exhibits a copy of the notice. **R116.7**

Response of acquitted person

8.—(1) If the acquitted person wishes to respond to the application, he shall, within 28 days of service on him of notice under rule 6, file in the Crown Office a witness statement or affidavit which— **R116.8**

(a) deals with the conditions in section 55(1), (2), and (4) of the Act; and

(b) exhibits any relevant documents (which may include a copy of any record of court proceedings).

(2) The acquitted person shall, within 4 days of the filing of the documents mentioned in paragraph (1), serve copies of them on the prosecutor.

Evidence

9.—(1) A witness statement or affidavit filed under rule 5, 7, 8 of this rule may contain statements of information or belief with the sources and grounds thereof. **R116.9**

(2) The prosecutor may, not later than 10 days after expiry of the period allowed under rule 8(1), apply for an order granting permission to file further evidence without notice being served on any other party.

(3) If the single judge grants permission, the order shall specify a period within which further evidence or records are to be filed, and the Crown Office shall serve a copy of the order on the prosecutor and on the acquitted person.

(4) The prosecutor shall, within 4 days of filing further evidence in the Crown Office, serve a copy of that evidence on the acquitted person.

Determination of the application

10.—(1) Subject to paragraph (3), the single judge shall determine whether or not to make an order under section 54(3) of the Act on the basis of the written material provided under rules 5, 7, 8 and 9 in the absence of the prosecutor, the acquitted person, or of any witness. **R116.10**

(2) The determination shall not be made, and any hearing under paragraph (3) shall not take place, before the expiry of—

(a) 10 days after the expiry of the period allowed under rule 8(1), or

(b) 10 days after the expiry of the period allowed by any order made under rule 9(3).

(3) The single judge may, of his own initiative or on the application of the prosecution or acquitted person, order a hearing of the application if he thinks fit.

(4) An application under paragraph (3) shall state whether a hearing is desired in order for a deponent for the other party to attend and be cross-examined, and, if so, the reasons for wishing the witness to attend.

(4) An application under paragraph (3) shall state whether a hearing is desired in order for a deponent for the other party to attend and be cross-examined, and, if so, the reasons for wishing the witness to attend.

(5) An application under paragraph (3) shall be made no later than 7 days after the expiry of the period allowed—

(a) under rule 8(1) or

(b) by any order made under rule 9(3).

(6) Where a hearing is ordered, the single judge may, of his own initiative or on the application of the prosecutor or acquitted person, order a witness to attend in order to be cross-examined.

(7) (7) The prosecutor or the acquitted person, as the case may be, shall within 4 days after filing the application under paragraph (3), serve a copy of it on the other party, and file in the Crown Office a witness statement or affidvit of service.

(8) A party served under paragraph (7) shall, within 5 days of service, file any representations he wishes to make as to whether or not a hearing should be ordered.

(9) Subject to paragraph (10) below—

(a) the single judge shall not determine an application for a hearing under paragraph (3) unless—

(i) a witness statement or affidavit of service has been filed as required by paragraph (7), and

(ii) the period for filing representations allowed under paragraph (8) has elapsed; or

(iii) representations have been filed under paragraph (8).

(b) The requirements imposed by sub-paragraph (a)(i) and (iii) are satisfied even though the witness statement or affidavit of service or, as the case may be, the representations are filed outside the time limits allowed.

(10) Where after an application for a hearing has been made—

(a) no witness statement or affidvit of service has been filed and

(b) no representations under paragraph (8) have been received after the expiry of 7 days from the filing of the application,

the single judge may reject the application.

(11) Where after a hearing is ordered, either the prosecution or the acquitted person desires a witness for the other party to attend the hearing in order to be cross-examined, he must apply for an order under paragraph (5) giving his reasons without notice being served on any other party.

(12) The Crown Office shall serve notice on the prosecutor and the acquitted person of any order made under the foregoing paragraphs of this rule and, where a hearing is ordered, the notice shall—

(a) set out the date, time and place of the hearing, and

(b) give details of any witness ordered to attend for cross-examination.

(13) A hearing ordered under paragraph (3) above shall be in public unless the single judge otherwise directs.

(14) The Crown Office shall serve notice of any order made under section 54(3) of the Act quashing the acquittal or of a decision not to make such an order on the prosecutor, the acquitted person and—

(a) where the court before which the acquittal or conviction occurred was a magistrates' court, on the justices' clerk;

(b) where the court before which the acquittal or conviction occurred was the Crown Court, on the appropriate officer of the Crown Court sitting at the place where the acquittal or conviction occurred.

SCHEDULE 2

Rule 50(4)

CCR ORDER 1

CITATION, APPLICATION AND INTERPRETATION

Application of RSC to county court proceedings

6. Where by virtue of these rules or section 76 of the Act or otherwise any **C1.6**
provision of the RSC is applied in relation to proceedings in a county court, that provision shall have effect with the necessary modifications and in particular—

(b) any reference in that provision to a Master, district judge of the Principal Registry of the Family Division, the Admiralty registrar, or a district judge or taxing officer shall be construed as a reference to the district judge of the county court; and

(d) any reference in that provision to an office of the Supreme Court having the conduct of the business of a division or court or a district registry shall be construed as a reference to the county court office.

Effect of rule—The CCR never were a comprehensive procedural code for the county courts. **C1.6.1**
Section 76 of the CCA states that "in any case provided for by or in pursuance of this Act, the general principles of practice of the High Court may be adopted and applied to proceedings in a county court". The only surviving rule in CCR, O.1, r.6, applies the RSC "with the necessary modifications". *Grepe v. Loam* (1888) 37 Ch.D. 168 is authority for the proposition that a judge in the county court has power—as in the High Court—to order that a litigant be prohibited from making any further application in the proceedings without permission but today the county court judge would no doubt prefer to use the case management powers in Pt 3 of the CPR.

CCR ORDER 3

COMMENCEMENT OF PROCEEDINGS

Appeals to county court

6.—(1) Where by or under any Act an appeal lies to a county court from any **C3.6**
order, decision or award of any tribunal or person, then, subject to any special provision made by or under the Act, the provisions of this rule shall apply.

(2) The appellant shall, within 21 days after the date of the order, decision or award, file—

(a) a request for the entry of the appeal, stating the names and addresses of the persons intended to be served (in this rule called "respondents") and the appellant's address for service, together with as many copies of the request as there are respondents; and

(b) a copy of the order, decision or award appealed against.

(3) Where the provision under which the appeal lies requires the appellant to give to the other parties notice in writing of his intention to appeal and of the grounds of his appeal, the appellant shall file a copy of such notice with the request, and in any other case he shall include in his request a statement of the grounds of the appeal.

(4) On the filing of the documents mentioned in paragraphs (2) and (3) the court officer shall—

(a) enter the appeal in the records of the court and fix the return day;

(b) prepare a notice to each respondent of the day on which the appeal will be heard and annex each copy of the request for the entry of the appeal to a copy of the notice; and

(c) deliver a notice of issue to the appellant.

(5) The return day shall be a day fixed for the hearing of the appeal by the judge (or, if the district judge has jurisdiction to hear the appeal, by the district judge) or, if the court so directs, a day fixed for a pre-trial review.

(6) The notice of the day of hearing shall be served—

(a) by the appellant delivering the notice to the respondent personally; or

(b) by the court sending it by first-class post to the respondent—

(i) at his address for service; or

(ii) where CPR rule 6.5(5) applies at the place of service specified in that rule.

(7) Unless the appellant otherwise requests, service shall be effected in accordance with paragraph (6)(b).

(8) Where a notice is served in accordance with paragraph (6)(b) the date of service shall, unless the contrary is shown, be deemed to be the seventh day after the date on which the notice was sent to the respondent.

(9) Where—

(a) a notice has been sent by post in accordance with paragraph (6)(b) to the respondent's address for service; and

(b) the notice has been returned to the court office undelivered, the court shall send notice of non-service to the appellant pursuant to CPR Rule 6.11 together with a notice informing him that he may request bailiff service at that address.

(10) If the appellant requests bailiff service under paragraph (9), it shall be effected by a bailiff of the court—

(a) inserting the notice, enclosed in an envelope addressed to the respondent, through the letter-box at the respondent's address for service;

(b) delivering the notice to some person, apparently not less than 16 years old, at the respondent's address for service; or

(c) delivering the notice to the respondent personally.

(11) Service of a notice shall be effected not less than 21 days before the hearing, but service may be effected at any time before the hearing on the appellant satisfying the court by witness statement or affidavit that the respondent is about to remove from his address for service.

C3.6.1 **Effect of rule**—Very few statutes give a right of appeal to the county court. It is, of course, a question of construction of the statute itself as to whether or not such a right exists. If it does, CCR, O.3, r.6 governs the procedure.

C3.6.2 **"Request for Entry of Appeal"**—It is surprising that this method of commencing proceedings in the county court has survived (at least for the time being) into the CPR. The relevant form is now numbered N201 (see Practice Direction—Forms—4PD–001). As to other documents required see O.3, r.6(2) and (3). The time limit is "within 21 days after the date of the order, decision or award" (see *Griffiths v. Secretary of State for the Environment* [1983] 2 A.C. 51).

C3.6.3 **"return day"**—Rule 6(5) provides for the fixing of a date for the hearing of the appeal or a pre-trial review. The latter is more likely as the court will wish to give any necessary case management directions and set a timetable for the hearing.

C3.6.4 **Service**—Note the provisions of r.6(6) to (11). Service by the county court bailiff is provided for if service by post fails.

CCR ORDER 4

VENUE FOR BRINGING PROCEEDINGS

Proceedings relating to land

C4.3 **3.** Proceedings—

(a) for the recovery of land;

(b) for the foreclosure or redemption of any mortgage or, subject to Order 31, rule 4, for enforcing any charge or lien on land; or

(c) for the recovery of moneys secured by a mortgage or charge on land,

may be commenced only in the court for the district in which the land or any part of the land is situated.

Effect of rule—Proceedings for the recovery of land are now governed by Pt 8, CPR and its supplementing Practice Direction. The effect of CCR, O.4, r.3 is to require such proceedings to be "commenced only in the court for the district in which the land or any part of the land is situated". The county courts were originally created to provide a local forum for the resolution of disputes. In the context of recovery of land this means "local" to the land itself. C4.3.1

CCR ORDER 5

CAUSES OF ACTION AND PARTIES

Representative proceedings

5.—(1) Where numerous persons have the same interest in any proceedings, not being such proceedings as are mentioned in rule 6, the proceedings may be begun and, unless the court otherwise orders, continued, by or against any one or more of them as representing all or all except one or more of them. C5.5

(2) At any stage of proceedings under this rule the court may—

(a) on the application of a claimant who is suing in a representative capacity, appoint him to represent all, or all except one or more, of the persons on whose behalf he sues;

(b) on the application of the claimant or of a defendant who is sued in a representative capacity, appoint any one or more of the defendants or other persons on whose behalf the defendants are sued to represent all, or all except one or more, of those persons.

Where in the exercise of the power conferred by sub-paragraph (b) the court appoints a person not named as a defendant, it shall make an order under CPR rule 19.1, adding that person as a defendant.

(3) An application under paragraph (2)—

(a) if made under sub-paragraph (a), may be made without notice being served on any other party;

(b) if made under sub-paragraph (b), shall be made on notice—

(i) where the applicant is the claimant, to the person sought to be appointed; or

(ii) where the applicant is a defendant, to the claimant and to any person, other than the applicant, sought to be appointed;

and in each case the notice shall state the facts on which the applicant relies and the names and addresses or, where appropriate a collective description, of the persons to be represented.

(4) Where an order is made granting an application under paragraph (2)(b), the court shall send notice of the order to the person to whom notice of the application was given and shall notify other persons affected by the order in such manner as the court may direct.

(5) A judgment or order given or made in proceedings under this rule shall be binding on all persons on whose behalf the claimant sues or, as the case may be, the defendant is sued but shall not be enforced against any person not a party to the proceedings except with the permission of the court.

(6) An application for permission under paragraph (5) shall be made on notice to the person against whom it is sought to enforce the judgment or order and, notwithstanding that the judgment or orders is binding on him, he may dispute liability to have it enforced against him on the ground that by reason of facts and matters particular to his case he is entitled to be exempted from such liability.

C5.5.1 **Effect of rule**—CCR, O.5, r.5 serves the same purpose for county courts as does RSC, O.15, r.12 in the High Court. See further commentary on RSC, O.15, r.12 in Sched. 1.

Representation of person or class

C5.6 **6.**—(1) In any proceedings concerning—

(a) the estate of a deceased person;

(b) property subject to a trust; or

(c) the construction of a written statement, including a statute,

the court may appoint one or more persons to represent any person (including an unborn person) or class who is or may be interested in or affected by the proceedings, if the person, the class or some member of the class cannot readily be ascertained or cannot be found or if it otherwise appears to the court expedient to exercise this power for the purpose of saving expense.

(2) A judgment or order given or made when a person or persons appointed under paragraph (1) is or are before the court shall be binding on the person or class so represented.

(3) Where, in proceedings to which paragraph (1) applies, a compromise is proposed and some of the persons who are interested in or who may be affected by the compromise (including unborn or unascertained persons) are not parties to the proceedings but—

(a) there is some person in the same interest before the court who assents to the compromise or on whose behalf the court sanctions the compromise; or

(b) the absent persons are represented by a person appointed under paragraph (1) who so assents,

the court, if satisfied that the compromise will be for the benefit of the absent persons and that it is expedient to exercise this power, may approve the compromise and order that it shall be binding on the absent persons, and they shall be bound accordingly except where the order has been obtained by fraud or non-disclosure of material facts.

C5.6.1 **Effect of rule**—CCR, O.5, r.6 serves the same purpose for county courts as does RSC, O.15, r.13 in the High Court. See further commentary on RSC, O.15, r.13 in Sched. 1.

Representation of estate where no personal representative

C5.7 **7.**—(1) Where in any proceedings it appears to the court that a deceased person who was interested in the matter in question in the proceedings has no personal representative, the court may, on the application of any party to the proceedings—

(a) proceed in the absence of a person representing the estate of the deceased person; or

(b) by order appoint a person to represent the estate for the purpose of the proceedings.

(2) Any such order, and any judgment or order subsequently given or made in the proceedings, shall bind the estate of the deceased person to the same extent as if a personal representative of that person had been a party to the proceedings.

(3) Before making an order under this rule, the court may require notice of the application for the order to be given to such of the persons having an interest in the estate as it thinks fit.

C5.7.1 **Effect of rule**—CCR, O.5, r.7 serves the same purpose for county courts as does RSC, O.15, r.15 in the High Court. See further commentary on RSC, O.15, r.15 in Sched. 1.

Proceedings against estates

C5.8 **8.**—(1) Where any person against whom a claim would have laid has died but the cause of action survives, the claim may, if no grant of probate or administration has been made, be brought against the estate of the deceased.

(2) Without prejudice to the generality of paragraph (1), a claim brought against "the personal representatives of A.B. deceased" shall be treated, for the purposes of that paragraph, as having been brought against his estate.

(3) A claim purporting to have been commenced against a person shall be treated, if he was dead at its commencement, as having been commenced against his estate in accordance with paragraph (1), whether or not a grant of probate or administration was made before its commencement.

(4) In any such claim as is referred to in paragraph (1) or (3)—

(a) the claimant shall, where the court fixed a date for the hearing when it issued the claim, on or before that date, or, in any other case within the time allowed for service of the claim form, apply to the court for an order appointing a person to represent the deceased's estate for the purpose of the proceedings or, if a grant of probate or administration has been made, for an order that the personal representative of the deceased be made a party to the proceedings, and in either case for an order that the proceedings be carried on against the person so appointed or, as the case may be, against the personal representative, as if he had been substituted for the estate;

(b) the court may, at any stage of the proceedings and on such terms as it thinks just and either of its own motion or on application, make any such order as is mentioned in sub-paragraph (a) and allow such amendments (if any) to be made and make such other order as the court thinks necessary in order to ensure that all matters in dispute in the proceedings may be effectually and completely determined and adjudicated upon.

(5) Before making an order under paragraph (4) the court may require notice to be given to any insurer of the deceased who has an interest in the proceedings and to such (if any) of the persons having an interest in the estate as it thinks fit.

(6) Where an order is made under paragraph (4), the person against whom the proceedings are to be carried on shall be served with a copy of the order, together with a copy of the application notice if any.

(7) Where no grant of probate or administration has been made, any judgment or order given or made in the proceedings shall bind the estate to the same extent as it would have been bound if a grant had been made and a personal representative of the deceased had been a party to the proceedings.

Effect of rule—CCR, O.5, r.8 serves the same purpose for the county courts as does RSC, O.15, r.6A in the High Court. See further commentary on RSC, O.15, r.6A in Sched. 1. **C5.8.1**

Partners may sue and be sued in firm name

9.—(1) Subject to the provisions of any enactment, any two or more persons claiming to be entitled, or alleged to be liable, as partners in respect of a cause of action and carrying on business within England or Wales may sue or be sued in the name of the firm of which they were partners when the cause of action arose. **C5.9**

(2) Where partners sue or are sued in the name of the firm, the partners shall, on demand made in writing by any other party, forthwith deliver to the party making the demand and file a statement of the names and places of residence of all the persons who were partners in the firm when the cause of action arose.

(3) If the partners fail to comply with such a demand, the court, on application by any other party, may order the partners to furnish him with such a statement and to verify it on oath and may direct that in default—

(a) if the partners are claimants, the proceedings be stayed on such terms as the court thinks fit; or

(b) if the partners are defendants, they be debarred from defending the claim.

(4) When the names and places of residence of the partners have been stated in compliance with a demand or order under this rule, the proceedings shall continue in the name of the firm.

C5.9.1 **Effect of rule**—It is clearly an administrative convenience for partners to be able to sue or be sued in the firm name and CCR, O.5, r.9 so provides. The rule is the same in the High Court (see RSC, O.81, r.1, in Sched. 1, and commentary thereon).

It would seem that actions between a firm and one of its members, or between two firms with a common member, are maintainable in the firm's name: see CCR, O.25, r.10.

Defendant carrying on business in another name

C5.10 **10.**—(1) A person carrying on business in England or Wales in a name other than his own name may, whether or not he is within the jurisdiction, be sued—

(a) in his own name, followed by the words "trading as A.B.", or

(b) in his business name, followed by the words "(a trading name)".

(2) Where a person is sued in his business name in accordance with paragraph (1)(b), the provisions of these rules relating to claims against firms shall, subject to the provisions of any enactment, apply as if he were a partner and the name in which he carried on business were the name of his firm.

C5.10.1 **Effect of rule**—CCR, O.5, r.10 enables a sole trader, carrying on business in a name other than his own to be sued in that name as if it were a firm name. However, unlike partners, a sole trader cannot sue in his business name.

RSC, O.81, r.9 is to like effect for High Court proceedings.

Failure to proceed after death of party

C5.12 **12.**—(1) If, after the death of a claimant or defendant in any claim or matter, the cause of action survives but no order is made substituting any person in whom the cause of action vests or, as the case may be, the personal representatives of the deceased defendant, the defendant or, as the case may be, those representatives may apply to the court for an order that unless the claim is proceeded with within such time as may be specified in the order the claim shall be struck out as against the claimant or defendant who has died; but where it is the claimant who has died, the court shall not make an order unless satisfied that notice of the application has been given to the personal representatives (if any) of the deceased claimant and to any other interested person who the court considers should be notified.

(2) Where a counterclaim is made by a defendant to any claim this rule shall apply in relation to the counterclaim as if the counterclaim were a separate claim and as if the defendant making a counterclaim were a claimant and the person against whom it is made a defendant.

C5.12.1 **Effect of rule**—CCR, O.5, r.12 is to the same effect as RSC, O.15, r.9: see commentary thereon in Sched. 1.

Claim to money in court where change in parties after judgment

C5.13 **13.**—(1) Where any change has taken place after judgment, by death, assignment or otherwise, in the parties to any claim and there is money standing in court to the credit of the claim, any person claiming to be entitled to the money may give to the court notice of his claim, accompanied by a witness statement or affidavit verifying the facts stated in the notice.

(2) The district judge may, if satisfied as to the entitlement of the person giving notice, cause the money to be paid to him or may refer the claim to the judge and may require the claimant to give notice of the claim to any other person.

(3) It shall not be necessary for notice to be given under this rule where the person claiming to be entitled to the money in court has obtained permission under Order 26, rule 5, to issue a warrant of execution.

Effect of rule—CCR, O.5, r.13 only applies where "there is money standing in court to the credit of the claim" and a change has taken place after judgment. The rule derives from the time when all monies due under a county court judgment had to be paid into court (and not, as is usually the case now, direct to the judgment creditor) and consequently is of limited practical significance. Nevertheless, where it does apply it provides a simple procedure whereby "any person claiming to be entitled to the money" can obtain an order for payment out upon satisfying the district judge. A witness statement or affidavit is required (see Pt 32, CPR and its Supplementing Practice Direction). C5.13.1

Bankruptcy of claimant

14. Rules 11 and 13 shall not apply to any case for which provision is made by section 49 of the Act. C5.14

"Section 49 of the Act"—Section 49 of the CCA 1984 states that the bankruptcy of the claimant in any case which the trustee might maintain for the benefit of the creditors shall not cause the action to abate it, within such reasonable time as the court orders, the trustee elects to continue the action and to give security for the costs of the action. Where the trustee does not elect to continue the action on those terms the defendant may avail himself of the bankruptcy as a defence to the action. C5.14.1

CCR ORDER 6

PARTICULARS OF CLAIM

Recovery of land

3.—(1) In a claim for recovery of land the particulars of claim shall— C6.3

(a) identify the land sought to be recovered;
(b) state whether the land consists of or includes a dwelling-house;
(c) give details about the agreement or tenancy, if any, under which the land is held, stating when it commenced and the amount of money payable by way of rent or licence fee;
(d) in a case to which section 138 of the Act applies (forfeiture for non-payment of rent), state the daily rate at which the rent in arrear is to be calculated; and
(e) state the ground on which possession is claimed, whether statutory or otherwise.

(2) In proceedings for forfeiture where the claimant knows of any person entitled to claim relief against forfeiture as underlessee (including a mortgagee) under section 146(4) of the Law of Property Act 1925 or under section 138(9C) of the County Courts Act 1984, the particulars of claim shall give the name and address of that person and the claimant shall file a copy of the particulars of claim for service on him.

(3) Where possession of land which consists of or includes a dwelling-house is claimed because of non-payment of rent, the particulars of claim shall be in the prescribed form and shall also—

(a) state the amount due at the commencement of the proceedings;
(b) give—
  (i) (whether by means of a schedule or otherwise) particulars of all the payments which have been missed altogether; and
  (ii) where a history of late or under-payments is relied upon, sufficient details to establish the claimant's case;
(c) state any previous steps which the claimant has taken to recover arrears of rent and, in the case of court proceedings, state—
  (i) the dates when proceedings were commenced and concluded; and

(ii) the dates and terms of any orders made;

(d) give such relevant information as is known by the claimant about the defendant's circumstances and, in particular, whether (and, if so, what) payments on his behalf are made direct to the claimant by or under the Social Security Contributions and Benefits Act 1992; and

(e) if the claimant intends as part of his case to rely on his own financial or other circumstances, give details of all relevant facts or matters.

Related Sources

C6.3.1
- Pt 8—Alternative Procedure for Claims
- Practice Direction—Alternative Procedure for Claims (see 8PD–001)
- CCR, O.6, r.5—mortgage claim
- CCR, O.6, r.5A—mortgage claim—dwelling house.

C6.3.2 **Effect of rule**—A claim for recovery of land is now made by the Pt 8 procedure of the CPR. CCR, O.6, r.3 sets out additional pleading requirements in such cases.

Mortgage claim

C6.5 **5.**—(1) Where a claimant claims as mortgagee payment of moneys secured by a mortgage of real or leasehold property or possession of such property, the particulars of claim shall contain the information required under this rule and, as the case may be, by rule 5A.

(2) Where there is more than one loan secured by the mortgage, the information required under the following paragraphs of this rule and under rule 5A shall be provided in respect of each loan agreement.

(3) The particulars shall state the date of the mortgage and identify the land sought to be recovered.

(4) Where possession of the property is claimed, the particulars of claim shall state whether or not the property consists of or includes a dwelling-house within the meaning of section 21 of the Act.

(5) The particulars shall state whether or not the loan which is secured by the mortgage is a regulated consumer credit agreement and, if so, specify the date on which any notice required by section 76 or section 87 of the Consumer Credit Act 1974 was given.

(6) The particulars shall show the state of account between the claimant and the defendant by including—

(a) the amount of the advance and of any periodic repayment and any payment of interest required to be made;

(b) the amount which would have to be paid (after taking into account any adjustment for early settlement) in order to redeem the mortgage at a stated date not more than 14 days after the commencement of proceedings specifying the amount of solicitor's costs and administrative charges which would be payable;

(c) where the loan which is secured by the mortgage is a regulated consumer credit agreement, the total amount outstanding under the terms of the mortgage;

(d) the rate of interest payable—

(i) at the commencement of the mortgage;

(ii) immediately before any arrears referred to in sub-paragraph (e) accrued; and

(iii) where it differs from that provided under (ii) above, at the commencement of the proceedings; and

(e) the amount of any interest or instalments in arrear at the commencement of the proceedings.

(7) The particulars of claim shall state any previous steps which the claimant has taken to recover the moneys secured by the mortgage or the mortgaged property and, in the case of court proceedings, state—

(a) the dates when proceedings were commenced and concluded; and
(b) the dates and terms of any orders made.

(8) In this rule "mortgage" includes a legal or equitable mortgage and a legal or equitable charge, and references to the mortgaged property and mortgagee shall be construed accordingly.

Related Sources C6.5.1

- Pt 8—Alternative Procedure for Claims
- Practice Direction—Alternative Procedure for Claims (see 8PD–001)
- CCR, O.6, r.3—recovery of land
- CCR, O.6, r.5A—mortgage claim—dwelling house

Effect of rule—A mortgage action is now commenced using the "Alternative Procedure for Claims" pursuant to Pt 8, CPR (see, in particular, the Practice Direction which supplements Pt 8). The particulars of claim in such cases must, however, continue to comply with the pleading requirements of CCR, O.6, r.5 and, in the case of a dwelling-house, with CCR, O.6, r.5A. C6.5.2

Mortgage claim—dwelling-house

5A.—(1) This rule applies where a claimant claims as mortgagee possession of land which consists of or includes a dwelling-house and in such a case the particulars of claim shall be in the prescribed form. C6.5A

(2) Where the claimant's claim is brought because of failure to make the periodic payments due, the particulars of claim shall—

(a) give details (whether by means of a schedule or otherwise) of all the payments which have been missed altogether;
(b) where a history of late or under-payments is relied upon, provide sufficient details to establish the claimant case;
(c) give details of any other payments required to be made as a term of the mortgage (such as for insurance premiums, legal costs, default interest, penalties, administrative or other charges) together with any other sums claimed stating the nature and amount of each such charge, whether any payment is in arrear and whether or not it is included in the amount of any periodic payment;
(d) give such relevant information as is known by the claimant about the defendant's circumstances and, in particular, whether (and, if so, what) payments on his behalf are made direct to the claimant by or under the Social Security Contributions and Benefits Act 1992.

(3) In a claim to which this rule applies, the claimant shall state in his particulars of claim whether there is any person on whom notice of the claim is required to be served in accordance with section 8(3) of the Matrimonial Homes Act 1983 and, if so, he shall state the name and address of that person and shall file a copy of the particulars of claim for service of that person.

(4) In this rule "mortgage" has the same meaning as in rule 5(8).

Effect of rule—See "Related Sources" and "effect of rule" in commentary to CCR, O.6, r.5 above. C6.5A.1

"Matrimonial Homes Act 1983"—This Act has been repealed but is re-enacted with minor amendments in Sched. 4 to Family Law Act 1996. "Rights of occupation" under the MHA are now known as "matrimonial home rights". C6.5A.2

In practice a land registry or land charges search is required in all cases so that the claimant can satisfy the requirements of CCR, O.6, r.5A(3). It is wrong to suggest that no search for "matrimonial home rights" is required merely because the mortgagors are husband and wife: it is perfectly possible that, unbeknown to the mortgagee, the mortgagors have divorced and there could be a new non-owning spouse with registered matrimonial home rights. Thus the district judge will insist on a search in all cases.

Hire-purchase

6.—(1) Where a claimant claims the delivery of goods let under a hire-purchase agreement or a conditional sale agreement to a person other than a body corporate, he shall in his particulars state in the order following— C6.6

(a) the date of the agreement and the parties to it with the number of the agreement or sufficient particulars to enable the debtor to identify the agreement;
(b) where the claimant was not one of the original parties to the agreement, the means by which the rights and duties of the creditor under the agreement passed to him;
(c) whether the agreement is a regulated agreement and, if it is not a regulated agreement, the reason why;
(d) the place where the agreement was signed by the debtor (if known);
(e) the goods claimed;
(f) the total price of the goods;
(g) the paid-up sum;
(h) the unpaid balance of the total price;
(i) whether a default notice or a notice under section 76(1) or section 98(1) of the Consumer Credit Act 1974 has been served on the debtor, and if it has, the date on which it was so served;
(j) the date when the right to demand delivery of the goods accrued;
(k) the amount (if any) claimed as an alternative to the delivery of the goods; and
(l) the amount (if any) claimed in addition to the delivery of the goods or any claim under sub-paragraph (k), stating the cause of action in respect of which each such claim is made.

(2) Where a claimant's claim arises out of a hire-purchase agreement or a conditional sale agreement but is not for the delivery of goods, he shall in his particulars state in the order following—

(a) the date of the agreement and the parties to it with the number of the agreement or sufficient particulars to enable the debtor to identify the agreement;
(b) where the claimant was not one of the original parties to the agreement, the means by which the rights and duties of the creditor under the agreement passed to him;
(c) whether the agreement is a regulated agreement and, if it is not a regulated agreement, the reason why;
(d) the place where the agreement was signed by the debtor (if known);
(e) the goods let under the agreement;
(f) the amount of the total price;
(g) the paid-up sum;
(h) the amount (if any) claimed as being due and unpaid in respect of any instalment or instalments of the total price; and
(i) the nature and amount of any other claim and the circumstances in which it arises.

(3) Expressions used in this rule which are defined by the Consumer Credit Act 1974 have the same meanings in this rule as they have in that Act.

C6.6.1 **History of rule**—Amended by Civil Procedure (Amendment) Rules 1999 (S.I. 1999 No. 1008).

Related Sources

C6.6.2
- Pt 7—How to Start Proceedings—the Claim Form
- Practice Direction—How to Start Proceedings—The Claim Form—7PD–001
- Practice Direction—Consumer Credit Act Claim—7BPD–001

C6.6.3 **Effect of rule**—As is obvious from the inclusion of CCR, O.6, r.6 in Sched. 2, the pleading requirements in hire-purchase claims have not changed. Prior to the CPR such cases were brought by means of a "fixed-date action". Rule 7.9(a) CPR provides that a Practice Direction "shall set out the circumstances in which the court may give a fixed date for a hearing when it issues a claim" and Practice Direction—Consumer Credit Act Claim (7BPD–001) has been made accordingly.

CCR ORDER 7

SERVICE OF DOCUMENTS

Recovery of land

15.—(1) Where, in the case of a claim form for the recovery of land which is to be served by bailiff, the court is of opinion that it is impracticable to serve the claim form in accordance with any of the foregoing provisions of CPR Part 6, the claim form may be served in a manner authorised by this rule. C7.15

(2) The claim form may be served on any person on the premises who is the husband or wife of the defendant or on any person who has or appears to have the authority of the defendant—

(a) to reside or carry on business in the premises or to manage them on behalf of the defendant or to receive any rents or profits of the premises or to pay any outgoings in respect of the premises; or

(b) to safeguard or deal with the premises or with the furniture or other goods on the premises, and service on any such person shall be effected in the manner required for service of the notice of the day of hearing in accordance with Order 3, rule 6.

(3) Paragraph (2) shall apply to a man and woman who are living with each other in the same household as husband and wife as it applies to the parties to a marriage.

(4) Where the premises are vacant or are occupied only by virtue of the presence of furniture or other goods, the claim form may be served by affixing it to some conspicuous part of the premises.

(5) Unless the court otherwise orders, service of a claim form in accordance with this rule shall be good service on the defendant, but if a claim for the recovery of money is joined with the claim for recovery of land, the court shall order the claim form to be marked "not served" with respect to the money claim unless in special circumstances the court thinks it just to hear and determine both claims.

Related Source C7.15.1

- Part 6—Service of Documents
- Practice Direction—Service (see 6PD–001)

Effect of rule—It is for the court to choose the method of service (r.6.3 of the CPR) and service will normally be by first-class post. Service by the county court bailiff is not retained by Part 6 as a general method of service but CCR, O.7, r.15 clearly envisages it in certain actions for the recovery of land. C7.15.2

If postal service fails the court gives notice in Form N216 (notice of non-service) to the claimant. It is then open to a claimant to attempt personal service; service pursuant to CCR, O.7, r.15(4) where appropriate (e.g. where the Post Office has returned the claim form to the court as the premises appear to be vacant) or to seek an order pursuant to CPR, r.6.8 (service by an alternative method).

Actions for recovery of land should be commenced using the "Alternative Procedure for Claims" in Pt 8: see Practice Direction which supplements Pt 8.

Mortgage possession claims

15A.—(1) After the issue of the claim form in a mortgage possession claim, the claimant shall not less than 14 days before the hearing send to the address of the property sought to be recovered a notice addressed to the occupiers which— C7.15A

(a) states that possession proceedings have been commenced in respect of the property;

(b) shows the name and address of the claimant, of the defendant and of the court which issued the claim form; and

(c) gives details of the case number and of the hearing date.

(2) The claimant shall either—

(a) not less than 14 days before the hearing, file a certificate stating that a notice has been sent in accordance with paragraph (1); or

(b) exhibit the notice to any witness statement or affidavit used at the hearing.

(3) In this rule "mortgage possession claim" means a claim in which the claimant claims as mortgagee possession of land which consists of or includes a dwelling-house and "mortgage" has the same meaning as in Order 6, rule 5(8).

C7.15A.1 **Effect of rule**—The purpose of CCR, O.7, r.15A is to require the claimant to give notice to "the occupiers" of the fact that a claim for possession of the property is to be heard by the court. Usually the occupiers will be well aware of this having been served with the claim form as defendants to the mortgage possession claim but this is not always so as the occupiers could be tenants of the defendants (whether or not the tenancy has been authorized by the mortgagee) who have no idea that they are in danger of being evicted because their landlord is in arrears with his mortgage. The rule give no protection to the occupiers but does at least give them notice so that they can make representations to the court.

Note the strict requirements of r.15A(2). The court will insist upon compliance with the rule in view of its purpose and importance.

CCR ORDER 13

APPLICATIONS AND ORDERS IN THE COURSE OF PROCEEDINGS

General provisions

C13.1 **1.**—(10) An appeal shall lie to a judge from any order made by a district judge in the course of proceedings.

(11) An appeal under paragraph (10) shall be made on notice, which shall be filed and served on the opposite party within 5 days after the order appealed from or such further time as the judge may allow.

C13.1.1 **History of rule**—Amended by Civil Procedure (Amendment) Rules 1999 (S.I. 1999 No. 1008).

Related Sources

C13.1.2
- Pt 23—General Rules about Applications for Court Orders
- Practice Direction—Applications—23PD–001
- CCR, O.37—Rehearing, Setting Aside and Appeal from District Judge.

C13.1.3 **Effect of rule**—CCR, O.13, r.1 gives a right of appeal from a district judge to a circuit judge from "any order made ... in the course of proceedings". This would include, for example, directions or any case management decision of the district judge. For a case management system to work properly it is essential that appellant courts have confidence in those who have to manage cases and consequently appeals on case management decisions ought not to be entered lightly.

The appeal is now a true appeal and no longer takes the form of a complete re-hearing.

An appeal from a district judge should be heard by the circuit judge nominated to be the designated Civil Judge for the court in question wherever possible: if this is not possible by the circuit judge who acts in the D.C.J.'s absence.

Note the strict time limit in O.13, r.1(11).

CCR ORDER 16

TRANSFER OF PROCEEDINGS

Interpleader proceedings under execution

C16.7 **7.**—(1) This rule applies to interpleader proceedings under an execution which are ordered to be transferred from the High Court.

(2) Notice of the hearings or pre-trial review of the proceedings shall be given by the court officer to the sheriff as well as to every other party to the proceedings.

(3) The interpleader claimant shall, within 8 days of the receipt by him of the notice referred to in paragraph (2), file in triplicate particulars of any goods alleged to be his property and the grounds of his interpleader claim and the court officer shall send a copy to the execution creditor and to the sheriff, but the judge may hear the proceedings or, as the case may be, the district judge may proceed with the pre-trial review, if he thinks fit, notwithstanding that the particulars have not been filed.

(4) Subject to any directions in the order of the High Court, damages may be claimed against the execution creditor in the same manner as in interpleader proceedings commenced in a county court.

(5) On any day fixed for the pre-trial review of the proceedings or for the hearing of any application by the sheriff or other party for directions the court may order the sheriff—

(a) to postpone the sale of the goods seized;
(b) to remain in possession of such goods until the hearing of the proceedings; or
(c) to hand over possession of such goods to the district judge,

and, where a direction is given under sub-paragraph (c), the district judge shall be allowed reasonable charges for keeping possession of the goods, not exceeding those which might be allowed to the sheriff, and, if the district judge is directed to sell the goods, such charges for the sale as would be allowed under an execution issued by the county court.

(6) No order made in the proceedings shall prejudice or affect the rights of the sheriff to any proper charges and the judge may make such order with respect to them as may be just.

(7) The charges referred to in paragraphs (5) and (6) shall ultimately be borne in such manner as the judge shall direct.

(8) The order made at the hearing of the proceedings shall direct how any money in the hands of the sheriff is to be disposed of.

Related Sources C16.7.1

- RSC, O.17—Interpleader
- CCR, O.33—Interpleader Proceedings

Effect of rule—CCR, O.16, r.7 applies only to interpleader proceedings under an execution which are transferred from the High Court to the county court. Generally, it is not convenient so to order. In the High Court interpleaders are heard by a master or district judge. In the county court the district judge (as successor to the "high bailiff") cannot hear an interpleader under execution. Although there is no reason for this limitation on transfer from the High Court (the sheriff, not the bailiff, will have levied) O.16, r.7 clearly envisages the hearing being before a circuit judge. C16.7.2

See further commentary to RSC, O.17 and CCR, O.33.

CCR ORDER 19

REFERENCE TO EUROPEAN COURT

Making and transmission of order

15.—(1) In this rule "the European Court" means the Court of Justice of the European Communities and "order" means an order referring a question to the European Court for a preliminary ruling under article 177 of the Treaty establishing the European Economic Community, article 150 of the Treaty establishing the European Atomic Energy Community or article 41 of the Treaty establishing the European Coal and Steel Community. C19.15

(2) An order may be made by the judge before or at the trial or hearing of any claim and either of his own initiative or on the application of any party.

(3) An order shall set out in a schedule the request for the preliminary ruling of the European Court, and the judge may give directions as to the manner and form in which the schedule is to be prepared.

(4) The proceedings in which an order is made shall, unless the judge otherwise orders, be stayed until the European Court has given a preliminary ruling on the question referred to it.

(5) When an order has been made, the court officer shall send a copy thereof to the Senior Master for transmission to the Registrar of the European Court; but, unless the judge otherwise orders, the copy shall not be sent to the Senior Master until the time for appealing to the Court of Appeal against the order has expired or, if an appeal is entered within that time, until the appeal has been determined or otherwise disposed of.

(6) Nothing in these rules shall authorise the district judge to make an order.

Related Sources

C19.15.1 • RSC, O.14—References to the European Court

C19.15.2 **Effect of rule**—See commentary to RSC, O.114 in Sched. 1, O.114, r.1(1) includes references to the ECJ of questions under the Conventions referred to in the Civil Jurisdiction and Judgments Act 1982 and the Contracts (Applicable Law) Act 1990, s.1.

CCR Order 22

Judgments and Orders

Certificate of judgment

C22.8 **8.**—(1) Any person who wishes to have a certificate of any judgment or order given or made in a claim shall make a request in writing to the court stating—

(a) if he is a party to the claim, whether the certificate—

(i) is required for the purpose of taking proceedings on the judgment or order in another court;

(ii) is required for the purpose of enforcing the judgment or order in the High Court; or

(iii) is for the purpose of evidence only;

(b) if he is not a party to the claim, the purpose for which the certificate is required, the capacity in which he asks for it and any other facts showing that the certificate may properly be granted.

(1A) Where the certificate is required for the purpose of enforcing the judgment or order in the High Court, the applicant shall also either—

(a) state that it is intended to enforce the judgment or order by execution against goods; or

(b) confirm that an application has been made for an order under section 42 of the Act (transfer to High Court by order of a county court) and attach a copy of the application to the request for a certificate.

(2) Where the request is made by a person who is not a party to the claim, the request shall be referred to the district judge, who may, if he thinks fit, refer it to the judge.

(3) Without prejudice to paragraph (2), for the purposes of section 12(2) of the Act a certificate under this rule may be signed by the court manager or any other officer of the court acting on his behalf.

Related Sources

C22.8.1 • Art. 8—High Court and County Courts Jurisdiction Order 1991 (SCP Mainwork, Vol. 2—20B–252)

- QB Masters Practice Direction 32—Enforcement in the High Court of County Court Judgments (SCP 1999, Vol. 2—2A–100)
- Civil Jurisdiction and Judgments Act 1982 (SCP 1999, Vol. 2—7B–1)
- Sched. 4—Title II of 1968 Convention as Modified for Allocation of Jurisdiction within U.K. (SCP 1999, Vol. 2—7B–137)

Effect of rule—CCR, O.22, r.8 is a self-contained and straightforward procedure for obtaining a certificate of judgment. In practice, such a certificate is required mainly for the purpose of enforcing the judgment either elsewhere within the U.K. (*i.e.* outside England and Wales) or abroad. **C22.8.2**

Variation of payment

10.—(1) Where a judgment or order has been given or made for the payment of money, the person entitled to the benefit of the judgment or order or, as the case may be, the person liable to make the payment (in this rule referred to as "the judgment creditor" and "the debtor" respectively) may apply in accordance with the provisions of this rule for a variation in the date or rate of payment. **C22.10**

(2) The judgment creditor may apply in writing, without notice being served on any other party, for an order that the money, if payable in one sum, be paid at a later date than that by which it is due or by instalments or, if the money is already payable by instalments, that it be paid by the same or smaller instalments, and the court officer may make an order accordingly unless no payment has been made under the judgment or order for 6 years before the date of the application in which case he shall refer the application to the district judge.

(3) The judgment creditor may apply to the district judge on notice for an order that the money, if payable in one sum, be paid at an earlier date than that by which it is due or, if the money is payable by instalments, that it be paid in one sum or by larger instalments, and any such application shall be made in writing stating the proposed terms and the grounds on which it is made.

(4) Where an application is made under paragraph (3)—

(a) the proceedings shall be automatically transferred to the debtor's home court if the judgment or order was not given or made in that court; and

(b) the court officer shall fix a day for the hearing of the application before the district judge and give to the judgment creditor and the debtor not less than 8 days' notice of the day so fixed,

and at the hearing the district judge may make such order as seems just.

(5) The debtor may apply for an order that the money, if payable in one sum, be paid at a later date than that by which it is due or by instalments or, if the money is already payable by instalments, that it be paid by smaller instalments, and any such application shall be in the appropriate form stating the proposed terms, the grounds on which it is made and including a signed statement of the debtor's means.

(6) Where an application is made under paragraph (5), the court officer shall—

(a) send the judgment creditor a copy of the debtor's application (and statement of means); and

(b) require the judgment creditor to notify the court in writing, within 14 days of service of notification upon him, giving his reasons for any objection he may have to the granting of the application.

(7) If the judgment creditor does not notify the court of any objection within the time stated, the court officer shall make an order in the terms applied for.

(8) Upon receipt of a notice from the judgment creditor under paragraph (6), the court officer may determine the date and rate of payment and make an order accordingly.

(9) Any party affected by an order made under paragraph (8) may, within

14 days of service of the order on him and giving his reasons, apply on notice for the order to be re-considered and, where such an application is made—

(a) the proceedings shall be automatically transferred to the debtor's home court if the judgment or order was not given or made in that court; and

(b) the court officer shall fix a day for the hearing of the application before the district judge and give to the judgment creditor and the debtor not less than 8 days' notice of the day so fixed.

(10) On hearing an application under paragraph (9), the district judge may confirm the order or set it aside and make such new order as he thinks fit and the order so made shall be entered in the records of the court.

(11) Any order made under any of the foregoing paragraphs may be varied from time to time by a subsequent order made under any of those paragraphs.

C22.10.1 **Effect of rule**—It has always been a feature of the county courts to provide for payment of a judgment debt by instalments. It used not to be possible for a High Court judgment to provide for payment by instalments (though a similar result could be achieved by applying for a stay of execution pursuant to RSC, O.47, r.1) but it is now (see CPR, r.40.11(a)).

Inevitably changes of circumstances can occur which render it appropriate to review an order for payment by instalments. CCR, O.22, r.10 provides for either a creditor or debtor to seek a review of an instalment order. Subject to the provisions of the rule, an application is considered by the "court officer" or, if necessary, by the district judge.

Set-off of cross-judgments

C22.11 **11.**—(1) An application under section 72 of the Act for permission to set off any sums, including costs, payable under several judgments or orders each of which was obtained in a county court shall be made in accordance with this rule.

(2) Where the judgments or orders have been obtained in the same county court, the application may be made to that court on the day when the last judgment or order is obtained, if both parties are present, and in any other case shall be made on notice.

(3) Where the judgments or orders have been obtained in different county courts, the application may be made to either of them on notice, and notice shall be given to the other court.

(4) The district judge of the court to which the application is made and the district judge of any other court to which notice is given under paragraph (3) shall forthwith stay execution on any judgment or order in his court to which the application relates and any money paid into court under the judgment or order shall be retained until the application has been disposed of.

(5) The application may be heard and determined by the court and any order giving permission shall direct how any money paid into court is to be dealt with.

(6) Where the judgments or orders have been obtained in different courts, the court in which an order giving permission is made shall send a copy of the order to the other court, which shall deal with any money paid into that court in accordance with the order.

(7) The court officer or, as the case may be, each of the court officers affected shall enter satisfaction in the records of his court for any sums ordered to be set off, and execution or other process for the enforcement of any judgment or order not wholly satisfied shall issue only for the balance remaining payable.

(8) Where an order is made by the High Court giving permission to set off sums payable under several judgments and orders obtained respectively in the High Court and a county court, the court officer of the county court shall, on receipt of a copy of the order, proceed in accordance with paragraph (7).

C22.11.1 **"section 72 of the Act"**—See SCP 1999, Vol. 2, para. 20A–745—"set off in cases of cross judgments in county courts and High Court. The section deals with the situation where parties have obtained judgments against one another ("cross-judgments"), one obtained in a county court and the other in a county court or in the High Court.

Order of appellate court

13. Where the Court of Appeal or High Court has heard and determined an appeal from a county court, the party entitled to the benefit of the order of the Court of Appeal or High Court shall deposit the order or an office copy thereof in the office of the county court. C22.13

CCR ORDER 24

SUMMARY PROCEEDINGS FOR THE RECOVERY OF LAND

Contents C24.0.1

Part I—Land

Editorial Introduction

CCR, O.24, Pt I is modelled on RSC, O.113. It provides a fast and economical procedure for obtaining an order for possession against squatters. C24.0.2

Interim possession orders are available only in the county court (not the High Court) and are governed by O.24, Pt II. There are several additional limitations which apply to Pt II—importantly, the proceedings must not include a claim other than for the recovery of land; "premises" is defined to exclude open land; and the applicant must commence proceedings within 24 hours of the date on when he knew, or ought reasonably to have known, that the respondent, or any of the respondents, was in occupation. An interim possession order compels the respondent to vacate within 24 hours of service of the order. The order is enforceable by the police, not county court bailiffs.

Related Sources C24.0.3

- Criminal Justice and Public Order Act 1994, Pt V
- RSC, O.113—Summary Proceedings for Possession of Land

Forms C24.0.4

- N8(1)—Notice to respondent when a matter will be heard under O.24
- N36—Order for possession under O.24
- N51—Warrant of restitution (O.24, r.6(1))
- N52—Warrant of possession under O.24
- N130—Application for possession order including application for interim possession order
- N131—Notice of application for interim possession order
- N132—Affidavit of service of notice of application for interim possession order
- N133—Affidavit of occupier to oppose the making of an interim possession order

- N134—Interim possession order
- N135—Affidavit of service of interim possession order
- N136—Order for possession
- N312—Originating Application for Possession under O.24

PART I—LAND

Proceedings to be by claim form

C24.1 **1.**—(1) Where a person claims possession of land which he alleges is occupied solely by a person or persons (not being a tenant or tenants holding over after the termination of the tenancy) who entered into or remained in occupation without his licence or consent or that of any predecessor in title of his, the proceedings may be brought by claim form in accordance with the provisions of this Order.

(2) Where proceedings of the type referred to in paragraph (1) are brought, the court will fix a day for the hearing when it issues the claim form.

C24.1.1 **Effect of rule**—Proceedings under CCR, O.24 are now commenced by claim form (see Pt 7 of the CPR) and the court fixes a hearing date upon issue. The defendant is entitled to 5 days or 2 days notice (see CCR, O.24, r.5) and service is effected pursuant to CCR, O.24, r.3. The hearing date will be the earliest possible date having made due allowance for the service and notice requirements. Note the requirements for a witness statement or affidavit in CCR, O.24, r.2.

Witness statement or affidavit in support

C24.2 **2.**—(1) The applicant shall file in support of the claim form a witness statement or affidavit stating—

(a) his interest in the land;

(b) the circumstances in which the land has been occupied without licence or consent and in which his claim to possession arises; and

(c) that he does not know the name of any person occupying the land who is not named in the claim form.

(2) Where the applicant considers that service in accordance with rule 3(2)(b) may be necessary, he shall provide, together with the claim form, sufficient stakes and sealable transparent envelopes for such service.

C24.2.1 **"witness statement"**—see Pt 22 of the CPR—Statements of Truth: Pt 32 of the CPR—Evidence and, in particular, the Practice Direction Supplementing Pt 32 (paras 17.1 *et seq.*).

C24.2.2 **"his interest in the land"**—Note the wording of CCR, O.24, r.2(1)(a): this means that the witness statement (or affidavit) must be by the claimant personally and not, for example, by his solicitor.

Service of claim form

C24.3 **3.**—(1) Where any person in occupation of the land is named in the claim form, the application shall be served on him—

(a) by delivering to him personally a copy of the claim form, together with the notice of the return day and a copy of the witness statement or affidavit in support;

(b) by an officer of the court leaving the documents mentioned in sub-paragraph (a), or sending them to him, at the premises;

(c) in accordance with CPR rule 6.4(2); or

(d) in such other manner as the court may direct.

(2) Where any person not named as a respondent is in occupation of the land, the claim form shall be served (whether or not it is also required to be

served in accordance with paragraph (1)), unless the court otherwise directs, by—

(a) affixing a copy of each of the documents mentioned in paragraph (1)(a) to the main door or other conspicuous part of the premises and, if practicable, inserting through the letterbox at the premises a copy of those documents enclosed in a sealed transparent envelope addressed to "the occupiers", or

(b) placing stakes in the ground at conspicuous parts of the occupied land, to each of which shall be affixed a sealed transparent envelope addressed to "the occupiers" and containing a copy of each of the documents mentioned in paragraph (1)(a).

Effect of rule—Note the differing methods of service according to whether or not there is a named defendant (in most cases there is not: the defendant is "Persons Unknown"—see *e.g. McPhail v. Persons Unknown* [1973] Ch. 447) and whether the land includes a "main door". Thus, for example, where there are no premises (*e.g.* caravans trespassing on open land) service is effected by placing stakes in the ground at conspicuous parts of the occupied land to each of which is affixed a sealed transparent envelope addressed to "the occupiers" containing a copy of the claim form, notice of the "return day" (*i.e.* the hearing date) and the witness statement (or affidavit) in support. C24.3.1

Application by occupier to be made a party

4. A person not named as a respondent who is in occupation of the land and wishes to be heard on the question whether an order for possession should be made may apply at any stage of the proceedings to be joined as respondent, and the notice of the return day shall contain a notice to that effect. C24.4

Hearing of claim

5.—(1) Except in case of urgency and by permission of the court, the day fixed for the hearing of the claim— C24.5

(a) in the case of residential premises, shall not be less than 5 days after the day of service, and

(b) in the case of other land, shall not be less than 2 days after the day of service.

(3) An order for possession in proceedings under this order shall be to the effect that the applicant do recover possession of the land mentioned in the claim form.

(4) Nothing in this order shall prevent the court from ordering possession to be given on a specified date in the exercise of any power which could have been exercised if possession had been sought otherwise than in accordance with this order.

Effect of rule—The hearing is a summary *trial.* Thus if the claimant proves his case the district judge must make an order for possession forthwith (see *GLC v. Jenkins* [1975] 1 W.L.R. 155; *McPhail v. Persons Unknown* [1973] Ch. 447). The defendant cannot prevent judgment merely by raising a triable issue. However, if the defendant raises a substantial defence, possibly requiring oral evidence, the case is not suitable for summary trial: see *Eyles v. Wells* (1991) CA, Transcript 376, and commentary to RSC, O.113. C24.5.1

"do recover possession"—The order provides that the claimant "do recover possession" and is therefore enforceable against all occupiers of the land (*R. v. Wandsworth County Court, ex p. London Borough of Wandsworth* [1995] 1 W.L.R. 1314). The court has no power to suspend the order for possession (*McPhail v. Persons Unknown* [1973] Ch. 447). C24.5.2

Warrant of possession

6.—(1) Subject to paragraphs (2) and (3), a warrant of possession to enforce an order for possession under this order may be issued at any time after the making of the order and subject to the provisions of order 26, rule 17, a warrant of restitution may be issued in aid of the warrant of possession. C24.6

(2) No warrant of possession shall be issued after the expiry of 3 months

from the date of the order without the permission of the court, and an application for such permission may be made without notice being served on any other party unless the court otherwise directs.

(3) Nothing in this rule shall authorise the issue of a warrant of possession before the date on which possession is ordered to be given.

C24.6.1 **Effect of rule**—See commentary to RSC, O.113—"writ of possession".

In *Wiltshire County Council v. Fraser* [1986] 1 W.L.R. 109 it was held that a warrant of restitution will issue to recover land from occupants who were neither parties to the original proceedings nor dispossessed by the original order provided there is a plain and sufficient nexus between the order for possession and the need to effect further recovery of land.

In the county court warrants are executed by the county court bailiffs.

Setting aside order

C24.7 **7.** The judge or district judge may, on such terms as he thinks just, set aside or vary any order made in proceedings under this order.

PART II—INTERIM POSSESSION ORDERS

Definitions and interpretation

C24.8 **8.**—(1) In this Part of this order—

(a) "applicant" means a person who applies for an interim possession order;

(b) "premises" means premises within the meaning of section 12 of the Criminal Law Act 1977; and

(c) "respondent" means a person against whom an application for an interim possession order is made, whether or not that person is named in the application or order.

(2) Where a rule in this Part of this order requires an act to be done within a specified number of hours, CPR rule 2.8(4) shall not apply to the calculation of the period of time within which the act must be done.

C24.8.1 **"Interim Possession Orders"**—are unique to the county court (see *Editorial Introduction* to CCR, O.24).

Conditions for interim possession order application

C24.9 **9.** In proceedings for possession under Part I of this order, an application may be made for an interim possession order where the following conditions are satisfied—

(a) the only claim made in the proceedings is for the recovery of premises;

(b) the claim is made by a person who—

(i) has an immediate right to possession of the premises; and

(ii) has had such a right throughout the period of unlawful occupation complained of;

(c) the claim is made against a person (not being a tenant holding over after the termination of the tenancy) who entered the premises without the applicant's consent and has not subsequently been granted such consent, but no application for an interim possession order may be made against a person who entered the premises with the consent of the person who, at the time of entry, had an immediate right to possession of the premises; and

(d) the claim is made within 28 days of the date on which the applicant first knew, or ought reasonably to have known, that the respondent, or any of the respondents, was in occupation.

Issue of the applications

C24.10 **10.**—(1) In proceedings in which an application for an interim possession order is made, unless otherwise provided, rules 2 to 7 shall not apply.

(2) The applicant shall file—

(a) a claim form;

(b) a witness statement or affidavit in support; and

(c) an application notice,

each of which shall be in the appropriate prescribed form, together with sufficient copies for service on the respondent.

(3) The witness statement or affidavit shall be sworn by the applicant personally or, where the application for an interim possession order is made by a body corporate, shall be sworn by an officer of the body corporate duly authorised to swear the witness statement or affidavit on its behalf.

(4) On the filing of the documents mentioned in paragraph (2), the court shall—

(a) issue the claim form and the application for an interim possession order;

(b) fix an appointment for the application to be considered; and

(c) insert the time of that appointment in the application notice filed under paragraph (2) and in the copy to be served on the respondent.

(5) The time fixed for consideration of the application for an interim possession order shall be as soon as possible after the documents have been filed, but not less than 3 days after the date on which the application for an interim possession order is issued.

Service of the notice of application

11.—(1) Within 24 hours of the issue of the application for an interim possession order, the applicant shall serve the following documents on the respondent, namely— **C24.11**

(a) the application notice; and

(b) the prescribed form of respondent's witness statement or affidavit, which shall be attached to the application notice.

(2) The applicant shall serve the documents mentioned in paragraph (1) by fixing a copy of them to the main door or other conspicuous part of the premises and, if practicable, inserting through the letter-box at the premises a copy of the documents in a sealed, transparent envelope addressed to "the occupiers".

(3) Additionally (but not alternatively), the applicant may place stakes in the ground at conspicuous parts of the premises to each of which shall be fixed a sealed transparent envelope addressed to "the occupiers" and containing a copy of the documents.

(4) At or before the time fixed for consideration of the application for an interim possession order, the applicant shall file a witness statement or affidavit of service in the prescribed form in relation to the documents mentioned in paragraph (1).

(5) At any time before the time fixed for consideration of the application for an interim possession order the respondent may file a witness statement or affidavit in the prescribed form in response to the application.

Consideration of the application

12.—(1) If the respondent has filed a witness affidavit in accordance with rule 11(5), he may attend before the court when the application for an interim possession order is considered to answer such questions on his witness statement or affidavit or on the applicant's witness statement or affidavit as the court may put to him. **C24.12**

(2) The parties' witness statements or affidavits shall be read in evidence and no oral evidence shall be adduced except in response to questions put by the court.

(3) If the court so directs, an application for an interim possession order may be dealt with in private and in the absence of one or both of the parties.

(4) In deciding whether to grant an interim possession order the court shall have regard to whether the applicant has given or is prepared to give undertakings in support of his application—

(a) to reinstate the respondent if, after an interim possession order has been made, the court holds that the applicant was not entitled to the order;

(b) to pay damages if, after an interim possession order has been made, the court holds that the applicant was not entitled to the order;

(c) not to damage the premises pending final determination of the possession proceedings;

(d) not to grant a right of occupation to any other person pending final determination of the possession proceedings; and

(e) not to damage or dispose of any of the respondent's possessions pending final determination of the possession proceedings.

(5) The court shall make an interim possession order if—

(a) the applicant has filed witness statement or affidavit of service of the notice of application; and

(b) the court is satisfied that—

(i) the conditions specified in rule 9 are met; and

(ii) any undertakings given by the applicant as a condition of making the order are adequate.

(6) An interim possession order shall be in a prescribed form and shall be to the effect that the respondent vacate the premises specified in the claim form within 24 hours of service of the order.

(7) On the making of an interim possession order, the court shall fix a return date for the hearing of the claim which shall be not less than 7 days after the date on which the interim possession order is made.

(8) Where an interim possession order is made, the court officer shall submit a draft of the order as soon as possible to the judge or district judge by whom it was made for approval, and when the draft order has been approved the court shall insert in the order the time limit for service under rule 13(1).

(9) Where the court does not make an interim possession order—

(a) the court officer shall fix a return date for the hearing of the claim;

(b) the court may give directions for the further conduct of the matter; and

(c) subject to such directions, the matter shall proceed in accordance with Part I of this order.

(10) When it has considered the application for an interim possession order, the court shall give a copy of the respondent's witness statement or affidavit (if any) to the applicant, if the applicant requests such a copy.

(11) The court shall serve any directions made under paragraph (9) on the parties and at the same time shall serve on the respondent a copy of the claim form and witness statement or affidavit in support.

Service and enforcement of the interim possession order

C24.13 **13.**—(1) An interim possession order must be served within 48 hours of the judge or district judge's approving the draft order under rule 12(8).

(2) The applicant shall serve copies of the claim form, the applicant's witness statement or affidavit and the interim possession order in accordance with rule 11(2) and (3) or in such other manner as the court may direct.

(3) Order 26, rule 17 (enforcement of warrant of possession) shall not apply to the enforcement of an interim possession order.

(4) If an interim possession order is not served within the time limit specified by this rule or by any order extending or abridging time, the applicant may apply to the court for directions for the application for

possession to continue under Part I of this order as if it had not included a claim for an interim possession order.

Matters arising after making of an interim possession order

14.—(1) Before the return date the applicant shall file a witness statement or affidavit of service in the prescribed form in relation to the documents specified in rule 13(2), and no final order for possession may be made unless such a witness statement or affidavit has been filed. C24.14

(2) The interim possession order shall expire on the return date.

(3) On the return date the court may make such order as appears appropriate and may in particular—

(a) make a final order for possession;
(b) dismiss the claim for possession;
(c) give directions for the application for possession to continue under Part I of this order as if it had not included a claim for an interim possession order.

(4) An order may be made on the return date in the absence of one or both of the parties.

(5) If the court holds that the applicant was not entitled to an interim possession order, the respondent may apply for relief pursuant to any undertakings given by the applicant.

(6) Unless it otherwise directs, the court shall serve a copy of any order or directions made under this rule on the parties.

(7) Unless the court otherwise directs, service on the respondent under paragraph (6) shall be in accordance with rule 11(2) and (3).

(8) Rule 6 (warrant of possession) shall apply to the enforcement of a final order for possession made under this rule.

Application to set aside an interim possession order

15.—(1) If the respondent has vacated the premises, he may apply on grounds of urgency for the interim possession order to be set aside before the return date. C24.15

(2) An application under this rule shall be supported by a witness statement or affidavit.

(3) On receipt of an application to set aside, the judge or district judge shall give directions as to—

(a) the date for the hearing; and
(b) the period of notice, if any, to be given to the applicant and the mode of service of any such notice.

(4) No application to set aside an interim possession order may be made under CPR Part 39.3.

(5) Where no notice is required under paragraph (3)(b), the only matter to be dealt with at the hearing shall be whether the interim possession order should be set aside (and the consequent application of any undertaking given under rule 12(4)(a)) and all other matters shall be dealt with on the return date.

(6) The court shall serve on the applicant a copy of any order made under paragraph (5) and, where no notice is required under paragraph (3)(b), the court shall at the same time serve a copy of the respondent's application to set aside and the witness statement or affidavit in support.

(7) Where notice is required under paragraph (3)(b), the court may treat the application as an application to bring forward the return date, in which case rule 14(2) to (8) shall apply accordingly.

CCR ORDER 25

ENFORCEMENT OF JUDGMENTS AND ORDERS: GENERAL

C25.0.1 **Contents**

Editorial Introduction

C25.0.2 CCR, Orders 25–35 inclusive, are concerned with enforcement of judgments. O.25, r.2 facilitates transfer for enforcement purposes (for oral examinations, see O.25, r.3; for charging orders see O.31; for attachment of earnings see O.27; and for judgment summons see O.28).

Unlike the High Court an affidavit is not required on application for an oral examination.

Interest on Judgment Debts (O.25, r.5A) differs from the High Court in two respects: Judgments far less than £5,000 carry no interest; interest ceases to run as soon as enforcement proceedings (including an oral examination) are issued unless the enforcement proceedings fail to produce any result.

Warrants are enforced by county court bailiffs (not sheriffs officers as in the High Court), hence the need for court records (O.25, r.7). Applications to suspend warrants are common. O.25, r.8 includes a "paper adjudication" procedure by a court clerk with reference to the district judge only if a party applies for re-consideration.

O.25, rr.9 and 10 are based on the equivalent RSC in RSC, O.81.

O.25, r.11 deals with enforcement of a High Court judgment in a county court (attachment of earnings, for example, is not available in the High Court—save for certain Family Division cases) while O.25, r.13 deals with transfer to the High Court for enforcement (which is necessary, for example, where it is sought to enforce by execution against goods a judgment for £5,000 or more and is possible if the judgment is for £1,000 or more).

Related Sources

C25.0.3
- CCR, O.26–O.35 inclusive
- Attachment of Earnings Act 1971 (see SCP 1999, Vol. 2, Section 21E)
- County Courts Act 1984, Pt V (see SCP 1999, Vol. 2, Section 20A)
- Charging Orders Act 1979 (see SCP 1999, Vol. 2, Section 21F)
- County Court Funds Rules 1987
- County Court (Interest on Judgment Debts) Order 1991 (S.I. 1991 No. 1184)
- High Court and County Courts Jurisdiction Order 1991 (see SCP 1999, Vol. 2, Section 20B)
- *Queen's Bench Masters' Practice Direction No. 32—Enforcement in the High Court of county court judgments* (see SCP 1999, Vol. 2, Section 2A, para. 2A–100)

Forms

C25.0.4
- N37—Order for oral examination of judgment debtor
- N38—Order for oral examination (person other than judgment debtor)
- N39—Order for debtor's attendance at an adjourned hearing or an oral examination
- N40—Warrant of committal—oral examination
- N41—Order suspending judgment or order and/or warrant of execution/committal
- N41A—Order suspending warrant (determination)
- N316—Request for oral examination
- N322—Order for recovery of money awarded by tribunal
- N322A—Application for order to recover money awarded by tribunal or other body
- N322H—Request to register a High Court judgment or order for enforcement
- N328—Notice of transfer of proceedings to the High Court
- See also complete list of "Forms of Enforcement" (see SCP 1999, Vol. 2, Section 1C)

Cognate RSC

C25.0.5
- RSC, O.45—Enforcement of Judgments and Orders: General
- RSC, O.47, r.1—Power to stay execution by writ of *fi-fa*

- RSC, O.48—Examination of Judgment Debtor, etc.
- RSC, O.81, r.5—Enforcement of judgment or order against firm
- RSC, O.81, r.6—Enforcing judgment or order in actions between partners, etc.

Judgment creditor and debtor

1. In this Order and Orders 26 to 29 "judgment creditor" means the person who has obtained or is entitled to enforce a judgment or order and "debtor" means the person against whom it was given or made. **C25.1**

Transfer of proceedings for enforcement

2.—(1) Where, with a view to enforcing a judgment or order obtained by him in a county court, a judgment creditor desires to apply for— **C25.2**

(a) the oral examination of the debtor;
(b) a charging order under section 1 of th eCharging Orders Act 1979;
(c) an attachment of earnings order; or
(d) the issue of a judgment summons,

and the application is required by any provision of these rules to be made to another county court, the judgment creditor shall make a request in writing to the court officer of the court in which the judgment or order was obtained for the transfer of the proceedings to the other court.

(2) On receipt of a request under paragraph (1), the court officer shall make an order transferring the proceedings to the other court and shall—

(a) make an entry of the transfer in the records in his court; and
(b) send to the court to which the proceedings have been transferred a certificate of the judgment or order stating the purpose for which it has been issued, and, if requested by that officer, all the documents in his custody relating to the proceedings.

(3) When the proceedings have been transferred to the other court—

(a) the court shall give notice of the transfer to the judgment creditor and the debtor;
(b) any payment which, by or under these rules or the Court Funds Rules 1987, is authorised or required to be made into court shall be made into that court; and
(c) subject to sub-paragraph (d), any subsequent steps in the proceedings shall be taken in that court, but
(d) any application or appeal under Order 37 shall be made to the court in which the judgment or order was obtained.

(4) If the judgment creditor desires to make a subsequent application for any of the remedies mentioned in paragraph (1)(a) to (d) and the application is required to be made to another court, he may make a request under paragraph (1) to the court to which the proceedings have been transferred and paragraphs (2) and (3) shall apply with the necessary modifications.

Effect of rule—It is usually necessary for enforcement proceedings to be taken in the judgment debtor's local county court—hence the straightforward provisions of CCR, O.25, r.2. (It is not necessary to transfer for the purpose of issuing a warrant—see CCR, O.26: the warrant itself is sent to the judgment debtors' local court as an administrative act for execution by bailiffs of the debtor's local court). **C25.2.1**

Oral examination of debtor

3.—(1) Where a person has obtained a judgment or order in a county court for the payment of money or where an order has been made under rule 12 of this order, the appropriate court may, on an application made by the judgment creditor without notice being served on any other party, order the debtor or, if the debtor is a body corporate, an officer thereof to attend before **C25.3**

the court officer and be orally examined as to the debtor's means of satisfying the judgment or order, and may also order the person to be examined to produce at the time and place appointed for the examination any books or documents in his possession relevant to the debtor's means.

(1A) An application under paragraph (1) shall certify the amount of money remaining due under the judgment, order or award (as that word is defined by rule 12(1) of this Order).

(2) The appropriate court for the purposes of paragraph (1) shall be the court for the district in which the person to be examined (or, if there are more such persons than one, any of them) resides or carries on business.

(3) The order shall be served in the manner required for service of the notice of the day of hearing in accordance with Order 3, rule 6 except that Order 3, rule 6(11) will not apply.

(4) If the person to be examined fails to attend at the time and place fixed for the examination, the court may adjourn the examination and make a further order for his attendance and any such order shall direct that any payments made thereafter shall be paid into court and not direct to the judgment creditor.

(5) Nothing in Order 29, rule 1(2) to (7) shall apply to an order made under paragraph (4), but Order 27, rules 7B and 8, shall apply, with the necessary modifications, as they apply to orders made under section 23(1) of the Attachment of Earnings Act 1971 except that for a period of 5 days specified in paragraph (1) of Order 27, rule 8 there shall be substituted a period of 10 days.

(5A) Where an examination has been adjourned, the judgment creditor, if requested to do so by the person to be examined not less than 7 days before the day fixed for the adjourned examination shall pay to him a sum reasonably sufficient to cover his expenses in travelling to and from the court unless such a sum was paid to him at the time of service of the order for oral examination.

(5B) The judgment creditor shall, not more than 4 days before the day fixed for the adjourned examination, file a certificate stating either that no request has been made under paragraph (5A) or that a sum has been paid in accordance with such a request.

(5C) Where the person to be examined has made a request under paragraph (5A), he shall not be committed to prison under Order 29, rule 1(1) for having failed to attend at the time and place fixed for the adjourned examination unless the judgment creditor has paid to him a sum reasonably sufficient to cover the travelling expenses before the day fixed for the adjourned examination.

(6) CPR rule 34.8 (evidence by deposition) shall apply the necessary modifications, to an examination under this rule as it applies to an examination under that Part save that CPR rule 34.8(6)(b) shall not apply.

(7) Nothing in this rule shall be construed as preventing the court, before deciding whether to make an order under paragraph (1), from giving the person to be examined an opportunity of making a statement in writing or a witness statement or affidavit as to the debtor's means.

Related Source

C25.3.1 • RSC, O.48—Examination of Judgment Debtor etc. (see commentary thereon).

C25.3.2 **Effect of rule**—It is for the judgment creditor to decide how best to enforce the judgment. If he does not already have necessary information upon which to base an informed decision, the judgment creditor can obtain (by applying without notice) an order bringing the debtor before the court for an oral examination as to means. CCR, O.25, r.3 thus serves the same purpose as RSC, O.48 (see commentary thereon).

Examination of debtor under judgment not for money

C25.4 **4.** Where any difficulty arises in or in connection with the enforcement of any judgment or order for some relief other than the payment of money, the court may make an order under rule 3 for the attendance of the debtor and for his examination on such questions as may be specified in the order, and that rule shall apply accordingly with the necessary modifications.

Effect of rule—CCR, O.25, r.3 (see above) provides for the oral examination as to means of a judgment debtor to enable a judgment creditor to better decide how to enforce the judgment. (This is still a decision for the judgment creditor rather than the court. The law on enforcement of judgments is currently unsatisfactory and in need of reform: see further RSC, O.45 and commentary thereon). In the case of a judgment or order for relief other than the payment of money, an oral examination will not usually be necessary as the appropriate means of enforcement will be obvious (*e.g.* warrant of possession of land; see CCR, O.26, r.17: warrant of delivery of goods; see CCR, O.26, r.16: committal to enforce an injunction; see CCR, O.29). However, "where any difficulty arises in or in connection with the enforcement of any judgment or order for some relief other than the payment of money" CCR, O.25, r.4 enables the court to make an order for the oral examination of the debtor "on such questions as may be specified in the order" and applies r.3 with the necessary modifications. C25.4.1

Provision of information

5.—(1) The requests and applications mentioned in paragraph (2) are— C25.5

(a) a request for a warrant of execution, delivery or possession;
(b) a request for a judgment summons or warrant of committal,
(c) an application for a garnishee order under Order 30, rule 1; and
(d) an application for a charging order.

(2) Where the judgment creditor has filed any request or application referred to in paragraph (1) or is seeking to enforce a judgment or order by making an application under rule 3 or under Order 27 or 32, he shall forthwith notify the court of any payment received from the debtor in respect of the judgment to be enforced after the date of the application and before—

(a) the final return to the warrant of execution, delivery or possession; or
(b) in any other case, the date fixed for the hearing of the application.

(3) Without prejudice to rule 8(9), where the judgment creditor applies to re-issue enforcement proceedings, he shall file a request in that behalf certifying the amount of money remaining due under the judgment or order and that the whole or part of any instalment due remains unpaid and stating why re-issue is necessary.

Effect of rule—Where the judgment creditor is seeking to enforce the judgment by any of the means listed in CCR, O.25, r.5(1), by oral examination under CCR, O.25, r.3 by attachment of earnings under CCR, O.27 or by the appointment of a receiver under CCR, O.32 and, in any of these situations, the debtor makes a payment, the creditor is required to notify the court of any such payment. C25.5.1

CCR, O.25, r.5(3) applies where the judgment creditor applies to re-issue enforcement proceedings.

Interest on judgment debts

5A. Where the judgment creditor claims interest pursuant to the County Courts (Interest on Judgment Debts) Order 1991 and takes proceedings to enforce payment under the relevant judgment (within the meaning of article 4(1) of that Order), any request or application for enforcement made in those proceedings shall be accompanied by two copies of a certificate giving details of— C25.5A

(a) the amount of interest claimed and the sum on which it is claimed;
(b) the dates from and to which interest has accrued; and
(c) the rate of interest which has been applied and, where more than one rate of interest has been applied, the relevant dates and rates.

County Court (Interest on Judgment Debts) Order 1991 (S.I. 1991 No. 1184)—Provides for certain county judgment debts to carry interest at the same rate as that payable on High Court judgments under the Judgments Act 1838, s.17. In general, only judgments for the payment of a sum of £5,000 or more will carry interest and the Order also provides for some types of judgment C25.5A.1

to be excluded from the scheme altogether (Art. 2). Where the judgment creditor applies to enforce payment of the judgment by execution or some other means, interest will not accrue as long as the enforcement process is wholly or partly successful (Art. 4). Provision is also made as to the appropriation of interest (Art. 6). See further, section 74 of the CCA 1984 SCP Mainwork, (Vol. 2, para. 20A–747). The current rate of interest on judgment debts is 8 per cent (since April 1, 1993—Judgment Debts (Rate of Interest) Order 1993 (S.I. 1993 No. 564)): for table of previous rates and further commentary generally see SCP 1999, Vol. 1, para. 42/1/17.

Description of parties

C25.6 **6.** Where the name or address of the judgment creditor or the debtor as given in the request for the issue of a warrant of execution or delivery, judgment summons or warrant of committal differs from his name or address in the judgment or order sought to be enforced and the judgment creditor satisfies the court officer that the name or address as given in the request is applicable to the person concerned, the judgment creditor or the debtor, as the case may be, shall be described in the warrant or judgment summons as "C.D. of [name and address as given in the request] suing [or sued] as A.D. of [name and address in the judgment or order]".

Related Sources

C25.6.1
- CCR, O.25, r.9—Enforcement of judgment or order against firm
- RSC, O.81, r.5—Enforcing judgment or order against firm

C25.6.2 **"satisfies the court officer"**—Although CCR, O.25, r.6 does not in terms require evidence, in practice the judgment creditor must explain the original misdescription and this is best done by affidavit or written statement. (The latter requires a "statement of truth"—see Pt 22, CPR and, in particular, its supplementing Practice Direction at para. 22PD–001).

Recording and giving information as to warrants and orders

C25.7 **7.**—(1) Subject to paragraph (1A), every district judge by whom a warrant or order is issued or received for execution shall from time to time state in the records of his court what has been done in the execution of the warrant or order.

(1A) Where a warrant of execution is is issued by a court ("the home court") is sent to another court for execution ("the foreign court"), paragraph (1) shall not apply to the district judge of the home court, but when such a warrant is returned to the home court under paragraph (7), the court officer of the home court shall state in the records of his court what has been done in the execution of the warrant or order.

(2) If the warrant or order has not been executed within one month from the date of its issue or receipt by him, the court officer of the court responsible for its execution shall, at the end of that month and every subsequent month during which the warrant remains outstanding, send notice of the reason for non-execution to the judgment creditor and, if the warrant or order was received from another court, to that court.

(3) The district judge responsible for executing a warrant or order shall give such information respecting it as may reasonably be required by the judgment creditor and, if the warrant or order was received by him from another court, by the district judge of that court.

(4) Where money is received in pursuance of a warrant of execution or committal sent by one court to another court, the foreign court shall, subject to paragraph (5) and to section 346 of Insolvency Act 1986 and section 326 of the Companies Act 1948, send the money to the judgment creditor in the manner prescribed by the Court Funds Rules 1987 and, where the money is received in pursuance of a warrant of committal, make a return to the home court.

(5) Where interpleader proceedings are pending, the court shall not

proceed in accordance with paragraph (4) until the interpleader proceedings are determined and the district judge shall then make a return showing how the money is to be disposed of and, if any money is payable to the judgment creditor, the court shall proceed in accordance with paragraph (4).

(6) Where a warrant of committal has been received from another court, the foreign court shall, on the execution of the warrant, send notice thereof to the home court.

(7) Where a warrant of execution has been received from another court, either—

(a) on the execution of the warrant; or
(b) if the warrant is not executed—
  (i) on the making of a final return to the warrant; or
  (ii) on suspension of the warrant under rule 8 (suspension of judgment or execution) or Order 26, rule 10 (withdrawal and suspension of warrant at creditor's request),

the foreign court shall return the warrant to the home court.

"District Judge"—Although this rule refers to the district judge the functions mentioned are in fact carried out by court staff (see CCR, O.26, r.1(1A)). C25.7.1

Suspension of judgment or execution

8.—(1) The power of the court to suspend or stay a judgment or order or to stay execution of any warrant may be exercised by the district judge or, in the case of the power to stay execution of a warrant of execution and in accordance with the provisions of this rule, by the court officer. C25.8

(2) An application by the debtor to stay execution of a warrant of execution shall be in the appropriate form stating the proposed terms, the grounds on which it is made and including a signed statement of the debtor's means.

(3) Where the debtor makes an application under paragraph (2), the court shall—

(a) send the judgment creditor a copy of the debtor's application (and statement of means); and
(b) require the creditor to notify the court in writing, within 14 days of service of notification upon him, giving his reasons for any objection he may have to the granting of the application.

(4) If the judgment creditor does not notify the court of any objection within the time stated, the court officer may make an order suspending the warrant on terms of payment.

(5) Upon receipt of a notice by the judgment creditor under paragraph (3)(b), the court officer may, if the judgment creditor objects only to the terms offered, determine the date and rate of payment and make an order suspending the warrant on terms of payment.

(6) Any party affected by an order made under paragraph (5) may, within 14 days of service of the order on him and giving his reasons, apply on notice for the order to be reconsidered and the court shall fix a day for the hearing of the application before the district judge and give to the judgment creditor and the debtor not less than 8 days' notice of the day so fixed.

(7) On hearing an application under paragraph (6), the district judge may confirm the order or set it aside and make such new order as he thinks fit and the order so made shall be entered in the records of the court.

(8) Where the judgment creditor states in his notice under paragraph (3)(b) that he wishes the bailiff to proceed to execute the warrant, the court shall fix a day for a hearing before the district judge of the debtor's application and give to the judgment creditor and to the debtor not less than 2 days' notice of the day so fixed.

(9) Subject to any directions given by the district judge, where a warrant of

execution has been suspended, it may be re-issued on the judgment creditor's filing a request pursuant to rule 5(3) showing that any condition subject to which the warrant was suspended has not been complied with.

(10) Where an order is made by the district judge suspending a warrant of execution, the debtor may be ordered to pay the costs of the warrant and any fees or expenses incurred before its suspension and the order may authorise the sale of a sufficient portion of any goods seized to cover such costs, fees and expenses and the expenses of sale.

Enforcement of judgment or order against firm

C25.9 **9.**—(1) Subject to paragraph (2), a judgment or order against a firm may be enforced against—

(a) any property of the firm;

(b) any person who admitted in the proceedings that he was a partner or was adjudged to be a partner;

(c) any person who was served as a partner with the claim form if—

(i) judgment was entered under CPR Part 12, in default of defence or under CPR Part 14 on admission; or

(iii) the person so served did not appear at the trial or hearing of the proceedings.

(2) A judgment or order may not be enforced under paragraph (1) against a member of the firm who was out of England and Wales when the claim form was issued unless he—

(a) was served within England and Wales with the claim form as a partner; or

(b) was, with the leave of the court under RSC Order 11, rule 1 served out of England and Wales with the claim form as a partner,

and, except as provided by paragraph (1)(a) and by the foregoing provisions of this paragraph, a judgment or order obtained against a firm shall not render liable, release or otherwise affect a member of the firm who was out of England and Wales when the claim form was issued.

(3) A judgment creditor who claims to be entitled to enforce a judgment or order against any other person as a partner may apply to the court for permission to do so by filing an application notice in accordance with CPR Part 23.

(4) An application notice under paragraph (3) shall be served on the alleged partner, not less than three days before the hearing of the application, in the manner required for service of the notice of the day of hearing in accordance with Order 3, rule 6 and on the hearing of the application, if the alleged partner does not dispute his liability, the court may, subject to paragraph (2), give permission to enforce the judgment or order against him and, if he disputes liability, the court may order that the question of his liability be tried and determined in such a manner as the court thinks fit.

(5) The foregoing provisions of this rule shall not apply where it is desired to enforce in a county court a judgment or order of the High Court, or a judgment, order, decree or award of any court or arbitrator which is or has become enforceable as if it were a judgment or order of the High Court, and in any such case the provisions of the RSC relating to the enforcement of a judgment or order against a firm shall apply.

C25.9.1 **"the provisions of the RSC"**—This is a reference to RSC, O.81, r.5—Enforcing judgment or order against firm.

Enforcing judgment between a firm and its members

C25.10 **10.**—(1) Execution to enforce a judgment or order given or made in—

(a) proceedings by or against a firm, in the name of the firm against or by a member of the firm; or

(b) proceedings by a firm in the name of the firm against a firm in the name of the firm where those firms have one or more members in common,

shall not issue without the leave of the court.

(2) On an application for leave the court may give such directions, including directions as to the taking of accounts and the making of inquiries, as may be just.

Enforcement of High Court judgment

11.—(1) A judgment creditor who desires to enforce a judgment or order of the High Court, or a judgment, order, decree or award of any court or arbitrator which is or has become enforceable as if it were a judgment or order of the High Court, shall file in the appropriate court (with such documents as are required to be filed for the purpose of enforcing a judgment or order of a county court)— **C25.11**

(a) an office copy of the judgment or order or, in the case of a judgment, order, decree or award of a court other than the High Court or an arbitrator, such evidence of the judgment, order, decree or award and of its enforceability as a judgment of the High Court as the district judge may require;

(b) a certificate verifying the amount due under the judgment, order, decree or award;

(c) where a writ of execution has been issued to enforce it, a copy of the sheriff's return to the writ; and

(d) a copy of the order to transfer the proceedings to the county court.

(2) In this rule the "appropriate court" means the county court in which the relevant enforcement proceedings might, by virtue of these rules, be brought if the judgment or order had been obtained in proceedings commenced in a county court.

Provided that if under these rules the court in which the relevant enforcement proceedings might be brought is identified by reference to the court in which the judgment or order has been obtained the appropriate court shall be the court for the district in which the debtor resides or carries on business.

(3) The provisions of this rule are without prejudice to Order 26, rule 2.

Enforcement of award of tribunal

12.—(1) This rule applies where any enactment (other than these rules) provides that if a county court so orders, a sum of money is recoverable as if payable under an order of a county court, and in this rule an application for such an order is referred to as an application to enforce an award and "award" means the award, order, agreement or decision which it is sought to enforce. **C25.12**

(2) Unless these rules otherwise provide, an application to enforce an award shall be made without notice by—

(a) certifying the amount remaining due to the applicant; and

(b) producing either the original or a copy of the award and by filing a copy.

(3) Unless otherwise provided, the application shall be made to the court for the district in which the person against whom the award was made resides or carries on business or, where that person does not reside or carry on business within England and Wales, to the court for the district in which the applicant resides or carries on business.

(4) The order may be made by the court officer.

Transfer to High Court for enforcement

13.—(1) Where the judgment creditor makes a request for a certificate of judgment under Order 22, rule 8(1) for the purpose of enforcing the **C25.13**

judgment or order in the High Court by execution against goods, the grant of a certificate by the court shall take effect as an order to transfer the proceedings to the High Court and the transfer shall have effect on the grant of that certificate.

(2) On the transfer of proceedings in accordance with paragraph (1), the court shall give notice to the debtor that the proceedings have been transferred and shall make an entry of that fact in the records of his court.

(3) In a case where a request for a certificate of judgment is made under Order 22, rule 8(1) for the purpose of enforcing a judgment or order in the High Court and—

(a) an application for a variation in the date or rate of payment of money due under a judgment or order;
(b) an application under either CPR rule 39.3(3) or CPR rule 13.4;
(c) a request for an administration order; or
(d) an application for a stay of execution under section 88 of the Act, is pending,

the request for the certificate shall not be dealt with until those proceedings are determined.

CCR ORDER 26

WARRANTS OF EXECUTION, DELIVERY AND POSSESSION

C26.0.1 **Contents**

Editorial Introduction

C26.0.2 County Court warrants are enforced by the court's own bailiffs, not by sheriff's officers as in the High Court. A warrant of execution is the equivalent of the High Court writ of *fieri facias*. Under O.26, r.1(2) where the order is for payment by instalments, the warrant can be (subject to r.1(3)) for the arrears of instalments or the whole outstanding sum. A warrant of delivery (the equivalent of the High Court's writ of delivery) is to enforce an order for delivery up of goods and a warrant of possession (the equivalent of the High Court's writ of possession) is to enforce an order for recovery of land.

In all three cases the procedure for the judgment creditor is very simple: the appropriate request form and prescribed fee are sent or taken to the office of the court which made the order.

Related Sources

C26.0.3
- CCR, O.25—Enforcement of Judgments and Orders—General
- County Courts Act 1984, Pt V (see SCP 1999, Vol. 2, Section 20A)
- Insolvency Act 1986, s.346

Forms

C26.0.4
- N42—Warrant of Execution
- N46—Warrant of Delivery and of Execution for damages and costs
- N48—Warrant of Delivery where, if goods are not returned, levy is to be made for their value
- N49—Warrant for Possession of Land
- N50—Warrant of restitution (O.26)

- N245—Notice of application for suspension of warrant (and for variation of an instalment)
- N246—Claimant's reply to defendant's application to vary instalment order
- N246A—Claimant's reply to defendant's application to suspend warrant of execution
- N323—Request for Warrant of Execution
- N324—Request for Warrant of delivery of goods
- N325—Request for Warrant for possession of land
- N317—Bailiff's report
- N317A—Bailiff's report to the claimant
- N318—Notice of return and remittance from foreign court
- N320—Request for return of, or to, warrant
- N323—Request for warrant of execution
- N324—Request for warrant of goods (sic)
- N325—Request for warrant for possession of land
- N326—Notice of issue of warrant of execution
- N327—Notice of issue of warrant of execution to enforce a judgment or order of the High Court
- N330—Notice of sale or payment under execution in respect of a judgment for a sum exceeding £500
- N331—Notice of withdrawal from possession, or payment over of moneys on a notice of bankruptcy or winding-up order
- N332—Inventory of goods removed
- N333—Notice of time when and where goods will be sold
- N334—Request to hold walking possession and authority to re-enter
- N335—Notice (to foreign court) of payment made
- N444—Details of sale under a warrant of execution
- N445—Notice for re-issue of warrant

Cognate RSC

- RSC, O.45—Enforcement of Judgments and Orders: General **C26.0.5**
- RSC, O.46—Writs of Execution: General
- RSC, O.47—Writs of *fieri facias*

Application for warrant of execution

1.—(1) A judgment creditor desiring a warrant of execution to be issued shall file a request in that behalf certifying— **C26.1**

(a) the amount remaining due under the judgment or order; and

(b) where the order made is for payment of a sum of money by instalments—

(i) that the whole or part of any instalment due remains unpaid; and

(ii) the amount for which the warrant is to be issued.

(1A) The court officer shall discharge the functions—

(a) under section 85(2) of the Act of issuing a warrant of execution;

(b) under section 85(3) of the Act of entering in the record mentioned in that subsection and on the warrant the precise time of the making of the application to issue the warrant; and

(c) under section 103(1) of the Act of sending the warrant of execution to another county court.

(2) Where the court has made an order for payment of a sum of money by instalments and default has been made in payment of such an instalment, a warrant of execution may be issued for the whole of the said sum of money and costs then remaining unpaid or, subject to paragraph (3), for such part as the judgment creditor may request, not being in the latter case less than £50 or the amount of one monthly instalment or, as the case may be, 4 weekly instalments, whichever is the greater.

(3) In any case to which paragraph (2) applies no warrant shall be issued unless at the time when it is issued—

(a) the whole or part of an instalment which has already become due remains unpaid; and

(b) any warrant previously issued for part of the said sum of money and costs has expired or has been satisfied or abandoned.

(4) Where a warrant is issued for the whole or part of the said sum of money and costs, the court officer shall, unless the district judge responsible for

execution of the warrant directs otherwise, send a warning notice to the person against whom the warrant is issued and, where such a notice is sent, the warrant shall not be levied until 7 days thereafter.

(5) Where judgment is given or an order made for payment otherwise than by instalments of a sum of money and costs to be assessed in accordance with CPR Part 47 (detailed assessment procedure) and default is made in payment of the sum of money before the costs have been assessed, a warrant of execution may issue for recovery of the sum of money and a separate warrant may issue subsequently for the recovery of the costs if default is made in payment of them.

Execution of High Court judgment

C26.2 **2.**—(1) Where it is desired to enforce by warrant of execution a judgment or order of the High Court, or a judgment, order, decree or award which is or has become enforceable as if it were a judgment of the High Court, the request referred to in rule 1(1) may be filed in any court in the district of which execution is to be levied.

(2) Subject to Order 25, rule 9(5), any restriction imposed by these rules on the issue of execution shall apply as if the judgment, order, decree or award were a judgment or order of the county court, but permission to issue execution shall not be required if permission has already been given by the High Court.

(3) Notice of the issue of the warrant shall be sent by the county court to the High Court.

Execution against farmer

C26.3 **3.** If after the issue of a warrant of execution the district judge for the district in which the warrant is to be executed has reason to believe that the debtor is a farmer, the execution creditor shall, if so required by the district judge, furnish him with an official certificate, dated not more than three days beforehand, or the result of a search at the Land Registry as to the existence of any charge registered against the debtor under the Agricultural Credits Act 1928.

Concurrent warrants

C26.4 **4.** Two or more warrants of execution may be issued concurrently for execution in different districts, but—

(a) no more shall be levied under all the warrants together than is authorised to be levied under one of them; and

(b) the costs of more than one such warrant shall not be allowed against the debtor except by order of the court.

Permission to issue certain warrants

C26.5 **5.**—(1) A warrant of execution shall not issue without the permission of the court where—

(a) six years or more have elapsed since the date of the judgment or order;

(b) any change has taken place, whether by death or otherwise in the parties entitled to enforce the judgment or order or liable to have it enforced against them;

(c) the judgment or order is against the assets of a deceased person coming into the hands of his executors or administrators after the date of the judgment or order and it is sought to issue execution against such assets; or

(d) any goods to be seized under a warrant of execution are in the hands of a receiver appointed by a court.

(2) An application for permission shall be supported by a witness statement

or affidavit establishing the applicant's right to relief and may be made without notice being served on any other party in the first instance but the court may direct the application notice to be served on such persons as it thinks fit.

(3) Where, by reason of one and the same event, a person seeks permission under paragraph (1)(b) to enforce more judgments or orders than one, he may make one application only, specifying in a schedule all the judgments or orders in respect of which it is made, and if the application notice is directed to be served on any person, it need set out only such part of the application as affects him.

(4) Paragraph (1) is without prejudice to any enactment, rule or direction by virtue of which a person is required to obtain the permission of the court for the issue of a warrant or to proceed to execution or otherwise to the enforcement of a judgment or order.

Duration and renewal of warrant

6.—(1) A warrant of execution shall, for the purpose of execution, be valid in the first instance for 12 months beginning with the date of its issue, but if not wholly executed, it may be renewed from time to time, by order of the court, for a period of 12 months at any one time, beginning with the day next following that on which it would otherwise expire, if an application for renewal is made before that day or such later day (if any) as the court may allow. **C26.6**

(2) A note of any such renewal shall be indorsed on the warrant and it shall be entitled to priority according to the time of its original issue or, where appropriate, its receipt by the district judge responsible for its execution.

Notice of levy

7. Any bailiff upon levying execution shall deliver to the debtor or leave at the place where execution is levied a notice of the warrant. **C26.7**

Bankruptcy or winding up of debtor

8.—(1) Where the district judge responsible for the execution of a warrant is required by any provision of the Insolvency Act 1986 or any other enactment relating to insolvency to retain the proceeds of sale of goods sold under the warrant or money paid in order to avoid a sale, the court shall, as soon as practicable after the sale or the receipt of the money, send notice to the execution creditor and, if the warrant issued out of another court, to that court. **C26.8**

(2) Where the district judge responsible for the execution of a warrant—

(a) receives notice that a bankruptcy order has been made against the debtor or, if the debtor is a company, that a provisional liquidator has been appointed or that an order has been made or a resolution passed for the winding up of the company; and

(b) withdraws from possession of goods seized or pays over to the official receiver or trustee in bankruptcy or, if the debtor is a company, to the liquidator the proceeds of sale of goods sold under the warrant or money paid in order to avoid a sale or seized or received in part satisfaction of the warrant,

the court shall send notice to the execution creditor and, if the warrant issued out of another court, to that court.

(3) Where the court officer of a court to which a warrant issued out of another court has been sent for execution receives any such notice as is referred to in paragraph (2)(a) after he has sent to the home court any money seized or received in part satisfaction of the warrant, he shall forward the notice to that court.

Withdrawal and suspension of warrant at creditor's request

C26.10 **10.**—(1) Where an execution creditor requests the district judge responsible for executing a warrant to withdraw from possession, he shall, subject to the following paragraphs of this rule, be treated as having abandoned the execution, and the court shall mark the warrant as withdrawn by request of the execution creditor.

(2) Where the request is made in consequence of a claim having been made under Order 33, rule 1, to goods seized under the warrant, the execution shall be treated as being abandoned in respect only of the goods claimed.

(3) If the district judge responsible for executing a warrant is requested by the execution creditor to suspend it in pursuance of an arrangement between him and the debtor, the court shall mark the warrant as suspended by request of the execution creditor and the execution creditor may subsequently apply to the district judge holding the warrant for it to be re-issued and, if he does so, the application shall be deemed for the purpose of section 85(3) of the Act to be an application to issue the warrant.

(4) Nothing in this rule shall prejudice any right of the execution creditor to apply for the issue of a fresh warrant or shall authorise the re-issue of a warrant which has been withdrawn or has expired or has been superseded by the issue of a fresh warrant.

Suspension of part warrant

C26.11 **11.** Where a warrant issued for part of a sum of money and costs payable under a judgment or order is suspended on payment of instalments, the judgment or order shall, unless the court otherwise directs, be treated as suspended on those terms as respects the whole of the sum of money and costs then remaining unpaid.

Inventory and notice where goods removed

C26.12 **12.**—(1) Where goods seized in execution are removed, the court shall forthwith deliver or send to the debtor a sufficient inventory of the goods removed and shall, not less than 4 days before the time fixed for the sale, give him notice of the time and place at which the goods will be sold.

(2) The inventory and notice shall be given to the debtor by delivering them to him personally or by sending them to him by post at his place of residence or, if his place of residence is not known, by leaving them for him, or sending them to him by post, at the place from which the goods were removed.

Account of sale

C26.13 **13.** Where goods are sold under an execution, the court shall furnish the debtor with a detailed account in writing of the sale and of the application of the proceeds.

Notification to foreign court of payment made

C26.14 **14.** Where, after a warrant has been sent to a foreign court for execution but before a final return has been made to the warrant, the home court is notified of a payment made in respect of the sum for which the warrant is issued, the home court shall send notice of the payment to the foreign court.

Order for private sale

C26.15 **15.**—(1) Subject to paragraph (6), an order of the court under section 97 of the Act that a sale under an execution may be made otherwise than by public auction may be made on the application of the execution creditor or the debtor or the district judge responsible for the execution of the warrant.

(2) Where he is not the applicant for an order under this rule, the district judge responsible for the execution of the warrant shall, on the demand of the

applicant, furnish him with a list containing the name and address of every execution creditor under any other warrant or writ of execution against the goods of the debtor of which the district judge has notice, and where the district judge is the applicant, he shall prepare such a list.

(3) Not less than 4 days before the day fixed for the hearing of the application, the applicant shall give notice of the application to each of the other persons by whom the application might have been made and to every person named in the list referred to in paragraph (2).

(4) The applicant shall produce the list to the court on the hearing of the application.

(5) Every person to whom notice of the application was given may attend and be heard on the hearing of the application.

(6) Where the district judge responsible for the execution of the warrant is the district judge by whom it was issued and he has no notice of any other warrant or writ of execution against the goods of the debtor, an order under this rule may be made by the court of its own motion with the consent of the execution creditor and the debtor or after giving them an opportunity of being heard.

Warrant of delivery

16.—(1) Except where an Act or rule provides otherwise, a judgment or order for the delivery of any goods shall be enforceable by warrant of delivery in accordance with this rule. **C26.16**

(2) If the judgment or order does not give the person against whom it was given or made the alternative of paying the value of the goods, it may be enforced by a warrant of specific delivery, that is to say, a warrant to recover the goods without alternative provision for recovery of their value.

(3) If the judgment or order is for the delivery of the goods or payment of their value, it may be enforced by a warrant of delivery to recover the goods of their value.

(4) Where a warrant of delivery is issued, the judgment creditor shall be entitled, by the same or a separate warrant, to execution against the debtor's goods for any money payable under the judgment or order which is to be enforced by the warrant of delivery.

(4A) Where a judgment or order is given or made for the delivery of goods or payment of their value and a warrant is issued to recover the goods or their value, money paid into court under the warrant shall be appropriated first to any sum of money and costs awarded.

(5) The foregoing provisions of this Order, so far as applicable, shall have effect, with the necessary modifications, in relation to warrants of delivery as they have effect in relation to warrants of execution.

Warrant of possession

17.—(1) A judgment or order for the recovery of land shall be enforceable by warrant of possession. **C26.17**

(2) Without prejudice to paragraph (3A), the person desiring a warrant of possession to be issued shall file a request in that behalf certifying that the land has not been vacated in accordance with the judgment or order for the recovery of the said land.

(3) Where a warrant of possession is issued, the judgment creditor shall be entitled, by the same or a separate warrant, to execution against the debtor's goods for any money payable under the judgment or order which is to be enforced by the warrant of possession.

(3A) In a case to which paragraph (3) applies or where an order for possession has been suspended on terms as to payment of a sum money by instalments, the judgment creditor shall in his request certify—

(a) the amount of money remaining due under the judgment or order; and

(b) that the whole or part of any instalment due remains unpaid.

(4) A warrant of restitution may be issued, with the permission of the court, in aid of any warrant of possession.

(5) An application for permission under paragraph (4) may be made without notice being served on any other party and shall be supported by evidence of wrongful re-entry into possession following the execution of the warrant of possession and of such further facts as would, in the High Court, enable the judgment creditor to have a writ of restitution issued.

(6) Rules 5 and 6 shall apply, with the necessary modifications, in relation to a warrant of possession and any further warrant in aid of such a warrant as they apply in relation to a warrant of execution.

C26.17.1 **Setting aside warrant of possession**—For circumstances in which warrant of possession may be suspended or set aside, see *Leicester City Council v. Aldwinckle* (1991) 24 HLR 40, CA.

In *London Borough of Hammersmith and Fulham v. Hill* [1994] Gazette No. 22 p. 35, CA, where a tenant was evicted from a secure tenancy without notice of warrant for possession, it was held, the warrant of possession could only be suspended or set aside in the circumstances set out in *Leicester City Council v. Aldwinckle* (1991) 24 HLR 40, CA.

C26.17.2 **Staying execution of warrant of possession**—Where mortgagees obtain a warrant for possession to enforce their security by sale forthwith and the mortgagor proposes to apply to the High Court under the Law of Property Act 1925, s.91(2) to enable him to sell the property in due course, on an application by the mortgagor a county court has no jurisdiction to stay the execution of the warrant (*Cheltenham and Gloucester Building Society v. Krausz* [1997] 1 All E.R. 21, CA). Where the court has power, under s.36 of the Administration of Justice Act 1970 and section 8 of the Administration of Justice Act 1973, to allow the mortgagor a "reasonable period" to pay sums due under the mortgage, in the absence of unusual circumstances, the outstanding term of the mortgage was the starting point in determining how long it would be reasonable to keep a mortgage. (*Western Bank Ltd v. Schindler* [1977] Ch. 1; *Cheltenham and Gloucester Building Society v. Norgan* [1996] 1 W.L.R. 343.) There is no rule that, for example, all arrears must be paid off within four years. Neither is there a rule that, where the mortgage is to be repaid by reselling the property a warrant can only be suspended if a sale will take place within a short period of time. Thus if there is evidence that completion of a sale could take place in six or nine months or even a year, the court may conclude that the mortgagor was "likely to be able within a reasonable period to pay any sums due under the mortgage" (*National and Provincial Building Society v. Lloyd* [1996] 1 All E.R. 630). However, where there is insufficient evidence to show either that the mortgagor could sell the property within three to five years or that the proceeds would be sufficient to discharge the mortgage debt, a warrant should not be suspended (*Bristol and West Building Society v. Ellis* (1996) 76 P. & C.R. 158, CA).

Section 36 of the Administration of Justice Act 1970 is at SCP 1999, Vol. 2, Section 20B; and section 8 of the Administration of Justice Act 1973 is also at SCP 1999, Vol. 2, Section 20B.

RSC, O.45, r.3. A warrant of possession is the county court equivalent of the writ of possession. The warrant is executed by a county court bailiff. A representative of the judgment creditor should be present when the warrant is executed to receive the premises from the bailiff and to secure them as appropriate.

Saving for enforcement by committal

C26.18 **18.** Nothing in rule 16 or 17 shall prejudice any power to enforce a judgment or order for the delivery of goods or the recovery of land by an order of committal.

C26.18.1 **"order of committal"**—see CCR, O.29 and RSC, O.52.

CCR ORDER 27

ATTACHMENT OF EARNINGS

Contents C27.0.1

Part I—General

Part II—Consolidated attachment of earnings orders

Editorial Introduction

By the Attachment of Earnings Act 1971 the High Court can make an attachment of earnings order only to secure payments under a High Court maintenance order. The county courts can make such orders to secure payments under a High Court or county court maintenance order, the payment of a judgment debt or payments under an administration order. Thus, the majority of attachment orders are made in the county court and, administratively, there is a centralised system for collection. The procedure is very effective where the debtor is in employment with sufficient earnings. For a creditor the procedure is very simple, usually involving only the completion of the Request for an Attachment of Earnings Order and payment of the prescribed fee: the court does the rest. C27.0.2

Related Sources

- Attachment of Earnings Act 1971 (see SCP 1999, Vol. 2, Section 21E; the Act does not apply to debtors who are members of Her Majesty's Armed Forces, but see analogous remedies under the Armed Forces Act 1971). C27.0.3

Forms C27.0.4

- N55—Notice of application for attachment of earnings order
- N55A—Notice of application for attachment of earnings order—maintenance
- N56—Reply to attachment of earnings application—statement of means
- N58—Order for debtor's attendance at adjournal hearing of attachment of earnings application—maintenance
- N59—Warrant of committal under s.23(1) Attachment of Earnings Act 1971
- N60—Attachment of earnings order—judgment debt
- N61—Order for production of Statement of Means
- N61A—Notice to employer for production of statement of earnings
- N62—Summons for offence under Attachment of Earnings Act 1971
- N63—Notice to show cause under s.23 Attachment of Earnings Act
- N64—Suspended attachment of earnings order
- N64A—Suspended attachment of earnings order—maintenance
- N65—Attachment of earnings order—maintenance
- N66—Consolidated attachment of earnings order
- N66A—Notice of application for consolidated attachment of earnings order
- N112A—Power of Arrest s.23 Attachment of Earnings Act 1971

- N118—Notice to defendant where committal order made but suspended under Attachment of Earnings Order 1971
- N337—Request for an Attachment of earnings order
- N338—Request for statement of earnings
- N339—Discharge of attachment of earnings order
- N340—Notice as to payment under attachment of earnings order made by High Court
- N341—Notice of intention to vary attachment of earnings order under s.10(2) Attachment of Earnings Act 1971
- N448—Request to defendant for employment details—attachment of earnings
- N449—Notice to employer—failure to make deductions under attachment of earnings order

PART I—GENERAL

Interpretation

C27.1 **1.**—(1) In this Order—

"the Act of 1971" means the Attachment of Earnings Act 1971 and, unless the context otherwise requires, expressions used in that Act have the same meanings as in that Act.

Index of orders

C27.2 **2.**—(1) The court officer of every court shall keep a nominal index of the debtors residing within the district of his court in respect of whom there are in force attachment of earnings orders which have been made by that court or of which the court officer has received notice from another court.

(2) Where a debtor in respect of whom a court has made an attachment of earnings order resides within the district of another court, the court officer of the first-mentioned court shall send a copy of the order to the court officer of the other court for entry in his index.

(3) The court officer shall, on the request of any person having a judgment or order against a person believed to be residing within the district of the court, cause a search to be made in the index of the court and issue a certificate of the result of the search.

Appropriate court

C27.3 **3.**—(1) Subject to paragraphs (2) and (3), an application for an attachment of earnings order may be made to the court for the district in which the debtor resides.

(2) If the debtor does not reside within England or Wales, or the creditor does not know where he resides, the application may be made to the court in which, or for the district in which, the judgment or order sought to be enforced was obtained.

(3) Where the creditor applies for attachment of earnings orders in respect of two or more debtors jointly liable under a judgment or order, the application may be made to the court for the district in which any of the debtors resides, so however that if the judgment or order was given or made by any such court, the application shall be made to that court.

Mode of applying

C27.4 **4.**—(1) A judgment creditor who desires to apply for an attachment of earnings order shall file his application certifying the amount of money remaining due under the judgment or order and that the whole or part of any instalment due remains unpaid and, where it is sought to enforce an order of a magistrates' court—

(a) a certified copy of the order; and

(b) a witness statement or affidavit verifying the amount due under the order or, if payments under the order are required to be made to the clerk to the magistrates' court, a certificate by that clerk to the same effect.

(2) On the filing of the documents mentioned in paragraph (1) the court

officer shall, where the order to be enforced is a maintenance order, fix a day for the hearing of the application.

Service and reply

5.—(1) Notice of the application together with a form of reply in the appropriate form, shall be served on the debtor in the manner required for service of the notice of the day of hearing in accordance with Order 3, rule 6 except that Order 3, rule 6(11) shall not apply. C27.5

(2) The debtor shall, within 8 days after service on him of the documents mentioned in paragraph (1), file a reply in the form provided, and the instruction to that effect in the notice to the debtor shall constitute a requirement imposed by virtue of section 14(4) of the Act of 1971:

Provided that no proceedings shall be taken for an offence alleged to have been committed under section 23(2)(c) or (f) of the Act of 1971 in relation to the requirement unless the said documents have been served on the debtor personally or the court is satisfied that they came to his knowledge in sufficient time for him to comply with the requirement.

(2A) Nothing in paragraph (2) shall require a defendant to file a reply if, within the period of time mentioned in that paragraph, he pays to the judgment creditor the money remaining due under the judgment or order and, where such payment is made, the judgment creditor shall so inform the court officer.

(3) On receipt of a reply the court officer shall send a copy to the applicant.

Notice to employer

6. Without prejudice to the powers conferred by section 14(1) of the Act of 1971, the court officer may, at any stage of the proceedings, send to any person appearing to have the debtor in his employment a notice requesting him to give to the court, within such period as may be specified in the notice, a statement of the debtor's earnings and anticipated earnings with such particulars as may be so specified. C27.6

Attachment of earnings order

7.—(1) On receipt of the debtor's reply, the court officer may, if he has sufficient information to do so, make an attachment of earnings order and a copy of the order shall be sent to the parties and to the debtor's employer. C27.7

(2) Where an order is made under paragraph (1), the judgment creditor or the debtor may, within 14 days of service of the order on him and giving his reasons, apply on notice for the order to be re-considered and the court officer shall fix a day for the hearing of the application and give to the judgment creditor and the debtor not less than 2 days' notice of the day so fixed.

(3) On hearing an application under paragraph (2), the district judge may confirm the order or set it aside and make such new order as he thinks fit and the order so made shall be entered in the records of the court.

(4) Where an order is not made under paragraph (1), the court officer shall refer the application to the district judge who shall, if he considers that he has sufficient information to do so without the attendance of the parties, determine the application.

(5) Where the district judge does not determine the application under paragraph (4), he shall direct that a day be fixed for the hearing of the application whereupon the court officer shall fix such a day and give to the judgment creditor and the debtor not less than 8 days' notice of the day so fixed.

(6) Where an order is made under paragraph (4), the judgment creditor or the debtor may, within 14 days of service of the order on him and giving his reasons, apply on notice for the order to be re-considered; and the court

officer shall fix a day for the hearing of the application and give to the judgment creditor and the debtor not less than 2 days' notice of the day so fixed.

(7) On hearing an application under paragraph (6), the district judge may confirm the order or set it aside and make such new order as he thinks fit and the order so made shall be entered in the records of the court.

(8) If the creditor does not appear at the hearing of the application under paragraph (5) but—

(a) the court has received a witness statement or affidavit of evidence from him; or
(b) the creditor requests the court in writing to proceed in his absence,

the court may proceed to hear the application and to make an order thereon.

(9) An attachment of earnings order may be made to secure the payment of a judgment debt if the debt is—

(a) of not less than £50; or
(b) for the amount remaining payable under a judgment for a sum of not less than £50.

Failure by debtor

C27.7A **7A.**—(1) If the debtor has failed to comply with rule 5(2) or to make payment to the judgment creditor, the court officer may issue an order under section 14(1) of the Act of 1971 which shall—

(a) be indorsed with or incorporate a notice warning the debtor of the consequences of disobedience to the order;
(b) be served on the debtor personally; and
(c) direct that any payments made thereafter shall be paid into the court and not direct to the judgment creditor.

(2) Without prejudice to rule 16, if the person served with an order made pursuant to paragraph (1) fails to obey it or to file a statement of his means or to make payment, the court officer shall issue a notice calling on that person to show good reason why he should not be imprisoned and any such notice shall be served on the debtor personally not less than 5 days before the hearing.

(3) Order 29, rule 1 shall apply, with the necessary modifications and with the substitution of references to the district judge for references to the judge, where a notice is issued under paragraph (2) or (4) of that rule.

(4) In this rule "statement of means" means a statement given under section 14(1) of the Act of 1971.

Suspended committal order

C27.7B **7B.**—(1) If the debtor fails to attend at an adjourned hearing of an application for an attachment of earnings order and a committal order is made, the judge or district judge may direct that the committal order shall be suspended so long as the debtor attends at the time and place specified in the committal order and paragraphs (2), (4) and (5) of Order 28, rule 7 shall apply, with the necessary modifications, where such a direction is given as they apply where a direction is given under paragraph (1) of that rule.

(2) Where a committal order is suspended under paragraph (1) and the debtor fails to attend at the time and place specified under paragraph (1), a certificate to that effect given by the court officer shall be sufficient authority for the issue of a warrant of committal.

Failure by debtor—maintenance orders

C27.8 **8.**—(1) An order made under section 23(1) of the Act of 1971 for the attendance of the debtor at an adjourned hearing of an application for an attachment of earnings order to secure payments under a maintenance order shall—

(a) be served on the debtor personally not less than 5 days before the day fixed for the adjourned hearing; and
(b) direct that any payments made thereafter shall be paid into the court and not direct to the judgment creditor.

(2) An application by a debtor for the revocation of an order committing him to prison and, if he is already in custody, for his discharge under subsection (7) of the said section 23 shall be made to the judge or district judge in writing without notice to any other party showing the reasons for the debtor's failure to attend the court or his refusal to be sworn or to give evidence, as the case may be, and containing an undertaking by the debtor to attend the court or to be sworn or to give evidence when next ordered or required to do so.

(3) The application shall, if the debtor has already been lodged in prison, be attested by the governor of the prison (or any other officer of the prison not below the rank of principal officer) and in any other case be made on witness statement or affidavit.

(4) Before dealing with the application the judge or district judge may, if he thinks fit, cause notice to be given to the judgment creditor that the application has been made and of a day and hour when he may attend and be heard.

Costs

9.—(1) Where costs are allowed to the judgment creditor on an application for an attachment of earnings order, there may be allowed— **C27.9**

(a) a charge of a solicitor for attending the hearing and, if the court so directs, for serving the application;
(b) if the court certifies that the case is fit for counsel, a fee to counsel; and
(c) the court fee on the issue of the application.

(2) For the purpose of paragraph (1)(a) a solicitor who has prepared on behalf of the judgment creditor a witness statement or affidavit or request under rule 7(8) shall be treated as having attended the hearing.

(3) The costs may be fixed and allowed without detailed assessment under CPR Part 47.

Contents and service of order

10.—(1) An attachment of earnings order shall contain such of the following particulars relating to the debtor as are known to the court, namely— **C27.10**

(a) his full name and address;
(b) his place of work; and
(c) the nature of his work and his works number, if any,

and those particulars shall be the prescribed particulars for the purposes of section 6(3) of the Act of 1971.

(2) An attachment of earnings order and any order varying or discharging such an order shall be served on the debtor and on the person to whom the order is directed, and CPR Part 6 and CPR rules 40.4 and 40.5, shall apply with the further modification that where the order is directed to a corporation which has requested the court that any communication relating to the debtor or to the class of persons to whom he belongs shall be directed to the corporation at a particular address, service may, if the district judge thinks fit, be effected on the corporation at that address.

(3) Where an attachment of earnings order is made to enforce a judgment or order of the High Court or a magistrates' court, a copy of the attachment of earnings order and of any order discharging it shall be sent by the court

officer of the county court to the court officer of the High Court, or, as the case may be, the clerk of the magistrates' court.

Application to determine whether particular payments are earnings

C27.11 **11.** An application to the court under section 16 of the Act of 1971 to determine whether payments to the debtor of a particular class or description are earnings for the purpose of an attachment of earnings order may be made to the district judge in writing and the court officer shall thereupon fix a date and time for the hearing of the application by the court and give notice thereof to the persons mentioned in the said section 16(2)(a), (b) and (c).

Notice of cesser

C27.12 **12.** Where an attachment of earnings order ceases to have effect under section 8(4) of the Act of 1971, the court officer of the court in which the matter is proceeding shall give notice of the cesser to the person to whom the order was directed.

Variation and discharge by court of own motion

C27.13 **13.**—(1) Subject to paragraph (9), the powers conferred by section 9(1) of the Act of 1971 may be exercised by the court of its own motion in the circumstances mentioned in the following paragraphs.

(2) Where it appears to the court that a person served with an attachment of earnings order directed to him has not the debtor in his employment, the court may discharge the order.

(3) Where an attachment of earnings order which has lapsed under section 9(4) of the Act of 1971 is again directed to a person who appears to the court to have the debtor in his employment, the court may make such consequential variations in the order as it thinks fit.

(4) Where, after making an attachment of earnings order, the court makes or is notified of the making of another such order in respect of the same debtor which is not to secure the payment of a judgment debt or payments under an administration order, the court may discharge or vary the first-mentioned order having regard to the priority accorded to the other order by paragraph 8 of Schedule 3 to the Act of 1971.

(5) Where, after making an attachment of earnings order, the court makes an order under section 4(1)(b) of the Act of 1971 or makes an administration order, the court may discharge the attachment of earnings order or, if it exercises the power conferred by section 5(3) of the said Act, may vary the order in such manner as it thinks fit.

(6) On making a consolidated attachment of earnings order the court may discharge any earlier attachment of earnings order made to secure the payment of a judgment debt by the same debtor.

(7) Where it appears to the court that a bankruptcy order has been made against a person in respect of whom an attachment of earnings order is in force to secure the payment of a judgment debt, the court may discharge the attachment of earnings order.

(8) Where an attachment or earnings order has been made to secure the payment of a judgment debt and the court grants permission to issue execution for the recovery of the debt, the court may discharge the order.

(9) Before varying or discharging an attachment of earnings order of its own motion under any of the foregoing paragraphs of this rule, the court shall, unless it thinks it unnecessary in the circumstances to do so, give the debtor and the person on whose application the order was made an opportunity of being heard on the question whether the order should be varied or discharged, and for that purpose the court officer may give them notice of a date, time and place at which the question will be considered.

Transfer of attachment order

14.—(1) Where the court by which the question of making a consolidated attachment order falls to be considered is not the court by which any attachment of earnings order has been made to secure the payment of a judgment debt by the debtor, the district judge of the last-mentioned court shall, at the request of the district judge of the first-mentioned court, transfer to that court the matter in which the attachment of earnings order was made. C27.14

(2) Without prejudice to paragraph (1), if in the opinion of the judge or district judge of any court by which an attachment of earnings order has been made, the matter could more conveniently proceed in some other court, whether by reason of the debtor having become resident in the district of that court or otherwise, he may order the matter to be transferred to that court.

(3) The court to which proceedings arising out of an attachment of earnings are transferred under this rule shall have the same jurisdiction in relation to the order as if it has been made by that court.

Exercise of power to obtain statement of earnings etc.

15.—(1) An order under section 14(1) of the Act of 1971 shall be indorsed with or incorporate a notice warning the person to whom it is directed of the consequences of disobedience to the order and shall be served on him personally. C27.15

(2) Order 34, rule 2, shall apply, with the necessary modifications, in relation to any penalty for failure to comply with an order under the said section 14(1) or, subject to the proviso to rule 5(2), any penalty for failure to comply with a requirement mentioned in that rule, as it applies in relation to a fine under section 55 of the County Courts Act 1984.

Offences

16.—(1) Where it is alleged that a person has committed any offence mentioned in section 23(2)(a), (b), (d), (e) or (f) of the Act of 1971 in relation to proceedings in, or to an attachment of earnings order made by, a county court, the district judge shall, unless it is decided to proceed against the alleged offender summarily, issue a summons calling upon him to show cause why he should not be punished for the alleged offence. C27.16

The summons shall be served on the alleged offender personally not less than 14 days before the return day.

(2) Order 34, rules 3 and 4, shall apply, with the necessary modifications, to proceedings for an offence under section 23(2) of the Act of 1971 as they apply to proceedings for offences under the County Courts Act 1984.

Maintenance orders

17.—(1) The foregoing rules of this Order shall apply in relation to maintenance payments as they apply in relation to a judgment debt, subject to the following paragraphs. C27.17

(2) An application for an attachment of earnings order to secure payments under a maintenance order made by a county court shall be made to that county court.

(3) Any application under section 32 of the Matrimonial Causes Act 1973 for permission to enforce the payment of arrears which became due more than 12 months before the application for an attachment of earnings order shall be made in that application.

(3A) Notice of the application together with a form of reply in the appropriate form shall be served in the manner required for service of the notice of the day of hearing in accordance with Order 3, rule 6.

(3B) Rule 5(2A) shall not apply.

(4) An application by the debtor for an attachment of earnings order to secure payments under a maintenance order may be made on the making of

the maintenance order or an order varying the maintenance order, and rules 4 and 5 shall not apply.

(5) Rule 7 shall have effect as if for paragraphs (1) to (8) there were substituted the following paragraph—

"(1) An application for an attachment of earnings order may be heard and determined by the district judge, who shall hear the application in private."

(6) Rule 9 shall apply as if for the reference to the amount payable under the relevant adjudication there were substituted a reference to the arrears due under the related maintenance order.

(7) Where an attachment of earnings order made by the High Court designates the court officer of a county court as the collecting officer, that officer shall, on receipt of a certified copy of the order from the court officer of the High Court, send to the person to whom the order is directed a notice as to the mode of payment.

(8) Where an attachment of earnings order made by a county court to secure payments under a maintenance order ceases to have effect and—

- (a) the related maintenance order was made by that court; or
- (b) the related maintenance order was an order of the High Court and—
    - (i) the court officer of the county court has received notice of the cessation from the court officer of the High Court; or
    - (ii) a committal order has been made in the county court for the enforcement of the related maintenance order,

the court officer of the county court shall give notice of the cessation to the person to whom the attachment of earnings order was directed.

(9) Where an attachment of earnings order has been made by a county court to secure payments under a maintenance order, notice under section 10(2) of the Act of 1971 to the debtor and to the person to whom the district judge is required to pay sums received under the order shall be in the form provided for that purpose, and if the debtor wishes to request the court to discharge the attachment of earnings order or to vary it otherwise than by making the appropriate variation, he shall apply to the court, within 14 days after the date of the notice, for the remedy desired.

(10) Rule 13 shall have effect as if for paragraphs (4) to (7) there were substituted the following paragraph:

"(4) Where it appears to the court by which an attachment of earnings order has been made that the related maintenance order has ceased to have effect, whether by virtue of the terms of the maintenance order or under section 28 of the Matrimonial Causes Act 1973 or otherwise, the court may discharge or vary the attachment of earnings order."

C27.17.1 **History of Rule**—Amended by Civil Procedure (Amendment) Rules 1999 (S.I. 1999 No. 1008).

PART II—CONSOLIDATED ATTACHMENT OF EARNINGS ORDERS

Cases in which consolidated order may be made

C27.18 **18.** Subject to the provisions of rules 19 to 21, the court may make a consolidated attachment order where—

- (a) two or more attachment of earnings orders are in force to secure the payment of judgment debts by the same debtor; or

(b) on an application for an attachment of earnings order to secure the payment of a judgment debt, or for a consolidated attachment order to secure the payment of two or more judgment debts, it appears to the court that an attachment of earnings order is already in force to secure the payment of a judgment debt by the same debtor.

Application for consolidated order

19.—(1) An application for a consolidated attachment order may be made— C27.19

(a) by the debtor in respect of whom the order is sought; or

(b) by any person who has obtained or is entitled to apply for an attachment of earnings order to secure the payment of a judgment debt by that debtor.

(2) An application under paragraph (1) may be made in the proceedings in which any attachment of earnings order (other than a priority order) is in force and rules 3, 4 and 5 of this order shall not apply.

(3) Where the judgment which it is sought to enforce was not given by the court which made the attachment of earnings order, the judgment shall be automatically transferred to the court which made the attachment of earnings order.

(3A) An application under paragraph (1)(b) shall certify the amount of money remaining due under the judgment or order and that the whole or part of any instalment due remains unpaid.

(3B) Where an application for a consolidated attachment of earnings order is made, the court officer shall—

(a) notify any party who may be affected by the application of its terms; and

(b) require him to notify the court in writing, within 14 days of service of notification upon him, giving his reasons for any objection he may have to the granting of the application.

(3C) If notice of any objection is not given within the time stated, the court officer shall make a consolidated attachment of earnings order.

(3D) If any party objects to the making of a consolidated attachment of earnings order, the court officer shall refer the application to the district judge who may grant the application after considering the objection made and the reasons given.

(3E) In the foregoing paragraphs of this rule, a party affected by the application means—

(a) where the application is made by the debtor, the creditor in the proceedings in which the application is made and any other creditor who has obtained an attachment of earnings order which is in force to secure the payment of a judgment debt by the debtor;

(b) where the application is made by the judgment creditor, the debtor and every person who, to the knowledge of the applicant, has obtained an attachment of earnings order which is in force to secure the payment of a judgment debt by the debtor.

(4) A person to whom two or more attachment of earnings orders are directed to secure the payment of judgment debts by the same debtor may request the court in writing to make a consolidated attachment order to secure the payment of those debts, and on receipt of such a request paragraphs (3B) to (3E) shall apply, with the necessary modifications, as if the request were an application by the judgment creditor.

Making of consolidated order by court of its own motion

20. Where an application is made for an attachment of earnings order to secure the payment of a judgment debt by a debtor in respect of whom an attachment of earnings order is already in force to secure the payment of C27.20

another judgment debt and no application is made for a consolidated attachment order, the court officer may make such an order of his own motion after giving all persons concerned an opportunity of submitting written objections.

Extension of consolidated order

C27.21 **21.**—(1) Where a consolidated attachment order is in force to secure the payment of two or more judgment debts, any creditor to whom another judgment debt is owed by the same judgment debtor may apply to the court by which the order was made for it to be extended so as to secure the payment of that debt as well as the first-mentioned debts and, if the application is granted, the court may either vary the order accordingly or may discharge it and make a new consolidated attachment order to secure payment of all the aforesaid judgment debts.

(2) An application under this rule shall be treated for the purposes of rules 19 and 20 as an application for a consolidated attachment order.

Payments under consolidated order

C27.22 **22.** Instead of complying with section 13 of the Act of 1971, a court officer who receives payments made to him in compliance with a consolidated attachment order shall, after deducting such court fees, if any, in respect of proceedings for or arising out of the order as are deductible from those payments, deal with the sums paid as he would if they had been paid by the debtor to satisfy the relevant adjudications in proportion to the amounts payable thereunder, and for that purpose dividends may from time to time be declared and distributed among the creditors entitled thereto.

CCR ORDER 28

JUDGMENT SUMMONSES

C28.0.1 **Contents**

Editorial Introduction

C28.0.2 A Judgment Summons is a means of obtaining an Order committing the debtor to prison but suspending the order so long as specified instalments are paid. The creditor must show that the debtor has the means to pay but has failed to do so. However, this method of enforcement is no longer available to ordinary creditors, it can be used only to enforce High Court or county court maintenance orders and judgments for payment of certain taxes, other sums or contributions due to the State. Thus, it is now quite rare. If the debtor is an employee, an attachment of earnings order invariably provides a better means of securing payment.

Related Sources

C28.0.3
- CCR, O.27—Attachment of Earnings
- Debtors Act 1869, s.5
- Attachment of Earnings Act 1971 (see SCP 1999, Vol. 2, Section 21E)

Forms

C28.0.4
- N67—Judgment Summons under Debtors Act 1869
- N69—Order for debtors' attendance at an adjourned hearing of a judgment summons

- N70—Order of commitment under s.110 County Courts Act 1984
- N71—Order revoking an order of commitment under s.110 County Courts Act 1984
- N72—Notice to debtor where committal order made, but directed to be suspended under debtors Act 1869
- N73—New order on Judgment Summons
- N74—Warrant of committal on a judgment
- N75—Indorsement on a warrant of committal sent to foreign court
- N76—Certificate to be indorsed on duplicate warrant of committal issued for re-arrest of debtor
- N342—Request for judgment summons
- N343—Notice of result of hearing of a judgment summons issued on a judgment or order of the High Court
- N344—Request for warrant of committal on judgment summons
- N345—Certificate of payment by prisoner under the Debtors Act 1869
- N346—Request by creditor for discharge of prisoner
- N347—Certificate for discharge of prison at plaintiff's request
- N348—Certificate by District Judge for discharge of defendant

Cognate RSC

- RSC, O.45—Enforcement of Judgments and Orders: General (see commentary thereon regarding the Debtors Act 1869) **C28.0.5**

Application for judgment summons

1.—(1) An application for the issue of a judgment summons may be made to the court for the district in which the debtor resides or carries on business or, if the summons is to issue against two or more persons jointly liable under the judgment or order sought to be enforced, in the court for the district in which any of the debtors resides or carries on business. **C28.1**

(2) The judgment creditor shall make his application by filing a request in that behalf certifying the amount of money remaining due under the judgment or order, the amount in respect of which the judgment summons is to issue and that the whole or part of any instalment due remains unpaid.

Mode of service

2.—(1) Subject to paragraph (2), a judgment summons shall be served personally on every debtor against whom it is issued. **C28.2**

(2) Where the judgment creditor or his solicitor gives a certificate for postal service in respect of a debtor residing or carrying on business within the district of the court, the judgment summons shall, unless the district judge otherwise directs, be served on that debtor by an officer of the court sending it to him by first-class post at the address stated in the request for the judgment summons and, unless the contrary is shown, the date of service shall be deemed to be the seventh day after the date on which the judgment summons was sent to the debtor.

(3) Where a judgment summons has been served on a debtor in accordance with paragraph (2), no order of commitment shall be made against him unless—

(a) he appears at the hearing; or

(b) the judge is satisfied that the summons came to his knowledge in sufficient time for him to appear at the hearing.

(4) Where a judgment summons is served personally, there may, if the judgment creditor so desires, be paid to the debtor at the time of service a sum reasonably sufficient to cover his expenses in travelling to and from the court.

Time for service

3.—(1) A judgment summons shall be served not less than 14 days before the day fixed for the hearing. **C28.3**

(2) A notice of non-service shall be sent pursuant to CPR rule 6.11, in respect of a judgment summons which has been sent by post under rule 2(2) and has been returned to the court office undelivered.

(3) CPR rules 7.5 and 7.6, shall apply, with the necessary modifications, to a judgment summons as they apply to a claim form.

Enforcement of debtor's attendance

C28.4 **4.**—(1) Order 27, rules 7B and 8, shall apply, with the necessary modifications, to an order made under section 110(1) of the Act for the attendance of the debtor at an adjourned hearing of a judgment summons as they apply to an order made under section 23(1) of the Attachment of Earnings Act 1971 for the attendance of the debtor at an adjourned hearing of an application for an attachment of earnings order.

(2) At the time of service of the order there shall be paid or tendered to the debtor a sum reasonably sufficient to cover his expenses in travelling to and from the court, unless such a sum was paid to him at the time of service of the judgment summons.

Evidence by witness statement or affidavit

C28.5 **5.** Where the judgment creditor does not reside or carry on business within the district of the court from which the judgment summons issued, evidence by witness statement or affidavit shall be admissible on his behalf without any notice having been given, unless the judge otherwise directs.

Suspension of committal order

C28.7 **7.**—(1) If on the hearing of a judgment summons a committal order is made, the judge may direct execution of the order to be suspended to enable the debtor to pay the amount due.

(2) A note of any direction given under paragraph (1) shall be entered in the records of the court and notice of the suspended committal order shall be sent to the debtor.

(3) Where a judgment summons is issued in respect of one or more but not all of the instalments payable under a judgment or order for payment by instalments and a committal order is made and suspended under paragraph (1), the judgment or order shall, unless the judge otherwise orders, be suspended for so long as the execution of the committal order is suspended.

(4) Where execution of a committal order is suspended under paragraph (1) and the debtor subsequently desires to apply for a further suspension, the debtor shall attend at or write to the court office and apply for the suspension he desires, stating the reasons for his inability to comply with the terms of the original suspension, and the court shall fix a day for the hearing of the application by the judge and give at least 3 days' notice thereof to the judgment creditor and the debtor.

(5) The district judge may suspend execution of the committal order pending the hearing of an application under paragraph (4).

New order on judgment summons

C28.8 **8.**—(1) Where on the hearing of a judgment summons, the judge makes a new order for payment of the amount of the judgment debt remaining unpaid, there shall be included in the amount payable under the order for the purpose of any enforcement proceedings, otherwise than by judgment summons, any amount in respect of which a committal order has already been made and the debtor imprisoned.

(2) No judgment summons under the new order shall include any amount in respect of which the debtor was imprisoned before the new order was made, and any amount subsequently paid shall be appropriated in the first instance to the amount due under the new order.

Notification of order on judgment of High Court

C28.9 **9.**—(1) Notice of the result of the hearing of a judgment summons on a judgment or order of the High Court shall be sent by the county court to the High Court.

(2) If a committal order or a new order for payment is made on the hearing,

the office copy of the judgment or order filed under Order 25, rule 11, shall be deemed to be a judgment or order of the court in which the judgment summons is heard, and if the judgment creditor subsequently desires to issue a judgment summons in another county court, Order 25, rule 2, shall apply with the necessary modifications.

Costs on judgment summons

10.—(1) No costs shall be allowed to the judgment creditor on the hearing of a judgment summons unless— C28.10

(a) a committal order is made; or
(b) the sum in respect of which the judgment summons was issued is paid before the hearing.

(2) Where costs are allowed to the judgment creditor,

(a) there may be allowed—
  (i) a charge of the judgment creditor's solicitor for attending the hearing and, if the judge so directs, for serving the judgment summons;
  (ii) a fee to counsel if the court certifies that the case is fit for counsel;
  (iii) any travelling expenses paid to the debtor; and
  (iv) the court fee on the issue of the judgment summons;
(b) the costs may be fixed and allowed without detailed assessment under CPR Part 47;

(3) For the purposes of paragraph (2)(a)(i) a solicitor who has prepared on behalf of the judgment creditor a witness statement or affidavit under rule 5 shall be treated as having attended the hearing.

Issue of warrant of committal

11.—(1) A judgment creditor desiring a warrant to be issued pursuant to a committal order shall file a request in that behalf. C28.11

(2) Where two or more debtors are to be committed in respect of the same judgment or order, a separate warrant of committal shall be issued for each of them.

(3) Where a warrant of committal is sent to a foreign court for execution, that court shall indorse on it a notice as to the effect of section 122(3) of the Act addressed to the governor of the prison of that court.

Notification to foreign court of part payment before debtor lodged in prison

12. Where, after a warrant of committal has been sent to a foreign court for execution but before the debtor is lodged in prison, the home court is notified that an amount which is less than the sum on payment of which the debtor is to be discharged has been paid, the home court shall send notice of the payment to the foreign court. C28.12

Payment after debtor lodged in prison

13.—(1) Where, after the debtor has been lodged in prison under a warrant of committal, payment is made of the sum on payment of which the debtor is to be discharged, then— C28.13

(a) if the payment is made to the court responsible for the execution of the warrant, the court officer shall make and sign a certificate of payment and send it by post or otherwise to the gaoler;
(b) if the payment is made to the court which issued the warrant of committal after the warrant has been sent to a foreign court for execution, the home court shall send notice of the payment to the foreign court, and the court officer at the foreign court shall make and sign a certificate of payment and send it by post or otherwise to the gaoler;

(c) if the payment is made to the gaoler, he shall sign a certificate of payment and send the amount to the court which made the committal order.

(2) Where, after the debtor has been lodged in prison under a warrant of committal, payment is made of an amount less than the sum on payment of which the debtor is to be discharged, then subject to paragraph (3), paragraph (1)(a) and (b) shall apply with the substitution of references to a notice of payment for the references to a certificate of payment and paragraph (1)(c) shall apply with the omission of the requirement to make and sign a certificate of payment.

(3) Where, after the making of a payment to which paragraph (2) relates, the balance of the sum on payment of which the debtor is to be discharged is paid, paragraph (1) shall apply without the modifications mentioned in paragraph (2).

C28.13.1 **History of rule**—Amended by Civil Procedure (Amendment) Rules 1999 (S.I. 1999 No. 1008).

Discharge of debtor otherwise than on payment

C28.14 **14.**—(1) Where the judgment creditor lodges with the district judge a request that a debtor lodged in prison under a warrant of committal may be discharged from custody, the district judge shall make an order for the discharge of the debtor in respect of the warrant of committal and the court shall send the gaoler a certificate of discharge.

(2) Where a debtor who has been lodged in prison under a warrant of committal desires to apply for his discharge under section 121 of the Act, the application shall be made to the judge in writing and without notice showing the reasons why the debtor alleges that he is unable to pay the sum in respect of which he has been committed and ought to be discharged and stating any offer which he desires to make as to the terms on which his discharge is to be ordered, and Order 27, rule 8(3) and (4), shall apply, with the necessary modifications, as it applies to an application by a debtor for his discharge from custody under section 23(7) of the Attachment of Earnings Act 1971.

(3) If in a case to which paragraph (2) relates the debtor is ordered to be discharged from custody on terms which include liability to re-arrest if the terms are not complied with, the judge may, on the application of the judgment creditor if the terms are not complied with, order the debtor to be re-arrested and imprisoned for such part of the term of imprisonment as remained unserved at the time of discharge.

(4) Where an order is made under paragraph (3), a duplicate warrant of committal shall be issued, indorsed with a certificate signed by the court officer as to the order of the judge.

CCR ORDER 29

COMMITTAL FOR BREACH OF ORDER OR UNDERTAKING

C29.0.1 **Contents**

C29.0.2 **Editorial Introduction**

A county court is a "superior" court not an "inferior" court for the purpose of contempt of court proceedings and has the same powers as the High Court under the Contempt of Court Act 1981. Breach of an injunction or undertaking can be punished as a contempt (fine and/or imprisonment for a fixed term up to two years). The Court's primary aim in committal proceedings is to secure future compliance with its order rather than to punish a past contempt.

CCR, O.29 has a more specific purpose and title (Committal for breach of order or undertaking) than RSC, O.52 (Committal). CCR, O.29, r.1 has the same title as RSC, O.45, r.5. See further RSC O.52 and commentary thereon. CCR, O.29 is now supplemented by a Practice Direction (see para. R52PD–001)

Related Sources

- Practice Direction supplementing RSC, O.52 and CCR, O.29 (para. R52PD–001) C29.0.3
- CCR, O.27, r.7B—Committal under Attachment of Earnings Act 1971
- CCR, O.28—Judgment Summons
- CCR, O.34—Penal and disciplinary provisions
- Administration of Justice Act 1960 (Appeal in cases of contempt of court: SCP 1999, Vol. 2, Section 20B)
- Attachment of Earnings Act 1971 (see SCP 1999, Vol. 2, Section 21E)
- Contempt of Court Act 1981 (see SCP 1999, Vol. 2, Section 13A)
- County Courts (Penalties for Contempt) Act 1983
- County Courts Act 1984 (see SCP 1999, Vol. 2, Section 20A)
- Failure to carry out an undertaking given to the court (see SCP 1999, Vol. 1, para. 52/1/9)
- Sequestration (available in county courts by virtue of section 38 of the County Courts Act 1984)

Forms

- N77—Notice as to consequences of disobedience to Court order ("penal notice") C29.0.4 (*Note—unless the "penal notice" has been endorsed on the order requiring a person to do or abstain from doing an act, and the order then personally served, it is not usually possible to enforce the order by commital*)
- N78—Notice to show cause why an order for your committal to prison should not be made
- N79—Committal or other order upon proof of disobedience of a court order or breach of an undertaking
- N80—Warrant of committal to prison
- N81—Notice to solicitor to how cause why undertaking should not be enforced by committal to prison
- N82—Order of committal for failure by solicitor to carry out undertaking
- N83—Order of discharge from custody under Warrant of Committal
- N117—General Form of Undertaking
- N319—Notice of execution of warrant of committal
- N329—Notes for completion of N79

Cognate RSC

- RSC, O.45, r.5—Enforcement of Judgment to do or abstain from doing any act C29.0.5
- RSC, O.52—Committals

Enforcement of judgment to do or abstain from doing any act

1.—(1) Where a person required by a judgment or order to do an act C29.1 refuses or neglects to do it within the time fixed by the judgment or order or any subsequent order, or where a person disobeys a judgment or order requiring him to abstain from doing an act, then, subject to the Debtors Acts 1869 and 1878 and to the provisions of these rules, the judgment or order may be enforced, by order of the judge, by a committal order against that person or, if that person is a body corporate, against any director or other officer of the body.

(2) Subject to paragraphs (6) and (7), a judgment or order shall not be enforced under paragraph (1) unless—

(a) a copy of the judgment or order has been served personally on the person required to do or abstain from doing the act in question and also, where that person is a body corporate, on the director or other officer of the body against whom a committal order is sought; and

(b) in the case of a judgment or order requiring a person to do an act, the copy has been so served before the expiration of the time within which he was required to do the act and was accompanied by a copy of any order, made between the date of the judgment or order and the date of service, fixing that time.

(3) Where a judgment or order enforceable by committal order under paragraph (1) has been given or made, the court officer shall, if the judgment or order is in the nature of an injunction, at the time when the judgment or order is drawn up, and in any other case on the request of the judgment

creditor, issue a copy of the judgment or order, indorsed with or incorporating a notice as to the consequences of disobedience, for service in accordance with paragraph (2).

(4) If the person served with the judgment or order fails to obey it, the judgment creditor may issue a claim form or, as the case may be, an application notice seeking the committal for contempt of court of that person and subject to paragraph (7), the claim form or application notice shall be served on him personally.

(4A) The claim form or application notice (as the case may be) shall—

(a) identify the provisions of the injunction or undertaking which it is alleged have been disobeyed or broken;
(b) list the ways in which it is alleged that the injunction has been disobeyed or the undertaking has been broken;
(c) be supported by an affidavit stating the grounds on which the application is made,

and unless service is dispensed with under paragraph (7), a copy of the affidavit shall be served with the claim form or application notice.

(5) If a committal order is made, the order shall be for the issue of a warrant of committal and, unless the judge otherwise orders—

(a) a copy of the order shall be served on the person to be committed either before or at the time of the execution of the warrant; or
(b) where the warrant has been signed by the judge, the order for issue of the warrant may be served on the person to be committed at any time within 36 hours after the execution of the warrant.

(6) A judgment or order requiring a person to abstain from doing an act may be enforced under paragraph (1) notwithstanding that service of a copy of the judgment or order has not been effected in accordance with paragraph (2) if the judge is satisfied that, pending such service, the person against whom it is sought to enforce the judgment or order has had notice thereof either—

(a) by being present when the judgment or order was given or made; or
(b) by being notified of the terms of the judgment or order whether by telephone, telegram or otherwise.

(7) Without prejudice to its powers under Part 6 of the CPR, the court may dispense with service of a copy of a judgment or order under paragraph (2) or a claim form or application notice under paragraph (4) if the court thinks it just to do so.

(8) Where service of the claim form or application notice has been dispensed with under paragraph (7) and a committal order is made in the absence of the respondent, the judge may on his own initiative fix a date and time when the person to be committed is to be brought before him or before the court.

C29.1.1 **"notice as to the consequences of disobedience"**—this is usually referred to as a "penal notice"; see Form N77.

C29.1.2 **"claim form or application notice"**—Application for a committal order is now made either by a claim form (see Pt 7, CPR) or application notice (see Pt 23, CPR—General Rules About Applications for Court Orders). It will invariably be more convenient to use the latter.

C29.1.3 **"committal order"**—Committal must be for a fixed term—see generally commentary to RSC, O.52.

C29.1.4 **Family Proceedings**—Order 29 applies to family proceedings as varied by the Family Proceedings Rules 1991 (S.I. 1991 No. 1247), rr.3.9A and 4.21A.

C29.1.5 **Contempt procedure**—In *M v. P (Contempt of Court: Committal Order), Butler v. Butler* [1992] 3 W.L.R. 813, CA, the Court of Appeal said that, in determining whether to reverse or vary a contempt order on appeal, the Court should ask itself whether, notwithstanding any departure from the proper procedure, the alleged contemnor had suffered any injustice. In *Nicholls v. Nicholls* [1997] 1 W.L.R. 314, Lord Woolf, M.R. said: "... in the future it should not be necessary to revisit authorities prior to *M v. P; Butler v. Butler* ...". As committal orders involve liberty of the subject it is particularly important that relevant rules are complied with. However, if the contemnor had a fair trial, and the order was made on valid grounds, a defect in the order would not result in its being set aside except where the interests of justice so require; they would not so require where no prejudice is caused by an error. If there was a procedural irregularity which had occasioned injustice the court would consider exercising its power to order a new trial. The court had to have regard to the interests of the other party as well as the contemnor.

Where a court commits for contempt otherwise than in the face of the court the committal must be for a fixed term and the court has no power to direct that the contemnor be brought back to court at a later date for a custodial sentence and in the meantime be detained (see *Delaney v. Delaney* [1996] 2 W.L.R. 74, CA, where Court of Appeal explains procedure to be adopted where judge initially uncertain what sentence to impose).

- RSC, O.52—see full commentary.

District Judges—A district judge has power to commit in respect of assaults on staff and contempts in the face of the court (County Courts Act 1984, ss.14 and 118); for breach of injunctions under Pt IV of the Family Law Act 1996 and the Housing Act 1996, but not generally for breach of orders. C29.1.6

Undertaking given by party

1A. Rule 1 (except paragraph (6)) shall apply to undertakings as it applies to orders with the necessary modifications and as if— C29.1A

(a) for paragraph (2) of that rule there were substituted the following—

"(2) A copy of the document recording the undertaking shall be delivered by the court officer to the party giving the undertaking—

(a) by handing a copy of the document to him before he leaves the court building; or

(b) where his place of residence is known, by posting a copy to him at his place of residence; or

(c) through his solicitor,

and, where delivery cannot be effected in this way, the court officer shall deliver a copy of the document to the party for whose benefit the undertaking is given and that party shall cause it to be served personally as soon as is practicable."

(b) in paragraph (7), the words from "a copy of" to "paragraph (2) or" were omitted.

Solicitor's undertaking

2.—(1) An undertaking given by a solicitor in relation to any proceeding in a county court may be enforced, by order of the judge of that court, by committal order against the solicitor. C29.2

(2) Where it appears to the judge that a solicitor has failed to carry out any such undertaking, he may of his own initiative direct the court officer to issue a notice calling on the solicitor to show cause why he should not be committed to prison.

(3) Where any party to the proceedings desires to have the undertaking enforced by committal order, the court officer shall, on the application of the party supported by an affidavit setting out the facts on which the application is based, issue such a notice as is referred to in paragraph (2).

Discharge of person in custody

3.—(1) Where a person in custody under a warrant or order, other than a warrant of committal to which Order 27, rule 8, or Order 28, rule 4 or 14, relates, desires to apply to the court for his discharge, he shall make his application in writing attested by the governor of the prison (or any other officer of the prison not below the rank of principal officer) showing that he has purged or is desirous of purging his contempt and shall, not less than one day before the application is made, serve notice of it on the party, if any, at whose instance the warrant or order was issued. C29.3

(2) If the committal order—
(a) does not direct that any application for discharge shall be made to a judge; or
(b) was made by the district judge under section 118 of the Act, any application for discharge may be made to the district judge.

(3) Nothing in paragraph (1) shall apply to an application made by the Official Solicitor in his official capacity for the discharge of a person in custody.

C29.3.1 **Para. (2) "Section 118 of the Act"**—The Courts and Legal Services Act 1990, s.74 extended the powers conferred by these sections to district judges as well as Circuit judges.

C29.3.2 **Appeals**—Appeals in contempt proceedings are provided for by the AJA 1960 (see s.13(2) in SCP 1999, Vol. 2, Section 20B at para. 20B–35). The applicant, as well as the contemnor can appeal (see *Wilson v. Webster* [1998] 1 F.L.R. 1097—14 day sentence of imprisonment increased to three months). See further, commentary to RSC, O.52.

CCR ORDER 30

GARNISHEE PROCEEDINGS

C30.0.1 **Contents**

Editorial Introduction

C30.0.2 CCR, O.30 is based on RSC, O.49. Where a judgment debtor is owed money by another, a judgment creditor can obtain an order that that other (the "garnishee") should pay the judgment creditor instead. The order is obtained in two stages; an "order to show cause"—(often referred to as a "garnishee order nisi") which has to be served on the garnishee and the debtor, which has the effect of "freezing" payment from the garnishee and which is obtained without notice—and, following a hearing, a garnishee order absolute. Application is made to the county court where judgment was obtained but, if necessary, is transferred to the garnishee's local court if the garnishee disputes his liability. Garnishee proceedings are common against "deposit taking institutions" (see further, commentary to RSC, O.49).

Related Sources

C30.0.3
- CCR, O.42, r.14—Attachment of debts due from the Crown
- County Courts Act 1984, s.109 (see SCP 1999, Vol. 2, Section 20A)

Forms

C30.0.4
- N84—Garnishee Order to show cause
- N85—Garnishee Order Absolute
- N349—Affidavit in support of application for garnishee order

Cognate RSC

C30.0.5
- RSC, O.49—Garnishee proceedings

Attachment of debt due to judgment debtor

C30.1 **1.**—(1) Where a person (in this Order called "the judgment creditor") has obtained in a county court a judgment or order for the payment of a sum of money amounting in value to at least £50 by some other person ("the judgment debtor") and any person within England and Wales ("the garnishee") is indebted to the judgment debtor, that court may, subject to the provisions of this Order and of any enactment, order the garnishee to pay the judgment creditor the amount of any debt due or accruing due from the garnishee to the judgment debtor or so much thereof as is sufficient to satisfy the judgment or order against the judgment debtor and the costs of the garnishee proceedings.

(2) An order under this rule shall in the first instance be an order to show cause, specifying the place and time for the further consideration of the matter (in this Order called "the return day") and in the meantime attaching the debt due or accruing due from the garnishee or so much of it as is sufficient for the purpose aforesaid.

(3) Among the conditions mentioned in section 108(3) of the Act (which enables any sum standing to the credit of a person in certain types of account to be attached notwithstanding that certain conditions applicable to the account in question have not been satisfied) there shall be included any condition that a receipt for money deposited in the account must be produced before any money is withdrawn.

(5) An order under this rule shall not require a payment which would reduce below £1 the amount standing in the name of the judgment debtor in an account with a building society or a credit union.

Application for order

2. An application for an order under rule 1 may be made without notice being served on any other party by filing a witness statement or affidavit— **C30.2**

(a) stating the name and last known address of the judgment debtor;
(b) identifying the judgment or order to be enforced and stating the amount of such judgment or order;
(c) stating that, to the best of the information or belief of the witness, the garnishee (giving his name and address) is indebted to the judgment debtor,
(d) where the garnishee is a deposit-taking institution having more than one place of business, giving the name and address of the branch at which the judgment debtor's account is believed to be held and the number of that account or, if it be the case, that all or part of this information is unknown to the witness; and
(e) certifying the amount of money remaining due under the judgment or order and that the whole or part of any instalment due remains unpaid.

Preparation, service and effect of order to show cause

3.—(1) An order under rule 1 to show cause shall be drawn up by the court with sufficient copies for service under this rule. **C30.3**

(2) Unless otherwise directed, a copy of the order shall be served—

(a) on the garnishee in the manner required for the notice of the day of hearing in accordance with Order 3, rule 6 at least 15 days before the return day; and
(b) on the judgment debtor in accordance with CPR Part 6, at least 7 days after a copy has been served on the garnishee and at least 7 days before the return day,

and as from such service on the garnishee the order shall bind in his hands any debt due or accruing due from the garnishee to the judgment debtor, or so much thereof as is sufficient to satisfy the judgment or order obtained by the judgment creditor against the judgment debtor, and the costs entered on the order to show cause.

Notice by deposit-taking institution denying indebtedness

5. Where the garnishee being a deposit-taking institution alleges that it does not hold any money to the credit of the judgment debtor, the garnishee **C30.5**

may, at any time before the return day, give notice to that effect to the court and to the judgment creditor and thereupon, subject to rule 8 the proceedings against the garnishee shall be stayed.

Order where no notice given, etc.

C30.7 **7.**—(1) Where the garnishee—

(a) does not give notice under rule 5; and

(b) does not on the return day appear or dispute the debt due or claimed to be due from him to the judgment debtor,

then, if the judgment debtor does not appear or show cause to the contrary, the court may, if it thinks fit, make an order absolute under rule 1 against the garnishee.

(2) An order absolute under rule 1 may be enforced in the same manner as any other order for the payment of money.

Directions where dispute as to notice under rule 5

C30.8 **8.** Where the garnishee in a notice given under rule 5 makes an allegation which the judgment creditor disputes, the court shall on the return day give directions for the determination of the question at issue.

Determination of liability in other cases

C30.9 **9.** Where in a case in which no notice has been given under rule 5 the garnishee on the return day disputes liability to pay the debt due or claimed to be due from him to the judgment debtor, the court may summarily determine the question at issue or order that any question necessary for determining the liability of the garnishee be tried in any manner in which any question or issue in proceedings may be tried.

Transfer of proceedings

C30.10 **10.** A garnishee who does not reside or carry on business within the district of the court in which the garnishee proceedings have been commenced and who desires to dispute liability for the debt due or claimed to be due from him to the judgment debtor may apply without notice being served on any other party in writing to that court for an order transferring the proceedings in which the judgment or order sought to be enforced was obtained to the court for the district in which the garnishee resides or carries on business, and the court applied to may, if it thinks fit, grant the application after considering any representations which it may give the judgment creditor and the judgment debtor an opportunity of making.

Discharge of garnishee

C30.11 **11.** Any payment made by a garnishee in compliance with an order absolute in garnishee proceedings, and any execution levied against him in pursuance of such an order, shall be a valid discharge of his liability to the judgment debtor to the extent of the amount paid or levied (otherwise than in respect of any costs ordered to be paid by the garnishee personally), notwithstanding that the garnishee proceedings are subsequently set aside or the judgment or order from which they arise is reversed.

Money in court

C30.12 **12.**—(1) Where money is standing to the credit of the judgment debtor in any county court, the judgment creditor shall not be entitled to take garnishee proceedings in respect of the money but may apply to the court on notice for an order that the money or so much of it as is sufficient to satisfy the judgment or order sought to be enforced and the costs of the application be paid to the judgment creditor.

(2) On receipt of notice of an application under paragraph (1) the court

officer shall retain the money in court until the application has been determined.

(3) The court hearing an application under paragraph (1) may make such order with respect to the money in court as it thinks just.

Costs of judgment creditor

13. Any costs allowed to the judgment creditor on an application for an order under rule 1 or 12 which in the former case are not ordered to be paid by the garnishee personally shall, unless the court otherwise directs be retained by the judgment creditor out of the money recovered by him under the order in priority to the amount due under the judgment or order obtained by him against the judgment debtor. **C30.13**

Attachment of debt owed by firm

14.—(1) An order may be made under rule 1 in relation to a debt due or accruing due from a firm carrying on business within England and Wales, notwithstanding that one or more members of the firm may be resident out of England and Wales. **C30.14**

(2) An order to show cause under rule 1 relating to such a debt shall be served on a member of the firm within England and Wales or on some other person having the control or management of the partnership business.

Powers of district judge

15. The powers conferred on the court by any provision of this order may be exercised by the judge or district judge. **C30.15**

CCR ORDER 31

CHARGING ORDERS

Contents **C31.0.1**

Editorial Introduction

The Charging Orders Act 1979, s.1 provides that where a judgment debtor is required to pay a sum of money to a judgment creditor then, for the purpose of enforcing that judgment or order the "appropriate court" may make an order (a "charging order") imposing on such property of the debtor as may be specified in the order, a charge for securing the payment of any money due or to become due under the judgment or order. Such an order must be made in accordance with the provisions of the 1979 Act. **C31.0.2**

Broadly, there are three kinds of charging order; a charging order on land (the most common); a charging order on securities; and a charging order over the debtor's interest in partnership property.

Jurisdiction of the county court to make a charging order over land is unlimited. If the judgment is a county court judgment, application should be made to the county court presently seised of the action. If the judgment is a High Court Judgment, application should be made to the debtor's local county court. A charging order on land is, in effect a mortgage over the land specified in the order and, subject to any prior mortgages and charges, the creditor becomes a secured creditor.

The order is obtained in a two-stage process. Application is made without notice by filing a witness statement or affidavit for a charging order nisi (the order should be registered at the Land Registry or the Land Charges Registry as appropriate). A hearing then takes place when, if the application is successful, a charging order absolute will be made (technically that order should also be registered, though in practice registration of the order nisi continues and is often relied on).

To enforce a charging order separate proceedings are necessary (see O.31, r.4) commenced by claim form.

Related Sources

C31.0.3
- Charging Orders Act 1979 (see SCP 1999, Vol. 2, Section 21F)
- County Courts Act, s.23 (see SCP 1999, Vol. 2, Section 20A)
- RSC, O.50—Charging Orders, Stop Orders, etc.
- RSC, O.88—Mortgage Actions (RSC, O.88 applies to enforcement of charging order by sale in the High Court—see RSC, O.50, r.9A: in the county court see CCR, O.31, r.4)

Forms

C31.0.4
- PF 101—Evidence in support of charging order (this is a High Court form in Table 2 of Practice Direction—Forms at 4PD–001. It should be adapted for use in the county court as a form is not provided for to use in the County Court. The Practice Direction wrongly refers to RSC, O.49—it should refer to RSC, O.50).
- N86—Charging Order Nisi
- N87—Charging Order Absolute
- N436—Order for sale of land under charging order

Application for charging order

C31.1 **1.**—(1) An application to a county court for a charging order under section 1 of the Charging Orders Act 1979 may be made—

(a) if the order is sought in respect of a fund in court, to the court where the money is lodged;

(b) subject to (a), if the judgment or order sought to be enforced is that of a county court, to the court in which the judgment or order was obtained or, if the proceedings have been transferred to another court under CPR rule 30.2(1)(b)(ii) or Order 25, rule 2, the court to which it has been transferred.

(c) subject to (a) and (b), to the court for the district in which the debtor resides or carries on business or, if there is no such district, to the court for the district in which the judgment creditor resides or carries on business.

(1A) An application for a charging order under paragraph 11 of Schedule 4 to the Local Government Finance Act 1992 shall be made to the court for the district in which the relevant dwelling (within the meaning of section 3 of that Act) is situated.

(2) The application may be made without notice being served on any other party by filing a witness statement or affidavit—

(a) stating the name and address of the debtor and, if known, of every creditor of his whom the applicant can identify;

(aa) certifying the amount of money remaining due under the judgment or order and that the whole or part of any instalment due remains unpaid;

(b) identifying the subject matter of the intended charge;

(c) either verifying the debtor's beneficial ownership of the asset to be charged or, where the asset is held by one or more trustees (including where the asset is land which is jointly owned) and the applicant relies on paragraph (b) of section 2(1) of the said Act of 1979, stating on which of the three grounds appearing in that paragraph the application is based and verifying the material facts;

(d) stating, in the case of securities other than securities in court, the name and address of the person or body to be served for the purpose of protecting the intended charge;

(e) stating, where the subject matter is an interest under a trust, or held by a trustee, the names and addresses of such trustees and beneficiaries as are known to the applicant.

Where the judgment or order to be enforced is a judgment or order of the

High Court or a judgment, order, decree or award of a court or arbitrator which is or has become enforceable as if it were a judgment or order of the High Court, the applicant shall file with his witness statement or affidavit the documents mentioned in Order 25, rule 11(a) and (c), and witness statement or the affidavit shall verify the amount unpaid at the date of the application.

(3) Subject to paragraph (1), an application may be made for a single charging order in respect of more than one judgment or order against a debtor.

(4) Upon the filing of the witness statement or affidavit mentioned in paragraph (2), the application shall be entered in the records of the court, and if, in the opinion of the district judge, a sufficient case for such an order is made in the witness statement or affidavit, the district judge shall make a charging order nisi fixing a day for the further consideration of the matter by the court.

(5) A copy of the order shall be sent by the court officer to the judgment creditor and, where funds in court are to be charged, shall be served by the court officer on the Accountant-General at the Court Funds Office.

(6) Copies of the order and of the witness statement or affidavit shall be served by the judgment creditor on—

(a) the debtor;
(b) the other creditors named in the witness statement or affidavit (unless the district judge otherwise directs); and
(c) where a trust is involved, on any trustee holding the asset to be charged, where the applicant relies on paragraph (b) of section 2(1) of the said Act of 1979 and on such other trustees and beneficiaries as the district judge may direct.

(7) Where an interest in securities not in court is to be charged, copies of the order nisi shall be served by the judgment creditor on the person or body required to be served in like circumstances by RSC Order 50, rule 2(1)(b).

(8) The documents required by the foregoing paragraphs to be served shall be served in accordance with CPR Part 6, not less than 7 days before the day fixed for the further consideration of the matter.

(9) Upon further consideration of the matter service required under paragraph (6) or (7) shall be proved by witness statement or affidavit.

Order on further consideration of application for charging order

2.—(1) On the day fixed under rule 1(4) for the further consideration of the matter, the court shall either make the order absolute, with or without modifications, or discharge it. C31.2

(2) If an order absolute is made, a copy shall be served by the court officer, in accordance with CPR Part 6 on each of the following persons, namely—

(a) the debtor;
(b) the applicant for the order;
(c) where funds in court are charged, the Accountant-General at the Court Funds Office; and
(d) unless otherwise directed, any person or body on whom a copy of the order nisi was served pursuant to rule 1(7).

(3) Every copy of an order served on a person or body under paragraph (2)(d) shall contain a stop notice.

Effect of charging order etc.

3.—(1) Where a charging order nisi or a charging order absolute has been made and served in accordance with rule 1 or 2, it shall have the same effect as an order made and served in like circumstances under RSC Order 50. C31.3

(2) The court may vary or discharge a charging order in the like circumstances and in accordance with the same procedure, with the necessary modifications, as a like order made by the High Court.

(3) The powers of the court under rule 2 or the last preceding paragraph, except the power to vary an order made by the judge, may be exercised by the district judge.

Enforcement of charging order by sale

C31.4 **4.**—(1) Proceedings in a county court for the enforcement of a charging order by sale of the property charged shall be commenced by a claim form, which shall be filed in the appropriate court, together with a witness statement or affidavit and a copy thereof—

(a) identifying the charging order sought to be enforced and the subject matter of the charge;
(b) specifying the amount in respect of which the charge was imposed and the balance outstanding at the date of the application;
(c) verifying, so far as known, the debtor's title to the property charged;
(d) identifying any prior incumbrances on the property charged, with, so far as known, the names and addresses of the incumbrancers and the amounts owing to them; and
(e) giving an estimate of the price which would be obtained on sale of the property.

(2) The appropriate court shall be—

(a) if the charging order was made by a county court, that court;
(b) in any other case, the court for the district in which the debtor resides or carries on business or, if there is no such district, the court for the district in which the judgment creditor resides or carries on business.

(3) A copy of the witness statement or affidavit filed under paragraph (1) shall be served on the respondent with a copy of the claim form and a notice to each respondent of the date of the hearing.

(4) The proceedings may be heard and determined by the district judge.

(5) The net proceeds of sale, after discharging any prior incumbrances and deducting the amount referred to in paragraph (1)(b) and the costs of the sale, shall be paid into court.

CCR ORDER 33

INTERPLEADER PROCEEDINGS

C33.0.1 **Contents**

Editorial Introduction

C33.0.2 As explained in the commentary to RSC, O.17, interpleading is a proceeding by which a person, from whom two or more persons claim the same property or debt, and who does not himself claim it, can protect himself from legal proceedings by calling upon the two claimants to interplead, that is to say, claim against one another, so that the title to the property or debt may be decided. Interpleaders are of two types. First there is execution interpleader where a sheriff or any other person charged with the execution of process under the authority of a court seizes or intends to seize goods by way of execution and a person other than the judgment debtor claims them. Here the sheriff etc. initiates the proceedings. The second type comprises all other interpleaders, principally stakeholders' interpleaders. A person who is a stakeholder, in the sense that he is under a liability in respect of a debt or any money or any goods, and who expects to be sued in relation thereto by two or more persons making adverse claims thereto, may apply to the court for relief by way of interpleader.

CCR, O.33, following the distinction between execution interpleader and stakeholder's interpleader, is divided into two Parts (see, respectively, rr.1 to 5 and rr.6 to 11). The cognate Order in the RSC is O.17 but it is not similarly divided. Consequently, direct comparison between the two Orders on a rule by rule basis cannot always be made. The effect of the two Orders are broadly the same. CCR, O.33 is a little more elaborate in places, partly because of the need to spell out the functions of the proper officer of the court and to take account of the role of the distict judge in execution (see County Courts Act 1984, s.101, interpleader by district judge). On the other hand the RSC contains more detailed provisions concerning the powers that the High Court may exercise in the disposing of an interpleader application; see O.17, r.5 (powers of Court hearing summons), r.6 (power to order sale of goods taken in execution), r.7 (power to stay proceedings), r.8 (other powers), r.9 (one order in several causes or matters) and r.10 (discovery). CCR, O.33 makes few express references to the disposal powers of a county court but the relevant RSC rules could be applied in county court interpleader proceedings by virtue of the County Courts Act 1984, s.76 in so far as it may be said that these rules constitute "general principles of practice in the High Court".

In the High Court interpleader under execution is heard and determined by a master or district judge, the sheriff having started the interpleader proceedings. However, in the county court the bailiff will have seized the goods in execution and as—due to an anomalous technicality—the district judge is responsible for the bailiffs (County Courts Act 1984, s.123) it is the district judge who must issue the interpleader. Consequently, in the County Court, an interpleader under execution must be determined by the circuit judge.

Related Sources

- County Courts Act 1984, ss.38, 76, 101 and 123 (see SCP 1999, Vol. 2, Section 20A) **C33.0.3**

Forms

- N88—Interpleader summons to execution creditor **C33.0.4**
- N88(1)—Interpleader summons to claimant claiming goods or rent under execution
- N89—Interpleader summons to person making adverse claims to debt
- N358—Notice of claim to goods taken in execution
- N359—Notice to claimant of goods taken in execution to make deposit or give security
- N360—Affidavit in support of interpleader summons other than an execution
- N361—Notice of application for relief in pending action
- N362—Order on interpleader summons under an execution where the claim is not established
- N363—Order on interpleader summons under an execution where the claim is established
- N364—Order on interpleader summons (other than execution) where there is an action
- N365—Order on an interpleader summons (other than execution) where there is no action

Cognate RSC

- RSC, O.17—Interpleader **C33.0.5**

PART I—UNDER EXECUTION

Notice of claim

1.—(A1) In this Part of this Order "the interpleader claimant" means any person making a claim to or in respect of goods seized in execution or the proceeds or value thereof and "the interpleader claim" means that claim. **C33.1**

(1) The interpleader claimant shall deliver to the bailiff holding the warrant of execution, or file in the office of the court for the district in which the goods were seized, notice of his claim stating—

(a) the grounds of the interpleader claim or, in the case of a claim for rent, the particulars required by section 102(2) of the Act; and

(b) the interpleader claimant's full name and address.

(2) On receipt of an interpleader claim made under this rule, the court shall—

(a) send notice thereof to the execution creditor; and

(b) except where the interpleader claim is to the proceeds or value of the goods, send to the interpleader claimant a notice requiring him to make a deposit or give security in accordance with section 100 of the Act.

Reply to interpleader claim

C33.2 **2.**—(1) Within 4 days after receiving notice of a claim under rule 1(2) the execution creditor shall give notice to the court officer informing him whether he admits or disputes the interpleader claim or requests the district judge to withdraw from possession of the goods or money claimed.

(2) If, within the period aforesaid, the execution creditor gives notice to the court admitting the claim or requesting the district judge to withdraw from possession of the goods or money claimed, the execution creditor shall not be liable to the district judge for any fees or expenses incurred after receipt of the notice.

Order protecting district judge

C33.3 **3.** Where the execution creditor gives the court such a notice as is mentioned in rule 2(2), the district judge shall withdraw from possession of the goods or money claimed and may apply to the judge, on notice to the interpleader claimant, for an order restraining the bringing of a claim against the district judge for or in respect of his having taken possession of the goods or money and on the hearing of the application the judge may make such order as may be just.

Issue of interpleader proceedings

C33.4 **4.**—(1) Where the execution creditor gives notice under rule 2(1) disputing an interpleader claim made under rule 1 or fails, within the period mentioned in rule 2(1), to give the notice required by that rule, the district judge shall, unless the interpleader claim is withdrawn, issue an interpleader notice to the execution creditor and the interpleader claimant.

(2) On the issue of an interpleader notice under paragraph (1) the court shall enter the proceedings in the records of the court, fix a day for the hearing by the judge and prepare sufficient copies of the notice for service under this rule.

(3) Subject to paragraph (4) the notice shall be served on the execution creditor and the interpleader claimant in the same manner required for service of the notice of the day of hearing in accordance with Order 3, rule 6.

(4) Service shall be effected not less than 14 days before the return day.

Claim for damages

C33.5 **5.** Where an interpleader proceedings under an execution the interpleader claimant claims from the execution creditor or the district judge, or the execution creditor claims from the district judge, damages arising or capable of arising out of the execution—

(a) the party claiming damages shall, within 8 days after service of the notice on him under rule 4(3), give notice of this claim to the court and to any other party against whom the claim is made, stating the amount and the grounds of the claim; and

(b) the party from whom damages are claimed may pay money into court in satisfaction of the claim as if the interpleader proceedings were a claim brought in accordance with CPR Part 7 by the person making the claim.

PART II—OTHERWISE THAN UNDER EXECUTION

Application for relief

C33.6 **6.**—(1) Where a person (in this Part of this Order called "the applicant") is under a liability in respect of a debt or any money or goods and he is, or expects to be, sued for or in respect of the debt, money or goods by two or more persons making adverse claims thereto ("the interpleader claimants"), he may apply to the court, in accordance with these rules, for relief by way of interpleader.

(2) The application shall be made to the court in which the claim is pending against the applicant or, if no claim is pending against him, to the court in which he might be sued.

(3) The application shall be made by filing a witness statement or affidavit showing that—

(a) the applicant claims no interest in the subject-matter in dispute other than for charges or costs;

(b) the applicant does not collude with any of the interpleader claimants; and

(c) the applicant is willing to pay or transfer the subject-matter into court or to dispose of it as the court may direct,

together with as many copies of the witness statement or affidavit as there are interpleader claimants.

Relief in pending claim

7. Where the applicant is a defendant in a pending claim— **C33.7**

(a) the witness statement or affidavit and copies required by rule 6(3) shall be filed within 14 days after service on him of the claim form;

(b) the return day of the application shall be a day fixed for the pre-trial review of the claim including the interpleader proceedings and, if a day has already been fixed for the pre-trail review or hearing of the claim, the court shall, if necessary, postpone it;

(c) the interpleader claimant, the applicant and the claimant in the claim shall be given notice of the application, which shall be prepared by the court together with sufficient copies for service;

(d) the notice to the interpleader claimant shall be served on him, together with a copy of the witness statement or affidavit filed under rule 6(3) and of the claim form and particulars of claim in the claim, not less than 21 days before the return day in the same manner as an interpleader notice in accordance with rule 4(3);

(e) the notices to the applicant and the claimant shall be sent to them by the court and the notice to the claimant shall be accompanied by a copy of the said witness statement or affidavit.

Relief otherwise than in pending claim

8. Where the applicant is not a defendant in a pending claim— **C33.8**

(a) the court shall enter the proceedings in the records of the court;

(b) the court shall fix a day for the pre-trial review or, if the court so directs, a day for the hearing of the proceedings and shall prepare and issue an interpleader notice, together with sufficient copies for service;

(c) the notice together with a copy of the witness statement or affidavit filed under rules 6(3), shall be served on each of the claimants not less than 21 days before the return day in the same manner as an interpleader notice to be served under rule 4(3); and

(d) the court shall deliver or send a notice of issue to the applicant.

Payment into court, etc.

9. Before or after the court proceeds under rule 7 or 8 the district judge may direct the applicant to bring the subject-matter of the proceedings into court, or to dispose of it in such manner as the district judge thinks fit, to abide the order of the court. **C33.9**

Reply by interpleader claimant

10.—(1) An interpleader claimant shall, within 14 days after service on him of the notice under rule 7(c) or the interpleader notice under rule 8(c), file— **C33.10**

(a) a notice that he makes no interpleader claim; or

(b) particulars stating the grounds of his interpleader claim to the subject matter,

together in either case with sufficient copies for service under paragraph (2).

(2) The court shall send to each of the other parties a copy of any notice or particulars filed under paragraph (1).

(3) The court may, if it thinks fit, hear the proceedings although no notice or particulars have been filed.

Order barring interpleader claim, etc.

C33.11 **11.**—(1) Where an interpleader claimant does not appear on any day fixed for a pre-trial review or the hearing of interpleader proceedings, or fails or refuses to comply with an order made in the proceedings, the court may make an order barring his interpleader claim.

(2) If, where the applicant is a defendant in a pending claim, the claimant does not appear on any day fixed for a pre-trial review or the hearing of the interpleader proceedings, the claim including the interpleader proceedings may be struck out.

(3) In any other case where a day is fixed for the hearing of interpleader proceedings, the court shall hear and determine the proceedings and give judgment finally determining the rights and claims of the parties.

(4) Where the court makes an order barring the interpleader claim of an interpleader claimant, the order shall declare the claimant, and all persons claiming under him, for ever barred from prosecuting his interpleader claim against the applicant and all persons claiming under him, but unless the interpleader claimant has filed a notice under rule 10 that he makes no interpleader claim, such an order shall not affect the rights of the claimants as between themselves.

CCR ORDER 34

PENAL AND DISCIPLINARY PROVISIONS

C34.0.1 **Contents**

Editorial Introduction

C34.0.2 CCR, O.34 conveniently sets out the procedure to enforce various penal and disciplinary provisions in the County Courts Act 1984. It had no directly equivalent rule in the RSC. Thus, for example, in the county court a witness who disobeys a witness summons can be fined under section 55 of the CCA 1984 whereas disobedience to a High Court subpoena (now also called a witness summons, see Pt 34 of the CPR) has always been dealt with as a contempt of court (see RSC, O.52).

For details of the courts powers see the various sections of the CCA mentioned in the rule. The courts powers are limited. In particular the court has no power to remand in custody or on bail (in contrast to Part IV of the Family Law Act 1996—Domestic Violence and Family Homes).

Section 74 of the Courts and Legal Services Act 1990 extended the powers conferred by sections 14, 55 and 118 of the CCA 1984 to district judges as well as circuit judges. The definition of "judge" in r.2.3 of the CPR includes a district judge. Accordingly the former CCR, O.35, r.5, dealing with the exercise of penal powers by district judges, is not included in Sched. 2 as it is not necessary.

Related Sources

C34.0.3
- CCR, O.26—Warrants of execution
- CCR, O.29—Committal for breach of Order or Undertaking
- RSC, O.52—Committal
- CCA 1984, s.14—Penalty for Assaulting Officers (SCP 1999, Vol. 2, Section 20A)
- CCA 1984, s.55—Penalty for neglecting or refusing to give evidence (SCP 1999, Vol. 2, section 20A)

- CCA 1984, s.92—Penalty for rescuing goods seized (SCP 1999, Vol. 2, Section 20A)
- CCA 1984, s.118—Power to commit for contempt (SCP 1999, Vol. 2, Section 20A)
- CCA 1984, s.124—Liability of bailiff for neglect to levy execution (SCP 1999, Vol. 2, Section 20A)
- Courts and Legal Services Act 1990, s.74—(SCP 1999, Vol. 2, Section 20B).

Forms

- N90—Summons for assaulting an officer of the court or rescuing goods C34.0.4
- N91—Order for committal and/or imposing a fine for assaulting an officer of the court of rescuing goods
- N366—Summons for neglect to levy execution
- N367—Notice of hearing to consider why fine should not be imposed
- N368—Order fining a witness for non-attendance
- N370—Order of committal or imposing a fine for insult or misbehaviour

Issue and service of summons for offence under section 14, 92 or 124 of the Act

1. Where— C34.1

(a) it is alleged that any person has committed an offence under section 14 or 92 of the Act by assaulting an officer of the court while in the execution of his duty, or by rescuing or attempting to rescue any goods seized in execution, and the alleged offender has not been taken into custody and brought before the judge; or

(b) a complaint is made against an officer of the court under section 124 of the Act for having lost the opportunity of levying execution,

the court officer shall issue a summons, which shall be served on the alleged offender personally not less than 8 days before the return day appointed in the summons.

Committal under section 14, 92 or 118 of the Act

1A. Rule 1(5) of Order 29 shall apply, with the necessary modifications, C34.1A where an order is made under section 14, 92 or 118 of the Act committing a person to prison.

Notice to show cause before or after fine under section 55 of the Act

2. Before or after imposing a fine on any person under section 55 of the Act C34.2 for disobeying a witness summons or refusing to be sworn or give evidence, the judge may direct the court officer to give to that person notice that if he has any cause to show why a fine should not be or should not have been imposed on him, he may show cause in person or by witness statement or affidavit or otherwise on a day named in the notice, and the judge after considering the cause shown may make such order as he thinks fit.

Non-payment of fine

3.—(1) If a fine is not paid in accordance with the order imposing it, the C34.3 court officer shall forthwith report the matter to the judge.

(2) Where by an order imposing a fine, the amount of the fine is directed to be paid by instalments and default is made in the payment of any instalment, the same proceedings may be taken as if default had been made in payment of the whole of the fine.

(3) If the judge makes an order for payment of a fine to be enforced by warrant of execution, the order shall be treated as an application made to the district judge for the issue of the warrant at the time when the order was received by him.

Repayment of fine

4. If, after a fine has been paid, the person on whom it was imposed shows C34.4 cause sufficient to satisfy the judge that, if it had been shown at an earlier date, he would not have imposed a fine or would have imposed a smaller fine or would not have ordered payment to be enforced, the judge may order the fine or any part thereof to be repaid.

CCR ORDER 35

ENFORCEMENT OF COUNTY COURT JUDGMENTS OUTSIDE ENGLAND AND WALES

C35.0.1 **Contents**

Part I—Enforcement outside United Kingdom

Part II—Enforcement in other parts of the United Kingdom

Editorial Introduction

C35.0.2 The various statutes under which county court judgments can be enforced outside the U.K. and in other parts of the U.K. are, of course, reciprocal. The cognate RSC, O.71, is entitled "Reciprocal Enforcement of Judgments". All the statutes referred to in CCR, O.35 are explained in the commentary to RSC, O.71. If proceedings are taken in a county court consider whether the courts for the country where it is intended to enforce it will recognise the judgment and, in particular, what attitude they might take to a default judgment. Before approaching the court outside England and Wales a certificate of the judgment must be obtained. Once registered the judgment can be enforced as if it were a judgment of the registering country. If it is intended to enforce in a country which does not have reciprocal enforcement arrangements (see countries listed in commentary to RSC, O.71) it is necessary to sue on that judgment in the country concerned.

Related Sources

C35.0.3
- Foreign Judgments (Reciprocal Enforcement) Act 1933 (see SCP 1999, Vol. 1, para. 71/1/4)
- Civil Jurisdiction and Judgments Act 1982 (see SCP 1999, Vol. 2, Section 7B)

Forms

C35.0.4
- N293—Certificate of Judgment or order
- See also forms noted under RSC, O.71

Cognate RSC

C35.0.5 RSC, O.71—Reciprocal Enforcement of Judgments, etc.

PART I—ENFORCEMENT OUTSIDE UNITED KINGDOM

Interpretation of Part I

C35.1 **1.** In this Part of this Order "the Act of 1933" means by Foreign Judgments (Reciprocal Enforcement) Act 1933, "the Act of 1982" means the Civil Jurisdiction and Judgments Act 1982 and expressions which are defined in those Acts have the same meaning in this Part of this Order as they have in those Acts.

Application under section 10 of the Act of 1933 for certified copy of county court judgment

C35.2 **2.**—(1) An application under section 10 of the Act of 1933 for a certified copy of a judgment of a county court may be made by a filing a witness statement or affidavit, made by a solicitor of the party entitled to enforce the judgment, or by the party himself, if he is acting in person.

(2) A witness statement or affidavit by which an application under section 10 of the Act of 1933 is made must—

(a) give particulars of the proceedings in which the judgment was obtained;

(b) have annexed to it evidence of service on the defendant of the claim form or other process by which the proceedings were begun (where service was effected otherwise than through the court), copies of the statements of case, if any, and a statement of the grounds on which the judgment was based;

(c) state whether the defendant did or did not object to the jurisdiction, and, if so, on what grounds;

(d) show that the judgment is not subject to any stay of execution;

(e) state that the time for appealing or applying for a re-hearing has expired, or, as the case may be, the date on which it will expire and in either case whether notice of appeal against the judgment has been given or an application for a re-hearing has been made; and

(f) state whether interest is recoverable on the judgment or part thereof and, if so, the rate and period in respect of which it is recoverable.

(3) The certified copy of the judgment shall be a sealed copy indorsed with a certificate signed by the district judge certifying that the copy is a true copy of a judgment obtained in the county court and that it is issued in accordance with section 10 of the Act of 1933.

(4) There shall also be issued a sealed certificate signed by the district judge and having annexed to it a copy of the claim form or other process by which the proceedings were begun and stating—

(a) the manner in which the claim form or other process was served on the defendant or that the defendant has delivered to the court an admission, defence or counterclaim;

(b) what objections, if any, were made to the jurisdiction;

(c) what statements of case, if any, were filed;

(d) the grounds on which the judgment was based;

(e) that the time for appealing or applying for a re-hearing has expired or, as the case may be, the date on which it will expire;

(f) whether notice of appeal against the judgment has been given or an application for a re-hearing has been made;

(g) whether interest is recoverable on the judgment or part thereof and, if such be the case, the rate of interest, the date from which interest is recoverable, and the date on which interest ceases to accrue; and

(h) such other particulars as it may be necessary to give the court in the foreign country in which it is sought to obtain execution of the judgment.

Application under section 12 of the Act of 1982 for certified copy of county court judgment

3.—(1) An application under section 12 of the Act of 1982 for a certified copy of a judgment of a county court may be made by filing a witness statement or affidavit made by a solicitor of the party entitled to enforce the judgment, or by the party himself, if he is acting in person. C35.3

(2) A witness statement or affidavit by which an application under section 12 of the Act of 1982 is made must—

(a) give particulars of the proceedings in which the judgment was obtained;

(b) have annexed to it evidence of service on the defendant of the claim form or other process by which the proceedings were begun (where service was effected otherwise than through the court), copies of the statements of case, if any, and a statement of the grounds on which the judgment was based together with, where appropriate, any document under which the applicant is entitled to legal aid or assistance by way of representation for the purposes of the proceedings;

(c) state whether the defendant did or did not object to the jurisdiction and, if so, on what grounds;

(d) show that the judgment has been served in accordance with CPR Part 6 and CPR rule 40.4 and is not subject to any stay of execution;

(e) state that the time for appealing or applying for a re-hearing has expired, or, as the case may be, the date on which it will expire and in either case whether notice of appeal against the judgment has been given or an application for a re-hearing has been made; and

(f) state—

(i) whether the judgment provides for the payment of a sum or sums of money;

(ii) whether interest is recoverable on the judgment or part thereof and, if such be the case, the rate of interest, the date from which interest is recoverable, and the date on which interest ceases to accrue.

(3) The certified copy of the judgment shall be a sealed copy and there shall be issued with the copy of the judgment a sealed certificate signed by the district judge and having annexed to it a copy of the claim form or other process by which the proceedings were begun.

PART II—ENFORCEMENT IN OTHER PARTS OF THE UNITED KINGDOM

Interpretation of Part II

C35.4 **4.** In this Part of the Order—

"the Act of 1982" means the Civil Jurisdiction and Judgments Act 1982,

"money provision" means a provision in any judgment to which section 18 of the Act of 1982 applies for the payment of one of more sums of money,

"non-money provision" means a provision in any judgment to which section 18 of the Act of 1982 applies for any relief or remedy not requiring payment of a sum of money.

Application for certificate of money provision

C35.5 **5.**—(1) A certificate in respect of any money provision contained in a judgment of the county court may be obtained by filing a witness statement or affidavit made by the solicitor of the party entitled to enforce the judgment, or by the party himself if he is acting in person, together with a form of certificate.

(2) A witness statement or affidavit by which an application under paragraph (1) is made must—

(a) give particulars of the judgment, stating the rate of payment, if any, specified under the money provisions contained in the judgment, the sum or aggregate of sums (including any costs or expenses) remaining unsatisfied, the rate of interest, if any, applicable and the date or time from which any such interest began to accrue;

(b) verify that the time for appealing against the judgment or for applying for a re-hearing has expired, or that any appeal or re-hearing has been finally disposed of and that enforcement of the judgment is not stayed or suspended; and

(c) state to the best of the information or belief of the witness the usual or last known address of the party entitled to enforce the judgment and of the party liable to execution on it.

(3) The proper officer shall enter on the certificate—

(a) the number of the proceedings;

(b) the amount remaining due under the judgment,
(c) the rate of interest payable on the judgment debt, and the date or time from which any such interest began to accrue;
(d) a note of the costs, if any, allowed for obtaining the certificate; and
(e) the date on which the certificate is issued.

Application for certified copy of judgment containing non-money provision

6.—(1) A certified copy of a judgment of a county court which contains any non-money provision may be obtained by filing a witness statement or affidavit made by the solicitor of the party entitled to enforce the judgment, or by the party himself, if he is acting in person. C35.6

(2) The requirements in paragraph (2) of rule 5 shall apply with the necessary modifications to a witness statement or affidavit made in an application under paragraph (1) of this rule.

(3) The certified copy of a judgment shall be a sealed copy to which shall be annexed a certificate signed by the court officer and stating that the conditions specified in paragraph (3)(a) and (b) of Schedule 7 to the Act of 1982 are satisfied in relation to the judgment.

CCR ORDER 37

REHEARING, SETTING ASIDE AND APPEAL FROM DISTRICT JUDGE

Contents C37.0.1

Editorial Introduction

Just three of the rules in CCR, O.37 have survived into the CPR. They are, of course, subject to the express provisions of the CPR (*e.g.* setting aside a judgment and rehearing is governed by CPR, r.27.11 in the case of claims on the small claims track and appeal under Pt 27 is governed by r.27.12). C37.0.2

The overriding objective of Pt 1 applies. Dealing with a case justly includes "saving expense" (r.1.1(1)(b)) and ordering a rehearing under CCR, O.37, r.1 necessarily involves increasing expense. It must be anticipated that ~~order~~ an order for a rehearing will be exceptional, on strong grounds and on terms as to costs. Note the unusually strict time limit in r.1(5). It is not sufficient to issue the application within 14 days of the trial; it must be served "not more than 14 days after the day of the trial" (see similarly, CCR, O.13, r.6).

Related Sources

- CPR, r.27.11—Setting Judgment Aside and re-hearing (small claims) C37.0.3
- CPR, r.27.12—Right of Appeal under Pt 27
- CCR, O.13, r.1—Applications and Orders in the Course of Proceedings
- CCR, O.24, r.7—Summary proceedings for recovery of land—setting aside
- CCR, O.44, r.3—Agricultural Holdings Act 1986—removal of arbitrator or setting aside award

Forms

- N244—Application notice (see Pt 23PD2.1) C37.0.4
- N285—General Form of Affidavit
- N372—Order for re-hearing

Rehearing (before the same Judge)

1.—(1) In any proceedings tried without a jury the judge shall have power on application to order a rehearing where no error of the court at the hearing is alleged. C37.1

(2) Unless the court otherwise orders, any application under paragraph (1) shall be made to the judge by whom the proceedings were tried.

(3) A rehearing may be ordered on any question without interfering with the finding or decision on any other question.

(4) Where the proceedings were tried by the district judge, the powers conferred on the judge by paragraphs (1) and (3) shall be exercisable by the district judge and paragraph (2) shall not apply.

(5) Any application for a rehearing under this rule shall be made on notice stating the grounds of the application and the notice shall be served on the opposite party not more than 14 days after the day of the trial and not less than 7 days before the day fixed for the hearing of the application.

(6) On receipt of the notice, the court officer shall, unless the court otherwise orders, retain any money in court until the application had been heard.

Appeal from district judge

C37.6 **6.**—(1) Any party affected by a judgment or final order of the district judge may, except where he has consented to the terms of the order, appeal from the judgment or order to the judge, who may, upon such terms as he thinks fit—

- (a) set aside or vary the judgment or order or any part of it;
- (b) give any other judgment or make any other order in substitution for the judgment or order appealed from;
- (c) remit the claim or any question in the claim to the district judge for rehearing or further consideration; or
- (d) order a new trial to take place before himself or another judge of the court on a day to be fixed.

(2) The appeal shall be made on notice, which shall state the grounds of the appeal and be served within 14 days after the day on which judgment or order appealed from was given or made.

Imposition of terms and stay of execution

C37.8 **8.**—(1) An application to the judge or district judge under any of the foregoing rules may be granted on such terms as he thinks reasonable.

(2) Notice of any such application shall not of itself operate as a stay of execution on the judgment or order to which it relates but the court may order a stay of execution pending the hearing of the application or any rehearing or new trial ordered on the application.

(3) If a judgment or order is set aside under any of the foregoing rules, any execution issued on the judgment or order shall cease to have effect unless the court otherwise orders.

CCR ORDER 38

COSTS

Fixed costs

C38.18 **18.**—(1) Appendix B shall effect for the purpose of showing the total amount which, in the several cases to which Appendix B applies, shall be allowed to the solicitor for the claimant as fixed costs without assessment (whether by the summary or the detailed procedure), unless the court otherwise orders.

(2) In a claim to which Appendix B or CPR Part 45 does not apply no

amount shall be entered on the claim form for the charges of the claimant's solicitor, but the words "to be assessed" shall be inserted.

APPENDIX B

PART I

CLAIMS FOR THE RECOVERY OF PROPERTY, APPLICATIONS TO ENFORCE AN AWARD

DIRECTIONS

1. The Tables in this Part of this Appendix show the amount to be entered on the claim form or application in respect of solicitors' charges— CB.1

(c) in a claim for the recovery of property, including land, with or without a claim for a sum of money (other than a claim to which CPR Part 45 applies), for the purpose of Part II of this Appendix or of fixing the amount which the plaintiff may receive in respect of solicitors' charges without assessment whether by the detailed or summary procedure in the event of the defendant giving up possession and paying the amount claimed, if any, and costs;

(e) in proceedings for the enforcement of a tribunal or other award, for the purposes only of Order 25, rule 12.

2. In addition to the amount entered in accordance with the relevant Table the appropriate court fees shall be entered on the application.

3. In the Tables the expression "claim" means—

(a) the sum of money claimed, or

(b) in relation to a claim for the recovery of land (with or without a claim for a sum of money), a sum exceeding £600 but not exceeding £2,000;

(c) in relation to a claim for the recovery of property other than money or land, the value of the property claimed or in the case of goods supplied under a hire purchase agreement, the unpaid balance of the total price.

4. The Tables do not apply where the application or the claim form is to be served out of England and Wales or where service by an alternative method is ordered.

TABLES OF FIXED COSTS

TABLE I

Where claim exceeds £25 but does not exceed £250

	Amount of charges £
(a) Where service is not by solicitor	30.75
(a) Where service is by solicitor	35.00

TABLE II

Where claim exceeds £250 but does not exceed £600

	Amount of charges £
(a) Where service is not by solicitor	41.00
(a) Where service is by solicitor	48.50

TABLE III

Where claim exceeds £600 but does not exceed £2,000

	Amount of charges £
(a) Where service is not by solicitor	69.50
(a) Where service is by solicitor	77.00

TABLE IV

Where claim exceeds £2,000

	Amount of charges £
(a) Where service is not by solicitor	75.50
(a) Where service is by solicitor	82.00

PART II

JUDGMENTS

DIRECTIONS

CB.2 Where an amount in respect of solicitors' charges has been entered on the claim form under Part I of this Appendix and judgment is given in the circumstances mentioned in paragraphs (d) in column 1 of the following Table, the amount to be included in the judgment in respect of the solicitors' charges shall, be the amount entered on the application or the claim form together with the amount shown in column 2 of the Table under the sum of money by reference to which the amount entered on the application or the claim form was fixed. Where judgment is given for a sum less than the amount claimed or for the delivery of goods of which the value or the balance of the total price is a sum less than the amount claimed, the foregoing paragraph shall, unless the court otherwise directs, have effect as if the amount entered on the application or the claim form had been fixed by reference to that sum.

FIXED COSTS ON JUDGMENTS

Column 1	*Column 2* *Sum of money*		
	A *Exceeding £25 but not exceeding £600*	B *Exceeding £600 but not exceeding £3,000*	C *Exceeding £3,000*
	£	£	£
(d) Where judgment is given in a fixed date action for— (i) delivery of goods where goods are not subject to a regulated agreement; or (ii) possession of land suspended on payment of arrears of rent, whether claimed or not, in addition to current rent, and the defendant has neither delivered a defence, admission or counterclaim, nor otherwise denied liability	38.50	57.25	70.75

(Delivery of goods claims subject to a regulated agreement are dealt with by CPR Part 45)

SCHEDULE 2

PART III

MISCELLANEOUS PROCEEDINGS

The following Table shows the amount to be allowed in respect of solicitors' charges in the circumstances mentioned. The appropriate court fee shall be allowed in addition. CB.3

	Amount to be allowed
3. For filing a request for the issue of a warrant of execution for a sum exceeding £25	£2.25
4. For service of any document required to be served personally (other than an application for an attachment of earnings order or a judgment summons unless allowed under Order 27, rule 9(1)(a), or Order 28, rule 10(2)(a)(i)), including copy and preparation of certificate of service	£8.50
5. For service by an alternative method, including attendances, making appointments to serve claim forms, preparing and attending to swear and file afidavits and to obtain order, and the fees paid for oaths	£25.00
6. For each attendance on the hearing of an application for an attachment of earnings order of a judgment summons where costs are allowed under Order 27, rule 9, or Order 28, rule 10	£8.50
7. For the costs of the judgment creditor when allowed in garnishee proceedings or an application under Order 30, rule 12—	
(a) where the money recovered is less than £70.00	one half of the amount recovered
(b) where the money recovered is not less than £70.00	£46.50
8. For the costs of the judgment creditor when allowed on an application for a charging order	£71.00
9. For obtaining a certificate of judgment where costs allowed under Order 35, rule 5(3)(d)	£8.00
10. Where an order for possession is made under rule 6 or rule 6A of Order 49 without the attendance of the plaintiff, for preparing and filing the application, the documents attached to the application and the request for possession	£79.50
11. On examination of a witness under CCR Order 25, rule 3 where any responsible representative of the solicitor attends, for each half-hour or part thereof	£15.00

CCR ORDER 39

ADMINISTRATION ORDERS

Contents

Editorial Introduction

An administration order can be made only against a person who has at least one High Court or county court judgment against him but whose total indebtedness does not exceed £5,000. C39.0.2

(Amendments to the CCA 1984, s.112 made by the CLSA 1990 have not been brought into force so the limit remains £5,000). It has been called "the poor man's bankruptcy". Like bankruptcy, a schedule of creditors is prepared, the debtor makes regular payments and a dividend is paid to creditors. Unlike bankruptcy, the order is administered by the county court and an administration order carries none of the legal disabilities of bankruptcy—though the order is registered at the Registry of County Court Judgments. While an administration order is in force no interest can accrue on a county court judgment and it is not possible to issue enforcement proceedings. If the debtor does not comply with the order it can be revoked. The court has the duty of enforcing the order: the usual method is an attachment of earnings order.

Administration Orders under the County Courts Act 1984 (dealt with in O.39) are not to be confused with the different, but identically entitled topic, of administration orders under the Insolvency Act 1986.

Related Sources

C39.0.3
- Attachment of Earnings Act 1971
- County Courts Act 1984, s.112 (amendments to s.112 and new ss.112A and 112B, effected by CLSA 1990, have never been brought into force)

Forms

C39.0.4
- N92—Request for administration order
- N93—List of creditors furnished under Attachment of Earnings Act 1971
- N94—Administration Order
- N95—Order revoking an administration order
- N95A—Order suspending or varying an administration order
- N270—Notes for guidance—administration order
- N373—Notice of application for an administration order
- N374—Notice of intention to review an administration order
- N374A—Notice of intention to revoke an administration order
- N375—Notice of further creditors' claim
- N376—Notice of hearing—administration order (by direction of the court)
- N377—Notice of dividend

Exercise of powers by district judge

C39.1 **1.** Any powers conferred on the court by Part VI of the Act, section 4 of the Attachment of Earnings Act 1971 or this Order may be exercised by the district judge or, in the circumstances mentioned in this Order, by the court officer.

Request and list of creditors

C39.2 **2.**—(1) A debtor who desires to obtain an administration order under Part VI of the Act shall file a request in that behalf in the court for the district in which he resides or carries on business.

(2) Where on his examination under Order 25, rule 3, or otherwise, a debtor furnishes to the court on oath a list of his creditors and the amounts which he owes to them respectively and sufficient particulars of his resources and needs, the court may proceed as if the debtor has filed a request under paragraph (1).

(3) Where a debtor is ordered to furnish a list under section 4(1)(b) of the said Act of 1971, then, unless otherwise directed, the list shall be filed within 14 days after the making of the order.

Verification on oath

C39.3 **3.** The statements in the request mentioned in rule 2(1) and the list mentioned in rule 2(3) shall be verified by the debtor on oath.

Orders made by the court officer

C39.5 **5.**—(1) The question whether an administration order should be made, and the terms of such an order, may be decided by the court officer in accordance with the provisions of this rule.

(2) On the filing of a request or list under rule 2, the court officer may, if he considers that the debtor's means are sufficient to discharge in full and within a reasonable period the total amount of the debts included in the list, determine the amount and frequency of the payments to be made under such an order ("the proposed rate") and—

(a) notify the debtor of the proposed rate requiring him to give written reasons for any objection he may have to the proposed rate within 14 days of service of notification upon him;
(b) send to each creditor mentioned in the list provided by the debtor a copy of the debtor's request or of the list together with the proposed rate;
(c) require any such creditor to give written reasons for any objection he may have to the making of an administration order within 14 days of service of the documents mentioned in sub-paragraph (b) upon him.

Objections under sub-paragraph (c) may be to the making of an order, to the proposed rate or to the inclusion of a particular debt in the order.

(3) Where no objection under paragraph (2)(a) or (c) is received within the time stated, the court officer may make an administration order providing for payment in full of the total amount of the debts included in the list.

(4) Where the debtor or a creditor notifies the court of any objection within the time stated, the court officer shall fix a day for a hearing at which the district judge will decide whether an administration order should be made and the court officer shall give not less than 14 days' notice of the day so fixed to the debtor and to each creditor mentioned in the list provided by the debtor.

(5) Where the court officer is unable to fix a rate under paragraph (2) (whether because he considers that the debtor's means are insufficient or otherwise), he shall refer the request to the district judge.

(6) Where the district judge considers that he is able to do so without the attendance of the parties, he may fix the proposed rate providing for payment of the debts included in the list in full or to such extent and within such a period as appears practicable in the circumstances of the case.

(7) Where the proposed rate is fixed under paragraph (6), paragraphs (2) to (4) shall apply with the necessary modifications as if the rate had been fixed by the court officer.

(8) Where the district judge does not fix the proposed rate under paragraph (6), he shall direct the court officer to fix a day for a hearing at which the district judge will decide whether an administration order should be made and the court officer shall give not less than 14 days' notice of the day so fixed to the debtor and to each creditor mentioned in the list provided by the debtor.

(9) Where an administration order is made under paragraph (3), the court officer may exercise the power of the court under section 5 of the Attachment of Earnings Act 1971 to make an attachment of earnings order to secure the payments required by the administration order.

Notice of objection by creditor

6.—(1) Any creditor to whom notice has been given under rule 5(8) and who objects to any debt included in the list furnished by the debtor shall, not less than 7 days before the day of hearing, give notice of his objection, stating the grounds thereof, to the court officer, to the debtor and to the creditor to whose debt he objects. **C39.6**

(2) Except with the permission of the court, no creditor may object to a debt unless he has given notice of his objection under paragraph (1).

Procedure on day of hearing

7. On the day of hearing— **C39.7**

(a) any creditor, whether or not he is mentioned in the list furnished by the debtor, may attend and prove his debt or, subject to rule 6, object to any debt included in that list;
(b) every debt included in that list shall be taken to be proved unless it is

objected to by a creditor or disallowed by the court or required by the court to be supported by evidence;

(c) any creditor whose debt is required by the court to be supported by evidence shall prove his debt;

(d) the court may adjourn proof of any debt and, if it does so, may either adjourn consideration of the question whether an administration order should be made or proceed to determine the question, in which case, if an administration order is made, the debt, when proved, shall be added to the debts scheduled to the order;

(e) any creditor whose debt is admitted or proved, and, with the permission of the court, any creditor the proof of whose debt has been adjourned, shall be entitled to be heard and to adduce evidence on the question whether an administration order should be made and, if so, in what terms.

Direction for order to be subject to review

C39.8 **8.**—(1) The court may, on making an administration order or at any subsequent time, direct that the order shall be subject to review at such time or at such intervals as the court may specify.

(2) Where the court has directed that an administration order shall be subject to review, the court officer shall give to the debtor and to every creditor who appeared when the order was made not less than 7 days' notice of any day appointed for such a review.

(3) Nothing in this rule shall require the court officer to fix a day for a review under rule 13A.

Service of order

C39.9 **9.** Where an administration order is made, the court officer shall send a copy to—

(a) the debtor;

(b) every creditor whose name was included in the list furnished by the debtor;

(c) any other creditor who has proved his debt; and

(d) every other court in which, to the knowledge of the district judge, judgment has been obtained against the debtor or proceedings are pending in respect of any debt scheduled to the order.

Subsequent objection by creditor

C39.10 **10.**—(1) After an administration order has been made, a creditor who has not received notice under rule 5 and who wishes to object to a debt scheduled to the order, or to the manner in which payment is directed to be made by instalments, shall give notice to the court officer of his objection and of the grounds thereof.

(2) On receipt of such notice the court shall consider the objection and may—

(a) allow it;

(b) dismiss it; or

(c) adjourn it for hearing on notice being given to such persons and on such terms as to security for costs or otherwise as the court thinks fit.

(3) Without prejudice to the generality of paragraph (2), the court may dismiss an objection if it is not satisfied that the creditor gave notice of it within a reasonable time of his becoming aware of the administration order.

Subsequent proof by creditor

C39.11 **11.**—(1) Any creditor whose debt is not scheduled to an administration order, and any person who after the date of the order became a creditor of the debtor, shall, if he wishes to prove his debt, send particulars of his claim to the court officer, who shall give notice of it to the debtor and to every creditor whose debt is so scheduled.

(2) If neither the debtor nor any creditor gives notice to the court officer, within 7 days after receipt of notice under paragraph (1), that he objects to the claim, then, unless it is required by the court to be supported by evidence, the claim shall be taken to be proved.

(3) If the debtor or a creditor gives notice of objection within the said period of 7 days or the court requires the claim to be supported by evidence, the court officer shall fix a day for consideration of the claim and give notice of it to the debtor, the creditor by whom the claim was made and the creditor, if any, making the objection, and on the hearing the court may either disallow the claim or allow it in whole or in part.

(4) If a claim is taken to be proved under paragraph (2) or allowed under paragraph (3), the debt shall be added to the schedule to the order and a copy of the order shall then be sent to the creditor by whom the claim was made.

Permission to present bankruptcy petition

12. An application by a creditor under section 112(4) of the Act for permission to present or join in a bankruptcy petition shall be made on notice to the debtor in accordance with CPR Part 23, but the court may, if it thinks fit, order that notice be given to any other creditor whose debt is scheduled to the administration order. C39.12

Conduct of order

13.—(1) The court manager or such other officer of the court as the court making an administration order shall from time to time appoint shall have the conduct of the order and shall take all proper steps to enforce the order (including exercising the power of the court under section 5 of the Attachment of Earnings Act 1971 to make an attachment of earnings order to secure payments required by the administration order) or to bring to the attention of the court any matter which may make it desirable to review the order. C39.13

(2) Without prejudice to section 115 of the Act, any creditor whose debt is scheduled to the order may, with the permission of the court, take proceedings to enforce the order.

(3) The debtor or, with the permission of the court, any such creditor may apply to the court to review the order.

(4) When on a matter being brought to its attention under paragraph (1) the court so directs or the debtor or a creditor applies for the review of an administration order, rule 8(2) shall apply as if the order were subject to review under that rule.

(5) Nothing in this rule shall require the court officer to fix a day for a review under rule 13A.

Review by court officer in default of payment

13A.—(1) Where it appears that the debtor is failing to make payments in accordance with the order, the court officer shall (either of his own initiative or on the application of a creditor whose debt is scheduled to the administration order) send a notice to the debtor— C39.13A

- (a) informing him of the amounts which are outstanding; and
- (b) requiring him (within 14 days of service of the notice upon him) to—
  - (i) make the payments as required by the order; or
  - (ii) explain his reasons for failing to make the payments; and
  - (iii) make a proposal for payment of the amounts outstanding; or

(iv) make a request to vary the order.

(2) If the debtor does not comply with paragraph (1)(b) within the time stated, the court officer shall revoke the administration order.

(3) The court officer shall refer a notice given by a debtor under paragraph (1)(b)(ii), (iii) or (iv) to the district judge who may—

(a) without requiring the attendance of the parties—

(i) revoke the administration order or vary it so as to provide for payment of the debts included in the order in full or to such extent and within such a period as appears practicable in the circumstances of the case; or

(ii) suspend the operation of the administration order for such time and on such terms as he thinks fit; or

(b) require the court officer to fix a day for the review of the administration order and to give to the debtor and to every creditor whose debt is scheduled to the administration order not less than 8 days' notice of the day so fixed.

(4) Any party affected by an order made under paragraph (2) or (3)(a) may, within 14 days of service of the order on him and giving his reasons, apply on notice for the district judge to consider the matter afresh and the court officer shall fix a day for the hearing of the application before the district judge and give to the debtor and to every creditor whose debt is scheduled to the administration order not less than 8 days' notice of the day so fixed.

(5) On hearing an application under paragraph (4), the district judge may confirm the order or set it aside and make such new order as he thinks fit and the order so made shall be entered in the records of the court.

Review of order

C39.14 **14.**—(1) On the review of an administration order the court may—

(a) if satisfied that the debtor is unable from any cause to pay any instalment due under the order, suspend the operation of the order for such time and on such terms as it thinks fit;

(b) if satisfied that there has been a material change in any relevant circumstances since the order was made, vary any provision of the order made by virtue of section 112(6) of the Act;

(c) if satisfied that the debtor has failed without reasonable cause to comply with any provision of the order or that it is otherwise just and expedient to do so, revoke the order, either forthwith or on failure to comply with any condition specified by the court; or

(d) make an attachment of earnings order to secure the payments required by the administration order or vary or discharge any such attachment of earnings order already made.

(2) The court officer shall send a copy of any order varying or revoking an administration order to the debtor, to every creditor whose debt is scheduled to the administration order and, if the administration order is revoked, to any other court to which a copy of the administration order was sent pursuant to rule 9.

Discharge of attachment of earnings order

C39.16 **16.** On the revocation of an administration order any attachment of earnings order made to secure the payments required by the administration order shall be discharged.

Declaration of dividends

C39.17 **17.**—(1) The officer having the conduct of an administration order shall from time to time declare dividends and distribute them among the creditors entitled to them.

(2) When a dividend is declared, notice shall be sent by the officer to each of the creditors.

Creditors to rank equally

18. All creditors scheduled under section 113(d) of the Act before an administration order is superseded under section 117(2) of the Act shall rank equally in proportion to the amount of their debts subject to the priority given by the said paragraph (d) to those scheduled as having been creditors before the date of the order, but no payment made to any creditor by way of dividend or otherwise shall be disturbed by reason of any subsequent proof by any creditor under the said paragraph (d). **C39.18**

Change of debtor's address

19.—(1) A debtor who changes his residence shall forthwith inform the court of his new address. **C39.19**

(2) Where the debtor becomes resident in the district of another court, the court in which the administration order is being conducted may transfer the proceedings to that other court.

CCR ORDER 42

PROCEEDINGS BY AND AGAINST THE CROWN

Contents **C42.0.1**

Editorial Introduction

Proceedings by and against the Crown are governed by the Crown Proceedings Act 1947. Section 35 states that any power to make rules of court shall include a power to make rules for the purpose of giving effect to the Act and any such rules may contain provisions to have effect, in relation to any proceedings by or against the Crown, in substitution for, or by way of addition to, any other provisions of the rules. Many such special provisions are found in CCR, O.42 and RSC, O.77. These two Orders need to be consolidated and included in the main body of the CPR but, in the meantime, in slightly amended form, both are now enacted in Sched. 2 and Sched. 1 respectively. The rules require careful study before commencing proceedings: note, for example, the pleading requirements (r.4), the lack of default judgment without permission (r.5(3)) and that no application can be made for summary judgment (r.5(5)). It is open to debate whether these special privileges for government departments (which is usually what "the Crown" means in practice) still have a place in a modern procedural code but that is a matter for Parliament not the Civil Procedure Rules Committee. **C42.0.2**

Related Sources

- Crown Proceedings Act 1947 (SCP 1999, Vol. 2, Section 21L) **C42.0.3**
- RSC, O.77—Proceedings by and against the Crown

Forms

- N390—Notice that a claim has been entered against the Crown **C42.0.4**
- N391—Crown Proceedings Act affidavit in support of application directing payment by Crown to judgment creditor
- N392—Crown Proceedings Act notice of application for order directing payment by the Crown to the judgment creditor

Application and interpretation

C42.1 **1.**—(1) These rules apply to any proceedings, so far as they are civil proceedings to which the Crown is a party, subject to the following rules of this Order.

(2) Except where the context otherwise requires, references in these rules to a claim for the recovery of land or other property shall be construed as including references to proceedings against the Crown for an order declaring that the claimant is entitled as against the Crown to the land or property or to the possession of it.

(3) In this Order—

"the Act of 1947" means the Crown Proceedings Act 1947;

"civil proceedings by the Crown" and "civil proceedings against the Crown" and "civil proceedings by or against the Crown" have the same respective meanings as in Part II of the Act of 1947 and do not include any of the proceedings specified in section 23(3) of that Act;

"civil proceedings to which the Crown is a party" has the same meaning as it has for the purposes of Part IV of the Act of 1947 by virtue of section 38(4) of that Act.

Particulars of claim in claim against the Crown

C42.4 **4.** The particulars of claim shall, in the case of civil proceedings against the Crown, include a statement of the circumstances in which the Crown's liability is said to have arisen and as to the government department and officers of the Crown concerned.

Subsequent procedure in claim

C42.5 **5.**—(1) If in a claim against the Crown the defendant considers that the particulars of claim do not contain a sufficient statement as required by rule 4, he may, before the time for delivering a defence has expired, file two copies of a demand for further information as specified in the demand and thereupon the court officer shall serve one copy on the claimant.

(2) Where the defendant files a demand under paragraph (1), the time for delivering a defence shall not expire until 4 days after the defendant has given notice to the court and the claimant that the defendant is satisfied with the information supplied in compliance with the demand or 4 days after the court has, on the application of the claimant of which not less than 7 days' notice has been given to the defendant, decided that no further information as to the matters referred to in rule 4 is reasonably required.

(3) Except with the permission of the court, no default judgment shall be entered under CPR Part 12 in a claim against the Crown.

(4) An application for leave under paragraph (3) shall be made on not less than 7 days' notice to the defendant.

(5) No application against the Crown shall be made under CPR Part 24 (summary judgment).

Subsequent procedure in fixed date claim

C42.6 **6.**—(1) In the case of a fixed date claim against the Crown, on the filing of the claim form the court shall—

(a) enter a plaint in the records of the court and deliver to the claimant a notice of issue omitting any reference to a return day;

(b) serve on the defendant a copy of the particulars of claim if they are filed with the claim form and the notice of issue and of the effect of paragraphs (3) and (5).

(2) Upon the service of the notice mentioned in paragraph (1)(b) all further proceedings in the claim shall be stayed except as provided in this rule.

(3) If the defendant considers that the particulars of claim do not contain a

sufficient statement as required by rule 4, he may, within 21 days after service on him of the particulars of claim, file in the court office two copies of a demand for further information as specified in the demand and thereupon the court shall serve one copy on the claimant.

(4) If within the said period the defendant does not file two copies of such a demand, then, subject to paragraph (5), the stay of proceedings provided for by paragraph (2) shall cease to have effect at the end of that period.

(5) If within the said period the defendant files a statement that no such demand will be made, the stay of proceedings provided for by paragraph (2) shall cease to have effect forthwith.

(6) If within the said period the defendant files two copies of such a demand, the stay of proceedings provided for by paragraph (2) shall cease to have effect when the defendant gives notice to the court and the claimant that the defendant is satisfied with the information supplied in compliance with the demand or when the court decides, on the application of the claimant of which not less than 7 days' notice has been given to the defendant, that no further information as to the matters referred to in rule 4, is reasonably required.

(7) When the stay of proceedings provided for by paragraph (2) ceases to have effect, the court shall fix a return day and give notice of it to the claimant and shall proceed to issue the claim form.

Service on the Crown

7.—(1) RSC Order 11 and any other provision of these rules relating to service of process out of England and Wales shall apply in relation to civil proceedings by the Crown but shall not apply in relation to civil proceedings against the Crown. **C42.7**

(2) Personal service of any document which is to be served on the Crown for the purpose of or in connection with civil proceedings by or against the Crown shall not be requisite.

(3) Any such document may be served on the Crown—

(a) by leaving the document at the office of the person to be served in accordance with section 18 of the Act of 1947, or any agent whom he has nominated for the purpose, but in either case with a member of the staff of that person or agent; or

(b) by posting it in a prepaid envelope addressed to the person to be served in accordance with the said section 18 or to any such agent as aforesaid.

"RSC, Order 11"—deals with Service of Process etc. out of the Jurisdiction and now applies to both High Court and County Court cases (the former CCR, O.8 is not re-enacted in Sched. 2). **C42.7.1**

"served in accordance with section 18 of the Act of 1947"—see the Crown Proceedings Act 1947 in SCP 1999, Vol. 2, Section 21L; at para 21L–41 and for a list of Government Departments and their respective solicitors and addresses for services see SCP 1999, Vol. 2, paras 21L–36 and 21L–37. **C42.7.1A**

Special provisions regarding orders made by the Court of its own initiative against the Crown

8.—(2) No order shall be made against the Crown by the court of its own initiative— **C42.8**

(a) (i) requiring the Crown to file or serve any statement of case or give any particulars which the court thinks necessary for defining the issues in the proceedings; and

(ii) at the same or any subsequent time directing that the claim be dismissed or the defendant be debarred from defending altogether or that anything in any statement of case of which particulars have been ordered be struck out unless the order is obeyed;

(b) ordering one or more questions or issues to be tried before the others; or

(c) at a hearing other than the trial.

C42.8.1 **Effect of rule**—CCR, O.42, r.8 is an extraordinary rule which deprives the Court of significant case management powers in cases where "the Crown" is a defendant.

Counterclaim in proceedings by or against the Crown

C42.9 **9.**—(1) In proceedings by the Crown for the recovery of taxes, duties or penalties the defendant shall not be entitled to avail himself of any set-off or counterclaim and accordingly the claim form to be served on the defendant and the forms for defending the claim, admitting the claim and acknowledging service, to accompany the claim form shall omit any reference to a counterclaim.

(2) In proceedings of any other nature by the Crown the defendant shall not be entitled to avail himself of any set-off or counterclaim arising out of a right or claim to repayment in respect of any taxes, duties or penalties.

(3) In any proceedings by the Crown the defendant shall not be entitled, and in any proceedings against the Crown the Crown shall not be entitled, without the permission of the court to be obtained on application of which not less than 7 days' notice has been given to the claimant, to make any counterclaim or claim in his statements of case to be entitled to any set-off if—

(a) the Crown sues or is sued in the name of a Government department and the subject-matter of the set-off or counterclaim does not relate to that department; or

(b) the Crown sues or is sued in the name of the Attorney-General.

Adjustment of liability under judgment for taxes

C42.10 **10.** Where the Crown has obtained a judgment for taxes but subsequently the tax liability is reduced, whether by reason of an appeal against an assessment or otherwise, and the Crown has given notice of the reduction to the court and to the debtor, the sum remaining unsatisfied under the judgment shall be reduced accordingly, but the amount of the reduction shall not rank as a payment under the judgment.

Part 20 claim against the Crown where the Crown is not already a party

C42.11 **11.**—(1) A Part 20 claim for service on the Crown where the Crown is not already a party shall not be issued without the permission of the court to be obtained on application in accordance with CPR Part 23.

(1A) An application notice under paragraph (1) must be served on the Crown and the claimant at least 7 days before the hearing.

(2) Permission shall not be granted under paragraph (1) unless the court is satisfied that the Crown is in possession of all such information as it reasonably requires as to the circumstances in which it is alleged that the liability of the Crown has arisen and as to the departments and officers of the Crown concerned.

Disclosure against the Crown

C42.12 **12.**—(2) Where in any proceedings an order of the court directs that a list of documents made in answer to an order for disclosure against the Crown shall be verified by witness statement or affidavit, the witness statement or affidavit shall be made by such officer of the Crown as the court may direct.

(3) The court may direct which officer of the Crown shall make the disclosure statement required by CPR rule 31.10(5).

Execution and satisfaction of orders against the Crown

13.—(1) Nothing in Orders 25 to 31 or RSC Order 30 (in so far as it applies to proceedings in the county court) shall apply in respect of any order against the Crown. **C42.13**

(2) A certificate issued under section 25(1) of the Act of 1947 shall be in the form used under Order 22, rule 8, with such variations as the circumstances of the case may require.

History of rule—Amended by Civil Procedure (Amendment) Rules 1999 (S.I. 1999 No. 1008). **C42.13.1**

Orders disapplied—CCR, O.42, r.13 disapplies the following Orders in respect of any order against the Crown: **C42.13.2**

CCR, O.25—Enforcement of Judgments and Orders: General
CCR, O.26—Warrants of Execution, Delivery and Possession
CCR, O.27—Attachment of Earnings
CCR, O.28—Judgment Summons
CCR, O.29—Committal for Breach or Order of Undertaking
CCR, O.30—Garnishee Proceedings
CCR, O.31—Charging Orders
RSC, O.30—Receivers

"section 25(1) of the Act of 1947"—see SCP 1999, Vol. 2, para. 21L–60. **C42.13.3**

Effect of rule—The Orders disapplied (see above) by r.13 are the enforcement provisions of the CCR. The successful claimant thus cannot enforce against the Crown in the usual way (see Part III of the CPA 1947—"Judgments and Execution" in SCP 1999, Vol. 2 at para. 21L–58). In practice the Crown will pay but if it refuses the remedy hitherto has been political rather than legal (but consider now the Human Rights Act 1998). **C42.13.4**

Attachment of debts, etc.

14.—(1) No order for the attachment of a debt under Order 30 or for the appointment of a receiver under RSC Order 30 shall be made or have effect in respect of any money due or accruing due, or alleged to be due or accruing due, from the Crown. **C42.14**

(2) Where such an order could have been obtained in a county court if the money had been due or accruing due from a subject, an application may be made to that county court in accordance with CPR Part 23, for an order under section 27 of the Act of 1947 restraining the person to whom the money is payable by the Crown from receiving the money and directing payment to the applicant or to the receiver.

(3) The application shall be supported by a witness statement or affidavit setting out the facts giving rise to it and in particular identifying the particular debt from the Crown in respect of which it is made.

(4) Notice of the application together with a copy of the witness statement or affidavit shall be served on the Crown and, unless the court otherwise directs, on the person to be restrained or his solicitor at least 7 days before the day fixed for the hearing.

(5) Order 30, rules 7 to 9, shall apply, with the necessary modifications, in relation to an application under the said section 27 as they apply in relation to an application for an order under Order 30, rule 1, except that the court shall not have power to issue execution against the Crown.

C42.14.1 **Attachment of moneys payable by the Crown**—See also section 27 of the Crown Proceedings Act 1947 in SCP 1999, Vol. 2 at para. 21L–73.

CCR ORDER 43

THE LANDLORD AND TENANT ACTS 1927, 1954, 1985 AND 1987

C43.0.1 **Contents**

Editorial Introduction

C43.0.2 The county court has full jurisdiction under the Landlord and Tenant Acts co-extensive with the High Court.

Part II of the Landlord and Tenant 1954 enables a business tenant to obtain a new tenancy. A tenancy to which Pt II applies will not come to an end unless terminated in accordnce with the Act. Although most cases are compromised a very large number of applications are issued in the county courts every year. Time limits under the Act are critical. The application to the court must be issued "not less than two nor more than four months" after the landlord's s.25 notice or, as the case may be, after the making of the tenant's s.26 request (see s.29). *The court has no power to extend these statutory time limits.* (Since the timetable is procedural it may be waived by the parties—see *Kammins Ballrooms Co. Ltd v. Zenith Investments (Torquay) Ltd* [1971] A.C. 850—but it very rarely is).

A tenancy which continues by virtue of Pt II does so on the same terms as before. Section 24A enables the court to fix an "interim rent" while the case continues. It is very rare for an application for an interim rent to be tried separately. Usually the application is heard with the application for the new tenancy as the same evidence is relevant to both. An application for an interim rent is usually made in the landlord's answer, though there is provision for a separate application.

The application is now made by "claim form" (O.43, r.2) but the claim form to be used in an application for a new tenancy is Form N397 which is an adaptation of the form of originating application in use before April 26, 1999.

Related Sources

C43.0.3
- Landlord and Tenant Acts 1927, 1954, 1985 and 1987
- High Court and County Courts Jurisdiction Order 1991 (see SCP 1999, Vol. 2, Section 20B)
- RSC, O.97—Landlord and Tenant Acts 1927, 1954 and 1987 (see Commentary to this Order).

Forms

C43.0.4
- N394—Claim Form for determining the right to compensation for improvement (Landlord and Tenant Act 1927)
- N395—Claim Form for cert. or determination of question other than compensation (Landlord and Tenant Act 1927)
- N396—Claim Form for statutory tenancy under Part I of the Landlord and Tenant Act 1954
- N397—Claim Form for new tenancy under Part II of the Landlord and Tenant Act 1954

- N398—Order an application for certificate as to improvement (Landlord and Tenant Act 1927)
- N399—Final order (Landlord and Tenant Act 1927)
- N400—Answer to claim form for new tenancy under Part II of the Landlord and Tenant Act 1954
- N401—Order an application for a new tenancy under Part II of the Landlord and Tenant Act 1954
- N402—Order substituting date in landlord's notice or tenant's request
- N403—Application for certificate of ground for refusing new tenancy
- N404—Certificate of ground for refusing new tenancy
- N404(1)—Order authorising agreement excluding Landlord and Tenant Act 1954
- N405—Notice of proceedings

Interpretation

1.—(1) In this order "the Act of 1927" means the Landlord and Tenant Act 1927, "the Act of 1954" means the Landlord and Tenant Act 1954, "the Act of 1985" means the Landlord and Tenant Act 1985 and "the Act of 1987" means the Landlord and Tenant Act 1987. **C43.1**

(2) In relation to any proceedings under the Act of 1954 any reference in this order to a landlord shall, if the interest of the landlord in question is subject to a mortgage and the mortgagee is in possession or a receiver appointed by the mortgagee or by the court is in receipt of the rents and profits, be construed as a reference to the mortgagee.

Commencement of proceedings and answer

2.—(1) Proceedings in a county court under the Act of 1927 or of 1954, or of 1985 or of 1987 shall be commenced by claim form and the respondent shall file an answer. **C43.2**

(2) The court shall fix a return day which, unless it otherwise directs, shall be a day fixed for the case management hearing of the proceedings.

Claim for compensation in respect of improvement

3.—(1) A claim under section 1 of the Act of 1927 for compensation in respect of any improvement, or a claim by a mesne landlord under section 8(1) of that Act, shall be in writing, signed by the claimant, his solicitor or agent, and shall contain— **C43.3**

(a) a statement of the name and address of the claimant and of the landlord against whom the claim is made;
(b) a description of the holding in respect of which the claim arises and of the trade or business carried on there;
(c) a concise statement of the nature of the claim;
(d) particulars of the improvement including the date when it was completed and the cost of it; and
(e) a statement of the amount claimed.

(2) Where any document relating to any proposed improvement, or to any claim, is sent to or served on a mesne landlord in pursuance of Part I of the Act of 1927, he shall forthwith serve on his immediate landlord a copy of the document, together with a notice in writing stating the date when the document was received by the mesne landlord, and if the immediate landlord is himself a mesne landlord, he shall, forthwith on receipt of the documents aforesaid, serve on his immediate landlord a similar copy and notice and so on from landlord to landlord.

(3) Any document required to be served under paragraph (2) shall be served in the manner prescribed by section 23 of the Act of 1927.

Proceedings under Part I of the Act of 1927

4.—(1) Subject to paragraph (2), the claim form by which proceedings under Part I of the Act of 1927 are commenced shall state— **C43.4**

(a) the nature of the claim or application or matter to be determined;
(b) the holding in respect of which the claim or application is made, its rateable value and the trade or business carried on there;
(c) particulars of the improvement or proposed improvement to which the claim or application relates; and
(d) if the claim is for payment of compensation, the amount claimed.

(2) In any case to which rule 3(1) relates the particulars required by paragraph (1) may, so far as they are contained in a claim made in accordance with that rule, be given by appending a copy of the claim to the claim form.

(3) The applicant's immediate landlord shall be made respondent to the application.

(4) Any certificate of the court under section 3 of the Act of 1927 that an improvement is a proper improvement or has been duly executed shall be embodied in an order.

Proceedings under Part I of the Act of 1954

C43.5 **5.**—(1) A respondent to an application under section 7 of the Act of 1954 who resists any of the applicant's proposals as to the terms of a statutory tenancy shall state in his answer the terms which he proposes in their place.

(2) The particulars in an application under section 13 of the Act of 1954 for the recovery of possession shall state, in addition to the matters set out in Order 6, rule 3—

(a) the date and terms of the lease under which the tenant holds or has held the property;
(b) the date of service upon the tenant of the landlord's notice to resume possession and the date of termination specified in the notice;
(c) where the tenant has notified the landlord that he is not willing to give up possession, the date of the notification; and
(d) where the claimant is not both the freeholder of the property comprised in the tenancy and the immediate landlord of the defendant, details of the interest constituting him the landlord for the purpose of proceedings under Part I of the Act of 1954.

(3) Where an order has been made under paragraph 1 of the Second Schedule to the Act of 1954 for the reduction of rent of any premises on the ground of failure by the landlord to do initial repairs, and it is subsequently agreed between the landlord and the tenant that the repairs to which the order relates have been carried out, the landlord shall file a copy of the agreement, and a note thereof shall be entered in the records of the court.

(4) Where the court makes an order for the recovery of possession of property in proceedings to which paragraph 9 of the Fifth Schedule to the Act of 1954 applies, the claimant shall, if the occupying tenant is not a party to the proceedings, forthwith notify him of the terms of the order and inform him of his rights to obtain relief under sub-paragraph (2) of that paragraph.

(5) If a copy of a notice under section 16(2) of the Act of 1954 or paragraph 9(2) or 10(2) of the Fifth Schedule to that Act is lodged in court, a note of the lodgment shall be entered in the records of the court.

Application for new tenancy under section 24 of the Act of 1954

C43.6 **6.**—(1) An application under section 24 of the Act of 1954 for a new tenancy shall state—

(a) the premises to which the application relates, their rateable value and the business carried on there;
(b) particulars of the applicant's current tenancy of the premises and of every notice or request given or made in respect of that tenancy under section 25 or 26 of that Act;
(c) the applicant's proposals as to the terms of the new tenancy applied

for, including, in particular, terms as to the duration thereof and as to the rent payable thereunder;

(d) the name and address of any person other than the respondent who, to the knowledge of the applicant, has an interest in reversion in the premises expectant (whether immediately or in not more than 14 years) on the termination of the applicant's current tenancy; and

(e) the name and address of any person having an interest in the premises other than a freehold interest or tenancy who, to the knowledge of the applicant, is likely to be affected by the grant of a new tenancy.

(2) The person who, in relation to the applicant's current tenancy, is the landlord as defined by section 44 of the Act of 1954 shall be made respondent to the application.

(3) A claim form under this rule must be served within 2 months after the date of issue whether served within or out of the jurisdiction and CPR rule 7.5(2) and 7.5(3) will not apply.

Answer to application for new tenancy under section 24 of the Act of 1954

7. Every answer by a respondent to an application to which rule 6 relates shall state— **C43.7**

(a) whether or not the respondent opposes the grant of a new tenancy and, if so, on what grounds;

(b) whether or not, if a new tenancy is granted, the respondent objects to any of the terms proposed by the applicant and, if so, the terms to which he objects and the terms which he proposes in so far as they differ from those proposed by the applicant;

(c) whether the respondent is a tenant under a lease having less than 14 years unexpired at the date of the termination of the applicant's current tenancy and, if he is, the name and address of any person who, to the knowledge of the respondent, has an interest in reversion in the premises expectant (whether immediately or in not more than 14 years from the said date) on the termination of the respondent's tenancy;

(d) the name and address of any person having an interest in the premises other than a freehold interest or tenancy who is likely to be affected by the grant of a new tenancy; and

(e) if the applicant's current tenancy is one to which section 32(2) of the Act of 1954 applies, whether the respondent requires that any new tenancy ordered to be granted shall be a tenancy of the whole of the property comprised in the applicant's current tenancy.

Order dismissing application under section 24 which is successfully opposed

8. Where the court hearing an application under section 24 of the Act of 1954 is precluded by section 31 of that Act from ordering the grant of a new tenancy by reason of any of the grounds specified in section 30(1) of that Act, the order dismissing the application shall state all the grounds by reason of which the court is so precluded. **C43.8**

Other applications under Part II of the Act of 1954

9. An application for an order under section 31(2)(b) of the Act of 1954 and, unless made at the hearing of the application under section 24, an application for a certificate under section 37(4) of that Act may be made to the district judge without notice being served on any other party. **C43.9**

Service of order in proceedings under Part II of the Act of 1954

10. A copy of any order made on an application to which rule 6 or 9 relates shall be sent by the court to every party to the proceedings. **C43.10**

Proof of determination of rateable value

C43.11 **11.** Where pursuant to section 37(5) of the Act of 1954 any dispute as to the rateable value of any premises has been referred to the Commissioners of Inland Revenue for decision by a valuation officer, whether for the purpose of section 37(2) or of section 63 of that Act, any document purporting to be a notification by the valuation officer of his decision shall be admissible in any proceedings in a county court as evidence of the matters contained therein.

Provisions as to assessors

C43.13 **13.**—(1) This rule applies to proceedings under Part I of the Act of 1927 or Part I or II of the Act of 1954, where an assessor is summoned by the judge under section 63(1) of the County Courts Act 1984, as extended by section 63 of the Act of 1954.

(3) Any report made by the assessor pursuant to paragraph (a) of section 63(6) of the Act of 1954 shall be filed by the assessor, together with a copy for each party to the proceedings, and thereupon the court shall send a copy to each party and shall, if the further consideration of the proceedings has not been adjourned to a day named, fix a day for further consideration and give notice thereof to all parties.

District judge's jurisdiction

C43.15 **15.**—(1) If on the day fixed for the hearing of an application under section 7 or section 24 of the Act of 1954 the district judge is satisfied that—

- (a) the parties to the application have agreed, in the case of an application under section 7, on the matters specified in subsection (2) of that section, or, in the case of an application under section 24, on the subject, period and terms of the new tenancy;
- (b) the owner of any reversionary interest in the property consents thereto; and
- (c) there are no other persons with interests in the property who are likely to be affected,

the district judge shall have power to make an order giving effect to the agreement.

(2) An application under section 38(4) of the Act of 1954 for the authorisation of an agreement may be heard and determined by the district judge and may be dealt with in private.

Application under section 12(2) of the Act of 1985

C43.16 **16.** An application under section 12(2) of the Act of 1985 for an order authorising the inclusion in a lease of provisions excluding or modifying the provisions of section 11 of that Act may be heard and determined by the district judge and may, if the court thinks fit, be dealt with in private.

Transfer to leasehold valuation tribunal

C43.16A **16A.** Where a question arising in proceedings is ordered to be transferred to a leasehold valuation tribunal for determination under section 31C of the Landlord and Tenant Act 1985 the court shall—

(a) send notice of the transfer to all parties to the proceedings; and

(b) send to the leasehold valuation tribunal copies certified by the district judge of all entries in the records of the court relating to the question, together with the order of transfer and all documents filed in the proceedings which relate to the question.

Application under section 19 of the Act of 1987

C43.17 **17.** A copy of the notice served under section 19(2)(a) of the Act of 1987 shall be appended to the claim form seeking an order under section 19(1) thereof, and an additional copy of the notice shall be filed.

Application for acquisition order under section 29 of the Act of 1987

19.—(1) An application for an acquisition order under section 29 of the Act of 1987 shall— C43.19

(a) identify the premises to which the application relates and give such details of them as are necessary to show that section 25 of the Act of 1987 applies to them;
(b) give such details of the applicants as are necessary to show that they constitute the requisite majority of qualifying tenants;
(c) state the names and addresses of the applicants and of the landlord of the premises, or, where the landlord cannot be found or his identity ascertained, the steps taken to find him or ascertain his identity;
(d) state the name and address of the person nominated by the applicants for the purposes of Part III of the Act of 1987;
(e) state the name and address of every person known to the applicants who is likely to be affected by the application, including, but not limited to, the other tenants of flats contained in the premises (whether or not they could have made an application), and mortgagee or superior landlord of the landlord, and any tenants' association; and
(f) state the grounds of the application,

and a copy of the notice served on the landlord under section 27 of the Act of 1987 shall be appended to the claim form unless the requirement to serve such a notice has been dispensed with, and an additional copy of the notice shall be filed.

(2) The respondents to an application for an acquisition order under section 29 of the Act of 1987 shall be the landlord of the premises and the nominated person, where he is not an applicant.

(3) A copy of the application shall be served on each of the persons named by the applicant under paragraph (1)(e), together with a notice stating that he may apply under rule 14 to be made a party to the proceedings.

(4) Where the nominated person pays money into court in accordance with an order under section 33(1) of the Act of 1987, he shall file a copy of the certificate of the surveyor selected under section 33(2)(a) thereof.

Application for order under section 38 or section 40 of the Act of 1987

20.—(1) An application for an order under section 38 or section 40 of the Act of 1987 shall state— C43.20

(a) the name and address of the applicant and of the other current parties to the lease or leases to which the application relates;
(b) the date of the lease or leases, the premises demised thereby, the relevant terms thereof and the variation sought;
(c) the name and address of every person who the applicant knows or has reason to believe is likely to be affected by the variation, including, but not limited to, the other tenants of flats contained in the premises of which the demised premises form a part, any previous parties to the lease, any mortgagee or superior landlord of the landlord, any mortgagee of the applicant, and any tenants' association; and
(d) the grounds of the application.

(2) The other current parties to the lease or leases shall be made respondents to the application.

(3) A copy of the application shall be served by the applicant on each of the persons named by the applicant under paragraph (1)(c) and by the respondent on any other person who he knows or has reason to believe is likely to be affected by the variation, together, in each case, with a notice stating that the person may apply to be made a party to the proceedings.

(4) An application under section 36 of the Act of 1987 shall be contained in the respondent's answer, and paragraphs (1) to (3) shall apply to such an application as if the respondent were the applicant.

C43.20.1 **History of rule**—Amended by the Civil Procedure (Amendment) Rules 1999 (S.I. 1999 No. 1008).

Service of documents in proceedings under the Act of 1987

C43.21 **21.**—(1) Where a claim form or answer is to be served in proceedings under the Act of 1987 it shall be served by the applicant or, as the case may be, by the respondent.

(2) Where a notice is to be served in or before proceedings under the Act of 1987, it shall be served in accordance with section 54 and, in the case of service on a landlord, it shall be served at the address furnished under section 48(1).

Tenants' associations

C43.22 **22.** In rules 18, 19 and 20 a reference to a tenants' association is a reference to a recognised tenants' association within the meaning of section 29 of the Act of 1985 which represents tenants of the flats of which the demised premises form a part.

CCR ORDER 44

THE AGRICULTURAL HOLDINGS ACT 1986

C44.0.1 **Contents**

Editorial Introduction

C44.0.2 The county court has a limited and diminishing jurisdiction under the AHA 1986. The Agricultural Tenancies Act 1995 applies to farm business tenancies beginning on and after September 1, 1995 and by s.4 the AHA 1986 applies only to tenancies created before September 1, 1995 or in pursuance of a contract made before September 1, 1995. The county court has no jurisdiction under the ATA 1995. Several sections of the AHA 1986 confer jurisdiction on the county court namely s.19 (disputes re distress levied on an agricultural holding); s.27 (enforcement of order made by Agricultural Land Tribunal); s.85 (recovery of a sum awarded as compensation) and Sched. 11 (control of arbitrations).

Related Sources

C44.0.3
- Agricultural Holdings Act 1986
- Agricultural Tenancies Act 1995
- RSC, O.94, r.7—Reference of question of law by Agricultural Land Tribunal

Order to arbitrator to state case

C44.1 **1.**—(1) An application under paragraph 26 of Schedule 11 to the Agricultural Holdings Act 1986 for an order directing an arbitrator to state, in the form of a special case for the opinion of the court, a question of law arising in the course of the arbitration shall include a concise statement of the question of law.

(2) The arbitrator shall not be made a respondent to the application, but if the judge grants the application, a copy of the order shall be served on the arbitrator.

Special case stated by arbitrator

C44.2 **2.**—(1) Where, pursuant to the said paragraph 26, an arbitrator states, in the form of a special case for the opinion of the court, any question of law arising in the course of the arbitration, the case shall contain a statement of such facts and reference to such documents as may be necessary to enable the judge to decide the question of law.

(2) The case shall be signed by the arbitrator and shall be lodged in the court office by the arbitrator or any party to the arbitration, together with a copy for the use of the judge.

(3) The court officer shall fix a day for the hearing of the special case and give notice thereof to the parties.

(4) On the hearing the judge shall be at liberty to draw any inferences of fact from the case and the documents referred to therein.

(5) The judge may remit the case to the arbitrator for restatement or further statement.

(6) A copy of the order made by the judge on the hearing shall be served on the parties to the arbitration and on the arbitrator.

Removal of arbitrator or setting aside award

3.—(1) An application under paragraph 27 of Schedule 11 to the said Act of 1986 for the removal of an arbitrator on the ground of his misconduct or for an order setting aside an award on the ground that the arbitrator has misconducted himself or that an arbitration or award has been improperly procured or that there is an error of law on the face of the award shall be made within 21 days after the date of the award. **C44.3**

(2) The arbitrator and all parties to the arbitration, other than the applicant, shall be made respondents.

Enforcement of order imposing penalty

4.—(1) When taking any proceedings for the enforcement in a county court of an order under section 27 of the Agricultural Holdings Act 1986, the party in whose favour the order was made shall file— **C44.4**

(a) a certified copy of the order; and

(b) a certificate specifying the amount due under the order and stating whether any previous proceedings have been taken for its enforcement and, if so, the nature of the proceedings and their result.

(2) Where it is desired to enforce the order by warrant of execution, the proceedings may be taken in any court in the district of which execution is to be levied.

CCR ORDER 45

THE REPRESENTATION OF THE PEOPLE ACT 1983

Contents

C45.0.1

Editorial Introduction

CCR, O.45, r.1 governs applications for a detailed assessment (formerly "taxation") of a returning officer's account pursuant to section 30 of the Representation of the People Act 1983. Appeal from a decision of a registration officer is governed by O.45, r.2: note that notice of appeal is given to the returning officer who is required to forward it to the appropriate county court (see O.45, r.2(2)). Order 45, r.3 provides a procedure for a selected appeal to be used as a test case: if the procedure of r.3 is followed the test case is binding on persons not parties to the appeal. **C45.0.2**

Related Sources

C45.0.3

- Pt 7 of the CPR How to start proceedings—the Claim Form
- CCR, O.3, r.6—Appeals to the County Court

- Representation of the People Act 1983
- RSC, O.94, r.5—Exercise of jurisdiction under Representation of the People Acts

Forms

C45.0.4 No specific forms are prescribed by Practice Direction—Forms (at 4PD–001) which supplements Part 4, (the previous forms N408 to N416 inc having been discontinued). Therefore, forms generally in use must be adapted to the case.

- N1—claim form
- N201—Request for entry of appeal

Application for detailed assessment of returning officer's account

C45.1 **1.**—(1) An application by the Secretary of State under section 30 of the Representation of the People Act 1983 for the detailed assessment of a returning officer's account shall be made by claim form and on issuing the claim form the court will fix a day for the hearing which shall be a day for proceeding with the detailed assessment if the application is granted.

(2) Where on the application the returning officer desires to apply to the court to examine any claim made against him in respect of matters charged in the account, the application shall be made in writing and filed, together with a copy thereof, within 7 days after service on the returning officer of the copy of the application for detailed assessment.

(3) On the filing of an application under paragraph (2) the court officer shall fix a day for the hearing and give notice thereof to the returning officer, and a copy of the application and of the notice shall be served on the claimant in the manner required for service of the notice of the day of hearing, in accordance with Order 3, rule 6.

(4) The examination and detailed assessment may, if the court thinks fit, take place on the same day, but the examination shall be determined before the detailed assessment is concluded.

(5) The application for detailed assessment and any application under paragraph (2) may be heard and determined by the district judge and a copy of the order made on the application shall be served on the Secretary of State and the returning officer and, in the case of an application under paragraph (2), on the claimant.

Appeal from decision of registration officer

C45.2 **2.**—(1) Where notice of appeal from a decision of a registration officer is given pursuant to regulations made under section 53 of the said Act of 1983, the registration officer shall, within 7 days after receipt of the notice by him, forward the notice by post to the court in which the appeal is required to be brought, together with the statement mentioned in those regulations.

(2) The appeal shall be brought in the court for the district in which the qualifying premises are situated.

In this paragraph "qualifying premises" means the premises in respect of which—

(a) the person whose right to be registered in the register of electors is in question on the appeal is entered on the electors' list or is registered or claims to be entitled to be registered; or

(b) the person whose right to vote by proxy or by post is in question on the appeal is or will be registered in the register of electors; or

(c) the elector whose proxy's right to vote by post is in question on the appeal is or will be registered in the register of electors,

as the case may be.

(3) The respondents to the appeal shall be the registration officer and the party (if any) in whose favour the decision of the registration officer was given.

(4) On the hearing of the appeal—

(a) the statement forwarded to the court by the registration officer and any document containing information furnished to the court by the registration officer pursuant to the regulations mentioned in paragraph (1) shall be admissible as evidence of the facts stated therein; and

(b) the judge shall have power to draw all inferences of fact which might have been drawn by the registration officer and to give any decision and make any order which ought to have been given or made by the registration officer.

(5) A respondent to an appeal other than the registration officer shall not be liable for or entitled to costs, unless he appears before the court in support of the decision of the registration officer.

Selected appeals

3.—(1) Where two or more appeals to which rule 2 relates involve the same point of law, the judge may direct that one appeal shall be heard in the first instance as a test case and thereupon the court shall send a notice of the direction to the parties to the selected appeal and the parties to the other appeals. **C45.3**

(2) If within 7 days after service of such notice on him any party to an appeal other than the selected appeal gives notice to the court that he desires the appeal to which he is a party to be heard—

(a) the appeal shall be heard after the selected appeal is disposed of;

(b) the court shall give the parties to the appeal notice of the day on which it will be heard;

(c) the party giving notice under this paragraph shall not be entitled to receive any costs occasioned by the separate hearing of the appeal to which he is a party, unless the judge otherwise orders.

(3) If no notice is given under paragraph (2) within the time limited—

(a) the decision on the selected appeal shall bind the parties to each other appeal without prejudice to their right to appeal to the Court of Appeal;

(b) an order similar to the order in the selected appeal shall be made in each other appeal without further hearing;

(c) the party to each other appeal who is in the same interest as the unsuccessful party to the selected appeal shall be liable for the costs of the selected appeal in the same manner and to the same extent as the unsuccessful party to that appeal and an order directing him to pay such costs may be made and enforced accordingly.

CCR ORDER 46

THE LEGITIMACY ACT 1976

Contents **C46.0.1**

Editorial Introduction

It is a surprise to find CCR, O.46 re-enacted in Sched. 2 of the CPR 1998 as, in practice, it is obsolete. The Order refers to a declaration of legitimacy under section 45(2) of the Matrimonial Causes Act 1973. That section was repealed and replaced by Part III of Family Law Act 1986 which came into force on April 4, 1988. Applications under the FLA 1986 are governed by the Family Proceedings Rules 1991 (S.I. 1991 No. 1247)—see rr.3.14 and 3.16. **C46.0.2**

Manner of application

1.—(1) An application to a county court under section 45(2) of the Matrimonial Causes Act 1973 for a declaration of legitimation by virtue of the Legitimacy Act 1976 shall be made by claim form— **C46.1**

(a) the grounds on which the applicant relies;

(b) the date and place of birth of the applicant and the maiden name of his mother and, if it be the case, that the applicant is known by a name other than that which appears in the certificate of his birth; and

(c) particulars of every person whose interest may be affected by the proceedings and his relationship, if any, to the applicant, including any person other than the applicant's father to whom his mother was married at the date of his birth.

(2) The application may be filed in the court for the district in which the applicant resides or the marriage leading to the legitimation was celebrated, or if neither the residence of the applicant nor the place of the marriage is in England or Wales, then in the Westminster County Court.

(3) The applicant shall file with the claim form—

(a) a witness statement or affidavit by him (or, if he is a child, by his litigation friend) verifying the application; and

(b) any birth, death or marriage certificate intended to be relied on at the hearing.

Preliminary consideration and service

C46.2 **2.**—(1) On the filing of the documents mentioned in rule 1, the court officer shall fix a day for a case management hearing and give notice thereof to the Attorney-General.

(2) It shall not be necessary to serve the application on the Attorney-General otherwise than by delivering a copy of it to him in accordance with section 45(6) of the Matrimonial Causes Act 1973.

(3) At the case management hearing the court shall give directions as to the persons, if any, other than the Attorney-General, who are to be made respondents to the application.

(4) Where in the opinion of the court it is impracticable to serve a respondent other than the Attorney-General in accordance with the rules relating to service or it is otherwise necessary or expedient to dispense with service of the claim form on any such respondent, the court may make an order dispensing with service on him.

Answer

C46.3 **3.**—(1) The Attorney-General may file an answer to the application within 14 days after directions have been given at the case management hearing.

(2) Any other respondent who wishes to oppose the application or to dispute any of the facts alleged in it shall, within 14 days after service of the application on him, file an answer to the application.

(3) A respondent who files an answer shall file with it as many copies as there are other parties to the proceedings and the court shall send one of the copies to each of those parties.

CCR ORDER 47

DOMESTIC AND MATRIMONIAL PROCEEDINGS

C47.0.1 **Contents**

Editorial Introduction

C47.0.2 The bulk of CCR, O.47 was repealed and replaced by the Family Proceedings Rules 1991 (S.I. 1991 No. 1247) as from October 14, 1991. Just one rule now survives into Sched. 2 of the CPR. Part III of the Family Law Reform Act 1969 is entitled "Provisions for use of blood tests in determining paternity". Section 25 defines "blood samples" and "blood tests" (the substitution of the term "bodily samples" is provided for in the Family Law Reform Act 1987—see s.33(1) and para. 21 of Sched. 2—but has never been brought into force). Note that the court cannot "order" a blood test: the court gives a "direction". Blood samples are used for DNA testing: the Court directs a blood sample and orders it to be submitted for DNA testing. Adverse inferences can be drawn if the direction is not complied with.

Related Sources C47.0.3

- Family Law Reform Act 1969
- Blood Tests (Evidence of Paternity) Regulations 1971 (S.I. 1971 No. 1861)
- RSC, O.112—Applications for use of blood tests in determining paternity.

Forms

No forms are prescribed by the Practice Direction—Forms (at 4PD–001) which supplements Part 4 but forms are prescribed in the Schedule to Blood Tests (Evidence of Paternity) Regulations 1971: see commentary to RSC, O.112 where the regulations and forms are set out. For a suggested form of words for a direction for a blood test see *Re H (Paternity: Blood Test)* (1996) 2 F.L.R. 65 *per* Ward L.J. at 83. C47.0.4

Family Law Reform Act 1969

5.—(1) In this rule— C47.5

"blood samples" and "blood tests" have the meanings assigned to them by section 25 of the Family Law Reform Act 1969; and

"direction" means a direction for the use of blood tests under section 20(1) of that Act.

(2) Except with the permission of the court, an application in any proceedings for a direction shall be made on notice to every party to the proceedings (other than the applicant) and to any other person from whom the direction involves the taking of blood samples.

(3) Where an application is made for a direction involving the taking of blood samples from a person who is not a party to the proceedings in which the application is made, the application notice shall be served on him personally and the court may at any time direct him to be made a party to the proceedings.

(4) Where an application is made for a direction in respect of a person (in this paragraph referred to as a person under disability) who is either—

(a) under 16; or

(b) suffering from mental disorder within the meaning of the Mental Health Act 1983 and incapable of understanding the nature and purpose of blood tests,

the notice of application shall state the name and address of the person having the care and control of the person under disability and shall be served on him instead of on the person under disability.

(5) Where the court gives a direction in any proceedings, the court officer shall send a copy to every party to the proceedings and to every other person from whom the direction involves the taking of blood samples, and, unless otherwise ordered, the proceedings shall stand adjourned until the court receives a report pursuant to the direction.

(6) On receipt by the court of a report made pursuant to a direction, the court officer shall send a copy to every party to the proceedings and to every other person from whom the direction involved the taking of blood samples.

CCR ORDER 48B

ENFORCEMENT OF PARKING PENALTIES UNDER THE ROAD TRAFFIC ACT 1991

Contents C48B.0.1

Editorial Introduction

The Road Traffic Act 1991 established a new regime for the enforcement of parking charges thereby removing such proceedings from the jurisdiction of magistrates courts. Initially the C48B.0.2

regime of the Act applied only to London but has now been extended to the whole of England and Wales. CCR, O.48B is to enable local authorities to request the issue of court orders to recover certain parking charges and to arrange for such orders to be enforced.

Related Sources

C48B.0.3
- Road Traffic Act 1991
- High Court and County Courts Jurisdiction Order 1991, art. 8A (SCP 1999, Vol. 2, Section 20B)
- Enforcement of Road Traffic Debts Order 1993 (S.I. 1993 No. 2073)
- Enforcement of Road Traffic Debts (Certified Bailiffs) Regulations 1993 (S.I. 1993 No. 2072)

Application and interpretation

C48B.1 **1.**—(1) This order applies for the recovery of—

(a) increased penalty charges provided for in parking charge certificates issued under paragraph 6 of Schedule 6 to the 1991 Act; and

(b) amounts payable by a person other than an authority under an adjudication of a parking adjudicator pursuant to section 73 of the 1991 Act.

(2) In this order, unless the context otherwise requires—

"authority" means the local authority which served the charge certificate;

"order" means an order made under paragraph 7 of Schedule 6 to the 1991 Act or, as the case may be, under section 73 of that Act;

"the Order" means the Enforcement of Road Traffic Debts Order 1993 made under section 78 of the 1991 Act as it applies to a local authority;

"relevant period" means the period of 21 days allowed for serving a statutory declaration by paragraph 8(1) of Schedule 6 to the 1991 Act or, where a longer period has been allowed pursuant to paragraph 8(4) of the said Schedule, that period;

"respondent" means the person on whom the charge certificate was served or, as the case may be, the person (other than an authority) by whom the amount due under an adjudication of a parking adjudicator is payable;

"specified debts" means the Part II debts specified in article 2 of the Order;

"statutory declaration" means a declaration in the appropriate form which complies with paragraph 8(2) of Schedule 6 to the 1991 Act; and

"the 1991 Act" means the Road Traffic Act 1991.

(3) Unless the context otherwise requires, expressions which are used in the 1991 Act have the same meaning in this order as they have in that Act.

(4) The references in paragraph (2) to a local authority mean—

(a) in England, a London authority, a county or district council or the Council of the Isles of Scilly; and

(b) in Wales, a county or county borough council.

Establishment of the parking enforcement centre

C48B.1A **1A.**—(1) There shall be a parking enforcement centre ("the Centre") situated at such place or places as the Lord Chancellor may determine and having such functions relating to proceedings under this order and other related matters as he may direct.

(2) For any purpose connected with the exercise of the Centre's functions—

(a) the Centre shall be deemed to be part of the office of the court whose name appears on the documents to which the functions relates or in whose name the documents are issued;

(b) any officer of the Centre shall, in exercising its functions, be deemed to act as the court officer of that court,

and these rules shall have effect accordingly.

Requests for orders

2.—(1) An authority which wishes to take proceedings under this order shall give notice to the court officer and, where the court officer so allows, requests for orders may be made, and such orders may be enforced, in accordance with the following provisions of this order. C48B.2

(2) An authority shall file a request for an order in the appropriate form scheduling the increased penalty charges in respect of which an order is sought.

(3) The authority shall in the request or in another manner approved by the court officer—

(a) certify—

(i) that 14 days have elapsed since service of the charge certificate;

(ii) the amount due under the charge certificate and the date on which the charge certificate was served; and

(iii) that the amount due remains unpaid;

(b) give the charge certificate number;

(c) specify (whether by reference to the appropriate code or otherwise) the grounds stated in the notice to owner on which the parking attendant who issued the penalty charge notice believed that a penalty charge was payable with respect to the vehicle;

(d) state—

(i) the name and address of the respondent and, where known, his title;

(ii) the registration number of the vehicle concerned;

(iii) (whether by reference to the appropriate charge certificate's number or otherwise) the authority's address for service;

(iv) the court fee.

(4) If satisfied that the request is in order, the court officer shall order that the increased charge (together with the court fee) may be recovered as if it were payable under a county court order by sealing the request and returning it to the authority.

(5) When the court officer so orders and on receipt of the sealed request, the authority may draw up the order and shall annex to any such order a form of statutory declaration for the respondent's use.

(6) Within 14 days of receipt of the sealed request, the authority shall serve the order (and the form of statutory declaration) on the respondent by—

(a) delivering the order to the respondent personally; or

(b) sending it by first-class post to the respondent at the address given in the request.

(6A) Where an order is served in accordance with paragraph (6)(b), the date of service shall, unless the contrary is shown, be deemed to be the seventh day after the date on which the order was sent to the respondent.

(6B) Subject to paragraphs (6C) and (6D), where partners are served in the name of their firm, service of an order shall be good service on all the partners, whether any of them is out of England and Wales or not, if the order is—

(a) delivered to a partner personally; or

(b) served by a court officer sending it by first class post to the firm at the address stated in the request.

(6C) Where the partnership has to the knowledge of the authority been dissolved before the service of the order, the order shall be served upon every person within the jurisdiction sought to be made liable.

(6D) Unless the authority, or its solicitor, otherwise requests, service on the partnership shall be effected in accordance with paragraph (6B)(b).

(6E) Where an order is served in accordance with paragraph (6B)(b) the date of service shall, unless the contrary is shown, be deemed to be the seventh day after the date on which the order was sent to the respondent.

(6F) Service on a corporation may be effected by serving it on the mayor, chairman or president of the body or the chief executive, clerk, secretary, treasurer or other similar officer thereof.

(6G) Service of an order on a company registered in England and Wales may be effected by serving it at the registered office or at any place of business of the company which has some real connection with an issue in the proceedings.

(6H) Where an order has been served under paragraph (6G) other than at the registered office, and after a request for a warrant of execution has been sealed, it appears to the court officer that the order did not come to the attention of the appropriate person within the company in due time, the court may, on application under CPR Part 23 or of its own initiative, set aside the warrant, and may give such directions as it considers appropriate.

(7) Where an authority requests an order in respect of amounts payable by a person other than an authority under an adjudication of a parking adjudicator pursuant to section 73 of the 1991 Act, paragraphs (2) and (3) shall apply with the necessary modifications and in addition the authority shall—

(a) state the date on which the adjudication was made;
(b) provide details of the order made on the adjudication; and
(c) certify the amount awarded by way of costs and that the amount remains unpaid.

Documents

C48B.3 **3.**—(1) Where by or under this order any document is required to be filed, that requirement shall be deemed to be satisfied if the information which would be contained in the document is delivered in computer-readable form but nothing in this paragraph shall be taken as enabling an authority to commence proceedings without supplying a written request in the appropriate form under rule 2(2).

(2) For the purposes of paragraph (1), information which would be contained in a document relating to one case may be combined with information of the same nature relating to another case.

(3) Where by or under this order or by virtue of any order a document which contains information is required to be produced, that requirement shall be deemed to be satisfied if a copy of the document is produced from the computer records kept for storing such information.

Functions of court officer

C48B.4 **4.**—(1) The functions of the district judge under paragraph 8(4) and (5)(d) of Schedule 6 to the 1991 Act (longer period for service of the statutory declaration and notice of effect of statutory declaration) may be exercised by the court officer.

(2) Where pursuant to paragraph 8(4) of Schedule 6 to the 1991 Act a longer period is allowed for service of the statutory declaration, the court officer shall notify the authority and the respondent accordingly.

Enforcement of orders

C48B.5 **5.**—(1) Subject to the Order and to this rule, the following provisions of Orders 25 to 27, 30 and 31 of these Rules shall apply for the enforcement of specified debts—

Order 25, rules 1, 2 (except paragraph (3)(b), (c) and (d)), 3, 5 (except paragraph (1)(a) and (b)) and 9;
Order 26, rule 5;
Order 27, rules 1 to 7, 7A, 9 to 16 and 18 to 22;
Order 30, rules 1 to 3, 5 and 7 to 15;

Order 31, rules 1 to 4.

(2) CPR rule 30.2(1)(b)(ii) (court may order transfer of proceedings to enforce judgment or order to another county court if proceedings could be more conveniently or fairly taken there) applies to proceedings under this order.

(3) An authority desiring to issue a warrant of execution shall file a request in that behalf in the appropriate form or in another manner approved by the court officer—

(a) certifying the amount remaining due under the order;
(b) specifying the date of service of the order on the respondent; and
(c) certifying that the relevant period has elapsed.

(4) The court shall seal the request and return it to the authority which shall, within 7 days of the sealing of the request, prepare the warrant in the appropriate form.

(5) No payment under a warrant shall be made to the court.

(6) A warrant shall, for the purpose of execution, be valid for 12 months beginning with the date of its issue and nothing in this rule or in Order 26 shall authorise an authority to renew a warrant.

(7) Where an order is deemed to have been revoked under paragraph 8(5) of Schedule 6 to the 1991 Act—

(a) the court shall serve a copy of the statutory declaration on the authority;
(b) any execution issued on the order shall cease to have effect; and
(c) on receipt of the court officer's notice under paragraph 8(5)(d) of Schedule 6, the authority shall forthwith inform any bailiff instructed to levy execution of the withdrawal of the warrant.

(8) In addition to the requirements of that rule, any application by an authority under Order 25, rule 2, shall—

(a) where the authority has not attempted to enforce by execution, give the reasons why no such attempt was made;
(b) certify that there has been no relevant return to the warrant of execution;
(c) specify the date of service of the order on the respondent; and
(d) certify that the relevant period has elapsed.

(9) An application under Order 30, rule 2 and (unless provided pursuant to an application under Order 25, rule 2) any application by an authority under Order 25, rule 3, Order 27, rule 4(1) or Order 31, rule 1(2) shall, in addition to the requirements of those rules—

(a) where the authority has not attempted to enforce by execution, give the reasons why no such attempt was made;
(b) certify that there has been no relevant return to the warrant of execution;
(c) specify the date of service of the order on the respondent; and
(d) certify that the relevant period has elapsed.

(10) In paragraphs (8) and (9) "no relevant return to the warrant" means that—

(a) the bailiff has been unable to seize goods because he has been denied access to the premises occupied by the respondent or because the goods have been removed from those premises;
(b) any goods seized under the warrant of execution are insufficient to satisfy the specified debt and the cost of execution; or
(c) the goods are insufficient to cover the cost of their removal and sale.

(11) If the court officer allows, an authority may combine information relating to one charge certificate with information concerning the same respondent in another charge certificate in any request made, or any application brought, under one of the provisions mentioned in paragraph (8) or (9) above.

CCR ORDER 48D

ENFORCEMENT OF FIXED PENALTIES UNDER THE ROAD TRAFFIC (VEHICLE EMISSIONS) (FIXED PENALTY) REGULATIONS 1997

Application and Interpretation

C48D.1 **1.**—(1) This Order applies for the recovery of fixed penalties as defined in regulation s.2(1)(b) and 9 of the 1997 Regulations.

(2) In this Order, unless the context otherwise requires—

"authority" means a participating authority as defined in regulation 2(1)(f) of the 1997 Regulations;

"order" means an order made under regulation 10(1) of the 1997 Regulations;

"the Order" means the Enforcement of Road Traffic Debts Order 1993;

"respondent" means the person on whom the fixed penalty notice was served;

"specified debts" means the Part II debts specified in article 2(1)(a) of the Order;

"the 1997 Regulations" means the Road Traffic (Vehicle Emissions) (Fixed Penalty) Regulations 1997.

(3) Unless the context otherwise requires, expressions which are used in the 1997 Regulations have the same meaning in this Order as they have in those Regulations.

The Parking Enforcement Centre

C48D.2 **2.** The parking enforcement centre established in rule 1A of Order 48B shall have such functions relating to proceedings under this Order and other related matters as the Lord Chancellor may direct.

Requests for Orders and Warrants of Execution

C48D.3 **3.**—(1) An authority which wishes to take proceedings under this Order shall give notice to the court officer and, where the court officer so allows, a combined request for an order and a warrant of execution may be made, and such an order may be enforced and a warrant executed in accordance with the following provisions of this Order.

(2) An authority shall file a combined request for an order and a warrant of execution in the appropriate form or in another manner approved by the court officer scheduling the fixed penalties in respect of which an order and warrant of execution are sought.

(3) The authority shall in the request or in another manner approved by the court officer—

(a) certify—

(i) that 56 days have elapsed since the issue of the fixed penalty notice,

(ii) the amount due under the fixed penalty notice and the date on which it was issued, and

(iii) that the amount due remains unpaid;

(b) give the number of the fixed penalty notice;

(c) specify (whether by reference to the appropriate code or otherwise) the grounds stated in the fixed penalty notice and in regulation 2(1)(d) of the 1997 Regulations on which the authorised person who issued the fixed penalty notice believed that a fixed penalty was payable with respect to that vehicle;

(d) state—

(i) the name and address of the respondent and where known, his title;

(ii) the registration number of the vehicle concerned;

(iii) (whether by reference to the appropriate fixed penalty notice number or otherwise) the authority's address for service;
(iv) the court fee.

(4) If satisfied that the combined request is in order, the court officer shall order that the fixed penalty (together with the court fee) may be recovered as if it were payable under a county court order by sealing the request and returning it to the authority.

(5) When the court officer so orders and on receipt of the sealed request, the authority shall, within 7 days of the sealing of the request, prepare the warrant in the appropriate form.

Documents

4.—(1) Rule 3 of Order 48B shall apply to this Order with the modification referred to in paragraph (2). **C48D.4**

(2) The reference to rule 2(2) in rule 3(1) of Order 48B shall be a reference to rule 3(2) of this Order.

Enforcement of Orders

5.—(1) Rule 5 of Order 48B shall apply to this Order with the modifications referred to in paragraphs (2), (3) and (4). **C48D.5**

(2) Paragraphs (3), (4) and (7) of rule 5 shall not apply.

(3) Sub-paragraphs (c) and (d) of rule 5(9) shall not apply.

(4) In paragraph (11) of rule 5, the references to the words "charge certificate" shall be references to the words "fixed penalty notice".

(5) Where a fixed penalty notice is withdrawn under regulation 12 of the 1997 Regulations—

(a) any order made or warrant issued in respect of that fixed penalty notice is deemed to be revoked;
(b) any execution issued on the order shall cease to have effect, and
(c) the authority shall forthwith inform any bailiff instructed to levy execution of the withdrawal of the warrant.

CCR ORDER 49

MISCELLANEOUS STATUTES

Contents **C49.0.1**

Editorial Introduction

C49.0.2 CCR, O.49 is a "rag-bag" order which has no direct equivalent in the RSC. Many statutes, on coming into force, create new rights and remedies and it is necessary to have machinery to enforce them. The modern trend is to confer jurisdiction on the county court. The RSC prefer having a separate Order for each new Act of Parliament (see RSC, Orders 95 to 115) whereas the CCR have O.49 dealing with "miscellaneous statutes" and separate rules therein for each statute. These statutes are arranged alphabetically within O.49. Some of these are very important and are part of the daily fare of the county courts (*e.g.* Consumer Credit Act 1974; Housing Act 1988) whilst, at the other end of the scale, some are obsolete in practice. The statutes are so diverse that no meaningful generalisations can be made (see the commentary on each rule, especially r.4 (Consumer Credit Act 1974) and r.6 (Housing Act 1988: assured tenancies), r.6A (Housing Act 1988: assured shorthold tenancies), and r.6B (Housing Act 1996: injunctions and powers of arrest).)

Related Sources

C49.0.3
- See the statutes listed in the contents list above.
- Consumer Credit Act 1974 (see SCP 1999, Vol. 2, Section 9A)
- Housing Act 1988 (see SCP 1999, Vol. 2, Section 8O)
- High Court and County Courts Jurisdiction Order 1991 (see SCP 1999, Vol. 2, Section 20B)

Forms

C49.0.4
- Relevant forms are listed in the commentary on each rule.

Access to Neighbouring Land Act 1992

C49.1 **1.**—(1) In this rule, "the 1992 Act" means the Access to Neighbouring Land Act 1992, a section referred to by number means the section so numbered in the 1992 Act and expressions which are defined in the 1992 Act have the same meaning in this rule as they have in that Act.

(2) An application for an access order under section 1 of the 1992 Act shall be made by the issue of a claim form which shall be filed in the court for the district in which the dominant land is situated.

(3) The application shall—

(a) identify the dominant land and the servient land and state whether the dominant land is or includes residential land;

(b) specify the works alleged to be necessary for the preservation of the whole or a part of the dominant land;

(c) state why entry upon the servient land is required and specify the area to which access is required by reference, if possible, to a plan annexed to the application;

(d) give the name of the person who will be carrying out the works if it is known at the time of the application;

(e) state the proposed date on which, or the dates between which, the works are to be started and their approximate duration, and

(f) state what (if any) provision has been made by way of insurance in the event of possible injury to persons or damage to property arising out of the proposed works.

(4) The respondents shall be the owner and the occupier of the servient land and any respondent who wishes to be heard on the application shall file an answer within 14 days after the date of service of the application on him.

(5) Order 24, rule 3 shall apply with the necessary modifications to service of the claim form under this rule.

(6) The court may direct that a copy of the claim form shall be served on any person who may be affected by the proposed entry and any such person may, within 14 days after service of the claim form on him, apply to be made a respondent to the application.

(7) The application may be heard and determined by the district judge.

C49.1.1 **History of rule**—Amended by Civil Procedure (Amendment) Rules 1999 (S.I. 1999 No. 1008).

C49.1.2 **Effect of rule**—The Access to Neighbouring Land Act 1992 created a right of access to adjoining land (the "servient land") for the purpose of carrying out works to the "dominant land". The High Court and County Courts Jurisdiction Order 1991 requires applications to be in the county court. An application is brought by claim form see O.49, r.1(2) and (3). Service is governed by CCR, O.24, r.3 (see O.49, r.1(5)) rather than Pt 6, CPR.

Administration of Justice Act 1970

1A. Any action by a mortgagee for possession of a dwelling-house, being a claim to which section 36 of the Administration of Justice Act 1970 applies, shall be dealt with by the court sitting in private unless the court otherwise directs. **C49.1A**

Effect of rule—This rule is no longer necessary. Actions by mortgages will be listed for hearing in private pursuant to r.39.2(3)(c) of the CPR and the Practice Direction supplementing Pt 39. **C49.1A.1**

Chancel Repairs Act 1932

2.—(1) A notice to repair under section 2 of the Chancel Repairs Act 1932 shall— **C49.2**

(a) identify the responsible authority by whom it is given and the chancel alleged to be in need of repair;

(b) state the repairs alleged to be necessary and the grounds on which the person to whom the notice is addressed is alleged to be liable to repair the chancel, and

(c) call upon that person to put the chancel in proper repair,

and shall be served in accordance with paragraph 1A.

(1A) The notice may be served—

(a) where no solicitor is acting for the person to be served, by delivering it to him personally, or by delivering it at, or sending it by first-class post to his address for service or, if he has no address for service by—

(i) by delivering it at his residence or by sending it by first class post to his last known residence, or

(ii) in the case of a proprietor of a business, delivering it at his place of business or sending it by first class post to his last known place of business.

(b) Where a solicitor is acting for the person to be served—

(i) by delivering it at, or sending it by first-class post to the solicitor's address for service; or

(ii) where the solicitor's address for service includes a numbered box at a document exchange, by leaving it at that document exchange or at a document exchange which transmits documents daily to that document exchange.

(c) For the purpose of this rule first class post means prepaid post or post in respect of which pre payment is not required.

(d) Any document which is left at a document exchange shall be deemed served on the second day after the day on which it was left, unless the contrary is shown.

(e) In determining for the purposes of this rule—

(i) whether a document exchange transmits documents daily to another document exchange, and

(ii) the second day after the day on which a document was left at a document exchange,

any day on which the court office is closed shall be excluded.

(2) Proceedings to recover the sum required to put a chancel in proper repair shall be started by a claim form.

(3) An application for the permission of the court under the proviso to subsection (2) of the said section 2 may be made in accordance with CPR Part 23.

(4) If the court is satisfied that the defendant has a defence to the claim on the merits, the court may, on an application made by the defendant in

accordance with CPR Part 23 order the claimant to give security for the defendant's costs.

(5) Where judgment is given for the payment of a sum of money in respect of repairs not yet executed, the court may order that the money be paid into court and dealt with in such manner as the court may direct for the purpose of ensuring that the money is spent in executing the repairs, but nothing in this paragraph shall prejudice a solicitor's lien for costs.

Related Sources

C49.2.1
- Chancel Repairs Act 1932
- Pt 23 of the CPR—General Rules about Applications for Court Orders
- RSC, O.23—Security for Costs

Forms

C49.2.2
- N425—Notice to repair
- N426—Notice of proceedings

Consumer Credit Act 1974

C49.4 **4.**—(1) In this rule "the Act" means the Consumer Credit Act 1974, a section referred to by number means the section so numbered in the Act and expressions which are defined in the Act have the same meaning in this rule as they have in the Act.

(2) This rule only applies to claims relating to land.

(Claims under the Act relating to money only shall be started by a claim form issued in accordance with CPR Part 7, and claims relating to recovery of goods shall be made in accordance with the procedure set out in the CPR Consumer Credit Act Practice direction.)

(3) Where in any claim relating to a regulated agreement the debtor or any surety has not been served with the claim form, the court may, on the claimant's application made in accordance with CPR Part 23 without notice, at or before the hearing of the claim, dispense with the requirement in section 141(5) that the debtor or surety, as the case may be, shall be made a party to the proceedings.

(4) Where a claim relating to a regulated agreement is brought by a person to whom a former creditor's rights and duties under the agreement have been passed by assignment or by operation of law, the requirement in section 141(5) that all parties to the agreement shall be made parties to the claim shall not apply to the former creditor unless the court so directs.

(5) An application under section 129(1)(b) may be made by a claim form and the claim form—

- (a) shall be filed in the court for the district in which the applicant resides or carries on business; and
- (b) shall state—
  - (i) the date of the agreement and the parties to it with the number of the agreement or sufficient particulars to enable the respondent to identify the agreement and details of any sureties;
  - (ii) if the respondent was not one of the original parties to the agreement, the name of the original party to the agreement;
  - (iii) the names and addresses of the persons intended to be served with the application;
  - (iv) the place where the agreement was signed by the applicant;
  - (v) details of the notice served by the respondent giving rise to the application;
  - (vi) the total unpaid balance admitted to be due under the agreement and the amount of any arrears (if known) together with the amount and frequency of the payments specified by the agreement;

(vii) the applicant's proposals as to payment of any arrears and of future instalments together with details of his means;

(viii) where the application relates to a breach of the agreement other than the non-payment of money, the applicant's proposals for remedying it.

(6) Any application under section 131 may be heard and determined by the judge or by the district judge.

(9) An application for an enforcement order may be made—

(a) by a claim form asking for permission to enforce the agreement in respect of which the order is sought, or

(b) if, apart from the need to obtain an enforcement order, the creditor is entitled to payment of the money or possession of land to which the agreement relates, by a claim to recover the money or land.

(10) A claim form under paragraph (9)(a) and the particulars of claim in a claim brought pursuant to paragraph (9)(b) shall state the circumstances rendering an enforcement order necessary.

(11) Paragraph (9) shall apply to an order under section 86(2), 92(2) or 126 as it applies to an enforcement order, so however that in the case of an order under section 86(2) the personal representatives of the deceased debtor or hirer shall be made parties to the proceedings in which the order is sought, or, if no grant of representation has been made to his estate, the applicant shall, forthwith after commencing the proceedings, apply to the court for directions as to what persons, if any, shall be made parties to the proceedings as being affected or likely to be affected by the enforcement of the agreement.

(14) An application to a county court under section 139(1)(a) for a credit agreement to be reopened shall be made by a claim form.

(15) Where in any such proceedings in a county court as are mentioned in section 139(1)(b) or (c), the debtor or a surety desires to have a credit agreement reopened, he shall, within 14 days after the service of the claim form on him, give notice to that effect to the court and to every other party to the proceedings and thereafter the debtor or surety, as the case may be, shall be treated as having delivered a defence or answer.

Editorial Note—The Consumer Credit Act 1974 is a comprehensive statute dealing with all forms of personal credit. The Act is in XII Pts with 193 sections and five Schedules. There is also a myriad of subordinate regulations. The Act is arranged as follows: **C49.4.1**

Pt I (ss.1 to 7)—Director General of Fair Trading
Pt II (ss.8 to 20)—Credit Agreements, Hire Agreements and Linked Transactions
Pt III (ss.21 to 42)—Licensing of Credit and Hire Businesses
Pt IV (ss.43 to 54)—Seeking Business
Pt V (ss.55 to 74)—Entry into Credit or Hire Agreements
Pt VI (ss.75 to 86)—Matters arising during currency of credit or hire agreements
Pt VII (ss.87 to 104)—Default and Termination
Pt VIII (ss.105 to 126)—Security
Pt IX (ss.127 to 144)—Judicial control
Pt X (ss.145 to 160)—Ancillary Credit Business
Pt XI (ss.161 to 173)—Enforcement of Act
Pt XII (ss.174 to 193)—Supplemental

For the purposes of the Act s.189(1) defines "court" as "in relation to England and Wales, the county court . . .". Thus, the county court has exclusive jurisdiction under the Act.

It is suggested that the following preliminary considerations arise:

(1) Is the credit provided within the Act? (see s.8(2)—the Act applies to a personal credit agreement for credit not exceeding £25,000. This limit can be changed by Order under s.181);

(2) Is the agreement exempt? (see s.16—for example, most first mortgages of land are exempt);

(3) Have all necessary formalities been complied with?—including, where appropriate, default and termination notices.

The powers of the court can be summarised as follows:

(1) to hear and determine an action by the creditor to enforce a regulated agreement and/or any security;

(2) to hear and determine applications to enforce agreements and securities which are enforceable only on a court order (see s.127);
(3) to make a time order allowing the debtor to pay by instalments over a longer period (see s.129);
(4) to make a protection order preserving any property of the creditor from damage or depreciation pending determination of proceedings (see s.131);
(5) to order repayment to a hirer under a consumer hire agreement of the whole or part of the sum paid by him in respect of goods repossessed by the owner or where an order has been made for their delivery to the owner (s.132);
(6) in proceedings by the creditor to recover goods (or an application for a time order or enforcement order) to order the return of goods or to make a "transfer order" (sometimes called a "split order") transferring title to certain goods to the debtor and directing return of remaining goods (s.133);
(7) to make conditional or suspend the operation of any term of an order (s.127);
(8) to include in any order such provision of the court thinks just for amending any agreement or security in consequence of a term of the order (s.136). This includes power to alter the interest rate (see *Southern and District Finance plc v. Barnes* [1996] 1 E.C.R. 679, CA).
(9) To re-open a credit agreement where the bargain is extortionate (s.137);
(10) to make declaratory orders (s.142).

Related Sources

C49.4.2
- Consumer Credit Act 1974 (see SCP 1999, Vol. 2, Section 9A)
- High Court and County Courts Jurisdiction Order 1991, Art. 8(1A) (see SCP 1999, Vol. 2, Section 20B)
- Pt 7 of the CPR—How to start proceedings—the Claim Form
- Rule 7.9 of the CPR—Fixed date and other claims
- Practice Direction—Consumer Credit Act Claim—7BPD–001
- CCR, O.6, r.6—Particulars of claim—hire purchase

Forms

C49.4.3
- N1(FD)—Notes for defendant (Consumer Credit Act cases)
- N32(1) HPCCA—Judgment for delivery of goods under s.133(1)(i)
- N32(2) HPCCA—Judgment for delivery of goods under s.133(1)(i) suspended on time order
- N32(3) HPCCA—Judgment for delivery of goods under s.133(1)(i)(ii)
- N32(4) CCA—Variation Order (return of goods). Order on application under s.130(6) or s.135(4)
- N32(5) CCA—Order for balance of purchase price (return of goods). Order on application under s.133(6)
- N33—Judgment for a delivery of goods let under a regulated consumer hire agreement
- N46—Warrant of delivery and execution for damages and costs
- N48—Warrant of delivery where, if goods are not returned, levy is to be made for their value
- N440—Notice of application for time order before proceedings have been instituted by creditor

Applications under section 114, 204 and 231 of the Copyright, Designs and Patents Act 1988

C49.4A **4A.** The CPR Patents Court practice direction shall apply with the necessary modifications to proceedings brought under sections 114(1), 204(1) and 231(1) of the Copyright, Designs and Patents Act 1988.

C49.4A.1 **Editorial note**—See CPR Patents Court Practice Direction (para. 49EPD–001)

Fair Trading Act 1973

C49.5 **5.**—(1) In this rule a section referred to by number means the section so numbered in the Fair Trading Act 1973 and "the Director" means the Director General of Fair Trading.

(2) Proceedings in a county court under section 35, 38 or 40 shall be started by a claim form.

(3) The respondent shall file an answer.

(4) Where in any proceedings under section 35 or 38 the Director intends to apply for a direction under section 40(2) that any order made against a body corporate (in this rule referred to as the "respondent body") which is a member of a group of interconnected bodies corporate shall be binding on all members of the group, he shall file notice of his intention together with as

many copies of the claim form and of the notice as are required for the purposes of paragraph (5).

(5) A copy of any notice under paragraph (4) shall be served on the respondent body and a copy of the notice together with a copy of the claim form and a notice of the return day shall be served on each of the bodies corporate specified in the notice under paragraph (4).

(6) The respondent body may at any time serve on the Director a notice containing particulars of any interconnected body corporate not mentioned in a notice under paragraph (4).

(7) With a view to deciding whether or in respect of which bodies notice should be given under paragraph (4) the Director may serve on the respondent body a notice requiring that body to give to him within 14 days after service of the notice particulars of any interconnected bodies corporate belonging to the same group as the respondent body and a copy of any such notice shall be filed.

(8) An application under section 40(3) shall be made on notice to the respondent body and every interconnected body belonging to the same group.

Effect of rule—Proceedings under the Fair Trading Act 1973 are brought by the Director-General of Fair Trading. Usually proceedings are taken in the Restrictive Practices Court but in certain circumstances the Director can proceed in the county court. **C49.5.1**

Housing Act 1988: assured tenancies

6.—(1) In this rule **C49.6**

"the 1988 Act" means the Housing Act 1988;

"dwelling-house" has the same meaning as in Part I of the 1988 Act;

a Ground referred to by number means the Ground so numbered in Schedule 2 to the 1988 Act;

"the requisite notice" means such a notice as is mentioned in any of those Grounds and

"the relevant date" means the beginning of the tenancy.

(2) This rule applies to proceedings brought by a landlord to recover possession of a dwelling-house which has been let on an assured tenancy in a case where all the conditions mentioned in paragraph (3) below are satisfied.

(3) The conditions referred to in paragraph (2) are these—

- (a) The tenancy and any agreement for the tenancy were entered into on or after 15th January 1989.
- (b) The proceedings are brought
  - (i) on Ground 1 (landlord occupation),
  - (ii) on Ground 3 (former holiday occupation),
  - (iii) on Ground 4 (former student letting) or
  - (iv) on Ground 5 (occupation by a minister of religion).
- (c) The only purpose of the proceedings is to recover possession of the dwelling-house and no other claim is made in the proceedings (such as for arrears of rent).
- (d) The tenancy is an assured tenancy within the meaning of the 1988 Act (and consequently is not a protected, statutory or housing association tenancy under the Rent Act 1977), and
  - (i) is the subject of a written agreement, or
  - (ii) is on the same terms (though not necessarily as to rent) as a tenancy which was the subject of a written agreement and arises by virtue of section 5 of the 1988 Act, or
  - (iii) relates to the same or substantially the same premises which were let to the same tenant and is on the same terms (though not necessarily as to rent or duration) as a tenancy which was the subject of a written agreement.

Where the tenancy in relation to which the proceedings are brought arises by virtue of section 5 of the 1988 Act but follows a tenancy which was the subject of an oral agreement, the condition mentioned in sub-paragraph (d)(ii) or (iii) above is not satisfied.

(e) The proceedings are brought against the tenant to whom the requisite notice was given.

(f) The tenant was given the requisite notice, not later than the relevant date.

(g) The tenant was given notice in accordance with section 8 of the 1988 Act that proceedings for possession would be brought.

(4) Where the conditions mentioned in paragraph (3) of this rule are satisfied, the landlord may bring possession proceedings under this rule instead of making a claim in accordance with Order 6, rule 3 (claim for recovery of land by claim form).

(5) The application must be made in the prescribed form, and a copy of the application, with a copy for each defendant, must be filed in the court for the district in which the dwelling-house is situated.

(6) The application shall include the following information and statements—

(a) a statement identifying the dwelling-house which is the subject matter of the proceedings;

(b) a statement identifying the nature of the tenancy, namely—

(i) whether it is the subject of a written agreement; or

(ii) whether the tenancy arises by virtue of section 5 of the 1988 Act, or

(iii) where it is the subject of an oral agreement whether the tenancy is periodic or for a fixed term and, if for a fixed term, the length of the term and the date of termination;

(c) a statement that the dwelling-house (or another dwelling-house) was not let to the tenant by the landlord (or any of his predecessors) before 15th January 1989;

(d) the date on which and the method by which the requisite notice was given to the tenant;

(e) a statement identifying the Ground on which possession is claimed giving sufficient particulars to substantiate the claimant's claim to be entitled to possession on that Ground;

(f) a statement that a notice was served on the tenant in accordance with section 8 of the 1988 Act,

(i) specifying the date on which and the method by which the notice was served; and

(ii) confirming that the period of notice required by section 8 of the 1988 Act has been given; and

(g) the amount of rent which is currently payable.

(7) Copies of the following documents shall be attached to the application—

(i) the first written tenancy agreement and the current (or most recent) written tenancy agreement;

(ii) the requisite notice (referred to in paragraph (6)(d) above); and

(iii) the notice served in accordance with section 8 of the 1988 Act, together with any other documents necessary to prove the claim.

(8) The statements made in the application and any documents attached to the application shall be verified by the claimant on oath.

(9) Service of the application and of the attachments shall be effected by an officer of the court sending them by first-class post to the defendant at the address stated in the application and paragraphs (8) and (9) of Order 3, rule 6 (Commencement of Proceedings) and Order 7, rule 15 (service of claim form for recovery of land) shall apply as they apply where service is effected under those rules.

(10) A defendant who wishes to oppose the claimant's application must, within 14 days after the service of the application on him, complete and deliver at the court office the form of reply which was attached to the application.

(11) On receipt of the defendant's reply the court shall—

(a) send a copy of it to the claimant;

(b) refer the reply and the claimant's application to the judge, and where a reply is received after the period mentioned in paragraph (10) but before a request is filed in accordance with paragraph (12) the reply shall be referred without delay to the judge.

(12) Where the period mentioned in paragraph (10) has expired without the defendant filing a reply, the claimant may file a written request for an order for possession and the court shall without delay refer the claimant's application to the judge.

(13) After considering the application and the defendant's reply (if any), the judge shall either—

(a) make an order for possession under paragraph (15) or

(b) fix a day for a hearing under paragraph (14) and give directions regarding the steps to be taken before and at the hearing.

(14) The court shall fix a day for the hearing of the application where the judge is not satisfied as to any of the following—

(a) that the requisite notice was given before the relevant date;

(b) that a notice was served in accordance with section 8 of the 1988 Act and that the time limits specified in the 1988 Act have been complied with;

(c) that service of the application was duly effected; or

(d) that the claimant has established that he is entitled to recover possession under the Ground relied on against the defendant.

(15) Except where paragraph (14) applies, the judge shall without delay make an order for possession without requiring the attendance of the parties.

(16) Where a hearing is fixed under paragraph (14)—

(a) the court shall give to all parties not less than 14 days' notice of the day fixed;

(b) the judge may give such directions regarding the steps to be taken before and at the hearing as may appear to him to be necessary or desirable.

(17) The court may, on application made on notice in accordance with CPR Part 23 within 14 days of service of the order or of its own initiative, set aside, vary or confirm any order made under paragraph (15).

(18) A district judge shall have power to hear and determine an application to which this rule applies and references in this rule to the judge shall include references to the district judge.

History of rule—Amended by Civil Procedure (Amendment) Rules 1999 (S.I. 1999 No. 1008) **C49.6.1**

Editorial Note—The Housing Act 1988 came into force on January 15, 1989. As from that date all housing tenancies are assured tenancies, assured shorthold tenancies or exempted tenancies. The Act had no effect on existing tenancies (such as protected or statutory tenancies under the Rent Acts) which remain governed by pre-January 15, 1989 law but obviously these diminish in importance with the passage of time. **C49.6.2**

Grounds for possession are in Sched. 2. It is important to distinguish mandatory grounds for possession from discretionary grounds.

Further, where the claim is for possession only (and does not, for example, include a claim for arrears of rent) there is an accelerated possession procedure for some of the mandatory ground cases (see O.49, r.6(3)) and most assured shorthold cases (see O.49, r.6A(4)).

The striking feature of the accelerated possession procedure is that no hearing is necessary and usually none is held. The district judge can make an order for possession after considering the papers (O.49, r.6(13) and O.49, r.6A(15)). Proceedings are in Form N5A which is entitled "Application for accelerated possession (assured tenancies) Housing Act 1988, s.8" and which includes an affidavit to support the application.

For non-accelerated possession cases proceedings are commenced in Form N5. The Practice Direction which supplements Part 4—Forms dated April 19, 1999 still describes Form N5 as "Summons for possession of property" rather than "Claim Form".

Proceedings for recovery of land are now governed by Pt 8 of the CPR—Alternative Procedure for Claims and its Supplementing Practice Direction.

Claims for possession are listed for hearing in private (Rule 39.2(3)(c) and the Practice Direction which supplements Part 39: 39PD–001).

Relevant sections of the Housing Act 1988 and related statutes are annotated in SCP 1999, Vol. 2 at Section 8—Housing.

Related Sources

C49.6.3
- Pt 8—Alternative Procedure for Claims
- Practice Direction supplementing Part 8 (see 8PD–001)
- CCR, O.4, r.3—Venue—proceedings relating to land
- CCR, O.6, r.3—Particulars of claim—recovery of land
- CCR, O.7, r.15—Service—recovery of land
- CCR, O.26—Warrants of execution, delivery and possession
- CCR, O.49, r.6A—Housing Act 1988—assured shorthold tenancies
- Housing Acts—see SCP 1999, Vol. 2, Section 8
- County Courts Act 1984, s.21—SCP 1999, Vol. 2, section 20A

Forms

C49.6.4
- N5—Summons (sic) for possession of property (see "Editorial Note", above)
- N5A—Application for accelerated possession (assured tenancies) Housing Act 1988, s.8
- N5B—Application for accelerated possession (assured tenancies) Housing Act 1988, s.21
- N11—Form of Reply—Possession Summons
- N11A—Form of Reply to application for accelerated possession (assured tenancies), Housing Act 1988, s.8
- N11B—Form of Reply to application for accelerated possession (assured tenancies) Housing Act 1988, s.21
- N11R—Form of Reply (rented property)
- N26—Order for possession (rented property)
- N26A—Order that claimant have possession (assured tenancies)
- N49—Warrant for Possession of Land
- N119—Particulars of claim for possession (rented property)
- N206A—Notice of issue of application (assured tenancies)
- N229—Notice of Admission in Possession Action

Housing Act 1988: assured shorthold tenancies

C49.6A **6A.**—(1) In this rule, "the 1988 Act" means the Housing Act 1988 and "dwelling-house" has the same meaning as in Part I of the 1988 Act.

(2) This rule applies to proceedings brought by a landlord under section 21 of the 1988 Act to recover possession of a dwelling-house let on an assured shorthold tenancy on the expiry or termination of that tenancy in a case where all the conditions mentioned in paragraph (3) below (or, as the case may be, paragraph (9)) are satisfied.

(3) The conditions referred to in paragraph (2) are these—

(a) The tenancy and any agreement for the tenancy were entered into on or after 15th January 1989.

(b) The only purpose of the proceedings is to recover possession of the dwelling-house and no other claim is made in the proceedings (such as for arrears of rent).

(c) The tenancy—

(i) was an assured shorthold tenancy and not a protected, statutory or housing association tenancy under the Rent Act 1977;

(ii) did not immediately follow an assured tenancy which was not an assured shorthold tenancy;

(iii) fulfilled the conditions provided by section 19A or section 20(1)(a) to (c) of the 1988 Act, and

(iv) was the subject of a written agreement.

(d) Where the tenancy and any agreement for the tenancy were entered into before 28th February 1997, a notice in writing was served on the tenant in accordance with section 20(2) of the 1988 Act and the proceedings are brought against the tenant on whom that notice was served.

(e) A notice in accordance with section 21(1)(b) of the 1988 Act was given to the tenant in writing.

(4) Where the conditions mentioned in paragraph (3) or paragraph (9) of this rule are satisfied, the landlord may bring possession proceedings under this rule instead of making a claim in accordance with Order 6, rule 3 (action for recovery of land by claim form).

(5) The application must be made in the prescribed form and a copy of the application, with a copy for each defendant, shall be filed in the court for the district in which the dwelling-house is situated.

(6) The application shall include the following information and statements—

(a) A statement identifying the dwelling-house which is the subject matter of the proceedings.

(b) A statement that the dwelling-house (or another dwelling-house) was not let to the tenant by the landlord (or any of his predecessors) before 15th January 1989.

(c) A statement that possession is claimed on the expiry of an assured shorthold tenancy under section 21 of the 1988 Act giving sufficient particulars to substantiate the claimant's claim to be entitled to possession.

(d) Where the tenancy and any agreement for the tenancy were entered into before 28th February 1997, a statement that a written notice was served on the tenant in accordance with section 20(2) of the 1988 Act.

(e) A statement that a notice in writing was given to the tenant in accordance with section 21(1) of the 1988 Act specifying the date on which, and the method by which, the notice was given.

(f) In a case where the original fixed term tenancy has expired, a statement that no other assured tenancy is in existence other than an assured shorthold periodic tenancy (whether statutory or not).

(g) A statement confirming that there is no power under the tenancy agreement for the landlord to determine the tenancy (within the meaning given for the purposes of Part I of the 1988 Act by section 45(4) of the 1988 Act) at a time earlier than six months from the beginning of the tenancy.

(h) A statement that no notice under section 20(5) of the 1988 Act has been served.

(7) Copies of the following documents shall be attached to the application—

(i) the first written tenancy agreement and the current (or most recent) written tenancy agreement;

(ii) where the tenancy and any agreement for the tenancy were entered into before 28th February 1997 the written notice served in accordance with section 20(2) of the 1988 Act; and

(iii) the notice in writing given in accordance with section 21 of the 1988 Act,

together with any other documents necessary to prove the claim.

(8) The statements made in the application and any documents attached to the application shall be verified by the claimant on oath.

(9) Where on the coming to an end of an assured shorthold tenancy (including a tenancy which was an assured shorthold but ceased to be assured before it came to an end) a new assured shorthold tenancy of the same or substantially the same premises (in this paragraph referred to as "the premises") comes into being under which the landlord and the tenant are the

same as at the coming to an end of the earlier tenancy, then the provisions of this rule apply to that tenancy but with the following conditions instead of those in paragraph (3)—

(a) The tenancy and any agreement for the tenancy were entered into on or after 15th January 1989.

(b) The only purpose of the proceedings is to recover possession of the dwelling-house and no other claim is made in the proceedings (such as for arrears of rent).

(c) The tenancy in relation to which the proceedings are brought—

(i) is an assured shorthold tenancy within the meaning of section 20 of the 1988 Act and consequently is not a protected, statutory or housing association tenancy under the Rent Act 1977;

(ii) did not immediately follow an assured tenancy which was not an assured shorthold tenancy; and

(aa) is the subject of a written agreement; or

(ab) is on the same terms (though not necessarily as to rent) as a tenancy which was the subject of a written agreement and arises by virtue of section 5 of the 1988 Act; or

(ac) relates to the same or substantially the same premises which were let to the same tenant and is on the same terms (though not necessarily as to rent or duration) as a tenancy which was the subject of a written agreement.

Where the tenancy in relation to which the proceedings are brought arises by virtue of section 5 of the 1988 Act but follows a tenancy which was the subject of an oral agreement, the conditions mentioned in sub-paragraph (c)(ii)(ab) or (ac) above is not satisfied.

(d) Where the agreement and any agreement for the tenancy were entered into before 28th February 1997, a written notice was served in accordance with section 20(2) of the 1988 Act on the tenant in relation to the first assured shorthold tenancy of the premises and the proceedings are brought against the tenant on whom that notice was served.

(e) A notice in writing was given to the tenant in accordance with section 21(4) of the 1988 Act.

(10) In a case to which paragraph (9) applies, the application shall include the following information and statements.

(a) A statement identifying the dwelling-house which is the subject matter of the proceedings.

(b) A statement identifying the nature of the tenancy, namely—

(i) whether it is the subject of a written agreement;

(ii) whether the tenancy arises by virtue of section 5 of the 1988 Act, or

(iii) where it is the subject of an oral agreement, that the tenancy is periodic, or for a fixed term, and if for a fixed term, the length of the term and the date of termination.

(c) A statement that the dwelling-house (or another dwelling-house) was not let to the tenant by the landlord (or any of his predecessors) before 15th January 1989.

(d) A statement that possession is claimed under section 21 of the 1988 Act giving sufficient particulars to substantiate the claimant's claim to be entitled to possession.

(e) Where the tenancy and any agreement for the tenancy were entered into before 28th February 1997, a statement that a written notice was served in accordance with section 20(2) of the 1988 Act in relation to the first assured shorthold tenancy of the premises on the tenant against whom the proceedings are brought.

(f) A statement that a notice in writing was given to the tenant in accordance with section 21(4) of the 1988 Act specifying the date on which, and the method by which, the notice was given.

(g) In a case where the tenancy is a fixed term tenancy which has expired, a statement that no other assured tenancy is in existence other than an assured shorthold periodic tenancy (whether statutory or not).

(h) A statement confirming that there was no power under the tenancy agreement for the landlord to determine (within the meaning given for the purposes of Part I of the 1988 Act by section 45(4) of the 1988 Act) the first assured shorthold tenancy of the premises to the tenant against whom the proceedings are brought at a time earlier than six months from the beginning of the tenancy.

(i) A statement that no notice under section 20(5) of the 1988 Act has been served.

(j) The amount of rent which is currently payable.

(11) Service of the application and of the attachments shall be effected by an officer of the court sending them by first-class post to the defendant at the address stated in the application and paragraphs (8) and (9) of Order 3, rule 6 (Commencement of Proceedings) and Order 7, rule 15 (service of claim form for recovery of land) shall apply as they apply where service is effected under those rules.

(12) A defendant who wishes to oppose the claimant's application must, within 14 days after the service of the application on him, complete and deliver at the court office the form of reply which was attached to the application.

(13) On receipt of the defendant's reply the court shall—

(a) send a copy of it to the claimant;

(b) refer the reply and the claimant's application to the judge and where a reply is received after the period mentioned in paragraph (12) but before a request is filed in accordance with paragraph (14) the reply shall be referred without delay to the judge.

(14) Where the period mentioned in paragraph (12) has expired without the defendant filing a reply, the claimant may file a written request for an order for possession and the court shall without delay refer any such request to the judge.

(15) After considering the application and the defendant's reply (if any), the judge shall either—

(a) make an order for possession under paragraph (17); or

(b) fix a day for a hearing under paragraph (16) and give directions regarding the steps to be taken before and at the hearing.

(16) The court shall fix a day for the hearing of the application where the judge is not satisfied as to any of the following—

(a) where the tenancy and any agreement for the tenancy were entered into before 28th February 1997 that a written notice was served in accordance with section 20 of the 1988 Act,

(b) that a written notice was given in accordance with section 21 of the 1988 Act,

(c) that service of the application was duly effected, or

(d) that the claimant has established that he is entitled to recover possession under section 21 of the 1988 Act against the defendant.

(17) Except where paragraph (16) applies, the judge shall without delay make an order for possession without requiring the attendance of the parties.

(18) Where a hearing is fixed under paragraph (16)—

(a) the court shall give to all parties not less than 14 days' notice of the day so fixed;

(b) the judge may give such directions regarding the steps to be taken before and at the hearing as may appear to him to be necessary or desirable.

(19) The court may, on application made on notice in accordance with CPR Part 23 within 14 days of service of the order or of its own initiative, set aside, vary or confirm any order made under paragraph (17).

(20) A district judge shall have power to hear and determine an application to which this rule applies and references in this rule to the judge shall include references to the district judge.

C49.6A.1 **History of rule**—Amended by Civil Procedure (Amendment) Rules 1999 (S.I. 1999 No. 1008).

C49.6A.2 **Editorial Note**—An assured shorthold tenancy is a species of assured tenancy. All the grounds for possession relevant to assured tenancies apply to assured shorthold tenancies.

A key feature of the assured shorthold is that the tenant has no security of tenure beyond the fixed term of the tenancy. Before February 28, 1997 the fixed term had to be for a minimum of six months. Although there is now no minimum term by s.21(5) of the Housing Act 1988 (inserted by s.99 of the Housing Act 1996) an order for possession cannot be made so as to take effect earlier than six months after the beginning of the tenancy. The court must make an order for possession if satisfied that the fixed term has come to an end and that the landlord has given not less than two month's notice in writing that he requires possession (s.21(1)).

When the Housing Act 1988 came into force on January 15, 1989, the concept of no security of tenure was controversial and contrary to the philosophy of the Rent Acts. Accordingly, to ensure that tenants understood the new law, s.20 required a notice to be given before the tenancy was granted. This requirement is reflected in CCR, O.49, r.6A (see paras (3)(d); (6)(d); (7)(ii); (9)(d) and (10)(e)). However, the assured shorthold proved so popular that the formalities were simplified by the Housing Act 1996. As from February 28, 1997 tenancies commencing on and after that date are assumed to be assured shorthold tenancies (s.19A of the Housing Act 1988) unless Sched. 2A applies, *e.g.* Notice is given that is *not* an assured shorthold. Hence the reference to that date in several rules. See also *Editorial Note* in commentary to CCR, O.49, r.6.

Related Sources

C49.6A.3
- CCR, O.49, r.6—Assured tenancies
- See "Related Sources" in commentary to CCR, O.49, r.6
- Housing Acts 1988 and 1996—SCP 1999, Vol 2, Section 8
- Accelerated possession—see *Editorial Note* in commentary to CCR, O.49, r.6

Forms

C49.6A.4
- See "Forms" in commentary to CCR, O.49, r.6
- Form N5B—Application for accelerated possession (assured tenancies) Housing Act 1988, s.21

Housing Act 1996: injunctions and powers of arrest

C49.6B **6B.**—(1) An application for an injunction under section 152 of the Housing Act 1996 may be made by a claim in the appropriate prescribed form and shall be commenced in the court for the district in which the respondent resides or the conduct complained of occurred.

(2) Every application shall—

(a) state the terms of the injunction applied for; and

(b) be supported by a witness statement or affidavit in which the grounds on which the application is made are set out.

(3) Every application made on notice must be served, together with a copy of the witness statement or affidavit, by the applicant on the respondent personally not less than 2 days before the date on which the application will be heard.

(4) Where an application is made without giving notice, the witness statement or affidavit in support shall explain why notice was not given and the application and witness statement or affidavit shall be served (with a copy of any order made by the court), on the respondent personally without delay.

(5) Unless otherwise directed, every application made on notice shall be heard in public.

(6) Where in exercise of the powers conferred by section 152(6) or 153(1) of the Housing Act 1996, a power of arrest to any provision of an injunction ("a relevant provision")—

(a) each relevant provision shall be set out in a separate clause of the injunction and no such clause shall refer to any form of conduct which would not entitle a constable to arrest the respondent under paragraph (a), (b) or (c) of section 152(1) or under paragraph (a), (b) or (c) of section 153(5) of the Housing Act 1996; and
(b) the applicant shall deliver a copy of the relevant provisions to the police officer for the time being in charge of any police station for the area where the conduct occurred.

(7) Where an order is made varying or discharging any relevant provision of an injunction to which a power of arrest has been attached, the court shall—
(a) immediately inform the police officer for the time being in charge of the police station to which a copy of the relevant provisions was delivered under paragraph (6); and
(b) deliver a copy of the order to any police officer so informed.

(8) The judge before whom a person is brought following his arrest may adjourn the proceedings and, where such an order is made, the arrested person shall be released and—
(a) be dealt with (whether by the same or another judge) within 14 days of the day on which he was arrested; and
(b) be given not less than 2 days' notice of the adjourned hearing.

Nothing in this paragraph shall prevent the issue of a notice under Order 29, rule 1(4) if the arrested person is not dealt with within the period mentioned in sub-paragraph (a).

(9) In relation to a person who is in custody under such an order and warrant of a county court, Order 29, rule 3, shall have effect as if the order and warrant were issued at the instance of the person who made the application.

(10) Order 29, rule 1 shall apply where an application is made to commit a person—
(a) for breach of an injunction granted; or
(b) arrested under a power of arrest attached to an injunction under Chapter III of Part V of the Housing Act 1996,

as if references in that rule to the judge included references to a district judge.

(11) In paragraph (8) "arrest" means the arrest of a person pursuant to a power of arrest which, in exercise of the powers conferred by section 152(6) or 153(1) of the Housing Act 1996, has been attached to an injunction.

(12) The jurisdiction of the court under sections 152 to 157 of the Housing Act 1996 may be exercised by a district judge.

History of rule—Amended by Civil Procedure (Amendment) Rules 1999 (S.I. No. 1008). **C49.6B.1**

Editorial Note—CCR, O.49, r.6B was inserted to provide a procedure for injunctions and powers of arrest pursuant to Chapter III of the Housing Act 1996. That Act introduced the concept of the "registered social landlord". One policy objective of the Act is to "crack down" on neighbours who are anti-social *e.g.* by indulging in criminal activities such as drug dealing, by racially harassing other tenants or by engaging in prostitution. Thus, in addition to amending the Grounds for Possession under the Housing Act 1985 and creating new "introductory tenancies", s.152 gives power to grant injunctions against "anti-social behaviour". Section 152(6) enables the court to attach a "power of arrest" to an injunction. Applications can be made without notice. **C49.6B.2**

Related Sources **C49.6B.3**
- Housing Act 1996, s.152—SCP 1999, Vol. 2, para. 8Q–65
- Housing Act 1996, s.153—SCP 1999, Vol. 2, para. 8Q–71
- Housing Act 1996, s.154—SCP 1999, Vol. 2, para. 8Q–81
- Housing Act 1996, s.155—SCP 1999, Vol. 2, para. 8Q–83
- Housing Act 1996, s.156—SCP 1999, Vol. 2, para. 8Q–86
- Housing Act 1996, s.157—SCP 1999, Vol. 2, para. 8Q–89
- Housing Act 1996, s.158—SCP 1999, Vol. 2, para. 8Q–91
- CCR, O.29—Committal

Forms

C49.6B.4
- N16—General Form of Injunction
- N16A—General Form of Application for Injunction
- N110A—Anti social behaviour injunction—power of arrest Housing Act 1996, ss.152, 153

Injunctions to prevent environmental harm: Town and Country Planning Act 1990 etc.

C49.7 **7.**—(1) An injunction under—

(a) section 187B or 214A of the Town and Country Planning Act 1990;

(b) section 44A of the Planning (Listed Buildings and Conservation Areas) Act 1990; or

(c) section 26AA of the Planning (Hazardous Substances) Act 1990,

may be granted against a person whose identity is unknown to the applicant; and in the following provisions of this rule such an injunction against such a person is referred to as "an injunction under paragraph (1)", and the person against whom it is sought is referred to as "the respondent".

(2) A applicant for an injunction under paragraph (1) shall describe the respondent by reference to—

(a) a photograph;

(b) a thing belonging to or in the possession of the respondent; or

(c) any other evidence,

with sufficient particularity to enable service to be effected, and the form of the claim form used shall be modified accordingly.

(3) An applicant for an injunction under paragraph (1) shall file evidence by witness statement or affidavit—

(a) verifying that he was unable to ascertain, within the time reasonably available to him, the respondent's identity.

(b) setting out the action taken to ascertain the respondent's identity and

(c) verifying the means by which the respondent has been described in the claim form and that the description is the best that the applicant is able to provide.

(4) Paragraph (2) is without prejudice to the power of the court to make an order in accordance with CPR Part 6 for service by an alternative method or dispensing with service.

Related Sources

C49.7.1
- Town and Country Planning Act 1990
- Planning (Listed Buildings and Conservation Areas) Act 1990
- Planning (Hazardous Substances) Act 1990
- RSC, O.110—Environmental Control Proceedings
- CCR, O.29—Committal

Form

C49.7.2
- N16—General Form of Injunction

Leasehold Reform Act 1967

C49.8 **8.**—(1) In this rule a section referred to by number means the section so numbered in the Leasehold Reform Act 1967 and "Schedule 2" means Schedule 2 to that Act.

(2) Where a tenant of a house and premises desires to pay money into court pursuant to section 11(4) or section 13(1) or (3)—

(a) he shall file in the office of the appropriate court a witness statement or affidavit stating—

(i) the reasons for the payment into court,

(ii) the house and premises to which the payment relates and the name and address of the landlord, and

(iii) so far as they are known to the tenant, the name and address of every person who is or may be interested in or entitled to the money;

(b) on the filing of the witness statement or affidavit the tenant shall pay the money into court and the court officer shall enter the matter in the records of the court and send notice of the payment to the landlord and to every person whose name and address are given in the witness statement or affidavit pursuant to sub-paragraph (a) (iii);
(c) any subsequent payment into court by the landlord pursuant to section 11(4) shall be made to the credit of the same account as the payment into court by the tenant and sub-paragraphs (a) and (b) shall apply as if for the references to the tenant and the landlord there were substituted references to the landlord and the tenant respectively;
(d) the appropriate court for the purposes of sub-paragraph (a) shall be the court for the district in which the property is situated or, if the payment into court is made by reason of a notice under section 13(3), any other county court specified in the notice.

(3) Where the proceedings on an application are ordered to be transferred to a leasehold valuation tribunal under section 21(3), the court shall—
(a) send notice of the transfer to all parties to the application; and
(b) send to the leasehold valuation tribunal copies certified by the district judge of all entries in the records of the court relating to the application, together with the order of transfer and all documents filed in the proceedings.

(4) Where an application is made under section 17 or 18 for an order for possession of a house and premises the respondent shall—
(a) forthwith after being served with the application, serve on every person in occupation of the property or part of it under an immediate or derivative sub-tenancy, a notice informing him of the proceedings and of his right under paragraph 3(4) of Schedule 2 to appear and be heard in the proceedings with the permission of the court, and
(b) within 14 days after being served with the application, file an answer stating the grounds, if any, on which he intends to oppose the application and giving particulars of every such sub-tenancy.

Editorial Note—The Leasehold Reform Act 1967 enables a lessee to acquire the freehold subject to the detailed provisions of the Act. See further the various sections quoted in the rule and the Act generally. **C49.8.1**

Related Sources
- Leasehold Reform, Housing and Urban Development Act 1993 **C49.8.2**
- CCR, O.49, r.9

Forms
- N8(4)—Notice to respondent in application under sections 17 and 18 of the Leasehold Reform Act 1967 **C49.8.3**

Leasehold Reform, Housing and Urban Development Act 1993

9.—(1) In this rule— **C49.9**
(a) "the 1993 Act" means the Leasehold Reform, Housing and Urban Development Act 1993;
(b) a section or Schedule referred to by number means the section or Schedule so numbered in the 1993 Act; and
(c) expressions used in this rule have the same meaning as they have in the 1993 Act.

(2) Where an application is made under section 23(1) by a person other than the reversioner—
(a) on the issue of the application, the applicant shall send a copy of the application to the reversioner;
(b) the applicant shall promptly inform the reversioner either—

(i) of the court's decision; or
(ii) that the application has been withdrawn.

(3) Where an application is made under section 26(1) or (2) or section 50(1) or (2) it shall be made by the issue of a claim form which must not be served on any other person to the district judge, who may grant or refuse it or give directions for its future conduct, including the addition as respondents of such persons as appear to have an interest in it.

(4) Where an application is made under section 26(3), it shall be made by the issue of a claim form and—

(a) the applicants shall serve notice of the application on any person who they know or have reason to believe is a relevant landlord, giving particulars of the application and the return date and informing that person of his right to be joined as a party to the proceedings;
(b) the landlord whom it is sought to appoint as the reversioner shall be a respondent to the application, and shall file an answer;
(c) a person on whom notice is served under sub-paragraph (a) shall be joined as a respondent to the proceedings when he gives notice in writing to the court of his wish to be added as party, and the court shall notify all other parties of the addition.

(5) Where a person wishes to pay money into court under section 27(3), section 51(3) or paragraph 4 of Schedule 8, rule 8(2) shall apply as it applies to payments into court made under the Leasehold Reform Act 1967, subject to the following modifications—

(a) references in rule 8 to the payment of money into court by a tenant shall be construed as references to the person or persons making a payment into court under the 1993 Act;
(b) the reference in rule 8(2)(a)(ii) to "house and premises" shall be construed as a reference to the interest or interests in the premises to which the payment into court relates, or, where the payment into court is made under section 51(3), to the flat to which it relates;
(c) the witness statement or affidavit filed by the tenant under rule 8(2)(a) shall include details of any vesting order; and
(d) the appropriate court for the purposes of that sub-paragraph shall be—
   (i) where a vesting order has been made, the court which made the vesting order; or
   (ii) where no such order has been made, the court in whose district the premises are situated.

(6) Where an order is made under section 91(4), rule 8(3) (transfer to leasehold valuation tribunal) shall apply as it applies on the making of an order under section 21(3) of the Leasehold Reform Act 1967.

(7) Where a relevant landlord acts independently under Schedule 1, paragraph 7, he shall be entitled to require any party to proceedings under the 1993 Act (as described in paragraph 7(1)(b) of Schedule 1) to supply him, on payment of the reasonable costs of copying, with copies of all documents which that party has served on the other parties to the proceedings.

C49.9.1 **Editorial Note**—The Leasehold Reform and Urban Development Act 1993 extends leasehold enfranchisement first granted by the Leasehold Reform Act 1967. It provides for collective enfranchisement of flats and rights of renewal of leases for tenants of flats (the 1967 Act is confined to houses).

Local Government Finance Act 1982

C49.10 **10.**—(1) In this rule a section referred to by number means the section so numbered in the Local Government Finance Act 1982.

(2) Proceedings in a county court under section 19 or section 20 shall be commenced in the court for the district in which the principal office of the

body to whose accounts the application relates (in this rule referred to as "the body concerned") is situated.

(3) A claim form for a declaration under section 19(1) shall state the facts on which the applicant intends to rely at the hearing of the application and the respondents to the application shall be the body concerned and any person against whom an order is sought under section 19(2).

(4) An appeal under section 19(4) or section 20(3) against a decision of an auditor shall be brought within 28 days of the receipt by the appellant of the auditor's statement of the reasons for his decision.

(5) The notice of appeal to which paragraph (4) relates shall state—

(a) the reasons stated by the auditor for his decision;
(b) the date on which the appellant received the auditor's statement;
(c) the facts on which the appellant intends to rely at the hearing of the appeal; and
(d) in the case of a decision not to apply for a declaration, such facts within the appellant's knowledge as will enable the court to consider whether to exercise the powers conferred on it by section 19(2).

(6) The respondents to the appeal shall be—

(i) the auditor who for the time being has responsibility for the audit of the accounts of the body concerned;
(ii) the body concerned; and
(iii) in the case of an appeal against a decision not to certify under section 20(1) that a sum or amount is due from any person, that person.

(7) The court may at any stage of an application or appeal under section 19 or section 20 direct that any officer or member of the body concerned be added to the proceedings as a respondent.

Editorial Note—It is surprising to find CCR, O.49, r.10 re-enacted in Sched. 2 as, in practice, it is obsolete. C49.10.1

Local Government (Miscellaneous Provisions) Act 1976

11. A person who appeals against a notice under section 21, 23 or 35 of the Local Government (Miscellaneous Provisions) Act 1976 shall state in his notice of appeal the grounds of the appeal and where one of those grounds is that it would have been fairer to serve the notice on another person or, as the case may be, that it would be reasonable for the whole or part of the expenses to which the notice relates to be paid by some other person, that person shall be made a respondent to the appeal, unless the court on application of the appellant made without notice, otherwise directs. C49.11

Related Source

- CCR, O.3, r.6—appeals to county court C49.11.1

Form

- N201—Request for entry of appeal C49.11.2

Mental Health Act 1983

12.—(1) In this rule— C49.12

a section referred to by number means the section so numbered in the Mental Health Act 1983 and "Part II" means Part II of that Act;

"place of residence" means, in relation to a patient who is receiving treatment as an in-patient in a hospital or other institution, that hospital or institution;

"hospital authority" means the managers of a hospital as defined in section 145(1).

(2) An application to a county court under Part II shall be made by a claim form filed in the court for the district in which the patients' place of residence

is situated or, in the case of an application made under section 30 for the discharge or variation of an order made under section 29, in that court or in the court which made the order.

(3) Where an application is made under section 29 for an order that the functions of the nearest relative of the patient shall be exercisable by some other person—

(a) the nearest relative shall be made a respondent to the application unless the application is made on the grounds set out in subsection (3)(a) of the said section or the court otherwise orders; and
(b) the court may order that any other person, not being the patient, shall be made a respondent.

(4) On the hearing of the application the court may accept as evidence of the facts stated therein any report made by a medical practitioner and any report made in the course of his official duties by—

(a) a probation officer; or
(b) an officer of a local authority or of a voluntary organisation exercising statutory functions on behalf of a local authority; or
(c) an officer of a hospital authority,

provided that the respondent shall be told the substance of any part of the report bearing on his fitness or conduct which the judge considers to be material for the fair determination of the application.

(5) Unless otherwise ordered, an application under Part II shall be heard and determined by the court sitting in private.

(6) For the purpose of determining the application the judge may interview the patient either in the presence of or separately from the parties and either at the court or elsewhere, or may direct the district judge to interview the patient and report to the judge in writing.

C49.12.1 **Editorial Note**—See the various sections in the Mental Health Act 1983 referred to in the rule. The procedure under CCR, O.49, r.12 is now by claim form (r.12(2)) and is heard in private (r.12(5)). Note the provisions as to evidence in r.12(3), and the provision to interview the patient in r.12(6). A report by the district judge is in Form N437.

Mobile Homes Act 1983

C49.13 **13.**—(1) An application—

(a) under section 1 or 2 of the Mobile Homes Act 1983; or
(b) pursuant to paragraph 4, 5 or 6 of Part I of Schedule 1 to that Act; or
(c) with respect to any question arising under paragraph 8(1) or 9 of the same Part of that Schedule,

shall be made by a claim form and the respondent shall file an answer.

(2) Any application to which paragraph 1(b) applies may include an application for an order enforcing the rights mentioned in section 3(1)(b) of the Caravan Sites Act 1968.

C49.13.1 **History of rule**—Amended by Civil Procedure (Amendment) Rules 1999 (S.I. 1999 No. 1008)

Related Sources

C49.13.2
- Mobile Homes Act 1983
- Caravan Sites Act 1968
- Pt 7—How to start Proceedings—the Claim Form

Post Office Act 1969

C49.15 **15.**—(1) An application under section 30(5) of the Post Office Act 1969 for permission to bring proceedings in the name of the sender or addresse of a postal packet or his personal representatives shall be made by a claim form.

(2) The respondents to the application shall be the Post Office and the person in whose name the applicant seeks to bring proceedings.

C49.15.1 **Editorial Note**—Section 30 of the Post Office Act 1969 imposes on the Post Office a limited liability in respect of registered inland postal packs.

Rentcharges Act 1977

16. Where for the purposes of section 9 of the Rentcharges Act 1977 the sum required to redeem a rentcharge is to be paid into the county court, it shall be paid into the court for the district in which the land affected by the rentcharge or any part thereof is situated. C49.16

Editorial Note—The Rentcharges Act 1977 creates a statutory procedure whereby the owner of land subject to rentcharge may apply to the Secretary of State for a certificate that the rentcharge has been redeemed. In defined circumstances, s.9 provides for the specified sum to redeem the rentcharge to be paid into court; CCR, O.49, r.16 creates the necessary procedure. C49.16.1

Sex Discrimination Act 1975 and Race Relations Act 1976

17.—(1) In this rule— C49.17

(a) "the Act of 1975" and "the Act of 1976" mean respectively the Sex Discrimination Act 1975 and the Race Relations Act 1976;

(b) in relation to proceedings under either of those Acts expressions which are used in the Act concerned have the same meanings in this rule as they have in that Act;

(c) in relation to proceedings under the Act of 1976 "court" means a designated county court and "district" means the district assigned to such a court for the purposes of that Act.

(2) A claimant who brings a claim under section 66 of the Act of 1975 or section 57 of the Act of 1976 shall forthwith give notice to the Commission of the commencement of the proceedings and file a copy of the notice.

(3) CPR Rule 35.15 shall have effect in relation to an assessor who is to be appointed in proceedings under section 66(1) of the Act of 1975.

(4) Proceedings under section 66, 71 or 72 of the Act of 1975 or section 57, 62 or 63 of the Act of 1976 may be commenced—

(a) in the court for the district in which the defendant resides or carries on business; or

(b) in the court for the district in which the act or any of the acts in respect of which the proceedings are brought took place.

(5) An appeal under section 68 of the Act of 1975 or section 59 of the Act of 1976 against a requirement of a non-discrimination notice shall be brought in the court for the district in which the acts to which the requirement relates were done.

(6) Where the claimant in any claim alleging discrimination has questioned the defendant under section 74 of the Act of 1975 or section 66 of the Act of 1976—

(a) either party may make an application to the court in accordance with CPR Part 23 to determine whether the question or any reply is admissible under that section; and

(b) CPR Rule 3.4, shall apply to the question and any answer as it applies to any statement of case.

(7) Where in any claim the Commission claim a charge for expenses incurred by them in providing the claimant with assistance under section 75 of the Act of 1975 or section 66 of the Act of 1976—

(a) the Commission shall, within 14 days after the determination of the claim, give notice of the claim to the court and the claimant and thereafter no money paid into court for the benefit of the claimant, so far as it relates to any costs or expenses, shall be paid out except in pursuance of an order of the court; and

(b) the court may order the expenses incurred by the Commission to be assessed whether by the summary or detailed procedure as if they were costs payable by the claimant to his own solicitor for work done in connection with the proceedings.

(8) Where an application is made for the removal or modification of any term of a contract to which section 77(2) of the Act of 1975 or section 72(2) of

the Act of 1976 applies, all persons affected shall be made respondents to the application, unless in any particular case the court otherwise directs, and the proceedings may be commenced—

(a) in the court for the district in which the respondent or any of the respondents resides or carries on business, or
(b) in the court for the district in which the contract was made.

C49.17.1 **Editorial Note**—Only county courts designated by the Lord Chancellor by Order pursuant to s.67 of the County Courts Act 1984 have jurisdiction in Race Relations cases. However, the districts of courts not so designated are assigned to a county court which is so designated. The judge hearing the case sits with assessors unless the parties agree to dispense with them.

Telecommunications Act 1984

C49.18A **18A.**—(1) CPR Rule 35.15 applies to proceedings under paragraph 5 of Schedule 2 to the Telecommunications Act 1984.

Related Source

C49.18A.1 • CPR, r.35.15—Assessors

Applications under section 19 of the Trade Marks Act 1994

C49.18B **18B.** The CPR Patents Court Practice direction shall apply with the necessary modifications to proceedings brought under section 19 of the Trade Marks Act 1994 in a county court.

Related Source

C49.18B.1 • Patents Court Practice Direction—para. 49EPD–001

Trade Union and Labour Relations Consolidation Act 1992

C49.19 **19.**—(1) Where a complainant desires to have an order of the Certification Officer under section 82 of the Trade Union and Labour Relations Consolidation Act 1992 recorded in the county court, he shall produce the order and a copy thereof to the court for the district in which he resides or the head or main office of the trade union is situate.

(2) The order shall be recorded by filing it, and the copy shall be sealed and dated and returned to the complainant.

(3) The sealed copy shall be treated as if it were the notice of issue in a claim begun by the complainant.

(4) The costs, if any, allowed for recording the order shall be recoverable as if they were payable under the order.

(5) The order shall not be enforced until proof is given to the satisfaction of the court that the order has not been obeyed and, if the order is for payment of money, of the amount remaining unpaid.

Trustee Act 1925, section 63

C49.20 **20.**—(1) Any person wishing to make a payment into court under section 63 of the Trustee Act 1925 shall make and file in the office of the appropriate court a witness statement or an affidavit setting out—

(a) a brief description of the trust and of the instrument creating it or, as the case may be, of the circumstances in which the trust arose;
(b) so far as known to him, the names and addresses of the persons interested in or entitled to the money or securities to be paid into court;
(c) his submission to answer all such inquiries relating to the application of such money or securities as the court may make or direct;
(d) his place of residence; and
(e) an address where he may be served with any notice or application relating to such money or securities.

(2) The appropriate court for the purposes of paragraph (1) shall be the court for the district in which the person or any of the persons making the payment into court resides.

(3) The costs incurred in the payment into court shall be assessed by the detailed procedure and the amount of the assessed costs may be retained by the person making the payment into court.

(4) The district judge may require, in addition to the witness statement or affidavit, such evidence as he thinks proper with regard to the matter in respect of which the payment into court is made.

(5) On the making of the payment into court the court shall send notice thereof to each person mentioned in the witness statement or affidavit pursuant to paragraph (1)(b).

(6) An application for the investment or payment out of court of any money or securities paid into court under paragraph (1) may be made without notice but on the hearing of the application the court may require notice to be served on such person as it thinks fit and fix a day for the further hearing.

(7) No witness statement or affidavit in support of the application shall be necessary in the first instance but the court may direct evidence to be adduced in such manner as it thinks fit.

(8) The application may be heard and determined by the district judge.

(9) Paragraphs (6) to (8) are without prejudice to any provision of the County Court Funds Rules enabling or requiring the court to transfer money from a deposit to an investment account of its own motion.

Form

- N432—Affidavit on payment into court under section 63 of the Trustee Act 1925 C49.20.1

MISCELLANEOUS PRACTICE DIRECTIONS

PRACTICE DIRECTION FOR THE COURT OF APPEAL (CIVIL DIVISION)

1. Introduction

1.1. Jurisdiction of the Court of Appeal

PD–001 **1.1.1.** The Court of Appeal is a superior court of record. It exercises all the jurisdiction conferred on it by the Supreme Court Act 1981. In any appeal to the Civil Division of the Court of Appeal, and in relation to the amendment, execution and enforcement of any judgment or order made on such appeal, it has the same authority and jurisdiction as the court or tribunal from which the appeal is brought. When rules of court permit, any incidental jurisdiction in any proceedings pending before the Civil Division of the Court of Appeal, not involving the determination of an appeal, may be exercised, with or without a hearing, by a single judge of that Court, or by the master.

1.2. Consolidated Practice Directions

1.2.1. This is a consolidation, with some amendments, of all the principal Practice Directions which apply to proceedings in the Court of Appeal (see the list at Annex A). It covers the process of instituting proceedings, documentation including skeleton arguments, the requirement for permission to appeal, judgments, case management and Alternative Dispute Resolution. It also deals with particular aspects of the current practice of the Court of Appeal, for example, the making of references to the European Court of Justice under Article 177 of the EC Treaty. It should be noted that permission to appeal is now required in the vast majority of cases. This consolidated Practice Direction applies equally to appeals to the Court in family cases. Further or amended directions may be issued once the new Civil Procedure Rules, governing the work of the Court of Appeal, have been made.

1.3. The Civil Appeals Office

1.3.1. The administrative work of the Civil Appeals Office is conducted under the direction of the Head of the Civil Appeals Office. When acting in a judicial capacity he is known as master. In this Practice Direction the term master is used with that specific meaning. Provision is also made for the appointment of deputy masters.

1.4. Litigants in person

1.4.1. All of this Practice Direction may be of relevance to litigants in person but the key points of which they need to be aware will be found at section 8.

2. Permission to Appeal

2.1. When is permission required?

PD–002 **2.1.1.** Most appeals require the permission of the court below (the court which made the decision which is challenged) or of the Court of Appeal to bring an appeal.

2.1.2. Since 1 January 1999, permission has been required for all appeals except appeals against:

(a) committal orders;

(b) refusals to grant *habeas corpus*; and

(c) secure accommodation orders made pursuant to section 25 of the Children Act 1989.

(see RSC Order 59 r.1B(1)(a)–(c))

2.1.3. The experience of the Court of Appeal is that many appeals and applications for permission to appeal are made which are quite hopeless. They demonstrate basic misconceptions as to the purpose of the civil appeal system and the different roles played by appellate Courts and courts below. The court below has a crucial role in determining applications for permission to appeal. This guidance indicates how applicants, and courts, should approach the matter.

2.2 From which court should permission to appeal be sought?

2.2.1. The court which has just reached a decision is often in the best position to judge whether there should be an appeal. It should not leave the decision to the Court of Appeal. Courts below can help to minimise the delay and expense which an appeal involves. Where the parties are present for delivery of the judgment, it should be routine for the judge below to ask whether either party wants permission to appeal and to deal with the matter then and there. However, if the court below is in doubt whether an appeal would have a realistic prospect of success or involves a point of general principle, the safe course is to refuse permission to appeal. It is always open to the Court of Appeal to grant it.

2.2.2. The advantages which flow from permission being considered by the court of first instance are lost if the application cannot be listed before the judge who made the decision which is the subject of the application. Where it is not possible for the application for permission to be listed before the same judge, or where undue delay would be caused by so listing it, the Court of Appeal will be sympathetic to applicants who claim that it was impracticable for them to make their application to the court below and will not require such an application to be made.

2.3. Oral or paper hearings

2.3.1 Many applications to the Court of Appeal for permission to appeal are considered in the first instance by a single Lord Justice on paper, but in some cases the Court directs that the application should proceed straight to an oral hearing. Usually, only applications for permission where the applicant is legally represented are dealt with on paper. However, some applications from litigants in person may be deemed suitable to be dealt with in the same way. Following a notification that the Lord Justice is minded to refuse permission to appeal and in the absence of a request for an oral hearing being received within 14 days, the application will be determined in open court without further reference to the applicant.

2.3.2 Whether the application is dealt with on paper or at a hearing the applicant should not burden the Court with documents which are not relevant to the application. The letter from the Civil Appeals Office acknowledging entry of the application in the records of the Court sets out the Court's requirements concerning application bundles.

2.4. Applications for permission listed for oral hearing

2.4.1. If the single Lord Justice, on consideration of the papers, grants permission or directs an oral hearing of the application, directions may be given on paper as to (1) the maximum time to be allowed to each party for oral argument on the appeal or the oral hearing of the application for permission, as the case may be; (2) the filing and service of skeleton arguments; and (3) other directions for the progress of the case.

2.4.2. Where an application for permission to appeal is listed for oral hearing, whether initially or after a decision on paper, the following directions will apply.

2.4.3. In all cases where the application is listed for an oral hearing at which the Court has directed that other parties are to have the opportunity to attend, the applicant's solicitors (or the applicant, if acting in person) must, on receipt of notification from the Civil Appeals Office that such a hearing has been directed, immediately supply the respondent's solicitors (or the respondent, if in person) with a copy of the application bundle (including a copy of the transcript or note of judgment) in exactly the same form as the bundles filed for the use of the Court of Appeal. For the purposes only of providing the copy of the application bundle to the respondent's side photocopies of transcripts of judgment and, where relevant, evidence, may be used. The costs of provision of that bundle shall be borne by the applicant initially, but will form part of the costs of the application.

2.5. Time allowed for oral hearings

2.5.1. In the absence of specific directions, the Court of Appeal will expect oral argument in support of applications for permission to appeal, or renewed applications for permission to apply for judicial review, to be confined to a maximum of 20 minutes.

2.6. Skeleton arguments for applications for permission to appeal

PD–003 **2.6.1.** In order to assist the Court of Appeal to deal efficiently with applications for permission to appeal, all represented applicants for permission must provide a skeleton argument and applicants in person are strongly encouraged to do so. Three copies of the skeleton argument must accompany the bundle of documents which the applicant's solicitors lodge with the Civil Appeals Office for the application. (These copies should be filed with, but not bound in, the bundle.) Where dates are of significance in relation to the proposed appeal, a chronology should be filed and served with the applicant's skeleton argument.

2.6.2 If the application is listed for oral hearing at which the Court has directed that other parties are to have the opportunity to attend, the respondent's skeleton argument must be filed and served within 14 days of receipt of the applicant's bundle. Where an application for permission to appeal is listed for hearing, with the appeal to follow if permission is granted, the timetable for skeleton arguments will be the same as in the case of an appeal, and the amount of time allowed for oral argument will depend on the time estimate for the appeal.

2.7. Renewed applications for permission to apply for judicial review

2.7.1. The applicant's advocate (and where any respondent will be represented at the Court of Appeal hearing, that party's advocate) must file four copies of their skeleton arguments with the Civil Appeals Office with the application bundles.

2.7.2. This applies only to renewed applications for permission to apply for judicial review. Where permission to apply has been granted and the substantive application for judicial review has been dealt with in the High Court, any application to the Court of Appeal for permission to appeal against that decision will be governed by the general provisions for such applications.

2.8. The general test for permission

2.8.1. There is no limit on the number of appeals the Court of Appeal is prepared to hear. It is therefore not relevant to consider whether the Court of Appeal might prefer to select for itself which appeals it would like to hear. The general rule applied by the Court of Appeal, and thus the relevant basis for first instance courts deciding whether to grant permission, is that permission will be given unless an appeal would have no real prospect of success. A fanciful prospect is insufficient. Permission may also be given in exceptional circumstances even though the case has no real prospect of success if there is an issue which, in the public interest, should be examined by the Court of Appeal. Examples are where a case raises questions of great public interest or questions of general policy, or where authority binding on the Court of Appeal may call for reconsideration. The approach will differ depending on the category and subject matter of the decision and the reason for seeking permission to appeal, as will be indicated below. However, if the issue to be raised on the appeal is of general importance that will be a factor in favour of granting permission. On the other hand, if the issues are not generally important and the costs of an appeal will far exceed what is at stake, that will be a factor which weighs against the grant of permission to appeal.

2.9. A point of law

2.9.1. Permission should not be granted unless the judge considers that there is a realistic prospect of the Court of Appeal coming to a different conclusion on a point of law which will materially affect the outcome of the case. An appeal on the grounds that there is no evidence to support a finding is an appeal on a point of law, but it is insufficient to show that there was little evidence.

2.10. A question of fact

2.10.1. The Court of Appeal will rarely interfere with a decision based on the judge's evaluation of oral evidence as to the primary facts or if an appeal would involve examining the fine detail of the judge's factual investigation. Permission is more likely to be appropriate where what is being challenged is the inference which the judge has drawn from the primary facts, or where the judge has not received any particular benefit from having actually seen the witnesses, and it is properly arguable that materially different inferences should be drawn from the evidence. In such a case the judge, if he grants permission, should expressly indicate that this is the basis on which permission is given.

2.10.2. If a case is one which has involved considering many witnesses and/or documents, it will be especially important that the trial court considers whether to grant permission and, where it refuses permission, gives its reasons for doing so. This is because in a case of this sort the Court of Appeal is less able to assess whether an appeal is appropriate.

2.11. Questions of discretion

2.11.1. The Court of Appeal does not interfere with the exercise of discretion by a judge unless satisfied the judge was wrong. The burden on an appellant is a heavy one (many family cases do not qualify for permission for this reason). It will be rare, therefore, for a trial judge to give permission on a pure question of discretion. He may do so if the case raises a point of general principle on which the opinion of a higher court is required. PD–004

2.12. Appeals from interlocutory orders

2.12.1 An interlocutory order is an order which does not entirely determine the proceedings. Where the application is for permission to appeal from an interlocutory order, additional considerations arise:

(a) the point may not be of sufficient significance to justify the costs of an appeal;

(b) the procedural consequences of an appeal (e.g. loss of the trial date) may outweigh the significance of the interlocutory issue;

(c) it may be more convenient to determine the point at or after the trial.

2.12.2. In all cases under (a) permission to appeal should be refused. In the case of (b) and (c) it will be necessary to consider whether to refuse permission or adjourn the application until after trial so as to preserve the appellants right to appeal.

2.13. Limited and conditional permission

2.13.1. Permission may be limited to one or more points. It may also be conditional, e.g. on some special order for costs. If a court grants permission on one or more issues only, it should expressly refuse permission on other issues. The reason for this is that the other issues can then only be raised with the permission of the Court of Appeal.

2.13.2. If an appellant wishes to raise additional issues for which there is no permission to appeal, written notice of this must be given to all other parties and the Court of Appeal within 28 days of permission being granted, or 28 days prior to the hearing, if this is earlier. Unless there are special reasons for making an application earlier, to avoid additional expense the application to raise an additional issue should be dealt with at the outset of the appeal and all parties should normally be prepared to argue the additional issues at that hearing. If, however, a respondent considers the additional issues will have a significant effect on the preparation necessary for, or the length of, the hearing, he may inform the appellant within 14 days of receiving the notice that he requires an application to be made prior to the hearing. An application should then be made in writing within 14 days accompanied, if necessary, by short written submissions, which should be served on the respondent. The respondent may deliver short written submissions within a further 14 days. The court will, where practicable, give its decision as to whether the additional issues can be argued prior to the hearing of the appeal.

2.14. Reasons

PD–005 **2.14.1.** When permission is refused by the court below, the Court gives short reasons which are primarily intended to inform the applicant why permission is refused. Where permission is granted, reasons may be given which are intended to identify for the benefit of the parties and the Court hearing the appeal why it was thought right to give permission. There may be only one issue that the judge or judges giving permission considered it was necessary to draw to the attention of the parties and the Court hearing the appeal. It is a misconception to assume that, because only one aspect of the proposed appeal was mentioned in any reasons which were given, permission was granted under a misapprehension that there were not other issues to be determined on any appeal unless the reasons make this clear.

2.14.2. When the Lord Justice is minded to refuse permission to appeal, his or her reasons for doing so will be sent to the applicant's solicitors (or the applicant, if in person). A letter will accompany the Lord Justice's comments informing the applicant of the right to seek an oral hearing. (An example of the letter that will be sent is at **Annex B** to this Practice Direction.) The Lord Justice will direct whether the oral hearing should be before one or two Lord Justices.

2.15. The Form

2.15.1. At **Annex C** to this Practice Direction is a generic example of the form which the judge should complete when he grants or refuses permission to appeal, giving his reasons. The reasons for the decision need only be brief, e.g. difficult point of law or pure question of fact. All parties will, on request, be given a copy of the form. It is the applicant's responsibility to annex the form to his notice of application where he has been refused permission, or to his notice of appeal where he has been granted permission.

2.16. Directions

2.16.1 When an application for permission to appeal is referred to the single Lord Justice on the papers alone and the Lord Justice decides to grant permission, the Lord Justice may give directions for the subsequent progress of the appeal.

2.17. Legally-aided applicants

2.17.1. In any case where the applicant is legally aided and the single Lord Justice is minded to refuse permission to appeal on paper, the applicant's solicitor must send to the relevant legal aid office a copy of the single Lord Justice's comments (together with any reasons he/she gave for refusing permission) as soon as it has been received from the Civil Appeals Office. The court will require confirmation that this has been done in any case where an application for permission to appeal is renewed before the full court on legal aid.

2.18. Applications to set aside grant of permission to appeal to the Court of Appeal

2.18.1. There is a heavy onus on a respondent who seeks to set aside permission. Before making such an application, the respondent must bear in mind that the fact that the appeal has no real prospect of success does not necessarily mean that permission should not have been given. The applicant will be required to establish that there was no good reason for giving permission, which may not be the same thing. In addition, it should be borne in mind, prior to making such an application, that this court is likely to be very unsympathetic to it being made if it will in effect involve the parties in exactly the same expense as determining the appeal itself, and will not necessarily save the time of the Court but risk the Court having to have two hearings when only one would be necessary had there been no application to set aside. **PD-006**

2.19. More than one level of appeal

2.19.1. Where there has already been one unsuccessful appeal to a court (not a tribunal) against the decision being challenged, for example from a District Judge to a Circuit Judge or from a Master to a High Court Judge, and the application is for permission for a further appeal to the Court of Appeal, a more restrictive approach to the test for permission to appeal should be adopted. Permission should be granted only if the case raises a point of principle or practice or the case is one which for some other compelling reason should be considered by the Court of Appeal.

3. Skeleton Arguments

3.1. Introduction

3.1.1. Skeleton arguments are, as their name implies, a very abbreviated note of the argument and in no way usurp any part of the function of oral argument in court. They are an *aid-memoire* for convenience of reference before and during the hearing. **PD-007**

3.2. When are they required?

3.2.1. Skeleton arguments are compulsory in the case of all appeals (and full-court applications) to the Civil Division of the Court of Appeal, and in the case of all applications for permission to appeal (heard by a single judge), except (i) in cases which are heard as a matter of great urgency and (ii) any individual case where the court otherwise directs. Litigants in person are strongly encouraged to provide skeleton arguments.

3.3. The necessity for skeleton arguments

3.3.1. Before the appeal is called on, the judges will normally have read the notice of appeal, any respondent's notice and the judgment appealed from. The purpose of this pre-reading is not to form any view of the merits of the appeal, but to familiarise themselves with the issues and scope of the dispute and thereby avoid the necessity for a lengthy, or often any, opening of the appeal.

3.3.2. This process is assisted by the provision of skeleton arguments, which are much more informative than a notice of appeal or a respondent's notice, being fuller. During the hearing of the appeal itself, skeleton arguments enable much time to be saved because they reduce or obviate the need for the judges to take a longhand note, sometimes at dictation speed, of the submissions and authorities and other documents referred to. Furthermore, in some circumstances a skeleton argument can do double duty not only as a note for the judges but also as a note from which counsel can argue the appeal. It cannot be over-emphasised that skeleton arguments are not formal documents. They are simply a tool to be used in the interests of greater efficiency.

3.4. Form and content

3.4.1. To facilitate filing of skeleton arguments in the Civil Appeals Office, advocates must ensure:

(a) that their names are typed at the end of their skeleton arguments; and

(b) that the correct Court of Appeal reference number is shown on the front page. Where a skeleton argument covers two or more appeals, or applications, which are due to be heard together the reference numbers for all of them must be given.

3.4.2. The skeleton arguments should contain a numbered list of the points which the advocate proposes to argue, stated in no more than one or two sentences, the object being to identify each point, not to argue it or to elaborate on it. Each listed point should be followed by full references to the material to which the advocate will refer in support of it, i.e. the relevant pages or passages in authorities, bundles of documents, witness statements, transcripts and the judgment under appeal. It should also contain anything which the advocate would expect to be taken down by the court during the hearing, such as propositions of law, chronologies of events, lists of *dramatis personae* and, where necessary, glossaries of terms. If more convenient, these can of course be annexed to the skeleton argument rather than being included in it. Both the court and the opposing advocate can then work on the material without writing it down, thus saving considerable time and labour.

3.5. Length

3.5.1. The purpose of a skeleton argument is to identify and summarise the points, not to argue them fully on paper. A skeleton argument should therefore be as succinct as possible. In the case of a normal length appeal against a final order (i.e. an appeal in the range of one to two days), skeleton arguments should not normally exceed 10 pages in the case of an appeal on law and 15 pages in the case of an appeal on fact.

3.5.2 In the case of points of law, the skeleton argument should state the point and cite the principal authority or authorities in support, with references to the particular page(s) where the principle concerned is enunciated. In the case of questions of fact, it should state briefly the basis on which it is contended that the Court of Appeal can interfere with the finding of fact concerned, with cross-references to the passages in the transcript or notes of evidence which bear on the point.

3.6. Chronologies

PD–008 **3.6.1.** The court wishes to emphasise the importance of advocates for the appellant preparing a written chronology of events relevant to the appeal. If practicable the chronology should be agreed with the respondent(s). This should be a separate document in order that it can readily be consulted in conjunction with other papers. The appellant's advocate's skeleton argument must be accompanied by the written chronology of events relevant to the appeal cross-referenced to the core bundle or appeal bundle.

3.7. Respondent's skeleton argument

3.7.1. In the case of respondents who wish only to contend that the judgment of the court below is correct for the reasons given, the respondent's advocate can send in a letter to that effect in place of a skeleton argument. Where, however, the respondent is going to rely on any authority or refer to any evidence which is not dealt with in the judgment of the court below, a respondent's skeleton argument must be filed. The respondent's advocate must always file a skeleton argument in any case where there is a respondent's notice.

3.8. Skeleton arguments and litigants in person

3.8.1. In the interests of avoiding placing undue burdens on them litigants in person are not obliged to file skeleton arguments in support of their appeals and applications, but are strongly encouraged to do so. Where the litigant in person does decide to put in a skeleton argument he/she must;

(a) file four copies of it with the Civil Appeals Office within the time limit which would apply if an advocate were acting; and

(b) provide the respondent's advocate with a copy of it no later than the date on which the copies are filed with the Civil Appeals Office.

3.9. Timetable for skeleton arguments

3.9.1. If any advocate does not have instructions or all necessary papers sufficiently far in advance to be able to complete and file the skeleton argument on time, he/she should write to the master immediately. PD-009

3.10. Applications for extensions of time to file skeleton arguments

3.10.1. Applications for extensions of time must be made by the advocate personally (not by his or her clerk, or instructing solicitor). Such applications should be made by letter or fax setting out the reasons why the prescribed timetable could not be complied with and what further time is required. Such letters should be filed with, or posted to, the Case Section Support and Documents Room (Room E307, Royal Courts of Justice, Strand, London WC2A 2LL); the fax number is 0171-936 6810. That office will then pass the letter or fax to the master or the relevant Lord Justice.

3.11. Skeleton arguments and time limits

3.11.1 The court expects the time limits to be strictly adhered to and extensions of time will only be granted if it is satisfied that there are good reasons for doing so.

3.12. Skeleton arguments and the Short Warned List

3.12.1. In the case of appeals and applications assigned to the Short Warned List, applications for extensions of time for filing skeleton arguments will normally be dealt with by the master and the letter or fax should therefore be addressed to him. Requests for cases to be removed from the Short Warned List and given a fixture will not automatically relieve advocates from the obligation to file skeleton arguments. In most instances, before deciding whether the case should be taken out of the Short Warned List, the master or supervising Lord Justice will need to see the skeleton arguments in order to assist him to determine whether the case is one which satisfies the test for being given a fixture or second fixture. Where skeleton arguments are required for that purpose, the Civil Appeals Listing Office will inform the advocates concerned.

3.13. Skeleton arguments for appeals and full court applications

3.13.1. Where permission to appeal is granted by the Court of Appeal, the appellant (and any respondent who has filed a skeleton argument in response to the permission application) may use the same skeleton arguments for the purposes of the appeal (subject to making any minor amendments which they consider necessary, such as changes to page references), or they may prepare fresh skeleton arguments for the purposes of the appeal.

3.13.2. The appellant's solicitors must include with the appeal bundle, or the bundle for any full court application, four copies of their skeleton argument. (These copies should be filed with, but not bound in, the bundle.) The appellant's solicitors must also include a copy of that skeleton argument with the set of bundles served on the respondent. Appellants are reminded of the obligation to serve a set of bundles on the respondent at the same time as the appeal bundles are filed with the Civil Appeals Office.

3.13.3. The respondent's solicitors must file with the Civil Appeals Office four copies of their skeleton argument within 21 days of the date on which the appellant's bundle was served on them or, if earlier, not later than 14 days before the appeal hearing. No supplemental or revised skeleton arguments may be filed without the permission of the Court. Permission will only be granted if there are good reasons for doing so.

3.14. Application or appeals in linked or similar cases

3.14.1. Where advocates are aware that an application or appeal in which they are instructed is linked with another case, or raises issues similar to or connected with, those raised in other applications and appeals, they should inform the master, by letter, as soon as practicable.

4. Case Management

4.1. Supervising Lords Justices

PD–010 **4.1.1.** A group of supervising Lords Justices maintain oversight of groups of appeals. This involves them in specific case management as well as keeping abreast of developments in their areas of litigation. They will welcome general information from the professional bodies and specialist associations about difficulties or initiatives of which the Court of Appeal should be aware. The membership of the team will change from time to time. The names of the current supervising Lords Justices and their areas of responsibility are set out in **Annex D**.

4.2. Case management

4.2.1. When it appears to the court that it would for any reason be advantageous to do so, the Court will invite the parties advocates and any party acting in person to attend a directions hearing held in advance of the main hearing. Such directions hearings may be conducted by the full Court, a single Lord Justice or the master.

4.2.2. Supervising Lords Justices will give directions concerning the progress and future conduct of appeals on their own initiative wherever they think fit, and most requests from parties for expedition or for other directions to be given will be referred to the relevant supervising Lord Justice.

4.2.3. So far as possible, directions will be given on paper, in the interests of saving costs. In those cases where a hearing is necessary, it will be conducted before the supervising Lord Justice in private (unless otherwise directed) and therefore both solicitors and counsel will have a right of audience. It will rarely be necessary for more than one counsel, or, where counsel has not been briefed, for more than one solicitor to attend on behalf of any particular party.

4.2.4. Directions hearings will not be allowed to develop into satellite litigation. They are intended to be a speedy and informal means of arriving at practical solutions to unresolved problems relating to the preparation for and future conduct of the appeal. Attempts at "point scoring" will not be tolerated.

The supervising Lord Justice will have read in advance the judgment under appeal, the notice of appeal and any respondent's notice, together with any correspondence or other documents which raise or define the issues to be decided at the directions hearing. Advocates should therefore proceed straightaway to make their points about those issues briefly and without any opening or preamble. The costs of such directions hearings will be in the discretion of the Court in the usual way. Although a shorthand note of the hearing will be taken, a detailed or lengthy judgment will not normally be given.

4.2.5. To ensure that all requests for directions are centrally monitored and correctly allocated, all requests for directions or rulings (whether relating to listing or any other matters) should be made to the Civil Appeals Listing Office. Those seeking directions or rulings must not approach the supervising Lord Justice either directly, or via his or her clerk.

4.2.6. If directions are requested or needed close to the hearing date, the matter will normally be referred to the presiding Lord Justice of the court in which the appeal is due to be heard. He or she will then make the necessary directions as a single Lord Justice or refer the matter to the full court.

4.2.7. The management of the list will continue to be dealt with by the listing officer under the oversight of the master. Subject to any direction given in any individual case by the full Court or by a Lord Justice, the master and deputy masters will continue to exercise their powers to give directions.

4.2.8. The Court may at any time give directions whether in individual cases or through information leaflets in relation to the documents to be produced. It may also give directions as to the manner in which documents are to be presented and as to other matters incidental to the conduct of the appeal, as appear best adapted to secure the just, expeditious and economical disposal of the appeal.

4.2.9. Directions regarding documentation may be given without a hearing. The master may at any time issue a notice requiring the parties to an appeal or application to attend before him. Any party given notice of an appeal or application may apply at any time for an appointment before the master.

5. Receiving and Processing Appeals and Applications

5.1. The principal features of the system

5.1.1. In the case of notices of appeal and applications which are filed by personal attendance at the Civil Appeals Office Registry, the staff on the counter will not carry out any check on whether permission to appeal is required or whether there is any other jurisdictional bar to the appeal or application being accepted. The counter staff will carry out a preliminary check on the following: **PD–011**

(a) whether the relevant time limits have been complied with;

(b) whether a copy of the order being appealed has been filed;

(c) in the case of applications (other than in time applications for permission to appeal), whether the statement of truth in the application notice has been signed and whether a witness statement or an affidavit in support of the application is included with the papers; and

(d) whether the correct court fee has been paid.

5.1.2. If the person dealing with the matter at the counter considers that the appeal is out of time, or that any of the other requirements listed above have not been complied with, he/she will inform the solicitor, or solicitor's clerk, of this and will not take the papers in. If the solicitor who has the conduct of the case considers that all relevant time limits and other formalities have been complied with, that solicitor (not the clerk) should telephone the Civil Appeals Office or send a letter or fax, and the matter will be referred to the master.

5.1.3. If the member of the staff at the counter considers that the time limits and other formalities have been complied with, he/she will accept the papers; but they will then be referred to an office lawyer and, if necessary, the master. If it is considered that, for any reason, the appeal or application has not been validly instituted or is one which the Court has no jurisdiction to entertain, the appellants/applicants solicitor (or the appellant/applicant if in person) will be informed of this, normally by letter or telephone. Any query concerning the office lawyer's decision will be referred to the master.

5.1.4. It follows from the arrangements set out above that the fact that the staff in the Civil Appeals Office have accepted the notice of appeal or application concerned must not be taken to be an indication, still less a guarantee, that the appeal or application is validly instituted or is one which the court has jurisdiction to entertain.

5.1.5. Appeals and applications filed by post will be similarly dealt with. The staff in the registry will carry out the preliminary check on time limits and formalities, and then the papers will be referred for legal scrutiny.

5.1.6. If, after the preliminary check, the appeal or application is considered to be in order, it will be set down (i.e. entered in the records of the Court of Appeal) and given a reference number. The appellant's/applicant's solicitors (or the appellant/applicant if in person) will then be informed by a letter from the Civil Appeals Office that the appeal/application has been set down; that letter will give the appeal/application reference number (which should be quoted when writing or telephoning) and will specify what further steps must be complied with by the appellant's/applicant's side and within what timetable. When an appeal is set down the appellant must inform the respondent of the reference number and the timetable.

5.1.7. It is important to emphasise that these procedures for vetting appeals and applications are intended to assist the court in the management of its case load and to ensure, so far as possible, that invalid appeals or applications are not accepted. They do not, however, relieve any party (whether represented or acting in person) of the obligation to comply with the requirements of all of the relevant rules and directions and that party's solicitor, or the party himself/herself, as the case may be, will remain solely responsible for all consequences, including the costs, of any failure to comply with any relevant requirement.

5.1.8. It is unwise for solicitors, or litigants in person, to leave it until the last day, or even close to the last day, of the period concerned before posting or bringing the requisite documents to the Civil Appeals Office.

5.2. Notice of appeal

PD–012 **5.2.1.** Except for appeals and decisions of the Social Security Commissioners on questions of law and appeals from certain tribunals (see RSC Order 59 rule 21 and Order 61), there is a single time limit for serving the notice of appeal of four weeks from the date on which the judgment or order of the court below was sealed or otherwise perfected, unless this limit is abridged or extended by order of the court below, the master, a Lord Justice or the Court of Appeal (see RSC Ord. 59 r. 4(1)). Such applications are ordinarily heard by the master.

5.3. Contents of Notice of Appeal

5.3.1. A notice of appeal which complies fully with RSC Ord. 59 r. 3 will both define and confine the area of controversy on the hearing of the appeal, thus saving both time and expense to the parties.

5.3.2. The notice of appeal must contain a certificate stating which track the case is currently allocated to in the Court below.

5.3.3. There is no form of notice of appeal fixed by statute or the rules. If a notice of appeal does not contain the following suggested statement or certificate, it will not for that reason alone be invalid. However the following suggestions are recommended in order to save the parties time, trouble and expense.

(a) On setting down an appeal to the Court of Appeal one copy of the notice of appeal should be endorsed with a certificate of the solicitors for the appellant (or the appellant himself if in person) stating the date or dates on which notice of appeal was served on the party or parties named as respondents and on the county court or tribunal as appropriate. The officer receiving the notice of appeal should satisfy himself that it was served in due time on the respondents and on the appropriate court or tribunal where required and must refuse to set the appeal down if it appears that the notice was served out of time. The copy of the notice of appeal containing the certificate as to service shall be in the custody of the officer in attendance on the Court of Appeal when the appeal comes on to be heard.

(b) Notices of appeal should contain, after the signature by the solicitor for the appellant, a statement as follows:

"No notice as to the date on which this appeal will be in the list for hearing will be given: it is the duty of solicitors to keep themselves informed as to the state of the lists. A respondent intending to appear in person should inform the Civil Appeals Office Registry, Royal Courts of Justice, WC2A 2LL, of that fact and give his address; if he does so he will be notified to the address given of the date when the appeal is expected to be heard." The form of the notice of appeal will be found at **Annex E**.

5.4. The list of appeals

5.4.1. RSC Ord. 59 r.3(4) requires the notice of appeal to specify the list of appeals in which the appellant proposes that the appeal shall be set down. There are final and interlocutory lists as described in **Annex F**.

5.5. Setting down the appeal

5.5.1. RSC Order 59 Rule 5 requires the appellant to 'set down' the appeal PD–013 within seven days after the later of (i) the date on which service of the notice of appeal was effected, or (ii) the date on which the judgment or order of the court below was sealed or otherwise perfected. The time limit is important and will be strictly enforced. 'Setting down' means filing the notice of appeal with the court, accompanied by the documents specified in RSC Ord. 59 r.5(1). Any application to extend time for setting down must be made to the master.

5.6. Respondent's Notice

5.6.1. RSC Ord.59 r.6 makes provision for the service of a respondents' notice within 21 days after the service of the notice of appeal and its subsequent filing. The content of any such notice is as important as that of the notice of appeal and for the same reason, it defines and confines the scope of the argument on the appeal, enables the members of the Court to inform themselves in advance of the hearing of what the appeal is about and so saves both time and expense. Again the time limit is important and will be strictly enforced, any application for an extension of time must be made to the master unless the appeal is before the Court itself at the time when the application is made.

5.7. Amendment of notice of appeal and respondent's notice

5.7.1. It can happen that, on reflection, it is thought desirable to amend such notices. Rule 7 allows this to be done without leave at any time before the appeal first appears in the documents list. An application for permission to amend should be made to the master on notice to all other parties, unless the appeal is already before the Court for some other purpose.

5.8. Appearance of appeal or application in the documents list

5.8.1. Once an appeal or application appears in the document list, the appellant has fourteen days in which to file the various documents specified at paragraph 7.2. and 7.3. A notice of appeal and respondent's notice may be amended as of right before the case enters the documents list, but thereafter only with permission.

5.9. Constitution of Courts

5.9.1. Section 54(4) of the Supreme Court Act 1981 and the Court of Appeal (Civil Division) Order 1982, SI 1982/543, have authorised the constitution of Courts consisting of two judges instead of three in certain specified circumstances, mainly appeals from interlocutory decisions, which includes most family and divorce matters, and appeals from the county courts. It will sometimes happen that, whilst an appeal is of such a nature that there is jurisdiction for a two-judge Court to hear it, issues of complexity or general importance arise such that a three-judge Court is desirable. Should this appear to the master to be the case, he will list the appeal for hearing by a three-judge Court. In addition the parties that this is the case may apply to the master for a special listing before a three judge Court, but should not adopt this course unless there are compelling reasons for so doing.

5.10. Documents needed for filing an application

5.10.1. Upon filing an application, the following documents are to be filed in duplicate in addition to the relevant court fee:

(a) the application notice;

(b) the order under appeal;

(c) in the case of an application for permission to appeal, the order of the court below refusing such permission and any written reasons given;

(d) any witness statement or affidavit in support of the application. In the case of an application for permission to appeal, the statement of truth must be signed or a witness statement or affidavit be filed only if the application is made after the expiry of the time limit or if a stay of execution or other remedy is requested;

(e) In the case of an application for permission to appeal, the draft notice of appeal or document stating the grounds of the proposed appeal.

5.10.2. The application notice must contain a certificate stating which track the case is currently allocated to in the Court below.

5.10.3. The forms of notice of application are at **Annex G**.

5.11. Internal appeals and referrals

PD–014 **5.11.1.** The master has power to refer matters to a single judge and the single judge power to refer matters to the Court of Appeal. The judicial decision of the master may be appealed to a single Lord Justice and the determination of the single Lord Justice may be appealed to the full Court of Appeal. However, in respect of a determination by the master, there is no right of appeal to the Court of Appeal without the leave of that Court if the master's determination has been reviewed by the single Lord Justice.

5.12. Time estimates

5.12.1. In all cases where there are solicitors acting for the appellant they must file with the Civil Appeals Office within 14 days after an appeal has been entered in the records of the Court, an estimate of the length of the appeal hearing (exclusive of judgment). That time estimate must be on the form sent to the solicitors with the letter from the Civil Appeals Office acknowledging that the appeal has been entered in the records of the Court. The procedure is as follows:

(a) form must be duly completed and signed by the appellant's advocate.

(b) Within that 14 day time limit the original of that completed form must be sent or delivered to the Civil Appeals Office and a photocopy must be sent to the respondent's advocate, either directly or through the respondent's solicitors.

(c) The respondent's advocate must consider the appellant's estimate as soon as it has been received and notify the Civil Appeals Office within 14 days (by filing the photocopy of the form with the respondent's section of it completed and signed) if his/her own estimate differs from that of the appellant's advocate. In the absence of such notification the respondent's advocate will be deemed to have accepted the estimate from the appellant's side.

5.12.2. Where the court directs that an application for permission to appeal shall be listed for hearing with the appeal to follow if permission is granted and the court has not specified what length of time is to be allowed for oral argument, the appellant's advocate must provide a certified time estimate of the length of the hearing on the assumption that permission will be granted and the court will hear argument on the appeal. The procedure is the same as in paragraph 5.12.1., except that (1) the time-limit will be 14 days after the date of the direction that the application be listed with appeal to follow, and (2) the estimate need not be on any special form.

5.12.3. A copy of the certified estimate must he placed and kept with each advocate's papers. Each time the advocate for any party is asked to give any advice or to deal with anything in connection with the appeal he/she must check whether the estimate is still correct. The fact that a time estimate has been filed in the case does not prevent the Court from allocating its own time estimate.

5.13. Revised estimates

5.13.1. If, for any other reason, the original estimate requires revision, the Civil Appeals Office should be informed immediately in writing by the advocate concerned.

5.14. Appeal bundles

5.14.1. On filing the appeal bundles with the Civil Appeals Office, the appellant's solicitors must supply the respondent's solicitors (or the respondent, if in person) with a set of the appeal bundles in exactly the same form as the bundles filed for the use of the Court of Appeal. The costs of provision of bundles for the respondent shall be borne by the appellant initially, but will form part of the costs of the appeal.

5.14.2. Appellants will not, however, be required to furnish respondents with transcripts of judgment and evidence. The appellant's solicitors (or the appellant, if in person) must notify the respondent's solicitors (or the respondent, if in person) of what transcripts have been provided for the court so that they can order transcripts for their own use and also make representations if they consider that further transcripts will be required. Respondents must order and pay for transcripts for the use of their solicitors and advocates (see Section 7 *Documentation*).

6. Listing and Hear-by Dates

6.1. Introduction

6.1.1. Listing is carried out for the whole of the Court of Appeal rather than for individual courts. In order to ensure, so far as possible, that cases are heard in their proper place in the list, each appeal is given a target date (known as its PD–015 "hear-by date"). Because some types of appeal are inherently more urgent than others (for instance, family cases) different hear-by dates are set for different species of appeals; a list of the current hear-by dates is annexed to this practice direction at **Annex H**. The aim is that appeals should be listed so that they are heard neither significantly earlier, nor significantly later, than their respective hear-by dates. In the interests of flexibility the listing officer has a discretion to fix the hearing date within a reasonable band on either side of the hear-by date. That system will not always apply to appeals assigned to the Short Warned List; such cases may be put into the list considerably earlier than their hear-by dates and may not be called on for hearing until some time thereafter.

6.1.2. In relation to applications for permission to appeal or renewed applications for permission to apply for judicial review it will not be possible, save in exceptional circumstances, to list such cases to suit advocates availability.

6.1.3. Appeals will only be expedited so as to be heard well in advance of their hear-by dates, or deferred significantly thereafter, if there is a judicial direction to that effect. Requests for expedition should be made to the master, initially by letter: see paragraph 6.6. below. Informal requests for listing significantly before the hear-by date may be made to the Listing Officer.

6.2. Fixtures

6.2.1. A "fixture" means a hearing date fixed in advance: it means that the hearing is fixed to begin on a specified date or on the next following sitting day at the option of the court. Appeals (other than (a) those assigned to the Short Warned List, (b) those given second fixtures; and (c) cases where special listing directions have been given) will be given fixtures. If it does not prove to be possible for the court concerned to take the appeal on the specified date or on the following sitting day, and the Listing Office is unable to transfer the appeal to another court, the hearing date will have to be rearranged.

6.3. Second fixtures

6.3.1. Some appeals are designated by the court as "second fixtures". A second fixture is a hearing date arranged in advance on the express basis that the list is fully booked for the period in question and therefore the case will be heard only if a suitable gap occurs in the list. Any second fixture for which space does not become available will be given a first fixture on the earliest convenient date.

6.4. The Short Warned List

6.4.1. Cases assigned to the Short Warned List are put "on call" from a specified date and will then be called on for hearing as and when gaps occur in the Court of Appeal list. Short Warned List cases are not called in chronological order of setting down or assignment to that list; which case will be called on will depend upon the length of the gap, the subject-matter of the case and the constitution of the court. Because the number of last-minute settlements in the Court of Appeal varies enormously, it is not possible to predict when any particular Short Warned List case will be called on for hearing.

6.5. Short Warned List (procedure)

6.5.1. The system applicable to cases assigned to the Short Warned List is as follows.

(a) The parties' solicitors are notified by letter from the Civil Appeals Office that the case has been assigned to the Short Warned List.

(b) It is the duty of the solicitors to all parties (whether appellants, or respondents) on receipt of that letter from the Civil Appeals Office to inform their advocates forthwith of the fact that the case has been assigned to the Short Warned List.

(c) The Listing Office will notify counsel's clerks by telephone of the date from which the case will be "on call" and it will remain in the Short Warned List liable to be called on either on half a day's notice or (if the master has so directed, on 48 hours' notice). The listing officers will put Short Warned List cases "on call" in such numbers and from such dates as the state of the list requires.

(d) It is the duty of solicitors to inform their lay clients when a case has been assigned to the Short Warned List and what the consequences of that will be. It is important that this is done so that the clients are not taken by surprise if, as is quite likely, they have to be represented at the Court of Appeal hearing by a different advocate. The supervising Lord Justice or the master will consider applications to remove appeals from the Short Warned List and give them a fixture or second fixture provided that the application is made at the correct time and on valid grounds. Any such application must be made as soon as the solicitors have been notified that the appeal has been assigned to that list (i.e. immediately on receipt of the letter referred to in paragraph (a) above). It is far too late to do so when, or after, the case has been put "on call".

6.5.2. It is not a valid ground for taking a case out of the Short Warned List that the parties' advocates of first choice may not be available to represent them at the appeal hearing. A case assigned to the Short Warned List will only be taken out of that list and given a fixture or second fixture if it is, viewed objectively, one which cannot be properly presented save by a particular advocate.

6.5.3. It follows that if any party's advocate of first choice is, for whatever reason, not available to appear on the date for which a Short Warned List case is called on, then a substitute advocate must be instructed immediately. Time should not be spent asking that the case should not be called on for that particular date because the advocate is unavailable.

6.5.4. Between 75 per cent and 80 per cent, of cases are given fixtures. The master is charged with the duty of selecting the minority of cases which, in his view, can reasonably be expected to be mastered by an advocate other than the one originally instructed on half a day's notice or, in the case of those so designated, on 48 hours' notice. These are then assigned to the Short Warned List and the assignment notified to the parties.

6.5.5. The supervising Lord Justice or the master will always consider applications to remove appeals from the Short Warned List on the grounds that they are not of the appropriate character. However, such applications must be made as soon as the parties are notified that the appeal has been assigned to that list. It is far too late to do so when, or after, notification is given that such an appeal is on call.

6.5.6. Once an appeal is "called on for hearing" it becomes the immediate personal professional duty of the advocate instructed in the appeal to take all practicable measures with a view to ensuring that his lay client is represented at the hearing by the advocate who is fully instructed and able to argue the appeal.

6.5.7. The court has power under section 51 of the Supreme Court Act 1981, as substituted by section 4 of the Courts and Legal Services Act 1990, to order the advocate who has failed in his duty to pay any "wasted costs". Further or alternatively the court has power to refer counsel's conduct either personally or vicariously by his clerk, to the Bar Council for consideration of whether disciplinary proceedings should be taken.

6.6. Expedition

6.6.1. In the interests of saving costs the supervising Lord Justice or master PD–016 decide as many requests for expedition as possible on paper without a hearing. Requests for expedition should initially be made to the master by letter (or, if time is short, by fax) setting out succinctly and in short compass the grounds on which expedition is sought, and, if it is granted, how soon the appeal needs to be heard. At the same time a copy of that letter (or fax) must be sent to the other party's solicitors so that they know at the earliest possible stage that an expedited hearing is being sought, and why.

6.6.2. Subject to the qualification referred to below, the letter to the master requesting expedition should be accompanied by a transcript or note of the judgment being appealed, draft grounds of appeal, and a realistic advocate's time estimate of the anticipated length of the appeal. Where, however, a very early hearing is needed (i.e. a hearing within days), the letter requesting expedition should be sent to the master (with copy to the other side) without waiting for the transcript or note of judgment and the draft grounds of appeal, so that the court has the maximum possible notice that such a high degree of expedition is sought.

6.6.3. Because of the immense pressures on its lists the Court of Appeal is no longer able to expedite as many cases as in the past. Attention is drawn to the current practice of the court as summarised in *Unilever Plc. v. Chefaro Proprietaries Ltd (Practice Note)* [1995] 1 WLR 243 and paragraph 6.7.

6.7. Orders for expedited hearing of an appeal

6.7.1. There is a time-lag between the date an appeal is set down and the date it is heard. The court has in general been sparing in its grant of applications for expedition, and has imposed a high threshold which a party must cross before its application for an expedited hearing will be granted. Where that threshold is crossed and an expedited hearing is ordered, the court will in fixing the date for that hearing give weight not to the wishes of the parties to that appeal but to the interests of other parties adversely affected by the order. It will do its utmost, for example, to avoid cancelling a fixture that has already been cancelled on a previous occasion. The greater the expedition ordered, the less regard can usually be had to the parties' preferences concerning dates.

6.7.2. Expedition will not normally be granted unless the party seeking it is willing, if necessary, to change advocate. In an appropriate case the respondent may also have to change advocate; this possible adverse consequence will cause the court to lean against the making of an order save in a clear case. In granting an application for expedition, the court may seek to mitigate the disruption caused to other parties by giving procedural directions not currently given in the ordinary run of cases with a view to ensuring that the appeal is heard in the minimum time necessary to achieve a just result.

6.7.3. The following guidance must be flexibly applied according to the facts of the particular application for expedition. However, some appeals are so urgent that justice can only be done if the appeal is heard immediately or within days. This category includes:

(a) appeals against committal orders, particularly if the adverse finding is challenged or the sentence is short;

(b) cases in which children are likely to suffer extraordinary prejudice (that is prejudice beyond that almost inevitably consequent on involvement in proceedings) if a decision is delayed;

(c) cases under the 1980 Hague Convention on the Civil Aspects of Child Abduction (Cmnd. 8281);

(d) asylum appeals concerning return to third countries, where the right to return may be jeopardised by delay;

(e) cases in which the execution of a possession order is imminent and which appear to have some merit;

(f) cases in which a decision is about to be taken or implemented which will be irrevocable or confer rights on third parties;

(g) cases in which the publication of allegedly unlawful material is imminent;

(h) appeals against judicial decisions made in the course of continuing proceedings.

6.7.4. In all these cases, not least (e), the court will expect the parties involved to approach it as soon as they learn of the order which it is sought to challenge. When the approach is left until the eleventh hour, or the necessary materials are not provided, it may well prove impracticable to arrange a hearing.

6.7.5. The court recognises the need to try to arrange expedited hearings where it appears that, without such expedition,

(a) a party may lose its livelihood, business or home or suffer irreparable loss or extraordinary hardship;

(b) the appeal will become futile;

(c) the resolution of numerous cases turning on the outcome of a case under appeal, will be unreasonably delayed, or the orderly management of class or multi-party litigation in a lower court will be disrupted;

(d) widespread divergences of practice are likely to continue, with the prospect of multiple appeals until the correct practice is laid down;

(e) there would be serious detriment to good public administration or to the interests of members of the public not concerned in the instant appeal.

6.7.6. When these criteria are not satisfied, the court will not ordinarily grant an expedited hearing of appeals on preliminary issues, or substantial interlocutory appeals (even where this means the loss of a trial date), or appeals concerning the construction of a standard document.

7. Documentation

7.1. Directions of the Court of Appeal concerning bundles of documents for the purpose of appeals and full court applications.

7.1.1. It is the duty of those acting for appellants to ensure that the bundles of documents filed for the use of the court comply with the relevant rules and directions. It is also their duty to file the bundles within the time limit prescribed by R.S.C. Ord. 59, r.9(1). Neglect of these duties may lead to the appeal or application being dismissed. For that reason, attention is drawn, in particular, to the following requirements. PD–017

7.2. Documents for applications

7.2.1. In general, the following are required:

(a) The document used to institute the application to the Court of Appeal.

(b) The notice of appeal or draft notice of appeal.

(c) The Order of the court below being appealed.

(d) Any order of the court below which refused permission to appeal and the form giving reasons.

(e) Any affidavit or witness statement lodged with the Civil Appeals Office in support of the application.

(f) Transcripts or notes of judgment (explained in more detail under appeals heading) save that in the case of applications for permission to appeal, in the absence of a transcript, the note of judgment does not need to be approved by the judge.

(g) Claim form, statements of case.

(h) Any application notice (or case management documentation) relevant to the subject of the appeal.

(i) If the order or judgment arose from an appeal from or setting aside of another judge's order (e.g. from District Judge to Circuit judge), the first order, the reasons given and the application notice used to appeal from that order.

(j) Relevant affidavits, witness statements, summaries, experts' reports and exhibits.

(k) Such other documents as the Court may direct.

7.3. Documents for appeals

7.3.1. In general, the following are required:

(a) The notice of appeal.

(b) Any respondent's notice.

(c) Any supplementary notice served under rule 7.

(d) The judgment or order of the court/tribunal below.

(e) The document by which the proceedings in the court below were begun (for civil courts, usually a claim form).

(f) Any application notice which led to the order which is the subject of the appeal.

(g) The statements of case (pleadings) if any, and in Admiralty cases, the preliminary acts, if any.

(h) The approved transcript of the judge's reasons for giving the judgment or making the order of the court/tribunal below. If that is not available, the advocates' note of the judge's reasons approved, wherever possible, by the judge.

(i) The parts of the transcript of evidence given in the court below which are relevant to any question at issue on the appeal. In the absence of an approved transcript, the relevant parts of the judge's note of the evidence.

(j) If the order or judgment arose from an appeal from or setting aside of another judge's order (e.g. from District Judge to Circuit judge), the first order, the reasons given and the application notice used to appeal from that order.

(k) The relevant affidavits, witness statements summaries, experts' reports, exhibits or parts of exhibits, as were in evidence in the court below.

(l) Any order, whether of the Court of Appeal or court below, granting permission to appeal and, in the case of the court below, the form giving reasons.

(m) Where permission to appeal was granted by the Court of Appeal at an oral hearing, the transcript of that decision.

7.4. Applications and Appeals

PD–018 **7.4.1.** Appellants/applicants are notified of the number of judges (including in Admiralty cases, assessors) due to hear their case. The appellant/applicant must provide sufficient copies and bundles for each judge.

7.5. Transcripts

7.5.1. All transcripts lodged (whether of evidence or of the judgment) must be official copies provided by the shorthandwriters or transcribers. Appellants are not permitted to file photocopies which they have had taken.

7.5.2. Where proceedings in any court have been officially recorded in shorthand, by stenographic machine, or on tape, official transcripts of the judgment, and, where relevant, the evidence, must be filed with the Court of Appeal, and, unless the court otherwise directs, notes of judgment or evidence will not be accepted. Normally the court will only accept notes in place of transcripts where the case requires such an urgent hearing that there is not time to obtain them.

7.5.3. Where, however, either in any division of the High Court or in a county court, the judge handed down his/her judgment, photocopies of the text of that handed down judgment (signed by the judge) can be lodged for the purposes of an appeal to the Court of Appeal in place of official transcripts of the judgment.

7.6. Transcripts of Court of Appeal judgments

7.6.1. Court of Appeal (Civil Division) transcripts are held in the Supreme Court Library. Parties requiring copies of them can obtain them from the shorthand writers or transcribers on payment of the usual charges. Advocates who propose to refer to such transcripts should satisfy themselves that arrangements are being made for copies to be available to the Court and to other advocates concerned.

7.7. Notes of judgment

7.7.1. In cases where the judge's judgment was not officially recorded and was not handed-down, the advocate or the solicitor who appeared for the appellant in the court below must prepare a note of the judge's judgment, agree it (if possible) with the advocate or solicitor who appeared for the respondent, and submit it to the judge for approval. If the parties' advocates (or solicitors) are not able to reach agreement about the note speedily, they should submit their rival notes of judgment to the judge, stating that they are unable to agree a note. In the case of an application for permission to appeal the applicant's advocate's note of judgment does not have to be approved by either the respondent's advocate or judge.

7.7.2. Where the note of judgment has not been received back from the judge by the time the bundles are ready to be filed, copies of the unapproved note of judgment should be filed with the bundles; the approved note of judgment should then be substituted as soon as it is to hand. In those cases where the appellant is appealing in person, advocates or solicitors for the respondent must make available their notes of judgment without charge, whether or not the appellant has made any note of the reasoned judgment.

7.8. County court notes of evidence

7.8.1. In county court cases, where the evidence was not officially recorded, a typed copy of the judge's notes of evidence must be obtained from the county court concerned and a photocopy of those notes must be included in each bundle. Directives have been sent to county courts asking them to arrange for the notes of evidence to be transcribed as soon as the notice of appeal has been served on the county court (unless the evidence was tape recorded). The notes should then be ready for despatch to the appellant's solicitors (or the appellant, if in person) as soon as they formally request them and make provision for the copying charges.

7.9. Transcripts at public expense

7.9.1. An appellant or respondent acting in person will not be required to pay for a transcript where a certificate is given under this paragraph. Otherwise, the appellant or respondent will pay for any transcript required for the Court of Appeal in the first instance. The Court may in certain circumstances certify that it is proper for the cost of a transcript to be borne by public funds. These circumstances are where it is satisfied that an appellant (or respondent) is in such poor financial circumstances that the cost of a transcript would be an excessive burden on him, and, in the case of a transcript of evidence, also that there is reasonable ground for the appeal. PD–019

7.9.2. Where the Court is of opinion that it is necessary to see a transcript of proceedings and judgment (with or without a transcript of the evidence) relating to an appellant whose financial circumstances are as described above, it may certify that transcripts or all or any part of the proceedings and judgment may properly be supplied for the use of the Court at the expense of public funds. The Court for these purposes includes both the judge (of whatever level) whose decision is under appeal, and the Court of Appeal, a single judge of the Court of Appeal or the master. An appellant for these purposes includes a person who is seeking permission to appeal to the Court of Appeal.

7.10. Core bundles

7.10.1. In cases where the appellant seeks to place before the court bundles of documents comprising more than 100 pages (exclusive of the judgment appealed against), the appellant's solicitors must prepare and file with the court the requisite number of copies of a core bundle containing the documents central to the appeal.

7.10.2. In all cases where the appellant or applicant is represented only core bundles are to be filed without any trial or other bundles. Core bundles must contain only those documents which the Lords Justices will need to pre-read or to which it will be necessary to refer at the hearing, either in support of, or in opposition to, the appeal or application. As soon as the appeal or application has been filed, the appellant's or applicant's solicitors must give careful consideration (with the advice of their advocate where appropriate) to the necessary content of the core bundles. If they are in any doubt concerning the documents which the other side will need, they must consult the respondent's solicitors at an early stage.

7.11. Time for filing Core Bundles

7.11.1. No later than the date stated in the letter from the Civil Appeals Office acknowledging entry of the case in the court's records, the appellant's solicitors must file with the Civil Appeals Office Case Section Support and Documents Room the number of sets of core bundles specified in that letter. No other bundles are to be filed.

7.11.2. One set of the full trial bundles should be brought to the Court of Appeal hearing, but not filed in advance.

7.12. Contents of Core Bundles

PD–020 **7.12.1.** Each core bundle must always include the notice of appeal, the order appealed against, any other relevant orders made in the court below, the respondent's notice (if any) and the note of judgment and notes of evidence (if relevant). If it is a case where there are transcripts of the judgment/evidence, then those should not be bound in the core bundle, but kept separate, see below. In addition, the core bundle should include such of the documents put in evidence in the court below as are central to the appeal.

7.13. Core Bundles and litigants in person

7.13.1. For information helpful to litigants in person see paragraph 8.2.

7.14. Pagination

7.14.1. Bundles must be paginated. At present, many bundles are numbered merely by document. This is incorrect. Each page must be numbered individually and consecutively, starting with page 1 at the top of the bundle and working continuously through to the end.

7.15. Index

7.15.1. There must be an index at the front of the bundle listing the documents and giving the page references for each. In the case of documents such as letters, invoices, bank statements etc., they can be shown in the index by a general description; it is not necessary to list every letter, invoice etc. separately. But if a letter or other such document is particularly important to the case, then it should be listed separately in the index so that attention is drawn to it. In particular in the case of appeals and applications in judicial review proceedings, the letter or other document which constitutes the decision sought to be reviewed must be separately itemised in the index (whether or not it forms part of the exhibit to an affidavit). Where each set of bundles consists of more than one file or bundle, an index covering all of them should be placed at the beginning of Bundle A; there should not be separate indexes for each physical bundle comprised in the set.

7.16. Binding of bundles

7.16.1. All the documents (with the exception of transcripts) must be bound together in some form (e.g. lever-arch files, ring-binders, plastic binders, or laced through holes in the top left-hand corner).

7.17. Legibility

7.17.1. All documents must be legible. In particular, care must be taken to ensure that the edges of pages are not cut off by the photocopying machine or rendered illegible by the binding. If it proves impossible to produce adequate copies of individual documents, or if manuscript documents are illegible, typewritten copies of the relevant pages should also be interleaved at the appropriate place in the bundle. **PD–021**

7.18. Applications for permission to adduce further evidence

7.18.1. Where (as is often the case) the court has directed that an application for permission to adduce further evidence is to be listed for hearing at the same time as the appeal, separate bundles must nevertheless be filed in respect of that application so that the further evidence can readily be distinguished from the evidence which was before the court below.

7.19. Time limits for filing documents

7.19.1. Time limits must be complied with and will be strictly enforced except where there are good grounds for granting an extension.

7.20. Responsibility of the solicitor on the record

7.20.1. The solicitor in charge of the case must personally satisfy himself/herself, and is responsible as an officer of the court for ensuring that the documentation is in order before it is delivered to the court. London agents too have a responsibility; they should be prepared to answer any questions which may arise as to the sufficiency of the documentation.

7.21. Affidavits

See Practice Direction to CPR Part 32.

8. Litigants in Person (Litigants without Lawyers)

8.1. Applications for permission to appeal and appeals by litigants in person

8.1.1. So that the Court of Appeal can check whether it has jurisdiction to hear an application for permission to appeal, or a full appeal, litigants in person should take or send to the Civil Appeal Office: **PD–022**

(a) a copy of the order or decision by the court against which he or she seeks to appeal; and

(b) details of his or her name, address and telephone number.

8.1.2. If the application or appeal is one where the Court of Appeal has jurisdiction, the Civil Appeals Office will provide the litigant with notes for guidance on how to proceed.

8.1.3. If the application or appeal is not one where the Court of Appeal has jurisdiction, the Civil Appeals Office will write to the litigant to explain the reasons why.

8.1.4. It is emphasised that the administrative and legal staff in the Civil Appeals Office will need time to deal with these matters. Litigants are therefore advised to make sure that they communicate with the Civil Appeals Office as soon as possible after the order or decision by the court against which they wish to appeal has been given, and well before the expiry of the time limit for serving notice of appeal. The provision of this information at short notice can be made only in urgent circumstances. A case will not be regarded as urgent merely because a party has left it too close to the expiry of the time limit before taking the necessary steps to make the application or file an appeal. A case will be treated as urgent only if a direction to the effect is made by the Court.

8.2. Appeal and application bundles

8.2.1. Information about how to prepare for applications or appeals by preparing sets or a set (bundles) of documents for the use of the Court of Appeal can be found in two leaflets, one for applications and one for appeals. The Civil Appeals Office will send a copy of the relevant leaflet to the litigant with the letter confirming the matter has entered the records of the Court of Appeal.

8.2.2. It is then the responsibility of the litigant to comply with the requirements set out in the leaflet. In particular, litigants should refer to the checklist in the leaflet, which highlights the key requirements. When the litigant is sure that his or her bundles of documents comply with the requirements in the leaflet, he or she should sign the checklist and return it to the Civil Appeals Office with the bundles.

8.2.3. In certain circumstances, the Court may require fewer documents than are required for formal bundles for an application. Except in cases which are so urgent that there is no time to do so, the Civil Appeals Office will write to litigants to tell them whether limited documentation or full bundles are required.

8.2.4. Paragraphs 7.5. and 7.9. gives details about obtaining transcripts of judgment for incorporation in the bundles. Litigants who require help with the preparation of their bundles can obtain this from the Citizens' Advice Bureau in the Royal Courts of Justice. In appropriate cases (for example, where for whatever reason the litigant is unable to prepare his or her own bundles) the Citizens' Advice Bureau may arrange for the bundles to be prepared for the litigant free of charge.

8.3. Skeleton arguments

8.3.1. Skeleton arguments are short written statements of the arguments in support of an application or appeal. Litigants in person are not obliged to send to the court skeleton arguments in support of their applications and appeals, but are strongly encouraged to do so. If they do, they should try to comply with the directions given in the section entitled 'skeleton arguments' (section 3). Many litigants in person find that setting out the arguments which they wish to raise in court in advance can be of great assistance when, at a hearing, the Court asks them to explain what their case is about.

8.3.2. A litigant who wishes to prepare a skeleton argument can obtain advice on how to do this from the Citizens' Advice Bureau in the Royal Courts of Justice. In appropriate cases the Citizens' Advice Bureau will prepare the skeleton argument for the litigant free of charge.

9. Reserved Judgments of the Court of Appeal

9.1. Availability of handed down judgments in advance of the hearing

PD–023 **9.1.1.** Unless the court otherwise orders—for example, if a judgment contains price-sensitive information—copies of the written judgment will now be made available in these cases to the parties' legal advisers at about 4 pm on the second working day before judgment is due to be pronounced on condition that the contents are not communicated to the parties themselves until one hour before the listed time for pronouncement of judgment. Delivery to legal advisers is made primarily to enable them to consider the judgment and decide what consequential orders they should seek. The condition is imposed to prevent the outcome of the case being publicly reported before judgment is given, since the judgment is confidential until then. Some judges may decide to allow the parties' legal advisers to communicate the contents of the judgment to their clients two hours before the listed time, in order that they may be able to submit minutes of the proposed order, agreed by their clients, to the judge before the judge comes into court, and it will be open to judges to permit more information about the result of a case to be communicated on a confidential basis to the client at an earlier stage if good reason is shown for making such a direction.

9.1.2. If, for any reason, a party's legal advisers have special grounds for seeking a relaxation of the usual condition restricting disclosure to the party itself, a request for relaxation of the condition may be made informally through the judge's clerk (or through the associate, if the judge has no clerk). A copy of the written judgment will be made available to any party who is not legally represented at the same time as to legal advisers. It must be treated as confidential until judgment is given.

9.1.3. Every page of every judgment which is made available in this way will be marked "Unapproved judgment: No permission is granted to copy or use in court". These words will carry the authority of the judge, and will mean what they say.

9.1.4. The time at which copies of the judgment are being made available to the parties' legal advisers has been brought forward in order to enable them to submit any written suggestions to the judge about typing errors, wrong references and other minor corrections of that kind in good time, so that, if the judge thinks fit, the judgment can be corrected before it is handed down formally in court. The parties' legal advisers are therefore being requested to submit a written list of corrections of this kind to the judge's clerk (or to the associate, if the judge has no clerk) by 12 noon on the day before judgment is handed down. If it is not possible to comply with this deadline, any later corrections approved by the judge will be included in the final text which the official shorthand writer (or the judge's clerk, in courts which lack an official shorthand writer) will incorporate into the approved official text of the judgment as soon as practicable. In divisions of the court which have two or more judges, the list should be submitted in each case to the judge who is to deliver the judgment in question. Lawyers are not being asked to carry out proof-reading for the judiciary, but a significant cause of the present delays is the fact that minor corrections of this type are being mentioned to the judge for the first time in court, when there is no time to make any necessary corrections to the text.

9.2. Availability of approved versions of handed down judgments

9.2.1. This course will make it very much easier for the judge to make any necessary corrections and to hand down the judgment formally as the approved judgment of the court without any need for the delay involved in requiring the court shorthand writer, in courts which have an official shorthand writer, to resubmit the judgment to the judge for approval. It will always be open to the judge to direct the shorthand writer at the time of the hearing in court to include in the text of the judgment any last minute corrections which are mentioned for the first time in court, or which it has proved impracticable to incorporate in the judgments handed down. In such an event the judge will make it clear whether the shorthand writer can publish the judgment, as corrected, as the approved judgment of the court without any further reference to the judge, or whether it should be resubmitted to the judge for approval. It will be open to judges, if they wish, to decline to approve their judgments at the time they are delivered, in which case the existing practice of submitting the judgment for their approval will continue.

PD–023

9.3. Handing down judgment in court: availability of uncorrected copies

9.3.1. When the court hands down its written judgment, it will pronounce judgment in open court. Copies of the written judgment will then be made available to accredited representatives of the media, and to accredited law reporters who are willing to comply with the restrictions on copying, who identify themselves as such. In cases of particular interest to the media, it is helpful if requests for copies can be intimated to the judge's clerk, or the presiding Lord Justice's clerk, in advance of judgment, so that the likely demand for copies can be accurately estimated. Because there will usually be insufficient time for the judge's clerk to prepare the necessary number of copies of the corrected judgment in advance, in most cases these uncorrected copies will similarly bear the warning "Unapproved Judgment: No permission is granted to copy or use in court". The purpose of these arrangements is to place no barrier in the way of accredited representatives of the media who wish to report the judgments of the court immediately in the usual way, or to accredited law reporters who wish to prepare a summary or digest of the judgment or to read it for the purpose of deciding whether to obtain an approved version for reporting purposes. Its purpose is to put a stop to the dissemination of unapproved, uncorrected, judgments for other purposes, while seeking to ensure that everyone who is interested in the judgment (other than the immediate parties) may be able to buy a copy of the approved judgment in most cases much more quickly than is possible at present.

9.3.2. If any member of the public (other than a party to the case) or any law reporter who is not willing to comply with the restrictions on copying, wishes to read the written judgment of the court on the occasion when it is handed down, a copy will be made available for him or her to read and note in court on request made to the associate or to the clerk to the judge or the presiding Lord Justice. The copy must not be removed from the court and must be handed back after reading. The object is to ensure that such a person is in no worse a position than if the judgment had been read aloud in full.

9.4. Availability of approved judgments

PD–024 **9.4.1.** In courts without an official shorthandwriter, the approved judgment should contain on its frontispiece the rubric "Judgment: Approved by the court for handing down (subject to editorial corrections)", and every page of a judgment which is handed down in this form will be marked in a similar manner. There will be no embargo on copying a judgment handed down in this form, so long as its status is made clear, and at present no charge will be made for permission to copy it. In future, all judgments delivered at the Royal Courts of Justice will be published in a common format. For cases decided in the two divisions of the Court of Appeal and in the Crown Office List, copies of the approved judgment can be ordered from the official shorthand writers, on payment of the appropriate fee. In the other courts in the Royal Courts of Justice, copies of the approved judgment can be ordered from the Mechanical Recording Department, on payment of the fee prescribed for copy documents. Disks containing the judgment will also be available from the official shorthandwriters, and the Mechanical Recording Department, where relevant, on payment of an appropriate charge. It is hoped that in most cases copies of the approved judgment will be available from these sources on the same day as the judgment is handed down: they should no longer be sought from judges' clerks.

9.5. Restrictions on disclosure or reporting

9.5.1. Anyone who is supplied with a copy of the handed-down judgment, or who reads it in court, will be bound by any direction which the court may have given in a child case under section 39 of the Children and Young Persons

Act 1933, or any other form of restriction on disclosure, or reporting, of information in the judgment.

9.6. Availability of approved versions of ex tempore judgments

9.6.1. Delays have also been experienced in the publication of approved versions of judgments which were not reserved, whether they are produced by the official shorthand writers or by contractors transcribing the tapes which have been mechanically recorded.

9.6.2. Sometimes the delay is caused in courts without an official shorthand writer because a transcript is bespoken by one of the parties a long time after the judgment was delivered. If a transcribed copy of such a judgment is to be required, in connection with an appeal, for example, it should be ordered as soon as practicable after judgment was delivered.

9.6.3. Delays are also sometimes caused in these cases because judgments are delivered to a judge for approval without supplying the judge with copies of the material quoted in the judgment. In future no judge should be invited to approve any such transcript unless the transcriber has been provided by the party ordering the transcript with copies of all the material from which the judge has quoted. If the transcript is ordered by a person who is not a party to the case (such as a law reporter), that person should make arrangements with one of the parties to ensure that the transcriber (and the judge) will have access to all the material quoted in the judgment.

9.6.4. From time to time delays are also caused because judges have been slow in returning approved transcripts to the transcribers. Judges should endeavour to return approved transcripts to the transcribers within two weeks of their being delivered to them for approval. If anyone encounters serious delay on this account, the relevant Head of Division should be informed.

9.6.5. Where a reserved written judgment has not been reported, reference must still be made in court to the approved official transcript (if this is available) and not to the approved transcript which is handed down, since this may have been subject to late revision after the text was prepared for handing down.

9.7. Advocates' fees and notes of judgments

9.7.1. Advocates' brief (or, where appropriate, refresher) fee includes
(a) remuneration for taking a note of the judgment of the court;
(b) having the note transcribed accurately;
(c) submitting the note to the judge for approval where appropriate;
(d) revising it if so requested by the judge, and
(e) providing any copies required for the Court of Appeal, instructing solicitors and lay client.

9.7.2. Accordingly, save in exceptional circumstances, there can be no justification for charging any additional fee for such work.

9.7.3. When required to attend on a later day to take a judgment not delivered at the end of the hearing, the advocate will, subject to the rules of the court, ordinarily be entitled to a further fee for such attendance. This note does not affect that entitlement.

10. Miscellaneous Directions

10.1. Citation of authority

10.1.1. When authority is cited, whether in written or oral submissions, the following practice should in general be followed. **PD–025**

10.1.2. If a case is reported in the official Law Reports published by the Incorporated Council of Law Reporting for England and Wales that report should be cited. These are the most authoritative reports; they contain a summary of argument; and they are the most readily available. If a case is not (or not yet) reported in the official Law Reports but is reported in the Weekly Law Reports or the All England Law Reports that report should be cited. If a case is not reported in any of these series of reports, a report in any of the specialist series of reports may be cited. Such reports may not be readily available: photostat copies of the leading authorities or the relevant parts of such authorities should be annexed to written submissions; and it is helpful if photostat copies of the frequently used series are made available in court. It is recognised that occasions arise when one report is fuller than another, or when there are discrepancies between reports. On such occasions, the practice outlined above need not be followed. It is always helpful if alternative references are given.

10.1.3. Where a reserved written judgment has not been reported, reference should be made to the official transcript (if this is available) and not the handed-down text of the judgment. If the judgment under appeal has been reported before the hearing and counsel wish to argue from the published report rather than from the official transcript, the court should be provided with photocopies of the report for the use of the judges in order that they may be able to annotate it as the argument proceeds.

10.1.4. Advocates are reminded that lists of authorities, including text which they wish to refer should be delivered to the Head Usher's office not later than 5.30 p.m. on the working day before the day when the hearing of the application or appeal is due to commence. Advocates should also seek confirmation that an adequate number of copies are available for the use of the court and, if this is not the case, should themselves provide an appropriate number of photocopies.

10.1.5. Where, as is often the case, one or other party chooses to provide photocopies of the principal authorities (including textbook extracts and academic articles) relied on, the benefit to the court is greatly enhanced if (i) a list of those authorities, and the photocopies, are lodged with the skeleton argument so that they can be used by the members of the court when preparing for the hearing; (ii) counsel liaise with each other so as to ensure, so far as possible, that the authorities provided are not duplicated. The photocopies need only include, for each law report, the headnote and the pages containing the particular passages relied on and, for each textbook and article, the title pages and the pages containing the particular passages relied on.

10.1.6. Permission to cite unreported cases will not usually be granted unless advocates are able to assure the court that the transcript in question contains a relevant statement of legal principle not found in reported authority and that the authority is not cited because of the phraseology used or as an illustration of the application of an established legal principle.

10.2. Hansard Extracts

10.2.1. *Application*—This Direction concerns both final and interlocutory hearings in which any party intends to refer to the reports of parliamentary proceedings as reported in the official reports of parliamentary proceedings as reported in the official reports of either House of Parliament, *Hansard.* No other report of parliamentary proceedings is to be cited.

10.2.2. *Documents to be serve*—Any party intending to refer to any extract from *Hansard* in support of any such argument as was permitted by the decisions in *Pepper v. Hart.* [1993] A.C. 593; [1992] 3 W.L.R. 1032, and *Pickstone v. Freemans plc* [1989] A.C. 66; [1988] CMLR 221, HL, or otherwise, must unless the judge otherwise directs, serve upon all other parties and the court copies of any such extract together with a brief summary of the argument intended to be based upon such report.

10.2.3. *Time for Service*—Unless the judge otherwise directs, service upon other parties to the proceedings and the court of the extract and summary of arguments referred to above is to be effected not less than five clear working days before the first day of the hearing. That applies whether or not there is a fixed date. Solicitors must keep themselves informed as to the state of the lists where no fixed date had been given.

10.2.4. *Methods of service*—A service on the court is to be effected by sending to the Court of Appeal, Civil Division, three copies to the Civil Appeals Office, Case Support Section, Room E307, Royal Courts of Justice, Strand, London WC2A 2LL.

10.2.5. *Failure to serve*—If any party fails to comply with this Practice Direction the court might make such order, relating to costs and otherwise, as is in all the circumstances appropriate.

10.3. Judicial Review, renewal of application for permission to apply.

10.3.1. A refusal in a non-criminal cause or matter by a Divisional Court of the Queen's Bench Division or by a single judge for permission to apply for judicial review is renewable to the Court of Appeal within 7 days of the decision. **PD–026**

10.3.2. If, following a refusal by the Divisional Court or a single judge, the Court of Appeal grants permission to apply for judicial review, the substantive application should be made to the Divisional Court unless the Court of Appeal otherwise orders. The Court of Appeal will not normally so order unless the court below is bound by authority or for some other reason an appeal to the Court of Appeal is inevitable.

10.3.3. Where the Court of Appeal grants a renewed application for permission to apply for judicial review, except where the Court of Appeal reserves the application to itself, the application should be set down in the Crown Office list to be heard by a single judge, unless a judge nominated to try cases in that list directs that the application is to be heard by a Divisional Court of the Queen's Bench Division.

10.4. Dismissal of appeals/applications by consent

10.4.1. Where an appellant is of full legal capacity and does not desire to prosecute an appeal, he may present a request signed by his solicitor stating that he is of full legal capacity and asking to have the appeal dismissed, in which case (subject to the request being initialled by a judge of the court or by the master) the appeal will be dismissed and struck out of the list, and an order will, if necessary, be drawn up directing payment of the costs by the appellant, such costs to be assessed in case the parties differ. Where the parties are of full legal capacity and a settlement has been reached disposing of the appeal, they may present a request signed by the solicitors for all parties to the appeal, stating that they are of full legal capacity, including the terms of settlement and asking that the appeal be dismissed by consent, in which case (subject to the request being initialled by a judge of the court or by the master) the appeal will be dismissed and struck out of the list and an order will, if necessary, be drawn up.

10.4.2. If the appellant desires to have the appeal dismissed without costs, his request must be accompanied by a consent signed by the respondents' solicitors stating that the respondents are of full legal capacity and consent to the dismissal of the appeal without costs, in which case (subject to the request being initialled by a judge of the court or by the master) the appeal will be dismissed and struck out of the list.

10.4.3. Where any party has no solicitor on the record, any such request or consent must be signed by him personally. All other applications as to the dismissal of an appeal and all applications for an order by consent reversing or varying the order under appeal will be placed in the list and dealt with in court.

10.4.4. Forms of request appear at **Annex I**.

10.5. Allowing appeals or applications by consent

10.5.1. In cases where parties who are of full legal capacity seek an order to allow the appeal by consent, a copy of the proposed consent order signed by the parties' solicitors (and stating that the parties are of full legal capacity), together with a document setting out the relevant history of the proceedings and the matters relied on as justifying the proposed order, should be sent to the master who will refer them to a Lord Justice for consideration. He or she will either make the order or direct that it should be referred to two Lords Justices for hearing in open court.

10.6. Structured Settlements and consent orders involving a party under a disability

10.6.1. The following guidance applies in respect of settlements which require the court's approval.

10.6.2. The types of case concerned are: (1) consent orders relating to appeals and applications where one of the parties is a child or a patient; and (2) structured settlements which are agreed upon at the Court of Appeal stage.

10.7. Procedure

PD–027 **10.7.1.** The following procedure should be adopted;

(a) In cases where a consent order needs approval because one of the parties is a child a copy of the proposed order signed by the parties' solicitors should be sent to the master, together with an opinion from the advocate acting on behalf of the child. If on consideration of the documents the court considers that the consent order should be approved, the matter will be listed, but without any party being represented, and the order will be made in open court (See *Hadfield v. Knowles* [1996] 1 WLR 1003).

(b) Where a party is a patient and the case is not covered by RSC, Ord. 59, r.23, the same procedure will be adopted, but the documents filed should also include any relevant reports prepared for the Court of Protection and a document evidencing formal approval by that court where required.

(c) The same procedure should be followed in the case of a structured settlement which has been negotiated in a case which is under appeal and the documents filed should include those which would be required in the case of a structured settlement dealt with at first instance.

10.7.2. If, in any of those categories of case, the court requires further documents before deciding whether to approve the order or settlement, the master or a member of his staff will notify the solicitors of what is required. In future the court will only list any such case for mention at a hearing to be attended by the parties' advocates if the court considers that there are problems about the proposed order or settlement which cannot be satisfactorily resolved in any other way or that, for some other special reason, such a hearing is necessary or desirable.

10.8. Sittings of Court of Appeal in vacation

10.8.1. The Court of Appeal will sit in vacation on such days as the Master of the Rolls may direct and may hear such appeals or applications as the court may direct. Details of the number of courts sitting in August and September will be published each year, normally before Easter.

10.9. Solicitor's rights of audience

10.9.1. In addition to the cases in which solicitors already have rights of audience in the Supreme Court, and without prejudice to the discretion of a judge to allow a solicitor to represent his client in open court in an emergency, a solicitor may appear in the Supreme Court in formal or unopposed proceedings, that is to say those proceedings where (a) by reason of agreement between the parties there is unlikely to be any argument and (b) the court will not be called on to exercise a discretion.

10.9.2. A solicitor may also represent his client in the Supreme Court when judgment is delivered in open court following a hearing in private at which that solicitor conducted the case for his client.

10.10. Admiralty Appeals: Assessors

10.10.1. The relevant practice direction has not been consolidated and will be found at [1965] 1 WLR 853.

10.11. Use of unofficial tape recorders in court

10.11.1. Section 9 of the Contempt of Court Act 1981 contains provisions governing the unofficial use of tape recorders in court. The relevant practice direction has not been consolidated but will be found at [1981] 1 WLR 1526.

11. Alternative Dispute Resolution (ADR)

11.1.1. A *pro bono* scheme commenced in 1997. The scheme has to take into account the fact that cases which have already been tried at first instance raise different issues, so far as ADR is concerned, to cases which have yet to be tried. PD-028

11.1.2. The scheme has recently been refined. Now in appropriate cases, as soon as an appeal set down with the Civil Appeals Office, a letter of invitation to consider ADR, signed by the Master of the Rolls, is sent to the parties' solicitors. The letter encloses an explanatory leaflet and a response form. A member of staff is available to answer queries, provide general information and help with specific cases.

11.1.3. The supervising Lords Justices responsible for particular categories of work are vigilant in their case management for those cases that appear suitable for referral to ADR. Recently a very substantial commercial appeal was compromised as result of a referral by the supervising Lord Justice. Equally, presiding Lords Justices are able to propose a referral to ADR at the determination of appeals which otherwise will lead to a re-hearing or the issue of further proceedings.

11.1.4. Legal aid covers the costs of ADR for an assisted party.

11.1.5. Further information is available from the Civil Appeals Office, Royal Courts of Justice, Strand, London, WC2A 2LL (tel. 0171 936 6486)].

12. Supply of Documents from Civil Appeals Office Files

12.1.1. The Civil Procedure Rules CPR rule 5.4 makes general provision for the supply of documents from court records. This note sets out the practice of the Court of Appeal (Civil Division). Requests must usually be made in writing.

12.1.2. The person making the request should,

(a) cite the Court of Appeal reference number;

(b) explain what efforts have been made to obtain the document from another party to the appeal and state what reasons have been given by that other party for refusing to supply a copy;

(c) enclose the prescribed fee.

12.1.3. The master may, in the first instance, determine a request without a hearing. He may also, instead of giving permission or supplying the document, give directions regarding the supply of the document by another person. He may also refer the application to a Lord Justice or the court.

12.1.4. Requests to see skeleton arguments may alternatively be made orally to the associate in at the time of the hearing in open court.

12.1.5. Below, guidance is set out in tabular form:

PD–029

INFORMATION	CAN THE INFORMATION BE RELEASED?
Listing of case	Yes, but only after 1500 hrs the day before the hearing when the information is made public. Otherwise leave of the court is required. The Court list comprises the name and number of the case. Apply to the Listing Office.
From which court the appeal came	Yes. Apply to the case section.
Notice of Appeal	At the discretion of the court. In general the Court will grant requests to see notices of appeal which have been served on the respondent, and respondent's notices after they have been served on the appellant. Notices of appeal relating to cases involving children will not normally be disclosed nor other notices of appeal which assert confidentiality or the existence of a reporting restriction.
Skeleton arguments	Yes, available in court from Court clerk. Representatives of the media or members of the public can read the skeleton arguments in the courtroom, but may not take copies away. Skeleton arguments cannot be read without the permission of the Court in any cases involving minor children or any other cases where the Court has imposed a reporting restriction.
Files, bundles and computer records	Documents on the Court file (other than skeleton arguments, see above) cannot be shown to anyone without the leave of the Court.
Court orders given or made in open court	Yes. Refer to Associates.
Judgment	Yes. Refer to official Shorthandwriters or Supreme Court Library.

13. Hearings in Private

13.1. Hearings in private

13.1.1. Exceptional circumstances will have to be shown before the court will be prepared to hear an application or appeal in private. Where the advocate forms the view that it is necessary, in the interests of justice, that a preliminary application or an appeal should be heard in private, he or she should approach the master indicating his or her view. The reasons should be put into writing, signed by the advocate and handed to the master. In so doing, it should be understood that the advocate is expressing his personal professional view and is not making a submission on behalf of his client. This will enable the court to make a preliminary decision as to whether the application should initially be made in private or in open court. This procedure will avoid the problem which arises where the very reasons which justify a hearing in private must themselves be put forward in private if they are to be put forward at all. PD–030

14. References to the European Court of Justice

14.1. References to the European Court of Justice by the Court of Appeal and the High Court under Article 177 of the EC Treaty

14.1.1. Before making a reference to the European Court of Justice under Article 77 of the EC Treaty the Court of Appeal should pay close attention to (a) the terms of that Article, (b) Order 114 of the Rules of the Supreme Court and (c) Practice Form 109 (at para. 1A–114 of Volume 2 of the Supreme Court Practice 1999). Close attention should also be paid to the Guidance of the European Court of Justice on References by National Courts for Preliminary Rulings: this is set out in paragraph 14.2. below. PD–031

14.1.2. It is the responsibility of the Court of Appeal, not the parties, to settle the terms of the reference. This should identify as clearly, succinctly and simply as the nature of the case permits the question to which the British court seeks an answer. It is very desirable that language should be used which lends itself readily to translation.

14.1.3. The referring court should, in a single document scheduled to the order:

(a) identify the parties and summarise the nature and history of the proceedings;

(b) summarise the salient facts, indicating whether these are proved or admitted or assumed;

(c) make reference to the rules of national law (substantive and procedural) relevant to the dispute;

(d) summarise the contentions of the parties so far as relevant;

(e) explain why a ruling of the European Court is sought, identifying the EC provisions whose effect is in issue;

(f) formulate, without avoidable complexity, the question(s) to which an answer is requested.

14.1.4. Where the document is in the form of a judgment, as will often be convenient, passages which are not relevant to the reference should be omitted from the text scheduled to the order. Incorporation of appendices, annexes or enclosures as part of the document should be avoided, unless the relevant passages lend themselves readily to translation and are clearly identified.

14.1.5. The referring court should ensure that the order of reference, when finalised, is promptly passed to the Senior Master of the Queen's Bench Division so that it may be transmitted to Luxembourg without avoidable delay. The title of the referring court should be Court of Appeal (Civil Division) (England & Wales).

14.2. Guidance of the European Court of Justice on References by National Courts for Preliminary Rulings

14.2.1. The development of the Community legal order is largely the result of cooperation between the Court of Justice of the European Communities and national courts and tribunals through the preliminary procedure under Article 177 E.C. and the corresponding provisions of the ECSC and Euratom treaties. In order to make this co-operation more effective, and so enable the Court of Justice better to meet the requirements of national courts by providing helpful answers to preliminary questions, this Note for Guidance is addressed to all interested parties, in particular to all national courts and tribunals. It must be emphasised that the Note is for guidance only and has no binding or interpretative effect in relation to the provisions governing the preliminary ruling procedure. It merely contains practical information which, in the light of experience in applying preliminary ruling procedure, may help to prevent the kind of difficulties which the Court has sometimes encountered.

14.2.2. Any court or tribunal of a Member State may ask the Court of Justice to interpret a rule of Community law, whether contained in the Treaties or in acts of secondary law, if it considers that this is necessary for it to give judgment in a case pending before it.

14.2.3. Courts or tribunals against whose decisions there is no judicial remedy under national law must refer questions of interpretation arising before them to the Court of Justice, unless the Court has already ruled on the point or unless the correct application of the rule of Community law is obvious.

14.2.4. The Court of Justice has jurisdiction to rule on the validity of acts of the Community institutions. National courts or tribunals may reject a plea challenging the validity of such an act. But where a national court (even one whose decision is still subject to appeal) intends to question the validity of a Community act, it must refer that question to the Court of Justice.

14.2.5. Where, however, a national court or tribunal has serious doubts about the validity of a Community act on which a national measure is based, it may, in exceptional cases, temporarily suspend application of the latter measure or grant other interim relief with respect to it. It must then refer the question of validity to the Court of Justice, stating the reasons for which it considers that the Community act is not valid.

14.2.6. Questions referred for a preliminary ruling must be limited to the interpretation or validity of a provision of Community law, since the Court of Justice does not have jurisdiction to interpret national law or assess its validity. It is for the referring court or tribunal to apply the relevant rule of Community law in the specific case pending before it.

14.2.7. The order of the national court or tribunal referring a question to the Court of Justice for a preliminary ruling may be in any form allowed by national procedural law. Reference of a question or questions to the Court of Justice generally involves stay of the national proceedings until the Court has given its ruling, but the decision to stay proceedings is one which it is for the national court alone to take in accordance with its own national law.

14.2.8. The order of reference containing the question or questions referred to the Court will have to be translated by the Court's translators into the other official languages of the Community. Questions concerning the interpretation or validity of Community law are frequently of general interest and the Member States and Community institutions are entitled to submit observations. It is therefore desirable that the reference should be drafted as clearly and precisely as possible.

14.2.9. The order for reference should contain a statement of reasons which is succinct but sufficiently complete to give the Court, and those to whom it must be notified (the Member States, the Commission and in certain cases the Council and the European Parliament), a clear understanding of the factual and legal context of the main proceedings.

14.2.10. In particular, it should include: PD–032

—a statement of the facts which are essential to a full understanding of the legal significance of the main proceedings;

—an exposition of the national law which may be applicable;

—a statement of the reasons which have prompted the national court to refer the question or questions to the Court of Justice; and

—where appropriate, a summary of the arguments of the parties.

14.2.11. The aim should be to put the Court of Justice in a position to give the national court an answer which will be of assistance to it.

14.2.12. The order for reference should also be accompanied by copies of any documents needed for a proper understanding of the case, especially the text of the applicable national provisions. However, as the case-file or documents annexed to the order for reference are not always translated in full into the other official languages of the Community, the national court should ensure that the order for reference itself includes all the relevant information.

14.2.13. A national court or tribunal may refer a question to the Court of Justice as soon as it finds that a ruling on the point or points of interpretation or validity is necessary to enable it to give judgment. It must be stressed, however, that it is not for the Court of Justice to decide issues of fact or to resolve disputes as to the interpretation or application of rules of national law. It is therefore desirable that a decision to refer should not be taken until the national proceedings have reached a stage where the national court is able to define, if only as a working hypothesis, the factual and legal context of the question; on any view, the administration of justice is likely to be best served if the reference is not made until both sides have been heard.

14.2.14. The order for reference and the relevant documents should be sent by the national court directly to the Court of Justice, by registered post, addressed to:

The Registry
Court of Justice of the European Communities
Bell L2925, Luxembourg
(352) 43031.

14.2.15. The Court Registry will remain in contact with the national court until judgment is given, and will send copies of the various documents (written observations, Report for the Hearing, Opinion of the Advocate General). The Court will also send its judgment to the national court. The Court would appreciate being informed about the application of its judgment in the national proceedings and being sent a copy of the national court's final decision.

14.2.16. Proceedings for a preliminary ruling before the Court of Justice are free of charge. The Court does not rule on costs.

Annexes
Annex A

Individual Practice Directions for Court of Appeal (Civil Division)

PD–033 (in chronological order)

1. (1926) W.N. 308 statutory orders private or local Acts should be supplied to the Court
2. Practice Direction (1938) WN 89
3. Practice Direction (CA: Dismissal of Appeal) (1983) 1 WLR 85
4. Practice Direction; Contents of Notice of Appeal [1953] 2 All ER 1510, [1953] 1 WLR 1503, 30/11/53
6. Practice Note; Application for Judicial Review substantive hearings [1956] 1 WLR 430
7. Transcripts of Court of Appeal Judgments [1978] 1 WLR 600 24/2/78
8. Use of unofficial tape recorders in court [1981] 3 All ER 848 19/11/81
9. Practice Note [1982] 3 All ER 376 CA practice and procedure
10. (Practice Direction: Judicial Review: Appeals) Lane LCJ, Donaldson MR [1982] 1 WLR 1375, 2/11/82
11. Practice Direction: Judicial Review: Appeals [1990] 1 All ER 128
12. Practice Note; Hearing of Anton Piller appeals in camera [1982] 3 All ER 924 5/11/82
13. Practice Note: Skeleton arguments [1983] 2 All ER 34 12/4/83
14. Practice Note: Affidavits, exhibits and documents [1983] 3 All ER 33 21/7/83
15. Practice Note: Estimate of length of hearing [1983] 3 All ER 544 28/10/83
16. Practice Direction (Court of Appeal: Applications to a single Judge) [1985] 1 WLR 739
17. Practice Note: Skeleton arguments [1985] 3 All ER 384 17/10/85
18. Practice Direction: Solicitor's rights of Audience [1986] 2 All ER 226 9/5/86
19. Practice Note: Appeal where judgment under appeal has been reported [1987] 1 All ER 928 13/3/87
20. September sittings in CA (CA sittings in the Long Vacation) (1987) 1 All ER 1067
21. Mode of Address of Lady Justice Butler-Sloss, Palmer v Palmer, Times, June 15,1988
22. Practice Note: Short Warned List [1989] 1 All ER 891 1/3/89
23. Practice Direction (QBD Service of Documents) [1985]
24. (Practice Statement: Fee note for Judgment) (1989) The Times, May 12
25. Practice Direction: Receiving and processing appeals and applications [1990] 3 All ER 981 24/10/90
26. PD (Appeals: Short Warned Lists; counsel's duty where appointments clash) (No.2) [1992] 1 WLR 485
27. Counsel's fee notes of judgments PN [1994] 1 All ER 96,13/12/93
28. Reserved judgments ON [1995] 3 All ER 247 22/6/95
29. PD (Citation of Authority) June 23,1995 (1995) 1 WLR 1096
30. July 26,1995 Bingham MR [1995] 1 WLR 1188. Practice Statement (CA: procedural changes) WB 59/9/36
31. Bingham MR on CA Procedure (Previous consolidation)
32. Citation of authorities PN [1996] 3 All ER 382
33. Practice Note sub nom *Hadfteld v. Knowles* [1996] 1 WLR 1003 (structured settlements and consent orders involving party under disability) 16/5/96
34. May 12, 1997 [1997] 1 WLR 1013 CA: Amended Procedure WB 59/9/66

35. Orders for expedited hearings, Unilever v Chefaro Proprietaries [1995] 1 WLR 243
36. Practice Registrar (unreported PN) 5/97
37. November 5, 1997 [1997] 1 WLR 1535 (CA procedure changes) (Skeleton Arguments and procedural changes) WB 59/9/35
38. November 7, 1997 modifies PD on skeletons
39. (Practice Note) [1997] 1 WLR 1538 on grounds for leave to App. 1084 WB 59/14/19
40. Practice Statement (Supreme Court; judgments) 22/4/98, [1998] 1 WLR 825 Bingham LCJ
41. Practice Statement (Supreme Court: judgments) (No.2) 2/12/98 Times 2 December 1998
42. Hear-by dates; revised table of dates 10/11/98
43. 11/98 Lord Woolf MR's PD on leave to appeal to CA.
44. Guidance on applications to the European Court of Justice under Article 177 EC 1/99.

Annex B

PD–034 Dear ,

Re:

The application for permission to appeal in this case has been assigned to a Lord Justice (a judge of the Court of Appeal), who has considered the papers filed in support of the application. On the basis of the information provided, the Lord Justice is minded to refuse me application for the reasons attached to this letter.

You have the right to seek an oral hearing of the application. The advocate or party appearing at an oral hearing would need to be prepared to deal with the reasons attached to this letter and to answer any further questions that may be asked about the application. The assigned Lord Justice has directed that any oral hearing shall be before a single Lord Justice/two Lords Justices.

Wherever possible the assigned Lord Justice will conduct the oral hearing, either sitting alone or with another Lord Justice as the case may be. The oral hearing will be conducted in public in open court, unless the Court directs otherwise.

If you wish to have an oral hearing, you must notify this Office in writing within 14 days of receiving this letter. In cases where a hearing before two Lords Justices has been directed a second set of the application bundle(s) must be lodged with that notification. If the Office has not received such notification within the 14 day time limit, the application will be dealt with on the basis of the information already submitted and without any further participation by you. It will be dealt with in open court, and you will be sent an order giving the Court's decision.

Where an applicant is legally aided, and the single Lord Justice is minded to refuse the application on the papers, the applicant's solicitor must send to the relevant Legal Aid Office a copy of this letter and its attachment as soon as they have been received. The Court will require confirmation that this has been done in any case where an application for permission to appeal proceeds to an oral hearing before the Court on legal aid.

Unrepresented litigants are advised that help with their application may be available from the Citizens' Advice Bureau at the Royal Courts of Justice.

Yours faithfully,

Listing Office

Enc.

Annex C

In the Court Application for Permission to Appeal to the Court of Appeal (Civil Division)

PD–035

Title of proceedings | Claim

CA Ref

Heard/tried before (insert name of Judge): | Court no.

Nature of hearing:

Date of hearing/judgment

Results of hearing (attach copy of order):

Claimant/Defendant's application for permission to appeal* | Allowed/ Refused*

Reasons for decision (*to be completed by the Judge*):

Judge's signature:

Note to the Applicant:

When completed, this form should be filed in the Civil Appeals Office on a renewed application for permission to appeal or when setting down an appeal.

*Delete as appropriate

Annex D

Current supervising Lords Justices

PD–036

Butler-Sloss LJ and Thorpe LJ	Family Appeals
Morritt LJ and Chadwick LJ	Appeals from the Chancery Division
Pill LJ	Appeals from the Lands Tribunal and cases involving issues relating to planning, highways, footpaths or the Countryside Act 1968
Aldous LJ	Patent appeals
Schiemann LJ	Public law appeals (including appeals from the Immigration Appeal Tribunal) and cases involving European Community law
Brooke LJ and Mantell LJ	Appeals from the county courts (other than family cases)
May LJ	Appeals from the Queen's Bench Division and appeals relating to civil procedure rules
Clarke LJ	Appeals from the Commercial court
Mummery LJ	Appeals from tribunals (other than the Immigration Appeal Tribunal and the Lands Tribunal)

Annex E

Notice of appeal

IN THE COURT OF APPEAL Lower Court reference (Claim No.) PD–037

ON APPEAL FROM THE
[HIGH COURT OF JUSTICE
(CHANCERY or QUEEN'S BENCH or FAMILY) DIVISION
[DIVISIONAL COURT]] [or]

____________________ COUNTY COURT

BETWEEN:

____________________ Claimant (Plaintiff)/Petitioner

and

____________________ Defendant/Respondent

TAKE NOTICE that the __________ will apply to the Court of Appeal to appeal from the judgment/order of the Honourable Mr/Mrs Justice/His/Her Honour Judge __________ made on the ______ day of __________ 19____. By that order the Judge ordered that

____

____

____

The [Claimant] (Plaintiff) [Defendant] proposes to ask the Court of Appeal FOR AN ORDER that the judgment/order be set aside [and that judgment be entered in the above-mentioned claim for the

____

____

____

____

or alternatively that a new trial may be ordered] AND FOR AN ORDER that the ______ be ordered (adjudged) to pay to the __________ his/her costs of this appeal and the costs of the proceedings in the court below

AND FURTHER TAKE NOTICE that the grounds of this appeal are that

1 ____________________

____

2 ____________________

____

AND FURTHER TAKE NOTICE that the above named __________ proposes that this appeal be assigned to the [(Chancery or Queen's Bench or Family] Division or County Courts] Final/Interlocutory List

I CERTIFY THAT THIS CLAIM IS CURRENTLY ALLOCATED TO THE SMALL CLAIMS/ FAST/MULTI-TRACK IN THE __________ COURT.

DATED this ________ day of __________ 19

(SIGNED) ____________________

(Address) ____________________

____

____

____

(Telephone No.) ______________________________

(Reference No.) ______________________________

TO the above named

and to Messrs ____________________ his/her Solicitors

(Address) ______________________________

____

____

____

(Solicitor's Reference) ____________________

[and to the District Judge of the ______________________________ County Court]

No notice as to the date on which this appeal will be in the list of hearing will be given: it is the duty of solicitors to keep themselves informed as to the state of the lists. A Respondent intending to appeal in person should inform the Civil Appeals Office, Room E330, Royal Courts of Justice, Strand, London WC2A 2LL, of that fact and give his address; if he does so he will be notified to the address given of the date when the appeal is expected to be heard.

I certify that a true copy of this notice was served on the ______________________________'s solicitors on the __________ day of __________ 19______ [and that a true copy of this notice was served on(upon) the District Judge of the ____________________ County Court on the ____________________ day of 19__________]

(Signed)

IN THE COURT OF APPEAL

ON APPEAL FROM THE
[HIGH COURT OF JUSTICE
(CHANCERY or QUEEN'S BENCH or
FAMILY) DIVISION
[DIVISIONAL COURT]] [or]

____________________ COUNTY COURT

Claimant
(Plaintiff)/Petitioner

v.

Defendant/Respondent

____

Notice of Appeal

____

(Address) ____________________

____

____

____

(Telephone No.) ____________________

Annex F

List of Court Lists PD–038

County Courts:
Final List; Interlocutory List;
Final List (Admiralty); Interlocutory List (Admiralty);

Final List (Family); Interlocutory List (Family)
Chancery Division:
Final List; Interlocutory List;
Final List (Bankruptcy); Interlocutory List (Bankruptcy);
Final List (Patents); Interlocutory List (Patents);
Final List (Revenue); Interlocutory List (Revenue)

Employment Appeal Tribunal:
Final List; Interlocutory List

Family Division:
Final List; Interlocutory List

Queen's Bench Division:
Final List; Interlocutory List;
Final List (Admiralty); Interlocutory List (Admiralty);
Final List (Commercial); Interlocutory List (Commercial);
Final List (Crown Office and Divisional Court);
Interlocutory List (Crown Office and Divisional Court)

Appeal Tribunals:
Final List (Lands Tribunal); Interlocutory List (Lands Tribunal);
Final List (Other tribunals); Interlocutory List (other tribunals);
Final List (Social Security Conmissioners);
Interlocutory List, (Social Security Commissioners)]
Final List (Immigration Appeal Tribunal)

Annex G(1)

Application notice

PD–039 IN THE COURT OF APPEAL   Lower Court reference (Claim No.)

ON APPEAL FROM THE
[HIGH COURT OF JUSTICE
(CHANCERY or QUEEN'S BENCH or FAMILY) DIVISION
[DIVISIONAL COURT]] [or]

______________________________ COUNTY COURT

BETWEEN:

______________________________ Claimant (Plaintiff)/Petitioner

and

______________________________ Defendant/Respondent

Section A

[*Complete this section in all cases*]

TAKE NOTICE that the Claimant (Plaintiff)/Defendant (in person) will apply to the Court of Appeal for an order that ______________________________

____

____

____

AND FOR AN ORDER that (*set out costs order applied for*) ______________________________

____

AND FURTHER TAKE NOTICE that the application will be heard at the Royal Courts of Justice, Strand, London WC2A 2LL on a date and at a time to be notified by the Civil Appeals Office

____

Section B

I(We) wish to rely on the following evidence in support of this application (*here set out the reasons why the application should be granted*) ______________________________

____

____

____

____

____

____

____

____

____

STATEMENT OF TRUTH

*(I believe) (The applicant believes) that the facts stated above are true

**delete as appropriate*

Signed ______________________________   Position or office held ______________________________

(Applicant) ('s Solicitor) ('s litigation friend)

Date   (if signing on behalf of firm or company)

Section C
[*Complete this section in all cases*]

I CERTIFY THAT THIS CLAIM IS CURRENTLY ALLOCATED TO THE SMALL CLAIMS/FAST/MULTI-TRACK IN THE ______________________________ COURT.

DATED this ______________ day of ______________ 19

(SIGNED) ______________________________

(Address) ______________________________

____

____

(Telephone No.) ______________________________

(Reference No.) ______________________________

TO: Messrs ______________________________

Solicitors for the Claimant (Plaintiff)/Defendant/Petitioner/Respondent whose address for service is:

(Address) ______________________________

____

____

____

(Solicitor's Reference) ______________________________

Annex G(2)

Application notice for permission to appeal

PD–040

(AND A STAY OF EXECUTION)

IN THE COURT OF APPEAL   Lower Court reference (Claim No.)

ON APPEAL FROM THE
[HIGH COURT OF JUSTICE
(CHANCERY or QUEEN'S BENCH or FAMILY) DIVISION
[DIVISIONAL COURT]] [or]

______________________________ COUNTY COURT

BETWEEN:

______________________________ Claimant (Plaintiff)/Petitioner

and

______________________________ Defendant/Respondent

Section A

[*Complete this section in all cases*]

_____ TAKE NOTICE that the Claimant (Plaintiff)/Defendant/Petitioner/Respondent (in person) will apply to the Court of Appeal for an order that he/she be granted permission to appeal from the order of ____________________

dated 19_____ (and that, if permission is granted, execution of the said order should be stayed pending the hearing of the Claimant's (Plaintiff's)/Defendant's/Petitioner's/Respondent's appeal).

AND FURTHER TAKE NOTICE that the grounds of the proposed appeal are as set out in the draft Notice of Appeal attached

Section B

[*To be completed only in cases where the application for permission to appeal is being made after the time for appealing has expired or where a stay of execution is applied for*]

I(We) wish to rely on the following evidence in support of this application (*here set out the reasons why the application was not made before the expiry of the time for appealing and/or why a stay of execution should be granted*)

STATEMENT OF TRUTH

*(I believe) (The applicant believes) that the facts stated above are true

**delete as appropriate*

Signed ______________________ Position or Office held ______________________

(Applicant) ('s Solicitor) ('s litigation friend) (if signing on behalf of firm or company)

Date

Section C

[*Complete this section in all cases*]

I CERTIFY THAT THIS CLAIM IS CURRENTLY ALLOCATED TO THE SMALL CLAIMS/ FAST/MULTI-TRACK IN THE ______________________ COURT.

DATED this ____________ day of ____________ 19

(SIGNED) ______________________

(Address) ______________________

____

____

(Telephone No.) ______________________

(Reference No.) ______________________

TO: Messrs ______________________

Solicitors for the Claimant (Plaintiff)/Defendant/Petitioner/Respondent whose address for service is:

(Address) ______________________

____

____

____

(Solicitor's Reference) ______________________

(Solicitor's Reference) ______________________

Annex H

Hear-by Dates

PD–041 The current Hear-by Dates are set out in the table below. They apply to all cases entered in the Court's records on or after 1 December 1998.

	TYPE OF CASE	HEAR-BY DATE
Family	Child cases	3 months
	Financial and other	6 months
Crown Office Cases and Immigration appeals	Immigration Appeals and Crown Office Interlocutory	3 months
	Other Crown Office final orders	9 months
High Court	Order 14	3 months
	Other interlocutory orders*	5 months
	Bankruptcy and Directors' Disqualification cases	5 months
	Limitation as a preliminary issue in personal injury cases	5 months
	All other preliminary issues	8 months
	Personal injury final orders	12 months
	Other final orders	15 months
County Court	Interlocutory orders	4 months
	Possession	4 months
	All preliminary issues	4 months
	Personal injury final orders	8 months
	Other final orders	12 months
Tribunals(other than immigration appeals)		12 months

It should be noted that expedition continues to be available in accordance with *Unilever v. Chefaro Ltd (Practice Note) (CA)* [1995] 1 WLR 246. In addition, from 16 November 1998 very serious or distressing personal injury cases will be treated as being in the category of urgent appeals set out in that *Practice Note.*

[1] Includes appeals confined to RSC Ord. 14A. For appeals referring to Ord. 14A and another issue, the Hear-by Date will be determined by the other issue.

Annex I(1)

Request for dismissal of an appeal

PLEASE NOTE: SECTION A IS TO BE COMPLETED WHERE THERE IS NO RESPONDENT'S NOTICE AND THE APPEAL IS BEING DISMISSED WITH COSTS; IN THAT CASE, ONLY THE APPELLANT'S SOLICITOR (OR THE APPELLANT, IF ACTING IN PERSON) NEED SIGN. **PD–042**

IN ALL OTHER CASES SECTION B MUST BE COMPLETED AND IT MUST BE SIGNED BY THE SOLICITORS FOR ALL PARTIES (AND BY ANY PARTY ACTING IN PERSON).

IN THE COURT OF APPEAL Appeal No

ON APPEAL FROM

BETWEEN:

Claimant
(Plaintiff)/Appellant
Petitioner/Respondent

and

Defendant/Appellant
Respondent/Respondent

Section A

WE, the solicitors* for the above-named Appellant, who is of full legal capacity, REQUEST the dismissal of the appeal in the above matter with costs.

DATED this day of 19

(Signed) ______________________
*(Solicitor for Appellant)

Section B

WE, the solicitors* for the above-named Respondent and Appellant, who are of full legal capacity, REQUEST the dismissal of the appeal [*and respondent's notice*]† in the above matter with no order as to costs [*or specify other costs order required*].

DATED this day of 19

(Signed) ______________________
*(Solicitor for Appellant)

(Signed) ______________________
*(Solicitor for Respondent)

**If any party is acting in person, please modify the wording as appropriate.*
†*Delete where not applicable.*

Annex I(2)

General form of request for dismissal of an application

PD–043 PLEASE NOTE: SECTION A IS TO BE COMPLETED WHERE THE APPLICATION IS BEING DISMISSED WITH COSTS; IN THAT CASE, ONLY THE APPLICANT'S SOLICITOR (OR THE APPLICANT, IF ACTING IN PERSON) NEED SIGN.

IN ALL OTHER CASES SECTION B MUST BE COMPLETED AND IT MUST BE SIGNED BY THE SOLICITORS FOR ALL PARTIES (AND BY ANY PARTY ACTING IN PERSON).

IN THE COURT OF APPEAL Application No

ON APPEAL FROM

BETWEEN:

Claimant
(Plaintiff)/Appellant
Petitioner/Respondent

and

Defendant/Applicant
Respondent/Respondent

Section A

WE, the solicitors* for the above-named Applicant, who is of full legal capacity, REQUEST the dismissal of the application in the above matter with costs.

DATED this day of 19

(Signed) ______________________
*(Solicitor for Applicant)

Section B

WE, the solicitors* for the above-named Respondent and Applicant, who are of full legal capacity, REQUEST the dismissal the application in the above matter with no order as to costs [*or specify other costs order required*].

DATED this day of 19

(Signed) ______________________
*(Solicitor for Applicant)

(Signed) ______________________
*(Solicitor for Respondent)

**If any party is acting in person, please modify the wording as appropriate.*

Annex I(3)

Request for a dismissal of an application which has not been served on any other party

PD–044

THIS FORM IS FOR USE ONLY FOR AN APPLICATION
WHICH HAS NOT BEEN SERVED ON ANY OTHER PARTY

IN THE COURT OF APPEAL Application No

ON APPEAL FROM

BETWEEN:

Claimant
(Plaintiff)/Applicant
Petitioner/Respondent

and

Defendant/Applicant

WE, the solicitors* for the above-named Applicant, who is of full legal capacity,

(1) CERTIFY that the applicant in the above matter has not been served on any other party and

(2) REQUEST the dismissal of the said application with no order for costs.

DATED this day of 19

(Signed) ______________________________
*(Solicitor for Applicant)

**If any party is acting in person, please modify the wording as appropriate.*

PRACTICE DIRECTION INSOLVENCY PROCEEDINGS

Part One

1. General

PD–045 **1.1** In this Practice Direction:

(1) "The Act" means the Insolvency Act 1986;

(2) "The Insolvency Rules" means the rules for the time being in force and made under s.411 and s.412 of the Act in relation to insolvency proceedings;

(3) "CPR" means the Civil Procedure Rules and "CPR" followed by a Part or rule by number means the Part or rule with that number in those Rules;

(4) "RSC" followed by an Order by number means the Order with that number set out in Schedule 1 to the CPR;

(5) "Insolvency proceedings" means any proceedings under the Act, the Insolvency Rules, the Administration of Insolvent Estates of Deceased Persons Order 1986 (S.I. 1986 No. 1999), the Insolvent Partnerships Order 1986 (S.I. 1986 No. 2124) or the Insolvent Partnerships Order 1994 (S.I. 1994 No. 2421).

1.2 This Practice Direction shall come into effect on 26th April 1999 and shall replace all previous Practice Notes and Practice Directions relating to insolvency proceedings.

1.3 Except where the Insolvency Rules otherwise provide, service of documents in insolvency proceedings in the High Court will be the responsibility of the parties and will not be undertaken by the court.

1.4 Where CPR Part 2.4 provides for the court to perform any act, that act may be performed by a Registrar in Bankruptcy for the purpose of insolvency proceedings in the High Court.

1.5 A writ of execution to enforce any order made in insolvency proceedings in the High Court may be issued on the authority of a Registrar.

Part Two

Companies

2. Advertisement of winding up petition

PD–046 **2.1** Insolvency Rule 4.11(2)(b) is mandatory, and designed to ensure that the class remedy of winding up by the court is made available to all creditors, and is not used as a means of putting pressure on the company to pay the petitioner's debt. Failure to comply with the rule, without good reason accepted by the court, may lead to the summary dismissal of the petition on the return date (Insolvency Rule 4.11(5)). If the court, in its discretion, grants an adjournment, this will be on condition that the petition is advertised in due time for the adjourned hearing. No further adjournment for the purpose of advertisement will normally be granted.

2.2 Copies of every advertisement published in connection with a winding up petition must be lodged with the Court as soon as possible after publication and in any event not later than the day specified in Insolvency Rule 4.14 of the Insolvency Rules 1986. This direction applies even if the advertisement is defective in any way (e.g. is published at a date not in accordance with the Insolvency Rules, or omits or misprints some important words) or if the petitioner decides not to pursue the petition (e.g. on receiving payment).

3. Certificate of compliance—time for filing

PD–047 **3.1** In the High Court in order to assist practitioners and the Court the time laid down by Insolvency Rule 4.14 of the Insolvency Rules 1986, for filing a certificate of compliance and a copy of the advertisement, is hereby extended to not later than 4.30 p.m. on the Friday preceding the day on which the petition is to be heard. Applications to file the certificate and the copy advertisement after 4.30 p.m. on the Friday will only be allowed if some good reason is shown for the delay.

4. Errors in petitions

4.1 Applications for leave to amend errors in petitions which are discovered subsequent to a winding up order being made should be made to the Court Manager in the High Court and to the District Judge in the county court. **PD-048**

4.2 Where the error is an error in the name of the company, the Court Manager in the High Court and the District Judge in the county court may make any necessary amendments to ensure that the winding up order is drawn with the correct name of the company inserted. If there is any doubt, e.g. where there might be another company in existence which could be confused with the company to be wound up, the Court Manager will refer the application to the Registrar and the District Judge may refer it to the Judge.

4.3 Where an error is an error in the registered office of the company and any director or member of the company claims that the company was unaware of the petition by reason of it having been served at the wrong registered office, it will be open to them to apply to rescind the winding up order in the usual way.

4.4 Where it is discovered that the company had been struck off the Register of Companies prior to the winding up order being made, the matter must be restored to the list before the order is entered to enable an order for the restoration of the name to be made as well as the order to wind up.

5. Distribution of business

5.1 The following applications shall be made direct to the Judge and, unless otherwise ordered, shall be heard in public— **PD-049**

(1) Applications to commit any person to prison for contempt;

(2) Applications for urgent interim relief (e.g. applications pursuant to s.127 of the Act prior to any winding up order being made);

(3) Applications to restrain the presentation or advertisement of a petition to wind up; or

(4) Applications for the appointment of a provisional liquidator;

(5) Petitions for administration orders or an interim order upon such a Petition;

(6) Applications after an administration order has been made pursuant to s.14(3) of the Act (for directions) or s.18(3) of the Act (to vary or discharge the order);

(7) Petitions to discharge administration orders and to wind up;

(8) Applications pursuant to s.5(3) of the Act (to stay a winding up or discharge an administration order or for directions) where a voluntary arrangement has been approved;

(9) Appeals from a decision made by a County Court or by a Registrar of the High Court.

5.2 Subject to paragraph 5.4 below all other applications shall be made to the Registrar or the District Judge in the first instance who may give any necessary directions and may, in the exercise of his discretion, either hear and determine it himself or refer it to the Judge.

5.3 The following matters will also be heard in public—

(1) Petitions to wind up;

(2) Public examinations;

(3) All matters and applications heard by the Judge, except those referred by the Registrar or the District Judge to be heard in private or so directed by the Judge to be heard.

5.4 In accordance with directions given by the Lord Chancellor the

Registrar has authorised certain applications in the High Court to be dealt with by the Court Manager of the Companies Court, pursuant to Insolvency Rule 13.2(2). The applications are:

(1) To extend or abridge time prescribed by the Insolvency Rules in connection with winding up (Insolvency Rule 4.3 and 12.9);

(2) For substituted service of winding up petitions (Insolvency Rule 4.8(6));

(3) To withdraw petitions (Insolvency Rule 4.15);

(4) For the substitution of a petitioner (Insolvency Rule 4.19);

(5) By the Official Receiver for limited disclosure of a statement of affairs (Insolvency Rule 4.35);

(6) By the Official Receiver for relief from duties imposed upon him by the rules (Insolvency Rule 4.47);

(7) By the Official Receiver for permission to give notice of a meeting by advertisement only (Insolvency Rule 4.59);

(8) To transfer proceedings from the High Court to a County Court (Insolvency Rule 7.11);

(9) For permission to amend any originating application.

[N.B. In District Registries all such applications must be made to the District Judge.]

6. Drawing up of orders

PD–050 **6.1** The Court will draw up all orders except orders on the application of the Official Receiver or for which the Treasury Solicitor is responsible under the existing practice.

7. Rescission of a winding up order

PD–051 **7.1** Any application for the rescission of a winding up order shall be made within seven days after the date on which the order was made (Insolvency Rule 7.47(4)). Notice of any such application must be given to the Official Receiver.

7.2 Applications will only be entertained if made (a) by a creditor, or (b) by a contributory, or (c) by the company jointly with a creditor or with a contributory. The application must be supported by written evidence of assets and liabilities.

7.3 In the case of an unsuccessful application the costs of the petitioning creditor, the supporting creditors and of the Official Receiver will normally be ordered to be paid by the creditor or the contributory making or joining in the application. The reason for this is that if the costs of an unsuccessful application are made payable by the company, they fall unfairly on the general body of creditors.

7.4 Cases in which the making of the winding up order has not been opposed may, if the application is made promptly, be dealt with on a statement by the applicants legal representative of the circumstances; but apart from such cases, the court will normally require any application to be supported by written evidence.

7.5 There is no need to issue a form of application (Form 7.2) as the petition is restored before the Court.

8. Restraint of presentation of a winding-up petition

PD–052 **8.1** An application to restrain presentation of a Winding-up petition must be made to the Judge by the issue of an Originating Application (Form 7.1).

Part Three

Personal Insolvency—Bankruptcy

9. Distribution of business

9.1 The following applications shall be made direct to the Judge and unless otherwise ordered shall be heard in public: **PD-053**

(1) Applications for the committal of any person to prison for contempt;

(2) Application for injunctions or for the modification or discharge of injunctions;

(3) Applications for interlocutory relief or directions after the matter has been referred to the Judge.

9.2 All other applications shall be made to the Registrar or the District Judge in the first instance. He shall give any necessary directions and may, if the application is within his jurisdiction to determine, in his discretion either hear and determine it himself or refer it to the Judge.

9.3 The following matters shall be heard in public:

(1) The public examination of debtors;

(2) Opposed applications for discharge or for the suspension or lifting of the suspension of discharge;

(3) Opposed applications for permission to be a director;

(4) In any case where the petition was presented or the receiving order or order for adjudication was made before the appointed day, those matters and applications specified in Rule 8 of the Bankruptcy Rules 1952;

(5) All matters and applications heard by the Judge, except matters and applications referred by the Registrar or the District Judge to be heard by the Judge in private or directed by the Judge to be so heard.

9.4 All petitions presented will be listed under the name of the debtor.

9.5 In accordance with Directions given by the Lord Chancellor the Registrar has authorised certain applications in the High Court to be dealt with by the Court Manager of the Bankruptcy Court pursuant to Insolvency Rule 13.2(2). The applications are:

(1) by petitioning creditors: to extend time for hearing petitions (s.376 of the Act).

(2) by the Official Receiver:

(a) To transfer proceedings from the High Court to a County Court (Insolvency Rule 7.13);

(b) to amend the full title of the proceedings (Insolvency Rule 6.35 and 6.47).

[N.B. In District Registries all such applications must be made to the District Judge.]

10. Service abroad of statutory demand

10.1 A statutory demand is not a document issued by the Court. Leave to serve out of the jurisdiction is not, therefore, required. **PD-054**

10.2 Insolvency Rule 6.3(2) ("Requirements as to service") applies to service of the statutory demand whether outside or within the jurisdiction.

10.3 A creditor wishing to serve a statutory demand outside the jurisdiction in a foreign country with which a civil procedure convention has been made (including the Hague Convention) may and, if the assistance of a British Consul is desired, must adopt the procedure prescribed by RSC Ord. 11 r.6. In the case of any doubt whether the country is a "convention country", enquiries should be made of the Queen's Bench Masters' Secretary Department, Room E216, Royal Courts of Justice.

10.4 In all other cases, service of the demand must be effected by private arrangement in accordance with Insolvency Rule 6.3(2) and local foreign law.

10.5 When a statutory demand is to be served out of the jurisdiction, the time limits of 21 days and 18 days respectively referred to in the demand must be amended. For this purpose reference should be made to the table set out in the practice direction supplementing RSC Ord. 11 in Schedule 1 to the CPR.

10.6 A creditor should amend the statutory demand as follows:

(1) For any reference to 18 days there must be substituted the appropriate number of days set out in the table plus 4 days, and

(2) for any reference to 21 days must be substituted the appropriate number of days in the table plus 7 days.

Attention is drawn to the fact that in all forms of the statutory demand the figure 18 and the figure 21 occurs in more than one place.

11. Substituted service

Statutory demands:

PD–055 **11.1** The creditor is under an obligation to do all that is reasonable to bring the statutory demand to the debtor's attention and, if practicable, to cause personal service to be effected. Where it is not possible to effect prompt personal service, service may be effected by other means such as first class post or by insertion through a letter box.

11.2 Advertisement can only be used as a means of substituted service where:

(1) The demand is based on a judgment or order of any Court;

(2) The debtor has absconded or is keeping out of the way with a view to avoiding service and,

(3) There is no real prospect of the sum due being recovered by execution or other process.

As there is no statutory form of advertisement, the Court will accept an advertisement in the following form:

STATUTORY DEMAND

(Debt for liquidated sum payable immediately following a judgment or order of the Court)

To (Block letters)

of

TAKE NOTICE that a statutory demand has been issued by:

Name of Creditor:

Address:

The creditor demands payment of £ the amount now due on a judgment or order of the (High Court of Justice Division) (........County Court) dated the day of 199 .

The statutory demand is an important document and it is deemed to have been served on you on the date of the first appearance of this advertisement. You must deal with this demand within 21 days of the service upon you or you could be made bankrupt and your property and goods taken away from you. If you are in any doubt as to your position, you should seek advice immediately from a solicitor or your nearest Citizens'

Advice Bureau. The statutory demand can be obtained or is available for inspection and collection from:

Name:

Address:

(Solicitor for) the Creditor

Tel. No. Reference:

You have only 21 days from the date of the first appearance of this advertisement before the creditor may present a Bankruptcy Petition. You have only 18 days within which to apply to the Court to set aside the demand.

11.3 In all cases where substituted service is effected, the creditor must have taken all those steps which would justify the Court making an order for substituted service of a petition. The steps to be taken to obtain an order for substituted service of a petition are set out below. Failure to comply with these requirements may result in the Court declining to file the petition: Insolvency Rule 6.11(g).

Petitions

11.4 In most cases, evidence of the following steps will suffice to justify an order for substituted service:

(1) One personal call at the residence and place of business of the debtor where both are known or at either of such places as is known. Where it is known that the debtor has more than one residential or business address, personal calls should be made at all the addresses.

(2) Should the creditor fail to effect service, a first class prepaid letter should be written to the debtor referring to the call(s), the purpose of the same and the failure to meet with the debtor, adding that a further call will be made for the same purpose on the day of 19 at hours at (place). At least two business days notice should be given of the appointment and copies of the letter sent to all known addresses of the debtor. The appointment letter should also state that

(a) in the event of the time and place not being convenient, the debtor is to name some other time and place reasonably convenient for the purpose;

(b) (Statutory Demands) if the debtor fails to keep the appointment the creditor proposes to serve the debtor by [advertisement] [post] [insertion through a letter box] or as the case may be, and that, in the event of a bankruptcy petition being presented, the Court will be asked to treat such service as service of the demand on the debtor;

(c) (Petitions) if the debtor fails to keep the appointment, application will be made to the Court for an order for substituted service either by advertisement, or in such other manner as the Court may think fit.

(3) In attending any appointment made by letter, inquiry should be made as to whether the debtor has received all letters left for him. If the debtor is away, inquiry should also be made as to whether or not letters are being forwarded to an address within the jurisdiction (England and Wales) or elsewhere.

(4) If the debtor is represented by a Solicitor, an attempt should be made to arrange an appointment for personal service through such Solicitor. The Insolvency Rules enable a Solicitor to accept service of a statutory demand on

behalf of his client but there is no similar provision in respect of service of a bankruptcy petition.

(5) The written evidence filed pursuant to Insolvency Rule 6.11 should deal with all the above matters including all relevant facts as to the debtor's whereabouts and whether the appointment letter(s) have been returned.

11.5 Where the Court makes an order for service by first class ordinary post, the order will normally provide that service be deemed to be effected on the seventh day after posting. The same method of calculating service may be applied to calculating the date of service of a statutory demand.

12. Setting aside a statutory demand

PD–056 **12.1** The application (Form 6.4) and written evidence in support (Form 6.5) exhibiting a copy of the statutory demand must be filed in Court within 18 days of service of the statutory demand on the debtor. Where service is effected by advertisement in a newspaper the period of 18 days is calculated from the date of the first appearance of the advertisement. Three copies of each document must be lodged with the application to enable the Court to serve notice of the hearing date on the applicant, the creditor and the person named in Part B of the statutory demand.

12.2 Where, to avoid expense, copies of the documents are not lodged with the application in the High Court, any order of the Registrar fixing a venue is conditional upon copies of the documents being lodged on the next business day after the Registrar's order otherwise the application will be deemed to have been dismissed.

12.3 Where the statutory demand is based on a judgment or order, the Court will not at this stage go behind the judgment or order and inquire into the validity of the debt nor, as a general rule, will it adjourn the application to await the result of an application to set aside the judgment or order.

12.4 Where the debtor (a) claims to have a counterclaim, set off or cross demand (whether or not he could have raised it in the action in which the judgment or order was obtained) which equals or exceeds the amount of the debt or debts specified in the statutory demand or (b) disputes the debt (not being a debt subject to a judgment or order) the Court will normally set aside the statutory demand if, in its opinion, on the evidence there is a genuine triable issue.

12.5 A debtor who wishes to apply to set aside a statutory demand after the expiration of 18 days from the date of service of the statutory demand must apply for an extension of time within which to apply. If the applicant wishes to apply for an injunction to restrain presentation of a petition the application must be made to the Judge. Paragraphs 1 and 2 of Form 6.5 (Affidavit in Support of Application to set Aside Statutory Demand) should be used in support of the application for an extension of time with the following additional paragraphs:

"3 That to the best of my knowledge and belief the creditor(s) named in the demand has/have not presented a petition against me.

4. That the reasons for my failure to apply to set aside the demand within 18 days after service are as follows: ... "

If application is made to restrain presentation of a bankruptcy petition the following additional paragraph should be added:

"5. Unless restrained by injunction the creditor(s) may present a bankruptcy petition against me."

13. Proof of service of a statutory demand

PD–057 **13.1** Insolvency Rule 6.11(3) provides that, if the Statutory Demand has been served personally, the written evidence must be provided by the person who effected that service. Insolvency Rule 6.11(4) provides that, if service of the demand (however effected) has been acknowledged in writing, the evidence of service must be provided by the creditor or by a person acting on his behalf. Insolvency Rule 6.11(5) provides that, if neither paragraphs (3) or (4) apply, the written evidence must be provided by a person having direct knowledge of the means adopted for serving the demand.

13.2 Form 6.11 (Evidence of personal service of the statutory demand): this form should only be used where the demand has been served personally and acknowledged in writing (see Insolvency Rule 6.11(4)). If the demand has not been acknowledged in writing, the written evidence should be provided by the Process Server and Paragraphs 2 and 3 (part of Form 6.11) should be omitted (See Insolvency Rule 6.11(3).)

13.3 Form 6.12 (Evidence of Substituted Service of the Statutory Demand): this form can be used whether or not service of the demand has been acknowledged in writing. Paragraphs 4 and 5 (part) provide for the alternatives. Practitioners are reminded, however, that the appropriate person to provide the written evidence may not be the same in both cases. If the demand has been acknowledged in writing, the appropriate person is the creditor or a person acting on his behalf. If the demand has not been acknowledged, that person must be someone having direct knowledge of the means adopted for serving the demand.

Practitioners may find it more convenient to allow process servers to carry out the necessary investigation whilst reserving to themselves the service of the demand. In these circumstances Paragraph 1 should be deleted and the following paragraph substituted:

> "1. Attempts have been made to serve the demand, full details of which are set out in the accompanying affidavit of . . .".

13.4 "Written evidence" means an affidavit or a witness statement.

14. Extension of hearing date of petition

14.1 Late applications for extension of hearing dates under Insolvency Rule 6.28, and failure to attend on the listed hearing of a petition, will be dealt with as follows: PD–058

(1) If an application is submitted less than two clear working days before the hearing date (for example, later than Monday for Thursday, or Wednesday for Monday) the costs of the application will not be allowed under Insolvency Rule 6.28(3).

(2) If the petition has not been served and no extension has been granted the time fixed for the hearing of the petition, and if no one attends for the hearing, the petition will be re-listed for hearing about 21 days later. The Court will notify the petitioning creditor's solicitors (or the petitioning creditor in person), and any known supporting or opposing creditors or their solicitors, of the new date and times. Written evidence should then be filed on behalf of the petitioning creditor explaining fully the reasons for the failure to apply for an extension or to appear at the hearing, and (if appropriate) giving reasons why the petition should not be dismissed.

(3) On the re-listed hearing the Court may dismiss the petition if not satisfied it should be adjourned or a further extension granted.

14.2 All applications for extension should include a statement of the date fixed for the hearing of the petition.

14.3 The petitioning creditor should attend (by solicitors or in person) on or before the hearing date to ascertain whether the application has reached the file and been dealt with. It should not be assumed that an extension will be granted.

15. Bankruptcy petition

To help in the completion of the form of a creditor's bankruptcy petition, attention is drawn to the following points: PD–059

15.1 The petition does not require dating, signing or witnessing.

15.2 In the title it is only necessary to recite the debtor's name e.g. Re John William Smith or Re J W Smith (Male). Any alias or trading name will appear in the body of the petition. This also applies to all other statutory forms other than those which require the "full title".

15.3 Where the petition is based on a statutory demand, only the debt claimed in the demand may be included in the petition.

15.4 In completing Paragraph 2 of the petition, attention is drawn to Insolvency Rule 6.8(1)(a) to (c), particularly where the "aggregate sum" is made up of a number of debts.

15.5 Date of service of the statutory demand (paragraph 4 of the petition):

(1) In the case of personal service, the date of service as set out in the affidavit of service should be recited and whether service is effected before/after 1700 hours on Monday to Friday or at any time on a Saturday or a Sunday: see CPR Part 6.7(2) and (3).

(2) In the case of substituted service (otherwise than by advertisement), the date alleged in the affidavit of service should be recited: see "11. Substituted Service" above.

(3) In the strictly limited case of service by advertisement under Insolvency Rule 6.3, the date to be alleged is the date of the advertisement's appearance or, as the case may be, its first appearance: see Insolvency Rules 6.3(3) and 6.11(8).

15.6 There is no need to include in the petition details of the person authorised to present it.

15.7 Certificates at the end of the petition:

(1) The period of search for prior petitions has been reduced to eighteen months.

(2) Where a statutory demand is based wholly or in part on a County Court judgment, the following certificate is to be added:

> "I/We certify that on the day of 19 I/We attended on the County Court and was/were informed by an officer of the Court that no money had been paid into Court in the action or matter v Claim No pursuant to the statutory demand."

This certificate will not be required when the demand also requires payment of a separate debt, not based on a County Court judgment, the amount of which exceeds the bankruptcy level (at present £750).

15.8 Deposit on petition: the deposit will be taken by the Court and forwarded to the Official Receiver. In the High Court, the petition fee and deposit should be handed to the Supreme Court Accounts Office, Fee Stamping Room, who will record the receipt and will impress two entries on the original petition, one in respect of the Court fee and the other in respect of the deposit. In the County Court, the petition fee and deposit should be handed to the duly authorised officer of the Court's staff who will record its receipt.

In all cases cheque(s) for the whole amount should be made payable to "HM Paymaster General".

15.9 On the hearing of a petition for a bankruptcy order, in order to satisfy the Court that the debt on which the petition is founded has not been paid or secured or compounded the Court will normally accept as sufficient a certificate signed by the person representing the petitioning creditor in the following form:

> "I certify that I have/my firm has made enquiries of the petitioning creditor(s) within the last business day prior to the hearing/adjourned hearing and to the best of my knowledge and belief the debt on which the petition is founded is still due and owing and has not been paid or secured or compounded save as to ....
>
> Signed .... Dated ...."

For convenience in the High Court this certificate will be incorporated in the attendance slip, which will be filed after the hearing. A fresh certificate will be required on each adjourned hearing.

16. Orders without attendance

16.1 In suitable cases the Court will normally be prepared to make orders under Part VIII of the Act (Individual Voluntary Arrangements), without the attendance of either party, provided there is no bankruptcy order in existence and (so far as is known) no pending petition. The orders are: **PD–060**

(1) A fourteen day interim order with the application adjourned 14 days for consideration of the nominee's report, where the papers are in order, and the nominee's signed consent to act includes a waiver of notice of the application or a consent by the nominee to the making of an interim order without attendance.

(2) A standard order on consideration of the nominee's report, extending the interim order to a date 7 weeks after the date of the proposed meeting, directing the meeting to be summoned and adjourning to a date about 3 weeks after the meeting. Such an Order may be made without attendance if the nominee's report has been delivered to the Court and complies with Section 256(1) of the Act and Insolvency Rule 5.10(2) and (3) and proposes a date for the meeting not less than 14 days from that on which the nominee's report is filed in Court under Insolvency Rule 5.10 nor more than 28 days from that on which that report is considered by the Court under Insolvency Rule 5.12.

(3) A "concertina" Order, combining orders as under (1) and (2) above. Such an order may be made without attendance if the initial application for an interim order is accompanied by a report of the nominee and the conditions set out in (1) and (2) above are satisfied.

(4) A final order on consideration of the Chairman's report. Such an order may be made without attendance if the Chairman's report has been filed and complies with Insolvency Rule 5.22(1). The order will record the effect of the Chairman's report and may discharge the interim order.

16.2 Provided that the conditions as under 16.1(2) and (4) above are satisfied and that the appropriate report has been lodged with the Court in due time the parties need not attend or be represented on the adjourned hearing for consideration of the Nominee's report or of the Chairman's report (as the case may be) unless they are notified by the Court that attendance is required. Sealed copies of the order made (in all four cases as above) will be posted by the Court to the applicant or his Solicitor and to the Nominee.

16.3 In suitable cases the Court may also make consent orders without attendance by the parties. The written consent of the parties will be required. Examples of such orders are as follows:

(1) <u>On applications to set aside a statutory demand</u>, orders:

- (a) dismissing the application, with or without an order for costs as may be agreed (permission will be given to present a petition on or after the seventh day after the date of the order, unless a different date is agreed);
- (b) setting aside the demand, with or without an order for costs as may be agreed; or
- (c) giving permission to withdraw the application with or without an order for costs as may be agreed.

(2) <u>On petitions</u>: where there is a list of supporting or opposing creditors in Form 6.21, or a statement signed by or on behalf of the petitioning creditor that no notices have been received from supporting or opposing creditors, orders:

- (a) dismissing the petition, with or without an order for costs as may be agreed, or

(b) if the petition has not been served, giving permission to withdraw the petition (with no order for costs).

(3) On other applications, orders:

(a) for sale of property, possession of property, disposal of proceeds of sale

(b) giving interim directions

(c) dismissing the application, with or without an order for costs as may be agreed

(d) giving permission to withdraw the application, with or without an order for costs as may be agreed.

If (as may often be the case with orders under subparagraphs (3)(a) or (b) above), an adjournment is required, whether generally with liberty to restore or to a fixed date, the order by consent may include an order for the adjournment. If adjournment to a date is requested, a time estimate should be given and the Court will fix the first available date and time on or after the date requested.

16.4 The above lists should not be regarded as exhaustive, nor should it be assumed that an order will be made without attendance as requested.

16.5 The procedure outlined above is designed to save time and costs but is not intended to discourage attendance.

16.6 Applications for consent orders without attendance should be lodged at least two clear working days (and preferably longer) before any fixed hearing date.

16.7 Whenever a document is lodged or a letter sent, the correct case number, code (if any) and year (for example 123/SD/99 or 234/99) should be quoted. A note should also be given of the date and time of the next hearing (if any).

16.8 Attention is drawn to Paragraph 4.4(4) of the Practice Direction relating to CPR Part 44.

Part Four

Appeals

17. Appeals

PD–061 **17.1** An appeal from a decision made in a County Court by a Circuit or District Judge or in the High Court by a Registrar in Bankruptcy lies without leave to a Single Judge of the High Court ("Single Judge"): Section 375(2) of the Act and Insolvency Rule 7.48(2).

17.2 Such appeals are set down and heard as follows:

(1) An appeal from the decision of the Registrar in Bankruptcy shall, or from any decision made in any County Court may, be set down and heard in London by a High Court Judge of the Chancery Division or by a person authorised to sit in that capacity.

(2) An appeal from a decision made in a County Court exercising jurisdiction over an area within the Northern and North Eastern Circuits may be set down in Manchester for hearing in Leeds, Liverpool, Manchester, Preston or Newcastle upon Tyne by a High Court Judge of the Chancery Division or a person authorised to sit in that capacity.

(3) An appeal from a decision made in the County Court exercising jurisdiction over an area within the Birmingham, Bristol or Cardiff Chancery District Registries may be set down in the Registry appropriate to the area in which the decision was made for hearing in Birmingham, Bristol or Cardiff by a High Court Judge or a person authorised to sit in that capacity.

17.3 The procedure and practice of the Supreme Court relating to appeals to the Court of Appeal (RSC Ord. 59) apply to appeals in insolvency proceedings: Insolvency Rule 7.49(1).

17.4 In relation to any appeal under s.375(2) of the Act to a single Judge of the Chancery Division of the High Court any reference to the Court of Appeal in the CPR is replaced by reference to that Judge and any reference to the Registrar of Civil Appeals is replaced by a reference to a Bankruptcy Registrar who deals with insolvency appeals referred to below as the Registrar of Bankruptcy Appeals: Insolvency Rule 7.49(2).

17.5 The following applications shall be made to the Single Judge:

(1) for injunctions pending a substantive hearing of the appeal;

(2) by way of appeal from the Registrar of Bankruptcy Appeals;

(3) for expedition or vacation of the hearing date of an appeal;

(4) for permission to issue a witness summons on an appeal;

(5) any application that may be dealt with or referred to the Single Judge by the Registrar of Bankruptcy Appeals.

17.6 The following applications may be made to a Bankruptcy Registrar who deals with Insolvency Proceedings (the Registrar of Bankruptcy Appeals):

(a) for extension of time for serving a notice of appeal;
(b) for extension of time for setting down a notice of appeal;
(c) for extension of time for serving a respondent's notice;
(d) for permission to amend a notice of appeal or a respondent's notice;
(e) for security for costs of an appeal;
(f) for permission to adduce further evidence on appeal;
(g) for service of a notice of appeal or respondent's notice by substituted service.

17.7 A form of notice of appeal appropriate to Insolvency Appeals to the Single Judge is set out in Atkins Court Forms, Volume 7, or may be obtained in London from the Fees Room, The Royal Courts of Justice or from the addresses set out in Paragraph 17.9(5) below.

17.8 Applications to the Registrar of Bankruptcy Appeals may be made on Bankruptcy Application Form 7.2 which may be obtained from the Fees Room, The Royal Courts of Justice, or from the addresses set out in Paragraph 17.9(5) below, and should be lodged at the address set out in Paragraph 17.9(5)(a) below.

17.9 The following practice applies to all appeals to a Single Judge of the High Court whether set down in London, or set down at one of the other venues referred to in Paragraph 17.2 above:

(1) a notice of appeal must be served not later than 28 days, such time to run:

(a) in the case of an appeal from an order made in the County Court from the date the order is made (RSC Order 59 rules 4 and 19);
(b) in the case of an appeal from an order made by a Registrar in Bankruptcy from the date on which the order is sealed or otherwise perfected (RSC Ord. 59 r.4(1)).

(2) notice of appeal must be served on all parties to the proceedings below who are directly affected by the appeal. This will include the Circuit or the District Judge of the appropriate County Court and where a bankruptcy order has been made the Official Receiver.

(3) notice of appeal must be served by the appellant or by the legal representative of the appellant and may be effected by the following methods:

(a) by leaving the document at the proper address of the person to be served;
(b) by post;
(c) through a document exchange;
(d) if both appellant and respondent are represented by solicitors by fax or by other electronic method together with a hard copy posted to the party concerned on the same day as the fax or other electronic method is sent;

(e) by substituted service with leave of the Court.

(4) after service the appellant must set down the notice of appeal within seven days of the later of (i) the date on which service of the notice of appeal was effected or (ii) the date on which the judgment or order of the Court below was sealed or otherwise perfected, by lodging the documents listed below:

(a) two copies of the notice of appeal, one of which must be endorsed with a certificate of the date and method of service and stamped with the appropriate fee,
(b) a copy of the order under appeal, and
(c) the estimate of time for the hearing.

(5) the above documents may be lodged personally or by post at the address of the appropriate venue listed below:

(a) If the appeal is to be set down and heard in London the documents must be lodged at Room 110, Thomas More Building, The Royal Courts of Justice, Strand, London WC2A 2LL.
(b) If the appeal is to be set down in Manchester the documents must be lodged at the Chancery Section, Courts of Justice, Crown Square, Manchester, M3 3FL.
(c) If the appeal is to be set down in Birmingham, the documents must be lodged at the Registry of the Chancery Division of the High Court, 33 Bull Street, Birmingham B4 6D5.
(d) If the appeal is to be set down in Bristol the documents must be lodged at the District Registry of the Chancery Division of the High Court, Third Floor, Greyfriars, Lewins Mead, Bristol BS1 2NR.
(e) If the appeal is to be set down in Cardiff the documents must be lodged at the District Registry in the Chancery Division of the High Court, First Floor, 2 Park Street, Cardiff CF1 1MR.

(6) If the documents are correct and in order the Court at which the documents are lodged will fix a hearing date and will also fix the place of hearing. That Court will send letters to all the parties to the appeal informing them of the date and place of hearing and indicating the time estimate given by the appellant. The parties will be invited to notify the Court of any alternative or revised time estimates. In the absence of any such notification the estimate of the appellant will be taken as agreed. The Court will also send to the appellant a document setting out the Court's requirement concerning the form and content of the bundle of documents for the use of the Single Judge. Such bundle of documents must be lodged by the appellant at the address of the appropriate venue as set out in subparagraph 17.9(5) above not later than 7 days before the date fixed for the hearing. Failure to do so may result in the appeal being dismissed by the Judge.

(7) Skeleton arguments, accompanied by a written chronology of events relevant to the appeal, should be lodged at the address of the appropriate venue as set out in sub-paragraph 17.9(5) above, at least two clear days before the date fixed for the hearing. Failure to lodge may result in an adverse costs order by the Single Judge on the hearing of the appeal.

(8) A notice of appeal and a respondent's notice may be amended:

(a) With the permission of the Registrar of Bankruptcy Appeals or of the Single Judge at any time;
(b) Without permission by supplementary notice served:
  (1) in the case of a notice of appeal not later than five days after setting down the notice of appeal, and
  (2) in the case of a respondent's notice not later than five days after setting down the respondent's notice.

After service two copies of the amended notice must be lodged at the address of the appropriate venue as set out in sub-paragraph 17.9(5) above, one copy endorsed with the date on which service was effected and stamped with the appropriate fee.

(9) Where an appellant does not wish to continue with the appeal or where the appeal has been settled, the appeal may be dismissed by consent on paper without a hearing. An order to that effect signed by each party or letters of consent from each party must be lodged not later than 24 hours before the date fixed for the hearing of the appeal at the address of the appropriate venue as set out in sub-paragraph 17.9(5) above and will be dealt with by the Single Judge.

17.10 An appeal from a decision made by the Single Judge lies to the Court of Appeal with the leave of that Judge or of the Court of Appeal (see Insolvency Rule 7.49(2)). Application for such leave to appeal should be made to the Single Judge at the conclusion of his judgment on the appeal. If a party fails to apply at that time he may apply to the Single Judge for permission. Such application together with draft intended grounds of appeal must be lodged at the address of the appropriate venue as set out in sub-paragraph 17.9(5) above within 28 days of the sealing of the Order made on the appeal. The application will first be considered by the Single Judge who heard the appeal who may refuse leave or give such directions as the single Judge thinks fit for the disposal of the application. Any application made after the 28 day period has expired must be made direct to the Court of Appeal.

GLOSSARY

Scope

G1.1 This glossary is a guide to the meaning of certain legal expressions as used in these Rules, but it does not give the expressions any meaning in the Rules which they do not otherwise have in the law.

Expression	**Meaning**
Affidavit	A written, sworn statement of evidence.
Alternative dispute resolution	Collective description of methods of resolving disputes otherwise than through the normal trial process.
Base rate	The interest rate set by the Bank of England which is used as the basis for other banks' rates.
Contribution	A right of someone to recover from a third person all or part of the amount which he himself is liable to pay.
Counterclaim	A claim brought by a defendant in response to the claimant's claim, which is included in the same proceedings as the claimant's claim.
Cross-examination (and see "evidence in chief")	Questioning of a witness by a party other than the party who called the witness.
Damages	A sum of money awarded by the court as compensation to the claimant.
• aggravated damages	Additional damages which the court may award as compensation for the defendant's objectionable behaviour.
• exemplary damages	Damages which go beyond compensating for actual loss and are awarded to show the court's disapproval of the defendant's behaviour.
Defence of tender before claim	A defence that, before the claimant started proceedings, the defendant unconditionally offered to the claimant the amount due or, if no specified amount is claimed, an amount sufficient to satisfy the claim.
Evidence in chief (and see "cross-examination")	The evidence given by a witness for the party who called him.
Indemnity	A right of someone to recover from a third party the whole amount which he himself is liable to pay.
Injunction	A court order prohibiting a person from doing something or requiring a person to do something.
Joint liability (and see "several liability")	Parties who are jointly liable share a single liability and each party can be held liable for the whole of it.
Limitation period	The period within which a person who has a right to claim against another person must start court proceedings to establish that right. The expiry of the period may be a defence to the claim.
List	Cases are allocated to different lists depending on the subject-matter of the case. The lists are used for administrative purposes and may also have their own procedures and judges.
Official copy	A copy of an official document, supplied and marked as such by the office which issued the original.
Practice form	Form to be used for a particular purpose in proceedings, the form and purpose being specified by a practice direction.

Pre-action protocol	Statements of understanding between legal practitioners and others about pre-action practice and which are approved by a relevant practice direction.
Privilege	The right of a party to refuse to disclose a document or produce a document or to refuse to answer questions on the ground of some special interest recognised by law.
Seal	A seal is a mark which the court puts on a document to indicate that the document has been issued by the court.
Service	Steps required by rules of court to bring documents used in court proceedings to a person's attention.
Set aside	Cancelling a judgment or order or a step taken by a party in the proceedings.
Several liability (and see "joint liability")	A person who is severally liable with others may remain liable for the whole claim even where judgment has been obtained against the others.
Stay	A stay imposes a halt on proceedings, apart from taking any steps allowed by the Rules or the terms of the stay. Proceedings can be continued if a stay is lifted.
Strike out	Striking out means the court ordering written material to be deleted so that it may no longer be relied upon.
Without prejudice	Negotiations with a view to a settlement are usually conducted "without prejudice" which means that the circumstances in which the content of those negotiations may be revealed to the court are very restricted.

SECTION B

PRE-ACTION PROTOCOLS

CONTENTS

PRACTICE DIRECTION—PROTOCOLS

General

1.1 This Practice Direction applies to the pre-action protocols which have been approved by the Head of Civil Justice. B0–001

1.2 The pre-action protocols which have been approved are specified in the Schedule to this Practice Direction. Other pre-action protocols may subsequently be added.

1.3 Pre-action protocols outline the steps parties should take to seek information from and to provide information to each other about a prospective legal claim.

1.4 The objectives of pre-action protocols are:

(1) to encourage the exchange of early and full information about the prospective legal claim,

(2) to enable parties to avoid litigation by agreeing a settlement of the claim before the commencement of proceedings,

(3) to support the efficient management of proceedings where litigation cannot be avoided.

Compliance with Protocols

2.1 The Civil Procedure Rules enable the court to take into account compliance or non-compliance with an applicable protocol when giving directions for the management of proceedings (see CPR, rules 3.1(4) and (5) and 3.9(e)) and when making orders for costs (see CPR, rule 44.3(5)(a)).

2.2 The court will expect all parties to have complied in substance with the terms of an approved protocol.

2.3 If, in the opinion of the court, non-compliance has led to the commencement of proceedings which might otherwise not have needed to be commenced, or has led to costs being incurred in the proceedings that might otherwise not have been incurred, the orders the court may make include:

(1) an order that the party at fault pay the costs of the proceedings, or part of those costs, of the other party or parties;

(2) an order that the party at fault pay those costs on an indemnity basis;

(3) if the party at fault is a claimant in whose favour an order for the payment of damages or some specified sum is subsequently made, an order depriving that party of interest on such sum and in respect of such period as may be specified, and/or awarding interest at a lower rate than that at which interest would otherwise have been awarded;

(4) if the party at fault is a defendant and an order for the payment of damages or some specified sum is subsequently made in favour of the claimant, an order awarding interest on such sum and in respect of such period as may be specified at a higher rate, not exceeding 10% above base rate (*cf.* CPR, rule 36.21(2)), than the rate at which interest would otherwise have been awarded.

2.4 The court will exercise its powers under paragraphs 2.1 and 2.3 with the object of placing the innocent party in no worse a position than he would have been in if the protocol had been complied with.

3.1 A claimant may be found to have failed to comply with a protocol by, for example:

(a) not having provided sufficient information to the defendant, or

(b) not having followed the procedure required by the protocol to be followed (e.g. not having followed the medical expert instruction procedure set out in the Personal Injury Protocol).

3.2 A defendant may be found to have failed to comply with a protocol by, for example:

(a) not making a preliminary response to the letter of claim within the time fixed for that purpose by the relevant protocol (21 days under the Personal Injury Protocol, 14 days under the Clinical Negligence Protocol),

(b) not making a full response within the time fixed for that purpose by the relevant protocol (3 months of the letter of claim under the Clinical Negligence Protocol, 3 months from the date of acknowledgement of the letter of claim under the Personal Injury Protocol),

(c) not disclosing documents required to be disclosed by the relevant protocol.

4 Pre-Action Behaviour in Other Cases

not making a full response within the time fixed for that purpose by the relevant protocol (3 months of the letter of claim under the Clinical Negligence Protocol, 3 months from the date of acknowledgement of the letter of claim under the Personal Injury Protocol),

Commencement

5.1 Compliance or non-compliance, as the case may be, with the protocols specified in the Schedule will be taken into account by the court in dealing with any proceedings commenced after 26 April 1999 but will not be taken into account by the court in dealing with proceedings started before that date.

5.2 Where, in respect of proceedings commenced after 26 April 1999, the parties have by work done before that date substantially achieved the object designed to be achieved by steps to be taken under a protocol, the parties need not take those steps and their failure to do so will not be treated, for the purposes of paragraphs 2 and 3, as non-compliance.

5.3 Where, in respect of proceedings commenced after 26 April 1999, the parties have not had time since the publication of the protocols in January 1999 to comply with the applicable provisions, their failure to have done so will not be treated, for the purposes of paragraphs 2 and 3, as non-compliance.

5.4 As and when an additional protocol is approved, a Practice Direction will specify the date after which compliance or non-compliance with that protocol will be taken into account by the court.

Schedule

1. Personal Injury Protocol.
2. Clinical Negligence Protocol.

PRE-ACTION PROTOCOLS FOR PERSONAL INJURY CLAIMS

1. Introduction

B1–001 **1.1** Lord Woolf in his final Access to Justice Report of July 1996 recommended the development of pre-action protocols:

"To build on and increase the benefits of early but well informed settlement which genuinely satisfy both parties to dispute."

1.2 The aims of pre-action protocols are:

- more pre-action contact between the parties
- better and earlier exchange of information
- better pre-action investigation by both sides
- to put the parties in a position where they may be able to settle cases fairly and early without litigation
- to enable proceedings to run to the court's timetable and efficiently, if litigation does become necessary.

1.3 The concept of protocols is relevant to a range of initiatives for good litigation and pre-litigation practice, especially:

- predictability in the time needed for steps pre-proceedings
- standardisation of relevant information, including documents to be disclosed.

1.4 The Court will be able to treat the standards set in protocols as the normal reasonable approach to pre-action conduct: If proceedings are issued, it will be for the court to decide whether non-compliance with a protocol should merit adverse consequences. Guidance on the court's likely approach will be given from time to time in practice directions.

1.5 If the court has to consider the question of compliance after proceedings have begun, it will not be concerned with minor infringements, *e.g.* failure by a short period to provide relevant information. One minor breach will not exempt the "innocent" party from following the protocol. The court will look at the effect of non-compliance on the other party when deciding whether to impose sanctions.

2. Notes of Guidance

2.1 The protocol has been kept deliberately simple to promote ease of use and general acceptability. The notes of guidance which follow relate particularly to issues which arose during the piloting of the protocol. **B1–002**

Scope of the Protocol

2.2 This protocol is intended to apply to all claims which include a claim for personal injury and to the entirety of those claims: not only to the personal injury element of a claim which also includes, for instance, property damage.

2.3 This protocol is primarily designed for those road traffic, tripping and slipping and accident at work cases which include an element of personal injury with a value of less than £15,000 which are likely to be allocated to the fast track. This is because time will be of the essence, after proceedings are issued, especially for the defendant, if a case is to be ready for trial within 30 weeks of allocation. Also, proportionality of work and costs to the value of what is in dispute is particularly important in lower value claims. For some claims within the value "scope" of the fast track some flexibility in the timescale of the protocol may be necessary—see also paragraph 3.8.

2.4 However, the "cards on the table" approach advocated by the protocol is equally appropriate to some higher value claims. The spirit, if not the letter of the protocol, should still be followed for multi-track type claims. In accordance with the sense of the civil justice reforms, the court will expect to see the spirit of reasonable pre-action behaviour applied in all cases, regardless of the existence of a specific protocol.

2.5 The timetable and the arrangements for disclosing documents and obtaining expert evidence may need to be varied to suit the circumstances of the case. Where one or both parties consider the detail of the protocol is not appropriate to the case, and proceedings are subsequently issued, the court will expect an explanation as to why the protocol has not been followed, or has been varied.

Early Notification

2.6 The claimant's legal representative may wish to notify the defendant and/or his insurer as soon as they know a claim is likely to be made, but before they are able to send a detailed letter of claim, particularly for instance, when the defendant has no or limited knowledge of the incident giving rise to the claim or where the claimant is incurring significant expenditure as a result of the accident which he hopes the defendant might pay for, in whole or in part.

If the claimant's representative chooses to do this, it will not start the timetable for responding.

The Letter of Claim

2.7 The specimen letter of claim at Annex A will usually be sent to the individual defendant. In practice, he/she may have no personal financial interest in the financial outcome of the claim/dispute because he/she is insured. Court imposed sanctions for non-compliance with the protocol may be ineffective against an insured. This is why the protocol emphasises the importance of passing the letter of claim to the insurer and the possibility that the insurance cover might be affected. If an insurer receives the letter of claim only after some delay by the insured, it would not be unreasonable for the insurer to ask the claimant for additional time to respond.

Reasons for Early Issue

2.8 The protocol recommends that a defendant be given three months to investigate and respond to a claim before proceedings are issued. This may not always be possible, particularly where a claimant only consults a solicitor close to the end of any relevant limitation period. In these circumstances, the claimant's solicitor should give as much notice of the intention to issue proceedings as is practicable and the parties should consider whether the court might be invited to extend time for service of the claimant's supporting documents and for service of any defence, or alternatively, to stay the proceedings while the recommended steps in the protocol are followed.

Status of Letters of Claim and Response

2.9 Letters of claim and response are not intended to have the same status as a statement of case in proceedings. Matters may come to light as a result of investigation after the letter of claim has been sent, or after the defendant has responded, particularly if disclosure of documents takes place outside the recommended three-month period. These circumstances could mean that the "pleaded" case of one or both parties is presented slightly differently than in the letter of claim and response. It would not be consistent with the spirit of the protocol for a party to "take a point" on this in the proceedings, provided that there was no obvious intention by the party who changed their position to mislead the other party.

Disclosure of Documents

2.10 The aim of the early disclosure of documents by the defendant is not to encourage "fishing expeditions" by the claimant, but to promote an early exchange of relevant information to help in clarifying or resolving issues in dispute. The claimant's solicitor can assist by identifying in the letter of claim or in a subsequent letter the particular categories of documents which they consider are relevant.

Experts

2.11 The protocol encourages joint selection of, and access to, experts. Most frequently this will apply to the medical expert, but on occasions also to liability experts, e.g. engineers. The protocol promotes the practice of the claimant obtaining a medical report, disclosing it to the defendant who then asks questions and/or agrees it and does not obtain his own report. But it maintains the flexibility for each party to obtain their own expert's report, if necessary after proceedings have commenced, with the leave of the court. It would also be for the court to decide whether the costs of more than one expert's report should be recoverable.

2.12 Some solicitors choose to obtain medical reports through medical agencies, rather than directly from a specific doctor or hospital. The defendant's prior consent to the action should be sought and, if the defendant so requests, the agency should be asked to provide in advance the names of the doctor(s) whom they are considering instructing.

Negotiations/Settlement

2.13 Parties and their legal representatives are encouraged to enter into discussions and/or negotiations prior to starting proceedings. The protocol does not specify when or how this might be done but parties should bear in mind that the courts increasingly take the view that litigation should be a last resort, and that claims should not be issued prematurely when a settlement is in reasonable prospect.

Stocktake

2.14 Where a claim is not resolved when the protocol has been followed, the parties might wish to carry out a "stocktake" of the issues in dispute, and the evidence that the court is likely to need to decide those issues, before proceedings are started. Where the defendant is insured and the pre-action steps have been conducted by the insurer, the insurer would normally be expected to nominate solicitors to act in the proceedings and the claimant's solicitor is recommended to invite the insurer to nominate solicitors to act in the proceedings and do so 7–14 days before the intended issue date.

3. The Protocol

Letter of Claim

3.1 The claimant shall send to the proposed defendant two copies of a letter B1–003
of claim, immediately sufficient information is available to substantiate a realistic claim and before issues of quantum are addressed in detail. One copy of the letter is for the defendants, the second for passing on to his insurers.

3.2 The letter shall contain a **clear summary of the facts** on which the claim is based together with an indication of the **nature of any injuries** suffered and of **any financial loss incurred**. In cases of road traffic accidents, the letter should provide the name and address of the hospital where treatment has been obtained and the claimant's hospital reference number.

3.3 Solicitors are recommended to use a **standard format** for such a letter—an example is at Annex A: this can be amended to suit the particular case.

3.4 The letter should ask for **details of the insurer** and that a copy should be sent by the proposed defendant to the insurer where appropriate. If the insurer is known, a copy shall be sent directly to the insurer. Details of the claimant's National Insurance number and date of birth should be supplied to the defendant's insurer once the defendant has responded to the letter of claim; and confirmed the identify of the insurer. This information should not be supplied in the letter of claim.

3.5 **Sufficient information** should be given in order to enable the defendant's insurer/solicitor to commence investigations and at least put a broad valuation on the "risk".

3.6 The **defendant should reply within 21 calendar days** of the date of posting of the letter identifying the insurer (if any). If there has been no reply by the defendant or insurer within 21 days, the claimant will be entitled to issue proceedings.

3.7 The **defendant** ('s insurers) will have a **maximum of three months** from the date of acknowledgment of the claim **to investigate**. No later than the end of that period the defendant (insurer) shall reply, stating whether liability is denied and, if so, giving reasons for their denial of liability.

3.8 Where the accident occurred outside England and Wales and/or where the defendant is outside the jurisdiction, the time periods of 21 days and three months may reasonably be extended up to 42 days and six months.

3.9 Where **liability is admitted**, the presumption is that the defendant will be bound by this admission for all claims with a total value of up to £15,000.

Documents

3.10 If the **defendant denies liability**, he should enclose with the letter of reply, **documents** in his possession which are **material to the issues** between the parties, and which would be likely to be ordered to be disclosed by the court, either on an application for pre-action disclosure, or on disclosure during proceedings.

3.11 Attached at Annex B are **specimen**, but non-exhaustive, **lists** of documents likely to be material in different types of claim. Where the claimant's investigation of the case is well advanced, the letter of claim could indicate which classes of documents are considered relevant for early disclosure. Alternatively these could be identified at a later stage.

3.12 Where the defendant admits primary liability, but alleges contributory negligence by the claimant, the defendant should give reasons supporting those allegations and disclose those documents from Annex B which are relevant to the issues in dispute. The claimant should respond to the allegations of contributory negligence before proceedings are issued.

Special Damages

3.13 The claimant will send to the defendant as soon as practicable a Schedule of Special Damages with supporting documents, particularly where the defendant has admitted liability.

Experts

3.14 Before any party instructs an expert he should give the other party a list of the **name**(s) of **one or more experts** in the relevant speciality whom he considers are suitable to instruct.

3.15 Where a medical expert is to be instructed the claimant's solicitor will organise access to relevant medical records—see specimen letter of instruction at Annex C.

3.16 **Within 14 days** the other party may indicate **an objection** to one or more of the named experts. The first party should then instruct a mutually acceptable expert.

3.17 If the second party objects to all the listed experts, the parties may then instruct **experts of their own choice**. It would be for the court to decide subsequently if proceedings are issued, whether either party had acted unreasonably.

3.18 If the **second party does not object to an expert nominated**, he shall not be entitled to rely on his own expert evidence within that particular speciality unless:

(a) the first party agrees,

(b) the court so directs, or

(c) the first party's expert report has been amended and the first party is not prepared to disclose the original report.

3.19 **Either party may send to an agreed expert written questions** on the report, relevant to the issues, via the first party's solicitors. The expert should send answers to the questions separately and directly to each party.

3.20 The cost of a report from an agreed expert will usually be paid by the instructing first party: the costs of the expert replying to questions will usually be borne by the party which asks the questions.

3.21 Where the defendant admits liability in whole or in part, before proceedings are issued, any medical report obtained by agreement under this protocol should be disclosed to the other party. The claimant should delay issuing proceedings for 21 days from disclosure of the report, to enable the parties to consider whether the claim is capable of settlement. The Civil Procedure Rules, Part 36 permit claimants and defendants to make offers to settle pre-proceedings.

Annex A

Letter of Claim

To B1–004

Defendant

Dear Sirs

Re: <u>Claimant's full name</u>
<u>Claimant's full address</u>
<u>Claimant's Clock or Works Number</u>
<u>Claimant's Employer</u> (*name and address*)

We are instructed by the above named to claim damages in connection with an *accident at work/road traffic accident/tripping accident* on day of (*year*) at *(place of accident which must be sufficiently detailed to establish location).*

Please confirm the identity of your insurers. Please note that the insurers will need to see this letter as soon as possible and it may affect your insurance cover and/or the conduct of any subsequent legal proceedings if you do not send this letter to them.

The circumstances of the accident are:
(brief outline)

The reason why we are alleging fault is:
(simple explanation e.g. defective machine, broken ground)

A description of our clients' injuries is as follows:
(brief outline)

(In cases of road traffic accidents)
Our client (state hospital reference number) received treatment for the injuries at (name and address of hospital).

He is employed as *(occupation)* and has had the following time off work *(dates of absence).* His approximate weekly income is *(insert if known).*

If you are our client's employers, please provide us with the usual earnings details which will enable us to calculate his financial loss.

We are obtaining a police report and will let you have a copy of the same upon your undertaking to meet half the fee.

We have also sent a letter of claim to *(name and address)* and a copy of that letter is attached. We understand their insurers are *(name, address and claims number if known).*

At this stage of our enquiries we would expect the documents contained in parts *(insert appropriate parts of standard disclosure list)* to be relevant to this action.

A copy of this letter is attached for you to send to your insurers. Finally we expect an acknowledgement of this letter within 21 days by yourselves or your insurers.

Yours faithfully

Annex B

Standard Disclosure Lists

Fast Track Disclosure

RTA Cases

Section A: In all cases where liability is at issue

B1–005 (i) Documents identifying nature, extent and location of damage to defendant's vehicle where there is any dispute about point of impact.
(ii) MOT certificate where relevant.
(iii) Maintenance records where vehicle defect is alleged or it is alleged by defendant that there was an unforeseen defect which caused or contributed to the accident.

Section B: Accident involving commercial vehicle as potential defendant

(i) Tachograph charts or entry from individual control book.
(ii) Maintenance and repair records required for operators' licence where vehicle defect is alleged or it is alleged by defendants that there was an unforeseen defect which caused or contributed to the accident.

Section C: Cases against local authorities where highway design defect is alleged

(i) Documents produced to comply with Section 39 of the Road Traffic Act 1988 in respect of the duty designed to promote road safety to include studies into road accidents in the relevant area and documents relating to measures recommended to prevent accidents in the relevant area.

Highway Tripping Claims

Documents from Highway Authority for a period of 12 months prior to the accident:

(i) Records of inspection for the relevant stretch of highway.
(ii) Maintenance records including records of independent contractors working in relevant area.
(iii) Records of the minutes of Highway Authority meetings where maintenance or repair policy has been discussed or decided.
(iv) Records of complaints about the state of highways.
(v) Records of other accidents which have occurred on the relevant stretch of highway.

Workplace Claims

(i) Accident book entry.
(ii) First aider report.
(iii) Surgery record.
(iv) Foreman/supervisor accident report.
(v) Safety representatives accident report.
(vi) RIDDOR report to HSE.
(vii) Other communications between defendants and HSE.
(viii) Minutes of Health and Safety Committee meeting(s) where accident/matter considered.
(ix) Report to DSS.
(x) Documents listed above relative to any previous accident/matter identified by the claimant and relied upon as proof of negligence.

(xi) Earnings information where defendant is employer.

Documents produced to comply with requirements of the Management of Health and Safety at Work Regulations 1992—

(i) Pre-accident Risk Assessment required by Regulation 3.
(ii) Post-accident Re-Assessment required by Regulation 3.
(iii) Accident Investigation Report prepared in implementing the requirements of Regulations 4, 6 and 9.
(vi) Health Surveillance Records in appropriate cases required by Regulation 5.
(v) Information provided to employees under Regulation 8.
(vi) Documents relating to the employees health and safety training required by Regulation 11.

Workplace Claims—Disclosure where specific regulations apply

Section A: Workplace (Health Safety and Welfare) Regulations 1992

(i) Repair and maintenance records required by Regulation 5. B1–006
(ii) Housekeeping records to comply with the requirements of Regulation 9.
(iii) Hazard warning signs or notices to comply with Regulation 17 (Traffic Routes).

Section B: Provision and Use of Work Equipment Regulations 1992

(i) Manufacturers' specifications and instructions in respect of relevant work equipment establishing its suitability to comply with Regulation 5.
(ii) Maintenance log/maintenance records required to comply with Regulation 6.
(iii) Documents providing information and instructions to employees to comply with Regulation 8.
(iv) Documents provided to the employee in respect of training for use to comply with Regulation 9.
(v) Any notice, sign or document relied upon as a defence to alleged breaches of Regulations 14 to 18 dealing with controls and control systems.
(vi) Instruction/training documents issued to comply with the requirements of Regulation 22 insofar as it deals with maintenance operations where the machinery is not shut down.
(vii) Copies of markings required to comply with Regulation 23.
(viii) Copies of warnings required to comply with Regulation 24.

Section C: Personal Protective Equipment at Work Regulations 1992

(i) Documents relating to the assessment of the Personal Protective Equipment to comply with Regulation 6.
(ii) Documents relating to the maintenance and replacement of Personal Protective Equipment to comply with Regulation 7.
(iii) Record of maintenance procedures for Personal Protective Equipment to comply with Regulation 7.
(iv) Records of tests and examinations of Personal Protective Equipment to comply with Regulation 7.
(v) Documents providing information, instruction and training in relation to the Personal Protective Equipment to comply with Regulation 9.
(vi) Instructions for use of Personal Protective Equipment to include the manufacturers' instructions to comply with Regulation 10.

Section D: Manual Handling Operations Regulations 1992

(i) Manual Handling Risk Assessment carried out to comply with the requirements of Regulation 4(1)(b)(i).

(ii) Re-assessment carried out post-accident to comply with requirements of Regulation 4(1)(b)(i).

(iii) Documents showing the information provided to the employee to give general indications related to the load and precise indications on the weight of the load and the heaviest side of the load if the centre of gravity was not positioned centrally to comply with Regulation 4(1)(b)(iii).

(iv) Documents relating to training in respect of manual handling operations and training records.

Section E: Health and Safety (Display Screen Equipment) Regulations 1992

(i) Analysis of work stations to assess and reduce risks carried out to comply with the requirements of Regulation 2.

(ii) Re-assessment of analysis of work stations to assess and reduce risks following development of symptoms by the claimant.

(iii) Documents detailing the provision of training including training records to comply with the requirements of Regulation 6.

(iv) Documents providing information to employees to comply with the requirements of Regulation 7.

Section F: Control of Substances Hazardous to Health Regulations 1988

(i) Risk assessment carried out to comply with the requirements of Regulation 6.

(ii) Reviewed risk assessment carried out to comply with the requirements of Regulation 6.

(iii) Copy labels from containers used for storage handling and disposal of carcinogenics to comply with the requirements of Regulation 7(2A)(h).

(iv) Warning signs identifying designation of areas and installations which may be contaminated by carcinogenics to comply with the requirements of Regulation 7(2A)(h).

(v) Documents relating to the assessment of the Personal Protective Equipment to comply with Regulation 7(3A).

(vi) Documents relating to the maintenance and replacement of Personal Protective Equipment to comply with Regulation 7(3A).

(vii) Record of maintenance procedures for Personal Protective Equipment to comply with Regulation 7(3A).

(viii) Records of tests and examinations of Personal Protective Equipment to comply with Regulation 7(3A).

(ix) Documents providing information, instruction and training in relation to the Personal Protective Equipment to comply with Regulation 7(3A).

(x) Instructions for use of Personal Protective Equipment to include the manufacturers' instructions to comply with Regulation 7(3A).

(xi) Air monitoring records for substances assigned a maximum exposure limit or occupational exposure standard to comply with the requirements of Regulation 7

(xii) Maintenance examination and test of control measures records to comply with Regulation 9.

(xiii) Monitoring records to comply with the requirements of Regulation 10.

(xiv) Health surveillance records to comply with the requirements of Regulation 11.

(xv) Documents detailing information, instruction and training including training records for employees to comply with the requirements of Regulation 12.

(xvi) Labels and Health and Safety data sheets supplied to the employers to comply with the CHIP Regulations.

Section G: Construction (Design and Management) Regulations 1994

(i) Notification of a project form (HSE F10) to comply with the requirements of Regulation 7.

(ii) Health and Safety Plan to comply with requirements of Regulation 15.

(iii) Health and Safety file to comply with the requirements of Regulations 12 and 14.

(iv) Information and training records provided to comply with the requirements of Regulation 17.

(v) Records of advice from and views of persons at work to comply with the requirements of Regulation 18.

Section H: Pressure Systems and Transportable Gas Containers Regulations 1989

(i) Information and specimen markings provided to comply with the requirements of Regulation 5.

(ii) Written statements specifying the safe operating limits of a system to comply with the requirements of Regulation 7.

(iii) Copy of the written scheme of examination required to comply with the requirements of Regulation 8.

(iv) Examination records required to comply with the requirements of Regulation 9.

(v) Instructions provided for the use of operator to comply with Regulation 11.

(vi) Records kept to comply with the requirements of Regulation 13.

(vii) Records kept to comply with the requirements of Regulation 22.

Section I: Lifting Plant and Equipment (Records of Test and Examination Etc.) Regulations 1992

(i) Record kept to comply with the requirements of Regulation 6.

Section J: The Noise at Work Regulations 1989

(i) Any risk assessment records required to comply with the requirements of Regulations 4 and 5.

(ii) Manufacturers' literature in respect of all ear protection made available to claimant to comply with the requirements of Regulation 8.

(iii) All documents provided to the employee for the provision of information to comply with Regulation 11.

Section K: Construction (Head Protection) Regulations 1989

(i) Pre-accident assessment of head protection required to comply with Regulation 3(4).

(ii) Post-accident re-assessment required to comply with Regulation 3(5).

Section L: The Construction (General Provisions) Regulations 1961

(i) Report prepared following inspections and examinations of excavations etc. to comply with the requirements of Regulation 9.

(ii) Report prepared following inspections and examinations of work in cofferdams and caissons to comply with the requirements of Regulations 17 and 18.

N.B. Further Standard Discovery lists will be required prior to full implementation.

Annex C

Letter of instruction to medical expert

B1–007 Dear Sir,

Re: *(Name and Address)*

D.O.B. –
Telephone No. –
Date of Accident –

We are acting for the above named in connection with injuries received in an accident which occurred on the above date. The main injuries appear to have been **(main injuries)**.

We should be obliged if you would examine our Client and let us have a full and detailed report dealing with any relevant pre-accident medical history, the injuries sustained, treatment received and present condition, dealing in particular with the capacity for work and giving a prognosis.

It is central to our assessment of the extent of our client's injuries to establish the extent and duration of any continuing disability. Accordingly, in the prognosis section we would ask you to specifically comment on any areas of continuing complaint or disability or impact on daily living. If there is such continuing disability you should comment upon the level of suffering or inconvenience caused and, if you are able, give your view as to when or if the complaint or disability is likely to resolve.

Please send our Client an appointment direct for this purpose. Should you be able to offer a cancellation appointment please contact our Client direct. We confirm we will be responsible for your reasonable fees.

We are obtaining the notes and records from our Client's GP and Hospitals attended and will forward them to you when they are to hand/or please request the GP and Hospital records direct and advise that any invoice for the provision of these records should be forwarded to us.

In order to comply with Court Rules we would be grateful if you would insert above your signature a statement that the contents are true to the best of your knowledge and belief.

In order to avoid further correspondence we can confirm that on the evidence we have there is no reason to suspect we may be pursuing a claim against the hospital or its staff.

We look forward to receiving your report within ____________ weeks. If you will not be able to prepare your report within this period please telephone us upon receipt of these instructions.

When acknowledging these instructions it would assist if you could give an estimate as to the likely time scale for the provision of your report and also an indication as to your fee.

Yours faithfully

PRE-ACTION PROTOCOL FOR THE RESOLUTION OF CLINICAL DISPUTES

Clinical Disputes Forum
Executive Summary

1 The Clinical Disputes Forum is a multi-disciplinary body which was formed in 1997, as a result of Lord Woolf's "Access to Justice" inquiry. One of the aims of the Forum is to find less adversarial and more cost-effective ways of resolving disputes about healthcare and medical treatment. The names and addresses of the Chairman and Secretary of the Forum can be found at Annex E. **B2–001**

2 This protocol is the Forum's first major initiative. It has been drawn up carefully, including extensive consultations with most of the key stakeholders in the medico-legal system.

3 The protocol—

- encourages a climate of openness when something has "gone wrong" with a patient's treatment or the patient is dissatisfied with that treatment and/or the outcome. This reflects the new and developing requirements for clinical governance within healthcare;
- provides **general guidance** on how this more open culture might be achieved when disputes arise;
- recommends **a timed sequence** of steps for patients and healthcare providers, and their advisers, to follow when a dispute arises. This should facilitate and speed up exchanging relevant information and increase the prospects that disputes can be resolved without resort to legal action.

4 This protocol has been prepared by a working party of the Clinical Disputes Forum. It has the support of the Lord Chancellor's Department, the Department of Health and NHS Executive, the Law Society, the Legal Aid Board and many other key organisations.

1. Why This Protocol?

Mistrust in Healthcare Disputes

1.1 The number of complaints and claims against hospitals, GPs, dentists and private healthcare providers is growing as patients become more prepared to question the treatment they are given, to seek explanations of what happened, and to seek appropriate redress. Patients may require further treatment, an apology, assurances about future action, or compensation. These trends are unlikely to change. The Patients Charter encourages patients to have high expectations, and a revised NHS Complaints Procedure was implemented in 1996. The Civil Justice Reforms and new Rules of Court should make litigation quicker, more user friendly and less expensive.

1.2 It is clearly in the interests of patients, healthcare professionals and providers that patients' concerns, complaints and claims arising from their treatment are resolved as quickly, efficiently and professionally as possible. A climate of mistrust and lack of openness can seriously damage the patient/clinician relationship, unnecessarily prolong disputes (especially litigation), and reduce the resources available for treating patients. It may also cause additional work for, and lower the morale of, healthcare professionals.

1.3 At present there is often mistrust by both sides. This can mean that patients fail to raise their concerns with the healthcare provider as early as possible. Sometimes patients may pursue a complaint or claim which has little merit, due to a lack of sufficient information and understanding. It can also mean that patients become reluctant, once advice has been taken on a potential claim, to disclose sufficient information to enable the provider to investigate that claim efficiently and, where appropriate, resolve it.

1.4 On the side of the healthcare provider this mistrust can be shown in a reluctance to be honest with patients, a failure to provide prompt clear explanations, especially of adverse outcomes (whether or not there may have been negligence) and a tendency to "close ranks" once a claim is made.

What Needs to Change

1.5 If that mistrust is to be removed, and a more co-operative culture is to develop—

- healthcare professionals and providers need to adopt a constructive approach to complaints and claims. They should accept that concerned patients are entitled to an explanation and an apology, if warranted, and to appropriate redress in the event of negligence. An overly defensive approach is not in the long term interest of their main goal: patient care;
- patients should recognise that unintended and/or unfortunate consequences of medical treatment can only be rectified if they are brought to the attention of the healthcare provider as soon as possible.

1.6 A protocol which sets out "ground rules" for the handling of disputes at their early stages should, if it is to be subscribed to, and followed—

- encourage greater openness between the parties;
- encourage parties to find the most appropriate way of resolving the particular dispute;
- reduce delay and costs;
- reduce the need for litigation.

Why This Protocol Now?

1.7 Lord Woolf in his "Access to Justice" report in July 1996, concluded that major causes of costs and delay in medical negligence litigation occur at the pre-action stage. He recommended that patients and their advisers, and healthcare providers, should work more closely together to try to resolve disputes co-operatively, rather than proceed to litigation. He specifically recommended a pre-action protocol for medical negligence cases.

1.8 A fuller summary of Lord Woolf's recommendations is at Annex D.

Where the Protocol Fits In

1.9 Protocols serve the needs of litigation and pre-litigation practice, especially—

- predictability in the time needed for steps pre-proceedings;
- standardisation of relevant information, including records and documents to be disclosed

1.10 Building upon Lord Woolf's recommendations, the Lord Chancellor's Department is now promoting the adoption of protocols in specific areas, including medical negligence.

1.11 It is recognised that contexts differ significantly. For example: patients tend to have an ongoing relationship with a GP, more so than with a hospital; clinical staff in the National Health Service are often employees, while those in the private sector may be contractors; providing records quickly may be relatively easy for GPs and dentists, but can be a complicated procedure in a large multi-department hospital. The protocol which follows is intended to be sufficiently broadly based, and flexible, to apply to all aspects of the health service: primary and secondary; public and private sectors.

Enforcement of the Protocol and Sanctions

1.12 The civil justice reforms will be implemented in April 1999. One new set of Court Rules and procedures is replacing the existing rules for both the High and county courts. This and the personal injury protocols are being published with the Rules, Practice Directions and key court forms. The courts will be able to treat the standards set in protocols as the normal reasonable approach to pre-action conduct.

1.13 If proceedings are issued it will be for the court to decide whether non-compliance with a protocol should merit sanctions. Guidance on the court's likely approach will be given from time to time in practice directions.

1.14 If the court has to consider the question of compliance after proceedings have begun it will not be concerned with minor infringements, *e.g.* failure by a short period to provide relevant information. One minor breach will not entitle the "innocent" party to abandon following the protocol. The court will look at the effect of non-compliance on the other party when deciding whether to impose sanctions.

2. The Aims of the Protocol

2.1 The **general** aims of the protocol are— B2–002

- to maintain/restore the patient/healthcare provider relationship;
- to resolve as many disputes as possible without litigation.

2.2 The **specific** objectives are—

Openness

- to encourage early communication of the perceived problem between patients and healthcare providers;
- to encourage patients to voice any concerns or dissatisfaction with their treatment as soon as practicable;
- to encourage healthcare providers to develop systems of early reporting and investigation for serious adverse treatment outcomes and to provide full and prompt explanations to dissatisfied patients;
- to ensure that sufficient information is disclosed by both parties to enable each to understand the other's perspective and case, and to encourage early resolution.

Timeliness

- to provide an early opportunity for healthcare providers to identify cases where an investigation is required and to carry out that investigation promptly;
- to encourage primary and private healthcare providers to involve their defence organisations or insurers at an early stage;
- To ensure that all relevant medical records are provided to patients or their appointed representatives on request, to a realistic timetable by any healthcare provider;
- to ensure that relevant records which are not in healthcare providers' possession are made available to them by patients and their advisers at an appropriate stage;
- where a resolution is not achievable to lay the ground to enable litigation to proceed on a reasonable timetable, at a reasonable and proportionate cost and to limit the matters in contention;
- to discourage the prolonged pursuit of unmeritorious claims and the prolonged defence of meritorious claims.

Awareness of Options

- to ensure that patients and healthcare providers are made aware of the available options to pursue and resolve disputes on what each might involve.

2.3 This protocol does not attempt to be prescriptive about a number of related clinical governance issues which will have a bearing on healthcare providers' ability to meet the standards within the protocol. Good clinical governance requires the following to be considered—

(a) **Clinical risk management:** the protocol does not provide any detailed guidance to healthcare providers on clinical risk management or the adoption of risk management systems and procedures. This must be a matter for the NHS Executive, the National Health Service Litigation Authority, individual trusts and providers, including GPs, dentists and the private sector. However, effective co-ordinated, focused clinical risk management strategies and procedures can help in managing risk and in the early identification and investigation of adverse outcomes.

(b) **Adverse outcome reporting:** the protocol does not provide any detailed guidance on which adverse outcomes should trigger an investigation. However, healthcare providers should have in place procedures for such investigations, including recording of statements of key witnesses. These procedures should also cover when and how to inform patients that an adverse outcome has occurred.

(c) **The professional's duty to report:** the protocol does not recommend changes to the codes of conduct of professionals in healthcare, or attempt to impose a specific duty to those professionals to report known adverse outcomes or untoward incidents. Lord Woolf in his final report suggested that the professional bodies might consider this. The General Medical Council is preparing guidance to doctors about their duty to report adverse incidents and to co-operate with inquiries.

3. The Protocol

B2–003 **3.1** This protocol is not a comprehensive code governing all the steps in clinical disputes. Rather it attempts to set out **a code of good practice** which parties should follow when litigation might be a possibility.

3.2 The **commitments** section of the protocol summarises the guiding principles which healthcare providers and patients and their advisers are invited to endorse when dealing with patient dissatisfaction with treatment and its outcome, and with potential complaints and claims.

3.3 The **steps** section sets out, in a more prescriptive form, a recommended sequence of actions to be followed if litigation is a prospect.

Good Practice Commitments

3.4 Healthcare providers should—

(i) ensure that **key staff**, including claims and litigation managers, are appropriately trained and have some knowledge of healthcare law, and of complaints procedures and civil litigation practice and procedure;

(ii) develop an approach to **clinical governance** that ensures that clinical practice is delivered to commonly accepted standards and that this is routinely monitored through a system of clinical audit and clinical risk management (particularly adverse outcome investigation);

(iii) set up **adverse outcome reporting systems** in all specialties to record and investigate unexpected serious adverse outcomes as soon as possible. Such systems can enable evidence to be gathered quickly, which makes it easier to provide an accurate explanation of what happened and to defend or settle any subsequent claims;

(iv) use the results of **adverse incidents and complaints positively** as a guide to how to improve services to patients in the future;

(v) ensure **that patients receive clear and comprehensible information** in an accessible form about how to raise their concerns or complaints;

(vi) establish **efficient and effective systems of recording and storing**

patient records, notes, diagnostic reports and X-rays, and to retain these in accordance with Department of Health guidance (currently for a minimum of eight years in the case of adults, and all obstetric and paediatric notes for children until they reach the age of 25);

(vii) **advise patients** of a serious adverse outcome and provide on request to the patient or the patient's representative an oral or written explanation of what happened, information on further steps open to the patient, including where appropriate an offer of future treatment to rectify the problem, an apology, changes in procedure which will benefit patients and/or compensation.

3.5 Patients and their advisers should—

(i) **report any concerns and dissatisfaction** to the healthcare provider as soon as is reasonable to enable that provider to offer clinical advice where possible, to advise the patient if anything has gone wrong and take appropriate action;

(ii) consider the **full range of options** available following an adverse outcome with which a patient is dissatisfied, including a request for an explanation, a meeting, a complaint, and other appropriate dispute resolution methods (including mediation) and negotiation, not only litigation;

(iii) **inform the healthcare provider when the patient is satisfied** that the matter has been concluded: legal advisers should notify the provider when they are no longer acting for the patient, particularly if proceedings have not started.

Protocol Steps

3.6 The steps of this protocol which follow have been kept deliberately simple. An illustration of the likely sequence of events in a number of healthcare situations is at Annex A.

Obtaining the Health Records

3.7 Any request for records by the **patient** or their adviser should—

- **provide sufficient information** to alert the healthcare provider where an adverse outcome has been serious or had serious consequences;
- be as **specific as possible** about the records which are required.

3.8 Requests for copies of the patient's clinical records should be made using the Law Society and Department of Health approved **standard forms** (enclosed at Annex B), adapted as necessary.

3.9 The copy records should be provided **within 40 days** of the request and for a cost not exceeding the charges permissible under the Access to Health Records Act 1990 (currently a maximum of £10 plus photocopying and postage).

3.10 In the rare circumstances that the healthcare provider is in difficulty in complying with the request within 40 days, the **problem should be explained** quickly and details given of what is being done to resolve it.

3.11 It will not be practicable for healthcare providers to investigate in detail each case when records are requested. But healthcare providers should **adopt a policy on which cases will be investigated** (see paragraph 3.5 on clinical governance and adverse outcome reporting).

3.12 If the healthcare provider fails to provide the health records within 40 days, the patient or their adviser can then apply to the court for an **order for pre-action disclosure**. The new Civil Procedure Rules should make pre-action applications to the court easier. The Court will also have the power to impose costs sanctions for unreasonable delay in providing records.

3.13 If either the patient or the healthcare provider considers **additional health records are required from a third party**, in the first instance these should be requested by or through the patient. Third party healthcare providers are expected to co-operate. The Civil Procedure Rules will enable patients and healthcare providers to apply to the court for pre-action disclosure by third parties.

Letter of Claim

3.14 Annex C1 to this protocol provides **a template for the recommended contents of a letter of claim**: the level of detail will need to be varied to suit the particular circumstances.

3.15 If, following the receipt and analysis of the records, and the receipt of any further advice (including from experts if necessary—see Section 4), the patient/adviser decides that there are grounds for a claim, they should then send, as soon as practicable, to the healthcare provider/potential defendant, a **letter of claim**.

3.16 This letter should contain a **clear summary of the facts** on which the claim is based, including the alleged adverse outcome, and the **main allegations of negligence**. It should also describe the **patient's injuries**, and present condition and prognosis. The **financial loss** incurred by the plaintiff should be outlined with an indication of the heads of damage to be claimed and the scale of the loss, unless this is impracticable.

3.17 In more complex cases a **chronology** of the relevant events should be provided, particularly if the patient has been treated by a number of different healthcare providers.

3.18 The letter of claim **should refer to any relevant documents**, including health records, and if possible enclose copies of any of those which will not already be in the potential defendant's possession, *e.g.* any relevant general practitioner records if the plaintiff's claim is against a hospital.

3.19 **Sufficient information** must be given to enable the healthcare provider defendant to **commence investigations** and to put an initial valuation on the claim.

3.20 Letters of claim are **not** intended to have the same formal status as a **pleading**, nor should any sanctions necessarily apply if the letter of claim and any subsequent statement of claim in the proceedings differ.

3.21 **Proceedings should not be issued until after three months from the letter of claim**, unless there is a limitation problem and/or the patient's position needs to be protected by early issue.

3.22 The patient or their adviser may want to make an **offer to settle** the claim at this early stage by putting forward an amount of compensation which would be satisfactory (possibly including any costs incurred to date). If an offer to settle is made, generally this should be supported by a medical report which deals with the injuries, condition and prognosis, and by a schedule of loss and supporting documentation. The level of detail necessary will depend on the value of the claim. Medical reports may not be necessary where there is no significant continuing injury, and a detailed schedule may not be necessary in a low value case. The Civil Procedure Rules are expected to set out the legal and procedural requirements for making offers to settle.

The Response

3.23 Attached at Annex C2 is a template for the suggested contents of the **letter of response**.

3.24 The healthcare provider should **acknowledge** the letter of claim **within 14 days of receipt** and should identify who will be dealing with the matter.

3.25 The heathcare provider should, **within three months** of the letter of claim, provide a **reasoned answer**—

- if the **claim is admitted** the healthcare provider should say so in clear terms;
- if only **part of the claim is admitted** the healthcare provider should

make clear which issues of breach of duty and/or causation are admitted and which are denied and why;

- if it is intended that any **admissions will be binding**;
- if the claim is denied, this should include specific comments on the allegations of negligence, and if a synopsis or chronology of relevant events has been provided and is disputed, the healthcare provider's version of those events;
- where additional documents are relied upon, *e.g.* an internal protocol, copies should be provided.

3.26 If the patient has made an offer to settle, the healthcare provider should **respond to that offer** in the response letter, preferably with reasons. The provider may make its own offer to settle at this stage, either as a counter-offer to the patient's, or of its own accord, but should accompany any offer by any supporting medical evidence, and/or by any other evidence in relation to the value of the claim which is in the healthcare provider's possession.

3.27 If the parties reach agreement on liability, but time is needed to resolve the value of the claim, they should aim to agree a reasonable period.

4. Experts

4.1 In clinical negligence disputes **expert opinions** may be needed: B2–004

- on breach of duty and causation
- on the patient's condition and prognosis
- to assist in valuing aspects of the claim

4.2 The civil justice reforms and the new **Civil Procedure Rules** will encourage economy in the use of experts and a **less adversarial expert culture**. It is recognised that in clinical negligence disputes, the parties and their advisers will require flexibility in their approach to expert evidence. Decisions on whether experts might be instructed jointly, and on whether reports might be disclosed sequentially or by exchange, should rest with the parties and their advisers. Sharing expert evidence may be appropriate on issues relating to the value of the claim. However, this protocol does not attempt to be prescriptive on issues in relation to expert evidence.

4.3 Obtaining expert evidence will often be an expensive step and may take time, especially in specialised areas of medicine where there are limited numbers of suitable experts. Patients and healthcare providers, and their advisers, will therefore need to consider carefully how best to obtain any necessary expert help quickly and cost-effectively. Assistance with locating a suitable expert is available from a number of sources.

5. Alternative Approaches to Settling Disputes

5.1 It would not be practicable for this protocol to address in any detail how a patient or their adviser, or healthcare provider, might decide which method to adopt to resolve the particular problem. But, the courts increasingly expect parties to try to settle their differences by agreement before issuing proceedings. B2–005

5.2 Most disputes are resolved by **discussion and negotiation**. Parties should bear in mind that carefully planned face-to-face meetings may be particularly helpful in exploring further treatment for the patient, in reaching understandings about what happened, and on both parties' positions, in narrowing the issues in dispute and, if the timing is right, in helping to settle the whole matter.

5.3 Summarised below are some other alternatives for resolving disputes:

- The revised **NHS Complaints Procedure** which was implemented in April 1996, is designed to provide patients with an explanation of what happened and an apology if appropriate. It is not designed to provide compensation for cases of negligence. However, patients might choose to use the procedure if their only, or main, goal is to obtain an explanation, or to obtain more information to help them decide what other action might be appropriate.

- **Mediation** may be appropriate in some cases: this is a form of facilitated negotiation assisted by an independent neutral party. It is expected that the new Civil Procedure Rules will give the court the power to stay proceedings for one month for settlement discussions or mediation.
- Other methods of resolving disputes include **arbitration, determination by an expert, and early neutral evaluation** by a medical or legal expert. The Lord Chancellor's Department has produced a booklet on **"Resolving Disputes Without Going to Court"**, LCD 1995, which lists a number of organisations that provide alternative dispute resolution services.

Annex A

Illustrative Flowchart

B2–006

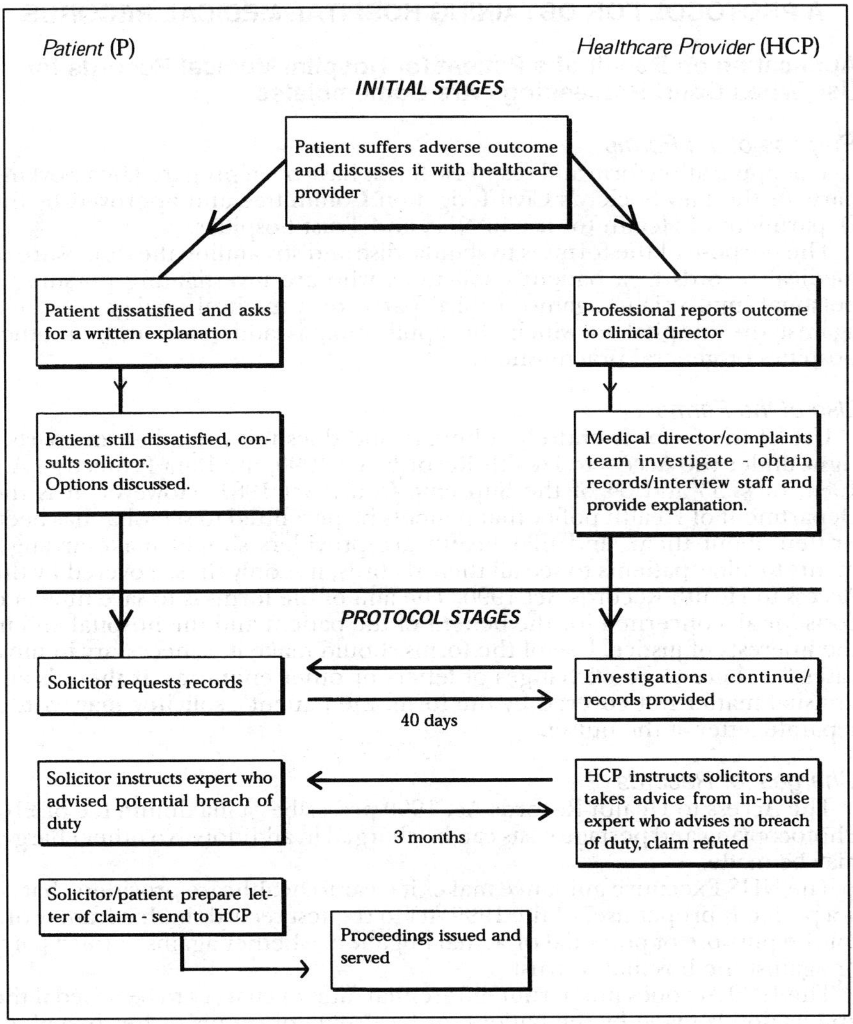

Annex B

Medical Negligence and Personal Injury Claims

A PROTOCOL FOR OBTAINING HOSPITAL MEDICAL RECORDS

Application on Behalf of a Patient for Hospital Medical Records for Use When Court Proceedings Are Contemplated

Purpose of the Forms

B2-007 This application form and response forms have been prepared by a working party of the Law Society's Civil Litigation Committee and approved by the Department of Health for use in NHS and Trust hospitals.

The purpose of the forms is to standardise and streamline the disclosure of medical records to a patient's solicitors, who are investigating pursuing a personal injury claim against a third party, or a medical negligence claim against the hospital to which the application is addressed and/or other hospitals or general practitioners.

Use of the Forms

Use of the forms is entirely voluntary and does not prejudice any party's right under the Access to Health Records Act 1990, the Data Protection Act 1984, or ss.33 and 34 of the Supreme Court Act 1981. However, it is the Department of Health policy that patients be permitted to see what has been written about them, and that healthcare providers should make arrangements to allow patients to see all their records, not only those covered by the Access to Health Records Act 1990. The aim of the forms is to save time and costs for all concerned for the benefit of the patient and the hospital and in the interests of justice. Use of the forms should make it unnecessary in most cases for there to be exchanges of letters or other enquiries. If there is any unusual matter not covered by the form, the patient's solicitor may write a separate letter at the outset.

Charges for Records

The Access to Health Records Act 1990 prescribes a maximum fee of £10. Photocopying and postage costs can be charged in addition. No other charges may be made.

The NHS Executive guidance makes it clear to healthcare providers that "it is a perfectly proper use" of the 1990 Act to request records in that framework for the purpose of potential or actual litigation, whether against a third party or against the hospital or trust.

The 1990 Act does not permit differential rates of charges to be levied if the application is made by the patient, or by a solicitor on his or her behalf, or whether the response to the application is made by the healthcare provider directly (the medical records manager or a claims manager) or by a solicitor.

The NHS Executive guidance recommend that the same practice should be followed with regard to charges when the records are provided under a voluntary agreement as under the 1990 Act, except that in those circumstances the £10 access fee will not be appropriate.

The NHS Executive Also Advises—

- that the cost of photocopying may include "the cost of staff time in making copies" and the costs of running the copier (but not costs of locating and sifting records).
- that the common practice of setting a standard rate for an application or charging an administration fee is not acceptable

because there will be cases when this fails to comply with the 1990 Act.

Records: What Might Be Included

X-rays and test results form part of the patient's records. Additional charges for copying X-rays are permissible. If there are large numbers of X-rays, the records officer should check with the patient/solicitor before arranging copying.

Reports on an "adverse incident" and reports on the patient made for risk management and audit purposes may form part of the records and be discloseable: the exception will be any specific record or report made solely or mainly in connection with an actual or potential claim.

Records: Quality Standards

When copying records healthcare providers should ensure—

1. All documents are legible, and complete, if necessary by photocopying at less than 100% size.
2. Documents larger than A4 in the original, *e.g.* ITU charts, should be reproduced in A3, or reduced to A4 where this retains readability.
3. Documents are only copied on one side of paper, unless the original is two sided.
4. Documents should not be unnecessarily shuffled or bound and holes should not be made in the copied papers.

Enquiries/Further Information

Any enquiries about the forms should be made initially to the solicitors making the request. Comments on the use and content of the forms should be made to the Secretary, Civil Litigation Committee. The Law Society, 113 Chancery Lane, London WC2A 1PL, telephone 0171 320 5739, or to the NHS Management Executive, Quarry House, Quarry Hill, Leeds LS2 7UE.

The Law Society

May 1998

B2–008

APPLICATION ON BEHALF OF A PATIENT FOR HOSPITAL MEDICAL RECORDS FOR USE WHEN COURT PROCEEDINGS ARE CONTEMPLATED

This should be completed as fully as possible

Insert Hospital Name and Address	**TO: Medical Records Officer** **Hospital**

1 (a)	Full name of patient (including previous surnames)	
(b)	Address now	
(c)	Address at start of treatment	
(d)	Date of birth (and death, if applicable)	
(e)	Hospital ref. no if available	
(f)	N.I. number, if available	
2	This application is made because the patient is considering	
(a)	a claim against your hospital as detailed in para 7 overleaf	YES/NO
(b)	pursuing an action against some one else	YES/NO

3	Department(s) where treatment was received	
4	Name(s) of consultant(s) at your hospital in charge of the treatment	
5	Whether treatment at your hospital was private or NHS, wholly or in part	
6	A description of the treatment received, with approximate dates	
7	If the answer to Q2(a) is "Yes" details of	
	(a) the likely nature of the claim,	
	(b) grounds for the claim,	
	(c) approximate dates of the events involved	
8	If the answer to Q2(b) is "Yes" insert	
	(a) the names of the proposed defendants	
	(b) whether legal proceedings yet begun	YES/NO
	(c) if appropriate, details of the claim and action number	
9	We confirm we will pay reasonable copying charges	
10	We request prior details of (a) photocopying and administration charges for medical records	YES/NO
	(b) number of and cost of copying x-ray and scan films	YES/NO

11	Any other relevant information, particular requirements, or any particular documents not required (e.g. copies of computerised records)	
	Signature of Solicitor	
	Name	
	Address	
	Ref.	
	Telephone Number	
	Fax number	

Please print name beneath each signature. Signature by child over 12 but under 18 years also requires signature by parent.

Signature of patient

Signature of parent or next friend if appropriate

Signature of personal representative where patient has died

B2–009

FIRST RESPONSE TO APPLICATION FOR HOSPITAL RECORDS

NAME OF PATIENT Our ref. Your ref.		
1	Date of receipt of patient's application	
2	We intend that copy medical records will be dispatched within 6 weeks of that date	YES/NO
3	We require pre-payment of photocopying charges	YES/NO
4	If estimate of photocopying charges requested or pre-payment required the amount will be	£/notified to you
5	The cost of x-ray and scan films will be	£/notified to you
6	If there is any problem, we shall write to you within those 6 weeks	YES/NO
7	Any other information	
	Please address further correspondence to	
	Signed	
	Direct telephone number	
	Direct fax number	
	Dated	

B2–010

SECOND RESPONSE ENCLOSING PATIENT'S HOSPITAL MEDICAL RECORDS

Address

Our Ref.
Your Ref.

	NAME OF PATIENT:	
1	We confirm that the enclosed copy medical records are all those within the control of the hospital, relevant to the application which you have made to the best of our knowledge and belief, subject to paras 2–5 below	YES/NO
2	Details of any other documents which have not yet been located	
3	Date by when it is expected that these will be supplied	
4	Details of any records which we are not producing	
5	The reasons for not doing so	
6	An invoice for copying and administration charges is attached	YES/NO
	Signed	
	Date	

Annex C

Templates for Letters of Claim and Response

C1 Letter of Claim

Essential Contents B2–011

1. Client's name, address, date of birth, etc.
2. Dates of allegedly negligent treatment

3. Events giving rise to the claim
- an outline of what happened, including details of other relevant treatments to the client by other healthcare providers.

4. Allegation of negligence and causal link with injuries
- an outline of the allegations or a more detailed list in a complex case an outline of the causal link between allegations and the injuries complained of.

5. The Client's injuries, condition and future prognosis

6. Request for clinical records (if not previously provided)
- use the Law Society form if appropriate or adapt;
- specify the records required;
- if other records are held by other providers, and may be relevant, say so;
- state what investigations have been carried out to date, *e.g.* information from client and witnesses, any complaint and the outcome, if any clinical records have been seen or expert's advice obtained.

7. The likely value of the claim
- an outline of the main heads of damage, or in straightforward cases the details of loss.

Optional Information

What investigations have been carried out
An offer to settle without supporting evidence
Suggestions for obtaining expert evidence
Suggestions for meetings, negotiations, discussion or mediation

Possible Enclosures

Chronology
Clinical records request form and client's authorisation
Expert report(s)
Schedules of loss and supporting evidence

C2 Letter of Response

Essential Contents

1. Provide requested records and invoice for copying
- explain if records are incomplete or extensive records are held and ask for further instructions;
- request additional records from third parties

2. Comments on events and/or chronology
- if events are disputed or the healthcare provider has further

information or documents on which they wish to rely, these should be provided, *e.g.* internal, protocol;
- details of any further information needed from the patient or a third party should be provided.

3. If breach of duty and causation are accepted
- suggestions might be made for resolving the claim and/or requests for further information;
- a response should be made to any offer to settle.

4. If breach of duty and/or causation are denied
- a bare denial will not be sufficient. If the healthcare provider has other explanations for what happened, these should be given at least in outline;
- suggestions might be made for the next steps, e.g. further investigations, obtaining expert evidence, meetings/negotiations or mediation, or an invitation to issue proceedings.

Optional Matters

An offer to settle if the patient has not made one, or a counter offer to the patient's with supporting evidence.

Possible Enclosures

Clinical records
Annotated chronology
Expert reports

Annex D

Lord Woolf's Recommendations

B2–012 **1.** Lord Woolf in his Access to Justice Report in July 1996, following a detailed review of the problems of medical negligence claims, identified that one of the major sources of **costs and delay** is **at the pre-litigation stage** because—

(a) Inadequate incident reporting and record keeping in hospitals, and mobility of staff, make it difficult to establish facts, often several years after the event.
(b) Claimants must incur the cost of an expert in order to establish whether they have a viable claim.
(c) There is often a long delay before a claim is made.
(d) Defendants do not have sufficient resources to carry out a full investigation of every incident, and do not consider it worthwhile to start an investigation as soon as they receive a request for records, because many cases do not proceed beyond that stage.
(e) Patients often give the Defendant little or no notice of a firm intention to pursue a claim. Consequently, many incidents are not investigated by the defendants until after proceedings have started.
(f) Doctors and other clinical staff are traditionally reluctant to admit negligence or apologise to, or negotiate with, claimants for fear of damage to their professional reputations or career prospects.

2. Lord Woolf acknowledged that under the present arrangements **healthcare providers**, faced with possible medical negligence claims, have a number of **practical problems** to contend with:—

(a) Difficulties of finding patients' records and tracing former staff, which can be exacerbated by late notification and be the healthcare provider's own failure to identify adverse incidents.
(b) The healthcare provider may have only treated the patient for a limited time or for a specific complaint: the patient's previous history may be relevant but the records may be in the possession of one of several other healthcare providers.
(c) The large number of potential claims do not proceed beyond the stage of a request for medical records, or an explanation; and that is difficult for healthcare providers to investigate fully every case whenever a patient asks to see the records.

Annex E

How to Contact the Forum

The Clinical Disputes Forum

Chairman B2–013
Dr Alastair Scotland
Director of Medical Education
Chelsea and Westminster Hospital
369 Fulham Road
London SW1 9NH
Telephone: 0181 746 8000

Secretary
Sarah Leigh
c/o Margaret Dangoor
3 Clydesdale Gardens
Richmond
Surrey
TW10 5EG
Telephone: 0181 241 1012

PRE-ACTION PROTOCOL FOR ROAD TRAFFIC ACCIDENTS

1. Introduction

1.1 The RTA Protocol forms the basis of the terms and conditions for the handling of all traffic accident claims between Solicitors and Insurers. B3–001

The objective is to set out a series of standards between the parties in respect of pre-issue conduct in handling all claims arising from a road traffic accident to include damage only and personal injury claims. The protocol includes procedures on general matters of conduct and early exchange of information; and an agreed level of costs.

The protocol is an opportunity to remove the uncertainty and mistrust between the parties, and to give stability and understanding between the parties with the common goal of improving the communication and speed of settlement of the claims handling process.

1.2 It is intended that the protocol be run initially under a pilot scheme. It is accepted by both parties that both clients consent must be sought prior to the claim being run under the pilot scheme.

1.3 The reference to the word "Solicitor" shall mean any employee of the firm of Solicitors handling the claim on behalf of the claimant and shall not be construed as a person passing themselves off as a Solicitor when they are not in fact a qualified Solicitor.

2. Part 1—Standards

2.1 Solicitors

B3–002 Solicitors in the pursuit of compensation for victims of a road traffic accident, agree as follows:

2.1.1 *To answer correspondence (including Fax and e-mail) received from Insurers within 7 working days and to abide by timetables set out under* items 3 to 8 *inclusive.*

2.1.2 To return all telephone calls, including voice mail messages, from Insurers (which are not immediately answered) within one working day at the latest and to attempt to return the call on the same day if practicable.

2.1.3 In all forms of communication, to be polite and courteous.

2.1.4 To nominate an individual within the ***Solicitor's office*** who will become the liaison officer in respect of the Protocol and to deal with any matter arising thereunder. To identify this contact name in the "Solicitor's initial letter" and to make known the name of such person to any Insurer who enquires.

2.2 Insurers

Insurers in the receipt of claims for compensation arising out of a road traffic accident, agree as follows:

2.2.1 *To answer correspondence (including Fax and e-mail) received from MASS Members within 7 working days and to abide by timetables set out under items 3 to 8 inclusive.*

2.2.2 To return all telephone calls, including voice mail messages, from Solicitors (which are not immediately answered) within one working day at the latest and to attempt to return the call on the same day if practicable.

2.2.3 In all forms of communication, to be polite and courteous.

2.2.4 To nominate an individual within the office who will become the liaison officer in respect of the Protocol and to deal with any matter arising thereunder. To identify this contact name in the "Insurer's first letter" and to make known the names of such person to any ***Solicitor*** who enquires.

2.2.5 Not to contact or communicate with the client direct without the consent of the ***Solicitor***.

3. Part 2—Claims Handling Procedures

B3–003 To facilitate a speedy and efficient claims service, ***Solicitors*** and Insurers will ensure the early release and exchange of information regarding claims, without prejudicing the interests of the client. It is agreed that this will be undertaken by a series of letters and procedures between the parties as follows:

3.1 The "Solicitor's initial letter" (Annex A)

3.1.1 The "Solicitor's initial letter" will be sent (where the Insurer is known) within 7 working days of notification of the claim or within 7 working days of identifying the Insurer. This letter will be clearly identified as the "Solicitor's initial letter" and will include the following information: name of Solicitor's nominated liaison officer; the contact name of the person dealing with the claim and their direct dial number, full name and address of all claimants; and where known, vehicle location; ***vehicle make*** and registration number; details of vehicle hire to include company, rates, type of vehicle, if appropriate, a copy of the engineer's report and estimate of repairs; details of injuries sustained, if any; date of birth and National Insurance Number; VAT Registered (Y/N); the reasons for the claim, *i.e.* allegations of negligence and the clients own insurance details, *i.e.* name, address, policy number and type of insurance.

3.2 The "Insurer's first letter" (Annex D)

3.2.1 The Insurer will respond within 7 working days upon receipt of the "Solicitor's initial letter". This letter will be clearly identified as the "Insurer's first letter" and will acknowledge receipt of the "Solicitor's initial letter"; provide the name of the Insurer's nominated liaison officer; the contact name of the person dealing with the claim and their direct dial number; and if appropriate, confirmation and details of the inspection process and the date by which the engineer's report will be available. The Insurer will also indicate the following: whether liability is under consideration; undisputed or disputed and if disputed, enclose copy of witness statements if available.

3.2.2 Where the Insurer is unable to trace the policy number, the Insurer will telephone the ***Solicitor*** to request any further information required to identify the insurers.

3.3 The "Solicitor's second letter" (Annex B)

3.3.1 The Solicitor will forward a "second letter" within 28 working days of receipt of the "Insurer's first letter". This letter will be clearly identified as the "Solicitor's second letter" and will contain a brief outline of the following: confirmation of whether pursuing (i) non injury claim or (ii) injury claim (to include: extent of the injuries, name and address of NHS hospital attended and commissioning of medical report); client's occupation and period off work (if appropriate); details of loss of use/car hire; storage; and vehicle location if not already advised in the "initial letter"; liability is/is not in issue; witness statements/details of witnesses (if available).

3.4 The "Insurer's second letter" (Annex E)

3.4.1 Within 14 working days of receipt of the "Solicitor's second letter", the Insurer will respond with the "Insurer's second letter". This letter will be clearly identified as the "Insurer's second letter" and will provide the following: confirmation of RTA cover; whether liability is in dispute and if in dispute, copy of witness summaries, if any; confirmation of inspection process; approval of repairs and if appropriate, delivery of an interim cheque for repairs; agree hire rate/propose replacement vehicle as stated in clause 3.9.1. (If liability in dispute **then** 3pi will obtain police report and forward a copy to the claimants Solicitor.)

3.5 Correspondence and telephone communication

All information contained in the above letters can be provided by telephone communication between the parties, provided that each party makes a detailed note of the information given, the date and time of the call and the parties to the conversation. It is also recommended that all subsequent communication be undertaken by telephone between the parties, noting all details in a similar manner.

3.6 Engineers' reports

3.6.1 The Insurer will forward a copy of the engineer's report to the ***Solicitor*** within 7 working days of receipt of the engineer's finding as indicated in the Insurer's "first letter".

3.6.2 If the Insurer has not confirmed in the Insurer's "first letter" that an engineer's report has been commissioned, then the ***Solicitor*** will be at liberty to arrange their own report and such report shall be an allowable disbursement in accordance with clause 7.1.

3.7 Repairable propositions (liability not in dispute)

3.7.1 In the event of the Insurer not undertaking the repairs, the client will elect to undertake one of the following:

(a) to receive a cheque for repairs to be taken by client;
(b) to receive cash in lieu.

3.7.2 The ***Solicitor*** will notify the Insurer of the elected option within 8 working days and the Insurer will within 7 working days either: (1) despatch a cheque or (ii) commence or authorise repairs.

3.7.3 Loss of use will be recoverable for a further 7 working days following receipt of the cheque by the ***Solicitor*** or completion of repairs whichever is the later and provided that the repairs are commenced promptly on receipt of the cheque. (For loss of use rates, see 7.2.2.)

3.8 Irreparable propositions (liability not in dispute)

3.8.1 All Insurers party to this Protocol adhere to the Motor Conference "Code of Practice for the Disposal of Motor Vehicle Salvage to Detect and Deter Criminal Activity" and copy of which is appended hereto.

3.8.2 If the vehicle is a write-off, the report or an accompanying letter will provide confirmation that an interim cheque will be sent within 7 working days. If the client disagrees with the Insurer's valuation and obtains a second report, the Insurer agrees to meet the costs of valuation if the agreed figure exceeds the first valuation by 15%.

3.8.3 The Insurer will not dispose of the vehicle without first obtaining the ***owner's*** consent.

3.8.4 If a courtesy vehicle has been provided or the client is hiring a vehicle, then the Insurer agrees that such hire shall continue and form part of the value of the claim until a period of 7 working days after receipt of the settlement cheque for the vehicle by the ***Solicitor***. (For hire rates, see 7.2.4.)

3.9 Hire

3.9.1 If the Client is already hiring a vehicle, then the insurer shall undertake either of the following:

(i) agree the hire rate, period and type of vehicle; or
(ii) provide a suitable replacement vehicle.

If (i) above, the solicitor will provide copy of the hire account to the Insurer upon request.

3.9.2 If a courtesy/replacement vehicle is provided by the Insurer, the Insurer shall be responsible for the insurance for the said vehicle and any deposit for the fuel shall not exceed £50. The client shall be responsible for all fuel consumption.

3.9.3 Where the Insurer has arranged a courtesy/replacement vehicle, a copy of the account as evidence of the period of replacement, shall be supplied to the Solicitor upon request.

3.9.4 The Insurer will arrange for courtesy/replacement vehicle delivery and collection.

3.10 Storage charges

3.10.1 Upon notification to the Insurer of the vehicle location, the Insurer shall be responsible for all storage charges until the Insurers engineer has inspected the vehicle and either an agreement has been made in accordance with clause 3.6 or a cheque paid in accordance with clause 3.7.

3.10.2 If the Insurer elects to move the vehicle to their own storage facility, the Clients consent must be obtained and 7 working days notice must be given in writing to the Solicitor, providing confirmation of vehicle location. This facility will allow access to the vehicle by the Solicitor's engineer if so required.

3.11 VAT

3.11.1 In all cases where the client is VAT registered, a separate, VAT only invoice will be forwarded by the Insurer or agent/repairer direct to the Client and the client will be responsible for discharging the VAT due.

3.11.2 The Insurer will pay the appropriate rate of VAT on the vehicle hire.

3.11.3 Where the claimant is VAT registered the insurer shall not be responsible for VAT on the Solicitors costs where the vehicle is being used for business purposes. VAT is to be collected by the Solicitor from the claimant.

3.12 Medical evidence

3.12.1 This section applies to instruction of medical experts. It is intended as a facility to reduce time, cost of instruction and dispute on expert evidence where there is direct or medical agency instruction.

3.12.2 Before the Solicitor or Insurer instructs an expert, the instructing party shall provide the other party with a list of the name(s) of one or more expert in the relevant speciality whom he considers suitable to instruct.

3.12.3 Where the instructing party intends to rely on an Agency selection, the instructing party shall request the Agency, to appoint a medical expert and:

(a) By way of Enquiry, provide to the instructing party with the names of alternative experts (prior to instruction of an expert) for disclosure to the other party.

(b) On receipt by the instructing Solicitor of details of the expert appointed, the name and location of the appointed expert should be disclosed to the other party.

3.12.4 Where details of an expert are disclosed to the other party under paragraphs 3.12.2 or 3.12.3 above, that party shall within 10 working days indicate any objection to one or more of the proposed experts. Should the instructing Solicitor receive no response within the expressed time limit, acceptance of the expert or experts disclosed is implied.

3.12.5 Where an objection is raised under 3.12.2 or 3.12.3 within the 10 working days time limit, the instructing Solicitor shall select and instruct another expert in the relevant speciality or request the Agency to so instruct.

3.12.6 If the other party objects to all the listed experts in 3.12.2 or 3.12.3 or to the second expert selected the parties may then instruct experts of their own choice within 5 working days. It would be for the court to decide subsequently if proceedings are issued whether either party acted unreasonably.

3.12.7 If the other party does not object to a nominted expert, then the other party shall not be entitled to rely on their own expert evidence within that particular speciality unless:

(a) the first party agrees;

(b) the Court so directs, or;

(c) the instructing party's expert report has been amended and the instructing party is not prepared to disclose the original report.

3.12.8 The instructed expert may be required to obtain all medical notes and records relating to the accident, the cost of which will be met by the instructing party in the first instance and reimbursed by the Insurer on request. For the avoidance of doubt the obtaining of medical records is discretionary but in any event the expert will be required to confirm whether he has reviewed the claimants GP records.

3.12.9 Upon receipt of the Client's consent to the medical report and its disclosure the Solicitor will forward a copy of the report to the Insurer within 10 working days.

3.12.10 Either party may send to the agreed expert written questions on the report relevant to the issues, via the instructing party. The expert should send answers to the questions separately and directly to each party. The cost incurred by the expert(s) in providing answers to the questions raised shall be paid by the party raising the relevant questions.

3.13 Claims where liability is not in dispute (non injury)

3.13.1 Upon receipt of the "Insurer's second letter" confirming liability is not in dispute and provided that full particulars of claims have been presented, the parties will contact one another within 15 working days to discuss settlement of the claim. Within this period no proceedings will be issued by the ***Solicitor***.

3.14 Claims where liability is not in dispute (injury)

3.14.1 Upon receipt of the ***Solicitor's*** medical report, the Insurer will undertake either of the following:

(i) Make an offer of settlement within 10 working days, where requested, or;

(ii) Advise the ***Solicitor*** if obtaining own medical report in accordance with the provisions set out in clause 3.12, and;

(iii) Forward a copy of the Insurer's medical report to the ***Solicitor*** within 10 working days from the date of receipt, provided the Insurer intends to rely upon this report.

3.14.2 If the offer of settlement is not accepted by the client, then a further 14 day period will be granted to allow for continued negotiation and during which period no proceedings will be issued by the ***Solicitor***.

3.15 Claims where liability is in dispute

3.15.1 The ***Solicitor*** will, within 10 working days of receipt of the "Insurer's second letter", in which liability is disputed and witness statements are attached, forward the "Solicitor's third letter" to be clearly identified as such and to include the ***Solicitor's*** own witness summaries (Annex C).

3.15.2 A further 10 working day period will be allowed for discussions and within which time, no proceedings will be issued.

3.15.3 If liability and/or settlement cannot be agreed within the 10 days discussion period, a police report, if such exists, will be obtained by the insurer and copied to the ***Solicitor*** within 7 working days.

3.15.4 If agreement cannot be reached within a further 10 day period from the exchange of the police report, then either party may issue proceedings, giving the appropriate notice.

3.15.5 In cases where a Claimant is unlikely to be able to return to pre-accident employment within 6 months, both sides will consider whether it is appropriate for a referral to be made to the Disability Assessment unit or similar body for immediate interim help and such assessment to be funded by the Insurer.

3.16 Settlement arrangement and interest

3.16.1 Upon confirmation of the client's agreement to the settlement offer, the insurer will forward a cheque within 10 working days. If at the end of this period no cheque has been received, the ***Solicitor*** will notify the Insurer of such by telephone. If the cheque is not received within 20 working days, interest will commence accruing at the rate of 25% per annum on a daily rate basis until receipt of the settlement cheque by the ***Solicitor***, such cheque to include the interest due. Exception to this clause applies only where receipt of a CRU certificate is pending and the Insurer has duly notified the ***Solicitor***. The Insurer will have made all attempts to have secured this certificate at the earliest opportunity. Interest will not be payable within this period and will commence accruing following 10 working days of receipt of the certificate.

4. Calculation of Time Periods

For the avoidance of doubt in the calculation of all time periods, days will be considered in working days and date of receipt will be assumed to be one day after the date of dispatch. **B3–004**

5. Part 36 Offers

5.1 In accordance with the spirit of the protocol it is suggested that Part 36 offers of settlement should not be made unless the claim involves other parties not operating their claim in accordance with this protocol. Parties would then be free to make such offers but only when the other party (not party to the protocol) makes a Part 36 offer of settlement. **B3–005**

6. Solicitor's Procedures

6.1 ***Solicitors*** further agree: **B3–006**

6.1.1 To abide by arrangements set up by Insurers for repairs, courtesy cars, hire vehicles, etc.

6.1.2 To report all offers in writing to the client within 3 working days of receipt.

6.1.3 If proceedings are issued and judgment is obtained, to serve a copy immediately on the known Insurer and allow the Insurer 7 working days to present proposals for settlement.

6.1.4 To welcome visits from Insurers' representatives and to supply the representative with a detailed schedule of claim (if available) prior to the visit.

6.1.5 To release signed forms of authority for release of relevant medical records when requested on an agreed standard form (Annex F).

7. Insurers' Procedures

7.1 ***Insurers*** further agree: **B3–007**

7.1.1 To pay costs as detailed in Annex G.

In addition, VAT at the prevailing rate and all reasonable disbursements will be paid. (N.B. paragraph 7.1.1 regarding payment of costs will not apply to claims from Northern Ireland and Scotland where own costs scales shall prevail.)

7.1.2 A cheque for the agreed costs will be dispatched at the same time as the settlement cheque in accordance with the time frame indicated in clause 3.16.1 above. If the costs cheque is not received within this period, the Insurer shall pay interest on the outstanding costs at the rate of 25% per annum calculated on a daily rate basis.

7.1.3 These cost schedules shall be reviewed on an annual basis in accordance with clause II.

7.1.4 In cases where the value of the claim exceeds £15,000, costs will be by agreement or detailed assessment and in default of agreement, Insurers will consent to an application for a detailed assessment.

7.2 Calculation of the value of the claim

7.2.1 In determining the value of a claim in accordance with the attached scale of costs, there shall be no deduction for any sum payable to the CRU.

7.2.2 For claims where no courtesy vehicle is provided or a hire vehicle obtained by the client and where loss of use and enjoyment of a vehicle is appropriate, the rate of £60 per week shall be calculated for loss of use claims unless there are exceptional circumstances (*i.e.*, where the size and type of vehicle would warrant a higher figure or where a client may be on holiday and a loss of use claim would not be applicable). Notice of any "exceptional circumstances" will be given in the ***Solicitor's*** "second letter".

7.2.3 The period for loss of use will expire following 7 working days of the receipt of the settlement cheque for the vehicle; or on the date of return of the vehicle following repair.

7.2.4 If a courtesy vehicle is provided by the Insurer, the Insurer will confirm the period of the loan and this will be displayed on the repair invoice. A rate of £20 per day will be applied for calculation of the value of the claim.

7.2.5 If the Insurer elects to provide a hire vehicle to the client, a daily rate of £20 will be applied in the calculation of the value of the claim. The Insurer will confirm the period of hire and provide such evidence if so requested by the ***Solicitor***.

Such period of hire will continue until the said vehicle has either been repaired or until the expiry of 7 working days following receipt of the settlement cheque for the vehicle by the ***Solicitor***. This period will, for the sake of clarity, also apply to claims where the client has obtained a hire vehicle.

7.2.6 In cases of contributory negligence, costs will be paid on the full value of the claim.

7.2.7 It is agreed that claims for insurer outlay can form part of the claim but that regardless of the value of the outlay the claim for costs, will be limited to £75 plus VAT and any reasonable disbursements (only on the basis that the Memorandum of Understanding has been followed), and shall not be added to the value of the balance of the claim in order to calculate the overall value of the claim.

7.3 Notification of a client's misdemeanour

If the Insurer discovers any evidence of wrong doing on the part of the client, immediate notification of such will be given to the ***Solicitor***.

8. Disputes

B3–008 All disputes must be referred to the liaison officers of each Organisation who will attempt to resolve the dispute. If agreement cannot be reached then either:—

1. The parties agree that the matter cannot be dealt with in accordance with this ***Protocol*** and the claim must be dealt with outside this ***Protocol***, or;
2. Notice is given in writing by either party that the dispute be resolved

by the Chairperson of MASS and the nominated Chairperson for the Insurers.

9. Breaches of the Agreement

If any party wishes to submit a complaint regarding breaches of this ***Protocol*** by any ***Solicitor*** or Insurer, then such complaint giving details must be made in writing and sent for the attention of ***the nominated Solicitors Chairperson and Insurers Chairperson.*** B3–009

The alleged responsible party will be advised of the complaint and will be given the opportunity to make representations on their account of any allegations.

The respective Chairpersons will then meet and discuss the complaint and decide its validity. If the complaint is upheld then the member found responsible will be advised of the disciplinary procedure which will be either:

(a) a written reprimand;
(b) suspension from the ***Protocol Pilot***;
(c) expulsion from the ***Protocol Pilot***.

10. Procedure

All those members of staff who handle road traffic accident claims ***within the offices of participating Solicitors*** and Insurers will be notified of the ***Protocol***, in terms and members. B3–010

All Solicitors and Insurers will advise their respective staff of the nominated liaison officer for each member and ensure that a list is available to all staff of such individuals and their role in the ***Protocol***.

Any agreed changes to this ***Protocol*** must be communicated to all relevant staff within 7 working days of the liaison officer being notified of the changes.

A liaison Sub-Committee ***comprising of two nominated representatives for Solicitors and two nominated representatives for Insurers*** to be set up to meet on a bi-annual basis to discuss the Protocol, resolve problems and suggest and agree any alterations or improvements to the Protocol.

The Sub-Committee should also consider a method of assessing compliance with the ***Protocol***.

B3–011 *Annex A (Clause 3.1)*

Our ref.: ABCD/12345
Please ask for: Mr A N Other

Date: within 7 working days of notification of claim or identification of Insurer

"Solicitor's Initial Letter" under the RTA Protocol Pilot

Dear Sirs,

Re: Our Client
Your Insured: (full details where known) **Claim Ref No:**
Accident Date:

We hereby notify you of a claim which our client/s wish to pursue against your above name insured.

1. Our client's details are as follows:
   Name & Address
   Injured—Y/N
   Date of Birth
   National Insurance Number
   VAT registered—Y/N

2. Clients' insurance details:
   Name of Insurer
   Address
   Policy No./Claim Ref. Policy Type
   Policy Excess

3. Allegations of negligence:

4. Vehicle registration number, model and location (if known) and contact name:

5. Details of vehicle hire, if any, to include Company, rates, type of vehicle:

6. Copy of the engineer's report and estimate of repairs, if available:

7. Outline details of heads of claim (if known):

8. The nominated liaison officer is .... and contact name dealing with this claim is .... and their direct dial number is:

Yours faithfully

XYZ Solicitors

Annex B (Clause 3.3) **B3–012**

Our ref.: ABCD/12345
Please ask for: Mr A N Other

Date: within 28 working days of receipt of the Insurer's "First letter"

"Solicitor's Second Letter" under the RTA Protocol Pilot

Dear Sirs,

Re: Our Client:
Your Insured:
Claim Ref No:
Accident Date:

Further to your "first letter" dated .... we confirm the following information:

1. Injury claim

There is no injury claim/Our client/s suffered the following injuries:

(a) Client 1

Treatment was/was not provided by a NHS Hospital—name and address of hospital

We are applying for a medical report/It is too soon to arrange a report/There is no medical report.

2. Heads of claim

(a) Loss of use/car hire details to include Company, rates, type of vehicle;
(b) Storage details;
(c) Vehicle location;
(d) Client's occupation;
(e) Period off work (if appropriate) and to include loss of earnings (approx);

Contact .... on tel: .... to arrange an inspection.

3. Liability is under consideration/is not in issue/is in issue and we enclose copies of witness statements/details of witnesses.

Your faithfully

XYZ Solicitors

B3–013 *Annex C (Clause 3.15)*

Our ref.: ABCD/12345
Please ask for: Mr A N Other

Date: within 10 working days of receipt of the Insurer's "second letter" in which liability is disputed

"Solicitor's Third Letter" under the RTA Protocol Pilot

Dear Sirs,

Re: Our Client Your Insured: Claim Ref No: Accident Date:

Further to your "second letter" dated .... in which liability is disputed, we now enclose a copy of our witness summaries, not previously available or disclosed, to include ....

Yours faithfully

XYZ Solicitors

Annex D (Clause 3.2) **B3–014**

ZYX Insurance Company

Our ref.: ABCD/12345
Please ask for: Mr A N Other

Date: within 7 working days of receipt of Solicitor's "initial letter"

"Insurer's First Letter" under the RTA Protocol Pilot

Dear Sirs,

Your reference:	**Incident date:**	**Insured:**
Our reference:	**Claim reference:**	
Liaison Officer:	**Claim handled by & Tel No:**	

We thank you for your "Solicitor's initial letter" dated .... and your interest is noted.

We confirm:

— (We are/are not the Road Traffic Act 1988 Insurers for the above (insured).)
— (Your client's vehicle is being inspected by our Engineer and we will have the inspection report by ....)
— (Liability is under consideration/is not in issue/is in issue and we enclose copies of witness statements/details of witnesses.)

The following information was missing from your letter, please provide it by return:

1.
2.
3.

Yours faithfully

<u>**XYZ Insurance Company**</u>

B3–015 *Annex E (Clause 3.4)*

ZYX Insurance Company

Our ref.: ABCD/12345
Please ask for: Mr A N Other

Date: within 14 working days of receipt of the "Solicitor's second letter"

"Insurer's Second Letter" under the RTA Protocol Pilot

Dear Sirs,

Your reference:	**Incident date:**	**Insured:**
Our reference:	**Claim reference:**	
Liaison Officer:	**Claim handled by & Tel No:**	

We thank you for your "Solicitor's second letter" dated ....

We confirm:

That we are/are not the Road Traffic Act 1988 Insurers for the above (insured).

(Liability is not in issue.)

(Liability is in issue and we enclose copies of witness summaries/details of witnesses.)

Your client's vehicle has been inspected and:

(The vehicle is repairable and we are prepared to offer by way of an interim payment a cheque for the sum of £.......... for the repairs/in lieu of repairs.)

(We authorise repairs to be carried out at ABC garage/ABC will provide a courtesy vehicle for the period whilst the vehicle is being repaired.)

Please notify us within 7 working days of your client's preferred option.

(The vehicle is not repairable and the salvage will be designated as .... in accordance with the code of practice for the disposal of motor vehicles under category ...., a cheque for the sum of £.......... is enclosed (salvage of £.......... has been deducted.)

(Hire rates of £.......... for the period of ..... days are agreed/we have arranged for "DEF" hire company to provide your client with a vehicle.)

Yours faithfully

XYZ Insurance Company

Annex F

Form of Authority for the Release of Medical Records (Clause 6.1.5.)

B3–016 This personal injury claim is regulated by the Road Traffic Act Protocol, which encourages joint selection of, and access to medical experts. The Protocol promotes the practice of the claimant obtaining a medical report, disclosing it to the defendant who then asks questions and/or agrees to it and does not obtain his own report. Any medical report obtained by agreement under the Protocol should be disclosed to the other party.

Please complete and return to:

Name of firm:

NAME IN FULL: (including former name if changed since the accident)

....

DATE OF BIRTH: ....

NATIONAL INSURANCE NUMBER: ....

ADDRESS AND POSTCODE: (including former address if changed since the accident)

....

....

CONTACT TELEPHONE NUMBER:

Home: .... Work: ....

HOSPITAL ATTENDED: (if known, please give Record Number on appointment card and name of Consultant attending)

....

....

GENERAL PRACTITIONER'S NAME AND ADDRESS:

....

....

I confirm that I am not involved in litigation with any G.P. or Hospital Authority and consent to the disclosure of the following, which may be required for the purpose of pursuing my claim for personal injury:

1. G.P. Records
2. Hospital Records
3. Works Medical Records

I understand that if the report is obtained from an agreed expert under the Road Traffic Accident Protocol, it is possible that the other party's representative may make an application to Court for the disclosure of the report even though I may not agree to the report being disclosed.

Signed: ....

B3–017

Annex G

Cost Schedules

RTA Protocol Costs Proposal

NON PI (Including Pi upto £1000)								
Value of claim £	1–500	501–1000	1001–1500	1501–2000	2001–2500	2501–3000		
Costs £	**50**	**150**	**213**	**263**	**288**	**313**		
20% of the value of the claim 3001–5000		4000	5000					
Costs £		**413**	**513**					
12.5% of the difference of value of claim 5001–10000				6000	7000	8000	9000	10000
Costs £				**638**	**763**	**888**	**1013**	**1138**
				11000	12000	13000	14000	15000
Costs £				**1263**	**1500**	**1625**	**1750**	**1875**

PI Claims

Value of claim	1000–2000	2001–3000	3001–4000	4001–5000	5000					
Costs £	**750**	**1000**	**1250**	**1500**						
17.5% of the difference of value of claim 5001–10000						6000	7000	8000	9000	10000
Costs £						**1675**	**1225**	**1400**	**1575**	**1750**
17.5% of the difference of value of claim 10001–15000				11000	12000	13000	14000	15000		
Costs £				**1925**	**2100**	**2275**	**2450**	**2625**		

Examples

1. SD £1000, GD £2000

	Costs:	SD	£ 150.00
		GD	£ 750.00
		Total	£ 900.00
Previous Protocol			£1050.00

2. SD £4000, GD £5000

	Costs:	SD	£ 413.00
		GD	£1500.00
		Total	£1913.00
Previous Protocol			£2550.00

3. SD £8000, GD £2000

	Costs:	SD	£ 800.00
		GD	£ 750.00
		Total	£1638.00
Previous Protocol			£2750.00

It is suggested that the SD claim and costs be paid at the time of payment of the SD claim. That the costs of GD be paid at the time the GD is paid.

Annex H

Code of Practice for the Disposal of Motor Vehicle Salvage to Detect and Deter Criminal Activities

Introduction

B3–018 This Code of Practice has been produced to give guidance to insurers on the steps to be taken in the treatment of salvage and recovered stolen vehicles. Representatives from the Police and DVLA have assisted in the preparation of this document and have given it their full support.

A side-effect of the Code will be to make vehicle histories much more transparent. This will do much to dispel public concern about the way in which the industry treats salvage.

Categorisation of Vehicle Salvage

Four categories of vehicle salvage have been defined. Details are given of the steps to be taken in advising DVLA and MIAFTR on each category, together with the consequential effects on actions by the police, database houses (Equifax—HPI and Experian) etc.

The inspecting engineer *must* decide and indicate to which of the four categories a particular item of salvage belongs. Other than to correct inputting errors, recategorisation or removal of MIAFTR data is prohibited.

Form V23 and MIAFTR

Form V23 should always be completed and returned to DVLA in respect of Category A, B, or C salvage. **It is vital that the current version of Form V23 is used and completed correctly and accurately, in particular the choice of tick boxes which indicate whether the vehicle is either scrap/break *or* other category of total loss.**

Similarly, care should be taken to ensure that notifications to MIAFTR are made properly and that amended/updated information is fed through quickly.

Conclusion

The categorisation of salvage as set out in this Code of Practice, together with the benefits of the V23 system and MIAFTR, will make it extremely difficult for criminals to ring vehicles or return dangerously repaired vehicles to the road.

B3–018

Code of Practice for the Disposal of Motor Vehicle Salvage to Detect and Deter Criminal Activities

	CATEGORY A	CATEGORY B	CATEGORY C	CATEGORY D
Definition	SCRAP only (ie with no economically salvageable parts and which is of value only for scrap metal) eg total burn outs	BREAK for spare parts (plus any residual scrap metal)	REPAIRABLE (V23 must be submitted) i.e. repair costs exceed PAV, AND PAV over £2,000 (£1,000 for motorcycles).	ALL OTHER REPAIRABLE VEHICLES
	These vehicles must never reappear on the road			
V23	Form V23 must be submitted to DVLA as soon as the categorisation decision is made and without waiting for V5			V23 not required
V5	A photocopy of the V5 should be given to the salvage buyer to assist in the identification of the salvage and the completion of the Notification of Destruction. For new style V5s (introduced 24 March 1997) complete the red section, signing on the insured's behalf, and return to DVLA. Shred the remaining parts of the V5. For pre-March 1997 V5s complete the V5/1 tear-off section and return to DVLA. Shred the remaining part of the V5.			V5 can be passed to new owner
	DVLA will not issue replacement V5 and notify any request to the police		DVLA will notify any relicensing activity to police for investigation	
MIAFTR "Loss type"	All total losses must be entered on MIAFTR as per the Code of Practice category - except that total burn-outs should be entered as "Fire".			
MIAFTR notes	Recovered stolen vehicles which are in a total loss condition must be categorised A, B, C or D as appropriate. Recovered stolen vehicles which are undamaged or with only minor damage must be notified to MIAFTR as recovered, not deleted. Any changes in a total loss category must be notified to MIAFTR.			
Database applications	All notifications to MIAFTR whether theft or damaged are passed to Equifax HPI and Experian for a finance check. The database houses use the information to provide a vehicle check service to the motor trade and the public. It is essential that loss information on MIAFTR is accurate and up to date.			
Document-ation	All insurer documentation to salvage dealers (eg invoices) in respect of individual items of salvage must categorise the salvage as either A, B, C or D			
Responsibili-ties of the primary salvage buyer in the treatment of salvage/ vehicles	**SALVAGE MUST BE CRUSHED. The vehicle identification number (VIN) plate must be removed at the earliest possible opportunity and either held in secure storage or securely disposed of. The stamped in VIN must be left in situ and not interfered with in any way.** Buyers of the salvage must complete and return to DVLA (with a copy to the insurer) a Notification of Destruction which confirms that the salvage has been/will be crushed. The vehicle must be de-identified immediately by the salvage buyer by removing all tax discs (old or new) and registration plates	Category B must be treated as Category A once salvageable parts have been removed. **THE SHELL/FRAME/ CHASSIS MUST BE CRUSHED.** Buyers of Category B salvage must complete and return to DVLA (with a copy to the insurer) a Notification of Destruction which confirms that shell/frame/chassis parts have been/will be crushed. Identification marks on engines and any other salvaged parts must not be erased. Air bags and seat belt components must be discharged and properly disposed of - these items must never be resold.	To be sold on for repair	

Note 1	It is imperative that the provisions of this Code of Practice are fully and expeditiously complied with in all circumstances by insurers
Note 2	Vehicles suffering water damage will usually be categorised A or B. It is for the inspecting engineer to determine, given the specific circumstances such as type of water (fresh, contaminated or salt), depth of submersion etc, whether a vehicle should be categorised A, B, C or D.
Note 3	All bodyshells (which must be categorised A or B) or the subject of replacement in service must be crushed (NB special arrangements may apply to manufacturers' bodyshell schemes)
Note 4	In the interests of environmental protection, insurers are strongly encouraged to utilise only the services of those salvage buyers/breakers who comply fully with the appropriate provisions of the Environmental Protection Act 1990
Note 5	The V23 marker should be considered a permanent part of a vehicle's history. In the rare event that it is necessary to recategorise a vehicle this can be achieved by writing to DVLA giving the reasons, together with the accident date
Note 6	Third party total losses should be categorised A, B, C or D and V23ed in the normal way. Insurers should endeavour to ensure that Category A and B vehicles do not return to the road

Flow Chart for Categorising Vehicles under Code

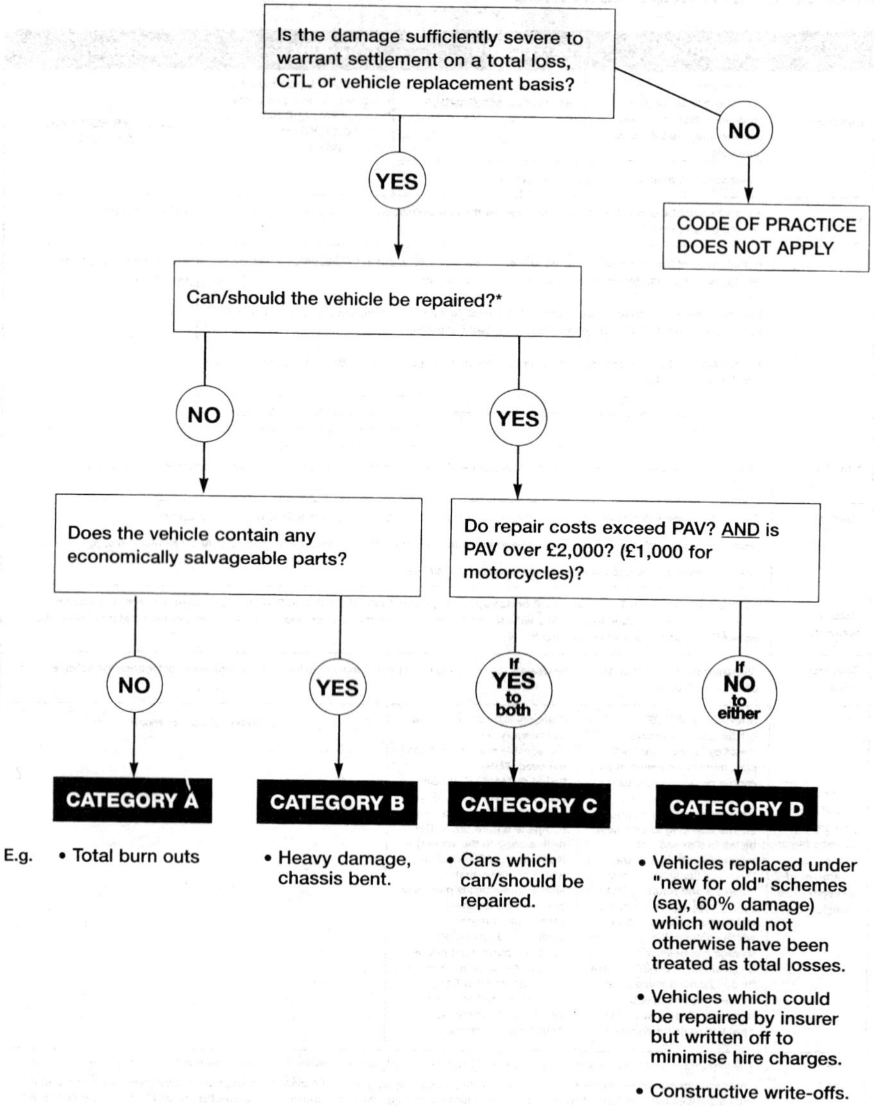

* Thatcham, Engineers Technical Sub-Committee is preparing guidance notes on categorisation.

SECTION C

FORMS

CONTENTS

N1 C1–001

Claim Form

N1 Claim Form	In the	
	Claim No.	

Claimant

Defendant(s)

SEAL

Brief details of claim

Value

Defendant's name and address

	£
Amount claimed	
Court fee	
Solicitor's costs	
Total amount	
Issue date	

The court office at

is open between 10 am and 4 pm Monday to Friday. When corresponding with the court, please address forms or letters to the Court Manager and quote the claim number.

Claim No.	

Particulars of Claim (attached) (to follow)

Statement of Truth
* (I believe) (The Claimant believes) that the facts stated in these particulars of claim are true.
* I am duly authorised by the claimant to sign this statement

Full name ______________________________

Name of claimant's solicitor's firm ______________________________

signed ______________________________
* (Claimant) (Litigation friend) (Claimant's solicitor)

position or office held ______________________________
(if signing on behalf of firm or company)

* delete as appropriate

Claimant's or claimant's solicitor's address to which documents or payments should be sent if different from overleaf including (if appropriate) details of DX, fax or e-mail.

C2–001

N1A

Notes for Claimant

Notes for claimant on completing a claim form

Further information may be obtained from the court in a series of free leaflets.

- Please read all of these guidance notes before you begin completing the claim form. The notes follow the order in which information is required on the form.
- Court staff can help you fill in the claim form and give information about procedure once it has been issued. But they cannot give legal advice. If you need legal advice, for example, about the likely success of your claim or the evidence you need to prove it, you should contact a solicitor or a Citizens Advice Bureau.
- If you are filling in the claim form by hand, please use black ink and write in block capitals.
- Copy the completed claim form and the defendant's notes for guidance so that you have one copy for yourself, one copy for the court and one copy for each defendant. Send or take the forms to the court office with the appropriate fee. The court will tell you how much this is.

Notes on completing the claim form

Heading

You must fill in the heading of the form to indicate whether you want the claim to be issued in a county court or in the High Court (The High Court means either a District Registry (attached to a county court) or the Royal Courts of Justice in London). There are restrictions on claims which may be issued in the High Court (see 'Value' overleaf).

Use whichever of the following is appropriate

'In the . . . . County Court'
(inserting the name of the court)

or

'In the High Court of Justice . Division'
(inserting eg. 'Queen's Bench' or 'Chancery' as appropriate)
'. . . . . District Registry'
(inserting the name of the District Registry)

or

'In the High Court of Justice . Division,
(inserting eg. 'Queen's Bench' or 'Chancery' as appropriate)
Royal Courts of Justice'

Claimant and defendant details

As the person issuing the claim, you are called the 'claimant'; the person you are suing is called the 'defendant'. Claimants who are under 18 years old (unless otherwise permitted by the court) and patients within the meaning of the Mental Health Act 1983, must have a litigation friend to issue and conduct court proceedings on their behalf. Court staff will tell you more about what you need to do if this applies to you.

You must provide the following information about yourself **and** the defendant according to the capacity in which you are suing and in which the defendant is being sued. When suing or being sued as:—

an individual:
All known forenames and surname, whether Mr, Mrs, Miss, Ms or other (e.g. Dr) and residential address (**including** postcode and telephone number) in England and Wales. Whether the defendant is a proprietor of a business, a partner in a firm or an individual sued in the name of a club or other unincorporated association, the address for service should be the usual or last known place of residence **or** principal place of business of the company, firm or club or other unincorporated association.

Where the individual is:
under 18 write '(a child by Mr Joe Bloggs his litigation friend)' after the name. If the child is conducting proceedings on their own behalf write '(a child)' after the child's name.

a patient within the meaning of the Mental Health Act 1983 write '(by Mr Joe Bloggs his litigation friend)' after the patient's name.

trading under another name you must add the words 'trading as' and the trading name e.g. 'Mr John Smith trading as Smith's Groceries'.

suing or being sued in a representative capacity you must say what that capacity is e.g. 'Mr Joe Bloggs as the representative of Mrs Sharon Bloggs (deceased)'.

suing or being sued in the name of a club or other unincorporated association add the words 'suing/sued on behalf of' followed by the name of the club or other unincorporated association.

a firm enter the name of the firm followed by the words 'a firm' e.g. 'Bandbox – a firm' and an address for service which is either a partner's residential address or the principal or last known place of business.

a corporation (other than a company) enter the full name of the corporation and the address which is either its principal office **or** any other place where the corporation carries on activities and which has a real connection with the claim.

a company registered in England and Wales enter the name of the company and an address which is either the company's registered office **or** any place of business that has a real, or the most, connection with the claim e.g. the shop where the goods were bought.

an overseas company (defined by s744 of the Companies Act 1985) enter the name of the company and either the address registered under s691 of the Act **or** the address of the place of business having a real, or the most, connection with the claim.

Brief details of claim

Note: The facts and full details about your claim and whether or not you are claiming interest, should be set out in the 'particulars of claim' ***(see note under 'Particulars of Claim').***
You must set out under **this** heading:
- a concise statement of the nature of your claim
- the remedy you are seeking e.g. payment of money; an order for return of goods or their value; an order to prevent a person doing an act; damages for personal injuries.

Value

If you are claiming a **fixed amount of money** (a 'specified amount') write the amount in the box at the bottom right-hand corner of the claim form against 'amount claimed'.
If you are *not* claiming a fixed amount of money (an 'unspecified amount') under 'Value' write "I expect to recover" followed by whichever of the following applies to your claim:
- "not more than £5,000" **or**
- "more than £5,000 but not more than £15,000" **or**
- "more than £15,000"

If you are **not able** to put a value on your claim, write "I cannot say how much I expect to recover".

Personal injuries
If your claim is for 'not more than £5,000' and includes a claim for personal injuries, you must also write "My claim includes a claim for personal injuries and the amount I expect to recover as damages for pain, suffering and loss of amenity is" followed by either:
- "not more than £1,000" **or**
- "more than £1,000"

Housing disrepair
If your claim is for 'not more than £5,000' and includes a claim for housing disrepair relating to residential premises, you must also write "My claim includes a claim against my landlord for housing disrepair relating to residential premises. The cost of the repairs or other work is estimated to be" followed by either:
- "not more than £1,000" **or**
- "more than £1,000"

If within this claim, you are making a claim for other damages, you must also write:
"I expect to recover as damages" followed by either:
- "not more than £1,000" **or**
- "more than £1,000"

Issuing in the High Court

You may only issue in the High Court if one of the following statements applies to your claim:–
"By law, my claim must be issued in the High Court.
The Act which provides this is ......(specify Act)"
or
"I expect to recover more than £15,000"
or
"My claim includes a claim for personal injuries and the value of the claim is £50,000 or more"
or
"My claim needs to be in a specialist High Court list, namely.....(state which list)".

If one of the statements does not apply and you wish to, or must by law, issue your claim in the High Court, write the words "I wish my claim to issue in the High Court because" followed by the relevant statement e.g. "I wish my claim to issue in the High Court because my claim includes a claim for personal injuries and the value of my claim is £50,000 or more."

Defendant's name and address

Enter in this box the full names and address of the defendant receiving the claim form (i.e. one claim form for each defendant). If the defendant is to be served outside England and Wales, you may need to obtain the court's permission.

Particulars of claim

You may include your particulars of claim on the claim form in the space provided or in a separate document which you should head 'Particulars of Claim'. It should include the names of the parties, the court, the claim number and your address for service and also contain a statement of truth. You should keep a copy for yourself, provide one for the court and one for each defendant. Separate particulars of claim can either be served
- with the claim form **or**
- within 14 days after the date on which the claim form was served.

If your particulars of claim are served separately from the claim form, they must be served with the forms on which the defendant may reply to your claim.

Your particulars of claim must include
- a concise statement of the facts on which you rely
- a statement (if applicable) to the effect that you are seeking aggravated damages or exemplary damages
- details of any interest which you are claiming
- any other matters required for your type of claim as set out in the relevant practice direction

Address for documents

Insert in this box the address at which you wish to receive documens and/or payments, if different from the address you have already given under the heading 'Claimant'. The address must be in England or Wales. If you are willing to accept service by DX, fax or e-mail, add details.

Statement of truth

This must be signed by you, by your solicitor or your litigation friend, as appropriate.
Where the claimant is a registered company or a corporation the claim must be signed by either the director, treasurer, secretary, chief executive, manager or other officer of the company or (in the case of a corporation) the mayor, chairman, president or town clerk.

N1C

C3–001

Notes for Defendant

Notes for defendant on replying to the claim form

Please read these notes carefully – they will help you decide what to do about this claim. Further information may be obtained from the court in a series of free leaflets

- If this claim form was received with the particulars of claim completed or attached, you must reply within 14 days of the date it was served on you. If the words 'particulars of claim to follow' are written in the particulars of claim box, you should not reply until after you are served with the particulars of claim (which should be no more than 14 days after you received the claim form). If the claim was sent by post, the date of service is taken as the second day after posting (see post mark). If the claim form was delivered or left at your address, the date of service will be the day after it was delivered.
- You may either
    - pay the amount claimed
    - admit that you owe all or part of the claim and ask for time to pay or
    - dispute the claim
- If you do not reply, judgment may be entered against you.
- The notes below tell you what to do.
- The response pack will tell you which forms to use for your reply. (The pack will accompany the particulars of claim if they are served after the claim form).
- Court staff can help you complete the forms of reply and tell you about court procedures. But they cannot give legal advice. If you need legal advice, for example about the likely success of disputing the claim, you should contact a solicitor or a Citizens Advice Bureau immediately.

Registration of Judgments: If the claim results in a judgment being made against you in a **county court**, your name and address may be entered in the Register of County Court Judgments. This may make it difficult for you to obtain credit.
Costs and Interest: Additional costs and interest may be added to the amount claimed on the front of the claim form if judgment is entered against you. In a county court, if judgment is for £5,000 or more, or is in respect of a debt which attracts contractual or statutory interest for late payment, the claimant may be entitled to further interest.

Your response and what happens next

How to pay

Do not bring any payments to the court – they will not be accepted.
When making payments to the claimant, quote the claimant's reference (if any) and the claim number.
Make sure that you keep records and can account for any payments made. Proof may be required if there is any disagreement. It is not safe to send cash unless you use registered post.

Admitting the Claim

Claim for specified amount

If you admit all the claim, take or send the money, including any interest and costs, to the claimant at the address given for payment on the claim form, within 14 days.
If you admit all the claim and you are asking for time to pay, complete Form N9A and send it to the claimant at the address given for payment on the claim form, within 14 days. The claimant will decide whether to accept your proposal for payment. If it is accepted, the claimant may request the court to enter judgment against you and you will be sent an order to pay. If your offer is <u>not</u> accepted, the court will decide how you should pay.
If you admit only part of the claim, complete Form N9A <u>and</u> Form N9B (see 'Disputing the Claim' overleaf) and send them to the court within 14 days. The claimant will decide whether to accept your part admission.
If it is accepted, the claimant may request the court to enter judgment against you and the court will send you an order to pay. If your part admission is <u>not</u> accepted, the case will proceed as a defended claim.

Claim for unspecified amount

If you admit liability for the whole claim but do not make an offer to satisfy the claim, complete Form N9C and send it to the court within 14 days. A copy will be sent to the claimant who may request the court to enter judgment against you for an amount to be decided by the court, and costs. The court will enter judgment and refer the court file to a judge for directions for management of the case. You and the claimant will be sent a copy of the court's order.
If you admit liability for the claim and offer an amount of money to satisfy the claim, complete Form N9C and send it to the court within 14 days. The claimant will be sent a copy and asked if the offer is acceptable. The claimant must reply to the court within 14 days and send you a copy. If a reply is not received, the claim will be stayed. If the amount you have offered is **accepted** –

- the claimant may request the court to enter judgment against you for that amount.
- if you have requested time to pay which is not accepted by the claimant, the rate of payment will be decided by the court.

If your offer in satisfaction is **not accepted** –

- the claimant may request the court to enter judgment against you for an amount to be decided by the court, and costs; and
- the court will enter judgment and refer the court file to a judge for directions for management of the case. You and the claimant will be sent a copy of the court's order.

Disputing the claim

If you are being sued as an individual for a specified amount of money and you dispute the claim, the claim may be transferred to your home court i.e. the one nearest your home or your solicitor's practice if different from the court where the claim was issued.

If you need longer than 14 days to prepare your defence or to contest the court's jurisdiction to try the claim, complete the Acknowledgement of Service form and send it to the court within 14 days. This will allow you 28 days from the date of service of the particulars of claim to file your defence or make an application to contest the court's jurisdiction. The court will tell the claimant that your Acknowledgment of Service has been received.

If the case proceeds as a defended claim, you and the claimant will be sent an Allocation Questionnaire. You will be told the date by which it must be returned to the court. The information you give on the form will help a judge decide whether your case should be dealt with in the small claims track, fast track or multi-track. After a judge has considered the completed questionnaires, you will be sent a notice of allocation setting out the judge's decision. The notice will tell you the track to which the claim has been allocated and what you have to do to prepare for the hearing or trial. **Leaflets telling you more about the tracks are available from the court office.**

Claim for specified amount

If you wish to dispute the full amount claimed or wish to claim against the claimant (a counterclaim), complete Form N9B and send it to the court within 14 days.

If you admit part of the claim, complete the Defence Form N9B and the Admission Form N9A and send them both to the court within 14 days. The claimant will decide whether to accept your part admission in satisfaction of the claim (see under 'Admitting the Claim – specified amount'). If the claimant does not accept the amount you have admitted, the case will proceed as a defended claim.

If you dispute the claim because you have already paid it, complete Form N9B and send it to the court within 14 days. The claimant will have to decide whether to proceed with the claim or withdraw it and notify the court and you within 28 days. If the claimant wishes to proceed, the case will proceed as a defended claim.

Claim for unspecified amount/return of goods/non-money claims

If you dispute the claim or wish to claim against the claimant (counterclaim), complete Form N9D and send it to the court within 14 days.

Personal injuries claims:

If the claim is for personal injuries and the claimant has attached a medical report to the particulars of claim, in your defence you should state whether you:

- agree with the report **or**
- dispute all or part of the report **and** give your reasons for doing so **or**
- nether agree nor dispute the report **or** have no knowledge of the report

Where you have obtained your own medical report, you should attach it to your defence.

If the claim is for personal injuries and the claimant has attached a schedule of past and future expenses and losses, in your defence you must state which of the items you:

- agree **or**
- dispute **and** supply alternative figures where appropriate **or**
- neither agree nor dispute or have no knowledge of

Address where notices can be sent

This must be either your solicitor's address, your own residential or business address in England and Wales or (if you live elsewhere) some other address within England and Wales.

Statement of truth

This must be signed by you, by your solicitor or your litigation friend, as appropriate.

Where the defendant is **a registered company or a corporation** the response must be signed by either the director, treasurer, secretary, chief executive, manager or other officer of the company **or** (in the case of a corporation) the mayor, chairman, president or town clerk.

N1(FD)

C4–001

Consumer Credit Act Claim

Notes for defendant on replying to the claim form (Consumer Credit Act claim)

Please read these notes carefully – they will help you decide what to do about this claim. You will have received a notice of hearing telling you when and where to come to court with the claim form. A leaflet is available from the court office about what happens when you come to a court hearing.

- You must reply to the claim form within 14 days of the date it was served on you. If the claim form was
    - sent by post, the date of service is taken as the second day after posting (see post mark)
    - delivered or left at your address, the date of service will be the day after it was delivered
    - handed to your personally, the date of service will be the day it was given to you
- You may either
    - pay the amount claimed
    - admit liability for the claim and offer to make payments to keep the goods
    - dispute the claim
- If you do not reply or attend the hearing, judgment may be entered against you.
- The notes below tell you what to do.
- Court staff can help you complete the forms of reply and tell you about court procedure. But they cannot give legal advice. If you need legal advice, for example about the likely success of disputing the claim, you should contact a solicitor or a Citizens Advice Bureau immediately.

Registration of Judgments: If the claim results in a judgment being made against you in a **county court**, your name and address may be entered in the Register of County Court Judgments. This may make it difficult for you to obtain credit.
Costs and Interest: Additional costs and interest may be added to the amount claimed on the front of the claim form if judgment is entered against you. In a county court, if judgment is for £5,000 or more, or is in respect of a debt which attracts contractual or statutory interest for late payment, the claimant may be entitled to further interest.

Your response and what happens next

How to pay

Do not bring any payments to the court – they will not be accepted.
When making payments to the claimant, quote the claimant's reference (if any) and the claim number.
Make sure that you keep records and can account for any payments made. Proof may be required if there is any disagreement. It is not safe to send cash unless you use registered post.

Admitting the Claim

If you admit liability for the claim and offer to make payments in order to keep the goods. Complete Form N9C and send it to the court within 14 days. **Remember** to keep a copy for yourself. The court will send a copy of your admission to the claimant and ask if your offer is acceptable.
If the claimant **accepts your offer** and asks the court to enter judgment before the date of the hearing, you will be sent a copy of the judgment and need not come to the hearing. If you do not hear from the court it is in your interests to attend the hearing.
If your offer is **not accepted**, you should attend the hearing. The court will treat your admission as evidence so remember to bring a copy of your admission with you to the hearing.

Disputing the claim

If you dispute the claim or wish to claim against the claimant (counterclaim), complete Form N9D and send it to the court within 14 days. **Remember** to keep a copy for yourself and to bring it with you to the hearing. The court will send a copy of your defence to the claimant. At the hearing the court may make a final order or judgment in the claim. If the court agrees that you have a valid defence (or counterclaim), it will tell you and the claimant what to do to prepare for a future hearing. If you send your defence to the court after the 14 days has expired, and you want to rely on it at the hearing, the court may take your failure to file it on time into account when deciding what order to make in respect of costs.

Statement of truth

This must be signed by you, by your solicitor or your litigation friend, as appropriate.
Where the defendant is **a registered company or a corporation** the response must be signed by either the director, treasurer, secretary, chief executive, manager or other officer of the company **or** (in the case of a corporation) the mayor, chairman, president or town clerk.

N9

Response Pack

Response Pack

You should read the 'notes for defendant' attached to the claim form which will tell you when and where to send the forms

Included in this pack are:

- either **Admission Form N9A** (if the claim is for a specified amount) or **Admission Form N9C** (if the claim for an unspecified amount or is not a claim for money)
- either **Defence and Counterclaim Form N9B** (if the claim is for a specified amount) or **Defence and Counterclaim Form N9D** (if the claim is for an unspecified amount or is not a claim for money)
- **Acknowledgment of service** (see below)

	Complete
If you admit the claim or the amount claimed and/or you want time to pay ▶	the admission form
If you admit part of the claim ▶	the admission form and the defence form
If you dispute the whole claim or wish to make a claim (a counterclaim) against the claimant ▶	the defence form
If you need 28 days (rather than 14) from the date of service to prepare your defence, or wish to contest the court's jurisdiction ▶	the acknowledgment of service
If you do nothing, judgment may be entered against you	

Acknowledgment of Service

Defendant's full name if different from the name given on the claim form

. . . .

. . . .

In the	
Claim No.	
Claimant (including ref.)	
Defendant	

Address to which documents about this claim should be sent (including reference if appropriate)

	if applicable	
	fax no.	
	DX no.	
Tel. no. Postcode	e-mail	

If you file an acknowledgment of service but do not file a defence within 28 days of the date of service of the claim form, or particulars of claim if served separately, judgment may be entered against you.

If you do not file an application within 28 days of the date of service of the claim form, or particulars of claim if served separately, it will be assumed that you accept the court's jurisdiction and judgment may be entered against you.

Tick the appropriate box

1. I intend to defend all of this claim ☐
2. I intend to defend part of this claim ☐
3. I intend to contest jurisdiction ☐

Signed (Defendant) (Defendant's Solicitor) (Litigation friend)

Position or office held (if signing on behalf of firm or company)

Date

The court office at

is open between 10 am and 4 pm Monday to Friday. When corresponding with the court, please address forms or letters to the Court Manager and quote the claim number.

N9A

C5–001

Admission (specified amount)

Admission (specified amount)

In the	
Claim No.	
Claimant (including ref.)	
Defendant	

- You have a limited number of days to complete and return this form
- Before completing this form, please read the notes for guidance attached to the claim form

When to fill in this form

- Only fill in this form if you are admitting all or some of the claim **and** you are asking for time to pay

How to fill in this form

- Tick the correct boxes and give as much information as you can. **Then sign and date the form.** If necessary provide details on a separate sheet, add the claim number and attach it to this form.
- Make your offer of payment in box 11 on the back of this form. **If you make no offer the claimant will decide how much and when you should pay.**
- If you are not an individual, you should ensure that you provide sufficient details about the assets and liabilities of your firm, company or corporation to support any offer of payment made in box 11.
- You can get help to complete this form at **any** county court office or Citizens Advice Brueau.

Where to send this form

- **If you admit the claim in full**
  Send the completed form to the address shown on the claim form as one to which documents should be sent.
- **If you admit only part of the claim**
  Send the form **to the court** at the address given on the claim form, together with the defence form (N9B).

How much of the claim to you admit?

☐ I admit the full amount claimed as shown on the claim form **or**

☐ I admit the amount of £

1 Personal details

Surname

Forename

☐ Mr ☐ Mrs ☐ Miss ☐ Ms

☐ Married ☐ Single ☐ Other *(specify)*

Age

Address

Postcode

Tel. no.

2 Dependants *(people you look after financially)*

Number of children in each age group

under 11 ☐ 11–15 ☐ 16–17 ☐ 18 & over ☐

Other dependants
(give details)

3 Employment

☐ **I am employed as a**
My employer is

Jobs other than main job *(give details)*

☐ **I am self employed as a**

Annual turnover is...................... £

☐ **I am not** in arrears with my national insurance contributions, income tax and VAT

☐ **I am** in arrears and I owe.......... £

Give details of:
(a) contracts and other work in hand
(b) any sums due for work done

☐ **I have been unemployed for** years months

☐ **I am a pensioner**

4 Bank account and savings

☐ **I have a bank account**

☐ The account is in credit by........ £

☐ The account is overdrawn by..... £

☐ **I have a savings or building society account**

The amount in the account is........ £

5 Residence

I live in ☐ my own house ☐ lodgings

☐ my jointly owned house ☐ council accommodation

☐ rented accommodation

6 Income

My usual take home pay (*including overtime, commission, bonuses etc*)	£	per
Income support	£	per
Child benefit(s)	£	per
Other state benefit(s)	£	per
My pension(s)	£	per
Others living in my home give me	£	per
Other income (*give details below*)		
	£	per
	£	per
	£	per
Total income	**£**	**per**

7 Expenses

(*Do not include any payments made by other members of the household out of their own income*)

I have regular expenses as follows:

Mortgage (*including second mortgage*)	£	per
Rent	£	per
Council tax	£	per
Gas	£	per
Electricity	£	per
Water charges	£	per
TV rental and licence	£	per
HP repayments	£	per
Mail order	£	per
Housekeeping, food, school meals	£	per
Travelling expenses	£	per
Children's clothing	£	per
Maintenance payments	£	per
Others (*not court orders or credit debts listed in boxes 9 and 10*)		
	£	per
	£	per
	£	per
Total expenses	**£**	**per**

8 Priority debts

(*This section is for arrears only. Do not include regular expenses listed in box 7.*)

Rent arrears	£	per
Mortgage arrears	£	per
Council tax/Community Charge arrears	£	per
Water charges arrears	£	per
Fuel debts: Gas	£	per
Electricity	£	per
Other	£	per
Maintenance arrears	£	per
Others (*give details below*)		
	£	per
	£	per
Total priority debts	**£**	**per**

9 Court orders

Court	Claim No.	£	per
Total court order instalments		**£**	**per**

Of the payments above, I am behind with payments to (*please list*)

10 Credit debts

Loans and credit card debts (*please list*)

	£	per
	£	per
	£	per

Of the payments above, I am behind with payments to (*please list*)

11 Offer of payment

☐ I can pay the amount admitted on

or

☐ I can pay by monthly instalments of £

If you cannot pay immediately, please give brief reasons below

12 Declaration

I declare that the details I have given above are true to the best of my knowledge

Signed

Date

Position or office held (if signing on behalf of firm or company)

N9B C6–001

Defence and Counterclaim (specified amount)

Defence and Counterclaim (specified amount)

- Fill in this form if you wish to dispute all or part of the claim and/or make a claim against the claimant (counterclaim).
- You have a limited number of days to complete and return this form to the court.
- Before completing this form, please read the notes for guidance attached to the claim form.
- Please ensure that all boxes at the top right of this form are completed. You can obtain the correct names and number from the claim form. The court cannot trace your case without this information.

How to fill in this form

- Complete sections 1 and 2. Tick the correct boxes and give the other detail asked for.
- Set out your defence in section 3. If necessary continue on a separate piece of paper making sure that the claim number is clearly shown on it. In your defence you must state which allegations in the particulars of claim you deny and your reasons for doing so. **If you fail to deny an allegation it may be taken that you admit it.**
- If you dispute only some of the allegations you must
  - specify which you admit and which you deny; and
  - give your own version of events if different from the claimant's.

In the	
Claim No.	
Claimant (including ref.)	
Defendant	

1. How much of the claim do you dispute?

☐ I dispute the full amount claimed as shown on the claim form

or

☐ I admit the amount of £

If you dispute only part of the claim you must **either**:

- pay the amount admitted to the person named at the address for payment on the claim form (see How to Pay in the notes on the back of, or attached to, the claim form). Then send this defence to the court

or

- complete the admission form **and** this defence form and send them to the court.

☐ I paid the amount admitted on (*date*)

or

☐ I enclose the completed form of admission (*go to section 2*)

- If you wish to make a claim against the claimant (a counterclaim) complete section 4.
- Complete and sign section 5 before sending this form to the court. Keep a copy of the claim form and this form.

Legal Aid

- You may be entitled to legal aid. Ask about the legal aid scheme at any county court office, Citizens Advice Bureau, legal advice centre or firm of solicitors displaying the legal aid sign.

2. Do you dispute this claim because you have already paid it? *Tick which ever applies*

☐ **No** (*go to section 3*)

☐ **Yes** I paid £ to the claimant

on (*before the claim form was issued*)

Give details of where and how you paid it in the box below (*then go to section 5*)

3. Defence

Defence (continued)

Claim No.

4. If you wish to make a claim against the claimant (a counterclaim)

If your claim is for a specific sum of money, how much are you claiming? £

My claim is for (*please specify nature of claim*)

- To start your counterclaim, you will have to pay a fee. Court staff will tell you how much you have to pay.
- You may not be able to make a counterclaim where the claimant is the Crown (e.g. a Government Department). Ask your local county court office for further information.

What are you reasons for making the counterclaim?
If you need to continue on a separate sheet put the claim number in the top right hand corner.

5. Signed
(To be signed by you or by your solicitor or litigation friend)

** delete as appropriate*

*(I believe) (The defendant believes) that the facts stated in this form are true. *I am duly authorised by the defendant to sign this statement

Position or office held (if signing on behalf of firm or company)

Date

Give an address to which notices about this case can be sent

Postcode

Tel. no.

if applicable	
fax no.	
DX no.	
e-mail	

N9C C7–001

Admission (unspecified amount and non-money claims)

Admission (unspecified amount, non-money and return of goods claims)

In the	
Claim No.	
Claimant (including ref.)	
Defendant	

- Before completing this form please read the notes for guidance attached to the claim form. If necessary provide details on a separate sheet, add the claim number and attach it to this form.
- If you are not an individual, you should ensure that you provide sufficient details about the assets and liabilities of your firm, company or corporation to support any offer of payment made.

In non-money claims only

☐ I admit liability for the whole claim (*Complete section 12*)

In return of goods cases only

Are the goods still in your possession?

☐ Yes ☐ No

Section A Response to claim (*tick one box only*)

☐ I admit liability for the whole claim but want the court to decide the amount I should pay / value of the goods

OR

☐ I admit liability for the claim and offer to pay [ ] in satisfaction of the claim (*complete sections B and 12*)

Section B How are you going to pay the amount you have admitted? (*tick one box only*)

☐ I offer to pay on (date) [ ]

OR

☐ I cannot pay the amount immediately because (state reason)

[ ]

AND

I offer to pay by instalments of £

per (week) (month)

starting (*date*) [ ]

1 Personal details

Surname [ ]

Forename [ ]

☐ Mr ☐ Mrs ☐ Miss ☐ Ms

☐ Married ☐ Single ☐ Other (*specify*) [ ]

Age [ ]

Address [ ]

Postcode [ ]

Tel. no.

2 Dependants (*people you look after financially*)

Number of children in each age group

under 11 ☐ 11–15 ☐ 16–17 ☐ 18 & over [ ]

Other dependants (*give details*) [ ]

3 Employment

☐ **I am employed as a** [ ]

My employer is [ ]

Jobs other than main job (*give details*) [ ]

☐ **I am self employed as a** [ ]

Annual turnover is...................... £

☐ **I am not** in arrears with my national insurance contributions, income tax and VAT

☐ **I am** in arrears and I owe....... £

Give details of:

(a) contracts and other work in hand [ ]

(b) any sums due for work done [ ]

☐ **I have been unemployed for** years months

☐ **I am a pensioner**

4 Bank account and savings

☐ **I have a bank account**

☐ The account is in credit by........ £

☐ The account is overdrawn by..... £

☐ **I have a savings or building society account**

The amount in the account is........ £

5 Residence

I live in ☐ my own property ☐ lodgings

☐ jointly owned house ☐ rented property

☐ council accommodation

6 Income

My usual take home pay (*including overtime, commission, bonuses etc*)	£	per
Income support	£	per
Child benefit(s)	£	per
Other state benefit(s)	£	per
My pension(s)	£	per
Others living in my home give me	£	per
Other income (*give details below*)		
	£	per
	£	per
	£	per
Total income	**£**	**per**

7 Expenses

(*Do not include any payments made by other members of the household out of their own income*)

I have regular expenses as follows:		
Mortgage (*including second mortgage*)	£	per
Rent	£	per
Council tax	£	per
Gas	£	per
Electricity	£	per
Water charges	£	per
TV rental and licence	£	per
HP repayments	£	per
Mail order	£	per
Housekeeping, food, school meals	£	per
Travelling expenses	£	per
Children's clothing	£	per
Maintenance payments	£	per
Others (*not court orders or credit debts listed in boxes 9 and 10*)		
	£	per
	£	per
	£	per
Total expenses	**£**	**per**

8 Priority debts

(*This section is for arrears only. Do not include regular expenses listed in box 7.*)

Rent arrears	£	per
Mortgage arrears	£	per
Council tax/Community Charge arrears	£	per
Water charges arrears	£	per
Fuel debts: Gas	£	per
Electricity	£	per
Other	£	per
Maintenance arrears	£	per
Others (*give details below*)		
	£	per
	£	per
Total priority debts	**£**	**per**

9 Court orders

Court	Claim No.	£	per
Total court order instalments		**£**	**per**

Of the payments above, I am behind with payments to (*please list*)

10 Credit debts

Loans and credit card debts (*please list*)

	£	per
	£	per
	£	per

Of the payments above, I am behind with payments to (*please list*)

11 Declaration

I declare that the details I have given above are true to the best of my knowledge

Signed

Date

Position or office held (if signing on behalf of firm or company)

N9D C8–001

Defence and Counterclaim (unspecified amount and non-money claims)

Defence and Counterclaim (unspecified amount, non-money and return of goods claims)

In the	
Claim No.	
Claimant (including ref.)	
Defendant	

- Fill in this form if you wish to dispute all or part of the claim and/or make a claim against the claimant (counterclaim)
- You have a limited number of days to complete and return this form to the court.
- Before completing this form, please read the notes for guidance attached to the claim form.
- Please ensure that all the boxes at the top right of this form are completed. You can obtain the correct names and number from the claim form. The court cannot trace your case without this information.

How to fill in this form

- Set out your defence in section 1. If necessary continue on a separate piece of paper making sure that the claim number is clearly shown on it. In your defence you must state which allegations in the particulars of claim you deny and your reasons for doing so. **If you fail to deny an allegation it may be taken that you admit it.**
- If you dispute only some of the allegations you must
  - specify which you admit and which you deny; and
  - give your own version of events if different from the claimant's.
- If the claim is for money and you dispute the claimant's statement of value, you must say why and if possible give your own statement of value.
- If you wish to make a claim against the claimant (a counterclaim) complete section 2.
- Complete and sign section 3 before returning this form.

Where to send this form

- send or take this form immediately to the court at the address given on the claim form.
- Keep a copy of the claim form and the defence form.

Legal Aid

- You may be entitled to legal aid. Ask about the legal aid scheme at any county court office, Citizens Advice Bureau, legal advice centre or firm of solicitors displaying the legal aid sign.

1. Defence

Defence (continued)

Claim No.

2. If you wish to make a claim against the claimant (a counterclaim)

If your claim is for a specific sum of money, how much are you claiming? £

My claim is for (*please specify*)

- To start your counterclaim, you will have to pay a fee. Court staff will tell you how much you have to pay.
- You may not be able to make a counterclaim where the claimant is the Crown (e.g. a Government Department). Ask at your local county court office for further information.

What are you reasons for making the counterclaim?
If you need to continue on a separate sheet put the claim number in the top right hand corner

3. Signed
(To be signed by you or by your solicitor or litigation friend)

** delete as appropriate*

*(I believe) (The defendant believes) that the facts stated in this form are true. *I am duly authorised by the defendant to sign this statement

Position or office held
(if signing on behalf of firm or company)

Date

Give an address to which notices about this case can be sent to you

Postcode

Tel. no.

if applicable	
fax no.	
DX no.	
e-mail	

N10

C9–001

Notice that Acknowledgment of Service has been filed

Notice that acknowledgment of service has been filed

In the	
Claim No.	
Claimant (including ref.)	
Defendant (including ref.)	
Date	

To the [Claimant]['s solicitor]

The defendant filed an Acknowledgment of Service on

The defendant responded to the claim indicating an intention to [defend all of the claim.] [defend part of the claim.] [contest the court's jurisdiction.]

The defendant has 28 days from the date of service of the claim form with particulars of claim, or of the particulars of claim, to file [a defence.] [an application to contest the court's jurisdiction.]

[The defendant's name has been corrected to read .]

[The defendant has given the following address for service of documents:]

[The acknowledgment was filed by the solicitors acting for the defendant who have given the following name and address for service of documents: .]

The court office at

is open between 10 am and 4 pm Monday to Friday. When corresponding with the court, please address forms or letters to the Court Manager and quote the claim number.

C10–001

N17

Judgment for Claimant (amount to be decided by the court)

Judgment for Claimant
(amount to be decided by the court)

In the	
Claim No.	
Claimant (including ref.)	
Defendant (including ref.)	
Date	

To the [Claimant][Defendant]['s solicitor]

[No [acknowledgment of service] [defence] having been filed] [The defendant having admitted liability] [The defendant having admitted liability and offered an amount in settlement which the claimant has not accepted], it is ordered that the defendant must pay the claimant an amount which the court will decide, and costs. To prepare for the hearing

[Master] [District Judge] orders that:

[You should attend the court at [am] [pm] on the of

at

when the court will make its decision.]

The court office at

is open between 10 am and 4 pm Monday to Friday. When corresponding with the court, please address forms or letters to the Court Manager and quote the claim number.

C11–001

N20

Witness Summons

C11–001

Witness Summons

In the	
Claim No.	
Claimant (including ref.)	
Defendant (including ref.)	
Issued on	

To

You are summoned to attend at (*court address*)

(am) (pm) on of at

(and each following day of the hearing until the court tells you that you are no longer required.)

☐ to give evidence in respect of the above claim

☐ to produce the following document(s) (*give details*)

The sum of £ is paid or offered to you with this summons. This is to cover your travelling expenses to and from court and includes an amount by way of compensation for loss of time.

This summons was issued on the application of the claimant (defendant) or the claimant's (defendant's) solicitor whose name, address and reference number is:

Do not ignore this summons
If you were offered money for travel expenses and compensation for loss of time, at the time it was served on you, and you
- fail to attend or produce documents as required by the summons; or
- refuse to take an oath or affirm for the purpose of answering questions about your evidence or the documents you have been asked to produce

you may be liable to a fine or imprisonment and may in addition be ordered to pay any costs resulting from your failure to attend or refusal to take an oath or affirm.

The court office at

is open between 10 am and 4 pm Monday to Friday. When corresponding with the court, please address forms or letters to the Court Manager and quote the claim number.

C12–001

Certificate of service

Claim No.	

I certify that the summons of which this is a true copy, was served by posting to ____________ ________________ (the witness) on ________________________ at the address stated on the summons in accordance with the request of the applicant or his solicitor.

I enclose a P.O. for £ for the witness's expenses and compensation for loss of time.

Signed ______________________

Officer of the Court

N21

C13–001

Order for Examination of Deponent (before the hearing)

Order for examination of deponent (before the hearing)

In the	
Claim No.	
Claimant (including ref.)	
Defendant (including ref.)	
Date	

To

Upon the application of the [claimant][defendant],[Master][District Judge] has **ordered you to attend**

at (am)(pm) on of

at

to be examined on oath.

[and] to produce the following document(s)]

[£ to cover your travelling expenses to and from the place of examination and compensation for your loss of time is attached]

[Sum to be offered or handed to deponent £ for travelling expenses to and from the place of examination (and compensation for loss of time)]

Do not ignore this order
If you were offered money for travel expenses and compensation for loss of time at the time it was served on you and you

- fail to attend or produce documents as required by the order; or
- refuse to take an oath or affirm for the purpose of the examination or to answer any lawful question or produce any document at the examination

you may be liable to fine and may in addition be ordered to pay any costs resulting from your failure to attend or refusal to take an oath or affirm.

The court office at

is open between 10 am and 4 pm Monday to Friday. When corresponding with the court, please address forms or letters to the Court Manager and quote the claim number.

C14–001

Certificate of service	**Claim No.**	

I certify that the order of which this is a true copy, was served by posting to ______________ ________________ (the deponent) on ________________________ at the address stated in the order.

I enclose a P.O. for £ for the deponent's expenses and compensation for loss of time.

Signed ________________________

Officer of the Court

N30 C15–001

Judgment for Claimant (in default)

Judgment for Claimant (in default)	In the ... County Court
To [Claimant][Defendant]['s solicitor]	Claim No.
	Claimant (including ref.)
	Defendant (including ref.)
	Date

Seal

To the Defendant

You have not replied to the claim form.

It is therefore ordered that you must pay the claimant £ for debt [and interest to date of judgment] and £ for costs [less £ which you have already paid]

You must pay to the claimant a total of £

[by instalments of £ per [week][month]

[the first payment to reach the claimant] by [and on or before this date each [week][month] until the debt has been paid]

Warning

If you ignore this order your goods may be removed and sold, or other enforcement proceedings may be taken against you. If this happens further costs will be added. If your circumstances change and you cannot pay, ask at the court office what you can do.

Notes for the defendant

If you did reply to the claim form and believe judgment has been entered wrongly in default, you may apply to the court office giving your reasons why the judgment should be set aside. An application form is available for you to use and you will need to pay a fee. A hearing may be arranged and you will be told when and where it will take place. If you live in, or your solicitor's business is in, another court's area, the claim may be transferred to that court.

This judgment has been registered on the Register of County Court Judgments. This may make it difficult for you to get credit. **If you pay in full within one month** you can ask the court to cancel the entry on the Register. You will need to give proof of payment. You can (for a fee) also obtain a Certificate of Cancellation from the court. If you pay the debt in full after one month you can ask the court to mark the entry on the Register as satisfied and (for a fee) obtain a Certificate of Satisfaction to prove that the debt has been paid.

If the judgment is for £5,000 or more, or is in respect of a debt which attracts contractual or statutory interest for late payment, the claimant may be entitled to further interest.

Address for payment

How to pay

- **Payment(s) must be made to the person named at the address for payment, giving the claimant's reference and claim number**
- **DO NOT bring or send payments to the court – they will not be accepted**
- You should allow at least 4 days for your payment to reach the claimant or his representative
- Make sure that you keep records and can account for all payments made. Proof may be required if there is any disagreement. It is not safe to send cash unless you use registered post
- Leaflets on registered judgments, how to pay and what to do if you cannot pay are available from the court

The court office at

is open between 10 am and 4 pm Monday to Friday. When corresponding with the court, please address forms or letters to the Court Manager and quote the claim number.

C16–001

N30(HC)

Judgment for Claimant (in default)

Judgment for Claimant (in default)

In the High Court of Justice	
Division **District Registry**	
Claim No.	
Claimant (including ref.)	
Defendant (including ref.)	
Date	

To [Claimant][Defendant]['s solicitor]

Seal

To the Defendant

You have not replied to the claim form.

It is therefore ordered that you must pay the claimant £ for debt [and interest to date of judgment] and £ for costs [less £ which you have already paid]

You must pay to the claimant a total of £

[by instalments of £ per [week][month]

[the first payment to reach the claimant] by [and on or before this date each [week][month] until the debt has been paid]

Warning

If you ignore this order your goods may be removed and sold, or other enforcement proceedings may be taken against you. If this happens further costs will be added. If your circumstances change and you cannot pay, ask at the court office what you can do.

Notes for the defendant

If you did reply to the claim form and believe judgment has been entered wrongly in default, you may apply to the court office giving your reasons why the judgment should be set aside. An application form is available for you to use and you will need to pay a fee. A hearing may be arranged and you will be told when and where it will take place. If you live in, or your solicitor's business is in, another court's area, the claim may be transferred to that court.

Address for payment

How to pay

- **Payment(s) must be made to the person named at the address for payment, giving the claimant's reference and claim number**
- **DO NOT bring or send payments to the court – they will not be accepted**
- You should allow at least 4 days for your payment to reach the claimant or his representative
- Make sure that you keep records and can account for all payments made. Proof may be required if there is any disagreement. It is not safe to send cash unless you use registered post

The court office at

is open between 10 am and 4.30 pm Monday to Friday. When corresponding with the court, please address forms or letters to the Court Manager and quote the claim number.

N30(1) C17–001

Judgment for Claimant (acceptance)

Judgment for Claimant (acceptance)

To [Claimant][Defendant]['s solicitor]

In the County Court	
Claim No.	
Claimant (including ref.)	
Defendant (including ref.)	
Date	

Seal

To the Defendant

You have made an offer of payment which the claimant has accepted.

It is therefore ordered that you must pay the claimant £ for debt [and interest to date of judgment] and £ for costs.

You must pay to the claimant a total of £

[by instalments of £ per [week][month]

[the first payment to reach the claimant] by [and on or before this date each [week][month] until the debt has been paid]

Warning

If you ignore this order your goods may be removed and sold, or other enforcement proceedings may be taken against you. If this happens further cost will be added. If your circumstances change and you cannot pay, ask at the court office what you can do.

Notes to defendant

If the payments are not what you offered, you should write at once to the court pointing this out.

This judgment has been recorded on the Register of County Court Judgments. This may make it difficult for you to get credit. **If you pay in full within one month you can ask the court to cancel the entry on the Register.** You will need to give proof of payment. You can (for a fee) also obtain a Certificate of Cancellation from the court. If you pay the debt in full after one month you can ask the court to mark the entry on the Register as satisfied and (for a fee) obtain a Certificate of Satisfaction to prove that the debt has been paid.

Address for payment

If the judgment is for £5,000 or more, or is in respect of a debt which attracts contractual or statutory interest for late payment, the claimant may be entitled to further interest.

How to pay

- **Payment(s) must be made to the person named at the address for payment, giving the claimant's reference and claim number**
- **DO NOT bring or send payments to the court – they will not be accepted**
- You should allow at least 4 days for your payment to reach the claimant or his representative.
- Make sure that you keep records and can account for all payments made. Proof may be required if there is any disagreement. It is not safe to send cash unless you use registered post.
- Leaflets on registered judgments, how to pay and what to do if you cannot pay are available from the court.

The court office at

is open between 10 am and 4 pm Monday to Friday. When corresponding with the court, please address forms or letters to the Court Manager and quote the claim number.

C18–001

N30(1)HC

Judgment for Claimant (acceptance)

Judgment for Claimant (acceptance)

In the High Court of Justice	
Division District Registry	
Claim No.	
Claimant (including ref.)	
Defendant (including ref.)	
Date	

To [Claimant][Defendant]['s solicitor]

Seal

To the Defendant

You have made an offer of payment which the claimant has accepted.

It is therefore ordered that you must pay the claimant £ for debt [and interest to date of judgment] and £ for costs.

You must pay to the claimant a total of £

[by instalments of £ per [week][month]

[the first payment to reach the claimant] by [and on or before this date each [week][month] until the debt has been paid]

Warning

If you ignore this order your goods may be removed and sold, or other enforcement proceedings may be taken against you. If this happens further costs will be added. If your circumstances change and you cannot pay, ask at the court office what you can do.

Note to the defendant

If the payments are not what you offered, you should write at once to the court pointing this out.

How to pay

- **Payment(s) must be made to the person named at the address for payment, giving the claimant's reference and claim number**
- **DO NOT bring or send payments to the court – they will not be accepted**
- You should allow at least 4 days for your payment to reach the claimant or his representative.
- Make sure that you keep records and can account for all payments made. Proof may be required if there is any disagreement. It is not safe to send cash unless you use registered post.

Address for payment

The court office at

is open between 10 am and 4.30 pm Monday to Friday. When corresponding with the court, please address forms or letters to the Court Manager and quote the claim number.

N30(2)

C19–001

Judgment for Claimant (after determination)

Judgment for Claimant (after determination)	**In the** **County Court**
To [Claimant][Defendant]['s solicitor]	**Claim No.**
	Claimant (including ref.)
	Defendant (including ref.)
	Date

Seal

To the Defendant

The claimant has objected to the rate of payment you offered.

The court has therefore decided the rate which you should pay. You must pay the claimant £ for debt [and interest to date of judgment] and £ for costs [less £ which you have already paid].

You must pay to the claimant a total of £

[by instalments of £ per [week][month]

[the first payment to reach the claimant] by [and on or before this date each [week][month] until the debt has been paid]

Warning

If you ignore this order your goods may be removed and sold, or other enforcement proceedings may be taken against you. If this happens further costs will be added. If your circumstances change and you cannot pay, ask at the court office what you can do.

Note to claimant and defendant

Either of you may object to the rate of payment fixed. You must apply to the court with your reasons within 16 days. The 16 days runs from the date on the envelope in which the judgment was posted. A form is available from the court. A hearing may be arranged and you will be told when and where it will take place. If you live in another court's area, the claim may be transferred to that court.

If judgment is for £5,000 or more, or is in respect of a debt which attracts contractual or statutory interest for late payment, the claimant may be entitled to further interest.

Address for payment

Note to the defendant

This judgment has been registered on the Register of County Court Judgments. This may make it difficult for you to get credit. **If you pay in full within one month you can ask the court to cancel the entry on the Register.** You will need to give proof of payment. You can (for a fee) also obtain a Certificate of Cancellation from the court. If you pay the debt in full after one month you can ask the court to mark the entry on the Register as satisfied and (for a fee) obtain a Certificate of Satisfaction to prove that the debt has been paid.

How to pay

- **Payment(s) must be made to the person named at the address for payment, giving the claimant's reference and claim number**
- **DO NOT bring or send payments to the court – they will not be accepted**
- You should allow at least 4 days for your payment to reach the claimant or his representative.
- Make sure that you keep records and can account for all payments made. Proof may be required if there is any disagreement. It is not safe to send cash unless you use registered post.
- Leaflets on registered judgments, how to pay and what to do if you cannot pay are available from the court.

The court office at

is open between 10 am and 4 pm Monday to Friday. When corresponding with the court, please address forms or letters to the Court Manager and quote the claim number.

C20–001

N30(2)HC

Judgment for Claimant (after determination)

Judgment for Claimant (after determination)

In the High Court of Justice	
Division District Registry	
Claim No.	
Claimant (including ref.)	
Defendant (including ref.)	
Date	

To [Claimant][Defendant]['s solicitor]

Seal

To the Defendant

The claimant has objected to the rate of payment you offered.

The court has therefore decided the rate at which you should pay. You must pay the claimant £ for debt [and interest to date of judgment] and £ for costs [less £ which you have already paid]

You must pay to the claimant a total of £

[by instalments of £ per [week][month]

[the first payment to reach the claimant] by [and on or before this date each [week][month] until the debt has been paid]

Warning

If you ignore this order your goods may be removed and sold, or other enforcement proceedings may be taken against you. If this happens further costs will be added. If your circumstances change and you cannot pay, ask at the court office what you can do.

Note to claimant and defendant

Either of you may object to the rate of payment fixed. You must apply to the court with your reasons within 16 days. The 16 days runs from the date on the envelope in which the judgment was posted. A form is available from the court. A hearing may be arranged and you will be told when and where it will take place. If you live in, or your solicitor's business is in, another court's area, the claim may be transferred to that court.

How to pay

- **Payment(s) must be made to the person named at the address for payment, giving the claimant's reference and claim number**
- **DO NOT bring or send payments to the court – they will not be accepted**
- You should allow at least 4 days for your payment to reach the claimant or his representative.
- Make sure that you keep records and can account for all payments made. Proof may be required if there is any disagreement. It is not safe to send cash unless you use registered post.

Address for payment

The court office at

is open between 10 am and 4.30 pm Monday to Friday. When corresponding with the court, please address forms or letters to the Court Manager and quote the claim number.

C21–001

N30(3)

Judgment for Claimant (after re-determination)

Judgment for Claimant (after re-determination)

In the	
County Court	
Claim No.	
Claimant (including ref.)	
Defendant (including ref.)	
Date	

To [Claimant][Defendant]['s solicitor]

Seal

To the Defendant

District Judge has considered the [claimant's][defendant's] application to change the rate of payment decided by the court and has ordered that you must pay the claimant £ for debt [and interest to date of judgment] and £ for costs.

You must pay to the claimant a total of £

[by instalments of £ per [week][month]

[the first payment to reach the claimant] by [and on or before this date each [week][month] until the debt has been paid]

Warning

If you ignore this order your goods may be removed and sold, or other enforcement proceedings may be taken against you. If this happens further costs will be added. If your circumstances change and you cannot pay, ask at the court office what you can do.

Note to the defendant

This judgment has been recorded on the Register of County Court Judgments. This may make it difficult for you to get credit. **If you pay in full within one month you can ask the court to cancel the entry on the Register.** You will need to give proof of payment. You can (for a fee) also obtain a Certificate of Cancellation from the court. If you pay the debt in full after one month you can ask the court to mark the entry on the Register as satisfied and (for a fee) obtain a certificate of Satisfaction to prove that the debt has been paid.
If judgment is for £5,000 or more, or is in respect of a debt which attracts contractual or statutory interest for late payment, the claimant may be entitled to further interest.

Address for payment

How to pay

- **Payment(s) must be made to the person named at the address for payment, giving the claimant's reference and claim number**
- **DO NOT bring or send payments to the court – they will not be accepted**
- You should allow at least 4 days for your payment to reach the claimant or his representative.
- Make sure that you keep records and can account for all payments made. Proof may be required if there is any disagreement. It is not safe to send cash unless you use registered post.
- Leaflets on registered judgments, how to pay and what to do if you cannot pay are available from the court.

The court office at

is open between 10 am and 4 pm Monday to Friday. When corresponding with the court, please address forms or letters to the Court Manager and quote the claim number.

C22–001

N30(3)HC

Judgment for Claimant (after re-determination)

Judgment for Claimant (after re-determination)	**In the High Court of Justice** **Division** **District Registry**

To [Claimant][Defendant]['s solicitor]

Claim No.	
Claimant (including ref.)	
Defendant (including ref.)	
Date	

Seal

To the Defendant

[Master][District Judge] has considered the [claimant's][defendant's] application to change the rate of payment decided by the court and has ordered that you must pay the claimant £ for debt [and interest to date of judgment] and £ for costs.

You must pay to the claimant a total of	£	
[by instalments of	£	per [week][month]
[the first payment to reach the claimant] by		[and on or before this date each [week][month] until the debt has been paid]

Warning

If you ignore this order your goods may be removed and sold, or other enforcement proceedings may be taken against you. If this happens further costs will be added. If your circumstances change and you cannot pay, ask at the court office what you can do.

How to pay

- **Payment(s) must be made to the person named at the address for payment, giving the claimant's reference and claim number**
- **DO NOT bring or send payments to the court – they will not be accepted**
- You should allow at least 4 days for your payment to reach the claimant or his representative.
- Make sure that you keep records and can account for all payments made. Proof may be required if there is any disagreement. It is not safe to send cash unless you use registered post.

Address for payment

The court office at

is open between 10 am and 4.30 pm Monday to Friday. When corresponding with the court, please address forms or letters to the Court Manager and quote the claim number.

N34

C23–001

Judgment for Claimant (after court decided amount)

Judgment for Claimant (after court decided amount)

In the	
County Court	
Claim No.	
Claimant (including ref.)	
Defendant (including ref.)	
Date	

To [Claimant][Defendant]['s solicitor]

Seal

To the Defendant

The claimant obtained judgment against you on for an amount to be decided by the court.

District Judge has decided the amount and ordered that you should pay £ [including interest to date of judgment] and £ for costs [with costs to be assessed].

You must pay to the claimant a total of £

[by instalments of £ per [week][month]

[the first payment to reach the claimant] by [and on or before this date each [week][month] until the debt has been paid]

If costs are to be assessed, you will be told when those costs have to be paid after the assessment has taken place.

Warning

If you ignore this order your goods may be removed and sold, or other enforcement proceedings may be taken against you. If this happens further costs will be added. If your circumstances change and you cannot pay, ask at the court office what you can do.

If judgment is for £5,000 or more, or is in respect of a debt which attracts contractual or statutory interest for late payment, the claimant may be entitled to further interest.

Address for payment

Note to the defendant

This judgment has been registered on the Register of County Court Judgments. This may make it difficult for you to get credit. **If you pay in full within one month** you can ask the court to cancel the entry on the Register. You will need to give proof of payment. You can (for a fee) also obtain a Certificate of Cancellation from the court. If you pay the debt in full after one month you can ask the court to mark the entry on the Register as satisfied and (for a fee) obtain a Certificate of Satisfaction to prove that the debt has been paid.

How to pay

- **Payment(s) must be made to the person named at the address for payment, giving the claimant's reference and claim number**
- **DO NOT bring or send payments to the court – they will not be accepted**
- You should allow at least 4 days for your payment to reach the claimant or his representative
- Make sure that you keep records and can account for all payments made. Proof may be required if there is any disagreement. It is not safe to send cash unless you use registered post.
- Leaflets on registered judgments, how to pay and what to do if you cannot pay are available from the court.

The court office at

is open between 10 am and 4 pm Monday to Friday. When corresponding with the court, please address forms or letters to the Court Manager and quote the claim number.

C24–001

N34HC

Judgment for Claimant (after court decided amount)

Judgment for Claimant
(after court decided amount)

To [Claimant][Defendant]['s solicitor]

In the High Court of Justice Division District Registry	
Claim No.	
Claimant (including ref.)	
Defendant (including ref.)	
Date	

Seal

To the Defendant

The Claimant obtained judgment against you on for an amount to be decided by the court.

[Master][District Judge] has decided the amount and ordered that you should pay £ [including interest to date of judgment] and £ for costs [with costs to be assessed]

You must pay to the claimant a total of £

[by instalments of £ per [week][month]

[the first payment to reach the claimant] by [and on or before this date each [week][month] until the debt has been paid]

If costs are to be assessed, you will be told when those costs have to be paid after the assessment has taken place.

Warning

If you ignore this order your goods may be removed and sold, or other enforcement proceedings may be taken against you. If this happens further costs will be added. If your circumstances change and you cannot pay, ask at the court office what you can do.

Address for payment

How to pay

- **Payment(s) must be made to the person named at the address for payment, giving the claimant's reference and claim number**
- **DO NOT bring or send payments to the court – they will not be accepted**
- You should allow at least 4 days for your payment to reach the claimant or his representative
- Make sure that you keep records and can account for all payments made. Proof may be required if there is any disagreement. It is not safe to send cash unless you use registered post
- Leaflets on how to pay and what to do if you cannot pay are available from the court

The court office at

is open between 10 am and 4.30 pm Monday to Friday. When corresponding with the court, please address forms or letters to the Court Manager and quote the claim number.

N150 C25–001

Allocation Questionnaire

Allocation questionnaire

In the	
Claim No.	
Last date for filing with court office	

To

SEAL

Please read the notes on page five before completing the questionnaire.

Please note the date by which it must be returned and the name of the court it should be returned to since this may be different from the court where proceedings were issued.

If you have settled this case (or if you settle it on a future date) and do not need to have it heard or tried, you must let the court know immediately.

A Settlement

Do you wish there to be a one month stay to attempt to settle the case? ☐ Yes ☐ No

B Track

Which track do you consider is most suitable for your case? (*Tick one box*) ☐ small claims ☐ fast track ☐ multi-track

If you think your case is suitable for a specialist list, say which:

If you have indicted a track which would not be the normal track for the case, please give brief reasons for you choice:

C Pre-action protocols

Have you complied with any pre-action protocol applicable to your claim?

☐ None applicable to this claim ☐ Yes ☐ No

If Yes, please say which protocol:

If No, please explain to what extent and for what reason it has no been complied with:

D Applications

If you have not already sent the court an application for summary judgment, do you intend to do so?

☐ Yes ☐ No

If you have not already issued a claim in the case against someone not yet a party, do you intend to apply for the court's permission to do so?

☐ Yes ☐ No

In either case, if Yes, please give details:

E Witnesses of fact

So far a you know at this stage, what witnesses of fact do you intend to call at the hearing?

Witness name	Witness to which facts

F Experts' evidence

Do you wish to use expert evidence at the hearing? ☐ Yes ☐ No

Have you already copied any experts' report(s) to the other party(ies)? ☐ None obtained as yet ☐ Yes ☐ No

Please list the experts whose evidence you think you will use:

Expert's name	Field of expertise (eg. orthopaedic surgeon, mechanical engineer)

Will you and the other party use the same expert(s)? ☐ Yes ☐ No

If No, please explain why not:

Do you want your expert(s) to give evidence orally at the hearing or trial? ☐ Yes ☐ No

If Yes, give the reasons why you think oral evidence is necessary:

G Location of trial

Is there any reason why your case needs to be heard at a particular court? ☐ Yes ☐ No

If Yes, give reasons (eg. particular facilities required, convenience of witnesses, etc.)

and specify the court:

H Representation and estimate of hearing/trial time

Do you expect to be represented by a solicitor or counsel at the hearing/trial? ☐ No ☐ Solicitor ☐ Counsel

How long do you estimate it will take to put your case to the court at the hearing/trial? days hours minutes

If there are days when you, your representative, expert or an essential witness will not be able to attend court, give details:

Name	Dates not available

I Costs (only relates to costs incurred by legal representatives)

What is your estimate of costs incurred to date £

What do you estimate the overall costs are likely to be £

J Other information

Have you attached documents you wish the judge to take into account when allocating the case? ☐ Yes ☐ No

Have they been served on the other parties? ☐ Yes ☐ No

If Yes, say when

Have the other parties agreed their content? ☐ Yes ☐ No

Have you attached a list of the directions you think appropriate for the management of your case? ☐ Yes ☐ No

Are they agreed with the other parties? ☐ Yes ☐ No

Are there any other facts which might affect the timetable the court will set? If so, please state

Signed Date

[Counsel][Solicitor][for the][Claimant][Defendant]

Notes for completing an allocation questionnaire

- If the case is not settled, a judge must allocate it to an appropriate case management track. To help the judge choose the most just and cost-effective track, you must now complete the attached questionnaire.
- If you fail to return the allocation questionnaire by the date given, the judge may make an order which leads to your claim or defence being struck out, or hold an allocation hearing. If there is an allocation hearing the judge may order any party who has not filed their questionnaire to pay, immediately, the costs of that hearing.
- If you wish to make an application, for example, for special directions, for summary judgment on the grounds that the other party has no reasonable chance of success in their claim or defence, or for permission to add another party to the claim, you should send it and any required fee with the completed allocation questionnaire. If a hearing is fixed for your application, it may also be used as an allocation hearing.
- Any other documents you wish the judge to take into account should be filed with the questionnaire. But you must confirm that the documents have been sent to the other party, or parties, saying when they would have received them and whether they agreed their contents.
- Use a separate sheet if you need more speace for your answers marking clearly which section the information refers to. Write the case number on it, sign and date it and attach it securely to the questionnaire.
- The letters below refer to the secitons of the questionnaire and tell you what information is needed.

A Settlement

If you think that you and the other party may be able to negotiate a settlement you should tick the 'Yes' box. The court may order a stay, whether or not all the other parties to the case agree. You should still complete the rest of the questionnaire, even if you are requesting a stay. Where a stay is granted it will be for an initial period of one month.

B Track

The basic guide by which cases are normally allocated to a track depends on the money value of the claim, although other factors such as the complexity of the case will also be considered:

Small Claims track	Claims values at £5,00 or less unless they include a claim for personal injuries worth over £1,000; or a claim for housing disrepair where the costs of the repairs or other work is more than £1,000 and any other claim for damages is more than £1,000
Fast track	Claims valued at more than £5,000 but not more than £15,000
Multi-track	Claims over £15,000

A leaflet available from the court office explains these limits in greater detail.

C Pre-action protocols

For certain kinds of claim, there are protocols which set out what ought to be done before court proceedings are issued. As at April 1999 there are protocols for clinical negligence and personal injury claims.

D Applications

If you intend to apply for summary judgment or for permission to add another party to the claim or make any other application you should, if you have not already done so, file the application with your completed allocation questionnaire.

E Witnesses of fact

Remember to include yourself, if you will be giving evidence; but not experts, who should be included in section F.

F Experts' evidence

Oral or written expert evidence will only be allowed at the trial with the court's permission. The judge will decide what permission it seems appropriate to give when the case is allocated to track.

G Location of trial

High Court cases are usually heard at the Royal Courts of Justice or certain Civil Trial Centres. Other multi-track cases are heard at the Civil Trial Centre for the court where they are proceeding. Fast track cases are usually heard either at the court in which they are proceeding or its Civil Trial Centre. The court office will tell you which is the Civil Trial Centre for any particular county court. Small claims cases are usually heard at the court in which they are proceeding.

H Representation and estimate of hearing time

If the case is allocated to the fast track, no more than one day will be allowed for the trial of the whole case.

I Costs

Estimates should be given using Form 1 which can be found in the Schedule of Costs Forms set out in the Civil Procedure Rules. The form should be attached to and returned with your completed questionnaire.

C26–001

N152

Notice that a [defence] [counterclaim] has been filed

Notice that a [defence] [counterclaim] has been filed

In the	
Claim No.	
Claimant (including ref.)	
Defendant (including ref.)	
Date	

To [Claimant][Defendant]['s solicitor]

[The defendant has filed a [defence][counterclaim], [a copy][copies] of which [is][are] enclosed with this notice. An allocation questionnaire is also enclosed which contains notes for guidance on how to complete it.]

[You have already been sent [a copy of a defence][copies of defences] received from [one][ ] of the defendants in this claim. The time for all the defendants to file their defences has now elapsed and I am enclosing an allocation questionnaire for you to complete. [No further defences have been received.] [A copy][Copies] of the final [defence][counterclaim] received [is][are] also enclosed.]]

You must complete the allocation questionnaire on or before

and return it to the court office at

[If you intend to defend the counterclaim, you must file a copy of your defence with your completed allocation questionnaire. Your defence must contain a statement of truth.]

The court office at

is open between 10 am and 4 pm Monday to Friday. When corresponding with the court, please address forms or letters to the Court Manager and quote the claim number.

N153 C27–001

Notice of Allocation or Listing Hearing

Notice of Allocation or Listing Hearing

In the	
Claim No.	
Claimant (including ref.)	
Defendant (including ref.)	
Date	

To [Claimant][Defendant]['s solicitor]

Seal

[Master][District Judge] has considered the statements of case and allocation [listing] questionnaires filed in this claim [counterclaim] and decided that a hearing is necessary before a final decision about [allocation][listing] can be made.

[Reasons for the hearing are as follows:—

]

The [Master][District Judge] orders you to attend at [am][pm] on the

of at

[The [Master][District Judge] directs the [claimant][defendant] to provide the following [further] information and send copies to the court and the other parties by .... :—

Note: If you fail to attend the hearing, the court may order you to pay the costs of the other party, or parties, that do attend. Failure to pay those costs within the time stated may lead to your statement of case being struck out.

The court office at

is open between 10 am and 4 pm Monday to Friday. Address all communications to the Court Manager quoting the claim number.

C28–001

N154

Notice of Allocation to the Fast Track

Notice of Allocation to the Fast Track	**In the**	
	Claim No.	
To [Claimant][Defendant]['s solicitor]	**Claimant** (including ref.)	
	Defendant (including ref.)	
	Date	

Seal

[Master] [District Judge] has considered the statements of case and allocation questionnaires filed, and allocated the [claim] [counterclaim] to **the fast track**.

The trial of this [claim] [counterclaim] will take place during the period commencing of and ending on of at a venue to be notified.

The [Master] [District Judge] orders that you and the other parties prepare for the trial as follows:—

[The reason[s] the judge has given for allocation to this task [is] [are] that .]

Notes:

- You and the other party, or parties, may agree to extend the time periods given in the directions above provided this **does not** affect the date given for returning the listing questionnaire or the date of the trial or trial period.
- If you do not comply with these directions, any other party to the claim will be entitled to apply to the court for an order that your statement of case (claim or defence) be struck out.
- Leaflets explaining more about what happens when your case is allocated to the fast track are available from the court office.

The court office at

is open between 10 am and 4 pm Monday to Friday. Address all communications to the Court Manager quoting the claim number.

N155 C29–001

Notice of Allocation to the Multi-track

Notice of Allocation to the Multi-track

In the	
Claim No.	
Claimant (including ref.)	
Defendant (including ref.)	
Date	

To [Claimant][Defendant]['s solicitor]

Seal

[Master][District Judge] has considered the statements of case and allocation questionnaires filed and allocated the claim [counterclaim] to **the multi-track**.

The [Master][District Judge] has ordered that:—

[The claim is being transferred to the [Civil Trial Centre at County Court] [Division of the Royal Courts of Justice] where all future applications, correspondence and so on will be dealt with]

[The reason[s] the judge has given for allocation to this task [is][are] that .]

Notes:

- You and the other party, or parties, may agree to extend the time periods given in the directions above provided this **does not** affect the date given any case management conference, for returning the listing questionnaire, for any pre trial review or the date of the trial or trial period.
- If you do not comply with these directions, any other party to the claim will be entitled to apply to the court for an order that your statement of case (claim or defence) be struck out.
- Leaflets explaining more about that happens when your case is allocated to the Multi-track are available from the court office.

The court office at

is open between 10 am and 4 pm Monday to Friday. Address all communications to the Court Manager quoting the claim number.

N156

Request for Further Information (allocation)

C30–001 **Order for Further Information (allocation)**

In the	
Claim No.	
Claimant (including ref.)	
Defendant (including ref.)	
Date	

To [Claimant][Defendant]['s solicitor]

Seal

[Master][District Judge] has considered the statements of case and allocation questionnaires filed and requires further information before making a final decision about allocation.

[The [Master][District Judge] orders the [claimant][defendant] to provide information about:—

This information and any accompanying documents should be delivered to the court and copied to the other parties on or before [ ]

Note: Where an allocation hearing is necessary because a party does not provide the information ordered above, the court may order that party to pay the costs of any other party attending the hearing.

The court office at

is open between 10 am and 4 pm Monday to Friday. Address all communications to the Court Manager quoting the claim number.

N157 C31–001

Notice of Allocation to the Small Claims Track

Notice of Allocation to the Small Claims Track

To [Claimant][Defendant]['s solicitor]

In the County Court	
Claim No.	
Claimant (including ref.)	
Defendant (including ref.)	
Date	

Seal

[District Judge] has considered the statements of case and allocation questionnaires filed and allocated the claim [counterclaim] to **the small claims track**.

The hearing of this claim [counterclaim] will take place at [am][pm] on the of at

The judge has estimated that the hearing of this claim [counterclaim] should take no longer than [mins][hours]. This is the total time for you, the other party [parties] and any witnesses to put your evidence and for the judge to reach a decision. To help prepare the claim [counterclaim] for hearing, the judge has ordered that you comply with the following directions:—

[The reason[s] the judge has given for allocation to this track [is][are] that .]

Note:

- If you cannot, or choose not to, attend the hearing, you must write and tell the court **at least 7 days before the date of the hearing**. The district judge will hear the case in your absence, but will take account of your statement of case and any other documents you have filed.
- If you do not attend the hearing and do not give notice that you will not attend, the district judge may strike out your claim, defence or counter claim. If the claimant attends but the defendant does not, the district judge may make a decision based on the evidence of the claimant only.
- Leaflets explaining more about what you should do and what happens when your case is allocated to the small claims track are available from the court office.

The court office at

is open between 10 am and 4 pm Monday to Friday. Address all communications to the Court Manager quoting the claim number.

C32–001

N158

Notice of Allocation to the Small Claims Track (preliminary hearing)

Notice of Allocation to the Small Claims Track (preliminary hearing)

In the	
Claim No.	
Claimant (including ref.)	
Defendant (including ref.)	
Date	

To [Claimant][Defendant]['s solicitor]

Seal

District Judge .... has considered the statements of case and allocation questionnaires filed and allocated the claim [counterclaim] to the **small claims track**.

Before the claim [counterclaim] is listed for hearing, the judge has ordered that a preliminary hearing should take place [because]:—

[special directions are needed in this claim [counterclaim] to prepare for the final hearing which the judge would prefer to explain to you in person.]

[to consider whether the [claim][counterclaim] can be disposed of because the [claimant][defendant] has no real prospect of success at a final hearing.]

The preliminary hearing will take place at [am][pm] on the of at

[The reason[s] the judge has given for allocation to this task [is][are] that .]

Note
- If you do not attend the hearing the court may make an order in your absence.
- If it is practical to do so and you and the other parties agree, the judge may decide to treat the preliminary hearing as a final hearing.
- Leaflets explaining more about what you should do and what happens when your case is allocated to the small claims track are available from the court office.

The court office at

is open between 10 am and 4 pm Monday to Friday. Address all communications to the Court Manager quoting the claim number.

N159

Notice of Allocation to the Small Claims Track (no hearing)

C33–001

Notice of Allocation to the Small Claims Track (no hearing)

To [Claimant][Defendant]['s solicitor]

In the	
County Court	
Claim No.	
Claimant (including ref.)	
Defendant (including ref.)	
Date	

Seal

District Judge has considered the statements of case and allocation questionnaires filed and allocated the claim [counterclaim] to the **small claims track.**

The judge proposes to deal with the claim [counterclaim] without a hearing, that is, on the papers alone but can only do this if all parties agree.

Please tell the court whether or not you agree to your case being dealt with in this way by completing the lower half of this form and returning a copy to the court on or before ______. You must at the same time send a copy of it to all other parties.

Leaflets explaining more about what you should do and what happens when your case is allocated to the Small Claims Track are available from the court office.

Reply to the court
Tick A or B and C

A ☐ I agree that the claim [counterclaim] should be dealt with on the papers alone.

or

B ☐ I do not agree that the claim [counterclaim] should be dealt with on the papers alone.

and

C ☐ I have sent a copy of this completed form to the other party.

In the	
County Court	
Claim No.	
Claimant (including ref.)	
Defendant (including ref.)	

Signed ______
(Claimant) (Defendant) ('s solicitor) ('s litigation friend)

Position or office held ______
(if signing on behalf of firm or company)

Date ______

The court office at

is open between 10 am and 4 pm Monday to Friday. Address all communications to the Court Manager quoting the claim number.

C34–001

N160

Notice of Allocation to the Small Claims Track (with parties' consent)

Notice of Allocation to the Small Claims Track (with parties' consent)

In the	
County Court	
Claim No.	
Claimant (including ref.)	
Defendant (including ref.)	
Date	

To [Claimant][Defendant]['s solicitor]

Seal

District Judge has considered the statements of case and allocation questionnaires filed and, with the consent of the parties, allocated the claim [counterclaim] to **the small claims track**.

The hearing of the claim [counterclaim] will take place at [am][pm] on the of at

The Judge has estimated that the hearing of this claim [counterclaim] should take no longer than mins/hours and has ordered that you must comply with the following directions which will tell you what to do to prepare for the trial:

Notes:
- If you cannot, or choose not to, attend the hearing, you must write and tell the court at **least 7 days before the date of the hearing**. The district judge will hear the case in your absence, but will take account of your statement of case and any other documents you have filed.
- As you have consented to your claim [counterclaim] being heard in the small claims track, any costs allowed to the successful party will be limited to the maximum sum which can be awarded in the fast track.
- If you do not attend the hearing and do not give notice that you will not attend, the district judge may strike out your claim, defence or counterclaim. If the claimant attends but the defendant does not, the district judge may make a decision based on the evidence of the claimant only.
- Leaflets telling you more about the small claims track are available from the court office.

The court office at

is open between 10 am and 4 pm Monday to Friday. When corresponding with the court, please address forms or letters to the Court Manager and quote the claim number.

N170 C35–001

Listing Questionnaire

Listing questionnaire

In the	
Claim No.	
Last date for filing with court office	

To

- The court will use the information which you and the other party(ies) provide to fix a date for trial (or to confirm the date and time if one has already been fixed), to confirm the estimated length of trial and to set a timetable for the trial itself. In multi-track cases the court will also decide whether to hold a pre-trial review.
- If you do not complete and return the questionnaire the procedural judge may
  - make an order which leads to your statement of case (claim or defence) being struck out.
  - decide to hold a listing hearing. You may be ordered to pay (immediately) the other parties' costs of attending.
  - if there is sufficient information, list the case for trial and give any appropriate directions.
  - separate estimates of costs incurred to date and those which will be incurred if the case proceeds to trial should be given using Form 1 in the Schedule of Costs Forms set out in the Civil Procedure Rules. This form should be attached to and returned with your completed questionnaire. (This relates only to costs incurred by legal representatives).

A Directions complied with

1. Have you complied with all the previous directions given by the court? ☐ Yes ☐ No
2. If no please explain which directions are outstanding and why.

Directions outstanding	Reasons directions outstanding

3. Are any further directions required to prepare the case for trial? ☐ Yes ☐ No (*If no, go to section B*)
4. If yes, please explain directions required and give reasons.

Directions required	Reasons required

B Experts

1. Has the court already given permission for you to use written expert evidence? ☐ Yes ☐ No (*If no, go to section B6*)

2. If yes, please give name and field of expertise.

Name of expert	Whether joint expert (*please tick, if appropriate*)	Field of expertise

3. Have the expert(s') report(s) been agreed with the other parties? ☐ Yes ☐ No

4. Have the experts met to discuss their reports? ☐ Yes ☐ No

5. Has the court already given permission for the expert(s) to give oral evidence at the trial? ☐ Yes ☐ No (*If yes go to Q8*)

6. If no, are you seeking that permission? ☐ Yes ☐ No (*If no, go to section C*)

7. Give your reasons for seeking permission.

8. What are the names, addresses and fields of expertise of your experts?

Expert 1	Expert 2	Expert 3	Expert 4

9. Please give details of any dates within the trial period when your expert(s) will not be available.

Name of expert	Dates not available

C Other witnesses

(If you are not calling other witnesses go to section D)

1. How many other witnesses (including yourself) will be giving evidence on your behalf at the trial? (*do not include experts – see section B above*) ☐ (*Give number*)

2. What are the names and addresses of your witnesses?

Witness 1	Witness 2	Witness 3	Witness 4

3. Please give details of any dates within the trial period when you or your witnesses will not be available?

Name of witness	Dates not available

4. Are any of the witness statements agreed? ☐ Yes ☐ No (*If no, go to question C6*)

5. If yes, give the name of the witness and the date of his or her statement

Name of witness	Date of statement

6. Do you or any of your witnesses need any special facilities? ☐ Yes ☐ No (*If no, go to question C8*)

7. If yes, what are they?

8. Will any of your witnesses be provided with an interpreter? ☐ Yes ☐ No (*If no, go to section D*)

9. If yes, say what type of interpreter e.g. language (stating which), deaf/blind etc.

D Legal representation

1. Who will be presenting your case at the hearing or trial? ☐ You ☐ Solicitor ☐ Counsel

2. Please give details of any dates within the trial period when the person presenting your case will not be available.

Name	Dates not available

E Other matters

1. How long do you estimate the trial will take, including cross-examination and closing arguments?

Minutes	Hours	Days

If your case is allocated to the fast track the maximum time allowed for the whole case will be no more than one day.

2. What is the estimated number of pages of evidence to be included in the trial bundle?

(*please give number*)

Fast track cases only

3. The court will normally give you 3 weeks notice in the fast track of the date fixed for a fast track trial unless, in exceptional circumstances, the court directs that shorter notice will be given. Would you be prepared to accept shorter notice of the date fixed for trial? ☐ Yes ☐ No

Signed

Claimant/defendant or Counsel/Solicitor for the claimant/defendant

Date

N171 C36–001

Notice of Date for Return of Listing Questionnaire

Notice of Date for Return of Listing Questionnaire

To [Claimant][Defendant]['s solicitor]

In the	
Claim No.	
Claimant (including ref.)	
Defendant (including ref.)	
Date	

Enclosed with this notice is a listing questionnaire which you must complete and return

on or before

to the court office at

Note: You should read the notes for guidance on the first page of the listing questionnaire and note particularly the possible sanctions for failure to complete and return it.

The court office at

is open between 10 am and 4 pm Monday to Friday. When corresponding with the court, please address forms or letters to the Court Manager and quote the claim number.

C37–001

N172

Notice of Trial Date

Notice of Trial Date

In the	
Claim No.	
Claimant (including ref.)	
Defendant (including ref.)	
Date	

To [Claimant][Defendant]['s solicitor]

The trial of the above claim [counterclaim] will take place at [am][pm]

on the of

at

[Any application in the case must be made to the court where the case is to be tried.]

[Master][District Judge] .... has ordered that:

Note for fast track cases: At the end of the trial, in addition to deciding which party will pay the costs of the case, the judge will also normally assess the amount to be paid. All parties should ensure that they bring all relevant information in respect of their costs to the trial to enable the judge to carry out that assessment.

The court office at

is open between 10 am and 4 pm Monday to Friday. When corresponding with the court, please address forms or letters to the Court Manager and quote the claim number.

N205A

C38–001

Notice of issue (specified amount) and request for judgment

Notice of Issue (specified amount)

To the Claimant['s Solicitor]

In the	
The court office at is open between 10 am & 4 pm Monday to Friday Tel:	
Claim No.	
Claimant (including ref.)	
Defendant(s)	
Issue fee	£

Your claim was issued on [ ].
The court sent it to the defendant by first class post on [ ] and it will be deemed to be served on [ ].
The defendant has until [ ] to reply.

The defendant may

- **Pay** you your total claim.
- **File an acknowledgement of service.** This will allow the defendant 28 days form the date of service of your particulars of claim to file a defence or contest the court's jurisdiction.
- **Dispute the whole claim.** The court will send you a copy of the defence.
- **Admit that all the money is owed.** The defendant will send you a completed admission form and you may ask the court to enter judgment using the request below.
- **Admit that only part of your claim is owed.** The court will send you a copy of the reply form and you will have to decide what to do next.
- **Not reply at all.** You may ask the court to enter judgment using the request below.

For further information please turn over

Note: If the claim is disputed and the defendant is an individual, the claim may be transferred to either the defendant's local court or, if he or she is represented, the one nearest the business address of the solicitor.

✂- -

Request for Judgment

In the	
Claim No.	
Claimant (including ref.)	
Defendant(s) (including ref.)	

- *Tick and complete either A or B. Remember to sign and date the form. Your signature certifies that the information you have given is correct.*
- *If the defendant has given an address on the form of admission to which correspondence should be sent, which is different from the address shown on the claim form, you must tell the court.*
- *Complete all the judgment details at C.*

A

☐ **The defendant has not filed an admission or defence to my claim or an application to contest the court's jurisdiction.**
Decide how and when you want the defendant to pay. You can ask for the judgment to be paid by instalments or in one payment.

B

☐ **The defendant admits that all the money is owed**
Tick only one box below and return the completed slip to the court.

☐ **I accept the defendant's proposal for payment**
Say how the defendant intends to pay. The court will send the defendant an order to pay. You will also be sent a copy.

☐ **The defendant has not made any proposal for payment**
Say how you want the defendant to pay. You can ask for the judgment to be paid by instalments or in one payment. The court will send the defendant an order to pay. You will also be sent a copy.

☐ **I do NOT accept the defendant's proposal for payment**
Say how you want the defendant to pay. Give your reasons for objecting to the defendant's offer of payment in Part D overleaf. Return this slip to the court **with the defendant's admission** (or a copy). The court will fix a rate of payment and send the defendant an order to pay. You will also be sent a copy.

C Judgment details

I would like the defendant to be ordered to pay

☐ (immediately)

☐ (by instalments of £ per month)

☐ (in full **by**)

Amount of claim as stated in claim form (including interest at date of issue)	
Interest since date of claim (if any)	
Period from......... to	
Rate ......%	
Court fees shown on claim	
Solicitor's costs (if any) on issuing claim	
Sub Total	
Solicitor's costs (if any) on entering judgment	
Sub Total	
Deduct amount (if any) paid since issue	
Amount payable by defendant	

I certify that the information given is correct

Signed.. **Date**.........................

(Claimant) (Claimant's solicitor) (Litigation friend)

Notes for Guidance

- The claim form must be served on the defendant within 4 months of the date of issue (6 months if you are serving outside England and Wales). You may be able to apply to extend the time for serving the claim form but the application must generally be made before the 4-month or 6-month period expires.

- If the defendant does not file an admission, defence or counterclaim; or if the defendant admits the whole claim with or without an offer of payment, you may ask for judgment. If you do not request judgment within 6 months of the end of the period for filing a defence, your claim will be stayed. This means that the only action you can take is to apply to a judge for an order lifting the stay.

- You should keep a record of any payments you receive from the defendant. If there is a hearing or you wish to take steps to enforce the judgment you will need to satisfy the court about the balance outstanding. You should give the defendant a receipt and payment in cash should always be acknowledged. You should tell the defendant how much he owes if he asks.

- **You must inform the court IMMEDIATELY if you receive any payment before a hearing date or after you have sent a request for enforcement to the court.**

- Further information in leaflet form can be obtained free of charge from the court.

Part D

Objections to the defendant's proposal for payment **Claim Number**

N205B C39-001

Notice of issue (unspecifed amount) and request for judgment

Notice of Issue (unspecified amount)

To the Claimant['s Solicitor]

In the	
The court office at is open between 10 am & 4 pm Monday to Friday Tel:	
Claim No.	
Claimant (including ref.)	
Defendant(s)	
Issue fee	£

Your claim was issued on [ ].

The court sent it to the defendant by first class post on [ ] and it will be deemed to be served on [ ].

The defendant has until [ ] to reply.

The defendant may either

- **Pay an amount into court to satisfy your claim.** This is called a 'payment in satisfaction'. The court will notify you of the payment and you will have to decide whether to accept the amount offered.
- **Offer to pay you an amount to satisfy your claim and/or ask for time to pay.** The court will send you a copy of the defendant's reply and you will have to decide what you want to do.
- **Admit liability for your claim but not offer an amount in satisfaction.** The court will send you a copy of the defendant's reply and you will be able to request judgment for amount to be decided by the court and costs.
- **File an acknowledgement of service.** This will allow the defendant 28 days from the date of service of your particulars of claim to file a defence or contest the court's jurisdiction. The court will send you a notice that an acknowledgment has been filed.
- **Dispute your claim.** The court will send you a copy of the defence and tell you what to do next.
- **Not reply at all.** You may ask the court to enter judgment for an amount to be decided by the court by completing the tear off portion on this form. A hearing will be arranged to determine the amount the defendant should pay you. **If you do not request judgment within 6 months of the date for filing a defence, your claim will be stayed. This means that the only action open to you would be to apply to a judge for an order lifting the stay.**

✂- -

Request for Judgment

Notes:

- The court will notify both you and the defendant of any steps you should take to prepare for the hearing at which the court will decide what amount you are entitled to.
- You should notify the court immediately if your claim is settled or you decide that you do not wish to proceed.

In the	
Claim No.	
Claimant (including ref)	
Defendant(s)	

To the court

The defendant has not filed an admission or defence to my claim, or an application to contest the court's jurisdiction and the time for doing so has expired.

I request that judgment be entered for an amount including costs, to be decided by the court.

Signed [ ] **Date** [ ]

(Claimant) (Claimant's solicitor) (Litigation friend)

C40–001

N205C

Notice of Issue (non-money claim)

Notice of Issue
(non-money claim)

In the	
Claim No.	
Claimant (including ref.)	
Defendant(s)	
Issue fee	£

To the Claimant['s Solicitor]

Your claim was issued on [ ].

[The court sent it to the defendant by the first class post on [ ] and it will be deemed served on [ ]. The defendant has until [ ] to reply.]

[The claim form [which includes particulars of claim] is returned to you, with the relevant response forms for you to serve them on the defendant[s].]

Notes for guidance

- The claim form and the particulars of claim, if served separately, must be served on the defendant within 4 months of the date of issue (6 months if you are serving outside England and Wales). You may be able to apply to extend the time for serving the claim form but the application must generally be made before the 4-month or 6-month period expires.
- You must inform the court immediately if your claim is settled or discontinued.

The defendant may
- **admit the truth of the whole or any part of your claim.** The court will send you a copy of the defendant's admission and tell you what to do next.
- **file an acknowledgement of service.** This will allow the defendant 28 days from the date of service of your particulars of claim to file a defence or contest the court's jurisdiction.
- **dispute the whole claim.** The court will send you a copy of the defence.
- **not reply at all.** You may make an application to the court for judgment. A fee may be payable.

The court office at

is open between 10 am and 4 pm Monday to Friday. When corresponding with the court, please address forms or letters to the Court Manager and quote the claim number.

C41–001

N208

Claim Form (CPR Part 8)

Claim Form (CPR Part 8)	In the	
	Claim No.	

Claimant

SEAL

Defendant(s)

Details of claim (see also overleaf)

Defendant's name and address

	£
Court fee	
Solicitor's costs	
Issue date	

The court office at

is open between 10 am and 4 pm Monday to Friday. When corresponding with the court, please address forms or letters to the Court Manager and quote the claim number.

Claim No.	

Details of claim (continued)

Statement of Truth
* (I believe)(The Claimant believes) that the facts stated in these particulars of claim are true.
* I am duly authorised by the claimant to sign this statement

Full name ______________________________

Name of claimant's solicitor's firm ______________________________

signed ____________________ position or office held ____________________
*(Claimant)(Litigation friend)(Claimant's solicitor) (if signing on behalf of firm or company)

* delete as appropriate

Claimant's or claimant's solicitor's address to which documents should be sent if different from overleaf. If you are prepared to accept service by DX, fax or e-mail, please add details.

C42–001

N208A

C42–001

Notes for Claimant (CPR Part 8)

Notes for claimant on completing a Part 8 claim form

- Please read all of these guidance notes before you begin completing the claim form. The notes follow the order in which information is required on the form.
- Court staff can help you fill in the claim form and give information about procedure once it has been issued. But they cannot give legal advice. If you need legal advice, for example, about the likely success of your claim or the evidence you need to prove it, you should contact a solicitor or a Citizens Advice Bureau.
- If you are filling in the claim form by hand, please use black ink and write in block capitals.
- You must file any written evidence to support your claim either in or with the claim form. Your written evidence must be verified by a statement of truth.
- Copy the completed claim form, the defendant's notes for guidance and your written evidence so that you have one copy for yourself, one copy for the court and one copy for each defendant. Send or take the forms and evidence to the court office with the appropriate fee. The court will tell you how much this is.

Notes on completing the claim form

Heading

You must fill in the heading of the form to indicate whether you want the claim to be issued in a county court or in the High Court (The High Court means either a District Registry (attached to a county court) or the Royal Courts of Justice in London).
Use whichever of the following is appropriate:

'In the . . . . County Court'
(inserting the name of the court)

or

'In the High Court of Justice . Division'
(inserting eg. 'Queen's Bench' or 'Chancery' as appropriate)
' . . . . District Registry'
(inserting the name of the District Registry)

or

'In the High Court of Justice . Division,
(inserting eg. 'Queen's Bench' or 'Chancery' as appropriate)
Royal Courts of Justice'

Claimant and defendant details

As the person issuing the claim, you are called the 'claimant'; the person you are suing is called the 'defendant'. Claimants who are under 18 years old (unless otherwise permitted by the court) and patients within the meaning of the Mental Health Act 1983 must have a litigation friend to issue and conduct court proceedings on their behalf. Court staff will tell you more about what you need to do if this applies to you.

You must provide the following information about yourself **and** the defendant according to the capacity in which you are suing and in which the defendant is being sued. When suing or being sued as:—

an individual:
All known forenames and surname, whether Mr, Mrs, Miss, Ms or Other (e.g. Dr) and residential address (**including** postcode and telephone and any fax or e-mail number) in England and Wales. Where the defendant is a proprietor of a business, a partner in a firm or an individual sued in the name of a club or other unincorporated association, the address for service should be the usual or last known place of residence **or** principal place of business of the company, firm or club or other unincorporated association.

Where the individual is:
under 18 write '(a child by Mr Joe Bloggs his litigation friend)' after the child's name.

a patient within the meaning of the Mental Health Act 1983 write '(by Mr Joe Bloggs his litigation friend)' after the patient's name.

trading under another name you must add the words 'trading as' and the trading name e.g. 'Mr John Smith trading as Smith's Groceries'.

suing or being sued in a representative capacity you must say what that capacity is e.g. 'Mr Joe Bloggs as the representative of Mrs Sharon Bloggs (deceased)'.

suing or being sued in the name of a club or other unincorporated association add the words 'suing/sued on behalf of' followed by the name of the club or other unincorported association.

a firm enter the name of the firm followed by the words 'a firm' e.g. 'Bandbox – a firm' and an address for service which is either a partner's residential address or the principal or last known place of business.

a corporation (other than a company) enter the full name of the corporation and the address which is either its principal office **or** any other place where the corporation carries on activities and which has a real connection with the claim.

a company registered in England and Wales enter the name of the company and an address which is either the company's registered office **or** any place of business that has a real, or the most, connection with the claim e.g. the shop where the goods were bought.

an overseas company (defined by s744 of the Companies Act 1985) enter the name of the company and either the address registered under s691 of the Act **or** the address of the place of business having a real, or the most, connection with the claim.

Details of claim

Under this heading you must set out either
- the question(s) you wish the court to decide;
or
- the remedy you are seeking and the legal basis for your claim; **and**
- if your claim is being made under a specific CPR Part or practice direction, you must state which.

Defendant's name and address

Enter in this box the full name and address of the defendant to be served with the claim form (i.e. one claim form for each defendant). If the defendant is to be served outside England and Wales, you may need to obtain the court's permission.

Address for documents

Insert in this box the address at which you wish to receive documents, if different from the address you have already given under the heading 'Claimant'. The address you give must be either that of your solicitors or your residential or business address and must be in England or Wales. If you live or carry on business outside of England and Wales, you can give some other address within England and Wales.

Statement of truth

This must be signed by you, by your solicitor or your litigation friend, as appropriate.
Where the claimant is a registered company or a corporation the claim must be signed by either the director, treasurer, secretary, chief executive, manager or other officer of the company or (in the case of a corporation) the mayor, chairman, president or town clerk.

N208C C43–001

Notes for Defendant (CPR Part 8)

Notes for defendant (Part 8 claim form)

Please read these notes carefully – they will help you decide what to do about this claim.

- You have 14 days from the date on which you were served with the claim form (see below) in which to respond to the claim by completing and returning the acknowledgement of service enclosed with this claim form.
- If you **do not return** the acknowledgment of service, you will be allowed to attend any hearing of this claim but you will **not** be allowed to take part in the hearing unless the court gives you permission to do so.

Court staff can tell you about procedures but they cannot give legal advice. If you need legal advice, you should contact a solicitor or Citizens Advice Bureau immediately

Responding to this claim

Time for responding

The completed acknowledgment of service must be returned to the court office within 14 days of the date on which the claim form was served on you. If the claim form was

- sent by post, the 14 days begins 2 days from the date of the postmark on the envelope.
- delivered or left at your address, the 14 days begins the day after it was delivered.
- handed to you personally, the 14 days begins on the day it was given to you.

Completing the acknowledgment of service

You should complete section A, B, **or** C as appropriate **and all** of section D.

Section A – contesting the claim
If you wish to contest the remedy sought by the claimant in the claim form, you should complete section A. If you seek a remedy different from that sought by the claimant, you should give full details in the space provided.

Section B – disputing the court's jurisdiction
You should indicate your intention by completing section B and filing an application disputing the court's jurisdiction within 14 days of filing of your acknowledgment of service at the court. The court will arrange a hearing date for the application and tell you and the claimant when and where to attend.

Section C – objecting to use of procedure
If you believe that the claimant should not have issued the claim under Part 8 because:

- there **is** a substantial dispute of fact involved and
- you do not agree that the rule or practice direction, stated does provide for the claimant to use this procedure

you should complete section C setting out your reasons in the space provided.

Written evidence

If you wish to file written evidence in reply to the claimant's written evidence, you must send it to the court with your acknowledgment of service. Your written evidence must be verified by a statement of truth or the court may disallow it.

Serving other parties

At the same time as you file your completed ackowledgment of service (and any written evidence) with the court, you must also send copies of both the form and any written evidence to any other party named on the claim form.

What happens next

The claimant may, within 14 days of receiving any written evidence from you, file further evidence in reply. On receipt of your acknowledgment of service and any evidence from the claimant in reply, the court file will be referred to the judge for directions for the disposal of the claim. The court will contact you and tell you what to do next.

Note: The court may already have given directions or arranged a hearing. If so, you will have received a copy with the claim form. You should comply with any directions and attend any hearing in addition to completing, filing and serving your acknowledgment of service.

Statement of truth

This must be signed by you, by your solicitor or your litigation friend, as appropriate. Where the claimant is a registered company or a corporation the claim must be signed by either the director, treasurer, secretary, chief executive, manager or other officer of the company or (in the case of a corporation) the mayor, chairman, president or town clerk.

C44–001

N209

Notice of Issue (CPR Part 8 claim)

Notice of Issue (Part 8 claim)

In the	
Claim No.	
Claimant (including ref.)	
Defendant(s)	
Issue fee	£

To the Claimant['s Solicitor]

Your claim was issued under Part 8 of the CPR on [ ].

The court sent it with a copy of your witness statement(s) to the defendant by the first class post on [ ] and it will be deemed served on [ ]. The defendant has until [ ] to reply.

[As you requested the claim form is returned to you, with copy[ies] of your witness statement(s) for you to serve on the defendant[s]].

Notes for guidance

Service of the claim form

- The claim form must be served on the defendant within 4 months of the date of issue (6 months if you are serving outside England & Wales). You may apply for an order extending the time for serving the claim form but the application must generally be made before the 4-month or 6-month period expires.

Replying to the claim form

- the defendant must file an acknowledgment of service with the court together with any written evidence to be relied on within 14 days of service of the claim form. At the same time, the defendant must send copies to you and all other parties.
- if the defendant files written evidence, you will have 14 days from receiving it in which to file any further evidence in reply. You must at the same time send copies to all other parties to the claim.

The defendant may

- contest your claim and seek a remedy different from that sought by yourself
- object to your using this procedure and set out his reasons for doing so
- dispute the court's jurisdiction

What happens next

- the court file will be referred to a judge for directions for the disposal of the claim 14 days after the expiry of the time for filing the acknowledgment of service
- the file will not be referred if the court has already arranged a hearing date or given directions

Failure to reply

- if an acknowledgment of services is not filed, the defendant may attend any hearing in the claim but may not take part at the hearing unless the court gives permission.

You must inform the court immediately if your claim is settled or discontinued.

The court office at

is open between 10 am and 4 pm Monday to Friday. When corresponding with the court, please address forms or letters to the Court Manager and quote the claim number.

N210 C45–001

Acknowledgment of Service (CPR Part 8)

Acknowledgment of Service
(Part 8 Claim)

You should read the 'notes for defendant' attached to the claim form which will tell you when and where to send this form.

In the	
Claim No.	
Claimant (including ref.)	
Defendant	

If you wish to contest the claim	complete section **A**
If you wish to dispute the court's jurisdiction	complete section **B**
If you believe the claimant should not have used this procedure	complete section **C**

A

☐ I intend to contest this claim
And (if applicable) I also seek the following different remedy to that claimed by the claimant:

B

☐ I intend to dispute jurisdiction
(you should file your application within 14 days of the date on which you file this acknowledgement of service with the court)

The court office at

is open between 10 am and 4 pm Monday to Friday. When corresponding with the court, please address forms or letters to the Court Manager and quote the claim number.

Claim No.	

C

☐ I object to the claimant issuing under this procedure

And my reasons for objecting are:

D

Signed (To be signed by you or by your solicitor or litigation friend)	*(I believe) (The defendant believes) that the facts stated in this form are true. *I am duly authorised by the defendant to sign this statement * *delete as appropriate*	**Position or office held** (if signing on behalf of firm or company)	
Date			

Give an address to which notices about this case can be sent	Postcode	if applicable	
		fax no.	
		DX no.	
	Tel. no.	e-mail	

C46–001

N211

Claim Form (CPR Part 20)

In the	
Claim No.	

Claim Form
(Additional claims – CPR Part 20)

Claimant(s)

Defendant(s)

SEAL

Part 20 Claimant(s)

Part 20 Defendant(s)

Brief details of claim

Value

Defendant's name and address

	£
Amount claimed	
Court fee	
Solicitor's costs	
Total amount	
Issue date	

The court office at

is open between 10 am and 4 pm Monday to Friday. When corresponding with the court, please address forms or letters to the Court Manager and quote the claim number.

Claim No.	

Particulars of Claim (attached)

Statement of Truth
*(I believe)(The Part 20 Claimant believes) that the facts stated in these particulars of claim are true.
*I am duly authorised by the Part 20 claimant to sign this statement

Full name ______________________________

Name of Part 20 claimant's solicitor's firm ______________________________

signed ______________________________
* (Part 20 Claimant) ('s solicitor) (Litigation friend)

position or office held ______________________________
(if signing on behalf of firm or company)

* delete as appropriate

Part 20 Claimant('s solicitor's) address to which documents or payments should be sent if different from overleaf. If you are prepared to accept service by DX, fax or e-mail, please add details.

N211A C47–001

Notes for Claimant (CPR Part 20)

Notes for Part 20 claimant on completing a Part 20 claim form

- Please read all of these guidance notes before you begin completing the claim form. The notes follow the order in which information is required on the form. Unless you issue your Part 20 claim before or at the same time as filing your defence to the main claim, (in other words the claim being brought against you as defendant) you will first need to obtain the court's permission to do so.
- Court staff can help you fill in the claim form and give information about procedure once it has been issued. But they cannot give legal advice. If you need legal advice, for example about the likely success of your claim or the evidence you need to prove it, you should contact a solicitor or a Citizens Advice Bureau.
- If you are filling in the claim form by hand, please use black ink and write in block capitals.
- When you have completed the claim form, copy the claim form and the defendant's notes for guidance so that you have one copy for yourself, one copy for the court, one copy for the Part 20 defendant and a copy for each of the other parties to the main claim. Send or take the forms to the court office with the appropriate fee, the court will tell you how much this is.
- Unless the court has ordered otherwise, the Part 20 defendant should be served with the claim form within 14 days of your defence being filed, together with copies of all the statements of case filed in the main claim. The parties to the main claim must also at the same time be served with copies of the Part 20 claim form and particulars of claim, if these are separate from the claim.
- The defendant is added as a party to the main claim once served with the Part 20 claim form.

Notes on completing the claim form

Heading

The name of the court and the claim number will be the same as on the claim form in the main claim. You should copy those details on to your Part 20 claim form.

Claimant and defendant details

You should copy the claimant and defendant details from the main claim in to the claimant and defendant boxes. You should enter your name in to the Part 20 claimant box and the name of the person you are claiming against in to the Part 20 defendant box. Claimants who are under 18 years old (unless otherwise permitted by the court), and patients within the meaning of the Mental Health Act 1983 must have a litigation friend to issue and conduct court proceedings on their behalf. Court staff will tell you more about what you need to do is this applies to you.

You must provide the following information about yourself **and** the Part 20 defendant according to the capacity in which you are suing and in which the defendant is being sued. When suing or being sued as:–

an individual:

All known forenames and surname, whether Mr, Mrs, Miss, Ms or Other (e.g. Dr) and residential address (**including** postcode, telephone and any fax or e-mail number) in England and Wales. Where the defendant is a proprietor of a business, a partner in a firm or an individual sued in the name of a club or other unincorporated association, the address for service should be the usual or last known place of residence **or** principal place of business of the company, firm or club or other unincorporated association.

Where the individual is:

under 18 write '(a child by Mr Joe Bloggs his litigation friend)' after the child's name.

a patient within the meaning of the Mental Health Act 1983 write '(by Mr Joe Bloggs his litigation friend)' after the patient's name.

trading under another name

you must add the words 'trading as' and the trading name e.g. 'Mr John Smith trading as Smith's Groceries'.

suing or being sued in a representative capacity

you must say what the capacity is e.g. 'Mr Joe Bloggs as the representative of Mrs Sharon Bloggs (deceased)'.

suing or being sued in the name of a club or other unincorporated association

add the words 'suing/sued on behalf of' followed by the name of the club or other unincorporated association.

a firm

enter the name of the firm followed by the words 'a firm' e.g. 'Bandbox – a firm' and an address for service which is either a partner's residential address or the principal or last known place of business.

a corporation (other than a company)

enter the full name of the corporation and the address which is either its principal office **or** any other place where the corporation carries on activities and which has a real connection with the claim.

a company registered in England and Wales

enter the name of the company and an address which is either the company's registered office **or** any place of business that has a real, or the most, connection with the claim e.g. the shop where the goods were bought.

an overseas company (defined by s744 of the Companies Act 1985)

enter the name of the company and either the address registered under s691 of the Act **or** the address of the place of business having a real, or the most connection with the claim.

C48–001

Brief details of claim

Note: The facts and full details about your claim and whether or not you are claiming interest, should be set out in the 'particulars of claim' (*see note under 'Particulars of Claim'*).

You must set out under **this** heading:

- a concise statement of the nature of your claim
- the remedy you are seeking

Value

Note:
If you are issuing your Part 20 claim in the High Court, you do not have to give a statement of value.

If you are issuing in the county court and claiming a fixed amount of money (a 'specified amount') write the amount in the box at the bottom right-hand corner of the claim form against 'amount claimed'.

If you are not claiming a fixed amount of money (an 'unspecified amount') under 'Value' write "I expect to recover" followed by whichever of the following applies to your claim:

- "not more than £5,000" **or**
- "more than £5,000 but not more than £15,000" **or**
- "more than £15,000"

If your claim is for 'not more than £5,000' and includes a claim for **personal injuries**, you must also write "My claim includes a claim for personal injuries and the amount I expect to recover as damages for pain, suffering and loss of amenity is" followed by either:

- "not more than £1,000" **or**
- "more than £1,000"

If your claim is for 'not more than £5,000' and includes a claim for **housing disrepair** relating to residential premises, you must also write "My claim includes a claim against my landlord for housing disrepair relating to residential premises. The costs of the repairs and other work is estimated to be" followed by either:

- "not more than £1,000" **or**
- "more than £1,000"

"I expect to recover as damages in respect of repairs and other work" followed by either;

- "not more than £1,000" **or**
- "more than £1,000"

If you are not able to put a value on your claim, write "I cannot say how much I expect to recover".

Defendant's name and address

Enter in this box the full names and address of the Part 20 defendant receiving the claim form (i.e. one claim form for each Part 20 defendant). If the defendant is to be served outside of England and Wales, you may need to obtain the court's permission.

Particulars of claim

You may include your particulars of claim on the claim form in the space provided or in a separate document which you should head 'Particulars of Claim'. It should include the names of the parties, the court, the claim number and your address for service and also contain a statement of truth. You should keep a copy for yourself, provide one for the court, one for each defendant and one for all other parties in the main claim. Separate particulars of claim **must** be served with the claim form. You should also attach copies of all statements of case already served in the main claim for service on the defendant.

Your particulars of claim must include

- a concise statement of the facts on which you rely
- a statement (if applicable) to the effect that you are seeking aggravated damages or exemplary damages
- details of any interest which you are claiming
- any other matters required for your type of claim as set out in the relevant practice direction

Address for documents

Insert in this box the address at which you wish to receive documents and/or payments, if different from the address you have already given under the heading 'Claimant'. The address you give must be either that of your solicitors or your residential or business address and must be in England or Wales. If you live or carry on business outside England and Wales, you can give some other address within England and Wales.

Statement of truth

This must be signed by you, by your solicitor or your litigation friend, as appropriate.
Where the claimant is a registered company or a corporation the claim must be signed by either the director, treasurer, secretary, chief executive, manager or other officer of the company or (in the case of a corporation) the mayor, chairman, president or town clerk.

N211C

C49–001

Notes for Defendant (CPR Part 20)

Notes for defendant on replying to the Part 20 claim form

Please read these notes carefully – they will help you decide what to do about this claim.

- You must reply to this claim form within 14 days of the date it was served on you. If the claim was
  - sent by post, the date of service is taken as the second day after posting (see post mark).
  - delivered or left at your address, the date of service will be the day after it was delivered.
  - handed to you personally, the 14 days begins on the day it was given to you.
- You may either
  - pay the amount claimed
  - admit the truth of all or part of the claim or
  - dispute the claim
- If you do not reply, the court will consider that you have admitted the claim and judgment may be entered against you.
- The notes below tell you what to do and which forms to use for your reply.
- Court staff can help you complete the forms of reply and tell you about court procedures. But they cannot give legal advice If you need legal advice, for example about the likely success of disputing the claim, you should contact a solicitor or a Citizens Advice Bureau immediately.

Registration of Judgments: If the claim results in a judgment being made against you in a **county court**, your name and address may be entered in the Register of County Court Judgments. This may make it difficult for you to obtain credit.
Costs and Interest: Additional costs and interest may be added to the amount claimed on the front of the claim form if judgment is entered against you. In a county court, if judgment is for £5,000 or more, or is in respect of a debt which attracts contractual or statutory interest for late payment, the claimant may be entitled to further interest.

Your response and what happens next

How to pay

Do not bring any payments to the court – they will not be accepted.
When making payments to the claimant, quote the claimant's reference (if any) and the claim number.
Make sure that you keep records and can account for any payments made. Proof may be required if there is any disagreement. It is not safe to send cash unless you use registered post.

Admitting the Claim

Claim for a specified amount
Complete Form N9A and send it to the claimant at the address given for payment on the claim form within 14 days. You should at the same time send a copy to all the other parties to the main claim (in other words the claim where the Part 20 claimant is the defendant).
Claim for an unspecified amount
Complete Form N9C and send it to the court within 14 days. A copy will be sent to the claimant.
What happens next
The claimant may apply to the court for judgment to be entered on your admission. The court will arrange a hearing and tell you and the claimant where and when to attend.

Disputing the claim

Complete the form of defence (either N9B if the claim is for a specified amount or N9D if the claim is for an unspecified amount) and return it to the court within 14 days. On receipt of your defence, the court will arrange a hearing and tell you and the claimant when and where to attend. At the hearing the judge will usually give directions as to the future case management of the claim but may make any other order, e.g. striking out all or part of a statement of case.
If you need longer than 14 days to prepare your defence, complete the acknowledgment of service Form N212 and return it to the court. This will allow you 28 days from the date of service of the claim form to file your defence.

Contesting the court's jurisdiction

Complete the acknowledgement of service Form N212 and return it to the court within 14 days. You should make an application to the court within 28 days of service of the claim. An application form (N244) can be obtained from the court and a fee may be payable.

If you do nothing

If you do nothing or you send an acknowledgement of service to the court but fail to send your defence, you will be considered to have admitted the claim and be bound by any judgment or decision made in the main claim where it relates to this claim against you.

Statement of truth

This must be signed by you, by your solicitor or your litigation friend, as appropriate.
Where the defendant is **a registered company or a corporation** the response must be signed by either the director, treasurer, secretary, chief executive, manager or other officer of the company **or** (in the case of a corporation) the mayor, chairman, president or town clerk.

C50–001

N212

Notice of Issue (CPR Part 20 claim)

Notice of Issue (Part 20 claim)

In the	
Claim No.	
Claimant (including ref.)	
Defendant(s) (including ref.)	
Part 20 Claimant (including ref.)	
Part 20 Defendant(s)	
Issue fee	£

To the Claimant ['s Solicitor]

Your Part 20 claim was issued on [ ].

[The court sent it and accompanying papers to the defendant by the first class post on [ ] and it will be deemed served on [ ]. The defendant has until [ ] to reply.

[As you requested the claim form [which includes particulars of claim] is returned to you, [with the relevant response forms] for you to serve them on the defendant[s]. You must also serve copies of any statements of case already filed in the main claim.]

Notes for guidance

Service

- The claim form must be served on the Part 20 defendant within 14 days of filing your defence to the main claim unless the court has directed otherwise.

Entering default judgment

- you will need the court's permission to enter judgment in default if you have **not** satisfied any default judgment against you in the main claim **or** you wish to obtain judgment for any remedy other than a contribution or an indemnity

The defendant may

- **admit the truth of the whole or any part of your claim.** You may apply to the court for judgment to be entered on the admission.
- **dispute all or part of your claim.** The court will arrange a hearing and tell you and the other parties to the claim when and where to attend. At the hearing the judge will usually give directions about the future case management of the claim but may make any other order considered appropriate, e.g. striking out all or part of a statement of case.
- **not reply at all.** The defendant will be considered to have admitted your claim and be bound by any judgment or decision made in the main claim where it relates to this claim.

You must inform the court immediately if your claim is settled or discontinued.

The court office at

is open between 10 am and 4 pm Monday to Friday. When corresponding with the court, please address forms or letters to the Court Manager and quote the claim number.

N213 C51–001

Acknowledgment of Service (CPR Part 20)

Acknowledgment of Service (Part 20 claim)

In the	
Claim No.	
Claimant (including ref.)	
Defendant(s) (including ref.)	
Part 20 Claimant (including ref.)	
Part 20 Defendant(s)	

Defendant's full name if different from the name given on the claim form

....

....

Address to which documents about this claim should be sent (including reference if appropriate)

		if applicable
	fax no.	
	DX no.	
Tel. no. Postcode	e-mail	

Tick the appropriate box

1. I intend to defend all of this claim ☐
2. I intend to defend part of this claim ☐
3. I intend to contest jurisdiction ☐

If you file an acknowledgment of service but do not file a defence within 28 days of the date of service of the claim form, you will be considered to have admitted the claim and will be bound by any judgment entered against the Part 20 claimant in the main claim.

If you do not file an application within 28 days of the date of service of the claim form, it will be assumed that you accept the court's jurisdiction and judgment may be entered against you.

Signed ______________

(Defendant) (Defendant's Solicitor) (Litigation friend)

Position or office held ______________

(if signing on behalf of firm or company)

Date ______________

The court office at

is open between 10 am and 4 pm Monday to Friday. When corresponding with the court, please address forms or letters to the Court Manager and quote the claim number.

C52–001

N215

Certificate of service

Certificate of service

In the	
Claim No.	
Claimant	
Defendant	

On the . . . . (*insert date*)

the . . . . (*insert title or description of documents served*)

a copy of which is attached to this notice was served on (*insert name of person served, including position i.e. partner, director if appropriate*) . . . .

Tick as appropriate

☐ by first class post

☐ by delivering to or leaving

☐ by fax machine (. . . . . time sent)
(*you may want to enclose a copy of the transmission sheet*)

☐ by other means (please specify)

☐ by Document Exchange

☐ by handing it to or leaving it with

☐ by e-mail

at (*insert address where service effected, include fax or DX number or e-mail address*)

being the defendant's:

☐ residence

☐ place of business

☐ registered office

☐ other (*please specify*) . . . .

The date of service is therefore deemed to be . . . . (*insert date – see over for guidance*)

I confirm that at the time of signing this Certificate the document has not been returned to me as undelivered.

Signed . . . .
(Claimant) (Defendant) ('s solicitor) ('s litigation friend)

Position or office held . . . .
(if signing on behalf of firm or company)

Date . . . .

Notes for guidance

Please note that these notes are only a guide and are not exhaustive
If you are in doubt you should refer to Part 6 of the rules

Where to serve

Nature of party to be served	Place of service
Individual	• usual or last known residence
Proprietor of business	• usual or last known residence; or • place of business or last known place of business
Individual who is suing or being sued in the name of a firm	• usual or last known residence; or • principal of last known place of business of the firm
Corporation (incorporated in England and Wales) other than a company	• principal office of the corporation; or • any place of within the jurisdiction where the corporation carries on its activities and which has a real connection with the claim
Company registered in England and Wales	• principal office of the company or corporation; or • any place of business of the company within the jurisdiction which has a real connection with the claim

Personal Service – A document is served personally on an individual by leaving it with that individual. A document is served personally on a company or other corporation by leaving it with a person holding a senior position within the company or corporation. In the case of a partnership, you must leave it with either a partner or a person having control or management at the principal place of business. Where a solicitor is authorised to accept service on behalf of a party, service must be effected on the solicitor, unless otherwise ordered.

Deemed Service – Part 6.7(1). A document which is served in accordance with these rules or any relevant practice direction shall be deemed to be served on the day shown in the following table.

Method of service	Deemed day of service
First class post	The second day after it was posted
Document exchange	The second day after it was left at the document exchange
Delivering the document to or leaving it at a permitted address	The day after it was delivered to or left at the permitted address
Fax	If it is transmitted on a business day before 4pm, on that day, or otherwise on the business day after the day on which it was transmitted
Other electronic method	The second day after the day on which it was transmitted

- If a document (other than a claim form) is served after 5 p.m. on a business day, or at any time on a Saturday, Sunday or a bank holiday, the document shall, for the purpose of calculating any period of time after service of the document, be treated as having been served on the next business day.
- In this context "business day" means any day except Saturday, Sunday or a bank holiday; and "bank holiday" includes Christmas Day and Good Friday.

Service of documents on children and patients – The rules relating to service on children and patients are contained in Part 6.6 of the rules.

Claim Forms – The general rules about service are subject to the special rules about service of claim forms contained in rules 6.12 to 6.16.

C53–001

N216

Notice of non-service

Notice of non-service

In the	
Claim No.	
Local No.	
Claimant (including ref.)	
Defendant	
Date	

Take Notice that the court has attempted to serve the

[claim form]

[particulars of claim]

[application for
please specify]

[[order][judgment] of *date*]

[*other to be specified*]

by first class post and the envelope has been returned by the Post Office marked:

["Not known at the address given"]

["Gone away"]

["No such address"]

["Insufficient address"]

[The document has been returned to the Home Court and any further correspondence should be sent there.]

You must now attempt service of the document yourself

The court office at

is open between 10 am and 4 pm Monday to Friday. Address all communications to the Court Manager and quote the claim number.

N217 C54–001

Order for Substituted Service

Order for Substituted Service

In the	
Claim No.	
Claimant (including ref.)	
Defendant	

Upon reading the evidence of

dated

Seal

[Master]
[District
Judge]

ORDERED

[that the delivery of a sealed copy of the issued in this claim, together with a sealed copy of this order, to an adult at

being the usual or last known address [or place of business] of the defendant]

[that the posting of a sealed copy of the issued in this claim, together with a sealed copy of this order, by [special delivery][recorded delivery] post addressed to the defendant at

being the usual or last known address [or place of business] of the defendant]

[that notice of the issued in this claim be published in the newspaper and that publication of such notice]

shall be deemed to be good and sufficient service of the on the defendant [on the day when they would be delivered in the ordinary course of post.]

Dated

The court office at

is open between 10 am and 4 pm Monday to Friday. Address all communications to the Court Manager quoting the claim number.

C55–001

N218

Notice of service on partner

Notice of service on partner

In the	
Claim No.	
Claimant (including ref.)	
Defendant	

The (claim form) (particulars of claim) served with this notice (is) (are) served on you

(tick only one box)

☐ as a partner of the business

☐ as a person having control or management of the partnership business

☐ as both a partner and as a person having control or management of the partnership business

named in the claim form (particulars of claim).

Signed ____________________ **Date** ____________

Claimant('s solicitor)

N225 C56–001

Request for judgment and reply to admission (specified amount)

Request for judgment and reply to admission (specified amount)

- Tick box A or B. If you tick box B you must complete the details in that part and in part C. Make sure that all the case details are given. Remember to sign and date the form. Your signature certifies that the information you have given is correct.
- If the defendant has given an address on the form of admission to which correspondence should be sent, which is different from the address shown on the claim form, you must tell the court.
- Return the completed form to the court.

In the	
Claim No.	
Claimant (including ref.)	
Defendant (including ref.)	

A ☐ The defendant has not filed an admission or defence to my claim

Complete all the judgment details at C. Decide how and when you want the defendant to pay. You can ask for the judgment to be paid by instalments or in one payment.

B ☐ The defendant admits that all the money is owed

Tick only **one** box below and complete all the judgment details at C.

☐ **I accept the defendant's proposal for payment**

Say how the defendant intends to pay. The court will send the defendant an order to pay. You will also be sent a copy.

☐ **The defendant has not made any proposal for payment**

Say how you want the defendant to pay. You can ask for the judgment to be paid by instalments or in one payment. The court will send the defendant an order to pay. You will also be sent a copy.

☐ **I do NOT accept the defendant's proposal for payment**

Say how you want the defendant to pay. Give your reasons for objecting to the defendant's offer of payment in the space opposite. (Continue on the back of this form if necessary.) Send this form to the court **with defendant's admission 9A.** The court will fix a rate of payment and send the defendant an order to pay. You will also be sent a copy.

C Judgment details

I would like the judgment to be paid

☐ (immediately)

☐ (by instalments of £ per month)

☐ (in full by)

Amount of claim as admitted (including interest at date of issue)	
Interest since date of claim (if any)	
Period from . . . . to	
Rate . . . . . . %	
Court fees shown on claim	
Solicitor's costs (if any) on issuing claim	
Sub Total	
Solicitor's costs (if any) on entering judgment	
Sub Total	
Deduct amount (if any) paid since issue	
Amount payable by defendant	

I certify that the information given is correct

Signed ____________________
(Claimant) (Claimant's solicitor) (Litigation friend)

Position or office held ____________________
(if signing on behalf of firm or company)

Date ____________________

The court office at

is open between 10 am and 4 pm Monday to Friday. When corresponding with the court, please address forms and letters to the Court Manager and quote the Claim number

C57–001

N225A

Notice of part admission (specified amount)

Notice of Part Admission (specified amount)

To the Claimant['s solicitor]

In the	
Claim No.	
Claimant (including ref.)	
Defendant (including ref.)	
Date	

The defendant has partly admitted your claim (see the attached forms N9A and N9B)

- **Please tell the court what you wish to do by completing the lower half of this form and returning it to the court on or before[ ]**
  At the same time you must send a copy to the defendant. If you do not return this form to the court by the date shown, your claim will be stayed. No further action will be taken by the court until the form is received.
- You must tick box A or B. If you tick box B you must also complete the details in that part and part C.
- Remember to sign and date the notice.

A ☐ I DO NOT accept the defendant's part admission

If you tick this box the claim will proceed as a defended claim. If the defendant is an individual and lives in, or the defendant's solicitor's business is in, another court's area, the claim may be transferred to that court. You and the defendant will be sent an allocation questionnaire and the date by which it must be returned to the court. The information you give will help a judge decide whether your case should be dealt with in the small claims, fast or multi-track. Leaflets telling you more about the tracks are available from the court office. You will be sent a notice of allocation setting out the judge's decision.

B ☐ I ACCEPT the amount admitted by the defendant in satisfaction of my claim

Tick only **one** box and follow the instructions given.

☐ **I accept the defendant's proposal for payment**
Complete all the judgment details at C. The court will enter judgment in accordance with the offer and will send the defendant an order to pay. You will also be sent a copy.

☐ **The defendant has not made any proposal for payment**
Complete all the judgment details at C. Say how you want the defendant to pay. You can ask for the judgment to be paid by instalments or in one payment. The court will send the defendant an order to pay. You will also be sent a copy.

☐ **I do NOT accept the defendant's proposal for payment**
Complete all the judgment details at C and say how you want the defendant to pay. Give your reasons for objecting to the defendant's offer of payment in the space opposite. (Continue on the back of this form if necessary.) The court will fix a rate of payment and send the defendant an order to pay. You will also be sent a copy.

C Judgment details

If you are not accepting the defendant's proposal for payment, say how you would like the judgment to be paid.

I would like the judgment to be paid

☐ (immediately)

☐ (by instalments of £ per month)

☐ (in full by)

Amount of claim as admitted	
Court fees entered on claim	
Solicitor's costs (if any) on issuing claim	
Sub Total	
Solicitor's costs (if any) on entering judgment	
Sub Total	
Deduct amount (if any) paid since issue	
Amount payable by defendant	

I certify that the information given is correct

Signed .... **Date** ....

N226

Notice of Admission (unspecified amount)

Notice of Admission (unspecified amount)

To the Claimant['s solicitor]

In the	
Claim No.	
Claimant (including ref.)	
Defendant (including ref.)	
Date	

Important notes for claimant

Enclosed with this notice is a copy of the defendant's admission of your claim (Form N9C).

- You must tick either A or C **or** complete B and D and return the form to the court **on or before [ ]**. At the same time you must send a copy to the defendant. If you do not return the form by this date, your claim will be stayed. No further action will be taken by the court until the form is received.
- Remember to sign and date the notice.

A ☐ I DO NOT accept the amount offered by the defendant in satisfaction on my claim. I wish judgment to be entered for an amount to be decided by the court.

The court will enter judgment and refer the court file to a judge for directions for management of the case. You and the defendant will be sent a copy of the court's order.

B ☐ I ACCEPT the amount admitted by the defendant in satisfaction of my claim

Tick only **one** box and follow the instructions given.

☐ **I accept the defendant's proposal for payment**

Complete all the judgment details at D. The court will enter judgment in accordance with the offer and will send the defendant an order to pay. You will also be sent a copy.

☐ **I do NOT accept the defendant's proposal for payment**

Complete all the judgment details at D and say how you want the defendant to pay. Give your reasons for objecting to the defendant's offer of payment in the space opposite. (Continue on the back of this form if necessary.) The court will fix a rate of payment and send the defendant an order to pay. You will also be sent a copy.

C ☐ The defendant has admitted liability but has not made any proposal for payment

The court will enter judgment and refer the court file to a judge for directions for management of the case. You and the defendant will be sent a copy of the court's order.

D Judgment details

If you are not accepting the defendant's proposal for payment, say how you would like the judgment to be paid.

I would like the judgment to be paid

☐ (immediately)

☐ (by instalments of £ per month)

☐ (in full by)

Enter amounts as shown	£	
Amount of offer		
Court fees entered on claim		
Solicitor's costs (if any) on issuing claim		
Solicitor's costs (if any) on entering judgment		
Sub Total		
Deduct amount (if any) paid since issue		
Balance payable by defendant		

I certify that the information given is correct

Signed .... **Date** ....

C59–001

N227

Request for judgment by default (amount to be decided by the court)

Request for judgment by default (amount to be decided by the court)	**In the**	
	Claim No.	
	Claimant (including ref.)	
	Defendant	

To the court

The defendant has not filed [an acknowledgment of service][a defence] to my claim and the time for doing so has expired.

I request judgment to be entered against the defendant for an amount to be decided by the court and costs.

Signed ____________________
(Claimant) (Claimant's Solicitor)
(Litigation friend)

Position or office held (if signing on behalf of firm or company) ____________________

Date ____________________

Note: The court will enter judgment and refer the court file who will give directions for the management of the case including its allocation to track.

The Court Manager

The court office at

is open between 10 am and 4 pm Monday to Friday. When corresponding with the court, please address forms or letters to the Court Manager and quote the claim number.

C60–001

N228

Notice of Admission in Return of Goods action (hire-purchase or conditional sale agreement)

Notice of Admission—
Return of Goods
(hire-purchase or conditional sale)
To the Claimant['s solicitor]

In the	
Claim No.	
Claimant (including ref.)	
Defendant (including ref.)	
Date	

Enclosed with this notice is a copy of the defendant's admission of your claim
- *Tick and complete either A or B and make sure that the judgment details at C are completed.*
- *Remember to sign and date the form. Your signature certifies that the information you have given is correct.*
- *Return the form to the court within 14 days.*

A ☐ I DO NOT accept the amount admitted by the defendant in satisfaction of my claim

You should attend court on the day fixed for the hearing. If you do not attend, an order may be made in your absence.

B ☐ I ACCEPT the amount admitted by the defendant in satisfaction of my claim

Tick only **one** box and follow the instructions given.

☐ **I accept the defendant's proposal for payment**

Complete all the judgment details at C. The court will make an order under sections 133 and 135 of the Consumer Credit Act 1974 for the return of the goods, suspended in accordance with the offer.
You will not have to attend court on the day fixed for the hearing.

☐ **The defendant has not made any proposal for payment**

Complete all the judgment details at C. Say how you want the defendant to pay. You can ask for the judgment to be paid by instalments or in one payment. The court will send the defendant an order to pay. You will also be sent a copy.

☐ **I do NOT accept the defendant's proposal for payment**

Complete all the judgment details at C and say how you want the defendant to pay. Give your reasons for objecting to the defendant's offer of payment in the space opposite. (Continue on the back of this form if necessary.) The court will fix a rate of payment and send the defendant an order to pay. You will also be sent a copy.

C Judgment details

If you are not accepting the defendant's offer, say how you would like the judgement to be paid.

I would like the judgment to be paid

☐ (immediately)

☐ (by instalments of £ per month)

☐ (in full by)

. . . .

List goods to be returned . . . .

Enter amounts as shown	£	
Amount of the unpaid balance of total price as stated in the claim .		
Deduct amount (if any) paid since issue		
Balance of total price		
Court fees entered on claim		
Solicitor's costs (if any) on issuing claim		
Solicitor's costs (if any) on entering judgment		
Total of fees and solicitor's costs		

I certify that the information given is correct

Signed . . . . **Date** . . . .

C61–001

N235

Certificate of suitability of litigation friend

Certificate of suitability of litigation friend	**In the**	
	Claim No.	
	Claimant (including ref.)	
	Defendant (including ref.)	

if you are acting

- **for a child**, you must serve a copy of the completed form on a parent or guardian of the child, or if there is no parent or guardian, the carer or the person with whom the child lives.
- **for a patient**, you must serve a copy of the completed form on the person authorised under Part VII of the Mental Health Act 1983 or, if no person is authorised, the carer or person with whom the patient lives unless you **are** that person. You must also complete a certificte of service (obtainable from the court office)

You should send the completed form to the court with the claim form (if acting for the claimant) or when you take the first step on the defendant's behalf in the claim together with the certificate of service (if applicable)

You do not need to complete this form if you do have an authorisation under Part VII of the Mental Health Act 1983 to conduct legal proceedings on the person's behalf.

I consent to act as litigation friend for .... (claimant) (defendant)

I believe that the above named person is a

☐ child ☐ patient (*give your reasons overleaf and attach a copy of any medical evidence in support*)

I am able to conduct proceedings on behalf of the above named person competently and fairly and I have no interests adverse to those of the above named person.

*I undertake to pay any costs which the above named claimant may be ordered to pay in these proceedings subject to any right I may have to be repaid from the assets of the claimant.

* delete if you are acting for the defendant

Please write your name in capital letters

☐ Mr ☐ ☐ Miss Surname ....

☐ Ms ☐ Other _______ Forenames ....

Address to which documents in this case are to be sent.

I certify that the information given in this form is correct

Signed ....

Date ....

The court office at

is open between 10 am and 4 pm Monday to Friday. When corresponding with the court, please address forms and letters to the Court Manager and quote the claim number.

Claim No.	

My reasons for believing that the (claimant)(defendant) is a patient are:—

C62–001

N236

Notice of Defence that Amount Claimed has been paid—Claimant's Reply

Notice of Defence that Amount Claimed Has Been Paid

In the	
Claim No.	
Claimant (including ref.)	
Defendant (including ref.)	

To the Claimant ['s solicitor]

The defendant says that the amount you are claiming has been paid (see attached Form N9B).

Please tell the court what you wish to do by completing the lower half of this form and returning it to the court on or before [ ]. You must send a copy of the completed form to the defendant as well as to the court.

- If you disagree with the defendant and wish to proceed with your claim, the court will contact you and tell you what to do next. If the defendant is an individual and lives in, or the defendant's solicitor's business is in, another court's area, the claim may be transferred to that court.
- If you do not return this form to the court by the date shown, your claim will be stayed. The only action which you will be able to take will be to apply to a judge for an order lifting the stay. A fee is payable on the application.

Claimant's Reply

In the	
Claim No.	
Claimant (including ref.)	
Defendant (including ref.)	

To the court

I have read Form N9B and

please tick 1 or 2 and 3

1. ☐ I wish to proceed with the claim

or

2. ☐ I do not wish to proceed with the claim.

3. ☐ I have sent a copy of this completed form to the defendant.

Signed

(Claimant) (Claimant's solicitor) (Litigation friend)

Date

Position or office held (if signing on behalf of firm or company)

The court office at

is open between 10 am and 4 pm Monday to Friday. Address all communication to the Court Manager quoting the claim number

N242A

C63–001

Notice of payment into court (in settlement)

Notice of Payment into court (in settlement—Part 36)

To the Claimant ('s solicitor)

In the	
Claim No.	
Claimant (including ref.)	
Defendant (including ref.)	

Take notice the defendant ____________________ has paid £ _______ (a further amount of £ ______) into court in settlement of
(tick as appropriate)
- ☐ the whole of your claim
- ☐ part of your claim *(give details below)*
- ☐ a certain issue or issues in your claim *(give details below)*

The (part) (issue or issues) to which it relates is (are): *(give details)*

- ☐ It is in addition to the amount of £ _______ already paid into court on
- ☐ It is not inclusive of interest and an additional amount of £ ______ is offered for interest *(give details of the rate(s) and period(s) for which the amount of interest is offered.)*

- ☐ It takes into account all (part) of the following counterclaim: *(give details of the party and the part of the counterclaim to which the payment relates)*

- ☐ It takes into account the interim payment(s) made in the following amount(s) on the following date(s): *(give details)*

Note: This notice will need to be modified where an offer of provisional damages is made (CPR Part 36.7) and/or where it is made in relation to a mixed (money and non-money) claim in settlement of the whole claim (CPR Part 36.4).

For cases where the Social Security (Recovery of Benefits) Act 1997 applies

The gross amount of the compensation payment is £ ____________________

The defendant has reduced this sum by £ ____________________ in accordance with section 8 of and Schedule 2 to the Social Security (Recovery of Benefits) Act 1997, which was calculated as follows:

Type of Benefit	Amount

The amount paid into court is the net amount after deduction of the amount of benefit.

Signed		Position held *(If signing on behalf of a firm or company)*	
	Defendant(s' solicitor)		

Date	

N243

C64–001

Notice of acceptance and request for payment

Notice of acceptance of payment into court (Part 36)

In the	
Claim No.	
Claimant (including ref.)	
Defendant (including ref.)	

Note: to the claimant
If you wish to accept the payment made into court without needing the court's permission you should:

- send this completed notice to the defendant not more than 21 days after you received this notice
- and at the same time send a copy to the court

**Delete as appropriate*

I accept the payment into court in settlement of (the whole of) (part of)*(certain issue(s) in)* my claim set out in the notice of payment into court received on *(insert date)*

I declare that:—

☐ it is not more than 21 days since I received the notice of payment into court
or
☐ it is more than 21 days since I received the notice and I have agreed the following costs provisions with the other party(ies) *(give details below)*
or
☐ the defendant's payment was made less than 21 days before the start of the trial and I have agreed the following costs provisions with the other party(ies) *(give details below)*

And I request payment of the money held in court to be made to

claimant's (solicitor's) full name and address (and ref.)

name and address of bank

sort code

title of account

account number

Signed

Claimant('s Solicitor)

Position held (If signing on behalf of a firm or company)

Date

C65–001

N244A

Notice of Hearing of Application

Notice of Hearing of Application

In the	
Claim No.	
Claimant (including ref.)	
Defendant (including ref.)	
Date	

To [Claimant] [Defendant] ['s solicitor]

The hearing of the [claimant's] [defendant's] application for

(see copy attached) will take place at [am] [pm] on the

of at

The court office at

is open between 10 am and 4 pm Monday to Friday. When corresponding with the court, please address forms or letters to the Court Manager and quote the claim number.

N252 C66–001

Notice of commencement of assessment of bill of costs

Notice of commencement of assessment of bill of costs

In the	
Claim No.	
Claimant (including Ref.)	
Defendant (including Ref.)	

To the claimant(defendant)

Following an ....(*insert name of document eg. order, judgment*) dated .... (copy attached) I have prepared my Bill of Costs for assessment. The Bill totals £.................... If you choose to dispute this bill and your objections are not upheld at the assessment hearing, the full amount payable (including the assessment fee) will be £....................... together with interest (*see note below*) I shall also seek the costs of the assessment hearing

You must send me any points of dispute by .... (*insert date 21 days from the date of service of the certificate*)

Your points of dispute must include
- details of the items in the bill of costs which are disputed
- concise details of the nature and grounds of the dispute for each item and, if you seek a reduction in those items, suggest, where practicable, a reduced figure

You must also serve copies of your points of dispute on all other parties to the assessment identified below.

I certify that I have also served the following (persons)(person) with a copy of this certificate and my Bill of Costs

If I have not received your points of dispute by the above date, I will ask the court to issue a default costs certificate for the full amount of my bill (see above) plus fixed costs and court fees as specified in the Costs Practice Direction and the Civil Courts Fees Order.

Signed .... **Date** ....
(Claimant) (Defendant) ('s Solicitor)

Note: interest may be added to all High Court judgments and certain County Court judgments under the Judgments Act 1838, the County Court Act 1984 and the Late Payment of Commercial Debts (Interest) Act 1998.

The court office at

is open between 10 am and 4 pm Monday to Friday. When corresponding with the court, please address forms or letters to the Court Manager and quote the claim number.

C67–001

N253

Notice of amount allowed on provisional assessment

Notice of amount allowed on provisional assessment (Legal Aid only)

To [Claimant][Defendant]['s solicitor]

In the	
Claim No.	
Claimant (including ref.)	
Defendant (including ref.)	
Date	

Take notice that the [claimant's][defendant's] bill of costs in this action has been provisionally assessed and is returned with this notice.

If you wish to be heard on the assessment, you must, within 14 days of the receipt of this notice inform the court in writing and return the bill of costs to the court. A date for assessment will then be fixed.

If you (and counsel, if any) accept the provisional assessment as final, please return the bill together with the balance of the assessment fee.

The court office at

is open between 10 am and 4 pm Monday to Friday. Address all communications to the Court Manager and quote the claim number.

N254 C68–001

Request for a Default Costs Certificate

Request for a Default Costs Certificate

In the	
Claim No.	
Claimant (including ref.)	
Defendant (including ref.)	

I certify that the attached Notice of Commencement was served on the paying party

.... (*and give details of any other party served with the notice*)

on (*insert date*)

I also certify that I have not received any points of dispute and that the time for receiving them has now elapsed.

I now request the court to issue a certificate for the amount of the bill of costs plus such fixed costs and court fees as are appropriate in this case.

Signed .... **Date** ....
(Claimant) (Defendant) ('s solicitor)

The court office at

is open between 10 am and 4 pm Monday to Friday. When corresponding with the court, please address forms or letters to the Court Manager and quote the claim number

C69–001

N255

Default Costs Certificate

Default Costs Certificate	In the County Court	
	Claim No.	
To [Claimant][Defendant]['s solicitor]	Claimant (including ref.)	
	Defendant (including ref.)	
	Date	

As you have not raised any points of dispute on the [defendant's][claimant's] bill of costs, the costs of the claim have been allowed and the total sum of £ is now payable. The VAT included in the total sum is £ . You must pay this amount to the [defendant][claimant] [within 14 days from the date of this order] [on or before [ ]].

The date from which any entitlement to interest under this certificate commences is [*date*].

Take Notice

To the defendant (claimant)

If you do not pay in accordance with this order your goods may be removed and sold or other enforcement proceedings may be taken against you. If your circumstances change and you cannot pay, ask at the court office about what you can do

Further interest may be added if judgment has been given for £5,000 or more or is in respect of a debt which attracts contractual or statutory interest for late payment.

Address for Payment

This judgment has been registered on the Register of County Court Judgments. This may make it difficult for you to get credit. **If you pay in full within one month** you can ask the court to cancel the entry on the Register. You will need to give proof of payment. You can (for a fee) also obtain a Certificate of Cancellation from the court. If you pay the debt in full after one month you can ask the court to mark the entry on the Register as satisfied and (for a fee) obtain a Certificate of Satisfaction to prove that the debt has been paid.

How to Pay

- **PAYMENT(S) MUST BE MADE to the person named at the address for payment, quoting their reference and the court case number**
- **DO NOT bring or send payments to the court. THEY WILL NOT BE ACCEPTED.**
- You should allow at least 4 days for your payment to reach the claimant (defendant) or his representative
- Make sure that you keep records and can account for all payments made. Proof may be required if there is any disagreement. It is not safe to send cash unless you use registered post.
- A leaflet giving further advice about payment can be obtained from the court.
- If you need more information you should contact the claimant (defendant) or his representative.

The court office at

is open between 10 am and 4 pm Monday to Friday. Address all communications to the Court Manager quoting the claim number

C70–001

N255HC

Default Costs Certificate

Default Costs Certificate

In the High Court of Justice	
Division **District Registry**	
Claim No.	
Claimant (including ref.)	
Defendant (including ref.)	
Date	

To [Claimant] [Defendant] ['s solicitor]

As you have not raised any points of dispute on the [defendant's] [claimant's] bill of costs, the costs of the claim have been allowed and the total sum of £ is now payable. The VAT included in the total sum is £ . You must pay this amount to the [defendant] [claimant] [within 14 days from the date of this order] [on or before [ ]].

The date from which any entitlement to interest under this certificate commences is [*date*].

Take Notice

To the defendant (claimant)

If you do not pay in accordance with this order your goods may be removed and sold or other enforcement proceedings may be taken against you. If your circumstances change and you cannot pay, ask at the court office about what you can do

Address for payment

How to Pay

- **PAYMENT(S) MUST BE MADE to the person named at the address for payment, quoting their reference and the court case number**
- **DO NOT bring or send payments to the court. THEY WILL NOT BE ACCEPTED.**
- You should allow at least 4 days for your payment to reach the claimant (defendant) or his representative
- Make sure that you keep records and can account for all payments made. Proof may be required if there is any disagreement. It is not safe to send cash unless you use registered post.
- A leaflet giving further advice about payment can be obtained from the court.
- If you need more information you should contact the claimant (defendant) or his representative.

The court office at

is open between 10 am and 4 pm Monday to Friday. Address all communications to the Court Manager quoting the claim number.

C71–001

N256

Final Costs Certificate

In the **County Court**	
Claim No.	
Claimant (including ref.)	
Defendant (including ref.)	
Date	

Final Costs Certificate

To [Claimant][Defendant]['s solicitor]

Upon the [claimant][defendant] filing a completed bill of costs in this claim

District Judge][ ] has assessed the total cost as £ [including £ for the costs of the detailed assessment. The VAT included in the total is £]

[And £] already having been paid under the interim costs certificate issued on [ ]]

You must pay [the balance of] £ to the [claimant][defendant] [within 14 days from the date of this order] [on or before [ ]]

The date from which any entitlement to interest under this certificate commences is [*date*].

Take Notice

To the defendant (claimant)

If you do not pay in accordance with this order your goods may be removed and sold or other enforcement proceedings may be taken against you. If your circumstances change and you cannot pay, ask at the court office about what you can do

Further interest may be added if judgment has been given for £5,000 or more or is in respect of a debt which attracts contractual or statutory interest for late payment.

Address for Payment

This judgment has been registered on the Register of County Court Judgments. This may make it difficult for you to get credit. **If you pay in full within one month** you can ask the court to cancel the entry on the Register. You will need to give proof of payment. You can (for a fee) also obtain a Certificate of Cancellation from the court. If you pay the debt in full after one month you can ask the court to mark the entry on the Register as satisfied and (for a fee) obtain a Certificate of Satisfaction to prove that the debt has been paid.

How to Pay

- **PAYMENT(S) MUST BE MADE to the person named at the address for payment, quoting their reference and the court case number**
- **DO NOT bring or send payments to the court. THEY WILL NOT BE ACCEPTED.**
- You should allow at least 4 days for your payment to reach the claimant (defendant) or his representative
- Make sure that you keep records and can account for all payments made. Proof may be required if there is any disagreement. It is not safe to send cash unless you use registered post.
- A leaflet giving further advice about payment can be obtained from the court.
- If you need more information you should contact the claimant (defendant) or his representative.

The court office at

is open between 10 am and 4 pm Monday to Friday. Address all communications to the Court Manager quoting the claim number.

N256(HC)
C72–001

Final Costs Certificate

Final Costs Certificate

In the High Court of Justice	
	Division **District Registry**
Claim No.	
Claimant (including ref.)	
Defendant (including ref.)	
Date	

To [Claimant] [Defendant] ['s solicitor]

Upon the [claimant] [defendant] filing a completed bill of costs in this claim

Master[ ] has assessed the total cost as £ [including £ for the costs of the detailed assessment. The VAT included in the total is £]

[And £] already having been paid under the interim costs certificate issued on [ ]]

You must pay [the balance of] £ to the [claimant] [defendant] [within 14 days from the date of this order] [on or before [ ]]

The date from which any entitlement to interest under this certificate commences is [*date*].

Take Notice

To the defendant (claimant)

If you do not pay in accordance with this order your goods may be removed and sold or other enforcement proceedings may be taken against you. If your circumstances change and you cannot pay, ask at the court office about what you can do

Address for payment

How to Pay

- **PAYMENT(S) MUST BE MADE to the person named at the address for payment, quoting their reference and the court case number**
- **DO NOT bring or send payments to the court. THEY WILL NOT BE ACCEPTED.**
- You should allow at least 4 days for your payment to reach the claimant (defendant) or his representative
- Make sure that you keep records and can account for all payments made. Proof may be required if there is any disagreement. It is not safe to send cash unless you use registered post.
- A leaflet giving further advice about payment can be obtained from the court.
- If you need more information you should contact the claimant (defendant) or his representative.

The court office at

is open between 10 am and 4 pm Monday to Friday. Address all communications to the Court Manager quoting the claim number.

C73–001

N257

Interim Costs Certificate

Interim costs certificate

In the	
Claim No.	
Claimant (including ref.)	
Defendant (including ref.)	
Date	

To [Claimant][Defendant]['s solicitor]

Upon application by the [claimant][defendant] for [a detailed assessment hearing] [the issue of an interim costs certificate by agreement].

[Master][District Judge][Costs Officer][ ] has ordered that you must pay

£ to the [claimant][defendant] [within 14 days from the date of this order]

[on or before [ ]] [into court to await the issue of a final costs certificate].

Take Notice

To the defendant (claimant)

If you do not pay in accordance with this order your goods may be removed and sold or other enforcement proceedings may be taken against you. If your circumstances change and you cannot pay, ask at the court office about what you can do

Address for payment

How to Pay

- **PAYMENT(S) MUST BE MADE to the person named at the address for payment, quoting their reference and the court case number**
- **DO NOT bring or send payments to the court. THEY WILL NOT BE ACCEPTED.**
- You should allow at least 4 days for your payment to reach the claimant (defendant) or his representative
- Make sure that you keep records and can account for all payments made. Proof may be required if there is any disagreement. It is not safe to send cash unless you use registered post.
- A leaflet giving further advice about payment can be obtained from the court.
- If you need more information you should contact the claimant (defendant) or his representative.

The court office at

is open between 10 am and 4 pm Monday to Friday. Address all communications to the Court Manager quoting the claim number.

N258 C74–001

Request for Detailed Assessment Hearing

Request for Detailed Assessment Hearing

In the	
Claim No.	
Claimant (including ref.)	
Defendant (including ref.)	

I certify that the attached Notice of Commencement was served on the paying party ....

(*and give details of any other party served with the notice*)

on (*insert date*)

I now ask the court to arrange an assessment hearing (provisionally assess the bill – legal aid case only)

I enclose copies of (*tick as appropriate*)

- ☐ Bill of Costs
- ☐ the paying party's points of dispute annotated as necessary in order to show which items have been agreed and their value and to show which items remain in dispute and their value;
- ☐ points in reply (if any);
- ☐ a copy of the authority for the assessment;
- ☐ a copy of all the orders made by the court relating to the costs of the proceedings which are to be assessed;
- ☐ any fee notes of counsel and receipts or accounts for other disbursements relating to items in dispute;
- ☐ [where solicitors' costs are disputed] the client care letter delivered to the receiving party or the solicitor's retainer.
- ☐ all civil legal aid certificates and amendments to them; notice of discharge or revocation and specific legal aid authorities;

I believe the hearing will take .... (*give estimate of time court should allow*).

I certify that the assisted person wishes to attend the assessment hearing (*delete if not applicable*).

I enclose the papers appropriate for a provisional assessment (legal aid case only).

I enclose my fee of £............

Signed .... **Date** ....

(Claimant) (Defendant) ('s solicitor)

The court office at

is open between 10 am and 4 pm Monday to Friday. When corresponding with the court, please address forms or letters to the Court Manager and quote the claim number.

C75–001

N265

List of Documents: Standard Disclosure

List of Documents:
Standard Disclosure

In the	
Claim No.	
Claimant (including ref.)	
Defendant (including ref.)	
Date	

Notes:

- The rules relating to standard disclosure are contained in Part 31 of the Civil Procedure Rules.
- Documents to be included under standard disclosure are contained in Rule 31.6
- A document has or will have been in your control if you have or have had possession, or a right of possession, of it **or** a right to inspect or take copies of it.

Disclosure Statement

I state that I have carried out a reasonable and proportionate search to locate all the documents which I am required to disclose under the order made by the court on [19] [20].

(I did not search for documents –

1 pre-dating . . . .

2 located elsewhere than . . . .
. . . .

3 in categories other than . . . .
. . . .)

I certify that I understand the duty of disclosure and to the best of my knowledge I have carried out that duty. I further certify that the list of documents set out in or attached to this form, is a complete list of all documents which are or have been in my control and which I am obliged under the order to disclose.

I understand that I must inform the court and the other parties immediately if any further document required to be disclosed by Rule 31.6 comes into my control at any time before the conclusion of the case.

(I have not permitted inspection of documents within the category or class of documents (as set out below) required to be disclosed under Rule 31(6)(b) or (c) on the grounds that to do so would be disproportionate to the issues in the case.)

Signed ______________________ **Date** ______________

(Claimant) (Defendant) ('s litigation friend)

Position or office held (*if signing on behalf of firm or company*)
Please state why you are the appropriate person to make the disclosure statement.

List and number here, in a convenient order, the documents (or bundles of documents if of the same nature, e.g. invoices) in your control, which you do not object to being inspected. Give a short description of each document or bundle so that it can be identified, and say if it is kept elsewhere, i.e. with a bank or solicitor

I have control of the documents numbered and listed here. I do not object to you inspecting them/producing copies.

List and number here, as above, the documents in your control which you object to being inspected. (Rule 31.19)

I have control of the documents numbered and listed here, but I object to you inspecting them:

Say what your objections are

I object to you inspecting these documents because:

List and number here, the documents you once had in your control, but which you no longer have. For each document listed, say when it was last in your control and where it is now.

I have had the documents numbered and listed below, but they are no longer in my control.

C76–001

N266

Notice to admit facts

Notice to admit facts

In the	
Claim No.	
Claimant (including ref.)	
Defendant (including ref.)	

I (We) give notice that you are requested to admit the following facts or part of case in this claim:

I (We) confirm that any admission of fact(s) or part of case will only be used in this claim.

Signed (Claimant) (Defendant) ('s solicitor)

Position or office held (If signing on behalf of firm or company)

Date

Admission of facts

I (We) admit the facts or part of case (set out above) (in the attached schedule) for the purposes of this claim only and on the basis that the admission will not be used on any other occasion or by any other person.

Signed (Claimant) (Defendant) ('s solicitor)

Position or office held (If signing on behalf of firm or company)

Date

The court office at

is open between 10 am and 4 pm Monday to Frida. Address all communication to the Court manager quoting the claim number

N268 C77–001

Notice to prove documents at trial

Notice to prove documents at trial

In the	
Claim No.	
Claimant (including ref.)	
Defendant (including ref.)	

I (We) give notice that you are requested to prove the following documents disclosed under CPR Part 31 in this claim at the trial:

Signed

(Claimant) (Defendant) ('s solicitor)

Position or office held
(If signing on behalf of firm or company)

Date

The court office at

is open between 10 am and 4 pm Monday to Friday. Address all communication to the Court manager quoting the claim number

C78–001

N279

Notice of discontinuance

Notice to discontinuance

Note: Where another party must consent to the proceedings being discontinued, a copy of their consent must be attached to, and served with, this form.

In the	
Claim No.	
Claimant (including ref.)	
Defendant (including ref.)	

To the court

The claimant (defendant)

(*tick only one box*)

☐ discontinues all of this (claim) (counterclaim)

☐ discontinues that part of this claim (counterclaim) relating to: (*specify which part*)

against the (defendant) (following defendants) (claimant) (following claimants)

(. . . . . (*enter name of Judge*) granted permission for the claimant to discontinue (all) (part) of this (claim) (counterclaim) by order dated . . . .)

I certify that I have served a copy of this notice on every other party to the proceedings.

Signed [ ]
(Claimant) (Claimant's solicitor) (Litigation friend)

Position or office held [ ]
(If signing on behalf of firm or company)

Date [ ]

The court office at

is open between 10 am and 4 pm Monday to Frida. When corresponding with the court, please address forms or letters to the Court Manager and quote the claim number

N292

C79–001

Order on settlement on behalf of child or patient

Order on settlement on behalf of child or patient

To [Claimant][Defendant]['s solicitor]

In the	
Claim No.	
Claimant (including ref.)	
Defendant (including ref.)	

Seal

An application was made on [date] by [counsel][solicitors] for the claimant [and was attended by[counsel][solicitors] for the defendant].

[Master][District Judge] approved the following terms of settlement and made them an Order of the Court.

BY CONSENT IT IS ORDERED that:–

The claimant may accept the sum of [£..........] in satisfaction of the claim[s].

(where the claim is in respect of a Fatal Accident)
[The said sum of [£..........] is apportioned as follows:–

a) under the Law Reform (Miscellaneous Provisions) Act 1934 the sum of [£..........]
b) under the Fatal Accidents Act 1976;
   (i) [£..........] to the personal claim of the claimant,
   (ii) [£..........] to the personal claim of the child dependant[s] [....................][....................]]

[The defendant pay the sum of [£..........] to the claimant's [solicitors] [litigation friend] on or before [..........].]

The defendant pay the [further] sum of [£..........] into the [office of this court] [Court Funds Office] on or before [..........][subject to a first charge under section 16(6) of the Legal Aid Act 1988] to be invested and accumulated in the Special Investment Account pending further order.

[The claimant's solicitor apply to the court for further investment directions on or before [..........].]

(where the claimant is a Patient)
[The claimant's solicitor to apply to the Court of Protection for the appointment of a receiver on or before [..........] and upon such appointment being made the sum of [£..........] [subject to a first charge under section 16(6) of the Legal Aid Act 1988] together with any interest accrued on that sum from the date of this order to be carried over to the Court of Protection to the credit of the claimant there to be dealt with as the Court of Protection thinks fit.]

[Any interest accrued up to the date of this order on any money in court paid in by or on behalf of the defendant be paid out to the defendant's solicitors.]

The defendant pay the claimant's costs be assessed with permission to request assessment to be dispensed with [and the claimant's solicitor waiving any claim to further costs].

[The claimant's costs be [assessed] in accordance with Regulation 107 of the Civil Legal Aid (General) Regulations 1989.]

Upon payment of the sum(s) and costs referred to above, the defendant be discharged from further liability in respect of all claims made by the claimant against him in these proceedings.

All further proceedings be stayed except that either party has permission to apply to the court for the purpose of carrying this order into effect.

The court office at

is open between 10 am and 4 pm Monday to Friday. When corresponding with the court, please address forms or letters to the Court Manager and quote the claim number

C80–001

N294

Claimant's application for a variation order

Claimant's Application for a Variation Order (without hearing)

In the	
Claim No.	
Claimant (including ref.)	
Defendant (including ref.)	

Defendant's address

Seal

I apply to the court for an order that the amount due and unpaid under the judgment or order in this claim be paid by instalments of £ for every month/week because
(*give your reason for making this application in the box below*)

Signed .... **Date** ....
Claimant('s solicitor)('s litigation friend)

Judgment details

Date of judgment or order

How payment was ordered

Outstanding debt
**including any interest where judgment was entered for £5,000 or more, or is in respect of a debt which attracts contractual or statutory interest for late payment*

AMOUNT REMAINING DUE* £

The court office at

is open between 10 am and 4 pm Monday to Friday. Address all communications to the Court Manager quoting the claim number.

N367 C81–001

Notice of hearing to consider why fine should not be imposed

Notice of hearing to consider why fine should not be imposed

In the	
Claim No.	
Claimant	
Defendant	
Date	

To

Seal

If there is any reason why you think a fine should not be imposed upon you for [your failure to attend as a witness summoned to attend this court] [your refusal to be sworn or give evidence] [your failure to produce documents] you should either attend the hearing

at [am] [pm] on

at

to give your reasons orally to the court **or**

set out your reasons in a witness statement

The court office at

is open between 10 am and 4 pm Monday to Friday. When corresponding with the court, please address forms or letters to the Court Manager and quote the claim number.

C82–001

N434

Notice of Change of Solicitor

Notice of change of solicitor

In the	
Claim No.	
Claimant (including ref.)	
Defendant	

Note: You should tick either box A **or** B as appropriate **and** box C. Complete details as necessary

I (We) give notice that

A ☐ my solicitor (*insert name and address*) ....
has ceased to act for me and I shall now be acting in person.

B ☐ we (*insert name of solicitor*) ....
have been instructed to act on behalf of the claimant (defendant) in this claim (in place of (*insert name and address of previous solicitors*) ....
....).

C ☐ I (we) have served notice of this change on every party to claim (and on the former solicitor).

Address to which documents about this claim should be sent (including any reference)

		if applicable	
		fax no.	
		DX no.	
Postcode		e-mail	

Signed

Defendant/Defendant's solicitor/ Litigation friend

Position or office held

If signing on behalf of firm or company

Date

The court office at

is open between 10 am and 4 pm Monday to Friday. When corresponding with the court, please address forms or letters to the Court Manager and quote the claim number.

SECTION D

PRACTICE GUIDES

CHANCERY GUIDE

(Incorporating the Chancery Division Practice Direction)

Contents

D1–001

CHANCERY GUIDE

CHAPTER 1

REFORM OF THE CIVIL JUSTICE SYSTEM

1.1 As from 26 April 1999 the new unified Civil Procedure Rules and the Practice Directions which supplement them come into force. The change goes well beyond the substituting of one set of rules for another and giving procedural steps and documents more modern names. The reforms are as a result of an enquiry by The Rt Hon. Lord Woolf M.R. into the civil justice system. In his final report entitled *Access to Justice* (HMSO, 1996) Lord Woolf identified many defects in the civil justice system, in particular that civil justice was too expensive and too slow and that there was inequality where parties had different resources. The aim of the civil justice reforms is to remove those defects and to improve access to justice through quicker, cheaper and more proportionate justice. As an integral part of the reforms, cases will be more closely monitored through to trial by the Judiciary and differences between High Court and County Court procedure will be removed. D1–002

1.2 To achieve these aims, all procedural decisions in future will be guided by the overriding objective stated in Civil Procedure Rule 1.1. The Court must deal with cases justly and dealing justly with a case is to include, so far as practicable, ensuring the parties are on an equal footing, saving expense, dealing with the case in ways which are proportionate to the sum at stake, the importance of the case, its complexity and each party's financial position, ensuring expedition and fairness and allotting to each case an appropriate share of the Court's resources. D1–003

CHAPTER 2

ABOUT THE CHANCERY DIVISION

2.1 The Chancery Division is one of the three parts, or Divisions, of the High Court of Justice, the other two being the Queen's Bench Division and the Family Division. The President of the Chancery Division is the Lord Chancellor. The effective head is the Vice Chancellor who is the Vice President of the Division and the Head of Civil Justice. There are currently seventeen High Court Judges attached to it. In addition, in the Royal Courts of Justice in London, there are five Masters (one of whom is the Chief Master), and six Bankruptcy Registrars (one of whom is the Chief Registrar). In the District Registries the work done by Masters in London is performed by District Judges. References in this Guide to a Master include, in the case of proceedings in a District Registry, references to a District Judge. D1–004

2.2 The Chancery Division undertakes civil work of most kinds and, in addition, it has specialist work, such as companies, patents and contentious probate. The range of cases heard in the Chancery Division is wide and varied. The major part of the case-load today involves business disputes of one kind or another. Often these are complex and involve substantial sums of money. D1–005

2.3 In many types of case (*e.g.* claims for professional negligence against solicitors, accountants, valuers or other professionals) the claimant has a choice whether to bring the claim in the Chancery Division or elsewhere in the High Court. But there are other types of case which in the High Court must be brought in the Chancery Division. The specialist work of the Chancery Division is dealt with in Section B of this Guide. D1–006

2.4 If a claim brought in the Chancery Division is a "commercial claim" within the meaning of paragraph 1.2 of the Practice Direction—Commercial Court supplementing CPR Part 49, the Court will in general, and to the extent that it is consistent with the CPR and relative Practice Directions, adopt the same practice as the Commercial Court. However, case management in such cases will usually be carried out by the Masters. D1–007

2.5 The terminology and practice in the Chancery Division has on occasion diverged from that used in civil work elsewhere. Most of these differences are removed by the new Civil Procedure Rules. D1–008

2.6 The principal changes in terminology introduced by the new Civil Procedure Rules are listed at the front of this Guide. D1–009

CHAPTER 3

ABOUT THIS GUIDE

3.1 The aim of this Guide is to provide additional practical information not already contained in the new Rules or the Practice Directions supplementing them. D1–010

D1–011 3.2 Litigants and their advisers are expected to take steps to familiarise themselves with the new Civil Procedure Rules. It is not the function of this Guide to summarise the Rules, nor should it be regarded as a substitute for the Rules.

D1–012 3.3 This Guide is published as part of a series of Guides to various civil courts. Where information is more readily available in another Guide this Guide may simply refer to it.

D1–013 3.4 Section A of this Guide is concerned with General Civil Work. Section B deals with Specialist Work.

D1–014 3.5 Section C of this Guide contains the Chancery Division Practice Directions updated to take account of the new Civil Procedure Rules and Practice Directions supplementing them. Practice Directions which are now superseded have been deleted.

D1–015 3.6 The (updated) Chancery Division Practice Orders will be published separately.

SECTION A

GENERAL CIVIL WORK

CHAPTER 4

STARTING PROCEEDINGS, SERVICE, ALLOCATION AND STATEMENTS OF CASE

D1–016 *Key Rules: CPR Parts 6, 7, 8, 9, 10, 15, 16, 18, 20 and 26* and *CPR Schedule 1*

How to start a claim

D1–016A 4.1 Claims are issued either out of Chancery Chambers or out of a District Registry. There is no Production Centre for Chancery claims.

D1–017 4.2 The claim form must be issued either as a Part 7 claim under CPR Part 7, or as a Part 8 claim under the alternative procedure for claims in CPR Part 8.

Service

D1–018 4.3 CPR Part 6 applies to the service of documents, including claim forms. Therefore, unless the claimant notifies the Court that he or she wishes to serve the claim form, it will be served by the Court. However, many solicitors will prefer to serve the claim form themselves and will notify the Court that they wish to do so.

Allocation

D1–019 4.4 All claims retained in the Chancery Division are allocated to the multi-track. Chapter 13 deals with transfer to the County Court.

Statements of case

D1–020 4.5 In addition to the matters which the PD supplementing CPR Part 16 requires to be set out specifically in the particulars of claim, a party must set out in any statement of case:

(1) full particulars of any allegation of fraud, dishonesty, malice or illegality;

(2) where any inference of fraud or dishonesty is alleged, the facts on the basis of which the inference is alleged.

Points of law may also be set out in any statement of case.

D1–021 4.6 Whenever a party gives particulars of his or her case, the guidelines in Appendix 1 should be followed.

D1–022 4.7 The guidelines apply to any particulars given in: the claim form; particulars of claim; defence; Part 20 claim; reply to a defence; and a response to a request for further information under Part 18.

D1–023 4.8 Parties should not attach copies of documents or any expert's report to their statement of case if they are bulky.

D1–024 4.9 Notwithstanding CPR rule 15.8, claimants should if possible serve any reply before they file their allocation questionnaire. This will enable other parties to consider the reply before they file their allocation questionnaire.

Part 8 claims

D1–025 4.10 This procedure will usually be used where there is no substantial dispute of fact, such as where the case raises only the question of the construction of a document or a statute. Part 8 claims will generally be disposed of on the written evidence. The features of the Part 8 procedure are:

- no particulars of claim
- no defence
- no allocation questionnaire
- no judgment in default

• normally no oral evidence

4.11 Defendants who wish to contest the claim or to take part in the proceedings should complete and file the acknowledgment of service in form N210 which accompanies the claim form. D1–026

4.12 Claimants must file the written evidenc on which they intend to rely with the claim form. Defendants are required to file and serve their evidence when they file their acknowledgment of service, namely within 14 days after service of the claim form (CPR rule 8.5(3)). By paragraph 5.6 of the PD supplementing CPR Part 8, a defendant's time for filing evidence may be extended by agreement for not more than 14 days from the filing of the acknowledgment of service. The claimant has 14 days for filing evidence in reply but this period may be extended by agreement for not more than 28 days from service of the defendant's evidence. Any longer extension either for the defendant or the claimant requires an application to the Court. If the parties are in agreement that such an extension should be granted the application should be made in writing. Any agreements extending time should be filed. D1–027

4.13 Defendants who acknowledge service but do not intend to file evidence should notify the Court in writing when they file their acknowledgment of service that they do not intend to file evidence. The purpose of this is so that the Court may know what each defendant's intention is when it considers the file. D1–028

4.14 The general rule (with the exception of, for example, mortgage claims and some claims under the Variation of Trusts Act 1958 or where a party has made a CPR Part 24 application) is that the Court file will be considered by the Court after the time for acknowledgment of service has expired, or, if the time for serving the defendant's evidence has been extended, after the expiry of that period. D1-029

4.15 It is likely that in many cases if the papers are in order the Court will not require any oral hearing, but will be able to deal with the matter on paper either by making the final order, or by directing a hearing before a Judge. D1–030

CHAPTER 5

THE COURT'S CASE MANAGEMENT POWERS

Key Rules: CPR rule 1.4, and Parts 3, 18, 29, 31, 35, 39 D1–031

5.1 A key feature of the civil justice reforms is that cases will be more closely monitored by the Court. Case management by the Court includes: identifying disputed issues at an early stage; fixing timetables; dealing with as many aspects of the case as possible on the same occasion; controlling costs; disposing of cases summarily where they disclose no case or defence; dealing with the case without the parties having to attend court; and giving directions to ensure that the trial of a case proceeds quickly and efficiently. The Court will expect the parties to co-operate with each other. Where appropriate the Court will encourage the parties to use alternative dispute resolution or otherwise help them settle the case. D1–031A

Directions

5.2 It is expected that parties and their advisers will endeavour to agree proposals for management of the case in accordance with CPR rule 29.4 and paragraphs 4.6 to 4.8 of the PD supplementing CPR Part 29. The Court will approve the parties' proposals, if they are suitable, and give directions accordingly. If it does not approve the agreed directions it will generally consult the parties or direct the holding of a case management conference, but it may give directions of its own initiative. If parties are unable to agree directions they should notify the Court of the matters on which they cannot agree. D1–032

5.3 In relatively straightforward claims the Court will give directions without holding a case management conference. D1–033

5.4 Any party who considers that a case management conference should be held before any directions are given should so state in his or her allocation questionnaire (or, in the case of a Part 8 claim, inform the Court in writing) and give reasons why he or she considers that a case management conference is required and supply a realistic time estimate for the length of the case management conference with a list of any dates or times inconvenient for him or her. D1–034

5.5 Wherever required by the CPR, or otherwise possible, the advocate(s) instructed or expected to be instructed to appear at the trial should attend any hearing at which case management directions are likely to be given. In order to help make this possible, the Court will endeavour so far as possible to give more than the minimum periods of notice of case management hearings provided in the CPR. D1–035

Applications for information and disclosure

5.6 Before a party applies to the Court for an order that another party provides him or her with D1–036 any further information or specific disclosure of documents he or she must communicate directly with the other party in an attempt to reach agreement or narrow the issues before the matter is raised with the Court. An application (separate from the case management conference) for a direction that a party provide further information or disclosure will not usually be heard without a prior written statement from the applicant that he or she has complied with the steps outlined in this paragraph.

Preliminary issues

D1–037 5.7 Costs can sometimes be saved by identifying decisive issues, or potentially decisive issues, and orering that they are tried first. The decision of one issue, although not itself decisive in law of the whole case, may enable the parties to settle the remainder of the dispute. In such cases a preliminary issue may be appropriate.

D1–038 5.8 At the allocation stage, at any case management conference and again at any PTR consideration will be given to the possibility of the trial of preliminary issues the resolution of which is likely to shorten proceedings. The Court may suggest the trial of a preliminary issue, but it will rarely make an order without the concurrence of at least one of the parties.

Trial timetable

D1–039 5.9 In order to assist the Court in setting a trial timetable (see CPR rule 29.8 and CPR rule 39.4) a draft trial timetable should be prepared by the advocate(s) for the claimant after consultation with the advocate(s) for all other parties. If there are differences of view between the advocate(s) for the claimant and the advocate(s) for other parties, these should be shown in the timetable. The draft trial timetable should be lodged with the Court.

D1–040 5.10 The trial timetable set by the Court will ordinarily fix the time for the oral submissions, witness evidence and expert evidence over the course of the trial. At any PTR (see below) the Judge may fix the trial timetable. If there is no PTR, then on the first day of the trial the Judge may fix the trial timetable. Trial timetables are always subject to any further order that may be made.

Pre-Trial Review

D1–041 5.11 In cases estimated to take more than 10 days and in other cases where the circumstances warrant it, the Court may direct that a PTR be held. (See CPR rule 29.7.)

D1–042 5.12 The PTR may be heard by a Master or a Judge. If it is to be heard by a Judge, the date and time should be fixed with the Clerk of the Lists. If the trial Judge has already been nominated, the application will if possible be heard by that Judge. The advocates' clerks must attend the Clerk of the Lists in sufficient time so that the PTR can be fixed for a date between 8 and 4 weeks before the trial date.

D1–043 5.13 A PTR should be attended by advocates who are to represent the parties at the trial.

D1–044 5.14 Not less than 7 days before the date fixed for the PTR the claimant, or another party if so directed by the Court, must circulate a list of matters to be considered at the PTR, including proposals as to how the case should be tried, to the other parties, who must respond with their comments at least 2 days before the PTR.

D1–045 5.15 The claimant, or another party if so directed by the Court, should deliver a bundle containing the listing questionnaires and the lists of matters to be considered and proposals served by the parties on each other and the trial timetable, together with the results of the discussions between the parties as to those matters, and any other documents the Court is likely to need in order to deal with the PTR, to the Listing Office by 10 a.m. on the day before the day fixed for the hearing of the PTR, or if the PTR is to be heard by a Master, to that Master.

D1–046 5.16 At the PTR the Court will review the state of preparation of the case, and deal with outstanding procedural matters, not limited to those apparent from the listing questionnaires or the lists of matters lodged by the parties. The Court may give directions as to how the case is to be tried, including directions as to the order in which witnesses are to be called (for example all witnesses of fact before all expert witnesses) or as to the time to be allowed for particular stages in the trial.

CHAPTER 6

DISCLOSURE OF DOCUMENTS AND EXPERT EVIDENCE

D1–047 *Key Rules: CPR Parts 18, 29, 31 and 35; PDs supplementing CPR Parts 31 and 35*

D1–047A 6.1 As part of its case management, the Court will give directions about the disclosure of documents and any expert evidence. Attention is drawn to paragraph 5.6 above (Applications for information and disclosure).

Disclosure of documents

General

6.2 Lord Woolf's conclusion in his final report on Access to Justice was that disclosure of documents should be retained but subject to controls.[1] Thus, under the new Civil Procedure Rules, the normal order for disclosure is an order for standard disclosure, that is disclosure of: D1–048

(a) *a party's own documents*—that is, the documents on which a party relies;

(b) *adverse documents*—that is, documents which adversely affect his or her own or another party's case or support another party's case; and

(c) *required documents*—that is, documents that a Practice Direction requires him or her to disclose.

6.3 The Court may make an order for specific disclosure if it is satisfied that standard disclosure is inadequate. In his final report on Access to Justice Lord Woolf said that when ordering such disclosure: D1–049

> the Court would have to be satisfied not only that it was necessary to do justice but that the cost of such disclosure would not be disproportionate to the benefit and that a party's ability to continue the litigation would not be impaired by an order for specific disclosure against him.[2]

6.4 The Court will therefore seek to ensure, so far as possible, that any specific disclosure ordered is tailored to the requirements of the particular case. The financial position of the parties, the importance of the case and the complexity of the issues will be taken into account when considering whether more than standard disclosure should be ordered. D1–050

6.5 If specific disclosure is sought, the parties should give careful thought to the ways in which such disclosure can be limited, for example by requiring disclosure in stages or by requiring disclosure simply of sufficient documents to show a specified matter and so on. They should also consider whether the need for disclosure could be avoided by requiring a party to provide information under CPR Part 18. D1–051

Expert evidence

General

6.6 In his report on *Access to Justice* Lord Woolf observed that expert evidence was one of the major generators of unnecessary cost in litigation and that there was wide agreement on a number of criticisms of expert evidence that he had made in his interim report (HMSO, 1995). In particular he had noted that experts sometimes acted in a partisan way rather than assisted the Court impartially. Lord Woolf made several recommendations designed to control the use of expert evidence, including the greater use of a single joint expert and restricting the number of experts to one expert for all parties. D1–052

6.7 Accordingly CPR Part 35 states that expert evidence must be restricted to what is reasonably required to resolve the proceedings and makes provision for the Court to direct that expert evidence is given by a single joint expert. D1–053

Duties of an expert

6.8 It is the duty of an expert to help the Court on the matters within his or her expertise and this duty overrides any obligation to the person from whom the expert has received instructions or by whom he or she is paid (CPR rule 35.3). Attention is drawn to the PD—Experts and Assessors supplementing CPR Part 35. D1–054

6.9 In fulfilment of this duty, an expert must for instance make it clear if a particular question or issue falls outside his or her expertise or he or she considers that insufficient data is available on which to express an opinion. Any material change of view by an expert should be communicated in writing (through legal representatives) to the other parties without delay, and when appropriate to the Court. D1–055

Single joint expert

6.10 The introduction to the PD—Experts and Assessors supplementing CPR Part 35 states that where possible matters requiring expert evidence should be dealt with bt a single expert. D1–056

6.11 In his final report on Access to Justice, Lord Woolf said: D1–057

> I do not think it would be appropriate to specify particular areas of litigation where a single expert should or should not be used. There are in all areas some large, complex and strongly contested cases where the full adversarial system, including oral cross-examination of opposing experts on particular issues, is the best way of producing a just result. That will apply particularly to issues on which there are several tenable schools of thought, or where the boundaries of knowledge are being extended. It does not, however, apply to all cases. As a general principle, I believe that single experts should be used wherever the case (or the

[1] Page 311, para. 134; see also pages 124 to 126, paras 37 to 46.
[2] Page 125, para. 40.

issues) is concerned with a substantially established area of knowledge and where it is not necessary for the Court directly to sample a range of opinions. The expert's duty to the Court will require him to set out in his report his view of the range of possible opinions. Too often under the present regime the experts are in fact agreed upon the range of opinion, but their reports only set out the extreme positions.

D1–058 6.12 In his report Lord Woolf also recommended that parties and procedural Judges should always consider whether a single expert could be appointed in a particular case (or to deal with a particular issue); and, if this is not considered appropriate, indicate why not.

D1–059 6.13 It is not necessarily a sufficient objection to the making by the Court of an order for a single joint expert that the parties have already appointed their own experts. An order for a single joint expert does not prevent a party from having his or her own expert to advise him or her, but he or she may well be unable to recover the cost of employing his or her own expert from the other party. The duty of an expert who is called to give evidence is to help the Court.

D1–060 6.14 When the use of a single joint expert is contemplated the Court will expect the parties to co-operate in developing and agreeing to the greatest possible extent, terms of reference for the expert. In most cases the terms of reference will (in particular) detail what the expert is asked to do, identify any documentary material he or she is asked to consider and specify any assumptions he or she is asked to make.

More than one expert—exchange of reports

D1–061 6.15 In an appropriate case the Court will direct that experts' reports are delivered sequentially.

Discussion between experts

D1–062 6.16 The Court will normally direct discussion between experts before trial. Sometimes it may be useful for there to be further discussions during the trial itself. The purpose of these discussions is to give the experts opportunity:

(a) to discuss the expert issues; and

(b) to identify the expert issues on which they share the same opinion and those on which there remains a difference of opinion between them (and what that difference is).

D1–063 6.17 Unless the Court otherwise directs, the procedure to be adopted at these discussions is a matter for the experts. It may be sufficient if the discussion takes place by telephone.

D1–064 6.18 Parties must not seek to restrict their expert's participation in any discussion directed by the Court, but they are not bound by any agreement on any issue reached by their expert unless they expressly so agree.

Written questions to experts

D1–065 6.19 It is emphasised that this procedure is only for the purpose generally of seeking clarification of an expert's report where the other party is unable to understand it. Written questions going beyond this can only be put with the agreement of the parties or with the permission of the Court. The procedure of putting written questions to experts is not intended to interfere with the procedure for an exchange of professional opinion in discussions between experts or to inhibit that exchange of professional opinion. If questions that are oppressive in number or content are put or questions are put without permission for any purpose other than clarification of an expert's report, the Court will not hesitate to disallow the questions and to make an appropriate order for costs against the party putting them.

Request by an expert to the Court for directions

D1–066 6.20 An expert may file with the Court a written request for directions to assist him or her in carrying out his or her function as expert: CPR rule 35.14. The expert should guard against accidentally informing the Court about, or about matters connected with, communications or potential communications between the parties that are without prejudice or privileged. The expert may properly be privy to the content of these communications because he or she has been asked to assist the party instructing him or her to evaluate them.

Assessors

D1–067 6.21 Under CPR rule 35.15 the Court may appoint an assessor to assist it in relation to any matter in which the assessor has skill and experience. The report of the assessor is made available to the parties. The remuneration of the assessor is determined by the Court and forms part of the costs of the proceedings.

CHAPTER 7

APPLICATIONS

D1–068 *Key Rules: CPR Parts 23 and 25, PDs supplementing CPR Parts 23 and 25*

D1–068A 7.1 This Chapter deals with applications to a Judge, including applications for interim remedies, and applications to a Master.

7.2 Only applications which need to be heard by a Judge (*e.g.* most applications for an injunction) should be made to a Judge. Any procedural application (*e.g.* for directions) should be made to a Master unless there is some special reason for making it to a Judge. Otherwise the application may be dismissed with costs. If an application is to be made to a Judge, the application notice should state that it is a Judge's application. D1–069

7.3 CPR Part 23 contains rules as to how an application may be made. In some circumstances it may be dealt with without a hearing, or by a telephone hearing. D1–070

Applications without notice

7.4 Generally it is wrong to make an application without giving prior notice to the respondent. There are exceptions, however, when, for instance, the giving of notice might frustrate the order (*e.g.* a search order) or there is such urgency that there has not been time to give notice. Even in an urgent case the applicant should notify the respondent informally of the application (unless secrecy is essential). An application made without giving notice which does not fall within the narrow classes of cases where absence of notice is justified, may be dismissed or adjourned until proper notice has been given. D1–071

Applications to a Judge

7.5 If an application is made to a Judge in existing proceedings, *e.g.* for an injunction, it should be made by application notice. Normally three clear days' notice to the other party is required but in an emergency or for other good reason the application can be made without giving notice to the other side. Except in an emergency a party notifies the Court of his or her wish to bring an application by delivering the requisite documents to the Listing Office and paying the appropriate fee. He or she should at the same time deliver a completed "Judge's Application Information Form" in the form of Appendix 5. D1–072

7.6 CDPD 3 contains information on the procedure that is followed. D1–073

7.7 There is a Judge available to hear applications each day in term and an application notice can be served for any day in term except the last. Special arrangements are made for hearing applications in vacation. D1–074

7.8 At the beginning of each day the Judge taking applications calls on each of the applications to be made that day in turn. This enables him or her to establish the identity of the parties, their state of readiness and their estimates of the duration of the hearing. On completion of this process, the Judge decides the order in which he or she will hear applications and gives any other directions that may be necessary. Sometimes cases are released to other Judges at this point. If cases are likely to take 2 hours or more, the Judge usually orders that they are given a subsequent fixed date for hearing (they are then called "applications by order") and hears any application for a court order to last until the application is heard fully. D1–075

7.9 Parties and their representatives should arrive at least ten minutes before the Court sits. This will assist the usher to take a note of the names of those proposing to address the Court and of their estimate of the hearing time. This information is given to the Judge before he or she sits. Parties should also allow time before the Court sits to agree any form of order with any other party if this has not already been done. If the form of the order is not agreed before the Court sits, the parties may have to wait until there is a convenient break in the list before they can ask the Court to make the agreed order. D1–076

The duty of disclosure

7.10 On all applications made in the absence of the respondent the applicant and his or her legal representatives owe a duty to the Court to disclose fully all matters relevant to the application, including matters, whether of fact or law, which are, or may be, adverse to it. If there is a failure to comply with this duty and an order is made, the Court may subsequently set aside the order on that ground alone. The disclosure if made orally must be confirmed by witness statement or affidavit. The representatives for the applicant must specifically direct the Court to passages in the evidence which disclose matters adverse to the application. D1–077

7.11 Where an urgent application is made, two copies of the order sought and an electronic copy on disk (in Word Perfect 5.1) and a completed Judge's Application Information Form in the form of Appendix 5 should, where possible, be included with the papers handed to the Judge's Clerk. If the proceedings have not yet been issued, every effort should be made to issue the claim form before the application is made. If this is not practicable, the party making the application must give an undertaking to the Court to issue the claim form forthwith even if the Court makes no order, unless the Court orders otherwise. D1–078

Freezing Injunctions and Search Orders

7.12 The grant of freezing injunctions (both domestic and world-wide) and search orders is a staple feature of the work of the Applications Judge. Applications for such orders are invariably made without notice in the first instance; and in a proper case the Court will sit in private in order to hear them. D1–079

7.13 Freezing injunctions and search orders are never granted as a matter of course. A strong case must be made out, and applications need to be prepared with great care. The application should always be accompanied by a draft of the order which the Court is to be invited to make. D1–080

Period for which an injunction/order appointing a receiver is made if the application was without notice

D1–081 7.14 When an application for an injunction is heard without notice, the Judge, if he or she decides that an injunction should be granted, will normally grant it for a limited period only—usually not more than seven days. The same applies to an interim order appointing a receiver. The applicant will be required to give the respondent notice of his or her intention to apply to the Court at the expiration of that period for the order to be continued. In the meantime the respondent will be entitled to apply, though generally only after giving notice to the applicant, for the order to be varied or discharged.

Opposed applications without notice

D1–082 7.15 These are applications of which proper notice has not been given to the respondents but made in the presence of both parties in advance of a full hearing of the application. The Judge may impose time limits on the parties if, having regard to the pressure of business or for any other reason, he or she considers it appropriate to do so. On these applications, the Judge may, in an appropriate case, make an order to continue until trial or further order as if proper notice had been given.

Implied cross-undertakings in damages where undertakings are given to the Court

D1–083 7.16 Often the party against whom an injunction is sought gives to the Court an undertaking which avoids the need for the Court to grant the injunction. In these cases, there is clearly an implied undertaking in damages by the party applying for the injunction in favour of the other. The position is less clear where the party applying for the injunction also gives an undertaking to the Court. The parties should consider and, if necessary, raise with the Judge whether the party in whose favour the undertaking is given must be taken to give a cross-undertaking in damages in those circumstances.

Orders on applications

D1–084 7.17 The Judge may direct the parties to agree, sign and deliver to the Court a statement of the terms of the Order made by the Court, particularly where complex undertakings are given.

D1–085 7.18 CDPD 8.B(ii) sets out the procedure for consent orders and undertakings when a party acts in person or his or her legal representatives do not attend the Court.

Agreed adjournments of Judge's applications

D1–086 7.19 Attention is drawn to the cost-saving procedure described in CDPD 3.C(i) whereby, if all parties to an application agree to do so, the application can be adjourned for not more than 14 days, on production to the Clerk of the Lists no later than 4.00 p.m. on the day before the hearing of the application, of the written consent of counsel or solicitors for all parties. The Clerk of the Lists may accept a written consent of counsel or solicitors sent to the Listing Office by fax in time. A litigant in person must attend before the Clerk of the Lists as well as signing a consent. Not more than three successive adjournments may be made and an application may not be adjourned to either of the last two Judge's application days of any law term. Undertakings previously given to the Court may be continued unchanged over the duration of any adjournment. If an existing undertaking is to be varied or a new undertaking given, the adjournment must be dealt with by the Judge.

Applications by order by agreement

D1–087 7.20 Attention is drawn to the procedure set out in CDPD 3 para C(iii) whereby a Judge's application may, without attendance before the Judge, be adjourned to be heard on a date to be fixed by the Clerk of the Lists. This procedure should be used where the parties are agreed that the hearing of the application will take two hours or more. The consent must contain an agreed timetable for written evidence, if written evidence is to be filed, or confirm that no additional written evidence will be filed, and any application arising trom the default of a party in abiding by the timetable and any application by the parties to extend the timetable must be made to the Judge. The application by order will initially at least, enter the Interim Hearings Warned List on the first Monday after the close of evidence.

Bundles and Skeleton Arguments

D1–088 7.21 See Chapter 8 below.

Applications to the Master

D1–089 7.22 Applications to the Master should be made by application notice. If the Master has directed a case management conference the parties should make all applications in the proceedings on that application. It is the duty of the parties to seek to agree directions if possible and to provide a draft of the order for consideration by the Master.

D1–090 7.23 Applications to the Master estimated to last in excess of two hours require the Master's directions before they are listed. The Master will require a time estimate signed by the applicant's representative (or if the party is acting in person signed by him or her) and that time estimate should have been specifically discussed with the respondent's representative. The time estimate must take into account not only the hearing time of the application but the time for the Master to give any judgment at the conclusion of the hearing. It should also take into account any further time that may be required for the Master to assess costs.

7.24 Prior to seeking the Master's directions for listing, the applicant should discuss with the respondent a timetable for the exchange of any evidence and invite the Master to make an order reflecting that timetable. **D1–091**

7.25 If the applicant considers that a bundle should be available for the Master on the application then this and the provision of skeleton arguments should similarly form part of the agreed listing directions. In matters of substance the parties should expect that the Master will require a bundle and skeleton arguments to be provided prior to the hearing. **D1–092**

7.26 The Masters may also allow applications to be made to them informally. **D1–093**

7.27 Attention is drawn to paragraphs 8.28 and 8.30 below. **D1–094**

CHAPTER 8

HEARINGS IN COURT

Key Rules: CPR Parts 29 and 39 **D1–095**

8.1 This Chapter deals with listing arrangements and contains guidelines on the preparation of cases for hearings in court. Guidelines about the conduct of trials are given in Chapter 9 of this Guide. **D1–095A**

Listing arrangements

8.2 Reference should also be made to CDPD 5 in Section C and to the Practice Direction on the Fixing of Trial Dates and Windows in the Multi-track in Section D. **D1–096**

Responsibility for listing

8.3 The Clerk of the Lists (Room W.16, Royal Courts of Justice) is in general responsible for listing. All applications relating to listing should, in the first instance, be made to the Clerk of the Lists. Any party dissatisfied with any decision of the Clerk of the Lists may, on one clear day's notice to all other parties, apply to the Judge in charge of the list. Any such application should be made within seven days of the decision of the Clerk of the Lists and be arranged through the Chancery Listing Office. **D1–097**

The Trial List

8.4 This comprises a list of all trials to be heard with witnesses. **D1–098**

The Interim Hearings List

8.5 This list comprises interim applications and appeals from Masters. **D1–099**

The General List

8.6 This list comprises other matters including revenue, bankruptcy and pension appeals, Part 8 proceedings, applications for judgment and all company matters. **D1–100**

Warned List—General and Interim Hearings Lists

8.7 On each Friday of term and on such other days as may be appropriate, the Clerk of the Lists will publish a Warned List, showing the matters that are liable to be heard in the following week. Any matters for which no date has been arranged will be liable to appear in the list for hearing with no warning save that given by the next day's list of cases, posted each afternoon outside Room W.15. Where a case is listed in the Warned List, the parties may agree to offer the case for a specified date, in accordance with the statement of Listing Office practice on offering cases issued by the Clerk of the Lists. **D1–101**

Estimate of duration

8.8 If after a case is listed the estimated length of the hearing is varied, or if the case is settled, withdrawn or discontinued, the solicitors for the parties must forthwith inform the Clerk of the Lists in writing. If the case is settled but the parties wish the Master to make a consent order, the solicitor must notify the Clerk of the Lists in writing, whereupon he or she will take the case out of the list and notify the Master. The Master may then make the consent order. **D1–102**

8.9 Seven days before the date for the hearing, the claimant's solicitors must inform the Clerk of the Lists whether there is any variation in the estimate of duration, and, in particular, whether the case is likely to be disposed of in some summary way. If the claimant is a litigant in person, this must be done by the solicitor for the first-named defendant who has instructed a solicitor. If a summary disposal is likely, the solicitor must keep the Clerk of the Lists informed of any developments as soon as they occur. **D1–103**

Applications after listing

8.10 After a case has been listed, any application in the case should be made to the Judge **D1–104** hearing applications if a hearing before a Master cannot be obtained in time for this not to delay the hearing of the case.

Daily list of cases

D1–105 8.11 This is available on **www.courtservice.gov.uk/highhome.htm**.

Preparation for Hearing in Court

D1–106 8.12 To ensure court time is used efficiently there must be adequate preparation of cases prior to the hearing. This covers, among other things, the preparation and exchange of skeleton arguments, the compiling of bundles of documents and the dealing out of court with queries which need not concern the Court. The parties should also use their best endeavours to agree before any hearing which are the issues or the main issues.

Estimates

D1–107 8.13 Realistic estimates of the length of time a hearing is expected to take must be given. Estimates play an essential role in the efficient listing of cases.

D1–108 8.14 In estimating the length of a hearing, sufficient time must be allowed for reading any documents required to be read, the length of the speeches, the time required to examine witnesses (if any) and if appropriate an immediate judgment, together with the summary assessment of costs, in cases where that may arise, and any application for permission to appeal.

D1–109 8.15 Except as mentioned below, a written estimate signed by the advocates for all the parties is required in the case of any hearing before a Judge. This should be delivered to the Clerk of the Lists:

(a) in the case of a trial, on the application to fix the trial date; and

(b) in any other case, as soon as possible after the application notice or case papers have been lodged with the Listing Office.

D1–110 8.16 If the estimate given in the application notice for an application to a Judge (other than applications by order) or for an application listed before the Companies Court Judge requires to be revised, the revised estimate should be given to the Court orally when the application is called on.

Changes in estimate

D1–111 8.17 The parties must inform the Court immediately of any material change in a time estimate. They should keep each other informed of any such change.

Inaccurate estimates

D1–112 8.18 Where estimates prove inaccurate, a hearing may have to be adjourned to a later date and the party responsible for the adjournment is likely to be ordered to pay the costs thrown away.

Bundles

D1–113 8.19 Bundles of documents for use in court will generally be required for all hearings if more than 25 pages are involved (and may be appropriate even if fewer pages are involved). The efficient preparation of bundles of documents is very important. Where bundles have been properly prepared, the case will be easier to understand and present, and time and costs are likely to be saved. Where documents are copied unnecessarily or bundled incompetently the cost may be disallowed.

D1–114 8.20 Where the provisions of this Guide as to the preparation or delivery of bundles are not followed, the bundle may be rejected by the Court or be made the subject of a special costs order.

D1–115 8.21 The claimant or applicant (as the case may be) should begin his or her preparation of the bundles in sufficient time to enable:

(1) the bundles to be agreed with the other parties (so far as possible);

(2) references to the bundles to be used in skeleton arguments; and

(3) the bundles to be delivered to the Court at the required time.

D1–116 8.22 The representatives for all parties involved must co-operate in agreeing bundles for use in court. The Court and the advocates should all have exactly the same bundles.

D1–117 8.23 When parties agree a bundle of documents, they should also make clear whether they are simply agreeing the contents of the bundle or whether in addition they are agreeing:

(a) that documents in the bundle may be treated as evidence of the facts stated in them even if a notice under the Civil Evidence Act 1995 has not been given; and/or

(b) that every document in the bundle is authentic even if not previously disclosed.

D1–118 8.24 Documents disclosed are in general to be admitted to be authentic under CPR rule 32.19.

D1–119 8.25 Detailed guidelines on the preparation of bundles are set out in Appendix 2. These should always be followed unless there is good reason not to do so.

D1–120 8.26 The general rule is that the claimant/applicant must ensure that one copy of a properly prepared bundle is delivered at the Listing Office at least two clear days before the hearing of an application and at least seven days before a trial. However, the Court may direct the delivery of bundles earlier than this. Where oral evidence is to be given a second copy of the bundle must be available in court for the use of the witnesses. In the case of bundles to be used on Judge's Applications (other than applications by order) the bundles must be delivered to the Clerk to the Applications Judge by 10 o'clock on the morning preceding the day of the hearing unless the

Court directs otherwise. A bundle delivered to the Court should always be in final form and parties should not make a request to alter a bundle after it has been delivered to the Court save for good reason.

8.27 If the case is one which does not require the preparation of a bundle, and the hearing is before a Judge, the advocate should check before the hearing starts that all the documents to which he or she wishes to refer and which ought to have been filed have been filed, and, if possible, indicate to the associate which they are. **D1–121**

8.28 In the case of a hearing before a Master or a Registrar, a bundle should be provided only if the nature of the application (as well as the number of pages) warrants it. The bundle should, if possible, be delivered two clear days in advance of the hearing. If the case is being heard in the Royal Courts of Justice the bundle should be delivered to Chancery Chambers Masters' Appointments, the Bankruptcy Registry or the Companies Court Issue Section as appropriate. **D1–122**

8.29 Bundles provided for the use of the Court should be removed promptly after the conclusion of the hearing unless the Court directs otherwise. **D1–123**

8.30 If a bundle of documents is not prepared for the use of the Court, but a party intends at any hearing to rely on the exhibits to a witness statement or affidavit filed on behalf of that party, that party must ensure that those exhibits are also filed with the Court in sufficient time to be available to be read by the Court in advance of the hearing. **D1–124**

Skeleton arguments

8.31 The general rule is that for the purpose of all hearings before a Judge skeleton arguments should be prepared. The exceptions to this general rule are where the application does not warrant one, for example because it is likely to be short, or where the application is so urgent that preparation of a skeleton argument is impracticable. **D1–125**

Time for delivery of skeleton arguments

8.32 **In the more substantial matters (e.g. trials and applications by order)**—not less than two clear days before the date or first date on which the application or trial is due to come on for hearing. **D1–126**

8.33 **On Judge's applications without notice**—with the papers which the Judge is asked to read on the application. **D1–127**

8.34 **On all other applications to a Judge, including interim applications**—as soon as possible and not later than 10 a.m. on the day preceding the hearing. **D1–128**

8.35 Where a case is liable to be placed in the Warned List, consideration should be given to the preparation of skeleton arguments as soon as the case is placed in the Warned List, so that the skeleton arguments are ready to be delivered to the Court on time. Preparation of skeleton arguments should not be left until notice is given that the case is to be heard. Notice may be given that the case is to be heard the next day. **D1–129**

Place to which skeleton arguments should be delivered

8.36 If the name of the Judge is not known, or the Judge is a Deputy Judge, skeleton arguments should be delivered to the Listing Office. **D1–130**

8.37 If the name of the Judge (other than a Deputy Judge) is known, skeleton arguments should be delivered to the Judge's clerk. **D1–131**

Content of skeleton arguments

8.38 Appendix 3 contains guidelines on the content of skeleton arguments and chronologies which should be followed wherever possible. The skeleton argument should identify any core document which the Judge should, if possible, read before the hearing starts. **D1–132**

8.39 In most cases before a Judge, a list of the persons involved in the facts of the case, a chronology and a list of issues will also be required. The chronology and list of issues should be agreed where possible. The claimant/applicant is responsible for preparing the list of persons involved and the chronology, and he or she should deliver these and his or her list of issues (if required) to the Court with his or her skeleton argument. **D1–133**

8.40 There is no general requirement for skeleton arguments before a Master or a Registrar. They should, however, be prepared on more complex or longer applications. They may be used on any other application if considered helpful. Skeleton arguments should be delivered personally to the Master or Registrar by 4 p.m. on the day before the hearing. A party may at the same time deliver any list of persons involved, list of issues and chronology, if considered helpful. **D1–134**

8.41 Unless the Court gives any direction, the parties shall, as between themselves, arrange for the delivery, exchange, or sequential service of skeleton argument and any list of persons involved, list of issues or chronology. Where there are no such arrangements, all such documents should, where possible, be given to the other parties (if any) in sufficient time before the hearing to enable them properly to consider them. **D1–135**

Failure to lodge bundles or skeleton arguments on time

8.42 Failure to lodge skeleton arguments and bundles in accordance with this Guide may result in: **D1–136**

(1) the matter not being heard on the date in question; and
(2) the costs of preparation being disallowed; and

(3) an adverse costs order being made.

D1–137 8.43 In the Royal Courts of Justice, a log will be maintained of all late skeletons and bundles.

Authorities

D1–138 8.44 Lists of authorities should be supplied to the usher by 9.00 a.m. on the first day of the hearing. Where photocopies of authorities are to be provided this should be indicated on the list. Delivery of skeleton arguments does not relieve a party of his or her duty to deliver his or her list of authorities to the usher by the time stated.

D1–139 8.45 Advocates should exchange lists of authorities by 4 p.m. on the day before the hearing.

D1–140 8.46 Excessive citation of authority should be avoided.

Oral argument

D1–141 8.47 The Court may indicate the issues on which it wishes to be addressed and those on which it wishes to be addressed only briefly.

Documents and authorities

D1–142 8.48 Only the key part of any document or authority should be read aloud in court.

8.49 At any hearing, handing in written material designed to reduce or remove the need for the
D1–143 Court to take a manuscript note will assist the Court and save time.

Adjournments

D1–144 8.50 As a timetable for the case will have been fixed at an early stage, applications for adjournment of a trial should only be necessary where there has been a change of circumstances not known when the timetable was fixed.

When to apply

(1) A party who seeks to have a hearing before a Judge adjourned must inform the Clerk of the Lists of his or her application as soon as possible.

(2) Applications for an adjournment immediately before a hearing begins should be avoided as they take up valuable time which could be used for dealing with effective business and, if successful, they may result in a loss of court time altogether.

How to apply

(3) If the application is agreed, the parties should, in writing, apply to the Chancery Listing Officer. The Officer will consult the Judge nominated for such matters. The Judge may grant the application on conditions and give directions as to a new hearing date. But the Judge may direct that the application be listed for a hearing and that all parties attend.

(4) If the adjournment is opposed the party asking for it should apply to the Judge nominated for such matters or to the Judge to whom the matter has been allocated. A hearing should be arranged, at the first opportunity, through the Chancery Listing Office.

(5) A short summary of the reasons for the adjournment should be delivered to the Listing Office, where possible by 12 noon on the day before the application is made. A witness statement or affidavit is not generally required.

(6) The party requesting an adjournment will, in general, be expected to show that he or she has conducted his or her own case diligently. Parties should take all reasonable steps to ensure that their cases are adequately prepared in sufficient time to enable a hearing before the Court to proceed. Likewise, they should take reasonable steps to prepare and serve any document (including any written evidence) required to be served on any other party in sufficient time to enable the other party similarly to be adequately prepared.

(7) If a failure to take reasonable steps necessitates an adjournment, the Court may disallow costs as between solicitor and client, or order the person responsible to pay the costs under CPR rule 48.7, or dismiss the application, or make any other order (including an order for the payment of costs on an indemnity basis).

CHAPTER 9

CONDUCT OF A TRIAL

D1–145 *Key Rules: CPR Parts 32 and 39*

D1–145A 9.1 An important aim of all concerned must be to ensure that at trial court time is used as efficiently as possible. Thorough preparation of the case prior to trial is the key to this.

9.2 Chapter 8 of this Guide applies to the conduct of a trial as well as other hearings in court. This Chapter contains matters which principally affect trials. D1–146

Time limits

9.3 The Court may at any time fix time limits for oral submissions, speeches and the examination and cross-examination of witnesses. D1–147

Opening speeches

9.4 The party opening the case should in general begin by making a short opening speech. D1–148

9.5 It is normally convenient for any outstanding procedural matters to be dealt with in the course of, or immediately after, the opening speech. D1–149

9.6 The Judge may ask or allow the other party to make a short speech at the end of the opening speech of the party opening the case. D1–150

9.7 The parties should be ready to give to the Judge at the start of or in the course of the opening a list of the documents which he or she needs to read. The Judge may decide to read the documents in his or her private room. D1–151

9.8 In some cases, before the case starts, the Judge may ask for a list of the essential documents he or she is required to read, and the start of the case may be deferred to enable him or her to read them. D1–152

9.9 Each party should provide written summaries of their opening speeches if the points are not covered in their skeleton arguments. The guidelines in Appendix 3 apply. A summary of an opening speech should be delivered to the Judge and the other parties no later than the time when the opening speech commences. D1–153

Witness statements

9.10 As to preparation of witness statements, the guidelines in Appendix 4 should be followed. D1–154

9.11 Unless the Court orders otherwise, a witness statement will stand as the witness' evidence in chief if he or she is called and confirms that he or she believes the facts stated in the statement are true: CPR rule 32.5. D1–155

9.12 A witness may be allowed to supplement his or her witness statement orally at the trial before submitting to cross-examination, but a party seeking to examine in chief a witness who has provided a witness statement must satisfy the Judge that there is good reason not to confine the evidence to the contents of his or her witness statement: see CPR rule 32.5(3) and (4). Where practicable a supplementary witness statement should be prepared and served on the other parties to deal with matters not dealt with in the original witness statement. Permission is required to adduce a supplementary witness statement at trial if any other party objects to it. D1–156

9.13 Witnesses are expected to have re-read their witness statements shortly before they are called to give evidence. D1–157

9.14 Where a party decides not to call a witness whose witness statement has been served to give oral evidence at trial, prompt notice of this decision should be given to all other parties. The party should make plain when he or she gives this notice whether he or she proposes to put, or seek to put, the witness statement in as hearsay evidence. If he or she does not put the witness statement in as hearsay evidence, CPR rule 32.5(5) allows any other party to put it in as hearsay evidence. D1–158

Cross-examination

9.15 The party cross-examining is not necessarily obliged to put his or her case to each witness even if they deal in chief with the same point. It may be sufficient if he or she puts it to one of the other side's witnesses. If that witness makes any admission or expresses any opinion or otherwise adds a qualification to his or her evidence, the party cross-examining can rely on it in argument but he or she cannot assume that other witnesses would have made the same admission or qualification and expressed the same opinion: see *Re Yarn Spinners' Agreement* [1959] 1 All E.R. 299 at 309 *per* Devlin J. D1–159

Expert evidence

9.16 The trial Judge may disallow expert evidence which is either not relevant or for any reason, or which he or she regards as excessive and disproportionate in all the circumstances, even though permission for he evidence had been given. D1–160

9.17 The evidence of experts (or of the experts on a particular topic) is commonly taken together at the same time and after the factual evidence has been given. If this is to be done it should be agreed by the parties before the trial and should be raised with the Judge at the PTR, if there is one, or otherwise at the start of the trial. Expert evidence should as far as possible be given by reference to the reports exchanged. D1–161

9.18 The evidence of experts must be impartial, complying with CPR rule 35.3. If it is not it may be disregarded. D1–162

Physical exhibits

9.19 Some cases involve a number of physical exhibits. The parties should endeavour to agree D1–163 the exhibits in advance and their system of labelling. Where it would be desirable, a scheme of display should be agreed (*e.g.* on a board with labels readable from a distance). Where witness statements refer to these, a note in the margin (which can be handwritten) of the exhibit number should be added.

Final speches

D1–164 9.20 The Judge may direct that the parties submit summaries of their final speeches before they begin. The guidelines in Appendix 3 apply. For this purpose the Court may grant an adjournment. The Court may require the written summaries to set out the principal findings of fact for which the party contends.

CHAPTER 10

JUDGMENTS, ORDERS AND PROCEEDINGS AFTER JUDGMENT

D1–165 *Key Rules: CPR Schedule 1 (incorporating RSC Order 44)*

Judgments

D1–165A 10.1 Where judgment is reserved, the Judge may deliver his or her judgment by handing down the written text without reading it out in open court. Where this course is adopted, the advocates will be supplied with the full text of the judgment in advance of delivery. In such cases, the advocates should familiarise themselves with the text of the judgment and be ready to deal with any points which may arise when judgment is deliverd. Any requirement to treat the text as confidential must be complied with.

D1–166 10.2 The judgment does not take effect until formally delivered in court. If the judgment is to be handed down in writing copies will then be made available to the parties and, if requested and so far as practicable, to the law reporters and the press.

D1–167 10.3 The Judge may direct that the written judgment may be used for all purposes as the text of the judgment, and that no transcript of the judgment need be made. Where such a direction is made, copies of the judgment may be obtained from the Mechanical Recording Department.

Orders

D1–168 10.4 It may often be possible for the Court to prepare and seal an order more quickly if a draft of the order is handed in. Speed may be particularly important where the order involves the grant of an interim injunction or the appointment of a receiver without notice.

D1–169 10.5 The Court may in any case direct the parties to agree and sign a statement of the terms of the order made by the Court. Where the proceedings are in the Royal Courts of Jutice, the statement should, when agreed and signed, be delivered to Chancery Chambers Registry and Issue Section (unless otherwise requested). In the case of any dispute or difficulty as to the contents of the order, the parties should mention the matter to the Judge who heard the application.

D1–170 10.6 Where a draft or an agreed statement of the terms of an order exists in electronic form, it is often helpful if the draft or agreed statement is provided to the Court on disk as well as in hard copy, particularly if the order needs to be drawn quickly. Any disk supplied for this purpose must be new and newly-formatted before writing the material on it so as to minimise the risk of transferring a computer virus. The current word processing system used by the Chancery Associates is WordPerfect 5.1 for DOS. Enquiries regarding the provision of disks should be made of the associate responsible for drawing the order in question.

D1–171 10.7 CDPD 8 contains further provisions about orders.

Proceedings after judgment

D1–172 10.8 RSC Order 44 still regulates proceedings under judgments and orders in the Chancery Division.

Directions

D1–173 10.9 Where a judgment or order directs further proceedings, such as accounts or inquiries, it will often give directions as to how the accounts and inquiries are to be conducted, for example:

For accounts

(a) who is to lodge the account and within what period;
(b) within what period objection is to be made;
(c) arrangements for inspection of vouchers or other relevant documents;

For inquiries

(d) whether the inquiry is to proceed on written evidence or with statements of case;
(e) directions for service of such evidence or statements; and
(f) directions as to disclosure.

10.10 If directions are not given in the judgment or order an application should be made to the appropriate Master as soon as possible asking for such directions. The application notice should be made in writing specifying the directions sought. Before making the application, applicants should write to the other parties setting out the directions they seek and inviting their response within 14 days. The application to the Court should not be made until after the expiry of that period unless there is some special urgency. The application must state that the other parties have been consulted and have attached to it copies of the applicant's letter to the other parties and of any response from them. The Master will then consider what directions are appropriate. In complex cases he or she may direct a case management conference. **D1–174**

10.11 If any inquiry is estimated to last more than two days and involves very large sums of money or strongly contested issues of fact or difficult points of law, the Master may direct that it be taken by a Judge. Accounts, however long they are estimated to take, will be taken before the Master. **D1–175**

CHAPTER 11

COSTS

Key Rules: CPR Parts 43 to 48 and the PD supplementing them **D1–176**

11.1 There are important new provisions on costs in the CPR, particularly with respect to: **D1–176A**

(1) *Informing the client of costs orders:* solicitors now have a duty to tell their clients, within 7 days, if an order for costs is made against them and they were not present at the hearing. Solicitors must also tell anyone else who has instructed them to act on the case or who is liable to pay their fees. They must inform these persons how the order came to be made (CPR rule 44.2; PD relating to CPR Part 44, para. 1).

(2) *Providing the Court with estimates of costs:* the Court can now order a party to file an estimate of costs and to serve it on the other parties. (PD supplementing CPR Part 43, para. 4.) This is to assist the Court in deciding what case management orders to make and also to inform other parties as to their potential liability for costs. In addition parties must file estimates of costs when they file their allocation questionnaire or listing questionnaire (PD relating to CPR Part 43, para. 4.5).

(3) *Summary assessment of costs:* there are new provisions about this, and an outline is given below. The new provisions mean that in many short cases the Court will now decide, at the end of the hearing, not only who is to pay the costs but also how much those costs should be. As a result the paying party may well have to pay the costs at a much earlier stage than before.

Summary assessment

11.2 When the Court orders a party to pay costs, the Court will in some circumstances make a summary assessment of those costs. In that event, detailed assessment of the costs by a costs Judge is unnecessary. For the detailed rules on summary assessment, see CPR rule 44.7 and the PD relating to CPR Part 44, paras 4.3–4.10, from which this outline is derived. **D1–177**

11.3 The Court will generally make a summary assessment of costs whenever the hearing lasts for less than one day. The Court that heard the application carries out the summary assessment. But the Court may decide not to assess costs summarily, for example because it orders the costs to be "costs in the case". **D1–178**

11.4 In order that the Court can assess costs summarily at the end of the hearing each party who intends to claim costs must, no later than 24 hours before the time fixed for the hearing, serve on the other party, and file with the Court, his or her statement of costs. Paragraph 4.5 of the PD relating to CPR Part 44 contains requirements about the information to be included in this statement, and the form of the statement. **D1–179**

11.5 Where the *receiving* party (the party to whom the costs are to be paid) is legally aided, the Court cannot assess costs summarily. But it is not prevented from assessing costs summarily by the fact that the *paying* party (the party by whom the costs are to be paid) is legally aided. A summary assessment of costs payable by an assisted person is not by itself a determination of the assisted person's liability to pay those costs (as to which see section 17 of the Legal Aid Act 1988). **D1–180**

11.6 The amount of costs to be paid by one person to another can be determined on the standard basis or the indemnity basis. The basis to be used is determined when the Court decides that a person should pay the costs of another. The usual basis is the standard basis. Costs that are unreasonably incurred or are unreasonable in amount are not allowed on either basis. **D1–181**

11.7 On the standard basis the Court only allows costs which are proportionate to the matters in issue. If it has any doubt as to whether the costs were reasonably incurred or reasonable and proportionate in amount, it resolves the doubt in favour of the *paying* party. **D1–182**

11.8 On the indemnity basis the Court resolves any doubt it may have as to whether the costs were reasonably incurred or were reasonable in amount in favour of the *receiving* party. **D1–183**

11.9 The Court must take into account all the circumstances, including the parties' conduct and the other matters mentioned in CPR rule 44.5. **D1–184**

11.10 A party must normally pay the costs awarded against him or her and summarily assessed within 14 days of the assessment. But the Court can extend that time (CPR rule 44.8, 3.1(2)(a)). The Court may therefore direct payment by instalment, or defer the liability to pay costs until the **D1–185** end of the proceedings so that the costs can then be set against any costs or judgment to which the paying party then becomes entitled.

D1–186 11.11 If the parties have agreed the amount of costs, they do not need to file a statement of the costs, and summary assessment is unnecessary.

Conditional fee agreements

D1–187 11.12 The Court should be informed, on any application for the payment of costs, if any party has entered into a conditional fee agreement. The Court can then consider whether, in the light of that agreement, to stay the payment of any costs which have been summarily assessed until the end of the action, or to decline to order the payment of costs on account under CPR rule 44.3(8).

Other provisions

D1–188 11.13 CPR Part 45 to 48, and the PDs relating to them, contain provisions regarding:

(1) special cases in which costs are payable (for example where the receiving party is a litigant in person);

(2) wasted costs;

(3) fixed costs (these are payable for instance if judgment for a sum of money is given in default); and

(4) detailed assessment.

CHAPTER 12

DISTRICT REGISTRIES

D1–189 12.1 A substantial number of Chancery cases are heard in the District Registries. Chancery Judges sit regularly in Birmingham, Bristol, Cardiff, Leeds, Liverpool, Manchester and Newcastle upon Tyne, and occasionally in Preston. Details of the arrangements for hearing cases in the District Registries are set out in CDPD 2.

D1–190 12.2 Outside London, the County Courts have exclusive jurisdiction in bankruptcy and proceedings in bankruptcy cannot therefore be brought in the District Registries.

CHAPTER 13

COUNTY COURTS

D1–191 *Key Rules: CPR Part 30; PD supplementing CPR Part 7 para. 2*

Unified procedure

D1–191A 13.1 A key feature of the civil justice reforms is the introduction of a unified procedure for the High Court and the County Court. The procedure to be followed in both courts is therefore the same.

Transfer to the County Court

D1–192 13.2 Any case which does not require to be heard by a High Court Judge, and falls within the jurisdiction of the County Court, may be transferred to the County Court.

D1–193 13.3 The jurisdiction of the County Court is set out in the High Court and County Court Jurisdiction Order 1991 as amended, and in enactments amended by that Order.

D1–194 13.4 The jurisdiction of the High Court to transfer cases to the County Court is contained in the County Courts Act 1984, section 40, as substituted by the Courts and Legal Services Act 1990, section 2(1). Under that section, the Court has jurisdiction in certain circumstances to strike out actions which ought to have been begun in the County Court.

D1–195 13.5 A claim with an estimated value of less than £50,000 will generally be transferred to a County Court, if the County Court has jurisdiction, unless it is either within a specialist list or is within the criteria of Article 7(5) of the High Court and County Court Jurisdiction Order 1991.

D1–196 13.6 If the case is one of a specifically Chancery nature a transfer from the Royal Courts of Justice will ordinarily be to the Central London County Court (Chancery List) ("the CLCC") where cases are heard by specialist Chancery Circuit Judges or recorders and a continuous Chancery List is maintained, unless the parties prefer a transfer to a local County Court.

D1–197 13.7 Even where the estimated value of the claim is more than £50,000 transfer to the CLCC may still be ordered if the criteria in Article 7(5) point in that direction, in particular having regard to the criteria in Article 7(5)(c), namely the complexity of the facts, legal issues, remedies or procedures involved.

D1–198 13.8 If a claim is transferred to the County Court at the allocation stage no other directions will usually be given and all case management will be left to the County Court.

D1–199 13.9 The Chancery List at the CLCC is managed by the Business Chancery & Patents Section at 26 Park Crescent W1. The telephone number of the section manager is 0171 917 7821. A guide to the Chancery List may be obtained from the section manager.

D1–200 13.10 As an alternative to starting the case in the Chancery Division and transferring to the

CLCC a case (if appropriate to be started there) may be started at the CLCC and a request made there for it to be transferred to the Chancery List. The request will receive judicial consideration and a transfer will be made if appropriate.

Patents County Court

13.11 See Chapter 23 below. **D1–201**

CHAPTER 14

USE OF INFORMATION TECHNOLOGY

Key Rules: CPR rule 1.4, CPR Part 6; PD supplementing CPR Part 6 **D1–202**

General

14.1 The CPR contains certain provisions about the use of information technology in the conduct of cases. Apart from these provisions, no standard practice has evolved or been prescribed for the use of information technology in civil cases, but it is possible to identify certain areas in which electronic techniques may be used which should encourage the efficient and economical conduct of litigation. **D1–202A**

14.2 It must be remembered, however, that it is unlikely that the number of litigants in person will diminish, and the number may well increase, in the future and that not all solicitors have available sophisticated IT facilities. Use of IT is acceptable only if no party to the case will be unfairly prejudiced and its use will save time or money. **D1–203**

14.3 A number of specific applications of information technology have been well worked out since the last edition of the Chancery Guide. The use of fax, the provision of skeleton arguments on disk, and daily transcripts on disk (with or without appropriate software) have become commonplace. Taking evidence by video link has become more common, and the available technology has improved considerably. There is still little experience of the intensive use of information technology in the ordinary course of the trial by, for example, providing documents as images to be displayed. **D1–204**

14.4 In any case in which it is proposed to use information technology in the preparation, management and presentation of a case in a manner which is not provided for by the CPR, it may be necessary for directions to be given by the Judge who is to hear the case. It is unlikely to be satisfactory for parties and their solicitors to agree to a particular application of information technology (as for example using imaging techniques to deal with disclosure) without the agreement of the Judge. Accordingly it is likely, particularly in heavy cases, that it will be desirable for a Judge to be nominated to conduct the case. Where a nomination is desired, application should be made to the Vice Chancellor in writing by letter addressed to his clerk for a Judge to be nominated. **D1–205**

14.5 In every case in which it is proposed to use information technology, the first step will be for the solicitors for all parties to determine whether it is possible to establish a common protocol for the electronic exchange and management of information. It is recommended that the protocol provided by the Official Referees Solicitors Association ("ORSA") be used. The ORSA protocol is comprehensive and has had success in the Technology and Construction Court. **D1–206**

14.6 It is expected that those Judges of the Chancery Division who use computers will be equipped with IBM compatible 486/Pentium machines using W95 or W98 and Word 6 for Windows. Any other requirements (spreadsheets and the like) must first be discussed with the clerk to the Judge concerned. **D1–205**

Provision of information on disk

(1) Skeleton arguments etc.

14.7 Skeleton arguments, chronologies, witness statements, experts' reports and other documents (if available in electronic form) should be provided on disk if the Judge requests this. Inquiries should be made of the Judge's clerk for this purpose. Disks provided to Judges must be checked for virus contamination and be clean. **D1–206**

(2) Transcripts

14.8 The various shorthand writers provide a number of different transcript services. These range from an immediately displayed transcript which follows the evidence as it is given (usually with about 10 seconds' delay) to provision of transcripts of a day's proceedings one or two days in arrears. The use of transcripts is always of assistance if they can be justified on the ground of cost and in long cases they are a considerable advantage. If an instantaneous service is proposed, inquiries should be made of the Judge's clerk and sufficient time for the installation of the equipment necessary and for any education of the Judge should be found. If special transcript-handling software is to be used by the parties, consideration should be given to making the software available to the Judge. **D1–207**

D1–208 14.9 If the shorthand writers make disks available (and nearly all do) the Judge should be provided with disks as they appear if he or she requires them.

Fax communications

D1–209 14.10 The use of fax in the service of documents is now authorised by CPR rule 6.2(1) and the PD supplementing CPR Part 6.

D1–210 14.11 Each of the Judges sitting in the Chancery Division may be reached by fax if the occasion warrants it. The fax number for communication with a particular Judge should be obtained from the Judge's clerk. Where the name of the Judge is not known, short documents may be sent to the listing office, whose fax number is given in Appendix 6. Written evidence should not be sent by fax to this number. ALL FAX MESSAGES SHOULD HAVE A COVER SHEET SETTING OUT THE NAME OF THE CASE, THE CASE NUMBER AND THE JUDGE'S NAME, IF KNOWN.

Evidence by video-link

D1–211 14.12 The Court may allow evidence to be taken using video-link: CPR rule 32.3. Experience has shown that normally taking evidence by this means is comparatively straightforward.

D1–212 14.13 Applications for permission to adduce evidence by video-link should be made as early in the proceedings as possible, and at least by the PTR.

D1–213 14.14 A protocol has been prepared as a guide to all persons who are involved in the use of video-conferencing equipment in civil proceedings in the High Court. It covers its use in courtrooms where the equipment may be installed, and also the situation where the Court assembles in a commercial studio or conference room containing video-conferencing equipment. Copies of the protocol (known as the Video-conferencing Protocol) may be obtained from the Bar Council. A charge of £2.50 will be made to cover expenses.

CHAPTER 15

MISCELLANEOUS MATTERS

D1–214 *Key Rules: CPR Parts 25 and 39; PD—Miscellaneous Provisions relating to Hearings supplementing CPR Part 39*

Litigants in person

D1–214A 15.1 The provisions of this Guide in general apply to litigants in person. Thus, for example, litigants in person should unless they have good reason for not doing so:

(1) prepare a written summary of their argument in the same circumstances as those in which a represented party is required to produce a skeleton argument;

(2) prepare a bundle of documents in the same way that a represented party is required to produce a bundle of documents; and

(3) be prepared to put forward their argument within a limited time if they are directed to do so by the Court.

D1–215 15.2 This means that litigants in person should identify in advance of the hearing those points which they consider to be their strongest points, and that they should put those points at the forefront of their oral and written submissions to the Court.

D1–216 15.3 It is not the function of Court officials to give legal advice. However, subject to that, they will do their best to assist any litigant. Litigants in person who need further assistance should consult a law centre, solicitor or the Citizens Advice Bureau. There is a Citizens Advice Bureau in the Main Entrance Hall of the Royal Courts of Justice.

D1–217 15.4 Where a litigant in person is the applicant, the Court may ask one of the represented parties to open the matter briefly and impartially, and to summarise the issues.

D1–218 15.5 It is the duty of an advocate to ensure that the Court is informed of all relevant decisions and enactments of which the advocate is aware (whether favourable or not to his or her case) and to draw the Court's attention to any material irregularity.

D1–219 15.6 Representatives for other parties must treat litigants in person with consideration. They should where possible be given photocopies of any authorities which are to be cited before the case starts in addition to the skeleton argument. They should be asked to give their names to the usher if they have not already done so. Representativs for other parties should explain the Court's order after the hearing if the litigant in person does not appear to understand it.

D1–220 15.7 If a litigant in person wishes to give oral evidence he or she will generally be required to do so from the witness box in the same manner as any other witness of fact.

D1–221 15.8 A litigant in person must give an address for service in England or Wales. If he or she is a claimant, the address will be in the claim form or other document by which the proceedings are brought. If he or she is a defendant, it will be in the acknowledgment of service form which he or she must send to the Court on being served with the proceedings. It is essential that any change of address should be notified in writing to Chancery Chambers and to all other parties to the case. Notice of hearing dates will be given by post to litigants at the address shown in the Court file. A litigant in person will generally be given a fixed date for trial on application. A litigant in person who wishes to apply for a fixed date should ask the Listing Office for a copy of its Guidance Notes for Litigants in Person.

15.9 Litigants in person may use the Supreme Court Library in the Queen's Building at the discretion of the Librarian. **D1–222**

Representation on behalf of companies

15.10 CPR rule 39.6 allows a company or other corporation to be represented at trial by an employee if the employee has been authorised by the company or corporation to appear on its behalf and the Court gives permission. **D1–223**

Out of hours emergency arrangements

15.11 An application should not be made out of hours unless it is essential. An explanation will be required as to why it was not made or could not be made during normal court hours. Applications made during legal vacations must also constitute vacation business. **D1–224**

15.12 There is always a Chancery Judge available to hear urgent out of hours applications. The following is a summary of the procedure: **D1–225**

(1) All requests for the Duty Chancery Judge to hear urgent matters are to be made through the Judge's clerk. There may be occasions when the Duty Judge is not immediately available. The clerk will be able to inform the applicant of the Judge's likely availability.

(2) Initial contact should be through the Security Office at the Royal Courts of Justice, who should be requested to contact the Duty Chancery Judge's clerk. The applicant must give a telephone number for the return call.

(3) When the clerk contacts the applicant, he or she will need to know:
- (a) the name of the party on whose behalf the application is to be made;
- (b) the name of the person who is to make the application;
- (c) the nature of the application;
- (d) the degree of urgency;
- (e) the contact telephone numbers.

(5) The Duty Judge will indicate to his or her clerk whether he or she is prepared to deal with the matter by telephone or whether it will be necessary for the matter to be dealt with in court. The clerk will inform the applicant and make the necessary arrangements. Applications for interim remedies will be heard by telephone only where the applicant is represented by counsel or solicitors (PD—Interim Injunctions supplementing CPR Part 25).

15.13 The Judges who will in appropriate cases hear out of hours applications vary according to when the application is made. **D1–226**

(1) *Weekdays.* Out of hours duty, during term time, is the responsibility of the Applications Judge. He or she is normally available from 4.15 p.m. until 10.15 a.m. Monday to Thursday.

(2) *Weekends.* A Chancery Division Judge is nominated by rota for weekends, commencing 4.15 p.m. Friday until 10.15 a.m. Monday.

(3) *Vacation.* The Vacation Judge also undertakes out of hours applications.

15.14 **Sealing orders out of hours.** In normal circumstances it will not be possible to issue a sealed order out of hours. The Judge may direct the applicant to lodge a draft of the order made, with the Orders and Accounts Section Office by 10.00 a.m. on the following working day. **D1–227**

15.15 **County Court matters.** Similar arrangements exist for making urgent applications out of hours in County Court matters in certain parts of England and Wales. Contact with the Circuit Judge on duty for the London County Courts can be made through the Security Office of the Royal Courts of Justice. **D1–228**

Vacation arrangements

15.16 There is a Chancery Judge available to hear applications in vacatiion. Applications must generally constitute vacation business in that, in particular, they require to be immediately or promptly heard. Special arrangements however exist in the Companies Court for certain schemes of arrangement and reductions of capital to be heard in the Long Vacation (see para. 8 of the PD—Applications under the Companies Act 1985 supplementing CPR Part 49). **D1–229**

15.17 In the Long Vacation, the Vacation Judge sits each day to hear vacation business. In other vacations there are no regular sittings. Mondays and Thursdays are made available for urgent interim applications on notice. The Judge is available on the remaining days for urgent business. **D1–230**

15.18 There is no distinction between term time and vacation so far as business before the Chancery Masters is concerned. They will deal with all types of business throughout the year, and when a Master is on holiday, his or her list will normally be taken by a deputy Master. **D1–231**

CHAPTER 16

SUGGESTIONS FOR IMPROVEMENT AND COURT USERS' COMMITTEES

16.1 Suggestions for improvements in this Guide or in the practice or procedure of the **D1–232**

Chancery Division are welcome. If they do not fall within the remit of the committees mentioned below, they should be sent to the Clerk to the Vice Chancellor.

Insolvency Court Users' Committee

D1–233 16.2 Proposals for change in insolvency matters fall within the remit of the Insolvency Court Users' Committee unless they relate to the Insolvency Rules 1986. The members of the Insolvency Court Users' Committee include members of the Bar, the Law Society, the Insolvency Service and the Society of Practitioners of Insolvency. Meetings of this committee are called when appropriate.

Insolvency Rules Committee

D1–234 16.3 The Insolvency Rules 1986 can only be changed by the Lord Chancellor with the concurrence of the Secretary of State for Trade and Indutry. The Insolvency Rules Committee must be consulted before any changes to the Rules are made. The Chairman of the Insolvency Rules Committee is Mr Justice Evans-Lombe. Proposals for changes in the Rules should be sent to The Insolvency Service, Room 502, PO Box 203, 21 Bloomsbury Street, London WC1B 3QW, with a copy to the Clerk to Mr Justice Evans-Lombe.

Intellectual Property Court Users' Committee

D1–235 16.4 This considers the problem and concerns of intellectual property litigation generally. Membership of the committee includes the principal Patent Judges, a representative of each of the Patent Bar Association, the Intellectual Property Lawyers Association, the Chartered Institute of Patent Agents, the Institute of Trade Mark Agents and the Trade Marks Designs and Patents Federation. It will also include one or more other Chancery Judges. The Chairman is Mr Justice Laddie. Anyone having views concerning the improvement of intellectual property litigation is invited to make his or her views known to the committee, preferably through the relevant professional representative on the committee.

Pension Litigation Court Users' Committee

D1–236 16.5 This consists of a Judge and a Master, two barristers and two solicitors. Its Chairman is Mr Justice Lloyd. Any suggestions for consideration by the committee should be sent to the Clerk to Mr Justice Lloyd.

CHAPTER 17

ALTERNATIVE DISPUTE RESOLUTION

D1–237 *Key Rules: CPR rules 3.1 and 26.4*

D1–237A 17.1 While emphasising the primary role of the Court as a forum for deciding cases, the Court encourages parties to consider the use of ADR (such as, but not confined to, mediation and conciliation) as a possible means of resolving disputes or particular issues.

D1–238 17.2 The settlement of disputes by means of ADR can:

(a) significantly help litigants to save costs;

(b) save litigants the delay of litigation in reaching finality in their disputes;

(c) enable litigants to achieve settlement of their disputes while preserving their existing commercial relationships and market reputation;

(d) provide litigants with a wider range of solutions than those offered by litigation; and

(e) make a substantial contribution to the more efficient use of judicial resources.

D1–239 17.3 The Court will in an appropriate case invite the parties to consider whether their dispute, or particular issues in it, could be resolved through ADR. The Court may also adjourn the case for a specified period of time to encourage and enable the parties to use ADR and for this purpose extend the time for compliance by the parties or any of them with any requirement under the CPR or this Guide or order of the Court. The Court may make such order as to the costs that the parties may incur by reason of the adjournment or their using or attempting to use ADR as may in all the circumstances seem appropriate.

D1–240 17.4 Legal representatives in all cases should consider with their clients and the other parties concerned the possibility of attempting to resolve the dispute or particular issues by ADR and they should ensure that their clients are fully informed as to the most cost effective means of resolving their dispute.

D1–241 17.5 Parties who consider that ADR might be an appropriate means of resolving their dispute, or particular issues in the dispute, may apply for directions at any stage.

D1–242 17.6 The Clerk to the Commercial Court keeps some published information as to individuals and bodies that offer ADR services. (The list also includes individuals and bodies that offer arbitration services.) If the parties are unable to agree upon a neutral individual, or panel of individuals, for ADR, they may refer to the Judge for assistance.

SECTION B

SPECIALIST WORK

CHAPTER 18

INTRODUCTION TO THE SPECIALIST WORK OF THE CHANCERY DIVISION

Key Rules: RSC Orders 88, 91, 93, 96, 97, 99, 106, 108 (see CPR Schedule 1); PD supplementing CPR Part 49—Commercial Court D1–243

18.1 As explained in Chapter 2 of this Guide, some proceedings in the High Court must be brought in the Chancery Division. These matters include: D1–243A
(a) the sale, exchange or partition of land, or the raising of charges on land;
(b) mortgage claims;
(c) the execution of trusts;
(d) the administration of the estates of deceased persons;
(e) bankruptcy;
(f) the dissolution of partnerships or the taking of partnership or other accounts;
(g) the rectification, setting aside or cancellation of deeds or other instruments in writing;
(h) contentious probate business;
(i) patents, trade marks, registered designs, copyright or design right;
(j) the appointment of a guardian of a minor's estate;
(k) jurisdiction under the Companies Act 1985 and the Insolvency Act 1986 relating to companies;
(l) some revenue matters;
(m) charities;
(n) some proceedings under the Solicitors Act 1974;
(o) proceedings under the Landlord and Tenant Acts 1927 (Part I), 1954 (Part II) and the Leasehold Reform Act 1967; and
(p) proceedings under other miscellaneous statutory jurisdictions.

18.2 There is a concurrent jurisdiction with the Family Division under the Inheritance (Provision for Family and Dependants) Act 1975. D1–244

18.3 Certain appeals lie to the Chancery Division including those from the Pensions Ombudsman, the Charity Commissioners, the Commons Commissioners, the Chief Land Registrar and many Revenue appeals. D1–245

18.4 The Chancery Judges are the nominated Judges of the Court of Protection but this Guide does not deal with the Court of Protection. D1–246

Commercial claims

18.5 Where a "commercial claim", within the meaning of paragraph 1.2 of the PD—Commercial Court supplementing CPR Part 49, is brought in the Chancery Division, the Court will in general and to the extent that it is consistent with the CPR and the relative Practice Directions, adopt the same practice as the Commercial Court. However, case management in such cases will usually be carried out by the Masters. D1–247

CHAPTER 19

THE BANKRUPTCY COURT

Key Rules: PD—Insolvency Proceedings; Insolvency Rules D1–248

19.1 The Bankruptcy Court is part of the Chancery Division. D1–248A

19.2 The procedure in the Bankruptcy Court is governed by the Insolvency Rules and the PD—Insolvency Proceedings. D1–248B

19.3 Proceedings in the Bankruptcy Court are issued in the Bankruptcy Issue and Search Room and they are dealt with by the Registrars in Bankruptcy, not the Masters. D1–249

19.4 The following publications regarding practice and procedure in the Bankruptcy Court are available free from the Bankruptcy Issue and Search Room and from Room 1.10 Thomas More Building, Royal Courts of Justice: D1–250
(a) Current Practice Direction and Practice Notes;
(b) A concise Guide to procedure in the Bankruptcy Court;

(c) *"I want to set aside my statutory demand—what do I do?"*
(d) *"I have a petition against me—what do I do?"*
(e) *"I want to appeal an order made by a District Judge or an order made by a Bankruptcy Registrar of the High Court—what can I do?"*
(f) *"I wish to apply for my Certificate of Discharge from Bankruptcy—what do I do?"*

CHAPTER 20

THE COMPANIES COURT

D1–251 *Key Rules: PD—Applications under the Companies Act 1985 supplementing CPR Part 49; PD—Insolvency; Insolvency Rules*

D1–251A 20.1 The Companies Court is a part of the Chancery Division. Applications in the High Court under the Companies Act 1985, the Insurance Companies Act 1982, the Insolvency Act 1986 in relation to companies registered in England and Wales, and the Company Directors Disqualification Act 1986, must be commenced in the Companies Court. There are many kinds of application brought in the Companies Court.

D1–252 20.2 Applications, other than in insolvency, are governed by the Civil Procedure Rules and PD—Applications under the Companies Act 1985, supplementing CPR Part 49.

D1–253 20.3 Applications in insolvency relating to companies are governed by the Insolvency Rules and PD—Insolvency.

D1–254 20.4 The Companies Court has a separate administrative procedure. Proceedings are issued in the Companies Court General Office, and they are dealt with by the Registrars attached to that Court or the Bankruptcy Court.

D1–255 20.5 Unopposed petitions for winding up, petitions for confirmation by the Court of reduction of capital, and interim applications for directions in proceedings by shareholders are among the principal matters heard by the Registrar of the Companies Court. The Registrar may direct that any case be heard by a Judge even if it is a kind of application which would normally be heard by him or her.

D1–256 20.6 Certain matters such as petitions for an administration order under Part II of the Insolvency Act 1986, petitions for approval by the Court of schemes of arrangement and applications for the appointment of provisional liquidators are heard by a Judge. Applications to be heard by the Companies Court Judge are generally listed for hearing on a Monday morning. The Judge will then determine the order in which he or she will hear the applications and may direct that they be heard later in the week. There is a Judge available to hear Companies matters each day in term time.

D1–257 20.7 Proceedings to wind up a company are commenced by presenting a petition to the Court. The presentation of a winding up petition can cause substantial damage to a company. A winding up petition should not be presented when it is known that a debt is disputed in good faith. Practitioners should make reasonable enquiries from their client as to the existence of any such dispute. The Court may order a petitioner to pay the company's costs of a petition based on a disputed debt on the indemnity basis.

Winding-up petitions

D1–258 20.8 When a winding up petition is presented to either the Companies Court, a Chancery District Registry or a County Court having jurisdiction, particulars including the name of the company and the petitioner's solicitors are entered in a computerised register. This is called the Central Registry of Winding Up Petitions. It may be searched by telephone on 0171 936 7328.

D1–259 20.9 If an order is made restraining advertisement while an application is made to the Court to stop the proceedings, the case is listed in the Daily Cause List by number only so that the name of the company is not given.

Proceedings for relief from unfairly prejudicial conduct under the Companies Act 1985, s.459

D1–260 20.10 Cases under the Companies Act 1985, s.459, are often liable to involve extensive factual enquiry and many of the measures summarised in Section A of this Guide which are designed to avoid unnecessary cost and delay are particularly relevant to them.

D1–261 20.11 Where applications are brought in the Companies Court and in a related case in the Chancery Division at the same time, special arrangements can be made on request to the Listing Officer for the applications to be heard by the same Judge.

D1–262 20.12 Inspection of the Court file in any insolvency proceedings is governed by Insolvency Rule 7.31.

D1–263 20.13 The following leaflets are available from the Companies Court General Office:
(a) Current Practice Directions and Practice Notes;

(b) *"I want to wind up a company: what do I do?"*
(c) *"I want to restore a company's name to the Register: what do I do?"*
(d) *"I want to extend time for registration of a charge or to rectify a mis-statement or omission in the registered particulars of a charge or of a memorandum of satisfaction: what do I do?"*

CHAPTER 21

MORTGAGE CLAIMS

Key Rules: RSC Order 88 (see CPR Schedule 1); PD supplementing CPR Part 8 (Part 8(B)) **D1–264**

21.1 In Greater London the High Court has concurrent jurisdiction with the County Court in mortgage possession claims for dwelling houses, and such claims are assigned to the Chancery Division. Lenders may take block bookings of such claims, timed at 12 an hour (or six a half-hour) and may book a whole day (or two whole days) at a time. This enables them to bring all their possession claims for Greater London at one time and place. This is not only beneficial to the lenders but is also likely to reduce the costs of the proceedings and therefore also benefit the borrowers. **D1–264A**

21.2 These claims are still subject to the special provisions of RSC Order 88. The effect of these is that not only is it impossible to obtain judgment in default, but it is also impossible to obtain judgment on a paper application. Even if (as is usually the case) the borrower fails to take any active part in the proceedings at all, judgment can only be obtained at a hearing of which notice has been given to the defendant. **D1–265**

21.3 Claimants must use the Part 8 claim form. If it is known that there is a dispute of fact (*e.g.* where a mortgagor is claiming that he or she is not bound by a mortgage purportedly executed by him or her because the signature is a forgery or was obtained by undue influence) an ordinary CPR Part 7 claim form can be used. **D1–266**

21.4 By CPR rule 8.5 the claimant's evidence in support of the claim must be filed and served at the same time as the claim form. On the other hand RSC Order 88, rule 4(2) provides that in a case where a defendant has failed to acknowledge service the claimant must serve a notice of appointment upon him not less than four clear days before the day fixed for the first hearing of the claim together with a copy of the witness statement or affidavit in support of the claim. In order to avoid unnecessary duplication of service of evidence and to reduce costs it will generally be considered sufficient if the claimant does not serve his evidence with the claim form but serves it with the notice of appointment; and this is so whether or not a defendant has acknowledged service. The Court will usually fix a date for the hearing at the same time as it issues the claim form. **D1–267**

21.5 By RSC Order 88, rule 5 where there is a claim for payment of the mortgage debt, this evidence in support must state **D1–268**

(a) the amount of the advance and the amount and dates of any periodic repayments and interest and a daily rate for interest;
(b) the amount which would have to be paid in order to redeem the mortgage at the date of commencement of the proceedings and at a stated date not more than 14 days after the date of commencement of the proceedings, specifying the amount of the solicitor's costs and administrative charges that will be payable, and
(c) the dates between which a particular rate of interest applied, the number of days in that period, and the capital on which the interest was calculated.

However compliance with (b) is only necessary if it appears that the borrower is seeking to refinance the loan and compliance with (c) may exceptionally be waived if it appears right to do so having regard to the cost and difficulty of compliance, unless the borrower requires compliance.

21.6 In claims for possession the requirements of RSC Order 88, rule 5(3) and (4) must be complied with strictly. In particular it is essential that particulars of every person who to the best of the claimant's knowledge is in occupation are given and no possession order will be made if with this requirement is not complied with. If someone other than the defendant is known to be in occupation a possession order will not be made unless this person has been given notice of the hearing. Although under CPR rule 8.5 a defendant who wishes to rely on written evidence is required to file and serve evidence in answer, the great majority of defendants are litigants in person and do not put in evidence but, if they take any active part in the proceedings, simply turn up at the hearing. The Master will consider their oral representations made at the hearing. **D1–269**

21.7 Because defendants normally do not file acknowledgments of service or put in evidence but an oral hearing is nonetheless necessary in all cases, the Masters give no preliminary consideration to mortgage possession cases when the time for acknowledging service has expired. The claimant should therefore take an appointment of sufficient length before the Master for the hearing of the claim as soon as the claim form has been served. Some points of detail relating to mortgages and possession claims are referred to in CPR rule 16.8 and in the PD supplementing CPR Part 16. **D1–270**

21.8 Outside Greater London the County Court has exclusive jurisdiction in mortgage possession cases relating to dwelling houses. **D1–271**

21.9 CDPD 7 contains further provisions about mortgages and possession orders. **D1–272**

CHAPTER 22

PARTNERSHIP ACTIONS AND RECEIVERS

D1–273 *Key Practice Directions: PDs supplementing CPR Parts 24 and 40*

Partnership actions

D1–273A 22.1 In actions for or arising out of the dissolution of a partnership often the only matters in dispute between the partners are matters of accounting. In such cases there will be no trial of the action. The Court will, if appropriate, make a summary order under paragraph 6 of the PD supplementing CPR Part 24 for the taking of an account. This will be taken before the Master.

D1–274 22.2 Only if there is a dispute as to the existence of a partnership (whether it is claimed that there never was a partnership or that the partnership is still continuing and has not been dissolved) or if there is a material dispute as to the terms of the partnership (*e.g.* as to the profit sharing ratios) will there be a trial, at which the Judge will decide those issues. In such cases there will be a two stage procedure with the Judge deciding these issues at the trial and ordering the winding up of the partnership which will involve the taking of the partnership accounts by the Master (see PD—Accounts, Inquiries etc. supplementing CPR Part 40).

D1–275 22.3 To avoid the expense of such a two stage procedure the parties may agree that disputes as to the terms of the partnership be determined by an inquiry by the Master held at the same time as he or she takes the accounts.

D1–276 22.4 The expense of taking an account in court is usually wholly disproportionate to the amount at stake. Parties are strongly encouraged to refer disputes on accounts to an accountant for determination or mediation. The Master can (whether before or after the reference to the accountant) decide any matters of principle arising on the accounts (*e.g.* the method for valuation of goodwill) or any substantial factual disputes (*e.g.* as to whether a partner has made a particular drawing or not).

D1–277 22.5 The functions of a receiver in a partnership action are limited. It is not his or her duty to wind up the partnership, like the liquidator of a company. His or her primary function is to get in the debts and preserve the assets pending winding up by the Court and he or she has no power of sale without the permission of the Court.

Receivers

D1–278 22.6 Copies of a guide to the procedure relating to receivers appointed by the Court can be obtained from an associate, or, if the order appointing the receiver is made by a Master, from the Master who makes the order.

CHAPTER 23

THE PATENTS COURT AND TRADE MARKS

D1–279 *Key Practice Directions: PD—Patents, etc. supplementing CPR Part 49*

D1–279A 23.1 PD—Patents, etc. supplementing CPR Part 49 deals with its particular procedures. The matters assigned to the Patents Court are essentially all those concerned with patents or registered designs.

D1–280 23.2 The Judges of the Patents Court are nominated by the Lord Chancellor. The following Judges of the Chancery Division are currently nominated:

Mr Justice Ferris
Mr Justice Jacob
Mr Justice Laddie
Mr Justice Neuberger
Mr Justice Pumfrey

There are also a number of senior practitioners who have been appointed to sit as Deputy High Court Judges to hear Patent Court matters.

D1–281 23.3 Mr Justice Laddie is the Judge in charge of the Patents List.

D1–282 23.4 In cases of great urgency, when a nominated Judge or Deputy Judge is not available an application can be made to other Judge of the High Court, preferably a Judge of the Chancery Division.

D1–283 23.5 The procedure of the Patents Court is broadly that of the Chancery Division as a whole, but there are exceptions.

D1–284 23.6 The Patents Court has its own Court Guide which is available from the Clerk in Charge of the Patents Court List (currently Mr Peter Smith, Clerk to Mr Justice Laddie, Room TM 7.02, Royal Court of Justice) and on the Patents Court Website (**www.open.gov.uk/courts/court/highhome.htm**). Although that Guide should be consulted for detailed guidance as to the procedure in the Patents Court, attention is drawn to the following particular matters.

(a) In patent actions proceeding in the Patents Court, dates are fixed by the Clerk in charge of the Patents Court List. It will be possible to fix a date at any time after allocation. A party wishing to apply in a patent matter without notice to the respondent(s) should contact the Clerk in charge of the Patents Court List.

(b) Short applications will normally be listed for hearing at 9.30 a.m. The Court also makes available a two hour slot from 9.00 a.m. to 11.00 a.m. on Tuesday mornings for the hearing and disposition of slightly more lengthy applications. All necessary documents and skeleton arguments must be provided to the Court by not later than 4.00 p.m. on the preceding working day.

(c) The Court's diary can be accessed on its Website. The Patents Court sits in September, in addition to term time.

(d) There are detailed provisions for lodging papers and time estimates with the Judge who is going to hear a patent matter. As far as time estimates are concerned, not only is it necessary, when setting down a patent action, to lodge a certificate stating the estimated length of the trial and an estimate of the time needed for the Judge to read the documents, but a separate time estimate must also be lodged by each party not less than one week before the commencement of the trial. The latter must state the estimated length of oral submissions, examination in chief (if any) and cross-examination.

(e) A simplified trial by written evidence is possible where the parties agree. This procedure is not suitable where cross-examination is likely on any issue of substance nor where any substantial disclosure is needed.

(f) Parties should lodge skeleton arguments in time for the Judge to read them before trial. That should normally be at least two days before commencement.

(g) All applications in a patent matter should be brought directly by application notice before the Patents Court, save that (i) consent orders (ii) orders on applications for extension of time (iii) applications for permission to serve out of the jurisdiction and (iv) applications for security for costs may be heard by a Master.

(h) There is at the moment no Pre-Action Protocol for patent matters.

(i) A general form of order for directions is annexed to the Patents Court Guide.

Patents County Court

23.7 Special provisions relate to the transfer of cases between the Patents Court and the Patents County Court. The Patents Court has no power to order the transfer to it of cases commenced in the Patents County Court which fall within the latter Court's special jurisdiction (*i.e.* matters relating to patents and designs). On the other hand it does have the power to transfer cases commenced in the High Court to the Patents County Court. In deciding whether to order such a transfer, regard must be had to all the circumstances including, in particular, the financial position of the parties and whether either party would be prejudiced by the proceedings continuing in one Court rather than the other. In practice transfers to the Patents County Court are rare. **D1–285**

Trademarks, copyright, design right and passing off

23.8 Proceedings in the High Court under the 1938 and 1994 Trade Marks Acts, the Olympic Symbol Protection Act 1995, the Olympic Association Right (Infringement Proceedings) Regulations 1995, the Copyright, Designs and Patents Act 1988, and for passing off are heard in the Chancery Division. Paragraphs 19 to 26 of the PD—Patents, etc. supplementing CPR Part 49 apply to these proceedings. They will be heard by any Chancery Judge save that in a suitable design right case may be transferred to one of the Patent Judges. **D1–286**

CHAPTER 24

PROBATE ACTIONS

Key Practice Directions: PD—Contentious Probate supplementing CPR Part 49 **D1–287**

24.1 Contentious probate proceedings are specialist proceedings within the meaning of CPR Part 49, and accordingly the CPR apply to them subject to the provisions of the relevant Practice Direction. The relevant Practice Direction is PD 49—Contentious Probate supplementing CPR Part 49. **D1–287A**

24.2 In general, contentious probate proceedings follow the same pattern as an ordinary claim but there are important differences and the PD should be carefully studied. Particular regard should be had to the following: **D1–288**

(1) a defendant must file an acknowledgment of service;

(2) the parties must at the outset of proceedings file affidavits or witness statements of scripts, and lodge the scripts at the Court (Room No. TM 709 Thomas More Building). Compliance with this provision is essential;

(3) the Court will generally ensure that all persons with any potential interest in the proceedings are joined as parties or served with notice under RSC Order 15, rule 13A; and

(4) the proceedings may not be discontinued without permission. Even if they are compromised, it will usually be necessary to have an order stating to whom the grant is to be made, either under paragraph 12 of the PD (leading to a grant in common form), after a trial on written evidence under paragraph 13.1 (leading to a grant in solemn form) or under Section 49 of the Administration of Justice Act 1985 and paragraph 13.2 of the PD (again leading to a grant in solemn form).

D1–289 24.3 CDPD 9 contains further provisions relating to contentious probate actions.

CHAPTER 25

REVENUE PROCEEDINGS

D1–290 *Key Rule: RSC Order 91 (see CPR Schedule 1)*

D1–290A 25.1 Several kinds of revenue proceedings are conducted in the Chancery Division. Usually they have the Inland Revenue on one side and a taxpayer on the other. The main instances are described in the following paragraphs.

Appeals, by the Inland Revenue or the taxpayer, from decisions of the General Commissioners (a first instance tribunal for tax appeals) relating to income tax, corporation tax or capital gains tax

D1–291 25.2 These appeals are conducted on the basis of a case stated, which is a document drawn up by the General Commissioners setting out the facts, the arguments, and the General Commissioners' decision. It is usually backed up by whatever documents were before the General Commissioners. In the Chancery Division these appeals are limited to questions of law. The Judge never hears evidence, and the appeal will almost certainly fail if the appellant's real complaint is that the General Commissioners got the facts wrong. The rules provide that when the party who is appealing from the General Commissioners receives from their clerk the Case Stated in its final form he or she has to transmit it to the High Court within 30 days. Appellants are reminded that the Court has no power to extend this time limit, which must be strictly observed or the Court cannot hear the appeal: *Petch v. Gurney* [1994] S.T.C. 689.

Appeals, by the Inland Revenue or the taxpayer, from decisions of the Special Commissioners (the other first instance tribunal for tax appeals) relating to the same three taxes—income tax, corporation tax and capital gains tax—or to inheritance tax

D1–292 25.3 These appeals are not conducted on the basis of a case stated, but rather on the basis of the Special Commissioners' decision and the papers which they had before them. Those papers may include a transcript of the evidence or the Special Commissioners' notes of the evidence, but, as with appeals from General Commissioners, appeals to the Chancery Division are limited to questions of law. The Judge never hears evidence, and the appeal will almost certainly fail if the appellant's real complaint is that the Special Commissioners got the facts wrong.

D1–293 25.4 Some inheritance tax appeals are exceptions to the normal and do not start before the Special Commissioners, so that the Chancery Division is the Court of first instance. These inheritance tax appeals, which start in the Chancery Division, have to be ones where the issues to be decided are wholly or mainly issues of law and there is no substantial dispute about the facts.

Stamp duty appeals

D1–294 25.5 These start in the Chancery Division, and are conducted on the basis of a case stated drawn up by the Inland Revenue. Usually there is no oral evidence, but there have been a few cases in which there has been.

CHAPTER 26

TRUSTS

D1–295 *Key Rules: RSC Order 85, 15 r.13A (see CPR Schedule 1), CPR Part 39*

Applications under the Variation of Trusts Act 1958

D1–295A 26.1 It will normally be appropriate for an application under the Variation of Trusts Act 1958 to be made by CPR Part 8 claim.

D1–296 26.2 The parties can have the case listed for hearing before a Judge without any preliminary consideration by the Master: see CDPDs 5.B(viii) and 12. The Master will not consider the file without an application.

D1–297 26.3 The application is heard by the Judge in private unless there is a contentious issue (see CPR rule 39.2(f) and the PD supplementing CPR Part 39, para. 1.5(11)).

Trustees' applications for directions

26.4 Applications to the Court by trustees for directions in relation to the administration of the trust are to be brought by Part 8 claim form. RSC Order 85 is relevant. References to trustees in this Chapter of the Guide include, where relevant, personal representatives. D1–298

26.5 If confidentiality of the directions sought is important (for example, where the directions relate to actual or proposed litigation with a third party who could find out what directions the claimants are seeking through access to the claim form under CPR rule 5.4) the statement of the remedy sought, for the purposes of CPR rule 8.2(b), may be expressed in general terms. The claimant must, in that case, state specifically in the application notice or written evidence what it is that he or she seeks to be allowed to do in an application notice or in the evidence, or produce a draft of the order sought. D1–299

26.6 The proceedings will normally be in private: CPR rule 39.2(3)(f). Accordingly the order made, and the other documents among the Court records (save a claim form which has been served), will not be open to inspection by third parties without the Court's permission: CPR rule 5.4(2). D1–300

26.7 RSC Order 85 rule 3(2) deals with the joining of beneficiaries as defendants. If the claimant is in doubt as to which beneficiaries to join as defendants, or whether to give notice to any person under RSC Order 15 rule 13A, he or she may apply to the Court for directions after issue of the claim form, whether or not before serving the claim form on the parties originally joined as defendants. This may be appropriate in a case concerning a pension scheme with many beneficiaries and a number of different categories of interest, especially if they may be differently affected by the action for which directions are sought, or in the case of a private trust with a large class of discretionary beneficiaries. D1–301

Evidence

26.8 Applications for directions whether or not to take or defend or pursue litigation (see *Re Beddoe* [1893] 1 Ch. 547) should be supported by evidence including instructions to, and the advice of, an appropriately qualified lawyer as to the prospects of success and other matters relevant to be taken into account, and a draft of any proposed statement of case. D1–302

26.9 On any such application the evidence should also state (i) whether any relevant Pre-Action Protocol has been followed, and (ii) whether the claimant has proposed or undertaken, or intends to propose, ADR, and (in each case) if not why not. D1–303

26.10 If a beneficiary of the trust is a party to the litigation about which directions are sought, with an interest opposed to that of the trustees, that beneficiary should be a defendant to the trustees' application, but any material which would be privileged as regards that beneficiary in the litigation should be put in evidence by being exhibited to the claimants' affidavit, should not be filed with the Court, and should not be served on the beneficiary, except that if the claimant's representatives consider that no harm would be done by the disclosure of all or some part of the material it should be served on that defendant. That defendant may also be excluded from part of the hearing, including that which is devoted to discussion of the material withheld: see *Re Moritz* [1960] Ch. 251; *Re Eaton* [1964] 1 W.L.R. 1269. D1–304

26.11 If the Court gives directions allowing the claimant to take, defend or pursue litigation it may do so up to a particular stage in the litigation, requiring the trustees, before they carry on beyond that point, to renew their application to the Court. In such a case the Court may sometimes direct that the case be dealt with at that stage without a hearing if the representative or representatives for the beneficiaries write and lodge an opinion stating that he or she or they support the continuation of the directions. Any such opinion will be considered by the Court and, if thought fit, the trustees will be given a direction allowing them to continue pursuing the proceedings without a hearing. D1–305

26.12 In a case of urgency, such as where a limitation period or period for service of proceedings is about to expire, the Court may give directions on a summary consideration of the evidence to cover the steps which need to be taken urgently, but limiting those directions so that the application needs to be renewed for fuller consideration at an early stage. D1–306

Hearing

26.13 In plain cases, the Master may give the directions sought. Otherwise he or she will refer the case to the Judge. D1–307

Applications considered without a hearing

26.14 There may be some cases, or types of case, other than the continuation of directions to trustees as mentioned at paragraph 26.11 above, in which the directions can be given without a hearing. One example is where personal representatives apply to be allowed to distribute the estate of a deceased Lloyd's name, following the decision in *Re Yorke deceased* [1997] 4 All E.R 907 see CDPD 12.9. D1–308

General

26.15 CDPD 12 contains further provisions about trusts. D1–309

SECTION C

CHANCERY DIVISION PRACTICE DIRECTIONS

D1–310 These Chancery Division Practice Directions (CDPDs) govern the practice to be followed in the Chancery Division. Apart from CDPD 5, Listing, they do not apply to the Bankruptcy Court, the Companies Court or the Patents Court which have their own Practice Directions. They apply to claims in District Registries save where inappropriate or where local directions apply.

These directions come into force on 26 April 1999. They replace the Directions printed in Part 2B of Volume 2 of the Supreme Court Practice.

D1–311 **Contents**

CDPD 1 APPEALS

A Contempt of Court: Appeals from Chancery Division

D1–312 Notices of appeal which by RSC, O.59, r.20(1) are required to be served on "the proper officer of the Court from whose order or decision the appeal is brought" may be served on the Chief Master of the Chancery Division and such service may be effected by leaving a copy of the notice of appeal with the Clerk of the Lists in Room W.16, Royal Courts of Justice, Strand, London WC2A 2LL.

B Dismissal by Consent

D1–313 In connection with cases stated on appeal from the Income Tax Commissioners and all appeals from Chancery Masters the Chancery Division adopts the practice of the Court of Appeal for the dismissal of appeals by consent as set out in the notes in RSC, O.59, r.1(15). A document signed by solicitors for all parties must be lodged with the Chancery Listing Office (Room W.15), Royal Courts of Justice, Strand, London WC2A 2LL, requesting dismissal of the appeal. The appeal can be dismissed without any hearing by an order made in the name of the Vice Chancellor. Any orders with directions as to costs will be drawn by the Chancery Associates.

C Masters

D1–314 (i) A litigant who is dissatisfied with a decision of a Master has a right of appeal from the Master to a Judge in chambers under RSC, O.58, r.1. The appeal is brought by a notice of appeal and this is issued out of Room W.15. It is not necessary to state the grounds of appeal. The Appellant opens the appeal, but, even if the appeal is against only part of the Master's order, the whole of the summons is treated as being before the Judge, who will make such order on it as he thinks fit.

(ii) The following documents must be lodged within 5 days after the judgment order or decision appealed against: (a) Two copies of the notice of appeal Form PF 110, containing the following information: (i) the name of the Master against whose decision the appeal is brought (ii) the terms of the order appealed against and the date of the order (iii) the relief sought on the appeal (iv) the name and address of the party issuing the notice of appeal, and the name and address of each party to whom the notice of appeal is addressed, together with their respective telephone numbers and references and (v) if the appeal is out of time and the Master has refused an extension, a request to the Judge to extend the time. (b) A cheque, or postal order or money order, crossed and made payable to HM Paymaster General for the fee of £100. In the case of a litigant in person, cash, a postal order or bankers' draft must be sent. (N.B.: The documents may be lodged by post.)

(iii) An appeal will be treated as having been made at the date and time of the actual receipt of the requisite documents at Chancery Chambers. No acknowledgment will be sent unless this is requested and a stamped addressed envelope is sent for this purpose.

For Listing of Appeals from Masters see CDPD 5.

CDPD 2 HEARINGS BY CHANCERY JUDGES OUT OF LONDON

A

The places at which Chancery Courts normally sit out of London are Birmingham, Bristol, Cardiff, Leeds, Liverpool, Manchester, Newcastle upon Tyne and Preston. Each of these places has a Chancery District Registry. D1–315

There are two Chancery Judges who have been appointed to supervise the arrangements for the hearing of Chancery cases out of London. Mr Justice Jacob is currently the Chancery Supervising Judge for Birmingham, Bristol and Cardiff and is concerned with Chancery hearings on the Western, Wales and Chester, and Midland and Oxford Circuits. Mr Justice Blackburne, as Vice Chancellor of the County Palatine of Lancaster, is concerned with Chancery hearings for the Northern and North Eastern Circuits. Both High Court Judges regularly take substantial Chancery matters for hearing outside London. Mr Justice Blackburne sits regularly in Manchester, Liverpool, Leeds and Newcastle and (as business may require) in Preston. If appropriate he will also sit at other court centres on the two circuits (*e.g.* Carlisle, Durham, Lancaster and Sheffield).

There are Specialist Circuit Judges who have the authority to exercise the powers of a Judge of the Chancery Division and who normally sit out of London. They exercise a general Chancery jurisdiction, subject to exceptions. Those exceptions are proceedings directly concerning revenue; proceedings before the Patents Court constituted as part of the Chancery Division under s.96 of the Patents Act 1977.

Arrangements can be made for other Judges of the Chancery Division (or a deputy High Court Judge) to hear cases at one of the above principal court centres, either where the case is proceeding in the District Registry but pressure on local judicial manpower calls for outside assistance, or where the case is proceeding in the Central Registry but circumstances make it appropriate that the case be tried at an out of London court centre.

Currently the Circuit Judges who sit regularly in Chancery out of London are:

His Honour Judge Weeks Q.C. (Bristol)
His Honour Judge Boggis Q.C. (Birmingham)

His Honour Judge Moseley Q.C. (Cardiff)
His Honour Judge Howarth (Manchester and Liverpool)
His Honour Judge Maddocks (Manchester and Liverpool)
His Honour Judge Behrens (Leeds and Newcastle)

Judge Howarth and Judge Maddocks also hear Preston cases but take them in either Manchester or Liverpool. Judge Cooke and Judge Gilliland Q.C. (who normally sits in Salford hearing Technology and Construction cases) also assist in the disposal of Chancery business on the Northern and North Eastern Circuits.

In addition certain other Circuit Judges are authorised to take Chancery cases on the same basis.

B Trials

D1–316 (i) If a Chancery case is proceeding in any District Registry other than a Chancery District Registry, the case should normally be transferred to the appropriate Chancery District Registry upon the first occasion the case comes before the court.

(ii) The venue of a Chancery trial out of London will normally be one of the centres mentioned above. However in many circumstances ((*e.g.* because of the number or age of local witnesses, the need for a site visit, or travel problems) arrangements can be made for the Chancery Court to sit elsewhere.

(iii) In cases of exceptional difficulty or importance the trial may be by a High Court Judge. Arrangements can also be made in exceptional circumstances for a High Court Judge to deal with any of the matters excepted from the jurisdiction of an authorised Circuit Judge. Such a Judge may be one of the Chancery Judges other than Jacob or Blackburne JJ.

(iv) Where it is desired that a hearing be outside one of the normal Chancery Centres, or be taken by a High Court Judge, inquiries should normally in the first instance be made to the Listing Officer for the area concerned. If the need arises, inquiries can also be made to clerk to Mr Justice Jacob (telephone 0171 936 6771, fax 0171 936 6650) or the clerk to Mr Justice Blackburne (telephone 0171 936 6512, fax 0171 936 7379). If no relevant clerk is available, inquiries should be made to the clerk in charge of the Chancery Lists in London.

C Applications

D1–317 (a) Subject to the following paragraphs any application should normally be made to a District Judge (unless it relates to a matter which a District Judge does not have power to hear).

(b) If the application relates to a matter which may significantly affect the conduct of the trial (*e.g.* relates to significant new evidence) and is made within 3 months before the date fixed for trial, the application should normally be made to a High Court Judge or Circuit Judge.

(c) A District Judge may of his or her own motion (for instance because of the complexity of the matter or the need for specialist attention) direct that an application be referred to High Court or Circuit Judge

(d) At any time if the parties agree that the matter is appropriate to be heard by a Judge (High Court or Circuit), the parties may jointly apply in writing to the District Judge for the application to be referred directly to a High Court or Circuit Judge. They will be informed of the result of their application by post or by telephone. If it is successful, details of availability and a time estimate must be lodged with the relevant Listing Officer who will fix a date for the hearing. If it is unsuccessful, oral application may be made to the District Judge.

D Application days before a Judge

D1–318 Normally one day a week is reserved for the hearing of applications and short appeals, including all interim matters. All matters will be called into Court at the commencement of the day in order to work out a running order. Matters will be heard without the court going into private session unless good reason is shown. Rights of audience are unaffected.

Applications days are: Monday in Birmingham, Thursday in Bristol and Friday in Cardiff. In Manchester and Liverpool application days are on either Tuesday or Thursday of each week. In Leeds and Newcastle applications are heard on average fortnightly.

E Applications out of hours and telephone applications

These are governed by the general rules, save that in the case of applications out of hours, the party applying should contact the relevant court office, the main relevant telephone numbers being: D1–319

Birmingham (Midland and Oxford Circuit):
West Side: 01399-618079
East Side: 01399-618078
Bristol: 01399-618088
Cardiff: 01399-618086
Manchester and Liverpool: 01399-618080
Leeds and Newcastle: 01399-618082
In case of difficulty, contact the Royal Courts of Justice on 0171-936-6260.

F Agreed interim orders

Normally a hearing will not be necessary. The procedure is as in the general rules. A Judge is unlikely to agree to more than two consent adjournments of an interim application. Applications to vacate a trial date will require substantial justification and a hearing, normally before the Trial Judge. D1–320

G Contacting the Court

The following are the Court addresses, telephone and fax numbers: D1–321

Birmingham:	The Priory Courts, 33 Bull Street, Birmingham B4 6DW. Telephone: 0121-681-3033. Fax: 0121-681-3121.
Bristol:	The Law Courts, Small Street, Bristol BS1 1DA. Telephone: 0117- 976-3098. Fax: 0117-976-3074.
Cardiff:	The Civil Justice Centre, 2 Park Street, Cardiff CF1 1ET. Telephone: 01222-376402. Fax: 01222-376470.
Leeds:	The Court House, 1 Oxford Row, Leeds LS1 3BG. Telephone: 0113-283-0040. Fax: 0113-244-8507.
Liverpool:	Queen Elizabeth II Law Courts, Derby Square, Liverpool L2 1XA. Telephone: 0151-473-7373. Fax: 0151-227-2806.
Manchester:	The Courts of Justice, Crown Square, Manchester M3 3FL. Telephone: 0161-954-1800. Fax: 0161-832-5179.
Newcastle:	The Law Courts, Quayside, Newcastle upon Tyne NE1 3LB. Telephone: 0191-201-2000. Fax: 0191-201-2001.
Preston:	The Law Courts, Openshaw Place, Ringway, Preston PR1 2LL. Telephone: 01772-832300. Fax: 01772-832-476.

In some centres resources do not permit the listing telephone numbers to be attended personally at all times. In cases of urgency, solicitors, counsel and counsel's clerks may come into the Chancery Court and leave messages with the member of staff sitting in Court.

H Local listing arrangements

D1–322 Listing arrangements may vary at different centres, depending on availability of Judges and courtrooms. The current details are as follows:

D1–323 Birmingham: shared and early listing

1. *The shared list*—The shared list is primarily for use by the three specialised lists of the Birmingham District Registry—those operated by the Chancery, Mercantile and Technology and Construction Courts.

The shared list is in addition to the normal lists of those Courts and allows better use to be made of judicial time. Given the settlement rate of trials in the three divisions, two additional cases, the fourth and fifth fixtures, will be listed at any one time, in addition to the three cases listed before the three specialist courts. Those two additional cases will be taken by any of the Section 9 Judges who become available. Cases are only entered into the shared list if there is a very strong expectation that they will be heard on the day fixed.

In order, therefore, for a case to enter the shared list it must be suitable for hearing before any of the Section 9 specialist Judges.

Suitability for listing a case in the shared list may be suggested by the District Judge at directions stage, or by the parties when setting the case down. It is likely that fourth and fifth fixtures will be allocated an earlier trial date than a case which has to be heard by the appropriate specialist Judge.

The final decision to list a case in the shared list will lie with Judge Boggis Q.C. for Chancery cases, Judge Lee Q.C. or Judge Gibbs Q.C. for Mercantile cases, and Judge Alton for Technology and Construction cases.

D1–324 2. *Early listing*—Where a case with a time estimate of two days or less is unable to be listed within the following three month period, the case will be listed in the usual way with as early a date as possible, but a note will be made of the case and put on the file. If due to settlement or adjournment of other cases, an earlier date becomes available, the parties will be informed that an earlier date has become available, and they will be given the opportunity to have their case brought forward to that earlier date.

Judge Boggis Q.C. will make the decision at setting down stage as to whether a case may be marked for the possibility of earlier hearing; suitable cases will be those which are to be argued on law alone and Applications by order.

If a case is listed in this way, the notice of hearing will inform the parties accordingly.

Bristol: reserve listing

In order to make available earlier hearing dates than would otherwise be possible, a reserve list is operated for Chancery cases listed to be heard in the Bristol District Registry. Cases in the reserve list are given a fixed date, usually as a second fixture. A second fixture will only be given when there is a very strong expectation of the case being heard on that date. Other Judges are called upon in the event of both first and second fixtures being effective.

Cardiff: reserve listing

Judge Moseley Q.C. sits both as a Chancery Judge and a Judge of the Technology and Construction Court. His list contains both categories of case. All cases are allocated a fixed starting date but some are first and some second fixtures. Other Judges are called upon in the event of both first and second fixtures being effective. A Mercantile Judge for Wales is due to be appointed shortly. His or her arrival may lead to a revision of present listing arrangements. Any discussions concerning listing should be with the Chancery Listing Clerk in Cardiff.

Manchester, Liverpool and Preston

1. *The shared list*—When sitting at the same court centre (as is usually the case) Judge Howarth and Judge Maddocks will assist each other in the disposal of their respective daily lists. If necessary and they are available at the relevant court centre, Judge Kershaw Q.C. and Judge Hegarty Q.C. (who are the local Mercantile Judges) will assist in the disposal of business.

2. *Second Fixtures*—To maximise the use of court resources, second (and sometimes third) fixtures are listed on each Judge's daily list. Parties to such fixtures are notified not later than 3.30 p.m. on the working day preceding the day for which the case is listed (and frequently considerably before then) if the second (or, as appropriate, third) fixture will be in the list for trial.

Leeds and Newcastle

1. *The shared list*—When sitting at the same time in Leeds or Newcastle Judge Behrens and Judge McGonigal (the principal Mercantile Judge on the North Eastern Circuit) will assist each other in the disposal of their respective daily lists.

2. *Second fixtures*—The same practice is adopted as is operated in Manchester and Liverpool.

CDPD 3 JUDGE'S APPLICATIONS

"Judge's Applications" means applications for interim remedies or other urgent applications made to a Judge. **D1–325**

All applications which are within the jurisdiction of the Master should be made to the Master and not the Judge unless there is a sufficient degree of urgency or other good reason which justifies making the application to the Judge.

A Application days

Every weekday (except the last day of each sittings) will be an application day. **D1–326**

B Applications Judge

(i) A Judge ("The applications Judge") will be assigned to hear Judge's applications on each application day. **D1–327**

(ii) If the volume of applications requires it any other Judge available to assist with applications will hear such Judge's applications as the applications Judge directs.

(iii) An application notice of a Judge's application, other than in the Patents Court, need not state the name of the Judge to whom the application will be made. It is sufficient to state "the Chancery Applications Judge" or, in the case of an application in the Companies Court, "the Companies Judge". The names of those Judges appear in the Daily Cause List and also in the Chancery Division term list.

C Adjournment of Judge's applications

D1–328 (i) If all parties to an application agree to do so it can be adjourned for not more than 14 days by counsel or solicitors attending before the Chancery Listing Officer (Room W.15) at any time before 4 p.m. on the day before the hearing of the application and producing a consent or consents signed by counsel or solicitors representing all parties agreeing to the adjournment. A litigant in person who is a party must attend before the Chancery Listing Officer as well as signing a consent.

(ii) Not more than three successive adjournments may be made and no adjournment shall be made to the last two applications days of any sitting.

(iii) The above procedure applies to Judge's applications which the parties agree should be adjourned to be heard as applications by order. In addition to the consents required under (i), above, an agreed time-table for the filing of any evidence must be produced to the Chancery Listing Officer. Any application arising from the default of a party in abiding by the time- table and any application by the parties to extend the time-table must be made in court.

(iv) Undertakings previously given to the court may be continued unchanged over the duration of any adjournment. Adjournments on which an undertaking is to be varied or a new undertaking given must be dealt with in court.

D Order of hearing

D1–329 The Judge hearing Judge's applications will continue to exercise his discretion as to the order in which he hears them, so that he may, for instance, give priority to any application that he considers to be sufficiently urgent, as may be the case with some applications made without notice. Subject to this:

(a) applications affecting the liberty of the subject will continue to take priority over all applications;
(b) ineffective applications that is to say matters which are to be adjourned or have been settled;
(c) all other applications listed, unlisted and made without notice will be heard in the order determined by the applications Judge;
(d) applications likely to last more than two hours will normally be made applications by order unless the state of work permits the Judge to deal with them as they arise;
(e) when another Judge is available to assist with applications, the applications Judge may transfer to him such applications as he considers appropriate, irrespective of priority;
(f) any application which at the end of the day is part heard will normally head the listed Judge's applications for the next court day, followed by any listed applications that have not been reached;
(g) the Judge will usually give effect to any variation in this order of priority which is agreed by all who are affected.

CDPD 4 LANDLORD AND TENANT

Grant of a New Business Tenancy—Claim Form

D1–330 (i) Where the parties are in negotiation on the grant of a new tenancy and neither side wishes to press on with the proceedings the tenant may request the Court not immediately to set a day for the hearing upon issue or service of the Claim Form but to await a request from either party that a hearing date be set. Either party may at any time thereafter request a hearing to be fixed.

(ii) It is of the greatest importance that the landlord should be informed promptly of the issue of the Claim Form, which must be served strictly within two calendar months from the date of issue. It is not to be assumed that the time will necessarily be extended if this requirement is not complied with.

(iii) If the landlord wishes the Court to determine an interim rent under s.24A of the Landlord and Tenant Act 1954, but is content that the determination should await the determination of the application for a new lease, and in reliance on the procedure specified above the tenant's Claim Form has not been brought on for hearing, he may likewise make an application for the determination of the interim rent which states the hearing as being for a day to be fixed instead of for a date and time. Such an application must be served promptly, and it may be brought on for hearing by either party on a date to be fixed by the Court on not less than three days' notice to the opposing party.

CDPD 5 LISTING

A General

(i) The Lists—There are three main lists in the Chancery Division: the Trial List, the General List and the Interim Hearings List. [There is also a Patents List which is controlled separately by the Judge in charge of the Patents List.] D1–331

The Trial List is for all trials to be heard with witnesses

The Interim Hearings List is for interim applications including appeals from Masters.

The General List is for other matters, including revenue, bankruptcy and pensions appeals, Part 8 proceedings, applications for judgment and all companies matters.

In the Royal Courts of Justice the fixing of trial dates and windows in the multi-track is regulated by a Practice Direction issued by the Vice Chancellor (this Practice Direction is set out in Section D of the Guide).

(ii) Responsibility for listing—The Clerk of the Lists (Room W.15, Royal Courts of Justice) is in general responsible for listing. All applications relating to listing should in the first instance be made to him. Any party dissatisfied with any decision of the Clerk of the Lists may, on one clear day's notice to all other parties, apply to the Judge in charge of the list. Any such application should be made within seven days of the decision of the Clerk of the Lists and be arranged through the Chancery Listing Officer. D1–332

(iii) General and Interim Hearings Lists D1–333

The warned lists—On each Friday of term and on such other days as may be appropriate, the Clerk of the Lists will publish a Warned List, showing the matters in the General and Interim Hearings Lists that are liable to be heard in the following week. Any matter for which no date has been fixed is liable to appear in the list for hearing with no warning save that given by the next day's cause list posted each afternoon outside Room W.15. The parties may by consent "offer" a case for a designated date following entry into the Warned List in accordance with the local directions notice issued by the Clerk of the Lists.

(iv) Estimates of duration—(a) If the estimated length of the trial is D1–334 varied, or the case settled, withdrawn or discontinued, the solicitors for the parties must forthwith inform the Clerk of the Lists in writing. If the case is settled but the parties wish the Master to make a consent order, the solicitor must notify the Clerk of the Lists in writing, whereupon he will take the case out of the list and notify the Master. The Master may then make the consent order.

(b) Seven days before the date for trial, the claimant's solicitors must inform the Clerk of the Lists whether there is any variation in the estimate of duration, and in particular whether the case is likely to be disposed of in some summary way. If the claimant is in person, this must be done by the solicitor for the first-named defendant who has instructed a solicitor. If a summary disposal is likely, the solicitor must keep the Clerk of the Lists informed of any developments as soon as they occur.

D1–335 **(v) General**

(a) *Unassigned cases*

I In addition to those cases listed to be heard by individual Judges, the Daily Cause List for each day may list one or more cases from any of the three main Lists to be heard on that day but not assigned to a particular Judge ("an unassigned case"). If on any day the case assigned to a particular Judge proves to be ineffective, he will hear an unassigned case. It is hoped that the great majority of unassigned cases will be heard on the day that they are listed but this cannot be absolutely guaranteed. It is not the practice to list cases as unassigned unless the parties consent and there are no witnesses.

II Solicitors and counsel engaged in cases listed as unassigned should communicate with the Chancery Listing Officer who will notify them as soon as possible which Judge is to hear the case.

(b) *Appeals from Masters*—Appeals from Masters will appear in the Interim Hearings List. Such appeals (stamped with the appropriate fee) must be lodged in Room W.15. On being notified that the case has been listed the solicitors should forthwith inform the Chancery Listing Officer whether they intend to instruct counsel and, if so, the names of counsel.

B Listing of Particular Business

D1–336 **(i) Bankruptcy**

(a) *Bankruptcy Appeals*—Notice of appeal from the decision of a Registrar or of a county court should be lodged in Room TM1.10. The appeal will be entered in the General List, usually with a fixed date. The date of hearing will be fixed by the Chancery Listing Officer in the usual manner.

(b) *Bankruptcy Applications*—All originating and ordinary applications to the Judge should be lodged with the Deputy Court Manager in Bankruptcy. Urgent applications without notice for (i) the committal of any person to prison for contempt, or (ii) injunctions or the modification or discharge of injunctions will be passed directly to the clerk of the Chancery Applications Judge for hearing by that Judge. All applications on notice for (i) and (ii) above, and applications referred to the Judge by the Registrar, will be listed by the Chancery Listing Officer. Applications estimated not to exceed two hours will be heard by the Applications Judge. The Listing Officer shall give at least three clear days notice of the hearing to the applicant and any respondents who attend before the Registrar. Applications over two hours will be heard on a fixed or floating date by such Judges as are available.

(ii) Companies Court—Applications and petitions adjourned by the Registrar and applications which are presently heard by the Companies Judge on each Monday of a term will be listed by the Chancery Clerk of the Lists. Any such applications and petitions which are estimated to exceed two hours will be liable to be stood over to a date to be fixed by the Chancery Clerk of the Lists. All such matters will be placed in the General List. **D1–337**

(iii) Applications adjourned to the Judge—Applications adjourned by the Master to the Judge will be added to the Interim Hearings List. **D1–338**

(iv) Judge's Applications **D1–339**

(a) *General Listing of Judge's Applications*

I The Chancery Listing Office is responsible for the listing of Judge's applications.

II A Judge's application will only be listed if (1) two copies of the Claim Form and (2) two copies of the application notice (one stamped with the appropriate fee) are lodged at the Chancery Listing Office, Room W.15 Royal Courts of Justice, before 12 noon on the day before the date for which notice of the application has been given or on the preceding Friday if the date for which notice has been given is a Monday.

(b) *Adjourning Judge's Applications*

I In Court

When a Judge's application is adjourned in court, the Associate in attendance will notify the Chancery Listing Office of the day to which it has been adjourned and the office will list the application for that day.

II Out of Court

If a Judge's application is by consent adjourned, the Chancery Listing Office will list the application for the day to which it has been adjourned. (For jurisdiction of Chancery Listing Officer to adjourn Judge's applications see CDPD 3).

(c) *Judge's Applications without notice*

I If it is desired to have an urgent hearing of a Judge's application listed, two copies of the order sought should be lodged as well as an application notice. If the application is to be made in private, it will be listed as "Application without notice" without naming the parties. Where, for example, publicity would defeat the object of hearing, if the application were heard in public, the Judge may hear the application in private (see CPR rule 39.2). Where an application is very urgent and the Applications Judge is unable to hear it promptly, it may be heard by any Judge who is available, though the request for this must be made to the Clerk to the Applications Judge, or, in default, to the Chancery Listing Officer.

II Urgent Judge's applications without notice

A party wishing to apply urgently to a Judge for remedies without notice to the respondent must notify the clerk to the Applications Judge by telephone.

(d) *Applications by order*—If a Judge directs that an application is to be an application by order (as will usually be done if the hearing is likely to exceed two hours), the solicitors or the clerks to counsel concerned should apply to the Chancery Listing Officer for a fixed or floating date for the hearing. Before so applying there must be lodged with the Clerk of the Lists a certificate signed by the advocate stating the estimated length of the hearing of the application. Applications by order may be entered in the Interim Hearings List and, if not fixed by arrangement with the Chancery Listing Officer, will be liable to be listed for hearing in accordance with the timetable fixed by the Judge.

(e) *Short service of Judge's applications*—Permission to serve short notice of a Judge's application may be obtained on application without notice to the Applications Judge. Such permission cannot be given by a Master.

D1–340 **(v) Revenue Appeals**—Appeals will be entered in the General List, usually with fixed dates, and will be heard by such Judges as are available. The dates for hearing shall be settled in the usual way on application to the Chancery Listing Officer. Where it would assist counsel and solicitors with their other commitments, the Chancery Listing Officer, if requested, will endeavour to fix two or more revenue appeals so that they will come on consecutively.

D1–341 **(vi) Short Applications**—An application for judgment in default made to a Judge (because the Master has no jurisdiction) should be made to the Applications Judge.

D1–342 **(vii) Summary judgment**—Where an application for summary judgment includes an application for an injunction, it usually has to be made to a Judge because in most cases the Master cannot grant an injunction save in terms agreed by the parties. In such cases the application should be made returnable before the Judge in the General List instead of the Master. The return date to be inserted in the application notice should be a Monday at least 14 clear days after the application notice has been served. The application notice should be issued in the Chancery Listing Office (Room W.15) when there must be lodged two copies of the application notice, and the witness statements or affidavits in support with the exhibits. On the return date the application will normally be adjourned to a date to be fixed if the hearing, whether opposed or unopposed, is likely to take longer than 30 minutes. The adjourned date will be fixed in the usual way through the Chancery Listing Officer, and a certificate signed by an advocate as to the estimated length of the hearing must be lodged with the Chancery Listing Officer.

D1–343 **(viii) Variation of Trusts: Application to a Judge**—Applications under the Variation of Trusts Act 1958 for hearing by a Judge may be listed for hearing in the General List without any direction by a Master on the lodgment (in Room W.15) of a certificate signed by advocates for all the parties, stating: (i) that the evidence is complete and has been filed; (ii) that the application is ready for hearing, and (iii) the estimated length of the hearing. The hearing will be in private unless there is a contentious issue (see CPR rule 39.2(f) and the PD supplementing CPR Part 39 para 1.5(11)).

CDPD 6 MASTERS

Arrangement of Business

D1–344 **(i) Assignment of cases**—Cases are assigned to Masters in accordance with the last digit of the claim number as follows:

0 and 1	Master Bragge	6 and 7	Chief Master Winegarten
2 and 3	Master Bowman	8 and 9	Master Moncaster
4 and 5	Master Bowles		

(ii) Oral applications without notice to the Masters—(a) Masters are normally available to hear oral applications without notice at 2.15 p.m. on working days. Notice should be given to the Master's Clerk in Room TM7.09 or by telephone on 0171 936 7391 or by fax on 0171 936 7422 by 4.30 p.m. on the previous day, except in cases of real emergency when notice may be given at any time, so that the file will be before the Master. D1–345

(b) If the assigned Master is not available on any particular day, the applicant will be informed and (except in cases of emergency), asked to come when the assigned Master is next available. Applications will only be heard by another Master in cases of emergency or when the assigned Master is on vacation.

CDPD 7 MORTGAGES AND POSSESSION ORDERS

A Mortgages

(i) RSC, O.88, r.5(2) requires that in mortgage claims a copy of the mortgage must be exhibited to the witness statement or affidavit in support of the claim, and the original mortgage or charge certificate must be produced at the hearing. D1–346

(ii) Most building society mortgages now incorporate standard mortgage conditions, and in such cases a copy of the relevant conditions must also be exhibited. D1–347

(iii) Some standard forms of building society mortgage are now so abbreviated that they give no particulars of the amount of the advance, the term of the loan, the rate of interest or the amount of the instalments, but all these matters are defined in the mortgage conditions by reference to the offer letter. Where the offer letter is thus in effect incorporated into the mortgage by reference, that also should be exhibited to the witness statement or affidavit. D1–348

(iv) Many bank mortgages, although expressed in the usual bank "all monies" form, are also qualified by an offer letter or other side letter, providing for repayment of the advance by instalments. In *Governor and Company of the Bank of Scotland v. Grimes* [1985] 1 Q.B. 1179, it was held that in such cases the mortgage may be treated as an instalment mortgage for the purposes of Administration of Justices Act 1970, s.36 and Administration of Justice Act 1973, s.8. In these cases also the relevant letter should be exhibited to the witness statement or affidavit in support. D1–349

B Suspended Possession Orders

(i) A suspended possession order is an order under which a person is entitled to a remedy subject to the fulfilment of a condition for the purposes of RSC, O.46, r.2(1)(d), so that O.46, r.4 accordingly applies. Permission to issue execution should not be given without notice and it follows that the Court must therefore direct an application for such permission to be made upon notice (r.4(1)). D1–350

(ii) Suspended orders are made frequently in mortgagees' possession claims by virtue of s.36 of the Administration of Justice Act 1970 and in such claims the defendant is often in default of acknowledging service of the claim form. D1–351

(iii) Where a defendant has not acknowledged service no special directions as to service are needed but a claimant requiring permission to issue execution on a suspended possession order when there has been a default of acknowledging service must send a copy of the application notice and of the witness statement or affidavit in support of the application to each defendant D1–352 in default at his last known address, so as to reach him not less than three clear days before the hearing, and will lodge with the Masters' clerk, at least one clear day before the hearing, the witness statement or affidavit in support of the application endorsed with a certificate by the claimant's solicitor in the form following or as near thereto as may be appropriate:

"I certify that on day the day of 19 a copy of the application notice herein dated 19 together with a true copy of the within document was sent by pre-paid letter post addressed to the defendant at his last known address being [insert address]. Claimant's Solicitor."

No further proof of service should normally be required in default cases.

D1–353 **(iv)** The same principles apply and the same practice will be followed where leave to issue execution is required because six years or more have elapsed since the date of an unsuspended possession order or because there has been a change in the party liable to execution. (See RSC, O.46, r.2).

D1–354 **(v)** Applications for permission to issue execution because of a change of the party entitled to execution or to issue a writ of restitution may be dealt with without notice.

CDPD 8 ORDERS

A Drafting of Orders

D1–355 **(i) Orders made by Masters**—Orders made by Masters will be drawn up by the court, and unless the court has any questions a sealed order will be sent to each party.

D1–356 **(ii) Orders made by Judges**

(a) *Agreed statements of the terms of order*—Where a Judge directs that a statement of the terms of the order be agreed and signed by counsel, the agreed statement may either be handed to the Associate in court or else lodged in Room TM3.07. In each case the claim number should be shown. Agreed statements will normally be adopted as the order of the Court.

(b) *Drafting by the Court*—The Court will draw up the order unless it directs or permits a party to draw it up or directs that an agreed statement of its terms be filed or that no order need be drawn up. Unless the Court has any questions it will seal and serve the order without reference to the parties. If the order is unusually complicated it may be necessary to submit a draft to the parties.

If the order is to be drawn up by a party two engrossments of the order proposed should be lodged at or posted to:

Order and Accounts Section
Room TM3.07 Thomas More Building
Royal Courts of Justice
Strand, London WC2A 2LL

(c) *Orders on application*—When the Court directs that an agreed statement of the terms of an order (formerly called "minutes of order") be filed, the statement, signed by counsel or solicitors who attended the hearing should be lodged in Room TM 3.07. The agreed statement will normally be adopted as the order of the Court.

D1–357 **(iii) Forms of order**—Recitals will be kept to a minimum, and the body of the order will be confined to setting out the decision of the Court and the directions required to give effect to it. If upon receipt of an order any party is of the opinion that it is not drawn in such a way as to give effect to the decision of the court, prompt notice must be given to the Order and Accounts Section in Room TM 3.07 and to all other parties setting out the reasons for dissatisfaction. If the differences cannot be resolved the objecting party may apply on notice for the order to be amended.

(iv) Copies of Orders—Copies of orders may be obtained from Room TM3.07 upon payment of the appropriate fee. D1–358

B Consent Orders

(i) Consent orders under the Inheritance (Provision for Family and Dependants) Act 1975—Every final order embodying terms of compromise made in proceedings in the Chancery Division under the 1975 Act shall contain a direction that a memorandum of the order shall be endorsed on or permanently annexed to the probate or letters of administration and a copy of the order shall be sent to the Principal Registry of the Family Division with the relevant grant of probate or letters of administration for endorsement, notwithstanding that any particular order may not, strictly speaking, be an order under the 1975 Act. D1–359

(ii) Consents by parties not attending the hearing—(a) Where the respondent to a Judge's application does not appear either by counsel or solicitors or in person, the applicant sometimes asks the Court to make a consent order, relying on a letter of consent from the respondent or his solicitors, or sometimes on a draft statement of agreed terms of order signed by the respondent's solicitors. D1–360

(b) If the remedy sought by the applicant falls wholly within the remedy or remedies claimed in the application notice, no difficulty normally arises, for the Court is able to grant the remedy even if there is no effective consent by the respondent.

(c) Where, however, the order sought goes outside the remedy or remedies claimed in the application notice, or even in the claim form, or when undertakings are proffered by the respondent, the practice has varied and it has become desirable to establish a simple and uniform procedure and so save costs. Subject always to the discretion of the Court, no order will normally be made in such cases unless a consent signed by or on behalf of the respondent is put before the Court in accordance with the following provisions: (1) Where there are solicitors on the record for the respondent, the Court will normally accept as sufficient a written consent signed by those solicitors on their headed notepaper. (2) Where there are solicitors for the respondent but they are not on the record, the court will normally accept as sufficient a written consent signed by those solicitors on their headed notepaper only if in the consent (or in some other document) the solicitors certify that they have fully explained to the respondent the effect of the order and that the respondent appeared to have understood the explanation. (3) Where there is a written consent signed by a respondent who is acting in person, the Court will normally not accept it as being sufficient unless the Court is satisfied that the respondent understands the effect of the order, either by reason of the circumstances (*e.g.* that the respondent is himself a barrister or solicitor) or by means of other material (*e.g.* that the respondent's consent is given in reply to a letter to him which sufficiently explained the effect of the order in simple language). (4) Where the respondent offers any undertaking to the Court (a) the letter or other document offering the undertaking must be signed by the respondent personally, (b) solicitors must certify on their headed notepaper that the signature is the signature of the respondent and (c) the solicitor must similarly certify, if the case falls within sub-para. (2) or sub-para. (3) above, that they have explained to the respondent the consequences of giving the undertaking and that the respondent appeared to understand the explanation.

(d) This procedure will apply generally to all applications in the Chancery Division, and it will apply whether the order is sought by a claimant or a defendant or by the applicant or the respondent.

D1–361 **(iii) Tomlin Order**—Where proceedings are to be stayed on agreed terms to be scheduled to the order, the draft order should be drawn so as to read as follows: "And the Claimant and the Defendant having agreed to the terms set forth in the schedule hereto, it is ordered that all further proceedings in this claim be stayed, except for the purpose of carrying such terms into effect. Liberty to apply as to carrying such terms into effect." This form of order is called a "Tomlin Order".

CDPD 9 PROBATE

A Verification of Original Will or Codicil

D1–362 **(i)** When the Court orders trial of a contentious probate claim on written evidence under paragraph 10 or 13 of the Contentious Probate Proceedings Practice Direction or when an application for summary judgment is made it is necessary for an attesting witness to sign a witness statement or swear an affidavit of due execution of any will or codicil sought to be admitted to probate. The will or codicil is at that stage in the Court's possession and cannot be handed out of court for use as an exhibit to the witness statement or affidavit, so that the attesting witness has to attend at the Royal Courts of Justice.

D1–363 **(ii)** Where an attesting witness is unable to visit the Royal Courts of Justice in order to sign his witness statement or swear his affidavit in the presence of an officer of the court the solicitor concerned may request from the Chancery Registry, Room TM7.09, Thomas More Building, Royal Courts of Justice, Strand, London WC2A 2LL a photographic copy of the will or codicil in question. This will be certified as authentic by the Court and may be exhibited to the witness statement or affidavit of due execution in lieu of the original. The witness statement or affidavit must in that case state that the exhibited document is an authenticated copy of the document signed in the witness's presence.

B Transmission of Scripts in Cases Tried Outside London

D1–364 When a probate claim is listed for trial outside London the solicitor for the party responsible for preparing the court bundle must write to the Chancery Registry, Room TM7.09, Thomas More Building, Royal Courts of Justice, Strand, London WC2A 2LL and request that the scripts be forwarded to the appropriate District Registry.

C Lodgment of Scripts

D1–365 When a party lodges an original script in Court he should at the same time lodge a copy thereof. If a script is not lodged by a party, *e.g.* when it is forwarded by the Family Division to the Chancery Division, the party relying on it should lodge a copy thereof in Chancery Chambers before the first hearing at which the script has to be considered. Photographic copies are preferred but typed copies are acceptable.

CDPD 10 SALE

Estate Agents' and Auctioneers' Charges

(i) The charges of estate agents and auctioneers selling freehold or leasehold property pursuant to orders of the Chancery Division will normally be considered reasonable by the Court if they do not exceed the rate of commission which that agent would normally charge on a sole agency basis, and they do not exceed 2½ per cent of the sale price; exclusive of value added tax. **D1–366**

(ii) These charges are to include all commission, valuations, expenses and other disbursements, including making affidavits, the cost of advertising and all other work except surveys. The allowance for a survey will be at the Court's discretion. **D1–367**

(iii) If (a) an agent's charges do not fall within the limits set out in para. (i) or (b) there is a sale of any investment property, business property or farm property or (c) a property is sold in lots or by valuation, an application must be made to the Court to authorise the fee to be charged. **D1–368**

CDPD 11 TITLE TO PROCEEDINGS

The general rule is that the title should contain only the parties to the proceedings, but there is one exception: where the proceedings relate to the administration of an estate or a probate claim they should be entitled "In the estate of AB deceased". **D1–369**

If proceedings are under an Act of Parliament, the Act need not be mentioned in the title but should be referred to in the body of the claim form.

CDPD 12 TRUSTS

A Application under s.48 of the Administration of Justice Act 1985

(i) Applications under s.48 of the Administration of Justice Act 1985 and RSC, O.93, r.21 should be made by Part 8 Claim Form (N 208). The claim need not be served on any other party. It should be supported by a witness statement or affidavit to which are exhibited: (a) copies of all relevant documents, (b) instructions to a person with a 10-year High Court qualification within the meaning of the Courts and Legal Services Act 1990 ("the qualified person"), (c) the qualified person's opinion, (d) draft terms of the desired order. **D1–370**

(ii) The witness statement or affidavit (or exhibits thereto) should state: (a) the names of all persons who are, or may be, affected by the order sought, (b) all surrounding circumstances admissible and relevant in construing the document, (c) the date of qualification of the qualified person and his experience in the construction of trust documents (d) the approximate value of the fund or property in question, (e) whether it is known to the applicant that a dispute exists and, if so, details of such dispute. **D1–371**

(iii) When the file is placed before the Master he will consider whether the evidence is complete and if it is send the file to the Judge. **D1–372**

(iv) The Judge will consider the papers and, if necessary, direct service of notices under RSC, O.15, r.13A or request such further information as he may desire. If the Judge is satisfied that the order sought is appropriate, the order will be made and sent to the claimant. **D1–373**

D1–374 **(v)** If following service of notices under O.15, r.13A any acknowledgment of service is received, the claimant must apply to the Master (on notice to the parties who have so acknowledged service) for directions. If the claimant desires to pursue the application to the court, in the ordinary case the Master will direct that the case proceeds as a Part 8 claim.

D1–375 **(vi)** If on the hearing of the claim the Judge is of the opinion that any party who entered an acknowledgment of service has no reasonably tenable argument contrary to the qualified person's opinion, in the exercise of his discretion he may order such party to pay any costs thrown away, or part thereof.

B Disability of Trustee

D1–376 **(i)** There must be medical evidence showing incapacity to act as a trustee at the date of issue of the claim form and that the incapacity is continuing at the date of signing the witness statement or swearing the affidavit. The witness statement or affidavit should also show incapacity to execute transfers, where a vesting order of stocks and shares is asked for.

D1–377 **(ii)** The trustee under disability should be made a defendant to the claim but need not be served unless he is sole trustee or has a beneficial interest.

C Funds

D1–378 Lodgment under s.63 of the Trustee Act 1925.

(i) Lodgment into the High Court of amounts of cash or securities of less than £500.00 under s.63 of the Trustee Act 1925, and r.14(1) of the Court Funds Rules 1987, will not be accepted by the Accountant-General unless the Chief Master (or Vacation Master) so signifies in writing.

D1–379 **(ii)** The Accountant-General will refer the applicant to the Chief Master (or Vacation Master) who will consider whether there is a more economical method of preserving the fund than lodging it in the High Court or, failing that, may suggest that the money be lodged in a county court (which has power to accept sums of up to £30,000 lodged under s.63 of the Trustee Act 1925).

D1–380 **(iii)** If the Chief Master (or the Vacation Master) decides that a particular lodgment should be made in the High Court, he will so signify on the back of the request (in respect of applications under r.14(1)(ii)(a)) or the office copy schedule to the affidavit (in respect of applications under r.14(1)(ii)(b)).

D Original Documents

D1–381 At the hearing of any case where a will is to be construed, the probate of the will must be in court at the opening of the case. When the construction of a document other than a will is to be considered, the original document must be similarly available. The court should not be asked to construe any document by reference to a mere copy.

E Property in Scotland

D1–382 In applications, for vesting orders under the Trustee Act 1925 any investments or property situate in Scotland should be set out in a separate schedule to the claim form, and the claim form should ask that the trustees may be at liberty to apply for a vesting order in Scotland in respect thereto.

The form of the order to be made in such cases will (with any necessary variation) be as follows:

> It is ordered that the   as Trustees be at liberty to take all steps that may be necessary to obtain a vesting order in Scotland relating to the securities specified in the schedule herein.

F Variation of Trusts

(i) Application to Judge—See Practice Direction CDPD 5.B(viii). D1–383

(ii) Counsel's Opinion—(a) Where any children or unborn beneficiaries will be affected by an arrangement under the Variation of Trusts Act 1958, evidence must normally be before the Court which shows that their litigation friends or the trustees support the arrangements as being in the interests of the children or unborn beneficiaries, and exhibits a case to counsel and counsel's written opinion to this effect. In complicated cases a written opinion is usually essential to the understanding of the litigation friends and the trustees, and to the consideration by the court of the merits and fiscal consequences of the arrangement. D1–384

(b) Where the interests of two or more children, or two or more of the children and unborn beneficiaries, are similar, a single written case to counsel and opinion will suffice; and no case to counsel and written opinion is required in respect of those who fall within the proviso to s.1(1) of the Act (Discretionary interests under protective trusts). Further, in proper cases the requirement of a case to counsel and a written opinion may at any stage be dispensed with by the Master or the Judge.

(iii) Stamp Duty—(a) An undertaking by solicitors with regard to stamping is not required to be included in an order under the Variation of Trusts Act 1958 whether made by a Judge or Master. D1–385

(b) The Commissioners of Inland Revenue consider that the stamp duty position of duplicate orders is as follows:

(i) Orders confined to the lifting of protective trusts. These orders are not liable for duty at all and should not be presented to a stamp office.

(ii) Orders affecting voluntary dispositions *inter vivos*. These orders may be certified under the Stamp Duty (Exempt Instruments) Regulations 1987 (S.I. 1987 No. 516), as within category L in the schedule to those regulations, in which case they should not be presented to a stamp office. Without such a certificate they attract 50p duty under the head "Conveyance or transfer of any kind not hereinbefore described."

(iii) Orders outside categories (i) and (ii) above that contain declarations of the trust, *i.e.* that effect no disposition of trust property. These orders attract 50p fixed duty under the head "Declaration of trust". They may be presented for stamping at any stamp office in the usual way, or sent for adjudication if preferred.

G Estates of Deceased Lloyd's Names

(i) Personal representatives who wish to apply to the Court for permission to distribute the estate of a deceased Lloyd's Name following the decision of Lindsay J. in *Re Yorke (deceased)* [1997] 4 All E.R. 907, may, until further notice and if appropriate in the particular estate, adopt the following procedure. D1–386

(ii) The procedure will be appropriate where: D1–387

(a) all liabilities of the estate in respect of syndicates of which the Name was a member have been reinsured (whether directly or indirectly) into the Equitas group and

(b) the only reason for delaying distribution of the estate is the possibility of personal liability to Lloyd's creditors.

(iii) In these circumstances personal representatives may apply by a Part 8 Claim Form (Form N208) headed "In the Matter of the Estate of [ ] deceased (a Lloyd's estate) and In the Matter of the Practice Direction dated November 21, 1997" for leave to distribute the estate on the footing that no or D1–388 no further provision need be made for Lloyd's creditors. The Claim Form need not be served on any other party.

D1–389 **(iv)** The Claim should be supported by a witness statement or an affidavit substantially in the form in the Chancery Masters' Practice Forms adapted as necessary to the particular circumstances and accompanied by draft minutes of the desired order substantially in the form in the Chancery Masters' Practice Forms. It should be supported by a Statement of Costs in the form specified in the Costs Practice Direction for the summary assessment of costs, or the signed consent of the residuary beneficiaries to the amount of costs claimed by the personal representatives.

D1–390 **(v)** The application will be considered in the first instance by the Master who, if satisfied that the papers are in order and that the relief sought should be granted, may make the order without requiring the attendance of the applicants and send it to them. If not so satisfied, the Master may give directions for the further disposal of the application, including the joinder of contingent creditors as defendants.

D1–391 **(vi)** The procedure described in this Practice Direction at present applies only to estates whose liabilities have been reinsured into Equitas. Extensions to the procedure to deal with other cases may be considered in due course.

APPENDICES TO THE CHANCERY DIVISION PRACTICE DIRECTIONS

Appendix 1

Queen's Bench Master's Practice Directions

D1–392 The Queen's Bench Master's Practice Directions specified in the appendix to these directions shall apply to the Chancery Divison.

Queen's Bench Practice Direction No.	Description
[*to be completed*].	

Appendix 2

Administration of Chancery Chambers and Companies and Bankruptcy Court

D1–393 This Appendix is set out at Appendix 6 to the Chancery Guide.

Appendix 3

Written Evidence Lodgment Form

D1–394 **Chancery Chambers**

TO FILING SECTION—ROOM TM3.07
CLAIM NO:
SHORT TITLE:

Herewith Affidavit or witness statement of ....
/or if other document specify ....

filed in respect of—

		Tick
1.	Application before Judge on	
2.	Application before Master on	
3.	Charging Order	
4.	Garnishee Order	
5.	Permission to issue [claim for] possession	
6.	Service by alternative method	
7.	Service out of Jurisdiction	
8.	Evidence	
9.	Oral examination of debtor	
10.	To enable a Master's order to be drawn	
11.	Other (Specify)	

Signed:

Solicitors for Claimant/Defendant
other (please specify)

Telephone No:

Ref

SECTION D

Practice Direction
Chancery and Queen's Bench Divisions

The Fixing of Trial Dates and Windows in the Multi-Track

Chancery and Queen's Bench Divisions
(excluding the Admiralty and Commercial Courts and the Technology and Construction Court)

The Fixing of Trial Dates and Windows in the Multi-Track

General

D1–395 The Royal Courts of Justice presents unique problems in terms of fixing trial dates. The number of Judges and Masters involved and their geographical location in tandem with the offices awaiting the installation of a fully integrated IT Support System scheduled for the summer of 2000 has caused, for the time being at least, a different approach to the fixing of trials in the Chancery and Queen's Bench Divisions. Moreover, the requirements of Judges to go on Circuit, sit in the Criminal Division of the Court of Appeal, deal with cases in the Crown Office and other lists make it difficult to fix dates for trials before particular Judges. Accordingly, the following will only apply to the Listing Offices in those Divisions in the Royal Courts of Justice.

Procedure

D1–396 (1) At as early an interim stage as practicable, the Court will give directions with a view to fixing the trial date or the week within which the trial is to begin (the trial window).

D1–397 (2) For that purpose the Court may:—

(a) direct that the trial do not begin earlier than a specified date calculated to provide enough time for the parties to complete any necessary preparations for trial; and/or

(b) direct that the trial date be within a specified period; and/or

(c) specify the trial date or window.

D1–398 (3) If direction under (2)(a) or (2)(b) are given the Court will direct the parties to attend upon the Listing Officer at such time as may be specified in order to fix the trial date or trial window.

D1–399 (4) The claimant must, unless some other party agrees to do so, take out an appointment with the Listing Officer within 7 days of obtaining the direction in paragraph (3) above and give notice of the appointment to all other parties. If an appointment is not taken out within the 7 days, the Listing Office will appoint a date for a listing hearing and give notice of the date to all parties.

D1–400 (5) At the listing hearing the Listing Officer will take account, in so far as it is practical to do so, of any difficulties the parties may have as to availability of counsel, experts and witnesses. The Listing Officer will, nevertheless, try to ensure the speedy disposal of the trial by arranging a firm trial date as soon as possible within the trial period or, as the case may be, after the "not before" date directed by the court under (2)(a) above. (If a case summary has been prepared (see the Multi-Track Practice Direction, paras 5.6 and 5.7) the claimant must produce a copy at the listing hearing together with a copy of the particulars of claim and any Orders relevant to the fixing of the trial date).

D1–401 (6) The Listing Officer will notify the Masters' Support staff of any trial date or trial window given. In accordance with rule 29.2(3) notice will also be given to all the parties.

D1–402 (7) A party who wishes to appeal a date or window allocated by the Listing Officer must, within 7 days of the allocation, make an application to the Judge nominated by each Division to hear such applications. The application notice should be filed in the Listing Office and served, giving one clear day's notice, on the other parties.

Issued by direction of the Vice Chancellor.

APPENDICES

APPENDIX 1

GUIDELINES ON STATEMENTS OF CASE

1. The document must be as brief and concise as possible. D1–403

2. The document must be set out in separate consecutively numbered paragraphs and sub-paragraphs. D1–404

3. So far as possible each paragraph or sub-paragraph should contain no more than one allegation. D1–405

4. The document should deal with the case on a point by point basis, to allow a point by point response.

5. Where the CPR require a party to give reasons (see CPR rule 16.5(2)), the allegation should be stated first and then the reasons listed one by one in separate numbered sub-paragraphs. D1–406

6. A party wishing to advance a positive case must identify that case in the document; a simple denial is not sufficient. D1–407

7. Any matter which if not stated might take another party by surprise should be stated. D1–408

8. Where they will assist, headings, abbreviations and definitions should be used and a glossary annexed. D1–409

9. Contentious headings, abbreviations, paraphrasing and definitions should not be used; every effort should be made to ensure that headings, abbreviations and definitions are in a form that will enable them to be adopted without issue by the other parties. D1–410 D1–411

10. Particulars of primary allegations should be stated as particulars and not as primary allegations. D1–412

11. Schedules or appendices should be used if this would be helpful, for example where lengthy particulars are necessary. D1–413

12. The names of any witness to be called may be given, and necessary documents (including an experts report) can be attached or served contemporaneously if not bulky (PD supplementing CPR Part 16; Guide para. 4.8). Otherwise evidence should not be included. D1–414

13. A response to particulars stated in a schedule should be stated in a corresponding schedule.

14. A party should not set out lengthy extracts from a document in his or her statement of case. If an extract has to be included, it should be placed in a schedule. D1–416

15. If solicitors or counsel drafted the statement of case, their name should appear at the end. D1–417

APPENDIX 2

GUIDELINES ON BUNDLES

Bundles of documents must comply with paragraph 3 of PD—Miscellaneous Provisions relating to Hearings supplementing CPR Part 39. These guidelines are additional to those requirements, and they should be followed wherever possible. D1–418

Duplicate copies

1. One copy, and one copy only, of each document on which any party intends to rely should be included. D1–419

2. If the same document is included in the chronological bundles and is also an exhibit to an affidavit, it should be included in the chronological bundle and where it would otherwise appear as an exhibit to an affidavit a sheet should instead be inserted. This sheet should state the page and bundle number in the chronological bundles where the documents can be found. D1–420

3. Where the Court considers that costs have been wasted by copying unnecessary documents, a special costs order may be made against the relevant person. D1–421

Pagination

4. This is covered by paragraph 3 of the PD. An exception to consecutive page numbering arises in the case of the core bundle. For this it may be preferable to retain the original numbering with each bundle represented by a separate divider. D1–422

5. Page numbers should be inserted in bold figures at the centre of the bottom of each page. D1–423

Chronological order

6. In general documents should be inserted in date order commencing with the earliest document. D1–424

Format and Organisation

7. Where possible, the documents should be in A4 format. Where a document has to be read D1–425

across rather than down the page, it should so be placed in the bundle as to ensure that the top of the text starts nearest the spine.

D1–426 8. Where any marking or writing in colour on a document is important, for example on a conveyancing plan, the document must be copied in colour or marked up correctly in colour.

D1–427 9. The size of any bundle should be tailored to its contents. There is no point having a large lever-arch file with just a few pages inside. On the other hand bundles should not be overloaded as they tend to break.

D1–428 10. Binders and files must be strong enough to withstand heavy use.

Staples etc.

D1–429 11. All staples, heavy metal clips etc. should be removed from documents in the bundle.

Statements of case

D1–430 12. Statements of case should be assembled in "chapter" form, *i.e.* claim form followed by particulars of claim, followed by further information, irrespective of date.

D1–431 13. Redundant documents, *e.g.* particulars of claim overtaken by amendments, requests for further information recited in the answers given, should generally be excluded. Backsheets to statements of case should also be omitted.

Witness statements and affidavits

D1–432 14. Where there are witness statements or affidavits from both sides, the claimant's/defendant's witness statements should be contained in separate bundles.

D1–433 15. The copies of the witness statements and affidavits in the bundles should have added to them, next to the reference to any document, the reference to that document in the bundles. This can be done in manuscript after the Court bundles have been prepared.

D1–434 16. Backsheets to affidavits should be omitted.

New documents

D1–435 17. Before a new document is introduced into bundles which have already been delivered to the Court—indeed before it is copied—steps should be taken to ensure that it carries an appropriate bundle/page number, so that it can be added to the Court documents.

D1–436 18. If it is expected that a large number of miscellaneous new documents will from time to time be introduced, there should be a special loose-leaf file for that purpose.

D1–437 19. An index should be produced for this file, updated as necessary.

Inter-solicitor correspondence

D1–438 20. It is seldom that all inter-solicitor correspondence is required. Only those letters which are likely to be referred to should be copied. They should normally be placed in a separate bundle.

Photocopy authorities

D1–439 21. If authorities, extracts from text-books etc. are photocopied for convenience for use in court, the photocopies should be placed in a separate bundle with an index and dividers. Reduced sized copies (*i.e.* two pages of original to each A4 sheet) should not be used. Where only a short passage from a long case is needed, the headnote and key pages only should be copied and the usher should be asked to have the full volume in Court.

APPENDIX 3

GUIDELINES ON SKELETON ARGUMENTS AND CHRONOLOGIES

D1–440 1. A skeleton argument should:

(1) concisely summarise the party's submissions in relation to each of the issues. It should cite the main authorities relied upon, which may be attached. It is not however the function of a skeleton argument to argue the case on paper;

(2) be as brief as the nature of the issues allows. It should not normally exceed 20 pages of double-spaced A4 paper and in many cases it should be much shorter than this;

(3) be divided into numbered paragraphs and paged consecutively. Any additional skeleton arguments coming from the same party should continue the numbering from the end of the previous documents;

(4) avoid formality and make use of abbreviations, *e.g.* C for Claimant, A/345 for bundle A page 345, 1.1.95 for 1st January 1995 etc.;

(5) identify any core documents which the Judge should if possible read before the heading starts.

2. Paragraph 1 also applies to written summaries of opening speeches and final speeches. D1–441

3. Chronologies should be non-contentious and agreed with the other parties if possible. If there is a material dispute about any event stated in the chronology, that should be stated. D1–442

APPENDIX 4

GUIDELINES ON WITNESS STATEMENTS

1. The function of a witness statement is to set out in writing the evidence in chief of the maker of the statement. Accordingly witness statements should, so far as possible, be expressed in the witness's own words. This guideline applies unless the perception or recollection of the witness of the events in question is not in issue. D1–443

2. Witness statements should be as concise as the circumstances of the case allow. They should be written in consecutively numbered paragraphs. They should present the evidence in an orderly and readily comprehensible manner. They should be signed by the witness, and contain a statement that he or she believes that the facts stated in his or her witness statement are true. D1–444

3. Inadmissible material should not be included. Irrelevant material should likewise not be included. D1–445

4. Any party on whom a witness statement is served who objects to the relevance or admissibility of material contained in a witness statement should notify the other party of his or her objection within 28 days after service of the witness statement in question and the parties concerned should attempt to resolve the matter as soon as possible. If it is not possible to resolve the matter, the party who objects should make an appropriate application, normally at the PTR, if there is one, or otherwise at trial. D1–446

5. It is incumbent on solicitors and counsel not to allow the costs of preparation of witness statements to be unnecessarily increased by over-elaboration of the statements. Any unnecessary elaboration may be the subject of a special order as to costs. D1–447

6. Witness statements must contain the truth, the whole truth and nothing but the truth on the issues covered. Great care must be taken in the preparation of witness statements. No pressure of any kind should be placed on a witness to give other than a true and complete account of his or her evidence. It is improper to serve a witness statement which is known to be false or which the maker does not in all respects actually believe to be true. In addition, a professional adviser may be under an obligation to check where practicable the truth of facts stated in a witness statement if he or she is put on enquiry as to their truth. If a party discovers that a witness statement which he or she has served is incorrect he or she must inform the other parties immediatley. D1–448

7. A witness statement should simply cover those issues, but only those issue, on which the party serving the statement wishes that witness to give evidence in chief. Thus it is not, for example, the function of a witness statement to provide a commentary on the documents in the trial bundle. Witness statements should not deal with other matters merely because they may arise in the course of the trial. D1–449

8. Occasionally a party who serves a witness statement wishes the witness making the statement to give additional evidence, for example to deal with events occurring, or matters discovered, after his or her statement was served or in response to matters dealt with by another party's witness. In these cases, a supplementary witness statement should if practicable be served as soon as possible. Permission to adduce the evidence contained in a supplementary witness statement will be needed unless the other party consents. However this need not be sought prior to service. D1–450

APPENDIX 5

JUDGE'S APPLICATION INFORMATION FORM

IN THE HIGH COURT OF JUSTICE D1–451

CHANCERY DIVISION

[– CLAIM NO. –]

[– CLAIMANT(S) –]

and

[– DEFENDANT(S) –]

Application Information

1. [– DATE APPLICATION TO BE HEARD –]
2. DETAILS OF SOLICITOR/PARTY LODGING THE APPLICATION
   a. [Name]
   b. [Address]
   c. [Telephone No.]
   d. [Reference]
   e. [Acting for Claimant(s)/Defendant(s)]
3. DETAILS OF COUNSEL/OR OTHER ADVOCATE
   a. [Name]
   b. [Address of Chambers/Firm]
   c. [Telephone No.]
4. DETAILS OF OTHER PARTY('S) (IES) SOLICITORS
   a. [Name]
   b. [Address]
   c. [Telephone No.]
   d. [Reference]
   e. [Acting for Claimant(s)/Defendant(s)]

APPENDIX 6

ADDRESSES, ROOM NUMBERS AND TELEPHONE AND FAX NUMBERS

D1–452 (*All telephone extension numbers and fax numbers should be prefixed by 0171 936 unless otherwise specified*)

1st Floor

TM1.10. Bankruptcy Registrars' Clerks, *ex parte* applications, Registrars' hearings and orders, setting down appeals from Registrars and District and Circuit Judges (6444).

Bankruptcy Registrars' Chambers (7386).

Bankruptcy Court Fax no.: (6378)

2nd Floor

D1–453 TM2.06. Deputy Court Manager (6863).

TM2.07. Court Manager, Companies, Bankruptcy and Restrictive Practices Courts (6870).

TM2.09. Companies Court General Office: issue of all winding-up petitions and all other Companies Court applications, filing of documents and requests for office copies (6294).

Central Searches: General Index (7328).

TM2.11. Bankruptcy Issue Room: issue of all petitions presented by creditors and debtors and applictions to set aside statutory demand and applications for interim orders; search room (6448).

Companies Court Fax no.: (6958).

3rd Floor

D1–454 TM3.07. Chancery Chambers Registry and Issue Section: issue and amendment of all Chancery process, filing affidavits and witness statements save those lodged within two days of a hearing before a Master which shall be filed in Room TM7.09; filing acknowledgments of service, searches of cause book; applications for office copy documents, including orders; transfers in and out (6148/6167).

TM3.08 and 3.09. Bankruptcy and Companies Registry. Filing affidavits and documents and bespeaking bankruptcy and company files for *ex parte* applications to be made in Chambers; requests for office copies, lodging applications for certificates of discharge in bankruptcy (6441).

4th Floor

D1–455 TM4.04. Companies Schemes and reductions (6365).

TM4.05. Companies Orders Section (Winding up Court) (6731).

TM4.09. Companies Orders Section (Registrars' Chamber and disqualification of directors (6822).

5th Floor

D1–456 Court 79.

TM5.06. Section Manager, Order and Accounts Section (6754).

TM5.07 and TM5.13. Associates: preparation of all Chancery Orders and Companies and Bankruptcy Court Orders.

TM5.06. Accounts: bills of costs for assessment; small payments; sales by private treaty or auction; settlement of payment and lodgement schedules (otherwise than part of an Order); accounts of receivers; judicial trustees; guardians and administrators; applications relating to security set by the court; references to costs Judges under O.62, r.24; matters arising out of accounts and inquiries ordered by the court (6059/6728).

Chancery Orders and Accounts Fax no.: (7049).

TM5.09. Lawyer, Chancery Chambers (6080).

6th Floor

Court 78. **D1–457**

TM6.04. Chancery Masters' Library.

TM6.05. Master Bowman.

TM6.06. Court Manager, Chancery Chambers (6075).

TM6.07. Master Bowles.

TM6.08. Secretary to Masters (6777).

TM6.09. Master Bragge.

7th Floor

TM7.04. Deputy Court Manager, Chancery Chambers. Certification of documents for use abroad (6523). **D1–458**

TM7.05. Deputy Master.

TM7.06. Master Moncaster.

TM7.06. Chief Master Winegarten.

TM7.09. Masters' Appointments. Issue of Master' applications, including applications without notice to Masters; filing affidavits and witness statements in proceedings before Masters (only if filed within two working days of hearing before the Master); applications to serve out of jurisdiction; filing stop notices; filing testamentary documents in contested probate cases; filing grants lodged under O.99, r.7; filing affidavits relating to funds paid into court under the Trustee Act 1925, Compulsory Purchase Act 1965 and the Lands Clauses Consolidation Act 1845.

Executive office in charge (6095).

Clerks to Chancery Masters (6702/7391).

Masters' Appointments Fax no.: (7422).

8th Floor

Court 77: Bankruptcy Court; public examinations. **D1–459**

TM8.09. Senior Court Manager (*p.m. only*) (6736).

Any difficulty in contacting the relevant office should be referred to the Chancery Chambers Registry and Issue Section.

Addresses, room numbers, telephone and fax numbers outside Thomas More Building

(*Prefaced by 0171 936 unless otherwise specified*) **D1–460**

RCJ Switchboard (6000).

RCJ Security Office (6260).

Fees Office (Rm E01) (6527).

W15. Chancery Division Clerk of the Lists; Chancery Judges' Listing Office (6778/6690).

W11. Chancery Judges' Listing General Office (Motions and Listing enquiries) (6816).

Chancery Judges' Listing Office Fax no.:[1] (7345) .

Central Registry of Winding up Petitions (7328).

Officer in charge of mechanical recording (Rm WB.11) (6154).

Head Usher: Fax no.: (6668).

Citizens Advice Bureau at Royal Courts of Justice (6880) (Fax: 7167).

Royal Courts of Justice, Strand, London WC2A 2LL.

Central London County Court:

Civil Trial Centre, Chancery List, 26 Park Crescent, London W1N 4HT
DX 97325 Regents Park 2
Tel. 0171 917 7860 (office)
917 7887 (section manager)
Fax (Business Chancery and Patents section) 0171 917 7935

[1] (*See section [13.4(3)].*)

Official Referees Solicitors Association (ORSA) (0171 490 4000)
c/o Messrs Masons, 30 Aylesbury Street, London EC1R 0EP

THE COMMERCIAL COURT GUIDE

CONTENTS

D2–001

Introduction

Practice Directions

THE COMMERCIAL COURT

D2–002 List of Judges as at 1 January 1999

The Hon Mr Justice Rix (Judge in charge of the Commercial List)

The Hon Mr Justice Cresswell
The Hon Mr Justice Colman
The Hon Mr Justice Mance
The Hon Mr Justice Longmore
The Hon Mr Justice Morison
The Hon Mr Justice Moore-Bick
The Hon Mr Justice Langley
The Hon Mr Justice Thomas
The Hon Mr Justice Toulson
The Hon Mr Justice Timothy Walker
The Hon Mr Justice David Steel

THE COMMERCIAL COURT GUIDE

INTRODUCTION

D2–003 The Commercial Court was brought into existence in 1895 to provide a Court in which there was a greater familiarity with the subject matter of commercial and mercantile disputes and to provide procedures which would enable those disputes to be determined justly expeditiously and efficiently and without unnecessary formality.

D2–004 These remain the objectives of the Commercial Court today; the Judges of the Court and practitioners in the Court seek to use their expertise and experience to further them.

D2–005 The work of the Commercial Court is highly diverse. As commercial and mercantile activity changes so too does the range of work the Court attracts. The procedure of the Court has to take account of the whole range of the Court's work. There is more need than ever for the Court's procedure to be flexible and responsive. But procedure alone is not enough. The Commercial Court expects expertise, efficiency, co-operation and realism from the legal representatives of the parties.

D2–006 The introduction of the Civil Procedure Rules on 26 April 1999 will see major changes in the way that the business of any Court is transacted. Approached in a constructive spirit, the introduction of these Rules presents a major opportunity to add to the strengths and advantages of the English jurisdiction as a forum for commercial and international litigation and dispute resolution.

D2–007 The "overriding objective" of the Civil Procedure Rules is to enable the Courts to deal with cases justly. As the body of this Guide emphasises, it too has as its purpose the service of the "overriding objective", but in the specialist context of commercial cases.

D2–008 Particular attention is drawn to Part D of the Guide relating to case management, Part F relating to applications, and Part H relating to expert evidence. Important Appendices include Appendix 4 relating to statements of case and Appendix 11 on bundle preparation.

D2–009 The Civil Procedure Rules apply to cases in the Commercial List subject to the provisions of this Guide. This Guide adapts some of the Civil Procedure Rules, and puts others in a particular context, in order that the special demands of the work of the Court can be met. To the same end it also introduces some further procedural requirements not found in the Civil Procedure Rules.

The Guide is being issued for the first time in a loose-leaf form. This is to enable changes, where necessary, to be effected rapidly and in a user friendly form. The Judges of the Commercial Court, together with the Commercial Court Committee, will be closely monitoring the working of the Guide in the context of the new Civil Procedure Rules as a whole. **D2–010**

This Guide is not a substitute for the Civil Procedure Rules, and does not attempt to cover all procedural points. It is not a litigation hand-book nor a blue-print to which all litigation must unthinkingly conform. It rather seeks to provide a modem and flexible framework within which litigation in the Commercial Court can be conducted with efficiency and in the interests of justice. **D2–011**

PRACTICE DIRECTIONS

PRACTICE DIRECTION—COMMERCIAL COURT

This Practice Direction supplements CPR Part 49 and replaces, with modifications, Order 72 of the Rules of the Supreme Court (see para. 49DPD–001). **D2–012**

PRACTICE DIRECTION—ARBITRATIONS

This Practice Direction supplements CPR Part 49 and replaces, with modifications, Order 73 of the Rules of the Supreme Court (see para. 49GPD–001 above). **D2–012A**

A. PRELIMINARY

A1 Status of the Guide

The Civil Procedure Rules and the Commercial Court Practice Direction

A1.1 This Guide is brought into force by the Practice Direction—Commercial Court ("the Commercial Court Practice Direction"). **D2–013**

A1.2 By Rule 49 of the Civil Procedure Rules ("CPR") the CPR apply to commercial proceedings subject to the relevant Practice Direction which applies to those proceedings. For commercial claims in the Commercial List, the Commercial Court Practice Direction is the relevant Practice Direction (see paragraph 1.1 of the Commercial Court Practice Direction). **D2–014**

The Guide

A1.3 Paragraph 9.5 of the Commercial Court Practice Direction provides that the practice set out in this Guide should be followed subject to the provisions of the Commercial Court Practice Direction or any other Commercial Court Practice Direction and to any order that may be made in an individual case. **D2–015**

A1.4 In matters for which specific provision is not made by this Guide, the parties, their solicitors and their counsel will be expected to act in accordance with the spirit of the Guide. **D2–016**

A1.5 Transitional arrangements are detailed in Appendix 20. **D2–017**

Other Practice Directions supplementing the CPR

A1.6 Practice Directions supplementing the CPR that are not Commercial Court Practice Directions also apply to proceedings in the Commercial List, save where otherwise provided in this Guide. For ease of reference, Appendix 1 sets out in schedule form the application of Practice Directions supplementing the CPR to proceedings in the Commercial List. **D2–018**

A2 Purpose of the Guide

D2–019 A2.1 The "overriding objective" of the CPR is to enable the Courts to deal with cases justly (see CPR 1.1).

D2–020 A2.2 The purpose of this Guide is to serve the "overriding objective" in the specialist context of commercial cases.

A3 Future development of the Guide

D2–021 A3.1 The Commercial Court has since it was first established sought periodically to adapt its procedure to the continually changing needs of the commercial community.

D2–022 A3.2 This Guide will be kept under review.

A4 Particular features of the Commercial Court

D2–023 A4.1 In principle, and the resources available to the Court permitting, the trial or other hearing of a case should take place at the earliest date for which the parties can be ready.

D2–024 A4.2 Pre-trial matters in the Commercial Court are dealt with by the Judges of the Court (see paragraph 2.2 of the Commercial Court Practice Direction).

D2–025 A4.3 The Commercial Court expects a high level of co-operation and realism from the legal representatives of the parties. This expectation applies to dealings (including correspondence) between legal representatives and to dealings with the Court.

A5 The Admiralty & Commercial Court Registry; the Commercial Court Listing Office

D2–026 A5.1 The Admiralty & Commercial Court Registry ("the Registry") is located at Room E200 in the Royal Courts of Justice, Strand, London WC2A 2LL. The Commercial Court Listing Office ("the Listing Office") is located at Room E201 in the Royal Courts of Justice, Strand, London WC2A 2LL.

D2–027 A5.2 It is important that there is close liaison between legal representatives of the parties and both the Registry and the Listing Office.

A6 The Commercial Court Committee

D2–028 A6.1 The success of the Court's ability to meet the special problems and continually changing needs of the commercial community depends in part upon a steady flow of information and constructive suggestions between the Court, litigants and professional advisers.

D2–029 A6.2 The Commercial Court Committee has assisted in this process for many years. It is expected to play an important part in helping to ensure that the Court remains responsive to the "overriding objective". All concerned with the Court are encouraged to make the fullest use of this important channel of communication.

A7 Specialist associations

D2–030 A7.1 There are a number of associations of legal representatives which liaise closely with the Commercial Court. These will also play an important part in helping to ensure that the Court remains responsive to the "overriding objective".

D2–031 A7.2 The associations include the Commercial Bar Association ("COMBAR"), the London Common Law and Commercial Bar Association ("LCLCBA"), the City of London Law Society, the London Solicitors Litigation Association and the Admiralty Solicitors Group.

B. COMMENCEMENT TRANSFER AND REMOVAL

B1 Commercial cases

D2–032 B1.1 Paragraph 1.2(1) of the Commercial Court Practice Direction describes a "commercial claim". A "commercial claim" includes any case arising out of trade and commerce in general, including any case relating to a business document or contract, the export or import of goods, the carriage of goods by land, sea, air or pipeline, the exploitation of oil and gas reserves, insurance and reinsurance, banking and financial services, the operation of markets and exchanges, business agency and arbitration.

B2 Starting a commercial case in the Commercial Court

D2–033 B2.1 Subject to certain exceptions for certain applications relating to arbitrations, the case will be begun by a claim form under CPR Part 7 or Part 8.

D2–034 B2.2 The exceptions for applications relating to arbitrations are identified in the Practice Direction—Arbitrations ("the Arbitration Practice Direction"), which replaces, with modifications, RSC Order 73 (and see also section M of and Appendix 19 to this Guide).

D2–035 B2.3 Save where specified, in this Guide references to a claim form are to a Part 7 claim form.

D2–036 B2.4 The Commercial Court may give a fixed date for trial (see paragraph D12 below). However it does not give a fixed date for a hearing when it issues a claim; CPR 7.9 and the Practice Direction supplementing it accordingly have no application in the Commercial Court.

D2–037 B2.5 There is no Production Centre for the issue of claim forms for the Commercial Court;

CPR 7.10 and the Practice Direction supplementing it accordingly have no application in the Commercial Court.

B3 The Part 7 claim form

The form

B3.1 In accordance with paragraph 3.1 of the Practice Direction supplementing CPR Part 7, a claimant must use practice form no. N1 to start a claim under CPR Part 7. Paragraph 3.4 of the Practice Direction supplementing CPR Part 7 contemplates that a different practice form may be approved for specialist proceedings. **D2–038**

Marking

B3 .2 In accordance with paragraph 3.2 of the Commercial Court Practice Direction, the claim form should be marked with the words "Queen's Bench Division, Commercial Court", and on the issue of the claim form out of the Registry the case will be entered in the Commercial List. The required marking should appear in the top right hand corner of the claim form. **D2–039**

Statement of value

B3.3 CPR 16.3 and 16.5(6) contain provisions dealing with the inclusion of a statement of value in a claim form. In the Commercial Court compliance with the requirement for marking at paragraph B3.2 above is sufficient to satisfy CPR 16.3(5). Thus— **D2–040**

a. CPR 16.3(1), 16.3(2)(a) and 16.3(7) apply; but
b. no other provision of CPR 16.3 applies; and
c. CPR 16.5(6) does not apply.

Compliance with the requirement for marking at paragraph B3.2 above is also sufficient to satisfy paragraph 3.6 of the Practice Direction supplementing CPR Part 7, and paragraph 2 of the Practice Direction supplementing CPR Part 16 (each of which deal with statement of value).

Particulars of claim and the claim form

B3.4 For cases entered in the Commercial List, whilst a claim form may contain or be accompanied by particulars of claim, there is no requirement for this. In many cases it will not be realistic and particulars of claim will instead be served after the claim form. **D2–041**

B3.5 In these circumstances, the requirement at paragraph 3.1 of the Practice Direction supplementing CPR Part 16 (that if practicable the particulars of claim should be set out in the claim form) does not apply in the Commercial Court. **D2–042**

B3.6 Further, for claim forms issued in the Commercial List it is the claim form (rather than the particulars of claim) that must be accompanied by the three forms specified in CPR 7.8(1), one of which is a form for acknowledging service. If the particulars of claim are not contained in or served with the claim form, the claimant must include a statement on the claim form that if an acknowledgment of service is filed that indicates an intention to defend the claim then the particulars of claim will follow. This is in place of the requirement at CPR 16.2(2), paragraph 3.3 of the Practice Direction supplementing CPR Part 16 and paragraph 5.1 of the Practice Direction supplementing CPR Part 7. **D2–043**

Statement of truth

B3.7 A claim form (being a statement of case) must be verified by a statement of truth (CPR 22.1). Unless the Court otherwise orders any amendment to a claim form must also be verified (CPR 22.1(2)). The required form of statement of truth is set out at paragraph 6.2 of the Practice Direction supplementing CPR Part 7. **D2–044**

Trial without service of particulars of claim or a defence

B3.8 The attention of the parties and their legal representatives is drawn to paragraph 5 of the Commercial Court Practice Direction. This allows a Commercial Judge to order before or after the issue of a claim form) that the case shall be tried without the service or filing of particulars of claim or of a defence or of any other statement of case. **D2–045**

Interest

B3.9 The claim form (and not only the particulars of claim) must include the matters required by CPR 16.4(1)(b) and (2) (each of which deals with interest). **D2–046**

B3.10 For the avoidance of doubt, in cases in the Commercial Court references to particulars of claim in CPR 12.6(1) (referring to claims for interest where there is a default judgment) and CPR **D2–047**

14.14(1)(a) (referring to claims for interest where there is a judgment on admissions) may be treated as references to the claim form.

Issue of a claim form where the Registry is closed

D2–048 B3.11 The facility exists in the Commercial Court for dealing with requests by fax for the issue of a Part 7 claim form where the Registry is closed to the public. The procedure is as set out in Appendix 3. Any further details may be obtained from the Registry. The applicable fax number is given at the end of the Guide.

B4 The Part 8 claim form

Form

D2–049 B4.1 In accordance with paragraph 3.1 of the Practice Direction supplementing CPR Part 7, a claimant must use practice form no. N208 to start a claim under CPR Part 8. Paragraph 3.4 of the Practice Direction supplementing CPR Part 7 contemplates that a different practice form may be approved for specialist proceedings.

D2–050 B4.2 Attention is drawn to the requirement under CPR 8.2(a) that where a claimant uses the Part 8 procedure his claim form must state that Part 8 applies. Similarly, paragraph 3.3 of the Practice Direction supplementing CPR Part 7 requires that the claim form state (if it be the case) that the claimant wishes his claim to proceed under CPR Part 8 or that the claimant's position is that the claim is required to proceed under CPR Part 8. Paragraph 2.2 of the Practice Direction supplementing CPR Part 8 is also in similar terms.

Marking and statement of truth

D2–051 B4.3 Paragraph B3.2 above (marking) and paragraph B3.7 above (statement of truth) apply also to a claim form filed under CPR Part 8.

Other matters

D2–052 B4.4 CPR Part 8 applies to proceedings commenced by the issue of a Part 8 claim form, save that case management of a claim under CPR Part 8 is dealt with as referred to at paragraph D7.20 below, and disputes as to jurisdiction are dealt with as referred to at paragraph B7.8 below.

D2–053 B4.5 The use of a Part 8 claim form in arbitration matters is governed by the Arbitration Practice Direction (see also Appendix 19).

B5 Service of the claim form

Service by the parties

D2–054 B5.1 In accordance with paragraph 8.3 of the Commercial Court Practice Direction, claim forms issued in the Commercial List are to be served by the parties, not by the Registry (*cf.* CPR 6.3).

Methods of service

D2–055 B5.2 Methods of service are set out in CPR Part 6, which is supplemented by a Practice Direction.

D2–056 B5.3 Paragraphs 2.1 and 3.1 of the Practice Direction supplementing CPR Part 6 concern service by document exchange and by fax. Satisfaction of the requirements at paragraph 2.1 or 3.1(3)(b) of that Practice Direction will not be sufficient to allow service of the claim form by document exchange or by fax on the legal representative of the defendant unless that legal representative has also confirmed in writing that he has instructions to accept service of a claim form on behalf of the defendant, or the Court otherwise orders.

Applications for an extension of time

D2–057 B5.4 Applications for an extension of time in which to serve a claim form are governed by CPR 7.6, save that CPR 7.6(3)(a) (referring to service of the claim form by the Court) has no application to claim forms issued in the Commercial List.

D2–058 B5.5 The evidence required on an application for an extension of time is set out at paragraph 7.2 of the Practice Direction supplementing CPR Part 7.

Certificate of service

D2–059 B5.6 In accordance with CPR 6.14(2) once the claimant has served the claim form he must file a certificate of service. Satisfaction of this requirement is, in particular, relevant to the claimant's ability to obtain judgment in default (see CPR Part 12) and the right of a non-party to search for, inspect and take a copy of the claim form (see CPR 5.4(2)(a)).

B6 Service of the claim form out of the jurisdiction

B6.1 Applications for permission to serve a claim form out of the jurisdiction continue to be governed by RSC Order 11. **D2–060**

B6.2 Appendix 17 contains the applicable practice (adapted from that previously set out in the Fourth Edition of the Guide). **D2–061**

B6.3 Service of process in some foreign countries may take a long time to complete; it is incumbent upon solicitors to take prompt steps to effect such service. **D2–062**

B7 Acknowledgment of service

Part 7 claims

B7.1 CPR 10.1(3) limits the circumstances in which a defendant may file an acknowledgment of service to the following: (a) if he is unable to file a defence within 14 days after service of the particulars of claim and (1)) if he wishes to dispute the Court's jurisdiction. In dealing with the general rule for the period for filing an acknowledgment of service, CPR 10.3(1) contemplates that an acknowledgment of service will follow rather than precede service of particulars of claim (even where service of those particulars of claim is to follow service of the claim form). **D2–063**

B7.2 In the Commercial Court the preparation of particulars of claim can frequently be a complex task. The number of commercial cases where there is a dispute as to jurisdiction is reasonably high and the expense of preparation of particulars of claim may be wasted where jurisdiction is successfully challenged. Accordingly, in order to save time and cost, and to ensure uniformity of procedure in cases where the claim form has been issued in the Commercial List, the procedure at paragraph B7.3 below will apply in the Commercial Court. (The procedure does not alter the provisions for acknowledgment of service of a Part 8 claim form (CPR 8.3)). **D2–064**

B7.3a. A defendant should file an acknowledgment of service in every case. **D2–065**

b. The period for filing the acknowledgment of service will be calculated from service of the claim form (whether or not particulars of claim are to follow service of the claim form, are contained in the claim form or accompany the claim form). CPR 9.1(2) (which provides that in certain circumstances the defendant need not respond to the claim until particulars of claim have been served on him) does not apply.

c. Save as provided at B7.4 below, or otherwise ordered by the Court, the period for filing the acknowledgment of service will be 14 days after service of the claim form.

B7.4 The time specified at B7.3c above: **D2–066**

a. is (in accordance with CPR 10.3(2)(a)) subject to RSC Order 11 rule 1A (which deals with the time for acknowledgment of service where a claim form is served out of the jurisdiction without the need for the Court's permission), save that sub-paragraphs (a) and (b) of rule 1A(2) should be replaced with the words "21 days after service of the claim form" and sub-paragraphs (a) and (b) of rule 1A(3) should be replaced with the words "31 days after service of the claim form" (a similar adjustment may be required to the periods to be set out in the Practice Direction contemplated by rule 1A(4));

b. is also (in accordance with CPR 10.3(2)(b)) subject to CPR 6.16(4) ("service of claim form on agent of principal who is overseas"), although in the Commercial Court the reference in that rule to "respond to the particulars of claim" should be replaced with the words "file an acknowledgement of service of the claim form";

c. is also subject to RSC Order 11 rule 4(4) (which deals with the time for acknowledgment of service where a claim form is served out of the jurisdiction with the Court's permission).

B7.5 For the avoidance of doubt, an acknowledgment of service which is followed by an application under CPR Part 11 to dispute the Court's jurisdiction (or that the Court should not exercise its jurisdiction) made within the period for filing a defence shall not constitute a submission by the defendant to the jurisdiction. **D2–067**

Default judgment

B7.6 Default judgment is governed by CPR Part 12, and the Practice Direction supplementing that Part. However, because in the Commercial Court the period for filing the acknowledgment of service will be calculated from service of the claim form, the reference to "particulars of claim" in paragraph 4.1(1) of the Practice Direction supplementing CPR Part 12 should be read in the Commercial Court as a reference to the claim form. **D2–068**

Admissions

B7.7 Admissions are governed by CPR Part 14, and the Practice Direction supplementing that **D2–069**

Part. However, again because in the Commercial Court the period for filing the acknowledgment of service will be calculated from service of the claim form, the references to "particulars of claim" in paragraphs 2.1, 3.1 and 3.2 of the Practice Direction supplementing CPR Part 14 should read in the Commercial Court as references to the claim form.

Part 8 claims

D2–070 B7.8 In a Part 8 claim where the defendant intends, under CPR Part 11, to dispute the Court's jurisdiction or argue that the Court should not exercise its jurisdiction:

a. only evidence in support of an application under CPR Part 11 need be served and filed when the acknowledgment of service is filed (or within 14 days thereafter: see CPR 8.3(4));

b. accordingly CPR 8.5(3) and (4), and paragraph 5.3 of the Practice Direction supplementing CPR Part 8, (which refer to the time for service and filing by a defendant of evidence in answer to the evidence served with the Part 8 claim form) do not apply where there is an application under CPR Part 11;

c. as with pargraph B7.5 above, an acknowledgment of service which is followed by an application under CPR Part 11 made within the period specified by CPR 8.3(4) shall not constitute a submission by the defendant to the jurisdiction;

d. if an application under CPR Part 11 is unsuccessful, and the Court then considers giving directions for filing and serving evidence in support and in answer to the Part 8 claim form, a defendant does not submit to the jurisdiction merely by requesting a particular period for filing and serving that evidence in answer.

Acknowledgment of service in a claim against a firm

D2–071 B7.9 Schedule 1 to the CPR includes, with modifications, provisions previously contained in RSC Order 81 in relation to acknowledgment of service in a claim against a firm (see also the note at the end of CPR Part 10).

D2–072 B7.10 It should be noted that paragraph 4.4 of the Practice Direction supplementing CPR Part 10 provides that in a claim against a firm the acknowledgment service may be signed by a person having the control or management of the partnership business, without requiring that that person be a partner.

B8 Transfer of cases to and removal of cases from the Commercial List

D2–072A B8.1 The procedure for transfer and removal is set out at paragraphs 4.1 to 4.5 of the Commercial Court Practice Direction.

D2–073 B8.2 Although an order to transfer a case to the Commercial List may be made at any stage, normally such an order is made at an early stage.

D2–074 B8.3 Although transfer to the Commercial List may be ordered for limited purposes only, normally a transferred case will remain in the Commercial List until its conclusion. (For the avoidance of doubt CPR 13.4(1) (referring to transfers to the defendant's home court of an application to set aside or vary a judgment) does not apply to a commercial case transferred to the Commercial List, just as it does not (by CPR 13.4(2)) apply to a case commenced in the Commercial List).

D2–075 B8.4 Although an order for removal of a case from the Commercial List may be made at any stage, such an order will not usually be made after a pre-trial timetable has been fixed at the Case Management Conference (paragraph D7 below).

D2–076 B8.5 Some commercial cases may more suitably, or as suitably, be dealt with in one of the Mercantile Courts established in certain regional trial centres or in the Business Lists at the Central London County Court or elsewhere. Parties should give serious consideration to the appropriateness of starting the case in such jurisdictions and the Commercial Judge may on his own initiative order transfer.

C. PARTICULARS OF CLAIM, DEFENCE AND REPLY

C1 Form, content, serving and filing

Form

D2–077 C1.1 Particulars of claim, the defence and any reply must (save where otherwise ordered) be drafted in a form that complies with Appendix 4

Content

C1.2 The matters required to be included in particulars of claim and in a defence are set out in CPR 16.4 and 16.5, and in the Practice Direction supplementing CPR Part 16. In the Commercial Court, particulars of claim, the defence and any reply should comply with the provisions there set out, with the following exceptions and additions: **D2–078**

a. In the circumstances of paragraphs B3.3 and B7.3 a. above, CPR 16.5(6) and 16.5(8) do not apply to cases in the Commercial Court.

b. The requirements at paragraph 10.3 of the Practice Direction supplementing CPR part 16 should be treated as applying to a defendant and his defence, and not simply to a claimant and his particulars of claim (unless the defence and the claim are based on the same written agreement). The alternative of attaching or serving only relevant pages or sections of the written agreement should be adopted where that is likely to be sufficiently useful to the Court and to the opposite party. In most cases, attaching or serving more than 20 pages of a written agreement will unduly increase the bulk of the particulars of claim or defence, but this will ultimately depend on the requirements of the particular case. Although paragraph 10.3(1) of the Practice Direction refers to a requirement that the original of the written agreement be available at the hearing, in the Commercial Court it will be sufficient if a true copy of the complete written agreement is available at the hearing, unless the Court requires or any party requests that the original be made available.

c. The requirements at paragraphs 10.4 to 11.1 of the Practice Direction supplementing CPR Part 16 should be treated as applying to defendant and his defence, and to a claimant and his reply (if any), and not simply to a claimant and his particulars of claim.

d. In addition to the requirement at pragraph 11.2 of the Practice Direction supplementing CPR Part 16:

  i. Full and specific details must be given of any allegation of fraud, dishonesty, malice or illegality.
  ii. Where an inference of fraud or dishonesty is alleged, the facts on the basis of which the inference is alleged must be listed.

e. Where reliance is intended to be placed on any statute, the statute and relevant sections must be stated.

f. Points of European Law or based on Human Rights legislation must be stated.

g. Any allegation of foreign law must be stated, with reference to any foreign legislation, legal decisions or legal texts relied upon.

h. The permission given at paragraph 11.3(1) and (2) of the Practice Direction supplementing CPR Part 16 applies to any statement of case.

i. The permission given at paragraph 11.3(3) of the Practice Direction supplementing CPR Part 16 is subject to the following points:

  i. it is emphasised that paragraph 11.3(3) gives a permission; it does not contain a requirement;
  ii. the permission given to serve or attach documents should be regarded in the Commercial Court as applying only to obviously critical documents referred to in the particulars of claim and which are necessary for a proper understanding of the particulars of claim;
  iii. if any documents are attached to or served with the particulars of claim the particulars of claim must refer to that fact;
  iv. whilst a claimant cannot be prevented from serving an expert's report at an early stage (including with his particulars of claim) an expert's report should ot be attached to the particulars of claim (and should not be filed with the particulars of claim at the Registry);
  v. it is possibly unlikely that an expert's report will be served with particulars of claim in the Commercial Court; claimants are reminded that an order of the Court granting permission will be required before any expert's report may be relies on and that any expert's report served by a claimant without such an order will be served at the claimant's risk as to costs.

Summaries

C1.3 If particulars of claim, a defence or a reply exceed 25 pages in length (excluding schedules) a summary of the document must also be prepared. **D2–079**

C1.4 The summary should not normally exceed 4 pages in length and is to be included in the case management bundle (see paragraph D6). The Court may also order a summary to be prepared in other circumstances. **D2–080**

C1.5 The paragraph numbering of any summary should cross refer to the paragraph numbering of the full version of the statement of case. **D2–081**

Length

C1.6 Parties serving statements of case should bear in mind that the Court will take into account the length of the document served when considering any application by another party for further time within which to respond to that document. **D2–082**

Statement of truth

D2–083 C1.7 Particulars of claim, a defence and any reply must be verified by a statement of truth (CPR 22.1). So too must any amendment, unless the Court otherwise orders (CPR 22.1(2)).

D2–084 C1.8 The required form of statement of truth is as follows:

a. particulars of claim: as set out in paragraph 6.2 of the Practice Direction supplementing CPR Part 7 or paragraph 3.4 of the Practice Direction supplementing CPR Part 16;

b. defence: as set out at paragraph 2.2 of the Practice Direction supplementing CPR Part 15 or paragraph 14.2 of the Practice Direction supplementing CPR Part 16;

c. reply: the statement of truth should follow the form for the particulars of claim, but substituting the word "reply" for the words "particulars of claim" (see paragraph 2.1 of the Practice Direction supplementing CPR Part 22).

Serving

D2–085 C1.9 All statements of case are served by the parties in the Commercial Court.

Filing

D2–086 C1.10 The statements of case filed with the Court (at the Registry) will form part of the permanent record of the Court.

C2 Serving and filing particulars of claim

D2–087 C2.1 CPR 7.4(1) and (2) provide that where particulars of claim are not contained in or served with the claim form they must be served within 14 days after service of the claim form and in any event no later than the latest time for serving a claim form. CPR 7.4(2) and (3) provide that the general rule is that a claim form must be served within 4 months after the date of issue, or 6 months where the claim form is to be served out of the jurisdiction. These provisions are also referred to at paragraph 3.2(2) of the Practice Direction supplementing CPR Part 16 and paragraph 5.1 of the Practice Direction supplementing CPR Part 7. CPR 7.6 contains provisions allowing aparty to apply for an order extending the period within which the claim form may be served.

D2–088 C2.2 CPR 7.4(1) and (2) (and the references to them in the paragraphs of the Practice Directions mentioned above) do not apply to cases in the Commercial Court. Service of particulars of claim within 14 days after service of the claim form, and in any event no later than the latest time for serving the claim form, would be unrealistic in many commercial cases, especially those involving defendants abroad. Such a requirement would also lose the advantage of the acknowledgment of service procedure described at paragraph B7 above. Further, in some cases the Court will wish to commence case management at a stage before service of particulars of claim, and in other cases the Court may decide (under paragraph 5 of the Commercial Court Practice Direction) to try a case without service of particulars of claim and of a defence.

D2–089 C2.3 For cases in the Commercial Court, in place of CPR 7.4(1) and (2) the procedure for serving the particulars of claim will mirror the essential elements of the procedure for serving a defence (see paragraph C3). The validity of the claim form is not affected by complying with this procedure in place of CPR 7.4(1) and (2).

D2–090 C2.4 Thus, subject to any contrary order of the Court and unless particulars of claim are contained in or accompany the claim form:

a. The general rule is that the period for serving particulars of claim is 28 days after acknowledgment of service.

b. The parties may agree extensions for serving the particulars of claim, but any such agreement must be evidenced in writing and will be subject to c. below, and to any subsequent order of the Court reducing the period for filing the particulars of claim to a period shorter than that agreed.

c. Where an extension is agreed the claimant must notify the Court in writing; the notification should be addressed to the Clerk of the Commercial Court.

d. Any notification of an agreed extension exceeding 6 weeks, or which when taken together with preceding extensions exceeds 6 weeks in total, should be accompanied by a brief statement (agreed by the claimant and the defendant) of the reasons for the longer extension. The reasons will be brought to the attention of the Judge in charge of the Commercial List who may decide (a) that he need take no action, leaving the agreed extension to take its course, (b) to call for further information or (c) to convene a Case Management Conference.

D2–091 C2.5 Particulars of claim must be served by the claimant on all other parties. A copy of the claim form will be filed with the Court (at the Registry) on issue. However in accordance with CPR 7.4(3), where the claimant serves particulars of claim separately from the claim form they must be filed within 7 days of service together with a certificate of service.

C3 Serving and filing a defence

D2–092 C3.1 Although defences will be filed in the Commercial Court they must also be served by the parties. The question of the time within which a defence must be filed is equally a question of the time within which a defence must be served. Service and filing should be done at the same time.

C3.2 CPR 15.4(1)(b) provides that, if the defendant files an acknowledgment of service under CPR Part 10, the general rule is that the period for filing a defence is 28 days after service of the particulars of claim. The general rule is subject to certain other rules specified in CPR 15.4(2). CPR 15.5(1) permits the defendant and the claimant to agree that the period specified in CPR 15.4 for filing a defence shall be extended by up to 28 days. D2–093

C3.3 The complexity of many cases in the Commercial Court, and the desirability of allowing proper time for a defence to be fully and accurately formulated so that the issues in the case may be reliably defined, means that (a) it will often be appropriate for a claimant to agree an extension and (b) it may on occasion be necessary for the extension to exceed 28 days. The particulars of claim, for example, may have taken many months to prepare. That said, there will clearly be cases in which an extension is not appropriate, not least in a case where there is urgency. D2–094

C3.4 In the circumstances, in cases in the Commercial Court parties may agree extensions of the period for filing (and thus serving a defence that exceeds 28 days. The length of extension must in all cases be specified. Any such agreement must be evidenced in writing and will be subject to paragraph C3.5, and to any subsequent order of the Court reducing the period for filing the defence to a period shorter than that agreed. D2–095

C3.5 Where an extension is agreed the defendant must, in accordance with CPR 15.5(2), notify the Court in writing; the notification should be addressed to the Clerk to the Commercial Court. Any notification of an agreed extension exceeding 6 weeks, or which when taken together with preceding extensions exceeds 6 weeks in total, should be accompanied by a brief statement (agreed by the claimant and the defendant) of the reasons for the longer extension. The reasons will be brought to the attention of the Judge in charge of the Commercial List who may decide (a) that he need take no action, leaving the agreed extension to take its course, (b) to call for further information or (c) to convene a Case Management Conference. D2–096

C3.6 In this as in all other areas the Commercial Court will expect co-operation and realism from the legal representatives of the parties. D2–097

C3.7 In the Commercial Court the defence must be served by the defendant on all other parties. D2–098

C3.8 The claimant must notify the Listing Office by letter when all defendants who intend to serve a defence have done so. This information is material to the fixing of the Case Management Conference (see paragraph D7.1 below). D2–099

C4 Serving and filing a reply

C4.1 Any reply will also be served at the same time as it is filed (CPR 15.8(b)). CPR 15.8(a), which requires a claimant to file any reply to the defence when he files his allocation questionnaire under CPR Part 26 does not apply in proceedings in the Commercial List, where there is no allocation questionnaire. D2–100

C4.2 Save as provided below, in the Commercial Court the period for serving and filing any reply is 21 days after service of the defence. The reply should be served before case management information sheets are provided to the Court (see paragraph D7.10). In the normal case, this will allow the parties to consider any reply before completing the case management information sheet, and allow time for the preparation of the case memorandum and the list of issues each of which is required for the Case Management Conference (see paragraphs D4–D7). D2–101

C4.3 In some commercial cases, a longer period than 21 days may be necessary for preparation, service and filing of a reply. In these cases, an application (on paper) for an extension of the period for serving and filing a reply and for a postponement of the Case Management Conference should be made. Only one such application may be made, and in this situation should be made promptly after service of the defence. The following procedure applies: D2–102

a. The applicant should first ascertain whether the application is opposed by the other parties.

b. The applicant should apply by letter to the Court stating:

   i. when the defence was served;
   ii. when the 21 day period for serving and filing the reply expires;
   iii. why an extension of the period is necessary;
   iv. the proposed date for service and filing of the reply, and proposed date by which the Case Management Conference would be held;
   v. whether the application is opposed.

c. The application should be sent (by fax, where possible) to all other parties at the same time as it is sent to the Court.

d. Any other parties wishing to make representations should do so by letter within two days (*i.e.* two clear days) of the date of the applicant's letter of application. The representations should be sent (by fax, where possible) to the applicant and all other parties at the same time as they are sent to the Court.

e. The Court will advise its decision by letter addressed to all parties and sent to the applicant. The applicant must forthwith copy the Court's letter to all other parties (by fax, where possible).

C4.4 In the Commercial Court any reply must be served by the claimant on all other parties. D2–103

C5 Amendment

C5.1 Amendment of statements of case is governed by CPR Part 17, and (save as provided below) by the Practice Direction supplementing CPR Part 17. D2–104

D2–105 C5.2 The endorsement required on an amended statement of case is set out at paragraph 2.1 of the Practice Direction supplementing CPR Part 17.

D2–106 C5.3 Paragraph 2.2 of the Practice Direction supplementing CPR Part 17 does not apply in the Commercial Court. Instead the following procedure applies in the Commercial Court:

a. Amendments to a statement of case should show the original text, unless the Court specifically orders otherwise or d. below applies.

b. Amendments may be shown by using footnotes or marginal notes, provided that this shows precisely where and when an amendment has been made.

c. There is no need, unless the Court specifically so orders, to show amendments by colour-coding.

d. Where there have been extensive amendments it may be better to prepare a fresh copy of the statement of case, although if this is done arrangements should be made to ensure that a copy showing where and when amendments have been made is also available.

D2–107 C5.4 Amendments to a statement of case must be verified by a statement of truth unless the Court otherwise orders (CPR 22.1(2))). To avoid uncertainty, this requirement applies to all amendments: the limitation expressed in paragraph 1.4 of the Practice Direction supplementing CPR Part 17 does not apply

D2–108 C5.5 Questions of amendment, and consequential amendment, should wherever possible be dealt with by consent. A party should consent to a proposed amendment unless he has substantial grounds for objecting to it.

D2–109 C5.6 Late amendments should be avoided and may be disallowed.

D. CASE MANAGEMENT IN THE COMMERCIAL COURT

D1 Generally

The CPR

D2–110 D1.1 All proceedings in the Commercial List will be subject to case management by the Court.

D2–111 D1.2 All proceedings in the Commercial List will proceed as if allocated to the mutli-track and the rules of the CPR relating to allocation will not apply to them (paragraph 6.1 of the Commercial Court Practice Direction). In particular CPR Part 26, and the Practice Direction supplementing that Part, do not apply.

D2–112 D1.3 With one exception, the Commercial Court case management procedure set out in this section of the Guide takes the place of CPR Part 29, and the Practice Direction supplementing that Part. The one exception is that the provisions dealing with failure to comply with case management directions (paragraph 7 of the Practice Direction supplementing CPR Part 29) do not apply to proceedings in the Commercial List.

Key features of case management in the Commercial Court

D2–113 D1.4 In summary, in a normal commercial case commenced by a Part 7 claim form, case management will include the following 10 key features:

(1) Statements of case will be exchanged within fixed or monitored time periods.

(2) A case memorandum, a list of issues and a case management bundle will be produced at an early point in the case.

(3) The case memorandum, list of issues and case management bundle will be amended and updated or revised on a running basis throughout the life of the case and will be used by the Court at every stage of the case.

(4) A mandatory Case Management Conference will be held shortly after statements of case have been served, if not before (and preceded by the parties lodging case management information sheets identifying their views on the requirements of the case).

(5) At the Case Management Conference the Court will (as necessary) discuss the issues in the case, and the requirements of the case with the advocates retained in the case, will set a pre-trial timetable (to include a progress monitoring date and, normally, a fixed trial date), consideration will be given to the possibility of the trial of preliminary issues, and (if appropriate) Alternative Dispute Resolution ("ADR") directions may be made.

(6) Before the progress monitoring date the parties will report to the Court (using a progress monitoring information sheet) on compliance with the pre-trial timetable.

(7) On or shortly after the progress monitoring date a Judge of the Court will (without a hearing) consider progress and either confirm the fixed trial date or, if necessary, reconvene the Case Management Conference in order to give further directions.

(8) If at the progress monitoring date all parties have indicated that they will be ready for trial, all parties will complete a pre-trial checklist.

(9) In many cases there will be a Pre-Trial Review; in all cases the parties will be required to prepare (for consideration by the Court) a trial timetable.

(10) There will, throughout the case, be regular reviews of the estimated length of trial.

Typical case management sequence

D1.5 An outline chart of the typical case management sequence for cases in the Commercial Court is at Appendix 2. D2–114

Case management throughout the case

D1.6 In undertaking case management the Court will be concerned to serve the "over-riding objective". D2–115

D1.7 The Court will be concerned with case management at all stages of a case, and not simply at the Case Management Conference. It may give or vary directions at any hearing. It may give or vary direction either on the application of a party or on its own initiative. D2–116

D1.8 The parties: D2–117

a. are encouraged to agree proposals, for consideration by the Court, for the management of the case;

b. should at all stages, and in particular whenever the case is to come before the Court for a hearing, consider whether there are other directions that the Court should be asked to give in the case or other matters in the case that the Court should be asked to deal with.

D1.9 Where a party needs to apply for a direction not included in the pre-trial timetable, or to vary any direction included in the pre-trial timetable, he must do so as soon as possible in order to minimise the changes that may be required to that timetable. D2–118

D1.10 The sanctions that the Court may order where parties do not comply with the requirements of this Guide which are designed to ensure effective case management of proceedings in the Commercial List may include orders for costs, including (where appropriate) wasted costs orders. D2–119

D2 Time

D2.1 Attention is drawn generally to the provisions at CPR 2.8 to 2.11 dealing with time. In particular by CPR 2.8(3) "Clear days" means that in computing the number of days (a) the day on which the period begins and (b) (if the end of the period is defined by reference to an event) the day on which the event occurs, are not included. By CPR 2.8(2) a period of time expressed as a number of days shall be computed as clear days. For convenience the reference to clear days is emphasised in the body of this Guide when any period of three days or less is referred to. D2–120

D2.2 CPR 2.11 provides that unless the CPR or a Practice Direction provide otherwise or the Court orders otherwise, the time specified by a rule or by the Court for a person to do any act may be varied by the written agreement of the parties. In the Commercial Court: D2–121

a. the period for serving and filing a reply may not be extended without an order of the Court (paragraph C4.3);

b. the date provided for the Case Management Conference in accordance with paragraph D7.1 may not be postponed without an order of the Court;

c. the pre-trial timetable may only be varied within the limits set at paragraph D7.18 below.

D2.3 CPR 2.9(1) provides that where the Court gives a judgment, order or direction which imposes a time limit for doing any act, the time of day (and not just the date) by which the act must be done must be included wherever practicable. In the Commercial Court, unless the Court otherwise requires, it is sufficient to include the date but when a date is included the time for compliance is 4.30 p.m. D2–122

D3 Two-Judge team system

D3.1 Those cases which appear to lend themselves to such a system (*e.g.* because of length or complexity or the possibility of frequent or numerous pre-trial applications) will be allocated at the Case Management Conference to a management team of two Judges. The Judge who takes the Case Management Conference will be one of the two Judges in the management team. Whilst the Two-Judge team system has its advantages, it will not be used in every case because, given the commitments of individual Judges at particular times, it can restrict the ability of the Commercial Court to deal with the individual case as promptly as is desirable. D2–123

D3.2 All applications in the case, and the trial, should normally be heard by one or other of the two Judges with the exception (in the absence of the agreement of the parties) of any application for an interim payment. The Listing Office will inform the parties to which two Judges the case has been allocated. D2–124

D4 Case memorandum

D4.1 After the service of the defence (and any reply), the solicitors and counsel for each party shall liaise with a view to producing a short agreed case memorandum. Unless otherwise ordered, the solicitors for the claimant are to have the responsibility for the carriage of the case memorandum. D2–125

D4.2 The case memorandum should contain: D2–126

a. a short and uncontroversial description of what the case is about;

b. a very short and uncontroversial summary of the material procedural history of the case since it was commenced.

D4.3 After the Case Management Conference, and until trial, the solicitors for each party shall D2–127 liaise from time to time (and in particular in advance of the stages referred to at paragraph D6.6 a.–c.) with a view to updating the case memorandum in order to ensure that the description and the summary it contains are kept up to date. Where appropriate, counsel should also be involved in this exercise. Unless otherwise ordered, the solicitors for the claimant are to have the responsibility for the carriage of any revising or updating of the case memorandum.

D2–128 D4.4 The case memorandum should not refer to any application for an interim payment, to any order for an interim payment, to any voluntary interim payment, or to any payment or offer under CPR Part 36 or 37.

D5 List of issues

D2–129 D5.1 After the service of the defence (and any reply), the solicitors and counsel for each party shall liaise with a view to producing an agreed list of the important issues in the case. The list should include both issues of fact and issue of law. A separate section of the document should list what is common ground between the parties (or some of them, specifying which).

D2–130 D5.2 Unless otherwise ordered, the solicitors and counsel for the claimant are to have the responsibility for the carriage of the list of issues.

D2–131 D5.3 After the Case Management Conference, and until trial, the solicitors and counsel for each party shall liaise from time to time with a view to revising the list of issues in order to ensure that it is kept up to date. In particular there should be prompt liaison on the service of any amended statement of case (or summary) in order to revise the list of issues if that is appropriate. Unless otherwise ordered, the solicitors and counsel for the claimant are to have the responsibility for the carriage of revision of the list of issues.

D6 Case management bundle

Preparation

D2–132 D6.1 Before the Case Management Conference (see paragraph D7), a case management bundle should be prepared by the solicitors for the claimant.

Contents

D2–133 D6.2 The case management bundle should only contain the documents listed below (where the documents have been created by the relevant time). Paragraph references are references to paragraphs of this Guide.

a. The claim form.

b. The case memorandum (see paragraph D4).

c. The list of issues (see paragraph D5).

d. The pre-trial timetable (see D7.15–D7.16), or the case management information sheet where no pre-trial timetable has been ordered at the relevant time (see paragraph D7.10).

e. The statements of case subsequent to the claim form (excluding any schedules, and where a summary has been prepared under paragraph C1.3 including that summary instead of the full statement of case).

f. The principal orders made in the case.

g. Any agreement in writing made by the parties to disclose documents without making a list or any agreement in writing that disclosure (or inspection or both) shall take place in stages.

D2–134 D6.3 The case management bundle should not include a copy of any order for an interim payment.

Lodging

D2–135 D6.4 The case management bundle should be lodged with the Registry at least 7 days before the (first) Case Management Conference (or earlier hearing at which the parties are represented and at which the business of the Case Management Conference may be transacted: see D7.3–4.

Preparation and upkeep

D2–136 D6.5 The preparation and upkeep of the case management bundle is (unless otherwise ordered, and subject to paragraph L2.4 where a litigant in person is involved) the responsibility of the claimant and must be undertaken in accordance with Appendix 11. It should not be necessary to prepare a fresh case management bundle for each application. Instead, the bundle once first prepared should be amended and updated on a running basis as the case progresses (see further paragraph D6.6). It is accepted that there may come a stage in some cases when it is more sensible to prepare a fresh bundle, but these instances should be rare.

D2–137 D6.6 The claimant (or other party responsible for the preparation and upkeep of the case management bundle) should then attend at the Registry in order to update the case management bundle at the following stages:

a. within 10 days of the Case Management Conference, in order to add the pre-trial timetable (or any other order made on the Case Management Conference) and an updated case memorandum;

b. within 10 days of an order being made on an application, if in the light of the order or the application it is necessary to add a copy of the order made (as a principal order in the case) or an updated case memorandum;

c. within 14 days of the service of any amended statement of case (or summary), in order to substitute a copy of the amended statement of case (or summary) for the statement of case (or summary) it replaces, an updated case memorandum and (if appropriate) a revised list of issues;

d. within 10 days of any other revision to the case memorandum or the list of issues, in order to add (as the case may be) the revised case memorandum or the revised list of issues.

D7 Case Management Conference

Timing

D7.1 A mandatory Case Management Conference is to take place on the first available date 6 weeks after all defendants who intend to serve a defence have done so, save as provided below. This timescale allows time, in the normal case, for the preparation and service of any reply (see paragraph C4.2). **D2–138**

D7.2 Immediately after all defendants who intend to serve a defence have done so, the parties must take steps to fix the date for the Case Management Conference with the Listing Office. When doing so they should bear in mind the need to allow time for the preparation and service of any reply, in cases where there is to be a reply. **D2–139**

D7.3 In some cases it may be appropriate for a Case Management Conference to take place at an earlier date. A request by any party for an early Case Management Conference should be made in writing to the Judge in charge of the Commercial List, on notice to all other parties, at the earliest possible opportunity. **D2–140**

D7.4 If before the date on which the Case Management Conference would be held in accordance with paragraph D7.1 there is a hearing in the case at which the parties are represented, the business of the Case Management Conference will normally be transacted at that hearing and there will be no separate Case Management Conference. **D2–141**

D7.5 Where a party wishes to obtain an order not routinely made at a Case Management Conference an the other party or parties concerned have not agreed to a proposal that such an order be made, wherever possible the application notice for such an order should be filed and served so that it may be dealt with at the same time as the Case Management Conference. **D2–142**

Application to postpone

D7.6 An application may be made to postpone the Case Management Conference. The application must be made within 21 days after all defendants who intend to serve a defence have done so. Failure, for good reason, to complete service of all statements of case may be accepted by the Court as a good ground for postponement. The application will be dealt with on paper (adapting the procedure at paragraph C4.3 above), unless the Court requires, or any party requests, an oral hearing. **D2–143**

Monitoring

D7.7 In accordance with paragraph C3 above the Registry will expect a defence to be served and filed by the latest of (a) 28 days after service of the particulars of claim (as certified by the certificate of service) or (b) any extended date for serving and filing a defence as notified to the Court in writing following agreement between the parties, or (c) any extended date for serving and filing a defence as ordered by the Court on an application. If within 28 days after the latest of these dates has passed for each defendant, the parties have not taken steps to fix the date for the Case Management Conference with the Listing Office, the Listing Office will inform the Judge in Charge of the Commercial List, and at his direction will take steps to fix a date for the Case Management Conference without further reference to the parties. **D2–144**

Attendance

D7.8 Clients need not attend a Case Management Conference unless the Court otherwise orders before the date for that Conference. A representative who has conduct of the case must attend from each firm of solicitors instructed in the case. **D2–145**

D7.9 For each party at least one of the advocates retained in the case should also attend. The Case Management Conference is a very significant stage in the case; it is not simply a substitute for the summons for directions under the former Rules of the Supreme Court. **D2–146**

Materials: case management information sheet and case management bundle

D7.10 A completed case management information sheet must be provided by each party to the Court (and copied to all other parties) at least 7 days before the Case Management Conference. In the Commercial Court the requirement to file a completed case management information **D2–147** sheet takes the place of the requirement to file an allocation questionnaire under CPR Part 26. A standard form of case management information sheet is at Appendix 6.

D2–148 D7.11 The case management bundle will also be provided to the Court at least 7 days before the Case Management Conference (see paragraph D6.4). Only where it is essential for the Court on the Case Management Conference to see the full version of a statement of case that has been summarised in accordance with paragraph C1.3 above should a copy of that statement of case be lodged for the Case Management Conference.

The hearing

D2–149 D7.12 As indicated above, the Case Management Conference is a very significant stage in the case; it is not simply a substitute for the summons for directions under the former Rules of the Supreme Court.

D2–150 D7.13 At the Case Management Conference the Commercial Judge will:

a. (as necessary) discuss the issues in the case, and the requirements of the case, with the advocates retained in the case;

b. (where practicable) fix the entire pre-trial timetable (or if it is not practicable to fix the entire pre-trial timetable, fix as much of the pre-trial timetable as it is practicable to fix);

c. (in appropriate cases) make ADR orders.

D2–151 D7.14 Although CPR 26.4 does not apply to proceedings in the Commercial List (see D1.2 above), the Court will be prepared to consider applications that the case is adjourned while the parties try to settle the case by ADR or by means other than ADR (for example, conventional negotiation). The case management information sheet asks the parties to indicate whether such an adjournment is sought. Where an adjournment has been granted and before the expiry of the adjournment an extension is desired by all parties, a Commercial Judge will generally be prepared to deal with a request for such an extention if it is made by letter from the legal representatives of one of the parties. The letter should confirm that all parties consent, explain the steps being taken, identify any mediator or other form of ADR tribunal or any expert assisting with the attempts to settle. An extension will generally be for no more than four weeks unless clear reasons are given to justify a longer time. However, more than one extension may be granted. Alternatively, an ADR order may be made without an order adjoining the case. The parties should give careful consideration to the possibilities of fitting ADR into the pre-trial timetable without the need for any or much delay to it.

The pre-trial timetable

D2–152 D7.15 The pre-trial timetable will include:

a. a progress monitoring date (see paragraph D8 below); and

b. a fixed date for trial (see paragraph D7.17 below) or, exceptionally, a provisional range of dates for the commencement of the trial.

D2–153 D7.16 A standard form of pre-trial timetable is at Appendix 8.

Fixing the trial date

D2–154 D7.17 When, at the Case Management Conference, the Judge directs that a date be fixed for trial the parties should liaise promptly with the Clerk to the Commercial Court for the purpose of obtaining the fixed date for trial. This date will be included in the pre-trial timetable.

Variations to the pre-trial timetable

D2–155 D7.18 The parties may (unless otherwise ordered) agree minor variations to the time periods set out in the pre-trial timetable, without the case needing to be brought back to the Court, provided always that:

a. the minor variation does not affect the structure of the pre-trial timetable;

b. the minor variation will have no effect on the fixed date for trial or the provisional range of dates for trial;

c. the minor variation is not to the progress monitoring date and will not means that any matter originally scheduled to be completed by the progress monitoring date will no longer be completed by that date.

D2–156 D7.19 If in any case it becomes apparent that variations to the pre-trial timetable are required, and the variations are not minor variations that have been agreed under paragraph D7.18 above, the parties should take the initiative to reconvene the Case Management Conference before the Court. The parties should not wait until the progress monitoring date.

Case Management Conference: Part 8 claims

D2–157 D7.20 In a case commenced by the filing of a Part 8 claim form, a Case Management Conference is to take place on the first available date 6 weeks after service and filing of the defendant's evidence. At that Case Management Conference the Court will make such pre-trial directions as are necessary, adapting (where useful in the context of the particular claim) those of the case management procedures used in the Commercial Court for a claim commenced by the issue of a Part 7 claim form.

Case Management Conference: Part 20 claims

D7.21 Part 20 claims are defined by CPR 20.2(1). They include a counterclaim and a claim by a defendant against any person for contribution or an indemnity or some other remedy. **D2–158**

D7.22 The procedure for Part 20 claims is set out in CPR Part 20 and in the Practice Direction supplementing that Part. However, in the Commercial Court case management in relation to a Part 20 claim will be as set out at paragraph D7.24–7.25 below, and paragraphs 5.1 to 5.4 of the Practice Direction supplementing CPR Part 20 will not apply. **D2–159**

D7.23 Where a party contemplates making a Part 20 claim that Part 20 claim should whenever possible be made before the Case Management Conference dealing with the main claim (where the Court's permission to make a Part 20 claim is not required), or permission should be sought at the Case Management Conference to make the Part 20 claim. **D2–160**

D7.24 If the Part 20 claim is a counterclaim by a defendant against a claimant (but not a claimant and some other person), the Case Management Conference dealing with the main claim will normally deal with the Part 20 claim when convened in accordance with paragraph D7.1–7.2 above. (As stated at paragraph D7.1 above the timescale for convening that Case Management Conference allows time, in the normal case, for the preparation and service of any reply; as provided by paragraph 6.2 of the Practice Direction supplementing CPR Part 20, the reply and the defence to counterclaim should normally for one document.) **D2–161**

D7.25 Where the Part 20 claim is not a counterclaim by a defendant against a claimant, the Case Management Conference dealing with the main claim will, unless the Court otherwise orders, be reconvened on service of any defence to the Part 20 claim. The reconvened Case Management Conference is to take place on the first available date 6 weeks after service of the defence to the Part 20 claim, unless an application to postpone is made and granted (see paragraph D7.6 above). All parties (*i.e.* parties to the main claim and parties to the Part 20 claim) must attend. There will not be a separate Case Management Conference for the Part 20 claim alone. **D2–162**

D8 Progress monitoring

Fixing the progress monitoring date

D8.1 The progress monitoring date will be fixed at the Case Management Conference and will normally be placed after the date in the pre-trial timetable for exchange of witness statements and expert reports. **D2–163**

Progress monitoring information sheet

D8.2 At least 3 days (*i.e.* three clear days) before the progress monitoring date the parties must each send to the Listing Office (with a copy to all other parties) a completed information sheet (a "progress monitoring information sheet") to inform the Court: **D2–164**

a. whether they have complied with the pre-trial timetable, and if they have not, the respects in which they have not;

b. whether they will be ready for a trial commencing on the fixed date (or, where applicable, within the provisional range of dates) specified in the pre-trial timetable, and if they will not be ready why they will not be ready.

D8.3 A standard form of progress monitoring information sheet is at Appendix 13. **D2–165**

Pre-trial checklist

D8.4 If in the progress monitoring information sheets all parties inform the Court that they will be ready for a trial commencing on the fixed date (or, where applicable, within the provisional range of dates) specified in the pre-trial timetable, then: **D2–166**

a. within 7 days of the progress monitoring date each party must send to the Listing Office (with a copy to all other parties) a completed checklist confirming final details for trial (a "pre-trial checklist");

b. the Court may confirm the fixed date for trial or (where a fixed date has not been given) order the date of the trial to be fixed within the provisional range of dates specified in the pre-trial timetable.

D8.5 A standard form of pre-trial checklist is at Appendix 14. **D2–167**

Reconvening the Case Management Conference

D8.6 If one or more parties inform the Court in the progress monitoring information sheets that they will not be ready for a trial commencing on the fixed date (or, where applicable, within the provisional range of dates) specified in the pre-trial timetable, or if in the view of the Court the **D2–168** information on the pre-trial checklists justifies this course, the Court may direct that the Case Management Conference be reconvened for further hearing.

D2–169 D8.7 At a reconvened hearing of the Case Management Conference the Court may make such orders as are appropriate, including:

a. further directions (including a new progress monitoring date and a revised pre-trial timetable);

b. orders for costs; and

c. "unless" orders, amongst other things to the effect that the claim or the defence be automatically struck out unless the claimant or the defendant has complied with specified directions by specified dates.

D9 Further information

D2–170 D9.1 CPR 18.1 provides that the Court may at any time order a party to (a) clarify any matter which is in dispute in the proceedings; or (b) give additional information in relation to any such matter, whether or not the matter is contained or referred to in a statement of case.

D2–171 D9.2 One way in which this power may be used in the Commercial Court is that at the Case Management Conference, or on an application, the Court may direct a party further to detail a specified part or parts of his statement of case. This may, for example, be necessary to help define the issues in the case, to avoid any other party being taken by surprise or to save costs.

D2–172 D9.3 Save that paragraph D9.4 below contains certain additional requirements, CPR Part 18 and the Practice Direction supplementing that Part apply in the Commercial Court in relation to further information.

D2–173 D9.4 If a party declines to provide the further information requested, the solicitors or counsel for the parties concerned must communicate directly with each other in an attempt to reach agreement before the matter is raised with the Court. No application (separate from the Case Management Conference) for a direction that a party provide further information will be listed in the Commercial Court without prior written certification from the proposed applicant that the steps outlined in this paragraph have been complied with.

D2–174 D9.5 Because it falls within the definition of a statement of case (see CPR 2.3(1)) a response providing further information under CPR Part 18 must be verified with a statement of truth whether it is given voluntary or in compliance with an order (see paragraph 3 of the Practice Direction supplementing CPR Part 18). The form of the statement of truth is set out at paragraph 2.1 of the Practice Direction supplementing CPR Part 22.

D10 Preliminary issues

D2–175 D10.1 Costs can sometimes be saved by identifying decisive issues, or potentially decisive issues, and ordering that they be tried first. The decision of one issue may enable the parties to settle the remainder of the dispute.

D2–176 D10.2 At the Case Management Conference, and again at the Pre-Trial Review, consideration will be given to the possibility of the trial of a preliminary issue or issues the resolution of which is likely to shorten the proceedings. An example is a relatively short question of law which can be tried without significant delay (though the implications of a possible appeal for the remainder of the case cannot be lost sight of). The Court may suggest the trial of a preliminary issue, but it will rarely make an order without the concurrence of at least one of the parties.

D2–177 D10.3 Where preliminary issues are ordered to be tried, particular consideration should be given by the parties and the Court as to whether the costs should be in the issues or in the case.

D2–178 D10.4 Where on an application by a claimant for summary judgment issues of law or construction may be determined in the defendant's favour, it will usually be in the interests of the parties for such issues to be determined conclusively rather than that the application for summary judgment should simply be dismissed.

D11 Fixed trial dates

D2–179 D11.1 In the Commercial Court most cases will be given fixed trial dates when the pre-trial timetable is set at the Case Management Conference. Fixed trial dates for cases in the Commercial Court may be given before the Case Management Conference if the availability of advocates and expert witnesses could not be ensured were the fixing of the trial date to be left to the Case Management Conference.

D2–180 D11.2 A fixed date for trial in the Commercial Court is given on the basis that if previous fixtures have been substantially underestimated or other urgent matters are required to be heard, the trial may be delayed for a few days. Where such delay might cause particular inconvenience to witnesses or others involved in the trial, the Clerk to the Commercial Court should be informed well in advance of the fixed date.

D12 Provisional and confirmed estimates of length of trial

D2–181 D12.1 A provisional estimate of the minimum and maximum lengths of the trial will be estimated at the Case Management Conference and appear in the pre-trial timetable.

D2–182 D12.2 In the event that at any stage a party changes the advocate(s) who are to appear for him at the trial, the Listing Office should be notified by the party of that fact within 14 days of the change. The new advocate(s) should in due course review the then current estimate of the minimum and maximum lengths of the trial, and submit to the Listing Office a signed note confirming his agreement with the estimate or stating any different estimate.

D12.3 A confirmed estimate of the minimum and maximum lengths of the trial, signed by the advocates who are to appear at the trial, should be attached to the pre-trial checklist. **D2–183**

D12.4 It is the duty of all advocates who are to appear at the trial to liaise with one another and seek to reach agreement on the estimated minimum and maximum lengths of trial. **D2–184**

D12.5 The provisional estimate and (after it is given) the confirmed estimate must be kept under review by the advocates who are to appear at trial. If at any stage it should appear that an estimate warrants revision, all advocates must liaise further with one another to seek to reach agreement on a revised estimate and a signed revised estimate (whether agreed to not) must be submitted by the advocates to the Clerk to the Commercial Court. **D2–185**

D12.6 Accurate estimation of trial length is of great importance to the efficient functioning of the Commercial Court. **D2–186**

D13 Pre-Trial Review and trial timetable

D13.1 In cases that will involve trials estimates to last 8 days or more, and in some other cases such as those involving a large number of parties, it will probably be desirable that the pre-trial timetable provide for a Pre-Trial Review. **D2–187**

D13.2 A Pre-Trial Review will normally be directed to be held between 8 and 4 weeks before the date fixed for trial. In a very heavy case the Pre-Trial Review may be directed to be held in parts, the first part being held several months before the date fixed for trial. **D2–188**

D13.3 The case management bundle (see paragraph D6) will be before the Court on the date fixed for the Pre-Trial Review and must have been kept updated in accordance with paragraph D6.5 and D6.6. Only where it is essential for the Court on the Pre-Trial Review to see the full version of a statement of case that has been summarised in accordance with paragraph C1.3 above should a copy of that statement of case be lodged for the Pre-Trial Review. **D2–189**

D13.4 The Pre-Trial Review will be held whenever possible before the Trial Judge. It should be attended by the advocates who are to appear at the trial. **D2–190**

D13.5 The purpose of the Pre-Trial Review is to enable an informed discussion and assessment to take place of what will be involved in the trial and agreement to be reached as to the best way for it to be conducted. The Court will also take the opportunity to make any appropriate directions. **D2–191**

D13.6 The possible advantages of preliminary issues should again be considered at the Pre-Trial Review, as should the organisation of the trial. It may be appropriate that at trial some issues or topics are dealt with together or before others. Agreement can be reached or, if necessary, directions given to cover the order in which witnesses are going to be called, the organisation of documents, and generally the programming of the trial. If there are any remaining questions concerning the manner in which witnesses should give their evidence, these too can be the subject of directions. **D2–192**

D13.7 Where a Pre-Trial Review is held, a trial timetable should be produced for discussion at that Pre-Trial Review (*cf.* CPR 39.4). The trial timetable should be prepared by the advocate(s) for the claimant after consultation with the advocate(s) for all other parties. If there are differences of view between the advocate(s) for the claimant and the advocate(s) for other parties, these should be shown. The trial timetable will schedule the oral submissions, witness evidence and expert evidence over the course of the trial. At the Pre-trial Review the Judge may fix the trial timetable, subject to any further order (including a further order at the trial itself). **D2–193**

D13.8 Arrangements for a trial timetable in cases where there is no Pre-Trial Review are provided at paragraph 15.8 below. **D2–194**

D14 Orders

D14.1 The following provisions take the place of CPR 40.3, which does not apply to proceedings in the Commercial Court: **D2–195**

a. Orders under CPR 3.4(2)(a) or (b) (striking out a statement of case), or under paragraphs 2 to 4 of the Practice Direction supplementing CPR 3.4, will be drawn up by the Commercial Court if they are made by a Commercial Judge on his own initiative rather than on the application of a party.

b. The drawing up of consent orders on applications is to be dealt with as described at paragraph F7 below.

c. All other orders made by the Commercial Court are to be drawn up in draft by the parties (rather than the Court) and dated in the draft with the date of the Judge's decision. The claimant is to have carriage of the drafting, unless the order was made on the application of another party in which case that other party is to have carriage of the drafting. Unless the Judge making the order otherwise directs, two copies of the draft, signed by the parties themselves, or by their solicitors or counsel must be lodged with the Registry within three days (*i.e.* three clear days) of the decision of the Court reflected in the draft. The Court expects the highest degree of co-operation between all parties and all legal representatives to ensure that orders accurately recording the decision of the Court are drawn up promptly.

D14.2 Where an order is to provide a time by which something is to be done the order should wherever possible state the particular date by which the thing is to be done rather than refer to a period of time from a particular date or event. **D2–196**

D2–197 D14.3 Orders that require to be served should be served by the parties, unless the Court otherwise directs.

E. DISCLOSURE IN CASES IN THE COMMERCIAL COURT

E1 Generally

D2–198 E1.1 The Court will seek to ensure so far as possible that the disclosure ordered in a particular case is tailored to the requirements of the particular case and that the disclosure ordered is no wider than appropriate. Anything wider than standard disclosure (see paragraph E3) always needs to be justified. The Court may consider in an appropriate case that even standard disclosure across the whole spectrum of the case is wider than required, but similarly a limitation on standard disclosure needs to be justified. Among other things, parties should give careful thought to the feasibility of limiting disclosure by the use of sampling methods.

D2–199 E1.2 Documents are often of particular importance in a commercial case, and of particular assistance in enabling the Court to deal with cases justly. Parties to litigation in the Commercial Court can expect that disclosure beyond standard disclosure may be required either in a case as a whole or on particular issues in a case.

D2–200 E1.3 The "overriding objective" includes, so far as is practicable, dealing with cases in ways which are proportionate to four factors: (i) the amount of money involved, (ii) the importance of the case, (iii) the complexity of the issues and (iv) the financial position of each party (see CPR 1.1(2)(c)). A high or a limited level of disclosure may be proportionate in a commercial case by reference to such factors.

D2–201 E1.4 Subject to the provisions of this section of the Guide, CPR Part 31 applies in the Commercial Court. The Practice Direction supplementing CPR Part 31 does not apply in the Commercial Court, although certain provisions from that Practice Direction are included in this section of the Guide.

E2 Procedure

D2–202 E2.1 At the Case Management Conference the Court will consider:

a. whether to dispense with or limit standard disclosure (CPR 31.5(2));

b. whether to order standard disclosure (CPR 31.5(1));

c. whether to order specific disclosure (CPR 31.12), including whether to make a special disclosure order (see paragraph E5).

D2–203 E2.2 CPR 31.10(8)(a) permits the parties to gree in writing to disclose documents without making a list. The Commercial Court will consider making an order in similar terms in an appropriate case on application made at the Case Management Conference. The Court may however still require each party to make a disclosure statement, even if disclosure is to be made without a list.

D2–204 E2.3 CPR 31.13 provides that the parties may agree in writing or the Court may direct that disclosure (or inspection or both) shall take place in stages. In some commercial cases this provision may be useful. Parties should give consideration to it before the Case Management Conference.

D2–205 E2.4 Where in any particular case the parties agree in writing to disclosure documents without making a list or agree in writing that disclosure (or inspection or both) shall take place in stages, a copy of their agreement should be added to the case management bundle (see paragraph D6.2 above).

D2–206 E2.5 The obligations imposed by an order for disclosure will continue until the proceedings come to an end. If, after a list of documents has been prepared and served, the (present or past) existence of further documents to which the order applies comes to the attention of the disclosing party, that party must prepare and serve a supplemental list.

E3 Standard disclosure

D2–207 E3.1 Standard disclosure is defined by CPR 31.6. Where standard disclosure is ordered a party is required to disclose only:

a. the documents on which he relies; and

b. the documents which—

(i) adversely affect his own case;

(ii) adversely affect another party's case; or

(iii) support another party's case; and

c. the documents which he is required to disclose by a relevant Practice Direction.

D2–208 E3.2 CPR 31.7(3) contemplates that where a party required to make a reasonable search for documents falling within CPR 31.6(b) or (c) has not searched for a category or class of document on the grounds that to do so would be unreasonable, he must state this in his disclosure statement and identify the category or class of document. CPR 31.6(b) refers to documents which adversely affect a party's own case, adversely affect another party's case or support another party's case. CPR 31.6(c) refers to documents which a party is required to disclose by a relevant Practice Direction.

D2–209 E3.3 In order that the Case Management Conference may deal fully with disclosure issues, in the Commercial Court a party who considers that to search for a category or class of document under CPR 31.6(b) would be unreasonable must, where practicable, also indicate this in advance in his case management information sheet (see Appendix 6). The Judge hearing the Case Management Conference may direct that, notwithstanding that the party considers that to search for a category or class of document under CPR 31.6(b) would be unreasonable, there is to be a search for all documents falling within CPR 31.6(b).

E3.4 In order to comply with CPR 31.10(3) (which requires the list to identify the documents in a convenient order and manner and as concisely as possible) it will normally be necesssary to list the documents in date order to number them consecutively and give each a concise description. However, where there is a large number of documents all falling within a particular category the disclosing party may (unless otherwise ordered) list those documents as a category rather than individually. D2–210

E3.5 CPR 31.7(1) requires a party giving standard disclosure to make a reasonable search for documents falling within CPR 31.6(b) or (c). By CPR 31.7(2) the factors relevant in deciding the reasonableness of a search include (a) the number of documents involved, (b) the nature and complexity of the proceedings, (c) the ease and expense of retrieval of any particular document, and (d) the significance of any document which is likely to be located during the search. CPR 31.10(5) requires that where standard disclosure is to be given a list of documents is to include a disclosure statement. The disclosure statement must, by CPR 31.10(6), set out among other things the extent of the search that has been made to locate documents which the party is required to disclose. D2–211

E3.6 In commercial cases the disclosure statement must, in addition to complying with the requirements of CPR 31.7(3) and 31.10(6) and unless the Court otherwise directs, also: D2–212

a. identify any respects in which the search has been limited;

b. set out in detail the facts considered in arriving at the decision that it was reasonable to limit the search in those respects;

c. specify by whom the search has been conducted.

E3.7 The form of disclosure statement for standard disclosure should begin with the following words: D2–213

> "[I/we], [name(s)] [the above named claimant/defendant *or if the party making disclosure is a company, firm or other organisation identify here the position of the person(s) making the disclosure statement and why he is/they are the appropriate person(s) to make it*] state that [I/we] have carried out a reasonable search to locate all the documents which [I am *or* the claimant/defendant is] required to disclose under [the order made by the Court *or* the agreement in writing made between the parties] on [ ] day of [ ]."

E3.8 The form of disclosure statement for standard disclosure should end with the following certificate: D2–214

> "[I/we] certify that [I/we] understand the duty of disclosure and to the best of [my/our] knowledge [I have *or* the above named claimant/defendant has] carried out that duty. [I/we] certify that the list above is a complete list of all documents which are or have been in [my *or* the claimant's/defendant's] control which [I am *or* the claimant/defendant is] obliged under [the said order *or* the said agreement in writing] to disclose."

E3.9 The Court may at any stage order that a disclosure statement be verified by affidavit or witness statement. D2–215

E4 Specific disclosure

E4.1 Specific disclosure is defined by CPR 31.12(2). An order for specific disclosure is an order that a party must do one or more of the following things: D2–216

a. disclose documents or classes of documents specified in the order;

b. carry out a search to the extent stated in the order;

c. disclosure any documents located as a result of that search.

E4.2 An application for specific disclosure may be made at the Case Management Conference, or by later application. D2–217

E4.3 Applications for ship's papers are dealt with by paragraphs 7.1 and 7.2 of the Commercial Court Practice Direction. D2–218

E4.4 The Court may at any stage order that specific disclosure be verified by affidavit or witness statement. D2–219

E5 Special disclosure order

E5.1 Amongst the range of orders that may be made under CPR 31.12(2) is an order that a party must carry out a search to the extent stated in the order and disclose any documents located as a result of that search. In an appropriate case, the Commercial Court may make an order for disclosure to be known as a "special disclosure order" in or substantially in the terms set out in Appendix 9. D2–220

E5.2 A special disclosure order may be made in relation to one or more issues, or in relation to the case a whole. As with any other application for specific disclosure, an application for a special disclosure order may be made at the Case Management Conference, or by later application. D2–221

E5.3 If a special disclosure order is made it may be made so a to apply to all parties or only to some parties. The Commercial Court will (where it is justified) be prepared to make such an order where, as in circumstances such as those described in paragraph E5.4 below, a fuller D2–222 understanding of a history of events or of states of mind is important to enable the Court to deal with the case justly, and the likely costs of implementing a special disclosure order are proportionate to the amount of money involved and the importance of the case.

D2–223 E5.4 Without limiting the circumstances in which it may be appropriate to make a special disclosure order, examples of cases where such an order may be appropriate include cases:

a. where fraud, dishonesty or misrepresentation is alleged;

b. where knowledge or lack of knowledge, or disclosure or non-disclosure, is in issue.

D2–224 E5.5 The Court may at any stage order that special disclosure be verified by affidavit or witness statement.

F. APPLICATIONS

F1 Generally

Types of application

D2–225 F1.1 There are four types of application:

a. applications without notice;

b. expedited applications;

c. ordinary applications;

d. heavy applications.

CPR Part 23

D2–226 F1.2 Save as provided in this section of the Guide, CPR Part 23 applies to applications in the Commercial Court.

D2–227 F1.3 The Practice Direction supplementing CPR Part 23 also applies, with the following exceptions:

a. paragraphs 1, 2.2 to 2.6 do not apply;

b. paragraphs 2.8 and 2.10 apply only if the proposed (additional) application will not increase the time estimate already given for the hearing for which a date has been fixed;

c. paragraph 3 is subject in all cases to the Judge agreeing that the application may proceed without an application notice being served;

d. the time period set out in paragraph 4.1 does not apply;

e. paragraph 8 does not apply;

f. the requirement of filing at paragraph 9.6 does not apply to exhibits.

D2–228 F1.4 Paragraph 10.4 of the Practice Direction supplementing CPR Part 23 provides that subject to any rule or Practice Direction a letter will generally be acceptable as a form in which the Court is provided with the material it needs to be satisfied that it is appropriate to make a consent order. In the Commercial Court in general a draft consent order signed by all parties will be required rather than a letter.

D2–229 F1.5 The requirement in paragraph 12.1 of the Practice Direction supplementing CPR Part 23 that a draft order be supplied on disk does not apply in the Commercial Court. Orders will be drawn up by the parties (see further paragraph D14 above).

Service

D2–230 F1.6 Application notices are served by the parties in the Commercial Court, and not by the Court.

Evidence

D2–231 F1.7 Particular attention is drawn to paragraph 9.1 of the Practice Direction supplementing CPR Part 23. This points out that even where no specific requirement for evidence is set out in the CPR or the Practice Directions supplementing the CPR it should be borne in mind that, as a practical matter, the Court will often need to be satisfied by evidence of the facts that are relied on in support of or for opposing the application.

Time periods

F1.8 The time periods set out in the provisions of the CPR dealing with applications do not apply to applications in the Commercial Court. Instead the time periods set out in this section of the Guide apply. **D2–232**

Hearing

F1.9 Applications will be heard in public in accordance with CPR 39.2, save where otherwise ordered under CPR 39.2(3) (but for arbitration applications see in particular paragraph 15 of the Arbitration Practice Direction). An application without notice for a freezing injunction or a search order will normally be held in private. **D2–233**

F1.10 Paragraph 2.9 of the Practice Direction supplementing CPR Part 23 deserves particular emphasis. It requires the parties to expect that at any hearing the Court may wish to review the conduct of the case as a whole and give any necessary case management directions. As the paragraph further indicates, the parties should be ready to assist the Court in this, and to answer any questions that the Court may ask for this purpose. **D2–234**

F1.11 Paragraphs 6.1 to 7 of the Practice Direction supplementing CPR Part 23 deal with the hearing of an application by telephone (other than an urgent application out of Court hours) and the hearing of an application using video conferencing facilities. In the Commercial Court these methods may be useful when a Commercial Judge is on circuit, but in most cases applications in the Commercial Court are more conveniently dealt with in person. **D2–235**

F2 Applications without notice

F2.1 An application should be made on notice, even if the notice has to be short, unless (for example) it is part of the applicant's case that notice would or might defeat the relief sought by the application. **D2–236**

F2.2 Where an application without notice does not involve the giving of undertakings to the Court, it will normally be made and dealt with on paper (as, for example, an application for permission to serve a claim form out of the jurisdiction, and an application for an extension of time in which to serve a claim form). **D2–237**

F2.3 Any application for an interim remedy will require an attendance. **D2–238**

F2.4 On all applications without notice it is the duty of the applicant and those representing him to make full and frank disclosure of all matters relevant to the application. **D2–239**

F2.5 The papers lodged for the application should include two copies of a draft of the order sought. Save in exceptional circumstances where time does not permit, all the evidence relied upon in support of the application without notice and any other relevant documents must be lodged in advance with the Clerk to the Commercial Court. If the application is urgent, this (and the reasons for the urgency) should be brought to the attention of the Clerk to the Commercial Court. **D2–240**

F3 Expedited applications

F3.1 The Commercial Court is able to offer the facility of an expedited application on notice in cases of sufficient urgency and importance. **D2–241**

F3.2 Where a party wishes to seek an expedited application, in the first instance an approach should be made to the Clerk to the Commercial Court, on notice to all other parties. **D2–242**

F4 Ordinary applications

F4.1 Applications on notice expected to involve an oral hearing lasting half a day or less are regarded as ordinary applications. **D2–243**

F4.2 Ordinary applications will generally be heard on Fridays, but may be heard on other days of the week. Where possible, the Listing Office will have regard to the availability of advocates when fixing hearing dates. **D2–244**

F4.3 Many ordinary applications, especially those in the non-Counsel list on Fridays, are very short indeed (*e.g.* applications to extend time). As in the past, it is likely that many if not most of such applications can be heard without evidence and on short (*i.e.* a few days) notice. The parties should however have in mind what is said in paragraph F1.7 above. **D2–245**

F4.4 Leaving aside the very short applications, unless otherwise directed or agreed the timetable for ordinary applications is as follows: **D2–246**

a. Evidence in support should be served with the application.

b. Evidence in answer should be served within 14 days thereafter.

c. Evidence in reply (if any) should be served within 7 days thereafter.

In appropriate cases, this timetable should be abridged by agreement and can be abridged by the Court.

F4.5 An ordinary application bundle (see paragraph F11) must be lodged with the Listing Office by 1 p.m. one clear day before the date fixed for the hearing. The case management bundle will also be required on the hearing; this bundle will be passed by the Listing Office to the **D2–247**

Judge. Only where it is essential for the Court on the hearing of the ordinary application to see the full version of a statement of case that has been summarised in accordance with paragraph C1.3 above should a copy of that statement of case be lodged for the ordinary application.

D2–248 F4.6 Skeleton arguments must be served on the advocates for all other parties to the application, and lodged with the Listing Office, by 1 p.m. the day before (*i.e.* the immediately proceding day) the date fixed for the hearing.

D2–249 F4.7 Thus for an application estimated for a half day or less and due to be heard on a Friday:

a. the ordinary application bundle will be lodged by 1 p.m. on Wednesday;

b. skeleton arguments will be lodged by 1 p.m. on Thursday.

D2–250 F4.8 Problems with the lodging of bundles should be notified to the Clerk to the Commercial Court as far in advance as possible. If the ordinary application bundle is not lodged by the time specified, the application may be stood out of the list without further warning.

D2–251 F4.9 The applicant should, as a matter of course, provide all other parties to the application with a copy of the ordinary application bundle, at the cost of the receiving party. Further copies should be supplied on request, again at the cost of the receiving party.

F5 Heavy applications

D2–252 F5.1 Applications expected to involve an oral hearing lasting more than half a day are regarded as heavy applications.

D2–253 F5.2 Heavy applications normally involve a greater volume of evidence and other documents and more extensive issues. They accordingly require a longer lead-time for preparation and exchange of evidence. Where possible the Listing Office will have regard to the availability of advocates when fixing hearing dates.

D2–254 F5.3 Unless otherwise directed or agreed:

a. Evidence in support should be served with the application.

b. Evidence in answer should be served within 28 days thereafter.

c. Evidence in reply (if any) should be served as soon as possible, and in any event within 14 days of service of the evidence in answer.

D2–255 F5.4 An evidence bundle (see paragraph F12) must be lodged with the Listing Office by 4 p.m. two days (*i.e.* two clear days) before the date fixed for the hearing. The case management bundle will also be required on the hearing; this bundle will be passed by the Listing Office to the Judge. Only where it is essential for the Court on the hearing of the heavy application to see the full version of a statement of case that has been summarised in accordance with paragraph C1.3 above should a copy of that statement of case be lodged for the heavy application.

D2–256 F5.5 Skeleton arguments must be served on the advocates for all other parties to the application, and lodged with the Listing Office, as follows:

a. Applicant's skeleton argument (with chronology unless one is unnecessary, and with a dramatis personae if one is warranted), by 4 p.m. two days (*i.e.* two clear days) before the hearing;

b. Respondent's skeleton argument, by 4 p.m. one day (*i.e.* one clear day) before the hearing.

D2–257 F5.6 A documents bundle (see paragraph F13) must be lodged with the Listing Office by 1 p.m. the day before (*i.e.* the immediately preceding day) the day fixed for the hearing (if not before: see paragraph F5.9).

D2–258 F5.7 Unless a longer or shorter period is ordered, not later than 1 p.m. the day before (*i.e.* the immediately preceding day) the date fixed for the hearing a single reading list approved by all advocates with the conduct of the application must be lodged with the Listing Office.

D2–259 F5.8 Thus for an application estimated for more than half a day and due to be heard on a Thursday:

a. the evidence bundle and the applicant's skeleton argument will be lodged by 4 p.m. on Monday;

b. the respondent's skeleton argument will be lodged by 4 p.m. on Tuesday;

c. the documents bundle and the reading list will be lodged by 1 p.m. on Wednesday (if not before: see paragraph F5.9).

D2–260 F5.9 Where a document bundle of the first type described at paragraph F13.2 is used it should be possible for the documents bundle to be lodged with the evidence bundle (*i.e.* by 4 p.m. on Monday in the example given above).

D2–261 F5.10 Problems should be notified to the Clerk to the Commercial Court as far in advance as possible. If the application bundles are not lodged by the time specified, the application may be stood out of the list without further warning.

D2–262 F5.11 The applicant should, as a matter of course, provide all other parties to the application with a copy of the evidence bundle and the documents bundle, at the cost of the receiving party. Further copies should be supplied on request, again at the cost of the receiving party.

F6 Evidence

D2–263 F6.1 In the Commercial Court evidence on any application may be given by affidavit or by witness statement, except where the Practice Direction supplementing CPR Part 32 requires an affidavit only (as, for example, in the case of an application for a freezing injunction or a search order: see paragraph 1.4 of the Practice Direction supplementing CPR Part 32). As contemplated by paragraphs 1.4(1) and 1.5 of the Practice Direction supplementing CPR Part 32 the Court may order that evidence be given by affidavit only.

D2–264 F6.2 Witness statements and affidavits must comply with the requirements of the Practice Direction supplementing CPR Part 32 (subject to the limited exception at paragraph F6.5 below).

F6.3 Witness statements must be verified by a statement of truth, signed by the maker of the statement (CPR 22.1). At hearings other than trial an applicant may rely on the application notice itself, and a party may rely on his statement of case, if the application notice or statement of case (as the case may be) is verified by a statement of truth (CPR 32.6(2)). D2–265 D2–266

F6.4 Proceedings for contempt of court may be brought against a person if he makes, or causes to be made, a false statement in a witness statement (or any other document verified by a statement of truth) without an honest belief in its truth (see CPR 32.14(1)). D2–267

F6.5 Although paragraph 13.1 of the Practice Direction supplementing CPR Part 32 refers to a requirement that the originals of exhibited documents be made available at the hearing, in the Commercial Court this will not be necessary, unless the Court requires or any party requests that the original be made available. Similarly in accordance with paragraph C1.2b above a true copy of any complete written agreement on which particulars of claim are based or a defence is based will be sufficient if made available at the hearing, again unless the Court requires or any party requests that the original be made available. D2–268

F7 Applications disposed of by consent

F7.1 Many applications are disposed of by consent in the Commercial Court. D2–269

F7.2 Consent orders may be submitted to the Court in draft for approval and initialling without the need for an attendance. Two copies of the draft should be lodged at the Registry. The copies should be undated. The order will be dated with the date on which the Judge initials it, but that does not prevent the parties acting on their agreement immediately if they wish. The parties should act promptly in lodging the copies at the Registry. If it is important that the orders are made by a particular date, that fact (and the reasons for it) should be notified in writing to the Clerk to the Commercial Court. D2–270

F7.3 For the avoidance of doubt, this consent order procedure is not however available for a Case Management Conference or a Pre-Trial Review. Whether or not the parties are agreed as between themselves on the directions that the Court should be asked to consider giving at a Case Management Conference or a Pre-Trial Review, attendance will be required. D2–271

F7.4 As with all orders in the Commercial Court (see paragraph D14.2 above), where an order provides a time by which something is to be done the order should wherever possible state the particular date by which the thing is to be done rather than specify a period of time from a particular date or event. D2–272

F8 Hearing dates, time estimates and time limits

F8.1 Dates for the hearing of applications to be attended by advocates are normally fixed after discussion with the clerks to each counsel, or with the solicitor, concerned. D2–273

F8.2 The efficient working of the Court depends on accurate estimates of the time needed for the oral hearing of an application. Over-estimating can be as wasteful as under-estimating. D2–274

F8.3 Subject to paragraph F8.4, the Clerk to the Commercial Court will not accept time estimates for the oral hearing of applications where those estimates exceed the following maxima: D2–275

Application to set aside service:	4 hours
Application for summary judgment:	4 hours
Application to set aside or vary interim remedy:	4 hours
Application to set aside or vary default judgment:	2 hours
Application to amend statement of case:	1 hour
Application for specific disclosure:	1 hour
Application for security for costs:	1 hour

F8.4 A longer time estimate will only be permitted upon application in writing by an advocate in the case to the Judge in charge of the Commercial List (or such other Judge as he may nominate) specifying the extra time required and giving reasons why that extra time is required. A copy of the written application should be sent to the advocates for all other parties in the case at the same time as it is sent to the Judge. D2–276

F8.5 If it is anticipated after a time estimate has been given that there is a material risk that the hearing of an application will over-run the time specified in paragraph F8.3 above, application for a longer hearing must be made in writing by an advocate in the case to the Judge in charge of the Commercial List (or such other Judge as he may nominate) specifying the extra time required and giving reasons why that extra time is required. Again a copy of the written application should be sent to the advocates for all other parties in the case at the same time as it is sent to the Judge. D2–277

F8.6 All time estimates should be given on the assumption that the Judge will have read in advance the skeleton arguments and at least the ordinary application bundle (on an ordinary application) or the evidence bundle (on a heavy application). A time estimate for an ordinary application should allow time for judgment and consequential matters; a time estimate for a heavy application should not. D2–278

F8.7 Save in the situation referred to at paragraph F8.8, a separate time estimate must be given for each application, including any application issued after, but to be heard at the same time as, another application. D2–279

F8.8 A separate time estimate need not be given for any application issued after but to be heard at the same time as another application where an advocate in the case certifies in writing that: D2–280

a. the determination of the application first issued will necessarily determine the application issued subsequently; or

b. the matters raised in the application issued subsequently are not contested.

D2–281 F8.9 If it is found at the hearing that the time required for the hearing has been significantly underestimated, the Judge hearing the application may adjourn the matter and may make any special costs orders (including orders for the immediate payment of costs and wasted costs orders) as may be appropriate.

D2–282 F8.10 Similarly, failure to comply with the requirements for lodging bundles for the application will normally result in the application not being heard on the date fixed (see further paragraphs F4.8 and F5.10 above), at the expense of the party in default. An order for immediate payment of costs may be made.

D2–283 F8.11 On the hearing of any application, every effort must be made to avoid the reading aloud of documents or authorities. The Court will expect simply to be referred to the actual passages relied on by the relevant party.

F9 Application bundles

D2–284 F9.1 The contents of the bundle(s) that require to be prepared for an application are outlined at paragraphs F9.2 to F13.7 below. The preparation of all application bundles must also be undertaken in accordance with Appendix 11.

D2–285 F9.2 It is essential that all documents which are necessary, but no more documents than are necessary, are provided to the Court in advance of the hearing of any application.

F10 The case management bundle

D2–286 F10.1 The case management bundle (see paragraph D6) will always be provided to the Judge (by the Listing Office). A copy should always be in the possession of the advocates in the case before and on the hearing of each application. This applies to all applications whether made in writing or orally.

D2–287 F10.2 Other application bundles should not contain documents which are in the case management bundle, with the limited exception referred to at F12.2b.

F11 The ordinary application bundle

D2–288 F11.1 On an ordinary application (see paragraph F4) there should normally be only one application bundle (the ordinary application bundle) other than the case management bundle.

D2–289 F11.2 The ordinary application bundle should contain the application and all affidavits sworn or witness statements verified on the application, but only those exhibits or parts of exhibits are are regarded by one or more of the advocates who are to appear on the hearing of the application to be necessary for the purpose of the hearing.

D2–290 F11.3 Even where a number of exhibits are regarded as necessary for the purpose of the hearing, if those exhibits contain a selection from the contemporaneous documentation or from the correspondence they should, in accordance with Appendix 11, nonetheless be placed in a single chronological sequence (and paginated as part of the single bundle).

F12 The evidence bundle (heavy applications)

D2–291 F12.1 An evidence bundle will be normally only be required on a heavy application.

D2–292 F12.2 An evidence bundle should contain:

a. the application and all affidavits sworn or witness statements verified on the application but no exhibits;

b. if there is a contract that is central to the dispute, a copy of that contract or of the material parts of it (even if this is also in the case management bundle because it is attached to a statement or case under paragraph C1.2b).

F13 The documents bundle (heavy applications)

D2–293 F13.1 A documents bundle will normally only be required on a heavy application.

D2–294 F13.2 A documents bundle should be of one of two types:

a. a bundle containing those documents taken from the exhibits to affidavits sworn or witness statements verified on the application as are agreed (before the preparation of skeleton arguments) by the advocates who are to appear on the hearing of the application to be necessary; or if this is not practicable,

b. a bundle containing those documents taken from the exhibits to affidavits sworn or witness statements verified on the application as are mentioned in skeleton arguments prepared for the hearing of the application.

D2–295 F13.3 If, in accordance with paragraph F12, the evidence bundle already contains a copy of any contract (or of the material parts of it) a further copy should not appear in the documents bundle. Instead a page should be inserted in the documents bundle to show the chronological position of the contract, and that page should be marked to show where in the evidence bundle the contract itself may be found.

D2–296 F13.4 Whichever type of documents bundle is used, the documents bundle should contain only the documents referred to at paragraph F13.2, in chronological order (save only where Appendix 11 provides otherwise).

D2–297 F13.5 A documents bundle of the first type described at paragraph F13.2 is preferable. This is because it will allow advocates to use the documents bundle pagination in their skeleton arguments.

F13.6 Whichever type of documents bundle is used, each document in the documents bundle should be marked (normally at the top centre) to show the exhibit page, exhibit number and affidavit or witness statement from which the document has been taken. (The documents bundle will also be paginated in its own right in accordance with Appendix 11.) **D2–298**

F13.7 On a heavy application the applicant's legal representatives should ensure that one full set of the complete exhibits to all affidavits sworn or witness statements verified on the application is brought to the hearing of the application. This will allow reference to any document that was excluded from the documents bundle. **D2–299**

F14 Skeleton arguments

F14.1 Save only where the application is so urgent that there is insufficient time for the preparation of a skeleton argument, a concise written skeleton argument should be provided to the Court and all other parties involved by the advocate(s) for each party to any contested application. **D2–300**

F14.2 Guidelines on the preparation of skeleton arguments are set out in Part 1 of Appendix 10. **D2–301**

F15 Chronologies, indices and dramatis personae

F15.1 For most applications it is of assistance for the applicant to provide a chronology. Dramatis personae are also often useful. So too are indices (*i.e.* a document that collates key references on particular points, or a substantive list of the contents of a particular bundle or bundles). **D2–302**

F15.2 Guidelines on the preparation of chronologies and indices are set out in Part 2 of Appendix 10. **D2–303**

F16 Authorities

F16.1 On some applications there will be *key* authorities that it would be useful, if possible, for the Judge to read before the oral hearing of the application. Copies of these key authorities should be provided with the application bundle(s). **D2–304**

F16.2 It is also useful if a composite bundle or bundles of the authorities on which the parties wish to rely, in chronological order of report, is or are provided to the Judge hearing the application as soon as possible after skeleton arguments have been exchanged. The bundle or bundles should not repeat copies of the key authorities already provided in accordance with paragraph F16.1. If such a bundle or bundles is or are not prepared, the advocate for each party must provide a list of authorities to the usher by 9 a.m. on the day of the hearing. **D2–305**

F16.3 Any advocate preparing a bundle of authorities should, unless otherwise agreed, provide one copy of the bundle to each other advocate (or team of advocates). Advocates should liaise in relation to the production of bundles of authorities to ensure that the same authority does not appear in more than one bundle. **D2–306**

F16.4 Unreported cases should normally only be cited where the advocate is ready to give an assurance that the transcript contains a statement of some principle of law, relevant to an issue on the application, and of which the substance, as distinct from some mere choice of phraseology, is not to be found in any judgment that has appeared in one of the generalised or specialised series of law reports. **D2–307**

F17 Costs

F17.1 Costs are dealt with generally at paragraph I13. **D2–308**

F17.2 Reference should be also be made to the directions relating to the summary assessment of costs for shorter hearings. These are to be contained in directions relating to CPR Part 44 under the Practice Direction supplementing CPR Parts 43–48. **D2–309**

F17.3 In carrying out a summary assessment of costs, the Court may have regard amongst other matters to: **D2–310**

a. advice (general or particular) from a Commercial [Taxing] Master or from the Chief [Taxing] Master on costs of specialist solicitors and counsel;

b. any survey published by the London Solicitors Litigation Association showing the average hourly expense rate for solicitors in London;

c. any information provided to the Commercial Court at its request by one or more of the specialist associations (referred to at paragraph A7) on average charges by specialist solicitors and counsel.

F18 Case memorandum

F18.1 Following the hearing of each application in the case, and unless the Court otherwise directs, the case memorandum (provided for at paragraph D4) should be updated to include very short and uncontroversial reference to the application and its outcome (see further paragraph D4.3 above). **D2–311**

F19 Particular types of application: interim injunctions

Generally

D2–312 F19.1 In addition to the general practice for applications set out in this section of the Guide, the Practice Direction supplementing CPR Part 25 applies to applications for interim injunctions, save as follows:

a. the time period at paragraph 2.2 of that Practice Direction does not apply;

b. paragraph 2.3 of that Practice Direction does not apply because application notices and evidence are not served by the Commercial Court;

c. whilst a draft of the order sought should be filed as required by paragraph 2.4 of that Practice Direction, it is not necessary for a disk to be provided.

D2–313 F19.2 As much notice as the circumstances permit must be given to the Clerk to the Commercial Court of the intention to make an application for an interim injunction.

D2–314 F19.3 Save in cases where the urgency is such that there has not been any opportunity to do so, the applicant must issue his claim form and finalise his evidence in support of the application before making the application. On applications on any weight, and unless the urgency means that this is not possible, the applicant should provide the Court at the earliest opportunity with a skeleton argument. An affidavit, and not a witness statement, is required on an application for a freezing injunction or a search order: see paragraph 3.1 of the Practice Direction supplementing CPR Part 25.

Security by the applicant

D2–315 F19.4 Where the applicant for the interim remedy is not able to show assets within the jurisdiction of the Court to provide substance to the undertakings given, particularly the undertakings in damages, the applicant for the interim remedy may be required as a condition of the grant of the interim remedy to back his undertakings by providing some readily available security within the jurisdiction, such as a payment into Court, or the provision of a bond by an insurance company or of a first demand guarantee or standby credit by a bank. Alternatively, the Judge may order a payment by way of such security to the applicant's solicitors to be held by the solicitors as officers of the Court pending further order. Sometimes the undertaking of a parent company may be acceptable. Applicants should be prepared to deal with this point; failure to anticipate a need to back the undertakings can be a cause of unsatisfactory delay.

Form of order

D2–316 F19.5 Example forms of wording for orders made on applications for a freezing injunction and for a search order are at Appendix 5. These are based on the forms accompanying the Practice Direction supplementing CPR Part 25. The forms should be used save to the extent that the Judge hearing a particular application considers there is good reason for adopting a different form.

D2–317 F19.6 A phrase indicating that an interim remedy is in force until judgment or further order is normally understood in the context of an interim remedy to cover the period up to the completion of the trial by the delivery of a final judgment; if an interim remedy continuing after judgment is required, say until judgment has been satisfied, an application to that effect must be made (see further paragraph J1).

D2–318 F19.7 It is good practice to draft an order for an interim remedy so that it includes a proviso which permits acts, which would otherwise be a breach of the order, to be done with the written consent of the claimant's solicitors. This enables the parties to agree in effect to the variations (or exhaustion) of the order for an interim remedy without the necessity of coming back to Court.

Freezing injunctions

D2–319 F19.8 Freezing injunctions in the Commercial Court made on an application without notice will now provide for a return date, unless the Judge otherwise orders (see paragraph 5.1(3) of the Practice Direction supplementing CPR Part 25). In the usual course, the return date given will be on a Friday (unless a date for a Case Management Conference has already been fixed, in which event the return date given will in the usual course be that date). In the event that, after service or notification of the injunction, one or more of the parties anticipate that more than 15 minutes will be required to deal with the matter on the return date the Listing Office should be informed forthwith and in any event no later than 1600 hrs on the Wednesday before the Friday fixed as the return date. If the parties agree, the return date may be postponed to a later date on which all parties will be ready to deal with any substantive issues: in this event, an agreed form of order extending the injunction to the postponed return date should be submitted for consideration by a Commercial Judge and if the order is made in the terms submitted there will be no need for the parties to attend on the day originally fixed as the return date.

D2–320 F19.9 The defendant or other interested party will continue also to have liberty to apply. A provision for the defendant to give notice of any application to discharge or vary the freezing injunction is usually included as a matter of convenience but it is not proper to attempt to fetter the right of the defendant to apply without notice or on short notice if need be.

F19.10 As regards freezing injunctions in respect of assets outside the jurisdiction of the English Courts, the standard wording in relation to effects on third parties may in some cases appropriately incorporate wording to enable overseas branches of banks or similar institutions which have offices within the jurisdiction to comply with what they reasonably believe to be their obligations under the laws of the country where the assets are located or under the proper law of the relevant banking or other contract relating to such assets. D2–321

F19.11 Any bank or third party served with, notified of or affected by a freezing injunction may apply to the Court without notice to any party for directions, or notify the Court in writing without notice to any party, in the event that the freezing injunction affects or may affect the position or the bank or third party under legislation, regulations or procedures aimed to prevent money laundering. D2–322

F19.12 By CPR 25.10 if (a) the Court has granted an interim injunction and (b) the claim is stayed other than by agreement between the parties, an interim injunction shall be set aside unless the Court orders that it should continue to have effect even though the claim is stayed. A freezing injunction is listed separately from an interim injunction in CPR 25.1(1). To avoid the risk of uncertainty about the position, in the Commercial Court a freezing injunction will not be set aside unless and until an order to that effect is made. D2–323

Search orders

F19.13 Attention is drawn to the detailed requirements in respect of search orders set out at paragraphs 7.1 to 8.3 of the Practice Direction supplementing CPR Part 25. In addition, the applicant for the search order should undertake not to inform any third party of the search order or of the case until after a specified date. D2–324

Applications to discharge or vary freezing injunctions or search orders

F19.14 Applications to discharge or vary freezing injunctions or search orders are treated as matters of urgency for listing purposes. Those representing applicants for discharge or variation should ascertain before a date is fixed for the hearing whether, having regard to the evidence which they wish to adduce, the claimant would wish to adduce further evidence in opposition. If so, all reasonable steps must be taken by all parties to agree upon the earliest practicable date at which they can be ready for the hearing, so as to avoid the last minute need to vacate a fixed date. In cases of difficulty the matter should be referred to a Commercial Judge who may be able to suggest temporary solutions pending the hearing. D2–325

F19.15 If a freezing injunction or a search order is discharged on an application to discharge or vary, or on the return date, the Judge will always consider whether it is appropriate that he should assess damages at once and direct immediate payment by the applicant for the freezing injunction or search order. D2–326

Applications under section 25 of the Civil Jurisdiction and Judgments Act 1982

F19.16 Paragraph 1.2 of the Practice Direction supplementing CPR Part 8 contemplates that a Practice Direction may require the use of the CPR Part 8 procedure for additional types of proceedings. In the Commercial Court a Part 8 claim form (rather than an application notice: *cf.* CPR 25.4(2)) should be used for an application under section 25 of the Civil Jurisdiction and Judgments Act 1982 ("Interim relief in England and Wales and Northern Ireland in the absence of substantive proceedings"). The modified Part 8 procedure used in the Commercial Court is referred to at paragraph B4 above. D2–327

F20 Particular types of application: security for costs

F20.1 Applications for security for costs continue to be governed by RSC Order 23. D2–328

F20.2 The applicable practice (adapted from that previously set out in the Fourth Edition of the Guide) is set out in Appendix 18. D2–329

G. ALTERNATIVE DISPUTE RESOLUTION ("ADR")

G1.1 Generally

G1.1 While emphasising the primary role of the Commercial Court as a forum for deciding commercial cases, the Court encourages parties to consider the use of ADR (such as, but not confined to, mediation and conciliation) as a possible means of resolving disputes or particular issues. D2–330

G1.2 Whilst the Commercial Court remains an entirely appropriate forum for resolving most of the disputes which are entered in the Commercial List, the view of the Commercial Court is that the settlement of disputes by means of ADR: D2–331

a. significantly helps litigants to save costs;

b. saves litigants the delay of litigation in reaching finality in their disputes;

c. enables litigants to achieve settlement of their disputes while preserving their existing commercial relationships and market reputation;

d. provides litigants with a wider range of solutions than those offered by litigation;

e. is likely to make a substantial contribution to the more efficient use of judicial resources.

D2–332 G1.3 The Commercial Judges will in appropriate cases invite the parties to consider whether their dispute, or particular issues in it, could be resolved through ADR.

D2–333 G1.4 Legal representatives in all cases should consider with their clients and the other parties concerned the possibility of attempting to resolve the dispute or particular issues by ADR. Whilst it is again emphasised that the Commercial Court will remain the appropriate forum for deciding most disputes in its List, legal representatives should ensure that parties are fully informed as to the most cost effective means of resolving their dispute.

D2–334 G1.5 Parties to a case pending before the Commercial Court who consider that ADR might be an appropriate means of resolving the dispute or particular issues in the dispute, may apply for directions at any stage, including before service of the defence and before the Case Management Conference.

D2–335 G1.6 At the Case Management Conference if it should appear to the Judge that the case before him or any of the issues arising in it are particularly appropriate for an attempt at settlement by means of ADR but that the parties have not previously attempted settlement by such means, he may invite the parties to use ADR.

D2–336 G1.7 The Judge may, if he considers it appropriate, adjourn the case for a specified period of time to encourage and enable the parties to use ADR. He may for this purpose extend the time for compliance by the parties or any of them with any requirement under the CPR or this Guide or order of the Court.

D2–337 G1.8 The Judge may further consider in an appropriate case making an ADR Order in the terms set out in Appendix 7.

D2–338 G1.9 The Clerk to the Commercial Court keeps some published information as to individuals and bodies that offer ADR services. (The list will also include individuals and bodies that offer arbitration services.) If the parties are unable to agree upon a neutral individual or panel of individuals for ADR, they may by consent refer to the Judge for assistance in reaching such agreement. The Commercial Court will not recommend any individual or body because it would be inappropriate to do so.

D2–339 G1.10 At the Case Management Conference or on any other hearing in the course of which the Judge invites the parties to resolve the dispute or particular issues in the dispute by ADR, he may on that occasion make such order as to the costs that the parties may incur by reason of their using or attempting to use ADR as may in all the circumstances seem appropriate.

G2 Early neutral evaluation facility for cases in the Commercial Court

D2–340 G2.1 A facility for a without prejudice, non-binding, early neutral evaluation by a Commercial Judge of a dispute, or of particular issues in it, is available in appropriate cases.

D2–341 G2.2 If, after discussion with the advocates representing the parties, it appears to the Judge that an early neutral evaluation is likely to assist in the resolution of the dispute, or particular issues in it, he may offer to provide that evaluation himself or to arrange for another Judge to do so.

D2–342 G2.3 If the parties accept the course offered, the Judge may thereupon give directions as to such preparatory steps for the evaluation and the form which it is to take as he considers appropriate. The parties will in that event be required to arrange for the evaluation hearing having regard to the availability of the Judge concerned.

D2–343 G2.4 Where early neutral evaluation is provided by a Judge, that Judge will, unless the parties otherwise agree, take no further part in the case either for the purpose of the hearing of applications or as the Judge at trial.

H. EVIDENCE FOR TRIAL

H1 Witnesses of fact

Preparation and form of witness statements

D2–344 H1.1 The pre-trial timetable will usually include directions for the service of witness statements.

D2–345 H1.2 Witness statements must comply with the requirements of the Practice Direction supplementing CPR Part 32. For the avoidance of doubt, all witness statements must be signed or initialled on each page, unless the Court otherwise orders.

H1.3 The following points are emphasised: D2-346
a. whilst it is recognised that in commercial cases, a witness statement will usually be prepared by legal representatives, the witness statement must, so far as practicable, be in the witness's own words;
b. the witness statement must indicate which of the statements made in it are made from the witness's own knowledge and which are matters of information and belief (giving the source for any matters of information and belief);
c. the witness statement must include a statement by the witness that he believes the matters in it are true; a witness statement is the equivalent of the oral evidence which that witness would, if called, give as his evidence in chief at the trial and proceedings for contempt of court may be brought against a person if he makes, or causes to be made, a false statement in a witness statement without an honest belief in its truth (see CPR 32.14(1));
d. a witness statement should not be longer than necessary and should not contain lengthy renditions of correspondence.
H1.4 The rules of any relevant professional body regarding the drafting of witness statements must also be observed. D2-347

Fluency of witness

H1.5 Where a witness is not sufficiently fluent in English to give his evidence in English, the witness statement should be in the witness's own language and a translation provided. D2-348
H1.6 Where a witness is not fluent in English but can make himself understood in broken English and can understand written English, provided that these matters are indicated in the witness statement the statement need not be in his own words. It must however be written so as to express as accurately as possible the substance of his evidence. D2-349

Witness statement as evidence in chief

H1.7 By CPR 32.5(2) where a witness is called to give oral evidence, his witness statement is to stand as his evidence in chief unless the Court orders otherwise. In an appropriate case the Trial Judge may require the whole or any part of the witness's evidence in chief to be given orally. D2-350

Additional evidence from a witness

H1.8 By CPR 32.5(3) a witness giving oral evidence at trial may with the permission of the Court amplify his witness statement and give evidence in relation to new matters which have arisen since the witness statement was served on the other parties. CPR 32.5(4) provides that this permission will be given only if the Court considers that there is good reason not to confine the evidence of the witness to the contents of his witness statement. In the Commercial Court a supplemental witness statement should normally be served where the witness proposes materially to add to, alter, correct or retract from what is in his original witness statement. Permission will be required for the service of a supplemental statement. D2-351

Notice of decision not to call a witness

H1.9 Where a party has decided not to call a witness whose witness statement has been served to give oral evidence at trial, prompt notice of this decision should be given to all other parties. The party should make plain when he gives this notice whether he proposes to put, or seek to put, the witness statement in as hearsay evidence. If he does not put the witness statement in as hearsay evidence, CPR 32.5(5) allows any other party to put it in as hearsay evidence. D2-352

Witness summonses

H1.10 CPR 34.2 to 34.7 deal with witness summonses, including a summons for a witness to attend court or to produce documents in advance of the date fixed for trial. As for service (CPR 34.6), in the Commercial Court witness summonses are to be served by the parties, not the Court. D2-353

H2 Expert witnesses

Application for permission

H2.1 Any application for permission to call an expert witness, or serve an expert's report, should normally be made at the Case Management Conference. D2-354

D2–355 H2.2 CPR Part 35 applies to proceedings in the Commercial List subject to the exceptions and further provisions contained in this section of the Guide and in Appendix 12. The Practice Direction supplementing CPR Part 35 also applies, again subject to the exceptions and further provisions contained in this section of the Guide and in Appendix 12.

Separate experts

D2–356 H2.3 In the Commercial Court, as in cases generally, the parties should bear in mind that expert evidence can lead to unnecessary expenditure, and they should be prepared to consider the use of single joint experts. However, cases in the Commercial Court frequently are of a size and of a complexity or nature such that the use of single joint experts is not appropriate. In such cases, parties will generally be given permission each to call one expert whom they have retained in each field requiring expert evidence. In this Guide these experts are called "separate experts". On occasion there will be questions about appropriate fields of expertise, and the Court will have to resolve such questions.

Single joint expert

D2–357 H2.4 CPR 35.7 permits the Court to direct that there be a single joint expert rather than separate experts. Such a direction may be made in the Commercial Court in an appropriate case. The complexity and value of the case are relevant here; some cases are more straightforward and of lower value than others. There is, however, no presumption in the Commercial Court in favour of single joint experts. And where in an appropriate case both parties wish to instruct separate experts a direction in favour of a single joint expert may possibly be infrequently made.

D2–358 H2.5 In some cases the appointment of a single joint expert to carry out an examination at the very beginning of a case may be appropriate. But even here the Commercial Court recognises that the use of separate experts may bring greater advantage, not least in providing the facility for each party to take separate expert advice. However in such a case whenever possible joint inspections by both experts are to be encouraged.

D2–359 H2.6 Occasionally in a complex commercial case where a meeting of separate experts is likely to involve unusual difficulties or complexities the use of a single joint expert may be combined with the use of (separate) experts retained by the parties. Here the function of the single joint expert might be, not to report or give evidence, but to chair and facilitate meetings of separate experts.

D2–360 H2.7 Paragraph 5 of the Practice Direction supplementing CPR Part 35 indicates that where the Court has directed that the evidence on a particular issue be given by one expert only but there are a number of disciplines relevant to that issue, a leading expert in the dominant discipline will prepare the general part of a report and will annex or incorporate the contents of any reports from experts in other disciplines. Use of this procedure may be infrequent in the Commercial Court. If reports from experts in a number of disciplines or fields are necessary on a particular issue, the Court will require to be persuaded before allowing evidence to be given other than directly by each expert in each discipline or field.

D2–361 H2.8 When the use of a single joint expert is contemplated, the Court will expect the parties to co-operate in developing, and agreeing to the greatest possible extent, terms of reference for that expert. In most cases the terms of reference will (in particular) detail what the expert is asked to do, identify any documentary materials he is asked to consider and specify any assumptions he is asked to make.

Requirements of general application in relation to expert evidence

D2–362 H2.9 The requirements of Appendix 12 will apply in relation to all aspects of expert evidence (including expert reports, meetings of experts and expert evidence given orally) unless the Court orders otherwise. Legal representatives should ensure that Appendix 12 is at the earliest point drawn to the attention of an expert retained by a party.

Form and content of expert's reports

D2–363 H2.10 The requirements at paragraphs 1.1 and 1.2 of the Practice Direction supplementing CPR Part 35 should be followed. Paragraphs 1.3 and 1.4 of the Practice Direction are addressed at paragraphs H2.14 and H2.15 below.

D2–364 H2.11 The expert should take care always to state clearly the questions or issues with which he is dealing in his report.

H2.12 In stating the substance of all material instructions on the basis of which his report is written (see CPR 35.10(3) and paragraph 1.2(3) of the Practice Direction supplementing CPR Part 35) an expert witness should state the facts or assumptions upon which his opinion is based. If any of the facts stated are within his own direct knowledge he should make clear which those are. If a stated assumption is, in the opinion of the expert witness, unreasonable or unlikely he should state that clearly. **D2–365**

H2.13 It is useful if a report contains a glossary of significant technical terms. **D2–366**

Statement of truth

H2.14 At the end of the expert's report there must be a statement that: **D2–367**

a. the expert understands his duty to the Court and has complied with that duty (see CPR 35.10(2));

b. the expert has read and understood Appendix 12 to the Commercial Court Guide;

c. he has complied and will continue to comply with Appendix 12 at all stages of his involvement in the case;

d. the assumptions upon which his opinion is based are not in his opinion unreasonable or unlikely assumptions (or, where in his opinion any assumption is unreasonable or unlikely, that is clearly stated);

e. the facts stated in his report that are facts within his own direct knowledge have been identified as such and are true;

f. the opinions expressed in his report represent his true professional opinion.

The report must be signed by the expert.

H2.15 In the Commercial Court the requirement for a statement in the terms indicated at paragraph H2.14 above takes the place of the requirement for a statement of truth in the terms provided by paragraph 1.4 of the Practice Direction supplementing CPR Part 35 (and see paragraph 1.3 of the Practice Direction supplementing CPR Part 22). As with any document verified by a statement of truth, proceedings for contempt of court may be brought against a person if he makes, or causes to be made, without an honest belief in its truth, a false statement in an expert's report verified by a statement of truth (see paragraph 1.5 of the Practice Direction supplementing CPR Part 35). **D2–368**

Request by an expert to the Court for directions

H2.16 An expert may file with the Court a written request for directions to assist him in carrying out his function as expert, but: **D2–369**

a. at least 7 days before he does so (or such shorter period as the Court may direct) he should provide a copy of his proposed request to the party instructing him;

b. at least 4 days before he does so (or such shorter period as the Court may direct) he should provide a copy of his proposed request to all other parties.

H2.17 In the Commercial Court this procedure takes the place of CPR 35.14. It is intended to reduce the risk of an expert accidentally informing the Court about, or about matters connected with, communications or potential communications between the parties that are without prejudice or privileged. The expert may properly be privy to the content of these communications because he has been asked to assist the party instructing him to evaluate them. The procedure does not prevent the expert from filing a request for directions, but ensures that one or other party can approach the Court first if the request proposed by the expert would result in his informing the Court about, or about matters connected with, communications or potential communications between the parties that are without prejudice or privileged. **D2–370**

Exchange of reports

H2.18 In commercial cases the Court will where appropriate direct that the reports of expert witnesses be exchanged sequentially rather than simultaneously. This is an issue that the Court will normally wish to consider at the Case Management Conference. **D2–371**

Meetings of expert witnesses

H2.19 A meeting or meetings of expert witnesses before trial will normally be ordered. Sometimes it may be useful for there to be further meetings during the trial itself. **D2–372**

H2.20 The purposes of meetings of experts are to give the experts the opportunity: **D2–373**

a. to discuss the expert issues;

b. to decide, with the benefit of that discussion, on which expert issues they share or can come to agree the same expert opinion and on which expert issues there remains a difference of expert opinion between them (and what that difference is).

(In the Commercial Court this description of the purpose of the meetings takes the place of the description at CPR 35.12(1).)

H2.21 Subject to paragraph H2.24 below, the content of the discussion between the experts at or in connection with a meeting is without prejudice, and in particular (in accordance with CPR 35.12(4)) shall not be referred to at the trial unless the parties agree. **D2–374**

D2–375 H2.22 Subject to any directions of the Court, the procedure to be adopted at these meetings is a matter for the experts, not the parties or their legal representatives.

D2–376 H2.23 Neither the parties nor their legal representatives should seek to restrict the freedom of experts to identify and acknowledge the expert issues on which they agree (*i.e.* on which they share the same expert opinion) at (or following further consideration after) meetings of experts.

D2–377 H2.24 At or following their meetings the experts should prepare a joint memorandum for the Court recording:

a. the fact that they have met and discussed the expert issues;

b. the expert issues on which they agree (*i.e.* on which they share the same expert opinion);

c. the expert issues where they there is a difference of expert opinion between them, and a summary of what that difference of expert opinion is.

(In the Commercial Court this automatic requirement applies notwithstanding the Court's powers under CPR 35.12(3).)

D2–378 H2.25 Where experts reach agreement on an expert issue during (or following further consideration after) their meetings the agreement shall not bind the parties unless the parties expressly agree to be bound by the agreement.

D2–379 H2.26 Following the preparation of the joint memorandum each expert may prepare a short supplemental report highlighting the reasons why the expert adheres to the views he does on the expert issues recorded in the memorandum as being issues where there is a difference of expert opinion.

Written questions to experts

D2–380 H2.27 CPR 35.6 contains a procedure allowing a party, without seeking the prior permission of the Court, to put written questions to an expert instructed by another party (or to a single joint expert) about the expert's report. By CPR 35.6(2)(c) the questions must be for the purpose only of clarification of the report unless the Court gives permission or the other party agrees.

D2–381 H2.28 The Commercial Court will pay close attention to the use of this procedure (especially where separate experts are instructed) to ensure that it remains an instrument for the helpful exchange of information. The Court will not allow it to interfere with the procedure for an exchange of professional opinion at a meeting of experts, or to inhibit that exchange of professional opinion. In cases where (for example) questions that are oppressive in number or content are put, or questions are put (without permission) for any purpose other than clarification of an expert's report, the Court will not hesitate to disallow the questions and to make an appropriate order for costs against the party putting the questions.

Inspection of documents in an expert's report

D2–382 H2.29 CPR 31.14(e) provides that (subject to CPR 35.10(4)) a party may inspect a document mentioned in an expert's report. In a commercial case an expert's report will frequently, and helpfully, list all or many of the relevant previous papers (published or unpublished) or books written by the expert or to which the expert has contributed. Requiring inspection of this material may often be unrealistic, and the collating and copying burden could be huge. Accordingly, and subject to paragraph H2.30 below, in the Commercial Court a party wishing to inspect a document in an expert report should (failing agreement) make an application to the Court for that facility. The Court will not accede to the application unless it is satisfied that inspection is appropriate for dealing with the case justly and that the document is not reasonably available to the party making the application from an alternative source.

D2–383 H2.30 There should however be no need for an application to the Court in the case of photographs, plans, analyses, measurements, survey reports or other similar documents, and any unpublished sources relied on by an expert witness. Unless already provided on inspection of documents at the stage of disclosure, these must be provided to all parties at the same time as the report of the expert.

Trial

D2–384 H2.31 At trial the evidence of expert witnesses is usually taken as a block, after the evidence of witnesses of fact has been given.

H3 Evidence by video link

D2–385 H3.1 In an appropriate case, permission may be given for the oral evidence of a witness to be given by video link. If permission is given the Court will give directions for the conduct of this part of the trial.

D2–386 H3.2 The party seeking permission should prepare and serve on all parties and lodge with the Court a memorandum dealing with the matters outlined in the Videoconferencing Protocol (Appendix 15), and setting out precisely what arrangements are proposed. Where the proposal involves transmission from a location with no existing video link facility, experience shows that the questions of feasibility, timing and cost will require particularly close investigation.

D2–387 H3.3 The question of permission, and of directions, should be raised at the earliest possible opportunity. It will normally be considered at the Case Management Conference or, at the latest, at any Pre-Trial Review although it is recognised that in some cases it may have to be considered at an even later point.

H3.4 In considering whether to give permission the Court will be concerned in particular to balance any potential savings of costs against the fact that the Court will not, if permission is given, observe the witness at first hand when the witness gives oral testimony. D2–388

H4 Taking evidence from abroad

H4.1 In an appropriate case, permission may be given for the evidence of a witness to be taken from abroad. CPR Part 34 contains provisions for the taking of evidence by deposition, and the issue of letters of request. D2–389

H4.2 In a very exceptional case, and subject in particular to all necessary approvals being obtained and diplomatic requirements satisfied, the Court may be prepared to consider conducting part of the proceedings abroad where that very exceptional course appears to be necessary. The opportunity for the oral evidence of a witness to be given by video link may well militate against taking this course. D2–390

I. TRIAL

I1 Facility for expedited trial

I1.1 The Commercial Court is able to offer the facility of an expedited trial in cases of sufficient urgency and importance. D2–391

I1.2 Where a party wishes to seek an expedited trial, an application should be made to the Judge in charge of the Commercial List, on notice to all parties, at the earliest possible opportunity. Normally the application will be made after issue and service of the claim form but before service of particulars of claim. D2–392

I2 Split trials

I2.1 It will sometimes be advantageous to try liability first. Questions of damages can if necessary be referred to (for example) a Judge of the Technology and Construction Court or to a Master, or the parties may choose to ask an arbitrator to decide them. The same approach can be applied to other factual questions. D2–393

I2.2 At the stage of final preparation for the trial, or even at the commencement of the trial itself, it may be advantageous to separate issues and to take them consecutively. D2–394

I3 Documents for trial

I3.1 Bundles of documents for the trial must be prepared in accordance with Appendix 11. D2–395

I3.2 The number, content and organisation of the trial bundles must be approved by the advocates with the conduct of the trial. D2–396

I3.3 Consideration must always be given to what documents are and are not relevant and necessary and only those that are relevant and necessary should be included in the trial bundles. D2–397

I3.4 The number content and organisation of the trial bundles should be agreed in accordance with the following procedure: D2–398

a. details of the claimant's proposals to be submitted to other parties at least 6 weeks before the date fixed for trial;

b. details of other parties' required additions and any suggestions for revision of claimant's proposals to be submitted to the claimant at least 4 weeks before the date fixed for trial.

The details at a. and b. should be supplied in a form that will be most convenient for the recipient to understand and respond to: the form to be used should be discussed between the parties before the details are supplied.

I3.5 It is for the claimant to prepare and lodge the trial bundles, save only where another party proposes a bundle that the claimant regards as unnecessary in which case it is for the party proposing the bundle to prepare and lodge it. D2–399

I3.6 Unless a longer or shorter period is ordered, preparation of the trial bundles must be completed not later than 3 weeks before the date fixed for trial. Any party preparing a trial bundle should, as a matter of course, provide all other parties who are to take part in the trial with a copy of the trial bundle, at the cost of the receiving party. Further copies should be supplied on request, again at the cost of the receiving party. D2–400

I3.7 Unless a longer or shorter period is ordered, a full set of the trial bundles must be lodged with the Listing Office at least 7 days before the date fixed for trial. D2–401

I3.8 Failure to comply with the requirements for lodging bundles for the trial will normally result (among other things) in the trial not commencing on the date fixed, at the expense of the party in default. An order for immediate payment of costs may be made. D2–402

D2–403 I3.9 Where oral evidence will be given at trial by a witness or witnesses, a clean unmarked set of all relevant trial bundles must be provided for use in the witness box. It is essential that these bundles are kept up to date throughout the trial.

I4 Information technology at trial

D2–404 I4.1 The use of information technology at trial is encouraged where it is likely substantially to save time and cost, or to increase accuracy.

D2–405 I4.2 Where information technology is to be used at trial the same system should be used by all of those parties who wish to use information technology, and provided to the Court. In a heavy case the Court may wish at a stage as early as the Case Management Conference to discuss with the parties the question of directions on the use of information technology.

I5 Reading lists, authorities and trial timetable

D2–406 I5.1 Unless a longer or shorter period is ordered, not later than 1 p.m. two days (*i.e.* two clear days) before the date fixed for trial a single reading list approved by all advocates with the conduct of the trial must be lodged with the Listing Office.

D2–407 I5.2 If any party objects to the Judge reading any document in advance of the trial, this objection and its grounds should be clearly stated in a letter accompanying the trial bundles and in the skeleton argument of that party.

D2–408 I5.3 In particular, consideration should be given as to whether there is any objection or reservation to the Judge reading witness statements before the trial.

D2–409 I5.4 In the absence of objection or reservation, the Judge will be free to read the witness statements and documents in advance.

D2–410 I5.5 It is rarely necessary to remove or omit from the trial bundles documents (including witness statements) in respect of which there is an objection or reservation; some annotation to indicate the objection or reservation is usually sufficient.

D2–411 I5.6 A composite bundle or bundles of the authorities referred to in the skeleton arguments, in chronological order of report, should be lodged with the Listing Office as soon as possible after skeleton arguments have been exchanged. Unless otherwise agreed, the preparation of the bundle or bundles of authorities is the responsibility of the claimant, who should provide copies of the bundle or bundles to all other parties. Advocates should liaise in relation to the production of bundles of authorities to ensure that the same authority does not appear in more than one bundle.

D2–412 I5.7 Unreported cases should normally only be cited where the advocate is ready to give an assurance that the transcript contains a statement of some principle of law, relevant to an issue on the application, and of which the substance, as distinct from some mere choice of phraseology, is not to be found in any judgment that has appeared in one of the general or specialised series of law reports.

D2–413 I5.8 The reading list should be accompanied by a trial timetable (*cf.* CPR 39.4). This trial timetable may have been fixed by the Judge at the Pre-Trial Review (paragraph D13.7 above). If it has not, the trial timetable should be prepared by the advocate(s) for the claimant after consultation with the advocate(s) for all other parties. If there are differences of view between the advocate(s) for the claimant and the advocate(s) for other parties, these should be shown. The trial timeable will schedule the oral submissions, witness evidence and expert evidence over the course of the trial. On the first day of the trial the Judge may fix the trial timetable, subject to any further order.

I6 Skeleton arguments, chronologies, dramatis personae and indices at trial

D2–414 I6.1 Written skeleton arguments should be prepared by each party. Guidelines on the preparation of skeleton arguments are set out in Part 1 of Appendix 10.

D2–415 I6.2 Unless otherwise ordered, the skeleton arguments should be served on all other parties and lodged with the Court as follows:

a. by 1 p.m. two days (*i.e.* two clear days) before the start of the trial (in the case of the claimant);

b. by 1 p.m. one day (*i.e.* one clear day) before the start of the trial (in the case of the defendant(s)).

D2–416 I6.3 In heavier cases, it will often be appropriate for skeleton arguments to served and lodged at earlier times than indicated at paragraph I6.2. The timetable should be discussed between the advocates, and may be the subject of direction in the pre-trial timetable or at any Pre-Trial Review.

D2–417 I6.4 The claimant should provide a chronology with his skeleton argument. Indices (*i.e.* documents that collate key references on particular points, or a substantive list of the contents of a particular bundle or bundles) and dramatis personae should also be provided where these are likely to be useful. Guidelines on the preparation of chronologies and indices are set out in Part 2 of Appendix 10.

I7 Trial sitting days and hearing trials in public

D2–418 I7.1 Trial sitting days will not normally include Fridays.

D2–419 I7.2 Where it is necessary in order to accommodate hearing evidence from certain witnesses or types of witness, the Court may agree to sit outside normal hours.

I7.3 CPR 39.2(1) provides that the general rule is that a hearing is to be in public. Parties to litigation in the Commercial Court should be aware that, in accordance with existing legal principle and the public interest that a trial be in public, the Court will, before acceding to any application that all or part of a trial be in private, require to be satisfied that the interests of justice require that course. **D2–420**

I8 Oral opening statements at trial

I8.1 Oral opening statements should be no longer than the circumstances require. Even in a very heavy case, oral opening statements may be very short. Oral opening statements should not, save at the request of the Judge, be developed. It should be possible for the claimant's case and the issues to be tried to be explained to the Court fairly shortly. **D2–421**

I8.2 The unnecessary reading out of documents is to be avoided. How documents are dealt with in the opening will depend on the circumstances. In some cases, the Judge may already have read the material documents, or be invited to rise and read them for himself. In other cases, the reading of documents may be left until witnesses of fact give oral evidence. In other cases the convenient course may be for the advocate to take the Judge through the material documents or some of them, providing the Judge with cross-references and answering any questions the Judge may have about the documents. **D2–422**

I8.3 At the conclusion of an oral opening statement for the claimant, advocates for other parties in the case will usually each be invited to make a short oral opening statement. **D2–423**

I9 Applications in the course of trial

I9.1 In the course of a trial, applications will normally be permitted to be made without the need for an application notice to be issued. **D2–424**

I10 Oral closing submissions at trial

I10.1 In all cases, whether or not closing submissions have been made in writing, an opportunity for oral closing submissions will be preserved. It is a matter for the advocate to consider how in all the circumstances these oral submissions should be presented. **D2–425**

I10.2 Unless otherwise agreed the claimant will make his oral closing submissions first, followed by the defendant(s), the claimant having a right of reply. **D2–426**

I11 Written closing submissions at trial

I11.1 In a more substantial trial, the Court will normally also require closing submissions in writing before oral closing submissions. **D2–427**

I11.2 In this event the Court will normally allow an appropriate period of time after the conclusion of the evidence in the case to allow the preparation of these submissions. Even in a less substantial trial a skeleton argument on matters of law will normally be required. **D2–428**

I12 Judgment

I12.1 Where possible the Judge will indicate in advance whether he intends to reserve judgment. **D2–429**

I12.2 Where judgment is reserved, a copy of the draft text marked "Unapproved Judgment. No permission is granted to copy or use in Court" will normally be supplied to the advocates two days (here meaning one clear day) before the judgment is to be delivered. This is in order to allow the advocates to inform the Court by noon on the day before (*i.e.* the immediately preceding day) judgment is handed down of any matters which require attention. All requirements to treat the text as confidential must be complied with. **D2–430**

I12.3 The judgment does not take effect until formally delivered in open court. Copies of the approved judgment marked "Approved by the Court for handing down (subject to editorial corrections)" will then or shortly after be made available to the parties and to law reporters and to any other person requesting to see a copy. The Judge may direct that the written judgment be used for all purposes as the text of the judgment and that no transcript need be made. Any editorial corrections made at the time of handing down will be incorporated in an approved official text as soon as possible, and the approved official text, so marked, will be available from the Judge's clerk. **D2–431**

I13 Costs

I13.1 CPR Parts 43 to 48 govern the assessment of costs of the case. **D2–432**

I13.2 The summary assessment procedure referred to at paragraph F17.2–F17.3 above applies also to trials of the short length indicated by the directions relating to CPR Part 44 there referred to. **D2–433**

I13.3 A procedure for "abridged" assessment of costs of a case (rather than of an individual hearing) is also available in cases in the Commercial Court to parties who might wish to use it. The procedure is detailed in Appendix 16. It allows the parties greater flexibility to resolve differences **D2–434** before the matter is brought before the [Taxing] Master and involves a simpler and quicker assessment process using summary bills of costs. It should be emphasised that the procedure necessarily involves a more "broad brush" approach to assessment of costs, and all parties' solicitors should advise their clients accordingly.

D2–435 I13.4 In order to take advantage of the procedure for abridged assessment, the consent of all parties concerned will be required to the following order:

"Assessment of costs awarded in the case shall be carried out in accordance with the abridged assessment procedure laid down in Appendix 16 to the Commercial Court Guide."

Consent to the procedure for abridged assessment may be given at any stage in the case up to and including judgment or settlement, but normally should be given before trial, at the Case Management Conference.

D2–436 I13.5 Where costs are referred to assessment under the procedure for abridged assessment, the assessment shall be carried out by the Supreme Court [Taxing] Office and a Commercial [Taxing] Master. The procedure detailed at Appendix 16 is to be strictly adhered to.

J. AFTER TRIAL

J1 Continuation, variation or discharge of interim remedies or of undertakings

D2–437 J1.1 Applications to continue, vary or discharge interim remedies or undertakings should be made to a Commercial Judge, even after trial. Paragraphs 1.2 and 1.4 of the Practice Direction supplementing CPR Part 25 (and concerning interim injunctions) do not apply to proceedings in the Commercial List or where the interim remedy in question was granted by a Commercial Judge.

D2–438 J1.2 If a party wishes to continue a freezing injunction after trial or judgment, the application should be made to a Commercial Judge. Care should be taken to ensure that the application is made before the existing freezing injunction has expired.

J2 Accounts and inquiries

D2–439 J2.1 The Court may order that accounts and inquiries be referred to (for example) a Judge of the Technology and Construction Court or to a Master. Alternatively the parties may choose to ask an arbitrator to conduct these.

J3 Enforcement

D2–440 J3.1 Unless the Judge orders otherwise, all proceedings for the enforcement of any judgment or order for the payment of money given or made in the Commercial Court will be referred automatically to a Master of the Queen's Bench Division (see paragraph 2.2(ii) of the Commercial Court Practice Direction).

D2–441 J3.2 Any applications in connection with enforcement of a judgment or order for the payment of money should accordingly be directed to the Registry (where they will be allocated to the Admiralty Registrar (or other Master taking the Admiralty List) or to another Queen's Bench Master) and should not (unless otherwise ordered) be made to a Commercial Judge.

J4 Assessment of damages or interest after a default judgment

D2–442 J4.1 Where there is a default judgment for damages or interest to be assessed, that assessment will, in the absence of a direction or order to the contrary, be heard and determined by the Admiralty Registrar (or other Master taking the Admiralty List) or by another Queen's Bench Master to whom the case is allocated by the Registry.

K. MULTI-PARTY DISPUTES

K1 Early consideration

D2–443 K1.1 Cases involving, or which are proposed to involve, a large number of claimants or of defendants require close case management from the earliest point. The same is true where there are, or are likely to be, a large number of separate cases involving the same or similar issues. Both classes of case are referred to as "multi-party" disputes.

D2–444 K1.2 In any of these situations, an application for early consideration of a multi-party dispute should be made to the Judge in charge of the Commercial List at the earliest possible opportunity. Normally the application will be made after issue and service of the, or of a specimen, claim form but before service of particulars of claim. In an appropriate case the application may be made even before issue of a claim form. It may be necessary for the application to be made without notice in the first instance.

D2–445 K1.3 Most multi-party disputes will be very different from any other dispute, and the differences will vary from case to case. It is not easy to decide when disputes become multi-party disputes, meriting special procedures. This will not depend simply on whether the head count of parties exceeds a particular number. Nor is it desirable that once litigation is classed as multi-party litigation it should then automatically attract fixed special procedures.

K2 Available procedures

K2.1 The Commercial Court has developed a range of procedures for the effective management and resolution of multi-party disputes. **D2–446**

K2.2 Multi-party disputes may be allocated to a single Judge, or to a Two-Judge team. **D2–447**

K2.3 In any multi-party dispute the procedure set out in this Guide may be adapted to meet the circumstances of the multi-party dispute. **D2–448**

K2.4 In a multi-party dispute a Judge may if appropriate (and among other things): **D2–449**

a. dispense with statements of case;

b. make an order that one person represent (as a party) other persons (whether ascertained or unascertained) or a class of persons (applications for representation orders continue to be governed by RSC Order 15);

c. determine whether claimants should be required to opt-in or opt-out of the multi-party dispute, and how latecomers should be dealt with;

d. direct the use of questionnaires;

e. direct that there be test cases or lead cases (either on all issues or on particular issues), "tiered preparation" of test cases or lead cases, and a stay of other cases in the meantime;

f. consider questions of expert evidence and of the use of ADR procedures at the earliest point;

g. advance or put back the usual time for pre-trial steps to be taken or to have effect (for example the disclosure of documents by one or more parties or a payment into court);

h. direct regular review meetings, including informal and without prejudice multi-party Case Management Conferences between the Judge, the parties and their legal representatives.

i. request the assistance of an advocate as amicus curiae, and hear evidence and submissions from outside bodies;

j. refer particular questions or issues of fact to a Judge of the Technology and Construction Court or a Master.

K2.5 Issues of legal representation, costs, and communication and decision taking within multi-party groups will also normally be considered at the earliest point. In an appropriate case a Judge may, for example: **D2–450**

a. direct that all parties on one side be represented by one firm of solicitors and one advocate or team of advocates, or that there be a lead firm of solicitors;

b. give directions to the single firm of solicitors (including directions (i) to ensure that there is effective communication with the many parties represented by that firm, (ii) to ensure that differences of opinion between the parties represented by that firm are fairly addressed, and (iii) on the question of the firm's undertaking early stages of negotiation without reference to every one of the parties represented by that firm);

c. direct (and direct the form of) publicity of an existing or contemplated multi-party dispute in order to identify the parties.

K2.6 Where necessary the exercise of powers identified at paragraph K2.5 above will need to be considered by a Judge other than the Judge who will try the multi-party dispute or a case or cases in it. **D2–451**

L. LITIGANTS IN PERSON

L1 The litigant in person

L1.1 Litigants in person appear less often in the Commercial Court than in some other Courts. Their position requires special consideration. **D2–452**

L2 Represented parties

L2.1 Where a litigant in person is involved in a case in the Commercial Court, the Court will expect solicitors and counsel for other parties to do what they reasonably can to ensure that the litigant in person has a fair opportunity to prepare and put his case. **D2–453**

L2.2 Of particular importance in a case where a litigant in person is involved is the duty of an advocate to ensure that the Court is informed of all relevant decisions and legislative provisions of which the advocate is aware (whether the effect is favourable or unfavourable towards the contention for which the advocate argues), and to bring any procedural irregularity to the attention of the Court during the hearing. **D2–454**

L2.3 Further, where a litigant in person is involved, the Court will expect solicitors and counsel for other parties in the case to ensure that the case memorandum, the list of issues and all bundles are prepared and provided to the Court in accordance with this Guide, even where the litigant in person is unwilling or unable to participate. **D2–455**

L2.4 If the claimant is a litigant in person the Judge will normally at the Case Management Conference direct which of the parties is to have responsibility for the preparation and upkeep of the case management bundle. The issue of the cost of provision of copies of application bundles and trial bundles to the litigant in person may also need to be addressed at the Case Management Conference. **D2–456**

L3 Companies without representation

D2–457 L3.1 CPR 39.6 allows a company or other corporation to be represented at trial by an employee if the employee has been authorised by the company or corporation to appear at trial on its behalf and the Court gives permission.

D2–458 L3.2 Whilst the Court will give permission in an appropriate case, the occasions when this happens are likely to be rare. The complexity of cases in the Commercial Court militates against the suitability of companies or corporations being represented by their employees.

M. ARBITRATIONS

M1 Applications relating to arbitrations

D2–459 M1.1 The Arbitration Practice Direction continues the procedure existing before the introduction of the CPR (*i.e.* the procedure under RSC Order 73), save for minor changes necessitated by the new forms of originating and subsidiary process.

D2–460 M1.2 The additional applicable practice for applications relating to arbitrations (adapted from that previously set out in the Fourth Edition of the Guide) is set out at Appendix 18.

M2 Orders for transfer

D2–461 M2.1 Orders for transfer to lists other than the Commercial List will normally be made, if no significant point of arbitration law or practice is raised:

a. in rent-review arbitrations to a Judge of the Chancery Division;

b. in building and civil engineering arbitrations to a Judge of the Technology and Construction Court.

Salvage arbitrations will normally be transferred to the Admiralty Judge.

D2–462 M2.2 Applications relating to arbitration which are not required by the CPR to be heard by a Commercial Judge should not normally be issued in the Commercial List unless they concern:

a. a commercial arbitration; or

b. a significant point of arbitration law or practice.

M3 Service of arbitration forms

D2–463 M3.1 In accordance with paragraph 8.3 of the Commercial Court Practice Direction, arbitration forms in the Commercial List are to be served by the parties, not by the Registry.

M4 Appointment of a Commercial Judge as sole arbitrator or umpire

D2–464 M4.1 Provision allowing the appointment of a Commercial Judge as sole arbitrator or as umpire is made under section 93 of the Arbitration Act 1996. The Act limits the circumstances in which a Judge may accept such an appointment.

D2–465 M4.2 Enquiries in this regard should be directed to the Judge in charge of the Commercial List or the Clerk to the Commercial Court.

N. OTHER MATTERS

N1 Out of hours emergency arrangements

D2–466 N1.1 When the Listing Office is closed, in an emergency solicitors or counsel's clerks should approach, through the security desk at the Royal Courts of Justice, the Clerk to the Queen's Bench Judge in Chambers by telephone (see also paragraph 2.2(i) of the Commercial Court Practice Direction). The telephone number of the security desk is included in the list of addresses and contact details included at the end of the Guide.

D2–467 N1.2 An urgent hearing when the Listing Office is closed will initially be dealt with by the Queen's Bench Judge in Chambers. Where appropriate, the Queen's Bench Judge in Chambers may decide to make orders allowing the matter to come before a Commercial Judge at the first available opportunity.

N2 Index of unreported decisions of the Commercial Court

D2–468 N2.1 An Index has been prepared on a subject-matter basis of unreported or not yet reported Commercial Court and Admiralty Court judgments, from 1995 onwards, whether given in open Court or available for publication following hearings in chambers. The Index is updated regularly.

D2–469 N2.2 The Index is provided as a service to litigants and to the legal profession, and to assist the Commercial Court and the Admiralty Court to maintain reasonable consistency of approach in those areas of commercial and admiralty law and procedure most frequently before those Courts.

D2–470 N2.3 The Index is available on disk to counsel and to solicitors from the Registry, free of charge, in exchange for new unused 1.44 MB disks. Except in special circumstances no more than one disk will be issued to each set of Chambers or firm of solicitors. Copies of the disk should not be made except for copies that are to be made available to members of the set of Chambers or firm of solicitors to which it has been issued.

N2.4 The judgments referred to in the Index are kept in the Registry. They may be consulted there. D2–471

N2.5 Copies of the judgments referred to in the Index may be obtained from the Registry (or where there is difficulty, from the clerk to the Judge) unless the judgment is in the form of a transcript, in which case copies should be obtained from the shorthand writers or other transcript agency. D2–472

O. GLOSSARY

D2–473

Abridged assessment of costs procedure	Procedure available by consent for a simpler and quicker assessment of costs of a case, using summary bills of costs [paragraphs I13.3–I13.5 and Appendix 16]
ADR Order	One particular form of order to encourage the use of alternative dispute resolution procedures in an appropriate case [paragraph G1.8 and Appendix 7]
Evidence bundle	Bundle of affidavits sworn or witness statements verified, but not exhibits, on a heavy application [paragraph F12 and Appendix 11]
Alternative Dispute Resolution	Collective description of alternative procedures to trial or binding arbitration for the resolution of disputes, and including mediation, conciliation and early neutral evaluation
Case management bundle	Bundle, amended and updated on a running basis, of the key documents that the Court will need to see at the Case Management Conference, on any application, on the progress monitoring date and on any Pre-Trial Review [paragraph D6 and Appendix 11]
Case Management Conference	Mandatory hearing for the control of cases and at which (where practicable or appropriate) the pre-trial timetable will be set, ADR orders may be made, and the progress monitoring date and fixed trial date (or provisional range of dates) will be set [paragraph D7]
Case management information sheet	Information sheet required to be completed by each party and provided to the Court and copied to all parties before the Case Management Conference [paragraph D7.10 and Appendix 6]
Case memorandum	Very short agreed memorandum containing a short and uncontroversial description of what the case is about and a very short and uncontroversial summary of the material procedural history of the case since it was commenced [paragraph D4]
Documents bundle	Bundle of documents (selected from exhibits) required on a heavy application [paragraph F13 and Appendix 11]
Early neutral evaluation	Without prejudice, non-binding, summary evaluation of the dispute or particular issues in it, undertaken by a Commercial Judge [paragraph G2]

Freezing injunction	Order, formerly known as a Mareva injunction, restraining (amongst other things) dealing with assets [paragraph F19 and Appendix 5]
Heavy application	An application, on notice, with an estimated hearing length of more than half a day [paragraph F5]
Interim remedies	Remedies granted prior to or in aid of judgment, and including freezing injunctions and search orders [paragraphs F2, F19, J1 and CPR Part 25]
Listing Office	The Commercial Court Listing Office [paragraph A5.1]
Ordinary application bundle	Bundle of documents required on an ordinary application [paragraph F11 and Appendix 11]
Ordinary application	An application, on notice, with an estimated hearing length of half a day or less [paragraph F4]
Pre-trial checklist	Checklist to detail and check readiness for trial [paragraph D8.4 and Appendix 14]
Pre-trial Review	Hearing, normally between 8 and 4 weeks before trial, to enable an informed discussion and assessment to take place of what will be involved in the trial and agreement to be reached as to the best way for it to be conducted [paragraph D13]
Pre-trial timetable	Directions normally covering the period from the Case Management Conference up to the trial [Appendix 8]
Progress monitoring date	Date at which the Court will review, without a hearing, progress in the case, using the case management bundle and completed progress monitoring information sheets [paragraph D8.1]
Progress monitoring information sheet	Information sheet to indicate readiness for trial [paragraph D8.2 and Appendix 13]

Registry	The Admiralty & Commercial Court Registry [paragraph A5.1]
Search order	Order, formerly known as an Anton Piller injunction, under section 7 of the Civil Procedure Act 1997 requiring a person to admit another party to premises for the purpose of preserving evidence etc [paragraph F19 and Appendix 5]
Special disclosure order	Form of disclosure order requiring wider disclosure of documents [paragraph E5 and Appendix 9]
Summary assessment of costs	Procedure for the summary assessment of costs of a shorter hearing [paragraphs F17.2–17.3 and I13.2]
Trial timetable	Proposed timetable for the conduct of the trial itself, to be prepared by the parties for consideration by the Court [paragraphs D13.7 and I5.8]

APPENDICES

CONTENTS

D2–474

APPENDIX 1

SCHEDULE OF APPLICATION OF OTHER PRACTICE DIRECTIONS TO PROCEEDINGS IN THE COMMERCIAL LIST

The primary sources for a statement of the practice and procedure of the Commercial Court are the Commercial Court Practice Direction, the Arbitration Practice Direction and this Guide. However a number of (non-specialist) Practice Directions supplement the CPR. This Schedule sets out the extent to which each of those Practice Directions can, broadly speaking, be expected to apply to proceedings in the Commercial List. In any case in which there is a conflict between the Guide and a provision in one of the (non-specialist) Practice Directions which this Appendix indicates can be expected to apply in the Commercial Court, the Commercial Court will be D2–475 influenced by its view of how best to serve the "overriding objective" in the particular circumstances, but can be expected to apply the Guide.

Rule/Part supplemented by the Practice Direction	*Subject of the Practice Direction*	*Application to proceedings in the Commercial List of the Practice Direction supplementing the Rule of Part*
Rule 3.4	Striking out a statement of case	Applies in full
Part 6	Service	Applies in full, subject to paragraph B5.3 of the Guide
Part 7	How to start proceedings—the claim form	Applies in full, subject to paragraph B3.3, B3.6 and C2.2 of the Guide
Rule 7.9	Consumer Credit Act claim	Applies in full
Rule 7.9	Fixed date claims	No application
Rule 7.10	Production Centre	No application
Part 8	Alternative procedure for claims	Applies in full, subject to paragraph B4 of the Guide
Part 10	Acknowledgment of service	Applies in full, subject to paragraph B7 of the Guide
Part 12	Default judgment	Applies in full, subject to paragraph B7.6 of the Guide
Part 14	Admissions	Applies in full, subject to paragraph B7.7 of the Guide
Part 15	Defence and reply	Applies in full
Part 16	Statements of case	Applies in part: see paragraphs B3.3, B3.5, B3.6, C1.2 and C2.2 of, and Appendix 4 to, the Guide
Part 17	Amendments to statements of case	Applies in part: see paragraph C5.3 and C5.4 of the Guide
Part 18	Further information	Applies in full, but note paragraph D9 of the Guide
Part 19	Addition and substitution of parties	Applies in full, subject to paragraph D14.3 of the Guide
Part 20	Counterclaims and other Part 20 claims	Applies in part: see paragraph D7.22 of the Guide
Part 21	Children and patients	Applies in full
Part 22	Statements of truth	Applies in full, subject to Appendix 12 (paragraph 12) to the Guide
Part 23	Applications	Applies in part: see paragraphs F1.3, F1.4, F1.5 and F1.11 of the Guide
Part 24	Summary disposal of claims	Applies in full
Part 25	Interim payments	Applies in full
Part 25	Accounts and inquiries	Applies in full
Part 25	Interim injunctions	Applies in part: see paragraphs F19 and J1 of the Guide
Part 26	Case management—preliminary stage: allocation and re-allocation	No application
Part 27	Small claims track	No application
Part 28	The fast track	No application
Part 29	The multi track	No application except for paragraph 7 of the Practice Direction; but see Sections D and I of the Guide
Part 30	Transfer	Applies in full, subject to paragraph B8 of the Guide
Part 31	Disclosure and inspection	See Section E of the Guide
Part 32	Written evidence	Applies in full, subject to paragraphs F6.5 of the Guide
Part 34	Depositions and court attendance by witnesses	Applies in full, subject to paragraph H1.10 of the Guide
Part 35	Experts and assessors	See Section H of and Appendix 12 to the Guide
Part 36	Offers to settle and payments into court	Applies in full
Part 37	Miscellaneous provisions about payments into Court	Applies in full
Part 39	Miscellaneous provisions relating to hearings	Applies in part: see paragraph F1.9 and Section I of, and Appendix 11 to, the Guide

Rule/Part supplemented by the Practice Direction	Subject of the Practice Direction	Application to proceedings in the Commercial List of the Practice Direction supplementing the Rule of Part
Part 51	Transitional arrangements	Applies subject to Appendix 20 to the Guide

Note: At the time of preparation of the Guide, other Practice Directions supplementing the CPR were not available. It is intended to issue any necessary guidance on the application (in the Commercial Court) of those other Practice Directions at a later point.

APPENDIX 2

OUTLINE CHART OF TYPICAL CASE MANAGEMENT SEQUENCE FOR CASES IN THE COMMERCIAL COURT

D2–477

1.	**Claim form** (CPR Part 7) issued, served and filed (paragraphs B2–B6).
2.	[**Applications** made, where necessary] (paragraphs F1–F5 and F19).
3.	[**Early Case Management Conference**, if appropriate] (paragraphs D7.3–D7.4).
4.	**Acknowledgment of service** filed (paragraph B7).
5.	[**Particulars of claim** served and filed, if they did not accompany the claim form and were not contained in the claim form] (paragraphs C1–C2 and Appendix 4).
6.	**Defence** served and filed (paragraphs C1, C3 and Appendix 4).
7.	**Reply** (if any) served and filed (paragraphs C1, C4 and Appendix 4).
8.	**Case memorandum** prepared (paragraph D4).
9.	**List of issues** prepared (paragraph D5).
10.	**Case management bundle** prepared (paragraph D6 and Appendix 11).
11.	**Provisional estimate of trial length** prepared (Appendix 6 and paragraph D12.1).
12.	**Case management information sheet** lodged and served (paragraph D7.10 and Appendix 6).
13.	[**Two-Judge team** identified, in appropriate cases and unless already identified at an earlier point] (paragraph D3).
14.	**Case Management Conference** (paragraph D7): a. **pre-trial timetable** set (Appendix 8); [b. **ADR Directions** made, if appropriate and if not already made] (paragraph G1.5–1.8, Appendix 7); c. **trial date fixed** (or, exceptionally, provisional range of dates for trial specified).
15.	[**ADR Directions** followed, where made] (Section G).
16.	Pre-trial timetable followed: **Disclosure, Inspection, Witness Statements, Expert Reports** (Sections E, H and Appendices 8 and 12).
17.	[**Applications** made, where necessary] (Section F).
18.	**Progress monitoring information sheet** lodged and served (paragraphs D8.2–8.3 and Appendix 13).
19.	**Progress monitoring date** (paragraph D8.1).
20.	[**Reconvened Case Management Conference**, if appropriate] (paragraphs D8.6–8.7).
21.	**Confirmed estimate of trial length** prepared (paragraph D12.3).

22.	**Pre-trial checklist** lodged and served (paragraph D8.4 and Appendix 14).
23.	**Fixed trial date confirmed** (or, where applicable, trial date fixed within provisional range of dates for trial) (paragraph D8.4).
24.	**Meetings of experts** (paragraph H2.20 and Appendix 12).
25.	[**Pre-Trial Review**, if ordered, with consideration of trial timetable] (paragraph D13).
26.	**Trial bundles** prepared and provided to the Court (paragraph I3 and Appendix 11).
27.	Written trial **skeleton arguments** exchanged, and provided to the Court (paragraph I6; see also paragraphs I5 and I6.4 for **trial timetable, reading list, authorities, chronology, indices and dramatis personae**).
28.	**Trial** commences.

APPENDIX 3

PROCEDURE FOR ISSUE OF CLAIM FORM WHERE REGISTRY CLOSED

D2–478 (see paragraph B3.11 of the Guide)

Procedure

The procedure is as follows:

a. The claim form must be signed by a solicitor acting on behalf of the claimant, and must not require the permission of the Court for its issue (unless such permission has already been given).

b. The solicitor causing the claim form to be issued ("the issuing solicitor") shall (i) endorse on the claim form the endorsement shown below and sign that endorsement, (ii) transmit a copy of the claim form so endorsed to the Registry by fax for issue under this paragraph and (iii) when he has received a transmission report stating that the transmission of the claim form to the Registry was completed in full and the time and the date of the transmission, complete and sign the certificate shown in below.

c. When the Registry is next open to the public after the issue of a claim form in accordance with this procedure the issuing solicitor or his agent shall attend and deliver to the Registry the document which was transmitted by fax (including the endorsement and the certificate), or if that document has been served, a true and certified copy of it, together with as many copies as the Registry shall require and the transmission report.

d. When the proper officer at the Registry has checked and is satisfied that the document delivered at c. fully accords with the document received at b., and that all proper fees for issue have been paid, he shall allocate a number to the case, and seal, mark as "original" and date the claim form with the date on which it was issued (being, as indicated below, the date when the fax is recorded at the Registry as having been received).

e. As soon as practicable thereafter the issuing solicitor shall inform any person served with the unsealed claim form of the case number, and (on request) shall serve any such person with a copy of the claim form sealed and dated under d. above (at such address in England and Wales as the person may request) and the person may, without paying a fee, inspect and take copies of the documents lodged at the Registry under b. and c. above.

The issue of a claim form in accordance with this procedure takes place when the fax is recorded at the Registry as having been received, and the claim form bearing the endorsement shall have the same effect for all purposes as a claim form issued under CPR Part 7. Unless otherwise ordered the sealed version of the claim form retained by the Registry shall be conclusive proof that the claim form was issued at the time and on the date stated. If the procedure at a. and b. is not complied with or the document delivered is not sealed under d., a Commercial Judge may declare (on his own initiative or on application) that the claim form shall be treated as not having been issued.

Endorsement

D2–479

1. This claim form is issued under paragraph B3.11 of the Commercial Court Guide and may be served notwithstanding that it does not bear the seal of the Court.
2. A true copy of this claim form and endorsement has been transmitted to the Admiralty and Commercial Registry, Royal Courts of Justice, Strand, London WC2A 2LL, at the time and date certified below by the undersigned solicitor.
3. It is the duty of the undersigned solicitor or his agent to attend at the Registry when it is next open to the public for the claim form to be sealed.

4. Any person upon whom this unsealed claim form is served will be notified by the undersigned solicitor of the number of the case and may require the undersigned solicitor to serve a copy of the sealed claim form at an address in England and Wales and may inspect without charge the documents which have been lodged at the Registry by the undersigned solicitor.
5. I, the undersigned solicitor, undertake to the Court, to the defendants named in this claim form, and to any other person upon whom this claim form may be served:
   (i) that the statement in paragraph 2 above is correct;
   (ii) that the time and date given in the certificate at the foot of this endorsement are correct;
   (iii) that this claim form is a claim form which may be issued under paragraph B3.11 of the Commercial Court Guide;
   (iv) that I will comply in all respects with the requirements of paragraph B3.11 of the Commercial Court Guide;
   (v) that I will indemnify any person served with the claim form before it is sealed against any loss suffered as a result of the claim form being or becoming invalid in accordance with paragraph B3.11 of the Commercial Court Guide.

(Signed)

Solicitor for the claimant *[Note: the endorsement may be signed in the name of the firm of solicitors rather than an individual solicitor, or by solicitors agents in their capacity as agents acting on behalf of their professional clients]*

Certificate

I, the undersigned solicitor certify that I have received a transmission report confirming that the transmission of a copy of this claim form to the Registry by fax was fully completed and that the time and date of transmission to the Registry were [time] [date]. **D2–480**

Dated [*]

(Signed)

Solicitor for the claimant *[Note: the certificate may be signed in the name of the firm of solicitors rather than an individual solicitor, or by solicitors agents in their capacity as agents acting on behalf of their professional clients]*

APPENDIX 4

STATEMENTS OF CASE IN THE COMMERCIAL COURT

The following points apply to all particulars of claim, defences and replies in cases in the Commercial Court save where otherwise ordered. So far as possible a Part 8 claim form, which will not contain or be followed by particulars of claim, should, where applicable, also comply with the following points. **D2–481**

1 The document must be as brief and concise as possible.

2 The document must be set out in separate consecutively numbered paragraphs and sub-paragraphs.

3 So far as possible each paragraph or sub-paragraph should contain no more than one allegation.

4 The document must deal with the case on a point by point basis, to allow a point by point response.

5 Where reasons are required to be stated in the document (see CPR 16.5(2)), the allegation should be stated first and then the reasons listed one by one in separate numbered sub-paragraphs.

6 A party wishing to advance a positive case should identify that case in the document; a simple denial is not sufficient.

7 Any matter which if not stated might take another party by surprise should be stated.

8 Where they will assist:

8.1 headings should be used; and

8.2 abbreviations and definitions should be established and used, and a glossary annexed.

9 Contentious headings, abbreviations and definitions should not be used; every effort should be made to ensure that headings, abbreviations and definitions are in a form that will enable them to be adopted without issue by the other parties.

10 Particulars of primary allegations should be stated as particulars and not as primary allegations.

11 Where possible schedules or appendices should be used, especially where lengthy particulars are necessary.

12 Evidence should not be included.

13 A response to particulars stated in a schedule should be stated in a corresponding schedule.

14 Where substantial parts of the content of a document need to be included, this should be done by simply including a reference to the document, or by quotation in a schedule.

15 Contentious paraphrasing should be avoided.
16 The document must be signed by the individual person or persons who drafted it.

APPENDIX 5

DRAFT FREEZING INJUNCTIONS AND DRAFT SEARCH ORDER

D2–482 Note: these Drafts are taken from the Practice Direction supplementing CPR Part 25, with minor adjustments

(1) Draft Freezing Injunction: England & Wales

****Freezing Injunction****
Order to restrain assets in
England and Wales

IN THE HIGH COURT OF JUSTICE
QUEEN'S BENCH DIVISION
COMMERCIAL COURT
Strand London WC2A 2LL

Before The Honourable Mr Justice [ ]

Claim No.

Dated

Applicant

Seal

Respondent

Name, address and reference of Respondent

PENAL NOTICE

IF YOU THE WITHIN NAMED [ ] DISOBEY THIS ORDER YOU MAY BE HELD TO BE IN CONTEMPT OF COURT AND LIABLE TO IMPRISONMENT OR FINED OR YOUR ASSETS SEIZED

IMPORTANT

Notice to the Respondent

D2–483 **You should read the terms of the Order and the Guidance Notes very carefully. You are advised to consult a Solicitor as soon as possible.**

This Order prohibits you, the Respondent, from dealing with your assets up to the amount stated in the Order, but subject to any exceptions set out at the end of the Order. You have a right to ask the Court to vary or discharge this Order.

If you disobey this Order you may be found guilty of Contempt of Court and may be sent to prison or fined. In the case of a Corporate Respondent, it may be fined, its Directors may be sent to prison or fmed or its assets may be seized.

THE ORDER

An application was made today [*date*] by [Counsel] [Solicitors] [*or as may be*] for the Applicant to Mr Justice [ ] who heard the application. The Judge read the affidavits listed in Schedule A and accepted the undertakings set out in Schedule B at the end of this Order. As a result of the application **IT IS ORDERED** that until [[ ] ("the return date")] [or further Order of the Court]:— D2–484

1. The Respondent must not remove from England and Wales or in any way dispose of or deal with or diminish the value of any of his assets which are in England and Wales whether in his own name or not and whether solely or jointly owned up to the value of £ .

   This prohibition includes the following assets in particular:—
   (a) the property known as [*title/address*] or the net sale money after payment of any mortgages if it has been sold;
   (b) the property and assets of the Respondent's business known as (or carried on at [*address*]) or the sale money if any of them have been sold; and
   (c) any money in the account numbered [*a/c number] at [title/address*]

2. If the total unincumbered value of the Respondent's assets in England and Wales exceeds £ , the Respondent may remove any of those assets from England and Wales or may dispose of or deal with them so long as the total unincumbered value of his assets still in England and Wales remains above £ .

3. Exceptions to this Order:—
   (1) This Order does not prohibit the Respondent from spending £ a week towards his ordinary living expenses [and £ a week towards his ordinary and proper business expenses] and also £ a week [*or* a reasonable sum] on legal advice and representation. But before spending any money the Respondent must tell the Applicant's legal representatives where the money is to come from.
   [(2) This Order does not prohibit the Respondent from dealing with or disposing of any of his assets in the ordinary and proper course of business.]
   (3) The Respondent may agree with the Applicant's legal representatives that the above spending limits should be increased or that this Order should be varied in any other respect, but any agreement must be in writing.
   (4) The Respondent may cause this Order to cease to have effect if the Respondent provides security by paying the sum of £ into Court or makes provision for security in that sum by another method agreed with the Applicant's legal representatives.

4. The Respondent must:—
   (1) Inform the Applicant in writing at once of all his assets in England and Wales and whether in his own name or not and whether solely or jointly owned, giving the value, location and details of all such assets.

   [The Respondent may be entitled to refuse to provide some or all of this information on the grounds that it may incriminate him. *This sentence may be inserted in cases not covered by the Theft Act 1968, s.31.*]

   (2) Confirm the information in an affidavit which must be served on the Applicant's legal representatives within [ ] days after this Order has been served on the Respondent.

[5. *Where an Order for substituted service or service out of the jurisdiction has been made—*

(1) The Applicant may issue and serve a Claim Form on the Respondent at [*address*] by [*method of service*]

(2) If the Respondent wishes to defend the Claim he must complete and return the Acknowledgment of Service within [ ] days of being served with the Claim Form.]

GUIDANCE NOTES

Effect of this Order

D2–485 (1) A Respondent who is an individual who is ordered not to do something must not do it himself or in any other way. He must not do it through others acting on his behalf or on his instructions or with his encouragement.

(2) A Respondent which is a corporation and which is ordered not to do something must not do it itself or by its directors, officers, employees or agents or in any other way.

Variation or discharge of this Order

D2–486 The Respondent (or anyone notified of this Order) may apply to the Court at any time to vary or discharge this Order (or so much of it as affects that person), but anyone wishing to do so must first inform the Applicant's legal representatives.

Parties other than the Applicant and Respondent

D2–487 1. **Effect of this Order:—**
It is a Contempt of Court for any person notified of this Order knowingly to assist in or permit a breach of this Order. Any person doing so may be sent to prison, fined or have his assets seized.

2. **Set off by Banks:—**
This injunction does not prevent any bank from exercising any right of set off it may have in respect of any facility which it gave to the Respondent before it was notified of this Order.

3. **Withdrawals by the Respondent:—**
No bank need enquire as to the application or proposed application of any money withdrawn by the Respondent if the withdrawal appears to be permitted by this Order.

Interpretation of this Order

D2–488 (1) In this Order, where there is more than one Respondent (unless otherwise stated), references to "the Respondent" means both or all of them.

(2) A requirement to serve on "the Respondent" means on each of them. However, the Order is effective against any Respondent on whom it is served.

(3) An Order requiring "the Respondent" to do or not to do anything applies to all Respondents.

Communications with the Court

All communications to the Court about this Order should be sent to the Commercial Court Clerk, the Listing Office, Room E201, Royal Courts of Justice, Strand, London WC2A 2LL quoting the case number. The telephone number is 0171 936 6826. The offices are open between 10 am and 4.30 pm Monday to Friday. D2–489

Schedule A

Affidavits:—

The Applicant relied on the following affidavits:

[*name*] [*number of affidavit*] [*date sworn*] [*filed on behalf of*]

(1)
(2)

Schedule B

Undertakings given to the Court by the Applicant:—

(1) If the Court later finds that this Order has caused loss to the Respondent, and decides that the Respondent should be compensated for that loss, the Applicant will comply with any Order the Court may make.

(2) The Applicant will on or before [*date*] cause a written guarantee in the sum of £ to be issued from a bank having a place of business within England or Wales, such guarantee being in respect of any Order the Court may make pursuant to paragraph (1) above. The Applicant will further, forthwith upon issue of the guarantee, cause a copy of it to be served on the Respondent.

(3) As soon as practicable the Applicant will [issue and serve on the Respondent a Claim Form in the form of the draft produced to the Court] [serve on the Respondent the Claim Form] claiming the appropriate relief, together with this Order.

(4) The Applicant will cause an affidavit to be sworn and filed [substantially in the terms of the draft affidavit produced to the Court] [confirming the substance of what was said to the Court by the Applicant's Counsel/Solicitors].

[(5) *Where a return date has been given*—As soon as practicable the Applicant will serve on the Respondent an Application for the return date together with a copy of the affidavits and exhibits containing the evidence relied on by the Applicant.]

(6) Anyone notified of this Order will be given a copy of it by the Applicant's legal representatives.

(7) The Applicant will pay the reasonable costs of anyone other than the Respondent which have been incurred as a result of this Order including the costs of ascertaining whether that person holds any of the Respondent's assets and if the Court later finds that this Order has caused such person loss, and decides that such person should be compensated for that loss, the Applicant will comply with any Order the Court may make.

(8) If for any reason this Order ceases to have effect (including in particular where the Respondent provides security as provided for above or the Applicant does not provide a bank guarantee as provided for above), the Applicant will forthwith take all reasonable steps to inform, in writing, any person or company to whom he has given notice of this Order, or who he has reasonable grounds for supposing may act upon this Order, that it has ceased to have effect.

Name and Address of Applicant's Legal Representatives

The Applicants Legal Representatives are:—

[Name, address, reference, fax and telephone numbers both in and out of office hours.]

(2) Draft Freezing Injunction: Worldwide

D2–490 ****Freezing Injunction****
Order to restrain assets worldwide

IN THE HIGH COURT OF JUSTICE
QUEEN'S BENCH DIVISION
COMMERCIAL COURT
Strand London WC2A 2LL

Before The Honourable Mr Justice [ ]

Claim No.

Dated

Applicant

Seal

Respondent

Name, address and reference of Respondent

PENAL NOTICE

D2–491 **IF YOU THE WITHIN NAMED [ ] DISOBEY THIS ORDER YOU MAY BE HELD TO BE IN CONTEMPT OF COURT AND LIABLE TO IMPRISONMENT OR FINED OR YOUR ASSETS SEIZED**

IMPORTANT

Notice to the Respondent

You should read the terms of the Order and the Guidance Notes very carefully. You are advised to consult a Solicitor as soon as possible. D2–492

This Order prohibits you, the Respondent, from dealing with your assets up to the amount stated in the Order, but subject to any exceptions set out at the end of the Order. You have a right to ask the Court to vary or discharge this order.

If you disobey this Order you may be found guilty of Contempt of Court and may be sent to prison or fined. In the case of a Corporate Respondent, it may be fined, its Directors may be sent to prison or fined or its assets may be seized.

THE ORDER

D2–493

An application was made today [*date*] by [Counsel] [Solicitors] [*or as may be*] for the Applicant to Mr Justice [ ] who heard the application. The Judge read the affidavits listed in Schedule A and accepted the undertakings set out in Schedule B at the end of this Order. As a result of the application **IT IS ORDERED** that until [[ ] ("the return date"]] [further Order of the Court]:—

1. The Respondent must not:—

(1) remove from England and Wales or in any way dispose of or deal with or diminish the value of any of his assets which are in England and Wales whether in his own name or not and whether solely or jointly owned up to the value of £ or

(2) in any way dispose of or deal with or diminish the value of any of his assets whether they are in or outside England or Wales whether in his own name or not and whether solely or jointly owned up to the same value. This prohibition includes the following assets in particular:—

(a) the property known as [*title/address*] or the net sale money after payment of any mortgages if it has been sold;

(b) the property and assets of the Respondent's business known as (or carried on at [*address*]) or the sale money if any of them have been sold; and

(c) any money in the account numbered [*a/c number*] at [*title/address*]

2. (1) If the total unincumbered value of the Respondent's assets in England and Wales exceeds £ , the Respondent may remove any of those assets from England and Wales or may dispose of or deal with them so long as the total unincumbered value of his assets still in England and Wales remains above £ .

(2) If the total unincumbered value of the Respondent's assets in England and Wales does not exceed £ , the Respondent must not remove any of those assets from England and Wales and must not dispose of or deal with any of them, but if he has other assets outside England and Wales the Respondent may dispose of or deal with those assets so long as the total unincumbered value of all his assets whether in or outside England and Wales remains above £ .

3. Exceptions to this Order:—

(1) This Order does not prohibit the Respondent from spending £ a week towards his ordinary living expenses [and £ a week

towards his ordinary and proper business expenses] and also £ a week [*or* a reasonable sum] on legal advice and representation. But before spending any money the Respondent must tell the Applicant's legal representative where the money is to come from.

[(2) This Order does not prohibit the Respondent from dealing with or disposing of any of his assets in the ordinary and proper course of business.]

(3) The Respondent may agree with the applicant's legal representatives that the above spending limits should be increased or that this Order should be varied in any other respect, but any agreement must be in writing.

(4) The Respondent may cause this order to cease to have effect if the Respondent provides security by paying the sum of £ into Court or makes provision for security in that sum by another method agreed with the Applicant's legal representatives.

4. The Respondent must:—

(1) Inform the Applicant in writing at once of all his assets whether in or outside England and Wales and whether in his own name or not and whether solely or jointly owned, giving the value, location and details of all such assets.

[The Respondent may be entitled to refuse to provide some or all of this information on the grounds that it may incriminate him. *This sentence may be inserted in cases not covered by the Theft Act 1968, s.31.*]

(2) Confirm the information in an affidavit which must be served on the Applicant's legal representatives within [ ] days after this Order has been served on the Respondent.

[5. *Where an Order for substituted service or service out of the jurisdiction has been made—*

(1) The Applicant may issue and serve a Claim Form on the Respondent at [*address*] by [*method of service*]

(2) If the Respondent wishes to defend the claim he must complete and return the Acknowledgment of Service within [ ] days of being served with the Claim Form.]

GUIDANCE NOTES

Effect of this Order

D2–494 (1) A Respondent who is an individual who is ordered not to do something must not do it himself or in any other way. He must not do it through others acting on his behalf or on his instructions or with his encouragement.

(2) A Respondent which is a corporation and which is ordered not to do something must not do it itself or by its directors, officers, employees or agents or in any other way.

Variation or discharge of this Order

The Respondent (or anyone notified of this Order) may apply to the Court at any time to vary or discharge this Order (or so much of it as affects that person), but anyone wishing to do so must first inform the Applicant's legal representatives.

Parties other than the Applicant and Respondent

1. **Effect of this Order:—** D2–495

It is a Contempt of Order for any person notified of this Order knowingly to assist in or permit a breach of this Order. Any person doing so may be sent to prison, fined or have his assets seized.

2. **Effect of this Order outside England and Wales:—**

The terms of this Order do not affect or concern anyone outside the jurisdiction of this Court until it is declared enforceable by or is enforced by a Court in the relevant country and then they are to affect him only to the extent they have been declared enforceable or have been enforced UNLESS the person is:

(i) a person to whom this Order is addressed or an officer or an agent appointed by power of attorney of that person; or

(ii) a person who is subject to the jurisdiction of this Court and (a) has been given written notice of this Order at his residence or place of business within the jurisdiction of this Court and (b) is able to prevent acts or omissions outside the jurisdiction of this Court which constitute or assist in a breach of the terms of this Order.

3. **Set off by Banks:—**

This injunction does not prevent any bank from exercising any right of set off it may have in respect of any facility which it gave to the Respondent before it was notified of this Order.

4. **Withdrawals by the Respondent:—**

No bank need enquire as to the application or proposed application of any money withdrawn by the Respondent if the withdrawal appears to be permitted by this Order.

Interpretation of this Order

(1) In this Order, where there is more than one Respondent (unless otherwise stated), references to "the Respondent" means both or all of them. D2–496

(2) A requirement to serve on "the Respondent" means on each of them. However, the Order is effective against any Respondent on whom it is served.

(3) An Order requiring "the Respondent" to do or not to do anything applies to all Respondents.

Communications with the Court

All communications to the Court about this Order should be sent to the Commercial Court Clerk, the Listing Office, Room E201, Royal Courts of D2–497

Justice, Strand, London WC2A 2LL quoting the case number. The telephone number is 0171 936 6826. The offices are open between 10 am and 4.30 pm Monday to Friday.

Schedule A

Affidavits:—

D2–498 The Applicant relied on the following affidavits:

[*name*] [*number of affidavit*]	[*date sworn*]	[*filed on behalf of*]

(1)

(2)

Schedule B

Undertakings given to the Court by the Applicant:—

D2–499 (1) If the Court later finds that this Order has caused loss to the Respondent, and decides that the Respondent should be compensated for that loss, the Applicant will comply with any Order the Court may make.

(2) The Applicant will on or before [*date*] cause a written guarantee in the sum of £ to be issued from a bank having a place of business within England or Wales, such guarantee being in respect of any Order the Court may make pursuant to paragraph (1) above. The Applicant will further, forthwith upon issue of the guarantee, cause a copy of it to be served on the Respondent.

[(3) As soon as practicable the applicant will [issue and serve on the Respondent a Claim Form in the form of the draft produced to the Court] [serve on the Respondent the Claim Form] claiming the appropriate relief, together with this Order.]

(4) The Applicant will cause an affidavit to be sworn and filed [substantially in the terms of the draft affidavit produced to the Court] [confirming the substance of what was said to the Court by the Applicant's Counsel/Solicitors].

[(5) *Where a return date has been given*—As soon as practicable the Applicant will serve on the Respondent an application for the return date together with a copy of the affidavits and exhibits containing the evidence relied on by the Applicant.]

(6) Anyone notified of this Order will be given a copy of it by the Applicant's legal representatives.

(7) The Applicant will pay the reasonable costs of anyone other than the Respondent which have been incurred as a result of this Order including the costs of ascertaining whether that person holds any of the Respondent's assets and if the Court later finds that this Order has caused such person loss, and decides that such person should be compensated for that loss, the Applicant will comply with any Order the Court may make.

(8) If for any reason this Order ceases to have effect (including in particular where the Respondent provides security as provided for above or the Applicant does not provide a bank guarantee as provided for above), the Applicant will forthwith take all reasonable steps to inform, in writing, any person or company to whom he has given notice of this Order, or who he has reasonable grounds for supposing may act upon this Order, that it has ceased to have effect.

[(9) The Applicant will not without the leave of the Court begin proceedings against the Respondent in any other jurisdiction or use information obtained as a result of an Order of the Court in this jurisdiction for the purpose of civil or criminal proceedings in any other jurisdiction.]

[(10) The Applicant will not without the leave of the Court seek to enforce this Order in any country outside England and Wales [or seek an Order of a similar nature including Orders conferring a charge or other security against the Respondent or the Respondent's assets].]

Name and Address of Applicant's Legal Representatives

The Applicant's Legal Representatives are:—

[Name, address, reference, fax and telephone numbers both in and out of office hours.]

(3) Draft Search Order

****Search Order**** **Order to preserve evidence and property**	**IN THE HIGH COURT OF JUSTICE** **QUEEN'S BENCH DIVISION** **COMMERCIAL COURT** **Strand London WC2A 2LL**

D2–500

Before The Honourable Mr Justice [ ]

Claim No.

Dated

Applicant

Seal

Respondent

Name, address and reference of Respondent

PENAL NOTICE

D2–501 **IF YOU THE WITHIN NAMED [ ] DISOBEY THIS ORDER YOU MAY BE HELD TO BE IN CONTEMPT OF COURT AND LIABLE TO IMPRISONMENT OR FINED OR YOUR ASSETS SEIZED**

IMPORTANT

Notice to the Respondent

D2–502 **You should read the terms of the Order and the Guldance Notes very carefully. You are advised to consult a Solicitor as soon as possible.**

This Order orders you, the Respondent, to allow the persons mentioned in the Order to enter the premises described in the Order and to search for, examine and remove or copy the articles specified in the Order. The persons so named will have no right to enter the premises or, having entered, to remain at the premises, unless you give your consent to their doing so. If, however, you withhold your consent you will be in breach of this Order and may be held to be in Contempt of Court.

The Order also requires you to hand over any of such articles which are under your control and to provide information to the Applicant's Solicitors, and prohibits you from doing certain acts.

If you, the Respondent, disobey this Order you may be found guilty of contempt of Court and may be sent to prison or fined. In the case of a Corporate Respondent, it may be fined, its Directors may be sent to prison or fined or its assets may be seized.

THE ORDER

D2–503 **AN APPLICATION** was made today [*date*] by [Counsel] [Solicitors] for the Applicant to Mr Justice [ ] who heard the application. The Judge read the affidavits listed in Schedule F at the end of this Order and accepted the undertakings by the Applicant, the Applicant's Solicitors and the Supervising Solicitor set forth in the Schedules at the end of this Order. As a result of the application **IT IS ORDERED** that until [[ ] ("the return date")] [or further Order of the Court]:—

1. (1) The Respondent must allow Mr/Mrs/Miss [ ] ("the Supervising Solicitor"), together with [ ] a Solicitor of the Supreme Court, and a partner in the firm of [ ] the Applicant's solicitors and up to [ ] other persons being [*their capacity*] accompanying them, to enter the premises mentioned in Schedule A to this Order and any other premises of the Respondent disclosed under paragraph 4(1) below and any vehicles under the Respondent's control on or around the premises so that they can search for, inspect, photograph or photocopy, and deliver into the safekeeping of the Applicant's Solicitors all the documents and articles which are listed in Schedule B to this Order ("the listed items") or which [ ] believes to be listed items.

   (2) The Respondent must allow those persons to remain on the premises until the search is complete, and to re-enter the premises on the same or the following day in order to complete the search.

2. (1) No item may be removed from the premises until a list of the items to be removed has been prepared, and a copy of the list has been

supplied to the person served with the Order, and he has been given a reasonable opportunity to check the list.

(2) The premises must not be searched, and items must not be removed from them, except in the presence of the Respondent or a person appearing to be a responsible employee of the Respondent or in control of the premises.

(3) If the Supervising Solicitor is satisfied that full compliance with paragraph 2(1) or (2) above is impracticable, he may permit the search to proceed and items to be removed without compliance with the impracticable requirements.

3. (1) The Respondent must immediately hand over to the Applicant's Solicitors any of the listed items which are in his possession or under his control save for any computer or hard disk integral to any computer.

(2) If any of the listed items exists only in computer readable form, the Respondent must immediately give the Applicant's Solicitors effective access to the computers, with all necessary passwords, to enable them to be searched, and cause the listed items to be printed out. A print out of the items must be given to the Applicant's Solicitors or displayed on the computer screen so that they can be read and copied. All reasonable steps shall be taken by the Applicant to ensure that no damage is done to any computer or data. The Applicant and his representatives may not themselves search the Respondent's computers unless they have sufficient expertise to do so without damaging the Respondent's system.

4. (1) The Respondent must immediately inform the Applicant's Solicitors:—

(a) where all the listed items are; and

(b) so far as he is aware

(i) the name and address of everyone who has supplied him, or offered to supply him, with listed items;

(ii) the name and address of everyone to whom he has supplied, or offered to supply, listed items; and

(iii) full details of the dates and quantities of every such supply and offer.

(2) Within [ ] days after being served with this Order the Respondent must swear an affidavit setting out the above information.

5. (1) Except for the purpose of obtaining legal advice, the Respondent or anyone else with knowledge of this Order must not directly or indirectly inform anyone of these proceedings or of the contents of this Order, or warn anyone that proceedings have been or may be brought against him by the Applicant until [[ ] the return date] [or further Order of the Court].

(2) The Respondent must not destroy, tamper with, cancel or part with possession, power, custody or control of the listed items otherwise than in accordance with the terms of this Order.

(3) [*Insert any negative injunctions.*]

[6. *Insert any further order.*]

GUIDANCE NOTES

Effect of this Order

D2–504 (1) A Respondent who is an individual who is ordered not to do something must not do it himself or in any other way. He must not do it through others acting on his behalf or on his instructions or with his encouragement.

(2) A Respondent which is a corporation and which is ordered not to do something must not do it itself or by its directors officers employees or agents or in any other way.

(3) This Order must be complied with either by the Respondent himself or by an employee of the Respondent or other person appearing to be in control of the premises and having authority to permit the premises to be entered and the search to proceed.

(4) This Order requires the Respondent or his employee or other person appearing to be in control of the premises and having that authority to permit entry to the premises immediately the Order is served upon him, except as stated below.

Respondent's Entitlements

D2–505 (1) Before you the Respondent or the person appearing to be in control of the premises allow anybody onto the premises to carry out this order you are entitled to have the solicitor who serves you with this Order explain to you what it means in everyday language.

(2) You are entitled to insist that there is nobody [or nobody except] present who could gain commercially from anything he might read or see on your premises.

(3) You are entitled to refuse to permit entry before 9:30 am or after 5:30 pm or at all on Saturday and Sunday unless the Court has ordered otherwise.

(4) Except in certain cases, you may be entitled to refuse to permit disclosure of any documents which may incriminate you ("incriminating documents") or to answer any questions if to do so may incriminate you. It may be prudent to take advice, because if you so refuse, your refusal may be taken into account by the Court at a later stage.

(5) You are entitled to refuse to permit disclosure of any documents passing between you and your Solicitors or Patent or Trade Mark Agents for the purpose of obtaining advice ("privileged documents").

(6) You are entitled to seek legal advice, and to ask the Court to vary or discharge this Order, provided you do so at once, and provided you do not disturb or move anything in the interim and that meanwhile you permit the Supervising Solicitor (who is a Solicitor acting independently of the Applicant) to enter, but not start to search.

(7) Before permitting entry to the premises by any person other than the Supervising Solicitor, you (or any other person appearing to be in control of the premises) may gather together any documents you

believe may be [incrimmating or] privileged and hand them to the Supervising Solicitor for the Supervising Solicitor to assess whether they are [incriminating or] privileged as claimed. If the Supervising Solicitor concludes that any of the documents may be [incriminating or] privileged documents or if there is any doubt as to their status the Supervising Solicitor shall exclude them from the search and shall retain the documents of doubtful status in his possession pending further order of the Court. While this is being done, you may refuse entry to the premises by any other person, and may refuse to permit the search to begin, for a short time (not to exceed two hours, unless the Supervising Solicitor agrees to a longer period). If you wish to take legal advice and gather documents as permitted, you must first inform the Supervising Solicitor and keep him informed of the steps being taken.

Restrictions on Service

Paragraph 1 of the Order is subject to the following restrictions:— D2–506

(1) This Order may only be served between 9:30 am and 5:30 pm on a weekday unless the Court has ordered otherwise.

(2) This Order may not be carried out at the same time as a police search warrant.

(3) This Order must be served by the Supervising Solicitor, and paragraph 1 of the Order must be carried out in his presence and under his supervision. Where the premises are likely to be occupied by an unaccompanied woman and the Supervising Solicitor is a man, at least one of the persons accompanying him as provided by paragraph 1 of the Order shall be a woman.

(4) This Order does not require the person served with the Order to allow anyone [or anyone except] to enter the premises who in the view of the Supervising Solicitor could gain commercially from anything he might read or see on the premises if the person served with the Order objects.

Variation or discharge of this Order

The Respondent (or anyone notified of this Order) may apply to the Court at any time to vary or discharge this Order (or so much of it as affects that person), but anyone wishing to do so must first inform the Applicant's Solicitors. D2–507

Interpretation of this Order

(1) In this Order, where there is more than one Respondent, references to "the Respondent" means both or all of them. D2–508

(2) A requirement to serve on "the Respondent" means on each of them. However, the Order is effective against any Respondent on whom it is served.

(3) An Order requiring "the Respondent" to do or not to do anything applies to all Respondents.

(4) Any other requirement that something shall be done to or in the presence of "the Respondent" means to or in the presence of any one of them or in the case of a firm or company a director or a person appearing to the Supervising Solicitor to be a responsible employee.

Communications with the Court

D2–509 All communications to the Court about this Order should be sent to the Commercial Court Clerk, the Listing Office, Room E201, Royal Courts of Justice, Strand, London WC2A 2LL quoting the case number. The telephone number is 0171 936 6826. The offices are open between 10 am and 4.30 pm Monday to Friday.

Schedule A

D2–510 The premises

Schedule B

D2–511 The listed items

Schedule C

D2–512 Undertakings given by the applicant:—

(1) If the Court later finds that this Order or carrying it out has caused loss to the Respondent, and decides that the Respondent should be compensated for that loss, the Applicant will comply with any Order the Court may make. Further, if the carrying out of this Order has been in breach of the terms of this Order or otherwise in a manner inconsistent with the Applicant's Solicitors' duties as Officers of the Court the Applicant will comply with any order for damages the Court may make.

[(2) As soon as practicable to issue a Claim Form [in the form of the draft produced to the Court] [claiming appropriate relief]].

[(3) To [swear and file an affidavit] [cause an affidavit to be sworn and filed] [substantially in the terms of the draft produced to the Court] [confirming the substance of what was said to the Court by the Applicant's Counsel/Solicitors].]

(4) To serve on the Respondent at the same time as this Order is served upon him (i) the Claim Form, or if not issued, the draft produced to the Court (ii) an Application for hearing on [date] (iii) copies of the affidavits [or draft affidavits] and exhibits capable of being copied containing the evidence relied on by the Applicant. [Copies of the confidential exhibits need not be served, but they must be made available for inspection by or on behalf of the Respondent in the presence of the Applicant's Solicitors while the Order is carried out. Afterwards they must be provided to a Solicitor representing the Respondent who gives a written undertaking not to permit the Respondent to see them or copies of them except in his presence and not to permit the Respondent to make or take away any note or record of the exhibits] and (iv) a note of any allegation of fact made orally to the Judge where such allegation is not contained in the affidavits or draft affidavits read by the Judge.

(5) To serve on the Respondent a copy of the Supervising Solicitor's report on the carrying out of this Order as soon as it is received.

(6) Not, without the leave of the Court, to use any information or documents obtained as a result of carrying out this Order nor to inform anyone else of these proceedings except for the purposes of these

proceedings (including adding further Respondents) or commencing civil proceedings in relation to the same or related subject matter to these proceedings until after the return date.

[(7) To maintain pending further order the sum of £ in an account controlled by the Applicant's Solicitors.]

[(8) To insure the items removed from the premises.]

Schedule D

Underkings given by the Applicant's Solicitors:— D2–513

(1) To answer at once to the best of their ability any question whether a particular item is a listed item.

(2) To return the originals of all documents obtained as a result of this Order (except original documents which belong to the Applicant) as soon as possible and in any event within two working days of their removal.

(3) While ownership of any item obtained as a result of this Order is in dispute, to deliver the article into the keeping of Solicitors acting for the Respondent within two working days from receiving a written undertaking by them to retain the article in safe keeping and to produce it to the Court when required.

(4) To retain in their own safe keeping all other items obtained as a result of this Order until the Courts direct otherwise.

Schedule E

Undertakings given by the Supervising Solicitor:— D2–514

(1) To offer to explain to the person served with the Order its meaning and effect fairly and in everyday language, and to inform him of his right to seek legal advice (such advice to include an explanation that the Respondent may be entitled to avail himself of [the privilege against self-incrimination or] [legal professional privilege]) and apply to vary or discharge the Order as mentioned in the Respondent's Entitlements above.

(2) To make and provide to the Applicant's Solicitors and to the Judge who made this Order (for the purposes of the Court file) a written report on the carrying out of the Order.

Schedule F

Affidavits:— D2–515

The Applicant relied on the following affidavits:—

[*name*] [*number of affidavit*] [*date sworn*] [*filed on behalf of*]

Name and Address of Applicant's Solicitors

The Applicant's Solicitors are:—

[Name, address, reference, fax and telephone numbers both in and out of office hours.]

APPENDIX 6

CASE MANAGEMENT INFORMATION SHEET

D2–516 Party lodging information sheet
Name of solicitors
Name(s) of advocates for trial

[Notes: This Sheet should normally be completed with the involvement of the advocate(s) instructed for trial. If the claimant is a litigant in person this fact should be noted at the foot of the sheet and proposals made as to which party is to have responsibility for the preparation and upkeep of the case management bundle.]

(1) By what date can you give standard disclosure?

(2) In relation to standard disclosure, do you contend in relation to any category or class of document under CPR 31.6(b) that to search for that category or class would be unreasonable? If so, what is the category or class and on what grounds do you so contend?

(3) Is specific disclosure required on any issue (specifying which)?

(4) Is a special disclosure order appropriate?

(5) By what dates can you (a) give specific disclosure or (b) comply with a special disclosure order?

(6) May the time periods for inspection at CPR 31.15 require adjustment, and if so by how much?

(7) Are amendments to or is information about any statement of case required? If yes, please give brief details of what is required.

(8) Can you make any additional admissions? If yes, please give brief details of the additional admissions.

(9) Are any of the issues in the case suitable for trial as preliminary issues?

(10)a. On the evidence of how many witnesses of fact do you intend to rely at trial (subject to the directions of the Court)? Please give their names, or explain why this is not being done.

b. By what date can you serve signed witness statements?

c. How many of these witnesses of fact do you intend to call to give oral evidence at trial (subject to the directions of the Court)? Please give their names, or explain why this is not being done.

d. Will interpreters be required for any witness?

e. Do you wish any witness to give oral evidence by video link? Please give his or her name, or explain why this is not being done. Please state the country and city from which the witness will be asked to give evidence by video link.

(11)a. On what issues may expert evidence be required?

b. Is this a case in which the use of a single joint expert might be suitable (see CPR 35.7)?

c. On the evidence of how many expert witnesses do you intend to rely at trial (subject to the directions of the Court)? Please give their names, or explain why this is not being done. Please identify each expert's field of expertise.

d. By what date can you serve signed expert reports?

e. When will the experts be available for a meeting or meetings of experts?

f. How many of these expert witnesses do you intend to call to give oral evidence at trial (subject to the directions of the Court)? Please give their names, or explain why this is not being done.

g. Will interpreters be required for any expert witness?

h. Do you wish any expert witness to give oral evidence by video link? Please give his or her name, or explain why this is not being done. Please state the country and city from which the witness will be asked to give evidence by video link.

(12) What are the advocates' present provisional estimates of the minimum and maximum lengths of the trial?

(13) What is the earliest date by which you believe you can be ready for trial?

(14) Is this a case in which a Pre-Trial Review is likely to be useful?

(15) Is there any way in which the Court can assist the parties to resolve their dispute or particular issues in it without the need for a trial or a full trial?

(16)a. Might some form of Alternative Dispute Resolution procedure assist to resolve or narrow the dispute or particular issues in it?
b. Has the question at a. been considered between the client and legal representatives (including the advocate(s) retained)?
c. Has the question at a. been explored with the other parties in the case?
d. Do you request that the case is adjourned while the parties try to settle the case by Alternative Dispute Resolution or other means?
e. Would an ADR order in the form of Appendix 7 to the Commercial Court Guide be appropriate?
f. Are any other special directions needed to allow for Alternative Dispute Resolution?
(17) What applications will you wish to make at the Case Management Conference?
(18) Does provision need to be made in the pre-trial timetable for any application or procedural step not otherwise dealt with above? If yes, please specify the application or procedural step.
(19) Are there, or are there likely in due course to be, any related proceedings (e.g. a Part 20 claim)? Please give brief details.

[Signature of solicitors]

Note: This information sheet must be lodged with the Clerk to the Commercial Court at least 7 days before the Case Management Conference (with a copy to all other parties): see paragraph D7.10 of the Commercial Court Guide.

APPENDIX 7

DRAFT ADR ORDER

1. On or before [*] the parties shall exchange lists of 3 neutral individuals who are available to conduct ADR procedures in this case prior to [*]. Each party may [in addition] [in the alternative] provide a list identifying the constitution of one or more panels of neutral individuals who are available to conduct ADR procedures in this case prior to [*]. D2–517
2. On or before [*] the parties shall in good faith endeavour to agree a neutral individual or panel from the lists so exchanged and provided.
3. Failing such agreement by [*] the Case Management Conference will be restored to enable the Court to facilitate agreement on a neutral individual or panel.
4. The parties shall take such serious steps as they may be advised to resolve their disputes by ADR procedures before the neutral individual or panel so chosen by no later than [*].
5. If the case is not finally settled, the parties shall inform the Court by letter prior to [disclosure of documents exchange of witness statements/exchange of experts' reports] what steps towards ADR have been taken and (without prejudice to matters of privilege) why such steps have failed. If the parties have failed to initiate ADR procedures the Case Management Conference is to be restored for further consideration of the case.
6. [Costs].

Note: The term "ADR procedures" is deliberately used in the draft ADR order. This is in order to emphasise that (save where otherwise provided) the parties are free to use the ADR procedure that they regard as most suitable, be it mediation, early neutral evaluation, non-binding arbitration etc.

APPENDIX 8

STANDARD PRE-TRIAL TIMETABLE

1. [Standard disclosure is to be made by [*], with inspection [*] days after notice.] [Specific disclosure is to be made by [*] in relation to the following issues: [*], with inspection [*] days after notice.] D2–518

[Special disclosure order is to be complied with by [*], with inspection [*] days after notice.]

2. Signed statements of witnesses of fact, and hearsay notices where required by CPR 33.2, are to be exchanged not later than [*].
3. Unless otherwise ordered, witness statements are to stand as the evidence in chief of the witness at trial.
4. Signed reports of experts:

a. are to be confined to one expert for each party from each of the following fields of expertise: [*];
b. are to be confined to the following issues: [*].
c. are to be exchanged [sequentially/simultaneously];
d. are to be exchanged not later than [date or dates for each report in each field of expertise].

5. The procedure set out in the Practice Direction supplementing CPR Part 35 is to apply in relation to experts, subject to the exceptions and further provisions contained in Section H of and Appendix 12 to the Commercial Court Guide.

a. The meeting of experts is to be by [*]

b. The joint memorandum of the experts is to be completed by [*].

c. Any short supplemental expert reports are to be exchanged [sequentially/simultaneously] by not later than [date or dates for each supplemental report].

6. [If the experts' reports cannot be agreed, the parties are to be at liberty to call expert witnesses at the trial, limited to those experts whose reports have been exchanged pursuant to 4. above.]

[*Or:* The parties are to be at liberty to apply to call as expert witnesses at the trial those experts whose reports they have exchanged pursuant to 4. above, such application to be made not earlier than [*] and not later than [*].]

7. Preparation of trial bundles to be completed in accordance with Appendix 11 to the Commercial Court Guide by not later than [*].

8. The provisional estimated length of the trial is [*].

9. The fixed trial date is [*: *Note, the date will be obtained from the Clerk to the Commercial Court for insertion into the pre-trial timetable: see paragraph D7.17 of the Commercial Court Guide*]

[*Or, exceptionally*: The provisional range of dates for trial is [*]]

10. The progress monitoring date is [*]. Each party is to lodge a completed progress monitoring information sheet with the Clerk to the Commercial Court at least 3 days before the progress monitoring date (with a copy to all other parties).

11. Each party is to lodge a completed pre-trial checklist with the Clerk to the Commercial Court as soon as all parties have informed the Court by a progress monitoring information sheet that they will be ready for a trial commencing [on the fixed date/within the provisional range of dates].

12. [There is to be a Pre-Trial Review not earlier than [*] and not later than [*]].

13. Save as varied by this order or further order, the practice and procedures set out in the Commercial Court Guide are to be followed.

14. Costs in the case.

15. Liberty to restore the Case Management Conference.

APPENDIX 9

DRAFT SPECIAL DISCLOSURE ORDER

D2–519 It is ordered that:

(1) On or before [*] each party shall carry out a thorough search for all documents relevant to [the issues listed in the Schedule to this order/the issues in the case], including (for the avoidance of doubt) all documents which may lead to a train of inquiry enabling a party to advance his own case or damage that of his opponent.

(2) On or before [*] each party shall disclose [by list]:

(a) any documents located as a result of the search by that party under (1) above, and

(b) any other documents relevant to [the issues listed in the Schedule to this order/the issues in the case] that were once but are no longer in his control (as defined by CPR 31.8(2)).

(3) The parties remain under a continuing obligation until the proceedings are concluded to disclose documents described in (1) above.

(4) Each party is at liberty to apply to the Court, on notice to all other parties, for further directions in relation to the carrying out of this order.

(5) Costs in the case.

APPENDIX 10

SKELETON ARGUMENTS, CHRONOLOGIES AND INDICES FOR CASES IN THE COMMERCIAL COURT

PART 1:

SKELETON ARGUMENTS

D2–520 1 A skeleton argument assists to indicate to the parties and to the Court what points are or are not in issue, and the nature of the argument about the points that are in issue. It also assists the Court in its advance reading. It is not a substitute for oral argument.

2 If there is, at the stage of preparation of a skeleton argument, no list of issues in accordance

with paragraph D5 of the Commercial Court Guide, the skeleton argument should begin with a brief outline of the issues which arise in the case. On any application the applicant's skeleton argument should list concisely the issues which arise for decision on the application.

3 Skeleton arguments should set out concisely:

3.1 the propositions of law advanced with references to the relevant authorities;

3.2 the submissions of fact to be made with references to the evidence.

4 On an application the applicant's skeleton argument should also set out concisely, and in neutral terms, the background to, nature of and facts of the case so far as relevant to the application.

5 A skeleton argument must be in numbered paragraphs and state the name of the advocate(s) who prepared it.

Note: On an application, it is helpful if the applicant's skeleton argument includes an estimate of likely pre-reading time by the Judge, on the assumption stated at paragraph F8.6 of the Commercial Court Guide.

PART 2:

CHRONOLOGIES AND INDICES

6 Chronologies and indices should, so far as possible, not be prepared in a tendentious form. **D2–521** The ideal is that the Court and all the parties should have a single point of reference that all find useful and are happy to work with.

7 Where there is disagreement about a particular event or description, it is useful if that fact is indicated and the competing versions shortly stated.

8 If time and circumstances allow its preparation, a chronology or index to which all parties have contributed and agreed can be invaluable.

9 Chronologies and indices once prepared can be easily updated and are of continuing usefulness throughout the life of the case.

APPENDIX 11

BUNDLE PREPARATION FOR CASES IN THE COMMERCIAL COURT

1 The preparation of bundles requires a high level of co-operation between legal representa- **D2–522** tives for all parties; it is the duty of all legal representatives to co-operate to this high level.

2 The bundles that will need to be prepared at various stages of a case in the Commercial Court are identified at paragraphs D6, F11–F13 and I3 of the Commercial Court Guide.

3 Bundles should be prepared as follows for cases in the Commercial Court:

3.1 No more than one copy of any one document should be included, unless there is good reason for doing otherwise.

3.2 Contemporaneous documents, and correspondence, should be included in chronological order.

3.3 Where a contract or similar document is central to the case that contract or similar document may be included in a separate place (and must be included in the evidence bundle on a heavy application: see paragraph F12.2 b. of the Guide) provided that a page is inserted in the chronological run of documents to indicate (i) the place the contract or similar document would have appeared had it appeared chronologically and (ii) where it may be found instead.

3.4 Documents in manuscript, or not fully legible, should be transcribed; the transcription should be marked and placed adjacent to the document transcribed.

3.5 Documents in a foreign language should be translated; the translation should be marked and placed adjacent to the document transcribed.

3.6 Where an unstructured document, or clause, is liable to be subject to close analysis, thought should be given to introducing artificial paragraph or line numbers in manuscript so as to ease reference to particular passages.

3.7 Where a document has to be read across rather than down the page, it should be so placed in the bundle as to ensure that the top of the text starts nearest the spine.

3.8 Bundles should be thoroughly checked for the legibility of all contents.

3.9 No bundle should contain more than 300 pages.

3.10 Bundles should not be overfilled, and should allow sufficient room for later insertions. Subject to this, the size of file used should not be a size that is larger than necessary for the present and anticipated contents.

3.11 Bundles should be paginated, in the bottom right hand corner and in a form that can clearly be distinguished from any existing pagination on the document.

3.12 Bundles should be indexed, save that a chronological bundle of contemporaneous documents need not be indexed if an index is unlikely to be useful.

3.13 Marked bundle dividers should be used where suitable.

3.14 Bundles should be numbered and named on the outside and on the inside front cover, the label to include the short title of the case, and a description of the bundle (including its number, where relevant).

3.15 The use of different bundle colours for bundles dealing with different subjects is often useful.

D2–523 4 Documents within bundles should be marked as follows:

4.1 When copy documents from exhibits have been included in the bundle(s), then unless clearly unnecessary, the copy of the affidavit or witness statement to which the documents were exhibited should be marked in the right hand margin (in manuscript if need be) to show where the document referred to may be found in the bundle(s).

4.2 Unless clearly unnecessary, where copy documents in a bundle are taken from the disclosure of more than one party the documents should be marked in the top right hand corner (in manuscript if need be) to show from which party's disclosure the copy document has been taken.

4.3 Statements of case and witness statements contained in trial bundles should (where they refer to a document) include a page reference in the right hand margin (in manuscript if need be) identifying the location of a copy of that document elsewhere in the trial bundles. (Unless otherwise agreed this is the responsibility of the party tendering the statement of case or witness statement.)

5 For the trial a handy sized core bundle should (unless clearly unnecessary or not useful in the particular case) also be provided containing the really important documents in the case. The documents in this bundle should normally be paginated but should also bear a page reference identifying the location of a copy of that document elsewhere in the trial bundles. Allowing sufficient room for insertions (see 3.10 above) is particularly important in the case of this bundle.

6 Large documents, such as plans, should be placed into an easily accessible file.

7 When agreeing bundles for trial, the parties should also settle through their legal representatives, and record in correspondence, whether the agreement of bundles:

7.1 extends no further than agreement of the composition and preparation of the bundles; or

7.2 includes agreement that the documents in the bundles are authentic (see further CPR 32.19); or

7.3 includes agreement that the documents may be treated as evidence of the facts stated in them.

The Court will normally expect parties to agree that the documents or at any rate the great majority of them may be treated as evidence of the facts stated in them. A party not willing so to agree should, when the trial bundles are lodged, write a letter to the Court (with a copy to all other parties) stating that it is not willing so to agree, and explaining why it is not willing so to agree.

Note: Where the Court is of the opinion that costs have been wasted by the copying of unnecessary documents, the Court will have no hesitation in making a special order for costs against the person responsible.

APPENDIX 12

EXPERT EVIDENCE IN CASES IN THE COMMERCIAL COURT: REQUIREMENTS OF GENERAL APPLICATION

D2–524 1 It is the duty of an expert to help the Court on the matters within his expertise (CPR 35.3(1)). This duty is paramount and overrides any obligation to the person from whom the expert has received instructions or by whom he is paid (CPR 35.3(2)).

2 Expert evidence presented to the Court should be, and should be seen to be, the independent product of the expert uninfluenced by the exigencies of litigation.

3 An expert witness should provide independent assistance to the Court by way of objective unbiased opinion in relation to matters within his expertise. An expert witness should never assume the role of an advocate.

4 An expert witness should not omit to consider material facts which could detract from his concluded opinion.

5 An expert witness should make it clear when a particular question or issue falls outside his expertise.

6 If an expert's opinion is not properly researched because he considers that insufficient data is available, then this must be stated with an indication that the opinion is no more than a provisional one.

7 In a case where an expert witness who has prepared a report could not assert that the report contained the truth, the whole truth and nothing but the truth without some qualification, that qualification should be stated in the report.

8 If, after exchange of reports, an expert witness changes his view on a material matter having

read another expert's report or for any other reason, such change of view should be communicated in writing (through legal representatives) to the other side without delay, and when appropriate to the Court.

APPENDIX 13

PROGRESS MONITORING INFORMATION SHEET

[SHORT TITLE OF CASE and FOLIO NUMBER] D2–525

Fixed trial date/provisional range of dates for trial specified in the pre-trial timetable

Party lodging information sheet
Name of solicitors
Name(s) of advocates for trial
[**Note:** this information sheet should normally be completed with the involvement of the advocate(s) instructed for trial]
(1) Have you complied with the pre-trial timetable in all respects?
(2) If you have not complied, in what respects have you not complied?
(3) Will you be ready for a trial commencing on the fixed date (or, where applicable, within the provisional range of dates) specified in the pre-trial timetable?
(4) If you will not be ready, why will you not be ready?

[Signature of solicitors]

Note: This information sheet must be lodged with the Clerk to the Commercial Court at least 3 days before the progress monitoring date (with a copy to all other parties): see paragraph D8.2 of the Commercial Court Guide.

APPENDIX 14

PRE-TRIAL CHECKLIST

[SHORT TITLE OF CASE and FOLIO NUMBER] D2–526

a. Fixed trial date/provisional range of dates for trial specified in the pre-trial timetable
b. Whether Pre-Trial Review ordered
c. Party lodging checklist
d. Name of solicitors
e. Name(s) of advocates for trial
[**Note:** this checklist should normally be completed with the involvement of the advocate(s) instructed for trial]
(1) Have all parties informed the Court by a progress monitoring sheet that they will be ready for a trial commencing on the fixed date (or, where applicable, within the provisional range of dates) specified in the pre-trial timetable?
(2) What, if any, directions in the pre-trial timetable still remain to be carried out?
(3) For any direction identified in answer to (2) above, what is the current position in relation to carrying out that direction and by what date will it have been carried out?
(4) What, if any, further directions are necessary?
(5) Will you not later than 3 weeks before the date fixed for trial have completed preparation of trial bundles in accordance with Appendix 11 to the Commercial Court Guide?
(6)a. Which witnesses of fact do you intend to call?
b. (Where directions for expert evidence have been given) which expert witness(es) do you intend to call?
c. Will interpreters be required for any witness of fact or expert witness, and have any necessary directions already been given?
h. Do you wish any witness of fact or expert witness to give oral evidence by video link? Please state the name of the witness, and the country and city from which the witness will be asked to give

evidence by video link. Have any necessary directions already been given, and what is the current position on compliance with those directions?

(7) If a Pre-Trial Review has not been ordered, is it your view that it would be useful to have one?

(8) What are the advocates' confirmed estimates of the minimum and maximum lengths of the trial? (A confirmed estimate of length signed by the advocates should be attached).

(9)a. Might some form of Alternative Dispute Resolution procedure now assist to resolve or narrow the dispute or particular issues in it?

b. Has the question at a. been considered between the client and legal representatives (including the advocate(s) retained)?

c. Has the question at a. been explored with the other parties in the case?

[Signature of solicitors]

Note: This Checklist must be lodged with the Clerk to the Commercial Court (with a copy to all other parties) as soon as all parties have informed the Court by a progress monitoring sheet that they will be ready for a trial commencing on the fixed trial date or within the provisional range of dates specified in the pre-trial timetable: see paragraph D8.4 of the Commercial Court Guide.

APPENDIX 15

VIDEOCONFERENCING PROTOCOL

PROTOCOL FOR THE USE OF VIDEOCONFERENCING EQUIPMENT IN CIVIL PROCEEDINGS

D2–527 Based, with permission, upon the protocol of the Federal Court of Australia

Videoconferencing generally

D2–528 1. This protocol has been prepared as a guide to all persons who are involved in the use of videoconferencing (VCF) equipment in civil proceedings in the High Court. It covers its use in courtrooms where the equipment might be permanently placed in situ or where it might operate from a mobile unit. It also covers the situation where the court assembles in a commercial studio or conference room in which VCF equipment is installed for the hearing of evidence, as, for example, when the court assembles in the studio operated by the Bar Council.

The overall aim in the High Court is to make the VCF setting as close as possible to the usual practice in a trial court where evidence is taken in open court. There are a number of significant differences which must be understood by all persons using the system, to gain the maximum benefit from VCF. Matters which are taken for granted when examining a witness—matters such as the administration of an oath of affirmation to a witness, objections during evidence being adduced from a witness, and ensuring that the witness understands who the other people are in the courtroom and their respective roles—all these examples take on quite a different dimension when the witness is at a remote locality. It is best to work on the basis that the witness knows nothing of courtroom practice.

Matters to be considered by the Judge before authorising the taking of evidence by video conference

D2–529 2. The convenience of video conferencing should not be allowed to dictate its use. If other methods for taking evidence provide a satisfactory service at less overall cost, then these should be used.

Accordingly, in the interests of efficiency, the advocate should be required to make available to the Court a comparison of the costs of (a) taking the evidence on commission overseas, (b) bringing the witness to the UK, if this is possible, and (c) taking the evidence by video conference.

An estimate of the cost of taking evidence on commission overseas should take into account (a) the possible time required in the overseas location; (1)) the cost of the air and any other fares involved; (c) the cost of subsistence during the period overseas including the cost of hotel accommodation during the relevant period; (d) the total number of persons required to travel to the overseas location; (e) the daily and total cost for the appointment of a local assessor to supervise the taking of the evidence; (f) whether there is a need to appoint local counsel for the taking of the evidence; (g) the cost of local accommodation in which to hear the evidence; and (h) any other associated costs.

An evaluation of the possibility and cost of bringing the witness to the UK should consider the possibility and/or likelihood that the witness may not be willing to travel to the UK for reasons of health, family relationships, business commitments or some other reason.

An estimate of the cost of taking the evidence by video conferencing should include the total charges for the UK studio, the other end studio, the line charges for the estimated period, and any costs likely to be incurred by the witnesses in giving their evidence.

Permission from the foreign country

3. It should not be assumed that all foreign governments will agree with their nationals being examined before a High Court judge by means of VCF. Appropriate enquiries should be made of the Foreign Office in London, to ensure that the particular country raises no objection at diplomatic level to an examination being held, if there is any doubt. **D2–530**

Time zone differences

4. Time zone differences need to be addressed when a witness from an overseas country is to be examined in England by VCF. This requires careful co-ordination to ensure that if possible a witness in a overseas country has access to VCF during normal business hours. Out of hours transmissions normally incur additional hearing costs for building and studio access. **D2–531**

Co-ordination of picture with sound

5. There are millisecond delays between the receipt of the picture and the receipt of the accompanying sound. This is the case even with the most advanced Integrated Services Digital Networking (ISDN) communication. Where both systems are linked on the SG3 proprietary algorithm and the transmission is by cable the delay is barely noticeable. Persons, whether Judges, advocates or witnesses need to appreciate this time gap. If due allowance is not made for it, there is a tendency to 'speak over' the witness or other person whose voice continues to be heard for a millisecond or so after he or she appears on the screen to have fmished speaking. Experience has shown that where allowance is made for this, the speaker can quickly reach an understanding where neither is aware that a gap exists: for it fits naturally within the normal pace of court speech. Barristers have commented that it tends to encourage them to refrain from cutting off a witness before the witness has finished an answer. **D2–532**

Picture quality

6. Picture quality is good, but not as good as a television picture. The amount of information which can be sent by VCF on ISDN transmission is only 128 kbs, as compared to 2 mbs (i.e. 16 times 128 kbs) which can be sent by analogue television transmission. (The quid pro quo is that the cost of digital transmission such as occurs in VCF on ISDN lines is in the order of one tenth of the cost of analogue transmission). The computer is geared to recompose only those parts of the image which move, and all movement has a tendency to appear somewhat jerky. The lesson from this is that persons appearing on VCF monitors should endeavour to keep their movements to a minimum so as to enhance the quality of the picture being received by the viewers. **D2–533**

Informing the Judge what is to take place

7. It can be disconcerting to a judge to be informed by an advocate that the next day the trial is to take place at the VCF studio, without any prior warning. It is the duty of an advocate to ensure that the judge is told as soon as practical of any arrangements which have been made for the taking of evidence by VCF. If such arrangements involve the court sitting at unusual hours because of time zone differences, the arrangements should not be finalised without the concurrence of the judge. Advocates should also ensure that the judge is aware of this protocol well in advance of the transmission. **D2–534**

Informing witnesses what is to take place

8. The potential witness in the location remote from the courtroom should be informed of the significant differences mentioned in paragraphs 5 and 6 above (co-ordination of picture with sound, and picture quality). The witness should also be advised before the transmission commences of the name of the presiding judge and the names of the advocates who will be conducting the examination and the cross-examination. The names can be shown on the document camera if required. It is useful for the judge, at the commencement of the transmission, to have the camera focus on himself. Room arrangements can be made for the royal coat of arms to be present above the judge's bench. The judge can then ask the advocates to identify themselves to the witness. This takes but a few minutes. It is less likely for the witness to be confused if practices are explained beforehand; *e.g.* taking an oath or affirmation; not responding until directed to do so by a judge when an objection is taken. Where possible some indication could be given of the manner in which the witness can be given a copy of the evidence adduced. If there is to be an interpreter it has been found more appropriate for the interpreter to be present in the UK rather than at the far end. **D2–535**

Monitoring in the place where the witness is located

9. There is usually no need for an official from a local court to be present at the location of the witness, unless it is thought necessary to ensure that the witness does not take direction or **D2–536**

guidance from any other person in the room, or to ensure that documents are only shown to the witness at particular times. If an official is present, and something improper does take place, the official should bring whatever has occurred to the notice of the judge by moving to the camera location where he or she will be visible to the judge and explaining what has occurred.

The judge may, of course, have given leave in unusual circumstances for the witness to consult with a lawyer during the VCF transmission. If this is the case, this consultation may take place without the court official intervening. The lawyer should remember to cover the microphone in front of the witness if the conversation is not to be relayed to the receiving courtroom.

Court reporting transcript

D2–537 10. The parties should ensure that the Mechanical Recording Department is informed in good time of the arrangements which have been made for the VCF transmission, so that there is sufficient time to set up equipment to record the evidence in case a transcript is needed. This can usually be arranged through the court usher. The equipment should be set up and tested before the VCF transmission to ensure there is no interference during the transmission.

Familiarisation with the equipment

D2–538 11. It is recommended that the judge, practitioners and witness should arrive at their respective VCF venues about 20 minutes prior to the transmission commencing. This is particularly important in the early stages of becoming familiar with the use of VCF equipment.

If transmission is not to take place from a courtroom but from a conference room or a studio, the judge will need to determine who is to sit where. For example, barristers will need to have instructing solicitors in close proximity. Care must be taken to ensure the number of microphones is adequate for the speakers and that the panning (and pre-set, if fitted) of the camera for the bar table encompasses all legal representatives. Again, care needs to be taken with placing microphones and with panning of the camera to ensure that the viewer can see all people seated at the conference bench or table.

There will be a need for the judge to communicate the manner in which the proceeding is to be conducted to the remote locality. There is a need for advocates to indicate whether or not an authority or document camera will be needed during the transmission. It is too late after a transmission starts to ask for a document camera to be used; early consideration by the advocates, with notification to the judge and to the panel operator of the intention to use the equipment, is necessary. The panel operator will need to know the number and size of documents or objects if their images are to be sent by document camera.

The judge will need to tell the far end operator to pan to the witness during the admission of the oath or affirmation and to have the camera remain on the witness during the currency of the examination. This is not necessary if the judge operates on far end control (see 13, control of cameras).

Cost of transmission

D2–539 12. Payment of the cost of transmission from the Court and from the remote location should be determined before transmission. Every endeavour should be made to keep the transmission to a minimum because of the cost involved.

Control of cameras

D2–540 13. The judge should determine who is to control the cameras before the transmission starts as some equipment has 'far end' control, i.e. the London equipment can control the movement of the New York camera from the control pad in London, and likewise movement of the London camera can be controlled from New York. This facility is usually available where the equipment at both locations meets H261 compliance and is made by the same manufacturer. Thus far end control is possible if, say, PictureTel equipment is used in London and in New York, but it is not presently possible if, say, PictureTel equipment is used in London and CLI equipment is used in New York.

Order of proceedings

D2–541 14. The intention is that the examination of the witness at the remote locality will be following as closely as possible the practice when the witness is in the courtroom. During examination, cross-examination and re-examination, the witness would see the legal representative asking the question and the legal representative, the judge and everybody else would see the witness. If objections are taken, the witness would variously see opposing practitioners or the Judge.

Administration of the oath

D2–542 15. Generally, there are no difficulties with either the voluntary giving of evidence in noncriminal matters or the admission of oaths in the United States. 28 U.S.C. S1782(b) states: "This chapter does not preclude a person within the United States from voluntarily giving his testimony or his statement, or producing a document or other thing, for use in a proceeding in a foreign or international tribunal before any person and in any manner acceptable to him."

Particular countries may have a requirement that any oath or affirmation to be taken by a witness accords with local custom, and not the usual form of oath or affirmation taken in England. It is necessary for this requirement to be addressed in the event that some unforeseen consequences flow from the evidence being adduced from the foreign national (or even an English national residing temporarily in that country).

Assuming that there is no local custom for the administration of the oath, the witness should be asked before the trial to ensure that he brings to the remote location a copy of the New Testament (or whatever book is appropriate for his religion). At the trial the associate in England asks the witness to hold the New Testament in his uplifted hand, and the associate then speaks the words of the oath for the witness to repeat.

Witness viewing documents

16. Most facilities have a document or overhead camera. Thus a witness can be shown the image of documents transmitted from the courtroom and asked to identify them. It is useful for practitioners to agree on documents to be shown to the witness beforehand, if this is possible. Of course, in appropriate cases it should be possible for copies of agreed documents to be sent by post or facsimile to the remote location, and so avoid the necessity of using the document camera. Unless there is some reason why the witness should not see the documents in advance, they can be sent directly to him, to bring with him to the studio. If it is more appropriate, the documents can instead be sent to the local court officer, who can show them to the witness as directed by the advocates or the judge. **D2–543**

Court dress

17. The judge will need to decide whether court dress is appropriate when using the VCF facilities. It might be appropriate when transmitting from courtroom to courtroom. It might not be appropriate when a commercial facility is used at either or both ends of the transmission. Apart from the difficulty occasioned by lack of changing room facilities, consider the position of the witness at the remote location endeavouring to know who is addressing him or her. The witness would have had indicated to him or her who the various persons are; the judge and a number of advocates. As the screen changes to indicate a change of speaker, the witness would have some initial difficulty knowing which of several people was speaking when all are robed somewhat identically. A further criterion which may be useful in deciding whether or not to use court dress is whether the witnesses are witnesses of fact or expert witnesses: robes might be thought to be appropriate in the case of witnesses of fact, but not so necessary in the case of expert witnesses. **D2–544**

APPENDIX 16

PROCEDURE FOR ABRIDGED ASSESSMENT OF COSTS OF A CASE

Note: this procedure is available to deal with the assessment of costs of a case; for the assessment of costs of an individual hearing see paragraph F17 of the Guide. **D2–545**

1 Within 3 months of the order for assessment of costs, a schedule bill of costs (signed by a partner) together with requisite vouchers shall be drawn up by the solicitors for the receiving party and served on the solicitors for the paying party ("the Schedule Bill"). The Schedule Bill should briefly summarise the main areas and items of costs, and take the form of a schedule used in security for costs applications.

2 The paying party's solicitors and/or costs draftsman shall within 21 days of receipt of the Schedule Bill draw up and serve on the solicitors for the receiving party a list ("the response") identifying those items:

2.1 which are agreed;

2.2 which are disputed (and stating briefly the grounds of objection and the appropriate figure contended for);

2.3 in respect of which further information is required (and stating briefly the nature of the flirther information required).

3 The receiving party's solicitors shall within 21 days of receipt of the response draw up and serve a reply to points under 2.2 and 2.3 thereto in writing if so advised ("the reply").

4 If agreement cannot thereafter be reached between the parties within 7 days of the receipt of the reply (or failing service thereof, within 28 days of the service of the response), the solicitors for the receiving party shall within a further 7 days lodge with the Supreme Court [Taxing] Office the following:

4.1 the requisite document for commencement of assessment proceedings;

4.2 a copy of the order of the Court abridging assessment of costs;

4.3 any available transcript of the judgment;

4.4 the documents exchanged between the parties, namely:

a. the Schedule Bill and supporting vouchers;
b. the response with any supporting documents;
c. the reply (if any) with any supporting documents.

4.5 a letter marked "For the Attention of the Commercial [Taxing] Master" containing a request that a date be fixed for the hearing of the assessment;

4.6 a cheque in respect of the lodgement fee calculated in accordance with the current scale of fees;

4.7 a time estimate for the assessment which, save in exceptional circumstances, is to be limited to half a day.

5 Within 21 days of such lodgment, the Commercial [Taxing] Master shall fix a date for the hearing of such assessment which shall be as early as conveniently possible but in any event no more than 3 months ahead, unless agreed by the parties. Any interest awarded on taxed costs beyond that 3 month period shall be at the discretion of the Commercial [Taxing] Master.

6 The Commercial [Taxing] Master may require any party to provide any further information he considers necessary for the assessment and to have the fee earner who had the conduct of the case present at the assessment.

7 The assessment shall be heard and determined by the Commercial [Taxing] Master on the basis of the material lodged under paragraph 4. above and any oral submissions, confined to the points raised in the material lodged, made by the parties at the hearing. A party seeking the drawing up and service of a detailed Bill of Costs or part thereof or a detailed response or reply, must apply to a Commercial Judge for an order. Such an order will only be granted in exceptional cases.

8 Nothing in this Appendix shall prevent a party from bringing the matter before the Commercial [Taxing] Master at an earlier stage (by serving the requisite documents for the commencement of assessment) in order to obtain orders, e.g. delays in service etc.

9 The Commercial [Taxing] Master may, in the exercise of his discretion as to the costs of the assessment, take into account a written offer made "without prejudice save as to the costs of the assessment" and received more than 21 days prior to the date of the assessment hearing provided that the same has not been communicated to him until the question of the costs of the assessment proceedings falls to be decided.

10 For the avoidance of doubt, nothing in this Appendix shall abrogate or otherwise affect the powers or discretion of the Commercial [Taxing] Master.

11 In relation to the abridged assessment of costs procedure, the Commercial [Taxing] Master's decision shall be final.

12 This abridged assessment of costs procedure shall be available for use, by consent, in relation to the assessment of costs of arbitration and ADR, although an order of the Court constituting the necessary taxing instrument will be required.

APPENDIX 17

SERVICE OUT OF THE JURISDICTION: RELATED PRACTICE

Service out of the jurisdiction without permission

D2–546 1 Before issuing a claim form or seeking permission to serve out of the jurisdiction, it is necessary to consider whether the jurisdiction of the English Courts is affected by the Civil Jurisdiction and Judgments Act 1982. Where each claim in the claim form is a claim which the Court has by virtue of the Civil Jurisdiction and Judgments Act 1982 power to hear and determine, service of the claim form out of the jurisdiction may be effected without permission provided that the requirements of RSC O.11 r. 1(2) are satisfied and the claim form is endorsed before issue with a statement that the Court has power under the Act to hear and determine the claim against the defendant, and that no proceedings involving the same claim are pending between the parties in Scotland, Northern Ireland or another convention country; care must be taken to see that the statement is endorsed only when the statement is correct.

Application for permission: affidavit or witness statement

D2–547 2 On applications for permission under O.11 r. 1(1), the affidavit or witness statement required by O.11 r.4 must, amongst other things:

2.1 identify the paragraph or paragraphs of O.11 r. 1(1) relied on as giving the Court jurisdiction to order service out, together with a summary of the facts relied on as bringing the case within each such paragraph;

2.2 state the belief of the deponent that there is a good claim and state in what place or country the defendant is or probably may be found;

2.3 summarise the considerations relied upon as showing that the case is a proper one in which to subject a party outside the jurisdiction to proceedings within it;

2.4 draw attention to any features which might reasonably be thought to weigh against the making of the order sought;

2.5 state the deponent's grounds of belief and sources of information;

2.6 exhibit copies of the documents referred to and any other significant documents.

Application for permission: copies of draft order

D2–548 3 The documents submitted with the application must include a two copies of a draft of the order sought, which should also state the time for acknowledgement of service which is applicable in accordance with any applicable Practice Direction.

Application for permission: copy or draft of claim form

4 A copy or draft of the claim form which it is sought to issue and serve must be provided for the Judge to initial. It should be remembered that if the endorsement to the claim form includes causes of action or claims not covered by the grounds on which permission to serve out of the jurisdiction can properly be granted, permission will be refused unless the draft is amended to restrict it to proper claims. Where the application is for the issue of a concurrent claim form, the documents submitted must also include a copy of the original claim form. **D2–549**

Arbitration matters

5 Service out of the jurisdiction in arbitration matters is governed by the Arbitration Practice Direction. As to the 1968 Convention on Jurisdiction in the context of arbitration, see Article 1(4). **D2–500**

APPENDIX 18

SECURITY FOR COSTS: RELATED PRACTICE

First applications

1 First applications for security should not be made later than at the Case Management Conference and in any event any application should not be left until close to the trial (or other relevant hearing) date. Delay to the prejudice of the other party or the administration of justice will probably cause the application to fail, as will any use of the application to harass the other party. Where it is intended to make an application for security at the Case Management Conference the procedure, and timetable for evidence, for an ordinary application must be followed (see paragraph F4 of the Guide). **D2–551**

Successive applications

2 Successive applications for security can be granted where the circumstances warrant. If a claimant wishes to seek to preclude any further application it is incumbent on him to make that clear. **D2–552**

Evidence

3 An affidavit or witness statement in support of an application for security for costs should deal not only with the residence of the claimant (or other respondent to the application) and the location of his assets but also with the actual practical difficulties (if any) of enforcing an order for costs against him. **D2–553**

Investigation of the merits of the case

4 Investigation of the merits of the case on an application for security are strongly discouraged in the Commercial Court. Only in those cases where it can be shown without detailed investigation of evidence or law that the claim is certain or almost certain to fail will submissions as to the merits be entertained. **D2–554**

Undertaking by the applicant

5 In appropriate cases an order for security for costs may only be made on terms that the applicant gives an undertaking to comply with any order that the Court may make if the Court later finds that the order for security for costs has caused loss to the claimant and that the claimant should be compensated for such loss. Such undertakings are intended to compensate claimants in cases where no order for costs is ultimately made in favour of the applicant. **D2–555**

Stay of proceedings

6 In the Commercial Court it is not usually convenient or appropriate to order an automatic stay of the proceedings pending the provision of the security. It leads to delay and may disrupt the preparation of the case for trial, or other hearing. Experience shows that it is usually better to give the claimant (or other relevant party) a reasonable time within which to provide the security and the other party liberty to apply to the Court in the event of default. This enables the Court to put the claimant to his election and then if appropriate, to dismiss the case. **D2–556**

Amount of security

7 Where the dispute on an application for security for costs relates to the correct evaluation of the amount of costs likely to be allowed to a successful defendant on an assessment of costs, parties should consider whether it would be advantageous for the Judge hearing the application to sit with a [Taxing] Master as an informal assessor. The Judge himself may take such an initiative. **D2–557**

8 Applications of this type will be comparatively rare because disputes on amount more usually depend upon such matters as predicting the likely length of the trial or what expert evidence will be required; in deciding such matters the Judge will not need the assistance of an assessor. When an application is believed to be suitable for the involvement of an assessor, it is important that the parties communicate that fact to the Court as soon as possible after the issue of the application and in any event well before any return date.

APPENDIX 19

ARBITRATION MATTERS: RELATED PRACTICE

Generally

D2–558 1 The procedure to be used in arbitration matters differs according to whether or not the Arbitration Act 1996 applies to the arbitration matter to be raised. The 1996 Act applies in general to all arbitrations commenced on or after 31st January 1997 and to applications to the court made on or after that date in respect of arbitrations yet to be commenced.

2 Part I of the Arbitration Practice Direction applies to arbitration matters covered by the 1996 Act, whereas Part II of the Arbitration Practice Direction applies to matters covered by the Arbitration Acts 1950, 1975 and 1979. Part III of the Arbitration Practice Direction relates to enforcement of arbitration awards and contains a procedural regime of universal application regardless of the date when the arbitration was commenced.

3 The Commercial Court will continue to have primary responsibility for the administration and monitoring of the supervisory jurisdiction over arbitration and awards under the 1996 Act. Although such applications can be made not only in the Commercial Court but also in the Mercantile Courts, and the Business Lists at the Central London County Court or elsewhere, the decision whether to retain the application in a Mercantile List or Business List or to transfer it to the Commercial Court or to some other court is to be taken by the Mercantile Judge or Business List Judge, but in consultation with the Judge in charge of the Commercial List.

4 In giving effect to the 1996 Act and to the Arbitration Practice Direction the Judges of the Commercial Court will endeavour as far as possible to achieve consistency in matters of construction both of the Act and of the Arbitration Practice Direction. In order to facilitate consistency of approach, arrangements have been made for decisions on matters of construction and application to be circulated between the Judges immediately they are given. Members of the profession who identify particular problems in the working of the Arbitration Practice Direction are strongly encouraged to bring them to the attention of the Judge in charge of the Commercial List to enable the Judges to carry out their function of monitoring the effective working of the 1996 Act and the Arbitration Practice Direction.

Commencement

D2–559 5 In respect of arbitrations to which the 1996 Act does not apply arbitration matters are normally raised in proceedings commenced by an arbitration claim form under CPR Part 8 (paragraphs 24–25 of the Arbitration Practice Direction), or in some cases by an application notice (paragraph 25(3) of the Arbitration Practice Direction).

6 In respect of arbitrations to which the 1996 Act does apply arbitration matters are raised in proceedings commenced by an arbitration claim form in the required practice form. The same practice form is used as the application notice for applications under section 9 of the 1996 Act to stay legal proceedings (paragraph 6 of the Arbitration Practice Direction).

7 The required practice form is to be used for all applications in respect of arbitration to which the 1996 Act applies except enforcement and including applications to stay judicial proceedings, to determine issues as to jurisdiction, to enforce peremptory orders, to make orders in support of arbitral proceedings, to challenge awards on the grounds of want of jurisdiction or serious irregularity and including appeals on a question of law arising out of an award. The form is also to be used at the permission to appeal stage under section 69 of the 1996 Act.

8 Applications for permission to enforce an award (whether under the 1996 Act or not) are made by an arbitration claim form in the required practice form: paragraph 31 of the Arbitration Practice Direction.

Progress

D2–560 9 In arbitration matters it is the particular duty of the Court to see that court proceedings are not a cause of delay.

10 A hearing date must (where applicable) be applied for promptly after the issue of the required practice form (whether serving as an arbitration claim form or an application notice) or after obtaining permission to appeal under the Arbitration Acts 1979 and 1996.

11 The duty to apply promptly for a date for hearing exists even if the case may be transferred to the Chancery Division or to the Technology and Construction Court or to a Mercantile Court or Business List. The duty to act promptly persists after transfer.

12 A failure to act with all deliberate speed founds the Court's discretion to strike out. When it comes to the attention of the Court that delay is occurring, the Court may itself direct that the matter be listed for hearing.

Directions under Part I of the Arbitration Practice Direction

13 Paragraph 13 of the Arbitration Practice Direction contains a comprehensive series of directions relating to arbitration applications under Part I of the Arbitration Practice Direction. These directions will apply automatically unless the Court otherwise orders. The Judges of the Commercial Court will require strict compliance with these directions except with the permission of the Court. Parties who do not comply will risk the dates for hearings being vacated and/or adverse costs orders. D2–561

Requirements on applications by way of appeal under s.1(2) of the 1979 Act

14 For applications by way of appeal under s.1(2) of the 1979 Act please see paragraph 27 of the Arbitration Practice Direction, in particular at (6) to (9). Paragraphs 15 to 18 below amplify the practice. D2–562

15 Every arbitration application form used to appeal against an arbitration award under s.1(2) of the 1979 Act shall contain a succinct statement in numbered paragraphs of each ground upon which it is sought to contend that the arbitral tribunal erred in law. Reference shall be made to the paragraph or passage of the award and reasons where each alleged error is to be found. A copy of the award and reasons forming part of the award and any documents expressly incorporated in the award or such reasons shall accompany the arbitration application form when the same is issued unless the appeal arises from a minor part only of the award and reasons in which case the relevant extracts shall accompany the arbitration claim form.

16 Any respondent to an application by way of appeal under s.1(2) of the 1979 Act who contends that the award should be upheld on grounds not or not fully expressed in the award and reasons should provide to the applicant and to the Court not later than two clear days before the application for permission to appeal is listed for argument a succinct statement of such grounds in numbered paragraphs, with reference where appropriate to any relevant paragraphs or passage of the award and reasons.

17 Any statement provided under paragraphs 15 and 16 should contain specific reference to any authority relied on. A copy should be provided with the statement of any authority not contained in the Law Reports, the Weekly Law Reports, the All England Law Reports, Lloyd's Law Reports or the English Reports.

18 Where the applicant contends that any question of law arising out of an award concerns a term of contract or an event which is not a one-off clause or event, he shall serve on the respondent with his application and lodge with the Court an affidavit or witness statement setting out the facts relied on in support of his contention. A respondent who challenges that contention shall provide to the applicant and to the Court, not later than two days before the application is listed for argument, an affidavit or witness statement setting out the facts upon which he relies.

Evidence on applications for permission to enforce an award

19 Applications for permission to enforce an award must be supported by affidavit or witness statement (see paragraph 31 of the Arbitration Practice Direction) and two copies of a draft order must be provided. Care must be taken to see that the affidavit or witness statement and the draft order meet the requirements of the rule. D2–563

Determination of applications

20 For applications for permission to appeal under the 1979 Act there will be a hearing but it will not be expected to last more than half an hour. Any permission to appeal may be given on terms; these may restrict the points on which permission to appeal is given or require the provision of security etc. For the hearing of the substantive appeal the parties are expected to lodge skeleton arguments in the same way as for other contested hearings. D2–564

21 For applications for permission to appeal under the 1996 Act there will normally be no oral hearing of the application, unless the Court considers that one is required as provided by section 69(5) of the 1996 Act.

22 Substantive appeals and preliminary points of law are heard in public unless otherwise ordered.

23 All other arbitration applications are heard in private unless the Court orders that the hearing be in public.

Service on overseas parties and service out of the jurisdiction

24 For arbitration applications under Part I of the Arbitration Practice Direction, where an D2–565

overseas party has been represented by an English solicitor who was authorised to accept service of notices or documents in the arbitration and has not determined that solicitor's authority to act in the arbitration, the arbitration claim form can, with the Court's authorisation, be served on that solicitor and it will be unnecessary to obtain permission to serve the party outside the jurisdiction (see paragraph 7(2) of the Arbitration Practice Direction).

25 Service out of the jurisdiction is covered by paragraph 8 of the Arbitration Practice Direction (1996 Act arbitrations) and paragraph 29 of the Arbitration Practice Direction (1950–1979 Act arbitrations).

Security for costs

D2–566 26 The matters stated in Appendix 18 to the Commercial Court Guide are applicable to applications under section 12(6) of the Arbitration Act 1950 for the Court to exercise its power, for the purpose of and in relation to a reference, to make an order that a claimant give security for costs.

Multiple applications

D2–567 27 Where applications are being made to set aside or remit under the 1950 Act and for permission to appeal under the 1979 Act the Court may direct that one application be heard before the other or that they may be heard together if that is appropriate. Multiple relief applications under the 1996 Act will be similarly dealt with.

APPENDIX 20

TRANSITIONAL ARRANGEMENTS

General

D2–568 1. The Practice Direction supplementing CPR Part 51 ("the Transitional Arrangements Practice Direction") will apply to proceedings in the Commercial Court, subject to:

a. any order made by a Commercial Judge;
b. the provisions set out below.

Resolving points of doubt over applicability of CPR or RSC

D2–569 2. Where the parties are in doubt whether the CPR (and related Practice Directions) or the RSC (and related practice) apply they may refer the point to the Court. In the first instance the point should be raised by letter addressed to the Clerk to the Commercial Court, who will refer it to the Judge in Charge of the Commercial List. In an appropriate case it may be necessary for there to be a short informal hearing before the Judge in Charge of the Commercial List. If the point is a complex one, or one of some potential general importance or application, the Judge in Charge of the Commercial List may require that the point be raised by an application commenced by an application notice.

Applications made on and after 26 April 1999 in existing proceedings

D2–570 3. As contemplated by paragraph 14 of the Transitional Arrangements Practice Direction, all applications made on and after 26 April 1999 in existing proceedings (as defmed by the Transitional Arrangements Practice Direction) should nonetheless be made by application notice and in accordance with Section F of the Guide and CPR Part 23. However for applications in existing proceedings of a minor nature and estimated to last 30 minutes or less, it will not be obligatory for a case management bundle (with enclosed case memorandum and list of issues) to be prepared for the application if one does not already exist.

4. It should be noted that paragraph 14(2) to (4) of the Transitional Arrangements Practice Direction apply only where the application is made (i.e. the application notice is received by the Court: CPR 23.5) on or after 26 April 1999, and not to an application issued under the RSC before 26 April 1999 but not yet heard. For an application issued under the RSC before 26 April 1999 but not yet heard see paragraph 15(3) of the Transitional Arrangements Practice Direction, and the treatment of the summons for directions at paragraph 5 below.

Case Management Conferences in existing proceedings

D2–571 5. Where in existing proceedings a summons for directions under the RSC has been issued but not heard before 26 April 1999, the hearing will be treated as a Case Management Conference. Where a summons for directions would, but for the CPR, have been issued and heard after 26 April 1999 a Case Management Conference is to be convened instead.

6. The Judge in Charge of the Commercial List, or any other Commercial Judge, may require a plaintiff (claimant) to take steps to convene a Case Management Conference in any existing proceedings at any stage.

7. Where one or more of the parties is of the view that, despite the fact that directions given under or automatically applying under the RSC have still to be complied with, existing proceedings are at a stage where a Case Management Conference would be useful they should

liaise with the Listing Office in order to convene one. Until the Case Management Conference can be heard the parties should continue to follow the directions given under or applying under the RSC.

8. The critical area on the transition from RSC to CPR is in the matter of discovery/disclosure. Discovery comes before the summons for directions under the RSC but disclosure comes after the Case Management Conference under the CPR. The general rule for the transition is that given by paragraph 6(1) of the Transitional Arrangements Practice Direction, namely that where automatic discovery under RSC Ord. 24 has begun to apply before 26 April 1999 such automatic directions will continue to apply after 26 April 1999. However in the Commercial Court discovery may be so critical an area that the question of how it is to proceed in a complex claim needs to be considered carefully at an early stage. The parties should give careful consideration to whether in such cases a Case Management Conference should be convened at an early time in order that directions as to how (among other things) disclosure should proceed can be given.

9. For any Case Management Conference in existing proceedings, a case memorandum, list of issues and case management bundle will be required in accordance with the Guide. The contents of the case management bundle should follow the list at paragraph D6.2 of the Guide as closely as the circumstances permit.

First time before a Judge on or after 26 April 1999

10. Subject to any order to the contrary, paragraph 15(1) and (2) of the Transitional Arrangements Practice Direction will not apply where the existing proceedings come before a Commercial Judge on an application estimated to last 30 minutes or less. This is because there is unlikely to be enough time to deal satisfactorily with all of the matters there specified (for the proceedings as a whole) without some risk to the efficient conduct of the Court's business. On such an application the Commercial Judge may however direct that a Case Management Conference is to be convened, and at and from that Case Management Conference the provisions of paragraph 15(1) and (2) of the Transitional Arrangements Practice Direction will apply. **D2–572**

11. On the first occasion that existing proceedings come before a Judge on or after 26 April 1999 the parties should be in a position to advise the Judge how much progress has been made towards carrying out the next stage or stages required (whether by the RSC or by order) to be carried out. This will assist the Judge in deciding (as appropriate) whether a Case Management Conference should be convened or at what point the CPR (and related Practice Directions) should start to apply to the proceedings as a whole (for the application or other hearing itself, see paragraphs 15(3) and (4) of the Transitional Arrangements Practice Direction). For example, if substantial work has been undertaken in preparing to give discovery under the RSC the Court may decide that discovery should be completed under the RSC before the CPR start to apply.

Stay of proceedings

12. Paragraph 7(5) of the Transitional Arrangements Practice Direction applies to proceedings in the Commercial List subject to the modification that for existing proceedings the period of 6 months provided by CPR 15.11(1)(a) shall be treated as commencing on 26 April 1999. **D2–573**

Other matters

13. Paragraph 16 of the Transitional Arrangements Practice Direction does not apply to proceedings in the Commercial List. **D2–574**

ADDRESSES AND CONTACT DETAILS

D2–575

The Admiralty & Commercial Registry:	Room E200 Royal Courts of Justice Strand London WC2A 2LL Tel: 0171 936 6112 Fax: 0171 936 6245 DX 44450 STRAND
The Commercial Court Listing Office:	Room E201 Royal Courts of Justice Strand London WC2A 2LL Tel: 0171 936 6826 Fax: 0171 936 6245 DX 44450 STRAND
The Secretary to the Commercial Court Committee:	Mrs Maureen Myers Room E201 Royal Courts of Justice Strand London WC2A 2LL

	Tel: 0171 936 6826 Fax: 0171 936 6245 DX 44450 STRAND
Out of hours emergency number (security office at Royal Courts of Justice):	0171 936 6000
Fax number for the procedure under paragraph B3.11 of the Guide for the issue of claim forms when the Registry is closed	0171 936 6667

THE MERCANTILE COURTS GUIDE

Contents D3–001

THE MERCANTILE COURTS GUIDE

The Guide

1.1 This Guide to the practice of the Mercantile Courts is issued with the approval of the Head of Civil Justice pursuant to paragraphs 5.5 and 5.6 of the Mercantile Courts & Business Lists Practice Direction. D3–002

1.2 It applies to proceedings in any Mercantile Court. D3–003

1.3 It is concerned mainly with case management, but also with preparation for trial, and the conduct of trials, in Mercantile Courts. On matters not covered by the Guide reference should be made to the CPR and the Practice Directions supplementing the CPR. D3–004

Case Management

2. All cases proceeding in a Mercantile Court will be subject to case management by the court. D3–005

3. The case management procedures set out in CPR Part 29 (except for rules 29.2(1), 29.3(1), 29.6 and 29.8) and its accompanying Practice Direction (except for paragraphs 1, 2, 3.1 to 3.3, 4.1 and 4.3–4.5) apply to proceedings in Mercantile Courts. The management procedures set out in this Guide complement those management procedures. D3–006

4.1 A **case management conference** will be held at which the court will give directions for the conduct of the case—normally through to trial, including the fixing of a trial date or for the taking of steps to fix the trial date. D3–007

4.2 If a case management conference has not been held earlier, the claimant must apply to the mercantile listing officer within 14 days of the service of the defence or defences, (or, if there is a counterclaim, of the service of the defence to counterclaim),or within 14 days after the expiry of the time for service, to fix a date for a case management conference. Before applying the claimant should consult with the other parties as to any dates to be avoided and the time likely to be required for the hearing. D3–008

4.3 The date given for the case management conference will normally be within 4 weeks (or less) of the date on which the application to fix a date was made.

4.4 If the claimant fails to apply for a date for the case management conference to be fixed, it is the duty of the other parties to do so. D3–009

4.5 The claimant (or other applicant for the date of the conference to be fixed) shall supply to the court not less than 7 days before the date a file (**the Case Management File**) containing: D3–010

- an index,
- the claim form,
- the statements of case (excluding schedules of more than 15 pages in length),
- any orders already made,

- a short and uncontroversial summary of what the case is about (case summary)—see paragraph 5.7 of the Part 29 Practice Direction,
- a list of issues if this is appropriate given the complexity of the case.

D3–011 4.6 Not less than 7 days before the date of the case management conference each party shall provide to the court a **case management information sheet** in the form set out in the Appendix hereto, and shall provide copies to the other parties.

D3–012 4.7 The claimant or other party who has applied for the date shall also at the same time provide to the court and the other parties a draft order setting out the directions which that party considers appropriate. A standard form of order is contained in the Appendix hereto.

D3–013 4.8 Where any other party intends to apply for a direction of which it is helpful to give specific notice beyond that to be provided on the case management information sheet, that party shall give written notice of it to the court and to the other parties together with its case management information sheet.

D3–014 4.9 It shall be the duty of the parties to attend the case management conference by a representative who is properly familiar with the party's case for the purpose of the conference. If counsel has been instructed in the case but will not be appearing at the conference, the solicitor should discuss the case with him for the purpose of the conference (see CPR 29.3(2)).

D3–015 4.10 Any party may by written request to the judge ask that the case management conference be held earlier than provided for above, stating the reasons.

D3–016 4.11 The court will on its own initiative arrange a case management conference if at any time it appears appropriate.

D3–017 4.12 At the conference the court may fix a progress monitoring date or dates and make provision for the court to be informed as to the progress of the case at the date or dates fixed. On receipt of such information the court may, if it seems appropriate, or if no or insufficient information is provided, arrange a further case management conference with a view to making such further orders as may be necessary.

D3–018 4.13 In straightforward cases the parties may submit agreed directions not less than 7 days in advance of the conference for the approval of the judge. The judge may then make the directions proposed, or he may make them with alterations, or he may require the case management conference to proceed. The parties must assume that the conference will proceed until informed by the court that it is not required (see also paragraph 4.6 of the Part 29 Practice Direction).

D3–019 4.14 Where the case has been transferred to the mercantile list after the date for applying for a case management conference in accordance with paragraph 4.2 above has passed, and the court has not given directions when making the order for transfer (as provided for at paragraph 3.3 of the Mercantile & Business Lists Practice Direction), the case must be listed for a case management conference on the earliest possible date. It is the duty of the claimant, or, in default, of the other parties, to apply for a date.

The Case Management File

D3–020 5.1 Paragraph 4.5 above provides for the provision to the court of a **case management file**.

D3–021 5.2 At the conclusion of any hearing the court may retain the case management file or it may return it to the party providing it (normally the claimant).

D3–022 5.3 Where the file is retained by the court, it is the duty of the claimant to update the case management file as the case proceeds so that its contents will provide an up-to-date picture of the progress of the case.

D3–023 5.4 When any other hearing is to take place, it is the duty of the claimant (or of the party who has applied for the hearing) to provide the court with a file appropriate for the hearing to the court not less than 7 days before the hearing. This may be done by up-dating and adding to the case management file, or by providing a fresh file containing only those documents required for the hearing. Where a hearing is to take place before the first case management conference, an appropriate file shall be similarly provided.

D3–024 5.5 All notices of hearings issued by the court (other than of trials) will have attached a notice as follows:

> "Paragraphs 4.5 and 5 of the Mercantile Courts Guide require the provision to the court of an appropriate file for any hearing 7 days before the hearing. Failure to comply with this direction may result in the hearing being adjourned at the expense of the party in default. Where a case management file has been retained by the court, this file may be added to to provide the file for the hearing."

Time Estimates

D3–025 6.1 The provision of accurate and up-to-date estimates is essential for the efficient management of court time. Failure may result in disruption to the disadvantage of the parties and to other court users. The court will normally take steps to protect the interests of the other court users.

D3–026 6.2 **Case management conferences and applications**. The claimant or other party applying to the court for a date for a hearing must provide an estimate of the time required. The estimate should normally have been discussed with the other parties. If it appears to any party that the estimate is, or has become, too short or too long, that party shall communicate with the other parties and then with the court.

D3–027 6.3 **Trials**. It is the duty of the parties' representatives (solicitors and counsel) to keep under review any estimates given to the court of the likely length of the trial, and to arrange for the court to be informed if they change. This should not be left to the pre-trial review.

Pre-trial Reviews and Pre-trial Check Lists

7.1 At the first case management conference or at any time thereafter the court may provide for the holding of a **pre-trial review**. D3–028

7.2 Not less than 7 days before the date of the review each party shall provide to the court a completed **pre-trial check list** in the form set out in the Appendix hereto, and shall provide copies to the other parties. D3–029

7.3 The parties should, if possible, be represented at the review by the advocates who will be appearing at the trial. Where the action is not complex and is plainly in good order for trial, the advocate for trial need not appear where, for example, by reason of travel unjustified expense would be incurred. Any representatives appearing must be fully informed for the purposes of the review. D3–030

7.4 At the pre-trial review the court will give such directions as may be appropriate: D3–031

- for the further preparation of the case for trial,
- as to the conduct of the trial.

7.5a Where no pre-trial review has yet been provided for, each party shall provide to the court a completed **pre-trial check list** in the form set out in the Schedule hereto not less than 6 weeks before the trial date, and shall provide copies to the other parties. D3–032

7.5b The court will then consider whether a pre-trial review should be held or, if it considers that in the circumstances no hearing is necessary, may give directions as at 7.4 of its own motion. D3–033

Timetables

8. The court may fix, or may require the parties to provide, a **timetable** for the trial, providing for speeches and for each witness to be heard within the period set aside for the trial. D3–034

Variations by agreement

9. CPR 2.11 provides that, subject to the Rules, a Practice Direction or court order, the time specified by a rule or by the court for a person to do any act may be varied by the written agreement of the parties. A party must apply to the court if he wishes to vary the date fixed for: D3–035

(a) a case management conference;

(b) a pre-trial review;

(c) the filing of a case management check-list, progress monitoring information, a pre-trial check list;

(d) the trial, or the trial priod.

(2) Parties may not vary by agreement the time set for any step in the proceedings where that would jeopardise the proper preparation of the case for trial commencing on the trial date.

Where parties vary by agreement the time set for any step in the proceedings, the claimant (or by agreement another party) must write to the court informing it:

(a) of the agreed variation;

(b) of the reason why it was necessary;

(c) as to the effect of the variation on the preparation of the case for trial commencing on the trial date.

Any variation made by agreement is subject to any subsequent order.

Orders

10.1 Unless the court otherwise orders, all orders made in a Mercantile Court are to be drawn up in draft by the parties (compare CPR 40.3). D3–036

10.2 The claimant shall be responsible for preparing the draft and submitting it to the court for sealing, unless the order was made on the application of another party who shall then be responsible. The draft must be submitted within 3 clear days of the decision, with an appropriate number of copies allowing for one to be retained by the court. The sealed orders will be returned to the party submitting the draft, who shall be responsible for service of the order on the other parties. D3–037

10.3 Orders shall be dated with the date of the decision save for consent orders submitted for approval, which shall be left undated. D3–038

Experts

11.1 The provisions of CPR 35 and the Practice Direction supplementing it apply to proceedings in Mercantile Courts save that paragraphs 1.2(7) and 1.3 are replaced by paragraph 11.2 below. D3–039

11.2 At the end of the expert's report there must be a statement that: D3–040

(a) the expert understands his duty to the court and has complied with that duty (see CPR 35.10(2);

(b) the expert has read and understood Part B to the Appendix to this Guide (which is in the same form as Appendix 12 to the Commercial Court Guide);

(c) he has complied, and will continue to comply, with Part B at all stages of his involvement in the case;

(d) the assumptions on which his opinion is based are not in his opinion unreasonable or unlikely assumptions (or, where in his opinion any assumption is unreasonable or unlikely, that is clearly stated);

(e) the facts stated in his report that are facts within his own direct knowledge have been identified as such and are true;

(f) the opinions expressed in his report represent his true professional opinion.

Speeches at trial

D3–041 12.1 Subject to directions given in the particular case, the practice at trials in Mercantile Courts is as follows.

D3–042 12.2 The opening speech should be no longer than the circumstances require and should not normally develop submissions. Other advocates may be invited to make brief opening statements, outlining or clarifying their positions, based on their skeleton arguments. The prolonged reading out of documents in court will be avoided.

D3–043 12.3 Parties may normally assume that the judge will have read the statements of case and orders, the witness statements and experts reports, any file of core documents and the skeleton arguments; likewise documents included in any short reading list.

D3–044 12.4.a The advocate for the claimant will make the first closing speech. It is then that submissions on fact and law should be fully developed.

D3–045 12.4.b The advocate for the defendant will make the second closing speech.

D3–046 12.4.c The advocate for the claimant will make the final speech. This is by way of reply to the defendant's speech and is not a repetition of points made in the claimant's first closing speech.

D3–047 12.5 The use of skeleton arguments in conjunction with closing speeches will depend on the circumstances. They will often be helpful, in particular where there are complex issues of fact or issues of law.

APPENDIX A(1)

CASE MANAGEMENT INFORMATION SHEET
MERCANTILE COURTS

D3–048 [Title of Case]

[This information sheet must be lodged with Mercantile Listing at least 7 days before the Case Management Conference, and copies supplied to all other parties: see paragraph 4.6 of the Mercantile Courts Guide.]

D3–049 Party lodging:
Solicitors:
Advocate(s) for trial
Date:

Substance of case

D3–050 1. What in about 20 words maximum is the case about?
Please provide a separate concise list of issues in a complex case.

Parties

D3–051 2. Are all parties still effective?
3. Do you intend to add any further party?

Statements of Case

D3–052 4. Do you intend to amend your statement of case?
5. Do you require any "further information" – CPR 18?

Disclosure

D3–053 6. By what date can you give standard disclosure?
7. Do you contend that to search for any type of document falling within CPR 32.6(b) would be unreasonable within CPR 31.7(2); if so, what type and on what grounds?

8. Is any specific disclosure required – CPR 31.12?
9. Is a full disclosure order appropriate?
10. By what date could you give (1) any specific disclosure referred to at 3. (2) give full disclosure?
11. Is a full disclosure order appropriate?
12. By what date could you give full disclosure?

Admissions

13. Can you make any additional admissions? D3–054

Preliminary issues

14. Are any issues suitable for trial as preliminary issues? D3–055
If yes, which?

Witness of fact

15. On how many witnesses of fact do you intend to rely at the trial (subject to the court's direction)? D3–056
16. Please name them, or explain why you do not.
17. Which of them will be called to give oral evidence?
18. When can you serve their witness statements?
19. Will any require an interpreter?

Expert evidence

20. Are there issues requiring expert evidence? D3–057
21. If yes, what issues?
22. Might a joint single expert be suitable on an issues (see CPR 35.7)?
23. What experts do you intend (subject to the court's direction) to call? Please give the number, their names and expertise.
24. By what date can you serve signed expert reports?
25. Should there be meetings of experts of like disciplines, of all disciplines? By when?
26. Which experts, if any, do you intend not to call at the trial?
27. Will any require an interpreter?

Trial

28. What are the advocates' present estimates of the length of the trial? D3–058
29. What is the earliest date that you think the case can be ready for trial?
30. Where should the trial be held?
31. Is a Pre-Trial Review advisable?

A.D.R.

32. Might some form of Alternative Dispute Resolution assist to resolve the dispute or some part of it? D3–059
33. Hs this been considered with the client?
34. Has this been considered with the other parties?
35. Do you want the case to be stayed pending A.D.R. or other means of settlement – see CPR 26.4; or any other directions relating to A.D.R.?

Other applications

36. What applications, if any, not covered above, will you be making at the conference? D3–060

Costs

37. What, do you estimate, are your costs to date? D3–061
38. What, do you estimate, will be your costs to end of trial?

[Signature of party/solicitor]

APPENDIX A(2)

STANDARD DIRECTIONS IN MERCANTILE COURTS

D3–062 [Title of action with Judge's name]

Order for Directions
(made on

1. Standard disclosure is to be made by [..............].
Inspection on 48 hours notice to be completed by [..............].

2. Signed statements of witnesses of fact and hearsay notices when required by CPR 33.2 are to be exchanged not later then [..............].

Unless otherwise ordered, the witness statement shall stand as the evidence in chief of the witness at trial.

3. Each party shall have leave to call at the trial expert witnesses as follows:

Number	Expertise	Issue(s) to be covered

whose reports shall have been exchanged by [..............].

4. Experts of like disciplines shall meet without prejudice to identify the issues between them and to attempt to reach agreement on such issues, and shall prepare a joint statement pursuant to CPR 35.12(3), by [..............].

5. The action shall be tried in [..............] by judge alone, estimated length .... days, [commencing on ....] [not before ....
[The claimant shall apply to the mercantile listing officer to fix a date for the trial, no later than ...., and shall have available inconvenient dates for all parties.]

6. Signed pre-trial check lists to be filed and served by [..............] [not less than 7 days before the pre-trial review].

7. There be a pre-trial review on [..............].

8. Trial bundles shall be agreed, prepared and delivered to counsel not less than .... before the trial date, and to the court not less than ....

9. Costs in the cause.

DATED

APPENDIX A(3)

PRE-TRIAL CHECK LIST MERCANTIL COURTS

D3–063 [Title of Action]

Where a Pre-trial Review has been ordered, this check list must be lodged with Mercantile Listing at least 7 days before the Pre-trial Review, and copies supplies to all other parties.

Where a Pre-trial Review has not been ordered, it must be lodged not less than 6 weeks the trial date and copies supplied to all other parties.

See paragraphs 5.5(2) and 5.6 of the Mercantile Courts Practice Direction.

D3–063A a. Trial Date:
b. Whether Pre-trial Review ordered:

c. Date of Review:
d. Party lodging:
e. Solicitors:
f. Advocate(s) for trial:
g. Date lodged:

[Note: this checklist should normally be completed with the inovolvement of the advocate(s) instructed for trial.]

1. Have all the directions made to date been carried out? D3–064
2. If not, what remains to be carried out? When will it be carried out?
3. Do you intend to take any further steps regarding:
 a. statements of case?
 b. disclosure?
 c. witnesses and witness statements?
 d. experts and expert reports?

If yes in any case, what and by when?

4. Will the preparation of trial bundles be completed not later than 3 weeks before the date fixed for trial?

If not, what is the position?

5. What witnesses of fact do you intend to call? D3–065
6. (Where directions for expert evidence have been given) what experts do you intend to call?
7. Is any interpreter needed; for whom?
8. If a Pre-trial Review has not been ordered, do you think one would be useful?
9. What are the advocate(s)' confirmed estimates of the minimum and maximum lengths of the trial? A confirmed estimate signed by the advocate(s) and dated must be attached.

10. a. Might some form of alternative dispute resolution now assist? D3–066
 b. Has the question been considered with the client?
 c. Has the question been explored with the other parties to the case?

[Signature of party/solicitor]

APPENDIX B

EXPERT EVIDENCE IN THE MERCANTILE COURTS

[This incorporates the text of Appendix 12 from the Commercial Court Guide, with references to the Mercantile Courts substituted for references to the Commercial Court.] D3–067

Part 1: General

1. It is the duty of an expert to help the Court on the matters within his expertise (CPR 35.3(1)). D3–068
This duty is paramount and overrides any obligation to the person from whom the expert has received instructions or by whom he is paid (CPR 35.3(2)).

2. Expert evidence presented to the Court should be, and should be seen to be, the independent product of the expert uninfluenced by the exigencies of litigation.

3. An expert witness should provide independent assistance to the Court by way of objective unbiased opinion evidence in relatin to matters within his expertise. An expert witness should never assume the role of an advocate.

4. An expert witness should state the facts or assumptions on which his opinion is based. (In the Mercantile Courts this requirement takes the place of the requirement at CPR 35.10(3) that the expert's report state the substance of all material instructions). If any of the facts stated are within his own direct knowledge he should make clear which those are. If a stated assumption is in the opinion of the expert witness unreasonable or unlikely he should state that clearly.

5. An expert witness should not omit to consider material facts which could detract from his concluded opinion.

6. An expert witness should make it clear when a particular question or issue falls outside his expertise.

7. If an expert's opinion is not properly researched because he considers that insufficient data is available, then this must be stated with an indication that the opinion is no more than a provisional one.

8. An expert may file with the Court a written request for directions to assist him in carrying out his function as expert, but:

8.1 at least 7 days before he does so (or such shorter period as the Court may direct) he should provide a copy of his proposed request to the party instructing him;

8.2 at least 4 days before he does so (or such shorter period as the court may direct) he should provide a copy of his proposed request to all other parties.
(In the Mercantile Courts this paragraph takes the place of CPR 35.14. This is in order to reduce the risk of an expert accidentally informing the Court about, or about matters connected with, communications or potential communications between the parties that are without prejudice or privileged. The expert may properly be privy to the content of these communications because he has been asked to assist the party instructing him to evaluate them. Paragraph 8 does not prevent the expert from filing a request for directions, but ensures that one or other party can approach the Court first if the request proposed by the expert would result in his informing the Court about, or about matters connected with, communications or potential communications that are without prejudice or privileged.)

D3–069 **Part 2: Reports**

9. An expert's report must:
9.1 be addressed to the Court;
9.2 give details of the expert's qualifications;
9.3 state clearly the questions or issues with which he is dealing in his report;
9.4 give details of any literature or other material on which the expert has relied in making the report;
9.5 say who carried out any test or experiment which the expert has used for the report and whether or not the test or experiment has been carried out under the expert's supervision;
9.6 give the qualifications of the person who carried out any such test or experiment;
9.7 Where there is a range of opinion on the matter dealt with in the report:
(a) summarise the range of opinion, and
(b) give reasons for his own opinion;
9.8 give a summary of the conclusions reached.
10. Where an expert refers to photographs, plans, calculations, analyses, measurements, survey reports or other similar documents, and any unpublished sources relied on, these must be provided to all parties at the same time as the report.
11. It is useful if a report contains a glossary of significant technical terms.
12. At the end of the report there must be a statement that:
12.1 the expert understands his duty to the Court aned has complied with that duty (see CPR 35.10(2));
12.2 the expert has read and understood Part B to the Appendix to the Mercantile Courts Guide, 'Expert evidence in the Mercantile Courts';
12.3 he has complied with and will continue to comply with Part B at all stages of his involvement in the case;
12.4 the assumptions on which his opinion is based are not in his opinion unreasonable or unlikely assumptions (or, where in his opinion any assumption is unreasonable or unlikely, that is clearly stated);
12.5 the facts stated in his report that are facts within his own direct knowledge have been identified as such and are true;
12.6 the opinions expressed in his report represent his true professional opinion.
(In the Mercantile Courts the requirement for a statement in the more specific terms indicated above replaces the requirement for a statement of truth in the terms provided by paragraph 1.4 of the Practice Direction supplementing CPR Part 35 (cf. paragraph 1.3 of the Practice Direction Supplementing CPR Part 22). As with any document verified by a statement of truth, proceedings for contempt of court may be brought against a person if he makes, without an honest belief in its truth, a false statement in an expert's report verified by a statement in the more specific terms indicated above.)
13. The report must be signed by the expert.
14. In a case where an expert witness who has prepared a report could not assert that the report contained the truth, the whole truth and nothing but the truth without some qualification, that qualification should be stated in the report.
15. If, after an exchange of reports, an expert witness changes his view on a material matter having read another expert's report or for any other reason, such change of view should be communicated in writing (through legal representatives) to the other side without delay, and when appropriate to the Court.

D3–070 **Part 3: Meetings**

16. The purposes of meetings of experts are to give experts the opportunity:
16.1 to discuss the expert issues;
16.2 to decide, with the benefit of that discussion, on which expert issues they share the same expert opinion and on which expert issues there is a difference of expert opinion between them (and what that difference is).
(In the Mercantile Courts this description of the purpose of meetings takes the place of the description at CPR 35.12(1).)

17. The content of the discussion between the experts at or in connection with a meeting is without prejudice, and in particular (in accordance with CPR 35.12(4)) shall not be referred to at the trial unless the parties agree.

18. Subject to any directions of the Court, the procedure to be adopted at these meetings is a matter for the experts, not the parties or their legal representatives.

19. Neither the parties nor their legal representatives should seek to restrict the freedom of experts to identify and acknowledge the expert issues on which they agree (i.e. on which they share the same expert opinion) at (or following further consideration after) the meetings of experts.

20. At or following their meetings the experts should prepare a joint memorandum for the Court recording:

20.1 the fact that they have met and discussed the expert issues;

20.2 the expert issues on which they agree (i.e. on which they share the same expert opinion);

20.3 the expert issues on which there is a difference of expert opinion between them, and a summary of what that difference of expert opinion is.

(In the Mercantile Courts this automatic requirement applies notwithstanding the Court's powers under CPR 35.12(3).)

21. Where experts reach agreement on an expert issue during (or following further consideration after) their meetings the agreement shall not bind the parties unless the parties expressly agree to be bound by the agreement.

22. Following the preparation of the joint memorandum each expert may prepare a short supplemental report highlighting the reasons why the expert adheres to the views he does on the expert issues recorded in the memorandum as being issues where there is a difference of expert opinion.

PATENTS COURT GUIDE

D4–001 This is an explanation of the modern practice in the Patents Court for the conduct of patent actions. The general guidance applicable to all matters in the Chancery Division, as set out in the *Chancery Guide*, also apply to patent actions unless specifically mentioned below. The words "Practice Direction" refer to the *Practice Direction—Patents etc.* which supplements CPR Part 49 and replaces, with modifications, RSC Order 104, Order 100, and Order 93, and CCR Order 48A and Order 49A.

General

D4–002 1. All actions proceeding in the Patents Court are allocated to the multi-track (see Practice Direction paragraph 2.4). In actions proceeding in the Patents Court, dates will continue to be fixed by the Clerk in charge of the Patents list. The present practice of fixing only on "setting down" is obsolete, and it will be possible to fix at any time. The Court will expect the trial date to be fixed at the hearing of the first Case Management conference, at which the directions for conduct of the case to trial will be given. Paragraph 2.5 of the Practice Direction states when the application for directions is to be made: in summary, the application is to be made 14 days from the filing of the Defence or acknowledgement of service, whichever it the earlier. Note that the Practice Direction requires that a Defence in which invalidity is alleged is to be served within 42 days of service of the Claim and normally no acknowledgement of service will be required if that time limit is met.

Before issuing an application notice the applicant should apply to the Clerk in Charge of the Patents Courts List for a return date.

Clerk in Charge of the Patents List

D4–003 2. The clerk to one of the principal assigned patent judges will be in charge of the patents list. Until further notice the clerk in charge of the *patents list* will be the clerk to Laddie J. He is located in Room TM 7.02 in the Royal Courts of Justice. He can be contacted there or by telephone (0171 936 6518) or fax (0171 936 6439).

Short Applications

D4–004 3. These will normally be listed for hearing at 9.30 a.m. Parties should liaise with the clerk in charge of the patent list. In addition to these arrangements, the Court will make available a two hour slot from 9.00 a.m. to 11.00 a.m. on Tuesday mornings so as to speed up the hearing and disposition of slightly more lengthy applications. Parties and their representatives will be expected to continue to assist the Court to dispose efficiently of business. In the case of any of the applications referred to in this paragraph, the parties must provide to the Court by not later than 4.00 p.m. on the preceding working day all necessary documents and skeleton arguments. They should also provide drafts of any Order which the Court will be invited to make. It is important for the Court to be provided with accurate estimates of duration so that, where possible, more than one application can be listed for hearing. Parties will be kept to their estimates and, where necessary to achieve this, guillotines are likely to be imposed on oral submissions.

September sittings

D4–005 4. The Patents Court will sit in September.

Appeals from the Comptroller

D4–006 5. These are governed by the Practice Direction. The Practice Direction refers to the "Clerk or other person in charge of the Patents list". This is the clerk referred to in paragraph 2 above. The appellant has the conduct of the appeal and he or his representative should within two weeks of lodging the appeal contact the clerk in charge of the Patents Court List with a view to arranging a date for a hearing. Any party appealing from a decision of the Comptroller shall ensure that the appeal is set down as soon as reasonably practical after service of the notice of appeal. Parties are reminded that the provisions relating to the service of skeleton arguments set out in the Chancery Guide apply to appeals from the Comptroller.

Applications without notice

D4–007 6. A party wishing to apply without notice to the respondent(s) should contact the Clerk in Charge of the Patents Court List, or in his absence the clerk to Pumfrey J (0171-936 7482, fax 0171-936 6593) or in his absence Chancery Listing. In cases of emergency in vacation or out of normal court hours the application should be made to the duty Chancery Judge.

Documents

D4–008 7. (a) If it is known which judge will be taking the case, papers for the case should be lodged directly with that judge's clerk. Faxed documents of significance (and particularly skeleton arguments) should be followed up by clean direct prints.

(b) It is the responsibility of both parties to any applications to the Patents Court to ensure that all relevant documents are lodged with the Clerk of the Judge who will be taking the case by noon two days before the date fixed for hearing unless some longer or shorter period has been ordered by the judge or is prescribed by this Guide.

(c) The judges request that all important documents also be supplied to them on disk in a format convenient for the judge's use (normally Microsoft Word 6 for Windows). These will include skeleton arguments, the witness statements and expert reports.

(d) Bundling is of considerable importance and should be approached intelligently. The general guidance given in the Chancery Guide should be followed, though where documents bear their own internal numbering and are within a tabbed file, the whole file need not be paginated.

Simplified Trial

8. Attention is drawn to the ability and willingness of the Patents Court to hear actions on written evidence, if that is the wish of the parties. It is suggested that in appropriate cases solicitors acting for one of the parties should, after close of pleadings, write to the solicitors acting for the other party requesting agreement to a "Simplified Trial". That letter should point out that refusal may be brought to the attention of the judge after judgment and could result in an adverse order on costs. **D4–009**

If the parties agree to a Simplified Trial, one of them should within 14 days after close of pleadings apply for directions which should include:

(1) the filing of evidence by witness statement,

(2) the trial to be heard on written evidence alone,

(3) limitation of experts,

(4) setting down.

If agreed directions are sought, no attendance at Court is necessary.

A Simplified Trial would not be suitable where cross-examination is likely on any issue of substance nor where any substantial disclosure is needed.

Reading Guide and Time estimates

9. Judges hearing patent actions will normally read the basic documents in the action before the action is called on for trial in accordance with the Reading Guide provided by the parties (see below). The documents read will rarely include disclosed documents. **D4–010**

A party applying for a date for a patent action must lodge a certificate stating the estimated length of the trial and an estimate of the time needed for the judge to read the documents. The certificate should also identify in general terms the area of technology and include an assessment of the complexity of the technical issues involved indicated on a scale of 1 to 5 (1 is easiest and 5 is most complex).

Not less than 1 week before commencement of the trial, each party must lodge a certificate stating the estimated length of its oral submissions, its examination in chief (if any) of its own witnesses and its cross-examination of witnesses of any other party.

The documents in the form to be used at trial must be lodged by the claimant's solicitors at least four days before the date for trial together with a "Reading Guide" for the judge.

The "Reading Guide" should be short, non-contentious and if possible agreed. It should not contain argument. It should shortly set out the issues, the parts of the documents that need to be read on each issue and the most convenient order that they should be read. If thought appropriate, the relevant passages in text books and cases should be referred to.

Parties are reminded of the court's power to limit the duration of submissions and cross-examination. This power will be exercised in any case where it is considered that a case is not being conducted with reasonable expedition.

Narrowing of issues

10. As early as possible the patentee should identify which of the claims of its patent are contended to have independent validity and which of those claims are said to be infringed and should communicate a list of those claims to the other party. This position should be kept under constant review. If there is any reduction or increase in the number of claims said to have independent validity the patentee must forthwith notify the other parties. **D4–011**

Admissions

11. With a view to early elimination of non-issues, practitioners are reminded of the necessity of making admissions in accordance with CPR Rule 32.18 at an early stage. This may be done even without waiting for a notice to admit facts. It can be done as early as in a defence or reply. For instance in a defence a party may admit the acts complained of or that his article/process has certain of the features of a claim. In a reply a patentee may be able to admit prior publication of cited documents. **D4–012**

The notice to admit facts required by the Practice Direction may also include a request to identify points not in dispute. Technically a request seeking admissions in respect of particular integers of a claim may involve a mixed question of fact and law and so not be within the rule. By asking whether or not the defendant disputes that his article/process has certain features of the claim the real dispute can be narrowed. Thus the ambit of disclosure and of witness and expert statements will be narrowed.

Documents referred to in statements of case

12. It is desirable that copies of documents referred to in a statement of case (*e.g.* **D4–013**

advertisements referred to in Particulars of Infringements or documents cited in Particulars of Objections) are served with the statement of case. Where any such document requires translation, a translation should be served at the same time.

Skeleton arguments, pre-trial and post evidence

D4–014 13. In addition to the Reading Guide parties should lodge skeleton arguments in time for the judge to read them before trial. That should normally be at least two days before commencement of the trial, but in substantial cases a longer period (to be discussed with the clerk to the judge concerned) may be needed. It is desirable that each party should summarise what it contends to be the common general knowledge of the man skilled in the art.

Following the evidence in a substantial trial a short adjournment may be granted to enable the parties to summarise their arguments in writing before oral argument.

In trials where a transcript of evidence is being made and supplied to the judge, the transcript should be accompanied by a version on disk.

Jurisdiction of Masters

D4–015 14. All applications in a patent application should be brought directly by application notice before the Patents Court, save that (i) consent orders (ii) orders on applications for extension of time (iii) applications for leave to serve out of the jurisdiction and (iv) applications for security for costs may be heard by a Master. However if a matter which a Master may hear is anticipated to be substantial it should normally be taken direct to a patent judge. Further, if a Master is of the view that any application requires the attention of the Patents Court, then he will adjourn the application to come on before the Patents Court.

Agreed Orders

D4–016 15. The court is normally willing to make consent orders without the need for the attendance of any parties. A draft of the agreed order and the written consent of all the parties' respective solicitors or counsel should be supplied to the Clerk in charge of the Patents List. Where a draft has been substantially amended by hand, it is helpful for a disk of the unamended version to be supplied in accordance with [*insert reference*] of the Chancery Guide. Unless the judge considers a hearing is needed he will make the order in the agreed terms by initialling it. It will be drawn up accordingly and sent to the parties. This procedure applies to all orders.

Telephone Applications

D4–017 16. For short (20 minutes or less) matters before the Patents Court, the patents judges are willing, unless a matter of general public importance is involved, to hear applications by telephone conference in accordance with the Practice Direction under CPR Part 23.

It is possible for the application to be recorded, and if recording by the Patents Court rather than by British Telecom (or other service provider) is requested arrangements should be made with the Clerk in charge of the Patents list. The recording will not be transcribed. The tape will be kept by for a period of six months. Arrangements for transcription, if needed, must be made by the parties.

This procedure may be used for most short disputed matters. The parties should use it where it will save costs. The procedure is not a substitute for the even cheaper procedure of an agreed order.

Case Management conferences and Pre-trial reviews in patent actions

D4–018 17. At present, there is no experience of the use of Pre-trial reviews or of case management conferences in patent actions, but it is expected that the case management conference will resemble the current application for directions, but with substantially more judicial input. Attention is drawn to CPR Rule 29.4 (Agreed proposals for the management of the proceedings).

Patents judges able and willing to sit out of London

D4–019 18. If the parties so desire, for the purpose of saving time or costs, the Patents Court will sit out of London. If such a sitting is desired a request should be made in the first instance to the Clerk in charge of the Patents list whether the matter is proceeding in a district registry or in London.

Intellectual Property Court Users' Committee

D4–020 19. This considers the problems and concerns of intellectual property litigation generally. Membership of the committee includes the principal patent judges, a representative of each of the Patent Bar Association, the Intellectual Property Lawyers Association, the Chartered Institute of Patent Agents, the Institute of Trade Mark Agents and the Trade Marks Designs and Patents Federation. It will also include one or more other Chancery judges. Anyone having views concerning the improvement of intellectual property litigation is invited to make his or her views known to the committee, preferably through the relevant professional representative on the committee.

Orders following judgment

D4–021 20. Where a judgment is made available in draft before being given in open court and it is desired to ask the court for an order when judgment is given, the parties should, in advance of that occasion, exchange drafts of the desired consequential order. It is highly undesirable that one party should spring a proposal on the other for the first time when judgment is given.

Applications for interim remedies: trial dates

21. When an application for an interim remedy is made the claimant should, where practicable make prior inquiries and investigations as to the estimated length of trial and possible trial dates. **D4–022**

Specimen minute of order for directions

22. The general form minute of order for directions annexed to this Practice Direction has the approval of the Patents Judges. It is intended only as a guide and may need adaptation for particular circumstances. **D4–023**

Standard Form Minute of Order for Directions

(* indicates a provision which may be necessary when a rule has not been compiled with, for example, standard disclosure in accordance with the Practice Direction) **D4–024**

[RECITALS AS NECESSARY]

Transfer

1. [This Action and Counterclaim be transferred to the Patents County Court.] (*If this order is made, no other Order will generally be necessary, though it may be desirable for procedural orders to be made at this time to save the costs of a further conference in the County Court.*) **D4–025**

Proof of Documents

2. Legible copies of the specification of the Patent in suit [and any patent specifications or other documents cited in the Particulars of Objections] may be used at the trial without further proof thereof or of their contents. **D4–026**

Amendments to Pleadings

3. The Claimants have leave to amend their Particulars of Claim [and Particulars of Infringement] as shown in red on the copy [annexed to the Application Notice/as signed by the solicitors for the parties/annexed hereto] and [to re-serve the same on or before [*date*]/and that re-service be dispensed with] and that the Defendants have leave to serve a consequentially amended Defence within [*number*] days [thereafter/hereafter] and that the Claimants have leave to serve a consequentially amended Reply (if so advised) within [*number*] days thereafter. **D4–027**

4. (a) The Defendants have leave to amend their Defence [and Counterclaim and Particulars of Objections] as shown in red on the copy [annexed to the Application notice/as signed by the solicitors for the parties/annexed hereto] and [to reserve the same within [*number*] days/on or before [*date*]] [and that re-service be dispensed with] and that the Claimants have leave to serve a consequentially amended Reply (if so advised) within [*number*] days thereafter.

(b) The Claimants do on or before [*date*] elect whether they will discontinue this Claim and withdraw their Defence to Counterclaim and consent to an Order for the revocation of Patent No. [*NUMBER*] ("the patent in suit") AND IF the Claimants shall so elect and give notice thereof in the time aforesaid IT IS ORDERED THAT the patent in suit be revoked [and that it be referred to the costs officer to assess the costs of the Defendants and this Action and Counterclaim up to and including [*date*] being the date of delivery of the [amended] Particulars of Objections and Counterclaim to the date of this Order [except so far as the same have been increased by the failure of the Defendants originally to deliver the Defence and Counterclaim in its amended form], and to assess the costs of the Claimants in this Action and Counterclaim from [*date*] [insofar as they have been increased by the failure of the Defendants aforesaid] AND IT IS ORDERED that the said costs officer is to set off the costs of the Defendants and of the Claimants when so assessed as aforesaid and to certify to which of them the balance after such set-off is due.]/[*Order for payment of sums determined by the Court on a summary assessment*]

Further Information and Clarification

5. (a) The [Claimants/Defendants] do on or before [date] serve on the [Defendants/ **D4–028**

Claimants] the Further Information or Clarification of the [*specify Statement of case*] as requested by the [Claimants/Defendants] by their Request served on the [Defendants/Claimants] on [date] [and/or]

(b) The [Claimants/Defendants] do on or before [date] serve on the [Defendants/Claimants] a response to their Request for Further Information or Clarification of the [*identify statement of case*] served on the [Defendants/Claimants] on [*date*].

Admissions*

D4–029 6. The [Claimants/Defendants] do on or before [*date*] state in writing whether or not they admit the facts specified in the [Defendants'/Claimants'] Notice to Admit facts dated [*date*].

Security

D4–030 7. The Claimants do provide security for the Defendants' costs in the sum of £[*state sum*] by [*specify manner in which security to be given*] and that in the meantime all further proceedings be stayed.

Lists of Documents*

D4–031 8.(a) The Claimants and the Defendants respectively do on or before [*state date*] make and serve on the other of them a list in accordance with form N265 of the documents in their control which they are required to disclose in accordance with the obligation of standard disclosure as modified by the Practice Direction—Patents etc. in accordance with CPR Part 31

(b) In respect of those issues identified in Schedule [*number*] hereto disclosure shall be limited to those [documents/categories of documents] listed in Schedule [*number*].

Inspection*

D4–032 9. If any party wishes to inspect or have copies of such documents as are in another party's control it shall give notice in writing that it wishes to do so and such inspection shall be allowed at all reasonable times upon reasonable notice and any copies shall be provided within [*number*] working days of the request upon the undertaking of the party requesting the copies to pay the reasonable copying charges.

Experiments*

D4–033 10.(a) Where a party desires to establish any fact by experimental proof, including an experiment conducted for the purposes of litigation or otherwise not being an experiment conducted in the normal course of research, that party shall on or before [*date*] serve on all the other parties a notice stating the facts which it desires to establish and giving full particulars of the experiments proposed to establish them.

(b) A party upon whom a notice is served under the preceding subparagraph shall within [*number*] days serve on the party serving the notice a notice stating in respect of each fact whether or not that party admits it.

(c) Where any fact which a party wishes to establish by experimental proof is not admitted that party shall apply to the Court for further directions in respect of such experiments.

[Or where paragraph 10 of the Practice Direction has been complied with.]

D4–034 10.(a) The Claimants/Defendants are to afford to the other parties an opportunity, if so requested, of inspecting a repetition of the experiments identified in paragraphs [*specify them*] of the Notice[s] of Experiments served on [*date*]. Any such inspection must be requested within [*number*] days of the date of this Order and shall take place within [*number*] days of the date of the request.

(b) If any party shall wish to establish any fact in reply to experimental proof that party shall on or before [*date*] serve on all the other parties a notice stating the facts which it desires to establish and giving full particulars of the experiments proposed to establish them.

(c) A party upon whom a notice is served under the preceding subparagraph shall within [*number*] days serve on the party serving the notice a notice stating in respect of each fact whether or not that party admits it.

(d) Where any fact which a party wishes to establish by experimental proof in reply is not admitted the party may apply to the Court for further directions in respect of such experiments.

Notice of Models, etc.

D4–035 11.(a) If any party wishes to rely at the trial of this action upon any model, apparatus, drawing, photograph, cinematograph or video film whether or not the same is contained in a witness statement, affidavit or expert's report that party shall on or before [*date*] give notice thereof to all the other parties; shall afford the other parties an opportunity within [*number*] days of the service of such notice of inspecting the same and shall, if so requested, furnish the other party with copies of any such drawing or photograph and a sufficient drawing photograph or other illustration of any model or apparatus.

(b) If any party wishes to rely upon any such materials in reply to any matter of which notice was given under sub-paragraph (a) of this paragraph, that party shall within [*number*] days after the last inspection to be made in pursuance of the said sub-paragraph (a) give to the other parties a like notice, and if so requested within [*number*] days of delivery of such notice shall afford like opportunities of inspection which shall take place within [number] days of such request; and shall in like manner furnish copies of any drawing or photograph and illustration of any such model or apparatus.

(c) No further or other model apparatus drawing photograph cinematograph or video film shall be relied upon in evidence by either party save with consent or by leave of the Court.

Written evidence

12. (a) Each party may call up to [*number*] expert witnesses in this Action and Counterclaim provided that the said party: **D4–036**

(i) supplies the name of such expert to the other parties and to the Court on or before [*date*]; and

(ii) no later than [*date*/ [*number* days] before the date set for the hearing of this Action and Counterclaim] serve upon the other parties a report of each such expert comprising the evidence which that expert intends to give at trial.

(b) Each party shall on or before [*date*] serve on the other parties [*signed*] written statements of the oral evidence which the party intends to lead on any issues of fact to be decided at the trial, such statements to stand as the evidence in chief of the witness unless the Court otherwise directs;

(c) The parties shall [*here insert the particular directions sought, e.g. within 21 days after service of the other party's expert reports and written statements state in writing the facts and matters in those reports and statements which are admitted*].

Admissibility of evidence

13. A party who objects to any statements of any witness being read by the judge prior to the hearing of the trial, shall serve upon each other party a notice in writing to that effect setting out the grounds of the objection. **D4–037**

Non-compliance

14. Where either party fails to comply with the directions relating to experiments and written evidence it shall not be entitled to adduce evidence to which such directions relate without the leave of the Court. **D4–038**

Trial Bundles

15. Each party shall no later than [*number*] days before the date fixed for the trial of this Action and Counterclaim serve upon the parties a list of all the documents to be included in the trial bundles. The Claimants shall no later than [*number*] days before the date fixed for trial serve upon the Defendants an index of the bundles for use at trial. **D4–039**

Trial

16. The trial of these proceedings shall be before an Assigned Judge alone in [London], estimated length [*number*] days and a pre-reading estimate for the judge of [*number*] days. **D4–040**

Liberty to Apply

17. The parties are to be at liberty on two days' notice to apply for further directions and generally. **D4–041**

Costs

18. The costs of this Application are to be costs in the Action and Counterclaim. **D4–042**

SECTION E

FEES ORDERS

CONTENTS

THE SUPREME COURT FEES ORDER 1999

(S.I. 1999 No. 687) E1–001

8th March 1999	– – –	*8th March 1999*
11th March 1999		*11st March 1999*
26th April 1999		*26th April 1999*

The Lord Chancellor, in exercise of the powers conferred on him by section 130 of the Supreme Court Act 1981, sections 414 and 415 of the Insolvency Act 1986, and section 128 of the Finance Act 1990, with the concurrence of the Lord Chief Justice, the Master of the Rolls, the President of the Family Division, the Vice-Chancellor and the Treasury under section 130(2) of the Supreme Court Act 1981, and with the sanction of the Treasury under sections 414(1) and 415(1) of the Insolvency Act 1986, makes the following Order:

Citation and commencement

1. This Order may be cited as the Supreme Court Fees Order 1999 and shall come into force on 26th April 1999. E1–002

Interpretation

2. In this Order, unless the context otherwise requires— E1–003

(a) a fee referred to by number means the fee so numbered in Schedule 1 to this Order;
(b) "the CPR" means the Civil Procedure Rules 1998; and
(c) expressions also used in the CPR have the same meaning as in those Rules.

Fees to be taken

3. The fees set out in column 2 of Schedule 1 to this Order shall be taken in the Supreme Court in respect of the items described in column 1 in accordance with and subject to the directions specified in column 1. E1–004

4. The provisions of this Order shall not apply to— E1–005

(a) non-contentious probate business;
(b) proceedings in the Court of Protection, except in so far as any fee prescribed in section 1 of Schedule 1 is applicable;
(c) the enrolment of documents;
(d) criminal proceedings (except proceedings on the Crown side of the Queen's Bench Division to which the fees contained in Schedule 1 are applicable);
(e) proceedings by sheriffs, under-sheriffs, deputy-sheriffs or other officers of the sheriff; and
(f) family proceedings.

Exemptions, reductions and remissions

5.—(1) No fee shall be payable under this Order by a party who, at the time when a fee would otherwise become payable— E1–006

(a) is in receipt of any qualifying benefit, and
(b) is not in receipt of representation under Part IV of the Legal Aid Act 1988 for the purposes of the proceedings.

(2) The following are qualifying benefits for the purposes of paragraph (1)(a) above—

(a) income support;

(b) family credit and disability working allowance under Part VII of the Social Security Contributions and Benefits Act 1992; and

(c) income-based jobseeker's allowance under the Jobseekers Act 1995.

E1–007 **6.** Where it appears to the Lord Chancellor that the payment of any fee prescribed by this Order would, owing to the exceptional circumstances of the particular case, involve undue financial hardship, he may reduce or remit the fee in that case.

E1–008 **7.** Where by any convention entered into by Her Majesty with any foreign power it is provided that no fee shall be required to be paid in respect of any proceedings, the fees specified in this Order shall not be taken in respect of those proceedings.

Revocations

E1–009 **8.** The Orders specified in Schedule 2 shall be revoked, except as to any fee or other sum due or payable under those Orders before the commencement of this Order.

SCHEDULE 1

FEES TO BE TAKEN

E1–010

Column 1 Number and description of fee	*Column 2* Amount of fee
Section 1. Fees payable in the High Court only	
1. Commencement of proceedings	
1.1 On the commencement of originating proceedings (including originating proceedings issued after leave to issue is granted) to recover a sum of money, where the sum claimed:	
(a) does not exceed £50,000	£300
(b) exceeds £50,000 or is not limited	£400
1.2 On the commencement of originating proceedings for any other remedy or relief (including originating proceedings issued after leave to issue is granted)	£120
Fees 1.1 and 1.2 Recovery of land or goods Where a claim for money is additional or alternative to a claim for recovery of land or goods, only fee 1.2 shall be payable.	

Column 1 Number and description of fee	*Column 2* Amount of fee
Fees 1.1 and 1.2 Claims other than recovery of land or goods Where a claim for money is additional to a non money claim (other than a claim for recovery of land or goods) then fee 1.1 shall be payable in addition to fee 1.2. Where a claim for money is alternative to a non money claim (other than a claim for recovery of land or goods), only fee 1.1 shall be payable.	
Fees 1.1 and 1.2 Generally Where more than one non money claim is made in the same proceedings, fee 1.2 shall be payable once only, in addition to any fee which may be payable under fee 1.1.	
Fees 1.1 and 1.2 shall not be payable where fee 1.5(b) or fee 6 apply	
Fees 1.1 and 1.2 Amendment of claim or counterclaim Where the claim or counterclaim is amended, and the fee paid before amendment is less than that which would have been payable if the document, as amended, had been so drawn in the first instance, the party amending the document shall pay the difference.	
1.3 On the filing of proceedings against a party or parties not named in the originating proceedings	£30
Fee 1.3 shall be payable by a defendant who adds or substitutes a party or parties to the proceedings or by a claimant who adds or substitutes a defendant or defendants.	
1.4 On the filing of a counterclaim	The same fee as if the relief or remedy sought were the subject of separate proceedings
1.5(a) On an application for leave to issue originating proceedings	£30
(b) On an application for an order under Part III of the Solicitors Act 1974 for the assessment of costs payable to a solicitor by his client	£30

Column 1 Number and description of fee	*Column 2* Amount of fee
2. General Fees	
2.1 On the claimant filing an allocation questionnaire; or • where the court dispenses with the need for an allocation questionnaire, within 14 days of the date of despatch of the notice of allocation to track; or • where the CPR or a Practice Direction provide for automatic allocation or provide that the rules on allocation shall not apply, within 28 days of the filing of the defence (or the filing of the last defence if there is more than one defendant), or within 28 days of the expiry of the time permitted for filing all defences if sooner Fee 2.1 shall be payable by the claimant except where the action is proceeding on the counterclaim alone, when it shall be payable by the defendant— • on the defendant filing an allocation questionnaire; or • where the court dispenses with the need for an allocation questionnaire, within 14 days of the date of despatch of the notice of allocation to track; or • where the CPR or a Practice Direction provide for automatic allocation or provide that the rules on allocation shall not apply, within 28 days of the filing of the defence to the counterclaim (or the filing of the last defence to the counterclaim if there is more than one party entitled to file a defence to a counterclaim), or within 28 days of the expiry of the time permitted for filing all defences to the counterclaim if sooner	£80
2.2 On the claimant filing a listing questionnaire; or	£400

Column 1 Number and description of fee	*Column 2* Amount of fee
• where the court fixes the trial date or trial week without the need for a listing questionnaire, within 14 days of the date of despatch of the notice (or the date when oral notice is given if no written notice is given) of the trial week or the trial date if no trial week is fixed	
Fee 2.2 shall be payable by the claimant except where the action is proceeding on the counterclaim alone, when it shall be payable by the defendant—	
• on the defendant filing a listing questionnaire; or	
• where the court fixes the trial date or trial week without the need for a listing questionnaire, within 14 days of the date of despatch of the notice (or the date when oral notice is given if no written notice is given) of the trial week or the trial date if no trial week is fixed	
Where the court receives notice in writing—	
• before the trial date has been fixed or,	
• where a trial date has been fixed, at least 7 days before the trial date,	
from the party who paid fee 2.2 that the case is settled or discontinued, fee 2.2 shall be refunded.	
Fees 2.1 and 2.2 Generally Fees 2.1 and 2.2 shall be payable once only in the same proceedings.	
Fees 2.1 and 2.2 shall be payable as appropriate where the court allocates a case to a track for a trial of the assessment of damages.	
Fee 2.1 shall not be payable where the procedure in Part 8 of the CPR is used.	

Column 1 Number and description of fee	*Column 2* Amount of fee
2.3 Where no other fee is specified, on filing a notice of appeal (including an appeal against an allocation decision), or a case stated or a special case for the opinion of the High Court pursuant to statute, or a notice of cross appeal, or a respondent's notice of appeal	£100
2.4 On an application on notice where no other fee is specified	£50
2.5 On an application by consent or without notice for a judgment or order where no other fee is specified	£25
For the purpose of fee 2.5 a request for a judgment or order on admission or in default shall not constitute an application and no fee shall be payable.	
2.6 On an application for a summons or order for a witness to attend court to be examined on oath, other than an application for which fee 3.2 is payable	£30
2.7 On an application to vary a judgment or suspend enforcement (where more than one remedy is sought in the same application only one fee shall be payable)	£25
3. Enforcement	
3.1 On sealing a writ of execution/possession/delivery	£20
Where the recovery of a sum of money is sought in addition to a writ of possession and delivery, no further fee is payable.	
3.2 On an application to question a judgment debtor or other person on oath in connection with enforcement of a judgment.	£40
3.3 On an application for a garnishee order nisi or a charging order nisi, or the appointment of a receiver by way of equitable execution	£50
Fee 3.3 shall be payable in respect of each party against whom the order is sought.	

Column 1 Number and description of fee	*Column 2* Amount of fee
3.4 On an application for a judgment summons	£80
3.5 On a request or application to register a judgment or order, or for leave to enforce an arbitration award, or for a certified copy of a judgment or order for use abroad	£30
4. Miscellaneous proceedings or matters	
Bills of Sale	
4.1 On filing any document under the Bills of Sale Acts 1878 and 1882	£10
Searches	
4.2 For an official certificate of the research of a search for each name, in any register or index held by the court; or in the Court Funds Office, for an official certificate of the result of a search of unclaimed balances for a specified period of up to 50 years.	£5
4.3 On a search in person of the bankruptcy and companies records, including inspection, for each 15 minutes or part of 15 minutes	£5
Judge sitting as arbitrator	
4.4 On the appointment of—	
(a) a judge of the Commercial Court as an arbitrator or umpire under section 93 of the Arbitration Act 1996; or	£1,800
(b) a judge of the Technology and Construction Court as an arbitrator or umpire under section 93 of the Arbitration Act 1996	£1,400
4.5 For every day or part of a day (after the first day) of the hearing before—	
(a) a judge of the Commercial Court; or	£1,800
(b) a judge of the Technology and Construction Court, so appointed as arbitrator or umpire	£1,400

Column 1 Number and description of fee	*Column 2* Amount of fee
Where fee 4.5 has been paid on the appointment of a judge of the Commercial Court or a judge of the Technology and Construction Court or a judge of the Technology and Construction Court as an arbitrator or umpire but the arbitration does not proceed to a hearing or an award, the fee shall be refunded.	
5. Fees payable in Admiralty Matters In the Admiralty Registrar and Marshal's Office—	
5.1 On the issue of a warrant for the arrest of a ship or goods	£100
5.2 On the sale of a ship or goods— subject to a minimum fee of £200,	
(a) for every £100 or fraction of £100 of the price up to £100,000	£1
(b) for every £100 or fraction of £100 of the price exceeding £100,000	50p
Where there is sufficient proceeds of sale in court, fee 5.2 shall be taken by transfer from the proceeds of sale in court.	
5.3 On entering a reference for hearing by the Registrar	£50
6. Companies Act 1985 and Insolvency Act 1986	
6.1 On entering a bankruptcy petition:	
(a) if presented by a debtor or the personal representative of a deceased debtor	£120
(b) if presented by a creditor or other person	£150
6.2 On entering a petition for an administration order	£100
6.3 On entering any other petition	£150
One fee only is payable where more than one petition is presented in relation to a partnership.	

Column 1 Number and description of fee	*Column 2* Amount of fee
6.4(a) On a request for a certificate of discharge from bankruptcy	£50
(b) and after the first certificate for each copy	£1
Requests and applications with no fee No fee is payable on a request or on an application to the Court by the Official Receiver when applying only in the capacity of Official Receiver to the case (and not as trustee or liquidator), or on an application to set aside a statutory demand.	
Section 2. Fees payable in both the High Court and in the Court of Appeal	
7. Copy Documents	
7.1 On a request for a copy of any document (including a faxed copy where requested) or for examining a plain copy and marking it as an office copy:	
(a) per page for the first five pages of each document	£1
(b) per page for subsequent pages	25p
Fee 7.1 is payable whether or not the copy is issues as an office copy.	
7.2 Where copies of any document are made available on a computer disk or in other electronic form, for each such copy	£3
8. Affidavits	
8.1 On taking an affidavit or an affirmation or attestation upon honour in lieu of an affidavit or a declaration except for the purpose of receipt of dividends from the Accountant General and for a declaration by a shorthand writer appointed in insolvency proceedings	
—for each person making any of the above	£5
8.2 For each exhibit referred to in an affidavit, affirmation, attestation or declaration for which fee 8.1 is payable	£2

Column 1 Number and description of fee	*Column 2* Amount of fee
Section 3. Fees payable in the Court of Appeal only **9. Fees payable in appeals to the Court of Appeal**	
9.1 On filing a notice of appeal	£200
9.2 On filing a respondent's notice	£100
9.3 On filing any application notice	£100
Section 4. Fees payable on the determination of costs **10. Determination of costs**	
Transitional Provision	
Where a bill of costs or a request for detailed assessment or a request for a detailed assessment hearing is filed pursuant to an order made by the court before the coming into operation of this Order, or an application is made to review a taxing officer's decision made before the coming into operation of this Order, the fees payable shall be those which applied immediately before this Order came into force.	
10.1 On the filing of a request for detailed assessment where the party filing the request is legally aided and no other party is ordered to pay the costs of the proceedings	£120
10.2 On the filing of a request for a detailed assessment hearing in any case where fee 10.1 does not apply; or on the filing of a request for a hearing date for the assessment of costs payable to a solicitor by his client pursuant to an order under Part III of the Solicitors Act 1974	£160
10.3 On an application for the issue of a default costs certificate	£40
10.4 On an appeal against a decision made in detailed assessment proceedings or on an application to set aside a default costs certificate	£50
10.5 On applying for the court's approval of a Legal Aid Assessment Certificate	£20

Column 1 Number and description of fee	*Column 2* Amount of fee
Fee 10.5 is payable at the time of applying for the court's approval and is recoverable only against the Legal Aid Fund.	

SCHEDULE 2

ORDERS REVOKED

E1–011

Title	*Reference*
The Supreme Court Fees Order 1980	S.I. 1980/821
The Supreme Court Fees (Amendment) Order 1980	S.I. 1980/1060
The Supreme Court Fees (Amendment) Order 1982	S.I. 1982/1707
The Supreme Court Fees (Amendment) Order 1983	S.I. 1983/1680
The Supreme Court Fees (Amendment) Order 1986	S.I. 1986/637
The Supreme Court Fees (Amendment No. 2) Order 1986	S.I. 1986/2144
The Supreme Court Fees (Amendment) Order 1988	S.I. 1988/510
The Supreme Court Fees (Amendment) Order 1990	S.I. 1990/1460
The Supreme Court Fees (Amendment) Order 1993	S.I. 1993/3191
The Supreme Court Fees (Amendment) Order 1995	S.I. 1995/2629
The Supreme Court Fees (Amendment) Order 1996	S.I. 1996/3191
The Supreme Court Fees (Amendment) Order 1997	S.I. 1997/2672

EXPLANATORY NOTE

E1–012 *(This note is not part of the Order)*

This Order revokes the Supreme Court Fees Order 1980 and replaces it by specifying new fees for proceedings in the Supreme Court following the introduction of the Civil Procedure Rules 1998 which come into force on the same date as this Order.

In particular, the fee structure in this Order specifies fees payable at the two new stages of allocation and listing introduced by the Civil Procedure Rules. Where there are procedures similar to previous procedures, the fees have in most cases been increased.

The table of comparison below shows the comparison between the old fees and the new fees. The table also shows where new fees have been introduced.

TABLE OF COMPARISON

Number and summary of new fee (*for full description see Schedule 1*)	Amount of new fee (*for full details see Schedule 1*)	Amount of old fee	Number of old fee
Section 1. Fees payable in the High Court only			
1. Commencement of proceedings			
1.1 Money claim			
(a) not exceeding £50,000	£300	£120–500	1
(b) exceeds £50,000 or is not limited	£400	£120–500	1
1.2 Non money claim	£120	£50–120	1; 2
1.3 Filing proceedings against new party	£30	New fee	New fee
1.4 Filing counterclaim	same fee as originating proceedings	New fee	New fee
1.5 (a) Leave to issue originating proceedings	£30	New fee	New fee
(b) Application for assessment of costs under Solicitors Act	£30	£50	2(b)
2. General Fees			
2.1 On allocation	£80	New fee	New fee
2.2 On listing	£400	New fee	New fee
2.3 Appeal (other than in Court of Appeal)	£100	£50	9 and 11
2.4 Application on notice	£50	£30–50	5A; 5B
2.5 Application for order, no notice given	£25	£20–30	5AA; 5C
2.6 Witness summons	£30	£10	7
2.7 Application to suspend or vary judgment or order	£25	New fee	New fee
3. Enforcement			
3.1 Sealing a writ of execution/possession/delivery	£20	£20	12
3.2 Oral examination	£40	£35	14

Number and summary of new fee (*for full description see Schedule 1*)	Amount of new fee (*for full details see Schedule 1*)	Amount of old fee	Number of old fee
3.3 Garnishee order, charging order, appointment of receiver	£50	£60	13
3.4 Judgment summons	£80	£50	5B
3.5 Application to register a judgment or order	£30	£30	16(a)–(g); 17
4. Miscellaneous proceedings or matters			
Bills of Sale			
4.1 Filing any document under the Bills of Sale Acts	£10	£10	21(a); (b)
Searches			
4.2 For an official certificate of the result of a search	£5	£5	24(a); 28(a); (b)
4.3 Personal search in bankruptcy/companies records (per 15 minutes)	£5	£5	24(b)
Judge sitting as arbitrator			
4.4 Appointment as arbitrator or umpire of—			
(a) judge of the Commercial Court	£1,800	£1,800	25(a)(i)
(b) judge of the Technology and Construction Court	£1,400	£1,400	25(a)(ii)
4.5 for every day or part of a day (after the first day) of hearing			
(a) before a judge of the Commercial Court; or	£1,800	£1,800	25(b)(i)
(b) before a judge of the Technology and Construction Court	£1,400	£1,400	25(b)(ii)
5. Fees payable in Admiralty Matters			
5.1 On the issue of a warrant for the arrest of a ship or goods	£100	£100	26(a)
5.2 On the sale of a ship or goods (minimum fee £200);			
(a) for every £100 or fraction of £100 of the price up to £100,000	£1	£1	26(b)(i)
(b) for every £100 or fraction of £100 of the price over £100,000	50p	50p	26(b)(ii)

Number and summary of new fee (*for full description see Schedule 1*)	Amount of new fee (*for full details see Schedule 1*)	Amount of old fee	Number of old fee
5.3 On entering a reference for hearing by the Registrar	£50	£50	26(c)
6. Companies Act 1985 and Insolvency Act 1986			
6.1 On entering a bankruptcy petition:			
(a) if presented by a debtor or the personal representative of a deceased debtor	£120	£50	30(b)(i)
(b) if presented by a creditor or other person	£150	£80	30(b)(ii)
6.2 Petition for an administration order	£100	£120	30(c)
6.3 Any other petition	£150	£80	30(a)
6.4(a) Request for a certificate of discharge from bankruptcy	£50	New fee	New fee
(b) after the first certificate, for each copy	£1	New fee	New fee
Section 2. Fees payable in both the High Court and in the Court of Appeal			
7. Copy Documents			
7.1(a) Copy per page for the first five pages of each document	£1	£1	18(a)
7.1(b) Copy per page for subsequent pages	25p	25p	18(b)
7.2 Electronic copy	£3	New fee	New fee
8. Affidavits			
8.1 Taking an affidavit/affirmation or attestation	£5	£5	23(a)
8.2 For each exhibit referred to in an affidavit	£2	£2	23(b)
Section 3. Fees payable in the Court of Appeal only			
9. Fees payable in appeals to the Court of Appeal			
9.1 On filing a notice of appeal	£200	£200	27(a)
9.2 On filing a respondent's notice	£100	£150	27(b)
9.3 On filing any application notice	£100	£100	27(c)

Number and summary of new fee (*for full description see Schedule 1*)	Amount of new fee (*for full details see Schedule 1*)	Amount of old fee	Number of old fee
Section 4. Fees payable on the determination of costs **10. Determination of costs** Old fees apply where documents filed pursuant to a court order, or application made for review of taxing officer's decision, made before this Order came into force.			
10.1 Filing request for detailed assessment—legal aid only cases	£120	No specific fee	No specific fee
10.2 Filing request for detailed assessment hearing/request for hearing date for assessment under Part III Solicitors Act 1974	£160	scale fees (estimated average £720)	29(a); (b); (c); (d)
10.3 Issue of default costs certificate	£40	New fee	New fee
10.5 Applying for court's approval of a Legal Aid Assessment Certificate	£20	New fee	New fee

THE COUNTY COURT FEES ORDER 1999

(S.I. 1999 No. 689) E2–001

8th March 1999	– – –	*8th March 1999*
11th March 1999		*11st March 1999*
26th April 1999		*26th April 1999*

The Lord Chancellor, in exercise of the powers conferred on him by section 128 of the County Courts Act 1984, sections 414 and 415 of the Insolvency Act 1986 and section 128 of the Finance Act 1990, with the concurrency of the Treasury under section 128(1) of the County Courts Act 1984, and with the sanction of the Treasury under sections 414(1) and 415(1) of the Insolvency Act 1986, makes the following Order:

Citation and commencement

1. This Order may be cited as the County Court Fees Order 1999 and shall come into force on 26th April 1999. E2–002

Interpretation

E2–003 **2.** In this Order, unless the context otherwise requires—

(a) a fee referred to by number means the fee so numbered in Schedule 1 to this Order;
(b) "CCBC" means County Court Bulk Centre;
(c) "the CPR" means the Civil Procedure Rules 1998;
(d) expressions also used in the CPR have the same meaning as those Rules; and
(e) "CPC" means Claim Production Centre.

Fees to be taken

E2–004 **3.** The fees set out in column 2 of Schedule 1 to this Order shall be taken in county courts in respect of the items described in column 1 in accordance with and subject to the directions specified in column 1.

E2–005 **4.** The provisions of this Order shall not apply to family proceedings

Exemptions, reductions and remissions

E2–006 **5.**—(1) No fee shall be payable under this Order by a party who, at the time when a fee would otherwise become payable—

(a) is in receipt of any qualifying benefit, and
(b) is not in receipt of representation under Part IV and the Legal Aid Act 1988 for the purposes of the proceedings.

(2) The following are qualifying benefits for the purposes of paragraph (1)(a) above—

(a) income support;
(b) family credit and disability working allowance under Part VII of the Social Security Contributions and Benefits Act 1992; and
(c) income-based jobseeker's allowance under the Jobseekers Act 1995

(3) Paragraph (1) shall not apply to fee 4.8 (fee payable on a consolidated attachment of earnings order or an administration order).

E2–007 **6.** Where it appears to the Lord Chancellor that the payment of any fee prescribed by this Order would, owing to the exceptional circumstances of the particular case, involve undue financial hardship, he may reduce or remit the fee in that case.

E2–008 **7.** Where by any convention entered into by Her Majesty with any foreign power it is provided that no fee shall be required to be paid in respect of any proceedings, the fees specified in this Order shall not be taken in respect of those proceedings.

Revocations

E2–009 **8.** The Orders specified in Schedule 2 shall be revoked, except as to any fee or other sum due or payable under those Orders before the commencement of this Order.

SCHEDULE 1

FEES TO BE TAKEN

E2–010

Column 1 Number and description of fee	*Column 2* Amount of fee
1. Commencement of proceedings 1.1 On the commencement of originating proceedings (including originating proceedings issued after leave to issue is granted) to recover a sum of money, except in CPC cases, where the sum claimed:	(a) does not exceed £200 .... £20 (b) exceeds £200 but not £300 ...... £30 (c) exceeds £300 but not £400 ...... £40 (d) exceeds £400 but not £500 ...... £50 (e) exceeds £500 but not £1,000 ... £70 (f) exceeds £1,000 but not £5,000 .... £100 (g) exceeds £5,000 but not £15,000 .... £200 (h) exceeds £15,000 but not £50,000 .... £300 (i) exceeds £50,000 or not limited £400
1.2 On the commencement of originating proceedings to recover a sum of money in CPC cases, where the sum claimed:	(a) does not exceed £200 .... £15 (b) exceeds £200 but not £300 ...... £25 (c) exceeds £300 but not £400 ...... £35 (d) exceeds £400 but not £500 ...... £45 (e) exceeds £500 but not £1,000 ... £65 (f) exceeds £1,000 but not £5,000 .... £95 (g) exceeds £5,000 but not £15,000 .... £195 (h) exceeds £15,000 but not £50,000 .... £295 (i) exceeds £50,000 or not limited £395

Column 1 Number and description of fee	*Column 2* Amount of fee
1.3 On the commencement of originating proceedings for any other remedy or relief (including originating proceedings issued after leave to issue is granted)	£120
Fees 1.1 and 1.3 Recovery of land or goods Where a claim for money is additional or alternative to a claim for recovery of land or goods, only fee 1.3 shall be payable.	
Fees 1.1 and 1.3 Claims other than recovery of land or goods Where a claim for money is additional to a non money claim (other than a claim for recovery of land or goods) then fee 1.1 shall be payable in addition to fee 1.3. Where a claim for money is alternative to a non money claim (other than a claim for recovery of land or goods) then fee 1.1 or fee 1.3 shall be payable, whichever is the greater.	
Fees 1.1 and 1.3 Generally Where more than one non money claim is made in the same proceedings, fee 1.3 shall be payable once only, in addition to any fee which may be payable under fee 1.1.	
Fees 1.1 and 1.3 shall not be payable where fee 1.6(b) or fee 8 apply.	
Fees 1.1 and 1.3 Amendment of claim or counterclaim Where the claim or counterclaim is amended, and the fee paid before amendment is less than that which would have been payable if the document, as amended, had been so drawn in the first instance, the party amending the document shall pay the difference.	
1.4 On the filing of proceedings against a party or parties not named in the originating proceedings	£30
Fee 1.4 shall be payable by a defendant who adds or substitutes a party or parties to the proceedings or by a claimant who adds or substitutes a defendant or defendants.	

Column 1 Number and description of fee	*Column 2* Amount of fee
1.5 On the filing of a counterclaim	The same fee as if the relief or remedy sought were the subject of separate proceedings
1.6(a) On an application for leave to issue originating proceedings	£30
(b) On an application for an order under Part III of the Solicitors Act 1974 for the assessment of costs payable to a solicitor by his client	£30
2. General Fees 2.1 On the claimant filing an allocation questionnaire; or	£80
• where the court dispenses with the need for an allocation questionnaire, within 14 days of the date of despatch of the notice of allocation to track; or	
• where the CPR or a Practice Direction provide for an automatic allocation or provide that the rules on allocation shall not apply, within 28 days of the filing of the defence (or the filing of the last defence is there is more than one defendant), or within 28 days of the expiry of the time permitted for filing all defences if sooner	
Fee 2.1 shall be payable by the claimant except where the action is proceeding on the counterclaim alone, when it shall be payable by the defendant—	
• on the defendant filing an allocation questionnaire; or	
• where the court dispenses with the need for an allocation questionnaire, within 14 days of the date of despatch of the notice of allocation to track; or	

Column 1 Number and description of fee	*Column 2* Amount of fee
• where the CPR or a Practice Direction provide for automatic allocation or provide that the rules on allocation shall not apply, within 28 days of the filing of the defence to the counterclaim (or the filing of the last defence to the counterclaim if there is more than one party entitled to file a defence to a counterclaim), or within 28 days of the expiry of the time permitted for filing all defences to the counterclaim if sooner	
2.2 On the claimant filing a listing questionnaire; or	
• where the court fixes the trial date or trial week without the need for a listing questionnaire, within 14 days of the date of despatch of the notice (or the date when oral notice is given if no written notice is given) of the trial week or the trial date if no trial week is fixed:	
(a) if the case is on the multi-track	£300
(b) in any other case	£200
Fee 2.2 shall be payable by the claimant except where the action is proceeding on the counterclaim alone, when it shall be payable by the defendant—	
• on the defendant filing a listing questionnaire; or	
• where the court fixes the trial date or trial week without the need for a listing questionnaire, within 14 days of the date of despatch of the notice (or the date when oral notice is given if no written notice is given) of the trial week or the trial date if no trial week is fixed	
Where the court receives notice in writing—	
• before the trial date has been fixed, or	
• where a trial date has been fixed, at least 7 days before the trial date,	

Column 1 Number and description of fee	*Column 2* Amount of fee
from the party who paid fee 2.2 that the case is settled or discontinued, fee 2.2 shall be refunded.	
Fees 2.1 and 2.2 Generally Fees 2.1 and 2.2 shall be payable once only in the same proceedings.	
Fees 2.1 and 2.2 shall be payable as appropriate where the court allocates a case to a track for a trial of the assessment of damages.	
Fee 2.1 shall not be payable where the procedure in Part 8 of the CPR is used.	
Fee 2.2 shall not be payable in respect of a small claims hearing.	
2.3 On filing notice of appeal including an appeal against an allocation decision where no other fee is specified	£100
2.4 On an application on notice other than an application to fix the rate of payment before judgment where no other fee is specified	£50
2.5 On an application by consent or without notice for a judgment or order where no other fee is specified	£25
For the purpose of fee 2.5 a request for a judgment or order on admission or in default shall not constitute an application and no fee shall be payable	
2.6 On an application for a summons or order of a witness to attend court to be examined on oath, other than an application for which fee 4.3 is payable	£30
2.7 On an application to vary a judgment or suspend enforcement (where more than one remedy is sought in the same application only one fee shall be payable)	£25

Column 1 Number and description of fee	*Column 2* Amount of fee
3. Determination of costs Transitional provision Where a bill of costs or a request for detailed assessment or a request for a detailed assessment hearing is filed pursuant to an order made by the court before the coming into operation of this Order, or an application is made to the judge to review a taxation made before the coming into operation of this Order, the fees payable shall be those which applied immediately before this Order came into force.	
3.1 On the filing of a request for detailed assessment where the party filing the request is legally aided and no other party is ordered to pay the costs of the proceedings	£80
3.2 On the filing of a request for a detailed assessment hearing in any case where fee 3.1 does not apply; or on the filing of a request for a hearing date for the assessment of costs payable to a solicitor by his client pursuant to an order under Part III of the Solicitors Act 1974	£120
Where there is a combined party and party and legal aid determination of costs, fee 3.2 shall be attributed proportionately to the party and party and legal aid portions of the bill on the basis of the amount allowed.	
3.3 On an application for the issue of a default costs certificate	£40
3.4 On an appeal against a decision made in detailed assessment proceedings or on an application to set aside a default costs certificate	£50
3.5 On applying for the court's approval of a Legal Aid Assessment Certificate	£20
Fee 3.5 is payable at the time of applying for approval and is recoverable only against the Legal Aid Fund.	

Column 1 Number and description of fee	*Column 2* Amount of fee
4. Enforcement 4.1 On an application for or in relation to enforcement of a judgment or order of a county court or through a county court:	
in cases other than CCBC cases, by the issue of a warrant of execution against goods except a warrant to enforce payment of a fine;	(a) Where the amount for which the warrant issues does not exceed £125...............£25 (b) Where the amount for which the warrant issues exceeds £125 .£45
in CCBC cases, by the issue of a warrant of execution against goods except a warrant to enforce payment of a fine	(c) Where the amount for which the warrant issues does not exceed £125...............£20 (d) Where the amount for which the warrant issues exceeds £125 .£40
4.2 On a request for a further attempt at execution of a warrant at a new address following a notice of the reason for non-execution (except a further attempt following suspension and CCBC cases)	£20
4.3 On an application to question a judgment debtor or other person on oath in connection with enforcement of a judgment	£40
4.4 On an application for a garnishee order nisi or a charging order nisi, or the appointment of a receiver by way of equitable execution	£50
Fee 4.4 shall be payable in respect of each party against whom the order is sought.	
4.5 On an application for a judgment summons	£80

Column 1 Number and description of fee	*Column 2* Amount of fee
4.6 On the issue of a warrant of possession or a warrant of delivery	£80
Where the recovery of a sum of money is sought in addition, no further fee is payable.	
4.7 On an application for an attachment of earnings order (other than a consolidated attachment of earnings order) to secure payment of a judgment debt	£50
Fee 4.7 is payable for each defendant against whom an order is sought. Fee 4.7 is not payable where the attachment of earnings order is made on the hearing of a judgment summons.	
4.8 On a consolidated attachment of earnings order or on an administration order	for every £1 or part of a £1 of the money paid into court in respect of debts due to creditor 10p
Fee 4.8 shall be calculated on any money paid into court under any order at the rate in force at the time when the order was made (or, where the order has been amended, at the time of the last amendment before the date of payment).	
4.9 On the application for the recovery of a tribunal award	£30
4.10 On a request for an order to recover an increased penalty charge provided for in a parking charge certificate issued under paragraph 6 of Schedule 6 to the Road Traffic Act 1991 or on a request for an order to recover amounts payable by a person other than a London authority under an adjudication of a parking adjudicator pursuant to section 73 of the Road Traffic Act 1991;	£5
on a request to issue a warrant of execution to enforce such an order	
Fee 4.10 is payable on a request for an order but no further fee is payable on a request to issue a warrant of execution	

Column 1 Number and description of fee	*Column 2* Amount of fee
5. Sale 5.1 For removing or taking steps to remove goods to a place of deposit	The reasonable expenses incurred
Fee 5.1 is to include the reasonable expenses of feeding and caring for any animals.	
5.2 For advertising a sale by public auction pursuant to section 97 of the County Courts Act 1984	The reasonable expenses incurred
5.3 For the appraisement of goods	5p in the £1 or part of a £1 of the appraised value
5.4 For the sale of goods (including advertisements, catalogues, sale and commission and delivery of goods)	15p in the £1 or part of a £1 on the amount realised by the sale or such other sum as the district judge may consider to be justified in the circumstances
5.5 Where no sale takes place by reason of an execution being withdrawn, satisfied or stopped	(a) 10p in the £1 or part of a £1 on the value of the goods seized, the value to be the appraised value where the goods have been appraised or such other sum as the district judge may consider to be justified in the circumstances; and in addition (b) any sum payable under fee 5.1, 5.2 or 5.3
6. Copy documents 6.1 On a request for a copy of any documents (including a faxed copy where requested) or for examining a plain copy and marking it as an office copy;	
(a) per page for the first five pages of each document	£1

Column 1 Number and description of fee	*Column 2* Amount of fee
(b) per page for subsequent pages	25p
Fee 6.1 is payable whether or not the copy is issued as an office copy.	
6.2 Where copies of any document are made available on a computer disk or in other electronic form, for each such copy	£3
7. Registry of County Court Judgments 7.1 On a request for the issue of a certificate of satisfaction	£10
8. Companies Act 1985 and Insolvency Act 1986 8.1 On entering a bankruptcy petition:	
(a) if presented by a debtor or the personal representative of a deceased debtor	£120
(b) if presented by a creditor or other person	£150
8.2 On entering a petition for an administration order	£100
8.3 On entering any other petition	£150
One fee only is payable where more than one petition is presented in relation to a partnership.	
8.4(a) On a request for a certificate of discharge from bankruptcy	£50
(b) and after the first certificate, for each copy	£1
Request and applications with no fee No fee is payable on a request or on an application to the court by the Official Receiver when applying only in the capacity of Official Receiver to the case (and not as trustee or liquidator), or on an application to set aside a statutory demand.	

SCHEDULE 2

ORDERS REVOKED

E2–011

Title	*Reference*
The County Court Fees Order 1982	S.I. 1982/ 1706
The County Court Fees (Amendment) Order 1983	S.I. 1983/ 1681
The County Court Fees (Amendment) Order 1985	S.I. 1985/574
The County Court Fees (Amendment No. 2) Order 1985	S.I. 1985/ 1834
The County Court Fees (Amendment) Order 1986	S.I. 1986/633
The County Court Fees (Amendment No. 2) Order 1986	S.I. 1986/ 2143
The County Court Fees (Amendment) Order 1988	S.I. 1988/509
The County Court Fees (Amendment) Order 1992	S.I. 1992/ 2762
The County Court Fees (Amendment) Order 1994	S.I. 1994/ 1936
The County Court Fees (Amendment) Order 1995	S.I. 1995/ 2627
The County Court Fees (Amendment) Order 1996	S.I. 1996/ 3189
The County Court Fees (Amendment) Order 1997	S.I. 1997/787
The County Court Fees (Amendment) (No. 2) Order 1997	S.I. 1997/ 2670

EXPLANATORY NOTE

E2–012

(This note is not part of the Order)

This Order revokes the County Court Fees Order 1982 and replaces it by specifying new fees for proceedings in the county courts following the introduction of the Civil Procedure Rules 1998 which come into force on the same date as this Order.

In particular, the fee structure in this Order specifies fees payable at the two new stages of allocation and listing introduced by the Civil Procedure Rules. Where there are procedures similar to previous procedures, the fees have in most cases been increased.

The table of comparison below shows the comparison between the old fees and the new fees. The table also shows where new fees have been introduced.

TABLE OF COMPARISON

Number and summary of new fee (*for full description see Schedule 1*)	Amount of new fee (*for full details see Schedule 1*)	Amount of old fee	Number of old fee
1. Commencement of proceedings			1(i) & 1(ii)
1.1 & 1.2 Money claim			
(a) not exceeding £200	£20 (£15 CPC)	£10–£20 (£10–£15 CPC)	
(b) exceeds £200 but not £300	£30 (£25 CPC)	£30 (£25 CPC)	
(c) exceeds £300 but not £400	£40 (£35 CPC)	£40 (£35 CPC)	
(d) exceeds £400 but not £500	£50 (£45 CPC)	£50 (£45 CPC)	
(e) exceeds £500 but not £1,000	£70 (£65 CPC)	£60 (£55 CPC)	
(f) exceeds £1,000 but not £5,000	£100 (£95 CPC)	£80 (£65 CPC)	
(g) exceeds £5,000 but not £15,000	£200 (£195 CPC)	£100–£150 (£75 CPC)	
(h) exceeds £15,000 but not £50,000	£300 (£295 CPC)	£150 (£75 CPC)	
(i) exceeds £50,000 or not limited	£400 (£395 CPC)	£300–£500 (£75 CPC)	
1.3 Non money claim	£120	£80	1(iii)
1.4 Filing proceedings against new party	£30	New fee	New fee
1.5 Filing counterclaim	Same fee as originating proceedings	Same fee as originating proceedings	1(i)(ii); para. 3, schedule 1
1.6(a) Leave to issue originating proceedings	£30	New fee	New fee
(b) Application for order for assessment of costs under Solicitors Act	£30	New fee	New fee
2. General Fees			
2.1 On allocation	£80	New fee	New fee
2.2(a) On listing (multi-track)	£300	New fee	New fee
2.2(b) On listing (other)	£200	New fee	New fee
2.3 Appeal	£100	£20–£50	2B(i)(ii)
2.4 Application on notice	£50	£10–£30	2C(iii)(v)(vi)
2.5 Application for order, no notice given	£25	£10	2C(iv)

Number and summary of new fee (*for full description see Schedule 1*)	Amount of new fee (*for full details see Schedule 1*)	Amount of old fee	Number of old fee
2.6 Witness summons	£30	£20	2C(i)
2.7 Application to suspend, or vary judgment or order	£25	£10	2C(ii); 4(ix)
3. Determination of costs Old fees apply where documents filed pursuant to a court order, or application made for review of taxation, made before this Order came into force.			
3.1 Filing request for a detailed assessment—legal aid only cases	£80	No specific fee	No specific fee
3.2 Filing request for detailed assessment in any other case/request for hearing date for assessment pursuant to order under Part III of the Solicitors Act 1974	£120	scale fees (estimated average £300)	3(i) (ii)
3.3 Application for issue of the default costs certificate	£40	New fee	New fee
3.4 Appeal or application to set aside default costs certificate	£50	£50	3(iii)
3.5 Applying for court's approval of Legal Aid Assessment Certificate	£20	New fee	New fee
4. Enforcement			
4.1(a)(c) Execution up to £125	£25 (£30 CCBC)	£20 (£15 CCBC)	4(i)(a)(b)
4.1(b)(d) Execution over £125	£45 (£40 CCBC)	£40 (£35 CCBC)	
4.2 Further attempt at execution of warrant (not CCBC)	£20	£20	4(i)(c)
4.3 Oral examination	£40	£30	4(ii)
4.4 Garnishee order, or charging order, appointment of receiver	£50	£50	4(iii)(v)
4.5 Judgment summons	£80	£50	4(vi)
4.6 Warrant of possession or delivery	£80	£80	4(iv)
4.7 Attachment of earnings application	£50	£50	4(vii)
4.8 Consolidated attachment of earnings order/administration order	10p in the £	10p in the £	4(viii)

Number and summary of new fee (*for full description see Schedule 1*)	Amount of new fee (*for full details see Schedule 1*)	Amount of old fee	Number of old fee
4.9 Recovery of a tribunal award	£30	£30	4(A)i
4.10 Parking penalty charge	£5	£5	4(A)ii
5. Sale			
5.1 Taking steps to remove goods	reasonable expenses	reasonable expenses	5(i)
5.2 For advertising a sale by public auction	reasonable expenses	reasonable expenses	5(ii)
5.3 For the appraisement of goods	5p in the £	5p in the £	5(iii)
5.4 For the sale of goods	15p in the £	15p in the £	5(iv)
5.5 Stop sale fee	10p in the £ and fees 5.1, 5.2 or 5.3	10p in the £ and fees 5.1, 5.2 or 5.3	5(v)
6. Copy documents			
6.1(a) Copy per page for the first five pages	£1	£1	6(a)
6.1(b) Copy per page for subsequent pages	25p	25p	6(b)
6.2 Electronic copy	£3	New fee	New fee
7. Registry of County Court Judgments			
7.1 Certificate of satisfaction	£10	£3	7
8. Companies and Insolvency Acts			
8.1 On entering a bankruptcy petition:			
(a) by debtor/person representative of deceased debtor	£120	£50	9(i)(a)
(b) if presented by a creditor or other person	£150	£80	9(i)(b)
8.2 Petition for an administration order	£100	£80	9(ii)
8.3 Any other petition	£150	£80	9(ii)
8.4(a) Request for a certificate of discharge	£50	New fee	New fee
8.4(b) and after the first, for each copy	£1	New fee	New fee

INDEX

generally D2–028—D2–029

Commercial Court
Guide
features D2–023—D2–025
And see Commercial Court Guide
text D2–001—D2–481